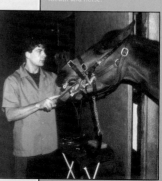

103rd
YEAR OF PUBLICATION

Raceform

HORSES

in Training 1996

ISBN 0 900611 54 5

INDEX TO GENERAL CONTENTS

Editor;   Len Bell; Orbit House, Albert Street, Eccles, Manchester, M30 0BL.
Tel: 0161 789 3237
Fax 0161 788 9152

Production Editor;   Alan Mosley; Eclipse Pedigrees, Weatherbys, Sanders Road, Wellingborough, NN8 4BX.

Subscription Orders;   Raceform Ltd., Compton, Newbury, Berkshire, RG20 6NL. Tel: 01635 578080
Fax: 01635 578101

Advertisements;   Tanya Liddiard; Compton, Newbury, Berkshire, RG20 6NL.
Tel: 01635 578128,   Fax: 01635 578101

Printed by Woolnough Bookbinding Ltd., Irthlingborough, Northamptonshire, NN9 5SE.
Distributed to the Newstrade by MMC, Octagon House, White Hart Meadows, Ripley, Woking, Surrey, GU23 6HR. Tel: 01483 211222

INDEX TO ADVERTISERS

1996

RACING FIXTURES

AND SALE DATES

Flat fixtures are in **Black Type**; Jump in Light Type; Irish in *Italic*; asterisk (☆) indicates an evening meeting; † indicates an All Weather meeting. Sale dates are at foot of fixtures.

Fixtures and sales dates are subject to alteration.

Owners names are shown against their horses where this information is available. In the case of Partnerships and Syndicates, the nominated owner is given alongside the horse with other owners listed below the team.

Foaling dates are shown for two-year-olds where these are provided.

Teams which have arrived too late for inclusion in Horses In Training 1996 will be published in the Raceform Update at the end of April.

JANUARY

Sun	Mon	Tues	Wed	Thur	Fri	Sat
	1	**2**	**3**	**4**	**5**	**6**
	Catterick Cheltenham Exeter Leicester Market Rasen **Southwell†** Uttoxeter Windsor *Fairyhouse* *Tramore*	Ayr **Lingfield†**	Lingfield Musselburgh **Wolverhampton†**	**Lingfield†** Nottingham Sedgefield *Thurles*	Newcastle **Southwell†** Towcester	Haydock **Lingfield†** Sandown Warwick *Naas*
7	**8**	**9**	**10**	**11**	**12**	**13**
	Lingfield **Southwell†**	Leicester **Lingfield†**	Kelso Plumpton **Wolverhampton†** *Punchestown*	**Lingfield†** Wetherby Wincanton *Tramore*	Ascot Musselburgh **Southwell†**	Ascot **Lingfield†** Newcastle Warwick *Leopardstown*
Fasig-Tipton *Sales*	Keeneland Sales	Keeneland Sales	Keeneland Sales	Keeneland Sales		
14	**15**	**16**	**17**	**18**	**19**	**20**
Navan	Fontwell **Southwell†**	Carlisle **Lingfield†**	Nottingham Windsor **Wolverhampton†** *Fairyhouse*	**Lingfield†** Ludlow Taunton *Tramore*	Catterick Kempton **Southwell†**	Catterick Haydock Kempton **Lingfield†** *Naas*
21	**22**	**23**	**24**	**25**	**26**	**27**
Leopardstown	Newton Abbot **Southwell†**	Leicester **Lingfield†**	Folkestone Sedgefield **Wolverhampton†**	Huntingdon **Lingfield†** Wincanton *Gowran Park*	Doncaster Lingfield **Southwell†**	Ayr Cheltenham Doncaster **Lingfield†** *Punchestown*
28	**29**	**30**	**31**			
	Plumpton **Southwell†**	**Lingfield†** Musselburgh Nottingham	Leicester Windsor **Wolverhampton†** *Down Royal* Doncaster Sales			

FEBRUARY

Sun	Mon	Tues	Wed	Thur	Fri	Sat
				1 Lingfield† Sedgefield Towcester *Punchestown* Doncaster Sales	**2** Folkestone Kelso **Southwell†**	**3** Chepstow **Lingfield†** Sandown Wetherby *Navan*
4 *Leopardstown* Fasig-Tipton Sales	**5** Fontwell **Southwell†**	**6** Carlisle **Lingfield†** Warwick Malvern Sales	**7** Ascot Ludlow **Wolverhampton†**	**8** Huntingdon **Lingfield†** Wincanton *Clonmel*	**9** Bangor-on-Dee Newbury **Southwell†**	**10** Ayr Catterick **Lingfield†** Newbury Uttoxeter *Navan*
11 *Punchestown*	**12** Hereford Plumpton **Southwell†** Goffs Sales	**13** Leicester **Lingfield†** Goffs Sales	**14** Lingfield Sedgefield **Wolverhampton†** *Fairyhouse*	**15** **Lingfield†** Sandown Taunton *Thurles* Deauville Sales	**16** Fakenham Sandown **Southwell†**	**17** Chepstow **Lingfield†** Newcastle Warwick Windsor *Gowran Park*
18 *Punchestown*	**19** Fontwell Musselburgh **Southwell†**	**20** **Lingfield†** Nottingham Ascot Sales	**21** Folkestone Sedgefield **Wolverhampton†**	**22** Huntingdon **Lingfield†** Wincanton *Clonmel*	**23** Haydock Kempton **Southwell†**	**24** Doncaster Haydock Kempton **Lingfield†** Musselburgh *Naas*
25 *Fairyhouse*	**26** Plumpton **Southwell†** Fasig-Tipton Sales	**27** Catterick Leicester **Lingfield†** Fasig-Tipton Sales	**28** Taunton Wetherby **Wolverhampton†** *Down Patrick*	**29** **Lingfield†** Ludlow Nottingham *Thurles*		

MARCH

Sun	Mon	Tues	Wed	Thur	Fri	Sat
31 *Curragh*					**1** Kelso Newbury **Southwell†**	**2** Doncaster **Lingfield†** Newbury Warwick **Wolverhampton** †☆ *Listowel*
3 *Leopardstown*	**4** Doncaster Windsor	**5** Leicester Sedgefield	**6** Bangor-on-Dee Catterick Lingfield **Wolverhampton†** Tattersalls (IRE) Sales	**7** Carlisle Towcester Wincanton Tattersalls (IRE) Sales	**8** Ayr Market Rasen Sandown	**9** Ayr Chepstow Sandown **Southwell†** *Navan*
10 *Naas*	**11** Plumpton Taunton	**12** Cheltenham Sedgefield	**13** Cheltenham Huntingdon Newton Abbot	**14** Cheltenham Hexham **Lingfield†**	**15** Fakenham Folkestone **Wolverhampton†**	**16** Hereford Lingfield Newcastle Uttoxeter **Wolverhampton** †☆ *Gowran Park*
17 *Limerick*	**18** Newcastle **Southwell†** *Down Royal* *Leopardstown* *Limerick*	**19** Fontwell Uttoxeter Ascot Sales	**20** Exeter Ludlow Towcester	**21** **Doncaster** Plumpton Wincanton Doncaster Sales	**22** **Doncaster** Kelso Newbury Doncaster Sales	**23** Bangor-on-Dee **Doncaster** **Lingfield†** Newbury *Clonmel* Doncaster Sales
24 *Naas*	**25** **Folkestone** Hexham Doncaster Sales	**26** **Newcastle** Sandown	**27** **Catterick** Chepstow **Lingfield†** *Downpatrick*	**28** Aintree **Leicester**	**29** Aintree **Lingfield†** Sedgefield	**30** Aintree **Beverley** Hereford **Wolverhampton** †☆ *Leopardstown*

18

APRIL

Sun	Mon	Tues	Wed	Thur	Fri	Sat
	1 Kelso **Southwell†**	**2** **Nottingham** Wolverhampton†	**3** Ascot **Hamilton** Ludlow *Down Royal*	**4** **Leicester** Lingfield **Musselburgh**	**5**	**6** Carlisle **Haydock** **Kempton** Newton Abbot Plumpton Towcester *Tipperary*
7 *Thurles* Plumpton Towcester Uttoxeter **Warwick** Wetherby Wincanton *Clonmel* *Fairyhouse*	**8** Carlisle Chepstow Fakenham Hereford Huntingdon Market Rasen **Newcastle** Newton Abbot **Nottingham**	**9** **Southwell†** Wetherby *Fairyhouse* Keeneland Sales	**10** Exeter **Ripon** Worcester *Fairyhouse*	**11** Cheltenham Fontwell **Hamilton** *Ballinrobe*	**12** **Beverley** **Brighton** **Nottingham**	**13** Ascot Newton Abbot Sedgefield **Warwick** **Wolverhampton** †☆ *Curragh* Goffs (France) Sales
14	**15** **Musselburgh** Southwell	**16** **Folkestone** **Newmarket** Goffs (France) Keeneland Tattersalls Sales	**17** Cheltenham **Newmarket** **Pontefract** *Gowran Park* Tattersalls Sales	**18** Ayr **Newmarket** **Ripon** *Tipperary* Tattersalls Sales	**19** Ayr **Newbury** Taunton☆ **Thirsk** Uttoxeter☆	**20** Ascot☆ Ayr Bangor-on-Dee **Newbury** Stratford☆ **Thirsk** *Leopardstown*
21	**22** **Brighton** Hexham☆ Newton Abbot☆ **Nottingham**	**23** **Folkestone** **Pontefract** *Punchestown*	**24** **Catterick** Chepstow☆ **Kempton**☆ Perth **Southwell†** *Punchestown*	**25** **Beverley** Exeter☆ Fontwell Perth Warwick☆ *Punchestown*	**26** Carlisle Ludlow☆ Perth **Sandown** Taunton☆	**27** Hexham☆ **Leicester** Market Rasen **Ripon** **Sandown** **Wolverhampton** †☆ Worcester☆ *Curragh* *Listowel*
28 *Listowel*	**29** **Pontefract** **Southwell†** *Sligo* Fasig-Tipton Sales	**30** Ascot☆ **Bath** Huntingdon☆ **Nottingham**				

MAY

Sun	Mon	Tues	Wed	Thur	Fri	Sat
			1 **Ascot** Cheltenham☆ Exeter Kelso☆	**2** **Hamilton** **Salisbury** **Wolverhampton†** *Tramore☆*	**3** Bangor-on-Dee☆ **Hamilton** **Newmarket** Newton Abbot Sedgefield☆ *Dundalk☆*	**4** **Haydock** Hereford Hexham☆ **Newmarket** Plumpton☆ **Thirsk** Uttoxeter Warwick☆ *Gowran Park*
5 **Newmarket** **Salisbury** *Gowran Park* *Down Royal* *Limerick* *Navan*	**6** **Doncaster** Exeter Fontwell Haydock **Kempton** Ludlow **Newcastle** Southwell Towcester **Warwick**	**7** **Chester**☆ **Doncaster**☆ Newton Abbot☆ Wincanton☆ Ascot Sales	**8** **Ayr** Chepstow **Chester** Uttoxeter☆ Wetherby☆	**9** **Brighton** **Chester** **Hamilton**☆ Sedgefield☆ **Southwell†** *Tipperary☆*	**10** **Beverley** **Carlisle** **Lingfield** Market Rasen☆ **Stratford**☆ *Downpatrick☆*	**11** **Bath** **Beverley** **Lingfield** Newcastle☆ **Warwick**☆ **Wolverhampton** †☆ Worcester *Downpatrick* *Leopardstown*
12 *Killarney*	**13** **Redcar** **Southwell†** Towcester☆ **Windsor**☆ *Killarney☆* Doncaster Sales	**14** Chepstow **York** *Killarney* Fasig-Tipton Doncaster Sales	**15** Hereford Huntingdon☆ Perth☆ **York** *Killarney* Doncaster Sales	**16** Aintree☆ Folkestone☆ Perth **Salisbury** **York** *Clonmel☆* *Laytown☆* Doncaster Sales	**17** **Newbury** **Newmarket** Newton Abbot☆ Stratford☆ **Thirsk**	**18** Bangor-on-Dee☆ Fakenham☆ **Hamilton**☆ **Lingfield**☆ **Newbury** Southwell **Thirsk** *Navan*
19 **Newbury** **Ripon** *Naas*	**20** **Bath** Musselburgh☆ Southwell **Windsor**☆ *Roscommon☆* Fasig-Tipton Sales	**21** **Beverley** **Goodwood** Goffs (France) Malvern Sales	**22** **Goodwood** Newcastle☆ Salisbury☆ Worcester *Leopardstown☆*	**23** Exeter☆ **Goodwood** **Newcastle** Uttoxeter☆ *Tipperary☆*	**24** **Brighton** **Haydock** **Nottingham** **Pontefract**☆ Towcester☆ *Dundalk☆*	**25** Cartmel **Doncaster** **Haydock** Hexham **Kempton** **Lingfield**☆ **Warwick**☆ **Wolverhampton** †☆ *Curragh*
26 *Curragh* Cartmel **Chepstow**	**27** Fontwell Hereford Huntingdon **Leicester** **Redcar** **Sandown** **Southwell†** Uttoxeter Wetherby *Kilbeggan☆*	**28** Hexham☆ **Leicester** **Redcar** Sandown☆	**29** Cartmel Folkestone **Newbury** **Ripon**☆ *Fairyhouse☆*	**30** **Brighton** Carlisle Hereford☆ **Musselburgh**☆ Uttoxeter *Clonmel☆*	**31** **Ayr** **Bath**☆ **Catterick** Stratford☆ **Wolverhampton†** *Down Royal☆* *Wexford☆*	

23

JUNE

Sun	Mon	Tues	Wed	Thur	Fri	Sat
30 Chepstow Doncaster *Curragh*						**1** Catterick Kempton☆ Lingfield Market Rasen☆ Newmarket Stratford *Naas*
2 *Sligo* *Tralee*	**3** Hamilton Leicester Thirsk☆ Windsor☆ *Leopardstown* *Tralee* Ascot Sales	**4** Brighton Pontefract Ascot Sales	**5** Beverley☆ Folkestone☆ Warwick Yarmouth *Navan*☆	**6** Beverley Chester☆ Goodwood Perth☆ Southwell† *Ballinrobe*☆ *Tipperary*☆	**7** Catterick Epsom Goodwood☆ Haydock☆ Perth *Dundalk*☆	**8** Doncaster Epsom Haydock Newmarket☆ Southwell☆ Wolverhampton †☆ Worcester *Curragh*
9 Epsom Uttoxeter	**10** Nottingham Pontefract Warwick☆ Windsor☆ *Roscommon*☆	**11** Redcar Salisbury Goffs Sales	**12** Beverley Hamilton☆ Kempton☆ Yarmouth *Leopardstown*☆ Goffs Sales	**13** Carlisle Chepstow☆ Newbury Yarmouth☆ *Clonmel*☆	**14** Goodwood☆ Market Rasen☆ Sandown Southwell† York	**15** Bath Leicester☆ Lingfield☆ Market Rasen Sandown York *Gowran Park*
16 *Gowran Park*	**17** Brighton Musselburgh Pontefract☆ Windsor☆ *Kilbeggan*☆	**18** Royal Ascot Thirsk *Tramore*☆	**19** Royal Ascot Nottingham☆ Ripon Worcester☆	**20** Royal Ascot Ripon☆ Southwell† Stratford☆ *Thurles*☆	**21** Royal Ascot Goodwood☆ Newmarket☆ Redcar *Wexford*☆	**22** Ascot Ayr Lingfield☆ Redcar Southwell Wolverhampton †☆ *Naas*
23	**24** Musselburgh Nottingham Warwick☆ Windsor☆ *Limerick*☆	**25** Lingfield Yarmouth *Sligo*☆ Malvern Sales	**26** Carlisle Chester☆ Kempton☆ Salisbury *Gowran Park*☆	**27** Carlisle Newbury☆ Salisbury Uttoxeter☆ *Tipperary* Tattersalls (IRE) Sales	**28** Folkestone Goodwood☆ Newcastle☆ Newmarket Wolverhampton† *Curragh*☆ Tattersalls (IRE) Sales	**29** Bath Doncaster☆ Lingfield☆ Newcastle Newmarket Worcester *Curragh*

JULY

Sun	Mon	Tues	Wed	Thur	Fri	Sat
	1 Musselburgh☆ Pontefract Southwell† Windsor☆ Doncaster Sales	**2** Chepstow Musselburgh *Bellewstown* Ascot Sales	**3** Catterick Epsom☆ Folkestone Yarmouth☆ *Bellewstown☆*	**4** Ayr☆ Catterick Haydock☆ Yarmouth *Bellewstown☆* Goffs (France) Sales	**5** Beverley☆ Hamilton☆ Haydock Sandown Warwick *Wexford☆*	**6** Beverley Carlisle☆ Chepstow Haydock Market Rasen Nottingham☆ Sandown Wolverhampton †☆ *Leopardstown*
7 *Dundalk*	**8** Bath Musselburgh Ripon☆ Windsor☆ *Roscommon☆*	**9** Newmarket Pontefract Tattersalls Sales	**10** Folkestone Kempton☆ Newmarket *Worcester☆* *Naas☆* Tattersalls Sales	**11** Chepstow☆ Newmarket Redcar☆ Wolverhampton† *Tipperary☆* Tattersalls Sales	**12** Chester☆ Hamilton☆ Lingfield York *Dundalk*	**13** Chester Lingfield Salisbury Southwell☆ Warwick☆ York *Down Royal* *Gowran Park*
14 *Curragh*	**15** Ayr Folkestone Windsor☆ Wolverhampton †☆ *Down Royal* *Killarney☆*	**16** Beverley Brighton *Killarney*	**17** Brighton☆ Doncaster☆ Redcar☆ Sandown *Killarney*	**18** Bath Leicester Redcar☆ *Worcester☆* *Killarney*	**19** Musselburgh Newbury Newmarket☆ Pontefract☆ Southwell *Kilbeggan☆*	**20** Ayr☆ Newbury Newmarket Nottingham Ripon☆ Warwick☆ *Leopardstown*
21 Ayr Stratford Yarmouth *Tipperary*	**22** Beverley☆ Musselburgh Southwell† Windsor☆ *Ballinrobe☆* Keeneland Sales	**23** Worcester Yarmouth *Ballinrobe* Keeneland Sales	**24** Bath Catterick Leicester☆ Sandown☆ *Naas☆* Fasig-Tipton Sales	**25** Brighton Catterick☆ Chepstow☆ Sandown *Wexford☆* Goffs (France) Sales	**26** ° Ascot Newmarket☆ Nottingham☆ Thirsk Wolverhampton† *Wexford☆*	**27** Ascot Lingfield☆ Newcastle Southwell☆ Stratford *Curragh*
28	**29** Brighton Newcastle Nottingham☆ Windsor☆ *Galway☆*	**30** Beverley Goodwood *Galway☆*	**31** Doncaster Epsom☆ Goodwood Stratford☆ *Galway*			

AUGUST

Sun	Mon	Tues	Wed	Thur	Fri	Sat
				1 Doncaster☆ Goodwood Salisbury☆ Yarmouth *Galway*	**2** Ascot☆ Bangor-on-Dee Goodwood Newmarket☆ Thirsk *Galway☆*	**3** Goodwood Hamilton☆ Market Rasen☆ Newmarket Newton Abbot Thirsk Windsor☆ *Galway*
4 Chester Lingfield Newcastle	**5** Brighton☆ Carlisle☆ Newton Abbot Ripon *Leopardstown* *Tipperary*	**6** Brighton Catterick *Roscommon☆* Ascot Fasig-Tipton Sales	**7** Brighton☆ Kempton☆ Newcastle Nottingham☆ *Fairyhouse☆* *Sligo☆* Fasig-Tipton Sales	**8** Bath Hamilton☆ Pontefract Yarmouth☆ *Sligo* Fasig-Tipton Sales	**9** Haydock☆ Newmarket☆ Plumpton Redcar Wolverhampton† *Kilbeggan☆*	**10** Ayr Haydock Lingfield☆ Market Rasen☆ Newmarket Redcar Worcester☆ *Gowran Park*
11 *Leopardstown*	**12** Leicester☆ Thirsk☆ Windsor Worcester Doncaster Fasig-Tipton Sales	**13** Bath Southwell *Wexford☆* Doncaster Sales	**14** Beverley Hamilton☆ Salisbury Sandown☆ Doncaster Fasig-Tipton Sales	**15** Beverley Newton Abbot☆ Salisbury Yarmouth☆ *Dundalk☆* *Tramore☆* Tattersalls (IRE) Sales	**16** Catterick☆ Folkestone Haydock☆ Newbury Southwell† *Tramore☆* Tattersalls (IRE) Sales	**17** Bangor-on-Dee Lingfield☆ Newbury Ripon Stratford Wolverhampton †☆ *Curragh* *Tramore* Deauville Sales
18 Brighton Pontefract *Roscommon* *Tramore* Deauville Sales	**19** Hamilton☆ Leicester☆ Plumpton☆ Windsor *Roscommon☆* Goffs Deauville Sales	**20** Folkestone York Goffs Deauville Fasig-Tipton Sales	**21** Ayr Exeter Hereford☆ Kempton☆ York Deauville Sales	**22** Cartmel☆ Salisbury☆ Yarmouth York *Tipperary☆* Deauville Sales	**23** Newmarket Sandown Thirsk *Kilbeggan☆*	**24** Beverley Cartmel Goodwood Hereford☆ Newmarket Windsor☆ *Leopardstown*
25 Goodwood Nottingham Redcar *Tralee* Cartmel Chepstow	**26** Epsom Fontwell Huntingdon Newcastle Newton Abbot Ripon Southwell Warwick *Downpatrick* *Tralee☆*	**27** Ripon Uttoxeter *Tralee☆*	**28** Brighton Carlisle Worcester *Tralee*	**29** Lingfield Musselburgh Sedgefield *Tralee*	**30** Chester Perth Sandown *Tralee*	**31** Chester Perth Ripon Sandown Wolverhampton †☆ *Curragh*

SEPTEMBER

Sun	Mon	Tues	Wed	Thur	Fri	Sat
1	**2** **Hamilton** Hexham *Sligo*	**3** **Brighton** **Pontefract** Ascot Sales	**4** **Brighton** Newton Abbot **York** *Dundalk*	**5** Plumpton **Salisbury** **York** *Clonmel*	**6** **Haydock** **Kempton** Sedgefield *Kilbeggan*☆ Tattersalls Sales	**7** **Haydock** **Kempton** Stratford **Thirsk** **Wolverhampton** †☆ *Fairyhouse*
8 *Ballinrobe* *Curragh*	**9** **Bath** **Southwell**† *Galway*☆ Keeneland Sales	**10** **Leicester** **Lingfield** *Galway*☆ Keeneland Doncaster Sales	**11** **Doncaster** **Epsom** Exeter *Galway* Keeneland Doncaster Sales	**12** **Chepstow** **Doncaster** Newton Abbot Keeneland Doncaster Sales	**13** **Doncaster** **Goodwood** Worcester *Down Patrick* Keeneland Doncaster Sales	**14** Bangor-on-Dee **Doncaster** **Goodwood** Sedgefield Worcester *Leopardstown* Keeneland Sales
15 Keeneland Sales	**16** Fontwell **Nottingham** *Roscommon* Keeneland Sales	**17** **Sandown** **Yarmouth** Keeneland Sales	**18** **Beverley** **Sandown** **Yarmouth**	**19** **Ayr** **Lingfield** **Yarmouth** *Gowran Park*	**20** **Ayr** Huntingdon **Newbury**	**21** **Ayr** Carlisle **Catterick** Market Rasen **Newbury** **Wolverhampton** †☆ *Curragh* *Down Royal*
22	**23** **Leicester** **Musselburgh** *Listowel* Fasig-Tipton Sales	**24** **Epsom** **Nottingham** *Listowel* Tattersalls (IRE) Sales	**25** **Chester** **Goodwood** Perth *Listowel* Tattersalls (IRE) Sales	**26** **Goodwood** Perth **Pontefract** *Listowel* Tattersalls (IRE) Sales	**27** **Folkestone** **Haydock** **Redcar** *Listowel* Goffs (France) Doncaster Sales	**28** **Ascot** **Haydock** **Redcar** Worcester *Listowel*
29 **Ascot** **Hamilton** Newton Abbot Fasig-Tipton Sales	**30** **Bath** **Hamilton** Fasig-Tipton Sales					

OCTOBER

Sun	Mon	Tues	Wed	Thur	Fri	Sat
		1 **Newmarket** Sedgefield Ascot Tattersalls Sales	**2** **Brighton** Exeter **Newcastle** Salisbury *Navan* Tattersalls Sales	**3** Cheltenham **Newmarket** Taunton *Punchestown* Tattersalls Sales	**4** Hexham **Lingfield** **Newmarket**	**5** Chepstow **Haydock** **Newmarket** Uttoxeter **Wolverhampton** †☆ *Curragh* *Down Royal* Goffs (France) Sales
6 **Haydock** Kelso Kempton *Tipperary*	**7** Fontwell **Pontefract**	**8** Redcar Warwick Goffs Sales	**9** **Nottingham** Towcester **York** Goffs Sales	**10** Ludlow Wincanton **York** *Thurles* Goffs Sales	**11** Ascot Carlisle Cheltenham Goffs Sales	**12** Ascot Bangor-on-Dee Hexham Worcester **York** *Fairyhouse*
13 *Naas*	**14** **Leicester** Newton Abbot *Roscommon* Tattersalls Fasig-Tipton Sales	**15** **Leicester** Sedgefield Tattersalls Fasig-Tipton Sales	**16** Exeter **Haydock** Wetherby *Navan* Tattersalls Sales	**17** **Newmarket** Redcar Taunton *Tipperary* Tattersalls Sales	**18** **Catterick** Hereford **Newmarket** *Downpatrick* Tattersalls Sales	**19** **Catterick** Kelso Kempton **Newmarket** Stratford **Wolverhampton** †☆ *Curragh*
20 *Limerick*	**21** **Folkestone** **Pontefract** Deauville Sales	**22** **Chepstow** Plumpton Deauville Sales	**23** Exeter **Newcastle** **Yarmouth** *Gowran Park* Doncaster Sales	**24** Ludlow **Newbury** Nottingham *Punchestown* Doncaster Sales	**25** **Doncaster** Fakenham Newbury Doncaster Sales	**26** Carlisle **Doncaster** Market Rasen **Newbury** Worcester *Down Royal* *Leopardstown* Doncaster Sales
27 Huntingdon Wetherby Wincanton *Galway* *Wexford*	**28** **Leicester** **Lingfield** *Galway* *Leopardstown* Tattersalls Sales	**29** **Leicester** **Redcar** Tattersalls Malvern Sales	**30** Cheltenham Fontwell **Yarmouth** Tattersalls Sales	**31** **Nottingham** Sedgefield Stratford *Gowran Park* Tattersalls Sales		

NOVEMBER

Sun	Mon	Tues	Wed	Thur	Fri	Sat
					1	**2**
					Bangor-on-Dee **Newmarket** Wetherby *Clonmel*	Ascot Kelso **Newmarket** Warwick **Wolverhampton** †☆
					Fasig-Tipton Tattersalls Goffs Sales	*Navan* Fasig-Tipton Sales
3	**4**	**5**	**6**	**7**	**8**	**9**
Punchestown	Newcastle Plumpton **Southwell†**	Exeter **Redcar**	Haydock Kempton Newton Abbot	**Lingfield†** Market Rasen **Musselburgh** *Clonmel*	Doncaster Hexham Uttoxeter	Chepstow **Doncaster** Newcastle Sandown Uttoxeter Wincanton *Naas*
Fasig-Tipton Keeneland Sales	Keeneland Tattersalls (IRE) Sales	Ascot Keeneland Tattersalls (IRE) Sales	Keeneland Tattersalls (IRE) Sales	Keeneland Tattersalls (IRE) Sales	Keeneland Tattersalls (IRE) Sales	Keeneland Tattersalls (IRE) Sales
10	**11**	**12**	**13**	**14**	**15**	**16**
Leopardstown	Carlisle **Folkestone** **Wolverhampton†**	**Lingfield†** Ludlow Sedgefield	Kelso Newbury Worcester *Fairyhouse*	**Lingfield†** Taunton Towcester *Thurles*	Ayr Cheltenham **Lingfield†**	Ayr Cheltenham Huntingdon Windsor **Wolverhampton** †☆ *Punchestown*
Keeneland Tattersalls (IRE) Sales	Tattersalls (IRE) Sales	Tattersalls (IRE) Sales	Tattersalls (IRE) Sales	Tattersalls (IRE) Goffs (France) Sales	Tattersalls (IRE) Sales	
17	**18**	**19**	**20**	**21**	**22**	**23**
Cheltenham Fontwell *Navan*	Leicester Plumpton **Southwell†**	**Lingfield†** Newton Abbot Wetherby	Haydock Hereford Kempton	Sedgefield Warwick Wincanton *Tipperary*	Aintree Ascot **Southwell†**	Aintree Ascot Catterick Market Rasen Towcester *Naas*
	Doncaster Sales	Fasig-Tipton Doncaster Sales	Doncaster Sales	Goffs Doncaster Sales	Goffs Sales	Goffs Sales
24	**25**	**26**	**27**	**28**	**29**	**30**
Clonmel	Catterick Folkestone **Wolverhampton†**	Cheltenham Huntingdon **Lingfield†**	Chepstow Hexham Windsor *Downpatrick*	Carlisle Taunton Uttoxeter	Bangor-on-Dee Newbury **Southwell†**	Haydock Newbury Newcastle Warwick **Wolverhampton** †☆ *Fairyhouse*
Goffs Sales	Tattersalls Sales	Tattersalls Sales	Tattersalls Sales	Tattersalls Sales	Tattersalls Sales	Tattersalls Sales

34

DECEMBER

Sun	Mon	Tues	Wed	Thur	Fri	Sat
1 *Fairyhouse*	**2** Kelso Worcester Tattersalls Sales	**3** Newcastle **Southwell†** Tattersalls Sales	**4** Catterick Fontwell Southwell Tattersalls Sales	**5** **Leicester** **Lingfield†** Windsor *Thurles* Goffs (France) Tattersalls Sales	**6** Exeter Hereford Market Rasen Tattersalls Sales	**7** Chepstow Sandown Towcester Wetherby **Wolverhampton** †☆ *Punchestown* Deauville Sales
8 *Clonmel* Tattersalls (IRE) Deauville Fasig-Tipton Sales	**9** Ludlow Musselburgh Tattersalls (IRE) Deauville Fasig-Tipton Ascot Sales	**10** Huntingdon Plumpton Sedgefield Ascot Goffs Sales	**11** Hexham Leicester **Lingfield†** Goffs Sales	**12** Fakenham Sandown Taunton *Clonmel* Goffs Sales	**13** Cheltenham Doncaster **Lingfield†** Goffs Sales	**14** Cheltenham Doncaster Haydock Lingfield **Wolverhampton** †☆ *Navan* Goffs Sales
15 *Thurles*	**16** Newton Abbot Warwick	**17** Folkestone Musselburgh	**18** Bangor-on-Dee Catterick Exeter	**19** Catterick Towcester **Wolverhampton†**	**20** Hereford Hexham **Lingfield†** Uttoxeter	**21** Ascot Haydock Lingfield Uttoxeter *Navan*
22	**23** Kelso Ludlow	**24**	**25** *Down Royal* *Leopardstown* *Limerick*	**26** Ayr Hereford Huntingdon Kempton Market Rasen Newton Abbot Sedgefield Wetherby Wincanton Wolverhampton	**27** Chepstow Kempton Leicester Musselburgh Wetherby *Leopardstown* *Limerick*	**28** Folkestone Huntingdon Newbury Newcastle *Leopardstown* *Limerick*
29 *Leopardstown* *Limerick*	**30** Carlisle Newbury Plumpton Stratford	**31** Catterick Fontwell **Lingfield†** Taunton Warwick *Punchestown*				

INDEX TO TRAINERS

† denotes Permit to train under N.H. Rules only

Name	Team No.	Name	Team No.
BATES, MR A. G.	043	BRAVERY, MR G. C.	081
BAUGH, MR B. P. J.	044	BRAZINGTON, MR R. G.	082
BEAUMONT, MR P.	045	BRENNAN, MR OWEN	083
BELL, MR M. L. W.	046	†BREWIS, MR R.	084
BELL, MR S. B.	047	BRIDGER, MR J. J.	085
BELMONT, MR FRANCOIS	048	BRIDGWATER, MR K. S.	086
BENNETT, MR J. A.	049	BRISBOURNE, MR W. M.	087
BENSTEAD, MR C. J.	050	BRITTAIN, MR C. E.	088
BERRY, MR J.	051	BRITTAIN, MR M. A.	089
BERRY, MR J. C. DE	052	BROAD, MR C. D.	090
BERRY, MR N.	053	BROMHEAD, MR H. DE	091
BETHELL, MR J. D.	054	†BROOKE, LADY SUSAN	092
†BETHELL, MR W. A.	055	BROOKS, MR C. P. E.	093
†BEVAN, MR E. G.	056	†BROOKS, MRS E. M.	094
BEVAN, MR P. J.	057	BROOKSHAW, MR S. A.	095
†BICKERTON, MRS P. F.	058	BROTHERTON, MR R.	096
BIELBY, MR M. P.	059	†BROWN, MR D. H.	097
BILL, MR T. T.	060	BROWN, MRS J.	098
BIRKETT, MR J. J.	061	†BROWN, MR R. L.	099
BISHOP, MR K.	062	†BROYD, MISS A. E.	100
†BLACK, MRS C. J.	063	BUCKLER, MR R. H.	101
†BLACKMORE, MR A. G.	064	BURCHELL, MR DAVID	102
BLANSHARD, MR M. T. W.	065	BURGOYNE, MR PAUL	103
BOLGER, MR J. S.	066	BURKE, MR K. R.	104
BOLLACK-BADEL, MRS M.	067	BUTLER, MR P.	105
BOLTON, MR M. J.	068	BYCROFT, MR N.	106
BOSLEY, MR J. R.	069		
BOSS, MR RONALD	070		
BOTTOMLEY, MR J. F.	071	**C**	
†BOUSFIELD, MR B.	072	CALDWELL, MR T. H.	107
BOWER, MISS J.	073	CALLAGHAN, MR N. A.	108
BOWER, MISS L. J.	074	CALVER, MR P.	109
BOWRING, MR S. R.	075	CAMACHO, MR M. J. C.	110
BRADBURNE, MRS S. C.	076	CAMBIDGE, MR B. R.	111
BRADLEY, MR J. M.	077	CAMPBELL, MR I.	112
†BRADLEY, MR P.	078	CAMPION, MR A. M.	113
BRADSTOCK, MR M. F.	079	CAMPION, MR S. W.	114
BRAMALL, MRS S. A.	080	CANDY, MR HENRY D.	115

Name	Team No.
†CAREY, MR D. N.	116
CARR, MR J. M.	117
CARR, MR T. J.	118
CARROLL, MR A. W.	119
CASEY, MR W. T.	120
CECIL, MR H. R. A.	121
CECIL, MRS J.	122
CHAMBERLAIN, MR A. J.	123
CHAMBERLAIN, MR N.	124
CHAMPION M.B.E., MR R.	125
CHANCE, MR N. T.	126
CHANNON, MR M.	127
CHAPMAN, MR DAVID W.	128
CHAPMAN, MR M. C.	129
CHAPPELL, MAJOR D. N.	130
CHAPPLE-HYAM, MR P. W.	131
CHARLES-JONES, MR G. F. H.	132
CHARLTON, MR J. I. A.	133
CHARLTON, MR ROGER J.	134
CHEESBROUGH, MR P.	135
†CHESNEY, DR D.	136
CHRISTIAN, MR S. P. L.	137
†CLARK, MR S. B.	138
CLARKE, MR PETER C.	139
CLAY, MR W.	140
CLEMENT, MR NICOLAS	141
CLEMENT, MR T. T.	142
†CLUTTERBUCK, MR K. F.	143
†CLYDE M.R.C.V.S., MR D. H.	144
COATHUP, MR S.	145
†COCKBURN, MR R. G.	146
COLE, MR P. F. I.	147
COLE, MR S. N.	148
COLLET, MR R.	149
COLLINGRIDGE, MR H. J.	150
COLLINS, MR C.	151
†COLLINS, MR R.	152
†COOMBE, MR M. J.	153

Name	Team No.
†COTON, MR F.	154
COTTRELL, MR L. G.	155
†CRAGGS, MR R.	156
CRAZE, MISS J. F.	157
CUMANI, MR L. M.	158
CUNDELL, MR P. D.	159
CUNNINGHAM, MR M.	160
CUNNINGHAM, MR W. S.	161
CUNNINGHAM-BROWN, MR K.	162
CURLEY, MR B. J.	163
†CURTIS, MR J. W. P.	164
CURTIS, MR ROGER	165
CUTHBERT, MR T. A. K.	166
CYZER, MR CHARLES	167

D

†DALTON, MR J. N.	168
DALTON, MR P. T.	169
†DAVIES, MR D. J.	170
†DAVIES, MR G. W. J.	171
†DAWE, MR N. J.	172
DE HAAN, MR B.	173
DICKIN, MR R.	174
†DIXON, MR J. E.	175
DODS, MR M. J. K.	176
DOUMEN, MR FRANCOIS	177
DOW, MR S. L.	178
†DOWSON, MRS H. B.	179
DOYLE, MISS JACQUELINE S.	180
DREWE, MR C. J.	181
†DU PLESSIS, MISS J. M.	182
†DUN, MR T. D. C.	183
DUNLOP, MR E. A. L.	184
DUNLOP, MR J. L.	185
DUNN, MR A. J. K.	186
DUTFIELD, MRS P. N.	187
DWYER, MR C. A.	188

Name	Team No.	Name	Team No.
DYER, MR T.	189	FETHERSTON-GODLEY, MR M.	221
		FFITCH-HEYES, MR J. R. G.	222
		FFRENCH DAVIS, MR D. J. S.	223
E		FIERRO, MR G.	224
EARLE, MR S. A.	190	FISHER, MR R. F.	225
EASTERBY, MR M. W.	191	FITZGERALD, MR J. G.	226
EASTERBY, MR T. D.	192	FLOOD, MR F.	227
ECCLES, MR P.	193	FLOWER, MR R. M.	228
†ECKLEY, MR B. J.	194	FORSTER, CAPT T. A.	229
ECKLEY, MR MALCOLM	195	†FOSTER, MR A.	230
EDDY, MR D.	196	FOSTER, MR A. G.	231
†EDWARDS, MR G. F.	197	FOWLER, MR J. R. H.	232
EDWARDS, MR J. A. C.	198	†FROST, MR K.	233
EGERTON, MR C. R.	199	FROST, MR R. G.	234
ELLERBY, MR M. W.	200		
†ELLIOTT, MR E. A.	201		
ELLISON, MR BRIAN	202	**G**	
ELSEY, MR C. C.	203	GANDOLFO, MR D. R.	235
ELSEY, MR C. W. C.	204	GASELEE, MR N. A.	236
EMBIRICOS, MISS A. E.	205	GEORGE, MR T. R.	237
†ENGLAND, MISS E. M. V.	206	GIFFORD, MR J. T.	238
ENRIGHT, MR G. P.	207	GLOVER, MR J. A.	239
ETHERINGTON, MR T. J.	208	GOLDIE, MR J. S.	240
†EUBANK, MR A.	209	GOLDIE, MR ROBERT H	241
EUSTACE, MR J. M. P.	210	GOLLINGS, MR S.	242
EVANS, MR P. D.	211	†GOODFELLOW, MRS A. C. D.	243
†EVANS, MR R. R.	212	GOSDEN, MR J. H. M.	244
EYRE, MR J. L.	213	GRAHAM, MR N. A.	245
		GRASSICK, MR L. P.	246
		GRASSICK, MR M. J.	247
F		†GRAY, MR FREDERICK	248
FABRE, MR A.	214	†GREATHEAD, MR T. R.	249
FAHEY, MR R. A.	215	†GREENWAY, MR V. G.	250
FAIRHURST, MR C. W.	216	†GRIFFIN, MR M. A.	251
FANSHAWE, MR J. R.	217	†GRIFFITHS, MR S. G.	252
FARRELL, MR P.	218	GRISSELL, MR D. M.	253
FELGATE, MR P. S.	219	GUBBY, MR BRIAN	254
FELLOWS, MR J.	220	GUEST, MR R.	255

Name	Team No.
H	
HAGGAS, MR W. J.	256
HAIGH, MR W. W.	257
HAINE, MRS D.	258
HALDANE, MR J. S.	259
HALL, MR L. MONTAGUE	260
HALL, MISS S. E.	261
HAM, MR G. A.	262
†HAMILTON, MRS A.	263
†HAMILTON-FAIRLEY, MRS A. J.	264
HAMMOND, MR J. E.	265
HAMMOND, MR M. D.	266
HANBURY, MR B.	267
HANNON, MR R.	268
†HARRIMAN, MR J.	269
HARRINGTON, MRS JESSICA	270
HARRIS, MR J. A.	271
HARRIS, MR J. L.	272
HARRIS, MR PETER W.	273
HARRIS, MR ROGER	274
†HARRIS, MR S. A.	275
HARRISON, MR R. A.	276
HARWOOD, MR GUY	277
HASLAM, MR PATRICK	278
HAYDEN, MR JOHN C	279
HAYDN JONES, MR D.	280
†HAYNES, MR H. E.	281
HAYNES, MR M. J.	282
HAYWARD, MR P. A.	283
HEAD, MRS C	284
HEATON-ELLIS, MR M. J. B.	285
HEDGER, MR P. R.	286
HELLENS, MR J. A.	287
HENDERSON, MR N. J.	288
HENDERSON, MRS R. G.	289
HERN C.V.O., MAJOR W. R.	290
HERRIES, LADY	291
HETHERTON, MR J	292
HEWITT, MRS A. R.	293
†HIATT, MR P. W.	294
HIDE, MR ANTHONY	295
HILLS, MR B. W.	296
HILLS, MR J. W.	297
HOAD, MR R. P. C.	298
HOBBS, MR P. J.	299
HODGES, MR R. J.	300
HOLLINSHEAD, MR R.	301
HOLMES, MR G	302
†HOMEWOOD, MR J. S.	303
HORGAN, MR CON	304
†HORLER, MISS C. J.	305
HOWE, MR H. S.	306
HOWLING, MR P.	307
HUBBARD, MR G. A.	308
†HUBBUCK, MR J. S.	309
HUGHES, MR D. T.	310
HUNTINGDON, LORD	311
I	
INCISA, DON E.	312
INGRAM, MR R.	313
IVORY, MR K. T.	314
J	
JACKSON, MR C. F. C.	315
†JACKSON, MR F. S.	316
JAMES, MR A. P.	317
JAMES, MR C. J.	318
JARVIS, MR A. P.	319
JARVIS, MR M. A.	320
JARVIS, MR W.	321
JEFFERSON, MR J. M.	322
†JEFFREY, MR T. E.	323
JENKINS, MR J. R. W.	324

Name	Team No.
JENKS, MR W. P.	325
†JESSOP, MR A. E. M.	326
†JESTIN, MR F.	327
JEWELL, MRS L. C.	328
JOHNSEY, MISS C.	329
JOHNSON, MR JOHN H.	330
†JOHNSON, MR P. R.	331
†JOHNSON, MR ROBERT W	332
†JOHNSON, MRS S. M.	333
JOHNSON HOUGHTON, MR G.	334
JOHNSON HOUGHTON, MR R.	335
JOHNSTON, MR M. S.	336
JONES, MR A. P.	337
JONES, MR C. H.	338
†JONES, MR G. ELWYN	339
JONES, MRS M. A.	340
†JONES, MR P. D.	341
†JONES, MR P. J.	342
JONES, MR R. W.	343
JONES, MR T. M.	344
JORDAN, MR F. T. J.	345
JORDAN, MRS J	346
†JOSEPH, MR J.	347
JUCKES, MR R. T.	348

K

Name	Team No.
KAUNTZE, MR M.	349
†KAVANAGH, MR H. M.	350
KELLEWAY, MISS G. M.	351
KELLEWAY, MR P. A.	352
KELLY, MR G. P.	353
KEMP, MR W. T.	354
†KENDALL, MRS M. A.	355
KETTLEWELL, MR S. E.	356
KING, MRS A. L. M.	357
KING, MR J. S.	358
†KINSEY, MR T. R.	359

Name	Team No.
†KIRBY, MR F.	360
†KIRBY, MR J.	361
KNIGHT, MISS H. C.	362
KNIGHT, MR S. G.	363

L

Name	Team No.
LAFFON-PARIAS, MR C.	364
LAMB, MR D. A.	365
†LAMB, MRS K. M.	366
†LAMYMAN, MRS S.	367
LE PENNEC, MR ROBIN	368
LEACH, MR M. R.	369
LEADBETTER, MR S. J.	370
LEAHY, MR AUGUSTINE	371
†LEDGER, MR R. R.	372
LEE, MR F. H.	373
LEE, MR RICHARD	374
LEIGH, MR J. P.	375
LEWIS, MR G.	376
LITTMODEN, MR N. P.	377
LLEWELLYN, MR B. J.	378
†LLOYD, MR F.	379
LLOYD-JAMES, MR L. R.	380
LODER, MR D. R.	381
LONG, MRS M. E.	382
†LUCKIN, MR P. D.	383
LUNGO, MR L.	384

M

Name	Team No.
MACAULEY, MRS N. J.	385
MACKIE, MR W. J. W.	386
MACTAGGART, MR A. B.	387
†MACTAGGART, MR A. H.	388
MADGWICK, MR M. J.	389
MANN, MR C. J.	390
MANN, MR W. G.	391

Name	Team No.	Name	Team No.
MARGARSON, MR GEORGE G.	392	MORGAN, MR K. A.	430
MARKS, MR D.	393	MORLEY, MR M. F. D.	431
†MARSHALL, MRS L. A.	394	MORRIS, MR D.	432
MARVIN, MR R. F.	395	MORRIS, MR M.	433
MCAULIFFE, MR K.	396	†MORTON, MR T.	434
MCCAIN, MR D.	397	†MOSCROP, MRS E.	435
MCCONNOCHIE, MR J. C.	398	MUGGERIDGE, MR M. P.	436
MCCORMACK, MR M.	399	MUIR, MR WILLIAM	437
MCCOURT, MRS M.	400	MULHOLLAND, MR A. B.	438
MCGOVERN, MR T. P.	401	MULLINS, MR J. W.	439
†MCINNES SKINNER, MRS C.	402	MULLINS, MR P.	440
MCKELLAR, MR R.	403	MURPHY, MR F.	441
†MCKENZIE-COLES, MR W. G.	404	MURPHY, MR P. G.	442
†MCKEOWN, MR W	405	MURRAY, MR B. W.	443
MCKIE, MRS V.	406	MURRAY SMITH, MR D. J. G.	444
MCMAHON, MR B. A.	407	MURTAGH, MR F. P.	445
MCMATH, MR B. J.	408	MUSSON, MR W. J.	446
†MCMILLAN, MR M. D.	409		
MEADE, MR MARTYN	410		
MEADE, MR N.	411	**N**	
MEAGHER, MR M. G.	412	NASH, MR C. T.	447
MEEHAN, MR B. J.	413	NAUGHTON, MRS A. M.	448
MELLOR, MR S.	414	NAUGHTON, MR T. J.	449
MILLIGAN, MISS M. K.	415	†NEAVES, MR A. S.	450
MILLMAN, MR B. R.	416	†NEEDHAM, MR J. L.	451
MILLS, MR T. G.	417	†NELSON, MR W. M.	452
†MITCHELL, MR C. W.	418	NEWCOMBE, MR A. G.	453
MITCHELL, MR N. R.	419	NICHOLLS, MR D.	454
MITCHELL, MR PAT	420	NICHOLLS, MR P. F.	455
MITCHELL, MR PHILIP	421	NICHOLSON, MR DAVID	456
MOFFATT, MR D.	422	†NIXON, MR G. R. S.	457
MONTEITH, MR PETER	423	†NOCK, MRS S.	458
MOORE, MR A.	424	NOLAN, MR D. A.	459
MOORE, MR A. L.	425	NORTON, MR J.	460
MOORE, MR G. L.	426		
MOORE, MR G. M.	427	**O**	
†MOORE, MR J. A.	428	O'BRIEN, MR CHARLES	461
MOORE, MR J. S.	429	O'BRIEN, MR D. C.	462

Name	Team No.	Name	Team No.
O'GORMAN, MR W. A.	463	†PLATER, MS L. C.	499
O'GRADY, MR E. J.	464	†POCOCK, MR ROBERT E.	500
O'NEILL, MR J. J.	465	POLGLASE, MR M. J.	501
O'NEILL, MR O.	466	POPHAM, MR C. L.	502
O'SHEA, MR J. G. M.	467	POULTON, MR J. C.	503
O'SULLIVAN, MR EUGENE M.	468	POULTON, MR J. R.	504
O'SULLIVAN, MR R. J.	469	PREECE, MR W. G.	505
†ODELL, MRS S. M.	470	PRENDERGAST, MR P.	506
†OGLE, MR M. B.	471	PRESCOTT BT, SIR MARK	507
OLD, MR J. A. B.	472	†PRICE, MRS A.	508
OLDROYD, MR G. R.	473	†PRICE, MR C. G.	509
OLIVER, MR H. J.	474	PRICE, MR RICHARD	510
OLIVER, MR J. K. M.	475	PRITCHARD, MR P. A.	511
†OWEN, MRS F. M.	476	†PRITCHARD, DR P. L. J.	512
OWEN JUN, MR EDWARD H.	477		
OXX, MR JOHN M.	478		

Q

Name	Team No.
QUINN, MR J. J.	513

P

Name	Team No.
PALLING, MR BRYN	479
PARKER, MR C.	480
PARKES, MR J. E.	481
PARROTT, MRS H.	482
†PATMAN, MISS R. J.	483
PAYNE, MR J. W.	484
PEACOCK, MR J. H.	485
PEACOCK, MR R. E.	486
PEARCE, MR B. A.	487
PEARCE, MR J.	488
PEASE, MR J. E.	489
PERRATT, MISS L. A.	490
PHILLIPS, MR R. T.	491
PICKERING, MR J. A.	492
†PIKE, MR S. L.	493
†PILE, MRS P. M.	494
†PILKINGTON, MRS T. D.	495
PIPE, MR MARTIN C	496
PITMAN, MRS J.	497
†PITTENDRIGH, MR S. I.	498

R

Name	Team No.
RAMSDEN, MRS J. R.	514
†RAW, MR W.	515
REED, MR W. G.	516
RETTER, MRS J. G.	517
REVELEY, MRS G. R.	518
†RICH, MR P. M.	519
RICHARDS, MR G. W.	520
†RICHARDS, MR GRAHAM	521
RICHARDS, MRS LYDIA	522
RITCHENS, MR P. C.	523
†ROBERTSON, MR DAVID	524
†ROBESON, MRS P.	525
†ROBINSON, MR S. J.	526
RODFORD, MR P. R.	527
ROE, MR C. G.	528
ROPER, MR W. M.	529
ROTHWELL, MR B. S.	530
ROUALLE, MR J. DE	531

Name	Team No.	Name	Team No.
ROUGET, MR J. C.	532	STACK, MR T.	568
ROWE, MR R.	533	STEWART, MR A. C.	569
†ROWLAND, MISS M. E.	534	†STIRK, MRS M. K.	570
ROWSELL, MR H. G. M.	535	†STODDART, MR D. R.	571
ROYER-DUPRE, MR A. DE	536	†STOREY, MR F. S.	572
†RUSSELL, MRS A.	537	STOREY, MR W.	573
RUSSELL, MISS L. V.	538	STOUTE, MR M.	574
†RYALL, MR B. J. M.	539	STREETER, MR A. P.	575
RYAN, MR M. J.	540	STRONGE, MR R. M.	576
		SWAN, CAPT. D.	577
S		†SWIERS, MR J. E.	578
SANDERS, MISS B.	541	SWINBANK, MRS A.	579
SAUNDERS, MR M. S.	542	†SWINDLEHURST, MR D. G.	580
SCARGILL, DR J. D.	543		
†SCOTT, MRS E.	544	**T**	
†SCRIVEN, MR B.	545	TATE, MR M.	581
†SCRIVENS, MRS J.	546	TATE, MR T. P.	582
SHEEHAN, MR J. J.	547	†TAYLOR, MRS L. C.	583
SHEPPARD, MR M. I.	548	†TEMPLE, MR B. M.	584
SHERWOOD, MR O. M. C.	549	THOM, MR D. T.	585
SHERWOOD, MR S. E. H.	550	†THOMAS, MRS D.	586
†SHIELS, MR R.	551	THOMPSON, MR RONALD	587
SIDDALL, MISS L. C.	552	†THOMSON, MR A. M.	588
†SIDEBOTTOM, MRS J.	553	THOMSON, MRS DOROTHY	589
SIMPSON, MR RODNEY	554	THOMSON JONES, MR H.	590
SLY, MRS P. M.	555	THOMSON JONES, MR T.	591
SMAGA, MR D.	556	THORNER, MR G. E.	592
SMART, MR B.	557	THORNTON, MR C. W.	593
SMITH, MR ALFRED	558	†TINNING, MR W. H.	594
SMITH, MR C.	559	TODHUNTER, MR D. M.	595
SMITH, MR DENYS	560	TOLLER, MR J. A. R.	596
SMITH, MR J. P.	561	TOMPKINS, MR M. H.	597
SMITH, MR JULIAN S.	562	†TOWNSLEY, MRS P. LAXTO	598
SMITH, MR N. A.	563	TUCK, MR J. C.	599
SMITH, MRS S. J.	564	†TUCKER, MR F. G.	600
†SNOOK, MR L. A.	565	TURNELL, MR ANDREW	601
SPEARING, MR J. L.	566	TURNER, MR W. G. M.	602
SPICER, MR R. C.	567	TWISTON-DAVIES, MR N. A.	603

Name	Team No.
	U
UPSON, MR J. R.	604
†UPSON, MR P. N.	605
USHER, MR M. D. I.	606
	W
†WADE, MR J.	607
†WAGGOTT, MR N.	608
WAINWRIGHT, MR J. S.	609
†WALEY-COHEN, MR ROBERT B	610
WALKER, MR N. J. H.	611
WALL, MR C. F.	612
WALL, MR T. R.	613
†WALTON, MRS K.	614
WALWYN, MR P. T.	615
WANE, MR M.	616
†WARD, MRS V. C.	617
WARING, MRS BARBARA	618
†WARNER, MR KEITH O.	619
WATSON, MR F.	620
WATSON, MR T. R.	621
WATTS, MR J. W.	622
†WEBB, MR H. J. M.	623
WEBBER, MR P. R.	624
WEEDON, MR C. V.	625
†WEGMANN, MR P.	626
WELD, MR D. K.	627
†WELLS, MR L.	628
WEYMES, MR E.	629
WHARTON, MR J. R. H.	630
WHILLANS, MR A. C.	631
WHITAKER, MR R. M.	632
†WHITE, MR G. F.	633
WHITE, MR J.	634
WHITEHOUSE, MISS K.	635
†WHYTE, MR J. W.	636
†WILKINSON, MRS J. V.	637

Name	Team No.
WILKINSON, MR M. J.	638
†WILLIAMS, MR A. J.	639
WILLIAMS, MR D. L.	640
WILLIAMS, MR R. J. R.	641
WILLIAMS, MR S. C.	642
WILLIAMS, MRS S. D.	643
WILLIAMS, MISS VENETIA	644
WILSON, MR A. J.	645
WILSON, MR D. A.	646
WILSON, CAPT J. H.	647
WILTON, MISS S. J.	648
WINGROVE, MR K. G.	649
†WINKWORTH, MR P.	650
†WONNACOTT, MISS L. J.	651
†WOOD, MR R. S.	652
WOODHOUSE, MR R. D. E.	653
WOODMAN, MR S.	654
†WOODROW, MRS A. M.	655
WOODS, MR S. P. C.	656
WRAGG, MR GEOFFREY	657
	Y
YARDLEY, MR F. J.	658
YARDLEY, MR G. H.	659
†YOUNG, MRS J. A. F.	660
†YOUNG, MR J. R. A.	661
†YOUNG, MR W. G.	662

ADDITIONAL TEAMS

DONNELLY, MR T. W.	663
HUGHES, MR P.	664
†LLOYD, MR D. M.	665
MAKIN, MR P. J.	666
†WHITE, MRS F. E.	667

PROPERTY OF HER MAJESTY

The Queen

Colours: Purple, gold braid, scarlet sleeves, black cap with gold fringe

Trained by **Lord Huntingdon**, West Ilsley Stables, Newbury

1 **BEYOND DOUBT**, 4, ch f Belmez (USA)—Highbrow
2 **MAGIC JUNCTION (USA)**, 5, b h Danzig Connection (USA)—Sleeping Beauty
3 **PHANTOM GOLD**, 4, b f Machiavellian (USA)—Trying For Gold (USA)
4 **PIQUANT**, 9, b br g Sharpo—Asnoura (MOR)
5 **RENOWN**, 4, b g Soviet Star (USA)—Starlet
6 **SHAFT OF LIGHT**, 4, gr g Sharrood (USA)—Reflection
7 **STEP ALOFT**, 4, b f Shirley Heights—Pas de Deux
8 **TWILIGHT SLEEP (USA)**, 4, b g Shadeed (USA)—Sleeping Beauty
9 **WHITECHAPEL (USA)**, 8, b g Arctic Tern (USA)—Christchurch (FR)

THREE-YEAR-OLDS

10 **ARABIAN STORY**, gr c Sharrood (USA)—Once Upon A Time
11 **DOCTOR GREEN (FR)**, b c Green Desert (USA)—Highbrow
12 **GIVE AND TAKE**, ch c Generous (IRE)—Starlet
13 **GOLDEN CHOICE**, ch f Midyan (USA)—Trying For Gold (USA)
14 **IDLE FANCY**, b f Mujtahid (USA)—Pizziri
15 **NOTE OF CAUTION (USA)**, b f Diesis—Silver Dollar
16 **PUNKAH (USA)**, b c Lear Fan (USA)—Gentle Persuasion
17 **RASH GIFT**, ch f Cadeaux Genereux—Nettle
18 **STATE CIRCUS**, b f Soviet Star (USA)—Wily Trick (USA)
19 **THREADNEEDLE (USA)**, b g Danzig Connection (USA)—Sleeping Beauty

TWO-YEAR-OLDS

20 **ARTHUR'S SEAT**, b c 29/4 Salse (USA)—Abbey Strand (USA) (Shadeed (USA))
21 **BEACON SILVER**, b f 8/3 Belmez (USA)—Nettle (Kris)
22 B f 27/1 Polish Precedent (USA)—Graphite (USA) (Mr Prospector (USA))
23 **HEBRIDES**, ch f 13/2 Gone West (USA)—Sleeping Beauty (Mill Reef (USA))
24 **JUGGLER**, b c 22/5 Soviet Star (USA)—Wily Trick (USA) (Clever Trick (USA))
25 **PETREL**, gr f 11/2 Petong—Brise de Mer (USA) (Bering)
26 **RUTLAND CHANTRY (USA)**, b c 11/4 Dixieland Band (USA)—Christchurch (FR)
(So Blessed)
27 **SPANISH KNOT (USA)**, b f 28/3 El Gran Senor (USA)—Ingenuity
(Clever Trick (USA))
28 **TEMPTING PROSPECT**, b f 19/2 Shirley Heights—Trying For Gold (USA)
(Northern Baby (CAN))
29 B c 2/5 Red Ransom (USA)—Turn To Money (USA) (Turn To Mars (USA))

Trained by **Mr I. A. Balding**, Park House, Kingsclere

THREE-YEAR-OLDS

30 **DANCING IMAGE**, ch g Salse (USA)—Reflection
31 **NIGHT WATCH (USA)**, b c Night Shift (USA)—Christchurch (FR)
32 **SHINE**, ch f Sharrood (USA)—Varnish
33 **VENDETTA**, b f Belmez (USA)—Storm Warning

PROPERTY OF HER MAJESTY

The Queen

Trained by **Mr I. A. Balding**, Park House, Kingsclere

TWO-YEAR-OLDS
34 **MAYFLOWER**, b f 2/2 Midyan (USA)—Chesnut Tree (USA) (Shadeed (USA))
35 **MISTER GLUM**, ch g 15/4 Ron's Victory (USA)—Australia Fair (AUS)
(Without Fear (FR))
36 **SABINA** b f 14/2 Prince Sabo—High Savannah (Rousillon (USA))

Trained by **Mr Roger J. Charlton**, Beckhampton

THREE-YEAR-OLDS
37 **HIGH NOTE**, b f Shirley Heights—Soprano
38 **KISSING GATE (USA)**, ch f Easy Goer (USA)—Love's Reward

TWO-YEAR-OLDS
39 **BROWBEAT**, ch c 9/3 Diesis—Gentle Persuasion (Bustino)
40 **GHILLIES BALL**, ch c 8/3 Groom Dancer (USA)—Highbrow (Shirley Heights)
41 **MOONSPELL**, b f 13/2 Batshoof—Shimmer (Bustino)
42 B c 15/2 Trempolino (USA)—Zonda (Fabulous Dancer (USA))

2

THE PROPERTY OF
H.M. QUEEN ELIZABETH THE QUEEN MOTHER

Colours: Blue, buff stripes, blue sleeves, black cap with gold tassel

Trained by **Mr N. J. Henderson**, Seven Barrows, Lambourn

1 **BOLD ROMEO**, 4, b g Bold Owl—First Romance
2 **BRAES OF MAR**, 6, b g Bustino—Barbella
3 **CLOSE HARMONY**, 4, ch f Bustino—Highland Lyric
4 **NEARCO BAY (NZ)**, 12, b g Double Nearco (USA)—Ahi Ua (NZ)
5 **STAMP DUTY**, 9, b g Sunyboy—Royal Seal

Trained by **Mr I. A. Balding**, Park House, Kingsclere

6 **BASS ROCK**, 8, b g Bellypha—Dunfermline
7 **BEWITCH** 6, b m Idiot's Delight—First Romance
8 **MOAT GARDEN (USA)**, 8, b g Sportin' Life (USA)—Round Tower

Trained by **Mr T. Thomson Jones**, The Croft, Upper Lambourn

9 **KEEL ROW**, 6, b m Relkino—Caserta
10 **NORMAN CONQUEROR**, 11, br g Royal Fountain—Constant Rose

3   MR M. J. AHERN, Swindon

Postal: **King Edward Place, Foxhill, Wanborough, Swindon, SN4 0DS.**

Phone: **(01488) 73559**

1 5, Ch g Black Minstrel—Boreen Princess **Mr Tom Segrue**
2 7, B g Rising—Brave Dorney **Mr Tom Segrue**
3 **BRIDEPARK ROSE (IRE)**, 8, b m Kemal (FR)—Elite Lady **Mr Tom Segrue**
4 **DEE EM AITCH**, 7, b g Lightning Dealer—Some Say **Mrs D. M. Hickman**
5 **ILEWIN**, 9, br g Ile de Bourbon (USA)—City Swinger **Middx Packaging Ltd**
6 **ILEWIN GERRY (IRE)**, 6, br g Strong Gale—Red Pine **Mr Tom Segrue**
7 **ILEWIN JANINE (IRE)**, 5, b m Soughaan (USA)—Mystery Queen **Mr Tom Segrue**
8 **KATIE'S KID**, 6, br g Balidar—Khahmens Delight **Mrs Susan J. Harraway**
9 **KAYTAK (FR)**, 9, b g Mouktar—Kaythama **T. J. Myles Co (Contractors)**
10 **MAYBE MOSES (IRE)**, 6, b g Le Moss—Jill Owens **T. J. Myles Co Contractors)**
11 **NEVEROLD (IRE)**, 6, br g Never So Bold—Fraulein Tobin (USA) **Mr Tom Segrue**
12 **PATONG BEACH**, 6, ch m Infantry—Winter Resort **Middx Packaging Ltd**
13 5, Ch g Phardante (FR)—Some Gale **T. J. Myles Co (Contractors)**
14 **VENUS VICTORIOUS (IRE)**, 5, ch m Tate Gallery (USA)—Persian Royale **Mr Tom Segrue**

Jockey (NH): M A Fitzgerald (10-0).

Conditional: M Kelly (9-10).

Lady Rider: Emma Folkes (8-0).

4   MR JONATHAN AKEHURST, Upper Lambourn

Postal: **Neardown Stables, Upper Lambourn, Hungerford, Berks, RG17 8QP.**

Phone: **(01488) 72688 FAX (01488) 72199 MOBILE (0860) 797111**

1 **ANILAFFED**, 6, b g Ilium—Hunt's Katie **Mrs Stella McLean**
2 **ANY MINUTE NOW (IRE)**, 6, b g Alzao (USA)—Miss Siddons **Mrs Susan Crane**
3 **CAROLES EXPRESS**, 8, ch m Scottish Reel—Peregrine Falcon **Mrs Susan Crane**
4 **EXPRESS ROUTING**, 4, b g Aragon—San Marguerite **The Alper Levy Partnership**
5 **FRONT PAGE**, 9, ch g Adonijah—Recent Events **Amity Finance Ltd**
6 **LORD OBERON (IRE)**, 8, b g Fairy King (USA)—Vaguely Jade **Ross, Pearce, Kehoe & Gocher**
7 **ROI DE LA MER (IRE)**, 5, b h Fairy King (USA)—Sea Mistress **Foundation Developments Ltd**
8 **SMART REBAL (IRE)**, 8, b g Final Straw—Tomfoolery **The Albert Arms**
9 **YOUNG LUCKY**, 5, b g Alleging (USA)—By Chance **The Young Lucky Partnership**

THREE-YEAR-OLDS

10 **BAKER**, b g Cigar—Bread 'n Honey **Mrs John Akehurst**
11 **GEE GEE TEE**, ch c Superlative—Glorietta (USA) **Mr John Trickett**
12 **MANDERELLA**, b f Clantime—Ascot Lass **Mrs M. J. Wells**
13 **NEWLANDS CORNER**, b f Forzando—Nice Lady **The Jolly Skolars**

TWO-YEAR-OLDS

14 **ADVANCE REPRO**, b f 11/2 Risk Me (FR)—Sunday Sport Gem (Lomond (USA)) **Advance Ltd**
15 B f 20/3 Midyan (USA)—Crymlyn (Welsh Pageant)
16 B c 19/4 Mazilier (USA)—Hen Night (Mummy's Game)
17 B c 19/4 Mac's Imp (USA)—Houwara (IRE) (Darshaan) **The Four Four Four Partnership**
18 **MARENGO**, b c 12/3 Never So Bold—Born To Dance (Dancing Brave (USA)) **Robert Lee International**
19 **MISS DARLING**, b f 25/2 Clantime—Slipperose (Persepolis (FR)) **Normandy Developments Ltd**
20 B c 3/1 Risk Me (FR)—Moonlight Princess (Alias Smith (USA)) **Mr C. Mulally**
21 **SOUTH WEST**, ch c 29/3 Sharpo—Ward One (Mr Flourocarbon) **Normandy Developments Ltd**
22 **TRY ME AND SEE**, ch c 11/3 Rock City—Al Raja (Kings Lake (USA)) **The Ashbourne Levy Partnership**

MR JONATHAN AKEHURST—continued

Other Owners: Mr Peter M. Crane, Mrs J. R. Foster, Mr Geoffrey C. Greenwood, Fraser Miller, Mr Bruce Montgomery, Mrs Jean Montgomery, Maxwell Morrison, Mr Andrew Ross, Mr B. G. Slade, Mr A. R. Travers.

Jockey (Flat): T R Quinn (w.a.).

Jockey (NH): Graham Bradley (w.a.).

Amateur: Miss Jane Allison.

5   MR R. P. J. AKEHURST, Epsom

Postal: **South Hatch Stables, 44 Burgh Heath Road, Epsom, Surrey, KT17 4LX.**
Phone: **(01372) 748800 FAX (01372) 739410**

1 **ABSOLUTELY FAYRE**, 5, ch h Absalom—June Fayre **The Bloodstock Brothers-Four Seasons**
2 **ADMIRAL'S WELL (IRE)**, 6, b h Sadler's Wells (USA)—Exotic Bride (USA) **Mr A. D. Spence**
3 **ANISTOP**, 4, b c Nomination—Pounelta **Mrs A. Valentine**
4 **ASTRAC (IRE)**, 5, b g Nordico (USA)—Shirleen **Mr C. J. Titcomb**
5 **BALANCE OF POWER**, 4, b g Ballacashtal (CAN)—Moreton's Martha **J. D. Falvey**
6 **BALLYNAKELLY**, 4, ch g Deploy—Musical Charm (USA) **Y. M. Y. Partnership**
7 **BIMSEY (IRE)**, 6, b h Horage—Cut It Out **Mr Aidan J. Ryan**
8 **BOLIVAR (IRE)**, 4, b g Kahyasi—Shuss (USA) **Bel Leisure Ltd**
9 **CHEZ CATALAN**, 5, b h Niniski (USA)—Miss Saint-Cloud **Dr G. Madan Mohan**
10 **CROFT SALLY**, 4, ch f Crofthall—Sannavally **Miss V. Pratt**
11 **DANCING SENSATION (USA)**, 9, b m Faliraki—Sweet Satina (USA) **Chelgate Public Relations**
12 **DARTER (IRE)**, 4, b c Darshaan—Mamouna (USA) **Mr A. D. Spence**
13 **DASHING DANCER (IRE)**, 5, ch g Conquering Hero (USA)—Santa Maria (GER) **P. F. Roberts**
14 **DOMULLA**, 6, br h Dominion—Ulla Laing **A. W. Boon**
15 **EDBAYSAAN (IRE)**, 6, b h Slip Anchor—Legend of Arabia **Sheikh Essa Bin Mubarak**
16 **ENGLISH INVADER**, 5, b h Rainbow Quest (USA)—Modica **M. J. Blackburn**
17 **EXHIBIT AIR (IRE)**, 6, b m Exhibitioner—Airy Queen (USA) **Mr A. J. Doyle**
18 **FAHS (USA)**, 4, br c Riverman (USA)—Tanwi **City Industrial Supplies Ltd**
19 **FIONN DE COOL (IRE)**, 5, b g Mazaad—Pink Fondant **Mr R. F. Kilby**
20 **FOREST STAR (USA)**, 7, b g Green Forest (USA)—Al Madina (USA) **Mrs A. Naughton**
21 **GREATEST**, 5, b g Superlative—Pillowing **Invoshire Ltd**
22 **JELLABY ASKHIR**, 4, b c Salse (USA)—Circus Act **Sheikh Essa Bin Mubarak**
23 **KADAMANN (IRE)**, 4, b c Doyoun—Kadissya (USA) **Sir Eric Parker**
24 **KETABI (USA)**, 5, ch g Alydar (USA)—Ivory Fields (USA) **Bob and Diana Whitney**
25 **KRAYYAN DAWN**, 6, ch h Krayyan—Tana Mist **R. E. Greatorex**
26 **LATAHAAB (USA)**, 5, b h Lyphard (USA)—Eye Drop (USA) **L. M. Bush**
27 **MEDITERRANEO**, 5, ch g Be My Guest (USA)—Model Bride (USA) **Bob and Diana Whitney**
28 **MIROSWAKI (USA)**, 6, b g Miswaki (USA)—Miroswava (FR) **Mrs A. Naughton**
29 **MISTER O'GRADY (IRE)**, 5, b g Mister Majestic—Judy O'Grady **City Industrial Supplies Ltd**
30 **MR BROWNING (USA)**, 5, br g Al Nasr (FR)—Crinoline **Mrs M. O'Shea**
31 **MRS DOUBTFIRE (IRE)**, 4, ch f Magical Strike (USA)—Eurynome **Mr R. N. C. Lynch**
32 **NEWPORT KNIGHT**, 5, ch g Bairn (USA)—Clara Barton **Muirmax Alper Partnership**
33 **NORSONG**, 4, b c Northern State (USA)—Winsong Melody **Fairy Story Partnership**
34 **PHARAMINEUX**, 10, ch g Pharly (FR)—Miss Longchamp **K. R. Snellings**
35 **PODDINGTON**, 5, b g Crofthall—Bold Gift **Miss V. Pratt**
36 **PROTON**, 6, b g Sure Blade (USA)—Banket **The Persian War Partnership**
37 **QUINTUS DECIMUS**, 6, b c Nordico (USA)—Lemon Balm **Penllyne Properties**
38 **REIMEI**, 7, b g Top Ville—Brilliant Reay **Mr I. Goldsmith**
39 **ROYAL CARLTON (IRE)**, 4, b g Mulholande (USA)—Saintly Angel **Mrs Ann Doyle**
40 **SEJAAL (IRE)**, 4, b g Persian Heights—Cremets **Mr J. Snow**
41 **SHADIRWAN (IRE)**, 5, b h Kahyasi—Shademah **Mr Clive Batt**

MR R. P. J. AKEHURST—continued

42 **SHARP PROSPECT**, 6, ch h Sharpo—Sabatina (USA) **Four Seasons Racing**
43 **SHUJAN (USA)**, 7, b h Diesis—Linda's Magic (USA) **Sir Eric Parker**
44 **SILVER GROOM (IRE)**, 6, gr g Shy Groom (USA)—Rustic Lawn **The Silver Darling Partnership**
45 **SPECIAL RISK (IRE)**, 6, br g Simply Great (FR)—Ahonita **M. E. Lee Partners**
46 **WAYNE COUNTY (IRE)**, 6, b h Sadler's Wells (USA)—Detroit (FR) **Mrs A. Naughton**
47 **WELL ARRANGED (IRE)**, 5, ch h Bold Arrangement—Eurynome **Mrs Anne-Marie Hamilton**
48 **WILDFIRE (SWI)**, 5, br g Beldale Flutter (USA)—Little White Star **Mr R. F. Kilby**
49 **WILLIE CONQUER**, 4, ch g Master Willie—Maryland Cookie (USA) **Mr R. Tooth**
50 **WISHING (USA)**, 5, b h Lyphard's Wish (FR)—Vivre Libre (USA) **Mr A. D. Spence**
51 **YEATH (IRE)**, 4, ch g Exhibitioner—Grain of Sand **Ruelles Partners**

THREE-YEAR-OLDS

52 **AMEER ALFAYAAFI (IRE)**, b g Mujtahid (USA)—Sharp Circle (IRE) **Lime St. Racing Syndicate**
53 **JOLI'S SON**, gr c Joli Wasfi (USA)—Hagen's Bargain **Mr C. Buckerfield**
54 **MACLOUD (IRE)**, br g Mac's Imp (USA)—Cloud Nine **Mr C. J. Titcomb**
55 **MARL**, ch f Lycius (USA)—Pamela Peach **Sir Eric Parker**
56 **POLONAISE PRINCE (USA)**, b c Alleged (USA)—La Polonaise (USA) **Four Seasons Racing**
57 **PRIMELTA**, b f Primo Dominie—Pounelta **Mrs A. Valentine**
58 **STRONZ (IRE)**, br c Classic Music (USA)—Carnival Fugue **Normandy Developments (London)**
59 **TRACI'S CASTLE (IRE)**, b f Ajraas (USA)—Mia Gigi **Fernray Ltd**

TWO-YEAR-OLDS

60 **LARKSTYLE**, ch c 23/3 Rock City—Bodham (Bustino) **Normandy Developments (London)**
61 **NOBLE STORY**, br f 25/1 Last Tycoon—Certain Story (Known Fact (USA)) **Fairy Story Partnership**
62 **NORTHERN PASS (USA)**, ch f 11/2 Crowning (USA)—North To Pine Pass (USA) (Holy War (USA)) **Fernray Ltd**
63 Ch c 11/4 Mac's Imp (USA)—Pepilin (Coquelin (USA))
64 **PEPPIATT**, ch c 31/3 Efisio—Fleur du Val (Valiyar) **Kevin Reddington & Partners**
65 **RAFFELINA (USA)**, gr f 14/3 Carson City (USA)—
                              Reine de Danse (Nureyev (USA)) **Normandy Developments (London)**
66 Ch c 13/5 Interrex (CAN)—Striking Image (IRE) (Flash of Steel) **Mr E. Duggan**
67 **SUCH BOLDNESS**, b c 14/2 Persian Bold—Bone China (IRE) (Sadler's Wells (USA)) **Mrs M. O'Shea**
68 B c 3/5 Deploy—Super Sally (Superlative) **Mr Clive Batt**
69 **SWINGING THE BLUES (IRE)**, b c 1/3 Bluebird (USA)—
                              Winsong Melody (Music Maestro) **Fairy Story Partnership**

Other Owners: Mr A. L. Alper, Aston House Stud, Mrs Mary Doyle, Food Brokers Ltd, Mr B. W. Greaves, Mr Paul V. Jackson, Jaytee Seafoods Ltd, Mr Alan Leiper, Mr Richard Levy, Mr J. K. Lomax, Mrs M. Lynch, Mr Nigel S. Scandrett, Mr Stephen G. Smith, Mr N. E. Stewart, Mr George Taiano, The Winning Line Racing Club, Mr James Thorburn-Muirhead, Mr Patrick Veitch.

Jockey (Flat): T R Quinn (w.a.).

Apprentices: T Ashley (8-0), D Denby (7-7).

Conditional: S Ryan (9-7).

6   MR D. S. ALDER, Belford

Postal: **Lucker Mill, Lucker, Belford, Northd, NE70 7JH.**

1 **ARCTIC MUSIC**, 7, b m Tudor Diver—Dundrum Melody VII **Mrs D. S. Alder**
2 **BAD TRADE**, 14, ch g Over The River (FR)—Churchtown Lass **Mr D. S. Alder**
3 **CAMPTOSAURUS (IRE)**, 7, br g Strong Gale—Baybush **Mrs D. S. Alder**
4 **INISHGLASS**, 6, b g Oats—Rock Dodger **Mrs D. S. Alder**
5 **MISS MCCORMICK (IRE)**, 7, gr m Roselier (FR)—Glens Hansel **Mrs D. S. Alder**
6 **ROYAL RANK (USA)**, 6, ch g Miswaki (USA)—Westminster Palace **Mr D. S. Alder**

7 MR HAMISH H ALEXANDER, Lanchester

Postal: **Partridge Close Stud, Lanchester, Co. Durham, DH7 3SZ.**

Phone: **(01207) 520066 OR (01207) 520896 FAX (01207) 520066**

1 **BALZINO (USA)**, 7, ch g Trempolino (USA)—Royal Procession (USA) **Hamish Alexander**
2 **HEATHERIDGE (IRE)**, 6, b m Carlingford Castle—Mrs Hill **Neil Kennedy**
3 **HOT PUNCH**, 7, ch g Dara Monarch—Glebehill **Mr Hamish Alexander**
4 **LEVEL EDGE**, 5, b m Beveled (USA)—Luaga **R. V. Jackson**
5 **PERCY PIT**, 7, b g Pitpan—Technical Merit **Mr Hamish Alexander**
6 **SARACEN PRINCE (USA)**, 4, ch g War (USA)—My Gallant Duchess (USA) **Alan Atkinson**
7 **WAIT YOU THERE**, 11, b g Nureyev (USA)—Ma Mere L'Oie (FR) **Mr Hamish Alexander**
8 **WELL BANK**, 9, b g Tudor Diver—Technical Merit **Mrs Doreen Swinburn**
9 **WHAT'S SECRETO (USA)**, 4, gr g Secreto (USA)—What A Shack (USA) **Alan Atkinson**

Jockeys (NH): B Storey (w.a.), L Wyer (w.a.).

Conditional: D Thomas.

Amateur: Mr S Swiers (10-4).

8 MR A. R. ALLAN, Cornhill-on-Tweed

Postal: **Pallinsburn Stables, Cornhill-on-Tweed, Northd, TD12 4SG.**

Phone: **CROOKHAM (01890) 820581**

1 **ADAMATIC (IRE)**, 5, b g Henbit (USA)—Arpal Magic **Mr Geoff Adam**
2 **ASTRALEON (IRE)**, 8, b g Caerleon (USA)—Noah's Acky Astra **Mr J. Stephenson**
3 **BIT O MAGIC (IRE)**, 4, ch g Henbit (USA)—Arpal Magic **Mr Geoff Adam**
4 **BORIS BROOK**, 5, ch g Meadowbrook—Crella **Mrs V. Scott-Watson**
5 **BRIAR'S DELIGHT**, 8, b g Idiot's Delight—Briar Park **Mr A. Clark**
6 **DOUBLING DICE**, 5, b g Jalmood—Much Too Risky **Mr R. Allan**
7 **FASTER RON (IRE)**, 5, b g Rontino—Ambitious Lady **Mrs V. Scott-Watson**
8 **HIGH PYRENEES**, 4, b g Shirley Heights—Twyla **Mr J. Stephenson**
9 **KING OF SHOW (IRE)**, 5, b g Green Desert (USA)—Don't Rush (USA) **Mr M. C. Boyd**
10 **LATVIAN**, 9, gr g Rousillon (USA)—Lorelene (FR) **Mr I. Bell**
11 **LISMORE LAD**, 7, b g Full Extent (USA)—Highlands Park **Mr J. J. Jeffrey**
12 **MY HANDY MAN**, 5, ch g Out of Hand—My Home **Mr I. Bell**
13 5, B m Risk Me (FR)—Queen's Lake **Mr James Baxter**
14 **TEACHER (IRE)**, 6, b g Caerleon (USA)—Clunk Click **Mr R. Allan**
15 **TRIENNIUM (USA)**, 7, ch g Vaguely Noble—Triple Tipple (USA) **Mr M. C. Boyd**
16 **VICTOR LASZLO**, 4, br g Ilium—Report 'em (USA) **Mr R. Allan**

Other Owners: Mr T. W. Beaty, Mr A. H. Dunlop, Mr Robert Gibbons, Mr L. Grant, Marion Grant, R. P. Adam Ltd, Mr I. Rodden, Mr I. Rutherford, Mr W. Thyne, Mr George B. Turnbull.

Jockeys (Flat): J Fortune (w.a.), J Weaver (w.a.).

Jockey (NH): B Storey (10-0, w.a.).

Conditional: Stephen Melrose (9-7).

Amateur: Andrew Robson (10-7).

9   MR C. N. ALLEN, Newmarket

Postal: **Shadowfax Stables, Hamilton Road, Newmarket, Suffolk, CB8 0NQ.**
Phone: **(01638) 667870 FAX (01638) 668005**

1 **ACHILLES HEEL**, 5, br g Superlative—Ela-Yianni-Mou **Four J's Syndicate**
2 **DARK ROMANCE (IRE)**, 7, b m Sarab—Narnia **Mr A. A. Goldson**
3 **GOOD SO FA (IRE)**, 4, b g Taufan (USA)—Future Shock **Mrs J. Williams**
4 **MIGHTY SENATE**, 4, b c Warning—Marseillaise **Four J's Syndicate**
5 **MISS MERCY (IRE)**, 4, b f Law Society (USA)—Missing You **Mr Jeff Lewis**
6 **RANZEL**, 6, b g Shirley Heights—Kanz (USA) **Eclipse Management Ltd**

THREE-YEAR-OLDS

7 **LADY PEPPERPOT (IRE)**, ch f Salt Dome (USA)—Idle Tale (USA) **Mrs Gill Forsyth**
8 **SPIRITO LIBRO (USA)**, b f Lear Fan (USA)—Teeming Shore (USA) **Camelot Racing**
9 **SYLVAN PRINCESS**, b f Sylvan Express—Ela-Yianni-Mou **Four J's Syndicate**

TWO-YEAR-OLDS

10 B c 5/4 Reprimand—Doppio (Dublin Taxi) **Camelot Racing Ltd**
11 B f 6/4 Lead On Time (USA)—Funoon (IRE) (Kris) **Camelot Racing Ltd**
12 B c 10/3 Sharpo—La Reine de France (Queen's Hussar) **Camelot Racing Ltd**
13 B c 23/3 Puissance—Miss Milton (Young Christopher) **Camelot Racing Ltd**
14 Ch f 20/2 Risk Me (FR)—Red Sails (Town And Country) **Chiquita Lodge Stud Ltd**
15 Ch f 15/1 Phone Trick (USA)—Song of You (USA) (Blushing Groom (FR)) **Chiquita Lodge Stud Ltd**

Other Owners: Mr J. R. Bamforth, Mr P. Charalambous, Mrs T. Charalambous, Mr Tom Mowbray.

Jockeys (Flat): L Dettori (8-4, w.a.), T Ives, J Quinn (7-7).

Jockeys (NH): D Bridgwater (w.a.), J McLaughlin (9-7).

Amateur: V Lukaniuk (9-0).

Lady Rider: Mrs R Allen (9-4).

10   MR J. S. ALLEN, Alcester

Postal: **Alne Park, Park Lane, Great Alne, Alcester, B49 6HU.**
Phone: **STABLES (01789) 488469 OFFICE (01789) 299492 FAX (01789) 415330**

1 **ALWAYS ALEX**, 9, b m Final Straw—Two High **Mrs Carol Allen**
2 5, Ch g Nicholas Bill—Rosalina **J. Allen**
3 4, B f Welsh Captain—Singing Hills **J. Allen**

TWO-YEAR-OLDS

4 B g 30/4 Welsh Captain—Singing Hills (Crash Course) **J. Allen**

Amateur: Mr Noel Bradley (9-7).

Lady Rider: Miss Ann Stockell (9-7).

11   MR ROGER ALLSOP, Ledbury

Postal: **Tattersalls, Hope End, Ledbury, Herefordshire, HR8 1JQ.**
Phone: **(01531) 632239 FAX (01684) 892337**

1 **AEOLIAN**, 5, b g Ovac (ITY)—Snare **Mrs Yvonne Allsop**
2 **BORO HILL (IRE)**, 7, ch g Arapahos (FR)—Marbles **Mr Roger Allsop**
3 **COLWALL**, 5, br g Derring Rose—Katebird **Mrs Yvonne Allsop**
4 **LEDBURIAN**, 6, br g Primitive Rising (USA)—Pretty Lass **Mrs Yvonne Allsop**
5 **MADAM POLLY**, 4, br f Buckley—Vonnage **Mrs Yvonne Allsop**
6 **MALVERNIAN**, 10, br g Fine Blade (USA)—Nesford **Mrs Yvonne Allsop**

Other Owners: Malvair Group Plc.

Amateur: Mr M Rimell.

12   MR R. H. ALNER, Blandford

Postal: **Locketts Farm, Droop, Blandford, Dorset, DT11 0EZ.**
Phone: **(01258) 817271 MOBILE (0860) 669959**

1 **ALACUE**, 6, b br m Al Amead—Chalk Your Cue **Mrs Barbara Daly**
2 **BEAUREPAIRE (IRE)**, 8, b g Beau Charmeur (FR)—Running Stream **Pell-mell Partners**
3 **BISHOPS HALL**, 10, br g Pimpernels Tune—Mariner's Dash **Mr T. J. Carroll**
4 **BLAKE'S WONDER (IRE)**, 6, gr g Sexton Blake—Wonderful Ana **The Sextet Partnership**
5 **BLUSTERY DAY**, 6, b g Reesh—Lindy Ann
6 **CANBRANO'S LAD**, 5, gr g Zambrano—Canny Member **Mr H. John Irish**
7 **COLUMCILLE**, 10, b m St Columbus—Damside **Mr R. Alner**
8 **COOL DAWN (IRE)**, 8, br g Over The River (FR)—Aran Tour **The Hon D. Harding**
9 **DECISIVE SPICE**, 7, ch g Vital Season—Opt Out **Mr H. Wellstead**
10 **FLYER'S NAP**, 10, b g Rolfe (USA)—English Flyer **Mr R. J. Tory**
11 **GILLAN COVE (IRE)**, 7, b g The Parson—Shanban **Forum Racing**
12 **HARWELL LAD (IRE)**, 7, b g Over The River (FR)—Gayles Approach **Mr H. Wellstead**
13 **HOPS AND POPS**, 9, b m Lighter—Panda Pops **The Happy Band**
14 **JUST DIMPLE (IRE)**, 5, b g Mister Lord (USA)—Cheers Don **Mr R. Alner**
15 **LETS RUMBLE (IRE)**, 7, b g Buckskin (FR)—Cherry Branch **Mr H. V. Perry**
16 **LIFT AND LOAD (USA)**, 9, b g Lyphard's Wish (FR)—Dorit (USA) **Mr R. W. Champion**
17 **LONICERA**, 6, br m Sulaafah (USA)—Cygne
18 **LORNA-GAIL**, 10, b m Callernish—Gilt Course **Mr H. V. Perry**
19 **MALWOOD CASTLE (IRE)**, 6, b g Bustineto—Boreen Nua **Mrs U. Wainwright**
20 **MASTER RYON**, 8, b g Rymer—Arctic Lion **Mr H. H. Richards**
21 **PHILATELIC (IRE)**, 5, br g Buckskin (FR)—Sami (FR) **Mr P. M. De Wilde**
22 **PURBECK POLLY**, 6, ch m Pollerton—Warwick Air **Mr H. V. Perry**
23 **REX TO THE RESCUE (IRE)**, 8, ch g Remainder Man—Cool Blue **Mr P. F. Gough**
24 **SECRET BID (IRE)**, 6, ch g Seclude (USA)—Trial Bid **The Droop Partners**
25 **SEVEN OF DIAMONDS**, 11, b g Comedy Star (USA)—Priceless Gem **Mr T. J. Keeping**
26 **SHAMARPHIL**, 10, b m Sunyboy—Chaffcombe **Miss Susan Pitman**
27 **SUPER TACTICS (IRE)**, 8, b g Furry Glen—Hilarys Pet **Mr H. V. Perry**
28 **VICOSA (IRE)**, 7, gr g General View—Mesena **Diamond Racing Ltd**
29 **WHIRLY (IRE)**, 7, b g Strong Gale—Divine Drapes **Pell-mell Partners**
30 **WHO AM I (IRE)**, 6, b g Supreme Leader—Bonny Joe **Mr James Burley**
31 **WINNIE LORRAINE**, 11, b m St Columbus—Win Green Hill **Mrs S. Fry**
32 **WINSPIT (IRE)**, 6, b g Desert of Wind (USA)—Celestial Drive **Mrs J. E. Purdie**

Other Owners: Mr H. S. Butt, Mr J. Chromiak, Mr B. Dennett, Mr Richard Gilder, Mr R. A. Gumm, Mr J. W. Horn, Mr M. T. Lockyer, Mr B. Nettley, Mr G. D. Nettley, Mr Anthony Pye-Jeary, Mrs E. J. Read, Mr S. G. Stickland, Mr Laurence Tarlo, Mr G. G. H. Tory, Mrs V. A. Tory, Mr D. F. Tucker, Mr Stephen T. Vass, Mr L. Warren.

Conditional: P Carey (9-7).

Amateur: Mr P Henley (9-10).

Lady Rider: Miss S Barraclough (9-7).

13   MR E. J. ALSTON, Preston

Postal: **Edges Farm Stables, Chapel Lane, Longton, Preston, PR4 5NA.**

Phone: **(01772) 612120 FAX (01772) 612120 MOBILE (0831) 680131**

1 **AMBIDEXTROUS (IRE)**, 4, b c Shareef Dancer (USA)—Amber Fizz (USA) **Mrs Carol P. McPhail**
2 **BOLD ELECT**, 8, b g Electric—Famous Band (USA) **Mr G. Lowe**
3 **BOUNDARY EXPRESS**, 4, b g Sylvan Express—Addison's Jubilee **Mrs Stella Barclay**
4 **BOWLAND PARK**, 5, b m Nicholas Bill—Macusla **Mrs Stella Barclay**
5 **CHINOUR (IRE)**, 8, b g Dalsaan—Chishtiya **Mr Frank McKevitt**
6 **CITIZEN BAND (IRE)**, 8, ch g M Double M (USA)—Last Act **Mr William Carroll**
7 **FLOATING LINE**, 8, ch g Bairn—County Line **Mr G. Lowe**
8 **FOUR LANE FLYER**, 4, b f Sayf El Arab (USA)—Collegian **4 Lane Accident Management**
9 **GOLDEN NUGGET**, 9, b g Furry Glen—Ivy Rambler **Mr William Carroll**
10 **GONDO**, 9, br g Mansingh (USA)—Secret Valentine **Mrs Helen O'Brien**
11 **GRACEFUL LADY**, 6, br m Bold Arrangement—Northern Lady **Mr S. Lee**
12 **GULF SHAADI**, 4, b c Shaadi—Ela Meem (USA) **The Bibby Halliday Partnership**
13 **HAWWAM**, 10, b g Glenstal (USA)—Hone **North West Racing Club Owners Club**
14 **KUMMEL KING**, 8, b g Absalom—Louise **Webb/Jones**
15 **LANCASHIRE LIFE (IRE)**, 5, b g Petorius—Parlais **Mrs D. Lawrence**
16 **MARGARETROSE ANNA**, 4, b f Handsome Sailor—Be Bold **Mrs Pam Slawson**
17 **MAROWINS**, 7, ch g Sweet Monday—Top Cover **Whitehills Racing Syndicate**
18 **MILL DANCER (IRE)**, 4, b f Broken Hearted—Theatral **Mrs Dot Jones**
19 **MOONLIGHT VENTURE**, 4, b g Jupiter Island—Moonlight Bay **Mr R. Smalley**
20 **NO COMEBACKS**, 8, b m Last Tycoon—Dead End **Mr Lionel Snowden**
21 **NORTHERN CHARMER**, 4, b g Charmer—Trading **The Bibby Halliday Partnership**
22 **RINUS MANOR (IRE)**, 5, b g Ballad Rock—Never Never Land **Mr A. M. Proos**
23 **RYMER'S RASCAL**, 4, b g Rymer—City Sound **Mr Brian Chambers**
24 **TANAH MERAH (IRE)**, 5, b g Alzao (USA)—Lady's Bridge (USA) **L.Mortimer (Bury) Ltd Crane & Plant Hire**
25 **ZIGGY'S DANCER (USA)**, 5, b h Ziggy's Boy (USA)—My Shy Dancer (USA) **Mr John Patrick Barry**

THREE-YEAR-OLDS

26 **RINUS MAGIC**, ch c Timeless Times (USA)—Callace **Mr A. M. Proos**

TWO-YEAR-OLDS

27 B c 19/2 Rambo Dancer (CAN)—Lariston Gale (Pas de Seul) **Mrs Carol P. McPhail**
28 B f 30/4 Petorius—Theatral (Orchestra) **Mr D. Hilton**
29 **WHITTLE TIMES**, ch f 12/2 Timeless Times (USA)—La Pepper (Workboy) **Whittle Partnership**

Other Owners: Mrs S. Y. Alston, Mr T. Bailey, Mr S. Bibby, Mr W. Brereton, Mr G. Brockbank, Mr D. Dowey, Mr P. D. Ebdon, Mrs Susan Gorton, Mr M. J. Halliday, Mr R. Halliday, Mrs Julie A. Jones, Mr P. Jones, Mr Michael Shaun Kelly, Mrs B Keogh, Mr Ian Lawrence, Mr D. Marshall, Mr J. Marshall, Mrs V. Nolan, Mr G. G. Sanderson, Mr Raymond Squire, Mr Alan Thorpe, Mr M. Twentyman, Mr A. C. Webb, Mrs D. E. Williams, Mr J. P. Wilson.

Jockey (Flat): K Fallon (8-1).

Apprentice: C Halliwell (7-0).

14   MR JACK ANDREWS, Ladybank

Postal: **Stratheden House, Ladybank, Cupar, Fife, KY7 7JS.**

1 **MELODY DANCER**, 5, b g Rambo Dancer (CAN)—Secret Song **Mr J. R. Andrews**

15   MR D. W. P. ARBUTHNOT, Compton

Postal: **Hamilton Stables, Compton, Newbury, Berks, RG16 0QT.**

Phone: **COMPTON (01635) 578427 FAX (01635) 578427 MOBILE (0836) 276464**

1 **DISTANT ECHO (IRE)**, 6, b g Seamanship—Ripperidge **Mr M. Fordham & Mr B. N. Fulton**
2 **FRANKLY FRAN**, 4, b f Petorius—Sunita **Mr Philip Banfield**
3 **JOHN LEE HOOKER**, 4, b g Superlative—Aunt Jemima **Mr Christopher Wright**
4 **LOVE LEGEND**, 11, ch g Glint of Gold—Sweet Emma **Mr George S. Thompson**
5 **MELASUS (IRE)**, 4, ch g Nashamaa—Sweet Camden **Mrs S. Watts**
6 **MONEY POINT SAM (IRE)**, 4, ch g Moscow Society (USA)—Ripperidge **Mr M. Fordham & Mr B. N. Fulton**
7 **NEVER SO RITE (IRE)**, 4, b f Nordico (USA)—Nephrite **Mr J. S. Gutkin**
8 **QUEST AGAIN**, 5, ch g Then Again—Eagle's Quest **Miss P. E. Decker**
9 **ROBELLION**, 5, b g Robellino (USA)—Tickled Trout **Mr George S. Thompson**
10 **SALTIS (IRE)**, b, ch g Salt Dome (USA)—Mrs Tittlemouse **Mr Noel Cronin**
11 **SECRETARY OF STATE**, 10, b g Alzao (USA)—Colonial Line (USA) **Mr W. H. Ponsonby**
12 **STRAT'S LEGACY**, 9, b g Chukaroo—State Romance **Mr Jack Blumenow**
13 **VERDE LUNA**, 4, b g Green Desert (USA)—Mamaluna (USA) **Mr J. A. Leek**

THREE-YEAR-OLDS

14 **CANADIAN JIVE**, b f Dominion—Ural Dancer **Mr T. C. Brown**
15 **DANDE FLYER**, b c Clantime—Lyndseylee **Dandelion Distribution Ltd**
16 **FARAWAY WATERS**, ch f Pharly (FR)—Gleaming Water **Mr R. Crutchley**
17 **MAC OATES**, b c Bairn (USA)—Bit of A Lass **Mr D. N. Larke**
18 **PREMIER GENERATION (IRE)**, b c Cadeaux Genereux—Bristle **Mrs W. A. Oram**

TWO-YEAR-OLDS

19 Ch f 28/3 Silver Kite (USA)—Brazilian Princess (Absalom) **Mr George S. Thompson**
20 B f 16/4 Nicholas (USA)—Eagle's Quest (Legal Eagle) **Mr D. W. P. Arbuthnot**
21 B c 23/4 Soviet Star (USA)—Gleaming Water (Kalaglow) **Mr J. S. Gutkin**
22 Ro c 13/4 Timeless Times (USA)—Misty Rocket (Roan Rocket) **Mr D. W. P. Arbuthnot**
23 B f 31/1 Mtoto—Pfalz (Pharly) **Mr Christopher Wright**
24 **PRESKIDUL (IRE)**, b f 2/2 Silver Kite (USA)—Dul Dul (USA) (Shadeed (USA)) **Mrs W. A. Oram**
25 B c 19/2 Alzao (USA)—Settlement (USA) (Irish River (FR)) **Mr Christopher Wright**
26 Ch f 12/4 Primo Dominie—Spirit of India (Indian King (USA)) **Mr Noel Cronin**
27 B c 17/5 Gildoran—Starawak (Star Appeal) **Mr J. S. Gutkin**
28 **TOI TOI (IRE)**, b f 1/4 In The Wings—Walliser (Niniski (USA)) **Mr Noel Cronin**

Other Owners: Mrs V. Bampton, Mr T. K. Bannister, Mr Terry Barwick, Mr J. M. H. Binney, Ms M. S. Brackenbury, Mr B. G. Brown, Mr Geoff Buck, Mr David Byrne, Mrs B. Cressey, Mr R. Cressey, Mr Stephen Crown, Mr C. A. Doyle, Mrs Alison Gamble, Mr Ray Harding, Dr Robin Holleyhead, Horris Vale Racing Partnership, Mrs Winifred Howie, Mr D. M. Hudson, Mr J. Kehoe, Mrs C. E. Kershaw, Mr W. Leadbeater, Mrs B. J. Lee, Mrs Judy Martin, Mr Bill Muirhead, Mr P. S. Mulligan, Mrs Judith Nicklin, Mr S. R. Noble, Miss L. Pearce, Mrs M. Peett, Mr Chris Poll, Mr T. S. Redman, Dr Brian J. Ridgewell, Mrs F. C. Saint Jean, H. R. H. Prince Fahd Salman, Mr Roddy Shand, Mr John Smith (Roehampton), Mr J. W. Taylor, Sir Gerald Whent, Lady Whent, Mr Godfrey Wilson, Mr Alan A. Wright, Mrs P. M. Yeomans.

Jockey (Flat): T Quinn (w.a.).

Lady Rider: Mrs D Arbuthnot (8-6).

16   MR R. W. ARMSTRONG, Newmarket

Postal: **St Gatien, Newmarket, Suffolk, CB8 8HJ.**

Phone: **(01638) 663333 FAX 662412 MOBILE (0850) 371474 CAR (0860) 959759**

1 **ABLE CHOICE (IRE)**, 6, b g Taufan (USA)—Great Land (USA) **Dr Cornel Li**
2 **AKIL (IRE)**, 4, b c Cyrano de Bergerac—Nonnita **Mr Hamdan Al Maktoum**
3 **BENFLEET**, 5, ch h Dominion—Penultimate **Mr C. G. Donovan**

MR R. W. ARMSTRONG—continued

4 **GABR**, 6, b h Green Desert (USA)—Ardassine **Mr Hamdan Al Maktoum**
5 **KUTTA**, 4, b c Old Vic—Ardassine **Mr Hamdan Al Maktoum**
6 **NORDINEX (IRE)**, 4, b g Nordico (USA)—Debbie's Next (USA) **Mr R. J. Arculli**
7 **RIVER KEEN (IRE)**, 4, ch c Keen—Immediate Impact **Dr Meou Tsen Geoffrey Yeh**
8 **SHEER DANZIG (IRE)**, 4, b c Roi Danzig (USA)—Sheer Audacity **Mr R. J. Arculli**

THREE-YEAR-OLDS

9 **ALBAHA (USA)**, br c Woodman (USA)—Linda's Magic (USA) **Mr Hamdan Al Maktoum**
10 **ALHALAL**, ch c Cadeaux Genereux—Vaguely **Mr Hamdan Al Maktoum**
11 **ALWARQA**, b f Old Vic—Ostora (USA) **Mr Hamdan Al Maktoum**
12 **ANTIGUAN JANE**, b f Shirley Heights—Dabbiana (CAN) **Mr Paul H. Locke**
13 **FORMIDABLE PARTNER**, b c Formidable (USA)—Brush Away **Mr George Ward**
14 **INTISAB**, b f Green Desert (USA)—Ardassine **Mr Hamdan Al Maktoum**
15 **JEZYAH (USA)**, ch f Chief's Crown (USA)—Empress Jackie (USA) **Mr Hamdan Al Maktoum**
16 **MAWWAL (USA)**, ch c Elmaamul (USA)—Dish Dash **Mr Hamdan Al Maktoum**
17 **MISTOOK (USA)**, b f Phone Trick (USA)—Princess Ivor (USA) **Wyck Hall Stud**
18 **MUJTAHIDA (IRE)**, b f Mujtahid (USA)—Domino's Nurse **Mr K. Hsu**
19 **MURHEB**, b g Mtoto—Masarrah **Mr Ahmed Al Shafar**
20 **MUTADARRA (IRE)**, ch c Mujtahid (USA)—Silver Echo **Mr Hamdan Al Maktoum**
21 **PATIALA (IRE)**, b f Nashwan (USA)—Catherine Parr (USA) **Wyck Hall Stud**
22 **RAISE A PRINCE (FR)**, b c Machiavellian (USA)—Enfant d'Amour (USA) **Mr George Tong**
23 **RUMBA RHYTHM (CAN)**, ch f Thorn Dance (USA)—Skoblikova **W. V. Robins**
24 **SAHHAR**, ch c Sayf El Arab (USA)—Native Magic **Mr R. J. Arculli**
25 **SHARP COMMAND**, ch c Sharpo—Bluish (USA) **Mr George Ward**
26 **TASDIK**, ch f Unfuwain (USA)—Stay Sharpe (USA) **Mr Hamdan Al Maktoum**
27 **WAHAB**, b c Unfuwain (USA)—Mileeha (USA) **Mr Hamdan Al Maktoum**

TWO-YEAR-OLDS

28 **BAAHETH (USA)**, ch c 10/3 Seeking The Gold—
                           Star Glimmer (USA) (General Assembly (USA)) **Mr Hamdan Al Maktoum**
29 **DUKHAN (USA)**, br c 6/4 Silver Hawk (USA)—Azayim (Be My Guest (USA)) **Mr Hamdan Al Maktoum**
30 B f 22/2 Saddlers' Hall (IRE)—False Lift (Grundy) **Mr Jeremy Gonpertz**
31 B c 18/5 Green Desert (USA)—Flying Bid (Auction Ring (USA)) **Mr George Tong**
32 Ch f 28/2 Woodman (USA)—Fond Romance (USA) (Fappiano (USA)) **Sceptre Racing**
33 B c 16/4 Lahib (USA)—Gezalle (Shareef Dancer (USA)) **Mr George Tong**
34 **GHAYAH (IRE)**, ch f 9/3 Night Shift (USA)—Blinding (IRE) (High Top) **Mr Hamdan Al Maktoum**
35 **HIRASAH (IRE)**, b f 5/2 Lahib (USA)—Mayaasa (USA) (Lyphard (USA)) **Mr Hamdan Al Maktoum**
36 **INDIHASH (USA)**, b f 17/5 Gulch (USA)—Linda's Magic (USA) (Far North (CAN)) **Mr Hamdan Al Maktoum**
37 B f 3/3 Warning—Ivoronica (Targowice (USA)) **Gene W-W Tsoi**
38 **KAMIN**, b c 12/3 Red Ransom (USA)—Sweet Rhapsody (USA) (Sea Bird II) **Mr Hamdan Al Maktoum**
39 **MAKHBAR**, ch c 4/4 Rudimentary (USA)—Primulette (Mummy's Pet) **Mr Hamdan Al Maktoum**
40 **MANAZIL (IRE)**, ch f 21/1 Generous (IRE)—Stay Sharpe (Sharpen Up) **Mr Hamdan Al Maktoum**
41 **MARAUD**, ch c 17/2 Midyan (USA)—Peak Squaw (USA) (Icecapade (USA)) **Wyck Hall Stud**
42 **MASRRAH (IRE)**, b c 8/5 Old Vic—Masarrah (Formidable (USA)) **Mr Ahmed Al Shafar**
43 **MUHAWWIL**, b c 15/4 Green Desert (USA)—Ardassine (Ahonoora) **Mr Hamdan Al Maktoum**
44 **MUJAZI (IRE)**, ch c 31/3 Mujtahid (USA)—Leaping Salmon (Salmon Leap (USA)) **Mr Hamdan Al Maktoum**
45 B c 24/5 Warning—Native Magic (Be My Native (USA))
46 **OLIVER**, b c 11/3 Priolo (USA)—Daniella Drine (USA) (Shelter Half (USA)) **Mr C. G. Donovan & Partners**
47 **RAAHA**, b f 16/4 Polar Falcon (USA)—Ostora (USA) (Blushing Groom (FR)) **Mr Hamdan Al Maktoum**
48 **REDDY BIRD (FR)**, b c 9/5 Bluebird (USA)—Real Gold (Yankee Gold) **Mr George Tong**
49 **SHARKIYAH (IRE)**, ch f 7/2 Polish Precedent—Peace Girl (Dominion) **Mr Hamdan Al Maktoum**
50 B f 23/3 Night Shift (USA)—Spire (Shirley Heights) **Sceptre Racing**
51 **SPRIOLO**, b f 28/2 Priolo (USA)—Springtime Sugar (Halo (USA)) **Wyck Hall Stud**
52 Ch c 26/3 Mujtahid (USA)—Supportive (IRE) (Nashamaa) **Mr H. C. Hart & Partners**

Other Owners: Mrs Robert Armstrong, Mr Francis Ward.

Jockeys (Flat): W Carson, Richard Hills, Russell Price.

17   MR J. R. ARNOLD, Upper Lambourn

Postal: **Cedar Lodge, Upper Lambourn, Hungerford, Berks, RG17 8QT**
Phone: **(01488) 73808 FAX (01488) 73826 E-mail: r-arnold @easynet.co.uk**

1 **BAKERS DAUGHTER**, 4, ch f Bairn (USA)—Tawnais **Mr J. R. Arnold**
2 **HIGHTIDE**, 4, b f Lugana Beach—Moon Charter **Mr Justin T. Arnold**
3 **LILAC RAIN**, 4, b f Petong—Dame Corley **Mr A. Ball**

THREE-YEAR-OLDS

4 **BRIGHT DIAMOND**, b f Never So Bold—Diamond House **Mr Trevor W. Stubbings**
5 **CLAN CHIEF**, b c Clantime—Mrs Meyrick **Mr P. G. Lowe**
6 **HIGH DESIRE (IRE)**, b f High Estate—Sweet Adelaide (USA) **Mr J. Gale**
7 **KING RUFUS**, ch c No Evil—Djanila **Mrs Audrey Pittendriegh**
8 **LETLUCE**, b f Aragon—Childish Prank **Mr A. H. Robinson**
9 **UNSPOKEN PRAYER**, br f Inca Chief (USA)—Dancing Doll (USA) **Mrs Sue A. Baker**

TWO-YEAR-OLDS

10 **CRYHAVOC**, b c 26/2 Polar Falcon (USA)—Sarabah (IRE) (Ela-Mana-Mou) **Mr A. H. Robinson**
11 B f 8/4 Keen—Miss Oasis (Green Desert (USA)) **Mr A. N. Brooke Rankin**

Other Owners: Mr Anthony R. Cersell, Mr J. D. Cotton, Exors Of The Late Mr Alan H. Oldham, Mr A. F. Rae Smith, Mrs
M. A. Rae Smith.

18   THE HON MRS R. ARTHUR, Hallington

Postal: **Bingfield East Quarter, Hallington, Newcastle Upon Tyne, NE19 2LH.**
Phone: **(01434) 672219**

1 **BUCK's DELIGHT (IRE)**, 8, br g Buckskin (FR)—Ethel's Delight **Mrs Richard Arthur**
2 **SERGEANT BILL (IRE)**, 4, ch g Persian Heights—Starlust **Mrs Richard Arthur**
3 **SWEET CALLERNISH (IRE)**, 7, br g Callernish—Winsome Doe **Mrs Richard Arthur**

19   MRS S. M. AUSTIN, Malton

Postal: **Burythorpe House, Burythorpe, Malton, North Yorks, YO17 9LB.**
Phone: **BURYTHORPE (01653) 658200**

1 **BLOTOFT**, 4, b g High Kicker (USA)—Foothold **Mr R. N. Forman**
2 **CHANTRY BELLINI**, 7, ch m Efisio—Lifestyle **Mrs J. J. Kirk Scott**
3 **CHORUS BOY**, 11, br g Sonnen Gold—Toccata **Mrs J. J. Kirk Scott**
4 **DUTCH BLUES**, 9, b g Dutch Treat—My Polyanna **Scotnorth Racing Ltd**
5 **FUTURE FAME (USA)**, 7, b g Stately Don (USA)—Hooplah **Mr A. Runacre**
6 **HUDSON BAY TRADER (USA)**, 9, b g Sir Ivor—Yukon Baby (USA) **Mr P. C. N. Curtis**
7 **KITTOCHSIDE LAD**, 6, br g Destroyer—Chalkies Pet **Scotnorth Racing Ltd**
8 **OUR RAINBOW**, 4, b f Primitive Rising (USA)—Cass Avon **Mr D. Ireland**
9 **POLLY TWO**, 6, b m Reesh—My Polyanna **Mr A. G. Forty**
10 **RICHMOND (IRE)**, 8, ch g Hatim (USA)—On The Road **Mrs S. M. Austin**
11 **RUN MILADY**, 8, b m Blakeney—Bewitched **Scotnorth Racing Ltd**
12 **SEA-AYR (IRE)**, 6, ch m Magical Wonder (USA)—Kunuz **Mr A. Runacre**
13 **SUN MARK (IRE)**, 5, ch g Red Sunset—Vivungi (USA) **Scotnorth Racing Ltd**
14 **TREVVEETHAN (IRE)**, 7, ch g On Your Mark—Carrick Slaney **Mr Ken Trevethan**
15 **TROODOS**, 10, b g Worlingworth—My Polyanna **Scotnorth Racing Ltd**

THREE-YEAR-OLDS

16 **ERIC'S BETT**, ro c Chilibang—Mira Lady **Mr R. D. Willis**

Other Owners: Miss Sallyanne Littlewood.

Jockey (NH): D Wilkinson (10-0).

20   MR M. AVISON, Nawton

Postal: **Little Manor Farm, High Lane, Nawton, York, YO6 5TU.**
Phone: **HELMSLEY (01439) 771672**

1 **EMMA'S VISION (IRE)**, 6, b m Vision (USA)—Julie Blake **Mrs J. Carr Evans**
2 **PALLINGHAM LAD (IRE)**, 6, b g Torenaga—Star Mill **Mr M. Avison**
3 **PRINCE SKYBURD**, 5, b g Domynsky—Burntwood Lady **Mrs P. M. A. Avison**
4 **SOUDONYM (IRE)**, 5, ch g Soudno—Frigid Lady **Mr K. Hanson**
5 **TWIN SWALLOW**, 5, b m Lightning Dealer—Second Swallow **Mr M. Avison**

21   MR N. G. AYLIFFE, Minehead

Postal: **Glebe Stables, Little Ham, Winsford, Minehead, TA24 7JH.**
Phone: **WINSFORD (0164385) 265**

1 **BALLYHAYS (IRE)**, 7, ch g Glow (USA)—Relanca **Mr D. Hooper**
2 **CYCLOPS**, 6, b g Naskracker (USA)—Go Penta **Mr J. R. Wootten**
3 **DANTE'S RUBICON (IRE)**, 5, ch g Common Grounds—Dromorehill **Mr R. A. Bimson**
4 **GIMINGHAM GLORY**, 4, b f Exodal (USA)—Carlton Glory **Mr D. F. Gillard**
5 **HILL CRUISE**, 7, ch g Cruise Missile—Danah's Lacquer **Mrs May Collins**
6 **KELLY'S DARLING**, 10, b g Pitskelly—Fair Darling **Miss C. A. Burrington**
7 **MARINE SOCIETY**, 8, b g Petoski—Miranda Julia **Bideford Tool Ltd**
8 **MILESTONE**, 4, b g Presidium—Light de Light (USA) **Miss N. L. Peskett**
9 **NINE O THREE (IRE)**, 7, b g Supreme Leader—Grenache **Bideford Tool Ltd**
10 **ROUTING**, 8, b g Rousillon (USA)—Tura **Mr Derek Jones**

Other Owners: Mrs S. L. Hooper.

Jockeys (NH): A P McCoy, B Powell.

22   MR J. W. F. AYNSLEY, Morpeth

Postal: **Rye Hill Farm, Thropton, Morpeth, Northd, NE65 7NG.**
Phone: **(01669) 620271**

1 **CHAIN LINE**, 6, br g Relkino—Housemistress **Mr J. W. F. Aynsley**
2 **RYE RUM (IRE)**, 5, br g Strong Gale—Eimers Pet **Mr J. W. F. Aynsley**

Jockeys (NH): R Hodge, P Niven, B Storey.

23   MR N. M. BABBAGE, Cheltenham

Postal: **1 Cleeve Cloud, Nutterswood, Cleeve Hill, Cheltenham, GL52 3PZ.**
Phone: **OFFICE (01242) 242699 HOME (01242) 580069**

1 **ALL CLAP HANDS**, 8, b g Lighter—Hands Off **Blacksmith Club**
2 **BADAWI (FR)**, 6, ch g Script Ohio (USA)—Beautiful Bedouin (USA) **Mr Glyn Harris**
3 **BARELY BLACK**, 8, br g Lidhame—Louisa Anne **Mr John Cantrill**
4 **BELLARA**, 4, b f Thowra (FR)—Sicilian Vespers **Mr B. Babbage**
5 **BUILT FOR COMFORT (IRE)**, 4, b f Nordico—Dewan's Niece (USA) **Mr D. Hiorns/Longdon Racing**
6 **COURTING NEWMARKET**, 8, b g Final Straw—Warm Wind **Mr Geo Taylor**
7 **FIREBIRD LAD**, 8, ch g Electric—Arbatina
8 **FLY GUARD (NZ)**, 9, gr g Imperial Guard—Fly (IRE)
9 **GARLANDHAYES**, 4, b f Adbass (USA)—Not Alone **Mr Geo Taylor**

MR N. M. BABBAGE—continued

10 **GREAT TERN**, 4, b f Simply Great (FR)—La Neva (FR) **Mr John Cantrill**
11 **HAYA YA KEFAAH**, 4, b g Kefaah (USA)—Hayat (IRE) **Mr Alan G. Craddock**
12 **KERRY JANE**, 6, gr m Nestor—Quaife Sport **Mr F. Page**
13 **KNIGHTSBRIDGE SCOT**, 5, ch g Scottish Reel—Marie Galante (FR) **Knightsbridge BC**
14 **MASTER M-E-N (IRE)**, 4, ch g My Generation—Secret Lightning (USA) **Mr R. Craddock**
15 **PIGALLE WONDER**, 8, br g Chief Singer—Hi-Tech Girl **D. G. & D. J. Robinson**
16 **SCENT OF POWER**, 6, b g Fairy King (USA)—Agreloui **Mr Gareth Gregory**
17 **SOUL TRADER**, 7, b m Faustus (USA)—Hot Case **Mr G. W. Hackling**
18 **WANNAPLANTATREE**, 5, b m Niniski (USA)—Cataclysmic **Mr A. Tombs**
19 **YOUNG TESS**, 6, b m Teenoso (USA)—Bundu (FR) **Mr Geo Taylor**

Other Owners: Mrs Sarah Babbage, Mr A. Blackmore, Mr Sean Bryan, Mr N. Evans, Mr A. Ewen, Mr R. C. F. Faiers, Mr B. Gladwin, Mr A. Grimmitt, Mr G. Leigh, Mr A. Payne, Mr J. Pellington, Mrs Jean Robinson, Mr R. Stevens, Mr K. Tombs, Mr P. V. Weston.

Conditional: M Smith.

Lady Rider: Miss C Pegnor.

24　　MR A. BAILEY, Tarporley

Postal: **Sandy Brow Stables, Little Budworth, Tarporley, Cheshire, CW6 9EG.**
Phone: **(01829) 760762 FAX (01829) 760370**

1 **BOLD STREET (IRE)**, 6, ch g Shy Groom (USA)—Ferry Lane **Codan Trust Company Limited**
2 **BUCKLEY BOYS**, 5, gr m Grey Desire—Strip Fast **The Buckley Boys Partnership**
3 **CRYSTAL LOOP**, 4, b f Dowsing (USA)—Gipping **Mr Roy Matthews**
4 **DAVID JAMES' GIRL**, 4, b f Faustus (USA)—Eagle's Quest **One In Ten Racing Club**
5 **DIWALI DANCER**, 6, gr g Petong—Dawn Dance (USA) **Mr B. E. Case**
6 **ELLE SHAPED (IRE)**, 6, b g Treasure Kay—Mamie's Joy **Simple Technology UK Ltd**
7 **EVERSET (FR)**, 8, b g Green Desert (USA)—Eversince (USA) **Mr Gordon Mytton**
8 **INDIAN RHAPSODY**, 4, b f Rock City—Indian Love Song **Mr G. G. Ashton**
9 **INTEABADUN**, 4, ch g Hubbly Bubbly (USA)—Madam Taylor **Esprit de Corps Racing**
10 **KILLICK**, 8, b m Slip Anchor—Enthralment (USA) **Esprit de Corps Racing**
11 **KING CURAN (USA)**, 5, b g Lear Fan (USA)—Runaway Lady (USA) **Mrs M. O'Donnell**
12 **KOMREYEV DANCER**, 4, b g Komaite (USA)—L'Ancressaan **Mr Denis Gallagher**
13 **LORD SKY**, 5, b g Emarati (USA)—Summer Sky **Mr Ray Bailey**
14 **MAPLE BAY (IRE)**, 7, b g Bold Arrangement—Cannon Boy (USA) **Mr Roy Matthews**
15 **MENTALASANYTHIN**, 7, b g Ballacashtal (CAN)—Lafrowda **Mrs M. O'Donnell**
16 **MOZEMO**, 9, ch g Remezzo—Mo Storeen **Codan Trust Company Limited**
17 **MY GALLERY (IRE)**, 5, ch m Tate Gallery (USA)—Sententious **Mr Gordon Mytton**
18 **NORDIC BREEZE (IRE)**, 4, b br g Nordico (USA)—Baby Clair **Mr Malcolm B. Jones**
19 **ONE FOR JEANNIE**, 4, b f Clantime—Miss Henry **Mrs J. Jones & Mrs J. P. Bailey**
20 **PROMISE FULFILLED (USA)**, 5, b m Bet Twice (USA)—Kind Prospect (USA) **Mr G. G. Ashton**
21 **SHOWTIME BLUES (IRE)**, 7, b g Kafu—Susan's Blues **Miss Anne Ewart**
22 **TIDAL REACH (USA)**, 4, b f Kris S (USA)—Davie Lady (USA) **Mr G. G. Ashton**
23 **WALK IN THE WILD**, 4, b f Bold Owl—Tripolitaine (FR) **Mr G. Coburn**

THREE-YEAR-OLDS

24 **AIRBORNE HARRIS (IRE)**, ch g Persian Heights—Excuse Slip (USA) **Mr G. G. Ashton**
25 **ARCTIC CYRANO (IRE)**, br g Cyrano de Bergerac—Scobys Baby **Mr J. McMullan**
26 **CRABBIE'S PRIDE**, ch g Red Sunset—Free Rein **Turks Head Racing Club**
27 **DOVEBRACE**, b g Dowsing (USA)—Naufrage **Mr David A. Jones**
28 **FLOOD'S FANCY**, ro f Then Again—Port Na Blath **Mrs M. O'Donnell**
29 **LE SPORT**, b g Dowsing (USA)—Tendency **Simple Technology UK Ltd**
30 **MARJORIE ROSE (IRE)**, b f Magical Strike (USA)—Arrapata **Lintscan Ltd (Corbett Bookmakers)**

MR A. BAILEY—continued

31 **MYTTONS MISTAKE,** b g Rambo Dancer (CAN)—Hi-Hunsley **Mr Gordon Mytton**
32 **ROXANE (IRE),** b f Cyrano de Bergerac—Janet Oliphant **Roxane Partnership**
33 **SO KEEN,** ch g Keen—Diana's Bow **Mr Ray Bailey**
34 **STEAL 'EM,** b f Efisio—Eastern Ember **Mr S. Hassett**

TWO-YEAR-OLDS

35 B f 24/5 Fairy King (USA)—Beautiful Secret (USA) (Secreto (USA)) **Mr M. Tabor**
36 **DIAMOND LADY,** ch f 13/3 Primo Dominie—June Fayre (Sagaro) **Mrs B. Higgins**
37 Gr f 2/5 Rambo Dancer (CAN)—Fancy Flight (FR) (Arctic Tern (USA)) **Mr Gordon Mytton**
38 Gr c 12/4 Absalom—Girl's Brigade (Brigadier Gerard) **Mr G. G. Ashton**
39 **GOLDEN SADDLE (IRE),** b f 5/3 Waajib—Flying Beckee (IRE) (Godswalk (USA)) **Mr F. Johnson**
40 Ch c 15/4 Mac's Imp (USA)—Katysue (King's Leap) **Mr A. Bailey**
41 Ch f 8/4 Statoblest—Princess Roxanne (Prince Tenderfoot (USA)) **Mrs M. O'Donnell**
42 Br f 13/3 High Estate—Respectfully (USA) (The Minstrel (CAN)) **Mr Gordon Mytton**
43 Ch f 24/2 Anshan—Waveguide (Double Form) **Mr N. C. Jones**

Other Owners: Mr D. Hildrop, Mr J. Parry, Mr J. A. Poirrette, Mr P. T. Quinn, Mr A. Thomson, Mrs C. A. Wallace, Mr T. S. Wallace, Mr J. D. Wynne.

Jockey (NH): T Kent.

Apprentices: Angela Gallimore (7-7), Iona Wands, Danny Wright (7-2).

Amateur: Miss Bridget Gatehouse.

Lady Rider: Miss E Gatehouse.

25   MR K. C. BAILEY, Upper Lambourn

Postal: **The Old Manor, Upper Lambourn, Hungerford, Berks, RG17 8RG**
Phone: **LAMBOURN (01488) 71483 FAX LAMBOURN (01488) 72978**

1 **ACT OF PARLIAMENT (IRE),** 8, br g Parliament—That's Show Biz **Mr J. Perriss**
2 **AH THERE YOU ARE,** 7, b g Netherkelly—Semi-Colon **Racing Club KCB**
3 **ALDERBROOK,** 7, b h Ardross—Twine **Mr E. Pick**
4 **AZTEC WARRIOR,** 5, b g El Conquistador—Jaunty Slave **Mrs J. Martin**
5 **BADGER'S LANE,** 5, b g Don't Forget Me—Rose Parade **Sir Gordon Brunton**
6 **BASIC PRINCIPLE (IRE),** 7, b g Runnett—Brown's Cay **Bloodstock & Stud Investment Co Ltd**
7 **BERTONE (IRE),** 7, b g Montelimar (USA)—Lady of Eilat **Mrs Harry J. Duffey**
8 **BETTY'S BOY (IRE),** 7, b g Cataldi—Decent Lady **Mr Richard Shaw**
9 **BIZIMKI,** 4, b f Ardross—Lady Shoco **M. Chavoush**
10 **BUCKLE DOWN,** 7, b g Buckley—Maladiction **J. Grist**
11 **CHINA MAIL (IRE),** 4, b g Slip Anchor—Fenney Mill **The Merlin Syndicate**
12 **CHIPARUS,** 7, b g Rymer—Stormation **Mr Arnie Kaplan**
13 **COACH (NZ),** 8, b br g Trubisc (AUS)—Fly (IRE) **Mr Stanley W. Clarke**
14 **COSA FUAIR (IRE),** 6, b g Roselier (FR)—Bold And True **Mr Martyn Booth**
15 **COUNTESS VERUSCHKA,** 10, br m Strong Gale—Rendezvous **Mr Huw Davies**
16 **CYRUS THE GREAT (IRE),** 4, ch g Persian Heights—Smart As Paint (USA) **Mr P. J. Vogt**
17 **DANDE DOVE,** 5, gr g Baron Blakeney—Ryans Dove **Dandelion Distribution Ltd**
18 **DARLEYFORDBAY,** 7, b g Riberetto—Decorum **Racing Club KCB**
19 **DEEL QUAY (IRE),** 5, b g Tidaro (USA)—Quayside Charm **Mrs Sharon C. Nelson**
20 **DELIGHT (FR),** 5, b g Vorias (USA)—Étoile du Berger III (FR) **G. Middlebrook**
21 **DOMINIE (IRE),** 8, b g Crash Course—Meneplete **Mr M. L. Shone**
22 **DRUMSTICK,** 10, ch g Henbit (USA)—Salustrina **Sarah Lady Allendale,E.Hawkings,M.Harris**
23 **DUKES MEADOW (IRE),** 6, ch g Glenstal (USA)—Mattira (FR) **Dukes Meadow Partnership**

MR K. C. BAILEY—continued

24 **EDINA (IRE)**, 6, b m The Parson—Dukes Darling **Mr Dennis Yardy**
25 **FAR SENIOR**, 10, ch g Al Sirat (USA)—Ross Lady **Mrs Harry J. Duffey**
26 **FAR SPRINGS (IRE)**, 5, b g Phardante (FR)—Ellasprings **Mr A. N. Solomons**
27 **FEEL THE POWER (IRE)**, 8, b g Torus—Donadea **Mr Martyn Booth**
28 **FELLOW COUNTRYMAN**, 9, b g Decent Fellow—Sonlaru **Mr A. D. Wardall**
29 **FULL OF FIRE**, 9, b g Monksfield—Sheila's Flame **Mr J. Michael Gillow**
30 **GAYE FAME**, 5, ch m Ardross—Gaye Memory **I. M. S. Racing**
31 **GLEMOT (IRE)**, 8, br g Strong Gale—Lady Nethertown **Mr Dennis Yardy**
32 **GOING AROUND**, 8, b g Baron Blakeney—Elect **The M.E.P. Partnership**
33 **GRANHAM PRIDE**, 6, ch g The Parson—Stand In **I. M. S. Racing**
34 **HAMILTON TERRACE (IRE)**, 7, b g Good Thyne (USA)—Highland Party **Mrs Sharon C. Nelson**
35 **HERBERT LODGE (IRE)**, 7, b g Montelimar (USA)—Mindyourbusiness **Mrs David Thompson**
36 **HOH MUSIC (IRE)**, 5, ch g Orchestra—Bells Hollow **D. F. Allport**
37 **IMPERIAL VINTAGE (IRE)**, 6, ch g Aristocracy—Monasootha **May We Never Be Found Out**
38 **INJECTABUCK (IRE)**, 6, b g Buckskin (FR)—Lovely Tartan **Dr D. B. A. Silk**
39 **KING COOL (IRE)**, 5, b g Supreme Leader—Sno-Sleigh **Mrs J. Martin**
40 **KING GIRSEACH (IRE)**, 7, b g King's Ride—Girseach **Blakeley Painters Ltd**
41 **LAKE OF LOUGHREA (IRE)**, 6, ch g Kings Lake (USA)—Polynesian Charm (USA) **Mrs Harry J. Duffey**
42 **LOBSTER COTTAGE**, 8, b g Southern Music—Seal Flower **Major-Gen. R. L. T. Burges**
43 **LUCIA FORTE**, 5, b m Neltino—Celtic Well **Mrs Lucia Farmer**
44 **LUCKY DOLLAR (IRE)**, 8, ch g Lord Ha Ha—Lucky Wish **Mr G. P. D. Milne**
45 **MAN-OF-THE-WORLD (IRE)**, 6, br g Mandalus—Rostrevor Lady **Mrs Charlotte Hopley**
46 **MASTER OATS**, 10, ch g Oats—Miss Poker Face **Mr P. A. Matthews**
47 **MITTENWALD (IRE)**, 7, b g Denel (FR)—Garden of Roses **Mr James Burley**
48 **MR BOJANGLES (IRE)**, 5, b g Orchestra—Lavarna Lady **Mrs D. Lousada**
49 **MR JAMBOREE**, 10, b g Martinmas—Miss Reliant **Mrs D. Lousada**
50 **MUSIC PLEASE**, 4, ch g Music Boy—Ask Mama **Mrs David Thompson**
51 **NORTHERN KINGDOM (USA)**, 7, b g Graustark—Wonder Mar (USA) **P. A. Deal**
52 **ODELL (IRE)**, 6, br g Torus—Indian Isle **Mrs Sharon C. Nelson**
53 **OVER THE STREAM**, 10, b g Over The River (FR)—Bola Stream **Mr J. D. Gordon**
54 **PEERS FOLLY (IRE)**, 6, ch g Remainder Man—Bola Stream **Lord Donoughue & Lord Swaythling**
55 **PORPHYRIOS**, 5, b g Mtoto—Tamassos **Mr Ian Bullerwell**
56 **PRICE'S HILL**, 9, gr g Furry Glen—Clever Milly **Mr G. D. W. Swire**
57 **QUINAG**, 5, ch m Tina's Pet—Erica Superba **Mr I. F. W. Buchan**
58 **RAMSTOWN LAD (IRE)**, 7, b g Mummy's Luck—Neasham **Mrs Christine Davies**
59 **RICHVILLE**, 10, b g Kemal (FR)—Golden Ingot **Major-Gen. R. L. T. Burges**
60 **SCOUNDREL**, 5, gr g Scallywag—Nicholcone **Mrs J. M. Corbett**
61 **SEEKIN CASH (USA)**, 7, b g Our Native (USA)—Tis Eloquent (USA) **Mrs David Thompson**
62 **SHARP PERFORMER (IRE)**, 7, br g Sharpo—Husnah (USA) **Mrs S. C. Ellen**
63 **SHERWOOD BOY**, 7, ch g Seclude (USA)—Madame Persian **P. Granger**
64 **SIMPLE ARITHMETIC**, 8, ch g Southern Music—Graphics Eska **Mrs Michael Motley**
65 **SNOWY PETREL (IRE)**, 4, b g Petorius—Bronzewing **Mrs J. Conroy**
66 **SPARKLING SPRING (IRE)**, 5, b g Strong Gale—Cherry Jubilee **Mr E. Benfield**
67 **STAC-POLLAIDH**, 6, b m Tina's Pet—Erica Superba **Mr I. F. W. Buchan**
68 **STARLIGHT FOOL**, 7, b g Idiot's Delight—Casa's Star **Mr Simon E. Bown**
69 **STORM DRUM**, 7, ch g Celestial Storm (USA)—Bushti Music **Mrs Shelley Fergusson**
70 **STRATHMINSTER**, 5, gr g Minster Son—Strathdearn **Mr Dennis Yardy**
71 **STRONG MEDICINE**, 9, b g Strong Gale—In The Forest **Dr D. B. A. Silk**
72 **TANTARA LODGE (IRE)**, 5, b g Import—Fashion Blade **The Toledo Partnership**
73 **THE BUD CLUB (IRE)**, 8, b g Le Moss—Tipperary Star **The Blue Chip Group**
74 **THE WHOLE HOG (IRE)**, 7, b g Cataldi—Beeston **Mrs Sharon C. Nelson**
75 **TRISQUARE (IRE)**, 5, b g Architect (USA)—Highlands Babe (USA) **Mr E. Benfield**
76 **UNHOLY ALLIANCE**, 9, b g Carlingford Castle—Rambling Love **Mrs Sharon C. Nelson**
77 **WARFIELD LAD (IRE)**, 7, b g King's Ride—Atlantic Hope **Mrs D. Todd**
78 **WATERFORD CASTLE**, 9, b g Le Bavard (FR)—Bob's Hansel **Sybil Lady Joseph**
79 **WHISPERING STEEL**, 10, b g Furry Glen—Shady Grove **Mr J. Michael Gillow**
80 **WISE APPROACH**, 9, bl g Strong Gale—Nocturnal Approach **Mrs S. Gee**
81 **ZEREDAR (NZ)**, 6, b g Isle of Man (NZ)—Zajal (NZ) **I. M. S. Racing**

MR K. C. BAILEY—continued

Other Owners: Mr R. H. Baines, Mr E. H. Ball, Mr J. R. Buchanan, Mrs Michael C. Byrne, Dr S. R. Cannon, Mr D. M. Clancy, Mr Kevin T. Clancy, Miss M. P. Clancy, Mrs David Clark, Mr G. W. Cleaver, Mr P. Fowler, Mr H. C. Hardy, Mr D. W. R. Harland, Major Basil Heaton, Mr C. Hellyer, Mr R. R. Hetherington, Mr A. J. Heyes, Mr D. A. Hibbert, Mr D. F. Hill, Mr Tony Hill, Mr M. W. Kwiatkowski, Mr M. H. G. Lang, Mr David Macfarlane, Mr Scott Marshall, Mr E. H. McMichael, Miss M. Noden, Major G. H. W. Oakford, Mr Craig Pearman, Prize Print Services Ltd, Mr R. K. Purkis, Mr Graham Radford, Mr Raymond J. Roberts, Mr D. G. Savala, Mr A. Scott, Mr G. A. Singh, Mrs I. M. Steinmann, Mr J. D. Steinmann, Air Commodore J. M. Stevenson, Mr Nick Tsappis, Mr Peter Wiegand, Mr Richard Williams.

Jockeys (NH): A Thornton (10-0), N Williamson (9-7).

Conditional: J Magee (10-0), T J Murphy (9-7).

26   MRS M. A. BAKER, Steyning

Postal: **Sweethill Farm, Ashurst, Steyning, West Sussex, BN44 3AY**

Phone: **(01403) 710252**

1 6, B g Orchestra—Grilse **Mrs M. A. Baker**

27   MR R. J. BAKER, Tiverton

Postal: **Steart House Racing Stables, Stoodleigh, Tiverton, Devon, EX16 9QA.**

Phone: **(01398) 351317**

1 **ARTHUR'S SPECIAL**, 6, gr m Sousa—Kynaston **Mr Arthur Souch**
2 **COEUR BATTANT (FR)**, 6, ch g General Holme (USA)—Feerie Boreale (FR) **Mr B. P. Jones**
3 **COOCHIE**, 7, b m King of Spain—York Street (USA) **Mr S. M. McCausland**
4 **DOMINION TREASURE**, 11, b br g Dominion—Chrysicabana **Mr R. J. Baker**
5 **DTOTO**, 4, b g Mtoto—Deposit **Mr W. H. Scott**
6 **DUKE OF DREAMS**, 6, gr g Efisio—Tame Duchess **Mrs V. W. Jones**
7 **FRAGRANCE MOUNTAIN**, 10, b m Le Moss—Bunny Brown **Mr S. M. McCausland**
8 **GUSHY**, 10, ch g Hard Fought—Be Gustful **Mr B. P. Jones**
9 **KINGSLEY SINGER**, 8, b g Chief Singer—Yelming **Duckhaven Stud**
10 **KIRBY MOORSIDE**, 5, b g Gay Meadow—Oujarater **Mr D. J. Minty**
11 **LEDOM LARK**, 7, b m Latest Model—Larkrose **Mr I. J. Webber**
12 **MU-TADIL**, 4, gr g Be My Chief (USA)—Inveraven **Mr B. P. Jones**
13 **MUTAWALI (IRE)**, 6, ch g Exactly Sharp (USA)—Ludovica **Mr John Warren**
14 **NO BONUS**, 12, ch g Baragoi—Lillytip **Mr J. K. Davis**
15 **NORTHERN STARLIGHT**, 5, b g Northern State (USA)—Ganadora **Mr Arthur Souch**
16 **OLD MASTER (IRE)**, 5, b g Tate Gallery (USA)—Nancy Drew **Mr S. M. McCausland**
17 **OPERA FESTIVAL (IRE)**, 6, ch g Buckskin (FR)—Glencairn Belle **Mr B. P. Jones**
18 **PERFAY (USA)**, 8, ch h Nodouble (USA)—Perfect Example (USA) **Mr N. F. Coleman**
19 **ROAD TO AU BON (USA)**, 8, b g Strawberry Road (AUS)—Village Lady (USA) **Mr M. H. Holland**
20 **SAAFI (IRE)**, 5, b h Primo Dominie—Baby's Smile **Mr A. White**
21 **SEVSO**, 7, b m Jupiter Island—Celestial Bride **Mr G. K. Hullett**
22 **STAR PLAYER**, 10, ch g Simply Great (FR)—Star Girl **Mr Paul Smith**
23 **TAP SHOES (IRE)**, 6, b g Nordance (USA)—Dance Fan **Mr R. J. Baker**

THREE-YEAR-OLDS

24 **DAYDREAM ISLAND**, ch f Never So Bold—La Belle Vie **Mr Robin Lawson**

Other Owners: Mr H. J. W. Davies, Mrs G. Hinton, Mr B. Samra, Mr A. D. Smith, Mrs J. M. Smith, P. K. & Mrs E. M. Smith, Mrs Marion Smith.

Jockey (NH): B Powell (w.a.).

28   MR G. B. BALDING, Andover

Postal: **Fyfield House Stables, Fyfield, Andover, Hants, SP11 8EW.**
Phone: **TEL (01264) 772278 FAX (01264) 771221**

1 **ASK THE GOVERNOR**, 10, b g Kambalda—Roman Run **Mrs D. Claessen-Brierton**
2 **BARBARY FALCON**, 6, b g El Conquistador—Dusty Run **Mr R. P. Shepherd**
3 **BEECH ROAD**, 14, ch g Nearly A Hand—North Bovey **Mr & Mrs Tony Geake**
4 **BERTRAGHBOY BAY**, 6, b g Destroyer—Fidessa **Mrs Derek Strauss**
5 **BEY D'AO (FR)**, 8, b g Baillamont (USA)—Ondoa (FR) **Bey D'ao Group**
6 **BILLY BARTER (IRE)**, 6, b g Tanfirion—Dia Glas **The Cornish Connection**
7 **BISHOPS TALE**, 6, b g Derring Rose—Lilac Silk **Highflyers**
8 **BLAIR CASTLE (IRE)**, 5, b g Waajib—Caimanite **Highflyers**
9 **BONITA BLAKENEY**, 6, gr m Baron Blakeney—Cashelmaer **John Hinchliffe & Leon Shack**
10 **BOOTS N ALL (IRE)**, 6, bl g Strong Statement (USA)—Sallstown **Mrs D. Tipper**
11 **BRAVE TORNADO**, 5, ch g Dominion—Accuracy **Miss B. Swire**
12 **BRYAN ROBSON (USA)**, 5, b g Topsider (USA)—Queen's Visit **Highflyers**
13 **CAMPECHE BAY (IRE)**, 7, b g Sandalay—Golden Goose **Mr J. M. Kinnear**
14 **CHARMER'S WELL (IRE)**, 8, b g Beau Charmeur (FR)—Palmers Well **M. Kerr-Dineen & M. S. Dalman**
15 **CHATTERTON (IRE)**, 6, b g Le Bavard (FR)—Clairellen **Mr Derek Strauss**
16 **CHILI HEIGHTS**, 6, gr g Chilibang—Highest Tender **Mr B. T. Attenborough**
17 5, Ch g Le Bavard (FR)—Clairellen **Mrs G. B. Balding**
18 **CLANCY'S EXPRESS**, 5, b g Faustus (USA)—Pink Pumpkin **Mrs J. A. Cleary**
19 **COASTING**, 10, b g Skyliner—Shantung Lassie (FR) **The Slipstream Partnership**
20 **CONTI D'ESTRUVAL (FR)**, 6, b g Synefos (USA)—Barbara Conti (ITY) **Mr Bernard Keay**
21 **DAKOTA GIRL**, 5, b m Northern State (USA)—Marielou (FR) **Dr J. M. Leigh**
22 **DOONLOUGHAN**, 11, br g Callernish—Cora Swan **Mr D. Strauss**
23 **DREAM HERE**, 8, b g Heres—Dream Buck **Mr A. Gadd**
24 **ELY ISLAND**, 9, b g Teofane—Court Fancy **Mr J. G. Thatcher**
25 **FAIR BROTHER**, 10, ch g Le Bavard (FR)—Fair People **Mrs S. Watts**
26 **FATHER DOWLING**, 9, br g Teofane—Stream Flyer **Mrs E. A. Haycock**
27 **FONTAINEROUGE (IRE)**, 6, gr g Millfontaine—How Are You **Mrs D. Tipper**
28 **FOOLS ERRAND (IRE)**, 6, b g Fools Holme (USA)—Zalazula **Mrs David Russell**
29 **GAVASKAR (IRE)**, 7, b g Indian King (USA)—Sovereign Bloom **Highflyers**
30 **GENERAL SALUTE (IRE)**, 6, gr g Salluceva—Fortina's General **Lord Chetwode**
31 **GERRY'S PRIDE (IRE)**, 5, br g Corvaro—Doll Acre **Gerry Heard**
32 **GOLDENSWIFT (IRE)**, 6, ch m Meneval (USA)—Golden Seekers **Mrs S. Watts**
33 **GOWLAUN**, 7, b g Electric—Tura **Highflyers**
34 **INTERMAGIC**, 6, ch g Interrex (CAN)—Tina's Magic **Mrs J. A. Cleary**
35 **JEWEL THIEF**, 6, b g Green Ruby (USA)—Miss Display **Mrs G. B. Balding**
36 **JIMMY'S CROSS (IRE)**, 6, ch g Phardante (FR)—Foredefine **Leslie Garratt Racing**
37 **KENDAL CAVALIER**, 6, gr g Roselier (FR)—Kenda **Mr Michael Wingfield Digby**
38 **LADY LACEY**, 9, b m Kampala—Cecily **Mrs K. L. Perrin**
39 **LADY MUCKY DUCK (IRE)**, 6, b m Buckskin (FR)—Stolen Gold
40 **MAJOR BUGLER (IRE)**, 7, b g Thatching—Bugle Sound **Mr Colin J. Buckle**
41 **MASTER HOPEFULL (NZ)**, 7, ch g Lanfranco—Eyelure (NZ) **Mr M. Padfield**
42 5, Ch g Zaffaran (USA)—Misclaire **Mrs G. B. Balding**
43 **MOORLOUGH BAY (IRE)**, 6, ch g Abednego—Monica's Pet **Mrs G. B. Balding**
44 **MORLEY STREET**, 12, ch g Deep Run—High Board **Michael Jackson Bloodstock Ltd**
45 **PAMPILLO (FR)**, 8, ch g Vacarme (USA)—Lady Chloe (FR) **The Lucky Ladies Partnership**
46 **PHAR FROM FUNNY**, 5, ch g Phardante (FR)—Joca **Mrs E. A. Haycock**
47 **PILGRIM'S MISSION (IRE)**, 6, b g Carlingford Castle—Hill Invader **Mr J. M. Kinnear**
48 **PLATINI (IRE)**, 5, b g Gallic League—Tardy (USA) **Highflyers**
49 **POLDEN PRIDE**, 8, b g Vital Season—Bybrook **Mr D. F. Lockyer**
50 **PUKKA SAHIB**, 9, b g Jalmood (USA)—So True **Miss B. Swire**
51 **PURBECK RAMBLER**, 5, b g Don't Forget Me—Sheer Nectar **Miss M. Lane**
52 **QUOTE**, 9, ch m Oats—Queen Hill **Mrs T. Sims**
53 **RAISE THE LIMIT (IRE)**, 7, br m Rising—Knowing Card **Mr Theo Waddington**
54 **ROBSAND (IRE)**, 7, b g Sandalay—Remindful **Sir Brian McGrath**
55 **ROCKY PARK**, 10, ch g Derrylin—Songe d'Inde **Mr & Mrs Tony Geake**
56 **ROMANY CREEK (IRE)**, 7, b g Trimmingham—Rare Picture **Duke of Atholl**

MR G. B. BALDING—continued

57 **ROXBURGH HOUSE (IRE)**, 7, b g Miner's Lamp—Loughamaire **M. Aiken W. Craig J. Craig C. Meredith**
58 **SEA FREEDOM**, 5, b h Slip Anchor—Rostova **Miss B. Swire**
59 **SEVEN BROOKS**, 6, ch g Seven Hearts—Eddie Brooks **Mr A. Gadd**
60 **SO HOPEFUL (NZ)**, 7, b g Little Brown Jug (NZ)—Red Highland (NZ) **Mr M. Padfield**
61 **SORCIERE**, 5, ch m Hubbly Bubbly (USA)—Fernessa **Mr M. Henriques**
62 **SOUTHAMPTON**, 6, b g Ballacashtal (CAN)—Petingo Gold **Highflyers**
63 **SUPER SERENADE**, 7, b g Beldale Flutter (USA)—Super Melody **Mrs G. B. Balding**
64 **TARIAN (USA)**, 4, b c Lyphard (USA)—Chain Fern (USA) **The Loopy Partnership**
65 **TEETOTALLER (IRE)**, 5, gr g Taufan (USA)—Mainly Dry **Highflyers**
66 **THE CAUMRUE (IRE)**, 8, b g Torus—Remindful **The On The Run Partnership**
67 **THE FLYING DOCTOR (IRE)**, 6, b g Camden Town—Sparkling Opera **The Rumble Racing Club**
68 **THE REVEREND BERT (IRE)**, 8, b g Decent Fellow—Best of Kin **M. Kerr-Dineen & M. S. Dalman**
69 **TOM PINCH (IRE)**, 7, b g Mandalus—Spanish Royale **Mrs G. B. Balding**
70 **TUG OF PEACE**, 9, b g Tug of War—Ardglass Pride **Mr P. Richardson**
71 **VICAR OF BRAY**, 9, b g The Parson—Fanfare Beauty **The Cleric Partnership**
72 **VICTORY TEAM (IRE)**, 4, b g Danehill (USA)—Hogan's Sister (USA) **Mr R. J. Lavelle**
73 **WIMPOLE STREET (IRE)**, 5, b br g Decent Fellow—Caherelly Cross **Mrs G. B. Balding**
74 **WISE STATEMENT (IRE)**, 7, ch g Strong Statement (USA)—Larkins Maid **Mr M. C. Humby**
75 5, B g Torus—Worldling **Mr & Mrs Tony Geake**

THREE-YEAR-OLDS

76 **AMELANCHIER**, ch f Cigar—Frost In Summer **Skeltools Ltd**
77 B g Prince Rupert (FR)—Banasiya **Michael Jackson Bloodstock Ltd**
78 **BELLATOR**, b g Simply Great (FR)—Jupiter's Message **Mr P. Richardson**
79 **CA'D'ORO**, ch g Cadeaux Genereux—Palace Street (USA) **Miss B. Swire**
80 **CALANDRELLA**, b f Sizzling Melody—Maravilla **Mrs G. B. Balding**
81 **DAY TRIPPER**, b g Forzando—Solo Vacation **Mrs G. B. Balding**
82 **ERUPT**, b g Beveled (USA)—Sparklingsovereign **Mr P. Richardson**
83 **INDIAN NECTAR**, b f Indian Ridge—Sheer Nectar **Dr J. M. Leigh**
84 **KORALOONA (IRE)**, b g Archway (IRE)—Polynesian Charm (USA) **Mr Bernard Keay**
85 **PHONETIC**, b g Shavian—So True **Miss B. Swire**
86 **REITERATE**, b f Then Again—Indubitable **Miss B. Swire**
87 **RIVERS MAGIC**, b g Dominion—Rivers Maid **Mr Rex L. Mead**

TWO-YEAR-OLDS

88 **CUGINA**, b f 16/3 Distant Relative—Indubitable (Sharpo) **Miss B. Swire**
89 **HIBERNICA (IRE)**, b f 13/3 Law Society—Brave Ivy (Decoy Boy) **Mr Theo Waddington**
90 **PALAEMON**, b c 1/2 Slip Anchor—Palace Street (USA) (Secreto (USA)) **Miss B. Swire**
91 **PEVERIL PENDRAGON**, b g 18/5 Emarati (USA)—Princess Siham (Chabrias (FR)) **Mrs E. A. Haycock**
92 **STAR PRECISION**, ch f 29/3 Shavian—Accuracy (Gunner B) **Miss B. Swire**

Other Owners: Mr P. J. G. Aldous, Mr Jonathan N. Baines, Mr Clive Bull, Mr F. J. Bush, Mrs A. M. Cleary, Mr Toby Davis, Mr P. C. Dutton, Mr David Erwin, Mr L. D. Faulkner, Mr R. W. Ford, Mrs B. J. Forrester, Mr James Frampton, Mr L. J. Garrett, Mrs P. D. Gulliver, Mr J. H. C. Harris, Mr John Hawkins, Mr J. M. Hooper, Mr S. Hosgood, Mr Robert Hunter, Mrs Karen Johnson, Mr Henry Kelly, Wing Comdr J. H. King, Mr C. Mynard, Mr T. J. Neal, Miss D. Neale, Miss D. V. Pares Wilson, Mrs C. A. Parry, Mr N. H. Poyntz-Wright, Mr Graeme Reed, Mrs Margaret Renshaw, Dr M. J. Ripley, Dr W. M. Robarts, Mr H. L. Rosevear, Mr M. J. Sechiari, Mr A. J. Sutton, Mr C. Swiderski, Mr Gerry Whatling, Mr J. B. Williams, Mr J. C. Worrow.

Jockey (Flat): J Williams (8-4, w.a.).

Jockeys (NH): B Clifford (10-0), A P McCoy (10-0).

Apprentice: R Gordon.

Conditional: R Arnold (9-7), B Fenton (9-7).

Amateur: Mr A Balding (10-7).

29 MR I. A. BALDING, Kingsclere

Postal: **Park House, Kingsclere, Newbury, Berks, RG20 5PY.**

Phone: **KINGSCLERE (01635) OFFICE 298210 HOME 298274 FAX 298305**

1 **BLAZE AWAY (USA)**, 5, b h Polish Navy—Battle Drum (USA) **Mr Paul Mellon**
2 **BLUE SIREN**, 5, ch m Bluebird (USA)—Manx Millenium **Mr J. C. Smith**
3 **BRANDON BRIDGE**, 5, b g Primo Dominie—Victoria Mill **Tunnel Vision**
4 **BRANDON COURT (IRE)**, 5, b g Law Society (USA)—Dance Date (IRE) **Mr R. P. B. Michaelson**
5 **BRANDON PRINCE (IRE)**, 8, b g Shernazar—Chanson de Paris (USA) **Mr I. A. Balding**
6 **CRYSTAL SPIRIT**, 5, b g Kris—Crown Treasure (USA) **Mr Paul Mellon**
7 **DENOMINATION (USA)**, 4, br g Danzig Connection (USA)—Christchurch (FR) **Mr Peter Oldfield**
8 **DIVINER (IRE)**, 7, b g Lancastrian—Paupers Spring **Mr Peter Oldfield**
9 **EUPHONIC**, 6, b g Elegant Air—Monalda (FR) **P. Stamp & Partners**
10 **GOLDEN ARROW (IRE)**, 5, ch g Glint of Gold—Sheer Luck **Mr Paul Mellon**
11 **GREY SHOT**, 4, gr g Sharrood (USA)—Optaria **Mr J. C. Smith**
12 **HOH EXPRESS**, 4, b g Waajib—Tissue Paper **Mr D. F. Allport**
13 **JAYANNPEE**, 5, ch g Doulab (USA)—Amina **J. A. Paniccia**
14 **KILCORAN BAY**, 4, b g Robellino (USA)—Catkin (USA) **Mr Nigel Harris**
15 **PAY HOMAGE**, 4, b g Primo Dominie—Embraceable Slew (USA) **Miss A. V. Hill**
16 **ROKEBY BOWL**, 4, b c Salse (USA)—Rose Bowl (USA) **Mr Paul Mellon**
17 **SEA THUNDER**, 4, gr f Salse (USA)—Money Moon **Greenfield Stud**
18 **SHAARID (USA)**, 8, b g El Gran Senor (USA)—Summer Silence (USA) **Mr Peter Oldfield**
19 **SHREWD ALIBI**, 5, gr g Sharrood (USA)—Alsiba **Tunnel Vision**
20 **SILENTLY**, 4, b g Slip Anchor—Land of Ivory (USA) **Mr Paul Mellon**
21 **SINISSIPI (USA)**, 6, b g Kris S (USA)—Illustrious Joanne (USA) **Robert & Elizabeth Hitchins**
22 **SPINNING**, 9, b br g Glint of Gold—Strathspey **Mr Paul Mellon**
23 **SPRING TO ACTION**, 6, b g Shareef Dancer (USA)—Light Duty **D. F. Allport & R. P. B. Michaelson**

THREE-YEAR-OLDS

24 **AGILE**, b c Shareef Dancer (USA)—Hence (USA) **Robert & Elizabeth Hitchins**
25 **AMAZING BAY**, b f Mazilier (USA)—Petriece **Mr J. C. Smith**
26 **BALLET HIGH (IRE)**, b c Sadler's Wells (USA)—
Marie d'Argonne (FR) **Sir Andrew Lloyd Webber & G. Strawbridge**
27 **BANDIT GIRL**, b f Robellino (USA)—Manx Millenium **Mr J. C. Smith**
28 **BOLD BUSTER**, b g Bustino—Truly Bold **Robert & Elizabeth Hitchins**
29 **BRANDON MAGIC**, ch c Primo Dominie—Silk Stocking **Mr R. P. B. Michaelson**
30 **CANONS PARK**, ch g Keen—Low Line **Mr G. M. Smart**
31 **COH SHO NO**, b f Old Vic—Castle Peak **Baron von Oppenheim**
32 **DASHING BLUE**, ch c Dashing Blade—Blubella **Mrs Duncan Allen**
33 **DOUBLE BLUFF (IRE)**, gr g Sharrood (USA)—Timely Raise (USA) **Mr J. C. Smith**
34 **DRAMATIC MOMENT**, b f Belmez (USA)—Drama School **Mrs R. Plummer & Partners**
35 **FITZWILLIAM (USA)**, b c Rahy (USA)—Early Lunch (USA) **Mr Paul Mellon**
36 **GIANT NIPPER**, b f Nashwan (USA)—Flamingo Pond **Exors of the late Mrs E. Longton**
37 **GRAND MUSICA**, b g Puissance—Vera Musica (USA) **Mach 3 Racing**
38 **HIGH CUT**, b f Dashing Blade—High Habit **Mr J. C. Smith**
39 **HIGHLAND RHAPSODY (IRE)**, ch f Kris—Farewell Song (USA) **Mrs Christopher Hanbury**
40 **JONA HOLLEY**, b g Sharpo—Spurned (USA) **Mr I. A. Balding**
41 **LILLIBELLA**, b f Reprimand—Clarandal **Mr S. Hastings-Bass**
42 **MAGIC LAHR (GER)**, ch g Dashing Blade—Miraflores (GER) **Mr G. M. Smart**
43 **NOTAIRE (IRE)**, b g Law Society (USA)—La Toulzanie (FR) **Mr M. E. Wates**
44 **PIKE CREEK (USA)**, b f Alwasmi (USA)—Regal Heights (USA) **Mr George Strawbridge**
45 **REGAL EAGLE**, b g Shirley Heights—On The Tiles **Mr J. C. Smith**
46 **SHERNA (IRE)**, ch f Eurobus—Zulu Hut **Sir Harry Moore**
47 **SKILLINGTON (USA)**, b c Danzig (USA)—Annie Edge **Mr George Strawbridge**
48 **SOCIETY MAGIC (USA)**, b g Imp Society (USA)—Lady Kirtling (USA) **Miss A. V. Hill**
49 **TAGULA (IRE)**, b c Taufan (USA)—Twin Island (IRE) **Robert & Elizabeth Hitchins**
50 **VICTORY MILL**, b f Ron's Victory (USA)—Victoria Mill **Mrs I. A. Balding**
51 **VOLA VIA (USA)**, b br g Known Fact (USA)—Pinking Shears (USA) **Mr G. M. Smart**
52 **WARBROOK**, b c Warrshan (USA)—Bracey Brook **Mr J. C. Smith**

MR I. A. BALDING—continued

TWO-YEAR-OLDS

53 **AL AZHAR**, b c 9/2 Alzao (USA)—Upend (Main Reef) **Al Muallim Partnership**
54 B f 17/3 Danzig (USA)—Annie Edge (Nebbiolo) **Mr George Strawbridge**
55 **ANQUILLA**, ch f 23/5 Arazi (USA)—Fiesta Fun (Welsh Pageant) **Heatherwold Stud**
56 **BORDER FALCON**, ch c 9/5 Polar Falcon (USA)—Tender Loving Care (Final Straw) **Sir William Purves**
57 **BRANDON JACK**, ch c 28/1 Cadeaux Genereux—Waitingformargaret (Kris) **Mr R. P. B. Michaelson**
58 **BRANDON PRINCESS**, b f 27/2 Waajib—Bless The Match (So Blessed) **Mr R. P. B. Michaelson**
59 **CAPTAIN WILLIAM (IRE)**, b c 1/3 Shernazar—Our Galadrial (Salmon Leap (USA)) **Mr David R. Watson**
60 **CHICKAMAUGA (USA)**, gr f 8/3 Wild Again (USA)—Gray And Red (USA) (Wolf Power (SAF)) **Mr Paul Mellon**
61 Ch f 1/3 Sharpo—Clouded Vision (So Blessed) **Mr M. E. Wates**
62 **DEAD AIM (IRE)**, b c 13/2 Sadler's Wells (USA)—Dead Certain (Absalom) **Al Muallim Partnership**
63 B f 13/4 Rock Hopper—Drama School (Young Generation) **Mr C. H. Bothway & S. Ellen**
64 **DULCINEA**, ch f 23/3 Selkirk (USA)—Ahohoney (Ahonoora) **Miss K. Rausing**
65 **EVIDENTLY (IRE)**, b f 8/5 Slip Anchor—Evocatrice (Persepolis (FR)) **Baron von Oppenheim**
66 **GLEN OGIL**, ch c 27/3 Thatching—Cormorant Bay (Don't Forget Me) **Mr G. M. Smart**
67 **GOLDEN GODDESS**, ch f 28/2 Formidable—Tame Duchess (Saritamer (USA)) **Mr Nigel Harris**
68 **GOLD ROBBER**, b c 29/3 Robellino (USA)—Bracey Brook (Gay Fandango (USA)) **Mr J. C. Smith**
69 **GRANDPA LEX (IRE)**, gr c 7/4 Kalaglow—Bustling Nelly (Bustino) **Maverick Productions**
70 **GREEN BOULEVARD (USA)**, ch f 6/3 Green Forest (USA)—Assez Cuite (USA) (Graustark) **R. F. Scully**
71 **GUILLOTINE (IRE)**, br c 3/2 Dashing Blade—Parisana (FR) (Gift Card (FR)) **Mr J. C. Smith**
72 **HANDLEY CROSS (USA)**, b r c 7/4 Houston (USA)—Imaginary Lady (USA) (Marfa (USA)) **Mr Paul Mellon**
73 **HIGHLY PRIZED**, b c 18/4 Shirley Heights—On The Tiles (Thatch (USA)) **Mr J. C. Smith**
74 Ch g 10/2 Selkirk (USA)—Historiette (Chief's Crown (USA)) **Miss K. Rausing**
75 **HOH DANCER**, ch f 5/5 Indian Ridge—Alteza Real (Mansingh (USA)) **D. F. Allport & R. P. B. Michaelson**
76 **HOH EXPLORER (IRE)**, ch c 22/5 Shahrastani (USA)—
                     Heart's Harmony (Blushing Groom (FR)) **D. F. Allport/Hoh Supply Ltd**
77 B f 26/2 Efisio—Island Mill (Mill Reef (USA)) **Mrs I. A. Balding**
78 **JORROCKS (USA)**, b c 14/4 Rubiano (USA)—Perla Fina (USA) (Gallant Man) **Mr Paul Mellon**
79 **JUNCTION CITY (USA)**, b c 14/2 Forty Niner (USA)—
                     Key Witness (USA) (Key To The Mint (USA)) **Mr Paul Mellon**
80 **KAREN'S HAT (USA)**, ch f 28/4 Theatrical—Miss Carlotita (ARG) (Masqued Dancer (USA)) **R. F. Scully**
81 **KING ARTHUR**, b c 21/3 Aragon—Periquito (USA) (Olden Times) **Mr J. C. Smith**
82 **LADY PRECIOUS**, ch f 6/4 Dashing Blade—Sheer Luck (Shergar) **Mr G. M. Smart**
83 **LOCHANGEL**, ch f 5/4 Night Shift (USA)—Peckitts Well (Lochnager) **Mr J. C. Smith**
84 **MARIE DORA (FR)**, gr f 20/3 Kendor (FR)—Marie de Vez (FR) (Crystal Palace (FR)) **Lord Roborough**
85 **MOREDUN (IRE)**, b c 5/5 Waajib—Izba (Thatching) **Mr G. M. Smart**
86 **MR SPONGE (USA)**, ch c 10/3 Summer Squall (USA)—Dinner Surprise (USA) (Lyphard (USA)) **Mr Paul Mellon**
87 **NOBBY BEACH**, ch c 8/5 Sharpo—Sunshine Coast (Posse (USA)) **Mr R. P. B. Michaelson**
88 **NORMAN CONQUEST (USA)**, ch c 1/4 Miswaki (USA)—Grand Luxe (CAN) (Sir Ivor) **R. F. Scully**
89 **PAPUA**, ch c 21/3 Green Dancer (USA)—Fairy Tern (Mill Reef (USA)) **Robert & Elizabeth Hitchins**
90 **ROBELLITA**, b c 12/3 Robellino (USA)—Miellita (King Emperor (USA)) **Mr J. C. Smith**
91 **ROSY OUTLOOK (USA)**, b f 21/1 Trempolino—Rosyphard (USA) (Lyphard (USA)) **Mr J. C. Smith**
92 **SAUSALITO BAY**, b c 29/4 Salse (USA)—Cantico (Green Dancer (USA)) **Mr J. C. Smith**
93 **SHIFTING TIME**, b f 31/3 Night Shift (USA)—Timely Raise (USA) (Raise A Man (USA)) **Mr J. C. Smith**
94 **SLIPSTREAM STAR**, b f 16/3 Slip Anchor—Alsiba (Northfields (USA)) **Mr J. C. Smith**
95 **SPEEDBALL (IRE)**, b c 26/1 Waajib—Lady Taufan (IRE) (Taufan (USA)) **Mr J. C. Smith**
96 B c 20/4 Selkirk (USA)—Spurned (USA) (Robellino (USA)) **Mr George Strawbridge**
97 **SUDEST (IRE)**, br c 1/2 Taufan (USA)—Frill (Henbit (USA)) **Robert & Elizabeth Hitchins**
98 Ch c 14/1 Green Forest (USA)—Tea And Scandals (USA) (Key To The Kingdom (USA)) **Mr J. C. Smith**
99 **TIKOPIA**, b c 26/2 Saddlers' Hall (IRE)—Shesadelight (Shirley Heights) **Robert & Elizabeth Hitchins**
100 **TISIMA (FR)**, ch f 13/4 Selkirk (USA)—
                     Georgia Stephens (USA) (The Minstrel (CAN)) **Robert & Elizabeth Hitchins**

Other Owners: The Queen, Queen Elizabeth, Mr Nagy Azar, Mr M. Djojomartono, Major A. Everett, Mrs Peter Hastings, Mr C. J. Kershaw, Mr R. Leah, Mr R. D. Mackinnon, Mrs Francesca Schwarzenbach, Mr Urs E. Schwarzenbach, Mr J. Y. Smart, Stamford Bridge Partnership, Mr A. M. Tolhurst.

Jockey (Flat): L Dettori (8-6, w.a.).

Jockey (NH): J Osborne (10-0, w.a.).

Apprentices: M Dwyer (7-7), D Griffiths (8-5), C Scudder (8-2).

Amateur: Mr Andrew Balding (11-0).

30   MR J. BALDING, Doncaster

Postal: **Mayflower Stables, Saracens Lane, Scrooby, Doncaster.**

Phone: **HOME (01302) 710096**

1 **MONIS (IRE),** 5, ch g Waajib—Gratify **Five Star Racing**
2 **PERFECT BRAVE,** 5, b g Indian Ridge—Perfect Timing **Mr G. Ashton**
3 **PURSUANCE (IRE),** 4, b c Glenstal (USA)—Pocket **Spring Hill Stud**

THREE-YEAR-OLDS

4 **CHALICE,** b f Governor General—Eucharis **Mrs J. T. Balding**
5 **GENERAL EQUATION,** b g Governor General—Logarithm **Make Our Day**
6 **GOLBORNE LAD,** ch g Jester—Taskalady **Mrs Stephen Allen**
7 **MADAM ZANDO,** ch f Forzando—Madam Trilby **Mr T. Jones**
8 **SPORTING FANTASY,** b g Primo Dominie—Runelia **Mrs J. Everitt**
9 **THORNTOUN JEWEL (IRE),** b f Durgam (USA)—Blue Bouquet **Classic Racing**

TWO-YEAR-OLDS

10 **BABY BE,** b f 20/3 Bold Arrangement—B Grade (Lucky Wednesday) **Mrs O. Tunstall**
11 **DYCE,** b f 28/1 Green Ruby (USA)—Miss Display (Touch Paper) **Mr T. Jones**

Other Owners: Mr Graham W. Backhouse, Miss C. Balding, Mr Peter Balding, Mr J. D. Cooke, Mr N. T. Davies, Mrs A. C. Digby, Mrs J. E. Gilderson, Mr A. C. Hall, Mr M. Hill, Mrs Catherine Lane, Mr Robert Lane, Mr H. Leather, Mr M. K. McGuire, Mr M. G. White.

Jockey (Flat): Claire Balding (7-7).

Apprentice: Jason Edmunds (7-12).

31   MR J. E. BANKS, Newmarket

Postal: **Jamesfield Place, Hamilton Road, Newmarket, Suffolk, CB8 7JQ.**

Phone: **HOME (01638) 661472 YARD (01638) 667997**

1 **BEAUMONT (IRE),** 6, br g Be My Native (USA)—Say Yes **Mr P. Cunningham**
2 **FAILTE RO,** 4, bl f Macmillion—Safe Passage **Mrs Patricia E. Cunningham**
3 **HIMALAYAN BLUE,** 4, b g Hallgate—Orange Parade **Miss C. Fagerstrom**
4 **LIXOS,** 5, b g Soviet Star (USA)—Lypharita (FR) **Miss C. Fagerstrom**
5 **TRAIKEY (IRE),** 4, b c Scenic—Swordlestown Miss (USA) **Sheik Ahmad Yousuf Al Sabah**

THREE-YEAR-OLDS

6 **HE'S MY LOVE (IRE),** ch c Be My Guest (USA)—Taken By Force **Sheik Ahmad Yousuf Al Sabah**
7 **JUST MILLIE (USA),** ch f Elmaamul (USA)—La Plus Belle (USA) **Mr E. Carter**
8 **LUNAR GRIS,** gr f Absalom—Sliprail (USA) **Mr David Hallums**
9 **MAGIC HEIGHTS,** gr c Deploy—Lady Regent **Mr E. Carter**
10 **MISSILE TOE (IRE),** b c Exactly Sharp (USA)—Debach Dust **Stag and Huntsman**
11 **ROYAL ACTION,** b c Royal Academy (USA)—Ivor's Honey **Mr E. Carter**
12 **SHE'S MY LOVE,** ch f Most Welcome—Stripanoora **Sheik Ahmad Yousuf Al Sabah**
13 **SLIEVENAMON,** br c Warning—Twice A Fool (USA) **Mr P. Cunningham**
14 **TITCHWELL LASS,** ch f Lead On Time (USA)—Bodham **Mr John Rutter**
15 **WATCH THE FIRE,** b f Statoblest—Thulium **Mr E. Carter**

Other Owners: Mr J. E. Banks, Mr Peter Charter, Mr R. Sabey, Mrs Jenny Smith, Hon W. H. Smith.

Jockey (NH): Shaun Keightley (9-2).

Apprentice: M Bridge (8-7).

Conditional: R Barret.

Amateur: Mr J. G. Townson (10-10).

32   MR J. BARCLAY, Leslie

Postal: **Kinneston, Leslie, Fife, KY6 3JJ.**
Phone: **(01592) 840331 FAX (01592) 840866**

1 **BELLS HILL LAD**, 9, ch g Buckskin (FR)—Laiton Peni **Mrs Kathryn Collins**
2 **CARDENDEN (IRE)**, 8, b g Bustomi—Nana **Mr Nicholas Alexander**
3 **CLASSICAL CHOICE (IRE)**, 5, ch g Nashwan (USA)—Easy To Copy (USA) **Kinneston Racing**
4 **EMERALD SEA (USA)**, 9, ch g Coastal (USA)—Emerald Reef **Mrs Cyril Alexander**
5 **PREMIER COUNTY**, 10, br g Decent Fellow—Far Away **Miss Alison Bruce**
6 **SEEKING GOLD (IRE)**, 7, b m Lancastrian—Platinum Gold **Gilry**
7 **SKYE WEDDING (IRE)**, 7, b br m Fine Blade (USA)—Nimble Ninepence **Mr Nicholas Alexander**
8 **SOLSGIRTH**, 5, br g Ardross—Lillies Brig **Mrs Cyril Alexander**

Other Owners: Mr David Alexander, Mr Jamie Alexander, Mr Michael Alexander, Mr Edward Baxter, Mr John Drysdale, Mr Marco Gabellone, Mr S. J. Lucas, Mr David Stanistreet, Mr W. G. Stewart, Mr Barry Williams.

33   MR W. L. BARKER, Richmond

Postal: **Greenbury Grange, Scorton, Richmond, North Yorks, DL10 6EP.**
Phone: **(01325) 378266 FAX (01748) 818910**

1 **BRAMBLES WAY**, 7, ch g Clantime—Streets Ahead
2 **COUP DE CATHERINE**, 10, br g Warpath—What A Coup **Mr W. L. Barker**
3 **DANGEROUS PLOY**, 4, b c Deploy—Protected (FR) **Mr W. L. Barker**
4 **MASKIN BROOK**, 8, b g Meadowbrook—Miss Maskin **Mr W. L. Barker**
5 **OUR BAIRN**, 4, b f Bairn (USA)—Bewitched **Hawston Racing**
6 **SHARP SENSATION**, 6, ch g Crofthall—Pink Sensation **Mrs A. Harker**
7 **SHYNON**, 6, gr g Nishapour (FR)—Sunset Ray **Mrs F. Bentley**
8 **TANCRED MISCHIEF**, 5, b m Northern State (USA)—Mischievous Miss **Mr W. L. Barker**

THREE-YEAR-OLDS

9 **POLISH LADY (IRE)**, b f Posen (USA)—Dame Ross **Mr David Hawes**
10 B g Lochnager—Red Squaw **Mr W. L. Barker**
11 **SIMPLY SILLY (IRE)**, b f Simply Great (FR)—Zany **Mr David Hawes**

TWO-YEAR-OLDS

12 Ch c 3/5 Prince Daniel (USA)—Absolutely Blue (Absalom) **Mr David Hawes**
13 **LADY MAGICIAN**, ch f 3/5 Lord Bud—Miss Merlin (Manacle) **Mr George H. Leggott**

Other Owners: Mr Jack Collins, Mrs J. Hawes.

Jockeys (NH): G Harker (10-0), R Supple.

34   MR M. A. BARNES, Penrith

Postal: **Bank House, Little Salkeld, Penrith, Cumbria, CA10 1NN.**
Phone: **(01768) 881257**

1 **AITCHTEE-P**, 8, gr g Belfort (FR)—Lucky Donation **Mr & Mrs Cooper**
2 **BEAUCADEAU**, 10, b g Alzao (USA)—Pretty Gift **Mr T. A. Barnes**
3 **CONSTRUCTIVIST (IRE)**, 7, b g Fools Holme (USA)—Spire **Mr M. Barnes**
4 **DERWENT LAD**, 7, br g Lidhame—Swifter Justice **Mr J. G. Graham**
5 **GALLANTS DELIGHT**, 6, b m Idiot's Delight—Miss Gallant **Mrs C. Johnston**
6 **GONE ASHORE (IRE)**, 5, b g Dry Dock—Fandango Girl
7 **HOWYOUDOING**, 6, ch g Meadowbrook—Reigate Head **Mr & Mrs Handley**
8 **LOWOOD GHYLL (IRE)**, 8, ch g Kemal (FR)—Baobab **Mr & Mrs Brennan**

MR M. A. BARNES—continued

9 **NIJWAY**, 6, b g Nijin (USA)—Runaway Girl (FR) **Mr T. A. Barnes**
10 **NORTH PRIDE (USA)**, 11, ch g Northjet—Necie's Pride (USA) **Mr John Wills**
11 **PAPERISING**, 4, b g Primitive Rising (USA)—Eye Bee Aitch **The Jockeys Whips**
12 **POSITIVE ACTION**, 10, b g Croghan Hill—Auragne (FR) **Mr G. Campbell**
13 **REBEL KING**, 6, b g Doc Marten—Cape Farewell **Mr M. Barnes**
14 **STRICTLY PERSONAL (USA)**, 6, b br g Secreto—Tash (USA) **Mrs Jean Maloney**
15 **SUMMER GHYLL**, 6, gr m Scallywag—Summer Path **Mr Francis James Mason**
16 **WEE WIZARD (IRE)**, 7, gr g Tender King—Zanskar **Armstrong-Greenwell**

Other Owners: Mr P. Bailey, Mr R. Burgan, Mrs J. Campbell, Mr J. M. Elliott, Mr Robert J. Elliott, Mr R. H. Hayton, Mr J. H. Millican, Mr J. G. White.

Jockeys (NH): A Dobbin (w.a.), P Waggott (10-6).

35   MR R. E. BARR, Middlesbrough

Postal: **Carr House Farm, Seamer, Stokesley, Middlesbrough, TS9 5LL.**

Phone: **STOKESLEY (01642) 710687**

1 **CATCH THE PIGEON**, 7, b m Wonderful Surprise—Cheeky Pigeon **Mrs R. E. Barr & Mr D. Thomson**
2 **CATTON LADY**, 6, b m Chas Sawyer—Carpenters Gloss **Mrs M. Dodgson**
3 **DIZZY DEALER**, 9, b m Le Bavard (FR)—Dizzy Dot **Mrs R. E. Barr**
4 **JIMMY SPRITE**, 5, b g Silly Prices—Little Mittens **Mr R. E. Barr**
5 **LORD NICK**, 6, b g Silly Prices—Cheeky Pigeon **Mrs R. E. Barr & Mr P. Cartmell**
6 **NITE SPRITE**, 6, b m Silly Prices—Little Mittens **Mr R. E. Barr**
7 **PENNY PEPPERMINT**, 4, b br f Move Off—Cheeky Pigeon **Mrs R. E. Barr**
8 **STARLIGHT WONDER**, 10, ch m Star Appeal—My Lady Muriel (USA) **Mr I. G. Thomson & Mr R. E. Barr**
9 **THATCHED (IRE)**, 6, b g Thatching—Shadia (USA) **Mr C. W. Marwood & Mr R. E. Barr**

THREE-YEAR-OLDS

10 **MAGGIE SIMPSON**, ch f Say Primula—Little Mittens **Mr R. E. Barr**
11 **TOEJAM**, ch g Move Off—Cheeky Pigeon **Mrs R. E. Barr**

Other Owners: Mr J. C. Garbutt.

Jockey (Flat): Stuart Webster.

Jockey (NH): N Smith (10-0).

Apprentice: P Fessey.

36   MR M. F. BARRACLOUGH, Claverdon

Postal: **Arden Park Stables, Manor Lane, Claverdon, Warwick, CV35 8NH.**

Phone: **(01926) 843332**

1 **BARQAISH**, 9, br g Jalmood (USA)—Adeebah (USA) **Arden Racing Club**
2 **CLUB ELITE**, 4, b f Salse (USA)—Little Bittern (USA) **Mr Ken Dale**
3 **ERICOLIN (IRE)**, 6, ch g Ahonoora—Pixie Erin **Ms Caron Stokell**
4 **HARD TO GET**, 9, b g Rousillon (USA)—Elusive **Ms Caron Stokell**
5 **KAI TAK MAC**, 6, b g Macmillion—Chayze **Mr R. J. Buxton**
6 **LAAL (USA)**, 4, b g Shirley Heights—Afaff (USA) **Mr M. F. Barraclough**

MR M. F. BARRACLOUGH—continued

7 **RELATED SOUND**, 10, b g Uncle Pokey—Darling June **Mr Nigel Wall**
8 5, Ch g True Song—Sussex Queen **Arden Racing Club**
9 **TIM SOLDIER (FR)**, 9, ch g Tip Moss (FR)—Pali Dancer (FR) **Mr N. Jinks**
10 5, Ch m Doctor Wall—Vanda's Creation **Arden Racing Club**
11 **VELVET ASITY**, 8, ch m Superlative—The Firebird **Mr R. J. Buxton**
12 **WEEHEBY (USA)**, 7, ch g Woodman (USA)—Fearless Dame (USA) **The D. A. N. A. Partnership**

THREE-YEAR-OLDS

13 **QUEEN'S CHARTER**, ch f Welsh Captain—Sussex Queen **Arden Racing Club**

Other Owners: Mr D. J. Griffin, Mr A. Lucas, Mr A. Peters, Mrs Eileen A. Stokell.

Jockey (NH): S McNeill (10-0, w.a.).

Lady Rider: Ms Ann Stokell (9-7).

37   MR L. J. BARRATT, Oswestry

Postal: **Bromwich Park, Oswestry, Salop, SY11 4JQ.**
Phone: **(01691) 610209**

1 **CALDERVALE**, 6, b g Midyan (USA)—Linguistic **Mr L. J. Barratt**
2 **EASBY JESTER**, 5, b g Idiot's Delight—Khatti Hawk **Mr L. J. Barratt**
3 **EPICA**, 5, b g Picea—Aladyat **Mr L. J. Barratt**
4 **LUCKNAM STYLE**, 8, b g Macmillion—Mrs Currie **Mr L. J. Barratt**
5 **MR LOWRY**, 4, b g Rambo Dancer (CAN)—Be Royal **Mr Doug Brereton**
6 **OUR MICA**, 6, gr g Belfort (FR)—Aristata **Mr L. J. Barratt**
7 **REGAL RAMBLER (CAN)**, 5, ch g Regal Classic (CAN)—Rushing Rachel (USA) **Mr P. L. Loake**

THREE-YEAR-OLDS

8 **A MILLION AT LAST (IRE)**, b g Cyrano de Bergerac—Any Price **Mr Ray Bailey**
9 **ASHIK (IRE)**, b g Marju (IRE)—Wakayi **Mr L. J. Barratt**
10 **I SAY DANCER (IRE)**, b f Distinctly North (USA)—Lady Marigot **Mr Doug Brereton**
11 **LADY RAMBO**, b f Rambo Dancer (CAN)—Albaciyna **Mr L. J. Barratt**
12 **RAKA KING**, b g Rakaposhi King—Spartan Native **Mr L. J. Barratt**

TWO-YEAR-OLDS

13 **MY TRACEY**, ch f 1/3 Risk Me (FR)—Tricky Tracey (Formidable (USA)) **Mr L. J. Barratt**
14 **SHARP SUSY**, b f 14/4 Beveled (USA)—Sharp Anne (Belfort (FR)) **Mr L. J. Barratt**

Lady Rider: Miss Diana Jones.

38   MR T. D. BARRON, Thirsk

Postal: **Maunby House, Maunby, Thirsk, N. Yorks, YO7 4HD.**
Phone: **(01845) 587435**

1 **ALLINSON'S MATE (IRE)**, 8, b g Fayruz—Piney Pass **Mr Peter Jones**
2 **ASHOVER**, 6, gr g Petong—Shiny Kay **Mr Timothy Cox**
3 **AT THE SAVOY (IRE)**, 5, gr g Exhibitioner—Hat And Gloves **Mr Stephen Woodall**
4 **BLUE BOMBER**, 5, b g Tina's Pet—Warm Wind **Mr Geoffrey Martin**
5 **COASTAL BLUFF**, 4, gr g Standaan (FR)—Combattente **Mrs D. E. Sharp**
6 **DANA POINT (IRE)**, 4, br g Phardante (FR)—Wallpark Princess **Mr J. Baggott**

MR T. D. BARRON—continued

7 **FOR THE PRESENT**, 6, b g Then Again—Axe Valley **Mrs J. Hazell**
8 **IN A MOMENT (USA)**, 5, ch g Moment of Hope (USA)—Teenage Fling (USA) **Mrs E. Dresser**
9 **KILERNAN**, 5, ch g K-Battery—Lekuti **Mr J. O. Hall**
10 **MCKELLAR (IRE)**, 7, b h Lomond (USA)—Local Belle **M. P. Burke Developments Ltd**
11 **MUSICAL SEASON**, 4, b c Merdon Melody—Earles-Field **Mr P. D. Savill**
12 **NISHAMIRA (IRE)**, 4, gr f Lashkari—Nishila (USA) **Mr I. Fox**
13 **PALO BLANCO**, 5, b m Precocious—Linpac Mapleleaf **Mr J. G. Brown**
14 **POLLY PARTICULAR**, 4, b f Beveled (USA)—Ballafort **Mr J. M. Ranson**
15 **SADDLEHOME (USA)**, 7, b g Aragon—Kesarini (USA) **Mr W. H. Clarke**
16 **THATCHER'S ERA (IRE)**, 4, ch f Never So Bold—Prima Domina (FR) **Mr Peter Jones**

THREE-YEAR-OLDS

17 **BIT OF BOTHER (IRE)**, b c Millfontaine—Mother White **Mr J. Baggott**
18 **BLUE DUCK (IRE)**, ch g Magical Wonder (USA)—Grave Error **Miss N. J. Barron**
19 **DIRAB**, ch c Groom Dancer (USA)—Double Celt **Mr A. Gorrie**
20 **FLIGHTY**, b f Reprimand—Flight of Pleasure (USA) **Mr A. Gorrie**
21 **FRONTMAN (IRE)**, ch c Imperial Frontier (USA)—Countess Kildare **Mrs J. Hazell**
22 **KRYSTAL MAX (IRE)**, b g Classic Music (USA)—Lake Isle (IRE) **The Oakfield Nurseries Partnership**
23 **KUNUCU (IRE)**, ch f Bluebird (USA)—Kunuz **Mr P. D. Savill**
24 **MALLIA**, b c Statoblest—Pronetta (USA) **Mr H. T. Duddin**
25 Br f Crofthall—Melaura Belle **Mrs J. Hazell**
26 **MIDDLE EAST**, b g Beveled (USA)—Godara **Mr T. Hazell**
27 **SZLOTO**, ch c Polish Patriot (USA)—Swinging Gold **Mr Geoffrey Martin**
28 **TRULY BAY**, b c Reprimand—Daymer Bay **The Oakfield Nurseries Partnership**

TWO-YEAR-OLDS

29 Ch c Polar Falcon (USA)—Comhail (USA) (Nodouble (USA))
30 Ch f Deploy—Glorietta (USA) (Shadeed (USA)) **Mr Peter Jones**
31 Ch c Magical Wonder (USA)—Ice On Fire (Thatching)
32 B c Superpower—Martyrdom (USA) (Exceller (USA)) **Lady Burnham**
33 **PATSY JO**, ch f Absalom—Tawny (Grey Ghost) **Mr J. Baggott**
34 Gr f Absalom—Riverain (Bustino) **J. Hazell**
35 B g Classic Music (USA)—Robin Red Breast (Red Alert) **The Oakfield Nurseries Partnership**
36 **ROSE BURTON**, b f Lucky Wednesday—Holly Burton (King Emperor (USA)) **Mrs R. M. West**
37 **SLIEMA CREEK**, gr g Beveled (USA)—Sea Farer Lake (Gairloch) **Mr J. M. Ranson & Mrs E. Ranson**
38 **SODA**, gr c Belfort (FR)—Bella Seville (King of Spain)
39 B c Then Again—Tarazando (Forzando) **Lady Burnham**
40 **ZIGSE**, b c Emarati (USA)—Primrose Way (Young Generation) **Mr J. Baggott**

Other Owners: Mrs M. Baggott, Mr J. R. Barr, Mrs Christine Barron, Mrs I. M. Boyle, Mr E. Buck, Mr B. Church, Mr Dave Scott, Mr Kevin Shaw, Mrs S. Sturman, Mr Ken Topham.

Jockey (Flat): J Fortune (8-2).

Apprentice: Kimberly Hart (7-10).

39 MR A. K. BARROW, Bridgwater

Postal: **Marsh Mills Farm, Over Stowey, Bridgwater, Somerset, TA5 1HG.**
Phone: **(01278) 732522 MOBILE (0860) 879115**

1 **BOLD REINE (FR)**, 7, b br m Policeman (FR)—Labold **Mr A. Barrow**
2 **BROWN AND MILD**, 5, b g Idiot's Delight—Catherine Tudor **Mr C. W. Cooper**
3 **CAROMANDOO (IRE)**, 8, b g Simply Great (FR)—Tanimara **Mrs R. T. H. Heeley**
4 **IRISH DOMINION**, 6, b g Dominion—Irish Cookie **Mr John Collier**
5 **JHAL FREZI**, 8, b g Netherkelly—Warham Trout **Mrs R. T. H. Heeley**

MR A. K. BARROW—continued

  6 **JUST BY CHANCE**, 4, b g Teenoso (USA)—Skerryvore **Duckhaven Stud**
  7 **L'UOMO PIU**, 12, b g Paddy's Stream—Easter Vigil **Mr C. J. Spencer**
  8 **MISS PIMPERNEL**, 6, b m Blakeney—New Edition **Mr Don Hazzard**
  9 **MO'S CHARLTON IMP**, 5, b m Impecunious—Starfun **Mrs Maureen Emery**
10 **SAN DIEGO CHARGER (IRE)**, 5, ch g Jareer (USA)—Great Dora **In The Pink Partnership**
11 **STRIFFOLINO**, 4, b g Robellino (USA)—Tizona **Mr C. W. Cooper**
12 **VEEAAR (IRE)**, 5, ch g Exhibitioner—Wiasma **Marsh Mills Partnership**
13 **YES WE ARE**, 10, br m Strong Gale—Are You Sure **Mr J. J. Whelan**

Other Owners: Ms B. Cooper, Mr Alan Harrington, Mrs P. Hooper, Mr A. S. Kirke, Mr S. J. Norton, Mr A. D. Smith, Mr A. P. Smith, Mrs J. M. Smith, Mr D. Tidball, Unity Farm Holiday Centre Ltd.

Jockey (Flat): N Adams (7-8).

Jockey (NH): B Powell (10-0).

40   MR C. R. BARWELL, Tiverton

Postal: **Ashfields, Stoodleigh, Tiverton, Devon, EX16 9QF.**
Phone: **OAKFORD (01398) 351333 MOBILE (0836) 599699**

  1 **BALLAGH COUNTESS**, 9, br m King's Ride—Countess Spray **Dragon Industrial Services D. J. Evans**
  2 **BOURNEL**, 8, ch m Sunley Builds—Golden Granite **Mr Nicholas Bowden**
  3 **COMMUTER COUNTRY**, 5, gr g Town And Country—Landed Lady **Mr D. Tylden-Wright**
  4 **DUHALLOW LODGE**, 9, ch g Deep Run—Ballyhoura Lady **Mr Harvey Spack**
  5 **FIVEPERCENT**, 8, ch g Leander—Guinea A Minute **The Hole In The Wall Gang**
  6 **GRATUITY**, 11, b g Torus—Craeve **Mr Robin Barwell**
  7 **HAYS LODGE**, 4, gr f Chief Singer—Sheer Gold **Lady Harris**
  8 5, Ch g Phardante (FR)—Kix **Mr Robin Barwell**
  9 **MAYFIELD PARK**, 11, b g Park Row—Arctic Lee **Mr Robin Barwell**
10 **NEW STATESMAN**, 8, br g Politico (USA)—Nova Ray **Mr L. J. Garrett**
11 **PACIFIC OVERTURE**, 4, br f Southern Music—Morning Miss **Mr Robin Barwell**
12 5, Ch g Black Minstrel—Pearly Lady **Mr Robin Barwell**
13 **SEMINOLE WIND**, 5, gr g Bold Owl—Slap Bang **The Hole In The Wall Gang**
14 **SPECIAL ACCOUNT**, 10, b g Le Moss—Liffey's Choice **Mr Tony Fiorillo**
15 **STEEL MOSS (IRE)**, 7, ch g Le Moss—Iron Star **Mr Tony Fiorillo**

THREE-YEAR-OLDS

16 **ANDSOME BOY**, ch g Out of Hand—My Home **The Select Partnership**
17 **CURTIS THE SECOND**, b f Thowra (FR)—Bay Jade **Mr Michael Smith**
18 **DRAMATIC ACT**, gr f Tragic Role (USA)—Curious Feeling **Michael Smith Racing Partnership**
19 **MORNING SIR**, b g Southern Music—Morning Miss **Rudry Park Syndicate**

Other Owners: Mr B. C. Allen, Mrs L. Allen, Mr R. C. Allen, Mr Phil Cook, Mr D. W. E. Coombs, Mrs L. Field, Mr Patrick Fuller, Mr Paul Laird, Mrs Angie Malde, Mrs T. G. Williams.

Jockeys (NH): Brian Clifford (10-0), Adrian Maguire (10-0, w.a.).

Conditional: I Hudson (9-7).

Amateur: Mr Richard White (10-10).

Lady Rider: Miss J Southcombe (9-0).

41   MR P. BARY, Chantilly

Postal: **5 Chemin des Aigles, 60500 Chantilly, France.**

Phone: **44 57 14 03 FAX: 44 58 56 12**

1 **ARAWAK D'AROCO (FR)**, 4, ch c Manganate—Arizona **M. Al Thani**
2 **EL ANGELO (USA)**, 4, b c El Gran Senor—Angela Serra **N. Incisa Della Roch**
3 **FAIDEELA (IRE)**, 4, b c Green Desert—Point of Honour **Y. Nishiura**
4 **KRAJINA (FR)**, 4, b f Holst—Turkeina **Mme D. G. Jacob**
5 **OIKLEUS (GER)**, 4, br c Acatenango—Opeia **E. Wanke**
7 **RAINBOW DANCER (FR)**, 5, b h Rainbow Quest—Ramanouche **D. Tsui**
8 **WELSH RUN (IRE)**, 4, b c Caerleon—Atropa **J. L. Bouchard**

THREE-YEAR-OLDS

9 **ABETH'S BOY (FR)**, ch c Northern Fashion—Celtic Crown **J. Forsythe**
10 **AL QUEST (FR)**, b c Rainbow Quest—Aldbourne **I. M. Fares**
11 **ARBATRAX (IRE)**, b c Mtoto—Caprarola **Mme L. Boutin**
12 **BELLE D'ARGENT (USA)**, b f Silver Hawk—Seattle Belle **Mme V. Riva**
13 **BINT BADDI (FR)**, b f Shareef Dancer—Baddi Baddi **I. M. Fares**
14 **CACHET NOIR (FR)**, b c Theatrical—Irish Wisdom **J. Garcia-Roady**
15 **CELTIC BIRD (FR)**, ch c Pampabird—Amour Celtique **Mme A. Vilay**
16 **CRACKERJACK (FR)**, b c Comrade In Arms—Ceiling **Mme H. Devin**
17 **DONNA VITTORIA (IRE)**, b f Sadler's Wells—Katie Koo **SC Super King**
18 **DONUSA (USA)**, ch f Woodman—Everything Nice **Ecurie A.M.A.**
19 **ETERNITY RANGE (USA)**, b c Majestic Light—Northern Eternity **Mme L. Boutin**
20 **EURYNOME (GER)**, ch f Acatenango—Eidothea **E. Wanke**
21 **GIOLA (IRE)**, ch f Priolo—Gipsy Road **Skymarc Farm**
22 **GOLD BRIDE (USA)**, ch f Unbridled—Golden Era **Skymarc Farm**
23 **GRAND VIZIR**, b c Bering—Perfect Tune **Mme D. G. Jacob**
24 **GREEN PLANET**, b c Green Desert—Interval **K. Abdulla**
25 **GREEN SAILS (IRE)**, b f Slip Anchor—Gemmologie **Skymarc Farm**
26 **HEAVENLY STAR (IRE)**, b f Alzao—Heavenly Music **Skymarc Farm**
27 **HILARY (FR)**, ch f Tropular—Caramiss **S. Trifa**
28 **HILL SILVER (USA)**, b f Alysheba—Hot Silver **Skymarc Farm**
29 **HONOR OF BAINO (FR)**, gr c Highest Honor—Baino Bluff **I. M. Fares**
30 **HORS PARIS (FR)**, br g Vaguely Pleasant—Star Blue **K. Nader**
31 **KARLASKA (FR)**, br f Lashkari—Kariya **Scuderia Pieffegi**
32 **KEN FIGHT (FR)**, b c Highest Honor—Fight Right **Mme D. G. Jacob**
33 **L'ADDITION (FR)**, b f Private Account—Add **Mme L. Boutin**
34 **LA DEVINETTE (FR)**, b f Scenic—Cupids Hill **Mme H. Devin**
35 **LE PIRATE (FR)**, b f Priolo—L'Americaine **Skymarc Farm**
36 **LOOPHOLE (FR)**, b f Groom Dancer—Luvia **Mme A. O'Reilly**
37 **MADMOUD (FR)**, b f Siberian Express—Full of Passion **I. Diab**
38 **MAZE GARDEN (USA)**, ch f Riverman—Itsamazing **K. Abdulla**
39 **MESSIRE D'ARTOIS (FR)**, b c Kaldoun—Miss Bregand **Y. Nishiura**
40 **NOMADIC WELCOME**, ch c Generous—Nomadic Pleasure **K. Abdulla**
41 **PORTO NOVO (FR)**, gr c Highest Honor—Plytroca **M. House**
42 **PREVAIL (USA)**, b f Danzig—Primevere **Skymarc Farm**
43 **PRIVATE GIFT (USA)**, b c Pirate Army—Salem Witchcraft **L. C. Bary**
44 **QUEEN OF DANCE (USA)**, b f Sadler's Wells—Lem's Peace **Scuderia Pieffegi**
45 **QUICKENING**, b f Warning—Quickstepping **K. Abdulla**
46 **RAGMAR (FR)**, ch c Tropular—Reggae **J. L. Bouchard**
47 **RASPBERRY RIPPLE (FR)**, b f Nashamaa—Rip Roaring **Mme H. Devin**
48 **RAVELLO (IRE)**, b c Machiavellian—Stellina **Mme L. Boutin**
49 **REINE DE FLEURY (FR)**, b f Lead On Time—Beaujolaise **Mme D. G. Jacob**
50 **REINE WELLS (IRE)**, b f Sadler's Wells—Rivoltade **Scuderia Pieffegi**
51 **SECRET NOIR (FR)**, br c Nashwan—Secret Dancer **J. L. Bouchard**
52 **SHAREEF PROSPECT (FR)**, b c Shareef Dancer—Prospector's Star **I. M. Fares**
53 **SHEN DA SHI (FR)**, ch f Tagel—Skodatatra **J. L. Bouchard**
54 **SHINING MOLLY (FR)**, b f Shining Steel—Molly Martine **J. L. Bouchard**
55 **STELLA MARIX (FR)**, gr f Linamix—Pointe Argentee **Mme D. G. Jacob**
56 **TRIPLE LINE (FR)**, ro c Linamix—Double Line **M. House**

MR P. BARY—continued

57 **VAL D'OA (FR)**, gr c Linamix—Sibelle d'Oa **Mme L. Boutin**
58 **VITABA (USA)**, ch f Northern Baby—Vitola **J. L. Bouchard**
59 **WEST COAST (USA)**, br c Gone West—Aglasini **K. Abdulla**
60 **WITHOUT WARNING (FR)**, b f Warning—Obertura **K. Abdulla**
61 **ZELYCHKI (FR)**, b c Zelphi—Kamonia **P. Deshayes**

TWO-YEAR-OLDS

62 B c Woodman—Absurde **Mme A. O'Reilly**
63 B c Epervier Bleu—Alcove **Mr Yong Nam Seng**
64 **ALEXANCO (USA)**, ch c Conquistador Cielo—Lucky State **J. Garcia Roady**
65 **AMALICA (FR)**, b f Always Fair—Anahita **J. L. Bouchard**
66 B c Lyphard—Angela Serra **N. Incisa Della Roch**
67 B f Ela-Mana-Mou—Anna Commena **Scuderia Pieffegi**
68 Ch c Blushing John—Atalazia **K. Yano**
69 B f Highest Honor—Baino Bluff **I. M. Fares**
70 **BRILLIANCE (FR)**, b f Priolo—Briesta **Skymarc Farm**
71 B c Known Fact—Catty **E. Puerari**
72 **CELTIC EXIT (FR)**, b c Exit To Nowhere—Amour Celtique **Mme A. Vilay**
73 **CEPACOYA (FR)**, b f Fijar Tango—Ranga **K. Nader**
74 **CLAUDIA OF NOWHERE (FR)**, b f Exit To Nowhere—Clodette **J. L. Bouchard**
75 **EN HAUSSE (FR)**, ch f Sicyos—Cotation **G. Larrieu**
76 **EPEOS (GER)**, br c Acatenango—Eidothea **E. Wanke**
77 **ERINYS (FR)**, br f Kendor—Enodia **E. Wanke**
78 **FABULOUS FLIRT (FR)**, ch f Caerleon—Green Danube **J. Garcia-Roady**
79 Ch f Highest Honor—Formidable Flight **I. M. Fares**
80 B c Marignan—France Direct **P. Kwok**
81 **GALLIPOLI (FR)**, b c Efisio—Gemmologie **Mme D. Jacob**
82 **GOLDEN WINGS (USA)**, b f Devil's Bag—Golden Era **Skymarc Farm**
83 **HAIFA (FR)**, br f Vaguely Pleasant—High Try **E. Aoun**
84 B f Slew O' Gold—Imperturbable Lady **K. Abdulla**
85 **INTEMPORELLE (FR)**, b f Caerwent—Sainte Hermine **Mr Yong Nam Seng**
86 B f Riverman—Itsamazing **K. Abdulla**
87 B f Pursuit of Love—Kalandariya **Scuderia Pieffegi**
88 B f Alleged—Lake Country **K. Abdulla**
89 **LA PANTHERE (USA)**, ch f Pine Bluff—La Tritona **Mme A. O'Reilly**
90 **LAURENTINE (FR)**, b f Private Account—La Sky **Scuderia Pieffegi**
91 **LIBRIA (IRE)**, b f Bering—L'Americaine **Skymarc Farm**
92 B f Highest Honor—Noble Tiara **I. M. Fares**
93 B c Highest Honor—Numidie **I. M. Fares**
94 **OA BALDIXE (FR)**, gr c Linamix—Bal d'Oa **F. Prat**
95 **ORMENA (GER)**, ch f Acatenango—Opeia **E. Wanke**
96 **PINWHEEL (FR)**, ch f Mujtahid—Peggy Finch **Skymarc Farm**
97 **PRIADA (USA)**, b f Dayjur—Primevere **Skymarc Farm**
98 Ch f Highest Honor—Quiet Thoughts **I. M. Fares**
99 **REGAUDIE (FR)**, ch c Vaguely Pleasant—Carmissa **P. Bary**
100 B c Dancing Dissident—Rhein Honey **E. Puerari**
101 **SANG CHAUD (FR)**, ch c Sanglamore—Folle Poursuite **Mme A. Vilay**
102 Gr c Highest Honor—Santiki **I. M. Fares**
103 **SCARLET STAR**, b f Priolo—Star Change **Skymarc Farm**
104 b f Machiavellian—Seranda **Mme A. O'Reilly**
105 B f Bering—Shardazar **I. M. Fares**
106 **SPECTRE (USA)**, b f St Jovite—Secret Form **Mme A. O'Reilly**
107 **STREET LINA (FR)**, gr f Linamix—Street Opera **Mme D. Jacob**
108 B c Lyphard—Sylph **K. Abdulla**
109 **VERTIGE (USA)**, b f Gulch—Verria **Mme A. O'Reilly**
110 **ZACINTA**, b f Hawkster—Portuguese **Sc. A. M. A.**

Jockeys (Flat): D Boeuf, F Grenet (8-7), O Peslier, P L Pouive, K Vaillant.

Apprentice: S Ladjadj.

MR P. BARY—continued

Late Namings
ARCHIPOVA, Ela-Mana-Mou — Anna Commena
FORM FORMIDABLE (FR), Highest Honor — Formidable Flight
GOOD THINKING (FR), Highest Honor — Quiet Thoughts
HIGH NORMANDY (FR), Highest Honor — Numidie
HIGH TIARA (FR), Highest Honor — Noble Tiara
KRILOVA, Pursuit Of Love — Kalandariya
LIBANOOR (FR), Highest Honor — Baino Bluff
SENATOR (FR), Highest Honor — Santiki
SHAHRAZAD (FR). Bering — Shardazar
SHINE ON ME, Machiavellian — Seranda

42   MR R. BASTIMAN, Wetherby

Postal: **The Grange Stables, Grange Park, Wetherby, Yorkshire, LS22 5DY.**
Phone: **(01937) 583050**

1 **BECKYHANNAH,** 6, b m Rambling River—Munequita **Mr Terry Pitts**
2 **BLACK ICE BOY (IRE),** 5, b g Law Society (USA)—Hogan's Sister (USA) **Omega Racing Club**
3 **DANCING DESTINY,** 4, b f Dancing Brave (USA)—Tender Loving Care **Mrs P. Bastiman**
4 **DEPUTY TIM,** 13, ch g Crofter (USA)—Kindle **Mrs P. Bastiman**
5 **FIRST OPTION,** 6, ch g Primo Dominie—Merrywren **Omega Racing Club**
6 **GOLDEN TORQUE,** 9, br g Taufan (USA)—Brightelmstone **Mr Trevor J. Smith**
7 **HELLO HOBSON'S (IRE),** 6, b m Fayruz—Castleforbes **Mrs P. Bastiman**
8 **HERE'S HONOUR (IRE),** 4, ch g King of Clubs—Coronea **V. Chandler Equus Ltd**
9 **HILLZAH (USA),** 8, ch g Blushing Groom (FR)—Glamour Girl (ARG) **Mrs P. Churm**
10 **HOWARD THE DUCK,** 6, ch g Baron Blakeney—One More Try **V. Chandler Equus Ltd**
11 **NEVER SO FIT,** 5, b g Never So Bold—Darine **Mrs N. Skelton**
12 **NO WORD,** 9, b br g Oats—Rapenna **Mr S. P. Hudson**
13 **SPEED OIL,** 7, br g Java Tiger—Maydrum **Mr John Howie**
14 **SUPER ROCKY,** 7, b g Clantime—Starproof **Mr I. B. Barker**
15 **TURGENEV (IRE),** 7, b g Sadler's Wells (USA)—Tilia (ITY) **Mrs Bridget Tranmer**

THREE-YEAR-OLDS

16 **KHABAR,** b g Forzando—Ella Mon Amour

Other Owners: Mr E. D. Atkinson, Mr A. D. Bastiman, Mrs C. B. Bastiman, Mr Robin Bastiman, Mr G. F. Bradley, Mr R. C. Copcutt, Mr Peter Frankland, Mr Greg Lancaster, Mrs Judith Marshall.

Jockeys (Flat): K Fallon (w.a.), D McKeown (w.a.).

Jockey (NH): M Dwyer (w.a.).

Apprentice: H J Bastiman (8-9).

Conditional: H J Bastiman (9-7).

Amateur: Mr Ian Baker (9-7).

Lady Rider: Miss T Ager (8-0).

43   MR A. G. BATES, Maisons-Laffitte

Postal: **1 Avenue Champaubert, 78600 Maisons-Laffitte, France.**
Phone: **1-39 62 77 77/1-39 62 03 14 FAX 139620314**

1 **CORBEAULIEU**, 5, b h Akarad—Kenyatta **Robert Fournier Sarloveze**
2 **PAMVER**, 6, b br g Pampabird—Viverba **Adolf Bader**
3 **SEA PLANE**, 7, gr g Nishapour—Pirogue **Robert Fournier Sarloveze**

THREE-YEAR-OLDS

4 **GAZETTE ROYALE**, b f Garde Royale—My Mistress **Alain Bates**
5 **LAURIS SOVEREIGN**, b c Round Sovereign—Lauris **Alain Bates**
6 **LUX HONOR**, gr c Highest Honor—Luxurious **J. C. Cheuvreux**

TWO-YEAR-OLDS

7 **SICYERA (FR)**, b f 25/4 Mister Sicy (FR)—Huntera (FR) (Huntercombe) **Alain Bates**

Lady Rider: Mrs Chantal Bates.

44   MR B. P. J. BAUGH, Little Haywood

Postal: **2 Crompton Close, Little Haywood, Stafford, ST18 0YS.**
Phone: **STABLES (01782) 723524 HOME (01889) 882114**

1 **BETABETCORBETT**, 5, b g Prince Sabo—Leprechaun Lady **Mrs Diane Baugh**
2 **FIREFIGHTER**, 7, ch g Sharpo—Courtesy Call **Mr J. W. Meredith**
3 **FLORISMART**, 4, b c Never So Bold—Spoilt Again **Mrs Diane Baugh**
4 **GIORDANO (IRE)**, 6, br g Cyrano de Bergerac—Kitterland **Mr M. J. Lyons**
5 **HORSETRADER**, 4, b g Aragon—Grovette **Mr John W. Meredith**
6 **REED MY LIPS (IRE)**, 5, br g Thatching—Taunsa **Messrs Chrimes, Winn & Wilson**
7 **SEYMOUR MANORS**, 7, ch m Seymour Hicks (FR)—Saucy Eater **Mr E. Bennion**
8 **TEXAS SCRAMBLE**, 7, b g Norwick (USA)—Orange Parade **Messrs Chrimes, Winn & Wilson**
9 **TTYFRAN**, 6, b g Petong—So It Goes **Mrs Diane Baugh**

THREE-YEAR-OLDS

10 **BOFFY (IRE)**, ch c Mac's Imp (USA)—No Dowry **Mr Stan Baugh**
11 **MAYSIMP (IRE)**, ch f Mac's Imp (USA)—Splendid Yankee **Mrs Joan M. Chrimes**

TWO-YEAR-OLDS

12 **GABLESEA**, b c 14/5 Beveled (USA)—Me Spede (Valiyar) **Messrs Chrimes Winn Wilson**
13 **JOYFUL JOY**, b f 27/3 River God (USA)—Joyfulness (FR) (Cure The Blues (USA)) **Mr E. Bennion**
14 B f Be My Native—Radalgo **Mr Ray Robinson**
15 B c 25/4 Mac's Imp (USA)—Sassalin (Sassafras (FR)) **Mr F. Dobby**
16 **STRAVANO**, b f 24/3 Handsome Sailor—La Stravaganza (Slip Anchor) **Mr E. Bennion**
17 B g 19/3 Arzanni—View Halloa (Al Sirat (USA)) **Working Class Hero Racing Club**

Other Owners: Mrs C. Hannam, Mr W. G. Hannam, Mr David Horne, Mr Gerry Powtney.

Jockey (Flat): W Lord (8-0).

Jockey (NH): Gary Lyons (10-0).

45   MR P. BEAUMONT, Brandsby

Postal: **Foulrice Farm, Brandsby, York, YO6 4SB.**
Phone: **BRANDSBY (01347) 888208 FAX (01347) 888208**

1 **ANY DREAM WOULD DO**, 7, b m Efisio—Pasha's Dream **Mrs C. M. G. Cawte**
2 **APPLAUDER**, 7, b g Scorpio (FR)—Prim Catherine **Mrs J. M. Plummer**
3 **BEGGARS BANQUET (IRE)**, 6, b g Callernish—Mo Storeen **Mr E. H. Ruddock**
4 **BLACKDALE BOY**, 5, ch g K-Battery—Sovereign Gal **Mr Ian Mosey**
5 **BOB NELSON**, 9, b g Le Moss—Caplight **Mrs C. M. Clarke**
6 **CHERRY DEE**, 5, ch m Ardross—Merry Cherry **Mr George Dilger**
7 **CHORUS LINE (IRE)**, 7, b m Torus—Right Chimes **Mrs A. P. Stead**
8 **CROWTHER HOMES**, 6, br m Neltino—Fair Sara **Mrs G. E. Barclay**
9 **DRUMDONNA (IRE)**, 6, b m Drumalis—Decoy Duck **Mrs M. R. Beaumont**
10 **EMILYMOORE**, 5, ch m Primitive Rising—Malmo **Mrs E. Dixon**
11 5, Ch g Hard Fought—Find The Sun **Mr C. N. Wilmot-Smith**
12 **FLICKERING LIGHT**, 5, b m Baron Blakeney—Palmerston Girl **Mrs Jos Wilson**
13 **GALE FORCE (IRE)**, 5, b g Strong Gale—Stay As You Are **Mr George Dilger**
14 **GRATE DEEL (IRE)**, 6, ch g The Parson—Cahernane Girl **Mrs M. Ashby**
15 **GRAZEMBER**, 9, b g Oats—Mellie **Mrs M. Ashby**
16 **IRISH GENT**, 10, br g Andretti—Seana Sheo **The Morley Stud**
17 **ISLAND CHIEF (IRE)**, 7, b g Carlingford Castle—Run Piggy Run **Mr George Dilger**
18 **JODAMI**, 11, b g Crash Course—Masterstown Lucy **Mr J. N. Yeadon**
19 **KING PIN**, 4, b g King's Ride—Bowling Fort **Mr J. N. Hinchcliffe**
20 **KINGS SERMON (IRE)**, 7, br g King's Ride—Sunday Sermon **Mrs P. A. H. Hartley**
21 **MIDDLEHAM PEARL**, 6, b m Loch Pearl—Twice Nice **Mr J. N. Hinchcliffe**
22 **NEW CHARGES**, 9, b g Shernazar—Wise Blood **Mrs M. R. Beaumont**
23 **NIKI DEE (IRE)**, 6, b g Phardante (FR)—Curragh Breeze **Mr George Dilger**
24 **ROMALDKIRK**, 4, b g Jalmood (USA)—Palace Tor **The Morley Stud**
25 **SCALLYMAC (IRE)**, 7, br g Oats—Maggies Girl **Mr John Veitch**
26 **SCRABO VIEW (IRE)**, 8, ch g Denel (FR)—Patricias Choice **Mr Robin Mellish**
27 **SHAHGRAM (IRE)**, 8, gr g Top Ville—Sharmada (FR) **Wise Owl Discount Drug Stores Ltd**
28 **TEMPLE GARTH**, 7, b g Baron Blakeney—Future Chance **Mrs Jos Wilson**
29 **TOPOTHENORTHRACING (IRE)**, 6, b m Tremblant—Waving Penant **The Foulrice Twenty**
30 **TWEEDSWOOD (IRE)**, 6, b g Strong Gale—Paulas Fancy **Mr J. N. Yeadon**
31 **URIZEN**, 11, ch g High Line—Off The Reel (USA) **Mrs P. A. H. Hartley**
32 **WESTWELL BOY**, 10, b g Kambalda—Lady Ashton **Mr D. N. Yeadon**
33 **YOUNG KENNY**, 5, b g Ardross—Deirdres Dream **Mr J. G. Read**

Other Owners: Mr G. Armstrong, Mrs M. W. Bird, Mr Paul Clarkson, Mr P. Clews, Mr G. L. Comer, Mrs Maureen Dilger, Mrs Anthea L. Farrell, Mr D. Hall, Mr Gordon Hall, Mr P. A. H. Hartley, Mr B. Heywood, Mrs V. Nolan, Mr H. Phipps, Mr G. Ratcliffe, Mr James Ritchie, Mr P. Sawyer, Mr F. T. Scotto, Mrs S. A. Search, C. H. & D. W. Stephenson Ltd, Mr M. P. Sutton, Mr D. W. Thompson, Mr A. Thorpe, Mr Malcolm Tulloch, Mr S. Vowles, Mr J. P. Wilson, Mr J. F. Wright.

Jockeys (NH): M Dwyer (w.a.), R Supple.

Conditional: B D Gratton (9-7).

Lady Rider: Mrs A L Farrell.

46   MR M. L. W. BELL, Newmarket

Postal: **Fitzroy House, Newmarket, Suffolk, CB8 0JT.**
Phone: **(01638) 666567 FAX (01638) 668000 MOBILE (0802) 264514**

1 **ALLEZ CYRANO (IRE)**, 5, b g Alzao (USA)—Miss Bergerac **Mr S. Carter**
2 **BLOCKADE (USA)**, 7, b g Imperial Falcon (CAN)—Stolen Date (USA) **Mr A. M. Warrender**
3 **CIM BOM BOM (IRE)**, 4, b c Dowsing (USA)—Nekhbet **Mr Yucel Birol**
4 **DOMITIA (USA)**, 4, ch f Arctic Tern (USA)—Fast Trek (FR) **Mr M. Desmond Fitzgerald**
5 **GRAND SELECTION (IRE)**, 4, b g Cricket Ball (USA)—Sine Labe (USA) **Mr M. B. Hawtin**

MR M. L. W. BELL—continued

6 **HOH MAGIC**, 4, ch f Cadeaux Genereux—Gunner's Belle **Mr D. F. Allport**
7 **LOCOROTONDO (IRE)**, 5, b m Broken Hearted—Rahwah **The P 1 Partnership**
8 **PARONOMASIA**, 4, b g Precocious—The Crying Game **Mr Paddy Barrett**
9 **PRINCELY HUSH (IRE)**, 4, b c Prince Sabo—So Kind **Mr P. A. Philipps**
10 **SARASOTA STORM**, 4, b g Petoski—Challanging **Mr B. J. Warren**
11 **TORREY PINES**, 4, b g Red Sunset—Yukon Baby (USA) **Mr J. G. Moore**

THREE-YEAR-OLDS

12 **A LIKELY TALE (USA)**, b c Alleged (USA)—Thatsallshewrote (USA) **Mr Nasser Abdullah**
13 **ANTONIA BIN (IRE)**, gr f Sadler's Wells (USA)—Lady Capulet (USA) **Mr Luciano Gaucci**
14 **BEAU BRUNO**, b g Thatching—Lady Lorelei **Mrs John Van Geest**
15 **DANKESTON (USA)**, b c Elmaamul (USA)—Last Request **Mr Luciano Gaucci**
16 **DATUM (USA)**, br c Dayjur (USA)—My Ballerina (USA) **H.R.H. Prince Fahd Salman**
17 **DELPHINE**, b br f Formidable (USA)—Archaic **Vintage Racing**
18 **DESERT SKIMMER (USA)**, ch f Shadeed (USA)—Massorah (FR) **Mr T. F. Harris**
19 **DISALLOWED (IRE)**, b f Distinctly North (USA)—Miss Allowed (USA) **Mr J. M. Ratcliffe**
20 **DISTANT STORM**, ch g Pharly (FR)—Candle In The Wind **Mr B. R. H. Burrough**
21 **DOCTOR BRAVIOUS (IRE)**, b c Priolo (USA)—Sharp Slipper **Mr Luciano Gaucci**
22 **FANCIULLA DEL WEST (USA)**, b f Manila (USA)—La Venta (USA) **Sir Andrew Lloyd Webber**
23 **FERVENT FAN (IRE)**, b f Soviet Lad (USA)—Shannon Lady **Major W. R. Paton-Smith**
24 **FLASH IN THE PAN (IRE)**, ch f Bluebird (USA)—Tomona **Lady Newman**
25 **FOUR WEDDINGS (USA)**, b g Runaway Groom (CAN)—Kitty's Best (USA) **Mr R. P. B. Michaelson**
26 **GO WITH THE WIND**, b c Unfuwain (USA)—Cominna **Mrs B. Long**
27 **GREEN BOPPER (USA)**, b c Green Dancer (USA)—Wayage (USA) **Mr T. F. Harris**
28 **HAMLET (IRE)**, b c Danehill (USA)—Blasted Heath **Mr M. B. Hawtin**
29 **HOH RETURNS (IRE)**, b f Fairy King (USA)—Cipriani **Mr D. F. Allport**
30 **MANCINI**, b br g Nomination—Roman Blue **Mrs Anne Yearley**
31 **NAVAL GAMES**, b c Slip Anchor—Plaything **Mrs S. J. Davis**
32 **PALOMA BAY (IRE)**, b f Alzao (USA)—Adventurine **Mrs E. A. Harris**
33 **PRINCELY AFFAIR**, b g Prince Sabo—Shillay **Mr M. C. Talbot-Ponsonby**
34 **PRINCELY SOUND**, b c Prince Sabo—Sound of The Sea **Mr G. W. Byrne**
35 **RED TIE AFFAIR (USA)**, b c Miswaki (USA)—Quiet Rendezvous **Mr Terry Neill**
36 **ROSE OF SIBERIA (USA)**, gr f Siberian Express (USA)—Exuberine (FR) **Mrs J. M. Corbett**
37 **SAMUEL SCOTT**, b g Shareef Dancer (USA)—Revisit **Richard Green (Fine Paintings)**
38 **SHERMOOD**, b f Shere Khan—Jalebird Blues **Mr K. F. Saunders**
39 **SILVER WING (USA)**, b f Silver Hawk (USA)—Cojinx (USA) **Cheveley Park Stud**
40 **SNOW FALCON**, b g Polar Falcon (USA)—Cameroun **Mrs G. Rowland-Clark**
41 **TRUANCY**, b c Polar Falcon (USA)—Zalfa **Cheveley Park Stud**
42 **WHITE PLAINS (IRE)**, b c Nordico (USA)—Flying Diva **Deln Ltd**

TWO-YEAR-OLDS

43 **ARANTXA**, b f 18/5 Sharpo—Amalancher (USA) (Alleged (USA)) **Mrs Anne Yearley**
44 **AUCTION HALL**, b f 26/3 Saddlers' Hall (IRE)—Single Bid (Auction Ring) **Cheveley Park Stud**
45 **AURELIAN**, ch c 22/4 Ron's Victory (USA)—Rive-Jumelle (IRE) (M Double M (USA)) **Mr M. Desmond Fitzgerald**
46 **AURORA BAY (IRE)**, b f 25/2 Night Shift (USA)—Dimmer (Kalaglow) **Mrs A. M. Byrne**
47 **BLUE MOVIE (IRE)**, ch c 29/1 Bluebird (USA)—Zoom Lens (IRE) (Caerleon (USA)) **Mr C. J. Wates**
48 **BLUES MAGIC (IRE)**, ch c 22/2 Imp Society (USA)—
                                                 Fairy Folk (IRE) (Fairy King (USA)) **Stamford Bridge Partnership**
49 **CALL THE BIRD (IRE)**, b c 28/1 Bluebird (USA)—Top Call (High Top) **Mr Luciano Gaucci**
50 Ch c 3/3 Common Grounds—Classic Ring (IRE) (Auction Ring (USA)) **Mr Mahmood Al-Shuaibi**
51 **CUESTA REY (USA)**, ch c 23/4 Lord At War (ARG)—Ms Hobby (USA) (Northern Prospect (USA)) **Mr K. Y. Lim**
52 **DANCING QUEEN (IRE)**, b f 21/4 Sadler's Wells (USA)—Bay Shade (USA) (Sharpen Up) **Mrs E. A. Harris**
53 B f 30/4 St Jovite (USA)—Dictina (FR) (Dictus (FR)) **Mr A. Rizzo**
54 **DOUBLY-H (IRE)**, b c 24/4 Be My Guest (USA)—Pursue (Auction Ring (USA)) **Mr G. L. H. Lederman**
55 B f 3/3 Slip Anchor—Doumayna (Kouban (FR)) **Mr B. R. H. Burrough**
56 **EASTERN EMBLEM (IRE)**, b c 8/4 Caerleon (USA)—Miss Garuda (Persian Bold) **Mr J. L. C. Pearce**
57 **ENAVIUS (IRE)**, b c 3/3 Lycius (USA)—Enaya (Caerleon (USA)) **Mr Luciano Gaucci**
58 Ch f 4/2 Elmaamul (USA)—Fair Sousanne (Busted) **Sporting Quest**
59 **HINT OF VICTORY**, ch c 7/4 Ron's Victory (USA)—May Hinton (Main Reef) **Sir Thomas Pilkington**
60 **HOH FLYER (USA)**, b f 20/4 Northern Flagship—Beautiful Bedouin (USA) (His Majesty (USA)) **Mr D. F. Allport**

MR M. L. W. BELL—continued

61 IECHYD-DA (IRE), b c 28/4 Sharp Victor (USA)—Key Partner (Law Society (USA)) **Mr K. J. Mercer**
62 B f 19/5 Night Shift (USA)—Indian Jubilee (Indian King (USA)) **Sir Andrew Lloyd Webber**
63 IVAN LUIS (FR), b c 11/5 Lycius (USA)—Zivania (IRE) (Shernazar) **Mr Luciano Gaucci**
64 KENWOOD MELODY, ch c 9/4 Lead On Time (USA)—Baddi Baddi (USA) (Sharpen Up) **Mr K. Y. Lim**
65 Ch f 2/4 Diesis—Lajna (Be My Guest (USA)) **Mr T. F. Harris**
66 MELIKSAH (IRE), ch c 19/1 Thatching—Lady of Shalott (Kings Lake (USA)) **Mr Yucel Birol**
67 MIDYAN CALL, b c 18/4 Midyan (USA)—Early Call (Kind of Hush) **Mr Luciano Gaucci**
68 MOM'S COVE (USA), b c 27/4 Irish River (FR)—Mom's The Word (USA) (Danzig (USA)) **Mr K. Y. Lim**
69 B f 30/3 Old Vic—Mrs Warren (USA) (Hail To Reason) **Mr Saif Ali**
70 MS ZIMAN, b f 3/2 Mystiko (USA)—Leave Her Be (USA) (Known Fact (USA)) **Mr K. Y. Lim**
71 B f 1/4 Anshan—Naturally Fresh (Thatching) **Miss S. Farr**
72 NO CHIEF, b c 12/2 Be My Chief (USA)—Carmelina (Habitat) **Mr Luciano Gaucci**
73 PISUM SATIVUM, ch f 19/3 Ron's Victory (USA)—Trojan Desert (Troy) **Mr Paddy Barrett**
74 POKER PRINCESS, br f 23/2 Waajib—Mory Kante (USA) (Icecapade) **Mr M. B. Hawtin**
75 QUEST EXPRESS, ch c 30/4 Rudimentary (USA)—
                                            Swordlestown Miss (USA) (Apalachee (USA)) **Mr D. F. Allport**
76 ROYAL BELUGA, b f 27/3 Soviet Star (USA)—Allegedly Blue (USA) (Alleged (USA)) **Mr T. F. Harris**
77 B c 6/4 Puissance—Safidar (Roan Rocket) **Sporting Quest**
78 SEQUOIA PRINCE (USA), ch c 4/4 Woodman (USA)—Loren's Baby (USA) (Czaravich (USA)) **Mr Terry Neill**
79 SHARP POPPET, ch f 5/4 Statoblest—Razor Blade (Sharp Edge) **Mr R. A. Baker**
80 SILENT MIRACLE (IRE), b f 21/3 Night Shift (USA)—Curie Point (USA) (Sharpen Up) **Mr M. A. Khan**
81 SOLAR STORM, ch c 13/5 Polar Falcon (USA)—Sister Sophie (USA) (Effervescing (USA)) **Mr T. F. Harris**
82 SOLFEGIETTO, b f 24/3 Music Boy—Maria Isabella (FR) (Young Generation) **Cheveley Park Stud**
83 SPARTACUS, b c 8/3 Persian Bold—Pravolo (Fools Holme (USA)) **Highclere Thoroughbreds Ltd**
84 STAR TURN (IRE), ch c 16/5 Night Shift (USA)—Ringtail (Auction Ring (USA)) **Innlaw Racing**
85 TRADING ACES, b f 15/2 Be My Chief (USA)—Corn Futures (Nomination) **Mr R. P. B. Michaelson**
86 WELL DONE, gr f 4/2 Petong—Mrs Darling (Mummy's Pet) **Mr Yucel Birol**
87 WOODERINE (USA), ch f 7/4 Woodman (USA)—Exuberine (FR) (Be My Guest (USA)) **Mr Luciano Gaucci**
88 ZEST (USA), gr f 20/4 Zilzal (USA)—Toveris (Homing) **Mr W. J. P. Jackson**

Other Owners: Mrs B. W. Bell, Lady Blyth, Mrs Monica Caine, Mr I. Cameron, Mrs J. Campion, Mr Peter Coe, Mr H. Credig, Mr Terence Cullen, Lady D'Avigdor-Goldsmid, Mr Alex Gorrie, Mr Geoffrey C. Greenwood, Mr R. Guy, Hoh Supply Limited, Mr Mike Igo, Mrs D. Joly, Mr P. Kelly, Mr R. D. A. Kelly, Mrs S. M. Lim, Mrs John Magnier, Mr Peter V. McCalmont, Mr Jeff McDonald, Mr T. F. McGee, Mrs S. Mercer, Mr J. R. Mitchell, Mr K. Mitchell, M. L. W. Bell Racing Ltd, Mr John C. Moore, Mr R. Pilkington, Mr David F. Powell, Mr Barry Pryor, Mr J. J. Ratcliffe, Mr T. S. Redman, Mr S. C. Sampson, Mr Alasdair Simpson, Mr Anthony Trace, Miss Carolyn Walton, Mr P. R. Whelan, Mr Christopher Wright.

Jockey (Flat): M Fenton (8-1).

Apprentices: G Faulkner (7-12), R Mullen (7-0).

Amateur: Mr R Wakley (10-0).

Lady Rider: Mrs L Lawson (8-6).

47   MR S. B. BELL, Driffield

Postal: **Hall Farm, Burton Fleming, Driffield, North Humberside, YO25 0PT.**
Phone: **(01262) 470519**

1 AQUASEEKER, 6, b g Dowsing (USA)—Patois **Mr C. H. P. Bell**
2 CORBLEU (IRE), 6, b g Corvaro (USA)—Another Daisy **Mr David Woodcock**
3 RED JAM JAR, 11, ch g Windjammer (USA)—Macaw **Mr C. H. P. Bell**
4 RUDI'S PRIDE (IRE), 5, b g Conquering Hero (USA)—Belle-Cote **Mrs Cheryl L. Owen**

MR S. B. BELL—continued

5 SIRERIC (IRE), 6, b g Asir—Twice Regal **Mr C. H. P. Bell**
6 THE PUB, 10, br g Riki Lash—Melerings **Mr Geoff Pickering**
7 TIMMOSS (IRE), 5, b g Le Moss—Tangaroa **Mr S. B. Bell**
8 TOP TATT, 6, b g Supreme Leader—Liebeslied **Mr C. H. P. Bell**
9 WOODBINE, 6, b g Idiot's Delight—Grange Hill Girl **Mrs Cheryl L. Owen**

Jockeys (NH): K Johnson, N Smith.

48   MR FRANCOIS BELMONT, Lamorlaye

Postal: **21b Rue Charles Pratt, 60260 Lamorlaye, France.**
Phone: **44 21 51 24   FAX 44 21 51 68**

1 CARAYANN II, 6, ch g Port Etienne (FR)—Djaipour II (FR) **B. van Dalfsen**
2 KALMAR, 4, b g Al Nasr (FR)—Kalmia **M. Charlton**
3 LE MAGE, 6, b g Top Ville—La Mirande (FR) **P. Coussaune**
4 TROPICAL KING (GER), 6, ch h Lagunas—Tanami (GER) **G. Weil**

THREE-YEAR-OLDS
5 FLUTIXOA (FR), gr f Linamix (FR)—Flutiskoa **Mme J. Belmont**

Other Owners: Mme De Chateaufou, C. Curtis, D. Dundon, M. Greaney, W. Gunther, O. Lecerf, A. F. S. Li, N. Ohana, L. De Quatre-Barbe, G. Von Finck, H. Von Finck.

Jockeys (Flat): D Boeuf, T Jarnet.

Jockeys (NH): D Mescam, D Vincent.

Amateur: L Maynard.

49   MR J. A. BENNETT, Wantage

Postal: **Miller Place Stables, 2 Filley Alley, Letcombe Bassett, Wantage, Oxon, OX12 9LT.**
Phone: **(01235) 763162**

1 ASKING, 4, b g Skyliner—Ma Famille **Miss J. C. Blackwell & Partners**
2 DARLING MADELINE, 5, b m Ilium—Madame Ruby (FR) **Mr D. Spenceley**
3 GOOD FETCH, 5, b m Siberian Express (USA)—Exceptional Beauty **Mr D. Spenceley**
4 KARIBU (GER), 5, b g Dancing Brave (USA)—Kaiserstadt (GER) **Mr D. Spenceley**
5 PARISIAN, 11, b g Shirley Heights—Miss Paris **Miss J. C. Blackwell**
6 RUBHAHUNISH (IRE), 5, b h Darshaan—Captive Island **Lone Star Racing Partnership**
7 SAXON MAGIC, 6, ch m Faustus (USA)—Wessex Kingdom **Miss J. C. Blackwell & Partners**
8 SHARP HOLLY (IRE), 4, b f Exactly Sharp (USA)—Children's Hour **Mr D. Spenceley & Partners**
9 TOPANGA, 4, b g Dancing Brave (USA)—Trampship **Mr J. McGuigan & Partners**

THREE-YEAR-OLDS
10 LOCKET, b f Precocious—Bracelet **Mr Jeff Plumb**
11 Ch f Jareer (USA)—Soie Gentille **Mr D. Spenceley**
12 TOUCH OF SNOW, b f Touch of Grey—Snow Huntress **Mr T. M. Jennings**

TWO-YEAR-OLDS
13 Ch c 19/4 Tina's Pet—Edraianthus (Windjammer (USA)) **Miller Place Partnership**

MR J. A. BENNETT—continued

Other Owners: Mr N. Abell, Mr R. Bartlett, Mrs Sara Clarke, Mrs V. E. Cudd, Mr G. J. Daly, Mrs Jane Geden, Mr A. L. Gray, Mrs I. A. Hancock, Mr Keith Hatwood, Mr T. Hopton, Mr B. P. Hoye, Mrs Julia Hucker, Mr F. Keeble, Mr M. K. King, Mrs S. G. King, Mrs L. Leyland, Mr N. E. Linter, Mr M. Reynolds, Mr L. G. Ryder, Mr N. P. Sherriff, Mr Frederick Smith, Mr B. G. Thorogood, Mr P. Trounce, Mr P. D. Tugwell, Mr M. T. R. Twigg.

Jockey (NH): L Harvey (w.a.).

50   MR C. J. BENSTEAD, Epsom

Postal: **The Limes, Shepherds Walk, Epsom, Surrey, KT18 6DF.**
Phone: **ASHTEAD (01372) 273152 FAX (01372) 274752**

1 DEEVEE, 7, b h Hallgate—Lady Woodpecker **Mr D. Turner**
2 EAST SHEEN, 4, b f Salse (USA)—Madam Cody **Mr D. Turner**
3 VANOLA, 4, b f Salse (USA)—Salilia **Del Roy**

THREE-YEAR-OLDS

4 ALHAWA (USA), ch c Mt Livermore—Petrava (NZ) **Mr Hamdan Al Maktoum**
5 EFFICACIOUS (IRE), ch f Efisio—Bushti Music **Mr R. Lamb**
6 FASIL (IRE), ch c Polish Patriot (USA)—Apple Peel **Mr Hamdan Al Maktoum**
7 ITKAN (IRE), b f Marju (IRE)—Boldabsa **Mr Hamdan Al Maktoum**
8 RUWY, b f Soviet Star (USA)—Psylla **Mr Hamdan Al Maktoum**

TWO-YEAR-OLDS

9 AJNAD (IRE), b c 23/4 Efisio—Lotte Lenta (Gorytus (USA)) **Mr Hamdan Al Maktoum**
10 ARDENT, b c 13/2 Aragon—Forest of Arden (Tap On Wood) **Mr R. Lamb**
11 FLYING COLOURS (IRE), b f 2/2 Fairy King (USA)—Crazed Rainbow (USA) (Graustark) **Mrs R. W. S. Baker**
12 JANDAL, ch c 10/4 Arazi (USA)—Littlefield (Bay Express) **Mr Hamdan Al Maktoum**
13 LAWZ (IRE), br c 1/5 Lahib (USA)—Sea Port (Averof) **Mr Hamdan Al Maktoum**
14 MARSAD (IRE), ch c 29/3 Fayruz—Broad Haven (IRE) (Be My Guest (USA)) **Mr Hamdan Al Maktoum**
15 MUKADDAR (USA), ch c 18/4 Elmaamul (USA)—
                Both Sides Now (USA) (Topsider (USA)) **Mr Hamdan Al Maktoum**

51   MR J. BERRY, Cockerham

Postal: **Moss Side Racing Stable, Crimbles Lane, Cockerham, Lancaster, LA2 OES.**
Phone: **FORTON (01524) 791179 FAX (01524) 791958 MOBILE (0374) 747718**

1 AMRON, 9, b g Bold Owl—Sweet Minuet **Mr R. Peebles**
2 ANSELLMAN, 6, gr g Absalom—Grace Poole **Ansells of Watford**
3 BEST OF ALL (IRE), 4, b f Try My Best (USA)—Skisette **Mr Robert Aird**
4 BOLSHOI (IRE), 4, br c Royal Academy (USA)—Mainly Dry **Mrs David Brown**
5 CARLISLE BANDITO'S (IRE), 4, b g Exhibitioner—Welsh Rhyme **Mr J. Berry**
6 CEE-JAY-AY, 9, gr g Free State—Raffinrula **Mr Richard Jinks**
7 FLASHING SABRE, 4, b g Statoblest—Placid Pet **Mr Chris Deuters**
8 GARNOCK VALLEY, 6, b g Dowsing (USA)—Sunley Sinner **Mr Robert Aird**
9 GLEN GARNOCK (IRE), 4, gr c Danehill (USA)—Inanna **Mr Robert Aird**
10 HONEY TRADER, 4, b g Beveled (USA)—Lizzie Bee **Mrs Chris Deuters**
11 LAGO DI VARANO, 4, b g Clantime—On The Record **Mr Norman Jackson**
12 LAUREL DELIGHT, 6, ch m Presidium—Foudroyer **Laurel Leisure Ltd**
13 LUCKY PARKES, 6, b m Full Extent (USA)—Summerhill Spruce **Mr J. Heler**
14 MIND GAMES, 4, b c Puissance—Aryaf (CAN) **Mr Rob Hughes**
15 MONKEY'S WEDDING, 5, b g Skyliner—Munequita **Mr J. Tolbol**
16 MOST UPPITTY, 4, gr f Absalom—Hyatti **Mr J. Berry**
17 NORTHERN GREY, 4, gr g Puissance—Sharp Anne **Mr R. Leah**

MR J. BERRY—continued

18 **PALACEGATE EPISODE (IRE)**, 6, b m Drumalis—Pasadena Lady **Palacegate Corporation Ltd**
19 **PALACEGATE JACK (IRE)**, 5, gr g Neshad (USA)—Pasadena Lady **Palacegate Corporation Ltd**
20 **PALACEGATE TOUCH**, 6, gr g Petong—Dancing Chimes **Palacegate Corporation Ltd**
21 **PENTRE FFYNNON (IRE)**, 4, ch g Ballad Rock—One Better **Lord Mostyn**
22 **PERSIAN FAYRE**, 4, b c Persian Heights—Dominion Fayre **Mr Murray Grubb**
23 **SELHURSTPARK FLYER (IRE)**, 5, b g Northiam (USA)—Wisdom To Know **Mr Chris Deuters**
24 **SMOLENSK (IRE)**, 4, b g Ela-Mana-Mou—Merry Twinkle **Mr Chris Deuters**
25 **TUSCAN DAWN**, 6, ch g Clantime—Excavator Lady **Mrs Chris Deuters**

THREE-YEAR-OLDS

26 **ALBERT THE BEAR**, b g Puissance—Florentynna Bay **Mr Chris Deuters**
27 **AMOEBA (IRE)**, b f Distinctly North (USA)—Lady Ingrid **Mr Sam Berry**
28 **ARC OF THE DIVER (IRE)**, ch g Archway (IRE)—Inner Pearl **R. E. M. Partnership**
29 **BALINSKY (IRE)**, b f Skyliner—Ballinacurra **Mrs Julie Martin**
30 **CHILIBANG BANG**, b f Chilibang—Quenlyn **Mr Ian Crawford**
31 **CRAIGNAIRN**, b c Merdon Melody—Bri-Ette **Mr Murray Grubb**
32 **DANAMICH (IRE)**, b g Fayruz—Galapagos **M. P. Burke Developments Limited**
33 **GI LA HIGH**, gr f Rich Charlie—Gem of Gold **Mr Basheer Kielany**
34 **GWESPYR**, ch g Sharpo—Boozy **Lord Mostyn**
35 **HAUTE CUISINE**, b g Petong—Nevis **Paris House Gourmets**
37 **LIMERICK PRINCESS (IRE)**, ch f Polish Patriot (USA)—Princess of Nashua **Mr T. Doherty**
38 **MADRINA**, b f Waajib—Mainly Sunset **Skyline Racing Ltd**
39 **MANOLO (FR)**, b g Cricket Ball (USA)—Malouna (FR) **Lucayan Stud**
40 **MILETRIAN CITY**, gr g Petong—Blueit (FR) **Miletrian Plc**
41 **MISS BIGWIG**, b f Distinctly North (USA)—Jacqui Joy **Bigwigs Entertainments**
42 **MONSIEUR CULSYTH**, b c Mon Tresor—Regal Salute **Forsyth Cully Racing**
43 **MY MELODY PARKES**, b f Teenoso (USA)—Summerhill Spruce **Mr J. Heler**
44 **NO MONKEY NUTS**, ch g Clantime—Portvally **The Monkey Partnership**
45 **PALACEGATE CHIEF**, b c Inca Chief (USA)—Sports Post Lady (IRE) **Palacegate Corporation Ltd**
46 **PEKAY**, b c Puissance—K-Sera **Mr T. G. & Mrs M. E. Holdcroft**
47 **PHANTOM DANCER (IRE)**, b g Distinctly North (USA)—Angel of Music **Mr J. Berry**
48 **PLAYMAKER**, b g Primo Dominie—Salacious **Mr Rob Hughes**
49 **POWER GAME**, b c Puissance—Play The Game **Mr Rob Hughes**
50 **QUINTA BOY**, b g Puissance—Figment **Highgrove Developments Ltd**
51 **RIVER TERN**, b f Puissance—Millaine **Mr T. G. & Mrs M. E. Holdcroft**
52 **STANDOWN**, b g Reprimand—Ashdown **Mrs Chris Deuters**
53 **SWIFTY NIFTY (IRE)**, b f Runnett—Swift Verdict **Mrs Norma Peebles**
54 **TROIKA (IRE)**, ch f Roi Danzig (USA)—Trojan Relation **Mrs Chris Deuters**
55 **TROPICAL BEACH**, b g Lugana Beach—Hitravelscene **Mr J. Unsworth**
56 **WHICKSEY PERRY**, b g Presidium—Phamilla (IRE) **Mr J. Henderson**
57 **WHOTHEHELLISHARRY**, ch g Rich Charlie—Ballagarrow Girl **Mrs Julie Martin**

TWO-YEAR-OLDS

58 **ANTONIA'S CHOICE**, ch f 22/2 Music Boy—Mainly Sunset (Red Sunset) **Mrs Chris Deuters**
59 **ASTRAL CROWN (IRE)**, b f 10/4 Astronef—Current Bay (Tyrant (USA)) **Cave Racing**
60 **AZTEC TRAVELLER**, b g 13/4 Timeless Times (USA)—Chief Dancer (Chief Singer) **John Brown & Partners**
61 **BARNBURGH BOY**, ch c 19/3 Shalford (IRE)—Tuxford Hideaway (Cawston's Clown) **M P Burke Developments**
62 **BOLD RISK**, b c 8/3 Midyan (USA)—Madam Bold (Never So Bold) **Lostford Manor Stud**
63 B g 30/3 Merdon Melody—Bri-Ette (Brittany) **Mr J. Tolbol**
64 **CHANGED TO BAILEYS (IRE)**, b c 1/4 Distinctly North—Blue Czarina (Sandhurst Prince) **G. R. Baileys Ltd**
65 **COME TOO MAMMA'S**, ch f 9/3 La Grange Music—
                    Purchased By Phone (IRE) (Wolverlife) **John Brown & Partners**
66 **EAGER TO PLEASE**, ch g 3/5 Keen—Ackcontent (Key To Content (USA)) **Totally Original Partnership**
67 **ENCHANTICA**, ch f 5/4 Timeless Times (USA)—North Pine (Import) **Mrs B. C. Ansell**
68 **FOR OLD TIMES SAKE**, ch c 9/5 Efisio—
                    Blue Birds Fly (Rainbow Quest (USA)) **Mr & Mrs P. Venner, Mr & Mrs G. Blum**
69 **FREDRIK THE FIERCE (IRE)**, b c 21/4 Puissance—Hollia (Touch Boy) **Mr Chris Deuters**
70 **FRUITANA (IRE)**, b c 26/4 Distinctly North—Tadjnama (USA) (Exceller (USA)) **Comerford Bros Ltd**
71 **FULL TRACEABILITY**, b f 30/3 Ron's Victory (USA)—Miss Petella (Dunphy) **Jack Clayton & Partner**
72 **GORRAN**, b c 9/3 Belfort (FR)—Con Carni (Blakeney) **Mr Scott Gibbons**

MR J. BERRY—continued

73 **HUMBLE PRINCE (IRE)**, b c 24/3 Anita's Prince—Humble Mission (Shack (USA)) **Richard Milner**
74 **I CAN'T REMEMBER**, br c 25/3 Petong—Glenfield Portion (Mummy's Pet) **Manny Bernstein Ltd**
75 **I'M STILL HERE**, gr g 9/4 Skyliner—Miss Colenca (Petong) **J. K. M. Oliver & J. M. Berry**
76 **JINGLE (GER)**, ch f 21/2 Suave Dancer (USA)—Jacqueline d'Or (Kris) **Mr Basheer Kielany**
77 **MARYLEBONE (IRE)**, ch c 28/4 River Falls—Pasadena Lady (Captain James) **Cricketers Syndicate**
78 **MY GIRL**, b f 28/1 Mon Tresor—Lady of Itatiba (BEL) (King of Macedon) **Mr T. G. Holdcroft**
79 **NAIVASHA**, gr f 5/5 Petong—Nevis (Connaught) **Mrs Joy Hobby**
80 **NANT-Y-GAMER (FR)**, b c 4/2 Warning—Norfolk Lily (Blakeney) **Lord Mostyn**
81 **NORTHERN SAL**, ch f 30/1 Aragon—Sister Sal (Bairn (USA)) **Mr Ray Robinson**
82 B f 9/3 Distinctly North—North Kildare (USA) (Northjet) **Dr Jene Tsoi**
83 **OLYMPIC SPIRIT**, b f 18/5 Puissance—Stripanoora (Ahonoora) **William Hill Ltd**
84 **PRESENTIMENT**, b c 20/2 Puissance—Octavia (Sallust) **Mr & Mrs Deuters, T. & M. Holdcroft**
85 **PRINCE OF PARKES**, b c 30/1 Full Extent (USA)—Summerhill Spruce (Windjammer (USA)) **Mr J. Heler**
86 **READ YOUR CONTRACT (IRE)**, ch c 13/5 Imp Society (USA)—
                                        Princess of Nashua (Crowned Prince (USA)) **Academy Leasing Ltd**
87 B f 2/5 River Falls—Rockeater (Roan Rocket) **Mr Basheer Kielany**
88 **ROSE MILL**, b f 14/3 Puissance—Amber Mill (Doulab (USA)) **Mr T. G. & Mrs M. E. Holdcroft**
89 Ch c 7/5 Shalford (IRE)—Sally St Clair (Sallust) **Mrs S. Magnier**
90 **TORONTO**, b c 21/3 Puissance—Impala Lass (Kampala) **John Hulme & T. G. Holdcroft**

Other Owners: Peter Barclay, Mr Roy Breeze, Mr William Burns, Mr B. E. Chandler, Mr P. E. T. Chandler, Mr J. Conway, Mr David Fish, Mr J. A. Forsyth, Mr B. H. Gollins, Mr T. Herbert-Jackson, Mr A. S. Hill, Mr J. Laughton, Mrs P. Laughton, Mr W. R. Lofthouse, Mr David R. Martin, Ms C. M. Parker, Mr Raymond Parker, Mrs A. E. Robertson, Mr John C. Shaw, Mr G. Tiribocchi, Mr Neil Warburton, Mrs Jean Wilson.

Jockeys (Flat): J Carroll (8-2), Gary Carter, L Charnock (w.a.), Kevin Darley (w.a.).

Jockey (NH): M Moloney.

Apprentices: Paul Fessey (7-2), Carl Lowther (7-12), Paul Roberts (8-2), Joanne Webster (7-13).

Amateur: R Hale.

52   MR J. C. DE BERRY, Newmarket

Postal: **17 Warrington Street, Newmarket, Suffolk, CB8 8BA.**
Phone: **(01638) 660663 FAX (01638) 660663**

1 **BLACK HILL (IRE)**, 7, br g Black Minstrel—Land of Smiles **Mr Anthony M. Smith**
2 **CANARY FALCON**, 5, ch g Polish Precedent (USA)—Pumpona (USA) **Mrs N. Aqil**
3 **CAPTAIN NAVAR (IRE)**, 6, gr g Sexton Blake—Too Vague **Mr Anthony M. Smith**
4 **ELRAAS (USA)**, 4, b g Gulch (USA)—Full Card (USA) **Mrs N. Aqil**
5 **FLOTATION**, 9, b g Salmon Leap (USA)—Bold Miss **Mr P. G. Tingey**
6 **GALLIC VICTORY (IRE)**, 5, b g Gallic League—Sally St Clair **Mr Anthony M. Smith**
7 **STATISTICIAN**, 4, br g Statoblest—Sharp Lady **Mr Anthony M. Smith**
8 **TIFASI (IRE)**, 6, b g Shardari—Tikrara (USA) **Mr Anthony M. Smith**

THREE-YEAR-OLDS

9 **BEAR TO DANCE**, b f Rambo Dancer (CAN)—Pooh Wee **Mrs Caroline Berry**
10 **FURTHER FUTURE (IRE)**, br c Doubletour (USA)—Tamara's Reef **Mr John Berry**
11 **MEG'S MEMORY (IRE)**, b f Superlative—Meanz Beanz **Mrs Anthony Veale**
12 **OLD ROMA (IRE)**, b f Old Vic—Romantic Past (USA) **1997 Syndicate**
13 **SHIMMY DANCING**, b f Rambo Dancer (CAN)—Sharp Lady
14 **SUPREME ILLUSION (AUS)**, ch f Rory's Jester (AUS)—Counterfeit Coin (AUS)
15 **VEESEY**, b f Rock City—Travel On **Mrs V. Bampton**

MR J. C. DE BERRY—continued

TWO-YEAR-OLDS

16 **IL PRINCIPE (IRE)**, b c 12/5 Ela-Mana-Mou—Seattle Siren (USA) (Seattle Slew (USA)) **1997 Syndicate**
17 **LARGESSE**, br c 17/4 Cadeaux Genereux—Vilanika (FR) (Top Ville) **Mrs Rosemary Moszkowicz**
18 **SEASIDE (IRE)**, b f 11/3 Salt Dome (USA)—Cipriani (Habitat) **1997 Syndicate**

Other Owners: Mr W. Benter, Mr C. De P. Berry, Mr A. K. Collins, Mr J. Dumas, Mr G. Grimstone, Mrs C. Luxton, Mr H. Moszkowicz, Mr L. Pipe, Mr L. C. Wadey, Mr A. Walter, Woodditton Stud Ltd, Mr N. S. Yong.

Jockeys (Flat): K Fallon (8-4, w.a.), M Fenton (8-1, w.a.).

Jockeys (NH): I Lawrence (10-0), V Smith (10-0).

Amateur: Mr C McEntee (8-7).

53   MR N. BERRY, Upper Lambourn

Postal: **Frenchmans House, Upper Lambourn, Newbury, Berks, RG16 7QT.**
Phone: **(01488) 72817 FAX (01488) 72817 MOBILE (0378) 841236**

1 **AIR OF MYSTERY**, 4, ch f Ballad Rock—Keep Looking (USA) **The London Bridge Partnership**
2 **ASHKERNAZY (IRE)**, 5, ch m Salt Dome (USA)—Eskaroon **London Bridge II**
3 **BIT ON THE SIDE (IRE)**, 7, b m Vision (USA)—Mistress (USA) **Mr Mike Hawkett**
4 **COMEDY RIVER**, 9, br g Comedy Star (USA)—Hopeful Waters **Mr Norman Berry**
5 5, Ch g Hotfoot—Four Lawns **Mr L. M. Shepherd**
6 **GENERAL GUBBINS**, 5, b g Mashhor Dancer (USA)—Crag Hall **Mr Peter Urquhart**
7 **OPENING RANGE**, 5, b m Nordico (USA)—Waveguide **Mr J. Bull**
8 **PLACID LAD**, 9, b g Bustomi—Worling-Pearl **Mr Trevor W. Stubbings**
9 **RAMBOLD**, 5, b m Rambo Dancer (CAN)—Boldie **Mr Ron Collins**
10 **SOBELOVED**, 4, gr g Beveled (USA)—Miss Solo **Mr M. T. Lawrance**
11 **WHITELOCK QUEST**, 8, b g Rainbow Quest (USA)—Sagar **Mrs J. Eales**
12 **WOODYARD**, 7, b g King of Spain—Bustle Along **Heavyweight Racing**

THREE-YEAR-OLDS

13 **FAIRLY SURE (IRE)**, b f Red Sunset—Mirabiliary (USA) **Mr B. Beale**
14 **IMPETUOUS LADY (USA)**, br f Imp Society (USA)—Urakawa (USA) **Mr Mike Hawkett**
15 Ch f Mac's Imp (USA)—Star Heading **Mr B. Beale**
16 **WHITE SWAN WATER (IRE)**, b f Mac's Imp (USA)—Lyphards Goddess (IRE) **Heavyweight Racing**

Other Owners: Mr David Batten, Mrs Sarah Beale, Mr A. A. Campbell, Mr W. H. Cooper, Mrs Elizabeth Corley, Mr G. M. Eales, Mr D. J. Field, Mr A. D. Gipp, Mr C. Gregson, Mr Keith Hoffman, Mr P. Kersey, Miss Heather Robbie, Mr Chris Romain, Mrs I. Shine, Mr J. Shine.

Jockeys (Flat): N Adams (7-7, w.a.), R Perham (8-2, w.a.).

Conditional: A Bates (9-7).

54   MR J. D. BETHELL, Middleham

Postal: **Clarendon House, Middleham, Leyburn, North Yorkshire, DL8 4PE.**
Phone: **WENSLEYDALE (01969) 622962 OFFICE 623321 HOME FAX (01969) 622157**

1 **DOUBLE ECHO (IRE)**, 8, b g Glow (USA)—Piculet **Mrs John Lee**
2 **EL BAILADOR (IRE)**, 5, b g Dance of Life (USA)—Sharp Ego (USA) **Mrs John Lee**
3 **FLAMBORO**, 4, ch g Handsome Sailor—Scottish Legend **Footballers' Racing Club**
4 **HUNTERS OF BRORA**, 6, b m Sharpo—Nihad **Mr Robert Gibbons**
5 **JUNDI (IRE)**, 5, b g Sadler's Wells (USA)—Royal Sister II
6 **TRUE BIRD (IRE)**, 4, b f In The Wings—I Want My Say (USA) **Mr T. R. Lock**

MR J. D. BETHELL—continued

THREE-YEAR-OLDS

7 **ALFAYZA,** b f Danehill (USA)—Dahlawise (IRE) **Al Dahlawi Stud Co Ltd**
8 **BEN'A'VACHEI BOY,** gr g Rock City—Vacherin (USA) **Chequers Racing Club**
9 **CATHERINE'S CHOICE,** ch g Primo Dominie—Bambolona **Chequers Racing Club**
10 **DAIRA,** br f Daring March—Ile de Reine **Mr L. B. Holliday**
11 **JUNGLE FRESH,** b g Rambo Dancer (CAN)—Report 'em (USA) **Mr Robert Gibbons**
12 **KUDOS BLUE,** b f Elmaamul (USA)—Don't Be Shy (IRE) **Mr M. Bebb**
13 **MINERAL WATER,** ch g Weldnaas (USA)—Joud **Mr Robert Gibbons**
14 **SHEEMORE (IRE),** b g Don't Forget Me—Curie Abu **Mrs M. B. Allwright**
15 **SNOWY MANTLE,** b f Siberian Express (USA)—Mollified **Mrs G. Fane**
16 **TABRIZ,** b f Persian Heights—Faisalah
17 **WILLISA,** ch f Polar Falcon (USA)—Ghassanah **Al Dahlawi Stud Co Ltd**
18 **WINSTON,** b c Safawan—Lady Leman **Mr J. Galvanoni**

TWO-YEAR-OLDS

19 **IBIN ST JAMES,** b c Salse (USA)—St James's Antigua (IRE) (Law Society) (USA)) **Al Dahlawi Stud Co Ltd**
20 Ch c Common Grounds—Impropriety (Law Society (USA))
21 **KEIRA MARIE (IRE),** b f Waajib—Porto Alegre (Habitat) **Mr John A. Blakey**
22 B c Old Vic—Late Matinee (Red Sunset)
23 B c Presidium—Madam Muffin (Sparkler) **Mr T. R. Lock**
24 Ch f Chilibang—Mollified (Lombard (GER)) **Mrs G. Fane**
25 **RETURN OF AMIN,** ch c Salse (USA)—Ghassanah (Pas de Seul) **Al Dahlawi Stud Co Ltd**
26 **RICH GROUND,** gr c Common Grounds—Gratclo (Belfort (FR)) **Mrs T. Vickers**
27 **ROTOR MAN,** b c River Falls—Need For Cash (USA) (Raise A Native) **Mrs John Lee**
28 B c Taufan (USA)—Take My Pledge (IRE) (Ahonoora)

Other Owners: Mr P. Ashford, Mr J. D. Bethell, Mrs James Bethell, Mr Harold Brown, Mr Steven Brown, Mr Steven L. Collier, Mrs J. M. Corbett, Mr N. D. Fisher, Mrs Penelope Lamming, Mrs Vivian Oakes, Mr J. Savage, Mr David Shirley, The Dante Partnership, The Oakes Partnership, The Pheasant Partnership, Mr Michael J. Tobin, Mr Richard Whiteley.

55 MR W. A. BETHELL, Hull

Postal: **Arnold Manor, Arnold, Hull, North Humberside, HU11 5HP.**

Phone: **(01964) 562996**

1 **COTTAGE CRAFT,** 7, b g Idiot's Delight—Jimmys Cottage **Mr W. A. Bethell**
2 **MALAWI,** 6, ch g Northern State (USA)—Nyeri **Mr R. A. Bethell**
3 **QUIET MISTRESS,** 6, b m Kind of Hush—Miss Acrow **Mr R. A. Bethell**
4 **SAFARI PARK,** 7, ch m Absalom—Nyeri **Mr R. A. Bethell**
5 **SQUIRES TALE (IRE),** 8, b g Kemal (FR)—Darren's Heather **Mr R. A. Bethell**
6 **THE TARTAN DYER,** 9, b g Kambalda—Moongello **Mr W. A. Bethell**
7 **UBU VAL (FR),** 10, b g Kashneb (FR)—Lady Val (FR) **Mr W. A. Bethell**

Jockey (NH): A S Smith (10-0, w.a.).

56 MR E. G. BEVAN, Hereford

Postal: **Pullen Farm, Ullingswick, HR1 3JQ.**

1 **DERRING COURT,** 6, b m Derring Rose—Foolish Hooley **Mr E. G. Bevan**
2 **LITTLE COURT,** 5, b g Little Wolf—Foolish Hooley **Mr E. G. Bevan**

57   MR P. J. BEVAN, Uttoxeter

Postal: **The Stables, Black Pitts Farm, Kingstone, Uttoxeter, ST14 8QW.**
Phone: **HOME (01889) 500670 STABLES (01889) 500647**

1 **BETTERGETON**, 4, ch c Rakaposhi King—Celtic Tore (IRE) **Mr Derek Boulton**
2 **FAIR FLYER (IRE)**, 7, b g Tilt Up (USA)—Fair Siobahn **Mrs P. J. Bevan**
3 **GIPSY RAMBLER**, 11, gr g Move Off—Gipsy Silver **Mrs Margaret Underwood**
4 **HEART OF SPAIN**, 6, b g Aragon—Hearten **Mr F. A. Jackson**
5 **IRISH AMBITION (IRE)**, 4, b f Glow (USA)—On The Fringe (USA) **Mrs Elisabeth Draper**
6 **KATY KOO**, 4, b f Presidium—Francis Furness **Mr N. D. Alsop**
7 **MY HANDSOME PRINCE**, 4, b g Handsome Sailor—My Serenade (USA) **Mr D. B. Holmes**
8 **MY ROSSINI**, 7, b g Ardross—My Tootsie **Mrs Cherry Eaton**
9 **SOMETHING SPEEDY (IRE)**, 4, b f Sayf El Arab (USA)—Fabulous Pet **Mrs P. J. Bevan**
10 **SWISS MOUNTAIN**, 6, b br m Formidable (USA)—Helvetique (FR) **Mr N. D. Alsop**
11 **THE ANGEL LEEK**, 6, b m Sonnen Gold—Muskcat Rambler **Steve Lilley Racing Ltd**

THREE-YEAR-OLDS

12 **MAN ON A MISSION**, ch c Hatim (USA)—Colly Cone **Mr Derek Boulton**

Other Owners: Mr L. E. Goddard, Mr H. Holland.

Jockey (Flat): N Carlisle (w.a.).

58   MRS P. F. BICKERTON, Market Drayton

Postal: **3 Pixley Cottages, Hinstock, Market Drayton, Shropshire, TF9 2TN.**
Phone: **(01952) 550384 MOBILE (0860) 401750**

1 **CASHEL QUAY (IRE)**, 6, ch g Quayside—Magar's Pride **Mr David Bickerton**
2 **LADY RENTON**, 5, ch m Rolfe (USA)—Rentons Gift **Mr David Bickerton**
3 **MAY GIFT**, 4, b f Reesh—Rentons Gift **Mr David Bickerton**

59   MR M. P. BIELBY, Grimsby

Postal: **College Farm, The Avenue, East Ravendale, Grimsby, South Humberside, DN37 0RX.**
Phone: **PHONE/FAX (01472) 827872 HOME (01472) 814634 MOBILE (0831) 555533**

1 **ALKARINE**, 4, gr g Alias Smith (USA)—Colly Cone **Mr J. F. Coupland**
2 4, Ch f Crofthall—Bollin Gorgeous **Dr A. K. Srivastava**
3 **BROWNLOWS**, 4, b g Prince Sabo—Glockenmadel (GER) **Mr J. F. Coupland**
4 **CANNY LAD**, 6, b g Green Ruby (USA)—Young Whip **Mrs M. Dunning**
5 **COLLEGE DON**, 5, gr g Kalaglow—Westerlake **Mr J. F. Coupland**
6 **DUBLIN INDEMNITY (USA)**, 7, b g Alphabatim (USA)—Sailongal (USA) **Miss H. M. Dunning**
7 **IRIE MON (IRE)**, 4, b g Waajib—Achafalaya (USA) **Sotby Farming Co Ltd**
8 **JAYFCEE**, 4, b g K-Battery—Marie Zephyr **Mr J. F. Coupland**
9 **MOUNTGATE**, 4, b c Merdon Melody—Young Whip **Mr J. F. Coupland**
10 **PRIMO PANACHE**, 4, ch f Primo Dominie—Royal Agnes **Mrs E. A. Coupland**
11 **UNDAWATERSCUBADIVA**, 4, ch g Keen—Northern Scene **Mr J. F. Coupland**

THREE-YEAR-OLDS

12 **ALIS PRINCESS**, ch f Sayf El Arab (USA)—Princess Zeddera **Mr J. F. Coupland**
13 **CELIA'S RAINBOW**, gr f Belfort (FR)—Mrs Skinner **Mrs Anna Fisher**
14 **CHIEF CONNECTIONS**, b c Inca Chief (USA)—Ballafort **Mr C. J. Boland**
15 **ECCENTRIC DANCER**, b f Rambo Dancer (CAN)—Lady Eccentric (IRE) **Mr J. F. Coupland**
16 **ELLE MAC**, b f Merdon Melody—Tripolitaine (FR) **Mr J. F. Coupland**
17 **ILLUSIVE GOLD (IRE)**, b f Magical Strike (USA)—Snappy Dresser **Mr J. F. Coupland**

TWO-YEAR-OLDS

18 B f 1/4 Rock Hopper—Gleeful (Sayf El Arab (USA)) **Mr Kevin McDonnell**
19 **GULLIVERS GOLD**, ch c 4/4 Environment Friend—Penny In My Shoe (USA) (Sir Ivor) **Mr J. F. Coupland**

MR M. P. BIELBY—continued

20 **LORD MEON**, b c 20/3 Merdon Melody—Swallow Bay (Penmarric (USA)) **Mr J. F. Coupland**
21 **MELODIC SQUAW**, b f 28/2 Merdon Melody—Young Whip (Bold Owl) **Mr J. F. Coupland**
22 **SUNDANCE LAD**, b c 27/4 Rambo Dancer (CAN)—Sun Worshipper (Sun Prince) **Mr J. F. Coupland**
23 **VALMAS**, b c 5/3 Mas Media—Valiyma (Top Ville) **Mr J. F. Coupland**

Other Owners: Mrs S. Boland, Mr Brian Dunning, Mr A. Glover, Mr E. J. Judge, Mrs C. Lawson, Mr J. Lawson, Mr B. Womersley.

Jockey (Flat): J Weaver (w.a.).

Jockey (NH): M Brennan (10-0, w.a.).

Lady Rider: Miss Rachel Judge (9-7).

60   MR T. T. BILL, Ashby-de-la-Zouch

Postal: **Manor Farm, Smisby, Ashby-de-la-Zouch, Leics, LE6 5TA.**
Phone: **(01530) 415881 FAX (01530) 411914 MOBILE (0378) 294866**

1 **BLUE PENNANT**, 5, b m Jupiter Island—Tudor Whisper **Mr P. Kirkland**
2 **DRUMMER'S DREAM (IRE)**, 8, b m Drumalis—Peaches And Cream (FR) **Mr P. S. Daly**
3 **JIMMY O'DEA**, 9, br g Funny Man—Premier Nell **Mr J. S. Harlow**
4 **MARSHALL PINDARI**, 6, b h Son of Shaka—Off The Pill **Mrs J. Salt**
5 **MISS TUT (IRE)**, 5, br m Phardante (FR)—Lady Tut **Mr T. T. Bill**
6 **MORSKI**, 7, ch g Morston (FR)—Lady Gainsborough **Mr W. Meah**
7 **SEPTEMBER SAND**, 8, b m Oats—Booly Bay **Mr T. T. Bill**
8 **THE FORTIES**, 11, ch g Bybicello—Fanny Adams **Alan Merritt A.F.M. (Holdings) Ltd**

Other Owners: Mr J. J. R. Boulton, Harlow Bros Ltd.

Jockey (NH): J Railton (10-0).

> At the time of going to press, Godolphin had not
> decided which of their horses would be
> returning to Europe for the 1996 Flat racing
> season. An up-to-date list will be published,
> along with other late teams, in Raceform Update
> at the end of April.

61   MR J. J. BIRKETT, Workington

Postal: **Garfield House, High Seaton, Workington, Cumbria, CA14 1PD.**

Phone: **(01900) 604189**

1 **BALATA BAY**, 5, ch g Chief Singer—Lets Fall In Love (USA) **The Claret and Blue Partnership**
2 **BITACRACK**, 9, ch g Le Bavard (FR)—Gothic Arch **The Claret & Blue Partnership**
3 **BROUGHPARK AZALEA**, 7, b g Song—Slip The Ferret **Mr Brian McNichol**
4 **CAPTAIN TANCRED (IRE)**, 8, b g The Parson—Tudor Lady **Mr Alf Preston**
5 **DALUSMAN (IRE)**, 8, b g Mandalus—Good Surprise **Mr J. Mason**
6 **IRISH FLASHER**, 9, b g Exhibitioner—Miss Portal **Mr L. Leyland**
7 **JAUNTY GIG**, 10, b g Dunphy—Hazel Gig **Mr Keith Thomas**
8 **LIABILITY ORDER**, 7, b g Norwick (USA)—Starky's Pet **Mr Alf Preston**
9 **NINE PIPES (IRE)**, 5, b g Sure Blade (USA)—Winning Look **Nine Pipes Racing**
10 **POP IN THERE (IRE)**, 8, b g Monksfield—Why Don't Ye **Mr T. Irving**
11 **SHEER GIFT**, 7, b m Sheer Grit—Merry Madam **Mr Alf Preston**
12 **SIR DICKIE COX (IRE)**, 5, b g Nordico (USA)—Arthur's Daughter **Mr M. Cullerton**
13 **TASHREEF**, 6, b g Shareef Dancer (USA)—Lune de Minuit (USA) **Mr Sid Alcock**
14 **WALLS COURT**, 9, ch g Cardinal Flower—Anega **The Claret & Blue Partnership**
15 **YOUNG GALA**, 7, b m Young Man (FR)—Spring Gala **Mrs S. McNichol**

Other Owners: Mrs K. P. Birkett, Mr R. Brough, Mr G. Crellin, Mr B. Forster, Mr Grahame Gordon, Mr Brian Greslow, Mr Keith Harding, Mr W. Irving, Mr Laurence McDowell, Mr Brian McNichol, Mr B. Stuart, Mr D. M. Stuart, Mr I. Wilcock, Mrs L. Woods.

Jockey (NH): L O'Hara (10-0).

Conditional: B Harding (10-0), D J Moffatt (10-0).

Amateur: Mr S Johnston (9-7).

Lady Rider: Miss F Barnes (9-7).

62   MR K. BISHOP, Bridgwater

Postal: **Barford Park Stables, Spaxton, Bridgwater, Somerset, TA5 1AF.**

Phone: **SPAXTON (01278671) 437 FAX 01278671437**

1 **CARNIVAL KID**, 6, b g Latest Model—Easter Carnival **Mrs M. D. Best**
2 **COUNTRY RAMBLER**, 8, b g Relkino—Vacuna **Mr J. G. Charlton**
3 **CREDO BOY**, 7, ch g Royal Vulcan—Welsh Cloud **Mr K. Bishop**
4 **FLASHFEET**, 6, b g Rousillon (USA)—Miellita **Mr P. D. Purdy**
5 **HILL TRIX**, 10, b g Le Moss—Up To Trix **Mrs E. K. Ellis**
6 **KONGIES MELODY**, 5, b m Sousa—Pullandese **Mr B. R. King**
7 **LAJADHAL (FR)**, 7, gr g Bellypha—Rose d'Amour (USA) **Mr P. D. Purdy**
8 **MR KEWMILL**, 13, b g Homing—Muninga **Mr P. D. Purdy**
9 **NASEER (USA)**, 7, b g Hero's Honor (USA)—Sweet Delilah (USA) **Mr P. D. Purdy**
10 **NAUGHTY NICKY**, 8, b m Monksfield—Mary Escart **Mr K. Bishop**
11 **ONE VOICE (USA)**, 6, ch h Affirmed (USA)—Elk's Ellie (USA) **Mr P. D. Purdy**
12 **PRIVILEGEDTOSERVE**, 7, b m King's Ride—Bellavard **Business Forms Express**
13 **RED POINT**, 5, b m Reference Point—Red Shoes **Business Forms Express**
14 **RIPSNORTER (IRE)**, 7, ch g Rousillon (USA)—Formulate **Mr P. D. Purdy**
15 **STEEPLE JACK**, 9, b g Pardigras—Mountain Mear **Mr K. Bishop**
16 **TUDOR TOWN**, 8, b g Town And Country—Cottage Melody **Mr P. D. Purdy**
17 **VERRO (USA)**, 9, ch g Irish River (FR)—Royal Rafale (USA) **Mr P. D. Purdy**

Other Owners: Mrs Diana C. Kirkman, Mr C. J. Macey, Mr C. H. Roberts.

Jockey (NH): R Greene (10-0).

63   MRS C. J. BLACK, Oswestry

Postal: **Tedsmore Hall, West Felton, Oswestry, Salop, SY11 4HD.**
Phone: **(01691) 610208**

1 **EVEN BLUE (IRE)**, 8, b g Gianchi—The Blue Pound **Mrs C. J. Black**
2 **MANVULANE (IRE)**, 6, b g Mandalus—La Vulane **Mrs C. J. Black**

64   MR A. G. BLACKMORE, Hertford

Postal: **'Chasers', Stockings Lane, Little Berkhamsted, Hertford, SG13 8LW.**
Phone: **(01707) 875060**

1 **HIGHLAND FLAME**, 7, ch g Dunbeath (USA)—Blakesware Saint **Mr A. G. Blackmore**
2 **PHYSICAL FUN**, 5, b g Phardante (FR)—Running Game **Mr A. G. Blackmore**

Jockey (NH): R Dunwoody (10-2, w.a.).

Conditional: G Hogan (9-10).

Lady Rider: Miss Gee Armytage (9-7).

65   MR M. T. W. BLANSHARD, Upper Lambourn

Postal: **Lethornes Stables, Upper Lambourn, Hungerford, Berkshire, RG17 8QT**
Phone: **LAMBOURN (01488) 71091 FAX (01488) 73497 MOBILE (0385) 370093**

1 **BAJAN ROSE**, 4, b f Dashing Blade—Supreme Rose
2 **BOWDEN ROSE**, 4, ch f Dashing Blade—Elegant Rose
3 **DUELLO**, 5, b g Sure Blade (USA)—Royal Loft
4 **MINT A MILLION (IRE)**, 5, b g Thatching—Often
5 **ROMALITO**, 6, b g Robellino (USA)—Princess Zita
6 **RUNIC SYMBOL**, 5, b g Warning—Pagan Deity
7 **SEA SPOUSE**, 5, ch g Jalmood (USA)—Bambolona
8 **TRIPLE TIE (USA)**, 5, ch m The Minstrel (CAN)—Tea And Roses (USA)
9 **WELSHMAN**, 10, ch g Final Straw—Joie de Galles

THREE-YEAR-OLDS

10 **BEN BOWDEN**, br g Sharrood (USA)—Elegant Rose
11 **POLLY GOLIGHTLY**, ch f Weldnaas (USA)—Polly's Teahouse
12 **PUBLIC OFFERING**, b f Warrshan (USA)—Money Supply
13 **RAMBLING BEAR**, ch c Sharrood (USA)—Supreme Rose
14 **ZDENKA**, b f Dominion—Short And Sharp

TWO-YEAR-OLDS

15 **GORE HILL**, b f 25/3 Be My Chief (USA)—Hollow Heart (Wolver Hollow)
16 **JAVA BAY**, b f 8/3 Statoblest—Flopsy (Welsh Pageant)
17 B f 10/5 Midyan (USA)—Orange Hill (High Top)
18 B f 10/5 Beveled (USA)—Pallomere (Blue Cashmere)
19 **SAFFRON ROSE**, b f 6/4 Polar Falcon (USA)—Tweedling (USA) (Sir Ivor)
20 Ch f 28/4 Beveled (USA)—Shapina (Sharp Edge)
21 B f 25/5 Beveled (USA)—Supreme Rose (Frimley Park)

Other Owners: Mr M. Blanshard, Mr Daniel Bradshaw, Mr C. R. Buttery, Mrs Elsa Dean, Mr Charles Farr, Mrs Barbara Garland, H. C. Promotions Ltd, Mrs Michael Hill, Mr Stanley Hinton, Mr Peter J. Kinden, Mr C. McKenna, Miss Frances Murphy, Mr J. A. Oliver, Lady Page, Mr Charles Philipson, Seven Seas Racing, Mr D. Sloan, Mr David Sykes, The Cheapside Syndicate, The Lower Bowden Syndicate, Mr A. R. B. Ward, Mrs C. Ward.

Jockeys (Flat): R Cochrane (w.a.), J Quinn (w.a).

Jockey (NH): D Gallagher.

66   MR J. S. BOLGER, Carlow

Postal: **Glebe House, Coolcullen, Carlow, Ireland.**

Phone: **(056) 43150 OR 43158 FAX (056) 43256**

1 **AILLEACHT (USA)**, 4, br f Chief's Crown—Poster Beauty **Mrs J. S. Bolger**
2 **AL MOHAAJIR (USA)**, 5, ch h Cadeaux Genereux—Lady In White **M. Al Maktoum**
3 **BLITZER (IRE)**, 4, b c Nordico—Special Display **D. H. W. Dobson**
4 **CELLADONIA (IRE)**, 4, b c Green Desert—Gayle Gal **D. H. W. Dobson**
5 **CLIFDON FOG (IRE)**, 5, b g Darshaan—Lake Mist **J. P. Hill**
6 **DANAA MINNI (IRE)**, 4, ch c Caerleon—Ivory Home **M. Al Maktoum**
7 **DIAMOND DISPLAY (IRE)**, 5, b m Shardari—Special Display **D. H. W. Dobson**
8 **DON'T CARE (IRE)**, 5, b m Nordico—Eyeliner **Mrs Una Manning**
9 **IDRIS (IRE)**, 6, b h Ahonoora—Idara **M. H. Keogh**
10 **MOHAAJIR (USA)**, 5, b h Sadler's Wells—Very Charming **M. Al Maktoum**
11 **PEACE PROCESS (IRE)**, 4, b c Danehill—Angor **A. G. Moylan**
12 **RIVER PROJECT (IRE)**, 4, b c Project Manager—Sweet **Mrs J. S. Bolger**

THREE-YEAR-OLDS

13 **ANALISA (IRE)**, b f Don't Forget Me—Volnost **D. H. W. Dobson**
14 **APACHE TWIST (IRE)**, b c Digamist—Mystery Treat **G. Monaghan**
15 **BLUES PROJECT (IRE)**, ch c Project Manager—Gorm **Mrs J. S. Bolger**
16 **CANADIAN PATRIOT (IRE)**, b c Polish Patriot—Gradille **D. H. W. Dobson**
17 **CANADIAN PROJECT (IRE)**, ch f Project Manager—Gayle Gal **D. H. W. Dobson**
18 **CAPELLINO (IRE)**, ch f Imperial Frontier—Easy To Please **D. H. W. Dobson**
19 **CATALYST (IRE)**, b f Sadler's Wells—Welsh Love **D. H. W. Dobson**
20 **CEIRSEACH (IRE)**, br f Don't Forget Me—Beparoe Jo Jo **Mrs J. S. Bolger**
21 **CELTIC PROJECT (IRE)**, ch c Project Manager—Diandra **D. H. W. Dobson**
22 **C K R RACING (IRE)**, b f Imperial Frontier—Flying Tribute **C. K. R. Racing Club**
23 **COIS NA FARKAIGE (IRE)**, b c Nashamaa—Persian Sparkler **Niall Quinn**
24 **DAFWAN (IRE)**, b f Nashwan—Dafrah **M. Al Maktoum**
25 **DATHUIL (IRE)**, b f Royal Academy—Smaoineamh **D. H. W. Dobson**
26 **DEED OF LOVE (USA)**, br c Shadeed—Widaad **M. Al Maktoum**
27 **DREAM BAY (USA)**, b f Mr Prospector—Nazoo **M. Al Maktoum**
28 **DURRAH GREEN (IRE)**, b f Green Desert—Durrah **D. H. W. Dobson**
29 **FIREBALL (IRE)**, b f Double Schwartz—Law Student **Niall Quinn**
30 **FRANZISKA (IRE)**, b f Sadler's Wells—Belle Epoque **Mrs C. Shubotham**
31 **IDENTIFY (IRE)**, b f Persian Bold—Nordic Pride **M. W. J. Smurfit**
32 **JUBILEE SCHOLAR (IRE)**, b c Royal Academy—Jaljuli **Ballylinch Stud**
33 **KAYONOORA (IRE)**, b f Treasure Kay—Noora Abu **Mrs C. Shubotham**
34 **MACHALINI (IRE)**, b c Machiavellian—Trescalini **M. Al Maktoum**
35 **MAZARINE (IRE)**, ch f Maelstrom Lake—Gravina **D. H. W. Dobson**
36 **MEGASCENE (IRE)**, b f Scenic—Megastart **D. H. W. Dobson**
37 **PARK PETARD**, gr f Petong—What A Pet **S. Burns**
38 **PENKA (IRE)**, br f Don't Forget Me—Junito **Mrs J. S. Bolger**
39 **POLISH DOME**, ch c Polish Precedent—Dome Lawel **M. Al Maktoum**
40 **PRIORY BELLE (IRE)**, ch f Priolo—Ingabelle **Ballylinch Stud**
41 **REVONDA (IRE)**, b f Sadler's Wells—Vaigly Star **M. Al Maktoum**
42 **RIZZOLI (IRE)**, b g Nordico—Malvern Beauty **D. H. W. Dobson**
43 **SEA LEOPARD**, b c Nordico—Water Splash **M. Al Maktoum**
44 **SHEFFIELD (USA)**, b f Dayjur—Formidable Lady **H. De Kwiatkowski**
45 **SLIABH BAWN (USA)**, b f Compliance—Andy's Bonus **Mrs J. S. Bolger**
46 **SOVIET DREAMER (IRE)**, ch c Soviet Star—Splendid Girl **M. Al Maktoum**
47 **TIRANO (IRE)**, b f Tirol—Allegheny River **T. F. Brennan**
48 **TREASURE (IRE)**, b f Treasure Kay—Mothers Blessing **Mrs P. O'Rourke**
49 **VIA BOLERO (IRE)**, ch c Imperial Frontier—Closette **D. H. W. Dobson**
50 **VICE PRESIDENT (IRE)**, b f Polish Precedent—Don't Rush **M. Al Maktoum**
51 **WELSH PROJECT (IRE)**, b c Project Manager—Tasha **Seamus McGowan**
52 **WORTH AVENUE (IRE)**, b c Treasure Kay—Marqueterie **Niall Quinn**
53 **ZAMPA (IRE)**, b c Danehill—Ancor **J. Moynihan**

MR J. S. BOLGER—continued

TWO-YEAR-OLDS

54 **ACADELLI (IRE)**, b f 6/2 Royal Academy—Petronelli (Sir Ivor) **D. H. W. Dobson**
55 Ch f 2/2 Cadeaux Genereux—Al Yazi (Danzig) **M. Al Maktoum**
56 B f 5/5 St Jovite—Amenity (Luthier) **D. H. W. Dobson**
57 Ch c 11/4 Gulch—Aminata (Glenstal) **Ballylinch Stud**
58 F 18/5 Last Tycoon—Angor (Lorenzaccio) **Mrs C. Shubotham**
59 Ch c 12/2 Soviet Star—Anjaab (Alydar) **M. Al Maktoum**
60 **ARANELLA (IRE)**, b f 14/4 Sadler's Wells—La Meilleure (Lord Gayle) **Mrs C. Shubotham**
61 **ARTS PROJECT (IRE)**, b f 23/5 Project Manager—Amparo (Taufan) **Mrs J. S. Bolger**
62 **AZRA (IRE)**, b f 8/5 Danehill—Easy To Please (What A Guest) **D. H. W. Dobson**
63 F 28/1 High Estate—Battle On (Blakeney) **D. H. W. Dobson**
64 B f 9/2 Last Tycoon—Bold-E-Be (Persian Bold) **Mrs J. S. Bolger**
65 **CISTE (IRE)**, b f 20/4 Treasure Kay—Mothers Blessing (Wolver Hollow) **Mrs P. O'Rourke**
66 **DISPLAY PROJECT (IRE)**, br f 25/5 Project Manager—Nordic Display (Nordico) **D. H. W. Dobson**
67 **EASTERN PROJECT (IRE)**, b c 20/4 Project Manager—Diandra (Shardari) **D. H. W. Dobson**
68 B c 15/3 Blushing John—Eliza Blue (Icecapade) **John Gaines**
69 B f 17/4 Project Manager—Favourite Niece (Busted) **Mrs J. S. Bolger**
70 **FINE PROJECT (IRE)**, b f 26/5 Project Manager—Heike (Glenstal) **D. H. W. Dobson**
71 B f 11/5 Project Manager—Flying Tribute (Fighting Fit) **Mrs J. S. Bolger**
72 **HASSIBA (IRE)**, b f 28/1 Salt Dome—Secretary Bird (Kris) **D. H. W. Dobson**
73 **HAZY HABIT (IRE)**, b f 11/4 Treasure Kay—Hazy Lady (Habitat) **D. H. W. Dobson**
74 Ch f 12/3 Don't Forget Me—High Beat (High Top) **D. H. W. Dobson**
75 B f 12/5 Last Tycoon—High Glider (High Top) **D. H. W. Dobson**
76 B c 25/4 Shirley Heights—Jammaayil (Lomond) **M. Al Maktoum**
77 B f 31/3 Shirley Heights—Jet Ski Lady (Vaguely Noble) **M. Al Maktoum**
78 B c 19/4 Last Tycoon—Join The Party (Be My Guest) **D. H. W. Dobson**
79 **JUNIKAY (IRE)**, br c 22/2 Treasure Kay—Junijo (Junius) **Mrs J. S. Bolger**
80 B c 27/2 Danzig—Kentucky Lill (Raise A Native) **M. Al Maktoum**
81 B f 3/5 Maledetto—Law Student (Precocious) **Mrs J. S. Bolger**
82 **LEGAL PROJECT (IRE)**, br c 5/2 Project Manager—Nordic Tiara (Nordico) **R. J. O'Brien**
83 F 22/3 Indian Ridge—Liebside Lass (Be My Guest) **Sporting Quest Syndicate**
84 B c 20/2 Woodman—Lucky Song (Seattle Song) **Ballylinch Stud**
85 **MALATUKO (IRE)**, b f 10/2 Maledetto—Miss Tuko (Good Times) **D. H. W. Dobson**
86 B c 20/4 Treasure Kay—Marqueterie (Well Decorated) **Sporting Quest Syndicate**
87 **MISS MARGAUX (IRE)**, b f 8/3 Royal Academy—Irish Call (Irish River) **Frank A. Wall**
88 Br c 23/3 Project Manager—Motus (Anfield) **Mrs J. S. Bolger**
89 B f 13/2 Alwasmi—My Princessa (Lines of Power) **D. H. W. Dobson**
90 B f 13/5 Sadler's Wells—Nordic Pageant (Nordico) **D. H. W. Dobson**
91 B f 11/4 Kenmare—Pennine Music (Pennine Walk) **P. O'Donovan**
92 B f 31/3 St Jovite—Primarily (Lord At War) **D. H. W. Dobson**
93 B c 28/2 Polish Precedent—Pumpona (Sharpen Up) **M. Al Maktoum**
94 **RINCE FADA (IRE)**, b f 30/3 Exit To Nowhere—Society Ball (Law Society) **D. H. W. Dobson**
95 **RUSSIAN PROJECT (IRE)**, b f Project Manager—Mariussa (Fools Holme) **D. H. W. Dobson**
96 B f 4/5 Quest For Fame—Sacred Squaw (Olden Times) **Mrs J. S. Bolger**
97 **SADLERS HOME (IRE)**, b f 11/4 Sadler's Wells—Ivory Home (Home Guard) **P. J. P. Gleeson**
98 **SAPONARIA (IRE)**, ch f 15/3 Pursuit of Love—Suva (Northjet) **D. H. W. Dobson**
99 B f 15/5 Royal Academy—Saviour (Majestic Light) **Mrs J. S. Bolger**
100 B f 12/3 Septieme Ciel—Secret Password (Secreto) **D. H. W. Dobson**
101 Gr f 12/5 Persian Bold—Secret Sunday (Secreto) **M. W. J Smurfit**
102 B c 25/1 Roanoke—September Kaper (Peterhof) **D. H. W. Dobson**
103 **SMART PROJECT (IRE)**, ch c 15/5 Project Manager—Malvern Beauty (Shirley Heights) **D. H. W. Dobson**
104 B c 28/4 Anita's Prince—Song Beam (Song) **D. H. W. Dobson**
105 **SONG PROJECT (IRE)**, b f 7/5 Project Manager—For Going (Balidar) **Mrs J. S. Bolger**
106 **SPECIAL MENTION (IRE)**, b f 10/4 Nashwan—Special Display (Welsh Pageant) **D. H. W. Dobson**
107 **STEFKA (IRE)**, b f 19/4 Pursuit of Love—Secala (Secretariat) **D. H. W. Dobson**
108 B f 1/4 Nordico—Sure Flyer (Sure Blade) **F. Bolger**
109 **SWEET PROJECT (IRE)**, ch f 27/2 Project Manager—Sweet (Pitskelly) **Mrs J. S. Bolger**
110 **VIA VERBANO (IRE)**, b f 7/5 Caerleon—Closette (Fabulous Dancer) **D. H. W. Dobson**

MR J. S. BOLGER—continued

111 B c 18/5 Last Tycoon—Volnost (Lyphard) **D. H. W. Dobson**
112 B f 8/4 Rainbow Quest—Water Splash (Little Current) **M. Al Maktoum**
113 B f 25/5 Sheikh Albadou—Welsh Garden (Welsh Saint) **Mrs J. D. Cantillon**
114 **ZAMBELLO (IRE)**, ch c 18/5 Shalford—Fit The Halo (Dance In Time) **D. H. W. Dobson**

Jockeys (Flat): C Everard (8-11), K J Manning (8-7).

Apprentices: T E Durcan (8-8), J A Heffernan (8-0).

Late Namings
SAIBHREAS, Last Tycoon — Bold-E-Be
GALKINA, High Estate — Battle On
LEOLA, Last Tycoon — High Glider
AMADA, Sadler's Wells — Nordic Pageant
BEAMINGALLOVER, Anita's Prince — Song Beam
MOSCONI, Last Tycoon — Volnost

67   MRS MYRIAM BOLLACK-BADEL, Lamorlaye

Postal: **20 Rue Blanche, 60260 Lamorlaye, France.**

Phone: **(33) 44 21 49 66/44 21 55 34 FAX (33) 44 21 33 67 MOBILE 07 89 17 37**

1 **ALENOU**, 4, b f Warrshan—Jalopy **Mr G. Halphen**
2 **ALLESPAGNE (USA)**, 5, b m Trempolino—Teresa **Mr J. Castellano**
3 **ALWAYS EARNEST (USA)**, 8, b g Alleged—Nettie Cometti **Mrs C. Bourg**
4 **CUMBRALES (IRE)**, 5, b h Exactly Sharp—Summer Bloom **Mrs G. Cabrero**
5 **EGIPCIO**, 4, br c Java Gold—Teresa **Cuadra Rosales**
6 **FREE LIFE**, 4, b c Shaadi—Dance Empress **Mr R. Ades**
7 **GONE PROFESSIONAL (USA)**, 4, b f Gone West—Professional Dance **Mr J. C. Smith**
8 **MESHUGGAH**, 5, br m Rousillon—Fabulous Luba **Mr G. Halphen**
9 **PAPPA'S PET**, 5, b g Petong—What A Pet **Mrs L. Chira**
10 **RADICOFANI (FR)**, 10, b h Big John—Romullia **Mrs M. Bollack-Badel**
11 **SOVIET PRINCESS (FR)**, 5, b m Soviet Lad—Black Princess **Mr G. Halphen**
12 **TUMBLEWEED CHAPEL**, 4, b c Warrshan—Panama Princess **Mrs M. Bollack-Badel**
13 **WARSHANOR**, 4, b c Warrshan—Sweet Home **Mrs L. Volterra**
14 **WINBURG (USA)**, 5, b g Alleged—Winver **Mrs M. Bollack-Badel**

THREE-YEAR-OLDS

15 **AQUATINTE (FR)**, br f Sarhoob—Spring Quest **Dr F. Krief**
16 **AUSSIE**, b c Sharrood—Arita **Mr G. Halphen**
17 **BRUME DOREE (FR)**, ch f Always Fair—Divine Madness **Dr F. Krief**
18 **EVEN HANDED**, b g Then Again—Trecauldah **Mrs M. Bollack-Badel**
19 **GRUNGE (FR)**, br f Mille Balles—Tres Speciale **Mr H. Philippart**
20 **HALCON**, b c Rainbow Quest—Teresa **Cuadra Rosales**
21 **INVIGORATING**, ch f Polar Falcon—Vitality **Scuderia Mirabella**
22 **IRISH WOMAN (FR)**, ch f Assert—Irish Beauty **Mr T. Attias**
23 **MADAME WESTWOOD (IRE)**, ch f Don't Forget Me—Exotic **Mrs M. Goodbody**
24 **MALABARISTA**, gr f Assert—Karosa **Mr J. Herold**
25 **NOK**, b f Warrshan—Ringed Aureole **Mr G. Halphen**
26 **PINOCCHIO BOY (IRE)**, b c Soviet Lad—Trust Sally **Mrs M. Bollack-Badel**
27 **RACING PEARL**, b f Dancing Spree—Rose Pearl **Mrs D. Malingue**
28 **SAKTI (AUS)**, gr f Kenmare—Sakala **Mr G. Halphen**
29 **SEPOY (IRE)**, ch c Common Grounds—Song Of The Glens **Dr F. Krief**
30 **STICKS MCKENZIE**, ch c Hadeer—Tithing **Scuderia Mirabella**
31 **SUNDAY NIGHT BLUES (FR)**, b c Dancing Spree—Pauvresse **Dr F. Krief**
32 **ZAYINE (IRE)**, b f Polish Patriot—The Woman In Red **Mr G. Halphen**

MRS MYRIAM BOLLACK-BADEL—continued

TWO-YEAR-OLDS

33 B f 19/4 Rudimentary—Desert Ditty (Green Desert) **Mr G. Halphen**
34 Ch f 7/5 Pistolet Bleu—Nuit de Lune (Crystal Palace) **Mr G. Halphen**
35 B f 23/2 Bluebird—Shebasis (General Holme) **Mr G. Halphen**
36 SHLOMO, b c 19/2 Belmez—Chicobin (J O Tobin) **Mrs M. Bollack-Badel**
37 THEATRE KING, b c 4/2 Old Vic—Draft Board (Rainbow Quest) **Mr J. C. Smith**

68   MR M. J. BOLTON, Shrewton

Postal: **The Cleeve, Elston Lane, Shrewton, Wilts, SP3 4HL.**

Phone: **(01980) 621059**

1 COASTGUARDS HAVEN, 4, b g Superpower—Marton Maid **Mrs S. P. Elphick**
2 DANCING BAREFOOT, 7, ch m Scallywag—High Venture **Mr J. T. Heritage**
3 DARING KING, 6, b g King of Spain—Annacando **Cleeve Stables**
4 DAWES OF NELSON, 11, b br g Krayyan—Killyhevlin **Mr M. J. Bolton**
5 DURRINGTON, 10, b g Crooner—Glanfield **Mrs S. P. Elphick**
6 ORCHESTON, 6, b m Nearly A Hand—Glanfield **Mrs S. P. Elphick**
7 ROCQUAINE BAY, 9, b m Morston (FR)—Queen's Royale **Mr D. C. Woollard**
8 THE NOBLE OAK (IRE), 8, ch g The Noble Player (USA)—Sea Palace **Cleeve Stables**
9 VANBOROUGH LAD, 7, b g Precocious—Lustrous **Mr A. R. M. Galbraith**

THREE-YEAR-OLDS

10 PETROS GEM, br f Sulaafah (USA)—Dancing Ballerina **Mrs R. A. Murrell**
11 PETROS PRIDE, b f Safawan—Hala **Mrs R. A. Murrell**

Jockey (NH): P Hide (10-0).

Amateur: Dr J R J Naylor (10-7).

69   MR J. R. BOSLEY, Wantage

Postal: **Manor Farm Racing Stables, Kingston Lisle, Wantage, Oxon, OX12 9QL.**

Phone: **HOME (01367) 820587 OFFICE (01367) 820115**

1 BAY FAIR, 4, b f Arctic Lord—Bampton Fair **Mr J. R. Bosley**
2 CHUKKARIO, 10, b g Chukaroo—River Damsel **Mr R. Cheetham**
3 ISLAND JEWEL, 8, ch g Jupiter Island—Diamond Talk **Mr M. F. Cartwright**
4 KADIRI (IRE), 5, b g Darshaan—Kadissya (USA) **Mr J. R. Bosley**
5 LADYMALORD, 4, br f Arctic Lord—Lady Catcher **Mr J. R. Bosley**
6 MAJBOOR YAFOOZ (USA), 6, b g Silver Hawk (USA)—Forced To Fly (USA) **Miss J. M. Bodycote**
7 PERSIAN BUD (IRE), 8, b br g Persian Bold—Awakening Rose **The Blowingstone Partnership**
8 PUSEY STREET BOY, 9, ch g Vaigly Great—Pusey Street **C. R. Marks (Banbury)**
9 RIVERTINO, 12, ch g Ivotino (USA)—River Damsel **Mr R. Cheetham**
10 SHARED GOLD, 6, b g Sharrood (USA)—Gold Paper (FR) **Mr P. A. Deal**
11 SILVER AGE (USA), 10, b g Silver Hawk (USA)—Our Paige (USA) **Mrs S. J. Bird**
12 SMART LORD, 5, br g Arctic Lord—Lady Catcher **Mr J. R. Bosley**
13 WINDRUSH BOY, 6, br g Dowsing (USA)—Bridge Street Lady **Mr J. R. Bosley**

THREE-YEAR-OLDS

14 BUDDING ANNIE, b f Lord Bud—Gold Paper (FR) **Mr P. A. Deal**
15 PUSEY STREET GIRL, ch f Gildoran—Pusey Street **C. R. Marks (Banbury)**
16 TABLETS OF STONE (IRE), b g Contract Law (USA)—Remember Mulvilla **Mr A. K. Collins**
17 TATHMIN, b g Weldnaas (USA)—Alcassa (FR)

Other Owners: Mr John B. Benson, Mr J. P. Carrington, Mr Angus Crichton-Miller, Mrs Florrie Kuler, Mrs B. A. Long, Mr J. F. Long, Mr A. J. Marshall, Mrs J. Spragg.

Jockey (Flat): Aimee Cook (w.a.).

Jockey (NH): M Bosley (10-2).

Lady Rider: Mrs Sarah Bosley (8-7).

70   MR RONALD BOSS, Newmarket

Postal: **Phoenix Lodge Stables, Rowley Drive, Newmarket, Suffolk, CB8 0NH.**
Phone: **OFFICE (01638) 661335 HOME (01638) 570320 FAX NO (01638) 560804**

1 **ACCESS ADVENTURER (IRE)**, 5, b g Al Hareb (USA)—Olwyn **Miss Elaine D. Williams**
2 **DIEBIEDALE**, 4, b f Dominion—Welwyn **Mr T. J. Wells**
3 **DON PEPE**, 5, br g Dowsing (USA)—Unique Treasure **Mrs Elaine Aird**
4 **FLIRTY GERTIE**, 4, ch f Prince Sabo—Red Tapsi **Mrs G. F. R. Boss**
5 **PELLEMAN**, 4, b g Distant Relative—Lillemor **Mr M. Berger**
6 **QUEEN OF ALL BIRDS (IRE)**, 5, b m Bluebird (USA)—Blue Bouquet **Mr John Arnou**
7 **WELSH MIST**, 5, b m Damister (USA)—Welwyn **Mr Peter Asquith**

THREE-YEAR-OLDS

8 **APICELLA**, ch c Pharly (FR)—Sixslip (USA) **Mr A. J. Thompson**
9 **BILLADDIE**, b g Touch of Grey—Young Lady **Mr Richard J. Gurr**
10 **CLASSY CHIEF**, b c Be My Chief (USA)—Jalopy **Mr Keith Sturgis**
11 **EL PASEO**, ch c Shavian—Collide **Mr R. B. Root**
12 **LASSEMAN**, ch c Cadeaux Genereux—Lillemor **Mr M. Berger**
13 **MY MILLIE**, ch f Midyan (USA)—Madam Millie **Mr Peter Asquith**
14 **PRIDDY FAIR**, b f North Briton—Rainbow Ring **Mr Peter Asquith**

TWO-YEAR-OLDS

15 **AMID THE STARS**, b f 10/2 Midyan (USA)—Celebrity (Troy) **Mr Peter Asquith**
16 B c 4/2 Merdon Melody—Balidilemma (Balidar) **Mrs Joan Root & Mr R. B. Root**
17 **BIBA (IRE)**, ch f 26/3 Superlative—Fahrenheit (Mount Hagen (FR)) **Mr A. M. Foustok**
18 B f 16/3 Selkirk (USA)—Clytie (USA) (El Gran Senor (USA)) **Mrs Joan Root & Mr R. B. Root**
19 B c 28/2 Phountzi (USA)—Diavalezza (Connaught)
20 Ch c 27/2 Pursuit Of Love—Fairy Fans (Petong)
21 B f 14/2 Access Travel—Forest Fairy (Faustus (USA)) **Miss E. D. & Miss D. A. Williams**
22 Ch c 20/4 Timeless Times (USA)—Meadmore Magic (Mansingh (USA)) **Ms Lynn Bell**

Other Owners: Mr Robert Aird, Mrs Elaine Holmes, Mr Winston Muktarsingh.

71   MR J. F. BOTTOMLEY, Malton

Postal: **23 Woodlands Avenue, Norton, Malton, North Yorks, YO17 9DB.**
Phone: **HOME (01653) 693511 YARD (01653) 697002 FAX (01653) 600292**

1 **COMTEC'S LEGEND**, 6, ch m Legend of France (USA)—Comtec Princess **Qualitair Holdings Limited**
2 **QUALITAIR PRIDE**, 4, b f Siberian Express (USA)—Qualitairess **Qualitair Holdings Limited**
3 **QUALITAIR RIDGE**, 4, ch f Indian Ridge—Comtec Princess **Qualitair Holdings Limited**
4 **ROYAL CITIZEN (IRE)**, 7, b g Caerleon (USA)—Taking Steps **Mr John F. Bottomley**
5 **SASKIA'S HERO**, 9, ch g Bairn (USA)—Comtec Princess **Qualitair Holdings Limited**
6 **SWYNFORD KING**, 4, b g Jalmood (USA)—Maputo Princess **Qualitair Holdings Limited**
7 **SWYNFORD PRIDE**, 4, ch g Siberian Express (USA)—Qualitair Princess **Qualitair Holdings Limited**

THREE-YEAR-OLDS

8 Ch g Statoblest—Comtec Princess **Qualitair Holdings Limited**
9 B f Deploy—Qualitairess **Qualitair Holdings Limited**
10 **SWYNFORD DREAM**, b g Statoblest—Qualitair Dream **Qualitair Holdings Limited**

TWO-YEAR-OLDS

11 Ch c 8/4 Charmer—Qualitairess (Kampala) **Qualitair Holdings Limited**

Other Owners: Mr P. Bottomley, Mr D. Garraton, Mrs O. K. Steele.

Jockeys (Flat): G Bardwell (7-7), J Lowe.

Jockeys (NH): D Byrne (10-0, w.a.), R Marley (10-0).

Lady Rider: Mrs L Pearce (w.a.).

72 MR B. BOUSFIELD, Brough

Postal: **Glaslyn House, Brough, Kirkby Stephen, Cumbria, CA17 4BT.**

1 **ARTHUR BEE**, 9, ch g Say Primula—Reigate Head **Mrs D. A. Bousfield**
2 **WHATDIDYOUSAY**, 8, ch g Say Primula—Reigate Head **Mrs D. A. Bousfield**

73 MISS J. BOWER, Grantham

Postal: **Kirby House Stables, Woolsthorpe By Belvoir, Grantham, Lincolnshire, NG32 1NT.**
Phone: **YARD/FAX (01476) 870898 HOUSE (01476) 870933**

1 **CHEEKY MOUSE (IRE)**, 8, b m Torus—Stormy Breeze **Mr J. Pownall**
2 **COSMIC FLASH**, 6, gr m Neltino—The Beginning
3 **GOLD CAP (FR)**, 11, ch g Noir Et Or—Alkmaar (USA) **Mr G. Meadows**
4 **LORD NASKRA (USA)**, 7, b g Naskra (USA)—Corvallis (USA) **Mr J. Pownall**
5 **MURPHY'S RUN (IRE)**, 6, b g Runnett—O'Hara (GER) **Miss J. Bower**
6 **QUAKER BOB**, 11, b g Oats—Bobette **Mr Geoff Meadows**
7 **SNEAKY WHISKY**, 9, b m Gabitat—Rosalia **Mrs T. P. Everington**
8 **STAGHOUND**, 14, gr g Buckskin (FR)—Blue Delphinium **Mr Geoff Meadows**
9 **THE BRUSH MAN (IRE)**, 7, b g The Parson—Bright Record **Mr I. Rosan**
10 **VALIANT MAN**, 5, br g Valiyar—Redcross **Miss Mr J. Rose**

Other Owners: Mrs D. Bower.

Jockey (NH): R Dunwoody (w.a).

Conditional: J J Hanson (9-9).

Amateur: J Apiafi (11-0).

74 MISS L. J. BOWER, Alresford

Postal: **'Greendowns', Preshaw Road, Beauworth, Alresford, SO24 0PB.**
Phone: **(01962) 771827**

1 **DUKES HOPE**, 9, b m Idiot's Delight—Furrette **Miss J. Wilkinson**
2 **DUPAD**, 6, br g Roman Glory—Sealac **Mr John W. Potter**
3 5, B m Derring Rose—Furrette **Miss L. J. Bower**
4 **HOLTERMANN (USA)**, 12, b g Mr Prospector (USA)—Royal Graustark (USA) **Miss M. Edwards**
5 **LIGHT O'THE MILL**, 7, b m Electric—Furrette **Mr M. V. Kirby**
6 **MASTER COMEDY**, 12, b g Comedy Star (USA)—Romardia **Miss J. Wilkinson**
7 **MICKY BROWN**, 5, b g Town And Country—Avenmore Star **Mr M. V. Kirby**
8 **MR ZIEGFELD (USA)**, 7, b g Fred Astaire (USA)—I Assume (USA) **Mr Adrian Hardman**
9 **NO SECRET SO CLOSE**, 6, b m Good Times (ITY)—Furrette **Major M. A. Villiers**
10 **SANDRO**, 7, b g Niniski (USA)—Miller's Creek (USA) **Mr Adrian Hardman**
11 **TAKE THE MICK**, 6, b g Hello Sunshine—Avenmore Star **Mr M. V. Kirby**
12 **THE WRONG REASONS**, 6, b m Idiot's Delight—Rosea Plena **Major M. A. Villiers**

Jockey (Flat): Tyrone Williams.

Jockeys (NH): Luke Harvey, A Maguire, N Williamson.

Amateur: Mr Chris Bonner (9-7).

75 MR S. R. BOWRING, Edwinstowe

Postal: **Fir Tree Farm, Edwinstowe, Mansfield, Notts, NG21 9JG.**

Phone: **MANSFIELD (01623) 822451**

1 **AQUADO,** 7, b g Green Desert (USA)—Meliora **Mr K. Nicholls**
2 **ASMARINA,** 6, b m Ascendant—Marina Plata **Mr S. R. Bowring**
3 **AUCKLAND CASTLE,** 5, b g Chilibang—Palace Tor **Collins Chauffeur Driven Executive Cars**
4 **BROADSTAIRS BEAUTY (IRE),** 6, ch g Dominion Royale—Holy Water **Mrs Judy Hunt**
5 **CHADWELL HALL,** 5, b h Kala Shikari—Cherrywood Blessin **Mr D. H. Bowring**
6 **CHEERFUL GROOM (IRE),** 5, ch g Shy Groom (USA)—Carange **Mr Bill Cahill**
7 **FORZAIR,** 4, b g Forzando—Persian Air **Charterhouse Holdings Plc**
8 **GENESIS FOUR,** 6, b g Dreams To Reality (USA)—Relma **Mrs M. Fanous**
9 **GREY AGAIN,** 4, gr f Unfuwain (USA)—Grey Goddess **Green Diamond Racing**
10 **IRCHESTER LASS,** 4, ch f Presidium—Fool's Errand **South Forest Racing**
11 **KOMIAMAITE,** 4, b g Komaite (USA)—Mia Scintilla **Mrs Zoe Grant**
12 **MATTHEW DAVID,** 6, ch h Indian Forest (USA)—Mazurkanova **Mrs Katherine Fogg**
13 **MR MORIARTY (IRE),** 5, ch g Tate Gallery (USA)—Bernica (FR) **Mr D. H. Bowring**
14 **NOBLE CANONIRE,** 4, b f Gunner B—Lucky Candy **Mr Roland Wheatley**
15 **PORTEND,** 4, b g Komaite (USA)—Token of Truth **Mr D. H. Bowring**
16 **SAILORMAITE,** 5, ch g Komaite (USA)—Marina Plata **Mr S. R. Bowring**
17 **SANDMOOR DENIM,** 9, b g Red Sunset—Holernzaye **Mr E. H. Lunness**
18 **SQUARE DEAL (FR),** 5, b g Sharpo—River Dove (USA) **Mr P. Flanagan**
19 **STRIP CARTOON (IRE),** 8, ch g Tate Gallery (USA)—Reveal **Mrs Irene Pryce**
20 **SWEET MATE,** 4, ch g Komaite (USA)—Be My Sweet **Mrs P. A. Barratt**

THREE-YEAR-OLDS

21 **ANTONIAS MELODY,** b f Rambo Dancer (CAN)—Ayodessa **Mrs B. D. Georgiou**
22 **BLONDANE,** b g Danehill (USA)—Whos The Blonde **P. A. B. S. Racing**
23 **BRIGANOONE,** b g Cyrano de Bergerac—Zareeta **Mr G. E. Griffiths**
24 **FIRST MAITE,** b c Komaite (USA)—Marina Plata **Mr S. R. Bowring**
25 **GINAS GIRL,** gr f Risk Me (FR)—Grey Cree **Mrs M. Fanous**
26 **GUNNER B SPECIAL,** ch g Gunner B—Sola Mia **Mrs P. A. Barratt**
27 **MAITEAMIA,** ch g Komaite (USA)—Mia Scintilla **Mrs Zoe Grant**
28 **ONEFOURSEVEN,** b g Jumbo Hirt (USA)—Dominance **Mr J. Roundtree**
29 **THEATRE MAGIC,** b g Sayf El Arab (USA)—Miss Orient **Green Diamond Racing**

TWO-YEAR-OLDS

30 B c 16/4 Komaite (USA)—Marina Plata (Julio Mariner) **Mr S. R. Bowring**
31 **SUPERAPPAROS,** b c 8/5 Superpower—Ayodessa **(Lochnager)**

Other Owners: Mr P. J. Burke, Mr J. Curtis, Mr Paul J. Dixon, Mr R. Hardstaff, Mr B. Hopkinson, Mr A. L. Hunt, Mr D. Larratt, Mr Tudur J. Lewis, Mr A. E. Noone, Mr Fred O'Brien, Mr Terence G. Robinson, Mr G. M. Sheppard, Mr G. L. Tanner, Mr John White, Mrs M. S. Wildman.

Apprentice: C Teague (8-0).

Conditional: C Teague.

76 MRS S. C. BRADBURNE, Cupar

Postal: **Cunnoquhie Cottage, Ladybank, Cupar, Fife, KY15 7RU.**

Phone: **(01337) 810325** FAX **(01337) 810486** MOBILE **(0374) 418003 (0468) 325117**

1 **ABSAILOR,** 12, b g Kambalda—Tarsilogue **Mr C. Latilla-Campbell**
2 **AMNESIA (IRE),** 5, b m Don't Forget Me—Amboselli **Mr G. Lochtie**
3 **ASK ME LATER (IRE),** 7, b g Phardante (FR)—Dancing Bush **Mr Timothy Hardie**
4 **BLUE CHARM (IRE),** 6, b g Duky—Blue Rinse **Mrs M. C. Lindsay**

MRS S. C. BRADBURNE—continued

5 **CHARMING GALE**, 9, b br m Strong Gale—Evas Charm **Mrs John Etherton**
6 **CORSTON RACER**, 8, ch g Scallywag—Corston Lass **Mr A. S. Lyburn**
7 **FINE TUNE (IRE)**, 6, b g Aristocracy—Tuney Two
8 **FRENCH PROJECT (IRE)**, 4, b f Project Manager—Malia **Fife Steeplechasing Partnership**
9 **KINCARDINE BRIDGE (USA)**, 7, b g Tiffany Ice (USA)—Priestess (USA) **Mr J. G. Bradburne**
10 **LADY TALLULAH (IRE)**, 5, ch m Executive Perk—Torekulu **Fife Steeplechasing Partnership**
11 **NATIVE CROWN (IRE)**, 8, b g Be My Native (USA)—Crystal Halo **Mr Tom Carruthers**
12 **SONSIE MO**, 11, b g Lighter—Charlotte Amalie **Mr Timothy Hardie**
13 **WILLIE SPARKLE**, 10, b g Roi Guillaume (FR)—Adamay **Mr Timothy Hardie**

Other Owners: The Hon Thomas Cochrane, Mr D. E. Harman.

Conditional: A Watt (9-0).

Amateur: Mr Mark Bradburne (10-2).

Lady Rider: Miss Lorna Bradburne (9-4).

77   MR J. M. BRADLEY, Chepstow

Postal: **Meads Farm, Sedbury Park, Chepstow, Gwent, NP6 7HN.**
Phone: **(01291) 622486**

1 **AQUA AMBER**, 4, ch c Librate—Misty Glen **Miss D. Hill & Mr D. Smith**
2 **ASTERIX**, 8, ch g Prince Sabo—Gentle Gael **Mr C. Hunt**
3 **ASTROLABE**, 4, b g Rainbow Quest (USA)—Sextant **Mr C. Hunt**
4 **ATHENIAN ALLIANCE**, 7, ch m Ayyabaan—Springaliance **Mr J. M. Bradley**
5 **BALLYMAC GIRL**, 8, gr m Niniski (USA)—Alruccaba **Mr Lee Bowles**
6 **BLAZE OF OAK (USA)**, 5, ch g Green Forest—Magic Robe (USA) **Mr E. A. Hayward**
7 **BORRISMORE FLASH (IRE)**, 8, ch g Le Moss—Deep Goddess **Mr Lee Bowles**
8 **CHRIS'S GLEN**, 7, ch g Librate—Misty Glen **The Tote End Racing Club**
9 **DOTS DEE**, 7, ch m Librate—Dejote **Mr J. M. Kearney**
10 **DREAMS END**, 8, ch h Rainbow Quest (USA)—Be Easy **Mr T. G. Price**
11 **ITS GRAND**, 7, b g Sula Bula—Light of Zion **Avon & West Racing Club Ltd**
12 **JASON'S BOY**, 6, b g Librate—Misty Glen **Mr W. E. Jones**
13 **MAGGOTS GREEN**, 9, ch m Pas de Seul—Fabled Lady **Mr E. A. Hayward**
14 **MAGICAL BID (IRE)**, 4, b g Magical Strike (USA)—Fortera (FR) **Mr Gwilym Fry**
15 **MR CUBE (IRE)**, 6, ch h Tate Gallery (USA)—Truly Thankful (CAN) **Mr R. Miles**
16 **OFFAS IMAGE**, 8, ch g Norwick (USA)—Eridantini **Mr J. M. Bradley**
17 **OKAY BABY**, 4, b f Treasure Kay—Miss Tuko **Mr R. Miles**
18 **OPAL'S TENSPOT**, 9, b g Royal Boxer—Opal Lady **Miss J. Mailes**
19 **RACHEL ANN**, 4, b f Ikdam—Gregorys Girl **Mr W. D. Morris**
20 **RAFTERS**, 7, b g Celestial Storm (USA)—Echoing **Mr M. B. Carver**
21 **ROYAL ACCLAIM**, 11, ch g Tender King—Glimmer **Mr J. M. Bradley**
22 **SEVERN MILL**, 5, ch g Librate—Staryllis Girl **Mr E. A. Hayward**
23 **SIZZONNIE**, 6, b g Sizzling Melody—Cri Connie **Mr John Wallis**
24 **SO INTREPID (IRE)**, 6, ch h Never So Bold—Double River (USA) **Mr E. A. Hayward**
25 **SOOTY TERN**, 9, br h Wassl—High Tern **Mr J. M. Bradley**
26 **SOPHIES DREAM**, 5, ch g Librate—Misty Glen **Mr W. E. Jones**
27 **TONY'S MIST**, 6, b g Digamist (USA)—Tinas Image **Mr E. A. Hayward**
28 **ZINGIBAR**, 4, b g Caerleon (USA)—Duende **Mr D. Holpen**

THREE-YEAR-OLDS

29 **DEEDEEJAY**, b f Cigar—Miss Patdonna **Mr T. J. & D. Price**

MR J. M. BRADLEY—continued

Other Owners: Mr C. D. Baldwin, Mrs R. Bradley, Mr P. Charlton, Mr G. Clothier, Mr A. D. Lewis, Mr M. Marsh, Mr S. McManaman, Mr G. Penrice, Mr S. Phillips, Mr D. Price, Mr T. Price, Mr N. Tanner.

Jockey (NH): R Farrant.

Apprentice: S Drowne.

Conditional: Guy Lewis.

78   MR P. BRADLEY, Forsbrook

Postal: **New Park, 117 Draycott Old Road, Forsbrook, Stoke-on-Trent, ST11 9AL.**
Phone: **(01782) 392191 (01782) 324637   FAX (01782) 598427**

1 **CRIMINAL RECORD (USA)**, 6, b g Fighting Fit (USA)—Charlie's Angel (USA) **Mr Paul Bradley**
2 **LOCAL CUSTOMER**, 11, b g Le Bavard (FR)—Penny Bar **Mr Paul Bradley**
3 **MERRYHILL MADAM**, 7, b m Prince Sabo—Western Line **Mr P. J. Bradley**
4 **MUST BE MAGICAL (USA)**, 8, ch g Temperence Hill (USA)—Honorine (USA) **Mr Paul Bradley**
5 **NEVER SO BLUE (IRE)**, 5, br h Never So Bold—Saneena **Mr P. J. Bradley**
6 **OH RUBY (IRE)**, 5, ch m Dunbeath (USA)—Lyric Opera **Mr Paul Bradley**
7 **SALDA**, 7, b g Bustino—Martinova **Mr Paul Bradley**
8 **STRAWBERRY FOOL**, 7, b m Idiot's Delight—Record Red **Mr Paul Bradley**
9 **TEJANO GOLD (USA)**, 6, ch g Tejano (USA)—Nelli Forli (USA) **Mr Paul Bradley**
10 **TOUGH DEAL (IRE)**, 8, b g Sheer Grit—Ballyeel **Mr Paul Bradley**

79   MR M. F. BRADSTOCK, Wantage

Postal: **The Old Manor House, Letcombe Bassett, Wantage, Oxon, OX12 9LP.**
Phone: **(01235) 760780 FAX (01235) 760754**

1 **ARDSCUD**, 9, b g Le Bavard (FR)—Tudor Lady **Mr Mark Bradstock**
2 **BRAIDA BOY**, 10, b g Kampala—Braida (FR) **Mr Mark Bradstock**
3 **DO RIGHTLY (IRE)**, 7, ch g Teofane—Lady Hiltop **Mr J. M. Fitzpatrick**
4 **LORD ANTRIM (IRE)**, 7, b g Ovac (ITY)—Moate Gypsy **Mr J. B. Dowler**
5 **LUGS BRANNIGAN (IRE)**, 7, b g Supreme Leader—Maria Tudor **Mr J. B. Dowler**
6 **MEDIANE (USA)**, 11, b g Dust Commander (USA)—Mlle Quille (USA) **White City All Stars C. C.**
7 **MONTAGNARD**, 12, b g Strong Gale—Louisa Stuart (FR) **Mr N. A. Gill**
8 **MR WILLIS**, 5, b g Bustomi—The Red Mare **B. L. Willis Developments**
9 **OJONNYO (IRE)**, 6, br g Spin of A Coin—Follow Lightly **Mr S. P. Tindall**
10 **PIERRE BLANCO (USA)**, 7, b g Sovereign Don (USA)—Kiss Off (USA) **N. Stewart**
11 **PRUSSIAN STORM (IRE)**, 7, b m Strong Gale—Let's Compromise **Mr Chris Deuters**
12 **ROYAL TRUMP (IRE)**, 7, b g King Persian—Four Queens **Mr J. M. Fitzpatrick**
13 **SOME DAY SOON**, 11, b g Beau Charmeur (FR)—Our Day **Mr K. Powell**
14 **WIXOE WONDER (IRE)**, 6, ch h Hatim (USA)—Jumana **Mr P. J. D. Pottinger**

Other Owners: Mr Alex Beard, Mr Barry Church, Mr G. A. Cowell, Mrs Chris Deuters, Mr C. Elgram, Mr N. C. J. Miles, Mr P. A. Oborne, Mr A. F. Rae Smith, Miss K. A. Stringer, Mr G. L. Unsworth, Mr Alan Waller.

Jockey (NH): P Holley (10-0).

Conditional: Katherine R Hambidge (9-0).

80   MRS S. A. BRAMALL, Thirsk

Postal: **Burtree House, Hutton Sessay, Thirsk, N. Yorks, YO1 3AY.**

Phone: **THIRSK (01845) 401333**

1 **ABLE PLAYER (USA)**, 9, b br g Solford (USA)—Grecian Snow (CAN) **Miss K. S. Bramall**
2 **ADRIEN (FR)**, 8, br g Imyar—Hermione R (FR) **Miss K. S. Bramall**
3 **ANTONIN (FR)**, 8, ch g Italic (FR)—Pin'hup (FR) **G. R. Bailey Ltd (Baileys Horse Feeds)**
4 **BAILEYS BRIDGE (IRE)**, 5, ch g Over The River (FR)—Tabithat Bay **G. R. Bailey Ltd (Baileys Horse Feeds)**
5 **BANGABUNNY**, 6, ch g Gunner B—Olympian Princess **Miss Anna Bramall**
6 **BEAUCHAMP GRACE**, 7, b m Ardross—Buss **Mrs S. A. Bramall**
7 **BLUE IRISH (IRE)**, 5, gr g Roselier (FR)—Grannie No **Mrs S. A. Bramall**
8 **BOLD STATEMENT**, 4, ch g Kris—Bold Fantasy **Mrs S. A. Bramall**
9 **CANAILLOU II (FR)**, 6, b g Le Riverain (FR)—Julie (FR) **Mr M. Stanners**
10 **CAPTAIN CHAOS (IRE)**, 5, b g Phardante (FR)—Asigh Glen **Miss K. S. Bramall**
11 **CAVALLO (FR)**, 6, b g Quart de Vin (FR)—Leuconea (FR) **Panther Racing Ltd**
12 **CESAR DU MANOIR (FR)**, 6, ch g Le Nain Jaune (FR)—Kalighte (FR) **Mr L. H. Froomes**
13 **COLONEL GEORGE**, 4, b g Petoski—Pagan Deity **Mrs Sandra Scott Bell**
14 **DRUMCLIFFE (IRE)**, 5, br g Strong Gale—Kadaga **Mrs S. A. Bramall**
15 **ETAT MAJOR (FR)**, 4, b g Mont Basile (FR)—P'Tite Poi (FR) **Mrs S. A. Bramall**
16 **GALANT DES EPEIRES (FR)**, 5, ch g Galant Vert (FR)—Marie de Bethisy (FR) **Mrs S. A. Bramall**
17 **HURDY**, 9, ch g Arapahos (FR)—Demelza Carne **Leading Star Racing**
18 **MILLIEWELL (IRE)**, 7, b m Denel (FR)—Weaver's Fool **Mr M. Stanners**
19 **MONKEY AGO**, 9, b g Black Minstrel—Arctic Sue **Mrs B. Gerber**
20 **MONOKRATIC (IRE)**, 7, b g King's Ride—Multeen **Leading Star Racing**
21 **PP O'REILLY (IRE)**, 6, br g Dancing Lights (USA)—Weaver's Fool **Mrs S. A. Bramall**
22 **SPANISH FAIR (IRE)**, 8, b g Spanish Place (USA)—Bonne Fair **Mrs S. A. Bramall**
23 **THE GOOFER**, 9, b g Be My Native (USA)—Siliferous **Mrs Paula Stringer**
24 **TUGRA (FR)**, 8, b m Baby Turk—Ramsar **Mrs S. A. Bramall**
25 **VELEDA II (FR)**, 9, ch g Olmeto—Herbe Fine (FR) **Mr L. H. Froomes**
26 **VIVA BELLA (FR)**, 9, b g Cap Martin (FR)—Moldau (FR) **Mr L. H. Froomes**
27 **VULPIN DE LAUGERE (FR)**, 9, b g Olmeto—Quisling II (FR) **Mr M. Stanners**
28 **WILD BROOK (IRE)**, 6, b g Mandalus—My Lily **Mrs S. A. Bramall**

Other Owners: Mr D. C. A. Bramall, Mr Richard J. Cohen, Mrs A. Ellis, Mr C. R. Galloway, Mrs Paula Stringer, Mrs Sue Waite.

Jockey (NH): J Burke (10-5).

81   MR G. C. BRAVERY, Newmarket

Postal: **Albert House Stables, Bury Road, Newmarket, Suffolk, CB8 8DU.**

Phone: **(01638) 668985 FAX (01638) 668985 STABLES (01440) 901 HOME**

1 **AYDISUN**, 4, gr g Aydimour—Briglen **Aydi Racing**
2 **BLATANT OUTBURST**, 6, b g War Hero—Miss Metro **Miss Bobby Quibell**
3 **DOVEDON LAD**, 4, ch c Statoblest—Miss Petella **Michael C. Whatley and Whatley Lane & Co**
4 **EXPLOSIVE POWER**, 5, br h Prince Sabo—Erwarton Seabreeze **Mr H. T. Short**
5 **HIGHLY REPUTABLE (IRE)**, 6, ch g Persian Heights—Reputation
6 **IRISH EMERALD**, 9, b g Taufan (USA)—Gaelic Jewel **Mrs F. E. Bravery**
7 5, B g Persian Mews—Jeanarie **Mr D. B. Clark**
8 5, B m Persian Mews—Ladycastle **Mr D. B. Clark**
9 5, Gr m Celio Rufo—Mandias Slave **Mr D. B. Clark**
10 **MARTINOSKY**, 10, b g Martinmas—Bewitched **Mr D. B. Clark**
11 **RISKY ROMEO**, 4, b g Charmer—Chances Are **Miss Sonja Quince**
12 **SILVER HUNTER (USA)**, 5, b g Silver Hawk (USA)—Martha Queen (USA) **Bravery Racing**
13 **SOUND TRICK (USA)**, 4, b f Phone Trick (USA)—Lettre d'Amour (USA) **Mr Michael N. Hwang**

MR G. C. BRAVERY—continued

THREE-YEAR-OLDS

14 **GO TOO MOOR (IRE)**, b g Posen (USA)—Gulistan **Mr Jeff Goodman**
15 **INFANTRY DANCER**, ch f Infantry—Electropet **Mr H. T. Short**
16 **RABICAN (IRE)**, b c Distinctly North (USA)—Kaysama (FR) **Mr Michael N. Hwang**

TWO-YEAR-OLDS

17 B f 4/4 Maledetto (IRE)—Actuate (IRE) (Shardari) **Mr J. J. May**
18 B c 28/4 Treasure Kay—Contraflow (Rainbow Quest (USA))
19 B f 21/4 Emarati (USA)—Dewberry (Bay Express)
20 B f 8/3 Reprimand—Formidable Dancer (Formidable (USA)) **Mr Jeff Goodman**
21 B f 20/3 Rock City—Sun Street (Ile de Bourbon (USA)) **Mr J. J. May**

Other Owners: Mr D. Amos, Mr Ettore Landi, Mrs P. J. Lewis, Mr A. D. Mackrill, Mrs M. Powell, Mr Michael C. Whatley.

Jockey (Flat): M Hills (w.a.).

Amateur: Mr K Santana (9-2).

82   MR R. G. BRAZINGTON, Redmarley

Postal: **Chapel Farm, Redmarley, Glos, GL19 3JF.**

Phone: **(01452) 840384**

1 **AIOLI**, 10, b m Tyrnavos—Coco de Mer **Mr R. G. Brazington**
2 4, Ch c Buckley—Assumption **Mr R. G. Brazington**
3 5, B h Vouchsafe—Assumption **Mr R. G. Brazington**
4 **CALLYR**, 9, b g Julio Mariner—Midnight Pansy **Mr R. G. Brazington**
5 **CREDIT CALL (IRE)**, 8, br g Rhoman Rule (USA)—Maiacourt **Mr R. G. Brazington**
6 **DOTTEREL (IRE)**, 8, b g Rhoman Rule (USA)—Miysam **Mr R. G. Brazington**
7 5, B m Vouchsafe—Hail A Cab **Mr R. G. Brazington**
8 **HEPBURN (IRE)**, 8, b m Pitskelly—Bradden **Mr R. G. Brazington**
9 6, Br g Buckley—Ionian Isle (FR) **Mr R. G. Brazington**
10 **JIMBALOU**, 13, b g Jimsun—Midnight Pansy **Mr R. G. Brazington**
11 **MARINERS MEMORY**, 8, b g Julio Mariner—Midnight Pansy **Mr R. G. Brazington**
12 5, B h Vouchsafe—Midnight Lily **Mr R. G. Brazington**
13 6, B g Buckley—Midnight Lily **Mr R. G. Brazington**
14 **TAXI LAD**, 12, ch g Dublin Taxi—Midnight Pansy **Mr R. G. Brazington**

Other Owners: Mr Bill Davies.

Jockey (NH): W Humphreys (10-0).

83   MR OWEN BRENNAN, Worksop

Postal: **Sloswicks Farm, Broad Lane, Worksop, Notts, S80 3NJ.**

Phone: **WORKSOP (01909) 473950**

1 **ARDENT LOVE (IRE)**, 7, b m Ardross—Love Match (USA) **Mrs Pat Brennan**
2 **ARTIC WINGS (IRE)**, 8, b m Mazaad—Evening Flight **Lady Anne Bentinck**
3 **BARNEY'S GIFT (IRE)**, 8, ch g Exhibitioner—Run-A-Line **Mr Richard J. Marshall**
4 **BOSTON ROVER**, 11, b g Ovac (ITY)—Vulgan Ten **Mr O. Brennan**
5 **CASH CHASE (IRE)**, 8, gr m Sexton Blake—Sugar Shaker **Mr Stephen Ryan**
6 **DARK PHOENIX (IRE)**, 6, b m Camden Town—Hopeful Dawn **Mrs Pat Brennan**

MR OWEN BRENNAN—continued

7 **DARK SILHOUETTE (IRE)**, 7, b g Good Thyne (USA)—Primrose Walk **Mr O. Brennan**
8 **DOMINOS RING (IRE)**, 7, b g Auction Ring (USA)—Domino's Nurse **Mrs Jenny Carrington**
9 **DUGORT STRAND (IRE)**, 5, b br g Entitled—Soltina **Achill Nottingham Syndicate**
10 **FAR OUT**, 10, b g Raga Navarro (ITY)—Spaced Out **Mr O. Brennan**
11 **FIONAS DANCER (IRE)**, 5, ch m Dancing Lights (USA)—Farsett Path **Mr O. Brennan**
12 **INVASION**, 12, b g Kings Lake (USA)—St Padina **Lady Anne Bentinck**
13 **JOLLY HEART**, 6, b g Kambalda—Wrens Lass **Lady Anne Bentinck**
14 **LINDA'S PRINCE (IRE)**, 7, b g Prince Bee—Linda Martin **Mr J. Witherow**
15 **MARSH'S LAW**, 9, b g Kala Shikari—My Music **Mrs Violet J. Hannigan**
16 **ORCHARD KING**, 6, ch g Rymer—Sprats Hill **Mr Kevin Orchard**
17 **OUR LAUGHTER**, 6, ch m Relkino—Sound of Laughter **Mrs B. A. Burgass**
18 **PINECONE PETER**, 9, ch g Kings Lake (USA)—Cornish Heroine (USA) **Mrs B. A. Burgass**
19 **SHALIK (IRE)**, 6, ch g Pauper—Jasmine Girl **Miss Cindy Brennan**
20 **SLOE BRANDY**, 6, b m Hotfoot—Emblazon **Mrs Jenny Carrington**
21 **SPEAKER WEATHERILL (IRE)**, 7, b g Strong Gale—Arctic Verb **Lady Anne Bentinck**
22 **SUVLA BAY (IRE)**, 8, b g Kemal (FR)—Miss Lacemore **Lady Anne Bentinck**
23 **TEEJAY'S FUTURE (IRE)**, 5, b m Buckskin (FR)—Lolos Run VII **Mr J. C. Hind**

Other Owners: Mr Michael Condon, Mr Brian Culley, D. King, Mr Phillip J. Mann, Mr M. Molloy, Mr Billy Scott, Mr P. Vesey, Mr A. E. Walton.

Jockey (NH): M J Brennan (9-7).

Conditional: S O'Donnell.

84   MR R. BREWIS, Belford

Postal: **Chester Hill, Belford, Northd, NE70 7EF.**
Phone: **(01668 213) 239**

1 **BILLSBROOK**, 6, b g Meadowbrook—Carney **Mr R. Brewis**
2 **BILOELA**, 6, ch m Nicholas Bill—Maple Syrup **Mr R. Brewis**
3 **BLUFF KNOLL**, 13, b g New Brig—Tacitina **Mr R. Brewis**
4 **CARNETTO**, 9, b m Le Coq d'Or—Carney **Mrs R. Brewis**
5 **NICK ROSS**, 5, b g Ardross—Nicolini **Mr R. Brewis**
6 **RISING MILL**, 5, b g Primitive Rising (USA)—Milly L'Attaque **Miss R. G. Brewis**
7 **VICARIDGE**, 9, b g The Parson—Streamon **Mr R. Brewis**

Jockey (NH): G Harker.

Amateur: Mr A W Robson.

85   MR J. J. BRIDGER, Liphook

Postal: **Upper Hatch Farm, Wheatsheaf Enclosure, Liphook, Hants, GU30 7EL.**
Phone: **LIPHOOK (01428) 722528 FAX (01428) 722528**

1 **CLOCK WATCHERS**, 8, b g Sula Bula—Hale Lane **Mr Shere & Mr H. Milam**
2 **COUNTRY BOY**, 5, b g Town And Country—Hollomoore **Tarragon Racing II**
3 **DERISBAY (IRE)**, 8, b g Gorytus (USA)—Current Bay **Miss Julie Self**
4 **DESERT WATER (IRE)**, 4, b g Green Desert (USA)—Ozone Friendly (USA) **Miss Julie Self**
5 **JOHNS JOY**, 11, b g Martin John—Saybya **Miss Julie Self**
6 **KALAKATE**, 11, gr g Kalaglow—Old Kate **Mr J. J. Bridger**
7 **KNOTTY SCOT**, 4, b f Scottish Reel—Ballyreef **Tarragon Racing**
8 **MOURNE ENDEAVOUR**, 11, ch g Parva Stella—Fair Eva **Miss Julie Self**

MR J. J. BRIDGER—continued

  9 READYPOWER, 4, b g Newski (USA)—Bay Runner **Miss Julie Self**
10 RUSSIAN RIVER, 4, b g Sulaafah (USA)—Ninotchka **Mrs R. M. Maclean**
11 SCISSOR RIDGE, 4, ch g Indian Ridge—Golden Scissors **Mr Donald J. Smith**
12 SMUGGLER'S POINT (USA), 6, b g Lyphard (USA)—Smuggly (USA) **Mr Martin Hickey**
13 SOMERSET DANCER (USA), 9, br g Green Dancer (USA)—Distant Song (FR) **Miss Julie Self**
14 SOVIET UNION, 4, b g Soviet Star (USA)—Chalon **Mr J. J. Bridger**
15 THORNIWAMA, 5, b m Hadeer—Hidden Asset **Miss Rachel Bridger**
16 THORNY BISHOP, 5, b g Belfort (FR)—Hill of Fare **Mr Terry Thorn**
17 THUNDEROUS, 4, b g Green Desert (USA)—Mixed Applause (USA) **Miss Julie Self**
18 TONRIN, 4, b g General Wade—Hot Tramp **Mr J. J. Bridger**
19 TOUCHING TIMES, 8, b g Touching Wood (USA)—Pagan Deity **Miss Julie Self**

THREE-YEAR-OLDS

20 DANCING JACK, ch c Clantime—Sun Follower **Mrs J. M. Stamp**
21 JEMSILVERTHORN (IRE), b c Maelstrom Lake—Fairy Don **Mr Terry Thorn**

TWO-YEAR-OLDS

22 B f 11/3 Puissance—Panienka (POL) (Dom Racine (FR)) **Mr J. J. Bridger**
23 Ch c 24/4 Durandal—Sun Follower (Relkino) **Mrs J. M. Stamp & Mrs J. Hitchman**
24 Ch f 28/2 Superlative—What A Looker (USA) (Raise A Native) **Mr J. J. Bridger**

Other Owners: Mr J. Bishop, Mr Paul Cheatle, Mr Steve Cheatle, Mr W. Woods.

Conditional: Rachel Bridger (9-0).

Amateur: Mr David Bridger (10-0).

Lady Rider: Miss Madeleine Bridger (9-0).

86   MR K. S. BRIDGWATER, Lapworth

Postal: **Bear House Farm, Old Warwick Road, Lapworth, Solihull, Warwickshire, B94 6AZ.**
Phone: **LAPWORTH (01564) 782895 FAX (01564) 782895**

  1 ADVENTUROUS LADY, 6, b m Roman Warrior—Marchiness Drake **Miss E. E. Hill**
  2 BERTS CHOICE, 5, b g Revlow—Miss Burgundy **Mr W. Sanderson**
  3 CAPTAIN CHROME, 9, b g Welsh Captain—Chrome Mag **Mrs Marion Gibbs**
  4 CAPTAIN SINBAD, 4, b g Welsh Captain—Lane Patrol **Mrs Mary Bridgwater**
  5 CASTLERICHARDKING, 11, b br g Matching Pair—Dont Rock **Joy & Jim Barker**
  6 CROCKNAMOHILL (IRE), 5, br g Strong Gale—Rusty Iron **Mrs C. Kelly**
  7 DEAL WITH HONOR, 7, b m Idiot's Delight—Vulgan's Honor **Mr Phil Price**
  8 DRAKES ADVENTURE, 4, br f Green Adventure (USA)—Marchiness Drake **Miss E. E. Hill**
  9 DRAKES COUNTRY, 8, b m Town And Country—Marchiness Drake **Miss E. E. Hill**
10 JUBILEE ROYALE (IRE), 5, ch g Dominion Royale—Genesee **Mr R. Paul Russell**
11 LUMO (IRE), 5, ch g Phardante (FR)—Fair Vic **Mr Arnie Kaplan**
12 MADAM CORA, 4, b f Gildoran—Lawnswood Miss **Mr R. Paul Russell**
13 MOST BEAUTIFUL, 5, ch m Most Welcome—Sorebelle **Joy & Jim Barker**
14 MR CIP (IRE), 5, ch g Stetchworth (USA)—Auragne (FR) **Coventry Industrial Pipework Ltd**
15 PEACE TRIBUTE (IRE), 7, br g Nomination—Olderfleet **Ms Caroline F. Breay**
16 PERTEMPS ZOLA, 7, b m Oats—Little Buskinbelle **Mr P. W. Pettitt**
17 PHILS FORTUNE, 4, ch f Kinglet—Crimson Sol **Daltagh Construction Ltd**
18 SECRET LIASON, 10, b g Ballacashtal (CAN)—Midnight Mistress **Mr Patrick Ward**
19 SIR PAGEANT, 7, b g Pharly (FR)—National Dress **The Dirty Dozen**
20 SPEARHEAD AGAIN (IRE), 7, b g Strong Gale—Afford The Queen **Mr Len Jakeman**
21 SWEETS (IRE), 5, b m Persian Heights—Osmunda **Mr R. W. Neale**

MR K. S. BRIDGWATER—continued

THREE-YEAR-OLDS

22 **CROWN AND CUSHION**, b g High Adventure—Soulieana **Mr Sydney Scarsbrook**
23 **IMPENDING DANGER**, ch g Fearless Action (USA)—Crimson Sol **Daltagh Construction Ltd**

Other Owners: Mrs Y. M. Ambery, Mr S. Baggott, Mr K. W. Bradley, Mr Bryan Curtiss, Mr J. Gilbert, Mrs B. D. Neale, Mr M. R. Paul, Miss S. C. Skinner, Mr B. Wirdman.

Jockey (NH): D Bridgwater.

87   MR W. M. BRISBOURNE, Nesscliffe

Postal: **Ness Strange Stables, Great Ness, Nesscliffe, Nr Shrewsbury, Shropshire, SY4 2LE.**
Phone: **NESSCLIFFE (01743741) 536 OR 360 MOBILE (0836) 694989**

1 **ANDY COIN**, 5, ch m Andy Rew—Legal Coin **Mr Bob Moseley**
2 **BARRYBEN**, 7, b br g Seymour Hicks (FR)—Ensigns Kit **Mrs Mary Brisbourne**
3 **CALLING (USA)**, 5, ch g Phone Trick (USA)—Sweet Singer (USA) **Mrs S. J. Edwards**
4 **DELMOUR**, 5, b g Seymour Hicks (FR)—Delbounty **Mr D. Slingsby**
5 **HILL FARM DANCER**, 5, ch m Gunner B—Loadplan Lass **Mr Dennis Newton**
6 **HILL FARM KATIE**, 5, b m Derrylin—Kate Brook **Mark & Pam Brisbourne**
7 **IVY LILIAN (IRE)**, 4, b f Cyrano de Bergerac—Catherine Clare **Mr M. E. Hughes**
8 **LITTLE SERENA**, 6, b m Primitive Rising (USA)—Navos **Mr A. Von Dinther**
9 **POLLI PUI**, 4, b f Puissance—Wing of Freedom **Mr M. E. Hughes**
10 **RAINDEER QUEST**, 4, ch f Hadeer—Rainbow Ring **Mr Steve MacDonald**
11 **ROYRACE**, 4, b g Wace (USA)—Royal Tycoon **Mr Andrew Evans**
12 4, B f Portogon—Scallymere **Mr Tudor Bebb**
13 **THROWER**, 5, b g Thowra (FR)—Atlantic Line **Mr Mark Owen**

THREE-YEAR-OLDS

14 **BACKWOODS**, ch g In The Wings—Kates Cabin **Mr Peter Kirk**
15 **CHILLINGTON**, gr g Chilibang—Saskia's Pride **Mr D. J. Kirkland**
16 B f Pallards Pride—Delbounty **Mark & Pam Brisbourne**
17 **EASTER COIN**, ch f Andy Rew—Legal Coin **Mr Bob Moseley**
18 Br f River God (USA)—Ensigns Kit **D. M. Brisbourne & Sons**
19 **FEET ON FIRE**, b f Nomination—Peregrine Falcon **Mr B. L. Benson**
20 **LADY BENSON (IRE)**, b f Pennine Walk—Sit Elnaas (USA) **Mr B. L. Benson**
21 **TYCOON TED**, b g Starch Reduced—Royal Tycoon **D. M. Brisbourne & Sons**

TWO-YEAR-OLDS

22 Br c 31/7 Nalchik (USA)—Delbounty (Bounteous) **D. M. Brisbourne & Sons**
23 B f 10/5 Imp Society (USA)—Rusty Goddess (Hard Fought) **Mr B. L. Benson**
24 **TYCOON TINA**, b f 9/5 Tina's Pet—Royal Tycoon (Tycoon II) **Mr Antony Brisbourne**

Other Owners: Mrs S. J. Edwards, Mr Robin Evans, Mr Antony Ewen, Mr Robert Moseley, Mrs Bernice Newton, Mrs Ann Slingsby, Mr Peter Wright.

Jockeys (Flat): Martin Dwyer (7-5), A Garth (7-10), S Maloney (7-13).

Jockeys (NH): R Massey (9-10), S Wynne (10-0).

Lady Rider: Diana Jones (9-5).

88 MR C. E. BRITTAIN, Newmarket

Postal: 'Carlburg', 49 Bury Road, Newmarket, Suffolk, CB8 7BY.

Phone: OFFICE (01638) 664347 HOME (01638) 663739 FAX (01638) 661744

1 ACCONDY (IRE), 4, gr c Sadler's Wells (USA)—As You Desire Me The Dayspring Company Limited
2 AGOER, 4, ch f Hadeer—Abuzz Mrs C. E. Brittain
3 ALANEES, 5, b g Cadeaux Genereux—Dabaweyaa Mr Mohamed Obaida
4 AUTUMN AFFAIR, 4, b f Lugana Beach—Miss Chalk Mr Ray Richards
5 BAY OF ISLANDS, 4, b g Jupiter Island—Lawyer's Wave (USA) Bloomsbury Stud
6 BERNARD SEVEN (IRE), 4, b c Taufan (USA)—Madame Nureyev (USA) Mr Bernard Butt
7 BIN NASHWAN (USA), 4, b c Nashwan (USA)—Dabaweyaa Mr Mohamed Obaida
8 CHATHAM ISLAND, 8, ch g Jupiter Island—Floreal Mr B. H. Voak
9 COOL JAZZ, 5, b h Lead On Time (USA)—Amber Fizz (USA) Mr Saeed Manana
10 CZARNA (IRE), 5, b h Polish Precedent (USA)—Noble Dust (USA) Ovidstown Investments Ltd
11 ERTLON, 6, b g Shareef Dancer (USA)—Sharpina Mr C. E. Brittain
12 HORESTI, 4, b c Nijinsky (CAN)—Sushila The Dayspring Company Limited
13 IONIO (USA), 5, ch g Silver Hawk (USA)—Private View (USA) The Dayspring Company Limited
14 KORAMBI, 4, ch g Kris—Green Lucia Mr B. H. Voak
15 LADY NASH, 4, b f Nashwan (USA)—Je Comprend (USA) Mrs J. Costelloe
16 LUSO, 4, b c Salse (USA)—Lucayan Princess Mr Saeed Manana
17 MISTER FIRE EYES (IRE), 4, b g Petorius—Surfing Mr C. T. Olley
18 MR MARTINI (IRE), 6, b h Pennine Walk—Arab Art Parrot Racing
19 MUSETTA (IRE), 4, b f Cadeaux Genereux—Monaiya Mr B. H. Voak
20 NEEDLE GUN (IRE), 6, b br h Sure Blade (USA)—Lucayan Princess Mr Saeed Manana
21 PINKERTON POLKA, 4, b f Shareef Dancer (USA)—Holy Day Miss E. G. Macgregor
22 PINKERTON'S PAL, 5, ch g Dominion—White Domino Miss E. G. MacGregor
23 PUNISHMENT, 5, b h Midyan (USA)—In The Shade Mr A. J. Richards
24 RUBBIYATI, 4, ch f Cadeaux Genereux—Ibtisamm (USA) Wyck Hall Stud
25 SACRED MIRROR (IRE), 5, b m Shaadi (USA)—Heavenly Abode (FR) Mr C. E. Brittain
26 SECRET ALY (CAN), 6, b g Secreto (USA)—Bouffant (USA) Mr B. H. Voak
27 SHAMBO, 9, b h Lafontaine (USA)—Lucky Appeal Mrs C. E. Brittain
28 SIEVE OF TIME (USA), 5, br g Arctic Tern (USA)—Got A Cold (USA) Mr B. H. Voak
29 TARTE AUX POMMES (USA), 4, b f Local Talent (USA)—My Mother's Eyes (FR) Mr A. J. Richards
30 TIRRA-LIRRA (IRE), 4, b f Tirol—Run My Beauty Mr C. E. Brittain
31 TOY PRINCESS (USA), 4, b f Arctic Tern (USA)—Princess Toy Mr C. E. Brittain
32 TUDOR ISLAND, 7, b g Jupiter Island—Catherine Howard The Hon D. Sieff
33 UNCHANGED, 4, b f Unfuwain (USA)—Favorable Exchange (USA) Mr M. J. Simmonds
34 UPPER MOUNT CLAIR, 6, b m Ela-Mana-Mou—Sun Street Mr C. E. Brittain
35 WAHEM (IRE), 6, b g Lomond (USA)—Pro Patria Mr C. E. Brittain
36 WESTERN HORIZON (USA), 4, ch f Gone West (USA)—Norette Wyck Hall Stud
37 ZELIBA, 4, br f Doyoun—Zia (USA) Mr C. E. Brittain

THREE-YEAR-OLDS

38 ACHARNE, ch c Pharly (FR)—Sibley Parrot Racing
39 AMBASSADORI (USA), b c Lear Fan (USA)—Czar's Bride (USA) The Thoroughbred Corporation
40 AMFORTAS (IRE), b c Caerleon (USA)—High Spirited Mr B. H. Voak
41 ARNHEM, b c Damister (USA)—Baltic Leap (USA) Mr W. J. Gredley
42 BABINDA, b c Old Vic—Babita Mr Saeed Manana
43 BURNT OFFERING, b c Old Vic—Burnt Amber Mr A. J. Richards
44 CASTANA, ch f Minster Son—Surpassing The Dayspring Company Limited
45 DIEGO, b c Belmez (USA)—True Queen (USA) Mr C. E. Brittain
46 DUBAI COLLEGE (IRE), b c Old Vic—Murooj (USA) Mr A. Merza
47 EWAR BOLD, b c Bold Arrangement—Monaneigue Lady Mr A. J. Richards
48 EWAR SUNRISE, ch f Shavian—Sunset Reef Mr A. J. Richards
49 FLAMANDA, b f Niniski (USA)—Nemesia The Dayspring Company Limited
50 GALAPINO, b c Charmer—Carousella The Dayspring Company Limited
51 GULF TYCOON, b f Cadeaux Genereux—Shihama (USA) Mr Mohamed Obaida
52 HENRY THE FIFTH, b c Village Star (FR)—Microcosme Mr A. J. Richards
53 HIPPY, b f Damister (USA)—Breakaway Mr D. Sieff
54 INFLUENCE PEDLER, b g Keen—La Vie En Primrose Mr C. E. Brittain
55 ITCHY FEET (IRE), b g Polish Patriot (USA)—Chilblains Mr C. E. Brittain

MR C. E. BRITTAIN—continued

56 LET'S GO, b g Keen—Daima Mr C. E. Brittain
57 LUCKY ARCHER, b c North Briton—Preobrajenska Mr W. J. Gredley
58 LUCKY HOOF, b f Batshoof—Lucky Omen Mr R. N. Khan
59 LUNDA (IRE), b f Soviet Star (USA)—Lucayan Princess Mr Saeed Manana
60 LYZIA (IRE), ch f Lycius (USA)—Zia (USA) Sheikh Marwan Al Maktoum
61 MAGELLAN (USA), b c Hansel (USA)—Dabaweyaa Mr Mohamed Obaida
62 MELTEMISON, b c Charmer—Salchow The Dayspring Company Limited
63 MILETRIAN FIT-OUT, b g Most Welcome—White Domino Miletrian Plc
64 MISS UNIVERSAL, ch f Lycius (USA)—Madame Nureyev (USA) Mr Bernard Butt
65 NAISSANT, b f Shaadi (USA)—Nophe (USA) Sheikh Marwan Al Maktoum
66 NORTH CYCLONE (USA), b c Gulch (USA)—Dubian Mr Mohamed Obaida
67 PARTITA, b f Polish Precedent (USA)—Pharian Mr Saeed Manana
68 PETRIKOV (IRE), ch f In The Wings—Pripet (USA) Sheikh Marwan Al Maktoum
69 PRIMROSE PATH, b f Shaadi (USA)—Crimson Conquest (USA) Sheikh Marwan Al Maktoum
70 PROMISSORY, b f Caerleon (USA)—Tricky Note Mr B. H. Voak
71 QASIDA (IRE), b c Lycius (USA)—Arab Heritage Sheikh Mohammed Obaid Al Maktoum
72 SORARA, ch f Aragon—Sorebelle Mr R. N. Khan
73 SPARTAN HEARTBEAT, b c Shareef Dancer (USA)—Helen's Dream Mr C. T. Olley
74 SYLVA PARADISE (IRE), b c Dancing Dissident (USA)—Brentsville (USA) Eddy Grimstead Honda Limited
75 UONI, ch f Minster Son—Maid of Essex The Dayspring Company Limited
76 WORLD PREMIER, b c Shareef Dancer (USA)—Abuzz Mrs C. E. Brittain
77 ZELAYA (IRE), b f Shaadi (USA)—Zizania Mr Ali Saeed

TWO-YEAR-OLDS

78 AIR EXPRESS (IRE), b c 26/4 Salse (USA)—Ibtisamm (USA) (Caucasus (USA)) Mr Mohamed Obaida
79 B f 11/4 Mtoto—Aquaglow (Caerleon (USA)) Mr C. E. Brittain
80 B br c 19/5 Mtoto—Bedouin Veil (USA) (Shareef Dancer (USA)) Mr C. E. Brittain
81 B c 14/3 Nashwan (USA)—Bevel (USA) (Mr Prospector (USA)) Saeed Manana
82 BIN CYCLONE (USA), b c 13/4 Shadeed—Dubian (High Line) Mohammed Obaida
83 Gr c 2/3 Mystiko (USA)—Black Ivor (USA) (Sir Ivor) Mr C. E. Brittain
84 Ch f 23/4 Archway (IRE)—Ceann-Na-Bann (Doulab (USA)) Mr C. E. Brittain
85 B f 2/1 Soviet Star (USA)—Crimson Quest (USA) (Diesis) Sheikh Marwan Al Maktoum
86 DEAR DRUE, b f 16/4 Jupiter Island—Top And Tail (Tilt Up (USA)) Bloomsbury Stud
87 EWAR ARRANGEMENT, b c 15/3 Bold Arrangement—Emily Allan (IRE) (Shirley Heights) Mr A. J. Richards
88 EWAR SNOWFLAKE, b f 8/3 Snow Chief (USA)—Petillante (Petong) Mr A. J. Richards
89 FRENCH MIST, b f 7/3 Mystiko (USA)—Flambera (FR) (Akarad (FR)) Mrs A. M. Upsdell
90 Ch f 18/2 Lycius (USA)—Heavenly Abode (FR) (Habitat) Saeed Manana
91 JOUST, b c 27/4 Keen—Tudorealm (Palace Music (USA)) Wyck Hall Stud
92 B f 8/4 Nashwan (USA)—Lagta (Kris) Saeed Manana
93 MACARONI BEACH, ch f 24/3 Jupiter Island—Real Princess (Aragon) The Hon D. Sieff
94 Gr c 27/2 With Approval (CAN)—Mingan Isle (USA) (Lord Avie (USA)) Saeed Manana
95 Ch f 3/2 Primo Dominie—Monaiya (Shareef Dancer (USA)) Mr B. H. Voak
96 NEMISTO, b c 24/1 Mystiko (USA)—Nemesia (Mill Reef (USA)) The Dayspring Company Limited
97 B f 16/2 Warrshan (USA)—Nophe (USA) (Super Concorde (USA)) Sheikh Marwan Al Maktoum
98 NORTH WHITE PLAINS, b c 17/5 Shareef Dancer (USA)—Clare Court (Glint of Gold) Mr G. Branchini
99 OUR WAY, ch f 8/5 Forzando—Hanglands (Bustino) Mr J. Ward-Hill
100 PETALUTHIS, b f 24/4 Terimon—Carousella (Rousillon (USA)) The Dayspring Company Limited
101 B f 4/5 Lycius (USA)—Pripet (USA) (Alleged (USA)) Sheikh Marwan Al Maktoum
102 PUZZLEMENT, gr c 19/4 Mystiko (USA)—Abuzz (Absalom) Mrs C. E. Brittain
103 B f 24/4 Lycius (USA)—She's The Tops (Shernazar) Saeed Manana
104 B c 2/3 Cadeaux Genereux—Shihama (USA) (Shadeed (USA)) Mr Mohamed Obaida
105 SODA POP (IRE), b c 5/4 River Falls—Riviere Salee (FR) (Luthier) Mr A. J. Richards
106 SPARTAN ROYALE, b c 15/4 Shareef Dancer (USA)—Cormorant Creek (Gorytus (USA)) Mr C. T. Olley
107 SUPERCHARMER, ch c 13/2 Charmer—Surpassing (Superlative) The Dayspring Company Limited
108 TIRAGE, ch c 16/4 Charmer—Maid of Essex (Bustino) The Dayspring Company Limited
109 B f 7/4 Warning—Troy Moon (Troy) Kings Bloodstock Limited
110 B c 21/3 Rock Hopper—Willowbank (Gay Fandango (USA)) Mr C. E. Brittain
111 WORD OF WARNING, b f 1/2 Warning—Usherette (FR) (Persian Bold) Mr A. J. Richards
112 ZARETSKI, b c 17/3 Pursuit of Love—Tolstoya (Northfields (USA)) Mr B. H. Voak
113 B c 18/3 Mujtahid (USA)—Zia (USA) (Shareef Dancer (USA)) Sheikh Marwan Al Maktoum
114 B c 13/4 Belmez (USA)—Zizania (Ahonoora) Ali Saeed

MR C. E. BRITTAIN—continued

Other Owners: Dorspring Limited, Miss I. G. Macgregor, Sheikh Mohammed, Mr M. C. Olley, Mr Robin Olley, Mr R. A. Pledger, Mrs E. W. Richards, Mr S. A. Richards, Mr R. Tibiletti.

Jockey (Flat): Brett Doyle (8-0).

89   MR M. A. BRITTAIN, Warthill

Postal: **Northgate Lodge, Warthill, York, YO3 9XR.**

Phone: **(01759) 371472 FAX (01759) 372915**

1 **AMIARGE**, 6, b g Reference Point—Scotia Rose **Miss D. J. Woods**
2 **EIRE LEATH-SCEAL**, 9, b g Legend of France (USA)—Killarney Belle (USA) **Mr Mel Brittain**
3 **GOLD DESIRE**, 6, b g Grey Desire—Glory Gold **Mr Mel Brittain**
4 **MEDIA EXPRESS**, 4, b c Sayf El Arab (USA)—Far Claim (USA) **Mr Tim Dean**
5 **PENDOLINO (IRE)**, 5, b g Thatching—Pendulina **Mr Ian Booth**
6 **PETER QUINCE**, 6, b h Kris—Our Reverie (USA) **Mr Mel Brittain**
7 **PORTITE SOPHIE**, 5, b m Doulab (USA)—Impropriety **Ms Maureen Hanlon**
8 **RAKIS (IRE)**, 6, b br g Alzao (USA)—Bristle **Mr P. G. Shorrock**
9 **SEE YOU AGAIN**, 4, b c Then Again—Down The Valley **Mr Tim Dean**
10 **TARTAN GEM (IRE)**, 5, ch h Lomond (USA)—Red Jade **Consultco Ltd**
11 **TOP PRIZE**, 8, b g High Top—Raffle
12 **TRY NEXT DOOR**, 9, b g Le Bavard (FR)—Winterwood **Mr M. S. Griffiths**

THREE-YEAR-OLDS

13 **BABYSHOOZ**, b f Efisio—Payvashooz **Mr M. J. Paver**
14 **MY ACHATES**, b f Prince Sabo—Persian Air **Mr G. G. Ashton**

TWO-YEAR-OLDS

15 **NOIRIE**, br c 12/2 Warning—Callipoli (USA) (Green Dancer (USA)) **Miss D. J. Woods**
16 Ch c 5/6 Thatching—Scuba Diver (Kings Lake (USA)) **Consultco Ltd**

Other Owners: Mr R. Abson, Eclipse Management Ltd, Wing Comdr K. E. Matson, Woodberry Limited.

Jockey (Flat): John Lowe (7-7).

90   MR C. D. BROAD, Westbury-on-Severn

Postal: **Tudor Stables, Elton, Westbury-on-Severn, Glos, GL14 1JH.**

Phone: **OFFICE (01452) 760835 FAX 760835 CAR (0836) 622858 HOME (01452) 760447**

1 **AMAHSAN (IRE)**, 4, ch g Nashamaa—Singing Filly **Mrs A. J. Broad**
2 **APRIL SEVENTH (IRE)**, 5, br g Stalker—Ring-Em-All **Park Industrial Supplies (Wales) Ltd**
3 **ARADIA'S DIOMOND**, 5, ch m Naskracker (USA)—Eight of Diamonds **Martha Spiers**
4 **BELL STAFFBOY (IRE)**, 7, b g Phardante (FR)—Trumpster **K. W. Bell & Son Ltd**
5 **DESIGN (IRE)**, 6, b m Millfontaine—Playwright **Mr K. W. Bell**
6 **HAWKFIELD (IRE)**, 7, b g Persian Bold—Oh Carol **The Hedonists**
7 **JIM VALENTINE**, 10, br g Furry Glen—Duessa **Mr R. H. L. Barnes**
8 **LANDED GENTRY (USA)**, 7, b g Vaguely Noble—Phydilla (FR) **K. W. Bell & Son Ltd**
9 **LUCKY DAWN (IRE)**, 7, b g Lancastrian—Slave Light **K. W. Bell & Son Ltd**
10 **MARINERS COVE**, 8, b g Julio Mariner—Ionian Isle (FR) **Mr Ray Cawthorn**
11 **MASTER MURPHY**, 7, b g Aragon—Magnifica **Mrs Sandy Herridge**
12 **MICHELLE'S ELLA (IRE)**, 4, b f Ela-Mana-Mou—Bustina (FR) **Mr Paul M. Hicks**
13 **MUDAHIM**, 10, b g Shareef Dancer (USA)—Mariska (FR) **Mr K. W. Bell**
14 **OLD MONEY**, 10, b g Furry Glen—Many Views **Uncle Jacks Pub**
15 4, Gr f Roselier (FR)—Over The Pond (IRE) **Mr Tom Kearns**

MR C. D. BROAD—continued

16 **RELUCKINO**, 6, b g Buckley—Releta **Mr M. G. Lilwall**
17 **SEIZE THE DAY (IRE)**, 8, b g Lomond (USA)—Cheerful Heart **Veterans of Trelleborgs**
18 **TWICE SHY (IRE)**, 5, gr g Sandalay—Nesford **Mr T. C. Couchman**

THREE-YEAR-OLDS
19 **HE'S GOT WINGS (IRE)**, b c In The Wings—Mariella **Mr Paul M. Hicks**

Other Owners: Castle Farm Stud, Mr T. Connop, Mr Paul De Weck, Miss F. Fenley, Mr J. W. Howarth, Mr J. Hughes, Mr Gordon E. Innes, Mr C. G. Major, Mr Ian D. Newman, Mr V. J. Pennington, Mr D. C. Pooley, Mr B. S. Port, Mr S. D. Reeve, Mr John Strang, Mr Jeffrey H. Wright.

Jockeys (Flat): M Fenton (w.a.), M Wigham.

Jockeys (NH): C Llewellyn (10-0, w.a.), W Marston (9-7).

Amateur: Mr A Wintle (10-7).

91   MR H. DE BROMHEAD, Knockeen

Postal: **Knockeen, Waterford, Ireland.**
Phone: **(051) 75726 FAX (051) 75726**

1 **BISHOPS HALL**, 10, br g Pimpernels Tune—Mariner's Dash **Joseph Carroll**
2 **BUCKISH (IRE)**, 6, b g Buckskin (FR)—Serbelle **Mr Charles Carroll**
3 **CORYMANDEL (IRE)**, 7, b g Mandalus—Curry Lunch **M. J. E. Thornhill**
4 4, Br f Brush Aside (USA)—Dikler Gale (IRE) **S. A. Aldridge**
5 5, B m Mandalus—Fifi L'Amour **S. A. Aldridge**
6 **FISSURE SEAL**, 10, ch g Tug of War—Annies Pet **Delton Syndicate**
7 4, B g King's Ride—Golden Cherry (IRE) **M. J. E. Thornhill**
8 6, B g Meneval (USA)—Kandy Kate **Dr Con O'Keeffe**
9 **MENESONIC (IRE)**, 6, b g Meneval (USA)—Kandy Kate **Mrs C. O'Keeffe**
10 **OAKS PRIDE (USA)**, 5, ch g Afleet (CAN)—Field Point Road (USA) **Thomas Liang**
11 5, B g Supreme Leader—Palazon
12 **PHAREIGN (IRE)**, 5, br g Phardante (FR)—Lena's Reign **K. Casey**
13 **PRIZE OF PEACE (IRE)**, 6, ch m Torus—Sheelin Bavard **Mr T. J. Carroll**
14 **STELLA NOVA (IRE)**, 6, b m Mandalus—Mistress Nova **Mrs R. Baly**

Jockey (Flat): Joanna Morgan.

Jockeys (NH): G Bradley, T Horgan, C O'Dwyer, P A Roche, C F Swan.

Amateur: Mr M D Carey.

92   LADY SUSAN BROOKE, Bromyard

Postal: **Wootton Farm, Pencombe, Bromyard, Herefordshire, HR7 4RR.**
Phone: **(01885) 400615**

1 **DERRING BUD**, 12, br g Derring Rose—Tarune **Lady Susan Brooke**
2 **GAELIC SUNRISE**, 9, b g Mr Big John—Sorrel Dawn **Lady Susan Brooke**
3 **GREY WATCH**, 6, gr m Petong—Royal Custody **Lady Susan Brooke**
4 **HIGHWAY FIVE (IRE)**, 8, ch g Carlingford Castle—Final Triumph **Lady Susan Brooke**

Jockey (NH): R Johnson.

Amateur: Mr M Jackson.

Lady Rider: Miss Emma James.

93   MR C. P. E. BROOKS, Lambourn

Postal: **Uplands Stables, Lambourn, Newbury, Berks, RG16 7QH.**

Phone: **(01488) 72077 FAX (01488) 71206**

1 **AARDWOLF**, 5, b g Dancing Brave (USA)—Pretoria **Lady Camilla Dempster**
2 **ABSOLUTELY AVERAGE (IRE)**, 6, b g Montelimar (USA)—Dr Shadad **Uplands Bloodstock**
3 **AMERICAN LORD (IRE)**, 5, b g Lord Americo—Princess Isabella **Uplands Bloodstock**
4 **BIG BEN DUN**, 10, b g The Parson—Shanban **Uplands Bloodstock**
5 **BLACK HUMOUR**, 12, b g Buckskin (FR)—Artiste Gaye **Lady Lloyd Webber**
6 **BOKARO (FR)**, 10, b g Air du Nord (USA)—Tzara (FR) **Dr A. J. F. O'Reilly**
7 **BOOTS N ALL (IRE)**, 6, br g Strong Statement (USA)—Sallstown **Mrs David V. Tipper**
8 **CONEY ROAD**, 7, gr g Grey Desire—Miss Diaward **Mrs M. C. Grant**
9 5, B g Lord Americo—Coolbawn Lady **Uplands Bloodstock**
10 **COULDNT BE BETTER**, 9, br g Oats—Belle Bavard **Mr R. A. B. Whittle**
11 **COUNTRY STAR (IRE)**, 5, b g Persian Bold—Sugar Plum Fairy **H.R.H. Prince Fahd Salman**
12 **CROSS THE RUBICON (IRE)**, 5, ch g Over The River (FR)—One Way Only **Mrs S. Towler**
13 **DARK STRANGER (IRE)**, 5, b g Iveday (FR)—Abeille Royale (USA) **Mr Terry Neill**
14 **DARREN THE BRAVE**, 8, ch g Sunyboy—Stey Brae **Mr D. Allport**
15 **DESERT HARVEST**, 4, b g Green Desert (USA)—Mill On The Floss **Alec J. Tuckermann**
16 **DONTFORGET INSIGHT (IRE)**, 5, b g Don't Forget Me—Starlust **Mr Terry Neill**
17 **FLORIDA SKY**, 9, b g Florida Son—Eskylane **Uplands Bloodstock**
18 **FONTAINEROUGE (IRE)**, 6, gr g Millfontaine—How Are You **Mrs David V. Tipper**
19 **FORT GALE (IRE)**, 5, b br g Strong Gale—Only Gorgeous **Michael Jackson Bloodstock Ltd**
20 **FOXTROT ROMEO**, 6, ch g Town And Country—Forest Frolic **Lady Cobham**
21 **FRIZZBALL (IRE)**, 4, br f Orchestra—Credit Card **Uplands Bloodstock**
22 **GAROLO (FR)**, 6, b g Garde Royale—Valgoya (FR) **Lady Lloyd Webber**
23 **GILT EDGE (IRE)**, 5, b g Dromod Hill—Gilt Course **Mrs G. Abecassis**
24 **GOOD INSIGHT (IRE)**, 8, ch g Good Thyne (USA)—Gentle Down (USA) **Mr Terry Neill**
25 **GOODSHOT RICH**, 12, b g Roscoe Blake—Hunter's Treasure **Mrs S. Towler**
26 **GO UNIVERSAL (IRE)**, 8, br g Teofane—Lady Dorcet **Universal Conference & Incentive Trv Ltd**
27 5, B g Idiot's Delight—Graeme's Gem **Mr W. Phillips**
28 **GREAT STUFF (IRE)**, 5, b br g Dromod Hill—Little Loch **Uplands Bloodstock**
29 **HANG'EM OUT TO DRY (IRE)**, 5, b g Executive Perk—Obsession **Torrance & Davies Racing Club**
30 **HARVEST VIEW (IRE)**, 6, b m Good Thyne (USA)—In View Lass **Dr P. P. Brown**
31 **HERMITE DU MANOIR (FR)**, 6, b g Bardamu (FR)—Hulotte Violet (FR) **Uplands Bloodstock**
32 **INDONESIAN (IRE)**, 4, b br c Alzao (USA)—Miss Garuda **Uplands Bloodstock**
33 4, B g Aristocracy—Lady Go Marching (USA) **Uplands Bloodstock**
34 5, B g Good Thyne (USA)—Lady Morgan **Mr Anthony Pye-Jeary**
35 **LE GINNO (FR)**, 9, ch g Concorde Jr (USA)—Fromentel (FR) **Irish World Partnership**
36 **LONESOME GLORY (USA)**, 8, ch g Transworld (USA)—Stronghold (FR) **Mrs Walter M. Jeffords Jr**
37 **LYNTON LAD**, 4, b g Superpower—House Maid **Uplands Bloodstock**
38 **MAN MOOD (FR)**, 5, b g Brinkmanship (USA)—Miss Mood **Steel Plate & Sections Ltd**
39 **MARLOUSION (IRE)**, 4, ch f Montelimar (USA)—Ware Princess **Mrs B. Mead**
40 **MERE CLASS**, 10, b g Class Distinction—Cuckmere Grange **Mrs P. Elsbury**
41 **MERRY PANTO (IRE)**, 7, ch g Lepanto (GER)—Merry Penny **Uplands Bloodstock**
42 4, Ch g Orchestra—Midnight Mistress **Uplands Bloodstock**
43 4, Ch g Saxon Farm—Milworth **Uplands Bloodstock**
44 **MR FLANAGAN**, 10, b g Idiot's Delight—Here We Go **Mrs Richard Stanley**
45 **MR PRESIDENT (IRE)**, 7, b g Supreme Leader—I've No Idea **Mrs B. Mead**
46 **MR PRIMETIME (IRE)**, 4, b g Phardante (FR)—Bavette **Anglia Telecom Centres Plc**
47 **MR STACKHOUSE (IRE)**, 5, gr g Step Together (USA)—Best Dressed **Mrs B. Mead**
48 **MYWEND'S (IRE)**, 6, ch g The Parson—People **Uplands Bloodstock**
49 **MY YOUNG MAN**, 11, b g Young Man (FR)—Hampsruth **Mrs Margaret McKenna**
50 **NELL VALLEY**, 5, b m Neltino—Loughnavalley **Mrs J. Thornton**
51 **NICE TONE (IRE)**, 5, ch g Orchestra—Tacova **Uplands Bloodstock**
52 **NICKY WILDE**, 6, br g Strong Gale—Dark Trix **Mr A. L. Brodin**
53 5, Ch g Over The River (FR)—November Tide **Uplands Bloodstock**
54 **PADRE MIO (IRE)**, 8, b g The Parson—Mwanamio **Lady Lloyd Webber**
55 **PRETORIA DANCER**, 4, b c Dancing Brave (USA)—Pretoria **Lady Camilla Dempster**
56 4, B g Tremblant—Queens Tricks **Uplands Bloodstock**
57 5, Ch g Orchestra—Rare Currency **Uplands Bloodstock**

MR C. P. E. BROOKS—continued

58 **RIVER BOUNTY**, 10, ch g Over The River (FR)—Billie Gibb **Uplands Bloodstock**
59 **SOUND REVEILLE**, 8, b g Relkino—Loughnavalley **Mrs G. Abecassis**
60 **STRAWBERRY ANGEL (USA)**, 5, ch m Red Attack (USA)—Stronghold (FR) **Mrs Walter M. Jeffords Jr**
61 **STROKESAVER (IRE)**, 6, ch g Orange Reef—Silver Love (USA) **The Bow Lane Partnership**
62 **SUNY BAY (IRE)**, 7, gr g Roselier (FR)—Suny Salome **Uplands Bloodstock**
63 4, B g The Noble Player (USA)—Suny Salome **Uplands Bloodstock**
64 **TIME ENOUGH (IRE)**, 7, ch g Callernish—Easter Gazette **The Lewis Partnership**
65 5, B m Tragic Role (USA)—Toumanova **Uplands Bloodstock**
66 **UNCLE JAMES (IRE)**, 5, br g Young Man (FR)—Hampsruth **Mrs W. Tulloch**
67 **UNIVERSAL MAGIC (IRE)**, 7, ch g Le Bavard (FR)—Autumn Magic **Universal Conference & Incentive Trv Ltd**
68 **UPLANDS (IRE)**, 6, br g Callernish—Rich Belle **Uplands Bloodstock**
69 **VENICE BEACH**, 4, b g Shirley Heights—Bold And Beautiful **Miss J. Bines**
70 **VERY VERY ORDINARY**, 10, b g Furry Glen—Very Very **Uplands Bloodstock**
71 **WILDE MUSIC (IRE)**, 6, b g Orchestra—Run For Shelter **Mr A. L. Brodin**
72 **WOODBURY FAIR (IRE)**, 8, ch g Over The River (FR)—Noble Lynn **Lady Cobham**
73 **YOUBETTERBELIEVEIT (IRE)**, 7, ch g The Parson—Emperors Twinkle **Uplands Bloodstock**

Other Owners: Mr T. F. M. Bebb, Mr D. W. H. Bell, Mrs Robert Brooks, Mr C. P. Burns, C. Buttery, Mr M. Byrne, Mr P. Cowan, Mr Nigel Dempster, A. Eaves, Mrs J. Stuart Evans, Mrs Miriam Francome, Mr John Halliday, Mr John Rhys Harris, Sir Andrew Lloyd Webber, R. B. Michaelson, Mr M. J. Morrison, M. Myers, Miss M. Talbot, Neil Waite, Mrs C. A. Waters, Harry Watton.

Jockeys (NH): G Bradley (10-2), D Gallagher (10-0).

Conditional: M Berry (10-0).

Amateur: Mr E James (10-0).

94   MRS E. M. BROOKS, Bideford

Postal: **The Barton, Monkleigh, Bideford, Devon, EX39 5JX.**

Phone: **(01805) 623156**

1 **BARTON ROSE**, 5, b g Derring Rose—Barton Sauce **Mrs J. Brooks**
2 **EXPRESSO DRUMMER**, 6, b g Sergeant Drummer (USA)—Free Expression **Mrs J. Brooks**
3 **LIBERTY JAMES**, 9, ch g Remezzo—Lady Cheval **Mrs J. Brooks**
4 **SAUCY'S WOLF**, 6, ch g Little Wolf—Barton Sauce **Mrs J. Brooks**
5 **TINTERN CHERRY**, 4, ch f Northern Game—Tintern Memory **Mrs J. Brooks**
6 **TINTERNDRUMMERGIRL**, 5, b m Sergeant Drummer (USA)—Tintern Memory **Mrs J. Brooks**

Jockeys (NH): W J McFarland, Guy Upton.

Amateur: Mr Tom Greed.

95   MR S. A. BROOKSHAW, Shrewsbury

Postal: **Preston Farm, Uffington, Shrewsbury, Shropshire, SY4 4TB.**

Phone: **PHONE & FAX (01743) 709227 MOBILE (0802) 364837**

1 **ARCTIC RED**, 9, ch g Deep Run—Snow Sweet **Mr A. Stennett**
2 **BARTON RELIC (USA)**, 5, b g Garcia (USA)—Morning Order (NZ) **Mr Stanley W. Clarke**
3 **BARTON SANTA (IRE)**, 7, b g Cataldi—Galloping Santa **Mrs H. J. Clarke**
4 **BARTON SCAMP**, 4, ch g Sadeem (USA)—Hachimitsu **Mrs H. J. Clarke**

MR S. A. BROOKSHAW—continued

5 BARTON WARD, 5, gr g Malaspina—Lily Mab (FR) **Mrs H. J. Clarke**
6 4, B g Super Imposing (NZ)—Carlyle Ace (NZ) **Mr Stanley W. Clarke**
7 GREY DANTE (IRE), 5, gr m Phardante (FR)—Grey Squirrell **Mr J. W. Beddoes**
8 HONEST WORD, 11, ch g Touching Wood (USA)—Amerella **Mrs H. J. Clarke**
9 LORD GYLLENE (NZ), 8, b g Ring The Bell (NZ)—Dentelle (NZ) **Mr Stanley W. Clarke**
10 MICHERADO (FR), 6, ch g Un Desperado (FR)—Quality Stripe (USA) **Mr Stanley W. Clarke**
11 4, Ch g Sadeem (USA)—Miss Lightening **Mrs H. J. Clarke**
12 ROLLING BALL (FR), 13, b g Quart de Vin (FR)—Etoile du Berger III (FR) **Mrs H. J. Clarke**
13 4, B g Lyphento (USA)—Somerford Glory **Mrs H. J. Clarke**
14 SQUIRRELLSDAUGHTER, 9, gr m Black Minstrel—Grey Squirrell **Mr J. W. Beddoes**
15 SWARF (IRE), 6, ch g Ore—Highly Acceptable **Mr A. Stennett**

Other Owners: Mr F. S. Brettell, Mrs J. M. Stennett.

96   MR R. BROTHERTON, Pershore

Postal: **Mill End Racing Stables, Netherton Road, Elmley Castle, Pershore, WR10 3JF.**
Phone: **EVESHAM (01386) 710772 MOBILE (0850) 027453**

1 ADMIRALTY WAY, 10, b g Petorius—Captive Flower **Mrs A. Burton**
2 ARKINDALE AMBER, 5, b g Superpower—Najat **Mrs A. Burton**
3 EXHIBITION PRINCE (IRE), 5, b g Exhibitioner—Glenardina **Mr Colin Keable**
4 FREE DANCER, 6, b m Shareef Dancer (USA)—Free Touch **Mrs V. E. Hayward**
5 GORDON, 5, b g Governor General—Red Spider **Mrs C. N. Pitt**
6 HOT DOG, 6, br m Sulaafah (USA)—Flying Portion **Mr Hugh Phipps**
7 KHAZARI, 8, ch g Shahrastani (USA)—Kozana **Mrs A. Burton**
8 KING ACRYLIC (IRE), 5, b g King of Clubs—Maynooth Belle **Mrs A. Burton**
9 MR POPPLETON, 7, ch g Ballacashtal (CAN)—Greenstead Lady **The Final Furlong Partnership**
10 PETITE BIJOU, 5, b m Tina's Pet—Highland Lassie **Mrs Carol Newman**
11 POLLYKENDU (IRE), 8, b br g Pollerton—Moykendu **Baskerville Racing Club**
12 ROGER DE MOWBRAY, 6, b g Grey Desire—Richesse (FR) **Baskerville Racing Club**
13 SAFE SECRET, 5, b m Seclude (USA)—Safe Passage **The Hall Orson Barker Partnership**
14 SELDOM IN, 10, ch g Mummy's Game—Pinzamber **Baskerville Racing Club**
15 TURRET, 5, b m Shirley Heights—Moogie **Mrs Tessa Byrne**
16 WILL IT LAST, 10, b m Roi Guillaume (FR)—Golden Annie **Mrs Theresa Walshe**

THREE-YEAR-OLDS

17 MS JONES (IRE), ch f Headin' Up—Deep Joy **Mrs Theresa Walshe**

Other Owners: Mr S. J. Barker, Mrs Janis Barton, Mr John W. Barton, Mr B. J. Byrne, Mr J. R. Hall, Miss S. E. Hayward, Mrs Susan Keable, Miss M. T. Orson, Mrs Philippa Phipps.

Jockeys (Flat): A Mackay (7-8), R Price (7-12).

Jockeys (NH): L J Harvey, C Llewellyn.

Conditional: T Eley.

97   MR D. H. BROWN, Maltby

Postal: **The Grove, Blyth Road, Roche Abbey, Maltby, S66 8NW.**
Phone: **(01709) 812854**

1 ICARUS (USA), 10, b g Wind And Wuthering (USA)—Cedar Waxwing (USA) **Mr D. H. Brown**
2 LA FONTAINBLEAU (IRE), 8, gr g Lafontaine (USA)—Alsong **Mr D. H. Brown**

Amateur: Mr A Rebori (10-7).

98   MRS J. BROWN, York

Postal: **The Old Chapel, Scackleton, Hovingham, York, YO6 5NB.**

1 **BIRD WATCHER**, 7, b g Bluebird (USA)—Grayfoot **Mr E. E. Newbould**
2 **COOL STEEL (IRE)**, 4, gr g Absalom—Formidable Task **Mr H. R. Hewitt**
3 **DARK DAWN**, 12, b g Pollerton—Cacador's Pet **Mrs J. M. Newitt**
4 **FIFTYSEVENCHANNELS (IRE)**, 7, b g Bustineto—Allitess **Mr John A. Cooper**
5 **FRYUP SATELLITE**, 5, br g Leading Star—Comedy Imp **Mr John Lees**
6 **HEAVENS ABOVE**, 4, br g Celestial Storm (USA)—Regal Wonder **R. & G. Leonard**
7 4, B g Hallgate—Hydrangea **Mr T. Fawcett**
8 **MR FUDGE**, 9, gr g Broadsword (USA)—Blades **Mr Paul Clifton**
9 4, B g Lord Bud—Trailing Rose **Mr R. Burridge**
10 **YOUNG DUBLINER (IRE)**, 7, br g Strong Gale—Desert Maid **Mr John A. Cooper**

Other Owners: Mrs H. Sedgwick.

99   MR R. L. BROWN, Abergavenny

Postal: **The Firs, Grosmont, Abergavenny, Gwent, NP7 8LY.**

1 **DRAKESTONE**, 5, b g Motivate—Lyricist **Mr R. L. Brown**
2 **MISS MOTIVATE**, 5, b m Motivate—Rustys Special **Mr S. R. Brown**
3 **PROJECT'S MATE**, 9, br g Rustingo—Lyricist **Mr R. L. Brown**

THREE-YEAR-OLDS

4 **STARTINGO**, b c Rustingo—Spartan's Girl **Mr R. L. Brown**

TWO-YEAR-OLDS

5 B f 21/4 Rustingo—Lyricist (Averof) **Mr R. L. Brown**
6 Ch f 24/7 Man Among Men (IRE)—Rustys Special (Rustingo) **Mr R. L. Brown**

100   MISS A. E. BROYD, Crickhowell

Postal: **Penrhiw Farm, Llangenny, Crickhowell, Powys, NP8 1HD.**
Phone: **(01873) 812292**

1 **AMBASSADOR ROYALE (IRE)**, 8, gr g Pennine Walk—Hayati **Miss Alison Broyd**
2 **ISLAND CUB**, 5, b g Little Wolf—Orkney Annie **Miss Alison Broyd**
3 **ORCADIAN ROSE**, 6, br m Derring Rose—Orkney Annie **Miss Alison Broyd**
4 **SYLVESTER (IRE)**, 6, ch g Shy Groom (USA)—Single Viking **Miss Alison Broyd**

101   MR R. H. BUCKLER, Bridport

Postal: **Melplash Court Farm, Melplash, Bridport, Dorset, DT6 3UH.**
Phone: **HOME (01308) 488318 MOBILE (0831) 806360 FAX (01308) 488403**

1 **AMBER REALM**, 8, ch m Southern Music—Thrupence **Mrs Dunn**
2 **ANGELO'S DOUBLE (IRE)**, 8, b g M Double M (USA)—Bebe Altesse (GER) **Mr J. Henwood**
3 **BALLYEDWARD (IRE)**, 6, b g Roselier (FR)—Paico Ana **Mr Nick Elliott**
4 **BAYBELLINA (IRE)**, 5, b m Robellino (USA)—Brosna (USA) **Mr Jack Bugler**
5 **BROCKTON LIGHT**, 4, b f Be My Chief (USA)—Lovers Light **Mrs D. A. La Trobe**
6 **CALLERMINE**, 7, ch m Callernish—Lady Vulmid **Supermare Scaffolding**
7 **COOL CHARACTER (IRE)**, 8, b g Furry Glen—Raise The Standard **Mr Nick Elliott**
8 **COOLE DODGER**, 11, ro gr g Scallywag—Coole Streak **Mrs B. M. Searle**
9 **COURT MASTER (IRE)**, 8, b br g Bustineto—Moycarkey **Vice Admiral Sir Fitzroy Talbot**

MR R. H. BUCKLER—continued

10 DIX SEPT MAI (FR), 5, ch g Cap Martin (FR)—Jakotte de Nereuil (FR) Mr R. H. Buckler
11 FLOW, 7, b m Over The River (FR)—Thrupence Mrs Dunn & Mrs Collier
12 FRANK NAYLAR, 5, b g All Fair—The Deer Hound Mr J. A. G. Meaden
13 GOLDEN OPAL, 11, b g Golden Love—Coquito Mr R. H. Buckler
14 GROUND NUT (IRE), 6, ch g Fools Holme (USA)—Corn Seed Mrs R. L. Haskins
15 HE KNOWS THE RULES, 4, b g Tirol—Falls of Lora Mr J. Henwood
16 KINGS CHERRY (IRE), 8, b g King's Ride—Another Cherry Mr T. J. Swaffield
17 MANDEVILLE GEORGE, 5, b g Emarati (USA)—Stately Gala Mr B. C. Knibbs
18 MEL (IRE), 6, ch g Millfontaine—Nataf Mr R. H. Buckler & Mrs R. L. Haskins
19 MISS DISKIN (IRE), 7, b m Sexton Blake—Knapping Mr Martyn Forrester
20 PADDYSWAY, 9, b g Paddy's Stream—Lastway Mr R. T. C. Searle
21 PRINCE TEETON, 7, b g Prince of Peace—Princess Teeton Mrs S. H. Richards
22 RHOMAN FUN (IRE), 7, b g Rhoman Rule (USA)—Fun Martyrs To Racing Partnership
23 RHYTHM AND BLUES, 6, b g Myjinski (USA)—Pitskelly Blues Mrs Peter Gregson
24 SEASAMACAMILE, 9, b m Lafontaine (USA)—Crisp Star Mr M. West
25 SEE ENOUGH, 8, ch g Sharp Deal—See-O-Duf Mr J. A. G. Meaden
26 ST VILLE, 10, b g Top Ville—Dame Julian Melplash Racing
27 TAKE BY STORM (IRE), 7, b g Bluebird (USA)—Laurel Express Mrs Robert Blackburn
28 TOUR LEADER (NZ), 7, ch g Nassipour (USA)—Colleen (NZ) Mr Peter Jones
29 WELL BRIEFED, 9, br g Miner's Lamp—In Brief Mr Peter Jones

Other Owners: Mr J. R. Barr, Mrs Marian Birks, Mrs I. M. Buckler, Mrs P. J. Buckler, Mr M. Channon, Mrs H. T. Edwards, Mrs Carol Fairbairn, Mr Frank Habberfield, Mrs J. P. Rabbetts, Mrs J. I. Searle, Mr M. A. F. Searle, Mrs L. M. Stobart, Mr J. P. Windsor.

Jockey (NH): B Powell (10-0).

Conditional: Gerrard Supple (9-7).

Amateur: Mr B Dixon (10-4).

102   MR DAVID BURCHELL, Ebbw Vale

Postal: Drysiog Farm, Briery Hill, Ebbw Vale, Gwent, NP3 6BU.
Phone: EBBW VALE (01495) 302551 MOBILE (0831) 601214 FAX (01495) 352464

1 APRIL'S MODEL LADY, 10, b m Shaab—Dream Lady Miss E. S. McKechnie
2 BOLD ACRE, 6, ch g Never So Bold—Nicola Wynn Mrs Marion C. Morgan
3 CASTLE SECRET, 10, b g Castle Keep—Baffle Mrs Ruth Burchell
4 CHANNEL PASTIME, 12, b g Turn Back The Time (USA)—Channel Ten Mrs Sandra Worthington
5 COAST ALONG (IRE), 4, b g Satco (FR)—Golden Flats Mr T. G. Brooks
6 COLETTE'S CHOICE (IRE), 7, b m Alzao (USA)—Madrilon (FR) Mr J. A. Cooper
7 CUPRONICKEL (IRE), 4, b f Distant Relative—One Half Silver (CAN) Exors of the late Mrs J. M. Snape
8 DESERT POWER, 7, b g Green Desert (USA)—Rivers Maid Mr Rhys Thomas Williams
9 FORGETFUL, 7, b m Don't Forget Me—Peak Squaw (USA) The Equus Club
10 HARRY, 6, ch g Risk Me (FR)—Relko's Pride Mr Simon T. Lewis
11 HEIGHTH OF FAME, 5, b g Shirley Heights—Land of Ivory (USA) Mr Simon T. Lewis
12 HOLY JOE, 14, b g The Parson—Doonasleen Mr Simon T. Lewis
13 PATS LADS, 4, ch g Prince des Coeurs (USA)—Jealous Sandy Mr John O'Malley
14 PETITJEAN (IRE), 5, b g Last Tycoon—Working Model Mr Rhys Thomas Williams
15 PHARLY REEF, 4, b g Pharly (FR)—Hay Reef Mr Vivian Guy
16 PONTYNYSWEN, 8, b g Ballacashtal (CAN)—Tropingay Mr J. L. Thomas
17 QUICK SILVER BOY, 6, gr g Kalaglow—Safidar Mr P. Riddick
18 REIGNING ROYAL, 5, ch m Tina's Pet—Regency Brighton Mr Lyn Phillips
19 SLIP A COIN, 5, b m Slip Anchor—Luck Penny Mr Eamonn O'Malley
20 STAGE FRIGHT, 5, b g Sure Blade (USA)—First Act Mr Rhys Thomas Williams
21 TECHNOLOGICAL RISK, 5, ch g Risk Me (FR)—Technology (FR) Mr Rhys Thomas Williams

MR DAVID BURCHELL—continued

Other Owners: Mr J. S. Aitchison, Mr P. M. Baldowski, Mrs C. Berridge, Mr J. Bruce, Mr R. F. Denmead, Mr C. Garland, Mr A. M. Harris, Mr D. A. Liscombe, Mr K. W. Martin, Mr F. D. J. McDevitt, Mr A. R. Mitchell, Mr R. T. Wilkins.

Jockey (NH): D J Burchell (10-0).

Conditional: John Prior (10-0).

Amateurs: Mr S Blackwell (10-0), Mr N Miles (10-0).

Lady Rider: Miss Emily Jones.

103   MR PAUL BURGOYNE, Lambourn

Postal: **Frenchmans Lodge, Lambourn, Berks, RG17 8QT.**

Phone: **LAMBOURN (01488) 71980**

1 **BANKONIT (IRE)**, 8, b g Horage—Tardy (USA) **Mrs A. J. America**
2 **DON'T GIVE UP**, 8, b h Nomination—Tug Along **Don't Give Up Partnership**
3 **DOODIES POOL (IRE)**, 6, b g Mazaad—Barncogue **Mr S. J. Edwards**
4 **HALBERT**, 7, b g Song—Stoneydale **Mr T. Barker**
5 **PHARAOH'S DANCER**, 9, b g Fairy King (USA)—Marie Louise **Pharaohs Computers Ltd**
6 **PROUD BRIGADIER (IRE)**, 8, b g Auction Ring (USA)—Naughty One Gerard **Mr S. J. Edwards**
7 **REQUESTED**, 9, b g Rainbow Quest (USA)—Melody Hour **Mr P. Burgoyne**
8 **ROCK THE BARNEY (IRE)**, 7, ch h Coquelin (USA)—Lady Loire **Mrs Satu Marks**
9 **ROCKY WATERS (USA)**, 7, b br g Rocky Marriage (USA)—Running Melody **Mr P. Chomiak**
10 **SOAKING**, 6, b g Dowsing (USA)—Moaning Low **Mr Philip Saunders**
11 **TAUTEN (IRE)**, 6, br m Taufan (USA)—Pitaka **Mr T. Barker**
12 **UNDERWYCHWOOD (IRE)**, 8, b g Try My Best (USA)—Sooner Or Later **Partnership**

Other Owners: Mr O'Sullivan.

Jockeys (Flat): T Quinn (w.a.), M Wigham (w.a.).

Jockey (NH): I Lawrence (w.a.).

Apprentice: D McCabe.

Lady Rider: Miss M O'Sullivan.

104   MR K. R. BURKE, Wantage

Postal: **Ginge Stables, Ginge, Wantage, Oxon, OX12 8QS.**

Phone: **OFFICE (01235) 821455**

1 **BODANTREE**, 5, b g Rambo Dancer (CAN)—Snow Tree **Mr R. S. Brookhouse**
2 **BRESIL (USA)**, 7, ch g Bering—Clever Bidder (USA) **Mr P. Sweeting**
3 **CHELSEA NATIVE**, 9, br m Be My Native (USA)—Chelsea Charmer **Mr J. H. Carter**

MR K. R. BURKE—continued

4 **CORLY SPECIAL**, 9, b g Lyphard's Special (USA)—Courreges **Mr P. A. Brazier**
5 **DARING DESTINY**, 5, b m Daring March—Raunchy Rita **Mrs A. Wright & Partners**
6 **EALING COURT**, 7, ch g Blazing Saddles (AUS)—Fille de General **Mr R. S. Brookhouse**
7 **EULOGY (FR)**, 9, b g Esprit du Nord (USA)—Louange **G-Express Limited**
8 **FULL SHILLING (USA)**, 7, b br g Sovereign Dancer (USA)—Full Virtue (USA) **Mr Barry Hawkins**
9 **MISS NOSEY OATS**, 8, b m Oats—Miss Poker Face **Mr P. A. Matthews**
10 **MONTEGO REEF**, 6, b g Miramar Reef—Raunchy Rita **Mrs Elaine M. Burke**
11 **MR BEAN**, 6, b g Salse (USA)—Goody Blake **Mr Brendan J. Toner**
12 **MUCH SOUGHT AFTER**, 7, b g Adonijah—Lady Clementine **The MSA Partnership**
13 **NATIONAL FLAG (FR)**, 6, b g Sure Blade (USA)—On The Staff (USA) **Mr Raymond Singer**
14 **NORTHERN TRIAL (USA)**, 8, b g Far North (CAN)—Make An Attempt (USA) **Mr Denis McCarthy**
15 **PETMER**, 9, gr g Tina's Pet—Merency **Mr Adrian Duckworth**
16 **SIAN WYN**, 6, br m Hotfoot—Curzon House **D. & G. Robinson**
17 **TAEL OF SILVER**, 4, b f Today And Tomorrow—Schula **Mrs Elaine M. Burke**
18 **VILLAINS BRIEF (IRE)**, 7, b g Torus—Larrys Glen **Mr J. A. Mackrell**
19 **WINDWARD ARIOM**, 10, ch g Pas de Seul—Deja Vu (FR) **Mr Andrew Shaw**
20 **ZAHID (USA)**, 5, ch g Storm Cat (USA)—Time An' Care (USA) **G-Express Limited**
21 **ZAMIL (USA)**, 11, b g Lyphard (USA)—Wayward Lass (USA) **Mr David Whyte**

THREE-YEAR-OLDS

22 **SMILING BESS**, b f Salse (USA)—Wanda **Mr E. J. Mangan**
23 **WELSH MELODY**, b f Merdon Melody—Young Whip **Mr M. Deren**
24 **YOUNG FREDERICK (IRE)**, ch g Polish Patriot (USA)—Notre Histoire **Mrs Elaine M. Burke**

TWO-YEAR-OLDS

25 Ch c 5/4 Never So Bold—Fire Sprite (Mummy's Game) **Mrs Elaine M. Burke**
26 B c 6/3 Superpower—Malindi (Mansingh (USA)) **Mrs Elaine M. Burke**
27 Ch f 14/3 Sharp Victor (USA)—Nurse Jo (USA) (J O Tobin (USA)) **Mr M. Deren**
28 B f 23/3 River Falls—Sevens Are Wild (Petorius) **Mr M. Deren**

Other Owners: Aston House Stud, S. L. Chapman & Partners, Mr K. Craddock, Mrs M. B. Craddock, Mr John G. Davis, Mrs Susan Davis, Mr W. P. J. Jackson, Mr Stephen S. James, Mr Glenn Martin, Mr T. Nicholson, Mr K. Powell, Mr Robert Russell, Mr F. A. Summerlin, Mr J. Weal, Ms Jane Withey.

Jockeys (Flat): J Quinn (w.a.), J Tate (w.a.).

Jockeys (NH): R Dunwoody (w.a.), M Fitzgerald (w.a.), N Williamson (w.a.).

Conditional: A Larnach.

Amateur: Mr E Burke (9-7).

105   MR P. BUTLER, Lewes

Postal: **Homewood Gate Racing Stables, Novington Lane, East Chiltington, Lewes, BN7 3AU.**
Phone: **(01273) 890124 OR (01273) 477254 MOBILE (0850) 114099**

1 **APOLLO VENTURE**, 8, b g Sunyboy—Hillside Venture **Mr D. Evans**
2 **CHURCHTOWN PORT (IRE)**, 6, gr g Peacock (FR)—Portane Miss **Mr John Plackett**
3 **FREEBYJOVE**, 6, ch m King Among Kings—London Chimes **Miss N. Ni Luasa**
4 **HOLIDAY ISLAND**, 7, ch g Good Times (ITY)—Green Island **Mr P. Bell**
5 **LITTLE LUKE (IRE)**, 5, b h Somethingfabulous (USA)—Yours Sincerely (USA) **Mrs Barbara Armstrong**
6 **NATHIR (USA)**, 10, b g Diesis—As You Would (USA) **Mrs Janet Coleman**
7 **POWDER MILL RUN**, 9, b g Deep Run—Seabury Heights **Miss M. Bryant**
8 **PRECIOUS WONDER**, 7, b g Precocious—B M Wonder **Mr D. J. Butler**

MR P. BUTLER—continued

9 **PRINCE ROONEY (IRE)**, 8, b h Dayeem (USA)—Fourth Degree **Mr P. Butler**
10 **SILLY POINT**, 4, ch f Weld—Silly Games **Miss N. Ni Luasa**
11 **STONEHAM GIRL**, 4, b f Nomination—Persian Tapestry **Mrs Liz Monnington**
12 **WILLOW GALE**, 9, b m Strong Gale—Tric Willow **Mr John Plackett**

THREE-YEAR-OLDS

13 **RED SKY DELIGHT (IRE)**, b f Skyliner—Blazing Sunset **Miss M. Bryant**

Other Owners: Mrs J. M. Bonard, Mr Jerry Laurence, Mr Ian Moody, Mr Alan J. Wood.

Conditional: S Arnold (9-7).

Lady Rider: Mrs E L Butler (8-7).

106   MR N. BYCROFT, Brandsby

Postal: **Cotman Rise, Brandsby, York, YO6 4RN.**

Phone: **(01347) 888641**

1 **BLUE LUGANA**, 4, b g Lugana Beach—Two Friendly **Mr D. Wright**
2 **CAROL AGAIN**, 4, b f Kind of Hush—Lady Carol **Mr J. G. Lumsden**
3 **CHILL WIND**, 7, gr g Siberian Express (USA)—Springwell **Mr E. H. Daley**
4 **CRAIGIE BOY**, 6, b g Crofthall—Lady Carol **Mr Bernard F. Rayner**
5 **DOUBLE GLOW**, 4, b f Presidium—Glow Again **Dr Horace Ngan**
6 **KIRKADIAN**, 6, b m Norwick (USA)—Pushkar **Mr G. J. Allison**
7 **MACAROON LADY**, 5, b m Prince Sabo—Cookie Time **Mr N. Bycroft**
8 **NEBRANGUS (IRE)**, 4, ch g Nashamaa—Choral Park **Mr Bernard F. Rayner**
9 **PENNY'S WISHING**, 4, b f Clantime—Lady Pennington **Mrs N. Bycroft**
10 **PLUM DENNIS**, 5, b g Robellino (USA)—Kaleidophone **Mrs N. Bycroft**
11 **PRINCE BALTASAR**, 7, ch g Claude Monet (USA)—Farababy (FR) **Mr J. G. Allison**
12 **RICH GLOW**, 5, b g Rich Charlie—Mayglow **Mr M. J. Bateson**
13 **SHOTLEY AGAIN**, 6, b g Then Again—Sweet Candice **Mr J. A. Swinburne**
14 **SKI PATH**, 7, ch m Celtic Cone—Obergurgl **Mr D. Pickles**
15 **SWANDALE FLYER**, 4, ch g Weldnaas (USA)—Misfire **Mr A. Carruthers**

THREE-YEAR-OLDS

16 **BALLYKISSANGEL**, ro g Hadeer—April Wind **Kendall White & Co Ltd**
17 **DEREK'S BO**, b f Rambo Dancer (CAN)—Mother Hubbard **Mrs H. A. Bycroft**
18 **EFIPETITE**, ch f Efisio—Petite Elite **Mr T. Umpleby**
19 **GENERAL GLOW**, b g Presidium—Glow Again **Mr J. G. K. White**
20 **JIVE BABY**, b g Crowning Honors (CAN)—Jive Music **Mr E. H. Daley**
21 **PATHAZE**, b f Totem (USA)—Stilvella **Mr N. Warriner**
22 **THE ODDFELLOW**, b g Efisio—Agnes Jane **Mr D. Maloney**

TWO-YEAR-OLDS

23 **ALISADARA**, b f 11/4 Nomination—Nishara (Nishapour (FR)) **Mr T. G. Allison**
24 **CHILLED WINE**, b f 5/2 Chilibang—Persian Joy (Persian Bold) **Mr R. Midgley**
25 **GLENSTONE BOY**, b c 2/4 Nomination—Magic Tower (Tower Walk) **Mr R. Midgley**
26 **JIVE BOOGIE**, b br c 27/4 Nomination—Jive Music (Music Boy) **Mr E. H. Daley**
27 **ODDFELLOWS GIRL**, b f 23/2 Nomination—Kaleidophone (Kalaglow) **Mr D. Maloney**

Other Owners: Mr J. Allan, Mr T. Barnes, B. C. D. Steels & Co Ltd, Mr P. Brennan, Mr M. Bush, Mrs S. Diver, Mr A. M. Gant, Mr T. Greaves, Mr F. Harman, Mr T. McCartney, Mr D. R. Moore, Mr W. G. Moore, Mr James O'Reilly, Mr Paul Quinn, Mr E. Ruddock, Mrs K. J. Spencer, Mrs M. Swinburne.

Jockey (Flat): S Maloney (8-0).

Conditional: D Towler (9-7).

Lady Rider: Miss Amanda Bycroft (7-10).

107   MR T. H. CALDWELL, Warrington

Postal: **Burley Heyes Cottage, Arley Road, Appleton, Warrington, WA4 4RR.**

Phone: **ARLEY (01565) 777275 FAX (01565) 777275**

1 **BLAZE OF MAJESTY (USA)**, 8, b g Majestic Light (USA)—Uncommitted (USA) **Mr T. H. Caldwell**
2 **COBBS CROSS**, 6, ch g Bairn (USA)—Trapani **Mr T. H. Caldwell**
3 **CULRAIN**, 5, b g Hadeer—La Vie En Primrose **Mr A. McDonald**
4 **DOLIKOS**, 9, b g Camden Town—Wolveriana **Mrs Pat Wharfe**
5 **KEEPHERGOING (IRE)**, 7, b m Carlingford Castle—Green Dream **Mr T. F. Harrington**
6 **KINGS CAY (IRE)**, 5, b g Taufan (USA)—Provocation **Mr R. S. G. Jones**
7 **MARJAN (IRE)**, 5, ch m Classic Secret (USA)—Powder Lass **Mr R. J. Pfeiffer**
8 **NIGHTS IMAGE (IRE)**, 6, br g Corvaro (USA)—Lysanders Lady **Mr T. H. Caldwell**
9 **OUT OF FAVOUR (IRE)**, 5, ch g Persian Heights—Peaches And Cream (FR) **Mr M. J. Pipe**
10 **RIVERBANK RED**, 5, ch m Lighter—Gypsy Louise **Mr G. J. Wheildon**
11 **RIVERBANK ROSE**, 5, b m Lighter—Queen of Gypsy's **Mr G. J. Wheildon**
12 **THE COTTONWOOL KID**, 4, b g Blakeney—Relatively Smart **Mr T. F. Harrington**
13 **VIOWEN (IRE)**, 7, b m Denel (FR)—Vulgan Ten **Mr A. McDonald**

TWO-YEAR-OLDS

14 Gr g 8/3 Fools Holme (USA)—Phar Lapa (Grundy) **Mrs Pat Wharfe**

Other Owners: Mrs M. R. Wheildon.

Jockey (NH): P A Caldwell (10-0).

Lady Rider: Pat Wharfe (9-7).

108   MR N. A. CALLAGHAN, Newmarket

Postal: **22 Hamilton Road, Newmarket, Suffolk, CB8 0NY.**

Phone: **HOME (01638) 664040 STABLES (01638) 663441 FAX (01638) 668446**

1 **BATTLESHIP BRUCE**, 4, b g Mazilier (USA)—Quick Profit **Mr T. A. Foreman**
2 **BE WARNED**, 5, b g Warning—Sagar **Midcourts**
3 **FAIRY WIND (IRE)**, 4, b f Fairy King (USA)—Decadence **Mr N. A. Callaghan**
4 **GOLDEN TOUCH (USA)**, 4, ch c Elmaamul (USA)—Tour d'Argent (USA) **Mrs Rita Godfrey**
5 **KAAFIH HOMM (IRE)**, 5, b g Kefaah (USA)—Shereeka **Gallagher Materials Ltd**
6 **LA SORRELA (IRE)**, 4, ch f Cadeaux Genereux—Miss Silca Key **Midcourts**
7 **MANDY'S BET (USA)**, 4, ch f Elmaamul (USA)—Dols Jaminque (USA) **Mr J. W. Smith**
8 **MANEREE**, 9, b m Mandalus—Damberee **Mr M. Tabor**
9 **NO KOMPARISON**, 4, b c Komaite (USA)—Lady Keyser **Mr A. Smith**
10 **POURQUOI PAS (IRE)**, 4, b f Nordico (USA)—Mystery Lady (USA) **Mr A. Smith**
11 **ROYAL DERBI**, 11, b g Derrylin—Royal Birthday **Mr M. Tabor**
12 **TARAWA (IRE)**, 4, br g Caerleon (USA)—Sagar **Mrs J. Callaghan**
13 **TREMPLIN (USA)**, 4, gr c Trempolino (USA)—Stresa **Mr M. Tabor**

THREE-YEAR-OLDS

14 **ANCIENT QUEST**, b c Rainbow Quest (USA)—Racquette **Midcourts**
15 **ARABIAN EXPRESS**, b f Common Grounds—Little Preston (IRE) **Transarabin Aviation Services**
16 **ARLINGTON LADY**, b f Prince Sabo—Flitcham **Mr J. R. Bostock**
17 **BALPARE**, ch f Charmer—Balinese **Mrs J. Callaghan**
18 **CADEAU ELEGANT**, ch f Cadeaux Genereux—Wasimah **Mr T. A. Foreman**
19 **DANEHILL DANCER (IRE)**, b c Danehill (USA)—Mira Adonde (USA) **Mr M. Tabor**
20 **JEANNE CUTRONA**, b f Risk Me (FR)—Veuve Perrin **Mr Michael Hill**
21 **JERRY CUTRONA (IRE)**, br g Distinctly North (USA)—Foulkesmills **Mr Michael Hill**
22 **NELLY'S COUSIN**, b f Distant Relative—Glint of Victory **Kais Al Said**
23 **SOVEREIGN PRINCE (IRE)**, b c Bluebird (USA)—Everything Nice **Mr M. Tabor**
24 **TAS HOSTESS**, b f Cyrano de Bergerac—Fiorini **Transarabin Aviation Services**

MR N. A. CALLAGHAN—continued

TWO-YEAR-OLDS

25 B c 26/2 High Estate—Aneeda (Rainbow Quest (USA)) **Gallagher Materials Ltd**
26 **BARNWOOD CRACKERS**, ch c 25/2 Be My Chief (USA)—Tartique Twist (USA) (Arctic Tern (USA)) **Mr Y. Nasib**
27 **BATTLE GROUND (IRE)**, b c 2/4 Common Grounds—Last Gunboat (Dominion) **Mr T. A. Foreman**
28 B c 28/2 Rudimentary (USA)—Best Girl Friend (Sharrood (USA))
29 **BOLD ORIENTAL (IRE)**, b c 17/4 Tirol—Miss Java (Persian Bold) **Mr M. Tabor**
30 **DANETIME (IRE)**, b c 27/3 Danehill (USA)—Alleghany River (USA) (Lear Fan (USA)) **Mr M. Tabor**
31 B f 22/2 Classic Music (USA)—Gentle Freedom (Wolver Hollow) **Gallagher Materials Ltd**
32 Ch c 16/2 Prince Sabo—Island Mead (Pharly (FR)) **John Remblance**
33 Ch c 25/2 Lycius (USA)—Little Red Rose (Precocious) **Gallagher Materials Ltd**
34 **PLAISIR D'AMOUR (IRE)**, b f 30/1 Danehill (USA)—Mira Adonde (USA) (Sharpen Up) **Mr M. Tabor**
35 **PURCHASING POWER (IRE)**, b c 3/4 Danehill (USA)—Purchasepaperchase (Young Generation) **Mr M. Tabor**
36 Ch c 1/3 Decoy—Unique Treasure (Young Generation) **Motcombs Club**

Other Owners: Mr B. H. McCuaig.

109   MR P. CALVER, Ripon

Postal: **Whitcliffe Grange Farm, Ripon, N. Yorks, HG4 3AS.**
Phone: **RIPON (01765) 600313 FAX (01765) 603431**

1 4, Ch g Alfie Dickins—Dessassis **Mr P. Calver**
2 **FULL O'PRAISE (NZ)**, 9, br g Church Parade—Adios Belle (NZ) **Lord Zetland**
3 **KID ORY**, 5, ch g Rich Charlie—Woomargama **Mrs C. Calver**
4 **PERRYSTON VIEW**, 4, b c Primo Dominie—Eastern Ember **Mrs Janis MacPherson**
5 **SOMERTON BOY (IRE)**, 6, b h Thatching—Bonnie Bess **Mrs Janis MacPherson**
6 **TIMES LEADER**, 7, b g Politico (USA)—Our Hard Times **Mrs D. M. Hall**
7 **VAN DER GRASS**, 7, ch g Van Der Linden (FR)—Fanny Keyser **Mr F. Grass**
8 **VILLAGE REINDEER (NZ)**, 9, b g Le Grand Seigneur (CAN)—Riggane (NZ) **Mr J. R. Chester**
9 **WAFIR (IRE)**, 4, b c Scenic—Taniokey **Mrs Janis MacPherson**

THREE-YEAR-OLDS

10 **CLASH OF SWORDS**, b c Shaadi (USA)—Swept Away **Mrs Janis MacPherson**
11 **ESCOBAR (IRE)**, br c Cyrano de Bergerac—Gale Force Seven **Mrs Janis MacPherson**
12 **FIRLE PHANTASY**, ch g Pharly (FR)—Shamasiya (FR) **Mr D. B. Stanley**
13 **FORGIE (IRE)**, b g Don't Forget Me—Damia **Mrs Janis MacPherson**
14 **GILLING DANCER (IRE)**, b c Dancing Dissident (USA)—Rahwah **Lord Zetland**
15 **KATY-Q (IRE)**, b f Taufan (USA)—Swift Chorus **Lord Zetland**
16 **RICCARTON**, b c Nomination—Legendary Dancer **Mr Kenneth MacPherson**
17 **TAFFS WELL**, b c Dowsing (USA)—Zahiah **Mr D. Hefin Jones**
18 **THE JOLLY BARMAID (IRE)**, b f Don't Forget Me—Gay Broad **Mr J. L. Woolford**

TWO-YEAR-OLDS

19 Ch c 21/4 Ela-Mana-Mou—Glasson Lady (GER) (Priamos (GER)) **Mrs Janis MacPherson**
20 B c 1/3 Deploy—Highly Polished (High Top) **Mrs Janis MacPherson**
21 B f 17/3 Then Again—Royal Resort (King of Spain) **Mrs C. Calver**

110   MR M. J. C. CAMACHO, Malton

Postal: **Star Cottage, Welham Road, Norton, Malton, YO17 9DU.**
Phone: **MALTON (01653) 694901 FAX (01653) 694901**

1 **ALABANG**, 5, ch g Valiyar—Seleter **Mr H. Roberts**
2 **AVRO ANSON**, 8, b g Ardross—Tremellick **Mr B. P. Skirton**
3 **BOROCAY**, 8, b g Lochnager—Maybehandy **Mrs S. Camacho**
4 **ELITE BLISS (IRE)**, 4, b f Tirol—Krismas River **Elite Racing Club**
5 **EL NIDO**, 8, ch g Adonijah—Seleter **Mrs S. Camacho**

MR M. J. C. CAMACHO—continued

6 **FAIREY FIREFLY**, 5, b m Hallgate—Tremellick **Mr B. P. Skirton**
7 **HEE'S A DANCER**, 4, b g Rambo Dancer (CAN)—Heemee **Mr B. S. Adamson**
8 **HI NOD**, 6, b h Valiyar—Vikris **Mr Brian Nordan**
9 **HI ROCK**, 4, ch f Hard Fought—Miss Racine **Filey Hi Flyers**
10 **MASTER NOVA**, 6, b g Ra Nova—Maid of The Manor **Matthews Racing & Breeding**
11 **MISTER NOVA**, 7, b g Ra Nova—Homing Hill **Matthews Racing & Breeding**
12 **NORDAN RAIDER**, 8, ch m Domynsky—Vikris **Miss J. A. Camacho**
13 **RAINBOWS RHAPSODY**, 5, b m Handsome Sailor—Rainbow Trout **Mrs S. Camacho**
14 **ROYAL CREST**, 5, b g Midyan (USA)—Lola Black (FR) **Elite Racing Club**
15 **SARASI**, 4, ch g Midyan (USA)—Early Call **The Blue Chip Group**
16 **SEA DEVIL**, 10, gr g Absalom—Miss Poinciana **Mr A. N. Goacher**
17 **TESSAJOE**, 4, ch g Clantime—Busted Love **Riley Partnership**

THREE-YEAR-OLDS

18 **ADLER (IRE)**, b g Warning—Orangerie (FR) **G. B. Turnbull Ltd**
19 **ANY COLOUR**, b f Anshan—Council Rock **Mr Christian Preiser**
20 **CHAMPAGNE WARRIOR (IRE)**, b f Waajib—Late Swallow **M. K. Slinger & A. Stuart**
21 **DANCING RAINBOW**, b f Rambo Dancer (CAN)—Heemee **Mr B. S. Adamson**
22 **FIASCO**, ch f Dunbeath (USA)—Rainbow Trout **Mr Edmund Smith**
23 **KINGDOM PRINCESS**, br f Forzando—Song of Hope **G. B. Turnbull Ltd**
24 **LAPU-LAPU**, b f Prince Sabo—Seleter **Mrs S. Camacho**
25 **LATIN LOVER (GER)**, br g Roi Danzig (USA)—Lago Real **Mr Dunstan French**
26 **MARSAYAS (IRE)**, ch g Classic Music (USA)—Babiana (CAN) **Mr M. Gleason**
27 **TAGATAY**, b g Nomination—Salala **Mrs S. Camacho**

TWO-YEAR-OLDS

28 **AVRO AVIAN**, b f 29/5 Ardross—Tremellick **Mr B. P. Skirton**
29 Ch c 23/4 Keen—Calachuchi **Mrs S. Camacho**
30 Br f 11/4 Primo Dominie—Corman-Style **Elite Racing**
31 **HIO NOD**, b c 7/5 Precocious—Vikris **Mr B. Nordan**
32 **KINGDOM EMPEROR**, br c 8/3 Forzando—Wrangbrook **G. B. Turnbull Ltd**
33 **KINGDOM PEARL**, ch f 24/3 Statoblest—Sunfleet **G. B. Turnbull Ltd**
34 B c 4/5 Efisio—Seleter **Mrs S. Camacho**
35 B f 14/2 Be My Guest—Welcome Addition **Mr A. Greenwood**
36 **WHIRL POOL**, b f 2/4 Superpower—Rainbow Trout **Mr E. Smith**

Other Owners: Mrs Joan Fay, Mr R. A. Flowerdew, Mr B. Harland, Mr Tony Hill, Miss M. Noden, Mr Chris Nordan, Mrs Fran Normington, Mrs Veronika Preiser, Mr David Riley, Mr Francis Riley, Mr W. Riley, Mrs D. Timmins.

Jockey (Flat): L Charnock (7-7).

Jockey (NH): M Dwyer (w.a.).

111   MR B. R. CAMBIDGE, Bishopswood

Postal: **Park Oak Farm, Tong Road, Bishopswood, Brewood, ST19 9AP.**
Phone: **WESTON-UNDER-LIZARD (01952 850) 249**

1 **BEAUFAN**, 9, br g Taufan (USA)—Beaume (FR) **Mr D. Craddock**
2 **BEAU QUEST**, 9, b g Rainbow Quest (USA)—Elegant Tern (USA) **Mr B. R. Cambidge**
3 **BREEZED WELL**, 10, b g Wolverlife—Precious Baby **Mrs H. Noonan**
4 **FOXY LASS**, 7, ch m Celtic Cone—Hunters Glen **Mr B. R. Cambidge**
5 **GLENDRONACH**, 4, b f Seymour Hicks (FR)—Iriri (USA) **Mr B. R. Cambidge**
6 **PRINCETHORPE**, 9, b g Ring Bidder—Sparkling Jenny **Mr G. A. Farndon**
7 **RIMOUSKI**, 8, b h Sure Blade (USA)—Rimosa's Pet **Mr John Steventon**
8 **SEAMERE**, 13, b g Crofter (USA)—Whistling Waltz **Mr B. R. Cambidge**
9 **SPICE AND SUGAR**, 6, ch m Chilibang—Pretty Miss **Mr A. S. Blackham**
10 **TIMELY EXAMPLE (USA)**, 5, ch h Timeless Moment (USA)—Dearest Mongo (USA) **Mr D. Craddock**

Amateur: Mr J R Cambidge (10-0).

112   MR I. CAMPBELL, Newmarket

Postal: **32 Elizabeth Avenue, Newmarket, Suffolk.**
Phone: **NEWMARKET (01638) 660605/660829 MOBILE (0850) 409004**

1 **AS MUSTARD,** 4, ch f Keen—Anna Karietta **Direct Bloodstock**
2 **CHEVALIER (USA),** 4, b c Danzig (USA)—Royal Touch **Mr S. Anrude**
3 **LAHOOB (USA),** 7, b g Miswaki (USA)—Sure Locked (USA) **Ian Campbell**
4 **REGGAE BEAT,** 11, b g Be My Native (USA)—Invery Lady **Ian Campbell**
5 **RUSTY REEL,** 6, ch g Scottish Reel—Blakeney Heights
6 **SWINGING TICH,** 7, b m Swing Easy (USA)—Little Tich **Ian Campbell Racing Club**
7 **TAP ON TOOTSIE,** 4, b f Faustus (USA)—My Tootsie **Mr R. Cowper**

THREE-YEAR-OLDS

8 B f Glacial Storm (USA)—Moonlight Romance **Mr J. Kent**

TWO-YEAR-OLDS

9 Ch c 25/3 Backchat (USA)—Book Review (Balidar) **Mr Eamonn O'Malley**
10 Ch c 23/2 Ron's Victory (USA)—Ceramic (USA) (Raja Baba (USA)) **Mrs C. Grady**
11 Ch c 27/4 Scottish Reel—Make A Signal (Royal Gunner (USA)) **Mr Eamonn O'Malley**

Other Owners: Mr K. Brown, Mr E. Campbell, Mr Kevin Elliott, Mr J. McCaul, Miss J. Southern.

113   MR A. M. CAMPION, Tunworth

Postal: **Tunworth Down Stables, Tunworth, Nr Basingstoke, Hants, RG25 2LE.**
Phone: **(01256) 463376 FAX (01256) 332968**

1 6, Br g Strong Gale—Cala Conta **Praemar Trading Inc**
2 **DAZZLER,** 4, ch g Zalazl (USA)—Mrs Danvers **The Soldiers Field Partnership**
3 **EZALBA,** 4, b f Formidable (USA)—Pleasure Island **Mr A. M. Campion**
4 **FOTOEXPRESS,** 8, ch g Librate—Rosefox **The Fotoexpress Partnership**
5 **GABRIEL'S LADY,** 5, b m Valiyar—Autumn Harvest **Gabriels Farm Partnership**
6 **GEMMA'S WAGER (IRE),** 6, b m Phardante (FR)—Lady's Wager **Mr & Mrs Barry Noakes**
7 **GENERAL AVERAGE,** 6, ch g Northern Game—Holm Andrea **Mrs Lyn How**
8 **KIROV ROYALE,** 5, b m Rambo Dancer (CAN)—Gay Princess **Mrs Deenagh Howard-Brown**
9 4, B f Rambo Dancer (CAN)—Llanddona
10 **LUDO'S ORCHESTRA (IRE),** 5, ch g Orchestra—Madam Milan **Mr & Mrs Barry Noakes**
11 **MOON DEVIL (IRE),** 6, br g Strong Gale—Moynalvey Lass **Mr P. G. Goulandris**
12 **MY WARRIOR,** 8, b g Roman Warrior—My Darling **Mr A. M. Campion**
13 **NEFARIOUS,** 10, b g Netherkelly—Black Baize **Lady Kleinwort**
14 **RAINCHECK,** 5, b g Mtoto—Lashing (USA) **Mrs Georgina Worsley**
15 **TYPHOON (IRE),** 6, br g Strong Gale—Bally Decent **The Cissbury Ring**

THREE-YEAR-OLDS

16 B c Crowning Honors (CAN)—Mummys Colleen
17 **TEOFILO STEPHENSON (IRE),** b c Taufan (USA)—Crufty Wood **Dr Antonio Bacci**

Other Owners: Mrs R. A. Aisher, Mr R. Ewing, Lady Rosemary Hardy, Mrs Michael Hill, Mrs J. Howell, Mr Colin Irving-Bell, Mr S. Pearson, Mr J. F. Sclater, Mr C. Sullivan.

Jockey (NH): Mark Richards (w.a.).

114   MR S. W. CAMPION, Wragby

Postal: **Tichbourne Stables, Glebe Farm, West Barkwith, Lincoln, LN3 5LF.**

Phone: **(01673) 858919   MOBILE (0585) 676482**

1 **CYPRUS POINT**, 5, b m Unfuwain (USA)—Sunshine Coast **Mr Peter W. Haddock**
2 **EVE'S TREASURE**, 6, ch m Bustino—Before Long **Mr N. J. Dixon**
3 **FIERY FOOTSTEPS**, 4, ro f Chilibang—Dancing Daughter **Mr David P. Milthorp**
4 **GAYTON RUN (IRE)**, 7, b g Commanche Run—Arkova **Hugh Bourn Developments (Wragby) Ltd**
5 **KAJOSTAR**, 6, ch m Country Classic—Rasimareem **Mr R. Fereday**
6 **LOCH MARINER**, 4, b br f Lochnager—Sky Mariner **Mrs S. Campion**
7 **PILLOW TALK (IRE)**, 5, b m Taufan (USA)—Concave **Mr A. E. Blee**
8 **RAVE-ON-HADLEY (IRE)**, 6, b g Commanche Run—Fleet Fact **Mrs S. Campion**
9 **RED HOT RISK**, 4, b g Risk Me (FR)—Hot Sunday Sport **Mrs C. D. Buckland & Mrs D. Dukes**
10 **TWICE IN ONE NIGHT**, 7, b g Pitpan—Again Kathleen **Mr S. W. Campion**

THREE-YEAR-OLDS

11 Ch g Blow The Whistle—Cheeky Monkey **Mr Milson Robinson**
12 **KAI'S LADY (IRE)**, b f Jareer (USA)—Rathnaleen **Mr S. W. Campion**
13 B f Superlative—Mrs Magic **Mrs H. E. Gillatt**
14 Ch g Presidium—Mylotta **Mrs H. E. Gillatt**

Jockeys (Flat): G Carter (w.a.), S D Williams (w.a.).

Jockeys (NH): A S Smith (w.a.), A Thornton (w.a.).

Conditional: P Midgeley (10-5, w.a.).

Lady Riders: Mrs S J Campion (8-10), Miss R Judge (9-0).

115   MR HENRY D. CANDY, Wantage

Postal: **Kingstone Warren, Wantage, Oxon, OX12 9QF.**

Phone: **FARINGDON (01367) 820276/514 FAX (01367) 820500 MOBILE (0836) 211264**

1 **BEAUCHAMP JADE**, 4, gr f Kalaglow—Beauchamp Buzz **Mr E. Penser**
2 **EVENINGPERFORMANCE**, 5, b m Night Shift (USA)—Classic Design **Mrs David Blackburn**
3 **EXEMPTION**, 5, ch g Ballad Rock—Great Exception **Mr T. A. F. Frost**
4 **RIPARIUS (USA)**, 5, b g Riverman (USA)—Sweet Simone (FR) **Mrs David Blackburn**
5 **SHARP CONSUL (IRE)**, 4, br g Exactly Sharp (USA)—Alicia Markova **Mrs David Blackburn**
6 **SPANDREL**, 4, ch f Pharly (FR)—Oxslip **Major M. G. Wyatt**
7 **TAPPETO**, 4, b g Liboi (USA)—Persian Carpet (FR) **Mrs David Blackburn**
8 **TOP BANANA**, 5, ch g Pharly (FR)—Oxslip **Major M. G. Wyatt**

THREE-YEAR-OLDS

9 **AGE OF REALITY (USA)**, b f Alleged (USA)—Isticanna (USA) **H.R.H. Prince Fahd Salman**
10 **BEAUCHAMP KATE**, b f Petoski—Beauchamp Buzz **Mr E. Penser**
11 **BEAUCHAMP KNIGHT**, ch g Chilibang—Beauchamp Cactus **Mr E. Penser**
12 **FOND EMBRACE**, b f Emarati (USA)—Detente **Commander G. G. Marten**
13 **FUNNY WAVE**, b f Lugana Beach—Comedy Lady **Kingstone Warren Partners**
14 **GENEROSA**, b f Generous (IRE)—Hotel Street (USA) **H.R.H. Prince Fahd Salman**
15 **ICENI (IRE)**, b f Distinctly North (USA)—Princess Galicia **Mrs C. M. Poland**
16 **INDIRA**, b f Indian Ridge—Princess Rosananti (IRE) **Mrs J. E. L. Wright**
17 **MAGIC SOLUTION (IRE)**, b f Magical Wonder (USA)—Brook's Dilemma **Kingstone Warren Partners**
18 **MOURNE MOUNTAINS**, b c Scenic—Orlaith **Girsonfield Ltd**
19 **PLEADING**, b c Never So Bold—Ask Mama **Mr Simon Broke**
20 **SERAPE**, b f Primo Dominie—Absaloute Service **Major M. G. Wyatt**

MR HENRY D. CANDY—continued

21 **SPEED ON**, b g Sharpo—Pretty Poppy **Mr P. A. Deal**
22 **THE POLYMATH**, ch g Sharpo—Nisha **Girsonfield Ltd**
23 **WELL DRAWN**, b c Dowsing (USA)—Classic Design **Mrs David Blackburn**

TWO-YEAR-OLDS

24 **ATTITUDE**, b c 27/2 Priolo (USA)—Parfum d'Automne (FR) (Sharpen Up) **Girsonfield Ltd**
25 **CRYSTAL HEARTED**, b c 25/4 Broken Hearted—Crystal Fountain (Great Nephew) **Mrs C. M. Poland**
26 **FARLEY GREEN**, b f 21/3 Pharly (FR)—Ring Cycle (Auction Ring (USA)) **Major M. G. Wyatt**
27 **FOR LARA (IRE)**, ch f 18/3 Soviet Star (USA)—On The Staff (USA) (Master Willie) **Mrs Robert Langton**
28 **IN YOUR DREAMS**, b f 29/4 Suave Dancer (USA)—By Charter (Shirley Heights) **Mr R. Barnett**
29 **JOZA**, b f 18/2 Marju (IRE)—Gold Runner (Runnett) **H.R.H. Prince Fahd Salman**
30 **LARK'S RISE**, b f 6/2 Niniski (USA)—Line of Cards (High Line) **Major M. G. Wyatt**
31 **MADE BOLD**, b f 30/4 Never So Bold—Classical Vintage (Stradavinsky) **Kingstone Warren Partners**
32 **MARY CULI**, gr f 15/2 Liboi (USA)—Copper Trader (Faustus (USA)) **Mrs David Blackburn**
33 **OXBANE**, b f 3/3 Soviet Star (USA)—Oxslip (Owen Dudley) **Major M. G. Wyatt**
34 **PENNYS FROM HEAVEN**, gr c 24/5 Generous (IRE)—
                                Heavenly Cause (USA) (Grey Dawn II) **H.R.H. Prince Fahd Salman**
35 **QUIBBLING**, b f 19/4 Salse (USA)—Great Exception (Grundy) **Mr T. A. F. Frost**
36 **RINGTIME (IRE)**, b f 16/4 Tirol—Lovat Spring (USA) (Storm Bird (CAN)) **Mr R. Pennant Jones**
37 **STAHR**, b c 8/3 Liboi (USA)—Celia Brady (Last Tycoon) **Mrs David Blackburn**
38 Ch f 13/3 Waajib—Staiconme (USA) (Pancho Villa (USA)) **Lord Chelsea**
39 **WITH A WILL**, b c 1/4 Rambo Dancer (CAN)—Henceforth (Full of Hope) **Mr Henry Candy**

Other Owners: Mr Michael Poland, Mr P. J. L. Wright.

Apprentices: Lee James (7-10), N Rance.

Lady Rider: Mrs C Dunwoody (8-7).

116   MR D. N. CAREY, Brynmawr

Postal: **'Tyr-sais', Golf View Stables, Nantyglo, Brynmawr, NP3 4NL.**
Phone: **(01495) 310794 MOBILE (0836) 504167**

1 **GILBERT (IRE)**, 8, br g Dalsaan—Pennyala **Mrs A. Carey**
2 **LORCANJO**, 5, b m Hallgate—Perfect Double **Mrs A. Carey**
3 **SHE KNEW THE RULES (IRE)**, 6, ch m Jamesmead—Falls of Lora **Mr D. N. Carey**

Jockey (NH): B Powell.

117   MR J. M. CARR, Malton

Postal: **18 Whitewall, Norton, Malton, North Yorks, YO17 9EH.**
Phone: **HOME (01653) 694671 OFFICE (01653) 692695**

1 **DANCE OF JOY**, 4, b f Shareef Dancer (USA)—Lady Habitat **Mrs Tina Carr**
2 **HERE COMES A STAR**, 8, b g Night Shift—Rapidus **Mrs June Goodridge**
3 **JOHNNY KELLY**, 9, ch g Over The River (FR)—Monaleigh **Mr F. Carr**
4 **KAITAK (IRE)**, 5, ch g Broken Hearted—Klairelle **Mr C. J. Murphy**
5 **MONNEDELL (IRE)**, 4, b g Montekin—Peggy Dell **Mr F. Carr**
6 **RIVER WYE (IRE)**, 4, b g Jareer (USA)—Sun Gift **Mr Eddie Ho**
7 **SWERVIN MERVIN**, 8, ch g Dominion—Brilliant Rosa **Mrs Tina Carr**

MR J. M. CARR—continued

THREE-YEAR-OLDS

8 **KILLMESSAN-TOWN (IRE)**, ch g Jareer (USA)—Perfect Chance **Frank Carr & Partners**
9 **NOIR ESPRIT**, b c Prince Daniel (USA)—Danse d'Esprit **Messrs J. T. Robson and R. Jeffs**
10 **SCOTTS LOT (IRE)**, ch g Pennine Walk—Sarahlee **Mr F. Carr**

TWO-YEAR-OLDS

11 Ch f 25/4 Indian Ridge—Orion Dream (Skyliner) **Mr C. J. Murphy**
12 **STAR OF THE ROAD**, b c 26/4 Risk Me (FR)—Astrid Gilberto (Runnett) **Mrs June Goodridge**

Other Owners: Mrs Sylvia Vokes.

Jockey (Flat): S Morris (8-0).

Jockey (NH): N Smith (10-0).

Lady Rider: Mrs T A Carr (9-7).

118   MR T. J. CARR, Saltburn-by-Sea

Postal: **Ridge House Stables, Ridge House Farm, Stanghow, Saltburn-by-Sea, TS12 3LD.**
Phone: **(01287) 660506**

1 **ARITAM (IRE)**, 7, b g Aristocracy—Tamu **Mr R. Dalton**
2 **CASH BOX (IRE)**, 8, ch g Carlingford Castle—Cash Discount **Dr T. A. Wadrop**
3 **CHARLYCIA**, 8, b m Good Times (ITY)—Gallic Law **Mrs V. Chilton**
4 **CLASSIC BLUES (IRE)**, 5, b br g Jeu de Paille (FR)—Singing Blues **Mr J. J. McInerney**
5 **EVEN CLOSE**, 6, b g K-Battery—Stubbs Daughter **Mr R. Dalton**
6 **HILLVIEW AUCTION**, 9, b br g Royal Auction (USA)—Hillview Maid **Mr J. J. McInerney**
7 **PARLIAMENT HOUSE (IRE)**, 6, ch g Parliament—Sabie Star **Mr J. J. McInerney**
8 **PIEREX (IRE)**, 5, b m Executive Perk—Deep Pier **Mr P. R. Warwick**
9 **VINES CROSS**, 8, b g General David—Vinobia **Mr J. A. Keith**
10 **WOODVILLA (IRE)**, 8, ch g Selko—Lady Herbert **Josttigo Racing**

Other Owners: Mr Peter Carr, Mr Tim Carr, Mr G. Halsall, Mr John Newman (Doncaster), Mr W. E. Robson, Mr S. M. Taylor.

119   MR A. W. CARROLL, Worcester

Postal: **Mill House, Kington, Ely Ford, Flavell, WR7 4DG.**
Phone: **(01386) 793459 FAX (01386) 792303**

1 **ALL OVER RED ROVER**, 4, b g Newski (USA)—Earth Wood **Mr Gary J. Roberts**
2 **CHOWPOR**, 5, b m Nishapour (FR)—Salchow **Mr T. V. Cullen**
3 **DAMCADA (IRE)**, 8, b br g Damister (USA)—Tiptoe **E4 Racing**
4 **KALZARI (USA)**, 11, b g Riverman (USA)—Kamisha (FR) **Mr Dennis Deacon**
5 **KINGSWOOD KITCHENS**, 16, b g General Ironside—Tyrone Typhoon **Mr Stuart Bruce**
6 **KUMARI KING (IRE)**, 6, ch g Colwyn—Raj Kumari **The Killoughery Family**
7 **MASTER SHOWMAN (IRE)**, 5, b g Alzao (USA)—Arctic Winter (CAN) **Mr Dennis Deacon**
8 **MY PREROGATIVE**, 7, gr m Sula Bula—Lavender Lace **Mr Dennis Deacon**
9 **OUR SLIMBRIDGE**, 8, b br g Top Ville—Bird Point (USA) **Mr A. W. Carroll**
10 **QUEEN OF SHANNON (IRE)**, 8, b m Nordico (USA)—Raj Kumari **Mr Gordon W. Day**
11 **SASTRUGI (IRE)**, 4, br c Bluebird (USA)—Royal Wolff **Mr Gary J. Roberts**
12 **SHANNON LAD (IRE)**, 6, ch g Montelimar (USA)—Dusty Busty **The Killoughery Family**
13 **WAR FLOWER (IRE)**, 8, ch m Cardinal Flower—Purdey Good **Mr Stuart Bruce**

MR A. W. CARROLL—continued

Other Owners: Mr T. J. Collins, Mr R. E. Gibbins, Mr C. J. Gibbons, Mr E. T. Gibbons, Mr Raymond Thomas, Mr G. Wiltshire.

Jockeys (NH): W Marston (10-0), B Powell (10-0).

Amateur: L Brown (10-7).

120   MR W. T. CASEY, Dorking

Postal: **Henfold House Cottage, Beare Green, Dorking, Surrey, RH5 4RW.**

Phone: **(01306) 631529 FAX (01306) 631529**

 1 **BAY BOB (IRE)**, 7, b h Bob Back (USA)—Princess Peppy **Mr Ricki Gache**
 2 **COOL SPOT (IRE)**, 8, ch g Boyne Valley—Beagle Bay **S. P. Racing**
 3 **EVEN FLOW (IRE)**, 7, b g Mandalus—Mariners Chain **Mr A. T. A. Wates**
 4 **FINE IDEA (IRE)**, 7, b br g Idea (USA)—Brookland Lass **S. P. Racing**
 5 **FLIGHT LIEUTENANT (USA)**, 7, b g Marfa (USA)—Lt Golden Girl (USA) **Mrs Laura Pegg**
 6 **GRASS ISLAND (IRE)**, 7, b g The Parson—Helenium **Mr B. McHugh Civil Engineering Ltd**
 7 **KRATON GARDEN (USA)**, 4, b g Sovereign Dancer (USA)—Kenanga **Mr C. M. Wilson**
 8 **LEITRIM COTTAGE (IRE)**, 5, b g Yashgan—New Talent **Mr B. McHugh Civil Engineering Ltd**
 9 **LITTLE ROWLEY**, 7, ch g Little Wolf—Not Negotiable **Mr J. A. Judd**
10 **PARLIAMENTARIAN (IRE)**, 7, br g Idiot's Delight—Elect **Mr A. T. A. Wates**
11 **RED CHANNEL (IRE)**, 6, b g Import—Winscarlet North **Mr David Wates**
12 **REPEAT THE DOSE**, 11, b g Abednego—Bahia de Palma **Mr A. T. A. Wates**
13 **ROUGH QUEST**, 10, b g Crash Course—Our Quest **Mr A. T. A. Wates**
14 **SILVERFORT LAD (IRE)**, 7, gr g Roselier (FR)—Sweet Run **Mr A. T. A. Wates**
15 5, B g High Kicker (USA)—Snap Tin **Alan Jackson**

Other Owners: Mr J. Connor, Mr Leslie Holder, Mr David Howe, Mr K. C. Mackenzie, Mr J. G. M. Wates, Lady Wates.

Jockey (Flat): J Reid (w.a.).

Jockeys (NH): R Dunwoody (w.a.), M Fitzgerald (w.a.).

Amateur: Mr Stephen Laird.

Teams which have arrived too late for inclusion in Horses In Training 1996 will be published in the Raceform Update at the end of April.

121   MR H. R. A. CECIL, Newmarket

Postal: **Warren Place, Newmarket, Suffolk, CB8 8QQ.**

Phone: **(01638) HOUSE 662387 OFFICE 662192 FAX 669005**

1 **ALDEVONIE**, 4, b f Green Desert (USA)—Kintail **Sir David Wills**
2 **ARIYAM**, 4, b f Dancing Brave (USA)—Laluche (USA) **Mr Brian Agnew**
3 **BAL HARBOUR**, 5, b h Shirley Heights—Balabina (USA) **Mr K. Abdulla**
4 **BALLIOL BOY**, 4, b c Nashwan (USA)—Fiesta Fun **Mr Wafic Said**
5 **BEQUEATH**, 4, ch c Rainbow Quest (USA)—Balabina (USA) **Mr K. Abdulla**
6 **CLAN BEN (IRE)**, 4, ch c Bluebird (USA)—Trina's Girl **Angus Dundee Plc**
7 **CORRADINI**, 4, b c Rainbow Quest (USA)—Cruising Height **Mr K. Abdulla**
8 **DACHA (IRE)**, 4, b c Soviet Star (USA)—Shadywood **Cliveden Stud**
9 **EVA LUNA (USA)**, 4, b f Alleged (USA)—Media Luna **Mr K. Abdulla**
10 **FLORID (USA)**, 5, ch h The Minstrel (CAN)—Kenanga **Lord Howard de Walden**
11 **GENERAL ASSEMBLY (IRE)**, 4, b c Pharly (FR)—Hastening **H.R.H. Prince Fahd Salman**
12 **LOST LAGOON (USA)**, 4, ch c Riverman (USA)—Lost Virtue (USA) **Mr K. Abdulla**
13 **MINDS MUSIC (USA)**, 4, ch c Silver Hawk (USA)—Misinskie (USA) **Mr S. S. Niarchos**
14 **PRUSSIAN BLUE (USA)**, 4, b c Polish Navy (USA)—Lit'l Rose **Mr L. Marinopoulos**
15 **SEBASTIAN**, 4, b c Sadler's Wells (USA)—Sandy Island **Lord Howard de Walden**
16 **SPEED TO LEAD (IRE)**, 4, b f Darshaan—Instant Desire (USA) **Buckram Oak Holdings**
17 **VITUS**, 4, b c Dancing Brave (USA)—Sancta **Lord Howard de Walden**

THREE-YEAR-OLDS

18 **AKHLA (USA)**, ch f Nashwan (USA)—Beautiful River (USA) **Mr L. Marinopoulos**
19 **ALI-ROYAL (IRE)**, b c Royal Academy (USA)—Alidiva **Greenbay Stables Ltd**
20 **ANNECY (USA)**, b f Mr Prospector (USA)—Lake Country (CAN) **Mr K. Abdulla**
21 **ATTALOS**, ch c Cadeaux Genereux—Messaria **Mrs H. G. Cambanis**
22 **BALLADUR (USA)**, b c Nureyev (USA)—Ballinderry **Mr K. Abdulla**
23 **BENATOM (USA)**, gr c Hawkster (USA)—Dance Til Two (USA) **Mr T. F. Harris**
24 **BIRDLIP (USA)**, ch f Sanglamore (USA)—Seven Springs (USA) **Mr K. Abdulla**
25 **BIRSAY**, b f Bustino—Surf Bird **Mr L. B. Holliday**
26 **BOSRA SHAM (USA)**, ch f Woodman (USA)—Korveya (USA) **Mr Wafic Said**
27 **BRIGHSTONE**, ch c Cadeaux Genereux—High Fountain **Mr Michael Poland**
28 **BRIGHT WATER**, b c Caerleon (USA)—Shining Water **Mr K. Abdulla**
29 **CANON CAN (USA)**, ch g Green Dancer (USA)—Lady Argyle (USA) **Canon (Anglia) O. A. Ltd**
30 **CENSOR**, b c Kris—Mixed Applause (USA) **Lord Howard de Walden**
31 **CHABROL (CAN)**, b c El Gran Senor (USA)—Off The Record (USA) **Mr L. Marinopoulos**
32 **CITY OF STARS (FR)**, b c Top Ville—Star of The Future (USA) **Mr K. Abdulla**
33 **CLEVER CLICHE**, b c Danehill (USA)—Beacon Hill **Mr Ivan Allan**
34 **COUNT BASIE**, b c Batshoof—Quiet Harbour **Lucayan Stud**
35 **DARING VERSE (USA)**, ch f Opening Verse (USA)—Power Bidder (USA) **Mrs Gale Brophy**
36 **DAWNA**, b f Polish Precedent (USA)—Welsh Daylight **Mr K. Abdulla**
37 **DEGREE**, b f Warning—Krill **Mr K. Abdulla**
38 **DISTANT OASIS (USA)**, b f Green Desert (USA)—Just You Wait **H.R.H. Prince Fahd Salman**
39 **DIVINE QUEST**, ch f Kris—Dance Quest (FR) **Lady Howard de Walden**
40 **DOUBLE NINER (USA)**, b c Forty Niner (USA)—Sure Locked (USA) **Mr S. Khaled**
41 **DOVALY**, b c Lycius (USA)—Sedova (USA) **Mr K. Abdulla**
42 **DUSHYANTOR (USA)**, b c Sadler's Wells (USA)—Slightly Dangerous (USA) **Mr K. Abdulla**
43 **FARASAN (IRE)**, b c Fairy King (USA)—Gracieuse Majeste (FR) **Prince A. A. Faisal**
44 **FLAMING JUNE (USA)**, ch f Storm Bird (CAN)—Affirmative Fable (USA) **Sir Andrew Lloyd Webber**
45 **FLYING LEGEND**, b c Alleged (USA)—L'Extravagante (CAN) **Mr Jim Browne**
46 **FOREST BUCK (USA)**, ch c Green Forest (USA)—Perlee (FR) **Buckram Oak Holdings**
47 **GENEROSUS (FR)**, ch c Generous (IRE)—Minya **H.R.H. Prince Fahd Salman**
48 **GINGER FOX (USA)**, ch c Diesis—Over Your Shoulder (USA) **H.R.H. Prince Fahd Salman**
49 **GLEN PARKER (IRE)**, ch c Bluebird (USA)—Trina's Girl **Angus Dundee Plc**
50 **GREAT CHIEF**, ch c Be My Chief (USA)—Padelia **Mrs Mark Burrell**
51 **INGRINA**, b f Warning—Naswara (USA) **Prince Khalid Al Saud**
52 **KING'S ACADEMY (IRE)**, b c Royal Academy (USA)—Regal Beauty (USA) **Mr Michael Poland**
53 **KINLOCHEWE**, b f Old Vic—Reuval **Sir David Wills**
54 **LADY CARLA**, b f Caerleon (USA)—Shirley Superstar **Mr Wafic Said**
55 **LEAR EXPRESS (USA)**, b c Lear Fan (USA)—Sheer Enchantment (USA) **Thoroughbred Corporation**

MR H. R. A. CECIL—continued

56 **LUMINOUS (USA)**, b f Majestic Light (USA)—Rapping (USA) **Cliveden Stud**
57 **MAGNIFICENT STYLE (USA)**, b f Silver Hawk (USA)—Mia Karina (USA) **Buckram Oak Holdings**
58 **MARINO CASINO (USA)**, b f Alleged (USA)—In Hot Pursuit (USA) **Mrs John Magnier**
59 **OMARA (USA)**, br f Storm Cat (USA)—Alamosa **F. Hinojosa**
60 **PALIO FLYER**, b f Slip Anchor—Moviegoer **Mrs E. A. Harris**
61 **PAPAHA (FR)**, b f Green Desert (USA)—Turban **Mr T. F. Harris**
62 **PEP TALK (USA)**, ch c Lyphard (USA)—Peplum (USA) **Mr K. Abdulla**
63 **PHANTOM QUEST**, b c Rainbow Quest (USA)—Illusory **Mr K. Abdulla**
64 **PLACE DE L'OPERA**, b f Sadler's Wells (USA)—Madame Dubois **Cliveden Stud**
65 **PRIVATE AUDIENCE (USA)**, b c Private Account (USA)—Monroe (USA) **Mr K. Abdulla**
66 **PSICOSSIS**, b c Slip Anchor—Precious Jade **Mr Eduardo Hinojosa**
67 **QUESTONIA**, b f Rainbow Quest (USA)—Danthonia (USA) **Mr K. Abdulla**
68 **QUOTA**, b f Rainbow Quest (USA)—Armeria (USA) **Mr K. Abdulla**
69 **RED ROBBO (CAN)**, b c Red Ransom (USA)—Aunt Jobiska (USA) **Lucayan Stud**
70 **SANDY FLOSS (IRE)**, b c Green Desert (USA)—Mill On The Floss **Cliveden Stud**
71 **SARDONIC**, b f Kris—Sardegna **Lord Howard de Walden**
72 **SEA WEDDING**, ch f Groom Dancer (USA)—Cruising Height **Mr K. Abdulla**
73 **SERIOUS ACCOUNT (USA)**, b c Danzig (USA)—Topicount (USA) **Mr Robert H. Smith**
74 **SET ADRIFT**, b c Slip Anchor—Cephira (FR) **Lord Howard de Walden**
75 **SHERPAS (IRE)**, b c Shirley Heights—Ala Mahlik **Mr K. Abdulla**
76 **SIDE NOTE**, b c Warning—Sarah Siddons (FR) **Mr K. Abdulla**
77 **SILVER DOME (USA)**, b br c Silver Hawk (USA)—Pink Topaze (FR) **Buckram Oak Holdings**
78 **SINGAPORE STING (USA)**, b f Dayjur (USA)—Ambassador of Luck (USA) **Mr B. Gover**
79 **SOLAR CRYSTAL (IRE)**, b f Alzao (USA)—Crystal Spray **Mr Michael Poland**
80 **STARK LOMOND (USA)**, b c Lomond (USA)—Stark Home (USA) **Mr S. Khaled**
81 **STORM CARD**, ch f Zalazl (USA)—Trikymia **Mr L. Marinopoulos**
82 **STORM SHELTER (USA)**, b f Storm Bird (CAN)—Dockage (CAN) **Mr K. Abdulla**
83 **STORM TROOPER (USA)**, b c Diesis—Stormette (USA) **H.R.H. Prince Fahd Salman**
84 **SUBTERFUGE**, b f Machiavellian (USA)—Sandy Island **Lord Howard de Walden**
85 **TORREMOLINOS (USA)**, ch c Trempolino (USA)—Honor Guard (USA) **Thoroughbred Corporation**
86 **TRAMLINE**, b c Shirley Heights—Trampship **Mr K. Abdulla**
87 **TURNING WHEEL (USA)**, b f Seeking The Gold (USA)—Misinskie (USA) **Mr S. S. Niarchos**
88 **UNREAL CITY (IRE)**, b c Rock City—Tolmi **Mr L. Marinopoulos**
89 **UNREFLECTED (USA)**, b br c Majestic Light (USA)—Look (USA) **Mr L. Marinopoulos**
90 **VALEDICTORY**, b c Slip Anchor—Khandjar **Lord Howard de Walden**
91 Gr f Handsome Sailor—Vico Equense **Queenholme**
92 **VIRIDIS (USA)**, b f Green Dancer (USA)—Vachti (FR) **Lord Howard de Walden**
93 **WELCOME PARADE**, b c Generous (IRE)—Jubilee Trail **Mr K. Abdulla**
94 **YAMUNA (USA)**, b f Forty Niner (USA)—Nimble Feet (USA) **Mr K. Abdulla**

TWO-YEAR-OLDS

95 **AGINOR**, b c 19/3 Slip Anchor—Fairy Feet (Sadler's Wells (USA)) **Mrs I. Tsatos**
96 **ALANIS**, b f 1/4 Warning—Pithara (GR) (Never So Bold) **Mr L. Marinopoulos**
97 B f 14/2 Nureyev (USA)—All At Sea (USA) (Riverman (USA)) **Mr K. Abdulla**
98 **ANUBIS**, b c 29/3 Caerleon (USA)—Point of Honour (Kris) **Mrs John Magnier**
99 **ARLETTY**, b f 13/5 Rainbow Quest (USA)—Mixed Applause (USA) (Nijinsky (CAN)) **Lord Howard de Walden**
100 B c 25/1 Rainbow Quest (USA)—Armeria (USA) (Northern Dancer) **Mr K. Abdulla**
101 Br c 24/3 Seattle Slew (USA)—Artiste (Artaius (USA)) **Mr K. Abdulla**
102 **AWESOME WELLS (IRE)**, b c 21/4 Sadler's Wells (USA)—Shadywood (Habitat) **Cliveden Stud**
103 B f 5/3 Shirley Heights—Balabina (USA) (Nijinsky (CAN)) **Mr K. Abdulla**
104 **BELMONTEE**, b c 26/3 Belmez (USA)—Annie Albright (USA) (Verbatim (USA)) **Mr Eduardo Hinojosa**
105 Br c 10/3 Magical Wonder (USA)—Black Fighter (USA) (Secretariat (USA)) **Buckram Oak Holdings**
106 **BLANCHE DUBOIS**, ch f 1/3 Nashwan (USA)—Madame Dubois (Legend of France (USA)) **Cliveden Stud**
107 **CARISBROOKE**, b c 6/5 Kahyasi—Dayanata (Shirley Heights) **Mr Michael Poland**
108 **CATCHABLE**, b c 2/2 Pursuit Of Love—Catawba (Mill Reef (USA)) **Lord Howard de Walden**
109 **CHANGE FOR A BUCK (USA)**, ch f 15/3 Time For A Change—
Pearl Bracelet (USA) (Lyphard (USA)) **Buckram Oak Holdings**
110 **COURTSHIP**, b c 28/4 Groom Dancer (USA)—Dance Quest (FR) (Green Dancer (USA)) **Lord Howard de Walden**
111 B f 7/3 Machiavellian (USA)—Dangora (USA) (Sovereign Dancer (USA)) **Mr K. Abdulla**
112 **DARNAWAY**, b c 14/3 Green Desert (USA)—Reuval (Sharpen Up) **Sir David Wills**

DARLEY STUD MANAGEMENT
STALLIONS FOR 1996

Standing at Dalham Hall Stud, Newmarket

ARAZI 1989 by Blushing Groom - Danseur Fabuleux
Champion 2yo in Europe and North America. 1st 2-y-olds 1996

LION CAVERN 1989 by Mr Prospector - Secrettame
Dual GW, own brother to **GONE WEST**. **1st Yearlings 1996**

MACHIAVELLIAN 1987 by Mr Prospector - Coup de Folie
Classic Sire of 7 individual Stakes Winners from his 1st crop

POLISH PRECEDENT 1986 by Danzig - Past Example
Classic Sire of PURE GRAIN and GWs RED ROUTE, RIYADIAN etc

SHAREEF DANCER 1980 by Northern Dancer - Sweet Alliance
A Leading European Sire of 27 individual GW/SWs of 50 races

WOLFHOUND 1989 by Nureyev - Lassie Dear
Champion European Sprinter. 1st Yearlings 1996

Standing at Aston Upthorpe Stud, Oxfordshire

MTOTO 1983 by Busted - Amazer
Sire of GW/SWs PRESENTING, FARU, TOTOSTAR, LOBBYIST

Standing at The Royal Studs, Norfolk

BELMEZ 1987 by El Gran Senor - Grace Note
Sire of dual GW CARAMBA and GP Pedraza

Standing at Ragusa Stud, Co. Kildare

IN THE WINGS 1986 by Sadler's Wells - High Hawk
Classic Sire of WINGED LOVE and SWs SINGSPIEL, IRISH WINGS etc

LYCIUS 1988 by Mr Prospector - Lypatia
A Leading 1st Season Sire, 12 Winners incl GWs MEDIA NOX, AYLESBURY

Enquiries to: Stud Office
Darley Stud Management Company Ltd.,
Dalham Hall Stud, Duchess Drive, Newmarket, Suffolk. CB8 9HD
Telephone: Newmarket (01638) 730070.
Fax: (01638) 730167.

MR H. R. A. CECIL—continued

113 Ch c 2/3 Zilzal (USA)—Dockage (CAN) (Riverman (USA)) **Mr K. Abdulla**
114 B f 25/5 Nureyev (USA)—Don't Sulk (USA) (Graustark) **Mr S. S. Niarchos**
115 Ch c 14/1 Nashwan (USA)—Double River (USA) (Irish River (FR)) **Mr K. Abdulla**
116 **ELAYSHA (USA),** b f 17/4 Gulch (USA)—Key Flyer (USA) (Nijinsky (CAN)) **H.R.H. Prince Fahd Salman**
117 **FASCINATING RHYTHM,** b f 2/2 Slip Anchor—Pick of The Pops (High Top) **Helena Springfield Ltd**
118 **FIJI,** b f 14/4 Rainbow Quest (USA)—Island Jamboree (USA) (Explodent (USA)) **H.R.H. Prince Fahd Salman**
119 Ch c 22/1 Royal Academy (USA)—Final Farewell (USA) (Proud Truth (USA)) **Mr Wafic Said**
120 **FLAMING WEST (USA),** ch c 2/2 Gone West (USA)—Flaming Torch (Rousillon (USA)) **Mr K. Abdulla**
121 Ch f 11/2 Magical Wonder (USA)—Forest Treasure (USA) (Green Forest (USA)) **Buckram Oak Holdings**
122 **GENTILESSE (IRE),** gr f 24/3 Generous (IRE)—As You Desire Me (Kalamoun) **H.R.H. Prince Fahd Salman**
123 **GOOD TIME (IRE),** ch c 15/4 Generous (IRE)—Honor To Her (USA) (Sir Ivor) **H.R.H. Prince Fahd Salman**
124 **GREGARIOUS,** b f 17/1 Pursuit Of Love—Anafi (Slip Anchor) **Mr L. Marinopoulos**
125 **HARRY WOLTON,** b c 21/4 Distant Relative—Tashinsky (USA) (Nijinsky (USA)) **Old Road Securities Plc**
126 **HIGH INTRIGUE (IRE),** b br c 7/3 Shirley Heights—Mild Intrigue (USA) (Sir Ivor) **Mrs E. A. Harris**
127 **HIGH ROLLER (IRE),** b c 2/3 Generous (IRE)—Helpless Haze (USA) (Vaguely Noble) **Baron G. von Ullmann**
128 Br c 8/5 Known Fact—Houseproud (USA) (Riverman (USA)) **Mr K. Abdulla**
129 Ch c 25/4 Polish Precedent—Illusory (Kings Lake (USA)) **Mr K. Abdulla**
130 Ch c 6/2 Machiavellian (USA)—Instant Desire (USA) (Northern Dancer) **Buckram Oak Holdings**
131 **ISMAROS,** ch c 20/4 Selkirk (USA)—Trikymia (Final Straw) **Mr L. Marinopoulos**
132 B f 31/1 Generous (IRE)—Jubilee Trail (Shareef Dancer (USA)) **Mr K. Abdulla**
133 **KASCH,** b c 16/1 Classic Music (USA)—Avra (FR) (Mendez (USA)) **Mr L. Marinopoulos**
134 B f 21/4 Mr Prospector (USA)—Kingscote (Kings Lake (USA)) **Mr K. Abdulla**
135 **KINNINO,** b c 2/2 Polish Precedent—On Tiptoes (Shareef Dancer (USA)) **Mr Eduardo Hinojosa**
136 **KYLE RHEA,** b f 26/3 In The Wings—Rynechra (Blakeney) **Sir David Wills**
137 **LYPHIELO (USA),** b f 15/5 Lyphard (USA)—

                    Miss Concielo (USA) (Conquistador Cielo (USA)) **Mr Robert H. Smith**
138 **MACHIAVELLI,** b c 25/5 Machiavellian (USA)—

                    Forest Blossom (USA) (Green Forest (USA)) **H.R.H. Prince Fahd Salman**
139 **MIDNIGHT WATCH (USA),** b c 18/3 Capote (USA)—

                    Midnight Air (USA) (Green Dancer (USA)) **H.R.H. Prince Fahd Salman**
140 Ch c 13/2 Shadeed (USA)—Million Stories (USA) (Exclusive Native (USA)) **Buckram Oak Holdings**
141 **MILLY OF THE VALLY,** b f 3/5 Caerleon (USA)—Mill On The Floss (Mill Reef (USA)) **Cliveden Stud**
142 Ch f 23/4 Nureyev (USA)—Modena (Roberto (USA)) **Mr K. Abdulla**
143 B f 2/4 Known Fact (USA)—Monroe (USA) (Sir Ivor) **Mr K. Abdulla**
144 **MYRTLEBANK,** ch f 2/2 Salse (USA)—Magical Veil (Majestic Light (USA)) **Sir David Wills**
145 **MYSTICAL HEIGHTS (IRE),** b f 17/3 High Estate—Richly Deserved (IRE) (Kings Lake (USA)) **Mr T. F. Harris**
146 B c 2/5 El Gran Senor (USA)—Nashmeel (USA) (Blushing Groom (USA)) **Mr K. Abdulla**
147 B f 22/4 Sadler's Wells (USA)—Nawara (Welsh Pageant) **Mr Wafic Said**
148 B f 27/1 Riverman (USA)—Nimble Feet (USA) (Danzig (USA)) **Mr K. Abdulla**
149 Ch c 5/2 Kris—Northshiel (Northfields (USA)) **Mr Ivan Allan**
150 **OCEAN EXPRESS (IRE),** b f 26/5 Royal Academy (USA)—Ocean Air (Elegant Air) **Greenbay Stables Ltd**
151 **OUT WEST (USA),** br f 8/2 Gone West (USA)—Chellingoua (USA) (Sharpen Up) **Buckram Oak Holdings**
152 B c 5/6 Nureyev (USA)—Pasadoble (USA) (Prove Out (USA)) **Mr S. S. Niarchos**
153 B f 2/4 Gone West (USA)—Peplum (USA) (Nijinsky (CAN)) **Mr K. Abdulla**
154 **PROSPECT STREET,** b f 1/4 Risk Me (FR)—Desert Gem (Green Desert (USA)) **Mr L. Marinopoulos**
155 B c 4/2 Alleged (USA)—Queens Only (USA) (Marshua's Dancer (USA)) **Mr K. Abdulla**
156 B f 13/3 Fairy King (USA)—Qui Suis Je (IRE) (Pennine Walk) **Mr M. B. Javett**
157 Ch c 26/2 Polish Precedent—Rafha (Kris) **Prince A. A. Faisal**
158 **ROYAL ALIBI,** b c 3/3 Royal Academy (USA)—Excellent Alibi (USA) (Exceller (USA)) **Mr T. F. Harris**
159 B f 20/4 Green Desert (USA)—Royal Climber (Kings Lake (USA)) **Sir Andrew Lloyd Webber**
160 **SANTORINI (FR),** b c 21/2 Exit To Nowhere (USA)—Light of Hope (USA) (Lyphard (USA)) **Mr S. S. Niarchos**
161 **SCOTTISH ROYAL (IRE),** b f 1/4 Night Shift (USA)—Foolish Lady (USA) (Foolish Pleasure (USA)) **Mr T. Hillman**
162 **SELFISH,** ch f 16/2 Bluebird (USA)—Sariza (Posse (USA)) **Mr L. Marinopoulos**
163 **SERPENTARA,** ch f 13/2 Kris—Sardegna (Pharly (FR)) **Lady Howard de Walden**
164 **SHINE ON,** b f 20/3 Mujtahid (USA)—Soyata (Bustino) **Mr L. Marinopoulos**
165 Br c 20/2 Caerleon (USA)—Shining Water (Kalaglow) **Mr K. Abdulla**
166 B c 8/2 Lyphard (USA)—Shirley Valentine (Shirley Heights) **Mr K. Abdulla**
167 **SLEEPYTIME (IRE),** b f 20/2 Royal Academy (USA)—Alidiva (Chief Singer) **Greenbay Stables Ltd**
168 B f 8/5 Danzig (USA)—Slightly Dangerous (USA) (Roberto (USA)) **Mr K. Abdulla**
169 **SOLEIL BLEU (IRE),** b f 27/2 Waajib—Sun On The Spey (Glint of Gold) **Mr Eduardo Hinojosa**

MR H. R. A. CECIL—continued

170 Ch c 6/4 Lycius (USA)—Star Ridge (USA) (Storm Bird (CAN)) **Buckram Oak Holdings**
171 STREET GENERAL, b c 12/5 Generous (IRE)—Hotel Street (USA) (Alleged (USA)) **Mr Luciano Gaucci**
172 SWEETEN UP, b f 14/3 Shirley Heights—Honeybeta (Habitat) **Cliveden Stud**
173 B f 13/3 Last Tycoon—Valley Lights (IRE) (Dance of Life (USA)) **Lucayan Stud**
174 VANISHING TRICK (USA), ch f 19/2 Gone West (USA)—Wand (IRE) (Reference Point) **Cliveden Stud**
175 Br c 11/2 Danzig (USA)—Wavering Girl (USA) (Wavering Monarch (USA)) **Thoroughbred Corporation**
176 WILD FOR GOLD (USA), b c 15/1 Wild Again (USA)—Vindaria (USA) (Roi Dagobert) **Buckram Oak Holdings**

Other Owners: Mr Peter Burrell, Mrs Stanley Cayzer, Mrs Henry Cecil, Mr W. H. Ferguson, Mrs David Nagle.

Jockeys (Flat): Pat Eddery (8-4, w.a.), A McGlone (7-11), W Ryan (8-2).

Late Namings

GRIMALDI (USA), Lyphard — Shirley Valentine
FLEET RIVER (USA), Riverman — Nimble Feet
LIGHT PROGRAMME, El Gran Senor — Nashmeel
JUBILEE WALK, Generous — Jubilee Trail
DRAGONADA (USA), Nureyev — Don't Sulk
PATMOS (USA), Nureyev — Pasadoble

122   MRS J. CECIL, Newmarket

Postal: **Southgate, Hamilton Road, Newmarket, Suffolk, CB8 0NQ.**
Phone: **OFFICE (01638) 560634 HOUSE   662420 FAX 560636**

1 ADAMTON, 4, b g Domynsky—Berwyn **Tripleprint**
2 ALBEMINE (USA), 7, b g Al Nasr (FR)—Lady Be Mine (USA) **Mr George Ward**
3 BEHAVIOUR, 4, b c Warning—Berry's Dream **Oceanic Limited**
4 DOMAPPEL, 4, b g Domynsky—Appelania **Mr M. C. Banks**
5 FOIL STONE, 5, b g Slip Anchor—Doumayna **Lord Howard de Walden**
6 FOREST CAT (IRE), 4, b f Petorius—Forest of Arden **Mr George Ward**
7 GONDOLIER, 8, b g Slip Anchor—Grimpola (GER) **Lord Howard de Walden**
8 ISAIAH, 7, gr g Bellypha—Judeah **Mrs D. MacRae**
9 JACK LEADER, 5, b g Ziggy's Boy—Mrs Leader (USA) **Mrs D. MacRae**
10 JERMYN STREET (USA), 5, b h Alleged (USA)—My Mother Mary (USA) **Mr John Bray**
11 KING OF MUNSTER (AUS), 4, gr g Kenmare (FR)—Artistic Princess (AUS) **Lord Howard de Walden**
12 LADY OF LEISURE (USA), 4, b f Diesis—Lyrebird (USA) **Mrs Anna L. Sanders**
13 LOMBARDIC (USA), 5, b h Private Account (USA)—If Winter Comes (USA) **Bonusprint**
14 OBELOS (USA), 5, ch h Diesis—Fair Sousanne **Lord Howard de Walden**
15 PATER NOSTER (USA), 7, b h Stately Don (USA)—Sainera (USA) **Mr Martin Myers**
16 QUILLWORK (USA), 4, b f Val de L'Orne (FR)—Quaff (USA) **Mr George L. Ohrstrom**
17 RESTRUCTURE (IRE), 4, b c Danehill (USA)—Twine **Mr Martin Myers**
18 RORY, 5, b g Dowsing (USA)—Crymlyn **Mrs J. Cecil**
19 SESAME SEED (IRE), 8, b g Wassl—Halva **Mr Raymond Tooth**
20 STICKS AND STONES (IRE), 4, b g Waajib—Maiacourt **Mr Martin Myers**
21 TILSTON, 5, b g Dunbeath (USA)—Cribyn **Julie Cecil**
22 TRIPPIANO, 6, b g Fappiano (USA)—Hence (USA) **Mrs J. Cecil**

THREE-YEAR-OLDS

23 BONANZA PEAK (USA), b c Houston (USA)—Bunnicula (USA) **Golden Arrow SA, Gavin Oram & Lee Eaton**
24 CALLALOO, b c Mtoto—Catawba **Lord Howard de Walden**
25 CHILTERN COURT (USA), b f Topsider (USA)—Ghillie (USA) **Bernard Gover**
26 DARK TRUFFLE, br f Deploy—River Dove (USA) **Southgate Racing**
27 DEAR JOHN (IRE), b g Caerleon (USA)—Alligatrix (USA) **Mr Raymond Tooth**
28 DEAR LIFE (USA), b f Lear Fan (USA)—Charming Life (NZ) **Lady Howard de Walden**
29 DRAGONCELLO (USA), b f Diesis—Spicy Life (USA) **Golden Arrow SA and Raju Mahboobani**
30 DRAGON'S BACK (IRE), ch c Digamist (USA)—Classic Choice **Wozgot Partnership**
31 FLY FISHING (USA), ch c Miswaki (USA)—Sharp Flick (USA) **Lord Howard de Walden**
32 FOREST HEIGHTS, b f Slip Anchor—Forest Blossom (USA) **Mr George Ward**

MRS J. CECIL—continued

33 **KAABA**, b f Darshaan—Konigsalpen (GER) **Lord Howard de Walden**
34 **LACRYMA CRISTI (IRE)**, b c Green Desert (USA)—L'Anno d'Oro **Golden Arrow SA**
35 **LITTLE MURRAY**, b c Mon Tresor—Highland Daisy **Mr Anthony Cherry-Downes**
36 **MAGAZINE GAP**, ch c Weldnaas (USA)—Divissima **Mrs Anna L. Sanders**
37 **MIRY LEADER**, ch f Polar Falcon (USA)—Mrs Leader (USA) **Mrs D. Macrae**
38 **OOPS PETTIE**, ch f Machiavellian (USA)—Miquette (FR) **Mrs D. Macrae**
39 **OSTIA**, b f Slip Anchor—Sarsina **Lord Howard de Walden**
40 **SMART PLAY (USA)**, gr c Sovereign Dancer (USA)—Casessa (USA) **Mrs George Ward**
41 **SNOWPOLES**, b f High Estate—Bronzewing **Sir Thomas Pilkington**
42 **SOLITAIRE (FR)**, b f Sadler's Wells (USA)—Helpless Haze (USA) **Mr S. S. Niarchos**
43 **SOUTH WIND**, b f Tina's Pet—Warm Wind **Southgate Racing**
44 **TARKHEENA (USA)**, b f Alleged—Comtesse de Loir (FR) **Mr George L. Ohrstrom**
45 **TROPICAL DANCE (USA)**, ch f Thorn Dance (USA)—Missuma (USA) **Mr George Ward**
46 **TSARSKAYA (USA)**, ch f Elmaamul (USA)—Wyandra **Golden Arrow SA and Daniel Zigal**

TWO-YEAR-OLDS

47 **AGONY AUNT**, b f Formidable (USA)—Loch Clair (IRE) (Lomond (USA)) **Capt J. MacDonald-Buchanan**
48 **AYBEEGIRL**, b f 24/2 Mazilier (USA)—So It Goes (Free State) **Stephen R. Hobson**
49 **CEREMONY**, ch f 17/1 Be My Chief (USA)—Khrisma (Kris) **Lord Howard de Walden**
50 **ISLE OF CORREGIDOR (USA)**, b c 5/4 Manila (USA)—
                                       Comtesse de Loir (FR) (Val de Loir (FR)) **George L. Ohrstrom**
51 **KINGFISHER MILL (USA)**, ch c 4/3 Riverman (USA)—
                                       Charming Life (NZ) (Sir Tristram) **Lord Howard de Walden**
52 Ch c 4/5 Gone West (USA)—Lightning Fire (Kris) **S. S. Niarchos**
53 B c 12/2 Fayruz—Lightning Laser (Monseigneur (USA)) **Martin Myers**
54 **MATRONA (USA)**, b f 21/2 Woodman (USA)—Happy Bride (IRE) (Royal Match) **Golden Arrow SA**
55 **NAMBUCCA**, b f 8/2 Shirley Heights—Cephira (FR) (Abdos) **Lord Howard de Walden**
56 **NORTHERN ANGEL (IRE)**, b c 28/3 Waajib—Angel Divine (Ahonoora) **James H. Stone**
57 B c 5/3 Salse (USA)—One Last Glimpse (Relko) **Stephen R. Hobson**
58 **POLEAXE**, b f 3/2 Selkirk (USA)—Sarmatia (USA) (Danzig (USA)) **Lady Howard de Walden**
59 B c 30/4 Warning—Rattle Along (Tap On Wood) **Bernard Gover**
60 **ROSA ROYALE**, b f 23/3 Arazi (USA)—Gussy Marlowe (Final Straw) **Mrs J. Van Geest**
61 **WITCHING HOUR (IRE)**, b f 9/5 Alzao (USA)—Itching (IRE) (Thatching) **Greenbay Stables Ltd**

Other Owners: Mr P. M. Burrell, Mrs Penelope Butler, Mr J. N. W. Dudley, Mr Malcolm Glenn, Rupert Hambro, Mr T. Hillman, John Humphreys (Turf Accountants) Ltd, Mr Bryan Keatley, Mrs Ronald K. Kirk, Mr William Nott, Mr O. H. Rosselli, Mr Ian Tomlin, Mr David Wilson, Major R. G. Wilson.

Jockey (NH): T J Kent (10-0).

Lady Rider: Jennie Crossley (8-7).

123   MR A. J. CHAMBERLAIN, Swindon

Postal: **North End Farm, Ashton Keynes, Swindon, Wilts, SN6 6QR.**
Phone: **(01285) 861347 MOBILE (0585) 823498**

1 **BEE BEAT**, 8, ch g Bairn (USA)—Thorny Rose
2 **BILLI BEE**, 4, b g Buckley—Kessie-Bee **Mr G. J. Chamberlain**
3 **BITE THE BULLET**, 5, ch g Ballacashtal (CAN)—Longgoo **Mr R. Drinkwater**
4 **GOVERNORS FORTUNE**, 4, b g Governor General—Fortune's Fancy **Mr E. H. Lodge**
5 **GREENHILL SURPRISE**, 4, b g Lugana Beach—Mitala Maria **Mr I. Plank**
6 **HANDCROSS**, 5, b g Handsome Sailor—Standard Breakfast **Mr A. J. Chamberlain**
7 **JIMMY-JADE**, 7, ch g Oats—Newella **Mr G. J. Chamberlain**
8 **LAUNDRYMAN**, 13, b g Celtic Cone—Lovely Laura **Mr A. J. Chamberlain**
9 **LENEY MOSS (IRE)**, 6, br m Le Moss—Castle Leney **Mr D. P. Travers-Clark**
10 **MISS KIVE**, 10, b m Kabour—Final Cast **Mr S. P. Howe**

MR A. J. CHAMBERLAIN—continued

11 **OPEN SESAME**, 10, b g Be My Guest (USA)—Syrian Sea (USA) **Mr A. J. Chamberlain**
12 **SOCKS DOWNE**, 17, b br g Paddy's Stream—Kincsem **Mr A. J. Chamberlain**
13 **THE GORROCK**, 7, b g Petoski—Aquarula **Mr A. J. Chamberlain**
14 **VISION OF WONDER**, 12, b g Tyrnavos—Valeur

THREE-YEAR-OLDS

15 **MISS BLUES SINGER**, b f Sula Bula—Lady Blues Singer **Mr E. H. Lodge**

Other Owners: Mr G. Gardiner, Mr M. Gerard, Mr P. King, Mr J. Thorne.

Jockey (Flat): R Perham (w.a.).

Jockeys (NH): B Powell (10-0, w.a.), A Tory.

Amateurs: Mr S Howe (9-10), Mr J Juckes (10-0), Mr Y Mehmet (9-7), Miss D Olding (10-4).

Lady Rider: Miss Lorna Vincent (w.a.).

124   MR N. CHAMBERLAIN, West Auckland

Postal: **Acrum Lodge, Staindrop Road, West Auckland, Bishop Auckland, DL14 9PB.**
Phone: **(01388) OFFICE 834636 HOUSE 832465**

1 **ADMISSION (IRE)**, 6, b g Glow (USA)—Admit **Mr N. Chamberlain**
2 **BITTER MOON**, 5, b m Rambling River—Elitist **Mr R. W. Chamberlain**
3 **DANCING RIVER**, 10, b g Niniski (USA)—River Chimes **Mr N. Chamberlain**
4 **GYMCRAK CYRANO (IRE)**, 7, b m Cyrano de Bergerac—Sun Gift **Mr N. Chamberlain**
5 **HYA PRIM**, 5, ch g Say Primula—Rilin **Mr N. Chamberlain**
6 **IMULARI**, 5, b g Say Primula—Ribera **Mr N. Chamberlain**
7 **KRALINGEN**, 4, ch f Move Off—Elitist **Mr R. W. Chamberlain**
8 **MARCHWOOD**, 9, ch g Black Minstrel—Lisnagrough **Mr N. Chamberlain**
9 **PAINT YOUR WAGON**, 6, b g Move Off—Gipsy Silk **Mr N. Chamberlain**
10 **PUBLIC WAY (IRE)**, 6, b g Common Grounds—Kilpeacon **Mr N. Chamberlain**
11 **SOUTHERN MINSTREL**, 13, ch g Black Minstrel—Jadida (FR) **Mr N. Chamberlain**
12 **TAKE A RIGHT**, 4, b g Skyliner—Miss Colenca **Mr N. Chamberlain**
13 **THRUSHWOOD**, 4, b f Move Off—Spring Garden **Mr N. Chamberlain**

THREE-YEAR-OLDS

14 **BROKEN ENGLISH**, ch f Say Primula—Elitist **Mr R. W. Chamberlain**
15 B f Say Primula—Spring Garden **Mr N. Chamberlain**

TWO-YEAR-OLDS

16 Ch f 22/3 Minster Son—Spring Garden (Silly Prices) **Mr N. Chamberlain**

Conditional: J Supple (9-7).

Lady Rider: Miss C Metcalfe (9-7).

125   MR R. CHAMPION M.B.E., Newmarket

Postal: **Bechers, Hamilton Road, Newmarket, Suffolk, CB8 7JQ.**
Phone: **(01638) 666546 FAX (01638) 561989**

1 **PATS MINSTREL**, 11, b g Black Minstrel—Lohunda Park **Mr K. J. Hunt**
2 **SPUMANTE**, 4, ch g Executive Man—Midler **Mr Terry Rowley**
3 **THE MINISTER (IRE)**, 7, br g Black Minstrel—Miss Hi-Land **Mrs P. S. Hunt and Mr C. Wallington**

MR R. CHAMPION M.B.E.—continued

THREE-YEAR-OLDS

4 TINA KATERINA, ch f Executive Man—Tria Romantica **Mr Terry Rowley**

Other Owners: Mrs T. Cassidy, Mrs D. F. Champion, Mrs C. A. Sasse.

Jockeys (NH): A Maguire (w.a.), B Powell.

126   MR N. T. CHANCE, Lambourn

Postal: **Folly House Stables, Lambourn, Newbury, Berks, RG16 7QG.**

Phone: **OFFICE (01488) 73436 MOBILE (0385) 300168**

1 AH SHUSH (IRE), 8, ch g Le Moss—Pampered Finch VII **Mr M. Worcester**
2 CAILIN GLAS (IRE), 7, ch m Mister Lord (USA)—Emerald Flair **Mr M. Worcester**
3 CRAMPSCASTLE (IRE), 6, ch g Orchestra—Just The Thing **Mr M. Worcester**
4 GRACEFIELD (IRE), 6, b g Stalker—Viva La Weavers **Mr M. Worcester**
5 HACKETTS CROSS (IRE), 8, b g Rusticaro (FR)—Anglesea Market **Mr B. R. Rudge**
6 5, Gr g Torus—Lady Barnaby **Mr M. Worcester**
7 LORD MILLS (IRE), 5, b g Lord Americo—Salt Mills **Mr M. Worcester**
8 MARCHING MARQUIS (IRE), 5, b g Aristocracy—Lady Go Marching (USA) **Mr M. Worcester**
9 MEAD COURT (IRE), 6, ch g Torus—Winning Fare **Mr M. Worcester**
10 MIDNIGHT CALLER, 10, br g Callernish—Miss Pitpan **Mr M. Worcester**
11 MR MULLIGAN (IRE), 8, ch g Torus—Miss Manhattan **Mr M. Worcester**
12 MRS JONES (IRE), 6, gr m Roselier (FR)—Glen of Hawthorn **Mr M. Worcester**
13 NUPDOWN BOY (IRE), 7, ch g Orchestra—Fiona's Blue **Mr M. Worcester**
14 NUPDOWN EXPRESS (IRE), 6, b g Good Thyne (USA)—Meadow Rhapsody **Mr M. Worcester**
15 PALIAPOUR (IRE), 5, br g Doyoun—Palitana **Mrs M. Chance**
16 ROYAL THIMBLE (IRE), 5, b m Prince Rupert (FR)—Tootsie Roll **Mrs M. Chance**

THREE-YEAR-OLDS

17 WITHY CLOSE (IRE), b g Petorius—Tender Pearl **Mr M. Worcester**

Jockey (Flat): J F Egan (w.a.).

Jockey (NH): R Johnson.

Apprentice: L Hagan.

Conditional: D Finnegan (9-7).

Amateur: Mr R F Coonan (10-0).

127   MR M. CHANNON, Upper Lambourn

Postal: **Kingsdown, Upper Lambourn, Hungerford, Berks, RG17 8QX.**

Phone: **(01488) 71149 FAX (01488) 73235**

1 CHAMPAGNE GRANDY, 6, ch m Vaigly Great—Monstrosa **Grandy Girls**
2 DANEGOLD (IRE), 4, b g Danehill (USA)—Cistus **The Dream Team**
3 DOMICKSKY, 8, b g Dominion—Mumruffin **Miss Melanie Hacker**
4 FANTASY RACING (IRE), 4, b f Tirol—Highland Girl (USA) **Aldridge Racing Limited**

MR M. CHANNON—continued

5 **GIGGLESWICK GIRL**, 5, b m Full Extent (USA)—Foligno **Mr M. Bishop**
6 **JACKATACK (IRE)**, 4, b g Astronef—Redwood Hut **Mr Peter Taplin**
7 **KATYA (IRE)**, 4, b f Dancing Dissident (USA)—Park Elect **Mr J. W. Mitchell**
8 **KNOBBLEENEEZE**, 6, ch g Aragon—Proud Miss (USA) **Mr Anthony Andrews**
9 **ROCKFORCE**, 4, ch g Rock City—Sleepline Princess **Mr G. Z. Mizel**
10 **SILCA BLANKA (IRE)**, 4, b c Law Society (USA)—Reality **Mr P. D. Savill**
11 **WELTON ARSENAL**, 4, b g Statoblest—Miller's Gait **Business Forms Express**

THREE-YEAR-OLDS

12 **AMBER RING**, ch f Belmez (USA)—Ring of Pearl **Pinecrest Racing**
13 **ANNA SOLEIL (IRE)**, b g Red Sunset—Flying Anna **Mr M. St Quinton**
14 **ARCH ENEMY (IRE)**, gr c Archway (IRE)—Rosserk **Mr P. D. Savill**
15 **BELZAO**, b c Alzao (USA)—Belle Enfant **Mr J. Mitchell**
16 **BOOZEROO**, ch g Never So Bold—Show Home **Mrs D. Hanson**
17 **CD SUPER TARGETING (IRE)**, ch f Polish Patriot (USA)—Hazy Bird **Circular Distributors Ltd**
18 **CISERANO (IRE)**, ch f Mujtahid (USA)—Blue Persian **Mr K. Dack**
19 **CORNICHE QUEST (IRE)**, b f Salt Dome (USA)—Angel Divine **A. and M. Racing Partners**
20 **DUNGEON PRINCESS (IRE)**, b f Danehill (USA)—Taplow **The Classicstone Partnership**
21 **FLYING HAROLD**, b c Gildoran—Anytime Anywhere **Mr Malcolm P. Allen**
22 **FLYING SQUAW**, b f Be My Chief (USA)—Sea Fret **Mr M. A. Foy**
23 **FOREVER NOBLE (IRE)**, b g Forzando—Pagan Queen **The Gap Partnership**
24 **HENCARLAM (IRE)**, b g Astronef—War Ballad (FR) **Mr J. Carey**
25 **HIGH PRIORITY (IRE)**, b c Marju (IRE)—Blinding (IRE) **Mrs E. Sheehan**
26 **LADY CAROLINE LAMB (IRE)**, b f Contract Law (USA)—Tuft Hill **Mr W. H. Ponsonby**
27 **MILETRIAN REFURB (IRE)**, b g Anita's Prince—Lady of Man **Miletrian Plc**
28 **MIRONOV**, b c Marju (IRE)—Marquina (FR)
29 **ON THE WILDSIDE**, ch f Charmer—No Control **Mr W. H. Ponsonby**
30 **PARIS JOELLE (IRE)**, b f Fairy King (USA)—Gentle Freedom **Mr R. M. Brehaut**
31 **PETERREX**, b g Interrex (CAN)—Standard Rose **Mr P. Taplin**
32 **POLY LAD (IRE)**, b c Alzao (USA)—Lady of Shalott **Sheet & Roll Convertors Ltd**
33 **POLY MY SON (IRE)**, ch c Be My Guest (USA)—Green Memory (USA) **Sheet & Roll Convertors Ltd**
34 **REPERTORY**, b c Anshan—Susie's Baby **Mr Chris Scott**
35 **RIVERBOURNE (USA)**, b c Riverman (USA)—Umaimah (USA) **Mrs N. Crook**
36 **STONEY END (USA)**, b c High Brite (USA)—Cranareen (CAN) **Mr M. Myers**
37 **SUNLEY SECURE**, b g Warrshan (USA)—Brown Velvet **Mr R. J. Sunley Tice**
38 **TOTALLY YOURS (IRE)**, b f Classic Music (USA)—Dominia **Mr M. R. Channon**
39 **WARNING REEF**, b c Warning—Horseshoe Reef **Mr P. Sheehan**
40 **WHISPERING DAWN**, b f Then Again—Summer Sky **Mr W. H. Ponsonby**

TWO-YEAR-OLDS

41 B c 13/4 Priolo (USA)—Ah Ya Zein (Artaius (USA)) **Mr Chris Scott & Partners**
42 **ANCHOR BLEU**, b c 10/4 Statoblest—Princess Rosananti (Shareef Dancer (USA)) **Surrey Laminators Ltd**
43 B c 23/2 Beveled (USA)—Baino Charm (Diesis) **Maygain Ltd**
44 **BAUBIGNY (USA)**, b c 23/2 Shadeed (USA)—
                    Pearl Essence (USA) (Conquistador Cielo (USA)) **Mr R. M. Brehaut**
45 B f 21/5 Suave Dancer (USA)—Blink Naskra (USA) (Naskra (USA)) **Sheet & Roll Convertors Ltd**
46 B c 17/5 Mtoto—Bold As Love (Lomond (USA)) **Mr A. Merza**
47 B f 29/3 Deerhound (USA)—Bouncing Slew (USA) (Seattle Slew (USA))
48 **BRAVEHEART (IRE)**, br c 28/2 Mujadil (USA)—Salonniere (FR) (Bikala) **Mr W. H. Ponsonby**
49 **CAUDA EQUINA**, b c 27/1 Statoblest—Sea Fret (Habat) **Mr M. A. Foy**
50 B c 27/4 Persian Bold—Cloud Peak (USA) (Storm Bird (USA)) **Aldridge Racing Limited**
51 **DANEHILL PRINCE**, b c 26/2 Danehill (USA)—Santarem (El Gran Senor (USA)) **Mr S. Crown**
52 B f 10/3 Rock City—Dash (Connaught)
53 B c 12/2 Warrshan (USA)—Emerald Ring (Auction Ring (USA)) **Mrs G. Rowland-Clarke**
54 **EPAULETTE**, b f 25/2 Warrshan (USA)—Dame Helene (USA) (Sir Ivor) **Mr & Mrs J. Knight**
55 **FLOOD'S HOT STUFF**, gr f 22/2 Chilibang—Tiszta Sharok (Song) **Richard Flood Bloodstock Ltd**
56 Ch f 25/4 Ballacashtal (CAN)—Foligno (Crofter (USA)) **Sheet & Roll Convertors Ltd**
57 **FRENCH KISS**, b c 17/4 Petorius—Cerosia (Pitskelly) **Mr T. S. M. Cunningham**
58 Ch f 15/3 Statoblest—Furry Dance (USA) (Nureyev (USA))
59 Ch f 22/3 Beveled (USA)—Golden October (Young Generation)

MR M. CHANNON—continued

60 Ch f 15/4 Rock City—Golden Scissors (Kalaglow) **Mrs J. Keegan**
61 **IRISH FICTION (IRE)**, b c 18/2 Classic Music (USA)—Wasmette (IRE) (Wassl) **Mr M. A. Foy**
62 B f 5/5 Reprimand—Ivory Bride (Domynsky) **Mrs J. Keegan**
63 Ch f 21/3 Be My Chief (USA)—Jennies' Gem (Sayf El Arab (USA)) **Mr Brian Lovrey**
64 B c 18/3 Puissance—Jobiska (Dunbeath (USA)) **Maygain Ltd**
65 **LAMORNA**, ch f 1/4 Shavian—Malibasta (Auction Ring (USA)) **Mr W. H. Ponsonby**
66 Ch c 13/5 Imperial Frontier—Lilac Lass (Virginia Boy)
67 **MALADERIE (IRE)**, b c 14/2 Thatching—Native Melody (Tudor Music) **Mr R. M. Brehaut**
68 B f 6/5 Dunbeath (USA)—Matching Lines (Thatching) **Mrs J. Keegan**
69 **MEILLEUR (IRE)**, b c 1/2 Nordico (USA)—Lucy Limelight (Hot Spark) **Mr Alec Tuckerman**
70 B c 19/5 Akarad (FR)—Miss Ivory Coast (USA) (Sir Ivor)
71 **M R POLY**, b c 20/5 Green Desert (USA)—Report 'em (USA) (Staff Writer (USA)) **Sheet & Roll Convertors Ltd**
72 **MUCHEA**, ch c 16/4 Shalford (IRE)—Bargouzine (Hotfoot) **Albion Investments**
73 B c 16/4 Polar Falcon (USA)—Nastassia (FR) (Noble Decree (USA)) **Allevamento La Nuova Sbarra S.R.L.**
74 Ch f 25/3 Polar Falcon (USA)—Night Transaction (Tina's Pet) **Aldridge Racing Limited**
75 Ch f 11/4 Sharpo—Norska (Northfields (USA))
76 B c 19/4 Jareer (USA)—Precious Egg (Home Guard (USA)) **Mr M. R. Channon**
77 B f 11/4 Lahib (USA)—Queens Welcome (Northfields (USA)) **Maygain Ltd**
78 **QUERTIER (IRE)**, ch c 14/3 Bluebird—Ganna (ITY) (Molvedo) **Mr R. M. Brehaut**
79 **RECONDITE (IRE)**, b c 9/3 Polish Patriot (USA)—Recherchee (Rainbow Quest (USA)) **Mr P. D. Savill**
80 B c 23/4 Bluebird (USA)—Ring of Light (Auction Ring (USA)) **Mr J. W. Mitchell**
81 **RUSSIAN SABLE**, b f 9/3 Statoblest—Princess Zita (Manado) **Mr T. S. M. Cunningham**
82 **SAUNDERS WREN**, b f 8/3 Handsome Sailor—Saunders Lass (Hillandale) **Charles Saunders Ltd**
83 **SHADES OF LOVE**, b c 30/4 Pursuit Of Love—Shadiliya (Red Alert) **The Pursuers - Four Seasons Racing**
84 **SILANKKA**, b f 7/2 Slip Anchor—Mary Sunley (Known Fact (USA)) **Simon Legg and Partners**
85 B c 6/3 Fairy King (USA)—Silly Tune (IRE) (Coquelin (USA)) **Maygain Ltd**
86 **STATESMAN**, b c 31/1 Doyoun—Affair of State (IRE) (Tate Gallery (USA)) **Mr S. Crown**
87 **SUN O'TIROL**, b c 20/4 Tirol—Nous (Le Johnstan) **Mrs A. Barwick**
88 **THE REAL McCOY**, b c 10/3 Deploy—Mukhayyalah (Dancing Brave (USA)) **Mrs N. Mathias**
89 **VASARI (IRE)**, ch c 3/3 Imperial Frontier—Why Not Glow (IRE) (Glow (USA)) **Mr Alec Tuckerman**
90 **VICTORIA'S DREAM (IRE)**, b f 14/2 Royal Academy (USA)—
                                      Woodland Garden (Godswalk (USA)) **Mrs Victoria Tuckerman**
91 **WAIT FOR ROSIE**, b f 18/4 Reprimand—Turbo Rose (Taufan (USA)) **Mrs Beryl Thorne**

Other Owners: Mr R. W. Allen, Mr Don Baker, Mr Chris Barrett, Mr Terry Barwick, Mr T. C. Brown, Mr Martin Clark, Mr A. K. Collins, Mr David Evans, Mr A. Eyres, Mrs A. V. Ferguson, Mr R. G. Giles, Mr Michael Johnson, Mrs A. M. Jones, Mr M. R. Jones, Mr Peter F. Jordan, Mrs Carole Kay, Miss E. A. Lake, Mrs J. Littler, Mr R. L. Maynard, Mrs Betty D. M. Mitchell, Mr P. S. Mulligan, Mrs Tessa Mulligan, Mr D. J. Peers, Mr E. J. Peett, Mr Peter Petyt, Dr Brian J. Ridgewell, Mr C. I. Robinson, Mrs F. C. Saint Jean, Mr S. A. Smith, Mr John Smith (Roehampton), Mrs S. Stafford, Mr Harold E. St Quinton, Mr John B. Sunley, Mr P. Trant, Mr J. M. Viegas, Mr Roy Warman, Lady Whent.

Jockeys (Flat): Richard Hughes (8-5), Candy Morris (8-1).

Apprentices: J Dennis (7-12), A Eddery (7-11), D Fergus Sweeney (7-7), Peter Murphy (7-10).

Amateur: Joanna Winter (9-0).

128   MR DAVID W. CHAPMAN, York

Postal: **Mowbray House Farm, Stillington, York, YO6 1LT.**
Phone: **(01347) 21683 CAR PHONE (0836) 760590 FAX (01347) 23018**

1 **AMBER BATTLE**, 6, gr g Kabour—Amber Vale **Mr David W. Chapman**
2 **BOWCLIFFE GRANGE (IRE)**, 4, b g Dominion Royale—Cala-Vadella **Mr David W. Chapman**
3 **CHEEKY CHAPPY**, 5, b g Sayf El Arab (USA)—Guilty Guest (USA) **Mrs Jeanne Chapman**
4 **CLAQUE**, 4, ch c Kris—Mixed Applause (USA) **Mr Michael Hill**
5 **DESERT INVADER (IRE)**, 5, br g Lead On Time (USA)—Aljood **Mr Michael Hill**
6 **GREAT BEAR**, 4, ch g Dominion—Bay Bay **Mr J. M. Chapman**
7 **GREEN'S BID**, 6, gr g Siberian Express (USA)—Arianna Aldini **Mr J. M. Chapman**

MR DAVID W. CHAPMAN—continued

8 **KABANCY**, 5, b g Kabour—Nikancy **Mr Bill Waddington**
9 **KABCAST**, 11, b g Kabour—Final Cast **Mrs M. M. Marshall**
10 **KALAR**, 7, b g Kabour—Wind And Reign **Mr E. Stockdale**
11 **MOWLAIE**, 5, ch g Nashwan (USA)—Durrah (USA) **Mr J. M. Chapman**
12 **NO SUBMISSION (USA)**, 10, b h Melyno—Creeping Kate (USA) **Mr T. S. Redman**
13 **PALACEGATE JO (IRE)**, 5, b m Drumalis—Welsh Rhyme **Mr David W. Chapman**
14 **SEA-DEER**, 7, ch g Hadeer—Hi-Tech Girl **Miss N. F. Thesiger**
15 **SHADOW JURY**, 6, ch g Doulab (USA)—Texita **Mrs Jeanne Chapman**
16 **SUPERCOOL**, 5, ch g Superlative—Florentynna Bay **Mr David W. Chapman**
17 **TEMPERING**, 10, b g Kris—Mixed Applause (USA) **Mr Richard Berenson**

THREE-YEAR-OLDS

18 **BELACQUA (USA)**, gr f Northern Flagship (USA)—Wake The Town (FR) **Mrs Jeanne Chapman**
19 **POSITIVE INDICATOR (IRE)**, b f Superpower—Cresalin **Mrs Jeanne Chapman**

Other Owners: Mr K. E. Monaghan.

Jockey (NH): R Garritty (w.a.).

Lady Rider: Miss Ruth Clark (9-7).

129 MR M. C. CHAPMAN, Market Rasen

Postal: **Woodland Racing Stables, Woodland Lane, Willingham Road, Market Rasen, LN8 3RE.**
Phone: **(01673) 843663 TELEX (01673) 843663**

1 **AWESOME VENTURE**, 6, b g Formidable (USA)—Pine Ridge **Market Rasen Racing Club**
2 **BALAAT (USA)**, 8, b g Northern Baby (CAN)—Bar J Gal (USA) **Mr Alan Mann**
3 **BRITANNIA MILLS**, 5, gr m Nordico (USA)—May Fox **Mr Alan Mann**
4 **BUZZARDS HALL**, 6, ch m Buzzards Bay—Nikoola Eve **Mr D. C. G. Cooper**
5 **KARINSKA**, 6, b m Master Willie—Kaiserchronik (GER) **Mr Geoff Whiting**
6 **KINDAKOOLA**, 5, b br g Kind of Hush—Nikoola Eve **Mr D. C. G. Cooper**
7 **MILO BOY**, 5, b g Jester—Miss Cervinia **Mr A. J. M. Norris**
8 **NADWATY (IRE)**, 4, b f Prince Sabo—Faisalah **Mrs B. Ward**
9 **NASHAAT (USA)**, 8, b g El Gran Senor (USA)—Absentia (USA) **Mr Tony Satchell**
10 **NON VINTAGE (IRE)**, 5, ch g Shy Groom (USA)—Great Alexandra **Mr Alan Mann**
11 **RECORD LOVER (IRE)**, 6, b g Alzao (USA)—Spun Gold **Mr Alan Mann**
12 **RULLY**, 7, ch g Rousillon (USA)—Hysterical **Mr Stanley W. Clarke**
13 **RUPPLES**, 9, b g Muscatite—Miss Annie **Exors of the late Mr C. Hague**
14 **SEA GOD**, 5, ch g Rainbow Quest (USA)—Sea Pageant **Mrs B. Ward**
15 **SPANISH STRIPPER**, 5, b g El Gran Senor (USA)—Gourmet Dinner (USA) **Mr Tony Satchell**
16 **SPROWSTON BOY**, 13, ch g Dominion—Cavalier's Blush **Mr Geoff Whiting**

THREE-YEAR-OLDS

17 **DOWN THE YARD**, b f Batshoof—Sequin Lady **Mr Geoff Whiting**
18 **MULHOLLANDE LAD (IRE)**, ch g Mulhollande (USA)—La Kumbha (FR) **Mr Mattie O'Toole**
19 **SEEKING DESTINY (IRE)**, b g Two Timing (USA)—Heads We Called (IRE) **Mr Mattie O'Toole**
20 **WINDWARD DANCER**, gr f Contest (USA)—Miss Val **Mr Bill Starling**

Other Owners: Mr A. R. Barnes, Mr R. Beresford, Mr K. D. Blanch, Mr F. W. Brown, Mr S. Hall, Mr T. J. Hayward, Mrs T. Mann, Mr Michael Neal, Mr T. Ranshaw, Mr K. C. West.

Jockey (NH): W Worthington (10-0).

Amateur: Mr M Mackley (10-4).

130 MAJOR D. N. CHAPPELL, Whitsbury

Postal: **Whitsbury Manor Racing Stables, Whitsbury, Fordingbridge, Hants, SP6 3QQ.**
Phone: **(01725) 518708 FAX 518747 HOME 518274 CAR (0374) 258364**

1 **ACE PLAYER (NZ)**, 8, b g Full On Aces (AUS)—C'Est La Vie (NZ) **Mr R. P. B. Michaelson**
2 **BRIEF GLIMPSE (IRE)**, 4, b f Taufan (USA)—Mini Look (FR) **Whiteways Racing**
3 **BRIMPTON BERTIE**, 7, ch g Music Boy—Lady of Bath **Whiteways Racing**
4 **CAPE MERINO**, 5, ch m Clantime—Laena **Mrs D. Ellis**
5 **CASSIMERE**, 4, ch f Clantime—Poshteen **Mrs D. Ellis**
6 **CHARTER**, 5, b h Reference Point—Winter Queen **Mrs Sheila Morris & Mrs Norma Paskin**
7 **JUDGE ADVOCATE (IRE)**, 4, b c Contract Law (USA)—Brigadina **Whiteways Racing**
8 **MISS TICKLEPENNY**, 4, b f Distant Relative—Aphrosina **Mr E. D. Evers**
9 **MONTY**, 4, ch g Colmore Row—Sussarando **Whiteways Racing**
10 **NOBLE FORESTER (IRE)**, 8, b g Lord Ha Ha—Diana Harwell **Major P. Pusinelli**
11 **PRINTERS QUILL**, 4, b g Squill (USA)—On Impulse **Mrs B. Woodford**
12 **QUARRY HOUSE (IRE)**, 8, b g The Parson—April Sal **Mrs E. Chappell**
13 **THATCHERELLA**, 5, br m Thatching—Ella Mon Amour **Mr J. H. Widdows**
14 **WHITE SHOOT (IRE)**, 5, ch m Carmelite House (USA)—Irish Kick **R.O.M. Racing**

THREE-YEAR-OLDS

15 **ALL STAND**, ch f Dominion—Now In Session (USA)
16 **CLASSIC LOOK**, b br f Classic Music (USA)—Mini Look (FR)
17 **DWINGELOO (IRE)**, b f Dancing Dissident (USA)—Thank One's Stars **Mrs Maxwell**
18 **OLIVER ROCK**, b g Shareef Dancer (USA)—Short Rations **Stamford Bridge Partnership**
19 **PERSIAN DAWN**, br f Anshan—Visible Form **R.O.M. Racing**
20 **RIVERS MAGIC**, b g Dominion—Rivers Maid **Mr R. Mead**
21 **SANTELLA KATIE**, ch f Anshan—Mary Bankes (USA) **Mr Roy Taiano**
22 **SOVEREIGNS COURT**, b g Statoblest—Clare Celeste **Whiteways Racing**
23 **STOLEN MUSIC (IRE)**, b f Taufan (USA)—Causa Sua **Whiteways Racing**
24 **TURIA**, b f Slip Anchor—Tura **Mr T. D. Rootes**

TWO-YEAR-OLDS

25 **DRAGON BIRD**, b f 1/5 Chilibang—Charm Bird (Daring March) **Mr J. H. Widdows**
26 **GIFT TOKEN**, b f 12/5 Batshoof—Visible Form (Formidable (USA)) **Mrs D. Ellis**
27 **LIVIUS (IRE)**, b c 10/2 Alzao (USA)—Marie de Beaujeu (FR) (Kenmare (FR)) **Mr C. J. Condon**
28 **LUCKY DIP**, b f 30/4 Tirol—Miss Loving (Northfields) **Mr C. J. Harper**
29 **NASH POINT**, b c 17/4 Robellino (USA)—Embroideress (Stanford) **Mr R. P. B. Michaelson**
30 B c 24/4 Prince Sabo—On Impulse (Jellaby) **Mrs B. Woodford**
31 B f 8/5 Midyan (USA)—Take Heart (Electric) **Mr C. J. Harper**
32 B c 26/2 Reprimand—Tribal Lady (Absalom)

Other Owners: Mr David Alport, Mr D. Fisher, Mr John Lucas, Mrs Francesca Schwarzenbach, Mr Urs E. Schwarzenbach, Sir William R. Stuttaford, Mr Andrew Tolehurst, Mr A. J. B. Vaux, Victor Chandler (Equus) Ltd, Miss Sarah White.

131 MR P. W. CHAPPLE-HYAM, Marlborough

Postal: **Manton House Estate, Manton, Marlborough, SN8 1PN.**
Phone: **(01672) 514901 OR 515294 FAX (01672) 514907**

1 **COURT OF HONOUR (IRE)**, 4, b c Law Society (USA)—Captive Island **Mr R. E. Sangster**
2 **DEFENCE COUNSEL (IRE)**, 4, b c Darshaan—Maryinsky (USA) **Mr R. E. Sangster**
3 **GENERAL MONASH (USA)**, 4, b c Thorn Dance (USA)—Zummerudd **Mr R. E. Sangster**
4 **HOWQUA RIVER**, 4, b g Petong—Deep Blue Sea **Mrs Jane Chapple-Hyam**
5 **PAINTER'S ROW (IRE)**, 4, b c Royal Academy (USA)—
Road To The Top **Lord Weinstock & The Hon Simon Weinstock**
6 **PRINCE ARTHUR (IRE)**, 4, b c Fairy King (USA)—Daniela Samuel (USA) **Mr M. Tabor**
7 **SONG OF TARA (IRE)**, 4, b c Sadler's Wells (USA)—Flame of Tara **Dr A. J. F. O'Reilly**
8 **SPANISH GRANDEE (USA)**, 8, b g El Gran Senor (USA)—Stealthy Lady **Mr R. E. Sangster**
9 **SPECTRUM (IRE)**, 4, b c Rainbow Quest (USA)—River Dancer **Lord Weinstock & The Hon Simon Weinstock**
10 **VARNISHING DAY (IRE)**, 4, b c Royal Academy (USA)—Red Letter Day **Mr R. E. Sangster**

MR P. W. CHAPPLE-HYAM—continued

THREE-YEAR-OLDS

11 **AILESBURY HILL (USA)**, ch f Woodman (USA)—Golden Oriole (USA) **Mr R. E. Sangster**
12 **ALPINE TWIST (USA)**, b f Seattle Dancer (USA)—Polar Bird **Mr R. E. Sangster**
13 **ASTOR PLACE (IRE)**, b c Sadler's Wells (USA)—Broadway Joan (USA) **Mr R. E. Sangster**
14 **AXFORD (USA)**, ch c Woodman (USA)—Timely **Mr R. E. Sangster**
15 **BACKDROP (IRE)**, b c Scenic—Knapping **Mr R. E. Sangster**
16 **CABARET (IRE)**, b f Sadler's Wells (USA)—Chamonis (USA) **Mr Ivan Allan**
17 **CAMPORESE (IRE)**, b f Saddler's Wells (USA)—Campestral (USA) **Mr M. Tabor**
18 **CHALAMONT (IRE)**, ch f Kris—Durtal **Mr R. E. Sangster**
19 **CHARMING TRIBUTE (AUS)**, ch f Rory's Jester (AUS)—Spectacular Gift (USA) **Mr R. E. Sangster**
20 **CHIEF CONTENDER (IRE)**, b c Sadler's Wells (USA)—Minnie Hauk (USA) **Mrs John Magnier**
21 **COMIC'S FUTURE (USA)**, b c Carnivalay (USA)—Destiny's Hour (USA)
22 **COYOTE BLUFF (IRE)**, gr c Fayruz—Ikala **Mr P. W. Chapple-Hyam**
23 **CREST WING (USA)**, b c Storm Bird (CAN)—Purify (USA) **Mr R. E. Sangster**
24 **DESERT BOY (IRE)**, br c Green Desert (USA)—City Fortress **Lord Weinstock & The Hon Simon Weinstock**
25 **DETACHMENT (USA)**, b c Night Shift (USA)—Mumble Peg **Mr R. E. Sangster**
26 **ELITE FORCE (IRE)**, b g Fairy King (USA)—La Petruschka **Mr R. E. Sangster**
27 **HERON ISLAND (USA)**, b c Shirley Heights—Dalawara (USA) **Mr R. E. Sangster**
28 **HIGH BAROQUE (IRE)**, b c High Estate—Alpine Symphony **Mr M. Tabor**
29 **HISMAGICMOMENT (USA)**, b c Proud Birdie (USA)—Affirmed Ambience (USA) **Mr M. Tabor**
30 **INNER CIRCLE (USA)**, ch f El Gran Senor (USA)—Conquistress (USA) **Mr M. Tabor**
31 **LA PELLEGRINA (IRE)**, b f Be My Guest (USA)—Spanish Habit **Mr R. E. Sangster**
32 **LATIN REIGN (USA)**, b br c El Gran Senor (USA)—Love Bunny (USA) **Mr R. E. Sangster**
33 **LEGAL RIGHT (USA)**, b c Alleged (USA)—Rose Red (USA) **Mr R. E. Sangster**
34 **LIONIZE (USA)**, ch c Storm Cat (USA)—Pedestal **Mr M. Tabor**
35 **LOTHLORIEN (USA)**, ch f Woodman (USA)—Fairy Dancer (USA) **Mr R. E. Sangster**
36 **MAZUREK**, b c Sadler's Wells (USA)—Maria Waleska **Mr R. E. Sangster**
37 **MERIBEL (IRE)**, b f Nashwan (USA)—Dark Lomond **Mr R. E. Sangster**
38 **MUSICK HOUSE (IRE)**, b c Sadler's Wells (USA)—Hot Princess **Mr R. E. Sangster**
39 **NAMOUNA (IRE)**, b f Sadler's Wells (USA)—Amaranda (USA) **Mr R. E. Sangster**
40 **NASH HOUSE (IRE)**, b c Nashwan (USA)—River Dancer **Lord Weinstock & The Hon Simon Weinstock**
41 **NIGHT PARADE (USA)**, b c Rory's Jester (AUS)—Nocturnal Song (USA) **Mr R. E. Sangster**
42 **OCEAN GROVE (IRE)**, b f Fairy King (USA)—Leyete Gulf (IRE) **Mr R. E. Sangster**
43 **ORINOCO RIVER (USA)**, ch c El Gran Senor (USA)—Miss Lilian **Mr R. E. Sangster**
44 **POLARIS FLIGHT (USA)**, b c Northern Flagship (USA)—Anytimeatall (USA) **Mr Richard S. Kaster**
45 **REGAL ARCHIVE (USA)**, b c Fairy King (USA)—Marseillaise **Mrs B. V. Sangster**
46 **REINHARDT (IRE)**, b g Bluebird (USA)—Rhein Bridge **Mr R. E. Sangster**
47 **ROYAL COURT (IRE)**, b c Sadler's Wells (USA)—Rose of Jericho (USA) **Mr R. E. Sangster**
48 **SALSINA**, b f Salse (USA)—Aphrosina **Mr B. V. Sangster**
49 **SEA SPRAY (IRE)**, b f Royal Academy (USA)—Sailor's Mate **Lord Weinstock & The Hon Simon Weinstock**
50 **SILK MASQUE (USA)**, b f Woodman (USA)—Silk Slippers (USA) **Mr R. E. Sangster**
51 **SKI ACADEMY (IRE)**, b c Royal Academy (USA)—Cochineal (USA) **Mr R. E. Sangster**
52 **SMILIN N WISHIN (USA)**, b f Lyphard's Wish (FR)—Smilin Michele (USA) **Mr R. E. Sangster**
53 **SMOOTH ASSET (IRE)**, b f Fairy King (USA)—Sofala **Mr A. K. Collins**
54 **SOLO SYMPHONY (IRE)**, ch f Fayruz—Keen Note **Mr B. V. Sangster**
55 **STATE THEATRE (IRE)**, b c Sadler's Wells (USA)—Fruition **Mr R. E. Sangster**
56 **TAKING LIBERTIES (IRE)**, b f Royal Academy (USA)—Lady Liberty (NZ) **Mr R. E. Sangster**
57 **TILLYARD (IRE)**, b f Caerleon (USA)—Royal Heroine **Mr R. E. Sangster**
58 **UPPER GALLERY (IRE)**, b c Sadler's Wells (USA)—Elevate **Mr R. E. Sangster**
59 **WILD RUMOUR (IRE)**, b f Sadler's Wells (USA)—Gossiping (USA) **Mr R. E. Sangster**
60 **WOODBOROUGH (USA)**, ch c Woodman (USA)—Performing Arts **Mr R. E. Sangster**

TWO-YEAR-OLDS

61 B c 23/3 Nureyev (USA)—Absentia (USA) (Raise A Cup (USA)) **Mr R. E. Sangster**
62 **AUTUMN TIME (IRE)**, b f 22/3 Last Tycoon—Cochineal (USA) (Vaguely Noble) **Mr R. E. Sangster**
63 **BURUNDI (IRE)**, b c 23/4 Danehill (USA)—Sofala (Home Guard (USA)) **Mr R. E. Sangster**
64 **CAPTAIN COLLINS (IRE)**, gr c 24/2 El Gran Senor (USA)—Kanmary (Kenmare (FR)) **Mr R. E. Sangster**
65 B c 19/5 Distinctly North—Caring (Crowned Prince) **Mr Ivan Allan**
66 **CARMINE LAKE (IRE)**, ch f 9/2 Royal Academy (USA)—Castillian Queen (Diesis) **Mr R. E. Sangster**
67 B f 30/4 Danehill (USA)—Chamonis (USA) (Affirmed (USA)) **Mr Ivan Allan**

MR P. W. CHAPPLE-HYAM—continued

68 CITY HALL (IRE), b c 29/4 Generous (IRE)—City Fortress (Troy) **Lord Weinstock & The Hon Simon Weinstock**
69 COMIC OPERA (IRE), b f 12/2 Royal Academy (USA)—Miss Toshiba (USA) (Sir Ivor) **Mr R. E. Sangster**
70 COPPERBEECH (IRE), ch f 26/3 Common Grounds—Caimanite (Tap On Wood) **J. Wilson & Dr Anne Gillespie**
71 CORAL SPRINGS (USA), br f 15/2 Minshaanshu Amad—
                                    Distinctiveness (USA) (Distinctive (USA)) **Mr R. E. Sangster**
72 CRYSTAL CROSSING (IRE), b f 5/3 Royal Academy (USA)—Never So Fair (Never So Bold) **Mr R. E. Sangster**
73 CUNNING VIXEN (IRE), b br f 19/2 Machiavellian (USA)—
                                    Sailor's Mate (Shirley Heights) **Lord Weinstock & The Hon Simon Weinstock**
74 DANCES WITH DREAMS, b f 29/3 Be My Chief (USA)—
                                    Oh So Well (IRE) (Sadler's Wells (USA)) **J. Wilson & Dr Anne Gillespie**
75 DAYLIGHT IN DUBAI (USA), ch c 4/4 Twilight Agenda (USA)—
                                    Lady Godolphin (USA) (Son Ange (USA)) **P. D. Savill**
76 Br f 23/3 Nureyev (USA)—Detroit (FR) (Riverman (USA)) **Mr R. E. Sangster**
77 EQUAL RIGHTS (IRE), b c 7/3 Royal Academy (USA)—Lady Liberty (Noble Bijou (USA)) **Mr R. E. Sangster**
78 ETOILE (FR), gr f 26/1 Kris—La Luna (USA) (Lyphard (USA)) **Mrs C. Waters**
79 FINAL STAGE (IRE), ch c 30/3 Shalford (IRE)—Alpine Symphony (Northern Dancer) **Mr R. E. Sangster**
80 FOREIGN RULE (IRE), b c 22/4 Danehill (USA)—Guida Centrale (Teenoso (USA)) **Mr R. E. Sangster**
81 GRAPEVINE (IRE), b f 24/4 Sadler's Wells (USA)—Gossiping (USA) (Chati (USA)) **Mr R. E. Sangster**
82 GULF HARBOUR (IRE), b c 7/6 Caerleon (USA)—Jackie Berry (Connaught) **Mr R. E. Sangster**
83 HIGH EXTREME (IRE), b c 11/5 Danehill (USA)—Rustic Lawn (Rusticaro (FR)) **Mr R. E. Sangster**
84 HURRICANE STATE (USA), ch c 19/2 Miswaki (USA)—Regal State (Affirmed (USA)) **Mr B. V. Sangster**
85 B c 22/2 Storm Bird (CAN)—Ice Prospect (USA) (Icecapade (USA)) **Mr R. E. Sangster**
86 B c 4/4 Storm Bird (CAN)—Ivory Idol (Alydar (USA)) **Mr Ivan Allan**
87 KARASAVINA (IRE), b f 27/5 Sadler's Wells (USA)—Clandestina (Secretariat (USA)) **Mr R. E. Sangster**
88 KINSHIP (IRE), ch c 17/2 In The Wings—
                                    Happy Kin (Bold Hitter (USA)) **Lord Weinstock & The Hon Simon Weinstock**
89 B br c 19/4 Danzig (USA)—Lassie's Lady (Alydar (USA)) **Mr M. Tabor**
90 B c 13/4 Sadler's Wells (USA)—Minnie Hauk (USA) (Sir Ivor) **R. Santulli**
91 NATIVE RHYTHM (IRE), ch f 2/3 Lycius (USA)—Perfect Time (IRE) (Dance of Life (USA)) **Mr B. V. Sangster**
92 NILE VALLEY (IRE), b f 1/5 Royal Academy (USA)—Sphinx (GER) (Alpenkonig (GER)) **Mr R. E. Sangster**
93 Ch c 5/4 El Gran Senor (USA)—Numeral (USA) (Alleged (USA)) **Syndicate**
94 B f 27/2 Gone West (USA)—Out On The Town (USA) (Spend A Buck (USA)) **Mr B. V. Sangster**
95 PANAMA CITY (USA), b c 16/5 El Gran Senor (USA)—Obeah (Cure The Blues (USA)) **Mr R. E. Sangster**
96 B f 30/3 Alleged (USA)—Performing Arts (The Minstrel (CAN)) **Mr R. E. Sangster**
97 B f 19/3 Storm Bird (CAN)—Polar Bird (Thatching) **Mr R. E. Sangster**
98 POLISH WARRIOR (IRE), ch c 29/4 Polish Patriot (USA)—Opuntia (Rousillon (USA)) **Mrs D. Weatherby**
99 RAVEN MASTER (USA), b c 1/5 Shalford (IRE)—Face The Facts (Lomond (USA)) **Mr R. E. Sangster**
100 REVOQUE (IRE), b c 21/1 Fairy King (USA)—La Bella Fontana (Lafontaine (USA)) **Mr R. E. Sangster**
101 RICKENBACKER (IRE), b c 8/2 Bluebird (USA)—Sodium's Niece (Northfields (USA)) **Mr R. E. Sangster**
102 ROMANOV (IRE), b c 1/3 Nureyev (USA)—Morning Devotion (Affirmed (USA)) **Mr R. E. Sangster**
103 B c 14/4 Sadler's Wells (USA)—Rose of Jericho (USA) (Alleged (USA)) **Mr R. E. Sangster**
104 Ch f 20/3 Woodman (USA)—Rose Red (USA) (Northern Dancer) **Mr R. E. Sangster**
105 SEA MIST (IRE), ch f 22/4 Shalford (IRE)—Somnifere (USA) (Nijinsky (USA)) **Mr R. E. Sangster**
106 SELF RULE (USA), b c 28/1 Pleasant Colony (USA)—Musicale (USA) (The Minstrel (CAN)) **Mr R. E. Sangster**
107 SINGLE EMPIRE (IRE), ch c 23/4 Kris—Captive Island (Northfields (USA)) **Mr R. E. Sangster**
108 B br f 21/4 Warning—Sistabelle (Bellypha) **Mr M. Tabor**
109 B c 12/4 Woodman (USA)—Star Pastures (Northfields (USA)) **Mr R. E. Sangster**
110 STONE FLOWER (USA), b f 6/4 Storm Bird (CAN)—
                                    Lively Living (USA) (Key To The Mint (USA)) **Mr R. E. Sangster**
111 TRULY ROYALE (IRE), b f 25/2 Sadler's Wells (USA)—Hot Princess (Hot Spark) **Mr R. E. Sangster**
112 VILLARICA (IRE), b f 19/2 Fairy King (USA)—Bolivia (GER) (Windwurf (GER)) **Mr R. E. Sangster**
113 WARSAW ROAD (IRE), b c 19/3 Polish Precedent—
                                    Road To The Top (Shirley Heights) **Lord Weinstock & The Hon Simon Weinstock**

Other Owners: Bloomsbury Stud, Mr T. Hyde, Mr John T. L. Jones Jr, Mrs John Magnier, Sheikh Mohammed, Mr R. Morgan-Jones, Mrs Jacqueline O'Brien, Mr M. V. O'Brien, Miss P. F. O'Kelly, Miss K. Rausing, H.R.H. Prince Fahd Salman, Mr Gary A. Tanaka.

Jockey (Flat): J Reid (w.a.).

Apprentices: Ryan Cody-Boutcher (7-7), Robert Havlin (7-12).

Lady Rider: Mrs Jane Chapple-Hyam.

132   MR G. F. H. CHARLES-JONES, Wantage

Postal: **The Coach House Stables, Letcombe Regis, Wantage, Oxon, OX12 9LH.**
Phone: **(01235) 767713 CAR (0836) 275292**

1 **BALLYSHEILA**, 4, b f Ayres Rock—Baltana **Mr B. K. Wells**
2 **BURFIELD BOY (IRE)**, 5, b g Eve's Error—Lady Wolver **Mr G. C. Farr**
3 **CEDAR RUN**, 13, b g Billion (USA)—Sapele **Mrs Jessica Charles-Jones**
4 **COBBLERS COOLER**, 11, b g Posse (USA)—Melaleuca **Mrs Jessica Charles-Jones**
5 **CODE OF SILENCE**, 4, br g Adbass (USA)—Keep Silent **Mr G. C. Farr**
6 **HUISH (IRE)**, 5, br g Orchestra—Lysanders Lady **Mr S. P. Tindall**
7 **ITALIAN MAN (IRE)**, 8, b g Don Orazio—Via Del Tabacco **Miss Barbara Murphy**
8 **PRECIOUS JUNO (IRE)**, 7, b m Good Thyne (USA)—Crashing Juno **Miss Barbara Murphy**
9 **SEE YOU ALWAYS (IRE)**, 6, b g Royal Fountain—Lohunda Park **Miss Barbara Murphy**
10 **TROUBLE AT MILL**, 6, ch g White Mill—Rusty Fern **Mr J. L. Brown**
11 **WHATMORECANIASKFOR (IRE)**, 8, ch m Le Bavard (FR)—Blackrath Girl **Mrs Jessica Charles-Jones**
12 **WHIPPERS DELIGHT (IRE)**, 8, ch g King Persian—Crashing Juno **Mr S. P. Tindall**

THREE-YEAR-OLDS

13 **RACHEL'S BOY**, b g Rustingo—Carreg Goch **Mr M. Brown**
14 **VELVET JONES**, gr g Sharrood (USA)—Cradle of Love (USA) **Miss Barbara Murphy**

Other Owners: Mr Clive Brace.

Jockey (NH): W McFarland (10-0).

Conditional: Paul Thompson (9-7).

Amateur: Mr A Charles-Jones (10-0).

133   MR J. I. A. CHARLTON, Stocksfield

Postal: **Mickley Grange, Stocksfield, Northd, NE43 7TB.**
Phone: **(01661) 843247 MOBILE (0850) 007415**

1 **CLAIRABELL (IRE)**, 5, b m Buckskin (FR)—Orient Breeze **Mr W. F. Trueman**
2 **EMERALD CHARM (IRE)**, 8, b m Mister Lord (USA)—Ko Mear **Mrs P. Boynton**
3 **FREETOME**, 8, b m Silly Prices—Who's Free **Mr J. I. A. Charlton**
4 **GAELIC CHARM (IRE)**, 8, b m Deep Run—Jungle Charm **Mrs P. Boynton**
5 **GOLDEN ISLE**, 12, b g Golden Fleece (USA)—Dunette (FR) **Mr John Hogg**
6 **HAGAR**, 7, ch g Viking (USA)—Blue Mistral (USA) **Mr J. I. A. Charlton**
7 **LEIGHTEN LASS (IRE)**, 5, b m Henbit (USA)—Biddy's Opinion **Mrs Susan Corbett**
8 **LORD DORCET (IRE)**, 6, b g Remainder Man—Lady Dorcet **Mr John Hogg**
9 **MULLINGAR (IRE)**, 7, b g Orchestra—Bramble Rose **Mr J. I. A. Charlton**
10 5, Ch g Radical—On The Dry **Mr J. I. A. Charlton**
11 **RADICAL CHOICE (IRE)**, 7, b g Radical—Shule Doe **Mr J. I. A. Charlton**
12 5, B g Nearly A Nose (USA)—Roaming Free **Mr J. I. A. Charlton**
13 **SHAWWELL**, 9, ro g Alias Smith (USA)—Besciamella **Mrs J. J. Straker**
14 **SKI LADY**, 8, b m Myjinski (USA)—Lady Jay **Mr J. W. Robson**
15 **STRONG APPROACH**, 11, br g Strong Gale—Smart Fashion **Mrs R. C. Carr**

TWO-YEAR-OLDS

16 Ch g 16/6 Roselier (FR)—Cathedral Street (Boreen Beag) **Mr J. I. A. Charlton**
17 B g 30/4 Commanche Run—Deverell's Lady (Sterling Bay (SWE)) **Mr J. I. A. Charlton**

Other Owners: Mr Ian C. Carr, Mr Frank Corbett, Mrs Susan Corbett, Mrs R. E. D. Nelson, Mr I. H. Pearson, Mr T. E. Robinson.

Jockey (Flat): Jane Findlay (8-0).

Jockey (NH): B Storey (10-0, w.a.).

134   MR ROGER J. CHARLTON, Beckhampton

Postal: Beckhampton House, Marlborough, Wilts, SN8 1QR.

Phone: **OFFICE (01672) 539533 FAX (01672) 539456 HOME (01672) 539330**

1 **BARON FERDINAND**, 6, ch g Ferdinand (USA)—In Perpetuity **Lady Rothschild**
2 **CAP JULUCA (IRE)**, 4, b c Mtoto—Tabyan (USA) **Mr Martin Myers**
3 **DON CORLEONE**, 4, b c Caerleon (USA)—Dance By Night **Mr Wafic Said**
4 **EASY LISTENING (USA)**, 4, b g Easy Goer (USA)—Queen of Song (USA) **Mr K. Abdulla**
5 **EVERGLADES (IRE)**, 8, b g Green Desert (USA)—Glowing With Pride **Mrs S. Lussier**
6 **MYRTLE QUEST**, 4, b g Rainbow Quest (USA)—Wryneck **Miss M. Sheriffe**
7 **ROYAL CIRCLE**, 4, b f Sadler's Wells (USA)—Queen Midas **Cliveden Stud**
8 **SOURCE OF LIGHT**, 7, b g Rainbow Quest (USA)—De Stael (USA) **Mr K. Abdulla**
9 **SPOUT**, 4, b f Salse (USA)—Arderelle (USA) **Lady Rothschild**

THREE-YEAR-OLDS

10 **AIR QUEST**, b c Rainbow Quest (USA)—Aryenne (FR) **Mr K. Abdulla**
11 **ARIADNE'S WAY**, b f Anshan—Shorthouse **Mrs Alexandra J. Chandris**
12 **ARIETTA'S WAY (IRE)**, b f Darshaan—Captive Island **Mrs Alexandra J. Chandris**
13 **BISCAY**, b f Unfuwain (USA)—Bay Bay **Lady Rothschild**
14 **CHALCUCHIMA**, gr g Reprimand—Ica **Mr Michael Pescod**
15 **CHIEF MOUSE**, b g Be My Chief (USA)—Top Mouse **Lady Vestey**
16 **DOMBEY**, b c Dominion—Arderelle (FR) **Lady Rothschild**
17 **DON VITO**, ch c Generous (IRE)—Dance By Night **Mr Wafic Said**
18 **EXPEDITIOUS WAY (GR)**, br c Wadood (USA)—Maid of Milan **Mrs Alexandra J. Chandris**
19 **FENCER'S QUEST (IRE)**, ch c Bluebird (USA)—Fighting Run **Mr James D. Wolfensohn**
20 **FINE DETAIL (IRE)**, b f Shirley Heights—De Stael (USA) **Mr K. Abdullah**
21 **FLYING GREEN (FR)**, ch g Persian Bold—Flying Sauce **Mr S. M. De Zoete**
22 **GAIN LINE (USA)**, b c Dayjur (USA)—Safe Play (USA) **Mr K. Abdulla**
23 **GOOSEBERRY PIE**, b f Green Desert (USA)—Supper Time **Mrs A. Skiffington**
24 **HIGHLAND GIFT (IRE)**, b f Generous (IRE)—Scots Lass **Lord Weinstock & The Hon Simon Weinstock**
25 **HIGH SUMMER (USA)**, ch f Nureyev (USA)—Miss Summer **Mr K. Abdulla**
26 **INCHYRE**, b f Shirley Heights—Inchmurrin **Mr A. E. Oppenheimer**
27 **INSINCERITY**, ch f Machiavellian (USA)—Queen Midas **Cliveden Stud**
28 **JACKSON HILL**, b c Priolo (USA)—Orange Hill **Mr James D. Wolfensohn**
29 **KING ALEX**, b c Rainbow Quest (USA)—Alexandrie (USA) **Mr Wafic Said**
30 **LATIN QUARTER (USA)**, b c Zilzal (USA)—Artiste **Mr K. Abdulla**
31 **LITTLE BLACK DRESS (USA)**, b f Black Tie Affair (USA)—Seattle Kat (USA) **Mr G. Howard-Spink**
32 **MEDFEE**, b f Alzao (USA)—Liaison (USA) **Mr K. Abdulla**
33 **MYSTIC KNIGHT**, b c Caerleon (USA)—Nuryana **Lady Oppenheimer**
34 **ON THE PISTE**, gr f Shirley Heights—Snowing **Cliveden Stud**
35 **PALAMON (USA)**, ch c Sanglamore (USA)—Gantlette **Mr Michael Pescod**
36 **PRIVATE SONG (USA)**, b c Private Account (USA)—Queen of Song (USA) **Mr K. Abdulla**
37 **PROMPT**, b f Old Vic—In Perpetuity **Lady Rothschild**
38 **REVEUSE DE JOUR (IRE)**, b f Sadler's Wells (USA)—Magic of Life (USA) **Mr S. S. Niarchos**
39 **SPLINTER (IRE)**, b c Warning—Sharpthorne (USA) **Mr K. Abdulla**
40 **SUMMER SPELL (USA)**, b br c Alleged (USA)—Summertime Lady (USA) **W. V. & Mrs E. S. Robins**
41 **TIUTCHEV**, b g Soviet Star (USA)—Cut Ahead **Lady Rothschild**
42 **TRAFALGAR LADY (USA)**, b f Fairy King (USA)—Tremulous (USA) **Mr W. L. Armitage**
43 **VICTIM OF LOVE**, b f Damister (USA)—Tantalizing Song (CAN) **Mr N. Bryce-Smith**
44 **VICTORIAN STYLE**, ch f Nashwan (USA)—Victoriana (USA) **Mr K. Abdulla**
45 **WAYPOINT**, b f Cadeaux Genereux—Princess Athena **Mr Ray Richards**
46 **WIXIM (USA)**, ch c Diesis—River Lullaby (USA) **Mr K. Abdulla**
47 **YALTA (IRE)**, b c Soviet Star (USA)—Gay Hellene **Lord Weinstock & The Hon Simon Weinstock**
48 **YUKON HOPE (USA)**, b f Forty Niner (USA)—Sahara Forest **Cliveden Stud**

TWO-YEAR-OLDS

49 **ABACAXI (IRE)**, b c 17/5 Alzao (USA)—Judicial (USA) (Law Society (USA)) **Lord Vestey**
50 B c 29/3 Sadler's Wells (USA)—Ala Mahlik (Ahonoora) **Mr K. Abdulla**
51 **ALARMIST**, b c 7/3 Warning—Wryneck (Niniski (USA)) **Miss M. Sheriffe/Beckhampton Stables Ltd**
52 B c 12/3 Lyphard (USA)—Alvernia (USA) (Alydar (USA)) **Mr K. Abdulla**

MR ROGER J. CHARLTON—continued

53 **ANCHORED IN LOVE,** b f 27/2 Alzao (USA)—Lyndonville (IRE) (Top Ville) **Mr G. Howard-Spink**
54 **AR HYD Y KNOS,** b f 16/1 Alzao (USA)—Top Table (Shirley Heights) **Mr Derek D. Clee**
55 **AWAY TO ME,** ch f 4/4 Exit To Nowhere—La Nureyeva (USA) (Nureyev (USA)) **The Hon. Mrs D. Joly**
56 **BOSS LADY (IRE),** b f 13/5 Last Tycoon—Queen Helen (Troy) **Lord Weinstock & The Hon Simon Weinstock**
57 **BOW STREET,** ch f 9/4 Rainbow Quest (USA)—In Perpetuity (Great Nephew) **Lady Rothschild**
58 **BURNING TRUTH (USA),** ch c 8/2 Known Fact (USA)—Galega (Sure Blade (USA)) **Mr K. Abdulla**
59 B c 4/1 Be My Guest (USA)—Cantanta (Top Ville) **Mr K. Abdulla**
60 B f 19/1 Dayjur (USA)—Chain Fern (USA) (Blushing Groom (FR)) **Mr K. Abdulla**
61 **COUNTDOWN,** ch c 8/3 Polar Falcon (USA)—Princess Athena (Ahonoora) **Mr Ray Richards**
62 **DANZAS,** b c 4/4 Polish Precedent—Dancing Rocks (Green Dancer (USA)) **Mr A. E. Oppenheimer**
63 B f 12/1 Sadler's Wells (USA)—Darayna (IRE) (Shernazar) **Mrs Alexandra J. Chandris**
64 B f 21/4 Kenmare (FR)—De Stael (USA) (Nijinsky (CAN)) **Mr K. Abdulla**
65 **DIXIE EYES BLAZING (USA),** b f 5/3 Gone West (USA)—
                                              Mariakova (USA) (The Minstrel (CAN)) **Mr G. Howard-Spink**
66 B f 26/4 Pursuit of Love—Eastern Shore (Sun Prince) **Duke of Roxburghe**
67 B f 15/4 Generous (IRE)—Gay Fantastic (Ela-Mana-Mou) **Dr C. Stelling**
68 **GRECIAN BRIDE (IRE),** ch f 8/2 Groom Dancer (USA)—
                                              Greektown (Ela-Mana-Mou) **Lord Weinstock & The Hon Simon Weinstock**
69 **GREEK MOON (IRE),** b f 20/5 Shirley Heights—
                                              Gay Hellene (Ela-Mana-Mou) **Lord Weinstock & The Hon Simon Weinstock**
70 **HIDDEN AGENDA (FR),** b f 28/2 Machiavellian (USA)—Ever Genial (Brigadier Gerard) **Cliveden Stud**
71 **ICY GUEST (USA),** b f 20/4 Clever Trick (USA)—Minstrel Guest (Be My Guest (USA)) **Dr C. Stelling**
72 **INCHOLM,** b c 1/2 Rainbow Quest (USA)—Inchmurrin (Lomond (USA)) **Mr A. E. Oppenheimer**
73 Ch f 12/2 Pursuit Of Love—Intermission (Stage Door Johnny) **Mr K. Abdulla**
74 B c 22/3 Distant Relative—Jamaican Punch (IRE) (Shareef Dancer (USA)) **Mr Wafic Said**
75 B f 19/1 Generous (IRE)—Kajall (USA) (Vaguely Noble) **Mr K. Abdulla**
76 B f 4/2 Lyphard (USA)—Key Dancer (USA) (Nijinsky (CAN)) **Mr K. Abdulla**
77 **LA RONDE,** b f 11/3 Common Grounds—Spun Gold (Thatch (USA)) **Mr N. Bryce-Smith**
78 **LEGENDARY LOVER (IRE),** b c 11/4 Fairy King (USA)—
                                              Broken Romance (IRE) (Ela-Mana-Mou) **Mr Martin Myers**
79 **MAGDALA (IRE),** b f 27/1 Sadler's Wells (USA)—Dalawara (IRE) (Top Ville) **Golden Arrow S. A.**
80 **MAID OF CAMELOT,** br f 22/2 Caerleon (USA)—
                                              Waterfowl Creek (IRE) (Be My Guest (USA)) **Mr A. E. Oppenheimer**
81 **MESSINA (IRE),** b f 28/2 Sadler's Wells (USA)—Magic of Life (USA) (Seattle Slew (USA)) **Mr S. S. Niarchos**
82 Ch c 7/3 Lahib (USA)—Ministra (USA) (Deputy Minister (CAN)) **Mr K. Abdulla**
83 B c 23/2 Quest For Fame—Nifty Fifty (USA) (Honey Jay (USA)) **Mr K. Abdulla**
84 B c 28/2 Sanglamore (USA)—Nurica (USA) (Nureyev (USA)) **Mr K. Abdulla**
85 B c 20/1 Woodman (USA)—Opera Queen (IRE) (Sadler's Wells (USA)) **Mr Wafic Said**
86 **POLYPHONY (USA),** b c 18/5 Cox's Ridge (USA)—Populi (USA) (Star Envoy (USA)) **Mr K. Abdulla**
87 **PRAY (IRE),** b f 19/3 Priolo (USA)—Lady Zi (Manado) **Lady Rothschild**
88 **PRIME MINISTER,** ch c 15/5 Be My Chief (USA)—Classic Design (Busted) **Highclere Thoroughbred Racing Ltd**
89 B c 6/3 Easy Goer (USA)—Queen of Song (His Majesty (USA)) **Mr K. Abdulla**
90 **RIVER PILOT,** b c 9/5 Unfuwain (USA)—Cut Ahead (Kalaglow) **Lady Rothschild**
91 **SAHARA RIVER (USA),** b f 24/2 Riverman (USA)—Sahara Forest (Green Desert (USA)) **Cliveden Stud**
92 Br f 26/1 Warning—Scribbling (USA) (Secretariat (USA)) **Mr K. Abdulla**
93 **SHOP AROUND,** b f 18/3 Rainbow Quest (USA)—Select Sale (Auction Ring (USA)) **Cliveden Stud**
94 **SILVER WHIRL (USA),** br f 16/3 Silver Hawk (USA)—
                                              With A Twist (Fappiano (USA)) **W. V. & Mrs E. S. Robins**
95 **SILVER WIJET (USA),** ch c 3/4 Silver Hawk (USA)—Nijit (Nijinsky (CAN)) **W. V. & Mrs E. S. Robins**
96 **SKEW,** ch f 2/5 Niniski (USA)—Arderelle (FR) (Pharly (FR)) **Lady Rothschild**
97 Ch c 28/1 Diesis—Social Wish (USA) (Lyphard's Wish (FR)) **Mr K. Abdulla**
98 Br c 18/3 Polish Precedent—Sudeley (Dancing Brave (USA)) **Mr K. Abdulla**
99 B f 14/2 Alysheba (USA)—Sunerta (USA) (Roberto (USA)) **Mr K. Abdulla**
100 **SWORD ARM,** b c 25/1 Be My Guest (USA)—Gai Bulga (Kris) **Mr A. E. Oppenheimer**
101 **TAYOVULLIN (IRE),** ch f 20/3 Shalford (IRE)—Fifth Quarter (Cure The Blues (USA)) **Mr A. J. Morrison**
102 **TIDEWATER,** b f 15/1 Shirley Heights—Widows Walk (Habitat) **Mr A. E. Oppenheimer**
103 B f 20/1 Warning—Victoriana (USA) (Storm Bird (CAN)) **Mr K. Abdulla**
104 **WITCHING WELL (IRE),** b f Night Shift—Diamond Spring (Vaguely Noble) **Mr N. Bryce-Smith**

Other Owners: The Queen, Mrs Susan Armitage, Beckhampton Stables Ltd, Mrs M. Bryce-Smith, Hascombe & Valiant Studs, Lady S. M. Rothschild.

Apprentice: Robin Brisland (7-7).

135   MR P. CHEESBROUGH, Bishop Auckland

Postal: **Crawleas, Leasingthorne, Bishop Auckland, Co. Durham, DL14 8EL.**

Phone: **(01388) 720213**

1 **ARIADLER (IRE)**, 8, b g Mister Lord (USA)—Arianrhod **Mr J. A. Stephenson**
2 **BAVARD'S BRIG**, 6, b g Le Bavard (FR)—Sailing Brig **Mr A. S. Corner**
3 **COOL WEATHER (IRE)**, 8, b g Kemal (FR)—Arctic Tack **Mr P. McDonagh**
4 5, Ch g Balinger—Crash Approach **Mr J. A. Stephenson**
5 **DEEP DECISION**, 10, b g Deep Run—Another Dutchess **Mr Alan Cairns**
6 **FORWARD GLEN**, 9, br g Sexton Blake—Daring Glen **Mr P. Cheesbrough**
7 **HEDDON HAUGH (IRE)**, 8, br g Seclude (USA)—Miss Kambalda **Mr I. D. Cheesbrough**
8 **MALTA MAN (IRE)**, 6, b g Lafontaine (USA)—Maltese Queen **Mr J. A. Stephenson**
9 **OVER STATED (IRE)**, 6, b g Strong Statement (USA)—Croase River **Mr J. A. Stephenson**
10 **ROAD BY THE RIVER (IRE)**, 8, ch g Over The River (FR)—Ahadoon **T. P. M. McDonagh Ltd**
11 **STRONGALONG (IRE)**, 6, b g Strong Gale—Cailin Cainnteach **Mr J. A. Stephenson**
12 **STRONG MEASURE (IRE)**, 8, b g Strong Gale—Inch Tape **Leading Star Racing**
13 **STRONG SOUND**, 9, b g Strong Gale—Jazz Music **Mrs H. Scotto**
14 **STYLISH ROSE (IRE)**, 6, b m Don't Forget Me—Cottage Style **Mr T. McDonagh**
15 **TICO GOLD**, 8, ch g Politico (USA)—Derigold **Miss S. J. Turner**
16 6, B g Meneval (USA)—Top Riggin **Mr J. A. Stephenson**
17 **TRUE SCOT (IRE)**, 6, b g Sheer Grit—Highland Worker **Mr J. A. Stephenson**

Other Owners: Mr P. Blanchard, Mr B. Bowles, Mr K. G. Fairbairn, Mr Keith Gammack, Mr Malcolm B. Jones, Mrs M. M. Lewitt, Mr M. McDonagh, T. F. McDonagh & Partners, Mrs W. A. Stephenson.

136   DR D. CHESNEY, Dorchester

Postal: **Cowden, Charminster, Dorchester, Dorset, DT2 9RN.**

Phone: **(01305) 265450 FAX (01305) 250684**

1 **BORIS BAGLEY**, 8, ch g Rymer—Lady Christine **Dr D. Chesney**
2 **MARKSMAN SPARKS**, 6, b g Gunner B—Forty Watts **Dr D. Chesney**
3 4, Ch g Nicholas Bill—Polly Washdish **Dr D. Chesney**

137   MR S. P. L. CHRISTIAN, Severn Stoke

Postal: **The Racing Stables, Kinnersley, Severn Stoke, Worcs, WR8 9JR.**

Phone: **(01905) 371426 FAX (01905) 371553**

1 **BOMBARDIER (IRE)**, 5, b g Royal Fountain—Magic Deer **Mr M. Olden**
2 **CABIN HILL**, 10, ch g Roselier (FR)—Bluejama **The Kinnersley Crew**
3 **CAIPIRINHA (IRE)**, 8, br m Strong Gale—Arctic Moonshine **Karen Roydon Racing Ltd**
4 **CAMITROV (FR)**, 6, b g Sharken (FR)—Emitrovna (FR) **Mr Jim Lewis**
5 **CARRY THE CARD (IRE)**, 5, b g Yashgan—Windy Run **Mr Simon Christian**
6 **GUTTERIDGE (IRE)**, 6, b g Roselier (FR)—Buck's Fairy **BCD Steels Ltd**
7 **HALONA**, 6, b m Pollerton—Premier Susan **Mrs Z. S. Clark**
8 **HAZEL GALE (IRE)**, 7, br m Strong Gale—Morry's Lady **Mr J. R. Holmes**
9 **HE FLIES BY NIGHT**, 7, b g Bold Owl—Premier Susan **Mrs Z. S. Clark**
10 **LADY REBECCA**, 4, b f Rolfe (USA)—Needwood Fortune **The Kinnersley Optimists**
11 **LIME STREET BLUES (IRE)**, 5, b g Digamist (USA)—Royal Daughter **Cheltenham Racing Ltd**
12 **MAURACHAS (IRE)**, 6, ch g Good Thyne (USA)—Fodder Beet VII **Mr R. W. Guilding**
13 **NAKIR (FR)**, 8, b g Nikos—Nabita (FR) **Mr Jim Lewis**
14 **QUADRAPOL**, 7, br m Pollerton—Dream World **Mr C. D. Harrison**
15 **ROYAL REIGN**, 7, b m Ilium—Lac Royale **Mr Simon Christian, Mr W. Smith**
16 **VALERIOS KING (IRE)**, 7, b g Strong Gale—Ariannrun **Valerio's Olympia Group Ltd**
17 **YOUR RISK (IRE)**, 6, b g Tale Quale—Give Us A Breeze **The Sterling Bears**

MR S. P. L. CHRISTIAN—continued

Other Owners: Mr Nigel Babbage, Mr Nicholas Charles Beecroft, Mr Ted Breen, Mr M. Checketts, Mr R. Clarke, Mr G. E. Copeland, Mr D. H. Driscoll, Mr Patrick Hall, Mr G. Heffernan, Dr D. Perks, Mr E. C. Stephens, Mr Ashley Tabony, Mr R. J. Tompkins.

Jockeys (NH): J Osborne (10-0, w.a.), G Upton (10-2).

138   MR S. B. CLARK, Sutton-on-the-Forest

Postal: **Ride Away, Stillington Road, Sutton-on-the-Forest, York, YO6 1EH.**
Phone: **HOME (01347) 810700 CAR (0860) 786104 FAX (01347) 810746**

1 **DEEP DAWN**, 13, br g Deep Run—Sharpaway **Mr S. B. Clark**
2 **MARDOOD**, 11, b g Ela-Mana-Mou—Tigeen **Mr S. B. Clark**

Lady Rider: Miss Ruth Clark (9-7).

139   MR PETER C. CLARKE, Hailsham

Postal: **Merryweathers Farm Stables, Chilsham Lane, Bodle Street, Hailsham, BN27 4QH.**
Phone: **(01323) 832098 FAX (01323) 833852 MOBILE (0836) 744510**

1 **BEE DEE BOY**, 8, b g Julio Mariner—H And K Gambler **Mrs E. M. R. Ludlow**
2 **INSURE**, 18, b g Dusky Boy—Shady Tree **Mr Peter C. Clarke**
3 **LITTLE WOBBLY**, 6, ch m Cruise Missile—Jameena **Miss C. M. Morris**
4 **MISS PARKES**, 7, ch m Mummy's Game—Bonne Baiser **Mr Peter C. Clarke**
5 **SILENT SOVEREIGN**, 7, ch g Kind of Hush—Regency Brighton **Mr D. A. Morris**
6 **STRAIGHT LACED (USA)**, 9, b g Alleged (USA)—Swoonmist (USA) **Mrs E. M. R. Ludlow**
7 **TELF**, 16, ch g Le Bavard (FR)—Vulplume **Mrs E. M. R. Ludlow**
8 **VICTORY ANTHEM**, 10, ch g Tug of War—Anvil Chorus **P. Gray Limited**

THREE-YEAR-OLDS

9 **CARWYN'S CHOICE**, b f Then Again—Over My Head **Second Chance Racing**
10 **PEEGRAYCO CHOICE**, b f Bold Fox—Unjha

Other Owners: Mr K. R. Sprange, Mr R. K. Sprange.

Jockey (Flat): N Adams.

Jockey (NH): B Powell.

Conditional: B Fenton.

Amateur: Mr P C Clarke (10-4).

140   MR W. CLAY, Stoke-on-Trent

Postal: **Saverley House Farm, Saverley Green, Cresswell, Stoke-on-Trent, ST11 9QX.**
Phone: **(01782) 392131**

1 **ASTRAL INVASION (USA)**, 5, ch g Risen Star (USA)—Santiki **Ed Weetman, Reynolds and Dean**
2 **BANANA COVE (IRE)**, 5, b g Shirley Heights—Tapaculo **Mr G. F. Cheney**
3 **BEECHFIELD FLYER**, 5, ch g Northern State (USA)—Djimbaran Bay **Mrs M. Robertson**

MR W. CLAY—continued

4 **CAVIL**, 4, b c Reprimand—Lagta **Mr D. Ashbrook**
5 **CHARLIESMEDARLIN**, 5, b g Macmillion—Top Cover **Middleton Scriven Investments Ltd**
6 **CHARTERFORHARDWARE**, 10, b g Furry Glen—Vulgan Thistle **Charter Racing Ltd**
7 **COURT CIRCULAR**, 7, b g Miswaki (USA)—Round Tower **Mr P. Lines**
8 **ERLEMO**, 7, b g Mummy's Game—Empress Catherine **Mr T. F. O'Malley**
9 **FRANS LAD**, 4, ch g Music Boy—Moberry **Mr W. Robinson**
10 **GREENACRES STAR**, 6, ch m Seymour Hicks (FR)—Greenacres Girl **Mr M. J. Talbot**
11 **JASONS FARM**, 6, ch g Saxon Farm—Quay Seat **Mr T. R. Darlington**
12 **KADARI**, 7, b m Commanche Run—Thoughtful **Mr H. Clewlow**
13 **LUKS AKURA**, 8, b g Dominion—Pacificus (USA) **Middleton Scriven Investments Ltd**
14 **MAMNOON (USA)**, 5, b g Nijinsky (CAN)—Continual (USA) **Lucky Seven Racing Club**
15 **MAN OF THE GRANGE**, 10, b br g Mandalus—Lass O Grange **Mr Richard J. Marshall**
16 **NIGHT BOAT**, 5, b g Night Shift (USA)—Billante (USA) **M. Bray-Cotton, V. Lockley & J. Davies**
17 **NORTHERN NATION**, 8, b g Nomination—Ballagarrow Girl **Ed Weetman (Haulage & Storage) Ltd**
18 **ORANGE EXTREME**, 5, b m Superlative—Suddenly Amber (USA) **Mr J. Craystone**
19 **PERIROYAL**, 6, ch g Royal Vulcan—Periplus **Mr V. Wilson**
20 **PINXTON POPPY**, 6, b m Son of Shaka—Penwood **Mr J. C. Archer**
21 **POLLERTON'S PRIDE**, 9, b m Pollerton—Arctic Snow Cat **Mr G. A. Greaves**
22 **PRUSSIA**, 5, b h Roi Danzig (USA)—Vagrant Maid (USA) **The Prussia Partnership**
23 **RIVERBANK RED**, 5, ch m Lighter—Gypsy Louise **Mr G. Wheildon**
24 **RIVERBANK ROSE**, 5, b m Lighter—Queen of Gypsy's **Mr G. Wheildon**
25 **SAYANT**, 11, b g Sayyaf—Bodnant **Mr T. Walker**
26 **SCOTTISH WEDDING**, 6, b m Scottish Reel—Pearl Wedding **Mrs G. A. Weetman**
27 **SINGING SCALLY**, 5, gr m Scallywag—Singing Kettle **Mr S. Adams**
28 **SKITTLE ALLEY**, 10, b g Adonijah—Skittish (USA) **Mr P. Riley**
29 **TEST MATCH**, 9, ch g Glenstal (USA)—Reprint **Mr K. J. Oulton**
30 **VIAGGIO**, 8, b g High Line—Al Washl (USA) **Mr K. G. Martin**
31 **WORLD WITHOUT END (USA)**, 7, ch g World Appeal (USA)—Mardie's Bid (USA) **B. A. S. Limited**

Other Owners: Mr N. Brown, Mr Dave Lane, Mr R. Parton, Mr T. J. Smith.

Amateur: Guy Lewis (9-11).

141   MR NICOLAS CLEMENT, Chantilly

Postal: **37, Avenue de Joinville, 60500 Chantilly, France.**
Phone: **44 57 59 60** FAX **44 57 70 84**

1 **DEBBIE'S LAW (IRE)**, 5, b m Law Society—Debbie's Next **Mme D. Norton**
2 **LADY BINN (IRE)**, 4, b f Bluebird—Sexy Lady **M. Binn**
3 **LUDGATE (USA)**, 4, b f Lyphard—Hatton Gardens **Lord Matthews**
4 **OPHIRA**, 4, b f Old Vic—Sephira **P. N. Rossier**
5 **SACRED FIRE**, 4, b c Saumarez—Miracle of Love **S. Niarchos**

THREE-YEAR-OLDS

6 **ADMIRALTY (FR)**, b g Green Desert—Absolute **Mme O'Reilly**
7 **ANTIOPA (FR)**, ch f Dancing Spree—Anahita **Mme P. Chedeville**
8 **BELGETTI (FR)**, br f Dancing Spree—Parannda **M. Binn**
9 **BLUE GOOSE**, ch f Belmez—Tundra Goose **Sheikh Mohammed**
10 **BRITANY (FR)**, b f Galetto—Bid Fair **A. Leonardi**
11 **CHRONOGRAPH**, b c Rainbow Quest—Zabelina **B. Freiha & G. Farha**
12 **COMMANCHE COURT (IRE)**, ch c Commanche Run—Sorceress **A. Crichton**
13 **COMME UNE FABLE (FR)**, b f Priolo—Lyceana **Ecurie Skymarc**
14 **ESAMIX (FR)**, gr c Linamix—Eau de Nuit **Mme G. de Chatelperron**
15 **FLYWAY (FR)**, b c Priolo—Flying Circus **Mme O'Reilly**
16 **HONORED (USA)**, ch c Academy Award—Stated **J. Mack Robinson**
17 **JASMINOLA (FR)**, b f Seattle Dancer—Jasm **M. Binn**

MR NICOLAS CLEMENT—continued

18 **JOYEUX DANSEUR (USA)**, b c Nureyev—Fabuleux Jane **Wayne B. Hughes**
19 **LAGOS (FR)**, gr c Linamix—Nashra **D. M. Kendall**
20 **LANDLER**, b c Shareef Dancer—Les Dancelles **Sheikh Mohammed**
21 **LITANEA (FR)**, gr f Linamix—Celeste Grimm **Ecurie Skymarc**
22 **MAROUSSIE (FR)**, br f Saumarez—Madiyma **J. F. Malle**
23 **MEDIANTE (FR)**, gr f Linamix—Takalaia **P. N. Rossier**
24 **O'TANGO (FR)**, br f Fijar Tango—Overdose **A. F. S. Li**
25 **PAIX ROYALE**, ch f Royal Academy—Play Or Pay **Ecurie Skymarc**
26 **POLENT**, b f Polish Precedent—Awaasif **Sheikh Mohammed**
27 **PRINCESSE BILBAO (FR)**, br f Highest Honor—Princesse Player **J. F. Malle**
28 **PRIVACY**, b f Priolo—Copt Hall Princess **Ecurie Skymarc**
29 **PURE SWING**, b c Shareef Dancer—Mrs Warren **Saif Ali**
30 **STAGE PASS**, ch c In The Wings—Sateen **Sheikh Mohammed**
31 **THISVI (FR)**, b f Saumarez—Pressure **C. Karpidas**
32 **VOL AU VENT**, b c In The Wings—Valuable **Mme O'Reilly**

TWO-YEAR-OLDS

33 Ch f 4/3 Blushing John—Andora (Conquistador Cielo) **Mme de Moratalla**
34 **ANGE ROUGE**, ch f 4/2 Priolo—Arriance (Gay Mecene) **Ecurie Skymarc**
35 Ch f 6/2 Imp Society—Barncogue (Monseigneur) **A. Crichton**
36 Ch f 7/1 Blushing John—Campechito (Olden Times) **A. Crichton**
37 **CARAVAGGIO (FR)**, ch c 27/2 Priolo—Charara (Top Command) **P. Le Blan**
38 **CAZAROONIE (FR)**, b f 25/3 Lahib—Guapa (Shareef Dancer) **M. Binn**
39 **COSTAR COMING (FR)**, br c 26/5 Pampabird—Nashra (Brustolon) **P. N. Rossier**
40 **CRASY DEB (FR)**, b f 29/1 Exit To Nowhere—Muirfield (Crystal Glitters) **A. de Ganay**
41 **CRAVATTE NOIRE (USA)**, b f Black Tie Affair—Nuryette (Nureyev) **Ecurie Skymarc**
42 **DESIDERIO (FR)**, b c 29/4 Pistolet Bleu—Rose River (Riverman) **P. N. Rossier**
43 **DIX HUIT CARATS (FR)**, b c 8/2 Kenmare—Dictania (Iron Duke) **C. Karpidas**
44 **ELMO (FR)**, gr c Linamix—Salve (Sallust) **P. N. Rossier**
45 B c 8/5 El Gran Senor—Gondole (Riverman) **S. Niarchos**
46 **HARKNESS WARRIOR (USA)**, b c 20/3 Geiger Counter—Judaire's Mint (Key To The Mint) **M. Silver**
47 **HEAVEN'S COMMAND**, b f 29/1 Priolo—Heavenly Music (Seattle Song) **Ecurie Skymarc**
48 **HERODOTOS (FR)**, gr c 5/5 Kaldoun—Griotte (Sir Ivor) **C. Karpidas**
49 B f 5/4 Local Talent—Hint of Intrigue (Far Out East) **A. Crichton**
50 **LACE FLOWER**, b f 5/2 Old Vic—Lighted Glitters (Crystal Glitters) **Mme O'Reilly**
51 **LA DEUXIEME FOIS (IRE)**, b f 3/2 Mujadil—Choral Park (Music Boy) **Ecurie Panache Blanc**
52 **LUCKY DREAM**, b c 1/2 Homme de Loi—Lady of The House (Habitat) **Mme M. Guerrico**
53 **LYRIQUE (USA)**, b c 17/3 Alleged—Lirica (Blushing Groom) **Mme O'Reilly**
54 **MAKE MY DAY (FR)**, b f 11/4 Akarad—Masada (Jimmy Reppin) **S. Svenby**
55 **NOUVEL ESPOIR (FR)**, b c 7/3 Saumarez—Fiasco Argento (Silver Hawk) **J. F. Malle**
56 Ch c 17/2 Arazi—Optimistic Lass (Mr Prospector) **Sheikh Mohammed**
57 **PARTIE (FR)**, br f 14/2 L'Emigrant—Parga (Gay Mecene) **Mme O'Reilly**
58 **PAVENTIA (USA)**, ch f 7/2 Trempolino—Patricia (Assert) **Sheikh Mohammed**
59 **QUICKFAST (FR)**, b c 8/4 Exit To Nowhere—Sparkling Plenty (Crystal Glitters) **J. F. Malle**
60 **STOWAWAY (USA)**, ch c 24/5 Strawberry Road—Slam Bid (Forli) **Ecurie Skymarc**
61 Ch f 27/3 Groom Dancer—Tsar Maiden (Nijinsky) **Sheikh Mohammed**

142 MR T. T. CLEMENT, Newmarket

Postal: **Calder Park, Hamilton Road, Newmarket, Suffolk.**

Phone: **(01638) 561384**

1 **ADONISIS**, 4, b c Emarati (USA)—Kind Lady **The John Peters Adonisis Syndicate**
2 **ARABIAN FLIGHT**, 4, ch c Sayf El Arab (USA)—Smooth Flight **Mrs C. Clement**
3 **COMMANDER TOM**, 7, ch g Jester—Girl Commander **Miss R. J. Bryant**
4 **EZEKIEL**, 5, ch g Be My Guest (USA)—Judeah **Mr N. J. Hurrell**
5 **JONBEL**, 8, b g Norwick (USA)—Two Shots **Mr Ian Pattle**
6 **LE BAM BAM**, 4, ch c Emarati (USA)—Lady Lustre **John Peters Le Bam Bam Syndicate**

MR T. T. CLEMENT—continued

7 **L'ENCHERE**, 11, b m Lafontaine (USA)—Lady Bidder **Racing Thoroughbreds Plc**
8 **LUNAR PRINCE**, 6, b g Mansingh (USA)—Lunate **Mr R. Ghyllebert**
9 **MAGIC LEADER (IRE)**, 4, b br g Architect (USA)—Magic Rotation (USA) **Mr Ian Pattle**
10 **MD THOMPSON**, 4, ch f Siberian Express (USA)—Zipperti Do **Mr Maurice Kirby**
11 **PATTLES PIPEDREAM (IRE)**, 4, b g Classic Secret (USA)—Melting Snows **Mr Ian Pattle**
12 **QUIET AMUSEMENT (USA)**, 5, ch m Regal And Royal (USA)—My Little Guest **Mr Roger Langley**
13 **QUIVIRA**, 5, ch m Rainbow Quest (USA)—Nobly Born (USA) **Mr Maurice Kirby**
14 **SCORPIUS**, 6, b h Soviet Star (USA)—Sally Brown **Mrs C. Clement**
15 **TROJAN RED**, 6, ch h Trojan Legend—Equatious **Mrs Iris S. Robert**
16 **WONDERFUL DAY**, 5, b m Niniski (USA)—Zipperti Do **Mr Maurice Kirby**
17 **ZESTI**, 4, br g Charmer—Lutine Royal **Miss R. J. Bryant**

THREE-YEAR-OLDS

18 **CASINO CHIP**, br c Daring March—Important Guest **Mr C. Deadman**
19 **KAYJEMIR**, ch f La Grange Music—Copper Burn **Mr J. Knowles**
20 **ORDAINED**, b f Mtoto—In The Habit (USA) **Mr Roger Langley**
21 **PLENTY OF SUNSHINE**, ch f Pharly (FR)—Zipperti Do **Mr Maurice Kirby**
22 B g Puissance—Rose Barton **Treasure Seekers Partnership**
23 **RUSHCUTTER BAY**, br c Mon Tresor—Llwy Bren **Treasure Seekers Partnership**
24 **STATIC LOVE**, b f Statoblest—Run For Love **Mr Maurice Kirby**

Other Owners: Mr F. B. Barnes, Mr S. F. P. Gilligan, Mr John Peters, Mrs Katherine Peters, Miss J. Pettingale, Mr G. D. Thompson.

Amateurs: Mr R Barrett (9-0), Mr V Lukaniuk (9-0).

143   MR K. F. CLUTTERBUCK, Royston

Postal: **The Greenings, Foxfield Farm, Fowlmere Road, Melbourn, SG8 6EZ.**
Phone: **(01763) 263143**

1 5, B g Persian Mews—Auntie Bee **Mr K. F. Clutterbuck**
2 **JIMSTRO**, 11, b g Jimsun—Bistro Blue **Mr K. F. Clutterbuck**
3 **MY-CE-BON**, 5, gr m Abutammam—Satin Silk (USA) **Mr K. F. Clutterbuck**
4 **PRETTY BOY GEORGE**, 7, ch g St Columbus—Sea Farmer **Mr K. F. Clutterbuck**
5 **SADEEMAR**, 4, ch f Sadeem (USA)—Cauchemar **Mr K. F. Clutterbuck**
6 4, B f Abutammam—Satin Silk (USA) **Mr K. F. Clutterbuck**
7 **THATS SHOWBUSINESS**, 6, ch m Celtic Cone—Cauchemar **Mr K. F. Clutterbuck**
8 **THEYDON PRIDE**, 7, ch g Oats—Cavaleuse **Mr K. F. Clutterbuck**
9 **WILLINGLY (IRE)**, 6, ch m Master Willie—Soon To Be **Mr K. F. Clutterbuck**

144   MR D. H. CLYDE M.R.C.V.S., Antrim

Postal: **Craigs Stud, Ballyclare, Co. Antrim, BT39 9DE, Ireland.**
Phone: **(01960) 322327**

1 **ABDULLAH BULBUL**, 8, b g Tina's Pet—Shercol **D. H. Clyde**
2 **BONNY WOOD GREEN (IRE)**, 8, b g Bustomi—Red House Lady
3 **CLOONYQUIN (IRE)**, 6, b g Bustomi—Mattress
4 **COULTERS HILL (IRE)**, 8, b g Bustomi—Birdcage
5 6, B m Bustomi—Donnabimba
6 **KATHERINE KATH**, 5, b m Merdon Melody—Krafty Kate
7 **MRS BROLLY (IRE)**, 5, br m Bustomi—Worling-Pearl
8 **SUDDEN SALLY (IRE)**, 5, br m Bustomi—Donnabimba
9 **THE DARGLE (IRE)**, 6, b g Bustomi—Worling-Pearl

Lady Rider: Miss E Hyndman (9-0).

145   MR S. COATHUP, Neston

Postal: **The Crows Nest, New Hall Farm, Chester High Road, Neston, L64 3TE.**
Phone: **(0151) 3368911**

1 **BUSHEHR (IRE)**, 4, b c Persian Bold—Shejrah (USA) **Mrs J. Coathup**
2 **COME ON CHARLIE**, 7, b g Reesh—Karyobinga **Mr Sidney Eaton**
3 **GHOSTLY GLOW**, 7, gr g Kalaglow—Amerella **Mr Douglas W. Jones**
4 **INTO THE MYSTIC**, 14, br g Kemal (FR)—Rochetta **Mrs J. Coathup**
5 **JALORE**, 7, gr g Jalmood (USA)—Lorelene (FR) **Wirral Racing II**
6 **MRSUNVALLEYPEANUTS**, 10, b g Le Moss—Quit The Hassle **Sun Valley Ltd**
7 **PATS DELIGHT**, 4, ch f Crofthall—Petroc Concert **Patrick Fennelly / Nancy Brook**
8 **ROYAL CELT**, 12, ch m Celtic Cone—Doubly Royal **Mr G. J. White**
9 **TARSID**, 4, ch c Indian Forest (USA)—Small Fee **Mr Sidney Eaton**
10 **THE TITAN GHOST**, 7, ch g Nicholas Bill—Holloway Wonder **Mr R. Cowie**

Other Owners: Dr N. M. Brook, Mr W. G. Graham, Mr J. J. McIntyre, Mr Clive R. Tomlinson, Mr G. M. Wilkins.

Jockey (Flat): T Williams (w.a).

Jockeys (NH): R Dunwoody (w.a), R Greene (w.a.).

Conditional: Mark Brown (9-0).

146   MR R. G. COCKBURN, Carlisle

Postal: **Stonecroft, High Ireby, Carlisle, Cumbria, CA5 1HF.**

1 **ELASTIC**, 10, b m Ela-Mana-Mou—Queen of The Dance **Mrs D. Cockburn**
2 **MY MISSILE**, 6, ch m Kabour—Miss Emily **Mrs D. Cockburn**
3 **SILVER SHILLING**, 9, gr g Sonnen Gold—Continental Divide **Mrs D. Cockburn**

147   MR P. F. I. COLE, Whatcombe

Postal: **Whatcombe Estate, Whatcombe, Wantage, Oxon, OX12 9NW.**
Phone: **(01488) 638433 FAX (01488) 638609**

1 **CHAHAYA TIMOR (IRE)**, 4, b g Slip Anchor—Roxy Hart **H.R.H. Sultan Ahmad Shah**
2 **DANCE SO SUITE**, 4, b g Shareef Dancer (USA)—Three Piece **Mr J. S. Gutkin**
3 **GENERAL SIR PETER (IRE)**, 4, br g Last Tycoon—Nashya **Mr Yahya Nasib**
4 **GREEN PERFUME (USA)**, 4, b c Naevus (USA)—Pretty Is (USA) **Lord Sondes**
5 **INDRAPURA (IRE)**, 4, b g Gallic League—Stella Ann **H.R.H. Sultan Ahmad Shah**
6 **INZAR (USA)**, 4, b c Warning—Czar's Bride (USA) **H.R.H. Prince Fahd Salman**
7 **MERIT (IRE)**, 4, b c Rainbow Quest (USA)—Fur Hat **H.R.H. Prince Fahd Salman**
8 **MONARCH**, 4, b c Sadler's Wells (USA)—Bint Pasha (USA) **H.R.H. Prince Fahd Salman**
9 **MONTJOY (USA)**, 4, b c Manila (USA)—Wendy's Ten (USA) **Sir George Meyrick**
10 **PERSIAN ELITE (IRE)**, 5, ch g Persian Heights—Late Sally **Elite Racing Club**
11 **POSIDONAS**, 4, b c Slip Anchor—Tamassos **Mr Athos Christodoulou**
12 **PRECEDE (IRE)**, 4, b c Polish Precedent (USA)—Height of Passion **Mr Anthony Speelman**
13 **RIYADIAN**, 4, ch c Polish Precedent (USA)—Knight's Baroness **H.R.H. Prince Fahd Salman**
14 **ROMIOS (IRE)**, 4, ch c Common Grounds—Domino's Nurse **Mr C. Shiacolas**
15 **ROYAL SCIMITAR (USA)**, 4, ch c Diesis—Princess of Man **H.R.H. Prince Fahd Salman**
16 **SALMON LADDER (USA)**, 4, b c Bering—Ballerina Princess (USA) **Mr M. Arbib**
17 **SERIOUS OPTION (IRE)**, 5, b g Reprimand—Top Bloom **Lord Portman**
18 **SILENCE IN COURT (IRE)**, 5, b h Law Society (USA)—Fair Flutter **Mr Peter G. Freeman**
19 **SPECIAL BEAT**, 4, b f Bustino—Special Guest **Mr C. Marner**

MR P. F. I. COLE—continued

20 STAR MANAGER (USA), 6, b g Lyphard (USA)—Angel Clare (FR) **Mr M. Arbib**
21 STRATEGIC CHOICE (USA), 5, b h Alleged (USA)—Danlu (USA) **Mr M. Arbib**
22 SWEET PAVLOVA (USA), 4, b f Zilzal (USA)—Meringue Pie (USA) **Mr M. Arbib**

THREE-YEAR-OLDS

23 ALZANTI, b c Alzao (USA)—Mumtaz Flyer (USA) **Elite Racing Club**
24 AMBER FORT, gr g Indian Ridge—Lammastide **Lord Portman**
25 BARON HRABOVSKY, ch g Prince Sabo—Joli's Girl **Black Run Racing Club**
26 BRECON, b br c High Estate—No Can Tell (USA) **Mr D. J. Deer**
27 BRILLIANT RED, b c Royal Academy (USA)—Red Comes Up (USA) **H.R.H. Prince Fahd Salman**
28 CASCADIA (IRE), br f Caerleon (USA)—Flood (USA) **H.R.H. Prince Fahd Salman**
29 CEBWOB, br f Rock City—Island Ruler **Mr C. M. Budgett**
30 CHALK DUST (USA), b f Unbridled—Charmie Carmie (USA) **Mr Christopher Wright**
31 CHARWELTON, b f Indian Ridge—Bazaar Promise **Mr Bernard Gover**
32 CORPORAL NYM (USA), gr c Cozzene (USA)—Fiji Fan (USA) **Sir George Meyrick**
33 CRAZY CHIEF, b c Indian Ridge—Bizarre Lady **Mr David J. Simpson**
34 DISMISSED (USA), b c Dayjur—Bemissed (USA) **H.R.H. Prince Fahd Salman**
35 EL OPERA (IRE), b f Sadler's Wells (USA)—Ridge The Times (USA) **Mr Faisal Salman**
36 EMY COASTING (USA), b f El Gran Senor (USA)—Coast Patrol (USA) **Mr Craig B. Singer**
37 EVIDENCE IN CHIEF, b f Be My Chief (USA)—Ominous **Mr Raymond Tooth**
38 FAIRLIGHT DOWN (USA), b f Dayjur (USA)—Stresa **Sir Andrew Lloyd Webber**
39 FILMORE WEST, b c In The Wings—Sistabelle **Mr Christopher Wright**
40 FIRST LAW, ch f Primo Dominie—Barsham **Mr Raymond Tooth**
41 GENTILHOMME, ch c Generous (IRE)—Bold Flawless (USA) **H.R.H. Prince Fahd Salman**
42 INFAMOUS (USA), ch c Diesis—Name And Fame (USA) **H.R.H. Prince Fahd Salman**
43 KUALA LIPIS (USA), b c Lear Fan (USA)—Caerna (USA) **H.R.H. Sultan Ahmad Shah**
44 KUANTAN (USA), b g Gone West (USA)—Cuddly Doll (USA) **H.R.H. Sultan Ahmad Shah**
45 LEAR JET (USA), b c Lear Fan (USA)—Lajna **H.R.H. Prince Fahd Salman**
46 LEONINE (IRE), gr c Danehill (USA)—Inanna **H.R.H. Prince Fahd Salman**
47 LIONEL EDWARDS (IRE), b g Polish Patriot (USA)—Western Heights **Richard Green (Fine Paintings)**
48 MA BELLE POULE, b f Slip Anchor—The Kings Daughter **Mr M. J. Simmonds**
49 MACMORRIS (USA), b c Silver Hawk (USA)—Andover Cottage (USA) **Sir George Meyrick**
50 MAGIC MELODY, b f Petong—Miss Rossi **Mr M. Olden**
51 MILTON, ch c Groom Dancer (USA)—Gold Flair **H.R.H. Prince Fahd Salman**
52 MOST WANTED (IRE), ch f Priolo (USA)—Dewan's Niece **Mr Christopher Wright**
53 MOUNTAIN DREAM, b c Batshoof—Echoing **Mr I. Helou**
54 OLEAMA (IRE), b f Alzao (USA)—Buraida **H.R.H. Prince Fahd Salman**
55 PACIFIC GROVE, b f Persian Bold—Dazzling Heights **Elite Racing Club**
56 PERFECT GIFT, ch f Generous (IRE)—Knight's Baroness **H.R.H. Prince Fahd Salman**
57 PRESENT ARMS (USA), b c Affirmed (USA)—Au Printemps (USA) **H.R.H. Prince Fahd Salman**
58 QUEEN'S INSIGNIA (USA), b f Gold Crest (USA)—Years (USA) **Mr W. H. Ponsonby**
59 RED LEO (USA), b c Crafty Prospector (USA)—Lucky Brook **Mr Terry Neill**
60 ROUGE RANCON (USA), b f Red Ransom (USA)—Lady O'Lyph **Mr Christopher Wright**
61 SIBBERTOFT (IRE), b f Shaadi (USA)—Rossnagran **Mr Bernard Gover**
62 SMILE FOREVER (USA), b f Sunshine Forever (USA)—Awenita **Blandford Thoroughbreds**
63 SQUANDAMANIA, b c Ela-Mana-Mou—Garden Pink (FR) **Mr M. Arbib**
64 SUPAMOVA (USA), b f Seattle Slew (USA)—Maximova (FR) **Mr M. Arbib**
65 SWEET TIMES, ch f Riverman (USA)—Affection Affirmed (USA) **H.R.H. Prince Fahd Salman**
66 SWIFT FANDANGO (USA), b c Lear Fan (USA)—Danlu (USA) **Mr M. Arbib**
67 TRILBY, b f In The Wings—Fur Hat **H.R.H. Prince Fahd Salman**
68 TWENTYFORTEN (IRE), ch c Be My Guest (USA)—Safe Home **H.R.H. Sultan Ahmad Shah**
69 WHITE SEA (IRE), ch f Soviet Lad (USA)—Bilander **Mr T. M. Hely-Hutchinson**

TWO-YEAR-OLDS

70 AZORES, b c 8/3 Polish Precedent—Shirley Superstar (Shirley Heights) **H.R.H. Prince Fahd Salman**
71 BADLESMERE (USA), b c 13/3 Geiger Counter—Arising (USA) (Secreto (USA)) **Lord Sondes**
72 B f 9/2 Personal Flag (USA)—Balakhna (FR) (Tyrant (USA)) **Mr Christopher Wright**
73 BARRIER KING, b c Sovereign Dancer (USA)—Coastal Jewel (IRE) (Kris) **Allsport Barrier Systems Ltd**
74 B c 10/5 Polar Falcon (USA)—Barsham (Be My Guest (USA)) **P. F. I. Cole Ltd**
75 BELGRAVIA, b c 31/3 Rainbow Quest (USA)—
          Affection Affirmed (USA) (Affirmed (USA)) **H.R.H. Prince Fahd Salman**

MR P. F. I. COLE—continued

76 **BINTANG TIMOR (USA)**, ch c 1/2 Mt Livermore (USA)—
Frisky Kitten (USA) (Isopach (USA)) **H.R.H. Sultan Ahmad Shah**
77 **CALAMANDER (IRE)**, b f 21/4 Alzao (USA)—
Local Custom (IRE) (Be My Native (USA)) **The Philip Blacker Studio Partnership**
78 **CLEAR THE AIR**, ch f 24/3 Salse (USA)—Belle Enfant (Beldale Flutter (USA)) **Mr W. H. Ponsonby**
79 **DAME LAURA (IRE)**, b f 10/4 Royal Academy (USA)—Aunty (FR) (Riverman (USA))
80 B f 17/2 Robellino (USA)—Danzig Harbour (USA) (Private Account (USA)) **P. F. I. Cole Ltd**
81 **DARK GREEN (USA)**, ch c 25/1 Green Dancer (USA)—
Ardisia (USA) (Affirmed (USA)) **H.R.H. Prince Fahd Salman**
82 **DEEP WATER (USA)**, b c 18/1 Diesis—Water Course (USA) (Irish River (FR)) **H.R.H. Prince Fahd Salman**
83 C 5/2 Red Ransom (USA)—Dream Creek (USA) (The Minstrel (CAN)) **Al Muallim Partnership**
84 **ELRIYADH (USA)**, b c 3/2 Time For A Change—
All My Memories (USA) (Little Current (USA)) **H.R.H. Prince Fahd Salman**
85 B c 30/3 Polar Falcon (USA)—Epure (Bellypha) **Mr Christopher Wright**
86 **FAIR RELATION**, b f 28/4 Distant Relative—Gold Flair (Tap On Wood) **H.R.H. Prince Fahd Salman**
87 **FAREWELL MY LOVE (IRE)**, b f 14/3 Waajib—So Long Boys (FR) (Beldale Flutter (USA)) **Mr W. H. Ponsonby**
88 **FLAME OF GLORY**, ch c 7/5 Polish Precedent—Danishkada (Thatch) **H.R.H. Prince Fahd Salman**
89 **FLETCHER**, b c 24/1 Salse (USA)—Ballet Classique (USA) (Sadler's Wells (USA)) **H.R.H. Prince Fahd Salman**
90 **FORETELL**, b f 4/3 Tirol—Foreno (Formidable (USA)) **Mr W. H. Ponsonby**
91 **GRANNY'S PET**, ch c 9/2 Selkirk (USA)—Patsy Western (Precocious) **Mrs D. M. Arbib**
92 B c 2/4 Tirol—Hemline (Sharpo) **Mr J. S. Gutkin**
93 **HINT**, b c 12/3 Warning—Throw Away Line (USA) (Assert) **Highclere Thoroughbred Racing Ltd**
94 **ISLE OF MAN (USA)**, b c 19/3 Manila—Princess of Man (Green God) **H.R.H. Prince Fahd Salman**
95 **JAYZAN**, b c 26/2 Selkirk (USA)—Land of Ivory (USA) (The Minstrel (CAN)) **H.R.H. Prince Fahd Salman**
96 **JUDE**, b f 12/2 Darshaan—Alruccaba (Crystal Palace (FR)) **H.R.H. Prince Fahd Salman**
97 **LONDON LIGHTS**, b c 23/2 Slip Anchor—Pageantry (Welsh Pageant) **H.R.H. Prince Fahd Salman**
98 **LOUJU (USA)**, br f 13/2 Silver Hawk (USA)—Secretarial Queen (USA) (Secretariat (USA)) **Mr Terry Neill**
99 **MAGNOLIA**, gr f 22/4 Petong—Daffodil Fields (Try My Best (USA)) **Mr Christopher Wright**
100 **MAJESTY (IRE)**, b c 26/4 Sadler's Wells (USA)—
Princesse Timide (USA) (Blushing Groom (FR)) **H.R.H. Prince Fahd Salman**
101 **MAYFAIR**, b f 2/3 Green Desert—Emaline (FR) (Empery (USA)) **H.R.H. Prince Fahd Salman**
102 Gr f 23/4 El Gran Senor (USA)—Mist A Risin (USA) (Raise A Native) **Sir Andrew Lloyd Webber**
103 **MONTFORT (USA)**, b c 11/2 Manila—Sable Coated (Caerleon (USA)) **Sir George Meyrick**
104 **MORE SILVER (USA)**, b f 9/4 Silver Hawk (USA)—Dancing Lt (USA) (San Feliou (FR)) **Brereton C. Jones**
105 **NATALIA BAY (IRE)**, b f 17/2 Dancing Dissident—Bayazida (Bustino) **The Philip Blacker Studio Partnership**
106 **OLD COLONY**, b f 24/2 Pleasant Colony (USA)—
Annoconnor (USA) (Nureyev (USA)) **H.R.H. Prince Fahd Salman**
107 **OLIVO (IRE)**, ch c 1/3 Priolo (USA)—Honourable Sheba (USA) (Roberto (USA)) **Mr Anthony Speelman**
108 **OVATION**, ch f 19/4 Generous (IRE)—Bint Pasha (USA) (Affirmed (USA)) **H.R.H. Prince Fahd Salman**
109 **PUTRA (IRE)**, ch c 10/4 Dixie Brass (USA)—Olatha (USA) (Miswaki (USA)) **H.R.H. Sultan Ahmad Shah**
110 B c 29/1 Housebuster (USA)—Queluz (USA) (Saratoga Six (USA)) **Richard Green (Fine Paintings)**
111 B c 18/4 Persian Bold—Regina St Cyr (IRE) (Doulab (USA)) **P. F. I. Cole Ltd**
112 Ch f 18/2 Night Shift (USA)—Revisit (Busted) **Richard Green (Fine Paintings)**
113 **REWARD**, gr c 9/5 Highest Honor (FR)—Intimate Guest (Be My Guest (USA)) **H.R.H. Prince Fahd Salman**
114 B f 9/5 Miswaki (USA)—Rose O'Riley (USA) (Nijinsky (CAN)) **Mr Christopher Wright**
115 B f 24/2 Mt Livermore (USA)—Saratoga Sizzle (USA) (Saratoga Six (USA)) **G. J. Beck**
116 Ch c 14/2 Primo Dominie—Scales of Justice (Final Straw) **Mr Christopher Wright**
117 B f 9/2 Petong—Scossa (USA) (Shadeed (USA)) **M. Olden**
118 B f 21/1 Woodman (USA)—Seattle Belle (Seattle Slew (USA)) **Mr Christopher Wright**
119 **SECRET SOURCE (USA)**, b c 1/3 Alleged (USA)—Lake Dianchi (USA) (Dansons (USA)) **Mr M. Arbib**
120 **SHEER FOLLY (USA)**, ch c 25/3 Woodman (USA)—
Why So Much (USA) (Northern Baby (CAN)) **Al Muallim Partnership**
121 **SLIP THE NET (IRE)**, b c 18/2 Slip Anchor—Circus Ring (High Top) **Mr J. S. Gutkin**
122 **SMART BOY (IRE)**, ch c 22/3 Polish Patriot (USA)—Bouffant (High Top) **H.R.H. Sultan Ahmad Shah**
123 **SMART KID (IRE)**, b c 29/1 Lahib (USA)—Diamond Lake (Kings Lake (USA)) **H.R.H. Sultan Ahmad Shah**
124 **SNOW PARTRIDGE (USA)**, ch c 10/3 Arctic Tern (USA)—Lady Sharp (FR) (Sharpman) **Mr M. Arbib**
125 **SONG MIST (IRE)**, gr f 23/3 Kenmare (FR)—Farewell Song (USA) (The Minstrel (CAN)) **Mrs C. Hanbury**
126 **STURGEON (IRE)**, ch c 23/2 Caerleon (USA)—Ridge The Times (USA) (Riva Ridge (USA)) **Mr M. Arbib**
127 **SWING WEST (USA)**, b c 12/3 Gone West (USA)—Danlu (USA) (Danzig (USA)) **Mr M. Arbib**
128 **TABASCO JAZZ**, b f 7/3 Salse (USA)—Melody Park (Music Boy) **Lord Portman**
129 B f 18/4 Law Society (USA)—Tamassos (Dance In Time (CAN)) **Mr Athos Christodoulou**

MR P. F. I. COLE—continued

130 **TAMRAH (USA)**, ch f 8/3 Gone West (USA)—River Jig (USA) (Irish River (FR)) **H.R.H. Prince Fahd Salman**
131 **TASIK CHINI (USA)**, b c 20/4 St Jovite (USA)—Ten Hail Marys (USA) (Halo (USA)) **H.R.H. Sultan Ahmad Shah**
132 **THE WEST (USA)**, ch c 20/1 Gone West (USA)—
                             Lady For Two (USA) (Storm Bird (CAN)) **H.R.H. Prince Fahd Salman**
133 **TROOPER**, b c 25/3 Rock Hopper—Silica (USA) (Mr Prospector (USA)) **H.R.H. Prince Fahd Salman**
134 **TUSCANY**, b c 25/2 Pursuit of Love—
                             Jhansi Ki Rani (USA) (Far North (CAN)) **Highclere Thoroughbred Racing Ltd**
135 **WATERCOLOUR (IRE)**, b f 31/3 Groom Dancer (USA)—
                             River Nomad (Gorytus (USA)) **Highclere Thoroughbred Racing Ltd**
136 **WINDSOR CASTLE**, b c 13/3 Generous (IRE)—One Way Street (Habitat) **H.R.H. Prince Fahd Salman**
137 **WIRA (IRE)**, ch c 27/4 Lahib (USA)—Mother Courage (Busted) **H.R.H. Sultan Ahmad Shah**
138 B c 20/3 Rock Hopper—Wish You Well (Sadler's Wells (USA)) **Mr Christopher Wright**
139 **YORKSHIRE (IRE)**, ch c 26/2 Generous (IRE)—Ausherra (USA) (Diesis) **H.R.H. Prince Fahd Salman**
140 **YOUNG MARCIUS (USA)**, ch c Green Dancer (USA)—Manhatten Miss (Artaius (USA)) **C. J. Wates**

Other Owners: Mr Mark Beattie, Ms M. S. Brackenbury, Mr D. C. Broomfield, Mrs J. M. Corbett, Lord Donoughmore, Mr Les Draper, Sir Mervyn Dunnington-Jefferson, Mr Alan C. Elliot, Mr Tony Hill, Dr John Ind, Mr K. Longden, Mr Charles Meyrick, Mr G. W. Meyrick, Miss M. Noden, Mr G. W. Pilkington, Mr S. Pittom, Mrs J. Price, Mrs F. C. Saint Jean, Mrs F. Schwarzenbach, Mr David Antony Sparkes, Mr J. W. Taylor.

Jockeys (Flat): T R Quinn (8-4), C Rutter (7-10).

Apprentices: James Bosley (7-0), David O'Neill (7-10).

148   MR S. N. COLE, Tiverton

Postal: **West Batsworthy Farm, Rackenford, Tiverton, Devon, EX16 8EG.**

Phone: **PHONE & FAX (01884) 881205 MOBILE (0835) 038963**

1 **BILLY**, 4, b f Nicholas Bill—Ty-With-Belle **Mr J. Reed**
2 **CEDARS ROSSLARE**, 11, b g Black Minstrel—Sea Guest **Mrs G. O. Green**
3 **COME ON PADDY**, 8, b g Sula Bula—Pharaoh's Bride **Mr M. G. Willey**
4 **COME ON TOBY**, 10, b g Dubassoff (USA)—Pharaoh's Bride **Mrs Anita Cole**
5 **DUALITY**, 5, b m Dreams To Reality (USA)—Sleepline Princess **Mrs G. O. Green**
6 **IMPERIAL FORTE**, 6, b m Midyan (USA)—Sunfleet **Mrs G. O. Green**
7 **LUCKY MO**, 6, ch m Zambrano—Come On Lucky **Mrs M. Willey**
8 **THE FLYING FIDDLE**, 4, ch f Northern State (USA)—Miss Flossa (FR) **Mr A. T. Wilson**

THREE-YEAR-OLDS

9 B f Northern Game—Mamamere **Mrs Anita Cole**
10 **SUNRISE SPECIAL (IRE)**, b c Petorius—Break of Day **Mr J. Reed**

TWO-YEAR-OLDS

11 B f Almoojid—Mamamere (Tres Gate) **Mrs Anita Cole**

Jockey (NH): R Bellamy.

149   MR R. COLLET, Chantilly

Postal: **32, Avenue Marie Amelie, 60500 Chantilly, France.**

Phone: **44 57 06 72 FAX 44 57 32 25**

1 **AKWABA (FR)**, 6, gr m Zino—Bublichka (USA)
2 **BIHAC (FR)**, 4, b c L'Emigrant—Boldnika
3 **DANLODY (IRE)**, 4, b g Danehill—Cajun Melody
4 **DODECANESE (USA)**, 4, b c Nijinsky—Konafa

MR R. COLLET—continued

5 **ERGANI (FR)**, 6, b g Lashkari—Eunomia (FR)
6 **FALINDOR (FR)**, 7, b g Fast Topaze—Serbie
7 **GRAND MONARQUE (USA)**, 4, b c Fortunate Prospect—Sandy Baby
8 **LAS CAJAS (FR)**, 8, b g Lashkari—Mi Casa Su Casa
9 **MINERVITTA**, 4, b f Warrshan—Marie de Sologne
10 **MON DOMINO**, 7, b g Dominion—Arderelle
11 **PETOSIVA (IRE)**, 4, b c Petorius—Siva
12 **RUN AND GUN (IRE)**, 8, b g Lomond (USA)—Charming Life
13 **SADERLINA (IRE)**, 4, b f Sadler's Wells—Dinalina
14 **SETTLER (FR)**, 4, b f Darshaan—Aborigine
15 **SILICON GLORY (FR)**, 4, b f Le Glorieux—Siliciana
16 **SLIPPER MAN (IRE)**, 4, b c Ela-Mana-Mou—Chaussons Roses
17 **STRIKE OIL (FR)**, 8, b g Fabulous Dancer—All Found
18 **TYCOON KING (IRE)**, 4, b c Last Tycoon—Park Express
19 **VOLOCHINE (IRE)**, 5, ch h Soviet Star (USA)—Harmless Albatross
20 **WHEEL OF POWER (IRE)**, 4, b g Darshaan—North Forland

THREE-YEAR-OLDS

21 **ABATTEUR (USA)**, b g Riverman—Amenity
22 **ADMIRE FRANCE (USA)**, b f Septieme Ciel—Logiciel
23 **ALLEGED CHALLENGE (USA)**, b c Alleged—Twin Cities
24 **AYKOKU SAKY (FR)**, b f Baby Turk—Axiane
25 **BAL DE DES SIRENES (IRE)**, b f Warning—Save Me The Waltz
26 **BERGUENE (FR)**, b f Apeldoorn—Danse du Sud
27 **CALITTO (FR)**, b g Galetto—Callia
28 **CHATEAU LA RIVIERE (USA)**, b f Irish River—Chateaubaby
29 **DANISH MALODY (IRE)**, b c Danehill—Cajun Melody
30 **EL GRAND RESULT (USA)**, b c El Gran Senor—Happy Result
31 **EXACTLY LIGHT (IRE)**, b g Exactly Sharp—Chaussons Roses
32 **FLAG D'ANTIBES (USA)**, b c Alleged—Breath Taking
33 **HIGH MARE (FR)**, b f Highest Honor—Belle Et Chere
34 **HONOR THE COFFEE (FR)**, b f Highest Honor—Turkish Coffee
35 **KYRA CROWN (IRE)**, b f Astronef—Kentucky Crown
36 **LEONILA (IRE)**, b f Caerleon—Dinalina
37 **NO QUEST (IRE)**, b f Rainbow Quest—No Disgrace
38 **SHIGERU SAMURAI (USA)**, b f Bering—La Carene
39 **SIMON DU DESERT (FR)**, b c Kaldoun—Kanaletto
40 **TRULY GENEROUS (IRE)**, b f Generous—Arctique Royale
41 **VILCABAMBA (USA)**, b f Green Dancer—Mary Davies
42 **YAMAMOTO (FR)**, b c Kendor—Yamuna

TWO-YEAR-OLDS

43 **ANTARCTIQUE (IRE)**, b c Sadler's Wells—Arctique Royal (Royal And Regal)
44 **CATFRIEND (USA)**, b c Capote—Beware of The Cat (Caveat)
45 **CHIMERE (FR)**, b f Soviet Lad—Onthecomet (Chief Singer)
46 **CHOSEN PRINCESS (USA)**, b f Alleged—Lady Be Gay (Sir Gaylord)
47 **ELTON MIST (IRE)**, b f Priolo—Naiadoora (Ahonoora)
48 **GALA SOIREE (IRE)**, b f Night Shift—Galla Placida (Crystal Palace)
49 **GRACIE LADY (IRE)**, b f Generous—No Disgrace (Djakao)
50 B f Trempolino—Hata (Kaldoun)
51 B f Waajib—Kentucky Crown (Gulf Pearl)
52 **NIGHT PLAYER (IRE)**, b c Night Shift—Racquette (Ballymore)
53 **PETIT PUSCHKO (FR)**, b c Kendor—Peaceful Water (General Assembly)
54 **RISEN PRINCE (FR)**, b c General Assembly—Secret Blade (Secreto)
55 **SELF FEEDER (IRE)**, b c Lycius—Last Drama (Last Tycoon)
56 **SPEED FRIEND (FR)**, b c Unfuwain—Batchelor's Button (Kenmare)
57 **SWALINA**, b f Sadler's Wells (USA)—Dinalina (Top Ville)
58 B f Exit To Nowhere—Toujours Elle (FR) (Lyphard)
59 **TYCOON'S SON (IRE)**, b c Last Tycoon—Chaussons Roses (Lyphard)
60 **VALET DE COEUR (USA)**, b c Chief's Crown—Color of Love (Conquistador Cielo)

MR R. COLLET—continued

61 VEILED THREAT (IRE), b f Be My Guest—Primrose Valley (Mill Reef)
62 ZELINSKY (FR), b c Dreams To Reality—Parannda (Bold Lad)

Jockeys (Flat): T Jarnet, O Peslier, E Saint-Martin.

Apprentices: C Hanotel, S Jesus, S Maillot.

Amateurs: Mr Rodolphe Collet, Mr De Chevigny, Mr H Nagger.

150   MR H. J. COLLINGRIDGE, Newmarket

Postal: **Beverley House Stables, Exeter Road, Newmarket, Suffolk, CB8 8LR.**
Phone: **(01638) 665454 FAX (01638) 560830**

1 BELLATEENA, 4, b f Nomination—Bella Travaille **Mr N. H. Gardner**
2 CHALKY DANCER, 4, br c Adbass (USA)—Tiny Feet **Mr T. E. Claydon**
3 DOLLY DOLITTLE, 5, ch m Infantry—Lost Moment **Mrs D. A. Carter**
4 DOREEN'S DELIGHT, 10, ch h Bay Express—Elizabeth Howard **Mrs D. A. Carter**
5 D SEVEN, 6, ch h Homeboy—Elizabeth Howard **Mrs D. A. Carter**
6 ETOILE DU NORD, 4, b br g Tragic Role (USA)—Daisy Topper **Miss Z. Whitmore**
7 FORGE GOLD, 6, b g Buzzards Bay—Korresia **Mr R. H. Coombes**
8 KIROV PROTEGE (IRE), 4, b g Dancing Dissident (USA)—Still River **Group 1 Racing (1994) Ltd**
9 KRAZY KAYE, 6, b m Idiot's Delight—Lady Kaye Michelle **Mrs D. A. Carter**
10 MEGHDOOT, 4, b f Celestial Storm (USA)—Greenhills Joy **CSGJ Racing Syndicate**
11 MR TAYLOR, 11, b g Martinmas—Miss Reliant **Mr H. J. Collingridge**
12 NORTH-WEST ONE (IRE), 8, b g Camden Town—Shahrazad **Miss Jenny Reekie**
13 PAT'S SPLENDOUR, 5, b m Primitive Rising (USA)—Northern Venture **Mrs Patricia Lunn**
14 PENGAMON, 4, b c Efisio—Dolly Bevan **Mrs A. Smallman**
15 SOUTH EASTERN FRED, 5, b h Primo Dominie—Soheir **South Eastern Electrical Plc**
16 TAYLORS PRINCE, 9, ch g Sandhurst Prince—Maiden's Dance **Mr H. J. Collingridge**
17 TAYLORS REVIVAL, 5, b m Sizzling Melody—Taylors Pet
18 UP AND ABOVE, 7, b g Cruise Missile—Brandy's Honour **Mr J. P. Morrogh-Ryan**
19 WYCHWOOD SANDY, 5, b g Mansingh (USA)—Do-Run-Do **Mr R. H. Coombes**
20 YOXALL LODGE, 6, b h Aragon—Opal Fancy **Miss Ann Featherstone**

THREE-YEAR-OLDS

21 Ch g Mac's Imp (USA)—Bluemore **G. B. Amy**
22 INAMINIT, gr c Timeless Times (USA)—Dolly Bevan **Miss A. Smallman**
23 KOLI, b f Sayf El Arab (USA)—Miss Willow **P. J. Byrnes**

TWO-YEAR-OLDS

24 B f 9/5 Chilibang—Dolly Bevan (Another Realm)

Other Owners: Mr Robin Adair, Mr L. Audus, Mrs P. A. L. Butler, Mr J. H. Davies, Mr Christopher Davis, Mr I. C. Dell, Mr Jeremy Edge, Mrs J. E. Garlick, Mr C. A. Harrison, Mr B. C. Holcroft, Mr B. A. Hughes, Mr Michael Linnane, Mr R. L. Maynard, Mr D. M. McLean, Miss S. F. Phillips, Mrs Penny Rattigan, Mrs Wendy Smyth, Mr Adam Stirling, Mr P. Tong.

Jockeys (Flat): J Quinn (7-7), M Rimmer (8-7).

Apprentice: C Hawksley.

Amateur: Mr P Close (9-7).

151   MR C. COLLINS, The Curragh

Postal: **Conyngham Lodge, The Curragh, Co. Kildare, Ireland.**

Phone: **THE CURRAGH (045) 441239   FAX NO (045) 441605**

1 **AULD SCALL (IRE)**, 4, b f Shernazar—Eye In The Sky
2 **BELMARTIN**, 10, gr g Bellypha—Martinova
3 5, B m Cataldi—Caffra Mills
4 **CRYPTIC MYTH**, 4, b f Carlingford Castle—Cryptic Gold
5 **FLORAL EMBLEM (IRE)**, 4, b f Shernazar—Hostess
6 **GARTER ROYALE (IRE)**, 4, ch f Garde Royale—Halba
7 **JINGLING SILVER (IRE)**, 5, b g Posen (USA)—Ashley Springs
8 **LADIES GALLERY (IRE)**, 6, b m Welsh Term—Knotty Gal
9 **LOGSTOWN (IRE)**, 4, b f Keen—No Distractions
10 **MONALEA (IRE)**, 5, b g Torus—Firhouse Fancy
11 **PRINCESS CATALDI (IRE)**, 6, b m Cataldi—Firhouse Fancy
12 **SOREZE**, 4, br f Gallic League—Run Bonnie
13 **TENDER RIVER**, 6, b g Tender King—Still River
14 **THE BOWER (IRE)**, 7, br g Don't Forget Me—Nyama (USA)
15 **VIOLETS WILD (IRE)**, 4, b f Imperial Frontier (USA)—Our Ena

THREE-YEAR-OLDS

16 **ALMATY (IRE)**, b c Dancing Dissident—Almaaseh (IRE)
17 **ANNAGH BELL (IRE)**, b f Cyrano de Bergerac—Homosassa
18 **CLASSIC MIX (IRE)**, b f Classic Secret—Fovea (IRE)
19 **CORN ABBEY (IRE)**, b c Runnett—Connaught Rose
20 **DAVENPORT WEEKEND (IRE)**, b br g Mac's Imp—White Caps
21 **DISTANT SHORE (IRE)**, b f Jareer (USA)—Sea Mistress
22 **ELIZA ORZESZKOWA (IRE)**, b f Polish Patriot (USA)—Martinova
23 **FORSAKE ME NOT (IRE)**, b g Don't Forget Me—Run My Beauty
24 **GREAT OUTLOOK (IRE)**, b f Simply Great (FR)—Out And About
25 **HIGH HOPE HENRY (USA)**, b c Known Fact (USA)—Parquill (USA)
26 **KIMU (IRE)**, b c Ela-Mana-Mou—Kifenia
27 Br c Broken Hearted—Linanbless
28 **LOWER THE TONE (IRE)**, ch f Phone Trick (USA)—Spring Daffodil
29 **LUDGROVE**, b br c Royal Academy (USA)—Top of The League
30 **NASHCASH (IRE)**, ch c Nashamaa—Six Penny Express
31 **REAL GUEST (IRE)**, b f Be My Guest (USA)—You Make Me Real (USA)
32 **SIMONS CASTLE (IRE)**, b g Scenic—Miss Toot
33 **SNIFFLE (IRE)**, b f Shernazar—Piffle
34 **SONHOS (IRE)**, ch f Machiavellian (USA)—Sorbus
35 **TIRALLE (IRE)**, b f Tirol—Gezalle
36 **TRAVEL NORTH (IRE)**, b f Distinctly North—Travel Away
37 B f Pennine Walk—Waterstown Girl

TWO-YEAR-OLDS

38 Ch f 29/4 Classic Music (USA)—Best Niece (Vaigly Great)
39 B g 20/5 Be My Native (USA)—Caffra Mills (Pitpan)
40 **FEATHER BED (IRE)**, b f 17/2 Fools Holme (USA)—Piffle (Shirley Heights)
41 Ch c 13/4 Caerleon (USA)—Heaven High (High Line)
42 **IOLANTA (IRE)**, b f 13/4 Danehill (USA)—Kifenia (IRE) (Hatim (USA))
43 **LADY ASSASSIN (IRE)**, ch f 15/3 Polish Patriot (USA)—Jambo Jambo (IRE) (Kafu)
44 Ch f 23/4 Indian Ridge—Lovers Light (Grundy)
45 B c 26/4 Dancing Dissident—Marphousha (FR) (Shirley Heights)
46 **MR LIGHTFOOT (IRE)**, b c 20/2 Dancing Dissident—Lundylux (Grundy)
47 **MYSTIC MAGIC (IRE)**, b c 8/2 Magical Wonder (USA)—Rahwah (Northern Baby (CAN))
48 **RAPHANE (USA)**, b c 11/3 Rahy (USA)—Fast Nellie (USA) (Ack Ack (USA))
49 Ch f 11/2 Be My Guest (USA)—Raysiya (Cure The Blues (USA))
50 **RUM BABA (IRE)**, b c 10/4 Tirol—Rum Cay (USA) (Our Native (USA))
51 **SHALERINA (USA)**, ch f 20/4 Shalford (IRE)—Icterina (USA) (Secreto (USA))
52 **SIMPANY (IRE)**, ch c 16/2 Imp Society (USA)—Volany (IRE) (Be My Native (USA))

MR C. COLLINS—continued

53 B c 14/4 Last Tycoon—Sister Ursula (Ela-Mana-Mou)
54 B f 18/3 Bluebird (USA)—Small Is Beautiful (Condorcet (FR))
55 B f 21/4 Imperial Frontier—Sudaf (Welsh Saint)
56 B c 13/4 Kylian (USA)—Tarsa (Ballad Rock)
57 TWO BANDITS (IRE), b c 4/3 Thatching—Summerhill (Habitat)
58 B c 16/5 Simply Great (FR)—Waterstown Girl (Ahonoora)
59 Ch f 10/3 Be My Guest (USA)—You Make Me Real (USA) (Give Me Strength (USA))

Owners: R. J. Barry, Lady Sarah Barry, Mrs C. Burns, Mrs Kathleen Colgan, Mrs C. Collins, Danilo Corridori, Hugh Curley, Mrs B. J. Eastwood, Prof J. Fennelly, Lord Harrington, Nicholas Hartery, The Hon D. F. Howard, Cyril Humphris, G. W. Jennings, Mrs Catherine Lauterpacht, Mrs H. D. McCalmont, Mr Hugh D. McCalmont, A. McLean, John McLoughlin, Mrs H. R. Norton, Donal O'Buachalla, Mrs St J. O'Connell, John Perrotta, Mr Gerard Purcell, Mrs K. Quinn, Ribot Racing Syndicate, Mrs A. W. Riddell Martin, Peter Savill, Edward St George, True Blue Racing Club.

Jockey (Flat): P V Gilson (w.a.).

Apprentices: Richard Farmer, John Mullins, Mary Williamson.

Lady Riders: Miss Sheena Collins, Miss Tracey Collins.

152   MR R. COLLINS, Stockton-on-Tees

Postal: **Collins (seafoods) Ltd, 30 Northfield Way, Aycliffe Industrial Estate, Newton Aycliffe, DL5 6UF.**
Phone: **(01325) 315544 FAX (01325) 314935**

1 KENMARE RIVER (IRE), 6, b g Over The River (FR)—Comeallye **Mr Richard Collins**
2 SHALLOW RIVER (IRE), 5, b g Over The River (FR)—Rule The Waves **Mr Richard Collins**

153   MR M. J. COOMBE, Weymouth

Postal: **Sea Barn Farm, Fleet, Weymouth, Dorset, DT3 4ED.**
Phone: **(01305) 782218   FAX (01305) 775396**

1 CAPTAIN DIMITRIS, 11, ch g Dubassoff (USA)—Proud Gipsy **Mrs N. M. Coombe**
2 GLEN MIRAGE, 11, b g Furry Glen—By Mistake **Mr J. Coombe**
3 HAN LINE, 8, ch g Capricorn Line—Nine Hans **Mr J. Coombe**
4 MATCH HANS, 11, ch m Royal Match—Nine Hans **Mr J. Coombe**
5 MIDNIGHT GALAXY, 7, b g Natroun (FR)—Sister Jinks **Mr J. Coombe**
6 PALACE WOLF (NZ), 12, b g Star Wolf—Castle Star (NZ) **Mrs N. M. Coombe**
7 SEA BARN, 13, ch g Julio Mariner—Zakyna **Mrs N. M. Coombe**

Lady Rider: Miss M Coombe (9-0).

154   MR F. COTON, Nottingham

Postal: **Chapel Farm, Epperstone, Nottingham, NG14 6AE.**
Phone: **NOTTINGHAM (01159) 663048**

1 EMERALD VENTURE, 9, b g Seclude (USA)—No Time For Tears **Mr F. Coton**
2 O'SLO, 5, gr m Ovac (ITY)—Not Easy **Mr F. Coton**
3 SEASIDE DREAMER, 6, b g Electric—Guilty Guest (USA) **Mr F. Coton**
4 VICKYBERTO, 7, b m Laxton—Silberto **Mr F. Coton**

MR F. COTON—continued

THREE-YEAR-OLDS

5 B f Roscoe Blake—Bella Banus **Mr F. Coton**

Lady Rider: Georgina Adkin (9-7).

155   MR L. G. COTTRELL, Cullompton

Postal: **Sprinters, Dulford, Cullompton, Devon, EX15 2DX.**

Phone: **KENTISBEARE (01884) 266320**

1 **AMAZON HEIGHTS**, 4, b f Heights of Gold—Formidable Lady **Mrs D. Jenks**
2 **CAPE PIGEON (USA)**, 11, ch g Storm Bird (CAN)—Someway Somehow (USA) **Mr E. J. S. Gadsden**
3 **CONSPICUOUS (IRE)**, 6, b g Alzao (USA)—Mystery Lady (USA) **Mrs Jenny Hopkins**
4 **DEVON PEASANT**, 4, b f Deploy—Serration **Mrs B. Skinner**
5 **FORMIDABLE LASS**, 5, ch m Formidable—Stock Hill Lass **Mr E. J. S. Gadsden**
6 **KOATHARY (USA)**, 5, b g Capote (USA)—Jeffo (USA) **Mr E. J. S. Gadsden**
7 **MONTSERRAT**, 4, b f Aragon—Follow The Stars **Mrs Anne Yearley**
8 **PRIDE OF BRITAIN (CAN)**, 7, ch m Linkage (USA)—Witches Alibhai (USA) **Pride of Britain Limited**
9 **PURPLE FLING**, 5, ch g Music Boy—Divine Fling **Mr H. C. Seymour**
10 **SPREAD THE WORD**, 4, b f Deploy—Apply **Mr John Boswell**
11 **SUPREME THOUGHT**, 4, b f Emarati (USA)—Who's That Girl **Mr Derek Simester**

THREE-YEAR-OLDS

12 **SHINING CLOUD**, ch f Indian Ridge—Hardiheroine **Mrs Anne Yearley**

TWO-YEAR-OLDS

13 **HARDIPRINCESS**, b f 5/2 Keen—Hardiheroine (Sandhurst Prince) **Mrs Anne Yearley**
14 **RIVERSMEET**, b c 17/5 Soviet Star (USA)—Zepha (Great Nephew) **Mr Henry Seymour OBE**
15 **ROSENKAVALIER (IRE)**, b c 19/3 Classic Music (USA)—Top Bloom (Thatch (USA)) **Mr G. W. Swire**

Other Owners: Mr D. J. Cole, Mr A. J. Cottrell, Mrs Nerys Dutfield, Lady Fortescue, Mr Gerald Gordon, Mr K. J. McCarten, Mr Terence M. Molossi, Mrs Simon Mounsey, Mr R. Neillands, Mrs Ruth Perry, Mr David F. Powell.

Jockeys (Flat): L Dettori (w.a.), A Munro (w.a.), J Quinn, M Roberts (w.a.).

Jockey (NH): S McNeill.

Amateur: Mr L Jefford (10-0).

156   MR R. CRAGGS, Sedgefield

Postal: **East Close Farm, Sedgefield, Stockton-on-Tees, Cleveland, TS21 3HW.**

Phone: **(01740) 620239 FAX (01740) 623476**

1 **BLUE DOMAIN**, 5, b g Dominion—Blue Rag **Mr Ray Craggs**
2 4, B g Green Ruby (USA)—Esilam **Mr Ray Craggs**
3 **GULER-A**, 8, b g King of Spain—Wayleave **Mr Ray Craggs**
4 **HIGHLAND PARK**, 10, ch g Simply Great (FR)—Perchance **Mr Ray Craggs**
5 **LITTLE RED**, 5, b g Dreams To Reality (USA)—Qualitairess **Mr Ray Craggs**
6 **RASIN CHARGE**, 5, b g Governor General—Airlanka **Mr Ray Craggs**
7 **RASIN LUCK**, 6, b m Primitive Rising (USA)—Delamere **Mr Ray Craggs**
8 **RASIN STANDARDS**, 6, b g Relkino—Growing Wild **Mr Ray Craggs**
9 **SUPERHOO**, 5, b g Superlative—Boo Hoo **Mr Ray Craggs**

TWO-YEAR-OLDS

10 Ch g 9/4 Interrex (CAN)—Kimbolton Katie (Aragon) **Mr Ray Craggs**

157   MISS J. F. CRAZE, York

Postal: **Nook House, Stray Lane, York Road, Elvington, York, YO4 5AX.**
Phone: **(01904) 608458 MOBILE (0585) 683359**

1 **BLYTON STAR (IRE)**, 8, b g Horage—Saintly Angel **Mrs J. Addleshaw**
2 **LADY SILK**, 5, ch m Prince Sabo—Adduce (USA) **Mr Mel Jackson & Mr K. West**
3 **LE BAL**, 4, b f Rambo Dancer (CAN)—Skarberg (FR) **Mrs Valerie Dixon**
4 **THE INSTITUTE BOY**, 6, b g Fairy King (USA)—To Oneiro **Mrs J. Addleshaw**

THREE-YEAR-OLDS

5 **LADY BLY**, b f Skyliner—Sveltissima **Mrs J. Addleshaw**
6 **LILA PEDIGO (IRE)**, b f Classic Secret (USA)—Miss Goldie **Mr G. Dove & Mr R. Cooper**
7 **MYSTIC TIMES**, b f Timeless Times (USA)—Chikala **Mr D. Franks**
8 **ORANGE AND BLUE**, br f Prince Sabo—Mazarine Blue **Orange and Blue Partners**
9 **PETARINA**, gr f Petong—Katharina **Petarina Partnership**
10 **QUEENS CHECK**, b f Komaite (USA)—Ski Baby **Mr W. Cooper & Mr N. Cooper**

Other Owners: Mr T. M. Jackson.

Jockeys (Flat): N Kennedy (7-10), Stuart Webster (8-4).

Amateur: Mr W Wenyon (9-0).

158   MR L. M. CUMANI, Newmarket

Postal: **Bedford House Stables, Bury Road, Newmarket, Suffolk, CB8 7BX.**
Phone: **NEWMARKET (01638) 665432 FAX (01638) 667160**

1 **BEND WAVY (IRE)**, 4, ch c Kefaah (USA)—Prosodie (FR) **Lord Portsmouth**
2 **CHIEF BURUNDI (USA)**, 4, b g Alleged (USA)—Lantana Lady (CAN) **Mr P. A. Leonard**
3 **LUCKY DI (USA)**, 4, b c Diesis—Lucky Song (USA) **Mrs Virginia Knott Bender**
4 **MIDNIGHT LEGEND**, 5, b h Night Shift (USA)—Myth **Umm Qarn Racing**
5 **SMART ALEC**, 4, b c Diesis—Ahead **Mr Gerald W. Leigh**
6 **SOUTH SEA BUBBLE (IRE)**, 4, b f Bustino—Night At Sea **Lady Juliet De Chair**
7 **SUPLIZI (IRE)**, 5, b h Alzao (USA)—Sphinx (GER) **Scuderia Rencati Srl**
8 **SURANOM (IRE)**, 4, b c Alzao (USA)—Gracieuse Majeste (FR) **Scuderia Rencati Srl**

THREE-YEAR-OLDS

9 **ADELAIDE (IRE)**, b f Alzao (USA)—Al Joharah **Sultan Al Kabeer**
10 **AGLIENTU**, b c Fairy King (USA)—Arbela (IRE) **Mr Piero Riccardi**
11 **AL SHADEEDAH (USA)**, br f Nureyev (USA)—Copperama (AUS) **Umm Qarn Racing**
12 **BALALAIKA**, b f Sadler's Wells (USA)—Bella Colora **Helena Springfield Ltd**
13 **BOURBONIST (FR)**, b c Soviet Star (USA)—Bourbon Topsy **Sheikh Mohammed**
14 **CHINENSIS (IRE)**, ch c Lycius (USA)—Chinese Justice (USA) **Sheikh Mohammed**
15 **CONSORDINO**, b f Alzao (USA)—Consolation **Sheikh Mohammed**
16 **CROWN COURT (USA)**, b c Chief's Crown (USA)—
Bold Courtesan (USA) **Lord De La Warr & Mr Michael Kerr-Dineen**
17 **DARLEITH**, b g Darshaan—Lomond Blossom **Sheikh Mohammed**
18 **ELA-YIE-MOU (IRE)**, ch c Kris—Green Lucia **Mr Andreas Michael**
19 **ELMI ELMAK (IRE)**, b c Fairy King (USA)—Ascensiontide **Sheikh Ahmed Al Maktoum**
20 **FLAMANDS (IRE)**, b f Sadler's Wells (USA)—Fleur Royale **Sultan Al Kabeer**
21 **FREEQUENT**, ch c Rainbow Quest (USA)—Free Guest **Fittocks Stud**
22 **HEADMASTER**, b c Kris—Ghislaine (USA) **Mr Gerald W. Leigh**
23 **HOUSE OF RICHES**, b c Shirley Heights—Pelf (USA) **Sheikh Mohammed**
24 **HOW LONG**, b c Alzao (USA)—Fresh **Dr M. Boffa**
25 **HUMOURLESS**, ch c Nashwan (USA)—Sans Blague (USA) **Sheikh Mohammed**
26 **KAYF**, ch f Nashwan (USA)—Northshiel **Sheikh Ahmed Al Maktoum**

MR L. M. CUMANI—continued

27 **KELTOI,** b c Soviet Star (USA)—Celtic Assembly (USA) **Sheikh Mohammed**
28 **KILVINE,** b c Shaadi (USA)—Kilavea (USA) **Sheikh Mohammed**
29 **MEZZANOTTE (IRE),** b c Midyan (USA)—Late Evening (USA) **Mr P. A. Leonard**
30 **MIGWAR,** b c Unfuwain (USA)—Pick of The Pops **Umm Qarn Racing**
31 **MONS,** b c Deploy—Morina (USA) **Mrs E. H. Vestey**
32 **MOUNT ROW,** b f Alzao (USA)—Temple Row **Lord Hartington**
33 **OLD IRISH,** gr c Old Vic—Dunoof **Sheikh Mohammed**
34 **PANATA (IRE),** b f Tirol—Rince Deas (IRE) **Mrs Angie Silver**
35 **PAOJIUNIC (IRE),** ch c Mac's Imp (USA)—Audenhove (GER) **Mr Paolo Riccardi**
36 **PAPERING (IRE),** b f Shaadi (USA)—Wrapping **Sheikh Mohammed**
37 **PASSAGE CREEPING (IRE),** b f Persian Bold—Tiptoe **Mr T. M. Brudenell**
38 **PEGRAM (IRE),** b c Cadeaux Genereux—Pertinent **Sultan Al Kabeer**
39 **PETROLIO (IRE),** b c Scenic—Petrolea Girl **Sultan Al Kabeer**
40 **POLISH QUEEN,** b f Polish Precedent (USA)—Indian Queen **Sheikh Mohammed**
41 **PRIMA VERDE,** b f Leading Counsel (USA)—Bold Green (FR) **The Lawster Partnership**
42 **PUCE,** b f Darshaan—Souk (IRE) **Fittocks Stud**
43 **ROBAMASET (IRE),** b c Caerleon (USA)—Smageta **Scuderia Rencati Srl**
44 **SEA OF STONE (USA),** ch f Sanglamore (USA)—Ocean Ballad **Sheikh Mohammed**
45 **SECOND BARRAGE,** b c Royal Academy (USA)—Proudfoot (IRE) **Mr M. Marchetti**
46 **SECONDMENT,** b c Shernazar—Designate (USA) **Sheikh Mohammed**
47 **SELECT FEW,** b c Alzao (USA)—Elect (USA) **Sheikh Mohammed**
48 **SLEETING,** ch c Lycius (USA)—Pluvial **Lord Hartington**
49 **SOUFRIERE (IRE),** b br f Caerleon (USA)—Shelbiana (USA) **Sultan Al Kabeer**
50 **SPILLO,** b c Midyan (USA)—Myth **Teknagro Srl**
51 **THREESOME (USA),** ch f Seattle Dancer (USA)—Triode (USA) **Fittocks Stud**
52 **UMBERSTON (IRE),** b c Nabeel Dancer (USA)—Pivotal Walk (IRE) **Mr Paul G. S. Silver**

TWO-YEAR-OLDS

53 **AL BLU (IRE),** b c 10/3 Exit To Nowhere (USA)—Kiri (Kris) **Scuderia Rencati Srl**
54 **ALLORA,** b f 21/2 Then Again—Vaula (Henbit (Aust)) **Mr P. A. Leonard**
55 Ch c 1/5 Nashwan (USA)—Alwathba (USA) (Lyphard (USA)) **Sheikh Ahmed Al Maktoum**
56 B br c 19/3 Hermitage (USA)—Ardy Arnie (USA) (Hold Your Peace (USA)) **Lord De La Warr & Partners**
57 B c 2/2 Shirley Heights—Avila (Ajdal (USA)) **Sheikh Mohammed**
58 B c 3/3 Cadeaux Genereux—Ballad Opera (Sadler's Wells (USA)) **Sheikh Mohammed**
59 Ch f 18/4 Blushing John (USA)—Beat (USA) (Nijinsky (CAN)) **Sheikh Mohammed**
60 Ch c 22/4 Trempolino (USA)—Blue Daisy (USA) (Shahrastani (USA)) **Sheikh Mohammed**
61 **BOLSTER,** b c 18/2 Batshoof—Flight of Pleasure (Roberto (USA)) **Lord Hartington**
62 **BOMBAZINE (IRE),** ch f 2/4 Generous—Brocade (Habitat) **Mr Gerald W. Leigh**
63 **BRAVE KRIS (IRE),** b f 10/2 Kris—Famosa (Dancing Brave) **Mr Robert H. Smith**
64 B f 25/3 Soviet Star (USA)—Burning Ambition (Troy) **Sheikh Mohammed**
65 Ch f 30/3 Arazi (USA)—Carnival Spirit (Kris) **Sheikh Mohammed**
66 B c 8/6 Irish River (FR)—Chaleur (CAN) (Rouge Sang (USA)) **Lord De La Warr & Partners**
67 **CORETTA (IRE),** b f 11/2 Caerleon (USA)—Free At Last (Shirley Heights) **Mr Gerald W. Leigh**
68 **DALRIADA (IRE),** ch f 1/5 Lomond—Douce Amie (USA) (Saratoga Six (USA)) **Sultan Al Kabeer**
69 B c 11/4 Slip Anchor—Dance Flower (CAN) (Northern Dancer) **Sheikh Mohammed**
70 **DARAPOUR (IRE),** b c 22/3 Fairy King—Dawala (IRE) (Lashkari) **H. H. The Aga Khan**
71 **DIXIE JAMBOREE (USA),** b br c 5/4 Dixie Brass (USA)—Glimmering (Troy) **W. V. & E. S. Robins**
72 **DR MARTENS (IRE),** b c 6/4 Mtoto—Suyayeb (USA) (The Minstrel (CAN)) **The R. Griggs Group Ltd**
73 **ETNA,** b f 21/2 Salse (USA)—Top Sovereign (High Top) **Lord Hartington**
74 **EUROLINK WINDSONG (IRE),** b f 24/3 Polish Patriot (USA)—Delvecchia (Glint of Gold) **The Eurolink Group Plc**
75 **FARNESE (IRE),** b c 14/2 Alzao (USA)—Flaxen Hair (Thatch) (USA)) **Sultan Al Kabeer**
76 B f 12/5 Kaldoun (FR)—Folia (Sadler's Wells (USA)) **Sheikh Mohammed**
77 **GREAT OVATION (IRE),** b c 15/2 High Estate—Wild Applause (IRE) (Sadler's Wells (USA)) **Mrs E. H. Vestey**
78 B c 22/4 Alleged (USA)—Hello Memphis (USA) (Super Concorde (USA)) **Lord De La Warr & Partners**
79 B c 10/3 Caerleon (USA)—Infamy (Shirley Heights) **Mr M. Tabor**
80 B c 16/2 Batshoof—Isotonic (Absalom) **Umm Qarn Racing**
81 **JANARA,** b f 16/2 Aragon—Aimee Jane (USA) (Our Native (USA)) **Paul G. S. Silver & Guy Chisenhale-Marsh**
82 B c 23/3 Midyan (USA)—Juliette Marny (Blakeney) **Mr M. Marchetti**
83 B f 29/3 Slip Anchor—Kadissya (USA) (Blushing Groom (FR)) **H. H. The Aga Khan**
84 Ch c 20/5 Seattle Dancer (USA)—Kaiserfahrt (GER) (Frontal) **Sheikh Mohammed**

MR L. M. CUMANI—continued

85 B f 8/3 Lear Fan (USA)—Kazoo (Shareef Dancer (USA)) **Sheikh Mohammed**
86 B f 24/3 Groom Dancer (USA)—Kiliniski (Niniski (USA)) **Sheikh Mohammed**
87 **LAJATTA**, ch c 7/4 Superlative—Lady Keyser (Le Johnstan) **Mr Paolo Riccardi**
88 B c 1/3 Fairy King (USA)—Le Melody (Levmoss) **Lord De La Warr & Partners**
89 **LIMA**, b f 26/2 Distant Relative—Lady Kris (IRE) (Kris) **Sultan Al Kabeer**
90 **LISTED ACCOUNT (USA)**, b f 3/5 Private Account (USA)—Sypharina (FR) (Lyphard (USA)) **Mr Robert H. Smith**
91 B c 28/3 El Gran Senor (USA)—Madiriya (IRE) (Diesis) **H. H. The Aga Khan**
92 **MONACO (IRE)**, b c 3/4 Classic Music (USA)—Larosterna (Busted) **Mark Blundell Racing**
93 **MYSTICAL**, b f 8/3 Mystiko (USA)—Midnight Imperial (Night Shift (USA)) **Consultco Ltd**
94 B f 7/5 Silver Hawk (USA)—Nikishka (USA) (Nijinsky (CAN)) **Sheikh Ahmed Al Maktoum**
95 B f 30/3 Soviet Star (USA)—Olivana (GER) (Sparkler) **Sheikh Mohammed**
96 **ONE SO WONDERFUL**, b f 4/5 Nashwan (USA)—Someone Special (Habitat) **Helena Springfield Ltd**
97 **PENTATEUCHE**, b c 19/2 Primo Dominie—Rivers Maid (Rarity) **Lord De La Warr & Partners**
98 B c 13/5 Saumarez—Perfect Production (USA) (Theatrical) **Umm Qarn Racing**
99 Ch f 30/1 Soviet Star (USA)—Queen Midas (Glint of Gold) **Umm Qarn Racing**
100 B f 23/4 Sadler's Wells (USA)—River Memories (USA) (Riverman (USA)) **Sheikh Mohammed**
101 B f 13/3 Kahyasi—Riyda (Be My Guest (USA)) **H. H. The Aga Khan**
102 **RUFALDA (IRE)**, b f 20/3 Sadler's Wells (USA)—Smageta (High Top) **Scuderia Rencati Srl**
103 **RUSSIAN OLIVE**, b f 23/2 Primo Dominie—Cottonwood (Teenoso (USA)) **Lord Carnarvon**
104 B f 13/2 Sadler's Wells (USA)—Samya's Flame (Artaius (USA)) **Sheikh Ahmed Al Maktoum**
105 **SCOSS**, b c 3/4 Batshoof—Misguided (Homing) **Scuderia Rencati Srl**
106 **SHADIANN (IRE)**, b c 24/3 Darshaan—Shakanda (IRE) (Shernazar) **H. H. The Aga Khan**
107 **SHADOW LEAD**, b c 13/2 Midyan (USA)—Shadow Bird (Martinmas) **Mr H. C. Chung**
108 **SHARBADARID (IRE)**, b c 23/3 Night Shift (USA)—Sharenara (USA) (Vaguely Noble) **H. H. The Aga Khan**
109 **SHIRAZAN (IRE)**, b c 22/4 Doyoun—Sharaniya (USA) (Alleged (USA)) **H. H. The Aga Khan**
110 **SHOUK**, b f 31/3 Shirley Heights—Souk (IRE) (Ahonoora) **Fittocks Stud**
111 **SILVERANI (IRE)**, b c 22/3 High Estate—Rose Society (Caerleon (USA)) **Mr Paul G. S. Silver**
112 **SILVER SIREN (USA)**, b br f 7/5 Silver Hawk (USA)—Male Strike (CAN) (Speak John) **W. V. & E. S. Robins**
113 **SILVER WONDER (USA)**, ch c 31/3 Silver Hawk (USA)—
                                          Upper Class Lady (USA) (Upper Nile (USA)) **W. V. & E. S. Robins**
114 B f 2/5 Polish Patriot (USA)—Soxoph (Hotfoot) **Mr M. Marchetti**
115 **SPEREMM (IRE)**, b f 18/4 Sadler's Wells (USA)—Forli's Treat (Forli (ARG)) **Scuderia Rencati Srl**
116 **STILETT (IRE)**, b c 5/4 Tirol—Legal Steps (IRE) (Law Society (USA)) **Scuderia Rencati Srl**
117 **STRACHIN**, b c 1/2 Salse (USA)—Collage (Ela-Mana-Mou) **Scuderia Rencati Srl**
118 **STRILLO (IRE)**, b c 21/4 Safawan—Silvers Era (Balidar) **Teknagro Srl**
119 **TABERANN (IRE)**, b c 5/4 Doyoun—Tabessa (USA) (Shahrastani (USA)) **H. H. The Aga Khan**
120 **TAHARA (IRE)**, ch f 11/4 Caerleon (USA)—Tarwiya (IRE) (Dominion) **H. H. The Aga Khan**
121 B c 18/2 Kendor (FR)—Tanz (IRE) (Sadler's Wells (USA)) **Sheikh Mohammed**
122 B c 26/4 Lahib (USA)—Tight Spin (High Top) **Sheikh Mohammed**
123 **TIMISSA (IRE)**, b f 9/3 Kahyasi—Timissara (USA) (Shahrastani (USA)) **H. H. The Aga Khan**
124 Ch c 23/2 Old Vic—Winter Queen (Welsh Pageant) **Sheikh Mohammed**

Other Owners: Mr A. M. Abdulla, Mr J. R. Boughey, Mr P. A. Deal, Sheikh Abdullah Bin Khalifa, Mrs H. Michael, Mr G. C. Mordaunt, Mr P. Seabrook, Mrs Amanda Skiffington, Mr E. H. Vestey, Lord Vestey, Mrs Timothy Von Halle, Miss Helena Weinfeld, Mr M. Weinfeld, Mr Simon Weinstock.

Apprentices: R Ffrench (7-3), J Hunnam (7-4), G Mitchell (8-0).

Lady Rider: Mrs S Cumani (9-0).

159   MR P. D. CUNDELL, Newbury

Postal: **Roden House, Compton, Newbury, Berks, RG20 6QR.**
Phone: **(01635) 578267 FAX (01635) 578267**

1 **EASTER BABY**, 10, ch m Derrylin—Saintly Miss **Mr P. D. Cundell**
2 **GREAT HALL**, 7, gr g Hallgate—Lily of France **Miss M. C. Fraser**

MR P. D. CUNDELL—continued

3 **HAPPY BRAVE**, 4, b g Daring March—Fille de Phaeton **Mr P. D. Cundell**
4 **LEIGH CROFTER**, 7, ch g Son of Shaka—Ganadora **Mr Peter Dimmock**
5 **REPEAT OFFER**, 4, b g Then Again—Bloffa **Mr D. M. Brick**
6 **RUSTY HALL**, 4, ch f Risk Me (FR)—Happy Snap **Mr P. D. Cundell**
7 **SPEEDY SNAPS PRIDE**, 4, gr g Hallgate—Pineapple's Pride **Mr P. D. Cundell**

THREE-YEAR-OLDS

8 B g Skyliner—Fille de Phaeton **Mr P. D. Cundell**

TWO-YEAR-OLDS

9 B f 4/5 Kylian (USA)—Easter Baby (Derrylin) **Mr K. S. Cundell**
10 **NITWITTY**, b g 3/4 Nomination—Dawn Ditty (Song) **Unity Farm Holiday Centre Ltd**
11 B g 25/4 Kylian (USA)—Precious Caroline (IRE) (The Noble Player) **Mr P. D. Cundell**
12 **SUPER ROOSTER**, gr g 3/5 Superlative—Mummy's Chick (Mummy's Pet) **Unity Farm Holiday Centre Ltd**

Other Owners: Mrs S. M. Booker, Mrs M. Hill, Mrs M. Young.

160   MR M. CUNNINGHAM, Navan

Postal: **Gormanstown Stables, Kildalkey, Navan, Co.Meath, Ireland.**
Phone: **(046) 31672 FAX (046) 31467**

1 **APPLEFORT (IRE)**, 6, b g Over The River (FR)—Sweet Apple **Herb M. Stanley**
2 5, B m Celio Rufo—Atlantic Hope **Francis Connon**
3 **BALLERIN DANCER (IRE)**, 5, gr m Commanche Run—Shangri-La **John McLarnon**
4 **BAMAPOUR (IRE)**, 6, b g Shardari—Banana Peel **Michael Hilary Burke**
5 **CABLE BEACH (IRE)**, 7, ch g Lepanto (GER)—Aliceion **Herb Stanley**
6 **CAITRIONA'S CHOICE (IRE)**, 5, b h Carmelite House (USA)—Muligatawny **Seamus MacCrosain**
7 **CORRAVOGGY (IRE)**, 7, ch g Buckskin (FR)—Tipperary Star **Mrs B. Lynch**
8 **DERRYMOYLE (IRE)**, 7, b g Callernish—Luminous Lady **Herb Stanley**
9 **EOINS LAD (IRE)**, 5, ch h The Noble Player (USA)—Dulcet Dido **Seamus MacCrosain**
10 **FIDDLERS TUNE**, 6, b g Relkino—Fiddlers Bee **Herb M. Stanley**
11 **KALONA**, 9, gr g Rough Lad—Bienfait **Seamus MacCrosain**
12 **MERRY CHANTER (IRE)**, 4, gr g Wood Chanter—Idle Taxi **John McLarnon**
13 6, B m Supreme Leader—Never Be Late **Mrs Michael Cunningham**
14 **NOELEENS DELIGHT (IRE)**, 7, ch m Le Bavard (FR)—Graham Dieu **Noel McGrady**
15 **NOELS DANCER (IRE)**, 6, ch g Nordance (USA)—Royal Desire **Noel McGrady**
16 **PANICKED (IRE)**, 6, ch g Parliament—Grange Kova **H. J. O'Brien**
17 **SHARLENE (IRE)**, 5, b br m Supreme Leader—Glissade **David P. Lavin**

THREE-YEAR-OLDS

18 B f Kefaah (USA)—Lyphard's Lady **Philip Fleming**
19 **PECAN (IRE)**, b f Magical Strike (USA)—Firdaunt **Mrs Michael Cunningham**
20 **PLAYPRINT**, ch c Persian Heights—Tawnais **Seamus MacCrosain**

TWO-YEAR-OLDS

21 B c 16/4 Common Grounds—Karayasha (Posse (USA)) **Seamus MacCrosain**
22 B c 17/4 Cyrano De Bergerac—Lyphard's Lady (Lyphard's Special (USA)) **Philip Fleming**
23 B f 24/3 Glacial Storm (USA)—Panalpina (Petorius) **Seamus McCrosain**
24 B f 27/3 Doubletour (USA)—We've Just Begun (USA) (Huguenot (USA)) **Mrs Michael Cunningham**

Lady Rider: Miss Tara Cunningham (9-0).

161 MR W. S. CUNNINGHAM, Yarm

Postal: **Embleton Farm, Garbutts Lane, Hutton Rudby, Yarm, TS15 0DN.**
Phone: **(01642) 701290 MOBILE (0585) 158703**

1 **BOLD AMUSEMENT**, 6, ch g Never So Bold—Hysterical **Mr David Bell**
2 **CHARLVIC**, 6, ch g Pollerton—Sharp Vixen **Mr Dave Scott**
3 **CRAIGSTOWN (IRE)**, 8, b g Green Shoon—Only Gorgeous **Mr David Slater**
4 **DEEP CALL**, 9, br g Callernish—Rise An Run **Mr Russel H. Lee**
5 **DE JORDAAN**, 9, br g Callernish—Gorge **The Trunley Partnership**
6 **ELEMENT OF RISK (IRE)**, 6, b g Strong Gale—Little Credit **The Trunley Partnership**
7 **KENILWORTH LAD**, 8, br g Ring Bidder—Lucky Joker **Mr David Bell**
8 **LUGER (IRE)**, 8, b g Farhaan—Divine Wonder **Mr R. Lee**
9 **MAYBE O'GRADY (IRE)**, 7, b g Strong Gale—Rosie O'Grady **Mr D. J. Bell**
10 **MITHRAIC (IRE)**, 4, b g Kefaah (USA)—Persian's Glory **Mrs Vicky Cunningham**
11 **RUSTINO**, 10, ch g Bustino—Miss Britain **Cadiz Ltd**
12 **SAMAKA HARA (IRE)**, 4, b g Taufan (USA)—Aunt Hester (IRE) **Mr Dave Scott**
13 **SPLENDID OCCASION (IRE)**, 6, b br g Supreme Leader—Little Bride **Mr David Slater**

THREE-YEAR-OLDS

14 **BLAZING IMP (USA)**, ch c Imp Society (USA)—Marital (USA) **Mrs Eileen Hawkey**

TWO-YEAR-OLDS

15 B f 7/5 Rock Hopper—The Fink Sisters (Tap On Wood) **Mr D. J. Bell**

Other Owners: Mr P. Adams, Mrs Ann Bell, Eclipse Management (Newmarket), Mr Ian Sanderson, Mr A. D. Tate.

162 MR K. CUNNINGHAM-BROWN, Stockbridge

Postal: **Danebury Place, Stockbridge, Hants, SO20 6JX.**
Phone: **(01264) 781061 FAX (01264) 781709/781061**

1 **AL CORNICHE (IRE)**, 4, b f Bluebird (USA)—Naxos (USA) **Mr D. Bass**
2 **BESSY (IRE)**, 4, b f Fayruz—Grecian Blue **Mrs Beth Cunningham-Brown**
3 **BOLD EFFORT (FR)**, 4, b g Bold Arrangement—Malham Tarn **Mr A. J. Richards**
4 **BRECKLAND (IRE)**, 6, b h Trojan Fen—Rose Noir **Danebury Racing Stables Limited**
5 **DANCING PADDY**, 8, b g Nordance (USA)—Ninotchka **Bychance Racing**
6 **DYNAMIS (IRE)**, 5, b m Dancing Brave (USA)—Diasprina (GER) **Mr D. Bass**
7 **EL GRANDO**, 6, b g King of Spain—Easterly Wind **Mr M. D. Brunton**
8 **FRISKY MISS (IRE)**, 5, b m Fayruz—Moira My Girl **Mr D. Bass**
9 **INDIAN FIRE**, 6, ch g Indian Forest (USA)—Saintly Game **Mr S. Pedersen**
10 **JOLTO**, 7, b g Noalto—Joytime **Mrs G. M. Gooderham**
11 **KING UBAD (USA)**, 7, ch g Trempolino—Glitter (FR) **Mr A. J. Richards**
12 **KOMODO (USA)**, 4, ch g Ferdinand (USA)—Platonic Interest (USA) **Mr A. J. Richards**
13 **LADY ELIZABETH (FR)**, 4, b f Bold Arrangement—Top Fille (FR) **Mr A. J. Richards**
14 **LADY KATE (USA)**, 4, ch f Trempolino (USA)—Glitter (FR) **Mr A. J. Richards**
15 **LEES PLEASE (IRE)**, 4, b c Glenstal (USA)—Perfect Choice **Mr M. D. Brunton**
16 **LONELY VIGIL (FR)**, 4, b f Noblequest (FR)—Castaway (FR) **Mr A. J. Richards**
17 **MODESTO (USA)**, 8, b g Al Nasr (FR)—Modena (USA) **Mr D. Bass**
18 **NORLING (IRE)**, 6, ch g Nashamaa—Now Then **Mr S. Pedersen**
19 **PRESIDENTIAL (FR)**, 5, b g Village Star (FR)—Pokhara (FR) **Mr A. J. Richards**
20 **PRINCE NASHA (IRE)**, 6, ch g Norwick (USA)—Merokette **Mr S. Pedersen**
21 **SHELTERED COVE (IRE)**, 5, ch g Bold Arrangement—Racing Home (FR) **Mr A. J. Richards**
22 **SHY PADDY (IRE)**, 4, b g Shy Groom (USA)—Griqualand **Danebury Racing Stables Limited**
23 **VICTORIA STREET**, 4, b f Old Vic—Sunset Reef **Mr A. J. Richards**

THREE-YEAR-OLDS

24 **MY MOTHER'S LOCAL (USA)**, b f Local Talent (USA)—My Mother's Eyes (FR) **Mr A. J. Richards**
25 **SANDPIPER**, b f Green Desert (USA)—Sojourn
26 **SLIPARIS**, b f Slip Anchor—Parisian Express (FR) **Mr D. Bass**
27 **VILLAGE NATIVE (FR)**, ch c Village Star (FR)—Zedative (FR) **Mr A. J. Richards**

MR K. CUNNINGHAM-BROWN—continued

TWO-YEAR-OLDS

28 B c 16/3 Mac's Imp (USA)—Holly Bird (Runnett) **Danebury Racing Stables**
29 Ch c 28/3 Ron's Victory (USA)—Magical Spirit (Top Ville) **Mark Barrett**
30 Ch f 12/4 Risk Me (FR)—Ramz (IRE) (The Minstrel (CAN)) **Tiletrio Racing**
31 **VILLAGE PUB (FR)**, ch c 7/5 Village Star (FR)—Sloe Berry (Sharpo) **Mr A. J. Richards**

Other Owners: Mr G. J. Cronin, Mr K. O. Cunningham-Brown, Ewar Stud Farms France, Mr G. H. Galley, Mrs G. M. Gooderham, Mr M. Green, Mrs D. M. Read, Mr P. S. Wilkinson.

Jockeys (Flat): L Dettori, T R Quinn, J Weaver.

Jockeys (NH): R Dunwoody, A Maguire, D O'Sullivan.

163   MR B. J. CURLEY, Newmarket

Postal: **White Horse Stables, Stetchworth, Newmarket, Suffolk.**
Phone: **(01638) 508251**

1 **ALL TALK NO ACTION (IRE)**, 7, ch g Orchestra—Clarrie **Mrs B. J. Curley**
2 **JOHNSTONS BUCK (IRE)**, 7, b g Buckskin (FR)—Another Crash **Mrs B. J. Curley**
3 **MOYNSHA HOUSE (IRE)**, 8, b g Carlingford Castle—Verbana **Mrs B. J. Curley**
4 **MY MAN IN DUNDALK (IRE)**, 7, ch g Orchestra—Marla **Mrs B. J. Curley**
5 **MY MAN ON DUNDRUM (IRE)**, 7, ch g Orchestra—Pargio **Mrs B. J. Curley**

Jockey (NH): E Murphy (9-3).

Conditional: F McGirr (9-7).

164   MR J. W. P. CURTIS, Driffield

Postal: **Manor House, Beeford, Driffield, N. Humberside, YO25 8BD.**
Phone: **(01262) 488225**

1 **ALICAT (IRE)**, 5, b g Cataldi—Sweet Result **Mrs M. E. Curtis**
2 **CLEVER BOY (IRE)**, 5, b g Kambalda—Fast And Clever **Mrs M. E. Curtis**
3 **DARK OAK**, 10, br g Kambalda—Dusky Jo **Mrs M. E. Curtis**
4 **DEVON CASTLE (IRE)**, 6, ch g Carlingford Castle—Oula-Ka Fu-Fu **Mr J. W. P. Curtis**
5 **FINAL BEAT (IRE)**, 7, ch g Orchestra—Market Romance **Mrs M. E. Curtis**
6 **MERRYHILL GOLD**, 5, b g Glint of Gold—Phlox **Mrs M. E. Curtis**
7 **OLD ALE (IRE)**, 6, b g Tale Quale—Golden Mela **Mr J. W. P. Curtis**
8 **OVER THE CORRIB (IRE)**, 6, ch g Over The River (FR)—Glencorrin **Mr J. W. P. Curtis**
9 **PRINCE YAZA**, 9, br g Ya Zaman (USA)—Frances Jordan **Mrs M. E. Curtis**

165   MR ROGER CURTIS, Lambourn

Postal: **Delamere House Stables, Baydon Road, Lambourn, Berkshire, RG16 7NT.**
Phone: **(01488) 73007 MOBILE (0836) 320690 FAX (01488) 73909**

1 **AL JINN**, 5, ch g Hadeer—Mrs Musgrove
2 **ANOTHER MONK (IRE)**, 5, b g Supreme Leader—Royal Demon **Mr D. W. Hoskyns**

MR ROGER CURTIS—continued

3 **BARON ALLFOURS**, 4, gr g Baron Blakeney—Georgian Quickstep **Tony Waters**
4 **CALL ME CITIZEN**, 10, b g Carlingford Castle—Kelenem
5 **CAPTAIN COE**, 6, b g Uncle Pokey—Hazeldean **Heart of the South Racing (2)**
6 **CLIFTON**, 7, b g Idiot's Delight—Lost For Words **Mrs G. Fletcher**
7 **COMPUTERAID LADY**, 6, b br m Shaab—Gypsy Field **Mr M. O'Brien**
8 **DEPTFORD BELLE**, 6, b g Sula Bula—Gemini Stone **Heart Of The South Racing (1)**
9 **EQUITY PLAYER**, 11, ch g Gala Performance (USA)—Eden Dale **The Mrs S Partnership**
10 **EXPRESS TRAVEL (IRE)**, 8, b g New Express—Agher Glebe **Mr Michael J. Low**
11 **FUNCHEON GALE**, 9, b g Strong Gale—Funcheon Breeze **Kings Of The Road Partnership**
12 **HILLWALK**, 10, b g Croghan Hill—Bell Walks Fancy **Mr M. L. Shone**
13 4, Gr g Pragmatic—Kelly's Delight (IRE) **William Dillon**
14 5, B m Town And Country—Kindled Spirit
15 **KREEF**, 4, b g Kris—Pelf (USA) **H. J. S. Racing**
16 **LAC DE GRAS (IRE)**, 5, gr g Henbit (USA)—I've No Idea **Michael Burwell**
17 **MAZZARELLO (IRE)**, 6, ch g Hatim (USA)—Royal Demon **Mr D. W. Hoskyns**
18 **MIRADOR**, 5, b m Town And Country—Wild Jewel **Mrs J. Whitehead and John McGivern**
19 **MISS MUIRE**, 10, ch m Scallywag—Coroin Muire **H. J. S. Racing**
20 **OH SO HANDY**, 8, b g Nearly A Hand—Geordie Lass **Mrs R. A. Smith**
21 **OUROWNFELLOW (IRE)**, 7, ch g Arapahos (FR)—Dara's March **Kings Of The Road Partnership**
22 **OXFORD QUILL**, 9, b g Balliol—No Ink **Mr T. F. Parrett**
23 4, Ch g Joli Wasfi (USA)—Popsi's Poppet **Mrs K. M. Curtis**
24 **ST ATHANS LAD**, 11, b g Crooner—Greasby Girl **Geyer Estates (St Athans Hotel)**
25 **THE SUBSTITUTE**, 4, b f Colmore Row—Snow Chief **Woodcote Racing Stables Ltd**
26 **YOUDONTSAY**, 4, ch f Most Welcome—Fabulous Luba **Mr T. W. Nicholls**

THREE-YEAR-OLDS

27 **YOUNG MAZAAD (IRE)**, b c Mazaad—Lucky Charm (IRE) **Mr T. F. Parrett**

TWO-YEAR-OLDS

28 B c Full Extent (USA)—Wild Jewel (Great Heron (USA)) **Mrs K. M. Curtis**

Other Owners: Mr D. Auer, Mr Hector H. Brown, Mr S. B. Glazer, Mr Roger Graham, Mr H. Green, Mr Roger Harding, Mrs Loretta Harris, Mr Peter Jeffs, Mrs Sylvia E. M. McGarvie, Mrs Caroline Penny, Mr John Penny, Mr Michael Riley, Mr P. A. Sells, Ms V. Staveacre, Mr S. D. Swaden, Mr D. Warren, Mr C. J. Wood.

Jockey (NH): Derrick Morris (10-0).

166   MR T. A. K. CUTHBERT, Carlisle

Postal: **26 Eden Grange, Little Corby, Carlisle, Cumbria, CA4 8OW.**
Phone: **(01228) 560822 STABLES (01228) 561317**

1 **DANCER DICKINS**, 5, b g Alfie Dickins—Doreen's Darling **Mr G. Eubank**
2 **JIM'S WISH (IRE)**, 8, b g Heraldiste (USA)—Fete Champetre **Mr T. A. K. Cuthbert**
3 **JOE'S BIT OF GOLD**, 4, gr f Gold Song—Katie Grey **Mr W. Hurst**
4 **JUSTICE LEA**, 16, b g Kinglet—Evada **Mr J. J. Sweeney**
5 **MARZOCCO**, 8, ch g Formidable (USA)—Top Heights **Mr T. A. K. Cuthbert**
6 **MIGHTY SUPREMO (USA)**, 15, b g Raja Baba (USA)—Glut's Kin (USA) **Mr T. A. K. Cuthbert**
7 **MILS MIJ**, 11, br g Slim Jim—Katie Grey **Mr W. Hurst**
8 **MR FLUORINE (IRE)**, 7, b g Mr Fluorocarbon—Madonna Who **Miss Helen E. Cuthbert**
9 **OTTER BOY**, 7, b g Davout—Fragrant Friday **Mr T. A. K. Cuthbert**
10 **PRIESTS MEADOW (IRE)**, 7, ch g Cardinal Flower—Miss Taurus **Mr Nigel Dean**
11 **STAGS FELL**, 11, gr g Step Together (USA)—Honey's Queen **Mrs Joyce Cuthbert**
12 **SWANK GILBERT**, 10, b g Balliol—Song To Singo **Mrs Joyce Cuthbert**

Other Owners: Mr I. C. Copeland.

Jockey (NH): Carol Cuthbert (9-7).

167   MR CHARLES CYZER, Horsham

Postal: **Elliotts, Maplehurst, Horsham, West Sussex, RH13 6QX.**

Phone: **(01403) 730255 FAX (01403) 730787**

1 **ALL THE JOYS**, 5, b br m Adbass (USA)—Joytime
2 **ART FORM (USA)**, 9, b g Little Current (USA)—Christi Dawn (USA)
3 **BOLD RESOLUTION (IRE)**, 8, b g Shardari—Valmarine (FR)
4 **BRAVE SPY**, 5, b g Law Society (USA)—Contralto
5 **ENDLESS FANTASY**, 4, b f Kalaglow—Headrest
6 **GOLDEN PUNCH (USA)**, 5, b g Seattle Song (USA)—Pagan Winter (USA)
7 **MASTER PLANNER**, 7, b g Night Shift (USA)—Shaky Puddin
8 **MISS HAVERSHAM**, 4, b f Salse (USA)—Rustic Stile
9 **OFFICE HOURS**, 4, b g Danehill (USA)—Charmina (FR)
10 **PRINCELY GAIT**, 5, b g Darshaan—Roussalka
11 **REMEMBER THIS (IRE)**, 6, b g Don't Forget Me—Regal Twin (USA)
12 **SALLY SLADE**, 4, b f Dowsing (USA)—Single Gal
13 **ULTIMATE WARRIOR**, 6, b g Master Willie—Fighting Lady
14 **UNCHARTED WATERS**, 5, b m Celestial Storm (USA)—Try The Duchess

THREE-YEAR-OLDS

15 **BATTLE SPARK (USA)**, b g Gold Seam (USA)—Flick Your Bick (USA)
16 **BOWLED OVER**, b g Batshoof—Swift Linnet
17 **CHOCOLATE ICE**, b g Shareef Dancer (USA)—Creake
18 **DUNCOMBE HALL**, b g Salse (USA)—Springs Welcome
19 **HARBET HOUSE (FR)**, b g Bikala—Light of Hope (USA)
20 **LOVE AND KISSES**, ch f Salse (USA)—Soba
21 **MOVE DARLING**, ch f Rock City—Larive
22 **QUIET ARCH (IRE)**, b g Archway (IRE)—My Natalie
23 **STEAMROLLER STANLY**, b g Shirley Heights—Miss Demure
24 **STONE ISLAND**, b g Rambo Dancer (CAN)—Single Gal
25 **TIME FOR TEA (IRE)**, ch f Imperial Frontier (USA)—Glowing Embers

TWO-YEAR-OLDS

26 **ACROSS THE WATER**, b f 10/3 Slip Anchor—Stara (Star Appeal)
27 **ACTION STATIONS**, b c 9/2 High Estate—Toast (IRE) (Be My Guest (USA))
28 **AQUAVITA**, b gr f 9/4 Kalaglow—Aigua Blava (USA) (Solford (USA))
29 **BEHIND THE SCENES**, ch c 27/3 Kris—Free Guest (Be My Guest (USA))
30 **BOOK AT BEDTIME (IRE)**, b f 23/4 Mtoto—Akila (FR) (Top Ville)
31 **CASTLES BURNING (USA)**, b br c 25/1 Minshaanshu Amad—Major Overhaul (Known Fact (USA))
32 **CHEEK TO CHEEK**, b f 3/2 Shavian—Intoxication (Great Nephew)
33 **DANDY REGENT (USA)**, b c 25/2 Green Desert (USA)—Tahilla (Moorestyle)
34 **DAYLIGHT DREAMS**, b f 9/4 Indian Ridge—Singing Nelly (Pharly (FR))
35 **INSPIRATIONAL (IRE)**, ch f 12/4 Lahib (USA)—Sun Breiz (FR) (Boran)
36 **MYSTICAL ISLAND**, b f 26/1 Deploy—Do Run Run (Commanche Run)
37 **NITE BITES**, b c 17/2 Thatching—Buraida (Balidar)
38 **PRINCESS TOPAZ**, b f 15/2 Midyan—Diamond Princess (Horage)
39 **RASPBERRY SAUCE**, b f 8/5 Niniski (USA)—Sobranie (High Top)
40 **REHEARSAL (IRE)**, b c 2/5 Royal Academy (USA)—Yashville (Top Ville)
41 **RICH IN LOVE (IRE)**, b f 12/4 Alzao (USA)—Chief's Quest (USA) (Chief's Crown (USA))
42 **RISE 'N SHINE**, ch f 11/5 Night Shift (USA)—Clunk Click (Star Appeal)
43 **SIGNED AND SEALED (USA)**, b c 13/2 Rahy (USA)—Heaven's Mine (USA) (Graustark)
44 **SIGNS AND WONDERS**, b f 31/1 Danehill (USA)—Front Line Romance (Caerleon (USA))
45 **SIPOWITZ**, b c 21/4 Warrshan (USA)—Springs Welcome (Blakeney)
46 **SPACE RACE**, b c 28/3 Rock Hopper—Melanoura (Imperial Fling (USA))

Owners: Amity Finance Ltd, Miss J. P. Bentley, Mr M. Caine, Mr Stephen Crown, Mr R. M. Cyzer, Mr R. Gander, Mrs G. M. Gooderham, Mr M. J. Morrison, Mr R. Parsons, Mr J. Wenman.

168   MR J. N. DALTON, Shifnal

Postal: **Sutton House Farm, Shifnal, Shropshire, TF11 9NF.**
Phone: **(01952) 730656 FAX (01952) 730261**

1 **FANCYTALKINTINKER (IRE)**, 6, b g Bold Owl—Our Ena **Mr J. N. Dalton**
2 **MY SENOR**, 7, b g Jalmood (USA)—San Marguerite **Mr J. N. Dalton**
3 **SANDFORD THYNE (IRE)**, 6, ch m Good Thyne (USA)—Dippy Girl **Mr J. N. Dalton**
4 **SHOON WIND**, 13, b g Green Shoon—Gone **Mr J. N. Dalton**

Amateur: Mr A N Dalton (10-12).

169   MR P. T. DALTON, Burton-on-Trent

Postal: **Dovecote Cottage, Bretby Park, Bretby, Burton-on-Trent, DE15 0RB.**
Phone: **HOME (01283) 221922 OFFICE 221922 FAX 224679 MOBILE (0374) 240753**

1 **ANYTIME BABY**, 4, b f Bairn (USA)—Cindys Gold **Messinger Stud Limited**
2 **BENVENUTO**, 5, b g Neltino—Rydewells Daughter **Mrs Lucia Farmer**
3 **DOOLAR (USA)**, 9, b g Spend A Buck (USA)—Surera (ARG) **Mrs Lucia Farmer**
4 **GLAMANGLITZ**, 6, ch g Town And Country—Pretty Useful **Mrs Julie Martin**
5 **IRISH LUCK (IRE)**, 6, b g Mister Lord (USA)—Glenarold Lass **Mrs Lucia Farmer**
6 **SAILOR JIM**, 9, gr g Scallywag—Madge Hill **Mr R. A. H. Perkins**
7 **SALTZ (IRE)**, 4, b g Salt Dome (USA)—Heather Hut **Mrs Julie Martin**
8 **STORMING RUN (IRE)**, 8, b g Strong Gale—Beauty Run **Mr R. A. H. Perkins**
9 **VAZON EXPRESS**, 10, b g Le Bavard (FR)—Grangecon Express **Mr R. A. H. Perkins**

THREE-YEAR-OLDS

10 **FRIENDLY DREAMS (IRE)**, gr f Midyan (USA)—Friendly Thoughts (USA) **Mrs Julie Martin**
11 **NEW REGIME (IRE)**, b f Glenstal (USA)—Gay Refrain **Mrs Julie Martin**
12 **PRECIOUS ISLAND**, b f Jupiter Island—Burmese Ruby **Mrs Jeffrey Robinson**
13 **TOPAGLOW (IRE)**, ch g Topanoora—River Glow **Mrs Julie Martin**

Other Owners: Mr David R. Martin, Miss Charlotte A. I. Perkins, Miss Melissa Perkins, Mrs R. S. Perkins.

Jockey (NH): W J Marston (10-0, w.a.).

Amateur: Miss J Wormall (9-0).

170   MR D. J. DAVIES, Neath

Postal: **Ynys Dwfnant Farm, Clyne, Resolven, Neath, SA11 4BN.**
Phone: **(01639) 710774**

1 **BELL GLASS (FR)**, 10, gr g Bellypha—Greener Pastures **Mr D. Davies**
2 **DEER MARNY**, 7, ch m Hadeer—Juliette Mariner **Mr D. Davies**
3 **GLYNN BRAE (IRE)**, 6, b g Spin of A Coin—Bright Toro **Mr D. Davies**

171   MR G. W. J. DAVIES, Abergavenny

Postal: **Home Farm, Llwyndu, Abergavenny, Gwent.**
Phone: **(0873) 852292**

1 4, Ch g Rustingo—Delta Rose **Mrs D. M. Davies**
2 **ROC AGE**, 5, ch m Rustingo—La Chica **Mr M. W. Davies**
3 **VOLCANIC ROC**, 6, b g Rustingo—La Chica **Mr M. W. Davies**

Conditional: Richard Davies (9-12, w.a.).

172   MR N. J. DAWE, Bridgwater

Postal: **Chantry Cottage, Sea Lane, Kilve, Bridgwater, TA5 1EG.**
Phone: **(01278) 741457**

1 **CHANTRY LAD,** 4, b g Fearless Action (USA)—Auto Connection **Mrs Jacqui Dawe**

THREE-YEAR-OLDS

2 B g Full Extent (USA)—Discreet Charm **Mrs Jacqui Dawe**
3 **MILTON ABBOT,** b g Full Extent (USA)—Auto Connection **Mrs Jacqui Dawe**

173   MR B. DE HAAN, Lambourn

Postal: **Fair View, Long Hedge, Lambourn, Newbury, RG16 7NA.**
Phone: **(01488) 72163 (0831) 104574 MOBILE**

1 **ASCOT LAD,** 11, ch g Broadsword (USA)—Aunt Livia **Mr J. C. Berry**
2 **BEACON FLIGHT (IRE),** 5, br g Phardante (FR)—Flying Pegus **The Heyfleet Partnership**
3 **CHARLIE'S FOLLY,** 5, ch g Capitano—Cavity **Mr Duncan Heath**
4 **EDEN ROC,** 6, b g Dragon Palace (USA)—Aunt Livia **Mr Stephen L. Ross**
5 **IVORY COASTER (NZ),** 5, b g Ivory Hunter (USA)—Rajah's Girl (NZ) **Mr D. Andrews & Partners**
6 **LAURA LYE (IRE),** 6, b m Carlingford Castle—Pennyala **Mr Duncan Heath**
7 **PADRINO,** 5, b g Teenoso (USA)—Power Happy **Padrino Partnership**
8 **SPRING SUNRISE,** 6, b m Robellino (USA)—Saniette **Mrs D. Vaughan**
9 **VLADIVOSTOK,** 6, gr g Siberian Express (USA)—Tsungani **Mr G. & L. Johnson**

Other Owners: Mr R. S. Allen, Mrs Richard Allen, Duke Of Devonshire, Mr C. W. Foreman, Mrs M. A. Foreman, Mr E R. Jervis, Mrs Joan Marie Jervis, Mrs E. Tatman, Mr Nicholas Tatman.

174   MR R. DICKIN, Stratford-on-Avon

Postal: **Alscot Racing Stables, Alscot Park, Stratford-on-Avon, Warwickshire, CV37 8BL.**
Phone: **TEL: (01789) 450052 FAX (01789) 450053 MOBILE (0374) 742430**

1 **BALLY PARSON,** 10, b g The Parson—Ballyadam Lass **Mr G. Hutsby**
2 **BLESSED MEMORY,** 5, ch m Rahy (USA)—Rummann (USA) **Mrs M. Payne**
3 **COLONEL COLT,** 5, b g Saint Andrews (FR)—Vallee des Sauges (USA) **Mr Pete Holder**
4 **DIXTON HILL,** 8, b g Pitpan—Miss Silly **Dixton Hill Partnership**
5 **DR ROCKET,** 11, b g Ragapan—Lady Hansel **The Rocketeers**
6 **DUBAI FALCON (USA),** 5, b g Woodman (USA)—Keeper's Charm (USA) **Mr H. Burford**
7 **ERIN'S LAD,** 5, br h Bold Owl—Vernair (USA) **Mr Anthony Smith**
8 **HURRYUP,** 9, b g Duky—Delay **Mr Allan Bennett**
9 **KADASTROF (FR),** 6, ch h Port Etienne (FR)—Kadastra (FR) **Mr A. P. Paton**
10 **KAMERLING (FR),** 4, br g Super Green (USA)—Kadastra (FR)
11 **KARLINE KA (FR),** 5, ch m Franc Parler—Kadastra (FR) **Mr A. P. Paton & Mr C. P. Paton**
12 **KASAYID,** 9, br g Niniski (USA)—Raabihah **Mrs C. M. Dickin**
13 **K C'S DANCER,** 11, ch g Buckskin (FR)—Lorna Lass **King of Clubs Ltd (Gloucester)**
14 **KETFORD BRIDGE,** 9, ch g Hardboy—Unsinkable Sarah **Mrs T. L. Benge**
15 **KYTTON CASTLE,** 9, ch m Carlingford Castle—Ballykytton **Joint Partnership**
16 **LODESTONE LAD (IRE),** 6, br g Norwick (USA)—Gentle Star **Mrs D. L. Weaver**
17 **LO-FLYING MISSILE,** 8, gr g Cruise Missile—Lo-Incost **Mr Brian Clifford**
18 **MAGGIE MARNE,** 6, b m Relkino—Penny Venus **Mrs M. A. Walters**
19 **MANARD,** 5, b m Ardross—Sweet Mandy **Mr Tony Walpole**
20 **MISS FERN,** 11, b m Cruise Missile—Fernshaw **Mrs Peter Andrews**
21 **MR GORDON BENNETT,** 5, b g Vin St Benet—Paphidia **Mr N. D. Edden**
22 **NUNSON,** 7, ch g Celtic Cone—Nunswalk **Mrs C. Williams**
23 **PATSCILLA,** 5, br m Squill (USA)—Fortune Teller **Mr S. Holmes**
24 4, B g Strong Gale—Poor Elsie **Mrs P. Andrews**
25 **RARE OCCURANCE,** 6, b g Damister (USA)—Superior Quality **Mr R. H. Harris & Partners**

MR R. DICKIN—continued

26 **RING THE BANK**, 9, ch m Ring Bidder—Ladybank **The Battyball Partnership**
27 **SAGAMAN (GER)**, 10, b g Solo Dancer (GER)—Scholastika (GER) **Mr M. Doocey**
28 **SILENT CRACKER**, 4, br g Teenoso (USA)—Silent Surrender **Mr R. C. G. Smith**
29 **STEY SUNY**, 9, ch g Sunyboy—Stey Brae **Mr R. C. G. Smith**
30 **THE FLYING FOOTMAN**, 10, b g Furry Glen—Ballygoman Maid **Mrs James West**
31 **TIME LEADER**, 4, ch g Lead On Time (USA)—Green Leaf (USA) **Mr H. Gott & Partners**

THREE-YEAR-OLDS

32 **ALISTOVER**, b f Zalazl (USA)—Song of Gold **Mr A. P. Paton**
33 **COME ON IN**, b g Most Welcome—Lominda (IRE) **Mrs C. M. Dickin & Mrs C. Weaver**
34 **NORTHERN SKY**, b f North Col—Emma Wright **Mr P. Thorne**
35 **SILENT ROSE**, b br f Petoski—Silent Surrender **Mr R. C. G. Smith**

TWO-YEAR-OLDS

36 Ch f 16/2 Most Welcome—Larive (Blakeney) **Mrs C. M. Dickin**
37 Ch c 11/2 Regal Intention (CAN)—Prairie Sky (USA) (Gone West (USA)) **Mr R. H. Harris & Mr W. Sanderson**

Other Owners: Mr D. L. Abbott, Mrs Pat Beck, Mr R. B. Begy, Mr R. Cawthorn, Mr A. Clift, Mrs P. M. Crawford, Mr R. E. Daniel, Mr P. Doyle, Mrs J. Duckett, Mr W. P. Evans, Mr M. Fleming, Flisher Foods, Miss M. Gledhill, Mr Derek C. Holder, Mr K. Jones, Mr Michael Kopsch, Captain B. Lennon-Smith, Mr J. De Lisle-Wells, Mr B. Veasey, Mr Waller, Miss Emma West, Mr P. D. Whitehouse.

Jockeys (Flat): T Quinn (8-4, w.a.), C Rutter (7-10).

Jockeys (NH): Robert Bellamy (10-0), Richard Dunwoody, D Meredith (10-0), B Powell.

Apprentice: Michelle Thomas.

Conditional: Philip Hughes (9-10).

Lady Rider: Miss Sally Duckett (9-7).

175   MR J. E. DIXON, Carlisle

Postal: **Moor End, Thursby, Carlisle, Cumbria, CA5 6QP.**
Phone: **DALSTON (01228) 710318**

1 **AMBER HOLLY**, 7, ch m Import—Holly Lodge **Mrs E. M. Dixon**
2 **ANOTHER FOUNTAIN**, 10, b g Royal Fountain—Another Joyful **Mrs E. M. Dixon**
3 **ANOTHER MEADOW**, 8, b g Meadowbrook—Another Joyful **Mrs E. M. Dixon**
4 **CROFTON LAKE**, 8, ch g Alias Smith (USA)—Joyful Star **Mrs E. M. Dixon**
5 **DARK FOUNTAIN**, 9, br g Royal Fountain—Another Joyful **Mrs E. M. Dixon**
6 **JOYFUL IMP**, 9, b m Import—Joyful Star **Mrs E. M. Dixon**
7 **JUMBO STAR**, 6, ch g Jumbo Hirt (USA)—Joyful Star **Mrs E. M. Dixon**

176   MR M. J. K. DODS, Darlington

Postal: **Denton Hall, Piercebridge, Darlington, Co Durham, DL2 3TY.**
Phone: **(01325) 374270 FAX (01325) 374020 MOBILE (0860) 411590**

1 **BALLON**, 6, b m Persian Bold—La Vosgienne **Whitworth Racing**
2 **BIRCHWOOD SUN**, 6, b g Bluebird (USA)—Shapely Test (USA) **Mr A. G. Watson**
3 **BLUE GRIT**, 10, b g Thatching—Northern Wisdom **Mr C. Michael Wilson**
4 **CALL TO THE BAR (IRE)**, 7, b g Kafu—Papun (USA) **Mr M. J. K. Dods**
5 **CURIE CRUSADER (IRE)**, 5, gr g Belfort (FR)—Katysue **Three Plus One Racing**
6 **DR EDGAR**, 4, b g Most Welcome—African Dancer **Mr A. G. Watson**
7 **FORGOTTEN BOY (IRE)**, 4, b g Don't Forget Me—Lunulae **Mr K. Chapman**

MR M. J. K. DODS—continued

8 **FRENCH GRIT (IRE)**, 4, b c Common Grounds—Charbatte (FR) **Mr C. Michael Wilson**
9 **HEATHYARDS MAGIC (IRE)**, 4, b g Magical Strike (USA)—Idle Gossip **Mr M. J. K. Dods**
10 **HENRY THE HAWK**, 5, b g Doulab (USA)—Plum Blossom (USA) **Mr S. Barras**
11 **KING CHESTNUT**, 5, ch g Efisio—Sweet Colleen **Mr C. Graham**
12 **LOSTRIS (IRE)**, 5, b m Pennine Walk—Herila (FR) **Mr K. Knox**
13 **MACCONACHIE**, 9, b g Good Times (ITY)—High Point Lady (CAN) **Mr M. C. J. Sunley**
14 **MAMICA**, 6, b g Idiot's Delight—Fishermans Lass **Mrs C. E. Dods**
15 **NED'S BONANZA**, 7, b g Green Ruby (USA)—Miss Display **Mr Ned Jones**
16 **QUILLING**, 4, ch g Thatching—Quillotern (USA) **Mr A. G. Watson**
17 **THOMAS RAND**, 7, b g Macmillion—Play It Sam **Mr N. A. Riddell**
18 **WALWORTH LADY**, 5, gr m Belfort (FR)—Manna Green **Mr Vernon Spinks**

THREE-YEAR-OLDS

19 **DAREROCK**, b g Daring March—Marock Morley **Whitworth Racing**
20 **ENERGY MAN**, b g Hadeer—Cataclysmic **Mr A. J. Henderson**
21 **FISIOSTAR**, b g Efisio—Sweet Colleen
22 **JUNGLE JEAN**, b f Dowsing (USA)—Noble Lustre (USA) **Mr M. C. J. Sunley**
23 **MADONNA DA ROSSI**, b f Mtoto—Granny's Bank **Smith & Allan Oils Racing Club**
24 **NED'S CONTESSA (IRE)**, ch f Persian Heights—Beechwood (USA) **Mr Ned Jones**
25 **POLISH SAGA**, ch f Polish Patriot (USA)—Sagar **Mr J. A. Wynn-Williams**
26 **TURBO NORTH**, b g Nordico (USA)—Turbo Rose **Mr A. G. Watson**

TWO-YEAR-OLDS

27 **BOLD ENGAGEMENT**, b f 13/4 Never So Bold—Diamond House (Habitat) **Smith & Allan Oils Racing Club**
28 B c 21/3 Common Grounds—Saint Navarro (Raga Navarro (ITY)) **Mr J. Hamilton**
29 B f 18/2 Silver Kite (USA)—Sudbury (IRE) (Auction Ring (USA)) **Mr M. J. K. Dods**
30 B f 23/5 Efisio—Sweet Colleen (Connaught) **Mr G. Graham & Partners**

Other Owners: Mr J. Beadle, Mr P. W. Boylett, Mr F. Burnside, Mr Neil Cooper, Mr M. S. Geddes, Mr T. Hebdon, Mr M. Henfrey, Mrs J. W. Hutchinson, Mrs L. Jones, Mr D. Kirsopp, Mrs P. A. Knox, Mr J. A. Pratt, Mrs Tracey Profitt.

Jockey (Flat): Dale Gibson.

Jockey (NH): T Reed (w.a.).

Lady Riders: Mrs C Dods (8-0), Miss E Maude (8-0).

177   MR FRANCOIS DOUMEN, Lamorlaye

Postal: **19 Rue Charles Pratt, 60260 Lamorlaye, France.**
Phone: **(00 33) 44214501 FAX (00 33) 44212341**

1 **ALGAN (FR)**, 8, b g Le Pontet (FR)—Djaipour II **Marquesa de Moratalla**
2 **BABA AU RHUM (IRE)**, 4, b g Baba Karam—Spring About **J. Poynton**
3 **BELLE CHAUMIERE**, 5, b m Gildoran—Sunny Cottage **Mr C. Botton**
4 **BILBAO V (FR)**, 7, b br g Bad Conduct (USA)—Seville **Marquesa de Moratalla**
5 **BILLIARD NONANTAIS (FR)**, 6, gr g Concorde Jr (USA)—Belle Nonantaise **Mr A. Wandeler**
6 **BOTTOM'S UP (FR)**, 4, b g Quart de Vin—Sclos **Mme F. Doumen**
7 **BOUL MICH (FR)**, 4, b c French Stress (USA)—Marie des Ruelles **Mr Gordon**
8 **BURGIN (FR)**, 9, b g Recitation (USA)—Rose of Ireland **Ecurie D'Ecouves**
9 **CIEL DE BRION (FR)**, 6, b g Shafoun—Jupe de Laine **Mr Henri De Pracomtal**
10 **CLAIYMAD DES IFS (FR)**, 6, b g Maiymad—Fridoline **Mr C. Hansard**
11 **CORPS ET AME (IRE)**, 6, b g Corvaro (USA)—Welsh Tan **Mr C. Botton**
12 **CORTON (FR)**, 6, br g Brezzo (FR)—Isis (FR) **Marquesa de Moratalla**
13 **DAN ROYAL (FR)**, 5, b g Video Rock—Lady Royale **Marquesa de Moratalla**
14 **DELIRE D'ESTRUVAL (FR)**, 5, b g Synefos (USA)—Magic **Mr Jim Brewer**
15 **DELUCK (IRE)**, 4, b g Denel—Sometime Lucky **Mr C. Botton**
16 **DORMEUIL (FR)**, 5, b g Quart de Vin—Dobetre **Marquesa de Moratalla**
17 **ELEVE D'ESTRUVAL (FR)**, 4, ch g Quart de Vin—Vocation **Mrs M. Fricker**

MR FRANCOIS DOUMEN—continued

18 **ELOI II (FR)**, 4, ch g Video Rock—Judelle **Ecurie D'Ecouves**
19 **FRENCH FELLOW (FR)**, 4, b g Quart de Vin—L'Oranaise **Marquesa de Moratalla**
20 **GREAT EXPECTATIONS (FR)**, 5, ch g Village Star—Balnica **Mrs K. Taplin**
21 **HOLY DRAGON (FR)**, 5, b g Comrade In Arms—Pasta **Marc De Montfort**
22 **JIMKANA (FR)**, 4, b f Double Bed (FR)—Jimka (FR) **Miss D. Platt**
23 **LAKE POWELL (FR)**, 6, b g Rose Laurel—Mille Feuilles **Marquesa de Moratalla**
24 **MARBELLA (GER)**, 6, b m Peloponnes—Mantilla **H. Hack**
25 **MON LUTTEUR (FR)**, 6, ch g King Luthier—Urdite (FR) **J. Poynton**
26 **OVERCRAFT (FR)**, 4, b g Lashkari—Quintefolle **Marquesa de Moratalla**
27 **POLLY UMRIGAR (IRE)**, 5, b g Phardante—Flashey Blond **J. Poynton**
28 **QUARTZ (FR)**, 7, ch g Saint Estephe (FR)—Quintefolle (FR) **Marquesa de Moratalla**
29 **ROYALTINO (FR)**, 4, b g Neltino—Royal Well **Mr Henri De Pracomtal**
30 **SO FAR SO BOLD (IRE)**, 6, br g Phardante (FR)—Blajina **J. Poynton**
31 **SOV SOV (FR)**, 4, ch c Sicyos (USA)—Noujoud **Ecurie D'Ecouves**
32 4, B c Be My Guest (USA)—Stapara **F. Doumen**
33 **SUNRISE SONG (FR)**, 5, gr m General Holme (USA)—Marissiya **Mr J. Percepied**
34 **SYVANIE (FR)**, 4, b f Sicyos (USA)—Avanie (USA) **Mrs E. Reeves**
35 **TAWAKAL (USA)**, 4, ch g Slew O' Gold—Cadeaux d'Amie **Marquesa de Moratalla**
36 **TOKOLOSH (IRE)**, 6, ch m Phardante—Same Token **Mme F. Doumen**
37 **TOSCA'S KING (GER)**, 6, b g Alpenkonig—Tosca Carla **Ecurie D'Ecouves**
38 **VAL D'ALENE (FR)**, 9, b g Quart de Vin—Faribole **Marc De Montfort**
39 **VISON (FR)**, 9, b g R B Chesne—Cigale II **Mr B. Legentil**
40 **VOL PAR NUIT (USA)**, 5, ch g Cozzene—Hedonic **Mr D. McIntyre**
41 **WARSAW CONCERTO (IRE)**, 6, ch g Orchestra—Warsaw **Mrs M. Levesque**

THREE-YEAR-OLDS

42 **ADIEU MON AMOUR (FR)**, b c Double Bed—Majuba **Ecurie D'Ecouves**
43 **ALARICO (FR)**, ch c Kadrou—Calabria **J. Poynton**
44 **BLEU A L'AME (FR)**, b g Double Bed—Sclos **Ecurie D'Ecouves**
45 **CABARET CLUB (FR)**, b f Top Ville—Riosamba **Mr R. Barby**
46 **DAME LA CHANCE (FR)**, ch f Sarhoob—Worlds Above **Mr T. Bailey**
47 **FOLLOW BERRY**, b g Tagel—Gennevilliers **J. Poynton**
48 **GIGAWATT (FR)**, b f Double Bed—Jimra **Ecurie D'Ecouves**
49 **GIPSIE DANCER (FR)**, ch f General Holme—Figure Libre **Miss D. Platt**
50 **L'ANNEE FOLLE (FR)**, b f Gai Lizza—Gairloch **Ecurie D'Ecouves**
51 **MY CONTESTED BED (FR)**, b g Double Bed—No Contest **Ecurie D'Ecouves**
52 **RED DIVAN (FR)**, b f Tip Moss—Hornblower Girl **Mr J. Killer**
53 **TAGAMET (FR)**, b f Double Bed—Gobern **Mr J. Killer**
54 **THE LOVER (FR)**, ch g Double Bed—Guards Gala **Mr J. Killer**
55 **THE TROLLOP (FR)**, b f Double Bed—La Belle Polonaise **Mr J. Killer**
56 **TOP GLORY (FR)**, b g Le Glorieux—Top Slipper **Mr Henri De Pracomtal**

TWO-YEAR-OLDS

57 **DANS LE CONTEXTE (FR)**, gr c 25/3 Gairloch—Pollys Mira **Ecurie D'Ecouves**
58 **DREAM BUSINESS (FR)**, b f 11/5 Double Bed—Sclos **Ecurie D'Ecouves**
59 **INKATHA (FR)**, gr c 22/3 Double Bed—Majuba **Ecurie D'Ecouves**
60 **INSIDER (FR)**, b c 16/2 Double Bed—Avaine **Mr M. Somerset-Leeke**
61 **IN ZE POCKET (FR)**, b f 20/3 Double Bed—No Contest **Mr J. Killer**
62 **JIM ET TONIC (FR)**, ch g 12/3 Double Bed—Jimka **Ecurie D'Ecouves**
63 **LALA I TOU (FR)**, b f 12/4 Suave Dancer—Lala **J. Poynton**
64 **MATINEE LOVER (FR)**, b c 22/3 Double Bed—Hornblower Girl **Mr M. Somerset-Leeke**
65 **OFF GUARD (FR)**, b f 25/4 Bakharoff—Guard's Gala **Mr J. Killer**
66 **RAIKABAG JUNCTION (FR)**, b c 27/2 Double Bed—La Belle Polonaise **Mr J. Killer**
67 **RAJPOUTE (FR)**, b c 1/2 Double Bed—Gai Lizza **Ecurie D'Ecouves**
68 **SIR HOLMFREY (FR)**, ch c 13/2 General Holme—Free Hair **Mr Henri De Pracomtal**

Jockey (Flat): Gerald Mosse (8-5, w.a.).

Jockeys (NH): Philippe Chevalier (10-0), Adam Kondrat (10-0).

Apprentice: Thierry Majorcrick.

Amateur: Mr Thierry Doumen (9-0).

178   MR S. L. DOW, Epsom

Postal: **Clear Height Stables, Derby Stables Road, Epsom, Surrey, KT18 5LB.**
Phone: **EPSOM (01372) 721490 FAX (01372) 748099 MOBILE (0860) 800109**

1 **ALLTHRUTHENIGHT (IRE)**, 7, ch h Precocious—Time For Pleasure **Mr G. Steinberg**
2 **BAG OF TRICKS (IRE)**, 6, br g Chief Singer—Bag Lady **Eurostrait Ltd**
3 **BIT OF ROUGH (IRE)**, 6, b g Roselier (FR)—Win Em All **The Fairway Partnership**
4 **CELTIC FIREFLY**, 4, ch f Cruise Missile—Celtic Art **Brighthelm Racing**
5 **CHAKALAK**, 8, b g Damister (USA)—Wig And Gown **Mr P. Chakko**
6 **CHIEF'S SONG**, 6, b g Chief Singer—Tizzy **Mrs Anne Devine**
7 **CONFRONTER**, 7, ch g Bluebird (USA)—Grace Darling (USA) **Hatfield Ltd**
8 **COURBARIL**, 4, b g Warrshan (USA)—Free On Board **Mr G. Steinberg**
9 **DARK HONEY**, 11, b g Marechal (FR)—Caillou **Mr Roger Sayer**
10 **DOCTOR DEATH (IRE)**, 5, ch g Thatching—Deepwater Blues **Mr R. N. Whittaker**
11 **DOLLIVER (USA)**, 4, b g Northern Baby (CAN)—Mabira **Mr D. G. Churston**
12 **EDAN HEIGHTS**, 4, b g Heights of Gold—Edna **Mr T. Mountain**
13 **FACE THE FUTURE**, 7, ch g Ahonoora—Chiltern Red **Future Prospectors - Four Seasons Racing**
14 **GAMEFULL GOLD**, 7, b m Mummy's Game—Speed The Plough **Mrs Caroline Martin**
15 **GLOBAL DANCER**, 5, b g Night Shift (USA)—Early Call **Cornish Arms-Charmandean Investments Plc**
16 **GREENSIDE CHAT (IRE)**, 6, b g Le Bavard (FR)—Elite Lady **The Fairway Partnership**
17 **ILANDRA (IRE)**, 4, b f Roi Danzig (USA)—Island Goddess **Chelgate Public Relations Ltd**
18 **ISMENO**, 5, b g Ela-Mana-Mou—Seattle Siren (USA) **Mrs A. M. Upsdell**
19 **IT'STHEBUSINESS**, 4, b c Most Welcome—Douceur (USA) **Eurostrait Ltd**
20 **JO MAXIMUS**, 4, b g Prince Sabo—Final Call **Mr J. A. Kelly**
21 **MENAS GOLD**, 4, br f Heights of Gold—Tolomena **Mr T. Mountain**
22 **MO'S MAIN MAN (IRE)**, 4, b g Taufan (USA)—Broadway Rosie **Hatfield Limited**
23 **MO'S STAR**, 4, b f Most Welcome—Star Face **Mrs A. M. Upsdell**
24 **NAGNAGNAG (IRE)**, 4, b f Red Sunset—Rubina Park **Sir Clement Freud**
25 **NATIVE CHIEFTAN**, 7, b g Trojan Fen—Habituee **Mr Ralph Cross**
26 **NORTHERN VILLAGE**, 9, ch g Norwick (USA)—Merokette **Mrs Heather Chakko**
27 **NO SPEECHES (IRE)**, 5, b g Last Tycoon—Wood Violet (USA) **Top Class Racing**
28 **PENNINE WIND (IRE)**, 4, b g Pennine Walk—Wintina **Mr F. K. Wilsdon**
29 **ROCKVILLE PIKE (IRE)**, 4, b g Glenstal (USA)—Sound Pet **Mr H. Nass**
30 **ROISIN CLOVER**, 5, ch m Faustus (USA)—Valiyen **Brighthelm Racing**
31 **SCHARNHORST**, 4, b g Tacheron—Stardyn **Mackenzie Print**
32 **SHINING DANCER**, 4, b f Rainbow Quest (USA)—Strike Home **The Lalemaha Partnership**
33 **SHOOFK**, 5, ch g Dunbeath (USA)—River Reem (USA) **Mr Sean Devine**
34 **SIR THOMAS BEECHAM**, 6, b g Daring March—Balinese **Mrs Heather Chakko**
35 **SLIGHTLY SPECIAL (IRE)**, 4, ch g Digamist (USA)—Tunguska **Mr T. M. J. Keep**
36 **SOVIET BRIDE (IRE)**, 4, b f Soviet Star (USA)—Nihad **Mr T. Shepherd**
37 **STOLEN MELODY**, 4, b f Robellino (USA)—Song of Hope **Mrs A. M. Upsdell**
38 **WAKEEL (USA)**, 4, b g Gulch (USA)—Raahia (CAN) **Mrs J. M. A. Churston**
39 **WALNUT BURL (IRE)**, 6, b h Taufan (USA)—Hay Knot **Mr G. Steinberg**
40 **WATER HAZARD (IRE)**, 4, b c Maelstrom Lake—Simply Inch **Nulli Secundus Racing Club**
41 **YOUNG ERN**, 6, b h Efisio—Stardyn **Mr M. F. Kentish**

THREE-YEAR-OLDS

42 **ASKING FOR KINGS (IRE)**, b g Thatching—Lady Donna **Mrs G. R. Smith**
43 **DAILY RISK**, ch g Risk Me (FR)—Give Me A Day **Mr D. G. Churston**
44 **ED'S FOLLY (IRE)**, b c Fayruz—Tabriya **Mr Eddie Davess**
45 **ELEGANTISSIMA**, b f Polish Precedent (USA)—Ela Meem (USA) **Bryan Taker & David Wilson**
46 **GET TOUGH**, b c Petong—Mrs Waddilove **Gravy Boys Racing**
47 **LA MODISTE**, b f Most Welcome—Dismiss **Mrs G. R. Smith**
48 **LANCASHIRE LEGEND**, gr g Belfort (FR)—Peters Pet Girl **Bryan Taker & David Wilson**
49 **MAPLE BURL**, b g Dominion—Carn Maire **Mr G. Steinberg**
50 **MERANTI**, b c Puissance—Sorrowful **Mr G. Steinberg**
51 **MIMOSA**, ch f Midyan (USA)—Figini **Mr G. Steinberg**
52 **MYSTIC DAWN**, b f Aragon—Ahonita **Mrs A. M. Upsdell**
53 **NAILS TAILS**, b c Efisio—Northern Dynasty **Mr M. F. Kentish**
54 **NIGHTSWIMMING (IRE)**, b g Mac's Imp (USA)—Kilnahard **Mr J. Etheridge**
55 **PREMIER NIGHT**, b f Old Vic—Warm Welcome **Mr D. G. Churston**

MR S. L. DOW—continued

56 QUEENS FANCY, ch f Infantry—Sagareina **Mr Ken Butler**
57 STEP ON DEGAS, b f Superpower—Vivid Impression **Mr A. Kazamia**
58 TIAMA (IRE), b f Last Tycoon—Soyata **Mr G. Steinberg**
59 TWICE REMOVED, b f Distant Relative—Nigel's Dream **Eurostrait Ltd**
60 WOT NO FAX, ch g Sharrood (USA)—Priors Dean **Kerniquips Racing Partnership**

TWO-YEAR-OLDS

61 CHAKRA, gr c Mystiko (USA)—Maracuja (USA) (Riverman (USA)) **Eurostrait Ltd**
62 EURO SUPERSTAR (FR), b c Rock City—Douceur (USA) (Shadeed (USA)) **Eurostrait Ltd**
63 HIPPIOS, b c 31/3 Formidable (USA)—Miss Doody (Gorytus (USA)) **Mr J. A. Kelly**
64 B c 25/2 High Estate—Just A Treat (IRE) (Glenstal (USA)) **Bryan Taker & David Wilson**
65 KAYZEE, b f 25/4 River Falls—Northern Amber (Shack (USA)) **Mr Hugh Doubtfire**
66 MYSTERY, b f Mystiko (USA)—Dismiss (Daring March) **Mrs G. R. Smith**
67 PALISANDER (IRE), ch c 26/2 Conquering Hero (USA)—Classic Choice (Patch) **Mr G. Steinberg**
68 PAPITA (IRE), b f 20/3 Law Society (USA)—Fantasise (FR) (General Assembly (USA)) **Mr G. Steinberg**
69 B c 23/1 Salt Dome (USA)—Play The Queen (IRE) (King of Clubs) **Future Prospectors - Four Seasons Racing**
70 TALISMAN (IRE), b c 4/5 Silver Kite (USA)—Sports Post Lady (IRE) (M Double M (USA)) **Mr X. Pullen**
71 THIRD PARTY, gr f Terimon—Party Game (Red Alert) **Mrs G. R. Smith**

Other Owners: Mr J. D. Ball, Mr H. Beaufort, Mr I. Blance, Mr Graham Brown, Mr Bruce Buckley, Mr Donald Burrough, Mr R. H. Chappell, Mr B. G. Desjardins, Mr M. B. Driver, Mr F. A. Ezen, Mrs S. Gadd, Mr B. Gee, Mr S. R. Harman, Mr J. R. Hayes, Mr I. Helou, Mr M. Hill, Mr Edward Hounslow, Mr Carl Hussey, Mr Paul G. Jacobs, Mr K. Kernahan, Mr P. Kernahan, Mr E. G. King, Mrs S. E. Lakin, Mr A. Lindsay, Mrs Janet Mackenzie, Mr N. G. Mackenzie, Mr J. E. Mills, Mr S. Munir, Mr Neil Munro, Mr D. Percival, Mr N. Pitt, Mrs Lesley Shepherd, Mr H. R. Siegle, Mrs L. Stone, Mrs Stovold.

Jockey (NH): A Dicken (10-0).

Apprentices: P Brookwood (8-4), A Daly (7-9).

Conditional: R Elkins (9-12).

Amateur: S Fetherston-Haugh (9-7).

179   MRS H. B. DOWSON, Pershore

Postal: **Lower Hill, Pershore, Worcs, WR10 3JR.**

1 EIGHTY EIGHT, 11, b g Doctor Wall—Pennulli **Mrs H. B. Dowson**

180   MISS JACQUELINE S. DOYLE, Eastbury

Postal: **Anniversary Cottage, Eastbury, Newbury, Berks, RG17 7QR.**
Phone: **(01488) 72222 MOBILE (0831) 880678**

1 BLUE AND ROYAL (IRE), 4, b g Bluebird (USA)—Cat Girl (USA) **Mr G. A. Libson**
2 BUCKMAN, 6, b g Buckley—Mango **The Legs Partnership**
3 FANTASTIC FLEET (IRE), 4, b c Woodman (USA)—Gay Fantastic **Mr Tom Ford**
4 FATACK, 7, b g Kris—Ma Petite Cherie (USA) **Mr Jeremy W. S. Barnett**
5 HADABET, 4, b g Hadeer—Betsy Bay (FR) **The Basics**
6 KALASADI (USA), 5, b g Shahrastani (USA)—Kassiyda **Mr G. A. Libson**
7 MEDITATOR, 12, ch g High Line—Thoughtful **Miss Jacqueline S. Doyle**
8 NAHLA, 6, b m Wassl—Bassita **The Safe Six**
9 NORTHERN SPRUCE (IRE), 4, ch g Astronef—Perle's Fashion **Jadecliff Ltd**

MISS JACQUELINE S. DOYLE—continued

10 **PORTSCATHO (IRE)**, 4, b g Common Grounds—Tweedling (USA) **Mr James**
11 **ROWHEDGE**, 10, ch g Tolomeo—Strident Note **Miss Jacqueline S. Doyle**
12 **WINNING WONDER**, 4, b f Charmer—Salchow **Jadecliff Ltd**

TWO-YEAR-OLDS

13 B f 15/4 Tina's Pet—Chinese Princess (Sunny Way) **Mr Tom Ford**

Other Owners: Mr W. Alsford, Mr P. Baum, Mr David L. Bayliss, Mr G. W. Bone, Mr J. Chapman, Mr F. A. Fisher, Mr K. Fletcher, Mr P. Gorman, Mr Stewart Gray, Mr A. J. Macgregor, Miss B. A. McAvenna, Mr M. J. McHale, Mr J. C. Newman, Mr G. P. O'Connor, Mr A. A. F. Panton, Mr T. C. Peters, Mr A. W. Regan, Mr D. J. Satchell, Mr D. Snow, Mr D. F. Sullivan, Value For Money Racing, Mr K. Washbourne.

Conditional: Sean Curran (9-12).

181   MR C. J. DREWE, Didcot

Postal: **Lower Cross Farm, Blewbury Road, East Hagbourne, Didcot, OX11 9ND.**
Phone: **(01235) 813124**

1 **BRAYDON FOREST**, 4, b c Presidium—Sleekit **Mrs Jenny Melbourne, Dr J. Melbourne**
2 **DO LETS**, 7, b m Pragmatic—Acushla Macree **Costcote Partnership**
3 **EXCELLED (IRE)**, 7, gr m Treasure Kay—Excelling Miss (USA) **Mrs J. Strange**
4 **FIRST AVENUE**, 12, b g Tina's Pet—Olympus Girl **Mr C. J. Drewe**
5 5, B g Amboise—Image of War **Mrs J. Strange**
6 **RAMBLING ON**, 6, b g Derring Rose—Into Song **Mrs J. Strange**
7 5, Ch m Over The River (FR)—Saroan Meed **Mrs Jenny Melbourne**
8 **WILL JAMES**, 10, ch g Raga Navarro (ITY)—Sleekit **Mrs Jenny Melbourne**

THREE-YEAR-OLDS

9 **NORTHERN SAGA (IRE)**, b g Distinctly North (USA)—Saga's Humour **Mr C. J. Drewe**
10 **SPA LANE**, ch g Presidium—Sleekit **Mr R. J. K. Roberts**

Other Owners: Mr R. Allen, Mr P. Benson, Mrs J. Drewe.

182   MISS J. M. DU PLESSIS, Saltash

Postal: **Higher Pill Farm, Saltash, Cornwall, PL12 6LS.**

1 **COMMANCHE CREEK**, 6, b g Commanche Run—Vice Vixen (CAN) **Miss J. du Plessis**
2 **KINGSMILL QUAY**, 7, b m Noble Imp—La Jolie Fille **Miss J. du Plessis**
3 **PILLMERE LAD**, 6, b g Karlinsky (USA)—La Jolie Fille **Miss J. du Plessis**
4 **TAMAR LASS**, 11, b m Shaab—La Jolie Fille **Mr David G. du Plessis**

183   MR T. D. C. DUN, Heriot

Postal: **Nether Brotherstone, Heriot, Midlothian, EH38 5YS.**
Phone: **(01875) 35225 FAX (01875) 835323**

1 **GALA WATER**, 10, ch m Politico (USA)—Royal Ruby **Mrs T. D. C. Dun**
2 **LAUDER SQUARE**, 8, gr g Pragmatic—Royal Ruby **Mrs T. D. C. Dun**

184   MR E. A. L. DUNLOP, Newmarket

Postal: **Gainsborough Stables, Hamilton Road, Newmarket, Suffolk, CB8 0TE.**

Phone: **TEL: (01638) 661998 FAX (01638) 667394**

1 **ALMUHIMM (USA)**, 4, ch g Diesis—Abeesh (USA) **Maktoum Al Maktoum**
2 **CADEAUX TRYST**, 4, b c Cadeaux Genereux—Trystero **Maktoum Al Maktoum**
3 **CLASSIC SKY (IRE)**, 5, b g Jareer (USA)—Nawadder **Mr Saeed Suhail**
4 **DIAMOND CROWN (USA)**, 4, b g Gone West (USA)—Elegant Champagne (USA) **Mr Saeed Suhail**
5 **HAWA AL NASAMAAT (USA)**, 4, b g Houston (USA)—Barrera Miss (USA) **Maktoum Al Maktoum**
6 **IKTAMAL (USA)**, 4, ch c Danzig Connection (USA)—Crystal Cup (USA) **Maktoum Al Maktoum**
7 **MONAASSIB (IRE)**, 5, ch g Cadeaux Genereux—Pluvial **Maktoum Al Maktoum**
8 **MUBARIZ (IRE)**, 4, b g Royal Academy (USA)—Ringtail **Mr Hamdan Al Maktoum**
9 **STORM BID (USA)**, 4, b br g Storm Cat (USA)—Slam Bid (USA) **Maktoum Al Maktoum**
10 **TOP GUIDE (USA)**, 5, ch g Diesis—Raahia (CAN) **Maktoum Al Maktoum**
11 **TOUCH A MILLION (USA)**, 4, b c Mr Prospector (USA)—Magic Gleam (USA) **Maktoum Al Maktoum**

THREE-YEAR-OLDS

12 **ABSOLUTE UTOPIA (USA)**, b g Mr Prospector (USA)—Magic Gleam (USA) **Maktoum Al Maktoum**
13 **ANTARCTIC STORM**, b g Emarati (USA)—Katie Scarlett **Mr Jimmy Strauss**
14 **BASOOD (USA)**, b f Woodman (USA)—Basoof (USA) **Maktoum Al Maktoum**
15 **BRIGHT DESERT**, b c Green Desert (USA)—Smarten Up **Maktoum Al Maktoum**
16 **CHEERFUL ASPECT (IRE)**, b g Cadeaux Genereux—Strike Home **Maktoum Al Maktoum**
17 **DAWAWIN (USA)**, b f Dixieland Band (USA)—Stalwart Moment (USA) **Mr Hamdan Al Maktoum**
18 **DUSTY GEMS (USA)**, b f Danzig (USA)—Dusty Dollar **Maktoum Al Maktoum**
19 **HANBITOOH (USA)**, b c Hansel (USA)—Bitooh **Maktoum Al Maktoum**
20 **JAMRAT JUMAIRAH (IRE)**, b f Polar Falcon (USA)—Coryana **Sheikh Ahmed Al Maktoum**
21 **LAZALI (USA)**, ch c Zilzal (USA)—Leyali **Maktoum Al Maktoum**
22 **LEAD STORY (IRE)**, b g Lead On Time (USA)—Mashmoon (USA) **Maktoum Al Maktoum**
23 **MINOLETTI**, b g Emarati (USA)—French Plait **Mrs John Dunlop**
24 **NIMBLE FOOT (USA)**, b f Nureyev (USA)—Worood (USA) **Maktoum Al Maktoum**
25 **RAPID RETREAT (IRE)**, ch f Polish Precedent (USA)—Rapide Pied (USA) **Maktoum Al Maktoum**
26 **SIHAFI (USA)**, ch c Elmaamul (USA)—Kit's Double (USA) **Mr Hamdan Al Maktoum**
27 **SILVER PREY (USA)**, b c Silver Hawk (USA)—Truly My Style (USA) **Maktoum Al Maktoum**
28 **TA RIB (USA)**, ch f Mr Prospector (USA)—Madame Secretary (USA) **Mr Hamdan Al Maktoum**
29 **THAKI**, b c Distant Relative—Highly Polished **Mr Hamdan Al Maktoum**
30 **WINTER ROMANCE**, ch c Cadeaux Genereux—Island Wedding (USA) **Maktoum Al Maktoum**
31 **ZILCLARE (IRE)**, ch f Zilzal (USA)—Clara Bow (USA) **Maktoum Al Maktoum**

TWO-YEAR-OLDS

32 B f 28/4 Rainbow Quest (USA)—Balwa (USA) (Danzig (USA)) **Sheikh Ahmed Al Maktoum**
33 Ch c 27/2 Generous (IRE)—Barari (Blushing Groom (FR)) **Maktoum Al Maktoum**
34 B c 4/3 Machiavellian (USA)—Bashoosh (USA) (Danzig (USA)) **Maktoum Al Maktoum**
35 B c 1/4 Zilzal (USA)—Bold'n Determined (USA) (Bold And Brave) **Maktoum Al Maktoum**
36 B f 20/2 Sadler's Wells (USA)—Continual (USA) (Damascus (USA)) **Maktoum Al Maktoum**
37 Ch f 17/3 Nabeel Dancer (USA)—Etoile d'Amore (USA) (The Minstrel (CAN)) **Maktoum Al Maktoum**
38 Br c 12/2 Wild Again (USA)—Foolish Miz (USA) (Foolish Pleasure (USA)) **Maktoum Al Maktoum**
39 B c 18/2 Kenmare (FR)—Green Flower (USA) (Fappiano (USA)) **Maktoum Al Maktoum**
40 F 13/4 Polish Precedent—Island Wedding (USA) (Blushing Groom (FR)) **Maktoum Al Maktoum**
41 B c 28/3 Rainbow Quest (USA)—Jameelaty (USA) (Nureyev (USA)) **Maktoum Al Maktoum**
42 **KAHAL**, b c 16/2 Machiavellian (USA)—Just A Mirage (Green Desert (USA)) **Mr Hamdan Al Maktoum**
43 **KHASAYES**, b f 6/3 Unfuwain (USA)—Hasana (USA) (Private Account (USA)) **Mr Hamdan Al Maktoum**
44 **KHAWAFI**, b f 23/2 Kris—Tabdea (USA) (Topsider (USA)) **Mr Hamdan Al Maktoum**
45 Br c 22/5 Darshaan—Mashmoon (USA) (Habitat) **Maktoum Al Maktoum**
46 Ch c 7/5 Cadeaux Genereux—Miss Fancy That (USA) (The Minstrel (CAN)) **Maktoum Al Maktoum**
47 Ch c 21/4 Diesis—Mlle Lyphard (USA) (Lyphard (USA)) **Maktoum Al Maktoum**
48 B c 30/3 Broad Brush (USA)—Monture Creek (USA) (Stop The Music (USA)) **Maktoum Al Maktoum**
49 **MORNING SUIT**, b c 27/4 Reprimand—Morica (Moorestyle) **The Serendipity Partnership**
50 **MUTASAWWAR**, ch c 24/4 Clantime—Keen Melody (USA) (Sharpen Up) **Mr Hamdan Al Maktoum**
51 B c 29/4 Silver Hawk (USA)—My Turbulent Beau (USA) (Beau's Eagle (USA)) **Maktoum Al Maktoum**
52 B c 15/3 Sheikh Albadou—One Fine Day (USA) (Quadratic (USA)) **Maktoum Al Maktoum**
53 Ch c 4/3 Rubiano (USA)—Overnight (USA) (Mr Leader (USA)) **Maktoum Al Maktoum**

MR E. A. L. DUNLOP—continued

54 Ch c 23/3 Dixieland Band (USA)—Parrish Empress (USA) (His Majesty (USA)) **Maktoum Al Maktoum**
55 B f 15/1 Nashwan (USA)—Reem Albaraari (Sadler's Wells (USA)) **Sheikh Ahmed Al Maktoum**
56 Ch c 21/3 Zilzal (USA)—Sanctuary (Welsh Pageant) **Maktoum Al Maktoum**
57 **TAYSEER (USA),** b c 28/2 Sheikh Albadou—Millfit (USA) (Blushing Groom (FR)) **Hilal Salem**
58 Ch c 1/3 Bold Ruckus (USA)—Trillium Woods (CAN) (Briartic (CAN)) **Maktoum Al Maktoum**
59 B c 8/5 Cadeaux Genereux—Trystero (Shareef Dancer (USA)) **Maktoum Al Maktoum**
60 Ch c 10/3 Eastern Echo (USA)—Visibly Different (USA) (Sir Ivor) **Maktoum Al Maktoum**
61 **WHITE HOT,** b c 30/1 Weldnaas (USA)—Glowing Reference (Reference Point) **The Serendipity Partnership**
62 B c 26/2 Shadeed (USA)—Widaad (USA) (Mr Prospector (USA)) **Maktoum Al Maktoum**
63 B f 1/3 Dayjur (USA)—Worood (USA) (Vaguely Noble) **Maktoum Al Maktoum**

Other Owners: Sir Anthony Page-Wood.

185   MR J. L. DUNLOP, Arundel

Postal: **Castle Stables, Arundel, West Sussex, BN18 9AB.**
Phone: **ARUNDEL (01903) 882194 TELEX-87475 RACDEL FAX (01903) 884173**

1 **ALFREDO ALFREDO (USA),** 4, b c Miswaki (USA)—Alleged Queen (USA) **Gerecon Italia**
2 **BEAUCHAMP JAZZ,** 4, ch c Nishapour (FR)—Afariya (FR) **Mr E. Penser**
3 **CAPTAIN HORATIUS (IRE),** 7, b h Taufan (USA)—One Last Glimpse **Mr D. R. Hunnisett**
4 **EDIPO RE,** 4, b c Slip Anchor—Lady Barrister **Gerecon Italia**
5 **EMERGING MARKET,** 4, b g Emarati (USA)—Flitteriss Park **Mr Philip Wroughton**
6 **HARLESTONE BROOK,** 6, ch g Jalmood (USA)—Harlestone Lake **Mr J. L. Dunlop**
7 **KRISTAL'S PARADISE (IRE),** 4, b f Bluebird (USA)—Kristal's Pride **Windflower Overseas Holdings Inc**
8 **MEDAILLE MILITAIRE,** 4, gr c Highest Honor (FR)—Lovely Noor (USA) **Mr James Hartnett**
9 **NWAAMIS (USA),** 4, b c Dayjur (USA)—Lady Cutlass (USA) **Mr Hamdan Al Maktoum**
10 **ORCHESTRA STALL,** 4, b g Old Vic—Blue Brocade **Hon. David Sieff**
11 **OTTO E MEZZO,** 4, b c Persian Bold—Carolside **Gerecon Italia**
12 **PAOLO IL CALDO (USA),** 4, b c Shadeed (USA)—Medley of Song (USA) **Gerecon Italia**
13 **PICCOLA BUDDHA (IRE),** 4, b c Royal Academy (USA)—Brosna (USA) **Gerecon Italia**
14 **PORTIERE DI NOTTE (USA),** 4, b c Green Forest (USA)—Minstrel Guest **Gerecon Italia**
15 **SALAMAN (FR),** 4, b g Saumarez—Merry Sharp **Lady Cohen**
16 **SON OF SHARP SHOT (IRE),** 6, b br h Sharp Shot—Gay Fantasy **Windflower Overseas Holdings Inc**
17 **SPECIAL DAWN (IRE),** 6, ch g Be My Guest (USA)—Dawn Star **Windflower Overseas Holdings Inc**
18 **SWALLOWS DREAM (IRE),** 5, ch g Bluebird (USA)—Gay Fantasy **Windflower Overseas Holdings Inc**
19 **TAIPAN (IRE),** 4, b c Last Tycoon—Alidiva **Lord Swaythling**

THREE-YEAR-OLDS

20 **ALICIA (IRE),** b f Darshaan—Tribal Rite **Ettore Landi**
21 **AL SHAFA,** b c Midyan (USA)—Thundercloud **Prince A. A. Faisal**
22 **AQUA STAR (IRE),** br c Village Star (FR)—First Water (FR) **David M. Adams**
23 **BEAUCHAMP KING,** gr c Nishapour (FR)—Afariya (FR) **Mr E. Penser**
24 **BECHSTEIN,** ch c Rainbow Quest (USA)—Anegada **Mr Benny Andersson**
25 **BINT SALSABIL (USA),** ch f Nashwan (USA)—Salsabil **Mr Hamdan Al Maktoum**
26 **CAMP FOLLOWER,** b c Warrshan (USA)—House Maid **Mr J. L. Dunlop**
27 **CASTAN (IRE),** b g Persian Bold—Erzsi **Mr James Hartnett**
28 **DELLA CASA (IRE),** ch f Royal Academy (USA)—Diamond Spring (USA) **Sultan Al Kabeer**
29 **ELSHABIBA (USA),** b br c Dayjur (USA)—Sweet Roberta (USA) **Mr Hamdan Al Maktoum**
30 **FAATEQ,** b c Caerleon (USA)—Treble (USA) **Mr Hamdan Al Maktoum**
31 **FIDDES (IRE),** b f Alzao (USA)—Kashteh **Stonethorn Stud Farms Limited**
32 **FIONA SHANN (USA),** b f Phone Trick (USA)—Aminata **Exors of the late Mrs E. Ogden White**
33 **FLAME OF HOPE,** b f Marju (IRE)—Tweedling **Duke of Marlborough**
34 **FLOCHECK (USA),** ch c Hansel (USA)—Eurobird **Stonethorn Stud Farms Limited**
35 **FREZELIERE,** b f Be My Chief (USA)—Anna Karietta **Lord Chelsea**
36 **GENERAL MACARTHUR,** b c Alzao (USA)—Royal Climber **Mr Ian Cameron**
37 **GOODWOOD ROCKET,** ch c Midyan (USA)—Feather-In-Her-Cap **Goodwood Racehorse Owners Group Limited**
38 **GRANULETTE (USA),** b f El Gran Senor (USA)—Tuca Tuca (USA) **Mr S. Khaled**
39 **GREEK ICON,** b f Thatching—Rosie Potts **Mr A. M. Cati**

MR J. L. DUNLOP—continued

40 **HARLESTONE HEATH,** b f Aragon—Harlestone Lake **Mr J. L. Dunlop**
41 **INSIYABI (USA),** b c Mr Prospector (USA)—Ashayer (USA) **Mr Hamdan Al Maktoum**
42 **JOHN-T,** b c Thatching—Ower (IRE) **Dr J. A. E. Hobby**
43 **KAHIR ALMAYDAN (IRE),** b c Distinctly North (USA)—Kilfenora **Mr Ahmed Al Shafar**
44 **LADY JOSHUA (IRE),** ch f Royal Academy (USA)—Claretta (USA) **Mrs A. E. Butler**
45 **LIBERATRICE (FR),** b f Assert—Liberale (FR) **Mr J. L. Dunlop**
46 **MANSAB (USA),** b c Housebuster (USA)—Epitome (USA) **Mr Hamdan Al Maktoum**
47 **MASEHAAB (IRE),** b c Mujtahid (USA)—Firefly Night **Mr Hamdan Al Maktoum**
48 **MAWARED (IRE),** ch c Nashwan (USA)—Harmless Albatross **Mr Hamdan Al Maktoum**
49 **MINNISAM,** ch c Niniski (USA)—Wise Speculation (USA) **Mrs C. Forrester**
50 **MISS PRISM,** b f Niniski (USA)—Reflected Glory (SWE) **Miss K. Rausing**
51 **MUBARHIN (USA),** b r c Silver Hawk (USA)—Upper Dancer (USA) **Mr Hamdan Al Maktoum**
52 **MUHTADI (IRE),** br c Marju (IRE)—Moon Parade **Mr Hamdan Al Maktoum**
53 **MUSHAHID (USA),** b c Wild Again (USA)—Playful Queen (USA) **Mr Hamdan Al Maktoum**
54 **NAJIYA,** b f Nashwan (USA)—The Perfect Life (IRE) **Mr Hamdan Al Maktoum**
55 **NILGIRI HILLS (IRE),** ch c Indian Ridge—Our Resolution **Mr A. J. Struthers**
56 **NINOTCHKA (USA),** b f Nijinsky (CAN)—Puget Sound **Miss K. Rausing**
57 **OBERON'S DART (IRE),** b c Fairy King (USA)—Key Maneuver (USA) **Mr Peter Wragg**
58 **PARROT JUNGLE (IRE),** b f High Estate—Palm Dove (USA) **Sultan Al Kabeer**
59 **PARSA (USA),** b f Risen Star (USA)—Pallanza (USA) **Mr J. L. Dunlop**
60 **POETIC DANCE (USA),** ch c Seattle Dancer (USA)—French Poem (USA) **Mr S. Khaled**
61 **POMPIER,** ch c Be My Chief (USA)—Fire Risk **Lord Swaythling**
62 **QUEEN BEE,** ch f Royal Academy (USA)—Honey Bridge **Mr Talal Bader**
63 **RISALAH,** b f Marju (IRE)—Alsaaybah (USA) **Mr Hamdan Al Maktoum**
64 **ROYAL DIVERSION (IRE),** b f Marju (IRE)—Royal Recreation (USA) **Mr P. Townsend & Susan Abbott Racing**
65 **Ch c** Thatching—Sabaah (USA) **Gerecon Italia**
66 **SALEEMAH (USA),** ch f Storm Bird (CAN)—Retire (USA) **Mr Hamdan Al Maktoum**
67 **SAMARA (IRE),** ch f Polish Patriot (USA)—Smeralda (GER) **Aylesfield Farms Stud**
68 **SAMIM (USA),** b c Nureyev (USA)—Histoire (FR) **Mr Hamdan Al Maktoum**
69 **SAMRAAN (USA),** br c Green Dancer (USA)—Sedra **Mr K. M. Al-Mudhaf**
70 **SATIN BELL,** b f Midyan (USA)—Silk Petal **N. M. H. Jones**
71 **SCARLET PLUME,** b f Warning—Circus Plume **Aylesfield Farms Stud**
72 **SERENDIPITY (FR),** b c Mtoto—Bint Damascus (USA) **Mr John Darby**
73 **SHARAF (IRE),** b c Sadler's Wells (USA)—Marie de Flandre (FR) **Mr Hamdan Al Maktoum**
74 **SHIP'S DANCER,** b f Shareef Dancer (USA)—Sunderland **Lady Juliet de Chair**
75 **SKI FOR GOLD,** b f Shirley Heights—Quest (USA) **Windflower Overseas Holdings Inc**
76 **B f** Last Tycoon—Starlust **Gerecon Italia**
77 **STATE OF CAUTION,** b c Reprimand—Hithermoor Lass **Mr George Ward**
78 **ST MAWES (FR),** ch c Shahrastani (USA)—Exemina (USA) **Lord Swaythling**
79 **ST RITA,** gr f Bustino—Able Mabel **Mrs M. Rickman**
80 **TAMNIA,** br f Green Desert (USA)—Tanouma (USA) **Prince A. A. Faisal**
81 **TASLIYA (USA),** ch f Gulch (USA)—Aghani (USA) **Mr Hamdan Al Maktoum**
82 **THE SWAN,** ch f Old Vic—El Vino **R. J. McAulay**
83 **THRACIAN,** b c Green Desert (USA)—Triple First **Hesmonds Stud Ltd**
84 **TRIA KEMATA,** b c Kris—Third Watch **Hesmonds Stud Ltd**
85 **TSARNISTA,** b f Soviet Star (USA)—Princess Genista **Mr I. H. Stewart-Brown**
86 **VEILED DANCER (IRE),** b f Shareef Dancer (USA)—Fatal Distraction **Mr Aubrey Ison**
87 **VERONICA FRANCO,** b f Darshaan—Maiden Eileen **Mr Cyril Humphris**
88 **WAHIBA SANDS,** b g Pharly (FR)—Lovely Noor (USA) **Mr J. L. Dunlop**

TWO-YEAR-OLDS

89 **AJAYIB (USA),** b f 19/4 Riverman (USA)—Maplejinsky (USA) (Nijinsky (CAN)) **Mr Hamdan Al Maktoum**
90 **B c** 13/5 Highest Honor (FR)—Aldbourne (Alzao (USA)) **Mr J. L. Dunlop**
91 **AMID ALBADU (USA),** b c 14/1 Sheikh Albadou—
　　　　　　　　　　　　Dream Play (Blushing Groom (FR)) **Mr Hamdan Al Maktoum**
92 **B f** 27/4 Fairy King (USA)—Audenhove (GER) (Marduk (GER)) **Mr Cyril Humphris**
93 **BAHHARE (USA),** b c 24/4 Woodman (USA)—Wasnah (USA) (Nijinsky (CAN)) **Mr Hamdan Al Maktoum**
94 **BARNUM SANDS,** b c 24/2 Green Desert (USA)—Circus Plume (High Top) **Aylesfield Farms Stud**
95 **BEAUCHAMP LION,** ch c 19/5 Be My Chief (USA)—Beauchamp Cactus (Niniski (USA)) **Mr E. Penser**
96 **BEN EWAR,** b c 14/4 Old Vic—Sunset Reef (Mill Reef (USA)) **Mr A. J. Richards**

MR J. L. DUNLOP—continued

97 B f 10/5 Lahib (USA)—Bequeath (USA) (Lyphard (USA)) **Mr Cyril Humphris**
98 **BLUE FORM**, b f 9/3 Formidable (USA)—Sculpture Bleue (Claude Monet (USA)) **Hesmonds Stud Ltd**
99 **BUBBLY**, b c 5/5 Rudimentary (USA)—Champagne Season (USA) (Vaguely Noble) **Lord Swaythling**
100 B f 17/3 Last Tycoon—Classic Beam (Cut Above) **Eurostrait Ltd**
101 **CONSPIRACY**, b f 7/3 Rudimentary (USA)—Roussalka (Habitat) **Lord Chelsea**
102 **DUST DANCER**, ch f 25/4 Suave Dancer (USA)—Galaxie Dust (USA) (Blushing Groom (FR)) **Hesmonds Stud Ltd**
103 **ELNADIM (USA)**, b c 24/4 Danzig (USA)—Elle Seule (USA) (Exclusive Native (USA)) **Mr Hamdan Al Maktoum**
104 **ESHTIAAL (USA)**, b c 21/4 Riverman (USA)—Lady Cutlass (USA) (Cutlass (USA)) **Mr Hamdan Al Maktoum**
105 **EUROLINK PEGASUS**, b c 23/3 Danehill (USA)—Lady Eurolink (Kala Shikari) **Eurolink Computer Group Plc**
106 **FANTASY GIRL (IRE)**, br f 29/1 Marju (IRE)—Persian Fantasy (Persian Bold) **Windflower Overseas Holdings Inc**
107 **FERNANDA**, b f 3/3 Be My Chief (USA)—Flaming Rose (USA) (Upper Nile) **Sultan Al Kabeer**
108 **FOLGORE (USA)**, ch f 5/3 Irish River (FR)—Florie (FR) (Gay Mecene (USA)) **Mr V. Schirone**
109 **GHATAAS**, b c 21/4 Sadler's Wells (USA)—Harmless Albatross (Pas de Seul) **Mr Hamdan Al Maktoum**
110 **GHAYYUR (USA)**, ch f 1/2 Riverman (USA)—New Trends (USA) (Lyphard (USA)) **Mr Hamdan Al Maktoum**
111 **GONZAGA (IRE)**, br c 2/4 Pistolet Bleu (IRE)—Gay Spring (FR) (Free Round (USA)) **Sultan Al Kabeer**
112 **GOODWOOD LASS**, b f 4/2 Alzao (USA)—Cutleaf (Kris) **Goodwood Racehorse Owners Group Limited**
113 B c 7/5 Danehill (USA)—Gracieuse Majeste (FR) (Saint Cyrien (FR)) **Mr D. Crowson**
114 **HADAWAH (USA)**, ch f 10/2 Riverman (USA)—Sajjaya (USA) (Blushing Groom (FR)) **Mr Hamdan Al Maktoum**
115 Gr f 12/2 Chilibang—Harlestone Lake (Riboboy (USA)) **Mr J. L. Dunlop**
116 B f 20/2 Shernazar—Hayat (IRE) (Sadler's Wells (USA)) **Mr J. L. Dunlop**
117 **HEAD GARDENER (IRE)**, b br c 5/4 Be My Chief (USA)—Silk Petal (Petorius) **Mr E. S. Tudor-Evans**
118 **HELLO (IRE)**, b c 23/3 Lycius (USA)—Itqan (IRE) (Sadler's Wells (USA)) **Mr P. Wroughton**
119 **HEN HARRIER**, ch f 8/2 Polar Falcon (USA)—Circus Feathers (Kris) **Sir Thomas Pilkington**
120 **IHTIYATI (USA)**, ch c 7/4 Chief's Crown (USA)—Native Twine (Be My Native (USA)) **Mr Hamdan Al Maktoum**
121 **INDIAN ROCKET**, b c 20/3 Indian Ridge—Selvi (Mummy's Pet) **Mr Khalil Al Sayegh**
122 **INIMITABLE**, b f 27/3 Polish Precedent—Saveur (Ardross) **Aylesfield Farms Stud**
123 **JAWHARI**, b c 18/3 Lahib (USA)—Lady of The Land (Wollow) **Mr Hamdan Al Maktoum**
124 **KENEMARA STAR (IRE)**, ch c 21/4 Kenmare (FR)—Dawn Star (High Line) **Windflower Overseas Holdings Inc**
125 B c 8/2 Highest Honor (FR)—Lady Liska (USA) (Diesis) **Mr D. Crowson**
126 **LADY OF THE LAKE**, b f 9/4 Caerleon (USA)—Llyn Gwynant (Persian Bold) **Capt. J. Macdonald-Buchanan**
127 B c 5/6 Ferdinand (USA)—Last Request (Dancer's Image (USA)) **Mr J. L. Dunlop**
128 B f 17/3 Rock Hopper—Lawful (Law Society (USA)) **Mr Cyril Humphris**
129 **MALABI (USA)**, b c 21/1 Danzig (USA)—Gmaasha (IRE) (Kris) **Mr Hamdan Al Maktoum**
130 **MAWHIBA (USA)**, b br f 9/5 Dayjur (USA)—Histoire (FR) (Riverman (USA)) **Mr Hamdan Al Maktoum**
131 **MOONLIGHT PARADISE (USA)**, b f 13/2 Irish River (FR)—
                        Ottomana (USA) (Strawberry Road (AUS)) **Sir Eric Parker**
132 Ch c 6/5 Mujtahid (USA)—Moonsilk (Solinus) **Mr J. L. Dunlop**
133 B c 25/2 Midyan (USA)—Moorish Idol (Aragon) **Mr M. C. C. Armitage**
134 **MORAN**, b c 7/4 Bustino—Ower (My Swallow) **Dr J. A. E. Hobby**
135 **MUHTAFEL**, b c 10/1 Nashwan (USA)—The Perfect Life (IRE) (Try My Best (USA)) **Mr Hamdan Al Maktoum**
136 **MUSHARAK**, b c 19/1 Mujtahid (USA)—Mahasin (USA) (Danzig (USA)) **Mr Hamdan Al Maktoum**
137 **NARISKIN (IRE)**, b c 23/4 Danehill (USA)—Nurah (USA) (Riverman (USA)) **Sultan Al Kabeer**
138 **NICK OF TIME**, b f 15/2 Mtoto—Nikitina (Nijinsky (CAN)) **Susan Abbott Racing**
139 **PALIO SKY**, b c 26/4 Niniski (USA)—Live Ammo (Home Guard (USA)) **Mr J. E. Nash**
140 **PASSI D'ORLANDO (IRE)**, ch c 8/3 Persian Bold—When Lit (Northfields (USA)) **Madame I. Tudini**
141 **PASSIFLORA**, ch f 23/1 Night Shift (USA)—Pineapple (Superlative) **Mrs K. Grieve & Susan Abbott Racing**
142 **POLENISTA**, b f 3/3 Polish Precedent—Princess Genista (Ile de Bourbon) **Mr I. H. Stewart-Brown**
143 B c 10/5 Sadler's Wells (USA)—Princess Tiara (Crowned Prince (USA)) **Mr J. L. Dunlop**
144 **RAINWATCH**, b c 24/4 Rainbow Quest (USA)—Third Watch (Slip Anchor) **Hesmonds Stud Ltd**
145 **RED WING**, b c 2/4 Reprimand—Bronzewing (Beldale Flutter (USA)) **Sir Thomas Pilkington**
146 Br c 18/5 Warning—Roxy Hart (High Top) **Mr J. L. Dunlop**
147 **SAHM (USA)**, b br c 16/2 Mr Prospector (USA)—Salsabil (Sadler's Wells (USA)) **Mr Hamdan Al Maktoum**
148 **SANDSTONE**, b c 4/4 Green Desert (USA)—Rose de Thai (USA) (Lear Fan (USA)) **Mr Peter S. Winfield**
149 **SHADDAD (USA)**, b c 4/4 Shadeed (USA)—Desirable (Lord Gayle (USA)) **Mr Hamdan Al Maktoum**
150 **SHARPEST**, ch c 6/4 Sharpo—Anna Karietta (Precocious) **Lord Chelsea**
151 **SHAWAF (USA)**, ch c 28/5 Mr Prospector (USA)—Shadayid (USA) (Shadeed (USA)) **Mr Hamdan Al Maktoum**
152 **SHELTERING SKY**, b c 13/3 Selkirk (USA)—
                        Shimmering Sea (Slip Anchor) **Mr V. Behrens & Susan Abbott Racing**
153 **SILVER PATRIARCH (IRE)**, gr c 8/5 Saddlers' Hall (IRE)—
                        Early Rising (USA) (Grey Dawn II) **Mr Peter S. Winfield**

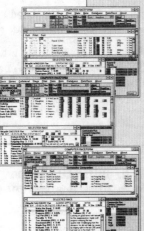

MR J. L. DUNLOP—continued

154 B c 31/1 Groom Dancer (USA)—Sonoma (FR) (Habitat) **Herr Focke**
155 B f 3/3 Waajib—Splendid Chance (Random Shot) **Watership Down Stud**
156 TANGO KING, b c 11/3 Suave Dancer (USA)—Be My Queen (Be My Guest (USA)) **Lord Swaythling**
157 B f 6/2 Warning—Tanouma (USA) (Miswaki (USA)) **Prince A. A. Faisal**
158 THE EUROLINK F B I (USA), b c 17/2 Red Ransom (USA)—
                                    Queen's Warning (USA) (Caveat (USA)) **Eurolink Computer Group Plc**
159 TRIPLE TERM, br c 31/3 Terimon—Triple Reef (Mill Reef (USA)) **Hesmonds Stud Ltd**
160 B f 13/4 Green Desert (USA)—Usaylah (Siberian Express (USA)) **Prince A. A. Faisal**
161 YAVLENSKY (IRE), b c 23/2 Caerleon (USA)—Schwanensee (USA) (Mr Leader (USA)) **Mr V. Schirone**

Other Owners: Mr Mohamed Azzam, Mr James Barber, Mr G. Bishop, Mrs Patrick Darling, Mr S. Fairbairn, Mr J. Flower, Mr T. Hyde, Mr & Mrs N. Macready, Mr M. J. Meacock, Mr Alberto Panetta, Mr I. A. D. Pilkington, Mr Anthony Pye-Jeary, Mr David Russell, Mr Jeremy Spurling, Mr & Mrs D. Thorp, Mr T. C. Wilson.

186   MR A. J. K. DUNN, Minehead

Postal: **The Maltings, Lynch, Allerford, Minehead, TA24 8HJ.**

Phone: **(01643) 863124**

1 ACROSS THE BOW (USA), 6, b g Fit To Fight (USA)—Crooning Water (USA) **Mr C. G. M. Lloyd-Baker**
2 ARJUNA, 11, b g Shirley Heights—Karsavina **Mr A. J. K. Dunn**
3 BELL ONE (USA), 7, ch g Lightning Leap (USA)—Ambrose Channel (USA) **Mrs J. P. Sellick**
4 FERNY BALL (IRE), 8, b g Hard Fought—Star Chamber (FR) **The Clumpy Group**
5 GREEN ISLAND (USA), 10, b g Key To The Mint (USA)—Emerald Reef **Mr J. E. Moloney**
6 HOLD THE FORT, 5, b g Baron Blakeney—Mizpah **Mr K. L. Sellick**
7 RIVER CONSORT (USA), 8, bl g Riverman (USA)—Queens Only (USA) **Mr H. H. Richards**
8 ROYAL CRAFTSMAN, 15, b br g Workboy—Royal Huntress **Mr A. J. K. Dunn**

Other Owners: Mr J. G. Daffurn, Mr A. R. Dunn, Mrs Hazel Leeves, Mr Peter Lister, Mrs J. McCarthy, Mrs C. A. Mitchell, Mr William Mitchell, Mrs P. A. Wills.

187   MRS P. N. DUTFIELD, Seaton

Postal: **Crabhayne Farm, Axmouth, Seaton, Devon, EX12 4BW.**

Phone: **(01297) 553560**

1 BIG THEO, 5, br g Tragic Role (USA)—Bolt Hole **Mr W. A. Harrison-Allan**
2 4, B f Mandalus—Clodagh's Treasure **Mrs Nerys Dutfield**
3 DESERT CALM (IRE), 7, br g Glow (USA)—Lancette **Mrs Nerys Dutfield**
4 4, B g Arctic Lord—Galley Bay **Mrs Nerys Dutfield**
5 GEMINI MIST, 5, b m Ardross—Festive Season **Mrs Nerys Dutfield**
6 POINTER, 4, b g Reference Point—Greenhill Lass **In For The Crack**
7 RAINBOW RUNNER, 5, ch g Northern State (USA)—Aldbury Girl **Mrs Nerys Dutfield**
8 ROYAL SEGOS, 9, b g High Line—Segos **Mrs Nerys Dutfield**
9 4, B f Lafontaine (USA)—Run For Shelter **Mrs Nerys Dutfield**
10 SUMMERHILL SPECIAL (IRE), 5, b m Roi Danzig (USA)—Special Thanks **Mrs Nerys Dutfield**
11 UP THE JUNCTION (IRE), 6, b m Treasure Kay—Lil's Charm **Mrs Nerys Dutfield & Mr Aidan Walsh**

THREE-YEAR-OLDS

12 PROVE THE POINT (IRE), b f Maelstrom Lake—In Review **Mrs Nerys Dutfield**

Other Owners: Mr John Boswell, Mr Simon Dutfield.

Conditional: Michael Hunt (9-7).

188   MR C. A. DWYER, Newmarket

Postal: **Cedar Lodge Racing Stables, Hamilton Road, Newmarket, Suffolk.**
Phone: **OFFICE & FAX (01638) 667857 MOBILE (0831) 579844 HOME (01638) 668869**

1 **COLLEGE NIGHT (IRE)**, 4, b f Night Shift (USA)—Gertrude Lawrence **Mrs Christine Dunnett**
2 **CYRANO'S LAD (IRE)**, 7, b br g Cyrano de Bergerac—Patiala **Mr M. M. Foulger**
3 **DUSTY POINT (IRE)**, 6, b g Reference Point—Noble Dust (USA) **Rochford Racing Ltd**
4 **JEAN DE FLORETTE (USA)**, 5, b g Our Native (USA)—The Branks (USA) **Mr John Purcell**
5 **KAYARTIS**, 7, b m Kaytu—Polyartis **Mrs Jenny Cornwell**
6 **LLOC**, 4, b f Absalom—Nosey **Mr John Purcell**
7 **NORTH ESK (USA)**, 7, ch g Apalachee (USA)—Six Dozen (USA) **Rochford Racing Ltd**
8 **SILKTAIL (IRE)**, 4, b f Jalmood (USA)—Silky (USA) **Mr John Purcell**
9 **SWEET SUPPOSIN (IRE)**, 5, b h Posen (USA)—Go Honey Go **Mrs Christine Rawson**
10 **WARDARA**, 4, ch f Sharpo—Ward One **Mrs Christine Rawson**
11 **YAVERLAND (IRE)**, 4, b c Astronef—Lautreamont **Mrs B. A. Blackwell**

THREE-YEAR-OLDS

12 **BADGER BAY (IRE)**, b f Salt Dome (USA)—Legit (IRE) **Mr M. E. Hall**
13 **GEORGIE BOY (USA)**, b c Zilzal (USA)—Stealthy Lady (USA) **Mrs D. M. Swinburn**
14 **ISITOFF**, b c Vague Shot—Plum Blossom (USA) **Rochford Racing Ltd**
15 **L A TOUCH**, b f Tina's Pet—Silvers Era **Mr C. A. Rosen**
16 **LITTLE NOGGINS (IRE)**, b f Salt Dome (USA)—Calash **Mr M. E. Hall**
17 **MUSICAL HEIGHTS (IRE)**, b f Roaring Riva—Littleton Song **Rochford Racing Ltd**
18 **PRINCE ZIZIM**, b c Shareef Dancer (USA)—Possessive Lady **Mr John Purcell**
19 **TOUCH OF FANTASY**, b f Never So Bold—Brera (IRE) **Mrs Christine Rawson**

TWO-YEAR-OLDS

20 B f 27/2 Runnett—Blue Elver (Kings Lake (USA)) **Mr M. E. Hall**
21 B f 28/4 Risk Me (FR)—Egnoussa (Swing Easy (USA)) **Mr G. Middlemass**
22 **JENNELLE**, b f 7/3 Nomination—Its A Romp (Hotfoot) **Mrs Jenny Cornwell**
23 B f 30/3 Grey Desire—Mazurkanova (Song) **Mrs E. Hawkey**
24 **SMALL RISK**, b f 5/3 Risk Me (FR)—Small Double (IRE) (Double Schwartz) **Mr M. Scaife**
25 B f 15/5 Treasure Kay—Thread of Gold (Huntercombe) **Mr M. E. Hall**
26 B c 7/4 Roaring Riva—Wolviston (Wolverlife) **Mr M. E. Hall**

Other Owners: Mrs Susan Bennett, Mrs S. E. A. Burton, Mrs Monica Caine, Mr M. L. Clements, Mr J. Denny, Mr D. Foley, Mr W. Green, Mr Chris Stasiak.

Jockeys (Flat): C Dwyer, M Wigham (w.a.).

Jockey (NH): V Smith.

Apprentices: S Downe (w.a.), J Stack (w.a.), N Varley (7-4, w.a.).

Lady Rider: Miss Louise Purcell (9-7).

189   MR T. DYER, Invergowrie

Postal: **1 Balruddery Meadows, Invergowrie, By Dundee, DD2 5LJ.**
Phone: **HOUSE (01382) 360622 STABLES 360594 FAX 360621 OFFICE 456662**

1 **BRUMON (IRE)**, 5, b g Sadler's Wells (USA)—Loveliest (USA) **Mr Mike Flynn**
2 **CHIEF MINISTER (IRE)**, 7, br g Rainbow Quest (USA)—Riverlily (FR) **Mr G. Shiel**
3 **DERRYVALE GIRL (IRE)**, 5, b m Noalto—Friars Action **Mr Daniel A. Couper**
4 **EXPLORE MONDIAL (IRE)**, 5, b g Alzao (USA)—Organdy **Mr Gordon Wallace**

MR T. DYER—continued

5 **FIRST BITE (IRE)**, 4, b c Be My Native (USA)—Saga's Humour **Mr G. Shiel**
6 **GYMCRAK GAMBLE**, 8, b g Beldale Flutter (USA)—Baridi **Mr Ian Herd**
7 **HILLTOWN BLUES**, 7, gr g Le Solaret (FR)—Herminda **Mrs Linda Dyer**
8 **HOME PARK (IRE)**, 6, ch g Shernazar—Home Address **Bahadur & Co**
9 **MARCO MAGNIFICO (USA)**, 6, b br g Bering—Viscosity (USA) **Mr S. Bruce**
10 **MIDDLE BAY (IRE)**, 5, ch h Le Bavard (FR)—Patricia's Joy **Mr S. Bruce**
11 **NAWTINOOKEY**, 6, gr m Uncle Pokey—Abrasive **Mr G. Mair**
12 **NICKY'S FEELINGS**, 4, b f Feelings (FR)—Polly Potter **Scottish Daily Record & Sunday Mail Ltd**
13 **ORD GALLERY (IRE)**, 7, ch g Tate Gallery (USA)—Red Magic **Mr G. Shiel**
14 **RACHAEL'S OWEN**, 6, ch g Oats—Polly Potter **Mrs Linda Dyer**
15 **RUNNING GREEN**, 5, b g Green Desert (USA)—Smeralda (GER) **Mrs Linda Dyer**
16 **SALDUBA**, 4, b f Fijar Tango (FR)—Silver Ore (FR) **Mr Graeme Renton**
17 **SHARP AT SIX (IRE)**, 6, ch g Sure Blade (USA)—Sixpenny **Mr G. Shiel**
18 **STASH THE CASH (IRE)**, 5, b g Persian Bold—Noble Girl **Mr G. Shiel**
19 **TAWAFIJ (USA)**, 7, ch g Diesis—Dancing Brownie (USA) **Mr Stephen Laidlaw**
20 **TONY'S FEELINGS**, 8, b g Feelings (FR)—Meg's Mantle **Mrs Linda Dyer**
21 **VINTAGE TAITTINGER (IRE)**, 4, b g Nordico (USA)—Kalonji **Mr S. Bruce**

THREE-YEAR-OLDS

22 **SUNDAY MAELSTROM (IRE)**, b f Distinctly North (USA)—
Make Your Mark **Scottish Daily Record & Sunday Mail Ltd**

Other Owners: Mr E. Bruce.

Jockey (Flat): M Fenton.

Jockeys (NH): A Dobbin, L Wyer.

Conditional: Alan Linton (10-0).

190   MR S. A. EARLE, Sturminster Newton

Postal: **Mappowder Court Racing, Mappowder, Sturminster Newton, Dorset, DT10 2EN.**
Phone: **(01258) 817814** FAX **(01258) 817814**

1 **AFTER THE FOX**, 9, b g Athens Treasure—The Deer Hound **Miss C. S. March**
2 **CASTLE CLAIRE**, 9, ch m Carlingford Castle—Last Trip **Mr Graham Brown**
3 **COTSWOLD CASTLE**, 10, ch g Carlingford Castle—Last Trip **Mr Graham Brown**
4 **CYRILL HENRY (IRE)**, 7, b g Mister Majestic—Stamina **Champagne and Dreams Partnership**
5 **DEXTRA DOVE**, 9, gr g Julio Mariner—Grey Dove **Dextra Lighting Systems**
6 **DEXTRA (IRE)**, 6, b g Torus—My Friend Fashion **Dextra Lighting Systems**
7 **FOUR THYME**, 6, b m Idiot's Delight—Quadro **Mrs R. Jenks**
8 **INKY SMUDGE**, 5, b g Ra Nova—Maid of The Manor **Mr G. Faber**
9 **JOHNYMOSS (IRE)**, 7, ch g Le Moss—Deep Pride **D & J Newell**
10 **LEOPARD LADY**, 4, b f Sulaafah (USA)—Swift Turtle **C M Dyer Syndicating (4)**
11 **LIGHTING DOVE**, 4, b f Town And Country—Celtic Dove **Dextra Lighting Systems**
12 **LITTLE BREEZE**, 6, b m Latest Model—Naughty Niece **Mrs B. Mills**
13 **MAGIC WIZARD**, 5, b g Teenoso (USA)—Brigannie Moon **C M Dyer Syndicating (1)**
14 **MARQUESA JUANA**, 5, b m Lepanto (GER)—Glorious Jane **The Maple Partnership**
15 **MIAMI SPLASH**, 9, ch g Miami Springs—Splash of Red **Mr G. D. Weekes**
16 **NORMAN'S DELIGHT (IRE)**, 5, b m Idiot's Delight—Thank Yourself **Mr Graham Brown**
17 **ORSWELL CHOICE**, 6, ch m Morgans Choice—Running Light **Mr R. M. E. Wright**
18 **PERTEMPS FLYER**, 5, b g Presidium—Brilliant Future **Pertemps Limited**
19 **PRESTON GUILD (IRE)**, 6, b g Mazaad—Dying Craft **The Crack Club**
20 **SILVERINO**, 10, gr g Relkino—Silver Tips **Mr S. N. Burfield**

MR S. A. EARLE—continued

21 **STRATUS**, 6, gr g Then Again—Splash of Red **Dextra Lighting Systems**
22 **THEFOURTHMUSKATEER**, 7, ch g Nearly A Hand—Wild Rushes **D & J Newell**
23 **WATERROW**, 8, br m Idiot's Delight—Waterside **Super Mare Scaffolding Ltd**
24 **YOUR WELL**, 10, ch g Le Moss—Triple Fire **D & J Newell**

THREE-YEAR-OLDS
25 B g Mac's Imp (USA)—Lady's Turn **Dextra Lighting Systems**

Other Owners: Mr R. J. A. Earle, Mrs D. Fox-Ledger, Mr M. L. Green, Mr R. M. Howard, Miss S. Koscinski, Mrs Constance Joyce Watts, Mrs R. L. Watts, Mr Timothy Watts, Mrs S. M. Weekes.

Jockeys (NH): C Maude (10-0), B Powell (10-7).

191   MR M. W. EASTERBY, Sheriff Hutton

Postal: **New House Farm, Sheriff Hutton, York, YO6 7TN.**

Phone: **(01347) 878368 FAX (01347) 878204**

1 **ADMIRALS SEAT**, 8, ch g Ardross—Sombreuil **Mr G. E. Shouler**
2 **ALJADEER (USA)**, 7, b br g Alleged (USA)—Return The Roses (USA) **Miss V. Foster**
3 **ARTWORLD (USA)**, 8, b g Blushing Groom (FR)—Folk Art (USA) **Major Watson**
4 **AUBURN BOY**, 9, ch g Sexton Blake—Milan Union **Mr G. E. Shouler**
5 **BALI TENDER**, 5, ch g Balidar—Highest Tender **Mr T. A. Hughes**
6 **BORNE**, 6, b g Bairn (USA)—Mummy's Glory **Early Morning Breakfast Syndicate**
7 **CALABRESE**, 11, ch g Monsanto (FR)—Salsafy **Major Watson**
8 **CIRCUS LINE**, 5, ch g High Line—Mrs Mills **Mrs P. A. H. Hartley**
9 **FLAT TOP**, 5, b g Blakeney—New Edition **Mr D. F. Spence**
10 **FOIST**, 4, b g Efisio—When The Saints **Mr D. F. Spence**
11 **HASTA LA VISTA**, 6, b g Superlative—Falcon Berry (FR) **Mr K. Hodgson**
12 **HOTSPUR STREET**, 4, b g Cadeaux Genereux—Excellent Alibi (USA) **Mr Stanley Clarke**
13 **ISSYIN**, 9, ch g Oats—Spiders Web **Mrs H. Brown**
14 **LADY SHERIFF**, 5, b m Taufan (USA)—Midaan **Mr E. J. Mangan**
15 **LEEDONS PARK**, 4, br g Precocious—Scottish Rose **Abbots Salford Caravan Park**
16 **MAID O'CANNIE**, 5, b m Efisio—Ichnusa **Mrs E. Rhind**
17 **MAJOR SNUGFIT**, 4, b g Tina's Pet—Sequoia **Mr A. Greenwood**
18 **MEADOW FOODS**, 4, ch c Handsome Sailor—Stern Lass **Tilstone Stud**
19 **MINSTER GLORY**, 5, b g Minster Son—Rapid Glory **Mr P. A. H. Hartley**
20 **PRIME PROPERTY (IRE)**, 4, b f Tirol—Busker **Alan Black & Co**
21 **PUREVALUE (IRE)**, 5, b br g Kefaah (USA)—Blaze of Light **Mr A. D. Simmons**
22 **SILVER STICK**, 9, gr g Absalom—Queen's Parade **Lord Manton**
23 **SOUTHERN CROSS**, 4, ch g Buckley—Muznah **Mr Urs E. Schwarzenbach**
24 **SPANISH STEPS (IRE)**, 4, b g Danehill (USA)—Belle Enfant **R.O.M. Racing**
25 **STOLEN KISS (IRE)**, 4, b f Taufan (USA)—Sweet Goodbye **R.O.M. Racing**
26 **STUFFED**, 4, ch g Clantime—Puff Pastry **Early Morning Breakfast Syndicate**
27 **TRESIDDER**, 14, b g Connaught—Twenty Two (FR) **Mr S. H. J. Brewer**
28 **VARYKINOV (IRE)**, 7, b g Roselier (FR)—Royal Handful **Bee Health Ltd**
29 **WESTCOURT PRINCESS**, 4, b f Emarati (USA)—Petrol **Mr K. Hodgson**

THREE-YEAR-OLDS
30 **BEE HEALTH BOY**, b g Superpower—Rekindle **Bee Health Ltd**
31 **BLESSINGINDISGUISE**, b g Kala Shikari—Blowing Bubbles **Mr A. Black**
32 **CONTRADICTORY**, br f Reprimand—Artistic Licence **Mr C. F. Buckton**
33 **DOUG'S FOLLY**, ch f Handsome Sailor—Stern Lass **Tilstone Stud**
34 **HARRIET'S BEAU**, b g Superpower—Pour Moi **Mr R. Watts**
35 **LA FANDANGO (IRE)**, b f Taufan (USA)—Cursory Look (USA) **Sheriff Racing Club**
36 **LUCKY BEA**, b g Lochnager—Knocksharry **Bee Health Ltd**
37 **MILL END LADY**, b f Tina's Pet—Azelly **Mr W. T. Allgood**

MR M. W. EASTERBY—continued

38 **MISTER JOEL**, b g Risk Me (FR)—Net Call **Mr Philip A. Jarvis**
39 **NORTHERN CLAN**, b c Clantime—Northern Line **Mrs E. Rhind**
40 **NORTHERN FALCON**, gr f Polar Falcon (USA)—Bishah (USA) **Mr & Mrs Hartley**
41 **PERCY PARK (USA)**, br g Rajab (USA)—Clayton's Miss (USA) **Mr K. Hodgson**
42 **WESTCOURT MAGIC**, b g Emarati (USA)—Magic Milly **Mr K. Hodgson**

TWO-YEAR-OLDS

43 **BOLERO BOY**, b c 18/4 Rambo Dancer (CAN)—Barrie Baby (Import) **Sheriff Racing Club**
44 **GIPSY PRINCESS**, b f 15/5 Prince Daniel (USA)—Gypsy's Barn Rat (Balliol) **Lady Manton**
45 **JEDI KNIGHT**, b c 12/5 Emarati (USA)—Hannie Caulder (Workboy) **Mr K. Hodgson**
46 **MILL END BOY**, ch c 7/4 Clantime—Annaceramic (Horage) **Mr W. Allgood**
47 **MILL END GIRL**, ch f 9/5 Superpower—Estefan (Taufan (USA)) **Mr W. Allgood**
48 **NOT A LOT**, ch c 15/4 Emarati (USA)—Spanish Chestnut (Philip of Spain) **Mr T. A. Hughes**
49 **TEDDY'S BOW (IRE)**, b f 19/2 Archway (IRE)—Gale Force Seven (Strong Gale) **Mrs A. Jarvis**
50 **THE DUBIOUS GOOSE**, b c 30/5 Yaheeb (USA)—Dunnington (Risk Me (FR)) **Mrs J. M. Davenport**
51 **WILLIAM'S WELL**, ch c 8/5 Superpower—Catherines Well (Junius (USA)) **Mr K. Hodgson**

Other Owners: Mr P. J. Berry, Mr C. Gardiner, Mr Andrew M. Hedley, Mr R. Mason, Mr R. J. McAlpine, Mr D. O. Pickering, Mr S. Ryan, Mrs Francesca Schwarzenbach, Mrs I. M. Silver, Mr M. J. Silver, Mr C. F. Spence, Mr Gordon Stead, Mr D. P. Travers-Clark.

Conditional: J Driscoll (10-0).

192   MR T. D. EASTERBY, Malton

Postal: **Habton Grange, Great Habton, Malton, North Yorks, YO17 0TY.**
Phone: **(01653) 668566 FAX (01653) 668621**

1 **BOLLIN FRANK**, 4, b c Rambo Dancer (CAN)—Bollin Emily **Sir Neil Westbrook**
2 **BOLLIN HARRY**, 4, b c Domynsky—Bollin Harriet **Sir Neil Westbrook**
3 **BRIDLE PATH (IRE)**, 5, b g Teenoso (USA)—Hilly Path **Mr Fred Wilson**
4 **CATARAS**, b g Silly Prices—Playing **Mr I. Bell**
5 **CHOPWELL CURTAINS**, 6, ch g Town And Country—Liquer Candy **Durham Drapes Ltd**
6 **CUMBRIAN CHALLENGE (IRE)**, 7, ch g Be My Native (USA)—Sixpenny **Cumbrian Industrials Ltd**
7 **CUMBRIAN RHAPSODY**, 6, ch m Sharrood (USA)—Bustellina **Cumbrian Industrials Ltd**
8 **CURRENT SPEECH (IRE)**, 5, b g Thatching—Lady Aladdin **Mr C. H. Stevens**
9 **DALLY BOY**, 4, b g Efisio—Gay Hostess (FR) **Mr T. H. Bennett**
10 **DAWN MISSION**, 4, b g Dunbeath (USA)—Bustellina **Mrs Jennifer E. Pallister**
11 **DURANO**, 5, b g Dunbeath (USA)—Norapa **Mr C. H. Stevens**
12 **DURHAM DRAPES**, 5, b m Taufan (USA)—Miss Bali Beach **Durham Drapes Ltd**
13 **EURO SCEPTIC (IRE)**, 4, ch g Classic Secret (USA)—Very Seldom **Mr C. H. Stevens**
14 **GOLDEN HELLO**, 5, b g Glint of Gold—Waltz **Mr G. E. Shouler**
15 5, Ch g Ardross—Grange Hill Girl **Scotton Developments Ltd**
16 **HABTON WHIN**, 10, b g Le Bavard (FR)—Bob's Hansel **Mr C. H. Stevens**
17 **INSTANTANEOUS**, 4, b f Rock City—Mainmast **Mr Reg Griffin**
18 **NEW BROOM (IRE)**, 4, b f Brush Aside (USA)—Qurrat Al Ain **Mrs J. B. Mountifield**
19 **PENBOLA (IRE)**, 4, b g Pennine Walk—Sciambola **Mr T. H. Bennett**
20 **RYE CROSSING (IRE)**, 6, b g Over The River (FR)—Aran Tour **Mr C. H. Stevens**
21 **SCOTTON BANKS (IRE)**, 7, b g Le Moss—Boherdee **Mr I. Bray**
22 **SHARE OPTIONS (IRE)**, 5, b br g Executive Perk—Shannon Belle **Mr Steve Hammond**
23 **SHARKASHKA (IRE)**, 6, ch m Shardari—Kashka (USA) **Mr C. H. Stevens**
24 **SHINING EDGE**, 4, ch g Beveled (USA)—Lustrous **Mr G. Graham**
25 **SILLY MONEY**, 5, b g Silly Prices—Playagain **Mrs J. P. Connew**
26 **SIMPLY DASHING (IRE)**, 5, br g Simply Great (FR)—Qurrat Al Ain **Mr Steve Hammond**
27 **THORNTON GATE**, 7, b g Hallgate—Lola Black (FR) **Mr T. H. Bennett**
28 **TOOGOOD TO BE TRUE**, 8, br g Sonnen Gold—Lady Relka **Mr Jim McGrath**

MR T. D. EASTERBY—continued

THREE-YEAR-OLDS

29 **BOLLIN DOROTHY,** b f Rambo Dancer (CAN)—Bollin Harriet **Lady Westbrook**
30 **BOLLIN JACOB,** b c Efisio—Bollin Emily **Sir Neil Westbrook**
31 **BOLLIN JOANNE,** b f Damister (USA)—Bollin Zola **Lady Westbrook**
32 **CAMIONNEUR (IRE),** b g Cyrano de Bergerac—Fact of Time **T. E. F. Freight (Scarborough) Ltd**
33 **CUMBRIAN MAESTRO,** b g Puissance—Flicker Toa Flame (USA) **Cumbrian Industrials Ltd**
34 **EURO EXPRESS,** ch g Domynsky—Teresa Deevey **Mr C. H. Stevens**
35 **EUROPEX,** bl g Dunbeath (USA)—Afrabela **Mr C. H. Stevens**
36 **GILDORAN SOUND,** b f Gildoran—Sound of Laughter **Mr J. J. Lawson**
37 **HARSH TIMES,** ch f Efisio—Larnem **Mr David Faulkner**
38 **JACKSON PARK,** gr g Domynsky—Hysteria **Mr C. H. Stevens**
39 **JO MELL,** b g Efisio—Militia Girl **C. H. Newton Jnr Ltd**
40 **RUSSIAN RASCAL (IRE),** b g Soviet Lad (USA)—Anglo Irish **Mr C. H. Stevens**
41 **SILVER WELCOME,** ch g Most Welcome—Silver Ore (FR) **Mr Peter Hurst**
42 **SIS GARDEN,** b f Damister (USA)—Miss Nanna **Mr Lin Cheng Lee**
43 **SUPERMISTER,** b g Damister (USA)—Superfina (USA) **Mr T. H. Bennett**
44 **SYLHALL,** ch f Sharpo—No Cards **Major M. G. Wyatt**
45 **TOO HASTY,** b c Dunbeath (USA)—Suggia **Mr C. H. Stevens**
46 B c Gunner B—Vitry **Scotton Developments Ltd**

TWO-YEAR-OLDS

47 **BOLLIN MILLIGAN,** b c 19/4 Efisio—Bollin Harriet (Lochnager) **Sir Neil Westbrook**
48 **BOLLIN TERRY,** b c 9/3 Terimon—Bollin Zola (Alzao (USA)) **Sir Neil Westbrook**
49 **CAJUN SUNSET (IRE),** b g 6/4 Red Sunset—Carcajou (High Top) **Mr P. D. Savill**
50 B f 18/1 Fools Holme (USA)—Calaloo Sioux (USA) (Our Native (USA)) **Mrs Marjorie Graham**
51 **CUMBRIAN QUEST,** b c 20/3 Be My Chief (USA)—Tinkerbird (Music Boy) **Cumbrian Industrials Ltd**
52 **DOUBLE ACTION,** br c 21/3 Reprimand—Final Shot (Dalsaan) **Mr C. H. Stevens**
53 **FLOATING DEVON,** br c 24/2 Simply Great (FR)—Devon Dancer (Shareef Dancer (USA)) **Mr C. D. Calvert**
54 **HIGH SPIRITS (IRE),** b c 26/4 Great Commotion (USA)—Spoilt Again (Mummy's Pet) **Mrs J. B. Mountifield**
55 **MAZIL,** ch c 24/3 Mazilier (USA)—Gymcrak Lovebird (Taufan (USA)) **Mrs J. B. Mountifield**
56 **MONARCH'S PURSUIT,** b c 12/3 Pursuit Of Love—Last Detail (Dara Monarch) **Mrs J. P. Connew**
57 B c 14/2 Pursuit Of Love—Rivers Rhapsody (Dominion) **Mr Reg Griffin**
58 B f 7/4 Tina's Pet—Springle (Le Johnstan) **Mr P. Bath**
59 Ch f 1/5 St Ninian—Who's That Lady (Nordance (USA)) **T. E. F. Freight (Scarborough) Ltd**
60 **YAM-SING,** b c 17/3 Aragon—Pushoff (USA) (Sauce Boat (USA)) **Mr T. H. Bennett**

Other Owners: Mr M. H. Easterby, Mr M. W. Easterby, Mr John M. Pinder, Sandmoor Textiles Co Ltd.

Jockeys (Flat): M Birch (8-2), S Maloney (7-9).

Jockeys (NH): R Garritty (10-0), L Wyer (10-0).

193   MR P. ECCLES, Lambourn

Postal: **Flat One, Stork House, Baydon Road, Lambourn, RG16 7NV.**

Phone: **(01488) 73483**

1 5, B g Detroit Sam (FR)—Bluehel **Mr J. P. J. Coles**
2 **DANTELEIGH,** 5, b m Phardante (FR)—Furraleigh **Mr J. P. J. Coles**
3 4, Ch f Afzal—Free Clare **Mr A. Holland**
4 **JARVEY (IRE),** 4, ch g Jareer (USA)—Blue Czarina **Mr B. Lewendon**
5 **MURPHY,** 12, ch g Touch Paper—Iamstopped **Mr J. P. J. Coles**
6 **ROLLING WATERS,** 6, b g Robellino (USA)—Idle Waters **Mrs Hilary Putt**
7 **RUBINS BOY,** 10, ch g Riberetto—Gaie Pretense (FR) **Mr J. Cooper**
8 **SPARKLIN'CHAMPAGNE,** 6, b g Pollerton—My Always **Mr J. P. J. Coles**
9 **SPARTS FAULT (IRE),** 6, ch g King Persian—Clonross Lady **Tidmarsh Racing Club**

MR P. ECCLES—continued

10 **STARSPORT (IRE)**, 5, ch g Salt Dome (USA)—Ivory Smooth (USA) **Mrs P. Carson**
11 **SUNGROVE'S BEST**, 9, ch g Buzzards Bay—Judann **Mr A. Holland**
12 **THUNDERING**, 11, b g Persian Bold—Am Stretchin' (USA) **Miss Victoria Jones**
13 **ZAJIRA (IRE)**, 6, b m Ela-Mana-Mou—Awsaaf (USA) **Mr F. J. Bush**

Other Owners: Mr C. Alexander, Mr J. F. Mitchell, Miss D. M. Stafford, Mr D. J. White.

194   MR B. J. ECKLEY, Brecon

Postal: **Closcedi Farm, Llanspyddid, Brecon, Powys, LD3 8NS.**
Phone: **(01874) 622422**

1 **ALICE SMITH**, 9, gr m Alias Smith (USA)—Dancing Jenny **Mrs J. H. E. Eckley**
2 **JAUNTY JUNE**, 5, b m Primitive Rising (USA)—Jaunty Jane **Mrs J. H. E. Eckley**

Jockey (NH): W J McFarland (10-0).

Lady Rider: Pip L Jones (9-0).

195   MR MALCOLM ECKLEY, Ludlow

Postal: **Alma House, Brimfield, Ludlow, Salop, SY8 4NG.**
Phone: **BRIMFIELD (01584) 711372**

1 **BENSTUN**, 5, b g Stunner Rascal (HOL)—Romany Empress **Mr A. D. Bennett**
2 **GYMCRAK DANCER**, 7, b m Pennine Walk—Silent Sun **Exors of the late Mrs J. M. Snape**
3 **OUT OF THE BLUE**, 4, b f Lochnager—Expletive **Mr W. Cowell**

THREE-YEAR-OLDS

4 Ch g Gunner B—Expletive **Mr Malcolm W. Eckley**

TWO-YEAR-OLDS

5 Ch f 5/4 Derrylin—Expletive (Shiny Tenth) **Mr Malcolm W. Eckley**
6 B f 9/5 Derrylin—Llacca Princess (Rymer) **Mr Malcolm W. Eckley**

Other Owners: Mr J. Rothwell, Mr H. M. Thursfield, Mr Mark Watson.

Jockeys (Flat): W Carson (7-9, w.a.), J Williams (8-4, w.a.).

Jockeys (NH): R Dunwoody (10-1, w.a.), M Fitzgerald (10-0, w.a.), A Maguire (10-0, w.a.).

Apprentice: D Moffat (7-0).

Conditional: G M Lee (9-7), D Meredith (9-7).

Lady Rider: Miss G Armytage (10-0).

196   MR D. EDDY, Newcastle Upon Tyne

Postal: **The Byerley Stud, Ingoe, Newcastle Upon Tyne, NE20 0SZ.**

Phone: **(01661) 886356**

1 BILLIBANG, 10, b g Derring Rose—Jurist **Mr James R. Adams**
2 JAHAZ (USA), 4, b g Reference Point—Hooriah (USA) **Mrs Karen McLintock**
3 LUCKER, 9, b g Anita's Prince—Musical Puss **Mr James R. Adams**
4 MAJIC RAIN, 11, bl g Northern Value (USA)—Dinsdale **Mr D. V. Tate**
5 MEESONS EXPRESS, 6, ch g Little Wolf—Final Answer **Mrs Karen McLintock**
6 NODFORM WONDER, 9, b g Cut Above—Wonder **Equiname Ltd**
7 PRINCE EQUINAME, 4, gr g Dominion—Moments Peace **Colin Barnfather and Frank Steele**
8 SHARIAKANNDI (FR), 4, b g Lashkari—Shapaara **Mr Kevin Elliott**
9 SHEFARID (IRE), 4, ch g Lashkari—Shashna **Equiname Ltd**
10 SUPER TRUCKER, 13, b g Lochnager—The Haulier **Mr James R. Adams**

Other Owners: Mrs I. Battla, Mr Charles Castle.

197   MR G. F. EDWARDS, Minehead

Postal: **Summering, Wheddon Cross, Minehead, Somerset, TA24 7AT.**

Phone: **(01643) 831549**

1 ABU MUSLAB, 12, b br g Ile de Bourbon (USA)—Eastern Shore **Mr G. F. Edwards**
2 CHICKABIDDY, 8, b m Henbit (USA)—Shoshoni **Mr G. F. Edwards**
3 DISTILLATION, 11, b g Celtic Cone—Cauldron **Mr G. F. Edwards**
4 LITTLE HOOLIGAN, 5, b br g Rabdan—Nutwood Emma **Mr G. F. Edwards**
5 THE MINDER (FR), 9, b br g Miller's Mate—Clarandal **Mr G. F. Edwards**

198   MR J. A. C. EDWARDS, Ross-on-Wye

Postal: **Caradoc Court, Sellack, Ross-on-Wye, Herefordshire, HR9 6LS.**

Phone: **(01989730) 259/315 FAX 329 HOUSE 639**

1 5, B g Cheval—A Weeks Notice (IRE) **Mr J. A. C. Edwards**
2 5, Ch g Over The River (FR)—Ballymore Status **Mr J. A. C. Edwards**
3 BECK AND CALL (IRE), 7, ch g Buckskin (FR)—Kilmurray Jet **Mr Peter J. Burch**
4 BETTER FUTURE (IRE), 7, br g Good Thyne (USA)—Little Else **Mr J. A. C. Edwards**
5 BODFARI PRODUCER (IRE), 6, b m The Wonder (FR)—Saltoki **Mr R. J. McAlpine**
6 CALLERNISH DAN (IRE), 6, ch g Callernish—Fairy River **Mrs Alurie O'Sullivan**
7 CARDINAL RULE (IRE), 7, ch g Carlingford Castle—Lady of Rathleek **Mr P. J. Burch & Mr E. Fenaroli**
8 CAREY'S COTTAGE (IRE), 6, ch g Sheer Grit—Straight Carl **The Cottage Partnership**
9 CAREYSVILLE (IRE), 5, b g Carmelite House (USA)—Kavali **Mr Geoffrey Johnson**
10 4, B br g Yashgan—Clerihan Miss **Mr J. A. C. Edwards**
11 COUNTRYMAN (IRE), 5, ch g Henbit (USA)—Riancoir Alainn **Mr Howard Parker**
12 CRACKING IDEA (IRE), 8, b g The Parson—Game Sunset **Mr Alan Parker**
13 DIRECT, 13, b g The Parson—Let The Hare Sit **Mr J. A. C. Edwards**
14 FATHER O'BRIEN, 9, b g The Parson—Tanala **Mrs G. Jenkinson**
15 FELDSPAR, 7, br g Green Ruby (USA)—Hill Vixen **Mrs J. P. Bissill**
16 FLAMING ROSE (IRE), 6, b m Roselier (FR)—Little Flame **Mr D. Williams**
17 FOURTH IN LINE (IRE), 8, b g Horage—Littoral Mes **Mrs G. Jenkinson**
18 GOLDEN DRUM (IRE), 6, ch g Black Minstrel—Four In A Row **Mr Howard Parker**
19 HAG'S WAY (IRE), 6, ch g Roselier (FR)—Lucifer's Way **Mrs Alurie O'Sullivan**
20 5, B m Governor General—Hill Vixen **Mrs J. P. Bissill**
21 JULTARA (IRE), 7, ch g Strong Statement (USA)—La Bise **Mr Roger Barby**
22 5, B g Lancastrian—Kilmurray Jet **Mr J. A. C. Edwards**
23 5, Gr g Over The River (FR)—Kilross **Mr J. A. C. Edwards**
24 5, Ch g Executive Perk—Little Flame **Lady A. Maxwell**

MR J. A. C. EDWARDS—continued

25 **LITTLE NICKERS (IRE)**, 6, b g Black Minstrel—Mehitabel **Mr Malcolm Sosna**
26 **LOTTERY TICKET (IRE)**, 7, b g The Parson—Beauty Run **Mr Alan Parker**
27 **MERLIN'S LAD**, 7, br g Rymer—Seal Marine **Mr H. Messer-Bennetts**
28 **MINERS FORTUNE (IRE)**, 8, b g Miner's Lamp—Banish Misfortune **Mr J. A. C. Edwards**
29 5, B g Over The River (FR)—Monalee Stream **Mrs Maureen J. Russell**
30 **MONSIEUR LE CURE**, 10, b g The Parson—Caramore Lady **Mr Hector H. Brown**
31 **OH LORD (IRE)**, 7, b g Mister Lord (USA)—Arctic Survivor **Mr J. A. C. Edwards**
32 4, B g Miner's Lamp—Petaluma Pet **Mr J. A. C. Edwards**
33 4, B f Supreme Leader—Protrial **Mr J. A. C. Edwards**
34 **RIOT LEADER (IRE)**, 6, b g Supreme Leader—Calamity Jane **The Riot Partnership**
35 **RIVERS END (IRE)**, 7, ch g Over The River (FR)—Ballymore Status **Mrs Douglas Graham**
36 5, B g Henbit (USA)—Secret Romance **Mr J. A. C. Edwards**
37 **SIGMA RUN (IRE)**, 7, b g The Parson—Splendid Run **B. G. S. Racing Partnership**
38 **SILK WORD**, 7, gr g Hasty Word—Ramas Silk **Silkword Racing Partnership**
39 **TARAMOSS**, 9, b g Le Moss—Birniebrig **Mr Howard Parker**
40 **TREATY BRIDGE**, 9, ch g Over The River (FR)—Diplomat's Tam **Mr J. A. C. Edwards**

THREE-YEAR-OLDS

41 B g Mandalus—Croom River (IRE) **Mr J. A. C. Edwards**

Other Owners: Mr Alan C. Elliot, Mr C. J. Green, Mrs M. D. Hartley, Mrs V. S. Hickman, Mr Barry McCormick, Mr D. O. Pickering, Mr David Snow, Mr Michael Stoddart, Mrs Richard Strachan, Mr Mike Wainford, Mr James Wilson.

Amateur: Mr M Daly.

199   MR C. R. EGERTON, Chaddleworth

Postal: **Heads Farm Stables, Chaddleworth, Newbury, Berks, RG16 0EE.**

Phone: **OFFICE (01488) 638771 HOME 638454 FAX 638832 MOBILE (0836) 740769**

1 **ADMIRAL VILLENEUVE**, 8, b g Top Ville—Great Tom **Mrs William Macauley**
2 **AVANTI EXPRESS (IRE)**, 6, b g Supreme Leader—Muckride Lady **Mrs Sarah Stevens**
3 **AZIZZI**, 4, ch g Indian Ridge—Princess Silca Key **Mr Abdul Rahman Mubarak**
4 **BARRON BAY (USA)**, 4, br g Track Barron (USA)—In Bay (ARG) **Elite Racing Club**
5 5, B g Orchestra—Breakfast **Mr Charles Egerton**
6 **CAST OF THOUSANDS**, 5, b g Arctic Lord—Mogen **Mr J. F. Dean**
7 **CAST THE LINE**, 6, b g Pharly (FR)—Off The Reel (USA) **Mr D. P. Barrie**
8 **COUNTRYMASTER**, 7, b g Scottish Reel—Rhinestone **Mr Chris Brasher**
9 **DJEBEL PRINCE**, 9, b g Ile de Bourbon—Noirmont Girl **Elite Thoroughbreds I**
10 **DONT TELL THE WIFE**, 10, br g Derring Rose—Dame Sue **Elite Racing Club**
11 **ELITE HOPE (USA)**, 4, ch f Moment of Hope (USA)—Chervil (USA) **Elite Racing Club**
12 **FRONTAGER**, 6, ch g Irish River—Arriya **Mr Charles Egerton & Partners**
13 **HAWKER HUNTER**, 5, b br g Silver Hawk (USA)—Glorious Natalie (USA) **Dr G. Madan Mohan**
14 **JAMEEL ASMAR**, 4, br c Rock City—Barsham **Mr P. A. Leonard**
15 **KALANSKI**, 10, ro g Niniski (USA)—Kalazero **Mr I. Kerman**
16 **LUMBERJACK (USA)**, 12, b g Big Spruce (USA)—Snip **Elite Racing Club**
17 **MAID FOR DREAMING (IRE)**, 5, br m Strong Gale—Star Chamber (FR) **Mr Chris Brasher**
18 4, B g Idiot's Delight—Mayfield **Sir Reginald Sheffield**
19 **MAY SUNSET (IRE)**, 6, b g Tremblant—Donegal Queen **Mrs B. V. Sangster**
20 **MCGILLYCUDDY REEKS (IRE)**, 5, b m Kefaah (USA)—Kilvarnet **Elite Racing Club**
21 **MOUNT SERRATH (IRE)**, 8, b br g Mandalus—Hopeful Secret **Mrs J. D. Clegg**
22 **MYSILV**, 6, ch m Bustino—Miss By Miles **Elite Racing Club**
23 **PARADISE NAVY**, 7, b g Slip Anchor—Ivory Waltz (USA) **Elite Racing Club**
24 **PERSIAN ELITE (IRE)**, 5, ch g Persian Heights—Late Sally **Elite Racing Club**
25 **RAGGED KINGDOM (IRE)**, 7, b g King's Ride—Golden Robe **Mrs Ronald Snow and Mrs David Oddie**
26 **RIVER LOSSIE**, 7, b g Bustino—Forres **Mr Chris Brasher**
27 **ROYAL IRISH**, 12, ch g Le Bavard (FR)—Leuze **Dr G. Madan Mohan**

MR C. R. EGERTON—continued

28 RUMI, 5, ch m Nishapour (FR)—Seldom **Elite Racing Club**
29 SILENT GUNS (NZ), 7, b g Guns of Navarone—Acol (NZ) **Lord Clinton**
30 SNOWTOWN ACTRESS (IRE), 6, b m Over The River (FR)—Constant Actress **Mr John Hussey**
31 STAR MYSTERY, 5, b g Insan (USA)—Emaline (FR) **Mr Charles Egerton**
32 STAR OF GOLD, 4, b g Night Shift (USA)—Sure Gold **Mr Austin Allison & Mr Andy Hayes**
33 STAY WITH ME (FR), 6, b g Nikos—Live With Me **Mrs Sandra A. Roe**
34 ST VALERY, 4, b f Statoblest—Fleur du Val **Olympic Racing 1994**
36 THEFIELDSOFATHENRY (IRE), 6, b g King Persian—Clodianus **Elite Racing Club**
38 5, Br g Dowsing—True Ring **Rhydian Morgan Jones**
39 WHITEBONNET (IRE), 6, b g Rainbow Quest (USA)—Dawn Is Breaking **The Blue Chip Group**

THREE-YEAR-OLDS

40 EARLY WARNING, br f Warning—Ile de Danse **The Blue Chip Group**
41 MY MARIAM, ch f Salse (USA)—Birch Creek **Mr Abdul Rahman Mubarak**
42 B g Taufan—Noble Treasure **Mr Abdul Rahman Mubarak**

TWO-YEAR-OLDS

43 B c 2/2 Robellino (USA)—Catkin (USA) (Sir Ivor) **Mr Chris Brasher**
44 B c 3/5 Green Desert (USA)—Missed Again (High Top) **Mr Abdul Rahman Mubarak**

Other Owners: Mrs S. A. Allan, Mr Brian Allen, Mr S. Bowrett, Mr D. L. Brooks, Michael Buckley, Mr I. Clay, Mr T. E. S. Egerton, Mrs Thomas Egerton, Mr N. V. Evans, Mrs V. Graham, Mr A. Hayes, Mrs M. Hill, Colin Ingleby-Mackenzie, Mr P. B. Mitford-Slade, Olympic Bloodstock Ltd, Mr M. J. Rees, Mr P. G. Ring, R. E. Sangster, Mr N. K. Siegel, Anthony Speelman, Mr C. C. Speke.

Jockeys (NH): J A McCarthy, J Osborne (10-0, w.a.).

Additional Horses

WOODRISING, 4 bf Nomination—Bodham **The Blue Chip Group**
2 bc 29/1 High Estate—Princess Pavlova **Mr Charles Egerton**

200　　　MR M. W. ELLERBY, Pickering

Postal: **Westgate Carr Farm, Westgate Carr Road, Pickering, North Yorks, YO18 8LX.**
Phone: **(01751) 74092**

1 CHOSEN MAN, 4, br g Dowsing (USA)—Town Lady **Mrs H. J. Ellerby**
2 CLEDESCHAMPS, 7, b m Doc Marten—Cape Farewell **Mrs H. J. Ellerby**
3 SHANNARA (IRE), 5, b m Treasure Kay—Elegant Owl **Mrs H. J. Ellerby**

THREE-YEAR-OLDS

4 Ch c Noblissimo (FR)—Cape Farewell **Mrs H. J. Ellerby**
5 B f Flying Tyke—Carrula **Mrs H. J. Ellerby**
6 B f Presidium—Light de Light (USA) **Mrs H. J. Ellerby**
7 B c Timeless Times (USA)—Miss Sherbrooke
8 WYDALE, b c Rich Charlie—Julia Mawe **Mrs H. J. Ellerby**

TWO-YEAR-OLDS

9 Ch f 9/4 Timeless Times (USA)—Miss Sherbrooke (Workboy) **Mrs H. J. Ellerby**

Jockey (Flat): S Morris (8-0).

Apprentices: Claire Balding (7-0), C Teague (7-0).

Conditional: F Leahy (9-7), N Smith (9-7).

201   MR E. A. ELLIOTT, Rushyford

Postal: **Planting House, Windlestone Park, Rushyford, Co. Durham, DL17 0LZ.**

Phone: **(01388) 720383**

1 **BALLYVAUGHAN (IRE)**, 6, ch g Carlingford Castle—Fahy Quay **Mrs Anne E. Elliott**
2 **BARNSTORMER**, 10, ch g Carlingford Castle—Sue Bell **Mr Eric A. Elliott**
3 **BELLWAY**, 15, ch g Orchestra—Victorian Era **Mr Eric A. Elliott**
4 **SELDOM BUT SEVERE (IRE)**, 6, br g Hawaiian Return (USA)—Goldfoot **Mr Eric A. Elliott**

202   MR BRIAN ELLISON, Lanchester

Postal: **Low Meadow Farm, Lanchester, Co. Durham.**

Phone: **HOME (01207) 501399 OFFICE (01207) 529991 MOBILE (0802) 852150**

1 **BHAVNAGAR (IRE)**, 5, gr g Darshaan—Banana Peel **Mr E. J. Berry**
2 **CLOVER GIRL**, 5, b m Spin of A Coin—Byerley Rose **Mr K. Brown**
3 **FARMER'S HAND**, 9, ch g Nearly A Hand—Farm Consultation **Mr K. Morton**
4 **FATEHALKHAIR (IRE)**, 4, ch c Kris—Midway Lady (USA) **Mrs Gwen Smith**
5 **GO SILLY**, 10, b g Silly Prices—Allez Stanwick **Ferrogragh**
6 **IVAN THE TERRIBLE (IRE)**, 8, ch g Siberian Express (USA)—Chrisanthy **Mrs Jean Stapleton**
7 **KITTY WATERJET**, 4, ch f Golden Lahab (USA)—Key Harvest **Mr Leslie R. Smith**
8 **LEDWYCHE ROSE**, 6, b m Derring Rose—Ledwyche **Mrs Ellison**
9 **MUSWELL BROOK (IRE)**, 6, br g Nashamaa—Motus **Mr Philip Serbert**
10 **RONNIE THE BUTCHER (IRE)**, 5, b g Northiam (USA)—Goirtin **Mr Ronald McCulloch**
11 5, Ch m Le Moss—Santa Jo **Toshiba (UK) Ltd**
12 **SHAMSHOM AL ARAB (IRE)**, 8, gr g Glenstal (USA)—Love Locket **Mrs Susan J. Ellison**
13 **TOSHIBA TALK (IRE)**, 4, ch g Horage—Court Ballet **Toshiba (UK) Ltd**
14 **URBAN DANCING (USA)**, 7, ch g Nureyev (USA)—Afifa (USA) **Mr R. McCulloch**
15 **WHITEGATESPRINCESS (IRE)**, 5, b m Valiyar—Whitegates Lady **Red Onion**

THREE-YEAR-OLDS

16 **GO-GO-POWER-RANGER**, ch g Golden Lahab (USA)—Nibelunga **Mr Fred Hayne**
17 B f Golden Lahab (USA)—Homing Hill **Mr Serbett**
18 B g Electric—Santa Jo **T. Batey**

Other Owners: Mrs N. B. Bowden, Mr R. W. L. Bowden, Mr Brian Chicken, Miss Abigail Strangeway, Mr Raymond Wagner.

Jockey (Flat): N Kennedy.

Conditional: B Harding.

Lady Rider: Jane Morton.

203   MR C. C. ELSEY, Lambourn

Postal: **Upshire Farm Racing Stables, Hungerford Hill, Lambourn, Newbury, RG16 7XZ.**

Phone: **LAMBOURN (01488) OFFICE 71242 HOME 72859**

1 **ACE CHAPEL (IRE)**, 4, br g Simply Great (FR)—Sistina **Mr Paul G. Jacobs**
2 **BY THE BAY**, 4, b f Shareef Dancer (USA)—Beryl's Jewel **Mr Richard Berenson**
3 **DIAMOND BANGLE**, 4, b f Chilibang—My Diamond Ring **Mrs Marion Wickham**
4 **DR FRANCES (IRE)**, 4, b f Pennine Walk—Pounding Beat **Mr Richard Berenson**
5 **KINTWYN**, 6, b g Doulab (USA)—Harriet Emma (USA) **Mrs F. E. Bacon**

MR C. C. ELSEY—continued

6 **KISSAVOS**, 10, ch g Cure The Blues (USA)—Hairbrush (USA) **Mr C. C. Elsey**
7 **LETS BE FRANK**, 5, b g Malaspina—Letitica **Mrs M. M. Stobart**
8 **PRINCESS DANIELLE**, 4, b f Prince Daniel—Bells of St Martin **Mrs Marion Wickham**

THREE-YEAR-OLDS

9 **CINDY KATE (IRE)**, b f Sayf El Arab (USA)—Marton Maid **Mr R. P. Clarke**
10 **DEVIOCK**, b f Shareef Dancer (USA)—Devon Defender **Mr Paul G. Jacobs**
11 **LONGWICK LAD**, gr c Chilibang—Bells of St Martin **Mrs Marion Wickham**
12 **TAHYA (USA)**, ch f Elmaamul (USA)—Tatwij (USA) **Mr C. C. Elsey**

Other Owners: Mrs Ann Chapman, Mrs M. E. Olsson, Mr Bob Till.

Jockeys (Flat): D Harrison (w.a.), C Rutter.

Jockeys (NH): G Bradley (w.a.), M Richards (w.a.).

Amateur: Miss A Elsey.

204   MR C. W. C. ELSEY, Malton

Postal: **Highfield House, Beverley Road, Malton, N. Yorks, YO17 9PJ.**
Phone: **(01653) 693149 FAX (01653) 600260**

1 **BATTERY BOY**, 4, b g K-Battery—Bonny's Pet **Mrs M. C. Butler**
2 **EAU BENITE**, 5, br g Monsanto (FR)—Hopeful Waters **Group One Racing**
3 **FORTIS PAVIOR (IRE)**, 6, b g Salt Dome (USA)—Heather Lil **Mr O. R. Dukes**
4 **PHILGUN**, 7, b g K-Battery—Andalucia **Mr C. W. C. Elsey**
5 **PHILMIST**, 4, b f Hard Fought—Andalucia **Mr C. D. Barber-Lomax**

THREE-YEAR-OLDS

6 **BALLET DE COUR**, b c Thowra (FR)—Chaleureuse **Group One Racing Partnership**
7 **CERISE (IRE)**, b f Red Sunset—Noble Nancy **Russell Bradley & Partners**
8 **ISLAY BROWN (IRE)**, b f Petorius—Speedy Action **Mr Andrew Smith**
9 **KAZIMIERA (IRE)**, b f Polish Patriot (USA)—Cartier Bijoux
10 **NDR'S CASH FOR FUN**, b g Ballacashtal (CAN)—Basic Fun **Group One Racing**

TWO-YEAR-OLDS

11 B f 16/1 Prince Sabo—Kajetana (FR) (Caro) **Mrs M. C. Butler**
12 **MOLLY DRUMMOND**, b f 10/2 Sizzling Melody—
                                        Miss Drummond (The Brianstan) **Group One Racing Partnership**
13 B f 13/4 K-Battery—Ribonny (FR) (Fast Hilarious (USA)) **Mrs M. C. Butler**

Other Owners: Mr John D. Butterworth, Mr L. Gudgeon, Mrs Avril Stanhope, Mr P. Towey.

Lady Rider: Miss Annie Elsey (9-0).

205   MISS A. E. EMBIRICOS, Newmarket

Postal: **The Old Twelve Stables, Moulton Paddocks, Newmarket, Suffolk, CB8 8QJ.**
Phone: **(01638) 660048**

1 **ANDROS PRINCE**, 11, b g Blakeney—Ribamba **Mr A. Zafiropulo**
2 **CHANGE THE REIGN**, 9, b g King's Ride—Reformed Rule **Mr E. D. Nicolson**
3 **COTTESMORE**, 5, b g Broadsword (USA)—Celestial Bride **Mrs S. N. J. Embiricos**

MISS A. E. EMBIRICOS—continued

4 **CROSSING THE STYX**, 10, b g Lucifer (USA)—Glad Rain **Chasers**
5 **DUNHILL IDOL**, 9, b g Tug of War—Indian Idol **Chasers**
6 **FABULOUS FRANCY (IRE)**, 8, ch g Remainder Man—Francie's Treble **Mr E. D. Nicolson**
7 5, B m Petoski—Fair Atlanta
8 **FIFTH FUSILIER**, 9, ch g Sunley Builds—Creggana **Chasers**
9 **FIGHTING TROUT**, 9, b m Broadsword (USA)—Warham Trout **Mr R. J. Lyles**
10 **GANDOUGE GLEN**, 9, b g Furry Glen—Gandouge Lady **Mr S. N. J. Embiricos**
11 **GREENWAY LADY**, 4, ch f Prince Daniel (USA)—Lady Ector (USA) **Bradnock Syndicate**
12 **HALL BANK COTTAGE**, 6, br m Tina's Pet—Cresta Leap **Mr F. Le Fleming**
13 **HIJACK**, 5, b g Cigar—Ballirumba **Mr Ian Evans**
14 **JOHNNY WILL**, 11, b g Salluceva—Hellfire Hostess **Chasers**
15 **LADY WOODSTOCK**, 4, b f Chilibang—Vent du Soir **Miss A. Embiricos**
16 **LORD VICK (IRE)**, 7, ch g Mister Lord (USA)—Vickies Gold **Mrs S. N. J. Embiricos**
17 **NANDURA**, 5, b m Nordico (USA)—The Ranee **Chasers**
18 5, B br m Jolly Jake (NZ)—Night Invader
19 **RAGLAN ROAD**, 12, b g Furry Glen—Princess Concorde **Chasers**
20 **SPECIAL TOPIC**, 6, ch m Very Special—Elevena (AUS) **Major R. G. Wilson**
21 **STAR OF DAVID (IRE)**, 8, b g Mister Lord (USA)—Knockantota Star **Mrs S. N. J. Embiricos**
22 **TOP WAVE**, 8, br g High Top—Sea Fret **Mr A. K. Collins**

Other Owners: Mr D. H. Crisp, Mr John Green, Mr Tim Jones, Mrs S. Shaw.

Jockeys (NH): J Bryan (10-0), J R Kavanagh (9-7).

Amateur: Mr T McCarthy (9-10).

Lady Rider: Miss A E Embiricos (10-6).

206   MISS E. M. V. ENGLAND, Rugby

Postal: **Grove Cottage, Priors Hardwick, Rugby, Warwickshire, CV23 8SN.**
Phone: **(01327) 260437**

1 **JANE CHILD**, 8, ch m Chabrias (FR)—Staboe Lady **Miss E. M. V. England**
2 **SIDNEY**, 7, b g Chabrias (FR)—Staboe Lady **Miss E. M. V. England**
3 **THE ELOPER**, 8, b g Idiot's Delight—Night Action **Miss E. M. V. England**
4 **TOP TARGET**, 10, ch g Cruise Missile—Topte **Miss E. M. V. England**
5 **TRY ME NOW**, 10, b g Try My Best (USA)—Sapientia (FR) **Miss E. M. V. England**

Jockey (NH): Robbie Supple.

207   MR G. P. ENRIGHT, Lewes

Postal: **The Oaks, Old Lewes Racecourse, Lewes, East Sussex, BN7 1UR.**
Phone: **LEWES (01273) 479183 FAX (01273) 479183**

1 **AEDEAN**, 7, ch g Risk Me (FR)—Finlandaise (FR) **Mr M. B. Orpen-Palmer**
2 **DUTCH**, 4, ch c Nicholas Bill—Dutch Princess **Mr Leonard Fuller**
3 **FLOW BACK**, 4, gr g Royal Academy (USA)—Flo Russell (USA) **Mr D. Leon**
4 **FROZEN SEA (USA)**, 5, ch h Diesis—Ocean Ballad **The Oaks Partners**
5 **LE SORCIER**, 4, ch g Prince des Coeurs (USA)—Pink N' Perky **The Witch Racing Club**
6 **MULL HOUSE**, 9, b g Local Suitor (USA)—Foudre **Mr Brian Beagley**
7 **NIDOMI**, 9, ch g Dominion—Nicholas Grey **Mr D. Leon**
8 **PALACE GUARD**, 4, br g Daring March—Royal Brush **Mr Chris Wall**

MR G. P. ENRIGHT—continued

9 **POLLY MINOR**, 9, b m Sunley Builds—Polly Major **The Witch Racing Club II**
10 **REAL MADRID**, 5, b g Dreams To Reality (USA)—Spanish Princess **Mr Chris Wall**

THREE-YEAR-OLDS

11 **DUTCH DYANE**, b f Midyan (USA)—Double Dutch **Mr Leonard Fuller**
12 **EL PRESIDENTE**, b c Presidium—Spanish Princess **Mr Chris Wall**

Other Owners: Mr A. O. Ashford, Mr E. Benfield, Mr John M. Pegler, Miss P. A. Ross, Mr Gerry Ryan, Sir Milton Sharp.

Jockey (Flat): N Adams.

Jockey (NH): M Perrett (10-0).

Lady Rider: Mrs M Enright (8-7).

208   MR T. J. ETHERINGTON, Malton

Postal: **Wold House, Langton Road, Norton, Malton, YO17 9QG.**
Phone: **MALTON (01653) 693049 (HOME) 692842 (OFFICE)**

1 **BE BRAVE**, 6, b g Never So Bold—Boo **Mrs Stephanie Parsons**
2 **CAPICHE (IRE)**, 7, b g Phardante (FR)—Sainthill **T. J. Etherington**
3 **DERRY'S DELIGHT**, 9, br m Mufrij—Derry Island **Miss Jayne Sunley**
4 **HEATHCOTE PLACE (USA)**, 5, b g Seattle Dancer (USA)—Mary L (USA) **Mr Edward Shouler**
5 **KING RAT (IRE)**, 5, ch g King of Clubs—Mrs Tittlemouse **Mr Paul Daniels**
6 **OWENS QUEST (IRE)**, 6, b m Black Minstrel—Our Quest **London Racing Club Owners Group**
7 **PENMAR**, 4, b g Reprimand—Latakia **Mr and Mrs G. Liversidge**
8 **ROCHARISARE**, 7, b g Mummy's Game—Sharseal **H. S. S.**
9 **SOBA UP**, 6, ch m Persian Heights—Soba **Mrs M. Hills**

THREE-YEAR-OLDS

10 **HALLIKELD**, ch f Bustino—Spring Sparkle **Mr W. R. Green**
11 **MOONRAKING**, gr g Rusticaro (FR)—Lunaire **Mr Richard Hoiles and Mr Ian Bartlett**
12 **PRINCIPAL BOY (IRE)**, br g Cyrano de Bergerac—Shenley Lass **Mr Chris Moreno**
13 **ZALOTTI (IRE)**, ch f Polish Patriot (USA)—Honest Penny (USA) **Mr P. D. Savill**

TWO-YEAR-OLDS

14 Ch f 31/1 Sanglamore (USA)—Eclipsing (IRE) (Baillamont (USA)) **Mr W. R. Green**
15 Ch c 25/4 Imp Society (USA)—Halimah (Be My Guest (USA)) **T. J. Etherington**
16 B c 4/5 Then Again—Moon Risk (Risk Me (FR)) **Mr Pat Pain**
17 **RHEINBOLD**, b c 22/4 Never So Bold—Rheinbloom (Rheingold) **Mr G. E. Oliver**
18 Gr c 22/3 Efisio—Strawberry Pink (Absalom) **Debbie McGhee and Sylvia O'Horan**
19 **ZALOTTO (IRE)**, b c 22/3 Polish Patriot (USA)—Honest Penny (USA) (Honest Pleasure (USA)) **Mr P. D. Savill**

Other Owners: Exors Of The Late Mr M. J. Clothier, Mr J. Etherington, Mr R. H. Hudson, Mr K. G. Hunt, Mr M. O'Horan, Mr P. F. Whitehead.

Jockey (Flat): K Darley (w.a.).

Jockey (NH): A Thornton.

Conditional: R Rourke (9-7).

209   MR A. EUBANK, Cockermouth

Postal: **Millstone Moor, Cockermouth, Cumbria, CA13 0QA.**

Phone: **(01900) 823027**

1 **LITTLE BROMLEY**, 9, ch m Riberetto—Bromley Rose **Mr A. Eubank**
2 **ONLY CHANCE**, 5, ch g Slim Jim—Bromley Rose **Mr A. Eubank**
3 **ROSE'S DOUBLE**, 6, ch m Respect—Bromley Rose **Mrs A. Eubank**

Conditional: A Manners (w.a.).

Amateur: Mr R Hale (w.a.).

210   MR J. M. P. EUSTACE, Newmarket

Postal: **Park Lodge Stables, Park Lane, Newmarket, Suffolk, CB8 8AX.**

Phone: **TEL (01638) 664277 FAX (01638) 664156 MOBILE (0802) 243764**

1 **BROCKTON FLAME**, 4, b f Emarati (USA)—Minne Love **Mrs D. A. La Trobe**
2 **INVEST WISELY**, 4, ch g Dashing Blade—Saniette **Mr J. C. Smith**
3 **LOCHBUIE**, 4, ch c Forzando—Nigel's Dream **Mr R. Carstairs**
4 **MASTER OF PASSION**, 7, b g Primo Dominie—Crime of Passion **Mr & Mrs Michael Kwee**
5 **MIDYAN BLUE (IRE)**, 6, ch g Midyan (USA)—Jarretiere **Mr Keith H. Palmer**
6 **PRIME OF LIFE (IRE)**, 6, b g Midyan (USA)—Ominous **Mrs T. S. Matthews**

THREE-YEAR-OLDS

7 **COMPASS POINTER**, gr c Mazilier (USA)—Woodleys **Park Lane Racing**
8 **KENDIG**, ch c Efisio—Zaius **Mr R. Carstairs**
9 **MAGIC MAIL**, b c Aragon—Blue Rhythm **Mr Gary Coull**
10 **PHILISTAR**, ch c Bairn (USA)—Philgwyn **Mr & Mrs A. W. Hobbs**
11 **SIMPLE ALTERNATIVE**, b g Then Again—Simply Jane **Mr R. Carstairs**

TWO-YEAR-OLDS

12 B f 8/2 Emarati (USA)—Bentinck Hotel (Red God) **Park Lane Racing & Mrs D. A. La Trobe**
13 **EASTERN EAGLE (IRE)**, b c 24/4 Polish Patriot (USA)—Lady's Turn (Rymer) **Anglo Welsh Partnership**
14 B c 24/1 Statoblest—Frasquita (Song) **Mr J. C. Smith**
15 **HIGHWAY ROBBER (IRE)**, b c 2/4 Robellino (USA)—High Habit (Slip Anchor) **Mr J. C. Smith**
16 **IRISH PET**, br f 22/3 Petong—Crystal's Solo (USA) (Crystal Water (USA)) **Mr J. C. Smith**
17 B f 2/4 Royal Academy (USA)—Last Ball (IRE) (Last Tycoon) **Mr & Mrs Michael Kwee**
18 **MADAME CHINNERY**, b f 16/2 Weldnaas (USA)—Bel Esprit (Sagaro) **The Chinnery Partnership**
19 **NOBLE INVESTMENT**, b c 6/2 Shirley Heights—Noble Destiny (Dancing Brave (USA)) **Mr J. C. Smith**
20 **REFUSE TO LOSE**, ch c 24/2 Emarati (USA)—Petrol (Troy) **Mr J. C. Smith**
21 Ch c 29/1 Primo Dominie—True Nora (Ahonoora) **The MacDougall Partnership**
22 B c 12/3 Saddlers' Hall (IRE)—Warning Light (High Top) **Mr Peter Kan**
23 B c 16/3 High Estate—Water Pixie (IRE) (Dance of Life (USA)) **Mr Gary Coull**
24 B f 8/2 Pursuit of Love—Wizardry (Shirley Heights) **Mr Gary Coull**

Other Owners: D. Batten, G. Canner, Mr & Mrs A. Chappell, C. Curtis, Major T. R. H. Eustace, Mrs M. W. F. Ewbank, A. Frost, J. George, R. Gibson, R. Jack, E. Mahoney, S. Marsh, K. Mercer, A. M. Mitchell, T. Oakley, C. Rash, Mr & Mrs B. Tebbutt, E. Voute, N. Wright.

211   MR P. D. EVANS, Welshpool

Postal: **Long Mountain Farm, Leighton, Welshpool, Powys, SY21 8JB.**
Phone: **(01938) 5701288 (0802) 367773 (0860) 599101**

1 **BARGASH,** 4, ch g Sharpo—Anchor Inn **Mr John Pugh**
2 **BEAUMAN,** 6, b g Rainbow Quest (USA)—Gliding **Mr M. W. Lawrence**
3 **BEST KEPT SECRET,** 5, b g Petong—Glenfield Portion **Tern Hill Communications**
4 **BONNY MELODY,** 5, b m Sizzling Melody—Bonny Quiver **Mrs E. A. Dawson**
5 **BROOKHEAD LADY,** 5, b m Petong—Lewista **Mr J. E. Abbey**
6 **DANNISTAR,** 4, br f Puissance—Loadplan Lass **Mr John Pugh**
7 **DUGGAN,** 9, b g Dunbeath (USA)—Silka (ITY) **Mr P. D. Evans**
8 **FOUR OF SPADES,** 5, ch g Faustus (USA)—Fall To Pieces (USA) **Mrs Anna L. Sanders**
9 **LITTLE IBNR,** 5, b g Formidable (USA)—Zalatia **Swinnerton Transport Ltd**
10 **MASTER BEVELED,** 6, b g Beveled (USA)—Miss Anniversary **Mrs E. J. Williams**
11 **RASAYEL (USA),** 6, b m Bering—Reham **Pentans Haulage & Cold Storage Ltd**
12 **WENTBRIDGE LAD (IRE),** 6, b g Coquelin (USA)—Cathryn's Song **Mr John Pugh**

THREE-YEAR-OLDS

13 **DON'T TELL ANYONE,** gr g Petong—Glenfield Portion **Tern Hill Communications**
14 **GAGAJULU,** b f Al Hareb (USA)—Rion River (IRE) **Mr R. F. F. Mason**
15 **MARINO STREET,** b f Totem (USA)—Demerger **Miss J. Oakey**
16 **MONTRESTAR,** ch g Mon Tresor—Wing of Freedom **Mr John Pugh**
17 **ORIEL LAD,** b g Colmore Row—Consistent Queen **Kendall White & Co Ltd**

TWO-YEAR-OLDS

18 **CHAMPAGNE ON ICE,** b f 16/4 Efisio—Nip In The Air (USA) (Northern Dancer) **Treble Chance Partnership**
19 **COCOLOBA (IRE),** b f 30/4 Distinctly North—Born To Fly (IRE) (Last Tycoon) **Mr M. W. Lawrence**
20 B g 12/4 Roi Danzig (USA)—Empress Wu (High Line) **Mr J. E. Abbey**
21 B f 9/5 Waajib—Havana Blade (USA) (Blade (USA)) **Mr John Pugh**
22 B f 8/3 Presidium—Heavenly Queen (Scottish Reel) **Mr J. E. Abbey**
23 B f 3/6 Beveled (USA)—Lonely Shore (Blakeney) **Mrs E. A. Dawson**
24 **MISS FUGIT PENANCE,** br f 16/4 Puissance—Figment (Posse (USA)) **Mr D. Simpson**
25 Gr f 30/4 Petong—Odilese (Mummy's Pet) **Mr J. E. Abbey**
26 **PERFECT BLISS,** ch f 20/2 Superlative—Nikatino (Bustino) **Mr R. F. Mason**
27 Ch f 26/4 Suave Dancer (USA)—Princess Arabella (Crowned Prince (USA)) **Mr John Pugh**
28 **ROCKAROUNDTHECLOCK,** b g 20/3 Rock City—Times (Junius (USA)) **Treble Chance Partnership**
29 **SWINO,** b g 14/4 Forzando—St Helena (Monsanto (FR)) **Swinnerton Transport Ltd**
30 **TAOME (IRE),** b f 7/4 Roi Danzig (USA)—Blue Bell Lady (Dunphy) **Mr M. W. Lawrence**
31 **WEET EES GIRL (IRE),** ro f 24/5 Common Grounds—Kastiliya (Kalamoun) **Ed Weetman Haulage & Storage Ltd**
32 B g 8/2 Emarati (USA)—White African (Carwhite) **Mr D. Maloney**

Other Owners: Mr L. Perry, Mr G. Weaver, Mr J. G. White, Mrs L. A. Windsor.

Apprentice: Hayley Williams (8-0).

Amateurs: Mr A Evans (9-7), Mr W McLaughlin (10-0).

212   MR R. R. EVANS, Stratford-upon-Avon

Postal: **Oxstalls Farm, Warwick Road, Stratford-upon-Avon, Warwicks, CV37 4NR.**
Phone: **(01789) 205277**

1 **ALBEIT,** 6, ch m Mandrake Major—Sioux Be It **Mrs Richard Evans**
2 **CYMRAES,** 6, br m Welsh Captain—Charlotte Mary **Mrs Richard Evans**

Lady Rider: Miss C Evans.

213   MR J. L. EYRE, Hambleton

Postal: **Hambleton House, Sutton Bank, Thirsk, North Yorks, YO7 2HA.**

Phone: **(01845) 597481**

1 **ARIAN SPIRIT (IRE)**, 5, b m High Estate—Astral Way **Mr Martin West**
2 **BARREL OF HOPE**, 4, b c Distant Relative—Musianica **Mr Peter J. Watson**
3 **CALDER KING**, 5, ch g Rakaposhi King—Name The Game **Mr J. L. Eyre**
4 **CAPTAIN MOR**, 14, b g Welsh Captain—Oona More **Mrs Corrina Hirst**
5 **CASHMERE LADY**, 4, b f Hubbly Bubbly (USA)—Choir **Mrs Sybil Howe**
6 **CASHMIRIE**, 4, b f Domynsky—Betrothed **Mr Ernest Spencer**
7 **CELESTIAL CHOIR**, 6, b m Celestial Storm (USA)—Choir **Mrs Carole Sykes**
8 **COLOSSE**, 4, b f Reprimand—French Cutie (USA) **Diamond Racing Ltd**
9 **EVAN 'ELP US**, 4, ch g Executive Man—Recent Events **Mr E. J. Ashton**
10 **FAR AHEAD**, 4, b g Soviet Star (USA)—Cut Ahead **Sunpak Potatoes**
11 **FENWICK'S BROTHER**, 6, ch g Domitor—Topsey Lorac **Mr Martin Firth**
12 **FLOWER OF NAP**, 5, ch m Kinglet—Luceva **Mr Tony Sweetman**
13 **GOODBYE MILLIE**, 6, b br m Sayf El Arab (USA)—Leprechaun Lady **Mr K. Meynell**
14 **GREEK NIGHT OUT (IRE)**, 5, b m Ela-Mana-Mou—Ce Soir **Sunpak Potatoes**
15 **KIRA**, 6, b m Starry Night (USA)—Irish Limerick **Mr J. E. Wilson**
16 **LANGTONIAN**, 7, br g Primo Dominie—Yankee Special **Mr Roy Peebles**
17 **LOCHON**, 5, br g Lochnager—Sky Mariner **Mr J. Lynam**
18 **MAHOOL (USA)**, 7, b g Alydar (USA)—Tax Dodge (USA) **Mrs Kate Watson**
19 **MURRAY'S MAZDA (IRE)**, 7, ch g M Double M (USA)—Lamya **Mr Murray Grubb**
20 **OLD HABITS (IRE)**, 7, b g Nordance (USA)—Layer Cake **Mr R. W. Thomson**
21 **PC'S CRUISER (IRE)**, 4, b g Homo Sapien—Ivy Holme **PC Racing Partners**
22 **PEEP O DAY**, 5, b m Domynsky—Betrothed **Mr John L. Holdroyd**
23 **PINE ESSENCE (USA)**, 5, ch m Green Forest (USA)—Paradise Coffee **Mr K. Meynell**
24 **PINE RIDGE LAD (IRE)**, 6, gr g Taufan (USA)—Rosserk **Whitestonecliffe Racing Partnership**
25 **PRIZEFIGHTER**, 5, b g Rambo Dancer (CAN)—Jaisalmer **Diamond Racing Ltd**
26 **RACHAEL'S DAWN**, 6, b m Rakaposhi King—Edwina's Dawn **Mrs C. A. Ward**
27 **SAINT AMIGO**, 4, gr c Presidium—Little Token **Mr E. Richmond**
28 **VISHNU (USA)**, 6, b g Storm Bird (CAN)—Vachti (FR) **Mr N. C. White**
29 **WIGBERTO (IRE)**, 4, ch c Old Vic—Royal Loft **Sunpak Potatoes**
30 **YACHT CLUB**, 14, b g New Member—Sparflow **Mr Ernest Spencer**

THREE-YEAR-OLDS

31 **AGENT**, ch c Anshan—Maria Cappuccini **Mr M. Gleason**
32 **CANDY'S DELIGHT**, b f Dunbeath—Simply Candy (IRE) **Mr Jeff Slaney**
33 **MELS BABY (IRE)**, br g Contract Law (USA)—Launch The Raft **Mr John Roberts (Wakefield)**
34 **OCEAN STREAM (IRE)**, b c Waajib—Kilboy Concorde **Mr M. Gleason**
35 **PETERS FOLLY**, b f King Among Kings—Santo Star **Mr Malcolm Prescott**
36 **THE FULLBANGLADESH**, ch f Hubbly Bubbly (USA)—Oakhurst **Mr David Campbell**
37 **WHITLEY GRANGE BOY**, b g Hubbly Bubbly (USA)—Choir **Mrs Carole Sykes**

Other Owners: Miss N. J. Cassidy, Mr D. Clarkson, Mr J. H. Eden, Mr T. S. Ely, Mr P. Hampshire, Mr Paul Hemingway, Mr B. Hooper, Mr A. H. Jackson, Mr John Johnson, Mr J. McCormack, Mr John Morley, Mr Michael Anthony O'Donnell, Mr Tony Parrish, Mr P. C. Smith, Mr M. G. St Quinton, Mr Frank Thornton, Ms Melanie Jayne Tyrrell, Mrs Linda Waddington, Mrs S. J. Yates, Mr Tony Yates.

Jockeys (Flat): K Fallon (8-3), R Lappin (8-1).

Apprentice: G Macdonald (7-12).

Conditional: C Elliot (10-0).

Lady Rider: Mrs Corrina Hirst (9-0).

214 MR A. FABRE, Chantilly

Postal: **14 Avenue de Bourbon, 60500 Chantilly, France.**

Phone: **44 57 04 98**

1 **AFFIDAVIT (USA)**, 4, b c Affirmed—Narwala **Sheikh Mohammed**
2 **BOBINSKI**, 4, br c Polish Precedent—Cockade **Mr R. McCreery**
3 **COPENT GARDEN (IRE)**, 4, b c Sadler's Wells—Ameridienne **Mr T. Wada**
4 **DE QUEST**, 4, b c Rainbow Quest—De Stael **Mr K. Abdulla**
5 **DIAMOND MIX (IRE)**, 4, b c Linamix—Diamond Seal **Mr J. L. Lagardere**
6 **FREEDOM CRY**, 5, b h Soviet Star—Falling Star **Mr D. Wildenstein**
7 **GOLDMARK (USA)**, 4, b c Lyphard—Gold Rose **Sheikh Mohammed**
8 **HELEN OF SPAIN**, 4, b f Sadler's Wells—Port Helene **Sheikh Mohammed**
9 **HOMME D'HONNEUR (FR)**, 4, b c Sadler's Wells—Luth de Saron **Mme Paul de Moussac**
10 **HOUSAMIX (FR)**, 4, b br c Linamix—Housatonic **Mr J. L. Lagardere**
11 **MUNCIE (IRE)**, 4, b f Sadler's Wells—Martingale **Mr D. Wildenstein**
12 **PENNEKAMP (USA)**, 4, b c Bering—Coral Dance **Sheikh Mohammed**
13 **POPLAR BLUFF (IRE)**, 4, b c Dowsing—Plume Bleu Pale **Mr D. Wildenstein**
14 **RESTIV STAR (FR)**, 4, b f Soviet Star—Restiver **Mr J. L. Lagardere**
15 **RIO VERDE (USA)**, 4, b c Nureyev—River Rose **Sheikh Mohammed**
16 **SENNEVILLE (USA)**, 4, b g Alysheba—Special Happening **Mr D. Wildenstein**
17 **SUNSHACK**, 5, b h Rainbow Quest—Suntrap **Mr K. Abdulla**
18 **SURESNES (USA)**, 4, b c Lomond—Saison **Mr D. Wildenstein**
19 **SWAIN (IRE)**, 4, b c Nashwan—Love Smitten **Sheikh Mohammed**
20 **TAMISE (USA)**, 4, b f Time For A Change—Tanapa **Mr D. Wildenstein**
21 **VETHEUIL (USA)**, 4, b c Riverman—Venise **Mr D. Wildenstein**
22 **WALK ON MIX (FR)**, 4, gr c Linamix—Walk On Air **Mr J. L. Lagardere**

THREE-YEAR-OLDS

23 **ALAMO BAY (USA)**, b c Nureyev—Albertine **Mr D. Wildenstein**
24 **ANASAZI (IRE)**, b f Sadler's Wells—Navajo Princess **Mr K. Abdulla**
25 **ANDROID (USA)**, b c Riverman—Action Francaise **Mr D. Wildenstein**
26 **ANZIYAN (USA)**, b c Danzig—Razyana **Mr K. Abdulla**
27 **ASSARANXA (FR)**, b f Linamix—Assaraayir **Mr J. L. Lagardere**
28 **ATELIER**, b f Warning—Stiletta **Mr K. Abdulla**
29 **BADDAMIX (FR)**, b c Linamix—Baddana **Mr J. L. Lagardere**
30 **BARQUE BLEUE (USA)**, b f Steinlen—Blithe Spirit **Mr D. Wildenstein**
31 **BARRICADE (USA)**, b c Riverman—Balleta **Mr K. Abdulla**
32 **BATTLE DORE (USA)**, b c Sanglamore—Nashmeel **Mr K. Abdulla**
33 **BLUEDONIX (FR)**, b c Linamix—Blue Mandolin **Mr J. L. Lagardere**
34 **BLUE HIBISCUS (USA)**, b c Woodman—Bonshamile **Mr D. Wildenstein**
35 **BLUE SADDLE (IRE)**, b c Sadler's Wells—Before Dawn **Mr D. Wildenstein**
36 **BOLD FAITH**, b f Warning—Bold And Beautiful **Mr K. Abdulla**
37 **BOURBON DYNASTY (FR)**, b c Rainbow Quest—Bourbon Girl **Mr K. Abdulla**
38 **BRIGHT FUTURE (FR)**, b f Akarad—Belle Bleue **Mr D. Wildenstein**
39 **BRIGHT SPELLS (USA)**, b f Alleged—Sunny Bay **Mr K. Abdulla**
40 **CHELSEA (USA)**, b f Miswaki—Prodigious **Mr K. Abdulla**
41 **CLOCHE DU ROI (FR)**, b f Fairy King—Cloche d'Or **Mr J. L. Lagardere**
42 **DALINDA (USA)**, b f Nureyev—Daloma **Sheikh Mohammed**
43 **DANCE FINALE (USA)**, b c Green Dancer—Tempus Fugit **Wafic Said**
44 **DARING BID (IRE)**, b c Darshaan—Friendly Finance **Sheikh Mohammed**
45 **DAWN AURORA (USA)**, b f Night Shift—Morning Colors **Sheikh Mohammed**
46 **DELEGATE**, b c Polish Precedent—Dangora **Mr K. Abdulla**
47 **DIAMOND FOR KING (FR)**, b c Fairy King—Diamond Seal **Mr J. L. Lagardere**
48 **DRESSAGE**, b f Sadler's Wells—Dial Dream **Sheikh Mohammed**
49 **EAST WOOD**, b c Sadler's Wells—Escaline **Mme Y. Seydoux**
50 **EUDOXE (IRE)**, b c Be My Guest—Violence **Mr Edouard Rothschild**
51 **FAIRHONOR (FR)**, b c Hero's Honor—Fairolan **Jean-Gerard Verdier**
52 **FATU HIVA (USA)**, b f Steinlen—Flying Blue Colors **Mr D. Wildenstein**
53 **FIRST FLAME**, b c Polish Precedent—Fatah Flare **Sheikh Mohammed**
54 **FLYING PEGASUS (IRE)**, b c In The Wings—Mill Princess **Wafic Said**

MR A. FABRE—continued

55 **FOLLYWAXA (FR)**, b f Linamix—Wicked Folly **Mr J. L. Lagardere**
56 **FOR VALOUR (USA)**, b c Trempolino—Glitter **Mr A. J. Richards**
57 **FRANCE ENCHANTEE (FR)**, b f French Stress—Luth Enchantee **Mme Paul de Moussac**
58 **GANYMEDE (FR)**, b f Kendor—Luth d'Or **Mme Paul de Moussac**
59 **GOLD OF ARABIA (USA)**, b c Seeking The Gold—Twitchet **Sheikh Mohammed**
60 **GOULT (FR)**, b c Sadler's Wells—Djallybrook **Wafic Said**
61 **GRAPE TREE ROAD**, b c Caerleon—One Way Street **M. Tabor**
62 **GREEN CAR**, b c Dowsing—Girouette **Mr D. Wildenstein**
63 **GREEN RING**, b c Groom Dancer—Emerald **Mr K. Abdulla**
64 **GUIGNOL (USA)**, b c Lear Fan—Gold Bird **Mr D. Wildenstein**
65 **HANDSOME DANCER**, b c Nijinsky—It's In The Air **Maktoum Al Maktoum**
66 **HELSINKI**, b f Machiavellian—Helen Street **Sheikh Mohammed**
67 **HOMME DE COEUR**, b c Generous—Luth de Saron **Mme Paul de Moussac**
68 **HONNEUR ROYAL (IRE)**, b g Hero's Honor—Pomme Royale **Mme Paul de Moussac**
69 **HOUSA DANCER (FR)**, b f Fabulous Dancer—Housatonic **Mr J. L. Lagardere**
70 **HYMENEE (USA)**, b f Chief's Crown—Hippodamia **Mr D. Wildenstein**
71 **INDIAN TWIST (IRE)**, b c Persian Bold—Danse Indienne **Mr Edouard Rothschild**
72 **JURATA (IRE)**, b f Polish Precedent—Port Helene **Sheikh Mohammed**
73 **KARMITYCIA (FR)**, b f Last Tycoon—Karmichah **Mr J. L. Lagardere**
74 **LADY MARGOT (IRE)**, b f Sadler's Wells—Bold Lady **Wafic Said**
75 **LAFITTE THE PIRATE**, b c Sadler's Wells—Reprocolor **M. Tabor**
76 **LA GARTEMPE (FR)**, b f French Stress—Light of Realm **Mme Paul de Moussac**
77 **LEGAL OPINION (IRE)**, b f Polish Precedent—Golden Opinion **Sheikh Mohammed**
78 **LOUP SOLITAIRE (USA)**, b c Lear Fan—Louveterie **Mr D. Wildenstein**
79 **LUNA DANCER (IRE)**, b f Groom Dancer—Luna Blue **Mr J. L. Lagardere**
80 **LUNAREVA (USA)**, b f Nureyev—Louve Bleue **Mr D. Wildenstein**
81 **LUNA WELLS (IRE)**, b f Sadler's Wells—Lunadix **Mr J. L. Lagardere**
82 **LYDENBURG (IRE)**, b c Lycius—Whitehaven **Sheikh Mohammed**
83 **MAMBO DRUMMER**, b g Tirol—Martingale **Mr D. Wildenstein**
84 **MAORI KING (USA)**, b g Steinlen—Mersey **Mr D. Wildenstein**
85 **MARTINIQUAIS (IRE)**, b c Simply Great—Majolique **Mr D. Wildenstein**
86 **MASSATIXA (FR)**, b f Linamix—Miss Satin **Mr J. L. Lagardere**
87 **MEDIA NOX**, b f Lycius—Sky Love **Mr K. Abdulla**
88 **MER DU SUD**, b f Bluebird—Make Plans **Mr D. Wildenstein**
89 **MISOLIDIX**, b c Linamix—Miss d'Ouilly **Mr J. L. Lagardere**
90 **MISS TAHITI**, b f Tirol—Mini Luthe **Mr D. Wildenstein**
91 **MONT D'ARBOIS (USA)**, b c Private Account—Meadow Dancer **Mme Paul de Moussac**
92 **MOON COLONY**, b c Top Ville—Honeymooning **Mr K. Abdulla**
93 **NANINJA (USA)**, b c Alysheba—Nijinsky's Lover **Mr D. Wildenstein**
94 **NEO CLASSIQUE (FR)**, b g In The Wings—Best Girl **Mme Paul de Moussac**
95 **NIGHT WATCH (FR)**, b c Soviet Star—Nuit de Lune **Mr D. Wildenstein**
96 **OTAITI**, b f Sadler's Wells—Ode **Mr D. Wildenstein**
97 **OVIRI (IRE)**, b c Shirley Heights—Onde Bleu Marine **Mr D. Wildenstein**
98 **PALAVERIX (IRE)**, b c Linamix—Palavera **Mr J. L. Lagardere**
99 **PALMERAIE (USA)**, b f Lear Fan—Petroleuse **Mr D. Wildenstein**
100 **PAREO BLEU (USA)**, b c Steinlen—Peinture Bleue **Mr D. Wildenstein**
101 **PATCH OF BLUE (USA)**, b f Siberian Express—Plume Bleu Pale **Mr D. Wildenstein**
102 **PINAFLORIX**, b c Linamix—Pinaflore **Mr J. L. Lagardere**
103 **POLAR LIGHTS (CAN)**, b c Trempolino—Quickshine **Sheikh Mohammed**
104 **QUEST FOR LADIES**, b f Rainbow Quest—Savoureuse Lady **Mme Paul de Moussac**
105 **QUORUM**, b c Sadler's Wells—Green Rock **Mr K. Abdulla**
106 **RADEVORE**, b c Generous—Bloudan **Mr K. Abdulla**
107 **REINE LASTY (FR)**, b f Last Tycoon—Reine Margie **Mr J. L. Lagardere**
108 **RESTINAMIX (FR)**, b c Linamix—Restiver **Mr J. L. Lagardere**
109 **RESTLESS CARL (IRE)**, b c Caerleon—Resless Kara **Mr J. L. Lagardere**
110 **RESTLESS MIXA (IRE)**, b f Linamix—Restless Girl **Mr J. L. Lagardere**
111 **RIVER DYLE (USA)**, b c Miswaki—Rixe River **Wafic Said**
112 **ROSE BOURBON (USA)**, b f Woodman—River Rose **Wafic Said**
113 **SANGRIA (USA)**, b f El Gran Senor—Champagne Cocktail **Mr D. Wildenstein**
114 **SAYYARAMIX (FR)**, b c Linamix—Sayyara **Mr J. L. Lagardere**

MR A. FABRE—continued

115 SELAGO (USA), b c Storm Cat—Mikaya Mme A. Plesch
116 SETTING SUN, b c Generous—Suntrap Mr K. Abdulla
117 SILVERSWORD (FR), b f Highest Honor—Silver Cobra Sheikh Mohammed
118 SI SEDUCTOR (USA), b c Diesis—Miss Evans Mme M. Miglietti
119 SOCIETY FAIR (FR), b f Always Fair—Society Bride Mr J. L. Lagardere
120 SOURIRE (USA), b g Dayjur—Southern Seas Mr D. Wildenstein
121 STAR VILLAGE (FR), b c Village Star—Top Fille Mr A. J. Richards
122 SUPREME COMMANDER (FR), b c Saumarez—Autocratic Wafic Said
123 SYMBOLI GENESISE (FR), b c Generous—Oriental Mr T. Wada
124 TALAMONE (USA), b c Trempolino—Dear Colleen Mme Paul de Moussac
125 TA MATETE (IRE), b c Caerleon—Triple Couronne Mr D. Wildenstein
126 TARATOR (USA), b c Green Dancer—Happy Gal Wafic Said
127 TEOBALDO (IRE), b c Green Desert—Oczy Czarnie Mr Edouard Rothschild
128 TRUST BALL (FR), b f Highest Honor—Terre de Feu Mr D. Wildenstein
129 TRYING TIMES (IRE), b c Sadler's Wells—Ozone Friendly Maktoum Al Maktoum
130 TULIPA (USA), b f Alleged—Black Tulip Sheikh Mohammed
131 VADSA HONOR (FR), b f Highest Honor—Vadsa Mr J. L. Lagardere
132 VAPORETTO (USA), b c Lear Fan—Venise Mr D. Wildenstein
133 WALK FAIRY (FR), b f Fairy King—Walk On Turf Mr J. L. Lagardere
134 WATER POET (IRE), b c Sadler's Wells—Love Smitten Sheikh Mohammed
135 WEST MEMPHIS (USA), b c Gone West—Dancing Slippers Sheikh Mohammed
136 WILD LIFE (FR), b f Nashwan—Walensee Mr D. Wildenstein
137 WILLSTAR (USA), b f Nureyev—Nijinsky Star Mr K. Abdulla
138 WLADISLAWA (USA), b f Capote—Color of Love Ecurie Demgalop

TWO-YEAR-OLDS

139 ACTION DE GRACE (USA), b f Riverman—Action Francaise Mr D. Wildenstein
140 B c Green Desert—African Peace Sheikh Mohammed
141 AGENT RUSSE (FR), b c Soviet Star—Banque Royale Mme Paul de Moussac
142 ALPHA PLUS (USA), b c Mr Prospector—Danzante Mr K. Abdulla
143 AMBITIEUSE (IRE), b f Caerleon—Allons Enfants Mr D. Wildenstein
144 ANCIENT RULE (IRE), b c Royal Academy—Allez Les Bleus Mr D. Wildenstein
145 ANGE BLEU (USA), b f Alleged—Albertine Mr D. Wildenstein
146 ARABIAN KING (FR), b c Arazi—Escaline Mme Y. Seydoux
147 ART ANCIEN (USA), b c Manila—All Along Mr D. Wildenstein
148 BALL OF FIRE (USA), b f Mining—Bonshamile Mr D. Wildenstein
149 B c Lycius—Barada Sheikh Mohammed
150 BARISTER (FR), b c Homme de Loi—Light of Realm Mme Paul de Moussac
151 BEFFOU (FR), b c Subotica—Averillannie Olivier Lecerf
152 B c Lyphard—Berceau Mr K. Abdulla
153 BIG VICTORY (IRE), b c Alzao—Batave Mr D. Wildenstein
154 BLUE SKY (IRE), b c Marignan—Belle Bleue Mr D. Wildenstein
155 CAD CAM (FR), b c Linamix—Camikala Mr J. L. Lagardere
156 B f El Gran Senor—Champagne Cocktail Mr Edouard Rothschild
157 CHANTEREINE (USA), b f Trempolino—Shoot A Line Mme Paul de Moussac
158 CHURCH LIFE (FR), b c Linamix—Church Missionary Mr J. L. Lagardere
159 B c Lear Fan—Coral Dance Maktoum Al Maktoum
160 B c Arazi—Coryana Wafic Said
161 DANGER REEF (USA), b c Nureyev—Danseuse du Soir Mr D. Wildenstein
162 B c Sadler's Wells—Darazina Wafic Said
163 EWAR CHIEFTAIN, b c Suave Dancer—Monaneigue Lady Mr A. J. Richards
164 B f Green Desert—Fawaayid Maktoum Al Maktoum
165 B f Sadler's Wells—Golden Opinion Sheikh Mohammed
166 GOLDEN SAND (USA), b f Riverman—Gold Bird Mr D. Wildenstein
167 B c Arazi—Grace Note Sheikh Mohammed
168 B c Royal Academy—Hastening M. Tabor
169 B c Caerleon—Homage Sheikh Mohammed
170 B f Belmez—Hooked Bid Sheikh Mohammed

MR A. FABRE—continued

171 B c Sadler's Wells—Ispahan **Sheikh Mohammed**
172 **KARDANSMIX (FR),** b c Linamix—Kardanskaia **Mr J. L. Lagardere**
173 **KENYAN (FR),** b c Marignan—Keniant **Mr D. Wildenstein**
174 **KEPSTER (USA),** b c Royal Academy—Zarissa **Wafic Said**
175 **KERGONAN (FR),** b c Subotica—Touville **Olivier Lecerf**
176 **KERMESSE (USA),** b f Irish River—Kemolina **Mr D. Wildenstein**
177 B c Seattle Dancer—Lady's Slipper **Sheikh Mohammed**
178 **LAST DREAM (IRE),** b f Alzao—Last Tango **Mr D. Wildenstein**
179 B c Kenmare—Legend of Arabia **Sheikh Mohammed**
180 **LOUP SAUVAGE (USA),** b c Riverman—Louveterie **Mr D. Wildenstein**
181 **LUNE ROUSSE (IRE),** b f Arazi—Louve Romaine **Mr D. Wildenstein**
182 **MALHAM VILLAGE (FR),** b c Village Star—Malham Tarn **Mr A. J. Richards**
183 B c Kris—Manureva **Wafic Said**
184 **MARADADI (USA),** b f Shadeed—Mersey **Mr D. Wildenstein**
185 **MARCIALE (USA),** b c Hansel—Destiny Dance **Sheikh Mohammed**
186 B c A P Indy—Maximova **Alfred S. Y. Hui**
187 B c Sadler's Wells—Millieme **Mrs Magnier**
188 B f Darshaan—Miss Fyor **Maktoum Al Maktoum**
189 **MONDIAL (IRE),** b c Alzao—Make Plans **Mr D. Wildenstein**
190 B f Nashwan—Musical Bliss **Sheikh Mohammed**
191 **NAGID (FR),** b c Cadoudal—Newness **Mme D. Wildenstein**
192 B f Seattle Slew—Navratilovna **Wafic Said**
193 B c Shining Steel—Neptuna **Mr Edouard Rothschild**
194 **NIGHT WARRIOR (USA),** b c Woodman—Nina North **Mr D. Wildenstein**
195 B c Seattle Dancer—Nom de Plume **Sheikh Mohammed**
196 **OL JOGI,** b c Sadler's Wells—Ode **Mr D. Wildenstein**
197 B c Bluebird—Or Vision **M. Tabor**
198 **PALME D'OR (IRE),** b f Sadler's Wells—Pampa Bella **Mr D. Wildenstein**
199 B c Darshaan—Pass The Peace **Sheikh Mohammed**
200 **PEACE TREATY (USA),** b f Time For A Change—Paulista **Mr D. Wildenstein**
201 **PEINTRE CELEBRE (USA),** b c Nureyev—Peinture Bleue **Mr D. Wildenstein**
202 B c Quest For Fame—Perfect Sister **Sheikh Mohammed**
203 **PILOT IN COMMAND (IRE),** b c Royal Academy—Pawneese **Mr D. Wildenstein**
204 B c Private Account—Prodigious **Mr K. Abdulla**
205 B f Danzig—Razyana **Mr K. Abdulla**
206 **REWARD (FR),** b c Fabulous Dancer—Restikala **Mr J. L. Lagardere**
207 B f Lyphard—River Lullaby **Mr K. Abdulla**
208 **RUWENZORI (IRE),** b f Alzao—Robertet **Mr D. Wildenstein**
209 **SCOUTMASTER (IRE),** b c Marignan—Seconde Bleue **Mr D. Wildenstein**
210 **SERENGETI PARK (USA),** b f Woodman—Special Happening **Mr D. Wildenstein**
211 **SIX ZERO (FR),** b c Linamix—Six Love **Mr J. L. Lagardere**
212 B f Diesis—Smooth Bore **M. Tabor**
213 B c Sadler's Wells—Snow Day **Wafic Said**
214 **SUPERCHARGER (FR),** b c Bering—Symphorine **Mr D. Wildenstein**
215 **SUPER CUB (USA),** b c Dynaformer—Shadowlawn **Mr D. Wildenstein**
216 **SUPERGIRL (USA),** b f Woodman—Southern Seas **Mr D. Wildenstein**
217 B f Sadler's Wells—Swan Heights **Mr Bin Abdullah**
218 **TIGER HIGHLANDS (IRE),** b c Bluebird—The Highlands **Patrick Offenstadt**
219 **TOUCH OF BLUE (FR),** b f Pistolet Bleu—Touch of Pink **Mr D. Wildenstein**
220 **TREASURE MINE (USA),** b f Forty Niner—Personal Business **Sheikh Mohammed**
221 **VALYFAIR (FR),** b c Always Fair—Vadsa **Mr J. L. Lagardere**
222 **VERTICAL SPEED (FR),** b c Bering—Victoire Bleue **Mr D. Wildenstein**
223 **VIGNE VIERGE (USA),** b f Diesis—Valhalla **Mr D. Wildenstein**
224 **VISIONARY (FR),** b c Linamix—Visor **Mr J. L. Lagardere**
225 **VORTEX (FR),** b c Linamix—Vadlava **Mr J. L. Lagardere**
226 **WEST SIDER,** b f Gone West—Fariedah **Prince Saud bin Khaled**
227 **WORLD CUP,** b c Epervier Bleu—Walensee **Mr D. Wildenstein**
228 B c Gone West—Zaizafon **Mr K. Abdulla**

215   MR R. A. FAHEY, Malton

Postal: **Manor House Farm, Butterwick, Brawby, Malton, YO17 0PS.**

Phone: **(01653) 628001 FAX (01653) 628001 MOBILE (0850) 270883**

1 **ACONORACE**, 4, b g Midyan (USA)—Saint Cynthia **The Butterwick Race Co.**
2 **BALLYRAG (USA)**, 5, ch g Silver Hawk (USA)—Dancing Rags (USA) **Mr J. C. Parsons**
3 **BELINDA BLUE**, 4, b f Belfort (FR)—Carrula **Mrs J. Jackson**
4 **DARK SHOT (IRE)**, 4, b c Rock City—Jeanne Avril **Mrs L. M. Fahey**
5 **DROMORE DREAM (IRE)**, 7, ch g Black Minstrel—Vickies Rambler **Mrs J. M. Newitt**
6 4, B g Roi Danzig (USA)—Girl On A Swing **Mr C. Raines**
7 **HIGH PREMIUM**, 8, b g Forzando—High Halo **Mr J. C. Parsons**
8 **KILGARIFF**, 10, ch g Le Bavard (FR)—Negrada **Mrs A. C. Brown**
9 **KNUCKLEBUSTER (IRE)**, 6, b g Bustineto—Diana Harwell **Mr A. N. Brooke Rankin**
10 **MBULWA**, 10, ch g Be My Guest (USA)—Bundu (FR) **Northumbria Leisure Ltd**
11 **MISS ZANZIBAR**, 4, b f Kefaah (USA)—Circe **The Butterwick Race Co.**
12 **MURPHY'S GOLD (IRE)**, 5, ch g Salt Dome (USA)—Winter Harvest **Mr D. A. Read**

THREE-YEAR-OLDS

13 **BUTTERWICK BELLE (IRE)**, b f Distinctly North (USA)—Forest Berries (IRE) **The Butterwick Race Co.**
14 **KIBRIS GOLD**, ch g Efisio—Milady Jade (IRE) **Mr D. A. Read**
15 **ROCKY'S METEOR**, b c Emarati (USA)—Hoop La **Mr P. S. Dhariwal**
16 **SIZZLING SYMPHONY**, b g Sizzling Melody—Polly Worth **Mr J. A. Campbell**
17 **THE BUTTERWICK KID**, ch g Interrex (CAN)—Ville Air **The Butterwick Race Co.**

TWO-YEAR-OLDS

18 Ch g Pharly (FR)—Almond Blossom (Grundy) **Mr P. Tingey**
19 B f Distinctly North (USA)—Cape of Storms (Fordham (USA)) **Mr C. Maessapp**
20 B g High Estate—Damezao (Alzao (USA)) **Mr R. A. Fahey**
21 Gr br f Kalaglow—El Rabab (USA) (Roberto (USA)) **Marathon Thoroughbred Racing**
22 Ch f Aragon—Good Woman (Good Times (ITY)) **Mr B. L. Parry**
23 Ch g Symbolic—Oxalis (Connaught) **Mrs M. W. Kenyon**
24 B f Rambo Dancer (CAN)—Petiller (Monsanto (FR)) **Mrs A. C. Brown**

Other Owners: A & K Lingerie Ltd., Mrs M. A. Brown, R. I. Chambers Esq., Mr William A. Davies, L. Foster Esq., Mr J. J. Gilmartin, D. Lanelois Esq., Miss C. Raines, Mrs E. Stoker, J. Wallis Esq..

Jockeys (Flat): A Culhane, J Quinn (w.a.).

Jockey (NH): L Wyer.

216   MR C. W. FAIRHURST, Middleham

Postal: **Glasgow House, Middleham, Leyburn, North Yorks, DL8 4QG.**

Phone: **(01969) 622039 FAX (01969) 622039**

1 **BOGART**, 5, gr g Belfort (FR)—Larnem **A. P. Development Products (NE) Ltd**
2 **BRISAS**, 9, ch g Vaigly Great—Legal Sound **Mr C. W. Fairhurst**
3 **BULSARA**, 4, b g Dowsing (USA)—Taiga **Twinacre Nurseries Ltd**
4 **CRIMSON BROCADE**, 5, b m Daring March—Stellaris **Mr J. G. Brearley**
5 **HIGHFIELD FIZZ**, 4, b f Efisio—Jendor **Mrs P. J. Taylor-Garthwaite**
6 **JENDORCET**, 6, b m Grey Ghost—Jendor **Mrs P. J. Taylor-Garthwaite**
7 **LARN FORT**, 6, gr g Belfort (FR)—Larnem **A. P. Development Products (NE) Ltd**
8 **PASH**, 4, b f Hallgate—Pashmina **Mr C. D. Barber-Lomax**
9 **PRIDE OF MAY (IRE)**, 5, b g Law Society (USA)—Aztec Princess **Glasgow House Partnership**
10 **PRUDENT PET**, 4, b f Distant Relative—Philgwyn **The McLain & Rodda Partnership**

MR C. W. FAIRHURST—continued

THREE-YEAR-OLDS

11 **AUTOBERRY**, b g Auto Bird (FR)—Sister Racine **Mr D. H. Berry & Mrs E. M. Berry**
12 **CLARY SAGE**, b f Sayf El Arab (USA)—Supergreen **Mr M. Handy**
13 **RAMSEY HOPE**, b c Timeless Times (USA)—Marfen **Mr C. D. Barber-Lomax**
14 **WINN CALEY**, ch f Beveled (USA)—Responder **Twinacre Nurseries Ltd**

TWO-YEAR-OLDS

15 **BARRESBO**, b c 15/3 Barrys Gamble—Bo' Babbity (Strong Gale) **North Cheshire Trading & Storage Ltd**
16 **FINE TIMES**, b c 2/3 Timeless Times (USA)—Marfen (Lochnager) **The Glasgow House Four**
17 B c 12/4 Warrshan (USA)—Lahin (Rainbow Quest (USA))
18 B f 18/2 Timeless Times (USA)—Lindrake's Pride (Mandrake Major) **Mr C. D. Barber-Lomax**
19 Gr f 19/4 Barrys Gamble—Ping Pong (Petong)
20 **RISSAGA**, ch f 8/3 Meqdaam (USA)—Crosby Place (Crooner) **Mr D. Bunn**

Other Owners: Mrs J. M. Brearley, Mr Brian Cann, Daleside Nurseries Ltd, Mrs P. J. Dobson, Mr W. J. Dobson, Mr D. M. Gardner, Mr J. T. Gardner, Mr G. D. Geraghty, Mr M. J. Grace, Mr D. G. Kirk, Mr Barry Kitching, Mr Des Redhead, Mr A. Robertson.

Apprentice: J Gracey (8-0).

Lady Rider: Mrs S Bosley (8-7, w.a.).

217   MR J. R. FANSHAWE, Newmarket

Postal: **Pegasus Stables, Snailwell Road, Newmarket, Suffolk, CB8 7DJ.**
Phone: **(01638) 664525 FAX (01638) 664523**

1 **ALMOND ROCK**, 4, b g Soviet Star (USA)—Banket **C.I.T. Racing Ltd**
2 **APOLLONO**, 4, b g Cyrano de Bergerac—Daima **Mr J. K. Ruggles & Mrs A. R. Ruggles**
3 **BARFORD LAD**, 9, b g Nicholas Bill—Grace Poole **Barford Bloodstock**
4 **BARFORD SOVEREIGN**, 4, b f Unfuwain (USA)—Barford Lady **Barford Bloodstock**
5 **BISHOP OF CASHEL**, 4, b c Warning—Ballet Classique (USA) **Cheveley Park Stud**
6 **BLOMBERG (IRE)**, 4, b c Indian Ridge—Daniella Drive (USA) **Comet Group Plc**
7 **BLUE ZULU (IRE)**, 4, gr f Don't Forget Me—Aldern Stream **T. & J. Vestey**
8 **BOLD GAIT**, 5, ch g Persian Bold—Miller's Gait **Mrs I. Phillips**
9 **BON LUCK (IRE)**, 4, ch g Waajib—Elle Va Bon **Mr J. K. Ruggles and Mrs A. R. Ruggles**
10 **ELLIE ARDENSKY**, 4, b f Slip Anchor—Circus Ring **The Snailwell Stud Company Limited**
11 **FIRED EARTH (IRE)**, 8, b g Soughaan (USA)—Terracotta (GER) **Mrs J. Fanshawe**
12 **THE TOISEACH (IRE)**, 5, b g Phardante (FR)—Owens Toi **T. and J. Vestey**
13 **TINASHAAN (IRE)**, 4, b f Darshaan—Catina **Mrs James McAllister**

THREE-YEAR-OLDS

14 **ALISURA**, br f Lead On Time (USA)—Iosifa **Mohammed Al Nabouda**
15 **ALWAYS HAPPY**, ch f Sharrood (USA)—Convivial **Cheveley Park Stud**
16 **BOAT O'BRIG**, b c Slip Anchor—Advie Bridge **Sir David Wills**
17 **DILAZAR (USA)**, ch c Zilzal (USA)—Dictina (FR) **Mr Mana Al Maktoum**
18 **FAMILY MAN**, ch c Indian Ridge—Auntie Gladys **Mr James Fanshawe**
19 **FORENTIA**, b f Formidable (USA)—Clarentia **Mrs Nicolas Kairis**
20 **FRISSON**, b f Slip Anchor—Comic Talent **Cheveley Park Stud**
21 **JAMAHEER (IRE)**, b f Don't Forget Me—Ward of Court (IRE) **Mr Abdulla Al Khalifa**
22 **KALAO TUA (IRE)**, b f Shaadi (USA)—Lisa's Favourite **Mr J. K. Ruggles & Mrs A. R. Ruggles**
23 **MAJOR QUALITY**, b c Sizzling Melody—Bonne de Berry **Mrs Mary Watt**
24 **MILFORD SOUND**, b c Batshoof—Nafis (USA) **C.I.T. Racing Ltd**
25 **MISHAWEER**, b f Primo Dominie—Ideal Home **Mr Abdulla Al Khalifa**
26 **NUNSHARPA**, b f Sharpo—Missed Blessing **Mr T. D. Holland-Martin**
27 **PREMIER CENSURE**, b f Reprimand—Mrs Thatcher **Mr W. J. Gredley**
28 **RED SALUTE**, b f Soviet Star (USA)—Sweet Slew (USA) **Cheveley Park Stud**

MR J. R. FANSHAWE—continued

29 **SALMIS**, b f Salse (USA)—Misguided **Sally Vere Nicoll, Dexa'tex and Partners**
30 **SEEKING FORTUNE (USA)**, b f Seeking The Gold (USA)—Gabfest (USA) **Cheveley Park Stud**
31 **SOAKED**, b c Dowsing (USA)—Water Well **Mr W. J. Gredley**
32 **SPECIAL OASIS**, b f Green Desert (USA)—Someone Special **Helena Springfield Ltd**
33 **TART (FR)**, br f Warning—Sharp Girl (FR) **Lord Vestey**
34 **THEA (USA)**, br f Marju (IRE)—Switched On **T. & J. Vestey**
35 **TOFFEE**, ch f Midyan (USA)—Vaula **Mrs Mary Watt**
36 **TONIC CHORD**, b f La Grange Music—Tight **Mrs E. Fanshawe**
37 **WANDERING STAR (USA)**, b f Red Ransom (USA)—Beautiful Bedouin (USA) **Mrs Nigel Elwes**

TWO-YEAR-OLDS

38 **ACADEMY STAR**, b f 30/4 Royal Academy (USA)—Startino (Bustino) **Mr James McAllister**
39 **ARCTIC OWL**, b c 29/3 Most Welcome—Short Rations (Lorenzaccio) **The Owl Society**
40 **BE VALIANT**, b c 8/5 Petong—Fetlar (Pharly (FR)) **Dr Catherine Wills**
41 **BLANE WATER (USA)**, b f 20/2 Lomond (USA)—Triode (USA) (Sharpen Up) **CIT Racing Ltd**
42 B f 5/2 Zilzal (USA)—Bridal Wreath (USA) (Stop The Music (USA)) **Mr Mana Al Maktoum**
43 **CERTAINTY**, b f 5/2 Belmez (USA)—La Carlotta (USA) (J O Tobin (USA)) **Dr Catherine Wills**
44 **ETERNITY**, b f 5/5 Suave Dancer (USA)—Chellita (Habitat) **Dr Catherine Wills**
45 Ch c 9/4 Music Boy—Fleeting Affair (Hotfoot) **Mr Raymond Tooth**
46 **FLOATING CHARGE**, b c 16/3 Sharpo—Poyle Fizz (Damister) **Mr S. D. Swaden**
47 **HEAVENLY RAY (USA)**, ch f 27/5 Rahy (USA)—Highest Truth (USA) (Alydar (USA)) **Cheveley Park Stud**
48 **INVERMARK**, b c 20/2 Machiavellian (USA)—Apple Cross (Glint of Gold) **Sir David Wills**
49 B c 12/4 Salse (USA)—Jamarj (Tyrnavos) **Mrs I. Phillips**
50 B f 28/4 Classic Music (USA)—Lake Isle (IRE) (Caerleon (USA)) **Mr N. Forman Hardy**
51 B c 18/3 Rambo Dancer (CAN)—Minwah (USA) (Diesis) **Mr Mana Al Maktoum**
52 **MISS SWEETLY**, ch f 21/3 Rudimentary (USA)—Bonne de Berry (Habitat) **The Hon. Mrs Mary Watt**
53 **PERFECT POPPY**, b f 25/1 Shareef Dancer (USA)—Benazir (High Top) **Mr J. M. Greetham**
54 **REEDS**, b c 22/2 Thatching—Bayadere (Green Dancer (USA)) **Mrs D. Haynes**
55 **SADDLERS' HOPE**, b f 5/2 Saddlers' Hall (IRE)—Hope And Glory (Well Decorated (USA)) **Cheveley Park Stud**
56 **SERENITY**, b f 14/3 Selkirk (USA)—Mystery Ship (Decoy Boy) **Dr Catherine Wills**
57 B c 13/3 Green Desert (USA)—Shaft of Sunlight (Sparkler) **Mr Khalifa Nasser**
58 **SUNNY RETREAT**, b f Saddlers' Hall (IRE)—Sanctuary Cove (Habitat) **Cheveley Park Stud**
59 **TOP**, gr f 6/3 Shirley Heights—Whirl (Bellypha) **Lord Halifax**
60 B c 9/3 Persian Bold—Ustka (Lomond (USA)) **Barford Bloodstock**
61 **VRENNAN**, ch f 7/4 Suave Dancer (USA)—Advie Bridge (High Line) **Sir David Wills**
62 **WARNINGFORD**, b c 21/3 Warning—Barford Lady (Stanford) **Barford Bloodstock and Dexatex Ltd**

Other Owners: Mrs Bruce Bossom, Lord Derby, Mrs Christine Handscombe, Mr T. I. Handscombe, Mr S. J. Richmond-Watson, Mr D. I. Russell, Mrs David Russell.

Jockey (Flat): David Harrison (8-0).

Apprentice: N Varley (7-7).

218　　　　MR P. FARRELL, Taunton

Postal: **Yard House, Burnworthy Stables, Burnworthy Manor, Churchstanton, TA3 7DR.**
Phone: **(01823) 601111 MOBILE (0421) 623044 FAX (01823) 601112**

1 6, Ch m Orchestra—Bailieboro **Mrs H. L. Farrell**
2 **BRAVO STAR (USA)**, 11, b g The Minstrel (CAN)—Stellarette (CAN) **Wyvern Racing**
3 **ELEANORA MUSE**, 6, b m Idiots Delight—Lavilla **Mr M. Trott & Mrs P. J. Steels**
4 **FISIANNA**, 7, b m Efisio—Jianna **Mrs Eve Baker**
5 **FURRY DAY**, 10, b g Furry Glen—Bright Company **Wyvern Racing**
6 **GOLDEN SPHINX (IRE)**, 6, ch m Carmelite House (USA)—Golden Carrier **Mr Paddy Farrell**
7 6, Ch g Salluceva—Moredee **Mrs A. Denning**
8 **REELING**, 10, br m Relkino—Mother Brown **Mrs Suzanne Fletcher**

MR P. FARRELL—continued

9 SNICKERSNEE, 8, b g Kris—Cat Girl (USA) **Mr Paddy Farrell**
10 UP THE TEMPO (IRE), 7, ch m Orchestra—Bailieboro **Wyvern Racing**
11 7, B m Southern Music—Wades Gazel
12 6, B m Derring Rose—Wayward Kate **Mrs Suzanne Fletcher**

THREE-YEAR-OLDS

13 B g Pablond—Cilerna Jet **Mrs Eve Baker**

Other Owners: Mr John Farmer, Mr N. Rixon, Miss A. Staddon.

219   MR P. S. FELGATE, Melton Mowbray

Postal: **Grimston Stud, Grimston, Melton Mowbray, Leics, LE14 3BZ.**
Phone: **(01664) 812019**

1 DOUBLE SPLENDOUR (IRE), 6, b g Double Schwartz—
                                Princess Pamela **Yorkshire Racing Club Owners Group 1990**
2 HIGHBORN (IRE), 7, b br g Double Schwartz—High State **Yorkshire Racing Club Owners Group 1990**
3 LOTTIES BID, 4, b f Ring Bidder—Gleneagle **Mr S. J. Beard**
4 MACS MAHARANEE, 9, b m Indian King (USA)—High State
5 NO QUARTER GIVEN, 11, b g Don—Maggie Mine **Mr P. S. Felgate**
6 SAMANA CAY, 4, ch f Pharly (FR)—Brown's Cay **Mr Michael Ng**
7 SELMESTON (IRE), 4, b g Double Schwartz—Baracuda (FR) **Mr Chris Wright**
8 5, B g Electric—Tarary
9 THE REAL WHIZZBANG (IRE), 5, b br h New Express—Gail's Crystal **Mr S. J. Beard**

THREE-YEAR-OLDS

10 CINNAMON STICK (IRE), ch g Don't Forget Me—Gothic Lady **Miss Johanna Milward**
11 LAGAN, b g Shareef Dancer (USA)—Lagta **Wild Racing**
12 SEANCHAI (IRE), b g Treasure Kay—Blue Infanta **Louth Racing**
13 B g Roi Danzig (USA)—Silvera
14 WELCOME LU, ch f Most Welcome—Odile **Mr M. F. Hyman**

Other Owners: Mr C. J. Ashworth, Mr J. S. Aspery, Mr R. Davidson, Mr Wayham Moran, Mr D. O. Pickering, Miss Kim Turner, Mr J. N. Wild, Mr N. R. Wild.

Jockey (Flat): G Hind.

Apprentice: P McCabe.

Lady Riders: Mrs Margaret Crawford, Mrs J Saunders.

220   MR J. FELLOWS, Chantilly

Postal: **4 Avenue du General Leclerc, 60500 Chantilly, France.**
Phone: **OFFICE 44582061 FAX 44581078**

1 AMERICAN GLORY, 4, b f Baby Turk—Santa Musica **Mme P. Vandervoort-Kumble**
2 BALL OF KIEV (FR), 5, b h Cricket Ball (USA)—Marie de Kiev (FR) **Ecurie Namour**
3 BIRD OF KIEV (FR), 6, b m Pampabird—Marie de Kiev (FR) **Ecurie Namour**
4 CLIVEDON PLACE (FR), 4, b c Pennine Walk—Beaute Dangereuse (USA) **M. Shone**
5 FAST SWINGER (FR), 4, b f Cricket Ball—Pregassona (FR) **A. Sommer**
6 GAIO (FR), 6, b h Caerwent—Gironde (USA) **Ecurie Linghfield**
7 GO DARLY (FR), 6, ch g Darly (FR)—Corfine (FR) **Mme J. Diot**
8 HAPPY REALM, 4, b c Saumarez—Air de Noblesse (USA) **R. Scully**

MR J. FELLOWS—continued

9 **HUGUENANT (FR)**, 4, b c Cricket Ball (USA)—Vindelonde (FR) **Ecurie Namour**
10 **MARIZADO (FR)**, 5, b g Un Desperado (FR)—Lady Mariza **Ecurie Namour**
11 **MAUJ (FR)**, 4, gr c Highest Honor (FR)—Ruling Honor (USA) **C. Poli**
12 **NATIDJA (FR)**, 7, b m Shardari—Nabita (FR) **Ecurie Namour**
13 **ORNAIS (FR)**, 4, b c Funambule (USA)—Moiree (FR) **C. Poli**
14 **OUYOUNI (FR)**, 4, b c Zayyani—Cara Maria (FR) **Ecurie Namour**
15 **POLISH POWER (USA)**, 4, ch c Polish Navy (USA)—Impatiente (USA) **Ecurie Namour**
16 **SAFELY SAY (USA)**, 6, ch h Affirmed (USA)—Assez Cuite (USA) **Mme P. Vandervoort-Kumble**
17 **SAMOSATE (FR)**, 4, ch f Galetto (FR)—Sara Lee (FR) **C. Poli**
18 **SAPERLIPOUPETTE (FR)**, 4, gr f Highest Honor (FR)—Emmanuelle (FR) **Mme P. Vandervoort-Kumble**
19 **SUPERABLE**, 7, b g Superlative—Coral Heights **Ecurie Namour**
20 **TIBERSEN (FR)**, 4, b f Posen (USA)—Tiberly (FR) **Ecurie Namour**

THREE-YEAR-OLDS

21 **LITTLE KAROO (FR)**, b c Le Glorieux—Sandmiss **Mme P. Vandervoort-Kumble**
22 **LORILAI (USA)**, b f Arctic Tern (USA)—Lorilla (USA) **Y. Nasib**
23 **NICE RIVER (FR)**, gr f R. B. chesne—Split River (USA) **Mme P. Vandervoort-Kumble**
24 **SALVINAXIA (FR)**, b f Linamix (FR)—Salve **Mme P. Vandervoort-Kumble**
25 **SNOWFLAKE (FR)**, gr f Kadrou (FR)—Snowdrop **Mme P. Vandervoort-Kumble**
26 **TIKVATI (FR)**, b c Lashkari—Vatipan (FR) **Ecurie Namour**
27 **VENDREDI SOIR (USA)**, b c Trempolino (USA)—Bruxelles **R. Scully**
28 **ZAHRANI (FR)**, b c Zayyani—Scented Rose **Ecurie Namour**
29 **ZARABIA (FR)**, b f Zayyani—Sonabie (FR) **Mme P. Vandervoort-Kumble**

TWO-YEAR-OLDS

30 **DOUBLE SCOTCH (FR)**, b c Caerwent—Galgarine (FR) (Frere Basile (FR)) **Mme P. Vandervoort-Kumble**
31 **SHENZEN (FR)**, ch f Fabulous Dancer (USA)—Simple Simone (FR) (Arctic Tern (USA)) **R. Scully**
32 **SIX FOUR KILO (USA)**, b c A P Indy (USA)—Star Standing (CAN) (Assert) **P. Augustus**
33 **SOUTH SEA (USA)**, b f Java Gold (USA)—So Romantic (USA) (El Gran Senor (USA)) **P. Augustus**
34 **SYDNEY OPERA (USA)**, b c Risen Star (USA)—L'Incestueuse (USA) (Lypheor) **R. Scully**

221   MR M. J. FETHERSTON-GODLEY, East Ilsley

Postal: **Kennett House, East Ilsley, Newbury, Berks, RG20 7LW.**

Phone: **(01635) 281 250 FAX (01635) 281 250**

1 **BLUSHING GRENADIER (IRE)**, 4, ch g Salt Dome (USA)—La Duse
2 **MACFARLANE**, 8, br g Kala Shikari—Tarvie **Mr P. Fetherston-Godley**
3 **NAKED WELCOME**, 4, ch c Most Welcome—Stripanoora **The Most Welcome Partnership**
4 **ROYALE FIGURINE (IRE)**, 5, ch m Dominion Royale—Cree's Figurine **Mr Craig Pearman**
5 **SHANGHAI LIL**, 4, b f Petong—Toccata **Mr M. J. Fetherston-Godley**

THREE-YEAR-OLDS

6 **COTYTTO**, b br f Puissance—Drudwen **The Pavilion Enders**
7 B f Forzando—Eaves **Mr M. J. Fetherston-Godley**
8 **ESKIMO KISS (IRE)**, b f Distinctly North (USA)—Felicitas **Mrs Alexander Scott**
9 **LAVENDER DELLA (IRE)**, gr f Shernazar—All In White (FR) **Abigail Limited**
10 **LITTLE KENNY**, b f Warning—Tarvie **Mr P. Fetherston-Godley**
11 **NAKED EMPEROR**, b g Dominion Royale—Torville Gold **The Most Welcome Partnership**
12 **NAME OF OUR FATHER (USA)**, b c Northern Baby (CAN)—
                                        Ten Hail Marys (USA) **Boase, Cleaver, Pearman, Scott & Todd**
13 **XENOPHON OF CUNAXA (IRE)**, b g Cyrano de Bergerac—Annais Nin **Abigail Limited**

TWO-YEAR-OLDS

14 Ch f 24/2 Beveled (USA)—Beyond The Moon (IRE) (Ballad Rock) **Mr Philip C. Nelson**
15 Gr f 12/2 Rudimentary (USA)—Inshirah (USA) (Caro) **Derek & Jean Klee**
16 B c 16/5 Most Welcome—Mount Ida (USA) (Conquistador Cielo (USA)) **Mr M. J. Fetherston-Godley**
17 Ch f 13/2 Belmez (USA)—Nafis (USA) (Nodouble (USA)) **Coriolan Partnership**

MR M. J. FETHERSTON-GODLEY—continued

18 B c 28/4 Waajib—Selchis (Main Reef) **Mr M. J. Fetherston-Godley**
19 Br f 23/3 Warning—Tarvie (Swing Easy (USA)) **Mr P. Fetherston-Godley**
20 B f 26/1 Petong—Volcalmeh (Lidhame) **Mr Julian Sheffield**

Other Owners: Mrs R. Buck, Ms P. J. Carter, Mr R. J. Domzalski, Mr David Harrison, Mrs E. W. Pitman, Mrs Amanda Simmons, Mr R. A. Simmons, Mr W. L. Smith.

222   MR J. R. G. FFITCH-HEYES, Lewes

Postal: **The Racing Stables, Old Lewes Racecourse, Lewes, E. Sussex, BN7 1UR.**
Phone: **(01273) 480804 FAX (01273) 478709 MOBILE (0831) 499322**

1 **BALLESTRO (IRE)**, 4, b g Astronef—Balaine (GER) **Joint Venture Racing**
2 **CREDIT CONTROLLER (IRE)**, 7, b g Dromod Hill—Fotopan **Mr Roger J. Spencer**
3 **JUST A SINGLE (IRE)**, 5, b g Adbass (USA)—Sniggy **Mr Roger J. Spencer**
4 **MANOLETE**, 5, b g Hard Fought—Andalucia **Miss J. A. Ewer**
5 **MUHTASHIM (IRE)**, 6, b g Caerleon (USA)—Baccalaureate **Mrs Jenny Willment**
6 **PA'S EMILY**, 4, b f Tinoco—Camping Out **Mr J. R. Elliott**
7 **SHERBLU**, 5, ch g Cigar—Glyn Blue **Mr C. Bennett**
8 **SOLAR WARRIOR**, 6, b g Le Solaret (FR)—Per Ardua **Mr Brian Eacott**
9 **THE QUADS**, 4, b g Tinoco—Queen's Royale **J. Duddy**
10 **THE WEST'S ASLEEP**, 11, ch g Mr Fordette—Ballinphonta **Mr Roger J. Spencer**
11 **YO KIRI-B**, 5, b m Night Shift (USA)—Briar Creek **Miss L. A. Elliott**
12 **YO-MATE**, 5, b h Komaite (USA)—Silent Sun **Miss L. A. Elliott**
13 **ZACAROON**, 5, b m Last Tycoon—Samaza (USA) **Mr C. Harradine**

THREE-YEAR-OLDS

14 **MOGIN**, ch f Komaite (USA)—Misdevious (USA) **Miss L. A. Elliott**
15 **YOUNG BUTT**, ch c Bold Owl—Cymbal **Mr G. R. Butterfield**

Other Owners: Mr Tom J. Bellamy, Mr A. Capaldi, Mr A. S. Champion, Mr R. F. Champion, Mrs B. M. L. Davis, Mr John Ffitch-Heyes, Mr G. Field, Mr J. Gregory, Mrs D. R. Hunnisett, Mr T. V. Kett, Mr G. P. Lewis, Mr L. S. Newman.

Jockey (NH): A Maguire.

Apprentice: John Neaves (9-12).

223   MR D. J. S. FFRENCH DAVIS, Upper Lambourn

Postal: **The Top Yard, Saxon House Stables, Upper Lambourn, Hungerford, Berks, RG17 8QH**
Phone: **OFFICE (01488) 71208 FAX 71214 MOBILE (0831) 118764 HOME (01488) 72342**

1 **ANDRE'S AFFAIR**, 5, b g Sulaafah (USA)—Andrea Dawn **Mr David Milburn**
2 **BARBRALLEN**, 4, b f Rambo Dancer (CAN)—Barrie Baby **Mr Peter J. Allen**
3 **DANCES WITH HOOVES**, 4, b c Dancing Dissident (USA)—Princesse Legere (USA) **Mr V. Squeglia**
4 **DAYTONA BEACH (IRE)**, 6, ch g Bluebird (USA)—Water Spirit (USA) **Mrs Mary Moloney**
5 **FLY IN AMBER (IRE)**, 5, b m Doubletour (USA)—Amber Gift **Mr Conor ffrench Davis**
6 **HAWAII STORM (FR)**, 8, b g Plugged Nickle (USA)—Slewvindaloo (USA) **Mr C. C. Capel**
7 **LYRICAL SEAL**, 6, b m Dubassoff (USA)—Sea-Rosemary **Mrs J. Dening**
8 **MAENAD**, 5, gr m Sharrood (USA)—Now In Session (USA) **Exors of the late Mrs C. A. Robinson**
9 **MISS GRUNTLED**, 5, b m Arctic Lord—Sweet Move **Mrs M. Duff**
10 **ROLLTHEGOLD**, 4, br g Tragic Role (USA)—Goldust (FR) **Mrs G. Kindersley**
11 **YOUR MOST WELCOME**, 5, b m Most Welcome—Blues Player **Mrs J. E. Lambert**

MR D. J. S. FFRENCH DAVIS—continued

THREE-YEAR-OLDS

12 ARCH ANGEL (IRE), ch f Archway (IRE)—Saintly Guest **Mr R. J. Lorenz**
13 BATH KNIGHT, b g Full Extent (USA)—Mybella Ann **Mr Paul De Weck**
14 WINDSWEPT (IRE), b f Taufan (USA)—Sutica **Miss Henrietta Senn**

TWO-YEAR-OLDS

15 Ch c 14/1 Diesis—High Sevens (Master Willie) **Mrs Mary Moloney**
16 Ch f 25/1 Forzando—Indian Summer (Young Generation)
17 B f 28/3 Polar Falcon (USA)—Tarasova (USA) (Green Forest (USA))

Other Owners: Mr James Blackshaw, Mrs P. Carson, Mr D. J. Ffrench Davis, Mr G. J. Head, Miss M. K. Rossbrook, Mrs M. J. Sharman.

Jockey (Flat): T Quinn (w.a.).

Jockey (NH): S McNeill.

---

224   MR G. FIERRO, Hednesford

Postal: 'Woodview', Rugeley Road, Hazel Slade Stables, Hednesford, WS12 5PH.
Phone: **(01543) 879611 MOBILE (0374) 784478**

1 CROOKED COUNSEL, 10, b g Workboy—Bacchantina **Mr G. Fierro**
2 DARU (USA), 7, gr g Caro—Frau Daruma (ARG) **Mrs J. Hughes**
3 DESERT FORCE (IRE), 7, b g Lomond (USA)—St Padina **Mr G. Fierro**
4 EDEN STREAM, 9, b g Paddy's Stream—Surplus Silk **Mr R. M. Kirkland**
5 ILUSTRE (IRE), 4, ch g Al Hareb (USA)—Time For Pleasure **Mr G. Fierro**
6 JOHN THE BAPTIST, 9, ch g Deep Run—Woodford Princess **Mr G. Fierro**
7 KALISKO (FR), 6, b g Cadoudal (FR)—Mista (FR) **Mr G. Fierro**
8 MARROWFAT LADY (IRE), 5, b m Astronef—Lady Topknot **Mr G. Fierro**
9 MISTY GREY, 7, gr g Scallywag—Finwood **Mr G. Fierro**
10 RANGER SLOANE, 4, ch g Gunner B—Lucky Amy **Mr G. Fierro**
11 T'NIEL, 5, ch m Librate—Classy Colleen **Mr G. Fierro**

Other Owners: Mr G.E. Sloane.

Conditional: Shaun Lycett (10-0).

---

225   MR R. F. FISHER, Ulverston

Postal: Great Head House, Priory Road, Ulverston, Cumbria, LA12 9RX.
Phone: **ULVERSTON (01229) 585664 FAX (01229) 585079**

1 BALLYALLIA CASTLE (IRE), 7, ch g Carlingford Castle—Clonsilla **S. P. Marsh**
2 CORPORAL KIRKWOOD (IRE), 6, br g Royal Fountain—The Black Bridge **Great Head House Estates Limited**
3 DE-VEERS CURRIE (IRE), 4, b f Glenstal (USA)—Regent Star **A. Antonelli**
4 ELI PECKANPAH (IRE), 6, b g Supreme Leader—Grove Girl **Great Head House Estates Limited**
5 EMBRYONIC (IRE), 4, b c Prince Rupert (FR)—Belle Viking (FR) **Mrs D. Miller**
6 KIERCHEM (IRE), 5, b g Mazaad—Smashing Gale **Mrs D. Miller**
7 PARIAH (IRE), 7, b g Derring Rose—Proverb Lady **Mrs D. Miller**
8 PRIME PAINTER, 6, b h Robellino—Sharp Lady **Great Head House Estates Limited**
9 RAZMAK, 4, b c Sizzling Melody—Martin-Lavell Post **Great Head House Estates Limited**
10 REBECCAS SECRET (IRE), 5, ch g Classic Secret (USA)—Cordon **Great Head House Estates Limited**

MR R. F. FISHER—continued

11 **ROOSECOTE**, 5, b g Bold Owl—Spare Wheel
12 **SLAUGHT SON (IRE)**, 8, br g Roselier (FR)—Stream Flyer **Mrs D. Miller**
13 **STONE CROSS (IRE)**, 4, b g Pennine Walk—Micro Mover **Mrs D. Miller**

THREE-YEAR-OLDS

14 **WILLIE HORNE**, b c Batshoof—Folle Idee (USA) **Great Head House Estates Limited**

Jockeys (Flat): N Connorton, K Fallon.

Jockeys (NH): M Dwyer, P Niven.

Conditional: F Leahy.

Amateur: Mr Richard Ford (10-7).

226   MR J. G. FITZGERALD, Malton

Postal: **Norton Grange, Norton, Malton, North Yorks, YO17 9EA.**
Phone: MALTON (01653) 692718 FAX MALTON (01653) 600214

1 **AGISTMENT**, 5, ch g Niniski (USA)—Cryptomeria **Marquesa de Moratalla**
2 **ALZULU (IRE)**, 5, b g Alzao (USA)—Congress Lady **Mr D. Buckle**
3 **AMIGOS**, 8, ch g Nordance (USA)—Hi Gorgeous **Mr Peter O'Sullevan**
4 **ASLAN (IRE)**, 8, gr g Ela-Mana-Mou—Celestial Path **Mr Raymond Anderson Green**
5 **ASTINGS (FR)**, 8, b g Brezzo (FR)—Osca **Mr W. A. A. Farrell**
6 **AUNTIE ALICE**, 6, b m Uncle Pokey—Fortalice **The East Riding Partnership**
7 **BALLAD MINSTREL (IRE)**, 4, gr g Ballad Rock—Sashi Woo **Mr Norman Jackson**
8 **BANOFFI (IRE)**, 7, ch g Be My Native (USA)—Jam Treacle (USA) **Mr W. Hancock**
9 **BARBAROJA**, 5, ch g Efisio—Bias **Marquesa de Moratalla**
10 **BOLD PURSUIT (IRE)**, 7, b g Thatching—Pursue **Mr R. J. Wragg**
11 **BONZER**, 7, b g Electric—Lady Doubloon **Mr Peter Rawson**
12 **CAMPASPE**, 4, b f Dominion—Lady River (FR) **Mr J. G. FitzGerald**
13 **CHINA KING (IRE)**, 5, b g King's Ride—China Jill **Mrs B. V. Eve**
14 **CLAVERHOUSE (IRE)**, 7, b g Buckskin (FR)—Baby Isle **Mrs Peter Corbett**
15 **CORONA GOLD**, 6, b g Chilibang—Miss Alkie **Mr T. J. FitzGerald**
16 **COVER POINT (IRE)**, 5, b g Northiam (USA)—Angie **Mrs Anne Henson**
17 **DARI SOUND (IRE)**, 8, b g Shardari—Bugle Sound **Mrs K. D. Leckenby**
18 **DOMAN**, 7, ch g Domynsky—Mantina **Mr W. R. Lofthouse**
19 **DORADUS**, 8, br g Shirley Heights—Sextant **Lady Halifax**
20 **DUAL IMAGE**, 9, b g Alzao (USA)—Odette Odile **Datum Building Supplies Limited**
21 5, B g Phardante (FR)—Fairy Hollow
22 **HEATHVIEW**, 9, b g Pitpan—Whosview **Mr J. G. FitzGerald**
23 **HIGH PADRE**, 10, b g The Parson—High Energy **Mr J. S. Murdoch**
24 **INTENDANT**, 4, b g Distant Relative—Bunduq **Marquesa de Moratalla**
25 **JAVA RED (IRE)**, 4, b g Red Sunset—Coffee Bean **Mr J. G. FitzGerald**
26 **KENILWORTH (IRE)**, 8, b g Kemal (FR)—Araglin Dora **Mrs D. D. Osborne**
27 **MANDICAT (IRE)**, 6, b g Mandalus—Apicat **Lady Lloyd Webber**
28 **NATIVE FIELD (IRE)**, 7, b g Be My Native (USA)—Broomfield Ceili **Mr R. L. White**
29 **NATIVE MISSION**, 9, ch g Be My Native (USA)—Sister Ida **Mr G. E. Shouler**
30 5, B g Hymns On High—Nevada Run
31 **NEWLANDS-GENERAL**, 10, ch g Oats—Spartiquick **Mr W. Hancock**
32 **NIJMEGEN**, 8, b g Niniski (USA)—Petty Purse **Mr W. Hancock**
33 **NINETY-FIVE**, 4, ch f Superpower—Vanishing Trick **The Exors of Mr M. H. Wrigley**
34 **NOBLE ORANGE**, 5, b g Ardross—Sip of Orange **Mrs R. A. G. Haggie**
35 **OUR ROBERT**, 4, b g Faustus (USA)—Duck Soup **Mr Tony Fawcett**
36 **OUR WYN-STON**, 4, ch g Hard Fought—Wyn-Bank **Mrs Shirley France**

MR J. G. FITZGERALD—continued

37 **PHILHARMONIC (IRE)**, 8, b g Orchestra—High Fi **Mr C. C. Longstaff**
38 **QUANGO**, 4, b g Charmer—Quaranta **Mr L. Milligan**
39 5, B g Satco (FR)—Quantas
40 **RICHARDSON**, 9, b g Strong Gale—Queen's Pet **Mr R. Haggas**
41 **RUSTIC AIR**, 9, ch g Crash Course—Country Tune **Mrs B. V. Eve**
42 **SILVER PRIDE**, 6, b g Silver Season—La Furze **Mr A. Bayman**
43 5, Ch m Ardross—Sister Claire
44 **SOUNDS FYNE (IRE)**, 7, b g Good Thyne (USA)—Sounds Familiar **Mr Peter O'Sullevan**
45 **SPARROW HALL**, 9, b g Fine Blade (USA)—Churchtown Breeze **Mr Peter Hall**
46 **STONE THE CROWS (IRE)**, 6, b g Phardante (FR)—Terrama Sioux **Mrs Anne Henson**
47 **SUNKALA SHINE**, 8, ch g Kalaglow—Allander Girl **Mr J. G. Fitzgerald**
48 **THURSDAY NIGHT (IRE)**, 5, ch g Montelimar (USA)—Alsazia (FR) **Mr R. Haggas**
49 **TRAINGLOT**, 9, ch g Dominion—Mary Green **Marquesa de Moratalla**
50 **UNCLE ERNIE**, 11, b g Uncle Pokey—Ladyfold **Lady Lloyd Webber**
51 **URANUS COLLONGES (FR)**, 10, b g El Badr—Flika (FR) **Halewood International Ltd**
52 **WAKING (CAN)**, 5, ch g Rahy (USA)—Dreamsend (USA) **Mrs H. Sedgwick**
53 **WESTERLY (IRE)**, 5, br g Strong Gale—Moonlight Romance **Mr J. G. FitzGerald**
54 **WHIP HAND (IRE)**, 5, b g Bob Back (USA)—Praise The Lord **Lady Lloyd Webber**

THREE-YEAR-OLDS

55 **LANDFALL**, b g Most Welcome—Sextant **Mr J. G. FitzGerald**
56 **LA VOLTA**, b f Komaite (USA)—Khadino **Sir Andrew Lloyd Webber**
57 **MOONCUSSER**, b g Forzando—Ragged Moon **Marquesa de Moratalla**
58 **OVERSMAN**, b c Keen—Jamaican Punch (IRE) **Marquesa de Moratalla**
59 **OXGANG (IRE)**, b c Taufan (USA)—Casla **Marquesa de Moratalla**
60 **SILENT SYSTEM (IRE)**, gr c Petong—Light Thatch **Marquesa de Moratalla**
61 **SIX CLERKS (IRE)**, b c Shadeed (USA)—Skidmore Girl (USA) **Marquesa de Moratalla**

TWO-YEAR-OLDS

62 B f 6/3 Henbit (USA)—Butter Knife (IRE) (Sure Blade (USA)) **Marquesa de Moratalla**
63 B c 29/4 Magical Wonder (USA)—Gay Krystyna (Malinowski (USA))
64 B c 28/3 Komaite (USA)—Khadine (Astec)
65 B f 25/2 Komaite (USA)—Khadino (Relkino)
66 Gr f 18/4 Absalom—Lady River (FR) (Sir Gaylord) **Mr J. G. FitzGerald**
67 B g 29/3 Charmer—Misowni (Niniski (USA)) **Mr Norman Jackson**
68 **MOONRAKER (IRE)**, b c 19/2 Classic Secret (USA)—Moona (USA) (Lear Fan (USA)) **Mr J. Dick**
69 B c 22/2 Machiavellian (USA)—Seductress (Known Fact (USA)) **Marquesa de Moratalla**
70 B f 10/5 Skyliner—Shawiniga (Lyphard's Wish (FR))
71 **SYMONDS INN**, ch c 5/2 In The Wings—Shining Eyes (USA) (Mr Prospector (USA)) **Marquesa de Moratalla**

Other Owners: Mr R. Burridge, Mr Peter Corbett, Mrs C. M. Dufton, Mrs Anita Green, Mrs C. C. Longstaff, Mrs L. Patten, Mrs P. M. White.

Jockeys (NH): D Byrne (10-0), W Dwan (9-7), M Dwyer (10-3).

Conditional: E Callaghan (9-7), F Leahy (9-7).

227   MR F. FLOOD, Grangecon

Postal: **Ballynure, Grangecon, Co. Wicklow, Ireland.**

Phone: **(045) 53136**

1 **ANNADOT (IRE)**, 6, gr m Roselier (FR)—Galliano **Mr R. Kelly**
2 **ANNIDA (IRE)**, 5, ch m Torus—Subiacco **Mr J. Coppola**
3 **BALLYGAR BOY (IRE)**, 6, b g Roselier—Knock Off **Mr R. McConn**
4 **BETTYS THE BOSS (IRE)**, 8, b m Deep Run—Even More **South Teffia R. C.**
5 **CAPTAIN BRANDY**, 11, ch g Step Together—Manhattan Brandy **Mr M. A. Cooney**

MR F. FLOOD—continued

6 **CARRICKDALE BOY (IRE)**, 5, ch g Buckskin (FR)—Eurolink Sea Baby **Mr P. McParland**
7 **CIARA'S PRINCE (IRE)**, 5, br g Good Thyne (USA)—Sparkling Opera **Mr R. McConn**
8 **CREDIT TRANSFER (IRE)**, 8, b m Kemal (FR)—Speedy Lady **Mr H. Dunne**
9 **DAMODAR**, 7, br g Damister (USA)—Obertura (USA) **Caldbeck Ltd**
10 **DAWN ADAMS (IRE)**, 8, b m Kemal (FR)—Light of Day **Mr J. Sheehan**
11 **FINCHPALM (IRE)**, 6, b g Mandalus—Milan Pride **Mr A. Doyle**
12 **GLENBALLYMA (IRE)**, 7, b m Ela-Mana-Mou—Ashken **Mr J. Byrne**
13 **GLENHAVEN ARTIST (IRE)**, 6, b m Supreme Leader—Loving Artist **M. D. Cahill**
14 **HENRY G'S (IRE)**, 6, b m The Parson—Break The Bank **Mr T. Fennesy**
15 **HERSILIA (IRE)**, 5, br m Mandalus—Milan Pride **Mr F. J. O'Reilly**
16 **JO JO BOY (IRE)**, 7, ch g Good Thyne (USA)—Sparkling Opera **Mr R. McConn**
17 **KNOCKAULIN**, 5, ch g Buckley—Two Shares **Mrs K. L. Urquhart**
18 **KNOCKTHOMAS (IRE)**, 7, gr g Good Thyne (USA)—Fortuity **Mr R. McConn**
19 **MICK O DWYER**, 9, br g Orchestra—Gracious View **Mr P. J. Whealan**
20 **MOYGANNON COURT (IRE)**, 7, b g Tumble Gold—Wrong Decision **Mr P. McAteer**
21 **PEACE TIME GIRL (IRE)**, 6, br m Buckskin (FR)—Sabatta VII **Mr L. Kelly**
22 **POKONO TRAIL (IRE)**, 7, ch g Aristocracy—Frank's Choice **Mr R. Murphy**
23 **PRE ORDAINED (IRE)**, 4, br g Iron Duke (FR)—Miyana (FR) **Dr J. B. O'Connor**
24 **QUENNIE MO GHRA (IRE)**, 5, br m Mandalus—Orient Conquest **D. R. Club**
25 4, Br f Roselier (FR)—Rathvilly Flyer **Mr J. Coogan**
26 **REUTER**, 8, br g Scorpio (FR)—Pendella **Mr J. Coogan**
27 **ROSSBEIGH CREEK**, 9, ch g Crash Course—Smile Away **Mr H. Ferguson**
28 **SALEMHADY (IRE)**, 7, ch g Lancastrian—Lucille Lady **Mrs H. L. McParland**
29 **SHILLELAGH OAK**, 6, ch g Nishapour (FR)—Sweet Ecstasy **Shillelagh R. C.**
30 4, Ch f Good Thyne (USA)—Sparkling Opera **Mr R. McConn**
31 **SPEED BOARD**, 4, b g Waajib—Pitty Pal (USA) **The Web R. C.**
32 **STRONG HICKS (IRE)**, 8, ch g Seymour Hicks (FR)—Deep Foliage **Garristown R. C.**
33 **TARBERT ILEX (IRE)**, 6, b g Aristocracy—Frank's Choice **Mr M. Holly**
34 **THE VILLAGE FANCY (IRE)**, 5, br g Castle Keep—Advantage **Mr K. McGinn**
35 **UNA'S CHOICE (IRE)**, 8, ch g Beau Charmeur (FR)—Laurabeg **Mr D. Cahill**

Other Owners: P. J. Donovan, Mrs T. Flood, Mr S. Lawlor, Mr R. McGearty, Mr D. B. Sanger.

Jockey (NH): F J Flood (9-9).

Apprentice: L Fleming (8-2).

Amateurs: Mr H F Cleary (10-0), Mr P J Faulkner (9-0).

228 MR R. M. FLOWER, Jevington

Postal: **Devonshire House, Jevington, East Sussex, BN26 5QB.**
Phone: **(01323) 488771 488522 FAX (01323) 488099**

1 **AUTUMN COVER**, 4, gr g Nomination—Respray **Mr G. A. Alexander**
2 **DELIFFIN**, 10, b g Wolverlife—Teletype **Mrs G. M. Temmerman**
3 **DUCKEY FUZZ**, 8, b g Ardross—Twine **Mr R. M. Flower**
4 **FORT KNOX (IRE)**, 5, b g Treasure Kay—Single Viking **Miss C. Markowiak**
5 **HALF TONE**, 4, gr c Touch of Grey—Demilinga **Mrs G. M. Temmerman**
6 **PADDY'S STORM**, 4, b g Celestial Storm (USA)—Hot Tan **Mrs G. M. Temmerman**
7 **PUDGY POPPET**, 5, b m Danehill (USA)—Top Heights **Mr G. A. Tanaka**
8 **SHARP IMP**, 6, b g Sharpo—Implore **Mrs G. M. Temmerman**
9 **SHAYNES DOMAIN**, 5, b g Dominion—Glen Na Smole **Mr R. M. Flower**
10 **SOOJAMA (IRE)**, 6, b g Mansooj—Pyjama Game **Mr N. G. Castleton**

MR R. M. FLOWER—continued

THREE-YEAR-OLDS

11 B f Touch of Grey—Cabinet Shuffle **Miss C. Markowiak**
12 COLOUR COUNSELLOR, gr g Touch of Grey—Bourton Downs **Mr R. M. Flower**
13 EMBROIDERED, b f Charmer—Emblazon **Mr M. Waghorn**
14 EXECUTIVE OFFICER, b g Be My Chief (USA)—Caro's Niece (USA) **Mr M. Waghorn**
15 B c Touch of Grey—Foggy Dew **Tandnac Racing**
16 GREY LEGEND, gr c Touch of Grey—Northwold Star (USA) **Mr Jan Rieck**
17 B f Charmer—Hound Song **Tandnac Racing**

TWO-YEAR-OLDS

18 B c 20/4 Touch of Grey—Northwold Star (USA) (Monteverdi) **Miss C. Markowiak**

Other Owners: Mrs J. Gawthorpe, Mr T. M. Jennings, Miss Victoria Markowiak.

229   CAPT T. A. FORSTER, Ludlow

Postal: **Downton Hall Stables, Ludlow, Shropshire, SY8 3DX.**

Phone: **(01584) 873688 OFFICE (01584) 874034 HOME (01584) 873525 FAX**

1 ARTURO, 5, b g Gildoran—Metaxa **Lady Lewinton**
2 AUT EVEN (IRE), 6, b g Corvaro (USA)—Mistress Boosh **Anne Duchess of Westminster**
3 BIRONI, 7, b g Scorpio (FR)—Stern Lass **Mrs M. Wiggin**
4 BOLD DOLPHIN, 6, b g Idiot's Delight—Brave Remark **Mr S. Preston**
5 BRIERY GALE, 6, b m Strong Gale—Oranella **Mrs Helen Plumbly**
6 BUNGEE JUMPER, 6, b g Idiot's Delight—Catherine Bridge **Mr J. B. Sumner**
7 CLASS OF NINETYTWO (IRE), 7, b g Lancastrian—Lothian Lassie **Lord Cadogan**
8 COONAWARA, 10, b g Corvaro (USA)—Why Don't Ye **Mr Simon Sainsbury**
9 CORRIB SONG, b g Pitpan—Platinum Blond **Mrs D. K. Price**
10 CRIMSON KING (IRE), 5, b g Good Thyne (USA)—That's Mine **Mr Simon Sainsbury**
11 DANTES SUN (IRE), 7, b g Phardante (FR)—Shine Your Light **Anne Duchess of Westminster**
12 DON DU CADRAN (FR), 7, b g Dom Pasquini (FR)—Bel du Cadran (FR) **Lord Cadogan**
13 DUBLIN FLYER, 10, b g Rymer—Dublin Express **Mr J. B. Sumner**
14 EASTERN RIVER, 10, ch g Over The River (FR)—Oriental Infanta **Gamston Equine**
15 EEZ-AWAY (IRE), 7, b br g Spin of A Coin—Derring Way **Million In Mind Partnership (5)**
16 FOULKSCOURT DUKE (IRE), 8, b g Furry Glen—Last Princess **Mr Simon Sainsbury**
17 FUN WHILE IT LASTS, 5, b m Idiot's Delight—Henry's True Love **Mrs Philip Humphries-Cuff**
18 GALES OF LAUGHTER, 7, br g Strong Gale—Joca **Lord Leverhulme**
19 GENERAL WOLFE, 7, ch g Rolfe (USA)—Pillbox **The Winning Line**
20 GROUP HAT (IRE), 8, b g Mister Lord (USA)—Arctic Sue **Lady Pilkington**
21 HEARTS ARE WILD, 9, ch g Scallywag—Henry's True Love **Mr T. F. F. Nixon**
22 LADY HIGH SHERIFF (IRE), 6, b m Lancastrian—Pitalina **Mrs Michael Ward-Thomas**
23 LATEST THYNE (IRE), 6, b br g Good Thyne (USA)—I'm The Latest **Mr Simon Sainsbury**
24 LUCKY ESCAPE, 5, b g Then Again—Lucky Love **Mr G. C. Myddelton**
25 MAAMUR (USA), 8, gr g Robellino (USA)—Tiger Trap (USA) **Mrs A. L. Wood**
26 MAJORS LEGACY (IRE), 7, b br g Roselier (FR)—Sugarstown **Mrs G. Leigh**
27 MARTHA'S DAUGHTER, 7, br m Majestic Maharaj—Lady Martha **Mr M. Ward-Thomas**
28 MARTHA'S SON, 9, b g Idiot's Delight—Lady Martha **Mr M. Ward-Thomas**
29 MUSIC THERAPY (IRE), 6, b g Roselier (FR)—Suny Salome **Mr R. Van Gelder**
30 NICKLUP, 9, ch m Netherkelly—Voolin **Lord Cadogan**
31 NOTHINGTODOWITHME, 6, ch g Relkino—Lasses Nightshade **Captain Miles Gosling**
32 OATS ALOFT, 5, b g Oats—High Affair **Major H. R. M. Porter**
33 6, B g El Conquistador—Pepe Lew **Mr G. J. Phillips**
34 POPPEA (IRE), 7, br m Strong Gale—Lepida **Anne Duchess of Westminster**
35 POSTMAN'S PATH, 10, ch g Over The River (FR)—Coolbawn Lady **Mrs A. Reid Scott**
36 RECTORY GARDEN (IRE), 7, b g The Parson—Peace Run **Lord Cadogan**
37 ROYAL SILVER, 5, gr g Kalaglow—Avon Royale **Broughton Homes Ltd**
38 RUBY VISION (IRE), 7, gr m Vision (USA)—Blue Alicia **Mr G. J. G. Roberts**
39 RUFFTRADE, 9, b g Sunley Builds—Caribs Love **Mrs John Nesbitt**

CAPT T. A. FORSTER—continued

40 **SAIL BY THE STARS**, 7, b m Celtic Cone—Henry's True Love **Mr T. F. F. Nixon**
41 **SECOND CALL**, 7, ch m Kind of Hush—Matinata **Mr M. Ward-Thomas**
42 **SILVER STANDARD**, 6, b g Jupiter Island—One Half Silver (CAN) **Mr G. W. Lugg**
43 **SUN SURFER (FR)**, 8, ch g R B Chesne—Sweet Cashmere (FR) **Mr Simon Sainsbury**
44 **TEINEIN (FR)**, 5, b g Dancehall (USA)—Sweet Titania (FR) **Mr Simon Sainsbury**
45 **THE GO AHEAD (IRE)**, 6, b g Le Bavard (FR)—Cantafleur **Lady Knutsford**
46 **THREE PHILOSOPHERS (IRE)**, 7, b br g Strong Gale—Branstown Lady **Anne Duchess of Westminster**
47 **THREE SAINTS (IRE)**, 7, b g Rising—Oh Dora **Lady Cadogan**
48 **VALIANT (IRE)**, 5, b g Salluceva—Torreya **Mrs H. Jones**
49 **WANDERING LIGHT (IRE)**, 7, b g Royal Fountain—Pleaseme **Anne Duchess of Westminster**
50 **WYNBERG**, 5, b g Robellino (USA)—Pellinora (USA) **Mrs D. Pridden**

Other Owners: Miss J. I. Abel-Smith, Mrs C. H. Antrobus, Lady Barlow, Mr Ben Brooks, Mrs Thomas Buckley, Mrs Martin Bunting, Mrs Ian Cameron, Mrs A. S. Clowes, Mr A. Crichton-Brown, Mr J. H. Day, Mr R. B. Denny, Countess Of Eglinton & Winton, Mrs J. R. Fox, Mr Graham Goode, Mr P. J. Hartigan, Mr R. L. C. Hartley, Mr D. Minton, Mrs S. E. Morgan, Sir Philip Payne-Gallwey, Miss Annie Price, Mrs D. K. Price, Miss Gillian Price, Mrs A. L. Rook, Mrs G. Rowan-Hamilton, Mr Denys Simmons, Mrs C. A. Smith-Bingham, Mr N. E. Stewart, The Hon Mrs A. H. Todd, Mr Patrick Veitch, Major P. G. Verdin, Mrs P. M. Wiggin, Lord Zetland.

Jockey (NH): S Wynne (10-0).

230   MR A. FOSTER, Saltash

Postal: **Cutlinwith Farm, Tideford, Saltash, Cornwall, PL12 5HX.**

Phone: **(01752) 851713**

1 5, Ch g Nearly A Hand—Jerpoint Jessy **Miss S. Prout**
2 **MY OLD CHINA**, 7, b m Shaab—Meldon Lady **Mrs Gertrude M. Foster**
3 5, Ch m Shaab—Rose of Peace **Miss S. Prout**
4 **SOLDIER-B**, 6, ch g Gunner B—Meldon Lady **Mrs Gertrude M. Foster**

231   MR A. G. FOSTER, Lambourn

Postal: **Bourne House Stables, Oxford Street, Lambourn, Newbury, RG16 7XS.**

Phone: **TELEPHONE (01488) 73765 FAX (01488) 72005**

1 **EN VACANCES (IRE)**, 4, b f Old Vic—Welcome Break **Lambourn Valley Racing**
2 **I'M TOBY**, 9, b g Celtic Cone—Easter Tinkle **Mr D. H. Armitage**
3 **KEDGE ANCHOR MAN**, 5, b g Bustino—Jenny Mere **Mr Anthony M. Green**
4 **KNOCKBRIT LADY (IRE)**, 5, b m Creative Plan (USA)—Rose of Cloneen **Mr D. H. Armitage**
5 **MASTER GOODENOUGH (IRE)**, 5, ch g Torus—Hilary's Pet **The Moonrakers Partnership**
6 **RAYLEO (IRE)**, 7, ch g Gorytus (USA)—Vagrant Maid (USA) **Mrs Rosemary Moszkowicz**
7 **TENNESSEE KING (IRE)**, 6, gr g Tender King—Monrovia (FR) **Mr D. H. Armitage**

THREE-YEAR-OLDS

8 **COOL CAPER**, b c Inca Chief (USA)—Rekindled Flame (IRE) **Mr K. G. Knox**
9 **LILLI CLAIRE**, ch f Beveled (USA)—Lillicara (FR) **Mr C. Leafe**
10 **MADAM MARASH (IRE)**, br f Astronef—Ballybannon **Mrs C. Skipworth**
11 **WELLIRAN**, ch g Hadeer—Iranian **Mr K. G. Knox**

TWO-YEAR-OLDS

12 **INTERREGNUM**, ch f 23/2 Interrex (CAN)—Lillicara (FR) (Caracolero) **The Repent At Leisure Partnership**
13 **ROYAL EMBLEM**, gr f 10/3 Presidium—Lily of France (Monsanto) **Lambourn Valley Racing**
14 **SIMPLE LOGIC**, ch f 29/3 Aragon—Dancing Chimes (London Bells) **Miss Juliet E. Reed**
15 B f 19/4 Robellino (USA)—Son Et Lumiere (Rainbow Quest (USA)) **Mr R. W. & Mrs J. R. Fidler**

Other Owners: Bonapartes Partnership, R. W. And Mrs J. R. Fidler, Mr Henry Moszkowicz, Miss Juliet E. Reed, S. W. Transport (Swindon) Ltd, The Repent At Leisure Partnership.

232   MR J. R. H. FOWLER, Summerhill
Postal: Rahinston, Summerhill, Co. Meath, Ireland.
Phone: (0405) 57014 FAX (0405) 57537

1 **BACARDI (IRE)**, 4, ch f Be My Native (USA)—Sipped **T. A. Gillam**
2 **BRASS BAND (IRE)**, 5, br m Orchestra—Credit Card **Lady J. Fowler**
3 **CHESTER TRIX (IRE)**, 6, ch g Lancastrian—Merry Run **J. Rearden**
4 **COOL IT (IRE)**, 6, b g Maculata—Cool As Ice **Lady J. Fowler**
5 **DEIREFORE (IRE)**, 6, b m Callernish—Lovely Pine **C. Hanley**
6 **ELECTRIC LAD (IRE)**, 5, ch g Electric—Fahy Away **J. G. Graham**
7 **GRATE BRITISH (IRE)**, 4, br g Astronef—Stapelea (FR) **True Blue Racing**
8 **HAPPY HANGOVER (IRE)**, 6, ch g Sheer Grit—Rising Dipper **Miss D. Duggan**
9 **HEAD CHAPLAIN (IRE)**, 5, b g The Parson—Arctic Run **M. D. McGrath**
10 **HI KNIGHT (IRE)**, 6, b g King's Ride—Le Nuit **M. D. McGrath**
11 **JAPAMA (IRE)**, 5, ch g Nashamaa—Le Nuit **M. D. McGrath**
12 **LET US PRAY (IRE)**, 6, b m The Parson—Loge **B. D. Smith**
13 **MAID FOR DANCING (IRE)**, 7, b m Crash Course—La Flamenca **Mrs B. J. Fowler**
14 **MAYDAY DREAM (IRE)**, 6, b m Tremblant—Missing Note **J. Liggett**
15 **OPERA HAT (IRE)**, 8, br m Strong Gale—Tops O'Crush **Mrs T. K. Cooper**
16 **OUT OF FASHION (IRE)**, 6, b m Lancastrian—Sparkling Fashion **Out Of Fashion Syndicate**
17 **PRODIGAL PRINCE**, 8, ch g Oats—Olympian Princess **Miss L. Wood**
18 **SHINING WILLOW**, 6, b m Strong Gale—Lady Buck **S. P. Tindall**
19 **SILVER RIVER (IRE)**, 4, br f Strong Gale—Another Agent **Mrs C. A. Waters**
20 **SQUIRREL ISLAND (IRE)**, 6, b m King's Ride—Tante Marie **Mrs B. Brubaker**
21 **WILD VENTURE (IRE)**, 8, ch m Le Bavard (FR)—Fast Adventure **Lady J. Fowler**

Jockeys (NH): D P Fagan (9-7), C O'Dwyer (10-0, w.a.), A Powell (10-4, w.a.).

Amateurs: Mr A Coonan (10-0), Mr A F Doherty (10-0).

Lady Rider: Miss W Fox (9-7).

233   MR K. FROST, Doncaster
Postal: Folds Farm, Folds Lane, Tickhill, Doncaster, DN11 9RH.
Phone: TEL/FAX (01302) 743348

1 **RIVER RED**, 10, ch g Over The River (FR)—Monasootha **Mr K. Frost**

234   MR R. G. FROST, Buckfastleigh
Postal: Hawson Stables, Buckfastleigh, Devon, TQ11 0HP.
Phone: (01364) 642267

1 **ABAVARD (IRE)**, 7, ch g Le Bavard (FR)—Heroanda **Mr D. G. Henderson**
2 **BE DECENT**, 6, ch m Decent Fellow—Bush Radio **Mr P. Tosh**
3 **BISHOPS CASTLE (IRE)**, 8, ch g Carlingford Castle—Dancing Princess **A.E.C. Electric Fencing Ltd (Hotline)**
4 **BLUE CLANCY (IRE)**, 7, b g Hardboy—Blue Lilly **Mrs C. Loze**
5 **BOLD CHOICE**, 10, b g Auction Ring (USA)—Inner Pearl **Mr Jack Joseph**
6 **CABOCHON**, 9, b g Jalmood (USA)—Lightning Legacy (USA) **Mr Jack Joseph**
7 **CLEAR IDEA (IRE)**, 8, ch g Try My Best (USA)—Sloane Ranger **A.E.C. Electric Fencing Ltd (Hotline)**
8 **COME DANCE WITH ME (IRE)**, 6, ch m Rising—Dance For Gold **Mrs G. A. Robarts**
9 **DRY SEA**, 5, b g Green Desert (USA)—Prickle **The Blue Ball Lads**
10 **FEVER PITCH**, 6, gr g Kalaglow—Seragsbee **Four No Trumps Partnership**
11 **HOLDIMCLOSE**, 6, b g Teamwork—Holdmetight **Mrs C. Loze**

MR R. G. FROST—continued

12 **HOLD YOUR RANKS**, 9, b g Ranksborough—Holdmetight **Mr Brian Seward**
13 **IMALIGHT**, 7, b m Idiot's Delight—Armagnac Princess **Mr J. H. Nesbit**
14 **MIRAMAC**, 15, br g Relkino—Magical **Mr R. G. Frost**
15 **MISS FIRECRACKER**, 7, br m Relkino—Firella **Mrs Richard Stanley**
16 **MISS FOXY**, 6, br m High Season—Foxy Fort **Mr P. A. Tylor**
17 **MR COTTON SOCKS**, 8, ch g Sunyboy—Here We Go **Agriwise**
18 **MR PLAYFULL**, 6, br g Teamwork—Blue Nursery **Mr P. A. Tylor**
19 **MR WOODLARK**, 9, b g Ranksborough—Presceena Wood **Mr P. A. Tylor**
20 **PLUM FANCY**, 8, b m Prince of Peace—Hot Fancy **Mrs J. C. Welch**
21 **POOH STICK**, 6, b g Teamwork—Moorland Nell **Mr D. S. Mutton**
22 **PRUDENT PEGGY**, 9, br m Kambalda—Arctic Raheen **Mrs J. McCormack**
23 **STEER POINT**, 5, b g Shaab—Chronicle Lady **Mrs J. R. Bastard**

Other Owners: Mrs J. Clague, Mr Paul Hargreaves, Mrs J. Hubbard, Mr S. J. Hubbard, Mr J. R. Lavelle, Mrs R. J. Lavelle, Mr R. Newton, Mr Terry Sanders, Dr M. J. L. Scott.

Jockeys (NH): R Darke (10-0), J Frost (10-0).

Amateur: Mr A Wonnacott (11-0).

235   MR D. R. GANDOLFO, Wantage

Postal: **Downs Stables, Manor Road, Wantage, Oxon, OX12 8NF.**

Phone: **TEL (01235) 763242 FAX (01235) 764149**

1 **ARDCRONEY CHIEF**, 10, ch g Connaught—Duresme **Mr W. H. Dore**
2 **AROUND THE GALE (IRE)**, 5, b g Strong Gale—Ring Road **Mr T. J. Whitley**
3 **BALANAK (USA)**, 5, b g Shahrastani (USA)—Banque Privee (USA) **Mr W. H. Dore**
4 **BIETSCHHORN BARD**, 6, b g Rymer—Chalet Waldegg **Mr A. W. F. Clapperton**
5 **BROGEEN LADY (IRE)**, 6, br m Phardante (FR)—Dewy Clover **Starlight Racing**
6 **CAPTAIN DOLFORD**, 9, ch g Le Moss—Niatpac **Mr R. E. Brinkworth**
7 **CHAPS**, 6, b g Buckley—Winnetka **G. C. Hartigan**
8 **COME ON PENNY**, 5, b m Rakaposhi King—Gokatiego **Mr A. E. Frost**
9 **CURRAHEEN VIEW (IRE)**, 7, b br m Pragmatic—Real View **Mr W. H. Dore**
10 **DANTES CAVALIER (IRE)**, 6, b g Phardante (FR)—Ring Road **Mr W. H. Dore**
11 **DEYMIAR (IRE)**, 4, b c Doyoun—Dedra **Mr T. J. Whitley**
12 **FAST THOUGHTS**, 9, b g Feelings (FR)—Heldigvis **Mr W. H. Dore**
13 **GALES CAVALIER (IRE)**, 8, b g Strong Gale—Ring Road **Starlight Racing**
14 **GARRYLOUGH (IRE)**, 7, ch m Monksfield—Clonyn **Mr T. J. Whitley**
15 **GENERAL TONIC**, 9, ch g Callernish—Jude Lacy **Starlight Racing**
16 **HARDY WEATHER (IRE)**, 7, br g Strong Gale—Hardy Colleen **Starlight Racing**
17 **KHALIDI (IRE)**, 7, b g Shernazar—Khaiyla **Mr T. J. Whitley**
18 5, B m Pragmatic—Landa's Tipple **Mr D. R. Gandolfo**
19 **LETTERLUNA**, 4, ch f Shavian—Alteza Real **Mrs David Moon**
20 **LOGICAL STEP (IRE)**, 6, b g Pragmatic—Stepalong **Mr A. E. Smith**
21 **LONZA VALLEY**, 7, b g Pragmatic—Nautical Step **Mr A. W. F. Clapperton**
22 **LOTSCHBERG EXPRESS**, 4, ch f Rymer—Chalet Waldegg **Mr A. W. F. Clapperton**
23 **LUKE WARM**, 6, ch g Nearly A Hand—Hot 'n Scopey **Mr D. R. Gandolfo**
24 **MOMENT OF GLORY (IRE)**, 5, ch g Harp Islet (USA)—No Distractions **Mr David O. Moon**
25 **MOUSE BIRD (USA)**, 6, b g Glow (USA)—Irish Bird (USA) **Mr Osbert Pierce**
26 **NADJATI (USA)**, 7, ch g Assert—Najidiya (USA) **Mr T. J. Whitley**
27 **NOBLE EYRE**, 15, br g Aristocracy—Jane Eyre **Mr D. R. Gandolfo**
28 **PLAYING TRUANT**, 8, b g Teenoso (USA)—Elusive **Mr David O. Moon**
29 4, B g Weld—Purple Silk **Mr D. R. Gandolfo**
30 **RAKAPOSHI QUEEN**, 5, b m Rakaposhi King—Domtony **Mrs D. J. Hues**
31 **REALLY A RASCAL**, 9, b g Scallywag—Rockefillee **Mr T. J. Whitley**

MR D. R. GANDOLFO—continued

32 **RIVER LEVEN**, 7, b g Nearly A Hand—Ana Mendoza **Mr R. E. Brinkworth**
33 **SECOND STEP (IRE)**, 5, b g Phardante (FR)—Stepalong **Mr A. E. Smith**
34 **SELATAN (IRE)**, 4, ch g Shernazar—Seleret (USA) **Mr T. J. Whitley**
35 **SEYMOURSWIFT**, 6, b m Seymour Hicks (FR)—Swift Sentence **Starlight Racing**
36 **SPRING MUSLIN**, 4, b f Ra Nova—Wood Heath **Mr D. R. Gandolfo**
37 **THE LANCER (IRE)**, 7, b g Lancastrian—Bucktina **Mr A. E. Frost**
38 **THE WAYWARD BISHOP (IRE)**, 7, b g The Parson—Miss Lucille **Mrs L. C. Taylor**
39 **TIPPING ALONG (IRE)**, 7, ch g Rising—Gone **Mr D. R. Gandolfo**
40 **TRYING AGAIN**, 8, b g Northern Game—Wood Heath **Mr W. H. Dore**
41 **UPHAM RASCAL**, 5, ch g Gunner B—Upham Kelly **Mr R. E. Brinkworth**
42 5, Ch g Rakaposhi King—Upham Reunion **Mr T. J. Whitley**

THREE-YEAR-OLDS

43 Ch f Sula Bula—Anyone's Fancy **Mr W. H. Dore**
44 **COURTING DANGER**, b g Tina's Pet—Court Town **Miss E. A. Gandolfo**
45 B g Scottish Reel—Miss Wrensborough **Mr A. W. F. Clapperton**

Other Owners: Mr H. Candler, Mr J. Deeley, Mr George Ennor, Mr Stephen Freud, Mr C. Mackenzie, Mr G. C. Reilly, Mr Patrick Renahan.

Jockeys (NH): M Dwyer (w.a.), D Leahy (10-0).

Apprentice: Sophie Mitchell (8-5).

Conditional: A Dowling (9-7), Sophie Mitchell (9-7).

236   MR N. A. GASELEE, Upper Lambourn

Postal: **Saxon Cottage, Upper Lambourn, Hungerford, Berks, RG17 8QN.**
Phone: **LAMBOURN (01488) 71503 FAX (01488) 71585**

1 **ACT OF FAITH**, 6, b g Oats—Ruby's Vision **Mrs R. W. S. Baker**
2 **ADMIRAL BRUNY (IRE)**, 5, b g Strong Gale—Rhymaround **Mr & Mrs R. E. Morris-Adams**
3 **BAVARD DIEU (IRE)**, 8, ch g Le Bavard (FR)—Graham Dieu **Sagvaro Stables**
4 **BUCKET OF GOLD**, 6, b g Buckskin (FR)—Among The Gold **Mrs F. D. McInnes Skinner**
5 **CASTLE COURT (IRE)**, 8, ch g Deep Run—Mawbeg Holly **Mrs David Thompson**
6 **COMMERCIAL ARTIST**, 10, b g Furry Glen—Blue Suede Shoes **Mrs David Thompson**
7 **DESTINY CALLS**, 6, ch g Lord Avie (USA)—Miss Renege (USA) **Mr Simon Harrap**
8 **ERCKULE**, 6, b g Petoski—Mytinia **The Saxon Partnership**
9 **FLIPPANCE**, 6, b g Relkino—Stey Brae **Mr C. L. Rykens**
10 **FORTUNE**, 5, ch g Gildoran—Caer-Gai **Mr Robert Cooper**
11 **GAMBLER'S GOLD (IRE)**, 5, b m Idiot's Delight—Among The Gold **Mrs F. D. McInnes Skinner**
12 **INDIAN QUEST**, 7, b g Rainbow Quest (USA)—Hymettus **J. A. L. Racing**
13 **KENTISH PIPER**, 11, br g Black Minstrel—Toombeola **Mrs Tim Perkins**
14 **MAD THYME**, 9, b g Idiot's Delight—Another Breeze **Mr R. J. Jenks**
15 **MILLERSFORD**, 5, b g Meadowbrook—My Seer **Mrs Derek Fletcher & Mrs B. P. Hall**
16 **MR ENTERTAINER**, 13, gr g Neltino—Office Party **Mr M. A. Boddington**
17 **MR INVADER**, 9, br g Le Moss—Bruna Magli **Mr M. A. Boddington**
18 **MYSTIC ISLE (IRE)**, 6, b g Callernish—Sleemana **Mrs P. Furse**
19 **NO JOKER (IRE)**, 8, b g Jester—Canta Lair **Brigadier R. W. S. Hall**
20 **PARTY POLITICS**, 12, b g Politico (USA)—Spin Again **Mrs D. B. Thompson**
21 **PRINCE OF SALERNO**, 9, ch g Slippered—Daffydown Lady **Sir Christopher Walford**
22 **PROPOSE THE TOAST**, 6, b m Oats—Miss Evelin **Miss F. M. Fletcher**
23 **SPARKLING SPIRIT**, 8, b m Sparkling Boy—Spartan Spirit **The Horseflies**
24 **SPARTAN SILVER**, 10, ch g Warpath—Spartan Spirit **Lord Somerleyton**

MR N. A. GASELEE—continued

25 **SPINNAKER**, 6, gr g Neltino—Spin Again **Mr D. R. Stoddart**
26 **THE FROG PRINCE (IRE)**, 8, b g Le Johnstan—Fine Lass **Mr Robert Cooper**
27 **TITUS ANDRONICUS**, 9, b g Oats—Lavilla **Mrs Julian Belfrage**
28 **VICTOR BRAVO (NZ)**, 9, br g War Hawk—Regal Command (NZ) **Mrs R. D. Cowell**

Other Owners: Mr A. J. Armfield, Mr A. J. Baker, Mr Brian F. Baldock, Mr A. N. Brooke Rankin, Mr J. A. Cameron, Mr N. Davies, Mr G. R. Furse, Mr N. A. Gaselee, Mr M. G. S. Gibson, Mr C. A. Gidman, Mr L. J. Hawksworth, Viscount Head, Mr D. Hookins, Mr A. C. D. Ingleby-Mackenzie, Mr Denis Milne, Miss L. M. Neal, Mrs J. K. Newton, Mr M. A. F. Newton, Mrs Gordon Pepper, Major C. R. Philipson, Mr S. P. Scarsbrook, Mrs R. Sutcliffe-Smith, Mr R. H. Todd, Mrs Nicola Turner.

Jockey (NH): C Llewellyn (10-0, w.a.).

Conditional: Feargal Cooper (9-7).

237   MR T. R. GEORGE, Stroud

Postal: **Springbank, Slad, Stroud, Glos, GL6 7QE.**
Phone: **(01452) 814267 FAX (01452) 814246 MOBILE (0860) 487426**

1 **CARMEL'S JOY (IRE)**, 7, ch m Carlingford Castle—Bealaghanaffrin **Mr T. R. George**
2 **FELLOO (IRE)**, 7, br g Decent Fellow—Cuckaloo **Mrs J. Edwards-Heathcote**
3 **FRANK KNOWS**, 6, ch g Chilibang—Chance Match **Mrs C. Peacock**
4 **GENERAL PONGO**, 7, b g Kaytu—Charlotte Mary **Mrs J. K. Powell**
5 **GRIMMBEE**, 5, b m Gunner B—Folkland **Mrs J. K. Powell**
6 **GRUSHKO**, 6, b g Troy Fair—Elfen Queen **Mrs J. K. Powell**
7 **HIGH MOOD**, 6, b g Jalmood (USA)—Copt Hall Princess **Mr John French**
8 **HOLY WANDERER (USA)**, 7, b g Vaguely Noble—Bronzed Goddess (USA) **Mr Gain Partnership**
9 **LATE SHIFT**, 5, ch g Night Shift (USA)—Mrs Cullumbine **Mr M. J. Perkins**
10 **LET YOU KNOW (IRE)**, 6, b m Prince Regent (FR)—More Wise **The Full Brochure Partnership**
11 **LYPHARD'S FABLE (USA)**, 5, b g Al Nasr (FR)—Affirmative Fable (USA) **Mrs G. C. McFerran**
12 **MOBILE MESSENGER (NZ)**, 8, b g Ring The Bell (NZ)—Sleepy Slipper (NZ) **Mr A. E. Dean**
13 **NEWTON POINT**, 7, b g Blakeney—Assertive (USA) **PPS Racing Partnership**
14 **OTTER PRINCE**, 7, b g Riberetto—Saintly Princess **Mr M. R. C. Opperman**
15 **SABEEL**, 6, ch m Local Suitor (USA)—River Reem (USA) **Mr Peter Slip**
16 **SIMON JOSEPH**, 9, b br g Tower Walk—Lady Bess **Mrs G. C. McFerran**
17 **STUNNING STUFF**, 11, b g Boreen (FR)—Mayfield Grove **Mr Giles Gleadell**
18 **THATS THE LIFE**, 11, ch g Wolverlife—Culleenamore **Mr T. R. George**

Other Owners: Mr J. S. Cullis, Mr Edward Farquhar, Mr R. M. Fleming, Capt J. A. George, Mrs Sarah Gleadell, Miss C. Pegna, Mr E. W. Pegna, Mr Alex Snow, Dr M. Stoppard, Mr Mark Stroyan, Mr C. N. Walker.

238   MR J. T. GIFFORD, Findon

Postal: **The Downs, Findon, Worthing, W. Sussex, BN14 0RR.**
Phone: **FINDON (01903) 872226 FAX (01903) 877232**

1 **ANNIO CHILONE**, 10, b g Touching Wood (USA)—Alpine Alice **Miss J. Semple**
2 **ARMALA**, 11, ch g Deep Run—Bardicate **Mrs C. Houston**
3 **AROUND THE HORN**, 9, b br g Strong Gale—Tou Wan **Pell-mell Partners**
4 **AS DES CARRES (FR)**, 9, b g Le Pontet (FR)—Belle Nonataise (FR) **Mr Claude Cohen**
5 **BLUNDSAM BOY**, 6, ch g Celtic Cone—Be Spartan **Sir Christopher Wates**
6 **BOARDROOM SHUFFLE (IRE)**, 5, b g Executive Perk—Eurotin **Mr A. D. Weller**

MR J. T. GIFFORD—continued

7 **BOLLINGER**, 10, ch g Balinger—Jolly Regal **Mr W. E. Gale**
8 **BRADBURY STAR**, 11, b g Torus—Ware Princess **Mr James Campbell**
9 **BRAVE HIGHLANDER (IRE)**, 8, b g Sheer Grit—Deerpark Rose **Mr S. N. J. Embiricos**
10 **BRIEF GALE**, 9, b m Strong Gale—Lucky Chesnut **Mrs Carrie Zetter-Wells**
11 **BUCKSHOT (IRE)**, 8, b g Le Moss—Buckfast Lass **Mr B. M. Wootton**
12 **BUCK WILLOW**, 12, b g Kambalda—Da Capo **Mrs S. N. J. Embiricos**
13 **CIPRIANI QUEEN (IRE)**, 6, b m Seattle Dancer (USA)—Justsayno (USA) **Tor Royal Racing Club**
14 **CORSEWALL POINT (IRE)**, 5, b g Corvaro (USA)—Ross Maid **Mrs S. N. J. Embiricos**
15 **CYTHERE**, 12, gr g Le Soleil—Vinotino **Mr Ken Carr**
16 **DEEP SENSATION**, 11, ch g Deep Run—Bannow Bay **Mr R. F. Eliot**
17 **DENVER BAY**, 9, b g Julio Mariner—Night Action **Mr Bill Naylor**
18 **FOODBROKER STAR (IRE)**, 6, gr g Roselier (FR)—Stormy Breeze **Food Brokers Ltd**
19 **FRENCH CHARMER**, 11, b g Beau Charmeur (FR)—Shreelane **Mr H. T. Pelham**
20 **GENERAL JACKIE (IRE)**, 6, b g Supreme Leader—Carry On Jackie **Michael Jackson Bloodstock Ltd**
21 **GENTLE BREEZE (IRE)**, 4, b f Strong Gale—Truo's Last **Mr D. Trangmar**
22 **GIVUS A CALL (IRE)**, 6, ch g Callernish—Theinthing **Mr T. Benfield and Mr W. Brown**
23 **GLITTER ISLE (IRE)**, 6, gr g Roselier (FR)—Decent Dame **Mrs Timothy Pilkington**
24 **GOOD CALL (IRE)**, 7, b br g Callernish—Even Doogles **Mr R. F. Eliot**
25 **GROOVING (IRE)**, 7, b g Callernish—Sams Money **Mrs T. Brown**
26 **HEADWIND (IRE)**, 5, b g Strong Gale—Lady In Red **Pell-mell Partners**
27 **'IGGINS (IRE)**, 6, br g Strong Gale—Gale Flash **Peli-mell Partners**
28 **IT'S A GEM**, 7, ch g Funny Man—Seed Pearl **Capt F. Tyrwhitt-Drake**
29 **JAKES JUSTICE (IRE)**, 5, b g Jolly Jake (NZ)—Flachra's Kumar **D. and M. Evans**
30 **JUST 'N ACE (IRE)**, 5, b g Bustomi—Belace **Mrs Joseph Abensur**
31 **KATABATIC**, 13, br g Strong Gale—Garravogue **Pell-mell Partners**
32 **LAGHAM LAD**, 7, b g Don't Forget Me—Sweet Eliane **Mrs Sue Addington-Smith**
33 **LIVELY KNIGHT (IRE)**, 7, b g Remainder Man—Love The Irish **Mr A. D. Weller**
34 **LORD ROOBLE (IRE)**, 5, b g Jolly Jake (NZ)—Missing Note **The Findon Partnership**
35 **MAESTRO PAUL**, 10, b g Petorius—Muligatawny **Mr H. T. Pelham**
36 **MAJOR SUMMIT (IRE)**, 7, b br g Callernish—Bramble Hatch **Mr A. D. Weller**
37 **MANDYS MANTINO**, 6, br g Neltino—Mandy's Melody **Mr John Plackett**
38 **MARCHIES MAGIC**, 6, b g Ballacashtal (CAN)—Marchuna **The Marchuna Partnership**
39 **MARIUS (IRE)**, 6, b g Cyrano de Bergerac—Nesreen **Mrs Anthony Andrews**
40 **MR FELIX**, 6, b g Camden Town—Mohila **Felix Rosenstiel's Widow & Son**
41 **MR JERVIS (IRE)**, 7, b g M Double M (USA)—Amorosa (GER) **Felix Rosenstiel's Widow & Son**
42 **MR PERCY (IRE)**, 5, ch g John French—Rathvilly Flier **Felix Rosenstiel's Widow & Son**
43 **MY WIZARD**, 9, b g Ile de Bourbon (USA)—Palace Tor **Mrs Angela Brodie**
44 **NASONE (IRE)**, 5, b g Nearly A Nose (USA)—Skateaway **Mr John Plackett**
45 **NONE STIRRED (IRE)**, 6, b g Supreme Leader—Double Wrapped **Mr C. Frewin**
46 **NO PAIN NO GAIN (IRE)**, 8, ch g Orchestra—Clarrie **The Marvellous Partnership**
47 **ONE MORE MAN (IRE)**, 5, b g Remainder Man—Pampered Sally **Mr A. J. Ilsley**
48 **OVER THE POLE**, 9, b g Cruise Missile—Arctic Lee **Pell-mell Partners**
49 **PA D'OR (USA)**, 6, ch g Slew O' Gold (USA)—Padelia **The Peoples Express Partnership**
50 **POORS WOOD**, 9, b g Martinmas—Lyaaric **Mr A. D. Weller**
51 **QUAFF (IRE)**, 6, b g Buckskin (FR)—Raheen Pearl **Mr A. D. Weller**
52 **RAINBOW CASTLE**, 9, b g Le Moss—Dont Rock **Findon Cricket Racing Club**
53 **REDEEMYOURSELF (IRE)**, 7, b g Royal Fountain—Reve Clair **Mrs T. Brown**
54 **ROWAN HEIGHTS**, 5, b m Idiot's Delight—Be Spartan **Sir Christopher Wates**
55 **ROYAL RAVEN (IRE)**, 5, b g Castle Keep—Decent Dame **Mr A. D. Weller**
56 **RUN HENRY RUN (IRE)**, 6, b g Henbit (USA)—Run Piggy Run **Mrs John Shipley**
57 **RUN UP THE FLAG**, 9, ch g Deep Run—Trianqo **Pell-mell Partners**
58 **SAFEGLIDE (IRE)**, 6, b h Mandalus—Snowey Arctic **P. H. Betts (Holdings) Ltd**
59 **SAN FERNANDO**, 10, b g Bulldozer—Burren Orchid **Mrs S. N. J. Embiricos**
60 **SENDAI**, 10, b m Le Moss—Dark Harbour **Mrs M. N. Tufnell**
61 **SPUFFINGTON**, 8, b g Sula Bula—Pita **Mr Julian Clopet**
62 **STRONG PALADIN (IRE)**, 5, b g Strong Gale—Kalanshoe **Mrs Angela Brodie**
63 **SUGAR HILL (IRE)**, 6, b g Mister Lord (USA)—Beautys Belle **Mrs Timothy Pilkington**
64 **SUPREME KELLYCARRA (IRE)**, 5, b m Supreme Leader—Vamble **Littlejohn Tyres Ltd**
65 **THE WIDGET MAN**, 10, b g Callernish—Le Tricolore Token **Mr A. Ilsley**
66 **TOP JAVALIN (NZ)**, 9, ch g Veloso (NZ)—Buena Vista (AUS) **Mrs V. Thum**

MR J. T. GIFFORD—continued

67 **VINTAGE CLARET**, 7, gr g Funny Man—Vinotino **Mrs J. F. Hall**
68 **WEE WINDY (IRE)**, 7, b g Cheval—Vulrain **Mr W. E. Gale**
69 **WELSH COTTAGE**, 9, b g Balinger—Sunny Cottage **Parafix Tapes & Conversions Ltd**
70 **WYLAM**, 9, b g What A Guest—Wish You Wow **Mrs J. S. Wootton**
71 **YORKSHIRE GALE**, 10, br g Strong Gale—Mio Slipper **Mr Bill Naylor**

Other Owners: Mrs Joseph Abensur, Mrs Sue Addington-Smith, Mr A. G. Baker, Mr Jon Baldwin, Mrs J. A. Barrett, Mr S. P. Barrett, Mr J. Bayer, Mr E. Benfield, Mr G. H. L. Bird, Mr W. J. Brown, Mr Ken Carr, Mr Nigel Chamberlain, Mr J. Chromiak, Mr G. K. Duncan, Mr J. Dyer, Mr R. F. Eliot, Mrs D. J. Evans, Ms M. Evans, Mr Martin Fletcher, Food Brokers Ltd, Mrs J. T. Gifford, Mr Richard Gilder, Mr Raymond Anderson Green, Mr Jeremy Hancock, Mr S. Hurst, Mr R. J. Kershaw, Mr M. J. Marchant, Michael Jackson Bloodstock Ltd, Mr H. T. Pelham, Mr D. F. Pengelly, Mrs K. M. Pengelly, Mr T. J. Rawlings, Mrs Jackie Reip, Miss J. Semple, Mr B. T. Stewart-Brown, Mr N. F. Tebbutt, The Marchuna Partnership, Tor Royal Racing Club, Mr T. F. Tremlett, Mr T. F. Villiers-Smith, Mr R. C. Watts, Mr Ian Fenton White, Mr B. M. Wootton, Mrs Carrie Zetter-Wells.

Jockey (NH): P Hide (10-0).

Conditional: L Aspell (9-9), W Greatrex (9-7).

Amateur: Mr P O'Keeffe (10-4).

239   MR J. A. GLOVER, Worksop

Postal: **Pinewood Stables, Carburton, Worksop, Notts, S80 3BT.**
Phone: **WORKSOP (01909) 475425 (OFFICE) 475962 (HOUSE)**

1 **ALUMIA**, 4, b g Domynsky— **Lord Crawshaw**
2 **ALZOOMO (IRE)**, 4, b g Alzao (USA)—Fandangerina (USA) **Mr L. A. Jackson**
3 **ARC LAMP**, 10, b g Caerleon (USA)—Dazzling Light **Mr B. Bruce**
4 **ATHERTON GREEN (IRE)**, 6, ch g Shy Groom (USA)—Primacara **Atherton and Green**
5 **BROUGHTON'S PRIDE (IRE)**, 5, b m Superpower—French Quarter **Mrs Janet Morris**
6 **CLIFTON FOX**, 4, b c Deploy—Loveskate (USA) **P. and S. Partnership**
7 **COGENT**, 12, b g Le Bavard (FR)—Cottstown Breeze **Pell-mell Partners**
8 **CROFT POOL**, 5, b g Crofthall—Blackpool Belle **Countrywide Classics Limited**
9 **DISSENTOR (IRE)**, 4, b g Dancing Dissident (USA)—Helen's Dynasty **Mr Brian T. Eastick**
10 **KALAMATA**, 4, ch c Kalaglow—Good Try **Mr B. H. Farr**
11 **KIVETON TYCOON (IRE)**, 7, b g Last Tycoon—Zillionaire (USA) **K. P. H. (Equine) Ltd**
12 4, Ch c Kind of Hush—Light Your Fire **Lord Crawshaw**
13 **MAJOR YAASI (USA)**, 6, b g Arctic Tern (USA)—Dimant Rose (USA) **P. and S. Partnership**
14 **RAMBO'S HALL**, 11, b g Crofthall—Murton Crags **Mr B. Dixon**
15 **SCEPTICAL**, 8, b g Idiot's Delight—Lavilla **Mr David Jenkins**
16 **SOUPERFICIAL**, 5, gr g Petong—Duck Soup **Mr M. G. Ridley**
17 **TAKE THE LAST**, 6, b g Petoski—Latakia **Mr Michael F. Maguire**

THREE-YEAR-OLDS

18 **CARBURTON**, b c Rock City—Arminda **Mr B. H. Farr**
19 **LADY ECLAT**, b f Nomination—Romantic Saga **The Robin Hood Connection**
20 **MERCURY (IRE)**, b g Contract Law (USA)—Monrovia (FR)
21 **PENYGARN GUV'NOR**, b g Governor General—Alumia **M. G. Ridley Partnership**
22 **TOTAL PEACE (IRE)**, b c Soviet Lad (USA)—Que Tranquila **Total (Bloodstock) Ltd**

TWO-YEAR-OLDS

23 B f 8/3 Terimon—Arminda (Blakeney) **Mr B. H. Farr**
24 **LEGEND OF ARAGON**, b f 3/3 Aragon—Legendary Dancer (Shareef Dancer (USA)) **Mr S. J. Beard**
25 B c 5/3 Risk Me (FR)—Lompoa (Lomond (USA)) **Mr J. A. Glover**

MR J. A. GLOVER—continued

26 Ch c 9/5 Mystiko (USA)—South Shore (Caerleon (USA)) **Mr B. H. Farr**
27 B c 26/2 Full Extent (USA)—Sylvan Song (Song) **Mr J. A. Glover**
28 Ch c 12/5 Interrex (CAN)—Tricata (Electric) **Mr J. A. Glover**
29 B c 7/6 Timeless Times (USA)—Uptown Girl (Caruso) **Mr J. A. Glover**
30 B f 27/4 Tina's Pet—Villacana (Lord Gayle (USA)) **Mr J. A. Glover**

Other Owners: Mr Paul Bacon, Bassetlaw Bloodstock Agency Ltd, Mrs J. A. Beckett, Mrs Judith Beckett, Mr Colin G. R. Booth, Mr J. Chromiak, Mr A. J. Coleman, Mr M. Dews, Mr Richard Gilder, Mrs S. Glover, Mr Keith Green, Mrs S. Jackson, Mr Jeffrey Newton, Mr John Pumfrey, Mr Russell Rogers, Mr P. B. Short, Mr Gary J. Watson, Mr Paul Wheeler, Mr Richard C. Williams, Mr Noel Wilson.

Jockeys (Flat): M Birch (w.a.), Stephen Williams (8-4).

Jockeys (NH): T Reed, A S Smith.

Lady Rider: V Appleby.

240   MR J. S. GOLDIE, Glasgow

Postal: **Libo Hill Farm, Uplawmoor, Glasgow, G78 4BA.**

Phone: **(01505) 850212**

 1 **AUNTY NESSIE,** 4, b f Destroyer—Oorain Lass **Mr J. S. Goldie**
 2 **BRIGHT DESTINY,** 5, br g Destroyer—Bright Suggestion **Mr J. S. Goldie**
 3 **CARIBBEAN SURFER (USA),** 7, b g Summing (USA)—Caribbean Surfing (USA) **Mr M. Sawers**
 4 **CYMBALO,** 5, ch g Sharpo—Cynomis **Mr M. Sawers**
 5 **HARRKEN HEIGHTS (IRE),** 4, b f Belmez (USA)—In High Spirits **Mr M. Sawers**
 6 **KALKO,** 7, b g Kalaglow—Salchow **Mr J. S. Goldie**
 7 **KEEP BATTLING,** 6, b g Hard Fought—Keep Mum **Mr J. S. Goldie**
 8 **MARTHA BUCKLE,** 7, br m Lochnager—Bamdoro **Paterson's of Saturland Farm**
 9 **MR SLOAN,** 6, b g Destroyer—Bright Suggestion **Mr J. S. Goldie**
10 **NICHOLAS PLANT,** 7, ch g Nicholas Bill—Bustilly **Mrs M. F. Paterson**
11 **PHOTINIA,** 11, b g Tender King—Permutation **Mr M. Sawers**
12 **SECONDS AWAY,** 5, b g Hard Fought—Keep Mum **Mr J. S. Goldie**
13 **SYLVAN CELEBRATION,** 5, b m Sylvan Express—Footstool **Mr J. S. Goldie**
14 **TEEJAY'N'AITCH (IRE),** 4, b g Maelstrom Lake—Middle Verde (USA) **Mr J. S. Goldie**
15 **THISONESFORALICE,** 8, b g Lochnager—Bamdoro **Mrs Alice S. Goldie**
16 **VALIANT DASH,** 10, b g Valiyar—Dame Ashfield **Mr L. W. Dunbar**

THREE-YEAR-OLDS

17 B f Destroyer—Bright Suggestion **Mr J. S. Goldie**
18 Br f Destroyer—Oorain Lass **Mr J. S. Goldie**

TWO-YEAR-OLDS

19 B g Destroyer—Bright Suggestion (Magnate) **Mr J. S. Goldie**
20 Ch g Destroyer—Oorain Lass (Lord Nelson) **Mr J. S. Goldie**

Other Owners: Gm Engineering, Mr George Murray, Mrs Kathleen Murray, Mr Andrew Paterson, Mr Anthony Paterson, Mr Neal Paterson.

Jockeys (NH): F Leahy (9-7), Fraser Perratt (9-7, w.a.).

Amateur: Mr Ken Santana (9-2).

241   MR ROBERT H GOLDIE, Kilmarnock

Postal: **Harpercroft, Old Loans Road, Dundonald, Kilmarnock, KA2 9DD.**
Phone: **TROON (01292) 317222 FAX (01292) 313585**

1 **EASTER OATS**, 9, b m Oats—Ice Lass **Mrs R. H. Goldie**
2 **GLINT OF AYR**, 6, b m Glint of Gold—Iyamski (USA) **Mr Robert H. Goldie**
3 **JAVAMAN**, 4, b g Homo Sapien—Brownhill Lass **Mr W. McIntosh**
4 4, B g Torus—Mashin Time **Mrs R. H. Goldie**
5 **MISS CAVO**, 5, b m Ovac (ITY)—Ice Lass **Mrs R. H. Goldie**
6 **SUNY ZETA**, 12, b m Sunyboy—Blue Zeta **Mrs R. H. Goldie**
7 **THOMAS THE TANK**, 12, ch g Palm Track—Galah Bird **Mr Robert H. Goldie**

THREE-YEAR-OLDS

8 B g Primitive Rising (USA)—Ice Lass **Mrs R. H. Goldie**
9 B g Primitive Rising (USA)—Mashin Time **Mrs R. H. Goldie**

TWO-YEAR-OLDS

10 B f 26/5 Le Bavard (FR)—Ice Lass (Heroic Air) **Mrs R. H. Goldie**

Amateur: Professor S Love (10-7).

242   MR S. GOLLINGS, Louth

Postal: **Highfield House, Scamblesby, Louth, Lincs, LN11 9XT.**
Phone: **PHONE & FAX (01507) 343204**

1 **AUGUSTAN**, 5, b g Shareef Dancer (USA)—Krishnagar **Mr Nilesh Unadkat**
2 **CHRISTIAN FLIGHT (IRE)**, 7, b m Fayruz—Opening Flight **Mr Derek G. M. Holland**
3 **CLYDE GODDESS (IRE)**, 5, b m Scottish Reel—Clymene **Mr R. L. Houlton**
4 **DR CALIGARI (IRE)**, 4, b g My Generation—Mallabee **Mr Dave Mager, Mrs Sue Mager**
5 **EAST BARNS (IRE)**, 8, gr g Godswalk (USA)—Rocket Lass **Northern Bloodstock Racing**
6 **EMBEZZLER**, 4, b g Emarati (USA)—Double Touch (FR) **Mr Ralph Taylor**
7 **ENSHARP (USA)**, 10, b g Sharpen Up—Lulworth Cove **Mrs Jayne M. Gollings**
8 **IKIS GIRL**, 5, ch m Silver Hawk (USA)—Jealous One (USA) **Mr Ian K. I. Stewart**
9 **IN TRUTH**, 8, ch g Dreams To Reality (USA)—Persian Express **Mrs E. Houlton**
10 **IT IS NOW**, 4, ch g Blow The Whistle—Final Game **The Sheikh Mahands Partnership**
11 **NEW INN**, 5, b g Petoski—Pitroyal **Mr Ian K. I. Stewart**
12 **PASJA (IRE)**, 5, b m Posen (USA)—Camogie **Mr A. N. Barrett**
13 **VASILIEV**, 8, b g Sadler's Wells (USA)—Poquito Queen (CAN) **Mr R. L. Houlton**
14 **WE'RE JOKEN**, 4, b f Statoblest—Jay Gee Ell
15 **ZIPPY**, 9, ch g Lighter—Ballaquine **Mr A. H. French**

THREE-YEAR-OLDS

16 **BACKTIARI**, b g Backchat (USA)—Tiernee Quintana **Mr G. D. Dalrymple**
17 **ENIGMA BELL**, b c Rambo Dancer (CAN)—Skelton **Mr Ian K. I. Stewart**
18 **LORD HAASHIM**, b g Scorpio (FR)—Bantel Bouquet **Mr Nilesh Unadkat**
19 **MY CHEROKEE**, b f Warrshan (USA)—Conquista **Mrs Angela E. Allen**
20 **TRUTHFULLY**, ch f Weldnaas (USA)—Persian Express **Mrs E. Houlton**

TWO-YEAR-OLDS

21 **KHAIRUN NISAA**, b f 9/2 Never So Bold—Sea Clover (IRE) (Ela-Mana-Mou) **Mr Nilesh Unadkat**
22 B c 12/4 Terimon—Onika (Great Nephew)
23 B f 25/4 Emarati (USA)—Ration of Passion (Camden Town)
24 Ch f 1/3 Anshan—Santee Sioux (Dancing Brave (USA))
25 **SUPREME MAIMOON**, b c 27/4 Jareer (USA)—Princess Zena (Habitat) **Mr Nilesh Unadkat**

MR S. GOLLINGS—continued

Other Owners: Mr C. S. Bagley, Mr A. Crookes, Mr E. Goodall, Mr John Green, Mr D. Hanby, Mr Doug Kirk, Mrs Rita Taylor, Mr Bob Worth.

Jockey (Flat): Stephen Davies.

Jockeys (NH): A Dobbin, R Dunwoody, A Maguire, A S Smith.

Apprentice: Samantha-Jayne Rooks (8-0).

Lady Rider: Mrs Jayne M Gollings (9-0).

243   MRS A. C. D. GOODFELLOW, Earlston

Postal: **Leadervale House, Earlston, Berwickshire, TD4 6AJ.**

Phone: **EARLSTON (01896) 849541 MOBILE (0831) 133899 FAX (01896) 849541**

1 **CEILIDH BOY**, 10, b g Oats—Charlotte's Festival **Mrs J. D. Goodfellow**
2 **CHEAP KNIGHT (USA)**, 5, ch g Spend A Buck—Courtly Courier (USA) **Mrs J. D. Goodfellow**
3 **DEIRDRE'S PRIDE (IRE)**, 6, ch g Duky—Princess Mine **Mr J. D. Goodfellow**
4 **KILCOLGAN**, 9, ch g Le Bavard (FR)—Katula **Mr J. D. Goodfellow**
5 **MARY'S CASE (IRE)**, 6, b g Taufan (USA)—Second Service **Mrs J. D. Goodfellow**
6 **POLLY CINDERS**, 5, gr m Alias Smith (USA)—Political Prospect **Mr J. D. Goodfellow**
7 **STAN'S YOUR MAN**, 6, b g Young Man (FR)—Charlotte's Festival **Mrs J. D. Goodfellow**
8 **TOUGH TEST (IRE)**, 6, ch g Lancastrian—Take Beating **Mr J. D. Goodfellow**

Jockey (NH): B Storey.

244   MR J. H. M. GOSDEN, Newmarket

Postal: **Stanley House Stables, Bury Road, Newmarket, Suffolk, CB8 7DF.**

Phone: **(01638) 669944 FAX (01638) 669922**

1 **BAKERS' GATE (USA)**, 4, b br c Danzig (USA)—Alydaress (USA)
2 **CAPIAS (USA)**, 5, b h Alleged (USA)—Smooth Bore (USA)
3 **DAUNT**, 4, b c Darshaan—Minute Waltz
4 **DECORATED HERO**, 4, b g Warning—Bequeath (USA)
5 **FLEMENSFIRTH (USA)**, 4, b c Alleged (USA)—Etheldreda (USA)
6 **INQUISITOR (USA)**, 4, b c Alleged (USA)—Imperturbable Lady (CAN)
7 **ISTABRAQ (IRE)**, 4, b c Sadler's Wells (USA)—Betty's Secret (USA)
8 **LEAP FOR JOY**, 4, ch f Sharpo—Humble Pie
9 **PARTHIAN SPRINGS**, 5, b h Sadler's Wells (USA)—Princess Pati
10 **PRESENTING**, 4, br c Mtoto—d'Azy
11 **TAMURE (IRE)**, 4, b c Sadler's Wells (USA)—Three Tails

THREE-YEAR-OLDS

12 **AERLEON JANE**, ch f Caerleon (USA)—An Empress (USA)
13 **ALRAYYIH (USA)**, b br c Mr Prospector (USA)—Cheval Volant (USA)
14 **ALREEH (IRE)**, b f Priolo (USA)—Fleeting (USA)
15 **ALTAMURA (USA)**, b f El Gran Senor (USA)—Narwala
16 **AMBASSADRESS (USA)**, br f Alleged (USA)—Ancient Regime (USA)
17 **ANNABA (IRE)**, ch f In The Wings—Anna Matrushka
18 **APPLE MUSASHI**, b c Never So Bold—Third Movement
19 **ARCTIID (USA)**, b br c Silver Hawk (USA)—Arctic Eclipse (USA)

MR J. H. M. GOSDEN—continued

20 **ARKTIKOS (IRE)**, b c Sadler's Wells (USA)—Arctic Heroine (USA)
21 **ASH GLADE**, ch f Nashwan (USA)—Flit (USA)
22 **ATLANTIC STORM**, b c Dowsing (USA)—Tatouma (USA)
23 **ATTARIKH (IRE)**, b c Mujtahid (USA)—Silly Tune (IRE)
24 **AWAAMIR**, b f Green Desert (USA)—Kadwah (USA)
25 **BADIUS (IRE)**, b f Sadler's Wells (USA)—Bay Shade (USA)
26 **BADRI (USA)**, b c Topsider (USA)—Hedonic (USA)
27 **BENEFICENT (FR)**, b c Generous (IRE)—Phaleria (USA)
28 **BESWEETOME**, b f Mtoto—Actraphane
29 **CANYON CREEK (IRE)**, b c Mr Prospector (USA)—River Memories (USA)
30 **CATUMBELLA**, ch f Diesis—Benguela (USA)
31 **CHIRICO (USA)**, b c Danzig (USA)—Colour Chart (USA)
32 **COMMITTAL (IRE)**, b c Lycius (USA)—Just Cause
33 **DANCING DEBUT**, b f Polar Falcon (USA)—Exclusive Virtue (USA)
34 **DARLING FLAME (USA)**, b f Capote (USA)—My Darling One (USA)
35 **DAYDREAMER (USA)**, b c Alleged (USA)—Stardusk (USA)
36 **DERBY DARBAK (USA)**, b c Lyphard (USA)—Joy Returned (USA)
37 **DIAMOND DANCE (IRE)**, b f Sadler's Wells (USA)—Diamond Field (USA)
38 **DOMAK AMAAM (IRE)**, b c Dominion—La Courant (USA)
39 **DUCHESSE DE BERRI (USA)**, ch f Diesis—Berry Berry Good (USA)
40 **DUEL AT DAWN**, ch c Nashwan (USA)—Gayane
41 **EASY NUMBER (USA)**, ch f Easy Goer (USA)—Treizieme (USA)
42 **ELASHATH (USA)**, b c El Gran Senor (USA)—Gorgeoso (USA)
43 **ELSALEET (USA)**, b br c Storm Cat (USA)—Blushing Redhead (USA)
44 **ENRICHED (IRE)**, b f Generous (IRE)—Embla
45 **ESQUILINE (USA)**, ch f Gone West (USA)—Ville Eternelle (USA)
46 **GALB ALASAD (IRE)**, b c Royal Academy (USA)—Soleiade
47 **GREENSTEAD (USA)**, b c Green Dancer (USA)—Evening Air (USA)
48 **HERODIAN (USA)**, b br c Housebuster (USA)—Try Something New (USA)
49 **HIGHLY FINISHED (IRE)**, b c Top Ville—Lustre (USA)
50 **INTIDAB (USA)**, b c Phone Trick (USA)—Alqwani (USA)
51 **INTRODUCING**, b f Mtoto—d'Azy
52 **IRONHEART**, b c Lycius (USA)—Inshirah (USA)
53 **KABALEVSKY (USA)**, b c Nureyev (USA)—Beautiful Aly (USA)
54 **KARAMZIN (USA)**, ch f Nureyev (USA)—Kartajana
55 **KERRY RING**, b f Sadler's Wells (USA)—Kerrera
56 **KITTEN TRICKS (USA)**, b f Storm Cat (USA)—Tricky Game (USA)
57 **L'AMI LOUIS (USA)**, ch c Easy Goer (USA)—Jadana
58 **LIEFLING (USA)**, b f Alleged (USA)—Mata Cara
59 **LITUUS (USA)**, gr c El Gran Senor (USA)—Liturgism (USA)
60 **LORD OF MEN**, ch c Groom Dancer (USA)—Upper Strata
61 **MAIDEN CASTLE**, b c Darshaan—Noble Destiny
62 **MALLOOH**, gr c Niniski (USA)—Kalisha
63 **MASHMOUM**, ch f Lycius (USA)—Flaming Rose (USA)
64 **MEDIA STAR (USA)**, b c Lear Fan (USA)—Media Luna
65 **MISKY BAY**, b c Shareef Dancer (USA)—Rain Date
66 **MISRULE (USA)**, b f Miswaki (USA)—Crowning Ambition (USA)
67 **MUHANDIS**, b c Persian Bold—Night At Sea
68 **ONEFORTHEDITCH (USA)**, gr f With Approval (CAN)—Wee Dram (USA)
69 **POLISH LEGION**, b c Polish Precedent (USA)—Crystal Bright
70 **POMMARD (IRE)**, b c Darshaan—Pont-Aven
71 **RAHEEFA (USA)**, b br f Riverman (USA)—Oogie Poogie (USA)
72 **RESOUNDER (USA)**, b c Explodent (USA)—Rub Al Khali (USA)
73 **RETICENT**, b c Sadler's Wells (USA)—Shy Princess (USA)
74 **RING OF MUSIC**, b f Sadler's Wells (USA)—Glorious Song (CAN)
75 **RIVER CAPTAIN (USA)**, ch c Riverman (USA)—Katsura (USA)
76 **SACHO (IRE)**, b c Sadler's Wells (USA)—Oh So Sharp
77 **SANDHILL (IRE)**, b f Danehill (USA)—Sand Grouse (USA)
78 **SANTILLANA (USA)**, ch c El Gran Senor (USA)—Galway (FR)
79 **SAWA-ID**, b br c Anshan—Bermuda Lily

MR J. H. M. GOSDEN—continued

80 **SHANTOU (USA)**, b c Alleged (USA)—Shaima (USA)
81. **SHEMOZZLE (IRE)**, b f Shirley Heights—Reactress (USA)
82 **SHOSHONE**, ch f Be My Chief (USA)—Bridestones
83 **STRAZO (IRE)**, b c Alzao (USA)—Ministra (USA)
84 **SUMMER BEAUTY**, ch f Cadeaux Genereux—Try The Duchess
85 **TAHARQA (IRE)**, b c Sadler's Wells (USA)—Too Phar
86 **TEA COLONY (USA)**, b br f Pleasant Colony (USA)—Tea At Five (USA)
87 **TRIPLE LEAP**, b c Sadler's Wells (USA)—Three Tails
88 **TUMI (USA)**, ch f Diesis—Carotene (CAN)
89 **TURBULENT**, b f Rainbow Quest (USA)—Storm Weaver (USA)
90 **TWO TO TANGO (IRE)**, ch f Anshan—Marie de Sologne
91 **VOODOO ROCKET**, ch f Lycius (USA)—Vestal Flame
92 **WASHINGTON REEF (USA)**, b c Seattle Dancer (USA)—Broken Wave
93 **WATERWAVE (USA)**, ch c Irish River (FR)—Wajna (USA)
94 **WEST DEVON (USA)**, b f Gone West (USA)—Devon Diva (USA)
95 **WOLLSTONECRAFT (IRE)**, b f Danehill (USA)—Ivory Thread (USA)
96 **WOOD VINE (USA)**, ch f Woodman (USA)—Massaraat (USA)
97 **ZEHOOR ALSAFA (USA)**, b f Wild Again (USA)—Legion d'Honneur (USA)

TWO-YEAR-OLDS

98 Ch c 21/4 Persian Bold—Anjuli
99 B c 8/4 Sadler's Wells—Arctic Heroine
100 B f 5/5 El Prado—Aspara
101 Ch f 11/3 Generous—Bareilly
102 **BENNY THE DIP (USA)**, br c 25/3 Silver Hawk—Rascal Rascal
103 B c 8/2 Kris—Bonne Ile
104 **BOUT**, br f 4/2 Batshoof—Reyah
105 B c 3/5 Shareef Dancer—Bright Crocus
106 B c 21/2 Alzao—Brilleaux
107 B f 20/3 Defensive Play—Brisk Waters
108 B c 27/1 Explodent—Caithness
109 B f 8/3 Lear Fan—Carya
110 Ch f 3/2 Woodman—Catopetl
111 Ch c 28/1 Rainbow Quest—Cattermole
112 **CEANOTHUS**, ch f 2/4 Bluebird—Golden Bloom
113 B f 12/3 Machiavellian—Chief Ornament
114 B c 13/5 Sadler's Wells—Cocotte
115 B c 17/3 Lear Fan—Connecting Link
116 Ch f 18/3 Kris—Dance Machine
117 Br f 7/5 Caerleon—Embla
118 **ENCORE**, b f 19/1 Be My Guest—Lucia Tarditi
119 Br f 8/3 Riverman—Equate
120 B c 16/3 Red Ransom—Fan Mail
121 B f 9/4 Woodman—Fateful
122 **FINE QUILL**, ch f 3/3 Unfuwain—Quillotern
123 Br c 23/3 Caerleon—Flood
124 B c 17/4 Groom Dancer—Gold Bracelet
125 Ch f 13/5 Persian Bold—Good Policy
126 **HERITAGE**, b c 19/3 Danehill—Misty Halo
127 **HOME ALONE**, b c 18/2 Groom Dancer—Quiet Week-End
128 B f 2/3 Rainbow Quest—Idraak
129 Gr c 6/3 Alzao—Jazz
130 **KAFAF (USA)**, b f 30/4 Zilzal—Alqwani
131 **KARAWAN**, ch f 26/2 Kris—Sweetly
132 Ch c 29/4 Irish River—Katsura
133 **KHASSAH**, b f 14/3 Green Desert—Kadwah
134 B f 11/4 Sadler's Wells—Kissagram
135 **LADYBIRD**, b f 17/2 Polar Falcon—Classic Heights
136 B f 22/4 Lahib—La Romance
137 Ch f 19/3 Rahy—Late From Lunch

MR J. H. M. GOSDEN—continued

138 Ch c 3/2 Thatching—Loucoum
139 B f 13/4 Indian Ridge—Lunaire
140 B c 20/2 Darshaan—Lustre
141 MAFTOOL, ch c 2/3 Machiavellian—Majmu
142 Ch f 15/4 Storm Bird—Make Change
143 MAMALIK (USA), b c 23/2 Diesis—Have It Out
144 MARSUL (USA), b c 22/3 Cozzene—Beside
145 B c 25/1 Woodman—Mount Helena
146 B c 11/2 Diesis—Mystery Play
147 Ch f 21/3 Nashwan—Nadma
148 B c 20/3 Common Grounds—Nikki's Groom
149 B f 7/5 Sadler's Wells—Organza
150 B c 22/3 Polish Precedent—Outstandingly
151 Ch c 26/4 Caerleon—Ploy
152 Ch c 1/4 Indian Ridge—Red Rose Garden
153 B c 16/3 Alleged—Red Slippers
154 B c 13/3 Fairy King—Sable Lake
155 B c 5/4 Highest Honor—Samsova
156 B c 16/2 Danehill—Sand Grouse
157 SARAMAH (USA), ch f 21/3 Forty Niner—Cheval Volant
158 B c 5/2 Mr Prospector—Satin Flower
159 SEATTLE SWING, b f 2/3 Saddlers' Hall—Sweet Slew
160 B c 20/1 Darshaan—Shamshir
161 Br c 27/2 Storm Bird—Silver Clover
162 B c 15/5 Gone West—Social Column
163 SQUEAK, ch f 19/1 Selkirk—Santa Linda
164 B f 8/4 St Jovite—Sunday Best
165 Ch c 24/5 Machiavellian—Sweet Mover
166 THANKS, ch c 14/3 Persian Bold—Thakhayr
167 B c 22/2 Slip Anchor—Three Tails
168 Ch c 21/1 Pursuit Of Love—Trojan Crown
169 B f 8/4 Riverman—Trolley Song
170 B c 12/2 Fairy King—Undiscovered
171 Ch c 4/3 Polish Precedent—Upper Strata
172 B c 14/3 Primo Dominie—Valika
173 Ch c 12/1 Miswaki—Wellomond
174 B c 27/4 Persian Bold—Ziggy Belle

Jockey (Flat): L Dettori (8-4).

Owners: Sheikh Mohammed, Mr K. Abdulla, Mr Herbert Allen, Mr Doug Armitage, Mrs Alice Chandler, Cheveley Park Stud, Mr Nick Cowan, Mr Alan Gibson, Godolphin, Lady Harrison, Lord Hartington, Mr Kazuhiro Hasegawa, Mr Seisuke Hata, Hesmonds Stud, Highclere Thoroughbred Racing Ltd., Ms Rachel D. S. Hood, Mr Landon Knight, Mr Louis Lo, Mr Paul Locke, Sheikh Ahmed Al Maktoum, Mr Hamdan Al Maktoum, Sheikh Marwan Al Maktoum, Mr Mohammed Bin Hendi, Mr Mohammed Saeed, Mr R. Morgan-Jones, Mr Nabeel Mourad, Mr Rex Norton, Oak Cliff Foals of 1993 Plus 2 LLC, Platt Promotions, Mrs Snowden, Mr Anthony Speelman, Mr George Strawbridge, Mr Thomas P. Tathem, Mrs Shirley H. Taylor, Mrs C. A. Waters, Mr C. M. Watt, Mr Michael T. Willis, Mr Ronnie Wood.

245   MR N. A. GRAHAM, Newmarket

Postal: **Coronation Stables, Newmarket, Suffolk, CB8 9BB.**
Phone: **OFFICE (01638) 665202 FAX (01638) 667849**

1 ANASTINA, 4, ch f Thatching—Nikitina **Mr R. & Mrs A. Craddock**
2 BEST OF BOLD, 4, ch g Never So Bold—I'll Try **Mr Paul G. Jacobs**
3 CAVINA, 6, b m Ardross—Royal Yacht (USA) **Mr Paul G. Jacobs**
4 CRUMPTON HILL (IRE), 4, b g Thatching—Senane **Mr T. H. Chadney**
5 PLINTH, 5, b g Dowsing (USA)—Pedestal **Mr T. H. Chadney**

MR N. A. GRAHAM—continued

6 **RUSTY MUSKETEER**, 5, ch g Bustino—Mousquetade **Mr R. Greenwood**
7 **SIMAFAR (IRE)**, 5, b g Kahyasi—Sidama (FR) **Mr Paul G. Jacobs**
8 **TREHANE**, 4, b f Rock City—Trelissick **Mr B. H. March**

THREE-YEAR-OLDS

9 **BAILIWICK**, b g Dominion—Lady Barkley **Mrs Lesley Graham**
10 **BRIGHTER BYFAAH (IRE)**, ch g Kefaah (USA)—Bright Landing **Mr Rupert Hambro & Partners**
11 **BURJ**, b g Aragon—Aspark
12 **CONWY**, ch f Rock City—Degannwy **Mr James Miller**
13 **DESERT DUNES**, b c Unfuwain (USA)—Palm Springs **Bloomsbury Stud**
14 B c Nabeel Dancer (USA)—Fiddle-Faddle
15 **FIRBUR**, b g Be My Chief—La Masse **Mr Paul G. Jacobs**
16 **FURSAN (USA)**, b c Fred Astaire (USA)—Ancient Art (USA) **Mr Hamdan Al Maktoum**
17 **TAKE NOTE (IRE)**, b c Don't Forget Me—Verthumna **Mr T. H. Chadney**
18 **THRILLING DAY**, b f Groom Dancer (USA)—Pushoff (USA) **Bloomsbury Stud**

TWO-YEAR-OLDS

19 B c 20/4 Distinctly North—Bold Kate (Bold Lad (IRE)) **Mr G. Mazza**
20 Gr c 1/3 Pursuit Of Love—Crodelle (IRE) (Formidable (USA)) **Mr J. L. Moore**
21 **FAUNA (IRE)**, b f 15/3 Taufan (USA)—Labwa (USA) (Lyphard (USA)) **Lord Swaythling**
22 **HAMLEYS**, ch f 20/1 Superlative—Child's Play (USA) (Sharpen Up) **Bloomsbury Stud**
23 **JAZA**, b c 12/4 Pursuit Of Love—Nordica (Northfields (USA)) **Mr Hamdan Al Maktoum**
24 B f 2/4 Night Shift (USA)—Late Evening (USA) (Riverman (USA)) **Mr M. Scotney**
25 **MUTAHADETH**, ch c 9/3 Rudimentary (USA)—
                              Music In My Life (IRE) (Law Society (USA)) **Mr Hamdan Al Maktoum**
26 **PLEASURE BOAT**, ch c 18/5 Suave Dancer (USA)—Pilot (Kris) **Mr R. D. Hollingsworth**
27 **SALOME**, ch f 5/4 Risk Me (FR)—Dancing Belle (Dance In Time (CAN)) **Mrs Lesley Graham**
28 **SANDYSTONES**, b f 4/5 Selkirk (USA)—Sharanella (Shareef Dancer (USA))
29 B f 26/2 Common Grounds—Tasskeen (FR) (Lyphard (USA)) **Coronation Partnership**

Other Owners: Mr John T. Brown, Mr P. A. Deal, Mrs Janet Ford, Mrs S. Jay, Mrs Laura Jones, Mr J. Marett, Mr M. J. Silver, Sir John Swaine, Mr Michael Warner.

246   MR L. P. GRASSICK, Cheltenham

Postal: **Postlip Racing Stables, Winchcombe, Cheltenham, Glos. GL54 5AQ**
Phone: **(01242) 603124**

1 **ALPHA LEATHER**, 5, gr g Zambrano—Harvey's Choice **High Roost Racing**
2 **ARTFUL ARTHUR**, 10, b g Rolfe (USA)—Light of Zion **Mrs Pat Beck**
3 **BLACKGUARD (USA)**, 10, ch g Irish River (FR)—Principle (USA) **Mr D. W. Phipps & Mrs C. A. Davis**
4 **BROWN SAUCE (NZ)**, 10, b g Wolverton—Gold Leaf (NZ) **Mr J. A. T. de Giles**
5 **BUSINESS IS ROSIE**, 6, b m Derring Rose—Comedy Spring **Mr Richard Cook**
6 **CASTLE WARRIOR**, 9, b g Castle Keep—Christines Lady **Miss V. J. Paxton**
7 **FIGHT TO WIN (USA)**, 8, b g Fit To Fight (USA)—Spark of Life (USA) **Mr B. Partridge**
8 **HIGHTECH TOUCH**, 6, b g Sunley Builds—Caribs Love
9 **HUBERT**, 6, b g Rolfe (USA)—Pilicina **Mr L. H. Ballinger**
10 **INDIAN BAY**, 5, b h Chauve Souris—Jamra **High Roost Racing**
11 **MISS CRUSTY**, 8, gr m Belfort (FR)—Blue Empress **Mr L. H. Ballinger**

THREE-YEAR-OLDS

12 **GRAND FIASCO**, gr f Zambrano—Lady Crusty **Mr L. P. Grassick**
13 **POSTLIP ROYALE**, b f Zambrano—Wilhelmina Crusty **Mrs Pat Beck & Mr Alan Waller**

Other Owners: Mr J. Davies, Mr John English, Mrs P. H. Grassick, Mr John Whiffen, Mrs Pat Whiffen.

Amateur: J R Grassick (9-7).

247   MR M. J. GRASSICK, Curragh

Postal: **Fenpark Stables, Pollardstown, Curragh, Co. Kildare, Ireland**
Phone: **HOME (045) 436956 YARD (045) 434483 FAX (045) 434483**

1 CRYSTAL BIRD (IRE), 4, ch f Ela-Mana-Mou—Irish Bird (USA) Mrs H. Focke
2 FINAL REMINDER (IRE), 5, ch g Don't Forget Me—Pleasant Review (USA) Mrs S. Grassick
3 FLAUNT (IRE), 4, b g Persian Bold—Fuchsia Belle Mr Albert Finney
4 GLADIATORIAL (IRE), 4, b g Mazaad—Arena Mrs J. Magnier
5 HI-HANDSOME (IRE), 5, b g High Estate—Bonnie Bess P. X. Clarke
6 LESSONS LASS (IRE), 4, b f Doyoun—Badraya Mr Ken Campbell
7 MASCOT, 5, b m Mashhor Dancer (USA)—Kirby's Princess Mr R. Weiss
8 PROPITIOUS (IRE), 4, b f Doyoun—Northern Chance Mrs C. Grassick
9 5, B g Seclude—Rose Deer Mrs D. Fortune
10 SARAH BLUE (IRE), 6, b m Bob Back (USA)—Blue Lookout Mrs S. Grassick
11 SIR TRUE BLUE (IRE), 4, b c Bluebird (USA)—Very Sophisticated (USA) Mr J. Crowley
12 SONG FOR AFRICA (IRE), 5, b m Orchestra—Live Aid Mrs S. Grassick
13 STRAWBERRY BELLE (IRE), 5, b m Vision (USA)—Cuckoo Weir Mr B. Hartelust
14 THE KEEGSTER (IRE), 5, ch g Tate Gallery (USA)—Stapara Mr J. Crowley
15 VISTULA (IRE), 4, b f Posen (USA)—Tajniak (USA) Mrs S. Grassick

THREE-YEAR-OLDS

16 ARCHWAY BELLE (IRE), ch f Archway (IRE)—Quilting Mrs F. Prendergast
17 BELLFAN (IRE), b g Taufan (USA)—Fuchsia Belle Mr Albert Finney
18 DADDY'S HAT (IRE), b f Dancing Dissident (USA)—Hat And Gloves Reudi Weiss
19 FLAME OF ATHENS (IRE), b c Royal Academy (USA)—Flame of Tara Miss P. F. O'Kelly
20 JUNE BRILLY (IRE), b f Fayruz—Robinia (USA) Mrs C. Grassick
21 MY NIECE (IRE), b f Don't Forget Me—Bonny's Niece (FR) Mr M. J. Grassick
22 PICARD (IRE), b g Durgam (USA)—Miners Society Mrs D. Fortune
23 QUEEN'S MUSIC (USA), ch f Dixieland Band (USA)—Sticky Habit Mrs T. Pabst
24 REKONDO (IRE), b c Two Timing (USA)—Tuesday Morning Ricardo Sanz
25 RINCE ABHANN (IRE), b f Dancing Dissident (USA)—Ballysnip Mrs M. J. Grassick
26 B g Durgam (USA)—Rose Deer Mrs D. Fortune
27 SILKS OF THE FIELD (IRE), ch f Polish Patriot (USA)—Very Sophisticated (USA) Robert Bloomer
28 B f Posen (USA)—Singing Millie Mr C. O'Loughlin
29 SISKIN (IRE), b f Royal Academy (USA)—Maellen D. Corrigan
30 THE GENT (IRE), b c Fairy King (USA)—Mosaique Bleue P. X. Clarke

TWO-YEAR-OLDS

31 Ch f 12/4 Shalford (IRE)—Belle-Cote (Coquelin (USA)) Mrs C. Grassick
32 Ch c 23/4 Classic Music (USA)—Bengala (FR) (Hard To Beat) Mr Char Kar Sun
33 B f 16/2 Royal Academy (USA)—Dingle Bay (Petingo) Mrs M. J. Grassick
34 B f 29/4 Doyoun—Fanellan (Try My Best (USA)) Mr W. Kinsella
35 B f 27/4 Bob Back (USA)—Fuchsia Belle (Vision (USA)) Mr Albert Finney
36 B f 3/5 Great Commotion (USA)—Idrak (Young Generation) Mr J. Davis
37 Br f 17/2 Darshaan—Jaldi (IRE) (Nordico (USA)) Mr Albert Finney
38 B f 27/2 Bluebird (USA)—Laser Show (IRE) (Wassl) Mr S. Mullin
39 Ch f 16/5 Ballad Rock—Minnie Tudor (Tudor Melody) Mr Ken Campbell
40 MOON ROSE (IRE), b f 2/3 Imperial Frontier—Crown Rose (Dara Monarch) Mr G. Delaney
41 B f 28/4 Tirol—Pickety Place (Prince Tenderfoot (USA)) Mr G. Hynes
42 B c 28/3 Don't Forget Me—Shadia (USA) (Naskra (USA)) Mr Char Kar Sun
43 SPIRIT OF TARA (IRE), b f 13/3 Sadler's Wells (USA)—Flame of Tara (Artaius (USA)) Miss P. K. O'Kelly
44 Ch c 21/4 Niniski (USA)—Top of The League (High Top) Ricardo Sanz
45 B f 3/5 Polish Patriot (USA)—Traumerei (GER) (Surumu (GER)) Miss S. Von Schilchel
46 WELSH LION (IRE), b c 4/3 Caerleon (USA)—Welsh Flame (Welsh Pageant) Miss P. F. O'Kelly

Other Owners: H. E. The President Of Ireland, Miss S. Schilcher.

Jockeys (Flat): T J Daly (8-0), L O'Shea (7-7).

Jockey (NH): P L Malone (9-7).

Apprentices: E Ahern (6-13), G Moylan (7-0).

Amateur: Mr R Neylon (9-12).

248   MR FREDERICK GRAY, Haywards Heath

Postal: **Drewitts, Warninglid, Haywards Heath, West Sussex, RH17 5TB.**
Phone: **(01444) 461235 FAX (01444) 461485**

1 **BOY BUSTER**, 7, b g Pitpan—Medway Melody **Mr Frederick Gray**
2 **CAPPUCCINO GIRL**, 9, ch m Broadsword (USA)—Coffee Bob **Mrs Jeanne Gray**
3 **LIZZIES LASS**, 11, br m Sandalay—Kiltegan **Mrs Liz Creber**
4 **OLIVIPET**, 7, b m Sula Bula—Gamlingay **Mr Frederick Gray**
5 **PROFESSION**, 5, b h Shareef Dancer (USA)—Mrs Warren (USA) **Mr Frederick Gray**
6 **SCOTTISH BALL**, 7, b m Ardross—Dance In Rome **Mr Frederick Gray**

Conditional: Paul John Stevens (9-7).

Amateur: Mr G Hogan.

249   MR T. R. GREATHEAD, Chipping Norton

Postal: **Chalford Oaks, Oxford Road, Chipping Norton, Oxon, OX7 5QP.**
Phone: **(01608) 642954**

1 **CERIDWEN**, 6, ch m Fearless Action (USA)—Bellecana **Mrs S. Greathead**
2 **CHARLAFRIVOLA**, 8, br g Persian Bold—Tattle **Mrs S. Greathead**
3 **LINCHMERE LAD (IRE)**, 8, b g Petorius—Adamantos **Mrs S. Greathead**
4 **LITTLE ROUSILLON**, 8, b g Rousillon (USA)—Carolside **Mrs S. Greathead**
5 **SECRET FORMULA**, 6, b g Sulaafah (USA)—Bidula **Mrs S. Greathead**

Jockey (NH): William Humphreys (9-13).

250   MR V. G. GREENWAY, Taunton

Postal: **Higher Vexford Farm, Lydeard St Lawrence, Taunton, Somerset, TA4 3QG.**
Phone: **(01984) 656548**

1 **BLADE OF FORTUNE**, 8, b g Beldale Flutter (USA)—Foil 'em (USA) **Mr V. G. Greenway & Partners**
2 **ON ALERT (NZ)**, 9, ch g Double Trouble (NZ)—Stand By (NZ) **Mr V. G. Greenway**
3 **VEXFORD MODEL**, 6, b m Latest Model—Suchong **Mr V. G. Greenway & Partners**

Other Owners: Mr M. G. Greenway, Mrs M. M. Greenway.

251   MR M. A. GRIFFIN, Liskeard

Postal: **Sportmans Arms Hotel, Station Road, Menheniot Station, Liskeard.**
Phone: **(01503) 240249**

1 **APARECIDA (FR)**, 10, b br m Direct Flight—Doll Poppy (FR) **Mr M. Griffin**
2 **BENJAMIN LANCASTER**, 12, b g Dubassoff (USA)—Lancaster Rose **Mr M. Griffin**
3 **BLAISE LANCASTER**, 7, b m Blakeney Point—Lancaster Rose **Mr M. Griffin**
4 5, B g Shaab—Lancaster Rose **Mr M. Griffin**
5 **ROSE LANCASTER**, 13, b m Oh Henry—Lancaster Rose **Mr M. Griffin**
6 **VAGANOVA (IRE)**, 7, b g Where To Dance (USA)—Modena **Mr M. Griffin**

Lady Rider: S Young (10-5).

252 MR S. G. GRIFFITHS, Carmarthen

Postal: **Rwyth Farm, Nantgaredig, Carmarthen, Dyfed, SA32 7LG.**
Phone: **(012672) 90321**

1 DINGLE WOOD (IRE), 6, ch g Jamesmead—Over View **Mr S. G. Griffiths**
2 FORESTAL, 4, b g Glenstal (USA)—Foreno **Mr S. G. Griffiths**

253 MR D. M. GRISSELL, Robertsbridge

Postal: **Brightling Park, Robertsbridge, East Sussex, TN32 5HH.**
Phone: **(01424) 838241 FAX (01424) 838378 MOBILE (0378) 498850**

1 BON VOYAGE (USA), 4, b c Riverman (USA)—Katsura (USA) **The Hon Mrs C. Yeates**
2 BUCKLAND LAD (IRE), 5, ch g Phardante (FR)—Belcraig **Mrs R. M. Hepburn**
3 ENVOPAKLEADA (IRE), 6, b g Supreme Leader—Rock Solid **Mr Frank Arthur**
4 FIRST INSTANCE (IRE), 6, b g Torus—Red-Leria **Pepin Racing**
5 GLENCARRIG GALE (IRE), 8, br g Strong Gale—Glencarrig Jewel **Petticoat Partnership**
6 HANDSOME NED, 10, br g Netherkelly—Beau Wonder **Mr M. J. Bridger**
7 JOJO (IRE), 6, ch g Buckskin (FR)—Autumn Queen **Mr John Grist**
8 LE CHAT NOIR, 13, br g Paico—June **Mr F. J. T. Parsons**
9 LITTLE CHINK (IRE), 6, b g Mandalus—Alice Minkthorn **Mrs Eric Boucher**
10 MR MATT (IRE), 8, b g Bustineto—Princesspry **Mrs Eric Boucher**
11 NORMARANGE (IRE), 6, ch g Lancastrian—Perdeal **Mr D. Curtis**
12 RIO TRUSKY, 7, b g Ballacashtal (CAN)—Polly's Song **Mrs John Grist**
13 SOLEIL DANCER (IRE), 8, b g Fairy King (USA)—Cooliney Dancer **Mrs John Grist**
14 THE WHIP, 9, ch g Fine Blade (USA)—Phayre Vulgan **The Hon Mrs C. Yeates**
15 TIN PAN ALLEY, 7, b g Pitpan—Also Kirsty **Mrs Christine Notley**

Other Owners: Mrs Denise Bloomfield, Mrs Elizabeth J. Bourne, Mrs Diana Cheveley, Mrs D. M. Grissell, Mrs R. Howell, Mr D. J. Instance, Mrs Lorna Keat, Mr Y. Matsuoka, His Honour Judge Peppitt, Exors Of The Late Mr P. D. Rylands, Mrs Judith Weller, Mr J. N. G. Winter.

254 MR BRIAN GUBBY, Bagshot

Postal: **Dukes Wood, Bracknell Road, Bagshot, Surrey, GU15 3JF.**
Phone: **DAY (01276) 63282 FAX (01276) 26964 HOME (01276) 471030**

1 EASY DOLLAR, 4, ch g Gabitat—Burglars Girl **Brian Gubby Ltd**
2 OUR EDDIE, 7, ch g Gabitat—Ragusa Girl **Brian Gubby Ltd**
3 SORISKY, 4, ch g Risk Me (FR)—Minabella **Brian Gubby Ltd**
4 TRIBAL PEACE (IRE), 4, ch g Red Sunset—Mirabiliary (USA) **Brian Gubby Ltd**

THREE-YEAR-OLDS

5 CORTES, ch f Roi Danzig (USA)—Jumra **Brian Gubby Ltd**
6 MULTI FRANCHISE, ch g Gabitat—Gabibti (IRE) **Brian Gubby Ltd**
7 MUMMY'S MUSIC, ch f La Grange Music—Anse Chastanet **Brian Gubby Ltd**
8 TRIBLE PET, b f Petong—Fire Sprite **Brian Gubby Ltd**

TWO-YEAR-OLDS

9 LUCAYAN BEACH, gr c 31/1 Cyrano de Bergerac—Mrs Gray (Red Sunset) **Brian Gubby Ltd**
10 OMAHA CITY (IRE), b g 11/5 Night Shift (USA)—Be Discreet (Junius (USA)) **Brian Gubby Ltd**
11 TULSA (IRE), b c 25/3 Priolo (USA)—Lagrion (USA) (Diesis) **Brian Gubby Ltd**
12 UTAH (IRE), b c 15/4 High Estate—Easy Romance (USA) (Northern Jove (CAN)) **Brian Gubby Ltd**

255   MR R. GUEST, Newmarket

Postal: **Chestnut Tree Stables, Exeter Road, Newmarket, Suffolk, CB8 8LR.**
Phone: **(01638) 661508 FAX (01638) 667317 MOBILE (0850) 745112**

1 **DANCING SIOUX**, 4, b c Nabeel Dancer (USA)—Sutosky **A. M. Jeffrey**
2 **MILLYANT**, 6, ch m Primo Dominie—Jubilee Song **Mr C. J. Mills**
3 **MISTER RM**, 4, b g Dominion—La Cabrilla **Mr J. W. Biswell**
4 **MOUSEHOLE**, 4, b g Statoblest—Alo Ez **Mrs Janet Kent**
5 **MY BOY JOSH**, 4, ch g Risk Me (FR)—Merry Kate **Huff 'N' Hitch Racing**
6 **MY CADEAUX**, 4, ch f Cadeaux Genereux—Jubilee Song **Mr C. J. Mills**
7 **PORTELET**, 4, b f Night Shift (USA)—Noirmant **Matthews Breeding & Racing**

THREE-YEAR-OLDS

8 **DEPICTION**, b g Hadeer—Depict **Matthews Breeding & Racing**
9 **HOSTILE NATIVE**, b c Formidable (USA)—Balatina **Mr S. Lury**
10 **INDIAN RELATIVE**, b f Distant Relative—Elegant Tern (USA) **Mr Vijay Mallya**
11 **KIND OF LIGHT**, b f Primo Dominie—Kind Thoughts **Mrs B. Mills**
12 **KRISTIANA**, ch f Kris—Noirmant **Matthews Breeding & Racing**
13 **LINDA'S JOY (IRE)**, b f Classic Secret (USA)—Enaam **Mr M. Hill**
14 **LOVELY PROSPECT**, b f Lycius (USA)—Lovely Lagoon **R. Axford & Partners**
15 **MONTECRISTO**, br g Warning—Sutosky **Matthews Breeding & Racing**
16 **MY EMMA**, b f Marju (IRE)—Pato **Matthews Breeding & Racing**
17 **PRESENT GENERATION**, ch c Cadeaux Genereux—Penny Mint **Mr S. Lury**
18 **SONGSHEET**, b f Dominion—Songstead **Matthews Breeding & Racing**
19 **TIME OF NIGHT (USA)**, gr f Night Shift (USA)—Tihama (USA) **M & L. B. Wackett**
20 **VELMEZ**, ch g Belmez (USA)—Current Raiser **Matthews Breeding & Racing**

TWO-YEAR-OLDS

21 B f 6/4 Distant Relative—Alkion (Fordham (USA)) **Mrs Homewood & Partners**
22 B f 10/4 Polar Falcon (USA)—Good Thinking (Raja Baba (USA)) **Mr C. J. Mills**
23 **JAY-GEE-EM**, b f 23/2 Aragon—Mana (GER) (Windwurf (GER)) **Matthews Breeding & Racing**
24 B f 5/3 Suave Dancer (USA)—Joma Kaanem (Double Form) **Mr Khalid M. Affara**
25 **JOVIAN**, gr f 1/3 Petong—What A Pet (Mummy's Pet) **Matthews Breeding & Racing**
26 **LUST**, ch f 3/6 Pursuit Of Love—Pato (High Top) **Matthews Breeding & Racing**
27 B f 28/4 Midyan (USA)—Miss Swansong (Young Generation) **Mr A. P. Davies & Partners**
28 B f 30/4 Night Shift (USA)—Old Domesday Book (High Top) **Mr C. J. Mills**
29 **PADDY LAD (IRE)**, b br c 22/4 Anita's Prince—Lady of Man (So Blessed) **M & G Hill Ltd**
30 Gr f 8/5 Petong—Pattis Pet (Mummy's Pet) **Mr C. J. Mills**
31 **RUN LUCY RUN**, b f 28/3 Risk Me (FR)—Pat Or Else (Alzao (USA)) **Matthews Breeding & Racing**
32 **SLIPSTREAM**, b c 20/5 Slip Anchor—Butosky (Busted) **Matthews Breeding & Racing**

Other Owners: Mrs Jenny Biswell, Bradmill Ltd, Mr R. Filgate, Mr David Hitchenor, Mr Peter Hughff, Mr J. Leahy, Mrs J. E. Lury, Mrs Leslie Mills.

256   MR W. J. HAGGAS, Newmarket

Postal: **Somerville Lodge, Fordham Road, Newmarket, Suffolk, CB8 7AA.**
Phone: **NEWMARKET (01638) 667013 FAX (01638) 660534**

1 **ABSOLUTE MAGIC**, 6, b g Doulab (USA)—Trickster **Mrs Barbara Bassett**
2 **FEN TERRIER**, 4, b f Emarati (USA)—Kinz **Jolly Farmers Racing**
3 **HAND CRAFT (IRE)**, 4, b g Dancing Dissident (USA)—Fair Flutter **Mrs M. M. Haggas**
4 **PATTO (USA)**, 5, b h Dixieland Band (USA)—Pasampsi (USA) **Mr B. Haggas**
5 **RAINBOW TOP**, 4, b c Rainbow Quest (USA)—Aigue **Mr B. Haggas**
6 **ROCK SYMPHONY**, 6, ch g Ballad Rock—Shamasiya (FR) **Mrs C. E. Feather**
7 **SILVER TZAR**, 4, gr g Dominion—Altaia (FR) **Mr P. A. Deal**
8 **YEAST**, 4, b g Salse (USA)—Orient **Mr B. Haggas**

MR W. J. HAGGAS—continued

THREE-YEAR-OLDS

9 **ALAMEIN (USA)**, ch c Roi Danzig (USA)—Pollination **Mr Henryk De Kwiatkowski**
10 **CRIMSON ROSELLA**, b f Polar Falcon (USA)—Double Finesse **Mrs P. D. Rossdale**
11 **D'NAAN (IRE)**, b g Royal Academy (USA)—Festive Season (USA) **Mr Adel M. Almojil**
12 **KINGS WITNESS (USA)**, b c Lear Fan (USA)—Allison's Deeds **Highclere Thoroughbred Racing Ltd**
13 **MISSILE**, b g Rock City—Fast Chick **Mr J. W. Bogie**
14 **SHAAMIT (IRE)**, b c Mtoto—Shomoose **Mr Khalifa Dasmal**
15 **SHEHAB (IRE)**, b g Persian Bold—Fenjaan **Mr Ali K. Al Jafleh**
16 **SHU GAA (IRE)**, ch g Salse (USA)—River Reem (USA) **Mr Ali K. Al Jafleh**
17 **SPLICING**, ch f Sharpo—Soluce **Mr A. Hirschfeld**
18 **TOTAL ALOOF**, b f Groom Dancer (USA)—Bashoosh (USA) **Total Asset Ltd**
19 **TUDOR FALCON**, b c Midyan (USA)—Tudorealm (USA) **Wyck Hall Stud**

TWO-YEAR-OLDS

20 **AJEEBAH**, b f 12/2 Mujtahid (USA)—Saffron (FR) (Fabulous Dancer (USA)) **Mr Ahmed Al Shafar**
21 **B c** 25/4 Warning—Aililsa (USA) (Alydar (USA)) **Mr J. Hulme**
22 **ALL IN LEATHER**, b f 1/2 Saddlers' Hall (IRE)—Ivana (IRE) (Taufan (USA)) **Cheveley Park Stud**
23 **CATWALK**, b f 2/2 Shirley Heights—Moogie (Young Generation) **Mr M. Brower**
24 **HAND SPUN**, b c 2/4 Midyan (USA)—Baileys By Name (Nomination) **Mrs M. M. Haggas**
25 **B f** 28/2 Statoblest—Lets Fall In Love (USA) (Northern Baby (CAN))
26 **B c** 20/3 Taufan (USA)—Miss Darcy (IRE) (Glow (USA))
27 **Ch f** 6/4 Rock City—Orlaith (Final Straw)
28 **PEN FRIEND**, b c 27/2 Robellino (USA)—Nibbs Point (IRE) (Sure Blade (USA)) **Mr B. Haggas**
29 **PRINCESS OF HEARTS**, b f 26/3 Prince Sabo—Constant Delight (Never So Bold) **Cheveley Park Stud**
30 **ROCHEA**, b f 12/5 Rock City—Pervenche (Latest Model) **Mrs M. M. C. Clark**
31 **ROYAL CRUSADE (USA)**, b c 25/4 Diesis—
                            Sainte Croix (USA) (Nijinsky (CAN)) **Highclere Thoroughbred Racing Ltd**
32 **SAHARA REEM**, b f 20/3 Don't Forget Me—River Reem (USA) (Irish River (FR)) **Mr Ali K. Al Jafleh**
33 **SECRET HAND (IRE)**, b c 30/4 Classic Secret (USA)—Ballysnip (Ballymore) **Mrs M. M. Haggas**
34 **SEVERITY**, b c 22/4 Reprimand—Neenah (Bold Lad (IRE)) **Mrs M. M. C. Clark**
35 **SHARAZAMATAZ**, b f 1/3 Shareef Dancer (USA)—Phylae (Habitat) **Mrs M. Southcott**
36 **SHARPO WASSL**, ch c 25/5 Sharpo—Wasslaweyeh (USA) (Damascus (USA)) **Mr Ali K. Al Jafleh**
37 **SPECULATOR (IRE)**, b c 16/5 Last Tycoon—Abbeydale (Huntercombe) **Highclere Thoroughbred Racing Ltd**
38 **STATE OF GOLD**, b c 10/5 High Estate—Mawaal Habeebee (Northfields (USA)) **Mr Ali K. Al Jafleh**
39 **TELEMANIA (IRE)**, b f 2/3 Mujtahid (USA)—African Dancer (USA) (El Gran Senor (USA)) **Mr J. D. Ashenheim**
40 **B c** 14/2 Don't Forget Me—Vian (USA) (Far Out East (USA))
41 **WAFA (IRE)**, ch f 16/2 Kefaah (USA)—Shomoose (Habitat) **Mr Khalifa Dasmal**
42 **WOBBLE**, ch c 24/2 Kris—Horseshoe Reef (Mill Reef (USA)) **Mr B. Haggas**

Other Owners: Mr M. E. H. Bradley, Mr J. S. Dale, Mr A. L. Deal, Fernedge Bloodstock Ltd, Mr J. Horne, Mr B. Lythe, Mr M. Pound, Mr N. Sagon, Mr P. C. Taylor, Tessona Racing Ltd, Mr W. J. Walters.

Apprentice: Elizabeth Turner (7-10).

257   MR W. W. HAIGH, Malton

Postal: **Spring Cottage Stables, Langton Road, Norton, Malton, YO17 9PY.**

Phone: **MALTON (01653) 694428 MOBILE (0378) 342019**

1 **5**, B g Dubassoff (USA)—Flopsy Mopsy
2 **HULLBANK**, 6, b g Uncle Pokey—Dubavarna **Mrs P. Gibbon**
3 **LEGAL ISSUE (IRE)**, 4, b c Contract Law (USA)—Natuschka **Mr B. Valentine**
4 **MAJOR MOUSE**, 8, ch g All Systems Go—Tzu-Hsi **Mr N. Barber**
5 **MR TOWSER**, 5, b g Faustus (USA)—Saltina **Mrs I. Gibson**
6 **PEGASUS BAY**, 5, b g Tina's Pet—Mossberry Fair **Mr R. P. Dineen**
7 **PHARLY DANCER**, 7, b g Pharly (FR)—Martin-Lavell Mail **Mr A. Marucci**
8 **SHASHI (IRE)**, 4, br f Shaadi (USA)—Homely Touch **Mr B. Valentine**

MR W. W. HAIGH—continued

9 **SOLOMON'S DANCER (USA)**, 6, b br g Al Nasr (FR)—Infinite Wisdom (USA) **Mr W. W. Haigh**
10 **TORQUE CURVE**, 4, b g Puissance—Luck Penny **Mrs V. Haigh**
11 **TROUBADOUR SONG**, 4, b g King of Clubs—Silver Singing (USA) **Spring Cottage Racing Partnership**
12 **VANART**, 7, b g Precocious—Red Spider
13 **VOCAL COMMAND**, 4, b g Chief Singer—To Oneiro **Mr W. R. Thomas**

THREE-YEAR-OLDS

14 **BATOUTOFTHEBLUE**, br g Batshoof—Action Belle **Dr C. I. Emmerson**
15 **DAINTY DAMSEL**, b f Good Times (ITY)—Classy Lassy **Mr Harry Atkinson**
16 **PRETTY PRECEDENT**, b f Polish Precedent (USA)—Pretty Pol
17 **RAIN CLOUD**, ch f Totem (USA)—Cool Number **Mr W. W. Haigh**
18 **SURF CITY**, ch g Rock City—Waveguide **Mr A. W. Anderson**

TWO-YEAR-OLDS

19 B f 23/4 Syrtos—Breakfast In Bed (Tickled Pink)
20 **INDIAN AFFAIR**, b f 29/4 Indian Ridge—Steppey Lane (Tachypous)
21 **MADAM LUCY**, b f 23/3 Efisio—Our Aisling (Blakeney)
22 B f 11/2 Pharly (FR)—Manageress (Mandamus)

Other Owners: Mr C. L. Baker, Mr & Mrs P. Colson, Mr Tim Hawkins, Mr G. Parkinson, Mrs Marion Wickham.

Jockey (Flat): Dale Gibson (7-12, w.a.).

Jockey (NH): D Byrne (w.a.).

258   MRS D. HAINE, Newmarket

Postal: **San Remo, 92 Crockfords Road, Newmarket, Suffolk, CB8 9BG.**
Phone: **HOME** (01638) 561001 **STABLE** (01638) 662346

1 **ADARE QUEEN (IRE)**, 8, br m Spin of A Coin—Queen of The Firs **Mr Kevin Williams**
2 **CRACKLING FROST (IRE)**, 8, b b g Green Shoon—Moppet's Last **The Unlucky For Some Partnership**
3 **DESMOND GOLD (IRE)**, 8, b g Tumble Gold—Stylish Princess **J. Scanlon & J. Toner**
4 **FLAMEWOOD**, 7, b m Touching Wood (USA)—Alan's Girl **Mrs Solna Thomson Jones**
5 **FURL (IRE)**, 7, br m Strong Gale—Drom Lady **Mrs Solna Thomson Jones**
6 **HENRIETTA HOWARD (IRE)**, 6, b m King's Ride—Knockaville **Mrs Solna Thomson Jones**
7 **IMOLA**, 7, br m Netherkelly—Monza **Mr J. B. Fenwick**
8 **INFIRAAJ (USA)**, 4, b g Dayjur (USA)—Capricorn Belle **Mrs Diana Haine**
9 **JUST LIKE THAT**, 5, b m Gunner B—H And K Hattrick **H & K Commissions**
10 **KING'S RAINBOW (IRE)**, 7, b m King's Ride—Royalement **W. & E. Mumford (Racing)**
11 **MCGARRETTFIVEO (IRE)**, 6, ch g Hawaiian Return (USA)—Grotto Princess **Mrs Diana Haine**
12 **MILL O'THE RAGS (IRE)**, 7, b g Strong Gale—Lady Rag **Mr E. J. Fenaroli**
13 **OCEAN LEADER**, 9, b g Lord Ha Ha—Rough Tide **Sir Peter Gibbings**
14 **PEACE LORD (IRE)**, 6, ch g Callernish—French Academy **Sir Peter Gibbings**
15 **PEACEMAN**, 10, b g Martinmas—Miss Posy **Sir Peter Gibbings**
16 **SHARP BLADE**, 6, ch g Sure Blade (USA)—Compton Lady (USA) **Mrs Diana Haine**
17 **SPREE CROSS**, 10, b g Kemal (FR)—Danger Lady **Exors of the late Mr P. L. Mason**
18 **SUPREME SPIRIT (IRE)**, 7, b g Supreme Leader—Down All The Coves **Mr F. J. Haggas**

THREE-YEAR-OLDS

19 **KRASNIK (IRE)**, br g Roi Danzig (USA)—Kermesse (IRE) **Mrs Solna Thomson Jones**

TWO-YEAR-OLDS

20 Gr c Kendor (FR)—Oshawa (Alzao (USA)) **Mrs Solna Thomson Jones**

Other Owners: Mr Rex Carter, Mr Barry H. Collinson, Mrs Isabel M. Collinson, Lady Gibbings, Mr J. Leat, Mr Jeremy Mason, Mr W. H. Mellen, Mrs E. Mumford, Mr Walter W. Mumford, Mr T. W. Newton.

Amateur: Mr G Haine (9-7).

259   MR J. S. HALDANE, Kelso

Postal: **Hendersyde Stables, Kelso, Roxburghshire, TD5 7ST.**

Phone: **(01573) 224956**

1 **ANOTHER GIRL (IRE)**, 7, gr m Buckskin (FR)—Tinkletoes **Mr Simon Fraser**
2 **CRYSTADO (FR)**, 7, ch g Crystal Glitters (USA)—Kantado **Mr Jack Johnston**
3 **FRIENDLY KNIGHT**, 6, b g Horage—Be A Dancer **Mr G. J. Johnston**
4 **HIGHLANDMAN**, 10, b g Florida Son—Larne **Mrs Hugh Fraser**
5 **MEGANS MYSTERY (IRE)**, 6, b g Corvaro (USA)—Megans Choice **Mr J. S. Haldane**
6 **MISS GREENYARDS**, 5, b m Stalker—Isle Maree **Mr J. T. Blacklock**
7 **PADDY MORRISSEY**, 9, b g Strong Gale—Reynoldstown Rose **Mrs Hugh Fraser**
8 **RESPECTABLE LAURA**, 5, b m Respect—Laura Lyshill Wood **Mr J. S. Haldane**
9 **TUMLIN OOT (IRE)**, 7, b g Amazing Bust—Tumlin Brig **Mrs Hugh Fraser**

THREE-YEAR-OLDS

10 **BROGANS BRUSH**, ch c Jendali (USA)—Sweet 'n' Sharp **Mr G. J. Johnston**
11 **PEARLS OF THOUGHT (IRE)**, br f Persian Bold—Miss Loving **Mr J. S. Haldane**

TWO-YEAR-OLDS

12 B f 3/3 Environment Friend—Noble Singer (Vaguely Noble) **Mr J. S. Haldane**

Other Owners: Mr Anthony Green.

260   MR L. MONTAGUE HALL, Epsom

Postal: **Chartwell Stables, Motts Hill Lane, Tadworth, Epsom, Surrey, KT20 6BA.**

Phone: **(01737) 814847/370911 FAX (01737) 370911**

1 **FAST FORWARD FRED**, 5, gr g Sharrood (USA)—Sun Street **Mr G. R. H. Pickard & Partners**
2 **GLITTERAZZI**, 5, b g Midyan (USA)—Burnt Amber **Mrs P. J. Sheen**
3 **GLOW FORUM**, 5, b m Kalaglow—Beau's Delight (USA) **The Forum Ltd**
4 **MR STREAKY**, 5, gr g Sizzling Melody—Cawstons Prejudice **Chartwell Racing**
5 **ROBO MAGIC (USA)**, 4, b g Tejano (USA)—Bubble Magic (USA) **Mr A. D. Green and Partners**
6 **THE LAD**, 7, b g Bold Owl—Solbella **The Trebeth Partnership**
7 **WILL'S LEGACY**, 6, ch g Northern Tempest (USA)—Crosby Triangle **Miss J. D. Anstee**
8 **WOTTASHAMBLES**, 5, b br g Arrasas (USA)—Manawa **Dream On Racing Partnership**

THREE-YEAR-OLDS

9 **BLUE DELIGHT (IRE)**, b c Bluebird (USA)—Highly Delighted (USA) **E. and B. Productions (Theatre) Ltd**
10 **ILLEGALLY YOURS**, br f Be My Chief (USA)—Legal Precedent **Prestige Racing Management Ltd**
11 **MIJAS**, ch f Risk Me (FR)—Out of Harmony **Mr Minhinnick and Partners**
12 **ZAFORUM**, b c Deploy—Beau's Delight (USA) **The Forum Ltd**

Other Owners: Mr D. J. Campbell, Mr Carter, Mr R. Farrington, Mr R. Fuller, Mr Victor J. Hoare, Mr Johnston, Mr G. D Jones, Mr S. F. Lane, Mr G. A. McMullan, Mr R. G. Moody, Mrs J. Murray, Mr Stanford, Mr G. E. Thompson, M Patrick M. Williamson.

261   MISS S. E. HALL, Middleham

Postal: **Brecongill, Coverham, Leyburn, North Yorks, DL8 4TJ.**

Phone: **(01969) 640223 FAX (01969) 640223**

1 **BRECONGILL LAD**, 4, b g Clantime—Chikala **Three Horse Shoes Partnership**
2 **KEY TO MY HEART (IRE)**, 6, b h Broken Hearted—Originality **Mrs M. Pickering**
3 **KISSEL**, 4, b f Warning—Ice Chocolate (USA) **Mr R. Fenwick-Gibson**
4 **LEIF THE LUCKY (USA)**, 7, ch g Lemhi Gold (USA)—Corvine (USA) **Miss Betty Duxbury**
5 **LORD LAMB**, 4, gr g Dunbeath (USA)—Caroline Lamb **Mrs T. Hall**

MISS S. E. HALL—continued

6 **MOVING ARROW**, 5, ch g Indian Ridge—Another Move **Mr G. Westgarth**
7 **MY BUSTER**, 4, ch g Move Off—Young Lamb **Mrs T. Hall**
8 **ROYAL YORK**, 4, b f Bustino—Rustle of Silk **Mr R. Ogden**
9 **SHADES OF SILVER**, 4, gr f Sharrood (USA)—Arita **Mrs Joan Hodgson**
10 **SO AMAZING**, 4, b f Hallgate—Jussoli **Mr C. Platts**
11 **STYLISH WAYS (IRE)**, 4, b c Thatching—Style of Life (USA) **Ian Hall Racing**
12 **TARA RAMBLER (IRE)**, 7, ch g Arapahos (FR)—Tarabelle **Mr J. Hanson**
13 **TOPSAWYER**, 8, b g Kris—Catalpa **Mrs Joan Hodgson**
14 **UNCLE MOUSE**, 5, b g Hallgate—Miss Diaward **Miss S. E. Hall**

THREE-YEAR-OLDS

15 B c Sylvan Express—Another Move **Miss S. E. Hall**
16 **BEANO SCRIPT**, b g Prince Sabo—Souadah (USA) **Mr J. Hanson**
17 Ch c Digamist (USA)—Formidable Task **Mr C. Platts**
18 **GOLDRILL**, ch g Never So Bold—Irish Impulse (USA) **Miss Betty Duxbury**
19 **GULF OF SIAM**, ch g Prince Sabo—Jussoli **Mr J. Hanson**
20 **HOTCAKE**, b g Sizzling Melody—Bold Cookie **Miss S. E. Hall**
21 **MERRILY**, gr f Sharrood (USA)—Babycham Sparkle **Miss Betty Duxbury**
22 **NOT A WORD**, gr f Batshoof—Secret Gill **Mr R. Duggan**
23 **PHANTOM HAZE**, gr g Absalom—Caroline Lamb **Mrs Joan Hodgson**

TWO-YEAR-OLDS

24 B f 19/3 Rambo Dancer (CAN)—Bold Cookie (Never So Bold) **Miss S. E. Hall**
25 Gr f 28/2 Absalom—Formidable Task (Formidable (USA)) **Mr C. Platts**
26 B f 9/3 Hadeer—On The Record (Record Taken) **Miss S. E. Hall**
27 Ch c 22/4 Broken Hearted—Originality (Godswalk (USA)) **Mr C. Platts**
28 Ch g 7/4 Sylvan Express—Royal Girl (Kafu) **Miss S. E. Hall**
29 Gr g 15/3 Batshoof—Secret Gill (Most Secret) **Miss S. E. Hall**
30 **SILVER BUTTON**, b g 16/3 Silver Kite (USA)—Klairover (Smackover) **Miss Betty Duxbury**

Other Owners: Mrs Linda Diggle, Mr William Jarvis, Mr Ronald Martin, Mrs W. Martin, Mrs A. M. Murns, Mr R. Murns, Mr John Russell, Miss M. Thompson.

Jockey (Flat): J Weaver (w.a.).

Jockey (NH): N Bentley.

Amateur: Mr C Platts.

262   MR G. A. HAM, Axbridge

Postal: **Rose Farm, Rooksbridge, Axbridge, Somerset, BS26 2TH.**
Phone: **HOME (01934) 750331 EVENINGS (01934) 733117**

1 **AGANEROT (IRE)**, 6, b g Torenaga—Silly Company **Mr D. Walker**
2 **AN BUCHAILL LIATH (IRE)**, 7, gr g Roselier (FR)—Buckette Lady **Mrs Caroline Lyndon**
3 **ANOTHER HUBBLICK**, 5, ch g Nearly A Hand—Sue Lark **Mr T. Hubbard**
4 **ARTIC EXPLORER**, 5, b g Arctic Lord—Happy Wonder **Mr David Edwards**
5 **BRIDIE'S PRIDE**, 5, b g Alleging (USA)—Miss Monte Carlo **Mr K. C. White**
6 **GEORGE BUCKINGHAM**, 11, b g Royal Palace—Flying Idol **Mr Mike Cornish**
7 **GREENACRES ROSE**, 6, b m Derring Rose—New Cherry **Mr W. E. Catstrey**
8 **GREEN'S FAIR (IRE)**, 6, b g Carmelite House (USA)—Lockwood Girl **Mr N. G. Ahier**
9 **HI DUCHESS**, 9, ch m Carwhite—Good Larker **Mrs Caroline Lyndon**
10 **HIGH POST**, 7, b g Lidhame—Touch of Class (FR) **Mr C. Garland**
11 **LANSDOWNE**, 8, b g High Top—Fettle **Mr R. F. Denmead**

MR G. A. HAM—continued

12 **LAW FACULTY (IRE)**, 7, b g Law Society (USA)—Ask The Wind **North Liverpool Racing Partnership**
13 **NO SACRIFICE**, 4, b f Revlow—Cool Brae **Mr Mike Cornish**
14 **ORCHESTRAL DESIGNS (IRE)**, 5, b g Fappiano (USA)—Elegance In Design **Mr T. O. Coughlan**
15 **SHAMELESS LADY**, 6, b m Bold Owl—Spartan's Girl **Travail Employment Group Ltd**
16 **SUPER SPELL**, 10, ch g Smooth Stepper—Super Twig **Mr W. E. Catstrey**
17 **WOMAN OF THE ROAD**, 10, b m Boreen (FR)—Lady Darnley **Mrs S. Hutchings**

Other Owners: R. F. Denmead & Partners, Mr F. T. Glass, Mr David John Jones, Mr P. Jones, Mr J. M. Moran, Mrs Diane Oates, Mr R. T. Wilkins.

Jockeys (NH): S Burrough (10-0), A P McCoy (w.a.).

Amateur: Mr G Densley (10-6).

263   MRS A. HAMILTON, Newcastle Upon Tyne

Postal: **Claywalls Farm, Capheaton, Newcastle Upon Tyne, NE19 2BP.**
Phone: **(01830) 530219**

1 **BAVINGTON**, 5, b g Meadowbrook—Bargello's Lady **Mr Ian Hamilton**
2 **BELLS WILL RING (IRE)**, 6, b g Roselier (FR)—Chapel Bells **Mr Ian Hamilton**
3 **CLAYWALLS**, 5, b g Meadowbrook—Lady Manello **Mr Ian Hamilton**
4 **ROLY PRIOR**, 7, b g Celtic Cone—Moonduster **Mr Ian Hamilton**

THREE-YEAR-OLDS

5 B f Respect—Bargello's Lady **Mr Ian Hamilton**

TWO-YEAR-OLDS

6 B g 13/5 Milieu—Bargello's Lady (Bargello) **Mr Ian Hamilton**

264   MRS A. J. HAMILTON-FAIRLEY, Basingstoke

Postal: **Moor Place, Plough Lane, Bramshill, Basingstoke, RG25 0RF.**
Phone: **(01734) 326269**

1 **MISTER BLAKE**, 6, b g Damister (USA)—Larive **Mrs Richard Plummer**
2 **REFERENTIAL**, 5, b g Reference Point—Pelf (USA) **Mrs Richard Plummer**

265   MR J. E. HAMMOND, Chantilly

Postal: **25, Avenue de Joinville, 60500 Chantilly, France.**
Phone: **44 58 50 25 FAX 44 57 31 28**

1 **AGENT COOPER (FR)**, 7, ch g Kris—Northern Trick **S. Niarchos**
2 **ALMUNTASSER**, 4, b c Sadler's Wells—Ispahan **W. Said**
3 **ANOTHER FELIX**, 4, ch c Miswaki—Give Her The Gun **M. Charlton**
4 **BEYROUTH (USA)**, 4, b f Alleged—Lightning Fire **Ecurie Chalhoub**
5 **BLUE WATER (USA)**, 4, b f Bering—Shining Water **Rebecca Philipps**
6 **BOUCHE BEE (USA)**, 4, b f Naevus—Miss Henderson Co **A. Leonard**
7 **CELESTIAL WAY (USA)**, 5, ch h Diesis—Stellaria **M. Lynam**
8 **DIMITY**, 4, b f Soviet Star—Diminuendo **M. Al Maktoum**
9 **GENNY WREN (USA)**, 4, ch f Trempolino—Attirance **M. Lynam**

MR J. E. HAMMOND—continued

10 **GRECIAN DART (IRE)**, 4, b c Darshaan—Grecian Urn **A. Weinstock**
11 **MIESQUE'S SON (USA)**, 4, b c Mr Prospector—Miesque **S. Niarchos**
12 **NICOSIE (USA)**, 4, b c Northern Baby—Wayage **Ecurie Chalhoub**
13 **NORTON SOUND (USA)**, 5, b h Bering—Shining Water **Rebecca Philipps**
14 **PARFAIT GLACE (FR)**, 4, b c Pampabird—Star System **L. Oung**
15 **RUNNING FLAME**, 4, b c Assert—Fanning The Flame **M. Charlton**
16 **SCRIBE**, 6, b h Sadler's Wells—Northern Script **L. Oung**
17 **SOVEREIGN RULE (USA)**, 5, b h Sovereign Dancer—Surprise Special **L. Oung**
18 **STARRY EYED**, 4, b f Warning—Star of The Future
19 **SUAVE TERN (USA)**, 5, b h Arctic Tern—Suavite **Ecurie Chalhoub**
20 **TAGLIONI (USA)**, 4, ch c Woodman—Karri Valley **A. Leonard**
21 **TOMMELISE (USA)**, 4, b f Dayjur—Norland
22 **ULTIMATE GLORY (USA)**, 6, b h Our Native—Miss Ultimo **L. Oung**

THREE-YEAR-OLDS

23 **AKATIME (FR)**, b c Lead On Time—Akadya **Ecurie Chalhoub**
24 **ALBADA (USA)**, ch c Houston—Allegretta **Haras De La Perelle**
25 **AMOR'S PRINCESS (USA)**, ch f Sanglamore—Paddy's Princess **Haras De La Perelle**
26 **BACALL (USA)**, ch f Alysheba—Regal Gal **Tom Tatham**
27 **BACK OFF (IRE)**, gr c Waajib—Saltoki **L. Oung**
28 **BHAYDAMIX (FR)**, gr c Linamix—Bhaydana **L. Oung**
29 **BRINDLE**, b c Polar Falcon—Blade of Grass **L. Oung**
30 **BUENOS AIRES (FR)**, b c Saint Andrews—Pharlotte **Ecurie Chalhoub**
31 **BUTTERMERE**, ch c Polish Precedent—English Spring **M. Al Maktoum**
32 **BYZANTIUM (USA)**, b c Gulch—Bravemie **S. Niarchos**
33 **CARNIOLA**, b f Rainbow Quest—Carnival Spirit **M. Al Maktoum**
34 **CAXTON STAR**, ch c Soviet Star—Fiesta Fun **M. Charlton**
35 **CLURE (USA)**, ch c Theatrical—Garimpeiro **Alan Paulson**
36 **DARK AGE (IRE)**, b c Darshaan—Sarela **M. Al Maktoum**
37 **DISTANT THUNDER (USA)**, gr c Storm Cat—Am Wonderful **M. Lynam**
38 **DRAG QUEEN (IRE)**, b c Tirol—Queen of The Brush **L. Oung**
39 **FOLLE TEMPETE (FR)**, b f Fabulous Dancer—Belle Tempete **Simone Del Duca**
40 **FORT NOTTINGHAM (USA)**, b c Alleged—Aletta Maria **John Chandler**
41 **GEMSTONE (FR)**, b c Akarad—Noble Tiara **M. Al Maktoum**
42 **HARIM**, b c Nashwan—Harifa **M. Al Maktoum**
43 **HELIANTHUS**, b f Groom Dancer—Sunny Flower **Faisal Bin Salman**
44 **HIGHLY REGARDED (IRE)**, ch f Royal Academy—Society Royale **L. Oung**
45 **KALWHITE (FR)**, b f Kaldoun—White Wash **Ecurie Chalhoub**
46 **KEY LIGHT (USA)**, b f Theatrical—Top Nice **R. Witt**
47 **LADY LIEUTENANT (IRE)**, b f General Holme—Satin Pointe **M. Al Maktoum**
48 **LAND RIDE (USA)**, gr c Cozzene—Badgettland Rose **Ecurie Chalhoub**
49 **LISTE ROUGE (USA)**, b c Red Ransom—Bestseller's List **M. Charlton**
50 **MARELLE D'ETE (FR)**, gr f Kendor—Lutive **Y. Piaget**
51 **MAYSHIEL (IRE)**, b c Ela-Mana-Mou—Orillia **Cyril Humphris**
52 **MICHAELANGELO (FR)**, b c Lear Fan—Illusive Icicle **Ecurie NP Bloodstock**
53 **MONADIS (USA)**, ch f Miswaki—The Wheel Turns **Haras De La Perelle**
54 **MOON IS UP (USA)**, b f Woodman—Miesque **S. Niarchos**
55 **NEW YORK NEW YORK (FR)**, b c Le Glorieux—Treasure City **A. Richards**
56 **ON THE BEACH (USA)**, b f Cormorant—Street Walking
57 **PLEIN DE COULEURS**, b c Salse—Rainbow's End **L. Oung**
58 **POLAR COMMAND**, b c Polar Falcon—Queen's Visit **Cheveley Park Stud**
59 **POLAR STATE (IRE)**, b c Polar Falcon—Savahra **Ecurie Chalhoub**
60 **REVEALED (USA)**, b c Cryptoclearance—Gai Minois **L. Oung**
61 **RIVER BAY (USA)**, ch c Irish River—Buckeye Gal **Ecurie Chalhoub**
62 **SAUMAREINE (FR)**, b f Saumarez—Charming Queen **Haras De La Perelle**
63 **SCENE OF CHARGE (FR)**, b f Scenic—Charge Along **D. McIntyre**
64 **SEPTEUIL (USA)**, b c Lear Fan—Corita **Ecurie Chalhoub**
65 **SING WITH ME (FR)**, b f Hero's Honor—Live With Me **Ecurie Chalhoub**
66 **SPRIGHTLY**, b c Salse—Aunt Judy **L. Oung**
67 **STAGE MANNER**, b f In The Wings—Air Distingue **M. Al Maktoum**

MR J. E. HAMMOND—continued

68 **STAR PERFORMANCE (USA)**, b c Theatrical—Savannah Marsh **R. Witt**
69 **STONE TEMPLE (USA)**, b c Nureyev—Yemanja **S. Niarchos**
70 **SUPERNATURAL (FR)**, b c Fairy King—Eclat Nocturne **L. Oung**
71 **VAUTOUR ROUGE (USA)**, b c Sadler's Wells—Coup de Folie **S. Niarchos**
72 **VICOMTESSE MAG (FR)**, br f Highest Honor—Vigorine **Ecurie Chalhoub**
73 **VINGT ET UNE (FR)**, b f Sadler's Wells—Whakilyric **S. Niarchos**
74 **WIND OF ROSES (USA)**, ch f Lomond—Chimes of Freedom **S. Niarchos**
75 **WOODSPELL (USA)**, ch f Woodman—Beat **M. Al Maktoum**
76 **YOGTA (USA)**, ch f Riverman—Pasadoble **S. Niarchos**
77 **ZORYA (USA)**, gr f Relaunch—Ziska **M. Al Maktoum**

TWO-YEAR-OLDS

78 **ANNEMASSE (FR)**, b f 1/3 Suave Dancer—American Order **Ecurie Chalhoub**
79 B c 11/4 Kenmare—Ayah **M. Al Maktoum**
80 B c 3/4 Pistolet Bleu—Beaute Dangereuse **Ecurie Chalhoub**
81 **BRIARVILLE (IRE)**, b c 25/5 Top Ville—Bally Rose **A. Weinstock**
82 B f 20/2 Pistolet Bleu—Broken Sky **A. Wong**
83 B c 12/3 In The Wings—Catherine Parr **M. Al Maktoum**
84 **DARK WATER (FR)**, b f 15/3 Akarad—Little Deep Water **Simone Del Duca**
85 B c 27/3 Suave Dancer—Dial Dream **Ecurie Chalhoub**
86 B c 25/3 Miswaki—Earthland **M. Al Maktoum**
87 B c 21/2 Mujtahid—Far But Near **L. Oung**
88 **HONOURABLE (FR)**, b c 13/5 Hero's Honor—Donacika **A. Richards**
89 B c 14/4 Riverman—Konafa **S. Niarchos**
90 B c 5/3 Mtoto—Lambada **L. Oung**
91 **MILORD FONTENAILLE (FR)**, ch c 11/3 Nashamaa—Miss Fontenailles **Antonia Devin**
92 **MONSIEUR DANIEL (FR)**, b c 26/2 Fijar Tango—Avoise **L. Oung**
93 **PATRAS (IRE)**, ch c 3/5 Ela-Mana-Mou—Waterway **A. Weinstock**
94 B f 1/1 Groom Dancer—Sandbank **Rebecca Philipps**
95 B c 1/1 Machiavellian—Schezerade **S. Niarchos**
96 **SHADEYIEV (FR)**, b c 15/4 Exit To Nowhere—Touraille **A. Wong**
97 **SIR ALEC (FR)**, gr c 25/2 Rusticaro—Exiled **L. Oung**

266   MR M. D. HAMMOND, Middleham

Postal: **Tupgill Park Stables, Coverham, Middleham, Leyburn, DL8 4TJ.**

Phone: **(01969) 640228 FAX (01969) 640662**

1 **ALCIAN BLUE**, 5, b h Tina's Pet—Rhiannon **Rykneld Thoroughbred Co Ltd**
2 **ALLIMAC NOMIS**, 7, b g Daring March—Game For A Laugh **Wetherby Racing Bureau Plc**
3 **CAMPAIGN**, 5, b g Sure Blade (USA)—Just Cause **Spectrum**
4 **CLAY COUNTY**, 11, b g Sheer Grit—Make-Up **The County Set**
5 **CURRENT MONY (IRE)**, 5, ch g Electric—Killiney Rose **Mr Trevor Hemmings**
6 **DOMINANT SERENADE**, 7, b g Dominion—Sing Softly **North Briton Racing Club**
7 **ENCHANTED COTTAGE**, 4, b c Governor General—Mitsubishi Colour **David Kay Racing**
8 **ETHICAL NOTE (IRE)**, 5, ch h Orchestra—Ethel's Delight **Mr Trevor Hemmings**
9 **FURIETTO (IRE)**, 6, b g Lafontaine (USA)—Sesetta **Shirebrook Park Management Ltd**
10 **GONE AWAY (IRE)**, 7, b g Seclude (USA)—Im Leaving **Mr M. D. Hammond**
11 **KASIRAMA (IRE)**, 5, b g Asir—Queen of Swords **B. & K. Associates**
12 **LEGAL LORD**, 6, b g Strong Gale—Country Seat **Mr Trevor Hemmings**
13 **LORD FORTUNE (IRE)**, 6, b g Supreme Leader—All Profit **Mr Trevor Hemmings**
14 **MASTER OFTHE HOUSE**, 10, b g Kind of Hush—Miss Racine **Allerton Racing Club**
15 **MERRY ROSE**, 6, gr g Roselier (FR)—Velindre **Mr R. G. Ross**
16 **MONYMAN (IRE)**, 6, b g Mandalus—Superdora **Mr Trevor Hemmings**
17 **NATIVE MONY (IRE)**, 7, b g Bulldozer—Native Wings **Mr Trevor Hemmings**
18 **OUTSET (IRE)**, 6, ch g Persian Bold—It's Now Or Never **Mr Mark Kilner**
19 **PAGLIACCIO**, 8, b g Idiot's Delight—Stella Roma **Mr A. D. Stewart**
20 **PIMS GUNNER (IRE)**, 8, b g Montelimar (USA)—My Sweetie **Mr A. G. Chappell**

MR M. D. HAMMOND—continued

21 **PINK GIN,** 9, ch g Tickled Pink—Carrapateira **Mrs Margaret Francis**
22 **PORT IN A STORM,** 7, b g Blakeney—Crusader's Dream **John Doyle Construction**
23 **PROMITTO,** 6, ch m Roaring Riva—I Don't Mind **Yorkshire Born and Bred Racing**
24 **SARMATIAN (USA),** 5, br h Northern Flagship (USA)—Tracy L (USA) **Mr S. T. Brankin**
25 **SIR PETER LELY,** 9, b g Teenoso (USA)—Picture **John Doyle Construction Limited**
26 **TWIN CREEKS,** 5, b g Alzao (USA)—Double River (USA) **The Armchair Jockeys-Four Seasons Racing**
27 **UK HYGIENE (IRE),** 6, br g Lepanto (GER)—Proceeding **Mr A. J. Peake**
28 **UNPREJUDICE,** 5, b g North Briton—Interviewme (USA) **BDL Partners**
29 **VALIANT WARRIOR,** 8, br g Valiyar—Jouvencelle **Mr P. Sellars**
30 **WILMAN (IRE),** 6, b br g Supreme Leader—Kilcor Rose **Mr John Wilman**
31 **WISE ADVICE (IRE),** 6, b g Duky—Down The Aisle **Mr A. G. Chappell**

Other Owners: Mr T. Bosomworth, Mr Ben Brooks, Mr R. Butler, Mr B. Coulthard, Mr David Currie, Mr Philip Curry, Mrs M. A. Doohan, Mr A. Edgar, Mr J. M. Gahan, Mr George Godsman, Mr J. D. Gordon, Mr B. W. Greaves, Mr G. Hayton, Mr Richard Johnson, Mr B. Kennedy, Mr A. Kettles, Mr Cornelius Lysaght, Mr Charles Macmillan, Mr H. G. Owen, Mrs M. Powney-Jones, Mr A. R. Pryer, Mr Eddison Skeels, Mr Jimmy Smith, Mr Stephen G. Smith, Mr John Spencer, The Gemini Partnership (2), Mr G. Tuer, Mr D. M. Williams.

Jockey (Flat): J Marshall (7-7).

Jockeys (NH): A Dobbin (10-0, w.a), P Niven (w.a), B Storey (10-0, w.a).

Conditional: D Bentley (9-11), Kate Sellars (9-7).

Amateur: Mr C Bonner (9-10).

267 MR B. HANBURY, Newmarket

Postal: **Diomed Stables, Hamilton Road, Newmarket, Suffolk, CB8 OPD.**
Phone: **OFFICE (01638) 663193 YARD 664799 FAX 667209 HOME (01440) 820396**

1 **AMRAK AJEEB (IRE)**, 4, b c Danehill (USA)—Noble Dust (USA)
2 **BARDON HILL BOY (IRE)**, 4, b g Be My Native (USA)—Star With A Glimer
3 **BLUE BLAZER**, 6, b g Bluebird (USA)—View
4 **CHEYENNE SPIRIT**, 4, ch f Indian Ridge—Bazaar Promise
5 **EN ATTENDANT (FR)**, 8, ch g Bairn (USA)—Vizenia
6 **HAGWAH (USA)**, 4, b f Dancing Brave (USA)—Saraa Ree (USA)
7 **HUGWITY**, 4, ch c Cadeaux Genereux—Nuit d'Ete (USA)
8 **MARSOOM (CAN)**, 5, b h Wild Again (USA)—Sadwester (USA)
9 **MILLESIME (IRE)**, 4, ch g Glow (USA)—Persian Myth
10 **MOMENTS OF FORTUNE (USA)**, 4, b g Timeless Moment (USA)—How Fortunate (USA)
11 **MOONLIGHT QUEST**, 8, gr g Nishapour (FR)—Arabian Rose (USA)
12 **SAFEY ANA (USA)**, 5, b g Dixieland Band (USA)—Whatsoraire (USA)
13 **SOVEREIGN PAGE (USA)**, 7, ch g Caro—Tashinsky (USA)
14 **YET AGAIN**, 4, ch g Weldnaas (USA)—Brightelmstone
15 **ZAALEFF (USA)**, 4, ch c Zilzal (USA)—Continual (USA)

THREE-YEAR-OLDS

16 **AFRICAN SUN (IRE)**, b g Mtoto—Nuit d'Ete (USA)
17 **ALPINE HIDEAWAY (IRE)**, b c Tirol—Arbour (USA)
18 **BENT RAIWAND (USA)**, b f Cadeaux Genereux—Raiwand
19 **CARIBBEAN QUEST**, b f Rainbow Quest (USA)—Jammaayil (IRE)
20 **EAGLE CANYON (IRE)**, b br c Persian Bold—Chrism
21 **FYORS GIFT (IRE)**, b f Cadeaux Genereux—Miss Fyor (USA)
22 **KUWAM (IRE)**, b g Last Tycoon—Inshad
23 **MATIYA (IRE)**, b f Alzao (USA)—Purchasepaperchase
24 **MR WILD (USA)**, b g Wild Again (USA)—Minstress (USA)
25 **MY REEM (USA)**, ch f Chief's Crown (USA)—Fabulous Salt (USA)
26 **NO HIDING PLACE**, ch c Nabeel Dancer (USA)—Blushing Pink (USA)
27 **NO RETURN (USA)**, ch g Danzig Connection (USA)—Up To Juliet (USA)
28 **NORTHERN JUDGE**, ch g Highest Honor (FR)—Nordica
29 **PERSEPHONE**, ch f Lycius (USA)—Elarrih (USA)
30 **POLAR PROSPECT**, b c Polar Falcon (USA)—Littlemisstrouble (USA)
31 **RAMOOZ (USA)**, b c Rambo Dancer (CAN)—My Shafy
32 **RIVER FOREST (USA)**, ch g Diesis—Huronia (USA)
33 **SECRET GIFT**, ch f Cadeaux Genereux—Triste Oeil (USA)
34 **UHUD (IRE)**, b f Mujtahid (USA)—Princess of Zurich (IRE)
35 **WHAT A FUSS**, b g Great Commotion (USA)—Hafwah

TWO-YEAR-OLDS

36 B c 7/3 Lead On Time (USA)—Al Guswa (Shernazar)
37 **ASEF ALHIND**, ch c 4/5 Indian Ridge—Willowbed (Wollow)
38 Ch c 21/1 Salse (USA)—Bereeka (Main Reef)
39 b f 28/4 Indian Ridge—Branston Express (Bay Express)
40 B c 16/3 Dayjur (USA)—Copper Creek (IRE) (Habitat)
41 **CRESCENT'S WHISPER (IRE)**, ro c 10/3 Shalford (IRE)—Checkers (Habat)
42 B c 20/1 Green Desert (USA)—Fitnah (Kris)
43 B br c 7/3 Wild Again (USA)—Garvin's Gal (USA) (Seattle Slew (USA))
44 **GRANITE MOUNTAIN (USA)**, ch c 14/4 Mt Livermore (USA)—Desagiada (ARG) (Consultant's Bid (USA))
45 B c 1/4 Cadeaux Genereux—Hafwah (Gorytus (USA))
46 **HARIK**, ch c 16/4 Persian Bold—Yaqut (USA) (Northern Dancer)
47 **HIKMAH (USA)**, b f 13/3 Alleged (USA)—Followeveryrainbow (USA) (Mehmet (USA))
48 **IRTAB (IRE)**, b c 26/4 Lycius (USA)—Sharayif (IRE) (Green Desert (USA))
49 **JAFN**, ch f 7/2 Sharpo—Harold's Girl (FR) (Northfields (USA))
50 B c 31/1 Green Desert (USA)—Layaali (USA) (Diesis)
51 **MANWAL (IRE)**, b c 14/3 Bluebird (USA)—My My Marie (Artaius (USA))
52 **MESHHED (USA)**, ch f 15/3 Gulch (USA)—Umniyatee (Green Desert (USA))

MR B. HANBURY—continued

53 B f 18/2 Lahib (USA)—Murooj (USA) (Diesis)
54 B c 20/3 Sheikh Albadou—My Shafy (Rousillon (USA))
55 **NIGHT EXPRESS,** ch c 28/2 Night Shift (USA)—New Edition (Great Nephew)
56 **SWEET PATOOPIE,** b f 28/4 Indian Ridge—Patriotic (Hotfoot)
57 Gr c 27/3 Black Tie Affair—Tia Juanita (USA) (My Gallant (USA))
58 **TITHCAR,** b f 27/2 Cadeaux Genereux—Miznah (IRE) (Sadler's Wells (USA))
59 B f 29/1 Green Desert (USA)—Triste Oeil (USA) (Raise A Cup (USA))
60 Gr c 18/3 Petong—Very Nice (FR) (Green Dancer (USA))
61 Ch f 22/2 Cadeaux Genereux—Winnie Reckless (Local Suitor (USA))
62 **ZUGUDI,** b c 29/3 Night Shift (USA)—Overdrive (Shirley Heights)

Apprentices: P Bowe (8-8), J Stack (7-13).

Late Naming

NEUF A LA BANQUE, b f 28/4 Indian Ridge — Branston Express (Bay Express)

268   MR R. HANNON, Marlborough

Postal: **East Everleigh Stables, Marlborough, SN8 3EY.**

Phone: **(01264) 850 254 FAX (01264) 850 820**

1 **ALDANEH,** 4, ch f Indian Ridge—Maiyaasah **Sheikh Essa Bin Mubarak**
2 **ALRIFFA,** 5, b h Danehill (USA)—Sweet Soprano **Sheikh Essa Bin Mubarak**
3 **ASSESSOR (IRE),** 7, b h Niniski (USA)—Dingle Bay **Sultan Al Kabeer**
4 **ASTERITA,** 4, b f Rainbow Quest (USA)—Northshiel **Mr B. E. Nielsen**
5 **AT LIBERTY (IRE),** 4, b c Danehill (USA)—Music of The Night (USA) **Mr Bruce Adams**
6 **BAGSHOT,** 5, b h Rousillon (USA)—Czar's Bride (USA) **Mr George E. K. Teo**
7 **BLAZE OF SONG,** 4, ch c Jester—Intellect **Mr D. Boocock**
8 **COMMONER (USA),** 4, b c Far North (CAN)—Searching Around (USA) **Mr B. E. Nielsen**
9 **DESERT GREEN (FR),** 7, b g Green Desert (USA)—Green Leaf (USA) **Mrs P. Jubert**
10 **FAIRY KNIGHT,** 4, b c Fairy King (USA)—Vestal Flame **P. & S. Lever Partners**
11 **FIRE DOME (IRE),** 4, ch c Salt Dome (USA)—Penny Habit **Mr Mahmood Al-Shuaibi**
12 **MAJOR CHANGE,** 4, gr c Sharrood (USA)—May The Fourteenth **Mrs C. J. Powell**
13 **NOBLE SPRINTER (IRE),** 4, b c The Noble Player (USA)—Daybreaker **Khanmaher**
14 **RIGHT WIN (IRE),** 6, br h Law Society (USA)—Popular Win **Mr Conal Kavanagh**
15 **SERGEYEV (IRE),** 4, ch c Mulholland (USA)—Escape Path **Mr B. T. Stewart-Brown**
16 **SHOW FAITH (IRE),** 6, ch g Exhibitioner—Keep The Faith **Mr I. A. N. Wight & D. M. Wight**
17 **STONE RIDGE (IRE),** 4, b c Indian Ridge—Cut In Stone (USA) **Mrs Chris Harrington**
18 **VAUGRENIER (IRE),** 4, b c Scenic—Church Mountain **Mr Ivan Twigden**
19 **WAVIAN,** 4, b c Warning—Vian (USA) **Mr Saleh Al Homeizi**
20 **WET PATCH (IRE),** 4, b br g Common Grounds—Disco Girl (FR) **Mr Peter Hammond**
21 **WIJARA (IRE),** 4, b c Waajib—Nawara **Mr Mohamed Suhail**

THREE-YEAR-OLDS

22 **APACHE LEN (USA),** br c Rahy (USA)—Shining Skin (USA) **Mr Roy Taiano**
23 **AUTOBABBLE (IRE),** b c Glenstal (USA)—Almalat **Mr Bruce Adams**
24 **BALLPOINT,** ch c Indian Ridge—Ballaquine **Mr A. N. Solomons**
25 **BEARNAISE (IRE),** b f Cyrano de Bergerac—Gentle Guest (IRE) **Lord Carnarvon**
26 **BELIEVE ME,** b c Beveled (USA)—Pink Mex **Mr Bruce Adams**
27 **BOMBAY SAPPHIRE,** b f Be My Chief (USA)—Ginny Binny **Mr P. T. Tellwright**
28 **CAYMAN KAI (IRE),** ch c Imperial Frontier (USA)—Safiya (USA) **Mr I. A. N. Wight & D. M. Wight**
29 **CHARLIE CHANG (IRE),** b c Don't Forget Me—East River (FR) **Mr Jim Horgan**
30 **CLEMENTE,** b br c Robellino (USA)—Gravad Lax **Mr Robert P. Beahan**
31 **CLOUDS HILL (FR),** b c Sarhoob (USA)—Dana Dana (FR) **Mrs P. Jubert**
32 **CROSS THE BORDER,** b g Statoblest—Brave Advance (USA) **Mr P. D. Savill**
33 **CURRENT LEADER,** b g Primo Dominie—Trelissick **Mr P. D. Savill**
34 **DAUNTING DESTINY (BEL),** b c Formidable (USA)—Heavy Land (FR) **The Gold Buster Syndicate**
35 **DECISION MAKER (IRE),** b c Taufan (USA)—Vain Deb **The Boardroom Syndicate**

MR R. HANNON—continued

36 DIL DIL, b f Puissance—My Croft **Khanmaher**
37 DOMETTES (IRE), ch f Archway (IRE)—Superetta **Albion Investments**
38 FLAHUIL, b f Generous (IRE)—Sipsi Fach **Mr N. Hayes**
39 FLINT AND STEEL, b g Rock City—Brassy Nell **Mr Michael Broke**
40 FLYING PENNANT (IRE), gr c Waajib—Flying Beckee (IRE) **Mr C. M. Hamer**
41 FUTURE'S TRADER, b c Alzao (USA)—Awatef **Mr A. Hakim**
42 GENERAL ROSE, b c Governor General—Aleda Rose **Mr D. B. Gallop**
43 GOLDEN ACE (IRE), ch c Archway (IRE)—Gobolino **Mr George E. K. Teo**
44 GUMAIR (USA), ch c Summer Squall (USA)—Finisterre (AUS) **Sheikh Essa Bin Mubarak**
45 HONORABLE ESTATE (IRE), b f High Estate—Holy Devotion **R. A. Bernard**
46 KIROV LADY (IRE), b f Soviet Lad (USA)—Cestrefeld **Mr David Seale**
47 KISS ME AGAIN (IRE), b f Cyrano de Bergerac—Now Serving **Mr Bob Lalemant**
48 LA TANSANI, b c High Estate—Hana Marie **Mr Saleh Al Homeizi**
49 LOMBERTO, b c Robellino (USA)—Lamees (USA) **Mr Saleh Al Homeizi**
50 LONELY LEADER (IRE), ch c Royal Academy (USA)—Queen To Conquer (USA) **Mr Salem Suhail**
51 LOVE BATETA (IRE), b br f Caerleon (USA)—Marie Noelle (FR) **Sheik Ahmad Yousuf Al Sabah**
52 LUCKY LIONEL (USA), ch c Mt Livermore (USA)—Crafty Nan (USA) **Mr Antonio Balzarini**
53 MAJOR DUNDEE (IRE), b c Distinctly North (USA)—Indigo Blue (IRE) **Mr J. A. Leek**
54 MORE THAN YOU KNOW (IRE), ch f Kefaah (USA)—Foston Bridge **Mr Bob Lalemant**
55 MYRTLE, b f Batshoof—Greek Goddess **Lord Carnarvon**
56 NAVIGATE (USA), ch c Diesis—Libras Shiningstar (USA) **Highclere Thoroughbred Racing Ltd**
57 NIGHT HARMONY (IRE), ch c Digamist (USA)—Quaver **Mr T. J. Dale**
58 NORTHERN BALLET (IRE), b f Sadler's Wells (USA)—Miranisa **Mrs John Magnier**
59 ORTOLAN, gr c Prince Sabo—Kala Rosa **Mr J. A. Lazzari**
60 PAINT IT BLACK, ch c Double Schwartz—Tableaux (FR) **Mr Michael Pescod**
61 PHILOSOPHER (IRE), b c Royal Academy (USA)—Flyaway Bride (USA) **Mr Michael Kelly (New Jersey)**
62 PIGEON HOLE, b f Green Desert (USA)—Cubby Hole **Lord Carnarvon**
63 PLEASE SUZANNE, b f Cadeaux Genereux—Aquaglow **Mr Mohamed Suhail**
64 PRENDS CA (IRE), b f Reprimand—Cri de Coeur (USA) **Mr P. B. Adams**
65 REGIMENT (IRE), gr c Shaadi (USA)—Rossaldene **Highclere Thoroughbred Racing Ltd**
66 ROMAN GOLD (IRE), b c Petorius—Saffron (FR) **Mr George E. K. Teo**
67 ROYAL EXPOSE (USA), ch c Unzipped (USA)—Royal Tasha (USA) **Mr Mahmood Al-Shuaibi**
68 SANTELLA CAPE, b c Alzao (USA)—Kijafa (USA) **Mr Roy Taiano**
69 SEVEN CROWNS (USA), b c Chief's Crown (USA)—Ivory Dance (USA) **Mr Mahmood Al-Shuaibi**
70 SHAHA, b c Polish Precedent (USA)—Height of Passion **Mr Salem Suhail**
71 SHARP SHUFFLE (IRE), ch c Exactly Sharp (USA)—Style **Mrs H. F. Prendergast**
72 SLIP JIG (IRE), b c Marju (IRE)—Taking Steps **Mr John Horgan**
73 SPOTTED EAGLE, ch g Risk Me (FR)—Egnoussa **Lord Carnarvon**
74 STERLING FELLOW, b c Pharly (FR)—Favorable Exchange **Mr J. A. Leek**
75 VILLAGE KING (IRE), b c Roi Danzig (USA)—Honorine (USA) **Mr N. Ahamad**
76 WATCH ME (IRE), b f Green Desert (USA)—Fenny Rough **Mr Salem Suhail**
77 WHITE SETTLER, b c Polish Patriot (USA)—Oasis **J. Newsome**
78 WIGHT, gr f Sharrood (USA)—Wrangbrook **Mr G. Mazza**
79 WISAM, b c Shaadi (USA)—Moon Drop **Mr Mohamed Suhail**

TWO-YEAR-OLDS

80 ALARME BELLE, b f 26/2 Warning—Dazzlingly Radiant (Try My Best (USA)) **J. G. Davis**
81 ANOTHER NIGHT (IRE), ch c 30/4 Waajib—Little Me (Connaught) **Mr Bob Lalemant**
82 B f 1/5 Polish Patriot (USA)—Arbour (USA) (Graustark) **Mr Peter Hammond**
83 ARETHUSA, ch f 16/2 Primo Dominie—Downeaster Alexa (USA) (Red Ryder (USA)) **Lord Carnarvon**
84 B f 3/4 Night Shift (USA)—Art Age (Artaius (USA)) **P. Winfield**
85 Ch c 13/3 Maelstrom Lake—Baliana (CAN) (Riverman (USA)) **J. S. Threadwell**
86 BALLADARA, b c 25/4 Ballad Rock—Mochara (Last Fandango) **Mr D. Boocock**
87 BLUE JAY (IRE), br c 8/4 Bluebird (USA)—Alpine Spring (Head For Heights) **Lord Carnarvon**
88 B f 16/2 Green Desert (USA)—Blushing Storm (USA) (Blushing Groom (FR)) **Mr Mohamed Suhail**
89 BOLD SPRING (IRE), b c 28/2 Never So Bold—Oasis (Valiyar) **J. Newsome**
90 BRISKA (IRE), b f 14/4 River Falls—Calash (Indian King) **Lord Carnarvon**
91 CAVIAR ROYALE (IRE), ch c 26/3 Royal Academy (USA)—
                                      Petite Liquerelle (IRE) (Shernazar) **Mr George E. K. Teo**
92 CELEBRANT, b f 29/4 Saddlers' Hall (IRE)—Cathedra (So Blessed) **Cheveley Park Stud**

MR R. HANNON—continued

93 **CHAMPAGNE TOAST**, ch c 15/3 Mazilier (USA)—Saraswati (Mansingh (USA)) **The Boardroom Syndicate**
94 **CHERRY BLOSSOM (IRE)**, br f 26/3 Primo Dominie—Varnish (Final Straw) **Highclere Thoroughbred Racing Ltd**
95 **CHIEF PREDATOR (USA)**, ch c 6/4 Chief's Crown (USA)—
                                    Tsavorite (USA) (Halo (USA)) **Thurloe Thoroughbred Services**
96 Gr c 19/4 El Prado (IRE)—Chili Lee (USA) (Belted Earl (USA)) **Mr G. Howard-Spink**
97 **CORINTHIAN (IRE)**, b c 30/3 Lycius (USA)—
                                    Royal Recreation (USA) (His Majesty (USA)) **Highclere Thoroughbred Racing Ltd**
98 Br c 11/5 Known Fact (USA)—Cosmic Sea Queen (USA) (Determined Cosmic (USA)) **Mr George E. K. Teo**
99 **DALVIK (USA)**, b c 1/1 Cozzene (USA)—Danzigitty (USA) (Danzig (USA)) **Sultan Al Kabeer**
100 **DICKIE BIRD (IRE)**, ch c 22/3 Shalford (IRE)—Peace In The Woods (Tap On Wood) **Mr George E. K. Teo**
101 **DON SEBASTIAN**, br c 3/4 Indian Ridge—Bertrade (Homeboy) **Khanmaher**
102 **DOWRY**, b f 14/4 Rudimentary (USA)—Priceless Bond (USA) (Blushing Groom (FR)) **Cheveley Park Stud**
103 **FANNY'S CHOICE (IRE)**, b f 16/2 Fairy King (USA)—Gaychimes (Steel Heart) **Mr N. Ahamad**
104 **FASHION DISTRICT (IRE)**, ch f 17/4 Common Grounds—First Heiress (IRE) (Last Tycoon) **Sultan Al Kabeer**
105 B c 8/2 Puissance—Femme Formidable (Formidable (USA)) **Mr Saleh Al Homeizi**
106 B c 31/3 Pursuit Of Love—Figini (Glint of Gold) **Sheikh Essa Bin Mubarak**
107 **FIZZING**, b f 6/2 Efisio—Kentucky Starlet (USA) (Cox's Ridge (USA)) **W. Hawkings**
108 Ch f 3/3 Shalford (IRE)—God Speed Her (Pas de Seul) **Mrs John Magnier**
109 Ch c 10/4 Salt Dome (USA)—Good Behaviour (Artaius (USA)) **J. Shannon**
110 **GOPI**, b f 27/2 Marju (IRE)—Chandni (IRE) (Ahonoora) **Miss L. Regis**
111 **GREEN JEWEL**, gr f 8/2 Environment Friend—Emeraude (Kris) **T. Bucknall**
112 B f 17/4 Rainbow Quest (USA)—Hatton Gardens (Auction Ring (USA)) **Mr Mohamed Suhail**
113 **INDIAN RAPTURE**, ch f 27/1 Be My Chief—Moments Joy (Adonijah) **Mr A. F. Merritt**
114 Ch f 3/3 Shalford (IRE)—Indigo Blue (IRE) (Bluebird (USA)) **Mr Mahmood Al-Shuaibi**
115 B c 26/3 Dancing Dissident—Kafsa (IRE) (Vayrann) **J. S. Threadwell**
116 Ch c 19/1 Night Shift (USA)—Lassalia (Sallust) **Lucayan Stud**
117 **LATIN MASTER (IRE)**, ch c 1/5 Priolo (USA)—Salustrina (Sallust) **J. Perry**
118 **LIFE ON THE STREET**, b f 18/1 Statoblest—Brave Advance (USA) (Bold Laddie (USA)) **Mr P. D. Savill**
119 **LUDO**, gr c 25/1 Petong—Teacher's Game (Mummy's Game) **Mr Michael Pescod**
120 **MAGAONA (FR)**, b f 6/5 Slip Anchor—Movieland (USA) (Nureyev (USA)) **V. C. Matalon**
121 **MARIA DI CASTIGLIA**, b f 12/1 Danehill (USA)—Macrina Pompea (Don Roberto (USA)) **Mr G. Mazza**
122 **MASTERPIECE**, br c 2/3 Primo Dominie—Swift Return (Double Form) **Lady Tennant**
123 Ch f 22/3 Elmaamul (USA)—Migiyas (Kings Lake (USA)) **Mr T. A. Johnsey**
124 Ch c 28/4 Presidium—Missish (Mummy's Pet) **J. Palmer-Brown**
125 B f 6/5 Green Desert (USA)—Moon Drop (Dominion) **Mr Mohamed Suhail**
126 **ORONTES (USA)**, br c 6/5 Lomond (USA)—Chateau Princess (USA) (Majestic Prince (USA)) **Mr J. A. Lazzari**
127 **ORTELIUS**, br c 18/4 Rudimentary (USA)—Third Movement (Music Boy) **Mr I. A. N. Wight & D. M. Wight**
128 **PELHAM (IRE)**, b c 19/4 Archway (IRE)—Yavarro (Raga Navarro) **D. Lucie Smith**
129 **PERMISSION**, b f 18/4 Rudimentary (USA)—Ask Mama (Mummy's Pet) **Cheveley Park Stud**
130 Br c 18/1 Petong—Petriece (Mummy's Pet) **Mr Saleh Al Homeizi**
131 **POINT BREAK**, ch c 14/2 Sharpo—Sweet Quest (Rainbow Quest (USA)) **Kennet Valley Thoroughbreds**
132 **POWDER RIVER**, b c 24/1 Alzao (USA)—Nest (Sharpo) **Lord Carnarvon**
133 **RAINDANCING (IRE)**, b f 30/3 Tirol—Persian Song (Persian Bold) **Mr N. Hayes**
134 **RED EMBERS**, gr f 23/3 Saddlers' Hall (IRE)—Kala Rosa (Kalaglow) **Cheveley Park Stud**
135 Gr c 13/4 Great Commotion (USA)—Renzola (Dragonara Palace (USA)) **Lucayan Stud**
136 **RIVER KING**, b c 27/2 River Falls—Sialia (IRE) (Bluebird (USA)) **Highclere Thoroughbred Racing Ltd**
137 **ROFFEY SPINNEY (IRE)**, ch c 27/4 Masterclass (USA)—Crossed Line (Thatching) **Mrs D. F. Cock**
138 B f 10/3 Robellino (USA)—Rose Chanelle (Welsh Pageant) **Amity Finance**
139 **RUDI'S PET (IRE)**, ch c 15/5 Don't Forget Me—Pink Fondant (Northfields (USA)) **The Broadgate Partnership**
140 **RUMBUSTIOUS**, b f 24/3 Rambo Dancer (CAN)—Persian Alexandra (Persian Bold) **C. Curtis**
141 **SAND CAY (USA)**, ch c 12/4 Geiger Counter (USA)—
                                    Lily Lily Rose (Lyphoor) **Mr I. A. N. Wight & D. M. Wight**
142 **SECRET BALLOT (IRE)**, b c 13/3 Taufan (USA)—Ballet Society (FR) (Sadler's Wells) **Mr N. Ahamad**
143 **SENORITA MATILDA (USA)**, b f 6/2 El Gran Senor (USA)—Copperama (AUS) (Comeran (FR)) **Mr J. C. Smith**
144 **SHALL WE GO (IRE)**, b f 1/4 Shalford (IRE)—Grapette (Nebbiolo) **Kennet Valley Thoroughbreds**
145 **SHARP HAT**, ch c 29/4 Shavian—Madam Trilby (Grundy) **Mr J. C. Smith**
146 **SMOKEY PETE**, gr c 7/3 Petong—Quick Profit (Formidable (USA)) **J. G. Davis**
147 **SNOW EAGLE (IRE)**, b f 25/3 Polar Falcon (USA)—Icefern (Moorestyle) **Highclere Thoroughbred Racing Ltd**
148 Ch c 2/3 Indian Ridge—Souadah (USA) (General Holme (USA)) **Mr Saleh Al Homeizi**
149 **SPONDULICKS (IRE)**, b c 26/3 Silver Kite (USA)—Greek Music (Tachypous) **Barouche Stud**

MR R. HANNON—continued

150 TAUFAN ROOKIE (IRE), b c 11/3 Taufan (USA)—Royal Wolff (Prince Tenderfoot (USA)) **Meridian Stud**
151 Ch f 20/1 Miswaki (USA)—Tom's Lassie (USA) (Tom Rolfe) **Mr Mohamed Suhail**
152 TONY'S RIDGE, ch f 16/3 Indian Ridge—Polly's Pear (USA) (Sassafras (FR)) **A. Harrington**
153 TRIPLE HAY, ch c 25/3 Safawan—Davinia (Gold Form) **The Broadgate Partnership**
154 WILD HADEER, ch c 24/3 Hadeer—Wild Moon (USA) (Arctic Tern (USA)) **Khanmaher**
155 WOLF MOUNTAIN, ch c 16/4 Selkirk (USA)—Cubby Hole (Town And Country) **Lord Carnarvon**

Other Owners: Mr C. Aleong, Aston House Stud, Mr Victor Behrens, Mr Noel Browne, Mr Richard J. Cohen, Mr Michael Collins, Mr C. Cook, Mr R. J. Fuller, Mrs W. H. Gibson Fleming, Mr E. J. Gilbertson, Mr I. Goldsmith, Mr M. W. Grant, Mr C. D. Ham, Mr K. S. Jones, Mr Paul Jubert, Mr Peter Jubert, Mr J. Kavanagh, Mr A. M. Kneen, Mr Jose A. Maher, Mr Mana Al Maktoum, New Cavendish Import & Export Ltd, Mr L. Orlandi, Mr Peter R. Pritchard, Mr Robert Russell, Mr L. M. Salzman, Mr G. C. Sampson, Mr Pierpont Scott, Mr Ruthven Smith, Mr G. S. Stockil, Mr D. J. Toye.

Jockey (Flat): R Perham (8-4).

Apprentices: Mark Denaro (8-7), Enda Greehy (8-4), Dane O'Neill (8-0).

Lady Rider: Mrs Denise Machale (8-8).

269   MR J. HARRIMAN, Tredegar

Postal: **Hen-tafern (Old Britannia), Market Street, Tredegar, Gwent, NP2 3NH.**
Phone: **(0495) 723724**

1 GORT, 8, b g Teenoso (USA)—Stemegna **Mr John Harriman**

270   MRS JESSICA HARRINGTON, Kildare

Postal: **Commonstown Stables, Moone, Co. Kildare.**
Phone: **(0507) 24153 FAX (0507) 24292 CAR (088) 566129**

1 ABBEY GALE (IRE), 5, br m Strong Gale—Monks Lass (IRE) **Mrs A. Smyth**
2 AIN'T MISBEHAVIN', 9, br g Callernish—Well Mannered **Mrs J. Harrington**
3 BROCKLEY COURT, 9, b g Boreen (FR)—Arctic Free **Cronin Plc**
4 5, B m Supreme Leader—Caught In The Act **Mrs J. Harrington**
5 CHERKIZOVSKY (IRE), 6, br g Good Thyne (USA)—Regent's Gina **Mrs E. Queally**
6 DANCE BEAT (IRE), 5, br m Dancing Dissident (USA)—In My Time **Mrs E. Queally**
7 FAUSTDANTENO (IRE), 5, br g Phardante (FR)—Vermont Angel **Mrs E. Queally**
8 FIDDLING THE FACTS (IRE), 5, br m Orchestra—Facts 'n Fancies **Mrs G. Nicholl**
9 GRANGE COURT (IRE), 6, br g Bassa Selim—Tetlin (FR) **Cronin Plc**
10 GRENNANHILL (IRE), 7, br g Roselier (FR)—Polarogan **The H. Syndicate**
11 HEARNS HILL (IRE), 7, b g Lancastrian—Bigwood **George Kent**
12 IGOR BOY (IRE), 6, b g Aylesfield—Hidden Hand (USA) **Mrs E. Queally**
13 JACK CHAUCER, 4, ch g Kalaglow—Madison Girl **Liam Burke**
14 KNOCKBOY QUAY (IRE), 6, br g Quayside—Knockboy Star **Sean Walshe**
15 MISS ORCHESTRA (IRE), 5, b m Orchestra—Jims Monkey **The BB Horse Racing Club**
16 MUNNINGS (IRE), 5, ch g Roselier (FR)—James Rose **R. McElliott & Miss Zoe McElliott**
17 OCTOBER SYMPHONY (IRE), 5, br g Orchestra—Galmoy Girl **Mrs M. Foley**
18 OH SO GRUMPY, 8, b g Daring March—Gay Rhapsody **Mrs E. Queally**
19 4, Br g Don't Forget Me—Olwyn **Mrs D. Nagle & Partners**
20 PROLOGUE (IRE), 5, br g Mandalus—Advance Notice **R. McElliott**
21 5, Br g Derrylin—Raise The Dawn **Mrs J. Harrington**

MRS JESSICA HARRINGTON—continued

22 5, B g Supreme Leader—Rodeo Fun **Mrs R. Coleman & Partners**
23 ROSCOLVIN (IRE), 4, b g Prince Rupert (FR)—Chepstow House (USA) **Mrs J. Harrington**
24 SHIEFFER (IRE), 5, ch m Electric—Money Incinerator **Mrs J. Magnier & Mrs J. Horgan**
25 SKY LEADER (IRE), 6, b g Supreme Leader—Sky Is The Limit **R. A. B. Whittle**
26 SPACE TRUCKER (IRE), 5, b g Kambalda—Seat of Learning **Mrs E. Queally**
27 SPINDANTE (IRE), 6, br m Phardante (FR)—Spin of A Coin **Mrs E. Queally**
28 4, B g Boreen (FR)—Superfine **Harry Murphy & Mrs J. Harrington**
29 THATS FAR ENOUGH (IRE), 6, b g Carlingford Castle—Love And Idleness **Laurence Dempsy**
30 THE FLASHER (IRE), 5, gr g Cardinal Flower—Eye Flasher **G. V. Nicholl**
31 TOM KENNY (IRE), 6, b g Lhasa—Lady Hapsburg **David Nugent**
32 5, Ch g Ra Nova—True Divine **Adam Gurney**
33 UNKNOWN SOLDIER (IRE), 6, b g Supreme Leader—Money Incinerator **Mrs J. Magnier & Mrs J. Horgan**
34 VERITATIS SPLENDOR (IRE), 7, b g Supreme Leader—Gold Artiste **Mrs J. Harrington**
35 YOUR CALL (IRE), 7, b g Boreen Beag—In Brief **Mrs E. Queally**

THREE-YEAR-OLDS

36 KHAMBANI (IRE), br f Royal Academy (USA)—Tobira Celeste (USA) **Mrs D. Nagle & Mrs J. Magnier**
37 LOST ALPHABET (IRE), br g Don't Forget Me—Zenga **Mrs J. Harrington**
38 RENATA'S PRINCE (IRE), br c Prince Rupert (FR)—Maria Renata **Mrs E. Queally**

Jockey (NH): John Shortt (w.a.).

Conditional: B J Heffernan (9-0).

271 MR J. A. HARRIS, Edingley

Postal: **Carvers Croft, Carvers Hollow, Off Greaves Lane, Edingley.**
Phone: HOME **(01623) 882595** YARD **(01636) 816719** MOBILE **(0860) 698270**

1 ANCHORENA, 4, b f Slip Anchor—Canna **Joanne Francesca Wichelow**
2 ANYAR REEM, 5, br g Slip Anchor—Alruccaba **Mr Paul Murphy**
3 BIRTHPLACE (IRE), 6, br g Top Ville—Birthday Party (FR) **The Boden Cummings Partnership**
4 BURNTWOOD MELODY, 5, gr g Merdon Melody—Marwick **Mr Robert Fearnall**
5 CASTLE DIAMOND, 9, ch g Carlingford Castle—Miss Diamond **Mr Paul Murphy**
6 GREEN'S SEAGO (USA), 8, ch g Fighting Fit (USA)—Ornamental (USA) **Mr Steve McLaughlin**
7 HATTA RIVER (USA), 6, b h Irish River (FR)—Fallacieuse **Mr R. N. Fearnall**
8 LET'S GET LOST, 7, ch g Chief Singer—Lost In France **Mr Paul Murphy**
9 NEEDWOOD JOKER, 5, b g Picea—Mey Madam **Triple Diamond Partnership**
10 NITE-OWL DANCER, 4, b f Robellino (USA)—Lady Tap **Burntwood Sports Ltd**
11 RAFTER-J, 5, b br g Petoski—Coming Out **Mr W. Meah**
12 SMART GUEST, 4, ch c Be My Guest (USA)—Konbola **Mr Paul Murphy**
13 SWYNFORD FLYER, 7, b m Valiyar—Qualitairess **Mr David Pettifor**
14 TILLY OWL, 5, b m Formidable (USA)—Tilly Tavi **Burntwood Sports Ltd**
15 VICTORIA DAY, 4, b f Reference Point—Victoress (USA) **Mr Paul Murphy**

THREE-YEAR-OLDS

16 BITES, b f Risk Me (FR)—Sundaysport Splash **Mr W. Meah**
17 DONINGTON PARK, ch f Risk Me (FR)—Small Double (IRE) **Mr R. N. Fearnall**
18 KURY GIRL, b f Superlative—Azubah **D. Howlett**
19 NITEOWL RAIDER (IRE), ch c Standaan (FR)—Havana Moon **Burntwood Sports Ltd**
20 NORTH MOSS, b c Scorpio (FR)—Bint Al Arab **David McDuffie**
21 RENO'S TREASURE (USA), ch f Beau Genius (USA)—Ligia M (USA) **Mr David Pettifor**
22 SATURIBA (USA), b c Fighting Fit (USA)—My Popsicle (USA) **Mrs Annette Harris**
23 STAR REP, b f Reprimand—My Greatest Star **Chippenham Lodge Stud**

TWO-YEAR-OLDS

24 FRANDICKBOB, b c 17/2 Statoblest—Crimson Ring (Persian Bold) **Mr J. S. Fox, Mr Frank Beale**
25 SCOBI, ch c 26/2 Scottish Reel—Bint Al Arab (Ahonoora) **David McDuffie**

MR J. A. HARRIS—continued

Other Owners: Mr R. B. Johnstone, Mr Bob Landrey, Messinger Stud Limited, Mr G. R. Oliver, Mrs H. M. Oliver, Potwells Racing, Mr P. Winks.

Jockeys (Flat): Dale Gibson (w.a.), Steve Williams (w.a.).

Jockey (NH): Dean Gallagher (w.a.).

Amateur: Mr Joshua Apiafi (11-0).

272   MR J. L. HARRIS, Melton Mowbray

Postal: **Eastwell Hall Stables, Eastwell, Melton Mowbray, Leics, LE14 4EE.**
Phone: **(01949) 60671 MOBILE (0860) 277138 FAX (01949) 60671**

1 ABSOLUTE RULER (IRE), 5, ch g Absalom—Princess Biddy **Mr P. D. Roche**
2 BERTIE, 6, b g Teofane—Decki's Pride **Mr J. L. Harris**
3 CICERONE, 6, br g Tina's Pet—Emma Royale **Dr C. W. Ashpole**
4 DESERT ZONE (USA), 7, ch g Affirmed (USA)—Deloram (CAN) **Lavender Hill Leisure Limited**
5 DONIA (USA), 7, ch m Graustark—Katrinka (USA) **Mr J. S. Gowling**
6 DON'T GET CAUGHT (IRE), 4, b f Danehill (USA)—Be Discreet **Dr P. W. McGrath**
7 DOUBLE STAR, 5, b g Soviet Star (USA)—Startino **Mr J. L. Harris**
8 HARVEST REAPER, 4, gr g Bairn (USA)—Real Silver **Mr J. L. Harris**
9 IMLAK (IRE), 4, ch c Ela-Mana-Mou—Mashteen (USA) **Mr J. David Abell**
10 IOTA, 7, b br m Niniski (USA)—Iosifa **Lavender Hill Leisure Limited**
11 LITHE SPIRIT (IRE), 4, b f Dancing Dissident (USA)—Afternoon Nap (USA) **Mr J. L. Harris**
12 LITTLE BLACKFOOT, 8, b g Sicyos (USA)—Nip In The Air (USA) **Mr J. L. Harris**
13 MARY MACBLAIN, 7, b m Damister (USA)—Tzarina (USA) **Mr D. Jackson**
14 RAIN-N-SUN, 10, gr g Warpath—Sun Noddy **Mrs M. Bostock**
15 ROSE CHIME (IRE), 4, b br f Tirol—Repicado Rose (USA) **Mr J. South**
16 SCOTTISH PARK, 7, ch m Scottish Reel—Moss Agate **Cleartherm Ltd**
17 SEA VICTOR, 4, b g Slip Anchor—Victoriana (USA) **Mr J. David Abell**
18 SIR TASKER, 8, b h Lidhame—Susie's Baby **Mr J. F. Coupland**
19 STAR RAGE (IRE), 6, b g Horage—Star Bound **Mr J. David Abell**
20 SWORDKING (IRE), 7, ch g Kris—Reine Mathilde (USA) **Lavender Hill Leisure Limited**
21 TAUFELIANE, 5, b m Taufan (USA)—Sweet Eliane **Mr D. Eccleston**
22 TRISTAN'S COMET, 9, br g Sayf El Arab (USA)—Gleneagle **Mr D. Wilcox**
23 VINDALOO, 4, ch g Indian Ridge—Lovely Lagoon **Mr J. David Abell & Mrs J. Abell**
24 WORDSMITH (IRE), 6, b g Cyrano de Bergerac—Cordon **Mr A. K. Collins**

THREE-YEAR-OLDS

25 ALPHETON PRINCE, b g Prince of Cill Dara—Batsam Lady **Mr Tim Phillips**
26 DOUBLE IMPRESSION (IRE), b f Mac's Imp (USA)—Thalssa **Mr R. W. Huggins & Mr N. McGrath**
27 ELFIN QUEEN (IRE), br f Fairy King (USA)—West of Eden **Mr J. David Abell & Mrs J. Abell**
28 FLORRIE'M, ch f Tina's Pet—Rosie Dickins **Lavender Hill Leisure Limited**
29 INCANTRICE, ch f Faustus (USA)—Dependable **Mr J. Pattison & Mr J. L. Harris**
30 KILKENNY LASS (IRE), ch f Fayruz—African Cousin **Mr J. L. Harris**
31 LOZZIE, gr f Siberian Express (USA)—Fast Motion **Mr J. L. Harris**
32 MRS POLLOCK, b f Precocious—Power And Red **Mr Michael G. T. Stokes**

TWO-YEAR-OLDS

33 Br f 16/2 Timeless Times (USA)—Decki's Pride (Goldhills Pride) **Mr J. L. Harris**
34 B g 14/4 Clantime—Kasu (Try My Best (USA)) **Mr J. L. Harris**

Other Owners: Mr R. Atkinson, Burton Park Country Club, Mr Barry Franks, Mr J. G. Hutchinson, Miss R. Lipman, Mr N. G. Mead, Ms S. Miller, Mr William Smith, The Stubble Jumpers.

Apprentice: Jaroslav Kovarik (7-7).

273   MR PETER W. HARRIS, Berkhamsted

Postal: **Sallow Copse, Ringshall, Berkhamsted, Herts, HP4 1LZ.**

Phone: **(0144284) 2480 FAX (0144284) 2521**

1 **ABOVE THE CUT (USA)**, 4, ch c Topsider (USA)—Placer Queen **Mrs P. W. Harris**
2 **BOSTON ROCK**, 4, ch g Ballad Rock—Miss Boston (FR) **Mrs P. W. Harris**
3 **CAPTIVE SONG (IRE)**, 4, b c Danehill (USA)—Tony Award (USA) **Mrs Gillian Godfrey**
4 **DELTA SOLEIL (USA)**, 4, b c Riverman (USA)—Sunny Roberta (USA) **American Connection I**
5 **DESERT SPRING**, 4, b c Green Desert (USA)—Little Loch Broom **The Pendley Enthusiasts**
6 **EVER SO LYRICAL**, 6, b h Never So Bold—Lyra **The Pendley Punters**
7 **KINGS ASSEMBLY**, 4, b c Presidium—To The Point **The Everhopefuls I**
8 **POPPY CAREW (IRE)**, 4, b f Danehill (USA)—Why So Silent **Mrs P. W. Harris**
9 **PRIMO LARA**, 4, ch c Primo Dominie—Clara Barton **Thanet Leasing/Mrs P. W. Harris**
10 **SOTOBOY (IRE)**, 4, b c Danehill (USA)—Fire Flash **Mrs Marlene Hollis**
11 **SPENDER**, 7, b br g Last Tycoon—Lady Hester **The Entrepreneurs**
12 **STAR OF PERSIA (IRE)**, 4, gr c Persian Bold—Caranina (USA) **The Saturday Club**
13 **TO THE ROOF (IRE)**, 4, b g Thatching—Christine Daae **Mrs P. W. Harris**
14 **TWICE AS SHARP**, 4, ch c Sharpo—Shadiliya **Formula Twelve**
15 **UNFORGIVING MINUTE**, 7, b g Bellypha—Kindjal **Mrs P. W. Harris**

THREE-YEAR-OLDS

16 **ARCTIC FANCY (USA)**, ch c Arctic Tern (USA)—Fit And Fancy (USA) **The Cool Customers**
17 **CHAMPAGNE PRINCE**, b c Prince Sabo—Champagne Season (USA) **Magnum Force**
18 **DAISY BATES (IRE)**, b f Danehill (USA)—Martha Stevens (USA) **Mrs P. W. Harris**
19 **DASHING INVADER (USA)**, ch c Pirate Army (USA)—Cherie's Hope (USA) **The Mutineers**
20 **DREAMHILL (USA)**, b c Danehill (USA)—Keep The Thought (USA) **Stable Minds**
21 **ENCHANTED GUEST (IRE)**, ch f Be My Guest (USA)—Last Blessing **The Fillies Fanciers**
22 **FINAL STAB (IRE)**, b c Kris—Premier Rose **Mrs P. W. Harris**
23 **FOURDANED (IRE)**, b c Danehill (USA)—Pro Patria **Four Square**
24 **HAPPY AND BLESSED (IRE)**, b f Prince Sabo—Bless The Match **Mrs P. W. Harris**
25 **KELLY'S KAP**, b c Green Desert (USA)—Civility **Mrs Marlene Hollis**
26 **LEAD HIM ON (USA)**, b c Cahill Road (USA)—Wicked Ways (USA) **Mrs P. W. Harris & Mr Neil Rodway**
27 **MELT THE CLOUDS (CAN)**, ch c Diesis—Population **Mrs Gillian Godfrey**
28 **MY LEWICIA (IRE)**, b f Taufan (USA)—Christine Daae **Mr Graham Knight**
29 **NAVAL HUNTER (USA)**, ch c Jade Hunter (USA)—Navy Light (USA) **Mr Les Hooper**
30 **OCTAVIA HILL**, ch f Prince Sabo—Clara Barton **Mrs P. W. Harris**
31 **PASSING STRANGERS (USA)**, b c Lyphard (USA)—The Way We Were (USA) **Mrs P. W. Harris**
32 **PENDLEY ROSE**, ch f Prince Sabo—Rose Bouquet **The Roseates**
33 **PRIDE OF KASHMIR**, gr g Petong—Proper Madam **The New Recruits**
34 **RANDOM KINDNESS**, b g Alzao (USA)—Lady Tippins (USA) **Mrs P. W. Harris**
35 **SCANDATOR (IRE)**, b g Danehill (USA)—Rustic Lawn **The Patient Few**
36 **SEA DANE**, b c Danehill (USA)—Shimmering Sea **Carat Gold Connection**
37 **TAUFAN BOY**, b c Taufan (USA)—Lydia Maria **The Supreme Team**
38 **THAI MORNING**, gr c Petong—Bath **Thai Connection**
39 **UTMOST ZEAL**, b c Cozzene (USA)—Zealous Lady (USA) **Mrs P. W. Harris**
40 **VERIDIAN**, b c Green Desert (USA)—Alik (FR) **Mrs P. W. Harris**
41 **WHISPERED MELODY**, b f Primo Dominie—Sing Softly **Mrs P. W. Harris**

TWO-YEAR-OLDS

42 **CHINGACHGOOK**, b c 5/3 Superlative—Petomania (Petong) **Capital Partnership**
43 B c 14/4 Alzao (USA)—Christine Daae (Sadler's Wells (USA))
44 B c 6/3 Primo Dominie—Class Adorns (Sadler's Wells (USA))
45 Ch f 28/3 Kris—Connaught Bridge (Connaught) **Mrs P. W. Harris**
46 **DIAMOND FLAME**, b c 23/4 Suave Dancer (USA)—Eternal Flame (Primo Dominie)
47 B c 6/6 Danehill (USA)—Feather Glen (Glenstal (USA))
48 **FLYAWAY HILL (FR)**, b f 13/4 Danehill (USA)—Flyaway Bride (USA) (Blushing Groom (FR)) **Pendley Fliers**
49 **HILLINSKI (IRE)**, b c 8/3 Danehill (USA)—Llangollen (IRE) (Caerleon (USA))
50 B c 6/3 Danehill (USA)—Kilvarnet (Furry Glen)

MR PETER W. HARRIS—continued

51 B f 1/3 Waajib—Last Blessing (Final Straw)
52 B c 16/4 Primo Dominie—Lydia Maria (Dancing Brave (USA))
53 B c 11/2 Risk Me (FR)—Mandrake Madam (Mandrake Major)
54 B c 18/3 Thatching—Martha Stevens (USA) (Super Concorde (USA))
55 B f 10/4 Danehill (USA)—Noble Dust (USA) (Dust Commander (USA))
56 Ch c 15/5 Indian Ridge—Odile (Green Dancer (USA))
57 B c 8/3 Dixieland Band (USA)—Only A Rumour (Ela-Mana-Mou)
58 Ch c 19/2 Geiger Counter (USA)—Placer Queen (Habitat)
59 B c 7/2 Primo Dominie—Remany (Bellypha)
60 Ch c 16/3 Danzig Connection—Royal Fi Fi (USA) (Conquistador Cielo (USA))
61 B c 10/5 Danehill (USA)—Salette (Sallust)
62 B c 6/4 Superlative—Sing Softly (Luthier)
63 Ch c 30/4 Be My Guest (USA)—State Treasure (USA) (Secretariat (USA))
64 B c 19/4 Persian Bold—St Clair Star (Sallust)
65 B f 11/4 Danehill (USA)—Why So Silent (Mill Reef (USA)) **Mrs P. W. Harris**
66 **YOUNG PRECEDENT,** b c 23/4 Polish Precedent—Guyum (Rousillon (USA)) **Pendley Knights**

Other Owners: Raymond Amer, Miss Kathy Anderson, Mr S. Appelbee, Mr B. Arthurs, Mrs Brenda Aslett, Michael Aslett, Miss D. J. Atkins, Mr Mark Avery, Bob Barnes, Mr Jonathan Barthorpe, Sasha Bartusek, Mr P. Baxter, Mr Patrick Beaumont, Mr M. Beever, Mr B. Bell, Lol Benbow, Mrs Marjorie Binns, Terry Bird, Mrs Edna Bishop, Leslie Blackford, Mr R. Blackman, Mr A. K. Blackwell, Mr G. Blute, Mr P. Bones, Mr D. Booth, Mrs Carol Bowley, Eddy Bowley, Mr John Brady, Mr G. Briggs, Mrs Jennifer Brimble, Mrs B. V. Brown, Mr A. Budd, Chris Bushe, Mr R. Butler, Mr J. Byrne, Mr M. Byrne, Mr Colin Campbell, Mr I. Campbell, Mrs Sarah Carne, Mr J. Chilton, Mr D. Clark, Mr P. Clayton, Mr T. Cleary, Jerry Clement, Ms Jane Clemetson, Mrs Irene Clifford, Mr N. Cohen, Mr J. Conroy, Mr S. Coomes, Mr E. Cottam, Mr M. Crabb, Les Cross, Mr B. Cullom, Mr J. M. Curtis, Mr M. Danzebrink, Mrs Pamela Davies, Mrs Ericka Davis, Tony Depass, Mr John Derry, Alex Dixon-Kelly, Sam Dodd, Mr E. Dolan, Mr S. Donnelly, Mr John Donovan, Mrs Shirley Dore, Mr B. Ead, Mr C. Edwards, Mrs Susan Edwards, David Eldridge, Ms Glynne Rhys Evans, Mr N. Falkner, Miss Dee Fisher, Gerry Fitch, Mr D. Flower, Mr M. Ford, Miss Diane Foster, Bob Franks, Miss D. A. Fraser, Eddie Gibson, Mr W. Glaister, John Glennon, Mrs Joy Goff, Tony Grayston, Bill Greaves, Mrs Jean Greaves, Mr J. Green, Mr J. Grimson, Mr S. Grosvenor, Mrs Glenice Guntrip, Mrs Alexandra Hall, Mr K. Hall, Mr Andrew Harris, Mr John Harris, Mr Robert Harris, Mrs Terri Harris, Charles Harrison, Mr C. Hassan, Mr A. J. Haygarth, Mr S. Haymes, Mrs Carole Hilton, Tony Holdham, Mr M. Hollington, Mr D. Holman, Mr Ron Holmes, Mr J. Hon, Mrs Iris Horgan, Mrs Shirley Horn, Mrs Alison Hufford, Mr A. D. Hyson, Bill Johnson, Mr Paul Johnston, Mr Derek Jones, Mr M. Kavanagh, Mrs Beryl Kaye, Mr R. Keats, Mr Alan Keers, Mr D. Kirby, Mr S. Knight, Lee Lammin, Brett Lawrence, Ed Liley, Mr K. Liston, Mr David Long, Elaine Long, Miss Ange Lonsdale, Sandy Mair, Mr Brian Manfield, Phil Manning, Mr J. Marr, Miss Carol Mason, Mr J. Mason, Mrs Barbera May, Alf McDonald, Mr W. McGaffin, Mr C. McPhie, Max Merron, Mr S. Miller, Mrs S. A. Miller, Mrs Sue Mitchel, Mrs Anne Mitchell, Mr K. Mockler, Mr B. D. Moore, Mr Martin Moore, Mr S. Morgan, Mr Alastair Munro, Mrs Margaret Murray, Mr C. Naylor, Mr John Neary, Mr N. Newman, Terry Newsome, Mr A. Oakes, Mr Graham Parrish, Ms Jennifer Passey, Mr C. C. Pell, Mrs Terry Poffley, Mr M. Ponting, Mr Jonathan Porter, Mr S. Posthuma, Gerry Pottinger, Mr S. R. Povey, Mr M. Powell, Mr D. C. Pugsley, Mr L. Randall, Mr C. Rear, Ms Jane Reedy, Mrs Patricia Restall, Mr David Revell, Bill Rhodes, Mr M. Ridgway, Mr A. Rix, Mr T. Roberts, Mrs Sylvia Robinson, Mrs Joyce Robson, Mr D. W. Rogers, Mrs Diane Rogers, Meirion Roscoe, Mr E. Rossbacher, Mr P. Rowland, Mr D. Rusher, Miss Anita Russell, Mel Russell, Mrs Ruth Russell, Phil Rutter, Mr D. Savage, Mr B. Scutts, Mr B. Seal, Mr T. Sharman, Mr M. Shipperly, Mrs Benita Silverman, Mr A. Skinner, Mr Gary Smith, Mr Melvyn Smith, Mr Stephen G. Smith, Tony Smith, Mr A. Snow, Mrs Gillian Softley, Mr P. Softley, Ms Karen Stanford, Mr A. Stevens, Mr A. Suckling, Mr H. Sweet, Karen Swinden, Mr David Taylor, Mr K. Taylor, Mr G. Tebbutt, Mr M. Thatcher, The Management, Mr G. Theobald, Beryl Thorne, Mr B. Thorogood, Ms Barbara Tischler, Mr N. Tritton, Mr P. Truman, Mr P. Upperton, Mr N. Vaughan, Perry Wallington, Mr Thomas Walsh, Mr G. Warrell, Mr Roger Watson, Chris Weatherly, Mr A. Weller, Mr A. Welton, Laurence Wess, Mr M. Whalley, Mr N. Whitfield, Mr J. Whiting, Mr N. Whittome, Mr F. Williams, Mr F. Wingfield, Mr M. Winter, Mrs Anne Wormstone, Mr D. Wright, Mr B. Yeardley, Cheng Yoe.

Jockey (Flat): Gary Hind (8-0).

Lady Rider: Miss Annie Elsey.

274   MR ROGER HARRIS, Exning

Postal: **Priory Stables, 22 Church Street, Exning, Newmarket, CB8 7EH.**

Phone: **(0638) 578140 FAX (0638) 577429 MOBILE (0860) 574561**

1 **ANTIGUAN FLYER**, 7, b g Shirley Heights—Fleet Girl **Mr George Prodromou**
2 **CASTEL ROSSELO**, 6, br h Rousillon (USA)—On The House (FR) **Mr T. J. Dawson**
3 **CHARLIE BIGTIME**, 6, b g Norwick (USA)—Sea Aura **Mr T. J. Dawson**
4 **DANCE KING**, 4, b g Rambo Dancer (CAN)—Northern Venture **Mr T. Connors**
5 **DVORAK (IRE)**, 5, b g Darshaan—Grace Note (FR) **Mr T. J. Dawson**
6 **EVER FRIENDS**, 4, ch g Crever—Cappuccilli **Mr T. J. Dawson**
7 **HUMBERT'S LANDING (IRE)**, 5, b h Cyrano de Bergerac—Bilander **Mr A. O. Irish**
8 **OLD PROVENCE**, 6, b h Rainbow Quest (USA)—Orange Hill **Mr T. J. Dawson**
9 **SABELLA**, 5, ch m Prince Sabo—Pour Moi **Two Worlds Engineering A/S**
10 **SOMMARIVA STAR (DEN)**, 6, b g Monsanto (FR)—Comic Strip **Mrs Anne Dooks**

THREE-YEAR-OLDS

11 **CHARNWOOD JACK (USA)**, ch c Sanglamore (USA)—Hyroglyph (USA) **Mr T. J. Dawson**
12 **CHARNWOOD MEG (IRE)**, ch f Scenic—Cathryn's Song **Mr T. J. Dawson**
13 **CLASSIC AFFAIR (USA)**, ch f Trempolino (USA)—Coupole (USA) **Classic Bloodstock Plc**
14 **CLASSIC ARTISTE (USA)**, ch f Arctic Tern (USA)—Batan Gantlet **Classic Bloodstock Plc**
15 **CLASSIC BEAUTY (IRE)**, b f Fairy King (USA)—Working Model **Classic Bloodstock Plc**
16 **CLASSIC DAME (FR)**, gr f Highest Honor (FR)—Reem El Fala (FR) **Classic Bloodstock Plc**
17 **CLASSIC DELIGHT (USA)**, br f Green Forest (USA)—Weather Girl (USA) **Classic Bloodstock Plc**
18 **CLASSIC FORM (IRE)**, b f Alzao (USA)—Formulate **Classic Bloodstock Plc**
19 **CLASSIC LOVER (IRE)**, b f Taufan (USA)—Sound Pet **Classic Bloodstock Plc**
20 **CLASSIC PARISIAN (IRE)**, b f Persian Bold—Gay France (FR) **Classic Bloodstock Plc**
21 **CLASSIC RIBBON (IRE)**, br f Persian Bold—House Tie **Classic Bloodstock Plc**
22 **CLASSIC ROMANCE**, b f Cadeaux Genereux—What A Pity **Classic Bloodstock Plc**
23 **CLASSIC VICTORY**, b g Puissance—Seattle Mama (USA) **Classic Bloodstock Plc**
24 **FREEDOM RUN**, b c Polish Precedent (USA)—Ausherra (USA) **Mrs S. A. Harris**
25 **GENERAL SHABBA**, b c Master Willie—Kevins Lady **Mr T. J. Dawson**
26 **INDIAN BLUFF**, b g Indian Ridge—Hannie Caulder **Mr T. J. Dawson**
27 **KATIE IS MY LOVE (USA)**, ch f Talinum (USA)—Familiar (USA) **Mr T. J. Dawson**
28 **POPPY MY LOVE**, ch f Clantime—Yankeedoodledancer **Mr T. J. Dawson**
29 **PRINCESS RENATA (IRE)**, ch f Maelstrom Lake—Sajanjal **Mr T. J. Dawson**
30 **WORLDWIDE ELSIE (USA)**, b f Java Gold (USA)—Tender Camilla **Mr T. J. Dawson**

TWO-YEAR-OLDS

31 Ch f 8/4 Mystiko (USA)—Boogy Lady (IRE) (Glenstal (USA)) **Classic Bloodstock Plc**
32 **CLASSIC FAN (USA)**, b f 10/3 Lear Fan (USA)—Miss Boniface (Tap On Wood) **Classic Bloodstock II Plc**
33 B f 2/5 Trempolino (USA)—Madonna Sprite (Saint Cyrien (FR)) **Classic Bloodstock II Plc**
34 B f 16/4 Batshoof—No Jazz (Jaazeiro (USA)) **Mr T. J. Dawson**
35 B f 8/2 Theatrical—Out of Joint (USA) (Quack (USA)) **Classic Bloodstock II Plc**
36 B c 3/5 Pharly (FR)—Penny Blessing (So Blessed) **Classic Bloodstock Plc**
37 Ch f 19/3 Keen—Plie (Superlative) **Mr T. J. Dawson**
38 B f 14/1 Soviet Star (USA)—Point de Galle (USA) (Kris) **Classic Bloodstock II Plc**
39 B f 9/3 Risk Me (FR)—Spirit Away (Dominion) **Two Worlds Engineering A/S**

Other Owners: Mr M. K. Armitt

Jockeys (Flat): D Batteate, A Mackay, J McLaughlin (8-5).

Jockey (NH): J McLaughlin.

Lady Rider: Miss H Webster (8-7).

275   MR S. A. HARRIS, Doncaster

Postal: **5 Town View, Scawsby, Doncaster, South Yorks, DN5 7UF.**

Phone: **(01302) 724979**

1 **DALLAI (IRE)**, 5, b g Dance of Life (USA)—Wavetree **Mrs Debra Harris**
2 **KIND PRINCE**, 4, b g Kind of Hush—Silent Princess **Mrs Debra Harris**

276   MR R. A. HARRISON, Middleham

Postal: **Arundel House, Middleham, Leyburn, North Yorks, DL8 4PF.**

Phone: **(01969) 23788 MOBILE (0831) 644239**

1 **ASHDREN**, 9, b g Lochnager—Stellaris **Mr D. Broderick**
2 **DALERIA**, 5, b m Darshaan—Phaleria (USA) **Mr R. Fenwick-Gibson**
3 **DARIKA LAD**, 8, gr g Belfort (FR)—Lindrake's Pride **Mrs J. Rookes & Mr R. Rookes**
4 **FORGOTTEN EMPRESS**, 4, b f Dowsing (USA)—Vynz Girl **Mr R. Fenwick-Gibson**
5 **HANDMAIDEN**, 6, gr m Shardari—Flyaway Bride (USA) **Mr R. Fenwick-Gibson**
6 **MERRY MASTER**, 12, br g Le Coq d'Or—Merry Missus **Mr G. Lansbury**
7 **SKOLERN**, 12, b g Lochnager—Piethorne **Mr A. Harrison**
8 **TEE TEE TOO (IRE)**, 4, ch g Hatim (USA)—Scottish Welcome **Mrs Anna Dent**
9 **WHITE SORREL**, 5, ro h Chilibang—Midnight Imperial **Mr R. Fenwick-Gibson**

THREE-YEAR-OLDS

10 **ONE LIFE TO LIVE (IRE)**, gr c Classic Music (USA)—Fine Flame **Mr R. Fenwick-Gibson**
11 **RAPID LINER**, b c Skyliner—Stellaris **Mr D. Broderick**
12 **SLEEP STANDING (IRE)**, b f Standaan (FR)—Sleeping Car **Miss Alison Walley**

TWO-YEAR-OLDS

13 B c 24/2 Treasure Kay—Bally Pourri (IRE) (Law Society (USA))
14 B f 24/4 Classic Music (USA)—Hetty Green (Bay Express)
15 B f 29/5 Imperial Frontier—Pamphylia (Known Fact (USA))
16 B f 23/4 Night Shift (USA)—Thank You Note (What A Guest)

Other Owners: Mr H. A. Armytage, Mr P. H. Lewellen, Mr J. G. Rookes, Mr J. Tennant.

Jockeys (NH): D Bentley (w.a.), J Callaghan, B Storey (w.a.).

Lady Rider: Mrs G Harrison (8-0).

277   MR GUY HARWOOD, Pulborough

Postal: **Coombelands Stables, Pulborough, West Sussex, RH20 1BP.**

Phone: **PULBOROUGH (01798) 873011 FAX (01798) 875163**

1 **AEROKING (USA)**, 5, b g Lear Fan (USA)—Blue Grass Baby (USA) **The PBT Group**
2 **AMANCIO (USA)**, 5, b g Manila (USA)—Kerry Ring (USA) **Mr Paul H. Locke**
3 **ARTICULATE (IRE)**, 7, gr g Roselier (FR)—Bold Tavo **Mr Fred Cotton**
4 **BETTER OFFER (IRE)**, 4, b g Waajib—Camden's Gift **Mrs Wendy Sainer**
5 **BOUNDEN DUTY (USA)**, 10, b g His Majesty (USA)—Inward Bound (USA) **Mrs A. J. Perrett**
6 **BURNING (USA)**, 4, b c Bering—Larnica (USA) **Mr Khalifa Dasmal**
7 **CAPE BREEZE (IRE)**, 5, b m Strong Gale—Gale Flash **Mr Bernard Keay**
8 **CAPTAIN'S GUEST (IRE)**, 6, b g Be My Guest (USA)—Watership (USA) **Mr & Mrs K. J. Buchanan**
9 **CLINKING**, 5, b g Glint of Gold—Kai **Mr G. Harwood**
10 **FALSE CREEK**, 6, b g Uncle Pokey—Jennifer Wren **Mr Fred Cotton**
11 **FINE THYNE (IRE)**, 7, ch g Good Thyne (USA)—Bring Me Sunshine **Mr Peter Wiegand**

MR GUY HARWOOD—continued

12 **GRAPHIC DESIGNER (IRE)**, 7, b g Sheer Grit—Kates Princess **GPS (Print) Limited**
13 **HAUNTING MUSIC (IRE)**, 8, b g Cataldi—Theme Music **Mr Ron Miller**
14 **IMMENSE (IRE)**, 6, br g Strong Gale—Faultless Girl **Mrs Jenny Ells**
15 **KAYVEE**, 7, gr g Kaldoun (FR)—Secret Life (USA) **Mr J. H. Richmond-Watson**
16 **MELNIK**, 5, ch g Nashwan (USA)—Melodist (USA) **Mr Peter Wiegand**
17 **MUNTAFI**, 5, b g Unfuwain (USA)—Princess Sucree (USA) **The One Over Eight Partnership**
18 **MYSTIC HILL**, 5, b g Shirley Heights—Nuryana **Mrs S. L. Whitehead**
19 **PONTOON BRIDGE**, 9, ch g Carlingford Castle—Lumax **Mr Peter Wiegand**
20 **ROYAL SQUARE (CAN)**, 10, ch g Gregorian (USA)—Dance Crazy (USA) **Mrs C. A. Clevett**
21 **SEIGNEURIAL**, 4, b g Primo Dominie—Spinner **The PBT Group**
22 **SQUIRE CORRIE**, 4, b g Distant Relative—Fast Car (FR) **Mr G. Harwood**

THREE-YEAR-OLDS

23 **CANDLE SMOKE (USA)**, b br g Woodman (USA)—Light The Lights (FR) **Mr Anthony Speelman**
24 **CONSORT**, b c Groom Dancer (USA)—Darnelle **Mr K. Abdulla**
25 **FAR DAWN (USA)**, b c Sunshine Forever (USA)—Dawn's Reality (USA) **Mr Peter Wiegand**
26 **FILIAL (IRE)**, b c Danehill (USA)—Sephira **Mr K. Abdulla**
27 **HOOFPRINTS (IRE)**, b c Distinctly North (USA)—Sweet Reprieve **Mr Selwyn Lewis**
28 **MIDDAY COWBOY (USA)**, b c Houston (USA)—Perfect Isn't Easy (USA) **Mr Simon Karmel**
29 **MONTE FELICE (IRE)**, ch g Be My Guest (USA)—Elabella **Lady Harrison**
30 **NORTHERN FLEET**, b c Slip Anchor—Kamkova (USA) **Mr K. Abdulla**
31 **ORANGE ORDER (IRE)**, ch c Generous (IRE)—Fleur d'Oranger **Mr K. Abdulla**
32 **RENZO (IRE)**, b c Alzao (USA)—Watership (USA) **Mr K. J. Buchanan**
33 **SACRED LOCH (USA)**, ch c Lomond (USA)—Cypria Sacra (USA) **Mr Athos Christodoulou**
34 **TAKE NOTICE**, b c Warning—Metair **Mr K. Abdulla**

TWO-YEAR-OLDS

35 B c 11/2 Alleged (USA)—Fabulous Native (USA) (Le Fabuleux) **Mr K. Abdulla**
36 **METEOR STRIKE (USA)**, ch c 14/2 Lomond (USA)—Meteoric (High Line) **Mr K. Abdulla**
37 Br c 25/4 Alzao (USA)—Obertura (USA) (Roberto (USA)) **Mr K. Abdulla**
38 Ch c 23/5 Devil's Bag (USA)—Popularity (General Assembly (USA)) **Mr K. Abdulla**
39 **SUNDAY MARKET (USA)**, b c 19/2 Lear Fan (USA)—Sunday Bazaar (USA) (Nureyev (USA)) **Mr K. Abdulla**
40 **TOUGH ACT**, b c 1/3 Be My Chief (USA)—Forelino (Trempolino (USA)) **Mrs Wendy Sainer**
41 B c 10/3 Theatrical—Water Angel (USA) (Halo (USA)) **Mr K. Abdulla**

Other Owners: Mr T. L. Adams, Mr Peter Ballard, Mr Chris Bellis, Mrs Lola Black, Mrs S. Buchanan, Dr J. A. Chandler, Mr Stelios A. Christodoulou, Mr Seymour Cohn, Mr B. S. Creber, Mr Nick Elliott, Mr C. J. Ells, Mr John Farncombe, Major Charles Hennings, Mrs M. R. Landau, Mr P. J. Mellon, Sir Eric Parker, Mr Timothy J. Pope, Mr Paul A. Rhodes, Miss Paula Sarzi-Braga, Mrs Gaynor Scruton, Mr Peter Silvester, Tessona Limited, Mr A. P. Thompson, Mr David Todd, Mr S. Watt, Mrs D. Willis.

Jockey (Flat): A Clark (8-2).

Jockey (NH): M Perrett (10-0).

Apprentice: G Harwood (8-0).

Lady Rider: Miss Amanda Harwood (9-7).

278   MR PATRICK HASLAM, Middleham

Postal: **Castle Stables, Middleham, Leyburn, North Yorkshire, DL8 4QQ.**
Phone: **(01969) 624351 FAX (01969) 624463**

1 **MAC'S TAXI**, 4, b g Komaite (USA)—Orange Silk **Mr J. McMurdo**
2 **NIGEL'S LAD (IRE)**, 4, b g Dominion Royale—Back To Earth (FR) **Mr N. C. Dunnington**
3 **PAGEBOY**, 7, b g Tina's Pet—Edwins' Princess **Lord Scarsdale**
4 **PARKLIFE (IRE)**, 4, ch g Double Schwartz—Silk Trade **Mr Darren Croft**

International Horse Dentistry

Robin Abel Smith M/Eqd
Certified Master Equine Dentist

Director of World-Wide
Association of
Equine Dentistry

Barleythorpe, Oakham,
Rutland, LE15 7EQ
Telephone/Fax : (01664) 454787

Car Telephone: (0836) 637704

MR PATRICK HASLAM—continued

5 PIPE MAJOR (IRE), 4, b c Tirol—Annsfield Lady **Lord Scarsdale**
6 PROPHETS HONOUR, 4, ch g Deploy—Cat's Claw (USA) **Mr S. A. B. Dinsmore**
7 RED SPECTACLE (IRE), 4, b g Red Sunset—Buz Kashi **Mr David H. Morgan**
8 SUMMER VILLA, 4, b f Nomination—Maravilla **Mr K. E. Williamson**
9 TALENTED TING (IRE), 7, ch g Hatim (USA)—An Tig Gaelige **Mr Martin Wickens**
10 ULTRA BEET, 4, b g Puissance—Cassiar **Pet Express Ltd T/A Nutrimix**

THREE-YEAR-OLDS

11 CASTLE GOVERNOR, b g Governor General—Sorcha (IRE) **Patrick Haslam Racing Club**
12 CHINA CASTLE, b g Sayf El Arab (USA)—Honey Plum **Mr J. M. Davis**
13 COPPER BRIGHT, b g Mon Tresor—Arabian Nymph **Mr Gerald Selby**
14 OLD HUSH WING (IRE), b g Tirol—Saneena **Mr S. A. B. Dinsmore**
15 SHEPHERDS DEAN (IRE), b f Tirol—Royal Episode **Ray Tutton Partnership**
16 ULTRA BARLEY, ch g Beveled (USA)—Chapter One **Pet Express Ltd T/A Nutrimix**

TWO-YEAR-OLDS

17 BEN'S RIDGE, b c 27/3 Indian Ridge—Fen Princess (IRE) (Trojan Fen) **Mr S. A. B. Dinsmore**
18 B c 28/5 Selkirk (USA)—Choke Cherry (Connaught) **Middleham Park Racing VI**
19 Ch c 26/3 Hatim (USA)—Floating Note (Music Boy) **Mr Martin Wickens**
20 FLYING GROUSE (IRE), b c 15/3 Robellino (USA)—
                         Amenaide (Known Fact (USA)) **The Glorious Twelfth Syndicate**
21 GADROON, ch c 25/3 Cadeaux Genereux—Greensward Blaze (Sagaro) **Lord Scarsdale**
22 GOING FOR BROKE, b c 8/2 Simply Great (FR)—Empty Purse (Pennine Walk) **Dunnington, Smart & Brock**
23 Ch c 4/2 Midyan (USA)—Good As Gold (IRE) (Glint of Gold) **Mr S. A. B. Dinsmore**
24 HEBE (IRE), b f 17/1 Tirol—Inseyab (Persian Bold) **Mrs M. E. F. Haslam**
25 Ch g 7/3 Interrex (CAN)—Nellie O'Dowd (USA) (Diesis) **Mr S. A. B. Dinsmore**
26 B c 30/3 Contract Law (USA)—Secret Hideaway (USA) (Key To The Mint (USA)) **Mr S. A. B. Dinsmore**
27 SIOUXROUGE, b c 23/4 Indian Ridge—Scarlett Holly (Red Sunset) **Mr Les Buckley & Middleham Park Racing**
28 B f 25/4 Merdon Melody—Thabeh (Shareef Dancer (USA)) **Mrs M. McSweeney**
29 ULTRA BOY, b c 15/2 Music Boy—Golden Award (Last Tycoon) **Pet Express Ltd T/A Nutrimix**
30 WEDDING MUSIC, b f 5/3 Music Boy—Diamond Wedding (USA) (Diamond Shoal) **Mrs M. E. F. Haslam**

Other Owners: Mrs E. Auburn, Mr D. J. Bamber, Mr Chris Barry, Mr David Barter, Mrs E. Brock, Mr J. F. Brock, Mr A. N. Brooke-Rankin, Mr A. P. Brookes, Mr J. L. Butterworth, Mr R. K. Carvill, Mr Gary Chapman, Mr G. Cole, Mrs N. Corner, Mr J. Coyle, Mr T. A. Daniel, Mr Ron Davison, Mr J. E. Edge, Miss Audrey Forbes, Mr W. Foster, Mr Alan Gleadall, Mr N. P. Green, Mr H. Guss, Mrs J. M. Hargreaves, Mr J. A. Harvey, Mr P. C. Haslam, Mr P. Higgins, Mr S. Higgins, Mr Nick Hodge, Mr J. Jarvis, Mrs Peter Lambert, Mrs F. Lord, Mrs J. Malkin, Mr P. J. McSweeney, Middleham Park Racing I, Middleham Park Racing V, Mr Michael Barrington Moore, Viscount Mountagarret, Mrs E. Muir, Mrs Marilyn Muse-Hodgson, Mr Peter O'Reilly, Mr T. S. Palin, Mr Stan Phillips, Mr A. Piller, Mr J. A. Preece, Mr David Schofield, Mrs S. Searle, Mr J. M. Smart, Mr W. N. Smith, Mr D. Snookes, Mr J. Soulsby, Mr G. L. Swales, Mr J. Swinglehurst, Mr Barrie Tudor, Mr Ray Tutton, Mr G. Wedd, Mr A. C. Williams, Mr G. Wood, Mrs M. Wyvill, Colonel E. C. York.

Jockey (Flat): J Weaver (8-4, w.a.).

Jockeys (NH): J Callaghan (10-0), M Foster (10-0).

Apprentice: Carol Davison (7-7).

Conditional: Sarah Bainbridge (9-0).

279   MR JOHN C HAYDEN, Kildare

Postal: **Castlemartin Abbey House Stables, Kilcullen, Co. Kildare, Ireland.**

Phone: **(045) 481598 FAX (045) 481598**

1 4, B g Mandalus—Disetta
2 **JACK YEATS**, 4, b g Don't Forget Me—Petty Session
3 **KING OF THE OCEAN (IRE)**, 4, b g King's Ride—Jacqueline's Glen
4 **MAGICAL FUN**, 4, b g Magical Strike (USA)—Roundstone Lass
5 4, B g Montelimar (USA)—Mindyourbusiness
6 **RELIC IMAGE (IRE)**, 4, b f Maelstrom Lake—Relic Spirit
7 **ROSIE'S GUEST (IRE)**, 4, ch f Be My Guest (USA)—Rose A Village
8 **SUSIE'S DELIGHT (IRE)**, 6, b m Bulldozer—Betty's Delight

THREE-YEAR-OLDS

9 **ARISTOCRATIQUE**, gr f Cadeaux Genereux—Well Off
10 **PRIOLINA (IRE)**, b f Priolo (USA)—Salustrina
11 **SET THE MOUSETRAP (IRE)**, ch c Krayyan—Emma Louise
12 **SLAYJAY (IRE)**, ch f Mujtahid (USA)—Fire Flash
13 **THE DIRECTOR**, b g Prince Rupert (FR)—Caroll's Canyon (IRE)

TWO-YEAR-OLDS

14 **ARC (IRE)**, b c 7/5 Archway (IRE)—Columbian Sand (IRE)
15 B f 26/4 River Falls—Camden's Gift
16 Gr f 26/5 Common Grounds—Island Goddess
17 B c 19/5 Montelimar (USA)—Mindyourbusiness
18 B c 7/3 Mon Tresor—Play The Game
19 B f 25/4 Dancing Dissident—Roundstone Lass

Other Owners: Mr T. Bruton, Castlemartin Racing Club, Mr E. Gilmartin, J. P. Hardiman, Mrs B. Hayden, Mrs G. Hayden, Mr S. Hayden, Mr J. Keeling, Mr E. McAllister, Mr P. McCutcheon, Mr J. Moore, Dr. A. J. O'Reilly, Mrs Chryss O'Reilly, Mr F. O'Toole, Mr R. O'Toole, Mr S. Ridgeway, F. Salter, Mr F. Stynes, Mr J. Sutton, T. P. Waters.

Jockeys (Flat): J P Murtagh (w.a.), Willie Supple (w.a.).

Amateur: Mr P M Kelly.

280   MR D. HAYDN JONES, Pontypridd

Postal: **Garth Paddocks, Efail Isaf, Pontypridd, Mid Glam, CF38 1SN.**

Phone: **(01443) 202515 FAX (01443) 201877**

1 **AFRICAN-PARD (IRE)**, 4, b g Don't Forget Me—Petite Realm **Mr Gerald Weeks**
2 **ASKERN**, 5, gr g Sharrood (USA)—Silk Stocking **Mrs M. O'Donnell**
3 **BELLEMINETTE (IRE)**, 5, ch m Simply Great (FR)—Kitty's Sister **Mrs Judy Mihalop**
4 **BEX HILL**, 4, ch f Grey Desire—Pour Moi **J. S. Fox and Sons**
5 **DAWALIB (USA)**, 6, ch g Danzig Connection (USA)—Centavos (USA) **Jack Brown (Bookmaker) Ltd**
6 **DELROB**, 5, b m Reprimand—Stoneydale **Mrs E. M. Haydn Jones**
7 **DRAGONFLIGHT**, 5, b h Formidable (USA)—Lappet **Mrs Jacqueline Wilkinson**
8 **HALFABOB (IRE)**, 4, ch g Broken Hearted—Hasten **Mr J. G. Moore**
9 **JOHNS ACT (USA)**, 6, b g Late Act (USA)—Deluxe Type (USA) **Jack Brown (Bookmaker) Ltd**
10 **LAUREATE**, 4, br f Statoblest—Indian Wells **Mr D. Haydn Jones**
11 **PERSIAN AFFAIR (IRE)**, 5, b g Persian Heights—Lady Chesterfield (USA) **Mrs M. O'Donnell**
12 **PREMIER DANCE**, 9, ch g Bairn (USA)—Gigiolina **J. S. Fox and Sons**
13 **Q FACTOR**, 4, br f Tragic Role (USA)—Dominiana **Mr H. G. Collis**
14 **QUINZIL MARTIN**, 8, b g Song—Quaranta **Monolithic Refractories Ltd**
15 **SAND STAR**, 4, b f Lugana Beach—Overseas **Mrs T. M. Parry**
16 **SNAKE PLISSKEN (IRE)**, 5, ch g Reasonable (FR)—Shalie **Mrs M. O'Donnell**
17 **TIMBER BROKER**, 5, ch g Jalmood (USA)—La Petite Noblesse **North Cheshire Trading & Storage Ltd**

MR D. HAYDN JONES—continued

THREE-YEAR-OLDS

18 **CAPILANO PRINCESS**, b f Tragic Role (USA)—Lady Capilano **Mr H. G. Collis**
19 **MONO LADY (IRE)**, b f Polish Patriot (USA)—Phylella **Monolithic Refractories Ltd**
20 **NATAL RIDGE**, b c Indian Ridge—Song Grove **Mr Gerald Weeks**
21 **NATURAL KEY**, ch f Safawan—No Sharps Or Flats (USA) **Mrs M. O'Donnell**
22 **SANS DIABLO (IRE)**, b f Mac's Imp (USA)—Second Movement **Mrs Judy Mihalop**

TWO-YEAR-OLDS

23 **FLEUVE D'OR (IRE)**, gr f 20/5 Last Tycoon—Aldern Stream (Godswalk (USA)) **Mrs Judy Mihalop**
24 B f 20/5 Petorius—Night of Gaiety (What A Guest)
25 **SELLETTE (IRE)**, ch f 28/4 Selkirk (USA)—Near The End (Shirley Heights) **Mrs Judy Mihalop**

Other Owners: Mr R. H. Fox, Mr R. W. Fox, Mr P. Steele-Mortimer, Mr A. Thomson.

Jockey (Flat): John Reid (8-4, w.a.).

281   MR H. E. HAYNES, Swindon

Postal: **Red Down Farm, Highworth, Swindon, Wilts, SN6 7SH.**
Phone: **(01793) 762437**

1 **CALL THE BUREAU**, 7, ch g Gorytus (USA)—Mount of Light **Miss Sally R. Haynes**
2 **COOL HARRY (USA)**, 5, b br g Sir Harry Lewis (USA)—No Chili **Mrs H. E. Haynes**
3 **HOW'S BETTY**, 11, b m New Member—Brown Gull **Mrs H. E. Haynes**
4 **OUT FOR A DUCK**, 5, b g Cricket Ball (USA)—Patchinia **Miss Sally R. Haynes**
5 **PECHE D'OR**, 12, ch g Glint of Gold—Fishermans Bridge **Mrs H. E. Haynes**
6 **ROYAL GLINT**, 7, b m Glint of Gold—Princess Matilda **Mrs H. E. Haynes**

Lady Rider: Miss Fiona Haynes (9-5).

282   MR M. J. HAYNES, Epsom

Postal: **21 Chantry Hurst, Epsom, Surrey, KT18 7BW.**
Phone: HOME **EPSOM (013727) 22664** STABLES **BURGH HEATH (01737) 351140**

1 **ARAMON**, 6, b g Aragon—Princess Mona **Mr J. P. Saunders**
2 **BANDAR PERAK**, 5, b g Aragon—Noire Small (USA) **Mr T. W. King**
3 **KINGSFOLD PET**, 7, b g Tina's Pet—Bella Lisa **Mr G. E. Nye**
4 **OUTSTAYED WELCOME**, 4, b g Be My Guest (USA)—Between Time **Mrs B. Bell**
5 **POPSI'S LEGACY**, 9, ch m Little Wolf—Popsi's Poppet **M. J. Haynes**
6 **PYRRHIC DANCE**, 6, b g Sovereign Dancer (USA)—Cherubim (USA) **Mr T. W. King**
7 **SCENT OF BATTLE**, 8, ch g Rousillon (USA)—Light O'Battle **Mr W. G. Carpenter**
8 **STAR FIGHTER**, 4, gr c Siberian Express (USA)—Eezepeeze **Miss Susan Flynn**
9 **WIZZARD STAR**, 4, ch f Prince Sabo—Wizzard Art **Mr David Myers**
10 **YOUNG AT HEART (IRE)**, 5, ch g Classic Secret (USA)—Yenillik **Indexstream Ltd T/A Matthews Racing**

THREE-YEAR-OLDS

11 **ASHANTI DANCER (IRE)**, b f Dancing Dissident (USA)—Shanntabariya (IRE) **Mrs B. Bell**
12 **IDLE ROCKS (IRE)**, b c Roi Danzig (USA)—Viceroy Princess **Mr T. W. King**
13 **LINCON TWENTY ONE**, ch f Sharpo—Angels Are Blue **D. M. Butler**
14 **MAD ALEX**, b g Risk Me (FR)—Princess Mona **Mr J. P. Saunders**
15 **NATIVE SONG**, b f Hatim (USA)—Ivors Melody **Invicta BS**

MR M. J. HAYNES—continued

TWO-YEAR-OLDS

16 **AMARELLA (IRE)**, ch f 14/3 Soviet Lad—Eight Mile Rock (Dominion) **G. Steinberg**
17 **PADAUK**, b c 30/4 Warrshan (USA)—Free On Board (Free State) **G. Steinberg**
18 B f 16/4 Emarati (USA)—Pearl Pet (Mummy's Pet)
19 **SERENADE (IRE)**, gr g 2/4 Classic Music (USA)—Friendly Thoughts (USA) (Al Hattab (USA)) **Ansells Of Watford**
20 **SWIFT REFUSAL**, ch f 9/4 Emarati (USA)—Dark Hush (Kind of Hush) **Wheatmill Partners**

Other Owners: Mr J. A. Butt, Mrs J. B. Carpenter, Mrs Maureen Day, Mr M. A. Evans, Mrs V. Ford, Mr D. J. Gander, Mr M. J. Haynes.

Lady Rider: Miss Y Haynes (9-7).

283   MR P. A. HAYWARD, Netheravon

Postal: **Copperfield, Haxton, Netheravon, Wilts, SP4 9PY.**

Phone: **(01980) 670585**

1 **COURAGEOUS KNIGHT**, 7, gr g Midyan (USA)—Little Mercy **Mr L. Kirkwood**
2 **EMPERORS WOOD**, 5, b g Then Again—Silver Empress **Moonraker Racing**
3 **GRANBY BELL**, 5, b g Ballacashtal (CAN)—Betbellof **Mr H. A. Watton**
4 **I RECALL (IRE)**, 5, b g Don't Forget Me—Sable Lake **Mr P. Hayward**
5 **KASHAN (IRE)**, 8, b g Darshaan—Kamanika (FR) **Mr H. A. Watton**
6 **LEOPARD LADY**, 4, b f Sulaafah (USA)—Swift Turtle **C. M. Dyer Syndicating (3)**
7 **PEGGOTTY**, 8, gr m Capricorn Line—Silver Empress **Mr P. Hayward**
8 **PRESS AGAIN**, 4, ch f Then Again—Silver Empress **Mr J. Sawyer**
9 **SHOODAH (IRE)**, 5, ch g Common Grounds—Tunguska **Mr P. Hayward**
10 **SPRING TO GLORY**, 9, b g Teenoso (USA)—English Spring (USA) **Mr A. J. Byrne**

THREE-YEAR-OLDS

11 **LITTLE MILLIE**, b f Colmore Row—Little Kraker **Mr T. K. Pearce**

TWO-YEAR-OLDS

12 **JEST-A-KRAK**, b f 28/5 Jester—Little Kraker (Godswalk (USA)) **Mr T. K. Pearce**
13 B f 13/5 Full Extent (USA)—Sharp N' Easy (Swing Easy (USA)) **Mr P. Hayward**
14 Gr c 22/4 Then Again—Silver Empress (Octavo (USA)) **Mr P. Hayward**

Other Owners: Ms J. A. Hodges, Mr V. Holmes, Mr D. Oborne, Mr R. E. Scott.

Jockey (Flat): R Street (7-7).

284   MRS C. HEAD, Chantilly

Postal: **32 Avenue du General Leclerc, 60500 Chantilly, France.**

Phone: **44 57 01 01 FAX 44 58 53 33**

1 **ANABAA**, 4, b c Danzig—Balbonella **Mrs Alec Head**
2 **BABA THONG (USA)**, 4, b g Nureyev (USA)—Madame Premier (USA) **Mr J. Wertheimer**
3 **BAZAJET (USA)**, 4, b g Shahrastani (USA)—Belle Sultane (USA) **Mr J. Wertheimer**
4 **BEAU MANOIR (USA)**, 4, b c Bering—Bernis Heights (USA) **Mrs Alec Head**
5 **BOLD VIRGIN (USA)**, 4, b f Sadler's Wells (USA)—Careless Virgin (USA) **Mr J. Wertheimer**
6 **ENODE (FR)**, 4, ch g Antheus (USA)—Luth Commander (CAN) **Mr J. Wertheimer**
7 **FIFTY FOUR (USA)**, 4, ch c Lyphard (USA)—Partygoer (USA) **Mr J. Wertheimer**
8 **FORTY BELLES (USA)**, 5, ch m Forty Niner (USA)—Bellarida (FR) **Mr J. Wertheimer**
9 **FUN BOARD (FR)**, 4, b f Saumarez—La Dorga (USA) **Mr J. Wertheimer**

MRS C. HEAD—continued

10 **GANASHEBA (USA)**, 4, ch f Alysheba (USA)—Gana Facil (USA) **Mr J. Wertheimer**
11 **GOLDEN HANOOF (USA)**, 4, b f Slew O' Gold (USA)—Hanoof (USA) **Gainsborough Stud**
12 **LABBASEA (IRE)**, 4, b c Last Tycoon—Basilea (FR) **Gainsborough Stud**
13 **LAKALDA**, 4, gr f Kaldoun (FR)—La Luna (USA) **Mr J. Wertheimer**
14 **ORNY FANCY (USA)**, 4, b f Val de L'Orne (FR)—Minstrel Girl (FR) **Mr J. Wertheimer**
15 **OSLO CONNECTION**, 4, b c Trempolino—Allegretta **Mr Faisal Abu Khadra**
16 **POLIGLOTE**, 4, b c Sadler's Wells—Alexandrie (USA) **Mr J. Wertheimer**
17 **QUESTAN**, 4, b c Rainbow Quest (USA)—Vallee Dansante (USA) **Mr J. Wertheimer**
18 **ROUNG BEND (USA)**, 4, b c Caerwent—Blue River (FR) **Mr J. Wertheimer**
19 **SAND REEF**, 5, b h Reference Point—Reine d'Egypte (USA) **Mr J. Wertheimer**
20 **SAVELLI (USA)**, 5, b h Bering—Sans Prix **Mrs Alec Head**
21 **SERVIABLE (IRE)**, 4, b c Royal Academy—Habituee **Gainsborough Stud**
22 **SILVERING (USA)**, 4, b c Polish Precedent (USA)—Silvermine (FR) **Mrs Alec Head**
23 **SKY TIME (FR)**, 4, ch c Lead On Time (USA)—Haute Autorite ((USA) **Mr J. Wertheimer**
24 **SMART PROSPECTOR (USA)**, 4, b c Houston (USA)—Your Serve (USA) **Mr J. Wertheimer**
25 **SPICILEGE (USA)**, 4, ch g Lyphard (USA)—Grabelst (USA) **Mr J. Wertheimer**
26 **STRICTLY COOL (USA)**, 4, ch f Bering—Strictly Raised (USA) **Mr J. Wertheimer**
27 **SURFING DUBB (FR)**, 4, b c Alleged (USA)—Mysouko (FR) **Mr J. Wertheimer**

THREE-YEAR-OLDS

28 **ALL FOR SHOW**, b c Mr Prospector—Aliya **Gainsborough Stud**
29 **ALYPHARD**, b c Lyphard—Blue River **Mr J. Wertheimer**
30 **ANSWERED PRAYER**, b f Green Desert—Jet Ski Lady **Gainsborough Stud**
31 **AUTORITAIRE**, b c Lead On Time—Haute Autorite **Mr J. Wertheimer**
32 **A VOTRE SANTE**, b f Irish River—Mrs Jenny **Mr Marshall W. Jenny**
33 **BAULDING**, b f Bering—Spaulding **Mrs Morange**
34 **BLUESHAAN**, b c Darshaan—Pale Blue **Mr J. Wertheimer**
35 **BLUSHING GLEAM**, b f Caerleon—Blushing Away **Mr J. Wertheimer**
36 **BOLD BOLD**, b f Sadler's Wells—Jasmina **Mr J. Wertheimer**
37 **BRAVALMA**, b f Danzig—Brave Raj **Mr J. Wertheimer**
38 **BUBBLING HEIGHTS**, b f Darshaan—Bubbling Danseuse **Mr J. Wertheimer**
39 **CLASSIC MIX**, b c Danzig—Bambee T T **Gainsborough Stud**
40 **CLOUD FOREST**, b c Green Forest—Abeer **Prince Khalid Abdulla**
41 **DANCING KRIS**, b c Kris—Liska's Dance **Mr J. Wertheimer**
42 **DARK NILE**, b c Riverman—Ixtapa **Prince Khalid Abdulla**
43 **DELTATOWN**, b f Sanglamore—Daeltown **Prince Khalid Abdulla**
44 **DIRECVIL**, b f Top Ville—L'Irlandaise **Mr J. Wertheimer**
45 **DJINN**, b c Mr Prospector—Divine Danse **Ecurie Aland**
46 **ECOUTE**, b f Manila—Soundings **Mr J. Wertheimer**
47 **EGYPTOMAN**, b c Antheus—Reine d'Egypte **Mr J. Wertheimer**
48 **ELECTRIC TALENT**, b f Capote—Catch On Quick **Mr J. Wertheimer**
49 **FORT LAMY**, b c Antheus—Foolish Valley **Mrs Alec Head**
50 **FULTON**, b c Saint Cyrien—Funny Pearl **Mrs Alec Head**
51 **GOING GREEN**, b c Green Dancer—Partygoer **Mr J. Wertheimer**
52 **GOLDEN FLIRT**, b c Slew O' Gold—Quemora **Mr J. Wertheimer**
53 **GOLDEN HAPPINESS**, b f Sanglamore—Ma Petite Jolie **Gainsborough Stud**
54 **GOLD LEAP**, b f Seeking The Gold—Ivory Slippers **Mr J. Wertheimer**
55 **HIGHEST DREAM**, b f Highest Honor—Ring Beaune **Mr J. Wertheimer**
56 **HILL DANCER**, b c Groom Dancer—Mysouko **Mr J. Wertheimer**
57 **HOIST TO HEAVEN**, b c Alleged—Heaven Knows **Mr J. Wertheimer**
58 **HUMOOL**, b c Seattle Slew—Rumoosh **Gainsborough Stud**
59 **INGMAR**, b c Irish River—Minstrel Girl **Mr J. Wertheimer**
60 **IRIKA**, b f Irish River—Princesse Kathy **Mr J. Wertheimer**
61 **KENTUCKY FALL**, b f Lead On Time—Autumn Tint **Prince Khalid Abdulla**
62 **KISTENA**, b f Miswaki—Mabrova **Mr J. Wertheimer**
63 **KRISSANTE**, b f Kris—Vallee Dansante **Mr J. Wertheimer**
64 **L'AFRICAIN BLEU**, b c Saint Cyrien—Afrique Bleu Azur **Mr J. Wertheimer**
65 **LAPIDAIRE**, b c Saumarez—Legataire **Mrs Alec Head**
66 **LASCASES**, b c Generous—Young Hostess **Mr J. Wertheimer**
67 **LE TRITON**, b c El Gran Senor—La Tritona **Gainsborough Stud**

BALLYLINCH
STUD

Mount Juliet, Thomastown, County Kilkenny, Ireland. Telephone: 056-24217 Fax: 056-24624

SIRES FOR 1996

BOB BACK by Roberto ex Toter Back
Group 1 winner and Proven Classic Sire

POSEN by Danzig ex Michelle Mon Amour
Group 2 winner and Proven Stakes Sire

Breeders in 1995 of:
PRIORY BELLE
Moyglare Stakes *Group 1*

WILD BLUEBELL
Coolmore Concorde Stakes *Group 3*

Other Services

Boarding, Foaling, Sales Preparation, Breaking,
Resident Vet and Laboratory

MRS C. HEAD—continued

68 **L'HARNONIE,** b f Bering—False Image **R Romanet**
69 **LYPHOON,** b c Lyphard—Green Moon **Mr J. Wertheimer**
70 **LYPINK,** b f Lyphard—Pink Valley **Mr J. Wertheimer**
71 **MAGIC KING,** b c Fairy King—Magic Spell **Mr J. Wertheimer**
72 **MAHALIA,** b f Danehill—Maresca **Mr G. A. Oldham**
73 **MALAISIE,** b f Bering—Mother of Pearl **Mrs Alec Head**
74 **MISTRA,** b f Rainbow Quest—Mackla **Mr G. A. Oldham**
75 **MOLDAVA,** b f Saumarez—Mondovision **Mrs Alec Head**
76 **MORE FUN,** b c Sanglamore—Arewehavingfunyet **Prince Khalid Abdulla**
77 **NATURAL GOLD,** b f Mr Prospector—Riviere d'Or **Mr J. Wertheimer**
78 **NOBEL TYCOON,** b c Last Tycoon—Charmante Dame **Mr J. Wertheimer**
79 **NORTHERN BRIDE,** b f Antheus—Egyptale **Mr J. Wertheimer**
80 **OCCUPANDISTE,** b f Kaldoun—Only Seule **Mr J. Wertheimer**
81 **PAPALMA,** b f Dixieland Band—Papal Decree **Mr J. Wertheimer**
82 **PARTICULIER,** b c Septieme Ciel—Perle Fine **Mr J. Jones**
83 **PAST THE HILL,** b c Danehill—Passerella **Gainsborough Stud**
84 **PERALTA,** b f Green Desert—Olbia **Mr G. A. Oldham**
85 **PINK REASON,** b f Lear Fan—Hersande **Mr J. Wertheimer**
86 **PLANETAIRE,** b c Lead On Time—Private Rive **Mrs Alec Head**
87 **PRECIOUS RING,** b c Bering—Most Precious **Gainsborough Stud**
88 **QUESTINA,** b f Rainbow Quest—Soviet Squaw **Mr J. Wertheimer**
89 **RADIO ACTIVE,** b f Alleged—Fariedah **Prince Saud Bin Khaled**
90 **SAHARAN,** b c Bering—Desert Holly **Gainsborough Stud**
91 **SCOTCH MIST,** b f Polish Precedent—Shimmer **Aylesfield Farm**
92 **SEA HILL,** b f Seattle Slew—Featherhill **Mr J. Wertheimer**
93 **SEATTLE SPECIAL,** b f Nureyev—O'Slewmova **Mr J. Wertheimer**
94 **SENSATION,** b f Soviet Star—Outstandingly **Sheikh Mohammed**
95 **SEPTIEME BRIGADE,** b c Septieme Ciel—Brigade Speciale **Gainsborough Stud**
96 **SET IN MOTION,** b f Mr Prospector—Cadeaux d'Amie **Gainsborough Stud**
97 **SILVERSTORM,** b c Saumarez—Silvermine **Mrs Alec Head**
98 **SILWANA,** b f Nashwan—Riviere d'Argent **Mr J. Wertheimer**
99 **SOLDAT,** b c Bering—Sans Prix **Mrs Alec Head**
100 **SPANISH FALLS,** b f Belmez—Flamenco Wave **Sheikh Mohammed**
101 **SPECIAL REEF,** b c Shirley Heights—Mona Stella **Mr J. Wertheimer**
102 **STEPNEYEV,** b c Nureyev—Athyka **Mr J. Wertheimer**
103 **STRICT TRICK,** b c Phone Trick—Strictly Raised **Mr J. Wertheimer**
104 **SYPHA,** b f Saumarez—Syphaly **Mrs Alec Head**
105 **TRIOMPHALE,** b f Nureyev—Time Deposit **Mrs Alec Head**
106 **TRUE FLARE,** b f Capote—Proflare **Prince Khalid Abdulla**
107 **TRYATRICK,** b f Phone Trick—Bilakna **Mr J. Wertheimer**
108 **TURKISHMAN,** b c Riverman—Solveig **Mr J. Wertheimer**
109 **TYCOON PRINCE,** b c Last Tycoon—Princesse Vali **Gainsborough Stud**
110 **UNDERSTOOD,** b c Green Desert—Untold **Sheikh Mohammed**
111 B c Lyphard—Viva Zapata **Mr J. Wertheimer**
112 **WELL WALPI,** b c Sadler's Wells—Apachee **Mr J. Wertheimer**
113 **WEST BROOKLYN,** b f Gone West—Brooklyn's Dance **Mr J. Wertheimer**
114 **WHENBY,** b f Bering—Nether Poppleton **Mrs C. Head**
115 **XAYMARA,** b f Sanglamore—Nimble Folly **Prince Khalid Abdulla**
116 **ZAPATAFAR,** b c Lyphard—Viva Zapata **Mr J. Wertheimer**
117 **ZILAREE,** b c Zilzal—Saraa Ree
118 **ZILUM,** b c Zilzal—Avum **Gainsborough Stud**

TWO-YEAR-OLDS

119 **ADVANCE,** b f Shernazar—Green Light **Aylesfield Farm**
120 B c Known Fact—Arewehavingfunyet **Prince Khalid Abdulla**
121 B f Green Forest—Autumn Glory **Prince Khalid Abdulla**
122 **BACK TO MANILA,** b c Manila—Go Solo **Mr J. Wertheimer**
123 B f Zilzal—Balbonella **Gainsborough Stud**
124 **BALDEMARA,** b f Sanglamore—Bamieres **Gainsborough Stud**
125 B f Zilzal—Bialy **Gainsborough Stud**

MRS C. HEAD—continued

126 **BLADE AE**, b c Cox's Ridge—Compulsory **Mr J. Wertheimer**
127 **CHIC**, b c Al Nasr—Time For Romance **Mrs Martine Head**
128 **CIRINO**, b c Gone West—Lacovia **Mr G. A. Oldham**
129 **COSPICUA**, b f High Estate—Stellina **Mr G. A. Oldham**
130 **CRY THE BLUES**, ch f Shahrastani—Pale Blue **Mr J. Wertheimer**
131 **DAME KIRI**, b f Old Vic—Aborigine **Aylesfield Farm**
132 **DANISSIMA**, b f Fabulous Dancer—Dalyane **Mr Wattinne**
133 **DELIMARA**, b f In The Wings—Mariella **Mr G. A. Oldham**
134 **DESTIN**, b c Sillery—Dixiella **Mrs Alec Head**
135 **DEVIL'S CALL**, ch f Phone Trick—La Pitie **Mr J. Wertheimer**
136 **DISSERTATION**, b f Sillery—Devalois **Mrs Alec Head**
137 **DIVIN DANSEUR**, b c Nureyev—Divine Danse **Ecurie Aland**
138 **EBULLISANTE**, b f Lead On Time—Bubbling Danseuse **Mr J. Wertheimer**
139 B c Sanglamore—Emerald **Prince Khalid Abdulla**
140 B c Rainbow Quest—Filigree **Aylesfield Farm**
141 **FILM NOIR**, b c Alleged—Black Princess **Mr J. Wertheimer**
142 B c Sadler's Wells—Foreign Courier **Gainsborough Stud**
143 **FRESHMAN**, b c Sillery—Finicia **Mrs Morange**
144 **FUMARELLI**, ch c Trempolino—Bellarida **Mr J. Wertheimer**
145 **GINGERBOY**, b c Hansel—Grabelst **Mr J. Wertheimer**
146 **GOLD DODGER**, b f Slew O'Gold—Brooklyn's Dance **Mr J. Wertheimer**
147 **GOLDNAYA**, b f Goldneyev—Mabrova **Mr J. Wertheimer**
148 **GREEN BEND**, b f Riverman—Vallee Dansante **Mr J. Wertheimer**
149 **GREEN PUTT**, b c Green Dancer—Animatrice **Mr J. Wertheimer**
150 B c Groom Dancer—Guillem **Prince Khalid Abdulla**
151 **HANKSLEW**, b c Seattle Slew—Fabulous Hostess **Mr J. Wertheimer**
152 **HAPAX**, b c Bering—Hanalei **Mrs Alec Head**
153 B f Danzig—Hiaam **Gainsborough Stud**
154 **HIGHEST HIGH**, b c Highest Honor—Haute Autorite **Mr J. Wertheimer**
155 **HIGHSHAAN**, b f Pistolet Bleu—Renashaan **Mr J. Wertheimer**
156 **HIPPARQUE**, b c Highest Honor—Hylandra **Mr W. Saunders**
157 B c Riverman—Ixtapa **Prince Khalid Abdulla**
158 **IZIBI**, b f Saint Cyrien—Vallee des Fleurs **Mr J. Wertheimer**
159 **KELTSHAAN**, b f Pleasant Colony—Featherhill **Mr J. Wertheimer**
160 **L'ANTILLAISE**, b f Generous—Liska's Dance **Ecurie Aland**
161 **LEADVILLE**, b f Saumarez—Legataire **Mrs Alec Head**
162 **LIEUTENANTE**, b f Sanglamore—La Generale **Mrs Alec Head**
163 **LISHAWAY**, b f Polish Precedent—Blushing Away **Mr J. Wertheimer**
164 **LONELY TYCOON**, b c Last Tycoon—Only Seule **Mr J. Wertheimer**
165 **LONG BAY**, b f Saumarez—Beautiful Time **Mrs Alec Head**
166 **LYTE SPLASH**, b f Lyphard—Belle Sultane **Mr J. Wertheimer**
167 B c Bluebird—Majieda **Gainsborough Stud**
168 **MAJINSKAYA**, gr f Marignan—Makarova **Mr J. Wertheimer**
169 **MARATHON**, b c Diesis—Most Precious **Ecurie Aland**
170 **MARETHEA**, b f Bering—Maralinga **Mrs Alec Head**
171 **MARJORIEN**, b c Machiavellian—Green Rosy **Gainsborough Stud**
172 **MASTER**, b c Bering—Milesime **Gainsborough Stud**
173 **MATEYEV**, ch c Woodman—Angelina Ballerina **Mr J. Wertheimer**
174 B f Nureyev—Mercantile **Mr J. Jones**
175 B f Bering—Music Folies **Mr Carey**
176 **MY PINK**, b f Slew O'Gold—Pink Valley **Mr J. Wertheimer**
177 **MYTHOLOGIE**, b f Bering—Mondovision **Mrs Alec Head**
178 **NASHABA**, ch f Nashwan—Reine d'Egypte **Mr J. Wertheimer**
179 **NIJINSTIC**, ch c Caerleon—Young Hostess **Mr J. Wertheimer**
180 B f Riverman—Nimble Folly **Prince Khalid Abdulla**
181 **ONEREUSE**, b f Sanglamore—J'Ai Deux Amours **Mr J. Wertheimer**
182 B f Nashwan—Ordina **Prince Khalid Abdulla**
183 **PALERMO**, b c Green Desert—Caprarola **Mr G. A. Oldham**
184 **PAS DE REPONSE**, b f Danzig—Soundings **Mr J. Wertheimer**
185 B f Nureyev—Perfect Tune **Mrs Morange**

MRS C. HEAD—continued

186 PHYSICIEN, b c Sillery—Philycia **Mrs Alec Head**
187 PINK SAND, ch f Dancing Spree—Hersande **Mr J. Wertheimer**
188 PLIRIANA, b f Bering—Plania **Mr O'Reilly**
189 B c Unfuwain—Plume Magique **Gainsborough Stud**
190 POLISHNAYA, ch f Soviet Lad—Polish Looks **Mr J. Wertheimer**
191 PRETENDANT, b c Seeking The Gold—Pallanza **Mr J. Wertheimer**
192 B f Trempolino—Proflare **Prince Khalid Abdulla**
193 PUERTO RICO, b c Saumarez—Private River **Mrs Alec Head**
194 QUESTNEYEV, b c Rainbow Quest—Mona Stella **Mr J. Wertheimer**
195 RAHEED, b c Rahy—Samra **Prince Saud Bin Khaled**
196 RAINGAY, b c Saumarez—Solveig **Mr J. Wertheimer**
197 B f Slew O'Gold—Reine des Iles **Ecurie Aland**
198 RINGSHAAN, b f Darshaan—Ring Beaune **Mr J. Wertheimer**
199 RIPOSTO, b c Night Shift—Kahara **Mr G. A. Oldham**
200 ROME, b f Sillery—Redden Queen **Mrs Alec Head**
201 ROYALE ROSE, b f Bering—Rose Blanche **Mrs Alec Head**
202 SADLER'S DANCER, b c Sadler's Wells—Dearly Loved **Mr J. Wertheimer**
203 SEE GOLD, b f Goldneyev—Moquerie **Mr J. Wertheimer**
204 B c Bering—Shimmer **Aylesfield Farm**
205 SHIRLEY BLUE, b f Shirley Heights—Blue River **Mr J. Wertheimer**
206 SICULO, b c Highest Honor—Vanya **Mr G. A. Oldham**
207 SILVER FUN, b f Saumarez—Riviere d'Argent **Mr J. Wertheimer**
208 SILVER PEAK, ch f Sillery—Gerbera **Mr J. Wertheimer**
209 SKY, b c Bering—Silvermine **Mrs Alec Head**
210 SLEW FEMALE, b f Seattle Slew—Female Star **Mr J. Wertheimer**
211 B f Pleasant Colony—Sous Entendu **Gainsborough Stud**
212 SOVIET ARTIC, ch f Bering—Soviet Squaw **Mr J. Wertheimer**
213 SPACE GROOM, ch c Rahy—Space Angel **Mr J. Wertheimer**
214 SPANISH WELLS, b c Kaldoun—Funny Pearl **Mrs Alec Head**
215 SPECIAL DISCOUNT, b c Nureyev—Look Sensational **Mr J. Wertheimer**
216 B f Arazi—Splendid Girl **Gainsborough Stud**
217 B c Zilzal—Starstruck Gal **Gainsborough Stud**
218 STEINER, b c Kaldoun—Rivala **Mr J. Wertheimer**
219 STINGY, ch c Generous—L'Irlandaise **Mr J. Wertheimer**
220 TALK BAND, b f Dixieland Band—Lawyer Talk **Mr J. Wertheimer**
221 B c Nashwan—Touch And Love **Gainsborough Stud**
222 TOUJOURS IRISH, ch f Irish River—Princesse Kathy **Mr J. Wertheimer**
223 TRESORIERE, b f Lyphard—Time To Deposit **Mrs Alec Head**
224 URN DANCER, b c Groom Dancer—Grecian Beauty **Mr J. Wertheimer**
225 VASSIA, b f Machiavellian—Dom Ludge **Mrs Alec Head**
226 VERT VAL, b f Septieme Ciel—Valthea **Mr J. Wertheimer**
227 B c Shadeed—Ville d'Amore **Gainsborough Stud**
228 WAKIGOER, ch f Miswaki—Partygoer **Mr J. Wertheimer**
229 WELLKA, b f Sadler's Wells—Athyka **Mr J. Wertheimer**
230 WESTERN SMART, b f Gone West—Smartly Styled **Mr J. Wertheimer**
231 YXENERY, b f Sillery—Polyxena **Mr J. Wertheimer**

Jockeys (Flat): O Doleuze (7-2), Freddy Head (8-7).

Apprentices: N Guesdon, R Libert.

Amateur: Mr P Hamel.

Lady Rider: Dominique Clerc.

285   MR M. J. B. HEATON-ELLIS, Wroughton

Postal: **Barbury Castle Farm, Wroughton, Wilts, SN4 0QZ.**

Phone: **(01793) 815009 FAX (01793) 845080**

1 **ABSOLUTELY EQUINAME (IRE)**, 5, gr g Roselier (FR)—Cotton Gale **Mr F. J. Sainsbury**
2 **ARTFUL DANE (IRE)**, 4, b c Danehill (USA)—Art Age **S. P. Lansdown Racing**
3 **GODMERSHAM PARK**, 4, b g Warrshan (USA)—Brown Velvet **Mr W. H. Patterson**
4 **HIGH ALLTITUDE (IRE)**, 8, b g Coquelin (USA)—Donna Cressida **Mr F. J. Sainsbury**
5 **LILY OF LUGANA**, 4, b f Lugana Beach—Glimmer **Mr A. P. Holland**
6 **LORD HIGH ADMIRAL (CAN)**, 8, b g Bering—Baltic Sea (CAN) **Elite Racing Club**
7 **MICK THE YANK (IRE)**, 6, b g Millfontaine—Pampered Rose **S. P. Lansdown Racing**
8 **MULLITOVER**, 6, ch g Interrex (CAN)—Atlantic Air **Mrs D. B. Mulley**
9 **NORTHERN CELADON (IRE)**, 5, b h Classic Secret (USA)—Exemplary **The Over The Bridge Partnership**
10 **RATHKEAL (IRE)**, 5, b g Roselier (FR)—Fandango Lady **S. P. Lansdown Racing**
11 **RUPERT'S PRINCESS (IRE)**, 4, b f Prince Rupert (FR)—Llanelli **Mr F. J. Sainsbury**
12 **SICARIAN**, 4, b c Kris—Sharka **Mr F. J. Sainsbury**
13 **SPEEDY CLASSIC (USA)**, 7, br g Storm Cat (USA)—Shadows Lengthen **Stainless Design Services**
14 **THUNDER RIVER (IRE)**, 6, ch g Thatching—In For More **Mr T. H. Luckock**
15 **VENDOON (IRE)**, 6, b g Sanchi Steeple—Lovely Venture **Mrs Francoise Jansen**

THREE-YEAR-OLDS

16 **ARTERXERXES**, b c Anshan—Hanglands **Mr P. G. Lowe & Partners**
17 **DANISH CIRCUS (IRE)**, b c Danehill (USA)—Circus Maid (IRE) **Mr S. Svenby**
18 **FAYRE HOLLY (IRE)**, b f Fayruz—Holly Bird **The Double Barrels**
19 **FREDDIE'S RECALL**, b f Warrshan (USA)—Coir 'a' Ghaill **Mrs H. Murat**
20 **GIRL OF MY DREAMS (IRE)**, b f Marju (IRE)—Stylish Girl (USA) **Mrs Caroline Parker**
21 **JOHN'S LAW (IRE)**, b g Contract Law (USA)—Vieux Carre **Mr R. J. Downes**
22 **LADY OF LIMERICK (IRE)**, b f Thatching—Aunt Hester (IRE) **Mr K. Maeda**
23 **MARLEY'S SONG (IRE)**, b c Classic Music (USA)—Steady The Buffs **Mrs Caroline Parker**
24 **STAR OF RING (IRE)**, b c Taufan (USA)—Karine **Mrs Caroline Parker**
25 **STILL HERE (IRE)**, b g Astronef—Covey's Quick Step **Mr A. K. Collins**
26 **VENI VIDI VICI (IRE)**, b c Fayruz—Divine Apsara **Mr R. A. Bicker**
27 **WELSH MOUNTAIN**, b c Welsh Captain—Miss Nelski **Mr F. J. Sainsbury**

TWO-YEAR-OLDS

28 Ch c 19/4 Nebos (GER)—Baie des Anges (Pas de Seul) **Mr Michael Watt**
29 **BRAVE ENVOY**, b c 7/4 High Estate—Restless Anna (Thatching) **Mrs M. De Zulueta**
30 B f 15/2 River Falls—Burren Breeze (IRE) (Mazaad) **S. P. Lansdown Racing**
31 **CHANDLER'S HALL**, b c 23/4 Saddlers' Hall (IRE)—Queen's Visit (Top Command (USA)) **Sir Peter Cazalet**
32 **DIAMOND GLINT**, gr c 25/2 Absalom—Rosy Diamond (Jalmood (USA)) **Mr F. J. Sainsbury**
33 B f 5/3 River Falls—Double Grange (IRE) (Double Schwartz) **The Double Barrels**
34 B c 31/3 Ballad Rock—Eeduff (Auction Ring (USA)) **Mr Nat Parker & Partners**
35 Br c 15/5 Warning—Erwinna (IRE) (Lyphard (USA)) **Mrs J. Joynson & Partners**
36 Ch c 19/3 Bluebird (USA)—Senane (Vitiges (FR)) **Mr K. Maeda**
37 **SILVER SECRET**, gr c 27/2 Absalom—Secret Dance (Sadler's Wells (USA)) **Mr F. J. Sainsbury**
38 **WOODY'S BOY (IRE)**, ch c 10/4 Roi Danzig (USA)—Smashing Gale (Lord Gayle (USA)) **Mr Vic Woodason**

Other Owners: Mr Haydn Ames, The Hon Adam Barker, Mr David Bowen, Mrs A. N. Campbell-Harris, The Hon Mrs C. Colman, Lt Gen Sam Cowan Cbe, Mr J. M. Davidson, Mr Mel Davies, Mr T. M. Dawson, Mr David Ferrell, Mr D. Gold, Mr P. A. Green, The Hon Jolyon Grey, Mr J. M. Jeyes, Mr John Manser, Mr B. T. Nugent, Mr Roddy Owen, Mrs Parker, Mr R. Pennant-Jones, Mr Nigel Pugh, Mr David Shorthouse, Mr B. H. Simpson, Mr John B. Sunley, Mr S. P. Tindall, Mr Philip L. Treadgold, Mr C. A. W. Williams, Mrs D. Yeats Brown, Mr E. Yeats Brown.

Jockeys (Flat): M Roberts (w.a), W Woods (w.a).

Jockey (NH): D Gallagher (w.a).

Apprentices: S Drowne (8-0), Jonjo Fowle (7-2).

286   MR P. R. HEDGER, Chichester

Postal: **Eastmere Stables, Eastgate Lane, Eastergate, Chichester, PO20 6SJ.**

Phone: **(01243) 543863**

1 **CALL ME RIVER (IRE)**, 8, ch g Over The River (FR)—Larkins Mills **The Larkin Around Partnership**
2 **CASTLE KING**, 9, b g Crash Course—Caherelly Cross **Mr E. Whelan**
3 **DANTE'S VIEW (USA)**, 8, ch g Cox's Ridge (USA)—Only Star (USA) **Mr J. J. Whelan**
4 **DARZEE**, 6, b g Darshaan—Royal Lorna (USA) **Mr Tony Walsh**
5 **GENERAL SHIRLEY (IRE)**, 5, b g Shirley Heights—Adjala **Mr P. R. Hedger**
6 **GINGER JIM**, 5, ch g Jalmood (USA)—Stratch (FR) **Mrs Gina Webster**
7 **HOSTILE WITNESS (IRE)**, 6, br g Law Society (USA)—No Time To Dance **The Pink Panthers**
8 **INTENTION (USA)**, 6, b g Shahrastani (USA)—Mimi Baker (USA) **The Spoofers**
9 **KEDWICK (IRE)**, 7, b g Be My Guest (USA)—Lady Pavlova **Mrs Joyce Griffiths**
10 **LE DENSTAN**, 9, b g Valuta—Sweet Canyon (NZ) **Mr S. Powell**
11 **PRIDE OF HAYLING (IRE)**, 5, ch m Bold Arrangement—Malham Tarn **Mr Bill Broomfield**
12 **REVERSE THRUST**, 5, b g Ilium—Flying Straight **Mrs M. N. Tufnell**
13 **ROBIN ISLAND**, 4, b g Robellino (USA)—Irish Isle **Mr John Lemon**
14 **ROCKUSA**, 4, b f Rock City—Miss Derby (USA) **Deja Vu**
15 **SECRET SPRING (FR)**, 4, b c Dowsing (USA)—Nordica **Mr M. K. George**
16 **SMART IN SABLE**, 9, br m Roscoe Blake—Cool Down **Mrs Jacqueline Elizabeth Hooker**
17 **SUPER GOSSIP (IRE)**, 7, ch g Le Bavard (FR)—Super Amber **P. R. Hedger**
18 **SUPREME STAR (USA)**, 5, b g Gulch (USA)—Just A Game **Mr J. J. Whelan**
19 **THE NIGELSTAN**, 15, b g Fine Blade (USA)—Owenette **Mr P. R. Hedger**
20 **TU DEAR**, 5, b m Lighter—Nelodor **Mrs A. E. Wadman**

Other Owners: Ms. L. Angell, Mr B. G. A. Button, Mr R. B. Felmingham, Mr A. U. Gauna, Mr Mark Hewitt, Mr A. K. Johnson, Mr K. A. Little, Mr M. G. Malone, Mr K. D. Ott, Mr A. Ross, Mr P. A. Sheehan, Mr Chris Silverthorne, Mr David Tapper, Mr R. L. Tappin, Mr Douglas A. Tyler.

Jockey (NH): M Richards (10-0, w.a.).

Conditional: M Clinton (9-7).

287   MR J. A. HELLENS, Chester-le-Street

Postal: **Felledge Farm, Walldridge Lane, Chester Moor, Chester-le-Street, DH2 3RX.**

Phone: **(01913) 885403**

1 **BLACK MAGIC WOMAN**, 8, b m Uncle Pokey—Munster Glen **Mr J. A. Hellens**
2 **BLOND MOSS**, 6, b g Pablond—Moss Pink (USA) **Miss L. Wilson**
3 **BROOMHILL DUKER (IRE)**, 6, br g Strong Gale—Distant Castle **Mr G. F. Bear**
4 **BUYERS DREAM (IRE)**, 6, b g Adonijah—Twist And Shout **Mr C. Hill**
5 **CLASSIC STATEMENT**, 10, ch g Mill Reef (USA)—Lady Graustark (USA) **Mr John Sisterson**
6 **CONTACT HELLENS (IRE)**, 7, gr g Roselier (FR)—Oonagh's Teddy **John Hellens (Contracts) Ltd**
7 **CROSS CANNON**, 10, b g Kambalda—Cushla **Mr J. A. Hellens**
8 **DURHAM GLINT**, 5, b g Glint of Gold—Jem Jen **Mr Eddy Luke**
9 **HERBALIST**, 7, b g Mandrake Major—Mohican **Mr C. Hill**
10 **HILLHEAD (IRE)**, 7, br g Aristocracy—Serpentine Artiste **Mr J. A. Hellens**
11 **JENDEE (IRE)**, 8, b g Dara Monarch—Bunch of Blue **The Avenue Racing Partnership**
12 **LORD BERTRAM (IRE)**, 8, b g Teofane—Satlan **Mr J. A. Hellens**
13 **PHILEAS FOGG (IRE)**, 7, gr g Roselier (FR)—Julie's Gi-Gi **Mr John Sisterson**
14 **POSTED ABROAD (IRE)**, 4, b g Cyrano de Bergerac—Postie **Mr David M. Fulton**
15 **PREMIER FIRST (IRE)**, 7, br g Good Thyne (USA)—Bowerina **Premier Trade Frames Ltd**
16 **RUSTIC WARRIOR**, 6, b g Broadsword (USA)—Lavender Tiger **Mrs M. Tindale**
17 **VAYRUA (FR)**, 11, ch g Vayrann—Nabua (FR) **John Hellens (Contracts) Ltd**
18 **WEAVER GEORGE (IRE)**, 6, b g Flash of Steel—Nephrite **Regent Decorators Ltd**

Other Owners: Mr Peter Bromley, Mr J. R. Brown, Mr P. S. Elliott, Mr B. Hughes, Mr K. Jonas, Mr B. T. Newton, Mr D. Robinson, Mr T. Robson, Mr James Thompson, Mr Arthur Turner, Mr R. F. Turner.

Conditional: Scott Taylor (9-7).

288   MR N. J. HENDERSON, Lambourn

Postal: **Seven Barrows, Lambourn, Newbury, Berks, RG16 7UJ.**

Phone: **LAMBOURN (01488) 72259 OR 72300 FAX (01488) 72596**

1 **ACROBATE (USA)**, 7, ch g Arctic Tern (USA)—Musical Medicine (FR) **Mr Raymond Tooth**
2 **AIRTRAK (IRE)**, 7, b g Strong Gale—Deep Khaletta **Amtrak Express Parcels Limited**
3 **ALLEZ WIJINS (USA)**, 7, br g Alleged (USA)—Dance Machine **Mrs Christopher Hanbury**
4 **AMTRAK EXPRESS**, 9, ch g Black Minstrel—Four In A Row **Amtrak Express Parcels Limited**
5 **APPROACH THE STARS (IRE)**, 8, b br g Strong Gale—Golden Approach **Mrs Shirley Robins**
6 **ARABIAN BOLD (IRE)**, 8, br g Persian Bold—Bodham **Sheikh Amin Dahlawi**
7 **BARNA BOY (IRE)**, 8, b g Torus—Barna Beauty **Mr Lynn Wilson**
8 **BAYARIYKA (IRE)**, 5, b m Slip Anchor—Bayazida **Paddock Potential Racing**
9 **BIG MATT (IRE)**, 8, b g Furry Glen—Stoirin **Mr T. Benfield & Mr W. Brown**
10 **BRAVE PATRIARCH (IRE)**, 5, gr g Alzao (USA)—Early Rising (USA) **Mr Peter S. Winfield**
11 **CAMERA MAN**, 6, ch g Scorpio (FR)—Something To Hide **Mrs P. Shaw**
12 **CHERYL'S LAD (IRE)**, 6, b g Mister Majestic—Two's Company **Mrs Elaine Baines**
13 **CONQUERING LEADER (IRE)**, 7, b m Supreme Leader—Fair Invader **Mrs R. A. Proctor**
14 **CONVENT GARDEN**, 6, b m The Parson—Spartan Daisy **Mrs D. A. Henderson**
15 **CORALETTE (IRE)**, 6, ch g Le Moss—Myralette **Lady Lloyd Webber**
16 **CRAIGHILL (IRE)**, 7, br g Dromod Hill—Walnut Hill **Mr J. R. Henderson**
17 **DEAR DO**, 9, b br g Swinging Rebel—Earlsgift **Mr C. J. Edwards**
18 **EBULLIENT EQUINAME (IRE)**, 5, b g Zaffaran (USA)—Corvina **Mr Lynn Wilson**
19 **ELFLAA (IRE)**, 5, b br g Sure Blade (USA)—Miss Gris (USA) **Mr Raymond Tooth**
20 **FREELINE LUSTRE (IRE)**, 6, b g Supreme Leader—My Serena **Mr Irving Struel**
21 **GARNWIN (IRE)**, 6, b g Strong Gale—Lisnamandra **Pioneer Heat-Treatment**
22 **GLENTOWER (IRE)**, 8, b g Furry Glen—Helens Tower **Lord Swaythling**
23 **GOLDEN SPINNER**, 9, ch g Noalto—Madame Russe **Sir Peter Miller**
24 **HOODED HAWK (IRE)**, 5, b g Henbit (USA)—Kessella **Exors of the Late Mrs L. M. Davies**
25 **HUNTING LORE (IRE)**, 5, b g Lafontaine (USA)—Millies Luck **Mr Milton Ritzenberg**
26 **JACK RUSSELL (IRE)**, 7, b g The Parson—My Duchess **Mr Robert Waley-Cohen**
27 **JOBSAGOODUN**, 5, b g Rakaposhi King—Donna Farina **Mr D. J. W. Ross**
28 **JOURNEYS FRIEND (IRE)**, 8, b g Green Shoon—Carry On Polly **Mr Peter S. Winfield**
29 **KILLUSTY CASTLE (IRE)**, 6, br g Castle Keep—Galloping Gold VII **Mr W. H. Ponsonby**
30 **KIMANICKY (IRE)**, 6, b g Phardante (FR)—Kitty Frisk **Mrs Elaine Baines**
31 **LADY PETA (IRE)**, 6, b g The Parson—Smooth Run **Mr B. M. Collins**
32 **LITENING CONDUCTOR**, 6, br g Strong Gale—Music Interpreter **Count K. Goess-Saurau**
33 **LIXWM**, 7, b m Scorpio (FR)—Connaughts' Trump **Lord Mostyn**
34 **MAN OF WISLEY (IRE)**, 6, b g Mandalus—Sabura **The Wisley Golf Partnership**
35 **MILLIE THE MAORI (IRE)**, 5, gr m Roselier (FR)—Miss Lucille **Mr Peter Urquhart**
36 **MNEMONIC**, 4, b f Mtoto—Neenah **Mr N. J. Henderson**
37 **MOUNTAIN PATH**, 6, b g Rakaposhi King—Donna Farina **Mr Anthony Speelman**
38 **MUTUAL MEMORIES**, 8, b g Relkino—Mindblowing **The Tilley Wright Partnership**
39 **NEW ALBION (USA)**, 5, b br g Pleasant Colony (USA)—Grand Bonheur (USA) **The Barrow Boys**
40 **NOVA RUN**, 7, ch g Ra Nova—Sound Run **Mr S. Keeling**
41 **OUR KRIS**, 4, b c Kris—Our Reverie (USA) **Million In Mind Partnership (5)**
42 **PASHTO**, 9, b g Persian Bold—Epure **Mr Raymond Tooth**
43 **PHILIP'S WOODY**, 8, b g Sula Bula—Pine Gypsy **Mr B. R. Wilsdon**
44 **PLUNDER BAY (USA)**, 5, b g Cutlass (USA)—La Ninouchka (USA) **Mrs Shirley Robins**
45 **POINTED REMARK (IRE)**, 5, ch g Exactly Sharp (USA)—King's Chase **Mrs Michael Ennever**
46 **POLAR REGION**, 10, b g Alzao (USA)—Bonny Hollow **Mr C. Marner**
47 **RIDING CROP (IRE)**, 6, b g King's Ride—Vintage Harvest **The Barrow Boys**
48 **ROBERT SAMUEL**, 5, b g Another Sam—Dracons Girl **Mrs R. Murdoch**
49 **SALMON BREEZE (IRE)**, 5, ch g Kambalda—Channel Breeze **The Salmon Racing Partnership**
50 **SECURON LADY**, 5, b m Derrylin—Thevicarsdaughter **Mrs R. A. Proctor**
51 **SOLAR KESTREL (IRE)**, 8, b g Decent Fellow—The Tonne **Mr Richard Unwin**
52 **SORBIERE**, 9, b g Deep Run—Irish Mint **Mrs R. A. Proctor**
53 **SOVEREIGNS PARADE**, 4, ch g Chromite (USA)—Queen's Visit **Mr Raymond Tooth**
54 **SUBLIME FELLOW (IRE)**, 6, b g Phardante (FR)—Whakapohane **Lady Annabel Goldsmith**
55 **THINKING TWICE (USA)**, 7, ch g Kris—Good Thinking (USA) **Mr Ed McGrath**
56 **THUMBS UP**, 10, b g Fidel—Misclaire **Mr Michael Buckley**

MR N. J. HENDERSON—continued

57 **TRAVADO**, 10, br g Strong Gale—Adelina **Mrs P. Sherwood**
58 **TREMBLE**, 7, b g Tremblant—Bird's Custard **Mrs E. Roberts**
59 **TUDOR FABLE (IRE)**, 8, b g Lafontaine (USA)—Welsh Pride **Mr J. E. H. Collins**
60 **WALTER'S DREAM (IRE)**, 6, b br g Strong Gale—Wonder Alice **Mrs Elaine Baines**
61 **WAYFARERS WAY (USA)**, 5, ch g Manastash Ridge (USA)—Miss Daytona (USA) **Lady Tennant**
62 **WESTERLY GALE (IRE)**, 6, br g Strong Gale—Alix **Mr R. S. Dawes**
63 **WHATTABOB (IRE)**, 7, ch g Bob Back (USA)—Out And About **Mrs Margaret Turner**
64 **WHO IS EQUINAME (IRE)**, 6, b g Bob Back (USA)—Instanter **Mr Lynn Wilson**
65 **WINDY WAYS**, 11, br g Strong Gale—Woodville Grove **Mr N. J. Henderson**
66 **WINTER SQUALL (IRE)**, 8, gr g Celio Rufo—No Honey **Mrs Shirley Robins**
67 **WONDER MAN (FR)**, 11, ch g The Wonder (FR)—Juvenilia (FR) **Mrs Shirley Robins**
68 **WONDER MAN (FR)**, 6, b g Strong Gale—Woodford Princess **Lady Lloyd Webber**
69 **ZANYMAN**, 10, b g Idiot's Delight—Noble Leaf **Mrs P. Shaw**

Other Owners: Queen Elizabeth, Mr J. Adeane, Mr M. Arbib, Earl Of Arran, Mr E. Benfield, Dr J. J. Bourke, Ms M. S. Brackenbury, Mrs Maureen Broadway, Mr Mike Bromley, Mr Ben Brooks, Mr P. R. Burling, Mr David Byrne, Mr N. C. Clark, Mr Mark Coley, Mr Gerald Cooper, Mr S. R. Counsell, Mrs J. M. F. Dibben, Mr A. Eyres, Mr Philip Freedman, Mrs Susan Gilchrist, Mr Graham Goode, Mr C. M. Hamer, Mr Christopher Heath, Mr M. B. J. Kimmins, Sir Timothy Kitson, Mr K. G. Knox, Mr Gavin Macechern, Mrs Hugh Maitland-Jones, Mr K. G. Manley, E. B. McGrath & Partners, Mr D. R. Midwood, Mr D. Minton, Mr G. C. Mordaunt, Mr M. J. Morris, Mr D. S. Mossman, Miss J. S. Murdoch, Mr R. P. North, Lord Pembroke, Mr David F. Price, Mr W. V. Robins, Mrs Basil Samuel, Mrs W. J. Sherwood & Mrs K. Ennever, Mr John Tilley, Mrs June Tilley, Mr B. Townsley, Mr R. Van Gelder, Mr Michael White, Dr Alan Whitworth, Mr J. G. W. Wilson, Mr R. D. A. Woodall, Mr & Mrs P. J. L. Wright.

Jockeys (NH): M A Fitzgerald (10-0), J R Kavanagh (10-0).

Amateur: Mr C Vigors (10-4).

289   MRS R. G. HENDERSON, Okehampton

Postal: **Heath Hills, Folly Gate, Okehampton, Devon, EX20 3AE.**
Phone: **(01837) 52914**

1 **ABSCURE**, 7, b m Absalom—Villajoyosa (FR) **Mrs S. Joint**
2 **BLAZING MIRACLE**, 4, b f Shaab—Cottage Blaze **Mrs R. G. Henderson**
3 **BROWN ROBBER**, 8, gr g Baron Blakeney—Brown Veil **Mr W. J. Henderson**
4 **FIDDLERS PIKE**, 15, b g Turnpike—Fiddlers Bee **Mrs R. G. Henderson**
5 **FORTITUDE STAR**, 6, b m Morgans Choice—Fort Courage **Mrs Jean Saunders**
6 **IL SAURO**, 6, b g Idiot's Delight—Rely-On-Pearl **Mr W. P. Ponsford**
7 **I REMEMBER YOU (IRE)**, 6, ch g Don't Forget Me—Non Casual **Mrs R. G. Henderson**
8 4, B g Prince of Peace—Meldon Lady **Mrs A. Furness**

Other Owners: Mr M. G. Smale.

Conditional: D Salter (9-9).

Amateur: Mr W J Henderson (10-0).

Lady Rider: Mrs R G Henderson (10-0).

290 MAJOR W. R. HERN C.V.O., Lambourn

Postal: **Kingwood House Stables, Lambourn, Newbury, Berks, RG16 7RS.**

Phone: **OFFICE (01488) 73300 FAX 71728 HOME (01635) 281251 TELEX 848362**

1 **AL NUFOOTH (IRE)**, 4, b g Green Desert (USA)—Reine Maid (USA) **Mr Hamdan Al Maktoum**
2 **CUFF LINK (IRE)**, 6, ch g Caerleon (USA)—Corinth Canal **Lord Weinstock & The Hon Simon Weinstock**
3 **FARRINGDON HILL**, 5, b g Minster Son—Firgrove **Mr J. R. Wallis**
4 **GEORGE BULL**, 4, b g Petoski—Firgrove **The Hopeful Partnership**
5 **ISM**, 4, b g Petong—Brigado **Mrs W. R. Hern & Partners**
6 **LANKRIDGE**, 6, b g Alzao (USA)—Free Dance (FR) **Mrs Hugh Dalgety**
7 **MUTAZZ (USA)**, 4, b c Woodman (USA)—Ghashtah (USA) **The All-Round Partnership**
8 **POLISH CONSUL**, 5, ch g Polish Precedent (USA)—Consolation **Lord Chelsea**
9 **ZEETARO**, 5, b g Taufan (USA)—Gem Bracelet (USA) **The Dayspring Company Limited**
10 **ZINE LANE**, 4, ch g Minster Son—Pine **The Hopeful Partnership**

THREE-YEAR-OLDS

11 **ALHAARTH (IRE)**, b c Unfuwain (USA)—Irish Valley (USA) **Mr Hamdan Al Maktoum**
12 **BAASM**, br g Polar Falcon (USA)—Sariah **Mr Hamdan Al Maktoum**
13 **BARIJA (USA)**, ch f Phone Trick (USA)—Viva Aviva (USA) **Mr Hamdan Al Maktoum**
14 **CUE CALL (IRE)**, br f In The Wings—Arousal **Lord Weinstock & The Hon Simon Weinstock**
15 **GHAZWAT (USA)**, b f Riverman (USA)—Ghashtah (USA) **Mr Hamdan Al Maktoum**
16 **HAL HOO YAROOM**, b c Belmez (USA)—Princess Nawaal (USA) **Sheikh Ahmed Al Maktoum**
17 **HAYAAIN**, b c Shirley Heights—Littlefield **Mr Hamdan Al Maktoum**
18 **LABEED (USA)**, b c Riverman (USA)—Gracious Beauty (USA) **Mr Hamdan Al Maktoum**
19 **MAJDAK JEREEB (IRE)**, b c Alzao (USA)—Aunty (FR) **Sheikh Ahmed Al Maktoum**
20 **MAMDOOH (USA)**, b br c Dayjur (USA)—Life's Magic (USA) **Mr Hamdan Al Maktoum**
21 **MIN ALHAWA (USA)**, b f Riverman (USA)—Saffaanh (USA) **Mr Hamdan Al Maktoum**
22 **MIN ELREEH (USA)**, b f Danzig (USA)—Roseate Tern **Mr Hamdan Al Maktoum**
23 **MUHASSIL (IRE)**, ch g Persian Bold—Nouvelle Star (AUS) **Mr Hamdan Al Maktoum**
24 **MUKABIR (USA)**, b c Dayjur (USA)—Copper Creek **Mr Hamdan Al Maktoum**
25 **MUKHLLES (USA)**, b c Diesis—Serenely (USA) **Mr Hamdan Al Maktoum**
26 **MUTARRATTAB**, b c Robellino (USA)—Idle Waters **Mr Hamdan Al Maktoum**
27 **NASEEM ALSAHAR**, ch f Nashwan (USA)—El Fabuloso (FR) **Sheikh Ahmed Al Maktoum**
28 **NO-AMAN**, b c Nashwan (USA)—Ghanimah **Mr Hamdan Al Maktoum**
29 **RAGSAK JAMEEL (USA)**, b g Northern Baby (CAN)—Dream Play (USA) **Sheikh Ahmed Al Maktoum**
30 **RASMIAH**, b f Sadler's Wells (USA)—Reine Maid (USA) **Mr Hamdan Al Maktoum**
31 **SHAWKEY (IRE)**, ch c Nashwan (USA)—Rosia Bay **Mr Hamdan Al Maktoum**
32 **ZUHAIR**, ch c Mujtahid (USA)—Ghzaala (USA) **Mr Hamdan Al Maktoum**

TWO-YEAR-OLDS

33 **AL AMLAH (USA)**, ch f 26/3 Riverman (USA)—Saffaanh (USA) (Shareef Dancer (USA))
34 **BUTRINTO**, ch c 12/4 Anshan—Bay Bay (Bay Express)
35 **ELHAFID (USA)**, ch c 24/3 Nureyev (USA)—Shy Dame (USA) (Damascus (USA))
36 **ELRAYAHIN**, ch f 18/4 Riverman (USA)—Gracious Beauty (USA) (Nijinsky (CAN))
37 **FALAK (USA)**, b c 2/2 Diesis—Tafrah (IRE) (Sadler's Wells (USA))
38 **FALLAH**, b c 6/4 Salse (USA)—Alpine Sunset (Auction Ring (USA))
39 **FLAGSHIP**, ch f 18/2 Rainbow Quest (USA)—Bireme (Grundy)
40 **IKDAM (USA)**, b f 4/2 Dayjur (USA)—Orca (ARG) (Southern Halo (USA))
41 **INJAZAAT (USA)**, b br f 30/1 Dayjur (USA)—Basma (USA) (Grey Dawn)
42 **JUWWI (USA)**, ch c 1/4 Mujtahid (USA)—Nouvelle Star (AUS) (Luskin Star (AUS))
43 **KHAFAAQ**, b c 19/3 Green Desert (USA)—Ghanimah (Caerleon (USA))
44 B c 8/3 Belmez (USA)—Leipzig (Relkino)
45 **MADMUN (IRE)**, ch c 18/3 Cadeaux Genereux—Kates Cabin (Habitat)
46 **MASHARIK (IRE)**, b br f 4/5 Caerleon (USA)—Rosia Bay (High Top)
47 **MUKDAR (USA)**, b br c 27/4 Gulch (USA)—Give Thanks (Relko)
48 **MUTI (USA)**, b c 15/3 El Gran Senor (USA)—Marie de Chantilly (USA) (Alleged (USA))
49 B f 26/2 Lycius (USA)—Princess Nawaal (USA) (Seattle Slew (USA))
50 **RASHIK**, ch c 9/4 Cadeaux Genereux—Ghzaall (USA) (Northern Dancer)
51 **RIGHT WING**, b c 4/4 In The Wings—Nekhbet (Artaius (USA))
52 **ROYAL CASTLE (IRE)**, b c 19/3 Caerleon (USA)—Sun Princess (English Prince)
53 **SARAYIR (USA)**, b f 7/4 Mr Prospector (USA)—Height of Fashion (FR) (Bustino)

MAJOR W. R. HERN C.V.O.—continued

54 **SHAYA**, ch c 10/1 Nashwan (USA)—Gharam (USA) (Green Dancer (USA))
55 B f 3/5 Irish River (FR)—Spit Curl (USA) (Northern Dancer)
56 **TAMYIZ (IRE)**, b f 7/3 Caerleon (USA)—Reine Maid (USA) (Mr Prospector (USA))
57 **TELLION**, b c 19/3 Mystiko (USA)—Salchow (Niniski (USA))
58 **WA-AD (USA)**, b br c 2/2 Nashwan (USA)—Elhasna (USA) (Danzig (USA))

Other Owners: Mrs E. M. Barling, Mrs Donald Black, Lady D'Avigdor-Goldsmid, Mrs P. A. Holliday, R. D. Hollingsworth, Sir Philip Payne-Gallwey, Miss Diana Rennie, Lady Rothschild, Mrs V. N. Wallis.

Jockeys (Flat): W Carson (7-11, w.a.), B Procter (8-3).

291   LADY HERRIES, Littlehampton

Postal: **Angmering Park, Littlehampton, West Sussex, BN16 4EX.**
Phone: **HOME (01903) 871421 YARD (01903) 871460 FAX (01903) 871609**

1 **AMAZE**, 7, b g Natroun (FR)—Entrancing **Lady Katherine Phillips**
2 **ANDANITO (IRE)**, 5, b g Darshaan—Newquay **Bonusprint**
3 **ARCTIC THUNDER (USA)**, 5, b g Far North (CAN)—Flying Cloud (USA) **Merthyr Motor Auctions**
4 **BAJAN (IRE)**, 5, b g Taufan (USA)—Thatcherite **Mr Tim Sinclair**
5 **BELLA SEDONA**, 4, ch f Belmez (USA)—My Surprise **Mr E. Reitel**
6 **BILLY MOONSHINE**, 4, ch g Nicholas Bill—Indian Moonshine **Mrs C. Stupple**
7 **BRANDONHURST**, 6, b g Elegant Air—Wolverina **Lady Sarah Clutton**
8 **CASTLE CAVALIER**, 8, b g Castle Keep—Peteona **Lady Mary Mumford**
9 **CASTLE COURAGEOUS**, 9, b g Castle Keep—Peteona **Lady Mary Mumford**
10 **CELTIC SWING**, 4, br c Damister (USA)—Celtic Ring **Mr P. D. Savill**
11 **CLOUDED ELEGANCE**, 6, b g Elegant Air—Clouded Vision **Lady Sarah Clutton**
12 **CORE BUSINESS**, 5, ch m Starry Night (USA)—Sirenivo (USA) **Mrs E. Reffo**
13 **DAMARITA**, 5, ch m Starry Night (USA)—Sirenivo (USA) **The Classic Link Syndicate**
14 **DARAYDAN (IRE)**, 4, b c Kahyasi—Delsy (FR) **Mr P. D. Savill**
15 **GLORIANA**, 4, b f Formidable (USA)—Tudor Pilgrim **Mr David Blacker**
16 **GREEN GREEN DESERT (FR)**, 5, b g Green Desert (USA)—Green Leaf (USA) **Mr P. D. Savill**
17 **GULF WATER (USA)**, 6, br g Al Nasr (FR)—Paddle (FR) **Lady Herries**
18 **ISLE OF PEARLS (USA)**, 6, b g Theatrical—Margaritaville (USA) **Mrs Berta Lazarus**
19 **JAWAAL**, 6, ch g Soviet Star (USA)—Pencil Sharpener (USA) **Mr T. G. Fox**
20 **KING OF BABYLON (IRE)**, 4, b g Persian Heights—My My Marie **Mr Richard J. Cohen**
21 **LUCAYAN SUNSHINE (USA)**, 4, b f Sunshine Forever (USA)—Be Bop A Lu (USA) **Lucayan Stud**
22 **MAIDMENT**, 5, b m Insan (USA)—Lady Garardina **Mrs B. V. Chennells**
23 **MARALINGA (IRE)**, 4, ch c Simply Great (FR)—Bellinzona **Mr D. K. R. & Mrs J. B. C. Oliver**
24 **MEANT TO BE**, 6, b m Morston (FR)—Lady Gerardina **Lady Mary Mumford**
25 **MENEBUCK**, 10, b g Buckskin (FR)—Meneplete **Lady Sarah Clutton**
26 **MINNESOTA VIKING**, 5, b g Northern State (USA)—Miskin **Mr Charles Green**
27 **MISWAKI DANCER (USA)**, 6, ch g Miswaki (USA)—Simply Divine (USA) **The High Flying Partnership**
28 **MOSCOW MIST (IRE)**, 5, b g Soviet Star (USA)—Ivory Dawn (USA) **Merthyr Motor Auctions**
29 **NANTON POINT (USA)**, 4, b g Darshaan—Migiyas (USA) **Mr L. G. Lazarus**
30 **NIGHT CITY**, 5, b g Dominion—Chiming Melody **Mr E. Reitel**
31 **OCEAN PARK**, 5, b g Dominion—Chiming Melody **Mr E. Reitel**
32 **PRAGUE SPRING**, 4, b f Salse (USA)—Wassl's Sister **All At Sea Partnership**
33 **RASAK**, 4, b g Kris—Lypharita (FR) **Lady Herries**
34 **RIVER NORTH (IRE)**, 6, ch g Lomond (USA)—Petillante (USA) **Mr P. D. Savill**
35 **SAFETY IN NUMBERS**, 6, b g Slip Anchor—Winter Queen **Mrs Sylvia Cohen**
36 **SALAMANDER KING**, 4, b g Distant Relative—Spirit of The Wind (USA) **H.R.H. Princess Michael of Kent**
37 **SERIOUS**, 6, b g Shadeed (USA)—Azallya (FR) **Mrs Denis Haynes**
38 **TAUFAN'S MELODY**, 5, b g Taufan (USA)—Glorious Fate **All At Sea Partnership**
39 **TIBETAN**, 4, b g Reference Point—Winter Queen **Lady Herries**

LADY HERRIES—continued

40 **TOE THE LINE**, 8, b g High Line—Maiden's Walk **Lady Sarah Clutton**
41 **TYKEYVOR (IRE)**, 6, b g Last Tycoon—Ivoronica **Seymour Bloodstock (UK) Ltd**
42 **ZAJKO (USA)**, 6, b g Nureyev (USA)—Hope For All (USA) **Sir Roger Gibbs**

THREE-YEAR-OLDS

43 **AETHRA (USA)**, ch f Trempolino (USA)—All For Hope (USA) **Hesmonds Stud**
44 **AJCOMBE (IRE)**, b g Arjaas (USA)—Whichcombe **Lady Herries**
45 **ARAVINDA (IRE)**, b f Superpower—Surmise (USA) **Who'd A Thought It**
46 **BEAR HUG**, b c Polar Falcon (USA)—Tender Loving Care **Mr L. G. Lazarus**
47 **DANISH RHAPSODY (IRE)**, b g Danehill (USA)—Ardmelody **Mr P. D. Savill**
48 **DOUBLE UP**, ch f Weldnaas (USA)—Bel Esprit **Mrs L. Stevens**
49 **FANCY HEIGHTS**, b f Shirley Heights—Miss Fancy That (USA) **Maktoum Al Maktoum**
50 **GOLDEN FAWN**, ch f Crowning Honours (CAN)—Hill of Fare **Sir Colin Cowdrey**
51 **GRAND SPLENDOUR**, b f Shirley Heights—Mayaasa (FR) **Miss H. Al Maktoum**
52 **GRETNA GREEN (USA)**, b f Hansel (USA)—Greenland Park **Maktoum Al Maktoum**
53 **HARBOUR DUES**, b c Slip Anchor—Quillotern (USA) **Hesmonds Stud**
54 **HEIGHT OF HEIGHTS (IRE)**, b c Shirley Heights—Azallya (FR) **Mrs Denis Haynes**
55 **INFATUATION**, b g Music Boy—Fleeting Affair **Lady Katharine Phillips**
56 **KENTUCKY FALL (FR)**, b f Lead On Time (USA)—Autumn Tint (USA) **Mrs Edna Green**
57 **KITTY KITTY CANCAN**, b f Warrshan (USA)—Kittycatoo Katango (USA) **Mr G. Herridge**
58 **MEDIEVAL LADY**, ch f Efisio—Ritsurin **Mr Jerrard Williamson**
59 **MOON MISCHIEF**, b c Be My Chief (USA)—Castle Moon **Sir Roger Gibbs**
60 **OPALETTE**, b f Sharrood (USA)—Height of Folly **Angmering Park Stud**
61 **PARSIS (USA)**, b c Diesis—Par Excellance (CAN) **Maktoum Al Maktoum**
62 **PURPLE FLIGHT**, b g Polar Falcon (USA)—Purple Prose **Sir Colin Cowdrey**
63 **ROCK FALCON (IRE)**, ch g Polar Falcon (USA)—Rockfest (USA) **Lady Herries**
64 **ROSEBERRY AVENUE (IRE)**, b c Sadler's Wells (USA)—Lady's Bridge (USA) **Mr P. D. Savill**
65 **RUSSIAN WRITER**, b g Soviet Star (USA)—Speed Writing (USA) **Bonusprint**
66 **TRIBAL MOON (IRE)**, b c Ela-Mana-Mou—Silk Blend **Mr P. D. Savill**
67 **WEST HUMBLE**, ch f Pharly (FR)—Humble Pie **Mrs P. J. Sheen**
68 **YIPSILANTI**, ch c Master Willie—Reel Foyle (USA) **Seymour Bloodstock (UK) Ltd**

TWO-YEAR-OLDS

69 **ALAMEDA**, b c 7/3 Formidable (USA)—Albiflora (USA) (Manila (USA)) **Hesmonds Stud**
70 **BEST MAN**, ch c 14/5 Lahib (USA)—Model Bride (USA) (Blushing Groom (FR)) **J. Lazzari**
71 B c 28/2 Saddlers' Hall (IRE)—Blonde Prospect (USA) (Mr Prospector (USA)) **Stephen Dunlop**
72 Gr c 24/3 Reprimand—Castle Moon (Kalamoun) **Angmering Park Stud**
73 **DRAGON LORD**, b c 16/3 Warning—Cockatoo Island (High Top) **Mr P. D. Savill**
74 B g 27/3 Lahib (USA)—Fluella (Welsh Pageant) **Lady Herries**
75 Ch c 26/4 Polish Precedent—Galava (CAN) (Graustark) **Maktoum Al Maktoum**
76 B f 29/1 Midyan (USA)—Height of Folly (Shirley Heights) **Angmering Park Stud**
77 Ch c 6/2 Formidable (USA)—Lovers Tryst (Castle Keep) **Lady Herries**
78 B c 7/2 Polish Precedent—Meis El-Reem (Auction Ring (USA)) **Maktoum Al Maktoum**
79 **MOWELGA**, ch c 26/4 Most Welcome—Galactic Miss (Damister (USA)) **Hesmonds Stud**
80 B f 13/5 Slip Anchor—Tajfah (USA) (Shadeed (USA)) **Maktoum Al Maktoum**
81 **TINTINARA**, b f 27/3 Selkirk (USA)—Mystic Crystal (IRE) (Caerleon (USA)) **Mr D. K. R. & Mrs J. B. C. Oliver**

Other Owners: Mr Victor Behrens, Mr Brian Blacker, M. Broke, Mrs Wendy Brown, Mr John M. D. Knight, Lady Legard, Group Capt A. Mumford, Mr Peter Willett.

Jockey (NH): E Murphy (10-0).

Apprentices: Paul Doe (7-0), John McAuley (7-0), John O'Dwyer (8-0), Richard Smith (7-10).

Lady Rider: Mrs M Cowdrey.

292   MR J. HETHERTON, Malton

Postal: **Highfield Stables, Beverley Road, Malton, North Yorks, YO17 9PJ.**

Phone: **OFFICE (01653) 696778 CAR (0831) 168608**

1 **ALL ON**, 5, ch m Dunbeath (USA)—Fresh Line **Mr N. Hetherton**
2 4, B g Rakaposhi King—Audrina **Mr Garry West**
3 **EXCLUSION**, 7, ch g Ballad Rock—Great Exception **Mr J. Byrne & Mr J. Hetherton**
4 **GUARDS BRIGADE**, 5, b g Bustino—Light Duty **Mr C. D. Barber-Lomax**
5 **HANCOCK**, 4, b g Jester—Fresh Line **Mr N. Hetherton**
6 **MANFUL**, 4, b g Efisio—Mandrian **Mr C. D. Barber-Lomax**
7 **PANTHER (IRE)**, 6, ch g Primo Dominie—High Profile **Mr K. C. West**
8 **RENNYHOLME**, 5, ch g Rich Charlie—Jacqui Joy **Mr G. Cosburn**

THREE-YEAR-OLDS

9 **COQUETTISH**, b f Precocious—Cold Line **Mr N. Hetherton**
10 Gr f Superlative—Lady of The Lodge
11 **MANOY**, b g Precocious—Redcross Miss **Mr C. D. Barber-Lomax**
12 **PHILGEM**, b f Precocious—Andalucia **Mr C. D. Barber-Lomax**
13 **TOTEM DANCER**, b f Mtoto—Ballad Opera **Diamond Racing Ltd**

TWO-YEAR-OLDS

14 Ch c 17/5 K-Battery—Andalucia (Rheingold) **Mr C. D. Barber-Lomax**
15 **IMPETUS**, b g 22/5 Puissance—Cold Line (Exdirectory) **Mr N. Hetherton**

Other Owners: Mrs C. Ashworth, John Rose.

293   MRS A. R. HEWITT, Malpas

Postal: **The White House, Duckington, Malpas, Cheshire, SY14 8LH.**

Phone: **BROXTON (01829) 782314**

1 **CAPTAIN CAVEMAN**, 11, gr g Scallywag—Canadian Pacific **Mr G. Lowe**
2 **CONNAPIGHI**, 7, ch m Respighi—Queen of Connaught **Mr R. P. R. Williams**
3 5, B g Golden Heights—Grange Ratcliffe VII **Mrs A. R. Hewitt**
4 **LAURA BEE**, 7, ch m Saxon Farm—Celtic View **Mr G. S. Williams**
5 **RAGDON**, 5, b g Portogon—Just A Whisper **Miss M. A. De Quincey**
6 **REAL CLAIRE**, 7, b m Dreams To Reality (USA)—La Clairiere (USA) **Mr R. Kinsey & Mr K. Benson**
7 **SEYMOUR'S DOUBLE**, 5, b g Seymour Hicks (FR)—Ida Spider **Mr D. W. Heys**
8 **SEYMOUR SPY**, 7, b g Seymour Hicks (FR)—Ida Spider **Mrs June Burnett**
9 **SPY'S DELIGHT**, 10, b g Idiot's Delight—Ida Spider **Mr W. Graham Woolley**

THREE-YEAR-OLDS

10 **THE DISTAFF SPY**, b f Seymour Hicks (FR)—Ida Spider **Mr D. W. Heys**

Jockey (NH): S Wynne (w.a.).

294   MR P. W. HIATT, Banbury

Postal: **Six Ash Farm, Hook Norton, Banbury, Oxon, OX15 5BU.**

Phone: **(01608) 737255**

1 **BIG TREAT (IRE)**, 4, b g Be My Guest—Cavurina **Mr P. W. Hiatt**
2 **CANARY BLUE (IRE)**, 5, b m Bluebird (USA)—Norfolk Bonnet **Mr P. W. Hiatt**
3 **GARLANDE D'OR**, 4, b f Belfort (FR)—Torville Gold **Mr P. W. Hiatt**
4 **JUNGLE HIGHWAY**, 7, b m Java Tiger—Amber Highway **Mr P. W. Hiatt**
5 **NEVER SO LOST**, 6, ch g Never So Bold—Lost In France **Mr P. W. Hiatt**
6 **ROYAL CIRCUS**, 7, b g Kris—Circus Ring **Mr P. W. Hiatt**

Jockeys (NH): D Bridgwater (9-9), D J Burchell (10-3).

Conditional: E Husband (9-11).

295 MR ANTHONY HIDE, Newmarket

Postal: **Machell Place, Old Station Road, Newmarket, Suffolk, CB8 8DW.**

Phone: **NEWMARKET (01638) 662063 FAX (01638) 560756**

1 DIAMOND PROSPECTOR, 7, b g Jalmood (USA)—Lady Andrea **Mr M. C. Bletsoe**
2 HOUSE DEED, 6, b m Presidium—Miss Deed **Mr J. Jiggens**
3 MEDIATE (IRE), 4, b g Thatching—Unheard Melody **Mr Gerald Tams**
4 MELODY WHEEL, 4, b f Merdon Melody—Spare Wheel **Mrs D. Bruce**
5 MY LEARNED FRIEND, 5, b br g Broken Hearted—Circe **Mrs J. Roberts**
6 OTTAVIO FARNESE, 4, ch g Scottish Reel—Sense of Pride **Mr Cyril Humphris**
7 PERSIAN SMOKE, 5, b m Persian Bold—Gauloise **Mrs Andrew Normand**
8 PRUDENT PRINCESS, 4, b f Puissance—Princess Story **Miss V. R. Jarvis**
9 SAMBA SHARPLY, 5, b g Rambo Dancer (CAN)—Sharper Still **Miss V. R. Jarvis**
10 SCENIC DANCER, 8, b g Shareef Dancer (USA)—Bridestones **Mr Anthony Hide**
11 VIRTUAL REALITY, 5, b g Diamond Shoal—Warning Bell **Ash Partnership**

THREE-YEAR-OLDS

12 CLIO, ch f Scottish Reel—Clymene **Mr Cyril Humphris**
13 ELL ELL EFF, ch f Pharly (FR)—Yen (AUS) **Ms Lucy Franklin**
14 ON THE GREEN, br f Pharly (FR)—Regal Wonder
15 RUSSIAN ROSE (IRE), br f Soviet Lad (USA)—Thornbeam **Ash Partnership**
16 SOLDIER MAK, ch g Infantry—Truly Blest **Mr I. A. Low**
17 WOLF CLEUGH (IRE), b f Last Tycoon—Santa Roseanna **Mr Cyril Humphris**

TWO-YEAR-OLDS

18 INKWELL, b c 15/2 Relief Pitcher—Fragrant Hackette (Simply Great (FR)) **M. Cartwright**

Other Owners: Mr J. Austin, Mrs M. E. Austin, Mr D. H. Bletsoe, Mrs M. Hayes, Mr M. G. H. Heald, Mr David F. Howard, Mr J. L. Napier, Mr J. Roberts, Mr Andrew Singleton, Tessona Racing Limited, Mr D. W. Tonge, Mrs B. Wilkinson.

Jockeys (Flat): J Williams, W Woods.

Jockey (NH): P Hide (9-11).

Amateur: Miss L J Hide (8-4).

296 MR B. W. HILLS, Lambourn

Postal: **South Bank Stables, Lambourn, Newbury, Berks, RG17 7LL.**

Phone: **OFFICE LAMBOURN (01488) 71548 FAX LAMBOURN (01488) 72823**

1 BOWCLIFFE COURT (IRE), 4, b g Slip Anchor—Res Nova (USA) **Mr J. Hanson**
2 CHARLIE SILLETT, 4, ch c Handsome Sailor—Bystrouska **Mr John Sillett**
3 FURTHER FLIGHT, 10, gr g Pharly (FR)—Flying Nelly **Mr S. Wingfield Digby**
4 JOBIE, 6, b g Precocious—Lingering **Mr J. A. Redmond**
5 JUYUSH (USA), 4, b c Silver Hawk (USA)—Silken Doll (USA) **Mr Hamdan Al Maktoum**
6 KEVASINGO, 4, b g Superpower—Katharina **Mrs J. R. Woodhouse**
7 MOONAX (IRE), 5, ch h Caerleon (USA)—Moonsilk **Godolphin**
8 SANMARTINO (IRE), 4, b c Salse (USA)—Oscura (USA) **Mr K. Abdulla**
9 TYPHOON EIGHT (IRE), 4, b c High Estate—Dance Date (IRE) **Mr Michael Siu**
10 WARNING STAR, 4, b f Warning—Blade of Grass **Mr Stephen Crown**

THREE-YEAR-OLDS

11 ALESSANDRA, ch f Generous (IRE)—Kiss **Mr D. J. Deer**
12 AMBASSADOR (USA), b c Hansel (USA)—Taba (ARG) **Maktoum Al Maktoum**

MR B. W. HILLS—continued

13 **APRIL THE EIGHTH**, b c Statoblest—Miami Melody **Mr Michael Siu**
14 **AUNTY JANE**, b f Distant Relative—Aloha Jane (USA) **Mr Paul H. Locke**
15 **BODFARI LASS**, b f Tirol—Sugar Loch **Tilstone Lodge Stud**
16 **BOLD ENOUGH**, ch f Bold Arrangement—Sweet Enough **Mr Ray Richards**
17 **BUSY FLIGHT**, br c Pharly (FR)—Bustling Nelly **Mr S. Wingfield Digby**
18 **CEILIDH STAR (IRE)**, b f Soviet Star (USA)—Highland Ball **Mr John C. Grant**
19 **CIRCLED (USA)**, gr f Cozzene (USA)—Hold The Hula (USA) **Mrs J. M. Corbett**
20 **COVERED GIRL (IRE)**, b f Thatching—Tootle **Southbank Bloodstock**
21 **COXSWAIN**, b f Shirley Heights—Pilot **Mr R. D. Hollingsworth**
22 **DARK DEED (USA)**, ch f Known Fact (USA)—Sin Lucha (USA) **Mr K. Abdulla**
23 **DIAMOND BEACH**, b c Lugana Beach—Cannon Boy (USA) **Mr Ray Richards**
24 **FIJON (IRE)**, b f Doyoun—Tasskeen (USA) **Mrs J. C. Raper**
25 **FILLY MIGNONNE (IRE)**, ch f Nashwan (USA)—Christabelle (USA) **Mr Wafic Said**
26 **FLORENTINO (IRE)**, b c Machiavellian (USA)—Helens Dreamgirl **Lady Harrison**
27 **FLY TIP (IRE)**, b f Bluebird (USA)—Sharp Deposit **Mr D. E. McDowell**
28 **GOLD DISC (USA)**, ch c Slew O' Gold (USA)—Singing (USA) **Mr K. Abdulla**
29 **GREY GALAVA**, gr f Generous (IRE)—Galava (CAN) **Maktoum Al Maktoum**
30 **GULLIVER**, b c Rainbow Quest (USA)—Minskip (USA) **Mr K. Abdulla**
31 **HIGH ATLAS**, b f Shirley Heights—Balliasta (USA) **Mr K. Abdulla**
32 **LEITH ACADEMY (USA)**, b f Academy Award—Uvula (USA) **Newbyth Stud**
33 **LEPIKHA (USA)**, ch f El Gran Senor (USA)—Hortensia (FR) **Mr R. E. Sangster**
34 **LIGHT REFLECTIONS**, b c Rainbow Quest (USA)—Tajtah (USA) **Maktoum Al Maktoum**
35 **MADAME STEINLEN**, b f Steinlen—Equadif (FR) **Sir Eric Parker**
36 **MOODY'S CAT (IRE)**, b f Alzao (USA)—Zamayem **K. Al-Said**
37 **MUBHIJ (IRE)**, ch c Mujtahid (USA)—Abhaaj **Mr Hamdan Al Maktoum**
38 **MY BRANCH**, b f Distant Relative—Pay The Bank **Mr Wafic Said**
39 **NEREUS**, b c Shareef Dancer (USA)—Lady of The Sea **Sheikh Mohammed**
40 **NUZU (IRE)**, b c Belmez (USA)—Nutria (GER) **Sheikh Mohammed**
41 **ONE POUND**, b g Shareef Dancer (USA)—Beloved Visitor (USA) **Mr Michael Goodbody**
42 **POLINESSO**, b c Polish Precedent (USA)—Lypharita (FR) **Sheikh Mohammed**
43 **POLISH SPRING (IRE)**, ch f Polish Precedent (USA)—Diavolina (USA) **Marston Stud**
44 **PRINCE OF MY HEART**, ch c Prince Daniel (USA)—Blue Room **Mr G. J. Hicks**
45 **PROJECTION (USA)**, b c Topsider (USA)—Image of Reality (USA) **Mr K. Abdulla**
46 **PROUD LOOK**, b c Dayjur (USA)—Very Charming (USA) **Maktoum Al Maktoum**
47 **ROYAL APPLAUSE**, b c Waajib—Flying Melody **Maktoum Al Maktoum**
48 **ROYAL JADE**, b f Last Tycoon—Imperial Jade **Mr D. J. Deer**
49 **RUZNAMA (USA)**, ch f Forty Niner (USA)—Last Feather (USA) **Mr Hamdan Al Maktoum**
50 **SABOT**, b c Polar Falcon (USA)—Power Take Off **Mr J. Hanson**
51 **SALTY GIRL (IRE)**, b f Scenic—Sodium's Niece **Mr N. N. Browne**
52 **SANDICLIFFE (USA)**, b f Imp Society (USA)—Sad Song (USA) **Sandicliffe Motor Group**
53 **SHADOW CASTING**, b f Warning—Fanciful (FR) **Mr K. Abdulla**
54 **SHADY GIRL (IRE)**, b f Shaadi (USA)—Octavia Girl **Mr John Leat**
55 **SINKING SUN**, gr f Danehill (USA)—Oscura (USA) **Mr K. Abdulla**
56 **STATOYORK**, b c Statoblest—Ultimate Dream **Mr Seymour Cohn**
57 **STELLAR LINE (USA)**, ch g Zilzal (USA)—Stellaria (USA) **Mr K. Abdulla**
58 **STORY LINE**, ch f In The Wings—Known Line **Broughton Homes Ltd**
59 **TAWKIL (USA)**, b c Riverman (USA)—Lyphette (FR) **Mr Hamdan Al Maktoum**
60 **THREE HILLS**, b c Danehill (USA)—Three Stars **Mr K. Abdulla**
61 **TINTARA (IRE)**, b f Caerleon (USA)—Justsayno (USA) **Mr R. E. Sangster**
62 **VILLEGGIATURA**, b c Machiavellian (USA)—Hug Me **Maktoum Al Maktoum**
63 B g Fairy King (USA)—Whist Awhile
64 **WILAWANDER**, ch c Nashwan (USA)—Wilayif (USA) **Maktoum Al Maktoum**
65 **WINDYEDGE (USA)**, ch c Woodman (USA)—Abeesh (USA) **Maktoum Al Maktoum**
66 **WITCH OF FIFE (USA)**, b f Lear Fan (USA)—Fife (IRE) **Sheikh Mohammed**

TWO-YEAR-OLDS

67 **AMYAS (IRE)**, b c 26/4 Waajib—Art Duo (Artaius (USA)) **Mrs J. M. Corbett**
68 **AWASH**, b c 27/3 Reprimand—Wave Dancer (Dance In Time (CAN)) **Mr R. D. Hollingsworth**
69 B f 24/2 Common Grounds—Boldabsa (Persian Bold)
70 **BOOJUM**, b f 30/4 Mujtahid (USA)—Haboobti (Habitat) **Mrs A. D. Bourne**
71 B f 20/2 Old Vic—Burning Desire (Kalaglow) **Broughton Homes Ltd**

MR B. W. HILLS—continued

72 **CADEAUX CHER,** ch c 3/4 Cadeaux Genereux—Home Truth (Known Fact (USA)) **Mr N. N. Browne**
73 **COBLE,** b c 5/6 Slip Anchor—Main Sail (Blakeney) **Mr R. D. Hollingsworth**
74 Ch c 24/3 Selkirk (USA)—Daki (USA) (Miswaki (USA)) **Mr K. Abdulla**
75 B f 13/3 Warning—Dance It (USA) (Believe It (USA)) **K. Al-Said**
76 **DAVOSKI,** b c 29/3 Niniski (USA)—Pamela Peach (Habitat) **Mr Robert Ogden**
77 **DORADO BEACH,** b f 27/5 Lugana Beach—Cannon Boy (USA) (Canonero (USA)) **Mr Ray Richards**
78 B c 19/2 Common Grounds—Dorado Llave (USA) (Well Decorated (USA)) **Mr A. L. R. Morton**
79 B c 12/5 Classic Music—Duende (High Top) **Mr Pip Elson**
80 Gr f 29/4 Machiavellian (USA)—Dunoof (Shirley Heights) **Sheikh Mohammed**
81 **ENTICE (FR),** b f 2/3 Selkirk (USA)—Loure (USA) (Lyphard (USA)) **Sheikh Mohammed**
82 B f 29/1 Green Desert (USA)—Eternal (Kris) **Mr K. Abdulla**
83 **FARINGDON FUTURE,** b c 20/1 Distant Relative—Lady Dowery (USA) (Manila (USA)) **Mr R. A. N. Bonnycastle**
84 B c 24/3 Simply Majestic (USA)—Fashion Front (Habitat) **Newbyth Stud**
85 B c 19/3 Gone West (USA)—Fife (IRE) (Lomond (USA)) **Sheikh Mohammed**
86 B c 15/5 Crafty Prospector—Forever Waving (USA) (Hoist The Flag (USA)) **Maktoum Al Maktoum**
87 **GOOD REPUTATION,** ch f 11/3 Bluebird (USA)—Reputation (Tower Walk) **Mr R. E. Sangster**
88 B f 21/3 Fairy King (USA)—Happy Smile (IRE) (Royal Match) **Sceptre Racing**
89 B c 19/3 Green Desert (USA)—Hayati (Hotfoot) **Maktoum Al Maktoum**
90 B f 4/4 Nashwan (USA)—Height of Passion (Shirley Heights) **Sheikh Mohammed**
91 **HIGHWAY,** gr c 7/4 Salse (USA)—Ivory Lane (USA) (Sir Ivor) **Mr Guy Reed**
92 **IN COMMAND (IRE),** b c 28/2 Sadler's Wells (USA)—
                              Flying Melody (Auction Ring (USA)) **Maktoum Al Maktoum**
93 **ITTIFAK (USA),** b f 5/4 Danzig (USA)—Last Feather (USA) (Vaguely Noble) **Mr Hamdan Al Maktoum**
94 **JONFY (IRE),** b c 5/5 Waajib—Hyland Rose (Steel Heart) **Mr J. C. Raper**
95 Ch c 29/5 Sharpo—Kerali (High Line) **Mr K. Abdulla**
96 B c 25/3 Sanglamore (USA)—Livry (USA) (Lyphard (USA)) **Mr K. Abdulla**
97 **LOOKOUT,** b f 9/5 Salse (USA)—Sea Pageant (Welsh Pageant) **Mr R. D. Hollingsworth**

MR B. W. HILLS—continued

 98 B c 20/2 Soviet Star (USA)—Lower The Tone (USA) (Master Willie) **Sheikh Mohammed**
 99 B c 23/4 Gone West (USA)—Ma Petite Jolie (USA) (Northern Dancer) **Miss H. Al Maktoum**
100 B c 26/1 Sadler's Wells (USA)—Marie de Flandre (FR) (Crystal Palace (FR)) **Mr Wafic Said**
101 B f 28/2 Rainbow Quest (USA)—Minskip (USA) (The Minstrel (CAN)) **Mr K. Abdulla**
102 MISTY RAIN, b f 16/2 Polar Falcon (USA)—Ballerine (USA) (Lyphard's Wish (FR)) **Mr Ray Richards**
103 MITHAK (USA), b c 13/2 Silver Hawk (USA)—
                                  Kapalua Butterfly (USA) (Stage Door Johnny) **Mr Hamdan Al Maktoum**
104 MY VALENTINA, b f 14/2 Royal Academy (USA)—Imperial Jade (Lochnager) **Mr D. J. Deer**
105 NATIVE PRINCESS (IRE), ch f 28/4 Shalford (IRE)—Jealous One (Raise A Native) **Mr Stephen Crown**
106 NATURAL EIGHT (IRE), b c 30/4 In The Wings—Fenny Rough (Home Guard (USA)) **Mrs Melody Siu**
107 NIGHTBIRD (IRE), b f 11/2 Night Shift (USA)—Pippas Song (Reference Point) **Mr S. P. Tindall**
108 Ch c 25/2 Mujtahid (USA)—Nimieza (USA) (Nijinsky (CAN)) **Sheikh Mohammed**
109 NUBILE, b f 24/3 Pursuit of Love—Trojan Lady (USA) (Irish River (FR)) **Mr J. Hanson**
110 B c 17/3 Sadler's Wells (USA)—Ozone Friendly (USA) (Green Forest (USA)) **Maktoum Al Maktoum**
111 B f 21/5 Distant Relative—Pay The Bank (High Top) **Mr Wafic Said**
112 PRAIRIE FALCON (IRE), b c 27/2 Alzao (USA)—Sea Harrier (Grundy) **Lady Harrison**
113 B c 7/2 Deploy—Questionable (Rainbow Quest (USA)) **Mr K. Abdulla**
114 SABOTINI, b f 15/2 Prince Sabo—Low Line (High Line) **Mrs E. Roberts**
115 B f 20/4 Diesis—Sedulous (Tap On Wood) **Mr J. Peter Williams**
116 SHOWBOAT, b c 27/3 Warning—Boathouse (Habitat) **Mr R. D. Hollingsworth**
117 Br f 13/2 Warning—Silly Bold (Rousillon (USA)) **Mr K. Abdulla**
118 B c 30/4 Irish River (FR)—Singing (USA) (The Minstrel (CAN)) **Mr K. Abdulla**
119 Ch f 9/1 Irish River (FR)—Sin Lucha (USA) (Northfields (USA)) **Mr K. Abdulla**
120 SPARGO EXPRESS, b c 12/4 Mystiko (USA)—Noora's Rose (NZ) (Ahonoora) **Mr A. L. R. Morton**
121 STATE FAIR, b c 16/2 Shirley Heights—Lobinda (Shareef Dancer (USA)) **Mr Ray Richards**
122 THE FLY, gr c 2/5 Pharly (FR)—Nelly Do Da (Derring-Do) **Mrs J. M. Corbett**
123 Ch f 21/4 Common Grounds—The Saltings (FR) (Morston (FR)) **Sceptre Racing**
124 VALAGALORE, b f 24/4 Generous (IRE)—Victoria Cross (USA) (Spectacular Bid (USA)) **Mrs A. D. Bourne**
125 VARDA (IRE), b f 2/2 Taufan (USA)—Almond Flower (IRE) (Alzao (USA)) **Mr J. Hanson**
126 B f 29/1 Warning—Well Beyond (IRE) (Don't Forget Me) **Mr K. Abdulla**
127 Ch c 24/4 Common Grounds—Welsh Fantasy (Welsh Pageant) **Tilstone Lodge Stud**
128 Ch f 10/5 Rainbow Quest (USA)—Wilayif (USA) (Danzig (USA)) **Maktoum Al Maktoum**
129 ZAAHIR (IRE), b c 5/4 Marju (IRE)—Abhaaj (Kris) **Mr Hamdan Al Maktoum**
130 ZA-IM, b c 3/5 Green Desert (USA)—Al Bahathri (USA) (Blushing Groom (FR)) **Mr Hamdan Al Maktoum**

Other Owners: Mr A. K. Collins, Mr B. W. Hills, Mr Paul McNamara, Mr J. Mercer, Mr D. O. Pickering, Mr Kenneth B. Rawlings, Mrs Allen Russell-Smith, Lady Richard Wellesley, Mr Christopher Wright.

Apprentices: Gary Brace (8-0), J D Smith (8-0).

Amateur: Mr C B Hills (9-7).

297   MR J. W. HILLS, Lambourn

Postal: **Hill House Stables, Folly Road, Lambourn, Newbury, RG17 8QE.**

Phone: **(01488) 73144 FAX (01488) 73099**

1 ANN'S PEARL (IRE), 5, br m Cyrano de Bergerac—Pariscene **Mrs Paul Levinson**
2 AWESOME POWER, 10, b g Vision (USA)—Majestic Nurse **Mr Garrett J. Freyne**
3 CAROL'S DREAM (USA), 4, ch c Risen Star (USA)—Merle Halton (USA) **Mrs Carol Lane**
4 GLIDE PATH (USA), 7, ch h Stalwart (USA)—Jolly Polka (USA) **The Jampot Partnership**
5 MISS LAUGHTER, 4, b f Sulaafah (USA)—Miss Comedy **Miss J. Wilkinson**
6 OKEEDOKEE (FR), 6, gr g Kaldoun (FR)—Multitude (USA) **Mr Michael Gates**
7 SHERIFF, 5, b g Midyan (USA)—Daisy Warwick (USA) **Mr Christopher P. J. Brown**

MR J. W. HILLS—continued

THREE-YEAR-OLDS

8 **AL ABRAQ (IRE)**, b c Reprimand—Dazzling Maid (IRE) **Mr Ziad A. Galadari**
9 **ALZABELLA (IRE)**, b f Alzao (USA)—Believer **Mr Michael Wauchope**
10 **BOLD PATRIOT (IRE)**, b c Polish Patriot (USA)—Don't Be Cruel **Racegoers Club Owners Group (1995)**
11 **BRIGHT ECLIPSE (USA)**, br c Sunny's Halo (CAN)—Miss Lantana (USA) **Mr J. W. Robb**
12 **CLASSIC DEFENCE (IRE)**, b c Cyrano de Bergerac—My Alanna **Mr J. W. Robb**
13 **CODE RED**, b c Warning—For Action (USA) **Mr Abdulla Al Khalifa**
14 **COMMIN' UP**, b f Primo Dominie—Ridalia **Abbott Racing Partners**
15 **DALWHINNIE**, b f Persian Bold—Land Line **Ibra Racing Company**
16 **DIMINUTIVE (USA)**, b c Diesis—Graceful Darby (USA) **Gainsbury Partnership**
17 **DIVINA LUNA**, b f Dowsing (USA)—Famosa **Mr D. J. Deer**
18 **EVENING IN PARIS**, ch f Be My Chief (USA)—Photocall **John Good**
19 **HAREB (USA)**, b c Diesis—All At Once (USA) **Mr Ziad A. Galadari**
20 **IBERIAN DANCER (CAN)**, b f El Gran Senor (USA)—Cutty (USA) **Mr G. R. Collister**
21 **JAMAICAN FLIGHT (USA)**, b c Sunshine Forever (USA)—Kalamona (USA) **The Jampot Partnership**
22 **MAID TO LAST**, b f Groom Dancer (USA)—Derniere Danse **Julian Richmond-Watson**
23 **MAX'S MAGIC (USA)**, b c Chief's Crown (USA)—Pattyville (USA) **Mr Freddy Bienstock**
24 **MIGHTY PHANTOM (USA)**, b f Lear Fan (USA)—Migiyas **Mr Michael Wauchope**
25 **MOHANNAD (IRE)**, b c Royal Academy (USA)—Pudibunda **Mr Ziad A. Galadari**
26 **NIMBLE (IRE)**, b f Danehill (USA)—Sierra Leone (ITY) **Highclere Thoroughbred Racing Ltd**
27 **OH WHATAKNIGHT**, b f Primo Dominie—Carolside **Mr & Mrs D. Clee**
28 **ROSES IN THE SNOW (IRE)**, gr f Be My Guest (USA)—Desert Bluebell **Mr G. Howard-Spink**
29 **SAFECRACKER**, ch c Sayf El Arab (USA)—My Polished Corner (USA) **Mrs R. F. Lowe**
30 **SCARPETTA (USA)**, ch f Seattle Dancer (USA)—Pump (USA) **Mr James Barber (Susan Abbott Racing)**
31 **SONDOS**, b f Dowsing (USA)—Krameria **Mr Ziad A. Galadari**
32 **THE LEGIONS PRIDE**, b c Rambo Dancer (CAN)—Immaculate Girl **Royal British Legion Racing Club**
33 **TOP**, b c Weldnaas (USA)—Daisy Topper **Mr J. Davies**
34 **TWILIGHT TIME**, b f Aragon—In The Shade **Mr G. Howard-Spink**
35 **URGENT LIAISON (IRE)**, b f High Estate—Itching (IRE) **N. N. Browne & Partners**

TWO-YEAR-OLDS

36 Br c 17/5 Red Ransom (USA)—Akamare (FR) (Akarad (FR)) **Mr N. N. Brolone**
37 **ARRIVING**, b c 17/2 Most Welcome—Affirmation (Tina's Pet) **Wyck Hall Stud**
38 Br c 10/2 Danzatore (USA)—Cardamine (USA) (Secretariat (USA)) **Mr Ziad Galadari**
39 **CAVIAR ROYALE (IRE)**, ch c 26/3 Royal Academy (USA)—Petite Liquerelle (Shernazar)
40 **CHIEF'S DREAM (USA)**, b c 14/2 Chief's Crown (USA)—Chase The Dream (USA) (Sir Ivor) **Mr Ziad Galadari**
41 B c 14/5 Cyrano de Bergerac—Dazzling Maid (IRE) (Tate Gallery (USA)) **Mr J. W. Hills**
42 B c 28/3 Wild Again (USA)—Fabrina (USA) (Storm Bird (USA)) **Sultan Al Kabeer**
43 B c 8/4 Known Fact (USA)—Free Spirit (USA) (Avatar (USA)) **W. Patterson & Partners**
44 Ch c 19/2 Lahib (USA)—Gentle Guest (IRE) (Be My Guest (USA)) **Mr J. Halokes & Partners**
45 **KRISTOPHER**, ch c 23/3 Kris—Derniere Danse (Gay Mecene) (USA) **Mr Julian Richmond-Watson**
46 B f 9/4 Rainbow Quest (USA)—Luth Celtique (FR) (Thatch (USA)) **Sultan Al Kabeer**
47 B c 5/5 Law Society (USA)—Majestic Nurse (On Your Mark) **Mr Garrett Freyne**
48 B c 18/3 Sadler's Wells (USA)—Producer (USA) (Nashua) **Freddy Bienstock**
49 **PROTOCOL (IRE)**, b c 23/4 Taufan (USA)—
                    Ukraine's Affair (USA) (The Minstrel (CAN)) **Highclere Thoroughbred Racing Ltd**
50 B c 5/4 Fairy King (USA)—Quality of Life (Auction Ring (IRE)) **C. R. Nelson & Partners**
51 **REUNION (IRE)**, b f 25/2 Be My Guest (USA)—Phyella (Persian Bold) **Highclere Thoroughbred Racing Ltd**
52 **SHAMES (USA)**, b c 15/4 Quest For Fame—Munchkin Michele (USA) (Naked Sky (USA)) **Mr Ziad Galadari**
53 B c 27/3 Sadler's Wells (USA)—Sharata (IRE) (Darshaan) **N. B. F. Hubbard**
54 **SPANISH WARRIOR**, b c 19/3 Warrshan (USA)—Spanish Heart (King of Spain) **Avon Industries**
55 B f 11/3 Midyan (USA)—Vielle (Ribero) **Mr Gareth Noble**

Other Owners: J. Ansell, Astaire & Partners (Holdings) Ltd, Mr Derek Auburn, N. Biggin, Miss D. Birks, A. Black, Miss J. Bradford, Mrs Joan Buckingham, Mr Keith Buckingham, Mr C. Buttery, Dr J. Chandler, David Chapman, Mr R. Chapman, Mrs N. Clarke, Mr Derek Clee, Bill Coleman, Mr P. Cooper, Mr Robert Cottam, Mr N. Dallas, Mr D. Dring, Sir Simon Dunning, Lady Fairbairn, M. Fielding, L. Godfrey, Mr Brian Hall, Miss Wendy Hall, J. Hamilton, Lady Frances Hanmer, Mr A. Hawkes, M. Hawkes, J. Hobhouse, Mr Hophouse, Mr D. Hopson, Mrs S. Hopson, Mr R. Hunter, Group Capt. Peter Johnson, Mr J. Locory, Gary Lowe, Mr S. Marsh, Mr Terry Milson, Mr T. Morning, J. O'Neill, Lt. Gen. Sir

MR J. W. HILLS—continued

David Scott-Barrett, Hugh Scott-Barrett, Karen Scott-Barrett, Mr Ken Sharp, Mrs W. Shirley, Mr J. Simpson, D. Snushall, The Losers Owners Group, Mr D. Thorpe, Mrs W. Tulloch, Mrs Lucinda Waterhouse, Miss Z. Whitmore, Mr Christopher Wright.

Jockeys (Flat): M Hills (8-0), R Hills (8-0).

Apprentice: M Henry (7-8).

Lady Rider: Miss Eve Johnson Houghton (9-7).

298   MR R. P. C. HOAD, Lewes

Postal: **Windmill Lodge Stables, Spital Road, Lewes, East Sussex, BN7 1LS.**

Phone: **(01273) 477124 MOBILE (0585) 252783**

1 **CARFAX,** 11, ch g Tachypous—Montana Moss **Mrs V. E. Maunders**
2 **CELTIC LILLEY,** 6, ch m Celtic Cone—Pal Alley **Miss J. E. Reed**
3 **COURAGE-MON-BRAVE,** 8, gr g Bold Owl—Bri-Ette **Mrs Alison Gamble**
4 **DESERT PRESIDENT,** 5, ch g Polish Precedent (USA)—Majestic Kahala (USA) **Mr P. M. Mooney**
5 **ELBURG (IRE),** 6, b g Ela-Mana-Mou—Iosifa **Mrs Alison Gamble**
6 **FATTASH (USA),** 4, ch g Tejano (USA)—Green Pompadour (USA) **Mr Michael Tobitt**
7 **GIANO,** 8, ch g True Song—Lavenham Rose **Mr John Galvanoni**
8 **GUNNER JOHN,** 5, b g Gunner B—Hilly-Down Lass **Mr John Galvanoni**
9 **HEAD FOR HEAVEN,** 6, b g Persian Heights—Believer **Nairn - O'Connell Racing**
10 **ILE DE SOO,** 10, br g Ile de Bourbon (USA)—Bloomsday **Mr R. C. Hawkins**
11 **NAMASTE,** 8, b g Petoski—View **Mr John Galvanoni**
12 **NIVASHA,** 4, b f Shavian—Rheinza **Mills Racing**
13 **SPLENDID THYNE,** 4, ch c Good Thyne (USA)—Mrs Jennifer **Mr John Galvanoni**
14 **THE OIL BARON,** 10, gr g Absalom—Ruby's Chance **Mrs J. J. T. Gunn**
15 **WOODLANDS BOY (IRE),** 8, b g Hawaiian Return (USA)—Annie Sue VI **Mr Stan Moore**

Other Owners: Mrs J. Hoad, Mr R. P. C. Hoad, Mr George Tobitt.

Lady Rider: Lois Macintoish (8-0).

299   MR P. J. HOBBS, Minehead

Postal: **Sandhill, Bilbrook, Minehead, Somerset, TA24 6HA.**

Phone: **(01984) 640366 CAR (0860) 729795 FAX (01984) 641124**

1 **AAL EL AAL,** 9, br h High Top—Last Card (USA) **Six Horse Power**
2 **ALFIE THE GREAT (IRE),** 7, b g Supreme Leader—Last Round **The Margaret Street Partnership**
3 **ALWAYS REMEMBER,** 9, b g Town And Country—Try To Remember **Mrs S. C. Cockshott**
4 **AMLAH (USA),** 4, gr c Storm Bird (CAN)—Old Mother Hubbard (USA) **Mr Salvo Giannini**
5 **ASHMEAD RAMBLER (IRE),** 6, b g Henbit (USA)—Bramble Lane **The Guiburn Set**
6 **ASHWELL BOY (IRE),** 5, b g Strong Gale—Billys Pet **A. B. S. Racing**
7 **BADASTAN (IRE),** 7, b g Shardari—Badalushka **Mr Salvo Giannini**
8 **BANKROLL,** 9, b g Chief Singer—Very Nice (FR) **Mr Ian S. Steers**
9 **BELLS LIFE (IRE),** 7, b g The Parson—Affability **Mr R. Gibbs**
10 **BLUE RAVEN,** 5, ch g Monsanto (FR)—Caswell Bay **Mr David Brace**
11 **BORN TO PLEASE (IRE),** 4, ch g Waajib—Gratify **Mr P. J. Hobbs**
12 **BORROWED AND BLUE,** 6, b m Local Suitor (USA)—Abielle **Mr Brian Cooper**

MR P. J. HOBBS—continued

13 **BRAVE BUCK (IRE)**, 5, ch g Buckskin (FR)—Free Choice **Mr Peter Luff**
14 **CERTAIN ANGLE**, 7, ch g Saxon Farm—Cytisus **The Plyform Syndicate**
15 **CHARGED**, 7, ch g Scottish Reel—Abielle **Mr Brian Cooper**
16 **CHOICE BAR**, 6, b m Morgans Choice—Evening Bar **Mrs A. Frank**
17 **CLARIFICATION**, 5, b g Teenoso (USA)—Greenhill Jazz Time **Mr H. R. C. Catherwood**
18 **CLERIHUE**, 7, br m Rymer—Funny Baby **Col R. J. Martin**
19 **CLEVER SHEPHERD**, 11, b g Broadsword (USA)—Reluctant Maid **Miss H. L. Cope**
20 **CLIFTON BEAT (USA)**, 5, b h Danzatore (CAN)—Amenity (FR) **Mr D. B. O'Connor**
21 **CONNAUGHT CRACKER**, 6, ch g Gunner B—Burlington Belle **Connaught Group Ltd**
22 **CONNAUGHT'S PRIDE**, 5, ch m Hubbly Bubbly (USA)—Burlington Belle **Connaught Group Ltd**
23 **CRACK ON**, 6, ch g Gunner B—Wing On **Mr D. R. Peppiatt**
24 **CRANE HILL**, 6, b g Dancing Brave (USA)—Consolation **Mr Rod Hamilton**
25 **CREGG BOREEN**, 9, ch g Boreen (FR)—Denys Eyre **Mr Rod Hamilton**
26 **CRU EXCEPTIONNEL**, 8, b g Scottish Reel—Elton Abbess **Mr B. K. Peppiatt**
27 **CURRENT AFFAIR (IRE)**, 5, b g Electric—Good Oh **Travail Employment Group Ltd**
28 **DISTANT MEMORY**, 7, gr g Don't Forget Me—Canton Silk **Mrs Ann Weston**
29 **DOUBLE PENDANT (IRE)**, 5, b g Double Schwartz—Emerald Pendant **The Baad Boys**
30 **DR LEUNT (IRE)**, 5, ch g Kefaah (USA)—Not Mistaken (USA) **Mr Peter Emery**
31 **EDGEMOOR PRINCE**, 5, b g Broadsword (USA)—Stubbin Moor **The Racing Hares**
32 **ELAINE TULLY (IRE)**, 8, b m Persian Bold—Hanna Alta (FR) **Mrs P. G. Wilkins**
33 **FATHER POWER (IRE)**, 8, b g The Parson—Believe It Or Not **Mr Peter Bowling**
34 **FAUSTINO**, 4, br g Faustus (USA)—Hot Case **The Bilbrook 4**
35 **GOLD CAP (FR)**, 11, ch g Noir Et Or—Alkmaar (USA) **Mr Geoff Meadows**
36 **GREENBACK (BEL)**, 5, b h Absalom—Batalya (Bel) **Mr Jack Joseph**
37 **GREENHILL RAFFLES**, 10, ch g Scallywag—Burlington Belle **Mr D. A. Price**
38 **GREENHIL TARE AWAY**, 8, b g Oats—Burlington Belle **Mrs P. F. Payne**
39 **GROOMS GOLD (IRE)**, 4, ch c Groom Dancer (USA)—Gortynia (FR) **Mrs J. Coward**
40 **HENLEY WOOD**, 11, b g Leander—Allengrove **Mr A. J. Scrimgeour**
41 **HYLTERS CHANCE (IRE)**, 5, ch g Zaffaran (USA)—Stickey Stream **Mrs Karola Vann**
42 **JAYDEEBEE**, 5, b m Buckley—Miss Poker Face **Mr J. D. Brownrigg**
43 **JENZSOPH (IRE)**, 5, b m Glow (USA)—Taken By Force **Superset Two**
44 **KAREN'S TYPHOON (IRE)**, 5, b g Strong Gale—Pops Girl **Six Horse Power**
45 **KEANO (IRE)**, 7, ch g Phardante (FR)—Nickel Run **Midavon Partnership**
46 **KIBREET**, 9, ch g Try My Best (USA)—Princess Pageant **Mrs Jill Emery**
47 **KIND CLERIC**, 5, b g Supreme Leader—Preacher's Gem **The Hammer Partnership**
48 **LASATA**, 11, b g Buckskin (FR)—De Lafield **Mr P. Lamb**
49 **LUCKY LANE**, 12, b g Mart Lane—O Token **Mr Rod Hamilton**
50 **MELLION PRIDE (IRE)**, 8, b g Sheer Grit—Saucy Slave **St Mellion Estates Ltd**
51 **MENDIP PRINCE (IRE)**, 6, b g King's Ride—Atlantic Hope **Three Ply Racing**
52 **MUSKORA (IRE)**, 7, b g Muscatite—Singing Wren **Mr N. C. Savery**
53 **MUTUAL TRUST**, 4, ch g Pollerton—Giolla's Bone **Mr Mark Bowling**
54 **NORDIC MINE (IRE)**, 6, b g Nordico (USA)—Tower Belle **Mr N. C. Savery**
55 **ORSWELL LAD**, 7, b g Pragmatic—Craftsmans Made **Mr R. M. E. Wright**
56 **PENNCALER (IRE)**, 6, ch g Callernish—Pennyland **Mrs Anona Taylor**
57 **PHAEDAIR**, 6, b g Strong Gale—Festive Season **Capt. E. J. Edwards-Heathcote**
58 **PLEASURE SHARED (IRE)**, 8, ch g Kemal (FR)—Love-In-A-Mist **Mr Tony Eaves**
59 **RAMSTAR**, 8, ch g Import—Meggies Dene **Mr A. Loze**
60 **REAL PROGRESS (IRE)**, 8, ch g Ashford (USA)—Dulcet Dido **Mr A. Stennett**
61 **ROCA MURADA (IRE)**, 7, br g Cyrano de Bergerac—Keppols **Connaught Group Ltd**
62 **ROYAL AG NAG**, 6, b m Nicholas Bill—Murex **Royal Agricultural College - Union Club**
63 **SAMLEE (IRE)**, 7, b g Good Thyne (USA)—Annie Buskins **Mr S. Martin**
64 **SAXON DUKE**, 5, b g Saxon Farm—Bucks Princess **Saxon Duke Partnership**
65 **SAXON MEAD**, 6, ch g Saxon Farm—Great Chance **Mr H. R. C. Catherwood**
66 **SHIRLEY'S TRAIN (USA)**, 7, br g Malinowski (USA)—Tiger Trap (USA) **Superset Two**
67 **SORREL HILL**, 9, b g Mandalus—Lamb's Head **Mr C. H. Vicary**
68 **SPARKLING YASMIN**, 4, b f Derring Rose—Kate Kimberley **Mr Victor G. Palmer**
69 **THE BOBTAIL FOX (IRE)**, 7, b g Supreme Leader—Tiepoless **Racing Club of Wales**
70 **TREVAYLOR (NZ)**, 12, ch g Rapier II—Regal Bride (NZ) **Mr G. N. Noye**
71 **WARNER'S SPORTS**, 7, b g Strong Gale—Cala Conta **Terry Warner Sports**
72 **WINSFORD HILL**, 5, ch g Nearly A Hand—Gay Ticket **Six Horse Power**

MR P. J. HOBBS—continued

Other Owners: Mr James Burley, Mr R. Coaten, Mrs Jo Cooney, Mr P. A. Deal, Miss I. D. Du Pre, Mr R. E. Evans, Mrs Anne Fisher, Mrs J. Gibbs, Mrs M. C. Grant, Mr Michael Gray, Mr J. R. Hall, Mr A. J. Heappey, Mrs Mary Hill, Mrs Michelle K. Isaacs, Prof A. Jones, Mr Phil Lake, Mr Donald Last, Mr C. Lewis, Mr Chris Llewellyn, Mr M. J. Ogborne, Mrs Izabel Palmer, Mr L. Perring, Mr J. A. Pickford, Mr M. Popham, Mr P. G. Rattenberry, Mr Alan J. Schneider, Mr I. L. Shaw, Mr A. N. Sheppard, Mrs Beryl Sheppard, Mr M. Sherling, Mrs R. O. Steed, Mrs J. M. Stennett, Miss Janet Stephens, Mr D. Veysey, Mrs H. K. Viney, Mr C. J. M. Walker, Mr J. T. Warner, Mr C. K. Watkins, Mr James T. Whiting, Mr A. Windle, Mr Andrew P. Wyer.

Conditional: M Moran (9-7), G Tormey (9-7).

Amateurs: Mr J Creignton (10-7), Mr S Mulcaire (10-0).

Lady Rider: Mrs S L Hobbs (9-0).

300   MR R. J. HODGES, Somerton

Postal: **Cedar Lodge, Charlton Adam, Somerton, Somerset, TA11 7AR.**
Phone: **CHARLTON MACKRELL (0145822) 3922**

1   **ABTAAL**, 6, b h Green Desert (USA)—Stufida **Mr P. Slade**
2   **ALMAPA**, 4, ch g Absalom—More Fun **Mr P. Slade**
3   **COMMANCHERO**, 9, gr g Telsmoss—Count On Me **Mr J. W. Mursell**
4   **CORPUS**, 7, ch g Ballacashtal (CAN)—Millingdale **Mr J. Newsome**
5   **CORRIN HILL**, 9, b g Petorius—Pete's Money (USA) **Mr Bob Froome**
6   **DAWN CHANCE**, 10, gr g Lighter—Main Chance **Mr G. Small**
7   **DORMY THREE**, 6, b g Morston (FR)—Dominant **Mr P. Slade**
8   **EVENING RAIN**, 10, b g Hays—Fine Form (USA) **The Gardens Entertainments Ltd**
9   **FENWICK**, 9, b g Magnolia Lad—Isobel's Choice **Major A. W. C. Pearn**
10 **GLOWING PATH**, 6, b g Kalaglow—Top Tina **Mr P. Slade**
11 **HAPPY HORSE (NZ)**, 9, ch g Gaiter (NZ)—Silver Valley (NZ) **Major Ian Manning**
12 **HARD TO FIGURE**, 10, gr g Telsmoss—Count On Me **Mr J. W. Mursell**
13 **HIGH BARON**, 9, gr g Baron Blakeney—High Finesse **Miss C. A. James**
14 **HIGHTOWN CAVALIER**, 5, b g Thowra (FR)—Hightown Fontana **Miss R. Dobson**
15 **HOW'S YER FATHER**, 10, b g Daring March—Dawn Ditty **Unity Farm Holiday Centre Ltd**
16 **INDIAN RUN (IRE)**, 7, b g Commanche Run—Excitingly (USA) **Mr P. Slade**
17 **J BRAND**, 9, b g Persian Bold—Napa Valley **Mr Terry Pasquale**
18 **JURZ (IRE)**, 8, b g Pennine Walk—Kawkeb (USA) **Mr P. Slade**
19 **KLOSTERS**, 4, ch f Royal Match—Snowy Autumn **Mr J. F. Tucker**
20 **LINE OF CONQUEST**, 6, b g El Conquistador—High Finesse **Miss C. A. James**
21 **MADRAJ (IRE)**, 8, b br g Double Schwartz—Poka Poka (FR) **Mr P. Slade**
22 **MAI PEN RAI**, 8, ch g All Systems Go—Jersey Maid **Mr R. T. Sercombe**
23 **MEDINAS SWAN SONG**, 8, b g Nearly A Hand—Miss Medina **Mrs Stanley Perry**
24 **MELLING**, 5, b g Thowra (FR)—Miss Melmore **Miss R. Dobson**
25 **MISS SPENT YOUTH**, 5, ch m Sylvan Express—Cedar Lady **Mr J. W. Mursell**
26 **MISTER JOLSON**, 7, br g Latest Model—Impromptu **Mr Bob Froome**
27 **MORSTOCK**, 6, gr g Beveled (USA)—Miss Melmore **Mrs M. Fairbairn**
28 **MUSTAHIL (IRE)**, 7, gr g Sure Blade (USA)—Zumurrudah (USA) **Unity Farm Holiday Centre Ltd**
29 **NOEPROB (USA)**, 6, b m Majestic Shore (USA)—Heat Haze (USA) **Mrs P. A. Bradshaw**
30 **NORTHERN SADDLER**, 9, ch g Norwick (USA)—Miss Saddler **Mr Richard J. Evans**
31 **NORTHERN SINGER**, 6, ch g Norwick (USA)—Be Lyrical **Mr Joe Panes**
32 **PALACEGATE GOLD (IRE)**, 7, b g Sarab—Habilite **Mr R. J. Hodges**
33 **PERSISTENT GUNNER**, 6, ch m Gunner B—Miss Saddler **Mr P. Slade**
34 **POWDER BOY**, 11, ch g Tarrago (ITY)—Powder Princess **Mr Don Hurford**
35 **SAILEP (FR)**, 4, ch c Holst (USA)—Sweet Cashmere (FR) **Mr P. Slade**
36 **SHY MYSTIC**, 6, ch m Shy Groom (USA)—Misowni

MR R. J. HODGES—continued

37 **SMILEY FACE**, 4, b g Colmore Row—Count On Me **Mr J. W. Mursell**
38 **SMILING CHIEF (IRE)**, 8, ch g Montelimar (USA)—Victa **Mrs E. A. Tucker**
39 **SPORTS VIEW**, 7, b g Mashhor Dancer (USA)—Persian Express **Mr J. T. Warner**
40 **SULABELL**, 4, b f Sulaafah (USA)—Miss Bluebell **Mr G. Small**
41 **TRUE FIDDLER**, 6, b g El Conquistador—True Finesse **Miss C. A. James**

THREE-YEAR-OLDS

42 **FINSBURY FLYER (IRE)**, ch g Al Hareb (USA)—Jazirah **Mr P. Slade**

Other Owners: Mr A. J. Coleman, Mr J. N. Coventry, Mrs E. J. Edwards, Mrs A. M. Evans, Exors Of The Late Mrs K. M. Burge, Mr V. S. Fox, Mr Andrew Gifford, Mrs Linda Goddard, Mr Percy J. Harris, Hightown Finance & Bloodstock Agency, Mrs Ann Hurford, Mr A. C. James, Mrs E. M. J. James, Mr R. E. James, Mr S. E. James, Mr G. Keirle, Mr Ron Osborne, Mr C. A. G. Perry, Mrs K. Sellars, Mr K. Small, Mr Paul Wheeler, Mr C. M. Wilson.

301   MR R. HOLLINSHEAD, Upper Longdon

Postal: **Lodge Farm, Upper Longdon, Rugeley, Staffs, WS15 1QF.**
Phone: **ARMITAGE (01543) 490298 FAX (01543) 490490**

1 **ALBERTITO (FR)**, 9, b g Esprit du Nord—Aranita **Miss B. Connop**
2 **ALL APOLOGIES (IRE)**, 4, b c Common Grounds—Living Rough **Mr Gabriel Mulholland**
3 **ARC BRIGHT (IRE)**, 6, b h Trempolino—Brillante (FR) **Mr J. E. Bigg**
4 **ARRYSU**, 5, b g Derring Rose—New Dawning **Miss Sandra E. Bowerman**
5 **BOLD ARISTOCRAT (IRE)**, 5, b h Bold Arrangement—Wyn Mipet **Mrs J. Hughes**
6 **CASTLEREA LAD**, 7, b h Efisio—Halo **Mrs Tess Graham**
7 **CHADLEIGH LANE (USA)**, 4, ch g Imp Society (USA)—Beauty Hour (USA) **Mr J. E. Bigg**
8 **CROSS TALK (IRE)**, 4, b c Darshaan—Liaison (USA) **Mr J. E. Bigg**
9 **CUANGO (IRE)**, 5, b br h Mtoto—Barinia **Barouche Stud Ltd**
10 **DODDINGTON FLYER**, 4, b c Distant Relative—Tino-Ella **Mr J. F. Bower**
11 **DUKE VALENTINO**, 4, br c Machiavellian (USA)—Aldhabyih **Mr J. E. Bigg**
12 **EASTLEIGH**, 7, b g Efisio—Blue Jane **Mr J. E. Bigg**
13 **FLYING IMP**, 5, b g Faustus (USA)—Quenlyn **Mrs Jane Galpin**
14 **FOOLS OF PRIDE (IRE)**, 4, ch f Al Hareb (USA)—I'll Take Paris (USA) **Mr L. A. Morgan**
15 **HEATHYARDS BOY**, 6, b g Sayf El Arab (USA)—French Cooking **Mr L. A. Morgan**
16 **HEATHYARDS LADY (USA)**, 5, b m Mining (USA)—Dubiously (USA) **Mr L. A. Morgan**
17 **HEATHYARDS ROCK**, 4, br g Rock City—Prudence **Mr L. A. Morgan**
18 **IF ONLY**, 6, b g Lightning Dealer—Pentland Beauty **Mr R. B. Hill**
19 **INDIAHRA**, 5, b m Indian Ridge—Mavahra **Mr P. J. Lawton**
20 **IN THE MONEY (IRE)**, 7, b h Top Ville—Rensaler (USA) **Mr J. E. Bigg**
21 **KING RAMBO**, 5, b g Rambo Dancer (CAN)—Infanta Maria **The Miracle Partnership**
22 **LIFE IS PRECIOUS (IRE)**, 4, b f Shernazar—Neelam (USA) **Mr Ed Weetman**
23 **MARADATA (IRE)**, 4, ch f Shardari—Maridana (USA) **Mr R. Hollinshead**
24 **NOUFARI (FR)**, 5, b g Kahyasi—Noufiyla **Ed Weetman (Haulage & Storage) Ltd**
25 **RESPECTABLE JONES**, 10, ch g Tina's Pet—Jonesee **Miss Sarah Hollinshead**
26 **RI RA**, 6, b m Derring Rose—Cat Meadow **Miss Sandra E. Bowerman**
27 **RISKY ROSE**, 4, b f Risk Me (FR)—Moharabuiee **Mr M. Johnson**
28 **ROSCOMMON LAD (IRE)**, 4, b g Groom Dancer (USA)—Preoccupy **David Manning Associates**
29 **ROUSITTO**, 8, ch g Rousillon (USA)—Helenetta **The Three R's**
30 **SHAKIYR (FR)**, 5, gr g Lashkari—Shakamyin **L & R Roadlines**
31 **STYLISH BLAKE**, 7, ch g Blakeney Point—Roaring Style **Mr J. Doxey**
32 **TANIYAR (FR)**, 4, b g Glenstal (USA)—Taeesha **Mrs J. Hughes**

THREE-YEAR-OLDS

33 **BLUNTSWOOD HALL**, b g Governor General—Miss Sarajane **Mr J. Smyth**
34 **CRISSEM (IRE)**, b f Thatching—Deer Emily **Mrs Christine Johnson**
35 **DANCING CAVALIER**, b c Nalchik (USA)—Miss Admington **The Three R's**
36 **DHES-C**, b f Lochnager—Keep Cool (FR) **Dhes-C Partnership**
37 **HEATHYARDS JADE**, b f Damister (USA)—French Cooking **Mrs B. L. Morgan**
38 **HEATHYARDS ROSE (IRE)**, b f Conquering Hero (USA)—Another Gayle **Mr L. A. Morgan**

MR R. HOLLINSHEAD—continued

39 **LAWNSWOOD CAPTAIN (IRE)**, ro c Maelstrom Lake—Morgiana **Mr R. Hollinshead**
40 **LIA FAIL (IRE)**, b f Soviet Lad (USA)—Sympathy **Mr Noel Sweeney**
41 **LOCH STYLE**, b g Lochnager—Simply Style **Mr J. B. Wilcox**
42 **OAKLEY FOLLY**, b f Puissance—Brown's Cay **Mr & Mrs T. G. Holdcroft**
43 **POTENZA**, b g Puissance—Indivisible **Mrs A. Mutch**
44 **RICHARD HOUSE LAD**, b c Warrshan (USA)—Sirenivo (USA) **Mr D. Morrall**
45 **SCENICRIS (IRE)**, b f Scenic—Princesse Smile **Mrs Christine Johnson**
46 **SHARP MONTY**, b g Mon Tresor—Sharp Anne **Mr R. Leah**
47 **SKELTON COUNTESS (IRE)**, ch f Imperial Frontier (USA)—Running Brook **Mr G. Bailey**
48 **SOSTENUTO**, b f Northern State (USA)—Pride of Ayr **Mrs B. E. Woodward**
49 **SUALTACH (IRE)**, b c Marju (IRE)—Astra Adastra **Mr Noel Sweeney**
50 **U-NO-HARRY (IRE)**, b c Mansooj—Lady Roberta (USA) **Mr D. Coppenhall**
51 **WEET-A-MINUTE (IRE)**, ro c Nabeel Dancer (USA)—Ludovica **Ed Weetman (Haulage & Storage) Ltd**
52 **WEETMAN'S WEIGH (IRE)**, b c Archway (IRE)—Indian Sand **Ed Weetman (Haulage & Storage) Ltd**

TWO-YEAR-OLDS

53 B br f 27/4 Ela-Mana-Mou—Bay Empress (Empery (USA))
54 **DANEHILL PRINCESS (IRE)**, b f 19/4 Danehill (USA)—Top Glad (USA) (I'm Glad (ARG)) **Mr J. D. Graham**
55 Ch c 16/3 Imperial Frontier—Desert Gale (Taufan (USA))
56 **DIVIDE AND RULE**, b c 28/4 Puissance—Indivisible (Remainder Man) **Mrs A. Mutch**
57 **FOOT BATTALION (IRE)**, b c 13/2 Batshoof—Roxy Music (IRE) (Song) **Mr A. S. Hill**
58 **GET THE POINT**, b c 9/4 Sadler's Wells (USA)—Tolmi (Great Nephew) **Mr J. E. Bigg**
59 **HEATHYARDS PEARL (USA)**, gr ro f 12/3 Mining (USA)—
                                        Dance Dance Dance (IRE) (Dance of Life (USA)) **Mr L. A. Morgan**
60 B f 27/3 Nomination—Moharabuiee (Pas de Seul)
61 B c 15/5 Contract Law (USA)—Mrs Lucky (Royal Match)
62 Gr c 21/5 Contract Law (USA)—Mrs Mutton (Dancer's Image (USA))
63 **MUJOVA (IRE)**, b c 22/3 Mujadil (USA)—Kirsova (Absalom) **Mr J. D. Graham**
64 **NORTHERN PRINCESS**, b f 7/3 Nomination—Glenstal Princess (Glenstal (USA)) **Mr J. D. Graham**
65 **PAGEL (IRE)**, b c 24/3 Polish Patriot (USA)—Fanfan (IRE) (Taufan (USA)) **Mr P. D. Savill**
66 B c 24/3 Bluebird (USA)—Sallymiss (Tanfirion) **Mr G. Johnson**
67 **THE WYANDOTTE INN**, ch c 24/2 Ballacashtal (CAN)—Carolynchristensen (Sweet Revenge) **Mr G. A. Farndon**
68 B c 9/3 Thorn Dance (USA)—Thought Provoker (USA) (Exceller (USA))
69 **VERASICA**, b f 13/1 Handsome Sailor—Vera Musica (USA) (Stop The Music (USA)) **Mr R. Leah**
70 **WEET A BIT (IRE)**, b c 1/5 Archway (IRE)—Aridje (Mummy's Pet) **Ed Weetman (Haulage & Storage) Ltd**
71 **WHISPER LOW (IRE)**, ch f 22/4 Shalford (IRE)—Idle Gossip (Runnett) **Mr D. Lowe**

Other Owners: Mrs W. L. Bailey, Mr D. R. Horne, Mr John M. Jackson, Mrs Judith Kassar, Mr Ray Robinson, Mr A. Singh, Mr G. Singh.

Jockey (NH): G Lyons (10-2).

Apprentices: F Lynch (7-10), C L Russell (7-12).

Conditional: M W Martin (9-7).

Amateur: Mr M Rimell (10-0).

Lady Rider: Mrs Jane Galpin (8-7).

302   MR G. HOLMES, Pickering

Postal: **Burlington House, Newton Upon Rawcliffe, Pickering, North Yorks, YO18 8QA.**

Phone: **(01751) 473446/476534**

1 **GYMCRAK DIAMOND (IRE)**, 6, b g Taufan (USA)—Down The Line **The Gymcrak Thoroughbred Racing Club**
2 **GYMCRAK FLYER**, 5, b m Aragon—Intellect **The Gymcrak Thoroughbred Racing Club**
3 **GYMCRAK HERO (IRE)**, 4, b g Taufan (USA)—Jamie's Girl **The Gymcrak Thoroughbred Racing Club**
4 **GYMCRAK PREMIERE**, 8, ch g Primo Dominie—Oraston **The Gymcrak Thoroughbred Racing Club**
5 **GYMCRAK SOVEREIGN**, 8, b g Ballacashtal (CAN)—Get Involved **The Gymcrak Thoroughbred Racing Club**
6 **GYMCRAK TIGER (IRE)**, 6, b g Colmore Row—Gossip **The Gymcrak Thoroughbred Racing Club**
7 **GYMCRAK TYCOON**, 7, b g Last Tycoon—Brazen Faced **The Gymcrak Thoroughbred Racing Club**
8 **RED EIKON**, 5, ch g French Gondolier (USA)—Loudoun Lass VII **Mrs Diana Reid**

THREE-YEAR-OLDS

9 **GYMCRAK GEM (IRE)**, b f Don't Forget Me—Santa Patricia (IRE) **The Gymcrak Thoroughbred Racing Club**
10 Br f Lord Bud—Pretty Soon

TWO-YEAR-OLDS

11 B br f 1/4 Rock Hopper—Bit O' May (Mummy's Pet)
12 B g 18/3 Derrylin—Emerin (King Emperor (USA))
13 Ch f 19/4 Nomadic Way (USA)—Pretty Soon (Tina's Pet)

Other Owners: Mr S. Binns, Mr M. Briggs, Mr Peter Cowles, Mr V. Dymoke White, Mr C. B. Ellmes, Miss J. N. Gaunt, Mr R. Goodwin, Mr A. H. Hewes, Mr Gordon Holmes, Mrs J. L. Holmes, Mrs C. Horne, Mr & Mrs D. Johnson, Mr Michael Laws, Mr Derek Leek, Mr H. Magee, Mr G. W. Singleton, Mrs M. Singleton, Mr Duncan R. Smith, Mr Raymond Smith, Mr L. J. Sweet, Mr Brian Taylor, Mrs M. Walker, Mr I. Whittingham, Mr G. J. Williams.

Jockey (Flat): K Fallon.

Jockeys (NH): M Dwyer (w.a.), R Garrity, L Wyer (w.a.).

303   MR J. S. HOMEWOOD, Ashford

Postal: **Pett Farm, Charing, Ashford, Kent, TN27 0DS.**

Phone: **HOME (01233) 713897   MOBILE (0836) 514194   FAX (01233) 714193**

1 **MAJESTIC GOLD**, 8, b g Majestic Maharaj—Balas **Mr J. S. Homewood**
2 **ONEOFUS**, 7, b g Lochnager—Mountain Child **Mrs D. C. Homewood**
3 **PETT LAD**, 8, b g Remainder Man—Winter Lodge **Mr J. S. Homewood**
4 **SURGICAL SPIRIT**, 6, b m Lighter—Sheba Queen **Mr J. S. Homewood**

Jockey (NH): Mark Richards (10-0).

304   MR CON HORGAN, Pulborough

Postal: **Recitation House, 3 Coombelands Stables, Pulborough, West Sussex, RH20 1BP.**

Phone: **OFFICE (01798) 874511   FAX (01798) 874511   MOBILE (0850) 365459**

1 **BELFRY GREEN (IRE)**, 6, gr g Doulab (USA)—Checkers **Mr John Kelsey-Fry**
2 **CLASSIC PET (IRE)**, 4, b f Petorius—Checkers **Friary Bloodstock Company Ltd**
3 **CRESTED KNIGHT (IRE)**, 4, gr g Night Shift (USA)—Casual (USA) **Mrs B. Sumner**
4 **PISTOL (IRE)**, 6, ch g Glenstal (USA)—First Wind **Mrs B. Sumner**
5 **RISING SPRAY**, 5, ch g Waajib—Rose Bouquet **Mr J. T. Heritage**
6 **RISK MASTER**, 7, b g Risk Me (FR)—Trigamy **Mrs B. Sumner**
7 **THATCHMASTER (IRE)**, 5, b g Thatching—Key Maneuver (USA) **Mrs B. Sumner**

MR CON HORGAN—continued

THREE-YEAR-OLDS

8 **ALZEUS (IRE)**, b g Alzao (USA)—Rentina **Mrs B. Sumner**
9 **COUNTRY THATCH**, b c Thatching—Alencon **Mrs B. Sumner**
10 **SAM ROCKETT**, b c Petong—Art Deco **Miss Monica Campbell**
11 **SOVEREIGN CREST (IRE)**, gr c Priolo (USA)—Abergwrle **Mrs B. Sumner**
12 **VICTOR BLUM (USA)**, b g Dr Blum (USA)—Victoria Elena (USA) **Mr R. Del Rosario**
13 **WARREN KNIGHT**, b c Weldnaas (USA)—Trigamy **Mrs B. Sumner**

TWO-YEAR-OLDS

14 Gr c 28/4 Kenmare (FR)—Gold Necklace (Golden Fleece (USA))
15 B c 17/1 Indian Ridge—Halvoya (Bay Express)
16 Ch gr c 2/4 Shalford (IRE)—Hat And Gloves (Wolver Hollow) **Mr B. Tantoc**
17 **PRINCE ZANDO**, b c 18/3 Forzando—Paradise Forum (Prince Sabo) **Mrs B. Sumner**
18 **REGAL ACADEMY (IRE)**, b f 9/1 Royal Academy (USA)—Polistatic (Free State) **Mrs B. Sumner**

Other Owners: Mr E. J. Bevan, Mrs S. Greenaway, Mr J. L. Harrison, Mr C. A. Horgan, Mr Tony Longden.

---

305   MISS C. J. HORLER, Bath

Postal: **Highchurch Stables, Hemington, Bath, Somerset, BA3 5XT.**
Phone: **(01373) 834216 MOBILE (0585) 486687 OFFICE (01373) 834188**

1 **CHANCE DE LA VIE**, 7, b g Town And Country—Little Charter **Miss Carol Horler**
2 **CHARTER SPRINGS**, 10, b g Miami Springs—Little Charter **Miss Carol Horler**
3 **ROTAMOLE**, 6, b g Sulaafah (USA)—Charanda **Miss Carol Horler**
4 **SPRING SAINT**, 7, ch g Midyan (USA)—Lady of Chalon **Miss Carol Horler**

Jockey (NH): Guy Upton.

---

306   MR H. S. HOWE, Tiverton

Postal: **The Old Smithy, Oakfordbridge, Tiverton, Devon, EX16 9JA.**
Phone: **(01398) 351224**

1 **ANOTHER BULA (IRE)**, 5, br g Cardinal Flower—Celtic Lace **H. S. Howe**
2 **APACHEE FLOWER**, 6, ch m Formidable (USA)—Molucella **Kate Spurway**
3 **BULLANGUERO (IRE)**, 7, ch g Be My Guest (USA)—Timid Bride (USA) **Secret Partnership**
4 **DONT BEAT THE BABY**, 8, b m Sulaafah (USA)—Molucella **Kate Spurway**
5 **DUNKERY BEACON**, 10, b g Casino Boy—Crown Member VII **Graham Kinson**
6 **FROG HOPPER**, 5, ch g Out of Hand—Dorothy Jane **Mr R. T. Grant**
7 **HIDDEN FLOWER**, 7, b m Blakeney—Molucella **Kate Spurway**
8 **MISS SOUTER**, 7, b m Sulaafah (USA)—Glenn's Slipper **Secret Partnership**
9 5, Gr g Step Together—Popsi's Darling **H. S. Howe**
10 **STORM POINT (IRE)**, 8, ch g Kambalda—Glenbrien Dusty **Secret Partnership**
11 **STRATTON FLYER**, 6, b m Mas Media—Empress Valley **Melvyn Worthington**

Other Owners: Mr C. Butler, Caroline Butler, Mr K. Crabb, Mr W. Evans, Q. J. Jones, D. Lockyer.

Jockeys (NH): D Bridgwater, A P McCoy, B Powell.

307   MR P. HOWLING, Newmarket

Postal: **Wellbottom Lodge, Moulton Paddocks, Bury Road, Newmarket, CB8 7PJ.**

Phone: **MOBILE (0836) 721029 (01638) 668503**

1 **CRADLE DAYS**, 7, b g Dance of Life (USA)—Dream Chaser **Mr Robert Baker**
2 **DAANIERA (IRE)**, 6, gr g Standaan (FR)—Right Cash **Mr G. Mann**
3 **HENRY WESTON**, 4, b c Statoblest—Young Tearaway **Mr K. Weston**
4 **HOPEFUL BID (IRE)**, 7, b g Auction Ring (USA)—Irish Kick **Mrs R. Parrish**
5 **JUDGEMENT CALL**, 9, b g Alzao (USA)—Syllabub **Mr K. Weston**
6 **JUNIOR BEN (IRE)**, 4, b c Tirol—Piney Pass **Mr B. R. Allen**
7 **LUCKY COIN**, 4, b f Hadeer—Lucky Omen **Mrs J. M. Khan**
8 **NAME THE TUNE**, 5, b h Chief Singer—Try To Remember **Mr C. Hammond**
9 **RASMI (CAN)**, 5, ch h Riverman (USA)—Snow Blossom (CAN) **Mr C. Hammond**
10 **ROCKY TWO**, 5, b h Cree Song—Holloway Wonder **Mr B. Bennett**
11 **SAMSOLOM**, 8, b g Absalom—Norfolk Serenade **Mr C. Hammond**
12 **SOLO PRIZE**, 4, b g Chief Singer—Raffle **Mr C. N. Wright**
13 **SUPER HIGH**, 4, b c Superlative—Nell of The North (USA) **Mrs J. M. Khan**
14 **SWEET MAGIC**, 5, ch g Sweet Monday—Charm Bird **Mr C. Hammond**
15 **TEE-EMM**, 6, b g Lidhame—Tower Glades **Mr Robert H. Carey**
16 **WESTERN COUNTRY**, 4, ch g Beveled (USA)—Country Singer **Mr B. Azemoudah**
17 **WHAT A NIGHTMARE (IRE)**, 4, gr g Petorius—Mysterious Lady **Six Furlongs Racing Ltd**

THREE-YEAR-OLDS

18 **BOUTON D'OR**, b f Mazilier (USA)—Cow Pastures **Mr J. Weston**
19 **IN TUNE**, b c Prince Sabo—Singing Nelly **Mr C. Hammond**
20 **MUSIC IN MOTION**, b f Batshoof—Falaka **Mr J. Hammond**
21 **RUDI'S BOY**, ch c Sayf El Arab (USA)—Miss Broughton **Mr M. Mazzonelli**
22 **SEA DANZIG**, ch g Roi Danzig (USA)—Tosara **Mr P. Cook**
23 **SHAVINSKY**, b c Shavian—Alteza Real **Mrs J. M. Khan**
24 **SQUARE MILE MISS (IRE)**, b f Last Tycoon—Call Me Miss **Mr P. Rawson**
25 **SWEET AMORET**, b f Forzando—Primrose Way **Mr Robert Baker**
26 **SWEET SEVENTEEN**, gr f Touch of Grey—Westminster Waltz **Mr D. Weedon**

TWO-YEAR-OLDS

27 Ch c 8/5 Ballad Rock—Havana Moon
28 B c 21/4 Statoblest—Jeanne Avril
29 Ch c 14/3 Don't Forget Me—Joanne's Joy

Other Owners: Mrs Maureen Bennett, Mrs P. Del Rio, Mr R. Del Rio, Mr P. Gwilliam, Mr R. N. Khan, Mr Laci Nester-Smith, Mr M. C. North, Mrs E. M. Oxley, Mr J. T. Rourke, Del Roy, Mr Elliott Simmonds, Mrs J. Weston, Mr P. D. Woodward.

Jockeys (Flat): Paul Eddery (8-2), J Quinn (7-7).

Apprentice: D Biggs (8-3).

308   MR G. A. HUBBARD, Woodbridge

Postal: **Worlingworth Hall, Worlingworth, Woodbridge, Suffolk, IP13 7NS.**

Phone: **(01728) 628243 (01728) 628554 ASST TRAINER (01473) 230168**

1 **BEDFIELD (IRE)**, 8, b g Buckskin (FR)—McNutt **Mr G. A. Hubbard**
2 **CUDDY DALE**, 13, b g Deep Run—Verbana **Mr G. A. Hubbard**
3 **ERNEST WILLIAM (IRE)**, 4, b br g Phardante (FR)—Minerstown (IRE) **Mr G. A. Hubbard**
4 **EXECUTIVE KING (IRE)**, 5, br g Executive Perk—Leith Hill **Mr G. A. Hubbard**
5 **FINKLE STREET (IRE)**, 8, b br g Strong Gale—Super Cailin **Mr G. A. Hubbard**

MR G. A. HUBBARD—continued

6 **GIPSY GEOF (IRE)**, 5, b g Miner's Lamp—Princess Menelek **Mr G. A. Hubbard**
7 **HI HEDLEY (IRE)**, 6, b g Henbit (USA)—Verbana **Mr G. A. Hubbard**
8 **JAVELIN COOL (IRE)**, 5, gr g Roselier (FR)—Wonderful Lilly **Mr G. A. Hubbard**
9 **LORD KHALICE (IRE)**, 5, b br g King's Ride—Khalice **Mr G. A. Hubbard**
10 **MERILENA (IRE)**, 6, b m Roselier (FR)—Scotsman Ice **Mr G. A. Hubbard**
11 **MONKS SOHAM (IRE)**, 8, b g The Parson—Kadaga **Mr G. A. Hubbard**
12 **PETTAUGH (IRE)**, 8, b g The Parson—Bright Record **Mr G. A. Hubbard**
13 **RUN FOR DANTE (IRE)**, 6, b g Phardante (FR)—Shallow Run **Mr G. A. Hubbard**
14 **SABRECOOL (IRE)**, 5, b g Lord Americo—Minerstown (IRE) **Mr G. A. Hubbard**
15 **SCOLE**, 11, b g Deep Run—Verbana **Mr G. A. Hubbard**
16 **SIBTON ABBEY**, 11, b g Strong Gale—Bally Decent **Mr G. A. Hubbard**
17 **SIMWELL (IRE)**, 8, ch g Over The River (FR)—Fairyslave **Mr G. A. Hubbard**
18 **SOUTHOLT (IRE)**, 8, b g Deep Run—Girseach **Mr G. A. Hubbard**
19 **STRONG JOHN (IRE)**, 8, b g Strong Gale—Deep Khaletta **Mr G. A. Hubbard**
20 **STRONG PROMISE (IRE)**, 5, b br g Strong Gale—Let's Compromise **Mr G. A. Hubbard**
21 **SUPER RAPIER (IRE)**, 4, b br g Strong Gale—Misty Venture **Mr G. A. Hubbard**
22 **THERMECON (IRE)**, 5, ch g Phardante (FR)—Brosna Girl **Mr G. A. Hubbard**
23 **VANDALUS (IRE)**, 8, b g Mandalus—Varamond **Mr G. A. Hubbard**
24 **WOODBRIDGE (IRE)**, 7, b g Royal Fountain—Monday's Pet **Mr G. A. Hubbard**

THREE-YEAR-OLDS

25 **AMBROSIA (IRE)**, ch f Strong Gale—Scotsman Ice **Mr G. A. Hubbard**
26 **CAPSOFF (IRE)**, b f Mazaad—Minerstown (IRE) **Mr G. A. Hubbard**

Jockey (NH): Pat Verling (9-7).

Conditional: Grant Bazin (10-2).

309   MR J. S. HUBBUCK, Hexham

Postal: **High House Farm, Highford Lane, Hexham, Northd, NE46 2LZ.**

1 **ANOTHER NICK**, 10, ch g Nicholas Bill—Another Move **Mr J. S. Hubbuck**
2 **BLAZING DAWN**, 9, b g Deep Run—Men's Fun **Mr J. S. Hubbuck**

310   MR D. T. HUGHES, Kildare

Postal: **Osborne Lodge, Kildare, Co. Kildare, Ireland.**

Phone: **(045) 521490 FAX (045) 521643 MOBILE (088) 534098**

1 **AEGEAN FANFARE**, 7, b g Trojan Fen—Sweet Melody **John P. Iburg**
2 **AGITATO (IRE)**, 7, ch g Orchestra—Gail Borden **Dr Joseph Masterson**
3 **AMAKANE LADY (IRE)**, 7, b m King Persian—Kitty Ellis **Thierry Delcros**
4 **BALLYNAGUSSAUN (IRE)**, 6, b m Air Display (USA)—Fethard Lady **L. Byrne**
5 **BOCKMANN'S CHOICE (IRE)**, 8, ch m Orchestra—Madrilon (FR) **Damien Hanlon**
6 **BUCK THE WEST (IRE)**, 6, b g Buckskin (FR)—Try Another **Mrs D. T. Hughes**
7 **CONQUEST OF LIGHT (IRE)**, 7, b g Pollerton—Blueola **Matthew McBride**
8 **CUBAN QUESTION**, 9, ch g Fidel—Straight Shot **Lawrence Byrne**
9 **DANCING CLODAGH (IRE)**, 4, b f Dancing Dissident (USA)—An Tig Gaelige **Sportsman's Inn Syndicate**
10 **DEIREADH AN SCEAL (IRE)**, 6, b g Burslem—Raubritter **Mrs Annette Noule**
11 **EXECUTIVE LAWYER (IRE)**, 5, b g Executive Perk—Aluda Queen **Mrs Mary Ward**
12 **FINAL RUN**, 8, b m Deep Run—Many Larks **Mark O'Connor**
13 **FIRE KING**, 10, b g Furry Glen—Foolish Lady **Mrs K. M. Berry**
14 **FIX THE SPEC (IRE)**, 6, ch g Burslem—Foolish Lady **T. J. Culhane**
15 **GUEST PERFORMANCE (IRE)**, 4, b g Be My Guest (USA)—Bold And Bright (FR) **Sean Mulryan**
16 **HEMISPHERE (IRE)**, 7, b g Dominion—Welsh Fantasy **Kevin McNulty**

MR D. T. HUGHES—continued

17 **INDIAN MAGIC (IRE)**, 7, b m Montelimar (USA)—Indian Beauty **Mrs D. T. Hughes**
18 **JOHNNY'S DREAM (IRE)**, 6, b g Trimmingham—Maypole Hie **Mrs T. M. Moriarty**
19 **LEOPOLD BLOOM**, 10, b g Le Moss—Barhopper **John P. Iburg**
20 **MIDNIGHT HOUR (IRE)**, 7, gr g Roselier (FR)—Shirowen **Mrs D. T. Hughes**
21 **MILE MILL (IRE)**, 5, b g Montekin—Owvane **Rory Mackey**
22 **MISTY MOMENTS (IRE)**, 5, b g Supreme Leader—Con Lady **Mrs T. M. Moriarty**
23 **PAPUITE (IRE)**, 5, b m Executive Perk—Amaprincess **G. Devlin**
24 **RETURN AGAIN (IRE)**, 6, b m Top Ville—Perfect Guest **James Barton**
25 **ROUNDWOOD (IRE)**, 7, b g Orchestra—Another Bless **M. P. Whelan**
26 **RUM FUN (IRE)**, 5, br g Burslem—Ivy Holme **Maureen Graham**
27 **STATE PRINCESS (IRE)**, 6, b m Flash of Steel—An Tig Gaelige **Sportsman's Inn Syndicate**
28 **TOO MANY CHIEFS (IRE)**, 7, b g Treasure Hunter—Young Express **Mrs James Nicholson**
29 **TRY ONCE MORE (IRE)**, 5, b g Cataldi—Good Court **Mrs D. T. Hughes**
30 **WOLF ELLA (IRE)**, 7, b g Wolverlife—Kessella **Miss Rhona McCarthy**

THREE-YEAR-OLDS

31 Ch c Gold Seam (USA)—More Berries (FR) **Mrs D. T. Hughes**
32 **SWEET SEPTEMBER (IRE)**, b f Persian Heights—Mrs Foodbroker **M. J. Connolly**

Apprentice: P Dobbs (7-0).

Conditional: Garrett Cotter (9-0).

Amateurs: Mr A Dempsey (9-7), Mr G Kearns (9-7).

311   LORD HUNTINGDON, West Ilsley

Postal: **West Ilsley Stables, Newbury, Berkshire, RG20 7AE.**
Phone: **OFFICE (01635) 281747 HOME (01635) 281725 FAX (01635) 281720**

1 **AL WIDYAN (IRE)**, 4, b c Slip Anchor—Rafha **Mr P. A. Leonard**
2 **ARABRIDE**, 4, ch f Unfuwain (USA)—Model Bride (USA) **Mr Yoshio Asakawa**
3 **COUNTRY LOVER**, 5, ch g Thatching—Fair Country **Sir Gordon Brunton**
4 **DISCORD**, 10, b g Niniski (USA)—Apple Peel **Mr Yoshio Asakawa**
5 **EASY JET (POL)**, 4, b c Robellino (USA)—Etourdie (USA) **Crown Partnership**
6 **KING PARROT (IRE)**, 8, br g King of Spain—Red Lory **Lord Huntingdon**
7 **PENNY DROPS**, 7, b m Sharpo—Darine **Mr Stanley J. Sharp**
8 **PRESENT SITUATION**, 5, ch g Cadeaux Genereux—Storm Warning **Mr Chris van Hoorn**
9 **PRINCE OF INDIA**, 4, b c Night Shift (USA)—Indian Queen **Sir Gordon Brunton**
10 **SHAMROCK FAIR (IRE)**, 4, ch f Shavian—Fair Country **Sir Gordon Brunton**
11 **SHE SAID NO**, 4, ch f Beveled (USA)—She Said Yes **Mr J. R. Bailey**
12 **SNOW PRINCESS (IRE)**, 4, b f Ela-Mana-Mou—Karelia (USA) **Lord Weinstock & The Hon Simon Weinstock**
13 **STINGING REPLY**, 4, ch f Belmez (USA)—Nettle **The Flying Fast Partnership**
14 **TOSKI**, 5, b g Petoski—First Pleasure **Mr J. Rose**

THREE-YEAR-OLDS

15 **ATTICA (USA)**, b f Nicholas (USA)—St Honore (USA) **Mr Henryk De Kwiatkowski**
16 **BANNERET (USA)**, b c Imperial Falcon (CAN)—Dashing Partner **Mrs Shirley Robins**
17 **BELLO CARATTERE**, b c Caerleon (USA)—Hyabella **Mark & Helena Weinfeld**
18 **CABALLUS (USA)**, b c Danzig Connection (USA)—Rutledge Place (USA) **Mrs Shirley Robins**
19 **CRANDON BOULEVARD**, b c Niniski (USA)—Last Clear Chance (USA) **Mr M. L. Oberstein**
20 **DRESS CIRCLE**, ch f Old Vic—Taj Victory **Sir Gordon Brunton**
21 **DUMMER GOLF TIME**, ch c Clantime—Chablisse **Coriolan Partnership**
22 **FARAWAY LASS**, b f Distant Relative—Vague Lass **Mr J. Rose**
23 **HURTLEBERRY (IRE)**, b f Tirol—Allberry **Mrs Ian Pilkington**
24 **IN THE BAND**, b f Sharrood (USA)—Upper Caen **Mr Tim Corby**

LORD HUNTINGDON—continued

25 **LA PERRUCHE (IRE)**, b f Cyrano de Bergerac—Red Lory **Mr G. W. Mooratoff**
26 **MONGOL WARRIOR (USA)**, b c Deputy Minister (CAN)—Surely Georgie's (USA) **Mr Henryk De Kwiatkowski**
27 **OSCAR ROSE**, b g Aragon—Mossy Rose **Mr Stanley J. Sharp**
28 **PERSUASION**, b f Batshoof—Primetta **Countess of Lonsdale**
29 **PRINCE KINSKY**, ch c Master Willie—Princess Lieven **Mrs J. L. Hislop**
30 **QUINELLA**, b f Generous (IRE)—Bempton **Lord Halifax**
31 **REPLOY**, gr f Deploy—Nelly Do Da **Mr S. Wingfield Digby**
32 **ROSE SHOW**, b f Belmez (USA)—Rose Parade **Sir Gordon Brunton**
33 **ROSE TINT (IRE)**, b f Salse (USA)—Sally Rose **Lord Weinstock & The Hon Simon Weinstock**
34 **SERENUS (USA)**, b c Sunshine Forever (USA)—Curl And Set (USA) **Mrs Shirley Robins**
35 **SPENCER STALLONE**, b c Rambo Dancer (CAN)—Armour of Light **Lord Crawshaw**
36 **SWEET WILHELMINA**, b f Indian Ridge—Henpot (IRE) **Mr Chris van Hoorn**
37 **TORMOUNT (USA)**, b c Local Talent (USA)—Virginia Hills (USA) **Coriolan Partnership**
38 **TWELVE CLUB**, ch g Sharrood (USA)—Persian Victory (IRE) **Sir Gordon Brunton**
39 **WESTERN SONATA (IRE)**, b f Alzao (USA)—Musique Classique (USA) **Mr Ken Nishikawa**

TWO-YEAR-OLDS

40 B c 9/4 Sharpo—Anodyne (Dominion) **Mr George Ward**
41 B c 11/3 Caerleon (USA)—Belize Tropical (IRE) (Baillamont (USA)) **Mr G. Cosmelli**
42 **BYZANTIUM**, b c 13/5 Shirley Heights—Dulceata (IRE) (Rousillon (USA)) **Mr R. van Gelder**
43 **FAIR FINNISH (IRE)**, b c 17/4 Commanche Run—
                        Karelia (Sir Ivor) **Lord Weinstock & The Hon Simon Weinstock**
44 **FARLEY MOUNT**, b c 30/3 Pharly (FR)—Mossy Rose (King of Spain) **Mr Stanley J. Sharp**
45 Ch f 20/3 Risk Me (FR)—Farras (Song) **Lord Huntingdon**
46 **GAILY GRECIAN (IRE)**, b f 20/3 Ela-Mana-Mou—
                        Gay Milly (FR) (Mill Reef (USA)) **Lord Weinstock & The Hon Simon Weinstock**
47 Ch f 20/4 Sunshine Forever—Ice House (Northfields (USA)) **Coriolan Partnership**
48 Gr c 28/3 Petong—Kimberley Park (Try My Best (USA)) **Mr Tim Corby**
49 **PERSEVERE**, b f 15/3 Pursuit Of Love—Seastream (USA) (Alleged (USA)) **Mrs Amschel Rothschild**
50 **REAR WINDOW**, b c 14/4 Night Shift (USA)—Last Clear Chance (USA) (Alleged (USA)) **Mr M. L. Oberstein**
51 **SPARTAN GIRL (IRE)**, ch f 21/3 Ela-Mana-Mou—
                        Well Head (IRE) (Sadler's Wells (USA)) **Lord Weinstock & The Hon Simon Weinstock**
52 **SWING AND BRAVE (IRE)**, b f 15/4 Arctic Tern (USA)—Sweet Snow (USA) (Lyphard (USA)) **Pietro Somaini**
53 **TINKERBELL**, ch f 31/1 Sharpo—Chasing Moonbeams (Final Straw) **Lord Carnarvon**
54 **VERITY**, ch f 1/4 Pharly (FR)—Persian Victory (IRE) (Persian Bold) **Sir Gordon Brunton**
55 **VISCOUMTESS BRAVE (IRE)**, br f 21/4 Law Society (USA)—
                        Vadrouille (USA) (Foolish Pleasure (USA)) **Pietro Somaini**
56 **YONKELMAN (USA)**, ch c 21/3 Woodman (USA)—Kafiyah (USA) (Shadeed (USA)) **Mr George A. Moore**

Other Owners: The Queen, Mr K. H. Fischer, Mr Geoffrey C. Greenwood, Mrs Peter Hastings, Mr S. Hastings-Bass, Mr I. A. Hislop, Maverick Productions Ltd, Mr T. Nakao, Mr David Neuberger, Lady Newman, Mr Ray Pollard, Mr W. V. Robins, Mr John E. Rose, Mrs Amanda Simmons, Mr R. A. Simmons, Mr H. R. Slack, Mr D. Tylden-Wright.

Apprentices: Aimee Cook (7-13), Jason Wilkinson (7-10).

312   DON E. INCISA, Middleham

Postal: **Thorngill, Coverham, Middleham, Leyburn, DL8 4TJ.**
Phone: **WENSLEYDALE (01969) 640653 FAX (01969) 640694**

1 **BARDIA**, 6, b m Jalmood (USA)—Bauhinia **Don Enrico Incisa**
2 **BATTLE COLOURS (IRE)**, 7, b g Petorius—Streamertail **Mrs Christine Cawley**
3 **DON'T CRY**, 8, b m Dominion—Black Veil **Don Enrico Incisa**
4 **ISLAND CASCADE**, 4, b f Hadeer—Island Mill **Don Enrico Incisa**
5 **LE TEMERAIRE**, 10, b g Top Ville—La Mirande (FR) **Don Enrico Incisa**
6 **NOBBY BARNES**, 7, b g Nordance (USA)—Loving Doll **Don Enrico Incisa**
7 **PLEASURE TRICK (USA)**, 5, br g Clever Trick (USA)—Pleasure Garden (USA) **Don Enrico Incisa**
8 **RANKAIDADE**, 5, b m Governor General—Keep Cool (FR) **Don Enrico Incisa**
9 **TUTU SIXTYSIX**, 5, br m Petong—Odilese **Don Enrico Incisa**

DON E. INCISA—continued
THREE-YEAR-OLDS

10 **OARE BUDGIE**, ch f Midyan (USA)—Port Vasco **Don Enrico Incisa**
11 **SASSETTA (IRE)**, ch f Soviet Lad (USA)—Sun Gift **Mrs C Cawley**

TWO-YEAR-OLDS

12 **MAREMMA**, b f 17/2 Robellino (USA)—Maiden Way (Shareef Dancer (USA)) **Don Enrico Incisa**

Other Owners: Razza Dormello Olgiata.

Jockey (Flat): Kim Tinkler (7-7).

313   MR R. INGRAM, Epsom

Postal: **Wendover Stables, Burgh Heath Road, Epsom, Surrey, KT17 4LX.**
Phone: **STABLES (01372) 748505 HOME (01372) 749157 MOBILE (0374) 239372**

1 **BEAVER BROOK**, 6, gr g Bairn (USA)—Lucky Song **Mr C. G. Adams**
2 **COALISLAND**, 6, br g Kind of Hush—Hit The Line **Mr P. McKernan**
3 **FORGOTTEN DANCER (IRE)**, 5, ch g Don't Forget Me—Dancing Diana **Mr Roger Ingram**
4 **JO N JACK (IRE)**, 8, ch g Gorytus (USA)—Dancing Song **Mr C. G. Adams**
5 **KINNEGAD KID**, 7, b m Formidable (USA)—Recamier **Mr J. B. Wilcox**
6 **LA BOSSETTE (IRE)**, 4, b f Cyrano de Bergerac—Bosquet **Mrs A. V. Cappuccini**
7 **LABUDD (USA)**, 6, ch h Deputy Minister (CAN)—Delightful Vie (USA) **Mr Peter Isaac & Partners**
8 **PERSIAN CONQUEST (IRE)**, 4, b g Don't Forget Me—Alaroos (IRE) **Mrs A. V. Cappuccini**
9 **TOMAL**, 4, b g King Among Kings—Jacinda **Toilley Partnership**
10 **TONDRES (USA)**, 5, br g Chief's Crown—Icing **Lawrence Plc**
11 **TOTAL RACH (IRE)**, 4, b f Nordico (USA)—Miss Kelly **Mrs A. V. Cappuccini**
12 **TRAPPER NORMAN**, 4, b g Mazilier (USA)—Free Skip **Mr H. G. Norman**
13 **TUIGAMALA**, 5, b g Welsh Captain—Nelliellamay **Mr Roger Ingram**
14 **WARM HEARTED (USA)**, 4, ch g Known Fact (USA)—Lovin' Lass (USA) **Mrs A. V. Cappuccini**

THREE-YEAR-OLDS

15 **BLUE FLYER (IRE)**, b g Bluebird (USA)—Born To Fly (IRE) **Mrs A. V. Cappuccini**
16 **LORD ELLANGOWAN (IRE)**, ch c Astronef—Gossip **Ellangowan Racing Partners**
17 **RIFIFI**, ch c Aragon—Bundled Up (USA) **Mr Roger Ingram**

Other Owners: Mr C. G. Adams, Mr Luke Devine, Mr Roger Ingram, C. Loutte, Ms Linda Pearce, Mr Andrew Ross.

Jockey (Flat): A McGlone (8-2, w.a.).

Jockey (NH): A Maguire (10-0).

Amateur: Mr P Killick (10-7).

314   MR K. T. IVORY, Radlett

Postal: **Harper Lodge Farm, Harper Lane, Radlett, Herts, WD7 7HU.**
Phone: **(01923) 855337**

1 **BOLD FRONTIER**, 4, gr g Chief Singer—Mumtaz Flyer (USA) **Mr K. T. Ivory**
2 **CHANCEY FELLA**, 5, ch g Sylvan Express—Musical Piece **Mrs Valerie Hubbard**
3 **DELIGHT OF DAWN**, 4, b f Never So Bold—Vogos Angel **Mr K. T. Ivory**
4 **MYFONTAINE**, 9, b h Persepolis (FR)—Mortefontaine (FR) **Mr K. T. Ivory**

MR K. T. IVORY—continued

5 **OUR SHADEE (USA)**, 6, b g Shadeed (USA)—Nuppence **Mr K. T. Ivory**
6 **SWING LUCKY**, 11, b g Swing Easy (USA)—Bounding **Mr Roy Skeggs**

THREE-YEAR-OLDS

7 **IVORY'S GRAB HIRE**, b g Shavian—Knees Up (USA) **Mr Dean Ivory**
8 **LAHIK (IRE)**, b g Lycius (USA)—Sangala (FR) **Mr Dean Ivory**
9 **MINDRACE**, b g Tina's Pet—High Velocity
10 **NEVER THINK TWICE**, b g Never So Bold—Hope And Glory (USA) **Mr K. T. Ivory**

TWO-YEAR-OLDS

11 **ANOKATO**, b g Tina's Pet—High Velocity (Frimley Park) **Mr K. T. Ivory**
12 **HELLO DOLLY (IRE)**, b f Mujadil (USA)—Great Leighs (Vaigly Great) **Mr K. T. Ivory**
13 **IVORY DAWN**, b f Batshoof—Cradle of Love (USA) (Roberto) **Mr Dean Ivory**
14 **KICK ON**, b g Rock City—Burglar Tip (Burglar) **Mr Dean Ivory**

Jockey (Flat): R Cochrane (w.a.).

Jockey (NH): Mark Richards (10-0).

Apprentice: C Scally (7-13).

315   MR C. F. C. JACKSON, Malvern

Postal: **Whitehouse Farm, Tanhouse Lane, Cradley, Malvern, WR13 5JX.**

Phone: **(01886) 880463**

1 **ASTROMIS (IRE)**, 5, b m Torus—Fast Money **Mr Tom Hayes**
2 **CHESTERTON SONG**, 10, ch m True Song—Chestertons Choice **Mr C. F. C. Jackson**
3 **FLYING FASCINATION**, 8, ch m Flying Tyke—Charming Thought (USA) **Mrs Jackie S. Wassall**
4 **FRED FUGGLES**, 4, ch g Green Adventure (USA)—Wald Konigin **B. H. R. W. Racing Partnership**
5 **GAELGOIR**, 12, gr g Godswalk (USA)—Sagosha **Mr C. F. C. Jackson**
6 **IMATOFF**, 6, ch g Respect—Belsprit Lady **Miss P. Elizabeth Porter**
7 **MOONLIGHTER**, 6, b m Lighter—Skidmore **Gold Top Racing**
8 **NERO'S GEM**, 5, b m Little Wolf—Miss Nero **Mr R. Yates**
9 **ROO'S LEAP (IRE)**, 8, b m Leap High (USA)—Island More **Mr Tom Hayes**
10 **SIMPLY A SEQUEL (IRE)**, 5, ch h Simply Great (FR)—Salique **Mr D. Craddock**
11 **TANCRED WALK**, 17, b g Farm Walk—Darling Do **Mr D. J. Pardy**
12 **VISCOUNT TULLY**, 11, b g Blakeney—Cymbal **Mr D. Craddock**
13 **ZALINA**, 10, b m Tyrnavos—Cymbal **Mr C. F. C. Jackson**

Other Owners: Mr P. Holland, Mr J. Ranford.

Jockeys (Flat): A McGlone (w.a.), W Newnes (w.a.).

Jockey (NH): W Humphreys.

Lady Rider: Miss S Jackson.

316   MR F. S. JACKSON, Gonalston

Postal: **Holme Farm, Gonalston, Nottinghamshire, NG14 7JA.**

Phone: **(0115) 9663970/(0115) 9663832**

1 **CARLY-J**, 5, b m Cruise Missile—Porto Louise **Mr F. S. Jackson**
2 **GONALSTON PERCY**, 8, gr g Dawn Johnny (USA)—Porto Louise **Mr F. S. Jackson**
3 4, Ch g Remezzo—Porto Louise **Mr F. S. Jackson**
4 **ROYAL MILE**, 11, b g Tyrnavos—Royal Rib **Mr F. S. Jackson**

THREE-YEAR-OLDS

5 Ch g Jendali (USA)—Porto Louise **Mr F. S. Jackson**
6 Ch g Jendali (USA)—Scotgavotte (FR) **Mr F. S. Jackson**

TWO-YEAR-OLDS

7 Ch f 6/6   Jendali (USA)—Scotgavotte (FR) (Dunbeath (USA))

317   MR A. P. JAMES, Tenbury Wells

Postal: **Elliotte House Farm, Vine Lane, Kyre, Tenbury Wells, WR15 8RL.**

Phone: **KYRE (01885) 410240 MOBILE (0836) 533049 FAX (01885) 410240**

1 **CELESTIAL WATERS**, 4, b f Monsanto (FR)—Hopeful Waters **Group 1 Racing (1994) Ltd**
2 4, B g Derring Rose—Daffodil **Mr T. N. Siviter**
3 **EXCLUSIVE ASSEMBLY**, 4, ch g Welndaas (USA)—Pretty Pollyanna **The Exclusive Connection Partnership**
4 **FORBURIES (IRE)**, 7, b m Boreen Beag—Madam George **C. T. & R. G. Bouston**
5 **HONG KONG DESIGNER**, 4, br g Dunbeath (USA)—Pokey's Pet **Group 1 Racing (1994) Ltd**
6 **INNOCENT PRINCESS (NZ)**, 9, ch m Full On Aces (AUS)—Kia Court (NZ) **Mrs Amanda James**
7 **IT'S SO EASY**, 5, b m Shaadi (USA)—Carmelina **Group 1 Racing (1994) Ltd**
8 **PACIFIC POWER**, 6, b br g Damister (USA)—Nell of The North (USA) **Group 1 Racing (1994) Ltd**
9 **PETTY BRIDGE**, 12, b g Weavers' Hall—Royal Cup **C. T. & R. G. Bouston**
10 **RUBY ESTATE (IRE)**, 5, b m High Estate—Tuesday Morning **Mr Carleton Wright**
11 **SEYMOUR DREAMS**, 7, b m Seymour Hicks (FR)—Sweetheart **Mr P. Morris**
12 **WALLY'S DREAM**, 7, b g Rymer—Cupids Bower **Mr Carleton Wright**

THREE-YEAR-OLDS

13 **COMMANCHE CUP (IRE)**, b c Commanche Run—Royal Cup **C. T. & R. G. Bouston**
14 **PEGGY ESS**, b f Seymour Hicks (FR)—Daffodil **Mr T. N. Siviter**

TWO-YEAR-OLDS

15 B c 20/5 Derrylin—Daffodil (Welsh Pageant) **Mr T. N. Siviter**
16 B f 10/4 Scallywag—Lullaby Baby (Kind of Hush) **Mr T. N. Siviter**

Other Owners: Cllr Eddie Clein, Mr A. Evans, Mr D. Filer, Mr Tom Green, Mr W. Macquarie, Mr N. McGeorge, Mr G. Page-Jones, Mr Andrew Parker, Mr T. Perkins, Dr Anne E. Ramkaran, Mr Martin Tunley, Dr M. Voikhansky, Mr Ken Weale, Mrs J. C. Wright.

318   MR C. J. JAMES, Newbury

Postal: **Mask Cottage, East Garston, Newbury, Berks, RG17 7EU.**

Phone: **GREAT SHEFFORD (01488) 648280**

1 **ARCATURA**, 4, b g Beveled (USA)—Bar Gold **Mr A. G. Waldie**
2 **BORRETO**, 12, b br g Treboro (USA)—Fiji Express **Mr C. James**
3 **CAWARRA BOY**, 8, b g Martinmas—Cawarra Belle **Mrs Margaret Kenyon Holden**
4 **DANNY RHY**, 7, ch m Rymer—Danny d'Albi **Mr C. James**
5 **DUSK IN DAYTONA**, 4, b f Beveled (USA)—Mount of Light **Mr C. James**
6 **ESPY**, 13, b g Pitpan—Minorette **Mr C. James**

MR C. J. JAMES—continued

7 **GREY CHARMER (IRE)**, 7, gr h Alzao (USA)—Sashi Woo **Mrs Gail Gaisford**
8 **JACK HILL**, 7, br g Lidhame—Alice Hill **Mrs J. N. Humphreys**
9 **MIRAMARE**, 6, br g Sulaafah (USA)—Skilla **Major R. P. Thorman**
10 **MISTER CHRISTIAN (NZ)**, 15, b g Captain Jason (NZ)—Grisette (NZ) **Mr C. James**
11 **PARTY BEDLAM**, 7, b br m Prince of Peace—Ceile **Mrs S. M. Walters**
12 **RANDOM**, 5, ch m Beveled (USA)—Martian Melody **Mr A. G. Waldie**
13 **TAMANDU**, 6, b m Petoski—Gohar (USA) **Mr R. A. Shaw**
14 **TIME FOR A FLUTTER**, 7, b m Beldale Flutter (USA)—Time Warp **Miss N. Carroll**
15 4, Ch f Nearly A Hand—Tinsel Rose **Major R. P. Thorman**
16 **WITH INTENT**, 4, b g Governor General—Don't Loiter **Mrs Pat Mountain**
17 **YOUR OPINION**, 10, gr g Cut Above—Dance Mistress **Mr C. James**

THREE-YEAR-OLDS

18 **CRAVEN COTTAGE**, b g Inca Chief (USA)—Seymour Ann **Mrs Beryl Williams**
19 **DEPRECIATE**, ch c Beveled (USA)—Shiny Penny **Mr V. R. Bedley**
20 **MARAEINCA**, b f Inca Chief (USA)—Countess Mariga **Mrs J. E. M. Powell**

TWO-YEAR-OLDS

21 **BEVILED CRYSTAL**, ro f 19/3 Beveled (USA)—Countess Mariga (Amboise) **Mrs J. E. M. Powell**
22 **PAMPASA (FR)**, b f 30/3 Pampabird—Dounasa (Kaldoun (FR)) **Mr N. Cowan**
23 B f 2/4 Inca Chief (USA)—Plectrum (Adonijah) **Mrs Carol J. Welch**
24 B f 19/4 Interrex (CAN)—Shiny Penny (Glint of Gold) **Mr V. R. Bedley**

Other Owners: Miss A. Braithwaite, Mrs C. J. James, Dr John Keen, Miss Janet King, Mr Tim Smee, Mr Cyril Townsend, Mrs Frances Wyman.

Amateurs: Mr E James (10-2), Mr Mark Walters (10-0).

Lady Rider: Miss C A Corbett (8-7).

319   MR A. P. JARVIS, Aston Upthorpe

Postal: **The Thatch, Frimley Stables, Aston Upthorpe, Didcot, OX11 9EG.**
Phone: **(01235) 851341 FAX (01235) 851361**

1 **ANOTHER JADE**, 6, ch m Beveled (USA)—Zamindara **Mrs Ann Jarvis**
2 **BLACK STATEMENT (IRE)**, 6, br g Strong Statement (USA)—Gambell And Dream **Mr Bill Naylor**
3 **BOTHSIDESNOW (IRE)**, 6, b g Exhibitioner—Caroline's Mark **Mrs Ann Jarvis**
4 **CALVARO (IRE)**, 5, b g Corvaro (USA)—Jukebox Katie **Mr Bill Naylor**
5 **CHAIRMANS CHOICE**, 6, ch g Executive Man—Revida Girl **Mrs D. B. Brazier**
6 **DOUCE MAISON (IRE)**, 5, b m Fools Holme (USA)—Cardomine **Mrs Ann Jarvis**
7 **DULZURA**, 8, b m Daring March—Comedy Lady **Mrs D. B. Brazier**
8 **EFFICACY**, 5, b m Efisio—Lady Killane **Mrs Ann Jarvis**
9 **ELEGANT KING (IRE)**, 7, b g Tender King—Malvern Beauty **Mr A. L. R. Morton**
10 **FAIRELAINE**, 4, b f Zalazl (USA)—Blue And White **Mr Martyn Booth**
11 **FLYING MISSILE (FR)**, 10, b g Gay Mecene (USA)—Tintagel **Mrs Ann Jarvis**
12 **FUTURE KING**, 9, b g Dynastic—Forthcoming **Mr Martyn Booth**
13 **LE MEILLE (IRE)**, 7, ch g Le Bavard (FR)—Glens Princess **Mr N. J. Mitchell**
14 **LENNOX LEWIS**, 4, b c Superpower—Song's Best **Mrs Ann Jarvis**
15 **MAGIC CAVE**, 8, b m Kemal (FR)—Blue Grotto **Mrs D. B. Brazier**
16 **MONICASMAN (IRE)**, 6, br g Callernish—Sengirrefcha **Mr Ambrose Turnbull**
17 **NOBLE BALLERINA (USA)**, 4, b f Green Dancer (USA)—Noble Devorcee (USA) **Mr Ambrose Turnbull**
18 **PROUD IMAGE**, 4, b g Zalazl (USA)—Fleur de Foret (USA) **Mr L. Fust**
19 **RISING MAN**, 5, b g Primitive Rising (USA)—Dream Again **Mr Bill Naylor**
20 **SACRED SPIRIT**, 4, b g Totem (USA)—Dream Again **Mrs Ann Jarvis**
21 **SAME DIFFERENCE (IRE)**, 8, b g Seymour Hicks (FR)—Santa Fe (GER) **Mr Ambrose Turnbull**

MR A. P. JARVIS—continued

22 **SECRET MISS**, 4, ch f Beveled (USA)—Zamindara **Mr N. Coverdale**
23 **SUE'S RETURN**, 4, b f Beveled (USA)—Return To Tara **Mr A. L. R. Morton**
24 **WHO'S THE BEST (IRE)**, 6, b g Wassl—Rip Roaring **Mrs Ann Jarvis**
25 **YOUNG RYAN**, 5, ch g High Kicker (USA)—Rankstreet **Mr Terence P. Lyons II**
26 4, Ch c Orchestra—Zaydeen **Mr A. L. R. Morton**

THREE-YEAR-OLDS

27 **ASTUTI (IRE)**, b f Waajib—Aunty Eileen **Mrs D. B. Brazier**
28 **BEENY**, b c Lugana Beach—Child Star **Mr J. D. Rogers**
29 Ch g Colmore Row—Broadway Stomp (USA)
30 **DIVINE MISS-P**, ch f Safawan—Faw **Mr L. Fust**
31 **EUROBOX BOY**, ch g Savahra Sound—Princess Poquito **Mr N. Coverdale**
32 **GALWAY BLADE**, b c Faustus (USA)—Slipperose **Mr T. Blade**
33 Ch f Bold Arrangement—Key To Enchantment
34 **KING OF PERU**, b c Inca Chief (USA)—Julie's Star (IRE) **Mr L. Fust**
35 **MAN OF WIT (IRE)**, b c Fayruz—Laughing Matter **Mr L. Fust**
36 **MATTIMEO (IRE)**, b g Prince Rupert (FR)—Herila (FR) **Mrs Monica Keogh**
37 **MORNING SURPRISE**, b br f Tragic Role (USA)—Fleur de Foret (USA) **Mrs D. B. Brazier**
38 **NORWEGIAN BLUE (IRE)**, b c Mac's Imp (USA)—Opening Day **Mr Ambrose Turnbull**
39 **OUR WORLEY (IRE)**, b f Mac's Imp (USA)—Castleforbes **Mr J. D. Rogers**
40 B c Nordico (USA)—Postscript **Mr L. Fust**
41 **SO SELECT**, ch f Northern State (USA)—Zamindara **Mr N. J. Mitchell**
42 **SPHINX LEVELV (IRE)**, ch c Digamist (USA)—Fantoccini **Mr A. L. R. Morton**
43 **STATE APPROVAL**, b c Pharly (FR)—Tabeeba **Mrs Ann Jarvis**
44 **URGENT SWIFT**, ch c Beveled (USA)—Good Natured **Mr L. Fust**
45 **YEZZA (IRE)**, b f Distinctly North (USA)—Small Paradise **Mrs Monica Keogh**

TWO-YEAR-OLDS

46 B f 22/2 Petorius—Alberjas (IRE) (Sure Blade (USA)) **Mrs Ann Jarvis**
47 B f 1/6 Dromod Hill—Dear France (USA) (Affirmed (USA))
48 B c 11/4 Imp Society (USA)—Karamana (Habitat) **Mrs Ann Jarvis**
49 B br f 26/2 Petorius—Laughing Matter (Lochnager) **Mr N. J. Mitchell**
50 Ch f 17/4 Beveled (USA)—Return To Tara (Homing)
51 **ROMAN IMP (IRE)**, ch c 9/3 Imp Society (USA)—Luvi Ullmann (Thatching) **Mr Ambrose Turnbull**
52 **SELECT CHOICE (IRE)**, b c 28/5 Waajib—Stella Ann (Ahonoora) **Mr N. J. Mitchell**
53 **SELECT STAR (IRE)**, b br c 15/1 Arcane (USA)—Chevrefeuille (Ile de Bourbon) **Mr N. J. Mitchell**
54 **SKIPPY WAS A KIWI (IRE)**, b f 29/4 River Falls—Hit For Six (Tap On Wood) **Mrs Ann Jarvis**
55 B c 17/5 Bering—Whitecairn (Sure Blade (USA)) **Mr L. Fust**

Other Owners: Mrs C. Barclay, Ms Rosie Bliss, Mr A. Ewen, Mr M. I. Glass, Mrs Joyce May, Mr S. M. McAnulty, Mr D. W. W. Norris.

Conditional: Pat Morris (9-7).

Lady Rider: Mrs E Burke.

320   MR M. A. JARVIS, Newmarket

Postal: **Kremlin House Stables, Fordham Road, Newmarket, Suffolk, CB8 7AQ.**
Phone: **(01638) OFFICE 661702 HOME 662519 FAX 667018**

1 **NORTHERN UNION (CAN)**, 5, b h Alwasmi (USA)—Loving Cup (USA) **Mr Raymond Anderson Green**

THREE-YEAR-OLDS

2 **ABEYR**, ch f Unfuwain (USA)—Haboobti **Sheikh Ahmed Al Maktoum**
3 **BLUE IRIS**, b f Petong—Bo' Babbity **Mr M. A. Jarvis**
4 **DANCE STAR**, b f Damister (USA)—Glen Dancer **Mr N. S. Yong**

MR M. A. JARVIS—continued

5 **LAKELINE LEGEND (IRE)**, ch c Caerleon (USA)—Bottom Line **Mr Jerry Sung**
6 **LARRY LAMBRUSCO**, b g Executive Man—Freudenau **Mr Christopher P. Ranson**
7 **MAGIC ROLE**, b c Tragic Role (USA)—Athens By Night (USA) **Mr T. G. Holdcroft**
8 **MISTER WOODSTICK (IRE)**, b g Distinctly North (USA)—Crannog **Mr John E. Sims**
9 **NAAMAN (IRE)**, b f Marju (IRE)—Shaiybaniyda **Mr K. G. Powter**
10 **NEZOOL ALMATAR (IRE)**, b f Last Tycoon—Rowa **Sheikh Ahmed Al Maktoum**
11 **POLAR PRINCE (IRE)**, b c Distinctly North (USA)—Staff Approved **Mrs Christine Stevenson**
12 **RET FREM (IRE)**, b g Posen (USA)—New Light **Mrs Anita Green**
13 **SABRAK (IRE)**, b c Fairy King (USA)—Embryo **Sheikh Ahmed Al Maktoum**
14 **SHOOTING LIGHT (IRE)**, b g Shernazar—Church Light **Lord Harrington**
15 **SYLVELLA**, b f Lear Fan (USA)—Suprematie (FR) **Mr Jack Fisher**
16 **THE BOOZING BRIEF (USA)**, b g Turkoman (USA)—Evening Silk (USA) **Mrs Anita Green**

TWO-YEAR-OLDS

17 **ADMONISH**, b f 28/2 Warning—Ashdown (Pharly (FR)) **Mr Alan Gibson**
18 **BLUE LAMP (USA)**, ch f 24/3 Shadeed (USA)—Matter of Time (Habitat) **Mrs Beryl Sims**
19 Ch c 29/3 Caerleon (USA)—Bottom Line (Double Jump) **Mr Jerry Sung**
20 Ch f 24/4 Tina's Pet—Cold Blow (Posse (USA))
21 **COSMIC PRINCE (IRE)**, b c 22/3 Teenoso (USA)—Windmill Princess (Gorytus (USA)) **Mr Bob Young**
22 **CZAR'S FORTUNE**, b f 23/2 Nicholas (USA)—Miss Primula (Dominion) **The Fortune In Mind Partnership**
23 **DEEP FINESSE**, b c 12/2 Reprimand—Babycham Sparkle (So Blessed) **Mr John E. Sims**
24 Ch f 3/4 Arazi (USA)—Gesedeh (Ela-Mana-Mou) **Sheikh Ahmed Al Maktoum**
25 **HERMANUS**, b c 25/3 Lugana Beach—Hitravelscene (Mansingh (USA)) **Mr J. Gilman**
26 **IN THE SKY (IRE)**, ch f 15/2 Imp Society (USA)—Susan's Angel (Lord Gayle (USA)) **Mr Matthew Sharkey**
27 B c 26/2 Slip Anchor—On Credit (FR) (No Pass No Sale) **Mr Bin Hindi Mohammed**
28 B br c 27/3 A P Indy (USA)—Real Jenny (USA) (Valid Appeal) **Sheikh Ahmed Al Maktoum**
29 **REMSKI**, b c 6/4 Risk Me (FR)—Dona Krista (King of Spain) **Mr A. D. Latter**
30 **RHAPSODY IN WHITE (IRE)**, b c 20/4 Contract Law (USA)—
　　　　　　　　　　　　　　　　　　　Lux Aeterna (Sandhurst Prince) **Mrs Christine Stevenson**
31 B c 13/5 In The Wings—Rowa (Great Nephew) **Sheikh Ahmed Al Maktoum**
32 **SUPERBELLE**, b f 9/2 Damister (USA)—Nell of The North (USA) (Canadian Gil (CAN)) **Mr N. S. Yong**
33 B br f 18/3 Soviet Lad (USA)—Tallow Hill (Dunphy) **Four Seasons Racing Ltd**
34 **TELLOFF**, b f 28/2 Reprimand—La Primavera (Northfields (USA)) **Mr T. G. Warner**
35 B f 11/4 Fayruz—Timiya (High Top) **Mrs Avril Light**
36 B c 5/3 Night Shift (USA)—Veronica (Persian Bold) **Sheikh Ahmed Al Maktoum**

Other Owners: Mr D. Fisher, Mrs Gay Jarvis, Mrs Greta Sarfaty Marchant, Mr R. P. Marchant, Sqn Ldr R. A. Milsom, Mr M. Sinclair, Mr Peter J. Stevenson.

Apprentice: C Eblet (7-7).

321　　　MR W. JARVIS, Newmarket

Postal: **Phantom House Stables, Fordham Road, Newmarket, Suffolk, CB8 7AA.**
Phone: **HOME (01638) 662677 OFFICE (01638) 669873 FAX (01638) 667328**

1 **CONTRAFIRE (IRE)**, 4, b g Contract Law (USA)—Fiery Song **Miss V. R. Jarvis**
2 **LAP OF LUXURY**, 7, gr m Sharrood (USA)—Lap of Honour **Mr I. C. Hill Wood & Partners**
3 **LORD OLIVER (IRE)**, 6, b g The Noble Player (USA)—Burkina **Miss V. R. Jarvis**
4 **MA PETITE ANGLAISE**, 4, b f Reprimand—Astolat **Mr K. P. Seow**
5 **MR FROSTY**, 4, b g Absalom—Chadenshe **Mr D. G. Wright and Partners**
6 **ZYGO (USA)**, 4, b c Diesis—La Papagena **Lord Howard de Walden**

THREE-YEAR-OLDS

7 **ALPINE PANTHER (IRE)**, b c Tirol—Kentucky Wildcat **Mr P. D. Savill**
8 **CAPSTONE**, b f Shirley Heights—Doumayna **Lord Howard de Walden**
9 **COUNTRY DANCING**, b f Thatching—Sugar Plum Fairy **Mr Michael Page**
10 **EL BARDADOR (IRE)**, b c Thatching—Osmunda **Mr Howard Spooner**

MR W. JARVIS—continued

11 FARHANA, b f Fayruz—Fahrenheit Mr A. Foustok
12 FOG CITY, b c Damister (USA)—Front Line Romance Mr Jerry Sung
13 GRYADA, b f Shirley Heights—Grimpola (GER) Lord Howard de Walden
14 KING JADE, b g Damister (USA)—Our Marie (USA) Mr N. S. Yong
15 LA PAPAYA (USA), b f Alleged (USA)—La Papagena Lord Howard de Walden
16 LAY THE BLAME, b c Reprimand—Rose And The Ring Mr Anthony Foster
17 LINE DANCER, b c Shareef Dancer (USA)—Note Book Mr Adam Gurney & Mr V. O'Donoghue
18 LOOSE TALK, ch f Thatching—Brazen Faced Mr & Mrs John Davis
19 MIDNIGHT BLUE, br f Be My Chief (USA)—Guyum Sussex-Essex Racing
20 REACT, b f Reprimand—Shehana (USA) H. R. H. Prince Fahd Salman
21 RED NYMPH, b f Sharpo—Red Gloves The Who Needs Partners Partnership
22 SCHERMA, b f Green Desert (USA)—Escrime (USA) Lord Howard de Walden
23 SECCO, ch c Kris—Secala (USA) Lady Howard de Walden
24 SUITOR, b c Groom Dancer (USA)—Meliora Lord Howard de Walden
25 SULAWESI (IRE), b f In The Wings—Royal Loft Mr James H. Slade
26 SWEET NATURE (IRE), b f Classic Secret (USA)—So Kind Mrs Doris N. Allen and Partners
27 WITH CARE, b f Warning—Benazir Mr J. M. Greetham

TWO-YEAR-OLDS

28 BACHELORS PAD, b c 21/2 Pursuit of Love—Note Book (Mummy's Pet) Mrs Doris N. Allen
29 BEGUINE (USA), br f 3/3 Green Dancer (USA)—La Papagena (Habitat) Lord Howard de Walden
30 BRIGGS TURN, b g 28/4 Rudimentary (USA)—Turnabout (Tyrnavos) Mr J. M. Ratcliffe & Mr F. W. Briggs
31 BROADGATE FLYER, br c 27/2 Silver Kite (USA)—
                             Fabulous Pet (Somethingfabulous (USA)) The Broadgate Partnership
32 COLD STEEL, b c 21/2 Warrshan (USA)—Rengaine (FR) (Music Boy) Mrs Doris N. Allen
33 B c 21/2 Anshan—Dance On The Stage (Dancing Brave (USA)) Mr Howard Spooner
34 ENGAGEMENT, b c 28/3 Pursuit of Love—Escrime (USA) (Sharpen Up) Lord Howard de Walden
35 FIRST PAGE, b f 26/2 Rudimentary (USA)—Miss Paige (AUS) (Luskin Star (AUS)) Lady Howard de Walden
36 FOREVER PHOEBE, b f 22/3 Rock Hopper—Historical Fact (Reform) Mr J. M. Greetham
37 FORTUNE HUNTER (IRE), ch c 29/4 Lycius (USA)—Cardomine (Dom Racine (USA)) Highclere Thoroughbreds
38 FUR WILL FLY, b f 12/3 Petong—Bumpkin (Free State) Mr Anthony Hogarth
39 GANGA, ch f 21/5 Generous (IRE)—Congress Lady (General Assembly (USA)) Mr Hernadez Font
40 GO HENCE, b c 13/2 Be My Chief (USA)—Hence (USA) (Mr Prospector (USA)) Mr P. E. Burrell & Mr W. Jarvis
41 JESUSA, b f 5/5 Kalaglow—Chadenshe (Taufan (USA)) Mr D. G. Wright
42 KALIMAT, b f 31/3 Be My Guest (USA)—Kantado (Saulingo) Mr A. M. Foustok
43 B c 19/5 Sharpo—Ktolo (Tolomeo) R. K. Bids Ltd
44 B f 26/2 Warning—Last Exit (Dominion) Mrs C. Gurney
45 B c 22/5 Never So Bold—Mill d'Art (Artaius (USA)) Lucky Seven Racing
46 MISH MISH, ch f 29/1 Groom Dancer (USA)—Kirsten (Kris) Lord Howard de Walden
47 B f 20/4 Reprimand—Pleasuring (Good Times (ITY)) Mr W. McGregor
48 ROLLING STONE, b c 24/3 Northern Amethyst—First Sapphire (Simply Great (FR)) Mr Brian Cooper
49 B c 20/2 Superlative—Rosa Why (IRE) (Damister (USA)) Mr Jerry Sung
50 SHOW OFF, ch f 6/3 Efisio—Brazen Faced (Bold And Free) Mr and Mrs John Davis
51 Ch f 7/5 Fayruz—So Kind (Kind of Hush)
52 STAR BERRY, b f 17/2 In The Wings—Top Berry (High Top) Mr P. E. Burrell
53 SUBMARINE, b c 3/2 Slip Anchor—Meliora (Crowned Prince (USA)) Lord Howard de Walden
54 WING OF A PRAYER, b c 12/4 Statoblest—Queen Angel (Anfield) Thurloe Thoroughbreds

322   MR J. M. JEFFERSON, Malton

Postal: Newstead Cottage Stables, Norton, Malton, N. Yorks, YO17 9PJ.

Phone: (01653) 697225

1 ANABRANCH, 5, b m Kind of Hush—An-Go-Look Mrs M. Barker
2 ARDLUSSA BAY, 8, b m Miramar Reef—Coliemore The Caledonian Racing Club
3 BEN CRUACHAN, 6, b g King's Ride—Vale of Peace The Caledonian Racing Club
4 BRIDEN, 4, gr f Minster Son—Tilly Topaz D. Cable & B. Hough
5 BRIDLED TERN, 5, b m Gildoran—Scrambird Mr G. Griffin

MR J. M. JEFFERSON—continued

6 **DANBYS GORSE**, 4, ch g Presidium—Dohty Baby **D. T. Todd**
7 **DATO STAR (IRE)**, 5, br g Accordion—Newgate Fairy **Kath Riley, Mrs M. Guthrie & Joe Donald**
8 **GO-INFORMAL**, 5, ch g Primitive Rising—Sable Hill **Mr R. G. Marshall**
9 **KINGS MASQUERADE**, 5, b g Rakaposhi King—Maskwood **Yorkshire Racing Club Owners Group**
10 5, B m Loch Pearl—Lady Carousel **Mr Barry Seal**
11 **MAGIC BLOOM**, 10, b m Full of Hope—Mantavella **Mr P. Nelson**
12 **MOREOF A GUNNER**, 6, ch g Gunner B—Coliemore **Mrs M. E. Dixon & Mrs A. Hamilton**
13 **NORTHERN SQUIRE**, 8, b g Uncle Pokey—Kit's Future **Mrs J. M. Davenport**
14 **PENTLAND SQUIRE**, 5, b g Belfort (FR)—Sparkler Superb **Mrs M. Dixon, Brian Gordon & J. Harrison**
15 **PERSIAN HOUSE**, 9, ch g Persian Bold—Sarissa **Mrs J. M. Davenport**
16 **PHILBECKY**, 5, b m Exorbitant—Beare Lady **Mr G. Stephenson**
17 4, Ch g Gunner B—Pugilistic **Mr J. Donald & Partners**
18 **ROBERT THE BRAVE**, 4, b g Alias Smith (USA)—An-Go-Look **Mrs M. Barker**
19 **SCAR**, 8, b g Skyliner—Looking For Gold **Brian Gordon**
20 **STRATHMORE LODGE**, 7, b m Skyliner—Coliemore **J. M. Jefferson**
21 **SUAS LEAT (IRE)**, 6, b br g Clearly Bust—Paico Lane **Marten Julian (Turf Club) Ltd**
22 **SUSELJA (IRE)**, 5, b m Mon Tresor—Stifen **Mr John Donald**
23 **THE KILLALOE RUN**, 5, ch m Insan (USA)—Thatchville **Mr J. M. Jefferson**
24 **THE TIGER HUNTER**, 5, b g Primitive Rising (USA)—Highland Waters **Mrs J. M. Davenport**
25 **TULLYMURRY TOFF (IRE)**, 5, b g King's Ride—Cooleogan **Mr John H. Wilson**

THREE-YEAR-OLDS

26 **ANN'S MUSIC**, b f Clantime—An-Go-Look **Mrs M. Barker**
27 **ANSWERS-TO-THOMAS**, b c Komaite (USA)—Launde Abbey **Mr J. Donald**
28 **SNOW DOMINO (IRE)**, ch g Habyom—Magic Picture **Mr G. Wilson**

Other Owners: Mr J. Griese, Mr C. W. Holmes, Mr J. H. Riley.

Jockey (Flat): K Fallon.

Jockey (NH): M Dwyer.

Conditional: M Newton (9-7).

Amateur: Mr W Wenyon.

323   MR T. E. JEFFREY, Alnwick

Postal: **Cold Harbour Farm, Christon Bank, Alnwick, Northd, NE66 3HB.**

1 **RICH LIBERTY**, 8, ch m Liberated—Rich Discovery **Mr T. E. Jeffrey**

Amateur: Mr T Jeffrey (10-0).

324   MR J. R. W. JENKINS, Royston

Postal: **Kings Ride, Baldock Road, Royston, Herts, SG8 9NN.**
Phone: **(01763) 241141 FAX (01763) 248223 HOME (01763) 246611**

1 **ANCHOR CROWN**, 4, b f Slip Anchor—Doumayna **Mr Bob Dix**
2 **ARCTIC LIFE (IRE)**, 7, b g Roselier (FR)—Miss Dollar **Mrs T. McCoubrey**
3 **BIGWHEEL BILL (IRE)**, 7, br g Last Tycoon—Get Ahead **Famestar Ltd**
4 **BIRTHDAY BOY (IRE)**, 4, b g Scenic—Thank You Note **Mr T. R. Pearson**
5 **BROMFYLDE FAYEMAID (IRE)**, 4, b f Treasure Kay—Fayes Ben **Mrs Stedman**
6 **CIRCUS COLOURS**, 6, b g Rainbow Quest (USA)—Circus Plume **Mr S. Powell**
7 **CREWS CASTLE**, 9, ch g Carlingford Castle—Crews Girl **Mrs T. McCoubrey**
8 **DAS ISLAND**, 4, b c Presidium—Phamilla (IRE) **Mrs Eliza Long**

MR J. R. W. JENKINS—continued

9 **DAWN FLIGHT**, 7, b g Precocious—Sea Kestrel **Mrs Carol Davis**
10 **DESERT CHALLENGER (IRE)**, 6, b g Sadler's Wells (USA)—Verily **Andrews Freight Services Ltd**
11 **DJAIS (FR)**, 7, ch g Vacarme (USA)—Dame de Carreau (FR) **Mr T. Long**
12 **DURSHAN (USA)**, 7, ch g Shahrastani (USA)—Dukayna **Mr O. J. Donnelly**
13 **FAMOUS DANCER**, 8, b g Top Ville—Dancing Place (FR) **Mr B. T. Buckley**
14 **FIERCE**, 8, ch g Carwhite—Nosey **Mr P. W. Piper**
15 **FLAPPING FREDA (IRE)**, 8, ch m Carlingford Castle—Just Darina **Mr F. G. Newberry**
16 **GONE BY (IRE)**, 8, ch g Whistling Deer—French Strata (USA) **Mrs T. McCoubrey**
17 **JIMBO**, 5, b h Salse (USA)—Darnelle **Mr T. Long**
18 **LAKMON**, 10, br g Final Straw—Tanagrea **Mr R. Fox**
19 **LAST SPIN**, 4, b f Unfuwain (USA)—Spin **Mrs Eliza Long**
20 **LORD WELLINGTON (IRE)**, 5, b g Taufan (USA)—Merrie Laughter **Mrs T. McCoubrey**
21 **LUCKY TUCKY**, 5, b g Alleging (USA)—Romana **L. E. Tuckwell Ltd**
22 **MONTONE (IRE)**, 6, b g Pennine Walk—Aztec Princess **Mr B. Shirazi**
23 **MOST WELCOME NEWS**, 4, b g Most Welcome—In The Papers **Mr S. Powell**
24 **NAWAR (FR)**, 6, b g Kahyasi—Nabita (FR) **Mr T. Long**
25 **OMIDJOY (IRE)**, 6, ch m Nishapour (FR)—Fancy Finish **Mr R. M. Ellis**
26 **PLATO'S REPUBLIC (USA)**, 5, b br g Woodman (USA)—Jura Mist (USA) **Mrs Eliza Long**
27 **RISK A MILLION**, 4, ch f Risk Me (FR)—Romana **Mr M. J. Moore**
28 **SCRIPT**, 5, b g Squill (USA)—Vitry **Mr R. M. Ellis**
29 **SENSITIVE KING (IRE)**, 8, b g Tender King—Jumana **Mrs Jennefer M. Morris**
30 **SHAMSHADAL (IRE)**, 6, b g Darshaan—Shabarana (FR) **Mr Robin C. Williams**
31 **SPIKEY (NZ)**, 10, b g Valuta—Sweet Canyon (NZ) **Mr S. Powell**
32 **STONEY VALLEY**, 6, b g Caerleon (USA)—Startino **Ellis & Partners (Stockbrokers) Ltd**
33 **SWEET WILLIAM**, 6, br g Soldier Rose—Kanpy Belle **Mr P. B. Allingham**
34 **THANE (IRE)**, 7, b g Flair Path—Thalictrum **Mr Charles Stewart**
35 **THE STAGER (IRE)**, 4, b c Danehill (USA)—Wedgewood Blue (USA) **Mr T. Long**
36 **TIM (IRE)**, 6, b g Sexton Blake—Wingau (FR) **Mr P. W. Piper**
37 **TOMMYKNOCKER (IRE)**, 4, ch g Woodman (USA)—Repercutionist (USA) **Mr T. Long**
38 **TOP SPIN**, 7, b g Niniski (USA)—Spin **Mrs Eliza Long**
39 **TUKANO (CAN)**, 5, ch g Halo (USA)—Northern Prancer (USA) **Mrs T. McCoubrey**
40 **VICEROY RULER**, 5, gr g Faustus (USA)—Viceroy Princess **Mr J. McBarron**
41 **WANSTEAD (IRE)**, 4, ch g Be My Native (USA)—All The Same **Mr Bernard H. Hutchinson**

THREE-YEAR-OLDS

42 B f Actinium (FR)—Bingdon Builders
43 **FORTUITIOUS (IRE)**, b f Polish Patriot (USA)—Echo Cove **Mr T. Long**
44 B f Niniski (USA)—Ivory Gull (USA) **Mr T. Long**
45 Ch f Imp Society (USA)—Lady Limbo (USA) **Mr T. Long**
46 **NAWAJI (USA)**, b f Trempolino (USA)—Nobile Decretum (USA) **Mr Tareq Al-Mazeedi**
47 **ON THE HOME RUN**, b f Governor General—In The Papers **Mr S. Powell**
48 **PRINCE OF FLORENCE (IRE)**, ch c Bluebird (USA)—Seme de Lys (USA) **Mr M. Jaber**
49 **SHEATH KEFAAH**, ch c Kefaah (USA)—Wasslaweyeh (USA) **Mr M. Jaber**
50 **VERULAM (IRE)**, br c Marju (IRE)—Hot Curry (USA) **Mr M. Jaber**
51 **X-RAY (IRE)**, b g Actinium (FR)—Charter Lights **Mr R. M. Ellis**

TWO-YEAR-OLDS

52 B c 15/4 Jendali (USA)—Blakeness (Blakeney) **Mr A. Al-Radi**
53 B c 10/3 Risk Me (FR)—Brown Taw (Whistlefield) **Mr Greg Mowlen**
54 Br f Adbass (USA)—Doubtfire (Jalmood (USA)) **Mrs Hayfaa Al Salam**
55 B f 2/3 Jendali (USA)—Lallax (Laxton) **Mrs Hayfaa Al Salam**
56 **MISS ST KITTS**, ch f 8/2 Risk Me (FR)—
                                So Beguiling (Woodman (USA)) **Mr Peter Routledge & Mrs Jean Routledge**
57 Ch c 11/4 Jendali (USA)—Sweet 'n' Sharp (Sharpo) **Mr A. Al-Radi**

Other Owners: Andrews Freight Services Ltd, Mr B. T. Buckley, Mrs James Burridge, Mrs Carol Davis, Mr Bob Dix, Mr D. H. W. Dobson, Mr O. J. Donnelly, Ellis & Partners (Stockbrokers) Ltd, Famestar Ltd, Mr Doug Hagger, Mr R. A. Hazelby, Mrs Wendy Jenkins, L. E. Tuckwell Ltd, Mrs J. M. Martin, Miss Ruth Martin, Mr M. J. Moore, Mrs Jennefer M. Morris, Mr F. G. Newberry, Mr T. H. Ounsley, Mr T. R. Pearson, Mr P. W. Piper, Exors Of The Late Mr John Shipley, Mr B. Shirazi, Mr H. B. Shouler, Mr Charles Stewart, Mr Paul Walker, Mr Robin C. Williams.

325   MR W. P. JENKS, Bridgnorth

Postal: **Wadeley Farm, Glazeley, Bridgnorth, Shropshire, WV16 6AD.**

Phone: **OFFICE (01746) 789288 FAX (01746) 789535**

1 **BOURDONNER**, 4, b g Pharly (FR)—Buzzbomb **Million In Mind Partnership (5)**
2 **DANZIG ISLAND (IRE)**, 5, b g Roi Danzig (USA)—Island Morn (USA) **The Glazeley Partnership**
3 **EDWARD SEYMOUR (USA)**, 9, b g Northern Baby (CAN)—Regal Leader (USA) **Mr W. Jenks**
4 **EL CORDOBES (IRE)**, 5, b g Torus—Queens Tricks **Mrs M. A. Hickman**
5 **GLAMOUR GAME**, 5, ch m Nashwan (USA)—Sharpina **Mr P. A. Howell**
6 **GOOD GOING GAME**, 5, b m Supreme Leader—Mrs Popple **Mr D. R. Obank**
7 **HIGH LOW (USA)**, 8, b g Clever Trick (USA)—En Tiempo (USA) **Mr Mario Lanfranchi**
8 **HOODWINKER (IRE)**, 7, b g Supreme Leader—Merrybash **Mr P. A. Howell**
9 **ICE COLD IN ALEX**, 5, b g Arctic Lord—Cobusino **Mr Jeremy Beasley**
10 **IRONS IN THE FIRE (IRE)**, 7, b g Starlan—Coach Road **Mr Mario Lanfranchi**
11 **KALADROSS**, 5, ch g Ardross—Calametta **Mrs J. M. Howell**
12 **QUITE A MAN**, 8, ch g Leading Man—Quite Cute **Mr R. Everall**
13 **REAL POPCORN (IRE)**, 5, ch m Jareer (USA)—Avidal Park **Mr Peter Barclay**
14 **ROSMARINO**, 6, br g Persian Bold—No More Rosies **Mr Roy Howell**
15 5, B m Baron Blakeney—Stella Romana **Mr W. Jenks**

Other Owners: Mrs D. E. Bromley, Mr Ben Brooks, Mr Graham Goode, Mrs J. M. Howell, Mr W. R. Milner, Mr D. Minton, Mr A. J. Whitehead.

Jockey (Flat): W Carson.

Jockeys (NH): Tom Jenks (9-11), S Wynne (10-0).

Amateur: Mr R Burton (10-4).

Lady Rider: Miss A Sykes (9-7).

326   MR A. E. M. JESSOP, Chelmsford

Postal: **Flemings Farm, Warren Road, South Hanningfield, Chelmsford.**

Phone: **(01268) 710210**

1 **ARTIC MEADOW**, 5, ch m Little Wolf—Meadow Maid **Mr Alan Jessop**
2 **FLEMINGS DELIGHT**, 6, b m Idiot's Delight—Meadow Maid **Mrs Gloria Jessop**
3 **FLEMINGS GLORY**, 6, ch g Bold Owl—How Blue **Mrs Gloria Jessop**
4 **GOVERNORS BLUE**, 5, b m Governor General—How Blue **Mrs Gloria Jessop**
5 **MY LISA TOO**, 7, b m K-Battery—Arkengarthdale **Mrs Gloria Jessop**
6 **SWISS TACTIC (IRE)**, 7, br g Strong Gale—Julia's Pauper **Mrs Gloria Jessop**
7 **THE WEATHERMAN**, 8, b g Official—Deep Depression **Mrs Gloria Jessop**

327   MR F. JESTIN, Wigton

Postal: **Hilltop, Brocklebank, Wigton, Cumbria, CA7 8DL.**

Phone: **(016974) 78439**

1 **BDOORE (IRE)**, 8, b m Petoski—Princess Biddy **Mr F. Jestin**
2 **SPECTRE BROWN**, 6, b g Respect—My Goddess **Mr F. Jestin**
3 **SPEKTRA**, 4, br f Respect—My Goddess **Mrs E. Jestin**
4 **TWICE WEEKLY**, 7, b m Young Man (FR)—My Goddess **Mr F. Jestin**
5 **WINTER RAMBLE**, 10, ch g Avocat—Little Anthea **Mr F. Jestin**

Amateurs: Mr H Finegan (10-7), Mr F Jestin (11-7).

Lady Rider: Mrs J Thurlow (9-0).

328 MRS L. C. JEWELL, Sutton Valence

Postal: **Southfield Stables, South Lane, Sutton Valence, Maidstone, ME17 3AZ.**

Phone: **(01622) 842788 MOBILE (0585) 379773**

1 CHALLENGER ROW (IRE), 6, b g Colmore Row—Tunguska **Mr Victor Semple**
2 CHARTER LANE (IRE), 6, b g Toravich (USA)—Ulster Belle **Mrs A. Emanuel**
3 CLEVER DICK, 11, b g Cosmo—Princess Albertina (FR) **Mrs P. S. Donkin**
4 5, Ch g Royal Vulcan—Dark Rosheen
5 DEVON MISSILE, 7, b h Cruise Missile—Delegation **Miss K. Wratten**
6 EMALLEN (IRE), 8, b g Prince Regent (FR)—Peperonia **Mr Peter J. Allen**
7 GALLANT LORD (IRE), 7, ch g Mister Lord (USA)—Knockantota Star **Mr Peter J. Allen**
8 ISHMA (IRE), 5, b g Kambalda—Scat-Cat **Mr Darren Page**
9 JEWEL TRADER, 4, b c Green Ruby (USA)—Maiden Bidder **Mr J. S. S. Hollins**
10 JUST A BEAU, 5, b g Just A Monarch—Piphue Rosie **Mrs P. S. Donkin**
11 KENTISH MAN (IRE), 6, b g Lancastrian—Southern Dandy **Mr D. N. Yeadon**
12 LETS GO NOW (IRE), 6, b g Montekin—Lady Penthony **Mrs A. Emanuel**
13 MOUNT LODGE (IRE), 5, b g Lancastrian—Heather-Can **Mr Victor Semple**
14 PONTEVECCHIO BELLA, 10, ch m Main Reef—Linguist **Mrs Helen Clarke**
15 RAFIQ (IRE), 5, b g Jareer (USA)—Trendy Princess **Miss Anna Daly**
16 RUSTIC GENT (IRE), 8, gr g Rusticaro (FR)—Namur **Sadlers Estate Agents**
17 RUTH'S GAMBLE, 8, b g Kabour—Hilly's Daughter **Mrs A. Emanuel**
18 SANTA PONSA BAY, 9, b g Kemal (FR)—Kasperova **Mrs C. M. Sloan**
19 TIGANA, 4, b f Lugana Beach—Tina's Beauty **Mrs C. M. Sloan**
20 TRENDY AUCTIONEER (IRE), 8, b g Mazaad—Trendy Princess **The Trendy Partnership**
21 VICTORY GATE (USA), 11, b g Lydian (FR)—Pago Miss (USA) **Mrs P. S. Donkin**

Other Owners: Mr A. Birthwright, Mr Frank Brawn, Mrs Linda Jewell, Mr Brian Matthews, Mrs Linda Matthews, Mrs P. B. Mitford-Slade, Mr R. B. Morton, Mr John Sparke, Mr Malcom J. Spencer, Mr K. A. Wood.

Jockey (Flat): J Williams (8-3, w.a.).

Jockeys (NH): D Leahy (10-0), J A Railton (10-2).

Conditional: W Walsh (9-7).

329 MISS C. JOHNSEY, Chepstow

Postal: **Devauden Court, Devauden, Chepstow, Gwent, NP6 6PL.**

Phone: **(01291) 650248 OR (01291) 650695 MOBILE (0585) 723300**

1 BOHEMIAN HARMONY, 6, ch g Brotherly (USA)—Capinza Gin **Mrs S. C. Harper**
2 CAPTAIN COOKIE, 6, ch g Relkino—Pharaoh's Lady **Mr T. A. Johnsey**
3 CLASSICATION (IRE), 5, b g King's Ride—Laurestown Rose **Mr T. A. Johnsey**
4 DON'T MEAN A THING (IRE), 4, b c Treasure Kay—Traminer **Mr T. A. Johnsey**
5 FANCY NANCY (IRE), 5, b m Buckskin (FR)—Lils Melody **Mr T. A. Johnsey**
6 LEGAL ARTIST (IRE), 6, b g Tate Gallery (USA)—Dowdstown Miss **Mr T. A. Johnsey & Partners**
7 MAJOR BUSH, 9, b g Julio Mariner—Peperino **P. G. T. Racing**
8 RUSHAWAY, 5, b g Robellino (USA)—Brush Away **Wheeler Dealers**
9 SPRIGHTLY PIP (IRE), 5, gr g Roselier (FR)—Owen's Rose **Mr T. A. Johnsey**
10 SUMMIT, 5, b g Salse (USA)—Reltop **Mr T. A. Johnsey**
11 SUPREME MASTER, 6, b g Primo Dominie—French Surprise **Mr T. A. Johnsey**
12 UPSTREAM TORONTO (IRE), 5, ch g Chief Singer—Night Encounter **Mr T. A. Johnsey**

Other Owners: Mr A. Darlow, Mr P. F. Hicks, Mr R. Hutchins, Mr G. W. Stevens, Mr T. Thraves, Mr J. Williams.

Jockeys (NH): Dean Gallagher (w.a.), A P McCoy (w.a.).

330   MR JOHN H. JOHNSON, Crook

Postal: **White Lea Farm, Crook, Co Durham, DL15 9QN.**

Phone: **01388 762113 CAR PHONE 0860 31964 FAX 01388 768278 MOBILE 0589 280887**

1 **ABBEY LAMP (IRE)**, 7, b g Miner's Lamp—Abbey Lodge **Mr J. Howard Johnson**
2 **ABBEYLANDS (IRE)**, 8, gr g Cardinal Flower—Findabair **Mr Chris Heron**
3 **ABERCROMBY CHIEF**, 11, br g Buckskin (FR)—Free For Ever **Mr Ian Davidson**
4 **ALY DALEY (IRE)**, 8, ch g Roselier (FR)—Roses In June **Mr Michael Tobitt**
5 **ANDROS GALE (IRE)**, 7, b g Strong Gale—Sirrahdis **Mr J. Howard Johnson**
6 **ANOTHER CHAPTER**, 6, b m Respect—Taxi Freight **Mr J. Howard Johnson**
7 **BECKLEY FOUNTAIN (IRE)**, 8, br g Royal Fountain—Sweet Mystery **Mr J. Henderson (Co Durham)**
8 **BRANDY CROSS (IRE)**, 7, br g Strong Statement (USA)—Rescued **Mr M. Thompson**
9 **BRAVE AND TENDER (IRE)**, 7, b g Strong Gale—Brave Intention **Mrs A. Taylor (Co Durham)**
10 **CHAPEL WALK**, 5, ch m Move Off—Chapel Close **Mr T. Pickering**
11 **CHEATER (IRE)**, 5, b g Good Thyne (USA)—Cute Play **Mr J. Howard Johnson**
12 **CHOPWELL DRAPES (IRE)**, 6, br g Callernish—Sally Pond **Durham Drapes Ltd**
13 **CLAVERING (IRE)**, 6, br g Good Thyne (USA)—Caffra Mills **Mr Billy Maguire**
14 **DAISY DAYS (IRE)**, 6, ch m Carlingford Castle—Deceptive Day **Mr J. Howard Johnson**
15 **DIRECT ROUTE (IRE)**, 5, b g Executive Perk—Mursuma **Mr Thomas Harty**
16 **DOWN THE FELL**, 7, b g Say Primula—Sweet Dough **Mr J. Howard Johnson**
17 **DOWN THE ROAD**, 9, br g Roi Guillaume (FR)—Killanny Bridge **Mr R. J. Crake**
18 **DOWN THE TRACK**, 7, ch m Move Off—Cobby Castle **Mrs S. Johnson**
19 **DUKE OF PERTH**, 5, ch g Scottish Reel—Own Free Will **Mr W. M. G. Black**
20 **ELLIOTT'S WISH (IRE)**, 5, b g Strong Gale—Prying Lady **Mr D. M. Fulton**
21 **FORBES (IRE)**, 5, b g Strong Gale—Gold Label **Mrs M. W. Bird**
22 **FOUR DEEP (IRE)**, 8, ch g Deep Run—I'm Grannie **The Braw Partnership**
23 **GENERAL MUCK (IRE)**, 7, b g Supreme Leader—Muckride Lady **Mr J. Howard Johnson**
24 **GNOME'S TYCOON**, 5, b br g Strong Gale—Fairgoi **Flibbertigibbet**
25 **GRAND SCENERY (IRE)**, 8, ch g Carlingford Castle—Ballyhoura Lady **The Scottish Steeplechasing Partnership**
26 **HIGHLAND VIEW (IRE)**, 6, b g Phardante (FR)—Chatty Di **Mr R. W. L. Bowden**
27 **HIGH ROAD**, 9, ch g Town And Country—Nikali **Mr R. W. Huggins**
28 **HIS WAY (IRE)**, 7, br g His Turn—Bay Foulard **Mrs M. Humble**
29 **HOUGHTON**, 10, b g Horage—Deirdre Oge **Mr Gordon Brown**
30 **ITALIAN PRINCESS (IRE)**, 6, gr m Strong Gale—Helens Tower **Mrs J. M. Corbett**
31 **JOE WHITE**, 10, ch g Tampero (FR)—Fiery Rose **Mr J. Howard Johnson**
32 **KIBBY BANK**, 7, gr g Pragmatic—Alcide Inn **Mr J. Henderson (Co Durham)**
33 **KILLBALLY BOY (IRE)**, 6, b g Strong Gale—Rare Dream **Everaldo Partnership**
34 4, B g Executive Perk—Laud **Mr J. Howard Johnson**
35 **LETHAL COCKTAIL (IRE)**, 7, ch g Bob Back (USA)—Naughty Lass **Mrs J. M. Corbett**
36 **MINI CRUISE**, 6, ch g Cruise Missile—Mini Pie **Mr J. Hirst**
37 **MISTER MUDDYPAWS**, 6, b g Celtic Cone—Jane's Daughter **Mr J. Howard Johnson**
38 **MORCELI (IRE)**, 8, gr g Mouktar—Safiah (FR) **Mrs J. M. Corbett**
39 **MORNING IN MAY (IRE)**, 8, b g General Ironside—Orinda Way **Mr Maurice Hutchinson**
40 **MR HATCHET (IRE)**, 5, ch g Executive Perk—Aubretia (USA) **Mr J. Howard Johnson**
41 **OVER THE DEEL**, 10, ch g Over The River (FR)—Cahernane Girl **Mr George Tobitt**
42 **OVER THE ISLAND (IRE)**, 8, ch m Over The River (FR)—Sin Bin **The Braw Partnership**
43 **PRIMITIVE HEART**, 4, b g Primitive Rising (USA)—Country Carnival **Mr J. Howard Johnson**
44 **THE ODD TIME (IRE)**, 7, b g Stalker—Very Seldom **Mr T. W. Ellwood**
45 **THUNDERSTRUCK**, 10, b g Young Generation—Ringed Aureole **Mr D. Thomas Sheridan**
46 **TOM BRODIE**, 6, b g Ardross—Deep Line **Mrs M. W. Bird**
47 **WHITEGATES WILLIE**, 4, b g Buckskin (FR)—Whitegates Lady **Mr R. W. L. Bowden**

Other Owners: Mrs J. Allison, Mr J. G. Askew, Mr Michael Cosgrove, Mr D. G. Divilly, Mr J. Hirst, Miss Lucy S. Johnson, Mr R. M. Kirkland, Mr J. T. Moyle, Group Captain J. A. Prideaux, Mr R. G. Ross, Mr Robert Watson, Mr P. H. Wilkerson.

Jockey (NH): P Carberry (w.a.).

331   MR P. R. JOHNSON, Cannock

Postal: **Pinetrees Farm, Stafford Road, Huntington, Cannock, WS12 4PX.**

Phone: **(01543) 502962**

1 5, Ch m Henbit (USA)—Etoile de Lune **Mr P. R. Johnson**
2 **ON APPRO (IRE),** 7, br g Mandalus—Philis's Friend **Mr P. R. Johnson**
3 **SUPER BRUSH (IRE),** 4, br f Brush Aside (USA)—Flying Silver **Mr P. R. Johnson**

THREE-YEAR-OLDS

4 Gr f Scallywag—Headbee **Mr P. R. Johnson**

TWO-YEAR-OLDS

5 Ch c 18/2 Sula Bula—Penair (Good Times (ITY)) **Mr P. R. Johnson**

332   MR ROBERT W JOHNSON, Newcastle Upon Tyne

Postal: **Grange Farm, Newburn, Newcastle Upon Tyne, NE15 8QA.**

Phone: **(01912) 674464**

1 **DIXIE HIGHWAY,** 6, gr m Absalom—Kip's Sister **Mr Robert Johnson**
2 **INSAYNE,** 7, b g Say Primula—Inrange **Mr Robert Johnson**
3 5, B g Wylfa—Monks Rambler **Mr Robert Johnson**
4 **NIAD,** 12, b g Lighter—Taxi Freight **Mr Robert Johnson**
5 **SHINING BURN,** 5, b m Respect—Shining Bann **Mr Robert Johnson**
6 **SHINING PRICE,** 7, b m Silly Prices—Shining Bann **Mr Robert Johnson**
7 **UPWELL,** 12, b g Tanfirion—Debnic **Mr Robert Johnson**

Jockey (NH): K Johnson (10-0).

Amateur: Mr P Johnson (10-9).

333   MRS S. M. JOHNSON, Madley

Postal: **Carwardine Farm, Madley, Hereford, HR2 9JQ.**

Phone: **(01981) 250214**

1 **DERRING BRIDGE,** 6, b g Derring Rose—Bridge Ash **Mr I. K. Johnson**
2 **RUSTY BRIDGE,** 9, b g Rustingo—Bridge Ash **Mr I. K. Johnson**
3 5, B g Reprimand—Skiddaw (USA) **Mrs S. M. Johnson**
4 **SOUND FORECAST,** 8, b g Hill's Forecast—Miss Soundly **Mrs S. A. Evans**

Conditional: Richard Johnson (9-7).

Lady Rider: Miss Candy Thomas (10-0).

334   MR G. F. JOHNSON HOUGHTON, Newmarket

Postal: **19 Lisburn Road, Newmarket, Suffolk, CB8 8HS.**

Phone: **(01638) 669817 MOBILE (0585) 753154**

1 4, Ch g Le Bavard (FR)—Acushla Macree **Mrs R. F. Johnson Houghton**
2 **ALCOVE,** 5, ch g Faustus (USA)—Cubby Hole **Mrs G. T. Johnson Houghton**
3 **MESPIL ROAD (IRE),** 6, b m Mandalus—Able Dancer **M. Pearce**
4 **PEMBRIDGE PLACE,** 5, b g Niniski (USA)—Rose d'Amour (USA) **Mrs G. T. Johnson Houghton**

MR G. F. JOHNSON HOUGHTON—continued

5 **PROTOTYPE**, 5, b g Governor General—Sweet Enough **Mrs G. T. Johnson Houghton**
6 **SQUADDIE**, 4, ch g Infantry—Mendelita **Mr J. P. Power**
7 **TOO CLEVER BY HALF**, 8, b g Pragmatic—Acushla Macree **Mrs R. F. Johnson Houghton**
8 **TUG YOUR FORELOCK**, 5, b g Arctic Lord—Tuggles Owen **Mrs R. F. Johnson Houghton**

THREE-YEAR-OLDS

9 **SARASOTA RYDE**, gr f Komaite (USA)—Freedom Line **Capt Alan Smith**

Other Owners: Mr S. Astaire, Mr K. Santana, Santos Racing.

Jockey (NH): A Thornton (10-0).

Lady Rider: Eve Johnson Houghton (9-0).

335   MR R. F. JOHNSON HOUGHTON, Didcot

Postal: **Woodway, Blewbury, Didcot, Oxon, OX11 9EZ.**
Phone: **(01235) 850480 FAX (01235) 851045 MOBILE (0836) 599232**

1 **BRICK COURT (IRE)**, 4, ch f Bluebird (USA)—Palmyra (GER) **Mr R. F. Johnson Houghton**
2 **GLORIOUS ARAGON**, 4, b f Aragon—Gloria Maremmana **Lord Leverhulme**
3 **LATCHING (IRE)**, 4, ch f Thatching—Keepers Lock (USA) **Mr R. F. Johnson Houghton**
4 **MAESTROSO (IRE)**, 7, b g Mister Majestic—That's Easy **Mrs Trisha Keane**
5 **PARADISE WATERS**, 4, gr f Celestial Storm (USA)—Gleaming Water **Mr R. Crutchley**
6 **STREET KID**, 8, b g Teenoso (USA)—Chalkey Road **Mr G. P. P. Stewart**

THREE-YEAR-OLDS

7 **BAIZE**, ch f Efisio—Bayonne **Lady Rothschild**
8 **CENTRE STALLS (IRE)**, b c In The Wings—Lora's Guest **Mr Anthony Pye-Jeary**
9 Gr f Ardross—Charlotte Gray **Mr G. P. P. Stewart**
10 **FOREST ROBIN**, ch c Formidable (USA)—Blush Rambler (IRE) **Mrs Peter Robeson**
11 **GOLDEN POND (IRE)**, b f Don't Forget Me—Golden Bloom **Mr John Horgan**
12 **KEEPERS DAWN (IRE)**, b f Alzao (USA)—Keepers Lock (USA) **Mr Bob Lanigan**
13 **LAST BUT NOT LEAST**, b f Dominion—Almadanivah **Mr Keith Wills**
14 **SASSY STREET (IRE)**, b g Danehill (USA)—Sassy Lane **Mr R. F. Johnson Houghton**
15 **TART**, b f Tragic Role (USA)—Fee **Lady Rothschild**

TWO-YEAR-OLDS

16 **AGIFT**, b f 16/4 Cadeaux Genereux—Aspark (Sparkler) **Mrs Peter Robeson**
17 Ch gr c 24/3 Absalom—Blush Rambler (IRE) (Blushing Groom (FR)) **Mr C. W. Sumner**
18 **COWRIE**, b f 19/1 Efisio—Bawbee (Dunbeath (USA)) **Lady Rothschild**
19 Ch c 16/4 Handsome Sailor—Eye Sight (Roscoe Blake) **Lord Leverhulme**
20 **FASTNET**, ch f 10/4 Forzando—Lambay (Lorenzaccio) **Lady Rothschild**
21 Gr c 3/5 Kenmare (FR)—Greatest Pleasure (Be My Guest (USA)) **Mr Anthony Pye-Jeary**
22 B c 5/3 Marju (IRE)—Haneena (Habitat) **Mr Anthony Pye-Jeary**
23 Ch f 18/2 Ballad Rock—Haskeir (Final Straw) **Mrs Anthony Andrews**
24 **INFLATION**, b f 3/3 Primo Dominie—Fluctuate (Sharpen Up) **Mr John Rowles**
25 B c 27/3 Classic Music (USA)—La Toulzanie (FR) (Sanctus II) **Mr R. F. Johnson Houghton**
26 B c 24/2 Reprimand—Lyra (Blakeney) **Mr R. F. Johnson Houghton**
27 **PENNYWELL**, b f 4/5 Nicholas (USA)—Fee (Mandamus) **Lady Rothschild**
28 **RAKE HEY**, b c 23/3 Petong—Dancing Daughter (Dance In Time (CAN)) **Lord Leverhulme**
29 B f 26/4 Statoblest—Spinelle (Great Nephew) **Mr Jim Short**

Jockey (Flat): J Reid (w.a.).

Jockey (NH): G McCourt (w.a.).

Apprentice: Barry Smith (7-10).

Lady Rider: Miss E A Johnson Houghton (9-7).

336   MR M. S. JOHNSTON, Middleham

Postal: **Kingsley House Racing Stables, Middleham, Leyburn, North Yorks, DL8 4PH.**

Phone: **(01969) 22237 FAX (01969) 22484**

1 **ASHGORE**, 6, b g Efisio—Fair Atlanta **Mr Harvey Ashworth**
2 **BRANSTON ABBY (IRE)**, 7, ch m Risk Me (FR)—Tuxford Hideaway **Mr J. David Abell**
3 **CAVERS YANGOUS**, 5, b g Daring March—Rapid Lady **Mr F. G. Leithead**
4 **CELESTIAL KEY (USA)**, 6, br g Star de Naskra (USA)—Casa Key (USA) **Mr M. J. Brodrick**
5 **DEANO'S BEENO**, 4, b g Far North (CAN)—Sans Dot **Mr Paul Dean**
6 **DIAGHILEF (IRE)**, 4, b c Royal Academy (USA)—Miss Audimar (USA) **Mr C. C. Buckley**
7 **DOUBLE BLUE**, 7, ch g Town And Country—Australia Fair (AUS) **Mr R. W. Huggins**
8 **DOUBLE ECLIPSE (IRE)**, 4, b c Ela-Mana-Mou—Solac (FR) **The Middleham Partnership**
9 **DOUBLE QUICK (IRE)**, 4, b f Superpower—Haraabah (USA) **2nd Middleham Partnership**
10 **DOUBLE TRIGGER (IRE)**, 5, ch h Ela-Mana-Mou—Solac (FR) **Mr R. W. Huggins**
11 **EQUERRY**, 5, b g Midyan (USA)—Supreme Kingdom **Mr J. R. Good & Mrs P. Good**
12 **LOVEYOUMILLIONS (IRE)**, 4, b c Law Society (USA)—Warning Sound **Mr M. Doyle**
13 **MILNGAVIE (IRE)**, 6, ch g Pharly (FR)—Wig And Gown **Mr A. S. Robertson**
14 **MR OSCAR**, 4, b g Belfort (FR)—Moushka **Mr W. McKeown**
15 **NINIA (USA)**, 4, ch f Affirmed (USA)—Lajna **Mrs D. R. Schreiber**
16 **PERCY BRAITHWAITE (IRE)**, 4, b g Kahyasi—Nasseem (FR) **Brian Yeardley Continental Ltd**
17 **SAKHAROV**, 7, b g Bay Express—Supreme Kingdom **Mr J. R. Good & Mrs P. Good**
18 **STAR RAGE (IRE)**, 6, b g Horage—Star Bound **Mr J. D. Abell & Mrs J. Abell**
19 **THREE ARCH BRIDGE**, 4, ch f Sayf El Arab (USA)—Alanood **Mr R. N. Pennell & Mrs J. Pennell**
20 **TILER (IRE)**, 4, br g Ballad Rock—Fair Siobahn **Mrs C. Robinson**

THREE-YEAR-OLDS

21 **BAILEYS FIRST (IRE)**, b f Alzao (USA)—Maiden Concert **G. R. Bailey Ltd**
22 **BALIOS (IRE)**, b c Be My Guest (USA)—Clifden Bottoms **Mr & Mrs A. Mordain**
23 **BEACONTREE**, ch c Lycius (USA)—Beaconaire (USA) **Sheikh Mohammed**
24 **BIJOU D'INDE**, ch c Cadeaux Genereux—Pushkar **Mr J. S. Morrison**
25 **BOUNDARY BIRD (IRE)**, b g Tirol—Warning Sound **Mrs I. Bird**
26 **CLINCHER CLUB**, b f Polish Patriot (USA)—Merry Rous **Brian Yeardley Continental Ltd**
27 **DECRESCENDO (IRE)**, ch f Polish Precedent (USA)—Diminuendo (USA) **Sheikh Mohammed**
28 **DESERT FROLIC (IRE)**, b f Persian Bold—Try To Catch Me (USA) **Maktoum Al Maktoum**
29 **DESERT TIGER**, br f Green Desert (USA)—Desert Bride (USA) **Maktoum Al Maktoum**
30 **DISC OF GOLD (USA)**, ch f Silver Hawk (USA)—Equal Change (USA) **Sheikh Mohammed**
31 **DOMOOR**, b c Dominion—Corley Moor **The Braindon Partnership**
32 **DOUBLE AGENT**, ch g Niniski (USA)—Rexana **Mr R. W. Huggins**
33 **DOUBLE DASH (IRE)**, gr c Darshaan—Safka (USA) **The Middleham Partnership**
34 **DOUBLE DIAMOND (IRE)**, b c Last Tycoon—State Treasure (USA) **The 2nd Middleham Partnership**
35 **DOUBLE OSCAR (IRE)**, ch c Royal Academy (USA)—Broadway Rosie **Mr R. W. Huggins**
36 **DOUBLE-O-SEVEN**, b c Tirol—Anneli Rose **Mr R. W. Huggins**
37 **FREEDOM FLAME**, b f Darshaan—Fire And Shade (USA) **Sheikh Mohammed**
38 **GOTHENBERG (IRE)**, b c Polish Patriot (USA)—Be Discreet **Brian Yeardley Continental Ltd**
39 **GREEN BARRIES**, b c Green Desert (USA)—Barari (USA) **Maktoum Al Maktoum**
40 **HALEAKALA (IRE)**, ch f Kris—Haiati (USA) **Sheikh Mohammed**
41 **ITSINTHEPOST**, b f Risk Me (FR)—Where's The Money **First Class - Four Seasons**
42 **LALLANS (IRE)**, b c Old Vic—Laluche (USA) **Sheikh Mohammed**
43 **LOVE BIRD (IRE)**, b c Bluebird (USA)—Top Glad (USA) **Mr M. Doyle**
44 **MAGIC CAROUSEL**, b f Mtoto—Lap of Honour **Mrs S. O'Brien**
45 **MAID FOR BAILEYS (IRE)**, b f Marju (IRE)—Island Time (USA) **G. R. Bailey Ltd**
46 **MARCOMIR (USA)**, br c Dayjur (USA)—Mariella (USA) **Sheikh Mohammed**
47 **MASK FLOWER (USA)**, b f Dayjur (USA)—Nom de Plume (USA) **Sheikh Mohammed**
48 **MATTAWAN**, ch c Nashwan (USA)—Sweet Mover (USA) **Sheikh Mohammed**
49 **METAL BADGE (IRE)**, b c Doyoun—Sharaya (USA) **Chris Bryan and Partners**
50 **MIGHTY KEEN**, ch c Keen—Mary Martin **Greenland Park Ltd**
51 **MISS OFFSET**, ch f Timeless Times—Farinara **Hertford Offset Ltd**
52 **MISTER ASPECTO (IRE)**, b g Caerleon (USA)—Gironde (USA) **Aspecto Clothing Co Ltd**
53 **NOSE NO BOUNDS (IRE)**, b c Cyrano de Bergerac—Damezao **Ridings Racing**
54 **PLEASANT SURPRISE**, b c Cadeaux Genereux—Quiet Week-End **Mr Abdullah Ali**
55 **POLAR ECLIPSE**, ch c Polar Falcon (USA)—Princess Zepoli **Mr J. R. Good**

MR M. S. JOHNSTON—continued

56 **PRINCE ASLIA**, b c Aragon—Aslia **Mrs R. J. Daniels**
57 **RUSSIAN ROULETTE**, b f Niniski (USA)—Gaucherie (USA) **2nd Middleham Partnership**
58 **SHIRLEY SUE**, b f Shirley Heights—Dame Ashfield **Greenland Park Ltd**
59 **SHONTAINE**, b g Pharly (FR)—Hinari Televideo **Mr Paul Dean**
60 **SWEET ROBIN (IRE)**, b f Mujtahid (USA)—La Romance (USA) **Sheikh Mohammed**
61 **TADEO**, ch c Primo Dominie—Royal Passion **Mr J. R. Good**
62 **THORNTOUN ESTATE (IRE)**, b g Durgam (USA)—Furry Friend (USA) **Mr W. M. Johnstone**
63 **UNCONDITIONAL LOVE (IRE)**, b f Polish Patriot (USA)—Thatcherite **Mrs H. Conroy**
64 **VICTORIA BLUE**, ch f Old Vic—Itsamaza (USA) **Sheikh Mohammed**
65 **VICTORY BOUND (USA)**, ch c Bering—Furajet (USA) **Maktoum Al Maktoum**

TWO-YEAR-OLDS

66 Ch c 24/2 Imp Society (USA)—Best Academy (USA) (Roberto (USA)) **G. R. Bailey Ltd**
67 Ch c 17/5 Pursuit of Love—Blade of Grass (Kris) **Mr J. S. Morrison**
68 B c 6/5 Ela-Mana-Mou—Bold Miss (Bold Lad (IRE)) **Atlantic Racing Ltd**
69 B c 7/4 Lomond (USA)—Capriati (USA) (Diesis) **Mr R. Robinson**
70 B f 4/4 Arazi (USA)—Celtic Assembly (USA) (Secretariat (USA)) **Sheikh Mohammed**
71 B f 5/4 Suave Dancer (USA)—Cominna (Dominion) **Mr P. Wetzel**
72 B br c 7/2 Alleged (USA)—Danseuse Etoile (USA) (Buckpasser) **Mr R. W. Huggins**
73 **DARGO**, b c 10/5 Formidable (USA)—Mountain Memory (High Top) **Mrs R. J. Daniels**
74 Ch f 18/4 Risk Me (FR)—Dark Kristal (IRE) (Gorytus (USA)) **Mr J. D. Abell & Mrs J. Abell**
75 B f 21/1 Alzao (USA)—Dedicated Lady (IRE) (Pennine Walk) **Mr C. C. Buckley**
76 **DOUBLE DELIGHT**, ch f 21/2 Aragon—Relatively Easy (Relkino) **Harland & Co Racing Club**
77 B c 6/2 Primo Dominie—Egalite (FR) (Luthier) **Mr J. D. Abell & Mrs J. Abell**
78 Ch c 23/4 Indian Ridge—Fair And Wise (High Line) **Dr Fuk To Chang**
79 Ch c 9/4 Nashwan (USA)—Fire And Shade (USA) (Shadeed (USA)) **Sheikh Mohammed**
80 B c 28/1 Lear Fan (USA)—Florinda (CAN) (Vice Regent (CAN)) **Mr J. Clopet & Mr A. Farmer**
81 B c 11/4 Capote (USA)—Grana (USA) (Miswaki (USA)) **Gainsborough Stud Management**
82 Ch f 23/2 Soviet Star (USA)—Haebah (USA) (Alydar (USA)) **Gainsborough Stud Management**
83 B c 16/3 Ela-Mana-Mou—Happy Tidings (Hello Gorgeous (USA)) **Mr R. W. Huggins**
84 Ch f 7/5 Masterclass (USA)—Haraabah (USA) (Topsider (USA)) **Mr R. W. Huggins**
85 Ch c 29/4 Magical Wonder (USA)—Hardiona (FR) (Hard To Beat) **Stakis**
86 B c 29/5 Law Society (USA)—Heather Lark (Red Alert) **Mr J. D. Abell**
87 B f 27/2 Polish Patriot (USA)—Hot Curry (USA) (Sharpen Up) **Mr J. D. Abell**
88 B c 9/5 Lead On Time (USA)—Hud Hud (USA) (Alydar (USA)) **Gainsborough Stud Management**
89 B f 18/4 Lycius (USA)—Just Pretty (USA) (Danzig (USA)) **3rd Middleham Partnership**
90 B f 11/3 Taufan (USA)—Kilcoy (USA) (Secreto (USA)) **Mr R. W. Huggins**
91 B c 21/4 Night Shift (USA)—Laluche (USA) (Alleged (USA)) **Sheikh Mohammed**
92 **LYCIUS TOUCH**, b f 12/2 Lycius (USA)—Homely Touch (Touching Wood (USA)) **Mr A. Cutler**
93 B c 1/5 Caerleon (USA)—Marie Noelle (FR) (Brigadier Gerard) **Ms B. Lee**
94 B f 23/3 High Estate—Millingdale Lillie (Tumble Wind (USA)) **Knavesmire Partnership**
95 B c 13/5 Alleged (USA)—Minstrelete (USA) (Round Table) **Atlantic Racing Ltd**
96 B f 11/4 Statoblest—Moushka (Song) **Mr W. McKeown**
97 B c 18/3 Robellino (USA)—Night Jar (Night Shift (USA)) **Mr J. S. Morrison**
98 Ch c 25/4 Diesis—Nijana (USA) (Nijinsky (CAN)) **Mr G. Tiney**
99 B c 13/2 Imp Society (USA)—Petite Realm (Realm) **Dr Fuk To Chang**
100 B c 27/4 Marju (IRE)—Phazania (Tap On Wood) **Mr C. C. Buckley**
101 Ch f 12/4 Midyan (USA)—Pushkar (Northfields (USA)) **Mr J. S. Morrison**
102 B c 4/5 Sunny's Halo (CAN)—Quite Attractive (USA) (Well Decorated (USA)) **Mr P. D. Savill**
103 B f 2/5 Efisio—Rectitude (Runnymede) **Mr R. Smith**
104 B c 20/2 Bluebird (USA)—Rise And Fall (Mill Reef (USA)) **Mr P. D. Savill**
105 B c 22/3 Shavian—Shannon Princess (Connaught) **Harland & Co Racing Club**
106 B f 14/3 Royal Academy (USA)—Sharp Circle (IRE) (Sure Blade (USA)) **Mr R. C. Moules**
107 B f 22/3 Mujtahid (USA)—Shojoon (USA) (Danzig (USA)) **Sheikh Mohammed**
108 B c 16/5 Polish Patriot (USA)—Summer Dreams (CAN) (Victoria Park) **Brian Yeardley Continental Ltd**
109 B f 30/3 Royal Academy (USA)—Sweetbird (Ela-Mana-Mou) **Mr R. W. Huggins**
110 B c 2/5 Green Desert (USA)—Swept Away (Kris) **Sheikh Mohammed**
111 B c 13/5 Royal Academy (USA)—Terracotta Hut (Habitat) **Mr P. D. Savill**
112 Ch c 19/2 Imp Society (USA)—Thatcherite (Final Straw) **Aspecto Clothing Co Ltd**
113 B br f 17/2 Unfuwain (USA)—Three Stars (Star Appeal) **G. R. Bailey Ltd**

MR M. S. JOHNSTON—continued

114 TOUCH'N'GO, b c 13/5 Rainbow Quest (USA)—Mary Martin (Be My Guest (USA)) **Greenland Park Ltd**
115 B c 9/5 Sheikh Albadou—Wayward Lass (Hail The Pirates (USA)) **Sheikh Mohammed**
116 B c 23/3 Red Ransom (USA)—What Not To Do (USA) (What Luck (USA)) **Dr Fuk To Chang**
117 B c 30/1 Polish Patriot (USA)—Wild Sable (IRE) (Kris) **Harland & Co Racing Club**

Other Owners: Mr P. J. Biggins, Lady Bolton, Miss Nuala Cassidy, Mr C. Chan, Mr A. G. Chappell, Demor Investments Ltd, Mr Christopher Donald, Mr Tom Ford, Mr J. Forsyth, Miss V. Foster, Mrs P. J. Garthwaite, Mr J. Godfrey, G & P Partners, Mrs Jean Greaves, Mr C. H. Greensit, Mr W. A. Greensit, Mr H. J. Hambley, Mr R. Hamer, Mr J. H. Henderson (Co Durham), Mr J. E. Horrocks, Mr B. J. Howes, Mr Richard B. Huckerby, Mr G. Jenkinson, Mr J. C. Jess, Mr A. D. Latter, Mr R. A. Lee, Mark Johnston Racing Ltd, Mr Steve McMillan, N. Y. L. Racing, Mr A. R. Phair, Mrs Gillian Quinn, Mr Geoff Rawson, Mr A. W. Regan, Mr James T. Robinson, Mrs Jean Rogers, Mrs Marian Rogers, Mr David Scott, Mr P. Simpson, Mr Stephen G. Smith, The No Hassle Partnership, Mr D. C. Thomas, Mrs J. D. Trotter, Mr P. Venner, Mr V. Verheecke, Mr P. H. Wilkerson, Mr K. C. Worrall.

Jockeys (Flat): Jason Weaver (8-3), Tyrone Williams (7-10).

Apprentices: Oliver Casey (7-11), Sam Hyland, Brian Malligan (7-0), Keith Sked (7-7).

Lady Rider: Miss C Williams.

337   MR A. P. JONES, Eastbury

Postal: **Eastbury Cottage Stables, Eastbury, Lambourn, Newbury, RG16 7JJ.**

Phone: **PHONE & FAX (01488) 72637 MOBILE (0831) 167346**

1 BUDS OF MAY, 6, ch m Sula Bula—Rydwells-Star **C. J. & G. C. Pearce**
2 CAPITAIN, 7, b g Idiot's Delight—Crosa **Mr S. C. Jones**
3 COLWAY PRINCE (IRE), 8, b g Prince Tenderfoot (USA)—El Cerrito **Mr A. A. King**
4 COUNTRY STORE, 7, ch m Sunyboy—Pollys Owen **Mrs M. I. Barton**
5 DERRING VALLEY, 11, b g Derrylin—Chalke Valley **Mr A. A. King**
6 DISTANT HOME, 8, b g Homeboy—Distant Sound **Mr A. P. Jones**
7 EVAPORATE, 4, b f Insan (USA)—Mona **Mr A. A. King**
8 FRAZER NASH, 5, ch g Town And Country—Berlinetta **Mrs R. Legouix**
9 I HAVE HIM, 9, b g Orange Reef—Costerini **Mr Thomas Weller**
10 JUST ROSIE, 7, b m Sula Bula—Rosa Ruler **Plough Racing**
11 KILDEE LAD, 6, b g Presidium—National Time (USA) **Mr J. F. O'Donovan**
12 MR KIRBY, 14, b g Monksfield—Mayfield Grove **Mr A. P. Jones**
13 NIKI SU, 8, b m Sula Bula—Sweet Orchid **The Born Loosers Racing Club**
14 PARSON'S WAY, 9, b g The Parson—Daithis Coleen **Mr A. King**
15 ROMANY BLUES, 7, b m Oats—Romany Serenade **Mr Harry Sibley**
16 SECRET MISS, 4, ch f Beveled (USA)—Zamindara
17 SOLO GENT, 7, br g Le Bavard (FR)—Go-It-Alone **Mr A. A. King**
18 TINKER'S CUSS, 5, ch m Nearly A Hand—Little Member **Mr Alan Briars**
19 TRIOMING, 10, b g Horning—Third Generation **Mr A. P. Jones**
20 WHISKEY CASTLE (IRE), 7, ch g Carlingford Castle—Oremus **Mr Richard Burley**

THREE-YEAR-OLDS

21 FESTIVAL (FR), gr g Mourtazam—Oseille IV (FR) **Mr A. A. King**
22 FIN BEC (FR), b g Tip Moss (FR)—Tourbrune (FR) **Mr A. A. King**

TWO-YEAR-OLDS

23 INCANDESCENT, b f 1/3 Inca Chief (USA)—Heavenly State (Enchantment) **John Gaysford**
24 KILDEE BOY, b c 22/2 Interrex (CAN)—National Time (USA) (Lord Avie (USA)) **Mr J. F. O'Donovan**
25 Ch c 5/4 Beveled (USA)—Luly My Love (Hello Gorgeous (USA)) **Mr A. A. King**
26 B c 15/3 Beveled (USA)—Seymour Ann (Krayyan) **Mr S. C. Jones**

MR A. P. JONES—continued

Other Owners: Mr Michael Burley, Mr M. Candy, Mr R. O. Graves, Mr D. M. Hawkins, Mr Steven Hodges, Mr R. D. Nicholas, Dr R. D. Pearce, Mr Peter Penfold, Mr A. Scanlon, Mr G. Weller.

Jockey (Flat): B Doyle.

Jockeys (NH): G Brown, L Harvey, S McNeill, B Powell.

Conditional: S Curran.

Amateur: Mr S Bush.

338   MR C. H. JONES, Cheltenham

Postal: **The Flat, Grove Farm House, Cold Aston, Cheltenham, GL54 3BN.**
Phone: **(01451) 821277 MOBILE (0973) 404770**

1 **ALTO PRINCESS**, 7, b m Noalto—Queen of The Hills **Miss B. Small**
2 **AVRIL ETOILE**, 6, ch m Sharpo—Alsiba **Miss B. Small**
3 **BELLDORAN**, 5, ch g Gildoran—Bellecana **Mrs Ann Taylor**
4, Ch g Fearless Action (USA)—Bishops Bell **Mrs Ann Taylor**
5 **COUNTRY CONCORDE**, 6, b g Ilium—Countrypop **Mr Bob Coles**
6 **COUNTRY PURSUITS**, 5, b m Fearless Action (USA)—Countrypop **Mr Bob Coles**
7, Ch g Fearless Action (USA)—Havaneza **Mrs Ann Taylor**
8 **LAKOTA**, 6, b m Infantry—Lost Legend **The Wishful Thinkers**
9 **POCONO KNIGHT**, 6, gr g Petong—Avahra **Mrs R. C. Jones**
10 **SIR CRUSTY**, 14, br g Gunner B—Brazen **Miss B. Small**
11 **SPARTAN GADFLY**, 8, ch m Rymer—Spartan Imp **Mr T. W. H. Dancer**
12 6, Ch m Rakaposhi King—Spartan Imp **Mr T. W. H. Dancer**
13 **TRUE CHIMES**, 5, ch g True Song—Ballytina **Mrs Ann Taylor**

Jockeys (NH): M Bosley (10-3), G Upton (10-1).

Amateur: Miss B Small (9-7).

339   MR G. ELWYN JONES, Lampeter

Postal: **Lluestnewydd, Bettws, Lampeter, Dyfed, SA48 8PB.**
Phone: **(01570) 493261**

1 **GLASGOW**, 7, b g Top Ville—Glasson Lady (GER) **Mr G. Elwyn Jones**
2 **GRAMPAS' GIRL (IRE)**, 6, b m Callernish—Miss Posy **Mr G. Elwyn Jones**
3 **MIDNIGHT JESTOR (IRE)**, 8, b m Jester—Midnight Patrol **Mr G. Elwyn Jones**

Amateur: Mr D Jones (10-7).

340   MRS M. A. JONES, Lambourn

Postal: **Stork House, Lambourn, Berkshire, RG17 8NU.**
Phone: **LAMBOURN (01488) 72409 MOBILE (0374) 492069 FAX (01488) 72409**

1 **BONNE NUIT**, 5, b g Jeu de Paille (FR)—A Bit of Honey **Mr F. J. Sainsbury**
2 **BROWN ROCCHETTO**, 6, br m Relkino—Brown Veil **Mrs Sue Smith**
3 **EQUINOX**, 5, b g Chauve Souris—Contessa (HUN) **Equinox Syndicate**
4 **GLENFINN PRINCESS**, 8, ch m Ginger Boy—Lady Amazon **Mr Patrick McGinty**
5 **GRAMSCI (IRE)**, 8, br g Miramar Reef—Away And Gone **Mr C. Flear**

MRS M. A. JONES—continued

6 **INDIAN SUMMIT**, 6, gr m Scallywag—Dyna Drueni **Mr F. J. Sainsbury**
7 5, Gr g Cataldi—Languid **Mr Louis Jones**
8 **LAST DECADE (IRE)**, 8, b g Leap High (USA)—Another Decade **Mr Louis Jones**
9 **LIGHT VENEER**, 11, ch g Touching Wood (USA)—Oscilight **Mr Louis Jones**
10 5, Ch g Buckley—Malediction **Mr C. Flear**
11 **MANOLETE**, 5, b g Hard Fought—Andalucia **Mr Louis Jones**
12 **MELROY (IRE)**, 5, b g Le Bavard (FR)—Blackrath Beauty **Mr Louis Jones**
13 **MILL BAY SAM**, 5, b g Lighter—Emancipated **Mill Bay Eng Pump & Turbine Repair Co**
14 **MORE DASH THANCASH (IRE)**, 6, ch g Stalker—Gobolino **Mr F. J. Sainsbury**
15 **ROYAL SHREWSBURY**, 6, ch g Cruise Missile—Hay-Hay **Mr Louis Jones**
16 **SNOW BOARD**, 7, gr g Niniski (USA)—Troja **Mr F. J. Sainsbury**
17 **SPANISH BLAZE (IRE)**, 8, b g Spanish Place (USA)—The Blazing Star
18 **SWEET BEN**, 11, ch g Sweet Monday—Oolywig **Mr Louis Jones**
19 **TARROCK**, 6, ch g Arctic Tern (USA)—In The Habit (USA) **Mr F. J. Sainsbury**
20 **TREASURE AGAIN (IRE)**, 7, b g Treasure Hunter—Ten Again **Mr John Hugo Gwynne**
21 **TWISP**, 5, b g Shirley Heights—Twyla **Mr J. Llewellyn**
22 **ZAMBEZI SPIRIT (IRE)**, 7, b g Over The River (FR)—Chiminee Fly **Mr P. C. Townsend**

Other Owners: Mrs J. L. Brindley, Mr M. R. Cooper, Mrs P. Corbett, Mr L. M. Dodds, Mr W. J. George, Mr L. J. Gwynne, Mr John Randall.

Jockeys (NH): Graham Bradley (10-2), Derek Byrne (10-0), M A Fitzgerald (10-0).

Conditional: J Cook (9-7).

341 MR P. D. JONES, Kingsbridge

Postal: **Wotton Farm, Woodleigh, Kingsbridge, Devon, TQ7 4DP.**
Phone: **(01548) 550222**

1 **DHARAMSHALA (IRE)**, 8, b g Torenaga—Ambitious Lady **Mr P. D. Jones**
2 **FIRST DESIGN**, 9, b g Rustingo—Designer **Mr P. D. Jones**
3 **GLENCOE BOY**, 13, b g Pry—Rainella **Mr P. D. Jones**
4 **IT'S NOT MY FAULT (IRE)**, 8, b g Red Sunset—Glas Y Dorlan **Mr P. D. Jones**
5 **OLD DEER PARK**, 10, b g Blakeney—Hurry On Honey **Mrs Sally Jones**
6 **REALITY PARK**, 5, b g Dreams To Reality (USA)—Everingham Park **Mr P. D. Jones**
7 **TIME TO MOVE (IRE)**, 6, b m Cyrano de Bergerac—June Goddess **Mrs Sally Jones**

Jockeys (NH): M Fitzgerald (w.a.), V Slattery (10-0, w.a.).

Conditional: O Burrows (w.a.).

Amateur: Mr J Cullotty (9-7).

342 MR P. J. JONES, Marlborough

Postal: **Fox Twitchen, East Kennett, Marlborough, Wiltshire, SN8 4EY.**
Phone: **(06782861) 427**

1 **DANTE'S DELIGHT**, 8, b m Idiot's Delight—Super Princess **Mr P. J. Jones**
2 **HAPPY JACK**, 5, b g Pragmatic—Slipalong **Mr P. J. Jones**
3 **TANGO COUNTRY**, 7, b m Town And Country—Lucky Tango **Mr P. J. Jones**
4 **THE SMILING GIRL**, 6, b m Broadsword (USA)—Slipalong **Mr P. J. Jones**

Conditional: D Leahy (9-7, w.a.).

Amateur: Mr L Baker (9-7).

343   MR R. W. JONES, Newmarket

Postal: **Boyden End House, Wickhambrook, Newmarket, Suffolk, CB8 8XX.**

Phone: **(01440) 820342/820664 OR (0831) 481140   FAX (01440) 820958**

1 **CANOVAS HEART**, 7, b g Balidar—Worthy Venture **Print Finisher Club and Osborne Controls**
2 **EUPHYLLIA**, 4, b f Superpower—Anse Chastanet **Mr J. G. Vaughan**
3 **GOLDWYN (USA)**, 4, b c Rainbow Quest (USA)—Golden Treasury (USA) **Horses For Courses Racing Club**
4 **JACK BUTTON (IRE)**, 7, b g Kings Lake (USA)—Tallantire (USA) **A. and B. Racing**
5 **LOOKINGFORARAINBOW (IRE)**, 8, ch g Godswalk (USA)—Bridget Folly **Mr B. M. Saumtally**
6 **MUNAADEE (USA)**, 4, b c Green Dancer (USA)—Aliysa **Mrs J. Woods & Mrs S. Osborne**
7 **RED ADAIR (IRE)**, 4, ch g Waajib—Little Red Hut **Mackenzie Print**
8 **RUDOLPHINE (IRE)**, 5, ch g Persian Bold—Ruffling Point **Syndicate**
9 **SEVENTEENS LUCKY**, 4, gr g Touch of Grey—Westminster Waltz **Mr D. M. Cameron**
10 **SPARA TIR**, 4, b g Dowsing (USA)—Jetelle (USA) **Mr P. J. C. Simmonite**
11 **THE SCYTHIAN**, 4, ch g Komaite (USA)—City To City **Mr David S. Blake**
12 **WATCH ME GO (IRE)**, 7, b g On Your Mark—Nighty Night **Mr Bob Jones**

THREE-YEAR-OLDS

13 **LE TETEU (FR)**, b c Saint Andrews (FR)—Nouvelle Star (USA) **Mr P. J. C. Simmonite**
14 **SIEGE PERILOUS (IRE)**, b c Taufan (USA)—Carado **Mr S. Demanuele**

TWO-YEAR-OLDS

15 Ro c 13/3 Chilibang—Princess Fair (Crowned Prince (USA)) **Mr D. M. Cameron**

Other Owners: Ms Selena Close, Mr A. Collins, Mr Lou Giaracuni, Mrs Janet Mackenzie, Mr M. G. Mackenzie, Mr C. J. Molloy, Mr C. F. Monticolombi, Mr M. J. Osborne, Mr B. Robertshaw, Mr L. G. Snell, Mr R. Westrop.

Jockey (Flat): M Wigham (8-6).

Jockeys (NH): D Bridgwater (w.a.), V Smith (9-7).

Lady Riders: Miss Diana Jane Jones (9-4), Miss Gemma Jones (8-0).

344   MR T. M. JONES, Guildford

Postal: **Brook Farm, Albury, Guildford, Surrey, GU5 9DJ.**

Phone: **SHERE (01483) 202604 (01483) 203749**

1 **HALLIARD**, 5, b g Hallgate—Princess Blanco **The Rest Hill Partnership**
2 **LITTLE SECRET**, 4, ch g Waajib—Talking Shop **Mr T. M. Jones**
3 **MICHAELMAS PARK (IRE)**, 5, ch g Common Grounds—Fresh As A Daisy **Miss Maureen Stopher**
4 **STARCHY'S QUEST**, 4, b g Starch Reduced—Karousa Girl **Mr T. M. Jones**
5 **TROYSTAR**, 5, b g War Hero—Golden Columbine **Mr J. M. Boodle**

THREE-YEAR-OLDS

6 **DIGWANA (IRE)**, b g Digamist (USA)—Siwana (IRE) **Mr Mervyn J. Evans**
7 **LITTLE PILGRIM**, b g Precocious—Bonny Bright Eyes **Mr Richard L. Page**
8 **SWINGALONG GIRL**, ch f Weldnaas (USA)—Singalong Lass **Mr T. M. Jones**
9 **TITANIAS DREAM**, ch f Sula Bula—Moor Frolicking **Mr Mervyn J. Evans**

TWO-YEAR-OLDS

10 B g 12/2 Totem (USA)—Chess Mistress (USA) (Run The Gantlet (USA)) **Mr T. M. Jones**
11 **DOZEN ROSES**, b f 19/4 Rambo Dancer (CAN)—Andbracket (Import) **Mr T. M. Jones**
12 **FOXFORD LAD**, b g 9/5 Akid (USA)—Spring Rose (Blakeney) **Mrs Ann Brown**
13 **LITTLE PROGRESS**, b c 2/6 Rock City—Petite Hester (Wollow) **Mr Richard L. Page**

Other Owners: Mrs John Brookes, Mr Barrie Catchpole, Fleetwood Developments Limited.

Jockey (Flat): R Perham.

345   MR F. T. J. JORDAN, Leominster

Postal: **Butt Oak Farm, Risbury, Leominster, Herefordshire, HR6 0NQ.**

Phone: **PHONE AND FAX (01568) 760281**

1 **BRIGHT SAPPHIRE**, 10, b g Mummy's Pet—Bright Era **Mr D. Roderick**
2 **CARLINGFORD LASS (IRE)**, 6, ch m Carlingford Castle—Clanwilla **Mr R. Cooper**
3 **CRAZY HORSE DANCER (USA)**, 8, b g Barachois (CAN)—Why Pass (USA) **Mr F. Jordan**
4 **DRAGONMIST (IRE)**, 6, b m Digamist (USA)—Etage **Mr D. Roderick**
5 **EASY FOR ME**, 5, b g Mandrake Major—Beads **Supercraft Ind & Farm Buildings Ltd**
6 **FADI**, 5, b g Celestial Storm (USA)—Rachael Tennessee (USA) **Islands Racing Connection**
7 **FIRST BEE**, 5, b m Gunner B—Furstin **Mr D. Pugh**
8 **FIRST CRACK**, 11, b m Scallywag—Furstin **Mr D. Pugh**
9 **GEORGE LANE**, 8, b g Librate—Queen of The Kop **Amtrak Express Parcels Limited**
10 **GOLDEN MADJAMBO**, 10, ch g Northern Tempest (USA)—Shercol **Mr T. P. Roberts-Hindle**
11 **GUNNY'S GIRL**, 5, ch m Scallywag—Girl In Green **Mr Robert Gunthorpe**
12 **LIFE AT SEA (IRE)**, 5, b g Slip Anchor—Exclusive Life (USA) **Mr R. A. Hancocks**
13 **PEUTETRE**, 4, ch c Niniski (USA)—Marchinella **Mr R. V. Cliff**
14 **PRINCE OF SPADES**, 4, ch g Shavian—Diamond Princess
15 **ROSS SPORTING**, 4, b g Derring Rose—Cheetah's Spirit **Mr A. Price**
16 **SAINT CIEL (USA)**, 8, b h Skywalker (USA)—Holy Tobin (USA) **Tam Racing**
17 **SARAVILLE**, 9, ch m Kemal (FR)—Golden Ingot **Mr R. V. Cliff**
18 **SEVERN GALE**, 6, b m Strong Gale—Miss Apex **Mr R. M. Phillips**
19 **SHADY EMMA**, 4, ch f Gunner B—Shady Legacy **Mr D. Pugh**
20 **SHIFTING MOON**, 4, b g Night Shift (USA)—Moonscape **Mrs K. Roberts-Hindle**
21 **SILVER CONCORD**, 8, gr g Absalom—Boarding House **Mrs D. E. Cheshire**
22 **THE CHAIRMAN (IRE)**, 5, b g Last Tycoon—Bhama (FR) **Dr Ian R. Shenkin**
23 **THEM TIMES (IRE)**, 7, b m Petorius—Atropine **Miss L. M. Rochford**
24 **WOODYOU**, 6, b g Gabitat—Jeanne d'Accord **Mr F. Jordan**

THREE-YEAR-OLDS

25 B g Accordion—Anka (GER) **Mr H. Gibney**
26 B f Accordion—Boyne Water (IRE) **Mr H. Gibney**
27 Ch f Little Wolf—Cheetah's Spirit **Mr A. Price**
28 Br f Accordion—Fandikos (IRE) **Mr H. Gibney**
29 B f Accordion—Ritual Girl **Mrs Maureen Shenkin**
30 B f Accordion—River Low (IRE) **Mr H. Gibney**
31 B g Martin John—Twilight In Paris **Dr Ian R. Shenkin**

Other Owners: Mr M. J. Bevan, Mr T. J. Bingham, Mr P. J. A. Bomford, Mrs R. V. Cliff, Mrs Jean Haslam, Mr M. Kear, Mr John McPhee, Mr Paul Robson.

Jockey (NH): Jonathan Lodder (10-0).

Amateur: Mr G Shenkin (10-0).

Lady Rider: Miss V Lucas (8-0).

346   MRS J. JORDAN, Yarm

Postal: **Staindale Lodge, Picton, Yarm, Cleveland, TS15 0AE.**

Phone: **(01642) 701061**

1 **ALILISA (USA)**, 8, b m Alydar (USA)—Balletomane (USA) **Mr J. E. Hulme**
2 6, B g Corvaro (USA)—Dizzy Dot **Mr Roddy McGahon**
3 **DOCTOR'S REMEDY**, 10, br g Doc Marten—Champagne Party **Mr J. O. Addison**
4 **GORODENKA BOY**, 6, ch g Then Again—Simply Jane **Mr P. Szuszkewicz**

MRS J. JORDAN—continued

5 **MARLINGFORD**, 9, ch g Be My Guest (USA)—Inchmarlo (USA) **Miss J. Seaton**
6 **MELEREK**, 21, ch g Menelek—Maureen Og **Mrs J. Jordan**
7 **NUVEEN (IRE)**, 5, br g Al Nasr (FR)—Cactus Road (FR) **Mr P. Szuszkewicz**
8 **RED HOT PRINCE**, 5, b g Sizzling Melody—La Belle Princesse **Mr B. Phizacklea**
9 **SULAAH ROSE**, 7, b m Sula Bula—Dusky Damsel **Mr J. E. Hulme**

THREE-YEAR-OLDS

10 **DARING LAD**, b g Daring March—Kept Waiting **Mr J. O. Addison**
11 **THISONESFORMAGGIE**, ch f Scottish Reel—Touch My Heart **Mr M. W. Mitchell**

TWO-YEAR-OLDS

12 **PERFECT GRACE**, b f 31/3 Lord David S (USA)—Luce Bay (Bronze Hill) **Mrs M. Matthew**

Other Owners: Mr R. I. Graham, Martin Pound Racing Ltd.

347   MR J. JOSEPH, Amersham

Postal: **Cherry Tree Farm, Coleshill, Amersham, Bucks, HP7 OLX.**
Phone: **(0494) 722239**

1 **AL HAAL (USA)**, 7, b g Northern Baby (CAN)—Kit's Double (USA) **Mr Jack Joseph**
2 **ALLIED'S TEAM**, 9, b m Teamwork—Allied Beaumel **Mr Jack Joseph**
3 **ANIF (USA)**, 5, b g Riverman (USA)—Marnie's Majik (USA) **Mr Jack Joseph**
4 **BUNDERBURG (USA)**, 6, b br g Nureyev (USA)—Hortensia (FR) **Mr Jack Joseph**
5 **CAVO GRECO (USA)**, 7, b g Riverman (USA)—Cypria Sacra (USA) **Mr Jack Joseph**
6 **IVYCHURCH (USA)**, 10, ch g Sir Ivor—Sunday Purchase (USA) **Mr Jack Joseph**
7 **MILZIG (USA)**, 7, b g Ziggy's Boy—Legume (USA) **Mr Jack Joseph**
8 **SIESTA TIME (USA)**, 6, ch m Cure The Blues (USA)—Villa Rose (USA) **Mr Jack Joseph**
9 **THE EXECUTOR**, 6, ch g Vaigly Great—Fee **Mr Jack Joseph**
10 **WARSPITE**, 6, b g Slip Anchor—Valkyrie **Mr Jack Joseph**

Other Owners: Sarena Plastics.

348   MR R. T. JUCKES, Abberley

Postal: **The Cherryash, Worsley Racing Stables, Abberley, Worcester, WR6 6BQ**
Phone: **GREAT WITLEY (01299) 896471 OR (01299) 896522**

1 **FETTUCCINE**, 12, ch g Bybicello—Reel Keen **Mr J. Wilson Walker**
2 **FOX CHAPEL**, 9, b g Formidable (USA)—Hollow Heart **Mr Barry Hine**
3 **HARD TO BREAK**, 5, b g High Season—Frogmore Sweet **Mrs M. Minett**
4 **INSIOUXBORDINATE**, 4, ch g Mandrake Major—Siouxsie **Mr A. C. W. Price**
5 **KEDGE**, 6, b g Slip Anchor—Bercheba **Mr S. Hibbert**
6 **KENNINGTON KUWAIT**, 6, ch g Bairn (USA)—Mylotta **Kennington Service Station**
7 **LANCER (USA)**, 4, ch g Diesis—Last Bird (USA) **Mr A. C. W. Price**
8 **LOVE OF THE NORTH (IRE)**, 5, b g Nordico (USA)—Avec L'Amour **Mr R. T. Juckes**
9 **MEGAMUNCH (IRE)**, 8, ch g Deep Run—Raby **Mr R. K. Armstrong**
10 4, B g Starch Reduced—Otterden **Mr R. T. Juckes**
11 **SECRET SERENADE**, 5, b g Classic Secret (USA)—Norfolk Serenade **Mr A. C. W. Price**
12 **SLIPPERY MAX**, 12, b g Nicholas Bill—Noammo **Mr P. M. Clarke**
13 **SPEEDY SIOUX**, 7, ch m Mandrake Major—Sioux Be It **Mr G. A. Martin**
14 **STIFF DRINK**, 5, ch g Starch Reduced—Karousa Girl **The Good Fun Racing Club**
15 4, B f High Kicker (USA)—Welsh Flute **Mr R. T. Juckes**

THREE-YEAR-OLDS

16 **ABDUCTION**, ch g Risk Me (FR)—Spirit Away **Mr R. T. Juckes**
17 B f Lord Bud—Cookie Time **Mr R. T. Juckes**
18 **MARGI BOO**, ch f Risk Me (FR)—Louisianalightning **Mr A. C. W. Price**

MR R. T. JUCKES—continued

TWO-YEAR-OLDS

19 B c 2/2 Starch Reduced—Otterden (Crooner) **Mr R. T. Juckes**
20 Gr f 18/2 Teamster—Play It Sam (Mandamus) **Mr G. A. Martin**
21 Ch f 11/4 Sunley Builds—Windmill Sails (Pollerton) **Mr R. T. Juckes**

Other Owners: Mrs A. E. Barlow, Mr J. Barry, Mr B. Benton, Mrs Sue Hine, Mr K. C. Lewis, Mr D. Liyod, Mr S. Piggot.

Jockey (NH): A Thornton (w.a.).

Conditional: G Tormey (w.a.).

349   MR M. KAUNTZE, Ashbourne

Postal: **Bullstown, Ashbourne, Co. Meath, Ireland.**

Phone: **DUBLIN (01) 8350440 FAX DUBLIN (01) 8351606 MOBILE (088) 586273**

1 DANCE ACADEMY (IRE), 4, ch f Royal Academy (USA)—Gemaasheh **Mr M. Haga**
2 DEVIL'S HOLIDAY (USA), 6, b g Devil's Bag (USA)—Mizima (USA) **Mr M. Haga**
3 INAKA (IRE), 4, b f Ballad Rock—Our Village **Mr M. Haga**
4 JAKDUL, 5, b g Nordance (USA)—Melika Iran **Lt. Col. W. Newell**
5 MAKE AN EFFORT (IRE), 5, ch g Try My Best (USA)—Tiptoe **Mrs Michael Kauntze**
6 PERSIAN HALO (USA), 8, br g Sunny's Halo (CAN)—Persian Susan (USA) **Tematron Racing Club**
7 THE PUZZLER (IRE), 5, br g Sharpo—Enigma **Lady Wellesley**

THREE-YEAR-OLDS

8 ANCIENT CHINA, b c Old Vic—Shajan **Sheikh Mohammed**
9 BATH HOUSE BOY (IRE), b g Don't Forget Me—Domiciliate **Mrs Michael Kauntze**
10 BLUE BIT (IRE), b g Bluebird (USA)—Minnie Habit **Mrs E. M. Burke**
11 COSSACK COUNT (USA), ch c Nashwan (USA)—Russian Countess (USA) **Sheikh Mohammed**
12 COUVERTURE, b f Lear Fan (USA)—Sugar Hollow (USA) **Sheikh Mohammed**
13 ESCAMILLO, b c Old Vic—Flamenco (USA) **Sheikh Mohammed**
14 ESPIEL, b c Belmez—Ste Nitouche **Sheikh Mohammed**
15 JUST LOOKING, b f Marju (IRE)—Finlandia **Mr M. Haga**
16 KEAL RYAN, b g Petorius—Paddy's Joy **Eugene O'Connor**
17 NOBLE GRASS, b f Caerleon (USA)—Sine Labe (USA) **Mr M. Haga**
18 SONG OF THE SWORD, b g Kris—Melodist (USA) **Sheikh Mohammed**
19 B g Persian Heights—Spring Reel **M. C. Throsby**
20 THE TODDY TAPPER (IRE), b br g Digamist (USA)—Lockwood Girl **Mrs Michael Kauntze**
21 TIJUANA TANGO, ch f Tejano (USA)—Northern Prancer (USA) **C. S. Gaisford St. Lawrence**
22 TIROL HOPE, b f Tirol—Salique **M. Cattaneo**

TWO-YEAR-OLDS

23 B c 4/5 Pursuit of Love—Bambolona
24 BINNEAS, b br f 5/5 Roi Danzig (USA)—Lady Celina (FR) **Vincent Loughnane**
25 B br f 17/3 Tejano—Half Moon Hotel **E. Flynn**
26 B c 3/2 Alwuhush (USA)—Hoedown Honey
27 B f 9/4 Cyrano de Bergerac—Isa **Ardmol Chan Syndicate**
28 Ch f 14/2 A P Indy—Kooyonga **Mr M. Haga**

Other Owners: John Leat, Sir T. Pilkington.

Jockey (Flat): Warren O'Connor (8-5).

Lady Rider: Miss Sophia Kauntze (9-3).

350   MR H. M. KAVANAGH, Bodenham

Postal: **Mereside, Church Road, Bodenham, Hereford, HR1 3JU.**

Phone: **(01568) 797048**

1 **DARK DIAMOND**, 6, br g Good Times (ITY)—Flame **Mrs S. Kavanagh**

351   MISS G. M. KELLEWAY, Whitcombe

Postal: **Whitcombe Manor Racing Stables, Whitcombe, Dorset, DT2 8NY.**

Phone: **OFFICE (01305) 257353 FAX (01305) 257354 MOBILE (0585) 701415**

1 **AJDAR**, 5, b g Slip Anchor—Loucoum (FR) **Mrs S. Catt**
2 **ALJAZ**, 5, b g Al Nasr (FR)—Santa Linda (USA) **Mr D. C. Toogood**
3 **ALKATEB**, 4, ch g Rock City—Corley Moor **Miss L. Crowley**
4 **ALMUHTARAM**, 4, b g Rambo Dancer (CAN)—Mrs Mainwaring (FR) **Mr A. M. Al-Midani**
5 **ALWAYS GRACE**, 4, b f Never So Bold—Musical Sally (USA) **Easy Going Partnership**
6 **ANSAL BOY**, 4, b c Robellino (USA)—Son Et Lumiere **Mr E. Donnelly**
7 **AWASHA (IRE)**, 4, b f Fairy King (USA)—Foliage **Mr H. Al-Mutawa**
8 **DAILY STARLIGHT (USA)**, 4, br g Minshaanshu Amad (USA)—Appeal The Rule (USA) **Mr A. Al-Radi**
9 **DISCORSI**, 4, b g Machiavellian (USA)—Bustara **Mr S. May**
10 **FATHER DAN (IRE)**, 7, ch g Martin John—Sonia John **Wessex Fm (Whitcombe) Racing Club Ltd**
11 **FLOWING OCEAN**, 6, ch h Forzando—Boswellia **Mr F. Al-Nassar**
12 **FRIENDLY BRAVE (USA)**, 6, b g Well Decorated (USA)—
                              Companionship (USA) **Grid Thoroughbred Racing Partnership**
13 **GOLDEN POUND (USA)**, 4, b c Seeking The Gold (USA)—Coesse Express (USA) **Mr F. M. Kalla**
14 **HANIFA**, 4, ch f Master Willie—Antoinette Jane **Mr K. Mahdi**
15 **LORD JIM (IRE)**, 4, b c Kahyasi—Sarah Georgina **Mrs S. Y. Thomas**
16 **MOODY**, 4, ch f Risk Me (FR)—Bocas Rose **Mr Brian T. Eastick**
17 **NISYA**, 4, ch f Risk Me (FR)—Lompoa **Mr K. Mahdi**
18 **OPERA BUFF (IRE)**, 5, br g Rousillon (USA)—Obertura (USA) **Mr D. C. Toogood**
19 **PERFECT PAL (IRE)**, 5, ch g Mulhollande (USA)—Gone **Whitcombe Manor Racing Stables Limited**
20 **ROCK ON HONEY**, 4, b g Rock City—Be My Honey **Thai Racing**
21 **SAMWAR**, 4, b g Warning—Samaza (USA) **Maygain Ltd**
22 **STAR TALENT (USA)**, 5, b h Local Talent (USA)—Sedra **Mr R. Abdullah and Miss Jo Crowley**
23 **WAR REQUIEM (IRE)**, 6, b h Don't Forget Me—Ladiz **Whitcombe Manor Racing Stables Limited**

THREE-YEAR-OLDS

24 **ALFAHAD**, b c Doyoun—Moogie **Mr A. Al-Radi**
25 **ALMUSHTARAK (IRE)**, b c Fairy King (USA)—Exciting **Mr A. Al-Radi**
26 **ANAK-KU**, ch c Efisio—City Link Lass **H.R.H. Sultan Ahmad Shah**
27 **FORZA FIGLIO**, b c Warning—Wish You Well **Grid Thoroughbred Racing Partnership**
28 **GLOWING MOON**, b f Kalaglow—Julia Flyte **Mr B. T. Eastick**
29 **KRISCLIFFE**, ch c Kris—Lady Norcliffe (USA) **Mr P. Idris**
30 Br c Kalaglow—Sabrine **Whitcombe Manor Racing Stables Limited**
31 **SCENIC SPIRIT (IRE)**, b f Scenic—Quality of Life **Mr A. Al-Radi**
32 **SORBIE TOWER (IRE)**, b c Soviet Lad (USA)—Nozet **P. D. Q.**

TWO-YEAR-OLDS

33 B f 27/4 Alzao (USA)—Dawning Beauty (USA) (Well Decorated (USA)) **H.R.H. Sultan Ahmad Shah**
34 **DESERT WARRIOR (IRE)**, b c 11/3 Fairy King (USA)—Highland Girl (USA) (Sir Ivor) **Mr A. Al-Radi**
35 Gr c 3/5 Absalom—Inca Girl (Tribal Chief) **Mr P. Idris**
36 **MISS DALAL (USA)**, b f 7/4 Minshaanshu Amad—Appeal The Rule (USA) (Valid Appeal (USA)) **Mr A. Al-Radi**
37 **MUPPET**, b f 29/4 Law Society (USA)—Shaadin (USA) (Sharpen Up) **Mr D. C. Toogood**
38 B f 13/3 Sadler's Wells (USA)—Sweeping (Indian King (USA)) **H.R.H. Sultan Ahmad Shah**

MISS G. M. KELLEWAY—continued

Other Owners: Mr Peter R. Bolton, Mr M. J. Bolwell, Cavendish Racing Ltd, Mr Ron Dawson, Mr Paul Dean, Mrs M. Fairbairn, Mr J. F. Hanna, Mrs Liz Nelson, Mr James Robertson, Mr G. Sharp, Mr David Whitefield, Mr I. Wicks, Mr Chris Wilkinson, Mrs Christine Wood.

Jockey (Flat): R Cochrane.

Jockey (NH): A Maguire (w.a.).

Apprentices: D O'Neill, A Whelan.

Conditional: L Reynolds.

Amateur: Mr Marcus Armytage.

Lady Riders: Miss Sarah Kelleway (8-0), Miss Lucy Vollaro (8-7).

352   MR P. A. KELLEWAY, Newmarket

Postal: **Paul Kelleway Bloodstock, Shalfleet, 17 Bury Road, Newmarket, CB8 7BX.**

Phone: **(01638) 661461 FAX (01638) 666238 MOBILE (0836) 510233**

1 **ANCHOR CLEVER,** 4, b c Slip Anchor—Mountain Bluebird (USA) **Mr Osvaldo Pedroni**
2 **BARTOK (IRE),** 5, b h Fairy King—Euromill **Mr A. Balzarini**
3 **FRESH FRUIT DAILY,** 4, b f Reprimand—Dalmally **Mr Kevin Hudson**
4 **RISKY TU,** 5, ch m Risk Me (FR)—Sarah Gillian (USA) **Mr Lewis H. Norris**
5 **SASSIVER (USA),** 6, b g Riverman (USA)—Sassabunda **Mr P. A. Kelleway**

THREE-YEAR-OLDS

6 **CHARNWOOD NELL (USA),** ch f Arctic Tern (USA)—Aphilandra **Chancery Bourse Inv (Brick Kiln Stud)**
7 **CRYSTAL FAST (USA),** b c Fast Play (USA)—Crystal Cave (USA) **Mr Lewis H. Norris**
8 **CYRILLIC,** ch f Rock City—Lariston Gale **Chancery Bourse Inv (Brick Kiln Stud)**
9 **MISS PICKPOCKET (IRE),** b f Petorius—Fingers **Mr F. M. Kalla**
10 **MR SPECULATOR,** ch g Kefaah (USA)—Humanity **The Speculators**
11 **POSEN GOLD (IRE),** b f Posen (USA)—Golden Sunlight **Mr F. M. Kalla**
12 **TOMBA LA BOMBA (USA),** b br c Green Dancer (USA)—Easter Mary (USA) **Mr Osvaldo Pedroni**
13 **ZELZELAH (USA),** b f Timeless Moment (USA)—Allevition (USA) **Mr P. A. Kelleway**

TWO-YEAR-OLDS

14 B f 13/2 Septieme Ciel (USA)—Becomes A Rose (CAN) (Deputy Minister (CAN)) **M. Hurley & PLT Partnership**
15 **BOBBY SWIFT,** ch c 2/6 Wing Park—Satin Box (Jukebox) **Wing Park Progeny Syndicate**
16 Ch c 15/4 Indian Ridge—Clare Celeste (Coquelin (USA)) **Gerecon Italia spa**
17 B f 25/3 Imperial Frontier—Fantasy To Reality (IRE) (Jester) **Mr L. Madden & Partners**
18 Ch f 16/3 Beau Genius (CAN)—First Division (CHI) (Domineau (USA)) **Mr F. M. Kalla & PLT Partnership**
19 **GALIBIS (FR),** b c 11/3 Groom Dancer (USA)—Damasquine (USA) (Damascus (USA)) **Gerecon Italia spa**
20 **HALOWING (USA),** b f 19/2 Danzatore (CAN)—Halo Ho (USA) (Halo (USA)) **Mr R. Trontz & Partners**
21 **LOGICA (IRE),** b f 7/4 Priolo (USA)—Salagangai (Sallust) **Mr Osvaldo Pedroni**
22 **MAGIC SUNRISE (USA),** b f 2/3 Pleasant Colony (USA)—
                               Tewksbury Garden (USA) (Wolf Power (SAF)) **Mr R. Trontz & Partners**
23 B f 29/1 Twilight Agenda (USA)—Maikai (USA) (Never Bend) **Mr F. M. Kalla & PLT Partnership**
24 B c 26/3 Shirley Heights—Mountain Bluebird (USA) (Clever Trick (USA)) **Mr Osvaldo Pedroni**
25 **NERO VIC,** b f 5/4 Old Vic—Light And Light (Head For Heights) **Mr Osvaldo Pedroni**
26 **NOT FORGOTTEN (USA),** b br c 21/5 St Jovite (USA)—
                               Past Remembered (USA) (Solford (USA)) **Mr R. Trontz & Partners**
27 **PAULY SPATY,** b f 20/3 Saddlers' Hall (IRE)—Catherine Farrel (FR) (Bellypha) **Mr Osvaldo Pedroni**
28 Ch f 26/3 Septieme Ciel (USA)—Princess Verna (USA) (Al Hattab (USA)) **Mr Lewis H. Norris & PLT Partnership**
29 Ch c 20/2 Carnivalay (USA)—
                               Royal Millinery (USA) (Regal And Royal (USA)) **Mr R. Belderson & PLT Partnership**
30 Ch f 9/4 Stop The Music (USA)—
                               Time On End (USA) (Timeless Moment (USA)) **Mr Lewis H. Norris & PLT Partnership**
31 Ch c 4/4 Sharpo—Tower Glades (Tower Walk) **Gerecon Italia spa**

MR P. A. KELLEWAY—continued

32 WEST RIVER (USA), ch f 19/2 Gone West (USA)—Rix River (USA) (Irish River (FR)) **Mr Osvaldo Pedroni**
33 B f 26/4 Unfuwain (USA)—Whitstar (Whitstead) **Gerecon Italia spa**

Other Owners: Mr A. Cleary, Mrs G. E. Kelleway.

Apprentice: A Gibbons (7-7).

Lady Rider: Miss S Kelleway (7-10).

353   MR G. P. KELLY, Sheriff Hutton

Postal: **Golden Flatts Farm, Torrington Road, Sheriff Hutton, York, YO6 1RS.**
Phone: **STABLES (01347) 878518 HOME (01347) 878770**

1 BARON TWO SHOES, 10, gr g Baron Blakeney—Win Shoon Please **Mr R. Harland**
2 BIBBY BEAR, 7, b m Sunley Builds—Coin All **Mr R. Harland**
3 BITCH, 4, ch f Risk Me (FR)—Lightning Legend **Mr R. Naylor**
4 KING BOO, 10, b g Van Der Linden (FR)—Star Bella **Mr N. A. Crawshaw**
5 LADY KHADIJA, 10, b m Nicholas Bill—Chenkynowa **Mr A. Barrett**
6 LAUDIBLE, 11, ch g Formidable (USA)—Clouds **Mr G. P. Kelly**
7 OFF THE LATCH, 9, b g Mandalus—Candora **Mr G. P. Kelly**
8, Ch f Glacial Storm (USA)—Princess Sunshine **Mr A. Barrett**
9 ROYAL FAN, 13, br g Taufan (USA)—Miss Royal **Mr Phillip Kneafsey**
10 SPORTING SPIRIT, 6, br g Dunbeath (USA)—Silent Plea **Mr G. P. Kelly**

Other Owners: Mr M. W. Easterby, Mrs Norma Robinson.

Jockey (NH): J Driscoll.

Amateurs: Mr M Keswick (9-7), Mr C Mulhall (10-9).

Lady Riders: Miss Sarah Brotherton, Miss Alex Greeves.

354   MR W. T. KEMP, Duns

Postal: **Drake Myre, Grants House, Duns, Berwickshire, TD11 3RL.**
Phone: **(01361) 850242**

1 BRUZ, 5, b g Risk Me (FR)—My Croft **Miss Julie Melville**
2 COPPERHURST (IRE), 5, ch m Royal Vulcan—Little Katrina **Mr W. T. Kemp**
3 D'ARBLAY STREET (IRE), 7, b g Pauper—Lady Abednego VII **Green For Luck**
4 FARNDALE, 9, gr g Vaigly Great—Beloved Mistress **Mr A. J. Thurgood**
5 JACKMANII, 4, b g Most Welcome—Blue Flower (FR) **Mr I. Anderson**
6 PERSIANSKY (IRE), 6, b g Persian Bold—Astra Adastra **Mr W. T. Kemp**
7 RICANA, 4, ch f Rich Charlie—Woolcana **Mr W. T. Kemp**
8 WHIRLWIND ROMANCE (IRE), 5, br m Strong Gale—Forever Together **Mr J. B. Mitchell**
9 YOUNG STEVEN, 5, b g Singing Steven—Adoration (FR) **Mr A. J. Thurgood**

THREE-YEAR-OLDS
10 PHAR CLOSER, br f Phardante (FR)—Forever Together **Mr J. B. Mitchell**

MR W. T. KEMP—continued

TWO-YEAR-OLDS

11 B c 20/3 King Among Kings—Heavenly Pet (Petong)
12 B c 16/4 Rope Trick—Pilar (Godswalk (USA))
13 B c 11/5 Exactly Sharp (USA)—Reine de Chypre (FR) (Habitat)

Other Owners: Mr William Burns, Mr G. A. Fordham, Mr Paul Hone, Mr G. McGuinness, Mr Tommy Naughton.

Jockey (NH): S McDougall (10-0).

355   MRS M. A. KENDALL, Penrith

Postal: **Wood Side, Great Strickland, Penrith, Cumbria, CA10 4DX.**
Phone: **HACKTHORPE (01931) 712318**

1 ANOTHER DYER, 12, ch g Deep Run—Saint Society **Mrs M. A. Kendall**
2 MARKED CARD, 8, b g Busted—Winter Queen **Mrs M. A. Kendall**
3 NOSMO KING (IRE), 5, b g Nordico (USA)—Selenis **Mrs M. A. Kendall**
4 OBVIOUS RISK, 5, b g Risk Me (FR)—Gymnopedie **Mrs M. A. Kendall**
5 PERFECT BERTIE (IRE), 4, b g Cyrano de Bergerac—Perfect Chance **Mrs M. A. Kendall**

Lady Rider: Mrs M A Kendall (9-7).

356   MR S. E. KETTLEWELL, Middleham

Postal: **Tupgill Park Stables, Middleham, Leyburn, N. Yorkshire, DL8 4TJ.**
Phone: **OFFICE (01969) 640411 FAX 640494 HOSTEL 640295 MOBILE (0421) 614983**

1 BRIEF REUNION (USA), 5, ch g Arctic Tern (USA)—Sweetened Offer **Miss N. F. Thesiger**
2 CHIEF OF KHORASSAN (FR), 4, br g Nishapour (FR)—Amber's Image **Middleham Park Racing**
3 CRUISING KATE, 8, b m Cruise Missile—Katebird **Hollinbridge Racing**
4 EASBY JOKER, 8, b g Idiot's Delight—Be Spartan **Mr G. R. Orchard**
5 EUROTWIST, 7, b g Viking (USA)—Orange Bowl **Mr Raymond Gomersall**
6 FASIH, 4, b g Rock City—Nastassia (FR) **Mr J. Tennant**
7 4, B f Petong—Friendly Glen **Mr A. Williams**
8 GINJA NINJA (IRE), 4, ch g Jareer (USA)—Mallee **Mr J. Lancaster**
9 HIGHSPEED (IRE), 4, ch g Double Schwartz—High State **Mr D. Wright**
10 HOSTILE ACT, 11, b g Glenstal (USA)—Fandetta **Mr J. Titley**
11 HUSHABAB, 5, ch g Kind of Hush—Princess Arabrab **Mrs B. Powell**
12 IRON GENT (USA), 5, b g Greinton—Carrot Top **Mr J. S. Calvert**
13 JUST BOB, 7, b g Alleging (USA)—Diami **Mr J. Fotherby**
14 MALZOOM, 4, b g Statoblest—Plum Bold **Mr S. Lowe**
15 PRECIOUS HENRY, 7, b g Myjinski (USA)—Friendly Glen **Mr S. Kettlewell**
16 RESPECT A SECRET, 4, ch f Respect—Pendle's Secret **Mrs P. Simpson**
17 ROSEATE LODGE, 10, b g Habitat—Elegant Tern (USA) **Mrs D. Kettlewell**
18 ROSY LYDGATE, 5, br m Last Tycoon—Sing Softly **Mr D. Barker**
19 SHERQY (IRE), 4, br c Persian Bold—Turkish Treasure (USA) **Miss N. F. Thesiger**
20 WHATASHOWMAN (IRE), 4, b g Exhibitioner—Whatawoman **Mr J. Firth**
21 YAAKUM, 7, b g Glint of Gold—Nawadder **Mr I. Thompson**

THREE-YEAR-OLDS

22 GRAND POPO, b c Salse (USA)—Rose Cordial (USA) **Mr A. Craven**
23 JENNY'S CHARMER, ch g Charmer—Jenny Wyllie **The Glatton Partnership**

Other Owners: Mr T. E. Kettlewell, Mr S. J. Raby, Mr Ian Thompson.

Jockey (Flat): J Fortune.

Jockey (NH): R Garritty.

Apprentice: J Stockton (8-0).

Conditional: S Porritt (9-7).

Lady Rider: Mrs D Kettlewell (9-0).

357 MRS A. L. M. KING, Stratford-upon-Avon

Postal: **Ridgeway House, Moor Farm, Wilmcote, Stratford-upon-Avon, CV37 9XG.**
Phone: **OFFICE (01789) 205087 HOME 298346 FAX 205087**

1 **CHARMED LIFE**, 7, b g Legend of France (USA)—Tanagrea **Mr Peter A. Brazier**
2 **FOLLOWMEGIRLS**, 7, b m Sparkling Boy—Haddon Anna **Exors of the late Mr J. Martin**
3 **JOHN O'DREAMS**, 11, b g Indian King (USA)—Mississipi Shuffle **Mr Peter A. Brazier**
4 **LAMPER'S LIGHT**, 6, b m Idiot's Delight—Lampstone **Mr Nick Skelton**
5 **L'EGLISE BELLE**, 4, b f Minster Son—Haddon Anna **Mr H. A. Murphy**
6 4, B f Ring Bidder—Lucky Joker **Mr G. Farndon**
7 **MAGGIE STRAIT**, 4, b f Rolfe (USA)—Pink Swallow **Mr L. Gotch & Mrs A. King**
8 **THE DEACONESS**, 5, b m Minster Son—Haddon Anna **Mrs Jennie Clarke**

THREE-YEAR-OLDS

9 **BELDRAY PARK (IRE)**, b br c Superpower—Ride Bold (USA) **Stainless Threaded Fasteners Ltd**
10 **FAIRY PRINCE (IRE)**, b c Fairy King (USA)—Danger Ahead **Mr A. Stennett**
11 **MAY KING MAYHEM**, ch c Great Commotion (USA)—Queen Ranavalona **Mr S. J. Harrison**
12 **MAY QUEEN MEGAN**, gr f Petorius—Siva (FR) **Mr S. J. Harrison**
13 B c Ballacashtal (CAN)—Mio Mementa **Mr H. A. Murphy**

TWO-YEAR-OLDS

14 **TUKAPA**, b g 27/3 Risk Me (FR)—Haddon Anna (Dragonara Palace (USA)) **Mrs A. Martin**

Other Owners: Mrs Angela Fayers, Mr T. P. Hilliam, Mr Douglas King, Mrs J. M. Stennett.

Jockeys (Flat): A Garth, A Munro (w.a.), M Roberts (w.a.).

Jockey (NH): S McNeill (w.a.).

358 MR J. S. KING, Swindon

Postal: **Elm Cross House, Swindon Road, Broad Hinton, Swindon, SN4 9PF.**
Phone: **(01793) 731481 MOBILE (0836) 245393 & (0378) 976114**

1 **ACCESS SUN**, 9, b g Pharly (FR)—Princesse du Seine (FR) **Dajam Ltd**
2 **AKULITE**, 6, b g Rakaposhi King—Macusla **Mr S. Clough**
3 **A N C EXPRESS**, 8, gr g Pragmatic—Lost In Silence **Mr Mark O'Connor**
4 **CAPENWRAY (IRE)**, 7, br g Supreme Leader—Godetia **Mr B. K. Peppiatt**
5 **CHIEF CELT**, 10, ch g Celtic Cone—Chieftain's Lady **Mrs J. J. Peppiatt**
6 **CHUCKLESTONE**, 13, b g Chukaroo—Czar's Diamond **Mrs P. M. King**
7 **CLAYMORE LAD**, 6, b g Broadsword (USA)—Cannes Beach **Marlborough Racing Partnership**
8 **COOL GUNNER**, 6, b g Gunner B—Coolek **Mr Richard Peterson**
9 **DUBELLE**, 6, b m Dubassoff (USA)—Flopsy Mopsy **Mrs A. E. Lee**
10 **EHTEFAAL (USA)**, 5, b g Alysheba (USA)—Bolt From The Blue (USA) **Ms M. Horan**
11 4, B f Welsh Captain—Eloquence
12 **FORTUNES COURSE (IRE)**, 7, b m Crash Course—Night Rose **Mrs A. J. Garrett**
13 **FORTUNES GLEAM (IRE)**, 5, b m Tremblant—Night Rose **Mrs A. J. Garrett**
14 **FORTUNES ROSE (IRE)**, 4, b f Tremblant—Night Rose **Mrs A. J. Garrett**
15 **GILSTON LASS**, 9, b m Majestic Streak—Cannes Beach **Marlborough Racing Partnership**
16 **HILLSWICK**, 5, ch g Norwick (USA)—Quite Lucky **Mr M. G. A. Court**
17 **IL FURETTO**, 4, b g Emarati (USA)—Irresistable **Mrs Marygold O'Kelly**
18 **INCHCAILLOCH (IRE)**, 7, b g Lomond (USA)—Glowing With Pride **Mr F. J. Carter**
19 **LIGHTENING LAD**, 8, b g Pragmatic—Miss Lightening **Mr Richard Peterson**
20 **LITTLE TOM**, 11, b g Nearly A Hand—Lost In Silence **Mr Mark O'Connor**
21 **MANILA BAY (USA)**, 6, b g Manila (USA)—Betty Money (USA) **Dajam Ltd**
22 **MARCHMAN**, 11, b g Daring March—Saltation **Mrs P. M. King**

MR J. S. KING—continued

23 **MISTER ODDY**, 10, b g Dubassoff (USA)—Somerford Glory **Mrs R. M. Hill**
24 **MONUMENT**, 4, ch g Cadeaux Genereux—In Perpetuity **Ms M. Horan**
25 **MOYMET**, 10, b g Jester—Majesta **Mr E. J. Mangan**
26 **NIKAROO**, 10, b br m Chukaroo—Nikali **Mrs Carrie Janaway**
27 **QUIET DAWN**, 10, b m Lighter—Lost In Silence **Mrs P. M. King**
28 **RELATIVE CHANCE**, 7, b g Relkino—Chance A Look **Miss S. Douglas-Pennant**
29 **RIVAGE BLEU**, 9, b g Valiyar—Rose d'Aunou (FR) **Mr C. D. King**
30 **ROVESTAR**, 5, b g Le Solaret (FR)—Gilberts Choice **Mr G. Burr**
31 **SULLAMELL**, 5, b g Sulaafah (USA)—Melody Lane **Mr J. G. Hodder**
32 **TURPIN'S GREEN**, 13, b g Nearly A Hand—Maria's Piece **Mrs P. M. King**

Other Owners: Mr D. Braithwaite, Mr R. W. Brien, Mr P. A. Deal, Mr F. P. Forbes, Mr J. S. King, Mr Alan Lee, Mr J. Newsome, Mr Eric Penny, Mr D. R. Peppiatt, Mr H. K. Porter, Mrs A. M. Whatley.

359   MR T. R. KINSEY, Ashton

Postal: **Peel Hall, Ashton, Chester, CH3 8AY.**

1 **ALBERT BLAKE**, 9, b g Roscoe Blake—Ablula **Mrs T. R. Kinsey**
2 **FIBREGUIDE TECH**, 13, b g Uncle Pokey—Starcat **Mrs T. R. Kinsey**
3 **PO CAP EEL**, 6, b m Uncle Pokey—Hejera **Mrs T. R. Kinsey**
4 **SCORPOTINA**, 7, b m Scorpio (FR)—Ablula **Mrs T. R. Kinsey**
5 **STEEL GOLD**, 6, gr g Sonnen Gold—Ablula **Mrs T. R. Kinsey**

360   MR F. KIRBY, Northallerton

Postal: **High Whinholme Farm, Streetlam, Danby Wiske, Northallerton.**
Phone: **(01325) 378213 FAX (01325) 378213**

1 **DESPERATE DAYS (IRE)**, 7, b g Meneval (USA)—Grageelagh Lady **Mr Fred Kirby**
2 **MCLOUGHLIN (IRE)**, 7, ch g Orchestra—Boyne Bridge **Mr Fred Kirby**
3 **ORWELL ROSS (IRE)**, 8, b g Roselier (FR)—Orwell Brief **Mr Fred Kirby**

Jockey (NH): R J Supple (9-7).

361   MR J. KIRBY, Wantage

Postal: **Pewit Farm, The Ridgeway, Manor Road, Wantage, OX12 8LY.**
Phone: **PHONE/FAX (01235) 767987**

1 **THE BRATPACK (IRE)**, 6, b m Mister Majestic—Lady Probus **Mr John Kirby**
2 **TISSISAT (USA)**, 7, ch g Green Forest (USA)—Expansive **Mr John Kirby**

Jockey (NH): G Upton (10-2).

Conditional: S Mitchell (9-7).

362   MISS H. C. KNIGHT, Wantage

Postal: **West Lockinge Farm, Wantage, Oxon, OX12 8QF.**

Phone: **(01235) 833535 FAX 820110 MOBILE (0860) 110153 CAR (0589) 805597**

1 **BEST OF FRIENDS (IRE)**, 6, ch g King Persian—Alto Mira **J. McGrath & R. Griffin**
2 **BISHOPS ISLAND**, 10, b g The Parson—Gilded Empress **Lord Vestey**
3 **CAMINO**, 9, b g Carlingford Castle—Vamble **I. A. Castle**
4 **CAPO CASTANUM**, 7, ch g Sula Bula—Joscilla **Mr D. C. G. Gyle-Thompson**
5 **CAULKIN (IRE)**, 5, b g Dry Dock—Tondbad **Executive Racing**
6 **COLONEL BLAZER**, 4, b g Jupiter Island—Glen Dancer **Mr T. H. Shrimpton**
7 **COURT JOKER (IRE)**, 4, b g Fools Holme (USA)—Crimson Glen **The Court Jokers**
8 **COXWELL STEPTOE**, 6, b g Relkino—Stepout **Mr M. E. R. Allsopp**
9 **DEBUTANTE DAYS**, 4, ch f Dominion—Doogali **Mrs Shirley Brasher**
10 **DORKING RANGER**, 11, b g Full of Hope—Miss Melita **Mr I. D. MacDonald**
11 **DUSKY ROVER (IRE)**, 7, ch g Denel (FR)—Dream Away **Dr George Scott**
12 **EASTHORPE**, 8, b g Sweet Monday—Crammond Brig **Mr Martin Broughton**
13 **EDIMBOURG**, 10, b g Top Ville—Miss Brodie (FR) **Mrs Iva Winton**
14 **FACTOR TEN (IRE)**, 8, b g Kemal (FR)—Kissowen **Premier Crops Limited**
15 **FIDDLER'S LEAP (IRE)**, 4, br g Phardante (FR)—Chief Dilke **Mrs A. M. Davis**
16 **FULL OF OATS**, 10, b g Oats—Miss Melita **Mr I. D. MacDonald**
17 **GAELIC MILLION (IRE)**, 5, b m Strong Gale—Lanigans Tower **Million In Mind (5)**
18 **GONE FOR LUNCH**, 5, br g Presidium—Border Mouse **Gradely Partners**
19 **GREY SMOKE**, 6, ch g Alias Smith (USA)—Salira **Lord Chelsea**
20 **GROUSEMAN**, 10, gr g Buckskin (FR)—Fortina's General **Aquarius**
21 **ITS NEARLY TIME**, 13, br g Newski (USA)—Lavenanne **Mrs R. Brackenbury**
22 **KARSHI**, 6, b g Persian Bold—Kashmiri Snow **Lord Vestey**
23 **KINDLE'S DELIGHT**, 8, b g Idiot's Delight—Kindled Spirit **Castle Farm Stud**
24 **LACKENDARA**, 9, ch g Monksfield—Driven Snow **Opening Bid Partnership**
25 **LUCKY TANNER**, 5, b g Silly Prices—Go Gipsy **The Superioat Partnership**
26 **MAID FOR ADVENTURE (IRE)**, 5, b m Strong Gale—Fast Adventure **Chris Brasher**
27 **MASTER ORCHESTRA (IRE)**, 7, ch g Orchestra—Good Loss **The Hatchet Partnership**
28 **MILITARY LAW**, 5, ch g Infantry—Sister-In-Law **Mrs P. Scott-Dunn**
29 **MIM-LOU-AND**, 4, b g Glacial Storm (USA)—Tina's Melody
30 **MOVING OUT**, 8, b g Slip Anchor—New Generation **Mrs Shirley Brasher**
31 **MR PICKPOCKET (IRE)**, 8, b g Roselier (FR)—Gusserane Princess **Mr Roger Sayer**
32 **OATIS REGRETS**, 8, b g Oats—Joscilla **Mr D. C. G. Gyle-Thompson**
33 **OBAN**, 6, ch g Scottish Reel—Sun Goddess (FR) **Lord Hartington**
34 **O MY LOVE**, 5, b m Idiot's Delight—Real Beauty
35 **PERHAPS (USA)**, 5, b br m Lord Avie (USA)—Allegedly Flashing (USA) **Mr Harold Winton**
36 **PONGO WARING (IRE)**, 7, b g Strong Gale—Super Cailin **Mrs J. K. Peutherer**
37 **PRAIRIE GROVE**, 6, b g Primo Dominie—Fairy Fans **Mrs Marygold O'Kelly**
38 **QUEENFORD BELLE**, 6, ch m Celtic Cone—Belle Bavard **Executive Racing**
39 **RED BLAZER**, 5, ch g Bustino—Klewraye **Mr T. H. Shrimpton**
40 **REPARTEE**, 5, br m Idiot's Delight—Brave Remark **M. Chamberlayne**
41 **RIVER BAY (IRE)**, 5, b m Over The River (FR)—Derrynaflan **Riverwood Racing**
42 **RUN FAST FOR GOLD**, 9, ch m Deep Run—Goldyke **Mrs D. J. Hodges**
43 **SERIOUS DANGER (IRE)**, 5, b g Sure Blade (USA)—Sugarbird **Executive Racing**
44 **SINGLE SOURCING (IRE)**, 5, b g Good Thyne (USA)—Lady Albron **Mr V. J. Adams**
45 **SLINGSBY (IRE)**, 6, b g Heraldiste (USA)—Tasmania Star **Mrs Linda McCalla**
46 **SOUNDS LIKE FUN**, 5, b g Neltino—Blakeney Sound **Mrs H. Brown**
47 **STOMPIN**, 5, b g Alzao (USA)—Celebrity **The Voice Group Ltd**
48 **STRIKE A LIGHT (IRE)**, 4, b g Miner's Lamp—Rescued **Kendrick Strang Partnership**
49 **SUPREME LADY (IRE)**, 5, b m Supreme Leader—Tudor Lady **The Supreme Lady Partnership**
50 **TALK BACK (IRE)**, 4, br g Bob Back (USA)—Summit Talk **Mr V. McCalla**
51 **TARA THE GREY (IRE)**, 5, gr m Supreme Leader—Tara's Lady **Aquarius**
52 **TELLICHERRY**, 7, br m Strong Gale—Quadro **Solid State Supplies**
53 **THE GREY FRIAR**, 7, gr g Pragmatic—Misty Lough **Mr M. J. Howard**
54 **THE PADRE (IRE)**, 7, b g The Parson—Alexandra **T. H. Shrimpton**
55 **TIGHT FIST (IRE)**, 8, b g Doulab (USA)—Fussy Budget **Mrs A. M. Davis**
56 **TOO SHARP**, 8, b m True Song—Pinchapenny **Sir Anthony Scott**
57 **TOUREEN PRINCE**, 13, b g Cheval—Laugreen **Mr Paul Stamp**

MISS H. C. KNIGHT—continued

58 TRAIL BOSS (IRE), 5, b g The Noble Player (USA)—Jackson Miss **Mr Martin Broughton**
59 TRICKSOME, 9, ch g Nicholas Bill—Pranky **Lady Vestey**
60 UNCLE ALGY, 7, ch g Relkino—Great Aunt Emily **Mr Dwight Makins**
61 VALLINGALE (IRE), 5, b m Strong Gale—Knockarctic **Patrick Burling Developments Ltd**
62 WADE ROAD (IRE), 5, b g King's Ride—Branstown Lady **Lord Chelsea**
63 WILD WEST WIND (IRE), 6, br g Strong Gale—Taggs Castle **Lord Vestey**
64 YES MAN (IRE), 7, b g Remainder Man—Gleness **Azzmok Winton Wright**

Other Owners: Mr Mokbul Ali, Mr Peter Bedford, Mr Keith Benham, Mr S. G. Boyle, Mr S. W. Broughton, Mr A. J. Buckley, Mrs C. Clatworthy, Mrs D. Clatworthy, Club Ten, Mr Brian R. Cole, Mr M. W. Cuddigan, Dr B. J. Eppel, Mrs John Etherton, Mrs J. R. Foster, Mr T. G. Fox, Mr G. C. Green, Mr H. Harrison, Mr Brian M. Hartigan, Mr John Holmes, Mr J. Hornsey, Mr R. J. Jenks, Mrs Nicholas Jones, Mrs M. Kelsey Fry, Mr M. B. J. Kimmins, Mr E. C. Lavelle, Mr J. R. Lavelle, Mrs R. J. Lavelle, Exors Of The Late Mr A. G. Lewis, Mr John Loader, Mrs Penelope Makins, Mrs G. C. Maxwell, Dr Marc Mendelson, Mr R. E. Morris-Adams, Mr R. J. Parish, Mr N. Pickett, Mr Aziz-Ur Rahman, Mr Ian Rees, Mr John L. Robertson, Mr G. A. Rogers, Mrs K. Rogers, Mr W. S. Rogers, Dr M. J. L. Scott, Mr D. F. Sumpter, Mr K. Thompson, Mr Barry W. Turner, Mr Lester C. Whelpdale, Mr Jerry Wright.

Jockey (NH): J F Titley (10-0).

Conditional: G F Ryan (9-9).

Amateur: Mr J Culloty (9-7).

Lady Rider: Miss J Brackenbury.

363   MR S. G. KNIGHT, Taunton

Postal: **Vincents Farm, Lower West Hatch, Taunton, Somerset, TA3 5RJ.**
Phone: **(01823) 480320   MOBILE (0378) 549452**

1 ALICE SHORELARK, 5, ch m Newski (USA)—Alice Woodlark **Mrs J. M. Greed**
2 ASTROJOY (IRE), 4, ch f Astronef—Pharjoy (FR) **Mrs Val Rapkins**
3 AUDE LA BELLE (FR), 8, ch m Ela-Mana-Mou—Arjona (GER) **Mrs Val Rapkins**
4 CASPIAN BELUGA, 8, b br g Persian Bold—Miss Thames **Mr L. J. Hawkings**
5 HUISH CROSS, 4, ch f Absalom—Sisslip (USA) **Mr P. J. Wightman**
6 KETCHICAN, 4, b g Joligeneration—Fair Melys (FR) **Mr Terry Keiler**
7 LA BELLE DOMINIQUE, 4, b f Dominion—Love Street **Mr Richard Withers**
8 TANANA, 7, b m Teenoso (USA)—La Nureyeva (USA) **Mrs Ginny Withers**
9 TRUST DEED (USA), 8, ch g Shadeed (USA)—Karelia (USA) **Mr Malcolm Enticott**

THREE-YEAR-OLDS

10 CASHTAL LACE, ch f Ballacashtal (CAN)—Chantilly Lace (FR) **Mr Alan Samuel**
11 RIVIERE ROUGE, ch f Forzando—Furry Dance (USA) **Mr Richard Withers**

364   MR C. LAFFON-PARIAS, Chantilly

Postal: **38, Avenue du General Leclerc,. 60500 Chantilly, France.**
Phone: **(33) 44 57 53 75 FAX (33) 44 57 52 43**

1 ALAMTARA, 5, b h Cadeaux Genereux—Catalonda **Maktoum Al Maktoum**
2 BASHAAYEASH, 4, b c Fairy King—Queen Cake **Maktoum Al Maktoum**
3 KING COBRA, 7, ch h Ardross—Sibley **F. Sanz**
4 RAJILL, 4, b c Shirley Heights—Tea Rose **J. Gispert**
5 UN SOLITAIRE, 4, b c Bering—Holy Tobin **Mme Morange**
6 VAGAMO, 5, b h Nashwan—Dancing Vaguely **J. Gispert**
7 YUSTE, 4, b c Fabulous Dancer—Ternia **Mme Vidal**

THREE-YEAR-OLDS

8 BALDEMOSA, b f Lead On Time—Bamieres **Maktoum Al Maktoum**
9 CAS D'ESPECES, b c Septieme Ciel—Cashierette **J. T. L. Jones**

MR C. LAFFON-PARIAS—continued

10 **CRYSTAL DROP**, b f Cadeaux Genereux—Rimsh **Mme Cealy**
11 **EGEO**, ch c Kris—Robertiya **Mme Vidal**
12 **FORT LAMY**, b c Antheus—Foolish Valley **Mme A. Head**
13 **GAITERO**, b c Groom Dancer—First Waltz **Mme Vidal**
14 **HERE TO ETERNITY**, b f Fairy King—Echoes of Eternity **Maktoum Al Maktoum**
15 **LITCHANINE**, gr c Linamix—Margello **Mme Vukobrat**
16 **PHONE FEE**, b c Phone Trick—Doigts de Fee **Maktoum Al Maktoum**
17 **SPEED FINE**, b c Lear Fan—Crystal Cup **Abdullah Ali**
18 **STARMANIAC**, b c Septieme Ciel—Silver Lane **J. T. L. Jones**
19 **TERAINA**, b f Fabulous Dancer—Ternia **Mme Vidal**
20 **WAVY CHRIS**, ch f Persian Bold—Wavy Reef **J. Gonzalez**

TWO-YEAR-OLDS

21 Ch f Pursuit of Love—Baiser Vole **J. T. L. Jones**
22 **BUBRUCK**, ch c Bering—Robertiya **Mme Vidal**
23 Ch c Machiavellian—Enfant d'Amour **Khalifa Sultan**
24 B f Alzao—Future Past **Saeed Suhail**
25 **GIRIO**, ch c Cadeaux Genereux—Giranna **Salem Suhail**
26 Ch c Night Shift—Happy Landing **Salem Suhail**
27 Ch c Septieme Ciel—I Wish **J. T. L. Jones**
28 Ch f Nashwan—Mayaasa **Maktoum Al Maktoum**
29 **PHARELLIA**, ch f Sillery—Pharetra **Kulfan Khurbash**
30 B c Royal Academy—Proskona **Saeed Suhail**
31 Ch f Diesis—Raahia **Maktoum Al Maktoum**
32 Ch f Affirmed—Star Game **F. Hinojosa**
33 B c Irish River—Tanapa **F. Hinojosa**
34 Ch f Fabulous Dancer—Ternia **Mme Vidal**

365   MR D. A. LAMB, Seahouses

Postal: **East Fleetham, Seahouses, Northd.**

Phone: **(01665) 720260**

1 **AYLESBURY LAD (IRE)**, 7, ch g Remainder Man—Aylesbury Lady **Exors of the late Mr R. R. Lamb**
2 **BIT OF LIGHT**, 9, ch g Henbit (USA)—Welsh Daylight **Exors of the late Mr R. R. Lamb**
3 **BUSY BOY**, 9, b g Dominion—Baidedones **Exors of the late Mr R. R. Lamb**
4 **CALLERNOY (IRE)**, 6, b g Callernish—Pats'y Girl **Exors of the late Mr R. R. Lamb**
5 **DARK MIDNIGHT (IRE)**, 7, br g Petorius—Gaelic Jewel **Exors of the late Mr R. R. Lamb**
6 **FLEET POINT**, 7, br m Bybicello—Abergeen **Mr I. D. Jordon**
7 **GAME POINT**, 7, b m Broadsword (USA)—Running Game **Exors of the late Mr R. R. Lamb**
8 **GERMAN LEGEND**, 6, br g Faustus (USA)—Fairfields **Exors of the late Mr R. R. Lamb**
9 **KINGS MINSTRAL (IRE)**, 6, ch g Andretti—Tara Minstral VII **Exors of the late Mr R. R. Lamb**
10 **LAURIE-O**, 12, b g Deep Run—Eight of Diamonds **Mr D. A. Lamb**
11 **MANOR COURT (IRE)**, 8, ch g Remainder Man—Court Fancy **Exors of the late Mr R. R. Lamb**
12 **MUFID (USA)**, 7, ch g Woodman (USA)—Princess Laika (USA) **Mr D. G. Pryde**
13 **PERSIAN GRANGE (IRE)**, 6, ch g King Persian—Little Grange **Exors of the late Mr R. R. Lamb**
14 **PERSUASIVE TALENT (IRE)**, 5, ch g Exhibitioner—Giorradana **Exors of the late Mr R. R. Lamb**
15 **POTATO MAN**, 10, gr g Zambrano—Kit's Future **Mr Chris Foster**
16 **QUARTZ HILL (USA)**, 7, b g Crafty Prospector (USA)—Mom's Mia (USA) **Exors of the late Mr R. R. Lamb**
17 **SNOOK POINT**, 9, b g Bybicello—Tarisma **Mr I. D. Jordon**
18 **THE ENERGISER**, 10, ch g Energist—Be An Angel **Exors of the late Mr R. R. Lamb**
19 **TO BE THE BEST**, 6, ch g Superlative—Early Call **Exors of the late Mr R. R. Lamb**
20 **TRI MY WAY (IRE)**, 6, ch m It's The One (USA)—Jetting Ways (USA) **Exors of the late Mr R. R. Lamb**
21 **WOLFSVILLE**, 8, b g Little Wolf—Perryville **Exors of the late Mr R. R. Lamb**

Other Owners: Mr K. L. Larnach.

Conditional: A Manners (9-12).

366   MRS K. M. LAMB, Seahouses

Postal: **Burnhouse Farm, Seahouses, Northd, NE68 7UZ.**

Phone: **(01665) 720251**

1 **FISH QUAY**, 13, ch g Quayside—Winkle **Mrs K. M. Lamb**
2 **FOREVER SHY (IRE)**, 8, b g Sandalay—Cill Damhnait **Mrs K. M. Lamb**
3 **PANTO LADY**, 10, br m Lepanto (GER)—Dusky Damsel **Mrs K. M. Lamb**
4 **QUEENSBORO LAD (IRE)**, 8, b g Euphemism—Yukon Lil **Mrs K. M. Lamb**
5 **RUBISLAW**, 4, ch g Dunbeath (USA)—Larnem **Mrs K. M. Lamb**
6 **SON OF TEMPO (IRE)**, 7, b g Sandhurst Prince—Top Love (USA) **Mrs K. M. Lamb**

Lady Rider: Miss S Lamb (9-7).

367   MRS S. LAMYMAN, Lincoln

Postal: **Ruckland Manor, Louth, Lincs, LN11 8RQ.**

Phone: **(01507) 533260**

1 **ERNEST ARAGORN**, 7, b g Laxton—Passage To Freedom **Mr P. Lamyman**
2 **RESTANDBEJOYFUL**, 4, ch f Takachiho—Restandbethankful **Mr P. Lamyman**
3 **ROSIE (IRE)**, 6, gr m Roselier (FR)—Quetta's Dual **Mr P. Lamyman**

Other Owners: Mrs S. Lamyman.

368   MR ROBIN LE PENNEC, Jersey

Postal: **Green Bank Racing Stables, St Peter, Jersey.**

Phone: **HOME (01534) 499235 YARD (01534) 483800**

1 **AVANTI XIQUET**, 5, gr g Mashhor Dancer (USA)—Mummy's Chick **Green Bank Racing**
2 **DRINKS PARTY (IRE)**, 8, b m Camden Town—Holy Water **Mr A. J. Le Pennec & Mr P. H. A'Court**

TWO-YEAR-OLDS

3 Ch c 11/3 Prince Of Cill Dara—Come On Doll (True Song) **Green Bank Racing**
4 B c 29/5 Prince Of Cill Dara—Sacred River (Town Crier) **Green Bank Racing**

Other Owners: Mr C. Elliot, Miss P. Philo.

Jockey (NH): P Holley (10-0, w.a.).

369   MR M. R. LEACH, Newark

Postal: **Rose Cottage, Long Lane, Barnby In The Willows, Newark, NG24 2SG.**

Phone: **(01636) 626518**

THREE-YEAR-OLDS

1 **DANAS**, ch g Dawn Johnny (USA)—Dana's Turn **Mr A. Snipe**
2 **JENAXA**, ch f Jendali (USA)—Laxay **Mr A. Snipe**
3 **JENNFIELD**, b br f Jendali (USA)—Valiant Dancer **Mr A. Snipe**
4 **JENOPIS**, b f Jendali (USA)—Asoness **Mr A. Snipe**
5 **JENTAIN**, b br f Jendali (USA)—No Rejection **Mr A. Snipe**
6 **TOBY**, b g Jendali (USA)—Au Revoir Sailor **Mr A. Snipe**

TWO-YEAR-OLDS

7 B f 29/3 Jendali (USA)—Lovely Ears (Auction Ring (USA)) **Mr A. Snipe**
8 B c 1/5 Jendali (USA)—No Rejection (Mummy's Pet) **Mr A. Snipe**
9 B c 28/3 Jendali (USA)—Welsh Fashion (Welsh Saint) **Mr A. Snipe**

370   MR S. J. LEADBETTER, Berwick-upon-Tweed

Postal: **Ladykirk Stables, Berwick-upon-Tweed, TD15 ISU.**

Phone: **(01289) 382519**

1 BAGOTS PARK, 7, ro g Alias Smith (USA)—Newfield Green **Mr S. J. Leadbetter**
2 DAVARA, 10, gr g Dawn Johnny (USA)—News Belle **Mr D. W. Nicholson**
3 DUNDYVAN, 14, ch g Crimson Beau—Flora Day **Mr S. J. Leadbetter**
4 5, B g Detroit Sam—French Note **Mr D. H. Nicholson**
5 JUPITER LORD, 5, b g Jupiter Island—Angelic Appeal **Mrs B. Ward**
6 MAGIC LAW, 9, b m Majestic Current (USA)—Lawsuitlaw
7 MONTEIN, 5, b g Ovac (ITY)—River Bark **Mr D. Montgomerie**
8 PADDY HAYTON, 15, br g St Paddy—Natenka **Mr S. J. Leadbetter**
9 5, Gr g Alias Smith (USA)—River Song **Mr D. Darling**
10 ROBARA, 6, b br g Another Realm—Kate Kimberley **Mr D. W. Nicholson**
11 ROMAN SWORD, 8, br m Broadsword (USA)—Winnetka **Mr D. W. Nicholson**

THREE-YEAR-OLDS

12 QUICK MARCH, b f Daring March—Cabaletta **Mrs N. Napier**

Amateur: Mr R Shiels (10-10).

371   MR AUGUSTINE LEAHY, Kilmallock

Postal: **"Lorien" Clogher, Kilmallock, Co. Limerick, Ireland**

Phone: **(063) 90676 (088) 580296 FAX (063) 90676**

1 BEAU CYRANO (IRE), 4, b g Cyrano de Bergerac—Only Great **White Star Holdings**
2 BE MY FOLLY (IRE), 4, ch f Astronef—Folly Gale **Miss M. McGrath**
3 BE THE LORD (IRE), 6, b g Mister Lord (USA)—Highlight Lass **Mrs Joan Brosnan**
4 CLAHANE (IRE), 5, b g King's Ride—Niagara Lass **M. M. Power**
5 EDANA (IRE), 5, b m Supreme Leader—Tomona **Mrs Joan Brosnan**
6 GLOUNTHAUNE, 4, b g Charmer—Dora's Rocket **T. F. Roe**
7 GRIGORI RASPUTIN (IRE), 5, ch g Moscow Society (USA)—Emily Bishop (IRE) **Virginia Lady Petersham**
8 HAKI SAKI, 10, ch g Tug of War—Shannon Lek **M. M. Power**
9 HAKKINEN (IRE), 5, ch g Rising—Shenley Annabella **Winners Circle Racing Club**
10 HAWKE'S SPIRIT (IRE), 5, ch g Long Pond—Carrig Lady
11 INDESTRUCTIBLE (IRE), 8, ch g Duky—Chatty Actress **J. Quane**
12 MIDDLE MOGGS (IRE), 4, b f Mazaad—Grenane Bayleaf **Dr J. Mansergh Wallace**
13 PERSIAN MYSTIC (IRE), 4, ch c Bold Arrangement—Bombalurida **J. F. Dorrian**
14 PHARDY (IRE), 5, b g Phardante (FR)—Enchanted Lady **Gan Ceann Syndicate**
15 REGIT (IRE), 6, b g Duky—Shenley Annabella **Mrs E. Leahy**
16 RENNY (IRE), 5, b g Bold Arrangement—She Is The Boss
17 SEA FISHER (IRE), 5, b g Mulhollande (USA)—Escape Path **J. P. McManus**
18 ZOE BAIRD, 5, b m Aragon—Gentle Stream **Mrs E. Leahy**

THREE-YEAR-OLDS

19 RED ROSE WALK (IRE), b f Pennine Walk—Excitingly (USA)
20 Ch c Glenstal (USA)—Royal Aunt
21 SOVIET TOWN (IRE), b f Soviet Lad (USA)—Town Ablaze **Mrs E. Leahy**
22 Br g Topanoora—Zazu

TWO-YEAR-OLDS

23 B c 12/5 Silver Kite (USA)—Air Rina (USA) (Lear Fan (USA))
24 Ch c 9/4 Kenmare (FR)—Classic Opera (Lomond (USA))
25 B c 12/4 Fools Holme (USA)—Hotel du Lac (Lomond (USA))
26 B f 13/5 Don't Forget Me—Moon Festival (Be My Guest (USA))
27 B f 16/2 Alzao (USA)—Peinture (FR) (Valiyar)
28 B f 31/3 Soviet Lad (USA)—She Is The Boss (Skyliner)

MR AUGUSTINE LEAHY—continued

29 B f 16/4 Topanoora—Tender Always (Tender King)
30 B f 28/3 Last Tycoon—Tomona (Linacre)
31 Gr f 29/4 Batshoof—To Oneiro (Absalom)

Jockey (NH): G M O'Neill (10-0).

Apprentice: J E Casey (7-11).

Conditional: S P Cooke (9-0).

Lady Rider: S J Leahy (8-10).

372   MR R. R. LEDGER, Sittingbourne

Postal: **Sorrento, School Lane, Borden, Sittingbourne, ME9 8JS.**
Phone: **(01795) 423360**

1 DOMITOR'S LASS, 9, ch m Domitor (USA)—Spartan Flame **Mr R. R. Ledger**
2 TARTAN GLORY, 6, b m Roman Glory—Spartan Flame **Mr R. R. Ledger**
3 UPWARD SURGE (IRE), 6, ch g Kris—Sizes Vary **Mr R. R. Ledger**
4 WILTOSKI, 8, b g Petoski—Cojean (USA) **Mr R. R. Ledger**

Lady Rider: Mrs Nicky Ledger (9-0).

373   MR F. H. LEE, Wilmslow

Postal: **Little Stanneylands Farm, Stanneylands Road, Wilmslow, Cheshire, SK9 4ER.**
Phone: **(01625) 533250/530042 TELEX 635435 FAX (01625) 539489**

1 BAJAN FRONTIER (IRE), 4, ch f Imperial Frontier (USA)—Sajanjal **Mrs C. E. Collinson**
2 BEAU VENTURE (USA), 8, ch h Explodent (USA)—Old Westbury (USA) **Mrs A. L. Stacey**
3 ENCORE M'LADY (IRE), 5, b m Dancing Dissident (USA)—Diva Encore **Mr F. H. Lee**
4 MISS TRI COLOUR, 4, b f Shavian—Bourgeonette **Tri-Colour Printing Inks Ltd**
5 MOVE SMARTLY (IRE), 6, b h Smarten—Key Maneuver (USA) **Mr F. H. Lee**
6 PEACEFULL REPLY (USA), 6, b h Hold Your Peace (USA)—Drone Answer (USA) **Mr F. H. Lee**

THREE-YEAR-OLDS

7 DINO'S MISTRAL, b g Petong—Marquessa d'Howfen **Mr F. H. Lee**
8 Ch f Weld—Spring Drill **Mr D. Farr**

TWO-YEAR-OLDS

9 B c 26/2 Precocious—Mardessa (Ardross) **Mr F. M. Lee**

Other Owners: Mr Peter Barr, Mr Michael Caveney.

374   MR RICHARD LEE, Presteigne

Postal: **The Bell House, Byton, Presteigne, Powys, LD8 2HS.**
Phone: **(01544) 267672 FAX 260247 CAR (0831) 846550 MOBILE(0836) 537145**

1 BOBBY SOCKS, 10, b br g Blakeney Point—Countesswells **Risk Factor Partnership**
2 DABALARK, 7, ch g Crested Lark—The Dabber **Mr Harry Bibbey**
3 DEBT OF HONOR, 8, ch g Deep River—Vulgan's Honor **Mrs Bill Neale**

MR RICHARD LEE—continued

4 **DECIDED (CAN)**, 13, b g Affirmed (USA)—Expediency (USA) **Mrs C. Lee**
5 **FORMAESTRE (IRE)**, 6, b m Formidable (USA)—Maestrette **Mrs C. Lee**
6 **GOOD FOR A LOAN**, 9, b g Daring March—Game For A Laugh **Racing Investments**
7 **HANGOVER**, 10, b g Over The River (FR)—Falcade **Mr Richard Edwards**
8 **JOE BEGLEY (IRE)**, 7, ch g Stetchworth (USA)—Moll Burke **Marten Julian (Turf Club) Ltd**
9 **JOSHUA'S VISION (IRE)**, 5, b g Vision (USA)—Perle's Fashion **J & D Racing**
10 **LEESWOOD**, 8, b g Little Wolf—Tina's Gold **G.H.S. Bailey, N.C.D. Hall and D. Murray**
11 **LIFE'S A BREEZE**, 7, b g Aragon—Zahira **Mr Richard Lee**
12 **LITTLE GAINS**, 7, b g Nearly A Hand—Flavias Cottage **Mr Bob Brazier**
13 **LOVELARK**, 7, b m Crested Lark—Emily Love **Mr Harry Bibbey**
14 **MACGEORGE (IRE)**, 6, b g Mandalus—Colleen Donn **Mr J. H. Watson**
15 **MANAMOUR**, 9, br g Mandalus—Fifi L'Amour **Mr Will Roseff**
16 **PERFIK LARK**, 6, ch g Crested Lark—The Dabber **Mr Harry Bibbey**
17 **POT BLACKBIRD**, 7, ch m Crested Lark—Blacktop **Mr Harry Bibbey**
18 **RATATOUILLE ROAD (IRE)**, 6, b g King's Ride—Gothic Model **Winsbury Livestock**
19 **SUPER COIN**, 8, b g Scorpio (FR)—Penny Princess **Mr George Brookes**
20 **THE SHY PADRE (IRE)**, 7, br g The Parson—Kenodon **Mike Bateman and Dennis Coltart**
21 **TWICE THE GROOM (IRE)**, 6, b g Digamist (USA)—Monaco Lady **Mr M. J. Fairbrother**
22 **VALISKY**, 6, gr m Valiyar—Rocket Trip **Risk Another Partnership**

Other Owners: Mr N. Abbott, Mr F. J. Ayres, Mrs J. A. Beavan, Mr J. O. Beavan, Mr R. A. Beavan, Mr R. J. Beavan Mrs Joan Brookes, Mr J. C. Coales, Mr B. Connolly, Mr T. M. J. Curry, Mr P. A. Dickinson, Miss C. Fagerstrom, M Ernie Flello, Mr B. W. L. George, Mr W. J. George, Mr P. Gowman, Mr L. J. Gwynne, Mr R. L. C. Hartley, Mr B Hinchliff, Mr John M. Jackson, Mr K. Brian Jones, Mr B. Lynn, Mr Richard Money, Mr W. J. Perchard, Mr P. T. G Phillips, Mr W. Quinn, Mr J. Stewart, Mr Martin Stillwell.

Jockey (Flat): Pat Eddery.

Jockey (NH): A Maguire (10-0).

375   MR J. P. LEIGH, Gainsborough

Postal: **Mount House Stables, 12 Long Lane, Willoughton, Gainsborough, DN21 5SQ.**
Phone: **(01427) 668210**

1 **CATTLY HANG (IRE)**, 6, b g King's Ride—Lawless Secret **Mr W. G. N. Morgan**
2 **GENERAL GIGGS (IRE)**, 8, br g Sandalay—Cold Sea **Lord Yarborough**
3 **GORBY'S MYTH (IRE)**, 6, b g Bustino—Crusader's Dream **Mr J. M. Greetham**
4 **JOHNNIE THE JOKER**, 5, gr g Absalom—Magic Tower **Miss M. Carrington-Smith**
5 **MATT REID**, 12, ch g Abednego—Abbey Lodge **Mr W. G. N. Morgan**
6 **PENNY'S WISHING**, 4, b f Clantime—Lady Pennington **Mr K. Pennington**
7 **SERGIO (IRE)**, 4, ch g Doubletour (USA)—Shygate **Mr H. Thompson**

THREE-YEAR-OLDS

8 **CHILLAM**, ch g Chilibang—Tissue Paper **Mr Brian Plows**
9 **DANLORA**, b f Shareef Dancer (USA)—Loreef **Mr J. W. Rowles**
10 **HAYSONG (IRE)**, ch f Ballad Rock—Hay Knot **Mr J. W. Rowles**

TWO-YEAR-OLDS

11 **INFLATION**, b f 3/3 Primo Dominie—Fluctuate (Sharpen Up) **Mr J. W. Rowles**
12 **RADIANCY (IRE)**, ch f 8/3 Mujtahid (USA)—Bright Landing (Sun Prince) **Mr J. W. Rowles**
13 **ROCKIE THE JESTER**, b c 8/4 Rock Hopper—Magic Steps (Nomination) **Miss M. Carrington-Smith**

Other Owners: Mr H. T. Pickering, Mrs E. A. Quayle, Mr C. Tomkins.

376   MR G. LEWIS, Epsom

Postal: **Thirty Acre Barn, Shepherds Walk, Headley, Epsom, KT18 6BX.**
Phone: **ASHTEAD (01372) 277662 OR 277366 FAX (01372) 277366**

1 **AMANY (IRE)**, 4, b f Waajib—Treeline
2 **JARAAB**, 5, b g Sure Blade (USA)—Ostora (USA) **Mr S. I. Ross**
3 **JIBEREEN**, 4, b g Lugana Beach—Fashion Lover **Mr Peter Skelton**
4 **LIDHAMA (USA)**, 4, b f Sword Dance—Running Melody **Mr Abdulla Al Khalifa**
5 **LOKI (IRE)**, 8, ch g Thatching—Sigym **Mr Michael H. Watt**
6 **NIGHT DANCE**, 4, ch c Weldnaas (USA)—Shift Over (USA) **Mr G. V. Wright**
7 **THAT MAN AGAIN**, 4, ch g Prince Sabo—Milne's Way **Mrs R. Duffy**

THREE-YEAR-OLDS

8 **ANOTHERANNIVERSARY**, gr f Emarati (USA)—Final Call **Mr David Barker**
9 **BELLACARDIA**, b f Law Society (USA)—Clarista (USA) **Mrs Thelma Wade**
10 **BLUE DELIGHT (IRE)**, b c Bluebird (USA)—Highly Delighted (USA) **E & B Productions (Theatre) Ltd**
11 **BRENTABILITY (IRE)**, b g Dancing Dissident (USA)—Stanerra's Song (USA) **Mr David Barker**
12 **CARICATURE (IRE)**, b g Cyrano de Bergerac—That's Easy **White Bear Ltd**
13 **CIVIL LIBERTY**, b c Warning—Libertine **Midcourts**
14 **FLYFISHER (IRE)**, b c Batshoof—Inveraven **Highclere Thoroughbred Racing Ltd**
15 **MASTER LYNX (USA)**, b c Cutlass (USA)—La Ninouchka (USA) **Mr Peter Skelton**
16 **NO CLICHES**, ch c Risk Me (FR)—Always On A Sunday **Mr Michael H. Watt**
17 **PASSION FOR LIFE**, br g Charmer—Party Game **Mr David Waters**
18 **PRIDE OF BRIXTON**, b c Dominion—Caviar Blini **The Voice Group Ltd**
19 **PROVINCE**, b g Dominion—Shih Ching (USA) **Highclere Thoroughbred Racing Ltd**
20 **RISKING**, b f Risk Me (FR)—Dark Kristal (FR) **Mr Abdulla Al Khalifa**
21 **TROJAN RISK**, ch g Risk Me (FR)—Troyes **Mr Jim McCarthy**
22 **VERA'S FIRST (IRE)**, b f Exodal (USA)—Shades of Vera **Mrs Vera Mason**

TWO-YEAR-OLDS

23 Gr f 4/5 Petong—Always On A Sunday (Star Appeal)
24 **APPLE BRANDY (USA)**, ch f 27/2 Cox's Ridge (USA)—
                           Channel Three (USA) (Tri Jet (USA)) **Highclere Thoroughbred Racing Ltd**
25 Ch f 6/4 Risk Me (FR)—Bocas Rose (Jalmood (USA)) **Roldvale Ltd**
26 B f 1/5 Priolo—Calandra (USA) (Sir Ivor) **White Bear Ltd**
27 Ch c 7/4 Caerleon—Catina (Nureyev (USA)) **Mr John Manley**
28 Ch f 16/2 Risk Me (FR)—Celtic River (IRE) (Caerleon (USA)) **Roldvale Ltd**
29 B f 18/4 River Falls—Clifton Beach (Auction Ring (USA))
30 **DEBONAIR**, b f 5/2 Batshoof—Celestial Air (Rheingold) **Highclere Thoroughbred Racing Ltd**
31 B c 17/4 Maledetto (IRE)—Dublin Millennium (Dalsaan)
32 Ch c 2/3 Emarati (USA)—Exceptional Beauty (Sallust) **Mr Abdulla Al Khalifa**
33 Gr c 4/1 Sheikh Albadou—Fit And Ready (USA) (Fit To Fight (USA)) **Highclere Thoroughbred Racing Ltd**
34 Br c 6/3 Cyrano de Bergerac—Glass Minnow (IRE) (Alzao (USA)) **Mr J. M. Gosse**
35 **GUINEAS GALORE (IRE)**, br c 31/3 Classic Secret (USA)—Morning Stroll (Tower Walk) **Mr David Barker**
36 Gr c 23/3 Robellino (USA)—High Matinee (Shirley Heights) **Mr G. V. Wright**
37 Ch c 17/4 Thatching—Hooray Lady (Ahonoora) **Mr George A. Moore**
38 **HYPE ENERGY**, b f 9/4 Tina's Pet—Stoneyside (Tickled Pink) **Mr Robert Cox**
39 Ch c 29/4 River Falls—Kowalski (IRE) (Cyrano de Bergerac)
40 **LA CHATELAINE**, b f 18/3 Then Again—La Domaine (Dominion) **White Bear Ltd**
41 B c 29/4 River Falls—Little Red Hut (Habitat)
42 **MANTLES PRINCE**, ch c 8/3 Emarati (USA)—Miami Mouse (Miami Springs) **Mr David Barker**
43 Gr f 7/5 Mystiko (USA)—No Chili (Glint of Gold)
44 Ch c 10/3 Efisio—Prejudice (Young Generation)
45 Gr c 6/2 Risk Me (FR)—Princess Tara (Prince Sabo) **Mr John Manley**
46 B c 1/3 Silver Kite (USA)—Red Note (Rusticaro (FR))
47 **REFERENDUM (IRE)**, b c 21/2 Common Grounds—
                           Final Decision (Tap On Wood) **Highclere Thoroughbred Racing Ltd**
48 **REGAL REPRIMAND**, br c 17/3 Reprimand—Queen Caroline (USA) (Chief's Crown (USA)) **The Voice Group Ltd**
49 **RUDE AWAKENING**, b c 6/3 Rudimentary (USA)—Final Call (Town Crier) **Mr David Barker**
50 B c 31/3 Petorius—Sandra's Choice (Sandy Creek)

MR G. LEWIS—continued

51 B f 8/4 Classic Music (USA)—Second Movement (Music Boy)
52 STRATHMORE CLEAR, b c 3/4 Batshoof—Sunflower Seed (Mummy's Pet) **Food Brokers Ltd**

Other Owners: Mr John T. Duffy, Mrs Lyn Fatah, Mr Vic Fatah, Mr P. D. Jameson, Laurel (Leisure) Limited, Mrs Andry Muinos, Victor Chandler (Equus) Ltd.

Jockeys (Flat): Pat Eddery (8-4, w.a.), Paul Eddery (8-0).

Apprentice: A Whelan (7-12).

377   MR N. P. LITTMODEN, Wolverhampton

Postal: **Dunstall Park Stables, Wolverhampton Racecourse, Gorsebrook Road, Wolverhampton, WV6 0PE.**
Phone: **(01902) 688558 FAX (01902) 688558**

1 ANOTHERONE TO NOTE, 5, ch g Beveled (USA)—Dame Nellie **Mr T. Clarke**
2 ARRANGE A GAME, 9, ch g Le Bavard (FR)—Lucky Mary **Mr A. M. McArdle**
3 4, B f Weld—Baltic Call **M & D Burton**
4 CERTAIN WAY (IRE), 6, ch h Sure Blade—Ruffling Point **R. A. M. Racecourses Ltd**
5 CRETAN GIFT, 5, ch g Cadeaux Genereux—Caro's Niece (USA) **R. A. M. Racecourses Ltd**
6 6, B g Seymour Hicks—Cute Dancer **Mr M. Horton**
7 EVEZIO RUFO, 4, b c Blakeney—Empress Corina **Mr T. Clarke**
8 GARDEN WALK (IRE), 8, b g Le Moss—Paradise Ramble **Mr J. Collard**
9 HAVE A NIGHTCAP, 7, ch g Night Shift (USA)—Final Orders (USA) **R. A. M. Racecourses Ltd**
10 HIDDEN GOLD, 4, ch c Crowning Honors (CAN)—Affluent Lady **Ms Patricia Watson**
11 HUNZA STORY, 4, b f Rakaposhi King—Sense of Occasion **Mr M. S. Moule**
12 LASER LIGHT LADY, 4, b f Tragic Role (USA)—Raina Perera **R. A. M. Racecourses Ltd**
13 MAN OF MAY, 4, b c High Kicker (USA)—Faldwyn **Mr J. W. C. Coxon**
14 MEDIA MESSENGER, 7, b g Hadeer—Willow Court (USA) **Mr O. A. Gunter**
15 NEDDY TWO SOCKS, 5, b g Pitpan—Wings Ground **Mr J. R. Salter**
16 NOVEMBER SONG, 7, b m Scorpio (FR)—Auto Sam **Mr T. Clarke**
17 RECESSIONS OVER, 5, b g Komaite (USA)—Lucky Councillor **Mrs J. E. Lloyd**
18 ZALAMENT, 4, b f Zalazl (USA)—Key To Enchantment **Mr Nick Littmoden**

THREE-YEAR-OLDS

19 BORN A LADY, ch f Komaite (USA)—Lucky Candy **Mr D. Voivodich**
20 DENNIS WISE, ch c High Kicker (USA)—Poppin Gill **Cavendish Racing Ltd**
21 HI HOH (IRE), gr f Fayruz—Late Date **Mountview Ventures**
22 RADMORE BRANDY, b f Derrylin—Emerin **Mr J. R. Salter**
23 B f Thethingaboutitis (USA)—Rue de Remarque **M & D Burton**
24 Ch g Ballacashtal (CAN)—Storm of Plenty
25 SWEET SERANADE (IRE), b f Ballad Rock—Little Honey **Mr A. M. McArdle**
26 TALLULAH BELLE, b f Crowning Honors (CAN)—Fine A Leau (USA) **Miss Stephanie Clark**
27 TASHTAIYA, b f Totem (USA)—Bonita Estrella **Ms Patricia Watson**

TWO-YEAR-OLDS

28 D-DAY-SMOKE, ch c 7/6 Cigar—Little Pockthorpe **Mr N. Wolston Croft**
29 Gr f 13/5 Thethingaboutitis—Rue de Remarque **M & D Burton**
30 Gr g 2/3 Thethingaboutitis—Sovereign Love **R. A. M. Racecourses Ltd**
31 Ch c 31/5 Cigar—Sultans Gift **Mr N. Wolston Croft**

Other Owners: Mrs E. S. Bradley, Mr D. J. Moody, Mr J. Collard, Mr D. Voivodich, Mr R. Webb, Mr P. A. Whiteman.

Jockey (Flat): T G McLaughlin (8-2).

Apprentice: John Bramhill (7-4).

Amateur: Mr M Salaman (9-0).

378   MR B. J. LLEWELLYN, Bargoed

Postal: **Ffynonau Duon Farm, Pentwyn Fochriw, Bargoed, Mid Glam, CF8 9NR.**

Phone: **(01685) 841259 FAX (01685) 841259**

1 **BACKVIEW**, 4, ch g Backchat (USA)—Book Review **Mr Eamonn O'Malley**
2 **CUBAN NIGHTS (USA)**, 4, b g Our Native (USA)—Havana Moon (USA) **Mr Eamonn O'Malley**
3 **DAILY SPORT GIRL**, 7, b m Risk Me (FR)—Net Call **Mr B. J. Llewellyn**
4 **DANGER BABY**, 6, ch g Bairn (USA)—Swordlestown Miss (USA) **Mouse Racing**
5 **DEEP ISLE**, 10, ch g Deep Run—Baby Isle **Mr B. J. Llewellyn**
6 **FLASHMAN**, 6, b g Flash of Steel—Proper Madam **Mr Colin Simpson**
7 **GIGFY**, 4, b g Warrshan (USA)—Empty Purse **Mr B. J. Llewellyn**
8 **GUNMAKER**, 7, ch g Gunner B—Lucky Starkist **Mr B. J. Llewellyn**
9 **HELLO ME MAN (IRE)**, 8, b g Asir—Tide Gate **Mr B. J. Llewellyn**
10 **LORD NITROGEN (USA)**, 6, b br g Greinton—Jibber Jabber (USA) **Mr B. J. Llewellyn**
11 **LOVESCAPE**, 5, b m Precocious—Alpine Damsel **Mr Gary Mills**
12 **MIXED MOOD**, 4, br f Jalmood (USA)—Cool Combination **Millstream Associates**
13 **NORD LYS (IRE)**, 5, b g Nordico (USA)—Beach Light **Mr N. Heath**
14 **NORTHERN OPTIMIST**, 8, b m Northern Tempest (USA)—On A Bit **Mr Graham Hunt**
15 **OFF THE AIR (IRE)**, 5, b m Taufan (USA)—Milly Daydream **Mr Eamonn O'Malley**
16 **RECTORY BOY**, 13, b g Rustingo—Ron's Girl **Mr B. J. Llewellyn**
17 **ROOTSMAN (IRE)**, 6, b g Glenstal (USA)—Modena **Mrs J. Morgan**
18 **SHANAKEE**, 9, br g Wassl—Sheeog **Mr Alan J. Williams**
19 **STATION EXPRESS (IRE)**, 8, b g Rusticaro (FR)—Vallee d'O (FR) **Lodge Cross Partnership**
20 **STRIKE-A-POSE**, 6, ch m Blushing Scribe (USA)—My Bushbaby **Four Star Racing Club**
21 **WHITE LADY**, 5, ch m Risk Me (FR)—Cassiar **Mr E. Borg**

Other Owners: Mr Mark Bailey, Mr B. H. Berry, Mr Michael Berry, Mr John Berry (Trevethin), Mr J. M. Butts, Mr Barry H. Cahusac, Mr Gwerfyl Coombs, Mrs S. De Courcy-Parry, Mr Dilwyn Davies, Mr T. H. Gibbon, Mr John Jones (Pontypridd), Mrs D. McCabe, Mr John O'Malley, Mr G. E. Parr, Mr N. C. Richards, Mr M. T. R. Twigg, Mrs Paula Williams.

Jockey (Flat): Tyrone Williams.

Conditional: Guy Lewis.

Amateur: Mr John Lewis Llewellyn (9-9).

379   MR F. LLOYD, Bangor-on-Dee

Postal: **Althrey Woodhouse, Bangor-on-Dee, Wrexham, Clwyd, LL13 0DA.**

Phone: **(01978) 780356 FAX (01978) 780427**

1 **ALTHREY ARISTOCRAT (IRE)**, 6, ch g Aristocracy—Fairy Island **Mr F. Lloyd**
2 **ALTHREY BLUE (IRE)**, 7, b g Milk of The Barley—Hua Hin **Mr F. Lloyd**
3 **ALTHREY CAPTAIN (IRE)**, 6, ch g Hardboy—Shimering Star **Mr F. Lloyd**
4 **ALTHREY LEADER (IRE)**, 6, b g Supreme Leader—Shannon Belle **Mr F. Lloyd**
5 **ALTHREY LORD (IRE)**, 6, b g Le Moss—Pidgeon Lady **Mr F. Lloyd**
6 **ALTHREY RUN (IRE)**, 6, b g Phardante (FR)—Nickel Run **Mr F. Lloyd**
7 **ALTHREY SUPREME (IRE)**, 6, b g Supreme Leader—Caught In The Act **Mr F. Lloyd**
8 **ON THE TEAR**, 10, br g The Parson—Queen Menelek **Mr F. Lloyd**
9 **SWINHOE CROFT**, 14, b g Orange Bay—On A Bit **Mr F. Lloyd**

380 MR L. R. LLOYD-JAMES, Malton

Postal: 4 Wayfaring Close, Malton, North Yorks, YO17 9DW.

1 BRACKENTHWAITE, 6, ch g Faustus (USA)—Cosset Mr J. B. Slatcher
2 BURN BRIDGE (USA), 10, b g Linkage (USA)—Your Nuts (USA) Mr J. B. Slatcher
3 4, B f Kala Shikari—Cherrywood Blessin Mrs Cheryl L. Owen
4 GOOD VENTURE, 5, b m Good Times (ITY)—Sarah's Venture Mrs Cheryl L. Owen
5 MY CHERRYWELL, 6, br m Kirchner—Cherrywood Blessin Mrs Cheryl L. Owen
6 NORDIC SUN (IRE), 8, gr g Nordico (USA)—Cielsoleil (USA) Mr J. B. Slatcher
7 PASSION SUNDAY, 5, ch g Bairn (USA)—Holy Day Mr J. B. Slatcher
8 PLUM FIRST, 6, b g Nomination—Plum Bold Mr J. B. Slatcher
9 POLITICAL DOMAIN (IRE), 6, b g Shernazar—Irish Green Mr L. R. Lloyd-James
10 SHALMA, 4, ch f Cigar—Oujarater Mr L. R. Lloyd-James
11 SHE'S A MADAM, 5, b m Kabour—Mrs Buzby Miss L. M. Helliwell
12 UPEX LE GOLD TOO, 4, ch g Precocious—Restless Star Mr J. B. Slatcher

THREE-YEAR-OLDS

13 Ch g Primitive Rising (USA)—Mount Ailey Miss L. M. Helliwell
14 SHASAY, b f Thowra (FR)—Casbah Girl Mr J. B. Slatcher
15 Ch f Handsome Sailor—The Huyton Girls Mr L. R. Lloyd-James

Jockeys (Flat): R Cochrane (w.a.), T Williams (w.a.).

Jockey (NH): P Carberry (w.a.).

Apprentice: Kimberley Hart (w.a.).

381 MR D. R. LODER, Newmarket

Postal: Graham Lodge Stables, Birdcage Walk, Newmarket, Suffolk, CB8 0NF.
Phone: (01638) 662233 FAX (01638) 665596

1 BAHAMIAN SUNSHINE (USA), 5, ch h Sunshine Forever (USA)—Pride of Darby (USA)
2 BIN ROSIE, 4, b g Distant Relative—Come On Rosi
3 BONNE ETOILE, 4, b f Diesis—Bonne Ile
4 GRAND DU LAC (USA), 4, ch c Lac Ouimet (USA)—Vast Domain (CAN)
5 NIJO, 5, b g Top Ville—Nibabu (FR)
6 PRINCE OF ANDROS (USA), 6, b h Al Nasr (FR)—Her Radiance (USA)
7 SOUTHERN POWER (IRE), 5, b g Midyan (USA)—Tap The Line
8 SOVIET SHORE, 4, b c Soviet Star (USA)—Shore Line
9 STRUGGLER, 4, b c Night Shift (USA)—Dreamawhile
10 VERZEN (IRE), 4, ch c Salse (USA)—Virelai

THREE-YEAR-OLDS

11 APPLAUD (USA), ch f Rahy (USA)—Band (USA)
12 BAHAMIAN KNIGHT (CAN), b br c Ascot Knight (CAN)—Muskoka Command (USA)
13 BLUE DUSTER (USA), b f Danzig (USA)—Blue Note (FR)
14 BRIGHT HERITAGE (IRE), b c Ela-Mana-Mou—Mother of The Wind
15 CORNISH SNOW (USA), br c Storm Cat (USA)—Pleasantly Free (USA)
16 DEUX CARR (USA), b c Carr de Naskra (USA)—Deux Chance (USA)
17 DIMAKYA (USA), b f Dayjur (USA)—Reloy (USA)
18 EL PENITENTE (IRE), b c Ela-Mana-Mou—Penny Habit
19 GROUND GAME, b f Gildoran—Running Game
20 HAL'S PAL, br c Caerleon (USA)—Refinancing (USA)
21 LUCAYAN PRINCE (USA), br c Fast Play (USA)—Now That's Funny (USA)
22 MAID FOR THE HILLS, b f Indian Ridge—Stinging Nettle
23 MASTER BOOTS, br c Warning—Arpero

MR D. R. LODER—continued

24 **MELDORF,** ch c Lycius (USA)—Melanoura
25 **MOUNTAIN HOLLY,** b f Shirley Heights—Ela Romara
26 **NADOR,** ch c Rainbow Quest (USA)—Nadma (USA)
27 **NANDA,** ch f Nashwan (USA)—Pushy
28 **NANSHAN (IRE)** b f Nashwan (USA)—Pass The Peace
29 **NASRUDIN (USA),** b c Nureyev (USA)—Sunshine O'My Life (USA)
30 **NAVAL GAZER (IRE),** b f Sadler's Wells (USA)—Naval Light (USA)
31 **OVERRULED (IRE),** b f Last Tycoon—Overcall
32 **PEARL D'AZUR (USA),** b c Dayjur (USA)—Priceless Pearl (USA)
33 **POLSKA (USA),** b f Danzig (USA)—Aquaba (USA)
34 **PRANCING,** br f Prince Sabo—Valika
35 **RIO DUVIDA,** ch c Salse (USA)—Fluctuate
36 **ROYAL CANASKA,** ch c Royal Academy (USA)—North Telstar
37 **SEATTLE SAGA (USA),** b c Seattle Dancer (USA)—Sid's Kate (USA)
38 **SHANGHAI GIRL,** b f Distant Relative—Come On Rosi
39 **SIMPLY KATIE,** ch f Most Welcome—Rechanit (IRE)
40 **SOUTH SALEM (USA),** b c Salem Drive (USA)—Azzurrina
41 **ST ADELE (USA),** b f Pleasant Colony (USA)—Northern Sunset
42 **SUNSET WELLS (USA),** b f Sadler's Wells (USA)—Alysunset (USA)
43 **UNALLOYED (USA),** b f Silver Hawk (USA)—Copperhead (USA)
44 **WOOD MAGIC,** b g Shaadi (USA)—Majenica (USA)

TWO-YEAR-OLDS

45 **ALPINE TIME,** b f 5/4 Tirol—Millie Musique (Miller's Mate)
46 **ARD NA SIGHE (IRE),** b f 10/5 Kenmare (FR)—Lady Seymour (Tudor Melody)
47 **AS ONE (USA),** ch f 20/4 Affirmed (USA)—Twosome (USA) (One For All (USA))
48 B f 2/4 St Jovite (USA)—Azzurrina (Knightly Manner (USA))
49 B f 11/4 Salse (USA)—Birch Creek (Carwhite)
50 B c 13/2 Miswaki (USA)—Bold Jessie (Never So Bold)
51 Ch f 6/5 Mujtahid (USA)—Brentsville (USA) (Arctic Tern (USA))
52 **CABRAL,** ch c 21/3 Arctic Tern (USA)—Model Girl (FR) (Lyphard (USA))
53 **DREAM OF NURMI,** ch c 11/4 Pursuit of Love—Finlandaise (FR) (Arctic Tern (USA))
54 **E SHARP (USA),** b f 1/5 Diesis—Elvia (USA) (Roberto (USA))
55 B f 12/2 Lord At War (ARG)—Ever (USA) (What Luck (USA))
56 B c 16/2 In The Wings—First Kiss (Kris)
57 Ch c 15/5 Soviet Star (USA)—Flamenco Wave (USA) (Desert Wine (USA))
58 B c 28/3 Alzao (USA)—Flute (USA) (Woodman (USA))
59 Ch f 1/5 Kris—Hopeful Search (USA) (Vaguely Noble)
60 B c 31/3 Seattle Dancer (USA)—Kalikala (Darshaan)
61 Ch c 27/3 Salse (USA)—Key Tothe Minstrel (USA) (The Minstrel (CAN))
62 **LYRICAL BID (USA),** b f 11/2 Lyphard (USA)—Doctor Bid (USA) (Spectacular Bid (USA))
63 B f 17/3 St Jovite (USA)—Majestic Nature (USA) (Majestic Prince (USA))
64 B c 9/3 Night Shift (USA)—Merry Rous (Rousillon (USA))
65 **MIDNIGHT ANGEL,** gr f 2/2 Machiavellian (USA)—Night At Sea (Night Shift (USA))
66 B br f 7/2 Polish Precedent—Misallah (IRE) (Shirley Heights)
67 Gr f 16/4 Fairy King (USA)—Miss Toot (Ardross)
68 **NIGHTLARK (IRE),** b f 1/2 Night Shift (USA)—Overcall (Bustino)
69 Ch c 6/2 Known Fact (USA)—Novel Approach (USA) (Codex (USA))
70 **PRIMONDO,** ch c 10/2 Cadeaux Genereux—Clarentia (Ballad Rock)
71 **PROMINENT,** b c 23/4 Primo Dominie—Mary Bankes (USA) (Northern Baby (CAN))
72 B f 5/4 Thatching—Repique (USA) (Sharpen Up)
73 Ch c 9/5 Night Shift (USA)—Rivoltade (USA) (Sir Ivor)
74 **ROSE CARNIVAL,** b f 13/4 Salse (USA)—Jungle Rose (Shirley Heights)
75 B f 25/1 Doyoun—Santella Bell (Ballad Rock)
76 B c 9/3 Indian Ridge—Sarcita (Primo Dominie)
77 B c 20/4 Dixieland Band (USA)—Save The Doe (USA) (Spend A Buck (USA))
78 **SCARLET LAKE,** b f 8/3 Reprimand—Stinging Nettle (Sharpen Up)
79 **SEVA (IRE),** b f 17/1 Night Shift (USA)—Swallowcliffe (Caerleon (USA))
80 B c 13/4 Arazi (USA)—Shoot Clear (Bay Express)
81 B f 7/2 Mtoto—Silk Braid (USA) (Danzig (USA))

MR D. R. LODER—continued

82 B c 30/3 Common Grounds—Strike It Rich (FR) (Rheingold)
83 B f 18/5 Danehill (USA)—Sweet Soprano (High Line)
84 Gr c 29/3 Cozzene (USA)—Thirty Below (USA) (It's Freezing (USA))
85 **VITA BELLA (USA)**, ch f 25/4 Silver Hawk (USA)—Speaking of Sweets (USA) (Elocutionist (USA))
86 **WELLSPRING (IRE)**, b f 20/4 Caerleon (USA)—Marwell (Habitat)

Owners: Cuadra Africa, Saif Ali, Sheikh Ahmed Bin Saeed Al Maktoum, Mohammed Obaid Al Maktoum, Mr Chris Brasher, Cheveley Park Stud, Mrs P. T. Fenwick, Miss D. F. Fleming, Mr John Guest, Lady Harrison, Kirtlington Stud, Mr P. A. Leonard, Sir Andrew Lloyd Webber, Mr Edmund Loder, Mrs K. A. Loder, Lucayan Stud, Mrs S. Magnier, Mr Saeed Manana, Sheikh Mohammed, Mr B. E. Nielsen, Mrs Virginia Kraft Payson, Payson Partnership, Mr P. D. Player, Mr Ali Saeed, Mr Faisal Salman, Mrs June Sifton, Mrs D. Snowden, Mrs M. Taylor, Mr Michael Watt, Mr Peter Winfield, Dr Sinn Dung Wing, Mr Michael Worth.

382   MRS M. E. LONG, Woldingham

Postal: **Barn Yard Stables, Tilling Downs, Woldingham, Surrey, CR3 7JA.**

Phone: **(01883) 340064**

1 **BID FOR A RAINBOW**, 5, b g Sulaafah (USA)—Star Alert **Mrs Kate Breslin**
2 **HAWTHORNE GLEN**, 9, b g Furry Glen—Black Gnat **Mrs Gail Davison**
3 **RAINBOW LEGACY**, 4, b g Sulaafah (USA)—Star Alert **Mrs Gail Davison**
4 **ROSALEE ROYALE**, 4, ch f Out of Hand—Miss Ark Royal **Mrs Gail Davison**
5 **SAILS LEGEND**, 5, b h Hotfoot—Miss Polly Peck **Mrs Gail Davison**
6 **SPRINTFAYRE**, 8, b g Magnolia Lad—Headliner **Mrs Gail Davison**
7 **WILL I FLY**, 10, b g What A Guest—Monalda (FR) **Mr J. Stone**

THREE-YEAR-OLDS

8 **DANCING MAN**, ch c Executive Man—Lyne Dancer **Miss L. D. Martin**
9 **MOYLOUGH REBEL**, ch c Hotfoot—Stellajoe **Mr J. Stone**

TWO-YEAR-OLDS

10 B c 9/4 Tina's Pet—Absalantra (Absalom) **Mrs Gail Davison**
11 B f 23/4 Tina's Pet—Dumerica (Yukon Eric (CAN)) **Mrs Gail Davison**
12 B f 23/4 Tina's Pet—Miss Ark Royal (Broadsword (USA)) **Mrs Gail Davison**
13 B f 1/4 Tina's Pet—Stone Madness (Yukon Eric (CAN)) **Mr J. Stone**

Other Owners: Mr David Digby, Mrs C. J. Fortescue, Mr Cecil Holland, Mr J. Perfitt, Mr R. W. Savage.

Jockey (NH): D Gallagher (10-0).

Apprentices: T P Field (7-0), V Webb (7-0).

Amateur: Mr T McCarthy (10-0).

Lady Rider: Miss Leesa Long (9-7).

383   MR P. D. LUCKIN, Arundel

Postal: **Manor Farm, Tortington, Arundel, West Sussex, BN18 0BG.**

1 5, B g Town And Country—Eastern Air **Mr P. D. Luckin**
2 **KEELBY**, 11, b g Kemal (FR)—Peter's Pet **Mr P. D. Luckin**
3 **MY MUM SAID**, 4, ch f Formidable (USA)—Moorland Lady **Mr P. D. Luckin**

384   MR L. LUNGO, Carrutherstown

Postal: **Hetland Hill Farm, Carrutherstown, Dumfriesshire, DG1 4JX.**

Phone: **(01387) 840691 FAX (01387) 840323**

1 **ASHGROVE DANCER (IRE)**, 6, ch g Roselier (FR)—Leith Hill **Rycon Ltd**
2 **ASTRAL WEEKS (IRE)**, 5, ch g Astronef—Doon Belle **Kenmore Estates**
3 **ATTADALE**, 8, b g Ardross—Marypark **The Low Flyers (Thoroughbreds) Ltd**
4 **CASUAL PASS**, 13, ch g Formidable (USA)—Pitapat **Mr J. J. H. Walker**
5 **CELTIC GIANT**, 6, ch g Celtic Cone—Hester Ann **Mr R. J. Gilbert**
6 **CHERRY STONE**, 7, b g Celtic Cone—Cherry Opal **Mrs A. G. Martin**
7 **CHUMMY'S SAGA**, 6, ch g Caerleon (USA)—Sagar **Mrs I. Curran**
8 **CORSTON JOKER**, 6, b g Idiot's Delight—Corston Lass **Mr A. S. Lyburn**
9 **CORSTON RAMBO**, 9, b g Relkino—Corston Lass **Mr A. S. Lyburn**
10 **DORLIN CASTLE**, 8, b g Scorpio (FR)—Gorgeous Gertie **Mrs D. C. Greig**
11 **FORBIDDEN TIME (IRE)**, 8, b g Welsh Term—Good Court **Mrs J. K. Peutherer**
12 **FOREVER SILVER (IRE)**, 6, ch m Roselier (FR)—Gleann Oge **Mr D. J. Gordon Wright**
13 **GIVE IT LALDY**, 6, b g Mirror Boy—Marjoemin **Mackinnon Mills**
14 **GOLF LAND (IRE)**, 4, ch g Be My Native (USA)—Just Clara **Mrs J. K. Peutherer**
15 **IFALLELSEFAILS**, 8, b g Pollerton—Laurello **Mr R. J. Gilbert**
16 **KIRSTENBOSCH**, 9, b g Caerleon (USA)—Flower Petals **Mrs S. J. Matthews**
17 **KIRTLE SUPERSTAR**, 7, ch m Germont—Girostar **Mr R. B. Hope**
18 **LIVIO (USA)**, 5, b g Lyphard (USA)—Make Change (USA) **The Low Flyers (Thoroughbreds) Ltd**
19 **LOTHIAN PILOT**, 9, ro g Alias Smith (USA)—Lothian Lightning **Crawford, Wares & Hamilton**
20 **MAKE A BUCK**, 6, ch g Buckley—Gaye Memory **Mrs A. G. Martin**
21 **MENSHAAR (USA)**, 4, b g Hawkster (USA)—Klassy Imp (USA) **Mrs Barbara Lungo**
22 **MISTER TRICK (IRE)**, 6, br g Roselier (FR)—Fly Fuss **Mr Edward Birkbeck**
23 **MOMENT OF JUSTICE (USA)**, 5, ch g Timeless Moment (USA)—Court Quillo (USA) **Mr G. A. Martin**
24 **NODDLE (USA)**, 8, ch g Sagace (FR)—Formartin (USA) **Mr J. C. Galbraith**
25 **NOOSA SOUND (IRE)**, 6, br g Orchestra—Borecca **Mrs J. K. Peutherer**
26 **OAT COUTURE**, 8, b g Oats—Marjoemin **Mackinnon Mills**
27 **PALACE OF GOLD**, 6, b g Slip Anchor—Salacious **Mr Garry Hamilton**
28 **PARSON'S LODGE (IRE)**, 8, ch m The Parson—Loge **Mrs S. J. Matthews**
29 **PHAR ECHO (IRE)**, 5, b g Phardante (FR)—Borecca **S. H. C. Racing**
30 **PLANNING GAIN**, 5, ch g Blakeney—Romantiki (USA) **The Low Flyers (Thoroughbreds) Ltd**
31 **PLUMBOB (IRE)**, 7, br g Bob Back (USA)—Naujella **Kenmore Estates Ltd**
32 **POLLY STAR**, 6, b m Pollerton—Belle Comedienne **Mr I. W. Farley**
33 **SANTA CONCERTO (IRE)**, 7, ch g Orchestra—Sapristi **Mr John Corr**
34 **STAR MASTER**, 5, b g Rainbow Quest (USA)—Chellita **Mrs Barbara Lungo**
35 **SUPERTOP**, 8, b br g High Top—Myth **Mr R. J. Gilbert**
36 **SWANBISTER (IRE)**, 6, b g Roselier (FR)—Coolentallagh **Colonel D. C. Greig**
37 **THE NEXT WALTZ (IRE)**, 5, b g Buckskin (FR)—Loge **Mrs Michael Royds**
38 **THE STITCHER (IRE)**, 6, b g Denel (FR)—Garnerstown Lady **Mr J. K. Huddleston**

Other Owners: Mrs F. A. B. Burn, Mr Martin Carroll, Exors Of The Late Lt Cmdr W. H. Crawford, Mrs J. M. Crawford, Mr Tom Duffy, Mrs S. D. Gourlay, Mr Andrew Hamilton, Mrs E. P. Henry, Mrs A. S. J. Johnston, Mr G. A. Martin, Mr Norman McNeil, Mrs Beatrice Wares.

Jockey (NH): T Reed (10-5).

Conditional: Fraser Perratt (9-7).

385   MRS N. J. MACAULEY, Melton Mowbray

Postal: **The Sidings, Saltby Road, Sproxton, Melton Mowbray, LE14 4RA.**

Phone: **(01476) HOME 860578 OFFICE 860090 FAX 860611**

1 **BENTICO**, 7, b g Nordico (USA)—Bentinck Hotel **Mr G. Wiltshire**
2 **BOOST**, 4, b g Superpower—Sirene Bleu Marine (USA) **Mr G. Wiltshire**
3 **CEDAR GIRL**, 4, b f Then Again—Classic Times **Mrs A. L. Saunders**
4 **CELTIC LADY**, 5, b m Kabour—Lady Gilly **Mr S. Lee**

MRS N. J. MACAULEY—continued

 5 **CROWNING TINO**, 4, b f Crowning Honors (CAN)—Tino Reppin **Sandown Park Stud**
 6 **DIA GEORGY**, 5, b br h Reesh—Carpadia **Mrs Deborah Crowley**
 7 **ELTON LEDGER (IRE)**, 7, b g Cyrano de Bergerac—Princess of Nashua **The Posse**
 8 **FIABA**, 8, b m Precocious—Historia **Mr A. J. Peake**
 9 **GLORIOUS ISLAND**, 6, ch g Jupiter Island—Gloria Maremmana **Mr G. Wiltshire**
10 **GREENS PRIDE**, 4, b f Green Adventure (USA)—La Furze **Mr A. Bayman**
11 **JOYFUL TIMES**, 4, br f Doc Marten—Time For Joy **Joyful Times Racing**
12 **JUST LUCKY (IRE)**, 4, b g Fools Holme (USA)—Miss Victoria **Mr Jeffrey Ross**
13 **KARTTIKEYA (FR)**, 5, br g Darshaan—Karosa (FR) **Mr A. J. Peake**
14 **LAUGHING GAS (IRE)**, 7, ch g Lord Ha Ha—Magic Deer **Mr Ralph P. Peters**
15 **MAID WELCOME**, 9, br m Mummy's Pet—Carolynchristensen **Mrs Anna L. Sanders**
16 **MONTAGUE DAWSON (IRE)**, 4, ch g Doulab (USA)—Annacloy **Mr G. Wiltshire**
17 **P G TIPS (IRE)**, 5, ch g Don't Forget Me—Amenaide
18 **PRINCE RUDOLF (IRE)**, 4, b g Cyrano de Bergerac—Princess Raisa **Mr J. Heritage**
19 **RIVAL BID (USA)**, 8, b g Cannonade (USA)—Love Triangle (USA) **Mr G. Wiltshire**
20 **SCYLLA**, 4, b f Rock City—Hearten **Mr D. Cooper**
21 **SHUTTLECOCK**, 5, ch g Pharly (FR)—Upper Sister **Mrs Anna L. Sanders**
22 **SOMMERSBY (IRE)**, 5, b g Vision (USA)—Echoing **Mr A. J. Peake**
23 **SPRINGTIME AFFAIR**, 5, br m Danzig Connection (USA)—Springtime Sugar (USA) **Mr G. Wiltshire**
24 **SUIVEZ**, 6, b g Persian Bold—Butterfly Kiss **Mr G. Wiltshire**

THREE-YEAR-OLDS

25 **BELOW THE RED LINE**, b c Reprimand—Good Try **Mr Brian Pollins**
26 **ETERNALLY GRATEFUL**, b f Picea—Carpadia **Mrs Deborah Crowley**
27 **GOVERNORS DREAM**, b f Governor General—Friendly Miss **Mr P. W. Saunders**
28 **NAPIER STAR**, b f Inca Chief (USA)—America Star **Mr P. M. Heaton**
29 Gr f Timeless Times (USA)—Pilar
30 **SHANOORA (IRE)**, gr f Don't Forget Me—Shalara
31 **SILKY SMOOTH (IRE)**, b f Thatching—Smoo **Mr Brian Pollins**
32 **WATER CHESTNUT**, ch g Most Welcome—Water Pageant **Mr S. Thompson**

TWO-YEAR-OLDS

33 **UNFORGETABLE CHARM (IRE)**, b f Don't Forget Me—Polynesian Charm (USA) (What A Pleasure (USA))

Other Owners: Mr Donald Cooper, Mr G. P. Cope, Mr J. Crowley, Mr Kim Fear, Mrs S. M. Graves, Mr C. Wagstaff, Mrs E. Wagstaff.

Jockeys (NH): R Johnson, S Wynne.

Apprentices: A Sanders, S Sanders (w.a.).

Conditional: E Husband.

386   MR W. J. W. MACKIE, Church Broughton

Postal: **The Bungalow, Barton Blount, Church Broughton, Derby, DE6 5AN.**
Phone: **BURTON-ON-TRENT (01283) 585 604 MOBILE (0831) 888434**

1 **ABSALOM'S PILLAR**, 6, ch g Absalom—Collapse **Mr Peter C. Sherlock**
2 **BUCKS SURPRISE**, 8, ch g Hard Fought—Lady Buck **Mrs L. E. Morton**
3 **CHARLEY LAMBERT (IRE)**, 5, b g Strong Gale—Frankford Run **Mr Peter C. Sherlock**
4 **CIRACUSA (IRE)**, 4, b g Kahyasi—Miranisa **Mr Tim Kelly**
5 **COUTURE STOCKINGS**, 12, b g Free State—Miss Couture **Couture Marketing Ltd**
6 **DIVERTIMIENTO**, 5, b g Night Shift (USA)—Aunt Jemima **Mr B. J. Wood**
7 **HUNTERS' HEAVEN (USA)**, 5, b g Seeking The Gold (USA)—Rose of Virginia (USA) **Mr A. J. Winterton**

MR W. J. W. MACKIE—continued

8 **MASTER OF THE ROCK**, 7, b g Alzao (USA)—Come True (FR) **Mrs Sue Adams**
9 **MR SETASIDE**, 11, br g Royal Fountain—Cregg Park **Mr F. A. Dickinson**
10 **MRS ROBINSON (IRE)**, 5, b m The Parson—Celtic Connection **Mr Peter C. Sherlock**
11 **NAHRI (USA)**, 5, ch g Riverman (USA)—Welden (USA) **Mrs Sue Adams**
12 **PATROCLUS**, 11, b g Tyrnavos—Athenia Princess **Applied Signs Ltd**
13 **QUIXOTRY**, 5, ro g Risk Me (FR)—Grey Charter **Mr F. A. Dickinson**
14 **SLAPY DAM**, 4, b g Deploy—Key To The River (USA) **Rose And Crown, Boylestone**
15 **STAR SELECTION**, 5, b g Rainbow Quest (USA)—Selection Board **Mr R. M. Mitchell**
16 **TIAPHENA**, 5, b m Derrylin—Velda **Mrs J. Small**
17 **TRECENTO**, 5, b m Precious Metal—Tudor Tempest **Mr F. A. Dickinson**

Other Owners: Mr S. P. Adams, Mr N. Brown, Mr Bill Cahill, Mrs J. Mackie, Mr Denis Mulvihill, Mr A. J. Wall.

387   MR A. B. MACTAGGART, Hawick

Postal: **Greendale, Hawick, Roxburghshire, TD9 7NT.**
Phone: **(01450) 372086 FAX (01450) 372086 MOBILE (0860) 139698**

1 **ALNBROOK**, 5, ch g Meadowbrook—Spring Onion **Mr W. Amos**
2 **BARNABY WILLOW**, 4, ch g Dominion—Joli's Girl **Mr J. M. Rudkin**
3 **CAGIE'S TRIUMPH**, 7, b m Germont—Lindean Highlight VII **Mrs Hilary MacTaggart**
4 **CARZARA**, 9, b m Zambrano—Miss Appleyard **Mrs I. A. Forrest**
5 **DARK BUOY**, 7, b g Idiot's Delight—Matilda Mile **Mr R. J. Cowper**
6 **GOLDEN REVERIE (USA)**, 8, b g Golden Act (USA)—Our Reverie (USA) **Mr John Robertson**
7 **HOBKIRK**, 7, b g Niniski (USA)—Banda Sea **Mr W. Amos**
8 **MASTER SANDY (USA)**, 9, b g Master Willie—Whose Broad (USA) **Miss I. Forrest**
9 4, Ch g Rakaposhi King—Mendick Adventure **Mrs S. MacTaggart**
10 **MERRY MERMAID**, 6, ch m Bairn (USA)—Manna Green **Miss J. Campbell**
11 **RUMBLEINTHEJUNGLE**, 5, b g Fort Nayef—Pansy Potter **Mrs H. MacTaggart**
12 **SIDE OF HILL**, 11, b g Furry Glen—Fiuggi **Mr J. M. Rudkin**
13 **THE PATTERS MAGIC**, 9, ch g Cardinal Flower—Carlins Daughter **Mr R. J. Cowper**
14 **WELL APPOINTED (IRE)**, 7, b g Petorius—So Stylish **Drumlanrig Racing**

THREE-YEAR-OLDS

15 **CHEENY'S GOLD**, b f Tumble Gold—Cheeny's Brig **Mr B. MacTaggart**

TWO-YEAR-OLDS

16 **CHEENY'S D'OR**, b f 6/3 Le Coq D'Or—Cheeny's Brig (New Brig) **Mr B. MacTaggart**
17 **DALTON LADY**, b f 3/5 Roscoe Blake—Drom Lady (Royalty) **Mr R. Armstrong & Mr B. MacTaggart**
18 **ROBBIE'S ADVENTURE**, ch c Le Coq d'Or—Mendick Adventure (Mandrake Major) **Mrs S. MacTaggart**

Other Owners: Mr A. Dawson, Mr Andrew Minto, Mr David Morrison.

Jockey (NH): B Storey (10-0, w.a.).

Conditional: G Lee (9-7, w.a.).

388   MR A. H. MACTAGGART, Hawick

Postal: **Hallrule, Bonchester Bridge, Hawick, Roxburghshire, TD9 8JF.**
Phone: **(01450) 860314**

1 **OLIVE BRANCH**, 8, b m Le Moss—Olive Press **Mr A. H. Mactaggart**
2 **PRESS TO STING**, 7, b g Scorpio (FR)—Olive Press **Mr A. H. Mactaggart**

Amateur: Mr J Mactaggart (11-7).

389 MR M. J. MADGWICK, Denmead

Postal: **Forest Farm, Forest Road, Denmead, Hants, PO7 6UA.**

Phone: **(01705) 258313**

1 BETALONGABILL, 7, b br g Lir—Cornish Susie **Miss Judy Taylor**
2 HARRY'S BIRTHDAY (IRE), 4, b c Red Sunset—Great Land (USA) **Mr M. Madgwick**
3 JAAZIM, 6, ch h Night Shift (USA)—Mesmerize **Mr D. Knight**
4 LOCH PATRICK, 6, b g Beveled (USA)—Daisy Loch **Miss E. M. L. Coller**
5 MAY MISSILE, 5, b m Cruise Missile—Amber Marsh **Mr T. Smith**
6 MEMORY'S MUSIC, 4, b c Dance of Life (USA)—Sheer Luck **Mr W. V. Roker**
7 NORDANSK, 7, ch g Nordance (USA)—Free On Board **Mr D. Knight**
8 OUT LINE, 4, gr f Beveled (USA)—Free Range **Mrs D. M. Green**
9 POLICEMANS PRIDE (FR), 7, bl g Policeman (FR)—Proud Pet **Mr R. R. Dove**
10 ROYAL HAND, 6, b g Nearly A Hand—Royal Rushes **Mr H. George**
11 SHARED (IRE), 4, b br g Doyoun—Fenjaan **Mr C. P. Fulford**
12 SHAVANO, 4, ch g Indian Ridge—Out of Range **Mrs H. Veal**
13 SMART REMARK, 4, b g Broadsword (USA)—Miss Cervinia **Miss J. Smith**
14 THAMES SIDE, 5, gr g Beveled (USA)—Free Range **Mr D. Knight**
15 TIGER BLUE (IRE), 5, b g Henbit (USA)—Ballinlonig Star **Mrs H. Goody**
16 VICEROY OF INDIA (CAN), 9, b g Vice Regent (CAN)—Damascene Lady (USA) **Mr T. Smith**

TWO-YEAR-OLDS

17 B f 29/3 Tirol—Kottna (USA) (Lyphard (USA)) **Mr T. G. N. Burrage**

Other Owners: Mr A. G. Axton, Mrs C. Knight, Mrs Trish Tyler.

Jockeys (Flat): M Fenton (8-0), T Quinn (8-0).

Jockey (NH): R Dunwoody.

390 MR C. J. MANN, Upper Lambourn

Postal: **Kings Farm Stables, Upper Lambourn, Newbury, Berks, RG16 7QT.**

Phone: **(01488) 71717 FAX 73223 MOBILE (0374) 212833 OFFICE (01488) 73118**

1 ALQAIRAWAAN, 7, b g Ajdal (USA)—Clare Island **Mr J. Joseph**
2 BASIL STREET (IRE), 4, b g Glenstal (USA)—Pockatello **Don't Libel Me**
3 BIREQUEST, 5, ch g Rainbow Quest (USA)—Artic Mistral (CAN) **Pinnacle Racing Partnership**
4 BONJOUR, 6, br g Primo Dominie—Warm Welcome **The Tramp Partnership**
5 CELIBATE (IRE), 5, ch g Shy Groom (USA)—Dance Alone (USA) **Stamford Bridge Partnership**
6 CLIFTON SET, 5, b g Northern State (USA)—Brave Maiden **Mrs Christine Fennell**
7 CONVOY, 6, gr g Be My Guest (USA)—Be Easy **U. K. Home Computers**
8 DENHAM HILL (IRE), 5, ch g Electric—Barrow Breeze **Mr J. E. Brown**
9 ELGINTORUS (IRE), 6, b g Torus—Marble Owen **Mrs A. T. Pollard & Partners**
10 FITZROVIAN (IRE), 5, b g Millers Mate—Nuravia **U. K. Home Computers**
11 FRENCH MYLE (IRE), 8, ch g Le Bavard (FR)—Myle Avenue **Mr J. E. Brown**
12 FRIAR STREET (IRE), 6, b g Carmelite House (USA)—Madam Slaney **B.R.A.T.S**
13 GENERAL RUSTY (IRE), 8, gr g General Ironside—Auburn Queen **Mr Michael H. Watt**
14 INJUNCTION (IRE), 5, ch g Glenstal (USA)—Laide Festa (ITY) **Miss R. I. Still**
15 ITS A SNIP, 11, ch g Monksfield—Snipkin **The Icy Fire Partnership**
16 IVANHOE, 5, b g Bairn (USA)—Ural Dancer **Mr Godfrey Wilson**
17 KIPPANOUR (USA), 4, b g Alleged (USA)—Innsbruck **Mr Michael H. Watt**
18 L'EQUIPE (IRE), 6, b g Seattle Dancer (USA)—Nordic Dance (USA) **Mr Michael H. Watt**
19 LYPHANTASTIC (USA), 7, b g Lyphard's Wish (FR)—Tango Five Juliet (USA) **Jayflex-Lanz Partnership**
20 MEDWAY QUEEN, 7, b m Pitpan—Starboard Belle **Mrs S. Stanier**
21 MOUNTAIN REACH, 6, b g Wassl—Ural Dancer **Mr Godfrey Wilson**

MR C. J. MANN—continued

22 **MULTY (IRE)**, 4, b br g Posen (USA)—Geraldville **The Izz That Right Partnership**
23 **NESCAF (NZ)**, 6, b g Gold Blend (USA)—Urania (NZ) **Mr Michael H. Watt**
24 **RANGITIKEI (NZ)**, 5, b g Alleged Dash (USA)—Suelga (NZ) **Mrs J. M. Mayo**
25 **SANTELLA BOY (USA)**, 4, b g Turkoman (USA)—Dream Creek (USA) **The Link Leasing Partnership**
26 **SHEER ABILITY**, 10, b g Carlingford Castle—Auburn Queen **Mr Michael Devlin**
27 **SIREN SONG (IRE)**, 5, b g Warning—Nazwa **Mr Michael H. Watt**
28 **SWAN STREET (NZ)**, 5, b g Veloso (NZ)—Azatla (NZ) **Stamford Bridge Partnership**
29 **TALE OF ENDURANCE (IRE)**, 8, b g Ovac (ITY)—Black Tulip **C'est La Vie Racing Partnership**
30 **TORDO (IRE)**, 5, ch g Bob Back (USA)—New Light **Mr M. Myers**
31 **TOTAL JOY (IRE)**, 5, gr g Persian Bold—Caranina (USA) **Mr P. M. Warren**
32 **WRISTBURN**, 6, ch g Nearly A Hand—Loch Chastity **Stamford Bridge Partnership**

Other Owners: Mr Kevin Bays, Bothy Racing Partnership, Mr B. R. H. Burrough, Clifton Set Partnership, Mr Martin Cruddace, Mrs P. Dodd, Mr T. L. Fitzgerald-O'Connor, Mr J. E. Funnell, Mrs A. M. Gladwyn, Mr R. J. Gladwyn, Mr A. Granados, Mr James A. Hamilton, Mr J. F. Hansberry, Mr D. J. Hepsworth, Mr P. D. Hepsworth, Mr J. A. Kendall, Mrs E. F. McKee, Mr R. P. B. Michaelson, Mr M. J. Morrison, Mr Larry Murphy, Mr C. R. Nugent, Mrs P. A. O'Reilly, Mr D. R. Painter, Mr G. A. Parry, Mr J. M. Quinn, Mr A. M. Tolhurst, Mr R. J. Tomes, Sir Gerald Whent, Lady Whent, Mr G. Willey, Mr Michael J. Williams, Mrs Caroline Wilson, Mr R. P. Woolford, Mr I. W. Young, Mr P. H. Young.

Jockeys (NH): R Dunwoody (w.a.), J Railton.

Conditional: Muredach Kelly.

391   MR W. G. MANN, Leamington Spa

Postal: **The Cottage Stables, Bishops Itchington, Leamington Spa, Warwickshire, CV33 0QA.**

1 **BILLY THE BANDIT**, 6, b g Mansingh (USA)—Sweet Fragance (USA) **Mr R. C. Blackman**
2 **CANESTRELLI (USA)**, 11, b g Native Royalty (USA)—Princess Amelia **Mrs Anthea Checkley**
3 **CHRISTIAN SOLDIER**, 4, b g Tickled Pink—Super Princess **Mr O. J. Henley**
4 **COMMANCHE STORM (IRE)**, 4, b g Maelstrom Lake—Commanche Maid **Miss Katy McDaide**
5 **FAR BERRY LAD**, 10, ch g Torus—Honey Roast **Mrs J. Worthington**
6 **NOBLE INSIGHT**, 9, ch g The Noble Player (USA)—Instanter **Miss L. A. Lathe**
7 **SUKEY TAWDRY**, 10, gr m Wassl—Jenny Diver (USA) **Mr O. J. Henley**
8 **TALAB**, 11, b g Beldale Flutter (USA)—Glen Dancer **Mr O. J. Henley**
9 **TOP SLICE (IRE)**, 8, ch g Sandhurst Prince—Traumerei (GER) **Miss D. Thawley**

Other Owners: Mr M. J. Maloney, Mr A. S. McPherson.

Amateur: Mr D Verco (10-2).

392   MR GEORGE G. MARGARSON, Newmarket

Postal: **Machell Place, Old Station Road, Newmarket, Suffolk, CB8 0DW.**
Phone: **(01638) 668043 FAX (01638) 668043**

1 **DANEHILL CHIEF**, 4, b g Dunbeath (USA)—Calafuria
2 **GILT THRONE**, 9, b g Thatching—Nikara (FR)
3 **ROCKCRACKER (IRE)**, 4, ch g Ballad Rock—Forest Blaze (USA)
4 **SWALLOWDALE**, 4, ch f Statoblest—Rambadale

TWO-YEAR-OLDS

5 **CABCHARGE GEMINI**, b c High Kicker (USA)—Miss Noname (High Top)
6 B f 22/2 Music Boy—Carlton Glory (Blakeney)
7 **CORINCHILI**, ch f 25/2 Chilibang—Corinthia (USA) (Empery (USA))

MR GEORGE G. MARGARSON—continued

8 Ch c 26/1 Ron's Victory (USA)—Little Bittern (USA) (Riva Ridge (USA))
9 **SINGFORYOURSUPPER,** ch f 25/2 Superlative—Suzannah's Song (Song)
10 **SPEEDFIT,** gr c 19/5 Mystiko (USA)—Softly Spoken (Mummy's Pet)

Other Owners: Mr P. E. Axon, Computer Cab (Racing Club) Ltd, Mr J. D. Guest, Mrs S. M. Martin, Mrs Jill Sinclair, Mr J. Whiting, Mrs Patricia Williams.

Jockeys (Flat): D D Biggs (8-0, w.a.), A S Clark (8-2, w.a.).

Jockey (NH): J F McLaughlin.

Lady Rider: Mrs Jennie Crossley (8-7).

393   MR D. MARKS, Upper Lambourn

Postal: **Lethornes, Upper Lambourn, Hungerford, Berks, RG17 8QS**
Phone: **(01488) 71767 FAX (01488) 73783**

1 **BOLLINGTON (FR),** 7, ch g Lightning (FR)—Secret Hideaway (USA) **Mr D. Marks**
2 **CHILD STAR (FR),** 7, gr m Bellypha—Miss Shirley (FR) **Mr P. J. Pearson**
3 **DARIUS THE GREAT (IRE),** 4, ch c Persian Heights—Derring Dee **Mr C. R. Buttery**
4 **JAIPUR PRINCESS (IRE),** 4, ch f Shernazar—Jessamy Hall **Mr D. Marchant**
5 **LA MENORQUINA (USA),** 6, b m Woodman (USA)—Hail The Lady (USA) **Mr Joe Arden**
6 **OUR BESSIE,** 5, b m Persian Bold—Jamarj **Mr John N. Simpson**
7 **PARAMOUNT LEADER,** 4, b g Presidium—Dragusa **P. Oppenheimer**
8 **PRIVATE FIXTURE (IRE),** 5, ch g The Noble Player (USA)—Pennyala **Mr Richard P. Mooney**
9 **TENAYESTELIGN,** 8, gr m Bellypha—Opale **Mr G. J. King**

THREE-YEAR-OLDS

10 **DHULIKHEL,** b f Reprimand—Travel Storm **Mr G. J. King**

TWO-YEAR-OLDS

11 **CHILI BOUCHIER,** br f 23/2 Stop The Music (USA)—Low Approach (Artaius (USA)) **Mr John M. Simpson**

Other Owners: Mr D. J. Cremin, Mr M. Freti, Mr P. A. Heath, Mr John M. Jackson.

Jockey (Flat): P Eddery (w.a.).

Jockey (NH): J McCarthy (10-0, w.a.).

Lady Riders: Miss Amy Dronsfield (9-0), Miss Kelly Marks (9-0).

394   MRS L. A. MARSHALL, Morpeth

Postal: **Togston Hall Farmhouse, North Togston, Amble, Morpeth, NE65 0HR.**
Phone: **(01665) 712699**

1 **BY THE BYE,** 9, ch m Bybicello—Reel Keen **Mrs L. Marshall**
2 **CALLED TO ACCOUNT,** 7, b m Cool Guy (USA)—True Grit **Mrs L. Marshall**
3 **DONOVANS REEF,** 10, b g Cool Guy (USA)—Mother Machree **Mrs L. Marshall**
4 **MORE JOY,** 8, b g Lighter—Caubeen **Mrs L. Marshall**
5 **WHITER MORN,** 6, b m Alias Smith (USA)—Mother Machree **Mrs L. Marshall**

Amateurs: Mr K Whelan, Mr N Wilson.

395   MR R. F. MARVIN, Newark

Postal: **The Hunter Yard, Southwell Racecouse, Rolleston, Newark, NG25 0TS.**

Phone: **YARD (01302) 746577**

 1 **BEAUCHIEF**, 4, br g Kind of Hush—Firdale Rosie **Mr Tom Roberts**
 2 **BLACK BOY (IRE)**, 7, br g Auction Ring (USA)—Relic Spirit **Mr David G. Woods**
 3 **DRUSO (USA)**, 12, b g Raise A Cup (USA)—Pretty Pride **Mr Brian Parr**
 4 **JULIETSKI**, 8, gr m Niniski (USA)—Plum Blossom (USA) **Mr Robert McBurnie**
 5 **LEGEND OF SHARROW (IRE)**, 5, b g Heraldiste (USA)—Listooder Girl **Miss Megan Phipps**
 6 **LUKES BROTHER (IRE)**, 5, ch g Kirchner—Golden Baby **Miss Megan Phipps**
 7 **PARISIENNE KING (USA)**, 7, b g Key To The Kingdom (USA)—Paris Dawn (USA) **Mr David G. Woods**
 8 **QUICK ON THE DRAW**, 4, b f Kind of Hush—Shoot To Kill **Mr R. B. Boland**
 9 4, B g Komaite (USA)—Starkist **Mr R. W. Jaines**
10 **TOMMANION (IRE)**, 4, b g Maelstrom Lake—Saranita **Miss Megan Phipps**
11 **WASSL'S GUEST (IRE)**, 5, b m Be My Guest (USA)—Wassl's Sister **Mr Robert McBurnie**
12 4, B f Poetic Justice—Westamist

THREE-YEAR-OLDS

13 B c Inca Chief (USA)—Davemma **Mrs C. Humphrey**
14 B f Sylvan Express—Lady Homily **Mrs C. Humphrey**
15 B f Prince of Peace—Musical Moments

TWO-YEAR-OLDS

16 B c 19/2 Warrshan (USA)—Adorable Cherub (USA) (Halo (USA)) **Saloop Ltd**
17 B f 27/3 Mac's Imp (USA)—Genzyme Gene (Riboboy (USA)) **Mr R. W. Jaines**
18 B c 10/4 Warrshan (USA)—Mountain Harvest (FR) (Shirley Heights) **Mr R. W. Jaines**
19 B f 7/3 Superpower—Vico Equense (Absalom) **Mr E. Gray**

Other Owners: Mr Ray Pickworth.

Jockey (Flat): Francis Norton (8-0).

Jockey (NH): W Worthington (10-0).

Lady Riders: Mrs M Morris (9-0), Ms Megan Phipps (8-7).

396   MR K. MCAULIFFE, Lambourn

Postal: **Delamere Cottage Stables, Folly Road, Lambourn, Berks, RG17 8QE.**

Phone: **(01488) 73999 FAX (01488) 73888 MOBILE (0802) 368846**

 1 **CARE AND COMFORT**, 4, ch f Most Welcome—Whipp's Cross **Elite Racing Club**
 2 **DRIMARD (IRE)**, 5, ch g Ela-Mana-Mou—Babilla (USA) **Mr E. P. Jameson**
 3 **FALLAL (IRE)**, 4, b f Fayruz—Lady Bidder **Mr Jorg Vasicek**
 4 **FIORENZ (USA)**, 4, ch f Chromite (USA)—Christi Dawn (USA) **Mrs G. Lanzara**
 5 **HARRY WELSH (IRE)**, 4, gr g Treasure Kay—Excelling Miss (USA) **Mr Jorg Vasicek**
 6 **MISTER**, 4, ch g Risk Me (FR)—Beauvoir **Mr B. J. Kelly**
 7 **MONTANELLI (FR)**, 4, b g Dowsing (USA)—Honeymooning (USA) **Delamere Cottage Racing Syndicate**
 8 **NEWINGTON BUTTS (IRE)**, 6, br m Dowsing (USA)—Cloud Nine **Mr D. D. Davies**
 9 **PRECEDENCY**, 4, b g Polish Precedent (USA)—Allegedly Blue (USA) **Mr E. D. Kessly**
10 **WOLVER MURPHY (IRE)**, 4, b f Persian Heights—Wolverstar **Mr L. Murphy**

THREE-YEAR-OLDS

11 **ACCOUNTANCY JEWEL (IRE)**, b f Pennine Walk—Polyester Girl **D. Brennan Accountants**
12 **ANIMATION**, ch f Superlative—What A Looker (USA) **Mr E. P. Jameson**

MR K. MCAULIFFE—continued

13 **APARTMENTS ABROAD**, b f Prince Sabo—La Graciosa **Mr Peter Barclay**
14 Ch f Chromite (USA)—Christi Dawn (USA) **Mrs G. Lanzara**
15 **DESERT SCOUT**, b c Picea—Queens Pearl **Norman Hill Plant Hire Ltd**
16 **FOREST BOY**, b g Komaite (USA)—Khadine **Highgrove Developments Limited**
17 **LA BELLE KATHERINE (USA)**, b f Lyphard (USA)—Little Scioto (USA) **Mrs G. Lanzara**
18 B f Imperial Frontier (USA)—La Padma **Mr B. J. Kelly**
19 **MON PERE**, b g Belfort (FR)—Lady Ever-So-Sure **Mrs H. Raw**
20 **MY KIND**, ch f Mon Tresor—Kind of Shy **Elite Racing Club**
21 **NOT QUITE GREY**, gr g Absalom—Strawberry Song **Mr D. D. Davies**
22 **PEOPLE DIRECT**, ch f Ron's Victory (USA)—Ayr Classic **Mr Peter Barclay**
23 **REBOUNDER**, b c Reprimand—So Bold **Mr G. Tong**
24 **RIGHTEOUS GENT**, b g Superpower—Golden **Mrs H. Raw**
25 **SONIC MAIL**, b g Keen—Martin-Lavell Mail **Folly Road Racing Partners 1995**

TWO-YEAR-OLDS

26 B c 7/4 Chilibang—Anse Chastanet (Cavo Doro)
27 B f 20/3 Superpower—Chablisse (Radetzky) **Mr J. Raw & Highgrove Developments Ltd**
28 B c 9/3 Fayruz—Daybreaker (Thatching) **Srl General Horse Advertising**
29 B c 2/5 Emarati (USA)—Dominion Blue (Dominion) **Folly Road Racing Partners (1996)**
30 B c 28/4 Fayruz—Farriers Slipper (Prince Tenderfoot (USA)) **Srl General Horse Advertising**
31 Ch c La Grange Music—Golden (Don) **Mrs H. Raw**
32 **HOH DOWN (IRE)**, b f 30/4 Fairy King (USA)—
                              Tintomara (IRE) (Niniski (USA)) **Mr D. F. Allport & Hoh Supply Ltd**
33 B c 3/3 Treasure Kay—Poka Poka (FR) (King of Macedon)
34 B f 4/2 Common Grounds—Red Magic (Red God) **Mr A. Macgillivray**
35 B c 27/3 Arcane (USA)—Tales of Wisdom (Rousillon (USA)) **Delamere Cottage Racing Partners (1996)**

Other Owners: Chiquita Lodge Stud, Mr M. A. Kirby, Mrs J. Langmead, Mr J. P. McCann, Mr G. Melican, Mr A. N. Miller, Mr J. Wicks.

397   MR D. MCCAIN, Cholmondeley

Postal: **Bankhouse, Cholmondeley, Malpas, Cheshire, SY14 8AL.**
Phone: **(01829) 720352 OR (0836) 780879 FAX (01829) 720475**

1 **ABBEY MOSS**, 5, b g Executive Man—Mickley Vulstar
2 **ALICANTE**, 9, b g Alzao (USA)—Safe And Happy **Mr Alan Winstanley**
3 4, Ch f Le Moss—At First Sight
4 **BICKERTON POACHER**, 6, ch g Gabitat—On Tour **Mr D. McCain**
5 **CIRCULATION**, 10, b g Town And Country—Veinarde **Mr John Singleton**
6 **COME ON RISK ME**, 5, ch g Risk Me (FR)—Star Rose (FR) **Mr Harry Ormesher**
7 **COOLINNY (IRE)**, 7, b g Torus—Lady Driver **Mr D. McCain**
8 **CRAFTY CHAPLAIN**, 10, ch g The Parson—She's Clever **Mr D. A. Malam**
9 **DON LUIGI**, 5, b g Rakaposhi King—Lorien Lady **Mrs K. Lloyd**
10 **EBEN AL HABEEB (IRE)**, 5, ch g Nashwan (USA)—Family Style (USA) **The Cholmondeley Confederacy**
11 **ERICA**, 5, b m Rakaposhi King—Snippet **Mrs K. Lloyd**
12 **EUROLINK SHADOW**, 4, b g Be My Chief (USA)—Miss Top Ville (FR) **Mr A. J. Baxter**
13 **FARADAY**, 6, b g Electric—Muffet's Gold
14 **FOLLOW DE CALL**, 6, b g Callernish—Designer **Mr D. McCain**
15 4, B f Derrylin—Herald The Dawn
16 4, Ch g Gunner B—Kirsheda
17 **LAMBRINI (IRE)**, 6, b m Buckskin (FR)—Keeping Company **Halewood International Ltd**
18 4, B f Derrylin—Little Oats
19 **LOTHIAN COMMANDER**, 4, ch g Alias Smith (USA)—Lothian Lightning **Mr Roger Bellamy**
20 **NADIAD**, 10, b g Darshaan—Naveen **Mr L. A. Morgan**
21 **RAINHAM**, 9, b g Sadler's Wells (USA)—Edge of Town **Mr A. K. Collins**
22 **RINUS MAJESTIC (IRE)**, 4, b g Gallic League—Deepwater Blues **Mr A. M. Proos**
23 **RINUS MAJOR (IRE)**, 5, b g Don't Forget Me—Needy **Mr A. M. Proos**

MR D. MCCAIN—continued

24 RINUS MASTER (IRE), 5, ch g Jareer (USA)—Prodical Daughter **Mr A. M. Proos**
25 5, Ch m Executive Man—Saheej (USA)
26 4, B g Rakaposhi King—Snippet
27 4, B g Pablond—Sovereign's Oak
28 STRETCHIT, 6, b g Full Extent (USA)—Snippet **Mr Roger Bellamy**
29 SURE METAL, 13, b g Billion (USA)—Sujini **Mr L. A. Morgan**
30 THE SECRET GREY, 5, gr g Rakaposhi King—Locketts Lane **Mr J. Clayton & Mr James Bieley**
31 TRIBAL RULER, 11, b g Prince Tenderfoot (USA)—Candolcis **Mr John Singleton**
32 5, B g Rakaposhi King—Vulpro
33 5, B g Ballacashtal (CAN)—Whose Lady (USA)

THREE-YEAR-OLDS

34 B g Rakaposhi King—Divine Affair (IRE) **Mr A. A. Parkinson**
35 B g Pablond—Joyful's Girl
36 B f Henbit (USA)—Let Me Finish
37 Ch f Henbit (USA)—Miss Club Royal **Halewood International Ltd**

TWO-YEAR-OLDS

38 Br g 30/3 Gildoran—Fille de Soleile (Sunyboy)
39 B g 18/5 Precious Metal—My Solitaire (Sparkler)
40 B f 5/6 Le Moss—Snippet (Ragstone)
41 B g 31/5 Gildoran—Valiant Vision (Brave Invader (USA))

Other Owners: Mr Richard Abbott, Mr Roy Ashley, Mr James Bigley, Exors Of The Late Mr F. S. Markland, Mrs B. McCain, Mr I. N. Meadows, Mr G. Gary Salters, Mrs A. V. Winstanley.

Jockeys (NH): D McCain (Jnr) (10-4), G McCourt (w.a.).

Conditional: C Hoggart (9-7), D Walsh (9-9).

Amateur: Mr G Lake (9-0).

398   MR J. C. MCCONNOCHIE, Stratford-on-Avon

Postal: **Bankfield Racing Stables, Billesley Road, Wilmcote, Stratford-on-Avon, CV37 9XG.**
Phone: **(01789) 415607 MOBILE (0831) 788565**

1 ARMATEUR (FR), 8, b g Miller's Mate—Artistically (USA) **Major H. R. M. Porter**
2 BELLE BARONESS, 6, gr m Baron Blakeney—Ribobelle **Mr J. C. McConnochie**
3 CHAMPAGNE GOLD, 9, ch g Bairn (USA)—Halkissimo **Mr J. A. Bianchi**
4 COUNTERBALANCE, 9, b m Orchestra—Lysanders Lady **Derwent Dene Farm**
5 COUNTRY PARSON (IRE), 7, ch g The Parson—Fisalmar Isle VII **Major H. R. M. Porter**
6 DIAMOND FORT, 11, b g Mirror Boy—Fortina Lass **Mrs R. E. Stocks**
7 EVERSO IRISH, 7, b g Hatim (USA)—Ever So **Mr M. J. Clarke**
8 PEARL'S CHOICE (IRE), 8, b br m Deep Run—Vendevar **Mr J. C. McConnochie**
9 TWO STEP RHYTHM, 12, gr g Neltino—Niagara Rhythm **Mrs R. E. Stocks**

Other Owners: Mr S. Forster, Mr A. J. Stocks, Miss J. Wilkinson.

Jockeys (NH): R Bellamy, S McNeill, Mark Sharratt (10-0).

399   MR M. MCCORMACK, Wantage

Postal: **East Manton Stables, Sparsholt, Wantage, Oxon, OX12 9PJ.**
Phone: **CHILDREY (01235) 751433**

1 AN SPAILPIN FANACH (IRE), 7, b g Rymer—Sidhe Gaoth **Mr K. Styles**
2 JOSIFINA, 5, b m Master Willie—Superfina (USA) **Mr Andrew Shenston**
3 MAYLIN MAGIC, 5, b m Minster Son—Miss Felham **Mr F. Lipscomb**

MR M. MCCORMACK—continued

4 **MONTENDRE**, 9, b g Longleat (USA)—La Lutine **Mr David Mort**
5 **PAB'S CHOICE**, 5, ch m Telsmoss—Dido **Mr C. Papaioannou**
6 **SING UP**, 4, b c Sizzling Melody—Hellene **Unit Partnership**
7 **SPITFIRE BRIDGE (IRE)**, 4, b g Cyrano de Bergerac—Maria Renata **East Manton Racing Stables Limited**

THREE-YEAR-OLDS

8 **CHARTERHOUSE XPRES**, b c Clantime—Uptown Girl **Charterhouse Holdings Plc**
9 **HANK-A-CHIEF**, b c Inca Chief (USA)—Be Sharp **Sixpenny Racing Club**
10 **ISLA GLEN**, b f Be My Chief (USA)—Serration **Mr J. W. Wells**
11 **TWO SOCKS**, ch c Phountzi (USA)—Mrs Feathers **Mrs Satu Marks**

TWO-YEAR-OLDS

12 Br c Prince Sabo—Beautiful Orchid (Hays) **G. West**
13 Br c Superlative—Good Time Girl (Good Times (ITY)) **G. West**
14 B c Anshan—Great Splendour (Pharly (FR)) **Eastmanton Racing Stables Ltd**

Other Owners: D. Ackroyd, R. Batty, Mr J. W. B. Crawford, Mr R. K. Curtis, Mrs A. Hall, G. M. Harrison, Mr R. W. Hester, Isla Glen Partnership, Mr Colin W. McKerrow, J. Philips, Mr Nigel Rich, Mr Mohammad Shafiq, Mr D. P. Shea, Mr John Simms, Mr J. R. Stanton, Mr Peter Tafler, Mr D. I. Thomas, Mrs R. G. Wellman.

Jockey (Flat): J Reid (w.a.).

400 MRS M. MCCOURT, Wantage

Postal: **Antwick Stud, Letcombe Regis, Wantage, Oxon, OX12 9LH.**
Phone: **(01235) 764456 OFFICE (01235) 760896**

1 **ANNABEL'S BABY (IRE)**, 7, b m Alzao (USA)—Spyglass **Mrs M. McCourt**
2 **BARRANAK (IRE)**, 4, b g Cyrano de Bergerac—Saulonika **Mr M. Mac Carthy**
3 **CERTAIN SHOT**, 5, b g Little Wolf—Duckdown **Mr D. E. H. Horton**
4 **DANNY GALE (IRE)**, 5, b g Strong Gale—Mary The Rake **Mr Robert Cox**
5 **DONNA DEL LAGO**, 10, b m Kings Lake (USA)—Cannon Boy (USA) **Mr M. Mac Carthy**
6 **DRIVING FORCE**, 10, ch g Be My Native (USA)—Frederika (USA) **Mr B. J. Reid**
7 **FONTANAYS (IRE)**, 8, b g Wassl—Mombones **Pegasus Racing Partnership**
8 **HERESTHEDEAL (IRE)**, 7, b g Martin John—Newgate Princess **Pegasus Racing Partnership II**
9 **KIRI'S ROSE (IRE)**, 6, b m Roselier (FR)—Kiri's Return **Mrs M. McCourt**
10 **LANCE ARMSTRONG (IRE)**, 6, ch g Lancastrian—Wolver Rose **Mr G. L. Porter**
11 **LIKASHOT**, 7, b m Celtic Cone—Duckdown **Mr D. E. H. Horton**
12 **NATIVE RAMBLER (IRE)**, 6, ch g Le Bavard (FR)—Native Shot **Mr Robert Cox**
13 **POLLYDALUS (IRE)**, 5, b m Mandalus—Dandy Poll **In Touch Partnership**
14 **SISTER STEPHANIE (IRE)**, 7, b br m Phardante (FR)—Soul Lucy **The Antwick Partnership**
15 **THE MERRY NUN (IRE)**, 7, ch m Lancastrian—Katebeaujolais **Greycing Club**
16 **TROUBLE SHOOT (USA)**, 6, ch g Greinton—Troubles Trouble **Mr Robert Cox**
17 **UNCLE BERT (IRE)**, 6, b g Ovac (ITY)—Sweet Gum (USA) **Mr Alec Tuckerman**

THREE-YEAR-OLDS

18 **MRS KEEN**, b f Beveled (USA)—Haiti Mill **Mr J. F. Watson**
19 **NELLIE NORTH**, b f Northern State (USA)—Kimble Princess **Mr Geoffrey C. Greenwood**

Other Owners: Mr R. F. Batty, Mr John Bodinham, Mr Shaun Bradford, Mr A. Carney, Mr Jeremy Charles, Mr M. Connell, Mr J. P. Cooper, Mr David Curtis, Mr S. D. Gray, Mr Richard Hill, Mr John Mandeville, Mrs M. Moriarty, Mr Chris Page, Mr Irving Phillips, Mrs Victoria Tuckerman, Mr Andy Turner, Mrs Margaret Turner, Mr C. P. Walker, Mr J. D. Walton, Mr Christopher White.

Jockey (Flat): B Thomson (w.a.).

Jockeys (NH): D Gallagher, G McCourt (10-5).

401 MR T. P. MCGOVERN, Lewes

Postal: **Grandstand Stables, Old Lewes Racecourse, Lewes, East Sussex.**

Phone: **(01273) 487813**

1 **BALLYGRIFFIN LAD (IRE)**, 7, ch g Carlingford Castle—Calfstown Night **Mr Tommy Breen**
2 **LADY GHISLAINE (FR)**, 9, b m Lydian (FR)—Planeze (FR) **Cottage Rake Racing**
3 **LORD GLENVARA (IRE)**, 8, ch g Millfontaine—Ishtar **Mr Paul Gibbons**
4 **MILLMOUNT (IRE)**, 6, ch m Be My Guest (USA)—Cooliney Princess **Eastridge Racing**
5 **MR GENEAOLOGY (USA)**, 6, b g Procida (USA)—Que Mona (USA) **Cottage Rake Racing**
6 **NORTH BANNISTER**, 9, b g Baron Blakeney—Freuchie **Liam Og's Racing**
7 **NORTHERN HIGHLIGHT**, 5, ch g Pharly (FR)—Unearthed **Mrs J. Jennings**
8 **RIVA ROCK**, 6, b g Roaring Riva—Kivulini **Mr Phil Collins**
9 4, B f Cyrano de Bergerac—Sasha Lea **Mrs D. Watts**
10 **SIMPLY (IRE)**, 7, b g Simply Great (FR)—Be A Dancer **Mr Paul Gibbons**
11 **TOM COVEY**, 10, b g Record Run—Sasha Lea **Mrs D. Watts**
12 **WALKING TALL (IRE)**, 5, ch g Hatim (USA)—Futility **Mr Phil Collins**

Other Owners: Mr M. J. Adams, Mrs Carole Binny, Mrs K. Cunningham, Mr W. Cunningham, Mr T. K. O'Toole.

402 MRS C. MCINNES SKINNER, Melton Mowbray

Postal: **John O'Gaunt House, Melton Mowbray, Leics, LE14 2RE.**

Phone: **(01664) 454327**

1 **LITTLE TINCTURE (IRE)**, 6, ch g Meneval (USA)—Lakefield Lady **Mrs T. J. McInnes Skinner**
2 **LONDON HILL**, 8, b g Little Wolf—Bambag **Mrs T. J. McInnes Skinner**
3 **SHEELIN LAD (IRE)**, 8, ch g Orchestra—Aryumad **Mrs T. J. McInnes Skinner**
4 **YOUNG MINER**, 10, ch g Monksfield—Tassel Tip **Mrs T. J. McInnes Skinner**

Jockey (NH): G Upton (10-2, w.a.).

Lady Rider: Sophie Mitchell (w.a.).

403 MR R. MCKELLAR, Lesmahagow

Postal: **Dumbraxhill, Brocketsbrae, Lesmahagow, Lanark, M11 9YP.**

Phone: **(01555) 892356**

1 **BENJARONG**, 4, ch f Sharpo—Rose And The Ring **Mrs Margaret Brown**
2 **BERKELEY BOUNDER (USA)**, 4, b c Diesis—Top Socialite (USA) **Mr R. Hilley**
3 **CORKY'S GIRL**, 4, b f Today And Tomorrow—Rectory Maid **Miss S. A. Corcoran**
4 **DAWN ROCK**, 5, b g Norwick (USA)—Venetian Joy **Punters Haven Racing Club**
5 **ENDOWMENT**, 4, ch g Cadeaux Genereux—Palm Springs **Mr R. Hilley**
6 **HUTCHIES LADY**, 4, b f Efisio—Keep Mum **Mrs Linda Mckellar**
7 **KIRKIE CROSS**, 4, b f Efisio—Balgownie **Mr Alex Gorrie**
8 **MUZZ (IRE)**, 5, br g Gallic League—Cartier Bijoux **Mr Alex Gorrie**
9 **NABURN LOCH**, 6, b m Lochnager—Balgownie
10 **OPERATIC DANCER**, 5, b g Germont—Indian Dancer **Mr Peter Howell**
11 **SCHOOL OF SCIENCE**, 6, b g Then Again—Girl's Brigade **Mr Raymond White**
12 **SERIOUS HURRY**, 8, ch g Forzando—Lady Bequick **Miss S. A. Corcoran**
13 **STINGRAY CITY (USA)**, 7, b g Raft (USA)—Out of This World **Mr Peter McMahon**
14 **SUEDORO**, 6, b m Hard Fought—Bamdoro **Mr Ray Vardy**

THREE-YEAR-OLDS

15 **LENNOX LADY**, b f Dominion Royale—Balgownie **Mr Alex Gorrie**
16 **VALES ALES**, b g Dominion Royale—Keep Mum **Mr Willie Smith**

MR R. MCKELLAR—continued
TWO-YEAR-OLDS

17 B f 8/2 Crowning Honors (CAN)—Junuh (Jalmood (USA)) **Mrs Linda Mckellar**

Other Owners: Mr Jim Anderson, Mr J. W. Hazeldean, Mr Peter Henderson, Mr D. McGonagle.

Jockeys (Flat): J K Fanning, T Williams.

Apprentice: Ian Campbell (7-12).

Conditional: D Parker (w.a.).

Amateur: Mr R Hale (9-7, w.a.).

Lady Riders: Miss A Creedon (9-0), Mrs C Williams (9-0).

404   MR W. G. MCKENZIE-COLES, Taunton
Postal: **Bells Cottage, Lydeard St Lawrence, Taunton, Somerset, TA4 3RN.**
Phone: **LYDEARD ST LAWRENCE (01984) 667334**

1 AT IT AGAIN (IRE), 7, ch g Regular Guy—Pollys Grind **Mr W. G. McKenzie-Coles**
2 LOUIS RENEE (IRE), 5, ch g Cardinal Flower—Moon Lock **Mr W. G. McKenzie-Coles**
3 SUPREME CRUSADER (IRE), 5, br g Supreme Leader—Seanaphobal Lady **Mr W. G. McKenzie-Coles**
4 TOM TUGG (IRE), 6, b g Supreme Leader—Healys Pass **Mrs R. McKenzie-Coles**

Jockeys (NH): C Maude, W J McFarland.

405   MR W. MCKEOWN, Newcastle
Postal: **East Wideopen Farm, Wideopen, Newcastle Upon Tyne, NE13 6DW.**
Phone: **TEL (0191) 236 7545 FAX (0191) 236 2959**

1 ALAN'S PRIDE (IRE), 5, b m Supreme Leader—Mantilla Run **Mrs L. E. McKeown**
2 BOGARTS DISCO (IRE), 8, b g Forties Field (FR)—Kitty's Reject **Mrs L. E. McKeown**
3 CHARLIE TRUMPER (IRE), 8, ch g Denel (FR)—Karazend **Mr W. McKeown**
4 DOXFORD HUT, 12, b g Class Distinction—Tillside Brig **Mr W. McKeown**
5 ENVIRONMENTAL LAW, 5, b g Slip Anchor—Dame Margot (USA) **Mrs L. E. McKeown**
6 GODS SQUAD, 4, ro g Gods Solution—My Always **Mr W. McKeown**
7 JOCK'S BURN, 10, ch g Paddy's Stream—Fairyslave **Mrs L. E. McKeown**
8 JOG-ALONG, 7, b g Cool Guy (USA)—South Dakota **Mr W. McKeown**
9 LAGO LAGO (IRE), 4, b f Shernazar—Lagolette **Mr W. McKeown**
10 QATTARA (IRE), 6, b g Callernish—Javelot's Dancer **Mr W. McKeown**
11 SIR BOB (IRE), 4, br g Aristocracy—Wilden **Mrs L. E. McKeown**
12 STORMING LORNA (IRE), 6, b m Strong Gale—Furry Shamrock **Mr W. McKeown**

THREE-YEAR-OLDS
13 MR TITCH, b g Totem (USA)—Empress Nicki **Mrs L. E. McKeown**

406   MRS V. MCKIE, Twyford

Postal: 'Twyford Mill', Twyford, Buckingham, MK18 4HA.

Phone: STEEPLE CLAYDON (01296) 730707 FAX: (01296) 730806

1 5, B g Black Minstrel—Ashford Doll **Mrs Ian McKie**
2 BELONGA MICK (IRE), 6, b g Rowlandson—Swift Vulgan **Alfordshire Ltd**
3 CALL ME NOW (IRE), 6, b g Callernish—Tarrants Cross **Mr M. H. D. Barlow & Mrs Ian McKie**
4 FASHION MAKER (IRE), 6, b g Creative Plan (USA)—Cailin Alainn **Mr J. B. Sumner**
5 FENCING MASTER, 7, b g Broadsword (USA)—Adroit **Mr M. H. D. Barlow**
6 FILL THE BOOT (IRE), 6, br g Mandalus—Lady O' The Grange **Mrs Ian McKie**
7 GOING UNDER (IRE), 8, br g Miner's Lamp—Tawney Rose **Mrs Ian McKie**
8 4, B g Waajib—Kavali **Mrs Ian McKie**
9 5, B g Mister Lord (USA)—Ko Mear **Mrs Ian McKie**
10 MAKES ME GOOSEY (IRE), 8, b g Roselier (FR)—Clonmeen Official **Alfordshire Ltd**
11 NO LIGHT, 9, gr g Celio Rufo—Lady Templar **Alfordshire Ltd**
12 4, B g Strong Gale—Pallastown Run **Mr G. Payne**
13 QUICK QUOTE, 6, b m Oats—Spartiquick **Mr M. H. D. Barlow**
14 ROYAL DADDA, 6, br g Denel (FR)—Royal Typhoon **Mrs Ian McKie**
15 SPECIAL CHELLOW, 5, ch g Winter Words—Counter Measure **Mr K. Cooper**
16 THE MALAKARMA, 10, b g St Columbus—Impinge (USA) **Mr Charles Dixey**
17 TORIAN (IRE), 5, b g Torus—Brave Intention **Mrs Ian McKie**
18 5, B br g Corvaro (USA)—Welsh Tan **Mrs Ian McKie**

Jockey (NH): L Harvey (10-0).

Amateur: Mr T Byrne.

Lady Rider: Miss K Holmes (9-7).

407   MR B. A. MCMAHON, Tamworth

Postal: Woodside Farm, Hopwas Hill, Tamworth, Staffs, B78 3AR.

Phone: (01827) 62901 FAX (01827) 68361

1 BAND ON THE RUN, 9, ch h Song—Sylvanecte (FR) **Mr D. J. Allen**
2 COLOMBO KING (IRE), 4, ch g Thatching—Joanne's Joy **Mrs L. Mathew**
3 I'M YOUR LADY, 5, ch m Risk Me (FR)—Impala Lass **Mr Michael G. T. Stokes**
4 JALMAID, 4, ch f Jalmood (USA)—Misowni **Breeson**
5 KATY'S LAD, 9, b g Camden Town—Cathryn's Song **Mr J. W. Butler**
6 KUNG FRODE, 4, ch c Interrex (CAN)—Harmony Heights **Mrs J. McMahon**
7 MAYBANK (IRE), 4, gr g Contract Law (USA)—Katysue **Mr Soong & Mr Tsang**
8 ROVING MINSTREL, 5, ch h Cree Song—Klairove **Mrs J. McMahon & Mr T. Staunton**
9 SHEECKY, 5, b g Green Ruby—Beth of Houndhill **Mrs Angela Beard**
10 SING WITH THE BAND, 5, b m Chief Singer—Ra Ra Girl **Mr D. J. Allen**
11 SUPERBIT, 4, b c Superpower—On A Bit **Mr Neville H. Smith**
12 YOUNG BENSON, 4, b c Zalazl (USA)—Impala Lass **Mr Michael G. T. Stokes**

THREE-YEAR-OLDS

13 AMINGTON LASS, ch f Cree Song—Millfields House **Mr M. Higgins**
14 ANGUS MCCOATUP (IRE), ch c Mac's Imp (USA)—In For More **Mr D. J. Allen**
15 HIGHLAND FAWN, ch f Safawan—Highland Rowena **Mr T. Staunton**
16 HOLLOWAY MELODY, ch f Cree Song—Holloway Wonder **Mr R. Thornhill**
17 INCA BIRD, b f Inca Chief (USA)—Polly Oligant **Mr Lowe**
18 JACK JENNINGS, ch c Deploy—Lareyna **Mr G. Whitaker**
19 LOOK WHO'S CALLING (IRE), b c Al Hareb (USA)—House Call **Mr G. Edwards**
20 MA BULSIE, b f Beveled (USA)—Cool Run **Mr J. Blain**

MR B. A. MCMAHON—continued

21 **MULLAGH HILL LAD (IRE)**, b c Cyrano de Bergerac—Fantasie (FR) **The Bramble Partnership**
22 **NICHOLA'S PRINCESS**, b f Handsome Sailor—Barachois Princess (USA) **Mr J. P. Graham**
23 **PRINCESS EFISIO**, b f Efisio—Cutlass Princess (USA) **Mr J. P. Graham**
24 **PULGA CIRCO**, b f Tina's Pet—Pulga
25 **SAFA DANCER**, b f Safawan—Dalby Dancer **Mrs J. McMahon**
26 **SECRET VOUCHER**, b c Vouchsafe—Welsh Secret **Mr I. Guise & Mr J. R. Smith**
27 **VAN GURP**, ch c Generous (IRE)—Atlantic Flyer (USA) **Barouche Stud Ltd**
28 **YEOMAN OLIVER**, b c Precocious—Impala Lass **Mr Michael G. T. Stokes**

TWO-YEAR-OLDS

29 Ch c 8/2 Cadeaux Genereux—Chance All (FR) (Glenstal (USA)) **Mr Ian Guise**
30 **COURT HOUSE**, b c 12/2 Reprimand—Chalet Girl (Double Form) **Mr J. R. Smith**
31 **NOMINATOR LAD**, b c 25/2 Nomination—Ankara's Princess (USA) (Ankara (USA)) **J. P. Graham**
32 **OUT OF SIGHT (IRE)**, ch c 31/1 Salse (USA)—Starr Danias (USA) (Sensitive Prince (USA))
33 **PENPRIO (IRE)**, b c 16/4 Priolo—Pennine Mist (IRE) (Pennine Walk) **M. Sturgess & Patricia Sturgess**
34 **PHOENIX PRINCESS**, b f 16/4 Nomination—Princess Poquito (Hard Fought) **M. Chea**
35 **ROYAL SAFFRON**, ch c 23/3 Safawan—Purple Fan (Dalsaan) **G. Whitaker & R. L. Bedding**
36 **RUBY TUESDAY**, b f 11/2 Al Nasr (FR)—Habibay (Habitat) **Mr Peter G. Freeman**
37 **SILVER MOON**, gr f 3/2 Environment Friend—High And Bright (Shirley Heights) **M. Sturgess & Mrs J. McMahon**
38 **SPARE MY BLUSHES**, b f 28/2 Puissance—Juris Prudence (IRE) (Law Society (USA)) **D. J. Allen**
39 **THE GAY FOX**, gr c 21/2 Never So Bold—School Concert (Music Boy) **Mr G. Whitaker**
40 **VAN CHINO**, ch c 29/5 Suave Dancer—Atlantic Flyer (Storm Bird (CAN)) **Barouche Stud**

Other Owners: Mrs S. E. Allen, Mr Daniel Bracken, Mr R. C. Breese, Mr G. Charlesworth, Mr C. G. Conway, Mr A. Drummond-Brydson, Mr K. P. Holland, Mr T. E. Hollins, Mr Michael Lambe, Mrs Christine Wilson.

Jockeys (Flat): G Carter (w.a.), L Dettori (w.a.), T Quinn (w.a.).

Apprentice: L Newton.

Amateur: Mr E McMahon (10-9).

408   MR B. J. MCMATH, Newmarket

Postal: **Newmarket Equine Pool, Hamilton Road, Newmarket, Suffolk, CB8 0PD.**
Phone: **NEWMARKET (01638) 665868 MOBILE (0831) 337628 FAX (01638) 665868**

 1 **ACTION JACKSON**, 4, ch g Hadeer—Water Woo (USA) **Print Professionals Ltd**
 2 **CHIMBORAZO**, 5, ch g Salse (USA)—Pale Gold (FR) **Mrs Lisa Olley**
 3 **DERRING WELL**, 6, b m Derring Rose—Barwell **Mr T. J. Wyatt**
 4 **DOCKLANDS COURIER**, 4, b g Dominion—High Quail (USA) **Mrs Lisa Olley**
 5 **FAIRY FAY (IRE)**, 4, b f Fayruz—Isa **Mr Bob Williams**
 6 **MALINDI BAY**, 8, gr g Grey Desire—Malindi **Saracen Racing**
 7 **MEDLAND (IRE)**, 6, ch g Imperial Frontier (USA)—Miami Dancer **Mrs Lisa Olley**
 8 **NARBONNE**, 5, b m Rousillon (USA)—Historical Fact **Saracen Racing**
 9 **PERSIAN HAZE (IRE)**, 7, ch g Bold Arrangement—Crufty Wood **M. Williamson and Partners**
10 **TELEPHUS**, 7, b g Efisio—Mrs Bizz **The Knockout Partnership**
11 **YUVRAJ**, 12, b g Final Straw—Never Never Land **Mr R. Fincham**

THREE-YEAR-OLDS

12 **DOCKLANDS LIMO**, b c Most Welcome—Bugle Sound **Mrs Lisa Olley**

Other Owners: Mr M. Armitt, W. A. Barrell, B. Clarke, T. J. Dawson, Miss M. Dawson, Mr John Ellis, Mr G. W. Holland, D. Lewis, C. Maloney, Mr B. J. McMath.

Jockeys (Flat): R Cochrane (w.a.), E Johnson (7-7).

Jockeys (NH): S Keightley, V Smith.

409   MR M. D. MCMILLAN, Bibury

Postal: **The Glebe House, Bibury, Cirencester, Glos, GL7 5NS.**

Phone: **(01285) 740341 FAX (01285) 740592**

1 **ALI'S DELIGHT**, 5, br g Idiot's Delight—Almelikeh **Mr M. D. McMillan**
2 **REVE EN ROSE**, 10, b m Revlow—Bois de Rose **Mr M. D. McMillan**
Other Owners: Mrs A. T. McMillan.

410   MR MARTYN MEADE, Malmesbury

Postal: **Ladyswood, Sherston, Malmesbury, Wilts, SN16 0JL.**

Phone: **OFFICE (01666) 840880 HOME (01666) 840465 FAX (01666) 840073**

1 **ANJELIKA ROSS (IRE)**, 5, b m Ardross—Cindie Girl **Mrs B. Taylor**
2 **BELLA COOLA**, 4, b f Northern State (USA)—Trigamy **Mr Arthur E. Smith**
3 **BOMBADIL**, 4, b g Gunner B—Sugar Token **Mr T. Barrett**
4 **FLAG FEN (USA)**, 5, br g Riverman (USA)—Damascus Flag (USA) **Ladyswood Racing Club**
5 **FLAMMANT ROSE (IRE)**, 4, gr f Cyrano de Bergerac—Sweet Class **Mr Martyn Meade**
6 **HENRYS PORT**, 6, b g Royal Vulcan—Bright Swan
7 **LOST REALM**, 4, b g Reprimand—Clarandal **Mr Martyn Meade**
8 **LUMUMBA DAYS**, 10, gr g Neltino—Bright Swan **Mr Henry Taylor**
9 **NORNAX LAD (USA)**, 8, b g Northern Baby (CAN)—Naxos (USA) **Mrs B. Taylor**
10 **REDUNDANT PAL**, 13, ch g Redundant—Palesa **Ladyswood Racing Club**
11 **SOLDIER COVE (USA)**, 6, ch g Manila (USA)—Secret Form **Ladyswood Racing Club**
12 5, Ch m Gunner B—Swakara **Mr T. Barrett**
13 **WALK THE BEAT**, 6, b g Interrex (CAN)—Plaits **Country Life Partnership**
14 **WARNING SHOT**, 4, b g Dowsing (USA)—Warning Bell **Continental Racing**

THREE-YEAR-OLDS

15 **EDDIELEE (IRE)**, b f Dancing Dissident (USA)—Milly Daydream **Mr Martyn Meade**
16 **GEMOLLY (IRE)**, b f Be My Native (USA)—Hayhurst **Mr & Mrs S. Bayless**
17 B f Komaite (USA)—Lucky Monashka **Mr T. Barrett**
18 **LUCKY REVENGE**, b f Komaite (USA)—Sweet And Lucky **Ladyswood Racing Club**
19 **LUNAR MIST**, b f Komaite (USA)—Sugar Token **Ladyswood Racing Club**
20 B g Jareer (USA)—Steady Molly
21 **TOE TAPPIN MUSIC (USA)**, b g Show Dancer (USA)—Miss Garrett (USA) **Mr D. Caddy**
22 **WEEK TWO (IRE)**, b g Red Sunset—Great Land (USA) **Mr D. Caddy**
23 **WILFULL LAD (IRE)**, b g Distinctly North (USA)—Lisa's Music **Mr R. G. Hardie & Mr P. H. Ling**
24 **WILL DO**, b g Weldnaas (USA)—Philogyny **Mr Arthur E. Smith**
25 **WIRE ACT (USA)**, ro g Gate Dancer (USA)—Giovanelli (USA) **Ladyswood Racing Club**

TWO-YEAR-OLDS

26 B f 23/3 Conquering Hero (USA)—Alitos Choice (Baptism)
27 B f 3/3 Statoblest—Alo Ez (Alzao (USA)) **Mr T. H. Rossiter**
28 B f 21/4 Deploy—Berberana (Never So Bold)
29 B f 30/4 Astronef—Brandywell (Skyliner)
30 B f 3/4 Full Extent (USA)—By Chance (Le Johnstan) **Mr Robert Biggs**
31 B f 14/4 Unfuwain (USA)—Chrisanthy (So Blessed)
32 B f 4/4 Statoblest—Evening Star (Red Sunset) **Mr C. T. Bletsoe**
33 Ch f 4/3 Superlative—Glide Path (Sovereign Path)
34 Br c 18/3 Rock City—Go Tally-Ho (Gorytus (USA))
35 **HERECOMESTHEKNIGHT**, b g 15/3 Thatching—Storm Riding (USA) (Storm Bird (CAN)) **Mr & Mrs D. Clee**
36 B f 11/3 Fairy King—Kaiserlinde (GER) (Frontal)
37 B f 22/5 Komaite (USA)—Lucky Candy (Lucky Wednesday) **Mr T. Barrett**
38 **NO NANNETTE**, gr f 16/4 Reprimand—Jenny's Call (Petong) **Mrs B. Taylor**
39 B f 22/4 Suave Dancer (USA)—Our Reverie (USA) (J O Tobin (USA))
40 Br f 19/3 Tina's Pet—Pulga (Blakeney) **Mr R. West**
41 B f 22/2 Tina's Pet—Songlines (Night Shift (USA))
42 B f 29/4 Sillery (USA)—Top The Rest (Top Ville)
43 Ch f 17/4 Risk Me (FR)—Valldemosa (Music Boy)

Other Owners: Mrs Jane Bradbery, Mr Andrzej Bucko, Mr M. Freti, Lei (Bloodstock), Mr B. P. Ryan, Mrs H. Taylor, Mrs Phillippa Taylor.

411

MR N. MEADE, Navan

Postal: **Tu Va Stables, Castletown, Navan, Co. Meath, Ireland.**
Phone: **(046) 54197 or 54278 FAX (046) 54459**

1 **ALASAD,** 6, ch g Kris—Midway Lady (USA)
2 **ALWAYS A PAUPER (IRE),** 7, b g Pauper—Pickled Girl
3 **ANOTHER COQ HARDI (IRE),** 8, ch g Camden Town—Favant
4 **ANTRIM TOWN (IRE),** 5, br g Roselier (FR)—Rosalisa
5 **ATHA BEITHE (IRE),** 5, b g Mandalus—Russell's Touch
6 **BE MY HOPE (IRE),** 7, b m Be My Native (USA)—Diamond Gig
7 4, Gr f Roselier (FR)—Big Polly
8 5, B g Roselier (FR)—Big Polly
9 **BOB DEVANI,** 10, b g Mandalus—Russells Touch
10 **CALAWASSIE (IRE),** 6, b g Mandalus—Aryumad
11 **CLASSIC MATCH (IRE),** 8, ch g Ballad Rock—Ballymaloe Girl
12 **COQ HARDI AFFAIR (IRE),** 8, b g The Parson—Deep Fern
13 **DAWN ALERT (IRE),** 7, b g Strong Gale—Gamonda
14 **DEERE REPH (IRE),** 5, ch m Exhibitioner—Daring Belle
15 **DISTANT STAR (IRE),** 6, ch g Buckskin (FR)—Tipperary Star
16 5, Br m Phardante (FR)—Dream House
17 **EARP,** 4, b g Anita's Prince—Ottavia Abu
18 **EMBELLISHED (IRE),** 4, b c Scenic—Embroidery
19 **FIDDLERS BOW VI,** 8, b g Said To Be Fidel—Dam Unknown
20 **FONTAINE FABLES (IRE),** 6, b g Lafontaine (USA)—Garland Song
21 **FOR MOG (USA),** 7, ch g Mogambo (USA)—Forever Command (USA)
22 **GOVERNMENT GRANT (IRE),** 5, b g Be My Native (USA)—Rock Blues
23 **HEIST,** 7, ch g Homeboy—Pilfer
24 **HILL SOCIETY (IRE),** 4, b c Law Society (USA)—Sun Screen
25 **HILLSON (IRE),** 6, b g The Parson—Irish Hill Lass
26 **HOPEFUL DECISION (IRE),** 5, b m Boyne Valley—Wrong Decision
27 **JOHNNY SETASIDE (IRE),** 7, b g Remainder Man—Stormy Waters
28 **LADY BLAYNEY (IRE),** 4, gr f Mazaad—Standing Ovation
29 **MICK MAN (IRE),** 5, b g Electric—Belle Chanel
30 **MIDNIGHT SERVICE (IRE),** 7, b g The Parson—Stringfellows
31 **MINNESOTA FATS (IRE),** 4, b c Little Bighorn—Pepper Cannister
32 **MUBADIR (USA),** 8, ch g Nodouble (USA)—Hapai
33 **NOVELLO ALLEGRO (USA),** 8, b g Sir Ivor—Tants
34 **PERSIAN POWER (IRE),** 8, br h Persian Bold—Am Stretchin (USA)
35 **REGAL ACCESS (USA),** 5, br g Lear Fan (USA)—Low Approach
36 **SAVING BOND,** 4, ch c Digamist (USA)—Marine Life
37 **SHAWAHIN,** 4, b c Nashwan (USA)—Bempton
38 **SIGMA WIRELESS (IRE),** 7, b br g Henbit (USA)—Canelle
39 **STREET VIEW (IRE),** 4, br c Vision (USA)—Sweet Marjorie (FR)
40 **SWINGER (IRE),** 7, ch g Orchestra—Great Desire
41 **THE LATVIAN LARK,** 8, b g Buckskin (FR)—Dark Harbour
42 4, B g Executive Perk—Track Down
43 **TRY FOR EVER (IRE),** 4, b f Try My Best (USA)—Dame Ross
44 **WALT (IRE),** 6, b g King's Ride—Random What
45 **WESPERADA (IRE),** 4, ch g Waajib—Divine Apsara
46 **WOODY,** 5, ch h Insan (USA)—Gitee (FR)
47 **WYATT (IRE),** 6, br g Roselier (FR)—Big Polly
48 4, B br g Be My Native (USA)—Zalazula

THREE-YEAR-OLDS

49 B f Mac's Imp (USA)—Be Nimble
50 **FAIRY FOOTPRINT,** br f Persian Bold—Fairy Feet
51 **LUNA FLEUR (IRE),** b f Shardari—Medicosma (USA)
52 B c Homo Sapien—Maria Tudor
53 **NAXIA,** b f Fairy King (USA)—Ariadne
54 **SIGMA COMMS (IRE),** b c Don't Forget Me—River Serenade (USA)

MR N. MEADE—continued
TWO-YEAR-OLDS

55 B br f 28/3 Petorius—Delray Jet (USA) (Northjet)
56 B c 28/4 High Estate—El Pina (Be My Guest (USA))
57 B f 23/3 Classic Music (USA)—Herila (FR) (Bold Lad (USA))
58 B f 24/4 Dancing Dissident—Lady Tyrrel (Pall Mall)
59 B f 11/3 Royal Academy (USA)—Nouschka (Ahonoora)
60 B c 5/5 Royal Academy (USA)—Shyoushka (Shy Groom (USA))
61 Ch c 27/2 Silver Kite (USA)—Superflash (Superlative)

Apprentice: Patrick Stringer.

Conditional: Shane McGovern.

Amateur: Mr G Harford.

Lady Rider: Jacinta Lightholder.

412   MR M. G. MEAGHER, Ormskirk

Postal: **'Brookfields', Charity Lane, Westhead, Ormskirk.**
Phone: **(01695) 579334**

1 BRAILLE (IRE), 5, br g Vision (USA)—Winning Feature **The Winning Feature Partnership**
2 CRONK'S COURAGE, 10, ch g Krayyan—Iresine (GER) **Mr M. R. Johnson**
3 HAMILTON SILK, 4, b g K-Battery—Silver's Girl **Haydock Exhibitions Ltd**
4 J'ACCUSE (IRE), 6, ch g Torus—Glens Princess **Mr Ashley Tabony**
5 LINKSIDE, 11, b g Good Thyne (USA)—Laurel Wood **Mrs S. J. Le Gros**
6 MARBLE, 5, b m Petong—Hymettus **Mr George M. Thomson**
7 ROOD MUSIC, 5, ro g Sharrood (USA)—Rose Music **Mr M. R. Johnson**
8 SUVALU (USA), 4, b c Woodman (USA)—Danlu (USA) **Aim High Partnership**
9 TANSEEQ, 5, b g Green Desert (USA)—Kawkeb (USA) **Miss N. C. Taylor**

THREE-YEAR-OLDS

10 GAD YAKOUN, ch c Cadeaux Genereux—Summer Impressions (USA) **Mr M. R. Johnson**
11 HANNAHS BAY, b f Buzzards Bay—Hi-Hannah **Mr M. R. Johnson**
12 NEWBRIDGE BOY, b g Bustino—Martyrdom (USA) **Mr Alan Draper**
13 SOME HORSE (IRE), ch c Astronef—Daniela Lepida (ITY) **The Anfield Hombres**

TWO-YEAR-OLDS

14 B g 27/3 Roscoe Blake—Rainbow Lady (Jaazeiro (USA)) **Mr M. R. Johnson**
15 B f 27/3 Kris—Sextant (Star Appeal) **Carry On Partnership**

Other Owners: Mr C. P. Bayliss, Mr Allan Collier, Mr B. Collier, Mr Trevor Hemmings, Mr Bob Heywood, Mr G. B. Holly, Mr M. I. Lee, Mr W. B. Marshall, Mr L. G. McMullan, Mr J. Pickavance, Mr A. M. Quinn, Mr P. P. Richmond, Mr Neil Ruddock, Mr M. Saunders, Mrs P. Saunders.

Jockeys (Flat): J Fortune (8-3, w.a.), J Quinn (7-7, w.a.).

Jockey (NH): L Wyer (10-0, w.a.).

413   MR B. J. MEEHAN, Upper Lambourn

Postal: **Tumbleweed Cottage, Upper Lambourn, Newbury, Berks, RG16 7QT.**
Phone: **OFFICE (01488) 73656/73636 HOME 73125 FAX 73633 MOBILE (0836) 754254**

1 **ALONGWAYDOWN (IRE)**, 7, b g Supreme Leader—Trident Missile **The Three Bears Racing**
2 **AUDREY GRACE**, 5, b m Infantry—Fair Nic **Mr Paul Dean**
3 **DANCING HEART**, 4, b g Thowra (FR)—Miss Lawsuit **Vintage Services Limited**
4 **DANCING LAWYER**, 5, b g Thowra (FR)—Miss Lawsuit **Vintage Services Limited**
5 **ELLY FLEETFOOT (IRE)**, 4, b f Elmaamul (USA)—Fleetwood Fancy **Mr A. S. Reid**
6 **EMILY-MOU (IRE)**, 4, b f Cadeaux Genereux—Sarajill **Mr A. S. Reid**
7 **GENERAL MOUKTAR**, 6, ch g Hadeer—Fly The Coop **Mr A. S. Helaissi**
8 **GENTLE IRONY**, 4, b f Mazilier (USA)—Irenic **Mr A. S. Reid**
9 **GREYCOAT BOY**, 4, br g Pragmatic—Sirdar Girl **Mr N. W. Rimington**
10 **KHAYRAPOUR (IRE)**, 6, b g Kahyasi—Khayra (FR) **Miss J. Semple**
11 **PISTOLS AT DAWN (USA)**, 6, b g Al Nasr (FR)—Cannon Run (USA) **Mr G. Howard-Spink**
12 **ROCK OYSTER**, 4, b g Ballad Rock—Bombshell **Mr R. L. Harding**
13 **SHAHRANI**, 4, b g Lear Fan (USA)—Windmill Princess **Mr A. S. Helaissi**
14 **SHARPICAL**, 4, b g Sharpo—Magical Spirit **Mr A. S. Reid**
15 **SPEEDYBIRD (IRE)**, 4, b f Danehill (USA)—Mille Fleurs (USA) **Mr A. S. Reid**
16 **SUPER MALT (IRE)**, 8, ch m Milk of The Barley—Super Amber **Mr F. D. Allison**
17 **TART AND A HALF**, 4, b f Distant Relative—Vaigrant Wind **Mr & Mrs P. Boggis**
18 **TWICE PURPLE (IRE)**, 4, b g Then Again—Tyrian Belle **The Mathieson Partnership**
19 **WILLRACK FARRIER**, 4, b f Lugana Beach—Bonny Bright Eyes **Willrackers**
20 **ZELDA ZONK**, 4, b f Law Society (USA)—Massive Powder **Mrs Christine Painting**

THREE-YEAR-OLDS

21 **BAG AND A BIT**, b f Distant Relative—Vaigrant Wind **Mr & Mrs P. Boggis**
22 **BE MY BIRD**, b f Be My Chief (USA)—Million Heiress **Mr A. S. Reid**
23 **BLUE SUEDE HOOFS**, g f Nomination—Massive Powder **Mr Trevor Painting**
24 **CONDOR RIDGE**, b g Inca Chief (USA)—Second Flower **Adv Richard J. Michel**
25 **HALF AN INCH (IRE)**, gr g Petoski—Inch **Mr T. Dale & Mr C. Mills**
26 **HARTFIELDS BOY**, b g Shavian—Fallen Angel **Mr F. D. Allison**
27 **LAUGHING BUCCANEER**, ch g Weldnaas (USA)—Atlantic Line **Mr P. J. Orme**
28 **LONGHILL BOY**, b g Statoblest—Summer Eve **Vintage Services**
29 **OBERONS BOY (IRE)**, b g Fairy King (USA)—Bold Starlet **Mr Edward P. Winfield**
30 **SHAMAND (USA)**, br g Minshaanshu Amad (USA)—Rose And Betty (USA) **Mr Jim McCarthy**
31 **SHARP STOCK**, bc Tina's Pet—Mrewa **Mrs M. Fairbairn**
32 **SOUND CHECK**, b f Formidable (USA)—Imperatrice (USA) **Theobalds Stud**
33 **STAR ISLAND**, b g Jupiter Island—Gippeswyck Lady **High Seas Leisure Ltd**
34 **TUMBLEWEED RIDGE**, ch c Indian Ridge—Billie Blue **The Tumbleweed Partnership**
35 **VOLARE**, b f Prince Sabo—Nazmiah **Mr A. S. Helaissi**
36 **WARNING TIME**, b c Warning—Ballad Island **Mr F. C. T. Wilson**
37 **WHITE EMIR**, b g Emarati (USA)—White African **Mr Nigel Stafford**
38 **WINGED PRINCE**, b g Prince Daniel (USA)—Phyl **Mr P. J. Orme**

TWO-YEAR-OLDS

39 B c 3/4 Emarati (USA)—Abbotswood (Ahonoora) **The Three Bears Racing**
40 **BEGORRAT (IRE)**, ch c 10/3 Ballad Rock—Hada Rani (Jaazeiro (USA)) **Mr R. Bernard**
41 **CATHEDERAL CITY (IRE)**, b c 6/3 Prince Sabo—Choire Mhor (Dominion) **Kennet Valley Thoroughbreds**
42 B c 11/3 Petong—Cat's Claw (Sharpen Up) **Mr John Gutkin**
43 **CLARA BLISS (IRE)**, b f 16/5 Fayruz—Kinosium (Relkino) **Mr Gary Catchpole**
44 **CLASSIC MYSTERY (IRE)**, ch g 14/2 Classic Secret (USA)—
    Mystery Bid (Auction Ring (USA)) **Mr Gary Catchpole**
45 **CODE**, b c 7/5 Mystiko (USA)—Farewell Letter (USA) (Arts And Letters) **Miss Gloria Abbey**
46 **CORNCRAKE**, b f Nordico (USA)—Lemon Balm **J. T. & K. M. Thomas**
47 **DALMENY DANCER**, b c 14/4 Batshoof—Greek Goddess (Young Generation) **Thurloe Thoroughbreds**
48 B f 26/3 Last Tycoon—Forest Berries (IRE) (Thatching) **Mr F. C. T. Wilson**
49 **GROVEFAIR FLYER (IRE)**, b c 13/4 Astronef—Hitness (Hittite Glory) **Grovefair PLC**
50 **GROVEFAIR LAD (IRE)**, b c 14/4 Silver Kite (USA)—Cienaga (Tarboosh (USA)) **Grovefair Plc**
51 **GROVEFAIR MAIDEN (IRE)**, ch f 29/3 Red Sunset—Coffee Bean (Doulab (USA)) **Grovefair Plc**

MR B. J. MEEHAN—continued

52 **JOINT VENTURE (IRE)**, b g 5/4 Common Grounds—Renata's Ring (IRE) (Auction Ring (USA) **Mrs B. Bell**
53 **LADY GROVEFAIR (IRE)**, ch f 10/5 Shalford (IRE)—Zinovia (USA) (Ziggy's Boy (USA)) **Grovefair Plc**
54 B c 15/3 Mac's Imp (USA)—Marton Maid (Silly Season) **H. E. Lmendup Dorji**
55 **MASTERSTROKE**, b g 23/2 Timeless Times (USA)—Fauve (Dominion) **N. Attenborough**
56 B c 11/5 Fairy King (USA)—Melbourne Miss (Chaparral (FR) **The Harlequin Partnership**
57 **MERCILESS COP**, ch c 18/4 Efisio—Naturally Bold (Bold Lad (IRE)) **Mr Mario Lafranchi**
58 Ch c 26/4 Presidium—Miramede (Norwick (USA)) **Mrs Fairbairn**
59 **MR MAJICA**, b c 18/2 Rudimentary (USA)—Pellinora (USA) (King Pellinore (USA)) **Carl Metcalfe**
60 **NORTHERN GIRL (IRE)**, b f 25/4 Distinctly North—Auction Maid (IRE) (Auction Ring (USA)) **Mr K. Sim**
61 Ch f 9/4 Mujtahid (USA)—Piney River (Pharly (FR)) **Mr D. Rogers**
62 **PLATINUM PRINCESS (IRE)**, b f 21/2 Petardia—Soignee (Night Shift (USA)) **Mr Gary Catchpole**
63 **RUPERT'S DOUBLE (IRE)**, ch c 1/3 Silver Kite (USA)—Perfect Guest (What A Guest) **N. Harper**
64 **SAGACIOUS ARDENT**, b c 30/4 Keen—Nazmiah (Free State) **Mr A. S. Hebissi**
65 B f 13/4 Chilibang—Silent Sun (Blakeney) **Miss L. Elliott**
66 **SMART PROSPECT**, ch c 31/3 Superpower—Bustily (Busted) **Smart Racing**
67 **SPANIARDS INN**, b c 24/1 Dominion—Zelda (USA) (Sharpen Up) **Mr Schmidt Bodnor**
68 **TINKER'S SURPRISE (IRE)**, b g 28/3 Cyrano De Bergerac—Lils Fairy (Fairy King (USA)) **Mr S. Molloy**
69 **TITTA RUFFO**, b c 11/3 Reprimand—Hithermoor Lass (Red Alert) **Mr Stan Threadwell**
70 **TUMBLEWEED PEARL**, b f 19/4 Aragon—Billie Blue (Ballad Rock) **The Tumbleweed Partnership**
71 **TUMBLEWEED QUEST (USA)**, b f 26/3 Quest For Fame—
                    Hail The Dancer (USA) (Green Dancer (USA)) **The Second Tumbleweed Partnership**
72 **VICTORY DANCER**, b g 14/4 Ron's Victory (USA)—Villajoyosa (FR) (Satingo) **Alan Cunliffe**

Other Owners: Mr P. Abbott, Amity Finance Ltd, Mr N. Andrew, Mr S. Ashley, Mr B. J. Barnes, Mr C. P. Billot, Mr Robert Brown, Mr Geoff Buck, Mr N. C. Clark, Mr M. C. Dean, Mr Luigi Ferraris, Mr P. Ford, Mr E. J. S. Gadsden, Mrs P. Jubert, Mr Paul Jubert, Mr Peter Jubert, Mr S. Le Gassick, Mr A. C. Mathieson, Mrs Susan McCarthy, Mr A. S. Mill, Mr M. R. Pascall, Mr Richard Pitman, Mr W. Rack, Mr E. Robson, Mr C. F. Stear, Mr Wayne B. Sweeting, Mr Stephen Tucker, Mr Peter S. Winfield.

Jockey (Flat): B Doyle.

Jockey (NH): Brendan Powell.

Lady Rider: Miss Jane Allison.

414   MR S. MELLOR, Swindon

Postal: **Pollardstown Racing Stables, Foxhill, Wanborough, Swindon, SN4 0DR.**
Phone: **(01793) 790230 FAX (01793) 790871**

1 **ANLACE**, 7, b m Sure Blade (USA)—Ascot Strike (USA) **The Felix Bowness Partnership**
2 **ANOTHER BATCHWORTH**, 4, b f Beveled (USA)—Batchworth Dancer **Mrs Diana Price**
3 **BALLYMGYR (IRE)**, 7, ch g Town And Country—Channel Breeze **Mrs Rosemary Kavanagh**
4 **BOLD CHARLIE**, 4, ch g Weldnaas (USA)—Flirty Lady **Mrs J. Harmsworth**
5 **BONE SETTER (IRE)**, 6, b g Strong Gale—Princess Wager **Lord Leverhulme**
6 **BRONZE RUNNER**, 12, gr g Gunner B—Petingalyn **Austin Stroud & Co Ltd**
7 **CADDY'S FIRST**, 4, b g Petong—Love Scene **The Caddy's Four Partnership**
8 **COURT NAP (IRE)**, 4, ch g Waajib—Mirhar (FR) **Sir Michael Connell**
9 **DARK MENACE**, 4, b g Beveled (USA)—Sweet And Sure **Austin Stroud & Co Ltd**
10 **ERLKING (IRE)**, 6, b g Fairy King (USA)—Cape of Storms **Mr S. P. Tindall**
11 **EZZY'S BOY**, 8, b g Welsh Captain—Pearl Bound **Mr Stewart Wilson**
12 **HARDING**, 5, b g Dowsing (USA)—Orange Hill **Mr S. P. Tindall**
13 **HULLO MARY DOLL**, 7, br m Lidhame—Princess Story **Plough Jumpers (Ashton Keynes)**
14 **JAPACADA**, 6, b g Celtic Cone—Bird's Custard **Mrs Millie Mullen**
15 **KING'S COURTIER (IRE)**, 7, b g King's Ride—Glamorous Night **Mrs Hilary Thomas**

MR S. MELLOR—continued

16 **LEGIBLE**, 8, b g Sadler's Wells (USA)—Northern Script (USA) **Mr S. P. Tindall**
17 **MALIBU MAN**, 4, ch c Ballacashtal (CAN)—National Time (USA) **Church Racing Partnership**
18 **MASON (IRE)**, 4, ch g Simply Great (FR)—Viva Ronda **Mr S. P. Tindall**
19 **MISS THE BEAT**, 4, b f Music Boy—Bad Start (USA) **Mr Stan Mellor**
20 **MISTER RAIDER**, 4, ch g Ballacashtal (CAN)—Martian Melody **Raiders Partnership**
21 **NESSUN DORO**, 4, b g Hallgate—Barndoro **Paul Porter & Partners**
22 **OLDHILL WOOD (IRE)**, 6, ch g Salluceva—Davinsky Rose **Mr David Mullen**
23 **RED PHANTOM (IRE)**, 4, ch g Kefaah (USA)—Highland Culture **Plough Twenty (Ashton Keynes)**
24 **ROSEVEAR (IRE)**, 4, b f Contract Law (USA)—Caimanite **Interiors of Ascot Partnership**
25 **SEOD RIOGA (IRE)**, 7, br g Down The Hatch—Jackie's Pet **Mr S. P. Tindall**
26 **SHEPHERDS REST (IRE)**, 4, b g Accordion—Mandy's Last **The Odd Dozen**
27 **STORM FALCON (USA)**, 6, ch g Storm Bird (CAN)—Noble Natisha (USA) **Mr E. R. Dalby**
28 **STORM TIGER (IRE)**, 5, b g Strong Gale—Happy Party **W. R. Partnership**
29 **THE CHEESE BARON**, 5, b g Idiot's Delight—Stella Roma **T. D. J. Syder & S. M. D. Oliver**
30 **THE NAUGHTY VICAR**, 6, ch g The Parson—Kylogue Daisy **The Hell Raisers**
31 **TITAN EMPRESS**, 7, b m Oats—Stella Roma **Mr T. D. J. Syder**

Other Owners: Mr P. N. Austin, Mr Gary Baggs, My Sydney Baker, Mr D. P. Barnard, Mr D. G. Barnes, Mr Roy Baron, Mrs Janet Benney, Mr Alan Birchall, Mr R. C. Booker, Mr Felix Bowness, Mr M. C. Brittain, Mr D. Carroll, Mr Peter Church, Mrs Margaret F. Cook, Mr I. Edward, Mr A. K. Farmer, Mr M. Freti, Mr Tony Gammon, Mr John Guy, Mr M. Hall, Mr Terry Hardy, Mr Michael Harrold, Mrs E. B. Hill, Mr J. D. Horler, Mrs Moyra James, Mr John Kavanagh, Mr H. Kayne, Mrs A. Lawrence-Dorler, Mr J. A. Lloyd, Mr F. E. Maslin, Mr Noel McLoughlin, Mr Philip Michael, Mr Ben Miller, Mr N. U. Morgan, Mr C. Mortimer, Mr Chris Page, Mrs E. Plester, Mr P. A. Porter, Mr K. W. C. Readings, Dr S. M. Readings, Mr J. Rickard, Mr B. Ridge, Mr Christopher P. Riley, Mrs Daphne Rothwell, Mr B. Sanders, Mr E. A. Saunders, Mrs Phyllis Smith, Mr A. J. Stevens, Mr M. E. Thompsett, Mr Clive Wakefield, Mr Alan Waller, Mrs S. Warren, Mrs G. G. White, Mr James Wilson, Mr Stewart Wilson, Mr Doug Woodward.

Jockey (Flat): M Wigham (8-7, w.a.).

Jockeys (NH): N Mann (10-0), M Perrett (10-0).

Conditional: C Webb (9-7).

415   MISS M. K. MILLIGAN, Middleham

Postal: **Brough Farm, Middleham, Leyburn, North Yorkshire, DL8 4SG.**
Phone: **(01969) 23221 OFFICE (01969) 24105 HOME (01969) 23541 FAX**

1 **ANOTHER GEORGE**, 6, b g Fort Nayef—Worthy Heiress **Gerard Hayton & Tony Monk**
2 **BEAU MATELOT**, 4, ch g Handsome Sailor—Bellanoora **Mr A. Buckley**
3 **COMMANDEER (IRE)**, 6, b g Mandalus—Cantabryne **Mr A. G. Chappell**
4 **CULLANE LAKE (IRE)**, 6, b m Strong Statement (USA)—Gusserane Lark **Mrs J. M. L. Milligan**
5 **DOCKMASTER**, 5, b g Dominion—Surf Bird **Mr J. D. Gordon**
6 **DON'T TELL JUDY (IRE)**, 8, b g Strong Gale—Two In A Million **Mrs A. J. M. Cockburn**
7 **FAIR AND FANCY (FR)**, 5, b g Always Fair (USA)—Fancy Star (FR) **F and F Partnership**
8 **JOYRIDER**, 5, b g Risk Me (FR)—Villajoyosa (FR) **The Joyriders**
9 **KERAK**, 6, b g Rakaposhi King—Up Cooke **Mrs J. M. L. Milligan**
10 **MISTI HUNTER (IRE)**, 7, gr g Roselier (FR)—Lovely Stranger
11 **SWISS GOLD**, 6, ch g Balinger—Gold Gift **The Aunts**
12 **TACTIX**, 6, gr m Nearly A Hand—Steel Typhoon **Mr Dave Teasdale**
13 **TIGERSONG (USA)**, 6, b g Seattle Song (USA)—Tovalop (USA) **Mr J. D. Gordon**
14 **WESTERN GENERAL**, 5, ch g Cadeaux Genereux—Patsy Western **Mr J. D. Gordon**

THREE-YEAR-OLDS

15 **SHARVIC (IRE)**, b g Sharp Victor (USA)—Binnissima (USA) **Tony and Patsy Monk**

MISS M. K. MILLIGAN—continued

Other Owners: Mrs D. L. Barrett, Geoff Bridges, Mr Adrian Buckley, Mr Alan Buckley, Mrs Joan Buckley, Mrs J. M. Hall, Mr Ray Hanlon, Mr P. D. Jackson, Miss Kate Milligan, Ron Motion, Mrs S. Murray-Usher, Dr Roy Palmer, Racecourse Doctors, Mr B. J. Rae, Mrs Judith Robson, Mr M. J. Willan.

Jockey (NH): Richard Guest.

Lady Rider: Pauline Robson.

416   MR B. R. MILLMAN, Cullompton

Postal: **The Paddocks, Kentisbeare, Cullompton, Devon, EX15 2DX.**
Phone: **(01884) 266620 FAX (01884) 266620 MOBILE (0585) 168447**

1 **BATH TIMES,** 4, ch f Good Times (ITY)—Lady of Bath **Mr D. L. C. Hodges**
2 **CLIFTON MATCH,** 4, gr f Nicholas Bill—Brave Maiden **Oping Enterprises**
3 **CRACKING PROSPECT,** 5, ch g Hubbly Bubbly (USA)—Crackerjill **Mrs J. Gliddon**
4 **GAGOOS BABY,** 6, b g Prince of Peace—Dusky Heart **Mr Michael Lethbridge**
5 **HANDSON,** 4, ch g Out of Hand—My Home **Burrow Racing**
6 **JAILBREAKER,** 9, ch g Prince of Peace—Last Farewell **Mrs G. E. Willman**
7 **JUSTFORTHERECORD,** 4, br f Forzando—Classical Vintage **Mrs S. Joint**
8 **MASTER ERIC,** 6, ch g Sula Bula—Miss Lightening **Mr John Brookman**
9 **MAYBE TODAY,** 4, br f Today And Tomorrow—Sonairo **Mr J. P. Curnow**
10 **POLLY LEACH,** 6, b m Pollerton—Come On Gracie **Mr G. Willey**
11 **ROYAL SEATON,** 7, b g Blakeney—Aldbury Girl **Axminster Carpets Ltd**
12 **SUILE MOR,** 4, b f Satin Wood—Ra Ra **Hammy Racing**
13 **WORLD EXPRESS (IRE),** 6, b g Jareer (USA)—Eight Mile Rock **World Express Limited**

THREE-YEAR-OLDS

14 **ATLANTIC MIST,** ch g Elmaamul (USA)—Overdue Reaction **The Wardour Partnership**
15 **MASBRO BIRD,** b f Midyan (USA)—Grinning (IRE) **The Masbro Partnership**
16 **RUBY TWO SHOES,** b f Revlow—Miss Burgundy **Mrs S. J. Retter**
17 **THERHEA (IRE),** b g Pennine Walk—Arab Art **Mr Colin Lewis**

TWO-YEAR-OLDS

18 **BURBERRY QUEST,** b f 9/4 Thornberry (USA)—Flying Joker (Kalaglow) **Mr S. Horn**
19 B f 10/3 Jester—Dorothy Jane (He Loves Me) **Mrs C. Wildash**
20 **HERBSHAN DANCER,** b c 12/4 Warrshan (USA)—Herbary (USA) (Herbager) **Kingtroll Partnership**
21 **PERCHANCE TO DREAM (IRE),** b f 15/2 Bluebird (USA)—Foliage (Thatching) **Mrs S. Joint**
22 B f 24/4 Jurado (USA)—Tacheo (Tachypous)
23 **YANGTZE (IRE),** b c 1/5 River Falls—Sister Dympna (Grundy) **Mr A. Walsh**

Other Owners: Mrs Mary Abbott, Mr D. H. Bradford, Mr S. R. J. Bridges, Mr D. Condick, Mr J. P. Curnow, Mrs A. Dale, Mr B. Donnellan, Mr O. Donohue, Mr M. Dragisic, Mrs Nerys Dutfield, Mr John Earle, Mr N. Edkins, Mr David Fitzgerald, Mr John Fullam, Mr H. Gooding, Mr R. T. Grant, Mr H. Harris, Mr J. W. Haydon, Mr M. J. Iles, Mr D. J. Longhurst, Mr Jamie McPhee, Dr John Newman, Mrs A. North, Mrs D. Ogilvie, Mr T. D. O'Sullivan, Mr G. Palmer, Mrs M. Palmer, Mr G. R. Poole, Mr J. Taaffe, Mr M. R. Terry, Mr Alan Thomas, Mr N. W. Thompson, Mr J. R. Upton, Mr Peter Watkinson, Mr S. E. White, Dr A. Willman.

Jockey (Flat): D Holland (w.a.).

Jockey (NH): Darren Salter (9-7).

417   MR T. G. MILLS, Epsom

Postal: **Loretta Lodge, Tilley Lane, Headley, Epsom, KT18 6EP.**

Phone: **(01372) 377209 (01372) 386578**

1 **CAPTAIN'S DAY,** 4, ch g Ballacashtal (CAN)—Seymour Ann (GB) **Mr W. R. Norton**
2 **DOUBLE RUSH (IRE),** 4, b g Doulab (USA)—Stanza Dancer **Mr Tony Murray**
3 **GREENWICH AGAIN,** 4, b g Exodal (USA)—What A Challenge **John Humphreys (Turf Accountants) Ltd**
4 **IVY EDITH,** 6, b m Blakeney—Royal Birthday **Mr Glen Antill**
5 **JONSALAN,** 6, gr g Robellino (USA)—Nelly Do Da **Mr Alan E. Ward**
6 **PARK RIDGE,** 4, b g Indian Ridge—Aspark **Mrs T. G. Mills**

THREE-YEAR-OLDS

7 **BROTHER ROY,** b c Prince Sabo—Classic Heights **Mr T. G. Mills**
8 **LADY ISABELL,** b f Rambo Dancer (CAN)—Warning Bell **Mr T. Staplehurst**
9 **LAW DANCER (IRE),** b c Alzao (USA)—Judicial (USA) **Mr T. G. Mills**
10 **PETITE ANNIE,** b f Statoblest—Kuwait Night **Mr T. G. Mills**
11 **PROPER BLUE (USA),** b c Proper Reality (USA)—Blinking (USA) **Mr M. J. Legg**
12 **SHEILANA (IRE),** b f Bluebird (USA)—Shadia (USA) **Sherwoods Transport Ltd**
13 **SUPAROY,** b g Midyan (USA)—Champ d'Avril **Mrs T. G. Mills**

TWO-YEAR-OLDS

14 **BLUE RIVER (IRE),** ch c 29/3 River Falls—Royal Resident (Prince Regent (FR)) **Mr M. J. Legg**
15 B c 30/4 Soviet Star (USA)—Bourgeonette (Mummy's Pet) **Mrs Pauline Merrick**
16 B f 15/2 Mujadil (USA)—Elminya (IRE) (Sure Blade (USA))
17 **HAYES WAY (IRE),** b c 19/3 Lahib (USA)—Edgeaway (Ajdal (USA)) **Mr Alan E. Ward**
18 **JUST ALEX (IRE),** b c 23/3 River Falls—Picnic Basket (Pharly (FR)) **Mr Tony Murray**
19 B c 5/3 Be My Chief (USA)—Klewraye (Lord Gayle (USA)) **John Humphreys (Turf Accountants) Ltd**
20 **MY HERO (IRE),** b f 15/3 Bluebird (USA)—Risacca (ITY) (Sir Gaylord) **Mr W. J. Brown**
21 Ch f 3/4 Astronef—Numidia (Sallust)
22 **PASSION,** ch f 27/4 Risk Me (FR)—Gotcher (Jalmood (USA)) **Mr Paul Bourdon**
23 **TEAR WHITE (IRE),** b c 28/1 Mac's Imp (USA)—Exemplary (Sovereign Lord) **A. W. Lawson Ltd**
24 B c 24/3 Formidable (USA)—What A Challenge (Sallust)

Other Owners: Mr I. C. Childs, Mr Peter Hannon, Miss Karen Francesca Manzi, Mr Bob Merrick, Mr Tony Morgan, Mr T. J. Oswin, Mr Ernie Penfold, Mr Peter Pepper, Mr Christopher Wright.

Jockey (Flat): John Reid (w.a.).

Apprentices: James Cornally (7-7), Dominic Toole (7-7).

418   MR C. W. MITCHELL, Dorchester

Postal: **White House, Buckland Newton, Dorchester, Dorset, DT2 7DE.**

Phone: **(01300) 345276**

1 **DUCKLING,** 6, b m White Prince (USA)—Romful Donna **Mr C. W. Mitchell**
2 **MISS SECRET,** 6, b m El Conquistador—Harts Lane **Mr C. W. Mitchell**
3 **ROMFUL PRINCE,** 13, b g White Prince (USA)—Romfultears **Mr C. W. Mitchell**
4 **SPRING GROVE JUST,** 6, b g Pablond—Lady Tammany **Mr C. W. Mitchell**
5 **TEARFUL PRINCE,** 12, b g White Prince (USA)—Romfultears **Mr C. W. Mitchell**
6 **WALTER'S DESTINY,** 4, ch g White Prince (USA)—Tearful Sarah **Mr C. W. Mitchell**

419 MR N. R. MITCHELL, Dorchester

Postal: **East Hill Stables, Piddletrenthide, Dorchester, Dorset, DT2 7QY.**

Phone: **PIDDLETRENTHIDE (01300) 348739**

1 **ALWAYS READY,** 10, b g Tyrnavos—Merchantmens Girl **Mrs E. Mitchell**
2 **CLASSIC PAL (USA),** 5, b g Danzatore (CAN)—Welsh Garden **Mr P. C. Tory**
3 **DRESS DANCE (IRE),** 6, b g Nordance (USA)—Pitaya **Messrs J. & G. Goode**
4 **EXACT ANALYSIS (USA),** 10, b br g Berbatim (USA)—Mity Nice Girl **Mr N. R. Mitchell**
5 4, Ch g Nearly A Hand—Grey Receipt **Mr S. L. Mitchell**
6 **KALAMOSS,** 7, ch m Kalaglow—Moss Pink (USA) **Mr N. R. Mitchell**
7 **KEEP ME IN MIND (IRE),** 7, b g Don't Forget Me—Gold Trinket **Mr P. C. Tory**
8 **MAGGIE TEE,** 8, b m Lepanto (GER)—Grey Receipt **Mr R. L. Scorgie**
9 **MAREMMA GALE (IRE),** 8, b g Strong Gale—My Halo **Mr R. L. Scorgie**
10 **MILDRED SOPHIA,** 9, b m Crooner—Glanfield **Mr N. R. Mitchell**
11 **WINGS OF FIRE,** 4, gr g White Prince (USA)—Came Cottage **Mrs E. Mitchell**

THREE-YEAR-OLDS

12 Ch g Riverwise (USA)—Cutabovetherest **Mr N. R. Mitchell**
13 **RAISIN' RIVER,** b f Riverwise (USA)—Seymour Lady **Mr N. R. Mitchell**

Conditional: S Mitchell (8-0).

420 MR PAT MITCHELL, Newmarket

Postal: **Hamilton Stables, Hamilton Road, Newmarket, Suffolk, CB8 7JQ.**

Phone: **NEWMARKET (01638) 660013 FAX (01638) 660013**

1 **BEGGER'S OPERA,** 4, ch c North Briton—Operelle **Mr Sam McBride**
2 **FIRST HOME,** 9, b g Homing—Mill Wind **Mrs B. A. Mitchell**
3 **GENERAL MONTY,** 4, b g Vague Shot—State Free **Mrs Patricia Appleby**
4 **JAHANGIR (IRE),** 7, ch g Ballad Rock—Marsh Benham **Mrs R. S. Johnston**
5 **MERRIE LE BOW,** 4, b f Merdon Melody—Arch Sculptress **H2O Nightspot**
6 **MISSAL (IRE),** 7, b m Alzao (USA)—Priors Mistress **Mrs Doreen Smith**
7 **MOUJEEB (USA),** 6, b h Riverman (USA)—Capricorn Belle **Mrs Caroline Guignard**
8 **SALTANDO (IRE),** 5, b g Salt Dome (USA)—Ange de Feu **Mrs Sandy Herridge**
9 **SWEET CAROLINE,** 5, br m Squill (USA)—Think Ahead **Mrs R. S. Johnston**
10 **TAUBER,** 12, b g Taufan (USA)—Our Bernie **Mrs Catherine Reed**
11 **WADERS DREAM (IRE),** 7, b g Doulab (USA)—Sea Mistress **Mr Richard Berenson**
12 **YOUNG ROSE,** 4, b f Aragon—Primrose Way **Ms Sandra Stevens**

THREE-YEAR-OLDS

13 **HADADABBLE,** ch f Hadeer—Magnifica **The Fun Managers Partnership**

Other Owners: Miss J. A. Bunting, Castle Farm Stud, Mr A. A. Penney, Mr Paul Reed.

421 MR PHILIP MITCHELL, Epsom

Postal: **Downs House, Epsom Downs, Surrey, KT18 5ND.**

Phone: **(01372) 273729 FAX (01372) 278701 MOBILE (0836) 231462**

1 **AMWAJ (USA),** 4, b f Tejano (USA)—Thatsallshewrote **Mrs Fiona Reilly**
2 **ANALOGUE (IRE),** 4, b g Reference Point—Dancing Shadow **S. Holt**
3 **CULTURAL ICON (USA),** 4, b c Kris S (USA)—Sea Prospector (USA)
4 **EASY CHOICE (USA),** 4, b c Easy Goer (USA)—Monroe (USA) **Mr J. Morton**
5 **KAGUYAHIME,** 4, b f Distant Relative—Pushkar **Mrs Fiona Reilly**
6 **KYRENIA TIMES,** 4, b c Good Times (ITY)—Kyrenia Sunset (CYP) **Mr G. V. Eliades**

MR PHILIP MITCHELL—continued

7 **LEAR DANCER (USA)**, 5, b br g Lear Fan (USA)—Green Gown **Mrs R. A. Johnson**
8 **PANDROP**, 5, b m Sharrood (USA)—Trying For Gold (USA) **Mrs Fiona Reilly**
9 **PEDALTOTHEMETAL (IRE)**, 4, b f Nordico (USA)—Full Choke **Mr G. R. Harris**
10 **SALAM (IRE)**, 5, b g Sovereign Dancer (USA)—La Francaise (USA) **Mr Derek Crowson**
11 **TODD (USA)**, 5, b g Theatrical—Boldara (USA) **Mr J. Morton**

THREE-YEAR-OLDS

12 **AMADOUR (IRE)**, b c Contract Law (USA)—Truly Flattering **Mr Derek Crowson**
13 **FANCY DESIGN (IRE)**, b f Cyrano de Bergerac—Crimson Robes **Mr Derek Crowson**
14 **HEAVEN SENT (IRE)**, b f Fayruz—Folle Remont **Mrs Patricia Mitchell**
15 **KYRENIA VICTORY**, b f Ron's Victory (USA)—Kyrenia Sunset (CYP) **Mr G. V. Eliades**
16 **MAKASKAMINA**, b br g Mtoto—Flying Flo Jo (USA) **Mr J. R. Ali**
17 **MAM'SELLE BERGERAC (IRE)**, b f Cyrano de Bergerac—Miss Merryweather **Mr J. Morton**
18 **REALMS OF GLORY (IRE)**, b c Reprimand—Wasaif (IRE) **Mr Derek Crowson**
19 **RED RAJA**, b c Persian Heights—Jenny Splendid **Mr J. R. Ali**
20 **SOMER SOLO**, b f Prince Daniel (USA)—Shift Over (USA) **K. P. Foods Group Racing Partners**
21 **SOVIET KING (IRE)**, b c Soviet Lad (USA)—Finessing **Mrs Sharifah Mukti**
22 **SOVIET SAKTI (IRE)**, b c Soviet Lad (USA)—Hill's Realm (USA) **Mrs Sharifah Mukti**

TWO-YEAR-OLDS

23 B f 22/3 Picea—English Mint (Jalmood (USA)) **A. R. Pierce**
24 **LA BELLE AFFAIRE (USA)**, gr f 2/5 Black Tie Affair—Away's Halo (USA) (Sunny's Halo (USA)) **J. Lamote**
25 **MISS IMP (IRE)**, b f 29/4 Mac's Imp (USA)—Be Nimble (Wattiefield) **Mr W. R. Mann**
26 Ch f 6/3 El Prado (IRE)—Tour d'Argent (USA) (Halo (USA)) **A. R. Perry**

Other Owners: Mr Daniel Abbott, Mrs Belinda Boyd, Mrs V. M. Harris, Mr D. W. Johnson, Mrs E. Miles.

Jockey (Flat): S O'Gorman (w.a.).

Amateur: Mr R Teal (10-0).

422   MR D. MOFFATT, Cartmel

Postal: **Pit Farm Racing Stables, Cartmel, Grange-over-Sands, Cumbria, LA11 6PJ.**
Phone: **CARTMEL (015395) 36689 FAX (015395) 36236**

1 **ANASTASIA WINDSOR**, 5, b m Leading Star—Causanna **Mrs Gloria Bath**
2 **BOWLANDS GEM**, 6, ch g Nicholas Bill—Early Doors **Mrs Lynn Campion**
3 **DAVWILTIMO**, 6, b m Rakaposhi King—Lady Lawyer **W. G. R. B. Racing**
4 **DAYTIME DAWN (IRE)**, 5, b g Rashar (USA)—Ard Clos **Mr W. R. Burrow**
5 **GRANDMAN (IRE)**, 5, b g Executive Perk—Gerise **Mrs Eileen M. Milligan**
6 **GREAT GABLE**, 5, b g Torus—Kath's Venture **Cartmel Racing**
7 **HOME COUNTIES (IRE)**, 7, ch g Ela-Mana-Mou—Safe Home **Roxy Cinemas (Dalton) Ltd**
8 **INGRAM VALLEY**, 6, b m Balinger—Melodic Beat **Mr Ian Ives**
9 **LOCH SCAVAIG (IRE)**, 7, b m The Parson—Regent Star **Mrs G. A. Turnbull**
10 **MULLINS (IRE)**, 5, b g Mandalus—Nire's Pride **A. Milligan**
11 **PALACE RIVER (IRE)**, 8, b m Dragon Palace (USA)—Rosebrook **Mr G. R. Parrington**
12 **PATTERN ARMS**, 4, b g Governor General—Early Doors **Mrs Lynn Campion**
13 **RED FIVE**, 5, b g Clantime—Miami Dolphin **Mr J. W. Barrett**
14 **SEENTHELIGHT**, 4, ch f Rich Charlie—Ackabarrow **Mrs Jennie Moffatt**
15 **SHEROOT**, 4, b c Cigar—Act of Treason **The Sheroot Partnership**
16 **TALOS (IRE)**, 8, b g Taufan (USA)—Jovial Josie (USA) **Mrs G. Lister**
17 **VILPRANO**, 5, b g Ra Nova—Village Princess **The Vilprano Partnership**

THREE-YEAR-OLDS

18 **PRECIOUS GIRL**, ch f Precious Metal—Oh My Oh My **Mr P. G. Airey**
19 **PRINCESS BRIANA**, b f Daring March—Jersey Maid **Mr P. G. Airey**

MR D. MOFFATT—continued

TWO-YEAR-OLDS

20 B f 30/3 Barry's Gamble—Jersey Maid (On Your Mark) **Mr P. G. Airey & R. Whitton**
21 B gr f 10/4 Be My Chief (USA)—Lammastide (Martinmas) **Mr G. R. Parrington**
22 Ch f 30/3 Gunner B—Molly Carew (Jimmy Reppin) **A. Douglas**
23 B f 30/5 Sylvan Express—Oh My Oh My (Ballacashtal (CAN)) **Mr P. G. Airey & R. Whitton**
24 Ch f 15/4 Phardante (FR)—Red Leaf (Carry Off)

Other Owners: Mrs D. Askew, Mr K. Bowron, Mr T. Brockbank, Mr A. M. Busby, Miss M. Faragher, Mr P. E. Hewitt, Mr B. R. Jervis, Mr A. R. Mills, Mr Dudley Moffatt, Mr William Morrison, Dr H. W. Proctor, Mr J. D. Wilson.

Apprentice: Darren Moffatt (7-4, w.a.).

Conditional: D J Moffatt (10-4).

423   MR PETER MONTEITH, Rosewell

Postal: **Whitebog Farm, Rosewell, Midlothian, EH24 9AY.**

Phone: **(0131 440) 2309 MOBILE (0585) 211794**

1 ARAGON AYR, 8, b br h Aragon—Brig of Ayr **Kelso Members Lowflyers Club**
2 BELDINE, 11, gr g Belfort (FR)—Royal Celandine **Lt-Col W. L. Monteith**
3 BILL'S PRIDE, 5, gr m Precocious—Hazel Bank **Exors of the late Mr William McKinlay**
4 DONE WELL (USA), 4, b g Storm Bird (CAN)—Suspicious Toosome (USA) **Mr Allan W. Melville**
5 ELECTRIC COMMITTEE (IRE), 6, ch g Lancastrian—Mary Black **Mrs Maud Monteith**
6 EMERALD STORM, 9, br g Strong Gale—Emerald Flair **Mr T. P. Finch**
7 FLASH OF REALM (FR), 10, b g Super Moment (USA)—Light of Realm **Mr Allan W. Melville**
8 FUNNY CHOICE (IRE), 6, b m Commanche Run—Best of Fun **Kelso Members Lowflyers Club**
9 FUNNY ROSE, 6, b m Belfort (FR)—Scottish Rose **Mr P. Monteith**
10 HENRY HOOLET, 7, b g Bold Owl—Genervera **Matchsemi**
11 JUKE BOX BILLY (IRE), 8, ch g Kemal (FR)—Friendly Circle **Everaldo Partnership**
12 KILLIMOR LAD, 9, b g Tina's Pet—Jeldi **Mr C. Jenkins**
13 MASTER BAVARD (IRE), 8, ch g Le Bavard (FR)—Honey Come Back **Mr P. Monteith**
14 MONTRAVE, 7, ch g Netherkelly—Streakella **Mr D. St. Clair**
15 RUSTY BLADE, 7, b g Broadsword (USA)—Sea Sand **Mrs M. I. Nisbet**
16 SHARP SAND, 6, ch g Broadsword (USA)—Sea Sand **Mrs M. I. Nisbet**
17 SHONARA'S WAY, 5, b m Slip Anchor—Favorable Exchange (USA) **A. Gothrie**
18 SUNNY LEITH, 5, b g Feelings (FR)—Pinkie Hill **Mr G. M. Cowan**
19 TEA SHOCK (IRE), 5, b g Electric—Teanam **Mr John Pirie**
20 WILD ROSE OF YORK, 5, gr m Unfuwain (USA)—Chepstow Vale (USA) **Lt-Col W. L. Monteith**

Other Owners: Mr T. Alderson, Mr Iain J. Campbell, Mr J. Davis, Mr K. M. Everitt, Mrs Jetta Fisher, Mr Jim Kean, Mr G. W. Kemp, Mr Tom McConnell, Mr Patrick McDade, A. W. Melville & P. Monteith, Mr Geoffrey Parkhouse, Mr R. E. Sutter.

Jockey (NH): A. Dobbin.

424   MR A. MOORE, Brighton

Postal: **10 Holt View Road, Woodingdean, Brighton, E. Sussex, BN2 6DH.**

Phone: **BRIGHTON (01273) 681679**

1 APOLLO RED, 7, ch g Dominion—Woolpack **Mr A. Moore**
2 BARBASON, 4, ch c Polish Precedent (USA)—Barada (USA) **Mr F. L. Hill**
3 BE SURPRISED, 10, ch g Dubassoff (USA)—Buckenham Belle **Mr F. L. Hill**
4 BLUE CAPS BOY, 4, ch g Prince Sabo—Avon Royale **Mr Edward East**
5 CAPSIZE, 10, ch g Capitano—Fused Light **Mr F. L. Hill**
6 CHEWIT, 4, gr g Beveled (USA)—Sylvan Song **Ballard (1834) Limited**

MR A. MOORE—continued

7 **GUEST ALLIANCE (IRE)**, 4, ch g Zaffaran (USA)—Alhargah **Ballard (1834) Limited**
8 **HATTA SUNSHINE (USA)**, 6, b g Dixieland Band (USA)—Mountain Sunshine (USA) **Mr R. Kiernan**
9 **INVOCATION**, 9, ch g Kris—Royal Saint (USA) **Mr R. Kiernan**
10 **IRON N GOLD**, 4, ch g Heights of Gold—Southern Dynasty **A Family Affair Partnership**
11 **JULIASDARKINVADER**, 6, br g Lidhame—Una Donna (GER) **Mr A. Moore**
12 **KELLAIRE GIRL (IRE)**, 4, b f Gallic League—Frensham Manor **Mrs Elizabeth Kiernan**
13 **KENTAVRUS WAY (IRE)**, 5, b g Thatching—Phantom Row **Mr F. L. Hill**
14 **KENYATTA (USA)**, 7, b g Mogambo (USA)—Caranga (USA) **Mr A. Moore**
15 **LIFT BOY (USA)**, 7, b g Fighting Fit (USA)—Pressure Seat (USA) **Mr A. Moore**
16 **LOOSE CHANGE**, 5, br m Spin of A Coin—Lirchur **Mr C. F. Sparrowhawk**
17 **MORE BILLS (IRE)**, 4, b g Gallic League—Lady Portobello **Mr A. Moore**
18 **NAHRAWALI (IRE)**, 5, b g Kahyasi—Nashkara **Mr C. F. Sparrowhawk**
19 **NICK THE GOLD**, 5, ch m Nicholas Bill—Goldyke **Mrs Elizabeth Kiernan**
20 **ONE OFF THE RAIL (USA)**, 6, b h Rampage (USA)—Catty Queen (USA) **Mr K. Higson**
21 **ROGER'S PAL**, 9, ch g Lir—Amberush **Mr A. Moore**
22 **THE LITTLE FERRET**, 6, ch g Scottish Reel—Third Movement **Mr K. Higson**

THREE-YEAR-OLDS

23 **BE SATISFIED**, gr g Chilibang—Gentalyn **Mr F. L. Hill**
24 **BOSTON TEA PARTY**, b f Rambo Dancer (CAN)—Tea-Pot **Mr B. Smith**
25 **GENERAL HENRY**, b g Belmez (USA)—Western Star **Mr F. Willson**
26 **IRON AND STEEL**, ch g Dominion—Fairy Fortune **Ballard (1834) Limited**

Other Owners: Mr C. J. Pennick.

Jockeys (NH): D Gallagher (w.a), B Powell (w.a.).

Apprentice: A Whelan.

Conditional: M Batchelor.

Lady Riders: Mrs Jayne Moore, Ms Candy Morris (8-8).

425   MR A. L. MOORE, Naas

Postal: **Dereens, Naas, Co. Kildare, Ireland.**
Phone: **(045) 876292 FAX (045) 876292**

1 **ALL THE ACES**, 9, gr g Roselier (FR)—Alice Starr **J. P. McManus**
2 **AMBLE SPEEDY (IRE)**, 6, b g Lancastrian—Speedy Debbie **R. Minnis**
3 **ARDSHUIL**, 7, b g Pennine Walk—Ordina (FR) **N. McCarthy**
4 **ARISTODEMUS**, 7, b g Politico (USA)—Easter Jane **C. Nolan**
5 **BACK BAR (IRE)**, 8, b g Strong Gale—Ballingee Marge **P. J. McCarthy**
6 **CAVALIER D'OR (USA)**, 5, b g Diesis—Luth d'Or (FR) **J. P. McManus**
7 **CELTIC SUNRISE**, 8, b g Celtic Cone—Fille de Soleil **Mrs M. A. Brennan**
8 **COWANSTOWN LADY (IRE)**, 6, b m Strong Gale—Free Run **Lyreen Syndicate**
9 **DEE ELL**, 10, ch g Little Wolf—Sagora **Mrs A. L. T. Moore**
10 **DEEP HERITAGE**, 10, ch g Deep Run—Bunkilla **J. P. McManus**
11 **DIAMANTINO (FR)**, 5, ch g Altayan—Perle de Saisy (FR) **C. Jones**
12 **DOONANDORAS (IRE)**, 8, b g Cataldi—Welsh Beauty **E. P. King**
13 **FAMILY WAY**, 9, b g Deep Run—Miss Miller **J. P. McManus**
14 **FEATHERED GALE**, 9, b g Strong Gale—Farm Approach **E. P. King**
15 **GENERAL NORMAN**, 9, b g Sheer Grit—Merry Mirth **C. Hanbury**
16 **GOOD GLOW**, 6, b g Jalmood (USA)—Dame Scarlet **Miss E. Lawlor**

MR A. L. MOORE—continued

17 **HAVE TO THINK**, 8, b m Impecunious—Dusty Run **P. Law**
18 **HEAVY HUSTLER (IRE)**, 5, b g Strong Gale—Balingale **Mrs R. Hale**
19 **JEFFELL**, 6, gr g Alias Smith (USA)—Saleander **T. Bailey**
20 **KILSPINDIE**, 5, b g Niniski (USA)—Kilavea (USA) **Lyreen Syndicate**
21 **KLAIRON DAVIS (FR)**, 7, b g Rose Laurel—Styrene (FR) **C. Jones**
22 **LOW FRONT (IRE)**, 6, b g Strong Gale—Mildred's Ball **Mrs R. Jones**
23 **MAJOR RUMPUS**, 8, b g Politics (USA)—Premier Susan **F. Conroy**
24 **MANHATTAN CASTLE (IRE)**, 7, b g Strong Gale—Allamanda (FR) **P. Fitzpatrick**
25 **NORTHERN HIDE**, 10, b g Buckskin (FR)—Lovely Tyrone **T. Ryan**
26 **OWENBWEE (IRE)**, 5, b g Broussard (USA)—Cookstown Lady **F. Cruess-Callaghan**
27 **PAT HARTIGAN (IRE)**, 6, ch g Orchestra—Oriental Star **J. P. McManus**
28 **PROFESSOR STRONG (IRE)**, 8, b g Strong Gale—Chapter Four **Mrs H. Murphy**
29 **RIFAWAN (USA)**, 4, b g Cox's Ridge (USA)—Rifada **Mrs G. Gillyan**
30 **SCRIBBLER**, 10, ch g The Parson—Chapter Four **Mrs H. Murphy**
31 **STRONG DILEMMA (IRE)**, 8, b g Strong Gale—Minorette **J. Halliday**
32 **TARTHOOTH (IRE)**, 5, ch g Bob Back (USA)—Zoly (USA) **Mrs H. De Burgh**
33 **TURNING POINT (IRE)**, 6, ch g Bulldozer—Sinead's Princess **R. Jordan**
34 **VEREDARIUS (FR)**, 5, b g Le Nain Jaune (FR)—Villa Verde (FR) **Mrs A. L. T. Moore**
35 **WHALE OF A KNIGHT (IRE)**, 7, b g Buckskin (FR)—Three Ladies **S. Galvin**
36 **WYLDE HIDE**, 9, b g Strong Gale—Joint Master **J. P. McManus**

Jockeys (NH): C O'Brien (9-7), F Woods (9-7).

Conditional: T Hallen (9-7), D O'Sullivan (9-7).

Amateurs: Mr G Donnelly (10-4), Mr J D Moore (9-0), Mr M Moran (10-0).

Lady Rider: Miss A Moore (9-0).

426   MR G. L. MOORE, Epsom

Postal: **Ermyn Lodge, Shepherds Walk, Epsom, Surrey, KT18 6DF.**
Phone: **(01372) 271526 FAX (01372) 271526**

 1 **BO KNOWS BEST (IRE)**, 7, ch g Burslem—Do We Know **Mr David Humphreys**
 2 **CALL ME ALBI (IRE)**, 5, ch g Glenstal (USA)—Albeni **Mrs Rita Bates**
 3 **DAHIYAH (USA)**, 5, b g Ogygian (USA)—Sticky Prospect (USA) **Mr Bryan Pennick**
 4 **DEEPLY VALE (IRE)**, 5, b g Pennine Walk—Late Evening (USA) **Mr K. Higson**
 5 **EQUASION (IRE)**, 4, b f Cyrano de Bergerac—Konigin Kate (GER) **Mr K. Higson**
 6 **ERMYNS PET**, 5, gr g Petoski—Trois Vallees **Mr J. Daniels**
 7 **EURO FORUM**, 4, ch g Deploy—Unique Treasure **The Forum Ltd**
 8 **GLOW FORUM**, 5, b m Kalaglow—Beau's Delight (USA) **The Forum Ltd**
 9 **HARDY DANCER**, 4, ch c Pharly (FR)—Handy Dancer **Mr Peter L. Higson**
10 **MR NEVERMIND (IRE)**, 6, b g The Noble Player (USA)—Salacia **Mr K. Higson**
11 **NO EXTRAS (IRE)**, 6, b g Efisio—Parkland Rose **Mr K. Higson**
12 **NO PATTERN**, 4, ch c Rock City—Sunfleet **Mr K. Higson**
13 **OWDBETTS (IRE)**, 4, b f High Estate—Nora Yo Ya **Mr K. Higson**
14 **PEARL DAWN (IRE)**, 6, b m Jareer (USA)—Spy Girl **Mrs E. Keep**
15 **QUEENFISHER**, 4, b f Scottish Reel—Mavahra **Mr K. Higson**
16 **RISING DOUGH (IRE)**, 4, br g Dowsing (USA)—Shortning Bread **Mr Bryan Pennick**
17 **ROMAN REEL (USA)**, 5, ch g Sword Dance—Our Mimi (USA) **Mr K. Higson**
18 **SOPHIE MAY**, 5, b m Glint of Gold—Rosana Park **Mr J. Daniels**
19 **STOPPES BROW**, 4, b g Primo Dominie—So Bold **Mr C. J. Pennick**
20 **SWINGING SIXTIES (IRE)**, 5, b g Fairy King (USA)—La Bella Fontana **Mr K. Higson**
21 **TICKERTY'S GIFT**, 6, b g Formidable (USA)—Handy Dancer **Mr K. Higson**
22 **WAIKIKI BEACH (USA)**, 5, ch g Fighting Fit (USA)—Running Melody **Mr K. Higson**

MR G. L. MOORE—continued

23 **WARM SPELL**, 6, b g Northern State (USA)—Warm Wind **Mr K. Higson**
24 **ZAMALEK (USA)**, 4, b g Northern Baby (CAN)—Chellingoua (USA) **Mr David Humphreys**

THREE-YEAR-OLDS

25 **AGAIN TOGETHER**, b f Then Again—Starawak **Mr C. J. Pennick**
26 **BANZHAF (USA)**, ch c Rare Performer (USA)—Hang On For Effer (USA) **Mr Bryan Pennick**
27 **CARMARTHEN BAY**, ch c Prionsaa—Pattie's Grey **Mr D. R. W. Jones**
28 **DRIFTHOLME**, b f Safawan—Avahra **Pennine Partners**
29 **FLAGSTAFF (USA)**, b c Personal Flag (USA)—Shuffle Up (USA) **Mr C. J. Pennick**
30 **MOVING UP (IRE)**, ch f Don't Forget Me—Our Pet **Mr Jim Horgan**
31 **NO SYMPATHY**, ch f Ron's Victory (USA)—Ackcontent (USA) **Pennine Partners**
32 **PROUD MONK**, gr c Aragon—Silent Sister **Pennine Partners**
33 **QUAKERS FIELD**, b c Anshan—Nosey **Mr Bryan Pennick**
34 **ROWLANDSONS CHARM (IRE)**, b f Fayruz—Magic Gold **Allen & Associates**
35 **ROWLANDSONS STUD (IRE)**, b br c Distinctly North (USA)—Be My Million **Allen & Associates**
36 **TO THE WHIRE**, br f Rock City—Free Dance (FR) **Pennine Partners**
37 **WILLIE RUSHTON**, ch f Master Willie—Amberush **Pennine Partners**

TWO-YEAR-OLDS

38 B c 1/3 Shalford (IRE)—Bap's Miracle (Track Spare)
39 Gr c 22/5 Chilibang—Free Rein (Sagaro) **Mr C. J. Pennick**
40 **GROVEFAIR CHIEF (IRE)**, ch c 27/3 Indian Ridge—From The Rooftops (IRE) (Thatching) **Grovefair PLC**
41 **GROVEFAIR DANCER (IRE)**, ch f 19/2 Soviet Lad (USA)—Naval Artiste (Captain's Gig (USA)) **Grovefair PLC**
42 B c Rock Hopper—Handy Dancer **Mr K. Higson**
43 Ch f 7/5 Shalford (IRE)—Saintly Guest (What A Guest)
44 B g 29/3 Belmez (USA)—Sipsi Fach (Prince Sabo)

Other Owners: M. Morris, Rowlandsons Ltd (Jewellers), Mrs P. Sore.

Jockeys (Flat): B Rouse (8-4), S Whitworth (8-4).

Apprentices: A Lakeman (7-13), L Suthern (8-10).

Conditional: M Attwater (10-0).

Amateurs: K Goble (9-0), Mr J Keller (10-7).

Lady Rider: Mrs J Moore.

427   MR G. M. MOORE, Middleham

Postal: **Warwick Lodge Stables, Middleham, Leyburn, North Yorks, DL8 4PB.**
Phone: **WENSLEYDALE (01969) 623823**

1 **ADIB (USA)**, 6, b g Alleged (USA)—Santa's Sister (USA) **N. B. Mason (Farms) Ltd**
2 **ANORAK (USA)**, 6, b g Storm Bird (CAN)—Someway Somehow (USA) **Mrs Susan Moore**
3 **BOLD ACCOUNT (IRE)**, 6, b g Strong Statement (USA)—Ogan Spa **Mr John Robson**
4 **BOLD BOSS**, 7, b g Nomination—Mai Pussy **Mr J. Robson**
5 **BOLD FOUNTAIN (IRE)**, 5, b g Royal Fountain—Glitter On **Mr John Robson**
6 **BOWLANDS COUNTRY**, 5, b g Town And Country—Kilbride Madam **Mrs Lynn Campion**
7 **BURNT IMP (USA)**, 6, ch g Imp Society (USA)—Flaming Reason (USA) **N. B. Mason (Farms) Ltd**
8 **CLASSIC CREST (IRE)**, 5, ch g Persian Heights—Blunted **G. B., A. & G. Peacock**
9 **COOL LUKE (IRE)**, 7, b g Red Sunset—Watet Khet (FR) **Mr B. Batey**
10 **DEVILRY**, 6, b g Faustus (USA)—Ancestry **Mr Richard Johnson**

MR G. M. MOORE—continued

11 **DONT FORGET CURTIS (IRE)**, 4, b g Don't Forget Me—Norse Lady **Mr S. D. Swaden**
12 **FAMILIAR ART**, 5, b m Faustus (USA)—Mill d'Art **Mr M. Keating**
13 **FLASHY'S SON**, 8, b g Balidar—Flashy Looker **Mr M. K. Lee**
14 **GALE AHEAD (IRE)**, 6, br g Strong Gale—Caddy Girl **Mr John Robson**
15 **GLENUGIE**, 5, b g Insan (USA)—Excavator Lady **Mr Frazer Hines**
16 **HIGHFLYING**, 10, b g Shirley Heights—Nomadic Pleasure
17 **HOUSE OF DREAMS**, 4, b c Darshaan—Helens Dreamgirl **J. & M. Leisure Ltd**
18 **MAFTUN (USA)**, 4, ch c Elmaamul (USA)—Allesheny **Mrs Susan Moore**
19 **MAGUIRE**, 6, b g Prince Ragusa—Mary Maguire **Mr D. Leech**
20 **NONIOS (IRE)**, 5, b g Nashamaa—Bosquet **B. R. A. T. S.**
21 **OUT BY NIGHT (IRE)**, 5, b g Phardante (FR)—Love And Idleness **Mr A. J. Coupland**
22 **PACIFIC RAMBLER (IRE)**, 6, b g Riberetto—Cooleen **Mr D. J. Bushell**
23 **PAPARAZZO**, 5, b g Posen (USA)—Royale Warning (USA) **Mr Emmett Quinlan**
24 **PEBBLE BEACH (IRE)**, 6, gr g Roselier (FR)—Indian Idol **The Pebble Beach Partnership**
25 **ROCK FOUNDATION**, 4, b g Rock City—Runelia **Mr J. Watson**
26 **ROYAL VACATION**, 7, b g King of Spain—Crane Beach **Mr G. P. Edwards**
27 **SHANAVOGH**, 5, b g Idiot's Delight—Honeybuzzard (FR) **Mr Sean Graham**
28 **SIMAND**, 4, b f Reprimand—Emmylou **Ms Sigrid Walter**
29 **TALLYWAGGER**, 9, b g Mandalus—Boro Cent **Mr J. R. Featherstone**
30 **THALEROS**, 6, b g Green Desert (USA)—Graecia Magna (USA) **Mr M. Gleason**
31 **TWIN FALLS (IRE)**, 5, b g Trempolino (USA)—Twice A Fool (USA) **Mrs Susan Moore**
32 **WEE RIVER (IRE)**, 7, b g Over The River (FR)—Mahe Reef **Mr Sean Graham**
33 **XAIPETE (IRE)**, 4, b g Jolly Jake (NZ)—Rolfete (USA) **Mrs Susan Moore**

THREE-YEAR-OLDS

34 **BLOSSOM DEARIE**, b f Landyap (USA)—Jose Collins **Miss Jacquie Tarr**
35 **HOBBS CHOICE**, b f Superpower—Excavator Lady **Liz Hobbs MBE**
36 **IMP EXPRESS (IRE)**, b c Mac's Imp (USA)—Fair Chance **Mr G. E. Stevenson**
37 **NAPOLEON'S RETURN**, gr c Daring March—Miss Colenca **Mr N. Honeyman**
38 **TIME TO TANGO**, b f Timeless Times (USA)—Tangalooma **Mrs D. N. B. Pearson**
39 **VILLAGE OPERA**, gr f Rock City—Lucky Song **Mr M. Keating**

Other Owners: Mr Gordon Brown, Mrs J. M. Gray, Mr R. Grocott, Mr A. Gundersen, Mr M. W. Harrison, Mr P. Jenkinson, Mrs Bet Jones, Mr K. S. Kilmartin, Mr John Lishman, Mr Anthony J. Martin, Mr R. Murray, Mr D. Neale, Mr Alan Thompson, Mr James Keith Tranter, Mr Malcolm Wassall.

Jockeys (NH): N Bentley (10-0), J Callaghan (10-0).

Conditional: T Hogg (10-0), P Walsh (10-0).

428 MR J. A. MOORE, Darlington

Postal: **South View, Bolam, Darlington, Co Durham, DL2 2UP.**

1 **DASHMAR**, 9, b g Rare One—Ballinattin Girl **Mr J. A. Moore**
2 **HURRICANE ANDREW (IRE)**, 8, ch g Hawaiian Return (USA)—Viable **Mr J. A. Moore**
3 **JUST FOR ME (IRE)**, 7, b g Callernish—Just Reward **Mr J. A. Moore**
4 **TARTAN MIX (IRE)**, 5, b g Mandalus—Gentle Madam **Mr J. A. Moore**

429 MR J. S. MOORE, Hungerford

Postal: **Parsonage Farm Racing Stables, Newbury Road, East Garston, Hungerford, RG17 7ER.**
Phone: **HOME/YARD** (01488) 648822 **MOBILE** (0860) 811127 **FAX** (01488) 648185

1 **BILLS PLOUGHGIRL**, 4, gr f Risk Me (FR)—Petite Angel **Mrs P. M. Ratcliffe**
2 **BURNT SIENNA (IRE)**, 4, b f Don't Forget Me—Ribot Ann **Mr Alex Gorrie**
3 **CLASH OF CYMBALS**, 7, gr g Orchestra—Woodland View **The Wiltshire Partnership**
4 **DRAMATIC EVENT**, 11, b g Kind of Hush—Welsh Jane **Mr D. G. Sprackland**

MR J. S. MOORE—continued

5 **EMMA GRIMES (IRE)**, 5, b m Nordico (USA)—Keep The Faith **Mr J. K. Grimes**
6 **INISHMANN (IRE)**, 5, ch g Soughaan (USA)—Danova (FR) **Mr Paul Kwok**
7 **MA BELLA LUNA**, 7, b m Jalmood (USA)—Macarte (FR) **Mr M. J. Spore**
8 **PATSY GRIMES**, 6, b m Beveled (USA)—Blue Angel **Mr J. K. Grimes**
9 **RISKIE THINGS**, 5, ch m Risk Me (FR)—Foolish Things **Mr Terry Pasquale**
10 **STAPLEFORD LADY**, 8, ch m Bairn (USA)—Marie Galante (FR) **Mr C. Kyriakou**
11 **WITNEY-DE-BERGERAC (IRE)**, 4, b g Cyrano de Bergerac—Spy Girl **Mr Ernie Houghton**

THREE-YEAR-OLDS

12 **DON'T TELL VICKI**, b f Mazilier (USA)—Jans Contessa **Mrs V. Goodman**
13 **DUNMEBRAINS (IRE)**, ch f Rich Charlie—Branch Out **Mr P. Wootton**
14 **GETUPANDLIEDOWN**, ch f Rich Charlie—Naar Chamali **Mr P. Wootton**
15 **GOLDEN SILVER**, b f Precious Metal—Severals Princess **Mr D. G. Sprackland**
16 **ICHOR**, b f Primo Dominie—Adeebah (USA) **Mrs D. Strauss**
17 **LADY OF THE MIST (IRE)**, ch f Digamist (USA)—Stradey Lynn **Mr Ernie Houghton**
18 **LAKESIDE EXPRESS**, ch f Siberian Express (USA)—Jenny's Rocket **Mr C. W. Rogers**
19 **LAST TOKEN**, b g Nomination—Beretta **Mr Liam Doherty**
20 **LINDAS DELIGHT**, b f Batshoof—Agreloui **Mr Liam Doherty**
21 **MUSIC MISTRESS (IRE)**, ch f Classic Music (USA)—Blue Scholar **Mrs D. Strauss**
22 **QUEEN EMMA (IRE)**, b f Mac's Imp (USA)—Hinari Disk Deck **Mr Ernie Houghton**
23 **SALLY'S TWINS**, b f Dowsing (USA)—Bird of Love **Mr Liam Doherty**

TWO-YEAR-OLDS

24 B f 15/4 River Falls—Ballywhat (IRE)
25 Ch c 10/5 Superlative—Ever Reckless
26 Br f 11/5 Archway (IRE)—Indian Sand **Mr Ernie Houghton**
27 B f 10/1 River Falls—Katie's Delight
28 B f 10/4 Anita's Prince—Little Club **Mrs V. Goodman**
29 B f 18/4 Mujadil (USA)—Peace Mission **Mrs V. Goodman**
30 B f 30/5 Forzando—Sandy Looks **Mrs V. Goodman**
31 Br f 3/5 Don't Forget Me—Shoka (FR)

Other Owners: Mr J. Franklin, Mr Jonathan Fry, Mrs D. Hammerson, Mr A. Hunt, Mr J. S. Moore.

Jockey (Flat): A McGlone (8-0).

Jockey (NH): W McFarland (10-0).

Apprentice: H Fox (8-12)

Conditional: L McGrath (9-7).

Lady Rider: Mrs J S Moore (8-0).

430   MR K. A. MORGAN, Melton Mowbray

Postal: **Hall Farm Stables, Waltham On The Wolds, Melton Mowbray, Leics, LE14 4AJ.**
Phone: **(01664) 464711 OR 464488 FAX (01664) 464492 MOBILE(0860) 151341**

1 **ADMIRAL HOOD (USA)**, 5, b g Devil's Bag (USA)—De La Rose (USA) **Mr M. R. Parkes**
2 **BUCKMIST BLUE (IRE)**, 6, b m Buckskin (FR)—Grease Pot **Mr J. Cleeve**
3 **CORRIMULZIE (IRE)**, 5, ch g Phardante (FR)—Scott's Hill **Roemex Ltd**
4 **COUNT OF FLANDERS (IRE)**, 6, b g Green Desert (USA)—Marie de Flandre (FR) **Mrs C. A. Morgan**

MR K. A. MORGAN—continued

5 **DASH TO THE PHONE (USA)**, 4, b br c Phone Trick (USA)—Dashing Partner **Mrs M. Williams**
6 **FALCON'S IMAGE (USA)**, 5, b g Silver Hawk (USA)—Will of Victory **Mr T. R. Pryke**
7 **GAME DRIVE (IRE)**, 4, b c Dancing Brave (USA)—Twixt **Mrs C. A. Morgan**
8 **GEORGE ASHFORD (IRE)**, 6, b g Ashford (USA)—Running Feud **Mr B. Leatherday**
9 **GLANMERIN (IRE)**, 5, b g Lomond (USA)—Abalvina (FR) **Mr Rex Norton**
10 **HALLSTAR**, 4, b f Hallgate—Star Route **Miss Pauline Hall**
11 **HAPPY DAYS BILL**, 4, ch c Island Set (USA)—Fantasie Impromptu **Mr P. A. Stewart**
12 **KIND'A SMART**, 11, ch g Kind of Hush—Treasure Seeker **Mrs P. A. L. Butler**
13 **KING ATHELSTAN (USA)**, 8, b g Sovereign Dancer (USA)—Wimbledon Star (USA) **Mr Ian Guise**
14 **LIFE DANCING (IRE)**, 5, b m Dance of Life (USA)—Ringawoody **Mrs C. A. Morgan**
15 **LORD PALMERSTON (USA)**, 4, b g Hawkster (USA)—First Minister (USA) **Mr J. C. Fretwell**
16 **MEZZORAMIO**, 4, ch g Cadeaux Genereux—Hopeful Search (USA) **Mr T. R. Pryke**
17 **MOLONYS DRAM**, 5, b g Toirdealbhach—Conversant **Mr A. Grummitt**
18 **MOOBAKKR (USA)**, 5, b br g Mr Prospector (USA)—Without Feathers (USA) **Mr Ian Guise**
19 **MR VINCENT**, 6, ch g Nishapour (FR)—Brush Away **Mr J. A. Outwin**
20 **NIFAAF (USA)**, 4, b f Silver Hawk (USA)—Betty Money (USA) **Mrs C. A. Morgan**
21 **NOCATCHIM**, 7, b g Shardari—Solar **Mr R. E. Gray**
22 **NODDING AQUANTANCE**, 4, b g Dragonara (USA)—Sombreuil **Mrs P. A. L. Butler**
23 **ORCHID HOUSE**, 4, b f Town And Country—Tudor Orchid **Omega Racing Club**
24 **RATIFY**, 9, br g Shirley Heights—Rattle (FR) **Mr J. C. Fretwell**
25 **ROSSCOYNE**, 6, b m Ardross—Banking Coyne **Mr R. E. Gray**
26 **ROTHARI**, 4, b g Nashwan (USA)—Royal Lorna (USA) **Mr Michael Saunders**
27 **RUSSIAN BEAR**, 5, ch g Celestial Storm (USA)—Alma Ata **Mr P. Dobson**
28 **SHOOFE (USA)**, 8, ch g L'Emigrant (USA)—Bid For Manners (USA) **Mr J. A. Outwin**
29 **SYLVAN SABRE (IRE)**, 7, b g Flash of Steel—Flute (FR) **Mr J. C. Fretwell**
30 **TONNERRE**, 4, b c Unfuwain (USA)—Supper Time **Mr M. T. Basso & Mr Ian Guise**
31 **TOP WOLF**, 6, b g Little Wolf—Top Cover **Mr G. Horsford**
32 **WAMDHA (IRE)**, 6, b m Thatching—Donya **Mr T. R. Pryke**
33 **WASSL STREET (IRE)**, 4, b c Dancing Brave (USA)—One Way Street **Mr Rex Norton & Mr B. Leatherday**
34 **WEATHER ALERT (IRE)**, 5, b g Dance of Life (USA)—Ask The Wind **Mrs R. M. Burgess**
35 **WISDOM**, 4, b c Insan (USA)—Emaline (FR) **Mr T. R. Pryke**

THREE-YEAR-OLDS

36 B f Totem (USA)—Alma Ata **Mr P. Dobson & Mrs C. A. Morgan**
37 B f Jupiter Island—Fantasie Impromptu **Mr P. A. Stewart**

Other Owners: Mr S. Cavender, Mr W. A. Fouracres, Mr M. J. Harmer, Mr Michael Kenley, Mr Philip Kenley, Mr Alan Kerr, Mr P. G. Kerr, Mr W. B. Mawson, Mr C. P. Mitchell, Mr Bill Nuttell, Mr John O'Hara, Mr B. Parker, Mrs Ann Price, Mr John H. Price, Mr Alan J. Putland, Mr M. Rozenbroek, Mr R. A. Simcox, Mr Richard Simpson, Mrs P. Stark, Twinacre Nurseries Ltd, Mrs G. M. Wild, Mr J. Wild, Mr W. J. Williams, Mr Keith Wills.

Jockey (NH): Aidie Smith (9-12).

Conditional: R Massey (9-7).

Amateur: Mr R Barrett.

431   MR M. F. D. MORLEY, Newmarket

Postal: **High Havens Stables, Hamilton Road, Newmarket, Suffolk, CB8 ONQ.**
Phone: **NEWMARKET (01638) 667175 FAX (01638) 667913**

1 **BUROOJ**, 6, br h Danzig (USA)—Princess Sucree (USA) **Mr Hamdan Al Maktoum**
2 **CELERIC**, 4, b g Mtoto—Hot Spice **Mr Christopher Spence**
3 **DARLING CLOVER**, 4, ch f Minster Son—Lady Clementine **Mr K. Craddock**
4 **FAHAL (USA)**, 4, b c Silver Hawk (USA)—By Land By Sea (USA) **Mr Hamdan Al Maktoum**

MR M. F. D. MORLEY—continued

5 HAWKISH (USA), 7, b g Silver Hawk (USA)—Dive Royal (USA) Mrs M. F. D. Morley
6 TAJAR (USA), 4, b g Slew O' Gold (USA)—Mashaarif (USA) Mr Hamdan Al Maktoum

THREE-YEAR-OLDS

7 AKALIM, b c Petong—Tiszta Sharok Mr Hamdan Al Maktoum
8 ALSAHAH (IRE), b f Unfuwain (USA)—Princess Sucree (USA) Mr Hamdan Al Maktoum
9 ATRAF, b c Clantime—Flitteriss Park Mr Hamdan Al Maktoum
10 CALENDULA, b f Be My Guest (USA)—Sesame Mr Christopher Spence
11 DAWAM (IRE), b f Marju (IRE)—Atlantic Dream (USA) Mr Hamdan Al Maktoum
12 GIDDY, b br f Polar Falcon (USA)—Spin Turn Lord Hartington
13 NABHAAN (IRE), b c In The Wings—Miss Gris (USA) Mr Hamdan Al Maktoum
14 NAYIB, b c Bustino—Nicholas Grey Mr Hamdan Al Maktoum
15 PINE NEEDLE, ch f Kris—Fanny's Cove Lord Halifax
16 SPINNING MOUSE, b f Bustino—Minute Waltz Lord Hartington
17 SUFUF, b f Caerleon (USA)—Deira (NZ) Mr Hamdan Al Maktoum
18 TASHJIR (USA), ch f Slew O' Gold (USA)—Mashaarif (USA) Mr Hamdan Al Maktoum
19 TASWIB (USA), gr c Housebuster (USA)—Umbrella Rig (USA) Mr Hamdan Al Maktoum
20 TAWAFEK (USA), br c Silver Hawk (USA)—Tippy Tippy Toe (USA) Mr Hamdan Al Maktoum

TWO-YEAR-OLDS

21 ALMIAD (USA), b f 25/2 Silver Hawk (USA)—Mashaarif (USA) (Mr Prospector (USA)) Mr Hamdan Al Maktoum
22 BATSFORD, b f 6/5 Batshoof—Sandford Lady (Will Somers) Lord Hartington
23 BELUSHI, b f 26/4 Risk Me (FR)—Trigamy (Tribal Chief) Mrs Kate Watson & Partners
24 BICTON PARK, b c 2/3 Distant Relative—Merton Mill (Dominion) Lord Clinton
25 BOATER, b c 12/3 Batshoof—Velvet Beret (IRE) (Dominion) Lord Hartington
26 CINNAMON, b f 6/2 Robellino (USA)—Hot Spice (Hotfoot) Mr J. D. Morley
27 CLANCY, ch f 27/3 Clantime—Tendency (Ballad Rock) Mrs Mary Chapman
28 HADIDI, b c 25/4 Alzao (USA)—Sesame (Derrylin) Mr Hamdan Al Maktoum
29 HAKKANIYAH, b f 9/3 Machiavellian (USA)—Mousaiha (Shadeed (USA)) Mr Hamdan Al Maktoum
30 INTIKHAB (USA), b c 8/5 Red Ransom (USA)—
Crafty Example (USA) (Crafty Prospector (USA)) Mr Hamdan Al Maktoum
31 KAYFIYAH (IRE), b f 3/6 Marju (IRE)—Princess Sucree (USA) (Roberto (USA)) Mr Hamdan Al Maktoum
32 KHAYALI (IRE), b c 24/2 Unfuwain (USA)—Coven (Sassafras (FR)) Mr Hamdan Al Maktoum
33 LAWAHIK, b c 24/5 Lahib (USA)—Lightning Legacy (USA) (Super Concorde (USA)) Mr Hamdan Al Maktoum
34 MARADI (IRE), b c 1/4 Marju (IRE)—Tigora (Ahonoora) Mr Hamdan Al Maktoum
35 MUTABARI (USA), b c 23/2 Seeking The Gold—
Cagey Exuberance (USA) (Exuberant (USA)) Mr Hamdan Al Maktoum
36 PUN, b f 29/3 Batshoof—Keen Wit (Kenmare (FR)) Lord Hartington
37 SHIRTY, b c 14/4 Shirley Heights—Sassy Lassy (IRE) (Taufan (USA)) Lord Hartington
38 STRIDE, b f 26/4 Batshoof—The Strid (IRE) (Persian Bold) Lord Hartington
39 TALIB (USA), b c 25/3 Silver Hawk (USA)—Dance For Lucy (USA) (Dance Bid (USA)) Mr Hamdan Al Maktoum
40 TAUNT, b c 17/4 Robellino (USA)—Minute Waltz (Sadler's Wells (USA)) Lord Hartington

Other Owners: Mrs J. Gleason, Mr David Kelly, Mr Gordon Petrie.

432   MR D. MORRIS, Newmarket

Postal: Hackness Villa Stables, Exeter Road, Newmarket, Suffolk, CB8 8LP.
Phone: (01638) 667959

1 COVEN MOON, 6, ch m Crofthall—Mayspark Mrs Sara Pepper
2 GADGE, 5, br g Nomination—Queenstyle J. B. R. Leisure Ltd
3 KINDRED GREETING, 4, b g Most Welcome—Red Berry White House Racing Club
4 MR ROUGH, 5, b g Fayruz—Rheinbloom Mr Robin Akehurst
5 PARIS BABE, 4, b f Teenoso—Kala's Image Mrs S. I. Parry
6 SAIFAN, 7, ch g Beveled (USA)—Superfrost Miss L. Hawes
7 STUDIO THIRTY, 4, gr g Rock City—Chepstow Vale (USA) Mr Derek C. Holder
8 TOAT CHIEFTAIN, 4, b g Puissance—Tribal Lady D. & L. Racing

MR D. MORRIS—continued

THREE-YEAR-OLDS

9 **DEERLY**, b f Hadeer—Grafitti Gal (USA) **Mrs C. Holder**
10 **FARFESTE**, b f Jester—Our Horizon **Bob Tallentire and Jim Cameron**
11 **HIGHLIGHTS**, ch f Phountzi (USA)—Idella's Gold (FR) **Bloomsbury Stud**
12 **RED RUSTY (USA)**, ch g The Carpenter (USA)—Super Sisters (AUS) **Exors of the Late Mr R. E. Mason**

TWO-YEAR-OLDS

13 B f 3/2 Chilibang—Dear Person (Rainbow Quest (USA)) **D. & L. Racing**
14 B f 25/2 Jareer (USA)—Hellicroft (High Line) **D. & L. Racing**
15 B f 28/3 Puissance—Miss Echo (Chief Singer) **D. & L. Racing**

Other Owners: Mr Michael Fenton, Mr D. Morris, Mrs Linda Morris, Ms Wendy Smith.

Jockeys (Flat): Ray Cochrane, Jason Tate.

Jockey (NH): Nick Mann.

Apprentice: Carl Hodgson.

Lady Rider: Mrs L Morris (9-0).

433   MR M. MORRIS, Fethard

Postal: **Everardsgrange, Fethard, Co. Tipperary, Ireland.**
Phone: **(052) 31474 FAX (052) 31654**

1 **ALICE FREYNE (IRE)**, 6, b m Lancastrian—Samtimwen **Mr M. F. Morris**
2 **ANDROS DAWN (IRE)**, 6, b m Buckskin (FR)—Aillwee Dawn **A. J. O'Reilly**
3 **A WOMANS HEART (IRE)**, 7, b m Supreme Leader—Mary Black **Mrs Shanny Morris**
4 **BELVEDERIAN**, 9, b g Deep Run—Arctic Shine **A. J. O'Reilly**
5 **BETTER THANA BRIEF (IRE)**, 8, ch m Remainder Man—Grove Road **Mrs C. Whyte**
6 **BOOTS MADDEN (IRE)**, 6, b g The Parson—Little Welly **Mrs J. Magnier**
7 **CAPITULAR (IRE)**, 6, b br h The Parson—Scotch News **Mrs Lewis C. Murdock & Mrs P. Fanning**
8 **CELTIC WHO (IRE)**, 5, br g Strong Gale—Whoseview **Mrs P. Desmond**
9 **CRISTYS PICNIC (IRE)**, 6, b g Tremblant—My Maizey **The Albatross Racing Club**
10 **CROI**, 6, b g Lancastrian—Our Chrisy **Mr G. Fitzmaurice**
11 7, Ch g Scorpio—Embuscade **Mrs A. J. O'Reilly**
12 **EMPOWERMENT (IRE)**, 6, ch g Be My Native (USA)—Fun
13 **FEAR CLISTE (IRE)**, 5, b g Homo Sapien—Glenravel **Mr M. F. Morris**
14 **FERNHILL (IRE)**, 6, ch m Good Thyne (USA)—Highland Party **A. J. O'Reilly**
15 **FIFTH SYMPHONY (IRE)**, 7, ch g Orchestra—Bruleen **Mrs Miles Valentine**
16 **FIREBLENDS (IRE)**, 5, b m Phardante (FR)—Biowen **A. J. O'Reilly**
17 **FORCE THIRTEEN (IRE)**, 5, b g Strong Gale—Canta Lair **Mrs P. F. N. Fanning**
18 **FOR WILLIAM**, 10, b g Whistling Deer—Pampered Sue **Mr M. F. Morris**
19 **GIMME (IRE)**, 6, b g Sheer Grit—Barrow Breeze **The Albatross Racing Club**
20 **ILLEGAL ALIEN (IRE)**, 6, b h Duky—Dontellvi **Mr M. F. Morris**
21 **ITSAJUNGLEOUTTHERE (IRE)**, 6, ch g Callernish—Er In Doors **Mrs John Magnier**
22 **IT'S THE KLONDIKE**, 6, b g Derring Rose—Always Shining **The Albatross Racing Club**
23 **JOHN RUDD (IRE)**, 9, b g King's Ride—Lorna Doone **Mrs Miles Valentine**
24 **JOLLY JOHN (IRE)**, 5, b h Jolly Jake (NZ)—Golden Seekers **Mrs P. F. N. Fanning**
25 **KNOCKMUIRA (IRE)**, 6, b g Strong Gale—Bargara **Mrs Miles Valentine**
26 **LEVEL VIBES**, 7, ch g Scorpio (FR)—Embuscade **Mr M. F. Morris**
27 **MILLA'S DELIGHT (IRE)**, 5, br g Boreen (FR)—Brook Lady **Mr David Lloyd**
28 **MULLIGAN (IRE)**, 6, ch g Callernish—Anaglogs Pet **The Albatross Racing Club**
29 **MYFAVOURITEMARTIAN (IRE)**, 6, b g Strong Gale—Le Idol **Mrs Sharon Nelson**

MR M. MORRIS—continued

30 **NEVER THE REASON (IRE)**, 5, br g Strong Gale—Bargara **Mrs Miles Valentine**
31 **NEW CO**, 8, ch g Deep Run—True Minstrel **Mrs L. C. Ronan**
32 **OLYMPIC D'OR**, 8, ch g Boreen—Brook Lady **Mrs Dorine V. Reihill**
33 **PHARADISO (IRE)**, 5, ch h Phardante (FR)—Sugar Shaker **A. J. O'Reilly**
34 **PHARLINDO (IRE)**, 5, b g Phardante (FR)—Linda Martin **A. J. O'Reilly**
35 **PRECARIUM (IRE)**, 8, b g The Parson—Bonne Bouche **Mrs Lewis C. Murdock**
36 **ROARING SPRING (IRE)**, 6, b g Callernish—Sister Cecelia **Lady Lloyd Webber**
37 **RUA SKY (IRE)**, 7, b g Strong Gale—Rathara **Mr P. Hanley**
38 **SOUNDS GOOD (IRE)**, 5, b g Decent Fellow—Churchtown Breeze **Mr M. F. Morris**
39 **THREE BROWNIES**, 9, b g Strong Gale—Summerville Rose **Mrs A. M. Daly**
40 **VERUNA (IRE)**, 6, b m Strong Gale—Canta Lair **Mrs P. F. N. Fanning**
41 **WHAT A QUESTION (IRE)**, 8, b m The Parson—Er In Doors **Mrs John Magnier**

Jockeys (NH): Graham Bradley (w.a.), Martin Davey, Connor O'Dwyer.

Amateur: Mr Mark Cahill.

434   MR T. MORTON, Leominster

Postal: **Little London, Downwood, Shobdon, Leominster, HR6 9NH.**
Phone: **(01568) 708488**

1 **CELTIC WIND**, 9, ch m Celtic Cone—Cool Wind **Mr T. Morton**
2 **WASSLS MILLION**, 10, b g Wassl—Black Crow **Mr T. Morton**

435   MRS E. MOSCROP, Seaton Burn

Postal: **East Brenkley Stables, Brenkley, Seaton Burn, Newcastle Upon Tyne, NE13 6BT.**
Phone: **(0191) 2362145**

1 **MISTER POINT**, 14, ch g Ahonoora—Rozmeen (FR) **Mrs E. Moscrop**
2 **OLE OLE**, 10, br g Boreen (FR)—Night Caller **Mrs E. Moscrop**
3 **SHUT UP**, 7, b m Kind of Hush—Creetown Lady **Mr George R. Moscrop**
4 **TANGO IN PARIS (ARG)**, 6, ch g Bates Motel (USA)—What A Bang (USA) **Mrs E. Moscrop**

Amateur: Mr G R Moscrop (10-7).

436   MR M. P. MUGGERIDGE, Lambourn

Postal: **Charleston's Place Racing Stables, Eastbury, Nr. Lambourn, Berks.**
Phone: **HOME (01488) 648715 YARD (01488) 73532**

1 4, Br f Macmillion—Bel Creation **The Old Chestnut Tree Syndicate**
2 5, Ch m Scallywag—Devine Lady **Mr Stephen L. Darby**
3 **ELA PALIKARI MOU (IRE)**, 5, b g Lomond—Ionian Raja (USA) **Mr Andreas Michael**
4 **FIELDRIDGE**, 7, ch g Rousillon (USA)—Final Thought **The Charleston Partnership**
5 **FLY THE EAGLE**, 4, b g Rock City—Tittlemouse **Mr Stephen L. Darby**
6 **GRAND APPLAUSE (IRE)**, 6, gr g Mazaad—Standing Ovation **Mr M. J. Lewin**
7 **ONE TO NOTE**, 12, br g Star Appeal—Town Lady **Mr J. F. Mitchell**
8 **PAPER STAR**, 9, br m Strong Gale—Lynwood Lady **Gallery Racing**
9 **SPUMANTE**, 4, ch g Executive Man—Midler **The Charleston Partnership**

MR M. P. MUGGERIDGE—continued
THREE-YEAR-OLDS

10 OUR ADVENTURE, ch f Green Adventure (USA)—Honey Dipper **Mr A. F. Leighton**

Other Owners: Mrs M. Bennett, Mrs P. G. Lewin, Ms A. J. B. Smalldon.

Jockeys (NH): Simon McNeill, Brendan Powell.

Apprentice: Tom McLaughlin (8-0).

Conditional: Sean Curran (10-0).

Amateur: Mr Gary Brown (10-0).

437   MR WILLIAM MUIR, Lambourn

Postal: **Linkslade, Wantage Road, Lambourn, Hungerford, Berks, RG17 8UG.**

Phone: **OFFICE (01488) 73098 HOME 73748 FAX 73490 MOBILE (0831) 457074**

1 **ALESSIA,** 4, b f Caerleon (USA)—Kiss **Mr D. J. Deer**
2 **AVERTI (IRE),** 5, b h Warning—Imperial Jade **Mr D. J. Deer**
3 **ETHBAAT (USA),** 5, b br h Chief's Crown (USA)—Alchaasibiyeh (USA) **Fayzad Thoroughbred Limited**
4 **GOLD LUCK (USA),** 4, b f Slew O'Gold (USA)—Rambushka (USA) **Mr D. J. Deer**
5 **GREENSPAN (IRE),** 4, b c Be My Guest (USA)—Prima Ballerina (FR) **Mrs H. Levy**
6 **HIGHLY CHARMING (IRE),** 4, b c Shirley Heights—Charmante Dame (FR) **The Liar's Poker Partnership**
7 **HOW'S IT GOIN (IRE),** 5, ch g Kefaah (USA)—Cuirie **Mrs J. M. Muir**
8 **INHERENT MAGIC (IRE),** 7, ch m Magical Wonder (USA)—Flo Kelly **Mrs Danita Winstanly**
9 **JAGELLON (IRE),** 5, b h Danzig Connection (USA)—Heavenlyspun (USA) **Mr D. J. Deer**
10 **KRISTAL BREEZE,** 4, ch f Risk Me (FR)—Mistral's Dancer **Mr S. Lamb**
11 **MIAMI BANKER,** 10, ch g Miami Springs—Banking Coyne **Mr J. J. Amass**
12 **ORSAY,** 4, gr c Royal Academy (USA)—Bellifontaine (FR) **Mr D. J. Deer**
13 **PADISHAH (IRE),** 7, ch g Kris—Aunty (FR) **Perspicacious Punters Racing Club**
14 **PERILOUS PLIGHT,** 5, ch g Siberian Express (USA)—Loveskate (USA) **Mr J. Jannaway**
15 **RAISA POINT,** 5, b m Raised Socially (USA)—To The Point **Mr J. J. Amass**
16 **ROUFONTAINE,** 5, gr m Rousillon (USA)—Bellifontaine (FR) **Mr D. J. Deer**
17 **ROYAL PRINT (IRE),** 7, ch g Kings Lake (USA)—Reprint **Miss J. Halford**
18 **SHABANAZ,** 11, b g Imperial Fling (USA)—Claironcita **Fayzad Thoroughbred Limited**
19 **SLANEY PROJECT (IRE),** 4, b g Project Manager—Sundrive **Mrs D. Winstanly**
20 **SUE ME (IRE),** 4, b br g Contract Law (USA)—Pink Fondant **Mr Michael Payton**
21 **SUPERMICK,** 5, ch g Faustus—Lardana **Mrs J. M. Muir**
22 **TAKESHI (IRE),** 4, b f Cadeaux Genereux—Taplow **Mr J. Jannaway**

THREE-YEAR-OLDS

23 **AL'S ALIBI,** b c Alzao (USA)—Lady Kris (IRE) **The Sussex Stud Limited**
24 **BEAS RIVER (IRE),** b g Classic Music (USA)—Simple Annie **Mr A. J. de V. Patrick**
25 **BELLS OF HOLLAND,** b f Belmez (USA)—Annie Albright (USA) **Mr R. Haim**
26 **DARBY FLYER,** ch c Dominion Royale—Shining Wood **Mr S. Darby**
27 **D J CAT,** b g Ballad Rock—Four-Legged Friend **Mr J. O'Mulloy**
28 **DONA MARINA (IRE),** b f Belmez (USA)—Fantastic Bid (USA) **Mr D. J. Deer**
29 **EXTRA HOUR (IRE),** b g Cyrano de Bergerac—Renzola **Mr R. Haim**
30 **IMPINGTON (IRE),** b f Mac's Imp (USA)—Ultra **Mrs H. Levy**
31 **LOMU,** b g Floose—Sancilia **Mrs J. M. Muir**
32 **ONE SHOT (IRE),** b g Fayruz—La Gravotte (FR) **Mr R. Haim**
33 **PRIME PARTNER,** b g Formidable (USA)—Baileys By Name **Mr P. Bourke**
34 **RAWI,** ch c Forzando—Finally **Mrs Danita Winstanly**
35 **SHOULDBEGREY,** ch c Siberian Express (USA)—Miss Magnetism **Mr B. Levy**
36 **THREE WEEKS,** ch g Formidable (USA)—Zilda (FR) **Mr D. Wiltshire**
37 **WOODBURY LAD (USA),** ch c Woodman (USA)—Habibti **Fayzad Thoroughbred Ltd**

MR WILLIAM MUIR—continued

TWO-YEAR-OLDS

38 Ch c 31/1 Timeless Times (USA)—Arroganza (Crofthall)
39 B c 13/4 Night Shift (USA)—Avantage Service (IRE) (Exactly Sharp (USA))
40 B c 21/3 Roi Danzig (USA)—Avidal Park (Horage)
41 B c 1/4 Green Desert (USA)—Bermuda Classic (Double Form)
42 DAYRELLA, ch f 27/5 Beveled (USA)—Divissima (Music Boy) **Dulverton Equine**
43 Ch c 25/2 Faustus (USA)—Dependable (Formidable (USA))
44 B f 9/5 Emarati (USA)—Harmony Park (Music Boy)
45 Gr c 28/1 Timeless Times (USA)—Heaven-Liegh-Grey (Grey Desire)
46 B f 16/4 Shalford (IRE)—Kilfenora (Tribal Chief)
47 LITTLESTONE ROCKET, ch c 17/3 Safawan—Miss Hocroft (Dominion) **Mr J. Bailey**
48 B c 1/3 Midyan (USA)—Rock Face (Ballad Rock)
49 Br f 23/5 Komaite (USA)—Senorina Francesca (The Brianstan) **Mr P. Bourke**
50 B c 14/2 Reprimand—Spinner (Blue Cashmere)

Other Owners: Mrs D. Cunningham-Reid, Mr John Davies, Mrs M. E. Deer, Mr H. Dickson, Mr Robert M. Gibson, Mr M. P. Graham, Mr K. Jeffrey, Mr S. Kaemofer, Mr S. Meadows, Mr L. A. Pickett, Mrs J. A. Seaden, Mr P. Smith, Mr D. Wheatley.

Jockey (Flat): Jason Weaver (8-4, w.a.).

Jockey (NH): Mark Richards (10-0).

Apprentice: Robert Pooles.

438   MR A. B. MULHOLLAND, Hambleton

Postal: **Hambleton Lodge, Hambleton, Thirsk, North Yorkshire, YO7 2HA.**
Phone: **HOME (01845) 526379 OFFICE 597288 FAX 597288 MOBILE (0585) 437643**

1 ARAK (USA), 8, b g Clever Trick (USA)—Twilight Flight (USA) **David Crossland & Jayne McGivern**
2 DREAM WEDDING, 4, ch f Soviet Star (USA)—Island Wedding (USA) **David Crossland & Jayne McGivern**
3 GREENACRES LAD, 13, ch g Billion (USA)—Moon Lady **Miss Angela Bennett**
4 KOMLUCKY, 4, b f Komaite (USA)—Sweet And Lucky **Hambleton Racing Partnership**
5 LA DAMA (USA), 4, ch f Known Fact (USA)—Cypria Sacra (USA) **Miss Angela Bennett**
6 MY GODSON, 6, br g Valiyar—Blessit **Linkchallenge Limited**
7 THE PREMIER EXPRES, 6, gr g Siberian Express (USA)—Home And Away **Mrs Elizabeth Lewis**
8 4, Ch g Orchestra—White Jasmin **Bronzepatch (Ltd)**

THREE-YEAR-OLDS

9 AFISIAK, b f Efisio—Maestrette **David Crossland & Jayne McGivern**
10 DARK SOUND (IRE), b g Darshaan—Second Guess **The Barons Partnership**
11 DOMUSKY, ch f Domynsky—Roches Roost **Mr Charles Castle**
12 B c Imperial Frontier (USA)—English Lily **H. L. E. P. (Ltd)**
13 KULE POPSI, b f Mac's Imp (USA)—Flight Fantasy (USA) **Bronzepatch (Ltd)**
14 Ch f Komaite (USA)—Rapid Action **The Northern Partnership (1993)**
15 Ch f Keen—Tommys Dream **Mrs Joy Turner**

TWO-YEAR-OLDS

16 B c 26/4 Salt Dome (USA)—Daidis (Welsh Pageant) **Noel Finnagen**
17 Ch c 1/4 Mac's Imp (USA)—Ellaline (Corvaro (USA)) **Dr Noel Cogan**
18 B c Mac's Imp (USA)—Flight Fantasy (USA) (Air Forbes Won (USA)) **Bronzepatch (Ltd)**
19 B c 1/5 Jurado (USA)—Janeswood (IRE) (Henbit (USA)) **Noel Finnagen**
20 B c 28/4 Contract Law (USA)—La Sass (Sassafras (FR)) **Noel Finnagen**

Jockeys (Flat): M McAndrews (8-2), J Weaver (w.a.), T Williams (7-10).

Lady Rider: Carol Williams (8-4).

439   MR J. W. MULLINS, Amesbury

Postal: **Wilsford Stables, Wilsford-cum-lake, Amesbury, Salisbury, SP4 7BP.**

Phone: **(01980) 626344 FAX (01980) 626344 MOBILE (0831) 363832**

1 **AGAINST THE CLOCK**, 4, b g Puissance—Sara Sprint **Mr P. Everard**
2 **CASHFLOW CRISIS (IRE)**, 4, ch g The Noble Player (USA)—Crepe de Paille **Mr C. Tilly**
3 **EMBLEY BUOY**, 8, ch g Nearly A Hand—Busy Quay **Mrs Heather Bare**
4 **FAST RUN (IRE)**, 8, ch g Commanche Run—Starlite Night (USA) **Mr Ian M. McGready**
5 **GAME DILEMMA**, 5, b m Sulaafah (USA)—Stagbury **Mr Ian M. McGready**
6 **GINKA**, 5, b m Petoski—Pine **Mr Seamus Mullins**
7 **KENTFORD TINA**, 5, b m Nearly A Hand—Notina **Mr D. I. Bare**
8 **MADAM ROSE (IRE)**, 6, b br m Cardinal Flower—Misquested **Mrs Barbara Mills**
9 **MAGSOOD**, 11, ch g Mill Reef (USA)—Shark Song **Pipers Partnership**
10 5, B g Town And Country—Notinhand **Mrs Heather Bare**
11 **OUR WIZZER (IRE)**, 7, ch g Bulldozer—Straffan Lady **Mr Simon Lytle**
12 **POPPETS PET**, 9, b g Native Bazaar—Imperial Miss **Pipers Partnership**
13 **QUICK MILLION**, 5, b m Thowra (FR)—Miss Quick **Mrs Jane Simpson**
14 **REFERRAL FEE**, 9, b g Le Moss—Quick Romance **Mr Seamus Mullins**
15 **RENT DAY**, 7, b m Town And Country—Notinhand **Mr D. I. Bare**
16 **THIRD MELODY**, 10, b m Leander—Baynton Melody **Mr Brian S. Heath**
17 **WISSYWIS (IRE)**, 4, b f Waajib—Miss Sandman **P. Glynn Jones**
18 **ZEN OR**, 5, b m Porthmeor—Carmels Gold **Mrs M. L. Bruce**

THREE-YEAR-OLDS

19 **KENTFORD CONQUISTA**, b f El Conquistador—Notinhand **Mr D. I. Bare**

Other Owners: Mr H. R. Clark, Mr Christopher Leat, Mr D. J. Line, Mrs Sally Mullins, Mr Paul Shotter.

Conditional: S Curran.

Amateurs: Mr E Bailey, Mr O Ellwood (10-0).

Lady Rider: Miss V Mills (9-0).

440   MR P. MULLINS, Goresbridge

Postal: **Doninga, Goresbridge, Co. Kilkenny, Ireland.**

Phone: **(0503) 75121 FAX (0503) 75417**

1 **BART OWEN**, 11, br g Belfalas—Ten Again **Mrs S. McCarthy**
2 **BEAKSTOWN (IRE)**, 7, b g Orchestra—Little Shoon **Mr P. J. O'Meara**
3 **BORO VACATION (IRE)**, 7, b g Ovac (ITY)—Boro Quarter **Mr Jeremy P. Hill**
4 **BUCK THE TIDE (IRE)**, 7, b h Buckskin (FR)—Light The Lamp **Mrs Rionda Braga**
5 **BULWARK HILL (IRE)**, 6, br g Dromod Hill—Farina **Mr Thomas Mullins**
6 **CASTLEKELLYLEADER (IRE)**, 7, b g Supreme Leader—Cailin Donn **Mr E. Morrissey**
7 **CHIEF RANI (IRE)**, 6, ch g Salt Dome (USA)—Hada Rani **Mrs P. Mullins**
8 **DAMANCHER**, 4, gr c Damister (USA)—Amalancher (USA) **Mr Thomas Mullins**
9 **DEER PARTY (IRE)**, 8, ch g Whistling Deer—Highland Party **Mr Peter S. O'Neill**
10 **DERRYAD (IRE)**, 5, b m Ballad Rock—Redwood Hut **Mrs C. A. Moore**
11 **EVER SO BOLD**, 9, ch g Never So Bold—Spinelle **Ms Fiona Williams**
12 **EXECUTIVE STRESS (IRE)**, 5, b g Executive Perk—Mary Kate Finn **Mr E. Morrissey**
13 **FABULIST (IRE)**, 7, b m Lafontaine (USA)—Mag (USA) **Mrs C. A. Moore**
14 **GAILY RUNNING (IRE)**, 7, b g Strong Gale—Ketta's Lass **Mr Thomas Farrell**
15 **GALE TOI (IRE)**, 7, br g Strong Gale—Zitas Toi **Mrs M. O'Leary**
16 **GAMBOLLING DOC (IRE)**, 6, b g Burslem—Courreges **Mrs Margaret O'Leary**

MR P. MULLINS—continued

17 HELLO MONKEY, 9, ch g Exhibitioner—Matjup **Mrs Audrey Healy**
18 ICANTELYA (IRE), 7, b g Meneval (USA)—Sky Road **Mr Fergus P. Taaffe**
19 KEEP CLEAR (IRE), 6, b g Clearly Bust—Keep Dancing **Thomas Mullins**
20 NANNAKA (USA), 6, b m Exceller (USA)—Najidiya (USA) **Mrs P. Mullins**
21 NEAR GALE (IRE), 6, b m Strong Gale—Whisht **Mr P. F. Kehoe**
22 NOBLE THYNE (IRE), 6, b g Good Thyne (USA)—Tina O'Flynn **Colm O'Connell**
23 NO DUNCE (IRE), 6, b m Nordance (USA)—Dundovail **Mrs P. Mullins**
24 NO NEWS (IRE), 5, b g Persian Mews—Dundovail **Mrs P. Mullins**
25 NOREASTER (IRE), 5, b m Nordance (USA)—Winds Light **Mrs S. McCarthy**
26 NOTCOMPLAININGBUT, 5, b m Supreme Leader—Dorcetta **Mr C. A. Moore**
27 PARSKINT (IRE), 6, b m Buckskin (FR)—Parijatak **Mrs P. Mullins**
28 SHECOULDNTBEBETTER (IRE), 5, b m Royal Fountain—Mullawn **Thomas Mullins**
29 SPECKLED GLEN (IRE), 6, ch g Glen Quaich—Speckled Leinster **Mr Thomas Mullins**
30 SUDDEN STORM (IRE), 5, b m Strong Gale—Barello **G. Kingston**
31 TALINA'S LAW (IRE), 4, b f Law Society (USA)—Talina **Mr M. Donovan**
32 WHO'S TO SAY, 10, ch g Saher—Whisht **Mrs P. Mullins**

THREE-YEAR-OLDS

33 NORTH OF WHAT (IRE), b g Distinctly North (USA)—Whatyawant **Mrs P. Mullins**

Other Owners: Mr John Flynn, Mr George Mullins.

Jockey (NH): T P Treacy.

Amateurs: Mr A C Coyle, Mr Tom Mullins (10-11), Mr W P Mullins (10-11).

Lady Rider: Mrs Sandra McCarthy (9-0).

441   MR F. MURPHY, Middleham

Postal: **Oak Wood Stables, East Witton Road, Middleham, Leyburn, DL8 4PT.**
Phone: **TELEPHONE & FAX (01969) 622289 MOBILE (0421) 398034**

1 AINSI SOIT IL (FR), 5, b br g Amen (FR)—Crinolene (FR) **A-Men Partnership**
2 ALBERMARLE (IRE), 5, ch g Phardante (FR)—Clarahill **Mr Robert Ogden**
3 ANOTHER VENTURE (IRE), 6, br g Tanfirion—Fitz's Buck **Mr Richard Wheeler**
4 APPEARANCE MONEY (IRE), 5, b m Dancing Dissident (USA)—Fussy Budget **Irish Festival Racing Club**
5 AVENUE FOCH (IRE), 7, gr g Saint Estephe (FR)—Marie d'Irlande (FR) **Mr P. O'Donnell**
6 BUSKING ALONG (IRE), 7, br g Phardante (FR)—Buskins Reward **Mr Stanley Nixon**
7 CALIPO BELLO (IRE), 6, ch g Buckskin (FR)—Stradbally Beg **Express Caterers Partnership**
8 COLONEL IN CHIEF (IRE), 6, br g Strong Gale—Sirrahdis **Mr Robert Ogden**
9 CUSH SUPREME (IRE), 7, b g Supreme Leader—Nevada Hansel **Mr Robert Ogden**
10 DIABLE AU CORPS III (FR), 5, b g Pamponi (FR)—Psyche II (FR) **Mr Robert Ogden**
11 DISCO DES MOTTES (FR), 5, b g Useful—Video des Mottes (FR) **Mr Robert Ogden**
12 DONJUAN COLLONGES (FR), 5, ch g Trebrook (FR)—Tessy Collonges (FR) **Mr Robert Ogden**
13 EDELWEISS DU MOULIN (FR), 4, b g Lute Antique (FR)—Tulipe du Moulin (FR) **Mr Robert Ogden**
14 FRENCH HOLLY (USA), 5, b g Sir Ivor—Sans Dot **Mr K. Flood**
15 FRICKLEY, 10, b br g Furry Glen—Shallow Run **Mr Robert Ogden**
16 FROWN, 6, ch g Bustino—Highbrow **Mr Rhys Thomas Williams**
17 GEANEY OIL (IRE), 6, br g Callernish—Another Lady VI **Mr A. P. McLaughlin**
18 GENERAL JIMBO (IRE), 4, b g King Luthier—The Saltings (FR) **Mr Brett Badham**
19 GROSVENOR (IRE), 5, b g Henbit (USA)—Fair Invader **Mr Robert Ogden**
20 IRISH STAMP (IRE), 7, b g Niniski (USA)—Bayazida **Mr P. O'Donnell**
21 LOCH GARMAN (IRE), 6, b g Strong Statement (USA)—Mijette **Mrs R. D. Cairns**
22 4, B g Supreme Leader—Merry Breeze **Mr Brendan McEntaggartt**

MR F. MURPHY—continued

23 **ORLA'S CHOICE (IRE)**, 6, b g Roselier (FR)—Continuity Lass **Mr J. Byrne**
24 **OSCAIL AN DORAS (IRE)**, 7, ch g Avocat—Candora **Mr Rhys Thomas Williams**
25 **PADDY'S RETURN (IRE)**, 4, b g Kahyasi—Bayazida **Mr P. O'Donnell**
26 **POSTAGE STAMP**, 9, ch g The Noble Player (USA)—Takealetter **Mr P. O'Donnell**
27 **PRIME EXAMPLE (IRE)**, 5, ch g Orchestra—Vanessa's Princess **Mr Robert Ogden**
28 **RADANPOUR (IRE)**, 4, b g Kahyasi—Rajpoura **Mr Peter Bridson**
29 **RESTATE (IRE)**, 5, b m Soviet Star (USA)—Busca (USA) **Mrs K. Cunningham**
30 **RICH DESIRE**, 7, b m Grey Desire—Richesse (FR) **Miss Marie Kearns**
31 **ROYAL BANKER (IRE)**, 6, b g Roselier (FR)—Dottie's Wasp **Mr Robert Ogden**
32 **SAUNDERS COURT (IRE)**, 7, ch g Sandalay—Knockarone Star **Irish Festival Racing Club**
33 **STOP THE WALLER (IRE)**, 7, b g Lancastrian—Lisalway Lass **Mr Ray Burgan & Mr Nick Tanner**
34 **THE ADJUTANT (IRE)**, 8, ch g Deep Run—Inagh's Image **Mrs G. P. Seymour**
35 **TRICKLE LAD (IRE)**, 7, b g Denel (FR)—Miss Fanackapan **Mrs H. F. Prendergast**
36 **TWABLADE (IRE)**, 8, gr m Strong Gale—Grey Duchy **Mr M. Rowsell**

THREE-YEAR-OLDS

37 **DREAM OF MY LIFE (USA)**, gr g Danzatore (CAN)—Sureya **Mr C. Toscano**

Other Owners: Mr J. Ayres, Mr P. Cassidy, Express Caterers Partnership, Mr J. Fleming, Mr George Graham, Mr Brian Hunter, Mr W. D. Jamieson, Mr K. Knyeston, Mr A. P. McLaughlin, Mr F. Murphy, Mr Wayne Neville, Mr Stanley Nixon, Mr Steven Pattinson, Mr L. Seaton.

Jockeys (Flat): R Cochrane (8-3, w.a.), T Williams (7-10, w.a.).

Jockeys (NH): Paul Carberry (10-0), Mark Dwyer (10-2, w.a.), M Foster (w.a.), A Maguire (w.a.).

Apprentice: Michael Mathers (7-7).

Conditional: D J Kavanagh (9-7).

Lady Rider: Miss Elizabeth Doyle (9-4).

442   MR P. G. MURPHY, Bristol

Postal: **Racecourse Farm Racing Stables, Portbury, Bristol, Avon, BS20 9SN.**
Phone: **OFFICE** (01275) 373581 **FAX** (01275) 375053 **MOBILE** (0831) 410409

1 **COMEDY HOUR**, 5, gr m Homeboy—Laughing Home **Mr N. C. Rolfe**
2 **GENTLEMAN SID**, 6, b g Brotherly (USA)—Eugenes Chance **Miss J. Collison**
3 **GENUINE LEADER**, 4, b g Formidable (USA)—Glorietta (USA) **Mr Raymond Miquel**
4 **HAND OF STRAW (IRE)**, 4, b g Thatching—Call Me Miss **Mrs Louise Murphy**
5 **HANGING GROVE (IRE)**, 6, b g Asir—Churchlands Madam **Mr J. H. Forbes**
6 **JIGSAW BOY**, 7, ch g Homeboy—Chiparia **Mark Holder Bloodstock**
7 **LEGENDRA**, 6, ch m Legend of France (USA)—Obertura (USA) **Mrs Louise Murphy**
8 **MANZOOR SAYADAN (USA)**, 8, b g Shahrastani (USA)—Icing **Mrs A. B. Appleyard**
9 **PARADE RACER**, 5, b g Derring Rose—Dusky Damsel **Mr G. Golledge**
10 **REAGANESQUE (USA)**, 4, b g Nijinsky (CAN)—Basoof (USA) **Mrs John Spielman**
11 **RUNS IN THE FAMILY**, 4, b f Distant Relative—Stoneydale **Mr Geoffrey C. Greenwood**
12 **SEBASTOPOL**, 7, b g Royal Match—Saucy Sprite **Mr Derrick Page**
13 **SIR JOEY (USA)**, 7, ch g Honest Pleasure (USA)—Sougoli **Mrs Gwen Sims**
14 **SQUIRE YORK**, 6, b g Bairn (USA)—Alice Parry **Mr J. T. Powell-Tuck**
15 **WINSOME WOOSTER**, 5, ch m Primo Dominie—Bertrade **Miss Amanda J. Rawding**

MR P. G. MURPHY—continued

THREE-YEAR-OLDS

16 **ASTRA MARTIN**, ch f Doc Marten—Bertrade **Mr Geoffrey C. Greenwood**
17 **DANGEROUS WATERS**, b f Risk Me (FR)—Queen's Lake **Olympic Plumbing**
18 **DURALOCK FENCER**, b g General Wade—Madame Laffitte **Duralock (UK) Ltd**
19 **MEMBERS WELCOME (IRE)**, b g Eve's Error—Manuale Del Utente **Avon & West Racing Club Ltd**
20 **SIBERIAN MYSTIC**, gr f Siberian Express (USA)—Mystic Crystal (IRE) **The Syndicate**

TWO-YEAR-OLDS

21 B f 7/3 Mazilier (USA)—Adana (FR) (Green Dancer (USA)) **Mrs Pat Wyatt**

Other Owners: Mr R. S. Agate, Mr N. J. Allcock, Mr D. W. Armstrong, Mr K. Ball, Mr M. K. Barnett, Mr S. A. Barningham, Mr S. C. Botham, Mr M. A. H. Bradfield, Mrs Sandy Herridge, Mr Nolan Herring, Mr M. J. Holder, Mr K. Lloyd, Mr R. E. Maccallum, Mr Patrick Joseph O'Keeffe, Mr D. P. Parker, Mrs J. A. Rawding, Mr W. M. Rawding, Mr Frank Smith.

Jockey (Flat): J Williams (8-0).

Jockey (NH): E Murphy (w.a.).

Apprentice: R Waterfield.

Lady Rider: Miss A Plunkett (9-7).

443 MR B. W. MURRAY, Malton

Postal: **60 Parliament Street, Norton, Malton, North Yorks, YO17 9HE.**
Phone: **MALTON (01653) 692879 MOBILE (0831) 611841**

1 **INTREPID FORT**, 7, gr g Belfort (FR)—Dauntless Flight **Mr B. Murray**
2 **MAURANGI**, 5, bl g Warning—Spin Dry **Mr M. E. Foxton**
3 **MISTY IMAGE**, 4, gr f Kind of Hush—Misty Rocket **Mr D. Ford**
4 **NEWGATE BUBBLES**, 5, b m Hubbly Bubbly (USA)—Streets Ahead **Mr W. P. S. Johnson**
5 **ROYAL COMEDIAN**, 7, gr m Jester—Royal Huntress **Fir Trading Ltd**
6 **RUBY ROCK**, 4, b f Rock City—Resonation (CAN) **Mr J. M. Lacey**

THREE-YEAR-OLDS

7 **PARTY POSER**, b f Presidium—Pooka **Mr D. Ford**
8 **SUPREME SCHOLAR**, b f Superpower—Double Decree **Mr B. Murray**
9 **TICKA TICKA TIMING**, b c Timeless Times (USA)—Belltina **Mrs M. Lingwood**
10 **TIME TO FLY**, gr c Timeless Times (USA)—Dauntless Flight **Miss N. A. Harrod**

TWO-YEAR-OLDS

11 B f 19/4 Timeless Times (USA)—Dauntless Flight (Golden Mallard) **Miss N. A. Harrod**
12 Br f 13/3 Timeless Times (USA)—Hunting Gold (Sonnen Gold) **Miss N. A. Harrod**

Other Owners: Mr B. Cunningham.

Lady Rider: Miss A Elsey.

444   MR D. J. G. MURRAY SMITH, Lambourn

Postal: **Saxon House Stables, Lambourn, Hungerford, Berks, RG17 8QH.**
Phone: **OFFICE (01488) 71041 FAX (01488) 71065 HOME (01488) 71105**

1 **DENBRAE (IRE)**, 4, b g Sure Blade (USA)—Fencing **Mr Michael Mellersh**
2 **GRUNGE (IRE)**, 8, b br g Crash Course—Hills of Fashion **Mrs R. D. Cowell & Mrs S. Nash**
3 **JUST FOR A REASON**, 4, b g Siberian Express (USA)—Artaius Rose (FR) **Mr D. Murray Smith**
4 **KANCELSKIS (IRE)**, 7, ch g Buckskin (FR)—Left Hand Woman **Mrs Gina Edgedale**
5 **KYMIN (IRE)**, 4, b f Kahyasi—Akila (FR) **Diana Wilder**
6 **OLD ROUVEL (USA)**, 5, b h Riverman (USA)—Marie de Russy (FR) **Mrs R. D. Cowell**
7 **OSMOSIS**, 10, b g Green Shoon—Milparinka **Mr Michael Mellersh**
8 **PRINCE DANZIG (IRE)**, 5, ch g Roi Danzig (USA)—Veldt **Mr A. H. Ulrick**
9 **RIZAL (USA)**, 4, ch g Zilzal (USA)—Sigy (FR) **Diana Wilder**
10 **WOOLVERSTONE HALL (IRE)**, 4, b f Roi Danzig (USA)—Silver Mantle **Woolverstone Hall Partnership**

THREE-YEAR-OLDS

11 **BARANOV (IRE)**, b c Mulhollande (USA)—Silojoka **Mrs R. D. Cowell & Mrs S. Nash**
12 **BARONESS BLIXEN**, b f Cyrano de Bergerac—Provocation **Saxon House Partnership**
13 **JELALI (IRE)**, b c Last Tycoon—Lautreamont **The Fort Partnership**
14 **MIRANI (IRE)**, b f Danehill (USA)—Alriyaah **The Fort Partnership**
15 **NAKHAL**, b c Puissance—Rambadale **The Fort Partnership**
16 **NIKITA'S STAR (IRE)**, ch c Soviet Lad (USA)—Sally Chase **Nikita's Partners**
17 **ROSTAQ**, b c Keen—American Beauty **The Fort Partnership**

TWO-YEAR-OLDS

18 **PERSISTANT (IRE)**, b f 30/3 Polish Patriot (USA)—Sally Chase **D. Twomey**
19 **WOODLAND NYMPH**, gr f 6/5 Norton Challenger—Royal Meeting **Mr D. Murray Smith**

Other Owners: Mrs S. Ashcroft, Mr N. Jackson, Miss D. Lancia, Mrs Wendy Percival, Mrs R. Philps, Lady D. M. Watts.

Jockey (NH): Dean Gallagher (w.a.).

445   MR F. P. MURTAGH, Carlisle

Postal: **Hurst Farm, Ivegill, Carlisle, Cumbria, CA4 0NL.**
Phone: **(017684) 84362/84649 MOBILE (0421) 720250**

1 **BOLANEY GIRL (IRE)**, 7, b m Amazing Bust—French Note **Mr J. Proudfoot**
2 4, Ch f Buckley—H And K Gambler **Mr F. P. Murtagh**
3 **HURST FLYER**, 4, br gr f Neltino—True Missile **Mr J. Proudfoot**
4 **LYRIC LADY**, 8, ch m My Chopin—Lady Lily **Mr R. R. Bainbridge**
5 **MANX MONARCH**, 6, ch m Dara Monarch—Solemn Occasion (USA) **Mr John Lane**
6 **MILLIES IMAGE**, 5, ch m Mirror Boy—Sweet Millie **Mr M. H. Ford**
7 **MISS LAMPLIGHT**, 6, b m Jupiter Island—Lady With The Lamp **Mr Dennis Hutchinson**
8 **MOVIE MAKER (IRE)**, 8, b g Remainder Man—Night Moves **Mr J. Proudfoot**
9 **MR OPTIMISTIC**, 9, ch g King Persian—Saybya **Mrs J. D. Bulman**
10 **POLITICAL MISSILE**, 5, b g Cruise Missile—Lahtico VII **Mr Peter Diggle**
11 **ROYAL MIXTURE**, 4, b f Rakaposhi King—Princess Zenobia **Mr R. R. Bainbridge**

Other Owners: Mrs Mary Proudfoot.

Jockeys (NH): A Dobbin, R J Supple.

Lady Rider: Miss S Nichol (8-7).

446   MR W. J. MUSSON, Newmarket

Postal: **Saville House, St Mary's Square, Newmarket, Suffolk, CB8 0HZ.**

Phone: **(01638) 663371 FAX (01638) 667979**

1 **AUTHORSHIP (USA)**, 10, b g Balzac (USA)—Piap (USA) **Mr C. A. Roberts & Partners**
2 **BIT ON THE SIDE (IRE)**, 7, b m Vision (USA)—Mistress (USA) **Mr Mike Hawkett**
3 **BROUGHTONS CHAMP**, 4, b g Dowsing (USA)—Knees Up (USA) **Broughton Bloodstock**
4 **BROUGHTONS FORMULA**, 6, b g Night Shift (USA)—Forward Rally **Crawford Gray & Aylett**
5 **BROUGHTON'S PORT**, 6, b g Reesh—Tawnais **Broughton Thermal Insulation**
6 **BROUGHTONS TURMOIL**, 7, b g Petorius—Rustic Stile **Broughton & Westwood**
7 **CUBAN REEF**, 4, b f Dowsing (USA)—Cox's Pippin (USA) **Mr K. L. West**
8 **FERN'S GOVERNOR**, 4, b f Governor General—Sharp Venita **Fern Components Ltd**
9 **GENTLE IRONY**, 4, b f Mazilier (USA)—Ivenic **Mr A. S. Reid**
10 **GONE SAVAGE**, 8, b g Nomination—Trwyn Cilan **The On The Floor Partnership**
11 **I'LL BE BOUND**, 5, b g Beveled (USA)—Treasurebound **The C R Partnership**
12 **LADY SABINA**, 6, ch m Bairn (USA)—Calibina **Mr W. J. Musson**
13 **LOFTY DEED (USA)**, 6, b g Shadeed (USA)—Soar Aloft (USA) **Mrs P. A. Linton**
14 **NOBLE NEPTUNE**, 4, b g Governor General—Calibina **Mrs Rita Brown**
15 **NOTHING DOING (IRE)**, 7, b g Sarab—Spoons **Broughton Bloodstock**
16 **RISE UP SINGING**, 8, ch g Noalto—Incarnadine **Mrs Rita Brown**
17 **SWIFT SILVER**, 9, gr g Bairn (USA)—Asmalwi **The On The Floor Partnership**
18 **TURRILL HOUSE**, 4, b f Charmer—Megabucks **Mr J. R. Hawksley**

THREE-YEAR-OLDS

19 **DAUPHIN (IRE)**, b br c Astronef—Va Toujours **Mrs Rita Brown**
20 B f Bluebird (USA)—Finalist **Angley Stud Ltd**
21 **FOREIGN JUDGEMENT (USA)**, b c El Gran Senor (USA)—Numeral **Ms A. M. Jeffrey**
22 **FORMIDABLE FLAME**, ch g Formidable (USA)—Madiyla **Mrs Rita Brown**
23 **IMPETUOUS LADY (USA)**, b f Imp Society (USA)—Urakawa (USA) **Mr Mike Hawkett**
24 **KILLATTY LARK (IRE)**, ch f Noalto—Killatty Sky (IRE) **Mr B. Little**

TWO-YEAR-OLDS

25 B c 25/1 Reprimand—Artistic Licence (High Top)
26 B f 13/5 Komaite (USA)—Fair Dino (Thatch (USA)) **Mrs N. A. Ward**
27 B f 12/5 Rock Hopper—Kimble Blue (Blue Refrain)
28 B c 26/5 Batshoof—Lady Bequick (Sharpen Up)
29 B f 4/3 Statoblest—Lamees (USA) (Lomond (USA)) **Mrs N. A. Ward**
30 Br f 14/2 Petong—White's Pet (Mummy's Pet)

Other Owners: Mrs V. Albert, Mr Roger Aylett, Mr K. G. Balfour, Mr B. Beale, Mrs C. J. Broughton, Mr M. E. Broughton, Mrs Sarah Faulks, Mr B. N. Fulton, Mr J. Gilman, Mr T. Crawford Gray, Mrs Judy Musson, Mr Clive Pettigrew, Miss C. A. Roberts, Mr Saul Saywood, Miss Therese Sevremont, Mr A. T. Thompkins, Mr A. J. Westwood.

Apprentice: P A McCabe (7-12).

447   MR C. T. NASH, Wantage

Postal: **Raceyard Cottage, Kingston Lisle, Wantage, Oxon, OX12 9QH.**

Phone: **(01367) 820510 MOBILE (0836) 387987**

1 **AIR COMMAND (BAR)**, 6, br g Concorde Hero (USA)—Hubbardair **Mr Edwin Phillips**
2 **BADRAKHANI (FR)**, 10, b g Akarad (FR)—Burnished Gold **Mr P. J. Slade**
3 **BANNY HILL LAD**, 6, gr g Pragmatic—Four M's **Mr C. T. Nash**
4 **GOD SPEED YOU (IRE)**, 7, gr g Roselier (FR)—Pitmark **Wallop**
5 **JIMSISTER**, 6, ch m Relkino—Merry Minuet **Mrs B. Hobbs**
6 **LOCH NA KEAL**, 4, b f Weldnaas (USA)—Keyanloch **Mr M. J. Holley**
7 **MADAME PRESIDENT (IRE)**, 5, b m Supreme Leader—Deep Dollar **Sir Peter Miller**
8 5, B m Town And Country—Merry Minuet **Mrs S. Nash**

MR C. T. NASH—continued

9 MISS ROULETTE, 6, b m Mummy's Game—Madame Russe **Mrs J. F. Maitland-Jones**
10 MY KEY SILCA, 11, ch g Deep Run—La Flamenca **Mr Y. T. Tsang**
11 ROYAL RABBIT, 4, b g Prince Daniel (USA)—Lirchur
12 STEVE FORD, 7, gr g Another Realm—Sky Miss **Mr P. J. Morgan**
13 THE GAUFFER, 5, b g Ra Nova—Polygon **J. P. M. & J. W. Cook**
14 TRUSTINO, 8, b m Relkino—Game Trust **Mrs S. Nash**
15 ULURU (IRE), 8, b g Kris—Mountain Lodge
16 UPTON LASS (IRE), 7, b m Crash Course—Gorrue Lady **Mr L. G. Kimber**
17 WAR HEROINE, 6, b m War Hero—Lead Me On **Dr K. W. J. Bowen**

Other Owners: Mr A. N. Brooke Rankin, Mr N. Cassidy, Mr J. P. M. Cook, Mrs J. W. Cook, Mr Bernard Fox, Mr R. J. Graham, Mr P. M. Joslin, Mr M. Miller, Mrs K. Morgan, Mrs P. Pearce.

Jockey (Flat): R Perham.

Jockey (NH): J R Kavanagh (10-0).

Conditional: G Hogan (10-0).

Amateur: Mr P Phillips (9-7).

448   MRS A. M. NAUGHTON, Richmond

Postal: **High Gingerfield Lodge, Hurgill Road, Richmond, N. Yorkshire.**
Phone: **(01748) 822803 (0374) 133011 MOBILE**

1 BOWCLIFFE, 5, b g Petoski—Gwiffina **Mr Philip Davies**
2 CELTIC BREEZE, 13, b g Celtic Cone—Sipped **Mr Hugh Gething**
3 FLINTLOCK (IRE), 6, ch g Kris—Foolish Lady (USA) **Mrs J. Watters**
4 GABRIELLE GERARD, 4, ch f Roaring Riva—Mr Chris Cakemaker **Mr Ian P. Davies**
5 GREENFINCH (CAN), 5, gr g Green Dancer (USA)—Princess Verna (USA) **Jack The Lads**
6 HOMECREST, 4, b g Petoski—Homing Hill **Mrs M. Foster**
7 JARROW, 5, ch g Jalmood (USA)—Invite **Mr Hugh Gething**
8 KUDOS PRINCESS (IRE), 6, ch m Montekin—Hy Carol **Mr Dave Tuckwell**
9 ONE FOR THE POT, 11, ch g Nicholas Bill—Tea-Pot **Mr Philip Davies**
10 PALLIUM (IRE), 8, b g Try My Best (USA)—Jungle Gardenia **Mr W. J. Kelly**
11 SAYRAF DANCER (IRE), 7, b g Glad Dancer—Sayraf **Mr Dave Tuckwell**
12 SHAREOFTHEACTION, 5, gr g Sharrood (USA)—Action Belle **Mrs C. T. Woodley**
13 STAGGERING (IRE), 7, bl m Daring March—Sipped **Miss J. M. Thompson**
14 TEDBURROW, 4, b g Dowsing (USA)—Gwiffina **Mr Philip Davies**

Other Owners: Mr Peter J. Davies, Mr B. M. Johnson, Mr W. Johnson, Mr Michael O'Grady, Mr B. T. Price, Mr David Robinson.

449   MR T. J. NAUGHTON, Epsom

Postal: **The Durdans, Chalk Lane, Epsom, Surrey, KT18 7AX.**
Phone: **(01372) 745112 FAX (01372) 741944**

1 AIN'TLIFELIKETHAT, 9, gr h Godswalk (USA)—Blue Alicia **Mrs J. T. Naughton**
2 ALLMOSA, 7, b m Alleging (USA)—Wimosa **Durdans Four Two**
3 BON SECRET (IRE), 4, b c Classic Secret (USA)—Bon Retour **Mr F. R. Jackman**
4 CABCHARGE BLUE, 4, b f Midyan (USA)—Mashobra **Mr R. A. Popely & Mrs A. Wise**

MR T. J. NAUGHTON—continued

5 **COMANCHE COMPANION**, 6, b m Commanche Run—Constant Companion **The Allstars Club/Drofmor Racing**
6 **FABRIANA**, 6, b m Northern State (USA)—Fashion Flow **Mrs Payne & Partners**
7 **GO HEVER GOLF**, 4, ch g Efisio—Sweet Rosina **Hever Racing Club**
8 **HEVER GOLF LADY**, 4, b f Dominion—High Run (HOL) **Martin Lester Racing Services**
9 **HEVER GOLF ROSE**, 5, b m Efisio—Sweet Rosina **Mr M. P. Hanson**
10 **HEVER GOLF STAR**, 4, b g Efisio—Truly Bold **Mr M. P. Hanson**
11 **KNIGHTON**, 5, b g Precious Metal—Moon Chant **Just For The Crack Partnership**
12 **LANESRA BREEZE**, 4, b g Petoski—Constant Companion **Mrs A. Wise**
13 **MILOS**, 5, b g Efisio—Elkie Brooks **Mr R. A. Popely**
14 **MUCH TOO HIGH**, 4, b g Salse (USA)—Hi-Li **Mr E. J. Fenaroli**
15 **MYSTIC LEGEND**, 4, gr g Standaan (FR)—Mandy Girl **Mrs E. Sinclair**
16 **NORDANCE PRINCE (IRE)**, 5, b g Nordance (USA)—Shirleys Princess **Pinks Gym & Leisure Wear Ltd**
17 **NORDIC FLASH**, 9, b g Nordico (USA)—Rosemore **Mr D. Borrows**
18 **NORTHERN CONQUEROR (IRE)**, 8, ch g Mazaad—Gaylom **Mrs J. C. Naughton**
19 **ORANGE PLACE (IRE)**, 5, ch g Nordance (USA)—Little Red Hut **Mr George Micheal Archer**
20 **RISKY ROYAL**, 4, ch g Risk Me (FR)—Royal Clover **Mrs S. Sheldon & Mrs A. Wise**
21 **TYRIAN PURPLE (IRE)**, 8, b h Wassl—Sabrine **Mr T. O'Flaherty**

THREE-YEAR-OLDS

22 **ALLSTARS DANCER**, b f Primo Dominie—Danzig Harbour (USA) **The Allstars Club**
23 **ALLSTARS EXPRESS**, b c Rambo Dancer (CAN)—Aligote **The Allstars Club**
24 **ALLSTARS ROCKET**, b c Puissance—Sally Delight **The Allstars Club**
25 **CANE THEM**, ch c Risk Me (FR)—She's A Sport
26 **CHERRY GARDEN (IRE)**, b g Treasure Kay—Door To Door (USA) **The Allstars Club**
27 **DARING VENTURE**, b f Dowsing (USA)—Berberana **The Prospectors Club**
28 **EASTERN PROPHETS**, b c Emarati (USA)—Four Love **Hever Racing Club**
29 **FOLLOWTHEALLSTARS**, ch c Anshan—Angels Sing **The Allstars Club**
30 **GENERAL HAVEN**, ch c Hadeer—Verchinina **Mr A. Callard**
31 **HEVER GOLF CLASSIC**, b br c Bustino—Explosiva (USA) **Hever Racing Club III**
32 **HEVER GOLF DIAMOND**, b g Nomination—Cadi Ha **Mr M. Cunningham**
33 **HEVER GOLF EAGLE**, b c Aragon—Elkie Brooks **Hever Racing Club III**
34 **HEVER GOLF EXPRESS**, b g Primo Dominie—Everdene **Hever Racing Club II**
35 **HEVER GOLF HERO**, b c Robellino (USA)—Sweet Rosina **Hever Racing Club III**
36 **HEVER GOLF QUEEN**, b f Efisio—Blue Jane **Mr M. P. Hanson**
37 **HOMELAND**, b g Midyan (USA)—Little Loch Broom **Mrs E. Jackman & Mr F. R. Jackman**
38 **KEEN COMPANION**, b f Keen—Constant Companion **Drofmor Racing**
39 **MONEY HOUSE**, ch f Starch Reduced—Quite A Lark
40 **OLD SCHOOL HOUSE**, ch c Polar Falcon (USA)—Farewell Letter (USA)
41 **PREFECT**, b c Kendor (FR)—Ahohoney
42 **SCHOOL BOY**, b c Aragon—Grovehurst **The Allstars Club**
43 **SECRET COMMANDER**, ch g Ron's Victory (USA)—Louise **Mr John Lam**
44 B g Nordico (USA)—Sweet Miyabi (JPN) **Mrs E. Sinclair**
45 **TAKAPUNA (IRE)**, ch f Be My Native (USA)—Tenoria **Mrs E. Jackman & Mr F. R. Jackman**
46 **VICTORY COMMANDER**, b g Efisio—Gay Hostess (FR) **Mr John Lam**

TWO-YEAR-OLDS

47 **AMELIA JANE**, ch f 24/3 Efisio—Blue Jane (Blue Cashmere) **Pinks Gym & Leisure Wear Ltd**
48 B f 27/4 Taufan (USA)—Anagall (USA) (Irish River (FR)) **Hever Racing Club**
49 Ch f 7/4 Anshan—Bamian (USA) (Topsider (USA)) **Hever Racing Club**
50 B c 29/4 Distant Relative—Blue Rag (Ragusa) **Hever Racing Club**
51 Gr f 25/5 Salse (USA)—Brightness (Elegant Air) **Mrs A. Wise**
52 Ch g 10/4 Risk Me (FR)—Brig of Ayr (Brigadier Gerard)
53 B c 30/3 Precocious—Callas Star (Chief Singer)
54 B c 28/4 Mujadil (USA)—Clogher Head (Sandford Lad) **Hever Racing Club**
55 **DIZZY TILLY**, b f 23/2 Anshan—Nadema (Artaius (USA)) **Mrs Leech**
56 B f 23/3 Mujadil (USA)—Doon Belle (Ardoon) **Hever Racing Club**
57 Br c 30/4 Bustino—Explosiva (USA) (Explodent (USA))
58 B f 10/3 Silver Kite (USA)—Friendly Song (Song) **Hever Racing Club**
59 B c 14/3 Salt Dome (USA)—Glowlamp (IRE) (Glow (USA)) **Mr G. A. Archer**
60 Ch f 5/5 Efisio—Joyce's Best (Tolomeo)

MR T. J. NAUGHTON—continued

61 **KEEN ALERT,** b g 16/5 Keen—Miss Coco (Swing Easy (USA)) **Ms D. Stagg**
62 B f 23/2 High Estate—My Sister Ellen (Lyphard (USA)) **Hever Racing Club**
63 B c 21/2 Silver Kite (USA)—Peace Carrier (IRE) (Doulab (USA)) **Hever Racing Club**
64 B f 26/3 Warning—Song of Hope (Chief Singer) **Mr B. J. Fenaroli**
65 Ch f 24/3 Efisio—Teresa Deevey (Runnett) **Hever Racing Club**
66 Ch f 12/2 Ballad Rock—Track Twenty Nine (IRE) (Standaan (FR)) **Hever Racing Club**
67 B c 18/4 Efisio—Truly Bold (Bold Lad (IRE))
68 B c 10/3 Efisio—Zaius (Artaius (USA))

Other Owners: Mr A. Evendon, Mr P. Sheldon.

Jockeys (Flat): Pat Eddery (w.a.), J Weaver (w.a.).

Conditional: M Payne.

Lady Rider: Mrs J T Naughton (8-7).

450   MR A. S. NEAVES, Faversham

Postal: **Arnolds Oak Farm, Eastling, Faversham, Kent, ME13 0BD.**
Phone: **EASTLING (01793) 890274**

1 **BAN RI (IRE),** 6, gr m Gairloch—God Save (USA) **Mr A. S. Neaves**
2 **MASTER UPEX,** 4, b g Aragon—Little Egret **Mr A. S. Neaves**
3 **MISS CERTAIN,** 7, br m Kind of Hush—Demi Rock **Mr A. S. Neaves**
4 **SIMOCKI,** 5, b m Octogenarian—Royalty Miss **Mr A. S. Neaves**
5 **TOP HILL,** 5, b m Insan (USA)—Nuala **Mr A. S. Neaves**
6 **TOP MISS,** 7, b m Celestial Storm (USA)—Crimson Ring **Mr A. S. Neaves**
7 **TOTAL GENEVIEVE (IRE),** 4, br f Lesotho (USA)—Abbessingh **Mr A. S. Neaves**

THREE-YEAR-OLDS

8 **ALL LIGHT,** b f Risk Me (FR)—Brampton Grace **Mr A. S. Neaves**

451   MR J. L. NEEDHAM, Ludlow

Postal: **Gorsty Farm, Mary Knoll, Ludlow, Salop, SY8 2HD.**
Phone: **(01584) 874826/872112 FAX: (01584) 873256**

1 **ARIOSO,** 8, b m True Song—Most **Mr J. L. Needham**
2 **CARLINGFORD BELLE,** 10, ch m Carlingford Castle—Swiftly Belle **Mr J. L. Needham**
3 **HAL'S PRINCE,** 9, b g Le Moss—Hal's Pauper **Mr J. L. Needham**
4 **JUST FOR A LAUGH,** 9, b m Idiot's Delight—Mekhala **Mr J. L. Needham**
5 **LEINTHALL DOE,** 10, b m Oats—Cover Your Money **Mr J. L. Needham**
6 **LEINTHALL PRINCESS,** 10, b m Prince Regent (FR)—Due Consideration **Mr J. L. Needham**
7 **LEINTHALL THISTLE (IRE),** 7, b m Mandalus—Phantom Thistle **Mr J. L. Needham**
8 **LING (USA),** 11, b g Far North (CAN)—Zabolina **Mr J. L. Needham**
9 **ONE MORE DIME (IRE),** 6, b m Mandalus—Deep Dollar **Mr J. L. Needham**
10 **OVER THE WREKIN,** 9, ch g Over The River (FR)—Wrekin Rose **Mr J. L. Needham**
11 **PADDY IN PARIS,** 13, ch g Paddy's Stream—Wrekin Rose **Mr J. L. Needham**
12 **WESTERN SUN,** 6, b g Sunyboy—Running Valley **Mr J. L. Needham**

Jockeys (NH): D Gallagher, R Guest.

452   MR W. M. NELSON, Torthorwald

Postal: **Longrigg, Torthorwald, Dumfries, DG1 3PS.**
Phone: **(0138775) 237**

1 THISTLEHOLM, 10, ro g Hello Handsome—Private Path **Mr W. M. Nelson**

453   MR A. G. NEWCOMBE, Barnstaple

Postal: **Lower Delworthy Racing Stables, Yarnscombe, Barnstaple, Devon, EX31 3LT.**
Phone: **(01271) 858554 FAX (01271) 73460**

1 ALLO GEORGE, 10, ch g Buckskin (FR)—Dodgy Lady **Lavis Medical Systems**
2 BID FOR TOOLS (IRE), 4, b g Don't Forget Me—Running Feud **Bideford Tool Ltd**
3 CASUAL WATER (IRE), 5, b g Simply Great (FR)—Top Nurse **Mr G. H. Leatham**
4 CATS BOTTOM, 4, ch f Primo Dominie—Purple Fan
5 DELWORTHY DANCER, 7, b g Natroun (FR)—Traditional Miss **Mr A. G. Newcombe**
6 FAIRFIELD CHOICE, 5, b m Nomination—Beaufort Star **Mr Roger Johns**
7 GOODY FOUR SHOES, 8, gr m Blazing Saddles (AUS)—Bronzamer **Mr S. R. Barrett**
8 KRISTAL DIVA, 5, ch m Kris—Dame Ashfield **Mr Cliffe Rowlands**
9 MARINE SOCIETY, 8, b g Petoski—Miranda Julia **Bideford Tool Ltd**
10 MISLEMANI (IRE), 6, b g Kris—Meis El-Reem **Mrs Pamela Cann**
11 MISSED THE BOAT (IRE), 6, b g Cyrano de Bergerac—Lady Portobello **Mr R. Harding**
12 NABJELSEDR, 6, b g Never So Bold—Klewraye **Bois De Boulougne Racing Club**
13 NINE O THREE (IRE), 7, b g Supreme Leader—Grenache **Bideford Tool Ltd**
14 NITA'S CHOICE, 6, b m Valiyar—What's The Matter **Atlantic Racing Club**
15 OLIVIA VAL, 6, b m Valiyar—Traditional Miss **Atlantic Racing Club**
16 PALACE PARADE (USA), 6, ch g Cure The Blues (USA)—Parasail (USA) **Miss J. Monk**
17 PAPRIKA (IRE), 7, ch m The Parson—Barhopper **Lavis Medical Systems**
18 RAFFLES ROOSTER, 4, gro g Galetto (FR)—Singapore Girl (FR) **Mr A. G. Newcombe**
19 RUTHY'S ROMANCE, 5, b m Then Again—What's The Matter **Atlantic Racing Club**
20 STAY HAPPY (FR), 7, b g Chief Singer—Santa Aurora (GER) **Lavis Medical Systems**
21 SUPER HERO, 4, ch g Superlative—Beaute Fatale
22 TUDOR FLIGHT, 5, b m Forzando—Tudor Pilgrim **Bideford Tool Ltd**
23 VOICES IN THE SKY, 5, b m Petoski—Saltation **John Cairns**
24 WARM HEARTED (USA), 4, ch g Known Fact (USA)—Lovin' Lass (USA) **Mrs A. Capuccini**
25 WINGSPAN (USA), 12, b g Storm Bird (CAN)—Miss Renege (USA) **Lavis Medical Systems**

THREE-YEAR-OLDS

26 B f Common Grounds—Imperial Friend **Mr A. G. Newcombe**
27 B c Formidable (USA)—Revoke (USA) **Mr A. G. Newcombe**
28 SILVER HARROW, gr g Belmez (USA)—Dancing Diana
29 B f Forzando—What's The Matter **Mr A. G. Newcombe**

TWO-YEAR-OLDS

30 B f 27/1 Inca Chief (USA)—Let's Go Lochy (Lochnager) **Mr A. G. Newcombe**
31 B c 11/5 Forzando—What's The Matter (High Top) **Mr A. G. Newcombe**

Other Owners: Mr A. D. Smith, Mr M. J. Southall, Mr Howard Wetter.

454   MR D. NICHOLLS, Thirsk

Postal: **Tall Trees Farm, Sessay, Thirsk, North Yorkshire, YO7 3ND.**
Phone: **(01845) 501470 FAX (01845) 501666 MOBILE (0860) 226664**

1 ANONYM (IRE), 4, b g Nashamaa—Bonny Bertha **Mr V. P. Greaves**
2 AXEMAN (IRE), 4, b c Reprimand—Minnie Tudor **Mr John Barton**
3 BELLA PARKES, 5, b m Tina's Pet—Summerhill Spruce **Mr John Barton**

MR D. NICHOLLS—continued

4 **CHAMPAGNE N DREAMS,** 4, b f Rambo Dancer (CAN)—Pink Sensation **The Handy Grand Club**
5 **DEAUVILLE DANCER (IRE),** 4, ch g Al Hareb (USA)—Bru Ri (FR) **Miss V. H. Owen**
6 **FAIR AND FANCY (FR),** 5, b g Always Fair (USA)—Fancy Star (FR) **Mr Ron S. Motion**
7 **FARFIELDS PRINCE,** 4, b g Weldnaas (USA)—Coca **Mrs D. Bainbridge**
8 **GRAND CHAPEAU (IRE),** 4, b g Ballad Rock—All Hat **Mr V. P. Greaves**
9 **GREEK GOLD (IRE),** 7, b g Rainbow Quest (USA)—Gay Hellene **Wetherby Racing Bureau Plc**
10 **JAZILAH (FR),** 8, br g Persian Bold—Muznah **Mr S. Aitken**
11 **JOSEPH'S WINE (IRE),** 7, b g Smile (USA)—Femme Gendarme (USA) **Wetherby Racing Bureau Plc**
12 **LUNCH PARTY,** 4, b c Beveled (USA)—Crystal Sprite **Mr S. Aitken**
13 **MAYYAADA (IRE),** 4, b g Nabeel Dancer (USA)—Badiya (USA) **Mr S. Aitken**
14 **MUSEUM (IRE),** 5, b g Tate Gallery (USA)—Go Anywhere **Mr W. G. Swiers**
15 **NEW CENTURY (USA),** 4, gr c Manila (USA)—Casessa (USA) **Mr W. J. Kelly**
16 **NIGHT WINK (USA),** 4, ch g Rahy (USA)—Lady In White **Mrs Dyanne Benjamin**
17 **NIZAAL (USA),** 5, ch h Diesis—Shicklah (USA) **Mr S. Aitken**
18 **NOYAN,** 6, ch g Northern Baby (CAN)—Istiska (FR) **Mr C. H. McGhie**
19 **NUKUD (USA),** 4, b g Topsider (USA)—Summer Silence (USA) **Mr W. G. Swiers**
20 **PARLIAMENT PIECE,** 10, ch g Burslem—Sallywell **Mr G. A. Farndon**
21 **PLATINUM PLUS,** 4, ch c Hadeer—Verchinina **Mr S. Aitken**
22 **PRIDE OF PENDLE,** 7, ro m Grey Desire—Pendle's Secret **Mrs Linda Miller**
23 **PRIMULA BAIRN,** 6, b m Bairn (USA)—Miss Primula
24 **RAMBO WALTZER,** 4, b g Rambo Dancer (CAN)—Vindictive Lady (USA) **Keystone Partnership**
25 **ROUSSI (USA),** 4, b c Nureyev (USA)—Iva Reputation (USA) **A A Bloodstock**
26 **SAMAH,** 6, ch g Pennine Walk—Ghanayim (USA) **Mr S. Aitken**
27 **SARAWAT,** 8, b g Slip Anchor—Eljazzi **Mr S. Aitken**
28 **SENSE OF PRIORITY,** 7, ch g Primo Dominie—Sense of Pride **Mr S. Schofield**
29 **SIGAMA,** 10, ch g Stop The Music (USA)—Lady Speedwell (USA) **Mr I. W. Glenton**
30 **SLMAAT,** 5, ch m Sharpo—Wasslaweyeh (USA) **Mr G. A. Farndon**
31 **TABARD GARDEN,** 4, ch f Scottish Reel—Wigeon **Mr John Barton**
32 **TENOR,** 5, b g Music Boy—Songstead **Mr Geoffrey Thompson**
33 **VENTURE CAPITALIST,** 7, ch g Never So Bold—Brave Advance (USA) **Mr W. G. Swiers**
34 **WARHURST (IRE),** 5, b g Nordance (USA)—Pourboire **Mr V. Greaves**
35 **WATERLORD (IRE),** 6, b g Bob Back (USA)—Ringtail
36 **WHACKFORD SQUEERS,** 4, ch g Komaite (USA)—Manhunt **Trilby Racing**
37 **ZAIN DANCER,** 4, ch c Nabeel Dancer (USA)—Trojan Lady (USA) **Mr S. Aitken**

THREE-YEAR-OLDS

38 **CHEMCAST,** ch c Chilibang—Golden October **Mr B. L. Cassidy**
39 **CRYSTAL WARRIOR,** b f Warrshan (USA)—Crystal's Solo (USA) **Mr Ian W. Glenton**
40 **MAYFAIR BOW,** b f Lugana Beach—Bloomsbury Girl **Mr Raymond Bowden**
41 **MYSTICAL MIND,** gr g Emarati (USA)—Spanish Chestnut **Mr V. Greaves**
42 **PORTUGUESE LIL,** ch f Master Willie—Sabonis (USA) **Mr David Windle**
43 **SOUTH PAGODA (IRE),** b c Distinctly North (USA)—Lamya **Mr W. G. Swiers**
44 **THE WAD,** b c Emarati (USA)—Fair Melys (FR) **Mr W. J. Kelly**

TWO-YEAR-OLDS

45 B c 23/4 Ron's Victory (USA)—Raaya (Be My Guest (USA)) **Mr W. G. Swiers**

Other Owners: Mr E. C. Alton, Ardsley Racing, Mrs S. Bainbridge, Mr A. Barker, Mr Don Barrick, Mr S. Bean, Mr Terry Connors, Mr K. Cookson, Mr Kim Fear, Mr B. Hooper, Mrs Jennifer Houghton, Mr Ken Hudson, Mr A. McGregor, Mr T. G. Meynell, Mr F. O'Donoghue, Mr J. Oldfield, Mr W. Palfreeman, Mr Jeffrey Ross, Mr S. A. Short, Mr T. R. Stockdale, Mrs C. A. Wadsworth, Mr H. J. Walker, Mr Michael Watson, Mr John L. Wilkinson.

Jockey (Flat): Alex Greaves (8-4).

Jockey (NH): S Mason (10-0).

Amateur: Mrs A Perrett.

455 MR P. F. NICHOLLS, Shepton Mallet

Postal: **Heighes House, Manor Farm Stables, Ditcheat, Shepton Mallet, BA4 6RD.**

Phone: **(01749) 860656 FAX (01749) 860523 MOBILE (0860) 225692**

1 **BALLYDOUGAN (IRE)**, 8, ch g The Parson—Get My Pint **Mrs Robin Mathew**
2 **BEAU BABILLARD**, 9, b g Le Bavard (FR)—Mrs Jenner **Mrs C. I. A. Paterson**
3 **BELMONT KING (IRE)**, 8, b g Kemal (FR)—The Potwalluper **Mrs Billie Bond**
4 **BLUE LAWS (IRE)**, 6, b g Bluebird (USA)—Claretta (USA) **Mr Hordle**
5 **BOND JNR (IRE)**, 7, ch g Phardante (FR)—Sea Scope **Mr Paul K. Barber**
6 **BRACKENFIELD**, 10, ch g Le Moss—Stable Lass **T. and J. A. Curry**
7 **BRAMBLEHILL BUCK (IRE)**, 7, gr g Roselier (FR)—Buckybrill **Mr Paul K. Barber**
8 **CALL EQUINAME**, 6, gr g Belfort (FR)—Cherry Season **Mick Coburn, P. K. Barber, C. Lewis**
9 **CAPTAIN KHEDIVE**, 8, ch g Deep Run—Wing On **Khedive Partnership**
10 **CHERRYNUT**, 7, b g Idiot's Delight—Merry Cherry **Hunt & Co (Bournemouth) Ltd**
11 **CHILDHAY CHOCOLATE**, 8, b g Impecunious—Childhay **Mr T. C. Frost**
12 **CHIP AND RUN**, 10, b g Strong Gale—Pampered Run **Mr C. Murphy**
13 **CLAIRE-DE-LUNE (IRE)**, 7, ch m Le Bavard (FR)—Fine Artist **Mr G. D. F. Sims**
14 **COOLREE (IRE)**, 8, b g Gianchi—Positron **Mr B. T. R. Weston**
15 **COURT MELODY (IRE)**, 8, b g Whistling Deer—Overwood Grove **Mr Mick Coburn**
16 **DEEP BRAMBLE**, 9, ch g Deep Run—Bardicate **Mr Paul K. Barber**
17 **DESERT RUN (IRE)**, 8, ch g Deep Run—Another Dutchess **The Reynolds Family**
18 **GENERAL CRACK (IRE)**, 7, ch g Lancastrian—Barna Havna **Mr Paul K. Barber**
19 **HERBERT BUCHANAN (IRE)**, 6, ch g Henbit (USA)—Our Siveen **Five For Fun**
20 **IDEAL PARTNER (IRE)**, 7, ch g Ovac (ITY)—Castle Demon **T. and J. A. Curry**
21 **IKTASAB**, 4, ch g Cadeaux Genereux—Loucoum (FR) **T. and J. A. Curry**
22 **JAC DEL PRINCE**, 6, b g Teofane—Star Shell **Mr Derek Millward**
23 **JAMES THE FIRST**, 8, ch g Wolver Heights—Juliette Mariner **Mr B. L. Blinman**
24 **LAKE KARIBA**, 5, b g Persian Bold—Gold Bracelet **Mr Curry and Mr Barber**
25 **LARRY'S LORD (IRE)**, 5, b g Lord Chancellor (USA)—Archers Dream **Marten Julian (Turf Club) Ltd**
26 **MARTELL BOY (NZ)**, 9, b g Princes Gate—Amorae (NZ) **Mr David G. Jones**
27 **MR STRONG GALE (IRE)**, 5, b g Strong Gale—Fleeting Sunshine **Mrs Jackson and Mr Chappell**
28 **MYBLACKTHORN (IRE)**, 6, br m Mandalus—Green Apple **Mrs Mary Coburn**
29 **NEARLY AN EYE**, 5, ch g Nearly A Hand—Kitty Come Home **Mr J. A. Keighley and Mr Paul K. Barber**
30 **OTTOWA (IRE)**, 6, b g Roselier (FR)—Queenie Kelly **Mr Paul K. Barber**
31 **PAGET**, 9, b g Taufan (USA)—Haco **Mr J. G. Olds**
32 **SEE MORE BUSINESS (IRE)**, 6, b g Seymour Hicks (FR)—Miss Redlands **Mr J. A. Keighley**
33 **SIERRA NEVADA**, 5, ch g Nearly A Hand—Yellow Iris **Mr D. J. Nichols**
34 **STONEY BURKE (IRE)**, 7, b br g Niels—Stoney Broke **Mrs Marianne G. Barber**
35 **STORM RUN (IRE)**, 6, b g Strong Gale—Summerville Lass **Mr J. W. Aplin**
36 **STRAIGHT TALK**, 9, b g Ovac (ITY)—Golden Tipp **Mrs C. I. A. Paterson**
37 **SUNLEY BAY**, 10, gr g Sunley Builds—Menrise Bay **Mrs Carole Solman**
38 **SUPREME MUSIC (IRE)**, 7, b g Supreme Leader—Wraparound Sue **Mr Russell Dennis**
39 **TRELAWNEYS DREAM**, 6, b m Sula Bula—Balitree **W. H. Williams Turf Accountants Ltd**
40 **VICOMPT DE VALMONT**, 11, b g Beau Charmeur (FR)—Wish Again **Mr John C. Blackwell**
41 **WHAT'S IN ORBIT**, 11, br g Strong Gale—Jet Travel **Mr C. I. A. Paterson**
42 **WITH IMPUNITY**, 7, br g Sula Bula—Sleepline Comfort **Guest Leasing & Bloodstock Co Ltd**

Other Owners: Mrs B. C. Dice, Mr P. G. Fry, Mr A. J. Graham, Mr K. Harris, Mr R. Holbrook, Mrs M. E. Jones, Mr Colin Lewis, Mr E. N. Liddiard, Mrs Bridget Nicholls, Mr R. E. Nuttall, Mrs Frances Reynolds, Mr J. M. Reynolds, Mr J. V. Sinnott, Mr D. Viney, Mr B. T. Weisberg.

Jockey (NH): A P McCoy (10-0).

456   MR DAVID NICHOLSON, Temple Guiting

Postal: **Ford Farm Racing, Jackdaws Castle, Temple Guiting, Cheltenham, GL54 5XU.**

Phone: **(01386) 584209 (01386) 584219 FAX (01386) 584218**

1 **AIR SHOT,** 6, b g Gunner B—Dans Le Vent **Mrs Peter Prowting**
2 **ANZUM,** 5, b g Ardross—Muznah **The Old Foresters Partnership**
3 **ARTHUR'S MINSTREL,** 9, ch g Black Minstrel—Jadida (FR) **Mr Bernard Hathaway**
4 **BALLYEA BOY (IRE),** 6, gr g Sandalay—Nesford **Mr Denis Barry**
5 **BARONET (IRE),** 6, ro g Roselier (FR)—Shuil Agragh **Mrs David Thompson**
6 **BARTON BANK,** 10, br g Kambalda—Lucifer's Daughter **Mrs J. Mould**
7 5, B m King's Ride—Bellerose Abbey **Mrs A. L. Davies & Partners**
8 **BELSTONE FOX,** 11, br g Buckskin (FR)—Winter Fox **Mrs J. Skan**
9 **BIG ARTHUR (IRE),** 7, b g Royal Fountain—Rockholm Rosie **Lord Vestey**
10 **BILLYGOAT GRUFF,** 7, b g Afzal—Autumn Ballet **Mr Peter D. Cooper**
11 **BOSS'S BANK (IRE),** 6, b g Strong Gale—Dusty Hall **Mrs J. Mould**
12 **BUTTERCUP JOE,** 6, b g Scallywag—Evergreen Melody **Mr R. C. F. Faiers**
13 **CALL IT A DAY (IRE),** 6, b g Callernish—Arctic Bavard **Mrs Jane Lane**
14 **CASTLE SWEEP (IRE),** 5, b g Castle Keep—Fairy Shot **Lord Vestey**
15 **CERTAINLY STRONG (IRE),** 6, b m Strong Gale—Arctic Verb **Mr Nick Skelton**
16 **CHICODARI,** 4, b c Shardari—Chicobin (USA) **Brig C. B. Harvey**
17 **COOLE HILL (IRE),** 5, b br m Strong Gale—Cool Girl **Messrs B. Winfield and J. Potter**
18 **CORNER BOY,** 9, br g Callernish—Rescued **Mrs E. W. Wilson**
19 **DASHANTI,** 5, b g Rakaposhi King—Deep Line **Birch Hall Five Partnership**
20 **DETROIT DAVY (IRE),** 5, b g Detroit Sam (FR)—Pretty Damsel **Mrs Stewart Catherwood**
21 **DINO MALTA (FR),** 5, ch g Bad Conduct (USA)—Sri Lanka III (FR) **Lady Harris**
22 **DREAM RIDE (IRE),** 6, b g King's Ride—Night Dreamer **Gerry Mordaunt & Christopher Clarke**
23 **DUBLIN FREDDY,** 5, b g Ardross—Dublin Ferry **Mrs Claire Smith**
24 **DUKE'S MOUNT (IRE),** 6, b g King's Ride—Georgiana **Mrs Claire Smith**
25 **EUROLINKHELLRAISER (IRE),** 5, b br g Mandalus—Lady Lucifer **Eurolink Group Plc**
26 **FIXTURESSECRETARY (IRE),** 7, b g Lancastrian—Astrina's Daughter **Mr K. G. Manley**
27 **FLY BY NORTH (USA),** 8, b g Northern Horizon (USA)—Lazy E (CAN) **Ford Farm Racing**
28 **FLYING GUNNER,** 5, ch g Gunner B—Dans Le Vent **Mr R. Maryan Green**
29 **FOREST IVORY (NZ),** 5, ch g Ivory Hunter (USA)—Fair And Square (NZ) **The Old Foresters Partnership**
30 4, B g Bowling Pin—Fortina Lass **The Racegoers Club**
31 **GENERAL PERSHING,** 10, br g Persian Bold—St Colette **Mr J. E. Potter**
32 **HATCHAM BOY (IRE),** 6, br g Roselier (FR)—Auling **Mr Robert Benton**
33 **HATTA BREEZE,** 4, b f Night Shift (USA)—Jouvencelle **Mrs J. Mould**
34 **HEBRIDEAN,** 9, b g Norwick (USA)—Pushkar **Mr P. A. Deal**
35 **HENRY CONE,** 7, br g Celtic Cone—Misty Sunset **Mrs David J. Barrington**
36 **HILL OF TULLOW (IRE),** 7, b br g Roselier (FR)—Clonmeen Mist **Lady Harris**
37 **HURRICANE LAMP,** 5, b g Derrylin—Lampstone **Mr & Mrs F. C. Welch and Mr R. A. Barrs**
38 **IN THE ROUGH (IRE),** 5, b g Strong Gale—Cherrydawn **Mrs L. R. Lovell**
39 **JATHIB (CAN),** 5, ch g Trempolino (USA)—Noble Gaze (USA) **Horses For Courses Racing Club**
40 **JOHNNY-K (IRE),** 5, b g King's Ride—Queen Kate **Norwood Partners**
41 **KEMILLER (IRE),** 6, b br g King's Ride—Icy Gal **Mrs Stewart Catherwood**
42 **KING LUCIFER (IRE),** 7, b g King's Ride—Cahore **Mr J. A. H. West**
43 **KING OF CAMELOT (IRE),** 5, b g King's Ride—Radical Review **Mr Jerry Wright**
44 **LOVE THE BLUES,** 4, ch f Bluebird (USA)—Love Match (USA) **Mrs Claire Smith**
45 **MARTIN'S LAMP,** 9, b g Martinmas—Lampstone **Mr & Mrs F. C. Welch**
46 **MASTER HOPE (IRE),** 7, b g Strong Gale—Bunkilla **The Deeley Partnership**
47 **MELEAGRIS,** 12, b g True Song—Fritillaria **Mr D. J. Jackson**
48 **MENOO WHO (IRE),** 4, ch c Keen—Flying Anna **Jebel Ali Racing Stables**
49 **MIGHTY MOSS (IRE),** 5, b g Moscow Society (USA)—Derry Girl **Mr K. Hutsby**
50 **MINTY'S FOLLY (IRE),** 6, ch g Fools Holme (USA)—Sugarbird **Mrs Claire Smith**
51 **MISS OPTIMIST,** 6, b m Relkino—Sweet Optimist **The Plough Partnership**
52 **MOORCROFT BOY,** 11, ch g Roselier (FR)—Well Mannered **Mr K. G. Manley**
53 **MUSTHAVEASWIG,** 10, gr g Croghan Hill—Gin An Tonic **P. R. D. Fasteners Ltd**
54 **MY CHEEKY MAN,** 5, ch g Cisto (FR)—Regal Flutter **Mrs A. A. Shutes**
55 **MYLINK (IRE),** 6, b g Mandalus—The Brown Link **Mr S. Constable**
56 **PENROSE LAD (NZ),** 6, b g Captain Jason (NZ)—Salimah (NZ) **Mrs C. N. Weatherby**

MR DAVID NICHOLSON—continued

57 **PERCY SMOLLETT**, 8, br g Oats—Misty Sunset **Mr R. G. Murray**
58 **PHARANEAR (IRE)**, 6, b g Camden Town—Monas River **Stainless Threaded Fasteners Ltd**
59 **PICKET PIECE**, 5, br g Shareef Dancer (USA)—Jouvencelle **Mrs J. Mould**
60 **POTTER'S BAY (IRE)**, 7, br g Strong Gale—Polly Puttens **Mrs J. E. Potter**
61 **POTTER'S GALE (IRE)**, 5, br m Strong Gale—Polly Puttens **Mr J. E. Potter**
62 **PUTTY ROAD (IRE)**, 6, ch g Bob Back (USA)—Mill's Girl **Lady Harris**
63 **REINE DE LA CHASSE (FR)**, 4, ch f Ti King (FR)—Hunting Cottage **Million In Mind Partnership (5)**
64 **RELKEEL**, 7, b g Relkino—Secret Keel **Brig C. B. Harvey**
65 **RIVER JUNCTION (IRE)**, 5, b g Cyrano de Bergerac—Lovestream **The Superioat Partnership**
66 **ROLFE (NZ)**, 6, b g Tom's Shu (USA)—Tredia (NZ) **Mr S. W. Clarke**
67 **ROWINGTON**, 5, b g Ardross—Cherry Crest **Mrs Jane Lane**
68 **SANDYBRAES**, 11, ch g Kambalda—Kinsella's Choice **Mr K. Hutsby**
69 **SHANKAR (IRE)**, 5, gr g Shareef Dancer (USA)—Sibelle d'Oa (FR) **International Plywood Plc**
70 **SHEEPCOTE HILL (IRE)**, 5, b g Corvaro (USA)—Misty Boosh **Mr J. E. Brown**
71 **SHINING LIGHT (IRE)**, 7, b g Crash Course—Arumah **The Deeley Partnership**
72 **SIMPLE SIMON (IRE)**, 6, ch g Callernish—Simply Sally **Mrs M. A. Powis**
73 **SONIC STAR (IRE)**, 7, b g Euphemism—Daraheen Blade **Mr R. F. Nutland**
74 **SOUNDS STRONG (IRE)**, 7, br g Strong Gale—Jazz Bavard **Mrs David Thompson**
75 **SPLINTERS (IRE)**, 6, b g Dancing Lights (USA)—Mugra **Mrs J. Mould**
76 **ST MELLION FAIRWAY (IRE)**, 7, b g Mandalus—Kilbricken Bay **St Mellion Estates Ltd**
77 **STORM ALERT**, 10, b g Strong Gale—Jet Travel **Mrs D. Perrett**
78 **SUTHERLAND MOSS**, 5, b g Ardross—Caoimhe **Mrs Claire Smith**
79 **SWIVEL**, 4, ch f Salse (USA)—Spin Turn **Mrs Claire Smith**
80 **SYMPHONY'S SON (IRE)**, 5, b g Orchestra—Garden of Roses **Mrs J. Mould**
81 **TEELYNA**, 4, b f Teenoso (USA)—Lynda-B **Mrs Claire Smith**
82 **THE BINGER**, 5, ch g Ovac (ITY)—Little Ginger **Mrs M. P. Sutton & Mrs R. J. Skan**
83 **THE CAPTAIN'S WISH**, 5, ch g Infantry—The Lady's Wish **Miss A. J. Murray**

MR DAVID NICHOLSON—continued

84 **TURNING TRIX**, 9, b g Buckskin (FR)—Merry Run **Mr Mel Davies**
85 **TWICE A NIGHT**, 7, br m Oats—Celtic Cygnet **All in the Mind**
86 **VERY PROMISING**, 18, br g The Parson—No Hitch **Mr David Nicholson**
87 **VIKING FLAGSHIP**, 9, b g Viking (USA)—Fourth Degree **Roach Foods Limited**
88 **WHAT'S YOUR STORY (IRE)**, 7, ch g The Parson—Lolos Run VII **Mr Jerry Wright**
89 **WINDROSS**, 4, b g Ardross—Dans Le Vent **Mrs Peter Prowting**
90 **ZABADI (IRE)**, 4, b g Shahrastani (USA)—Zerzaya **Lady Harris**
91 **ZAITOON (IRE)**, 5, b g Waajib—Sawlah **Cheltenham Racing Ltd**

Other Owners: Mr A. M. Armitage, Mrs J. M. Bannister, Mrs Pam Bates, Lady Blyth, Mr Ben Brooks, Mr David Brown, Mrs H. J. Clarke, Ms Selena Close, Mr D. E. Cook, Mr J. S. Dale, Mr A. J. Davies, Mr D. I. B. Dick, Mr S. B. Duncombe, Mrs Sue Faccenda, Mr Christopher J. Fell, Mr Lou Giaracuni, Mr Graham Goode, Mrs G. Harper, Mr D. A. Howes, Mr Michael Jeffery, Mr W. Jenks, Konvekta Ltd, Mr Frank P. Krasovec, Sheikh Ahmed Al Maktoum, Mr Guy Massey, Mr D. Minton, Sheikh Mohammed, Mr J. B. R. Morris, Mr Charles F. Newman, Mr C. G. Nicholl, Mr B. A. O'Brien, Mrs S. B. Olink, Mr M. R. Oliver, Mr C. B. Smith, Mr M. R. Smith, Mr John G. Stevens, Mr D. J. Ward, Mr F. Welch, Mrs S. C. Welch, Exors Of The Late Lt Col W. Whetherly, Mr C. Williamson.

Jockey (Flat): Lindsay Charnock (7-10).

Jockeys (NH): Robert Bellamy (10-0), Adrian Maguire (10-0), Warren Marston (10-0).

Conditional: Xavier Aizpuru (9-7), Gerry Hogan (9-12), Richard Johnson (9-11), Robert Massey (9-9).

Amateurs: Mr Richard Burton (10-0), Mr Fred Hutsby (10-0), Mr Oliver McPhail (9-7), Mr Glenn Smith (9-9), Mr Robert Thornton (9-7).

457   MR G. R. S. NIXON, Selkirk

Postal: **Oakwood Farm, Ettrickbridge, Selkirk, TD7 5HJ.**

Phone: **(01750) 52245**

1 **POLITICAL MILLSTAR**, 4, b g Leading Star—Political Mill **Mr G. Nixon & Mrs S. Nixon**
2 **POLITICAL TOWER**, 9, b g Politico (USA)—Crosby Waves **Mr G. Nixon & Mrs S. Nixon**
3 **TURKISH TOWER**, 5, b g Idiot's Delight—Tringa (GER) **Mr G. Nixon & Mrs S. Nixon**

THREE-YEAR-OLDS

4 B f Rakaposhi King—Kilglass **Mr G. Nixon & Mrs S. Nixon**
5 Br f Respect—Political Mill **Mr G. Nixon & Mrs S. Nixon**
6 Br g Meadowbrook—Tringa (GER) **Mr G. Nixon & Mrs S. Nixon**

TWO-YEAR-OLDS

7 Ch g 24/3 Ardar—Kincherinchee (Dunbeath (USA)) **Mr G. Nixon & Mrs S. Nixon**
8 Br g 26/4 Mirror Boy—Political Mill (Politico (USA)) **Mr G. Nixon & Mrs S. Nixon**

458   MRS S. NOCK, Stow-on-the-Wold

Postal: **Smenham Farm, Icomb, Stow-on-the Wold, Cheltenham, GL54 1JT.**

1 **COOL RUNNER**, 6, b g Sunyboy—Nosey's Daughter **Mr Gerard Nock**
2 **DODGY DEALER (IRE)**, 6, ch g Salluceva—Donna Chimene **Mr Gerard Nock**
3 **OPERETTO (IRE)**, 6, b g Orchestra—Love From Judy **Mr Gerard Nock**
4 **SENOR EL BETRUTTI (IRE)**, 7, gr g Roselier (FR)—Rambling Gold **Mr Gerard Nock**

459   MR D. A. NOLAN, Wishaw

Postal: **Riverside Racing Stables, 227a Bonkle Road, Newmains, Wishaw, ML2 9QQ.**
Phone: **(01698) 381829 FAX (01698) 386674**

1 **AH JIM LAD**, 12, b g Jimsun—Gigante Rossa **Mr A. S. McPherson**
2 **BADDI QUEST**, 4, b c Rainbow Quest (USA)—Baddi Baddi (USA) **Mr J. P. Slattery**
3 **JABAROOT (IRE)**, 5, b g Sadler's Wells (USA)—Arctic Heroine (USA) **Mr J. P. Slattery**
4 **KENESHA (IRE)**, 6, br m Don't Forget Me—Calvino
5 **LOGANI**, 6, b m Domynsky—Vidette **Miss P. Hamilton**
6 **LORD ADVOCATE**, 8, br g Law Society (USA)—Kereolle **Mrs J. McFadyen-Murray**
7 **MINSK**, 10, ch m Kabour—Wedded Bliss **Mrs J. McFadyen-Murray**
8 **MISS HOSTESS**, 9, gr m Petong—Rosalina **Mrs J. McFadyen-Murray**
9 **RAPID MOVER**, 9, ch g Final Straw—Larive **Mrs J. McFadyen-Murray**
10 **SELF IMPORTANT (USA)**, 11, ch g Vigors (USA)—Dear Meme (USA) **Mrs J. McFadyen-Murray**
11 **SIX FOR LUCK**, 4, b g Handsome Sailor—Fire Sprite **Mrs J. McFadyen-Murray**
12 **UPPANCE**, 8, b m Kabour—Final Cast **Mrs J. McFadyen-Murray**
13 **VALLEY OF TIME (FR)**, 8, br m In Fijar (USA)—Vallee Sarthoise (FR) **Mrs J. McFadyen-Murray**

THREE-YEAR-OLDS

14 **JIMMY-S (IRE)**, b c Marju (IRE)—Amber Fizz (USA) **Mr J. P. Slattery**
15 **LORD CORNELIOUS**, b c Lochnager—Title **Mrs J. McFadyen-Murray**

Other Owners: Mr R. Nichol, Mr F. Sestin, Mrs L. Sestin, Shale Contracts Ltd.

Jockey (Flat): Lindsay Charnock (7-10).

Apprentice: Neil Varley (7-7).

Amateur: Adrian McPherson (10-0).

460   MR J. NORTON, Barnsley

Postal: **Globe Farm, High Hoyland, Barnsley, S. Yorks, S75 4BE.**
Phone: **(01226) 387633   FAX (01226) 387633**

1 **AHWAAL (USA)**, 4, b g Danzig (USA)—Miss Brio (CHI) **Mrs Sylvia Blakeley**
2 **BOLD ACTION (IRE)**, 5, b g Denel (FR)—Loughan-Na-Curry **Mrs Sylvia Blakeley**
3 **BRADLOR PENNY (IRE)**, 6, b g Roselier (FR)—Merry Penny **Bradlor Developments Limited**
4 **BRANCHER**, 5, gr g Lyphento (USA)—Sunlit **Mrs Sylvia Blakeley**
5 **DISSINGTON DENE**, 7, b g Denel (FR)—Greenpeace **D. A. & W. Wyllie**
6 **DOZEN DIRHAM (USA)**, 4, b g Dayjur (USA)—Capades (USA) **Mrs Sylvia Blakeley**
7 **EFAAD (IRE)**, 5, b g Shaadi (USA)—Krismas River **Mr J. Norton**
8 **GENERAL'S ORDERS (USA)**, 5, b g Java Gold (USA)—Close In (USA) **Mrs Sylvia Blakeley**
9 **INN AT THE TOP**, 4, b g Top Ville—Woolpack **Mrs Sylvia Blakeley**
10 **JIHAAD (USA)**, 6, b g Chief's Crown (USA)—Desirable **Mr Mattie O'Toole**
11 **JILLS JOY (IRE)**, 5, b g Law Society (USA)—Cooliney Princess **Mr R. Baker**
12 **KING'S ORDERS**, 4, gr f Rakaposhi King—Sunlit **Mrs Sylvia Blakeley**
13 **LESLEY'S ANGEL (IRE)**, 5, b g Common Grounds—Indian Swallow **Mrs Sylvia Blakeley**
14 **LISALEEN WREN (IRE)**, 7, br g The Parson—Kitty Wren **Mrs Sylvia Blakeley**
15 **LONE HAND (USA)**, 4, ch f Lomond (USA)—Tricky Fingers (USA) **Mrs Sylvia Blakeley**
16 **MUDLARK**, 4, b g Salse (USA)—Mortal Sin (USA) **Mr J. Norton**
17 **NORTON GALE (IRE)**, 5, ch m Le Bavard (FR)—Galeshula **Mrs Sylvia Blakeley**
18 **OLERON**, 4, b f Darshaan—Orangerie (FR) **Mrs Sylvia Blakeley**
19 **ONEOFTHEOLDONES**, 4, b c Deploy—Waveguide **Mr R. Baker**
20 **SAGAVILLE (IRE)**, 6, b g Mister Lord (USA)—Beautiful Glen **Mrs Sylvia Blakeley**
21 **SHARED RISK**, 4, ch g Risk Me (FR)—Late Idea **Mr Graham Brooksbank**

MR J. NORTON—continued

22 **STARNINA (IRE)**, 4, b f Caerleon (USA)—Kayrava **Mrs Sylvia Blakeley**
23 **SUDDEN SPIN**, 6, b g Doulab (USA)—Lightning Legacy (USA) **Mr Billy Parker**
24 **TEMPTING (IRE)**, 4, b f Waajib—Belela **Mr J. Norton**
25 **THREEOUTOFFOUR**, 11, b g Milford—Smiling **Mr R. Baker**
26 **TOM TYLER**, 4, b g Aragon—Lingering **Mr J. Norton**
27 **TREE OF TIME (USA)**, 5, br g Storm Cat (USA)—Timely Queen (USA) **Mrs Sylvia Blakeley**
28 **WILD CAT BAY**, 4, b g Never So Bold—Mardi Gras Belle (USA) **Mr J. Norton**
29 **YOUNG ARDROSS**, 5, b g Ardross—Celtic Silk **Mrs Sylvia Blakeley**

THREE-YEAR-OLDS

30 **APRIL'S JOY**, b f Mazilier (USA)—Ziobia **Mrs Sylvia Blakeley**
31 **LAST ACTION**, gr f Lyphento (USA)—Sunlit **Mrs Sylvia Blakeley**
32 **STAR DANCER**, ch f Groom Dancer (USA)—Pencarreg **Mrs Sylvia Blakeley**

TWO-YEAR-OLDS

33 B f 15/1 Classic Secret (USA)—Deverells Walk (IRE) (Godswalk (USA)) **Mrs Sylvia Blakeley**
34 **DISSINGTON TIMES**, ch g 8/6 Timeless Times (USA)—Zam's Slave (Zambrano) **D. A. & W. Wyllie**
35 Gr c 21/4 Green Ruby (USA)—Fara (Castle Keep) **Mrs Sylvia Blakeley**

Jockey (NH): W Fry (10-0).

Apprentice: Amy Gosden (7-8).

461　　MR CHARLES O'BRIEN, Kildare

Postal: **Ridge Manor Stables, Rathbride, Kildare, Ireland**
Phone: **(045) 522607 FAX (045) 522609**

1 **ALISIDORA (IRE)**, 4, ch f Nashwan (USA)—Christabelle (USA)
2 **AMERICA'S CUP (IRE)**, 4, b c Fairy King (USA)—Boat Race (USA)
3 **BURDEN OF PROOF (IRE)**, 4, b c Fairy King (USA)—Belle Passe
4 **FABRIANO (USA)**, 5, ch g El Gran Senor (USA)—Thorough
5 **IRISH ACADEMY (IRE)**, 4, ch c Royal Academy (USA)—Rosa Mundi (USA)
6 **MARQUETA (USA)**, 4, ch f Woodman (USA)—Russian Ballet (USA)
7 **ROYAL CANAL (USA)**, 4, b c Shirley Heights (USA)—Woodstream (USA)
8 **WOOD LEOPARD (USA)**, 4, ch c Woodman (USA)—Thorough
9 **YUKON GOLD (IRE)**, 7, b g Lomond (USA)—Exotic Bride (USA)

THREE-YEAR-OLDS

10 **BICYCLE THIEF (IRE)**, ch g Archway (IRE)—Push Bike
11 **CREWMAN (IRE)**, b g Fairy King (USA)—Boat Race (USA)
12 **DESERT MOUNTAIN (IRE)**, b c Alzao (USA)—Curie Point (USA)
13 **EPIGRAM (IRE)**, b g Royal Academy (USA)—Perlita (FR)
14 **HAPPY MEDIUM (IRE)**, b c Fairy King (USA)—Belle Origine (USA)
15 **LYRICAL LOOK (IRE)**, b f Royal Academy (USA)—Wood Violet (USA)
16 **MR DIGNITY (IRE)**, ch g Archway (IRE)—Forliana
17 **NASCIMENTO (USA)**, b c Green Dancer (USA)—Miss Pele (USA)
18 **PARIS MODEL (IRE)**, gr f Thatching—Aldern Stream
19 **PERFECT VENUE (IRE)**, b c Danehill (USA)—Welsh Fantasy
20 **SERENE SWING (USA)**, b f Seattle Dancer (USA)—Alyannock (USA)
21 **THIRD MILLENIUM (IRE)**, b c Fairy King (USA)—Fantasy Land
22 **THOROUGHLY (IRE)**, ch f Woodman (USA)—Thorough
23 **TRUTH OR DARE (IRE)**, b c Royal Academy (USA)—Rose de Thai (USA)
24 **WORLD STAGE (IRE)**, b c Sadler's Wells (USA)—Rosa Mundi (USA)

MR CHARLES O'BRIEN—continued

TWO-YEAR-OLDS

25 Gr c 20/3 Thatching—All Ashore (Nureyev (USA))
26 B f 27/4 Fairy King (USA)—Arcade (Rousillon (USA))
27 B f 21/3 Royal Academy (USA)—Boat Race (Seattle Slew (USA))
28 B c 16/4 Common Grounds—Concave (Connaught)
29 Ch c 14/4 Suave Dancer (USA)—Creake (Derring-Do)
30 B c 17/2 Last Tycoon—Dreamy River (USA) (Bates Motel (USA))
31 B c 13/3 Fairy King (USA)—It's All Academic (IRE) (Mazaad)
32 B f 2/2 Woodman (USA)—Karri Valley (USA) (Storm Bird (CAN))
33 B f 25/4 Fairy King (USA)—Key Maneuver (USA) (Key To Content (USA))
34 B f 11/4 Royal Academy (USA)—Lisadell (USA) (Forli (ARG))
35 B c 23/3 Sadler's Wells (USA)—Maiden Concert (Condorcet (FR))
36 B c 24/1 Night Shift (USA)—Mosaique Bleue (Shirley Heights)
37 Ch f 3/3 Woodman (USA)—Rua d'Oro (USA) (El Gran Senor (USA))
38 B c 29/4 Fabulous Dancer (USA)—Ruffle (FR) (High Line)
39 Ch c 1/2 Woodman (USA)—Russian Ballet (USA) (Nijinsky (CAN))
40 B c 20/2 Night Shift (USA)—Sheer Audacity (Troy)
41 B f 14/3 Thatching—Soltura (IRE) (Sadler's Wells (USA))
42 B f 11/5 Royal Academy (USA)—Ste Nitouche (FR) (Riverman (USA))
43 Ch f 20/3 Royal Academy (USA)—Wood Violet (USA) (Riverman (USA))

Owners: Mr B. P. Burns, Dr Anne Heffernan, Mr R. Lewis, Mrs John Magnier, Mr D. McCarthy, Mrs E. McClory, Mrs J. Myerscough, Dr M. V. O'Brien, Mrs M. V. O'Brien, Dr A. J. O'Reilly, Mr N. Pharaon, Ms P. Reddy, Ms M. M. Ridgway, Mr M. Tabor.

462   MR D. C. O'BRIEN, Tonbridge

Postal: **Knowles Bank, Capel, Tonbridge, Kent, TN11 0PU.**

1 AUGUST TWELFTH, 8, b g Full of Hope—Espanita **Mr D. C. O'Brien**
2 BLACK ARROW, 9, br g Full of Hope—Snow Damsel **Mr D. C. O'Brien**
3 DARK PHANTOM, 9, b g Daring March—Lady Henham **Mr D. C. O'Brien**
4 KELLY MAC, 6, b g Precocious—Ridalia **Mrs V. O'Brien**
5 MY JAZZMYN, 4, b f Chief Singer—Azaiyma **Mr Graham Pasquill**
6 PINOCCIO, 9, b g Full of Hope—White Oaks **Mr Bernard O'Brien**
7 REGAL AURA (IRE), 6, ch g Glow (USA)—Dignified Air (FR) **Mrs V. O'Brien**
8 SCORPIONS TALE, 9, ch g Full of Hope—Too Familiar **Mrs V. O'Brien**
9 TODAY'S FANCY, 8, b g Today And Tomorrow—Fancy Pages **Mr D. C. O'Brien**

THREE-YEAR-OLDS

10 GOLDEN WEDDING, b g Today And Tomorrow—Too Familiar **Mrs F. I. Davis**
11 PATCHY BOY, b g Today And Tomorrow—Lady Henham **Miss C. F. Sainty**
12 VALJESS, b f Today And Tomorrow—Emmer Green **Mrs R. M. Blake**
13 VITAL EVIDENCE, br f Today And Tomorrow—Vital Witness **Mrs V. O'Brien**

TWO-YEAR-OLDS

14 B f 24/4 Efisio—Capel Lass (The Brianstan) **Syndicate**
15 Ch f 20/4 Rock Hopper—Emmer Green (Music Boy) **Syndicate**
16 B f 27/3 Today And Tomorrow—Frimley Grove (Tower Walk) **Syndicate**
17 B f 1/4 Rock Hopper—Lady Henham (Breakspear II) **Syndicate**
18 B f 27/3 Timeless Times (USA)—Midnight Lass (Today And Tomorrow) **Syndicate**
19 B c 7/4 Today And Tomorrow—Miss Blizard (Vitiges (FR)) **Syndicate**
20 Gr f 30/3 Today And Tomorrow—Mossaka (FR) (Targowice (USA)) **Syndicate**
21 B c 28/2 Today And Tomorrow—Next-of-Kin (Great Nephew) **Syndicate**
22 B c 23/3 Today And Tomorrow—Nimble Dancer (Northern Wizard) **Syndicate**
23 B f 19/5 Ardross—Targow Girl (Targowice (USA)) **Syndicate**
24 B f 6/3 Lord Bud—Too Familiar (Oats) **Syndicate**

463   MR W. A. O'GORMAN, Newmarket

Postal: **Seven Springs, Hamilton Road, Newmarket, Suffolk, CB8 7JQ.**

Phone: **(01638) 663330 FAX (01638) 663160**

1 **AFRICAN CHIMES,** 9, b h Kampala—Rynville **Mr D. G. Wheatley**
2 **BERGE (IRE),** 5, b h Most Welcome—Miss Blitz **Mr S. Fustok**
3 **SASEEDO (USA),** 6, ch g Afleet (CAN)—Barbara's Moment (USA) **Mr S. Fustok**
4 **TAME DEER,** 4, ch c Hadeer—Ever Welcome **Red Seven Stable**
5 **WILD PALM,** 4, b c Darshaan—Tarasova (USA) **Mr S. Fustok**

THREE-YEAR-OLDS

6 **ARCTIC ZIPPER (USA),** gr g Unzipped (USA)—Arctic Fashion (USA) **Times of Wigan**
7 **BALLYMONEY (IRE),** b c Fayruz—Blunted **Mr W. A. O'Gorman**
8 **CHLOE'S ANCHOR,** b f Slip Anchor—Mademoiselle Chloe **Mr S. Fustok**
9 **DISTINCT BEAUTY (IRE),** ch f Pancho Villa (USA)—Beautiful Secret (USA) **Mr N. S. Yong**
10 **FOREMAN,** b c Timeless Times (USA)—Skiddaw Bird **Times of Wigan**
11 **GALINE,** b f Most Welcome—Tarasova (USA) **Mr S. Fustok**
12 **GIFT STAR (USA),** b g Star de Naskra (USA)—Super Kitten (USA) **Mr N. S. Yong**
13 **GOLDSEARCH (IRE),** ch f Fayruz—Win For Me **Mr N. S. Yong**
14 **MOFASA,** b c Shardari—Round Midnight **Mr S. Fustok**
15 **MUSIC GOLD (IRE),** b c Taufan (USA)—Nonnita **Mr N. S. Yong**
16 **QUALITAIR BEAUTY,** b f Damister (USA)—Mac's Princess (USA) **Qualitair Holdings Limited**
17 **QUALITY (IRE),** b c Rock City—Queens Welcome **Mr N. S. Yong**
18 **ROC DE FER (IRE),** br g Polar Falcon (USA)—Miss Blitz **Mr S. Fustok**
19 **SOBRE TIMES (USA),** b c Hooched (USA)—Saint Pea (USA) **Times of Wigan**
20 **SOCIETY TIMES (USA),** b c Imp Society (USA)—Mauna Loa (USA) **Times of Wigan**
21 **SUPERGOLD (IRE),** ch c Keen—Superflash **Mr N. S. Yong**
22 **TEN TIMES (USA),** b c On To Glory (USA)—Third And Ten (USA) **Times of Wigan**

TWO-YEAR-OLDS

23 **ARCTIC BLAST (USA),** gr c Unzipped (USA)—
                                        Arctic Fashion (USA) (The Knack) **Times Of Wigan & Mr W. A. O'Gorman**
24 B c Glitterman (USA)—Cut Test (USA) (Relaunch (USA)) **Mr T. Mohan**
25 **DESERT DIAMOND,** b c Suave Dancer (USA)—Mademoiselle Chloe (Night Shift (USA)) **Mr S. Fustok**
26 **EUROGOLD (IRE),** ch c Shalford (IRE)—Nesreen (The Parson) **Mr N. S. Yong**
27 B c d'Accord (USA)—Jazzborne (USA) (Sir Wimborne (USA)) **Mr W. A. O'Gorman**
28 **LIQUID GOLD (IRE),** br c Fairy King (USA)—Heavenward (USA) (Conquistador Cielo (USA)) **Mr N. S. Yong**
29 B f Dodge (USA)—Nesian's Burn (USA) (Big Burn (USA)) **Times Of Wigan**
30 **NIGHT RAIN,** b f Most Welcome—Saluti Tutti (Trojan Fen) **Mr S. Fustok**
31 **PRIME POWER (IRE),** b g Polish Patriot (USA)—Dont Be Cruel (Persian Bold) **Mr N. S. Yong**
32 B f Damister (USA)—Rocket Alert (Red Alert) **Mr Thomas R. Capehart**
33 **SAINT WHO (USA),** b g Hooched (USA)—
                                        Saint Pea (USA) (Christopher R (USA)) **Times Of Wigan & Mr W. A. O'Gorman**
34 **SUPERQUEST,** ch c Superlative—More Or Less (Morston (FR)) **Mr N. S. Yong**
35 Ch c Saratoga Six (USA)—Wajibird (USA) (Storm Bird (CAN)) **Mr T. Mohan**

Jockeys (Flat): Tony Ives (8-6), Emma O'Gorman (8-4).

464   MR E. J. O'GRADY, Thurles

Postal: **Killeens, Ballynonty, Thurles, Co. Tipperary, Ireland.**

Phone: **(052) 56156 FAX (052) 56466**

1 **ANKER RING (IRE),** 6, ch g Torus—Mrs Jenner **C. P. Millikin**
2 **BAGATELLE (IRE),** 6, br m Strong Gale—Decent Slave **Mrs S. L. Jackson**
3 **BALAWHAR (IRE),** 6, b g Doyoun—Bayazida **Michael Tabor**
4 **BE THE ONE (IRE),** 5, b m Supreme Leader—Homewrecker **J. J. Power**
5 **BLOWN AWAY (IRE),** 5, b m Strong Gale—Buck Away **B. Duffy**
6 **BOHOLA PETE (IRE),** 5, ch g Orchestra—Deep Link **K. Murphy**

MR E. J. O'GRADY—continued

7 CLASHBEG (IRE), 5, b m Jeu de Paille (FR)—Gentildonna P. McLoughney
8 CONNEMARA TRAIL (IRE), 6, b g Tremblant—Judy Loe Mrs John J. Fogarty
9 DEEP BIT (IRE), 5, b g Henbit (USA)—Deep Down L. Thompson
10 EDUARDO (IRE), 6, br g Denel (FR)—Palhiri Brian Lenaghan
11 EMPEROR GLEN (IRE), 8, b g Glenstal (USA)—Cooliney Princess J. M. O'Malley
12 FERN WATCH (IRE), 7, b g Le Moss—Hourly Rate John P. McManus
13 FLIP YOUR LID, 7, br g Lidhame—Lady Antonia W. A. Barrett
14 GAELTEACHT (IRE), 5, br g Strong Gale—Galliano N. A. McCarthy
15 GIMME FIVE, 9, b g Deep Run—Cill Dara John P. McManus
16 GLITTER PADDY (IRE), 5, br g Rising—Glitterati P. McLoughney
17 KERRY ORCHID, 8, gr g Absalom—Matinata P. Curling
18 LENNI LENAPE, 4, b c Be My Native—Judy Loe Dr J. Torsney
19 LOVING AROUND (IRE), 8, b m Furry Glen—Shannon Ville Marquess Of Tavistock
20 MALLARDSTOWN (IRE), 5, b g Buckskin (FR)—Decent Enough Dr James Fennelly
21 MUCKLEMEG (IRE), 8, br m Strong Gale—Quadro John P. McManus
22 MUSKIN MORE (IRE), 5, ch g Electric—Clontinty Queen Mrs L. McCallan
23 NANTUCKET BAY (IRE), 5, b h Ardross—Tara Dream K. Murphy
24 NO WHEN TO RUN (IRE), 8, b g Deep Run—Hourly Rate John P. McManus
25 OVERTIME (IRE), 5, br m Executive Perk—Hourly Rate John P. McManus
26 PRIDE OF TIPPERARY (IRE), 5, b m Supreme Leader—Moneyforusall V. Loughnane
27 REAL TAOISEACH (IRE), 6, b g Supreme Leader—Saintly Tune John Horgan
28 REASILVIA (IRE), 6, br m Supreme Leader—Quite Amazing P. Senezio
29 SEA GALE (IRE), 8, b m Strong Gale—Sea Scope B. D. Darrer
30 SERGEANT MULLARKEY (IRE), 8, b g Furry Glen—Cashelgarran Ray MacSharry
31 SESAME CRACKER, 5, b m Derrylin—Quadro R. Jenks
32 SHOREWOOD (IRE), 5, b g Reference Point—Shona (GER) L. Thompson
33 SOUND MAN (IRE), 8, b g Kemal (FR)—Frankford Run David A. Lloyd
34 TALES OF HEARSAY (GER), 6, gr g Celestial Storm (USA)—Trying Girl Michael Nugent
35 TIME FOR A RUN, 9, b g Deep Run—Hourly Rate John P. McManus
36 VENTANA CANYON (IRE), 7, b g Un Desperado (FR)—Adariya P. Myrescough
37 VESPER LADY (IRE), 5, b m Hymns On High—Anacarty Bruce Barham

THREE-YEAR-OLDS

38 ONE MORE SPIN (IRE), b br c Tirol—Manela Lady J. S. Gutkin
39 POLYGUEZA (FR), ch f Be My Guest (USA)—Polifontaine (FR) F. A. McNulty

Other Owners: Dermot Desmond, Miss M. Goodbody, John Magnier, Michael McGread, Mrs J. Myerscough.

Jockey (NH): A J Slattery (10-0).

Amateur: Mr P Fenton (10-0).

465   MR J. J. O'NEILL, Penrith

Postal: Ivy House, Skelton Wood End, Penrith, Cumbria, CA11 9UB.
Phone: (017684) 84555 FAX (017684) 84559

1 AMBLESIDE HARVEST, 9, b br g Decent Fellow—Watch The Birdie G. & P. Barker Ltd/Globe Engineering
2 ARDRONAN (IRE), 6, b g Roselier (FR)—Molly Coddle Mrs L. R. Joughin
3 AVOWHAT (IRE), 6, ch g Avocat—Welwhat Mr J. Clayton
4 BANG IN TROUBLE (IRE), 5, b g Glenstal (USA)—Vaguely Deesse (USA) Mrs L. R. Joughin
5 BEACHY HEAD, 8, gr g Damister (USA)—No More Rosies Mr M. Tabor
6 CAIRO PRINCE (IRE), 6, b h Darshaan—Sphinx (GER) Mr A. K. Collins
7 DIG DEEPER, 9, b g Seymour Hicks (FR)—Deep Foliage Mr Ian G. M. Dalgleish
8 DILLONS BRIDGE (IRE), 7, b g Le Bavard (FR)—Colour Clown Mrs A. R. Thompson
9 DOON RIDGE, 5, ch g Indian Ridge—Quisissanno Mr D. G. Rogers

MR J. J. O'NEILL—continued

10 **EAST HOUSTON**, 7, b g Reach—Patchinia **Highgreen Partnership**
11 **FRONT LINE**, 9, ch g High Line—Caroles Delight **Mr J. P. McManus**
12 **GENERAL CHAOS (IRE)**, 6, b g Taufan (USA)—Isa **Mr C. H. Stevens**
13 **GIVE BEST**, 5, ch g Dunbeath (USA)—Cold Line
14 **GRANDINARE (USA)**, 4, b br c El Gran Senor (USA)—Hail The Lady (USA) **Mr M. Tabor**
15 **HEY UP DOLLY (IRE)**, 4, b f Puissance—I Don't Mind **Mr A. Barry**
16 **IVY HOUSE (IRE)**, 8, b g Orchestra—Gracious View **Mrs L. R. Joughin**
17 **JENNIE'S PROSPECT**, 5, b g Rakaposhi King—Jennie Pat
18 **JIGGINSTOWN**, 9, b g Strong Gale—Galliano **Miss G. Joughin**
19 **JUST A GUESS (IRE)**, 5, ch g Classic Secret (USA)—Wild Justice **Mr P. G. Johnston**
20 **JUST ONE QUESTION (IRE)**, 6, b g Torus—Stormy Night **Anne Duchess of Westminster**
21 **JYMJAM JOHNNY (IRE)**, 7, b g Torus—Inventus **Mr Allan J. Schaverien**
22 **LORD OF THE WEST (IRE)**, 7, b g Mister Lord (USA)—Caroline's Girl **Anne Duchess of Westminster**
23 **LOVELY RASCAL**, 4, gr f Scallywag—Owen Belle **Mr S. S. G. Hayes**
24 **MAGSLAD**, 6, ch g Jumbo Hirt (USA)—Welsh Diamond **Mr David Alan Harrison**
25 **MAY DAY BELLE**, 5, gr m Scallywag—Owen Belle **Mr S. S. G. Hayes**
26 **NAUGHTY FUTURE**, 7, ch g Scallywag—Sea Rambler **Mr A. K. Collins**
27 **PRINCESS MAXINE (IRE)**, 7, b m Horage—Sallywell **Mr J. Clayton**
28 **RIVERDALE BOY (IRE)**, 6, b br g Mister Lord (USA)—Elgran Citizen **G. & P. Barker Ltd/Globe Engineering**
29 **ROSCOMMON JOE (IRE)**, 6, b g Simply Great (FR)—Kilvarnet **Mrs Carmel Sweeney**
30 **SEGALA (IRE)**, 5, b h Petorius—Cerosia **Mr F. S. Williams**
31 **SLIDEOFHILL (IRE)**, 7, ch g Le Bavard (FR)—Queen Weasel **Mr J. J. O'Neill**
32 **STEADFAST ELITE (IRE)**, 5, b m Glenstal (USA)—Etching **Mr J. Clayton**
33 **THUNDERHEART**, 5, b h Celestial Storm (USA)—Lorelene (FR) **Mr Ian G. M. Dalgleish**
34 **TIRA HEIGHTS (USA)**, 4, gr g Bering—Tira (FR) **Mr G. Tong**
35 **TO PROVE A POINT**, 4, b g Weldnaas (USA)—Run Little Lady (USA) **Mr J. J. O'Neill**
36 **TRONCHETTO (IRE)**, 7, b g Shernazar—Idle Days **Mr Ian G. M. Dalgleish**
37 **UNCLE KEENY (IRE)**, 6, b g Phardante (FR)—Honeyburn **Mr Richard Seed**
38 **VALLEY GARDEN**, 6, b g Valiyar—April **The Motley Crew**
39 **WAYUPHILL**, 9, b m Furry Glen—Queen Weasel **Mr D. Phelan**
40 **YOUNG ENDEAVOUR**, 4, b c Nashwan (USA)—Just Class **Mr E. Williams**
41 **ZUBOON (USA)**, 5, ch g The Minstrel (CAN)—Won't She Tell (USA) **Mr J. J. O'Neill**

THREE-YEAR-OLDS

42 **CRYSTAL FALLS (IRE)**, b r Alzao (USA)—Honourable Sheba (USA) **Mr C. H. Stevens**
43 **FINISTERRE (IRE)**, b g Salt Dome (USA)—Inisfail **Les Femmes Fatales**
44 **GLOBE RUNNER**, b c Adbass (USA)—Scenic Villa **G. & P. Barker Ltd/Globe Engineering**
45 **LARRYLUKEATHUGH**, b g Prince Sabo—Hidden Asset **Mr J. Clayton**
46 **RATTLE**, b g Mazilier (USA)—Snake Song **Miss G. Joughin**
47 **SHE'S SIMPLY GREAT (IRE)**, b f Simply Great (FR)—Petrine (IRE) **Mr Peter Mayo**
48 **WHAT JIM WANTS (IRE)**, b g Magical Strike (USA)—Sally Gone (IRE) **Mr J. Clayton**

TWO-YEAR-OLDS

49 **BARACHOIS LAD**, b c Nomination—Barachois Princess (USA) (Barachois (CAN)) **Mr J. D. Graham**
50 **FATHER EDDIE**, b c Aragon—Lady Philippa (IRE) (Taufan (USA)) **Mr C. H. Stevens**
51 **NIGHT FLIGHT**, gr c Night Shift (USA)—Ancestry (Persepolis (FR)) **Mr C. H. Stevens**
52 **TOP OF THE WIND (IRE)**, b f 28/4 Silver Kite (USA)—Domino's Nurse **Mr Jim McGrath**
53 **WAGGA MOON (IRE)**, b c Mac's Imp (USA)—Faapette (Runnett) **Mr C. H. Stevens**

Other Owners: Dr Linda Barber, Mr J. Bigley, Mr Graeme Butterworth, Mr J. R. Chambers, Mrs A. Chapman, Mr J. Gibbons, Mrs Judy Hunt, Mr Paddy Hunt, Mr A. B. Jamieson, Mrs Hilary Kerr, Mr R. P. McNaught, Mr R. Mentha, Mr C. J. Murphy, Mrs Mavis Murphy, Mr J. P. Nolan, Mr A. L. Orritt, Mr A. Parkinson, Mrs Agnes Parkinson, Mr Brian Robb, Mr G. Gary Salters, Mrs Maralyn Seed, Mrs D. Singleton, Mr John Singleton, Mr S. Stirling, My Cyril Taylor, Mr Ronald Taylor, Top Of The North Racing Club, Mr Derek Wilson, Mr K. Wilson.

Jockey (NH): Mark Dwyer (w.a.).

Conditional: R McGrath, A Roche.

Amateur: Mr L Corcorum.

Lady Rider: Miss Sarah Kerswell.

466   MR O. O'NEILL, Cheltenham

Postal: **Cleeve Lodge, Cleeve Hill, Cheltenham, Glos, GL52 3PW.**

Phone: **(01242) 673275**

1 **B MY LOVELY**, 6, ch m Gunner B—Poets Day **Mr Michael J. Brown**
2 **BOOLAVOGUE (IRE)**, 6, b m Torus—Easter Beauty **Mr Noel Murphy**
3 **CARLINGFORD LIGHTS (IRE)**, 8, ch g Carlingford Castle—Chinese Queen **Mr John Murray**
4 **CRUSTYGUN**, 6, b g Gunner B—Lady Crusty **Mr O. O'Neill**
5 **IMPECCABLE TIMING**, 13, ch g Paddy's Stream—Wynchy Comby **Mrs C. Mitchell**
6 **KATIE'S JOKER**, 10, b g Idiot's Delight—Roller Skate **Mr J. Russell**
7 **LEGUARD EXPRESS (IRE)**, 8, b g Double Schwartz—All Moss **Mr John C. Gilbert**
8 **STEVEADON**, 10, b g Don—Littoral **Miss H. Smith**
9 **WEST ORIENT**, 11, b g Strong Gale—Bean Giolla **Mrs H. Stewart**

Other Owners: Mrs M. Millar, Mrs L. J. O'Neill.

Jockey (Flat): J V Slattery (8-6).

Jockey (NH): J V Slattery (10-0).

Amateur: Mr A Mitchell (9-12).

467   MR J. G. M. O'SHEA, Redditch

Postal: **14 Romsley Close, Winyates East, Redditch, Worcs, B98 0PS.**

Phone: **(01527) 522480 MOBILE (0973) 459551**

1 **BIG PAT**, 7, b g Backchat (USA)—Fallonetta **Mr Gary Roberts**
2 **BOLTROSE**, 6, b g Electric—Garnette Rose **Mr Gary Roberts & V & T Associates**
3 **BOOK OF DREAMS (IRE)**, 8, b g Mandalus—Hare Path **Mrs B. J. Lockhart**
4 **BYE-BYE**, 4, ch f Superlative—Breakaway **Sean Murphy**
5 **CAPE COLONY**, 4, b g Dominion—Valiancy **Patrick Kelly**
6 **CHIEF GALE (IRE)**, 4, b g Strong Gale—Distant Lady **T. G. K. Construction Ltd**
7 4, B g Almutanabbi—Come On Clover **Mrs B. J. Lockhart**
8 **FLUIDITY (USA)**, 8, b g Robellino (USA)—Maple River (USA) **Patrick Kelly**
9 **GESNERA**, 8, br m Rusticaro (FR)—Joie d'Or (FR) **Mr V. M. Biggs**
10 **GO BALLISTIC**, 7, br g Celtic Cone—National Clover **Mrs B. J. Lockhart**
11 **GOVERNOR DANIEL**, 5, b g Governor General—Princess Semele **Mr Patrick Kelly**
12 **HERBALLISTIC**, 4, ch f Rolfe (USA)—National Clover **Mrs B. J. Lockhart**
13 **ISLAND VISION (IRE)**, 6, b g Vision (USA)—Verandah **Fumel Securities**
14 **LOUGH KENT (IRE)**, 8, b g Floriferous—Fancy Ride **T. G. K. Construction Ltd**
15 **MESP (IRE)**, 5, br m Strong Gale—Queenie Kelly **McMahon (Contractors Services) Ltd**
16 **RAINBOW WALK (IRE)**, 6, ch g Rainbow Quest (USA)—Widows Walk **T. G. K. Construction Ltd**
17 **RED VALERIAN**, 5, b g Robellino (USA)—Fleur Rouge **Mrs Alurie O'Sullivan**
18 **SHAHIK (USA)**, 6, b g Spectacular Bid (USA)—Sham Street (USA) **Mr S. Hunter**
19 **SPRING LOADED**, 5, b g Last Tycoon—Time For Romance **Mr J. P. McGowan**
20 **THOMAS SUPREME (IRE)**, 5, b g Supreme Leader—Ardmelard **T. G. K. Construction Ltd**
21 **TRADE WIND**, 5, b g Rambo Dancer (CAN)—Cadasi **Fumel Securities**
22 **TRUMPET**, 7, ch g Dominion—Soprano **Mr Costas Andreou**
23 **VIRIDIAN**, 11, b g Green Shoon—Cahermone Ivy **Patrick Moriarty**
24 **WAAZA (USA)**, 7, b g Danzig Connection (USA)—Nishig (USA) **Mr Peter Hughes**

MR J. G. M. O'SHEA—continued

THREE-YEAR-OLDS

25 B g Little Wolf—Come On Clover **Mrs B. J. Lockhart**
26 B g Jupiter Island—Princess Semele **Patrick Kelly**
27 ROUSHAN, ch c Anshan—Fleur Rouge **Mr R. J. Cummings**
28 B g Jupiter Island—The Mount **Patrick Kelly**

Jockeys (NH): M A Fitzgerald (10-0), A P McCoy (10-0).

Conditional: S Quiltey.

468   MR EUGENE M. O'SULLIVAN, Mallow

Postal: **Brittas, Lombardstown, Mallow, Co. Cork.**

Phone: **(022) 47116/47304**

 1 ANJLORE (IRE), 5, ch m Ore—Beyond It **Helen Taylor**
 2 ANOTHER CRACKER (IRE), 7, ch g Over The River (FR)—Bob's Hansel **Into The Brook R.S.**
 3 ANOTHER EXCUSE (IRE), 8, br g Mandalus—Alan's Rosalinda **Kilshannig R. S.**
 4 AS THINGS GO (IRE), 5, b g Asir—Wind Chimes **Limal Syndicate**
 5 BALLYHEST FOUNTAIN (IRE), 5, b m Royal Fountain—Ride The Waves **D. O'Reilly**
 6 BIT OF A CITIZEN (IRE), 5, b m Henbit (USA)—Boreen Citizen **E. J. O'Sullivan**
 7 BOSS MORTON (IRE), 5, b g Tremblant—Sandy Kelly **M. C. O'Sullivan**
 8 BROOK QUEEN (IRE), 7, b m Lafontaine (USA)—Nelly Don **T. O'Donnell**
 9 CITIZEN LEVEE, 10, b m Monksfield—Imperial Levee **E. J. O'Sullivan**
10 EARL OF MIRTH (IRE), 6, ch g Lord Ha Ha—Magic Deer **D. O'Reilly**
11 EASTFIELDS (IRE), 6, ch m Clearly Bust—Southfields **Charles P. Doyle**
12 EASY RUN (IRE), 8, ch m Deep Run—Skelmorlie **E. J. O'Sullivan**
13 FINNOW THYNE (IRE), 6, br g Good Thyne (USA)—Mother Cluck **Ivor Dulohery**
14 HAY DANCE, 5, b g Shareef Dancer (USA)—Hay Reef **Fiona O'Sullivan**
15 JACK'S WELL (IRE), 5, b g Henbit (USA)—Julias Well **John G. Linehan**
16 4, B g Supreme Leader—Kelenem **E. J. O'Sullivan**
17 LOVELY CITIZEN, 13, b g Golden Love—Kelenem **E. J. O'Sullivan**
18 MARIANNE'S CITIZEN (IRE), 6, b m Black Minstrel—Kelenem **E. J. O'Sullivan**
19 MAYPOLE FOUNTAIN (IRE), 6, br g Royal Fountain—Maypole Gayle
20 4, Br g Royal Fountain—Orangery **Fiona O'Sullivan**
21 RIVERDALE EXPRESS (IRE), 6, b g Clearly Bust—Ligarde **William O'Sullivan**
22 SAM VAUGHAN (IRE), 7, ch g Milk of The Barley—Kentstown Girl **Maura Moylan**
23 SPINNING MELODY (IRE), 5, b m Tremblant—Alan's Rosalinda **Mrs E. Meehan**
24 SPIRIT OF A KING (IRE), 5, b g King's Ride—Autumn Spirit **Limal Syndicate**
25 STOLBRYN GLEN (IRE), 8, gr g Parole—Glen Pearl **Fiona O'Sullivan**
26 STRONG CHERRY, 10, b m Strong Gale—Abbey Leaf **Helen Taylor**
27 TOOTH PICK (IRE), 6, b g Milk of The Barley—Kentstown Girl **Cormal R. S.**

Other Owners: Mr Denis A. Linehan, M. Madden, C. Meehan, D. N. O'Brien.

Jockey (Flat): D G O'Shea (7-0).

Jockey (NH): James Jones (9-7).

Amateurs: Brendan O'Sullivan (9-7),

Lady Rider: Fiona O'Sullivan (9-7).

469 MR R. J. O'SULLIVAN, Whitcombe

Postal: **Tithe Barn Cottage, Whitcombe Manor Racing Stables, Whitcombe, Dorchester, Dorset, DT2 8NY.**

Phone: **(01305) 267369**

1 **AGWA**, 7, b g Local Suitor (USA)—Meissarah (USA) **Mr I. A. Baker**
2 **AL SHAATI (FR)**, 6, b m Lead On Time (USA)—With You All **Mrs R. J. Doorgachurn**
3 **CRYSTAL HEIGHTS (FR)**, 8, ch g Crystal Glitters (USA)—Fahrenheit **Mr Jack Joseph**
4 **DANTEAN**, 4, b g Warning—Danthonia (USA) **Mr R. J. O'Sullivan**
5 **DIGPAST (IRE)**, 6, ch g Digamist (USA)—Starlit Way **Mr R. J. O'Sullivan**
6 **DINNER AT EIGHT**, 6, b g Slip Anchor—Periquito (USA) **Mr M. T. Bevan**
7 **DOCTOOR (USA)**, 6, ch g Cozzene (USA)—To The Top (USA) **Mr Alfred Walls**
8 **DUTOSKY**, 6, b m Doulab (USA)—Butosky **Mr D. A. Johnson**
9 **EL VOLADOR**, 9, br g Beldale Flutter (USA)—Pharjoy (FR) **Mr A. A. J. Peirce**
10 **HARLEQUIN WALK (IRE)**, 5, ch m Pennine Walk—Taniokey **Mr D. A. Johnson**
11 **IKHTIRAA (USA)**, 6, b g Imperial Falcon (CAN)—True Native (USA) **Mr I. Kerman**
12 **JOVIAL MAN (IRE)**, 7, b g Ela-Mana-Mou—Jovial Josie (USA) **Mrs Barbara Marchant**
13 **LA PETITE FUSEE**, 5, br m Cigar—Little Missile **Mr M. Bevan, Mr P. W. Saunders**
14 **LITTLE MISS RIBOT**, 6, b m Lighter—Little Missile **Mr Christopher Lane**
15 **MASNUN (USA)**, 11, gr g Nureyev (USA)—Careless Kitten (USA)
16 **PEE TEE CEE (IRE)**, 5, b g Broken Hearted—Lady Petrushka **Mr P. Trant**
17 **POLO KIT (IRE)**, 5, b g Trempolino (USA)—Nikitina **Mr M. J. Marchant**
18 **READY TO DRAW (IRE)**, 7, ch g On Your Mark—Mitsubishi Art **Mr A. Walls**
19 **SCOTONI**, 10, ch g Final Straw—Damyia (FR) **D. G. & D. J. Robinson**
20 **SIR NORMAN HOLT (IRE)**, 7, b g Ela-Mana-Mou—Ploy **Mr Jack Joseph**
21 **STRIDING EDGE**, 11, ch g Viking (USA)—Kospia **Mr Christopher Lane**
22 **TACHYCARDIA**, 4, ch f Weldnaas (USA)—Gold Ducat **Mr J. Bury**
23 **UNITED FRONT**, 4, br g Be My Chief (USA)—Julia Flyte **Mr T. Beresford**
24 **VOLUNTEER (IRE)**, 4, b g Midyan (USA)—Sistabelle **Mr M. J. Marchant**
25 **WILKINS**, 7, b g Master Willie—Segos **Mr Fred Honour**

Other Owners: Mr Michael R. Jaye, Mrs Virginia Malby, Mr K. Ovenden, Mr I. W. Page, Miss Deborah Penfold, Mr Bert Powis, Mr A. P. Sotiriou.

Amateur: K Santana (9-2).

470 MRS S. M. ODELL, Chipping Norton

Postal: **Little Brook House, Little Tew, Chipping Norton, Oxon, OX7 4JJ.**

1 **RYTON RUN**, 11, b g Deep Run—Money Spinner **Mr W. J. Odell**
2 **TOSS THE DICE**, 7, ch g Risk Me (FR)—Curfew **Mr W. J. Odell**

471 MR M. B. OGLE, Buckfastleigh

Postal: **Skerraton, Buckfastleigh, Devon, TQ11 0NB.**

Phone: **TEL: (01364) 642232 FAX (01364) 644282**

1 **CARROT BAY**, 10, b g Spitsbergen—Gold Harp **Mr M. B. Ogle**
2 **MALORY'S MISTAKE**, 6, ch m Right Regent—Lady Guinevere **Mr M. B. Ogle**
3 **WISE FLORIZEL**, 7, b g Right Regent—Sage Mountain **Mr M. B. Ogle**

472   MR J. A. B. OLD, Wroughton

Postal: **Upper Herdswick Farm, Hackpen, Burderop, Wroughton, SN1 0RH.**

Phone: **(01793) 845200 (OFFICE) CAR (0836) 721459 FAX (07193) 845201**

1 **ARFER MOLE (IRE)**, 8, b g Carlingford Castle—Sharpaway **Mr W. E. Sturt**
2 **ARKLEY ROYAL**, 5, b g Ardross—Lady Geneva **Mr John Bickel**
3 **BACKGAMMON**, 5, b g Midyan (USA)—Messaria **Mr W. E. Sturt**
4 **BOXGROVE MAN (IRE)**, 6, br g Mandalus—Kittykelvin **Sir Andrew Lloyd Webber**
5 **BRAVE EDWIN (IRE)**, 6, ch h Le Bavard (FR)—Peace Run **Mr W. E. Sturt**
6 **BUDDY HOLLY (NZ)**, 11, b g Leader of The Band (USA)—Annie Day (NZ) **Mr J. A. B. Old**
7 **CAPTAIN WALTER (IRE)**, 6, b h Supreme Leader—Deep Captain **Mr W. E. Sturt**
8 **CHAI-YO**, 6, b h Rakaposhi King—Ballysax Lass **Mr Nick Viney**
9 **COLLIER BAY**, 6, b g Green Desert (USA)—Cockatoo Island **Mr W. E. Sturt**
10 **CORRARDER**, 12, ch g True Song—Craig Maigy **Mrs E. T. Smyth-Osbourne**
11 **DANGEROUS GUEST (IRE)**, 4, b g Deploy—Guest List
12 **EL FREDDIE**, 6, b g El Conquistador—Unto Rose **Mrs Alison Smith**
13 **FRYS NO FOOL**, 6, b g Idiot's Delight—Scotch And Ice **Mr R. P. Fry**
14 **HARLEQUIN CHORUS**, 6, ch g Jester—Raise The Dawn **Harlequin Software Consultants Ltd**
15 **HARRY THE HORSE**, 8, ch g Capricorn Line—Laureppa **Mr J. L. Eddis**
16 **HOCANTELL**, 5, b m Primitive Rising (USA)—Princess Nora **Mrs K. B. Elliott**
17 **JEFFERIES**, 7, br g Sunyboy—Scotch Princess **Miss S. Blumberg**
18 **KATREE RUNNER**, 7, b g Scorpio (FR)—Last Run **Mr L. J. Fulford**
19 **KILLONE ABBOT (IRE)**, 7, ch g The Parson—Outdoor Girl **Lady Lloyd Webber**
20 **LAKE TEEREEN**, 11, ch g Callernish—Gusserane Lark **Mrs A. T. Grantham**
21 **MANDALAY**, 7, b g Mandalus—Hurricane Hattie **The Auld Alliance**
22 5, B m Town And Country—Mearlin **Mr J. A. B. Old**
23 5, Ch g Gildoran—Milltown Lady **Mr J. A. B. Old**
24 **MOLE BOARD**, 14, br g Deep Run—Sharpaway **Mr W. E. Sturt**
25 **PETE THE PARSON (IRE)**, 7, b g The Parson—Gemelek **Mr W. E. Sturt**
26 **PLASTIC SPACEAGE**, 13, b g The Parson—Chestnut Fire **Spaceage Plastics Limited**
27 **RED LIGHTER**, 7, ch g Lighter—Miss Redlands **Mr C. H. Antrobus**
28 **RIVER ISLAND (USA)**, 8, b g Spend A Buck (USA)—Promising Risk (USA) **The White Harte Partnership**
29 **SAND-DOLLAR**, 13, ch g Persian Bold—Late Spring **Mr R. P. Fry**
30 5, B g Rakaposhi King—Sayshar **Mr J. A. B. Old**
31 **SEATON**, 6, b m Town And Country—Sea Spice **Miss C. Foster**
32 **SIMPSON**, 11, ch g Royal Match—Black Penny **Mr K. R. Britten**
33 **SOOTHFAST (USA)**, 7, b g Riverman (USA)—Sookera (USA) **Mr W. E. Sturt**
34 **SPACEAGE GOLD**, 7, b g Sunyboy—Chancer's Last **Spaceage Plastics Limited**
35 **SPLINT**, 6, b g Relkino—Chancer's Last **Count K. Goess-Saurau**
36 **SUPREME GENOTIN (IRE)**, 7, b g Supreme Leader—Inagh's Image **Mr W. E. Sturt**
37 **THERMAL WARRIOR**, 8, ch g Leading Man—Quelles Amours **The Kentish Men**
38 6, B g Rakaposhi King—Thevicarsdaughter **Mr J. A. B. Old**
39 **THIRTY BELOW (IRE)**, 6, b g Strong Gale—Arctic Bavard
40 **THREE FARTHINGS**, 6, b g Derring Rose—Black Penny
41 **UPHAM SURPRISE**, 8, b g Sula Bula—Upham Lady **Mr J. A. B. Old**
42 **VIRBAZAR (FR)**, 9, br g Grandchant (FR)—Ortie II (FR) **Mrs E. T. Smyth-Osbourne**
43 **WISE KING**, 6, b g Rakaposhi King—Sunwise **Mr J. A. B. Old**
44 **WRECKLESS MAN**, 9, br g Mandalus—Wreck-Em-All **Mrs Anne-Marie Dartnall**
45 **YAHMI (IRE)**, 6, b g Law Society (USA)—Hogan's Sister (USA) **Mr W. E. Sturt**

Other Owners: Mr Charles Arkwright, Mr M. G. A. Court, Mrs C. R. Davison, Mr Roger M. Day, Mr A. Down, Mrs R. W. Farrant, Mr Richard C. Finch, Ms V. Franklin, Mrs K. Fulford, Mr C. F. Hacking, Mr Chris Jenkins, Mr H. B. Lowe, Mr C. J. Oakley, Ms S. A. Patrick, Mr Jan Rieck, Mr J. M. Sage, Mr Richard P. Smith, Mr Adrian Spooner, Mr D. Swan, Mr D. F. Turner, Mr C. M. Wilson, Mr W. Osborne Young.

Jockeys (NH): T Grantham (10-0), C Llewellyn (10-0, w.a.).

Conditional: David Creech (10-0).

Amateurs: Mr G Baines (9-7), Mr J Smyth-Osborne.

473   MR G. R. OLDROYD, York

Postal: **Common Farm, Upper Hemsley, York, YO4 1JX.**

Phone: **(01759) 373007**

1 **ANTARTICTERN (USA)**, 6, b g Arctic Tern (USA)—False Image (USA) **Mr J. F. Wright**
2 **BOLD JOKER**, 5, b g Jester—Bold Difference **Mr T. H. Morris**
3 **FLYING FREDDIE**, 5, b g Idiot's Delight—Bay Jade **Mr J. F. Wright**
4 **HORTON LADY**, 4, b f Midyan (USA)—Mohibbah (USA) **Mr M. Burrowes**
5 **KAGRAM QUEEN**, 8, b m Prince Ragusa—Arodstown Alice **Mr Robert E. Cook**
6 **LOOK AT ME**, 6, b g Kris—With Distinction (USA) **Mr Robert E. Cook**
7 **MANADEL**, 6, b m Governor General—Manabel **Mr P. Currey**
8 **MASTER GLEN**, 8, ch g Rabdan—Rage Glen **Mr Robert E. Cook**
9 **MU-ARRIK**, 8, b br h Aragon—Maravilla **Mr C. Raine**
10 **RUBY PLUS**, 5, b m Energy Plus—Irish Grace **Mrs D. Morris**
11 **STYLISH GENT**, 9, br g Vitiges (FR)—Squire's Daughter **Mr Robert E. Cook**

THREE-YEAR-OLDS

12 B f Rambo Dancer (CAN)—Andbracket **Mr W. B. Imison**
13 **DISPOL CONQUEROR (IRE)**, b c Conquering Hero (USA)—Country Niece **Mr W. B. Imison**
14 **DISPOL DUCHESS**, b f Rock City—Antum **Mr W. B. Imison**
15 B f Sharpo—Fabulous Rina (FR) **Mr W. B. Imison**
16 B g Risk Me (FR)—Gemma Kaye **Mr W. B. Imison**
17 **MYBOTYE**, br c Rambo Dancer (CAN)—Sigh **Mr Anthony Moroney**
18 **TOTALLY DIFFERENT**, b c Totem (USA)—Bold Difference **Mr T. H. Morris**
19 B f Jendali (USA)—Welsh Fashion **Mr W. B. Imison**

TWO-YEAR-OLDS

20 B f 24/4 Archway (IRE)—Golden Room (African Sky) **Mr E. B. Gale**
21 **THE WRIGHTONE (IRE)**, b f 23/4 Fayruz—Vote Barolo (Nebbiolo) **Mr C. Wright**
22 B br f 26/3 Fools Holme (USA)—Thornbeam (Beldale Flutter (USA)) **Mr J. Swailes**

Other Owners: Mrs G. M. Cook, Mr Paul L. Hudson, Mr Trevor Swailes.

Apprentice: A P Colgan (8-2).

Conditional: P Midgley (10-7).

Amateur: Mr Simon Walker (9-3).

474   MR H. J. OLIVER, Cheltenham

Postal: **Hunters Moon, Dixton, Cheltenham, Glos, GL52 4RB.**

Phone: **(01242) 679330   FAX (01242) 679330**

1 **A FEW DOLLARS MORE (IRE)**, 6, ch g Tremblant—Spanish Natalie **The T. O. O. O. E. Partnership**
2 **COSMIC FORCE (NZ)**, 12, b g Diagramatic (USA)—Cosmic Lass (NZ) **Ms J. M. Oliver**
3 4, B g Rashar (USA)—Densidal **Mr T. N. Siviter**
4 **FAIRY PARK**, 11, ch g Don—Laricina **Ms J. M. Oliver**
5 **IRISH WILDCARD (NZ)**, 8, b h Lyphard's Trick (USA)—Courageous Mahony (NZ) **Mr A. J. Baker**
6 **KING'S SHILLING (USA)**, 9, b g Fit To Fight (USA)—Pride's Crossing (USA) **Mr Keith M. Pinfield**
7 **MY SHENANDOAH (IRE)**, 5, br g Derrylin—Edwina's Dawn **Ms J. M. Oliver**
8 **NOT GUILTY (IRE)**, 4, b g Electric—Just Darina **Mrs J. M. Oliver**
9 **RIO DANCER (IRE)**, 7, b m Where To Dance (USA)—Rio Dulce **The Samurai Partnership**
10 **SILVER SUMAL**, 7, gr g Rymer—Heron's Mirage **Mr M. K. Penny**
11 **SUPER SHARP (NZ)**, 8, ch g Brilliant Invader (AUS)—Aspen Anne (NZ) **Mr M. K. Penny**
12 **THE CAMPDONIAN (IRE)**, 5, ch g Clearly Bust—Not At All **Mr P. J. R. Gardner**
13 **VISION OF LIGHT**, 6, gr m Lighter—Heron's Mirage **Mr M. K. Penny**

MR H. J. OLIVER—continued

THREE-YEAR-OLDS

14 RAPID LINER, b c Skyliner—Stellaris **Mr D. Broderick**

Other Owners: Mrs Verity Baldus, Mr N. Brookes, Mr Rob Brown, Mr P. J. R. Gardner, Mr D. A. Gascoigne, Mr Peter Gormley, Mr Ivor Potter.

Jockeys (NH): J Oliver (10-0), V Slattery (10-0).

Amateur: Mr N H Oliver (9-7).

475   MR J. K. M. OLIVER, Hawick

Postal: **Hassendean Bank, Hawick, Roxburghshire, TD9 8RX.**
Phone: **(01450) 870216 MOBILE (0374) 426017 FAX (01450) 870357**

1 ARCTIC SANDY (IRE), 6, ch g Sandalay—Reach Here **Mr Raymond Anderson Green**
2 BLUE SMOKE (IRE), 4, b c Posen (USA)—Raubritter **Mrs P. M. Guild**
3 BULA NUDAY, 11, b g Prince Regent (FR)—Arctic Free **Colonel D. C. Greig**
4 EVENING DUSK (IRE), 4, b f Phardante (FR)—Red Dusk **Mr J. K. M. Oliver**
5 FOXILAW, 7, ch m Alias Smith (USA)—Kippie Knowe **Mr J. K. M. Oliver**
6 GOLDEN FIDDLE (IRE), 8, b g Strong Gale—Belle Mackay **Mr W. Stuart Wilson**
7 HOWCLEUCH, 9, b m Buckskin (FR)—Swiftly Belle **The Howcleuch Partnership**
8 5, B m Mandalus—Mossfield **Mr J. K. M. Oliver**
9 SANDY ANDY, 10, ch g Sandalay—Fort Etna **Mr T. J. Summerfield**
10 T O O MAMMA'S (IRE), 5, ch m Classic Secret (USA)—Bohemian Rhapsody **Mr J. Berry**

TWO-YEAR-OLDS

11 Ch g 6/3 Be My Native (USA)—Phantom Thistle (Deep Run) **Mr J. K. M. Oliver**
12 B f 3/6 Phardante (FR)—Red Dusk (Deep Run) **Mr J. K. M. Oliver**

Other Owners: Miss L. M. Gold, Mr J. B. Richardson, Mr E. Rodgers, Mr P. R. Walker.

Jockeys (NH): T Reed (10-5), B Storey (w.a.).

Lady Rider: Miss Sandra Forster (10-0).

476   MRS F. M. OWEN, Rugeley

Postal: **Brick Kiln Farm, Hood Lane, Armitage, Rugeley, WS15 4AG.**
Phone: **(01543) 490320**

1 FION CORN, 9, br g Monsanto (FR)—Lady of Wales **Mrs Margaret Park**
2 LAWNSWOOD LADY, 4, b f Lochnager—Keep Cool (FR) **Mrs Margaret Park**
3 RAVENSPUR (IRE), 6, b g Reference Point—Royal Nugget (USA) **Mrs Margaret Park**
4 ROYALE CAMERON, 5, b g Saunter—Royale Gardner **Mrs Margaret Park**
5 SAUCY ISLA, 5, b m Devil To Play—Saucy Alice **Mrs Margaret Park**

477 MR EDWARD H OWEN JUN, Denbigh

Postal: **Y Wern, Llandyrnog, Denbigh, Clwyd, LL16 4HW.**

Phone: **LLANDYRNOG (01824) 790264**

1 **BOADICEA'S CHARIOT**, 9, b m Commanche Run—Indigine (USA) **Mrs F. Williams**
2 **FAST CRUISE**, 11, b m Cruise Missile—Speeder **Miss Tina Patel**
3 **INCEY WINCEY**, 4, b f Idiot's Delight—Muffet's Spider **Mrs Julia Owen**
4 **LIBRETTIST (IRE)**, 5, b m Black Minstrel—Novelist **Mrs S. M. Shone**
5 **MERRY NOELLE**, 6, b m Scorpio (FR)—Merry Jane **Mrs D. G. Scott**
6 **MISS BROWN**, 8, b m Relkino—Gadabout **Mr John A. Owen**
7 **THE LADY LETTY**, 8, ch m Cruise Missile—Plush **Mrs S. M. Shone**

THREE-YEAR-OLDS

8 **PAPER MAZE**, b f Mazilier (USA)—Westone Paperchase (USA) **Mrs F. Williams**

478 MR JOHN M. OXX, Kildare

Postal: **Creeve, Currabeg, Kildare, Ireland.**

Phone: **0455 521310 FAX 0455 522236**

1 **APPROVANCE (USA)**, 4, gr g With Approval (CAN)—Anniversary Wish (USA) **Sheikh Mohammed**
2 **TIMARIDA (IRE)**, 4, gr f Kalaglow—Triumphant **H. H. Aga Khan**
3 **TOM TOM (IRE)**, 4, b g Dancing Dissident—Ashanti **Miss E. M. & Mrs J. M. Oxx**

THREE-YEAR-OLDS

4 **AFARKA (IRE)**, b f Kahyasi—Afasara (IRE) **H. H. Aga Khan**
5 **ASMARA (USA)**, b f Lear Fan (USA)—Anaza **H. H. Aga Khan**
6 **AYLESBURY (IRE)**, ch c Lycius (USA)—Ayah (USA) **Sheikh Mohammed**
7 **AZINTER (IRE)**, b f Magical Strike (USA)—Madelon **Mrs C. Corballis**
8 **BAKIYA (USA)**, b f Trempolino (USA)—Banque Privee (USA) **H. H. Aga Khan**
9 **CASCATELLE BLEUE (IRE)**, b f Bluebird (USA)—Wuthering Falls **Mr R. Klaey**
10 **CHARLOCK (IRE)**, ch f Nureyev (USA)—Charmante (USA) **Sheikh Mohammed**
11 **DASHARAN (IRE)**, b c Shahrastani (USA)—Delsy (FR) **H. H. Aga Khan**
12 **DEYNAWARI (IRE)**, b c Doyoun—Denizliya (IRE) **H. H. Aga Khan**
13 **DISSIDENT PRINCE (IRE)**, b c Dancing Dissident—What A Candy (USA) **J. F. Malle**
14 **ESCHASSE (USA)**, ch f Zilzal (USA)—Skating **Sheikh Mohammed**
15 **EZANAK (IRE)**, b c Darshaan—Ezana **H. H. Aga Khan**
16 **GRIEF (IRE)**, ch g Broken Hearted—Crecora **Dundalk Racing Club**
17 **HARGHAR (USA)**, gr c El Gran Senor (USA)—Harouniya **H. H. Aga Khan**
18 **HISAR (IRE)**, br c Doyoun—Himaya (IRE) **H. H. Aga Khan**
19 **KARAKAM (IRE)**, ch c Rainbow Quest (USA)—Karaferya (USA) **H. H. Aga Khan**
20 **KASORA (IRE)**, b f Darshaan—Kozana **H. H. Aga Khan**
21 **KATIYSA (IRE)**, br f Doyoun—Katiyfa **H. H. Aga Khan**
22 **KERIALI (IRE)**, b c Irish River (FR)—Kerita **H. H. Aga Khan**
23 **KEY CHANGE (IRE)**, b f Darshaan—Kashka (USA) **Lady Clague**
24 **KHAIRAZ (IRE)**, gr c Kahyasi—Khairkana (IRE) **H. H. Aga Khan**
25 **KHALIKHOUM (IRE)**, b c Darshaan—Kahlisiyn **H. H. Aga Khan**
26 **KOHOUTEK**, b c Mtoto—Kalmia **Sheikh Mohammed**
27 **KUWAIT BAY (IRE)**, b c Mujtahid (USA)—Mexican Two Step **Mr Khaled D. S. Al-Sabah**
28 **LACINIA**, b f Groom Dancer (USA)—Pretty Lady **Sheikh Mohammed**
29 **MASAFIYA (IRE)**, b f Shernazar—Masarika **H. H. Aga Khan**
30 **MATANGI (IRE)**, b f Mtoto—Flawless Image (USA) **Skeikh Mohammed**
31 **MATSURI (IRE)**, b f Darshaan—Dance Festival **Sheikh Mohammed**
32 **MAZAMET (USA)**, b c Elmaamul (USA)—Miss Mazepah **Sheikh Mohammed**
33 **MERAWANG (IRE)**, b c Shahrastani (USA)—Modiyna **H. H. Aga Khan**
34 **MOONFIRE**, b f Sadler's Wells (USA)—Moon Cactus **Sheikh Mohammed**
35 **NOUKARI (IRE)**, b c Darshaan—Noufiyla **H. H. Aga Khan**
36 **OREJANA (IRE)**, b f Mujtahid (USA)—Madame du Barry (FR) **D. Hoefemeier**

MR JOHN M. OXX—continued

37 **ORIANE**, ch f Nashwan (USA)—Rappa Tap Tap (FR) **Lady Clague**
38 **POWER PLAY**, b c Nashwan (USA)—Game Plan **Sheikh Mohammed**
39 **PRAIRIE CHARM (IRE)**, b f Thatching—Prairie Venus (IRE) **Walter Vischer**
40 **PREDAPPIO**, b c Polish Precedent—Khalafiya **Sheikh Mohammed**
41 **RAIYOUN (IRE)**, b c Doyoun—Raymouna (IRE) **H. H. Aga Khan**
42 **RED ROBIN (IRE)**, b br c Bob Back (USA)—Toshair Flyer **Three Islands Syndicate**
43 **ROSE OF RAPTURE**, b f Old Vic—Romantic Age **Sheikh Mohammed**
44 **SAMAKAAN (IRE)**, b c Darshaan—Samarzana (USA) **H. H. Aga Khan**
45 **SANINKA (IRE)**, b br f Doyoun—Sanamia **H. H. Aga Khan**
46 **SARPADAR (IRE)**, b c Doyoun—Saraposa (IRE) **H. H. Aga Khan**
47 **SHADAPOUR (IRE)**, b c Doyoun—Shademah **H. H. Aga Khan**
48 **SHAMNEEZ (IRE)**, gr f Pharly (FR)—Shamiyda (USA) **H. H. Aga Khan**
49 **SHARAZAN (IRE)**, b c Akarad (FR)—Sharaniya (USA) **H. H. Aga Khan**
50 **SHARIYKA (IRE)**, b f Kahyasi—Shayraz **H. H. Aga Khan**
51 **SHERAKA (IRE)**, b f Doyoun—Sherzana **H. H. Aga Khan**
52 **SOCIALITE (IRE)**, b f Alzao (USA)—Merriment (USA) **J. P. Mangan**
53 **SOMMAR (IRE)**, br f Saumarez—Abha **Mr T. Wada**
54 **SUN BALLET (IRE)**, ch c In The Wings—Sunset Village (USA) **Sheikh Mohammed**
55 **SWEET TAVLA (IRE)**, b f Kendor (FR)—Tarlace **Mr T. Wada**
56 **SYMBOLI KILDARE (IRE)**, b c Kaldoun (FR)—Quiche **Mr T. Wada**
57 **TARAKHEL (USA)**, ch c Seattle Dancer (USA)—Tarafa **H. H. Aga Khan**
58 **TARQUINIA (IRE)**, b f In The Wings—Tarsila **Sheikh Mohammed**
59 **TARWARA (IRE)**, b f Dominion—Touraya **H. H. Aga Khan**
60 **TIKASHAR (IRE)**, b c Doyoun—Tikarna (FR) **H. H. Aga Khan**
61 **TIMIDJAR (IRE)**, b c Doyoun—Timissara (USA) **H. H. Aga Khan**
62 **WESTERN SEAS (IRE)**, b g Caerleon (USA)—My Potters (USA) **Lady Clague**
63 **WOODREN (USA)**, ch f Woodman (USA)—Whitethroat **Lady Clague**
64 **ZABARI (USA)**, b c Soviet Star (USA)—Zafadola (IRE) **Sheikh Mohammed**
65 **ZAFZALA (IRE)**, b f Kahyasi—Zerzaya **H. H. Aga Khan**
66 **ZAGREB FLYER**, b f Old Vic—Flying Clipper **Sheikh Mohammed**
67 **ZAYNAL (IRE)**, b c Shernazar—Zariya (USA) **H. H. Aga Khan**

TWO-YEAR-OLDS

68 **ALZARO (IRE)**, b c 25/4 Alzao (USA)—Merriment (USA) (Go Marching (USA)) **Mr J. P. Mangan**
69 B c 18/4 Seattle Dancer (USA)—Cielo's Love (USA) (Conquistador Cielo (USA)) **Sheikh Mohammed**
70 Ch f 20/3 Belmez (USA)—Crystal Bright (Bold Lad (IRE)) **Sheikh Mohammed**
71 B c 21/5 Top Ville—Cut Velvet (USA) (Northern Dancer) **Sheikh Mohammed**
72 **DABALI (IRE)**, b c 21/3 Doyoun—Dabiliya (Vayrann) **H. H. Aga Khan**
73 Ch f 7/3 Night Shift (USA)—Dabbing (USA) (Cure The Blues (USA)) **Lady Clague**
74 **DABTARA (IRE)**, b f 15/4 Kahyasi—Dabtiya (FR) (Shirley Heights) **H. H. Aga Khan**
75 Ch f 21/1 Lycius (USA)—Dance Date (IRE) (Sadler's Wells (USA)) **Lady Clague**
76 **DATHIYNA (IRE)**, b f 4/3 Kris—Dafayna (Habitat) **H. H. Aga Khan**
77 B c 26/3 Persian Bold—Equal Eloquence (USA) (Top Ville) **Lady Clague**
78 Br f 4/5 Be My Guest (USA)—Hazaradjat (IRE) (Darshaan) **H. H. Aga Khan**
79 **HAZARFEN (IRE)**, b c 28/4 Law Society (USA)—Hanzala (FR) (Akarad (FR)) **H. H. Aga Khan**
80 B f 4/4 Darshaan—Hebba (USA) (Nureyev (USA)) **Sheikh Mohammed**
81 B f 9/3 Danehill (USA)—Honey Buzzard (Sea Hawk II) **Mr T. Monaghan**
82 B c 15/5 Thatching—Isle of Glass (USA) (Affirmed (USA)) **Sheikh Mohammed**
83 B c 23/2 Shareef Dancer (USA)—Kalmia (Miller's Mate) **Sheikh Mohammed**
84 B f 6/5 Hansel (USA)—Katies First (USA) (Kris) **Sheikh Mohammed**
85 B f 23/4 Green Desert (USA)—Khanata (USA) (Riverman (USA)) **H. H. Aga Khan**
86 **KHARSHANI (IRE)**, gr c 14/2 Last Tycoon—Khalisiyn (Shakapour) **H. H. Aga Khan**
87 **LANCEA (IRE)**, ch f 10/1 Generous (IRE)—Knight's Baroness (Rainbow Quest (USA)) **Lady Clague**
88 B f 25/4 Shernazar—Marmana (Blushing Groom (FR)) **H. H. Aga Khan**
89 Ch c 6/5 Lycius (USA)—Most Amusing (Blushing Groom (FR)) **Sheikh Mohammed**
90 B c 29/1 Darshaan—My Potters (USA) (Irish River (FR)) **Lady Clague**
91 B f 15/5 Kenmare (FR)—Northern Chance (Northfields (USA)) **Lady Clague**
92 B c 7/3 Selkirk (USA)—Our Home (Habitat) **Sheikh Mohammed**
93 Ch f 13/5 Caerleon (USA)—Pebbles (Sharpen Up) **Sheikh Mohammed**
94 **PRAIRIE FLAME (IRE)**, b f 21/1 Marju (IRE)—Prairie Venus (GER) (Surumu (GER)) **Mr Walter Vischer**

EQUINE NUTRITIONAL CONSULTANCY

Helping Clients to Stay Lengths Ahead

Advisors to English and Irish Champion
Trainers and Leading Producers of
Thoroughbred Bloodstock

*While many companies are just trying to sell you
products – come to us for completely independent
advice on how to effectively maximise the benefits
of your feeding and supplemental programmes*

OUR REFERENCES AND THE CONSISTENT RESULTS OF OUR CLIENTS SPEAK FOR THEMSELVES

For more Information on how to join this elite group contact:
Pamela Kinslow BA MSc – ENC Limited – Jasmine Cottage,
East Garston, Berkshire UK RG17 7EX – Tel/Fax: 01488-648683

MR JOHN M. OXX—continued

95 B f 8/2 In The Wings—Pretoria (Habitat) **Sheikh Mohammed**
96 **RAYOUNI (IRE)**, b c 7/5 Zayyani—Raymouna (GER) (High Top) **H. H. Aga Khan**
97 B f 23/2 Generous (IRE)—Red Comes Up (USA) (Blushing Groom (FR)) **Lady Clague**
98 Ch c 15/5 Diesis—Royal Touch (Tap On Wood) **Sheikh Mohammed**
99 B f 30/4 Doyoun—Samarzana (USA) (Blushing Groom (FR)) **H. H. Aga Khan**
100 B f 22/5 Kahyasi—Saraposa (IRE) (Ahonoora) **H. H. Aga Khan**
101 **SHANTARINI (IRE)**, gr c 25/3 Pharly (FR)—Shanjarina (USA) (Blushing Groom (FR)) **H. H. Aga Khan**
102 B c 6/5 Nashwan (USA)—Sharka (Shareef Dancer (USA)) **Sheikh Mohammed**
103 **SHERIKYA (IRE)**, b f 16/5 Goldneyev (USA)—Sherzana (Great Nephew) **H. H. Aga Khan**
104 B c 16/3 Polish Precedent—Shy Princess (USA) (Irish River (FR)) **Sheikh Mohammed**
105 **SIRINNDI (IRE)**, b c 25/2 Shahrastani (USA)—Sinntara (IRE) (Lashkari) **H. H. Aga Khan**
106 **SOMERTON REEF**, gr c 15/3 Mystiko (USA)—Lady Reef (Mill Reef (USA)) **Mr B. Somerfield**
107 B c 13/2 In The Wings—Sunset Village (USA) (Spectacular Bid (USA)) **Sheikh Mohammed**
108 Br f 19/4 Doyoun—Touraya (Tap On Wood) **H. H. Aga Khan**
109 B f 19/2 In The Wings—Tribal Rite (Be My Native (USA)) **Mr S. Mullion**
110 B c 17/2 Slip Anchor—Welsh Dancer (Welsh Saint) **Lady Clague**
111 Gr f 14/4 Sadler's Wells (USA)—Zafadola (IRE) (Darshaan) **Sheikh Mohammed**

Jockeys (Flat): D Hogan (8-5), J P Murtagh (8-7), D G O'Shea (7-7).

Apprentices: J R Byrne (7-10), A F Egan (8-3), S O'Keeffe (7-10).

Lady Riders: Miss L Dykes (8-10), Miss L Robinson (8-9).

479   MR BRYN PALLING, Cowbridge

Postal: **Ty-wyth-newydd, Tredodridge, Cowbridge, South Glam, CF7 7UL.**

Phone: **COWBRIDGE (01446) 760122**

1 **ANITA'S CONTESSA (IRE)**, 4, b f Anita's Prince—Take More (GER) **Mrs Anita Quinn**
2 **BARON BRUCE**, 6, b g Green Ruby (USA)—Tender Manx **Mrs M. M. Palling**
3 **BOLD CYRANO (IRE)**, 5, b g Cyrano de Bergerac—Court Hussar **Millbrook Associates**
4 **CARRANITA (IRE)**, 6, b m Anita's Prince—Take More (GER) **Lamb Lane Associates**
5 **CHICKAWICKA (IRE)**, 5, b h Dance of Life (USA)—Shabby Doll **Mr Alan Davies**
6 **HAROLDON (IRE)**, 7, ch g Heraldiste (USA)—Cordon **Lamb Brook Associates**
7 **HAVANA MISS**, 4, b f Cigar—Miss Patdonna **Mrs L. Hedlund**
8 **HIGH CONCEPT (IRE)**, 4, b f Thatching—Keep The Thought (USA)
9 **I'LL SOON KNOW**, 9, ch m Known Fact (USA)—Soolyn
10 **JADY'S DREAM (IRE)**, 5, b m Dreams To Reality—Lemon Balm **Mr J. H. Davies & Mr M. G. Bridgeman**
11 **JAREER DO (IRE)**, 4, b f Jareer (USA)—Shining Bright (USA) **Mr A. L. Roberts**
12 **LAID BACK BEN**, 6, ch g Starch Reduced—Mrs Dumbfounded **Mr S. Sullivan**
13 **MR BERGERAC (IRE)**, 5, b g Cyrano de Bergerac—Makalu **Mr P. R. John**
14 **NOMINATION GOLD**, 6, b m Nomination—Sipapu **Mr A. L. Roberts**
15 **PACIFIC GIRL (IRE)**, 4, b f Emmson—Power Girl **Gill Salimeni**
16 **ROSE OF GLENN**, 5, b m Crofthall—May Kells **Mr K. M. Rideout**
17 **SUPER RITCHART**, 8, b g Starch Reduced—Karousa Girl **The Gradon Associates**
18 **WIZZO**, 6, b g Nicholas Bill—Ozra **Mr H. Weeks**

THREE-YEAR-OLDS

19 **BELLE'S BOY**, b c Nalchik (USA)—Ty-With-Belle **Mrs M. M. Palling**
20 **CROESO CYNNES**, ch f Most Welcome—Miss Taleca **Davies and Bridgeman**
21 **KOSSOLIAN**, b f Emarati (USA)—Cwm Deri (IRE) **Mr K. J. Mercer**
22 **NATATARL (IRE)**, ch f Roi Danzig (USA)—Little Me **Mr Alan Davies**
23 **QUINNTESSA**, ch f Risk Me (FR)—Nannie Annie **Arctic Partnership**
24 **SHANOORA (IRE)**, gr f Don't Forget Me—Shalara **Windsor Associates**
25 **TIME CLASH (IRE)**, b f Timeless Times (USA)—Ash Amour **Mrs D. J. Hughes**
26 **TYMEERA**, b f Timeless Times (USA)—Dear Glenda **Glenbrook Associates**

MR BRYN PALLING—continued
TWO-YEAR-OLDS

27 **CLASSIC SERVICES**, b c 24/5 Totem (USA)—Loving Doll (Godswalk (USA)) **Mrs D. J. Hughes**
28 B f 22/4 Anita's Prince—Diewitt (IRE) (Dara Monarch) **D. Brennan**
29 Ch f 24/2 Anshan—Heavenly Note (Chief Singer) **Mr A. Rhead**
30 B f 18/3 Forzando—Honeychurch (USA) (Bering) **Mr K. Mercer**
31 B f 8/2 Statoblest—La Pirouette (USA) (Kennedy Road (CAN))
32 B f 17/2 Mac's Imp (USA)—Morning Welcome (IRE) (Be My Guest (USA)) **D. Brennan**
33 Gr f 29/4 Good Times (ITY)—Ville Air (Town Crier) **Millbrook Association**
34 B f 30/3 Nalchik (USA)—Zoomar (Legend of France (USA)) **Mr John Hamilton Jones**

Other Owners: Mr D. Baker, Mr J. C. Bunyan, Mr G. Button, Mrs S. D. Button, Mr Huw Ceredig, Mr D. E. Crompton, Mr F. C. Crompton, Mr S. P. Crompton, Mr J. R. Davies, Mr Peter D. Davies, Mr Nigel B. Davis, Mr R. N. Edwards, Mr C. Evans, Mrs G. Gore, Mr Mike Hanley, Mr Anthony Howells, Mr Russell Lewis, Mr R. J. Maguire, Mrs S. Mercer, Mr K. L. Merriman, Mr David Reed, Mr G. W. Rees, Mr Ivor Rees, Mr P. A. Sutton, Mrs A. Taylor, Mr D. A. J. Thomas, Mr G. J. Thomas, Mrs K. Thomas, Mr P. J. Thomas, Mr M. A. Tilke, Mr E. B. Turner, Mrs Christine Weeks, Mr S. D. Williams, Mr Paul A. Young.

480 MR C. PARKER, Lockerbie

Postal: **Douglas Hall Farm, Lockerbie, Dumfriesshire, DG11 1AD.**
Phone: **(01576) 510232**

1 **BAREFOOT LANDING (USA)**, 5, b m Cozzene (USA)—River Flower (USA) **Mr M. C. MacKenzie**
2 **BOARDING SCHOOL**, 9, b g Glenstal (USA)—Amenity (FR) **Mr Raymond Anderson Green**
3 **CAITHNESS CLOUD**, 8, ch g Lomond (USA)—Moonscape **Mr Raymond Anderson Green**
4 **DOUBLE STANDARDS (IRE)**, 8, br g Entre Nous—Miss Minstrel VI **Mr Raymond Anderson Green**
5 **ISLAND RIVER (IRE)**, 8, ch g Over The River (FR)—Diana's Flyer **Jacksons Timber**
6 **JAUNTY GENERAL**, 5, b g Governor General—Ash Gayle **Mr E. Waugh**
7 **LIE DETECTOR**, 8, b g Nearly A Hand—Rose Ravine **Mr Raymond Anderson Green**
8 **LUPY MINSTREL**, 11, br g Black Minstrel—Lupreno **Mr Raymond Anderson Green**
9 **MASTER OF TROY**, 8, b g Trojan Fen—Gohar (USA) **Mr Chilton Fawcett**
10 **NEW CAPRICORN (USA)**, 6, ch g Green Forest (USA)—Size Six (USA) **Mr Raymond Anderson Green**
11 **PAPPA CHARLIE (USA)**, 5, b g Manila (USA)—Lassie's Lady (USA) **Mr Raymond Anderson Green**
12 **SANDRIFT**, 7, ch m Glint of Gold—Olivian **Mr Raymond Anderson Green**
13 **SHREWD THOUGHT (USA)**, 5, ch g Lyphard's Wish (FR)—Tamed Shrew (USA) **Mr Raymond Anderson Green**
14 **SNITTON LANE**, 10, b m Cruise Missile—Cala di Volpe **Mr Raymond Anderson Green**
15 **SOLBA (USA)**, 7, b g Solford (USA)—Pabapa **Mr Raymond Anderson Green**
16 **SPARKY GAYLE (IRE)**, 6, b g Strong Gale—Baybush **Mr Raymond Anderson Green**
17 **STORMY CORAL (IRE)**, 6, br g Strong Gale—Sciure (USA) **Mr Raymond Anderson Green**
18 **TRUMP**, 7, b g Last Tycoon—Fleeting Affair **Mr Raymond Anderson Green**

THREE-YEAR-OLDS

19 **COOL TACTICIAN**, gr c Petong—Thevetia **Mr E. Waugh**
20 **KEMO SABO**, b g Prince Sabo—Canoodle **Mr R. Nichol**
21 **NATURAL TALENT**, ch g Kris—Tropicaro (FR) **Mr Raymond Anderson Green**
22 **SHINEROLLA**, b g Thatching—Primrolla **Mr Raymond Anderson Green**

Other Owners: Mrs Anita Green, Mr Derrick Mossop, Mrs L. Mossop, Mr David A. Taglight, Mr J. Waugh.

Jockey (NH): Brian Storey.

Amateurs: Mr Andrew Parker (10-0), Mr David Parker (9-9).

Lady Rider: Miss Pauline Robson.

481   MR J. E. PARKES, Malton

Postal: **12 Whitewall Cottages, Norton, Malton, North Yorkshire, YO17 9EH.**

Phone: **(01653) 697570**

1 **ADALOALDO (USA)**, 4, ch g Arctic Tern (USA)—Alicia's Lady (USA) **Mr R. Flegg**
2 **ARECIBO (FR)**, 4, ch g Dancing Spree (USA)—Anahita (FR) **Mr W. A. Sellers**
3 4, Br f Buckskin (FR)—Hampton Grange **Mr Vince Dolan**
4 **HAUGHTON LAD (IRE)**, 7, b g Drumalis—I'm The Latest **Mr Vince Dolan**
5 **IJAB (CAN)**, 6, b g Ascot Knight (CAN)—Renounce (USA) **Mrs Lynn Parkes**
6 **KILNAMARTYRA GIRL**, 6, b m Arkan—Star Cove **Mr P. J. Cronin**
7 **LIAM'S LOSS (IRE)**, 7, ch g Denel (FR)—Karazend **Mr Niall Enright**
8 **LISNAVARAGH**, 9, b g Kemal (FR)—Weaver's Fool **Mrs C. Dolan**
9 **MILLTOWN CLASSIC (IRE)**, 4, b f Classic Secret (USA)—Houwara (IRE) **Mr J. Parkes**
10 **PIER THIRTY NINE**, 10, br g Torus—Mrs Optimistic **Mr Niall Enright**
11 **PUSH ON POLLY (IRE)**, 6, b m Salluceva—Brave Polly **Mr N. Finegan**
12 **QUEENSMEAD RULE (IRE)**, 6, b m Rhoman Rule (USA)—Stativa **Mr R. Flegg**
13 **SALINGER**, 8, b g Rousillon (USA)—Scholastika (GER) **Mr Vince Dolan**
14 **UNCLE BENJI (IRE)**, 7, b g Cataldi—Solfatara **Mr R. Flegg**

Other Owners: Mr P. Fiske.

Conditional: Raymond McCarthy (9-7).

482   MRS H. PARROTT, Mitcheldean

Postal: **Church Farm, Church Lane, Abenhall, Mitcheldean.**

Phone: **DEAN (01594) 542204 MOBILE (0860) 585876 FAX (01594) 544691**

1 **AMY'S BOY**, 7, ch g Stan Flashman—Blue Mist **Mr B. P. Moore**
2 **BRIGHT NOVEMBER**, 5, b g Niniski (USA)—Brigata **Mrs H. Parrott**
3 **CELTIC REG**, 6, ch g Celtic Cone—Another Molly **Mr T. J. Parrott**
4 **DARK ORCHARD (IRE)**, 5, b g Black Minstrel—Ballyheda's Love **Mr Colin Jones**
5 **FLAXLEY WOOD (IRE)**, 5, b br g Kambalda—Coolbawn Run **Mrs H. Parrott**
6 **KELLY'S FIDDLE**, 6, b m Netherkelly—Mayfield Monaveen **Mr T. J. Parrott**
7 **LOMAS (IRE)**, 5, b h Ela-Mana-Mou—Bold Miss **Mr T. J. Parrott**
8 **PILKINGTON (IRE)**, 6, b g Roselier (FR)—Little Bloom **Mr T. J. Parrott**

THREE-YEAR-OLDS

9 **KENNY DAVIS (IRE)**, b g Mazaad—Very Seldom **J. P. Group Limited**
10 **MAZILEO**, b g Mazilier (USA)—Embroglio (USA) **J. P. Group Limited**

Jockeys (Flat): T Sprake, J Williams (8-3).

Jockeys (NH): S Curran (9-7), L Harvey, P Hughes (10-0), D Leahy (9-7).

483   MISS R. J. PATMAN, Moreton-in-marsh

Postal: **Grove Farm, Chastleton, Moreton-in-marsh, Glos, GL56 0SZ.**

Phone: **(01608) 674492**

1 **FEARLESS HUSSAR**, 6, b g Fearless Action (USA)—Merebimur
2 **OUTFIELDER (IRE)**, 6, b g Mandalus—Prying Nell

Other Owners: Mr David M. Foster.

Jockey (NH): W Humphreys (10-0).

Amateur: Mr John Gallagher (10-4).

484 MR J. W. PAYNE, Newmarket

Postal: **Frankland Lodge, Hamilton Road, Newmarket, Suffolk, CB8 7JQ.**

Phone: **NEWMARKET (01638) 668675 FAX (01638) 668675 MOBILE (0850) 133116**

1 **AHLA**, 4, ch f Unfuwain (USA)—Rahik **Mr Marwan Tabsh**
2 **BASHFUL BRAVE**, 5, ch g Indian Ridge—Shy Dolly **Mrs G. M. Hay**
3 **GLEN MILLER**, 6, b g Music Boy—Blakeney Sound **Mr Marwan Tabsh**
4 **MAMLOUK**, 4, gr g Distant Relative—Nelly Do Da **Mr Gordon Smyth**
5 **RACING TELEGRAPH**, 6, b g Claude Monet (USA)—Near Enough **Mr Cliff Woof**
6 **RON'S SECRET**, 4, br f Efisio—Primrose Bank **Mrs Linda Popely**
7 **SARASONIA**, 5, b m Dunbeath (USA)—La Graciosa **Mrs J. W. Payne**
8 **SQUARED AWAY**, 4, b c Blakeney—Maureen Mhor **Mrs E. and Miss C. Lake**
9 **TIRLIE (IRE)**, 4, b g Tirol—Lisa's Favourite **Mr Gerald Cooper**
10 **YA MALAK**, 5, b g Fairy King (USA)—La Tuerta **Mr G. Jabre**

THREE-YEAR-OLDS

11 **DRAGONJOY**, b g Warrshan (USA)—Nazakat **Mr T. H. Barma**
12 **GENEROUS PRESENT**, ch c Cadeaux Genereux—Dance Move **Mr Alex Penman**
13 B c Double Schwartz—Kasarose **Mr Sean Gollogly**
14 **MISTER SEAN (IRE)**, b g Mac's Imp (USA)—Maid of Mourne **Mr Sean Gollogly**
15 **PHARAOH'S JOY**, b f Robellino (USA)—Joyce's Best **Pyramid Racing Club**
16 **WESTERN VENTURE (IRE)**, ch g Two Timing (USA)—Star Gazing (IRE) **Mr J. P. Power**
17 **YA MARHABA**, b g Efisio—Ichnusa **Mr G. Jabre**

TWO-YEAR-OLDS

18 **AL MUALLIM (USA)**, b c 19/4 Theatrical—Gerri N Jo Go (USA) (Top Command (USA)) **Al Muallim Partnership**
19 **DANCER'S CHIEF**, ch c 28/2 Suave Dancer (USA)—Kijafa (USA) (Chief's Crown (USA)) **Mr Marwan Tabsh**
20 B c 27/3 Red Ransom (USA)—Gaye's Delight (USA) (Imperial Falcon (CAN)) **Al Muallim Partnership**
21 **KWEILO**, b c 28/2 Mtoto—Hug Me (Shareef Dancer (USA)) **Mr Nagy El Azar**
22 **MECHILIE**, b f 24/4 Belmez (USA)—Tundra Goose (Habitat) **Colonel S. Lycett-Green**
23 B g 17/4 Petong—Nazakat (Known Fact (USA)) **Mr T. H. Barma**

Other Owners: Mrs Richard Casey, Mr D. E. Harman, Mr D. Popely, Mr Dennis Purkiss, Mr James P. C. Tien, Mr R. Wicks.

Lady Rider: Mrs Sally Cahill (7-12).

485 MR J. H. PEACOCK, Much Wenlock

Postal: **Atterley Farm Stables, Atterley, Much Wenlock, Shropshire, TF13 6BR.**

Phone: **(01952) 728037**

1 4, Ch f Radical—Belmont Lady **Mr I. D. McEwen**
2 **BLUSHING STAR**, 9, b g Le Bavard (FR)—Vulstar **Mr R. A. B. Brassey**
3 **CHAIN SHOT**, 11, b g Pas de Seul—Burnished **Mr H. F. McEwen**
4 **DANCE ON SIXPENCE**, 8, b g Lidhame—Burning Ambition **Wenlock Racing**
5 **LITTLE BERTHA**, 7, ch m Nearly A Hand—General's Daughter **Mr E. R. A. Jones**
6 **LUSTREMAN**, 9, ch g Sallust—Miss Speak Easy (USA) **Mrs Janet J. Peacock**
7 **RADAR KNIGHT**, 8, b g Beldale Flutter (USA)—Eurynome **Mr R. A. B. Brassey**
8 **RELAXED LAD**, 7, ro g Kalaglow—Relaxed **The Ironbridge Partnership**
9 **SCALLY'S SECRET**, 5, br m Scallywag—Andy's Secret **The Ironbridge Partnership**
10 **SEVEN WELLS**, 4, ch g Weld—Andy's Secret **The Ironbridge Partnership**
11 **TAUNTING (IRE)**, 8, b g Taufan (USA)—Dancing Decoy **Mr Brian Oxton**
12 4, Ch f Montelimar (USA)—The Parson Fox **Mr I. D. McEwen**

THREE-YEAR-OLDS

13 **BALMORAL PRINCESS**, b f Thethingaboutitis (USA)—Fair Balmoral **Mrs S. K. Maan**
14 B f The Dissident—Nemophilia **Mrs Janet J. Peacock**

MR J. H. PEACOCK—continued

Other Owners: Mr J. R. Adams, Mr P. C. Burgess, Mr R. W. Caron, Mr D. Edwards, Mr J. D. Evans, Mrs H. E. Hill, Mr I. W. Jones, Mr K. McEwen, Mr P. Oakley, Mr John Potter, Mr K. A. Pratt, Mr M. J. Pugh, Mr G. T. Ruff, Mr M. D. Thompson, Mr W. H. Todd.

Jockey (Flat): C Rutter (w.a.).

Jockey (NH): R Bellamy.

Lady Riders: Miss S Lea (9-7), Mrs Carman Peacock.

486   MR R. E. PEACOCK, Malmesbury

Postal: **Oliver House Stud, Chedglow, Malmesbury, Wilts, SN16 9EZ.**

Phone: **(01666) 577238**

1 **BURNING COST**, 6, br m Lochnager—Sophie Avenue **Mr R. E. Peacock**
2 **CALL MY GUEST (IRE)**, 6, b g Be My Guest (USA)—Overcall **Mr Derek D. Clee**
3 **CHRISTIAN WARRIOR**, 7, gr g Primo Dominie—Rashah **Miss P. Kissock-Smith**
4 **DISTINCTIVE LADY**, 6, ch m Primo Dominie—Kenton's Girl **Datum Building Supplies Limited**
5 **DREAM CARRIER (IRE)**, 8, b g Doulab (USA)—Dream Trader **Mr R. E. Peacock**
6 **FIGHTER SQUADRON**, 7, ch g Primo Dominie—Formidable Dancer **Mr R. E. Peacock**
7 **NUNS CONE**, 8, ch g Celtic Cone—Nunswalk **Mrs Alurie O'Sullivan**
8 **PHANAN**, 10, ch g Pharly (FR)—L'Ecossaise **Mr R. E. Peacock**
9 **SCBOO**, 7, b g Full Extent (USA)—Maygo **Mrs P. Hutchinson**
10 **SHEEP STEALER**, 8, gr g Absalom—Kilroe's Calin **Datum Building Supplies Limited**
11 **TOMMY TEMPEST**, 7, ch g Northern Tempest (USA)—Silently Yours (USA) **Mr Allan White**
12 **WRITTEN AGREEMENT**, 8, ch g Stanford—Covenant **Mr R. E. Peacock**

Other Owners: Mrs Jean P. Clee, Mr Mark Loveless.

Jockey (Flat): J Williams (8-3, w.a.).

Jockey (NH): S McNeill (10-0, w.a.).

Lady Rider: Mrs Carmen Peacock (9-4).

487   MR B. A. PEARCE, Limpsfield

Postal: **Brills Racing Stables, Grants Lane, Limpsfield, Oxted, RH8 0RH.**

Phone: **(01883) 730345**

1 **ANZIO (IRE)**, 5, b g Hatim (USA)—Highdrive **Mr Richard J. Gray**
2 **ASHTINA**, 11, b g Tina's Pet—Mrewa **Ms S. A. Joyner**
3 **BIG BAD WOLF (IRE)**, 8, gr g Orchestra—Perato
4 **CHEMIN-DE-FER**, 4, b g Darshaan—Whitehaven **Mr Richard J. Gray**
5 **CHOCOLATE CHIP**, 4, b g Hard Fought—Roses Galore (USA) **Mr Brian Arthur Pearce**
6 **DISTANT DYNASTY**, 6, br g Another Realm—Jianna **Mr M. V. Kirby**
7 **ELA-MENT (IRE)**, 4, b g Ela-Mana-Mou—Dorado Llave (USA) **Mr S. Kwai**
8 **HONEST DAVE**, 6, b g Derring Rose—Fille de Soleil **Mr D. Newman**
9 **HONG KONG DOLLAR**, 4, b g Superpower—Daleside Ladybird **Mr Ronnie Toft**

MR B. A. PEARCE—continued

10 **MEGA TID**, 4, b g Old Vic—Dunoof **Mr P. C. J. Saunders**
11 **MUTINIQUE**, 5, br m General Wade—Little Visitor **Mrs Maureen Bell**
12 **RES IPSA LOQUITUR**, 9, b g Law Society (USA)—Bubbling (USA) **Mr Brian Arthur Pearce**
13 **SIR OLIVER (IRE)**, 7, b g Auction Ring (USA)—Eurorose **Ms S. A. Joyner**

THREE-YEAR-OLDS

14 **LATZIO**, b f Arrasas (USA)—Remould **Mr Ronnie Toft**
15 **MIDNIGHT COOKIE**, b c Midyan (USA)—Midnight's Reward **Ms S. A. Joyner**
16 **MOI CANARD**, ch c Bold Owl—Royal Scots Greys **Mr Richard J. Gray**
17 **TARTAN EXPRESS (IRE)**, b g New Express—Running Feud **Mrs E. N. Nield**

Other Owners: Mr Nick Clark, Mr Martin J. Gibbs, Mr J. S. Scott.

Jockey (NH): Roger Rowell.

488   MR J. PEARCE, Newmarket

Postal: **Wroughton House, 37 Old Station Road, Newmarket, Suffolk, CB8 8DT.**
Phone: **NEWMARKET (01638) 664669 FAX (01638) 664669**

1 **ANJOU**, 4, b g Saumarez—Bourbon Topsy **Mr G. H. Tufts & Mr Jeff Pearce**
2 **BELLAS GATE BOY**, 4, b g Doulab (USA)—Celestial Air **Miss A. Meadows**
3 **BOLD HABIT**, 11, ch g Homing—Our Mother **Mr Arthur Old**
4 **BRILLIANT**, 8, ch m Never So Bold—Diamond Hill
5 **BURN OUT**, 4, b g Last Tycoon—Obertura (USA) **Al Yancy Partnership**
6 **CAN CAN CHARLIE**, 6, gr g Vaigly Great—Norton Princess **Mr G. H. Tufts**
7 **CHANTRO BAY**, 8, b g Chantro—Hannah's Song **U. K. Letterbox Marketing Ltd (N.L.M.)**
8 **CONIC HILL (IRE)**, 5, ch g Lomond (USA)—Krisalya **Mr & Mrs B. Crangle**
9 **ELPIDA (USA)**, 4, b c Trempolino (USA)—All For Hope (USA) **Mr A. J. Thompson**
10 **EQUESTRIANISM (IRE)**, 5, ch g Ballad Rock—Dawn's Meteor (USA)
11 **GOLD BLADE**, 7, ch g Rousillon (USA)—Sharp Girl (FR) **Mr Jeff Pearce**
12 **GUESSTIMATION (USA)**, 7, b g Known Fact (USA)—Best Guess (USA) **Exclusive Two Partnership**
13 **HARVEY WHITE (IRE)**, 4, b br g Petorius—Walkyria **The Harvey White Partnership**
14 **JOHN TUFTY**, 5, ch g Vin St Benet—Raffles Virginia **Mr G. H. Tufts**
15 **KILFINNY CROSS (IRE)**, 8, ch g Mister Lord (USA)—Anvil Chorus **Mr A. J. Thompson**
16 **LAMBSON**, 9, b g Petorius—Julie Be Quick (USA) **Mr Ian Hall**
17 **LORD LAMBSON**, 7, b g Today And Tomorrow—Sum Star **Mr Ian Hall**
18 **LUCY TUFTY**, 5, b m Vin St Benet—Manor Farm Toots **Mr G. H. Tufts**
19 **MYSTERIOUS MAID (USA)**, 9, ch m L'Emigrant (USA)—Body Heat (USA) **Mr A. J. Thompson & Partners**
20 **NAGOBELIA**, 8, b br g Enchantment—Lost Valley **U. K. Letterbox Marketing Ltd (N.L.M.)**
21 **PETOSKIN**, 4, b g Petoski—Farcical
22 **PILIB (IRE)**, 5, b g Salt Dome (USA)—Princess Elinor
23 **RETENDER (USA)**, 7, br g Storm Bird (CAN)—Dandy Bury (FR) **Mr Jeff Pearce**
24 **ROCK GROUP**, 4, b g Rock City—Norska **Mr J. R. Furlong & Partners**
25 **ROYAL LEGEND**, 4, b g Fairy King (USA)—Legend of Arabia
26 **STREAKY HAWK (USA)**, 4, b g Hawkster (USA)—Veroom Maid (USA)
27 **SUPER PARK**, 4, b c Superpower—Everingham Park
28 **TOP ROYAL**, 7, b g High Top—Maria Isabella (FR) **Mr & Mrs P. Routledge & Mr Jeff Pearce**
29 **TOUJOURS RIVIERA**, 6, ch g Rainbow Quest (USA)—Miss Beaulieu **Mr James Furlong**

THREE-YEAR-OLDS

30 **ATHENRY**, b c Siberian Express (USA)—Heresheis **Mr A. J. Thompson & Mr Jeff Pearce**
31 **ECTOMORPH (IRE)**, ch f Sharp Victor (USA)—Hail To You (USA) **Twoforthecrack Partnership**
32 **ESPERTO**, b g Risk Me (FR)—Astrid Gilberto **Mrs A. V. Holman-Chappell**
33 **JEAN PIERRE**, b c Anshan—Astolat **Mr P. D. Burnett & Mr J. L. Davidson**
34 **NOSEY NATIVE**, b g Cyrano de Bergerac—Native Flair **Mr J. R. Furlong**
35 **PROSPECTOR'S COVE**, b g Dowsing (USA)—Pearl Cove **Saracen Racing**
36 **RUSK**, b c Pharly (FR)—Springwell **Mrs J. Connew**

MR J. PEARCE—continued
TWO-YEAR-OLDS

37 ANNALETTA, b f 18/3 Belmez (USA)—A Priori (GER)
38 B f 24/4 Unfuwain (USA)—Branitska
39 COMMISSION, b c 29/3 Safawan—Heresheis
40 JUCINDA, gr f 19/2 Midyan (USA)—Catch The Sun **Mrs S. Watson & Partners**
41 SARABI, b f 12/2 Alzao (USA)—Sure Enough (IRE) **Twoforthecrack Partnership**

Other Owners: Mr P. Cunningham, Mr Richard De Lisle, Mr I. Fuhrmann, Mr G. T. Harvey, Mr Terry Harvey, Mr G. W. Holland, Mr Lance Lodge, Mr D. J. Maden, Mr B. J. McMath, Miss Islee S. Oliva, Qualitair Holdings Limited, Quintet Partnership, Mr David White, Mr P. Wymann.

Jockeys (Flat): Gary Bardwell (7-7, w.a.), John McLaughlin (8-7).

Jockey (NH): John McLaughlin (9-7).

Lady Rider: Mrs Lydia Pearce (8-7).

489   MR J. E. PEASE, Chantilly

Postal: **Villa Primerose, Chemin des Aigles, 60500 Chantilly, France.**
Phone: **44 58 19 96/44 57 23 09 FAX 44 57 59 90**

1 HUDO (USA), 6, b h Hero's Honor (USA)—Jardin de Nuit (USA) **S. S. Niarchos**
2 PHILANTHROP (FR), 4, b c Machiavellian (USA)—Shezerade (USA) **S. S. Niarchos**
3 THINK TWICE (USA), 4, b f Alleged (USA)—Charmie Carmie (USA) **George Strawbridge**

THREE-YEAR-OLDS

4 ABU'L FAZL (FR), b c Legend of France (USA)—Mevlana (IRE) **John Goelet**
5 BUCEPHALASS (FR), b f Akarad (FR)—Silicon Lady (FR) **John Goelet**
6 CIEL DE FEU (USA), ch f Blushing John (USA)—Northern Trick (USA) **S. S. Niarchos**
7 CONTARE, b f Shirley Heights—Balenare **George Strawbridge**
8 DEMI MONDE (USA), ch f Easy Goer (USA)—Awesome Account (USA) **G W Leigh**
9 ECCOLA, b f Seattle Dancer (USA)—Evocatrice **F. Von Oppenheim**
10 FABULOUS WHISPER (FR), b c Al Nasr (FR)—Fabulous Noble (FR) **Andre Ben Lassin**
11 FLURRY (FR), b f Groom Dancer (USA)—Snow Top **George Strawbridge**
12 FREESTYLE (USA), b c Silver Hawk (USA)—Snowbowl (USA) **George Strawbridge**
13 HANA (FR), b f Alleged (USA)—Quarter Deck (IRE) **Prince Badr Bin Abdulaziz**
14 LONELY BROOK (USA), b f El Gran Senor (USA)—Ariosa (USA) **George Strawbridge**
15 MAYOUMBE (FR), gr c Kaldoun (FR)—Moucha (FR) **Larry Roy**
16 MERCI MONSIEUR, ch c Cadeaux Genereux—Night Encounter **Simon Emmet**
17 METAPHOR (USA), ch f Woodman (USA)—Mystery Rays (USA) **S. S. Niarchos**
18 MIDNIGHT OASIS (USA), ch f Java Gold (USA)—Northernette (CAN) **S. S. Niarchos**
19 MOTZKI (FR), b f Le Glorieux—Madigan Mill **W. Wolf**
20 NOBLESSE OBLIGE, b c Salse (USA)—Fair Rosamunda **Sir Gordon Brunton**
21 PHILADELPHUS (FR), b g Pharly (FR)—Balsamine **H. Seymour & Partners**
22 POMME SECRET (FR), b c Assert—Thalestria (FR) **Mrs A. J. Richards**
23 RESONATOR (FR), b c Saumarez—Echoes (FR) **S. S. Niarchos**
24 ROYAUMONT (FR), gr c Kaldoun (FR)—Regent's Fawn (CAN) **George Strawbridge**
25 SERAC (USA), ch c Riverman (USA)—Franc Argument (USA) **George Strawbridge**
26 SHOWBOAT (USA), b f Theatrical—Fitzwilliam Place **George Strawbridge**
27 SILICON ARC (FR), b c Akarad (FR)—Siliciana **W. Wolf**
28 SPINNING WORLD (USA), ch c Nureyev (USA)—Imperfect Circle (USA) **S. S. Niarchos**
29 TITUS LIVIUS (FR), ch c Machiavellian (USA)—Party Doll **S. S. Niarchos**
30 WILLSTOWN (USA), b f Lear Fan (USA)—First Approach (USA) **George Strawbridge**
31 WITH FASCINATION (USA), b f Dayjur (USA)—Fran's Valentine (USA) **George Strawbridge**

MR J. E. PEASE—continued

TWO-YEAR-OLDS

32 **BUCK'S DREAM (FR)**, b c 27/4 Le Glorieux—Buckleby (Buckskin (FR)) **A. Dary**
33 **CANDIDLY**, b f 24/4 Rainbow Quest (USA)—Castle Peak (Darshaan) **F. Von Oppenheim**
34 B f 30/3 Mr Prospector (USA)—Coup de Folie (USA) (Halo (USA)) **S. S. Niarchos**
35 B f 13/4 Green Desert (USA)—Dazzling Heights (Shirley Heights) **Peter Pritchard**
36 Ch f 10/3 Silver Hawk (USA)—First Approach (USA) (Northern Fling (USA)) **George Strawbridge**
37 B f 8/5 Dayjur (USA)—Fitzwilliam Place (Thatching) **George Strawbridge**
38 B c 1/4 Gulch (USA)—Fran's Valentine (USA) (Saros) **George Strawbridge**
39 B f 25/4 Irish River (FR)—Glowing Ardour (Dancing Brave (USA)) **S. S. Niarchos**
40 B c 22/4 Machiavellian (USA)—Gwydion (USA) (Raise A Cup (USA)) **S. S. Niarchos**
41 **HOMING INSTINCT**, b f 13/3 Arctic Tern (USA)—Singapore Girl (FR) (Lyphard (USA)) **George Strawbridge**
42 B c 5/5 Sadler's Wells (USA)—Idyllic (USA) (Foolish Pleasure (USA)) **S. S. Niarchos**
43 **ITHACA**, b c 12/4 Groom Dancer (USA)—Ionian Sea (Slip Anchor) **George Strawbridge**
44 **KAIZEN (FR)**, b c 23/4 Saumarez—Karannja (USA) (Shahrastani (USA)) **J. D. Champalbert & A. Lyons**
45 **LEGENDE D'OR (FR)**, ch f 29/4 Diesis—Spectacular Bid (USA) (Spectacular Bid (USA)) **Saeed Manana**
46 **LUMINOSITY**, ch f 14/4 Sillery (USA)—Bague Bleue (IRE) (Last Tycoon) **George Strawbridge**
47 **NAHLIN**, b f 12/5 Slip Anchor—Alys (Blakeney) **T. D. Rootes**
48 Ch f 3/2 Sovereign Dancer—O My Darling (USA) (Mr Prospector (USA)) **Peter Pritchard**
49 **PISTOLE BLISS (FR)**, ch c 5/4 Pistolet Bleu (IRE)—Embraze Moi (FR) (Vacarme (USA)) **Larry Roy**
50 **PSYLLA (FR)**, b f 23/2 Fabulous Dancer (USA)—Silicon Lady (FR) (Mille Balles (FR)) **John Goelet**
51 B c 3/2 Slew O' Gold (USA)—Puppet Dance (USA) (Northern Dancer) **S. S. Niarchos**
52 B f 7/3 Danzig (USA)—Reiko (FR) (Targowice (USA)) **George Strawbridge**
53 **SILICON GIRL (FR)**, b f 28/3 Mille Balles (FR)—Siliciana (Silly Season) **W. Wolf**
54 **SNOWDRIFT (FR)**, b f 20/2 Polish Precedent—Snowtop (Thatching) **George Strawbridge**
55 **STILBE (FR)**, b f 25/2 Mille Balles (FR)—Mevlana (IRE) (Red Sunset) **John Goelet**
56 B c 17/3 Nureyev (USA)—Wings of Wishes (USA) (Alydar (USA)) **S. S. Niarchos**

Jockey (Flat): C Asmussen.

Apprentice: F Champagne.

---

490 MISS L. A. PERRATT, Ayr

Postal: **Cree Lodge, 47 Craigie Road, Ayr, KA8 0HD.**

Phone: **PHONE/FAX (01292) 266232**

1 **CALDER'S GROVE**, 6, b g Jupiter Island—Thatched Grove **Mr G. N. Perratt**
2 **CELEBRATION CAKE (IRE)**, 4, b g Mister Majestic—My Louise **Lightbody of Hamilton Ltd**
3 **DIET**, 10, b g Starch Reduced—Highland Rescue **Miss Linda A. Perratt**
4 **LEADING PRINCESS (IRE)**, 5, gr m Double Schwartz—Jenny Diver (USA) **Mrs Ruth S. S. Wyllie**
5 **MISS PIGALLE**, 5, b m Good Times (ITY)—Panayr **Miss Heather Galbraith**
6 **MISTER WESTSOUND**, 4, b g Cyrano de Bergerac—Captivate **Mr R. McLean**
7 **NORTHERN SPARK**, 8, b g Trojan Fen—Heavenly Spark **Scottish Daily Record & Sunday Mail Ltd**
8 **RECLUSE**, 5, b g Last Tycoon—Nomadic Pleasure **Mr T. P. Finch**
9 **RUNRIG (IRE)**, 6, b m Jalmood (USA)—Bluethroat **Mr D. Callaghan**
10 **STRATHTORE DREAM (IRE)**, 5, b br m Jareer (USA)—Beyond Words **Miss L. A. Perratt**
11 **SUNDAY MAIL TOO (IRE)**, 4, b f Fayruz—Slick Chick **Scottish Daily Record & Sunday Mail Ltd**
12 **TAM TAIN (IRE)**, 4, b g Contract Law (USA)—Valediction **Mr John Scanlon**

THREE-YEAR-OLDS

13 **AYE READY**, ch g Music Boy—Cindy's Princess **Mr David White (Bothwell)**
14 **DANCING DOT (IRE)**, b f Durgam (USA)—Canty's Gold **Mr C. J. C. McLaren**
15 **DISTINCTLY SWINGIN (IRE)**, b f Distinctly North (USA)—Swoon Alone **Mr David Sutherland**
16 **READY TEDDY (IRE)**, b f Fayruz—Racey Naskra (USA) **Mr David White (Bothwell)**
17 **TERMON**, b f Puissance—Alipura **Miss L. A. Perratt**
18 **WEE TINKERBELL**, ch f Timeless Times (USA)—Kiveton Komet **Mr T. P. Finch**

MISS L. A. PERRATT—continued

TWO-YEAR-OLDS

19 BRAVE MONTGOMERIE, ch c 10/2 Most Welcome—Just Precious (Ela-Mana-Mou) **Mr C. J. C. McLaren**
20 B f 28/2 Lapierre—Canty's Gold (Sonnen Gold) **Miss Linda Perratt**
21 Ch f 30/3 Shalford (IRE)—Debenham (Formidable (USA)) **Miss Linda Perratt**
22 Ch c 7/2 Durgam (USA)—Flash The Gold (Ahonoora) **Miss Linda Perratt**
23 B f 10/4 Rambo Dancer (CAN)—Kiveton Komet (Precocious) **Miss Linda Perratt**
24 Ch f 30/3 La Grange Music—Screenable (USA) (Silent Screen (USA)) **Miss Linda Perratt**
25 B f 17/3 High Estate—Wind of Change (FR) (Sicyos (USA)) **Miss Linda Perratt**

Other Owners: Mr James Campbell, Mrs M. S. J. Clydesdale, Mrs Renee Coutts, Globe Bar Syndicate, Mr L. Hamilton, Mr Ian Hay, Mrs Mary Murdoch, Mrs Helen Perratt, Mrs Christine Richard, Mr J. W. M. M. Richard, Mr Brian Russo, Mr Ronald Wyllie.

Jockeys (Flat): N Connorton (w.a.), G Duffield (w.a.), J K Fanning (w.a.).

Jockeys (NH): A Maguire (w.a.), G McCourt (w.a.), P Niven (w.a.), L O'Hara.

Amateurs: Mr James Dellahunt (10-10), Mr M Lightbody, Mr J J McLaren.

Lady Rider: Miss Linda A Perratt (9-0).

491   MR R. T. PHILLIPS, Lambourn

Postal: **Beechdown Farm, Sheepdrove, Lambourn, Newbury, Berkshire, RG17 7UN.**
Phone: **OFFICE (01488) 73072 HOME 73378 FAX (01488) 73500 MOBILE (0374) 832715**

1 ADILOV, 4, b g Soviet Star (USA)—Volida **Lord Vestey**
2 ARD RI CHERRY (IRE), 7, b g King's Ride—Another Cherry **Nut Club Partnership**
3 AWAYWITHTHEFAIRIES, 6, b m Idiot's Delight—Rose Mulholland **Count K. Goess-Saurau**
4 BRASS TACKS, 4, br f Prince Sabo—Brassy Nell **Elite Racing Club**
5 CORACO, 9, br g Oats—Coral Delight **Old Berks Two Partnership**
6 FROGMARCH (USA), 6, ch g Diesis—La Francaise (USA) **Mrs Helen Mills**
7 KILLISREW ABBEY (IRE), 7, ch m Good Thyne (USA)—Fair Freda **Mr Richard Phillips**
8 LUCKY LANDING (IRE), 7, b g Lancastrian—Twice Lucky **Lady D. Powell**
9 NICK THE BISCUIT, 5, b g Nicholas Bill—Maryland Cookie (USA) **Mr G. Middlebrook**
10 4, B g Arctic Lord—Save It Lass **Richard Phillips**
11 TIME WON'T WAIT (IRE), 7, b g Bulldozer—Time Will Wait **Old Berks Partnership**
12 WILLIE MAKEIT (IRE), 6, b g Coquelin (USA)—Turbina **Old Berks Three Partnership**
13 ZADOK, 4, ch g Exodal (USA)—Glenfinlass **Mrs Jenny Willment**

THREE-YEAR-OLDS

14 BOLDER STILL, ch c Never So Bold—Glenfinlass **Mrs Jenny Willment**
15 FOOTHILL (IRE), b c Tirol—Threshold **Mrs Johnny Mckeever**
16 KULSHI MOMKEN, ch c In The Wings—Gesedeh **Sheikh Ahmed Al Maktoum**
17 LAAZIM AFOOZ, b c Mtoto—Balwa (USA) **Sheikh Ahmed Al Maktoum**
18 SURE TO DREAM (IRE), b f Common Grounds—Hard To Stop **Dozen Dreamers Partnership**
19 SYLVAN HEIGHTS, b c Reprimand—Shibui **Mrs Jenny Willment**

TWO-YEAR-OLDS

20 FLEIDERMAUS (IRE), b c 20/3 Batshoof—Top Mouse (High Top) **Lord Vestey**
21 B g 9/5 Warning—Indian Pink (USA) (Seattle Slew (USA)) **Mrs Helen Mills**

Other Owners: Mr A. Blackman, Mr D. Bladon, Mr R. Blocker, Mr Paul Bowden, Mr John Clarke, Mr P. A. Deal, Mr Sallie Good, Mrs K. Green, Mr Tony Hill, Mr Jeremy Hulme, Mr J. Inverdale, Mr Nicholas Jones, Anna Kellagher, The Hon E. D. Leigh-Pemberton, Lady Lewinton, Mrs T. Loyd, Mr T. Milson, Miss M. Noden, Mr Oscar O'Herlihy, Miss A. Paulley, Lady Poole, Mr R. Richards, Mrs M. Richardson, Martin Rowe, Sybil Ruscoe, Mr D. Sanderson, Mrs F. Shekleton, Mr M. Sissons, Siobhan Stafford, Mr R. Thomas, Mrs Jenny Trier, Judith Watson, Lt. Col. A. Young.

492   MR J. A. PICKERING, Hinckley

Postal: **Cottage Farm, Wigston Parva, Hinckley, Leics, LE10 3AP.**

Phone: **(0455) 220535**

1 **BENJAMINS LAW**, 5, b br g Mtoto—Absaloute Service **Mr D. Lowe**
2 **DOWDENCY**, 4, b f Dowsing (USA)—Tendency **Mr P. W. Till**
3 **KHAKI LIGHT**, 8, b g Lighter—Blue Speckle **Miss A. B. Cottrell**
4 **LAST WORLD**, 4, b f Puissance—Flicker Toa Flame (USA) **Mr Peter P. O'Neill**
5 **MINNAMOO**, 6, ch m Royal Vulcan—Macs Park **Mrs J. A. Pickering**
6 **PRIORY PIPER**, 7, b g Maris Piper—Priory Girl **Mrs J. A. Pickering**
7 **SEATWIST**, 7, gr g Pragmatic—March At Dawn **Mrs J. A. Pickering**
8 **SIDEWINDER**, 18, ch g Country Retreat—Woodland Wedding **Mr J. A. Pickering**
9 **SPA KELLY**, 8, br g Netherkelly—Tarkon Spa **Mr J. A. Pickering**
10 **SUPREME NORMAN (IRE)**, 6, b g Supreme Leader—Please Oblige **Mr S. Kitching**

THREE-YEAR-OLDS

11 **SHOOT THE MINSTREL**, ch c Brotherly (USA)—Shoot To Win (FR)

Jockey (NH): Mark Sharratt (10-0).

Conditional: D J Dennis (9-7).

493   MR S. L. PIKE, Sidmouth

Postal: **Synderborough Farm, Sidbury, Sidmouth, Devon, EX10 0QJ.**

Phone: **(01395) 597485**

1 **FRONT COVER**, 6, b m Sunyboy—Roman Lilly **Mr Stewart Pike**
2 **PROUD SUN**, 8, ch g Sunyboy—Roman Lilly **Mr Stewart Pike**
3 **SWEATSHIRT**, 11, ch g Leander—Roman Lilly **Mr Stewart Pike**
4 **SYNDERBOROUGH LAD**, 10, ch g Rymer—Roman Lilly **Mr Stewart Pike**
5 **WINTER'S LANE**, 12, ch g Leander—Roman Lilly **Mr Stewart Pike**

Jockey (NH): M Fitzgerald.

Amateur: Mr M Felton.

494   MRS P. M. PILE, Leamington Spa

Postal: **Splash Leys, Avon Dassett, Leamington Spa, Warwickshire, CV33 0AZ.**

1 **GREY BLADE**, 4, gr f Dashing Blade—High Matinee **Mrs D. Mitchell**
2 **SILVER HOLLOW**, 11, gr g True Song—Wilspoon Hollow **Mrs P. M. Pile**

495   MRS T. D. PILKINGTON, Stow-on-the-Wold

Postal: **Hyde Mill, Stow-on-the-Wold, Cheltenham, Glos, GL54 1LA.**

Phone: **(01451) 830641**

1 **HYDEMILLA**, 6, b m Idiot's Delight—Bellaloo **Mrs T. D. Pilkington**
2 **ROSEHALL**, 5, b br m Ardross—Coral Delight **Mrs T. D. Pilkington**

496   MR MARTIN C PIPE, Wellington

Postal: **Pond House, Nicholashayne, Wellington, Somerset, TA21 9QY.**

Phone: **OFFICE (01884) 840715 FAX (01884) 841343**

1 **ACCOUNTANCY LADY**, 6, ch m Capitano—Loophole **Lord Donoughmore**
2 **AGRA (NZ)**, 8, b g Virginia Privateer (USA)—Polar Star (NZ) **Ramjet Racing**
3 **ALL CLEAR (IRE)**, 5, b g Castle Keep—Hustle Bustle **Mr A. J. Lomas**
4 **ALLEGATION**, 6, b g Dominion—Pageantry **Martin Pipe Racing Club**
5 **ALL FOR LUCK**, 11, b g Kemal (FR)—Lisgarvan **Mr B. J. Craig**
6 **ANNA BANNANNA**, 4, b f Prince Sabo—Top Berry **405200 Racing**
7 **BALASANI (FR)**, 10, b g Labus (FR)—Baykara **Mr M. D. Smith**
8 **BANJO (FR)**, 6, b g Beyssac (FR)—Fabinou (FR) **Mr Darren C. Mercer**
9 **BANNTOWN BILL (IRE)**, 7, gr g Roselier (FR)—Supple **Mr Eric Scarth**
10 **BELMORE CLOUD**, 7, gr m Baron Blakeney—Direct Call **Mrs Audrey J. Hartnett**
11 **BIG STRAND (IRE)**, 7, b g King's Ride—Tranquil Love **Mr E. C. Jones**
12 **BOOGIE BOPPER (IRE)**, 7, b g Taufan (USA)—Mey **Martin Pipe Racing Club**
13 **BORJITO (SPA)**, 5, b h Chayote (FR)—Tanaquil (FR) **Mrs Angie Malde**
14 **BORN TO BE WILD**, 4, gr f Pharly (FR)—Carose **Pond House Racing**
15 **CACHE FLEUR (FR)**, 10, ch g Kashneb (FR)—Blanche Fleur (FR) **Mr B. A. Kilpatrick**
16 **CADOUGOLD (FR)**, 5, b g Cadoudal (FR)—Fontaine Aux Faons (FR) **Mr D. A. Johnson**
17 **CALLING JAMAICA**, 4, b f Elmaamul (USA)—Tolstoya **405200 Racing**
18 **CELCIUS**, 12, b g Ile de Bourbon (USA)—Cistus **Martin Pipe Racing Club**
19 **CHALLENGER DU LUC (FR)**, 6, b g Chamberlin (FR)—Islande II (FR) **J. & J. Securities Limited**
20 **CHAPRASSI (FR)**, 7, ch g Tropular—Kirsten (FR) **Mr B. A. Kilpatrick**
21 **CHARLIE PARROT (IRE)**, 6, gr g Sexton Blake—Pranburi **Mrs Alison C. Farrant**
22 **CHARM DANCER**, 4, b f Rambo Dancer (CAN)—Skelton **Mrs R. Cobbold**
23 **CHATAM (USA)**, 12, b g Big Spruce (USA)—Cristalina (FR) **Mr Adrian F. Nolan**
24 **CHESTER'S CHAT**, 7, ch m Rabdan—Miss Quay **405200 Racing**
25 **COOL CLOWN**, 9, b g Idiot's Delight—Fabice **Mrs P. B. Browne**
26 **CROSA'S DELIGHT**, 9, b g Idiot's Delight—Crosa **Bisgrove Partnership**
27 **CYBORGO (FR)**, 6, b g Cyborg (FR)—Quintessence (FR) **County Stores (Somerset) Holdings Ltd**
28 **DIAMOND CUT (FR)**, 8, b g Fast Topaze (USA)—Sasetto (FR) **405200 Racing**
29 **DOLCE NOTTE (IRE)**, 6, b m Strong Gale—Caratasca (FR) **County Stores (Somerset) Holdings Ltd**
30 **DOM SAMOURAI (FR)**, 5, gr g Dom Pasquini (FR)—Miss Dianon (FR) **Mr B. A. Kilpatrick**
31 **DRABORGIE (FR)**, 5, b m Cyborg (FR)—Trapette (FR) **Mr Darren C. Mercer**
32 **ELITE REG**, 7, b g Electric—Coppice **Martin Pipe Racing Club**
33 **ENCORE UN PEU (FR)**, 9, ch g Nikos—Creme Caramel (FR) **Mr Vincent Nally**
34 **EVANGELICA (USA)**, 8, b m Dahar (USA)—Rebut (USA) **Martin Pipe Racing Club**
35 **EVER SMILE (FR)**, 9, ch g Be My Guest (USA)—Smiling (FR) **Mr David L'Estrange**
36 **FEELS LIKE GOLD (IRE)**, 8, b g Oats—Drom Lady **Independent Twine Manufacturing Co Ltd**
37 **FRAGRANT DAWN**, 12, br g Strong Gale—Aridje **D. & S. Mercer**
38 **GLENGARRIF GIRL (IRE)**, 6, b m Good Thyne (USA)—Mention of Money **Mr David L'Estrange**
39 **GRANVILLE AGAIN**, 10, ch g Deep Run—High Board **Mr Eric Scarth**
40 **GYSART (IRE)**, 7, br g Good Thyne (USA)—Cute Play **Mrs R. Cobbold**
41 **HABASHA (IRE)**, 6, b m Lashkari—Haughty Manner **Mr Terry Neill**
42 **INDIAN JOCKEY**, 4, b g Indian Ridge—Number Eleven **Mr Darren C. Mercer**
43 **KHATIR (CAN)**, 5, gr g Alwasmi (USA)—Perfect Poppy (USA) **Mr Frank A. Farrant**
44 **KISSAIR (IRE)**, 5, b g Most Welcome—Salonniere (FR) **Mr Terry Benson**
45 **LANDSKER MISSILE**, 7, b m Cruise Missile—Gemmerly Jane **Mrs J. K. L. Watts**
46 **LEMON'S MILL (USA)**, 7, b m Roberto (USA)—Mill Queen **Mr Stuart M. Mercer**
47 **LORD RELIC (NZ)**, 10, b g Zamazaan (FR)—Morning Order (NZ) **Mrs H. J. Clarke**
48 **MACK THE KNIFE**, 7, b g Kris—The Dancer (FR) **D. & G. Mercer**
49 **MAKE A STAND**, 5, ch g Master Willie—Make A Signal **Mr P. A. Deal**
50 **MIGHTY GALE (IRE)**, 5, b g Strong Gale—Swanee Mistress **Mrs L. M. Sewell**
51 **MONEGHETTI**, 5, ch g Faustus (USA)—The Victor Girls **Mr Philip G. Harvey**
52 **MORNING BLUSH (IRE)**, 6, ch m Glow (USA)—Sweetbird **Bisgrove Partnership**
53 **MOST EQUAL**, 6, ch g Presidium—Dissolution **Mr Heeru Kirpalani**
54 **MR BUREAUCRAT (NZ)**, 7, b br g Markella (FR)—Katex (NZ) **Mr Stanley W. Clarke**

MR MARTIN C PIPE—continued

55 **MUGONI BEACH**, 11, b g Equal Opportunity—Cuckoo Flower **Mr Jim Ennis**
56 **NORDIC CROWN (IRE)**, 5, b m Nordico (USA)—Fit The Halo **405200 Racing**
57 **NORDIC VALLEY (IRE)**, 5, b g Nordico (USA)—Malia **Pond House Racing**
58 **NORMAN'S CONVINCED (IRE)**, 6, b g Convinced—A Nice Alert **Somerset White Lining Ltd**
59 **PALOSANTO (IRE)**, 6, b g Torus—Winterwood **Mr B. A. Kilpatrick**
60 **PETER MONAMY**, 4, ch g Prince Sabo—Revisit **Richard Green (Fine Paintings)**
61 **POLITICAL PANTO (IRE)**, 5, b g Phardante (FR)—Madam's Well **Mr Sean Lucey**
62 **POND HOUSE (IRE)**, 7, b g Phardante (FR)—Arctic Tack **Mr C. R. Fleet**
63 **PREENKA GIRL (FR)**, 7, b m Ashtar—Princess du Chalet (FR) **Martin Pipe Racing Club**
64 **PREROGATIVE**, 6, ch g Dominion—Nettle **Mr D. A. Johnson**
65 **PRIDWELL**, 6, b g Sadler's Wells (USA)—Glowing With Pride **Mr Malcolm B. Jones**
66 **RAINBOW ROAD**, 5, b g Shareef Dancer (USA)—Chalky Road **405200 Racing**
67 **RIVERSIDE BOY**, 13, ch g Funny Man—Tamorina **Bisgrove Partnership**
68 **ROBERT'S TOY (IRE)**, 5, b g Salt Dome (USA)—Zazu **Mr Clive D. Smith**
69 **ROLLED GOLD**, 7, b g Rymer—Goldaw **Mr David Jenks**
70 **RUNAWAY PETE (USA)**, 6, b g Runaway Groom (CAN)—Pete's Damas (USA) **Perran Associates**
71 **SEASONAL SPLENDOUR (IRE)**, 6, b m Prince Rupert (FR)—Snoozy Time **Mr D. A. Johnson**
72 **SHALLAGAMBLE**, 6, b g Gambler's Cup (USA)—Marshalla **Mrs E. M. Beresford**
73 **SILVER SHRED**, 5, gr m Nishapour (FR)—Golden Curd (FR) **Mr D. M. Beresford**
74 **SOHRAB (IRE)**, 8, ch g Shernazar—On Show **Mrs Joanne Richards**
75 **SOLATIUM (IRE)**, 4, b g Rainbow Quest (USA)—Consolation **Mr Frank A. Farrant**
76 **SOPHISM (USA)**, 7, b g Al Nasr (FR)—Over The Waves **Mr A. J. Lomas**
77 **SOZZLED**, 5, gr g Absalom—The High Dancer **Mr J. D. Smeaden**
78 **STICKY MONEY**, 8, b m Relkino—Cover Your Money **Mrs D. Jenks**
79 **ST MELLION DRIVE**, 6, b g Gunner B—Safeguard **St Mellion Estates Ltd**
80 **SUPERIOR RISK (IRE)**, 7, b g Mandalus—Hal's Pauper **Mr Darren C. Mercer**
81 **SWEET GLOW (FR)**, 9, b g Crystal Glitters (USA)—Very Sweet **Mrs Marilyn Fairbrother**
82 **TEMPERATURE RISING**, 4, b f Then Again—Rather Warm **Seaborough Manor Limited**
83 **TERAO**, 10, b g Furry Glen—Bodyline **Mr B. A. Kilpatrick**
84 **THE BLACK MONK (IRE)**, 8, ch g Sexton Blake—Royal Demon **Martin Pipe Racing Club**
85 **TIPPING THE LINE**, 6, b g Baron Blakeney—Lily Mab (FR) **Mrs L. M. Sewell**
86 **TONYS GIFT**, 4, b f Midyan (USA)—Harmonical (USA) **The Blue Chip Group**
87 **TRAGIC HERO**, 4, b g Tragic Role (USA)—Pink Mex **Knight Hawks Partnership**
88 **VALIANT TOSKI**, 5, b h Petoski—Corvelle **Sir John Swaine**
89 **VARIO (FR)**, 4, br g Nerio (FR)—Karora (FR) **Knight Hawks Partnership**
90 **WHARFEDALE MUSIC**, 5, ch m Grey Desire—Flute Royale **Mr G. H. Senior**
91 **YUBRALEE (USA)**, 4, ch c Zilzal (USA)—Kentucky Lill (USA) **Mr D. A. Johnson**

Other Owners: Ms Debbie Aghdassi, Mr K. Barber, Mr D. A. Berstock, Mr G. C. Bisgrove, Miss H. A. Bisgrove, Mrs M. A. Bisgrove, Mr David Broadaway, Mr E. Carlisle, Mr L. Carver, Charles Eden Limited, Elite Racing Club, Mr Tony Fletcher, Mr Peter Fyvie, Mr J. Garratt, Mr Jonathan Goldsmith, Mr Tony Hill, Mr Michael R. Jaye, Mr A. Langham, Mr D. Lodge, Mr Grant Mercer, Merthyr Motor Auctions, Mr David J. Mills, Mr N. Morgan, Mr Steve Nelson, Mr James Neville, Mr Nick Newman, Mr P. Newton, Mr Michael Ng, Miss P. Noden, Dr B. Nolan, Mr Eugene O'Neill, Mrs Christine Painting, Mr Trevor Painting, Mr J. A. Palmer, Mr M. C. Pipe, Mrs Y. J. Reynolds, Mr Brian Simpkins, Mr R. Stanley, The Sun Punters Club, Mr P. Thompson, Mr R. H. Tiffany, Mr Bob Wheatley, Mr James S. Wilde, Mrs L. M. Wundke, Mr Roy Young.

Jockeys (NH): D Bridgwater (10-0), Jamie Evans (10-0), J Lower (10-4).

Conditional: O Burrows (9-7).

Amateur: Mr Ashley Farrant (10-12).

497   MRS J. PITMAN, Upper Lambourn

Postal: **Weathercock House, High Street, Upper Lambourn, Hungerford, Berks, RG17 8QT.**
Phone: **LAMBOURN (01488) 71714 FAX (01488) 72196**

1 **ANNIE RUTH (IRE)**, 5, ch m Good Thyne (USA)—Alamo Bay **Mrs Elizabeth Birks**
2 **ARITHMETIC**, 6, ch g Torus—Graphics Eska **Robert & Elizabeth Hitchins**
3 **BANK AVENUE**, 5, b g Buckley—Woodram Delight **Mr S. D. Hemstock**
4 **BATTLE CREEK (IRE)**, 6, b g Le Bavard (FR)—Tassel Tip **Blakeley Painters Ltd**
5 **BAYMATIC**, 7, b g Pragmatic—Cascade Bay VII **Mr G. I. Isaac**
6 **BROOMHILL BOY**, 7, b g Oats—Rose Window **Mr S. D. Hemstock**
7 **BUSTER BOB (IRE)**, 6, b br g Clearly Bust—Possible **Robert & Elizabeth Hitchins**
8 **CANTORIS FRATER**, 9, ch g Brotherly (USA)—Decoyanne **The Ley Partnership**
9 **CAYMANAS (IRE)**, 4, br g Celio Rufo—Bring Me Sunshine **Autofour Engineering**
10 **CELTIC LAIRD**, 8, ch g Celtic Cone—Anitacat **Robert & Elizabeth Hitchins**
11 **CHERRYMORE (IRE)**, 5, br g Cataldi—Cherry Bow **Robert & Elizabeth Hitchins**
12 **COKENNY BOY**, 11, b g Abednego—Northern Push **Mr S. D. Hemstock**
13 **CYPHRATIS (IRE)**, 5, b g Le Bavard (FR)—Torus Light **Mailcom Plc & Mr Pat Whelan**
14 **DARK CHALLENGER (IRE)**, 4, b br g Brush Aside (USA)—Great Aunt Emily **Legs Only Partnership**
15 **DO BE BRIEF**, 11, ch g Le Moss—Right Performance **Mr Errol Brown**
16 **DO BE HAVE (IRE)**, 8, b g Le Bavard (FR)—Darjoy **Peters and Lee**
17 **DUKE OF LANCASTER (IRE)**, 7, br g Lancastrian—Chake-Chake **Hunt Allen Partnership**
18 **EGYPT MILL PRINCE**, 10, b g Deep Run—Just Darina **Mr S. R. Webb**
19 **EVER BLESSED (IRE)**, 4, b g Lafontaine (USA)—Sanctify **The Ever Blessed Partnership**
20 **EYRE POINT (IRE)**, 7, b g Le Bavard (FR)—Betty Sue **Mailcom Plc**
21 **FAMBRIDGE**, 7, b g Baron Blakeney—Tye Bridge **Mr H. Gibbon**
22 **FILE CONCORD**, 12, br g Strong Gale—Lady Reporter **The Stationery Company Limited**
23 **FLYNN'S GIRL (IRE)**, 7, b m Mandalus—Flynn's Field **Robert & Elizabeth Hitchins**
24 **FRANKS JESTER**, 5, b g Idiot's Delight—Tropical Swing **Mrs J. Ollivant**
25 **GARRISON SAVANNAH**, 13, b g Random Shot—Merry Coin **Autofour Engineering**
26 **GILPA VALU**, 7, ch g Ovac (ITY)—More Cherry **Miss N. F. Thesiger**
27 **HARRY BOY (IRE)**, 7, b g Sexton Blake—Subiacco **Mrs T. Brown**
28 **IDIOT'S LADY**, 7, b m Idiot's Delight—Lady Ling **Mrs J. Ollivant**
29 **INDEFENCE (IRE)**, 5, b g Conquering Hero (USA)—Cathryn's Song **Indef Limited**
30 **JET BOYS (IRE)**, 6, b g Le Bavard (FR)—Fast Adventure **The Jet Stationery Company Limited**
31 **JET FILES (IRE)**, 5, ro g Roselier (FR)—Deepdecending **The Jet Stationery Company Limited**
32 **JET RULES (IRE)**, 6, b g Roselier (FR)—Bell Walks Fancy **The Jet Stationery Company Limited**
33 **JIBBER THE KIBBER (IRE)**, 7, br g Good Thyne (USA)—Mia's Girl **Mr J. Hitchins**
34 **JOYFUL PABS**, 4, b f Pablond—Joyful's Girl **Probus Stud Farm Partnership**
35 **JUST ALBERT (IRE)**, 6, b g Roselier (FR)—Carrigaun Lass **Mr A. E. T. Mines**
36 **LABURNUM GOLD (IRE)**, 5, b g Ragapan—Clashdermot Lady **Mr Arnie Kaplan**
37 **LADY NOSO**, 5, b m Teenoso (USA)—Canford Abbas **Mrs S. King**
38 **LAKE MISSION**, 11, b g Blakeney—Missed Blessing **Mr W. T. Montgomery**
39 **LORD LOFTY (IRE)**, 6, ch g Meneval (USA)—Deep Cristina **Salammi Racing**
40 **LORD REGAL (IRE)**, 5, b g Aristocracy—Regular Maid **Crombie Club Racing**
41 **LUCAYAN CAY (IRE)**, 5, ch g Al Hareb (USA)—Flying Melody **Peters and Lee**
42 **LUSTY LIGHT**, 10, b g Strong Gale—Pale Maid **Mr B. R. H. Burrough**
43 **MAGELLAN BAY (IRE)**, 8, b g Orchestra—Kintullagh **Autofour Engineering**
44 **MAILCOM**, 10, b g Strong Gale—Poll's Turn **Mailcom Plc**
45 **MASTER HARRY (IRE)**, 4, b g Strong Gale—Another Miller **Robert & Elizabeth Hitchins**
46 **MASTER PALLIETER (IRE)**, 5, gr g Henbit (USA)—Linen Thread **Mr Martin Van Doorne**
47 **MASTER TRIBE (IRE)**, 6, ch g Master Willie—Calaloo Sioux (USA) **Jebel Ali Racing Stables**
48 **MENTMORE TOWERS (IRE)**, 4, gr g Roselier (FR)—Decent Dame **Mr Philip Matton**
49 **MID-DAY MILLER**, 9, ch g Oats—Mid-Day Milli **Mr C. Cox**
50 **MISS BRECKNELL (IRE)**, 7, b m Supreme Leader—Just Darina **Mr Rex Johnson**
51 **MISTRIC**, 7, b m Buckley—Miss Poker Face **Mr S. D. Hemstock**
52 **NAHTHEN LAD (IRE)**, 7, b g Good Thyne (USA)—Current Call **Mr J. Shaw**
53 **NOBLE ATHLETE (IRE)**, 4, br g King's Ride—Bowerina **Mr G. & L. Johnson**
54 **PRINCEFUL (IRE)**, 5, b g Electric—Iram **Robert & Elizabeth Hitchins**
55 **ROBERO**, 5, b g Robellino (USA)—Copt Hall Princess **Robert & Elizabeth Hitchins**
56 **RONNIE'S DREAM (IRE)**, 4, b g Mandalus—Phantom Thistle **Mr G. Henfrey**

MRS J. PITMAN—continued

57 **ROSSELL ISLAND (IRE)**, 5, br g Strong Gale—Fraoch Ban **Robert & Elizabeth Hitchins**
58 **ROUYAN**, 10, b g Akarad (FR)—Rosy Moon (FR) **Mr Peter Mines**
59 **ROYAL ATHLETE**, 13, ch g Roselier (FR)—Darjoy **Mr G. & L. Johnson**
60 **SILVER THYNE (IRE)**, 4, br g Good Thyne (USA)—Fitz's Buck **Robert & Elizabeth Hitchins**
61 **SMITH'S BAND (IRE)**, 8, b g Orchestra—Pollys Flake **Mr Arthur Smith**
62 **SMITH TOO (IRE)**, 8, br g Roselier (FR)—Beau St **Smith Mansfield Meat Co Ltd**
63 **SUPERIOR FINISH**, 10, br g Oats—Emancipated **Mr G. Henfrey**
64 **TELUK (IRE)**, 5, ch g Sula Bula—Little Union **Jenny Pitman Racing Ltd**
65 **TENNESSEE TWIST (IRE)**, 6, b g Buckskin (FR)—Darjoy **Halewood International Ltd**
66 **TRAVEL BOUND**, 11, b g Belfalas—Sugar Shaker **Mr James Banister**
67 **VITAMAN (IRE)**, 7, b g King's Ride—Sea Cygnet **Larkhall Nat Hlth/Cantassium Vitamins**
68 **WILLSFORD**, 13, b g Beau Charmeur (FR)—Wish Again **Mr Arnie Kaplan**
69 **WREKENGALE (IRE)**, 6, br g Strong Gale—Wrekenogan **Robert & Elizabeth Hitchins**
70 **YOUNG BALDRIC**, 9, gr g Politico (USA)—No Don't **Blakeley Painters Ltd**

Other Owners: Mrs Richard Allen, Mr Stewart Andrew, Mr Mike Bateman, Mr E. G. M. Beard, Mr E. R. Beard, Mrs Kay Birchenhough, Mr S. J. Brittan, Mr D. A. Brown, Mrs H. R. Cross, Mr Roger Davies, Mrs L. Douglas, Mr Peter J. Douglas, Peter J. Douglas Engineering, Mr M. J. Farrell, Mr J. A. Gent, Mr P. Heath, Mr J. C. Hitchins, Mr Stewart R. Hunt, Mr T. P. Keary, Mrs J. M. Kennedy, Mr R. J. King, Mrs Christine Knight, Mrs David Laing, Mr C. J. R. Lee, Sheikh Ahmed Al Maktoum, Sheikh Mohammed, Mr N. Shulman, Mr M. A. Strong, Mr P. M. Tilley, Mr T. W. Upfield, Mr David P. Walker, Dr Robert Woodward.

Jockeys (NH): R Farrant (10-0), W Marston (10-0).

498   MR S. I. PITTENDRIGH, South Wylam

Postal: **Bradley Hall Farm, South Wylam, Northd, NE41 8SP.**

Phone: **(01661) 852676**

1 **ITS A DEAL**, 10, b g Lochnager—J J Caroline **Mr S. I. Pittendrigh**
2 **LIVE RUST (IRE)**, 6, ch g Air Display (USA)—Regretable **Mr S. I. Pittendrigh**
3 **MANDIKA**, 8, b g Flash of Steel—Bushti Music **Mr S. I. Pittendrigh**
4 **MOBILE MISS (IRE)**, 5, br m Classic Secret (USA)—Ellaline **Mr S. I. Pittendrigh**
5 **NOBODYS FLAME (IRE)**, 8, b g Dalsaan—Hamers Flame **Mr S. I. Pittendrigh**
6 **PERSIAN SYMPHONY (IRE)**, 5, ch m Persian Heights—River Serenade (USA) **Mr S. I. Pittendrigh**

Amateurs: Mr S I Pittendrigh (10-7), Mr C Wilson.

499   MS L. C. PLATER, Newcastle Upon Tyne

Postal: **The Stables, Little Harle, Kirkwhelpington, Newcastle Upon Tyne, NE19 2PD.**

Phone: **(01830) 540424**

1 **AUMALE (IRE)**, 5, ch g Be My Guest (USA)—Marie de Chantilly (USA)
2 4, B g Skyliner—Confident Vote
3 **CONNIE LEATHART**, 5, b m El Conquistador—Busy Quay
4 **JILLY GREY**, 11, gr m Grey Ghost—Mary McQuaker
5 5, Ch g Wood Chanter—More Energy
6 **PADAVENTURE**, 11, b g Belfalas—Cardamine
7 **ZOOT MONEY**, 4, gr f Scallywag—Moonduster

THREE-YEAR-OLDS

8 B g Past Glories—Mary McQuaker

Other Owners: Mr D. Sundin.

Jockey (NH): D Bentley.

Lady Rider: Ms P Robson (9-0).

500   MR ROBERT E POCOCK, Bridgwater

Postal: **Stringston Farm, Holford, Bridgwater, Somerset, TA5 1SX.**

1 DUST OF LIFE, 6, b m War Hero—Yellow Wagtail **Mr T. E. Pocock**
2 LOWER BITHAM, 9, ch m Julio Mariner—Peggy **Mr T. E. Pocock**
3 PRICKLY PATH, 6, ch m Royal Match—Thistle Blue **Mr T. E. Pocock**
4 ROSE GARDEN, 7, b m Pragmatic—Indian Rose **Mr T. E. Pocock**

501   MR M. J. POLGLASE, Newmarket

Postal: **Eve Lodge, Hamilton Road, Newmarket, Suffolk, CB8 0NY.**
Phone: **(01638) 560125 FAX (01638) 560859 EVENINGS (01638) 664459**

1 JARI (USA), 5, b g Dixieland Band (USA)—Dusty Heart (USA) **Mr M. J. Polglase & Mr H. Bond**
2 MANABAR, 4, b g Reprimand—Ring of Pearl **Mrs Anthony Polglase**
3 TAFAHHUS, 4, b g Green Desert (USA)—Mileeha (USA) **Mr Roger Newton**

THREE-YEAR-OLDS

4 Br f Respect—Now You Know **Mrs Donald Black**

TWO-YEAR-OLDS

5 B f 16/3 Keen—Festival Fanfare (Ile de Bourbon (USA)) **James Brown & Partners**
6 MISS BARCELONA (IRE), b f 6/3 Mac's Imp (USA)—National Ballet (Shareef Dancer (USA)) **Mr Brad Wetenhall**
7 SWIFT, ch c 16/5 Sharpo—Three Terns (USA) (Arctic Tern (USA)) **General Sir Geoffrey Howlett**

Other Owners: Mr Michael Brown, Mr T. Dean, Mr C. Hollingsworth, Mr Anthony Polglase.

Amateur: Ken Santana (9-2).

502   MR C. L. POPHAM, Taunton

Postal: **Bashford Racing Stables, West Bagborough, Taunton, Somerset, TA4 3EF.**
Phone: **(01823) 432769 (0831) 209875**

1 BAXWORTHY LORD, 5, b g Arctic Lord—Sugar Pea **Mr Richard Weeks**
2 BIG BANDS ARE BACK (USA), 4, b g Alleged (USA)—Jetta J (USA) **Mr A. G. Fear**
3 DAN DE LYON, 8, ch g Broadsword (USA)—Little Primrose **Mr A. Staple**
4 DONTDRESSFORDINNER, 6, b g Tina's Pet—Classic Times **The Dontdressfordinner Partnership**
5 EMRAL MISS, 8, b m Scorpio (FR)—Sugar Loch **Mrs Jonathan Bennett**
6 HE'S A KING (USA), 6, b g Key To The Kingdom (USA)—She's A Jay (USA) **Jill Emery And Partners**
7 HO LEE MOSES (IRE), 7, ch g Denel (FR)—Sofa River (FR) **Mr K. L. Dare**
8 HURRICANE BLAKE, 8, b g Blakeney—Nibelunga **Mr A. G. Fear**
9 KOO'S PROMISE, 5, bl m Lepanto (GER)—Koo-Ming **G. A. Warren Limited**
10 LUCKY AGAIN, 9, br g Ile de Bourbon (USA)—Soft Pedal **Mr Richard Weeks**
11 NEAT AND TIDY, 11, b g Dubassoff (USA)—Spic And Span **Miss L. A. Davis**
12 POSSOM PICKER, 6, b g El Conquistador—Sols Joker **Mr Henry T. Cole**
13 QUEENS CONTRACTOR, 6, br g Formidable (USA)—Salazie **Mr A. G. Fear**
14 RATHER SHARP, 10, b g Green Shoon—Rather Special **Mr C. L. Popham**
15 ROBINS PRIDE (IRE), 6, b g Treasure Hunter—Barney's Sister **Mr M. A. Long**
16 SANDS POINT, 6, br g Rakaposhi King—Jacqueline Jane **Mrs C. R. Hayton**
17 SUPREME FLAME (IRE), 6, b g Supreme Leader—Rossacurra **Mr Henry T. Cole**
18 TRAPEZE, 5, br g Shirley Heights—Fiesta Fun **Mr C. L. Popham**
19 ZITAS SON (IRE), 6, ch g The Parson—Zitas Toi **R. J. Heathman (County Contractors) Ltd**

Other Owners: Mr P. Littlejohns, Mr E. Morris, Mr P. F. Popham, Mr A. Skidmore, Mr Tony Wreford.

Jockeys (NH): T Dascombe, M A Fitzgerald (w.a.).

503   MR J. C. POULTON, Lewes

Postal: **Balmer Farm, Brighton Road, Lewes, East Sussex, BN7 3JN.**
Phone: **(01273) 603824/621303**

1 **BALMERDOWN**, 4, ch f Kabour—Boom Shanty **Mr Gerald West**
2 **BATA BULLETS**, 4, gr f Grey Desire—Barefoot Contessa
3 **BLURRED IMAGE (IRE)**, 5, ch g Exactly Sharp (USA)—Bear's Affair
4 **BRIGHTON BREEZY**, 6, b g Skyliner—Tree Mist **Mr J. C. Poulton**
5 **BRIGHT SEASON**, 8, b g Silly Prices—Cannes Beach **Mr M. C. Wells**
6 **DECIDING BID**, 10, ch g Valiyar—Final Call **Mr J. C. Poulton**
7 **DUKE OF LEE**, 6, b g Buckley—La Margarite **Mr Gerald West**
8 **EVERSO UMBLE**, 5, br g Grey Desire—Our Mandy **Mr Gerald West**
9 **GLAD SHE'S GONE**, 5, gr g Move Off—Absent Lady **Mr Gerald West**
10 **INCHYDONEY BOY (IRE)**, 7, b g Callernish—Inch Tape **Mr M. Lowry**
11 **ONE FOR MUM**, 5, gr m Absalom—Silly Games
12 **OUR LITTLE LADY**, 4, b f Queen's Soldier (USA)—Charlotte's Pearl
13 **PROPERO**, 11, b g Electric—Nadwa **Mr Gerald West**
14 **RUNNING SANDS**, 12, b g Record Run—Sirette **Mr J. C. Poulton**
15 **SABOTEUSE**, 4, b f Prince Sabo—Cloudless Sky **Mr Gerald West**

THREE-YEAR-OLDS

16 B g Derrylin—Early Run

Other Owners: Gordon House Partnership, Mr J. S. King, Mrs Jenny Smith.

Jockeys (NH): R Rowell (10-2), Andrew Thornton (w.a.).

Amateur: Mr J C Poulton (10-7).

Lady Rider: Miss Leesa Long (10-0).

504   MR J. R. POULTON, Lewes

Postal: **White Cottage, Stud Farm, Telscombe Village, Lewes, BN7 3HZ.**

1 **ARRASAS LADY**, 6, ch m Arrasas (USA)—Sharelle **Mr L. Best**
2 **CUCKMERE VENTURE**, 6, br m King of Spain—Kala Nashan **Mr R. C. Streeter**
3 **GENERAL BUNCHING**, 6, b g Kalaglow—Baino Charm (USA) **Mr T. Armour**
4 **JAYSMITH**, 10, ch g Ginger Boy—Medway Melody **Mr M. C. Wells**
5 **LADY POLY**, 8, b m Dunbeath (USA)—First Temptation (USA)
6 **OOZLEM (IRE)**, 7, b g Burslem—Fingers **Brooknight Guarding Ltd**
7 **PERCUSSION BIRD**, 4, b f Bold Owl—Cymbal **Mr J. R. Poulton**
8 4, Br f Arrasas (USA)—Romacina **Mr T. Armour**
9 **STEADY READY GO (IRE)**, 4, b c Night Shift (USA)—Smeralda (GER) **Mr T. Armour**
10 **SWEET ALLEGIANCE**, 6, b m Alleging (USA)—Child of Grace **The In-House Partnership**
11 **TAPESTRY ROSE**, 5, ch m Arrasas (USA)—Sharelle **Mr T. Armour**
12 **TENNYSON BAY**, 4, b g Allazzaz—Richards Folly **Mr Jamie Poulton**
13 **TIHEROS**, 4, ch g Risk Me (FR)—Farras **Mr T. Anthony**

THREE-YEAR-OLDS

14 **INTO DEBT**, b f Cigar—Serious Affair **Mrs Juliet Druce**
15 **ONE IN THE EYE**, br c Arrasas (USA)—Mingalles **Brooknight Guarding Ltd**
16 B c Arrasas (USA)—Romacina **Mr T. Armour**

Other Owners: Mr G. Gold, Miss Victoria Markowiak, Mr Robin Sarju.

505   MR W. G. PREECE, Telford

Postal: **Uppington Smithy, Uppington, Telford, Salop, TF6 5HN.**
Phone: **(01952) 740249 FAX (01952) 740434 MOBILE (0802) 358195**

1 **AWESTRUCK,** 6, b g Primo Dominie—Magic Kingdom **Mr D. Portman**
2 **BATTY'S ISLAND,** 7, b g Town And Country—Just Something **Mrs Mary Price**
3 **BIG VAL,** 6, b m Valiyar—Greenstead Lady **Mr R. Loughlin**
4 **CAHERASS COURT (IRE),** 5, b m Taufan (USA)—Grass Court **Mr Bill Preece**
5 **GOATSFUT (IRE),** 6, ch g Le Bavard (FR)—Kilbricken Glen **Mr D. Jones**
6 **GUNNER SID,** 5, ch g Gunner B—At Long Last **Mr Bill Preece**
7 **HUGH DANIELS,** 8, b g Adonijah—Golden Realm **Mr M. Ephgrave**
8 **JON'S CHOICE,** 8, b g Andy Rew—Whangarei **H. S. & E. M. Yates**
9 **LADY LOIS,** 5, b m Andy Rew—Right Formula **Mr S. A. Clear**
10 **MUSICAL VOCATION (IRE),** 5, ch m Orchestra—Kentucky Calling **Mr D. Portman**
11 **NAGARA SOUND,** 5, b g Lochnager—Safe 'n' Sound **The Grove Inn, Walcot Racing Club**
12 **NEWBURY COAT,** 6, b g Chilibang—Deanta In Eirinn **Mr M. Ephgrave**
13 **NIRVANA PRINCE,** 7, ch g Celestial Storm (USA)—Princess Sunshine **Mr D. Portman**
14 **PRETTY SCARCE,** 5, ch m Handsome Sailor—Not Enough **Mr S. A. Clear**
15 **RUGRAT,** 6, ro m Another Realm—Gay Hostess (FR) **Mr R. Loughlin**
16 **TROPWEN MARROY,** 7, b m Headin' Up—Tropwen Winbourne **Mr R. Pitchford**

THREE-YEAR-OLDS

17 **IMAGE MAKER (IRE),** gr f Nordico (USA)—Dream Trader **Mr J. B. Wilcox**

TWO-YEAR-OLDS

18 Ch c 22/4 Hadeer—Fly The Coop (Kris) **Mr Bill Preece**
19 B c 3/3 Prince Daniel (USA)—Hidden Asset (Hello Gorgeous (USA)) **Mr Bill Preece**

Other Owners: Miss J. L. Portman, Mrs E. J. Williams.

Lady Rider: Miss L Boswell (9-7).

506   MR P. PRENDERGAST, Kildare

Postal: **Melitta Lodge, Kildare, Co. Kildare, Ireland.**
Phone: **(045) 521288 OR 521401 FAX 353 45 521875**

1 **AVOID THE RUSH (IRE),** 6, b g Flash of Steel—Bonny Brae **Yoshiki Akazawa**
2 **CORRIB LEGEND,** 6, b g Over The River (FR)—Flutter Bug
3 4, B g Ardross—First Things First **Ms M. Horan**
4 **MACGILLYCUDDY,** 7, b br g Petorius—My Bonnie **Mrs Rita Hale**
5 **TAKE NO CHANCES,** 6, b m Thatching—Sovereign Pearl **Mr A. Walsh**
6 **TARAJAN (USA),** 4, ch g Shahrastani (USA)—Tarafa **Ms M. Horan**
7 4, B g Accordion—Temarie (FR) **Mrs Patrick Prendergast**
8 **THE AUGUSTINIAN,** 10, br g Deep Run—Shuill Donn **Mrs Patrick Prendergast**
9 **THOMOND PARK (IRE),** 8, b g Strong Gale—Tonduff Star **Mrs Patrick Prendergast**
10 **WINTER BELLE (USA),** 8, b g Sportin' Life (USA)—Belle O'Reason (USA) **Mr John Muldoon**

THREE-YEAR-OLDS

11 **MASTER ANGLER,** b c Governor General—Bright Stream **Mr J. D. Clague**

TWO-YEAR-OLDS

12 Ch c 19/4 Kris—Balenare (Pharly (FR)) **Ms M. Horan**
13 B c 3/4 Rambo Dancer (CAN)—Nicholess (Nicholas Bill) **Ms M. Horan**
14 Ch c 1/2 Soviet Lad (USA)—Special Meeting (Persian Bold) **Ms M. Horan**

507   SIR MARK PRESCOTT BT, Newmarket

Postal: **Heath House, Newmarket, Suffolk, CB8 8DU.**

Phone: **(01638) 662117 FAX (01638) 666572**

1 **ESPARTERO (IRE)**, 4, ch c Ballad Rock—Elabella **Mr Mario Lanfranchi**
2 **GIFTBOX (USA)**, 4, b c Halo (USA)—Arewehavingfunyet (USA) **Mr Charles Walker**
3 **NORTH REEF (IRE)**, 5, b h Danehill (USA)—Loreef **Mr W. E. Sturt**
4 **OTARU (IRE)**, 4, b f Indian Ridge—Radiant (USA) **Mrs N. Tomioka**
5 **SERIOUS FACT**, 4, b g Aragon—Plain Tree **Mr G. Moore**
6 **WIZARD KING**, 5, b h Shaadi (USA)—Broomstick Cottage **Sheikh Ahmed bin Saeed Al Maktoum**

THREE-YEAR-OLDS

7 **CIRCUS STAR**, b c Soviet Star (USA)—Circus Act **Mr Neil Greig**
8 **COACHELLA**, b f Warning—Cockatoo Island **Lord Derby**
9 **CREEKING**, b f Persian Bold—Miller's Creek (USA) **Cheveley Park Stud**
10 **EXALTED (IRE)**, b c High Estate—Heavenward (USA) **Mrs F. R. Watts**
11 **FAILED TO HIT**, b c Warrshan (USA)—Missed Again **Hesmonds Stud**
12 **FARMOST**, ch g Pharly (FR)—Dancing Meg (USA) **Mr W. E. Sturt**
13 **FROG**, b f Akarad (FR)—Best Girl Friend **Mr B. Haggas**
14 **LAST SECOND (IRE)**, gr f Alzao (USA)—Alruccaba **Mr Faisal Salman**
15 **LEARNING CURVE (IRE)**, gr f Archway (USA)—Children's Hour **Mr L. A. Larratt**
16 **NATTIER**, b f Prince Sabo—Naturally Fresh **Mr G. S. Shropshire**
17 **PASTERNAK**, b c Soviet Star (USA)—Princess Pati **Mr Graham Rock**
18 **PIVOTAL**, ch c Polar Falcon (USA)—Fearless Revival **Cheveley Park Stud**
19 **PRIOLO PRIMA**, b c Priolo (USA)—Jungle Rose **Petra Bloodstock**
20 **QUINZE**, b g Charmer—Quaranta **Lord Fairhaven**
21 **SERIOUS SENSATION**, ch g Be My Chief (USA)—Maiyaasah **Mr G. Moore**
22 **SERIOUS TRUST**, b c Alzao (USA)—Mill Line **Mr G. Moore**
23 **SILENT GUEST (IRE)**, b c Don't Forget Me—Guest House **Mr E. B. Rimmer**
24 **TRUTH**, b f Prince Sabo—Pursuit of Truth (USA) **Cheveley Park Stud**
25 **UPLIFT**, ch f Bustino—Relatively Easy **Capt. J. Macdonald-Buchanan**
26 **WARMING TRENDS**, b g Warning—Sunny Davis (USA) **Hesmonds Stud**

TWO-YEAR-OLDS

27 **ALL IS FAIR**, br f 25/2 Selkirk (USA)—Allegra (Niniski (USA)) **Miss K. Rausing**
28 **ARAPI**, b f Arazi (USA)—Princess Pati (Top Ville) **Hesmonds Stud**
29 B f 10/2 Petong—Bellyphax (Bellypha) **Mrs C. R. Philipson**
30 **BRAVE ACT**, b c 24/4 Persian Bold—Circus Act (Shirley Heights) **Mr W. E. Sturt**
31 **CARTOUCHE**, gr c Terimon—Emblazon (Wolver Hollow) **Lady Fairhaven**
32 **CATCH THE FLAME (USA)**, b f 6/2 Storm Bird (CAN)—
        Burnished Bright (USA) (Well Decorated (USA)) **Cheveley Park Stud**
33 **DAVIS ROCK**, ch f Rock City—Sunny Davis (Alydar (USA)) **Hesmonds Stud**
34 **DOMINANT AIR**, b c 18/2 Primo Dominie—Area Girl (Jareer (USA)) **Mr Neil Greig**
35 **DRIFT**, b c Slip Anchor—Norgabie (Northfields (USA)) **Mr B. Haggas**
36 **ENLISTED (IRE)**, b f Sadler's Wells (USA)—Impudent Miss (Persian Bold) **Mr Neil Greig**
37 **FERNY HILL (IRE)**, b c Danehill (USA)—Miss Allowed (Alleged (USA)) **Cheveley Park Stud**
38 **FLORENTINE DIAMOND (IRE)**, b f Primo Dominie—Poplina (USA) (Roberto (USA)) **Mr Faisal Salman**
39 **FLOTILLA**, b c Saddlers' Hall (IRE)—Aim For The Top (USA) (Irish River (FR)) **Cheveley Park Stud**
40 **HEAVENLY DANCER**, b f Warrshan (USA)—High Halo (High Top) **The Thurcoe Partnership**
41 **HYDE PARK (IRE)**, b c 27/4 Alzao (USA)—Park Elect (Ahonoora) **Mr Neil Greig**
42 **IL FALCO (FR)**, b c Polar Falcon (USA)—Scimitarila (USA) (Diesis) **Mr Alvaro Maccioni**
43 **KRABLOONIK (FR)**, b c 1/2 Bering—Key Role (Be My Guest) **Mrs F. R. Watts**
44 **MARYTAVY**, b f 10/3 Lycius (USA)—Rose Parade (Thatching) **Lord Roborough**
45 **MISSFORTUNA**, b f Priolo (USA)—Lucky Round (Auction Ring (USA)) **Canary Thoroughbreds**
46 **MUDFLAP**, b f 17/4 Slip Anchor—River's Rising (FR) (Mendez (FR)) **Major General Sir George Burns**
47 **MYTHICAL**, gr f 18/4 Mystiko (USA)—Geryea (USA) (Desert Wine (USA)) **Lord Fairhaven**
48 **PERPETUAL**, ch f 13/5 Prince Sabo—Brilliant Timing (USA) (The Minstrel (CAN)) **Cheveley Park Stud**
49 **PHILOSOPHIC**, b c 23/3 Be My Chief (USA)—Metaphysique (USA) (Law Society (USA)) **Mrs L. Burnet**
50 **PIETRO BEMBO (IRE)**, b c 17/3 Midyan (USA)—Cut No Ice (Great Nephew) **Mr Cyril Humphris**
51 **PIRATE'S GIRL**, b f 2/2 Mtoto—Maritime Lady (USA) (Polish Navy (USA)) **Cheveley Park Stud**

SIR MARK PRESCOTT BT—continued

52 **RED CAMELLIA**, b f 22/3 Polar Falcon (USA)—Cerise Bouquet (Mummy's Pet) **Cheveley Park Stud**
53 **RUDIMENTAL**, b c Rudimentary (USA)—Full Orchestra (Shirley Heights) **Cheveley Park Stud**
54 **SAEKO-BEAUTY**, b f 24/3 Warrshan (USA)—Jalopy (Jalmood (USA)) **Mr Shigeru Morinaka**
55 **SARARA (USA)**, ch f 13/5 Trempolino (USA)—Name And Fame (Arts And Letters) **Mrs Noriko Tomioka**
56 **SHARP BUT FAIR**, gr f Sharpo—Fair Minded (Shareef Dancer (USA)) **The Sharp But Fair Partnership**
57 **SHEPHERD'S DELIGHT**, b f 7/4 Prince Sabo—Montfort (Red Sunset) **Cheveley Park Stud**
58 **SUPERSPRING**, ch f 1/2 Superlative—Champ d'Avril (Northfields (USA)) **Mr David Hicks**
59 **THE IN-LAWS (IRE)**, ch f 15/3 Be My Guest (USA)—Amboselli (Raga Navarro (ITY)) **Mr G. D. Waters**
60 **UNION TOWN (IRE)**, b c Generous (IRE)—
Exclusive Life (USA) (Exclusive Native (USA)) **H.R.H. Prince Fahd Salman**

Other Owners: Mr J. Carroll, Mr Charles Catt, Mr David Coe, Mrs Sherry Collier, Dr St John Collier, Mr R. S. Dawes, The Hon Miss G. Douglas-Pennant, Mr Roger Ferris, Lady Margaret Fortescue, Mr David F. Howard, The Hon Miss Pearl Lawson-Johnston, Major C. R. Philipson, Mr G. B. Rimmer, Mr J. W. Rowles, Mrs Angela Stevens, Tessona Racing Limited, Mrs Ann Thurlow.

Jockeys (Flat): G Duffield (8-1), C Nutter (8-1).

508   MRS A. PRICE, Presteigne

Postal: **The Meeting House, Norton, Presteigne, Powys, LD8 2HA.**
Phone: **(01544) 267221**

1 **CWM ARCTIC**, 9, b m Cisto (FR)—Menel Arctic **Ms B. Brown**
2 **CWM BYE**, 5, ch g Hubbly Bubbly (USA)—To Oneiro **Ms B. Brown**
3 **FINAL ACE**, 9, ch g Sharpo—Palmella (USA) **Mrs A. Price**
4 **OPALS SON**, 5, b g Rabdan—Opal Fancy **Mrs A. Price**
5 **TRUE FRED**, 7, ch g True Song—Silver Spartan **Mrs A. Price**
6 **WATCHIT LAD**, 6, b g El-Birillo—Watch Lady **Mrs A. Price**

Amateur: Mr M Jackson (10-5).

509   MR C. G. PRICE, Hay-on-Wye

Postal: **Willow Croft, Hay-on-Wye, Hereford, HR3 5PN.**
Phone: **(01497) 820819 FAX (01497) 820776**

1 **CHIAROSCURO**, 10, b g Idiot's Delight—Lampshade **Mr Clive Price**
2 **DAMOCLES**, 4, b g Dashing Blade—Madam Trilby **Mr R. C. Price**
3 4, B g El Conquistador—Laura's Dream **Mr R. C. Price**
4 **LORELEI ROCK**, 5, b m Emarati (USA)—Singalong Lass **Mr R. C. Price**
5 **THINK IT OUT**, 5, ch m Master Willie—Fresh Thoughts **Mr R. C. Price**
6 **WAR O' THE ROSES**, 5, b m Derring Rose—Kincs **Mr Clive Price**

Jockey (NH): R Bellamy (9-7).

Amateur: Mr S Lloyd (10-7).

510   MR RICHARD PRICE, Leominster

Postal: **Eaton Hall Farm, Leominster, Herefordshire, HR6 0NA.**
Phone: **LEOMINSTER (0568) 615638/612333**

1 **AL SKEET (USA)**, 10, b g L'Emigrant (USA)—Processional (USA) **Mr R. J. Price**
2 **BLAZING DOVE**, 5, ch g Little Wolf—Shadey Dove **Mr J. T. Price**

MR RICHARD PRICE—continued

3 **CORN EXCHANGE**, 8, b g Oats—Travellers Cheque **Mr D. Wellon**
4 **DOVETTO**, 7, ch g Riberetto—Shadey Dove **Mr J. T. Price**
5 **FOXGROVE**, 10, b m Kinglet—Foxbury **Mrs C. W. Middleton**
6 **LITTLE GUNNER**, 6, ch g Gunner B—Love of Kings **A. W. Bailey**
7 **MISWISKERS**, 6, br m Reesh—That Space **Mr Tom Dawson**
8 **MORIARTY**, 9, b g Martinmas—Love Is Blind (USA) **Mr M. F. Oseman**
9 **PENIARTH**, 10, b m Oats—Rapenna **Mr Bill Davies**
10 **POSITIVE RESULT (IRE)**, 4, ch f Doulab (USA)—Second Service **Mr Hugh B. McGahon**
11 **PRIDEWOOD PICKER**, 9, b g Joshua—Guinea Feather **Mrs B. Morris**
12 **SISTER JIM**, 6, b m Oats—Midnight Pansy **Mr Bill Davies**
13 **TAAHHUB (IRE)**, 6, b g Nordico (USA)—Undiscovered **Mr A. E. Price**
14 **TANGO MAN (IRE)**, 4, ch g King Luthier—Amour Libre **Mr Hugh B. McGahon**
15 **TIP THE DOVE**, 7, br m Riberetto—Nimble Dove **Mr Cecil J. Price**

Other Owners: Mr P. E. Price.

511   MR P. A. PRITCHARD, Shipston-on-Stour

Postal: **The Gate House, Whatcote, Shipston-on-Stour, Warwickshire, CV36 5EF.**
Phone: **TYSOE (01295) 680689**

1 **BALLAD RULER**, 10, ch g Ballad Rock—Jessamy Hall **Woodlands (Worcestershire) Ltd**
2 **DEEP SONG**, 6, ch g True Song—Rapagain **Mr P. A. Pritchard**
3 **MALLYAN**, 9, b m Miramar Reef—Charlie's Sunshine **Mr Bryan Gordon**
4 **MUSICAL HIT**, 5, ch g True Song—Rapagain **Mrs E. M. Wharton**
5 **WOODLANDS ELECTRIC**, 6, b g Rich Charlie—Hallowed **Woodlands (Worcestershire) Ltd**
6 **WOODLANDS ENERGY**, 5, b m Risk Me (FR)—Hallowed **Woodlands (Worcestershire) Ltd**
7 **WOODLANDS GENHIRE**, 11, ch g Celtic Cone—Spartella **Woodlands (Worcestershire) Ltd**
8 **WOODLANDS LAD TOO**, 4, b c Risk Me (FR)—Hallowed **Woodlands (Worcestershire) Ltd**
9 **WOODLANDS POWER**, 8, b g Celtic Cone—Surely Right **Woodlands (Worcs) Ltd & Bryan Gordon**

THREE-YEAR-OLDS

10 Br c Rich Charlie—Hallowed **Woodlands (Worcestershire) Ltd**

TWO-YEAR-OLDS

11 B c 11/5 Risk Me (FR)—Hallowed (Wolver Hollow) **Woodlands (Worcestershire) Ltd**

Jockey (NH): R Davis (10-0).

Amateurs: Mr F Hutsby (10-0), Mr J Pritchard (10-7).

512   DR P. L. J. PRITCHARD, Purton

Postal: **Scrumpy Cottage, Purton, Berkeley, Glos, GL13 9HY.**
Phone: **(01453) 811881**

1 **GAMBLING ROYAL**, 13, ch g Royal Match—Chance Belle **Mrs T. Pritchard**
2 **KITTINGER**, 15, b g Crash Course—Mandaloch **Mrs T. Pritchard**
3 **MIDNIGHT MYSTIC**, 9, b m Black Minstrel—Magic Blaze **Mrs T. Pritchard**
4 **SANDMOOR PRINCE**, 13, b g Grundy—Princesse du Seine (FR) **Mrs T. Pritchard**

Amateur: Dr P L J Pritchard (9-11).

513   MR J. J. QUINN, Malton

Postal: **Bellwood Cottage Stables, Settrington, Malton, North Yorks, YO17 8NP.**
Phone: **(01944) 768370 MOBILE (0802) 406351 FAX (01944) 768370**

1 **B THE ONE**, 5, b g Gunner B—Half Asleep **Mr Andrew Page and Mr John Pollard**
2 **ERINY (USA)**, 7, b g Erins Isle—Memorable Girl (USA) **Lady Anne Bentinck**
3 **EYE OF THE STORM (IRE)**, 5, b g Strong Gale—Belon Brig **Mr John Stone**
4 **FLY TO THE END (USA)**, 6, b g Gulch (USA)—Bold Flora (USA) **Mr Ian Muir**
5 **HIGH PENHOWE**, 8, ch m Ardross—Spritely **Mrs M. J. Buck**
6 **INDICATOR**, 4, b g Reference Point—Comic Talent **Lady Anne Bentinck**
7 **IN GOOD FAITH**, 4, b g Beveled (USA)—Dulcidene **Mr Richard Dawson**
8 **LIEN DE FAMILLE (IRE)**, 6, b g Auction Ring (USA)—Soubrette **Mrs Marie Taylor**
9 **ORCHIDARMA**, 4, b g Reprimand—My Fair Orchid **Mr C. R. Galloway**
10 **REJOINUS**, 11, ch g Blue Refrain—Teesdale **Mr C. R. Galloway**
11 **ROBSERA (IRE)**, 5, b g Robellino (USA)—Que Sera **Mr Declan Kinahan**
12 **RON ON THE RUN (IRE)**, 6, b g Wassl—Celestial Path **'The Cow' Club**
13 **THE GOOFER**, 9, br g Be My Native (USA)—Siliferous **Mrs Paula Stringer & Mr C. R. Galloway**
14 **THE TOASTER**, 9, b g Furry Glen—Foolish Lady **Mrs Kay Owens**
15 **TRANSCENDENTAL (IRE)**, 6, b g Torenaga—Whistling Gold **Mrs S. Quinn**

THREE-YEAR-OLDS

16 **BABSY BABE**, b f Polish Patriot (USA)—Welcome Break **Mrs Carol Bloom**
17 **BASHTHEBOARDS**, b g Dancing Dissident (USA)—Vilanika (FR) **Hughes & Bloy**
18 **BOWLERS BOY**, ch g Risk Me (FR)—Snow Wonder **Bowlers Racing**
19 **COTTAGE PRINCE (IRE)**, b g Classic Secret (USA)—Susan's Blues **Mrs Kay Thomas**
20 **PERPETUAL LIGHT**, b f Petoski—Butosky **The Four Point Partnership**
21 **ROCKET GROUNDS (IRE)**, b f Common Grounds—Ginosa **Marple Vets Racing Club**
22 **THE BLACK DUBH (IRE)**, b g Classic Secret (USA)—Coral Cave **Bowlers Racing**

TWO-YEAR-OLDS

23 Gr c 25/5 Red Sunset—Chapter And Verse (Dancer's Image (USA)) **Mrs S. Quinn**
24 B f 17/3 Batshoof—Mia Fillia (Formidable (USA)) **Mrs Carol Bloom**
25 B g 7/4 Daring March—Mischievous Miss (Niniski (USA)) **Mrs S. Quinn**
26 B g 3/4 Precocious—Miss Racine (Dom Racine (FR)) **Mrs S. Quinn**

Other Owners: Mr S. Bowett, Mr N. J. Boyle, Mr P. R. Gooder, Mr Lol Grainger, Mr G. Griffin, Mr Paul Hogan, Mr D. Howell, Mr Jack Simmons, Mr J. E. Vowles.

Jockey (Flat): Mark Birch (8-4, w.a.).

Jockey (NH): Mark Dwyer (10-2, w.a.).

514   MRS J. R. RAMSDEN, Thirsk

Postal: **Breckenbrough Ltd, Breckenbrough House, Sandhutton, Thirsk, YO7 4EL.**
Phone: **(01845) 587226 FAX (01845) 587443**

1 **ADVANCE EAST**, 4, b g Polish Precedent (USA)—Startino **Mr Paul H. Locke**
2 **BARATO**, 5, ch g Efisio—Tentraco Lady **Mr David R. Young**
3 **BENZOE (IRE)**, 6, b g Taufan (USA)—Saintly Guest **Mr Tony Fawcett**
4 **CAPTAIN CARAT**, 5, gr g Handsome Sailor—Gem of Gold **Mr Colin Webster**
5 **CARLITO BRIGANTE**, 4, b g Robellino (USA)—Norpella **Mr Bernard Hathaway**
6 **COMMANDER GLEN (IRE)**, 4, b g Glenstal (USA)—Une Parisienne (FR) **Mr P. A. Leonard**
7 **DESERT LORE**, 5, b g Green Desert (USA)—Chinese Justice (USA) **Mr M. R. Charlton**
8 **FAME AGAIN**, 4, b f Then Again—Starawak **Mr M. R. Charlton**
9 **HALMANERROR**, 6, gr g Lochnager—Counter Coup **Mrs Joan Smith (Lincoln)**

MRS J. R. RAMSDEN—continued

11 **INSIDER TRADER**, 5, b g Dowsing (USA)—Careless Whisper **Mrs H. Carr**
12 **IT'S ACADEMIC**, 4, b f Royal Academy (USA)—It's Terrific **Mr J. R. Chester**
13 **MASTER CHARTER**, 4, ch g Master Willie—Irene's Charter **Mr Jonathan Ramsden**
14 **SELF EXPRESSION**, 8, b g Homing—Subtlety **Mr R. C. Moody**
15 **SUBTLE TOUCH (IRE)**, 5, b g Lomond (USA)—Lobbino **Mr F. Ellis**
16 **SUJUD (IRE)**, 4, b br f Shaadi (USA)—Sit Elnaas (USA) **Mr P. A. Leonard**
17 **SYCAMORE LODGE (IRE)**, 5, ch g Thatching—Bell Tower **Mrs J. R. Ramsden**
18 **TOP CEES**, 6, b g Shirley Heights—Sing Softly **Mr R. E. Sangster**
19 **TULU**, 5, ch m Nicholas Bill—Falcrello **Mr Mark Houlston**

THREE-YEAR-OLDS

21 **ALPINE JOKER**, b g Tirol—Whitstar **Mr G. F. Armitage**
22 **APPEAL AGAIN (IRE)**, br g Mujtahid (USA)—Diva Encore **Mr Colin Webster**
23 **ARABIAN HEIGHTS**, ch g Persian Heights—Arabian Rose (USA) **Mr P. A. Leonard**
24 **BRANSTON DANNI**, b f Ron's Victory (USA)—Softly Spoken **Mr J. David Abell**
25 **ETTERBY PARK (USA)**, b g Silver Hawk (USA)—Bonita Francita (CAN) **Crowther Homes Ltd**
26 **FAIRYWINGS**, b f Kris—Fairy Flax (IRE) **L. C. and A. E. Sigsworth**
27 **FALCON'S FLAME (USA)**, b br g Hawkster (USA)—Staunch Flame (USA) **Mr Colin Webster**
28 **HAWKSLEY HILL (IRE)**, ch c Rahy (USA)—Gaijin **Mr Hamish Alexander**
29 **KNOWN SECRET (USA)**, ch g Known Fact (USA)—Loa (USA) **Mr David McKenzie**
30 **LAWN ORDER**, b f Efisio—Zebra Grass **Mrs D. Ridley**
31 **MOCK TRIAL (IRE)**, b g Old Vic—Test Case **P. A. Leonard**
32 **NOBLE LORD**, ch g Lord Bud—Chasers' Bar **Mr J. E. Swiers**
33 **NORTHERN MOTTO**, b g Mtoto—Soulful (FR) **Mrs Alison Iles**
34 **OATEY**, ch f Master Willie—Oatfield **Mr R. Barnett**
35 **POLAR REFRAIN**, ch f Polar Falcon (USA)—Cut No Ice **Mr P. A. Leonard**
36 **ROAD RACER (IRE)**, br g Scenic—Rally **Mr J. E. Swiers**
37 **SANDBLASTER**, ch f Most Welcome—Honeychurch (USA) **Mr Graham Wood**
38 **SEATTLE ALLEY (USA)**, b c Seattle Dancer (USA)—Alyanaabi (USA) **Mr P. A. Leonard**
39 **SMARTER CHARTER**, br c Master Willie—Irene's Charter **Mrs Alison Iles**
40 **STRATEGIC PLOY**, b f Deploy—Wryneck **Mrs H. M. Carr**
41 Ch f Sanglamore (USA)—Syndaar (FR) **Mr L. Middlebrook**

TWO-YEAR-OLDS

42 **BISHOPS COURT**, ch c 24/2 Clantime—Indigo (Primo Dominie) **D. R. Brotherton**
43 **BOLD GAYLE**, ch f 24/2 Never So Bold—Storm Gayle (IRE) (Sadler's Wells (USA)) **Mr D. McKenzie**
44 **BRANSTON HARRIET (IRE)**, ro f 3/5 Petong—Food of Love (Music Boy) **Mr J. D. Abell**
45 **CAIRN DHU**, ch c 15/5 Presidium—My Precious Daisy (Sharpo) **Mr R. Thorburn**
46 **CAUTION**, b f 31/3 Warning—Fairy Flax (IRE) (Dancing Brave (USA)) **L. C. & A. E. Sysworth**
47 **CHEROKEE FLIGHT**, b c 23/1 Green Desert (USA)—Totham (Shernazar) **Mr P. A. Leonard**
48 **EPIC STAND**, b c 22/4 Presidium—Surf Bird (Shareef Dancer (USA)) **Mrs H. Carr**
49 **EXIT TO RIO (USA)**, ch c 2/3 Mining (USA)—Miami Vacation (USA) (Far North (CAN)) **Mr P. A. Leonard**
50 **FANTASY FLIGHT**, b f 15/3 Forzando—Ryewater Dream (Touching Wood (USA)) **Mr C. Webster**
51 Ch f 31/3 Tina's Pet—Fiddling (Music Boy) **Mr J. D. Abell**
52 **IRISH ACCORD (USA)**, b c 26/3 Cahill Road—Dimples (USA) (Smile (USA)) **Mr P. A. Leonard**
53 B c 7/4 Slip Anchor—Karavina (Karabas) **Mr M. Simmonds**
54 **KING UNO**, b c 28/4 Be My Chief (USA)—The King's Daughter (Indian King (USA)) **J & M Leisure (North) Ltd**
55 **MADISON MIST**, gr f 26/1 Mystiko (USA)—Hi-Li (High Top) **Mrs A. Iles**
56 **MADISON WELCOME (IRE)**, b c 7/4 Be My Guest (USA)—Subtle Change (IRE) (Law Society (USA)) **Mrs A. Iles**
57 **MOUCHE**, b f 24/2 Warning—Case For The Crown (USA) (Bates Motel (USA)) **Mr M. Simmonds**
58 **MUNGO PARK**, b c 9/3 Selkirk (USA)—River Dove (USA) (Riverman (USA)) **Mr P. A. Leonard**
59 **NO EXTRADITION**, b c 13/3 Midyan (USA)—Honey Pot (Hotfoot) **Mr P. A. Leonard**
60 **NO PRETENCE**, b c 7/5 Forzando—Minne Love (Homeric) **Mr B. Hathaway**
61 **ONLY JOSH (IRE)**, gr c 30/4 Waajib—Carlyle Suite (Icecapade (USA)) **Mr Tony Fawcett**
62 Ch f 18/2 Irish River (FR)—Princess Ivy (USA) (Lyphard's Wish (FR)) **Mr B. Hathaway**
63 **SILVER COLONY (USA)**, b f 29/3 Silver Hawk (USA)—

Colony Club (USA) (Tom Rolfe (USA)) **Mrs L. Middlebrook**
64 **STEP N GO (IRE)**, b f 15/5 Alzao (USA)—River Jet (USA) (Lear Fan (USA)) **Lord Petersham**
65 **SWISS COAST (IRE)**, b c 18/4 Mujadil (USA)—Rose A Village (River Beauty) **Mr B. Hathaway**
66 **TEST OF LOYALTY**, b c 21/2 Niniski (USA)—River Chimes (Forlorn River) **Mr B. Hathaway**

MRS J. R. RAMSDEN—continued

Other Owners: Mrs J. Abell, Sir Timothy Kitson, Mr P. R. C. Morrison, Mr G. E. Shouler, Ulceby Farms Ltd.

Jockey (Flat): K Fallon (8-4).

Jockey (NH): R Garritty (10-2).

Apprentices: S Buckley (8-4), T Finn (7-10), C West (7-10).

Amateur: Mr S Swiers (10-5).

Lady Rider: Miss E Ramsden (8-7).

515   MR W. RAW, Richmond

Postal: **Uckerby Mill, Scorton, Richmond, North Yorkshire, DL10 6DA.**

1 **ANOTHER RED,** 8, ch g Move Off—Daleena **Mr W. Raw**
2 **RED TRIX,** 4, ch f Primitive Rising (USA)—Daleena **Mr W. Raw**

Other Owners: Mrs E. D. Raw.

516   MR W. G. REED, Hexham

Postal: **Moss Kennels, Haydon Bridge, Hexham, Northd, NE47 6NL.**
Phone: **HALTWHISTLE (01434) 344201 MOBILE (0585) 934343**

1 **CELTIC COMMA,** 5, b m Celtic Cone—Lor Darnie **Miss Rosemary Jeffreys**
2 **JUST MOLLY,** 9, b m Furry Glen—Hansel's Trouble **Mr T. R. P. S. Norton**
3 **KIDLAW,** 8, b g Good Times (ITY)—Bedfellow **Mr J. Walby**
4 **MEADOWBURN,** 6, b m Meadowbrook—Miss Hubbard **Mr Geoffrey D. Dance**
5 **MISTER CASUAL,** 7, br g Damister (USA)—Something Casual **Mrs D. F. Culham**
6 **POLAR GALE (IRE),** 7, br g Strong Gale—Tanarpa **Mr James Stoddart**
7 **RIVER BEE,** 7, br g Meadowbrook—Brown Bee III **Mr J. Walby**
8 **SILVER PEARL,** 5, gr g Insan (USA)—Vanishing Trick **Mr Eric Scarth**
9 **STINGING BEE,** 5, b g Respect—Regal Bee **Mr W. G. Reed**
10 **STRONG DEEL (IRE),** 8, b g Strong Gale—Gorryelm **Mr J. Stephenson**
11 **THE STELL BURN,** 6, b m Respect—Little Swinburn **Mr W. G. Reed**

Other Owners: Mr J. N. Anthony, Mrs L. M. Joicey, Mrs G. Reed.

Jockey (NH): W T Reed (10-2).

517   MRS J. G. RETTER, Exeter

Postal: **Glebe Farm, Whitestone, Exeter, Devon, EX4 2HP.**
Phone: **(01392) 811410 MOBILE (0860) 248058 FAX (01392) 811410**

1 **ALLAHRAKHA,** 5, ch g Aragon—Bernigra Girl **Mr Martin Hill**
2 **BLACK HORSE LAD,** 12, ch g Orchestra—Little Peach **Mrs J. G. Retter**
3 **CRISTOSKI (IRE),** 4, b g Petoski—Cristalga

MRS J. G. RETTER—continued

4 GOT TO BE JOKING, 8, b g Homing—Rambert **Mr A. K. Collins**
5 IDIOM, 9, b g Idiot's Delight—Squiffy **Mrs J. Carrington**
6 KALOGY, 9, gr m Kalaglow—Coyote **Mrs B. Taylor**
7 MARIO'S DREAM (IRE), 8, ch g Boyne Valley—Its All A Dream **Mrs J. G. Retter**
8 PALLADIUM BOY, 6, b g Supreme Leader—Dear Jem **Palladium Ltd (Builders Merchants)**
9 PURBECK CAVALIER, 7, ch g Sula Bula—Party Miss **Mr B. Curtis**
10 RAFIKI, 11, br g Show-A-Leg—Drink Time **Mr J. P. Carrington**
11 SABAKI RIVER, 12, br g Idiot's Delight—Keen Lass **Mrs B. Taylor**

Other Owners: Mr Roy Crabbe, Mrs K. A. Stuart, Mr R. F. Woodward.

518   MRS G. R. REVELEY, Saltburn

Postal: **Groundhill Farm, Lingdale, Saltburn, Cleveland, TS12 3HD.**
Phone: **(01287) 650456 FAX (01287) 653095 MOBILE (0860) 686540**

1 AIRBORNE SUN, 5, ch g Infantry—Hardwick Sun **Mr Norton, Mr Pryke & Mr Fawcett**
2 ALI'S ALIBI, 9, br g Lucifer (USA)—Moppit-Up **Mrs Kearney**
3 ANGUS-G, 4, br g Chief Singer—Horton Line **Mr W. Ginzel**
4 ANSURO AGAIN, 7, b g Lochnager—Ansuro **Frickley Holdings Ltd**
5 APACHE RAIDER, 4, br g Dancing Brave (USA)—Calandra (USA) **Mrs E. A. Kettlewell/Mr E. W. Kettlewell**
6 ARDARROCH PRINCE, 5, b g Chief Singer—Queen's Eyot **Mr W. G. McHarg**
7 AVISHAYES (USA), 9, b g Al Nasr (FR)—Rose Goddess **Mr P. Davidson-Brown**
8 BARK'N'BITE, 4, b g Reprimand—Tree Mallow **Mr P. D. Savill**
9 BARTON HEIGHTS, 4, br g Primitive Rising (USA)—Changatre **Miss C. J. Raines**
10 BATABANOO, 7, ch g Bairn (USA)—For Instance **Mr P. D. Savill**
11 BAYROUGE (IRE), 8, br m Gorytus (USA)—Bay Tree (FR) **Mr A. Sharratt**
12 BILLY BUSHWACKER, 5, b g Most Welcome—Secret Valentine **Mr T. Child**
13 BONANZA, 9, ch g Glenstal (USA)—Forliana **Waldridge Developments Ltd**
14 BOWMANS LODGE, 5, b g Primitive Rising (USA)—Keldholme **Black Bull Partnership**
15 BRAVE BUCCANEER, 9, ch g Buckskin (FR)—Not So Dear **Mr Sean O'Shea**
16 BREAK THE RULES, 4, b g Dominion—Surf Bird **Mr P. D. Savill**
17 BROCTUNE BAY, 7, b g Midyan—Sweet Colleen **Mr Malcolm Bailey**
18 BROCTUNE GOLD, 5, b g Superpower—Golden Sunlight **Mrs Thwaites, Mrs Bailey**
19 BRODESSA, 10, gr g Scallywag—Jeanne du Barry **Mr R. W. S. Jevon, Mr B. Fairs**
20 CAB ON TARGET, 10, br g Strong Gale—Smart Fashion **Mr E. A. Murray**
21 CARBISDALE, 10, ch g Dunbeath (USA)—Kind Thoughts **Mrs M. Williams**
22 CARSON CITY, 9, ch g Carlingford Castle—Even More **J. A. L. Fish Ltd**
23 CELTIC CEILIDH, 5, ch m Scottish Reel—Show Home **Mrs M. Williams**
24 CHARITY CRUSADER, 5, b g Rousillon (USA)—Height of Folly **Express Marie Curie**
25 CHILL FACTOR, 6, br g Strong Gale—Icy Miss **Miss E. Shepherd**
26 CITTERN, 6, b g Ela-Mana-Mou—Seattle Serenade (USA) **Carnoustie Racing Club Ltd**
27 5, B br m Supreme Leader—Clonmello **Mr & Mrs Williams**
28 CRACKHILL FARM, 5, b g Formidable (USA)—Girl Friend **Mr P. D. Savill**
29 CURTELACE, 6, ch g Nishapour (FR)—Khandjar **Mr P. D. Savill**
30 CUTTHROAT KID (IRE), 6, b g Last Tycoon—Get Ahead **Mr P. D. Savill**
31 DECENT FAIRWAY (IRE), 7, b m Decent Fellow—Alhamdulillah **Mrs J. N. Askew**
32 DECENT PENNY (IRE), 7, b m Decent Fellow—Pencil **Mr G. G. Stevenson**
33 DESERT FIGHTER, 5, b g Green Desert (USA)—Jungle Rose **Mr A. Frame**
34 DURGAMS FIRST (IRE), 4, ch g Durgam (USA)—Miromaid **The Mary Reveley Racing Club**
35 EDEN DANCER, 4, b g Shareef Dancer (USA)—Dash
36 EFIZIA, 6, b m Efisio—Millie Grey **Mrs H. I. S. Calzini**
37 ERZADJAN (IRE), 6, b g Kahyasi—Ezana **Mr D. S. Hall**
38 ESSAYEFFSEE, 7, b g Precocious—Floreal **Mrs S. Murray**

MRS G. R. REVELEY—continued

39 **EXECUTIVE DESIGN**, 4, b g Unfuwain (USA)—Seven Seas (FR) **Mr W. H. Strawson**
40 **EXPRESS GIFT**, 7, br g Bay Express—Annes Gift **M. W. Horner, H. Young, and D. S. Arnold**
41 **FEARLESS WONDER**, 5, b g Formidable (USA)—Long View **Mr William A. Davies**
42 **FLYAWAY BLUES**, 4, b g Bluebird (USA)—Voltigeuse (USA) **Mr P. D. Savill**
43 **FOUNDRY LANE**, 5, b g Mtoto—Eider **Mr A. Sharratt**
44 **GALEN (IRE)**, 5, br g Roselier (FR)—Gaye Le Moss **Mr J. Renton & Mr A. Sharratt**
45 **GALLOWS HILL (IRE)**, 7, b g Strong Gale—Master Nidee **Mr D. S. Hall**
46 **GONE TO HEAVEN**, 4, b g Aragon—Divine Fling **Mr P. D. Savill**
47 **GRAND CRU**, 5, ch g Kabour—Hydrangea **Dr Glyn Meredith**
48 **HARFDECENT**, 5, ch g Primitive Rising (USA)—Grand Queen **Mr A. G. Knowles**
49 **HIGHBANK**, 4, b g Puissance—Highland Daisy **Mr Peter M. Dodd**
50 **HIGHBEATH**, 5, b g Dunbeath (USA)—Singing High **Mrs M. B. Scholey**
51 **HIGHLAND SPIN**, 5, ch g Dunbeath (USA)—In A Spin **Laurel Leisure Ltd**
52 **HIT THE CANVAS (USA)**, 5, ch g At The Threshold (USA)—Also Royal (USA) **Mr Jeremy Mitchell**
53 **JALCANTO**, 6, ch g Jalmood—Bella Canto **Mr William A. Davies**
54 **JOMOVE**, 7, ch g Move Off—Windlestrae **Raby Racing Ltd**
55 **JUST FRANKIE**, 12, ch g Tepukei—Harpalyce **Lady Susan Watson**
56 **KEEP YOUR DISTANCE**, 6, b g Elegant Air—Normanby Lass **Mr P. D. Savill**
57 **KIMBERLEY BOY**, 6, b g Mtoto—Diamond House **Mrs Susan McDonald**
58 **LINDISFARNE LADY**, 4, b f Jupiter Island—Harifa **Ken Matthews Racing**
59 **LINLATHEN**, 6, ch g Move Off—Loch Brandy **Mrs J. A. Niven**
60 **LOCHNAGRAIN (IRE)**, 8, b br g Strong Gale—Mountain Sedge **Lightbody of Hamilton Ltd**
61 **LUCIMAN (IRE)**, 6, b g Mandalus—Lucylet **Pamlyn Racing**
62 **MARRA'S ROSCOE**, 10, b br g Roscoe Blake—British Pet Queen **Mrs Dorothy Horner**
63 **MASTER BRACKEN**, 7, ch g Grey Desire—Maha **Express Marie Curie**
64 **MELOTTIE**, 11, b g Meldrum—Lottie Lehmann **Mrs Fulton**
65 **MERRY MASQUERADE (IRE)**, 5, b g King's Ride—Merry Madness **G. Brown, Lady Legard**
66 **MILL THYME**, 4, b f Thowra (FR)—Milinetta **Mrs Brigitte Pollard**
67 **MISS HUNTCLIFFE**, 9, ch m Deep Run—Woodcliffe **Mrs J. N. Askew**
68 **MONARU**, 10, b g Montekin—Raubritter **Mr R. Meredith**
69 **MONDRAGON**, 6, b g Niniski (USA)—La Lutine **Mr D. Young**
70 **MOONSHINE DANCER**, 6, b g Northern State (USA)—Double Birthday **Mr Peter Colquhoun**
71 **MORGANS HARBOUR**, 10, br g Radical—Parsfield **Mr P. C. W. Owen**
72 **MR BOSTON**, 11, b g Halyudh (USA)—Edith Rose **Mr M. K. Oldham**
73 **MR LURPAK**, 4, b g Minster Son—Ixia **M. D. Foods**
74 **MR PERSONALITY**, 4, ch g Bairn (USA)—Gentle Gain **Mrs Pam Goodall**
75 **MR TEES COMPONENTS**, 4, br g Strong Gale—Culinary **Tees Components Ltd**
76 **MR WOODCOCK**, 11, b g Sit In The Corner (USA)—Grey Bird **Mr P. A. Tylor**
77 **NORTH ARDAR**, 6, b g Ardar—Langwaite **Laurel Leisure Ltd**
78 **NOTABLE EXCEPTION**, 7, b g Top Ville—Shorthouse **Mr Roland Hope**
79 **OLD FART (IRE)**, 6, ch g Ela-Mana-Mou—Sea Port **Mr A. Flannigan**
80 **ONCE MORE FOR LUCK (IRE)**, 5, b g Petorius—Mrs Lucky **The Mary Reveley Racing Club**
81 **PENNY A DAY (IRE)**, 6, b g Supreme Leader—Mursuma **Mr J. Good**
82 **PINNY**, 5, b m Town and Country—The Plain Wain **Mrs Mary A. Meek**
83 **RANDOM HARVEST (IRE)**, 7, br g Strong Gale—Bavello **Mr C. C. Buckley**
84 **RHOSSILI BAY**, 8, b g Idiot's Delight—Hitting Supreme **Mrs M. Williams**
85 **RING OF VISION (IRE)**, 4, br g Scenic—Circus Lady **Mr P. D. Savill**
86 **ROAR ON TOUR**, 7, b g Dunbeath (USA)—Tickled Trout **Mrs S. D. Murray**
87 **ROBERTY LEA**, 8, b g Alleging (USA)—Rosy Lee (FR) **Wentdale Const Ltd**
88 **ROLLED NOTES**, 6, b m Oats—Rare Deal **Bealby - Roxburgh**
89 **ROSEBERRY TOPPING**, 7, gr g Nicholas Bill—Habitab **Mr Rex Norton**
90 **ROYAL EXPRESSION**, 4, b g Sylvan Express—Edwins' Princess **Mr Les De La Haye**
91 **ROY BOY**, 4, b g Emarati (USA)—Starky's Pet **Mr H. G. W. Brown**
92 **SAINT EXPRESS**, 6, ch g Clantime—Redgrave Design **Mr D. Hall**
93 **SATIN LOVER**, 8, ch g Tina's Pet—Canoodle **Mr D. S. Hall**
94 **SECOND COLOURS (USA)**, 6, b br g Timeless Moment (USA)—Ruffled Silk (USA) **Mr P. D. Savill**
95 **SEDVICTA**, 4, b g Primitive Rising (USA)—Annes Gift **The Mary Reveley Racing Club**
96 **SEVEN TOWERS (IRE)**, 7, b g Roselier (FR)—Ramble Bramble **Mrs E. A. Murray**
97 **SHAFFISHAYES**, 4, ch g Clantime—Mischievous Miss **Mr P. Davidson-Brown**

MRS G. R. REVELEY—continued

98 **SKIDDAW ROCK**, 6, b g Nishapour (FR)—Desrose **Mr John Wills**
99 **SMART APPROACH (IRE)**, 6, br m Buckskin (FR)—Smart Fashion **Mrs M. B. Thwaites**
100 **SON OF IRIS**, 8, br g Strong Gale—Sprats Hill **M.H.G. Systems Ltd**
101 **SOUPREME**, 4, ch f Northern State (USA)—Soupcon **The Soupreme Partnership**
102 **SOUTH WESTERLY (IRE)**, 8, br g Strong Gale—Kilclogher Lass **Mr W. H. Strawson**
103 **STAR PERFORMER (IRE)**, 5, b g Petorius—Whitstar **Mr P. D. Savill**
104 **STAY AWAKE**, 10, ch g Anfield—Djimbaran Bay **Mr Austin Donnellon**
105 **STRONG MINT (IRE)**, 5, br g Strong Gale—Derrygold **Mr Anderson, Mr Good & Lady Legard**
106 **SUFFOLK GIRL**, 4, ch f Statoblest—Miss Pisces **Lucayan Stud**
107 **SUGAR MILL**, 6, b g Slip Anchor—Great Tom **Mr C. C. Buckley**
108 **SUNDERLAND ECHO**, 7, br g Daring March—Incarnadine **Northeast Press Limited**
109 **SUPERPRIDE**, 4, b g Superpower—Lindrake's Pride **Mrs Muriel Ward**
110 **SURREY DANCER**, 8, br g Shareef Dancer (USA)—Juliette Marny **Laurel Leisure Ltd**
111 **SUSHI BAR (IRE)**, 5, gr g Petorius—Sashi Woo **Mr P. D. Savill**
112 **SWEET MIGNONETTE**, 8, b m Tina's Pet—Ixia **Mr Ron Whitehead**
113 **SWORD BEACH**, 12, ch g Scallywag—Bargello's Lady **Mrs S. J. Mason**
114 **THE GALLOPIN'MAJOR (IRE)**, 6, ch g Orchestra—Pedalo **Mr R. W. S. Jevon**
115 **TILLYBOY**, 6, b g Little Wolf—Redgrave Creative **The Mary Reveley Racing Club**
116 **TURNPOLE (IRE)**, 5, br g Satco (FR)—Mountain Chase **Mr W. J. Williams**
117 **UNCLE DOUG**, 5, b g Common Grounds—Taqa **Mr D. Saul**
118 **URON V (FR)**, 10, b g Cap Martin (FR)—Jolivette (FR) **Guy Faber and Peter Ambler**
119 **VIARDOT (IRE)**, 7, b g Sadler's Wells (USA)—Vive La Reine **The Mary Reveley Racing Club**
120 **WELSH MILL (IRE)**, 7, b g Caerleon (USA)—Gay Milly (FR) **Mr D. S. Hall**
121 **WHISKEY DITCH**, 5, ch m Kinglet—Trailing Rose **Mr R. Burridge**
122 **WHITE WILLOW**, 7, br g Touching Wood (USA)—Dimant Blanche (USA) **Mr H. North**
123 **WINDSWEPT LADY (IRE)**, 7, br m Strong Gale—Smithstown Lady **Mrs S. McDonald**
124 **WYNYARD LADY**, 5, ch m Say Primula—The White Lion **Lady Hall**

THREE-YEAR-OLDS

125 **AZTEC FLYER (USA)**, b g Alwasmi (USA)—Jetta J (USA) **Mr R. Meredith**
126 **COLWAY BRIDGE**, b c Colway Radial—Bell Bridge Girl **Mrs M. I. Jackson**
127 **DEADLINE TIME (IRE)**, b c Fayruz—Cut It Fine (USA) **Mr P. D. Savill**
128 **DUO MASTER**, b g Primo Dominie—Musical Sally (USA) **Mr P. D. Savill**
129 **FLYING NORTH (IRE)**, b g Distinctly North (USA)—North Kildare (USA) **Dr Glyn Meredith**
130 **JOE SHAW**, ch g Interrex (CAN)—Super Lady **Mr F. Gillespie**
131 **LEDGENDARY LINE**, b g Mtoto—Eider **Home & Away Partnership**
132 **MENTAL PRESSURE**, ch g Polar Falcon (USA)—Hysterical **Mr P. D. Savill**
133 B g Bairn (USA)—Mill d'Art **Mrs M. C. Reveley**
134 **NO MORE HASSLE (IRE)**, ch g Magical Wonder (USA)—Friendly Ann **No More Hassle Partnership**
135 **OPENING CHORUS**, ch g Music Boy—One Sharper **Mr P. D. Savill**
136 **SEDBERGH (USA)**, b c Northern Flagship (USA)—Crumbaugh Pike (USA) **Mr P. D. Savill**
137 B f Blakeney—Starky's Pet **Mr Brown**
138 **STOLEAMARCH**, br g Daring March—Pennine Star (IRE) **Mr E. Brown & Partners**
139 **TAUREAN FIRE**, ch g Tina's Pet—Golden Decoy **The Miles Apart Partnership**

TWO-YEAR-OLDS

140 **CATHEDRAL BELLE**, ch f 7/4 Minster Son—Corn Lily (Aragon) **Mrs S. McDonald**
141 **EMILY-JAYNE**, b f 1/4 Absalom—Tearful Reunion (Pas de Seul) **Waldridge Developments Ltd**
142 **GUARD A DREAM (IRE)**, ch g 12/5 Durgam (USA)—
　　　　　　Adarenna (FR) (Mill Reef (USA)) **The Mary Reveley Racing Club**
143 **KILCREGGAN**, b g 14/3 Landyap (USA)—Lehmans Lot (Oats) **Mr Good, Mr Anderson**
144 Ch c 29/4 Safawan—Ra Ra (Lord Gayle (USA)) **Mr D. Playforth & Partners**
145 Ch c 27/3 Rock Hopper—Thimbalina (Salmon Leap (USA)) **Mr A. Sharratt**

Other Owners: Mr D. Alton, Mr T. M. Andrews, Mr T. W. R. Bayley, Mrs S. M. V. Bealby, Mr T. J. Bird, Mrs Sue Blenkinsop, Mr H. Bowman, Mr M. Bradley, Mr David Buik, Mr Jeff Carling, Mr A. J. Coleman, Mrs J. Colling, Mr W. Crawford, Mr P. S. Dhariwal, Mr A. Emsley, Mr L. T. Foster, Mrs Marie Foster, Mr J. M. Garlick, Mr Alan Gauld, Mrs J. P. Goodall & Partners, Mr David Grant, Mr David A. Green, Mr A. F. S. Haynes, Mr R. Hebb, Mrs Lesley A. Hope, Mr H. Hurst, Mr N. Hurst, Mr Colin Jarvis, Mrs Lynne Jones, Mrs E. Jordan, Mr Joseph Kelly, Mr J. Laird, Mr Gary Peter

MRS G. R. REVELEY—continued

Lloyd, Mr C. Maesepp, Mr Malcolm McCall, Mr M. McClare, Mr Colin Metcalf, Mr Brian James Mitchell, Mr W. A. Money, Mr C. M. North, H. North & Partner, Mr M. J. Ogden, Mrs B. O'Shea, Mr S. O'Shea & Partners, Mr Gary Owers, Dr Roy Palmer, Mr D. Pearson, Mr Peter Phipps, Mr Bill Price, Mr T. R. Pryke, Mr H. A. Raby, Mr K. G. Reveley, Mr G. A. Robinson, Mr A. Roe, Mr Patrick Rooney, Mr D. G. Roxburgh, Mr L. M. Rutherford, Mrs H. Sedgwick, Mrs R. Semple, Mr R. Simpson, Mrs Richard Stanley, Mr C. E. Stedman, Mrs Margaret Stewart, Mr Jim Struth, Mr M. G. Tannahill, Mrs Dorothy Thompson, Mrs Mary Thompson, Mr R. C. Watts, Mr David Wild, Mr Ronald Wilkie, Mr Richard C. Williams, Mrs A. Wilson, Mr Noel Wilson, Mr Owen Watson Wilson, Mr David Wood, Mr J. T. Wood, Mr John Wood, Mr B. T. Woods, Mr Nigel Young.

Jockey (Flat): K Darley (8-1).

Jockeys (NH): R Hodge (10-0), P Niven (10-4), N Smith (10-0).

Apprentices: S Copp (8-5), G Parkin (8-1), K Prendergast (8-10).

Conditional: G Cahill, T J Comerford, M Herrington (9-7), G Lee (9-7), C McCormack.

Amateur: Mr M Naughton (9-7).

519   MR P. M. RICH, Usk

Postal: **Llangwendr Stables, Llangovan, Nr. Monmouth, Gwent, NP5 4BT.**
Phone: **(01291) 690864 FAX (01291) 690416**

1 **FERRUFINO (IRE)**, 8, b g Montekin—Fauchee **Mr P. M. Rich**
2 **NAIYSARI (IRE)**, 8, gr g Mouktar—Naiymat **Mr P. M. Rich**
3 **RICH TYCOON (IRE)**, 7, b g Buckskin (FR)—Stolen Gold **Mr P. M. Rich**
4 **ROYAL STANDARD**, 9, b g Sadler's Wells (USA)—Princess Tiara **Mr P. M. Rich**
5 **UNSUSPICIOUS (IRE)**, 6, ch g Caerleon (USA)—Lady's Bridge (USA) **Mr P. M. Rich**

520   MR G. W. RICHARDS, Greystoke

Postal: **The Stables, Greystoke, Penrith, Cumbria, CA11 0TG.**
Phone: **(017684) 83392 FAX (017684) 83933**

1 **ABBOT OF FURNESS**, 12, b g The Parson—Chestnut Fire **Lord Cavendish**
2 **ADDINGTON BOY (IRE)**, 8, br g Callernish—Ballaroe Bar **Gott Foods Limited**
3 **BELLE ROSE (IRE)**, 6, b br m Roselier (FR)—Golden Chestnut **The Belles**
4 **BETTER TIMES AHEAD**, 10, ro g Scallywag—City's Sister **Mr E. Briggs**
5 **CARLEY LAD (IRE)**, 8, br g Crash Course—Leveret **N. B. Mason (Farms) Ltd**
6 **DANCING DOVE (IRE)**, 8, ch m Denel (FR)—Curragh Breeze **Dr Kenneth S. Fraser**
7 **DARK HORIZON (IRE)**, 7, br m Strong Gale—Shady Doorknocker **Mrs Stewart Catherwood**
8 **DOMINO NIGHT (IRE)**, 6, b g Buckskin (FR)—Frying Pan **Mr R. Haggas**
9 **EARLYMORNING LIGHT (IRE)**, 7, gr g Idiot's Delight—Primrose Wood **Mrs Ann Starkie**
10 **ELATION**, 4, b g Sadler's Wells (USA)—Chellita **Mr R. Tyrer**
11 **ETERNAL CITY**, 5, b g Kind of Hush—Dark City **Mr R. Tyrer**
12 **FINCH'S GEM**, 8, ch g Saxon Farm—Glencaraig Gem **Mrs B. C. Finch**
13 **GENERAL COMMAND (IRE)**, 8, b g Strong Gale—Kylogue Daisy **Mr Robert Ogden**
14 **JOCKS CROSS (IRE)**, 5, ch g Riberetto—Shuil Le Dia **Mrs Gill Harrison**
15 **LANSBOROUGH**, 6, gr g Uncle Pokey—Young Lamb **Mr Robert Ogden**
16 **LOTHIAN COMMODORE**, 6, ro g Alias Smith (USA)—Lothian Lightning **Mr D. A. Whitaker**
17 **MCGREGOR THE THIRD**, 10, ch g Nearly A Hand—Arctic Dawn **Mrs D. A. Whitaker**
18 **NINFA (IRE)**, 8, b m The Parson—Lulu's Daughter **Lord Cavendish**
19 **ONE MAN (IRE)**, 8, gr g Remainder Man—Steal On **Mr J. Hales**
20 **ONESEVENFOUR (IRE)**, 7, ch g Jamesmead—Granny Grumble **Exors of the Late Mr G. Bartholomew**
21 **PARSONS BOY**, 7, ch g The Parson—Kylogue Daisy **Mr B. Ridge**

MR G. W. RICHARDS—continued

22 **PRECIPICE RUN**, 11, ch g Deep Run—Lothian Lassie **Cumbrian Racing Club**
23 **RAMPANT ROSIE (IRE)**, 8, b m Green Shoon—Ferrajo **Mr George J. H. Kemp**
24 **REAL TONIC**, 6, bl g Strong Gale—Primrose Wood **Mr Robert Ogden**
25 **SAVOY**, 9, ch g Callernish—Dream Daisy **Mr Robert Ogden**
26 **SKANE RIVER (IRE)**, 5, ch g Over The River (FR)—Miami High **Mr W. J. Peacock**
27 **SPANISH LIGHT (IRE)**, 7, b g Spanish Place (USA)—Arconist **Sir John Barlow**
28 **TARTAN TRADEWINDS**, 9, b g Strong Gale—Tipperary Special **Mackinnon Mills**
29 **TARTAN TYRANT**, 10, b g Tycoon II—Tina Fort **Mackinnon Mills**
30 **THE FINAL SPARK**, 5, b m Electric—Sailing Brig **The Belles**
31 **THE GREY MONK (IRE)**, 8, gr g Roselier (FR)—Ballybeg Maid **Mr Alistair Duff**
32 **THE TOYMAN (IRE)**, 7, br g Strong Gale—Halfsixagain **Mr J. Hales**
33 **THISTLE PRINCESS**, 7, gr m Belfort (FR)—Rueful Lady **Mr Joseph A. Gordon**
34 **UNGUIDED MISSILE (IRE)**, 8, br g Deep Run—Legaun **Mr D. E. Harrison**
35 **WHAAT FETTLE**, 11, br g Strong Gale—Double Century **Mackinnon Mills**
36 **WIND FORCE**, 11, br g Strong Gale—Richest **Mr J. N. G. Moreton**

Other Owners: Mr Roddy Duff, Greystoke Stables Ltd, Miss L. Hales, Mr Kenneth Kinch, Mr Kevin A. C. Kinch, Mr Roger Kinch, Mrs Susan Kinch, Mr E. R. Madden, Mrs Gordon Richards, Mrs T. R. Riley.

Jockeys (NH): A Dobbin (10-0), M Moloney (9-7).

Conditional: B Harding (9-7).

Amateur: Mr R Hale (9-7).

521   MR GRAHAM RICHARDS, Pontypridd

Postal: **1 Tynewydd Cottage, Llanfabon, Cilfynydd, Pontypridd, CF37 4HP.**
Phone: **(01443) 453189 FAX (01443) 453189**

1 **MINGAY**, 5, b g Gay Meadow—Miss Admington **Mr Graham Richards**

Jockey (NH): A Thornton.

Lady Rider: Miss Emily Jones.

522   MRS LYDIA RICHARDS, Arundel

Postal: **The Steddles, Yapton, Arundel, West Sussex, BN18 0DT.**
Phone: **HOME (01243) 553821**

1 **DEEPENDABLE**, 9, ch g Deep Run—Hester Ann **Mr Ron Stone**
2 **FICHU (USA)**, 8, b g Sharpen Up—Mousseline de Soie (FR) **Mrs Lydia Richards**
3 **JURASSIC CLASSIC**, 9, gr g Leading Man—Statfold Pride **Mr B. Seal**
4 **KEEN BID (IRE)**, 5, b g Alzao (USA)—Gaychimes **Mr B. Seal**
5 **KILLING TIME**, 5, b g Good Times (ITY)—Kelly's Bid **Mr B. Seal**
6 **KING'S GOLD**, 6, b g King of Spain—Goldyke **Mr G. C. Reilly**
7 **KNYAZ**, 6, b g Governor General—Aleda Rose **Mr Tony Clay**
8 **SHANUKE (IRE)**, 4, b f Contract Law (USA)—Auntie Ponny **Mr R. Howitt**
9 **TEATRADER**, 10, b g Baron Blakeney—Miss India **Mr B. Seal**

Other Owners: Mr K. L. Dalwood, Mr Tom Dearden, Mr Roger Rees, Mrs June Young.

Jockey (NH): M Richards (10-0).

523   MR P. C. RITCHENS, Tidworth

Postal: 'Hillview', 91 Parkhouse Road, Shipton Bellinger, Tidworth.

Phone: HOME (01980) 843088 YARD (01264) 781140

1 BLANCHLAND, 7, gr g Bellypha—Premier Rose Mr P. Ritchens
2 BLAZER MORINIERE (FR), 7, b g Montevideo—Kimberlite (FR) Mr Alan Kidd and Mr Andrew Johnson
3 CALGARY GIRL, 4, ch f Weld—Calgary Mrs B. Bishop
4 DANCING PIMPERNEL, 10, br g Baron Blakeney—Twist Mr G. R. Stevens
5 FROZEN DROP, 9, b g Le Bavard (FR)—Frozen Ground Mr Jock Cullen
6 HALLELUJA TIME, 4, b g Risk Me (FR)—Warm Wind Mrs Deborah Potter
7 KAIFOON (USA), 7, b h Woodman (USA)—Kitchen (USA) Mr John Pearl
8 MINITURE MELODY (IRE), 8, b m Kemal (FR)—Miss Fanackapan Mr P. Ritchens
9 MONKSANDER, 10, b g Monksfield—Maudie's Choice Mr John Pearl
10 RAQIB, 5, b g Slip Anchor—Reine Maid (USA) Mr Alan Kidd and Mr Andrew Johnson
11 ROCKY MELODY, 4, b g Music Boy—Summer Posy Mr Peter R. Davies
12 SUNSET AGAIN, 11, ch g Al Sirat (USA)—Noddy Mr John Hooper

Other Owners: Mrs B. D. Adams, Mr A. M. Beales, Mr D. Tye, Mr S. W. Ullyott.

Jockeys (NH): S Fox, A Tory.

524   MR DAVID ROBERTSON, Kilmarnock

Postal: Gateside Farm, Craigie, Kilmarnock, Ayrshire, KA1 5LR.

Phone: (01563) 860201

1 CANAAN VALLEY, 8, ch g Absalom—My Pink Parrot Mr D. Robertson
2 CRAIGIE RAMBLER (IRE), 7, b m Amazing Bust—Rambling Moss Mr D. Robertson
3 PIT PONY, 12, b g Hittite Glory—Watch Lady Mrs A. L. Robertson
4 RITA'S SISTER, 5, b m Meadowbrook—Miss Brig Mrs A. L. Robertson

Amateur: Mr D Robertson (10-5).

525   MRS P. ROBESON, Newport Pagnell

Postal: Fences Farm, Tyringham, Newport Pagnell, Bucks, MK16 9EN.

Phone: (01908) 611255 FAX (01908) 611255

1 ARCTIC TEAL, 12, b g Town And Country—Arctic Warbler Mrs P. Robeson
2 BLUEBILL, 5, gr m Baron Blakeney—Grouse Mrs P. Robeson
3 FIRECROWN, 6, b g Royal Vulcan—Grouse Mrs P. Robeson
4 REEDFINCH, 7, b g Rabdan—Tangara Mrs P. Robeson
5 SEDGE WARBLER, 9, ro m Scallywag—Arctic Warbler Mrs P. Robeson
6 TAWNY WARBLER, 4, b f Teenoso (USA)—Arctic Warbler Mrs P. Robeson
7 WREN WARBLER, 6, ch m Relkino—Arctic Warbler Mrs P. Robeson

Amateurs: Mr Richard Barret (9-7), Mr Stuart Edmunds (9-7).

526   MR S. J. ROBINSON, Darlington

Postal: Ketton Garage, Durham Road, Coatham Mundeville, Darlington, DL1 3LZ.

Phone: (01325) 311232 FAX (01325) 317952

1 DOC SPOT, 6, b g Doc Marten—Detonate Mr S. J. Robinson
2 DROMIN FOX, 10, b g The Parson—Kilcor Rose Mr S. J. Robinson
3 FAST STUDY, 11, b g Crash Course—Mary May Mr S. J. Robinson
4 OLYMPIC CLASS, 6, b g Strong Gale—Olympic Course Mr S. J. Robinson
5 SOME FLASH, 9, b g Quayside—Sirrahdis Mr S. J. Robinson

527   MR P. R. RODFORD, Martock

Postal: **Lavenoak House, Ash, Martock, Somerset, TA12 6NZ.**
Phone: **MARTOCK (01935) 823459**

1 **BRORA ROSE (IRE),** 8, b m Drumalis—Run Swift **Mr S. Watkins**
2 **DECEIT THE SECOND,** 4, ch g Bairn (USA)—Bushti Music **Mr E. T. Wey**
3 **DUNLIR,** 6, bl g Lir—Miss Black Glama **Mr B. R. Brereton**
4 **EMERALD MOON,** 9, b g Auction Ring (USA)—Skyway **Mr Paul C. N. Heywood**
5 **GOLDEN AFFAIR,** 5, ch m Golden Shields—Madame Rochas **Mr J. F. Symes**
6 **GOLDEN NEWS,** 5, b g Newski (USA)—Golden Rochas **Mr J. F. Symes**
7 **HENLEY REGATTA,** 8, br g Gorytus (USA)—Straw Boater **Mr E. T. Wey**
8 **MASKED MARTIN,** 5, b g Bustino—Mardi Gras Belle (USA) **Mr E. T. Wey**
9 **OATS N BARLEY,** 7, b g Oats—Doon Silver **Mr F. A. Landrigan**
10 **OUR NIKKI,** 6, gr m Absalom—Whisper Gently **Mr P. R. Rodford**
11 **SPINNING STEEL,** 9, b g Kinglet—Lasses Nightshade **Mrs C. A. Lewis-Jones**
12 **THE SHAW TRADER,** 7, ch g Noalto—Relkusa **Mrs Deborah Potter**

Other Owners: Mr D. Bell, Factorsecure Plc, Mr Geoff Lewis, Mr John Manley, Mr Mike Tebbut.

Jockey (NH): S Burrough (10-0).

Lady Rider: Miss S Cobden (9-7).

528   MR C. G. ROE, Chalford

Postal: **Hyde Park Farm, Lower Hyde, Chalford, Glos, GL6 8NZ.**
Phone: **(01453) 885487 FAX (01453) 88 5204**

1 **BIDE OUR TIME (USA),** 4, b c Timeless Moment (USA)—Had To Buy (USA) **Mr B. W. Parren**
2 **BLUE HAVANA,** 4, br f Cigar—Welsh Bluebell **Mr Harold Berlinski**
3 **CHEER'S BABY,** 6, b g Le Solaret (FR)—Marie Baby **Mrs Christine Matthew**
4 **JAIME'S JOY,** 6, b m Le Solaret (FR)—Tups **Roe Racing Ltd**
5 **LADY MARIE,** 7, b m Cruise Missile—Lady Amazon **Ms Caroline F. Breay**
6 **LE GRAND MAITRE,** 15, ch g Over The River (FR)—Cora Swan **Roe Racing Ltd**
7 **LLANELLY (FR),** 9, gr m Kenmare (FR)—Grey Valley (USA) **Roe Racing Ltd**
8 **MUMMY'S MOLE,** 5, gr g Le Solaret (FR)—Tups **Brann Ltd**
9 **PEACE TRIBUTE (IRE),** 7, br g Nomination—Olderfleet **Ms Caroline F. Breay**
10 **SUNGIA (IRE),** 7, b g Orchestra—Lysanders Lady **Ms Caroline F. Breay**
11 **THE OVERTRUMPER,** 9, b g Buzzards Bay—Nahawand **Mrs Lavinia Poppleton**
12 **TUPENNY SMOKE,** 4, b f Cigar—Tups **Roe Byfield Advertising**

Other Owners: Mr P. K. Davis, Mr J. W. Garofall, Rosemary Gordon.

Jockey (NH): W Humphreys (10-0).

Conditional: P Hughes (10-0).

529   MR W. M. ROPER, Co. Kildare

Postal: **Maddenstown Lodge, The Curragh, Co. Kildare, Ireland.**
Phone: **(045) 441798 MOBILE (088) 580688**

1 **ABIGAIL ROSE (BEL),** 4, gr f Abbey's Grey—Famille Rose **Mr D. McGowan**
2 6, Br g Tremblant—Burton Brown **Mr B. Burke**
3 4, B g Montelimar (USA)—Hurricane Dandy **Mr W. P. Roper**

MR W. M. ROPER—continued

4 **JIMMY O'GOBLIN**, 9, ch g Deep Run—Natural Shine **Mr F. Clarke**
5 **KINKY LADY**, 11, b m River Knight (FR)—Slinky Persin **Mrs M. Sinanan**
6 **MAORI'S DELIGHT**, 7, b m Idiot's Delight—Kath's Venture **Mr W. M. Roper**
7 **MUTAMANNI**, 6, b h Sadler's Wells (USA)—Betty's Secret (USA) **Mr W. M. Roper**
8 **ROCK POOL**, 7, ch g Ahonoora—Rockfest (USA) **D. Daly**
9 5, B g St Columbus—Slave's Bangle
10 **TALYGARN**, 5, gr g Faustus (USA)—Lucky Song **Mr Alan Cook**

THREE-YEAR-OLDS

11 **BROKEN RITES (IRE)**, b g Broken Hearted—Lady Wise **N. B. Wachman**
12 **CLEAR BLUE WATER (IRE)**, b c Dancing Dissident—Fair Song **Mr W. P. Roper**
13 **GOLDEN REPROACH**, ch f Magical Strike (USA)—No Reproach **Mr T. F. Long**
14 **QUOTE UNQUOTE**, b g Fayruz—Miss Quotation **Mr W. M. Roper**
15 **ROSY FUTURE (BEL)**, gr f Abbey's Grey—Famille Rose **Mr D. McGowan**

TWO-YEAR-OLDS

16 **HONOR'S STAG (USA)**, ch c 10/5 Blushing John (USA)—Bobbinette (USA) (Sir Ivor) **Mr W. P. Roper**
17 B f 20/5 Magical Strike (USA)—Killyhevlin (Green God) **Mr W. M. Roper**

Other Owners: Mr P. Finlay, Mr A. Hamilton, M. Killilea, D. Murphy, Mr R. J. Osborne, Mr K. Sinanan, Mr M. Taylor, Lord A. Weinstock, Hon S. A. Weinstock, M. Wyley.

530   MR B. S. ROTHWELL, Malton

Postal: **2 Honeysuckle Cottage, Musley Bank Stables, Malton, North Yorks, YO17 0TD.**
Phone: **HOME (01653) 696384 MOBILE (0378) 265300**

1 **BOLD TOP**, 4, ch g Bold Owl—Whirlygigger **Mrs G. M. Z. Spink**
2 **GALLARDINI (IRE)**, 7, b g Nordico (USA)—Sweet **Mr S. P. Hudson**
3 **GOLD PIGEON (IRE)**, 2, b m Goldhill—Bracka Pigeon **Contrac Promotions Ltd**
4 **JUST SUPPOSEN (IRE)**, 5, b g Posen (USA)—Snipe Singer **Consultco Ltd**
5 **LADY BLAKENEY**, 10, gr m Baron Blakeney—Queen of The Bogs **Mr J. B. Young**
6 **OCHOS RIOS (IRE)**, 5, br g Horage—Morgiana **Mrs H. A. Burn**
7 **QUEENS CONSUL (IRE)**, 6, gr m Kalaglow—Queens Connection **Miss Heather L. Davison**
8 **RARE PADDY**, 7, b m Royal Vulcan—Paddy's Gem **Mr Brian Rothwell**
9 **RISTON LADY (IRE)**, 6, b m Salt Dome (USA)—Trompe d'Oeil **Mrs G. M. Z. Spink**
10 **ROWDY YATES (IRE)**, 6, b g Kambalda—Mossy Game **Mr Steven Astaire**
11 **RUNFORACTION (IRE)**, 4, b f Contract Law (USA)—Prissy Miss **The Action Racing Club Ltd**
12 **WILLERFOSS (IRE)**, 6, b g Roselier (FR)—Some Gossip **Mr Michael Saunders**

THREE-YEAR-OLDS

13 **INPROMPTU MELODY (IRE)**, b f Mac's Imp (USA)—Greek Music **Contrac Promotions Ltd**
14 **IRISH OASIS (IRE)**, b g Mazaad—Alpenwind **Mr H. J. Harenberg**
15 **KLIPSPINGER**, ch f Formidable (USA)—Distant Relation **Mr Brian Rothwell**
16 **KRATZ (IRE)**, b g Prince Rupert (FR)—Some Spice **Mr Derek A. Smith**
17 **MILL HOUSE BOY (IRE)**, b g Astronef—Avantage Service (IRE) **Mr S. P. Hudson**

TWO-YEAR-OLDS

18 B g 8/5 Broken Hearted—Clubhouse Turn (IRE) (King of Clubs)
19 B f 9/3 Broken Hearted—Fiodoir (Weavers' Hall)
20 **RAHONA (IRE)**, b f 6/5 Sharp Victor (USA)—Hail To You (USA) (Hail To Reason) **Mr S. F. Moloney**

Other Owners: Mr F. Arnott, Mrs Brenda Bill, Mr David Hewson, Miss Alex McCabe, Mr Jeffrey Newton, Mrs B. Oughtred, Mr A. Spence, Mr E. St Quinton.

Jockey (Flat): M Fenton (8-1, w.a.).

Jockey (NH): R Supple (10-0, w.a.).

531   MR J. DE ROUALLE, Lamorlaye

Postal: 17 Rue Charles Pratt, 60260 Lamorlaye, France.

Phone: 44 21 37 37 FAX: 44 21 37 28

1 **EXTRA POINT**, 6, b h Reference Point—Fenella **J. Smadja**
2 **GOLFE JUAN (USA)**, 4, b c Lyphard—Green Moon **Sir J. Goldsmith**
3 **MANDAR**, 4, gr c Highest Honor—Marienthal **W. Nilsen**
4 **PARIS DANCER**, 4, ch c Paris Turf—Taboula Rasa **C. Gonzenbach**
5 **SPARKLINE**, 4, b f Akarad—Rhine Lane **Bnne de Forest**
6 **SUNDAY HORSE**, 4, b c Caerwent—Coincidence **J. Veil-Picard**
7 **SWIRA (IRE)**, 5, b m Dreams To Reality—Darment **L. Disaro**

THREE-YEAR-OLDS

8 **ALEXANDRE FARNESE**, gr c Caerwent—Coincidence **J-M Peycelon**
9 **ALYSHINO**, b g Alysheba—Shining Water **C. Gonzenbach**
10 **BONHEUR INEFFABLE**, b c Comrade In Arms—Mill Lady **J. Smadja**
11 **BOUYOUS ROULOUS**, b f Saint Andrews—Thirsty **Ecurie Claydia**
12 **BROWN LAD**, b c Garde Royale—Rhine Lane **Bnne de Forest**
13 **CUMBRES**, b f Kahyasi—Floripedes **Sir J. Goldsmith**
14 **DANCING JOY**, ch f Dancing Spree—Castle In The Air **Mme Tamagni**
15 **FAMOUS**, b g Tropular—Famous Horse **Ecurie Claydia**
16 **IL CASANOVA**, ch c Dancing Spree—Cox's Feather **C. Gonzenbach**
17 **IN YOUR DREAMS**, b f Always Fair—Pharsala **K-H Eng**
18 **LADY BUSINESS (IRE)**, b f Alzao—Ameridienne **Mme Tamagni**
19 **LOST AND FOUND**, b c Saumarez—Lighted Glory **W. Nilsen**
20 **MAILLOT (IRE)**, b c Bluebird—Special Thanks **P. Weill**
21 **MISS MARY GARDEN**, b f Assert—Heavenly Pearl **M. Dowling**
22 **MIXWAYDA**, gr f Linamix—Houwayda **K-H Eng**
23 **PIOU PIOUS (USA)**, ch f Bering—Pious **E. Lamarche**
24 **REMISE DE PEINE**, b f Fabulous Dancer—Glanost **Z. Hakam**
25 **RUPERT**, b c Kendor—Rudolfina **Z. Hakam**
26 **SPRONG**, b c Niniski—Samata **P. Baumgartner**
27 **SURGEON**, ch c Sharrood—Suva **K-H Eng**
28 **TAGELIA**, b f Tagel—Right River **C. Bardin**
29 **VIVE JAMES**, gr c Kendor—Rubelsanto **J. de Souza-Lage**
30 **ZOUKRIS**, b c Kris—Zoumorrod **W. Nilsen**

TWO-YEAR-OLDS

31 **ETOURDIS-MOI**, b f 15/1 Top Waltz—New River Gorge **Mr Brandebourger**
32 **FAIRLAY**, b f 20/4 Always Fair—Rhine Lane **Bnne de Forest**
33 **FEUER BALL**, b c 6/3 Galetto—Fahda Dream **Z. Hakam**
34 **FRENCH CONNECTION**, b f 22/3 Highest Honor—Eloisey **Mme Tamagni**
35 **GANELON**, b c 31/3 Exit To Nowhere—Gig **Z. Hakam**
36 **JERMIN**, b c 25/2 Zayyani—Jeromine **A. Schneider**
37 **JOY OF LIFE**, b f 16/4 Exit To Nowhere—Castle In The Air **Mme Tamagni**
38 **LE GRAND SEIZE**, b c 2/5 Akarad—Lidala **M. Dowling**
39 B f 12/4 Caerleon—Midnight Lady **Mme Tamagni**
40 **MONT D'ARNAUD**, b c 21/1 Double Bed—Mill Lady **Sir J. Goldsmith**
41 **MOTIV (IRE)**, b f 22/4 Akarad—Modiyna **K-H Eng**
42 **NAWAL**, b f 30/1 Homme De Loi—Lute String **Z. Hakam**
43 **PARTHE**, b c 22/3 Highest Honor—Plessaya **W. Nilsen**
44 **PIN PINICAILLE**, b c 13/3 Lead On Time—Coincidence **J. Baguenault**
45 **SCOTTISH SPRING**, b c 22/2 Kaldoun—Scottish Bride **Bnne de Forest**
46 **SILVER TAIL (USA)**, b c 13/3 Septieme Ciel—Brigade Speciale **W. Nilsen**
47 **SONETO**, b c 11/4 Kaldoun—Moucha **C. Berney**
48 **TATA NICOLE**, b f 28/5 Bakharoff—Comic Delivery **Mr Brandebourger**

Jockeys (Flat): Gerald Mosse, Olivier Peslier.

Apprentice: Antoine Sanglard.

532   MR J. C. ROUGET, Pau

Postal: **Chemin De La Foret, Bastard, 64000 Pau, France.**
Phone: **59 33 27 90 FAX 59 33 29 30**

1 ALFAHAR, 5, b h Al Nasr—Nonesuch Bay **L. de Quintanilla**
2 ATTENTION D'ANGERS, 5, b h Galetto—Karpa **P. V. Rayer**
3 BAINOBLESS, 5, gr g Highest Honor—Baino Bluff **J. C. Gour**
4 BOLD AND BLACK, 5, br g Never So Bold—Arminda **C. Gour**
5 CALAGUETO, 4, ch c Galetto—Calabria **A. Caro**
6 CARE OF PAPA, 6, b h Caerwent—Eagletown **L. de Quintanilla**
7 CAROFER, 5, ch g Dr Carter—Femme de Fer **P. Nogues**
8 CLEVER DAY, 6, b g Clever Trick—One Fine Day **C. Gour**
9 CLEVER TIGER, 7, gr g Clever Trick—She Tiger **M. Justov**
10 CLOSE CONFLICT, 5, br h High Estate—Catopetl **G. Tanaka**
11 COME ON JEEPY, 7, b g Comrade In Arms—Saadia **M. Daguzan-Garros**
12 COQ GAULOIS, 7, ch g Iron Duke—Celie **Marquis B. du Vivier**
13 FABULEUX VERMAND, 4, b g Fabulous Dancer—Marie de Vermand **C. Gour**
14 FARENDJ, 4, ch g Un Desperado—Touraille **L. Cattan**
15 FARU, 4, br c Mtoto—Fade **Sheikh Ahmed Al Maktoum**
16 FIK EL BARRAKI, 9, b g Crystal Glitters—Crillon **M. Daguzan-Garros**
17 GERSICA, 4, ch f Mille Balles—Heart Felt **Mrs J-F Dupont**
18 HALLE AUX GRAINS, 4, b f Shardari—Mo Pheata **C. Gour**
19 HECASIOS, 5, b g Sicyos—Hecalene **B. Ducasse**
20 HIGHEST BID, 4, b f Highest Honor—Bid Dancer **Ecurie I. M. Fares**
21 HUNTER STRAB, 4, ch g Huntercombe—Strabit **P. Nogues**
22 IPOH, 4, ch f Funambule—Irish Sea **Haras D'Etreham**
23 JOYFUL, 4, b f Green Desert—Optimistic Lass **Sheikh Mohammed**
24 LAMPOURDE, 4, br g Top Ville—Some Thing **Mrs R. Bousquet**
25 L'ILLUSION, 5, b m Mille Balles—Make It Sharp **Mrs J-F Dupont**
26 LIVERSAN, 5, b g Sure Blade—Pro Patria **M. Daguzan-Garros**
27 MACRUBY, 4, b g High Estate—Eight Mile Rock **J-C Gour**
28 MALAGAR, 7, bl g Highest Honor—Marie de Tracy **C. Gour**
29 MON HONNEUR, 4, gr g Highest Honor—Maralinga **C. Gour**
30 MORE HONOR, 4, br g Highest Honor—Saimore **Ecurie I. M. Fares**
31 PALATINE BOY, 4, b c Caerwent—La Palatine **C. Gour**
32 PAPIMENTO, 5, ch h Rainbow Quest—Papermoon **M. Daguzan-Garros**
33 POINT A LA LIGNE, 4, br f Akarad—Korinetta **Ecurie La Clauzade**
34 POTION D'AMOUR, 4, ch f Trempolino—Love Potion **R. C. McNair**
35 PUT FOR DOE, 7, b g Track Barron—Darbrielle **C. Gour**
36 QUEEN VILLE, 5, b m King of Macedon—Kadoutille **S. Boucheron**
37 REVE A TOI, 4, b g R B Chesne—Resilia **B. Belinguier**
38 ROI HO, 5, bl h Holst—Reine Ka **Mrs M. De Chambure**
39 ROOTS, 4, ch f Funambule—Ruma **Haras D'Etreham**
40 SALZEDO, 4, b g Caerwent—Surubinha **Marquis B. du Vivier**
41 SATIN DE SOIE, 6, b g Son of Silver—Surubinha **Marquis B. du Vivier**
42 SHANIKA, 5, br m Doyoun—Sassika **B. Ducasse**
43 TEMPS MODERNES, 4, b c Groom Dancer—Vieille France **C. Langlois-Meurinne**
44 TOUR DE TABLE, 6, ch g Fast Topaze—Dame des Roches **A. Caro**
45 TRUTH OR DIE, 5, b g Proud Truth—Baffling Ballerina **C. Gour**
46 UNA PERLA, 5, gr m Kendor—With You All **L. de Quintanilla**
47 WELCOME SIR, 4, b g Most Welcome—Round Midnight **C. Gour**

THREE-YEAR-OLDS

48 ACHERNOR, ch c Dancing Spree—Haumette **R. Bousquet**
49 AJAB ALZAMAAN, b f Rainbow Quest—Alwathba **Sheikh Ahmed Al Maktoum**
50 AKAVILLE, br f Akarad—Kadouville **S. Boucheron**
51 ALARCON, ch c Be My Chief—Collapse **A. Caro**
52 ALEXOR, ch g Brinkmanship—Rain Or Shine **J. P. Rios**
53 ALWAYS HIGHEST, br f Highest Honor—Never Late **Ecurie I. M. Fares**
54 ANDREW, br g Saint Andrews—Arcidia **Ecurie La Clauzade**
55 ARMAGH, br c Highest Honor—Missing Guest **R. Bousquet**

MR J. C. ROUGET—continued

56 **AUDIGNON,** br g Highest Honor—Juvenka **B. Ducasse**
57 **BAINO WARNING,** b f Warning—Baino Clinic **Ecurie I. M. Fares**
58 **BELY SAUCE,** ch f Lesotho—Back To One **H. Chamarty**
59 **BE MY ECHO,** ch c Eastern Echo—Dandera **C. Gour**
60 **BLACK LEO,** br c Leo Castelli—Betty Money **J. C. Gour**
61 **BOYASY,** ch f Mister Sicy—Boydara **R. Labeyrie**
62 **CAPABILITY,** ch f Nashwan—Victoress **Sheikh Mohammed**
63 **CAPODINEGRO,** b g Cyrano de Bergerac—Selvi **J. C. Gour**
64 **CHEEKYDUCK,** ch c Septieme Ciel—Bethrotal **Mrs M. de Chambure**
65 **CLIPTOMANIA,** br c Cryptoclearance—Marytavy **C. Gour**
66 **CONSTANCE DO,** ch f Risk Me—The Boozy News **Mrs A. Corcoral**
67 **COUT CONTACT,** br f Septieme Ciel—Company **J. T. L. Jones**
68 **CREEPSHOW,** b c Danehill—Servia **R. Bousquet**
69 **CRICKET GOAL,** br g Cricket Ball—Cilcaro **H. Chamarty**
70 **DANY BALL,** ch f Cricket Ball—Danirane **Ecurie La Clauzade**
71 **DI LUNA,** b f Fairy King—Histoire Douce **E. de Rothschild**
72 **DORSODURO,** gr c Highest Honor—Sioux City **J. P. Rios**
73 **ELISA WAR,** b f Warning—Elisa River **Ecurie I. M. Fares**
74 **FAC SIMILE,** b f Kaldoun—Indirasi **Mrs D. Steverlynck**
75 **FAUCON ROYAL,** br c Nikos—Aliscafi **H. Chamarty**
76 **FINE FELLOW,** br g Garde Royale—Resilia **B. Belinguier**
77 **FLIP FANTASIA,** b f Batshoof—Fade **R. Bousquet**
78 **FOLMANIE,** ch f Blushing John—Philarmonia **J. C. Gour**
79 **FRANC MIRACLE,** b g Legend of France—Reflect Miracle **Mrs J. F. Dupont**
80 **FUN HARBOUR,** ch c Funambule—Clef des Ondes **Marquis B. du Vivier**
81 **GELIGAUX MAXIMUM,** br f Kaldoun—Air Royal **B. Clin**
82 **GUEST OF ANCHOR,** b f Slip Anchor—Intimite Guest **Ecurie I. M. Fares**
83 **HIGHEST BABY,** b f Highest Honor—Lypheor Baby **Ecurie I. M. Fares**
84 **HIGHEST FOOD,** gr f Highest Honor—Food Corp **Ecurie I. M. Fares**
85 **HIGHEST HOLLOW,** b f Highest Honor—Sir Hollow **Ecurie I. M. Fares**
86 **HIGHEST WEDGE,** ch f Highest Honor—Wedge Cut **Ecurie I. M. Fares**
87 **HOOK LINE,** gr f Shaadi—Hooked Bid **Sheikh Mohammed**
88 **IBIN HONOR,** ch g Highest Honor—Ibin Atsil **Ecurie I. M. Fares**
89 **IRISH GASCON,** br c Cyrano de Bergerac—Get Ahead **J. C. Gour**
90 **ISSANOOR,** gr c Highest Honor—Noorissa **Ecurie I. M. Fares**
91 **ITSARA,** br f Caerwent—Brinosa **Ecurie Des Mousquetaires**
92 **JAUNATXO,** b c Lyphard's Wish—Femme de Fer **J. M. Soriano**
93 **JE REVE,** ch c Risk Me—First Fastnet **C. Gour**
94 **JUST RAINBOW,** ch f Rainbow Quest—Just Class **Ecurie I. M. Fares**
95 **KAILASA,** b f R B Chesne—Petite No **J. P. Hebrard**
96 **KANJI,** ch f Polish Patriot—Kamada **B. Belinguier**
97 **LA BELLE AFFAIRE,** b f Always Fair—Balalagka **J. F. Gribomont**
98 **LA MALLERET,** b f Summer Squall—Mousseline de Soie **Marquis B. du Vivier**
99 **LA MILITAIRE,** b f General Holme—Tanz **Sheikh Mohammed**
100 **LEAD THEM LADY,** br f Lead On Time—Lady Tamara **Ecurie I. M. Fares**
101 **LUROY,** br c Esprit du Nord—Lumiere du Feu **A. Caro**
102 **MACHINARI,** b c Machiavellian—Dafinah **Sheikh Mohammed**
103 **MALOUET,** gr c Kendor—Mi Longa **J. F. Gribomont**
104 **MANDARINO,** b g Trempolino—Hail The Dancer **Mrs M. de Chambure**
105 **MIMANSA,** ch f El Gran Senor—Mystical River **Sheikh Mohammed**
106 **MISS ST GERMAIN,** ch f Pampabird—Rodara **H. Chamarty**
107 **MISTER VALOIS,** b c Mister Sicy—Marie de Valois **H. Chamarty**
108 **NO WIN NO DEAL,** br f Machiavellian—Shenaleyah **Sheikh Ahmed Al Maktoum**
109 **ORIENTALIST,** ch c Afleet—Oriental Splendor **C. Gour**
110 **PARANOMELODY,** b f Cyrano de Bergerac—Stony Ground **J. C. Gour**
111 **PAR RAPPORT A CA,** ch g Regal Classic—Inside Line **C. Gour**
112 **PLAY FAIR,** b c Always Fair—Playing For Keeps **Ecurie I. M. Fares**
113 **PRINCE DE GIRAC,** gr g Lesotho—Inca Princess **Mrs A. Corcoral**
114 **PRINCE GUILLAUME,** b c Gairloch—Sudden Spirit **J. F. Gribomont**
115 **PSYCHOLADY,** b f Northern Baby—Ranchera **J. C. Gour**

MR J. C. ROUGET—continued

116 **RALLY FOR MTOTO**, b f Mtoto—Rally For Justice **Ecurie I. M. Fares**
117 **ROBROY**, ch c Goldneyev—Princess Mab **L. Cattan**
118 **ROI DES GENETS**, b c Baby Turk—Pomme d'Emeraude **A. Caro**
119 **SAINT MORITZ**, b g Midyan—Slew of Fortune **C. Gour**
120 **SANDALO**, ch c Royal Academy—Sassy Lassy **L. de Quintanilla**
121 **SATIN D'OR**, b c Tagel—Surubinka **Marquis B. du Vivier**
122 **SECRETO BOLD**, ch f Never So Bold—Bint Secreto **Ecurie I. M. Fares**
123 **SHARP PROSPECTOR**, b c Lycius—Welsh Note **B. Freiha**
124 **SIMPLY PRINCESS**, b f Simply Majestic—Night Fire **R. Bousquet**
125 **SURF CITY**, b c Groom Dancer—Serafica **J. C. Gour**
126 **SWEET LASS**, b f Belmez—Greenhill Lass **Sheikh Mohammed**
127 **THE SPECTATOR**, ch f General Holme—Ecran **Mrs R. Phillips**
128 **TINDERELLA VICTORY**, b f Al Nasr—Tinderella **Ecurie I. M. Fares**
129 **TORRENT DE LUNE**, b c Lesotho—Silver Fly **R. W. Denechere**
130 **TRINCAVEL**, ch c Magical Wonder—Reliable Rosie **R. Bousquet**
131 **UDINA**, b f Unfuwain—Tafila **Sheikh Mohammed**
132 **VALLYA STAR**, b f Saumarez—Lady Vallya **Ecurie La Clauzade**
133 **WAVEY**, b f Kris—Throw Away Line **G. Strawbridge**
134 **WINGED HUSSAR**, b c In The Wings—Akila **Sheikh Mohammed**
135 **XIANLANG**, b f Great Commotion—Down The Line **A. Lapoterie**
136 **ZOULOU BOY**, b g Danehill—Charara **J. C. Gour**

TWO-YEAR-OLDS

ALFALFA QUEEN, b f 7/5 Lashkari—Falafil (Fabulous Dancer) **Ecurie I. M. Fares**
ARME FATALE, ch f 23/3 Trempolino—Ville Eternelle (Slew O' Gold) **Abdul Aziz**
ASTRONOMIE, b f Cricket Ball—Arcidia (Al Nasr) **Ecurie La Clauzade**
BALLE DE GOLF, b f Homme de Loi—Baloa (Card King) **Marquis B. du Vivier**
BARAGUEY, ch c 2/3 Marignan—Liberty Nell (Weaver's Hall) **R. Bousquet**
BEAUTE BRUNE, b f 17/4 Kaldoun—Belle de Mai (Luthier) **R. Bousquet**
BONUS EVENTUS, ch c 16/4 Alwuhush—Femme de Fer (Dictus) **J. M. Soriano**
BRAVE, b c 23/3 Sanglamore—Boreale (Bellypha) **Mrs M. de Chambure**
CHLEPNYR, bc 16/4 Last Tycoon—Zircon Lady (Kings Lake) **R. Bousquet**
B f 31/1 Septieme Ciel—Company (Nureyev) **J. T. L. Jones**
CONSTELLATION, b f 17/3 Capote—Ambrosine (Mr Prospector) **B. Freiha**
DANCING ROSE, b f 12/3 Dancing Spree—Rose Bonbon (High Top) **E. de Rothschild**
DARLING SPREE, b c 27/3 Dancing Spree—Little Darling (Carvin) **H. Chamarty**
DE NOUVEAU, b c 2/4 Hero's Honor—Blue Design (Lightning) **A. Caro**
DIPIPERON, ch c 12/5 Houston—Spa Star (Saratoga Six) **C. Gour**
B f 25/3 Nashwan—Fair Rosamunda (Try My Best) **Sheikh Mohammed**
FLORISELLI, ch c 24/3 Afleet—Miracles Happen (Lear Fan) **Ecurie Des Mousquetaires**
B f 28/1 Top Ville—Glendera (Glenstal) **Sheikh Mohammed**
HELETTE, ch f 9/5 Be My Chief—Miss Butterfield (Cure The Blues) **M. Justou**
HOLLANDA, b f 10/4 Fabulous Dancer—Mona Mou (Luthier) **R. Bousquet**
INSIDON, b c 17/5 Kris—Boubskaia (Niniski) **J. C. Gour**
JO RIVER, ch c 13/2 Sanglamore—Jeanne de Laval (Gairloch) **B. Clin**
JOUMART, b c 1/5 Kendor—Dinner Out (Al Nasr) **Ecurie Des Mousquetaires**
JUSTFUL, gr c 20/3 Highest Honor—Just Class (Dominion) **Ecurie I. M. Fares**
KALDOUNSKA, b f 20/2 Kaldoun—Prologue (Fabulous Dancer) **Mme G. Forien**
KEEP PLAYING, ch c 4/6 Highest Honor—Playing For Keeps (Royal Match) **Ecurie I. M. Fares**
KIM, b c 20/3 Fabulous Dancer—Saimore (Ashmore) **L. Cattan**
LAKE ANNECY, b f 5/5 Kaldoun—Only Star (Nureyev) **B. Freiha**
LINAKENG, b c 30/3 Lesotho—Kenalya (Kenmare) **K. Benfell**
LISATINE, gr f 22/4 Linamix—Miss Satin (Satingo) **J. Laborde**
B f 4/2 Trempolino—Logiciel (Known Fact) **J. C. Rouget**
LOMA PREATA, b f 22/4 Zilzal—Halley's Comeback (Key To The Kingdom) **B. Clin**
MASSIMO, gr c 26/3 Lead On Time—Mi Longa (Caro) **J. F. Gribomont**
B f 10/5 Irish River—Mata Cara (Storm Bird) **Sheikh Mohammed**
MODERN TRAGEDY, gr f 26/3 Balleroy—Ciao Bella (Tower Walk) **J. C. Gour**
MON GASCON, b c 23/5 Saumarez—Marie de Tracy (Lightning) **Marquis B. du Vivier**
MUDEJAR, ch c 30/3 Bering—Vaguely Money (Vaguely Noble) **A. Caro**

MR J. C. ROUGET—continued

MY PRICKLY, ch c 8/5 Be My Guest—Prickle (Sharpen Up) **J. F. Dupont**
NEBLI, ch c 2/6 Blushing John—No One Bundles (Vice Regent) **A. Caro**
NIKO BOY, ch c 31/1 Nikos—Boydara (Darly) **Ecurie La Clauzade**
NOLEUS, b c 11/2 Tirol—Jolie Note (Fabulous Dancer) **R. Ades**
NOORMONDIALE, b c 28/3 Formidable—Lovely Noor (Fappiano) **Ecurie I. M. Fares**
OLYMPAX, b c 21/5 Never So Bold—Hedda Garbler (Stradavinsky) **J. C. Gour**
PARTIE PRIVEE, b f 15/4 Saumarez—Petite Soeur (Lyphard) **Haras D'Etreham**
B c 7/4 Hero's Honor—Perle d'Espagne (Kenmare) L. de Quintanilla
PRO SILBER, b c 24/2 Sanglamore—Pro Sugar (Miswaki) **Ecurie La Clauzade**
RAPETOU, ch c Septieme Ciel—River Rose (Riverman) **J. T. L. Jones**
RUNNING MAN, ch c 11/3 General Holme—Rudolfina (Pharly) **R. Bousquet**
SABIONETTA, b f Tirol—Pick Marie (Shadeed) **R. Ades**
SANDOVAL, ch c 16/5 Houston—Reassert Yourself (Caucasus) **J. C. Rouget**
B f 21/3 Subotica—Satanic Dance (Shareef Dancer) Sheikh Mohammed
SAUZET, ch f 17/2 Sillery—Sharp Sunrise (Sharpen Up) **A. Caro**
SHAKA, b c 30/3 Exit To Nowhere—Serafica (No Pass No Sale) **R. Bousquet**
B f 30/3 Green Desert—Sigy (Habitat) Sheikh Mohammed
SLEW GLORY, b f 5/5 Beaudelaire—Slew of Fortune (Seattle Slew) **Ecurie Du Panache-Blanc**
SUN KICKS, b c 16/3 Saumarez—For Kicks (Top Ville) **Ecurie La Clauzade**
SWEEPISIO, b f 30/1 Efisio—Sweep On (Sharpen Up) **Ecurie I. M. Fares**
B f 5/3 Shareef Dancer—Sword Lily (Mr Prospector) Mourad Nabeel
SYMBOLETHO, b c 10/4 Lesotho—Symbolique (Dancer's Image) **M. Daguzan-Garros**
VIVALAN, b c 4/5 Lear Fan—Dutchess Best (Blakeney) **C. Gour**
WIDUKING, ch c 9/4 Nikos—Bid Fair (Auction Ring) **C. Gour**
ZAZCA, b f Nashwan—Nibabu (Nishapour) **Sheikh Mohammed**

Jockeys (Flat): J R Dubosc, P H Dumortier, J B Eyquem.

533   MR R. ROWE, Pulborough

Postal: **Ashleigh House Stables, Sullington Lane, Storrington, Pulborough, RH20 4AE.**

Phone: **(01903) 742871**

1 **ASHBY HILL (IRE),** 5, ch m Executive Perk—Petite Deb **Mrs Meriel Humphrey**
2 **BLACK CHURCH,** 10, ch g Torus—Chantry Blue **Dr B. Alexander**
3 **BORODINO (IRE),** 4, b g Strong Gale—Boro Quarter **Mrs Philippa Cooper**
4 **CLOWATER LADY (IRE),** 7, br m Orchestra—Chief Dilke **The Paclin Partnership**
5 **CONGREGATION,** 10, ch g The Parson—Biowen **Mrs B. Sheils**
6 **EULOGY (IRE),** 6, ch g Paean—Daly Preacher **Mr Nicholas Cooper**
7 **FLORLESS GUY (IRE),** 8, b g Floriferous—Wine List **Mr Richard Rowe**
8 **FRESH CHOICE (IRE),** 6, b g Fresh Breeze (USA)—Levanter's Choice **Mr I. Kerman**
9 **GREEN WALK,** 9, b m Green Shoon—Princess Charmere **Mr C. Cornwell**
10 **HAWAIIAN YOUTH (IRE),** 8, ch g Hawaiian Return (USA)—Eternal Youth **Mr G. Redford**
11 **KARAR (IRE),** 6, b g Shardari—Karaferya (USA) **Mrs Margaret Sampson**
12 **KEY PLAYER (IRE),** 7, ch g Orchestra—Glenrula Queen **Mr W. Packham**
13 **KILORAN BAY,** 5, b m Lyphento (USA)—Love You Rosy **Mr N. Blair**
14 **LEAD VOCALIST (IRE),** 7, ch g Orchestra—Eternal Youth **Capt A. Pratt**
15 **MAZZINI (IRE),** 5, b g Celio Rufo—Dontellvi **Mr Nicholas Cooper**
16 **MEANUS MILLER (IRE),** 8, ch m Duky—Lough Gur Pet VII **Miss Genevieve Donovan**
17 **MERIVEL,** 9, b g Buckskin (FR)—Island Varra **Faulkner West & Co Ltd (Building Contrs)**
18 **MULLINTOR (IRE),** 5, b g King Luthier—Latin Verses **Mr Thomas Thompson**
19 **PARSONS KNOCK,** 6, b m The Parson—Knockeevan Girl **Clock House Racing**
20 **PAVLOVA (IRE),** 6, ch m Montelimar (USA)—Light Foot **Mrs Margaret McGlone**
21 **PEPPEROUE (IRE),** 7, b g Andy Rew—Peppardstown **Mr M. P. Sadler**
22 **PRAGADA,** 13, b g Pragmatic—Adare Lady **Mrs Margaret McGlone**
23 **PUNCH'S HOTEL,** 11, ch g Le Moss—Pops Girl **Mrs A. E. Dawes**
24 **RUSSIAN BART (IRE),** 6, b g Bulldozer—Coloressa's Pet **The Russian Bart Partnership**

MR R. ROWE—continued

25 SIR DANTE (IRE), 5, ch g Phardante (FR)—Tumvella **Mr Peter R. Wilby**
26 SIR TURTLE (IRE), 6, b g Supreme Leader—True Minstrel **Mr Peter R. Wilby**
27 SUFFOLK ROAD, 9, br g Yashgan—Maybird **Alpha Financial Futures**
28 TEPESTEDE (IRE), 5, b g Phardante (FR)—Quayville **Dr B. Alexander**
29 THE GOLFING CURATE, 11, ch g Avocat—Donnarabella **Mr Colin W. Poore**
30 THE REAL UNYOKE, 11, b g Callernish—Tudor Dancer **Mr Guy Luck**
31 THUHOOL, 8, b g Formidable (USA)—Wurud (USA) **Mr C. Cornwell**
32 TROJAN CALL, 9, b br g Trojan Fen—Breezy Answer **Mr A. A. V. Collins**
33 VODKA FIZZ, 11, ch g Don—Doon Royal **Dick Richardson Horse Racing Limited**
34 WHISTLING BUCK (IRE), 8, br g Whistling Deer—Buck Ends **Mr G. Redford**
35 YEOMAN WARRIOR, 9, b g Tug of War—Annies Pet **Mrs Heather Alwen**

THREE-YEAR-OLDS

36 A CHEF TOO FAR, b c Be My Chief (USA)—Epithet **Hon Mervyn Greenway**

Other Owners: Mr Patrick Bancroft, Mr Robin D. Barber, Mr J. C. H. Berry, Mr Richard J. B. Blake, Mr T. Boughton, Mr W. Clark, Mr David Coe, Mrs John Dawes, Mr A. R. Dowling, Mr Peter D. Edgar, Mr G. W. Elphick, Mr K. E. Gregory, Mr Christopher Hall, Mr K. C. Holliday, Mr Mark Hue Williams, Mr M. Humphreys, Mr Toby Humphreys, Mr M. I. Lewis, Mr Quin Lovis, Mrs J. A. C. Lundgren, Mr E. V. McGlone, Mr N. J. McKibbin, Mr C. J. Messer, Mr R. C. Murdoch, Mrs Robert Murdoch, Miss Henrietta Neville, Mr C. M. Owen, Mr S. Packham, Mr P. E. Paulson, Mr C. Platel, Mr James Scrimgeour, Mr R. J. Sharp, Mr Nigel R. Taylor, Mr Clive Turner, Mr A. P. Verrall, Mr Richard White, Mr Ian Wootton.

Jockey (NH): D O'Sullivan (10-2).

Conditional: Derek Carson (9-7).

Amateur: Mr Anthony Kinane (9-7).

534   MISS M. E. ROWLAND, Lower Blidworth

Postal: **Kirkfields, Calverton Road, Lower Blidworth, Nottingham, NG21 0NW.**
Phone: **(01623) 794831**

1 ABINGER, 4, ch g Absalom—Western Singer **Miss M. E. Rowland**
2 BUCKELLO (IRE), 5, b m Buckskin (FR)—Tengello **Miss M. E. Rowland**
3 DAHLIA'S BEST (USA), 6, b g Dahar (USA)—Eleanor's Best (USA) **Miss M. E. Rowland**
4 DOVER PATROL (IRE), 6, b h Dancing Brave (USA)—Britannia's Rule **Miss M. E. Rowland**
5 I'M A DREAMER (IRE), 6, b g Mister Majestic—Lady Wise **Miss M. E. Rowland**
6 KISMETIM, 6, b g Dowsing (USA)—Naufrage **Miss M. E. Rowland**
7 MILLENIUM LASS (IRE), 8, ch m Viking (USA)—Sandford Star **Miss M. E. Rowland**
8 NINE BARROW DOWN (IRE), 4, b g Danehill (USA)—Rising Spirits **Miss M. E. Rowland**
9 RIGHT ANGLE (IRE), 5, b g Shy Groom (USA)—Mamie's Joy **Miss M. E. Rowland**
10 VERY CHEERING, 13, b g Gleason (USA)—Cherry Joy **Miss M. E. Rowland**

Jockey (NH): Gary Lyons (10-2).

535   MR H. G. M. ROWSELL, Winchester

Postal: **West Stoke Farm, Stoke Charity, Winchester, Hants, SO21 3PN.**
Phone: **HOME (01962) 760419 OFFICE & FAX (01962) 760220**

1 CAMDEN'S RANSOM (USA), 9, b g Hostage (USA)—Camden Court (USA) **Mr E. Cobelli**
2 DE LA BILLIERE (IRE), 8, b h King of Clubs—Crazyfoot **Mr M. Green**
3 FARLEYER ROSE (IRE), 7, b br m Phardante (FR)—Dane-Jor's **Mr T. I. Fane**
4 GABRIEL'S LADY, 5, b m Valiyar—Autumn Harvest **Gabriel's Farm Partnership**
5 HEATON (NZ), 9, b g Veloso (NZ)—Honey Queen (NZ) **G. J. Rowsell**

MR H. G. M. ROWSELL—continued

6 **MY BOOKS ARE BEST (IRE)**, 7, gr m Sexton Blake—Rozifer **Mr M. Green**
7 **OPHIUCHUS**, 5, b m Nader—Scobitora
8 **SOLO VOLUMES**, 7, ch g Ballacashtal (CAN)—Miss Solo **Mr M. Green**

TWO-YEAR-OLDS

9 **FERGUS NO**, ch c 28/4 Be My Chief (USA)—Secret Freedom (USA) (Secreto (USA)) **Tessona Racing Limited**

Other Owners: Mrs Caroline Taylor.

Jockey (Flat): Brett Doyle (w.a.).

Jockey (NH): A Tory (10-0, w.a.).

536   MR A. DE ROYER-DUPRE, Chantilly

Postal: **3 Chemin des Aigles, 60500 Chantilly, France.**

Phone: **(4) 4580303 FAX (4) 4573938**

1 **BAHIAKARAD (FR)**, 5, b h Akarad—Bahia Laura **Melle M. C. de Saint Seine**
2 **BARAIYKA (FR)**, 5, ch m Shardari—Baykara **Doyen R. Cluzel**
3 **BREAKING STORY (FR)**, 4, ch c Shernazar—Zarzaya **Marquise de Moratalla**
4 **KASSANI (IRE)**, 4, b c Alleged—Kassiyda **H. H. Aga Khan**
5 **LAZY MOOD (IRE)**, 6, b h Assert—Grundys Flame **Oostvlaamse & Mr Van den Brook**
6 **MADAIYN (IRE)**, 4, b c Shernazar—Mill River **H. H. Aga Khan**
7 **MARIE DE KEN (FR)**, 4, gr f Kendor—Marie de Vez **Mr Adolf Bader**
8 **NEC PLUS ULTRA (FR)**, 5, b h Kendor—Quintefolle **Marquise de Moratalla**
9 **SAZAIYMAR (FR)**, 4, b g Doyoun—Samirza **H. H. Aga Khan**
10 **SHANNJAR (FR)**, 4, b c Doyoun—Shanjarina **H. H. Aga Khan**
11 **VALANOUR (IRE)**, 4, b c Lomond—Vearia **H. H. Aga Khan**

THREE-YEAR-OLDS

12 **ADJILANI (IRE)**, b c Lashkari—Adjriyna **H. H. Aga Khan**
13 **ALKAMI (USA)**, b c Alleged—Alimana **H. H. Aga Khan**
14 **ALMEDI (USA)**, b c Shahrastani—Aleema **H. H. Aga Khan**
15 **ANTALYA (IRE)**, b f Doyoun—Aneyza **H. H. Aga Khan**
16 **ASHKALANI (IRE)**, b c Soviet Star—Ashtarka **H. H. Aga Khan**
17 **BAYLAKAN (IRE)**, b c Darshaan—Balance **H. H. Aga Khan**
18 **BEHARIYA (IRE)**, b f Sadler's Wells—Behera **H. H. Aga Khan**
19 **BERRY ROSE (FR)**, ch f Dancing Spree—Lady Berry **Baron Guy de Rothschild**
20 **COUP DE FEU (FR)**, b c Dancing Spree—Emeraldine **Baron Guy de Rothschild**
21 **DARALBAYDA (IRE)**, b f Doyoun—Daralinda **H. H. Aga Khan**
22 **DARAZARI (IRE)**, b c Sadler's Wells—Darara **H. H. Aga Khan**
23 **DAROUGHA (IRE)**, b f Darshaan—Daroura **H. H. Aga Khan**
24 **DEVIL'S BONES**, b f Devil's Bag—Allicance **Mr Francois Fabre**
25 **DIBENOISE (FR)**, gr f Kendor—Boreale **Mr Francois Geffroy**
26 **DILIAPOUR (IRE)**, b c Akarad—Diya **H. H. Aga Khan**
27 **DJA DANCER**, b c Groom Dancer—Djaka Belle **Mr Adolf Bader**
28 **DOCTEUR GRADUS (FR)**, b c Always Fair—More Welsh **Oostvlaamse & Mr Van den Brook**
29 **DOUCEUR CREOLE**, gr f Highest Honor—Time For Romance **Mr Beniamino Arbib**
30 **DRY SACK**, b f In The Wings—Syzygy **Mr George Ohrstrom**
31 **DUNAYSIR (FR)**, b c Kahyasi—Dumayla **H. H. Aga Khan**
32 **EMBRACEABLE YOU (FR)**, ch c Ti King—Marcotte **Oostvlaamse & Mr Van den Brook**
33 **FABULEUX SARON**, gr c Sarhoob—Belle de Saron **Mr Beniamino Arbib**
34 **GAELIC SOVEREIGN**, b c Sovereign Dancer—Gaelic Bird **Mr Francois Fabre**
35 **HAMASYA (FR)**, b f Shernazar—Hilaya **H. H. Aga Khan**
36 **HAMIRPOUR (IRE)**, b c Shahrastani—Hamaliya **H. H. Aga Khan**

MR A. DE ROYER-DUPRE—continued

37 **HANSI (IRE)**, b c Doyoun—Hanzala **H. H. Aga Khan**
38 **HARAMAYDA (FR)**, b f Doyoun—Haratiyna **H. H. Aga Khan**
39 **HARIAPOUR (IRE)**, b c Darshaan—Haughty Manner **H. H. Aga Khan**
40 **HURMUZAN (IRE)**, b c Shahrastani—Huraymila **H. H. Aga Khan**
41 **ILKERI (IRE)**, b c Doyoun—Ilmiyya **H. H. Aga Khan**
42 **KARANPOUR (IRE)**, b c Darshaan—Karamita **H. H. Aga Khan**
43 **KAZARAN (IRE)**, b c Shardari—Khatima **H. H. Aga Khan**
44 **KAZAWARI (USA)**, b c Riverman—Kazaviyna **H. H. Aga Khan**
45 **KELEMAR (IRE)**, b c Doyoun—Karlafsha **H. H. Aga Khan**
46 **KHALISA (IRE)**, b f Persian Bold—Khaiyla **H. H. Aga Khan**
47 **KHARIBIYA (IRE)**, b f Shardari—Khalida **H. H. Aga Khan**
48 **KHARIZMI (FR)**, b c Lashkari—Khariyda **H. H. Aga Khan**
49 **KHAYDARIYA (IRE)**, b f Shardari—Khaydara **H. H. Aga Khan**
50 **LA CELESTINA (FR)**, b f Always Fair—Fleur de Ciel **Baron Guy de Rothschild**
51 **LANNKARAN (IRE)**, b c Shardari—Lankarana **H. H. Aga Khan**
52 **LELARI (IRE)**, b c Shahrastani—Lisana **H. H. Aga Khan**
53 **MANDALIKA (USA)**, b f Arctic Tern—Madiriya **H. H. Aga Khan**
54 **MANNDALIY (IRE)**, b c Akarad—Meadow Glen Lady **H. H. Aga Khan**
55 **MARWA (IRE)**, b f Shahrastani—Marmana **H. H. Aga Khan**
56 **MASALIKA (IRE)**, b f Kahyasi—Masamiyda **H. H. Aga Khan**
57 **MASSOURA (IRE)**, b f Shernazar—Masslama **H. H. Aga Khan**
58 **NAFSARI (IRE)**, b c Linamix—Nafzawa **H. H. Aga Khan**
59 **NASHANNDI (FR)**, b c Lashkari—Niece Divine **H. H. Aga Khan**
60 **NASHKAPOUR (IRE)**, b c Caerleon—Nashkara **H. H. Aga Khan**
61 **NORTHERN ORDER (FR)**, b c Caerleon—Irish Order **Marquise de Moratalla & Haras du Mezeray**
62 **PASSAGE (FR)**, b c Polish Precedent—Une Pensee **Baron Guy de Rothschild**
63 **PRETTY EARS (FR)**, b f Top Ville—Aytana **Mme Marie Ange Bousquet**
64 **SENAKHAN (IRE)**, b c Shardari—Sendana **H. H. Aga Khan**
65 **SEVRES ROSE (IRE)**, b c Caerleon—Indian Rose **Baron Guy de Rothschild**
66 **SHAMADARA (IRE)**, b f Kahyasi—Shamarzana **H. H. Aga Khan**
67 **SHAMARRA (FR)**, b f Zayyani—Shannfara **H. H. Aga Khan**
68 **SHANAB (IRE)**, b c Darshaan—Shashna **H. H. Aga Khan**
69 **SHARBAIYNI (FR)**, b c Akarad—Sharmada **H. H. Aga Khan**
70 **SHARBATA (IRE)**, b f Kahyasi—Shabarana **H. H. Aga Khan**
71 **SHAREMATA (IRE)**, b f Doyoun—Sharenara **H. H. Aga Khan**
72 **SHEREMA (USA)**, b f Riverman—Sherarda **H. H. Aga Khan**
73 **TANTATURA (FR)**, b f Akarad—Belle Doche **Marquise de Moratalla**
74 **TARKHAN (USA)**, b c Lomond—Tarikhana **H. H. Aga Khan**
75 **TIYANA (IRE)**, b f Zayyani—Triumphant **H. H. Aga Khan**
76 **TRADITIO (FR)**, b c General Holme—Jacobean Stairs **Marquise de Moratalla**
77 **VERBIER**, gr c Kendor—Viverba **Mr Adolf Bader**
78 **ZARANNDA (IRE)**, b f Last Tycoon—Zarna **H. H. Aga Khan**
79 **ZAYANA (IRE)**, b f Darshaan—Zaydiya **H. H. Aga Khan**

TWO-YEAR-OLDS

80 **AHLIYAT (USA)**, b f 22/2 Irish River—Alimana **H. H. Aga Khan**
81 **ANEYSAR (IRE)**, b c 13/4 Darshaan—Aneyza **H. H. Aga Khan**
82 **ASHAKIYR (IRE)**, b c 2/4 Thatching—Ashtarka **H. H. Aga Khan**
83 **ASTARABAD (USA)**, b c 2/2 Alleged—Anaza **H. H. Aga Khan**
84 **BANAWAR (USA)**, b c 31/3 Green Dancer—Banque Privee **H. H. Aga Khan**
85 **BRIDEPRICE**, b f Groom Dancer—Sardinella **Marquise de Moratalla**
86 **CIEL FLEURI**, b c General Holme—Fleur du Ciel **Baron Guy de Rothschild**
87 B c Lyphard—Clare Bridge **Mr Francois Fabre**
88 **DONKEY ENGINE**, b c Fairy King—City Ex **Marquise de Moratalla**
89 **DUBYANI (FR)**, b c 2/6 Zayyani—Dumayla **H. H. Aga Khan**
90 B f 19/4 Doyoun—Eviyrna **H. H. Aga Khan**
91 **GLORY ALLELUIA**, b c Subotica—Sudden Glory **Mssrs Fontaine, Grimbom & Cluzel**
92 **GRIFFON**, b c Cricket Ball—Grise Mine **Baron Guy de Rothschild**
93 **HARIFANA (FR)**, b f 17/4 Kahyasi—Haratiyna **H. H. Aga Khan**
94 **HEROS DE CAMERONE**, b c Subotica—Valreine **Mr Beniamino Arbib**

MR A. DE ROYER-DUPRE—continued

95 **JOYEUSE ENTREE**, b f Kendor—Cape of Good Hope **Marquise de Moratalla**
96 **KENBOURG**, b c Kendor—Duchesse du Bourg **Marquise de Moratalla**
97 **KERIBARI (USA)**, b c 7/5 Lomond—Kerita **H. H. Aga Khan**
98 **KHARALIYA (FR)**, b f 23/2 Doyoun—Khariyda **H. H. Aga Khan**
99 **KING ROSE**, b c Night Shift—Indian Rose **Baron Guy de Rothschild**
100 **LE VILLARET**, b c Fabulous Dancer—Vieille Villa **Mr Beniamino Arbib**
101 B c Be My Guest—Mika Red **Oostvlaamse & Mr Van den Brook**
102 **NADRAPOUR (FR)**, b c 11/2 Akarad—Nabagha **H. H. Aga Khan**
103 **NASIRABAD (IRE)**, b c 22/2 Shahrastani—Naziriya **H. H. Aga Khan**
104 **NOMBRE PREMIER**, b c Kendor—Sabiola **Marquise de Moratalla**
105 **NUIT DE FETE**, b f Night Shift—Hot Favourite **Marquise de Moratalla**
106 **OMBRE DE LUNE**, b f Polish Precedent—Reine du Ciel **Baron Guy de Rothschild**
107 **OUT OF NOWHERE**, b f Exit To Nowhere—More Welsh **Oostvlaamse & Mr Van den Brook**
108 **PETER OF SPAIN**, b c Highest Honor—La Tirana **Marquise de Moratalla**
109 **PIEPOWDER**, b f In The Wings—Tamarinda **Marquise de Moratalla**
110 **QUENDU**, b c Kendor—Quintefolle **Marquise de Moratalla**
111 **QUICK TRIP**, b c Cricket Ball—Tryptophane **Baron Guy de Rothschild**
112 **RAKISAPOUR (IRE)**, b c 20/4 Kahyasi—Rakisa **H. H. Aga Khan**
113 **ROSE FOR EVER**, b f Always Fair—Pinkie Rose **Baron Guy de Rothschild**
114 **SAFARID (FR)**, b c 8/2 Al Nasr—Safariyna **H. H. Aga Khan**
115 **SAMAPOUR (IRE)**, b c 8/3 Kahyasi—Samneeza **H. H. Aga Khan**
116 **SARATOVA**, b f Noblequest—Patney **Mr Walter Schmitt Ney**
117 **SHAMAD (IRE)**, b c 22/4 Subotica—Shamarzana **H. H. Aga Khan**
118 **SHARIYFA (FR)**, b f 17/2 Zayyani—Sherniya **H. H. Aga Khan**
119 B f 26/4 Trempolino—Sherarda **H. H. Aga Khan**
120 **TAJOUN (FR)**, b c 12/2 General Holme—Taeesha **H. H. Aga Khan**
121 B f 25/2 Trempolino—Tarafa **H. H. Aga Khan**
122 **TAVILDARAN (IRE)**, b c 11/3 Darshaan—Talwara **H. H. Aga Khan**
123 **TIRAAZ (USA)**, b c 3/4 Lear Fan—Tarikhana **H. H. Aga Khan**
124 **VISEGRAD**, b c Marignan—Crown Treasure **Mr Robert Bousquet**
125 **ZALAPOUR (FR)**, b c 5/4 Alzao—Zanata **H. H. Aga Khan**
126 **ZANDAKA (FR)**, b f 3/4 Doyoun—Zanadiyka **H. H. Aga Khan**

Jockey (Flat): Gerald Mosse.

Apprentice: Jeremy Cohen.

537   MRS A. RUSSELL, Kilmacolm

Postal: **Craiglinshaugh Farm, Off High Greenock Road, Kilmacolm, Renfrewshire, PA13 4TG.**
Phone: **HOME (01505) 872479   FAX (01505) 87 3060**

1 **CHOCOLATE DRUM (IRE)**, 5, br g Orchestra—Precious Petra **Mrs Ailsa Russell**
2 **MILTON ROOMS (IRE)**, 7, ch g Where To Dance (USA)—Raga Rine **Mrs Ailsa Russell**
3 **RIBBON LADY**, 6, b m Kinglet—Chaffcombe **Mrs Ailsa Russell**
4 **RISKY BUCK**, 6, b g Buckley—Miss Poker Face **Mrs Ailsa Russell**

538   MISS L. V. RUSSELL, Kinross

Postal: **Arlary House, Milnathort, Kinross, Tayside, KY13 7SJ.**
Phone: **OFFICE (01577) 862482   YARD (01577) 865512**

1 **FIVELEIGH BUILDS**, 9, b g Deep Run—Giolla Donn **Miss L. V. Russell & Miss E. C. A. Noble**
2 **GUNMETAL BOY**, 12, b g Warpath—Geranium **Mr Peter J. S. Russell**
3 **JAYDALAY (IRE)**, 6, b g Sandalay—Still Hoping **Mr M. F. B. Nicholson**
4 **KINFAUNS DANCER**, 8, b m Celtic Cone—New Dawning **Mr G. S. Brown**

MISS L. V. RUSSELL—continued

5 **LIVE AND LET LIVE,** 12, b g Comedy Star (USA)—Maid of Warwick **Mrs C. G. Greig & Mr P. J. S. Russell**
6 **ROCKET RUN (IRE),** 8, b g Orchestra—Roselita **Mr P. J. S. Russell, Mrs J. M. Grimston**
7 **SAND KING (NZ),** 10, gr g Beechcraft (NZ)—Gifted Girl (NZ) **Miss Lucinda V. Russell**
8 **ST ELMO'S FIRE (NZ),** 11, b g Grosvenor (NZ)—Star Quality (NZ) **Miss Lucinda V. Russell**
9 **THE LAUGHING LORD,** 10, b g Lord Ha Ha—Celtic Serenity **Mr Peter J. S. Russell**
10 **TWO FOR ONE (IRE),** 7, b br g Strong Gale—Shatana **Mrs C. G. Greig & Mr P. J. S. Russell**
11 **VAVASIR,** 10, b g Carlingford Castle—Decently **Mr M. F. B. Nicholson**
12 **WHITE DIAMOND,** 8, b g Touching Wood (USA)—Dimant Blanche (USA) **Mr Peter J. S. Russell**

539   MR B. J. M. RYALL, Yeovil

Postal: **Higher Farm, Rimpton, Yeovil, Somerset, BA22 8AD.**
Phone: **MARSTON MAGNA (01935) 850222**

1 **BOZO (IRE),** 5, b g Kefaah (USA)—Hossvend **Mr B. J. M. Ryall**
2 **COUNTRY KEEPER,** 8, b g Town And Country—Mariban **Mr B. J. M. Ryall**
3 **SPRING GRASS,** 8, br m Pardigras—Spring River **Mr B. J. M. Ryall**
4 **SPRING HEBE,** 6, b m Pragmatic—Spring River **Mr B. J. M. Ryall**
5 **SUKAAB,** 11, gr g Nishapour (FR)—Nye (FR) **Mr B. J. M. Ryall**
6 **WIN A HAND,** 6, b m Nearly A Hand—Mariban **Mr B. J. M. Ryall**

540   MR M. J. RYAN, Newmarket

Postal: **Cadland, 35 Old Station Road, Newmarket, Suffolk, CB8 8DT.**
Phone: **(01638) 664172 FAX 560248**

1 **BAYRAK (USA),** 6, b g Bering—Phydilla (FR)
2 **CHILLY LAD,** 5, ch g High Kicker (USA)—Miss Poll Flinders
3 **DUFFERTOES,** 4, ch g High Kicker (USA)—Miss Poll Flinders
4 **EL DON,** 4, b g High Kicker (USA)—Madam Gerard
5 **GOLDEN HADEER,** 5, ch h Hadeer—Verchinina
6 **HYLTERS GIRL,** 4, b f Dominion—Jolimo
7 **JOLIS ABSENT,** 6, b m Primo Dominie—Jolimo
8 **JOLI'S GREAT,** 8, ch m Vaigly Great—Jolimo
9 **JUST FLAMENCO,** 5, ch g Scorpio (FR)—Suzannah's Song
10 **JUST HARRY,** 5, ch h High Kicker (USA)—Dorame
11 **KINGCHIP BOY,** 7, b g Petong—Silk St James
12 **LA BRIEF,** 4, b f Law Society (USA)—Lady Warninglid
13 **LADY HIGHFIELD,** 5, br m High Kicker (USA)—Judy Burton
14 **MARONETTA,** 4, ch f Kristian—Suzannah's Song
15 **PIP'S DREAM,** 5, b m Glint of Gold—Arabian Rose (USA)
16 **PRIMA SILK,** 5, b m Primo Dominie—Silk St James
17 **SPENCER'S REVENGE,** 7, ch g Bay Express—Armour of Light
18 **STEVIE'S WONDER (IRE),** 6, ch g Don't Forget Me—Azurai
19 **THE MESTRAL,** 4, br f Formidable (USA)—Lariston Gale
20 **TOCCO JEWEL,** 6, br m Reesh—Blackpool Belle
21 **TURNER PRIZE (IRE),** 6, b h Tate Gallery (USA)—Pansoverina

THREE-YEAR-OLDS

22 **CONTRARIE,** b f Floose—Chanita
23 **DAFFODIL EXPRESS (IRE),** b f Skyliner—Miss Henry
24 **HAPPY TRAVELLER (IRE),** b c Treasure Kay—Elegant Owl
25 **INCAPOL,** b c Inca Chief (USA)—Miss Poll Flinders
26 **JOLIS PRESENT,** b c Prince Sabo—Jolimo
27 **MISS CAROTTENE,** b f Siberian Express (USA)—Silk St James
28 **PETITE HERITIERE,** b f Last Tycoon—Arianna Aldini
29 **SAMORELLE,** ch f High Kicker (USA)—Lemelasor
30 **SWEETNESS HERSELF,** ch f Unfuwain (USA)—No Sugar Baby (FR)

MR M. J. RYAN—continued

TWO-YEAR-OLDS

31 B c 4/5 Damister (USA)—Jolimo (Fortissimo)
32 B c 6/2 Sharpo—Langtry Lady (Pas de Seul)
33 B f 22/3 Never So Bold—Les Amis (Alzao (USA))
34 B f 19/4 Mystiko (USA)—Martin-Lavell Mail (Dominion)
35 B f 4/5 High Kicker (USA)—Mio Mementa (Streak)
36 B c 18/4 High Kicker (USA)—Miss Poll Flinders (Swing Easy (USA))
37 SILK ST JOHN, b c 8/4 Damister (USA)—Silk St James (Pas de Seul)

Owners: Mr Faiz Al-Mutawa, Mr P. E. Axon, Mr C. Baker, Mrs T. Baron, Mr D. Bell, Mr Tim Corby, C. R. S. Partnership, Mr P. J. Donnison, Enterprise Markets Ltd, Express Marie Curie Racing Club, Extraman Ltd, Four Jays Racing Partnership, Mr M. J. Harding, Mr S. J. Lavallin, Mrs M. J. Lavell, Mr P. Marron, Mrs S. M. Martin, Mr Don Morris, Mr Christopher Murray, Newmarket Consortium, Miss J. Nicholls, Mr Dan O'Donnell, Palacegate Corporation Ltd, Mr L. Perring, Mr J. A. Pickford, Mr A. S. Reid, Mrs M. J. Ryan, Mrs W. L. Sole, Mr D. Spencer, Mr A. Spier, The Happy Partnership, Three Ply Racing, Mrs Karola Vann, Mrs Patricia J. Williams.

Jockey (NH): John Ryan (10-0).

Apprentice: Mark Baird (7-0).

Amateur: Mr W Dixon (10-7, w.a.).

541   MISS B. SANDERS, Epsom

Postal: **Chalk Pit Stables, Headley Road, Epsom, Surrey, KT18 6BW.**
Phone: **ASHTEAD (01372) 278453 FAX (01372) 276137**

1 **CALAPAEZ,** 12, gr g Nishapour (FR)—Charter Belle **Mr T. J. Blake**
2 4, Ch f Nicholas Bill—Charossa **Leonard Fuller**
3 5, Gr g Malaspina—Charossa **Gallagher Materials Ltd & Mr T. J. Blake**
4 **HATTAAFEH (IRE),** 5, b m Mtoto—Monongelia **Mrs P. J. Sheen**
5 **LUNAR RISK,** 6, b g Risk Me (FR)—Moonlight Princess **Copyforce Ltd**
6 **MARLIN DANCER,** 11, b g Niniski (USA)—Mullet **Mr Robert Allen, Mr J. M. Quinn**
7 **MILLIES PRINCESS,** 5, b m Prince Sabo—Millie Belle **Mr Leonard Fuller**
8 **MR COPYFORCE,** 6, gr g Sharrood (USA)—Cappuccilli **Copyforce Ltd**
9 **MY DUTCH GIRL,** 4, b f Midyan (USA)—Double Dutch **Mr Leonard Fuller**
10 **WILD STRAWBERRY,** 7, ro m Ballacashtal (CAN)—Pts Fairway **Copyforce Ltd**

THREE-YEAR-OLDS

11 **BURSUL LADY,** b f Be My Chief (USA)—Neverdown **Gallagher Materials Ltd**
12 **MATTHIAS MYSTIQUE,** gr f Sharrood (USA)—Sheznice (IRE) **M. C. M. & Mrs J. Laycock**
13 **MYSTERY MATTHIAS,** b f Nicholas—Devils Dirge **M. C. M. & Mrs J. Laycock**
14 **SUPERIOR FORCE,** ch c Superlative—Gleeful **Copyforce Ltd**

Other Owners: Matthias Construction Materials Limited.

Lady Rider: Miss Holly Mitchell (8-12).

542   MR M. S. SAUNDERS, Wells

Postal: **Blue Mountain Farm, Wells Hill Bottom, Haydon, Wells, BA5 3EZ.**
Phone: **(01749) 841011**

1 **ASTRAL INVADER (IRE),** 4, ch g Astronef—Numidia **Mr M. S. Saunders**
2 **FABULOUS MTOTO,** 6, b h Mtoto—El Fabulous (FR) **Mrs Denise Saunders**
3 **FEELING HOPE,** 5, ch m Hadeer—Bonnie Hope (USA) **Mr Owen G. James**
4 **HARRY SPARKS,** 8, b g Electric—Queen's Treasure **Mr E. W. Jones**

MR M. S. SAUNDERS—continued

5 **INDIAN TEMPLE**, 5, ch g Minster Son—Indian Flower **Mr Derek Clarke**
6 **NAPOLEON STAR (IRE)**, 5, ch g Mulhollande (USA)—Lady Portobello **Napoleon's Racing Club**
7 **NOMADIC DANCER (IRE)**, 4, b f Nabeel Dancer (USA)—Loveshine (USA) **Mrs Denise Saunders**
8 **TINKER OSMASTON**, 5, br m Dunbeath (USA)—Miss Primula **Mr John Luff**

THREE-YEAR-OLDS

9 **CHARMED AGAIN**, b f Midyan (USA)—Charming **Mrs Denise Saunders**
10 **CONDITION RED**, b f Sayf El Arab (USA)—Forever Mary **Mr M. S. Saunders**
11 **DYANKO**, b g Midyan (USA)—Regain **N. R. & M. Pike & Sons**
12 **FORLIANO**, b g Forzando—Lucky Orphan **N. R. & M. Pike & Sons**
13 **HEIGHTS OF LOVE**, b f Persian Heights—Lets Fall In Love (USA) **Mr Derek Clarke**
14 **KEALBRA LADY**, b f Petong—Greensward Blaze **Mr B. Peacock**
15 **KINNESCASH (IRE)**, ch c Persian Heights—Gayla Orchestra **Mr Chris Scott**
16 **RED TIME**, br g Timeless Times (USA)—Crimson Dawn **Mr Peter Fyvie**
17 **SHARP NIGHT**, ch g Sharpo—Midnight Owl (FR) **Blue Mountain Racing Partnership**

Other Owners: Mr B. S. Hargreaves, Mr R. K. Kelly, Mr C. Omell, Mr Andrew Pike, Mr M. Rapley, Mr A. R. Thirkill, Mr A. Whiteoak, Mr David J. Wright.

Jockeys (Flat): J Egan, A McGlone.

Conditional: V Slattery (9-7).

Lady Rider: Miss K Jones.

543   DR J. D. SCARGILL, Newmarket

Postal: **Red House Stables, Hamilton Road, Newmarket, Suffolk, CB8 0TE.**
Phone: **(01638) 663254 FAX (01638) 667767**

1 **ABIGAILS BOY (HOL)**, 7, gr g Superlative—Heartbreaker **Mr Derek W. Johnson**
2 **GEOLLY (IRE)**, 4, b g Formidable (USA)—Four-Legged Friend **The Inn Crowd**
3 **HARRY THE CAB**, 7, ch g Hadeer—Hilly **Mrs Susan Scargill**
4 **HERR TRIGGER**, 5, gr g Sharrood (USA)—Four-Legged Friend **A. C. Edwards**
5 **JAWANI (IRE)**, 8, b g Last Tycoon—Fabled Lady **Mrs Susan Scargill**
6 **JUBA**, 4, b f Dowsing (USA)—Try The Duchess **Mr Tim Drew**
7 **MERSEYSIDE MAN**, 10, b g My Dad Tom (USA)—Chanita **Mrs Susan Scargill**
8 **OUR RITA**, 7, b m Hallgate—Ma Pierrette **Mr Jonathan Crisp**
9 **TEOROMA**, 6, ch h Teofane—Poppy Kelly **Mr Basil White**

THREE-YEAR-OLDS

10 **CALL ME MADGE**, b f Distant Relative—Apply **Robert A. Gladdis**
11 **HENRY COOPER**, b g Distant Relative—Miss Echo (GB) **Mr Ian Drury**
12 **HOME COOKIN'**, b f Salse (USA)—Home Fire **Galloping Gourmets**
13 **MYSTIC TEMPO (USA)**, ch f El Gran Senor (USA)—Doubling Time (USA) **Just Passing Through Partnership**
14 **ROGUE TRADER (IRE)**, b g Mazaad—Ruby Relic **House to House Partnership**
15 **SIGNS R US (IRE)**, b g Al Hareb (USA)—O La Bamba (IRE) **Mrs Susan Scargill**
16 **SUPAROSIE**, ch f Superlative—Rockin' Rosie **Mrs P. Reditt**
17 **TSARINA KAY**, b f Komaite (USA)—Lady Keyser **The Inn Crowd**

TWO-YEAR-OLDS

18 Br f 28/3 Superlative—Four-Legged Friend (Aragon) **Mr Jonathan Crisp**
19 **GO FOR GREEN**, br f 23/1 Petong—Guest List (Be My Guest (USA)) **Manor Farm Packers**
20 Ch c 29/4 Superpower—Out of Hours (Lochnager) **R. S. Cockerill (Farms) Ltd**
21 **ROCK IT ROSIE**, ch f Rock Hopper—Rockin' Rosie (Song) **Mrs P. Reditt**

DR J. D. SCARGILL—continued

22 RYLES DANCER, gr c 26/2 Chilibang—Bee Dee Dancer (Ballacashtal (CAN)) **Mr Frank Campbell**
23 Ch f 10/3 Superlative—Scravels Saran (IRE) (Indian King (USA)) **Mr Derek W. Johnson**
24 SILVER SPELL, gr f 18/4 Aragon—Silver Berry (Lorenzaccio) **Mrs P. Reditt**
25 VERINDER'S GIFT, gr c 13/3 Chilibang—A Nymph Too Far (IRE) (Precocious) **M. Gillanderson**

Other Owners: Mr Dave Andrews, Mr M. Bates, Mr M. Bennett, Mr P. Blythe, Mr G. Bridgford, Mrs Maureen Coppitters, Mr S. Cowan, Mr J. Custerson, Mr R. A. Dalton, Mr C. Dant, Mr D. Farey, Mr A. Fleming, Mr S. Fletcher, Mrs Moira Hurst, Mr M. Jakes, Mr R. Levitt, Mr R. Parker, Mr Colin Pell, Mr Adrian Richardson, Mr W. Rouse, Mrs Shirley Scargill, Mr J. Skelton, Mr A. Smith, Mr F. Spring, Mr P. Treacy, Mr M. Underwood, Mr G. Walshaw, Mr Graham Watts, Mr P. Williams, Mr C. A. Wotton.

Jockey (Flat): R Cochrane (w.a.).

Jockey (NH): N Mann.

544   MRS E. SCOTT, Taunton

Postal: **Home Farm, Nettlecombe, Williton, Taunton, TA4 4HS.**
Phone: **(01984) 640354**

1 BLUE NIGHT, 7, br m Latest Model—Midinette **Mrs E. Scott**
2 LATEST TARQUIN, 7, b m Latest Model—Gay Tarquin **Mrs E. Scott**

545   MR B. SCRIVEN, Taunton

Postal: **Cogload Farm, Durston, Taunton, Somerset, TA3 5AW.**
Phone: **NORTH CURRY (01823) 490208**

1 CONCINNITY (USA), 7, b g Hello Gorgeous (USA)—Cincinnity (USA) **Mr B. Scriven**
2 GABISH, 11, b g Try My Best (USA)—Crannog **Mr B. Scriven**
3 ROCQUAINE, 10, ch g Ballad Rock—Lola Sharp **Mr B. Scriven**

Conditional: R Johnson (9-7).

Amateur: Mr Robert Thornton (9-7).

546   MRS J. SCRIVENS, Bampton

Postal: **Barricane Stables, Bowden's Lane, Shillingford, Bampton, EX16 9BU.**
Phone: **(01398) 331232**

1 JAY JAYS DREAM, 10, b m Shaab—Traverser **Mrs J. Scrivens**
2 JAY JAY'S VOYAGE, 13, b g Saunter—Traverser **Mrs J. Scrivens**
3 MORDROS, 6, b g Interrex (CAN)—Jay Jays Dream **Mrs J. Scrivens**
4 TAILSPIN, 11, b g Young Generation—Mumtaz Flyer (USA) **Mrs J. Scrivens**

Amateur: Mr B Pollock (9-12).

547   MR J. J. SHEEHAN, Findon

Postal: **Woodmans Stables, London Road, Ashington, West Sussex, RH20 3AU.**

Phone: **YARD (01903) 893031 MOBILE (0459) 111898**

1 **COLERIDGE**, 8, gr g Bellypha—Quay Line **Mr P. J. Sheehan**
2 **IMPERIAL PROSPECT (USA)**, 4, b f Imperial Falcon (CAN)—One Tough Lady (USA) **Mrs Eileen Sheehan**
3 **KING OF TUNES (FR)**, 4, b c Chief Singer—Marcotte **Mrs Eileen Sheehan**
4 **MAFUTA (IRE)**, 4, b f Mtoto—Chrism **Mr John Sheehan**
5 **STATOGLOW**, 4, gr f Statoblest—Innerglow **Mrs Christina Dowling**
6 **WOODMANS LADY**, 4, b f Midyan (USA)—Diva Madonna **Mrs Christina Dowling**

THREE-YEAR-OLDS

7 **AJKUIT (IRE)**, b c Persian Heights—Hazar (IRE) **Mr P. J. Sheehan**
8 B f Warrshan (USA)—Lehzen **Mr John Sheehan**

TWO-YEAR-OLDS

9 B f Mujadil (USA)—Fleur-de-Luce **Mr John Sheehan**
10 Gr f Shavian—Innerglow **Mrs Christina Dowling**
11 B c Houston (USA)—Noble Devorcee (USA) **Mr John Sheehan**
12 **PARQUET**, ch f Lead On Time (USA)—Tocaronte (FR) **Mrs T. Harman**

Jockey (Flat): J Quinn.

Lady Rider: Miss C Hannaford.

548   MR M. I. SHEPPARD, Ledbury

Postal: **Home Farm Cottage, Eastnor, Ledbury, Herefordshire, HR8 1RD.**

Phone: **(01531) 634846**

1 **COUNTRY CHOICE (IRE)**, 6, b m Paean—Country Character **D. J. & C. B. Clapham**
2 **MASTER ERYL**, 13, gr g Anax—Blackberry Hill **Mrs Roger Guilding**
3 **NOW WE KNOW (IRE)**, 8, ch g Denel (FR)—Struell Course **R. Herbert, T. Doxsey and M. Drake**
4 **OATIS ROSE**, 6, b m Oats—Constant Rose **Mr A. L. C. Figg**
5 **PRIDE OF HEIGHTS**, 5, b m Golden Heights—Taffys Pride **Mrs C. A. Dance**
6 **SEEK THE FAITH (USA)**, 7, ch g Pilgrim (USA)—Bundler (USA) **Mr R. H. F. Matthews**
7 **SOUTHWICK PARK**, 4, ch f Little Wolf—Carry On Fighting **Mr David Hunt**

Other Owners: Mrs K. H. Bullock, Mr Gerald Kidd.

549   MR O. M. C. SHERWOOD, Upper Lambourn

Postal: **Rhonehurst, Upper Lambourn, Hungerford, Berks, RG17 8RG.**

Phone: **(01488) OFFICE 71411 HOSTEL 72263 FAX 72786**

1 **ABBEY STREET (IRE)**, 4, b c Old Vic—Racquette **Mr B. T. Stewart-Brown**
2 **AERION**, 5, b g Ardross—Swallowfield **P. Chamberlain, D. Addiscott Partnership**
3 **ALLTIME DANCER (IRE)**, 4, b g Waajib—Dance On Lady **Mr H. M. Heyman**
4 **ASK ME KINDLY (IRE)**, 8, b g Furry Glen—Kindly **Roach Foods Limited**
5 **AUBURN CASTLE**, 7, b g Good Times (ITY)—Glorious Jane **Rashleigh Arms Charlestown St Austell**
6 **BAS DE LAINE (FR)**, 10, b g Le Pontet (FR)—La Gaina (FR) **R. K. Bids Ltd**
7 **BEAR CLAW**, 7, b g Rymer—Carmarthen Honey **Roach Foods Limited**
8 **BERUDE NOT TO (IRE)**, 7, b g Roselier (FR)—Decent Debbie **Mr G. Addiscott**
9 **BLOWN WIND (IRE)**, 5, b g Strong Gale—Raise A Queen **Mr B. T. Stewart-Brown**
10 **BOLL WEEVIL**, 10, b g Boreen (FR)—Lavenham Lady **Mr John Bolsover**
11 **BRACEY RUN (IRE)**, 6, b g The Parson—Outdoor Ivy **Bonusprint**

MR O. M. C. SHERWOOD—continued

12 **BROWNSIDE BRIG**, 11, b g Goldhill—Tumlin Brig **I. A. Low**
13 **BUTLER'S TWITCH**, 9, ch g Electric—Lady Doubloon **Mr Christopher Heath**
14 **CALLISOE BAY (IRE)**, 7, b br g Callernish—Granagh Bay **Mr R. Waters**
15 **CELTIC TOWN**, 8, ch g Celtic Cone—Booterstown **Lady Helen Smith**
16 **CHARMING GIRL (USA)**, 5, b m L'Emigrant (USA)—Charming Pan (FR) **Mr C. Coxen**
17 **CHEROKEE CHIEF**, 5, ch g Rakaposhi King—Coole Pilate
18 **COOL AS A CUCUMBER (IRE)**, 5, ch g Ballad Rock—Siberian Princess **Rashleigh Arms Charlestown St Austell**
19 5, B g Roselier (FR)—Coolcanute **Mr B. T. Stewart-Brown**
20 **COPPER MINE**, 10, b g Kambalda—Devon Lark **Mr J. Dougall**
21 **COULTON**, 9, ch g Final Straw—Pontevecchio Due **Mr M. G. St Quinton**
22 **DACELO (FR)**, 5, b g Bad Conduct (USA)—Matuvu (FR) **B. R. Harris**
23 **DARK NIGHTINGALE**, 6, br m Strong Gale—First Things First **Miss Liz Clark**
24 **DESPERATE**, 8, ch g Saxon Farm—Menel Arctic **The Desperate Partnership**
25 **DOCS BOY**, 6, b g Rakaposhi King—Jennie Pat **Mr D. J. W. Ross**
26 **DONNINGTON (IRE)**, 6, b g Good Thyne (USA)—Eljay **Mr B. T. Stewart-Brown**
27 **DUTCH AUNTIE**, 5, b m Prince Sabo—Dutch Princess **Mr B. T. E. Shrubsall**
28 **EARLY DRINKER**, 8, b g Gabitat—Blow My Top **S. Channing Williams**
29 **EASY BREEZY**, 6, b g Strong Gale—Mill Shine **Mrs A. E. Goodwin**
30 **FATHER SKY**, 5, b g Dancing Brave (USA)—Flamenco Wave (USA) **Mr Kenneth Kornfeld**
31 **FORESHORE MAN**, 5, b g Derrylin—Royal Birthday **Roach Foods Ltd**
32 **FOXBOW (IRE)**, 6, b g Mandalus—Lady Bow **Mrs Shirley Robins**
33 **GREY FINCH**, 7, gr g Nishapour (FR)—Swiftsand **Economic Security**
34 **HIGH LEARIE**, 6, b g Petoski—Lady Doubloon **Mr Edward Harvey**
35 **HIM OF PRAISE (IRE)**, 6, b g Paean—Tamed **Mr M. G. St Quinton**
36 **KEEP IT ZIPPED (IRE)**, 6, gr g Roselier (FR)—Bodalmore Kit **Mrs Luisa Stewart-Brown**
37 **KINDLY MOVE**, 8, b g Move Off—Kindly Night **Chrissie Malkin Fan Club**
38 **KONVEKTA KING (IRE)**, 8, b g Mandalus—Realma **Konvekta Ltd**
39 **KONVEKTA QUEEN (IRE)**, 5, b m Lord Americo—Fair Argument **Konvekta Ltd**
40 **LARGE ACTION (IRE)**, 8, b g The Parson—Ballyadam Lass **Mr B. T. Stewart-Brown**
41 **LAST TRAIN**, 5, b m Strong Gale—Last Clear Chance (USA) **Mr M. L. Oberstein**
42 **LAYHAM LOW (IRE)**, 5, b g Mandalus—Tempestuous Girl **Mr I. A. Low**
43 **LEOTARD**, 9, b g Lyphard's Special (USA)—Tondbad **Mr Christopher Heath**
44 **LIBERTARIAN (IRE)**, 6, b g Supreme Leader—Liberty Calling **Mr J. Drugall**
46 **LYME GOLD (IRE)**, 7, ch g Phardante (FR)—Mad For Her Beer **Mr Nigel Chamberlain**
46 **MAHFIL**, 8, b g Head For Heights—Polavera (FR) **Mr M. R. Klein**
47 **MENELAVE (IRE)**, 6, b m Meneval (USA)—Harlave **R. B. Holt**
48 **MERLINS DREAM (IRE)**, 7, ch g Callernish—Mystical Moonshine **Mr W. S. Watt**
49 **MIDDAY BLUES**, 7, ch g Sweet Monday—Blue Speckle **The True Blues-Four Seasons Racing**
50 **MUSICAL MONARCH (NZ)**, 10, ch g Leader of The Band (USA)—Cheelbrite (NZ) **Mr Sid Williams**
51 **MYLAND (IRE)**, 7, br g Phardante (FR)—Own Acre **Bonusprint**
52 **NIGHT TIME**, 4, b c Night Shift (USA)—Gathering Place (USA) **Mr J. Palmer-Brown**
53 **RAMBLING OATS**, 7, gr g Oats—Ramelton **Mr R. J. Owen**
54 **READY MONEY CREEK (IRE)**, 5, b g Phardante (FR)—Chestnut Vale **Roach Foods Ltd**
55 **REAL GLEE (IRE)**, 7, ch g Phardante (FR)—Richest **Mr John Stone**
56 **REVEREND BROWN (IRE)**, 6, b g The Parson—Let The Hare Sit **Mr J. Palmer-Brown**
57 **RIVER THRUST (IRE)**, 6, br g Over The River (FR)—Ballygoman Maid **Knightsbridge Partnership**
58 **SIERRA BAY (IRE)**, 6, b g Castle Keep—Beau's Trout **Mr R. Waters**
59 **SILVER WEDGE (USA)**, 5, ch g Silver Hawk (USA)—Wedge Musical **Mrs Shirley Robins**
60 **SLANEY FRANCE (IRE)**, 8, b br g Over The River (FR)—Kitty Quin **Mr B. T. Stewart-Brown**
61 **SMART ROOKIE (IRE)**, 6, b br g King's Ride—Jim's Honey **Mrs Shirley Robins**
62 **SOUND CARRIER (USA)**, 8, br g Lord Gaylord (USA)—Bright Choice (USA) **Mr M. L. Oberstein**
63 **STRONG GROVE (IRE)**, 8, b br m Strong Gale—Woodville Grove **Roach Foods Limited**
64 **TARRAGON (IRE)**, 6, ch g Good Thyne (USA)—Vanda **Mr R. B. Holt**
65 **THE BOOLEY HOUSE (IRE)**, 6, b g Sheer Grit—Chalk It Down **The Booley Bunch**
66 **THE BOUNDER**, 6, b g Uncle Pokey—Young Romance **Mr B. T. Stewart-Brown**
67 **THE BULL BLACKMAN (IRE)**, 5, b g Executive Perk—Gay Seeker **Mrs John Magnier**
68 **WHISPERING TOM (IRE)**, 8, b g Furry Glen—Lady Iceberg
69 **YOUNG POKEY**, 11, b g Uncle Pokey—Young Romance **Mr O. M. C. Sherwood**
70 **YOUNG SNUGFIT**, 12, ch g Music Boy—Sinzinbra **Elite Racing Club**
71 **ZEPHYRUS (IRE)**, 6, gr g Celio Rufo—No Honey **Mrs Shirley Robins**

MR O. M. C. SHERWOOD—continued

Other Owners: Mr J. L. Beckwith, Mr Tom Casagranda, Mr Jeffrey Dartnall, Mr T. Dartnall, Mr R. F. Eliot, Mr J. S. English, Mr A. Higgins, Mr Tony Hill, Mr C. Hoddell, Mr C. Humphry, Mr R. D. A. Kelly, Mr E. N. Kronfeld, Prof David Lipsey, Mr I. Magee, Professor David Metcalf, Mrs C. J. Morcom, Mr R. G. Morcom, Mr Rodney Morcom, Mr C. I. C. Munro, Miss M. Noden, Mr R. B. Pearson, Mr David Pym, R. E. A. Bott (Wigmore St) Ltd, Mr J. Robertson, Mr W. V. Robins, Mr Neil Rodway, Mr N. Sheehan, Mr N. J. Sillett, Mr F. Simpson, Mr Stephen G. Smith, Mr P. M. Taylor, Mr Barry Ward, Mr Martin Wells.

Jockeys (NH): J McCarthy (10-0), J Osborne (10-0), M Richards (10-0).

Conditional: D Thomas.

Amateur: Mr A H Harvey (11-0).

550   MR S. E. H. SHERWOOD, East Ilsley

Postal: **Summerdown, East Ilsley, Newbury, Berks, RG20 7LB.**
Phone: **(01635) 281678 FAX (01635) 281746**

1 **BANK PLACE,** 9, ch g Sheer Grit—Shatana **Buman Doors Ltd**
2 **BULLENS BAY (IRE),** 7, b g Hallodri (ATA)—Coolgreen Lolly **Bullens Bay Partners**
3 **CARRIG DANCER (IRE),** 8, br m Cardinal Flower—Kilcronat Tune **Mr W. G. R. Fearon**
4 **COCO POINT (IRE),** 6, b m Good Thyne (USA)—Mrs Popple **Mrs Sally Morton**
5 **DANJING (IRE),** 4, b g Danehill (USA)—Beijing (USA) **Richard Green (Fine Paintings)**
6 **DERAB (USA),** 10, b g Alleged (USA)—Island Charm (USA) **Mrs E. Brown**
7 **DUSTY MILLER,** 10, b g Current Magic—Royal Barb **Watership Down Enterprises**
8 **ELY'S HARBOUR (IRE),** 5, gr g Roselier (FR)—Sweet Run **Mrs Jean R. Bishop**
9 **FAIRIES FAREWELL,** 6, ch m Broadsword (USA)—Fairies First **Mr N. E. C. Sherwood**
10 **FALMOUTH BAY (IRE),** 7, b g Miner's Lamp—Vita Veritas **Mr James Morton**
11 **FRONT STREET,** 9, b g Idiot's Delight—Nakomis (USA) **Mrs Jean R. Bishop**
12 **GALE WARGAME (IRE),** 5, br g Strong Gale—Game Sunset **Lady Lloyd Webber**
13 **HARINGTON HUNDREDS,** 6, ch g Tacheron—Spring Clear **Mrs Jean R. Bishop**
14 **KILCARNE BAY (IRE),** 6, b g Henbit (USA)—Thai Nang **The Compass Partnership**
15 **L'EGLISE BELLE,** 4, b f Minster Son—Haddon Anna
16 **LOOKOUT MOUNTAIN (IRE),** 8, b g Mandalus—Addies Lass **Pell-mell Partners**
17 **MORGANS HILL (IRE),** 4, b g Strong Gale—Tengello **Mrs Jean R. Bishop**
18 5, Ch g Camden Town—Poll's Best
19 **POLO RIDGE (IRE),** 4, gr g Phardante (FR)—Fane Bridge **Mr James Morton**
20 **RED LIGHT,** 4, b g Reprimand—Trull **Mr M. Desmond Fitzgerald**
21 **ROCCO,** 9, b g King's Ride—Ladycastle **M. L. Oberstein & Summerdown Racing**
22 **RUMBLE (USA),** 8, ch g Lugnaquilla—Sumba **Pell-mell Partners**
23 **RUSSELL DALUS,** 9, b g Mandalus—Russell's Touch **Watership Down Enterprises**
24 **SHIFT AGAIN (IRE),** 4, b f Siberian Express (USA)—Pushkinia (FR) **Mr R. J. Bassett**
25 **SIR LEONARD (IRE),** 6, b g Strong Gale—Boro Penny **Mrs Jean R. Bishop**
26 **SPRING GALE (IRE),** 5, b g Strong Gale—Orospring **The Pessimists**
27 **STELLAR FORCE (IRE),** 5, br g Strong Gale—Glenroe Star **Mrs R. J. Feilden**
28 **THE BRUD,** 8, b g Bustino—Tintagel **Mrs Jean R. Bishop**
29 **THE MINE CAPTAIN,** 9, b g Shaab—Bal Casek **Mr Gerald W. Evans**
30 **TIPP MARINER,** 11, ch g Sandalay—Knockbawn Lady **Mrs Jean R. Bishop**
31 **TWO GOOD JUDGES (IRE),** 6, b g Roselier (FR)—Allamanda **Mrs Jean R. Bishop**
32 **WELSH LOOT (IRE),** 5, b g Welsh Term—Lucky Money **Mr W. J. Bridge**

Other Owners: Viscountess Boyne, Mr David Buik, Mr F. J. Bush, Mr J. Chromiak, Mr P. F. A. Clark, Mr Richard Gilder, Miss Angela Graham, Mr Pat Gray, Mrs A. Haynes, Mr G. Lansbury, Mr P. H. Lewellen, Sir Andrew Lloyd Webber, Mrs Pat May, Mr Jeff McCarthy, Mrs M. McGuigan, Mr John McMullen, Mr D. G. Peters, Lady Plymouth, Mr Miles Rivett-Carnac, Mr S. Sherwood, Mr Robert Stigwood, Sir William Stuttaford, Mr C. Watts, Mrs S. Watts.

Jockeys (NH): J Osborne (10-0), M Richards (10-0), G Upton (10-0).

Conditional: S Curran (9-7).

551   MR R. SHIELS, Jedburgh

Postal: **Ramsacre, Thickside Farm, Jedburgh, Roxburghshire, TD8 6QY.**

Phone: **(01835) 864060**

1 4, Ch f Alias Smith (USA)—Lurdenlaw Rose **Mr R. Shiels**
2 **SMIDDY LAD**, 5, ch g Crofthall—Carrapateira **Mr R. Shiels**
3 **THE DELEGATOR**, 6, b g Le Coq d'Or—Lurdenlaw Rose **Mr R. Shiels**

THREE-YEAR-OLDS

4 B f Kind of Hush—Carrapateira **Mr R. Shiels**

Amateur: Mr Raymond Shiels (11-4).

552   MISS L. C. SIDDALL, Tadcaster

Postal: **Stonebridge Farm, Colton, Tadcaster, N. Yorks, LS24 8EP.**

Phone: **(01904) 744291 FAX (01904) 744291 MOBILE (0378) 216694/92**

1 **FEATHERSTONE LANE**, 5, b g Siberian Express (USA)—Try Gloria **Mr D. Parker**
2 **FRONTIER FLIGHT (USA)**, 6, b g Flying Paster (USA)—Sly Charmer (USA) **Miss L. C. Siddall**
3 **HIGH MIND (FR)**, 7, br g Highest Honor (FR)—Gondolina (FR) **Mr J. E. Wilson**
4 **INNOCENT GEORGE**, 7, b g Hallgate—Are You Guilty **Mr Edward C. Wilkin**
5 **LADY PLOY**, 4, b f Deploy—Quississanno **Mr Neville L. Warriner**
6 **LEAP IN THE DARK (IRE)**, 7, br h Shadeed (USA)—Star Guide (FR) **Mrs D. J. Morris**
7 **METAL BOYS**, 9, b g Krayyan—Idle Gossip **Miss L. C. Siddall**
8 **MISS ARAGON**, 8, b m Aragon—Lavenham Blue **Miss L. C. Siddall**
9 **MOONDANCE**, 4, ch f Siberian Express (USA)—Falling Star (FR) **Miss L. C. Siddall**
10 **MR CHRISTIE**, 4, b g Doulab (USA)—Hi There **David Mann Partnership**
11 **NOVA HILL**, 5, ch m Ra Nova—Homing Hill **Leading Star Racing**
12 **OAKBURY (IRE)**, 4, ch g Common Grounds—Doon Belle **Townville C. C. Racing Club**
13 **RASCALLY**, 6, gr m Scallywag—Blue Gift **Mr J. Townson**
14 **SHARMOOR**, 4, b f Shardari—Linpac North Moor **Mr T. W. Heseltine**
15 **TAKADOU (IRE)**, 5, br h Double Schwartz—Taka **Mr F. Tyldesley**
16 **THE OTHER MAN (IRE)**, 6, b g Remainder Man—Amelioras Gran **Stonebridge Racing**
17 **TITIAN GIRL**, 7, ch m Faustus (USA)—Redhead **A. J. Wilkinson**

THREE-YEAR-OLDS

18 **CHAVIN POINT**, b f Inca Chief (USA)—To The Point **Advance Stock**
19 **DONA FILIPA**, ch f Precocious—Quississanno **The Smile Group**
20 **FANCY CLANCY**, b f Clantime—Bold Sophie **Podso Racing**
21 **MEADOW BLUE**, b f Northern State (USA)—Cornflower (USA) **Mr M. Marklow**
22 **SUPERFRILLS**, b f Superpower—Pod's Daughter (IRE) **Podso Racing**

TWO-YEAR-OLDS

23 Ch c 25/3 Tina's Pet—Sparkling Hock (Hot Spark)
24 B c 1/3 Aragon—Sunley Silks (Formidable (USA)) **Mrs A. Wyatt**

Other Owners: Mr H. Banks, Mrs P. J. Clark, Mrs L. E. Crump, Mr M. Crump, Miss J. Goodyear, Mrs P. M. Hornby, Mr Ronnie Howe, Miss L. Ibbotson, Mrs Anne Shanks, Mr M. C. Simpson.

Apprentice: T Siddall (8-0).

553   MRS J. SIDEBOTTOM, Llandysul

Postal: **Rhydlewis Garage, Rhydlewis, Llandysul, Dyfed, SA44 5PE.**
Phone: **(01239) 851455**

1 BALLYHASTY LADY (IRE), 6, ch m Castle Keep—Ariawell **Mrs J. Sidebottom**
2 LADY BREYFAX, 6, ch m Ra Nova—Celtic Love **Mrs J. Sidebottom**
3 OLLIVER DUCKETT, 7, b g Bustino—Tatiana **Mrs J. Sidebottom**

Amateur: Mr J Jukes (10-0).

554   MR RODNEY SIMPSON, Wellington

Postal: **Orchard Court Racing Stables, West Buckland, Wellington, Somerset, TA21 9LE.**
Phone: **TEL/FAX (01823) 665156 MOBILE (0421) 012525 or (0802) 157210**

1 ARABOYBILL, 5, b g Aragon—Floral **Nigel Gay & Bernard G. Barry**
2 DURHAM, 5, ch g Caerleon (USA)—Sanctuary **The Secret Partnership**
3 FAEZ, 6, b g Mtoto—Ghanimah **The Secret Partnership**
4 KASTEL DOURIG (FR), 4, b g Esprit du Nord (USA)—Margelle (USA) **Mr M. Thole**
5 MALLASTANG (IRE), 8, b g Kemal (FR)—Evas Charm **Mr C. Duncan**
6 MISTER MAYBE, 5, b g Damister (USA)—Maybe So **Rod Simpson**
7 NIPPER REED, 6, b g Celestial Storm (USA)—Figrant (USA) **Mr G. Piper**
8 NUIN-TARA, 5, b m Petoski—Mira Lady **The Secret Partnership**
9 POWER SHARE, 5, ch g Superpower—Collegian **The Secret Partnership**
10 RESERVATION ROCK (IRE), 5, ch g Ballad Rock—Crazyfoot **Mr G. Piper**
11 TASHKENT, 4, b g Thowra (FR)—Royal Bat **Mr G. Piper**

THREE-YEAR-OLDS

12 SHEILAS DREAM, b f Inca Chief (USA)—Windlass **The Secret Partnership**
13 Ch f No Big Deal—Willie Marquesa **Mr G. Hodges**

Other Owners: Mr Shaun Millard, Mrs P. Thole.

Jockey (NH): Dean Gallagher (9-10).

Conditional: K Dempsey (9-12).

Amateur: Mr E Williams (10-2).

Lady Rider: Miss E Jones (8-4).

555   MRS P. M. SLY, Peterborough

Postal: **Singlecote, Thorney, Peterborough, PE6 0PB.**
Phone: **(01733) 270212**

1 BASSENHALLY, 6, ch g Celtic Cone—Milly Kelly **Thorney Racing Club**
2 BOLD REVIVAL, 4, b f Never So Bold—Convivial **Mrs P. Sly**
3 BUKEHORN, 5, b g Bold Owl—Milly Kelly **Mrs P. Sly**
4 CALL ME FLASH, 4, ch g Presidium—Relkisha **Mr F. Lipscomb**
5 CHICHELL'S HURST, 10, ch m Oats—Milly Kelly **Mrs P. Sly**
6 CRAZY WEATHER, 6, b g Idiot's Delight—Monsoon **Mr R. Brazier**

MRS P. M. SLY—continued

7 **FERRERS**, 5, b g Homeboy—Gay Twenties **Mr J. L. Burt**
8 **GRIFFINS BAR**, 8, b g Idiot's Delight—Milly Kelly **Mr M. S. Smith**
9 **IMA DELIGHT**, 9, b m Idiot's Delight—Milly Kelly **Mrs P. Sly**
10 **KLONDIKE (IRE)**, 6, b g Glint of Gold—Shannon Princess **Mr R. Brazier**
11 **NELTEGRITY**, 7, b g Neltino—Integrity **Mr T. Crowson**
12 **SALFRILL (IRE)**, 4, b f Salt Dome (USA)—Frill **Mr R. Brazier**
13 **SINGLESOLE**, 11, ch g Celtic Cone—Milly Kelly **Mrs P. Sly**
14 **SUPEROO**, 10, b g Superlative—Shirleen **Mrs P. Sly**

THREE-YEAR-OLDS

15 Ch f Never So Bold—Courtesy Call
16 **HOT DOGGING**, b f Petoski—Mehtab **Mrs P. Sly**
17 **LEBEDINSKI (IRE)**, ch f Soviet Lad (USA)—Excavate

TWO-YEAR-OLDS

18 Gr c 13/3 Petong—Mehtab

Other Owners: Mr F. Allan, Mr R. Andrew, Mrs Irene Dobney, Mrs J. Woollatt.

Jockey (Flat): A Culhane (w.a.).

Jockey (NH): R Marley.

Lady Rider: Miss Louise Allen (9-7).

556   MR D. SMAGA, Lamorlaye

Postal: **17 Voie de la Grange des Pres, 60260 Lamorlaye, France.**
Phone: **44-21-50-05 TELEX 150949 FAX 44 21 53 56**

1 **ADMISE (FR)**, 4, b f Highest Honor (FR)—Admiration (FR) **Alain Lequeux**
2 **ALDAMAR (FR)**, 4, b c Akarad (FR)—Avellaneda (USA) **Ecurie Seutet**
3 **ELBLEST**, 7, b h Ela-Mana-Mou—Much Blest **Mme F. Darty**
4 **ESSESSTEE (FR)**, 5, b h Perrault—Insistance **Baron T. Van Zuylen**
5 **INDIAN KEANE (IRE)**, 4, b c Sadler's Wells (USA)—Apachee (FR) **Ecurie du Club Galop**
6 **KING OF TROY (USA)**, 4, b c Shahrastani (USA)—Trojan Miss **Lord A. Weinstock**
7 **LEAGUE LEADER (IRE)**, 6, b h Shirley Heights—Happy Kin (USA) **Lord A. Weinstock**
8 **MARILDO**, 9, b h Romildo—Marike **David Smaga**
9 **MING DYNASTY (IRE)**, 5, b g Sadler's Wells (USA)—Marie Noelle (FR) **Mme O. A. Scemama**
10 **NEXT WINNER (FR)**, 6, b h Irish River (FR)—Pleasant Way (USA) **David Smaga**
11 **PALAIROS (FR)**, 6, b h Kahyasi—Glifahda (FR) **M. Lagasse**
12 **PECKINPAH'S SOUL (FR)**, 4, b c Zino—Nashra (FR) **Ecurie Leader**
13 **PERCUTANT**, 5, br h Perrault—Estada (FR) **Baron T. Van Zuylen**
14 **RINGING TONE (FR)**, 4, b g General Holme (USA)—Queen of The Ring (USA) **Lord A. Weinstock**
15 **SACREMENT (FR)**, 6, b g Lead On Time (USA)—Sentimentalite (USA) **Ecurie du Club Galop**
16 **STAR OF FEMME (FR)**, 4, b c Saint Cyrien—Femme Femme **David Smaga**
17 **TEC'S CHAMP (IRE)**, 4, b c Niniski (USA)—Noesis **Mr Hung Yat Fai**
18 **THE SHADOW**, 8, gr h Kaldoun—Evanescente **Baron T. Van Zuylen**
19 **TROJAN SEA (USA)**, 5, b h Bering—Trojan Miss **Lord A. Weinstock**
20 **TRUE BEARING (USA)**, 6, ch h Bering—Trojan Miss **Lord A. Weinstock**

THREE-YEAR-OLDS

21 **BAIKALA (FR)**, b f Sicyos (USA)—Willchris **David Smaga**
22 **BIG HONOR (FR)**, b c Highest Honor—Beautiful Time (FR) **Baron T. Van Zuylen**
23 **DI TULLIO (FR)**, b c Cricket Ball (USA)—The Faboulous (FR) **Tullio Attias**

MR D. SMAGA—continued

24 EXCLUSIVITY (FR), b f Highest Honor (FR)—Evanescente (FR) **Baron T. Van Zuylen**
25 INATTENDU (USA), b c Septieme Ciel—I Wich (FR) **Haras d'Étreham**
26 INFILTRATE (IRE), b f Bering—Trojan Miss **Lord A. Weinstock**
27 L'INSENSE (FR), b c Antheus (USA)—Estada (FR) **Baron T. Van Zuylen**
28 MISS EBENE (FR), b f Lead On Time (USA)—Miss Afrique (FR) **Ecurie Seutet**
29 MODERN TIMES (FR), b c Lead On Time (USA)—Glifahda (FR) **Baron T. Van Zuylen**
30 PLEASELOOKATMENOW (USA), b f Irish River (FR)—Pointed Path **Mme M. de Chambure**
31 ROYAL HOSTESS (IRE), b f Be My Guest (USA)—Edinburgh **Lord A. Weinstock**
32 SWEET BLUE EYES (USA), b f Seeking The Gold—Navratilovna (USA) **Ian D. Fair**
33 THE WIZZARD (FR), b c Pampabird (FR)—Emerald City **Baron T. Van Zuylen**
34 ZALAMALEC (USA), b f Septieme Ciel—Zolinana (FR) **Ecurie M3 Elevage**

TWO-YEAR-OLDS

35 ACHIEVER (FR), b g Bering—Queen of The Ring (USA) **Lord A. Weinstock**
36 AFRIKAL (FR), b c Kaldoun (FR)—Miss Afrique (FR) **Ecurie Seutet**
37 ALL'S WELL (FR), b f Always Fair (USA)—French Guichet (USA) **Baron T. Van Zuylen**
38 ALWAYS ALEXIS (FR), b c Lightning (FR)—Trenora (FR) **J. J. Taied**
39 AMANELLA (FR), b f Pampabird—Maranella (FR) **Baron T. Van Zuylen**
40 AMITIE FATALE (IRE), b f Night Shift (USA)—Adjarida **Ecurie M3 Elevage**
41 AVALOR (FR), b c Kendor (FR)—Avellaneda (FR) **Ecurie Seutet**
42 BOB DEL MARE (FR), b c Sanglamore (USA)—Femme Femme (USA) **Ecurie Leader**
43 CANTATA (IRE), b f Saddlers' Hall (IRE)—Victory Chorus **Lord A. Weinstock**
44 CASTADA (FR), b f Caerwent—Estada (FR) **Baron T. Van Zuylen**
45 B f Cadeaux Genereux—Dance Move **C. Stelling**
46 DART BOARD (IRE), b f Darshaan—Trojan Miss **Lord A. Weinstock**
47 DIAMETRALE, b f Septieme Ciel (USA)—Daisy Dance (FR) **J. T. L. Jones**
48 FUENJI (FR), b f Saumarez—Belle Et Chere (USA) **Mme O. A. Scemama**
49 GLIVANA (FR), b f Highest Honor (FR)—Glifahda (FR) **Baron T. Van Zuylen**
50 LARGESSE (FR), b f Saumarez—Leariva (USA) **Baron T. Van Zuylen**
51 PRESBOURG (FR), b c Sanglamore (USA)—Plytroca (USA) **Alain Lequeux**
52 B c Septieme Ciel (USA)—Reve de Reine (USA) **Ecurie Leader**
53 STAR CASTLE (IRE), b g Shahrastani (USA)—Edinburgh **Lord A. Weinstock**
54 VARXI (FR), b c Kaldoun (FR)—Girl of France **Baron T. Van Zuylen**
55 B c Saint Cyrien (FR)—Willchris (USA) **Mme O. A. Scemama**

Jockeys (Flat): G Guignard, F Head.

Apprentice: R Thomas.

557 MR B. SMART, Lambourn

Postal: **Sherwood Stables, Folly Road, Lambourn, Newbury, RG16 7QE.**

Phone: **LAMBOURN (01488) 71632 FAX (01488) 73859 MOBILE (0374) 946070**

1 BALLESWHIDDEN, 4, b g Robellino (USA)—Dame Scarlet **Mr Ian Henderson**
2 CALOGAN, 9, br g Callernish—Lady Tarsel **Mr K. H. Burks**
3 CARRICKROVADDY, 10, ch g Deroulede—Ballybeg Maid **Mrs Dianne J. Coleman**
4 FORTINA'S CONQUEST, 6, b g El Conquistador—Free Fortina **Mrs D. J. Hodges**
5 GANADOR, 4, gr f Weldnaas (USA)—Shakana **Mr B. Smart**
6 KATIE OLIVER, 4, b f Squill (USA)—Shih Ching (USA) **The Manlift Group**
7 MISTER LAWSON, 10, ch g Blushing Scribe (USA)—Nonpareil (FR) **Mr W. McKibbin**
8 MR TEIGH, 4, b g Komaite (USA)—Khadino **Hannah McAuliffe**
9 POLLY PECULIAR, 5, b m Squill (USA)—Pretty Pollyanna **Mr B. Smart**
10 PRESTIGE LAD, 4, ch g Weldnaas (USA)—Chic Antique **Prestige Racing Club**
11 PRESTIGE LADY, 5, b m Capitano—Nancherrow **Prestige Racing Club**
12 RUFUS, 10, ch g Cheval—Perdeal **Mrs Dianne J. Coleman**
13 SET-EM-ALIGHT, 6, b g Relkino—Dragon Fire **Mr R. A. Hughes**
14 SHARP DANCE, 7, b m Dance of Life (USA)—Sharp Jose (USA) **The Big Eaters Partnership**

MR B. SMART—continued

15 **SHARP GAZELLE**, 6, ch m Beveled (USA)—Shadha **Mr M. J. Samuel**
16 **SHARP 'N SMART**, 4, ch c Weldnaas (USA)—Scottish Lady **Mr K. H. Burks**
17 **SHARP THRILL**, 5, ch g Squill (USA)—Brightelmstone **Mr K. H. Burks**
18 **SUPER SAFFRON**, 6, b m Pollerton—Sagora **Mr R. B. Warren**
19 **THE NED**, 5, b g Kinglet—Galetzky **Mr Mike Perkins**

THREE-YEAR-OLDS

20 **HONESTLY**, ch f Weldnaas (USA)—Shadha **Mr B. Hoggart**
21 **MASTER MULLIGAN**, b c Then Again—Sagora **Mrs L. M. Dresher**
22 **MRS MCBADGER**, ch f Weldnaas (USA)—Scottish Lady **Mr Chris Badger**
23 **ONE DREAM**, b c Weldnaas (USA)—Superb Lady **One Dream Partnership**
24 **SIBERIAN HENRY**, b g Siberian Express (USA)—Semperflorens **Mr C. S. Tateson**
25 **SIL SILA (IRE)**, b f Marju (IRE)—Porto Alegre **Mr L. Alvarez Cervera**
26 **THREESOCKS**, ch f Weldnaas (USA)—Jeethgaya (USA) **Mr K. H. Burks**

TWO-YEAR-OLDS

27 B f 3/4 Forzando—Oakbrook Tern (USA) (Arctic Tern (USA)) **Gaelic 5 Partnership**
28 **POLGWYNNE**, ch f 25/2 Forzando—Trelissick (Electric)
29 B f 1/3 Robellino (USA)—Session (Reform) **Mrs P. A. Clark**
30 **TROIA (IRE)**, b f 8/4 Last Tycoon—Dubai Lady (Kris) **Mr J. Massey-Collier**

Other Owners: Mr Jason Brown, Mr David Bucknell, Mr I. Burt, Mr J. Carberry, Mr L. F. Chamberlain, Mr J. Crehan, Mr T. J. Crehan, Mr Edward Crisp, Mrs Bernice M. Cuthbert, Mr A. Flynn, Mr B. R. France, Mr J. A. Griffin, Mr T. Hanley, Mr Alan Haslam, Mr D. Johnson, Mr D. J. Jolly, Mr Alan Mason, Mr M. Pattimore, Mr John Pearce, Mr Robert Scott, Miss Christina Trent, Mr Mike Upstone, Mr D. R. Wright.

Jockeys (Flat): R Cochrane (w.a.), S Sanders (w.a.).

Jockeys (NH): R Dunwoody (w.a.), C Llewellyn (w.a.).

Conditional: M Molloy (9-7).

Lady Rider: Miss V Marshall (8-5).

558   MR ALFRED SMITH, Beverley

Postal: **Heath Racing Stables, Newbold Road, Beverley, N. Humberside, HU17 8EF.**
Phone: **(01482) 882520**

1 **BRACKEN**, 4, b f Cid's Kid—Miss Periwinkle **Mr A. H. Grant**
2 **CRAMBELLA (IRE)**, 4, b f Red Sunset—Simbella **Mrs Sheila Oakes**
3 **LITTLE CONKER**, 8, ch g All Systems Go—L'Irondelle **Mr Alfred Smith**
4 **MR EGLANTINE**, 4, ch g Mr Fluorocarbon—Sweet Rosa **Westwood Racing**
5 6, Ch m Primitive Rising (USA)—Ring of Flowers **Mr J. Bowden**
6 **TIP IT IN**, 7, gr g Le Solaret (FR)—Alidante **Mrs M. Dunning**

THREE-YEAR-OLDS

7 **LUGANA BOY**, b g Lugana Beach—Mischievous Tyke **Mr David Tate**

TWO-YEAR-OLDS

8 Ch c 9/4 Clantime—Allez-Oops (Moulin) **David Tate**
9 **BRIGHT GOLD**, ch c 6/4 Clantime—Miss Brightside (Crofthall) **Mr A. H. Grant**
10 **CAPTAIN FLINT**, b c 19/5 Bedford (USA)—Sun Yat Chen (Chou Chin Chow) **Mrs G. Wood**
11 **LOCKSILL**, b c 28/3 Silly Prices—Steelock (Lochnager) **Mrs G. Wood**
12 Ch c 10/5 Clantime—Mischievous Tyke (Flying Tyke) **David Tate**
13 **RISKY FLIGHT**, ch c 17/4 Risk Me (FR)—Stairway To Heaven (IRE) (Godswalk (USA)) **Mrs Sheila Oakes**

Other Owners: Mr P. Dixon, Mr K. A. Johnson, Mr M. Kelly, Mr Paul Laverack, Mr John Allan Milburn, Mr R. A. Nicklin, Mr J. Strudwick.

559 MR C. SMITH, Wellingore

Postal: **Thompsons Bottom Farm, Temple Bruer, Wellingore, Lincoln, LN5 0DE.**
Phone: **(01526) 833245 TELEPHONE AND FAX (0378) 149188 MOBILE**

1 **APRIL CITY**, 7, b m Lidhame—Gay City **Mr I. Gourley**
2 **BAHRAIN QUEEN (IRE)**, 8, ch m Caerleon (USA)—Bahrain Vee **Mr D. Thompson**
3 **BRANSTON KRISTY**, 4, b f Hallgate—Bare Spectacle **Mr J. Starbuck**
4 **CAN SHE CAN CAN**, 4, b f Sulaafah (USA)—Dominance **Mr Robinson**
5 **CAPTAIN TANDY (IRE)**, 7, ch g Boyne Valley—Its All A Dream **Mr D. Simms**
6 **CHEEKA**, 7, ch g Dawn Johnny (USA)—Lallax **Mr D. Thompson**
7 **COPPER CABLE**, 9, ch g True Song—Princess Mey **Dowager Lady Scott**
8 **MACS HERO**, 6, b g Scallywag—Celtic Kerry **Mrs P. Burrows & Mrs P. Stephens**
9 **MOSHAAJIR (USA)**, 6, b h Woodman (USA)—Hidden Trail (USA) **Mr Steve Macdonald**
10 **MRS JAWLEYFORD (USA)**, 8, b m Dixieland Band (USA)—Did She Agree (USA) **Mr C. Smith**
11 **MRS NORMAN**, 7, b m Lochnager—Economy Pep **Mr M. W. Flint**
12 **NEVER SAY SO**, 4, ch f Prince Sabo—So Rewarding **Mrs S. Lamyman**
13 **RAINDEER QUEST**, 4, ch f Hadeer—Rainbow Ring **Mr Steve Macdonald**
14 **ROTHERFIELD PARK (IRE)**, 4, b f High Estate—Alriyaah **Miss Rosie Dean**
15 **SADARAH (USA)**, 4, b c Dixieland Band (USA)—Chriso (USA) **Mr Terry Thorp**
16 **TIMBERLAND TUMBLER**, 4, gr f Lanhargy Lad—Stancombe Lass
17 **TRENTSIDE MIST**, 8, b g Laxton—Trent Lane **Mr J. Payne**
18 **TRENTSIDE VALOUR**, 11, b g Tudorville—Trent Valley **Mr J. Payne**
19 5, Ch g Say Primula—Trois Filles
20 **WALSHAM WITCH**, 6, b m Music Maestro—Makinlau **Mr J. Starbuck**

THREE-YEAR-OLDS

21 **KALA SUNRISE**, ch c Kalaglow—Belle of The Dawn **Mr A. E. Needham**
22 **PLEASURE TIME**, ch c Clantime—First Experience **The Temple Bruers**
23 **ROYAL RIGGER**, gr f Reprimand—Overdraft **Mrs Rita Smith**
24 **SAFIO**, ch c Efisio—Marcroft **Mrs M. A. Clayton**
25 **SNITCH**, ch g Blow The Whistle—Whispering Sea **Mr Gordon Batty**

TWO-YEAR-OLDS

26 **AMY**, b f 13/4 Timeless Times (USA)—Rion River (IRE) (Taufan (USA))
27 B f 13/4 Forzando—Katie Scarlett (Lochnager)
28 Ch f 24/4 Pharly (FR)—Miss Oriental (Habitat)

Other Owners: Mr P. Lamyman.

Jockey (NH): M Ranger (10-0).

Conditional: R Smith (9-7).

560 MR DENYS SMITH, Bishop Auckland

Postal: **Holdforth Farm, Bishop Auckland, Co Durham, DL14 6DJ.**
Phone: **(01388) 603317 OR 606180 FAX**

1 **CADEAUX PREMIERE**, 5, b g Cadeaux Genereux—Clare Island **Lumsden & Carroll Construction Ltd**
2 **CORNET**, 10, b g Coquelin (USA)—Corny Story **Duke of Sutherland**
3 **DENSBEN**, 12, b g Silly Prices—Eliza de Rich **Mrs Janet M. Pike**
4 **FINAL FLING**, 4, b f Last Tycoon—Lady Day (FR) **Duke of Sutherland**
5 **GEORGE DILLINGHAM**, 6, b g Top Ville—Premier Rose **J. Blair & Carlton Appointments Ltd**
6 **GUNNERDALE**, 4, b f Gunner B—Melody Moon **Mr David Curr**
7 **IMPERIAL BID (FR)**, 8, b g No Pass No Sale—Tzaritsa (USA) **Lord Durham**
8 **OAKLEY**, 7, ch g Nicholas Bill—Scrub Oak **Duke of Sutherland**
9 **REVE DE VALSE (USA)**, 9, ch g Conquistador Cielo (USA)—Dancing Vaguely (USA) **Mr K. Higson**

MR DENYS SMITH—continued

10 SPANISH VERDICT, 9, b g King of Spain—Counsel's Verdict Cox & Allen (Kendal) Ltd
11 STAIGUE FORT (IRE), 8, b g Torus—Lady Beecham Mr Denys Smith
12 TINKLERS FOLLY, 4, ch g Bairn (USA)—Lucky Straw Mr R. O. Manners
13 VAL DE RAMA (IRE), 7, b g Lafontaine (USA)—Port Magee Mr D. Morland

THREE-YEAR-OLDS

14 KARISMA (IRE), b g Tirol—Avra (FR) Mr D. Vic Roper
15 ROYAL CEILIDH (IRE), b f Prince Rupert (FR)—Isa Carlton Appointments (Aberdeen) Ltd

TWO-YEAR-OLDS

16 B c 14/4 Chilibang—Constant Companion (Pas de Seul) Mr Denys Smith
17 B c 22/4 Tina's Pet—Immodest Miss (Daring Display (USA)) Mr Denys Smith
18 B g 12/3 Prince Daniel (USA)—Rio Piedras (Kala Shikari) J. A. Bianchi & Mr Denys Smith

Other Owners: Mr Ian Darling, Mr Paul Darling, Mr J. F. Haigh, Lord Lambton, Mr C. J. Pennick, Mr J. R. Wharton.

Jockey (Flat): K Fallon (w.a.).

Jockey (NH): P Niven (w.a.).

Lady Rider: Miss Melanie Carson (8-5).

561　　　　MR J. P. SMITH, Rugeley

Postal: Coldwell Cottage, Coldwell, Gentleshaw, Rugeley, WS15 4NJ.

Phone: (01543) 686587

1 ARR EFF BEE, 9, b g Crooner—Miss Desla Mr P. R. Wheeler
2 BEE DEE BEST (IRE), 5, b g Try My Best (USA)—Eloquent Charm (USA) Mr Barry Foster
3 CERBERA, 7, b g Caruso—Sealed Contract Mr P. R. Wheeler
4 DARING RYDE, 5, b g Daring March—Mini Myra Mrs Linda Barrett
5 DESLA'S DEVIL, 4, b g Devil To Play—Miss Desla Mr Brian Marsh
6 LIVING PROOF, 12, ch g Known Fact (USA)—Lady Esmeralda
7 MY SWAN SONG, 11, b g Soul Singer—Palmaria Mr Brian McGowan
8 TUDOR BLUES, 9, ch m Sula Bula—Cottage Melody Mr Barry Foster

Other Owners: Mr D. A. Kippax.

562　　　　MR JULIAN S. SMITH, Tirley

Postal: Tirley Court, Tirley, Gloucester, GL19 4HA.

Phone: (01452) 780208 FAX (01452) 780 461

1 BENGAZEE (IRE), 8, b g Abednego—Sazek Mr David C. Hudd
2 DERRING TIRLEY, 6, b g Derring Rose—Tic-On-Rose Mr D. J. Eckley
3 HANDY LASS, 7, b m Nicholas Bill—Mandrian Mr G. Hackling
4 LITTLE JOE (IRE), 7, br g Cataldi—Linanbless Mr F. G. Smith
5 SENSE OF VALUE, 7, br m Trojan Fen—War Ballad (FR) Mr Donald Smith
6 TIRLEY LEADER, 7, b g Supreme Leader—Random Select Mr Donald Smith
7 TIRLEY MISSILE, 10, ch g Cruise Missile—Tic-On-Rose Mr J. D. Hankinson
8 TIRLEY WOLF, 6, ch g Little Wolf—Tudor Spartan Mr Donald Smith

Other Owners: Mr Ray Baverstock, Mr Roger F. Downes & Partners.

563 MR N. A. SMITH, Upton Snodsbury

Postal: **Court Farm Stables, Court Farm, Upton Snodsbury, Worcester, WR7 4NN.**

Phone: **OFFICE (01905) 381077**

1 **ALRIGHT GUVNOR**, 6, br m Governor General—Can't Be Wrong **Mrs J. Tarran**
2 **BILL'S JOY**, 5, b m Gabitat—Springs To Mind **Mr Edwin Smith**
3 **DEARDS SMASHER**, 7, b m Crash Course—Wunder Madchen **Mrs G. C. List**
4 **DESPERATE MAN**, 7, b g Ballacashtal (CAN)—Priors Dean **Mr N. A. Smith**
5 **GREEK CHIME (IRE)**, 7, gr g Bellypha—Corinth Canal **Mr P. L. Williams**
6 **KELLY OWENS**, 11, ch g Kemal (FR)—Jill Owens **Mr N. A. Smith**
7 **LADY PENDRAGON**, 7, b m Oats—Impressive Reward (USA) **Mr J. Aldersey**
8 **MAJOR NOVA**, 7, b g Ra Nova—Phyllis Jane **Mrs G. C. List**
9 **PETRACO (IRE)**, 8, b g Petorius—Merrie Moira **Mr Bernard Gover**
10 6, Ch m Oats—Springs To Mind **Miss E. Grainger & Mr J. Tarran**
11 **THE COVENTRY FLYER**, 7, b m Seymour Hicks (FR)—Easterly Gael **Coventry Arms Racing**
12 4, B g Lightning Dealer—White Linen **Mrs G. C. List**

THREE-YEAR-OLDS

13 **SKIPMAN (IRE)**, b c Posen (USA)—Near Miracle **Mr P. L. Williams**

Other Owners: Mr N. J. Barrowclough.

Jockey (Flat): S D Williams.

Jockey (NH): R Dunwoody (w.a.).

Amateurs: Mr N Bradley (10-0), Mr M Rodda (10-0).

564 MRS S. J. SMITH, Bingley

Postal: **Craiglands Farm, High Eldwick, Bingley, West Yorks, BD16 3BE.**

Phone: **BRADFORD (01274) 564930**

1 **ABSOLUTE FOLLY**, 4, gr g Absalom—Agreloui **Mrs S. Smith**
2 **AIRE VALLEY**, 7, b m Royal Vulcan—Loughnavalley **Mrs S. Smith**
3 **ALIAS CHUBB**, 5, gr g Alias Smith (USA)—Chubby Ears **Mrs S. Smith**
4 **AQUINAS**, 10, ch g Ahonoora—Latin Guest **The Secret Agents Racing Partnership**
5 **BALTIC BROWN**, 11, b m Le Moss—Riversfield Lady **Mr James McKeon**
6 **BASILICUS (FR)**, 7, b g Pamponi (FR)—Katy Collonge (FR) **Mr Trevor Hemmings**
7 **BIT OF A DREAM (IRE)**, 6, b g Henbit (USA)—Time And Patience **Michael Jackson Bloodstock Ltd**
8 **BRAMBLEBERRY**, 7, gr g Sharrood (USA)—Labista **Hampers Racing**
9 **CATAKIL (FR)**, 7, b g Bikala—Catacomb (USA) **Mrs S. Smith**
10 **CELTIC SILVER**, 8, gr g Celtic Cone—Rockin Berry **Mrs S. Smith**
11 **DEEP FAIR**, 9, br g Fidel—Run Fair **Mrs S. Smith**
12 **DESERT BRAVE (IRE)**, 6, b g Commanche Run—Desert Pet **Michael Jackson Bloodstock Ltd**
13 **DIDDY RYMER**, 6, b m Rymer—Doddycross **Mrs S. Smith**
14 **DREAM START**, 6, b g Dreams To Reality (USA)—Bad Start (USA) **Mrs S. Smith**
15 **EID (USA)**, 7, b g Northern Baby (CAN)—Millracer (USA) **Mr N. Wilby**
16 **EUPHORIC ILLUSION**, 5, ch g Rainbow Quest (USA)—High And Bright **Mrs S. Smith**
17 **EXEMPLAR (IRE)**, 8, b g Carlingford Castle—Mabbots Own **Mrs S. Smith**
18 **FAITHFUL HAND**, 6, ch g Nearly A Hand—Allende **Mrs Enid Brindle**
19 **FIVE FLAGS (IRE)**, 8, ch g Le Moss—Lovenos **Mrs S. Smith**
20 **GAELIC BLUE**, 6, ch g Celtic Cone—Giollaretta **Mr Trevor Hemmings**
21 **GATHERING TIME**, 10, ch g Deep Run—Noble Gathering **Mrs S. Smith**
22 **HARD TRY**, 4, ro g Sharrood (USA)—Trynova **Mrs S. Smith**
23 **KILTULLA (IRE)**, 6, br g Henbit (USA)—Sheer Vulgan **Mrs S. Smith**

MRS S. J. SMITH—continued

24 **LONE VENTURE**, 9, b g King's Ride—Strandhill **Mrs S. Smith**
25 **MAJOR SIOUX**, 5, ch g Mandrake Major—Sioux Be It **Mrs S. Smith**
26 **MILLERS GOLDENGIRL (IRE)**, 5, ch m Henbit (USA)—Millers Run **Mrs S. Smith**
27 **MONYMOSS (IRE)**, 7, b g Le Moss—El Scarsdale **Mr Trevor Hemmings**
28 **MONY-SKIP (IRE)**, 7, b g Strong Gale—Skiporetta **Mr Trevor Hemmings**
29 **MR GOLDFINGER**, 9, b g Beau Charmeur (FR)—Miss Dollar **Mrs S. Smith**
30 **NOVA CHAMP**, 8, ch g Nearly A Hand—Laval **Mrs C. E. Van Praag**
31 **OLD BETSY**, 6, b m Town And Country—Cilerna Jet **Mrs S. Smith**
32 **PERFECT LIGHT**, 7, b g Salmon Leap (USA)—Sheer Gold **Mr Russell Field**
33 **PERUVIAN GALE (IRE)**, 7, b g Strong Gale—Peruvian Lady **Mr J. L. Walbank**
34 **REGAL ROMPER (IRE)**, 8, b g Tender King—Fruit of Passion **Mrs S. Smith**
35 **RUA ROS (IRE)**, 6, gr m Roselier (FR)—Rescue Run **Mr R. Preston**
36 **SHUIL SAOR**, 9, b g Fairbairn—Shuil Comeragh **Mrs S. Smith**
37 **SUL FOSSO**, 4, b g Skyliner—Sveltissima **Mrs S. Smith**
38 **SUPER SNIPE**, 5, ch g Derrylin—Sweet Canyon (NZ) **Mr S. Powell**
39 **SUPPOSIN**, 8, b g Enchantment—Misty Rocket **Mr J. Kemp**
40 **TARGET LINE**, 6, b g Skyliner—Tree Breeze **Brampton Royal Oak**
41 **THE LAST FLING (IRE)**, 6, ch g Avocat—Highway's Last **Robert Waterson**
42 **TROY'S DREAM**, 5, b g Master Willie—Troja **Mr Trevor Hemmings**
43 **WHAT A DIFFERENCE (IRE)**, 7, ch g Carlingford Castle—Lantern Lady **Mr W. Raw**

Other Owners: Mr T. R. Benson, Miss Angela Brindle, Mr John Elcock, Mr Keith Hammill, Mr J. Laughton, Mrs B. Perrin, Mr D. A. Stephenson, Mr Richard Younger.

Jockey (NH): Richard Guest (10-0).

Conditional: L Donnelly, L McGrath, R Wilkinson (10-0).

Amateur: Mr Patrick Murray.

565   MR L. A. SNOOK, Sturminster Newton

Postal: **Lower Ridge Farm, Kings Stag, Sturminster Newton, Dorset, DT10 2AU.**
Phone: **TEL: (01258) 817364 FAX (01258) 817771**

1 **APRIL CRUISE**, 9, ch m Cruise Missile—April Belle **Mr Laurie Snook**
2 **MIGAVON**, 6, b m Sharrood (USA)—Migoletty **Mr Laurie Snook**
3 **MILLY BLACK (IRE)**, 8, b m Double Schwartz—Milly Lass (FR) **Mr Laurie Snook**
4 **ORCHARD LADY**, 6, ch m Rich Charlie—Ballagarrow Girl **Mr Laurie Snook**
5 **QUINTA ROYALE**, 9, b g Sayyaf—Royal Holly **Mr Laurie Snook**
6 **RAJADORA**, 4, b f Golden Heights—Raja Moulana **Mr Laurie Snook**
7 **RAMSBURY RIDGE**, 4, br f Golden Heights—Idyllic Glen **Mr Laurie Snook**
8 **TOM DIAMOND**, 4, ch g Right Regent—Shavegreen Holly VII **Mr Laurie Snook**

THREE-YEAR-OLDS

9 **COLONEL PETER**, b g Right Regent—Raja Moulana **Mr Laurie Snook**

566   MR J. L. SPEARING, Alcester

Postal: **Moor Hall Stables, Wixford, Alcester, Warwickshire, B49 6DL.**
Phone: **(01789) 772639**

1 **BICKERMAN**, 13, b h Mummy's Pet—Merry Weather **Mr B. Dowling**
2 **CASINO MAGIC**, 12, b g Casino Boy—Gypsy Girl **Mr J. Spearing**
3 **EL RUBIO**, 5, b g Tuam—Woodland Promise **Mrs A. Kemp**
4 **ESKIMO NEL (IRE)**, 5, ch m Shy Groom (USA)—North Lady **First Chance Racing**
5 **FINE HARVEST**, 10, b g Oats—Kayella **Miss A. Shirley-Priest**

MR J. L. SPEARING—continued

6 5, Gr m Derring Rose—Fonmon **Mr D. Spearing**
7 **FOREST MILL**, 4, ch f Aragon—Forest Blossom (USA) **Non-Stop Promotions & Marketing Ltd**
8 **HIGH DOMAIN (IRE)**, 5, b h Dominion Royale—Recline **Mr Stephen Borsberry**
9 **JARRWAH**, 8, ch m Niniski (USA)—Valiancy **Mr Alan C. Cadoret**
10 **JUCEA**, 7, b m Bluebird (USA)—Appleby Park **Mr A. A. Campbell**
11 **KING WILLIAM**, 11, b g Dara Monarch—Norman Delight (USA) **Group 1 Racing (1994) Ltd**
12 **LAWNSWOOD JUNIOR**, 9, gr g Bairn (USA)—Easymede **Mr Graham Treglown**
13 **MARINER'S AIR**, 9, ch m Julio Mariner—Havon Air **Mrs Peter Badger**
14 **MOONLIGHT AIR**, 5, b m Bold Owl—Havon Air **Mrs Peter Badger**
15 **NORTHERN ELATION (IRE)**, 6, b m Lancastrian—Pixelated **Group 1 Racing (1994) Ltd**
16 **POLONEZ PRIMA**, 9, ch g Thatching—Taiga **Mr D. J. Turney**
17 **SAATCHMO**, 4, b g Forzando—Into The Fire **Mr Graham Treglown**
18 **SUN CIRCUS**, 4, b f Statoblest—Carmen Maria **Mrs Robert Heathcote**

THREE-YEAR-OLDS

19 **INCATINKA**, gr f Inca Chief (USA)—Encore L'Amour (USA) **Mr M. V. S. Aram**
20 **MAGIC MELODY**, b f Petong—Miss Rossi **Mrs Marilyn Olden**
21 **PEACE HOUSE (IRE)**, ch f Magical Strike (USA)—Theda **Mrs Beryl Speller**
22 **ROZEL BAY**, ch f Beveled (USA)—Salinas **Mr Alan C. Cadoret**
23 **VAX NEW WAY**, gr c Siberian Express (USA)—Misty Arch **Vax Appliances Ltd**

TWO-YEAR-OLDS

24 Gr f 27/4 Chilibang—Foreign Mistress (Darshaan)
25 B c 27/3 Backchat (USA)—Girton Degree (Balliol) **Mr T. Pearson**
26 Ch f 25/3 Risk Me (FR)—Give Me A Day (Lucky Wednesday) **Mr C. Ross**
27 Gr f 20/2 Petong—Vax Lady (Millfontaine) **Vax Appliances Ltd**

Other Owners: Mr R. A. Beswick, Mr John F. Billington, Mr A. J. Brazier, Mrs Liz Brazier, Mr G. M. Eales, Group 1 Racing (1993) Ltd, Mr J. D. Groves, Mr Peter A. Head, Mr Barrie James, Mr M. J. Lilley, Mrs P. Lipscomb, Mr John Roberts, Mr C. P. Stansfield, Mrs Lynnette Turney, Mrs F. A. Veasey, Mrs Carol J. Welch.

Jockey (NH): D Bridgwater (w.a.).

Conditional: Shashi Righton (9-7).

Lady Riders: Miss Caroline Spearing (9-0), Miss Teresa Spearing (9-0).

567   MR R. C. SPICER, Spalding

Postal: **The Gallops, Dozens Bank, West Pinchbeck, Spalding, PE11 3ND.**
Phone: **(01775) 640068 MOBILE (0402) 258160**

1 **ALLEXTON LAD**, 5, b g Monsieure Edouarde—Miss Talli **Mr Peter Evans**
2 **CA IRA (IRE)**, 5, b m Dancing Dissident (USA)—Silver Mantle **Mr John Purcell**
3 **FRESH LOOK (IRE)**, 4, b f Alzao (USA)—Bag Lady **Mr John Purcell**
4 **GATE OF HEAVEN**, 6, b m Starry Night (USA)—Halatch **Mr John Purcell**
5 **JEAN DE FLORETTE (USA)**, 5, b g Our Native (USA)—The Branks (USA) **Mr John Purcell**
6 **JET JOCKEY**, 7, b g Relkino—Fen Mist **Mrs J. A. Nichols**
7 **KOO**, 10, b m Crofter (USA)—Sue's Dolly **Mr Peter Evans**
8 **LEAP OF FAITH (IRE)**, 5, b m Northiam (USA)—Greek Music **Mr John Purcell**
9 4, Ch f Presidium—Miss Talli **Mr P. J. Evans**
10 **PARSONS GIFT**, 8, b g The Parson—Rachels Baby **Mrs J. A. Nichols**
11 **RURAL LAD**, 7, b g Town And Country—French Plait **Mr Robert Baker**
12 **SOUND THE TRUMPET (IRE)**, 4, b g Fayruz—Red Note **Mr R. C. Spicer**
13 **VICTOR ROMEO**, 7, b g Nomination—Be My Sweet **Mr Peter Evans**

MR R. C. SPICER—continued

14 4, B f Presidium—We're In The Money **Mr P. J. Evans**
15 **YENGEMA**, 5, b m Petoski—Bundu (FR) **Mrs J. A. Nichols**

THREE-YEAR-OLDS

16 **CLASSIC DAISY**, b f Prince Sabo—Bloom of Youth (IRE) **Mr R. C. Spicer**
17 B c Daily Sport Soon—Koo **Mr P. J. Evans**
18 **PRINCE ZIZIM**, b c Shareef Dancer (USA)—Possessive Lady **Mr John Purcell**
19 **TOM SWIFT (IRE)**, b c Law Society (USA)—Debbie's Next (USA) **Mr P. Gwilliam**

TWO-YEAR-OLDS

20 B c 17/4 Ron's Victory (USA)—Shirlstar Investor (Some Hand) **Mr John Purcell**

Other Owners: Mr Elliott Simmonds.

568   MR T. STACK, Golden

Postal: **Thomastown Castle, Golden, Co. Tipperary, Ireland.**
Phone: **(062) 54129 FAX (062) 54399**

1 **CHARENTE RIVER (IRE)**, 4, b c Sadler's Wells—Fruition
2 **GALE AGAIN**, 9, br g Strong Gale—Going Again
3 **GOLIATH (IRE)**, 7, br g Supreme Leader—Miss Furlong
4 **HIGH IN THE CLOUDS (IRE)**, 4, b c Scenic—Miracle Drug (USA)
5 **JUNO MADONNA (IRE)**, 4, b f Sadler's Wells (USA)—Tough Lady
6 **MANETTI**, 4, b c Reference Point—Bex
7 **MASTER EXECUTIVE (IRE)**, 4, b c Executive Perk—Madam Owen
8 **ONE MAN BAND (IRE)**, 5, ch h Chief Singer—Star Attention
9 **SHINKOH ROSE (FR)**, 4, b f Warning—Sandpiper's Dream (USA)
10 **SIR SILVER SOX (USA)**, 4, gr c Corwyn Bay—Sox In The Box
11 **TAIDJA (IRE)**, 5, b m Shahrastani—Taysha
12 **THE TRAVELLINGLADY (IRE)**, 7, b m Callernish—Drumreagh

THREE-YEAR-OLDS

13 **AMERICAN RENAISANS (IRE)**, b c Sadler's Wells—Tough Lady
14 **ANTITHESIS (IRE)**, b f Fairy King—Music of The Night
15 **ARCUS (IRE)**, ch c Archway—Precision Chop
16 **BLENDING ELEMENT (IRE)**, ch f Great Commotion—Blue Wedding
17 **BOSS CROKER (IRE)**, b c Waajib—Maimiti
18 **CHILD OF FORTUNE (IRE)**, b f Fairy King—Elevated
19 **COHIBA**, b c Old Vic—Circus Ring
20 **DANCING BLUEBELL (IRE)**, b f Bluebird—Petite Liqueurelle
21 **DIESEL DAN (IRE)**, b c Mac's Imp—Elite Exhibition
22 **ESTRAGON (IRE)**, b c Thatching—Tickeridge
23 **GET A LIFE**, gr f Old Vic—Sandstream
24 **HEALTH AND WEALTH (IRE)**, b c Last Tycoon—Point of Honour
25 **HELSINGOR (IRE)**, b c Danehill—Assya
26 **HIGH POWERED (IRE)**, b c Danehill—Cartridge
27 **KRYSTALLOS (IRE)**, ch c Lycius—Dancing Crystal
28 **MALACODA (IRE)**, b c Fairy King—Squire's Daughter
29 **MISS BASHFUL (IRE)**, b f Shy Groom—Larosterna
30 **PRELUDE TO FAME (USA)**, b c Affirmed—Dance Call
31 **SHORT SHIFT (IRE)**, ch f Mac's Imp—Clipper Queen
32 **SIR ORACLE**, b c Niniski—Stedham
33 **SMERALDINA (IRE)**, b f Night Shift—Unyielding
34 **SOYINCA (IRE)**, ch f Caerleon—Spirits Dancing

MR T. STACK—continued
TWO-YEAR-OLDS

35 B c 11/3 Night Shift—Assya
36 **AUCTION HOUSE (IRE)**, b c 22/5 Waajib—Miss Sandman
37 **AUDREY'S PEARL (IRE)**, b f 14/5 Waajib—Inner Pearl
38 **BAPTISMAL ROCK (IRE)**, ch c 28/4 Ballad Rock—Flower From Heaven
39 **BLASKET ISLAND (IRE)**, b gr c 6/3 Kenmare—Starring Role
40 **BOAT SONG (IRE)**, b f 7/5 Shalford—Music of The Night
41 B f 29/5 Fairy King—Cartridge
42 B f 6/4 Bluebird—December Blossom
43 B f 25/4 Bluebird—Fiscal Folly
44 B f 27/4 Shirley Heights—Home Fire
45 B f 25/4 Night Shift—House of Queens
46 **LEESON (IRE)**, b c 30/4 Last Tycoon—Friendly Finance
47 Ch f 2/4 Thatching—Melinte
48 B f 24/2 Caerleon—Polista
49 **RECORD ENTRY**, b c 17/1 Emarati—Thorner Lane
50 **SABRE DANCER**, b c 3/5 Rambo Dancer—My Candy
51 Ch c 10/4 River Falls—Tatisha
52 B f 14/3 Kenmare—Tootling
53 B f 30/1 Rainbow Quest—Vice Vixen
54 **WELSH QUEEN (IRE)**, b f 16/4 Caerleon—Stellar Empress
55 **WHITE PAPER (IRE)**, b f 21/5 Marignan—Page Blanche

Owners: Mr M. A. Begley, Mr Peter Brennan, Mr P. A. Byrne, Mr T. Carden, S. Charlesworth, Ms W. Cousins, Mr K. Doyle, Mr D. B. Gallop, Ms Jane Geogan, Mr Hosokawa, Miss Y. Hosokawa, Mr Vincent Kilkenny, Miss C. Lynch, Mrs John Magnier, Mr John Magnier, Mr Raymond McArdle, Mr J. P. McManus, Mr J. O'Brien, Mr J. F. O'Malley, M. Parish, Mr Peter Pillar, Mrs J. Rowlinson, Mr R. E. Sangster, Mrs T. Stack, Mr Osamu Yasuda.

Jockey (Flat): P P O'Grady (7-12).

Apprentice: Michael Black (7-12).

Amateurs: Mr S Hennessy (10-0), Mr B Kinnane (10-0).

569   MR A. C. STEWART, Newmarket

Postal: **Clarehaven, Bury Road, Newmarket, Suffolk, CB8 7BY.**
Phone: **(01638) 667323 FAX (01638) 666389**

1 **FAKIH (USA)**, 4, b c Zilzal (USA)—Barakat
2 **MO-ADDAB (IRE)**, 6, b g Waajib—Tissue Paper
3 **NORTHERN FAN (IRE)**, 4, b c Lear Fan (USA)—Easy Romance (USA)

THREE-YEAR-OLDS

4 **AJAAD ALJAREE (IRE)**, b c Sadler's Wells (USA)—Impudent Miss
5 **ALL DONE**, ch f Northern State (USA)—Doogali
6 **ANGAAR (IRE)**, b c Fairy King (USA)—Decadence
7 **AREED AL OLA (USA)**, b c Chief's Crown (USA)—Ballerina Princess (USA)
8 **BARRACK YARD**, b c Forzando—Abbotswood
9 **BAYDAH**, b f Green Desert (USA)—Al Theraat (USA)
10 **BUDBY**, ch f Rock City—Lustrous
11 **CARINA CLARE**, b f Slip Anchor—Clare Island

MR A. C. STEWART—continued

12 **DABKA DANCER,** b c Cadeaux Genereux—Lady Shipley
13 **DIVINE,** b f Dowsing (USA)—Rectitude
14 **FAHIM,** b c Green Desert (USA)—Mahrah (USA)
15 **JUMAIRAH SUNSET,** ch f Be My Guest (USA)—Catalonda
16 **KAMARI (USA),** ch c Woodman (USA)—Karri Valley (USA)
17 **MANAYA,** b f Marju (IRE)—Almarai (USA)
18 **MUTANASSIB (IRE),** b c Mtoto—Lightning Legacy (USA)
19 **NAAZEQ,** ch f Nashwan (USA)—Gharam (USA)
20 **NAJM MUBEEN (IRE),** b c Last Tycoon—Ah Ya Zein
21 **NASEEM EL FAJR (IRE),** b f Green Desert (USA)—Flying Bid
22 **ROBUSTA (IRE),** b f Batshoof—Loucoum (FR)
23 **SABAAH ELFULL,** ch f Kris—Putupon
24 **SAFA (USA),** b f Green Dancer (USA)—Romanette (USA)
25 **SHAHRUR (USA),** b br c Riverman (USA)—Give Thanks
26 **SILVRETTA (IRE),** br f Tirol—Lepoushka
27 **TA AWUN (USA),** b f Housebuster (USA)—Barakat
28 **TANGO TEASER,** b br f Shareef Dancer (USA)—Ever Genial

TWO-YEAR-OLDS

29 **ALAKDAR (CAN),** ch c 18/1 Green Dancer (USA)—Population (General Assembly (USA))
30 **ALIFANDANGO,** b f 14/3 Alzao (USA)—Fandangerina (USA) (Grey Dawn II)
31 **ASSAILABLE,** b c 5/5 Salse (USA)—Unsuitable (Local Suitor (USA))
32 **BACCHUS,** b c 17/2 Prince Sabo—Bonica (Rousillon (USA))
33 Ch f 1/5 Sharpo—Baino Clinic (USA) (Sovereign Dancer (USA))
34 **BAKED ALASKA,** gr f 4/3 Green Desert (USA)—Snowing (USA) (Icecapade (USA))
35 **BLOWN-OVER,** ch f 10/2 Ron's Victory (USA)—Woodwind (FR) (Whistling Wind)
36 **FONTEYN,** b f 8/3 Aragon—Trull (Lomond (USA))
37 **GHARIB (USA),** b c 31/3 Dixieland Band (USA)—The Way We Were (USA) (Avatar (USA))
38 **HAWZAH,** b f 22/3 Green Desert (USA)—Mahrah (USA) (Vaguely Noble)
39 **HULAL,** b c 13/3 Arazi (USA)—Almarai (USA) (Vaguely Noble)
40 **IRSAL,** ch c 19/2 Nashwan (USA)—Amwag (USA) (El Gran Senor (USA))
41 **JALB (IRE),** b c 30/3 Robellino (USA)—Adjacent (IRE) (Doulab (USA))
42 Ch c 11/2 Rainbow Quest (USA)—Jasoorah (IRE) (Sadler's Wells (USA))
43 B c 25/4 Sadler's Wells (USA)—Maria Waleska (Filiberto (USA))
44 **MUKAWAMAH,** ch f 18/3 Kris—Al Theraab (USA) (Roberto (USA))
45 **MUMARIS (USA),** br c 2/2 Capote (USA)—Barakat (Bustino)
46 Ch c 4/2 Caerleon (USA)—Niamh Cinn Oir (IRE) (King of Clubs)
47 B f 13/4 Unfuwain (USA)—Positive Attitude (Red Sunset)
48 B c 8/5 Mtoto—Possessive Dancer (Shareef Dancer (USA))
49 **PRINCE ALEX (IRE),** b c 24/3 Night Shift (USA)—Finalist (Star Appeal)
50 B f 24/5 Salse (USA)—Sharmood (Sharpen Up)
51 **SHILLING (IRE),** b f 9/2 Bob Back (USA)—Quiche (Formidable (USA))
52 B c 5/2 Night Shift (USA)—Stylish Girl (Star de Naskra (USA))
53 B f 3/3 Kefaah (USA)—Top Treat (USA) (Topsider (USA))

Owners: Mr D. P. Barrie, Mrs B. Berrick, Mr I. Chamberlain, Cliveden Stud, Mr R. G. Collins, Earl Of Derby, Mr A. Dolbey, Mrs D. Domvile, Mr B. H. Farr, Mr N. J. Fish, Mr R. George, Gleadhill House Stud, Mr S. J. Hammond, Sir Stephen Hastings, Mr M. J. C. Hawkes, Sheikh Ahmed Al Maktoum, Mr Hamdan Al Maktoum, Hon Lady McAlpine, Normanby Stud Ltd, Mr M. J. Rees, Duchess Of Roxburghe, S. Corman Ltd, Mr & Mrs J. V. Sheffield, Snailwell Stud Company Ltd.

Jockey (Flat): M Roberts (w.a.).

Apprentice: M Humphries (7-11).

Amateur: Mr V Lukaniuk (9-0).

570   **MRS M. K. STIRK, Ripon**

Postal: **Sawpits Farm, Laverton, Kirkby Malzeard, Ripon, H G4 3SY.**
Phone: **(01765) 658447   FAX (01765) 658809**

1 SALVO, 5, ch g K-Battery—Saleander **Mrs M. Stirk**

Amateur: Mr S Swiers (10-5).

571   **MR D. R. STODDART, Towcester**

Postal: **Highfields, Adstone, Towcester, Northants, NN12 8DS.**
Phone: **HOME (01327) 860433 OFFICE & FAX (01327) 860305**

1 CHRISTMAS GORSE, 10, b g Celtic Cone—Spin Again **Mr D. R. Stoddart**
2 SHAAGNI ANA (USA), 5, ch g Ogygian (USA)—Poppycock (USA) **Mr D. R. Stoddart**

572   **MR F. S. STOREY, Carlisle**

Postal: **Low Dubwath, Kirklinton, Carlisle, Cumbria, CA6 6EF.**
Phone: **KIRKLINTON (0122 875) 331**

1 BEND SABLE (IRE), 6, b g Mtoto—Chrism **Mr F. S. Storey**
2 CANDID LAD, 9, b g Niniski (USA)—Helpless Haze (USA) **Mr F. S. Storey**
3 FAR HOWE, 4, ch f Respect—Unguarded **Mr F. S. Storey**

Jockey (NH): B Storey (9-10).

573   **MR W. STOREY, Consett**

Postal: **Grange Farm & Stud, Muggleswick, Consett, Co Durham, DH8 9DW.**
Phone: **(01207) 55259 OR (0860) 510441 FAX (01207) 55607**

1 CIRCLE BOY, 9, b g Carlingford Castle—Magic User **Shelway Ltd**
2 FANADIYR (IRE), 4, b g Kahyasi—Fair Fight **Mr D. Callaghan**
3 GREAT EASEBY (IRE), 6, ch g Caerleon (USA)—Kasala (USA) **Mr D. C. Batey**
4 ICANSPELL, 5, b g Petoski—Bewitched **Mr D. O. Cremin**
5 IZZA, 5, b m Unfuwain (USA)—Wantage Park **Mr D. C. Batey**
6 KARAYLAR (IRE), 4, b g Kahyasi—Karamana **Mr D. C. Batey**
7 KASHANA (IRE), 4, b f Shahrastani (USA)—Kashna (USA) **Mr A. Lister**
8 KING OF THE HORSE (IRE), 5, ch g Hatim (USA)—Milly Whiteway **Mr Alan Crook**
9 MASTER HYDE (USA), 7, gr g Trempolino (USA)—Sandspur (USA) **Mr D. Callaghan**
10 MR SLICK, 4, ch g Sharpo—Taj Victory **Mr John Herring**
11 NORTHANTS, 10, b g Northern Baby (CAN)—Astania (GER) **Mr C. B. Rennison**
12 SALLYOREALLY (IRE), 5, b m Common Grounds—Prosapia (USA) **Mr W. Storey**
13 SUNDAY NEWS'N'ECHO (USA), 5, b m Trempolino (USA)—Icy Pop **Mr D. C. Batey**
14 ZAMHAREER (USA), 5, b g Lear Fan (USA)—Awenita **Mr D. C. Batey**

Other Owners: Mr David Blythe, Mr C. A. Clark, Mr J. M. Elliott, Mr D. Neale, Mr Richard Thompson, Mr Foster Watson, Mr A. Whiting.

Lady Rider: Miss S Storey (8-7).

574   MR M. STOUTE, Newmarket

Postal: **Freemason Lodge, Bury Road, Newmarket, Suffolk, CB8 7BT.**

Phone: **NEWMARKET (01638) 663801 FAX (01638) 667276**

1 **AWESOME**, 4, b c Machiavellian (USA)—Blessed Event
2 **BLUSHING FLAME (USA)**, 5, b h Blushing Groom (FR)—Nearctic Flame
3 **CANDLE SMILE (USA)**, 4, b c Pleasant Colony (USA)—Silent Turn (USA)
4 **DANCE A DREAM**, 4, b f Sadler's Wells (USA)—Exclusive Order (USA)
5 **DESERT SHOT**, 6, b g Green Desert (USA)—Out of Shot
6 **ELA-ARISTOKRATI (IRE)**, 4, b c Danehill (USA)—Dubai Lady
7 **ELECTION DAY (IRE)**, 4, b c Sadler's Wells (USA)—Hellenic
8 **FIRE ON ICE (IRE)**, 4, b c Sadler's Wells (USA)—Foolish Lady (USA)
9 **FUJIYAMA CREST (IRE)**, 4, b g Roi Danzig (USA)—Snoozy Time
10 **HARBOUR ISLAND**, 4, b c Rainbow Quest (USA)—Quay Line
11 **MEZAAN (IRE)**, 4, ch c Royal Academy (USA)—Arctic Heroine (USA)
12 **PILSUDSKI (IRE)**, 4, b c Polish Precedent (USA)—Cocotte
13 **POLYDAMAS**, 4, b c Last Tycoon—Graecia Magna (USA)
14 **RED CARNIVAL (USA)**, 4, b f Mr Prospector (USA)—Seaside Attraction (USA)
15 **SACRAMENT**, 5, b h Shirley Heights—Blessed Event
16 **SANOOSEA (USA)**, 4, b c Storm Bird (CAN)—Nobiliare (USA)
17 **SINGSPIEL (IRE)**, 4, b c In The Wings—Glorious Song (CAN)
18 **SOVIET LINE (IRE)**, 6, b g Soviet Star (USA)—Shore Line
19 **STAR OF ZILZAL (USA)**, 4, b g Zilzal (USA)—Tell Me Sumthing (USA)
20 **STENCIL**, 4, ch c Nashwan (USA)—Colorspin (FR)

THREE-YEAR-OLDS

21 **BATHILDE (IRE)**, ch f Generous (IRE)—Bex (USA)
22 **BONARELLI (IRE)**, b c Dancing Dissident (USA)—Sovereign Dona
23 **BUSH ROSE**, b f Rainbow Quest (USA)—Bustara
24 **CARIBBEAN DANCER**, b f Shareef Dancer (USA)—Deposit
25 **CASTING FOR GOLD (IRE)**, ch f Hansel (USA)—Mesmerize
26 **CERDAN (USA)**, ch c Zilzal (USA)—Vie En Rose (USA)
27 **CLERKENWELL (USA)**, b c Sadler's Wells (USA)—Forlene
28 **CONGO MAN**, b c Rainbow Quest (USA)—African Dance (USA)
29 **DANCE ON A CLOUD (USA)**, b f Capote (USA)—Sharp Dance (USA)
30 **DANCE SEQUENCE (USA)**, ch f Mr Prospector (USA)—Dancing Tribute (USA)
31 **DARK WATERS (IRE)**, b c Darshaan—Grecian Sea (FR)
32 **DEFINED FEATURE (IRE)**, ch f Nabeel Dancer (USA)—Meissarah (USA)
33 **DEVIL'S DANCE (FR)**, b c Mujtahid (USA)—Dance of Leaves
34 **DON BOSIO (USA)**, b c El Gran Senor (USA)—Celtic Loot (USA)
35 **DOUBLE LEAF**, b c Sadler's Wells (USA)—Green Leaf (USA)
36 **DR MASSINI (IRE)**, b c Sadler's Wells (USA)—Argon Laser
37 **EXPENSIVE TASTE**, b f Cadeaux Genereux—Um Lardaff
38 **FINLANA**, b f Alzao (USA)—Insaf (USA)
39 **FLAME VALLEY (USA)**, b f Gulch (USA)—Lightning Fire
40 **GET AWAY WITH IT (IRE)**, b c Last Tycoon—Royal Sister II
41 **GOLD LANCE (USA)**, ch c Seeking The Gold (USA)—Lucky State (USA)
42 **GOLD SPATS (USA)**, b c Seeking The Gold (USA)—Foot Stone (USA)
43 **HAMMERSTEIN**, b c Kris—Musical Bliss (USA)
44 **INSATIABLE (IRE)**, b c Don't Forget Me—Petit Eclair
45 **IRISH SEA (USA)**, b g Zilzal (USA)—Dunkellin (USA)
46 **KASS ALHAWA**, b c Shirley Heights—Silver Braid (USA)
47 **KING OF THE EAST (IRE)**, b c Fairy King (USA)—Rising Tide
48 **KUTAISI (IRE)**, ch f Soviet Star (USA)—Mamouna (USA)
49 **KUTMAN (USA)**, b c Seattle Slew (USA)—Ouro Verde (USA)
50 **LADY LUCRE (IRE)**, b f Last Tycoon—Queen Helen
51 **MARIGLIANO (USA)**, b c Riverman (USA)—Mount Holyoke
52 **MENOO HAL BATAL (USA)**, b c Gone West (USA)—Bank On Love (USA)
53 **MOHAWK RIVER (IRE)**, b c Polish Precedent (USA)—High Hawk
54 **MULTICOLOURED (IRE)**, b c Rainbow Quest (USA)—Greektown

bloodstock matters

TAYLOR VINTERS

SOLICITORS

Contact: Jeremy Richardson or Rachel Flynn
119, High Street, Newmarket. Telephone (01638) 663571
(Our offices are directly opposite the Main Pedestrian Entrance to the Sale Ring)

MR M. STOUTE—continued

55 **NATIONAL TREASURE**, b f Shirley Heights—Brocade
56 **OBSESSIVE (USA)**, b br f Seeking The Gold (USA)—Secret Obsession (USA)
57 **ON FAIR STAGE (IRE)**, b f Sadler's Wells (USA)—Fair Salinia
58 **PROMPTLY (IRE)**, b f Lead On Time (USA)—Ghariba
59 **RAHEEN (USA)**, b c Danzig (USA)—Belle de Jour (USA)
60 **REALLY A DREAM (IRE)**, br f Last Tycoon—Ancestry
61 **RIVER DIVINE (USA)**, ch f Irish River (FR)—Etoile d'Amore (USA)
62 **ROCKY OASIS (USA)**, b c Gulch (USA)—Knoosh (USA)
63 **ROSSEL (USA)**, b g Blushing John (USA)—Northern Aspen (USA)
64 **ROYAL RESULT (USA)**, b br c Gone West (USA)—Norette
65 **RUSSIAN REQUEST (IRE)**, b f Soviet Star (USA)—I Want To Be (USA)
66 **SADLER'S REALM**, b c Sadler's Wells (USA)—Rensaler (USA)
67 **SANDABAR**, b c Green Desert (USA)—Children's Corner (FR)
68 **SERBIA (IRE)**, b f Thatching—So Directed
69 **SHANALADEE**, b c Darshaan—Sahara Baladee (USA)
70 **SILVER SHOWERS (USA)**, ch f Zilzal (USA)—Katies First (USA)
71 **SIROS (USA)**, ch g Rahy (USA)—Size Six (USA)
72 **TARNEEM (USA)**, b f Zilzal (USA)—Willowy Mood (USA)
73 **TERDAD (USA)**, ch c Lomond (USA)—Istiska (FR)
74 **TIME ALLOWED**, b f Sadler's Wells (USA)—Time Charter
75 **TRANQUIL DAYS (USA)**, b f Easy Goer (USA)—Kissogram Girl (USA)
76 **TRUE JOY (IRE)**, ch f Zilzal (USA)—Foreign Courier (USA)
77 **UNITUS (IRE)**, b c Soviet Star (USA)—Unite
78 **WEE HOPE (USA)**, b c Housebuster (USA)—Tell Me Sumthing (USA)
79 **WHITEWATER AFFAIR**, ch f Machiavellian (USA)—Much Too Risky
80 **YOM JAMEEL (IRE)**, b c Caerleon (USA)—Topping Girl

TWO-YEAR-OLDS

81 B c 27/4 Green Desert (USA)—Aliysa (Darshaan)
82 **ALPHABET**, b f 16/3 Saddlers' Hall (IRE)—A-To-Z (IRE) (Ahonoora)
83 B c 23/3 Royal Academy (USA)—Arctic Winter (CAN) (Briartic (CAN))
84 B c 22/4 Red Ransom (USA)—Attacat (USA) (Advocator)
85 **BALLARAT (IRE)**, b c 17/3 Sadler's Wells (USA)—Bex (USA) (Explodent (USA))
86 B f 27/4 Zilzal (USA)—Belle de Jour (USA) (Speak John)
87 B c 23/3 Mr Prospector (USA)—Bineyah (IRE) (Sadler's Wells (USA))
88 B f 10/3 Zilzal (USA)—Bitooh (Seattle Slew (USA))
89 **BRAVE AIR (FR)**, b f 11/3 Nashwan (USA)—Decided Air (IRE) (Sure Blade (USA))
90 B c 24/5 Caerleon (USA)—Bristle (Thatch (USA))
91 Ch c 26/3 Arazi (USA)—Bustara (Busted)
92 B c 22/1 Zilzal (USA)—Carduel (USA) (Buckpasser)
93 **CARIBBEAN STAR**, b f 13/3 Soviet Star (USA)—Whos The Blonde (Cure The Blues (USA))
94 B c 16/3 Danehill (USA)—Charmina (FR) (Nonoalco (USA))
95 **COLOMBIA (IRE)**, ch f 18/4 Mujtahid (USA)—Camarat (Ahonoora)
96 B c 29/3 Night Shift (USA)—Colorsnap (Shirley Heights)
97 B c 18/3 Sadler's Wells (USA)—Colorspin (FR) (High Top)
98 Ch c 14/3 Seeking The Gold—Crown Quest (USA) (Chief's Crown (USA))
99 Ch c 6/4 Arazi (USA)—Crystal Land (Kris)
100 **CURZON STREET**, b f 3/3 Night Shift (USA)—Pine Ridge (High Top)
101 B c 10/4 Silver Hawk (USA)—Dancing Grass (USA) (Northern Dancer)
102 B c 28/4 Shirley Heights—Dancing Vaguely (USA) (Vaguely Noble)
103 **DAZZLE**, b f 28/3 Gone West (USA)—Belle Et Deluree (USA) (The Minstrel (CAN))
104 **DELILAH (IRE)**, b f 23/4 Bluebird (USA)—Courtesane (USA) (Majestic Light (USA))
105 **DESERT BEAUTY (IRE)**, b f 4/2 Green Desert (USA)—Hellenic (Darshaan)
106 B c 16/5 Storm Cat (USA)—Diamond City (USA) (Mr Prospector (USA))
107 B f 23/4 Caerleon (USA)—Don't Rush (USA) (Alleged (USA))
108 B c 31/3 Storm Bird (CAN)—Fairy Footsteps (Mill Reef (USA))
109 B f 20/3 Night Shift (USA)—Fear Naught (Connaught)
110 Ch f 18/3 Shadeed (USA)—Fly To The Moon (USA) (Blushing Groom (FR))
111 Gr c 17/4 Zilzal (USA)—Future Bright (USA) (Lyphard's Wish (FR))
112 **GERSEY**, ch f 1/4 Generous (IRE)—River Spey (Mill Reef (USA))

MR M. STOUTE—continued

113 **GREEK PALACE (IRE),** b c 5/4 Royal Academy (USA)—Grecian Sea (FR) (Homeric)
114 Ch f 4/5 Arazi (USA)—Hawait Al Barr (Green Desert (USA))
115 B c 19/2 Soviet Star (USA)—Home Address (Habitat)
116 Ch f 27/4 Zilzal (USA)—Illgotten Gains (USA) (Search For Gold (USA))
117 **ILLUSION,** b c 13/5 Green Desert (USA)—Time Charter (Saritamer (USA))
118 **INK POT (USA),** ch f 15/3 Green Dancer (USA)—Refill (Mill Reef (USA))
119 **IRISH LIGHT (USA),** ch f 14/1 Irish River (FR)—Solar Star (USA) (Lear Fan (USA))
120 B c 13/1 Zilzal (USA)—Iva Reputation (USA) (Sir Ivor)
121 B f 23/1 Riverman (USA)—Ivrea (Sadler's Wells (USA))
122 B f 30/3 Seattle Slew (USA)—Jode (USA) (Danzig (USA))
123 B c 5/4 Shareef Dancer (USA)—Kallista (Zeddaan)
124 B f 4/2 Green Desert (USA)—Katakana (USA) (Diesis)
125 B c 18/4 Nureyev (USA)—Kristana (Kris)
126 B c 20/2 Mujtahid (USA)—Lady In Green (Shareef Dancer (USA))
127 Ch c 22/3 Arazi (USA)—Lastcomer (USA) (Kris)
128 **LATIN (FR),** b c 25/4 Ela-Mana-Mou—Cum Laude (Shareef Dancer (USA))
129 B f 11/3 Mtoto—Laughsome (Be My Guest (USA))
130 B c 1/5 Gone West (USA)—La Voyageuse (CAN) (Tentam (USA))
131 Ch c 23/5 Zilzal (USA)—Liberty Spirit (USA) (Graustark)
132 **MAGELLANO (USA),** b c 26/3 Miswaki (USA)—Mount Holyoke (Golden Fleece (USA))
133 Ch f 16/2 Zilzal (USA)—Manzanares (USA) (Sir Ivor)
134 B c 27/4 Polish Precedent—Mill Line (Mill Reef (USA))
135 Ch c 2/4 Kris—Pastorale (Nureyev (USA))
136 **PATRIOT GAMES (IRE),** b c 6/5 Polish Patriot (USA)—It's Now Or Never (High Line)
137 B c 6/5 Doyoun—Percy's Girl (IRE) (Blakeney)
138 Ch f 4/2 Woodman (USA)—Pixie Erin (Golden Fleece (USA))
139 **POLISH ROMANCE (USA),** b f 12/4 Danzig (USA)—Some Romance (USA) (Fappiano (USA))
140 B c 15/4 Green Desert (USA)—Possessive (Posse (USA))
141 B c 20/5 Suave Dancer (USA)—Prima Domina (FR) (Dominion)
142 B c 7/3 Zilzal (USA)—Questionablevirtue (USA) (Key To The Mint (USA))
143 **REGAL THUNDER (USA),** b c 15/2 Chief's Crown (USA)—Summertime Showers (USA) (Raise A Native)
144 B c 12/3 Danehill (USA)—Rince Deas (IRE) (Alzao (USA))
145 B c 19/3 Red Ransom (USA)—River Patrol (Rousillon (USA))
146 B f 2/2 Mtoto—Russian Countess (USA) (Nureyev (USA))
147 **SECRET RAPTURE (USA),** ch f 14/3 Woodman (USA)—Secret Obsession (USA) (Secretariat (USA))
148 Ch c 19/4 Groom Dancer (USA)—Shameem (USA) (Nureyev (USA))
149 **SILENCE REIGNS,** b c 7/4 Sadlers' Hall (IRE)—Rensaler (USA) (Stop The Music (USA))
150 **SOCIETY ROSE,** b f 18/3 Sadlers' Hall (IRE)—Ruthless Rose (USA) (Conquistador Cielo (USA))
151 **SPY KNOLL,** b c 15/2 Shirley Heights—Garden Pink (FR) (Bellypha)
152 B c 1/5 Lear Fan (USA)—Sweet Delilah (USA) (Super Concorde (USA))
153 **TECHNICOLOUR (IRE),** b f 3/4 Rainbow Quest (USA)—Grecian Urn (Ela-Mana-Mou)
154 Ch f 18/3 Be My Chief (USA)—Travel Mystery (Godswalk (USA))
155 B c 17/3 Sadler's Wells (USA)—Vaigly Star (Star Appeal)
156 **VIA SALERIA (IRE),** b f 5/5 Arazi (USA)—Alexandrie (USA) (Val de L'Orne (FR))
157 B f 10/3 Hawkster (USA)—Wall St Girl (USA) (Rich Cream (USA))
158 **WIND CHEETAH (USA),** b c 14/3 Storm Cat (USA)—Won't She Tell (USA) (Banner Sport (USA))
159 B c 14/3 Arazi (USA)—Zawaahy (USA) (El Gran Senor (USA))

Owners: Sultan Al Kabeer, Mr J. D. Ashenheim, Mr R. Barnett, Cheveley Park Stud, Mr Athos Christodoulou, Seymour Cohn, Mr J. M. Greetham, Mr S. Hanson, Lady Harrison, Mr Seisuke Hata, Helena Springfield Ltd, Hesmonds Stud, Highclere Thoroughbreds Ltd, Mr C. Ingleby-Mackenzie, Mr R. I. Khan, Mr Paul Locke, A. Macdonald-Buchanan, Capt J. Macdonald-Buchanan, Mr Maeada, Sheikh Ahmed Al Maktoum, Maktoum Al Maktoum, Mr Mana Al Maktoum, Mr Andreas Michael, Mrs H. Michael, Sheikh Mohammed, Mr Philip Newton, Mr Peter R. Pritchard, Mr J. Richmond Watson, Sir Evelyn De Rothschild, Mr P. D. Savill, Mr Pierpont Scott, Mr W. H. Scott, Basil Sellers, Dr K. Shimizu, Mr George Strawbridge, Mr Saeed Suhail, Mr Salem Suhail, Mrs Doreen M. Swinburn, Mr M. Tabor, Lord Weinstock, Mr Simon Weinstock, Mr James Wigan.

575   MR A. P. STREETER, Uttoxeter

Postal: **Hill House Farm, Poppits Lane, Stramshall, Uttoxeter, ST14 5EX.**

Phone: **OFFICE (01889) 568145 HOME (01782) 397819**

1 **ALASKAN HEIR**, 5, b g Northern State (USA)—Royal Meeting **Mr J. Burton**
2 **AQUADO**, 7, b g Green Desert (USA)—Meliora **Mr K. Nicholls**
3 **CENTAUR EXPRESS**, 4, b g Siberian Express (USA)—Gay Twenties **Centaur Racing**
4 **IRISH GROOM**, 9, b g Shy Groom (USA)—Romany Pageant **Mr J. T. Stimpson**
5 **LEGATEE**, 5, ch m Risk Me (FR)—Legal Sound **South Normanton Racing**
6 **MAZILLA**, 4, b f Mazilier (USA)—Mo Ceri **Mr M. Rhodes**
7 **NEWHALL PRINCE**, 8, b g Prince Ragusa—Doyles Folly **Mr B. W. Trubshaw**
8 **OPTIMISTIC AFFAIR**, 5, b g Derring Rose—Bantel Belle **Optimistic Racing**
9 **SALSKA**, 5, b m Salse (USA)—Anzeige (GER) **Mr P. L. Clinton**
10 **TILTY (USA)**, 6, b g Linkage (USA)—En Tiempo **Cheadle Racing**
11 **TOTAL ASSET**, 6, b g Dowsing (USA)—Fallen Angel **Mr E. Jackson**

THREE-YEAR-OLDS

12 **MY WEST END GIRL**, b f Dunbeath (USA)—Carnfield **Mr K. Nicholls**
13 **YOUNG DALESMAN**, br g Teenoso (USA)—Fabulous Molly **Mr B. J. Garrett**

TWO-YEAR-OLDS

14 **POT OF TEA**, b f 12/3 Tina's Pet—Ebony Park **Mr C. Adams**

Other Owners: Mr Brian Bailey, Mr T. Beck, Mr D. Bentley, Mr Joe Bland, Mr Frank Dronzek, Mr Tony Forbes, Mr R. Foster, Mr D. B. Holmes, Mr R. G. Johnson, Mr David Kastelan, Mr J. E. Lea, Mr Marek Pawlitta, Mr R. Pearce, Principal Racing, Mrs J. Salt, Mr C. Shaw, Target Racing, Mr N. Titterton, Mr Brian Wells, Mr W. Wibberley, Mr B. Wilne.

Jockey (Flat): S D Williams (8-5, w.a.).

Jockeys (NH): T Eley (10-0), G Lyons (10-2, w.a.).

576   MR R. M. STRONGE, Newbury

Postal: **Woods Folly, Beedon Common, Newbury, Berks, RG16 8TT.**

Phone: **PHONE/FAX: (01635) 248710**

1 **HERE HE COMES**, 10, b g Alzao (USA)—Nanette Brown, **Brooks & Thomas Partnership**
2 **JAMES IS SPECIAL (IRE)**, 8, b g Lyphard's Special (USA)—High Explosive **Diamant Precision Engineering Ltd**
3 **JOY FOR LIFE (IRE)**, 5, b m Satco (FR)—Joy's Toy **Mr Paul David Hodgkinson**
4 **LOCAL EXPRESS (IRE)**, 7, b g New Express—Empress of Persia **Diamant Precision Engineering Ltd**
5 **MONSIEUR BROOKS**, 6, b g Lidhame—Fille de Phaeton **Mrs Denise Brooks**
6 **PREMAZING**, 4, ch c Precocious—Amazing Journey (USA) **Mrs Denise Brooks**
7 **PYRRHIC VICTORY**, 5, ch g Groom Dancer (USA)—Victoress (USA) **The Claddagh Ring Partnership**
8 **ROSIE-B**, 6, b m Gunner B—Saucy Mop **Diamant Precision Engineering Ltd**
9 **SHADOW OF STEEL (IRE)**, 6, b m Flash of Steel—Salus **Miss Jane Ashby**
10 **TEEN JAY**, 6, b h Teenoso (USA)—Spoilt Again **Gemini Associates**
11 **ZHU JIANG**, 5, b g Nashwan (USA)—Made of Pearl (USA) **Mr Eddie Wilkinson**

Other Owners: Mr Albert Brown, Dr S. Mansoor, Miss M. Menga, Mr John Minogue, Mr David J. Thomas, Mr B. Thorne.

Jockey (NH): W McFarland (10-0).

577 CAPT. D. SWAN, Cloughjordon

Postal: **Modreeny, Cloughjordon, Co. Tipperary, Ireland.**

Phone: (0505) 42221 FAX (0505) 42128

1 **AN MAINEACH (IRE)**, 7, br g Lafontaine (USA)—Swanny Jane **C. Pettigrew**
2 **ANTON THE THIRD (IRE)**, 5, br g Phardante (FR)—Lady Flair **P. McGovern**
3 **BARNA LAD (IRE)**, 6, ch g Torus—Barna Beauty **M. J. Collison**
4 **BIT OF A SET TOO (IRE)**, 5, b m Henbit (USA)—Sesetta **Capt D. G. Swan**
5 **GLACIAL GIRL (IRE)**, 4, b f Glacial Storm (USA)—Zimuletta **Carl Finulane**
6 **KINGDOM GLORY (IRE)**, 5, gr g Wood Chanter—Ballybrennan **Simon Graham**
7 **LIKE A LION (IRE)**, 5, b g Farhaan—Marble Miller (IRE) **Mrs Orla Finulane**
8 **LITTLE ELLIOT (IRE)**, 8, b g Lafontaine (USA)—Light Whisper **Mrs T. M. Moriarty**
9 4, B f Executive Perk—Lucky Baloo **Kevin Clarke**
10 **LUCKY PERK (IRE)**, 5, br m Executive Perk—Lucky Baloo **Kevin Clarke**
11 **MR CONDUCTOR (IRE)**, 5, ch g Orchestra—Jubilaire **F. Kenny**
12 **NIGHTSCENE (IRE)**, 4, b f Scenic—Internet **Highcroney Syndicate**
13 **PERCY BRENNAN (IRE)**, 9, ch g Bon Sang (FR)—Jinane **Mrs W. Larkin**
14 **POUCHER (IRE)**, 6, b g Dock Leaf—Jacqueline Grey **J. R. Finn**
15 **TREASURE CHANT (IRE)**, 6, b g Treasure Hunter—Ring Twice **Michael V. Hough**
16 **TUSCANY HIGHWAY (IRE)**, 7, ch g Aristocracy—Johnnie's Lass **J. F. Keane**
17 **ZIMULANTE (IRE)**, 5, ch g Phardante (FR)—Zimuletta **Capt D. G. Swan**

THREE-YEAR-OLDS

18 Br g Be My Native—Atteses **Capt D. G. Swan**
19 **PERSIAN DREAM (IRE)**, b f Mazaad—Irish Dream **C. Pettigrew**

Jockey (NH): C F Swan (9-7, w.a.).

Conditional: Joseph Donnelly (10-0).

Lady Riders: Miss M L Olivefalk (9-7), Miss N Swan (9-7).

578 MR J. E. SWIERS, Helperby

Postal: **Norton House, Norton-le-clay, Helperby, York, YO6 2RS.**

Phone: (01423) 322153

1 **BLANC SEING (FR)**, 9, b g Shirley Heights—Blanche Reine (FR) **Mr J. E. Swiers**
2 **DEAR EMILY**, 8, b m Uncle Pokey—Malmar **Mr J. E. Swiers**
3 **GANTHORPE**, 7, b g Scorpio (FR)—Galah Bird **Mr J. E. Swiers**

579 MRS A. SWINBANK, Richmond

Postal: **Thorndale Farm, Melsonby, Richmond, North Yorks, DL10 5NJ.**

Phone: (01325) 377318 FAX (01325) 377796 MOBILE (0374) 129425

1 **ARCTICTALDI (IRE)**, 6, br g Cataldi—Arctic Sue **Mr G. A. Swinbank Panther Racing Ltd**
2 **BARIK (IRE)**, 6, b g Be My Guest (USA)—Smoo **Mr F. J. Sainsbury**
3 **CHOISTY (IRE)**, 6, ch g Callernish—Rosemount Rose **Hotel Brokers International**
4 **COLORFUL AMBITION**, 6, b g Slip Anchor—Reprocolor **Mr F. J. Sainsbury**
5 **IHTIMAAM (FR)**, 4, b g Polish Precedent (USA)—Haebeh (USA) **Upex Electrical Distributors Ltd**
6 **KANONA**, 5, ch g Gunner B—Pugilistic **Mr Colin Pringle**
7 **NOW YOUNG MAN (IRE)**, 7, br g Callernish—Claddagh Pride **Mrs Margaret Mitchell**
8 **PANGERAN (USA)**, 4, ch g Forty Niner (USA)—Smart Heiress (USA) **Mr G. A. Swinbank**
9 **SIERRA MADRONA (USA)**, 6, ch m Woodman (USA)—Senorita Poquito **Sims Cars Ltd**
10 **THE KHOINOA (IRE)**, 6, b g Supreme Leader—Fine Drapes **Mr M. Allison**

MRS A. SWINBANK—continued
THREE-YEAR-OLDS
11 **BROCKVILLE BAIRN**, b g Tina's Pet—Snow Chief **Mr Adam Menzies**
12 **DOMINO FLYER**, b c Warrshan (USA)—Great Dilemma **Mr S. Smith**
13 **LIMYSKI**, b g Petoski—Hachimitsu **Mrs Myra Nelson**
14 **SON OF ANSHAN**, b g Anshan—Anhaar **Mr G. A. Swinbank**
15 **TIROLS TYRANT (IRE)**, b g Tirol—Justitia **Mrs Margaret Mitchell**

TWO-YEAR-OLDS
16 B c 25/4 Dancing Dissident—Golden Sunlight (Ile de Bourbon (USA))
17 B c 16/3 Shalford (IRE)—Marazika (Great Nephew)

Other Owners: Mr C. Bradwell, Mr John Halliday, Mr D. P. McLaughlin, Mr J. D. McLaughlin, Mr E. Pakenham, Mrs A. Swinbank.

Jockey (Flat): N Connorton (w.a.).

Jockey (NH): J Railton (w.a.).

Amateur: Mr Chris Wilson (10-6).

580   MR D. G. SWINDLEHURST, Carlisle
Postal: **Lynefoot, Westlinton, Carlisle, Cumbria, CA6 6AJ.**
Phone: **(01228) 74289**

1 **GRANDERISE (IRE)**, 6, b g Digamist (USA)—Miss Morgan **Mr D. J. Swindlehurst**
2 **GROG (IRE)**, 7, b g Auction Ring (USA)—Any Price **Mr D. J. Swindlehurst**
3 **TALL MEASURE**, 10, b g High Top—Millimeter (USA) **Mr D. J. Swindlehurst**

Amateur: Mr D J Swindlehurst (10-4).

581   MR M. TATE, Kidderminster
Postal: **Winterfold Farm, Chaddesley Corbett, Kidderminster, Worcs, DY10 4PL.**
Phone: **(01562777) 243**

1 **BALLARD GIRL (IRE)**, 4, b f Ballad Rock—Little Cynthia **Mr M. Tate**
2 **BALLARD LIGHT (IRE)**, 4, b f Ballad Rock—Shikari Rose **Mr M. Tate**
3 **BESCABY GIRL**, 5, ch m Master Willie—Thatched Grove **Mr R. C. Smith**
4 **BOLD TIME MONKEY**, 5, ch m Bold Owl—Play For Time **Mr M. Tate**
5 **CLEMENCY (IRE)**, 4, ch f Kefaah (USA)—Supreme Crown (USA) **Mr M. Tate**
6 **NICKLE JOE**, 10, ro g Plugged Nickle (USA)—Travois (USA) **Mr M. Tate**
7 **PACIFIC SPIRIT**, 6, b m Governor General—Mossberry Fair **Mr M. Tate**
8 **RADIO CAROLINE**, 8, b g All Systems Go—Caroline Lamb **Mr S. B. Harris**
9 **SWEET TRENTINO (IRE)**, 5, b g High Estate—Sweet Adelaide (USA) **Hingley and Callow Oils Ltd**
10 **WESTCOAST**, 5, b g Handsome Sailor—Pichon **Mr M. Tate**

Other Owners: Mrs E. Tate.

Jockey (NH): W Marston.

Amateur: Mr R Rimell.

582   MR T. P. TATE, Tadcaster

Postal: **Castle Farm, Hazlewood, Tadcaster, North Yorks, LS24 9NJ.**
Phone: **(01937) 836036 FAX (01937) 530011**

1 **ASK TOM (IRE)**, 7, b g Strong Gale—On The Scratch **Mr B. T. Stewart-Brown**
2 **CLIVINE (FR)**, 6, ch g Italic (FR)—Quarvine Lulu (FR) **Mr S. Lycett Green**
3 **DRAGON ROSE**, 4, ch g Grey Desire—The Shrew **Mrs J. Young**
4 **ERNI (FR)**, 4, b g Un Numide (FR)—Quianoa (FR) **Mr T. P. Tate**
5 **FREQUENT VISION (IRE)**, 6, ch g Aristocracy—Kilmurray Lass **Mr T. P. Tate**
6 **LO STREGONE**, 10, b g The Parson—Somers Castle **Mrs Sylvia Clegg**
7 **NO MORE TRIX**, 10, b g Kemal (FR)—Blue Trix **The Roses Syndicate**
8 **NORDIC PRINCE (IRE)**, 5, b g Nordance (USA)—Royal Desire **Mrs S. L. Worthington**
9 **PRAISE BE (FR)**, 6, b g Baillamont (USA)—Louange **Mr T. P. Tate**
10 **RUALMIT (IRE)**, 7, b m Mister Lord (USA)—Demanoluma **Mr T. P. Tate**
11 **RULE OUT THE REST**, 5, ch g Scallywag—Saucy Eater **Mrs J. Young**
12 **SEPTEMBER BREEZE (IRE)**, 5, b m Henbit (USA)—Deepwater Woman **Mr T. P. Tate**
13 **SONNEN GIFT**, 6, b m Sonnen Gold—Hopeful Gift **Mr T. P. Tate**
14 **STORMHILL AMAZON**, 5, b m Gunner B—Little Brig **Mr S. Lycett Green**
15 **THREE WILD DAYS**, 4, b g Nishapour (FR)—Golden Curd (FR) **The Ivy Syndicate**
16 5, B g Cataldi—Turbulent Lass **Mr T. P. Tate**
17 **WEAPONS FREE**, 5, b g Idiot's Delight—Sea Kestrel **Mr B. T. Stewart-Brown**

TWO-YEAR-OLDS

18 B g 3/4 Law Society (USA)—Rubbiera (Pitskelly) **Mr T. P. Tate**

Other Owners: Mr D. M. W. Hodgkiss, Mrs S. Hodgkiss, The Ivy Syndicate, The Roses Syndicate.

Jockey (NH): R Garrity (10-0).

Conditional: W Fry (9-7).

583   MRS L. C. TAYLOR, Chipping Warden

Postal: **Blackgrounds Farm, Chipping Warden, Banbury, Oxon, OX17 1LZ.**
Phone: **(01295) 660267 FAX (01295) 660267**

1 **CHURCH LAW**, 9, br g Sexton Blake—Legal Argument **Mrs L. C. Taylor**
2 **DEACON'S FOLLY (IRE)**, 6, ch g Le Moss—Spring Chimes **Mrs L. C. Taylor**
3 **FIDDLERS GLEN (IRE)**, 8, b g Fidel—Glenava **Mrs L. C. Taylor**
4 **GRUNDON (IRE)**, 7, br g Mandalus—Buckskin Lady **Mrs L. C. Taylor**
5 **JACK THE TD (IRE)**, 7, b g Rochebrun (FR)—Lily of Dunmoon **Mrs L. C. Taylor**
6 **MUSIC SCORE**, 10, ch g Orchestra—Hansel Money **Mrs L. C. Taylor**

584   MR B. M. TEMPLE, Driffield

Postal: **Skeeting Farm, Driffield, North Humberside, YO25 7UX.**

1 **ACORN BROWN**, 5, ch g Claude Monet (USA)—Tiebell **Mr B. M. Temple**
2 **EASY RHYTHM**, 9, ch g Tudor Rhythm—Tiebell **Mr B. M. Temple**
3 **MANWELL**, 9, br g Tudor Rhythm—Tiemandee **Mr B. M. Temple**
4 **PRIMITIVE MAN**, 6, b g Primitive Rising (USA)—Tiemandee **Mr B. M. Temple**
5 4, B g Waki River (FR)—Tiebell **Mr B. M. Temple**

585   MR D. T. THOM, Newmarket

Postal: **Harraton Court, Exning, Newmarket, Suffolk, CB8 7HA.**

Phone: **HOME (01638) 577675 FAX (01638) 601675**

1 **BALL GOWN**, 6, b m Jalmood (USA)—Relatively Smart **Mr C. V. Lines**
2 **CAPTAIN MARMALADE**, 7, ch g Myjinski (USA)—Lady Seville **Mrs Alison Thom**
3 **DON'T DROP BOMBS (USA)**, 7, ch g Fighting Fit (USA)—Promised Star (USA) **Miss J. Feilden**
4 **GOLDEN FILIGREE**, 4, ch f Faustus (USA)—Muarij **Miss S. Graham**
5 **GOOD (IRE)**, 4, b g Persian Heights—Tres Bien **Mr W. F. Coleman**
6 **MISS CASHTAL (IRE)**, 5, b m Ballacashtal (CAN)—Midnight Mistress **Mrs A. G. Hooton**
7 **PUCK'S DELIGHT**, 6, b m Fairy King—Queenstyle **Mrs J. A. Purdy**
8 **SIZZLING ROMP**, 4, b f Sizzling Melody—Its A Romp **Mrs J. A. Martin**
9 **TIGER SHOOT**, 9, b g Indian King (USA)—Grand Occasion **C. V. Lines and Mason Brothers**

Other Owners: Mr Jack Ashurst, Mrs J. L. Beschizza, Mr J. M. Dyson, Mr P. J. Feilden, Mr Jamie Mason, Mr M. Mason, Mr N. Mason.

Jockey (NH): M Brennan.

Lady Rider: Miss Diana Jones (9-0).

586   MRS D. THOMAS, Bridgend

Postal: **Pen-y-lan Farm, Aberkenfig, Bridgend, Mid Glam, CF32 9AN.**

Phone: **(01656) 720254**

1 **BECKY'S LAD**, 6, ch g Gold Line—Karens Cottage **Mrs D. Thomas**
2 **SANDVILLE LAD**, 4, gr g Librate—Inglifield **Mrs D. Thomas**
3 **SEASONS**, 7, ch m Master Willie—Din Brown (USA) **Mrs D. Thomas**

587   MR RONALD THOMPSON, Doncaster

Postal: **No 2 Bungalow, Haggswood Racing Stable, Stainforth, Doncaster, DN7 5PS.**

Phone: **(01302) 845904 FAX (01302) 845904**

1 **BOBBY BLUE (IRE)**, 5, gr g Bob Back (USA)—Yuma (USA) **Haggswood Partnerships**
2 **HIGH FLOWN (USA)**, 4, b g Lear Fan (USA)—Isticanna (USA)
3 **M-I-FIVE (IRE)**, 5, ch g Classic Secret (USA)—B J Moon **Haggswood Partnerships**
4 **NORTHERN TROVE (USA)**, 4, b g Northern Jove (CAN)—Herbivorous (USA) **Cadiz Ltd**
5 **SKEDADDLE**, 4, b f Formidable (USA)—Norfolk Serenade **Haggswood Partnerships**
6 **STORM DANCE**, 5, b g Celestial Storm (USA)—Moonlight Fling **Haggswood Partnerships**
7 **THICK AS THIEVES**, 4, b c Shavian—Vivienda **Mrs Ronnie Hague**
8 **THORN OF GREATNESS (USA)**, 4, b g Image of Greatness (USA)—Two Roses (USA) **Cadiz Ltd**
9 **TOVARICH**, 5, b g Soviet Star (USA)—Pretty Lucky **Haggswood Partnerships**

THREE-YEAR-OLDS

10 **FERGAL (USA)**, ch c Inishpour—Campus (USA) **Cadiz Ltd**
11 B g Toledo (USA)—Liangold **Haggswood Partnerships**
12 **MELOS**, b f Emarati (USA)—Double Stretch **Mrs J. Carney**
13 **MIRUS**, ch g Tina's Pet—Water Stock **Mr J. Bradwell**
14 **SIKOSARKI (USA)**, ch f Inishpour—Miss Sarcastic (USA) **Cadiz Ltd**
15 **SOCIETY SUE (IRE)**, b f Mac's Imp (USA)—Ivory Wisdom (USA) **Haggswood Partnerships**

TWO-YEAR-OLDS

16 B c 9/3 Belfort (FR)—Divine Penny (Divine Gift) **Haggswood Partnerships**
17 B f 19/2 Lugana Beach—Saltina (Bustino) **Mrs J. Carney**
18 B f 12/4 Magical Wonder (USA)—Siwana (IRE) (Dom Racine (FR)) **Mrs J. Carney**
19 Ch f 11/4 Hatim (USA)—Sum Music (Music Boy) **Haggswood Partnerships**

Other Owners: Miss M. Chapman.

588   MR A. M. THOMSON, Greenlaw

Postal: **Lambden Burn, Greenlaw, Duns, Berwickshire, TD10   6UN.**
Phone: **(01361) 810514   FAX (01361) 810211**

1 **BENGHAZI,** 12, b br g Politico (USA)—Numerous **Mr A. M. Thomson**
2 **CELTIC MILE,** 7, b g Celtic Cone—Millymeeta **Mrs B. K. Thomson**
3 **CORNCASTLE,** 8, b br m Oats—Kitty Castle **Mr A. M. Thomson**
4 **CORNKITTY,** 9, b m Oats—Kitty Castle **Mr D. M. Thomson**
5 **MACMURPHY,** 11, ch g Deep Run—Millymeeta **Mr D. M. Thomson**
6 **MOLLYMEETA,** 8, b br m Deep Run—Millymeeta **Mr A. M. Thomson**
7 **YOUTHFUL INO,** 5, b m Teenoso (USA)—Polly Verry **Mrs B. K. Thomson**

Other Owners: Mrs M. C. Thomson.

589   MRS DOROTHY THOMSON, Milnathort

Postal: **Tillyrie Farm, Milnathort, Kinross, KY13 7RW.**
Phone: **(01577) 863418 FAX (01577) 863418**

1 **ALICHARGER,** 6, ch g Alias Smith (USA)—Amirati **Mr A. D. T. Fletcher**
2 **BLOOMING SPRING (IRE),** 7, b m Strong Gale—Ask The Boss **Mrs Jean McGregor**
3 **CELTIC WATERS,** 11, ch m Celtic Cone—Moonbreaker **Mrs Dorothy Thomson**
4 **DAY RETURN,** 7, b m Electric—Fly For Home **Duke of Atholl**
5 **FLOWER OF DUNBLANE,** 5, ch m Ardross—Anita's Choice **Mr Ian G. M. Dalgleish**
6 **KELPIE THE CELT,** 9, b br g Royal Fountain—Aunt Bertha **Mrs C. G. Braithwaite**
7 4, Gr f Sula Bula—Kissing Gate **Mrs R. Provan**
8 5, Ch m Alias Smith (USA)—Moonbreaker **Mrs Jean McGregor**
9 **MORE CHAMPAGNE,** 6, ch m Little Wolf—Anita's Choice **Tillyrie Cork Poppers**
10 **MUSIC BLITZ,** 5, b g Sizzling Melody—Sunny Waters **Mrs Daphne Pease**
11 **NORDISK LEGEND,** 4, b g Colmore Row—Nordic Rose (DEN) **Mrs E. G. Jorgensen**
12 **PEGGY GORDON,** 5, b m Feelings (FR)—Megan's Way **Frank Flynn and Richard Madden**
13 **STEPDAUGHTER,** 10, b m Relkino—Great Dancer **Mrs Daphne Pease**
14 **THROMEDOWNSOMETING,** 6, b m Teenoso (USA)—Shertango (USA) **Frank Flynn and Richard Madden**
15 5, Ch g Little Wolf—Tycoon Moon **Mrs Dorothy Thomson**

THREE-YEAR-OLDS

16 B f Teenoso (USA)—Anita's Choice **Mrs Dorothy Thomson**
17 B g Lighter—Moonbreaker **Mrs Dorothy Thomson**
18 **NORDIC GIFT (DEN),** ch g Bold Arrangement—Nordic Rose (DEN) **Mrs E. G. Jorgensen**
19 **RAISE A RIPPLE,** b c Primitive Rising (USA)—Bonnybrook **Mrs Sheila Hall**
20 B g Derrylin—Tycoon Moon **Mrs Dorothy Thomson**

Other Owners: Capt Ben Coutts.

Jockey (Flat): J Lowe.

Jockey (NH): Liam O'Hara.

590   MR H. THOMSON JONES, Newmarket

Postal: **Green Lodge, The Severals, Newmarket, Suffolk, CB8 7BS.**
Phone: **NEWMARKET (01638) 664884 OR 663640 FAX (01638) 660885**

1 **ALAMI (USA),** 4, b br c Danzig (USA)—Alchaasibiyeh (USA) **Mr Hamdan Al Maktoum**
2 **NIGGLE,** 4, b f Night Shift (USA)—Enchanted **Mrs H. T. Jones**
3 **SHERMAN (IRE),** 5, b h Caerleon (USA)—Aghsan **Mrs H. T. Jones**

MR H. THOMSON JONES—continued

THREE-YEAR-OLDS

4 **A-AASEM**, ch c Polish Precedent (USA)—Janbiya (IRE) **Mr Hamdan Al Maktoum**
5 **ABIR**, ch f Soviet Star (USA)—Nafhaat (USA) **Mr Hamdan Al Maktoum**
6 **AFAAN (IRE)**, ch c Cadeaux Genereux—Rawaabe (USA) **Mr Hamdan Al Maktoum**
7 **AJLAAN**, b c Unfuwain (USA)—Shurooq (USA) **Mr Hamdan Al Maktoum**
8 **ALFAHAAL (IRE)**, b c Green Desert (USA)—Fair of The Furze **Mr Hamdan Al Maktoum**
9 **ALSAHIB (USA)**, b c Slew O' Gold (USA)—Khwlah (USA) **Mr Hamdan Al Maktoum**
10 **AMANIY (USA)**, br f Dayjur (USA)—Muhbubh (USA) **Mr Hamdan Al Maktoum**
11 **ASHJAR (USA)**, b c Kris—Jathibiyah (USA) **Mr Hamdan Al Maktoum**
12 **ASMAHAAN (USA)**, b br f Dayjur (USA)—Albadeeah (USA) **Mr Hadi Al Tajir**
13 **DESERT CAT (IRE)**, b c Green Desert (USA)—Mahabba (USA) **Mr Hadi Al Tajir**
14 **DUBLIN RIVER (USA)**, b c Irish River (FR)—Vivre Libre (USA) **Mr Khalil Al Sayegh**
15 **HULM (USA)**, ch f Mujtahid (USA)—Sunley Princess **Mr Khalil Al Sayegh**
16 **ITTIFAK**, b c Marju (IRE)—Narjis (USA) **Mr Hamdan Al Maktoum**
17 **JIYUSH**, b c Generous (IRE)—Urjwan (USA) **Mr Hamdan Al Maktoum**
18 **LAAFEE**, gr g Machiavellian (USA)—Al Sylah **Mr Hamdan Al Maktoum**
19 **LUBABA (USA)**, b br f Woodman (USA)—Minifah (USA) **Mr Hamdan Al Maktoum**
20 **MARAWIS (USA)**, b c Danzig (USA)—Ra'a (USA) **Mr Hamdan Al Maktoum**
21 **MAWJUD**, b c Mujtahid (USA)—Elfaslah (IRE) **Mr Hamdan Al Maktoum**
22 **MAZEED (IRE)**, ch c Lycius (USA)—Maraatib (IRE) **Mr Hamdan Al Maktoum**
23 **MEZNH (IRE)**, ch f Mujtahid (USA)—Johara (USA) **Mr Hamdan Al Maktoum**
24 **MITHALI**, b c Unfuwain (USA)—Al Bahathri (USA) **Mr Hamdan Al Maktoum**
25 **MUTAMANNI (USA)**, b c Caerleon (USA)—Mathkurh (USA) **Mr Hamdan Al Maktoum**
26 **MUTASARRIF (IRE)**, b c Polish Patriot (USA)—Bouffant **Mr Hamdan Al Maktoum**
27 **SHARK (IRE)**, b c Tirol—Gay Appeal **Mr Hamdan Al Maktoum**
28 **TABL (IRE)**, b f Nashwan (USA)—Idle Gossip (USA) **Mr Hamdan Al Maktoum**
29 **TAMHID (USA)**, b br c Gulch (USA)—Futuh (USA) **Mr Hamdan Al Maktoum**
30 **WAASEF**, b c Warning—Thubut (USA) **Mr Hamdan Al Maktoum**
31 **YAROB (IRE)**, ch c Unfuwain (USA)—Azyaa **Mr Hamdan Al Maktoum**

TWO-YEAR-OLDS

32 **ABYAT (USA)**, gr f 2/5 Shadeed (USA)—Futuh (USA) (Diesis) **Mr Hamdan Al Maktoum**
33 **ALIKHLAS**, br f 9/3 Lahib (USA)—Mathaayl (USA) (Shadeed (USA)) **Mr Hamdan Al Maktoum**
34 **ALUMISIYAH (USA)**, b f 7/4 Danzig (USA)—Mathkurh (USA) (Riverman (USA)) **Mr Hamdan Al Maktoum**
35 **BAREEQ**, b c 8/5 Nashwan (USA)—Urjwan (USA) (Seattle Slew (USA)) **Mr Hamdan Al Maktoum**
36 **CHRISTMAS ROSE**, gr f 11/3 Absalom—Shall We Run (Hotfoot) **Mrs H. T. Jones**
37 **FAHRIS (IRE)**, ch c 27/3 Generous (IRE)—Janbiya (IRE) (Kris) **Mr Hamdan Al Maktoum**
38 **FAYIK**, ch c 15/2 Arazi (USA)—Elfaslah (IRE) (Green Desert (USA)) **Mr Hamdan Al Maktoum**
39 **GHALIB (IRE)**, ch c 2/2 Soviet Star (USA)—Nafhaat (USA) (Roberto (USA)) **Mr Hamdan Al Maktoum**
40 **HACHIYAH (IRE)**, gr f 24/2 Generous (IRE)—Himmah (USA) (Habitat) **Mr Hamdan Al Maktoum**
41 **HAJAT**, ch f 31/1 Mujtahid (USA)—Nur (USA) (Diesis) **Mr Hamdan Al Maktoum**
42 **JANIB (USA)**, ch c 11/2 Diesis—Shicklah (USA) (The Minstrel (CAN)) **Mr Hamdan Al Maktoum**
43 **KAFIL (USA)**, b c 4/4 Housebuster (USA)—Alchaasibiyeh (USA) (Seattle Slew (USA)) **Mr Hamdan Al Maktoum**
44 **KHALIK (USA)**, b c 30/3 Lear Fan (USA)—Silver Dollar (Shirley Heights) **Mr Hamdan Al Maktoum**
45 **KHARIR (IRE)**, b c 20/2 Machiavellian (USA)—Alkaffeyeh (IRE) (Sadler's Wells (USA)) **Mr Hamdan Al Maktoum**
46 **KHAYAL (USA)**, b c 14/2 Green Dancer (USA)—
Look Who's Dancing (USA) (Affirmed (USA)) **Mr Hamdan Al Maktoum**
47 **KHAZINAT EL DAR (USA)**, b br f 2/3 Slew O' Gold (USA)—Alghuzaylah (USA) (Habitat) **Mr Hamdan Al Maktoum**
48 **MAGHAS (IRE)**, ch c 28/4 Lahib (USA)—Rawaabe (USA) (Nureyev (USA)) **Mr Hamdan Al Maktoum**
49 **MAJJTHUB (USA)**, b c 16/4 Slew O' Gold (USA)—Jathibiyah (USA) (Nureyev (USA)) **Mr Hamdan Al Maktoum**
50 **MUSAFI (USA)**, br c 8/3 Dayjur (USA)—Ra'a (USA) (Diesis) **Mr Hamdan Al Maktoum**
51 **MUTRIBAH (USA)**, b f 13/1 Silver Hawk (USA)—Pattimech (USA) (Nureyev (USA)) **Mr Hamdan Al Maktoum**
52 **RUMUZ (IRE)**, b f 15/3 Marju (IRE)—Balqis (USA) (Advocator (USA)) **Mr Hamdan Al Maktoum**
53 **THAHABYAH (USA)**, b f 29/3 Sheikh Albadou—Golden Cap (Hagley (USA)) **Mr Hamdan Al Maktoum**
54 **WATER FLOWER**, b f 10/2 Environment Friend—Flower Girl (Pharly (FR)) **Mr W. J. Gredley**
55 **ZIBAK (USA)**, b br c 9/4 Capote (USA)—Minifah (USA) (Nureyev (USA)) **Mr Hamdan Al Maktoum**

Jockey (Flat): R Hills (8-0).

591   MR T. THOMSON JONES, Upper Lambourn

Postal: **The Croft, Upper Lambourn, Newbury, Berks, RG16 7QH.**
Phone: **LAMBOURN (01488) 71596 FAX (01488) 71146**

1 **ARFEY (IRE)**, 7, b g Burslem—Last Gunboat **Mr Martin Myers**
2 **BLAZON OF TROY**, 7, b g Trojan Fen—Mullet **Mr David F. Wilson**
3 **CANTE CHICO**, 4, b c Reference Point—Flamenco Wave (USA) **Mr Tim Thomson Jones**
4 **CHAPILLIERE (FR)**, 6, b g Tin Soldier (FR)—Matale (FR) **Mr Bryan Beacham**
5 **COLOSSUS OF ROADS**, 7, br g Rymer—Dear Jem **Mr David F. Wilson**
6 **DECIDE YOURSELF (IRE)**, 6, b g Tumble Gold—Wrong Decision **Mr David F. Wilson**
7 **DRUMMOND WARRIOR (IRE)**, 7, b g Rontino—Speckled Leinster **Mr David F. Wilson**
8 **ETON MANOR (IRE)**, 5, b m Strong Gale—Allgate **Mr Roy F. Reeve**
9 **FIDWAY**, 11, b g Fidel—Galway Maid **Mrs Lindsay Fallace**
10 **FORTUNES WOOD**, 10, b g Town And Country—Top Soprano **The Hon Mrs Townshend**
11 **I'M IN CLOVER (IRE)**, 7, ch g Good Thyne (USA)—Lady Cromer **Mr D. R. Peppiatt**
12 **JACKSON FLINT**, 8, b g Nishapour (FR)—Scamperdale **Mrs L. G. Turner**
13 **LINTON ROCKS**, 7, b g Town And Country—Top Soprano **The Hon Mrs Townshend**
14 **MASRUF (IRE)**, 4, b c Taufan (USA)—Queen's Share **Mr Hamdan Al Maktoum**
15 **PROFESSOR PAGE (IRE)**, 6, b g Spanish Place (USA)—Knight's Princess **Mr T. Thomson Jones**
16 **RED CARDINAL**, 10, b g Cardinal Flower—Deep Bonnie **Mr Harry Sibley**
17 **SARTORIUS**, 10, b g Henbit (USA)—Salvationist **Mr M. Popham**
18 **TAKE THE BUCKSKIN**, 9, b g Buckskin (FR)—Honeyburn **Mr David F. Wilson**
19 **THE BOILER WHITE (IRE)**, 8, ch g Deep Run—Cill Dara **Mr David F. Wilson**

THREE-YEAR-OLDS

20 **GHUSN**, b c Warning—North Page (FR) **Mr Hamdan Al Maktoum**
21 **JUBILEE PLACE (IRE)**, br f Prince Sabo—Labelon Lady **Mr Timothy N. Chick**

TWO-YEAR-OLDS

22 **MEQYAS (IRE)**, b c 9/5 Rock City—Baby Brew (Green God) **Mr Hamdan Al Maktoum**
23 **MUMKIN**, b c 17/3 Reprimand—Soon To Be (Hot Spark) **Mr Hamdan Al Maktoum**

Other Owners: Queen Elizabeth, Mrs Solna Thomson Jones, Mr Brian Lovrey, Mr B. K. Peppiatt, Miss Nicola Ridley, Mr P. D. Savill, Mrs P. Starkey.

592   MR G. E. THORNER, Wantage

Postal: **Upper Manor Farm, Letcombe Regis, Wantage, Oxon, OX12 9LD.**
Phone: **WANTAGE (01235) 763003**

1 **AWSAJ (IRE)**, 5, b g Astronef—Les Saintes **Mr G. E. Thorner**
2 **BLASTED**, 4, ch g Statoblest—Apprila **Miss A. Jones**
3 **CLARION CALL (IRE)**, 5, b g Don't Forget Me—Hillbrow **The Oh No Lawyers Partnership**
4 **FRANK IRISH**, 5, b m Saxon Farm—Ahalin Girl **Mr Frank R. Jarvey**
5 **GERGAASH**, 4, gr g Petong—Ashbocking **Mr G. Thorner**
6 **LASTO ADREE (IRE)**, 5, b g Shernazar—Summer Palace **Miss J. Newell**
7 **MACEDONAS**, 8, b g Niniski (USA)—Miss Saint-Cloud **Mr R. K. Wheate**
8 **MANABOUTTHEHOUSE**, 9, b g Homeboy—Miss Sunblest **Mr Frank R. Jarvey**
9 **MONKS JAY (IRE)**, 7, br g Monksfield—Boro Penny **Mr J. A. Cover**
10 **NEBAAL (USA)**, 6, b g Storm Cat (USA)—Primevere (USA) **Mr C. Humphry**
11 **NOBBY NORTH**, 4, b g Northern State (USA)—One Degree **The Silver and Blue Horse Racing Club**
12 **OLDEN DAYS**, 4, b g Old Vic—Olamic (USA) **Keith Ogden**
13 **STAUNCH RIVAL (USA)**, 9, b g Sir Ivor—Crystal Bright **Mr C. Humphry**
14 **WENTWORTH (USA)**, 4, b g Diesis—Line Call (USA) **Mr G. Thorner**
15 **XYLOTYMBOU**, 5, b m Town And Country—Glittering Gem **Mrs E. J. Crossman**

THREE-YEAR-OLDS

16 **MR HACKER**, b c Shannon Cottage (USA)—Aosta **Mr Bill Ivens**

MR G. E. THORNER—continued

Other Owners: Mr Thor N. Andersen, Mr J. W. Aplin, Mr N. Boyd, Mr Brian A. Crossman, Mr R. W. Hester, Mr Kirketerp Jensen, Mr Crispen Wall, Mr J. D. T. Wall, Mr M. Wilding.

Jockeys (NH): D Bridgwater, B Powell.

Conditional: Clare Thorner (10-0).

Amateur: Mr K Wheate (10-0).

593   MR C. W. THORNTON, Middleham

Postal: **Spigot Lodge, Middleham, Leyburn, N. Yorks, DL8 4TL.**

Phone: **(01969) 623350 LADS HOSTEL (01969) 622252 FAX (01969) 624374**

1 **ARRANGE**, 4, b g Deploy—Willowbed **Mr Guy Reed**
2 **BLOOD BROTHER**, 4, ch g Superlative—Two Moons **Mr Guy Reed**
3 **CHANTRY BEATH**, 5, ch g Dunbeath (USA)—Sallametti (USA) **Racegoers Club Spigot Lodge Owners Group**
4 **CITTADINO**, 6, b g Good Thyne (USA)—Slave's Bangle **Mr D. B. Dennison**
5 **EAU DE COLOGNE**, 4, b g Persian Bold—No More Rosies **Mr Guy Reed**
6 **FIVE TO SEVEN (USA)**, 7, br g Little Missouri (USA)—French Galaxy (USA) **The Five to Seven Partnership**
7 **LAST ROUNDUP**, 4, b g Good Times (ITY)—Washita **Mr Guy Reed**
8 **ME CHEROKEE**, 4, br f Persian Bold—Siouan **Mr Guy Reed**
9 **SECRET SERVICE (IRE)**, 4, b g Classic Secret (USA)—Mystery Bid **Mr Guy Reed**
10 **SIOUX TO SPEAK**, 4, b g Mandrake Major—Sioux Be It **Mr Guy Reed**
11 **SIOUX WARRIOR**, 4, br g Mandrake Major—Seminole **Mr Guy Reed**
12 **STAND TALL**, 4, b g Unfuwain (USA)—Antilla **Mr Guy Reed**
13 **TRUMBLE**, 4, b g Tragic Role (USA)—Sideloader Special **Mr Ben Pocock**
14 **WAR WHOOP**, 4, ch g Mandrake Major—Mohican **Mr Guy Reed**

THREE-YEAR-OLDS

15 **ALL IN GOOD TIME**, b g Shadeed (USA)—Good Thinking (USA) **Mr Guy Reed**
16 **COCOON (IRE)**, b f Cyrano de Bergerac—Arena **Mr Guy Reed**
17 **CONTRACT BRIDGE (IRE)**, b f Contract Law (USA)—Mystery Bid **Racegoers Club Spigot Lodge Owners Group**
18 **LOS ALAMOS**, b f Keen—Washita **Mr Guy Reed**
19 **MUSTANG**, ch c Thatching—Lassoo **Mr Guy Reed**
20 **RAJAH**, b br g Be My Chief (USA)—Pretty Thing **Mr Guy Reed**
21 **SOCIETY GIRL**, b f Shavian—Sirene Bleu Marine (USA) **Mr Guy Reed**
22 **TONTO**, b g Nomination—Brigado **Mr Guy Reed**

TWO-YEAR-OLDS

23 **AMICO**, b c 15/2 Efisio—Stormswept (USA) (Storm Bird (CAN)) **Mr Guy Reed**
24 **BUENA VISTA**, b f 21/2 Be My Chief (USA)—Florentynna Bay (Aragon) **Mr Guy Reed**
25 Ch f 13/2 Imp Society (USA)—Catherine Clare (Sallust) **Mr Guy Reed**
26 **COCHITI**, b f 5/2 Kris—Sweet Jaffa (Never So Bold) **Mr Guy Reed**
27 B c 30/4 Rambo Dancer (CAN)—Ozra (Red Alert) **Mr Guy Reed**
28 Ch f 21/2 Masterclass (USA)—Rebecca's Girl (IRE) (Nashamaa) **Mr Guy Reed**
29 **ROBBO**, b c 13/3 Robellino (USA)—Basha (USA) (Chief's Crown (USA)) **Mr Guy Reed**
30 **SAN FRANCISCO**, b c 16/4 Aragon—Sirene Bleu Marine (USA) (Secreto (USA)) **Mr Guy Reed**
31 **ZORBA**, b c 30/3 Shareef Dancer (USA)—Zabelina (USA) (Diesis) **Mr Guy Reed**

Other Owners: Mr E. G. Allen, Mrs Joy Bendall, Mr Simon Brown, Mr R. Brumpton, Mr L. Caley, Mr James Collins, Mr C. Pocock, Mr David Scott, Mr Alan Wyrill.

Jockey (Flat): Dean McKeown (w.a.).

Jockey (NH): D Wilkinson (10-0).

Apprentice: G Mills (7-7).

Conditional: Nathan Horrocks (9-7).

594   MR W. H. TINNING, Harrogate

Postal: **Lund Head Farm, Kirkby Overblow, Harrogate, N. Yorks, HG3 1HY.**
Phone: **LEEDS (01132) 886260**

1 CHADWICK'S GINGER, 8, ch m Crofthall—Knight Hunter **Mr W. H. Tinning**
2 GOLDMIRE, 6, b m Norwick (USA)—Orange Parade **Mr W. H. Tinning**

Conditional: D Parker (9-9).

595   MR D. M. TODHUNTER, Ulverston

Postal: **The North Lodge, Priory Road, Ulverston, Cumbria, LA12 9RX.**
Phone: **(01229) 580529**

1 CHIPPED OUT, 6, gr g Scallywag—City's Sister
2 HIGHLAND WAY (IRE), 8, b g Kemal (FR)—Peace Run **Mr J. D. Gordon**
3 I'M THE GAFFER, 5, ch g Lighter—City's Sister **Mr E. Briggs**
4 JUST LIKE DAD, 4, ch g Weld—Another City **Mr E. Briggs**
5 4, B g Feelings (FR)—Meg's Mantle **Mr K. Jackson**
6 4, B g Le Coq d'Or—Wedderburn **Mr K. Jackson**
7 WILLS TELMAR (IRE), 8, ch g Montelimar—Lady's Turn **Mr Bill Parkinson**

THREE-YEAR-OLDS

8 Ch g Nishapour (FR)—Share A Friend **Mr P. Fitzgerald**

Other Owners: Mr P. Dawson.

Jockey (NH): R Garrity.

596   MR J. A. R. TOLLER, Whitsbury

Postal: **Majors Farm, Whitsbury, Fordingbridge, Hants, SP6 3QP.**
Phone: **(01725) 518220 FAX (01725) 518520**

1 DIRECT DIAL (USA), 4, br c Phone Trick—Jig Jig (USA) **Blandford Thoroughbreds**
2 DRY POINT, 10, ch g Sharpo—X-Data **Lady Sophia Morrison**
3 FAIR ATTRACTION, 4, ch g Charmer—Fairfields **Ash Partnership**
4 LANDLORD, 4, b g Be My Chief (USA)—Pubby **Mr A. J. Morrison**
5 PAINTED HALL (USA), 4, br g Imperial Falcon (CAN)—Moon O'Gold (USA) **Duke of Devonshire**
6 RODERICK HUDSON, 4, b c Elmaamul—Moviegoer **Duke of Devonshire**

THREE-YEAR-OLDS

7 BEWITCHING (USA), ch f Imp Society (USA)—Mrs Magnum (USA) **Mr P. C. J. Dalby**
8 CHECHNYAN, b c Soviet Star (USA)—Eastern Shore **Blandford Thoroughbreds**
9 CROSS OF VALOUR, b g Never So Bold—X-Data **Mr P. C. J. Dalby**
10 EFFECTUAL, b c Efisio—Moharabuiee **Blandford Thoroughbreds**
11 ILLUMINATE, b c Marju (IRE)—Light Bee (USA) **Blandford Thoroughbreds**
12 INTIMATION, b f Warning—It's Terrific **Blandford Thoroughbreds**
13 KATATONIC (IRE), b c Waajib—Miss Kate (FR) **Blandford Thoroughbreds**
14 KIDSTON LASS (IRE), b f Alzao (USA)—Anthis (IRE) **Mr R. Bradley**
15 LITERARY SOCIETY (USA), ch c Runaway Groom (CAN)—Dancing Gull (USA) **Duke of Devonshire**
16 MELLORS (IRE), b c Common Grounds—Simply Beautiful (IRE) **Fortune In Mind Partnership**
17 MEMPHIS BEAU (IRE), ch g Ballad Rock—Texly (FR) **Blandford Thoroughbreds**
18 POLISH SWINGER (IRE), b c Polish Patriot (USA)—Girl On A Swing **Blandford Thoroughbreds**
19 SMILE FOREVER (USA), b f Sunshine Forever (USA)—Awenita **Blandford Thoroughbreds**
20 THE DILETTANTI (USA), br c Red Ransom (USA)—Rich Thought (USA) **Duke of Devonshire**
21 ZURS (IRE), b c Tirol—Needy **Blandford Thoroughbreds**

MR J. A. R. TOLLER—continued

TWO-YEAR-OLDS

22 **COMPTON PLACE**, ch c 20/4 Indian Ridge—Nosey (Nebbiolo) **Duke of Devonshire**
23 **FABLE**, ch f 15/3 Absalom—Fiction (Dominion) **G. H. Toller & Partners**
24 B f 16/3 Mac's Imp (USA)—Grade A Star (IRE) (Alzao (USA)) **W. Holy-Hastead & Partner**
25 **JUVENILIA (IRE)**, ch f 7/3 Masterclass (USA)—Amtico (Bairn (USA)) **G. B. Partnership**
26 **LIMELIGHT**, b f 6/5 Old Vic—Nellie Dean (Song) **Partnership**
27 **OTHER CLUB**, ch c 3/3 Kris—Tura (Northfields (USA)) **Duke of Devonshire**
28 Gr f 5/5 Absalom—Pearl Cove (Town And Country) **Partnership**
29 **SILVERY**, gr f 25/2 Petong—Petit Peu (IRE) (Kings Lake (USA)) **A. J. Morrison & Partners**
30 **ZIMIRI**, ch c 18/3 Keen—Annabrianna (Night Shift (USA)) **Forum Trustees**

Other Owners: Mr D. L. Brooks, Mr J. Findlay, Capt C. B. Toller, Mrs C. B. Toller, Mrs J. Toller, Mr Philip Wroughton.

597   MR M. H. TOMPKINS, Newmarket

Postal: **Flint Cottage Stables, Rayes Lane, Newmarket, CB8 7AB.**
Phone: **NEWMARKET (01638) 661434 FAX (01638) 668107**

1 **BELLROI (IRE)**, 5, b g Roi Danzig (USA)—Balela **Mrs G. A. E. Smith**
2 **BOBBY'S DREAM**, 4, b f Reference Point—Kiralyi (FR) **Mrs Patricia M. Kalman**
3 **BOB'S PLOY**, 4, b g Deploy—Santa Magdalena **Mrs M. Barwell**
4 **BURES (IRE)**, 5, b g Bold Arrangement—Grid (FR) **Mr John Wimbs**
5 **CLAIRESWAN (IRE)**, 4, ch g Rhoman Rule (USA)—Choclate Baby **Claire and Beryl**
6 **CLEAN EDGE (USA)**, 4, ch g Woodman (USA)—Najidiya (USA) **Mr Henry B. H. Chan**
7 **COOL EDGE (IRE)**, 5, ch g Nashamaa—Mochara **Mr Henry B. H. Chan**
8 **CUTHILL HOPE (IRE)**, 5, gr g Peacock (FR)—Sicilian Princess **Mrs Emma Gilchrist**
9 **EDEN'S CLOSE**, 7, ch g Green Dancer (USA)—Royal Agreement (USA) **Mrs M. Barwell**
10 **EDEN'S STAR (IRE)**, 4, b g Fools Holme (USA)—Flinging Star (USA) **Mrs M. Barwell**
11 **HALKOPOUS**, 10, b g Beldale Flutter (USA)—Salamina **Mr Athos Christodoulou**
12 **HELLO PETER (IRE)**, 4, b g Taufan (USA)—Apple Rings **Mr M. H. Tompkins**
13 **LEONTIOS (IRE)**, 4, b g Alzao (USA)—Akamantis **Fortune In Mind Partnership**
14 5, b g Strong Gale—Maid of Moyode **Mr D. Ashby**
15 **ON THE FLY**, 5, b g Bustino—My Greatest Star **Mrs Carol Davis**
16 **OVERPOWER**, 12, b g Try My Best (USA)—Just A Shadow **Mr M. P. Bowring**
17 **RINGMASTER (IRE)**, 4, b g Taufan (USA)—Salustrina **Mr M. H. Tompkins**
18 **SCHOOL MUM**, 4, b f Reprimand—Mother Brown **Mrs Bridget Blum**
19 **STAUNCH FRIEND (USA)**, 8, b g Secreto (USA)—Staunch Lady (USA) **Mr B. Schmidt-Bodner**
20 **TAKE COVER (IRE)**, 5, b g Meneval (USA)—Bad Weather **Adrienne and Michael Barnett**
21 **THE ATHELING (IRE)**, 6, b g Taufan (USA)—Shady Glade **Mr Ian Lochhead**
22 **THE FLYING PHANTOM**, 5, gr g Sharrood (USA)—Miss Flossa (FR) **P. H. Betts (Holdings) Ltd**
23 **TIME FOR ACTION (IRE)**, 4, b g Alzao (USA)—Beyond Words **Mrs G. A. E. Smith**
24 **TIME IS MONEY (IRE)**, 4, b g Sizzling Melody—Tiempo **Mrs M. H. Tompkins**
25 **VIRKON VENTURE (IRE)**, 8, b g Auction Ring (USA)—Madame Fair **Mr R. Auchincloss**
26 **VOILA PREMIERE (IRE)**, 4, b g Roi Danzig (USA)—Salustrina **Mr B. W. Gaule**
27 **WATCH MY LIPS**, 4, b g Vin St Benet—Manor Farm Toots **Miss D. J. Merson**
28 **WESTMINSTER (IRE)**, 4, ch g Nashamaa—Our Galadrial **Mr John Bull**
29 **ZIFFANY**, 4, b f Taufan (USA)—Bonnie Banks **Pamela, Lady Nelson of Stafford**

THREE-YEAR-OLDS

30 **AIR WING**, ch c Risk Me (FR)—Greenstead Lass **P. H. Betts (Holdings) Ltd**
31 **BELMARITA (IRE)**, ch f Belmez (USA)—Congress Lady **Mr G. A. Hubbard**
32 **BLURRED (IRE)**, ch g Al Hareb (USA)—I'll Take Paris **Mr A. B. Reason**
33 **BREYDON**, ch g Be My Guest (USA)—Palmella (USA) **Mr P. F. Riseborough**
34 **COWBOY DREAMS (IRE)**, b g Nashamaa—Shahrazad **Flint Fairyhouse Partnership**
35 **EVEN TOP (IRE)**, br c Topanoora—Skevena **Mr B. Schmidt-Bodner**
36 **FAG END (IRE)**, b f Treasure Kay—Gauloise Bleue (USA) **Mr Michael H. Keogh**
37 **FULL THROTTLE**, br g Daring March—Wheatley **Mrs M. H. Tompkins**
38 **HONEST GUEST (IRE)**, b f Be My Guest (USA)—Good Policy (IRE) **Mr Ian Lochhead**
39 **PARROT'S HILL (IRE)**, b g Nashamaa—Cryptic Gold **Mark Tompkins Elite**
40 **POETRY (IRE)**, gr f Treasure Kay—Silver Heart **Mr Michael H. Keogh**

MR M. H. TOMPKINS—continued

41 **POLISH RHYTHM (IRE)**, b f Polish Patriot (USA)—Clanjingle **Mr G. A. Hubbard**
42 **SKY DOME (IRE)**, ch c Bluebird (USA)—God Speed Her **Miss D. J. Merson**
43 **STOP PLAY (IRE)**, b f Distinctly North (USA)—Church Mountain **Mark Tompkins Racing**
44 **UNCLE GEORGE**, ch g Anshan—Son Et Lumiere **Mr J. A. Fuller**
45 **WELCOME ROYALE (IRE)**, ch g Be My Guest (USA)—Kirsova **Mrs G. A. E. Smith**

TWO-YEAR-OLDS

46 **BLOWING AWAY (IRE)**, b f 5/5 Last Tycoon—Taken By Force (Persian Bold) **Mark Tompkins Racing**
47 B f 5/4 Maledetto (IRE)—Blue Infanta (Chief Singer) **Mr Michael H. Keogh**
48 **CHYNNA**, b f 26/4 Golden Heights—What A Present (Pharly (FR)) **Mr M. J. Williams**
49 B f 29/3 Petorius—Cut It Fine (USA) (Big Spruce (USA)) **Mr J. H. Shannon**
50 B f 30/3 Lahib (USA)—Debach Delight (Great Nephew)
51 B g 2/5 Supreme Leader—Deep Kitty (IRE) (Deep Run) **Mr D. Ashby**
52 Ch f 10/2 Roi Danzig (USA)—Deloraine (Pharly (FR))
53 B g 25/5 Mandalus—Disetta (Distinctly (USA)) **Mr D. Ashby**
54 B c 28/2 Taufan (USA)—Eleganza (IRE) (Kings Lake (USA))
55 **FRANKIE**, b c 19/3 Shalford (IRE)—Twilight Secret (Vaigly Great) **Mr Richard R. Flatt**
56 B f 8/4 Treasure Kay—Gazettalong (Taufan (USA))
57 Ch c 18/1 Salt Dome (USA)—Insight (Ballad Rock) **Mr J. H. Shannon**
58 **JANIE'S BOY**, b c 20/2 Persian Bold—Cornelian (Great Nephew) **Mr R. Auchincloss**
59 B c 21/2 Old Vic—Jawaher (IRE) (Dancing Brave (USA))
60 **MUSICAL PURSUIT**, b c 18/4 Pursuit Of Love—Gay Music (FR) (Gay Mecene (USA)) **Mr B. Schmidt-Bodner**
61 Ch f 21/3 Topanoora—Partygoer (General Assembly (USA)) **Mr M. P. Bowring**
62 **SPANIARD'S MOUNT**, b c 15/5 Distant Relative—Confection (Formidable (USA)) **Mr B. Schmidt-Bodner**
63 **TURTLE MOON**, gr c 11/4 Absalom—Port Na Blath (On Your Mark) **Mr P. D. Savill**
64 **TYROLEAN DREAM (IRE)**, b c 3/3 Tirol—Heavenly Hope (Glenstal (USA)) **Mr Peter Heath**
65 B c 30/3 Astronef—Violet Somers (Will Somers) **Mr T. N. Claydon**

Other Owners: Mrs Sara J. Alldread, Mr K. Barwell, Mr B. G. Chan, Mr T. F. Dundon, Mr W. E. Dundon, Mr A. R. G. Else, Mr D. Fisher, Mrs C. F. Gaule, Mr P. S. Green, Mr R. V. Lewis, Mrs V. A. Lewis, Mrs Beryl Lockey, Mr S. M. McAnulty, Mr J. McGlinchey, Oceala Limited, P. H. Betts (Holdings) Ltd, Mr Colin Russell, Mr Robert F. Schlagman.

Jockey (Flat): Philip Robinson (8-0).

Jockey (NH): D Gallagher (10-0).

Apprentice: J Gotobed (7-7).

Conditional: P J Maher (9-7).

Amateur: Mr M Jenkins (10-7).

598   MRS P. LAXTO TOWNSLEY, Dunsfold

Postal: **Mendips, The Common, Dunsfold, Godalming, GU8 4LA.**
Phone: **(01483) 200849**

1 **DONT GAMBLE**, 10, gr g Spin of A Coin—Dontlike **Mrs Pru Townsley**
2 **ELL GEE**, 6, ch m Ra Nova—Evening Song **Mrs Pru Townsley**
3 **HALE'S MELODY**, 11, b m Dubassoff (USA)—Hale Lane **Mrs Pru Townsley**
4 **ZIP YOUR LIP**, 6, b g Ra Nova—Centaur Star **Mrs Pru Townsley**

Amateur: Mr P Townsley (11-0).

Lady Riders: Miss C Townsley (8-7), Miss L Townsley (9-7).

599   MR J. C. TUCK, Didmarton

Postal: **Manor Farm, Oldbury-on-the-hill, Didmarton, Badminton, GL9 1EA.**

Phone: **(01454) 238236**

1 **COOL CAT (IRE)**, 5, b h Cataldi—Artic Sue **Mumm Partnership**
2 **GUNNER B LUCKY**, 5, gr m Gunner B—Lucky Amy **A. J. & J. I. Whiting Partnership**
3 **HARLEQUIN BAY**, 6, b g Remezzo—New Columbine **Mr P. N. Baldwin**
4 **HUSH TINA**, 5, ch m Tina's Pet—Silent Dancer **Mr J. C. Tuck**
5 **JAVA SHRINE (USA)**, 5, b g Java Gold (USA)—Ivory Idol (USA) **Dr John Heathcock**
6 **LADY NESS**, 5, gr m Baron Blakeney—Philogyny **Knockdown Racing Club**
7 4, Br g Be My Native (USA)—Martialette **Mr R. A. J. Hatherell**
8 **MONDAY CLUB**, 12, ch g Remezzo—Jena **Mr J. C. Tuck**
9 **MR FLUTTS**, 10, b g Derrylin—Madam Flutterbye **Mr J. C. Tuck**
10 **PRIZE MATCH**, 7, ch m Royal Match—Prize Melody **Dr John Heathcock**
11 **ROALY**, 7, b m Energist—Top Feather **Mr James R. Tuck**
12 **WHAT'S THE JOKE**, 7, b m Mummy's Game—Smiling **Mr James R. Tuck**

THREE-YEAR-OLDS

13 Ch f Chilibang—Silent Dancer **Mr G. S. Tuck**

Other Owners: Mr Tim Green, Mr Arthur E. Smith.

Jockey (NH): Simon McNeill (10-0, w.a.).

Conditional: K Dempsey.

Amateurs: Jo Lewis,

600   MR F. G. TUCKER, Wedmore

Postal: **Mudgley Hill Farm, Mudgley, Wedmore, Somerset, BS28 4TZ.**

Phone: **(01934) 712684**

1 **DUNNICKS COUNTRY**, 6, ch m Town And Country—Celtic Beauty **Mr F. G. Tucker**
2 **DUNNICKS TOWN**, 4, b g Town And Country—Country Magic **Mr F. G. Tucker**
3 **DUNNICKS VIEW**, 7, b g Sula Bula—Country Magic **Mr F. G. Tucker**
4 **FREDS MELODY**, 11, br g Dubassoff (USA)—Sovereign Melody **Mr F. G. Tucker**

601   MR ANDREW TURNELL, Wantage

Postal: **Orchard Stables, East Hendred, Wantage, Oxon, OX12 8JP.**

Phone: **(01235) 833297 FAX (01235) 832827**

1 **ACAJOU III (FR)**, 8, b g Cap Martin (FR)—Roxane II (FR) **Mr Robert Ogden**
2 **ACT THE WAG (IRE)**, 7, ch g Over The River (FR)—Slyguff Lass **Mr Robert Ogden**
3 **APOLLO COLOSSO**, 6, br g Sunyboy—Culinary **Mr James R. Adam**
4 **BECKY'S REVENGE**, 6, b g Michael's Revenge—Isn't That Hard **Miss Harriet Wye**
5 **BOWL OF OATS**, 10, ch g Oats—Bishop's Bow **Mrs Anthony Morley**
6 **CARMEL**, 5, gr m Malaspina—Carrol's Cross **Orchard Lea Racing - Mrs H. Chittem**
7 **COUNTRY MEMBER**, 11, ch g New Member—Romany Serenade **Mrs C. C. Williams**
8 **CROWN EQUERRY (IRE)**, 6, b br g Strong Gale—Ballybrowney Gold **Mr Robert Ogden**
9 **EVENING RIOT (IRE)**, 7, ch g Riot Helmet—Evening Bun **Dr John Hollowood**
10 **FILS DE CRESSON (IRE)**, 6, b g Torus—Hellfire Hostess **Mr James R. Adam**
11 **FOX ON THE RUN**, 9, b g Le Moss—Chancy Gal **Mr Robert Ogden**

MR ANDREW TURNELL—continued

12 **FRED JEFFREY (IRE)**, 5, b g Supreme Leader—Shuil Ard **Mr L. G. Kimber**
13 **GARRISON COMMANDER (IRE)**, 7, b g Phardante (FR)—Rent A Card **Mr Robert Ogden**
14 **GIVENTIME**, 8, ch g Bustino—Duck Soup **Mr L. G. Kimber**
15 **GLENDOE (IRE)**, 5, b br g Lord Americo—Jazz Bavard **Mr K. C. B. Mackenzie**
16 **HAWAIIAN SAM (IRE)**, 6, b g Hawaiian Return (USA)—Thomastown Girl **Mr Robert K. Russell**
17 **HIGHLAND JACK**, 6, ch g Nearly A Hand—Highland Path **Mrs K. J. Gibbons**
18 **JUDICIOUS NORMAN (IRE)**, 5, br g Strong Gale—Smart Fashion **Mr James R. Adam**
19 **KINGDOM OF SHADES (USA)**, 6, ch g Risen Star (USA)—Dancers Countess (USA) **Mr Robert Ogden**
20 **LORINS GOLD**, 6, ch g Rich Charlie—Woolcana **Mrs M. R. Taylor**
21 **MAITRE DE MUSIQUE (FR)**, 5, ch g Quai Voltaire (USA)—Mativa (FR) **Mr Robert Ogden**
22 **MASTER PANGLOSS (IRE)**, 6, b g Pitpan—Wind Chimes **Equity Steeplechasing**
23 **MONNAIE FORTE (IRE)**, 6, b g Strong Gale—Money Run **Mr James R. Adam**
24 **MYSTIC COURT (IRE)**, 5, br g Mister Lord (USA)—Magic Money
25 **MYSTIC MANNA**, 10, b g Oats—Mystic Queen **Miss Carolyn A. B. Allsopp**
26 **OLD BRIDGE (IRE)**, 8, ch g Crash Course—What A Duchess **Mr K. C. B. Mackenzie**
27 **REESHLOCH**, 7, b g Reesh—Abalone **Mrs M. R. Taylor**
28 **RELKOWEN**, 6, ch m Relkino—Pollys Owen **Mrs M. I. Barton**
29 **RHYMING THOMAS**, 8, ch g Rymer—Gokatiego **Mr James R. Adam**
30 **RUBY'S GIRL**, 6, b m Sula Bula—Rugamour **Mr B. Higham**
31 **SLIPMATIC**, 7, b m Pragmatic—Slipalong **Mr Peter Sims**
32 **SNOWSHILL HARVEST (IRE)**, 5, b g Strong Gale—Slave-Lady **Mr H. Stephen Smith**
33 **SOCIETY GUEST**, 10, ch g High Line—Welcome Break **Robinson Webster (Holdings) Ltd**
34 **SQUIRE SILK**, 7, b g Natroun (FR)—Rustle of Silk **Mr Robert Ogden**
35 **STORMING ROY**, 6, b g Strong Gale—Book Token **Mr James R. Adam**
36 **THE PALADIN**, 6, b g Nearly A Hand—Romany Serenade **Mr R. K. Carvill**
37 **TOO PLUSH**, 7, b g Kaytu—Plush **Mrs C. C. Williams**
38 **TROUVAILLE (IRE)**, 5, b g King's Ride—Dream Run **Mr G. Payne**
39 **WHISPERING COURT (IRE)**, 6, ch g Avocat—Wind Over Spain **Court Jesters Partnership 2**

THREE-YEAR-OLDS

40 **CLAIRE'S DANCER (IRE)**, b g Classic Music (USA)—Midnight Patrol **Mrs Claire Hollowood**

Other Owners: Mr G. E. Botfield, Miss Jackie Burroughs, Mrs S. E. A. Gilbert, Miss V. J. Glynn, Mrs J. C. Greenland, Mrs Jenny Gregory, Miss Natalia Jaksic, Mr C. Keene, Mr Graham D. Kendrick, Mr Brian Kirk, Mr A. M. Morley, Mr David Salter, Mr Donald Salter, Mr Harry Sibley, Lord Sondes, Mr D. A. Speirs, Mr J. B. Stent, Mr Michael G. T. Stokes, Mr N. A. Woodcock.

Jockeys (NH): P Carberry (10-0), L Harvey (10-0), S McNeill (10-0).

Conditional: G S Crone (9-7), N S Willmington (9-7).

Amateur: Mr J Rees (9-7).

602　　MR W. G. M. TURNER, Sherborne

Postal: **Sigwells Farm, Sigwells, Corton Denham, Sherborne, DT9 4LN.**
Phone: **CORTON DENHAM (01963) 220523 FAX (01963) 220046**

1 **CHURCHTOWN CHANCE (IRE)**, 6, b m Fine Blade (USA)—Churchtown Breeze **Mr Paul B. Jordain**
2 **CNOCMA (IRE)**, 5, b m Tender King—Peggy Dell **Mr O. J. Stokes**
3 **COPPER COIL**, 6, ch g Undulate (USA)—April Rose **Mr R. A. Lloyd**
4 **DEE-LADY**, 4, b f Deploy—Bermuda Lily **Mrs M. S. Teversham**
5 **FANGIO**, 7, b g Nordance (USA)—Verily Jane **Mr Malcolm Heygate-Browne**
6 **FLEUR DE TAL**, 5, b m Primitive Rising (USA)—Penset **Mr John Woods**
7 **HALAM BELL**, 4, b f Kalaglow—Mevlevi **Mr T. Lightbowne**

MR W. G. M. TURNER—continued

  8 **JAMESWICK**, 6, b g Norwick (USA)—Auto Elegance **Mr R. A. Webb**
  9 **LA RESIDENCE**, 5, b g Doulab (USA)—Ideal Home **Mrs A. G. Sims**
 10 **LYING EYES**, 5, ch m Interrex (CAN)—Lysithea **Mr A. K. Holbrook**
 11 **MAYDAY KITTY**, 4, ch f Interrex (CAN)—T Catty (USA) **Mr T. Lightbowne**
 12 **MEDFORD**, 6, b g Pablond—Music Meadow **Mr P. F. Coombes**
 13 **MILLIE'S MODEL**, 7, br m Latest Model—Millie Gras **Miss J. Hodgkinson**
 14 **MOVE WITH EDES**, 4, b g Tragic Role (USA)—Good Time Girl **W. Ede & Co Partnership**
 15 **NAZZARO**, 7, b g Town And Country—Groundsel **Mr A. Morrish**
 16 **NICK THE DREAMER**, 11, ch g Nicholas Bill—Dream of Fortune **Somerset and Dorset Racing**
 17 **PEGASUS**, 6, b g Undulate (USA)—Bay Girl **Mr R. A. Lloyd**
 18 **SAFFRON RIVER**, 5, b m Sulaafah (USA)—Swift Turtle **Mr J. H. Stranger**
 19 **SLEEPTITE (FR)**, 6, gr g Double Bed (FR)—Rajan Grey **Mr David Chown**
 20 **SMOKEBRIDGE GRAS**, 9, b g Pardigras—Stalbridge Smoke **Miss J. Hodgkinson**
 21 **SOUTHERN RIDGE**, 5, b g Indian Ridge—Southern Sky **Mr Bill Brown**
 22 **ST KITTS**, 5, b m Tragic Role (USA)—T Catty (USA) **Mr T. Lightbowne**
 23 **TADELLAL (IRE)**, 5, ch m Glint of Gold—Meissarah (USA) **Mrs B. R. Stokes**
 24 **THE WAYWARD GUNNER**, 5, ch g Gunner B—Lady Letitia **Mr David Chown**
 25 **WESTFIELD**, 4, b g Lyphento (USA)—Wessex Flyer **Mrs A. G. Sims**

THREE-YEAR-OLDS

 26 **JESSICA'S SONG**, b f Colmore Row—Sideloader Special **Mr John Woods**
 27 **JOHAYRO**, ch c Clantime—Arroganza **Mr Frank Brady**
 28 **LADY BANKES (IRE)**, b f Alzao (USA)—Never So Fair **Mr T. Lightbowne**
 29 **POWER DON**, ch c Superpower—Donalee **Mr Frank Brady**
 30 **PRIMO LAD**, b c Primo Dominie—Zinzi **Mr P. F. Coombes**
 31 **SUBFUSK**, b f Lugana Beach—Hush It Up **Mrs J. M. Sexton**
 32 **THE FRISKY FARMER**, b c Emarati (USA)—Farceuse **Mr G. J. Bush**

TWO-YEAR-OLDS

 33 B f 26/3 Forzando—Down The Valley (Kampala)
 34 **EKATERINI PARITSI**, b f 22/5 Timeless Times (USA)—Wych Willow (Hard Fought)
 35 B f 18/3 Interrex (CAN)—Facetious (Malicious)
 36 **INDIAN SPARK**, ch c 26/4 Indian Ridge—Annes Gift (Ballymoss)
 37 B c 9/6 Meqdaam (USA)—Jokers High (USA) (Vaguely Noble)
 38 **JUST LOUI**, gr g 11/3 Lugana Beach—Absaloui (Absalom)
 39 Br f 1/2 Prince Sabo—Leprechaun Lady (Royal Blend)
 40 B g 7/4 Rolfe (USA)—Nicaline (High Line)
 41 Ch g 14/5 Interrex (CAN)—Raleigh Gazelle (Absalom)
 42 **SWEET EMMALINE**, b f 14/2 Emarati (USA)—Chapelfell (Pennine Walk)
 43 B f 20/3 Weldnaas (USA)—Ty High (IRE) (High Line)

Other Owners: Mr J. H. Bush, Mr N. A. Carpenter, Mr N. J. Coombs, Mr R. A. Coombs, Mr Richard Hedditch, Mr A. K. Holbrook, Mr F. Lewis, Mrs Janet Lockwood, Mr T. McComish, Mr A. C. Roberts, Mr M. J. Rogers, Mr Tony J. Smith, Mr R. Titt, Mr R. A. Webb, Mr Michael Woods.

Jockey (Flat): T Sprake (w.a.).

Jockey (NH): R Dunwoody (w.a.).

Conditional: T C Murphy (9-12), John Gerard Power.

603   MR N. A. TWISTON-DAVIES, Cheltenham

Postal: **Grange Hill Farm, Naunton, Cheltenham, Glos, GL54 3AY.**

Phone: **(01451) 850278 FAX (01451) 850101**

1 **ARCTIC KINSMAN**, 8, gr g Relkino—Arctic Advert **Mrs R. E. Hambro**
2 **BEATSON (IRE)**, 7, gr g Roselier (FR)—Toevarro **Mrs E. B. Gardiner**
3 **BETTER BYTHE GLASS (IRE)**, 7, br g Over The River (FR)—Money Buck **Bloodshot Syndicate**
4 **BETTER THAN BILLS (IRE)**, 5, br g Phardante (FR)—Mini Brennan **Mr John Chinn**
5 **BLESSED OLIVER**, 6, ch g Relkino—Oca **Mrs David Plunkett**
6 **BLUSTERY FELLOW**, 11, b g Strong Gale—Paulas Fancy **Mrs R. A. Humphries**
7 **BOARD MEMBER (IRE)**, 6, b br g Over The River (FR)—Alfuraat **Mr Howard Parker**
8 **BROWNED OFF**, 7, br g Move Off—Jenifer Browning **Mrs Lorna Berryman**
9 **BUCKHOUSE BOY**, 6, b g Relkino—Teapot Hall **The Bawtry Boys**
10 **CADES BAY**, 5, b h Unfuwain (USA)—Antilla **Mr R. D. Russell**
11 **CAMELOT KNIGHT**, 10, br g King's Ride—Jeanette Marie **Mr Michael Gates**
12 **CAMP BANK**, 6, b g Strong Gale—Rambling Gold **Mrs J. Mould**
13 **CARELESS FARMER**, 6, b m Waajib—Careless Whisper (USA) **Mr M. R. Gibson**
14 **CELTIC PRINCE**, 10, ch g Celtic Cone—Lothian Countess **Mrs J. Mould**
15 **CHIEF RAGER**, 7, ch g Relkino—Metaxa **Mr James Cheetham**
16 **CLEVER REMARK**, 7, b g Idiot's Delight—Brave Remark **Mrs Jan Smith**
17 **COOL VIRTUE (IRE)**, 5, b m Zaffaran (USA)—Arctic Straight **Mr Stephen Lambert**
18 **CORROUGE (USA)**, 7, b br h Alleged (USA)—Lake Country (CAN) **Mr Michael Gates**
19 **DENISE'S PROFILES**, 6, b g Royal Vulcan—Lovelyroseofclare **Exterior Profiles Ltd**
20 **DICTUM (IRE)**, 5, ch g Phardante (FR)—Secret Top **Mrs R. A. Humphries**
21 **DOC COTTRILL**, 6, b g Absalom—Bridal Wave **Bakers Arms Partnership**
22 **EARTH SUMMIT**, 8, b g Celtic Cone—Win Green Hill **The Summit Partnership**
23 **EASY BUCK**, 9, b g Swing Easy (USA)—Northern Empress **J. P. M. & J. W. Cook**
24 **EXTERIOR PROFILES (IRE)**, 6, b g Good Thyne (USA)—Best of Kin **Exterior Profiles Ltd**
25 **FEISTY BOSS (USA)**, 4, br g Fit To Fight (USA)—Fiesty Gal (USA) **Ms Josephine Collings**
26 **FLAPJACK LAD**, 7, b g Oats—Reperage (USA) **Mr H. B. Shouler**
27 **FREDDIE MUCK**, 6, b g Idiot's Delight—Muckertoo **Mrs C. Twiston-Davies**
28 **FRENCH BUCK (IRE)**, 6, br g Phardante (FR)—Flying Silver **Mrs C. M. Scott**
29 **FUZZY LOGIC (IRE)**, 8, b g Buckskin (FR)—Sister Cecelia **Cheltenham Racing Ltd**
30 **GALA'S PRIDE**, 9, b m Gala Performance (USA)—Miss He-Na-Su **Mr Audley Twiston-Davies**
31 **GHIA GNEUIAGH**, 10, b g Monksfield—Kindly **Mrs S. A. Scott**
32 **GOSPEL (IRE)**, 7, b m Le Bavard (FR)—Alfuraat **Mrs J. K. Powell**
33 **GRANGE BRAKE**, 10, b g Over The River (FR)—Arctic Brilliance **Mrs J. Mould**
34 **GREAT MARQUESS**, 9, b h Touching Wood (USA)—Fruition **The Great Marquess Partnership**
35 **GREG'S PROFILES**, 5, b br g Strong Gale—The Howlet **Exterior Profiles Ltd**
36 **GUINDA (IRE)**, 6, b m Corvaro (USA)—Our Cherry **Mrs J. K. Powell**
37 **HIT THE FAN**, 7, b g Lear Fan (USA)—Embroglio (USA) **Mr Michael J. Arnold**
38 **HOLY STING (IRE)**, 7, b g The Parson—Little Credit **Mr Gavin MacEchern**
39 **HUGE MISTAKE**, 7, b g Valiyar—Nicoletta **Windrush Racing**
40 **JUST ONE CANALETTO**, 8, ch g Claude Monet (USA)—Mary Shelley **Farmers Racing Partnership**
41 **LA BELLA VILLA**, 6, b m Relkino—Scotch Princess **PCJF Bloodstock**
42 **LONG REACH**, 8, br g Reach—Peperino **Mr Timothy J. Pope**
43 **MADAM MUCK**, 5, ch m Gunner B—Muckertoo **The Co-optimists**
44 **MADAM'S WALK**, 6, ch m Ardross—Emily Kent **Mrs J. Mould**
45 **MAHLER**, 6, b g Uncle Pokey—Dovey **English Badminton Partnership**
46 **MANKIND**, 5, b g Rakaposhi King—Mandarling **Mr James Fenlon**
47 **MAN OF MYSTERY**, 10, b g Torus—Queens Folly **PCJF Bloodstock**
48 **MARLINO (USA)**, 5, b g Slew O' Gold (USA)—Molly Moon (FR) **B. & T. Racing Club**
49 **MISTER MOROSE (IRE)**, 6, b g King's Ride—Girseach **Mrs J. Mould**
50 **MR MOTIVATOR**, 6, b g Rolfe (USA)—National Clover
51 **OCEAN HAWK (USA)**, 4, b g Hawkster (USA)—Society Sunrise (USA) **Miss Jean Broadhurst**
52 **PARIS FASHION (FR)**, 5, br m Northern Fashion (USA)—Paris Au Pair (USA) **Mr Peter Kelsall**
53 **PAT BUCKLEY**, 5, b g Buckley—Raheny **Mrs K. L. Urquhart**
54 **PENTLANDS FLYER (IRE)**, 5, b g Phardante (FR)—Bunkilla **Mrs M. W. Bird**
55 **PETER POINTER**, 8, br g Relkino—Housemistress **Mrs Ian McKie**
56 **POETIC FANCY**, 5, ch m Then Again—Massawa (FR) **Oxbridge Fanciers**

MR N. A. TWISTON-DAVIES—continued

57 PRU'S PROFILES (IRE), 5, b g Tale Quale—Hazy Hill **Exterior Profiles Ltd**
58 QUEEN OF SPADES (IRE), 6, b br m Strong Gale—Affordthe Queen **Mrs R. Vaughan**
59 RAISE AND GAIN (IRE), 5, ch g Rising—Bellus Mandy (IRE) **Mr W. Chinn**
60 ROMANCER (IRE), 5, br g Caerleon (USA)—Courtesane (USA) **Mr Matt Archer**
61 SAN GIORGIO, 7, b g Lighter—Gold Willow **Mr Peter Kelsall**
62 SCARLET RAMBLER, 7, ch g Blakeney Point—Rambling Rolls **E. V. Partnership**
63 SCHWARTZNDIGGER (IRE), 6, b g Double Schwartz—Sweet Nothings **Mrs Jan Smith**
64 SCOTBY (BEL), 6, gr g Scottish Reel—Two Seasons **Mr Mark G. Rimell**
65 SNOWSHILL SHAKER, 7, b g Son of Shaka—Knight Hunter **Mr Austin P. Knight**
66 SPEEDWELL PRINCE (IRE), 6, ch g Henbit (USA)—Eternal Fire **The Bar Fixtures Partnership**
67 SPRING DOUBLE (IRE), 5, br g Seclude (USA)—Solar Jet **Mrs Lorna Berryman**
68 STAR MARKET, 6, b g Celestial Storm (USA)—Think Ahead **Mrs P. Joynes**
69 SWING QUARTET (IRE), 6, b br m Orchestra—Sweetly Stung **Mr A. M. Armitage**
70 TAMERGALE (IRE), 7, b m Strong Gale—Miss Miller **Mrs R. Vaughan**
71 TENBIT (IRE), 6, b g Henbit (USA)—Lilardia **Mr Christopher Haycock**
72 TEXAN BABY (BEL), 7, b g Baby Turk—Texan Rose (FR) **Mr C. B. Sanderson**
73 THE PROMS (IRE), 5, b g Orchestra—Girseach **Mrs J. Mould**
74 TOMPETOO (IRE), 5, ch g Roselier (FR)—Express Course **Tom Pettifer Ltd**
75 TOTHEWOODS, 8, b g The Parson—Elsea Wood **Mrs Martin Scott & Mr Robert Cooper**
76 VINTAGE RED, 6, b g Sulaafah (USA)—Armonit **Special Reserve Racing**
77 VISAGA, 10, b g King's Ride—Subiacco **Mr L. Hellstenius**
78 WHERE'S WILLIE (FR), 7, br g Rahotep (FR)—Rambling **Mr David Langdon**
79 WISLEY WONDER (IRE), 6, ch g Phardante (FR)—Priscilla's Pride **The Wisley Golf Partnership**
80 YOUNG HUSTLER, 9, ch g Import—Davett **Mr Gavin MacEchern**
81 ZAMIRAH, 7, b m Trojan Fen—Sweet Pleasure **Mr N. A. Twiston-Davies**

Other Owners: Mr L. Arber, A. M. Armitage & Partners, M. J. Arnold & P. J. Horrocks, Mr Hugh Arthur, Mrs P. M. Arthur, Mr M. G. Bailey, Mr R. Bennett, Mr A. Bond, Mr A. E. Bowen-Jones, Mr Philip Brown, Mr Tom Brown, Mr A. Burrows, Mr William Campbell, Mr Andrew Clark, Mr J. F. Coakill, Mr A. J. Collins, Mr J. E. Collins, J. P. M. & J. W. Cook, Mr L. A. Cruickshank, Mrs A. J. Davies, Mr G. Dickinson, Mr J. W. Downer, Mr Ian Dunbar, I. Dunbar & Partners, Mr P. H. Earl, Mr Charles Fenby, Mr M. L. Fisher, Mr I. E. Foot, Mr Philip Freedman, Mr J. Gavin, Mr Ricky George, Mr M. R. Gibson, Mr Mike Gibson, Mr T. Gold Blyth, Mr G. C. Hallett, Mrs R. E. Hambro & D. Milne, Mr Michael Harman, Mrs Eileen Hawkey, Mr K. W. Hickman, Mr Alan R. Hill, Mr Alan Hirst, Mrs V. D. Hodgkiss, Mr P. G. Horrocks, Mr Adrian Huett, Mr P. John Huins, Mr H. Kaye, H. Kaye & Partners, Mr B. J. Lee, Mr Peter Mackenzie, Mr M. D. Macklin, Mr K. G. Manley, Mr David M. Mason, Mr Peter Maunder, Mrs G. Maxwell-Jones, Mr John McKenna, Mr F. J. Mills, Mr W. R. Mills, Mr Denis Milne, Mr Jan Molby, Mr M. C. Monk, Mr K. J. Mustow, Mr Anders W. Nielson, Mr David J. Pallen, Mr Alan Parker, Mr Nigel Payne, Mr N. Payne & Partners, Mr R. G. Perry, Mr D. G. Pether, Mr Nick Ponting, Mr Dean K. Pugh, Mr Kim K. Pugh, Mr Victor G. Pugh, Mr M. W. Robinson, Mr G. H. Robson, Mr Ian Rush, Mrs Valerie Sanderson, Mr C. M. F. Scott, Mr James Scott, Mrs Martin Scott & Mr Robert Cooper, Mrs J. Scott & Partners, Mrs Marilyn Scudamore, Mr D. F. Sheron, Mrs E. M. Shirley-Beavan, H. B. Shouler & T. H. Ounsley, Mr R. I. Sims, Mr R. Smith, Mr E. W. Southgate, Mr W. R. Starling, Mr Philip J. Surtees, Mr G. M. Thomson, Tom Pettifer Ltd, Mr R. Tookey, Mr P. A. Townsend, Mr Stephen Twohig, Mr S. D. Votier, Mr P. Wade, Mr Malcolm Wassall, Mr Paul Webber, Mr David Woodward, Mrs E. P. Wright, Mr Andrew P. Wyer, Mr S. M. Yassukovich, Mr P. Yates.

Jockeys (NH): T P Jenks (10-0), C Llewellyn (10-0).

Conditional: S Joynes (9-9), M Keithley (9-7), D Walsh (9-4).

Amateur: Mr M Rimell (10-0).

604 MR J. R. UPSON, Towcester

Postal: **Little Highfields, Adstone, Towcester, Northants, N12 8DS.**

Phone: **(01327) 860043 FAX (01327) 860043**

1 **ACTION AT LAST,** 5, b g Fearless Action (USA)—Wynall Serpent VII **Mr A. Lawrence**
2 **BLOWN A FUSE (IRE),** 5, b br g Electric—Liberty Calling **Mrs Diane Upson**
3 **BOWLES PATROL (IRE),** 4, br bl g Roselier (FR)—Another Dud **Mr John R. Upson**
4 **CATS RUN (IRE),** 8, ch g Deep Run—Zelamere **Mrs Ann Key**
5 **EAN MOR,** 5, b m Royal Vulcan—Pegs Promise **Mr John R. Upson**
6 **GILDORANS LASS,** 5, b m Gildoran—Lasses Nightshade **Mr G. Bodily**
7 **GO AGAIN (IRE),** 7, b g Febrino—Miss Avoca **The Three Horseshoes Sporting Club**
8 **LADY CONFESS,** 6, ch m Backchat (USA)—Special Branch **Mrs R. E. Tate**
9 **NAUTICAL GEORGE (IRE),** 6, b g Point North—Best Rose **Mrs Eva Ellis**
10 **NICK THE BEAK (IRE),** 7, ch g Duky—Rainy Weather **Sir Nicholas Wilson**
11 **NO MORALS,** 5, b g Royal Vulcan—Osmium **Mr W. M. Comerford**
12 **REFLEX HAMMER,** 5, b g Precious Metal—Khotso **Middleham Park Racing VII**
13 **RIVER CHALLENGE (IRE),** 5, ch g Over The River (FR)—Floppy Disk **Middleham Park Racing III**
14 **THE MILLMASTER (IRE),** 5, b g Mister Lord (USA)—Rolling Mill **Middleham Park Racing IV**
15 **TRUSS,** 9, b g Lyphard's Special (USA)—Trestle **The Three Horseshoes Sporting Club**
16 **YOUNG RADICAL (IRE),** 4, b g Radical—Fountain Blue **Mr N. Jones**

THREE-YEAR-OLDS

17 **GHOSTLY APPARITION,** gr g Gods Solution—Tawny **Mrs Diane Upson**

Other Owners: Mr J. Cayley, Mr T. S. Palin, Mr R. G. Smith, Mrs C. Steel, Mr C. Wallis.

Jockey (NH): Robbie Supple (10-0).

Conditional: C Davies (9-7), J Supple (9-11).

Amateur: Mr T Byrne (10-7).

605 MR P. N. UPSON, Folkestone

Postal: **New Barn Cottages, Lyminge, Folkestone, Kent, CT18 8DG.**

Phone: **(01303) 862776**

1 **MANSFIELD HOUSE,** 11, ch g Swing Easy (USA)—Pollinella **Mrs R. A. Upson**

Jockey (NH): M Richards (10-0, w.a.).

Conditional: G Hogan (10-0).

606 MR M. D. I. USHER, Swindon

Postal: **Foxhill Racing Stables, Foxhill, Wanborough, Swindon, SN4 0DS.**

Phone: **(01793) 791115 FAX (01793) 791149 CAR PHONE (0831) 873531**

1 **ALDWICK COLONNADE,** 9, ch m Kind of Hush—Money Supply **Coastguards Estate Agent of Bognor Regis**
2 **ALPINE STORM (IRE),** 4, b f Al Hareb (USA)—Alpine Dance (USA) **Mr R. J. O. Sowerby**
3 **AMNESTY BAY,** 4, b f Thatching—Sanctuary Cove **Clairtex Gwent**
4 **BAYIN (USA),** 7, b g Caro—Regatela (USA) **Mr Trevor Barker**
5 **DEARDAW,** 4, b f Tina's Pet—Faw **Miss D. G. Kerr**
6 **DODGY DANCER,** 6, b g Shareef Dancer (USA)—Fluctuate **Halewood International Ltd**
7 **FASTINI GOLD,** 4, b c Weldnaas (USA)—La Carlotta **Motolec Racing**
8 **LOUISVILLE BELLE (IRE),** 7, ch m Ahonoora—Lomond Fairy **Mrs M. P. Pearson**
9 **NAUTICAL JEWEL,** 4, b g Handsome Sailor—Kopjes **Sporting Partners**

MR M. D. I. USHER—continued

10 **PALEY PRINCE (USA)**, 10, b h Tilt Up (USA)—Apalachee Princess (USA) **Shirval Partners**
11 **REMAADI SUN**, 4, gr c Cadeaux Genereux—Catch The Sun **Mr Trevor Barker**
12 **RING THE CHIEF**, 4, b c Chief Singer—Lomond Ring **Clairtex Gwent**
13 **SPARKLING ROBERTA**, 5, b m Kind of Hush—Hitesca **Mr G. A. Summers**
14 **WHATEVER'S RIGHT (IRE)**, 7, b g Doulab (USA)—Souveniers **Mr M. S. C. Thurgood**
15 **ZERMATT (IRE)**, 6, b h Sadler's Wells (USA)—Chamonis (USA) **Clairtex Gwent**

THREE-YEAR-OLDS

16 **COASTGUARDS HERO**, ch g Chilibang—Aldwick Colonnade **Coastguards Estate Agent of Bognor Regis**
17 **KOWTOW**, b f Forzando—Aim To Please **Mr Trevor Barker**
18 **SPIRAL FLYER (IRE)**, b br f Contract Law (USA)—Souveniers **Mr M. S. C. Thurgood**

TWO-YEAR-OLDS

19 B f 13/5 Warrshan (USA)—Anhaar (Ela-Mana-Mou) **Charlestown Stud**
20 B c 22/3 Petoski—Hush It Up (Tina's Pet) **Charlestown Stud**

Other Owners: Mr I. E. Chant, Mr K. F. Clarke, Mr Bryan Fry, Mrs S. P. Fry, Mr M. Hopkins, Mr Graham King, Mr P. S. Pearson, Mr J. Seller, Mr K. Walton, Mr C. West-Meads, Mr P. Winfrow.

Apprentice: Corey Adamson (7-2).

Lady Rider: Mrs Ann Usher (7-7).

607   MR J. WADE, Mordon

Postal: **Howe Hills, Mordon, Sedgefield, Cleveland, TS21 2HF.**
Phone: **(01325) 313129 (01325) 315521 (01325) 320660 FAX**

1 **CALL THE SHOTS (IRE)**, 7, br g Callernish—Golden Strings **Mr John Wade**
2 **CASTLE RED (IRE)**, 5, b g Carlingford Castle—Pampered Russian **Mr John Wade**
3 **CHIEF RAIDER (IRE)**, 8, br g Strong Gale—Lochadoo **Mr John Wade**
4 **CLARES OWN**, 12, b g Al Sirat (USA)—Andonian **Mr John Wade**
5 **COOLTON HILL (IRE)**, 5, b g Coquelin (USA)—Woolton Hill **Mr John Wade**
6 **DEISE MARSHALL (IRE)**, 8, b g Euphemism—Rushing Wind **Mr John Wade**
7 **DON'T TELL TOM (IRE)**, 6, b g Strong Statement (USA)—Drop In **Mr John Wade**
8 **GREENFIELD MANOR**, 9, ch g Move Off—Kerosa **Mr John Wade**
9 **HICKSONS CHOICE (IRE)**, 8, br g Seymour Hicks (FR)—Gentle Rain **Mr John Wade**
10 **LEADER SAL (IRE)**, 7, br g Supreme Leader—Repetitive (USA) **Mr John Wade**
11 **LORD RULLAH (IRE)**, 5, b g Lord Americo—Pottlerath **Mr John Wade**
12 **MR REINER (IRE)**, 8, br g Vision (USA)—Yvonne's Choice **Mr John Wade**
13 **NICK THE BILL**, 5, b g Nicholas Bill—Another Treat **Mr John Wade**
14 **ONE MORE BILL**, 6, b g Silly Prices—Another Treat **Mr John Wade**
15 **OVERFLOWING RIVER (IRE)**, 7, ch g Over The River (FR)—Side Wink **Mr John Wade**
16 **RANDOM KING (IRE)**, 6, b g King Luthier—Avransha **Mr John Wade**
17 **RUSSIAN CASTLE (IRE)**, 7, b g Carlingford Castle—Pampered Russian **Mr John Wade**
18 **SELECTRIC (IRE)**, 5, b g Electric—Sweet Annabelle **Mr John Wade**
19 **SHELTON ABBEY**, 10, br g The Parson—Herald Holidolly **Mr John Wade**
20 **SHULTAN (IRE)**, 7, ch m Rymer—Double Cousin **Mr John Wade**
21 **SOUSON (IRE)**, 8, b g Soughaan (USA)—Down The Line **Mr John Wade**
22 **STRONG BLADE (IRE)**, 6, b g Strong Gale—Brickeen's Pet **Mr John Wade**
23 **TUDOR FELLOW (IRE)**, 7, ch g Decent Fellow—Canadian Tudor **Mr John Wade**

Jockey (NH): Kevin Jones (10-3).

Conditional: Diarmuid Ryan (9-7).

608   MR N. WAGGOTT, Spennymoor

Postal: **Ingledene, Vyners Close, Merrington Lane, Spennymoor, DL16 7HB.**

Phone: **(01388) 819012**

1 **BELIEVE IT,** 7, b g Bellypha—Hasty Key (USA) **Mrs J. Waggott**
2 **HIGHLAND MISS,** 6, gr m Highlands—Umtali **Mrs J. Waggott**
3 **JAMARSAM (IRE),** 8, b g The Parson—Park Blue **Mrs J. Waggott**
4 **LUCKY DOMINO,** 6, b g Primo Dominie—Ruff's Luck (USA) **Mr N. Waggott**
5 **NEED A LADDER,** 9, b g Highlands—Munster Glen **Mrs J. Waggott**
6 **POLAR WIND,** 7, ch g El Gran Senor (USA)—Tundra Goose **Mr N. Waggott**
7 **STYLISH INTERVAL,** 4, ch g Interrex (CAN)—Super Style **Mrs J. Waggott**

THREE-YEAR-OLDS

8 Ch g Highlands—Friendly Wonder **Miss T. Waggott**
9 B g Highlands—Munster Glen **Mr N. Waggott**

Other Owners: Mr G. L. Barker, Mr J. N. Hutchinson, The Butch Partnership.

Amateur: Mr N Waggott Jnr (11-0).

Lady Rider: Miss Tracy Waggott (9-7).

609   MR J. S. WAINWRIGHT, Malton

Postal: **Hanging Hill Farm, Kennythorpe, Malton, North Yorks, YO17 9LA.**

Phone: **(01653) 658537**

1 **BALLARD LADY (IRE),** 4, ch f Ballad Rock—First Blush **Mrs P. Wake**
2 **DANCING JAZZTIME,** 5, b m Clantime—Dance In Spain **Mr J. Gott**
3 **FINER FEELINGS,** 4, b f Feelings (FR)—High Caraval **Mr Dennis L. Dunbar**
4 **FRET (USA),** 6, b g Storm Bird (CAN)—Windy And Mild (USA) **Hopeful Enterprises**
5 **LEGAL BRIEF,** 4, b g Law Society (USA)—Ahonita **Wisma Partnership**
6 **MAJAL (IRE),** 7, b g Caerleon (USA)—Park Special **Mrs P. Wake**
7 **RAGAZZO (IRE),** 6, b g Runnett—Redecorate (USA) **Mr S. Pedersen**
8 **SENSO (IRE),** 5, b g Persian Heights—Flosshilde **Miss V. Foster**
9 **TAPATCH (IRE),** 8, b g Thatching—Knees Up (USA) **Miss V. Foster**
10 **WAVERLEY STAR,** 11, br g Pitskelly—Quelle Blague **Mr S. Pedersen**
11 **YOUNG BEN (IRE),** 4, ch g Fayruz—Jive **Mr J. H. Pickard**

THREE-YEAR-OLDS

12 **AUTOFYR,** br f Autobird (FR)—Fyrish **Mr Dennis L. Dunbar**

Other Owners: V. R. W. McCracken, Mr F. W. Wood.

Jockeys (Flat): L Charnock (7-10), J Fanning (7-10), D McKeown (8-3).

Conditional: P Midgley (10-6).

Amateur: Mr K Green (10-0).

610   MR ROBERT B WALEY-COHEN, Banbury

Postal: **Upton Viva, Banbury, Oxon, OX15 6HT.**

Phone: **OFFICE (0171) 244 6022 HOME (01295) 670242**

1 **BIBENDUM,** 10, b g Furry Glen—Bibs **Mr Robert Waley-Cohen**

611   MR N. J. H. WALKER, Wantage

Postal: **Kingston Lisle Farm Stables, Kingston Lisle, Wantage, Oxon, OX12 9QH.**
Phone: **(01367) 820068 FAX (01367) 820078**

1 **ARCHER (IRE)**, 8, b g Roselier (FR)—Suir Valley **Mr Paul Green**
2 **CHAN THE MAN**, 5, b g Krisinsky (USA)—Channel Ten **Mrs Sandra Worthington**
3 **EL ATREVIDO (FR)**, 6, ch g Rainbow Quest (USA)—Majestic Peck (USA) **Mr R. F. Batty**
4 **ELEMENTARY**, 13, b g Busted—Santa Vittoria **Mr Paul Green**
5 **FUNAMBULIEN (USA)**, 9, ch g L'Emigrant (USA)—Charming Pan (FR) **Mrs Jenny Green**
6 **GEISWAY (CAN)**, 6, br g Geiger Counter (USA)—Broadway Beauty (USA) **Mr Paul Green**
7 **GRANDES OREILLES (IRE)**, 4, b f Nordico (USA)—Top Knot **Mrs Lynsey Le Cornu**
8 **HELIOS**, 8, br g Blazing Saddles (AUS)—Mary Sunley **Mr D. H. Cowgill**
9 **HIGH PATRIARCH (IRE)**, 4, b g Alzao (USA)—Freesia **Mr Paul Green**
10 **HONEY MOUNT**, 5, b g Shirley Heights—Honeybeta **Mr Paul Green**
11 **KHATIM (USA)**, 4, b br c Topsider (USA)—Khwlah (USA) **Mr Paul Green**
12 **NEUWEST (USA)**, 4, b c Gone West (USA)—White Mischief **Mr Paul Green**
13 **NOBLELY (USA)**, 9, b g Lyphard (USA)—Nonoalca (FR) **Mr D. H. Cowgill**
14 **OUT ON A PROMISE (IRE)**, 4, b c Night Shift (USA)—Lovers' Parlour **Mr Paul Green**
15 **PISTOL RIVER (IRE)**, 6, b g Simply Great (FR)—Pampala **Mr Paul Green**
16 **RUSSIAN EMPIRE**, 6, b g Soviet Star (USA)—Lost Splendour (USA) **Mr J. Cooper**
17 **THOMAS CROWN (IRE)**, 4, ch c Last Tycoon—Upward Trend **Mr Paul Green**
18 **TORCH VERT (IRE)**, 4, b g Law Society (USA)—Arctic Winter (CAN) **Mr Paul Green**
19 **TYRONE BRIDGE**, 10, b g Kings Lake (USA)—Rhein Bridge **Mr Paul Green**
20 **UNSINKABLE BOXER (IRE)**, 7, b g Sheer Grit—Softly Sarah **Mr Paul Green**

THREE-YEAR-OLDS

21 **MELLOW MASTER**, b c Royal Academy (USA)—Upward Trend **Mr Paul Green**
22 **PRESUMING ED (IRE)**, b c Nordico (USA)—Top Knot **Mr Paul Green**

Other Owners: Mrs A. Brookes.

Jockey (Flat): J Stack.

612   MR C. F. WALL, Newmarket

Postal: **Induna Stables, Fordham Road, Newmarket, Suffolk, CB8 7AQ.**
Phone: **HOME (01638) 668896 OFFICE (01638) 661999 FAX (01638) 667279**

1 **ADMIRALS FLAME (IRE)**, 5, b g Doulab (USA)—Fan The Flame **Mrs C. A. Wall**
2 **ADMIRALS SECRET (USA)**, 7, ch g Secreto (USA)—Noble Mistress (USA) **Mrs C. A. Wall**
3 **ALMASI (IRE)**, 4, b f Petorius—Best Niece **The Equema Partners**
4 **DONNA VIOLA**, 4, b f Be My Chief (USA)—Countess Olivia **Mr K. D. Scott**
5 **LEADING SPIRIT (IRE)**, 4, b g Fairy King (USA)—Shopping (FR) **Induna Racing Partners Two**
6 **LOUGH ERNE**, 4, b f Never So Bold—Laugharne **Sir Stanley & Lady Grinstead**
7 **PRIZE PUPIL (IRE)**, 4, b c Royal Academy (USA)—Bestow **Mr Shunya Seki**

THREE-YEAR-OLDS

8 **ATOMIC SHELL (CAN)**, ch c Geiger Counter (USA)—In Your Sights (USA) **Mr Walter Grubmuller**
9 **BLESSED SPIRIT**, ch f Statoblest—Kukri **Mr W. R. Stuttaford**
10 **BLUEBERRY FIELDS**, gr f Shernazar—Be Easy **Mr A. E. Oppenheimer**
11 **CHARISSE DANCER**, b f Dancing Dissident—Cadisa **B. R. A. T. S.**
12 **CHARMING ADMIRAL (IRE)**, b g Shareef Dancer (USA)—Lilac Charm **Mr Walter Grubmuller**
13 **FAITH ALONE**, b f Safawan—Strapless **Mrs R. M. S. Neave**
14 **INDUNA MKUBWA**, ch c Be My Chief (USA)—Hyatti **Induna Racing Partners**
15 **IVOR'S DEED**, b c Shadeed (USA)—Gena Ivor (USA) **Mr Mervyn Ayers**
16 **LADY THIANG**, gr f Petong—Good Woman **Mr W. Wallick**
17 **MIDNIGHT ESCAPE**, b g Aragon—Executive Lady **Mr Mervyn Ayers**

MR C. F. WALL—continued

18 **MR SPEAKER (IRE)**, ch g Statoblest—Casting Vote (USA) **Mr David Allan**
19 **NEEDLE MATCH**, ch c Royal Academy (USA)—Miss Tatting (USA) **Mr Peter R. Pritchard**
20 **NORTHERN MIRACLE (IRE)**, b f Distinctly North (USA)—Danny's Miracle **Mr J. J. Ratcliffe**
21 **SHARP 'N' SHADY**, b f Sharpo—Shadiliya **Mr W. Wallick**
22 **THIRLMERE**, ch f Cadeaux Genereux—Laugharne **Sir Stanley & Lady Grinstead**

TWO-YEAR-OLDS

23 **MISS KALAGLOW**, b f 6/3 Kalaglow—Dame du Moulin (Shiny Tenth) **Mrs C. A. Wall**
24 **NOBLE ROCKET**, b f 9/5 Reprimand—Noble Lustre (USA) (Lyphard's Wish (FR)) **Mr David Allan**
25 **QUARTERSTAFF**, b c 16/4 Charmer—Quaranta (Hotfoot) **Mr Walter Grubmuller**
26 **REAL ESTATE**, b c 25/3 High Estate—Haitienne (FR) (Green Dancer (USA)) **Mr N. Ahamad**
27 **B c 21/3** Rudimentary (USA)—Revoke (USA) (Riverman (USA)) **Mr Walter Grubmuller**
28 **SALLY GREEN (IRE)**, b f 30/3 Common Grounds—Redwood Hut (Habitat) **Mr K. V. Stenborg**
29 **SAVU SEA (IRE)**, b f 14/1 Slip Anchor—Soemba (General Assembly (USA)) **Mr A. E. Oppenheimer**
30 **SUZIE DIAMOND (IRE)**, b f 5/3 Suave Dancer (USA)—Hot Lavender (CAN) (Shadeed (USA)) **Mr David Allan**
31 **TONIGHT'S PRIZE (IRE)**, b c 2/3 Night Shift (USA)—Bestow (Shirley Heights) **Mr Shunya Seki**
32 **TRIPLE HIGH**, b f 1/3 Reprimand—Rambadale (Vaigly Great) **Triple S Partners**
33 **B f 28/4** Dancing Dissident—Unspoiled (Tina's Pet) **The Boadicea Partners**

Other Owners: Mr S. Atkin, Mr T. Bater, Mr R. De Beaumont, Mr W. G. Bovill, Mr P. Brook, Mr R. Fraiser, Mr J. Gosling, Mr R. Grocott, Mr A. Gundersen, Mr C. J. A. Hughes, Mr Alan Martin, Mr A. J. Neal, Caroline Lady Newman, Mr A. E. Reeve, Prudence Lady Salt, Mr John E. Sims, Mr M. Sinclair, Miss R. Spence, Mrs S. Spence, Mrs R. A. Sunnucks, Mr M. Thompson, Mr M. Tilbrook, Mrs J. F. Toms, Mrs C. J. Walker, Mr J. H. Wall.

Jockeys (Flat): G Duffield, W Lord, W Woods (8-2, w.a.).

Apprentices: P Clarke (7-10), L Newton (7-12).

Lady Rider: Mrs Carole Wall (8-0).

613 MR T. R. WALL, Church Stretton

Postal: **Harton Manor, Harton, Church Stretton, Shropshire, SY6 7DL.**
Phone: **(01694) 724144 FAX (01694) 724144**

1 **ASHCAL LADY**, 5, b m Rolfe (USA)—Highlands Park **Mr Stephen Walker**
2 **BILL AND WIN**, 5, b g Faustus (USA)—Water Folly **Mr S. H. Pickering**
3 6, Ch g Rakaposhi King—Cristina Times **Mr E. A. Lee**
4 7, B g Idiot's Delight—Cristina Times **Mr E. A. Lee**
5 **DORMSTON BOYO**, 6, b g Sula Bula—March At Dawn **Mr T. W. Lowe**
6 **MISS CHARLIE**, 6, ch m Pharly (FR)—Close To You **Mr A. H. Bennett**
7 **QUEENS STROLLER (IRE)**, 5, b m Pennine Walk—Mount Isa **Mr P. Stringer**
8 **SISTER ELLY**, 6, b m Bairn (USA)—Arbor Lane **Mr R. Cave**
9 **STORM WARRIOR**, 11, b g Main Reef—Spadilla **Mrs J. A. Wall**
10 **VELVET HEART (IRE)**, 6, b m Damister (USA)—Bottom Line **Mr David M. Williams**
11 **VIZARD (IRE)**, 4, ch g Old Vic—Impudent Miss **Vizard Racing**

TWO-YEAR-OLDS

12 **B f** Warrshan (USA)—Aldwick Colonnade (Kind of Hush) **Mr R. Cave**
13 **B f** Rambo Dancer (CAN)—Warning Bell (Bustino) **Mr David M. Williams**

Other Owners: Mrs R. Lowe.

614   MRS K. WALTON, Middleham

Postal: **Sharp Hill Farm, Middleham, Leyburn, North Yorks, DL8 4QY.**

Phone: **(01969) 622250**

1 **GEMIKOSIX (FR)**, 6, b g Bikala—Gemia (FR) **Mrs K. Walton**
2 **NORTHUMBRIAN KING**, 10, b g Indian King (USA)—Tuna **Mrs K. Walton**

Jockey (NH): J Callaghan (10-0).

615   MR P. T. WALWYN, Lambourn

Postal: **Windsor House, Lambourn, Hungerford, Berks, RG17 8NR.**

Phone: **LAMBOURN (01488) 71347 FAX (01488) 72664**

1 **BEN GUNN**, 4, b g Faustus (USA)—Pirate Maid **Mr Michael White**
2 **MURAJJA (USA)**, 4, ch c Silver Hawk (USA)—Halholah (USA) **Mr Hamdan Al Maktoum**
3 **STALLED (IRE)**, 6, b g Glenstal (USA)—Chauffeuse **Mrs P. T. Walwyn**
4 **STORMY PETREL (IRE)**, 7, br m Strong Gale—Gorryelm **Mrs A. M. MacEwan**
5 **TOM MORGAN**, 5, b g Faustus (USA)—Pirate Maid **Mr Michael White**

THREE-YEAR-OLDS

6 **ALAJYAL (IRE)**, ch f Kris—Yaqut (USA) **Mr Hamdan Al Maktoum**
7 **ALAMBAR (IRE)**, b c Fairy King (USA)—Lightino **Mr Hamdan Al Maktoum**
8 **ARCADY**, b f Slip Anchor—Elysian **Mr A. D. G. Oldrey**
9 **AZWAH (USA)**, b f Danzig (USA)—Magic Slipper **Mr Hamdan Al Maktoum**
10 **BULLFINCH**, ch c Anshan—Lambay **Mr Robert Cooper**
11 **BULLPEN BELLE**, b f Relief Pitcher—Hopeful Waters **Mr J. D. A. Wallinger**
12 **FRAN GODFREY**, b f Taufan (USA)—One Last Glimpse **Mr S. W. E. J. Slack**
13 **HILAALA (USA)**, ch f Elmaamul (USA)—Halholah (USA) **Mr Hamdan Al Maktoum**
14 **IAMUS**, ch c Most Welcome—Icefern **Hesmonds Stud**
15 **IRISH KINSMAN**, b g Distant Relative—Inesdela **Mr P. J. H. Wills**
16 **KAWANIN**, ch f Generous (IRE)—Nahilah **Mr Hamdan Al Maktoum**
17 **MANALOJ (USA)**, ch c Gone West (FR)—Deviltante (USA) **Mr Hamdan Al Maktoum**
18 **MARJAANA (IRE)**, b f Shaadi (USA)—Funun (USA) **Mr Hamdan Al Maktoum**
19 **MISS PRAVDA**, ch f Soviet Star (USA)—Miss Paige (AUS) **Lord Howard de Walden**
20 **MUA-TAB**, ch f Polish Precedent (USA)—Alsabiha **Mr Hamdan Al Maktoum**
21 **RAED**, b c Nashwan (USA)—Awayed (USA) **Mr Hamdan Al Maktoum**
22 **SEIRENES**, b f Formidable (USA)—Seriema **Hesmonds Stud**
23 **SMITHEREENS**, ch f Primo Dominie—Splintering **Major & Mrs Kennard and Partners**
24 **TARF (USA)**, ch f Diesis—Tadwin **Mr Hamdan Al Maktoum**
25 **TAWAADED (IRE)**, ch f Nashwan (USA)—Thaidah (CAN) **Mr Hamdan Al Maktoum**
26 **TEMPTRESS**, br f Kalaglow—Circe **Mr A. D. G. Oldrey**

TWO-YEAR-OLDS

27 **ARRUHAN (IRE)**, b f 20/4 Mujtahid (USA)—Wakayi (Persian Bold) **Mr Hamdan Al Maktoum**
28 **ATNAB (USA)**, b br f 27/4 Riverman (USA)—Magic Slipper (Habitat) **Mr Hamdan Al Maktoum**
29 **BERT**, b c 9/3 Mujtahid (USA)—Keswa (Kings Lake (USA)) **Mr Rupert Hambro**
30 **BRAZILIA**, b f 10/3 Forzando—Dominio (IRE) (Dominion) **Major & Mrs Kennard and Partners**
31 **DANKA**, gr c 16/2 Petong—Angel Drummer (Dance In Time (CAN)) **Mr M. G. St Quinton**
32 **FARHAN (USA)**, b c 3/2 Lear Fan—Mafatin (IRE) (Sadler's Wells (USA)) **Mr Hamdan Al Maktoum**
33 **HANAJIR (IRE)**, b f 7/3 Cadeaux Genereux—Muhit (USA) (El Gran Senor (USA)) **Mr Hamdan Al Maktoum**
34 **HAPPY**, b c 24/3 Rock City—Joyful Thought (Green Desert (USA)) **Hesmonds Stud**
35 **HATTAB (IRE)**, b c 21/2 Marju (IRE)—Funun (USA) (Fappiano (USA)) **Mr Hamdan Al Maktoum**
36 **HUSUN (USA)**, b f 19/1 Sheikh Albadou—Tadwin (Never So Bold) **Mr Hamdan Al Maktoum**
37 **IJTINAB**, b c 28/2 Green Desert (USA)—Nahilah (Habitat) **Mr Hamdan Al Maktoum**
38 **IKHTISAR (USA)**, b br f 22/3 Slew O' Gold (USA)—Halholah (USA) (Secreto (USA)) **Mr Hamdan Al Maktoum**
39 **IRTIFA**, ch f 28/3 Lahib (USA)—Thaidah (CAN) (Vice Regent (CAN)) **Mr Hamdan Al Maktoum**
40 **KAWA-IB (IRE)**, b f 10/4 Nashwan (USA)—Awayed (USA) (Sir Ivor) **Mr Hamdan Al Maktoum**
41 **LABEQ (IRE)**, b c 25/2 Lycius (USA)—Ahbab (IRE) (Ajdal (USA)) **Mr Hamdan Al Maktoum**

MR P. T. WALWYN—continued

42 **MIDATLANTIC**, b c 21/4 Midyan (USA)—Secret Waters (Pharly (FR)) **Mrs Roger Waters**
43 **MISTER JAY**, b c 13/3 Batshoof—Portvasco (Sharpo) **Mrs Henry Keswick**
44 **MYSTIQUE**, b f 21/4 Mystiko (USA)—Sound of The Sea (Windjammer (USA)) **Hesmonds Stud**
45 **RIGHTY HO**, b c 25/3 Reprimand—Challanging (Mill Reef (USA)) **Eric Perry**
46 B f 1/2 Midyan (USA)—Scarlet Veil (Tyrnavos)
47 **TAJREBAH (USA)**, b f 18/3 Dayjur (USA)—Petrava (NZ) (Imposing (AUS)) **Mr Hamdan Al Maktoum**
48 **TEUTONIC LASS (IRE)**, b f 15/4 Night Shift (USA)—Highness Lady (GER) (Cagliostro (GER)) **Hesmonds Stud**

Other Owners: W. F. Macauley, Mr N. H. T. Wrigley.

Jockeys (Flat): W Carson (7-10), P Eddery (8-4, w.a.), R Hills (8-0).

Amateur: Mr P Macewan (10-7).

Lady Rider: Marchioness Of Blandford (9-5).

616   MR M. WANE, Richmond

Postal: **Barn House Racing Stables, Langdale, Melsonby, Richmond, DL10 5PW.**
Phone: **(01325) 718046**

1 **AL JINN**, 5, ch g Hadeer—Mrs Musgrove **Mr Greg Gregory**
2 **BACKHANDER (IRE)**, 4, b g Cadeaux Genereux—Chevrefeuille **Mrs C. Barlow**
3 **BLOW DRY (IRE)**, 6, b g Glenstal (USA)—Haco **Mr Gerard Moran**
4 **CHINA HAND (IRE)**, 4, ch g Salt Dome (USA)—China Blue **Penny Home Preservation**
5 **CONDIHAME**, 6, b g Lidhame—Connaught Queen **Mr F. Peckitt**
6 **DIAMOND CROWN (IRE)**, 5, ch g Kris—State Treasure (USA) **Mr J. M. Pickup**
7 **INVIGILATE**, 7, ch g Viking (USA)—Maria da Gloria **Mrs Karen S. Pratt**
8 **NEVER SO TRUE**, 5, b m Never So Bold—Cottage Pie **James S. Kennerley and Miss Jenny Hall**
9 **PAINTED LADY**, 4, b f Statoblest—Louise Moillon **Mr B. L. Davies**
10 **ROYAL DOME (IRE)**, 4, b g Salt Dome (USA)—Brook's Dilemma **Mr G. W. Jones**
11 **SWAN AT WHALLEY**, 4, b g Statoblest—My Precious Daisy **Capt H. H. Barlow**
12 **TEN PAST SIX**, 4, ch c Kris—Tashinsky (USA) **James S. Kennerley and Miss Jenny Hall**
13 **TERTIUM (IRE)**, 4, b c Nordico (USA)—Nouniya **Mr W. N. Smith**
14 **TOP SKIPPER (IRE)**, 4, b g Nordico (USA)—Scarlet Slipper **Mr James S. Kennerley**

THREE-YEAR-OLDS

15 **ABBOTT OF WHALLEY**, b g Marching On—La Pepper **Swan At Whalley Racing Club Ltd**
16 **HOH MAJESTIC (IRE)**, b g Soviet Lad (USA)—Sevens Are Wild **Capt H. H. Barlow**
17 **PRIDE OF WHALLEY (IRE)**, b f Fayruz—Wilderness **Swan At Whalley Racing Club Ltd**
18 **TRICKLEDOWN**, b f Dowsing—Pillowing **Mr S. P. Brotton**

TWO-YEAR-OLDS

19 **PRINCE DOME (IRE)**, ch c 27/1 Salt Dome (USA)—Blazing Glory (IRE) (Glow (USA)) **Mr G. W. Jones**

Other Owners: Mr B. R. Bradbury, Mrs B. Brotton, Mr M. J. Edmondson, Mrs P. E. Edmondson, Mr Matthew M. Elves, Mrs H. Wane, Mrs H. H. Wane.

617   MRS V. C. WARD, Grantham

Postal: **Aisby House, Aisby, Grantham, Lincs, NG32 3NF.**
Phone: **(01529) 455260**

1 **COUP DE VENT**, 6, ch g Viking (USA)—Callistro **Mrs V. C. Ward**
2 **DOCTOR DUNKLIN (USA)**, 7, gr g Family Doctor (USA)—Mis Jenifer's Idea (USA) **Mrs V. C. Ward**
3 **ESCADARO (USA)**, 7, b g Liloy (FR)—Mlle Chanteuse (USA) **Mrs V. C. Ward**

MRS V. C. WARD—continued

4 **GREEN CRUSADER**, 5, b g Green Desert (USA)—Hysterical **Mrs V. C. Ward**
5 **HAMADRYAD (IRE)**, 8, b g Fairy King (USA)—Clifden Bottoms **Mrs V. C. Ward**
6 **MISTER HOCHBERG**, 10, b g Croghan Hill—Brenclaric **Mrs V. C. Ward**
7 **SALMAN (USA)**, 10, b g Nain Bleu (FR)—H M S Pellinore (USA) **Mrs V. C. Ward**
8 **SOLOMAN SPRINGS (USA)**, 6, ch g Wajima (USA)—Malilla (CHI) **Mrs V. C. Ward**
9 **THE JEWELLER**, 9, ch g Le Bavard (FR)—Blackrath Gem **Mrs V. C. Ward**

618 MRS BARBARA WARING, Chippenham

Postal: **Lucknam Park Stud, Colerne, Chippenham, Wilts, SN14 8AZ.**
Phone: **BOX (01225) 742044 MOBILE (0860) 491636**

1 **ALTERMEERA**, 8, br g Noalto—Mac's Melody **Mr R. J. Simmons**
2 **AMILLIONMEMORIES**, 6, br g Macmillion—March Memories **S. H. Merritt & Elizabeth Burns**
3 **BUSTER**, 8, br g Macmillion—Valsette **Mrs Barbara Waring**
4 **FULL QUIVER**, 11, br g Gorytus (USA)—Much Pleasure **Mr Richard Parker**
5 **LILLY THE FILLY**, 5, br m Macmillion—March Memories **Racehorse Owners Bath Ltd**
6 **LUCKNAM DREAMER**, 8, b g Macmillion—River Damsel **Racehorse Owners Bath Ltd**
7 **ROSE OF MACMILLION**, 7, b m Macmillion—Tic-On-Rose **D. Jones M. Doran E. A. Davies**
8 **ROSS GRAHAM**, 8, gr g Macmillion—Play It Sam **Racehorse Owners Bath Ltd**
9 **TOMMY COOPER**, 5, br h Macmillion—My Charade **C. Griffin, E. Davies, B. Wilton**

THREE-YEAR-OLDS

10 **ABSOLUTELYSTUNNING**, br f Aragon—Dramatic Mood **Racehorse Owners Bath Ltd**
11 **BRONHALLOW**, b g Belmez (USA)—Grey Twig **Racehorse Owners Bath Ltd**
12 **LOUISIANA PURCHASE**, b g Macmillion—My Charade **Mr Ian Douglas**

Other Owners: Mr Mike Burns, Mr Harry Chisman, Mr R. Mercer.

Jockey (Flat): C Rutter.

Jockeys (NH): E Byrne (10-0), P Holley (9-7).

619 MR KEITH O. WARNER, Stafford

Postal: **Meadow View Cottage, The Pavement, Brewood, Stafford. ST19 9BZ**
Phone: **(01902) 850814 MOBILE (0831) 322199**

1 **APPLIANCEOFSCIENCE**, 9, b g Bairn (USA)—Moonlight Serenade **Mr M. K. Warner**
2 **EMPEROR CHANG (USA)**, 9, b g Wavering Monarch (USA)—Movin Mitzi (USA) **Mr K. O. Warner**
3 **MR PERSONALITY**, 4, ch g Bairn (USA)—Gentle Gain **Mr K. O. Warner**
4 **MY-UGLY-DUCKLING**, 9, ch g Longleat (USA)—Snow Goose **Mr K. O. Warner**

620 MR F. WATSON, Sedgefield

Postal: **Beacon Hill Farm, Sedgefield, Stockton-on-Tees, Cleveland, TS21 3HN.**
Phone: **(01740) 620582 MOBILE (0973) 632935**

1 **ALLEZ HOMBRE**, 5, br g Cadeaux Genereux—Aphrosina **M. D. Hetherington (Packaging) Ltd**
2 **BUNTY'S FRIEND**, 5, ch m Highlands—Buy Nordan **Mr F. Watson**
3 **GREAT ORATION (IRE)**, 7, b br g Simply Great (FR)—Spun Gold **M. D. Hetherington (Packaging) Ltd**
4 **HIGHLAND GEM**, 7, b m Highlands—Gemma Jean **Mr F. Watson**
5 **MOOFAJI**, 5, b h Night Shift (USA)—Three Piece **M. D. Hetherington (Packaging) Ltd**

MR F. WATSON—continued

6 PERSIAN LION, 7, br g Reesh—Parijoun Mr J. D. Blythe
7 RAASED, 4, b g Unfuwain (USA)—Sajjaya (USA) Mr F. Watson
8 RAMBO'S RUMTIME, 4, b f Rambo Dancer (CAN)—Errol Emerald Mr F. Watson
9 SHAMOKIN, 4, b c Green Desert (USA)—Shajan Marson Investments Ltd
10 THE BEACON RUSTLER, 6, b g Highlands—Unique Lady Mr F. Watson
11 THWAAB, 4, b g Dominion—Velvet Habit Mr F. Watson
12 TOPFORMER, 9, gr g Highlands—Umtali M. D. Hetherington (Packaging) Ltd

THREE-YEAR-OLDS

13 FINESTATETOBEIN, ch f Northern State (USA)—Haywain Mr F. Watson
14 INSIDEOUT, b c Macmillion—Parijoun Mr J. D. Blythe
15 PACKITIN, b g Rich Charlie—Sound Type M. D. Hetherington (Packaging) Ltd

621   MR T. R. WATSON, Gainsborough

Postal: School Yard Racing Stables, Northfield Lane, Willoughton, Gainsborough, DN21 5RT.

Phone: (01427) 667176 FAX (01427) 667176

1 ABDUL EMIR, 9, b g Ovac (ITY)—Azul Mrs R. T. Watson
2 AUNTIE LORNA, 7, b m Uncle Pokey—Bronze Tango Mr R. P. Brett
3 CUILLIN CAPER, 4, b f Scottish Reel—That Space Mr R. T. Watson
4 DOM PEDRO, 11, ch g Le Moss—Ursula's Choice Mr G. H. Dodsworth
5 GOLF BALL, 6, b g Pollerton—Blue Breeze (USA) Newitt and Co Ltd
6 KELLY THE BUCK, 8, b g Netherkelly—Buck's Bloom Robin C. B. Brett
7 MICK'S TYCOON (IRE), 8, b g Last Tycoon—Ladytown Mr G. H. Dodsworth
8 PUSHKA FAIR, 5, b g Salse (USA)—Orient Mr R. T. Watson
9 SEARCHLIGHT (IRE), 8, ch g Seymour Hicks (FR)—Night Caller Mrs R. T. Watson
10 SOCCER BALL, 6, b g Idiot's Delight—Over Beyond Newitt and Co Ltd

THREE-YEAR-OLDS

11 DESERT LYNX (IRE), b f Green Desert (USA)—Sweeping Mrs R. T. Watson
12 MR CARROT, ch g Robin-A-Tiptoe—Miss Flossa (FR) Mr R. P. Brett
13 PING-PONG BALL, b f Statoblest—Desert Ditty Newitt and Co Ltd
14 RHYTHMIC BALL, ch f Classic Music (USA)—Chrisanthy Newitt and Co Ltd
15 SAXIFRAGA, ch g Scottish Reel—Buck's Bloom Mrs R. T. Watson
16 UNIHOC BALL, ch f Indian Ridge—Soon To Be Newitt and Co Ltd

TWO-YEAR-OLDS

17 SOMETHING BLUE, b f 14/5 Petong—Blueit (FR) Miss S. Hoare

Other Owners: Mr F. T. Adams, Mrs J. Brett, Mr G. H. Dodsworth, Mrs R. Hoare, Mrs R. Ralli, Mr Michael Smith, Mr T. R. Watson.

622   MR J. W. WATTS, Richmond

Postal: Hurgill Lodge, Richmond, North Yorks, DL10 4TA.

Phone: (01748) 850444 FAX (01748) 850374 MOBILE (0836) 224721

1 COLWAY RAKE, 5, b g Salse (USA)—Barely Hot Mr R. Coleman
2 GOOD HAND (USA), 10, ch g Northjet—Ribonette (USA) Mrs M. M. Haggas
3 HABETA (USA), 10, ch h Habitat—Prise Mr R. D. Bickenson
4 MADLY SHARP, 5, ch g Sharpo—Madison Girl Lord Swaythling
5 SAGEBRUSH ROLLER, 8, br g Sharpo—Sunita Mr A. K. Collins

THREE-YEAR-OLDS

6 AMANITA, ch f Lead On Time (USA)—Amana River (USA) Sheikh Mohammed
7 AMUSING ASIDE (IRE), ch f In The Wings—Most Amusing Sheikh Mohammed

MR J. W. WATTS—continued

8 **BOLD FUTURE (IRE)**, b g Treasure Kay—Mother Courage **Mrs P. M. Watts**
9 **DIMINUET**, b f Dominion—Primulette **Mrs S. Cunliffe-Lister**
10 **LADYKIRK**, b f Slip Anchor—Lady Day (FR) **Duke of Sutherland**
11 **MYSTIC MAID (IRE)**, b f Mujtahid (USA)—Dandizette **Sheikh Mohammed**
12 **PERSIAN SECRET (FR)**, b f Persian Heights—Rahaam (USA) **Sheikh Mohammed**
13 **PHARMACY**, b f Mtoto—Anodyne **Lady Jane Kaplan**
14 **ROYAL MARK (IRE)**, b c Fairy King (USA)—Take Your Mark (USA) **Lord Swaythling**

TWO-YEAR-OLDS

15 Ch f 25/3 Polish Precedent—Amana River (USA) (Raise A Cup (USA)) **Sheikh Mohammed**
16 **BARITONE**, b c 11/3 Midyan (USA)—Zinzi (Song) **Lord Swaythling**
17 B c 4/4 Slip Anchor—Birthdays' Child (Caerleon (USA))
18 B c 7/3 Thatching—Calpella (Ajdal (USA)) **Sheikh Mohammed**
19 **COLWAY RITZ**, b c 22/4 Rudimentary (USA)—Million Heiress (Auction Ring) **Mr R. Coleman**
20 B c 8/4 Timeless Times (USA)—Crimson Dawn (Manado) **The Hurgill Lodge Partnership**
21 **DEMOLITION MAN**, br c 7/3 Primo Dominie—Town Lady (Town Crier) **Mrs K. Fritz**
22 **DENTON LAD**, b c 21/4 Prince Sabo—Dahlawise (IRE) (Caerleon (USA)) **Mrs M. Irwin**
23 Ch f 15/3 Emarati (USA)—Gitee (FR) (Carwhite) **The Hurgill Lodge Partnership**
24 Gr c 21/2 Old Vic—Integrity (Reform) **Sheikh Mohammed**
25 **LA LINEA**, gr f 25/3 Rock City—Altaia (FR) (Sicyos (USA)) **Sir Gordon Reece**
26 B f 19/5 Prince Sabo—Mortal Sin (USA) (Green Forest (USA)) **Duke of Sutherland**
27 B c 26/3 Mtoto—Nadina (Shirley Heights) **Sheikh Mohammed**
28 Gr c 13/4 Absalom—Sabonis (USA) (The Minstrel (CAN)) **The Hurgill Lodge Partnership**
29 **SHADED (IRE)**, b c 23/4 Night Shift (USA)—Sarsaparilla (FR) (Shirley Heights) **Lord Swaythling**
30 Ch c 11/5 Blushing John (USA)—Star Empress (USA) (Disciplinarian) **Miss Suzi Shoemaker**
31 B c 23/4 Silver Hawk (USA)—Sugar Hollow (USA) (Val de L'Orne (FR)) **Sheikh Mohammed**
32 B c 15/3 Rambo Dancer (CAN)—Try Vickers (USA) (Fuzzbuster (USA)) **The Hurgill Lodge Partnership**
33 Gr c 28/2 Ajraas (USA)—Winter Lady (Bonne Noel) **The Hurgill Lodge Partnership**

Other Owners: Mr C. C. Campbell Golding, Mrs B. J. Carrington, Mr J. P. Carrington, Lord Dalmeny, Lord Derby, Mr D. Dyer, Mr Warren Lee Primhak, Bryan Robson, Ron Wood Greeting Cards Ltd, Mr R. E. Sangster, Mrs D. M. Swinburn, The Earl Of Swinton, Mr Jeremy J. Thompson, Mr J. W. Watts, Viscountess Whitelaw, Mrs S. J. Wood.

623 MR H. J. M. WEBB, Faringdon

Postal: **Peartree Farm, Gt. Coxwell, Faringdon, Oxon, SN7 7NG.**

Phone: **(01367) 240173 FAX (01367) 240173**

1 **CATWALKER (IRE)**, 5, b g Reasonable (FR)—Norse Lady **Mrs I. M. Webb**
2 4, B g Green Adventure (USA)—Miss Inigo **Mr H. J. M. Webb**
3 **SUNDAY JIM**, 12, b g Jimsun—Berkeley Belle **Mr H. J. M. Webb**

THREE-YEAR-OLDS

4 B g Ballacashtal (CAN)—Miss Inigo **H. J. M. Webb**

624 MR P. R. WEBBER, Banbury

Postal: **Cropredy Lawn, Mollington, Banbury, Oxon, OX17 1DR.**

Phone: **(01295) 750226 FAX (01295) 758482 MOBILE (0836) 232465**

1 **ALTERNATION (FR)**, 7, ch m Electric—Alanood **Mr David Wade-Jones**
2 **BEL PROMISE (IRE)**, 7, ch m Soughaan (USA)—Linbel **Mrs M. Hartop**
3 **BOLD LOOK**, 5, b g Never So Bold—Madame Bovary **Miss Joanne Coward**
4 **BRAZIL OR BUST (IRE)**, 5, b g Bustino—Coffee **Mrs C. A. Waters**
5 **CROPREDY LAD**, 9, b g St Columbus—Lucky Story **Mr Richard Hall**
6 **DON'T MIND IF I DO (IRE)**, 5, gr g Roselier (FR)—Ginger Dee **Mrs J. Addison**
7 **ELFAST**, 13, b g Neltino—Niagara Rhythm **Mrs John Webber**
8 **EMERALD RULER**, 9, b g Tender King—Blue Gulf **Mr Roger Nicholls**

MR P. R. WEBBER—continued

9 **FLYING INSTRUCTOR**, 6, gr g Neltino—Flying Mistress **Lady Lyell**
10 **FRESHMANS ESSAY (IRE)**, 8, b g Mandalus—Mistress Nova **Mrs P. L. Aldersey**
11 **GOLDEN OLIVE (IRE)**, 7, ch m Roselier (FR)—Mary Deen **Mrs Mary Grant**
12 **JACOB'S WIFE**, 6, gr m Baron Blakeney—Vido **The Black Sheep Flock**
13 **JOHN DRUMM**, 5, gr g Alias Smith (USA)—Girl of Shiraz **Mr Andrew Jenkins**
14 **JOYFUL RUNNER (IRE)**, 6, b m Over The River (FR)—Joyful Anna **Mrs David Blackburn**
15 **LAND AFAR**, 9, b g Dominion—Jouvencelle **Mr T. J. Ford**
16 **LARKS TAIL**, 8, b m Crested Lark—Lucky Story **Mr P. S. Wilsdon**
17 **LIMITED LIABILITY**, 6, b g Bustino—Fine Asset **Miss Elizabeth Aldous**
18 **MID DAY CHASER (IRE)**, 5, b m Homo Sapien—Noon Hunting **Tavern Racing**
19 **MWEENISH**, 14, b g Callernish—No Trix **Mr Richard Hall**
20 **PEPPER'N THYNE (IRE)**, 6, b m Good Thyne (USA)—Peppardstownlady **Lady Lloyd Webber**
21 **REAL ALE**, 6, gr g Another Realm—Tentraco Lady **The Real Ale Racing Partnership**
22 **RICHELIEU (IRE)**, 4, ch c Kris—Madame Dubois **Mr P. A. Leonard**
23 **RULING MAN**, 6, br g Funny Man—Star Ruler **Mr S. E. Honour**
24 **SCOTTISH BAMBI**, 8, ch g Scottish Reel—Bambolona **Mr William J. Kelly**
25 **SKEOUGH (IRE)**, 8, b g Tanfirion—Birchwood **Mrs R. Wilson & Mrs C. Wilson**
26 **SPORTING RISK**, 4, b g Risk Me (FR)—Sunday Sport's Pet **Miss Joanne Coward**
27 **WHAT A STOREY**, 6, b g Crested Lark—Lucky Story **Mr P. S. Wilsdon**

TWO-YEAR-OLDS

28 B c 8/2 Alzao (USA)—Elevated (Shirley Heights) **Mr P. A. Leonard**
29 B f 15/4 Lahib (USA)—Karine (Habitat) **Mr P. Webber**
30 B f 25/5 Night Shift (USA)—Phantom Row (Adonijah) **Jan Steinmann**
31 B c 7/5 Akarad (FR)—Sioux City (Simply Great (FR)) **Mr P. A. Leonard**

Other Owners: Mr R. T. Anderson, Mr A. J. Barritt, Mr A. Bond, Mr Roger Brant, Major J. L. Damant, Miss M. L. Day, Mr N. J. Evans, Mrs C. Gale, Ms C. A. Gray, Mr K. P. Hills, Mr V. Kilkenny, Mr S. Laughton, Mr K. E. McCarthy, Mrs C. M. Meyrick, Mr G. C. Myddelton, Mr J. G. O'Neill, Mr D. E. Popham, Mr Trevor Rathbone, Mr D. Shockledge, Mr M. L. Sibley, Mr Vernon Taylor, Mrs M. Thomlinson, Mr J. Webber, Mr Godfrey Wilson.

Jockeys (NH): R Bellamy (10-0), G McCourt (10-9).

Amateur: Mr P Scott (9-7).

625   MR C. V. WEEDON, Chiddingfold

Postal: **Robins Farm, Fisher Lane, Chiddingfold, Surrey, GU8 4TB.**
Phone: **(0831) 115009 (01428) 683344**

1 **ALFION (IRE)**, 7, b g Saxon Farm—Knockeevan Girl **Mr Alf Chadwick**
2 5, B g King's Ride—Brownstown Lady **Mr Patrick Evans**
3 5, Ch g Electric—Dream Toi **Mr David Knox**
4 **EQUINIMITY**, 7, b m Lord Ballina (AUS)—Just Irene **Mr Tony Rooth**
5 **FASHION LEADER (IRE)**, 5, br g Supreme Leader—Record Halmony **Mr David Knox**
6 **FOEHN GALE (IRE)**, 5, b m Strong Gale—Woodford Princess **Mr David Knox**
7 **FOREST FEATHER (IRE)**, 8, b g Arapahos (FR)—Mistress Boreen **Mr David Knox**
8 **HEDGEHOPPER (IRE)**, 8, b g Henbit (USA)—Selham **Mr Tim Davis**
9 **INCULCATE (IRE)**, 5, b g Millfontaine—Last Thought **Swan Racing**
10 **INVER CLOUD (IRE)**, 7, b g Bustomi—Raise The Clouds **Mr Tony Rooth**
11 **LONESOME TRAIN (USA)**, 7, ch g Crafty Prospector (USA)—Alaki Miss (USA) **Mr Simon Gay**
12 **MIRACLE MAN**, 8, b g Kemal (FR)—Knockeevan Girl **Mr Patrick Evans**
13 **MRS BARTY (IRE)**, 6, b br m King's Ride—Black Rapper **Mr Martin N. Peters**
14 **RICH LIFE (IRE)**, 6, b g Dance of Life (USA)—Ringawoody **Mrs Susan Gay**
15 **SOU SOU WESTERLY (IRE)**, 5, b g Strong Gale—Fair Fashion **P & D Syndicate**
16 **STORMTRACKER (IRE)**, 7, br g Strong Gale—Stay As You Are **Mr Tim Davis**
17 **SWEETLISAJANE (IRE)**, 5, b m Strong Gale—Royal Secret **Mr Colin Weedon**

MR C. V. WEEDON—continued

Other Owners: Mr Barry Bethell, Mr C. H. Gay, Mrs A. D. Gray, Mr Colin D. Hale, Mr P. A. Heath, Mr Richard Lockwood, Mr John Marsh, Mrs Stephanie Marsh, Mr E. J. Pearce, Power Display (Engineering) Ltd, Star Racing, Mr Michael Street, Town And Country Tyre Services Limited.

Conditional: B T McGann (9-7).

626　　　MR P. WEGMANN, Gloucester

Postal: **Maisemore Park, Maisemore, Gloucester, GL2 8HX.**

Phone: **(01452) 301332 FAX (01452) 505002**

1 **CAPTAIN STOCKFORD**, 9, b g Grey Ghost—Stubbin Moor **Mr P. Wegmann**
2 **HASHAR (IRE)**, 8, b g Darshaan—Hazy Idea **Mr P. Wegmann**
3 **OWENS DELIGHT**, 6, b g Idiot's Delight—Tuggles Owen **Mr P. Wegmann**
4 **SARSTA GRAI**, 8, b m Blakeney—Horton Line **Mr P. Wegmann**
5 **SONNAURA**, 6, b m Sonnen Gold—Centaura **Mr P. Wegmann**
6 **STRONG GLEN (IRE)**, 8, br g Strong Gale—Merry And Bright **Mr P. Wegmann**

Apprentice: Simon Fowler (9-10).

Conditional: Simon Fowler (9-10).

627　MR D. K. WELD M.V.B. M.R.C.V.S., The Curragh

Postal: **Rosewell House, The Curragh, Co. Kildare, Irish Republic.**

Phone: **353-45-41273/41476 FAX 353-45-41119**

1 **ANY DREAM (IRE)**, 4, b f Shernazar—Danzig Lass (USA) **Mrs C. L. Weld**
2 **ARCHIVE FOOTAGE**, 4, b c Sadler's Wells (USA)—Trusted Partner (USA) **Moyglare Stud Farm**
3 **BLAZING SPECTACLE**, 6, b h Sadler's Wells—Temporary Lull (USA) **Michael J. Smurfit**
4 **CELTIC LORE**, 4, b g Caerleon (USA)—Slender Style (USA) **Moyglare Stud Farm**
5 **DEFINITE ARTICLE**, 4, br c Indian Ridge—Summer Fashion **Moyglare Stud Farm**
6 **FORTUNE AND FAME**, 9, b g Camden Town—Corrie Royal **Michael J. Smurfit**
7 **FREE TO SPEAK (IRE)**, 4, b c Be My Guest (USA)—Love For Poetry **Moyglare Stud Farm**
8 **MUNIF (IRE)**, 4, ch c Caerleon (USA)—Forest Lair **Hamdan Al Maktoum**
9 **NAUTICAL PET (IRE)**, 4, br c Petorius—Sea Mistress **Moyglare Stud Farm**
10 **PHARSTAR (IRE)**, 4, b g Phardante (FR)—Winter Fox **Mrs S. Robins**
11 **SILVIAN BLISS (USA)**, 4, ch c Green Forest (USA)—Welcome Proposal **Mr Jack Tierney**
12 **SOARING HIGH (IRE)**, 4, b f In The Wings—Too Phar **Frank Stronach**
13 **TRADE DISPUTE (IRE)**, 4, ro c Ela-Mana-Mou—Safety Feature **Mrs Gaynor Watt**
14 **TREBLE BOB (IRE)**, 6, b h Bob Back—Mittens **Michael J. Smurfit**
15 **VINTAGE CROP**, 9, ch g Rousillon (USA)—Overplay **Michael J. Smurfit**

THREE-YEAR-OLDS

16 **AHKAAM (USA)**, ch c Riverman (USA)—Rare Mint (USA) **Hamdan Al Maktoum**
17 **AMAZING SAIL (IRE)**, b c Alzao (USA)—Amazer **W. Howard Lester**
18 **ASTRELLINO (IRE)**, b c Bluebird (USA)—Rained Off **Thomas McDonagh**
19 **AWASSI (IRE)**, b c Fairy King (USA)—Phantom Row **Mr Michael Tabor**
20 **BAVARIO (USA)**, ch c Theatrical—Hawaiian Miss **Michael Watt**
21 **BELIEVE IN MYTHS**, b f Nijinsky (CAN)—Final Figure **Moyglare Stud Farm**
22 **CENTO (IRE)**, b g Shernazar—Callianire **Michael J. Smurfit**
23 **CLASS NOTE**, ch f Royal Academy—Golden Cay **Moyglare Stud Farm**
24 **CORDIAL KNIGHT (USA)**, b c Night Shift—Temperance Cordial **Mrs Joan Irvine Smith**
25 **DANCE DESIGN**, b f Sadler's Wells—Elegance In Design **Moyglare Stud Farm**
26 **DANCING FRED (USA)**, b c Fred Astaire (USA)—Grande Couture **Frank Stronach**
27 **DIALI (USA)**, b f Dayjur (USA)—Past Example (USA) **Hamdan Al Maktoum**

MR D. K. WELD M.V.B. M.R.C.V.S.—continued

28 **DREAM TYCOON (IRE)**, b f Last Tycoon—Grey Dream **Moyglare Stud Farm**
29 **EASY DEFINITION (IRE)**, br c Alzao (USA)—Easy To Copy **Moyglare Stud Farm**
30 **ENFANT PRODIGE (IRE)**, b f Dancing Dissident (USA)—Les Enfants **Mrs A. J. F. O'Reilly**
31 **ESCRITO (USA)**, b c Cox's Ridge—Lyphard's Starlite **Allen E. Paulson**
32 **FLAMING FEATHER**, b c Shirley Heights—Forest Flower **Mrs J. Maxwell Moran**
33 **FORCE OF WILL**, ch c Diesis—Clear Issue **Moyglare Stud Farm**
34 **FRIDOLIN (IRE)**, b c Danehill (USA)—Forli's Treat (USA) **Jochen Doehle**
35 **GAELIC SYMPHONY (IRE)**, b c Fayruz—Time Is Flying **Don Patsy Byrne Syndicate**
36 **GATES (USA)**, ch c Jade Hunter—Royal Herat **Michael Watt**
37 **GOD SPEED (IRE)**, ch f Be My Guest—Latest Chapter **Mrs C. L. Weld**
38 **GORDI (USA)**, ch c Theatrical—Royal Alydar **Allen E. Paulson**
39 **HAMAD (IRE)**, b c Sadler's Wells (USA)—Dead Certain **Mr Michael Tabor**
40 **HINT OF HUMOUR**, b f Woodman—High Competence **Moyglare Stud Farms**
41 **HI PLAINS DRIFTER (USA)**, b c Green Dancer (USA)—Allegedum (USA) **John D. Gunther**
42 **IN GENEROSITY**, b f Generous—Aptostar **Moyglare Stud Farm**
43 **J J BABOO (IRE)**, b c Be My Guest (USA)—Maricica **Jochen Doehle**
44 **JOKING REBUFF**, b c Dowsing (USA)—Perfect Welcome **Moyglare Stud Farm**
45 **LAYIK (IRE)**, b c Be My Guest (USA)—Forest Lair **Hamdan Al Maktoum**
46 **LIBROS (USA)**, ch c Blushing John—Gloria's Dancer **Allen E. Paulson**
47 **MITCH (USA)**, b c Jade Hunter—Ottomwa **Michael J. Smurfit**
48 **MODA (USA)**, ch f Theatrical—Gramatical **Allen E. Paulson**
49 **MUSICAL MAYHEM (IRE)**, b c Shernazar—Minstrels Folly **Moyglare Stud Farm**
50 **PARTY POLL (USA)**, b c Bering—Spark of Success **Moyglare Stud Farm**
51 **PEACE PRIZE**, ch c Polish Precedent—Sizes Vary **Moyglare Stud Farm**
52 **PECHORA**, ch f Thatching—Pechenga **Sheikh Mohammed**
53 **PERSICA**, ch f Persian Bold—Nadina **Sheikh Mohammed**
54 **PRO TRADER (USA)**, b br c Lyphard (USA)—Fuerza (USA) **John D. Gunther**
55 **REEM FEVER (IRE)**, b f Fairy King (USA)—Jungle Jezebel **Sheikh Ahmed Al Sabah**
56 **REGARDS**, b f Priolo (USA)—Hi Bettina **Woodlands Stud**
57 **RHUM DANCER (IRE)**, b c Eurobus—Audata (FR) **Mrs G. W. Jennings**
58 **RISKY MISSION**, br f Seattle Dancer—Slip Ashore **Moyglare Stud Farm**
59 **SMILE AWHILE**, b f Woodman—Rua d'Oro **Moyglare Stud Farm**
60 **STYLISH ALLURE (USA)**, b c Topsider (USA)—Excellent Fettle (USA) **Moyglare Stud Farm**
61 **SUPER GIFT**, b f Darshaan—Speciality Package **Moyglare Stud Farm**
62 **TAARISH**, b c Priolo (USA)—Strike It Rich **Hamdan Al Maktoum**
63 **TEHACHAPI (USA)**, b c Strawberry Road—Al Balessa **Allen E. Paulson**
64 **TOUCH JUDGE (USA)**, b c Nijinsky (CAN)—Hush Dear **Michael Watt**
65 **TRUST IN LUCK**, ch f Nashwan—Trusted Partner **Moyglare Stud Farm**
66 **ZAGREB (USA)**, b c Theatrical—Sophonisbe **Allen E. Paulson**
67 **ZALZIE**, b f Zalazl—Lucy Manette **Mrs A. J. F. O'Reilly**
68 **ZANKLE (USA)**, b c Opening Verse—Capre **J. J. King**

TWO-YEAR-OLDS

69 **ABSOLUTE GLEE (USA)**, gr f 16/3 Kenmare—Looking Brill (Sadler's Wells) **Moyglare Stud Farm**
70 **ACT OF DEFIANCE (IRE)**, b c 26/5 Caerleon (USA)—
                           Trusted Partner (USA) (Affirmed (USA)) **Moyglare Stud Farm**
71 **AGAINST THE BREEZE (USA)**, ch c 9/4 Diesis—Slip Ashore (Slip Anchor) **Moyglare Stud Farm**
72 **ANGELLINO (IRE)**, b c 9/3 Danehill (USA)—Commanche Belle (Shirley Heights) **Thomas McDonogh**
73 **ANID (USA)**, b br c 28/2 Irish River (FR)—Cousin Margaret (Topsider) **Hamdan Al Maktoum**
74 Gr c 11/3 Sadler's Wells (USA)—Anne de Beaujeu (Ahonoora) **Michael Watt**
75 Ch c 11/4 Night Shift (USA)—Bean Siamsa (Solinus) **Saleh Y Al Homaizi**
76 **BEAUTIFUL FIRE (IRE)**, b c 7/4 Selkirk—Beautiful France (Sadler's Wells) **Moyglare Stud Farm**
77 **CALL MY BLUFF (USA)**, b c 17/3 Deputy Minister—Clear Issue (Riverman) **Moyglare Stud Farm**
78 B f 19/2 Miswaki—Carnet Solaire (Sharpen Up) **Mrs A. J. F. O'Reilly**
79 **CRYPTIC PATTERN**, ch c 21/4 Green Dancer—Epicure's Garden (Affirmed) **Moyglare Stud Farm**
80 **DESERT EASE (IRE)**, b br f 9/2 Green Desert—Easy To Copy (Affirmed) **Moyglare Stud Farm**
81 **DOUCETTE (IRE)**, b f 12/5 Night Shift (USA)—Too Phar (Pharly) **Mrs C. L. Weld**
82 **FANCIFUL (USA)**, ch f 4/5 Mujtahid—Try My Rosie (Try My Best) **Mrs A. J. F. O'Reilly**
83 **FIGURE OF FUN**, b f 28/3 Woodman—High Competence (The Minstrel) **Moyglare Stud Farm**
84 B c 14/5 Sadler's Wells—Fleur Royale (Mill Reef) **Michael Watt**

MR D. K. WELD M.V.B. M.R.C.V.S.—continued

85 Gr f 11/3 Mr Prospector—Flowing (El Gran Senor) **Mrs J. Maxwell Moran**
86 B c 18/4 Caerleon (USA)—Go Honey Go (General Assembly) **Frank Stronach**
87 **GOLDEN CIRCLE (USA)**, b f 21/4 Theatrical—Golden Secretariat (Secretariat) **Mrs A. J. F. O'Reilly**
88 **GOLDEN LIGHTS (IRE)**, b c 28/1 Alleged—Spring To Light (Blushing Groom) **Moyglare Stud Farm**
89 **GRANNY KELLY (USA)**, ch f 23/2 Irish River—Deviltante (Devil's Bag) **Mrs J. Maxwell Moran**
90 B c 16/2 Shalford—Green Wings (General Assembly (USA)) **Mr Michael Tabor**
91 B f 27/3 St Jovite (USA)—Heaven Knows (USA) (Quadrangle) **Mrs A. J. F. O'Reilly**
92 **INCOMMUNICADO (IRE)**, b f 31/3 Sadler's Wells (USA)—
                             Apostar (USA) (Fappiano (USA)) **Moyglare Stud Farm**
93 **KATYDID (USA)**, ch f 4/6 Nureyev—Palm Reader (Sir Ivor) **Mrs J. Maxwell Moran**
94 B br c 19/5 St Jovite—Late Flowering (Nureyev) **Dean Grimm**
95 **MAGICAL CLICHE (USA)**, b f 1/5 Affirmed—Talking Picture (Speak John) **Moyglare Stud Farm**
96 **MANARAH**, b f 15/3 Marju (IRE)—Forest Lair (Habitat) **Hamdan Al Maktoum**
97 **MEDIA FRENZY (USA)**, b f 1/5 El Gran Senor—Ready For Action (Riverman) **Moyglare Stud Farm**
98 **MORE'S THE PITY**, ch c 15/3 Cadeaux Genereux—What A Pity (Blakeney) **Moyglare Stud Farm**
99 **MOVING ON UP**, b c 11/3 Salse—Thundercloud (Electric) **Moyglare Stud Farm**
100 **MUBADARA (IRE)**, b f 25/1 Lahib (USA)—Sweet Alma (Alzao) **Hamdan Al Maktoum**
101 **MUKARRAB (USA)**, b br c 24/4 Dayjur—Mahaasin (NZ) (Biscay (AUS)) **Hamdan Al Maktoum**
102 B c 29/1 El Gran Senor (USA)—Mystical River (Riverman (USA)) **Sheikh Mohammed**
103 **NITHA (IRE)**, b f 5/4 Dancing Dissident—Needy Thatch (Thatching) **Mrs A. J. F. O'Reilly**
104 **ORIENTAL STYLE (IRE)**, ro c 22/1 Indian Ridge—Bazaar Promise (Native Bazaar) **Moyglare Stud Farm**
105 **POETIC QUEST (IRE)**, ch c 7/2 Rainbow Quest—Love For Poetry (Lord Gayle) **Moyglare Stud Farm**
106 **POISED TO RALLY (IRE)**, br c 20/4 Green Dancer—Final Figure (Super Concorde) **Moyglare Stud Farm**
107 **RAFAHIYAH (USA)**, ch f 13/3 Irish River (FR)—Idle Hope (USA) (Valdez (USA)) **Hamdan Al Maktoum**
108 B br c 18/3 Riverman (USA)—Rossard (DEN) (Glacial) **Thomas T. S. Liang**
109 B c 2/4 Common Grounds—Sadie Jordan (USA) (Hail The Pirates) **Mrs A. J. F. O'Reilly**
110 **SHI-AR (IRE)**, ch c 14/3 Royal Academy (USA)—Welsh Love (Ela-Mana-Mou) **Hamdan Al Maktoum**
111 **SIMPLE IDEALS (USA)**, b br c 2/2 Woodman—Comfort And Style (Be My Guest) **Moyglare Stud Farm**
112 **SOCIAL HARMONY (IRE)**, b c 5/4 Polish Precedent—Latest Chapter (Ahonoora) **Moyglare Stud Farm**
113 **SPRING NIGHTS**, ch f 2/5 Nashwan—Seasonal Pickup (The Minstrel) **Moyglare Stud Farm**
114 **STAR PROFILE (IRE)**, b f 11/3 Sadler's Wells—Sandhurst Goddess (Sandhurst Prince) **Moyglare Stud Farm**
115 **STRIKING GOLD (IRE)**, b c 4/3 Sadler's Wells—Speciality Package (Blushing Groom) **Moyglare Stud Farm**
116 **SYMPHONY (IRE)**, b f 11/2 Cyrano de Bergerac—Silius (Junius) **Mrs C. L. Weld**
117 **TARRY FLYNN (IRE)**, br c 10/3 Kenmare (FR)—Danzig Lass (USA) (Danzig (USA)) **Mrs C. L. Weld**
118 **WENDY VAALA (USA)**, gr f 23/4 Dayjur—Balidaress (Balidar) **Mrs J. Maxwell Moran**
119 B br c 30/4 Theatrical—Wooing (Stage Door Johnny) **Michael J. Smurfit**
120 **YUDRIK (IRE)**, ch c 20/2 Lahib (USA)—Style of Life (USA) (The Minstrel (CAN)) **Hamdan Al Maktoum**

Jockeys (Flat): M J Kinane (8-3), P Shanahan (8-3).

Apprentices: D O'Donohoe (7-10), W Smith (7-10).

628   MR L. WELLS, Billingshurst

Postal: **Pallingham Manor Farm, Wisborough Green, Billingshurst, West Sussex, RH14 0EZ.**

1 **ANKOR GOLD**, 8, ch g Relkino—Arctic Fern **Mrs Carrie Zetter-Wells**
2 **BAT OUT OF HELL (IRE)**, 5, b g Orchestra—One Way Passage **Mrs Carrie Zetter-Wells**
3 **B FIFTY TWO (IRE)**, 5, b g Mandalus—Hyde's Pride **Mrs Carrie Zetter-Wells**
4 **COOLEGALE**, 10, br g Strong Gale—Napoleone III **Mrs Carrie Zetter-Wells**
5 **COUGAR RUN (IRE)**, 5, b br g Commanche Run—Orra Beg **Mrs Carrie Zetter-Wells**
6 **FANE PARK (IRE)**, 8, br g Mummy's Treasure—Random Princess **Mrs Carrie Zetter-Wells**
7 **HARROW WAY (IRE)**, 6, b g Strong Gale—Merry Miss **Mrs Carrie Zetter-Wells**
8 **MR RAKAPOSHI**, 6, b g Rakaposhi King—Miss Bell **Mrs Carrie Zetter-Wells**
9 **PITTS SPECIAL**, 6, b m Pitpan—Stuck For Words **Mrs Carrie Zetter-Wells**

629   MR E. WEYMES, Middleham

Postal: **Ashgill, Coverham, Leyburn, N. Yorks, DL8 4TJ.**

Phone: **(01969) 40229**

1 **DRUMMER HICKS**, 7, b br h Seymour Hicks (FR)—Musical Princess **Mrs N. Napier**
2 **IMPULSIVE AIR (IRE)**, 4, b g Try My Best (USA)—Tracy's Sundown **Mr T. A. Scothern & Mr M. Lee**
3 **MAUBEE**, 5, b g Nicholas Bill—Sigh **Mr Nigel Buckle**
4 **SAMSUNG LOVELYLADY (IRE)**, 4, b f Petorius—Kentucky Wildcat **Mr T. A. Scothern**
5 **SPECIAL-K**, 4, br f Treasure Kay—Lissi Gori (FR) **Mr G. Falshaw**

THREE-YEAR-OLDS

6 **CROSBY SUE**, b f Hotfoot—Lewista **Mrs P. M. Weymes**
7 **DICENTRA**, b f Rambo Dancer (CAN)—Be Noble **Mrs P. M. Weymes**
8 **VESHCA LADY (IRE)**, br f Contract Law (USA)—Genzyme Gene **Mr J. O'Malley**

TWO-YEAR-OLDS

9 **CROSBY NOD**, b c 31/3 Shalford (IRE)—Kirkby Belle (Bay Express) **Mr D. Raper & Mrs P. M. Weymes**
10 B f 16/2 Warning—Hardihostess (Be My Guest (USA)) **Mr T. A. Scothern & Mrs E. Palamountain**
11 Gr f 19/1 El Prado (IRE)—Jane Scott (USA) (Copelan (USA)) **Mr T. A. Scothern**
12 **MURRAY GREY**, gr f 2/2 Be My Chief (USA)—Couleur de Rose (Kalaglow) **Mrs A. Birkett & Mr H. Birkett**
13 **RAIVUE**, ch g 16/3 Beveled (USA)—Halka (Daring March) **Mrs A. Birkett & Mr H. Birkett**
14 B f 20/2 Mujadil (USA)—Romany Pageant (Welsh Pageant) **Mr T. A. Scothern**
15 B f 14/5 Statoblest—Sarong (Taj Dewan) **Mr T. A. Scothern**
16 **SIX SHOOTER**, b f 20/4 Damister (USA)—Ten To Six (Night Shift (USA)) **Mr G. Moorey**

Other Owners: Mrs M. Ashby, Mrs R. L. Heaton, Mr P. L. Pickford.

Amateur: Mr J Weymes (10-4).

630   MR J. R. H. WHARTON, Melton Mowbray

Postal: **Shipmans Barn Stud, Saxby Road, Melton Mowbray, Leics, LE14 4RZ.**

Phone: **HOME (01664) 69868 OFFICE (01664) 464334 MOBILE (0850) 252158**

1 **ANNIE KELLY**, 8, b m Oats—Deep Moppet **Mrs R. Hoare**
2 **ARMSTON**, 4, ch g Rock City—Silka (ITY) **Mr John Wharton**
3 **BESCABY (IRE)**, 5, ch g Dominion Royale—Elegant Act (USA) **Mr John Wharton**
4 **BLUE SIOUX**, 4, b f Indian Ridge—Blues Indigo **Mr J. L. Ashby**
5 **CONEYGREE**, 4, b f Northern State (USA)—Welsh Blossom **Mr P. M. Bradley**
6 **FIRST GOLD**, 7, gr g Absalom—Cindys Gold **Mr K. D. Standen**
7 **HORNPIPE**, 4, br g Handsome Sailor—Snake Song **Mr K. D. Standen**
8 **JOLLY HOKEY**, 4, b g Dominion—Judy's Dowry **Mrs V. McGeough**
9 **OUR TOM**, 4, br g Petong—Boa **Mr J. M. Berry**
10 **POPLIN**, 5, b m Derrylin—Poppy's Pride **Mrs M. Mann**
11 **SHARP FALCON (IRE)**, 5, gr m Shaadi (USA)—Honey Buzzard **Mr G. W. Mills**

THREE-YEAR-OLDS

12 **EBONY BOY**, bl c Sayf El Arab (USA)—Actress **Mr P. W. Lambert**
13 **FORECAST**, b c Formidable (USA)—Princess Matilda **Mr P. W. Lambert**
14 **FOREST FANTASY**, b f Rambo Dancer (CAN)—Another Treat **Mr W. Turner**
15 **GUY'S GAMBLE**, ch c Mazilier (USA)—Deep Blue Sea **Parkers of Peterborough Plc**
16 B c Dominion—Judy's Dowry **Mrs V. McGeough**
17 **KOTA**, b c Kris—Lady Be Mine (USA) **Mr P. W. Lambert**
18 **LYCETA**, b f Shirley Heights—Lycia (USA) **Mr P. W. Lambert**
19 **ROTHLEY IMP (IRE)**, b f Mac's Imp (USA)—Valediction **Crown Racing**
20 **RUSTIC SONG (IRE)**, b f Fayruz—Red Note **Mrs Lynn Tye**
21 **SIBERIAN ROSE**, b f Siberian Express (USA)—Deanta In China **Mr John R. Goddard**
22 **STILLY NIGHT (IRE)**, b f Martin John—Syndikos (USA) **Mr John Wharton**
23 **VICTORIA SIOUX**, ch f Ron's Victory (USA)—Blues Indigo **Mr J. L. Ashby**

MR J. R. H. WHARTON—continued

TWO-YEAR-OLDS

24 **BOLD WELCOME,** ch c 10/2 Most Welcome—Song's Best (Never So Bold) **Mr J. L. Ashby**
25 B f 23/2 Ron's Victory (USA)—Haunting (Lord Gayle (USA))
26 B f 16/4 Fayruz—Lorme (Glenstal (USA))

Other Owners: Mrs L. J. Berry, Mr Kenneth Kinch, Mr Kevin A. C. Kinch, Mr Roger Kinch, Mrs Susan Kinch, Mrs A. C. Lambert, Mr Geoffrey W. Mills, Mr J. H. Mills, Mr J. C. K. Steel, Dr Mary Underwood, Mr W. Wharton, Mrs Judy Wilson.

Jockey (NH): B Dalton (9-7).

631   MR A. C. WHILLANS, Hawick

Postal: **Esker House, Newmill-on-Slitrig, Hawick, TD9 9UQ.**
Phone: **(01450) 376642**

1 **CRYSTAL GIFT,** 4, b g Dominion—Grain Lady (USA) **Mrs L. M. Whillans**
2 **GOSPEL SONG,** 4, ch c King Among Kings—Market Blues **Mr Chas N. Whillans**
3 **MAJOR BELL,** 8, br g Silly Prices—Melaura Belle **Mr Ian T. Middlemiss**
4 **MR DEVIOUS,** 5, b g Superpower—Marton Maid
5 **NOORAN,** 5, b g Risk Me (FR)—Susie Hall **Mr Chas N. Whillans**
6 **PALACEGATE KING,** 7, ch g King Among Kings—Market Blues **Mr Chas N. Whillans**
7 **SANSOOL,** 10, b g Dominion—Young Diana **Mr A. C. Whillans**
8 **STORMIN GARY,** 5, b g Respect—Birniebrig **Mr C. Bird**
9 **SUPREME SOVIET,** 6, ch g Presidium—Sylvan Song **Mr Allan Gilchrist**

Other Owners: Mr D. Douglas.

632   MR R. M. WHITAKER, Leeds

Postal: **Hellwood Farm, Hellwood Lane, Scarcroft, Leeds, LS14 3BP.**
Phone: **(0113) 2892265 FAX (0113) 2892265**

1 **ANCRE VALLEY,** 7, gr m Van Der Linden (FR)—Menin **Mr C. A. Chapman**
2 **DINTINGDALE,** 5, b m Ardar—Barkston Ash **Mr C. A. Chapman**
3 **GANT BLEU (FR),** 9, ch g Crystal Glitters (USA)—Gold Honey
4 **JUST DISSIDENT (IRE),** 4, b g Dancing Dissident (USA)—Betty Bun **Mrs C. A. Hodgetts**
5 **OUR MAIN MAN,** 6, ch g Superlative—Ophrys **Mr Christopher Cooke**
6 **PERCY PARROT,** 4, b g Lochnager—Soltago **Mrs Juliet Thompson**
7 **REDSTELLA (USA),** 7, ch h Theatrical—Orange Squash **Mr R. M. Whitaker**
8 **RESOLUTE BAY,** 10, b g Crofthall—Spinner **Mr R. M. Whitaker**
9 **SILK COTTAGE,** 4, b g Superpower—Flute Royale **Mr Michael Ng**
10 **THE FED,** 6, ch g Clantime—Hyde Princess **Country Lane Partnership & Mr F. Downes**

THREE-YEAR-OLDS

11 **FERNWAY,** ch f Handsome Sailor—Redgrave Design **Mr R. M. Whitaker**
12 **GINGER HODGERS,** ch f Crofthall—Jarrettelle **Mr K. Hodgson**
13 **GOOL LEE SHAY (USA),** b c Explodent (USA)—Titled Miss (USA) **Mr W. Hattersley**
14 **OH WHATAKNIGHT,** b f Primo Dominie—Carolside **Mr Derek D. Clee**
15 **POWER PRINCESS,** b f Superpower—Hyde Princess **Mr F. Downes & Country Lane Partnership**
16 **ROCKY STREAM,** b f Reprimand—Pebble Creek (IRE) **Mr G. F. Pemberton**

TWO-YEAR-OLDS

17 Gr f 19/2 Reprimand—Fair Eleanor (Saritamer (USA))
18 **MELBOURNE PRINCESS,** ch f 2/2 Primo Dominie—Lurking (Formidable (USA)) **Mr D. Bardsley**
19 **STYLE DANCER (IRE),** b c 11/3 Dancing Dissident—Showing Style (Pas de Seul) **Mrs C. A. Hodgetts**
20 Ch c 7/2 Superpower—Yankeedoodledancer (Mashhor Dancer (USA))

MR R. M. WHITAKER—continued

Other Owners: Mrs Jose Button, Mrs Jean P. Clee, Mr D. Lodge, Miss E. A. Morley, Mr T. Richmond, Mr G. H. Senior, Mr R. H. Tiffany, Mrs S. C. Waring, Mr C. Michael Wilson.

Jockey (Flat): A Culhane (8-2).

Amateur: Mr Simon Richard Whitaker (11-7).

633   MR G. F. WHITE, Alnwick

Postal: **School House, Rennington, Alnwick, Northd, NE66 3RR.**

Phone: **OFFICE (01665) 603231 HOME (01665) 577430 FAX (01665) 510872**

1 **DELWOOD**, 4, br g Dancing High—Lorna's Choice **Mr G. F. White**
2 **DONSIDE**, 8, gr g Alias Smith (USA)—Delnadamph **Mr G. F. White**
3 4, Ch g Dancing High—Hallo Cheeky **Mr F. V. White**
4 5, Ch m Meadowbrook—Hallo Cheeky **Mr F. V. White**
5 **HARDIHERO**, 10, b g Henbit (USA)—Hardirondo **Mr G. F. White**
6 **HOUSELOPE BECK**, 6, ch g Meadowbrook—Hallo Cheeky **Mr F. V. White**
7 **TOP ACE**, 4, b g Statoblest—Innes House **Mr G. F. White**
8 **TRUE FAIR**, 13, b g Balinger—Aberfair **Mr G. F. White**

TWO-YEAR-OLDS

9 Ch g 17/5 Milieu—Lorna's Choice (Oats) **Mr G. F. White**

Jockey (NH): B Storey (10-0).

Amateur: Mr A Robson (10-9).

634   MR J. WHITE, Chinnor Hill

Postal: **Hillside, Chinnor Hill, Oxon.**

Phone: **(01844) 351548   FAX (01844) 351548   MOBILE (0831) 143356**

1 **ALKA INTERNATIONAL**, 4, b g Northern State (USA)—Cachucha **Highbrook Racing**
2 **BARRIE STIR**, 4, b g Law Society (USA)—Avahra **Waterloo**
3 **BELAFONTE**, 9, br g Derrylin—Ulla Laing **Miss K. George**
4 **BRINDLEY HOUSE**, 9, b g Deep Run—Annick (FR) **Mr S. B. Glazer**
5 **COME ON DANCER (IRE)**, 8, ch g Ahonoora—Crimson Royale **Mrs E. Reid**
6 **COUCHANT (IRE)**, 5, b g Petoski—Be Easy **Mr A. J. Allright**
7 **CUCHULLAINS GOLD (IRE)**, 8, ch g Denel (FR)—Rockford Lass **Mr M. A. McEvoy**
8 **DAYS OF THUNDER**, 8, ch g Vaigly Great—Silent Prayer **Mrs Joan Meredith**
9 **DON TOCINO**, 6, b g Dominion—Mrs Bacon **Mr Raymond McCadden**
10 **DOUBLE JEOPARDY**, 5, b g Polish Precedent (USA)—Infamy **Major B. Gatensbury**
11 **DRAGON GREEN**, 5, gr g Green Desert (USA)—Dunoof **Mr J. T. Morris**
12 **DUVEEN (IRE)**, 6, b g Tate Gallery (USA)—Wish You Were Here (USA) **Fat Boys Racing**
13 **EFHARISTO**, 7, b g Dominion—Excellent Alibi (USA) **Mr Adrian Fitzpatrick**
14 **ELUSIVE STAR**, 6, b m Ardross—Star Flower **Mr W. Ginzel**
15 **FLYING EAGLE**, 5, b g Shaadi (USA)—Fly Me (FR) **Mr T. F. Maycock**
16 **FRED'S BOY**, 6, b g Nishapour (FR)—Eider **Mr F. H. Williams**
17 **HAPPY HOSTAGE**, 5, b g Beveled (USA)—Run Amber Run **Mr A. J. Allright**
18 **IMAD (USA)**, 6, b br g Al Nasr (FR)—Dunoof **Mr Alan Brackley**
19 **INTO THE RED**, 12, ch g Over The River (FR)—Legal Fortune **Mr J. Huckle**
20 **KAMA SIMBA**, 4, b g Lear Fan (USA)—Dance It (USA) **Town and Country Tyre Services Limited**

MR J. WHITE—continued

21 KAMIKAZE, 6, gr g Kris—Infamy **Major B. Gatensbury**
22 LAKE DOMINION, 7, b g Primo Dominie—Piney Lake **Mrs Betty Bate and Mr Mark Campbell**
23 LINDEN'S LOTTO (IRE), 7, b g Kambalda—Linden **Crocketts Racing Club**
24 MAJOR'S LAW (IRE), 7, b g Law Society (USA)—Maryinsky (USA) **B. G. Racing**
25 MASTER HUNTER (IRE), 7, b br g Treasure Hunter—Hardyglass Lass **Mr M. A. McEvoy**
26 MOORISH, 6, b g Dominion—Remoosh **Mr Adrian Fitzpatrick**
27 MY BEST VALENTINE, 6, b h Try My Best (USA)—Pas de Calais **The Valentines**
28 NEW TRIBE (IRE), 5, b g Commanche Run—Red Partridge **Mr C. A. Robery**
29 RAGOSA, 5, ch m Ardross—No Sharing **Mrs C. A. Trendell**
30 RAMALLAH, 7, b g Ra Nova—Anglophil **Maidens Green Acres**
31 ROSGILL, 10, ch g Mill Reef (USA)—Speedy Rose **Brigadier Racing**
32 SAFETY (USA), 9, b g Topsider (USA)—Flare Pass (USA) **Mr Keith Sturgis**
33 SIMPLY GEORGE, 7, b g Simply Great (FR)—Grand Occasion **Mr Keith Sturgis**
34 SOUTHERNCROSSPATCH, 5, ch g Ra Nova—Southern Bird **Mrs P. I. Morgan**
35 SWEDISH INVADER, 5, b g Jareer (USA)—Nihad **Willwewontwe Club**
36 TAKE TWO, 8, b g Jupiter Island—Dancing Daughter **Major B. Gatensbury**
37 TELMAR SYSTEMS, 7, b g Don Enrico (USA)—Russola **Mr Richard Dodson**
38 THAT OLD FEELING (IRE), 4, b c Waajib—Swift Reply **Mrs P. Sherwood**
39 WAKT, 6, b m Akarad (FR)—Nasara (FR) **Mr B. Whitehorn**
40 WITHOUT A FLAG (USA), 6, ch g Stately Don (USA)—Northerly Cheer (USA) **Mrs P. Sherwood**

THREE-YEAR-OLDS

41 KINGS NIGHTCLUB, b f Shareef Dancer (USA)—Troy Moon **Kings Bloodstock Limited**
42 MARTINS FOLLY, ch f Beveled (USA)—Millingdale **Mr M. R. Pascall**

Other Owners: Mr Ian Andrews, Mr Paul W. Ballard, Mr A. Bennett, Mr Paul Bennett, Mr Don Billinghurst, Mr C. R. Black, Mr Phil Blair, Mr J. Bostel, Mr David Boyce, Mr Michael Boyce, Mrs Belinda Brackley, Mr Kenneth D. Bull, Mrs Irene Clifford, Mr D. G. Conopo, Mr J. P. Conopo, Mr N. K. Croft, Mr D. M. Drury, Mr J. Dungan, Mr B. Graham, Mr Neil Graham, Mr H. Green, Mr G. H. Griffith, Mr S. R. Griffiths, Mrs Loretta Harris, Mr R. J. Hawes, Mr Jeremy Hobbins, Mr G. M. Kelly, Mr J. Lamote, Mr R. J. Love, Mr Jim McGrath, Mr L. S. Muller, Mr J. Noone, Mr D. F. Parry, Mr A. R. Perry, Mr Mitchell Platts, Mr D. E. Popham, Mr D. Powell, Miss J. Rumford, Miss E. Saunders, Mr Bernard Shuck, Mr Timothy Siegfried, Mr H. Stephen Smith, Mr T. G. Stafferton, Ms Marie Steele, Mr K. R. Steeper, Mr J. Westley, Mr David White, Mr J. R. White, Mr R. Whitehorn, Miss Wendy Wood.

Jockeys (NH): A Maguire (w.a.), N Williamson (w.a.).

Conditional: A Bates, D Bohan, P McLoughlin.

635   MISS K. WHITEHOUSE, Church Stretton

Postal: **Lower Botvyle Farm, Church Stretton, Shropshire, SY6 6HG.**
Phone: **DAYTIME (01694) 722625 FAX (01694) 724295**

1 CASTLERICHARDKING, 11, b g Matching Pair—Dont Rock **Joy & Jim Barker**
2 COUNTESS MILLIE, 4, ch f Rakaposhi King—Countess Carlotti **Miss K. Whitehouse**
3 GOLDEN FISH, 4, b g Efisio—Fishpond **Mr D. Wright**
4 HOT BREEZE, 4, br g Hotfoot—Gunnard **The Wrinkly Tin Partnership**
5 KAHER (USA), 9, b g Our Native (USA)—June Bride (USA) **Mr F. J. Mills**
6 MY SISTER LUCY, 6, b m Farajullah—Woven Gold **Miss K. Whitehouse**
7 PENNANT COTTAGE (IRE), 8, b m Denel (FR)—The Hofsa **Mr P. J. Woolley**
8 RAGGERTY (IRE), 6, b g Prince Rupert (FR)—Princess Martina **Mrs C. J. Pennington**
9 RED BREAKER, 5, b g Starch Reduced—Otterden **Joy & Jim Barker**
10 SPIRITED STATEMENT (IRE), 6, br g Strong Statement (USA)—Somelli **Mr A. P. Gregory**
11 TIPSY QUEEN, 5, b m Rakaposhi King—Topsy Bee **Mrs R. E. Hambro**

TWO-YEAR-OLDS

12 Ch g 5/5 Headin' Up—Mrs Mouse **Miss K. Whitehouse**

Other Owners: Mr G. Heywood, Mr W. R. Mills.

636   MR J. W. WHYTE, Beccles

Postal: **Becks Green Farm, Becks Green Lane, Ilketshall St Andrew, Beccles, NR34 8NB.**
Phone: **(01986) 781221 FAX 781406**

1 **BEN CONNAN (IRE)**, 6, b g Lomond (USA)—Colourful (FR) **Mr John Whyte**
2 **DANRIBO**, 13, b g Riboboy (USA)—Sheridans Daughter **Mr John Whyte**
3 **GOOD OLD CHIPS**, 9, b g Oats—Etoile de Lune **Mr John Whyte**
4 **HOWARYAFXD**, 9, ch g Green Shoon—Pandos Pet **Mr John Whyte**
5 **PYRAMIS PRINCE (IRE)**, 6, b g Fairy King (USA)—Midnight Patrol **Mr John Whyte**
6 **SALISONG**, 7, gr g Song—Sylvanecte (FR) **Mr John Whyte**
7 **SOUNDS GOLDEN**, 8, br g Sonnen Gold—Tuneful Queen **Mrs John Whyte**

Amateur: Mr Matthew Gingell (10-7).

637   MRS J. V. WILKINSON, Blandford Forum

Postal: **Wrekin House, Ibberton, Blandford Forum, Dorset, DT11 0EN.**
Phone: **(01258) 817719**

1 **GYPSY BLUES**, 6, b m Sula Bula—Pine Gypsy **Mrs J. V. Wilkinson**
2 **WREKIN HILL**, 14, b g Duky—Cummin Hill **Mrs J. V. Wilkinson**

Amateur: Mrs J V Wilkinson (8-7).

638   MR M. J. WILKINSON, Banbury

Postal: **Trafford Bridge, Edgcote, Banbury, Oxon, OX17 1AG.**
Phone: **CHIPPING WARDEN (01295) 660713 CAR (0836) 613330 FAX (01295) 660767**

1 **APRIL WILLOW**, 9, ch g Alias Smith (USA)—Catherines April **Mrs P. N. Roberts**
2 **BARONCELLI**, 6, ch g Baron Blakeney—Toumanova **The Gardians**
3 **BENDOR MARK**, 7, b g Lighter—Montana **Mr C. J. Courage**
4 **BLACK STAG (IRE)**, 7, b g Phardante (FR)—Light Whisper **Mr T. Ovens**
5 **BONNIFER (IRE)**, 7, ch g Royal And Regal (USA)—Piper's Lady (CAN) **Towcester Members Race Club**
6 **BOOTS N ALL (IRE)**, 6, bl g Strong Statement (USA)—Sallstown **Mrs David V. Tipper**
7 **CAMDEN WAY (IRE)**, 6, b g Camden Town—Fuzzy Bug **Ms M. A. Madden**
8 **COULIN LOCH (IRE)**, 7, b g Long Pond—Flashy Gold **Mrs Leonie Harper**
9 **DISTINCTIVE (IRE)**, 7, ch g Orchestra—Zimuletta **Mr Jeremy Hancock**
10 **DODGEM (IRE)**, 8, b g Crash Course—Polrevagh **Mr D. J. Price**
11 **HICKORY WIND**, 9, ch g Dalsaan—Derrain **Horse & Rider Health**
12 **KEY TO MOYADE (IRE)**, 6, bl g Treasure Kay—Giorradana **Mrs Leonie Harper**
13 **KNOCKAVERRY (IRE)**, 8, b m Kemal (FR)—Ballinlough **Mrs W. Morrell**
14 **LAWBUSTER (IRE)**, 4, b g Contract Law (USA)—Tora Tora **Hopeful Racing**
15 **MISTER DRUM (IRE)**, 7, gr g Aristocracy—Pollyfaster **Mr Malcolm Batchelor**
16 **MONTEZUMAS REVENGE (IRE)**, 8, b g Commonty (USA)—Boonoonoonoos **Mr R. T. Macauley**
17 **MRS MONEYPENNY**, 7, b m Relkino—Quickapenny **Mr C. J. Courage**
18 **NETHERCOTE LAD**, 6, b g Mummy's Game—Infelice **Mr R. Neal**
19 **NO FIDDLING (IRE)**, 5, br g Glenstal (USA)—Gradille **Mr Malcolm Batchelor**
20 **RONANS GLEN**, 9, b br g Glen Quaich—Willabelle **Mrs W. Morrell**
21 **SAVUTI (IRE)**, 7, ch g Amoristic (USA)—Aprils Choice **Mrs David V. Tipper**
22 **SEABROOK LAD**, 5, b g Derrylin—Moll **Seabrook Partners**
23 **SEACHANGE**, 7, gr g Neltino—Maytide **Mr A. D. Steven**
24 **SIZZLING AFFAIR**, 7, b g Sizzling Melody—Vivchar **Mrs D. Ancil**

Other Owners: Mr D. Ancil, Mrs Anne Andrew, Mr Frank Andrew, Mr John Armstrong, Mr Douglas Baillie, Mrs Delyth Batchelor, Mr V. E. Broom, Mr James Campbell, Mr A. D. Chorlton, Mrs D. J. Chorlton, Mrs E. R. Courage, Mr R. C. Cox, Mr John Harper, Mrs Jo Hodges, Mr T. T. Moffat, Mr S. Pack, P.O.W.T.C. Ltd/speedy Snaps, Mr Craig Raymond, Mr Stephen Raymond, Mr R. R. Young.

Conditional: P Crowley.

639   MR A. J. WILLIAMS, Newport

Postal: **Hendrew Farm, Llandevaud, Newport, Gwent, NP6 2AB.**
Phone: **(01633) 400188**

1 **FLOATING RIVER (IRE)**, 8, ch m Over The River (FR)—Exemplary Fashion **Mr A. J. Williams**
2 4, B f Phardante (FR)—Kilistrano **Mr A. J. Williams**
3 **KING FOWLER (IRE)**, 6, gr g King's Ride—Chicchick **Mr A. J. Williams**
4 4, B f Phardante (FR)—Smashing Gale **Mr A. J. Williams**

THREE-YEAR-OLDS

5 B f Brush Aside (USA)—Kilistrano **Mr A. J. Williams**

Amateur: Mr A Wintle (10-2).

640   MR D. L. WILLIAMS, Newbury

Postal: **Hillside Stud, Great Shefford, Hungerford, Berkshire, RG17 7DL.**
Phone: **HOME/YARD (01488) 638636 FAX 638121 MOBILE (0421) 351572/792351**

1 **AMBER VALLEY (USA)**, 5, ch g Bering—Olatha (USA) **Berkshire Commercial Components Ltd**
2 **BATHWICK BOBBIE**, 9, b g Netherkelly—Sunwise **Mr W. Clifford**
3 **BLAAZIING JOE (IRE)**, 5, b g Alzao (USA)—Beijing (USA) **Berkshire Commercial Components Ltd**
4 **DERRYBELLE**, 5, ch m Derrylin—Pokey's Belle **Miss B. W. Palmer**
5 **HERMES HARVEST**, 8, b g Oats—Swift Messenger **Miss B. W. Palmer**
6 **HICKLETON LAD**, 12, ch g Black Minstrel—Lupreno **Miss B. W. Palmer & Mr P. F. Moore**
7 **JOBBER'S FIDDLE**, 4, b f Sizzling Melody—Island Mead **Berkshire Commercial Components Ltd**
8 **PENNINE PASS (IRE)**, 7, b g Pennine Walk—Red Realm **Mr P. F. Moore & Mrs P. J. Moore**
9 **SAINT KEYNE**, 6, b h Sadler's Wells (USA)—Sancta **Berkshire Commercial Components Ltd**
10 **SET THE FASHION**, 7, br g Green Desert (USA)—Prelude **Mr R. J. Matthews**
11 **SWIFT POKEY**, 6, b h Uncle Pokey—Swift Messenger **Miss B. W. Palmer**
12 **SYMBOL OF SUCCESS (IRE)**, 5, b g Red Sunset—Simbella **N. O. T. Racing Syndicate**
13 **TAUREAN TYCOON**, 12, b g Octogenarian—Eastling **The Laugh A Minute Racing Club**
14 **THALJANAH (IRE)**, 4, ch g In The Wings—Dawn Is Breaking **Mr W. Clifford**
15 **TOSKANO**, 4, b g Salse (USA)—Kukri **Berkshire Commercial Components Ltd**

Other Owners: Mr M. Bailey, Mr Gareth Cheshire, Mr Gwerfyl Coombes, Mrs Dawn McCabe, Miss Beverley Moore, Mrs Paula Williams, Mr M. G. Wooldridge.

Conditional: Michael Clarke (9-0).

Amateurs: Mr Andrew Balding (10-9), Miss Stephanie Higgins (8-10).

Additional Horse
DANGER BABY, 6 ch g Bairn (USA)—Swordlestown Miss (USA)

641   MR R. J. R. WILLIAMS, Newmarket

Postal: **Marriott Stables, Hamilton Road, Newmarket, Suffolk, CB8 0NY.**
Phone: **OFFICE (01638) 663218 HOME 665819 FAX 660145 MOBILE (0831) 493629**

1 **BRAMLEY MAY**, 6, b g Lidhame—Hailgaf **Mrs J. Spragg**
2 **BUDDY'S FRIEND (IRE)**, 8, ch h Jester—Hasta **Mr Colin G. R. Booth**
3 **CANNIZARO (IRE)**, 4, b f Gallic League—Paradise Regained **Wimbledon Racing Club**
4 **LA FILLE DE CIRQUE**, 4, ch f Cadeaux Genereux—Lady of The Land **Mr Richard I. Morris Jr**
5 **LEXUS (IRE)**, 8, b g Gorytus (USA)—Pepi Image (USA) **Marriott Stables Limited**

MR R. J. R. WILLIAMS—continued

6 **PREMIER BLUES (FR)**, 6, b m Law Society (USA)—Etoile d'Ocean (USA) **Mr Gerry Crean**
7 **TIROLETTE (IRE)**, 4, b f Tirol—Etage **Mr Richard I. Morris Jr**

THREE-YEAR-OLDS

8 **BELLAPHENTO**, b f Lyphento (USA)—Nautical Belle **Mr J. E. Sainsbury**
9 **CAPTURE THE MOMENT**, b f Keen—Shaieef (IRE) **The Really Keen Partnership**
10 **HOTLIPS HOULIHAN**, b f Risk Me (FR)—Lana's Pet **Mr Harry Ormesher**
11 **VIENNESE DANCER**, b f Prince Sabo—Harmony Park **The Super Trouper Partnership**

TWO-YEAR-OLDS

12 B f 11/4 Be My Chief (USA)—Echoing (Formidable (USA)) **Mr G. A. Libson and Partners**
13 **ETOILE DES NEIGE (FR)**, b f 15/5 Saint Cyrien (FR)—Snowdrop (FR) (Niniski (USA)) **Chiquita Lodge Stud**
14 B c 24/4 Rainbow Quest (USA)—Formosanta (Believe It (USA)) **Alexander MacGillivray**
15 B f 25/5 Subotica (FR)—Korinetta (FR) (Petingo) **Chiquita Lodge Stud**
16 B f 30/4 Risk Me (FR)—Lana's Pet (Tina's Pet) **Alexander MacGillivray**
17 **LE GRAND GOUSIER (USA)**, ch c 20/3 Strawberry Road (AUS)—
Sandy Baby (USA) (Al Hattab (USA)) **Alexander MacGillivray**
18 Gr c 2/4 Chilibang—Mazarine Blue (Bellypha)
19 **PIZZICATO**, b f 13/4 Statoblest—Musianica (Music Boy) **Richard I. Morris Jr**
20 **RADAR O'REILLY**, b c 26/2 Almoojid—Travel Bye (Miller's Mate) **Harry Ormesher**
21 B f 17/2 Mac's Imp (USA)—Sally Fay (IRE) (Fayruz)
22 **SMUGURS (IRE)**, ch f 10/4 Masterclass (USA)—Blue Vista (IRE) (Pennine Walk) **Mugs R Us Partnership**
23 Ch f 2/4 Classic Music (USA)—Spectacular Rise (USA) (Phone Trick (USA))
24 B c 7/4 Suave Dancer (USA)—Sunny Flower (FR) (Dom Racine (FR)) **Alexander MacGillivray**
25 B f 23/2 Alleged (USA)—Torrid Tango (USA) (Green Dancer (USA)) **Alexander MacGillivray**

Other Owners: Richard Abbott, Mr D. Bevan, Mr Geoffrey Taylor, Mr Derek Thompson.

Jockeys (Flat): D Biggs, R Cochrane.

Apprentice: Tracy Johnson (8-4).

642   MR S. C. WILLIAMS, Newmarket

Postal: **Trillium Place, Birdcage Walk, Newmarket, Suffolk, CB8 ONE.**
Phone: **YARD (01638) 663984 HOME & FAX (01638) 560143**

1 **CONCER UN**, 4, ch g Lord Bud—Drudwen **Miss L. J. Ward**
2 **FRAMED (IRE)**, 6, b g Tate Gallery (USA)—Golden Thread **Mr Luke McGarrigle**
3 **GREEN LAND (BEL)**, 4, b f Hero's Honor (USA)—Heavy Land (FR) **Mrs V. Vilain**
4 **REVERAND THICKNESS**, 5, b g Prince Sabo—Wollow Maid **Waresley Partnership**

THREE-YEAR-OLDS

5 **AFON ALWEN**, ch f Henbit (USA)—Brenig **Miss L. J. Ward**
6 **AMAZING GRACE (IRE)**, b f Polish Patriot (USA)—Sepideh **Mr D. A. Shekells**
7 **ATIENZA (USA)**, ch f Chief's Crown (USA)—Hattab Voladora (USA) **Mr W. J. de Ruiter**
8 **CHARMING BRIDE**, b f Charmer—Loredana **Mr D. A. Shekells**
9 **CLASSIC COLLEEN (IRE)**, b f Sadler's Wells (USA)—Nawara **Classic Bloodstock Plc**
10 **CLASSIC COLOURS (USA)**, ch c Blushing John (USA)—All Agleam (USA) **Classic Bloodstock Plc**
11 **CLASSIC EAGLE**, b c Unfuwain (USA)—La Lutine **Classic Bloodstock Plc**
12 **CLASSIC FIND (USA)**, b br c Lear Fan (USA)—Reve de Reine (USA) **Classic Bloodstock Plc**
13 **CLASSIC FLYER (IRE)**, b f Alzao (USA)—Sea Harrier **Classic Bloodstock Plc**
14 **CLASSIC JENNY (IRE)**, b f Green Desert (USA)—Eileen Jenny (IRE) **Classic Bloodstock Plc**
15 **CLASSIC LEADER**, b c Thatching—Tenderetta **Classic Bloodstock Plc**
16 **CLASSIC ROYALE (USA)**, b f Chief's Crown (USA)—Cuidado (USA) **Classic Bloodstock Plc**
17 **CLASSIC WARRIOR**, b c Sharpo—Petty Purse **Classic Bloodstock Plc**

MR S. C. WILLIAMS—continued

18 **DANICO**, ch c Most Welcome—Spica (USA) **Mr P. Geoghan**
19 **DIASAFINA**, b f Safawan—Diana Dee **Mr C. I. Henty**
20 **EBEN NAAS (USA)**, b c Dayjur (USA)—Regal State (USA) **Mr J. Lovitt**
21 **FAIRY HIGHLANDS (IRE)**, b f Fairy King (USA)—Breyani **Dr K. Rhode**
22 **GREEN GEM (BEL)**, b f Pharly (FR)—Batalya (BEL) **Mr Patrick Madelein**
23 **LUCITINO**, ch f Bustino—Lucky Fingers **Mrs A. Stacey**
24 **MYSTIQUE SMILE**, ch f Music Boy—Jay Gee Ell **Mr G. Thom**
25 **ON THE NOSE**, ch f Sharpo—Wollow Maid **Lomifa Partnership**
26 **SALSIAN**, b f Salse (USA)—Phylae **Mr I. A. Southcott**
27 **TRACEABILITY**, b g Puissance—Miss Petella **Mr J. Lovitt**

TWO-YEAR-OLDS

28 **ALLIED ACADEMY**, ch c 13/2 Royal Academy (USA)—Tsungani (Cure The Blues (USA)) **Mr I. A. Southcott**
29 **BOLDLY CLIFF (BEL)**, b c 2/4 Never So Bold—Miami Beach (Miami Springs)
30 Ch f 3/2 Mujtahid (USA)—Clear Procedure (USA) (The Minstrel (CAN)) **Mr D. A. Shekells**
31 **GREEN GROOM**, b c 31/3 Groom Dancer (USA)—Flying Sauce (Sauceboat (USA)) **Mr P. Madelein**
32 **NEON DEION (IRE)**, b c 28/1 Alzao (USA)—Sharnazad (IRE) (Track Barron (USA))
33 **SCARROTS**, b c 27/2 Mazilier (USA)—Bath (Runnett)
34 **WHEILDON**, ch c 29/3 Keen—Arabian Rose (USA) (Lyphard (USA))

Other Owners: Mr P. Dennis, Mr A. Gleeson, Mr P. Leach, Lloyd Bros, Mr J. Mears, Mr P. Norris, Mr M. Peacock, Mr A. Simpson, Mrs M. E. Southcott, Mr J. Sturnham, Mr M. Swannell, Mr B. Wyatt.

Jockey (Flat): Kevin Darley (w.a.).

Apprentice: D Williams (7-3).

643   MRS S. D. WILLIAMS, South Molton

Postal: **Hilltown, Mariansleigh, South Molton, Devon, EX36 4NS.**
Phone: **BISHOPS NYMPTON (01769) 550291 FAX (01769) 573661**

1 **AMBLESIDE (IRE)**, 5, b g Kambalda—Noellespir **Mr B. Yin**
2 **ARCTIC CHANTER**, 4, b g Arctic Lord—Callope (USA) **Mr Mike Rowe**
3 **BLASKET HERO**, 8, gr g Kalaglow—Glory Isle **Mrs Sarah D. Williams**
4 **CHANCE ENCOUNTER**, 6, b g Sulaafah (USA)—Bernigra Girl **Mr Ian Abrahams**
5 **JIMMY'S FANCY (IRE)**, 8, ch g Pimpernels Tune—Highway Girl **Mr S. A. Jones**
6 **LAUREN'S TREASURE (IRE)**, 5, b g Satco (FR)—Fern Glen **Mrs Sarah D. Williams**
7 **MANOR BOUND**, 6, ch m Baron Blakeney—Stormbound **Mrs Sarah D. Williams**
8 **MIDNIGHT LADY**, 10, gr m Foveros (GR)—Astrofengia (GR) **Mr G. Karatzlenis**
9 **MOULTAZIM (USA)**, 6, b g Diesis—Maysoon **Mr M. Oseman**
10 **NEWS FROM AFAR**, 5, b g Ardross—My Purple Prose **Christopher Shirley Brasher**
11 **RI NA MARA (IRE)**, 5, b g King's Ride—Aqua Pura **Mr Michael Sturgess**
12 **SECRET FOUR**, 10, b g My Top—Secret Top **The Premier Dozen Racing Partnership**
13 **SOUTHERNHAY BOY**, 5, b g Minster Son—Lady Andrea **Mr D. C. Coard**
14 **SPOROS (GR)**, 8, ch g Fanis (GR)—Hildarose (GR) **Mr G. Karatzlenis**
15 **YOUNG DUKE (IRE)**, 8, gr g Double Schwartz—Princess Pamela **Mr C. Budd**

Other Owners: Mr P. Masterson, Lord Roborough, Mrs S. J. Stovold, Mrs Pat Sturgess.

644 MISS VENETIA WILLIAMS, Hereford

Postal: **Aramstone, Kings Caple, Hereford, HR1 4TU.**

Phone: **(01432) 840646**

1 **BALLY CLOVER,** 9, ch g Deep Run—Miss de Jager **Mr James Williams**
2 **BORO EIGHT,** 10, b g Deep Run—Boro Nickel **Mr M. Murphy**
3 **CHANGE THE ACT,** 11, b g Furry Glen—Raise The Standard **Mr Christopher Foley**
4 **CHANNELS GATE,** 12, b g Fine Blue—Collies Pet **Cabalva Racing Partnership**
5 **DON'T LIGHT UP,** 10, b g Lighter—Hannah's Bar **Miss V. M. Williams**
6 **FORTRIA ROSIE DAWN,** 6, b m Derring Rose—Fortria **Mr M. J. Fenn**
7 **GLAISDALE (IRE),** 7, b g Lomond (USA)—Glass Slipper **Miss V. M. Williams**
8 **GUIDO (IRE),** 5, b g Supreme Leader—Cool Amanda **Mr P. Tompsett**
9 **HARRISTOWN LADY,** 9, b m Muscatite—Harristown Rose **Mr Stephen P. Berson**
10 **KAYTU'S CAROUSEL,** 7, ch m Kaytu—Touching Clouds **Miss A. C. Gibbons**
11 **KINGSWOOD MANOR,** 4, b g Exodal (USA)—Angelic Appeal **Mr Robert Allen**
12 **MONRUSH (IRE),** 5, b g Shirley Heights—Switched On **Mrs M. Devine**
13 **RAPHAEL BODINE (IRE),** 7, b g Crash Course—Noelbonne Femme **Mr Howard Parker**
14 **ROSENCRANTZ (IRE),** 4, b g Sadler's Wells (USA)—Rosananti **Mr F. Ransom**
15 **STORM NORTH,** 6, b g Slip Anchor—Artic Mistral (CAN) **Mr Irvin S. Naylor**
16 **WYE OATS,** 7, b m Oats—River Belle **Miss J. C. Andrews**

Other Owners: Mrs A. Devine, Mr W. J. Fenn, Mrs Revel Guest Albert, Mr J. J. Higginson, Mr P. Jennings, Mr H. Kaye, Mr Alan Parker, Mrs I. Phillips, Mrs A. T. Savage, Mr J. Williams.

645 MR A. J. WILSON, Cheltenham

Postal: **Glenfall Stables, Ham, Charlton Kings, Cheltenham, GL52 6NH.**

Phone: **(01242) 244713 OR (01242) 226319**

1 **FITZGANDHI,** 7, b g Majestic Maharaj—Belle Deirdrie **Mrs M. J. Wilson**
2 **GLENBROOK D'OR,** 12, b g Le Coq d'Or—Wedderburn **Mr Tim Leadbeater**
3 **GLENBROOK FORT,** 7, br m Fort Nayef—Wedderburn **Mr Tim Leadbeater**
4 **GREY STORY,** 8, gr g Scallywag—Fixby Story **Mr G. J. Phillips**
5 **HEIGHTH OF FAME,** 5, b g Shirley Heights—Land of Ivory (USA) **Simon T. Lewis**
6 **JEASSU,** 13, b g Whistlefield—Menhaden **The Up and Running Partnership**
7 **JUNGLE KING (NZ),** 7, ch g Kings Island—Jungle Licence (AUS) **A. M. Darlington**
8 **KINO'S CROSS,** 7, b g Relkino—Coral Delight **Mr N. V. Harvey**
9 **MR KERMIT,** 5, b g Rolfe (USA)—Sea Dart **Mr D. G. Blagden**
10 **NEEDWOOD MUPPET,** 9, b g Rolfe (USA)—Sea Dart **Mr D. G. Blagden**
11 **NEEDWOOD NATIVE,** 8, b g Rolfe (USA)—The Doe **Mr D. G. Blagden**
12 **PARTY LADY (IRE),** 7, ch m Sandalay—Lady Coleman **Mr Tim Leadbeater**
13 **ROYAL PIPER (NZ),** 9, b g Piperhill—Blue Ice (NZ) **A. M. Darlington**
14 **WOEFUL LAKE,** 5, b m Kinglet—Miss Horatio **Mrs J. E. Brookes**
15 **WOT NO GIN,** 7, b g Broadsword (USA)—Lawnswood Miss **Mr Malcolm Penney**
16 **YOUNG TYCOON (NZ),** 5, b g Young Runaway—Spare Money (NZ) **A. M. Darlington**

Other Owners: Mr D. B. Gallop, Mrs J. E. Mills.

646 MR D. A. WILSON, Epsom

Postal: **Cedar Point Racing Stables, Headley Road, Epsom, Surrey, KT18 6BH.**

Phone: **OFFICE (0372) 278327 MOBILE (0836) 226492 HOME/FAX (0372) 273839**

1 **AHJAY,** 6, br h Tina's Pet—City Link Rose **Mr R. J. Thomas**
2 **CHEVELEY DANCER (USA),** 8, b g Northern Baby (CAN)—Alwah (USA) **Mr G. A. Jackman**
3 **GREEN GOLIGHTLY (USA),** 5, b h Green Dancer (USA)—Polly Daniels (USA) **Mr T. S. M. S. Riley-Smith**

MR D. A. WILSON—continued

 4 HIGH FIVE (IRE), 6, b g High Line—Finger Lake **Mr D. A. Wilson**
 5 KESTON POND (IRE), 6, b g Taufan (USA)—Maria Renata **Mr T. S. M. S. Riley-Smith**
 6 PAIR OF JACKS (IRE), 6, ch g Music Boy—Lobbino **Mr D. A. Wilson**
 7 SHEPHERD MARKET (IRE), 5, b g Common Grounds—Dame Solitaire (CAN) **Mr T. S. M. S. Riley-Smith**

THREE-YEAR-OLDS

 8 GOVERNOR'S BID, b g Governor General—Maiden Bidder **Mr J. S. S. Hollins**
 9 SUNSET HARBOUR (IRE), br f Prince Sabo—City Link Pet **Mr R. J. Thomas**

Other Owners: Mr G. Steinberg.

Jockeys (Flat): G Carter (7-12), W Newnes (8-2), B Rouse (8-0), J Williams (8-3).

Jockeys (NH): D Bridgwater (9-7), C Llewellyn (10-0), A Maguire (10-0).

Apprentice: Rachael Moody (7-3).

Lady Riders: Elaine Bronson (9-0), Miss Diana Jones (9-0), Miss P Jones (9-0).

647   CAPT J. H. WILSON, Preston

Postal: **Moor Farm, Sollom, Tarleton, Preston, PR4 6HR.**

Phone: **(01772) 812780**

 1 MHEMEANLES, 6, br g Jalmood (USA)—Folle Idee (USA) **Mr G. A. Farndon**
 2 PERSONIMUS, 6, b g Ballacashtal (CAN)—Sea Charm **Mrs G. S. Rees**
 3 TREMENDISTO, 6, b g Petoski—Misty Halo **Capt James Wilson**

THREE-YEAR-OLDS

 4 AMY LEIGH (IRE), b f Imperial Frontier (USA)—Hollyberry (IRE) **Mr J. P. Hacking**
 5 JIMJAREER (IRE), br c Jareer (USA)—Onthecomet **Mr J. P. Hacking**
 6 KATIE KOMAITE, b f Komaite (USA)—City To City **Red Rose Partnership**
 7 NKAPEN ROCKS (SPA), b c Risk Me (FR)—Debutina Park **Lady Lilford**
 8 YUPPY GIRL (IRE), ch f Salt Dome (USA)—Sloane Ranger **Mr J. P. Hacking**

TWO-YEAR-OLDS

 9 Ch f 11/3 Superpower—Apocalypse (Auction Ring (USA))
 10 JUST VISITING, b f 6/4 Superlative—Just Julia (Natroun (FR)) **Mr & Mrs H. Moszkowicz**
 11 KOMASTA, b c 27/3 Komaite (USA)—Sky Fighter (Hard Fought) **F. Cunliffe**
 12 B c 8/2 Ballacashtal (CAN)—Nutwood Emma (Henbit (USA))
 13 Gr c 30/5 Always Fair (USA)—Restless Bethy (FR) (Bellypha)
 14 Ch c 29/4 Orchestra—Seapoint (Major Point) **Mrs C. Black**

Other Owners: Mr P. W. Phillips, Mr Michael M. Taylor.

Apprentice: Angela Hartley (7-7).

Lady Rider: Mrs G S Rees (8-10).

648 MISS S. J. WILTON, Stoke-on-Trent

Postal: **Round Meadow Racing Stables, Rownal Road, Wetley Rocks, Stoke-on-Trent, ST9 0BP.**
Phone: **HOME 0782 550861 OFFICE 0782 550115 FAX 0782 550158 MOBILE 0831 659666**

1 **ALAN BALL**, 10, b g Broadsword (USA)—Keshoon **Mr John Pointon**
2 **BACKSTABBER**, 6, ch g Flash of Steel—Guest List **Mr Ken Baker**
3 **BRER FOX (IRE)**, 7, b g Orchestra—Winter Fox **Gilberts Animal Feeds Products**
4 **CRIME CRACKER**, 5, b m Broadsword (USA)—Burley Hill Lass **Mr Martin Pointon**
5 **DANCING AT LAHARN (IRE)**, 6, b g Euphemism—Beau Lady **Gilberts Animal Feed Products**
6 **DANCING RANGER**, 5, b g Broadsword (USA)—Elegant Nell **Gilberts Animal Feed Products**
7 **GOING GREY**, 6, gr g Little Wolf—Lion And Lamb **Gilberts Animal Feed Products**
8 **GOOD CAUSE**, 12, ch h Kris—Goodwin Sands (USA) **Gilberts Animal Feed Products**
9 **GRANGEDEAL ILLEGAL**, 8, b g Town And Country—Burley Hill Lass **Gilberts Animal Feed Products**
10 **HIGH GRADE**, 8, b g High Top—Bright Sun
11 **INALTO**, 8, ch g Town And Country—Keshoon **Gilberts Animal Feed Products**
12 **LEGAL STREAK**, 9, b g Mr Fluorocarbon—Streakella **Gilberts Animal Feed Products**
13 **LORD FREDERICK**, 4, b g Wonderful Surprise—Romany Framboise **Mr Dave Dutton**
14 **MEADOW DANCER**, 5, ch m Broadsword (USA)—Lion And Lamb **Gilberts Animal Feed Products**
15 **MO ICHI DO**, 10, b g Lomond (USA)—Engageante (FR) **Miss Sue Wilton**
16 **NIGELSCHINAPALACE**, 7, b g Comrade In Arms—Ergo **Gilberts Animal Feed Products**
17 **SALTY SNACKS (IRE)**, 7, b g Callernish—Salty Sea **Gilberts Animal Feed Products**
18 **SMART DEBUTANTE (IRE)**, 7, b m Glenstal (USA)—Cecily **Gilberts Animal Feed Products**
19 **TOFTY'S TUNE**, 5, gr g Singing Steven—Sawk **The Ducking And Diving**

Other Owners: Mr Michael J. Dwyer, Mr Carl Pointon, Mr Peter Toft.

Jockey (NH): T Eley (10-0).

Conditional: M Kolosine (9-10), A Large (10-0).

649 MR K. G. WINGROVE, Newmarket

Postal: **Albert Cottage Stables, Albert Street, Newmarket, Suffolk, CB8 8DT.**
Phone: **(0589) 850700**

1 **BINLABOON (IRE)**, 5, b br h Polish Precedent (USA)—Aldhabyih **First In Racing Partnership**
2 **CHICAGO'S BEST**, 9, gr g Try My Best (USA)—Maryville Bick **Mr Alan Bosley**
3 **FIRE CARPET (USA)**, 6, b g Blushing Groom (FR)—Mystical Mood (USA) **Mr Alan Bosley**
4 **FLAMING SANDS (IRE)**, 7, ch m Sandalay—Shady Ahan **Mr M. M. Foulger**
5 **GREEN APACHE**, 4, b g Green Desert (USA)—Can Can Girl **First In Racing Partnership**
6 **NOBLE SOCIETY**, 8, b g Law Society (USA)—Be Noble **First In Racing Partnership**
7 **NOVELLINI**, 6, b m Relkino—Roseitess **Miss Catriona MacDonald**
8 **RAY RIVER**, 4, b g Waki River (FR)—Mrs Feathers **Mr Roger Nicholls**
9 **ROSMOJIQUE STAR (IRE)**, 4, b f Cyrano de Bergerac—Ring Dem Bells **Miss Catriona MacDonald**
10 **SIR EDWARD HENRY (IRE)**, 6, b g Taufan (USA)—Finessing **Mr R. J. Bateman**
11 **SISON (IRE)**, 6, b g Vacarme (USA)—Silent Sail **Mr M. M. Foulger**
12 **STRAW THATCH**, 7, b g Thatching—Lashing (USA) **Mr S. P. Burston**
13 **TURNER PRIZE (IRE)**, 6, b g Tate Gallery (USA)—Pansoverina **First In Racing Partnership**
14 **WATER DIVINER**, 6, b g Dowsing—Prudence **Mr K. G. Wingrove**

Other Owners: Mr M. E. Bradbury, Mr A. N. Bridges, Mr K. G. Wingrove.

Jockey (NH): John Ryan (10-0).

Apprentices: M Baird (7-0), P McCabe (7-8).

650　　MR P. WINKWORTH, Dunsfold

Postal: **Merton Place Stud, Dunsfold, Surrey. GU8 4NP**

Phone: **(01483) 200211 FAX (01483) 200878**

1 **ADDED DIMENSION (IRE)**, 5, b g Top Ville—Lassalia **Mrs Tessa Winkworth**
2 **ROSINA MAE**, 7, b m Rousillon (USA)—Dame Ashfield **Mr P. Winkworth**
3 4, B f Phardante (FR)—Rositary (FR) **Mr P. Winkworth**
4 **SO HUMBLE**, 5, b g Petoski—Altara (GER) **Mrs Tessa Winkworth**
5 **THE CARROT MAN**, 8, ch g True Song—Minor Furlong **Mrs Jill Winkworth**

Jockeys (NH): P Hide (w.a.), J R Kavanagh (w.a.).

651　　MISS L. J. WONNACOTT, Lifton

Postal: **Kellybeare, Lifton, Devon, PL16 0HQ.**

Phone: **(01566) 784278**

1 **FLEETING GLANCE**, 7, b m Lightning Dealer—Seabright Smile **Miss Linda Wonnacott**
2 **POLLOCK (FR)**, 13, b g Arctic Tern (USA)—Golden Gleam (FR) **Miss Linda Wonnacott**
3 **SKELTON PRINCESS (IRE)**, 5, b m Carmelite House (USA)—Fariha **Miss Linda Wonnacott**

Jockey (NH): D Morris.

Amateur: Mr J Culloty.

652　　MR R. S. WOOD, York

Postal: **Manor Farm, Nawton, York, YO6 5RD.**

Phone: **(01439) 771627**

1 **BLAZING HOLLY**, 4, br f Holly Buoy—Stuart's Gem **Mr R. S. Wood**
2 **DANCING HOLLY**, 9, br g Mufrij—Holly Doon **Mr R. S. Wood**
3 **OWES THE TILL**, 6, br m General David—Stuart's Gem **Mr R. S. Wood**

THREE-YEAR-OLDS

4 **GEM OF HOLLY**, br f Holly Buoy—Stuart's Gem **Mr R. S. Wood**

653　　MR R. D. E. WOODHOUSE, York

Postal: **Teal House, Welburn, York, YO6 7EJ.**

Phone: WHITWELL ON THE HILL **(01653618) 637**

1 **BOSTON BOMBER**, 5, b g Wonderful Surprise—Miss Anax **Mr R. D. E. Woodhouse**
2 **BOSTON MAN**, 5, b g True Song—Tempest Girl **Mr M. K. Oldham**
3 **DESERT MAN**, 5, b g Green Desert (USA)—Grayfoot **Mr David Scott**
4 **GAF**, 4, b g Wonderful Surprise—Jeanne du Barry **Mr G. A. Farndon**
5 **GRACE CARD**, 10, b g Ela-Mana-Mou—Val de Grace (FR) **Mr G. A. Farndon**
6 **MASTER BOSTON (IRE)**, 8, gr g Soughaan (USA)—Ballinoe Lass **Mr M. K. Oldham**
7 **PHARARE (IRE)**, 6, ch g Phardante (FR)—Shakie Lady **Mr C. F. Colquhoun**
8 **SHREWD JOHN**, 10, b g John French—Seal Shrew **Mr R. D. E. Woodhouse**
9 **TARO CARD (IRE)**, 5, b g Lancastrian—More Chat **Mr G. A. Farndon**
10 **TAROUDANT**, 9, b g Pharly (FR)—Melbourne Miss **Mr G. A. Farndon**

THREE-YEAR-OLDS

11 **KENILWORTH DANCER**, br g Shareef Dancer (USA)—Reltop **Mr G. A. Farndon**
12 **MY ARCHIE**, b c Silver Arch—My Alma (IRE) **Mr G. A. Farndon**

Jockey (Flat): N Connorton (7-8).

Jockeys (NH): M Dwyer (10-0), N Williamson (10-0).

654 MR S. WOODMAN, Chichester

Postal: **Parkers Barn Stables, East Lavant, Chichester, West Sussex, PO18 0AU.**

Phone: **OFFICE (01243) 527136**

1 **BY ARRANGEMENT (IRE)**, 7, b m Bold Arrangement—Eulalie **Mrs Sally Woodman**
2 **CHINA ROSE**, 5, b m Mossberry—Tennis Track **Mrs Tina Martin**
3 **CREDON**, 8, b g Sunyboy—Credo's Daughter **Fusilier Racing**
4 **KING CREDO**, 11, b g Kinglet—Credo's Daughter **Mr J. C. Bolam**
5 **MACNAMARA (IRE)**, 6, ch g Orchestra—Curraheen **Mr J. C. Bolam**
6 **MINKY MURRU**, 6, br m Mossberry—Tennis Track **Mrs Tina Martin**
7 **NIGHT IN A MILLION**, 5, br g Night Shift (USA)—Ridalia **Leith Hill Chasers**
8 **OUT OF ACES**, 6, b m Relkino—Gambling Wren **Mr Christian Wroe**
9 **SATIN NOIR (FR)**, 12, b g Polonium (FR)—Italienne (FR) **Mr Michael Kent**
10 **SMOKEY THUNDER (IRE)**, 6, br g Miners Lamp—Moorstown Lady **Mrs Fiona Gordon**
11 **STIPPLE**, 5, ch m Blushing Scribe (USA)—April **Mr Christian Wroe**

Other Owners: Mr G. Gornall, Miss Susan Jameson, Mr Andrew Lee, Mrs N. F. Maltby, Mr Brian Plaistowe, Ms Fiona Slomovic, Mr James Wilkinson.

Jockeys (NH): R Dunwoody (w.a.), A Maguire (w.a.).

655 MRS A. M. WOODROW, High Wycombe

Postal: **Crookswood Stud Farm, Horsleys Green, High Wycombe, Bucks, HP14 3XB.**

Phone: **(01494) 482557**

1 **MUALLAF (IRE)**, 4, b g Unfuwain (USA)—Honourable Sheba (USA) **Mrs Ann Woodrow & Mr John Woodrow**
2 **NIGHT FANCY**, 8, ch g Night Shift (USA)—Smooth Siren (USA) **Mrs Ann Woodrow**
3 **PEGMARINE (USA)**, 13, b g Text (USA)—Symbionese (USA) **Mrs Ann Woodrow**

Jockeys (NH): J A McCarthy (10-0), P McLoughlin, A Thornton (10-0).

656 MR S. P. C. WOODS, Newmarket

Postal: **La Grange Stables, Snailwell Road, Newmarket, Suffolk, CB8 7DP.**

Phone: **(01638) 561844 FAX (01638) 561352**

1 **ANOTHER TIME**, 4, ch g Clantime—Another Move **Mr D. Sullivan**
2 **BUBBLE WINGS (FR)**, 4, b f In The Wings—Bubble Prospector (USA) **Dr Frank S. B. Chao**
3 **CANTON VENTURE**, 4, ch g Arctic Tern (USA)—Ski Michaela (USA) **Dr Frank S. B. Chao**
4 **HOUGHTON VENTURE (USA)**, 4, ch c Groom Dancer (USA)—Perle Fine (USA) **Dr Frank S. B. Chao**
5 **JADE VENTURE**, 5, b m Never So Bold—Our Shirley **Dr Frank S. B. Chao**
6 **MISTLE CAT (USA)**, 6, gr h Storm Cat (USA)—Mistle Toe (USA) **Mr P. K. L. Chu**
7 **ORINOCO VENTURE (IRE)**, 5, br g Doyoun—Push A Button **Dr Frank S. B. Chao**
8 **PEARL VENTURE**, 4, b f Salse (USA)—Our Shirley **Dr Frank S. B. Chao**
9 **PRIMA COMINNA**, 4, ch f Unfuwain (USA)—Cominna **Dr Frank S. B. Chao**
10 **TRANS SIBERIA**, 5, gr g Siberian Express (USA)—Olivian **Mr H. Laska**

THREE-YEAR-OLDS

11 **ANCHOR VENTURE**, b c Slip Anchor—Ski Michaela (USA) **Dr Frank S. B. Chao**
12 **ANOTHER QUARTER (IRE)**, b f Distinctly North (USA)—Numidia **Mr Tony Murray**
13 **BALOUSTAR (USA)**, b f Green Forest (USA)—Ballerina Star (USA) **Mr R. M. E. Taylor**
14 **COINTOSSER (IRE)**, b f Nordico (USA)—Sure Flyer (IRE) **Mr Arashan Ali**
15 **COOL FIRE**, b c Colmore Row—Into The Fire **Mr D. Sullivan**
16 **FIKRA (USA)**, b f Gulch (USA)—Bolt From The Blue (USA) **Mr S. P. C. Woods**
17 **HALEBID**, b c Dowsing (USA)—Pink Robber (USA) **Mr S. P. C. Woods**

MR S. P. C. WOODS—continued

18 **HAMPI (USA)**, b f Runaway Groom (USA)—Foresighted Lady (USA) **Mr S. P. C. Woods**
19 **HANNALOU (FR)**, b f Shareef Dancer (USA)—Litani River (USA) **Mr Tony Murray**
20 **JUMP THE LIGHTS**, b g Siberian Express (USA)—Turtle Dove **Mr S. P. C. Woods**
21 **MARSARA**, ch f Never So Bold—Night Transaction **Mr Mark D. Johnson**
22 **NEED YOU BADLY**, b f Robellino (USA)—Persian Tapestry **Mr Arashan Ali**
23 **POLAR CHAMP**, b g Polar Falcon (USA)—Ceramic (USA) **Mr P. K. L. Chu**
24 **SCATHEBURY**, b g Aragon—Lady Bequick **Mr Mark D. Johnson**
25 **SHIRLEY VENTURE**, b f Be My Chief (USA)—Our Shirley **Dr Frank S. B. Chao**

TWO-YEAR-OLDS

26 B c 19/3 Sharpo—Aventina (Averof) **Mr Arashan Ali**
27 B f 3/5 Robellino (USA)—Carolside (Music Maestro) **Mr Arashan Ali**
28 **GEORGIA**, b f 9/4 Shirley Heights—Georgica (USA) (Raise A Native) **Dr Frank S. B. Chao**
29 **GREEN CARD (USA)**, b c 30/3 Green Dancer (USA)—Dunkellin (USA) (Irish River (FR)) **Mr P. K. L. Chu**
30 **JANGLYNYVE**, ch f 27/4 Sharpo—Wollow Maid (Wollow) **The Storm Again Syndicate**
31 B f 12/5 Distinctly North—Littleton Song (Song)
32 Ch c 21/5 Gold Alert (USA)—Mutterfly (USA) (Muttering (USA)) **A. Rutter**
33 B f 24/3 Pursuit Of Love—Our Shirley (Shirley Heights) **Dr Frank S. B. Chao**
34 Ch f 22/4 Risk Me (FR)—Princess Lily (Blakeney)
35 **PUSH A VENTURE**, b f 9/3 Shirley Heights—Push A Button (Bold Lad (IRE)) **Dr Frank S. B. Chao**
36 B c 9/3 Shirley Heights—Ski Michaela (USA) (Devil's Bag (USA)) **Dr Frank S. B. Chao**
37 **TIROL VENTURE**, b c 5/3 Thatching—Relatively Sharp (Sharpen Up) **Dr Frank S. B. Chao**
38 Ch c 7/4 Keen—Turtle Dove (Gyr (USA))
39 **UKRAINE VENTURE**, b f 29/1 Slip Anchor—Sherkraine (Shergar) **Dr Frank S. B. Chao**

Other Owners: Mr C. Callaghan, Mr R. A. Crawley, Mr Bob Goodes, Mr D. Raffel, Mr B. Stewart.

Jockey (Flat): W Woods (8-2).

Apprentice: J Moon (7-12).

657   MR GEOFFREY WRAGG, Newmarket

Postal: **Abington Place, Bury Road, Newmarket, Suffolk, CB8 7BT.**
Phone: **OFFICE (01638) 2328 FAX (01638) 663576 TELEX 94016161 WRAG G**

1 **ARCADIAN HEIGHTS**, 8, b g Shirley Heights—Miss Longchamp **Mr J. L. C. Pearce**
2 **CROSSILLION**, 8, b g Rousillon (USA)—Croda Rossa (ITY) **Mr G. Wragg**
3 **FIRST ISLAND (IRE)**, 4, ch c Dominion—Caymana (FR) **Mollers Racing**
4 **GRAND GUIGNOL**, 8, ch g Superlative—Boule de Suif **Mollers Racing**
5 **IBLIS (IRE)**, 4, b c Danehill (USA)—In Unison **Mrs Nicola Bscher**
6 **MOKUTI**, 4, b c Green Desert (USA)—Marie d'Argonne (FR) **Baron G. von Ullmann**
7 **PENTIRE**, 4, b c Be My Guest (USA)—Gull Nook **Mollers Racing**
8 **SADLER'S WALK**, 5, b g Sadler's Wells (USA)—Widows Walk **Mr A. E. Oppenheimer**
9 **SVELTANA**, 4, b f Soviet Star (USA)—Sally Brown **Mr D. W. Dennis**
10 **TATIKA**, 6, ch g Tate Gallery (USA)—Independentia **Mr G. Wragg**
11 **THE OLD CHAPEL**, 7, b g Lomond (USA)—Chapel Cottage **Baron G. von Ullmann**
12 **WILD RICE**, 4, b c Green Desert (USA)—On Show **Lady Oppenheimer**
13 **YOUNG BUSTER (IRE)**, 8, b h Teenoso (USA)—Bustara **Mollers Racing**

THREE-YEAR-OLDS

14 **ANTHELIA**, b f Distant Relative—Confection **Mrs Claude Lilley**
15 **BERENICE**, b f Groom Dancer (USA)—Belle Arrivee **Gestut Schlenderhan**
16 **CHARLOTTE CORDAY**, b f Kris—Dancing Rocks **Mr A. E. Oppenheimer**
17 **DANTESQUE (IRE)**, b c Danehill (USA)—I Want My Say (USA) **Mollers Racing**
18 **GERMANO**, b c Generous (IRE)—Gay Fantastic **Baron G. von Ullmann**

MR GEOFFREY WRAGG—continued

19 **HENRY ISLAND (IRE),** ch c Sharp Victor (USA)—Monterana **Mr H. H. Morriss**
20 **LARISSA (IRE),** b f Soviet Star (USA)—Pipitina **Sheikh Mohammed**
21 **MAWINGO (IRE),** b c Taufan (USA)—Tappen Zee **Mrs Claude Lilley**
22 **MEZZOGIORNO,** b f Unfuwain (USA)—Aigue **Mrs R. Philipps**
23 **MISS RIVIERA,** b f Kris—Miss Beaulieu **Mr J. L. C. Pearce**
24 **POLISH WIDOW,** b f Polish Precedent (USA)—Widows Walk **Mr A. E. Oppenheimer**
25 **PRIME LIGHT,** ch c Primo Dominie—Flopsy **Mollers Racing**
26 **PRIZE GIVING,** ch c Most Welcome—Glowing With Pride **Lady Oppenheimer**
27 **QUESTING STAR,** b f Rainbow Quest (USA)—Guest Artiste **Mr A. E. Oppenheimer**
28 **RADIANT STAR,** b c Rainbow Quest (USA)—Miss Kuta Beach **Mr J. L. C. Pearce**
29 **SASURU,** c Most Welcome—Sassalya **Lady Oppenheimer**
30 **SHENANGO (IRE),** b g Shernazar—Pipina (USA) **Sheikh Mohammed**
31 **STAR AND GARTER,** ch f Soviet Star (USA)—On Show **Mr A. E. Oppenheimer**
32 **STATELY DANCER,** b f Be My Guest (USA)—Wild Pavane **Mr A. E. Oppenheimer**
33 **TASSILI (IRE),** b c Old Vic—Topsy **Sheikh Mohammed**
34 **WELSH EMBLEM (IRE),** b c Mujtahid (USA)—David's Star **Mollers Racing**

TWO-YEAR-OLDS

35 **APACHE STAR,** b f 18/4 Arazi (USA)—Wild Pavane (Dancing Brave (USA)) **Mr A. E. Oppenheimer**
36 **BARROW CREEK,** ch c 8/2 Cadeaux Genereux—Breadcrumb (Final Straw) **Baron G. von Ullmann**
37 **EGOLI (USA),** ch f 19/2 Seeking The Gold—Krisalya (Kris) **Mr A. E. Oppenheimer**
38 **FABLED LIGHT (IRE),** b c 26/2 Alzao (USA)—Fabled Lifestyle (Kings Lake (USA)) **Mollers Racing**
39 **FINAL TRIAL (IRE),** b c 17/4 Last Tycoon—Perfect Alibi (Law Society (USA)) **Mollers Racing**
40 **FLINT KNAPPER,** ch c 25/1 Kris—Circe's Isle (Be My Guest (USA)) **Mr A. E. Oppenheimer**
41 **GREENAWAY BAY (USA),** ch c 15/2 Green Dancer (USA)—
Raise 'n Dance (USA) (Raise A Native) **Mollers Racing**
42 **GUERNICA,** b f 6/2 Unfuwain (USA)—Greenvera (USA) (Riverman (USA)) **Baron G. von Ullmann**
43 **LA CURAMALAL (IRE),** b f 15/3 Rainbow Quest (USA)—North Telstar (Sallust) **Count Federico Lichy-Thyssen**
44 **MARY CORNWALLIS,** ch f 18/2 Primo Dominie—Infanta Real (Formidable (USA)) **Mrs Claude Lilley**
45 **MISS GOLDEN SANDS,** ch f 3/2 Kris—Miss Kuta Beach (Bold Lad (IRE)) **Mr J. L. C. Pearce**
46 **MISS RIVIERA ROSE,** ch f 14/5 Niniski (USA)—Miss Beaulieu (Northfields (USA)) **Mr J. L. C. Pearce**
47 **MISS SANCERRE,** b f 19/2 Last Tycoon—Miss Bergerac (Bold Lad (IRE)) **Mr J. L. C. Pearce**
48 **MOONSHINER (USA),** b c 21/2 Irish River (FR)—Marling (IRE) (Lomond (USA)) **Baron G. von Ullmann**
49 **MOTET,** b c 19/5 Mtoto—Guest Artiste (Be My Guest (USA)) **Mr A. E. Oppenheimer**
50 **MUCH COMMENDED,** b f 7/4 Most Welcome—
Glowing With Pride (Ile de Bourbon (USA)) **Mr A. E. Oppenheimer**
51 **OCCAM (IRE),** ch c 24/5 Sharp Victor (USA)—Monterana (Sallust) **Mrs H. H. Morriss**
52 B c 11/4 Lear Fan (USA)—Oro Bianco (USA) (Lyphard's Wish (FR)) **Mr P. D. Savill**
53 **REBECCA SHARP,** b f 10/4 Machiavellian (USA)—Nuryana (Nureyev (USA)) **Mr A. E. Oppenheimer**
54 **RED GUARD,** ch c 14/2 Soviet Star (USA)—Zinzara (Stage Door Johnny) **Mr A. E. Oppenheimer**
55 **SALFORD SID,** b c 22/2 Don't Forget Me—Adjusting (IRE) (Busted) **Mr A. J. Thompson**
56 **SNOWCAP (IRE),** b f 15/5 Snow Chief (USA)—Very Subtle (USA) (Hoist The Silver (USA)) **Mr Ben Rochelle**
57 **ST RADEGUND,** b f 17/1 Green Desert (USA)—On The House (FR) (Be My Guest (USA)) **Mr A. E. Oppenheimer**
58 **THE FARAWAY TREE,** b f 12/5 Suave Dancer (USA)—Sassalya (Sassafras (FR)) **Mr A. E. Oppenheimer**
59 **THE PRINCE,** b c 26/3 Machiavellian (USA)—Mohican Girl (Dancing Brave (USA)) **Mr I. R. Macnicol**
60 **TWITCHER'S DELIGHT,** b br f 2/6 Polar Falcon (USA)—Loralane (Habitat) **Mr A. E. Oppenheimer**
61 **WATER GARDEN,** ch c 2/5 Most Welcome—On Show (Welsh Pageant) **Mr A. E. Oppenheimer**

Other Owners: Mrs Anthony Barrow, Bottisham Heath Stud, Mr S. W. S. Broke, Mr A. R. G. Cane, Mr James Charrington, Mr R. Cowell, Mr C. G. Hellyer, Lady De Ramsey, Mr S. J. Richmond Watson, Mr Gerard Strahan, Baroness Karin Von Ullmann.

Jockey (Flat): M Hills (8-0).

Apprentice: G E H Milligan (7-12).

658   MR F. J. YARDLEY, Stourport on Severn

Postal: **YC Group, YC Business Park, Nelsons Road, Stourport on Severn, Worcester, DY13 9PN.**
Phone: **WORCS (01905) 620477 FAX (01299) 824777**

1   4, B g Chief Singer—Absent Lover **Mr F. J. Yardley**
2   **ACHILTIBUIE**, 12, b g Roscoe Blake—Gorgeous Gertie **Maltsword Ltd**
3   **CHIEF INSPIRATION**, 4, gr g Chief Singer—Inspired Love **Maltsword Ltd**
4   **CRYSTAL HEART (IRE)**, 5, ch m Broken Hearted—Arachosia **Mr S. G. Pitt**
5   **ICE MAGIC**, 9, ch g Red Sunset—Free Rein **Mr F. J. Yardley**
6   **MECADO**, 9, b g Ballacashtal (CAN)—Parma Nova **Maltsword Ltd**
7   **NEVADA GOLD**, 10, ch g Kemal (FR)—French Note **Maltsword Ltd**
8   **ORCHARD GOLD**, 5, b h Glint of Gold—On The Top **Mr S. G. Pitt**
9   **PATS FOLLY**, 5, br m Macmillion—Cavo Varka **Mrs P. J. Holt**
10   **SALBUS**, 6, b g Salse (USA)—Busca (USA) **Mr Graham Parker**

THREE-YEAR-OLDS

11   Ch g Risk Me (FR)—Absent Lover **Mr F. J. Yardley**
12   B g Ile de Roi—Claudette **Maltsword Ltd**

Jockey (NH): D Gallagher (10-0).

Lady Rider: Miss Sarah Yardley (8-4).

659   MR G. H. YARDLEY, Malvern

Postal: **Upper Woodsfield Farm, Newland, Malvern, Worcs, WR13 5AQ.**
Phone: **WORCESTER (01905) 830245**

1   **BALLYRANEBOW (IRE)**, 8, ch m Carlingford Castle—Annes Luck **Mr J. T. Jones**
2   **DOUBLE LARK**, 7, b g Bairn (USA)—Straffan Girl **Mrs Carol Harrison**
3   **HO-JOE (IRE)**, 6, b g Burslem—Walkyria **Mr S. Ho**
4   **MISS CHEQUERS ISLE**, 10, ch m Cruise Missile—Chequers Girl
5   **SCHOLAR GREEN**, 4, b g Green Adventure (USA)—Quelle Chemise **Mr P. J. Jones**
6   **SNITTON STREAM**, 6, b g Domitor (USA)—Cala di Volpe **Mr M. P. Aldersey**
7   **STEEL GEM (IRE)**, 7, b h Flash of Steel—Ferjima's Gem (USA) **Mr Mervyn Jones**
8   **ZANDALEE**, 7, gr m Lucky Wednesday—Starkist **Mr J. T. Long**

Jockey (Flat): Russell Price (8-0).

Jockey (NH): W McFarland (10-0).

Conditional: D Leahy.

Lady Rider: Miss A Yardley (8-0).

660   MRS J. A. F. YOUNG, Calne

Postal: **Lower Bupton House, Bupton, Hilmarton, Calne, SN11 8SZ.**
Phone: **(01249) 760538/540**

1   **MARY BOROUGH**, 10, gr m Baron Blakeney—Risello **Mrs Judy Young**
2   **UNCLE BRUCE**, 6, b g Sula Bula—Saxon Belle **Mrs Judy Young**

Jockey (NH): Guy Upton (10-2).

Amateurs: Mr L Baker (9-0), Mr A Charles-Jones (10-0).

661   MR J. R. A. YOUNG, Oakham

Postal: **Brook House, Hambleton Road, Egleton, Oakham, LE15 8AE.**
Phone: **(01572) 770060 FAX (01572) 770051**

1 **GUNNER B SOMEBODY**, 5, b m Gunner B—My Name Is Nobody **Mr J. Young**
2 **THE ARCHORIAN**, 7, b g Sula Bula—My Name Is Nobody **Mr J. Young**
3 **THE HOBORIAN**, 9, b g Sula Bula—My Name Is Nobody **Mr J. Young**

662   MR W. G. YOUNG, Carluke

Postal: **Overton Farm, Crossford, Carluke, Lanarkshire, ML8 5QF.**
Phone: **(01555) 860226**

1 **GOOD PROFIT**, 7, ch g Meadowbrook—Night Profit **Mr W. G. Young**
2 **MEADOWLECK**, 7, b m Meadowbrook—Leckywil **Mr W. G. Young**
3 **MISS JEDD**, 9, gr m Scallywag—Leckywil **Mr W. G. Young**
4 **NORMANS PROFIT**, 6, ch g Meadowbrook—Night Profit **Mr W. G. Young**
5 **SOUND PROFIT**, 8, ch m Scallywag—Night Profit **Mr W. G. Young**

ADDITIONAL TEAMS

663   MR T. W. DONNELLY, Swadlincote

Postal: **Calke Abbey Racing Stables, Heath Lane, Boundary, Swadlincote, DE11 7AY.**
Phone: **(01283) 226046 MOBILE (0585) 405497**

BALLINDOO, 7, ch g Buzzards Bay—Model Lady **Mr R. J. Armson**
CAVATINA, 6, br m Chief Singer—Pennycuick **Hargate Stud and Racing Limited**
KALAMAZUZU, 6, b g Gunner B—Velda **Mr S. Taberner**
KINTAVI, 6, b g Efisio—Princess Tavi **Mr S. Taberner**
LAWFUL LOVE (IRE), 6, b g Law Society (USA)—Amata (USA) **Mrs D. E. Andrews**
MISS CAPULET, 9, b m Commanche Run—Judy Burton **C. I. P. Racing**
SANTARAY, 10, ch g Formidable (USA)—Stockingful **Mr S. Taberner**
TURSAL (IRE), 7, b g Fine Blade (USA)—Turlough Pet **Mr T. W. Donnelly**

Other Owners: Mr M. Bradford, Mr Peter Brain, Mr B. R. Britton, Mr Brian Edwards, Mr E. T. Fitchett, Mr R. W. Hickman, Mr R. F. Hill, Mr P. J. Vale, Mr R. Woods, Mr J. W. Woodward.

Conditional: T Eley.

Amateur: Mr R J Armson.

664   MR P. HUGHES, Bagenalstown

Postal: **Fenniscourt, Bagenalstown, Co. Carlow, Ireland.**

Phone: **(0503) 21250/21882**

ACES AND EIGHTS (IRE), 6, b g Phardante (FR)—No Battle **P. Hughes**
CLUB COUPE (IRE), 4, b g John French—Grainne Mac Cool **P. Hughes**
COOLANGATTA (IRE), 7, ch g Flair Path—Battle Again **P. Hughes**
FENIAN COURT (IRE), 5, ch m John French—Penny Maes **P. Hughes**
GET INTO IT (IRE), 7, b g Phardante (FR)—Lady Liznick **P. Hughes**
LACKEN RIVER (IRE), 4, ch f Over The River (FR)—Cassagh Run **P. Farrell**
5, B g Orchestra—Northern Dandy **M. P. Carroll**
4, B g King's Ride—Penny Holder **P. Hughes**
RARE STATEMENT (IRE), 6, b g Strong Statement—Kitty Run **P. Farrell**
STRONG HURRICANE, 9, b g Strong Gale—Gorryelm **Miss Esther Feeney**
WAIT NO LONGER, 10, b g Le Bavard—Knockaville **P. Hughes**
WHITE OAK BRIDGE (IRE), 7, b m Over The River (FR)—Grainne Mac Cool **J. M. Foley**

Other Owners: Seamus Hughes, A. Larken, Mrs G. T. McKoy.

Jockey (NH): Shane Broderick (w.a.).

Amateur: Mr T R Hughes (9-7).

665   MR D. M. LLOYD, Bridgend

Postal: **Avalon, Brynmenyn, Bridgend, Mid Glam, CF32 9LF.**

Phone: **(01656) 724654**

ARGAKIOS, 9, b g Busted—Salamina **Mr D. M. Lloyd**
VA UTU, 8, b g Balliol—Flame **Mr D. M. Lloyd**

666   MR P. J. MAKIN, Marlborough

Postal: **Bonita Racing Stables, Ogbourne Maisey, Marlborough, Wilts, SN8 1RY.**

Phone: **MARLBOROUGH (01672) 512973 FAX (01672) 514166**

CROWDED AVENUE, 4, b g Sizzling Melody—Lady Bequick **Mr T. W. Wellard**
DOUBLE BOUNCE, 6, b g Interrex (CAN)—Double Gift **Mrs P. Scott-Dunn**
FLIGHT MASTER, 4, ch g Master Willie—Mumtaz Mayfly **Mrs P. J. Makin**
GONE FOR A BURTON (IRE), 6, ch g Bustino—Crimbourne **Mr H. P. Carrington**
JERSEY BELLE, 4, b f Distant Relative—Hong Kong Girl **Mr D. A. Poole**
LITTLE SABOTEUR, 7, ch m Prince Sabo—Shoot To Win (FR) **Lady Walford**
LITTLE SCARLETT, 4, b f Mazilier (USA)—Scarlett Holly **Mrs P. J. Makin**
MAZIRAH, 5, b g Mazilier (USA)—Barbary Court **Mr A. W. Schiff**
MILTAK, 4, b f Risk Me (FR)—Tralee Maiden (IRE) **Mr Peter Haddock**
NAKAMI, 4, b g Dashing Blade—Dara's Bird **Mrs Toshiko Huddie**
OGGI, 5, gr g Efisio—Dolly Bevan **Skyline Racing Ltd**
PALATIAL STYLE, 9, b g Kampala—Stylish Princess **Skyline Racing Ltd**
PURPLE SPLASH, 6, b g Ahonoora—Quay Line **Sir Christopher Walford**
SHARP REBUFF, 5, b h Reprimand—Kukri **Mr D. M. Ahier**
SHINING EXAMPLE, 4, ch g Hadeer—Kick The Habit **Mr D. M. Ahier**
SPANIARDS CLOSE, 8, b g King of Spain—Avon Belle **Avon Industries Ltd**

MR P. J. MAKIN—continued

TONKA, 4, b c Mazilier (USA)—Royal Meeting **Mrs J. M. West**
TROPICAL JUNGLE (USA), 6, b g Majestic Shore (USA)—Diamond Oyster **Mr D. M. Ahier**
WILCUMA, 5, b g Most Welcome—Miss Top Ville (FR) **Mr T. G. Warner**
ZIDAC, 4, b br g Statoblest—Sule Skerry **Mr Brian Brackpool**

THREE-YEAR-OLDS

CHESTEINE, ch f Soviet Lad (USA)—Makalu
KACHUMBER, b g Governor General—La Jambalaya **Mrs P. J. Makin**
KINGS HARMONY (IRE), b g Nordico (USA)—Kingston Rose **Ten of Hearts**
LADY DIGNITY (IRE), b f Nordico (USA)—Royal Respect **Mr J. Garnsey**
MARISTAX, b f Reprimand—Marista **Mr T. G. Warner**
MAZCOBAR, ch c Mazilier (USA)—Barbary Court **Mr A. W. Schiff**
PLEASURELAND (IRE), ch c Don't Forget Me—Elminya (IRE) **Mrs Greta Sarfaty Marchant**
B f Puissance—Plum Bold **Skyline Racing Ltd**
REAL GEM, b f Formidable (USA)—Emerald Ring **Mrs P. J. Makin**
SCIMITAR, ch c Prince Sabo—Siokra **Mr R. P. Marchant**
THORDIS, b g Mazilier (USA)—Doppio **Mr Barrie C. Whitehouse**
WELVILLE, b c Most Welcome—Miss Top Ville (FR) **Mr T. G. Warner**

TWO-YEAR-OLDS

CIRCLE OF MAGIC, gr f 13/4 Midyan (USA)—Miss Witch (High Line) **Mr T. W. Wellard & Partners**
B f 23/2 Mujadil (USA)—Crimbourne (Mummy's Pet) **Bakewell Bloodstock**
Ch c 16/3 Don't Forget Me—Ella Mon Amour (Ela-Mana-Mou)
Ch c 29/4 Sharp Victor (USA)—Fabulous Deed (USA) (Shadeed (USA))
B c 18/4 Common Grounds—Grayfoot (Grundy)
B c 15/4 Mazilier (USA)—La Jambalaya (Reform) **Mrs P. J. Makin**
RACING HEART, b f 28/2 Pursuit of Love—Hearten (Hittite Glory) **Avon Industries Ltd**
B f 12/3 Cyrano de Bergerac—Shannon Lady (Monsanto) **Skyline Racing Ltd**
TRIBESMAN, b c 8/4 Be My Chief (USA)—Barbury Court (Grundy) **Mr A. W. Schiff**
Ch f 5/4 Gregorian (USA)—Valls d'Andorra (Free State) **Mr J. P. Carrington**
Ch f 15/3 Chilibang—Whirling Words (Sparkler)

Other Owners: Mr Jeremy Baker, Mr K. Brackpool, Mr Michael Broke, Mrs J. Carrington, Mr M. F. Cartwright, Mrs Ronda Cassidy, Mr Joseph Chan, Mrs Frank Clothier, Mr R. B. Denny, Mr H. R. Dobinson, Mrs L. Donald, Mr K. E. Gregory, Mr Peter Harriman, Mr Julian Hartnoll, Mr R. A. Henley, Mrs Moyra James, Mr P. J. Makin, Mrs S. Padovan, Mr John Rathmell, Mr Geoff Roberts, Mrs M. S. Rudler, Mr Derek Sadler, Mr Nicholas Schofield, Mr N. Taylor, Mr Roy Vandermeer, Mrs J. Veitch, Mrs Sarah Walker, Mrs C. A. Webster, Mrs L. Whitehouse.

667 MRS F. E. WHITE, Chelmsford

Postal: **The Lodge, Nipsells Farm, Nipsells Chase, Mayland, CM3 6EJ.**
Phone: **(01621) 742161 FAX 742161 MOBILE (0850) 209368 OR (0831) 719937**

KLEINELEABA (IRE), 7, b m Pollerton—Promising Very VII **Mr W. White**

Lady Rider: Miss S White (9-7).

STOP PRESS

ADDITIONS TO TEAMS

Trained by Mr B. P. J. Baugh, Little Haywood
FRUITFUL LADY, 3 b f Puissance—Tamango Lady **Mr Mark Pennell**

At the time of going to press, Godolphin had not decided which of their horses would be returning to Europe for the 1996 Flat racing season. An up-to-date list will be published, along with other late teams, in Raceform Update at the end of April.

INDEX TO HORSES

The Figure before the name of the horse refers to the number of the team in which it appears and **The Figure after** the horse supplies a ready reference to each animal. Horses are indexed strictly alphabetically, e.g. THE CARROT MAN appears in the T's, MR BEAN in the MR's, ST KITTS in the ST's etc.

LOCATION OF TRAINING QUARTERS

References show squares as on map
IN SEVERAL CASES THE NEAREST MAIN CENTRE IS SHOWN TO LOCATE SITUATION OF STABLES

Ahern, M. J., Swindon	F4
Akehurst, J., Upper Lambourn	F4
Akehurst, R. P. J., Epsom	F5
Alder, D. S., Belford	B4
Alexander, H. H., Lanchester	C4
Allan, A. R., Cornhill-on-Tweed	B3
Allen, C. N., Newmarket	E6
Allen, J. S., Alcester	E4
Allsop, R., Ledbury	E3
Alner, R. H., Blandford	G4
Alston, E. J., Preston	D3
Andrews, J., Ladybank	A3
Arbuthnot, D., Compton	F4
Armstrong, R. W., Newmarket	E6
Arnold, J. R., Upper Lambourn	F4
Arthur, The Hon. Mrs R., Hallington	C4
Austin, Mrs S. M., Malton	C5
Avison, M., Nawton	C4
Ayliffe, N. G., Minehead	F2
Aynsley, J. W. F., Morpeth	C4
Babbage, N. M., Cheltenham	F4
Bailey, A., Tarporley	D3
Bailey, K. C., Upper Lambourn	F4
Baker, Mrs M. A., Steyning	G5
Baker, R. J., Tiverton	G2
Balding, G. B., Andover	F4
Balding, I. A., Kingsclere	F4
Balding, J., Doncaster	D4
Banks, J. E., Newmarket	E6
Barclay, J., Leslie	A3
Barker, W. L., Richmond	C4
Barnes, M. A., Penrith	C3
Barr, R. E., Middlesbrough	C5
Barraclough, M. F., Claverdon	E4
Barratt, L. J., Oswestry	E2
Barron, T. D., Thirsk	C4
Barrow, A. K., Bridgwater	F3
Barwell, C. R., Tiverton	G2
Bastiman, R., Wetherby	D4
Baugh, B. P. J., Little Haywood	E4
Beaumont, P., Brandsby	C5
Bell, M. L. W., Newmarket	E6
Bell, S. B., Driffield	C5
Bennett, J. A., Wantage	F4
Benstead, C. J., Epsom	F5
Berry, J., Cockerham	C3
de Berry, J. C., Newmarket	E6
Berry, N., Upper Lambourn	F4
Bethell, J. D., Middleham	C4
Bethell, W. A., Hull	D5
Bevan, E. G., Hereford	E3
Bevan, P. J., Uttoxeter	E4
Bickerton, Mrs P. F., Market Drayton	E3
Bielby, M. P., Grimsby	D6
Bill, T. T., Ashby-de-la-Zouch	E4
Birkett, J. J., Workington	C2
Bishop, K., Bridgwater	F3
Black, Mrs C. J., Oswestry	E3
Blackmore, A. G., Hertford	F6
Blanshard, M. T. W., Upper Lambourn	F4
Bolton, M. J., Shrewton	F6
Bosley, J. R., Wantage	F4
Boss, R., Newmarket	E6
Bottomley, J. F., Malton	C5
Bousfield, B., Brough	C3
Bower, Miss J., Grantham	E5
Bower, Miss L. J., Alresford	F4
Bowring, S. R., Edwinstowe	E4
Bradburne, Mrs S. C., Cupar	A3
Bradley, J. M., Chepstow	F3
Bradley, P., Forsbrook	E4
Bradstock, M. F., Wantage	F4
Bramall, Mrs S. A., Thirsk	C4
Bravery, G. C., Newmarket	E6
Brazington, R. G., Redmarley	F3
Brennan, O., Worksop	D5
Brewis, R., Belford	B4
Bridger, J. J., Liphook	G5
Bridgwater, K. S., Lapworth	E4
Brisbourne, W. M., Nesscliffe	E3
Brittain, C. E., Newmarket	E6
Brittain, M. A., Warthill	D4
Broad, C. D., Westbury-on-Severn	F3
Brooke, Lady Susan, Bromyard	E3
Brooks, C. P. E., Lambourn	F4
Brooks, Mrs E M., Bideford	G2
Brookshaw, S. A., Shrewsbury	E3
Brotherton, R., Pershore	E3
Brown, D. H. Maltby	D4

FitzGerald, J. G., Malton C5
Flower, R. M., Jevington G6
Forster, Capt. T. A., Ludlow E3
Foster, A., Saltash G1
Foster, A. G., Lambourn F4
Frost, K., Doncaster D4
Frost, R. G., Buckfastleigh G2

Gandolfo, D. R., Wantage F4
Gaselee, N. A., Upper Lambourn F4
George, T. R., Stroud F4
Gifford, J. T., Findon G5
Glover, J. A., Worksop D5
Goldie, J. S., Glasgow B2
Goldie, R. H., Kilmarnock B1
Gollings, S., Louth D6
Goodfellow, Mrs A. C. D., Earlston B3
Gosden, J. H. M., Newmarket E6
Graham, N. A., Newmarket E6
Grassick, L. P., Cheltenham F4
Gray, F., Haywards Heath G5
Greathead, T. R., Chipping Norton E4
Greenway, V. G., Taunton G3
Griffin, M. A., Liskeard G1
Griffiths, S. G., Carmarthen F2
Grissell, D. M., Robertsbridge F6
Gubby, B., Bagshot F5
Guest, R., Newmarket E6

Haggas, W. J., Newmarket E6
Haigh, W. W., Malton C5
Haine, Mrs D., Newmarket E6
Haldane, J. S., Kelso B3
Hall, L. Montague, Epsom F5
Hall, Miss S. E., Middleham C4
Ham, G. A., Axbridge F3
Hamilton, Mrs A., Newcastle upon Tyne C4
Hamilton-Fairley, Mrs A. J., Basingstoke F4
Hammond, M. D., Middleham C4
Hanbury, B., Newmarket E6
Hannon, R., Marlborough F4
Harriman, J., Tredegar F3
Harris, J. A., Southwell D5
Harris, J. L., Melton Mowbray E5
Harris, P. W., Berkhamsted F5
Harris, Roger, Exning E6
Harris, S. A., Doncaster D4
Harrison, R. A., Middleham C4
Harwood, G., Pulborough G5
Haslam, Patrick, Middleham C4
Haydn Jones, D., Pontypridd F3
Haynes, H. E., Swindon F4
Haynes, M. J., Epsom F5
Hayward, P. A., Netheravon F4
Heaton-Ellis, Mr J. B., Wroughton F4
Hedger, P. R., Chichester G5
Hellens, J. A., Chester-le-Street C4
Henderson, N. J., Lambourn F4
Henderson, Mrs R. G., Okehampton G2
Hern, Major W. R., Lambourn F4
Herries, Lady, Littlehampton G5
Hetherton, J., Malton C5

Hewitt, Mrs A. R., Malpas D3
Hiatt, P. W., Banbury E4
Hide, A., Newmarket E6
Hills, B. W., Lambourn F4
Hills, J. W., Lambourn F4
Hoad, R. P. C., Lewes G6
Hobbs, P. J., Minehead F2
Hodges, R. J., Somerton F3
Hollinshead, R., Upper Longdon E4
Holmes, G., Pickering C5
Homewood, J. S., Ashford F7
Horgan, C., Pulborough G5
Horler, Miss C. J., Bath F3
Howe, H. S., Tiverton G2
Howling, P., Newmarket E6
Hubbard, G. A., Woodbridge E6
Hubbuck, J. S., Hexham C3
Huntingdon, Lord, West Ilsley F4

Incisa, Don Enrico, Middleham C4
Ingram, R., Epsom F5
Ivory, K. T., Radlett F5

Jackson, C. F. C. Malvern E3
Jackson, F. S., Gonalston D5
James, A. P., Tenbury Wells E3
James, C. J., Newbury F4
Jarvis, A. P., Aston Upthorpe F4
Jarvis, M. A., Newmarket E6
Jarvis, W., Newmarket E6
Jefferson, J. M., Malton C5
Jeffrey, T. E., Alnwick B4
Jenkins, J. R. W., Royston E6
Jenks, W. P., Bridgnorth E3
Jessop, A. E. M., Chelmsford F6
Jestin, F., Wigton C2
Jewell, Mrs L. C., Sutton Valence F6
Johnsey, Miss C., Chepstow F3
Johnson, John H., Crook C4
Johnson, P. R., Cannock E4
Johnson, R. W., Newcastle upon Tyne C4
Johnson, Mrs S. M., Madley F3
Johnson Houghton, G. F., Newmarket E6
Johnson Houghton, R. F., Didcot F4
Johnston, M. S., Middleham C4
Jones, A. P., Eastbury F4
Jones, C. H., Cheltenham F4
Jones, G. Elwyn, Lampeter E2
Jones, Mrs M. A., Lambourn F4
Jones, P. D., Kingsbridge G2
Jones, P. J., Marlborough F4
Jones, W., Newmarket E6
Jones, T. M., Guildford F5
Jordan, F. T. J., Leominster E3
Jordan, Mrs J., Yarm C5
Joseph, J., Amersham F5
Juckes, R. T., Abberley E3

Kavanagh, H. M., Bodenham E3
Kelleway, Miss G. M., Whitcombe G4
Kelleway, P. A., Newmarket E6
Kelly, G. P., Sheriff Hutton C4

Kemp, W. T., Duns....................................B3
Kendall, Mrs M. A., Penrith.........................C3
Kettlewell, S. E., Middleham.......................C4
King, Mrs A. L. M., Stratford-upon-Avon..........E4
King, J. S., Swindon..................................F4
Kinsey, T. R., Ashton.................................D3
Kirby, F., Northallerton..............................C4
Kirby, J., Wantage....................................F4
Knight, Miss H. C., Wantage.......................F4
Knight, S. G., Taunton................................G3

Lamb, D. A., Seahouses.............................B4
Lamb, Mrs K. M., Seahouses......................B4
Lamyman, Mrs S., Lincoln..........................D5
Leach, M. R., Newark................................D5
Leadbetter, S. J., Berwick-upon-Tweed.........B4
Ledger, R. R., Sittingbourne........................F6
Lee, F. H., Wilmslow.................................D3
Lee, R., Presteigne...................................E3
Leigh, J. P., Gainsborough..........................D5
Lewis, G., Epsom.....................................F5
Littmoden, N. P., Wolverhampton.................E3
Llewellyn, B. J., Bargoed............................F2
Lloyd, F., Bangor-on-Dee...........................E3
Lloyd-James, L. R., Malton..........................C5
Loder, D. R., Newmarket.............................E6
Long, Mrs M. E., Woldingham......................F5
Luckin, P. D., Arundel................................G5
Lungo, L., Carrutherstown...........................B2

Macauley, N. J., Melton Mowbray.................E5
Mackie, W. J. W., Church Broughton..............E4
Mactaggart, A. B., Hawick..........................B2
Mactaggart, A. H., Hawick..........................B2
Madgwick, M. J., Denmead..........................G4
Mann, C. J., Upper Lambourn......................F4
Mann, W. G., Leamington Spa......................E4
Margarson, George G., Newmarket................E6
Marks, D., Upper Lambourn.........................F4
Marshall, Mrs L. A., Morpeth.......................B4
Marvin, R. F., Newark................................D5
McAuliffe, K., Lambourn.............................F4
McCain, D., Cholmondeley..........................D3
McConnochie, J. C., Stratford-on-Avon...........E4
McCormack, M., Wantage...........................F4
McCourt, Mrs M., Wantage..........................F4
McGovern, T. P., Lewes.............................G6
McInnes-Skinner, Mrs C., Melton Mowbray......E5
McKellar, R., Lesmahagow..........................B2
McKenzie-Coles, W. G., Taunton...................F3
McKeown, N., Newcastle............................C4
McKie, Mrs V., Twyford..............................F5
McMahon, B. A., Tamworth.........................F5
McMath, B. J., Newmarket..........................E6
McMillan, M. D., Bibury..............................F4
Meade, M., Malmesbury.............................F4
Meagher, M. G., Ormskirk...........................D3
Meehan, B. J., Upper Lambourn....................F4
Mellor, S., Swindon...................................F4
Milligan, Miss M. K., Middleham...................C4
Millman, B. R., Cullompton..........................G3
Mills, T. G., Epsom...................................F5

Mitchell, C. W., Dorchester.........................G3
Mitchell, N. R., Dorchester..........................G3
Mitchell, Pat, Newmarket............................E6
Mitchell, Philip, Epsom...............................F5
Moffatt, D., Cartmel..................................C2
Monteith, P., Rosewell...............................B3
Moore, A., Brighton...................................G5
Moore, G. L., Epsom..................................F5
Moore, G. M., Middleham............................C4
Moore, J. A., Darlington..............................C4
Moore, J. S., Hungerford.............................F4
Morgan, K. A., Melton Mowbray....................E5
Morley, M. F. D., Newmarket........................E6
Morris, D., Newmarket................................E6
Morton, T., Leominster................................E3
Moscrop, Mrs E., Seaton Burn......................B4
Muggeridge, M. P., Lambourn.......................F4
Muir, W., Lambourn...................................F4
Mulholland, A. B., Hambleton.......................C4
Mullins, J. W., Amesbury............................F4
Murphy, F., Middleham...............................C4
Murphy, P. G., Bristol................................F3
Murray, B. W., Malton.................................C4
Murray-Smith, D. J. G., Lambourn..................F4
Murtagh, F. P., Carlisle...............................C3
Musson, W. J., Newmarket..........................E6

Nash, C. T., Wantage................................F4
Naughton, Mrs A. M., Richmond...................C4
Naughton, T. J., Epsom..............................F5
Neaves, A. S., Faversham...........................F6
Needham, J. L., Ludlow..............................E3
Nelson, W. M., Torthorwald.........................C2
Newcombe, A. G., Barnstaple......................F2
Nicholls, D., Thirsk...................................C4
Nicholls, P. F., Shepton Mallet.....................F3
Nicholson, D., Temple Guiting......................F4
Nixon, G. R. S., Selkirk..............................B3
Nock, Mrs S., Stow-on-the-Wold...................F4
Nolan, D. J., Wishaw.................................B2
Norton, J., Barnsley..................................D4

O'Brien, D. C., Tonbridge...........................F6
Odell, Mrs S. M., Chipping Norton.................F4
Ogle, M. B., Buckfastleigh...........................G2
O'Gorman, W. A., Newmarket......................E6
Old, J. A. B., Wroughton.............................F4
Oldroyd, G. R., York..................................C4
Oliver, H. J., Cheltenham............................F4
Oliver, J. K. M., Hawick..............................B3
O'Neill, J. J., Penrith.................................C3
O'Neill, O., Cheltenham..............................F4
O'Shea, J. G. M., Redditch..........................E4
O'Sullivan, R. J., Whitcombe.......................G4
Owen, Jnr., E. H., Denbigh..........................D2
Owen, Mrs F. M., Rugeley...........................E4

Palling, B., Cowbridge...............................F2
Parker, C., Lockerbie.................................B2
Parkes, J. E., Malton.................................C5
Parrott, Mrs H., Mitcheldean.......................F3
Patman, Miss R. J., Moreton-in-Marsh............E4

Payne, J. W., Newmarket E6
Peacock, J. H., Much Wenlock E3
Peacock, R. E., Malmesbury F3
Pearce, B. A., Limpsfield F5
Pearce, J., Newmarket E6
Perratt, Miss L. A., Ayr B1
Phillips, R. T., Lambourn F4
Pickering, J. A., Hinckley E4
Pike, S. L., Sidmouth G3
Pile, Mrs P. M., Leamington Spa E4
Pilkington, Mrs T. D., Stow-on-the-Wold F4
Pipe, M. C., Wellington G3
Pitman, Mrs J. S., Upper Lambourn F4
Pittendrigh, S. I., South Wylam B4
Plater, Ms L. C., Newcastle upon Tyne C4
Pocock, R. E., Bridgwater F3
Polglase, M. J., Newmarket E6
Popham, C. L., Taunton F3
Poulton, J. C., Lewes G6
Poulton, J. R., Lewes G6
Preece, W. G., Telford E3
Prescott, Sir M., Newmarket E6
Price, Mrs A., Presteigne E3
Price, C. G., Hay-on-Wye E3
Price, R. Leominster E3
Pritchard, P. A., Shipston-on-Stour F4
Pritchard, Dr. P. L. J., Purton F3

Quinn, J. J., Malton C5

Ramsden, Mrs J. R., Thirsk C4
Raw, W., Richmond C4
Reed, W. G. Hexham C3
Retter, Mrs J. G., Exeter G2
Reveley, Mrs G. R., Saltburn C5
Rich, P. M., Usk F3
Richards, Graham, Pontypridd F3
Richards, G. W., Greystoke C3
Richards, Mrs L., Arundel G5
Ritchens, P. C., Tidworth F4
Robertson, D., Kilmarnock B1
Robeson, Mrs P., Newport Pagnell E5
Robinson, S. J., Darlington C4
Rodford, P. R., Martock G3
Roe, C. G., Chalford F3
Rothwell, B. S., Malton C5
Rowe, R., Pulborough G5
Rowland, Miss M. E., Lower Blidworth D5
Rowsell, H. G. M., Winchester F4
Russell, Mrs A., Kilmacolm B2
Russell, Miss L. V., Kinross A3
Ryall, B. J. M., Yeovil G3
Ryan, M. J., Newmarket E6

Sanders, Miss B., Epsom F5
Saunders, M. S., Wells F3
Scargill, Dr. J., Newmarket E6
Scott, Mrs E., Taunton F3
Scriven, B., Taunton F3
Scrivens, Mrs J., Bampton G2
Sheehan, J. J., Findon G5
Sheppard, M. I., Ledbury E3

Sherwood, O. M. C., Upper Lambourn F4
Sherwood, S. E. H., East Ilsley F4
Shiels, R., Jedburgh B3
Siddall, Miss L. C., Tadcaster D4
Sidebottom, Mrs J., Llandysul E2
Simpson, R., Wellington G3
Sly, Mrs P. M., Peterborough E5
Smart, B., Lambourn F4
Smith, Alfred, Beverley D5
Smith, C., Wellingore D5
Smith, Denys, Bishop Auckland C4
Smith, J. P., Rugeley E4
Smith, Julian S., Tirley F4
Smith, N. A., Upton Snodsbury E3
Smith, Mrs S. J., Bingley D4
Snook, L. A., Sturminster Newton G3
Spearing, J. L., Alcester E4
Spicer, R. C., Spalding E6
Stewart, A. C., Newmarket E6
Stirk, Mrs M. K., Ripon C4
Stoddart, D. R., Towcester E5
Storey, F. S., Carlisle C3
Storey, W., Consett C4
Stoute, M., Newmarket E6
Streeter, A. P., Uttoxeter E4
Stronge, R. M., Newbury F4
Swiers, J. E., Helperby C4
Swinbank, Mrs A., Richmond C4
Swindlehurst, D. G., Carlisle C3

Tate, M., Kidderminster E3
Tate, T. P., Tadcaster D4
Taylor, Mrs L. C., Chipping Warden E5
Temple, B. M., Driffield F4
Thom, D. T., Newmarket E6
Thomas, Mrs D., Bridgend F2
Thompson, Ronald, Doncaster D4
Thomson, A. M., Greenlaw B4
Thomson, Mrs D., Milnathort A2
Thomson Jones, H., Newmarket E6
Thomson Jones, T., Upper Lambourn F4
Thorner, G. E., Wantage F4
Thornton, C. W., Middleham C4
Tinning, W. H., Harrogate C4
Todhunter, D. M., Ulverston C3
Toller, J. A. R., Whitsbury G4
Tompkins, M. H., Newmarket E6
Townsley, Mrs P. Laxto, Dunsfold F5
Tuck, J. C., Didmarton F3
Tucker, F. G., Wedmore F3
Turnell, A., Wantage F4
Turner, W. G. M., Sherborne F3
Twiston-Davies, N. A., Cheltenham F4

Upson, J. R., Towcester E5
Upson, P. N., Folkestone F7
Usher, M. D. I., Swindon F4

Wade, J., Mordon C4
Waggott, N., Spennymoor C4
Wainwright, J. S., Malton C5
Waley-Cohen, Robert B., Banbury E4

Walker, N. J. H., Wantage F4
Wall, C. F., Newmarket E6
Wall, T. R., Church Stretton E3
Walton, Mrs K., Middleham C4
Walwyn, P. T., Lambourn F4
Wane, M., Richmond C4
Ward, Mrs V. C., Grantham.................................E5
Waring, Mrs B., Chippenham F3
Warner, Keith O., Stafford E3
Watson, F., Sedgefield C4
Watson, T. R., Gainsborough D5
Watts, J. W., Richmond C4
Webb, H. J. M., Faringdon...................................F4
Webber, P. R., Banbury E4
Weedon, C. V., Chiddingfold G5
Wegmann, P., Gloucester F4
Wells, J., Billingshurst F5
Weymes, E., Middleham C4
Wharton, J. R. H., Melton Mowbray E5
Whillans, A. C., Hawick B3
Whitaker, R. M., Leeds D4
White, G. F., Alnwick B4
White, J., Chinnor Hill F5
Whitehouse, Miss K., Church Stretton E3
Whyte, J. W., Beccles E7
Wilkinson, Mrs J. V., Blandford Forum G3

Wilkinson, M. J., Banbury....................................E4
Williams, A. J., Newport F3
Williams, D. L., Newbury F4
Williams, R. J. R., Newmarket E6
Williams, S. C., Newmarket E6
Williams, Mrs S. D., South Molton G2
Williams, Miss Venetia, Hereford E3
Wilson, A. J., Cheltenham F4
Wilson, D. A., Epsom F5
Wilson, Capt. J. H., Preston.................................D3
Wilton, Miss S. J., Stoke-on-Trent E3
Wingrove, K. G., Newmarket E6
Winkworth, P., Dunsfold F5
Wonnacott, Miss L. J., Lifton G2
Wood, R. S., York C4
Woodhouse, R. D. E., York C4
Woodman, S., Chichester G5
Woodrow, Mrs A. M., High Wycombe....................F5
Woods, S. P. C., Newmarket E6
Wragg, G., Newmarket E6

Yardley, F. J., Stourport on Severn E3
Yardley, G. H., Malvern E3
Young, Mrs J. A. F., Calne F4
Young, J. R. A. Oakham E5
Young, W. G., Carluke B2

TRAINERS' VAT NUMBERS

TRAINER	REG NUMBER
Hamish H. Alexander	175984606
A. R. Allan	300750900
J. S. Allen	660853133
R. Allsop	594435118
R. H. Alner	634295432
D. W. P. Arbuthnot	314895146
R. W. Armstrong	334139375
J. R. Arnold	614780342
Mrs S. M. Austin	167413069
M. Avison	475485408
J. W. F. Aynsley	621192373
N. M. Babbage	650825538
K. C. Bailey	314664563
R. J. Baker	469685478
I. A. Balding	199094119
J. Balding	457758887
J. E. Banks	571150172
W. L. Barker	633223080
M. A. Barnes	621400401
M. F. Barraclough	109625667
A. K. Barrow	129915054
C. R. Barwell	585986658

TRAINER	REG NUMBER
J. A. Bennett	64187491₄
C. J. Benstead	20958026₃
J. Berry	334882733
J. C. De P. Berry	63810075₆
W. A. Bethell	59914040₆
E. G. Bevan	13351170₄
T. T. Bill	11501861₂
K. Bishop	37941123₆
Mrs C. J. Black	48907710₁
A. G. Blackmore	63228425₅
M. T. W. Blanshard	31433986₉
J. R. Bosley	19438234₀
Ronald Boss	29988735₉
J. F. Bottomley	59889075₀
S. R. Bowring	50927872₄
Mrs S. C. Bradburne	56132327₀
J. M. Bradley	27466433₃
P. Bradley	36816462₇
M. F. Bradstock	49147053₈
Mrs S. A. Bramall	48180035₄
G. C. Bravery	57129423₇
Owen Brennan	11756167₃

Foaling dates are shown for two-year-olds
where these are provided.

C. E. Brittain	102592304
M. A. Brittain	599146977
Lady Susan Brooke	647056430
D. H. Brown	600285285
Miss A. E. Broyd	615563149
R. H. Buckler	398770975
David Burchell	540651465
N. Bycroft	171213794
T. H. Caldwell	643608242
N. A. Callaghan	102933011
B. R. Cambidge	159314164
I. Campbell	571254645
A. M. Campion	587879646
S. W. Campion	526158055
J. M. Carr	490388953
W. T. Casey	485999065
Mrs J. Cecil	571088141
N. J. Chamberlain	628270144
R. Champion, M.B.E.	200286217
M. Channon	189661117
David W. Chapman	168959983
M. C. Chapman	344208574
Major D. N. Chappell	614533657
P. W. Chapple-Hyam	639328024
J. I. A. Charlton	176290937
P. Cheesbrough	258834717
S. P. L. Christian	479484974
K. F. Clutterbuck	636738704
P. F. I. Cole	314293378
S. N. Cole	121061826
H. J. Collingridge	104254807
R. Collins	546881407
L. G. Cottrell	140877853
R. Craggs	602268958
P. D. Cundell	614824055
Charles Cyzer	193494821
P. T. Dalton	616881224
B. De Haan	314859934
M. J. K. Dods	257933133
S. L. Dow	413544574
Miss J. S. Doyle	614635058
C. J. Drewe	362659921
Miss J. M. Du Plessis	643455339
Mrs P. N. Dutfield	634367727
C. A. Dwyer	638198012
T. Dyer	607670242
M. W. Easterby	169069725
Malcolm W. Eckley	133976644
J. A. C. Edwards	135768640
C. R. Egerton	569752780
C. C. Elsey	500802403
C. W. C. Elsey	167148645
G. P. Enright	435943923
A. Eubank	256413172
J. M. P. Eustace	521219779
P. D. Evans	489174986
J. L. Eyre	567150241
R. A. Fahey	598892254
C. W. Fairhurst	602285861
J. R. Fanshawe	521042309
P. S. Felgate	309389434
M. J. Fetherston-Godley	314028695
J. R. G. Ffitch-Heyes	423184865
G. Fierro	536880711
J. G. FitzGerald	167445835
Capt T. A. Forster	198928487
A. Foster	284376429
R. G. Frost	464882116
N. A. Gaselee	200779676
J. T. Gifford	192834929
J. A. Glover	570900256
J. S. Goldie	556428423
Robert H. Goldie	264621953
J. H. M. Gosden	637815906

N. A. Graham	521298456
Frederick Gray	620739940
M. A. Griffin	591157039
D. M. Grissell	192342270
R. Guest	521042211
W. J. Haggas	442932451
W. W. Haigh	256944328
Mrs D. Haine	344518947
J. S. Haldane	271440773
Miss S. E. Hall	602277467
G. A. Ham	469736784
M. D. Hammond	546958392
B. Hanbury	103810125
R. Hannon	188397010
J. L. Harris	117472769
Peter W. Harris	301872384
Roger Harris	442900665
Guy Harwood	620769830
Patrick Haslam	199936189
M. J. Haynes	211231925
M. J. B. Heaton-Ellis	576278007
P. R. Hedger	503611295
J. A. Hellens	605579624
N. J. Henderson	314065590
Mrs R. G. Henderson	631215678
Major W. R. Hern, C.V.O.	199315427
Lady Herries	321820494
J. Hetherton	598972355
Mrs A. R. Hewitt	334883338
P. W. Hiatt	119746644
Anthony Hide	289616800
B. W. Hills	385437325
J. W. Hills	569940094
P. J. Hobbs	357220859
R. J. Hodges	379438207
R. Hollinshead	100714234
G. Holmes	168634238
G. A. Hubbard	637802135
Lord Huntingdon	390634151
Don E. Incisa	602257083
K. T. Ivory	197200757
C. J. James	200940804
A. P. Jarvis	569954274
M. A. Jarvis	344445361
W. Jarvis	410611119
J. M. Jefferson	347619039
J. R. W. Jenkins	321802888
W. P. Jenks	632098837
Mrs L. C. Jewell	619190534
John H. Johnson	532645354
R. F. Johnson Houghton	199189886
A. P. Jones	537596404
P. J. Jones	468437411
W. R. Jones	344427265
T. M. Jones	211537989
T. Thomson Jones	491729023
J. Joseph	578594081
R. T. Juckes	275450647
Miss G. M. Kelleway	634657324
P. A. Kelleway	289689076
W. T. Kemp	202759770
Mrs A. L. M. King	398488080
Miss H. C. Knight	200516720
F. H. Lee	332025703
G. Lewis	210700431
F. Lloyd	625050964
L. R. Lloyd-James	599176181
D. R. Loder	571447728
W. J. W. Mackie	390480447
A. H. Mactaggart	300427024
C. J. Mann	614848525
D. Marks	199926095
K. McAuliffe	614826833
D. McCain	163949724
J. C. McConnochie	589597255

Trainer	VAT Number
Mrs C. A. P. McInnes Skinner	115347979
Mr W. J. McKeown	621277361
Mrs V. McKie	581014370
B. J. McMath	443021693
Martyn Meade	576029426
B. J. Meehan	614603958
S. Mellor	199598571
Miss M. K. Milligan	633271164
B. R. Millman	570248055
T. G. Mills	564116061
N. R. Mitchell	570325361
Pat Mitchell	192511569
Philip Mitchell	210994078
A. Moore	190606467
G. M. Moore	602113509
J. A. Moore	602275081
J. S. Moore	541696036
M. P. Muggeridge	568603025
William R. Muir	569863572
J. W. Mullins	504372669
F. Murphy	634496811
W. J. Musson	213080024
C. T. Nash	570064657
A. S. Neaves	203533507
W. M. Nelson	617359917
P. F. Nicholls	600891753
J. Norton	364180067
W. A. O'Gorman	521157284
J. J. O'Neill	257253650
O. O'Neill	275553829
R. J. O'Sullivan	230720311
J. A. B. Old	501801302
J. K. M. Oliver	270373273
J. E. Parkes	391888005
Mrs H. Parrott	535606251
J. W. Payne	521068184
R. E. Peacock	160348383
J. Pearce	443013104
R. T. Phillips	614622855
Mrs T. D. Pilkington	618259426
M. C. Pipe	130961289
M. J. Polglase	637800631
C. L. Popham	131287782
Sir Mark Prescott BT	102416525
P. A. Pritchard	377100172
Mrs J. R. Ramsden	444381746
W. G. Reed	621184371
Mrs J. G. Retter	510666761
Mrs G. R. Reveley	391822439
Graham Richards	615535939
Mrs P. Robeson	608630448
B. S. Rothwell	599172585
R. Rowe	397611812
Mrs A. Russell	617276629
Miss L. V. Russell	663751812
B. J. M. Ryall	186378909
M. J. Ryan	285407345
Miss B. Sanders	448745510
Mrs E. B. Scott	379454407
J. J. Sheehan	237456547
O. M. C. Sherwood	363042676
S. E. H. Sherwood	363406856
R. Shiels	593090919
Miss L. C. Siddall	431044695
Mrs P. M. Sly	486255319
B. Smart	450209482
Alfred Smith	168216456
Denys Smith	258094929
L. A. Snook	634363543
J. L. Spearing	275942326
A. C. Stewart	428074648
D. R. Stoddart	336058069
W. Storey	177757509
Mrs A. Swinbank	546764019
M. Tate	275382438
T. P. Tate	313539865
Mrs L. C. Taylor	623648926
D. T. Thom	103696770
Mrs Dorothy Thomson	561441459
J. A. R. Toller	334107589
M. H. Tompkins	334108488
J. C. Tuck	618276525
F. G. Tucker	131549581
Andrew Turnell	195199515
J. R. Upson	623653839
J. Wade	602275669
Robert B. Waley-Cohen	623686426
N. J. H. Walker	614816053
C. F. Wall	496701221
P. T. Walwyn	200416627
F. Watson	258841526
J. W. Watts	284940135
H. J. M. Webb	195351251
C. V. Weedon	212347206
E. Weymes	258248241
R. M. Whitaker	170674459
G. F. White	621220892
J. W. Whyte	410521022
Mrs J. V. Wilkinson	629228428
M. J. Wilkinson	443798217
A. J. Williams	136636167
D. L. Williams	551337849
Mrs S. D. Williams	631020504
A. J. Wilson	286154441
D. A. Wilson	563914425
R. S. Wood	313587459
R. D. E. Woodhouse	332320311
S. P. C. Woods	571402465
Geoffrey Wragg	102855589
F. J. Yardley	275327741
Mrs J. A. F. Young	639326814

Owners names are shown against their horses where this information is available. In the case of Partnerships and Syndicates, the nominated owner is given alongside the horse with other owners listed below the team.

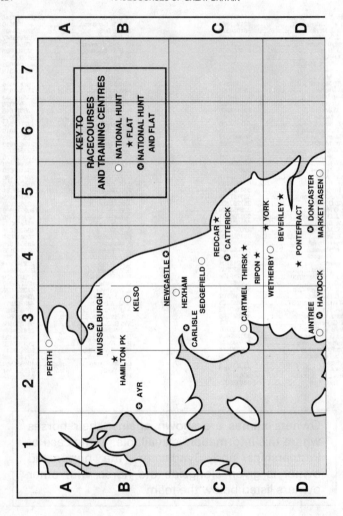

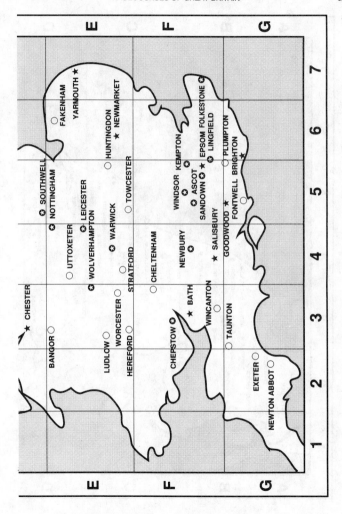

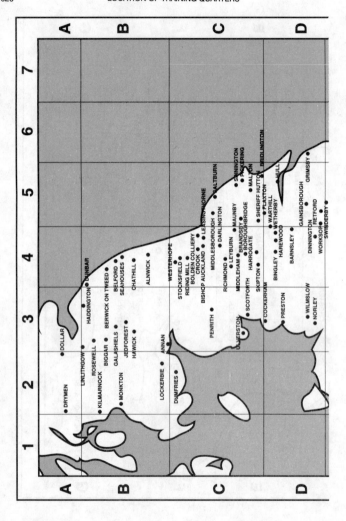

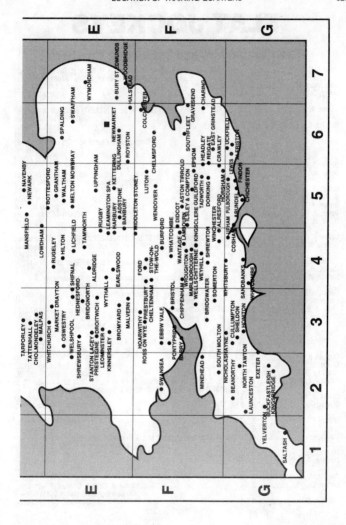

FLAT JOCKEYS

Their Employers and Telephone Numbers

Adams, N. M.	7	7	M. Saunders, A. Jones, A. K. Barrow, N. Berry, P. Clarke, G. Enroght (01488) 72004 or (0836) 787881 (car phone)
Asmussen, C.	8	3	J. E. Pease 1-47-20-07-50
Avery, C. M.	7	8	(0256) 463376
Bacon, A. E.	7	12	(0969) 22237 or agent (071251) 6666 (office hours) or (0402) 229168 (home)
Balding, C.	7	7	(01302) 710096
Ballantine, H.	7	7	(091265) 5265
Bardwell, G.	7	7	J. Bottomley, J. Pearce (01638) 668484 (agent)
Batteate, D. M.	8	1	(R. Harris)
Berry, R. J.	8	3	(03722) 77662
Biggs, D. D.	7	10	C. Cyzer, R. J. R. Williams (01638) 561287
Birch, M.	8	3	M. H. Easterby, J. Glover, J. J. Quinn, C. Booth (01653) 82578 or (0860) 245768 (car) or (0423) 526266 (agent)
Boeuf, D.	8	0	P. Bary 44 57 14 03
Bowker, Miss Julie	7	7	(0751) 76534
Brown, J. H.	8	1	(0653) 697768
Burke, P. A.	7	8	(0904) 647213 (agent)
Byrne, N.	8	11	01-6285480
Carberry, P.	9	0	N. Meade (046) 54197 or (01) 8256272 or (088) 571534 (mobile)
Carlisle, N. A.	7	8	(01832) 280132 or (0860) 392889and (01432) 274613 (agent) or (0589) 439345
Carroll, J.	8	2	J. Berry (01253) 812299 or (01253) 812299
Carroll, R.	8	4	D. K. Weld (045) 21863
Carson, W.	7	10	(Sheikh Hamdan al Maktoum's horses) R. Armstrong, W. R. Hern, P. Walwyn (01285) 658919 or (01385) 347676
Carter, G. A.	7	10	J. Berry, B. McMahon (01638) 668484 (agent) or 665950
Charnock, L.	7	10	M. Camacho, J. Berry, D.A Nolan, J. Wainwright (01653) 695004
Clark, A. S.	8	2	M. Dixon, G. Harwood, P. Blockley, (01222) 615594 or (01798) 873028
Cochrane, R.	8	6	R. J. R. Williams, J. D. Scargill, F. Murphy, Miss G. Kelleway, K. Ivory, B. McMath, M. Blanshard (01638) 743045
Comber, James	8	4	(0264) 773105 or (0638) 552666 (agent)
Connorton, N. B.	8	0	J. Dooler, Mrs. A. Swinbank, Miss S. Hall, R. Woodhouse, Miss L. A. Perratt, R. Fisher (01748) 824059 or (01751) 477142 (agent)
Coogan, B.	8	8	(045) 35090
Craine, S.	8	3	P. Hughes, T. Stack (045) 22032
Crossley, B. G.	7	13	(0638) 751367 or (0863) 366739
Culhane, P. A.	8	2	C. Booth, R. M. Whitaker, R. Fahey c/o (01937) 836171/582122 or (01977) 675129 and (0748) 825640 (agent) or (0831) 201425 (mobile)
Curant, J. A.	7	13	(01876) 0250
Curran, G.	8	8	(045) 2456
D'Arcy, P.	8	2	(0638) 750005/76686
Daly, T.J.	8	0	M.J. Grassick
Darley, K.	8	1	D. W. Chapman, J. Berry, Mrs G. Reveley, T. Etherington (01638) 741060 or (0836) 789919 (agent) or (0860) 926556 (car)
Davies, S.	7	7	S. Gollings (01638) 666350 (agent)
Dawson, S.	7	9	(0672) 40031 or (01903) 264336 agent
Day, N. P.	8	2	(0638) 666431, (0831) 336611 (mobile)
Deering, M.	7	10	P. Wigham (0653) 696065
Dettori, L.	8	4	J. Gosden, I. A. Balding, C. Allen, B. McMahon, K. Cunningham-Brown (01638) 667336
Dicks, A. C.	8	4	M. Saunders (0272) 519184

TONY HIND

agent for

J. FORTUNE   8-4

Can be contacted on

Tel: 01638 743756
Mobile: 0850 519333

SIMON DODDS

Agent for

D. McKeown	8-3
S. D. Williams	8-4
F. Norton	7-10

Tel: 01525 383633
Mobile: 0378 269618

Doleuze, O.	7	3	Mrs C. Head 44 57 20 36
Doyle, B.	7	11	C. E. Brittain, B. Meehan (01638) 664347 or (0836) 296860 and (01793) 870606 (agent) or (0374) 254523
Duffield, G. P.	8	1	Sir Mark Prescott (1st claim), Miss L. A. Perratt, C. F. Wall Duffy, (01638) 666350 and (0860) 539369 (agent)
Duggan, D.	8	10	(045) 21618
Dwyer, C. A.	8	8	C. A. Dwyer (01638) 668869
Eddery, J. D.	8	0	(045) 34855
Eddery, Pat	8	4	G. Lewis, H. Cecil, P. Walwyn, (01844) 290282 or (01844) 201427 and (01385) 317979 (agent)
Eddery, Paul	8	0	G. Lewis, T. J. Naughton, P. Howling (01884) 201427 (agent)
Egan, J. F.	7	12	M. S. Saunders, N. Chance (0802) 276798 and (01638) 561441 or (0370) 270820
Fallon, K. F.	8	4	Mrs L. Ramsden, E. J. Alston, R. Fisher, R. Bastiman, J. L. Eyre, D. Smith, G. Holmes, J. Jefferson, J. C. de Berry (01653) 693087 or (01751) 477142 (agent)
Fanning, J. K.	7	7	Miss L. A Perratt, J. Wainwright, R. McKellar (01751) 477142
Fenton, M.,	8	1	M. L. W. Bell, C. Broad, T. Dyer, J. C. de Berry (01638) 660669 and (0850) 377301 (mobile) (01638) 552666 or (0860) 343400 (agent)
Fortune, J. J.	8	2	T. D. Barron, S. Kettlewell, M. Meagher (01279) 725831 or (0850) 519333 (agent) or (01638) 743756
Garth, A.,	7	10	Mrs A. L. King, W. M. Brisbourne (01543) 490298
Geran, A. J.	7	9	(0638) 665293
Gibson, Dale	7	12	J. Harris, M. Dods, W. Haigh (01937) 842642 or (0831) 103354 (mobile) and (01531) 631593 or (0860) 370359 (agent)
Gilson, P. V.	8	5	(045) 31337 or (088) 568234 (mobile)
Greaves, Miss A.	8	1	D. Nicholls (01845) 501470 or (0347) 810825 (agent)

Name			Contact
Grenet, F.	8	7	P. Bary 44-21-44-10
Guest, E. J.	8	8	(01638) 721183
Harrison, D.	7	12	T. J. Naughton, J. Fanshawe, C. Elsey (01638) 666350
Head, F.	8	7	Mrs C. Head, D. Smaga
Hills, M.	8	1	G. Wragg, J. W. Hills, G. C. Bravery (01284) 850805
			or (0860) 235151 (agent)
Hills, R.	8	0	B. W. Hills, J. W. Hills, P. Walwyn, H. Thomson Jones, R. Armstrong
			(01284) 850805 or (01638) 570389 and (0860) 235151 (agent)
Hind, G.	8	0	J. M. Oxx (045) 21858
Hogan, D.	8	4	P. S. Felgate, P. W Harris (01638) 741060 or (0836) 789919 (mobile)
Holland, D. P.	8	2	B. R. Millman, M. Heaton-Ellis, T. J. Naughton (01403) 275150
			or (0831) 282788 (agent) (0850) 300449 (agent's mobile)
Hood, W.	8	5	G. Pritchard Gordon (0638) 778366/578366
Houston, Miss J.	7	7	(0638) 669839
Hughes, B. R.	8	0	D. T. Hughes (045) 21490 or (088) 594701
Hughes, R. D.	8	5	M. Channon (01222) 615594 (agent)
Ives, T. A.	8	5	C. Allen, W. A O'Gorman (01638) 500800
Johnson, E.	7	9	J. Hanson, B. McMath (01638) 720960 or (0831) 345360 (mobile)
Keightley, S. L.	9	0	(0638) 666070
Kelleway, Miss G. M.	8	3	(0860) 669511
Kennedy, N.	7	7	(01751) 477142 (agent)
Kent, T. J.	10	0	(0638) 668582
Kinane, M. J.	8	3	D. K. Weld (045) 21739 or (088) 567770
King, G. N.	7	10	
Lacy, T. F.	8	12	(0405) 37032
Lang, T. L.	8	2	(0296) 625310
Lappin, R.	8	1	J. L. Eyre (01845) 597481 (01969) 622477
Lequeux, A.	7	12	P. Bary 44-21-21-41
Lord, W.	8	1	(01638) 669846
Lowe, J. J.	7	7	M. Brittain, J. Bottomley, Mrs D. Thomson (01904) 708871 and
			(01904) 703766 or (0860) 766903 (car)
Lowry, P.	8	4	(045) 41957
Lucas, T. G.	8	6	(0347) 878697 or (0831) 197602 (mobile)
Mackay, A.	7	8	R. Brotherton, R Harris (01638) 560617 or (0454) 250814 (agent)
Maloney, S.	7	9	M. H. Easterby, N. Bycroft, W. M. Brisbourne (01751) 77142 (agent)
Manning, D.	8	0	(045) 34855
Manning, K. J.	8	7	(045) 22668 or (088) 567297
Manning, P. N.	8	7	(09276) 5337
Marshall, J.	7	7	M. Hammond (0969) 640228 or (0969) 24238
McDonnell, Miss K. S.	7	7	c/o (0488) 638463
McGlone, A.	7	11	H. Cecil, C. Jackson, R. Ingram, J. S. Moore, L. Holt,
			M. S. Saunders (01638) 731367 or (0836) 628159 or
			(01903) 264336 (agent)
McKeown, D.	8	3	C. Thornton, J. S. Wainwright, R. Bastiman (01977) 681247
			or (01525) 383633 and (0378) 269618 (agent)
McKinley, E. M.	9	7	(02357) 67713
McLaughlin, J.	8	7	J. Pearce (01638) 668115
McLaughin, T.	8	2	N. Littomden (01902) 688558
Mellor, Dana	7	7	(0793) 790230
Mercer, A.	8	0	(0748) 811103/5640 or (09442) 419 (agent)
Morris, A.	8	0	(0883) 344893 or (0372) 271526
Morris, Mrs C. L.	8	1	M. Channon (01273) 681679
Morris, S.	8	2	M. W. Ellerby, J. Carr (01653) 692098
Mosse, G.			F. Doumen
Munro, A.	7	12	L. G. Cottrell, Mrs A. L. M. King (0763) 289370 or (0850) 338815 (mobile)
			or (0536) 412144 or (0831) 630363 (agent's mobile)
Murray, J. G.	8	4	(09442) 419 (agent)

Murtagh, J. P.	8	5	(088) 586617 or (045) 22460
Newnes, W.	8	2	C. Jackson, Miss B. Sanders (01235751) 272 and (01638) 730320 (agent) or (0860) 766903 (mobile)
Nolan, A. J.	7	9	(045) 34193
Norton, F.	7	10	(0860) 758357 and (0378) 269618 (agent)
Nutter, C.	8	1	Sir Mark Prescott (01638) 668153
O'Connor, W.	8	5	M. Kauntze (045) 32877 or (088) 557494
O'Gorman, Miss E.	8	4	W. A. O'Gorman c/o (01638) 663330
O'Gorman, S. M.	7	12	P. Mitchell (0638) 730320 or (0860) 766903 (agent)
O'Grady, P. P.	7	12	(062) 54129
O'Reilly, J. F. P.	6	3	(0977) 648229
O'Shea, D. G.	7	7	J. Oxx, M. J. Grassick (088) 558649 (agent) or (045) 23565
Oldroyd, G.	8	7	(065381) 586
Perham, R.	8	4	R. Hannon, T. Jones, A. Chamberlain, C. Nash, N. Berry (01367) 820129 or (0836) 521636 or (01638) 660758 (agent)
Perks, S. J.	8	5	R. Hollinshead (0543) 490298
Perrett, M. E.	9	0	(079887) 4894 or (0367) 820214 (agent)
Peslier, O.			P. Bary 44-21-44-10
Poive, P. L.			P. Bary 44-21-44-10
Price, R. W.	7	11	R. Brotherton, G. Yardley, R. Armstrong (0454) 250814 (agent)
Procter, B.	8	3	W. R. Hern (01488) 71093
Proud, A.	7	10	(0969) 22237
Quinn, J. A.	7	7	C. Allen, L. G. Cottell, H. Collingridge, F. O'Mahony, M. Meagher, P. Howling, R. Fahey, K. Burke, M. Blanshard, P. Burgoyne, J. Sheehan (01638) 665454, (01638) 730445 or (0860) 883330 (mobile) or (01751) 477142 (agent)
Quinn, T. R.	8	2	P. Cole, R. Dickin, B. McMahon, R. P. J. Akehurst, J. Akehurst, D. Arbuthnot (0488) 684118 or (0831) 821100 (mobile)
Radmore, W.	7	7	(0635) 578879
Raymont, S.	7	13	(0249) 817007 and (01903) 264336 (agent)
Reid, J.	8	6	P. Chapple Hyam, T. G. Mills, L. Holt, D. Haydn Jones, W. T. Casey, R. Johnson-Houghton (036 782) 0214
Rimmer, Mark	8	4	H. Collingridge (01638) 500478 and (01432) 274613 (agent)
Roberts, M.	8	0	A. Stewart, M. Heaton Ellis, Mrs A. L. M. King (0860) 702322 or (01932) 343378 (fax)
Robinson, P.	8	2	M. Tompkins (01638) 668484 or (01638) 660946 (agent)
Roche, C.	8	4	J. Bolger (045) 21464 or (088) 557078
Roche, P. A.			H. de Bromhead (051) 86331
Rogers, T.	8	7	(0635) 864853 or (0831) 856969 or (0831) 865974 (agent)
Rouse, B. A.	8	3	G. Moore, F. O'Mahony, D. Wilson (01293) 871547
Rutter, C.	7	10	P. Cole, C. Wildman, R. Dickin, J. H. Peacock, Mrs B. Waring, C. Elsey (01235) 751614 or (0860) 370359 (agent)
Ryan, W.	8	2	H. Cecil, (01638) 741060 or (0836) 789919
Sedgwick, Paul	8	0	(0759) 71472
Shanahan, P.	8	3	(045) 21067/24545
Shoults, A. F.	8	0	(0709) 866276 (agent) (0831) 300935 (mobile)
Skingle, A.	7	13	c/o (0638) 668675
Slattery, J. V.	8	7	(01242) 603594 or (0850) 205872 (agent)
Smith, D. V.	7	13	(045) 33811
Smith, V.	10	0	(0638) 668972
Sprake, T. J.	7	11	W. Turner, Mrs H. Parrott, (01793) 870606 (agent)
Street, R.	7	7	P. Hayward (01488) 71412 and 71548
Stokell, Miss Ann	9	7	(092684) 333
Supple, W.	8	0	(045) 22583 or (088) 582645
Swan, C. F.	8	12	D. T. Hughes, M. Morris (045) 21490/22217
Swinburn, W. R.	8	6	(01440) 820277 (01536) 412144 (agent) or (0831) 630363

Tate, J.,	7	10	K. Burke, D. Morris (01638) 660758 (agent)
Tebbutt, M.	8	4	(0171) 8237538 or (0973) 781580 (agent)
Thomson, B.	8	3	(01488) 72671 and (01488) 73318 (agent)
Tinkler, Mrs K.	7	7	N. Tinkler, Don Enrico Incisa (01653) 658245
Tucker, A. P.	7	10	(0831) 865974
Vaillant, K.			P. Bary 44-21-44-10
Vincent, Miss Lorna	9	0	(0831) 532068 or (0836) 647725 (car)
Wall, T. R.	9	0	P. Blockley (074636) 569 or mobile (0860) 256211
Weaver, J.	8	4	M. Johnston, W. Muir, M. Bielby, P. Haslam (01375) 644059 and
			(0836) 230335 (agent)
Webster, S. G.	8	2	R. Barr, Miss J. Craze (01904) 608458
Wernham, R.	8	3	(0235) 833754
Wharton, W.	8	7	(036782) 710 or (0638) 665533
Whitworth, S.	8	4	(0850) 157198 (0672) 40961 or (0793) 870606 (agent)
Wigham, M.	8	2	P. Wigham, R. Jones, C. Broad, C. A. Dwyer (01638) 560507 or
			(0831) 456426 (mobile) or (0827) 66105
Wilkinson, D.	9	7	(0969) 22060
Williams, J. A. N.	8	3	G. Balding, A. Hide, P. Murphy, R. Peacock, Mrs H. Parrott,
			M. Eckley (01454) 218622 or (0836) 520252
Williams, T.	7	11	M. Johnston, R. Emery, R. Coathup, L. Lloyd-James (01969) 623271
			or (01635) 247532 agent
Williams, S. D.	8	4	N.Smith, J. Harris, A. L. Forbes, J. Glover, S. Campion,
			A. Streeter (01623) 823579 and (0589) 950832 or (0378) 269618 (agent)
Williamson, K	8	0	(0638) 661180
Wilson, T. G. A	7	7	(0638) 661999
Wood, M	7	13	(065385) 412 or (0836) 326084
Woods, W	8	2	S. Woods, A. Hide, M. Heaton-Ellis, C. Wall (01638) 711105 or
			(01638) 730320 (agent) or (0860) 766903 (mobile)

1995 RACEFORM APPRENTICE CHAMPIONSHIP

	1st	2nd	3rd
Seb Sanders	37	35	27
Dane O'Neill	32	41	30
John Stack	30	37	18
David McCabe	27	22	16
Matthew Henry	26	35	32
Jason Tate	24	22	32
Neil Varley	23	23	34
Paul Fessey	18	11	7
Patrick McCabe	17	17	17
Steven Drowne	16	16	19
Anthony Whelan	16	14	13
Alan Daly	14	20	14
Mark Baird	14	15	15
Joseph Smith	12	8	23
Colin Teague	11	8	11
Anthony Garth	10	8	17

Totals apply to Turf racing only

Adamson, C. N.	7	3	Mr M. Usher	(0793) 791113 and (0733) 261274 (agent)
Ahern, E.	7	3	Mr M. Grassick	(045) 34483
Ashley, T.	8	0	Mr R. Akehurst	c/o (01372) 748800
Baird, M.	7	3	Mr M. Ryan	(01638) 664172
Bannister, A. J.	7	2	Mr T. J Naughton	c/o (0372) 822803
Bastiman, H. J.	8	9	Mr R. Bastiman	(01937) 583050
Biggs, Miss D.	7	2	Mr Paul Howling	c/o (0142879) 4065
Black, M.	7	12	Mr T. Stack	(062) 54129

Bosley, J.	7	3	Mr P. Cole	c/o (01488) 638 433
Bowe, P.	8	8	Mr B. Hanbury	c/o (01638) 663193
Brace, G.	8	0	Mr B. W. Hills	c/o (01488) 71548
Bramhill, J.	7	4	Mr N. Littmoden	(01902) 688558 and (01543) 454390
Bridge, M.,	8	7	Mr J. Banks	(01638) 667997
Brisland, R.	7	7	Mr R. Charlton	(01672) 539533
Brookwood, P.	8	4	Mr S. Dow	(01372) 721490
Brown, S.	8	3	Mr W. Brisbourne	c/o (0743) 741536
Buckley, S.	8	4	Mrs L. Ramsden	c/o (01845) 587226
Campbell, I.	7	12	Mr R. McKellar	(01555) 892356
Casey, O.	7	11	Mr M. Johnston	c/o (01969) 22237
Cody-Butler, R.	7	7	Mr P. Chapple-Hyam	c/o (01672) 514901
Colgan, A. P.	8	2	Mr G. Oldroyd	(01759) 373007
Cook, Miss Aimee,	7	3	Lord Huntingdon	(01635) 281747
Copp, S.	8	5	Mrs G. R. Reveley	c/o (01287) 652000
Cornally, J.	7	7	Mr T. Mills	c/o (01372) 377209
Daly, A.,	7	9	Mr S. Dow	(01372) 721490
Davison, Miss C.	7	7	Mr P. Haslam	c/o (01969) 24351
Denaro, Mark	8	7	Mr R. Hannon	(01264) 850254 or (01638) 552017/667870
Denby, D.	7	7	Mr R. Akehurst	c/o (01372) 748800
Dennis, Jonathan	7	12	Mr M. Channon	
Doe, P.	7	0	Lady Herries	(01903) 871591
Drowne, S. J.	8	0	Mr M. Heaton-Ellis	(01793) 815009
Dwyer, M. J.	7	7	Mr I. Balding	(01635) 298210
Eddery, A. M.	7	11	Mr M. Channon	(01488) 71149
Edmunds, J.	7	12	Mr John Balding	c/o (0302) 710096
Faulkner, G.	7	12	Mr M. L. W. Bell	c/o (01638) 666567
Fergus-Sweeney, D.	7	7	Mr M. Channon	(0488) 71149
Fessey, P. J.	7	3	Mr J. Berry	(01524) 791179 and (01768) 892291 (agent) or (0374) 161202 (mobile)
Field, T. P.	7	3	Mrs M. Long	c/o (01883) 340064
Finn, T.	7	10	Mrs. L. Ramsden	c/o (0845) 587226
Fleming, L.	8	2	Mr F. Flood	(045) 403206
Fowle, J.	7	3	Mr M. Heaton-Ellis	c/o (01793) 815009
Fox, H.	8	12	Mr J. S. Moore	(01264) 889538
French, R.	7	3	Mr L. Cumani	(01638) 665432
Gallimore, Miss A.	7	7	Mr A. Bailey	(0829) 760762
Gibbs, D.	8	0	Mr G. Wragg	(01638) 667793
Gibbons, Miss A.	7	7	Mr P. Kelleway	(0638) 661461
Gordon, R.	7	7	Mr G. Balding	c/o (01264) 772278
Gosden, Miss A.	7	8	Mr J. Norton	c/o (0226) n387633
Gotobed, J. L.	7	11	Mr M. Tompkins	(01638) 661434
Gracey, J.	8	0	Mr C. Fairhurst	(01969) 622039
Grantham, I.	7	4	Mr A. Harrison	(01969) 23788
Greehy, E. P.	8	4	Mr R. Hannon	(01264) 850254
Griffiths, D. C.	8	4	Mr I. A. Balding	(01635) 298210
Halliday, Vincent	7	12	Mr T. J. Naughton	(04531) 631593 or (0860) 370359
Halligan, Brian	7	3	Mr M. Johnnston	
Halliwell, C.	7	0	Mr E. J. Alston	(01772) 612120
Hart, Miss K.	7	4	Mr T. Barron	(0845) 587435
Hartley, Miss A.	7	7	Capt J. Wilson	(01772) 812780
Harwood, Miss G. M.	8	0	Mr G. Harwood	(01798) 873011 and (01798) 872195
Havlin, R.	7	12	Mr P. Chapple-Hyam	(0850) 829449 or (01525) 383633 and (0378) 269618 (agent)
Hawksley, C.	7	3	Mr H. Collingridge	(01733) 263816 or (01638) 552407 and (0831) 865974 (agent)

Henry, M. P.	7	8	Mr J. Hills ....(0488) 73144
Humphries, M. B.	7	11	Mr A. Stewart ....(0113) 2711621 (agent)
Hunnam, Miss Jo	7	4	Mr L. Cumani ....(01638) 669506
Hyland, S.			Mr M. Johnston ....(01969) 622237
James, L.	7	10	Mr H. Candy ....c/o (01367) 820276
Johnson, Miss Tracy	8	4	Mr R. J. R. Williams ....c/o (01638) 663218
Kovarik, J.,	7	7	Mr J. Harris ....(01949) 863671
Lakeman, A.	7	13	Mr G. Moore ....(01372) 271526
Lanigan, S.	7	2	Mr J. Pearce ....(0454) 250814 (agent)
Lowther, C.	7	12	Mr J. Berry ....c/o (01524) 791179 and (01768) 892291 (agent) or (0374) 161202 (mobile)
Lynch, F.,	7	10	Mr R. Hollinshead ....(01543) 490298
MacDonald, G.	7	12	Mr J. L. Eyre ....(01845) 597481
Malligan, B.	7	3	Mr M. Johnston ....(01969) 622237
Marsden, Tony	8	4	Mr S. Norton ....(0924) 830450
Marshall, J.	7	10	Mr M. Hammond .. (0969) 640228 or (0969) 23054 and (0860) 942413
Mathers, M.	7	7	Mr F. Murphy ....(01969) 622289
McCabe, D. R.	7	10	Mr D. Loder ....(0440) 821000/821133 or (0836) 618318
McCabe, P. A.	7	12	Mr W. Musson .... c/o (01440) 821133 and (01440) 821000 or (0836) 618318 (agent)
Milligan, G.	7	12	Mr G. Wragg ....(01638) 660229
Mills, G.	8	0	Mr C. Thornton......................................(01969) 23350
Mitchell, G. C.	7	9	Mr L. Cumani ....(01638) 665432
Mitchell, Miss S.	8	5	Mr D. Gandolfo ....(01488) 681853 or 01468 267040
Moffatt, Darren	7	4	Mr D. Moffatt ....
Moody, Miss R.,	7	3	Mr D. A. Wilson .... c/o (01372) 278327
Moogan, R.	8	0	Mr R. P. J. Akehurst........................c/o (0372) 748800
Moon, J.	7	12	Mr S. Woods ....c/o (01638) 561844
Movington, Miss C.	7	2	....(0372) 271526
Moylan, G.	7	3	Mr M. Grassick ....(045) 34483
Mullen, R.	7	0	Mr M. Bell..(01638) 666567
Murphy, P. P.	7	10	Mr M. Channon ....(01488) 71149
Newton, L.	7	12	Mr B. McMahon ..... (0585) 360479 (mobile) and (0378) 269618 (agent)
O'Neill, David. W.	7	0	Mr P. Cole ....c/o (01488) 638 433
O'Neill, Dane. W.	8	0	Mr R. Hannon ....(01264) 850254 and (01635) 247532 (agent)
O'Shea, S. M.	7	3	Mr A. Leahy ....(063) 90676
Parkin, G.	8	1	Mrs G. R. Reveley ....(01287) 652000
Pooles, R.	7	5	Mr W. Muir ....c/o (01488) 73098
Prendergast, K.,	8	10	Mrs G.R. Reveley ....(01287) 652000
Rance, Miss R.,	7	0	Mr H. Candy ....c/o (01367)820500
Richardson, S.			Mr J. Glover ....c/o (0909) 475525
Roberts, Paul	8	2	Mr J. Berry ....c/o (01524) 791179 and (01768) 892291 (agent) or (0374) 161202 (mobile)
Rutter, K.	8	0	....(0245) 362394 (agent)
Rooks, Miss S-J	8	0	....(01507) 343204
Sanders, Miss A.	7	12	Mrs N. Macauley.............................c/o (01476) 860578
Sanders, S.	7	10	Mr R. Akehurst................................c/o (0372) 748800
Scally, C.	7	13	Mr K. T. Ivory ....c/o (01923) 855337
Scudder, C.	8	0	Mr I. Balding ....(01635) 298210
Sellars, Miss K.	9	7	Mr M. Hammond ....(0969) 640228 or (0969) 24489
Siddall, T.	8	0	Miss L. Siddall ....c/o (01904) 744291
Sked, K.	7	7	Mr M. Johnston ....c/o (01969) 22237
Smith, B.	7	10	Mr R. Johnson Houghton......................(01235) 850480

Smith, J. D.	8 0	Mr B. W. Hills	(01488) 71548
Smith, R.	7 10	Lady Herries	(01903) 871591
Stack, J. J.	7 13	Mr B. Hanbury	(01638) 660758
Stockton, J.	8 0	Mr S. Kettlewell	(01969) 640411
Stringer, P.		Mr N. Meade	c/o (046) 54197
Suthern, L.	8 10	Mr G. L. Moore	(01372) 271526 and (01386) 858279 (agent)
			or (0860) 934700
Sweeney D.F.,	7 7	Mr M. Channon	(01488) 71619 and (0374) 185301
			or (0378) 269618 (agent)
Teague, C.	7 3	Mr S. Bowring	(01623) 822451
Thomas, Miss Michelle	7 7	Mr R. Dickin	(01789) 450052
Toole, D.	7 0	Mr T. Mills	c/o (01372) 377209
Turner, Elizabeth	7 10	Mr W. J. Haggas	(01638) 664669
Varley, N.	7 7	Mr J. Fanshawe	(01454) 250814 or (0831) 865974 (agent)
Wall, Miss S.	7 7	Mr J. Jenkins	(01763) 241141
Wands, Miss I.	7 3	Mr A. Bailey	(01829) 760762
Waterfield, R. J.	7 9	Mr P. Murphy	c/o (0275) 372192
Webb, Charles	8 2	Mr C. Wall	(0638) 667763
Webb, Miss V.,	7 3	Mr M. Long	(01883) 340064
Webster, Miss J.	7 13	Mr J. Berry	c/o (01524) 791179 and (01768) 892291 (agent)
			or (0374) 161202 (mobile)
West, Miss C.	7 10	Mrs J.R. Ramsden	(01845) 587226
Whelan, A. W. E.	7 12	Mr G. Lewis	(01638) 660758 or (0860) 329555
Wilkinson, Jason	7 10	Lord Huntingdon	(01635) 281747 (office) or (01635) 281725
Williams, D.	7 3	Mr S. C. Williams	(01638)663984
Williams, Miss Hayley	8 0	Mr P. Evans	c/o (01398) 570288
Wright, D. T.	7 3	Mr A. Bailey	(0829) 760762 or (0831) 865974 (agent)
Wright, G. D.	8 0	Mr N. Bycroft	(01347) 888641

RACEFORM FLAT ANNUAL FOR 1996

£22 from Newsagents, Booksellers and W.H. Smith.
ISBN 0 900611 44 8

£24 by Post from the address below

RACEFORM LTD
COMPTON, NEWBURY, BERKSHIRE RG20 6NL
Access/Visa/Switch/Delta cardholders can order anytime
on
TEL: 01635 578 080

N.H. JOCKEYS

Weights, Phone Numbers, Stables

* Jockeys shown with an asterisk hold a "conditional" licence or a claiming licence. They are entitled to claim 7lb until they have won 15 races; thereafter 5lb until they have won 30 races; thereafter 3lb until they have won 55 races.

†Restricted to Conditional Jockeys Races and National Hunt Flat Races only.

Ahern, M. J., 10-0 .... (01763) 287219
†Aizpuru, X., 9-7.... (D. Nicholson) (01386) 584209
*Appleby, M., 9-7 .... (Mrs V. Hickman)
c/o (074634) 256
Armytage, Miss Gee, 9-7 ....(0163528) 273
*Arnold, R., 9-7....(G. B. Balding) (01264) 772278
Arnold, S., 9-7............. (P. Butler) (01273) 890124
*Aspell, L., 9-7............. (J. Gifford) (01903) 261799
Attwater, M., 10-0 (G. Moore) c/o (01372) 271526

*Bainbridge, S., 9-0..... (P. Haslam) ()1969) 24351
*Barret, R., ... (J. Banks) (01638) 661412
*Bastiman, H., 8-4,. (R. Bastiman) (01937) 583050
*Batchelor, M., 9-7 .... (A. Moore) (01273) 681679
*Bates, A., 9-7, ...(J. White, N. Berry)
*Bazin, G., 10-2....... (G. Hubbard) (01728) 628243
Bellamy, R. J., 10-0........(D. Nicholson, P. Webber,
S. Cole, R. Dickin, J. Peacock) (01451) 810563
or (0836) 241458 or (01531) 631593 and (agent)
Bentley, D. B., 9-7 ...(M. D. Hammond, R. Harrison,
L. Plater, G. Moore) (01989) 768974
Bentley, N. A., 9-11 (Miss S. Hall) (01969) 623054
or (0860) 199440 (mobile)
and (01347) 810825 (agent)
*Berry, M., 10-0, ...(C. Brooks) (01488) 72077
*Bohan, D., 9-7, ... (J. White) c/o (0831) 143356
Bosley, M. R., 10-3.............(J. Bosley, C. Jones)
(01367) 820115 (office) or (0367) 242224
and (0378) 938040 (mobile)
Bradley, G. J., 10-2.....(C. P. E. Brooks, M. Morris,
Mrs M. Jones, J. Akehurst, C. Elsey)
(01235) 751533 or mobile (0850) 350200
or agent (01235) 821250 or (0831) 547233
Brennan, M. J., 10-0 ....(O. Brennan, D. Thom,
M. Bielby) (01636) 636332
*Bridger, Miss R. J., 9-0......................(J. J. Bridger)
c/o (01428) 722528
Bridgwater, D., 10-0, ...(M. Pipe, G. Thorner)
(01386) 584597 or (0831) 635817 (Mobile)
and (01737) 761369 (agent)
Brown, G., 10-0......(Mrs A. Jones) (01488) 73385
*Brown, Kevin, 9-7 ..(A. J. Wilson) (01242) 244713
†Brown, M. P., 10-0..(S. Coathup) (0151) 3368911
Burchell, D. J., 10-0..............(D. Burchell, P. Hiatt)
(01495) 302551 or (0836) 329290 (car)
Burke, J. H., 10-0(Mrs S. Bramall) (01845) 537027
*Burns, R., 9-7
Burrough, S., 10-3 ....(P. Rodford, G. Ham,)
(0860) 869374 or (01823) 324618
and (01784) 241126 (agent)

*Burrows, O. J., 9-7 ....(P. Jones, M. Pipe)
(01548) 550222
Byrne, D. C., 10-0........(J. Fitzgerald, J. Bottomley,
W. Haigh, Mrs M. Jones) (01653) 600461 (home)
or (0836) 278374 (agent)
Bryan, J. 10-0...(01638) 667145 or (0802) 601590
Byrne, E. M., 10-0(Mrs B. Waring) (01275) 374102

*Cahill, G., 9-7(Mrs G. R. Reveley) (01287) 652000
and (01374) 161202 (agent)
Caldwell, P. A., 10-2...(T. Caldwell) (0831) 575879
and (01925) 861706
*Callaghan, E. G., 9-10 ....(J. Fitzgerald)
(01347) 810825
Callaghan, J.G., 10-0 ...(Mrs. K. Walton, P. Haslam,
R. Harrison, G. Moore) (01969) 622504
and (01751) 477142
Carberry, Paul, 10-0............(A Turnell, F. Murphy,
R. Lloyd-James, J. H. Johnson) (0831) 399633
and (01235) 821250 (agent)
*Carey, P. D., 9-7.........(R. Alner) (01258) 817271
*Carson, D. A., 9-7......(R. Rowe) (01903) 742871
Chevalier, P., 10-0................................(F. Doumen)
*Clarke, M. J., 9-0...(D. Williams) (01488) 638903
and (01287) 660506
Clay, Miss D., 10-0..............................(01782) 392131
*Cleary, M. G., 9-0 ....(D. Hughes) (045) 21490
Clifford, B., 10-0......(G. B. Balding) (01984) 40239
and (0374) 620549 or (01235) 921250 agent
(0860) 234342 (mobile)
Clinton, M., 9-7...........(P. Hedger) (01243) 543863
*Comerford, T.J. 9-6.............. (Mrs G. R. Reveley)
(01287) 652000

Collum, N., ...(C. Broad)
Cook, J., 9-7 ....(Mrs M. Jones) (01488) 73763
Cooper, F., 9-7 ...... (N. Gaselee) (012357)783223
*Cotter, G., 9-0................(D. Hughes) (045)21490
†Creech, D., 9-7 (P. Thompson) c/o (01488) 71483
Crosse, M., 10-2..............................(01444) 461586
*Crowley, P., 9-7...(M. Wilkinson) (01295) 660062
*Crone, G.S., 9-7........(A. Turnell) (01235) 833297
and (01235) 817573
*Curran, Sean, 9-12......................(S. Sherwood,
Miss Jacqueline S. Doyle, M. Muggeridge, J. Mullins,
Mrs A. Jones, Mrs H. Parrott) (01488) 722222
and (0374) 146169 (mobile)
Cuthbert, Miss C., 9-0...............(T. A. K. Cuthbert)
c/o (01228) 60822

Dalton, B. P., 9-7 ...... (J. Wharton) (01664) 464334

Darke, R., 10-2......... (R. Frost) (01364) 642951 or
(01364) 642267
*Dascombe, T. G., 9-7........... (01636) 816719 and
(01454) 250814 (agent) or (0831) 865974
Davey, M., 9-7....................(M. Morris) (052) 31909
Davies, C., 9-8.............. (J. Upson) (01327) 860043
Davis, R. J., 10-0 ....(P. Pritchard)
(01932) 243913 (agent) or (01989) 768974
or (0831) 592575 (Mobile)
*Dempsey, K., 9-12..............(J. Tuck, R. Simpson)
(01454) 238236 and (01823) 665156
Dicken, A., 10-0....................S. Dow
Dobbin, A., 10-0........ (G. Richards, W. Monteith,
F. Murtagh, S. Gollings, T. Dyer) (01768) 892291
and (0347) 161202 (agent)
*Donnelly, Joseph 10-0 ....(Capt. D. Swan)
(0505) 42306
Donnelly, Lorcan, 9-7 ....(Mrs S. Smith)
(01274) 564930
Dowling, A. 9-7..........(D. Gandolfo) (01235) 76420
Driscoll, J. P., 10-0............ (M. W. Easterby, G. Kelly)
(01347) 878794
*Dunne, C. P., 9-10...... (F. Flood) c/o (045) 53136
Dunwoody, T. R., 10-0.................(01367) 243111
or (0836) 502290 (car) and (01536) 85433 (agent)
Dwan, W. J., 10-0(J. G. FitzGerald) (01653) 692718
or (01751) 77142 (agent)
Dwyer, M. P., 10-2 ....(P. Beaumont, J. Jefferson,
M. Camacho, J. Fitzgerald, D. Gandolfo, J. J. O'Neill,
F. Murphy, R. Fisher, R. Woodhouse, J. Quinn)
(01944) 758841 or (01759) 371586 (agent)
or (0860) 502233 (mobile)

Elderfield, W. G., 10-0.....................(R. A. Bennett)
(01923) 563227
Eley, T., 10-0..............(A. Streeter, Miss S. Wilton)
(01332) 824696 and (mobile) (0585) 073823
Elkins, R., 9-12.............. (S. Dow) (01372) 721490
*Elliot, C., 10-0 .... (J. L. Eyre) (01845) 597481

Fagan, D. P., 9-7 ....(J. Fowler) (0405) 57401
Farrant, R., 10-0 .... (Mrs J. Pitman, J. Bradley)
(01367) 24480 (0850) 730733 (mobile)
*Fenton, B., 9-7.......................(G. Balding, P. Clarke)
(0374) 421118 (mobile)
and (01604) 711322 (agent)
or (0836) 266291 (agent)
Finnegan, D. 9-7 ....(N. Chance) (01488) 73436
FitzGerald, M. A., 10-2....... (N. Henderson, K. Burke,
P. Jones, W. Casey) (01367) 243208
or (0850) 742004 (mobile)
or (01737) 761369 (agent)
Flood, F., 9-9....................(F. Flood) (045) 403206
*Fortt, D., 9-9.(G. Ham, J. Glover) (01235) 833297
Foster, M. R., 10-0 ....(P. Haslam, F. Murphy)
(01430) 827756
*Fowler, S., 9-10... (P. Wermaan) (01242) 691955
or (01452) 301332
*Fox, S., 9-9 .... (A. Turnell) (01635) 247532
Frost, J. D., 10-4 ....(R. Frost, H. Howe)
(01364) 642267 or (01962) 772271 (agent)

Fry, W. S., 9-9............(T. P. Tate) (01226) 387633
or (01226) 390653

Gallagher, D. T., 10-0(M. Heaton-Ellis, M. Tompkins,
D. Murray-Smith, M. Blanshard, Mrs M. McCourt,
A. Moore, R. Simpson, J. Needham, C. Brooks,
M. Long, J. Harris, D. McCain) (01488) 73330
or (01737) 761369 (agent)
Garritty, R. J., 10-2...................(Mrs L. Ramsden,
M. H. Easterby, S. Kettlewell, T. Tate, G. Holmes)
(01653) 600221 or (01759) 371586 (agent)
†Gould, P. M., 9-7 (Mrs V. Aconley) (0653) 618594
Grantham, T., 10-0 .... (J. Old) (01903) 815360
or 742871
*Grattan, B. D., 9-7 (P. Beaumont) (01347) 888208
†Greatrex, W. 9-7 ....(J. Gifford) (01903) 872226
Greene, R. J., 10-0 .... (K. Bishop, S. Coathup)
Guest, R. C., 10-0... (Miss M. Milligan, J. Needham,
Mrs S. Smith) (01274) 564930
and (0830) 883303 (car) or (01932) 243913 (agent)

*Hallen, T., 9-7....................(A. Moore) (045) 76292
†Hambidge, Miss K. R., 9-0............ (M. Bradstock)
(01235) 760780
*Hanson, J., 9-9.. (Miss J. Bower) (01476) 870933
*Harding, B. P., 9-7 ....(J. Birkett, G. Richards,
B. Ellison) (01768) 483564
Harker, G. A., 10-2 .... (W. Barker, R. Brewis)
(01642) 780995 (01325) 378634
Harvey, L. J., 10-0 ....(Mrs V. McKie, Turnell,
R. Brotherton, Mrs H. Parrott, L. Bower)
(01235) 751608 or (0831) 399633
*Herrington, M., 9-7 ....(Mrs M. Reveley)
(01287) 652000
Hide, P. E., 10-0..(J. Gifford, A. Hide, P. Winkworth,
M. Bolton) (01903) 877323 or (0468) 233324
Hodge, R. J., 9-9 ....(Mrs G. Reveley)
(01287) 610955 or (01751) 477142 (agent)
*Hogan, G., 9-12 ....(D. Nicholson, C. Nash)
(01386) 584209
†Hogg, T., 10-0 .... (G. Moore) (01969) 623823
*Hoggart, C., 9-7.......(D. McCain) (01829) 720352
Holley, P., 10-0 .... (D. Elsworth, M. Bradstock,
Mrs B. Waring) (0860) 718654 (mobile)
and (01454) 250814 (agent)
†Horrocks, N., 9-7(C.W. Thornton) (01969) 623350
Hourigan, M., 9-7.......... (P. Hobbs, Mrs E. J. Taplin)
(0932) 243913 (0860) 234342 (agent)
*Huggan, C. H., 9-10........................(Mrs D. Haine)
(01638) 662346
*Hughes, P., 9-10(R. Dickin, C. Roe, Mrs H. Parrott)
c/o (01531) 890644
Humphreys, W., 10-0 (R. Brazington, T. Greathead,
C. Roe, W. Humphreys, Miss R. Patman)
(01451) 831515 or (0836) 777100
and (01451) 850069 (agent) or (0836) 774329
*Husband, E., 9-11 ....(Mrs N Macauley, P. Hiatt)

Jenks, T. P., 10-0 .... (W. Jenks) (01451) 831797
Johnson, K., 10-0 .... (R. Johnson) (01388) 721813
or (0374) 131121 (mobile)

*Johnson, R., 9-11 .(D. Nicholson, Mrs S. Johnson, Lady S. Brooke, B. Scriven, Mrs N. MacCauley) (01386) 584 374 or (01585) 765361
Jones, A. E., 10-0 .... (Mrs M. Easton) Great Shefford (0488) 648349 or (01235) 821250 (agent)
Jones, K., 10-0 .... (J. Wade) (0374) 986640
*Joynes, S., 9-11 .... (N. Twiston-Davies) (01451) 831397

*Kavanagh, D. J., 9-7 .... (01969) 622289
Kavanagh, J. R., 10-0 .... (N. Henderson, Miss A. Embiricos, C. Nash, P. Winkworth) (01367) 243968 or (0831) 376837 or (0860) 234342 or (01932) 243913 (agent)
*Keighley, M. H., 9-7 .... (N. Twiston-Davies) (01451) 850278
Keightley, S. L., 10-0 ....(J. Banks) (01638) 662838 or (0964) 551135 (agent)
Kelly, M., 9-7............ (W. P. Mullins) (0503) 21786
*Kelly, M., 9-10 .... (C. Mann, M.Ahern) (01488) 72982 or (01722) 714372 (agent)
Kent, T. J., 10-0 .... (Mrs J. Cecil, A. Bailey) (01638) 560634 or (0370) 418886 and (01440) 821133 (agent)
Kinane, J. K., 9-7 .... (045) 22725
Kinane, P. P., 9-7 .... (045) 22363
Kinane, T. Jun., 10-0 .... (045) 22231
*Knott, S., 9-7 .... (Mrs J. Pitman) (01488) 72196
†Kolosine, M., 9-10 .... (Miss S. Wilton)
Kondrat, A., 10-0 .... (F. Doumen)

†Lane, M. A. P., 9-7 .... (N. Henderson) (01488) 72259
†Large, A., 10-0 .... (Miss S. Wilton)
*Larnach, A. A., 9-12......................... (A. Burke) (0831) 211738
Lawrence, I. R., 9-7 .... (01635) 201554 (0836) 211479 (mobile)
Leahy, D., 10-0.................. (D. Gandolfo, P. Jones, Mrs L. C. Jewell, Mrs H. Parrott, G. Yardley) (0831) 323736 or (01367) 820214 (agent)
*Leahy, F. T., 9-7 ...... (J. Fitzgerald, M. W. Ellerby, R. Fisher) c/o (01653) 692718
*Lee, G. M., 9-7 .... (Mrs M. Reveley, M Eckley) (01751) 77142 (agent)
*Lewis, Guy, 9-11 .... (W. Clay, J. Bradley) (01749) 860656
*Linton, A., 10-0 .... (T. Dyer) (01382) 360594
Llewellyn, C., 10-0..................... (N. Twiston-Davies, R. Brotherton, C. Broad, N. Gaselee, B. Smart) (01235) 763410 or (0836) 783223 (mobile) or (01934) 641658 agent
Lodder, J., 10-0.......... (F. Jordan) (01568) 760281 or (085) 484556
Long, Miss Leesa, 9-7 ......(Mrs M. Long, F. Stone) (01273) 890244
Lower, J. A., 10-4 .... (M. Pipe) Wellington (01823) 473580
Lycett, S., 10-0............. (G. Fierro) (01543) 879611
Lyons, Gary, 10-2... (Miss M. Rowland, A. Streeter, B. Baugh), (01543) 876740 or (0831) 330265 (mobile)

*Magee, J., 10-0 ... (K. Bailey) c/o (01222) 615594
Maguire, A., 10-0.........(D. Nicholson, S. Woodman) (01737) 761369 and (01737) 768821 or (0860) 234342 (agent)
*Maher, P. J., 9-7........................... (M. Tompkins) c/o (01638) 661434
Malone, P. L., 9-7......(M. J. Grassick) (045) 74738
Mann, N. J. W., 10-0 .... (S. Mellor, D. Morris, Dr J. D. Scargill) (01638) 669356 or (0860) 927353 (mobile) or agent (0831) 865974
Manners, A., 9-12................... (D. Lamb, A. Eubank) (01665) 720297 or (0860) 884060
Marley, R. J., 10-0..........(J. Bottomley, Mrs P. Sly) (0831) 890339 or (01944) 738491
Marston, W. J., 10-0. (Mrs J. Pitman, D. Nicholson, C. Broad, M. Tate, P. Dalton) (01235) 821250 or (0831) 664745 agent
*Martin, M. W. 9-7 . (R. Hollinshead (01543) 49028
Mason, S. T., 10-0........................... (D. Nicholls) (0374) 857558 (mobile)
*Massey, R. I., 9-9 ... (D. Nicholson, W. Brisbourne, K. Morgan) (01386) 584 209/219
*Matthews, D., 10-0 .... (B. Llewellyn)
Maude, C. G., 10-0 .... (01823) 278466 or (0831) 094601 or (01793) 870606 (agent)
McCabe, A. J., 9-7......................... (D. Elsworth) c/o (07253) 504/520 or (0860) 718654 (mobile)
McCain, D. R., 10-4 ...(D. McCain) (01829) 720352 (01829) 720451 and (0836) 780879
McCarthy, J. A., 10-0..... (C. Egerton, A. Woodrow, D. Marks) (01488) 72263 or (01235) 762450 (agent)
*McCarthy, R., 9-7 (J. Parkes) c/o (01653) 697570
*McCormack, C., 9-7................ (Mrs G. R. Reveley) (01287) 652000
McCourt, G. M., 10-5....... (P. Webber, M. McCourt, R. Johnson-Houghton) (01235) 764456 or (0836) 749191 or (0374) 870760 and (01638) 668484 (agent)
McCoy, A. P., 10-0. (G. Ham, G. Balding, N. Ayliffe, P. Nicholls) (01264) 772278 (01932) 243913 (agent)
McDougall, S. J., 10-0 (W. Kemp) (01361) 850242
McFarland, W. J., 10-0 ...... (R. Stronge, G. Yardley, G. Charles-Jones, Mrs E. Brooks, J. S. Moore) (01488) 73374 or (0831) 317039 (Mobile) or (01225) 873882 (agent)
†McGann, B. T., 9-07 (C. Weedon) (01428) 683344
McGirr, F., 9-7 ....(B. Curley) (01638) 508251
McGovern, S., ... (N. Meade) (046) 54197
*McGrath, L., 9-7 ..(Mrs S. Smith) (01271) 564930
*McGrath, R., 9-7...(J. J. O'Neill) (017684) 54555
McLaughlin, J. F. S., 10-0(C. Allen) (01638) 668115
*McLoughlin, P. J., 9-7....................... (J. R. White, Mrs A. Woodrow) (01737) 761369 (agent) or (01296) 622058
McNeill, S. R O., 10-0(Mrs A. L. M. King, A. Turnell, M. Barraclough, Mrs M. Jones J. C. Tuck, D. Ffrench-Davis) (01488) 648861 or (0831) 107468
*Melrose, S., 9-7...........(R. Allan) (01890) 820581

Meredith, D., 10-0 .... (R. Dickin, M. Eckley)
    (0860) 458087/370359 or (01531) 631593
          or (0860) 370359 (agent)
*Midgley, P. T., 10-3 .... (G. Oldroyd, J. Wainwright,
    S. Campion) (01653) 698476 or (01759) 373007
          or (0860) 233041 (agent)
Mitchell, Miss S., 9-7 .... (D. Gandolfo, J. Kirby)
    (01488) 681853 and (0831) 169776 (mobile)
*Moffatt, D. J., 10-4 ... (J. Birkett) (015395) 36689
*Molloy, M., 9-7 .... (b. Smart) (01488) 71632
*Moran, M. P., 9-7 .... (P. Hobbs, K. Bishop)
Morris, Derrick, 10-0 (R. Curtis, Miss L. Wonnacott)
    (01488) 73897 and (01488) 73007
*Morris, P. S., 9-7... (A. P. Jarvis) (01235) 851341
Murphy, E. R., 10-0 ... (Lady Herries, P. G. Murphy,
    B. Curley) (01903) 871460 or (0860) 698152
*Murphy, T. J., 9-7 (K. Bailey) c/o (01235) 821250
*Murphy, T. C., 9-12 ...(W. Turner) (01963) 220523
*Neaves, J. P., 9-7 .... (J. Ffitch-Heyes)
    (01963) 251162 or (01477) 52857
*Newton, M. J., 9-7 ....(M. Jefferson)
    c/o (01653) 697225
Niven, P., 10-4 ..... (Mrs G. R. Reveley, R. F. Fisher,
    Denys Smith) (01751) 477142 (agent)
          or (0860) 260999 (car)
O'Brien, C., 9-7 .... (A. Moore) (045) 434789
O'Brien, K. F., 9-11 ....(045) 34789
*O'Donnell, S., 10-0 ....(01909) 473950
O'Dwyer, C. 10-0 .... (M. Morris, J. Fowler)
    (0188555) 692
O'Hara, L., 10-0. (Miss L. Perratt, Mrs D. Thomson,
    J. Birkett) (01759) 371586 (agent)
          or (0860) 596031 (mobile)
Oliver, Miss J., 10-0 .... (Mr H. Oliver)
    (01989) 65219 or (01235) 821250 (agent)
O'Neill, G. M., 10-3............ (A. Leahy) (061) 82394
          or (088) 588317
Osborne, J. A., 10-0 .... (S. E. H. Sherwood,
    O. Sherwood, R. Brotherton, S. Christian, R. Price,
    I. Balding, C. Egerton) (01488) 73139
          (0860) 533422 (car)
O'Sullivan, D. K., 10-4........ (K. Cunningham-Brown,
    R. Rowe) (01243) 267563 or (0374) 725718
    (01222) 615594 or (01903) 742871 (agent)
*O'Sullivan, D. W., 9-7..... (A. Moore) (045) 76292

*Parker, D., 9-9 .... (W. Tinning, R. McKellar)
    (01576) 510232
Pears, O., 10-0 ....(0850) 514068
*Perratt, W. F., 9-7 .... (L. Lungo, J. Goldie)
    (01387) 84673 or (0850) 434327 (mobile)
          or (01347) 822410 (agent)
Perrett, M. E., 10-0 .... (G. Enright, S. Mellor,
    G. Harwood) (01798) 874894
          or (0367) 820214 (agent)
Pittendrigh, S. I., 10-7 ....(01661) 852676
Porritt, S., 9-7 ....(01969) 640411
Powell, A., 10-4 .... (J. Fowler) (045) 23449

Powell, B. G., 9-7(B. Meehan, R. Buckler, N. Ayliffe,
    A. K. Barrow, D. Carey, A. Chamberlain, R. Baker)
    (01793) 782286 or (0860) 314745
         and (01793) 522359 (agent)
*Power, J. G., 9-7 ......(W. Turner) (01963) 220523
†Prior, J., 10-0 .... (D. Burchell) (01495) 302551
*Procter, A. R., 9-7 ....(R. Dean)
    (0454)   250814 and   (0831)   865974   (agent)

Railton, J. A., 10-2.........(C. Mann, Mrs L. C. Jewell,
    Mrs. A. Swinbank) (01367) 820794
          or (0374) 149336 (mobile)
          or (01793) 522359 (agent)
Ranger, M., 10-0 .... (C. Smith) (01526) 833245
Reed, W. T., 10-10(W. G. Reed, J. Glover, L. Lungo,
    J. Oliver, M. Dods) (01347) 810825
         and (01434) 344016 (agent)
*Reynolds, L. R., 9-7............... (Miss G. Kelleway)
Richards, M. R., 10-0 ....(K. Ivory, C. C. Elsey,
    O. Sherwood, Mrs L. Richards, W. Muir, P. Hedger,
    S. Sherwood, P. Upson) (01243) 553821
         or (0973) 198435 (mobile)
*Righton, S., 8-7 ..(J. L. Spearing) (01789) 772639
Robinson, M. I., 10-0........................(0507) 363525
         or (0472) 696710
Roche, A., 9-12 .... (J. J. O'Neill)
Rogers, H. ....(041) 533353
*Rourke, R. 9-7................................(01653) 692842
Rowell, R., 10-3 .... (J. Poulton) (01903) 213051
*Ryan, D. A., 9-7........... (J. Wade) (01325) 313129
Ryan, G. F. 9-9, ...(01235) 833535
Ryan, J. B. 10-0 .... (M. Ryan, K. Wingrove)
    (01932) 243913 or (0860) 234342 (agent)
*Ryan, S., 9-7 ... (R. Akehurst) c/o (01372) 748800

*Salter, D., 9-9 .... (B. Millman) (01823) 681054
         or (01884) 266620 agent
Sharratt, M., 10-0 .... (J. Pickering, J. McConnochie)
    (01430) 827756 (agent) or (0973) 699067 (mobile)
Sheridan, B., 9-10............ (D. K. Weld) (045) 71622
         or (088) 563633
Shortt, J., 10-0 .... (J. Harrington) (045) 85336
         or (088) 530672
Skyrme, D. V., 10-0 .... (W. J. L. Paul,
    R. S. C. Robinson, Miss K. George) (044282) 7830
         or (0836) 381957 (mobile)
         or (0793) 870606 (agent)
Slattery, A. J., 10-0.......... (E. O'Grady) (052) 56530
Slattery, J. V., 9-7(M. Saunders, P. Jones, O. O'Neill,
    H. Oliver) (01242) 603594 and (0831) 545789
         or (01432) 274613 (agent)
Sleator, P. M., 10-12(D. Clyde) (010) 353 45 53159
Smith, A. S., 10-0(K. Morgan, J. Glover, S. Campion,
    W. Bethell, S. Gollings) (0166478) 711/488
         or (0831) 272910
Smith, C. N., 10-0........ (Mrs G.R. Reveley, R. Barr)
    (01287) 639312
Smith, M., ... (N. Babbage) (01242) 242699
Smith, Miss R., 9-7. (Mr C. Smith) (01526) 833245
Smith, V., 10-0 .... (R. W. Jones, B. McMath,
    C. A. Dwyer, J. C. de Berry)
    (01638) 668972 or (0860) 386108 (mobile)

Stevens, M., 10-1 ..... (B. Stevens) (01962) 885154
or mobile (0385) 247709
†Stevens, P. J., 9-7 .... (F. Gray) (01444) 461324
Stokell, Miss Ann., 9-7 .... (M. Barraclough)
(092684) 3332
Storey, B., 10-0(F. Storey, A. Goodfellow, C. Parker,
J. Charlton, G. White, R. Harrison, A. Allan, J. Oliver)
(0122 875) 331 or (0860) 432881 (mobile)
*Supple, G., 9-7 .... (R. Buckler) (01308) 488502
*Supple, J. A., 9-11...... (N. Chamberlain, J. Upson)
(01327) 860043 and (0374) 699540 (agent)
Supple, R. J., 9-7 .... (J. Upson, B. Rothwell,
P. Beaumont, F. Murtagh, W. Barker)
(01628) 770766 (agent) (01788) 890909
and (0850) 120134 (mobile)
Swan, C. F. 9-7........ (Capt. D. Swan) (0505) 42410
or (088) 573194

*Taylor, S. D., 9-7 ......(J. Hellens) (0191) 3885403
or (0191) 3871474
*Teague, C., 9-7 .... (S. Bowring) (01623) 822451
*Thomas, D., 9-07.... (O. Sherwood, D. Thomas)
c/o (01488) 71411
*Thompson, P. A., 9-7...............(G. Charles-Jones)
(012357) 67713
Thornton, A. R., 10-0 .... (G. Johnson-Houghton,
Graham Richards, R. Juckes, A. Thornton, J. Poulton,
Mrs A. Woodrow) (01488) 73155
or (0831) 102065 (mobile)
Thornton, A., 10-0 ...... (S. Campion) (01488) 73155
or (0831) 102065 and (01737) 761369 (agent)
Titley, J. F., 10-0 .... (Miss H. C. Knight)
(01235) 821250 (agent)
*Tormey, G., 9-7 ....(P. Hobbs, R. Juckes)
c/o (01235) 821250
Tory. A. S., 10-0...........................(N. Chamberlain,
Mrs J. Renfree-Barons, P. Ritchens, H. Rowsell)
(01980) 629503 or (0831) 123956 (mobile)

*Towler, D. L., 9-7 ..... (N Bycroft) (01347) 888641
Treacy, T. P. 9-7............ (P. Mullins) (0503) 75121
and (088) 505298 (mobile)

Upton, Guy, 10-2 .... (Mrs J. Young, C. Jones,
S. Sherwood, J. Kirby, Mrs E. Brooks)
(01488) 681853 or (0385) 307872 (car)
or (01225) 834059 (agent)

Verling, P. M., 9-10.. (G. Hubbard) (0585) 5429988
or (01903) 208758 (agent)
Waggott, P., 10-0 ...... (M. Barnes) (01768) 881152
*Walsh, David, 9-9 .... (N. Twiston-Davies)
(01451) 850278
*Walsh, P., 10-0......... (G. Moore) (01969) 623823
Walsh, W., 9-7 ..... (Mrs L. Jewell) (01622) 842788
*Watt, A., 9-0. (Mrs S. Bradburne) (01337) 810325
Webb, C. 10-0 .... (S. Mellor, P. Eccles)
(01793) 790230
Wilkinson, D., 10-0 (Mrs S. M. Austin, C. Thornton)
(01969) 22060
*Wilkinson, R. D. J., 10-0 .... (Mrs S. Smith)
(01274) 564930
Williamson, N., 10-0 .... (K. Bailey)
(01488) 648437 or (0831) 343434 (mobile)
or (0932) 243913 (agent)
*Wilmington, N., 9-7... (A. Turnell) (01235) 833297
*Winter, D., 9-7..............................(0327) 860043
Woods, F., 9-7................. (A. Moore) (01) 350189
Worthington, W. M., 10-0.................... (R. Marvin,
M. C. Chapman) (01455) 619206
or (0673) 843663
Wyer, L. A., 10-0(M. H. Easterby, T. Dyer, R. Fahey,
M. Meagher, G. Holmes) (01653) 628877
or (0831) 218288 (Mobile)
or (01751) 477142 (agent)
Wynne, S., 10-0....(T. A. Forster, W. M. Brisbourne,
W. Jenks, A. Hewitt) (01584) 877672

AMATEUR RIDERS

Riding weights and telephone numbers.

Adkin, Mrs G., 9-7, ...(0115) 9664817
Ager, Miss T., 8-0,..............................(01937) 583050
Allen, Miss L. 9-7, ...c/o (01733) 211575
Allen, Mrs R., 9-4,...............................(01638) 667870
Allison, Miss J. K., 9-5,.......................(01638) 507067
Anderson, K., 10-0,..........................(01461 15) 482
Apiafi, J., 11-0,.........................(01476) 870933 and
....(01323) 509086
Appleby, C. E. J., 9-4,........................(01638) 660229
Arbuthnot, Mrs D., 8-6,.......................(01635) 578427
Armson, R. J., 11-0,...........................(01283) 226046
Armytage, M. D., 10-3,................(01367) 87637 or
....(0860) 507447 (car)

Bailey, E., 10-5,.................................(01272) 737099
Bailey Mrs T., 8-7, ...(01488) 71483
Baines, G., 9-7,...................................(01308) 488502
Baker, I., 9-7,......................................(01937) 583050
Baker, L., 9-7, ...(01672) 514013
Balding, A., 10-9,...................... (01264) 772278 and
....(01635) 298210
Barnes, Miss F., 9-7,..........................(01900) 604189
Barraclough, Miss S., 9-7,.............(071) 3818829 or
....(0831) 576806
Barrett, R., 9-0,...................................(01733) 893453
.......and (0589) 163191 (mobile) or (01908) 611369
Bevan, Miss H. L., 9-10 ... (01931) 716655/716787
....(017684) 83392
Black, Miss D., 9-7, ...(01930) 51354
Blackwell, S., 10-0,.............................(01495) 302551
Bonner, C., 9-7,..............................c/o (01969) 624238
Bosley, Miss Sarah Jane, 8-7, ...(01367) 820115 or
.......(0378) 938040 (mobile) and (0367) 242224
Boswell, Miss L., 9-7,.........................(01939) 210210
Brackenbury, Miss J., 9-12, ... (01548) 82325 and
....(01367) 243208
Bradburne, Miss Lorna, 9-4,..............(01337) 810325
Bradburne, M., 10-12,.........................(01337) 810325
Bradley, Mr N., 10-0,...........................(01789) 297057
Bridger, D., 10-0,................................(01428) 722528
Bridger, Miss Madeleine, 9-0,..c/o (01428) 722528
Bronson, Miss E., 8-7, ...(01689) 54749
Brown, G., 10-0,..................................(01488) 648953
Brown, L., 10-7, ...c/o (01386) 793459
Brown, Mr S. R., 8-9,..........................(01638) 662063
Burgess, Miss Carrie, 9-0, ... (015242) 22052 and
....(0421) 624799 (mobile)
Burke, Mrs E. M., 9-7,.........................(01235) 821455
Burnell, W., 10-0,................................(01937) 833564
Burton, R. 10-0,.........................c/o (01386) 584209/219
Bush, S., 10-7,....................................(01249) 782317
Butler, Mrs E. L., 8-7, ...(01273) 477254
Bycroft, Miss A. S., 7-10,...................(01347) 888641
Byrne, T., 10-10, ...(01327) 860043 or
....(01327) 860712

Cahill, M. ....(051) 647210
Cahill, Mrs S. M., 7-12,......................(0483) 38297
Cambidge, J. R., 10-0,.................c/o (0195276) 249
Campion, Mrs S. J., 8-10,...................(01673) 858919
Carr, Mrs T. A., 9-7,............................(01653) 694671
Carson, Melanie, 8-5,.........................(01388) 603317
Chapple-Hyam, Mrs Jane, 9-0, c/o (01672) 514901
Charles-Jones, A. S., 10-0,................(01993) 823265
Clark, Miss R. A., 9-7,..................(01347) 810700 or
....car (0850) 837123
Clarke, P. C., 10-4,.............................(0323) 832098
Cleary, H., 9-7,....................................(045) 403206
Close, P. L., 8-12,..............................(01638) 730480
Cobden, Miss S., 9-7,.........................(01935) 823391
Collins, Miss Sheena,.........................(045) 41239
Collins, Miss Tracey,..........................(045) 41239
Coombe, Miss M., 9-0,........................(01305) 782218
Coonan, R. F., 10-0,...........................(01488) 73436
Corbett, Miss C. A., 8-7,.....................(01488) 648280
Corcorum, L.,......................................(017684) 84555
Cowdrey, Mrs Maxine, 8-10, ... (01903) 871367 or
....(01903) 871460
Cowell, R. M. H., 10-3,.......................(01638) 730329
Coyle, A. C.,..................................c/o (0503) 75121
Creedon, Miss A., 9-0,........................(01387) 267278
Creignton, J., 10-7,.............................(01984) 40419
Crossley (rides as Goulding), Mrs Jennie, 8-7,
....(01638) 751367

Cuff, S. T., 9-0
Culloty, J., 9-7, ... (01363) 775231 and
....(01235) 833535
Cumani, Mrs S., 9-0,..........................(01638) 665432
Cunningham, Miss Tara, 9-0,..............(046) 31672
Curley, C., 10-0,.................................(01638) 508251

Dalton, A. N., 10-12,...........................(0195 271) 656
....and (01989) 62250
Daly, M., 10-4,............................(01989730) 259/315
Delahunt, J., 10-10,............................(01292) 266232
Dempsey, A., 9-7,...............................(045) 21490
Deniel, Miss A. J., 9-0,.......................(01653) 600461
....or (01653) 618594
Densley, G., 10-6,...............................(01934) 733117
Dixon, B., 10-4,...................................(01308) 488487
Dixon, W., 10-7,..................................(01638) 664172
Dods, Mrs C., 8-0,...............................(01325) 374270
Doherty, A., 10-0,................................(0405) 55321
Done, Miss L., 9-4,..............................(01969) 622289
Donnelly, G., 10-4,..............................(045) 76292
Dronsfield, Miss A., 9-0, ...c/o (01488) 71767
Duckett, Sally, 9-7,.............................(0531) 890644
Dudgeon, A. S., 10-7,.........................(01360) 22391
Dukes, J., 10-0,...................................(01559) 371534
Dunwoody, Mrs C., 8-7,.......................(01235) 59287
Durkan, J. P. P., 10-0,

THE OLD SPREAD EAGLE
HIGH STREET . EPSOM . SURREY . KT19 8DN

Specialist Racing Outfitters since 1898

Riding Department
Direct Line 01372 747 474 . Direct Fax Line 01372 743 129

RACING COLOURS

To order in pure silk, best jockey nylon or knitted National
Hunt. (Price List Available)
EXPRESS SERVICE AVAILABLE

PADDOCK RUGS

To order in melton, super cloth, medium or heavyweight
woollen cloths. (Price List Available)

JOCKEY'S CLOTHING includes

Exercise jodhpurs, race breeches, race boots, race whips,
jockey skulls, race goggles, Epsom range of jodhpurs boots,
waterproof suits, Puffa jackets and vests, Barbour wax
jackets, chaps, race mitts, safety body protectors.

RACE SADDLERY includes

Bates race saddles, full and half tree exercise saddles, irons,
race leathers, race bridles, blinkers, visors, girths, surcingles,
weight cloths etc.

MAIL ORDER
Please phone to discuss your mail order requirements.
All major credit cards accepted.

Mackley, M., 10-4,......................(01673) 843663
MacTaggart, J., 11-7, ...(01450) 860314
Mannish, M., 9-7, ...(0181) 340 5315
Marchioness of Blandford, 9-5,......(01608) 677558
Marks, Miss A. K., 9-0, ...(01488) 71767
Marshall, D. G., 10-0, ...(01 845) 1467
Marshall, Miss V., 8-5, ...(01488) 71632 or
                                                    (0374) 946120
Maude, Miss E., 8-0, ...(01325) 374270
McCarthy, Mrs S., 9-0, ...(056) 26425
McCarthy, T., 10-0, ...(01883) 742069
McEntee, C., 8-7, ...(01638) 660663
McGuigan, J. O., 9-10, ...(01382) 360594
McHale, Mrs D., 8-8, ...(01264) 850854
McLaren, J., 10-10, ...(0475) 84422
McLaughlin, Mr W., 10-0, ...(01938) 580273
McMahon, E., 10-9, ...(01827) 62901
McPhail, O., 9-7, ...c/o (01386) 584209/219
McPherson, A. S., 10-0, ...(01506) 842815
Mehmet, Y. T., 9-0, ...(01388) 834636
Metcalfe, Miss Claire, 9-7,............(01388) 832465
Miles, N., 10-0,(01495) 773847 or (01495) 302551
Mills, V., 9-0,
Mitchell, A., 9-12, ...(01454) 238236
Mitchell, Miss H. 8-12,..........c/o (01372) 278453
Mitchell, N., 11-2, ...(0300) 348739
Moore, Miss A., 9-0, ...c/o (045)76292
Moore, Mrs Jayne, 8-0, ...(01273) 620106
Moore, J. D., 9-0, ...c/o (045)76292
Moore, Mrs J. S., 8-0,..................(01264) 88538 or
                                                    (0264) 889738
Morris, Miss C., 8-8, ...(01793) 710469
Morris, Mrs L., 9-0, ...(01638) 667959
Morris, Mrs M., 9-0, ...(01623) 822714
Morton, J., 8-12,..........................(01207) 501399
Moscrop, G. R., 10-7, ...(0191) 2362145
Mulcaire, S., 10-0,........................(01984) 40419
Mulhall, C. A., 10-9,......................(01904) 708756
Mullins, T., 10-11,(0503) 75121 and (088) 555531
Mullins, W. P., 11-0, ...(0503) 21786 and
                                                    (088) 564940
Murray, P., 9-7, ...(01274) 564930

Naughton, Mrs J., 8-7, ...(01372) 745112
Naughton, M., 9-7,........................(01287) 652000
Naylor, Dr J. R. J., 10-7,........c/o (01980) 621059
Neylon, R., 9-12, ...(045) 24674/34483
Nichol, Miss S., 8-0,......................(017684) 84555

O'Keeffe, P. 10-4 ....(01903) 872852
Olding, Miss D., 10-4,..................(01388) 834636
Olivefalk, Miss M. L., 9-7, ...(0505) 42306
Oliver, N. H., 9-7,........................(01242) 679330
O'Sullivan William, 10-7,..............(022)47116
O'Sullivan, Brendan, 9-7,..............(022)47116
O'Sullivan, Miss Fiona, 9-7,..........(022)47116
O'Sullivan, Miss M.,....................(01488) 71980

Parker, A., 10-0, ...(01576) 300238 or
                                                    (01576) 5105232
Parker, D., 9-9,............................(01576) 510232
Payne, R. J., 10-7,........................(0398) 7244

Peacock, Mrs C., 9-4, ...(01952) 728037 or
                                                    (01666) 577238
Pearce, Lydia., 8-7,......................(01638) 664669
Pegnor, Miss C.,..........................(01242) 233090
Perratt, Miss L. A., 9-0,................(01292) 266232
Phillips, P., 9-7,....................c/o(01367) 820510
Phipps, Miss M., 8-7, ...(01623) 822714
Platts, C., 10-12,..........................(01274) 871522
Plunkett, Miss A., 9-7, ...c/o (01275) 373581
Pollock, B. N., 9-12, ...(01789) 266253 or
                                                    (0831) 834112
Portman, J., 10-2, ...(01235) 59205
Poulton, J. C., 10-7,....................(01273) 603824
Price, A., 10-0,............................(01495) 304794
Pritchard, J., 10-12,....................(01926) 632391
                                              or (0531) 634461
Pritchard, Dr P. L. J., 9-11,..........(01453) 811881
Pritchard-Gordon, P., 10-0, ...(01638) 662824
Purcell, Miss Louise., 9-7,............(01223) 812922
Purdy, Miss A., 9-7, ...(01367) 820658

Ramsden, Miss E., 8-7,............c/o (01845) 587226
Rebori, A. D., 10-7, ...(01709) 543229
Rees, Mrs G., 8-10,......................(01772) 812780
Rees, J., 9-7,(01235) 833297 and (01235) 769360
Rimell, M., 10-0,..........................(01451) 30417
Robinson, D. T., 9-7, ...(01507) 363525
Robson, A. W., 10-9, ...(01668) 213416
Robson, Miss P, 9-0, ...(0830) 30241
Rodda, M., 10-0, ...(01905) 381077

Salaman, M.,................................(01902) 688558
Santana, K., 9-2,..........................(0181 651) 6482
Saunders, Mrs J., 9-0, ...(060124) 739
Scott, P., 9-7,..............................(01295) 758218
Sharratt, Miss S., 10-2,................(01543) 490197
Sheenan, J. A., 9-7, ...(022) 47116
Shenkin, G., 10-0,........................(01568) 760605
Shiels, R., 11-4, ...(01835) 854060
Small, Miss B., 9-7, ...(01451) 821277
Smith, G., 9-9, ...c/o (01386) 584209/219
Spearing, Miss C. M., 9-0, ...(01789) 772639
Spearing, Miss T. S., 9-0, ...(01789) 772639
Stockell, Ms Ann, 9-7,..................(0192684) 2464
Storey, C., 10-2,..........................(069 77) 3810
Storey, Miss S., 8-7,....................(01207) 55259
Swan, Miss N., 9-7,......................(0505)42457
Swiers, S. J., 10-5,......................(01423) 324155
Swindlehurst, D., 10-4, ...(01228) 74376 and
                                                    (01228) 74289
Sykes, Miss A. 9-7, ...(01588) 638451

Thomas, Miss C., 10-0, ...(01544) 388980
Thompson, M., 10-7, ...(066 576) 272
Thorner, Miss C., 9-10, ...(01235) 763003
Thronton, R., 9-0, ...c/o (01836) 584209/219
Thurlow, Miss J., 9-0,..................(01697) 320576 or
                                                    (01900) 881331
Toal, N., 10-0, ...(0199421) 396
Townsley, Miss C., 8-7, ...(01483) 200849
Townsley, Miss L., 9-7,................(01483) 200849
Townsley, P., 11-0,......................(01483) 200849

Townson, J. G., 10-10, ... (01638) 660696) and
(0374) 824308) (mobile)
Trice-Rolph, J. C., 11-0, ...(01451) 32039

Usher, Mrs A., 7-7, ...(01793) 791115

Verco, D. I., 10-2, ... (97317) 150
Vigors, C., 10-4, ... (01488) 72561 and
(0402) 106220 (mobile)
Vollaro, Miss Lucy, 8-7

Waggot, N. jun., 11-0, ...(01388) 819012
Waggot, Miss T., 9-7, ...(01388) 819012
Wakley, R., 10-0, ...(01638) 666567
Walker, S., 9-3, ...(01430) 81295
Walters, M., 10-0 ....(01488) 648280
Waters, T., 10-0, ...(01273) 890244
Webster, Miss H., 8-7, ...(01969) 23788
Wenyon, W., 9-0, ...(01589) 138376

Weymes, J. R., 10-4, ...(01969) 40229
Wharf, P. Wharf., 9-7, ...(01565) 777275
Wheat, K., 10-0, ...(01235) 763003
Whitaker, S. R., 11-7, ...(01937) 582122
White, Miss S., 9-0, ...(01621) 742161
White, R., 10-10, ...(01984) 640532
Wikinson, Mrs J. V., 8-7, ...(01258) 817719
Williams, Miss C., ...(01969) 623271
Williams, E., 10-2, ...(01633) 680978
Wilson, C. R., 10-12, ...(01325) 374595
Winter, Miss J., 9-0, ...c/o (01488) 71149
Wintle, A., 10-7, ...(01452) 760377
Wonnacott, A. J., 11-0, ...(01364) 642267
Wormall, Miss J., 9-0, ...(01530) 260224

Yardley, Miss A., 8-0, ...(01905) 830245
Yardley, Miss S., 8-4, ...(01905) 620477
Young, Miss S., 10-5, ...(01579) 20159

If an entry is
incorrect or has been
omitted, please
notify the editor by
January 10th, 1997.

This will ensure it
appears correctly in
the 1997 edition.

RACECOURSES OF GREAT BRITAIN

AINTREE (N-H)

(Grand National Course) - Triangular, 2m 2f (16) 494y run-in with elbow. Perfectly flat. A severe test for both horse and rider, putting a premium on jumping ability, fitness and courage, although some of the fences were recently modified.

(Mildmay Course) - Rectangular, 1m 4f (8) 260y run-in. A very fast course with sharp bends.

Clerk of the Course: Mr C. H. Barnett, Aintree Racecourse, Aintree, Liverpool L9 5AS. Tel: (0151) 523 2600.

Photography: By prior permission only from Aintree Racecourse.

176 boxes allocated in strict rotation. A new Stable Lads' Hostel was opened for the 1995 Grand National meeting and facilities are available on the course for up to 100 stable staff.

By Car: North of the City, near the junction of the M57 and M58 with the A59 (Preston).

By Rail: Aintree Station is adjacent to the Stands, from Liverpool Central.

By Air: Liverpool (Speke) Airport is 10 miles. Helicopter landing facility by prior arrangement.

Leading Trainers (since 1991): M. C. Pipe 11-91 (12.1%), **D. Nicholson** 10-63 (15.9%), **N. A. Twiston-Davies** 8-49 (16.3%).

Leading Jockeys (since 1991): R. Dunwoody 10-66 (15.0%), **N. Williamson** 7-36 (19.0%), **G. Bradley** 6-21 (28.0%),

ASCOT (R.H.)

A triangular course of 1m 6f 34y. The course goes downhill from the mile and a half start for three furlongs into Swinley Bottom (the lowest part of the track): it soon joins the Old Mile (which starts on a chute) and is then uphill with a straight run-in of two and a half furlongs, the last 100y being level. The straight mile (Royal Hunt Cup Course) is downhill from the start, rises to the five furlong gate and then falls slightly to the junction of the courses. The whole course is of a galloping nature with easy turns but is nevertheless a testing one, especially on soft going.

Clerk of the Course and Secretary: Mr N. Cheyne, Ascot Racecourse, Ascot, Berkshire SL5 7JN. Tel: (01344) 22211.

Going Reports: (01344) 874567.

Free. Wood shavings (straw on request). No forage.

By Car: West of the town on the A329. Easy access from the M3 (Junc 3) and the M4 (Junc 6). Car parking adjoining the course and Ascot Heath. Contact the Secretary, Ascot Authority. Tel: (01990) 20768.

By Rail: Regular service from Waterloo to Ascot (500y from the racecourse).

By Air: Helicopter landing facility at the course. London (Heathrow) Airport 15 miles, White Waltam Airfield 12 miles.

Leading Trainers (since 1991): J. L. Dunlop 27-139 (19.4%), M. R. Stoute 24-183 (13.1%), J. H. M. Gosden 22-143 (15.4%).

Leading Jockeys (since 1991): Pat Eddery 36-241 (14.0%), W. Carson 36-256 (14.0%), L. Dettori 31-259 (11.0%).

ASCOT (N-H)

Triangular, 1m 6f (10) 240y run-in mostly uphill. A galloping course with an uphill finish, Ascot provides a real test of stamina. The fences are stiff and sound jumping is essential, especially for novices.

Clerk of the Course and Secretary: Mr N. Cheyne, Ascot Racecourse, Ascot, Berkshire SL5 7JN. Tel: (01344) 22211.

Going Reports: (01344) 874567.

Free. Wood shavings (straw on request). No forage.

By Car: West of the town on the A329. Easy access from the M3 (Junc 3) and the M4 (Junc 6). Car parking adjoining the course and Ascot Heath. Contact the Secretary, Ascot Authority. Tel: (01990) 20768.

By Rail: Regular service from Waterloo to Ascot (500y from the racecourse).

By Air: Helicopter landing facility at the course. London (Heathrow) Airport 15 miles, White Waltam Airfield 12 miles.

Leading Trainers (since 1991): M. C. Pipe 20-87 (23.0%), O. Sherwood 18-66 (27.3%), N. A. Twiston-Davies 16-104 (15.4%).

Leading Jockeys (since 1991): J. Osborne 34-115 (29.0%), R. Dunwoody 17-115 (14.0%), A. Maguire 17-89 (19.0%).

AYR (L.H.)

A wide, relatively flat oval track of just over 1m 4f. An extension to the back straight provides a 1m 3f course with a sweeping turn at the top of the straight course four furlongs from the winning post. The straight six furlongs falls slightly for some three and a half furlongs and then rises slightly. In general, this is a very fair galloping course.

Clerk of the Course: Mr S. R. Morshead, Racecourse Office, 2 Whitletts Road, Ayr. Tel: (01292) 264179. Home: (01655) 5277.

Secretary and Manager: Mr Mark Kershaw, address as above.

Free stabling and accommodation for lads and lasses. Tel: (01292) 262554.

By Car: East of the town on the A758. Free parking for buses and cars.

By Rail: Ayr Station (trains on the half hour from Glasgow Central). Journey time 55 minutes. Buses and taxis also to the course.

By Air: Prestwick International Airport (10 minutes by car). Glasgow Airport (1 hour).

Leading Trainers (since 1991): J. Berry 24-235 (10.2%), **Mrs M. Reveley** 22-106 (20.8%), **B. W. Hills** 22-59 (37.3%).

Leading Jockeys (since 1991): K. Darley 47-208 (22.0%), D. Holland 20-77 (25.0%), J. Carroll 19-142 (13.0%).

AYR (N-H)

Oval, 1m 4f (9) 210y run-in. Relatively flat and one of the fastest tracks in Great Britain. It is a well-drained course and the ground rarely becomes testing. Suits the long-striding galloper.

Clerk of the Course: Mr S. R. Morshead, Racecourse Office, 2 Whitletts Road, Ayr. Tel: (01292) 264179. Home: (01655) 5277.

Secretary and Manager: Mr Mark Kershaw, address as above.

Free stabling and accommodation for lads and lasses. Tel: (01292) 262554.

By Car: East of the town on the A758. Free parking for buses and cars.

By Rail: Ayr Station (trains on the half hour from Glasgow Central). Journey time 55 minutes. Buses and taxis also to the course.

By Air: Prestwick International Airport (10 minutes by car). Glasgow Airport (1 hour).

Leading Trainers (since 1991): G. Richards 57-258 (22.1%), **Mrs M. Reveley** 42-152 (27.6%), **J. J. O'Neill** 21-102 (20.6%).

Leading Jockeys (since 1991): P. Niven 38-156 (24.0%), **B. Storey** 25-176 (14.0%), **A. Dobbin** 21-110 (19.0%).

BANGOR-ON-DEE (N-H)

Circular, 1m 4f (9) 325y run-in. Apart from some `ridge and furrow', this is a flat course notable for three sharp bends, especially the paddock turn. Suits handy, speedy sorts and is ideal for front-runners.

Clerk of the Course: B. R. Davies, Shepherds Meadow, Eaton Bishop, Hereford, HR2 9UA. Tel: (01981) 250052 (Office), (01981) 580260 (Home), (01831) 602207 (Car).

Secretary and Manager: P. W. Ockleston, Chorlton Hall, Malpas, Cheshire, SY14 7ET. Tel: (01948) 860122 (Office), (01978) 780323 (Racedays).

Allotted on arrival. Shavings (straw on request). Applications to the Manager.

By Car: 5 miles South-East of Wrexham, off the B5069.
By Rail: Wrexham Station (bus or taxi to the course).
By Air: Helicopters may land by prior arrangement with Clerk of the Course at entirely their own risk.

Leading Trainers (since 1991): G. Richards 31-151 (20.5%), **M. C. Pipe** 26-91 (28.6%), **N. A. Twiston-Davies** 17-78 (21.8%).
Leading Jockeys (since 1991): R. Dunwoody 26-87 (29.0%), **A. Maguire** 13-75 (17.0%), **D. Bridgwater** 10-61 (16.0%).

BATH (L.H.)

An oval track of 1m 4f 25y with 1m 3f 150y, 1m 2f 50y and 1m starts set on chutes from the back straight and an uphill run-in of four furlongs, which bends to the left. There is no straight course but an extension provides for races of five furlongs and of 5f 167y, which run generally uphill and left-handed to a distinct left-handed curve about a furlong from the winning post.
Clerk of the Course: Mr R. D. Farrant, Tylers Farm, Gravel Hill Road, Yate, Bristol BS17 5BN. Tel: (01454) 313186.
Secretary: Captain C. B. Toller, Greenfields, Little Rissington, nr. Cheltenham, Gloucestershire. Tel: (01451) 820517.
Free stabling and accommodation for lads and lasses.
By Car: 2 miles North-West of the City (M4 Junc 18) at Lansdown. Unlimited free car and coach parking space immediately behind the stands. Special bus services operate from Bath to the racecourse.
By Rail: Bath Station (from Paddington), regular bus service from Bath to the course (3 miles).
By Air: Bristol or Colerne Airports. (no landing facilities at the course).

Leading Trainers (since 1991): P. F. I. Cole 21-130 (24.34%), **I. A. Balding** 17-108 (15.7%), **R. Hannon** 17-144 (11.8%).
Leading Jockeys (since 1991): T. Quinn 29-161 (18.0%), **Pat Eddery** 23-96 (23.0%), **J. Williams** 20-206 (9.0%).

BEVERLEY (R.H.)

An oval course of 1m 3f set on two levels. A chute to the back straight provides a mile and a quarter course, which has a straight run of some five furlongs to a steep downhill bend into the home turn and an uphill run-in of two and a half furlongs. The five furlong course, which rises throughout with a distinct jink after a furlong and a slight bend to the right at halfway, provides a severe test for juveniles at the start of the season. The downhill turn into the straight and the short run-in prevent this from being an entirely galloping track.
Clerk of the Course and Manager: Mr J. G. Cleverly, F.R.I.C.S., Glebe House, Settrington, York. Tel: (01944) 768203 (evenings), (01482) 867488/882645 (Office and course). Course foreman - Home (01430) 810409, Mobile (0585 678186).
Free.
By Car: 7 miles from the M62 (Junc 38) off the A1035. Free car parking opposite the course. Owners and Trainers use a separate enclosure.
By Rail: Beverley Station (Hull-Scarborough line). Occasional bus service to the course (1 mile).
By Air: Helicopter landings by prior arrangement. Light aircraft landing facilities at Linley Hill, Leven airport.

Leading Trainers (since 1991): M. H. Easterby 24-192 (12.5%), **J. Berry** 22-152 (14.5%), **M. Johnston** 21-104 (20.2%).
Leading Jockeys (since 1991): K. Darley 49-269 (18.0%), **W. Carson** 21-69 (30.0%), **M. Birch** 20-198 (10.0%).

BRIGHTON (L.H.)

The course forms a horseshoe of 1m 4f round with easy turns and a run-in of three and a half furlongs. The first three furlongs are slightly uphill. Then there is a gentle descent and rise to about four furlongs from home. From there the ground falls steeply until about two furlongs out; then a sharp rise with the last 100y level. This sharp track, reminiscent of Epsom with its pronounced gradients, is unsuitable for big, long-striding animals, but it suits sharp sorts and is something of a specialists' course.

Clerk of the Course: Mr G. R. Stickels, Lingfield Park 1991 Ltd., Lingfield, Surrey RH7 6PQ.
Tel: (01342) 834800 or (01273) 603580 (racedays).
Managers: Lingfield 1991 Ltd., address as above.
Stabling and accommodation available on request.

By Car: East of the town on the A27 (Lewes Road). There is a car park adjoining the course.
By Rail: Brighton Station (from Victoria on the hour, London Bridge or Portsmouth). Special bus service to the course from the station (approx 2 miles) and to the sea front.
By Air: No racecourse facilities.

Leading Trainers (since 1991): R. Hannon 44-234 (18.8%), **R. Akehurst** 26-113 (23.0%), **L. M. Cumani** 22-66 (33.3%).
Leading Jockeys (since 1991): T. Quinn 48-260 (18.0%), **W. Carson** 40-151 (26.0%), **M. Roberts** 25-106 (23.0%).

CARLISLE (R.H.)

A pear-shaped, undulating course of 1m 5f with an extension for a mile and a half start and a straight uphill run-in of three and a half furlongs. The six furlong course (which includes the five furlong) starts on a chute, bears right for the first furlong and a half and again at the turn into the straight. The rise to the winning post, although it begins to level out from `the distance', makes it a stiff test of stamina.

Clerk of the Course: Mr J. E. Fenwicke-Clennell, Toft Way, Sharperton, Morpeth, Northumberland NE65 7AE. Tel: (01669) 50369, Fax: (01669) 50339, Mobile: (01860) 737729.
Managing Director: Mr T. E. Robinson, Grandstand Office, Carlisle Racecourse, Durdar Road, Carlisle, Cumbria CA2 4TS. Tel: (01228) 22973.
Secretary & Club Secretary: Mrs Ann Bliss, Grandstand Office, Carlisle Racecourse, Durdar Road, Carlisle, Cumbria, CA2 4TS. Tel: (01228) 22973.
Stabling and accommodation available on request.

By Car: 2 miles south of the town (Durdar Road). Easy access from the M6 (Junc 42). The car park is free (adjacent to the course). Trackside car parking £3 (except premier meeting).
By Rail: Carlisle Station (2 miles from the course).
By Air: Helicopter landing facility by prior arrangement.

Leading Trainers (since 1991): J. Berry 22-119 (18.5%), **Mrs M. Reveley** 19-78 (24.4%), **Sir Mark Prescott** 15-36 (41.7%).
Leading Jockeys (since 1991): K. Darley 24-132 (18.0%), **G. Duffield** 20-86 (23.0%), **J. Carroll** 17-105 (16.0%).

CARLISLE (N-H)

Pear-shaped, 1m 5f (9) 300y run-in uphill. Undulating and a stiff test of stamina, ideally suited to the long-striding thorough stayer. Three mile chases start on a chute, and the first fence is only jumped once. Ground tends to be either very fast or very soft.

Clerk of the Course: Mr J. E. Fenwicke-Clennell, Toft Way, Sharperton, Morpeth, Northumberland NE65 7AE. Tel: (01669) 50369, Fax: (01669) 50339, Mobile: (01860) 737729.

Managing Director: Mr T. E. Robinson, Grandstand Office, Carlisle Racecourse, Durdar Road, Carlisle, Cumbria CA2 4TS. Tel: (01228) 22973.

Secretary & Club Secretary: Mrs Ann Bliss, Grandstand Office, Carlisle Racecourse, Durdar Road, Carlisle, Cumbria, CA2 4TS. Tel: (01228) 22973.

Stabling and accommodation available on request.

By Car: 2 miles south of the town (Durdar Road). Easy access from the M6 (Junc 42). The car park is free (adjacent to the course). Trackside car parking £3 (except premier meeting).

By Rail: Carlisle Station (2 miles from the course).

By Air: Helicopter landing facility by prior arrangement.

Leading Trainers (since 1991): G. Richards 33-199 (16.6%), **Mrs M. Reveley** 23-85 (27.1%), **M. D. Hammond** 17-114 (14.9%).

Leading Jockeys (since 1991): P. Niven 31-111 (27.0%), B. Storey 24-170 (14.0%), **A. Dobbin** 18-94 (19.0%).

CARTMEL (N-H)

Oval, 1m 1f (6) 800y run-in. Almost perfectly flat but very sharp, with the longest run-in in the country, approximately half a mile. The fences are stiff but fair.

Acting Clerk of the Course: Mr C. H. Barnett, Aintree Racecourse, Aintree, Liverpool L9 5AS. Tel: (0151) 523 2600.

Number of boxes and accommodation for lads ands lasses is limited. Prior booking is advisable. Apply to Mr J. Moorhouse, Cloggerbeck House, Cartmel. Tel: (01539) 536494.

By Car: 1 mile West of the town, 2 miles off the B5277 (Grange-Haverthwaite road). M36 (Junc 36).

By Rail: Cark and Cartmel Station (2 1/2 miles) (Carnforth-Barrow line).

By Air: Light aircraft facilities available at Cark Airport (4 miles from the course). Helicopter landing facility at the course, by prior arrangement only.

Leading Trainers (since 1991): G. Richards 16-53 (30.2%), **J. White** 14-54 (25.9%), **M. C. Chapman** 11-65 (16.9%).

Leading Jockeys (since 1991): P. Niven 7-15 (46.0%), D. J. Moffatt 7-33 (21.0%), **W. Worthington** 5-35 (14.0%).

CATTERICK (L.H.)

An oval, undulating course of 1m 180y with two chutes, one for seven furlong and another for five furlong starts, and a straight run-in of three furlongs. The five furlong course is downhill throughout, sharply at first, and jinks left-handed at the junction of the courses. The seven furlong track joins the round course at the six furlong gate and is slightly downhill to the home turn. This sharp track is entirely unsuitable for long-striding gallopers and is often a specialists' track for both horse and jockey.

Clerk of the Course: Mr S. C. Enderby, The Riding, Hexham, Northumberland NE46 4PF. Tel: (01434) 606881 (Office). Fax: (01434) 605814.
Secretary: Mr J. Sanderson, The Racecourse, Catterick Bridge, Richmond, North Yorkshire DL10 7PE. Tel: (01748) 811478. Fax: (01748) 811082.
Boxes are allotted on arrival. Contact Mr W. Scott, Racecourse Lodge, Catterick. Tel: (01748) 811478.
By Car: The course is adjacent to the A1, 1 mile North-West of the town on the A6136. There is a free car park.
By Rail: Darlington Station (special buses to course - 14 mile journey).

Leading Trainers (since 1991): J. Berry 35-209 (16.8%), **Mrs M. Reveley** 25-116 (21.6%), **B. W. Hills** 20-47 (42.6%).
Leading Jockeys (since 1991): K. Darley 35-171 (20.0%), **J. Carroll** 28-153 (18.0%), **J. Weaver** 15-91 (16.0%).

CATTERICK (N-H)

Oval, 1m 1f (9) 240y run-in. Undulating, sharp track that favours the handy, front-running sort, rather than the long-striding galloper.
Clerk of the Course: Mr S. C. Enderby, The Riding, Hexham, Northumberland NE46 4PF. Tel: (01434) 606881 (Office). Fax: (01434) 605814.
Secretary: Mr J. Sanderson, The Racecourse, Catterick Bridge, Richmond, North Yorkshire DL10 7PE. Tel: (01748) 811478. Fax: (01748) 811082.
Boxes are allotted on arrival. Contact Mr W. Scott, Racecourse Lodge, Catterick. Tel: (01748) 811478.
By Car: The course is adjacent to the A1, 1 mile North-West of the town on the A6136. There is a free car park.
By Rail: Darlington Station (special buses to course - 14 mile journey).

Leading Trainers (since 1991): Mrs M. Reveley 26-122 (21.3%), **M. H. Easterby** 15-94 (16.0%), **M. D. Hammond** 14-105 (13.3%).
Leading Jockeys (since 1991): M. Dwyer 19-68 (27.0%), **P. Niven** 16-89 (17.0%), **A. S. Smith** 13-42 (30.0%).

CHELTENHAM (N-H)

(Old Course) - Oval, 1m 4f (9) 350y run-in. A testing, undulating track with stiff fences. The ability to stay is essential as the going can get heavy in wet weather.
(New Course) - Oval, 1m 5f (10) 220y run-in. Undulating, stiff fences, testing course, uphill for the final half-mile.
(Park Course) - Oval, 1m 5f (9) 220y uphill run-in. Not as testing as the other two courses and designed to put less strain on the horses' legs in early and late-season.
Clerk of the Course: Major P. W. F. Arkwright, Shirley Farm, Little Wolford, Shipston-on-Stour, Warwickshire. Tel: (01608) 84460.
Club Secretary: Mrs R. Hammond, address and phone as Managing Director.
Managing Director: E. W. Gillespie, The Racecourse, Prestbury Park, Cheltenham, Gloucestershire. Tel: (01242) 513014.
Ample stabling and accommodation for lads. Apply to the Stable Manager (01242) 513014.
By Car: 11/2 miles North of the town on the A435. M5 (Junc 10 or 11).
By Rail: Cheltenham (Lansdowne) Station. Buses and taxis to course.
By Air: Helicopter landing site to the North-East of the stands.

Leading Trainers (since 1991 Park) M. C. Pipe 10-32 (31.3%), **N. A. Twiston-Davies** 8-40 (20.0%), **K. C. Bailey** 7-26 (26.9%)
Leading Jockeys (since 1991 Park): R. Dunwoody 5-26 (19.0%), **W. Marston** 4-14 (28.0%), **A. Maguire** 3-23 (13.0%).
Leading Trainers (since 1991 Old & New): D. Nicholson 39-192 (20.3%), **M. C. Pipe** 31-276 (11.2%), **N. A. Twiston-Davies** 27-186 (14.5%).
Leading Jockeys (since 1991 Old & New): R. Dunwoody 39-201 (19.0%), **J. Osborne** 23-151 (15.0%), **A. Maguire** 21-145 (14.0%).

CHEPSTOW (L.H.)

An oval, undulating course, about 2m in circumference with a straight run-in of five furlongs, which extends to make a straight mile. All races of up to a mile are run on the latter, which is downhill to the five furlong start and then rises sharply for two and a half furlongs before levelling out to the winning post. The changing gradients prevent this from being a really galloping track.
Clerk of the Course and Manager: Mr R. Farrant, Tylers Farm, Gravel Hill Road, Yate, nr Bristol BS17 5BN. Tel: (01291) 622260 (Office). (01454) 313186 (Home). (01850) 888380 (Mobile). Fax: (01291) 625550.
Secretary: G. C. Francis, 17 Welsh Street, Chepstow.
109 boxes, alloted on arrival. Limited accommodation for lads and lasses. Apply: (01291) 623414.
By Car: 1 mile North-West of the town on the A466. (1 mile from Junc 22 of the M4 (Severn Bridge)). There is a Free public car park opposite the Stands entrance.
By Rail: Chepstow Station (from Paddington, change at Gloucester or Newport). The course is 1 mile from station.
By Air: Helicopter landing facility in the centre of the course.

Leading Trainers (since 1991): R. Hannon 21-145 (14.5%), **H. R. A. Cecil** 12-40 (30.0%), **P. W. Chapple-Hyam** 10-43 (23.3%).
Laeding Jockeys (since 1991): J. Williams 17-122 (13.0%), **J. Reid** 17-103 (16.0%), **T. Quinn** 13-83 (15.0%).

CHEPSTOW (N-H)

Oval, 2m (11) 240y run-in. Many changing gradients, five fences in the home straight. Favours the long-striding front-runner, but stamina is important.
Clerk of the Course and Manager: Mr R. Farrant, Tylers Farm, Gravel Hill Road, Yate, nr Bristol BS17 5BN. Tel: (01291) 622260 (Office). (01454) 313186 (Home). (01850) 888380 (Mobile). Fax: (01291) 625550.
Secretary: G. C. Francis, 17 Welsh Street, Chepstow.
109 boxes, alloted on arrival. Limited accommodation for lads and lasses. Apply: (01291) 623414.
By Car: 1 mile North-West of the town on the A466. (1 mile from Junc 22 of the M4 (Severn Bridge)). There is a Free public car park opposite the Stands entrance.
By Rail: Chepstow Station (from Paddington, change at Gloucester or Newport). The course is 1 mile from station.
By Air: Helicopter landing facility in the centre of the course.

Leading Trainers (since 1991): M. C. Pipe 63-241 (26.1%), **N. A. Twiston-Davies** 24-111 (21.6%), **P. J. Hobbs** 19-84 (22.6%).
Leading Jockeys (since 1991): R. Dunwoody 30-114 (26.0%), **C. Llewellyn** 16-94 (17.0%), **A. Maguire** 15-83 (18.0%).

CHESTER (L.H.)

A perfectly flat, circular course, 1m 73y in circumference, with a sharp bend to a straight run-in of 230y. Long distance events are an extreme test of stamina, but for middle-distance races and sprints, the course greatly favours a sharp-actioned horse. Horses with previous winning form on this track are worthy of note.

Clerk of the Course: Mr C. H. Barnett, Aintree Racecourse, Aintree, Liverpool L9 5AS. Tel: (0151) 523 2600 or (01244) 323938 (racedays).

Secretary: Kidsons Impey, Steam Mill, Chester.CH3 5AN Tel: (01244) 327171.

Free stabling (175 boxes) and accommodation.

By Car: The course is near the centre of the city on the A548 (Queensferry Road). The Owners and Trainers car park is adjacent to the County Stand. There is a public car park in the centre of the course.

By Rail: Chester Station (3/4 mile from the course). Services from Euston, Paddington and Northgate.

By Air: Hawarden Airport (2 miles).

Leading Trainers (since 1991): M. R. Stoute 21-74 (28.4%), **A. Bailey** 17-147 (11.6%), **B. W. Hills** 16-73 (21.9%).

Leading Jockeys (since 1991): Pat Eddery 23-84 (27.0%), **W. R. Swinburn** 16-64 (25.0%), **D. Holland** 13-71 (18.0%).

DONCASTER (L.H.)

A pear-shaped track, about 1m 7f 110y in circumference with a distinct rise and fall to the mile marker. There is a level run-in of four and a half furlongs, extending to a straight mile, which tapers from a width of 88ft at the five-furlong pole to 60ft at the winning post. A round mile joins the straight course at a tangent. This good galloping track is suitable for strongly-built stayers and calls for stamina and courage.

Clerk of the Course (NH): Major C. L. Moore, Doncaster Racecourse, Leger Way, Doncaster.

Chief Executive & Clerk of Course (Flat): Mr J. Sanderson, International Racecourse Management Ltd., Grandstand, Leger Way, Doncaster DN2 6BB. Tel: (01302) 320066. Fax: (01302) 323271.

Free stabling and accommodation.

By Car: East of the town, off the A638 (M18 Junc 3 & 4). Club members car park reserved. Large public car park free and adjacent to the course.

By Rail: Doncaster Central Station (from King's Cross). Special bus service from the station (1 mile).

Leading Trainers (since 1991): J. H. M. Gosden 37-158 (23.4%), **B. W. Hills** 31-145 (21.4%), **H. R. A. Cecil** 28-107 (26.2%).

Leading Jockeys (since 1991): Pat Eddery 43-218 (19.0%), **W. Carson** 34-240 (14.0%), **K. Darley** 33-250 (13.0%).

DONCASTER (N-H)

Conical, 2m (11) 247y run-in. A very fair, flat track ideally suited to the long-striding galloper. The fences have been made noticeably stiffer of late.

Clerk of the Course (NH): Major C. L. Moore, Doncaster Racecourse, Leger Way, Doncaster.

Chief Executive & Clerk of Course (Flat): Mr J. Sanderson, International Racecourse Management Ltd., Grandstand, Leger Way, Doncaster DN2 6BB. Tel: (01302) 320066. Fax: (01302) 323271.
Free stabling and accommodation.
By Car: East of the town, off the A638 (M18 Junc 3 & 4). Club members car park reserved. Large public car park free and adjacent to the course.
By Rail: Doncaster Central Station (from King's Cross). Special bus service from the station (1 mile).

Leading Trainers (since 1991): Mrs M. Reveley 18-83 (21.7%), **J. G. FitzGerald** 12-80 (15.0%), **D. Nicholson** 10-48 (20.8%).
Leading Jockeys (since 1991): P. Niven 16-58 (27.0%), **L. Wyer** 8-39 (20.0%), **M. Dwyer** 8-55 (14.0%).

EPSOM (L.H.)

From the Derby start at the top of the Downs, the course climbs steadily for the first gently-bending four furlongs, then levels out for nearly two furlongs before falling sharply round the bend to Tattenham Corner and into the straight. This is of less than four furlongs and ends with a fairish rise of just over a furlong to the winning post. The City and Suburban course and the Epsom Mile are, respectively, the last 1m 2f 15y and the last 1m 110y of the Derby course. The five furlong course (Egmont Course) is perfectly straight and, running sharply downhill to the junction with the round course, is the fastest in the world. The Derby course is a unique test for the thoroughbred, the frequently fast early pace demanding stamina, and the bends and gradients calling for a faultless action. Well-balanced, medium-sized, handy sorts seem to do best over five furlongs.
Clerk of the Course & General Manager: Mr A. J. Cooper, The Grandstand, Epsom Downs, Surrey KT18 5LQ. Tel: (01372) 726311, Mobile (0374) 230850
Free stabling and accommodation.
By Car: 2 miles South of the town on the B290 (M25 Junc 8 & 9). For full car park particulars apply to: The Club Secretary, Epsom Grandstand, Epsom Downs, Surrey KT18 5LQ. Tel: (01372) 726311.
By Rail: Epsom, Epsom Downs or Tattenham Corner Stations (trains from London Bridge, Waterloo, Victoria). Regular bus services run to the course from Epsom and Morden Underground Station.
By Air: London (Heathrow) and London (Gatwick) are both within 20 miles of the course. Heliport (Derby Meeting only) apply to Hascombe Aviation. Tel: (01279) 680291.

Leading Trainers (since 1991): R. Hannon 16-143 (11.2%), **R. Akehurst** 15-85 (17.7%), **D. R. C. Elsworth** 10-49 (20.4%).
Leading Jockeys (since 1991): M. Roberts 22-99 (22.0%), **Pat Eddery** 16-102 (15.0%), **J. Reid** 16-92 (17.0%).

EXETER (N-H)

Oval, 2m (11) 300y run-in uphill. Undulating with a home straight of half a mile. A good test of stamina, suiting the handy, well-balanced sort. Has separate summer and winter courses, with different lay-outs of fences.
Clerk of the Course and Manager: N. G. P. Ansell, Pillhead House, Bideford, EX39 4NF (01237) 472574

Racecourse. (01392) 832599. Fax (01392) 833454.

28 boxes at Kennford (2 miles from the course) allotted on arrival; 69 loose boxes on the course. Sleeping accommodation and canteen for both lads and lasses. Apply to Mrs J. Browning. Tel: (01392) 832816.

By Car: The course is at Haldon, 5 miles South-West of Exeter on the A38 (Plymouth) road, 2 miles East of Chudleigh.

By Rail: Exeter (St Davids) Station.

Leading Trainers (since 1991): M. C. Pipe 100-328 (30.5%), **P. J. Hobbs** 32-157 (20.4%), **Miss H. C. Knight** 29-76 (38.2%).

Leading Jockeys (since 1991): R. Dunwoody 30-131 (22.0%), **J. Osborne** 20-68 (29.0%), **M. A. Fitzgerald** 20-121 (16.0%).

FAKENHAM (N-H)

Square, 1m (6) 200y run-in. On the turn almost throughout and undulating, suiting the handy front-runner. The going rarely becomes heavy.

Clerk of the Course: P. B. Firth, Fakenham Racecourse Ltd., The Racecourse, Fakenham, Norfolk NR21 7NY. Tel: (01328) 862388.

76 boxes allotted in rotation. Tel: (01328) 862388.

By Car: 1 mile South of the town on the B1146 (East Dereham) road.

By Rail: Norwich Station (26 miles) (Liverpool Street line), King's Lynn (22 miles) (Liverpool Street).

By Air: Helicopter landing facility in the centre of the course.

Leading Trainers (since 1991): O. Brennan 10-27 (37.0%), **M. J. Ryan** 10-28 (35.7%), **J. R. Jenkins** 9-44 (20.5%).

Leading Jockeys (since 1991): M. Brennan 9-33 (27.0%), **A. Maguire** 6-25 (24.0%), **Mr M. Armytage** 4-9 (44.0%).

FOLKESTONE (R.H.)

A circuit of 1m 3f, somewhat undulating, with a straight run-in of two and a half furlongs. Five and six furlong races start on an extension which joins the round course about three furlongs from the line and has a slight rise over the final furlong. Despite its gentle turns and its width, Folkestone can not be described as a galloping track.

Clerk of the Course: Mr G. R. Stickels, Lingfield Park 1991 Ltd., Lingfield, Surrey RH7 6PQ. Tel: (01342) 834800.

90 boxes allotted in rotation. Advance notice required for overnight accommodation.

By Car: 6 miles West of town at Westenhanger. Easy access from Junc 11 of the M20. Car park adjoins stands. (Free, except course enclosure £3).

By Rail: Westenhanger Station adjoins course. Trains from Charing Cross.

By Air: Helicopter landing facility by prior arrangement.

Leading Trainers (since 1991): R. Hannon 23-153 (15.0%), **R. Akehurst** 22-117 (18.8%), **J. Pearce** 19-61 (31.2%).

Leading Jockeys (since 1991): Pat Eddery 22-68 (32.0%), **T. Quinn** 20-149 (13.0%), **G. Duffield** 19-105 (18.0%).

FOLKESTONE (N-H)

Oval, 1m 3f (8) chases 220y run-in, hurdles 250y run-in. An undulating course with easy fences, not particularly suitable for the long-striding galloper.
Clerk of the Course: Mr G. R. Stickels, Lingfield Park 1991 Ltd., Lingfield, Surrey RH7 6PQ. Tel: (01342) 834800.
90 boxes allotted in rotation. Advance notice required for overnight accommodation.
By Car: 6 miles West of town at Westenhanger. Easy access from Junc 11 of the M20. Car park adjoins stands. (Free, except course enclosure £3).
By Rail: Westenhanger Station adjoins course. Trains from Charing Cross.
By Air: Helicopter landing facility by prior arrangement.

Leading Trainers (since 1991): J. T. Gifford 15-79 (19.0%), R. Rowe 11-55 (20.0%), **M. C. Pipe** 9-29 (31.0%).
Leading Jockeys (since 1991): A. Maguire 12-68 (17.0%), R. Dunwoody 7-43 (16.0%), **M. Richards** 6-24 (25.0%).

FONTWELL (N-H)

2m (7) 230y run-in with left-hand bend close home. The figure-of-eight chase course suits handy types and is something of a specialist's track. The hurdle course is oval, one mile round with nine hurdles per two and a quarter miles.
Clerk of the Course: C. E. Griggs, 11 Boltro Road, Haywards Heath, Sussex, RH16 1BP. Tel: (01444) 441111.
Secretaries: Messrs. Pratt & Co., 11 Boltro Road, Haywards Heath, Sussex RH16 1BP. Tel: (01444) 441111.
77 boxes. Limited accommodation for 16 lads and 3 girls only. If arriving the day before the meeting, contact: Mr R. Mant. Tel: (01243) 543335.
By Car: South of village at the junction of the A29 (Bognor) and A27 (Brighton-Chichester) roads.
By Rail: Barnham Station (2 miles). Brighton-Portsmouth line (access via London Victoria).
By Air: Helicopter landing facility by prior arrangement with the Clerk of the Course.

Leading Trainers (since 1991): J. T. Gifford 32-157 (20.4%), **M. C. Pipe** 27-85 (31.8%), **P. J. Hobbs** 23-64 (35.9%).
Leading Jockeys (since 1991): A. Maguire 25-148 (16.0%), Philip Hobbs 17-90 (18.0%), **D. Morris** 16-100 (16.0%).

Foaling dates are shown for two-year-olds where these are provided.

GOODWOOD (R.H.)

Set on the edge of the Downs, a straight six furlongs with a triangular loop on one side provides a variety of courses with the possibility of re-entering just above or below the five furlong gate. The Cup Course of about two and a half miles starts on a chute adjacent to the five furlong start and, running the reverse way of the course, turns left after about four furlongs and returns to the straight five furlong run-in by the top bend. The Stakes Course is the last 2m 3f, the Bentinck Course the last 1m 6f and the Gratwicke Course the last 1m 4f of the Cup Course. The Craven Course is 1m 2f, starting in almost the same spot as the Gratwicke Course but running in the reverse direction and returning to the five furlong run-in by the top bend. The Old Mile and seven furlong courses start on the Cup Course and join the five furlong course on the lower bend. The five and six furlong (Stewards' Cup) courses are perfectly straight, the first furlong of the latter being uphill and then slightly undulating to the finish. The sharp bends and downhill gradients suit the handy, well-balanced, neat-actioned sort over middle-distances and are against the big, long-striding horse.

Clerk of the Course and General Manager: Mr R. N. Fabricius, Goodwood Racecourse Limited, Chichester, Sussex. Tel: (01243) 774107, Racedays (01243) 774838.
Free stabling and accommodation for runners (115 well equipped boxes at Goodwood House). Subsidised canteen and recreational facilities.Tel: (01243 774157)
By Car: 6 miles North of Chichester between the A286 & A285. There is a car park adjacent to the course. Ample free car and coach parking.
By Rail: Chichester Station (from Victoria or London Bridge). Regular bus service to the course (6 miles).
By Air: Helicopter landing facility by prior arrangement with South Coast Helicopters. Tel: (01243) 779222. Goodwood Airport 2 miles (taxi to the course).

Leading Trainers (since 1991): R. Hannon 44-405 (10.9%), P. F. I. Cole 25-129 (19.4%), J. H. M. Gosden 23-126 (18.3%).
Leading Jockeys (since 1991): Pat Eddery 39-195 (20.0%), J. Reid 37-230 (16.0%), W. Carson 37-238 (15.0%).

HAMILTON (R.H.)

A straight six furlongs with a pear-shaped loop course of 1m 5f from a start in front of the stands and a run-in of five and a half furlongs. The turns are easy on the loop. The track is undulating with a dip (which can be very testing in wet weather) about three furlongs out and then rises to level out for the last 150y. A course where judgement and experience can make a considerable difference. Races are usually run at a true gallop here and form can be relied upon.

Clerk of the Course: Mr J. Fenwicke-Clennell, Toft Way, Sharperton, Morpeth, Northumberland NE65 7AE. Tel: (01669) 650369. Fax: (01669) 650339. Mobile: (0860) 737729.
Chief Executive and Secretary: Miss H. Dudgeon, The Racecourse, Bothwell Road, Hamilton ML5 0DW. Tel: (01698) 283806. Fax: (01698) 286621.
Free stabling (120 boxes) and accommodation on request. Tel: (01698) 284892.
By Car: Off the A74 on the B7071 (Hamilton-Bothwell road). (M74 Junc 5). Free parking for cars and buses.
By Rail: Hamilton West Station (1 mile).
By Air: Glasgow Airport (20 miles).

Leading Trainers (since 1991): J. Berry 55-289 (19.0%), Mrs M. Reveley 38-176 (21.6%), M. Johnston 32-187 (17.1%).
Leading Jockeys (since 1991): K. Darley 54-259 (20.0%), J. Carroll 46-236 (19.0%), J. Weaver 33-123 (26.0%).

HAYDOCK (L.H.)

An almost flat, oval track, 1m 5f round, with a run-in of four and a half furlongs and a straight six furlong course. The 1m 4f gate is set on a short chute. This course, which is of a galloping nature, suits the long-striding horse. On rain-affected turf, the going down the stands' rail in the straight is often faster and horses have often won races by being brought over to that side.

Clerk of the Course: Major P. W. F. Arkwright, Shirley Farm, Little Wolford, Shipston-on-Stour, Warwickshire. Tel: (01608) 684460.

Secretary: Mr F. Smith, Haydock Park Racecourse Company Limited, Newton-le-Willows, Merseyside WA12 0HQ. Tel: (01942) 725963.

Applications to be made to the Secretary for stabling and accommodation.

By Car: The course is on the A49 near Junc 23 of the M6.

By Rail: Newton-le-Willows Station (Manchester-Liverpool line) is 21/2 miles from the course. Earlstown 3 miles from the course. Warrington Bank Quay and Wigan are on the London to Carlisle/ Glasgow line.

By Air: Landing facilities in the centre of the course for helicopters and planes not exceeding 10,000lbs laden weight. Apply to the Sales Office

Leading Trainers (since 1991): J. L. Dunlop 27-112 (24.1%), J. H. M. Gosden 25-99 (25.3%), H. R. A. Cecil 22-62 (35.5%).

Leading Jockeys (since 1991): W. Ryan 30-148 (20.0%), J. Carroll 22-205 (10.0%), Pat Eddery 21-80 (26.0%).

HAYDOCK (N-H)

Oval, 1m 5f (10) 440y run-in. Flat, galloping chase course with stiff drop fences. The hurdle track, which is sharp, is inside the chase course and has some tight bends.

Clerk of the Course: Major P. W. F. Arkwright, Shirley Farm, Little Wolford, Shipston-on-Stour, Warwickshire. Tel: (01608) 684460.

Secretary: Mr F. Smith, Haydock Park Racecourse Company Limited, Newton-le-Willows, Merseyside WA12 0HQ. Tel: (01942) 725963.

Applications to be made to the Secretary for stabling and accommodation.

By Car: The course is on the A49 near Junc 23 of the M6.

By Rail: Newton-le-Willows Station (Manchester-Liverpool line) is 21/2 miles from the course. Earlstown 3 miles from the course. Warrington Bank Quay and Wigan are on the London to Carlisle/ Glasgow line.

By Air: Landing facilities in the centre of the course for helicopters and planes not exceeding 10,000lbs laden weight. Apply to the Sales Office.

Leading Trainers (since 1991): G. Richards 43-132 (32.6%), M. C. Pipe 36-145 (24.8%), J. G. FitzGerald 15-59 (25.4%).

Leading Trainers (since 1991): M. Dwyer 19-120 (15.0%), R. Dunwoody 17-63 (26.0%), G. McCourt 12-62 (19.0%).

HEREFORD (N-H)

Square, 1m 4f (9) 300y run-in. The turns, apart from the final one which is on falling ground, are easily negotiated, placing the emphasis on speed rather than stamina. A handy position round the home turn is vital, as winners rarely come from behind. The hurdle track is on the outside of the chase course. The fences have a reputation of being pretty stiff, but at the same time fair.

Clerk of the Course and Secretary: J. Williams, F.R.I.C.S., Shepherds Meadow, Eaton Bishop, Hereford. Tel: (01981) 250436 (Office). (01432) 273560.

100 boxes allocated on arrival. Apply to the Stabling Manager, The Racecourse House, Roman Road, Holmer, Hereford. Tel: (01432) 273560.

By Car: 1 mile North West of the City off the A49 (Leominster) road.

By Rail: Hereford Station (1 mile from the course).

By Air: Helicopter landing facility in the centre of the course by arrangement with the Clerk of the Course, and entirely at own risk.

Leading Trainers (since 1991): M. C. Pipe 39-130 (30.0%), N. A. Twiston-Davies 23-87 (26.4%), K. C. Bailey 17-91 (18.7%).
Leading Jockeys (since 1991): D. Bridgwater 21-109 (19.0%), R. Dunwoody 20-74 (27.0%), C. Llewellyn 13-49 (26.0%).

HEXHAM (N-H)

Oval, 1m 4f (10) 220y run-in. An undulating course that becomes very testing when the ground is soft, it has easy fences and a stiff uphill climb to the finishing straight, which is on a separate spur.

Clerk of the Course and Manager: S. C. Enderby, The Riding, Hexham. Tel: (01434) 606881 (Racecourse Office), (01434) 603738 (Course). Fax: (01434) 605814.

70 boxes allocated in rotation.

By Car: 11/2 miles South-West of the town off the B6305.

By Rail: Hexham Station (Newcastle-Carlisle line). Free bus to the course. A free bus is available from Hexham Station.

By Air: Helicopter landing facility in car park area (by special arrangement only).

Leading Trainers (since 1991): G. Richards 26-102 (25.5%), L. Lungo 22-73 (30.1%), P. Monteith 17-58 (29.3%).
Leading Jockeys (since 1991): T. Reed 26-110 (23.0%), P. Niven 19-77 (24.0%), A. Dobbin 17-81 (20.0%).

HUNTINGDON (N-H)

Oval, 1m 4f (9) 200y run-in. Perfectly flat, galloping track with a tricky open ditch in front of the stands. The two fences in the home straight can cause problems for novice chasers. Suits front runners.

Clerk of the Course: H. P. C. Bevan, The Old House, Little Everdon, Daventry, Northants NN11 3BG. Tel: (01327) 361266.

Manager: Adam Waterworth.

100 boxes available. Allotted on arrival.

By Car: The course is situated at Brampton, 2 miles West of Huntingdon on the A14. Easy access from the A1 (1/2 mile from the course).

By Rail: Huntingdon Station. Buses and taxis to course.
By Air: Helicopter landing facility by prior arrangement.

Leading Trainers (since 1991): F. Murphy 23-145 (15.9%), **D. Nicholson** 19-65 (29.2%),
J. T. Gifford 19-91 (20.9%).
Leading Jockeys (since 1991): A. Maguire 22-120 (18.0%), **R. Dunwoody** 16-110 (14.0%),
N. Williamson 13-51 (25.0%).

KELSO (N-H)

Oval, 1m 3f (9) 440y run-in uphill. Rather undulating with two downhill fences opposite the
stands, Kelso suits the nippy, front-running sort, though the uphill run to the finish helps the true
stayer. The hurdle course is smaller and very sharp with a tight turn away from the stands.
Clerk of the Course: Mr J. E. Fenwicke-Clennell, Toft Way, Sharperton, Morpeth,
Northumberland NE65 7AE. Tel: (01669) 650369. Fax: (01669) 650339.
Secretary: Mr Richard M. Landale, c/o Sale & Partners, 18-20 Glendale Road, Wooler,
Northumberland NE71 6DW. Tel: (01668) 281611. Fax: (01668) 281113
Racecourse: (01573) 224767. **Groundsman's Mobile:** (0374) 172527
81 boxes allotted in rotation. No reservations, accommodation for lads and lasses at the race-
course. Tel: (01573) 224822.
By Car: 1 mile North of the town, off the B6461.
By Rail: Berwick-upon-Tweed Station. 23 mile bus journey to Kelso.

Leading Trainers (since 1991): Mrs M. Reveley 45-147 (30.6%), **G. Richards** 36-147 (24.5%),
P. Monteith 22-139 (15.8%).
Leading Jockeys (since 1991): P. Niven 48-133 (36.0%), **B. Storey** 25-162 (15.0%),
A. Dobbin 23-108 (21.0%).

KEMPTON (R.H.)

A 1m 5f triangular course with a three and a half furlong straight run-in. The 1m 2f Jubilee
Course starts on an extension to the round course and sprint races are run over a separate
diagonal course. Kempton is a perfectly flat track which can not be described as either sharp or
galloping.
Clerk of the Course: Major R. M. O. Webster, Kempton Park, Sunbury-on-Thames. Tel:
(01932) 782292.
Allocated on arrival. Prior booking required for overnight stay.
By Car: On the A308 near Junc 1 of the M3. Main car park £2, Silver Ring and centre car park
free.
By Rail: Kempton Park Station (from Waterloo).
By Air: London (Heathrow) Airport 6 miles.

Leading Trainers (since 1991): R. Hannon 38-329 (11.6%), **J. L. Dunlop** 19-141 (13.5%),
R. Charlton 16-72 (22.2%).
Leading Trainers (since 1991): Pat Eddery 44-224 (19.0%), **T. Quinn** 28-228 (12.0%),
W. Carson 27-210 (12.0%).

KEMPTON (N-H)

Triangular, 1m 5f (10) 175y run-in. Practically flat; sharp course where the long run between the last obstacle on the far side and the first in the home straight switches the emphasis from jumping to speed.

Clerk of the Course: Major R. M. O. Webster, Kempton Park, Sunbury-on-Thames. Tel: (01932) 782292.

Allocated on arrival. Prior booking required for overnight stay.

By Car: On the A308 near Junc 1 of the M3. Main car park £2, Silver Ring and centre car park free.

By Rail: Kempton Park Station (from Waterloo).

By Air: London (Heathrow) Airport 6 miles.

Leading Trainers (since 1991): N. J. Henderson 21-76 (27.6%), **M. C. Pipe** 16-66 (24.2%), J. T. Gifford 16-118 (13.6%).

Leading Jockeys (since 1991): J. Osborne 25-137 (18.0%), R. Dunwoody 25-120 (20.0%), M. A. Fitzgerald 12-60 (20.0%).

LEICESTER (R.H.)

An oval track of approximately 1m 5f with a straight run-in of five furlongs. Races of a mile and less are run on a dead straight course which joins the round course five furlongs from the finish, the first half being downhill, followed by an ascent gradually levelling off to the winning post. The bends into the straight and after the winning post have been cambered to make a more galloping track.

Clerk of the Course: Captain N. E. S. Lees, The Racecourse, Leicester LE2 3AL. Tel: (01533) 716515 or (01638) 663482.

Secretary: D. C. Henson, Leicester Racecourse Co. Ltd., The Racecourse, Leicester: Tel: (01533) 716515 or (01604) 30757.

Allocated on arrival. Accommodation for one attendant per horse only. Canteen opens at 7.30a.m.

By Car: The course is 21/2 miles South-East of the City on the A6 (M1, Junc 21). The car park is free.

By Rail: Leicester Station (from St Pancras) is 21/2 miles.

By Air: Helicopter landing facility in the centre of the course.

Leading Trainers (since 1991): R. Hannon 30-194 (15.5%), **H. R. A. Cecil** 24-96 (25.0%), J. L. Dunlop 22-117 (18.8%).

Leading Jockeys (since 1991): L. Dettori 34-180 (18.0%), Pat Eddery 32-145 (22.0%), W. Carson 27-144 (18.0%).

LEICESTER (N-H)

Rectangular, 1m 6f (10) 250y run-in uphill. An undulating course with an elbow 150y from the finish, Leicester can demand a high degree of stamina, for the going can become extremely heavy and the last three furlongs are uphill.

Clerk of the Course: Captain N. E. S. Lees, The Racecourse, Leicester LE2 3AL. Tel: (01533) 716515 or (01638) 663482.

Secretary: D. C. Henson, Leicester Racecourse Co. Ltd., The Racecourse, Leicester. Tel: (01533) 716515 or (01604) 30757.

Allocated on arrival. Accommodation for one attendant per horse only. Canteen opens at 7.30a.m.

By Car: The course is 21/2 miles South-East of the City on the A6 (M1, Junc 21). The car park is free.
By Rail: Leicester Station (from St Pancras) is 21/2 miles.
By Air: Helicopter landing facility in the centre of the course.

Leading Trainers (since 1991): M. C. Pipe 26-91 (28.6%), **Mrs J. Pitman** 15-63 (23.8%), **D. Nicholson** 13-56 (23.2%).
Leading Jockeys (since 1991): R. Dunwoody 11-51 (21.0%), **A. Maguire** 9-47 (19.0%), **W. Marston** 8-51 (15.0%).

LINGFIELD (L.H.)

A 7f 140y straight course with a downhill gradient for about five furlongs, a slight rise and then a gradual fall to the winning post. The round turf course joins the straight at the four furlong post and then follows round the outside of the All-Weather tracks to the summit of a slight hill before turning downhill into the straight. The Derby Trial Course (1m 3f 106y) is very similar to the Epsom Derby Course and provides a good test for the Classic. The re-alignment of the turf course to accomodate the All-Weather tracks has made the turn out of the back straight much less pronounced. However, most of the characteristics remain. The Equitrack course favours the keen, free-running, sharp-actioned horse, particularly so in sprints, which are run on the turn.
Clerk of the Course: Mr G. R. Stickels, Lingfield Park Racecourse, Surrey RH7 6PQ.
200 boxes. For details of accommodation apply to the Manager.
By Car: South-East of the town off the A22 (M25 Junc 6). Ample free parking. Reserved car park £3.
By Rail: Lingfield Station (regular services from London Bridge and Victoria). 1/2m walk to the course.
By Air: London (Gatwick) Airport 10 miles. Helicopter landing facility south of wind-sock.

Leading Trainers (since 1991 Turf) R. Hannon 32-246 (13.0%), **R. Akehurst** 23-173 (13.3%), **G. L. Moore** 19-148 (12.8%).
Leading Trainers (since 1991 A.W) R. J. O'Sullivan 38-246 (15.5%), **Lord Huntingdon** 32-143 (22.4%), **W. A. O'Gorman** 32-170 (18.8%).

Leading Jockeys (since 1991 Turf) L. Dettori 33-159 (20.0%), **R. Cochrane** 30-153 (19.0%), **T. Quinn** 27-204 (13.0%).
Leading Jockeys (since 1991 A.W) T. Quinn 44-242 (18.0%), **J. Williams** 44-321 (13.0%), **D. Biggs** 42-396 (10.0%).

LINGFIELD (N-H)

Conical, 1m 5f (10) 200y run-in. Severely undulating with a tight downhill turn into the straight, the chase course suits front runners and those of doubtful resolution.
Clerk of the Course: Mr G. R. Stickels, Lingfield Park Racecourse, Surrey RH7 6PQ.
200 boxes. For details of accommodation apply to the Manager.
By Car: South-East of the town off the A22 (M25 Junc 6). Ample free parking. Reserved car park £3.
By Rail: Lingfield Station (regular services from London Bridge and Victoria). 1/2m walk to the course.
By Air: London (Gatwick) Airport 10 miles. Helicopter landing facility south of wind-sock.

Leading Trainers (since 1991): R. Akehurst 13-49 (26.5%), **Andrew Turnell** 11-31 (35.5%), **M. C. Pipe** 11-43 (25.6%).
Leading Jockeys (since 1991): A. Maguire 23-104 (22.0%), **A. Dicken** 20-58 (34.0%), D. O'Sullivan 13-97 (13.0%).

LUDLOW (N-H)

Oval, 1m 4f (9) 450y run-in. The chase course is flat and has quite sharp bends into and out of the home straight, although long-striding horses never seem to have any difficulties. The hurdle course is on the outside of the chase track and is not so sharp.
Secretary & Clerk of the Course: B. R. Davies. Tel: (01981) 580260 (Home), (01981) 250052 (Office), (01831) 602207 (Car), (01584) 77221 (racedays). **Registered Office:** Shepherds Meadow, Eaton Bishop, Hereford HR2 9UA. Fax: (01891) 250192.
Free and allocated on arrival. Shavings (straw) if required.
By Car: The course is situated at Bromfield, 2 miles North of Ludlow on the A49.
By Rail: Ludlow Station (Hereford-Shrewsbury line) 2 miles.
By Air: Helicopter landing facility in the centre of the course by arrangement with the Clerk of the Course and entirely at own risk.

Leading Trainers (since 1991): D. Nicholson 26-102 (25.5%), **M. C. Pipe** 20-89 (22.5%), **K. C. Bailey** 15-64 (23.4%).
Leading Trainers (since 1991): A. Maguire 13-80 (16.0%), **N. Williamson** 13-88 (14.0%), R. Dunwoody 12-38 (31.0%).

MARKET RASEN (N-H)

Oval, 1m 2f (8) 250y run-in. A sharp, undulating course with easy fences and a long run to the straight, Market Rasen favours the handy, front-running type.
General Manager and Clerk of the Course: Major C. L. Moore, The Racecourse, Market Rasen LN8 3EA. Tel: (01673) 843434.
99 boxes at the course, allocated on arrival. Accommodation for lads and lasses is by reservation only.
By Car: 1 mile East of the town on the A631. Free car parks and racecards.
By Rail: Market Rasen Station 1 mile (Lincoln-Grimsby line).
By Air: Helicopter landing facility by prior arrangement only.

Leading Trainers (since 1991): J. G. FitzGerald 24-115 (20.9%), **M. H. Easterby** 22-79 (27.9%), **Mrs M. Reveley** 22-87 (25.3%).
Leading Jockeys (since 1991): P. Niven 21-103 (20.0%), **L. Wyer** 20-105 (19.0%), A. S. Smith 18-113 (15.0%).

MUSSELBURGH (R.H.)
(formerly Edinburgh)

An oval of 1m 2f, with sharp bends and a straight, slightly undulating run-in of four furlongs. An extension provides a five furlong course, which bears slightly left and makes a distinct right-hand inclination after a furlong. Musselburgh is virtually flat but, with the turns being very sharp, handiness and manoeuverability are at a premium.

Clerk of the Course: Mr M. Kershaw, Racecourse Office, 2 Whitletts Road, Ayr. Tel: (01292) 264179 (Office). (0131) 665 2859 (Race days), (01563) 830096 (Home), (0850) 464258 (Mobile).
Free. Accommodation for one night in B & B provided.
By Car: The course is situated at Musselburgh, 5 miles East of Edinburgh on the A1. Car park, adjoining course, free for buses and cars.
By Rail: Waverley Station (Edinburgh). Local Rail service to Musselburgh.
By Air: Edinburgh (Turnhouse) Airport 30 minutes by car.

Leading Trainers (since 1991): J. Berry 40-200 (20.0%), **M. Johnston** 18-110 (16.4%), **Mrs M. Reveley** 11-80 (13.8%).
Leading Trainers (since 1991): K. Darley 35-164 (21.0%), **J. Carroll** 32-159 (20.0%), **J. Weaver** 29-111 (26.0%).

MUSSELBURGH (N-H)

Rectangular, 1m 3f (8) 150y run-in (variable). A virtually flat track with sharp turns, suiting the handy, front-running sort. Musselburgh drains well.
Clerk of the Course: Mr M. Kershaw, Racecourse Office, 2 Whitletts Road, Ayr. Tel: (01292) 264179 (Office). (0131) 665 2859 (Race days), (01563) 830096 (Home), (0850) 464258 (Mobile).
Free. Accommodation for one night in B & B provided.
By Car: The course is situated at Musselburgh, 5 miles East of Edinburgh on the A1. Car park, adjoining course, free for buses and cars.
By Rail: Waverley Station (Edinburgh). Local Rail service to Musselburgh.
By Air: Edinburgh (Turnhouse) Airport 30 minutes by car.

Leading Trainers (since 1991): M. D. Hammond 25-120 (20.8%), **Mrs M. Reveley** 16-72 (22.2%), **Howard Johnson** 15-95 (15.8%).
Leading Jockeys (since 1991): B. Storey 19-131 (14.0%), **T. Reed** 13-97 (13.0%), **P. Niven** 11-64 (17.0%).

NEWBURY (L.H.)

An oval track of about 1m 7f, 80 feet wide with a slightly undulating straight mile. The round mile and 7f 60y starts are set on a chute from the round course and both join the straight about five furlongs from the finish. Newbury is a good, galloping track, which is efficiently watered during dry periods.
Clerk of the Course: R. N. J. Pridham, 109 Greenham Road, Newbury, Berkshire RG14 7JE. Tel: (01635) 49511.
Chief Executive, Secretary and Club Secretary: Major General J. D. G. Pank, C.B.
Free stabling and accommodation for lads and lasses.
By Car: East of the town off the A34 (M4, Junc 12 or 13). Car park, adjoining enclosures, free.
By Rail: Newbury Racecourse Station, adjoins course.
By Air: Light Aircraft landing strip East/West. 830 metres by 30 metres wide. Helicopter landing facilities.

Leading Trainers (since 1991): R. Hannon 42-496 (8.5%), **P. W. Chapple-Hyam** 35-133 (26.3%), **J. H. M. Gosden** 33-145 (22.8%).
Leading Jockeys (since 1991): J. Reid 44-262 (16.0%), **Pat Eddery** 44-263 (16.0%), **L. Dettori** 41-217 (18.0%).

NEWBURY (N-H)

Oval, 1m 6f (11) 255y run-in. Slightly undulating, wide and galloping in nature. The fences are stiff and sound jumping is essential. One of the fairest tracks in the country.

Clerk of the Course: R. N. J. Pridham, 109 Greenham Road, Newbury, Berkshire RG14 7JE. Tel: (01635) 49511.

Chief Executive, Secretary and Club Secretary: Major General J. D. G. Pank, C.B.

Free stabling and accommodation for lads and lasses.

By Car: East of the town off the A34 (M4, Junc 12 or 13). Car park, adjoining enclosures, free.

By Rail: Newbury Racecourse Station, adjoins course.

By Air: Light Aircraft landing strip East/West. 830 metres by 30 metres wide. Helicopter landing facilities.

Leading Trainers (since 1991): N. J. Henderson 29-127 (22.8%), **D. Nicholson** 25-118 (21.2%), M. C. Pipe 21-95 (22.1%).

Leading Jockeys (since 1991): R. Dunwoody 41-165 (24.0%), **J. Osborne** 40-167 (23.0%), A. Maguire 19-119 (15.0%).

NEWCASTLE (L.H.)

An oval course of 1m 6f with a chute to provide a 1m 2f start and a straight run-in of four furlongs, gradually rising until levelling off in the final 100y. The run-in extends to allow a straight mile, which is against the collar all the way. Newcastle is a galloping track with the final climb making it a test of stamina and is not one for short runners.

Clerk of the Course: Mr James Hutchinson c/o High Gosforth Park plc, High Gosforth Park, Newcastle-upon-Tyne. NE3 5HP. Tel: (0191) 236 2020, (0191) 236 5508.

Free. It is essential to book accommodation in advance. Apply to the Manager. Tel: (0191) 217 0060 the day before racing, or the Racecourse Office otherwise.

By Car: 4 miles North of the city on the A6125 (near the A1). Car and coach park free.

By Rail: Newcastle Central Station (from King's Cross). Regular bus service to course from Four Lane Ends Metro Station.

By Air: Helicopter landing facility near the water jump. The Airport is 4 miles from the course.

Leading Trainers (since 1991): Mrs M. Reveley 25-174 (14.4%), **J. Berry** 24-170 (14.1%), M. R. Stoute 17-54 (31.5%).

Leading Trainers (since 1991): K. Darley 29-210 (13.0%), **J. Carroll** 21-150 (14.0%), M. Birch 17-159 (10.0%).

NEWCASTLE (N-H)

Oval, 1m 6f (11) 220y run-in. A gradually rising home straight of four furlongs makes this galloping track a true test of stamina, especially as the ground can become very heavy. The fences are rather stiff.

Clerk of the Course: Mr James Hutchinson c/o High Gosforth Park plc, High Gosforth Park, Newcastle-upon-Tyne. NE3 5HP. Tel: (0191) 236 2020, (0191) 236 5508.

Free. It is essential to book accommodation in advance. Apply to the Manager. Tel: (0191) 217 0060 the day before racing, or the Racecourse Office otherwise.

By Car: 4 miles North of the city on the A6125 (near the A1). Car and coach park free.

By Rail: Newcastle Central Station (from King's Cross). Regular bus service to course from Four Lane Ends Metro Station.

By Air: Helicopter landing facility near the water jump. The Airport is 4 miles from the course.

Leading Trainers (since 1991): Mrs M. Reveley 37-137 (27.0%), **Howard Johnson** 17-131 (13.0%), **M. D. Hammond** 15-125 (12.0%).
Leading Jockeys (since 1991): P. Niven 36-138 (26.0%), **T. Reed** 16-102 (15.0%), **L. Wyer** 15-92 (16.0%).

NEWMARKET

(Rowley Mile Course) - There is a straight course of ten furlongs with slight undulations as far as `The Bushes', about two furlongs from the finish. From that point it is downhill for a furlong to `The Dip', the final furlong being uphill. The Cesarewitch course starts on the Beacon Course, which turns right into the straight. The ten furlong straight is a wide, galloping track ideal for long-striding horses.

(July Course) - All races up to a mile inclusive are run on the straight Bunbury Mile, which has a steadily increasing downhill gradient after two furlongs, the final furlong being uphill. Races further than a mile start on the Cesarewitch course and turn right into the straight mile. Like the Rowley Mile course, this is a wide, galloping track.

Clerk of the Course: Captain N. E. S. Lees, Westfield House, The Links, Newmarket. Tel: (01638) 663482.
Free accommodation available at the Links Stables.
By Car: South-West of the town on the A1304 London Road (M11 Junc 9). Free car parking at the rear of the enclosure. Members car park £1 all days; Free courtesy bus service from Newmarket Station, Bus Station and High Street, commencing 90 minutes prior to the first race, and return trips up to 60 minutes after the last race.
By Rail: Infrequent rail service to Newmarket Station from Cambridge (Liverpool Street) or direct bus service from Cambridge (13 mile journey).
By Air: Landing facilities for light aircraft and helicopters on racedays at both racecourses. See Flight Guide. Cambridge Airport 11 miles.

Leading Trainers (since 1991 Rowley) J. H. M. Gosden 38-244 (15.6%), **H. R. A. Cecil** 37-200 (18.5%), **B. W. Hills** 30-243 (12.4%).
Leading Trainers (since 1991 July) R. Hannon 30-240 (12.5%), **H. R. A. Cecil** 22-104 (21.2%), **J. H. M. Gosden** 21-132 (15.9%).

Leading Jockeys (since 1991 Rowley): Pat Eddery 68-339 (20.0%), **W. Carson** 41-347 (11.0%), **L. Dettori** 40-337 (11.0%).
Leading Jockeys (since 1991 July): Pat Eddery 42-201 (20.0%), **L. Dettori** 40-221 (18.0%), **M. Roberts** 26-182 (14.0%).

NEWTON ABBOT (N-H)

Oval, 1m 2f (7) 300y run-in. Flat with two tight bends and a water jump situated three fences from home. The nippy, agile sort is favoured. The run-in can be very short on the hurdle course.
Clerk of the Course: Mr M. J. Trickey, The Racecourse, Kingsteignton Road, Newton Abbot. Tel: (01626) 53235 or (01374) 620717 (Mobile).
General Manager: Pat Masterson. Tel: (01626) 53235.
100 boxes, allocated on arrival.
By Car: North of the town on the A380. Torquay 6 miles, Exeter 17 miles.
By Rail: Newton Abbot Station (from Paddington) 3/4 mile.
By Air: Helicopter landing pad in the centre of the course.

Leading Trainers (since 1991): M. C. Pipe 105-385 (27.3%), **P. J. Hobbs** 43-154 (27.9%),
P. F. Nicholls 28-101 (27.7%).
Leading Jockeys (since 1991) R. Dunwoody 52-172 (30.0%), **M. A. Fitzgerald** 22-160 (13.0%),
D. Bridgwater 20-76 (26.0%).

NOTTINGHAM (L.H.)

A galloping oval track with a straight run-in of about five furlongs, from which a chute provides a
straight six furlongs. The turns on this flat course are easy.
Clerk of the Course and Manager: Major C. Moore, Hamilton House, Toft-next-Newton,
Market Rasen, Lincolnshire LN8 3NE. Tel: (01673) 878575.
Secretary: R. Goodman, Prestbury Park, Cheltenham, Gloucestershire GL50 4SH. Tel: (01242)
513014.
Free. 120 boxes allotted on arrival. New hostel for lads and lasses.
By Car: 2 miles East of the City on the B686. The car park is free. Silver Ring Picnic Car Park
£12 (admits car and four occupants).
By Rail: Nottingham (Midland) Station. Regular bus service to course (2 miles).
By Air: Helicopter landing facility in the centre of the course.

Leading Trainers (since 1991): H. R. A. Cecil 29-77 (37.7%), **J. L. Dunlop** 21-117 (18.0%),
P. F. I. Cole 16-82 (19.5%).
Leading Jockeys (since 1991): L. Dettori 30-153 (19.0%), **W. Carson** 28-167 (16.0%),
W. Ryan 24-177 (13.0%).

NOTTINGHAM (N-H)

Oval, 1m 4f (9) 240y run-in. Perfectly flat with easy turns and a home straight of about five fur-
longs. A good, galloping track. The run-in on the hurdle course is rather long, placing the
emphasis on flat speed.
Clerk of the Course and Manager: Major C. Moore, Hamilton House, Toft-next-Newton,
Market Rasen, Lincolnshire LN8 3NE. Tel: (01673) 878575.
Secretary: R. Goodman, Prestbury Park, Cheltenham, Gloucestershire GL50 4SH. Tel: (01242)
513014.
Free. 120 boxes allotted on arrival. New hostel for lads and lasses.
By Car: 2 miles East of the City on the B686. The car park is free. Silver Ring Picnic Car Park
£12 (admits car and four occupants).
By Rail: Nottingham (Midland) Station. Regular bus service to course (2 miles).
By Air: Helicopter landing facility in the centre of the course.

Leading Trainers (since 1991): D. Nicholson 17-74 (23.0%), **K. C. Bailey** 11-44 (25.0%),
J. G. FitzGerald 10-61 (16.4%).
Leading Jockeys (since 1991): J. Osborne 15-62 (24.0%), **G. McCourt** 13-59 (22.0%),
M. Dwyer 11-69 (15.0%).

PERTH (N-H)

Rectangular, 1m 2f (8) 283y run-in. A flat, easy track with sweeping turns. Not a course for the long-striding galloper. An efficient watering system ensures that the ground rarely gets hard.
Clerk of the Course: Mr S. R. Morshead, Racecourse Office, 2 Whitletts Road, Ayr. Tel: (01292) 264179 (Office), (01655) 5277 (Home).
Secretary: Miss I. J. C. Grant, Penrose Hill, Moffat, Dumfriesshire. Tel: (01683) 20131. Racedays (01738) 51597.
100 boxes and accommodation for lads and lasses. Apply to the Secretary. Stables Tel: (01738) 21604 (racedays only).
By Car: 4 miles North of the town off the A93.
By Rail: Perth Station (from Dundee) 4 miles. There are buses to the course.
By Air: Scone Airport (33/4 miles). Edinburgh Airport 45 minutes.

Leading Trainers (since 1991): G. Richards 25-141 (17.7%), **Mrs M. Reveley** 23-52 (44.2%), M. D. Hammond 21-89 (23.6%).
Leading Jockeys (since 1991): P. Niven 30-86 (34.0%), **M. Dwyer** 14-72 (19.0%), B. Storey 12-126 (9.0%).

PLUMPTON (N-H)

Oval, 1m 1f (7) 200y run-in uphill. A tight, undulating circuit with an uphill finish, Plumpton favours the handy, fast jumper. The ground often gets heavy, as the course is based on clay soil.
Clerk of the Course: Mr C. E. Griggs, 11 Boltro Road, Haywards Heath, Sussex, RH16 1BP. Tel: (01444) 441111.
75 boxes allocated in rotation. Advance notice is required for overnight arrival. Tel: (01273) 890383.
By Car: 2 miles North of the village off the B2116.
By Rail: Plumpton Station (from Victoria) adjoins course.
By Air: Helicopter landing facility by prior arrangement with the Clerk of the Course.

Leading Trainers (since 1991): J. White 45-167 (27.0%), **J. R. Jenkins** 14-89 (15.7%), C. R. Egerton 13-26 (50.0%).
Leading Jockeys (since 1991): A. Maguire 46-163 (28.0%), **R. Dunwoody** 20-103 (19.0%), J. Osborne 12-53 (22.0%).

PONTEFRACT (L.H.)

An oval, undulating course of 2m 133y with two sharp bends and a straight run-in of only two furlongs. There is a steep ascent over the last three furlongs. The undulations make it unsuitable for a long-striding horse, although a degree of stamina is called for. There have been a number of course specialists at Pontefract.
Clerk of the Course and Secretary: Mr J. Norman Gundill, 33 Ropergate, Pontefract, West Yorkshire. Tel: (01977) 703224 (Office), (01977) 620649 (Home), (01977) 702210 (racedays only).
Stabling and accommodation must be reserved. They will be allocated on a first come-first served basis. Tel: (01977) 702323)
By Car: 1 mile North of the town on the A639. Junc 32 of M62. Free car park adjacent to the course.

By Rail: Pontefract Station (Baghill), 11/2 miles from the course. Regular bus service from Leeds.
By Air: Helicopters by arrangement only. (Nearest airfield: Doncaster, Sherburn-in-Elmet, Yeadon (Leeds/Bradford).

Leading Trainers (since 1991): Mrs J. R. Ramsden 32-177 (18.1%), Mrs M. Reveley 25-133 (18.8%), R. Hollinshead 22-214 (10.3%).
Leading Jockeys (since 1991): K. Fallon 30-170 (17.0%), L. Dettori 25-126 (19.0%), K. Darley 20-206 (9.0%).

REDCAR (L.H.)

A perfectly flat, narrow, oval course of two miles with a straight run-in of five furlongs, which extends backwards to make a straight mile. Despite two very tight bends into and out of the back straight, Redcar is an excellent galloping course.
Clerk of the Course: Mr J. G. Cleverly F.R.I.C.S., Glebe House, Settrington, Malton, North Yorkshire. Tel: (01944) 768203. Office: (01482) 867488.
Racecourse Office; The Racecourse, Redcar, Cleveland TS10 2BY. Tel: (01642) 484068.
Groundsman; Mr J. Berry, The Racecourse, Redcar, Cleveland. Tel: (01642) 489861 (Stables on racedays only (01642) 484254).
By Car: In town off the A1085. Free parking adjoining the course for buses and cars.
By Rail: Redcar Station (1/4 mile from the course).
By Air: (None). Landing facilities at Turners Arms Farm (600y runway) Yearby, Cleveland. 2 miles South of the racecourse - transport available. Teeside airport (18 miles west of Redcar).

Leading Trainers (since 1991): Mrs M. Reveley 59-413 (14.3%), M. H. Easterby 22-221 (10.0%), J. Berry 19-169 (11.2%).
Leading Jockeys (since 1991): K. Darley 64-308 (20.0%), G. Duffield 20-117 (17.0%), Paul Eddery 18-76 (23.0%).

RIPON (R.H.)

An oval course of 1m 5f, joined to a straight six furlongs by a tightish bend at the five furlong point. The straight course is slightly on the ascent except for a shallow dip at the `distance' and, in general, this is a rather sharp track, a course where experience can be decisive.
Clerk of the Course: Mr J. M. Hutchinson, 77 North Street, Ripon HG4 1DS. Tel: (01765) 602156, evenings (01845) 567378, Mobile (0860) 679904.
Trainers requiring stabling (104 boxes available) are requested to contact Mr P. Bateson, The Racecourse, Ripon. Tel: (01765) 603696.
By Car: The course is situated 2 miles South-East of the city, near the A1. There is ample free parking for buses and cars. For reservations apply to the Secretary.
By Rail: Harrogate Station (11 miles). Bus service to Ripon.
By Air: Helicopters only on the course. Otherwise Leeds or Bradford airport.

Leading Trainers (since 1991): H. R. A. Cecil 24-49 (49.0%), J. Berry 23-154 (14.9%), M. Johnston 16-100 (16.0%).
Leading Jockeys (since 1991): K. Darley 33-170 (19.0%), W. Ryan 19-81 (23.0%), J. Weaver 16-72 (22.0%).

SALISBURY (R.H.)

The course consists of a loop with an arm of about four furlongs for the finish of all races. Contests of up to a mile are almost straight except for a slight right-hand bend at halfway. On the 1m 6f course, horses start opposite the stands, turn to the left around the loop and re-enter the straight at the seven furlong starting gate. The last half-mile is uphill, providing a stiff test of stamina.

Clerk of the Course: Mr R. I. Renton, Salisbury Racecourse, Netherhampton, Salisbury, Wiltshire SP2 8PN.

Secretary: The Bibury Club, Salisbury Racecourse, Netherhampton, Salisbury, Wiltshire. Tel: (01722) 326461.

Free stabling (112 boxes) and accommodation for lads and lasses, apply to the **Stabling Manager** (01722) 327327.

By Car: 3 miles South-West of the city on the A3094 at Netherhampton. Free car park adjoins the course.

By Rail: Salisbury Station is 31/2 miles (from Waterloo). Bus service to the course.

By Air: Helicopter landing facility near the ten furlong start.

Leading Trainers (since 1991): R. Hannon 52-368 (14.1%), P. F. I. Cole 17-106 (16.0%), J. L. Dunlop 15-130 (11.5%).

Leading Jockeys (since 1991): L. Dettori 26-119 (21.0%), J. Reid 24-168 (14.0%), Pat Eddery 24-123 (19.0%).

SANDOWN (R.H.)

An oval course of 1m 5f with a straight run-in of four furlongs. The ground is almost level until entering the straight, where it rises to the winning post. Five furlong contests are run on a separate straight course which cuts diagonally across the inside of the main circuit and is uphill all the way. The track suits long-striding horses and is a real test of stamina.

Clerk of the Course and Racecourse Manager: Mr A. J. Cooper, Sandown Park, Esher, Surrey. Tel: (01372) 463072.

Club Secretary: Miss Karen Winterbourne, Address and Tel as above.

Free stabling and accommodation for lads and lasses.

By Car: 4 miles South-West of Kingston-on-Thames, on the A307 (M25 Junc 10). The members' car park in More Lane £2. All other car parking is free.

By Rail: Esher Station (from Waterloo) adjoins the course.

By Air: London (Heathrow) Airport 12 miles.

Leading Trainers (since 1991): R. Hannon 41-347 (11.8%), M. R. Stoute 24-168 (14.3%), J. H. M. Gosden 21-111 (18.9%).

Leading Jockeys (since 1991): Pat Eddery 55-282 (19.0%), M. Roberts 42-261 (16.0%), L. Dettori 36-219 (16.0%).

SANDOWN (N-H)

Oval, 1m 5f (11) 220y run-in uphill. Features seven fences on the back straight, the last three (Railway Fences) are very close together and can often decide the outcome of races. The stiff uphill climb to the finish puts the emphasis very much on stamina, but accurate-jumping, free-running sorts are also favoured. Hurdle races are run on the Flat course.

Clerk of the Course and Racecourse Manager: Mr A. J. Cooper, Sandown Park, Esher, Surrey. Tel: (01372) 463072.
Club Secretary: Miss Karen Winterbourne, Address and Tel as above.
Free stabling and accommodation for lads and lasses.
By Car: 4 miles South-West of Kingston-on-Thames, on the A307 (M25 Junc 10). The members' car park in More Lane £2. All other car parking is free.
By Rail: Esher Station (from Waterloo) adjoins the course.
By Air: London (Heathrow) Airport 12 miles.

Leading Trainers (since 1991): J. T. Gifford 31-166 (18.7%), D. Nicholson 29-90 (32.2%), M. C. Pipe 15-82 (18.3%).
Leading Jockeys (since 1991): R. Dunwoody 33-122 (27.0%), A. Maguire 20-96 (20.0%), J. Osborne 15-108 (13.0%).

SEDGEFIELD (N-H)

Oval, 1m 2f (8) 200y run-in: Hurdles 200y run-in. Undulating with fairly tight turns. and does not suit the big, long-striding horse.
Clerk of the Course: J. G. Cleverly, F.R.I.C.S., Grandstand, York Road, Beverley, North Humberside HU17 8QZ. Tel: (01944) 768203 (Home), (01482) 867488 (Office).
Secretary: A. Brown, The Bungalow, Sedgefield Racecourse, Sedgefield, Stockton-on-Tees, Cleveland TS21 2HW. Tel: (01740) 621925.
Course Foreman: Sedgefield (01740) 20366 or 22629.
100 boxes filled in rotation. No forage.
By Car: 3/4 mile South-West of the town, near the junction of the A689 (Bishop Auckland) and the A177 (Durham) roads. The car park is free.
By Rail: Stockton-on-Tees Station (9 miles). Durham Station (12 miles).
By Air: Helicopter landing facility in car park area by prior arrangement only.

Leading Trainers (since 1991): Mrs M. Reveley 74-257 (28.8%), G. M. Moore 26-156 (16.7%), Howard Johnson 24-174 (13.8%).
Leading Jockeys (since 1991): P. Niven 62-187 (33.0%), M. Dwyer 27-130 (20.0%) L. Wyer 23-113 (20.0%).

SOUTHWELL (L.H.)

The All-Weather Fibresand track consists of an oval circuit, 1m 2f in circumference, with a three furlong straight and a spur to provide a five furlong turf straight that crosses the All-Weather track. The turf tracks are on the inside of the All-Weather track. A sharp, flat circuit, Southwell suits the keen, front-running sort.
Clerk of the Course: Mr A. J. Bealby, The Rookery, Bragborough Hall, Braunston, Daventry, Northamptonshire NN11 7HA. Tel: (01788) 891795. Fax: (01636) 812271.
110 boxes at the course.
By Car: The course is situated at Rolleston, 3 miles South of Southwell, 5 miles from Newark.
By Rail: Rolleston Station (Nottingham-Newark line) adjoins the course.

Leading Trainers (since 1991): D. W. Chapman 61-559 (10.9%), T. D. Barron 48-297 (16.2%), W. A. O'Gorman 45-249 (18.1%).
Leading Jockeys (since 1991): L. Dettori 42-191 (21.0%), J. Quinn 40-556 (7.0%), Dean McKeown 38-336 (11.0%).

SOUTHWELL (N-H)

Oval, 1m 1f (7) 220y run-in. A tight, flat track with a short run-in, admirably suited to front-run-ners.
Clerk of the Course: Mr A. J. Bealby, The Rookery, Bragborough Hall, Braunston, Daventry, Northamptonshire NN11 7HA. Tel: (01788) 891795. Fax: (01636) 812271.
110 boxes at the course.
By Car: The course is situated at Rolleston, 3 miles South of Southwell, 5 miles from Newark.
By Rail: Rolleston Station (Nottingham-Newark line) adjoins the course.

Leading Trainers (since 1991): K. C. Bailey 14-56 (25.0%), **Mrs M. Reveley** 13-33 (39.4%), **Mrs S. J. Smith** 9-69 (13.0%).
Leading Jockeys (since 1991): S. Wynne 24-127 (18.0%), **A. Maguire** 19-70 (27.0%), **R. Dunwoody** 19-57 (33.0%).

STRATFORD-ON-AVON (N-H)

Triangular, 1m 2f (8) 200y run-in. Virtually flat with two tight bends, and quite a short home straight. A sharp and turning course, Stratford-on-Avon suits the well-balanced, handy sort.
Clerk of the Course: James H. Sanderson Esq, Catterick Racecourse, Catterick Bridge, Richmond, N. Yorks, DL10 7PE. Tel: (01748) 811478. (01789) 267949 (Racedays), Fax: (01748) 811082.
Club Secretary: R. M. Dunstan, Rickstaddles, Snitterfield, Stratford-on-Avon, Warwickshire. Tel: (01789) 731322.
Company Secretary and Racecourse Manager: Mrs A. L. N. Gale, The Racecourse, Luddington Road, Stratford-on-Avon, Warwickshire. Tel: (01789) 267949.
92 boxes available. Allotted on arrival. Advance notice must be given for overnighters. Tel: (01789) 267949.
By Car: 1 mile from the town centre, off the A429 (Evesham road).
By Rail: Stratford-on-Avon Station (from Birmingham New Street or Leamington Spa) 1 mile.
By Air: Helicopter landing facility by prior arrangement.

Leading Trainers (since 1991): M. C. Pipe 29-125 (23.2%), **N. A. Twiston-Davies** 15-78 (19.2%), **K. C. Bailey** 15-77 (19.5%).
Leading Trainers (since 1991): A. Maguire 25-95 (26.0%), **R. Dunwoody** 19-102 (18.0%), **N. Williamson** 17-112 (15.0%).

TAUNTON (N-H)

Elongated oval, 1m 2f (8) 150y run-in uphill. Sharp turns, especially after the winning post, with a steady climb from the home bend. Suits the handy sort.
Clerk of the Course: Mr M. Trickey, The Racecourse, Taunton, Somerset TA3 7BL. Tel: (01823) 337172.
Approx. 100 boxes. Allotted on arrival. Advance bookings for long journeys. Apply to the Stable Manager, Mr H. J. Burnham on (01460) 234308 or (01823) 331195.
By Car: 2 miles South of the town on the B3170 (Honiton) road (M5 Junc 25). Free car park for Members. The public car parks are free or £3 on course.
By Rail: Taunton Station 2 1/2 miles. There are buses and taxis to course.

Leading Trainers (since 1991): M. C. Pipe 53-224 (23.7%), **R. J. Hodges** 23-228 (10.1%), **P. J. Hobbs** 22-108 (20.4%).
Leading Jockeys (since 1991): M. A. Fitzgerald 18-124 (14.0%), **J. Osborne** 11-43 (25.0), **R Dunwoody** 11-111 (9.0%).

THIRSK (L.H.)

An oval track of 1m 2f, with fairly tight turns and an undulating run-in of four furlongs. Races of five and six furlongs start on a straight, more undulating two furlong extension of the run-in. Though the turns on the round course are comparatively easy, the track is somewhat sharp. The going seldom rides heavy.

Managing Director/Company Director & Clerk of the Course: Mr Christopher Tetley, The Racecourse, Station Road, Thirsk, North Yorkshire YO7 1QL. Tel: (01845) 522276.
Registered Office: Thirsk Racecourse Limited, The Racecourse, Station Road, Thirsk, North Yorkshire YO7 1QL. Tel: (01845) 522276. Fax: (01845) 525353.
For stabling and accommodation apply to, The Racecourse, Station Road, Thirsk, North Yorkshire. Tel: (01845) 522276 or (01845) 522096 (racedays).
By Car: West of the town on the A61. Free car park adjacent to the course for buses and cars.
By Rail: Thirsk Station (from King's Cross). 1/2 mile from the course.
By Air: Helicopters only, landing on the hockey pitch. Prior arrangement required (01845) 522276. Fixed wing aircraft can land at RAF Leeming. Tel: (01677) 423041. Light aircraft at Bagby. Tel: (01845) 597385 or (01845) 537555.

Leading Trainers (since 1991): M. Johnston 16-97 (16.5%), **M. H. Easterby** 16-158 (10.1%), **J. L. Dunlop** 14-37 (37.8%).
Leading Jockeys (since 1991): G. Duffield 28-105 (26.0%), **J. Weaver** 17-87 (19.0%), **K. Fallon** 14-102 (13.0%).

TOWCESTER (N-H)

Square, 1m 6f (10) 200y run-in uphill. The final six furlongs are uphill. One of the most testing tracks in the country with the emphasis purely on stamina.

Clerk of the Course and Manager: Hugo Bevan, The Old House, Little Everdon, Daventry, Northamptonshire NN11 3BG. Tel: (01327) 361266.
Secretary: M. Chapman, Towcester Racecourse, Towcester, Northamptonshire NN12 7HS. Tel: (01327) 353414.
75 boxes available and allotted on arrival.
By Car: 1 mile South-East of the town on the A5 (Milton Keynes road). M1 (Junc 15) (from the South), M1 (Junc 16) (from the North).
By Rail: Northampton Station (Euston) 9 miles. Buses to Towcester.

Leading Trainers (since 1991): O.Brennan 27-120 (22.5%), **D. Nicholson** 19-62 (30.7%), **Capt T. A. Forster** 15-96 (15.6%).
Leading Jockeys (since 1991): M. Brennan 25-101 (24.0%), **R. Dunwoody** 22-106 (20.0%), **A. Maguire** 15-58 (25.0%).

UTTOXETER (N-H)

Oval, 1m 2f (8) 170y run-in. Few undulations, easy bends and fences and a flat home straight of over half a mile. Suits front-runners, especially the two mile hurdle course.
Clerk of the Course and Manager: Major D. McAallister, The Racecourse, Wood Lane, Uttoxeter. Tel: (01889) 562561.
90 boxes, allotted on arrival. Tel: (01889) 562561.
By Car: South-East of the town off the B5017 (Marchington Road).
By Rail: Uttoxeter Station (Crewe-Derby line) adjoins the course.

Leading Trainers (since 1991): M. C. Pipe 56-184 (30.4%), **K. C. Bailey** 24-108 (22.2%), **N. A. Twiston-Davies** 20-109 (18.4%).
Leading Jockeys (since 1991): R. Dunwoody 41-173 (23.0%), **J. Osborne** 29-95 (30.0%), **N. Williamson** 24-145 (16.0%).

WARWICK (L.H.)

A nearly circular track, 1m 6f 32y in circumference, with a distinct rise and fall levelling off a mile from home and a run-in of about two and a half furlongs. The five furlong course has a left-hand elbow at the junction with the round course. The mile course, straight for the first five furlongs, then turns into the home straight. This sharp track favours handiness and speed rather than staying power.
Racecourse Manager: Miss Lisa Rowl, Warwick Racecourse, Hampton Street, Warwick CV34 6HN. Tel: (01926) 491553. Fax (01926) 403223.
Clerk of the Course: P. R. McNeile, Warwick Racecourse Co. Ltd, Prestbury Park, Cheltenham, GL50 4SH. Tel: (01242) 513014, Fax: (01242) 224227. Racedays: (01926) 492301/ (0850) 091523.
112 boxes allocated on arrival or by reservation (01526) 493801.
By Car: West of the town on the B4095 adjacent to Junc 15 of the M40. Free parking (except the Members' Car Park, £5 to Daily Club Members).
By Rail: Warwick or Leamington Spa Station.

Leading Trainers (since 1991): P. F. I. Cole 15-93 (16.1%), **J. Berry** 15-111 (13.5%), **H. R. A. Cecil** 13-32 (40.6%).
Leading Jockeys (since 1991): Paul Eddery 18-97 (18.0%), **T. Quinn** 17-115 (14.0%), **W. Carson** 16-75 (21.0%).

WARWICK (N-H)

Circular, 1m 6f (10) 240y run-in. Undulating with tight bends, five quick fences in the back straight and a short home straight, Warwick favours handiness and speed rather than stamina.
Racecourse Manager: Miss Lisa Rowl, Warwick Racecourse, Hampton Street, Warwick CV34 6HN. Tel: (01926) 491553. Fax (01926) 403223.
Clerk of the Course: P. R. McNeile, Warwick Racecourse Co. Ltd, Prestbury Park, Cheltenham, GL50 4SH. Tel: (01242) 513014, Fax: (01242) 224227. Racedays: (01926) 492301/ (0850) 091523.
112 boxes allocated on arrival or by reservation (01526) 493801.
By Car: West of the town on the B4095 adjacent to Junc 15 of the M40. Free parking (except the Members' Car Park, £5 to Daily Club Members).
By Rail: Warwick or Leamington Spa Station.

Leading Trainers (since 1991): M. C. Pipe 39-146 (26.7%), **D. Nicholson** 25-112 (22.3%),
Mrs J. Pitman 17-94 (18.1%).
Leading Jockeys (since 1991): R. Dunwoody 37-93 (39.0%), **J. Osborne** 16-88 (18.0%),
A. Maguire 13-74 (17.0%).

WETHERBY (N-H)

Oval, 1m 4f (9) 200y run-in slightly uphill. A flat, very fair course which suits the long-striding gal-
loper. Good jumping is essential as the fences are stiff.
Clerk of the Course: C. M. Tetley, The Racecourse, Wetherby. Tel: (01937) 582035
Secretary: G. M. Hanson, The Racecourse, Wetherby. Tel: (01937) 582035. As from 1/9/95 -
Miss A. Dalby
98 boxes allocated on arrival. Accommodation for lads and lasses.
By Car: East of the town off the B1224 (York Road). Adjacent to the A1. Excellent bus and
coach facilities. Car park free.
By Rail: Leeds Station 12 miles. Buses to Wetherby.

Leading Trainers (since 1991): Mrs M. Reveley 52-179 (29.1%), **M. H. Easterby** 30-157 (19.1%),
G. Richards 25-131 (19.1%).
Leading Jockeys (since 1991): P. Niven 49-194 (25.0%), **L. Wyer** 38-158 (24.0%),
A. Maguire 20-73 (27.0%).

WINCANTON (N-H)

Rectangular, 1m 3f (9) 200y run-in. Good galloping course where the going rarely becomes
heavy. The home straight is mainly downhill.
Clerk of the Course and Manager: R. I. Renton, Wincanton Racecourse, Wincanton, Somerset
BA9 8BJ. Tel: (01963) 32344. Fax: (01963) 34668.
100 boxes allotted on arrival. Apply to the Stable Manager, Wincanton Racecourse. Tel: (01963)
32344.
By Car: 1 mile North of the town on the B3081.
By Rail: Gillingham Station (from Waterloo) or Castle Cary Station (from Paddington). Buses
and taxis to the course.
By Air: Helicopter landing area is situated in the centre of the course.

Leading Trainers (since 1991): M. C. Pipe 42-158 (26.6%), **Mrs J. Pitman** 23-86 (26.7%),
R. J. Hodges 19-189 (10.1%).
Leading Jockeys (since 1991): R. Dunwoody 33-157 (21.0%), **C. Llewellyn** 11-70 (15.0%),
J. Osborne 11-73 (15.0%).

Owners names are shown against their horses
where this information is available. In the case of
Partnerships and Syndicates, the nominated
owner is given alongside the horse with other
owners listed below the team.

WINDSOR (Fig.8)

In the form of a figure eight, Windsor has a circuit of 1m 4f 110y. Although both left and right-hand turns are met in races of a mile and a half, only right-hand turns occur in races up to 1m 70y. The five furlong course bends slightly to the right approaching halfway but is otherwise straight. The track is perfectly flat and its sharpness is largely offset by the long run-in.

Clerk of the Course and Director: Hugo Bevan, The Old House, Little Everdon, Daventry, Northamptonshire. Tel: (01327) 361266

Racecourse Manager: Mrs S. Dingle, The Racecourse, Windsor, Berkshire. Tel: (01753) 865234 or (01753) 864726; Stables (01753) 865350.

Reservation required for overnight stay and accommodation only. Tel: (01753) 865234.

By Car: North of the town on the A308 (M4 Junc 6). Car parks adjoin the course (£1, £1.50, £2).

By Rail: Windsor Central Station (from Paddington) or Windsor & Eton Riverside Station (from Waterloo).

By Air: London (Heathrow) Airport 15 minutes by car via the M4. Also White Waltham Airport (West London Aero Club) 15 minutes.

Leading Trainers (since 1991): R. Hannon 48-269 (17.8%), **H. R. A. Cecil** 13-41 (31.7%), **M. J. Heaton-Ellis** 12-70 (17.1%).

Leading Jockeys (since 1991): Pat Eddery 48-193 (24.0%), **L. Dettori** 24-137 (17.0%), **M. Roberts** 21-126 (16.0%).

WINDSOR (N-H)

1m 4f (7) 200y run-in. Perfectly flat but sharp, suited to front runners and those of doubtful stamina.

Clerk of the Course and Director: Hugo Bevan, The Old House, Little Everdon, Daventry, Northamptonshire. Tel: (01327) 361266

Racecourse Manager: Mrs S. Dingle, The Racecourse, Windsor, Berkshire. Tel: (01753) 865234 or (01753) 864726; Stables (01753) 865350.

Reservation required for overnight stay and accommodation only. Tel: (01753) 865234.

By Car: North of the town on the A308 (M4 Junc 6). Car parks adjoin the course (£1, £1.50, £2).

By Rail: Windsor Central Station (from Paddington) or Windsor & Eton Riverside Station (from Waterloo).

By Air: London (Heathrow) Airport 15 minutes by car via the M4. Also White Waltham Airport (West London Aero Club) 15 minutes.

Leading Trainers (since 1991): N. J. Henderson 12-63 (19.1%), **P. J. Hobbs** 10-58 (17.2%), **K. C. Bailey** 9-59 (15.3%).

Leading Jockeys (since 1991): N. Williamson 10-67 (14.0%), **R. Dunwoody** 8-61 (13.0%), **J. Osborne** 7-64 (10.0%).

WOLVERHAMPTON (L.H.)

An oval circuit, a mile in circumference with a run-in of 380y. The bends are tight and the seven furlong course, which starts on a chute, has already provoked some criticism as the run to the first bend is very short. The Fibresand surface consists of a blended mixture of silica sand and synthetic fibres set in a re-enforced sub-base. Initial impressions are that Wolverhampton rides slower that the All-Weather tracks at Lingfield and Southwell. Plans are in the pipeline to lay a turf track on the outside of the All-Weather track.

Clerk of the Course: Mr A. J. Bealby, The Rookery, Bragborough Hall, Braunston, Daventry, Northamptonshire NN11 7HA. Tel: (01788) 891795.

126 boxes allotted on arrival. Applications for lads and lasses accommodation must be made to Racecourse. Tel: (01902) 24481. Fax (01902) 716626

By Car: 1 mile North of town on the A449 (M54 Junc 2 or M6 Junc 12). Car parking at Dunstall Lane and Dunstall Enclosure (on the rails) £1.

By Rail: Wolverhampton Station (from Euston) 1 mile.

By Air: Halfpenny Green Airport 8 miles.

Leading Trainers (since 1991): J. Berry 39-270 (14.4%), R. Hollinshead 39-422 (9.2%), M. Johnston 31-126 (24.6%).

Leading Jockeys (since 1991): J. Weaver 46-223 (20.0%), L. Dettori 34-166 (20.0%), G. Carter 33-180 (18.0%).

WOLVERHAMPTON (N-H)

Clerk of the Course: Mr A. J. Bealby, The Rookery, Bragborough Hall, Braunston, Daventry, Northamptonshire NN11 7HA. Tel: (01788) 891795.

126 boxes allotted on arrival. Applications for lads and lasses accommodation must be made to Racecourse. Tel: (01902) 24481. Fax (01902) 716626

By Car: 1 mile North of town on the A449 (M54 Junc 2 or M6 Junc 12). Car parking at Dunstall Lane and Dunstall Enclosure (on the rails) £1.

By Rail: Wolverhampton Station (from Euston) 1 mile.

By Air: Halfpenny Green Airport 8 miles.

Leading Trainers (since 1991): D. Nicholson 12-40 (30.0%), M. C. Pipe 12-41 (29.3%), Miss H. C. Knight 8-29 (27.6%).

Leading Jockeys (since 1991): R. Dunwoody 15-63 (23.0%), J. Osborne 12-40 (30.0%).

WORCESTER (N.H)

Elongated oval, 1m 5f (9) 220y run-in. Flat with easy turns, Worcester is a very fair, galloping track.

Clerk of the Course: Hugo Bevan, The Old House, Little Everdon, Daventry, Northamptonshire NN11 3BG. Tel: (01327) 361266.

Manager: S. Brice, The Racecourse, Worcester. Tel: (01905) 25364 or (01684) 62033.

108 boxes allotted on arrival. Overnight accommodation for lads and lasses in Worcester.

By Car: West of the city off the A449 (Kidderminster road) (M5 Junc 8).

By Rail: Foregate Street Station, Worcester (from Paddington) 3/4 mile.

By Air: Helicopter landing facility in the centre of the course, by prior arrangement only.

Laeding Trainers (since 1991): M. C. Pipe 45-151 (29.8%), P. J. Hobbs 32-134 (23.9%), D. Nicholson 23-111 (20.7%).

Leading Jockeys (since 1991): R. Dunwoody 37-222 (16.0%), J. Osborne 29-114 (25.0%), A. Maguire 26-160 (16.0%).

YARMOUTH (L.H.)

An oblong course of about 1m 4f with a slight fall to a run-in of five furlongs. The straight mile joins the round course at the run-in and is perfectly level. The five, six and seven furlong courses form part of the straight mile.

Clerk of the Course: Mr D. C. Henson, F.R.I.C.S., 2 Lower Mounts, Northampton NN1 3DE. Tel: (01604) 30757. Fax: (01604) 30758.

Manager: Major T. M. Prior, The Racecourse, Jellicoe Road, Great Yarmouth, Norfolk NR30 4AV. Tel: (01493) 842527.

Stabling allocated on arrival. Tel: (01493) 855651.

By Car: 1 mile East of town centre (well sign-posted from A47 & A12). Large car park adjoining course £1.

By Rail: Great Yarmouth Station (1 mile). Bus service to the course.

By Air: Helicopter landing facilities available 300y from the course at North Denes Airfield. Tel: (01493) 851500. Fixed wing aircraft landing facilities are available at a private airfield in Ludham. Prior permission is required through Mr R. Collins. Tel: (01493) 843211. Fax: (01493) 859555.

Leading Trainers (since 1991): H. R. A. Cecil 27-102 (26.5%), M. R. Stoute 24-113 (21.2%), H. ThomsonJones 23-94 (24.5%).

Leading Jockeys (since 1991): M. Roberts 36-191 (18.0%), R. Hills 32-154 (20.0%), M. Hills 26-145 (17.0%).

YORK (L.H.)

From the two mile start at the bottom of the Knavesmire, this wide, U-shaped course runs parallel with the Tadcaster Road for five furlongs before bending left to pass under Knavesmire Wood and join the straight six furlongs round a sweeping turn in front of the five furlong gate. A new two furlong extension, set at a tangent, also joins the round course here and caters for seven furlong events. A fair, galloping course which calls for stamina and courage, especially in the wet weather when the going can be very testing. Because of the watering system, when the going is soft, much better ground can be found by racing wide in the back straight.

Manager, Clerk of the Course and Secretary: Mr J. L. Smith F.C.A., The Racecourse, York YO2 1EX. Tel: (01904) 620911. Fax: (01904) 611071.

Free.

By Car: 1 mile South-East of the city on the A1036. Car parking bookings can be made prior to race meetings (except August) for reserved car park (£2 (inc. VAT) per day). All other parking is free.

By Rail: 11/2 miles York Station (from King's Cross). Special bus service from station to the course.

By Air: Light aircraft and helicopter landing facilities available at Rufforth aerodrome (5,000ft tarmac runway). £20 landing fee-transport arranged to course. Leeds/Bradford airport (25 miles).

Leading Trainers (since 1991): J. H. M. Gosden 38-131 (29.0%), H. R. A. Cecil 28-110 (25.5%), M. R. Stoute 24-143 (16.8%).

Leading Jockeys (since 1991): Pat Eddery 46-234 (19.0%), L. Dettori 42-201 (20.0%), W. Carson 36-245 (14.0%).

RACEFORM STANDARD TIMES

The following represent the standard true-run race times for the various distances and courses brought to 9st.

ASCOT

5f.....................................59.5s	1m (rnd).........................1/39.6s	2m 45yds.........................3/26.5s
6f.....................................1/13.6s	1¼m.................................2/4.3s	2½m.................................4/19s
7f.....................................1/26.5s	1½m.................................2/29.5s	2¾m 34yds.....................4/48s
1m (str).........................1/39.2s		

AYR

5f.....................................57s	1m 1f..............................1/50.5s	1m 5f 13yds...................2/44.8s
6f.....................................1/9.8s	1¼m.................................2/4.6s	1m 7f..............................3/10.1s
7f.....................................1/24s	1¼m 192yds.................2/16.2s	2m 1f 105yds...............3/42.5s
1m.....................................1/36.8s		2½m 90yds.....................4/21s

BATH

5f 11yds.........................1/0.5s	1¼m 46yds......................2/7.7s	1m 5f 22yds...................2/45.7s
5f 161yds.......................1/9.3s	1m 3f 144yds 2/26.7s	2m 1f 34yds...................3/41s
1m 5yds.........................1/38.5s		

BEVERLEY

5f.....................................1/1.5s	1m 1f 207yds.................2/2.5s	2m 35yds.........................3/30.5s
7f 100yds.......................1/32s	1m 3f 216yds 2/31.5s	
1m 100yds.....................1/44s		

BRIGHTON

5f 59yds.........................1/0s	6f 209yds.......................1/20s	1m 1f 209yds 1/58s
5f 213 yds.....................1/8.4s	7f 214yds.......................1/32.2s	1m 3f 196yds 2/29s

CARLISLE

5f.....................................1/0.2s	6f 206yds.......................1/25.7s	1½m.................................2/31s
5f 207yds.......................1/12.3s	7f 214yds.......................1/39s	1¾m 32yds.....................3m

CATTERICK

5f.....................................57.5s	1m 3f 214yds.................2/31s	1m 5f 175yds 2/55.2s
5f 212yds.......................1/10.5s	1½m 44yds.....................2/34s	1m 7f 177yds 3/21s
7f.....................................1/23.2s		

CHEPSTOW

5f 16yds.........................57s	1m 14yds.........................1/32.5s	2m 49yds.........................3/28s
6f 16yds.........................1/9s	1¼m 36yds.....................2/4.3s	2m 2f 33yds...................3/52s
7f 16yds.........................1/20s	1½m 23yds.....................2/31.3s	

CHESTER

5f 16yds..................60s	1¼m 75yds.................2/8.7s	1m 5f 89yds 2/50s
6f 18yds................1/13.3s	1m 3f 79yds.................2/24s	1m 7f 195yds 3/22.9s
7f 2yds..................1/25.2s	1½m 66yds.................2/36.6s	2¼m 117yds.................3/58s
7f 122yds..............1/31.7s		

DONCASTER

5f..................58.4s	1m (str)..................1/36.5s	1½m..................2/30.6s
5f 140yds..................1/7s	1m (rnd)..................1/36.3s	1¾m 132yds..............3/3.6s
6f..................1/11s	1¼m 60yds..................2/7s	2m 110yds..................3/29s
7f..................1/23.4s		2¼m..................3/52.7s

EPSOM

5f..................54.5s	7f..................1/20.3s	1¼m 18yds..................2/4s
6f..................1/8s	1m 114yds..................1/42s	1½m 10yds..................2/35s

FOLKESTONE

5f..................58.6s	1m 1f 149yds 1/57.7s	1m 7f 92yds.............3/16.9s
6f..................1/11.7s	1½m..................2/31.2s	2m 93yds..................3/31s
6f 189yds..............1/21.6s		

GOODWOOD

5f..................56.7s	1m 1f..................1/50.7s	1¾m..................2/59s
6f..................1/10.2s	1¼m..................2/5s	2m..................3/24.5s
7f..................1/24.4s	1½m..................2/32s	2½m..................4/17s
1m..................1/37.6s		

HAMILTON

5f 4yds..................58.3s	1m 1f 36yds 1/54.3s	1½m 17yds..................2/32s
6f 5yds..................1/10s	1m 3f 16yds 2/19s	1m 5f 9yds..................2/45.7s
1m 65yds..................1/43.3s		

HAYDOCK

5f..................59s	1m 30yds..................1/40.4s	1¾m..................2/58.2s
6f..................1/11.7s	1¼m 120yds.............2/11.5s	2m 45yds..................3/27.2s
7f 30yds..................1/27.3s	1m 3f 200yds 2/28s	

KEMPTON

5f..................57.8s	1m (rnd)..................1/37.2s	1m 3f 30yds..................2/17.6s
6f..................1/11.3s	1m (Jubilee) 1/37s	1½m..................2/30.2s
7f (rnd)..................1/24.5s	1m 1f (rnd)..................1/50s	1¾m 92y..................3/3s
7f (Jubilee) 1/24.2s	1¼m (Jubilee) 2/2.5s	2m..................3/24.4s

LEICESTER

5f 2yds..................58.5s	7f 9yds..................1/22.5s	1m 1f 218yds 2/2.7s
5f 218yds..................1/10s	1m 8yds..................1/35s	1m 3f 183yds 2/28.8s

LINGFIELD (TURF)

5f.....................57s	7f 140yds.....................1/28s	1m 3f 106yds.....................2/22s
6f.....................1/9s	1m 1f.....................1/49.3s	1¾m.....................2/55.3s
7f.....................1/20.6s	1¼m.....................2/3s	2m.....................3/24s

LINGFIELD (AWT)

5f.....................58s	1m.....................1/37.4s	1m 5f.....................2/43.2s
6f.....................1/10.6s	1¼m.....................2/4.3s	2m.....................3/22s
7f.....................1/24s	1½m.....................2/30s	

MUSSELBURGH

5f.....................57.7s	1m 16yds.....................1/38.6s	1½m 31yds.....................2/32.5s
7f 15yds.....................1/26s	1m 3f 32yds.....................2/19.7s	1m 7f 16yds.....................3/10.5s

NEWBURY

5f 34yds.....................1/0.3s	1m (str).....................1/37s	1m 3f 5yds.....................2/16s
6f 8yds.....................1/11.8s	1m 7yds (rnd).....................1/36s	1½m 5yds.....................2/29.3s
7f.....................1/24.5s	1m 1f.....................1/49.2s	1m 5f 61yds.....................2/45.3s
7f 64yds.....................1/28.5s	1¼m 6yds.....................2/3s	2m.....................3/26.5s

NEWCASTLE

5f.....................58.4s	1m.....................1/39s	1½m 93yds.....................2/38.5s
6f.....................1/11.5s	1m 1f 9yds.....................1/52.3s	2m 19yds.....................3/25.5s
7f.....................1/24.3s	1¼m 32yds.....................2/6.7s	

NEWMARKET
(ROWLEY MILE COURSE)

5f.....................58.7s	1m 1f.....................1/49.7s	1¾m.....................2/56s
6f.....................1/11.3s	1¼m.....................2/2.6s	2m.....................3/23.3s
7f.....................1/23.7s	1½m.....................2/29.3s	2¼m.....................3/50s
1m.....................1/37s		

(JULY COURSE)

5f.....................59s	1m.....................1/37.7s	1¾m 175yds.....................3/6s
6f.....................1/11.5s	1¼m.....................2/2.4s	2m 24yds.....................3/23s
7f.....................1/24.4s	1½m.....................2/28.7s	

NOTTINGHAM

5f 13yds.....................58.7s	1m 1f 213yds.....................2/2.5s	2m 9yds.....................3/24.4s
6f 15yds.....................1/11s	1¾m 15yds.....................2/58.5s	2¼m 18yds.....................3/51.5s
1m 54yds.....................1/39.6s		

PONTEFRACT

5f.....................1/1.5s	1¼m 6yds.....................2/8.3s	2m 1f 216yds.....................3/52s
6f.....................1/14.3s	1½m 8yds.....................2/34.3s	2m 5f 122yds.....................4/40s
1m 4yds.....................1/42s	2m 1f 22yds.....................3/40s	

REDCAR

5f....................................56.7s	1m 1f.......................................1/49s	1¾m 19yds...................2/58s
6f.....................................1/9.3s	1¼m.......................................2/2.5s	2m 4yds........................3/25s
7f.......................................1/22s	1m 3f....................................2/15.7s	2m 3f................................4/5s
1m.....................................1/35s	1m 5f 135yds 2/51s	

RIPON

5f...58s	1m 1f....................................1/50.2s	2m...................................3/25s
6f...................................1/10.2s	1¼m.....................................2/3.5s	2m 1f 203yds 3/51.3s
1m.................................1/37.7s	1½m 60yds.........................2/34s	

SALISBURY

5f...60s	1m......................................1/39.3s	1½m...............................2/32.6s
6f...................................1/12.3s	1m 1f 209yds 2/4.7s	1¾m...............................2/58.2s
6f 212yds.......................1/25.7s		

SANDOWN

5f 6yds.............................59.8s	1m 1f....................................1/51.4s	1¾m...............................2/54.7s
7f 16yds.........................1/26.6s	1¼m 7yds..........................2/4.3s	2m 78yds......................3/30s
1m 14yds.......................1/39.2s	1m 3f 91yds 2/21.7s	

SOUTHWELL (AWT)

5f...57s	1m 3f......................................2/20s	1¾m...................................2/59s
6f...................................1/13.5s	1½m....................................2/32.5s	2m...................................3/26s
7f...................................1/26.8s	1m 5f......................................2/45s	2¼m...............................3/54s
1m.....................................1/40s		

SOUTHWELL (TURF)

6f...................................1/14.3s	1m 3f......................................2/22s	2m...................................3/27s
7f...................................1/27.2s	1½m....................................2/34.6s	

THIRSK

5f....................................57.2s	7f..1/22.7s	1½m...................................2/30s
6f.....................................1/9.7s	1m.....................................1/35.6s	2m...................................3/23s

WARWICK

5f...58s	1m..1/37s	1¾m 194yds...................3/9s
6f.....................................1/12s	1¼m 169yds..............2/13.5s	2m 20yds......................3/26s
7f...................................1/24.2s	1½m 115yds..............2/37.5s	2¼m 214yds...................4/4s

WINDSOR

5f 10yds...........................59s	1m 67yds....................1/41.6s	1m 3f 135yds 2/26s
5f 217yds....................1/10.5s	1¼m 7yds.........................2/4.9s	

WOLVERHAMPTON

5f...58s	1m 100y...............................1/44s	1½m...................................2/31s
6f...................................1/11.2s	1m 3f.....................................2/14s	1¾m 110yds...................3/6s
7f.....................................1/24s		

WOLVERHAMPTON (AWT)

5f....................................58.7s	1m 100yds....................1/45s	1¾m 166yds.................3/7.4s
6f....................................1/11.4s	1m 1f 79yds 1/56s	2m 46yds........................3/27s
7f....................................1/24.7s	1½m........................2/32.5s	

YARMOUTH

5f 43yds........................1/0.3s	1m 3yds.........................1/35.3s	1¾m 17yds.........................2/58s
6f 3yds.........................1/10.6s	1¼m 21yds....................2/4.4s	2m..............................3/23.5s
7f 3yds.........................1/22.8s	1m 3f 101yds 2/23s	2m 1f 170yds 3/47.5s
		2m 2f 51yds 3/54s

YORK

5f...57s	7f 202yds.......................1/36s	1m 3f 195yds 2/27s
6f...1/9.6s	1m 205yds....................1/49s	1m 5f 194yds 2/53.6s
6f 214yds...................1/21.5s	1¼m 85yds..................2/7.5s	1m 7f 195yds 3/20s

RACEFORM RECORD TIMES

As recorded by "Raceform" since 1936. Courses with electrical timing apparatus are indicated—(Electric).

ASCOT (Electric)

Distance	Time	Age	Weight	Going	Horse	Date	
5f	59.10	3	8-8	Firm	Orient	Jun 21,	1986
5f	59.72	2	8-8	Firm	Lyric Fantasy (IRE)	Jun 17,	1992
6f	72.53	4	9-4	Firm	Shalford (IRE)	Jun 17,	1992
6f	73.63	2	8-8	Firm	Minstrella (USA)	Jun 19,	1986
7f	85.94	3	9-1	Firm	Prince Ferdinand	Jun 17,	1992
7f	87.25	2	8-11	Fast	Celtic Swing	Oct 8,	1994
1m	98.58	3	9-0	Good to firm	Ridgewood Pearl	Jun 21,	1995
1m	100.92	2	8-7	Fast	Untold	Spt 26,	1985
1m	98.07	4	7-8	Firm	Colour Sergeant	Jun 17,	1992
1m 2f	123.31	4	9-1	Firm	Trepan (disq)	Jun 15,	1976
1m 4f	146.95	5	8-9	Firm	Stanerra	Jun 17,	1983
2m 45y	205.29	3	9-3	Firm	Landowner (IRE)	Jun 17,	1992
2m 4f	255.67	5	9-0	Firm	Royal Gait (disq)	Jun 16,	1988
2m 6f 34y	291.32	4	8-8	Firm	Otabari	Jun 20,	1986

AYR (Electric)

Distance	Time	Age	Weight	Going	Horse	Date	
5f	57.20	4	9-5	Fast	Sir Joey (USA)	Spt 16,	1993
5f	57.80	2	8-0	Hard	Monte Christo	May 17,	1946
6f	68.98	7	8-8	Fast	Sobering Thoughts	Spt 10,	1993
6f	69.73	2	7-10	Good	Sir Bert	Spt 17,	1969
7f	84.97	5	7-11	Firm	Sir Arthur Hobbs	Jun 19,	1992
7f	85.71	2	9-0	Fast	Jazeel (USA)	Spt 16,	1993
1m	96.00	4	7-13	Firm	Sufi	Spt 16,	1959
1m	99.21	2	9-0	Firm	Kribensis	Spt 17,	1986
1m 1f	115.25	3	7-10	Firm	Virkon Venture (IRE)	Spt 21,	1991
1m 2f	125.20	8	10-0	Fast	Knock Knock	Spt 18,	1993
1m 2f 192y	133.31	4	9-0	Good	Azzaam (USA)	Spt 18,	1991
1m 5f 13y	165.81	4	9-7	Fast	Eden's Close	Spt 18,	1993
1m 7f	193.16	3	9-4	Good	Romany Rye	Spt 19,	1991
2m 1f 105y	225.00	4	6-13	Good	Curry	Spt 16,	1955

> Foaling dates are shown for two-year-olds where these are provided.

BATH

Distance	Time	Age	Weight	Going	Horse	Date	
5f 11y	60.30	3	8-9	Hard	Katies First (USA)	May 21,	1990
5f 11y	60.80	2	8-11	Fast	Cheyenne Spirit	Aug 9,	1994
5f 161y	68.10	6	9-0	Firm	Madraco	May 22,	1989
5f 161y	70.00	2	8-13	Fast	Morocco (IRE)	Jly 22,	1991
1m 5y	98.20	4	9-9	Firm	Air Commodore (IRE)	Jly 1,	1995
1m 5y	100.70	2	8-11	Firm	Myhamet	Oct 2,	1989
1m 2f 46y	126.60	3	8-11	Good to firm	Easy Listening (USA)	May 22,	1995
1m 3f 144y	145.90	4	9-2	Firm	Alriffa	May 13,	1995
1m 5f 22y	167.30	4	10-0	Firm	Flown	Aug 13,	1991
2m 1f 34y	223.90	6	7-9	Fast	Patroclus	Jly 10,	1991

BEVERLEY

Distance	Time	Age	Weight	Going	Horse	Date	
5f	60.30	4	9-11	Firm	Eager Deva	Apr 25,	1991
5f	62.00	2	8-11	Firm	Persian Breeze	Jun 13,	1974
7f 100y	89.40	3	7-8	Firm	Who's Tef (IRE)	Jly 30,	1991
7f 100y	90.90	2	9-0	Firm	Majal (IRE)	Jly 30,	1991
1m 100y	102.30	3	8-4	Firm	Legal Case	Jun 14,	1989
1m 100y	103.30	2	9-0	Firm	Arden	Spt 24,	1986
1m 1f 207y	120.65	4	11-7	Good to firm	Ooh Ah Cantona	Jly 8,	1995
1m 3f 216y	150.60	3	8-1	Hard	Coinage	Jun 18,	1986
2m 35y	210.10	4	7-7	Firm	Between The Sheets	Spt 21,	1989

BRIGHTON

Distance	Time	Age	Weight	Going	Horse	Date	
5f 59y	59.40	3	8-9	Firm	Play Hever Golf	May 27,	1993
5f 59y	60.10	2	9-0	Firm	Bid For Blue	May 6,	1993
5f 213y	67.60	4	8-11	Firm	Dahiyah (USA)	May 11,	1995
5f 213y	68.50	2	8-9	Firm	Holetown	Spt 4,	1991
6f 209y	79.40	4	9-3	Firm	Sawaki	Spt 4,	1991
6f 209y	79.90	2	8-11	Hard	Rain Burst	Spt 15,	1988
7f 214y	90.90	5	8-12	Hard	Chase The Door	Jly 26,	1990
7f 214y	92.80	2	9-7	Firm	Asian Pete	Oct 3,	1989
1m 1f 209y	117.20	3	9-0	Firm	Get The Message	Apr 30,	1984
1m 3f 196y	145.80	4	8-2	Firm	New Zealand	Jly 4,	1985

CARLISLE

Distance	Time	Age	Weight	Going	Horse	Date	
5f	59.80	4	9-0	Hard	Brisas	Spt 10,	1991
5f	60.20	2	8-9	Hard	Metal Boys	Jun 1,	1989
5f 207y	71.80	6	8-13	Hard	Night Patrol	Aug 27,	1970
5f 207y	72.90	2	8-9	Hard	Parfait Amour	Spt 10,	1991
6f 206y	85.60	3	8-7	Firm	Cheerful Groom (IRE)	May 26,	1994
6f 206y	86.60	2	9-4	Hard	Sense Of Priority	Spt 10,	1991
7f 214y	87.60	7	8-0	Good	Northern Spark	Jun 1,	1995
7f 214y	104.60	2	8-8	Firm	Blue Garter	Spt 9,	1980
1m 4f	149.50	6	10-0	Firm	Batabanoo	Jun 29,	1995
1m 6f 32y	182.20	6	8-10	Firm	Explosive Speed (USA)	May 26,	1994

CATTERICK

Distance	Time	Age	Weight	Going	Horse	Date	
5f	57.10	4	8-7	Fast	Kabcast	Jly 7,	1989
5f	57.70	2	9-0	Fast	Verde Alitalia (IRE)	Spt 21,	1991
5f 212y	70.40	3	8-8	Firm	Triad Treble	May 31,	1984
5f 212y	71.40	2	9-4	Firm	Captain Nick	Jly 11,	1978
7f	83.00	4	7-12	Firm	Royal Ziska	Jun 9,	1973
7f	84.10	2	8-11	Firm	Lindas Fantasy	Spt 18,	1982
1m 3f 214y	154.80	3	8-0		Real Popcorn (IRE)	Jly 14,	1994
1m 5f 175y	174.80	3	8-5	Firm	Geryon	May 31,	1984
1m 7f 177y	200.80	4	7-11	Firm	Bean Boy	Jly 8,	1982

CHEPSTOW

Distance	Time	Age	Weight	Going	Horse	Date	
5f 16y	56.80	3	8-4	Firm	Torbay Express	Spt 15,	1979
5f 16y	57.60	2	8-11	Firm	Micro Love	Jly 8,	1986
6f 16y	68.80	4	8-6	Fast	African Rex (FR)	May 12,	1987
6f 16y	69.40	2	9-0	Fast	Royal Fi Fi (USA)	Spt 9,	1989
7f 16y	79.90	3	9-10	Firm	Prince Titian	Aug 29,	1978
7f 16y	81.40	2	8-11	Hard	Dijla	Aug 31,	1981
1m 14y	91.80	6	9-6	Firm	Traditional Miss	Jun 27,	1981
1m 14y	94.60	2	8-11	Fast	Glowing Ardour	Aug 27,	1990
1m 2f 36y	124.10	5	8-9	Hard	Leonidas (USA)	Jly 5,	1983
1m 4f 23y	151.00	7	9-6	Hard	Maintop	Aug 27,	1984
2m 49y	207.70	4	9-0	Fast	Wizzard Artist	Jly 1,	1989
2m 2f	240.20	8	9-1	Good to firm	Tamarpour (USA)	Jly 4,	1995
2m 2f 33y	239.50	8	9-5	Firm	Mardood	Jun 29,	1993

CHESTER (Electric)

Distance	Time	Age	Weight	Going	Horse	Date	
5f 16y	59.20	3	10-0	Firm	Althrey Don	Jly 10,	1964
5f 16y	60.40	2	8-11	Firm	Cynara	May 3,	1960
6f 18y	72.78	6	9-2	Good	Stack Rock	Jun 23,	1993
6f 18y	73.40	2	9-3	Good	Stung	Jly 27,	1968
7f 2y	85.27	3	9-3	Fast	Mizaaya	May 7,	1992
7f 2y	86.28	2	8-4	Fast	By Hand	Aug 31,	1991
7f 122y	92.00	6	8-5	Firm	Cee-Jay-Ay	May 6,	1993
7f 122y	95.00	2	9-0	Firm	Double Value	Spt 1,	1972
1m 2f 75y	127.98	3	8-10	Firm	Beneficial	May 10,	1993
1m 3f 79y	143.71	3	8-11	Fast	Braiswick	May 10,	1989
1m 4f 66y	154.21	3	8-11	Fast	Old Vic	May 9,	1989
1m 5f 89y	165.43	5	8-11	Firm	Rakaposhi King	May 7,	1987
1m 7f 195y	205.00	3	8-6	Firm	Seacourt	Spt 1,	1972
2m 2f 117y	237.28	4	9-8	Firm	Just David	May 6,	1987
2m 2f 147y	243.35	5	8-8	Good to firm	Top Cees	May 10,	1995

DONCASTER (Electric)

Distance	Time	Age	Weight	Going	Horse	Date	
5f	58.20	3	8-8	Firm	Sir Gatrick	Spt 10,	1959
5f	58.40	2	9-5	Firm	Sing Sing	Spt 11,	1959
5f 140y	66.20	3	9-2	Good	Welsh Abbot	Spt 12,	1958
5f 140y	68.00	2	8-10	Good	Crown Flatts	Oct 25,	1947
6f	69.74	3	8-9	Good to firm	Iltimas (USA)	Jly 26,	1995
6f	71.20	2	8-11	Firm	Paddy's Sister	Spt 9,	1959
7f	82.60	3	9-4	Hard	Pinolli	Jun 3,	1963
7f	84.40	2	9-0	Good	Chebs Lad	Spt 12,	1967
1m	97.18	8	9-6	Fast	Mellottie	Mar 25,	1993
1m	99.08	2	7-13	Firm	Wahem (IRE)	Spt 10,	1992
1m	95.34	3	9-0	Fast	Gneiss (USA)	May 2,	1994
1m	98.32	2	9-0	Firm	Sandy Creek	Oct 28,	1978
1m 2f 60y	125.48	3	8-8	Good to firm	Carlito Brigante	Jly 26,	1995
1m 2f 60y	133.47	2	8-8	Good	Yard Bird	Nov 6,	1981
1m 4f	149.95	3	9-4	Firm	Sherrifmuir	Jun 26,	1992
1m 6f 132y	182.22	3	8-3	Firm	Brier Creek (USA)	Spt 10,	1992
2m 110y	214.44	4	9-12	Firm	Farsi	Jun 12,	1992
2m 2f	235.60	6	9-3	Firm	Further Flight	Spt 10,	1992

EPSOM (Electric)

Distance	Time	Age	Weight	Going	Horse	Date	
5f	53.60	4	9-5	Firm	Indigenous	Jun 2,	1960
5f	55.20	2	8-9	Firm	Cerise	Jun 4,	1954
6f	67.91	5	7-7	Firm	Moor Lane	Jun 7,	1973
6f	67.85	2	8-11	Fast	Showbrook (IRE)	Jun 5,	1991
7f	80.15	4	8-7	Firm	Capistrano	Jun 7,	1972
7f	82.17	2	8-9	Fast	Shamrock Fair (IRE)	Aug 30,	1994
1m 114y	100.75	3	8-6	Fast	Sylva Honda	Jun 5,	1991
1m 114y	102.80	2	8-5	Fast	Nightstalker	Aug 30,	1988
1m 2f 18y	123.50	5	7-13	Good	Crossbow (unofficial)	Jun 7,	1967
1m 4f 10y	153.31	4	9-0	Firm	Bustino	Jun 7,	1975

FOLKESTONE

Distance	Time	Age	Weight	Going	Horse	Date	
5f	58.80	3	6-10	Good	Tammany	Aug 12,	1963
5f	58.60	2	8-11	Good	Sacque	Oct 9,	1990
6f	70.50	4	8-5	Firm	Zipperdi-Doo-Dah	Mar 31,	1976
6f	71.00	2	7-13	Hard	Fashion Model	Aug 31,	1970
6f 189y	81.30	3	8-9	Firm	Cielamour (USA)	Aug 9,	1988
6f 189y	84.10	2	9-7	Fast	Woodman's Mount(USA)	Spt 24,	1990
1m 1f 149y	117.80	4	8-11	Firm	Lord Raffles	Jun 2,	1980
1m 4f	153.30	4	8-8	Hard	Snow Blizzard	Jun 30,	1992
1m 7f 92y	203.10	3	9-11	Firm	Mata Askari	Spt 12,	1991
2m 93y	212.50	6	7-13	Firm	North West	Jly 21,	1981

GOODWOOD (Electric)

Distance	Time	Age	Weight	Going	Horse	Date	
5f	56.25	4	9-5	Good to firm	Hever Golf Rose	Jly 25,	1995
5f	57.53	2	8-12	Fast	Poets Cove	Aug 3,	1990
6f	69.58	4	8-3	Firm	For the Present	Jly 30,	1964
6f	70.08	2	9-7	Good to firm	April The Eighth	Jly 25,	1995
7f	83.88	3	8-7	Good to firm	Brief Glimpse (IRE)	Jly 25,	1995
7f	85.97	2	8-11	Fast	Maroof (USA)	Jly 30,	1992
1m	95.71	3	8-13	Firm	Distant View (USA)	Jly 27,	1994
1m	99.44	2	8-11	Fast	Seattle Rhyme (USA)	Spt 13,	1991
1m 1f	112.81	3	9-6	Firm	Vena (IRE)	Jly 27,	1995
1m 2f	124.96	3	8-6	Firm	Kartajana	Aug 4,	1990
1m 4f	151.57	3	8-10	Firm	Presenting	Jly 25,	1995
1m 6f	178.80	3	8-10	Firm	Secret Waters	Aug 2,	1990
2m	203.57	4	9-5	Firm	Tioman Island	Jly 28,	1994
2m 4f	251.75	3	7-10	Firm	Lucky Moon	Aug 2,	1990

HAMILTON

Distance	Time	Age	Weight	Going	Horse	Date	
5f 4y	58.00	5	8-6	Firm	Golden Sleigh	Spt 6,	1972
5f 4y	58.00	2	7-8	Firm	Fair Dandy	Spt 25,	1972
6f 5y	69.30	4	8-7	Firm	Marcus Game	Jly 11,	1974
6f 5y	70.10	2	7-5	Hard	Yoohoo	Spt 8,	1976
1m 65y	102.70	6	7-7	Firm	Cranley	Spt 25,	1972
1m 65y	105.80	2	8-11	Firm	Hopeful Subject	Spt 24,	1973
1m 1f 36y	114.20	3	8-2	Hard	Fairman	Aug 20,	1976
1m 3f 16y	140.50	3	9-3	Firm	Wang Feihoong	Jly 21,	1983
1m 4f 17y	152.00	4	7-4	Firm	Fine Point	Aug 24,	1981
1m 5f 9y	165.20	6	9-6	Firm	Mentalasanythin	Jun 14,	1995

HAYDOCK (Electric)

Distance	Time	Age	Weight	Going	Horse	Date	
5f	58.90	3	7-5	Firm	Fish and Chips	Jun 6,	1970
5f	59.20	2	9-4	Firm	Money For Nothing	Aug 12,	1964
6f	70.72	4	9-13	Firm	Sizzling Saga (IRE)	Jly 2,	1992
6f	71.63	2	8-11	Good to firm	Tamnia	Jly 8,	1995
7f 30y	87.21	4	9-4	Firm	Indian King	Jun 5,	1982
7f 30y	90.57	2	8-11	Hard	Go Grandly	Spt 30,	1972
1m 30y	100.35	3	7-7	Firm	Cashtal Dazzler	May 26,	1990
1m 30y	101.42	2	9-5	Firm	Suhailie (USA)	Oct 4,	1986
1m 2f 120y	129.59	4	9-3	Good	Urgent Request (IRE)	Aug 6,	1994
1m 3f 200y	146.40	5	8-2	Firm	New Member	Jly 4,	1970
1m 6f	179.90	4	9-10	Good	Soloman's Dancer	Aug 6,	1994
2m 45y	207.09	4	8-13	Firm	Prince of Peace	May 26,	1984

KEMPTON (Electric)

Distance	Time	Age	Weight	Going	Horse	Date	
5f	58.07	3	8-1	Firm	Silent Majority	Jun 25,	1986
5f	58.30	2	9-7	Firm	Schweppeshire Lad	Jun 3,	1978
6f	70.04	7	7-10	Firm	Jokist	Apr 6,	1990
6f	70.80	2	8-10	Good	Zabara	Spt 22,	1951
7f	83.83	4	9-11	Good to firm	Cameron Highland(IRE)	Jun 28,	1995
7f	87.52	2	8-6	Good	Duke of Ragusa	Spt 1,	1972
7f	83.79	3	8-11	Firm	Swiss Maid	Aug 19,	1978
7f	84.78	2	9-0	Good to firm	Canons Park	Jun 28,	1995
1m	95.39	3	8-12	Good to firm	Private Line (USA)	Jun 28,	1995
1m	102.50	2	7-4	Good	Batanolius	Oct 19,	1962
1m	95.81	4	9-1	Firm	County Broker	May 23,	1984
1m	103.40	2	7-0	Good	Fascinating	Nov 3,	1956
1m 1f	110.56	3	8-12	Fast	Sky Conqueror (USA)	Jun 29,	1988
1m 2f	119.53	4	9-6	Firm	Batshoof	Apr 6,	1990
1m 3f 30y	136.20	4	9-2	Firm	Shernazar	Spt 6,	1985
1m 4f	150.18	6	8-5	Firm	Going Going	Spt 7,	1985
1m 6f 92y	187.97	6	9-5	Good to firm	Wild Strawberry	Jun 14,	1995
2m	206.53	4	9-10	Good to firm	Latahaab (USA)	May 27,	1995

LEICESTER

Distance	Time	Age	Weight	Going	Horse	Date	
5f 2y	58.20	4	9-5	Fast	Lucky Parkes	Spt 6,	1994
5f 2y	58.40	2	9-0	Firm	Cutting Blade	Jun 9,	1986
5f 218y	69.40	3	8-12	Fast	Lakeland Beauty	May 29,	1990
5f 218y	70.20	2	8-11	Firm	Native Twine	Oct 16,	1989
7f 9y	80.80	3	8-7	Firm	Flower Bowl	Jun 9,	1986
7f 9y	83.20	2	8-9	Fast	Mandarina	Spt 6,	1994
1m 8y	93.80	3	9-0	Good to firm	Clifton Fox	May 29,	1995
1m 8y	95.80	2	9-0	Firm	Missionary Ridge	Oct 17,	1989
1m 1f 218y	122.40	3	8-11	Firm	Effigy	Nov 4,	1985
1m 1f 218y	127.20	2	8-13	Firm	Hardly Fair	Oct 21,	1985
1m 3f 183y	148.50	4	7-11	Hard	Gyroscope	Spt 21,	1964

LINGFIELD (Electric)

Distance	Time	Age	Weight	Going	Horse	Date	
5f	58.01	4	8-5	Standard	Little Saboteur	Feb 20,	1993
5f	59.27	2	9-2	Standard	Fort Hope	Jly 12,	1991
5f	56.24	3	9-1	Fast	Eveningperformance	Jly 25,	1994
5f	57.25	2	8-9	Fast	Quiz Time	Aug 6,	1994
6f	70.58	4	9-4	Standard	J Cheever Loophole	Nov 23,	1989
6f	71.65	2	9-7	Standard	Time's Arrow (IRE)	Jly 10,	1992
6f	68.20	6	9-10	Firm	Al Amead	Jly 2,	1986
6f	68.60	2	9-3	Firm	The Ritz	Jun 11,	1965
7f	82.99	3	9-3	Standard	Confronter	Jly 18,	1992
7f	84.00	2	8-12	Standard	Scottish Castle	Nov 2,	1990
7f	80.20	8	7-10	Hard	Polar Jest	Aug 19,	1955
7f	81.34	2	7-6	Firm	Mandav	Oct 3,	1980
7f 140y	86.73	3	8-6	Fast	Hiaam (USA)	Jly 11,	1987
7f 140y	89.93	2	8-12	Firm	Rather Warm	Nov 7,	1978
1m	96.32	5	9-5	Standard	Vanroy	Nov 30,	1989
1m	96.50	2	9-5	Standard	San Pier Niceto	Nov 30,	1989
1m 1f	112.40	4	9-2	Good to firm	Quandary (USA)	Jly 15,	1995
1m 2f	122.93	4	9-3	Standard	Rapporteur	Nov 2,	1990
1m 2f	127.50	2	8-11	Standard	Star Fighter	Nov 26,	1994
1m 2f	125.79	3	9-3	Firm	Aromatic	Jly 14,	1990
1m 3f 106y	143.95	3	8-5	Firm	Night-Shirt	Jly 14,	1990
1m 4f	149.30	4	8-6	Standard	Puff Puff	Nov 8,	1990
1m 5f	163.82	3	8-9	Standard	Ela Man Howa	Nov 26,	1994
1m 6f	183.20	4	8-3	Good to firm	Persian Smoke	Jly 15,	1995
2m	200.09	3	9-0	Standard	Yenoora (IRE)	Aug 8,	1992
2m	208.96	3	9-0	Firm	Lothian	Spt 20,	1990

MUSSELBURGH

Distance	Time	Age	Weight	Going	Horse	Date	
5f	57.40	4	7-2	Firm	Palm Court Joe	Jly 4,	1977
5f	57.50	2	8-2	Firm	Arasong	May 16,	1994
7f 15y	86.00	6	9-0	Firm	Show of Hands	Apr 19,	1982
7f 15y	87.50	2	9-1	Fast	Mubdi (USA)	Oct 6,	1986
1m 16y	98.30	4	8-13	Firm	Churchillian	Jly 11,	1977
1m 16y	100.90	2	8-11	Fast	Trompe d'Oeil	Oct 6,	1986
1m 3f 32y	139.70	3	8-10	Firm	Old Court	Jly 4,	1977
1m 4f 31y	152.20	5	7-9	Good	Glengrigor	Apr 15,	1946
1m 7f 16y	190.40	3	8-0	Good	Cunningham	Spt 21,	1953

NEWBURY (Electric)

Distance	Time	Age	Weight	Going	Horse	Date	
5f 34y	59.80	3	8-12	Good	Minstrel's Gallery	Jun 18,	1955
5f 34y	60.60	2	8-7	Firm	Zuccherene	Jun 25,	1959
6f 8y	70.79	3	8-9	Fast	Dancing Dissident(USA)	May 19,	1989
6f 8y	71.61	2	8-6	Firm	Bright Crocus (USA)	Jun 10,	1982
7f	83.84	5	9-3	Good to firm	Celestial Key (USA)	Jun 15,	1995
7f	85.80	2	9-0	Fast	Pencader (IRE)	Aug 14,	1993
7f 64y	86.28	3	8-11	Good	Inchinor	Aug 3,	1993
7f 64y	88.81	2	8-10	Fast	Duty Time	Aug 14,	1993
1m	95.76	4	9-0	Fast	Emperor Jones (USA)	May 13,	1994
1m	99.65	2	8-11	Fast	Zinaad	Spt 20,	1991
1m 7y	94.91	3	8-9	Fast	Philidor	May 16,	1992
1m 7y	97.29	2	8-11	Firm	Master Willie	Oct 1,	1979
1m 1f	109.65	3	8-0	Good to firm	Holtye (IRE)	May 21,	1995
1m 2f 6y	122.00	3	8-9	Firm	Sudden Love (FR)	May 13,	1988
1m 3f 5y	137.51	4	9-0	Fast	Hateel	May 19,	1990
1m 4f 5y	149.20	4	8-9	Hard	Vidi Vici	Jun 21,	1951
1m 5f 61y	165.15	5	8-11	Fast	Endoli (USA)	May 16,	1992
2m	206.41	3	7-13	Good	Sunyboy	Spt 8,	1973

NEWCASTLE (Electric)

Distance	Time	Age	Weight	Going	Horse	Date	
5f	58.00	4	9-2	Fast	Princess Oberon (IRE)	Jly 23,	1994
5f	59.20	2	8-2	Good	Dunce Cap	Aug 6,	1962
6f	71.21	3	9-2	Good	Tadwin	Jun 30,	1990
6f	72.67	2	9-0	Firm	Sundance Kid (USA)	Oct 3,	1989
7f	83.53	3	8-5	Firm	Beaudelaire (USA)	Jly 23,	1983
7f	85.29	2	9-0	Fast	Erhaab (USA)	Aug 30,	1993
1m	98.96	3	8-12	Firm	Jacamar	Jly 27,	1989
1m	99.97	2	9-0	Firm	Laxey Bay	Oct 3,	1989
1m	103.20	5	9-5	Good	Somerton Boy (IRE)	May 24,	1995
1m 1f 9y	112.30	3	6-3	Good	Ferniehurst	Jun 23,	1936
1m 2f 32y	126.59	3	8-11	Fast	Missionary Ridge	Jun 29,	1990
1m 4f 93y	157.30	5	8-12	Firm	Retender (USA)	Jun 25,	1994
2m 19y	202.00	4	7-12	Good	Nectar II	Jun 23,	1937

NEWMARKET (Electric)

Distance	Time	Age	Weight	Going	Horse	Date	
5f	56.81	6	9-2	Fast	Lochsong	Apr 30,	1994
5f	58.78	2	8-13	Good	Clifton Charlie	Oct 4,	1990
5f	58.52	4	9-6	Fast	Ned's Bonanza	Jly 6,	1993
5f	58.52	2	8-10	Good	Seductress	Jly 10,	1990
6f	70.25	4	9-8	Good to firm	Lake Coniston (IRE)	Apr 18,	1995
6f	70.14	2	9-0	Good	Lycius (USA)	Oct 4,	1990
6f	69.82	4	9-6	Good	Cadeaux Genereux	Jly 13,	1989
6f	70.61	2	8-10	Fast	Mujtahid (USA)	Jly 11,	1990
7f	82.24	4	9-5	Fast	Perfolia (USA)	Oct 18,	1991
7f	83.45	2	9-0	Fast	Dr Devious (IRE)	Oct 18,	1991
7f	83.56	3	8-12	Good	Inchinor	Jun 26,	1993
7f	84.93	2	8-7	Firm	Sexton Blake	Jly 30,	1977
1m	95.08	3	9-0	Fast	Mister Baileys	Apr 30,	1994
1m	96.74	2	9-0	Fast	Bold Pursuit (IRE)	Oct 18,	1991
1m	96.80	4	9-7	Hard	Pink Flower	Jun 6,	1944
1m	99.58	2	8-6	Good	Rowlandsons Rocks	Aug 26,	1994
1m 1f	107.45	3	8-3	Firm	Sin Timon	Oct 1,	1977
1m 2f	121.04	3	8-10	Good	Palace Music (USA)	Oct 20,	1984
1m 2f	124.65	2	9-4	Good	Highland Chieftain	Nov 2,	1985
1m 2f	122.31	4	9-1	Fast	Vallance	Aug 1,	1992
1m 4f	147.67	3	8-5	Fast	Kiveton Kabooz	Oct 17,	1991
1m 4f	146.70	3	8-1	Fast	Desert Team (USA)	Jly 6,	1993
1m 6f	174.34	5	8-6	Fast	Tudor Island	Spt 30,	1994
1m 6f 175y	186.07	3	8-10	Fast	Spring to Action	Jly 8,	1993
2m	203.12	3	8-4	Fast	Kikam	Oct 2,	1991
2m 24y	204.32	5	10-0	Fast	Jack Button	Aug 5,	1994

NOTTINGHAM

Distance	Time	Age	Weight	Going	Horse	Date	
5f 13y	58.40	6	8-8	Good	Minstrel King	Mar 29,	1960
5f 13y	57.90	2	8-9	Firm	Hoh Magic	May 13,	1994
6f 15y	70.00	4	9-2	Firm	Ajanac	Aug 8,	1988
6f 15y	71.40	2	8-11	Firm	Jameelapi (USA)	Aug 8,	1983
1m 54y	99.60	4	8-2	Fast	Blake's Treasure	Spt 2,	1991
1m 54y	100.80	2	9-0	Fast	King's Loch (IRE)	Spt 3,	1991
1m 1f 213y	122.30	3	8-8	Firm	Ayaabi	Jly 21,	1984
1m 1f 213y	125.60	2	9-0	Firm	Al Salite	Oct 28,	1985
1m 6f 15y	177.80	3	8-10	Firm	Buster Jo	Oct 1,	1985
2m 9y	204.00	5	7-7	Firm	Fet	Oct 5,	1936
2m 2f 18y	235.10	9	9-10	Fast	Pearl Run	May 1,	1990

PONTEFRACT

Distance	Time	Age	Weight	Going	Horse	Date	
5f	61.10	5	7-7	Hard	Regal Bingo	Spt 29,	1971
5f	61.40	2	8-9	Fast	Breakaway	Aug 6,	1987
6f	72.60	3	7-13	Firm	Merry One	Aug 29,	1970
6f	74.00	2	9-3	Firm	Fawzi	Spt 6,	1983
1m 4y	101.40	5	8-12	Firm	Nevison's Lad	May 14,	1965
1m 4y	102.80	2	9-13	Firm	Star Spray	Spt 6,	1983
1m 2f 6y	126.20	4	7-8	Hard	Happy Hector	Jly 9,	1979
1m 2f 6y	135.50	2	8-3	Firm	One Cal	Oct 10,	1977
1m 4f 8y	154.30	4	8-9	Hard	Ezra	Jun 23,	1975
2m 1f 22y	222.10	3	9-2	Firm	Night Eye (USA)	Spt 6,	1983
2m 1f 216y	231.10	3	8-8	Firm	Kudz (USA)	Spt 9,	1986
2m 5f 122y	287.80	4	8-4	Firm	Physical (USA)	May 14,	1984

REDCAR

Distance	Time	Age	Weight	Going	Horse	Date	
5f	56.50	3	9-7	Firm	Nazela	Aug 10,	1990
5f	57.10	2	9-0	Firm	Selhurstpark Flyer (IRE)	Jly 8,	1993
6f	68.60	3	9-2	Fast	Sizzling Saga (IRE)	Jun 21,	1991
6f	69.80	2	8-11	Firm	Futuh (USA)	Aug 11,	1990
7f	82.10	3	8-2	Firm	Marston	Jly 25,	1978
7f	81.90	2	8-11	Firm	Nagwa	Spt 27,	1975
1m	94.80	5	8-12	Firm	Genair (FR)	Aug 11,	1990
1m	96.70	2	8-8	Fast	Carbonate	Spt 15,	1987
1m 1f	108.50	5	8-12	Firm	Mellottie	Jly 25,	1990
1m 1f	113.80	2	9-0	Good	Double Trigger (IRE)	Spt 25,	1993
1m 2f	121.50	3	9-3	Firm	Inaad	May 29,	1989
1m 3f	137.00	3	8-9	Firm	Photo Call	Aug 7,	1990
1m 5f 135y	174.60	6	9-10	Firm	Brodessa	Jun 20,	1992
1m 6f 19y	179.90	3	8-6	Firm	Trainglot	Jly 25,	1990
2m 4y	204.90	3	9-3	Fast	Subsonic (IRE)	Oct 8,	1991
2m 3f	250.20	5	7-4	Fast	Seldom In	Aug 9,	1991

RIPON

Distance	Time	Age	Weight	Going	Horse	Date	
5f	57.60	5	8-10	Good	Broadstairs Beauty (IRE)	May 21,	1995
5f	57.80	2	8-8	Firm	Super Rocky	Aug 5,	1991
6f	69.80	5	7-0	Firm	Quoit	Jly 23,	1966
6f	71.00	2	8-11	Fast	Colway Bold	Aug 26,	1991
1m	97.00	4	7-10	Firm	Crown Witness	Aug 25,	1980
1m	101.20	2	7-2	Good	Roanstreak	Spt 5,	1970
1m 1f	110.80	4	8-3	Firm	Tarda	Aug 5,	1991
1m 2f	122.70	3	9-4	Firm	Swift Sword	Jly 20,	1991
1m 4f 60y	152.20	6	8-7	Firm	Cholo	Spt 27,	1941
2m	206.60	5	9-12	Fast	Encore Une Fois (IRE)	Aug 30,	1994
2m 1f 203y	231.30	3	7-8	Firm	Beechwood Seeker	Spt 1,	1981

SALISBURY (Electric)

Distance	Time	Age	Weight	Going	Horse	Date	
5f	59.40	3	8-11	Firm	Bellsabanging	May 5,	1993
5f	59.89	2	8-11	Fast	Blue Tango	Jun 25,	1985
6f	71.54	4	8-7	Fast	Prince Sky	Jun 25,	1986
6f	72.41	2	9-1	Fast	Basma (USA)	Spt 6,	1991
6f 212y	85.38	3	8-12	Firm	Moon King (IRE)	Jun 28,	1995
6f 212y	85.97	2	9-0	Firm	More Royal (USA)	Jun 29,	1995
1m	98.94	5	8-10	Firm	Weaver Bird	Jun 29,	1995
1m	103.86	2	9-3	Firm	Carocrest	Spt 1,	1983
1m 1f 209y	124.46	4	7-7	Fast	Kala Nashan	Jun 25,	1986
1m 4f	152.35	3	9-0	Firm	Master Charlie	May 5,	1993
1m 6f	178.01	4	10-0	Fast	Dancing Affair	Aug 16,	1984

SANDOWN (Electric)

Distance	Time	Age	Weight	Going	Horse	Date	
5f 6y	59.24	3	8-6	Fast	Lyndseylee	Jly 25,	1990
5f 6y	59.48	2	9-3	Firm	Times Time	Jly 22,	1982
7f 16y	86.36	3	9-0	Firm	Mawsuff	Jun 14,	1986
7f 16y	88.15	2	9-1	Firm	Attempt	Aug 19,	1983
1m 14y	99.08	3	8-8	Firm	Linda's Fantasy	Aug 19,	1983
1m 14y	101.14	2	8-11	Firm	Reference Point	Spt 23,	1986
1m 1f	114.23	3	8-13	Firm	Lovealoch (IRE)	Aug 30,	1991
1m 1f	117.74	2	8-7	Firm	Marius (IRE)	Spt 15,	1992
1m 2f 7y	122.14	4	8-11	Firm	Kalaglow	May 31,	1982
1m 3f 91y	141.61	4	8-3	Fast	Aylesfield	Jly 7,	1984
1m 6f	178.85	3	9-2	Fast	Sun of Spring	Aug 11,	1993
2m 78y	209.93	6	9-2	Firm	Sadeem (USA)	May 29,	1989

SOUTHWELL

Distance	Time	Age	Weight	Going	Horse	Date	
5f	57.70	3	9-6	Standard	Case Law	Aug 15,	1990
5f	59.00	2	9-0	Standard	Muzz (IRE)	Dec 16,	1993
6f	73.30	3	9-2	Standard	Rambo Express	Dec 18,	1990
6f	73.90	2	9-0	Standard	Superstrike	Jly 31,	1991
6f	74.10	4	9-12	Fast	Miss Haggis	Jly 26,	1993
6f	76.10	2	9-0	Fast	Darren Boy (IRE)	Jun 24,	1993
7f	86.80	5	8-4	Standard	Amenable	Dec 13,	1990
7f	87.00	2	8-4	Standard	Rejoice (IRE)	Nov 30,	1990
7f	87.10	3	8-3	Firm	Orient Air	Aug 14,	1991
7f	89.20	2	9-0	Good	Blaze Away (USA)	Aug 6,	1993
1m	77.00	4	9-12	Standard	Bella Parkes	Mar 3,	1995
1m	98.00	2	8-9	Standard	Alpha Rascal	Nov 13,	1990
1m 3f	141.50	4	9-7	Standard	Tempering	Dec 5,	1990
1m 3f	141.90	3	8-5	Firm	Pims Gunner (IRE)	Aug 15,	1991
1m 4f	154.10	4	9-12	Standard	Fast Chick	Nov 8,	1989
1m 4f	154.40	5	9-3	Firm	Corn Lily	Aug 10,	1991
1m 5f	172.80	4	9-9	Standard	Vishnu (USA)	Jan 1,	1994
1m 6f	181.60	3	7-7	Standard	Qualitair Aviator	Dec 1,	1991
2m	214.10	5	9-1	Fast	Triplicate	Spt 20,	1991
2m	217.80	4	9-12	Standard	Megan's Flight	Dec 6,	1989
2m 2f	245.30	4	9-1	Standard	Ceciliano (USA)	Aug 16,	1990

THIRSK

Distance	Time	Age	Weight	Going	Horse	Date	
5f	56.90	4	8-6	Firm	Singing Star	Aug 3,	1990
5f	57.40	2	9-1	Firm	Nifty Fifty (IRE)	Jly 19,	1991
6f	69.60	3	8-10	Firm	Cedar Grange	Spt 3,	1977
6f	69.90	2	9-5	Firm	Daarik	Jly 29,	1989
7f	82.60	5	6-11	Firm	Tuanwun	May 29,	1970
7f	84.60	2	8-12	Firm	Man of Harlech	Aug 2,	1975
1m	94.80	4	8-13	Firm	Yearsley	May 5,	1990
1m	99.10	2	9-0	Fast	Wild Fire	Spt 7,	1991
1m 4f	150.00	4	8-2	Firm	Casting Vote	Aug 1,	1964
2m	202.30	3	8-11	Firm	Tomaschek (USA)	Jly 17,	1981

WARWICK

Distance	Time	Age	Weight	Going	Horse	Date	
5f	57.80	5	9-4	Fast	Another Episode (IRE)	Aug 29,	1994
5f	58.70	2	8-9	Fast	Curie Express (IRE)	Jun 29,	1994
6f	71.80	4	9-5	Firm	Pride of Kilmallock	Jly 1,	1960
6f	72.10	2	7-7	Firm	Sum Mede	Jly 14,	1989
7f	83.80	6	7-12	Hard	Blackshore	May 19,	1956
7f	84.80	2	9-4	Firm	Nocino	Jly 28,	1979
1m	96.00	3	9-0	Firm	Academic World(USA)	Aug 25,	1975
1m	97.50	2	9-3	Firm	Perfect Stranger	Oct 14,	1986
1m 2f 169y	133.20	3	8-8	Firm	Classic Tale	Jly 7,	1987
1m 4f 115y	157.20	5	8-12	Hard	Noirmont Buoy	Jun 19,	1967
1m 6f 194y	188.90	4	9-1	Firm	Chucklestone	Jly 7,	1987
2m 20y	205.80	4	9-7	Fast	Sanamar (disq)	Aug 29,	1988
2m 2f 214y	243.90	5	9-10	Fast	Fitzpatrick	Aug 27,	1984

WINDSOR

Distance	Time	Age	Weight	Going	Horse	Date	
5f 10y	59.20	3	9-7	Fast	La Tuerta	Jly 15,	1985
5f 10y	58.90	2	9-0	Firm	Strictly Private	Jly 22,	1974
5f 217y	70.10	3	8-4	Firm	Sweet Relief	Spt 11,	1978
5f 217y	69.00	2	8-7	Fast	Options Open	Jly 25,	1994
1m 67y	101.50	4	7-2	Firm	Blowing Bubbles	Jly 16,	1984
1m 2f 7y	123.00	3	9-1	Firm	Moomba Masquerade	May 19,	1980
1m 3f 135y	141.50	3	9-2	Firm	Double Florin (USA)	May 19,	1980

WOLVERHAMPTON

Distance	Time	Age	Weight	Going	Horse	Date
5f	60.50	7	8-7	Standard	Sir Tasker	Jan 4, 1995
5f	63.60	2	7-13	Standard	Rotherfield Park (IRE)	Nov 12, 1994
5f	61.20	4	9-7	Standard	Lord Sky	Feb 22, 1995
5f	63.60	2	8-0	Standard	Afisiak	May 4, 1995
6f	74.10	3	8-13	Standard	Little Ibnr	Dec 10, 1994
6f	75.30	2	8-13	Standard	Petomi	Oct 15, 1994
6f	73.80	4	9-12	Standard	White Sorrel	Mar 8, 1995
6f	75.30	2	8-6	Standard	Worldwide Elsie (USA)	Jun 2, 1995
7f	87.30	4	10-0	Standard	Rocketeer (IRE)	Jan 4, 1995
7f	89.40	2	8-5	Standard	Master Millfield (IRE)	Dec 27, 1994
7f	88.30	6	9-12	Standard	Mahool (USA)	Mar 1, 1995
7f	93.20	2	8-8	Standard	Multi Franchise	Jun 30, 1995
1m	158.40	5	8-13	Standard	Johns Act (USA)	Mar 8, 1995
1m 100y	111.00	4	9-7	Standard	Sweet Supposin (IRE)	Jun 24, 1995
1m 100y	108.60	3	9-0	Standard	Contrafire (IRE)	Jan 4, 1995
1m 100y	110.60	2	9-0	Standard	Upper Grosvenor	Dec 27, 1993
1m 100y	109.30	3	8-6	Standard	Allemande (IRE)	Mar 8, 1995
1m 1f 79y	119.30	12	9-6	Standard	Aitch N'Bee	Jan 4, 1995
1m 1f 79y	120.50	5	8-10	Standard	Kintwyn	Mar 1, 1995
1m 4f	158.40	3	8-2	Standard	New Inn	Nov 26, 1994
1m 4f	161.40	5	9-2	Standard	Pistols At Dawn (USA)	May 4, 1995
1m 6f 166y	191.30	4	8-11	Standard	Noufari (FR)	Jan 4, 1995
1m 6f 166y	200.80	4	9-7	Standard	Jaraab	May 13, 1995
2m 46y	219.30	4	9-6	Standard	Secret Serenade	Jan 18, 1995
2m 46y	220.20	6	8-3	Standard	Child Star (FR)	Apr 1, 1995

YARMOUTH

Distance	Time	Age	Weight	Going	Horse	Date
5f 43y	60.20	3	8-11	Fast	Charm Bird	Spt 15, 1988
5f 43y	60.90	2	8-8	Firm	Aberbevine	Jun 14, 1967
6f 3y	70.40	4	8-4	Good	Denikin	Jly 4, 1951
6f 3y	70.40	2	9-0	Fast	Lanchester	Aug 15, 1988
7f 3y	82.20	3	8-7	Fast	Cielamour (USA)	Spt 15, 1988
7f 3y	82.20	2	9-0	Fast	Warrshan (USA)	Spt 14, 1988
1m 3y	94.60	3	8-11	Firm	Bonne Etoile	Jun 27, 1995
1m 3y	94.40	2	8-11	Fast	Alderney	Spt 14, 1988
1m 2f 21y	124.20	3	8-1	Firm	On The Foan	Aug 17, 1983
1m 3f 101y	143.00	3	8-9	Firm	Rahil (IRE)	Jly 1, 1993
1m 6f 17y	177.80	3	8-2	Fast	Barakat	Jly 24, 1990
2m	211.80	4	8-13	Good	Edge of Darkness	Aug 30, 1993
2m 2f 51y	247.00	3	8-3	Good	Danger Baby	Jly 21, 1993

YORK (Electric)

Distance	Time	Age	Weight	Going	Horse	Date	
5f	56.16	3	9-3	Fast	Dayjur (USA)	Aug 23,	1990
5f	57.39	2	7-8	Firm	Lyric Fantasy (USA)	Aug 20,	1992
6f	68.82	4	9-4	Fast	Shalford (IRE)	May 14,	1992
6f	69.84	2	9-0	Fast	Sharp N' Early	Aug 17,	1988
6f 214y	81.82	5	8-12	Fast	Dune River	Jly 9,	1994
6f 214y	82.98	2	8-10	Fast	Options Open	Aug 16,	1994
7f 202y	95.12	5	8-7	Fast	Lap of Luxury	Aug 19,	1994
7f 202y	98.51	2	8-11	Fast	Bocatower (disq)	Oct 8,	1986
1m 205y	108.89	6	8-4	Fast	No Comebacks	Jun 10,	1994
1m 205y	112.43	2	8-1	Firm	Oral Evidence	Oct 6,	1988
1m 2f 85y	126.18	3	9-0	Firm	Erhaab (USA)	May 11,	1994
1m 3f 195y	145.79	3	9-0	Fast	Diminuendo (USA)	Aug 16,	1988
1m 5f 194y	172.92	5	8-9	Firm	Mountain Kingdom	May 18,	1989
1m 7f 195y	198.49	3	8-0	Fast	Dam Busters (USA)	Aug 16,	1988

FLAT SPEED FIGURES 1995

The following list, based on Raceform Standard Times, shows Speed Figures of 30 and upwards, returned on British and selected Irish tracks and French tracks. All the ratings are given at 9st after allowances for going and distance behind winners. Additional information in parentheses following the Speed Figure shows the distance of the race in furlongs, course, state of going and the date on which the figure was recorded. Going abbreviations are: Hd (hard); F (firm); Gf (good-to-firm); Gs (good-to-soft); G (good); S (soft); Hy (heavy).

TWO-YEAR-OLDS

Abundant 48 (6f,Kem,G,Spt 2)
Academy of Dance (IRE) 31 (7f,Lei,G,Oct 9)
Acharne 49 (8f,Asc,G,Spt 23)
Admiral Jones (IRE) 45 (5f,Goo,GF,Jly 27)
Aerleon Jane 40 (7f,Goo,GF,Aug 26)
Aethra (USA) 46 (8f,Yar,F,Oct 25)
Ageeb (IRE) 39 (7f,Fol,G,Oct 16)
Agnella (IRE) 35 (6f,Fol,G,Jun 7)
Ailesbury Hill (USA) 43 (6f,Nwb,F,Jun 29)
Air Wing 30 (5f,San,GS,Spt 12)
Akalim 42 (6f,Nwm,G,Jly 22)
Al Abraq (IRE) 48 (7f,Nwm,G,Spt 26)
Al Shafa 44 (7f,Nwb,GS,Oct 21)
Al's Alibi 39 (7f,Fol,G,Oct 16)
Alambar (IRE) 35 (7f,Lin,G,Oct 23)
Alamein (USA) 30 (7f,Chs,GF,Jly 30)
Alhaarth (IRE) 59 (7f,Nwm,GF,Oct 13)
Alhawa (USA) 42 (7f,Lin,G,Oct 23)
Ali-Royal (IRE) 45 (7f,War,GS,Oct 3)
Allied Forces (USA) 56 (7f,Goo,F,Jly 26)
Almaty (IRE) 58 (5f,Goo,G,Jly 28)
Almushtarak (IRE) 40 (6f,Bri,G,Spt 20)
Altamura (USA) 31 (8f,Not,GF,Oct 19)
Always Happy 45 (8f,Don,GF,Nov 4)

Alzanti 47 (7f,Chs,GS,Spt 20)
Amanita 38 (7f,Nwm,G,Spt 26)
Amaniy (USA) 47 (6f,Ayr,G,Spt 15)
Amaretto Bay (IRE) 58 (6f,Nwb,GS,Oct 21)
Amazing Bay 37 (5f,Goo,G,Jly 28)
Amber Fort 35 (6f,Nwm,GF,Spt 30)
Amoeba (IRE) 31 (5f,Edi,S,Nov 2)
Amy Leigh 43 (5f,Cat,GF,Oct 14)
Ancestral Jane 35 (6f,Ayr,F,Aug 17)
Angaar (IRE) 37 (5f,Lin,S,Spt 28)
Angel Chimes 36 (5f,Bev,G,Spt 13)
Anotheranniversary 41 (5f,San,G,Jly 7)
Anthelia 40 (6f,Red,F,Oct 12)
Antonias Melody 35 (5f,Don,GF,Nov 3)
Apache Len (USA) 38 (7f,Red,F,Oct 31)
Applaud (USA) 40 (5f,Asc,F,Jun 23)
Apple Musashi 47 (6f,Lin,S,Spt 28)
April The Eighth 51 (6f,Goo,GF,Jly 25)
Arajaan (USA) 48 (6f,Yor,G,Oct 4)
Arctic Romancer (IRE) 40 (6f,Lin,GF,Aug 24)
Arctic Zipper (USA) 37 (7f,Chs,GS,Spt 20)
Ashjar (USA) 43 (7f,Lin,G,Oct 23)
Astor Place (IRE) 40 (7f,Nwm,G,Spt 28)
Astuti (IRE) 53 (7f,Nwm,G,Spt 26)

Athenry 47 (8f,Nwm,G,Spt 26)
Atraf 44 (6f,Ayr,G,Spt 16)
Aussie 30 (8f,San,GF,Aug 25)
Awaamir 31 (7f,Nwm,GF,Oct 28)
Axford (USA) 38 (7f,Nwb,G,Jly 15)
Aztec Flyer (USA) 30 (6f,Ayr,G,Jly 17)
Babinda 42 (6f,Pon,G,Spt 21)
Babsy Babe 38 (5f,Ayr,G,Spt 15)
Backdrop (IRE) 37 (7f,Hay,S,Oct 1)
Bahamian Knight (CAN) 52 (6f,Asc,GF,Jun 22)
Baileys First (IRE) 34 (6f,Ayr,F,Aug 17)
Baize 45 (5f,War,GF,Jun 12)
Balladur (USA) 41 (7f,Lei,G,Oct 10)
Ballpoint 31 (7f,Lin,G,Oct 23)
Bearnaise (IRE) 35 (6f,Fol,GF,Nov 6)
Beas River (IRE) 51 (6f,Fol,G,Oct 16)
Beauchamp King 60 (8f,Asc,S,Oct 7)
Beautiful Ballad (IRE) 35 (6f,Yor,G,Oct 7)
Bedside Mail 44 (6f,Lin,GF,Jly 15)
Bee Health Boy 43 (6f,Hay,S,Spt 30)
Belana 31 (7½f,Bev,GF,Aug 9)
Believe Me 49 (8f,Nwm,GF,Oct 27)
Bells of Holland 38 (6f,Fol,G,Oct 16)
Benatom (USA) 33 (10f,Pon,GF,Oct 2)
Bewitching 30 (5f,San,G,Apr 28)
Bijou d'Inde 56 (8f,Asc,G,Spt 23)
Bint Salsabil (USA) 48 (7f,Nwm,GF,Aug 5)
Bint Shadayid (USA) 78 (8f,Asc,S,Spt 24)
Blue Adelaide 35 (6f,Fol,GF,Nov 6)
Blue Duster (USA) 71 (6f,Nwm,G,Spt 26)
Blue Iris 45 (6f,Fol,G,Oct 16)
Blue Suede Hoofs 37 (6f,Lei,F,Oct 24)
Bold Enough 33 (6f,Lei,S,Spt 18)
Bold Times 32 (6f,Chs,GF,Jly 30)
Bollin Joanne 32 (5f,Hay,G,Jun 10)
Bonarelli (IRE) 51 (8f,Goo,G,Spt 8)
Born A Lady 34 (5f,Edi,G,Spt 18)
Bosra Sham (USA) 85 (8f,Asc,S,Spt 24)
Brandon Magic 59 (7f,Nwb,GS,Oct 19)
Brandonville 38 (7f,Fol,G,Oct 16)
Branston Danni 30 (6f,Ayr,G,Spt 16)
Brecon 38 (7f,Nwb,GS,Oct 21)
Brighstone 41 (8f,Don,GF,Nov 3)
Bright Diamond 32 (7f,Nwb,GS,Oct 21)
Bright Heritage (IRE) 48 (8f,Asc,S,Oct 7)
Bright Water 52 (8f,Yar,F,Oct 25)
Brilliant Red 41 (7f,Nwb,GS,Spt 15)
Bullfinch 47 (7f,Yor,G,Oct 7)
Busy Flight 60 (7f,Nwb,GS,Oct 19)
Cabcharge Striker 43 (7f,Nwc,F,Jun 30)
Capilano Princess 32 (7f,Don,GF,Nov 4)
Capture The Moment 33 (5f,Nwm,GF,Apr 19)
Carburton 45 (7f,Hay,S,Oct 1)
Caricature (IRE) 43 (6f,Eps,G,Spt 6)

Carmentalia 44 (8f,Goo,G,Spt 30)
Castan (IRE) 34 (6f,Lin,GF,Jly 15)
Cayman Kai (IRE) 66 (5f,Don,GS,Spt 9)
Cebwob 45 (7f,Lei,F,Oct 23)
Censor 30 (8f,Not,GF,Oct 26)
Centre Stalls (IRE) 52 (7f,Nwb,GS,Oct 19)
Centurion 35 (5f,Nwm,GF,Apr 20)
Cerdan (USA) 39 (6f,Nwm,GF,Oct 27)
Chalamont (IRE) 51 (6f,Not,GS,Spt 19)
Champagne Prince 49 (7f,Chs,GF,Aug 19)
Charwelton 35 (6f,Goo,GF,Jly 29)
Chemcast 33 (5f,Fol,GF,Spt 7)
Chief Mouse 32 (8f,Nwm,G,Spt 26)
Circled (USA) 30 (7f,Hay,GS,Oct 11)
Ciserano (IRE) 33 (6f,Goo,GF,Jun 16)
Civil Liberty 31 (7f,Goo,F,Jly 28)
Classic Ballet (FR) 42 (8f,Edi,S,Nov 2)
Classic Eagle 52 (8f,Chp,S,Oct 17)
Classic Lover (IRE) 33 (8f,Yar,GF,Oct 18)
Classy Chief 50 (8f,Don,GF,Nov 4)
Clerkenwell (USA) 33 (8f,Don,GS,Spt 8)
Clincher Club 44 (6f,Don,GS,Spt 9)
Coldstream 39 (7f,Nwc,G,Aug 28)
Comic Fantasy (AUS) 52 (5f,San,GS,Spt 13)
Committal (IRE) 53 (8f,Nwm,G,Spt 26)
Consordino 46 (7f,Yar,G,Spt 12)
Cornish Snow (USA) 44 (6f,Asc,S,Oct 6)
Corporal Nym (USA) 42 (6f,Kem,GF,May 27)
Craignairn 44 (6f,Cat,GF,Oct 13)
Crazy Chief 39 (6f,Nwb,GS,Oct 19)
Creative Account (USA) 54 (6f,Nwm,GF,Spt 30)
Cross The Border 51 (5f,Sal,GF,Aug 17)
Crystal Falls (IRE) 44 (7f,Hay,S,Oct 1)
Cumbrian Maestro 30 (8f,Ayr,G,Spt 15)
D'naan (IRE) 41 (8f,Yar,GF,Oct 18)
Dabka Dancer 32 (7f,Yar,G,Spt 13)
Daily Risk 42 (7f,Nwb,GS,Oct 21)
Dance On A Cloud (USA) 37 (7f,Lei,F,Oct 23)
Dance Sequence (USA) 55 (6f,Nwm,G,Spt 26)
Dance of The Moon 39 (5f,Nwm,GF,Apr 19)
Dande Flyer 40 (5f,Don,GF,Nov 3)
Danehill Dancer (IRE) 53 (7f,Nwm,GF,Oct 13)
Danesman (IRE) 40 (8f,Yar,G,Spt 14)
Danish Circus (IRE) 35 (7f,Lei,F,Oct 23)
Dankeston (USA) 45 (7f,Red,GF,Aug 23)
Dark Deed (USA) 38 (6f,Yar,G,Spt 13)
Darling Flame 56 (6f,Nwb,F,Jun 29)
Dashing Blue 56 (6f,Yor,G,Oct 4)
Daunting Destiny 42 (8f,Red,F,Oct 31)
Dawawin (USA) 39 (7f,Don,GF,Oct 20)
Deadline Time (IRE) 50 (7f,Nwb,GS,Oct 21)
Defined Feature (IRE) 49 (6f,Kem,G,Spt 2)
Degree 31 (7½f,Bev,GF,Spt 13)
Depreciate 49 (6f,Chs,G,Jly 15)

Desert Boy (IRE) 45 (6f,Yor,GF,Aug 17)
Desert Cat (IRE) 41 (7f,Hay,S,Oct 1)
Desert Lynx (IRE) 30 (6f,Not,GS,Spt 19)
Desert Tiger 47 (6f,Don,GF,Spt 6)
Detachment (USA) 38 (7f,Sal,F,Jun 29)
Diamond Beach 37 (7f,Nwc,G,Spt 27)
Diego 32 (8f,San,GS,Spt 12)
Dil Dil 34 (6f,Lei,S,Spt 18)
Dimakya (USA) 39 (6f,Red,G,Spt 23)
Diminutive (USA) 40 (7f,Sal,GF,Aug 17)
Disallowed (IRE) 39 (8f,Ayr,G,Spt 15)
Dismissed (USA) 47 (6f,Ayr,G,Jly 17)
Do Not Disturb (USA) 45 (8½f,Eps,GS,Spt 19)
Doctor Bravious (IRE) 34 (7f,Red,F,Oct 31)
Domak Amaam (IRE) 43 (6f,Nwc,GF,Oct 30)
Domettes (IRE) 33 (7f,Nwm,GF,Oct 12)
Don Micheletto 51 (7f,Lei,G,Oct 10)
Double Agent 32 (7f,San,GF,Jly 8)
Double Diamond (IRE) 48 (7f,Don,GF,Nov 4)
Double Leaf 37 (7f,Kem,G,Spt 1)
Double Oscar (IRE) 40 (6f,Nwb,GF,Jun 15)
Double Point (IRE) 45 (6f,Chs,G,Jly 15)
Dovebrace 52 (6f,Asc,GF,Jun 20)
Dublin River (USA) 39 (6f,Yar,GF,Jly 16)
Dungeon Master (IRE) 31 (5f,Nwm,GF,Apr 19)
Dushyantor (USA) 37 (8f,Not,GF,Oct 19)
Dwingeloo (IRE) 44 (5f,Cat,GF,Oct 14)
East India (IRE) 39 (8f,Chp,GF,Aug 28)
Eastern Paradise 43 (6f,Bri,G,Spt 20)
Eastern Prophets 57 (6f,Kem,G,Spt 2)
Ela-Yie-Mou (IRE) 32 (8f,Nwm,G,Spt 26)
Elite Force (IRE) 36 (6f,Nwb,GS,Spt 16)
Elshabiba (USA) 47 (6f,Nwm,GF,Oct 28)
Emperegrine (USA) 36 (7f,Cat,G,Spt 16)
Energy Man 34 (8f,Nwm,G,Spt 26)
Erupt 37 (6f,Not,GF,Oct 26)
Eurobox Boy 35 (7f,Lin,G,Oct 23)
Even Top (IRE) 52 (7f,Nwm,G,Spt 29)
Evening Chime (USA) 37 (5f,Hay,G,Jun 10)
Exalted (IRE) 46 (8f,Don,GF,Oct 20)
Expensive Taste 46 (7f,Nwm,G,Spt 26)
Extra Hour (IRE) 32 (6f,Eps,G,Spt 6)
Fag End (IRE) 45 (7f,Nwm,GF,Spt 30)
Fairlight Down (USA) 37 (7f,Lei,G,Oct 9)
Farhana 36 (6f,Nwm,GF,Oct 27)
Faraway Waters 42 (7f,Nwm,G,Spt 26)
Fenna 44 (6f,Lin,S,Spt 28)
First Fiddler 49 (5f,Asc,GF,Jun 22)
First Maite 46 (5f,Bev,G,Spt 13)
Flame Valley (USA) 36 (7f,Yar,GF,Aug 3)
Fly Fishing (USA) 41 (8f,Edi,S,Nov 2)
Fly Tip (IRE) 37 (6f,Nwb,GS,Oct 19)
Flyfisher (IRE) 45 (10f,Bat,GF,Spt 25)
Flying Green (FR) 39 (7f,Nwm,G,Spt 26)

Flying North (IRE) 32 (6f,Nwm,GF,Jly 29)
Flying Squaw 42 (6f,Goo,GF,May 25)
Fond Embrace 35 (5f,Nwb,GS,Spt 16)
Foreign Judgement (USA) 30 (7f,Don,GF,Oct 20)
Forentia 45 (6f,Nwm,GF,Jly 29)
Forest Buck (USA) 44 (8f,Lei,G,Oct 10)
Forest Robin 38 (7f,Don,GF,Oct 20)
Fourdaned (IRE) 42 (7f,Don,GF,Oct 20)
Frances Mary 39 (5f,Edi,S,Nov 2)
Frezeliere 45 (7f,Asc,S,Oct 6)
Friendly Forester (USA) 37 (8f,Bat,Hd,Spt 4)
Gagajulu 36 (5f,Not,F,Jly 8)
Galapino 40 (5f,San,GF,Apr 29)
General Macarthur 39 (8f,Lei,F,Oct 24)
General Rose 31 (7f,Don,GF,Nov 4)
Generosa 32 (7f,Sal,GF,Aug 31)
Gentilhomme 45 (10f,Bat,GF,Spt 25)
Germano 50 (7f,Don,GF,Oct 20)
Gi La High 36 (5f,Not,F,Jly 8)
Glen Parker (IRE) 36 (7f,Lin,G,Oct 23)
Golden Pond (IRE) 30 (7f,Cat,GF,Oct 14)
Goodwood Rocket 35 (8f,Goo,G,Spt 30)
Gothenberg (IRE) 44 (6f,Yor,GF,Aug 16)
Greek Icon 44 (7f,Nwm,GF,Spt 30)
Green Barries 44 (6f,Don,GF,Nov 3)
Green Bentley (IRE) 35 (7f,Yar,G,Spt 12)
Green Charter 31 (7f,Red,F,Oct 12)
Ground Game 33 (7f,Cat,GF,Oct 13)
Gryada 48 (7f,Yar,GF,Aug 3)
Gymcrak Gem (IRE) 38 (5f,Bev,G,Spt 13)
Hal's Pal 32 (7f,Yar,G,Spt 13)
Half An Inch (IRE) 35 (7f,Bri,G,Spt 26)
Hamlet (IRE) 36 (7f,Nwm,G,Spt 26)
Hammerstein 53 (8f,Asc,G,Spt 23)
Hear The Music (IRE) 49 (5f,Nwm,GF,Apr 19)
Helicon (IRE) 55 (8f,Nwm,G,Spt 26)
Henry The Fifth 37 (8f,Don,GF,Nov 3)
Herodian (USA) 41 (6f,Nwb,GS,Oct 19)
Heron Island (IRE) 49 (8f,Don,GS,Spt 8)
Hidden Oasis 57 (7f,Chs,GS,Spt 20)
High Cut 30 (5f,Yor,GF,May 16)
High Note 31 (7f,Lei,G,Oct 9)
High Priority (IRE) 45 (5f,Yor,GF,Aug 16)
High Target (IRE) 43 (7f,Nwm,G,Spt 26)
Hilaala (USA) 48 (7f,Cat,GF,Oct 13)
His Excellence (USA) 42 (7f,Nwm,G,Spt 26)
Hoh Returns (IRE) 40 (6f,Yar,G,Spt 13)
Home Shopping 51 (6f,Ayr,G,Spt 15)
Honest Guest (IRE) 50 (7f,Nwm,G,Spt 26)
Hoofprints (IRE) 30 (8f,Don,GF,Nov 4)
Humourless 35 (8f,Lei,G,Oct 10)
Iamus 54 (8f,Yor,G,Oct 4)
Imp Express (IRE) 35 (5f,Rip,GF,May 31)
In The Band 37 (8f,Don,GF,Nov 4)

Incarvillea (USA) 50 (5f,Nwm,GF,Apr 19)
Inchrory 56 (8f,Hay,GS,Oct 11)
Inchyre 30 (7f,Nwm,G,Aug 25)
Indian Relative 47 (7f,Cat,GF,Oct 13)
Insatiable (IRE) 46 (7f,Nwc,G,Spt 27)
Insiyabi (USA) 48 (6f,Asc,S,Oct 6)
Intidab (USA) 30 (7f,Yor,GF,Aug 30)
Introducing 38 (8f,Yar,F,Oct 25)
Inverlochy 31 (6f,Nwm,GF,Oct 13)
Ironheart 31 (7f,Nwm,GF,Jly 11)
It's A Ripper 34 (6f,Fol,GF,Oct 16)
Jack Jennings 61 (8f,Asc,G,Spt 23)
Jackson Hill 34 (7f,Don,GF,Nov 3)
Jaleel 31 (6f,Nwm,GF,Spt 30)
Jamrat Jumairah (IRE) 31 (7f,Red,F,Oct 12)
Jarah (USA) 50 (7f,Asc,GF,Jly 21)
Jerry Cutrona (IRE) 30 (7f,Fol,GF,Nov 6)
Jezyah (USA) 33 (7f,Lin,G,Oct 23)
Jiyush 42 (8f,Lei,G,Oct 10)
Jo Mell 50 (8f,Yor,GF,Oct 5)
Johayro 48 (5f,Cat,GF,Oct 14)
Juicy 32 (8f,Ayr,G,Spt 16)
Just Ice 48 (6f,Kem,GF,Aug 2)
Kahir Almaydan (IRE) 61 (6f,Nwb,G,Jly 15)
Kala Sunrise 44 (8f,Pon,F,Oct 16)
Kalao Tua (IRE) 34 (6f,Yar,GF,Jly 16)
Kamari (USA) 34 (7f,Hay,S,Oct 1)
Kandavu 34 (6f,Nwb,GF,Jun 15)
Karisma (IRE) 37 (8f,Yor,G,Oct 7)
Kass Alhawa 36 (7f,Nwm,GF,Aug 4)
Kazimiera (IRE) 33 (5f,Hay,G,Spt 1)
Keepers Dawn (IRE) 37 (16f,Not,GS,Spt 11)
Keiko 32 (6f,Fol,S,Spt 27)
Key To A Million (IRE) 49 (7f,Yar,GF,Aug 3)
Kilvine 38 (7f,Goo,G,Jly 29)
King of Peru 59 (6f,Nwm,GF,Spt 30)
King of The East (IRE) 49 (6f,Don,GS,Spt 9)
Kings Harmony (IRE) 36 (6f,Fol,GF,Nov 6)
Kings Witness (USA) 48 (7f,Asc,GF,Jly 21)
Kirov Lady (IRE) 31 (7f,Kem,G,Spt 1)
Kiss Me Again (IRE) 36 (6f,Wnd,GF,Aug 14)
Kossolian 30 (5f,War,G,Apr 17)
Krystal Max (IRE) 35 (5f,Hay,GF,Aug 11)
Kuantan (USA) 51 (5f,Asc,F,Jun 23)
Kunucu (IRE) 34 (5f,Ayr,G,Spt 14)
L'Ami Louis (USA) 50 (6f,Kem,GF,May 27)
La Modiste 36 (7f,Nwm,GF,Spt 30)
La Volta 35 (8f,Don,GF,Nov 3)
Laafee 47 (6f,Nwm,GF,Oct 28)
Labeed (USA) 40 (8f,Red,F,Oct 12)
Lac Dessert (USA) 34 (7f,San,GF,Jly 20)
Lacryma Cristi (IRE) 34 (6f,Wnd,GF,Jly 10)
Lady Carla 42 (8f,Lei,F,Oct 24)
Lady Caroline Lamb (IRE) 34 (5f,Red,G,Spt 23)

Ladykirk 33 (8f,Ayr,G,Spt 16)
Lakeline Legend (IRE) 36 (8f,Lei,G,Oct 10)
Lancashire Legend 30 (6f,Eps,G,Spt 6)
Larghetto (IRE) 32 (6f,Ham,F,Aug 14)
Last But Not Least 31 (6f,Fol,GF,Nov 6)
Last Second (IRE) 39 (6f,Red,G,Spt 23)
Latin Reign (USA) 43 (8f,Chp,S,Oct 17)
Laughing Buccaneer 37 (7f,Nwb,GS,Oct 21)
Lay The Blame 39 (6f,Not,GF,Oct 26)
Lear Jet (USA) 41 (8f,Nwb,GS,Spt 15)
Legal Right (USA) 34 (7f,Nwm,G,Spt 28)
Leonine (IRE) 45 (6f,Yor,GF,Aug 17)
Like A Hawk (USA) 54 (8f,Don,G,Spt 7)
Lila Pedigo (IRE) 30 (6f,Cat,G,Jun 3)
Limerick Princess (IRE) 46 (5f,Rip,GF,May 31)
Line Dancer 46 (7f,Nwb,GF,Aug 11)
Literary Society (USA) 33 (5f,Bev,GF,Spt 13)
Little Noggins (IRE) 45 (5f,Nwm,G,Spt 28)
Little Pilgrim 39 (6f,Asc,S,Oct 6)
Lomberto 57 (7f,Nwb,GS,Oct 19)
Lonely Leader (IRE) 39 (8f,Don,GS,Spt 8)
Longing (USA) 37 (8f,Goo,G,Spt 8)
Lord of Men 51 (7f,Nwm,GF,Aug 4)
Los Alamos 33 (8f,Edi,S,Nov 2)
Love Bird (IRE) 33 (8f,Ayr,G,Spt 16)
Lovely Prospect 38 (7f,Fol,S,Spt 27)
Lucayan Prince (USA) 43 (5f,Nwm,GF,Apr 20)
Lucky Lionel (USA) 65 (5f,Don,GS,Spt 9)
Lucky Rabbit 30 (6f,Yor,GF,Aug 16)
Lunar Mist 57 (6f,Nwb,GS,Oct 21)
Lydhurst (USA) 34 (8f,Nwm,G,Spt 26)
Lyzia (IRE) 47 (6f,Nwb,F,Jun 29)
Ma Belle Poule 38 (6f,Not,GS,Spt 19)
Madame Steinlen 30 (7f,Nwm,GF,Oct 14)
Maggi For Margaret 33 (5f,Don,G,Jly 1)
Magic Mill (IRE) 44 (7f,Red,F,Oct 31)
Magic Ron 32 (10f,Bat,GF,Spt 25)
Maid For Baileys (IRE) 45 (8f,War,GS,Oct 3)
Maid For The Hills 43 (6f,Nwm,GF,Jly 1)
Majdak Jereeb (IRE) 35 (7f,Nwm,GF,Aug 4)
Major Dundee (IRE) 30 (7f,Kem,GF,Aug 16)
Major Quality 36 (6f,Don,GF,Nov 3)
Mallia 37 (5f,Rip,GS,Apr 5)
Mansab (USA) 30 (6f,Nwc,GF,Oct 30)
Maple Burl 30 (6f,Nwb,GS,Oct 19)
Marawis (USA) 36 (6f,Don,GF,Nov 3)
Marigliano (USA) 31 (7f,Don,GF,Nov 3)
Marjaana (IRE) 32 (7f,Yar,G,Spt 12)
Marjorie Rose (IRE) 34 (6f,Hay,GF,Jly 8)
Mark of Esteem (IRE) 45 (7f,Goo,F,Jly 28)
Marl 48 (5f,Nwb,G,May 19)
Martara (IRE) 36 (5f,Eps,GS,Spt 19)
Masehaab (IRE) 42 (6f,Nwb,GF,May 21)
Matiya (IRE) 71 (8f,Asc,S,Spt 24)

Mawwal (USA) 52 (7f,Don,G,Spt 7)
May Queen Megan 33 (6f,Fol,GF,Nov 6)
Mazeed (IRE) 42 (6f,Hay,GF,Aug 4)
Meldorf 32 (6f,Nwc,G,Spt 27)
Melt The Clouds (CAN) 36 (7f,Don,GF,Oct 20)
Mental Pressure 35 (8f,Ayr,G,Spt 16)
Meranti 31 (6f,Bri,G,Spt 20)
Mezzogiorno 55 (7f,Nwm,G,Spt 26)
Mick's Love (IRE) 47 (8f,Nwb,GS,Spt 15)
Middle East 30 (6f,Don,GS,Spt 9)
Midnight Blue 62 (6f,Asc,S,Oct 6)
Miletrian Refurb (IRE) 37 (5f,Bri,G,Spt 26)
Mimosa 31 (6f,Goo,S,Spt 30)
Min Alhawa (USA) 51 (6f,Nwb,F,Jun 29)
Mindrace 37 (6f,Lei,F,Oct 24)
Misky Bay 34 (8f,Don,GF,Nov 4)
Miss Bigwig 54 (5f,Eps,GS,Spt 19)
Miss Riviera 40 (6f,Don,GF,Nov 3)
Miss Universal (IRE) 38 (7f,Nwm,G,Spt 26)
Missile 46 (7f,Fol,S,Spt 27)
Missile Toe (IRE) 36 (6f,Nwm,GF,Spt 30)
Mister Joel 35 (6f,Hay,S,Spt 30)
Modern Day (USA) 45 (7f,Red,GF,Aug 23)
Mongol Warrior (USA) 30 (6f,Nwb,G,Jly 14)
Mons 72 (8f,Asc,G,Spt 23)
Montecristo 34 (8f,Chp,GF,Aug 28)
Moody's Cat (IRE) 34 (7f,Yor,GF,Jly 14)
More Royal (USA) 62 (8f,Asc,G,Spt 23)
More Than You Know (IRE) 38 (7f,Sal,GF,Aug 31)
Mr Speaker (IRE) 33 (6f,Lei,S,Spt 18)
Mubhij (IRE) 64 (5f,Don,GS,Spt 9)
Muhandam (IRE) 30 (6f,Cat,G,Spt 16)
Muhandis 32 (6f,Goo,S,Spt 30)
Muhtadi (IRE) 32 (8f,Ayr,G,Spt 16)
Munketh (USA) 44 (7f,Nwb,GF,Aug 12)
Mushahid (USA) 51 (8f,Goo,G,Spt 8)
Music Gold (IRE) 58 (5f,Don,GF,Nov 3)
Mutadarra (IRE) 42 (6f,Nwm,GF,Oct 13)
Mutamanni (USA) 59 (8f,Asc,S,Oct 6)
My Branch 64 (6f,Nwm,G,Spt 26)
My Mariam 44 (7f,Nwm,G,Spt 26)
My Melody Parkes 49 (6f,Yor,GF,Aug 17)
Myrtle 48 (8f,Don,G,Spt 7)
Mystic Knight 46 (8f,Nwm,GF,Oct 13)
Mystic Tempo (USA) 31 (6f,Ayr,G,Jly 15)
Mystic Times 31 (5f,Rip,GF,May 31)
Mystique Smile 41 (5f,Chs,GF,May 11)
Myttons Mistake 41 (8f,Chs,G,Jly 15)
Nador 36 (7f,Nwb,GS,Oct 19)
Naissant 32 (6f,Goo,GF,Jly 25)
Najiya 56 (6f,Nwm,G,Spt 26)
Najm Mubeen (IRE) 31 (8f,Lin,G,Spt 14)
Napoleon's Return 31 (5f,Bri,G,Spt 26)

Naseem Alsahar 33 (8f,Don,GF,Oct 20)
Navigate (USA) 44 (6f,Goo,G,Jun 9)
Ned Al Sheeba 35 (6f,Nwm,GF,Jly 29)
Needham Star (USA) 45 (7f,Nwb,GS,Oct 21)
Nellie North 30 (6f,Nwb,GS,Oct 21)
Night Parade (USA) 48 (5f,Chs,GF,May 10)
Night Watch (USA) 36 (8f,Pon,G,Spt 21)
Nikita's Star (IRE) 40 (8f,Red,F,Oct 12)
Nilgiri Hills (IRE) 51 (6f,Lei,S,Spt 18)
No Cliches 32 (8f,Don,GF,Spt 6)
No Monkey Nuts 46 (5f,Don,GF,Nov 3)
Northern Fleet 38 (6f,Nwm,GF,Oct 27)
Northern Judge 33 (6f,Asc,S,Oct 6)
Northern Soul (USA) 50 (8f,Don,GF,Nov 4)
Norwegian Blue (IRE) 39 (5f,Hay,G,Spt 1)
Nose No Bounds (IRE) 35 (8f,Yor,GF,Oct 5)
Nosey Native 42 (8f,Yar,GF,Oct 18)

Oberons Boy (IRE) 46 (6f,Kem,GF,May 27)
Oblomov 48 (7f,Nwc,GF,Oct 30)
Obsessive (USA) 52 (7f,Nwm,GF,Spt 30)
Ocean Grove (IRE) 37 (7f,Goo,GF,Aug 26)
Ocean Stream (IRE) 40 (6f,Nwm,GF,Oct 27)
Oh Whataknight 34 (5f,Ayr,G,Spt 15)
Old Hat (IRE) 40 (6f,Asc,S,Oct 6)
Oleana (IRE) 38 (7f,Nwb,GS,Oct 21)
Omara (USA) 35 (6f,Nwm,G,May 19)
Opening Chorus 35 (5f,Red,G,Spt 23)
Opera 36 (8f,Don,GF,Spt 6)
Oriel Lad 40 (7f,Chs,GS,Spt 20)
Orinoco River (USA) 45 (8f,Nwm,G,Spt 26)
Ortolan 42 (5f,Sal,GF,May 7)
Overruled (IRE) 35 (8f,Don,GF,Oct 20)
Pacific Grove 49 (7f,Nwb,GS,Oct 21)
Paint It Black 36 (7f,Sal,GF,Aug 17)
Palamon (USA) 46 (8f,Nwm,G,Spt 26)
Paloma Bay (IRE) 49 (6f,Asc,GF,Jun 22)
Papaha (FR) 50 (7f,Nwm,G,Spt 26)
Parrot Jungle (IRE) 37 (7f,Red,F,Aug 5)
Passion For Life 42 (5f,Eps,GF,Jun 9)
Persian Secret (FR) 42 (6f,Nwm,GF,Jly 1)
Petrefuz (IRE) 30 (8f,Red,F,Oct 12)
Pharmacy 51 (6f,Ayr,F,Aug 17)
Pivotal 59 (5f,Fol,GF,Nov 6)
Playmaker 42 (5f,Rip,GS,Apr 5)
Pleading 38 (6f,Nwb,GS,Oct 19)
Pleasant Surprise 39 (7$\frac{1}{2}$f,Bev,GF,Aug 9)
Please Suzanne 40 (6f,Asc,G,Spt 23)
Poetry (IRE) 30 (7f,Fol,G,Oct 16)
Polar Eclipse 37 (7f,Hay,GS,Oct 11)
Polar Prince (IRE) 39 (7f,Hay,G,Spt 23)
Polar Spirit 37 (8f,Nwm,GF,Oct 28)
Polaris Flight (USA) 59 (6f,Nwb,G,Jly 15)
Polish Bear (IRE) 41 (6f,Nwb,GS,Oct 21)

Polish Legion 39 (5f,Nwb,GF,Apr 21)
Polish Spring (IRE) 30 (6f,Nwm,GF,Spt 30)
Polly Golightly 51 (5f,Don,GF,Nov 3)
Polska (USA) 40 (6f,Asc,G,Spt 23)
Poly By Staufan (IRE) 32 (5f,Bri,G,Spt 26)
Pommard (IRE) 35 (7f,San,GF,Jun 16)
Power Don 34 (5f,Bri,G,Spt 26)
Power Game 34 (6f,Cat,GF,Oct 13)
Prancing 43 (5f,Bev,GF,Aug 10)
Prends Ca (IRE) 46 (7f,Asc,S,Oct 6)
Present Arms (USA) 30 (8f,Chp,S,Oct 17)
Pride of Brixton 36 (6f,Bri,G,Spt 20)
Prima Volta 47 (6f,Nwm,GF,Oct 12)
Prince Aslia 56 (5f,Eps,GF,Jun 9)
Prince of Florence (IRE) 47 (8f,Yar,GF,Oct 18)
Prince of My Heart 57 (8f,Yor,G,Oct 4)
Priolo Prima 44 (6f,Pon,G,Spt 21)
Private Song (USA) 34 (7f,Don,GF,Nov 3)
Projection (USA) 42 (6f,Nwm,GF,Oct 13)
Promptly (IRE) 33 (6f,Nwm,GF,Aug 26)
Prospector's Cove 38 (7f,Edi,S,Nov 2)
Proud Monk 51 (7f,Nwb,GS,Oct 21)
Quakers Field 57 (7f,Nwb,GS,Oct 19)
Quality (IRE) 44 (7f,Nwc,GF,Oct 30)
Queen's Insignia (USA) 31 (8f,Goo,G,Spt 30)
Queens Check 41 (5f,Edi,S,Nov 2)
Rabican (IRE) 40 (6f,Nwm,GF,Jly 29)
Raed 39 (6f,Goo,GF,Jly 29)
Raheen (USA) 41 (6f,Yor,GF,Aug 17)
Rambling Bear 57 (6f,Kem,G,Spt 2)
Rambo Delight 34 (5f,Goo,GF,Jly 27)
Ramooz (USA) 52 (7f,Nwb,GS,Spt 15)
Ramsey Hope 40 (6f,Rip,GF,Aug 19)
Rayner (IRE) 31 (7f,Lin,G,Oct 23)
React 44 (7f,Nwm,G,Spt 26)
Rebel County (IRE) 39 (6f,Lin,S,Spt 28)
Red Nose (IRE) 43 (6f,Kem,GF,Aug 2)
Red Nymph 34 (6f,Nwm,G,Jly 22)
Red River Valley 44 (6f,Thi,GF,Aug 25)
Red Robbo (CAN) 31 (7f,Yor,GF,Aug 30)
Red Stream (USA) 43 (7f,Chs,GS,Spt 20)
Regiment (IRE) 37 (7f,San,G,Jly 7)
Reinhardt (IRE) 38 (7f,Goo,F,Jly 28)
Repatriate (AUS) 37 (5f,Don,GF,Nov 3)
Repertory 39 (5f,Chs,GF,May 10)
Resounder (USA) 50 (6f,Yor,G,Oct 7)
Rhumba Dancer 43 (7f,Asc,S,Oct 6)
Ribot's Secret (IRE) 39 (6f,Asc,GF,Jly 22)
Rio Duvida 62 (7f,Nwm,G,Spt 26)
Rock Sharp 37 (7f,Chs,GS,Spt 20)
Rocky Oasis (USA) 31 (7f,Don,G,Spt 7)
Roseberry Avenue (IRE) 32 (8f,Lei,F,Oct 24)
Roses In The Snow (IRE) 40 (7f,Nwm,G,Spt 26)
Rouge Rancon (USA) 63 (8f,Asc,S,Spt 24)

Royal Applause 71 (6f,Nwm,G,Spt 28)
Royal Ceilidh (IRE) 31 (7f,Cat,GF,Oct 14)
Royal Jade 37 (6f,Hay,GF,Aug 5)
Royal Mark (IRE) 43 (7f,Nwm,G,Spt 26)
Rumpipumpy 48 (7f,Nwm,G,Spt 26)
Rusk 37 (8f,Yor,G,Oct 7)
Russian Music 42 (6f,Yor,GF,Aug 17)
Russian Revival (USA) 63 (6f,Asc,GF,Jun 20)
Ruznama (USA) 58 (7f,Nwm,GF,Spt 30)
Sabot 48 (6f,Don,GS,Spt 9)
Safio 41 (5f,Asc,F,Jun 23)
Salmis 43 (7f,Fol,S,Spt 27)
Salty Girl (IRE) 30 (8f,Ayr,G,Spt 16)
Samara (IRE) 34 (6f,Lei,F,Oct 23)
Samim (USA) 45 (8f,Yor,GF,Oct 5)
Santillana (USA) 50 (8f,Edi,S,Nov 2)
Sapiston 52 (8f,Nwm,G,Spt 26)
Sasuru 43 (8f,Nwb,GS,Spt 15)
Sava River (IRE) 43 (7f,Nwb,GS,Spt 15)
Scarlet Plume 39 (7f,Goo,GF,Aug 26)
School Boy 37 (6f,Fol,S,Spt 27)
Sea Dane 50 (6f,Asc,GF,Jun 20)
Sea Spray (IRE) 40 (7f,Kem,G,Spt 1)
Second Time Lucky (IRE) 51 (7f,Nwb,GS,Oct 21)
Secret Voucher 39 (5f,Red,G,Spt 23)
Seirenes 33 (6f,Asc,G,Spt 23)
Select Few 36 (8f,Goo,G,Spt 29)
Semper (IRE) 31 (7f,Yor,GF,Jly 15)
Sepoy (IRE) 44 (6f,Ham,G,Spt 24)
Serendipity (FR) 49 (8f,Don,GF,Nov 4)
Shaamit (IRE) 57 (8f,Don,GF,Nov 4)
Shaniko (IRE) 38 (6f,Don,GS,Spt 9)
Sharaf (IRE) 40 (8f,Chp,S,Oct 17)
Sharp Pearl 34 (6f,Don,GS,Spt 9)
Sharp Shuffle (IRE) 42 (8f,Nwm,GF,Oct 28)
Sharp Stock 35 (5f,Fol,G,Oct 16)
Shawanni 62 (8f,Asc,S,Spt 24)
She's My Love 42 (7f,Yar,GF,Aug 3)
Sheilana (IRE) 30 (6f,Not,GS,Spt 11)
Shemozzle (IRE) 32 (7f,Nwc,GF,Oct 30)
Shining Cloud 33 (5f,San,GF,Jun 16)
Shontaine 40 (6f,Nwc,GF,Jly 24)
Sihafi (USA) 38 (6f,Yor,G,Oct 4)
Sil Sila (IRE) 57 (7f,Nwb,GS,Oct 21)
Silk Masque (USA) 33 (6f,Goo,GF,Jly 25)
Silver Harrow 36 (6f,Fol,G,Oct 16)
Silver Prey (USA) 36 (7f,Nwb,GF,Aug 12)
Silver Wing (USA) 37 (8f,Yor,G,Oct 7)
Singing Patriarch (IRE) 45 (7f,Nwm,G,Spt 26)
Singoalla (IRE) 30 (7f,Fol,S,Spt 27)
Sketchbook 57 (7f,Nwb,GS,Oct 19)
Ski Academy (IRE) 47 (8f,Goo,G,Spt 8)
Skillington (USA) 50 (7f,Asc,GF,Jly 21)
Smilin N Wishin (USA) 46 (8f,Chp,S,Oct 17)

Smithereens 36 (5f,Fol,GF,Nov 6)
Society Magic (USA) 33 (8f,Yor,G,Oct 4)
Solar Crystal (IRE) 56 (8f,Don,G,Spt 7)
Some Horse (IRE) 58 (6f,Don,GS,Spt 9)
Songsheet 41 (5f,Lin,G,Oct 23)
Sonic Mail 32 (5f,Sal,GF,Aug 17)
Sorbie Tower (IRE) 34 (6f,War,GS,Oct 3)
South Salem (USA) 62 (6f,Asc,GF,Jun 20)
Sovereign's Crown (USA) 50 (6f,Nwb,GS,Spt 16)
Soviet Style (AUS) 51 (5f,Lin,GF,Aug 5)
Spillo 44 (8f,Nwm,G,Spt 26)
Spirito Libro (USA) 32 (7f,Sal,F,Aug 9)
Splicing 32 (5f,War,GF,Jun 12)
Spring Campaign (IRE) 40 (8f,Yor,G,Oct 4)
St Mawes (FR) 32 (7f,Sal,F,Aug 9)
Staffin 47 (7f,Nwm,GF,Aug 5)
Standown 37 (6f,Nwm,GF,Oct 12)
State Approval 38 (8f,Nwm,GF,Oct 28)
State Theatre (IRE) 40 (8f,Nwm,G,Spt 26)
State of Caution 31 (7f,Lei,G,Oct 10)
Stately Dancer 30 (6f,Lei,F,Oct 23)
Stellar Line (USA) 35 (7f,Hay,G,Spt 23)
Stop Play (IRE) 44 (6f,Nwm,GF,Oct 12)
Storm Trooper (USA) 58 (8f,Asc,S,Oct 7)
Story Line 31 (7f,Asc,GS,Spt 24)
Supanova (USA) 44 (6f,Nwm,G,Spt 26)
Supreme Power 45 (5f,Eps,GS,Spt 19)
Surtees 36 (6f,Bri,G,Spt 20)
Sweet Robin (IRE) 51 (8f,Don,GF,Aug 18)
Swift Fandango (USA) 36 (7f,Yor,GF,Jly 15)
Swift Maiden 34 (7f,Nwb,GS,Oct 21)
Swynford Dream 47 (5f,Nwm,G,Spt 28)
Sylva Paradise (IRE) 42 (6f,Fol,S,Spt 27)
Ta Rib (USA) 37 (7f,Nwm,G,Aug 25)
Tabriz 36 (7f,Nwm,G,Spt 26)
Tadeo 61 (5f,Lin,G,Oct 23)
Tagula (IRE) 58 (6f,Asc,GF,Jun 20)
Take A Left 54 (5f,Rip,GF,May 31)
Tamhid (USA) 40 (6f,Yar,GF,Oct 18)
Tamnia 59 (6f,Hay,GF,Jly 8)
Tapintime (USA) 33 (8f,Red,GF,Oct 12)
Tarf (USA) 57 (5f,Sal,GF,Aug 17)
Tarneem (USA) 43 (7f,Don,GF,Oct 20)
Tasdik 31 (7f,Lei,G,Oct 9)
Tasliya (USA) 42 (7f,Nwc,GF,Oct 30)
Taufan Boy 30 (7f,San,G,Jly 7)
Tawaaded (IRE) 33 (6f,Asc,S,Oct 6)
Tawafek (USA) 32 (8f,Lei,F,Oct 24)
Tawkil (USA) 50 (7f,Chs,GF,Aug 18)
Terdad (USA) 37 (8f,Nwb,GS,Spt 15)
Thai Morning 41 (5f,Red,G,Spt 23)
The Boozing Brief (USA) 31 (8f,Bri,G,Oct 1)
The Imps (IRE) 35 (6f,Hay,S,Spt 30)
The Man 43 (6f,Eps,G,Spt 6)

Thea (USA) 44 (8f,Don,GF,Nov 4)
Therhea (IRE) 39 (7f,Chs,GF,Aug 19)
Thordis 41 (6f,Lei,F,Oct 24)
Thracian 53 (6f,Not,GS,Spt 19)
Threesome (USA) 36 (7f,Nwm,GF,Aug 4)
Thrilling Day 57 (6f,Hay,GF,Jly 8)
Times of Times (IRE) 39 (6f,Red,F,Oct 24)
Tina's Ridge 32 (6f,Eps,GF,Aug 28)
Too Hasty 34 (6f,Ayr,G,Spt 16)
Traceability 39 (7f,Sal,F,Aug 9)
Trafalgar Lady (USA) 34 (6f,Goo,S,Spt 30)
Tria Kemata 51 (7f,Yor,G,Oct 7)
Tropical Dance (USA) 52 (6f,Chs,GF,Aug 18)
Truancy 41 (6f,Not,GF,Jun 21)
Tsamista 35 (6f,Bri,G,Spt 20)
Tumbleweed Ridge 61 (7f,Nwb,GS,Oct 19)
Unconditional Love (IRE) 46 (5f,Asc,GF,May 3)
Unsold 40 (6f,Nwm,GF,Spt 30)
Vanishing Point 46 (8f,Yar,GF,Oct 18)
Vax New Way 37 (5f,Red,G,Spt 23)
Vera's First (IRE) 37 (6f,Kem,GF,Aug 2)
Verulam (IRE) 35 (8f,Chp,GF,Aug 28)
Victoria Regia (IRE) 46 (6f,Yor,G,Oct 4)
Vilayet 40 (7f,Yor,GF,Jly 14)
Village King (IRE) 43 (8f,Don,GF,Nov 4)
Village Native (FR) 43 (6f,Fol,G,Nov 6)
Villeggiatura 30 (7f,Sal,F,Aug 9)
Vola Via (USA) 45 (7f,Nwm,G,Spt 26)
Wahiba Sands 35 (7f,Don,GF,Nov 3)
Warbrook 48 (8f,Pon,F,Oct 16)
Warming Trends 45 (6f,Lei,S,Spt 18)
Warning Reef 39 (7f,Nwb,GF,Aug 12)
Warning Time 45 (6f,Yor,G,Oct 7)
Warren Knight 31 (6f,Asc,S,Oct 6)
Wavey 34 (7¹/₂f,Bev,G,Spt 13)
Wee Hope (USA) 34 (16f,Not,GS,Spt 11)
Weet-A-Minute (IRE) 56 (8f,Pon,F,Oct 16)
Welcome Royale (IRE) 40 (8f,Red,F,Oct 12)
Welsh Mountain 40 (5f,San,GF,Apr 29)
Welville 32 (6f,Goo,G,Spt 8)
West Humble 31 (7f,War,GS,Oct 3)
Westcourt Magic 52 (6f,Thi,GF,Aug 25)
What Fun 38 (6f,Asc,GF,Jun 20)
Whicksey Perry 42 (5f,San,GS,May 30)
White Emir 54 (6f,Nwm,GF,Oct 12)
White Plains (IRE) 40 (6f,Fol,GF,Nov 6)
White Sea (IRE) 51 (7f,Nwb,GS,Oct 21)
White Whispers 44 (6f,Don,GF,Spt 6)
Whittle Rock 33 (6f,Chs,GF,Aug 18)
Wilawander 43 (7f,Nwm,GF,Aug 4)
Wild Rumour (IRE) 33 (7f,Nwb,GS,Spt 15)
Wildwood Flower 43 (6f,Lei,F,Oct 23)
Wilfull Lad (IRE) 31 (5f,Ham,F,Jly 29)
Willisa 38 (6f,Hay,GF,Jly 8)

Willow Dale (IRE) 44 (5f,Nwb,GS,Spt 16)
Windswept (IRE) 30 (5f,Sal,GF,Aug 17)
Winter Quarters (USA) 38 (7f,Goo,G,Spt 9)
Winter Romance 50 (7f,Lei,G,Oct 10)
Wisam 48 (6f,Goo,GF,Jly 27)
Witch of Fife (USA) 46 (7f,Nwm,GF,Aug 5)
Wood Magic 43 (7¹/₂f,Chs,GS,Spt 20)
Woodborough (USA) 60 (6f,Nwm,G,Spt 28)

World Premier 59 (6f,Asc,GF,Jun 22)
Worldwide Elsie (USA) 35 (7f,Fol,GF,Nov 6)
Yarob (IRE) 47 (7f,Nwb,GF,Aug 11)
Zalotti (IRE) 37 (5f,Ayr,GF,Jun 3)
Zdenka 33 (7f,Fol,S,Spt 27)
Zelzelah (USA) 44 (8f,Asc,S,Spt 24)
Zuhair 41 (6f,Nwm,GF,Jly 12)

TWO-YEAR-OLDS - Sand

Agent 42 (6f,Sou,Std,Nov 20)
Arctic Romancer (IRE) 37 (6f,Lin,Std,Nov 14)
Ballymoney (IRE) 41 (6f,Sou,Std,Nov 20)
Catch The Lights 32 (8f,Lin,Std,Nov 14)
Charlie Chang (IRE) 35 (8f,Lin,Std,Nov 14)
Charterhouse Xpres 32 (6f,Wol,Std,Jly 22)
Coyote Bluff(IRE) 32 (6f,Wol,Std,Oct 14)
Double Diamond (IRE) 44 (7f,Sou,Std,Nov 16)
Fog City 39 (6f,Wol,Std,Oct 28)
Forest Boy 36 (6f,Wol,Std,Spt 30)
Fran Godfrey 31 (8f,Lin,Std,Nov 8)
Galine 37 (5f,Sou,Std,Nov 24)
Indian Relative 31 (6f,Wol,Std,Oct 28)
Itsinthepost 35 (6f,Lin,Std,Nov 14)
Jack Jennings 30 (7f,Sou,Std,Jly 13)
Kind of Light 41 (7f,Sou,Std,Nov 16)
Kings Harmony (IRE) 44 (6f,Sou,Std,Nov 20)
Krystal Max (IRE) 36 (5f,Sou,Std,Dec 1)
Lionel Edwards (IRE) 30 (7f,Sou,Std,Spt 4)
Mask Flower (USA) 31 (5f,Sou,Std,Nov 24)

Milton 30 (8f,Lin,Std,Nov 14)
Nose No Bounds (IRE) 33 (7f,Sou,Std,Spt 4)
Oberon's Dart (IRE) 35 (6f,Sou,Std,Nov 20)
Oblomov 35 (8f,Lin,Std,Nov 10)
Quality (IRE) 43 (8f,Sou,Std,Nov 20)
Red Acuisle (IRE) 32 (6f,Lin,Std,Nov 8)
Roman Gold (IRE) 47 (8f,Sou,Std,Nov 20)
Scathebury 38 (6f,Wol,Std,Jun 2)
Steamroller Stanly 31 (8f,Lin,Std,Nov 8)
Sweet Nature (IRE) 45 (6f,Wol,Std,Spt 30)
Sweet Wilhelmina 36 (8f,Lin,Std,Nov 30)
Tallulah Belle 30 (6f,Wol,Std,Spt 30)
Taufan Boy 36 (7f,Sou,Std,Spt 4)
Thordis 42 (6f,Wol,Std,Spt 30)
Tissue of Lies (USA) 33 (8f,Lin,Std,Nov 14)
Ultra Barley 41 (6f,Wol,Std,Oct 14)
Vera's First (IRE) 30 (7f,Sou,Std,Nov 16)
Wire Act (USA) 38 (6f,Wol,Std,Spt 30)
Wood Magic 31 (7f,Sou,Std,Spt 4)
Worldwide Elsie (USA) 42 (8¹/₂f,Wol,Std,Nov 13)

THREE-YEAR-OLDS AND UPWARDS

A Million to One (IRE) 50 (7f,War,GF,Jun 12)
A la Carte (IRE) 70 (8f,Asc,GF,Jun 21)
Able Choice (IRE) 36 (10f,Pon,G,Jun 12)
Able Sheriff 31 (5f,Nwm,GF,Spt 28)
Above the Cut (USA) 58 (8f,Yor,GF,Jly 14)
Absolute Magic 54 (7f,Chs,G,Jly 15)
Absolutely Fayre 57 (10f,San,G,May 29)
Abu Simbel (USA) 68 (8f,Yor,G,May 18)
Academy Life 46 (7f,Nwb,GF,Apr 21)
Access Adventurer (IRE) 66 (10f,Nwm,GF,May 7)
Achilles Heel 40 (12f,Don,G,Mar 23)
Ack's Again 53 (14f,Red,GF,Aug 27)
Acquittal (IRE) 38 (12f,Edi,GF,Aug 24)
Acting Brave 36 (12f,Nwm,GF,Oct 12)
Action Jackson 42 (8f,Nwm,GF,Jun 23)
Actual Fact (USA) 44 (6f,Kem,GF,May 27)
Adaloaldo (USA) 32 (12f,Cat,GF,Oct 14)
Adjareli (IRE) 72 (8f,Asc,GF,Jun 20)

Adjmal (IRE) 64 (6f,Asc,GF,Jun 22)
Admiral's Well (IRE) 70 (20f,Asc,GF,Jun 22)
Admirals Flame (IRE) 63 (8f,Red,F,Oct 12)
Admirals Secret (USA) 58 (11¹/₂f,Wnd,GF,Jly 24)
Adolescence (IRE) 71 (10¹/₂f,Hay,G,Jun 10)
Advance East 35 (12f,Pon,G,May 26)
Aeroking (USA) 66 (10f,San,GF,Jun 16)
Affidavit (USA) 69 (14¹/₂f,Don,GS,Spt 9)
African Chimes 57 (7f,Thi,GF,Apr 21)
African-Pard (IRE) 41 (8f,Chp,GF,Jly 13)
Afsaat 50 (8f,Rip,GF,Aug 19)
Agoer 34 (7f,Yar,F,Oct 25)
Agwa 63 (5f,San,GF,Jly 19)
Ahjay 41 (7f,Yar,F,Oct 25)
Ahla 59 (13f,Ayr,G,Spt 16)
Air Command (BAR) 37 (10¹/₂f,Hay,GS,Jun 9)
Air Commodore (IRE) 74 (8f,Bat,F,Jly 1)
Airport (USA) 78 (8f,Nwm,G,Spt 28)

Aitch N'Bee 44 (8f,War,F,May 8)
Akil (IRE) 76 (8f,Yor,G,Oct 4)
Al Nufooth (IRE) 32 (6f,Kem,GF,Apr 17)
Al Rawda (FR) 48 (6f,Kem,GF,May 8)
Al Safeer (IRE) 31 (10f,Sal,GF,May 7)
Al Widyan (IRE) 72 (12f,Don,GF,Nov 4)
Al Wujud (IRE) 57 (6f,Nwm,GF,Aug 4)
Alabang 40 (10f,Don,GF,May 9)
Alami (USA) 73 (7f,Nwm,GF,Apr 19)
Alanar (USA) 54 (10f,Don,G,May 27)
Alanees 65 (8f,San,G,Apr 28)
Alaraby (IRE) 53 (14f,Nwm,GF,Oct 13)
Alarming 45 (7f,Sal,G,Jly 27)
Alcian Blue 33 (18f,Pon,F,Oct 16)
Aldaneh 52 (8f,Lei,F,Oct 24)
Aldevonie 46 (8f,Chp,G,May 29)
Alessia 45 (10f,Nwm,GF,May 7)
Alfaaselah (GER) 32 (10f,Nwm,GF,May 7)
Aljawab (USA) 54 (10f,Not,GS,Spt 19)
Aljaz 50 (6f,Ham,Hy,Mar 31)
Aljazzaf 83 (10½f,Yor,GF,Aug 16)
Alkateb 67 (10f,Nwm,G,Spt 29)
All The Time 48 (7f,Nwb,GF,Apr 21)
All Time Great 56 (7f,Nwb,GF,Apr 21)
All the Joys 39 (12f,Nwm,GF,Oct 27)
Allemande (IRE) 70 (7f,Nwb,G,Jly 14)
Allesca 48 (11½f,San,GF,Jun 16)
Allez Cyrano (IRE) 51 (8f,Goo,F,Jly 27)
Allinson's Mate (IRE) 60 (7½f,Chs,GF,Aug 19)
Allmosa 32 (17f,Bat,G,Jun 2)
Allthruthenight (IRE) 61 (6f,Eps,GF,Jly 5)
Alltime Dancer (IRE) 32 (8f,San,GF,Jly 19)
Allwight Then (IRE) 43 (5f,War,F,Jly 7)
Allyana (IRE) 61 (5f,Nwm,G,Spt 28)
Almapa 33 (7f,Sal,G,May 18)
Almasi (IRE) 37 (6f,Wnd,GF,Jly 17)
Almizaj 37 (8f,Kem,GF,May 8)
Almond Rock 53 (8f,Sal,G,Jly 27)
Almuhimm (USA) 44 (10f,Nwb,GS,Oct 19)
Almuhtaram 44 (10f,Red,F,Oct 24)
Alriffa 67 (10f,Wnd,G,Aug 26)
Alusha 32 (10f,Sal,F,Aug 9)
Always Aloof (USA) 68 (16f,Kem,GF,Apr 17)
Alzianah 89 (6f,Asc,F,Jun 23)
Amanah (USA) 53 (8f,Rip,GS,Apr 5)
Amancio (USA) 67 (12f,Eps,GF,Jun 11)
Amrak Ajeeb (IRE) 63 (10½f,Hay,GF,Aug 4)
Amron 50 (6f,Don,GF,Mar 25)
Anam 53 (7f,Kem,G,Jun 3)
Anchor Clever 69 (14½f,Don,GS,Spt 9)
Anchorena 36 (11½f,San,GF,Aug 30)
Anegre (IRE) 34 (7f,Sal,G,May 18)
Angus-G 31 (8f,Pon,GF,Oct 2)
Anita's Contessa (IRE) 32 (7f,Fol,G,Oct 16)

Anjou 37 (12f,Cat,GF,Oct 13)
Anlace 40 (10f,Wnd,GF,Jly 10)
Ann's Pearl (IRE) 56 (5f,Chs,GF,Aug 19)
Anna of Brunswick 45 (11½f,Yar,G,Jly 18)
Anna-Jane 42 (7f,Kem,GF,Spt 1)
Anne D'Autriche (IRE) 41 (11½f,Yar,GF,Aug 3)
Annie Fay (IRE) 31 (6f,Yar,G,Jun 7)
Anniversarypresent 70 (7f,Nwm,GF,Jly 13)
Annus Mirabilis (FR) 84 (10½f,Yor,G,May 17)
Anonym (IRE) 46 (7f,Don,F,Jly 27)
Another Batchworth 37 (7f,Lin,F,Spt 5)
Another Fiddle (IRE) 55 (8f,Goo,G,Spt 8)
Another Jade 59 (6f,Bri,F,Jun 1)
Another Time 55 (10f,Red,F,Oct 24)
Ansellman 62 (5f,Nwm,GF,Aug 26)
Antartictern (USA) 33 (10f,Red,G,Spt 23)
Anzio (IRE) 56 (6f,Red,F,Oct 31)
Aoife Alainn (IRE) 37 (7f,Nwb,GF,May 20)
Apollono 54 (8½f,Eps,GF,Aug 28)
Aqaarid (USA) 68 (8f,Nwm,GF,May 7)
Aqua Rigia (IRE) 34 (10f,Bat,Hd,Aug 18)
Aquado 38 (5f,Ham,GF,May 20)
Araboybill 43 (10f,Bri,F,Aug 23)
Arabride 55 (8f,Asc,F,Jun 24)
Aragrove 66 (6f,Goo,G,Jly 28)
Arasong 38 (6f,Pon,GF,Aug 22)
Arc Bright (IRE) 34 (16f,Not,GF,Aug 2)
Arc Lamp 31 (6f,Leo,G,Aug 23)
Arcatura 40 (8f,Goo,G,Spt 8)
Arctic Charmer (USA) 40 (15f,Ayr,GF,Aug 5)
Arctic Thunder (USA) 75 (12f,Yor,GF,May 16)
Argyle Cavalier (IRE) 63 (13f,Ham,F,Jun 14)
Arian Spirit (IRE) 32 (16f,Red,GF,Jun 13)
Arndilly 59 (8f,Bat,GF,Jun 17)
Art Form (USA) 55 (20f,Asc,GF,Jun 20)
Art Tatum 30 (12f,Fol,GF,Apr 25)
Art of War 59 (6f,Ham,G,Spt 25)
Artful Dane (IRE) 48 (8f,Kem,GF,Jly 12)
Artic Courier 67 (12f,Eps,GF,Jun 10)
Arzani (USA) 45 (10f,Kem,GF,May 27)
As You Like It (USA) 40 (10f,San,GF,Aug 9)
Ashdren 40 (7f,Red,G,May 29)
Ashgore 31 (7f,Nwc,G,Aug 28)
Ashkernazy (IRE) 35 (5f,Not,GF,Aug 2)
Ashover 47 (12f,Yor,GF,Oct 5)
Ashtina 62 (5f,Eps,GF,Spt 6)
Askern 63 (10½f,Hay,GF,Aug 11)
Assessor (IRE) 57 (16f,Nwm,GF,Spt 30)
Assumpsit (IRE) 32 (6f,Goo,GF,May 25)
Asterita 61 (12f,Eps,GF,Jun 9)
Asterix 43 (8f,Chp,GF,Jly 4)
Astrac (IRE) 83 (6f,Asc,F,Jun 23)
Astral Invader (IRE) 40 (8f,Lei,GF,Apr 29)
Astral Weeks (IRE) 42 (8f,Lei,GF,May 29)

Astrolabe 46 (12f,Chs,GF,May 10)
Aswaat (IRE) 45 (7f,Red,G,Spt 23)
At Liberty (IRE) 64 (12f,Asc,GF,Jun 22)
At the Savoy (IRE) 35 (8f,Thi,GF,Aug 7)
Atlaal (USA) 43 (8f,Hay,G,Spt 22)
Atours (USA) 35 (16f,Nwb,GF,Aug 11)
Atticus (USA) 79 (8f,Asc,GF,Jun 20)
Audrey Grace 32 (8f,Yar,GF,Spt 14)
Augustan 51 (12f,Yor,GF,Aug 17)
Autumn Affair 67 (8f,Asc,S,Oct 6)
Autumn Cover 32 (8f,Nwm,GF,Jun 23)
Autumn Wings (FR) 38 (12f,Hay,GS,Oct 11)
Averti (IRE) 74 (5f,Lin,GF,Aug 24)
Avignon (IRE) 58 (10f,Don,G,Spt 6)
Avishayes (USA) 43 (8f,Nwm,GF,Aug 5)
Awayil (USA) 58 (6f,Yar,G,Spt 12)
Awesome Venture 50 (7f,Yar,F,Jun 27)
Axeman (IRE) 51 (7f,Nwm,GF,Apr 18)
Ayunli 55 (12f,Nwm,GF,Oct 27)
Azdihaar (USA) 45 (7f,Sal,F,Aug 10)
Baaderah (IRE) 57 (6f,Nwm,GS,Jun 3)
Backgammon 49 (12f,Kem,GF,Apr 15)
Backview 44 (10f,Bat,GF,May 22)
Baddi Quest 35 (11½f,Yar,G,Jly 18)
Bag of Tricks (IRE) 39 (12f,Fol,F,Jun 30)
Bagshot 61 (8f,Nwb,GF,May 21)
Bahamian Sunshine (USA) 70 (14f,Hay,G,Spt 22)
Bahith (USA) 57 (6f,Don,GF,Jly 26)
Bahri (USA) 95 (8f,Asc,G,Spt 23)
Baileys Sunset (IRE) 41 (5f,Nwm,G,Spt 28)
Bajan (IRE) 55 (10f,Yar,GF,Jly 6)
Bajan Rose 59 (5f,Nwm,G,Spt 28)
Bakers' Gate (USA) 39 (8f,Don,GF,May 9)
Bal Harbour 74 (12f,Asc,F,Jun 23)
Balance of Power 51 (6f,Fol,G,Oct 16)
Balanchine (USA) 83 (10f,Asc,GF,Jun 20)
Balasara (IRE) 62 (8f,Nwb,GF,Jun 15)
Ball Gown 60 (12f,Eps,GF,Jun 10)
Ballard Ring (IRE) 45 (7½f,Bev,GF,Apr 7)
Balliol Boy 58 (10f,San,GF,Apr 29)
Ballykett Nancy (IRE) 38 (12f,Asc,GS,Spt 24)
Ballymac Girl 44 (14f,Hay,S,Spt 30)
Baltic Raider 57 (10f,Kem,GF,Apr 15)
Bambara 47 (11½f,Chs,GF,May 10)
Banadam (USA) 40 (8f,Nwm,GF,May 7)
Band on the Run 70 (7f,Hay,G,Spt 2)
Bang in Trouble (IRE) 41 (17½f,Ayr,G,Spt 15)
Bangles 59 (5f,Sal,GF,Aug 31)
Banner (USA) 47 (6f,Cat,GF,Jly 19)
Barato 56 (6f,Red,G,Spt 23)
Barbaroja 62 (10½f,Yor,G,May 18)
Bardolph (USA) 55 (16f,Lin,Std,Aug 5)
Bardon Hill Boy (IRE) 53 (10f,Don,GS,Spt 9)
Barford Lad 53 (10f,Don,GF,May 9)

Barford Sovereign 38 (10f,Bev,GF,May 23)
Bargash 51 (6f,War,GF,Jly 15)
Baron Ferdinand 80 (10½f,Hay,GF,Aug 5)
Barossa Valley (IRE) 56 (5f,Nwb,F,Jun 29)
Barranak (IRE) 52 (5f,San,G,Spt 12)
Barrel of Hope 49 (7f,Yor,G,Oct 7)
Barti-Ddu 46 (12f,Chs,GF,May 11)
Barton Heights 30 (10f,Red,F,Aug 5)
Bashful Brave 54 (5f,Eps,G,Jly 26)
Bassmaat (USA) 51 (7½f,Chs,GF,Aug 19)
Bataan (USA) 45 (10f,Not,GF,May 2)
Batabanoo 68 (14f,Red,GF,Aug 27)
Battery Boy 30 (12½f,Nwc,GF,Apr 17)
Battle Colours (IRE) 47 (8f,Rip,GF,Jly 22)
Battleship Bruce 43 (8f,Asc,GF,May 3)
Bawader (USA) 49 (6f,Asc,F,Jun 23)
Bay of Islands 42 (10½f,Yor,GF,Aug 30)
Baydur (IRE) 47 (8f,Asc,GF,Jun 21)
Bayin (USA) 43 (6f,Yor,GF,Jun 17)
Bayrak (USA) 63 (12f,Thi,G,Jun 5)
Be Mindful 65 (7f,Nwm,GF,Apr 19)
Be Warned 61 (6f,Hay,GS,Oct 11)
Bean King 59 (16f,Nwb,GS,Oct 19)
Bearall (IRE) 38 (12f,Eps,GF,Jun 9)
Beau Matelot 32 (10f,Red,F,May 15)
Beau Venture (USA) 62 (5f,Hay,GF,Aug 5)
Beauchamp Hero 82 (12f,Asc,F,Jun 23)
Beauchamp Jade 53 (12f,Don,GF,Nov 4)
Beauchamp Jazz 70 (8f,Asc,GF,Jun 20)
Beauman 51 (10½f,Hay,GS,Jun 9)
Beaumont (IRE) 43 (10½f,Hay,G,Jun 10)
Beautete 42 (12f,Bri,G,Apr 6)
Bedevil (USA) 42 (16f,Nwc,G,May 25)
Bedivere (USA) 64 (8f,Asc,GF,Jun 23)
Bedouin Invader 46 (7f,Lin,F,Spt 5)
Bee Dee Best (IRE) 37 (6f,War,F,May 8)
Behaviour 70 (8f,Yor,GF,Aug 17)
Belfry Green (IRE) 75 (7f,Asc,GF,May 3)
Bella Parkes 40 (7f,Thi,GF,Apr 21)
Bellara 40 (14f,Not,GF,Aug 21)
Bellas Gate Boy 40 (8f,Kem,G,Jun 3)
Bellateena 33 (10f,Rip,G,Aug 28)
Belleminette (IRE) 40 (7f,Kem,GF,Aug 16)
Bells of Longwick 30 (6f,Hay,GS,Oct 11)
Ben Gunn 51 (7f,Goo,F,Jly 28)
Bencher Q C (USA) 66 (12f,Don,GS,Spt 8)
Bend Wavy (IRE) 42 (8f,Yar,GF,Oct 18)
Benfleet 77 (16f,Asc,G,Spt 23)
Benjamins Law 35 (14f,Hay,G,Spt 23)
Bentico 59 (8f,Lei,G,Oct 9)
Benzoe (IRE) 72 (6f,Thi,GF,Jly 28)
Bequeath 47 (10f,Sean,GF,Jun 16)
Berge (IRE) 48 (6f,Thi,GF,Apr 21)
Berkeley Bounder (USA) 44 (12f,Lei,G,Oct 10)

Bernard Seven (IRE) 66 (8f,Rip,GF,May 31)
Best Kept Secret 49 (7f,Red,G,May 29)
Best of All (IRE) 60 (8f,Edi,S,Nov 2)
Best of Bold 36 (8f,Lei,GF,May 30)
Better Offer (IRE) 68 (12f,Hay,G,Spt 2)
Bettergeton 64 (8f,Yor,GF,Aug 17)
Beware of Agents 36 (7f,Lei,G,Apr 6)
Bibliotheque (USA) 43 (8f,Yar,G,Spt 14)
Bide Our Time (USA) 42 (7f,Nwb,GF,Jun 15)
Big Pat 52 (12f,Asc,GF,Aug 23)
Big Treat (IRE) 30 (10f,San,GS,Spt 13)
Billy Bushwacker 62 (8f,Yor,GF,Aug 17)
Bimsey (IRE) 67 (14f,Not,GF,Oct 19)
Bin Ajwaad (IRE) 69 (7f,Goo,GS,Spt 30)
Bin Nashwan (USA) 71 (7f,Nwm,GF,Apr 19)
Bin Rosie 76 (8f,Nwm,G,Spt 28)
Bint Zamayem (IRE) 47 (11½f,Chs,GF,May 10)
Birchwood Sun 50 (7f,Nwc,G,Spt 27)
Birthday Boy (IRE) 39 (10f,Nwm,GF,Apr 18)
Bishop of Cashel 71 (8f,Asc,G,Spt 23)
Bit on the Side (IRE) 62 (12f,Don,GF,Oct 21)
Black Boy (IRE) 36 (5f,Yar,G,Spt 12)
Blanchland 35 (8f,Nwm,G,Jun 3)
Blasted 38 (7f,Don,GF,Oct 20)
Blaze Away (USA) 65 (18f,Nwm,GF,Oct 14)
Blaze of Oak (USA) 60 (9f,Yor,GF,Aug 30)
Blaze of Song 50 (8f,Chp,G,May 29)
Blisland 62 (10f,Goo,F,Jly 28)
Blockade (USA) 58 (8f,Goo,F,Jly 29)
Blomberg (IRE) 55 (8f,Yor,G,Oct 4)
Blow Dry (IRE) 40 (7f,Nwc,GF,Oct 30)
Blue And Royal (IRE) 30 (12f,Kem,GF,Jun 14)
Blue Blazer 59 (12f,Don,G,May 27)
Blue Bomber 62 (7f,Cat,GF,Oct 14)
Blue Grit 42 (8f,Nwm,G,Jun 3)
Blue Judge (IRE) 38 (14f,Not,G,Apr 24)
Blue Nile (IRE) 40 (10f,Nwm,G,Spt 26)
Blue Ocean (USA) 50 (7f,Nwm,G,Spt 29)
Blue Siren 54 (5f,Bev,GF,Apr 8)
Blue Zulu (IRE) 55 (8f,Nwm,G,Jly 22)
Blurred Image (IRE) 61 (6f,Goo,GF,Jun 23)
Blush Rambler (USA) 59 (12f,Lei,G,Jun 17)
Blushing Flame (USA) 84 (12f,Don,GF,Oct 21)
Blushing Grenadier (IRE) 43 (6f,Lei,S,Spt 18)
Bob's Ploy 62 (12f,Asc,GF,Jun 22)
Bobanlyn (IRE) 39 (10f,Red,G,Spt 23)
Bogart 37 (6f,Don,GF,May 9)
Bold Amusement 62 (9f,Yor,GF,Jun 17)
Bold Angel 54 (7½f,Chs,GF,Aug 19)
Bold Cyrano (IRE) 37 (6f,War,F,May 8)
Bold Effort (FR) 64 (6f,Yor,G,Oct 7)
Bold Gait 68 (16f,Nwc,F,Jly 1)
Bold Gem 32 (5f,Goo,G,Jun 9)
Bold Habit 47 (8f,Red,G,Spt 22)

Bold Look 52 (10f,San,GF,Aug 19)
Bold Mick 39 (10f,Rip,GF,Apr 29)
Bold Street (IRE) 40 (6f,Ayr,G,Jly 16)
Boldina Bay 42 (10f,Nwc,F,Jun 30)
Bollin Frank 37 (7½f,Bev,GF,Jly 18)
Bollin Harry 44 (6f,Hay,GF,Jly 8)
Boloardo 56 (12f,Yor,GF,Aug 17)
Bolshoi (IRE) 41 (5f,Bev,GF,Apr 7)
Bon Luck (IRE) 51 (7f,San,GF,Jun 16)
Bonita 33 (7f,Kem,GF,Jun 14)
Bonne Etoile 53 (8f,Yar,F,Jun 27)
Bonny Melody 32 (5f,Fol,GF,May 31)
Bookcase 53 (12f,Asc,GF,Jly 22)
Borrowby 31 (7½f,Bev,GF,May 13)
Bouche Bee (USA) 71 (7f,Goo,F,Jly 28)
Boundary Express 44 (12f,Hay,G,Spt 1)
Boursin (IRE) 50 (6f,Thi,G,Jly 21)
Bowcliffe 38 (10½f,Hay,GS,Jun 9)
Bowcliffe Court (IRE) 47 (14f,Nwm,G,Spt 29)
Bowden Rose 71 (5f,Bri,G,Oct 1)
Braille (IRE) 57 (10½f,Chs,GF,Aug 18)
Brandon Prince (IRE) 41 (18f,Don,G,Mar 24)
Brandonhurst 32 (10f,Lin,GF,May 20)
Branston Abby 75 (6f,Nwc,F,Jly 1)
Brass Tacks 43 (6f,Cat,G,Jun 2)
Brave Edge 89 (6f,Asc,F,Jun 23)
Brave Patriarch 36 (8f,Kem,GF,May 8)
Brave Princess 42 (7f,Nwb,GF,Apr 21)
Brave Revival 64 (8f,Nwm,G,May 5)
Brave Spy 46 (16f,Lin,Std,Aug 5)
Braydon Forest 43 (10f,Wnd,GF,Jly 10)
Break the Rules 51 (9f,Ham,F,Jly 29)
Breakfast Creek 32 (5f,Chs,G,Jun 4)
Brecongill Lad 49 (6f,Yor,G,Oct 7)
Breezed Well 33 (8f,War,G,May 27)
Bresil (USA) 34 (14f,Not,GF,Aug 12)
Brief Glimpse (IRE) 71 (7f,Goo,GF,Jly 25)
Brier Creek (USA) 53 (10f,Nwm,G,May 6)
Bring on the Choir 56 (8f,Nwm,GF,May 7)
Brisas 35 (5f,Crl,Hd,Aug 21)
Broadstairs Beauty (IRE) 63 (5f,Nwm,GF,Jly 11)
Broadway Flyer (USA) 83 (12f,Asc,GF,Jly 22)
Brockton Flame 46 (6f,Lei,F,Oct 23)
Broctune Bay 32 (14f,Nwm,G,Spt 29)
Broctune Gold 39 (6f,Red,F,May 15)
Brodessa 46 (16f,Red,GF,Jun 13)
Bronze Runner 35 (11½f,Wnd,GF,Jly 17)
Brookhead Lady 47 (6f,Hay,G,Spt 1)
Broom Isle 37 (13f,Ham,G,May 4)
Broughton Singer (IRE) 31 (10f,Lei,G,Oct 10)
Broughton's Pride (IRE) 43 (10f,Bev,GF,Aug 24)
Broughtons Formula 36 (11½f,Wnd,GF,Jly 29)
Broughtons Turmoil 54 (7f,Nwm,GF,Spt 30)
Brown Carpet 31 (11½f,Wnd,G,Jun 12)

Brown Eyed Girl 34 (7f,Yar,G,Jun 7)
Brumon (IRE) 46 (16f,Not,GF,Aug 2)
Bryan Robson (USA) 43 (6f,Kem,GF,Apr 17)
Buckley Boys 39 (11½f,Yar,G,Spt 12)
Buddy's Friend (IRE) 42 (7½f,Bev,G,Jun 7)
Built for Comfort (IRE) 32 (8f,War,GF,Apr 27)
Bulsara 33 (8f,Red,G,Spt 22)
Bunker (IRE) 32 (12f,Pon,GF,Jly 3)
Bunting 31 (11½f,Lin,F,May 13)
Bunty Boo 69 (5f,San,G,Jly 8)
Burning (USA) 71 (12f,Asc,GF,Jun 22)
Burnt Sienna (IRE) 31 (8f,Lei,F,Oct 24)
Burooj 79 (12f,Asc,G,Spt 23)
Bushehr (IRE) 44 (12f,Chp,GF,Jly 13)
Busy Banana 48 (8f,Crl,G,Apr 28)
By Arrangement (IRE) 31 (16½f,Fol,G,Jun 7)
By The Bay 36 (7f,Nwm,GF,Jly 29)
C-Yer-Simmie (IRE) 36 (5f,Don,GF,Jly 26)
Cadeaux Tryst 73 (7f,Nwm,GF,Jly 13)
Caerle Lad (IRE) 55 (9f,Goo,GF,Jun 16)
Calder King 47 (8f,Lei,G,Oct 9)
Caleman 65 (8f,Goo,F,Jly 25)
Call Me Albi (IRE) 38 (11½f,Wnd,GF,Jly 17)
Call Me I'm Blue (IRE) 66 (5f,Nwm,GS,Jun 3)
Call to the Bar (IRE) 34 (5f,Thi,GF,May 6)
Calling Collect (USA) 34 (7f,Nwm,GF,Apr 19)
Camden's Ransom (USA) 35 (10f,San,G,May 29)
Cameron Highland (IRE) 54 (7f,Kem,GF,Jun 28)
Can She Can Can 37 (14f,Not,GF,Jly 24)
Canary Falcon 37 (7f,Nwm,GF,Oct 28)
Candle Smile (USA) 55 (14f,Yor,GF,May 16)
Canny Lad 37 (8f,Pon,GF,Jly 28)
Canovas Heart 42 (5f,War,GS,Apr 1)
Cap And Gown (IRE) 54 (10f,Yar,GF,Aug 10)
Cap Juluca (IRE) 84 (8f,Yor,GF,Aug 17)
Cape Colony 37 (7f,Yar,G,Spt 12)
Cape Pigeon (USA) 46 (8f,Wnd,G,Jun 19)
Capias (USA) 84 (12f,Don,GF,Nov 4)
Captain Carat 52 (6f,Pon,GF,Aug 22)
Captain Horatius (IRE) 78 (10f,Kem,GF,Apr 17)
Captain Marmalade 36 (8f,Nwm,GF,Aug 5)
Captain Scarlet (IRE) 31 (12f,Goo,GF,Jun 9)
Captain's Day 62 (8f,Goo,F,Jly 25)
Caramba 50 (10½f,Yor,GF,May 16)
Care And Comfort 35 (8f,Nwm,GF,Jly 1)
Caribbean Surfer (USA) 31 (11f,Ayr,G,Spt 16)
Carlito Brigante 53 (10f,Don,GF,Jly 26)
Carnbrea Belle (IRE) 44 (16f,Not,GS,Spt 11)
Carnegie (IRE) 82 (12f,Asc,GF,Jly 22)
Carol's Dream (USA) 47 (8f,Rip,GF,Aug 19)
Carpathian 45 (12f,Eps,G,Jly 26)
Carranita (IRE) 73 (6f,Yar,G,Spt 13)
Cashmirie 31 (10f,Pon,GF,Jly 11)
Cask 57 (8f,Asc,F,Jun 24)

Castel Rosselo 64 (8f,Thi,GF,May 6)
Castle Courageous 63 (14f,Not,G,Apr 24)
Castlerea Lad 72 (6f,Asc,F,Jun 23)
Castoret 41 (11½f,Wnd,G,Jun 12)
Casual Water (IRE) 66 (12f,Don,GF,Oct 21)
Catercap (IRE) 44 (8f,Nwm,G,May 5)
Cats Bottom 45 (7f,Lei,G,Jun 17)
Cavatina 38 (7f,Lei,G,Spt 5)
Cavers Yangous 53 (6f,Ayr,G,Jly 16)
Cavil 42 (8f,Yar,GF,Aug 17)
Cayumanque (CHI) 62 (16½f,San,G,May 29)
Cedez le Passage (FR) 70 (12f,Asc,GF,Jun 21)
Cee-Jay-Ay 57 (7f,Chp,GS,Oct 10)
Celebration Cake (IRE) 33 (7f,Ayr,GF,Jun 3)
Celeric 77 (14f,Nwm,G,Spt 29)
Celestial Choir 64 (8f,Pon,GF,Aug 22)
Celestial Key (USA) 84 (7f,Nwm,GF,Aug 5)
Celtic Fringe 39 (8f,Not,GF,May 2)
Celtic Swing 94 (8f,Nwm,G,May 6)
Cemaes Bay 43 (5f,Bev,GF,Apr 27)
Cephista 34 (10f,Yar,GF,Jly 27)
Chadwell Hall 45 (5f,Yor,G,Oct 4)
Chahaya Timor (IRE) 31 (14½f,Don,GF,May 8)
Chairmans Choice 70 (8f,Goo,F,Jly 29)
Chakalak 48 (15½f,Fol,G,Jun 7)
Chaldon Herring 32 (11f,Edi,G,Apr 10)
Champagne Grandy 55 (7f,Nwb,GS,Spt 15)
Champagne N Dreams 34 (7f,Edi,F,Jun 26)
Chancey Fella 42 (7f,Nwm,G,Aug 25)
Chantry Beath 51 (12f,Rip,F,Jun 21)
Chantry Bellini 30 (8f,Pon,G,Jun 12)
Charity Crusader 71 (12f,Eps,GF,Jun 10)
Charlie Sillett 52 (7f,Don,GF,Nov 3)
Charnwood Forest (IRE) 81 (8f,Asc,GF,Jun 20)
Charnwood Queen 34 (6f,Fol,S,Spt 27)
Chatham Island 60 (10f,Nwm,GF,May 7)
Chattaroy (IRE) 68 (7f,Kem,G,Jun 3)
Cheeky Chappy 31 (5f,Edi,GF,Aug 24)
Cheeky Charm (USA) 33 (8f,Yar,GF,Oct 18)
Cherokee Rose (IRE) 66 (6f,Hay,G,Spt 2)
Cherrington 62 (14f,Goo,F,Jly 27)
Chevalier (USA) 42 (10f,Nwc,GF,Jly 24)
Chewit 37 (6f,Bri,G,Apr 6)
Cheyenne Spirit 75 (6f,Hay,GF,Jly 8)
Chez Catalan 38 (15½f,Fol,GF,Spt 7)
Chickawicka (IRE) 62 (6f,Nwb,GF,Aug 11)
Chief Bee 63 (12f,Asc,GS,Oct 6)
Chief Minister (IRE) 44 (16½f,Don,G,Jun 10)
Chief of Staff 57 (7f,Fol,G,Jun 7)
Chief's Lady 36 (7f,Nwm,G,Aug 25)
Chief's Song 44 (16½f,San,G,Apr 28)
Children's Choice (IRE) 50 (12f,Eps,GF,Jun 11)
Chili Heights 45 (7f,Nwb,G,Jly 14)
Chilly Billy 72 (8f,Nwm,G,May 6)

Chimanimani 36 (12f,Hay,GF,May 8)
Chimborazo 39 (14f,Not,GF,May 2)
Chiming In 38 (7½f,Bev,GF,Apr 8)
Chinour (IRE) 57 (6f,Nwc,GF,Jly 24)
Chita Rivera 31 (16½f,Fol,GF,Nov 6)
Chocolate Charlie 37 (10f,Wnd,GF,Jly 10)
Christian Flight (IRE) 34 (5f,Crl,F,May 12)
Christmas Kiss 60 (5f,Sal,F,Jun 28)
Chucklestone 33 (16½f,San,GF,Aug 18)
Cicerone 34 (8f,Yar,GF,Oct 18)
Cim Bom Bom (IRE) 66 (8f,San,GF,Apr 29)
Ciracusa (IRE) 41 (14f,Not,GF,Oct 19)
Citadeed (USA) 73 (7f,Nwm,GF,Apr 19)
Claireswan (IRE) 47 (14f,Yar,GF,Aug 10)
Clan Ben (IRE) 54 (8f,Nwm,GF,Oct 28)
Claque 33 (12f,Kem,GF,Jun 14)
Classic Cliche (IRE) 85 (10½f,Yor,G,May 17)
Classic Pet (IRE) 33 (5f,San,GF,Aug 30)
Classic Sky (IRE) 78 (7f,Asc,GF,May 3)
Classicy 66 (8f,Yor,G,May 18)
Clearly Devious 35 (8f,Pon,GF,Oct 2)
Cliburnel News (IRE) 47 (14f,Not,GF,Jun 12)
Clifton Fox 60 (8f,Lei,GF,May 29)
Cloette 31 (7f,Fol,G,Jly 5)
Clouded Elegance 64 (10f,Nwb,G,May 19)
Coastal Bluff 61 (5f,Nwc,G,Spt 27)
Coburg 59 (10f,San,GS,Spt 13)
Code of Law (USA) 34 (10f,Nwm,G,Spt 29)
Coffee 'n Cream 64 (5f,Hay,GF,Aug 5)
Coleridge 31 (15½f,Fol,GF,Spt 7)
College Don 49 (14f,Yor,GF,Aug 16)
College Night (IRE) 36 (10f,Yar,GF,Aug 10)
Colorful Ambition 62 (10½f,Hay,G,Jun 10)
Colosse 44 (12f,Ham,G,Spt 24)
Colston-C 42 (8f,Nwm,GF,Jun 23)
Colway Rake 51 (5f,San,G,Jly 8)
Colway Rock (USA) 47 (10½f,Hay,G,Jun 10)
Comanche Companion 65 (7f,Yor,G,Oct 7)
Comeonup 33 (7f,Chp,GS,Oct 10)
Commander Glen (IRE) 43 (8f,Bat,Hd,Spt 4)
Commoner (USA) 56 (10f,Kem,GF,Apr 15)
Concer Un 47 (8½f,Eps,GF,Aug 28)
Confronter 66 (8f,Yor,G,Oct 4)
Conic Hill (IRE) 33 (8f,Lei,GF,May 29)
Conspicuous (IRE) 47 (8f,Nwm,GF,Oct 28)
Contrafire (IRE) 57 (11f,Ayr,G,Spt 14)
Cool Edge (IRE) 70 (7f,Nwm,GF,Spt 30)
Cool Jazz 62 (6f,Don,GF,Spt 6)
Cool Luke (IRE) 48 (11f,Ham,S,Apr 12)
Corradini 57 (12f,Yor,GF,Jun 16)
Coryana Dancer (IRE) 40 (7f,Chs,GF,May 10)
Cosy Corner (IRE) 39 (10f,Nwm,GF,Spt 30)
Cotteir Chief (IRE) 85 (12f,Don,G,Mar 25)
Country Lover 63 (9f,Yor,GF,Jun 17)

Country Star (IRE) 59 (12f,Kem,G,Spt 2)
Courageous Dancer (IRE) 61 (8f,Asc,S,Oct 6)
Courbaril 44 (12f,Bri,F,Jly 31)
Coureur 40 (10f,Red,F,Oct 31)
Court Minstrel 32 (8f,Kem,GF,Jly 12)
Court Nap (IRE) 34 (8½f,Eps,GS,Spt 19)
Court of Honour (IRE) 77 (12f,Eps,GF,Jun 10)
Courting Newmarket 30 (9f,Lin,GF,Jun 24)
Cradle Days 38 (6f,Lei,GF,Apr 29)
Craigie Boy 43 (6f,Lei,S,Spt 18)
Crazy Paving (IRE) 34 (7f,Nwm,GF,Apr 19)
Credit Squeeze 70 (12f,Sal,GF,May 4)
Crees Sqaw 33 (7f,Red,G,Spt 23)
Crespo (IRE) 51 (12f,Kem,G,Jun 3)
Crested Knight (IRE) 36 (8f,Goo,GF,Jun 23)
Cretan Gift 56 (6f,Not,GS,Spt 19)
Croeso-I-Cymru 63 (6f,Goo,G,Spt 9)
Croft Imperial 59 (5f,Ayr,GF,Jun 3)
Croft Pool 63 (5f,Hay,G,Spt 23)
Croft Valley 63 (7f,Nwb,GF,Jun 15)
Crofters Ceilidh 37 (5f,Yor,GF,Jun 16)
Cross Talk (IRE) 38 (12f,Lei,F,Oct 24)
Crowded Avenue 74 (5f,Eps,GF,Spt 6)
Crown of Sheba (USA) 34 (7f,Yar,G,Jun 14)
Crumpton Hill (IRE) 54 (9f,Nwm,GF,Spt 30)
Crystal Blade 59 (12f,Yor,GF,Jly 14)
Crystal Cavern (USA) 49 (8f,Asc,S,Oct 6)
Crystal Heights (FR) 52 (7f,Bri,G,Oct 1)
Crystal Loop 51 (5f,Nwm,GF,Aug 26)
Crystal Magic 59 (5f,Nwb,GF,Apr 21)
Cuango (IRE) 67 (14f,Yor,G,May 17)
Cuba 37 (10f,San,GF,Jun 16)
Cuban Reef 30 (7f,Red,F,Oct 3)
Cuff Link (IRE) 67 (16½f,San,G,May 29)
Cumbrian Challenge (IRE) 55 (10½f,Yor,G,Oct 4)
Cumbrian Minstrel 30 (10f,Rip,GF,Aug 12)
Cumbrian Rhapsody 48 (17½f,Ayr,G,Spt 15)
Cumbrian Waltzer 60 (6f,Red,G,Spt 23)
Current Speech (IRE) 45 (8f,Ayr,G,Spt 15)
Curtelace 40 (10f,Lei,G,Oct 10)
Cutpurse Moll 54 (7f,Nwm,GF,Spt 30)
Cutthroat Kid (IRE) 58 (16f,Red,F,Jly 13)
Cyphell (IRE) 39 (10f,San,GF,Aug 19)
Cypress Avenue (IRE) 56 (14f,Yor,GF,May 16)
Cyrano's Lad (IRE) 74 (7f,Nwm,GF,Jun 23)
Cyrus the Great 61 (10f,Nwm,G,Spt 26)
Czarna (IRE) 62 (7f,Asc,GF,May 3)
Daawe (USA) 41 (9f,Yor,GF,Jun 17)
Dacha (IRE) 47 (12f,Lei,F,Oct 23)
Daffaq 40 (8f,Chp,G,May 29)
Dahik 70 (10f,Goo,F,Jly 28)
Dahiyah (USA) 50 (6f,Bri,F,May 11)
Dahlenburg (IRE) 43 (10f,Ayr,GF,Jun 2)
Daily Starlight (USA) 62 (14f,Nwm,G,Spt 29)

Daily Starshine (IRE) 34 (5f,Cat,G,Jun 9)
Dairine's Delight (IRE) 66 (5f,Nwm,G,Spt 28)
Dana Point (IRE) 46 (8f,Red,GF,Aug 23)
Dance Band (USA) 71 (8f,Asc,GF,Jly 22)
Dance King 39 (10f,Ayr,GF,Jun 2)
Dance So Suite 60 (10½f,Hay,S,Aug 30)
Dance Turn 76 (10f,Nwb,G,Jly 15)
Dance a Dream 70 (12f,Eps,GF,Jun 9)
Dances With Hooves 32 (8f,Nwb,G,Apr 22)
Dancing Destiny 40 (11f,War,GF,Jun 12)
Dancing Heart 46 (7f,Lin,GF,May 20)
Dancing Heights (IRE) 66 (9f,Yor,GF,Jun 17)
Dancing Lawyer 62 (7f,San,GF,Aug 30)
Dancing Sensation (USA) 58 (12f,Asc,GF,Jly 22)
Dancing Sioux 37 (5f,Chp,GS,Oct 10)
Danegold (IRE) 61 (8f,San,GS,Spt 13)
Danesrath (IRE) 52 (12f,Chs,GF,Aug 19)
Dangerous Guest (IRE) 47 (12f,Asc,GF,Jun 22)
Danjing (IRE) 57 (12f,Goo,GF,Aug 25)
Dante's Rubicon (IRE) 40 (6f,Thi,F,Jly 29)
Daraydan (IRE) 72 (16f,Goo,GS,Spt 30)
Darcey Bussell 46 (8f,Yar,GF,Oct 18)
Daring Destiny 71 (6f,Goo,F,Jly 29)
Daring Ryde 41 (8f,Chp,GS,Oct 10)
Dark Eyed Lady (IRE) 30 (5f,Bat,Hd,Aug 8)
Dark Menace 37 (5f,Bri,F,Aug 2)
Darling Clover 37 (10f,Yar,GF,Aug 3)
Darnay 99 (8f,Goo,GF,Aug 26)
Darren Boy (IRE) 48 (6f,Asc,F,Jun 23)
Darter (IRE) 44 (12f,Lei,F,Oct 24)
Dashing Dancer (IRE) 50 (6f,Lei,F,Oct 23)
Dashing Water 59 (7f,Goo,F,Jly 28)
Dato Star (IRE) 81 (12f,Don,GF,Nov 4)
Daunt 37 (8f,Lei,G,Apr 6)
David James' Girl 39 (7½f,Fol,GF,Spt 7)
Dawalib (USA) 48 (7f,Chs,G,Jun 8)
Dawlah 67 (10f,Don,G,May 29)
Dawn Flight 33 (15½f,Fol,GF,Spt 7)
Dawn Mission 35 (12½f,Nwc,GF,Apr 17)
Dawsha (IRE) 44 (10f,Eps,GF,Jun 9)
Daysman (USA) 43 (6f,Nwm,GF,Aug 5)
Daytona Beach (IRE) 56 (10½f,Chs,GF,Aug 18)
Deano's Beeno 56 (12f,Yor,GF,Aug 17)
Debutante Days 45 (10f,Ayr,G,Spt 15)
Deceit the Second 37 (10f,Don,GF,Oct 21)
Decorated Hero 69 (7f,Nwb,GF,Aug 12)
Dee-Lady 55 (8f,Don,GF,Mar 25)
Deeply Vale (IRE) 41 (7f,Lei,G,Oct 10)
Deevee 61 (8f,Asc,GF,May 3)
Delight of Dawn 46 (7f,Sal,GF,Aug 31)
Delightful Dancer (IRE) 30 (6f,Bri,F,May 11)
Delta One (IRE) 50 (7f,Goo,GF,Aug 25)
Delta Soleil (USA) 73 (7f,Nwm,GF,Spt 30)
Denbrae (IRE) 30 (7f,San,GF,Spt 13)

Denebola Way (GR) 34 (8f,Nwm,GF,Apr 20)
Densben 38 (6f,Hay,G,Spt 22)
Desert Courier 54 (7f,Nwm,GF,May 7)
Desert Green (FR) 77 (8f,Goo,F,Jly 27)
Desert Harvest 53 (7f,Nwb,GF,May 21)
Desert Invader (IRE) 41 (6f,Ayr,G,Jly 16)
Desert Power 43 (8f,Asc,GF,Jly 22)
Desert Shot 76 (9f,Nwm,GF,Apr 19)
Desert Style (IRE) 42 (6f,Asc,S,Spt 24)
Desert Time 60 (8f,San,GF,Aug 9)
Desert Zone (USA) 38 (8f,Nwm,G,Jun 3)
Devon Peasant 42 (10f,Nwb,GS,Oct 19)
Diaghilef (IRE) 85 (14f,Yor,GF,Aug 16)
Diamond Crown (IRE) 41 (12f,Crl,Hd,Aug 16)
Diamond Crown (USA) 30 (8f,Thi,GF,May 19)
Dictation (USA) 60 (6f,Nwm,G,Jly 21)
Didina 65 (7f,Yor,GF,Aug 17)
Diebiedale 39 (5f,Don,G,Jun 10)
Diet 37 (6f,Ayr,GF,Aug 5)
Diffident (FR) 85 (7f,Nwm,GF,Apr 19)
Direct Dial (USA) 37 (7f,Kem,G,Jun 3)
Distant Dynasty 31 (5f,Fol,GF,Apr 10)
Distant Princess 46 (7f,Yar,GF,Aug 10)
Divina Mia 39 (10f,San,GF,Aug 19)
Divine Pursuit 40 (8f,Goo,GF,May 23)
Dixit Dominus 30 (10½f,Hay,GS,Jun 9)
Doctor's Glory (USA) 57 (7f,San,G,May 29)
Doctor's Remedy 36 (12f,Crl,Hd,Aug 16)
Doddington Flyer 32 (14f,Not,G,May 26)
Dom One 32 (8f,Asc,GF,May 3)
Domappel 52 (10f,Nwm,G,Spt 26)
Domicksky 46 (5f,Rip,G,May 21)
Dominelle 30 (5f,Crl,Hd,Aug 16)
Domitia (USA) 46 (10f,Red,F,Oct 24)
Domulla 63 (6f,Nwb,GS,Oct 19)
Don Corleone 77 (12f,Asc,F,Jun 23)
Don Pepe 58 (7f,Ayr,F,Jun 24)
Don't Worry Me (IRE) 77 (5f,Lin,GF,Aug 24)
Done Well (USA) 56 (7f,Sal,F,Jun 28)
Donna Viola 62 (8f,Asc,S,Oct 6)
Dont Forget Curtis (IRE) 48 (9f,Kem,GF,Apr 15)
Dont Shoot Fairies 37 (12f,Lei,G,Oct 9)
Dontforget Insight (IRE) 59 (8f,Goo,F,Jly 29)
Doodies Pool (IRE) 35 (8f,Goo,G,Spt 29)
Dormy Three 59 (12f,Kem,G,Jun 3)
Dorothea Brooke (IRE) 65 (10f,Don,G,May 29)
Dosses Dan (IRE) 38 (7f,Hay,G,Apr 15)
Double Blue 79 (6f,Rip,GF,Aug 19)
Double Bounce 66 (7f,Nwm,GF,Spt 30)
Double Dagger 46 (14f,San,F,Jun 29)
Double Eclipse (IRE) 70 (16f,Asc,GF,Jun 21)
Double Matt (IRE) 60 (6f,Nwm,G,Jly 21)
Double Quick (IRE) 65 (5f,Nwm,G,Spt 28)
Double Rush (IRE) 37 (8½f,Eps,GS,Spt 19)

Double Splendour (IRE) 58 (6f,Nwc,GF,Oct 30)
Double Trigger (IRE) 86 (16½f,San,G,May 29)
Douce Maison (IRE) 56 (12f,Nwm,GF,Oct 27)
Dover Patrol (IRE) 64 (14f,Hay,G,Jun 10)
Dowsong 48 (8f,Chp,GS,Oct 10)
Doyce 49 (16f,Kem,GF,Apr 17)
Dr Caligari (IRE) 40 (8f,Pon,GF,Jly 28)
Dr Edgar 46 (10f,Fol,G,Oct 16)
Dr Zhivago 38 (11½f,San,GF,Aug 30)
Dragon Green 30 (11½f,Wnd,G,Jun 12)
Dream Ticket (USA) 46 (7f,Chs,GF,May 10)
Dream Wedding 30 (8f,War,GF,Apr 27)
Dreamboat (USA) 52 (7f,Red,G,Spt 23)
Dreamer (USA) 58 (10f,Kem,GF,Apr 15)
Dreams End 67 (12f,Don,G,Mar 25)
Drum Battle 42 (10½f,Hay,G,Spt 22)
Drummer Hicks 39 (11f,Ayr,GF,May 10)
Dry Point 59 (6f,Kem,GF,Jun 28)
Duchess of Alba 44 (10f,Eps,GF,Jly 5)
Ducking 47 (10f,Lei,GF,Oct 24)
Duello 49 (8½f,Eps,GS,Spt 19)
Duffertoes 50 (9f,Kem,GF,Apr 15)
Duke Valentino 37 (8f,Yar,GF,Oct 18)
Dune River 53 (7f,Yor,GF,Jly 15)
Dungeon Dancer 32 (8f,Bat,GF,May 22)
Durano 50 (10f,Rip,GF,Jly 22)
Durgams First (IRE) 39 (12f,Hay,GF,Jly 7)
Durham Drapes 46 (8f,Crl,Hd,Aug 16)
Durshan (USA) 43 (14½f,Kem,GF,Jun 14)
Dusty Point (IRE) 55 (14f,Yar,GF,Aug 10)
Dutosky 47 (10f,San,G,May 29)
Dvorak (IRE) 50 (12f,Don,GF,May 9)
Eagle Day (USA) 59 (6f,Bri,F,May 11)
Easy Dollar 71 (7f,Nwb,GF,Aug 11)
Easy Jet (POL) 59 (7f,Nwb,GF,May 21)
Easy Listening (USA) 55 (10f,Bat,GF,May 22)
Easy Option (IRE) 74 (5f,Kem,G,Jun 3)
Eau de Cologne 52 (16f,Nwb,GS,Oct 19)
Eben Al Habeeb (IRE) 49 (10f,Nwm,GF,May 7)
Edan Heights 51 (14f,Nwm,GF,Oct 13)
Edbaysaan (IRE) 47 (12f,Nwm,GF,Oct 12)
Eden's Close 37 (15f,Nwm,G,Jly 22)
Eden's Star (IRE) 46 (8f,War,F,Aug 28)
Eelious (USA) 48 (14f,Hay,GF,Aug 5)
Efizia 43 (10f,Red,F,Oct 31)
Efra 50 (6f,Fol,G,Oct 16)
Eid (USA) 41 (12f,Pon,G,May 26)
Eight Sharp (IRE) 37 (10½f,Yor,GF,May 16)
El Bailador (IRE) 58 (10f,Nwm,GF,May 7)
El Supremo (USA) 54 (10f,Asc,GF,Jly 22)
El Volador 34 (14f,Sal,GS,Spt 27)
El Yasaf (IRE) 68 (5f,Nwm,G,May 6)
Ela Man Howa 43 (12f,Sal,G,May 24)
Ela-Aristokrati (IRE) 70 (8f,San,GF,Apr 29)

Elation 39 (12f,Hay,G,Spt 1)
Elburg (IRE) 34 (21½f,Pon,F,May 1)
Elementary 49 (12f,Lei,G,Oct 10)
Elfin Laughter 40 (10f,Not,GF,Apr 17)
Elfland (IRE) 64 (6f,Nwm,G,May 6)
Elite Hope (USA) 58 (7f,Nwm,GF,Aug 5)
Elite Justice 34 (10f,Bri,F,Jly 20)
Elite Racing 57 (8½f,Eps,GF,Jly 5)
Elle Shaped (IRE) 67 (5f,Don,GF,Nov 4)
Ellie Ardensky 44 (9f,Rip,G,May 21)
Elly Fleetfoot (IRE) 37 (11½f,Lin,GF,Jun 27)
Elpidos 45 (8f,Lei,GF,Aug 14)
Eltish (USA) 83 (10f,Asc,GF,Jun 20)
Embankment (IRE) 55 (8f,Goo,F,Jly 27)
Embracing 59 (14f,Yor,GF,Aug 16)
Embryonic (IRE) 59 (13f,Ayr,G,Spt 16)
Emerging Market 59 (7f,Goo,F,Jly 28)
Emily-Mou (IRE) 51 (8½f,Eps,GF,Jly 5)
Emirates Express 64 (7f,Eps,GF,Jly 5)
Emma Grimes (IRE) 31 (12f,Nwm,GF,Oct 27)
Emperor Jones (USA) 93 (8f,Goo,GF,Aug 26)
Emphatic Candidate (IRE) 40 (7f,War,GF,Jun 12)
Empower (IRE) 47 (8f,Goo,GF,Jun 16)
Empty Quarter 69 (8f,Red,F,Oct 12)
En Attendant (FR) 81 (7f,Chs,GF,Aug 18)
En Vacances (IRE) 60 (16f,Nwb,GS,Oct 19)
Encore M'Lady (IRE) 41 (6f,Hay,GF,Jly 6)
Endless Light (USA) 63 (12f,Yor,GF,May 16)
Endless Wave 37 (5f,Not,GS,Spt 11)
Endowment 48 (12f,Sal,G,May 18)
English Invader 58 (12f,Bat,F,May 13)
Environment Friend 76 (12f,Asc,GF,Jly 22)
Environmentalist (IRE) 50 (16½f,Fol,GF,Nov 6)
Epagris 69 (7f,Goo,GF,Jly 25)
Eqtesaad (USA) 51 (8f,Asc,GF,May 3)
Equerry 48 (7f,Edi,G,Apr 10)
Equilibrium 31 (7f,Nwm,G,Aug 25)
Erin Bird (FR) 50 (10f,Goo,F,Jly 29)
Errant 31 (8f,Yar,F,Oct 18)
Ertlon 60 (7f,Yar,F,Oct 18)
Escarpment (USA) 58 (16f,Asc,GF,May 3)
Espartero (IRE) 72 (6f,Goo,GF,Jly 29)
Essayeffsee 44 (10f,Red,F,Oct 31)
Esthal (IRE) 30 (11½f,Wnd,G,Jun 12)
Ethbaat (USA) 48 (7f,Nwm,GF,Oct 14)
Euphyllia 53 (7f,Don,GF,Oct 20)
Euro Forum 33 (12f,Fol,S,Spt 27)
Euro Rebel 30 (7½f,Bev,GF,Apr 8)
Euro Sceptic (IRE) 39 (7½f,Bev,GF,Jun 14)
Euro Singer 30 (14f,Hay,S,Spt 30)
Eurolink Mischief 53 (11f,Red,F,Oct 31)
Eurolink Shadow 32 (14f,Not,GF,Oct 19)
Eurolink the Rebel (USA) 57 (10f,Don,GF,Oct 21)
Evan 'elp Us 45 (7f,Don,GF,Oct 20)

Evening Falls 34 (5f,San,G,Jly 8)
Eveningperformance 83 (5f,Kem,G,Jun 3)
Ever Friends 38 (14f,Not,GF,Oct 19)
Ever so Lyrical 47 (8f,Goo,F,Jun 30)
Everglades (IRE) 69 (6f,Asc,F,Jun 23)
Ewar Imperial 30 (10f,Lin,GF,Jun 27)
Executive Design 37 (14f,Hay,GF,Jly 6)
Exemption 53 (12f,Chp,G,May 29)
Exhibit Air (IRE) 35 (12f,Bri,F,Aug 1)
Express Gift 52 (12f,Pon,GF,Oct 2)
Express Routing 30 (7f,Lin,F,May 13)
Faal Mario (USA) 59 (14f,Hay,GF,May 8)
Fabillion 44 (14f,Not,GF,Oct 26)
Fabulous Mtoto 31 (14f,Not,GF,Oct 26)
Face the Future 51 (6f,Kem,GF,Jun 28)
Fahal (USA) 81 (10½f,Hay,GF,Aug 5)
Fair and Fancy (FR) 36 (14f,Not,GF,Oct 19)
Fairelaine 39 (8f,Goo,F,Jly 25)
Fairy Knight 57 (10f,Red,F,Oct 31)
Fairy Story (IRE) 60 (7f,Eps,GF,Jly 5)
Fairy Wind (IRE) 70 (5f,Nwm,GF,Jun 30)
Fakih (USA) 38 (7f,Lin,F,May 13)
Fame Again 61 (8f,Ayr,G,Spt 15)
Fangio 52 (5f,Lin,GF,Apr 7)
Fanjica (IRE) 53 (10f,Nwm,GF,May 7)
Fantasy Racing (IRE) 56 (6f,Red,G,Spt 23)
Far Ahead 34 (8f,Pon,GF,Oct 2)
Far Fetched (IRE) 32 (7f,Lei,G,Jun 5)
Farani 62 (7f,Nwb,GF,Apr 21)
Fard (IRE) 69 (6f,Nwm,GF,Jly 13)
Farringdon Hill 45 (12f,Nwb,G,May 19)
Fascination Waltz 38 (6f,Fol,S,Spt 27)
Fasih 47 (10f,Nwb,GS,Oct 19)
Fastini Gold 32 (8f,San,GS,Spt 13)
Fata (IRE) 40 (6f,Don,GF,Mar 25)
Father Dan (IRE) 38 (11½f,Wnd,GF,Aug 7)
Father Sky 40 (16f,Nwb,GF,Apr 21)
Faugeron 48 (16f,Not,GF,Jun 26)
Faustino 34 (12f,Bri,F,Jly 31)
Fawj (USA) 40 (7f,Kem,GF,Apr 17)
Fearless Wonder 40 (12f,Don,GF,May 9)
Featherstone Lane 42 (5f,Nwb,F,Jun 29)
Feinte 32 (7f,Nwm,G,May 5)
Felitza (IRE) 43 (7f,Yar,GF,Jly 16)
Fen Terrier 33 (12f,Fol,S,Spt 27)
Festive Lassie 38 (11f,Nwm,GF,Aug 23)
Ffynone (IRE) 48 (7f,San,G,May 29)
Field of Vision (IRE) 48 (8f,Edi,S,Nov 2)
Fieldridge 66 (10f,San,G,May 29)
Fiendish (USA) 52 (7f,Nwb,GF,Apr 21)
Fighter Squadron 33 (7f,Fol,G,Jun 7)
Fill the Bill (IRE) 40 (10f,Ayr,G,Jly 17)
Final Appearance (IRE) 41 (12f,Nwm,G,Spt 29)
Finjan 31 (8f,San,GF,Jly 19)

Finlaggan 58 (16f,Cat,GF,Oct 13)
Fionn de Cool (IRE) 61 (8f,San,GF,Aug 25)
Fire Dome (IRE) 60 (5f,Hay,S,Spt 30)
Fire Worshipper (IRE) 73 (12f,Don,G,Mar 25)
Fire on Ice (IRE) 55 (12f,Asc,G,Spt 23)
First Amendment (IRE) 41 (12f,Thi,F,May 20)
First Bid 37 (10f,Red,F,Jly 13)
First Bite (IRE) 30 (11f,Red,GF,Aug 27)
First Gold 48 (7f,Chp,GS,Oct 10)
First Island (IRE) 69 (7f,Asc,GF,Jun 21)
First Veil 53 (6f,Yar,G,Spt 12)
Fitzrovian (IRE) 62 (9f,Nwm,GF,Apr 19)
Five to Seven (USA) 30 (15f,Edi,S,Nov 2)
Flag Fen (USA) 35 (8f,Red,GF,Aug 22)
Flagbird (USA) 70 (10f,Nwm,GF,Spt 30)
Flair Lady 35 (8f,Edi,G,May 22)
Flame War (USA) 53 (12f,Lei,G,Jly 19)
Flash of Realm (FR) 47 (13f,Ayr,G,Spt 16)
Flashing Sabre 35 (5f,Edi,F,Jly 10)
Flashy's Son 56 (6f,Ayr,G,Jly 16)
Fleet Hill (IRE) 50 (8f,Nwm,GF,May 7)
Fleet Petite (IRE) 50 (6f,Nwm,G,Spt 29)
Flemensfirth (USA) 73 (8f,Asc,GF,Jun 20)
Flight Lieutenant (USA) 64 (12f,Eps,GF,Aug 28)
Flirty Gertie 41 (7f,Cat,G,Spt 16)
Floating Line 62 (14f,Nwm,G,Spt 29)
Florid (USA) 69 (12f,Goo,F,Jly 28)
Floridante (USA) 48 (8f,Nwb,GF,May 21)
Flowing Ocean 38 (8f,Don,G,Mar 24)
Flyaway Blues 36 (7f,Nwm,GF,Aug 26)
Followmegirls 37 (5f,Lei,S,Spt 18)
Folly Finnesse 32 (10f,Kem,GF,Apr 17)
For the Present 60 (5f,Rip,G,May 21)
Forest Cat (IRE) 67 (7f,San,G,May 29)
Foresworn (USA) 33 (12f,Nwm,GF,Apr 18)
Forever Diamonds 65 (8f,Rip,GF,May 31)
Forever Roses 45 (5f,Yar,G,Spt 12)
Formidable Liz 44 (6f,Thi,GF,Jly 28)
Fort Knox (IRE) 48 (8f,Nwm,GF,Aug 5)
Fortunes Course (IRE) 35 (14f,Not,GF,Oct 19)
Forzair 40 (6f,Wnd,GF,May 15)
Foundry Lane 73 (14f,Yor,G,May 17)
Four of Spades 41 (7f,Lin,GF,Jun 17)
Fox Sparrow 48 (12f,Thi,G,Apr 22)
Foxhound (USA) 69 (7f,Yor,GF,Aug 17)
Fraam 89 (8f,Goo,F,Jly 27)
Fragrant Belle (USA) 50 (10f,Asc,GF,Jly 22)
Francfurter 50 (10½f,Hay,G,Jun 10)
French Ginger 46 (6f,Lin,GF,May 20)
French Grit (IRE) 57 (6f,Nwm,G,Jun 3)
French Ivy (USA) 51 (16f,Asc,S,Oct 6)
Fresh Fruit Daily 51 (7f,Asc,G,Aug 23)
Fresh Look (IRE) 35 (10f,Yar,GF,Aug 3)
Fret (USA) 34 (12f,Don,G,Jun 10)

Friar Street (IRE) 36 (7f,Edi,G,Spt 18)
Friendly Brave (USA) 55 (6f,Lei,G,Jun 5)
Frisky Miss (IRE) 47 (7f,Kem,GF,Jun 14)
Frozen Sea (USA) 56 (12f,Asc,GF,Aug 23)
Fruitful Affair (IRE) 40 (14f,Yar,GF,Aug 10)
Frustration 38 (10f,Chp,GF,Jly 20)
Fujiyama Crest (IRE) 65 (16f,Asc,G,Spt 23)
Full Quiver 34 (14f,Sal,GS,Spt 27)
Further Flight 75 (16½f,San,G,May 29)
Future Act (USA) 65 (10f,Rip,GF,Jly 22)
Future Options 34 (8f,Sal,GF,Aug 17)
Gadge 53 (8f,Kem,GF,May 8)
Gallardini (IRE) 39 (10f,Don,G,Mar 24)
Gallows Corner (IRE) 46 (7f,Sal,GF,Aug 31)
Game Ploy (POL) 44 (10f,Nwm,G,Spt 26)
Gant Bleu (FR) 33 (7f,Red,G,May 29)
Garden of Heaven (USA) 57 (10½f,Yor,G,May 18)
Garnock Valley 48 (8f,Don,G,Mar 24)
Gay Gallanta (USA) 72 (8f,Asc,GF,Jun 21)
Geisway (CAN) 46 (10f,Nwm,G,May 6)
General Assembly (IRE) 52 (14f,Nwm,GS,Jun 3)
General Chaos (IRE) 36 (7f,Ayr,GF,Jun 24)
General Mouktar 64 (12f,Chs,GF,May 11)
General Sir Peter (IRE) 47 (5f,Don,GS,Spt 8)
Gentle Irony 31 (8f,Goo,G,Spt 8)
Gentleman Sid 38 (16½f,San,GF,Aug 18)
George Bull 45 (11½f,San,GS,Spt 12)
George Dillingham 51 (12f,Yor,GF,May 16)
Germane 47 (7f,Nwm,GF,Apr 18)
Germany (USA) 68 (10f,Nwm,GF,Oct 14)
Giggleswick Girl 51 (5f,Bat,Hd,Aug 8)
Ginger Jim 43 (14f,Sal,GF,Jly 6)
Ginger Tree (USA) 51 (5f,Nwm,G,Spt 28)
Girl From Ipanema 58 (8½f,Eps,GF,Jun 9)
Glide Path (USA) 83 (12f,Asc,GF,Jun 21)
Global Dancer 59 (12f,Eps,GF,Jun 10)
Gloriana 56 (10f,Red,F,Aug 5)
Glorious Aragon 52 (5f,Hay,G,Spt 23)
Glowing Jade 61 (7f,Don,G,May 27)
Go Hever Golf 66 (5f,Chs,GF,Jly 14)
Goalwah 52 (8f,Yar,F,Jun 27)
Godmersham Park 41 (7f,Nwb,GF,Jun 15)
Godwin (USA) 61 (12f,Yor,GF,May 16)
Gold Blade 42 (9f,Ham,F,Jly 14)
Gold Desire 31 (9f,Ham,G,May 4)
Golden Arrow (IRE) 59 (12f,Eps,GF,Aug 28)
Golden Ball (IRE) 68 (10f,Kem,GF,Apr 17)
Golden Envoy (USA) 40 (6f,Nwm,G,Jly 21)
Golden Fish 34 (8f,Thi,GF,Apr 7)
Golden Lady (IRE) 62 (5f,Chs,GF,May 9)
Golden Pound (USA) 54 (8f,Rip,GF,Aug 19)
Golden Torque 36 (11f,War,GS,Oct 3)
Gone Savage 53 (5f,Nwm,GF,Jly 11)

Gone for a Burton (IRE) 66 (12f,Nwb,G,May 19)
Good Hand (USA) 67 (16f,Red,F,Jly 13)
Good Match (USA) 30 (6f,Hay,G,May 26)
Goodbye Millie 31 (12f,Cat,GF,Oct 14)
Googly 44 (18f,Don,G,Mar 24)
Goonda 44 (10f,Nwb,G,Jly 14)
Gorinsky (IRE) 52 (5f,Yor,GF,Jly 14)
Gospel Song 40 (11f,Edi,GF,Jun 16)
Governor George (USA) 56 (7f,Nwm,GF,Apr 19)
Grand Applause (IRE) 40 (14f,Hay,G,Spt 23)
Grand Chapeau (IRE) 32 (6f,Goo,GF,Jun 16)
Grand Selection (IRE) 49 (12f,Goo,F,Jly 26)
Grand du Lac (USA) 58 (8f,Asc,F,Jun 24)
Grandinare (USA) 35 (10f,Wnd,GF,Jun 26)
Grate British (USA) 35 (12f,Hay,G,Spt 1)
Great Bear 45 (6f,Nwb,G,May 19)
Great Crusader 67 (14f,Yor,GF,Aug 15)
Great Deeds 41 (5f,San,G,Jly 8)
Great Easeby (IRE) 39 (14f,Red,F,Jun 24)
Great Hall 39 (6f,Wnd,G,Jly 3)
Great Inquest 56 (7f,Nwb,GF,May 21)
Great Marquess 39 (22f,Asc,F,Jun 23)
Greatest 53 (8f,Bri,F,Jun 1)
Greek Gold (IRE) 37 (8f,Rip,G,May 21)
Green Crusader 73 (10f,San,GF,Jun 16)
Green Golightly (USA) 40 (6f,Goo,GF,Jly 29)
Green Green Desert (FR) 68 (8f,Asc,GF,Jly 22)
Green Land (BEL) 39 (14½f,Don,GF,Oct 20)
Green Perfume (USA) 66 (7f,Nwb,GF,Aug 11)
Green Seed (IRE) 55 (7f,San,G,May 29)
Green's Bid 40 (7f,Crl,F,Jun 29)
Greenspan (IRE) 52 (10½f,Hay,S,Spt 30)
Greenwich Again 35 (8f,Lin,GF,Jly 14)
Grey Again 45 (7½f,Bev,GF,May 13)
Grey Charmer (IRE) 37 (5f,War,GS,Apr 1)
Grey Shot 74 (14f,Yor,GF,Aug 15)
Greycoat Boy 47 (16f,Nwb,GS,Oct 19)
Grooms Gold (IRE) 35 (12f,Chp,GF,Jly 20)
Guards Brigade 31 (10f,Ayr,GF,Jun 2)
Guesstimation (USA) 56 (9f,Yor,GF,Aug 30)
Gulf Shaadi 34 (8f,Goo,GF,Jun 16)
Gymcrak Flyer 42 (8f,Hay,G,Spt 2)
Gymcrak Premiere 63 (7f,Nwm,GF,Aug 5)
Gypsy Love (USA) 42 (9f,Goo,F,Jly 27)
H'Ani 35 (8f,Bri,G,Spt 26)
Habeta (USA) 30 (8f,Ham,F,Aug 9)
Hadabet 37 (10f,Nwm,GF,Jly 28)
Hadeel 56 (10f,Yar,GF,Aug 10)
Hadeyya Ramzeyah 48 (10f,San,GF,Jun 16)
Hagwah (USA) 52 (7f,Nwb,GF,May 20)
Hakika (USA) 69 (8f,Red,F,Oct 12)
Hakiki (IRE) 53 (6f,Goo,G,Spt 9)
Halbert 47 (5f,Hay,G,Spt 23)
Halkopous 75 (14f,Yor,G,May 17)

Halliard 44 (5f,War,G,Apr 17)
Halling (USA) 88 (10½f,Yor,GF,Aug 15)
Halmanerror 45 (6f,Pon,GF,Aug 13)
Ham N'Eggs 59 (8f,San,GF,Aug 25)
Hamilton Silk 39 (12f,Ham,G,Spt 24)
Hamsaat (IRE) 49 (8f,Hay,G,Jun 10)
Hand Craft (IRE) 55 (9f,Rip,GF,Aug 12)
Hand Woven 57 (9f,Ham,F,Jly 29)
Haniya (IRE) 56 (12f,Hay,G,Spt 22)
Hannah's Usher 30 (5f,Not,GS,Spt 11)
Harayir (USA) 94 (8f,Goo,GF,Aug 26)
Hard Love 40 (10f,Yar,GF,Jly 27)
Hard to Figure 88 (6f,Nwb,G,Jly 15)
Harding 30 (10f,Lei,F,Oct 24)
Harding Brown (USA) 36 (12f,Bri,F,Jly 31)
Hardy Dancer 59 (10f,Eps,GF,Jun 9)
Harlech (IRE) 38 (10½f,Yor,GF,Aug 30)
Harlestone Brook 77 (20f,Asc,GF,Jun 20)
Haroldon (IRE) 60 (12f,Hay,S,Oct 1)
Harry Browne (IRE) 54 (12f,Yor,GF,Oct 5)
Harry Welsh (IRE) 40 (14f,Not,GF,Oct 26)
Harry's Coming 40 (5f,Lin,GF,May 20)
Harry's Treat 35 (7f,Edi,F,Jun 26)
Harvest Reaper 37 (7f,Fol,G,Oct 16)
Harvey White (IRE) 36 (9f,Nwm,GF,Oct 27)
Hasta la Vista 36 (12f,Rip,GF,Aug 19)
Hatta Breeze 47 (8f,Lei,G,Oct 9)
Hatta River (USA) 45 (11f,Red,GF,Aug 23)
Hatta Sunshine (USA) 31 (9f,Goo,F,Jly 27)
Hattaafeh (IRE) 44 (12f,Nwm,GF,Oct 27)
Hawa Al Nasamaat (USA) 59 (7f,San,G,Jly 7)
Hawaash (IRE) 55 (7f,Nwm,GF,Oct 14)
Hawker's News (IRE) 50 (12f,Nwm,G,Spt 29)
Hawkish (USA) 33 (10f,Pon,F,Oct 16)
Hawwam 41 (8f,Hay,GF,Jly 8)
Hazard a Guess (IRE) 59 (12f,Asc,GF,Jun 21)
He Knows The Rules 31 (10f,Lei,S,Mar 30)
Head Turner 38 (15½f,Fol,GF,Apr 25)
Heart Broken 40 (6f,Crl,F,Jun 28)
Heart Lake 39 (6f,Nwm,GF,Jly 13)
Heath Robinson (IRE) 38 (10½f,Chs,GF,May 9)
Heathyards Lady (USA) 38 (7f,Lei,G,Spt 5)
Heathyards Magic (IRE) 33 (8f,Crl,F,Jun 29)
Heathyards Rock 62 (8f,Don,GF,Mar 25)
Heboob Alshemaal (IRE) 54 (10½f,Hay,S,Spt 30)
Hedera (USA) 38 (10f,Nwb,GF,Aug 11)
Helios 58 (8f,Goo,GF,Jun 9)
Hello Hobson's (IRE) 39 (6f,Nwb,GF,Jun 26)
Hello Mister 76 (6f,Nwm,GF,Oct 14)
Helmsman (USA) 67 (7f,Nwm,GF,Apr 19)
Henry Koehler 42 (7f,Nwb,G,Apr 22)
Here Comes Risky 43 (6f,Ayr,G,Spt 16)
Here Comes a Star 58 (5f,Crl,Hd,Aug 16)
Herr Trigger 58 (10f,Nwm,GF,May 7)

Hever Golf Rose 69 (7f,Lei,GF,Apr 29)
Hever Golf Star 48 (5f,Eps,GF,Spt 6)
Hey Up Dolly (IRE) 41 (7f,Chs,GF,May 10)
Hi Nod 76 (7f,Nwm,GF,Aug 5)
Hi Penny 32 (7f,Fol,G,Jun 7)
Hi Rock 38 (6f,Nwc,GF,Oct 30)
Hi-Aud 44 (12f,Kem,GF,Jun 14)
Hickory Blue 56 (5f,Lin,GF,May 12)
High Commotion (IRE) 30 (12f,Sal,GF,May 7)
High Domain (IRE) 52 (6f,Thi,G,Jly 21)
High Five (IRE) 30 (20f,Asc,GF,Jun 20)
High Flown (USA) 32 (12f,Pon,GF,Jly 3)
High Flying Adored (IRE) 57 (11½f,Lin,GF,Jun 27)
High Patriarch (IRE) 59 (10½f,Hay,G,Spt 22)
High Premium 63 (10f,Nwm,G,Spt 26)
High Priest 42 (5f,Lin,GF,Jun 24)
High Pyrenees 31 (10f,Nwc,G,May 25)
High Standard 45 (12f,Don,GF,Oct 21)
Highborn (IRE) 67 (7½f,Chs,GF,May 11)
Highbrook (USA) 51 (12f,Yor,GF,May 16)
Highfield Fizz 38 (11f,Red,G,Spt 22)
Highflying 80 (12f,Yor,GF,Aug 17)
Hill Farm Dancer 37 (13f,Ham,F,Jun 14)
Hillzah (USA) 54 (14f,Not,GF,Jun 21)
Himalayan Blue 32 (10f,Not,GF,Apr 17)
Hindaawee (USA) 36 (7f,Sal,F,Aug 10)
Hinton Rock (IRE) 62 (5f,Kem,G,Jun 3)
Hit the Canvas (USA) 45 (16½f,Don,F,Jly 27)
Hiwaya 48 (8½f,Eps,GF,Jun 9)
Ho-Joe (IRE) 53 (12f,Rip,F,Jun 21)
Hoh Express 78 (10½f,Yor,GF,Aug 16)
Hoh Magic 69 (6f,Nwm,GF,Jly 13)
Holtye (IRE) 70 (8f,Asc,GF,Jun 20)
Home Counties (IRE) 51 (10½f,Hay,G,Spt 23)
Honey Mount 53 (16f,Goo,G,Spt 9)
Honfleur (IRE) 46 (12f,Yor,GF,Jun 16)
Hong Kong Designer 32 (14f,San,G,Jly 7)
Hong Kong Dollar 30 (8f,Nwm,G,May 19)
Horesti 50 (8f,Nwm,GF,Apr 19)
Hot Snap 37 (5f,Nwm,GF,Jun 30)
Hotspur Street 42 (10f,Wnd,GF,Jly 10)
Houghton Venture (USA) 38 (7f,Hay,G,Apr 15)
House of Dreams 42 (10½f,Hay,G,Spt 22)
How's Yer Father 68 (6f,Fol,G,Jun 7)
How's it Goin (IRE) 36 (12f,Chp,GF,Jly 20)
Hugwity 50 (7f,Nwb,GF,May 21)
Hujjab (USA) 58 (8f,Rip,GF,May 31)
Hullbank 47 (14f,Red,F,Jun 24)
Humbel (USA) 72 (12f,Eps,GF,Jun 10)
Humbert's Landing (IRE) 64 (6f,Kem,GF,May 27)
Hunters of Brora (IRE) 69 (10½f,Yor,GF,Aug 16)
Hydrofoil 34 (12f,Bat,Hd,Jly 10)
I'm Outa Here (IRE) 40 (8f,Lin,GS,Jly 30)

I'm Your Lady 58 (5f,Hay,GS,May 27)
Iblis (IRE) 62 (7f,Nwm,GF,Apr 18)
Ihtiram (IRE) 75 (8f,San,GF,Apr 29)
Ikaab (USA) 56 (6f,Nwm,GF,Aug 4)
Ikis Girl 31 (7½f,Bev,GF,Apr 7)
Iktamal (USA) 71 (6f,Nwm,GF,Oct 14)
Iktasab 45 (7f,Ayr,G,Jly 17)
Il Trastevere (FR) 40 (7f,Red,F,Oct 3)
Iltimas (USA) 66 (5f,Sal,F,Aug 9)
Imad (USA) 50 (16½f,San,GF,Aug 18)
Imlak (IRE) 31 (10f,Not,GF,Apr 17)
Imperial Bid (FR) 51 (10f,Ayr,GF,Jun 2)
Impulsive Air (IRE) 58 (7f,Nwm,G,May 5)
In Camera (IRE) 72 (14½f,Don,GS,Spt 9)
In Good Faith 36 (12f,Hay,G,Spt 22)
In the Money (IRE) 47 (12f,Don,G,Mar 23)
Incha 37 (8f,War,F,Apr 27)
Inchcailloch (IRE) 51 (18f,Nwm,GF,Oct 14)
Inchkeith 42 (10f,Yar,G,Jun 14)
Indefence (IRE) 37 (9f,Nwc,G,May 24)
Inderaputeri 51 (8f,Bri,F,Aug 21)
Indescent Blue 31 (7f,Nwb,GF,Apr 21)
Indhar 75 (7f,Nwb,G,Jly 14)
Indiahra 34 (6f,Ham,F,Jun 5)
Indian Fly 83 (8f,Yor,GF,Aug 17)
Indian Jockey 33 (10½f,Chs,G,Jun 8)
Indian Light 61 (12f,Goo,F,Jly 25)
Indian Rhapsody 36 (7f,Nwm,G,Aug 25)
Indian Temple 32 (8f,Bat,G,Jun 2)
Indigo Time (IRE) 65 (12f,Asc,S,Oct 6)
Indonesian (IRE) 49 (12f,Don,GS,Spt 8)
Indrapura (IRE) 38 (7f,War,F,May 8)
Inherent Magic (IRE) 62 (5f,Hay,S,Spt 30)
Inn At the Top 44 (14f,Hay,G,Spt 23)
Innocence 47 (11½f,Yar,GF,Aug 17)
Inquisitor (USA) 76 (12f,Hay,G,Spt 2)
Insider Trader 57 (5f,Yor,G,Oct 4)
Instantaneous 38 (14f,Not,GF,Aug 21)
Intendant 45 (8f,Rip,GF,May 31)
Intiaash (IRE) 53 (5f,Nwm,GF,Jun 30)
Invest Wisely 61 (18f,Yar,G,Spt 14)
Invigilate 38 (5f,Thi,GF,Aug 25)
Invocation 38 (6f,Lin,F,May 13)
Inzar (USA) 77 (6f,Yar,GF,Aug 10)
Ionio (USA) 80 (10f,Asc,GF,Jun 20)
Iridal 49 (12f,Pon,GF,Jly 28)
Irie Mon (IRE) 34 (8f,Chp,GF,Jun 15)
Irish Groom 30 (11f,War,F,Aug 28)
Irkutsk (USA) 44 (12f,Goo,GF,Jun 9)
Iron Gent (USA) 33 (14f,Sal,GF,May 7)
Ironic (IRE) 36 (8f,Goo,G,Spt 8)
Island Blade (IRE) 40 (14f,Nwm,G,May 19)
Island Cascade 31 (10f,Ayr,GF,Jun 2)
Ism 44 (6f,Lei,S,Spt 18)

Ismeno 40 (12f,Chp,GF,Jly 13)
Istabraq (IRE) 77 (16f,Nwb,GS,Oct 19)
Istidaad (USA) 75 (12f,Asc,F,Jun 23)
It's Academic 51 (6f,Not,GS,Spt 11)
It'sthebusiness 31 (8½f,Eps,GS,Spt 19)
Itab (USA) 35 (8f,Thi,GF,May 19)
Ivan the Terrible (IRE) 46 (9f,Ham,G,May 4)
Ivor's Flutter 32 (16f,Nwc,F,Jly 1)
Jack Button (IRE) 54 (19f,Chs,GF,May 10)
Jackatack (IRE) 34 (8f,Chp,GS,Oct 10)
Jackmanii 33 (12½f,Nwc,GF,Apr 17)
Jade City 48 (5f,Fol,G,Jun 7)
Jade Pet 65 (5f,Lin,GF,Jly 1)
Jadwal (USA) 56 (14½f,Don,GF,Oct 20)
Jafeica (IRE) 63 (7f,Nwm,GF,Jly 13)
Jagellon (USA) 58 (10f,Nwb,GS,Oct 19)
Jalcanto 43 (14f,Red,F,Jly 12)
Jalfrezi 57 (10f,Goo,F,Jly 28)
Jalore 33 (16f,Cat,G,Jun 2)
Jam N Shadeed (USA) 56 (7f,San,G,Jly 7)
Jambia 55 (10f,Don,G,May 29)
Jameel Asmar 68 (12f,Yor,GF,Aug 17)
Jandeel (IRE) 62 (12f,Goo,GF,Aug 25)
Jaraab 48 (16f,Lin,Std,Aug 5)
Jato 57 (7f,Nwm,GF,Spt 30)
Jawaal 75 (8f,Yor,G,May 17)
Jawlaat (USA) 56 (6f,Hay,GF,Jly 6)
Jayannpee 74 (6f,Goo,GF,Jly 29)
Jellaby Askhir 66 (14½f,Don,GS,Spt 9)
Jemima Puddleduck 45 (12f,Lei,G,Apr 6)
Jibereen 66 (7f,Chp,GS,Oct 10)
Jigsaw Boy 35 (6f,Lei,GF,May 29)
Jo Maximus 48 (5f,San,GF,Jly 20)
Jobie 56 (5f,San,GF,Aug 30)
John Lee Hooker 40 (14f,San,G,Jly 7)
John O'Dreams 47 (5f,San,G,Spt 12)
Johnnie the Joker 39 (10f,Red,F,Oct 24)
Johns Act (USA) 62 (12f,Don,GF,Nov 4)
Join the Clan 70 (5f,Don,GF,Jly 2)
Jolto 56 (7f,Yor,G,Oct 7)
Joseph's Wine (IRE) 59 (10f,Don,G,Mar 24)
Jovie King (IRE) 32 (7f,Nwb,GF,Jun 15)
Jubran (USA) 57 (10f,Rip,F,Jun 22)
Jucea 52 (5f,Pon,G,Spt 21)
Judgement Call 33 (5f,San,GF,Aug 9)
Jumilla (USA) 45 (10f,Yar,G,Spt 12)
Jural 61 (14½f,Don,GS,Spt 9)
Just Bob 46 (5f,Edi,GF,Jun 16)
Just Dissident (IRE) 49 (5f,Don,G,Jun 10)
Just Fizzy 35 (8f,Pon,GF,Jly 28)
Just Flamenco 38 (10f,Wnd,GF,Jly 24)
Just Happy (USA) 89 (10f,Asc,GF,Jun 20)
Just Harry 53 (8f,Kem,G,Jly 12)
Just Like Me 48 (5f,San,GF,Aug 30)

Juyush (USA) 72 (10½f,Yor,G,May 17)
Kaafih Homm (IRE) 55 (12f,Bri,G,Spt 20)
Kabcast 37 (5f,Crl,Hd,Aug 21)
Kabil 53- (7f,Nwc,F,Jly 1)
Kadiri (IRE) 40 (15f,War,G,May 27)
Kaf 50 (8f,Red,F,Jun 24)
Kalabo (USA) 79 (12f,Asc,F,Jun 23)
Kalamata 47 (10f,Bat,GF,Spt 25)
Kalar 33 (5f,Thi,GF,Aug 25)
Kalou 60 (10f,Ayr,GF,Jun 2)
Kama Simba 33 (8f,Not,GF,Jun 26)
Kandyan 64 (10½f,Yor,GF,Aug 31)
Karaar 44 (8f,Hay,G,Jun 10)
Karayb (IRE) 43 (8f,Lei,G,Oct 10)
Karayib (USA) 47 (7f,San,G,May 29)
Karina Heights (USA) 49 (5f,Not,GF,Jun 12)
Karinska 40 (8f,Yar,GF,Jly 5)
Karttikeya (FR) 47 (12f,Kem,GF,Aug 16)
Kassbaan (USA) 58 (6f,Goo,GF,May 23)
Katie Oliver 36 (14f,Hay,G,Spt 22)
Katy's Lad 36 (10½f,Chs,GF,Jun 28)
Katya (IRE) 65 (5f,Sal,F,Aug 9)
Kayrawan (USA) 32 (6f,Kem,GF,Apr 17)
Kayvee 79 (7f,Nwm,GF,Aug 5)
Kazaki 53 (8f,Nwm,GF,Apr 19)
Keen To The Last (FR) 44 (8f,San,GF,Jly 20)
Keep Battling 41 (10f,Ayr,GF,Jun 2)
Keep Your Distance 59 (12f,Cat,GF,Oct 13)
Kelly Mac 44 (7f,Chp,GS,Oct 10)
Kemo Sabo 60 (7½f,Bev,GF,Aug 10)
Kenesha (IRE) 36 (5f,Crl,F,May 12)
Keston Pond (IRE) 66 (7f,Yar,F,Jun 27)
Kestrel Forboxes (IRE) 47 (8f,Goo,G,Spt 8)
Kevasingo 38 (8f,Sal,F,Jun 29)
Khamaseen 69 (12f,Don,G,Mar 25)
Khamseh 63 (7f,Chs,GF,Aug 18)
Khan 48 (7½f,Bev,GF,May 13)
Khatim (USA) 46 (7f,Yar,GF,Aug 17)
Khayrapour (IRE) 69 (8f,Goo,F,Jly 27)
Kid Ory 52 (7f,Red,GF,Aug 27)
Kilcoran Bay 48 (8f,Goo,GF,May 23)
Kildee Lad 56 (5f,San,G,Apr 28)
Kilernan 44 (12f,Rip,F,Jun 21)
Killick 58 (12f,Chs,GF,Jly 14)
Kilnamartyra Girl 44 (7½f,Bev,GF,Jun 14)
Kimberley Boy 35 (12f,Thi,GF,May 19)
Kimbridge Knight (IRE) 51 (12f,Asc,GF,Jun 22)
Kindergarten Boy (IRE) 48 (9f,Lin,GF,Jun 24)
King Chestnut 47 (7f,Red,GF,Aug 27)
King Curan (USA) 43 (10f,Ayr,F,Jun 24)
King Rambo 38 (5f,Pon,GF,Jly 28)
King Rat (IRE) 66 (7f,Red,GF,Aug 27)
King of Show (IRE) 43 (8f,Crl,G,Apr 28)
King of Tunes (FR) 43 (8f,Asc,S,Oct 6)

King's Crown 44 (9f,Rip,G,May 21)
Kingchip Boy 58 (8f,Goo,F,May 24)
Kings Assembly 49 (10f,Nwb,GS,Oct 19)
Kings Cay (IRE) 41 (10½f,Chs,G,Jun 8)
Kinoko 30 (16f,Cat,G,Spt 16)
Kintwyn 47 (8f,War,GS,Oct 3)
Kira 41 (6f,Lei,F,Oct 23)
Kismetim 30 (12f,Nwm,G,Spt 28)
Knave's Ash (USA) 79 (8f,Yor,GF,Aug 17)
Knayton Lass 47 (5f,Not,GF,Aug 2)
Knight Commander (USA) 53 (8f,Goo,F,Jly 29)
Knobbleeneeze 57 (8f,Chp,G,May 29)
Knotally Wood (USA) 46 (7f,Nwb,GF,May 21)
Koathary (USA) 56 (10f,San,G,May 29)
Komiamaite 31 (8f,Lei,G,Oct 9)
Komodo (USA) 45 (8f,San,G,May 30)
Komreyev Dancer 50 (10f,Rip,G,Aug 28)
Korambi 72 (12f,Don,GF,Nov 4)
Krayyan Dawn 34 (12f,Asc,GF,Aug 23)
Kristal's Paradise (IRE) 68 (16f,Goo,GS,Spt 30)
Kriva 34 (14f,Yar,G,Jly 18)
Krystallos 48 (8f,Asc,GF,Jun 20)
Kshessinskaya 54 (12f,Yor,GF,Aug 17)
Kummel King 38 (8f,Hay,G,Spt 2)
Kung Frode 44 (5f,Lei,S,Spt 18)
Kutta 59 (10f,Don,GS,Spt 9)
Kymin (IRE) 39 (12f,Bri,F,May 26)
La Belle Dominique 40 (5f,Don,G,Jun 10)
La Brief 31 (12f,Nwm,GF,Oct 27)
La Confederation 74 (12f,Yor,GF,Aug 16)
La Gran Senorita (USA) 39 (8f,San,GS,Spt 12)
La Menorquina (USA) 31 (16½f,Fol,G,Jun 7)
La Petite Fusee 54 (6f,Lin,G,Jun 3)
La Spezia 35 (12f,Nwb,G,May 19)
La Suquet 41 (5f,Not,GF,Apr 17)
Labibeh (USA) 64 (12f,Asc,S,Oct 7)
Labudd (USA) 46 (8f,Goo,G,Spt 29)
Lady Highfield 39 (10f,Lei,G,Oct 10)
Lady Lacey 34 (8f,Kem,G,Jun 3)
Lady Sheriff 66 (5f,Don,GF,Nov 4)
Lady-Bo-K 30 (6f,Crl,F,May 12)
Lago Di Varano 61 (5f,Yor,GF,Aug 16)
Lake Coniston (IRE) 96 (6f,Nwm,GF,Jly 13)
Lalindi (IRE) 55 (16f,War,GF,Jun 12)
Lammtarra (USA) 81 (12f,Eps,GF,Jun 10)
Lancashire Life (IRE) 39 (7½f,Bev,GF,Aug 24)
Lancer (USA) 43 (9f,Rip,GS,Apr 5)
Lancerette 35 (8f,Pon,GF,Oct 2)
Landlord 31 (7f,Lin,GF,Jun 17)
Lap of Luxury 65 (8f,Yor,GF,Aug 17)
Larn Fort 45 (10f,Pon,GF,Jly 11)
Larrocha (IRE) 74 (12f,Yor,GF,Aug 17)
Last Corner 44 (12f,Ham,G,Spt 24)
Last Laugh (IRE) 33 (12f,Nwb,G,May 31)

Last Roundup 41 (7f,Chs,GF,Aug 18)
Last Spin 31 (12f,Eps,GF,Jun 9)
Latahaab (USA) 59 (16f,Goo,GS,Spt 30)
Latching (IRE) 64 (5f,Nwm,G,Spt 28)
Latin Leader 48 (10f,Wnd,GF,Aug 14)
Latvian 60 (13f,Ham,F,Jun 14)
Lavender (IRE) 35 (10½f,Hay,GF,May 8)
Law Commission 53 (6f,Sal,F,Aug 10)
Laxford Bridge 68 (10½f,Chs,GF,May 9)
Leading Princess (IRE) 36 (5f,Nwc,GF,Oct 30)
Leading Spirit (IRE) 62 (12f,Ham,G,Spt 24)
Leap for Joy 52 (5f,Asc,G,Spt 23)
Lear Dancer (USA) 61 (16f,Goo,G,Spt 9)
Legal Fiction 42 (8f,Ayr,G,Spt 15)
Legal Issue (IRE) 42 (7f,Lei,G,Jly 19)
Legatee 41 (7f,Fol,G,Mar 27)
Legendary Leap 52 (10f,Goo,F,Jly 25)
Leif the Lucky (USA) 58 (8f,Don,GF,Mar 25)
Leigh Crofter 56 (5f,Lei,S,Spt 18)
Lennox Lewis 65 (6f,Hay,GS,May 27)
Leontios (IRE) 30 (10f,Nwm,GF,Apr 20)
Lepine (IRE) 59 (5f,Hay,GF,Aug 5)
Lesley's Fashion 50 (10½f,Chs,GF,May 9)
Lidhama (USA) 55 (12f,Nwm,GF,Oct 27)
Light Fantastic 37 (8f,Bri,F,Jun 1)
Limosa 36 (16½f,Fol,G,Jun 7)
Lincoln Treasure (IRE) 33 (7f,Nwm,GF,Aug 5)
Linger 47 (8f,War,GS,Oct 3)
Linney Head (USA) 80 (16½f,San,G,May 29)
Linpac West 70 (12f,Don,G,Mar 25)
Lion Tower 61 (10½f,Hay,G,Spt 22)
Lipizzaner (IRE) 60 (7f,Nwm,G,May 5)
Little Ibnr 42 (5f,Don,GF,Nov 4)
Little Saboteur 43 (5f,Lin,GF,May 27)
Llia 47 (10f,Nwm,GF,May 7)
Lloc 36 (5f,Nwm,GF,Jly 11)
Lobana (IRE) 36 (7f,Nwb,GF,Apr 21)
Loch Patrick 74 (5f,San,GF,Jun 17)
Lochon 45 (6f,Pon,GF,Aug 22)
Locorotondo (IRE) 57 (10f,Ayr,G,Spt 15)
Loki (IRE) 63 (10f,Nwm,G,Spt 26)
Lomas (IRE) 66 (7f,San,GF,Jun 16)
Lombardic (USA) 61 (12f,Yor,GF,Jly 14)
Lookingforarainbow (IRE) 63 (12f,Thi,G,Jun 5)
Lord Hastie (USA) 52 (12f,Yor,GF,Aug 17)
Lord High Admiral (CAN) 78 (5f,Hay,GS,May 27)
Lord Jim (IRE) 57 (14f,Yor,GF,May 16)
Lord Oberon (IRE) 43 (8f,Chp,GF,Jly 8)
Lord Olivier (IRE) 62 (6f,Nwm,GF,May 7)
Lord Vivienne (IRE) 38 (10f,Pon,GF,Jly 11)
Lorelei Lee (IRE) 43 (8½f,Bev,G,Jly 18)
Lost Lagoon (USA) 46 (10f,San,GF,Aug 9)
Lough Erne 42 (6f,Rip,GF,May 31)
Louis' Queen (IRE) 56 (8f,Asc,S,Oct 6)

Louisville Belle (IRE) 43 (6f,Nwm,G,Jly 21)
Love Legend 40 (7f,Chp,GF,Jun 15)
Love The Blues 44 (10f,San,GS,Spt 13)
Lovely Lyca 49 (10f,Goo,GF,Jun 16)
Lovely Me (IRE) 43 (5f,Thi,GF,Aug 25)
Lovely Millie (IRE) 55 (7f,Don,G,Spt 7)
Loveyoumillions (IRE) 57 (6f,Hay,GS,May 27)
Loving Legacy 41 (10f,Yar,GF,Jly 27)
Lowawatha 30 (10f,Wnd,G,Jun 12)
Loyalize (USA) 63 (6f,Hay,GS,May 27)
Lucayan Sunshine (USA) 61 (12f,Asc,S,Oct 6)
Lucidity 39 (10f,Rip,G,Aug 28)
Lucky Coin 38 (11½f,Lin,GF,Aug 24)
Lucky Di (USA) 59 (8f,Rip,GS,Apr 5)
Lucky Parkes 84 (5f,Lin,GF,Aug 24)
Lucky Quest 35 (14f,Sal,GS,Spt 27)
Lucky Soph (USA) 35 (7f,Nwm,G,May 5)
Lucky Tucky 43 (7f,Yar,F,Jun 27)
Ludgate (USA) 63 (10½f,Yor,G,May 17)
Lunar Mission (IRE) 45 (10f,Don,GF,Oct 21)
Luso 68 (14½f,Don,GS,Spt 9)
Lyford Law (IRE) 40 (7f,Lei,G,Jun 17)
Lynton Lad 45 (8f,Not,GF,Oct 26)
Lyrikos (USA) 61 (8f,Nwb,G,Apr 22)
Ma Petite Anglaise 51 (7½f,Chs,GF,Aug 19)
Mac's Taxi 41 (7f,Cat,G,Apr 26)
Macfarlane 51 (5f,Chs,G,Jun 8)
Mack the Knife 58 (12f,Nwm,G,Spt 29)
Mackook (USA) 58 (8f,Asc,F,Jun 24)
Macoumba (USA) 59 (8f,Nwm,GF,May 7)
Macs Maharanee 59 (6f,Nwm,G,Jly 21)
Mad Militant (IRE) 52 (12f,Chs,GF,May 11)
Madly Sharp 73 (7f,Nwm,GF,Jly 13)
Maeterlinck (IRE) 55 (10f,Don,GF,Jly 2)
Magic Junction (USA) 55 (10½f,Yor,G,Oct 4)
Magic Orb 63 (6f,Don,G,Jun 10)
Magic Pearl 36 (5f,Yor,GF,Jun 16)
Magical Manoeuvers 39 (6f,Not,G,Apr 24)
Magical Retreat (USA) 79 (12f,Yor,GF,Aug 16)
Magna Carta 32 (7f,Yor,G,May 18)
Magnificent Devil (USA) 53 (5f,San,G,Jly 8)
Maiandros (GR) 58 (7f,War,F,May 8)
Maid O'Cannie 43 (6f,Lei,S,Spt 18)
Maid for Walking 51 (6f,Yar,G,Jun 14)
Main Offender 51 (10f,Not,GF,Oct 26)
Majboor Yafooz (USA) 31 (10f,Wnd,GF,May 15)
Majestic Role (FR) 65 (12f,Yor,GF,Aug 17)
Major Change 59 (9f,San,G,Jun 17)
Major Mouse 35 (8f,Rip,GF,May 31)
Make Time 45 (7f,Yar,GF,Aug 10)
Make a Stand 51 (14f,Nwm,G,Spt 29)
Makri 32 (7f,Kem,G,Jun 3)
Malibu Man 46 (6f,Not,GS,Spt 19)
Mamlakah (IRE) 68 (8f,Asc,GF,Jun 21)

Mamnoon (USA) 39 (12f,Chs,GF,May 11)
Manabar 30 (8f,Thi,G,Jun 5)
Mandarina (USA) 55 (8f,Asc,F,Jun 24)
Manful 48 (10½f,Hay,G,Apr 15)
Maple Bay (IRE) 39 (6f,Hay,G,Spt 1)
Maralinga (IRE) 64 (12f,Chs,GF,May 9)
Marchant Ming (IRE) 48 (11½f,Yar,GF,Aug 17)
Marchman 38 (8f,Bat,F,Jly 1)
Marguerite Bay (IRE) 32 (7f,Goo,F,May 24)
Marha 57 (6f,Yar,GF,Aug 10)
Marocco (USA) 57 (7f,Nwb,GF,May 21)
Maronetta 31 (11f,Red,G,Spt 22)
Marrowfat Lady (IRE) 39 (7f,Fol,G,Jly 5)
Marsoom (CAN) 90 (12f,Asc,GF,Jun 21)
Martinosky 35 (7f,Fol,G,Mar 27)
Mary's Case (USA) 45 (8f,Yar,GF,Oct 18)
Marzipan (IRE) 40 (10f,Bat,Hd,Aug 3)
Masafah (USA) 57 (6f,Yar,G,Jun 7)
Masnad (USA) 33 (7f,War,G,Apr 17)
Masruf (IRE) 43 (6f,Hay,GF,Jly 8)
Master Beveled 57 (8f,Yor,GF,Aug 30)
Master Charter 44 (7f,Don,GF,Oct 20)
Master Hyde (USA) 45 (12f,Yor,GF,Aug 17)
Master M-E-N (IRE) 35 (8f,Bat,Hd,Spt 4)
Master Millfield (IRE) 47 (8f,War,GS,Oct 3)
Master Ofthe House 52 (8f,Red,GF,Aug 23)
Master Planner 78 (5f,Nwm,G,Jly 22)
Master of Passion 68 (6f,Asc,F,Jun 23)
Masuri Kabisa (USA) 30 (12f,Nwm,GF,Oct 27)
Matamoros 33 (13½f,Red,F,Oct 12)
Maurangi 44 (9f,Yor,GF,Jun 17)
Maydaan (IRE) 51 (6f,Chp,G,May 29)
Mayreau 42 (12f,Bat,Hd,Spt 4)
Mbulwa 49 (7f,Nwc,GF,Oct 30)
Meant to Be 66 (16f,Asc,S,Oct 6)
Medaille Militaire 78 (10½f,Yor,GF,Aug 16)
Media Express 53 (6f,Not,G,Apr 24)
Mediation (IRE) 66 (7f,Asc,GF,Jun 21)
Medieval Miss 38 (8½f,Eps,GF,Jly 5)
Medway (IRE) 35 (12f,Fol,S,Spt 27)
Meghdoot 40 (10f,San,GS,Spt 13)
Melasus (IRE) 46 (7f,Kem,G,Jun 3)
Mellottie 80 (8f,Goo,F,Jly 29)
Melodic Drive 46 (6f,Red,F,Jun 23)
Menas Gold 53 (8f,Nwm,GF,May 7)
Menshood (IRE) 33 (10f,Don,G,Mar 23)
Mentalasanythin 67 (13f,Ham,F,Jun 14)
Mentor (GR) 65 (12f,Chs,GF,Jly 14)
Mercadier 37 (14f,Goo,F,May 24)
Merit (IRE) 37 (15f,Edi,S,Nov 2)
Merlin's Fancy 32 (8f,Lei,G,Oct 9)
Merry Festival (USA) 59 (10½f,Hay,G,Spt 22)
Metal Boys 43 (5f,San,GF,Jun 16)
Mezaan (IRE) 69 (10½f,Yor,GF,Aug 16)

Mhemeanles 36 (10f,Pon,G,Jun 12)
Miami Banker 37 (5f,Eps,GF,Spt 6)
Miasma (USA) 48 (8f,Bat,GF,Spt 25)
Michellisa 47 (8f,Lei,G,Oct 9)
Microlite (USA) 43 (12f,Crl,F,Jly 8)
Midnight Break 42 (5f,Nwm,G,Spt 28)
Midnight Jazz (IRE) 49 (7f,Yar,GF,Jly 27)
Midnight Legend 79 (12f,Asc,F,Jun 23)
Midnight Spell 37 (7f,Fol,GF,Apr 10)
Midwich Cuckoo 50 (7f,San,G,Jly 7)
Midyan Blue (IRE) 68 (14f,Yor,GF,Aug 16)
Mighty Kingdom (IRE) 35 (8f,Bat,Hd,Spt 4)
Mighty Squaw 47 (7f,Nwb,GF,Apr 21)
Mihriz (IRE) 58 (8f,Lei,GF,Apr 29)
Mill Dancer (IRE) 31 (10f,Lei,S,Spt 18)
Millesime (IRE) 45 (5f,Yar,GF,Aug 3)
Million Dancer 32 (12f,Nwb,G,May 31)
Millstream (USA) 64 (6f,Nwm,GF,Jly 13)
Millyant 64 (5f,Yor,GF,Aug 17)
Mind Games 74 (5f,Nwm,G,May 6)
Minds Music (USA) 75 (14½f,Don,GS,Spt 9)
Minnesota Viking 49 (12f,Nwm,GF,Jly 28)
Miriam 37 (5f,Lin,GF,May 21)
Misbelief 81 (14f,Yor,GF,Aug 16)
Mislemani (IRE) 46 (8f,Nwm,GF,Aug 5)
Miss Aragon 37 (6f,Nwm,G,Jly 21)
Miss Charlie 46 (7f,Chs,GF,Aug 19)
Miss Felixstowe (USA) 31 (10f,Rip,GF,Aug 12)
Miss Movie World 47 (5f,Thi,G,Jun 5)
Miss Pin Up 68 (12f,Asc,GF,Jly 22)
Miss Whittingham (IRE) 36 (6f,Thi,GF,Apr 21)
Miss Zanzibar 35 (10f,Nwm,GF,Jly 28)
Missed Flight 80 (8f,San,G,Apr 28)
Missed the Boat (IRE) 30 (13f,Bat,Hd,Spt 4)
Missel 41 (8f,Kem,GF,Apr 15)
Mister Fire Eyes (IRE) 45 (8f,Not,GF,Oct 19)
Mister Jolson 58 (6f,Kem,GF,May 27)
Mister O'Grady (IRE) 33 (9f,Lin,GF,Jun 24)
Mister Raider 39 (5f,Not,GF,Apr 17)
Mister Rm 47 (7f,Nwb,GS,Spt 15)
Mister Westsound 47 (7f,Red,F,Oct 3)
Mistertopogigo (IRE) 67 (5f,Thi,GF,Apr 21)
Mistinguett (IRE) 48 (10½f,Hay,GS,Oct 11)
Mistle Cat (USA) 84 (7f,Lei,GF,Apr 29)
Mistress Thames 40 (6f,Fol,G,Oct 16)
Misty Silks 58 (8f,Lei,G,Oct 9)
Mizyan (IRE) 54 (14f,Not,GF,May 2)
Mo's Star 36 (8f,Goo,G,Spt 8)
Mo-Addab (IRE) 62 (8f,Pon,G,Apr 25)
Moccasin Run (USA) 66 (7f,Goo,GF,Aug 26)
Modajjaj 31 (10½f,Yor,GF,Oct 5)
Modest Hope (USA) 47 (14f,Yar,GF,Aug 10)
Mokhtar (IRE) 52 (12f,Nwm,GF,Jun 23)
Mokuti 34 (8f,Yar,G,Jun 7)

Moments of Fortune (USA) 61 (8f,Don,GF,Mar 25)
Monaassib (IRE) 67 (7f,Red,F,Oct 3)
Monarch 56 (12f,Asc,GF,Jun 22)
Mondragon 66 (16f,Red,F,Jly 13)
Moneefa 59 (8f,Asc,S,Oct 6)
Monis (IRE) 31 (5f,Pon,G,Spt 21)
Monkey Wench (IRE) 37 (11f,Ayr,GF,May 10)
Montendre 80 (6f,Nwb,G,Jly 15)
Montjoy (USA) 77 (10f,Nwm,GF,Oct 14)
Montone (IRE) 47 (10f,San,GF,Aug 19)
Montserrat 49 (6f,Nwm,GF,Oct 28)
Monty 35 (6f,Nwm,GF,Oct 28)
Monument 41 (8f,Hay,G,Jun 10)
Moody 39 (5f,Nwm,G,Spt 28)
Moofaji 38 (11f,Ayr,GF,May 10)
Moon King (IRE) 53 (7f,Nwb,G,Apr 22)
Moon Mistress 55 (10f,Don,GS,Spt 9)
Moon Strike (FR) 54 (7f,Lin,F,May 13)
Moonax (IRE) 68 (20f,Asc,GF,Jun 22)
Moonlight Calypso 37 (11f,Ham,GF,May 5)
Moonlight Quest 68 (16f,Goo,GS,Spt 30)
Moonlight Saunter (USA) 43 (6f,Nwm,GF,Aug 4)
Moonshell (IRE) 72 (12f,Eps,GF,Jun 9)
Moonshine Dancer 35 (16f,Cat,G,Spt 16)
Morocco (IRE) 54 (7f,Bri,G,Oct 1)
Moscow Mist (IRE) 39 (10f,Kem,G,Apr 26)
Moshaajir (USA) 41 (14f,Hay,G,Spt 22)
Motakabber (IRE) 53 (10½f,Yor,GF,Oct 5)
Moujeeb (USA) 47 (5f,Lin,GF,May 27)
Mountains of Mist (IRE) 33 (10f,Nwb,GF,May 20)
Mountgate 53 (7f,Nwm,GF,Oct 28)
Mousehole 58 (5f,Nwm,GF,Jun 30)
Move Smartly (IRE) 38 (8f,Hay,GF,Jly 8)
Move With Edes 37 (7f,Yar,GF,Jly 5)
Moving Arrow 82 (8f,Yor,G,Oct 4)
Mowlaie 58 (12f,Kem,GF,May 8)
Mr Bean 56 (12f,Eps,GF,Jun 11)
Mr Bergerac (IRE) 68 (5f,San,GF,Aug 18)
Mr Browning (USA) 55 (12f,Fol,F,Jun 30)
Mr Christie 40 (10½f,Hay,G,Spt 22)
Mr Confusion (IRE) 63 (10½f,Yor,G,May 18)
Mr Cube (IRE) 46 (7f,Kem,GF,Jly 12)
Mr Geneaology (USA) 57 (14f,Not,GF,Aug 21)
Mr Mactavish 35 (14f,Not,G,May 26)
Mr Martini (IRE) 77 (8f,Kem,GF,May 8)
Mr Medley 39 (8f,Nwb,GS,Spt 15)
Mr Nevermind (IRE) 52 (7f,Fol,G,Jun 7)
Mr Oscar 61 (5f,Lei,G,Spt 5)
Mr Rough 43 (7½f,Chs,GF,Aug 19)
Mr Teigh 36 (5f,Don,G,Jun 10)
Mr Towser 48 (12f,Thi,G,Jun 5)
Mu-Arrik 32 (6f,Red,G,Spt 23)
Mubariz (IRE) 35 (7f,Lin,F,May 13)

Much Too High 37 (16½f,Fol,G,Jun 7)
Muchtarak (IRE) 46 (7f,Lin,GF,Jly 15)
Mufarej (USA) 47 (7f,Lin,F,Spt 5)
Muferr (USA) 55 (10f,Rip,G,May 21)
Muhab (USA) 56 (8f,Asc,GF,Jun 20)
Muhtarram (USA) 97 (10f,Asc,GF,Jun 20)
Mukallad (IRE) 33 (8f,Chp,G,May 29)
Mukhatab 53 (8f,Red,GF,Aug 27)
Muktabas (IRE) 40 (7f,Sal,F,Aug 10)
Mulciber 48 (10f,Bat,Hd,Jly 10)
Mullitover 72 (7f,Nwm,GF,Spt 30)
Munif (IRE) 49 (12f,Asc,S,Spt 24)
Muntafi 32 (16f,Nwb,GF,May 21)
Munwar 70 (9f,Nwm,GF,Apr 20)
Murajja (USA) 65 (10½f,Hay,G,Apr 15)
Murphy's Gold (IRE) 50 (7½f,Bev,GF,Jun 14)
Murray's Mazda (IRE) 31 (6f,Thi,F,Jly 29)
Musetta (IRE) 65 (12f,Eps,GF,Jun 9)
Museum (IRE) 42 (9f,Red,F,Oct 3)
Music Maker 41 (10f,Kem,GF,Aug 16)
Musica 31 (5f,Bri,F,May 26)
Musical Season 45 (6f,Yor,GF,Jly 15)
Mustn't Grumble (IRE) 41 (6f,Hay,G,Spt 22)
Mutabassim (IRE) 55 (7f,Yar,GF,Aug 17)
Mutakddim (USA) 72 (8f,San,G,Apr 28)
Mutazz (USA) 34 (14f,Hay,GS,Jun 9)
Muzrak (CAN) 49 (13f,Ham,F,Jun 14)
My Abbey 31 (5f,Chs,GF,Aug 19)
My Best Valentine 60 (6f,Goo,GF,Aug 26)
My Cadeaux 55 (6f,Nwm,G,Jly 21)
My First Romance 30 (7f,Nwm,G,May 5)
My Gallery (IRE) 40 (8f,Rip,F,Jun 22)
My Gina 60 (9f,Ham,G,Spt 24)
My Handsome Prince 33 (8f,Rip,GF,May 31)
My Handy Man 37 (8f,Ham,F,Jly 7)
My Kerry Dancer (USA) 36 (11f,Ayr,GF,May 10)
My Learned Friend 71 (12f,Don,GF,Oct 21)
My Rossini 38 (14f,Hay,S,Spt 30)
Myasha (USA) 46 (5f,Lin,GF,Apr 7)
Myfontaine 49 (11f,War,GF,Jun 12)
Myrtle Quest 45 (8f,Asc,GF,Jun 20)
Myself 69 (8f,Asc,GF,Jun 21)
Mystic Hill 72 (12f,Asc,GF,Jun 21)
Mystic Lure 48 (6f,Nwm,G,Jly 21)
Naawy 35 (16f,Cat,G,Jun 2)
Nadwaty (IRE) 31 (5f,Pon,G,Spt 21)
Nagnagnag (IRE) 50 (7f,Eps,GF,Jun 11)
Najmat Alshemaal (IRE) 57 (11½f,Chs,GF,May 10)
Naked Welcome 69 (12f,Don,GF,Nov 4)
Nakita 36 (8f,War,F,May 8)
Name the Tune 60 (5f,Hay,GS,May 27)
Nanton Point (USA) 51 (18f,Nwm,GF,Oct 14)
Napoleon Star (IRE) 51 (6f,Bri,GF,Jun 19)

Narbonne 45 (8f,Nwm,GF,Jun 23)
Nash Terrace (IRE) 70 (12f,Sal,G,May 18)
Nashaat (USA) 54 (8f,Nwb,GF,May 21)
Nashotah 43 (10f,San,GF,Jun 16)
Nautical Pet (IRE) 69 (7f,Asc,GF,Jun 21)
Nawaasi 49 (6f,Red,GF,Aug 23)
Nawar (FR) 65 (20f,Asc,GF,Jun 20)
Ned's Bonanza 60 (6f,Thi,GF,Jly 28)
Needle Gun (IRE) 90 (10f,Asc,GF,Jun 20)
Negative Equity 39 (12f,Nwb,G,May 31)
Neither Nor 69 (7f,San,G,May 29)
Nero Kris 30 (8f,Nwm,GF,May 7)
Neuwest (USA) 56 (7f,Red,G,Spt 23)
Never Explain (IRE) 53 (8f,Nwb,G,Jly 15)
Never So Fit 34 (9f,Ham,S,Apr 12)
Never Such Bliss 32 (5f,Bev,GF,Apr 27)
Never so Rite (IRE) 38 (8f,Crl,Hd,Aug 16)
Never so True 36 (9f,Ham,F,Aug 14)
Neverending (IRE) 61 (8f,Yor,G,May 18)
New Capricorn (USA) 54 (7f,Nwb,GF,Jun 15)
New Century (USA) 63 (8f,Yor,G,Oct 4)
New Inn 52 (14f,Not,GF,May 2)
New Reputation 73 (14f,Hay,G,Spt 22)
Newport Knight 42 (12f,Fol,GF,Spt 7)
Nickitoto 41 (14f,Red,GF,Aug 23)
Nicolotte 88 (8f,Goo,F,Jly 26)
Nigel's Lad (IRE) 65 (9f,Ham,G,Spt 24)
Niggle 37 (8f,Nwm,G,May 5)
Night Asset 47 (6f,Bri,F,Jun 1)
Night City 69 (8f,Asc,GF,Jun 21)
Night Dance 57 (8f,Nwb,G,Jly 15)
Night Flare (FR) 40 (8f,San,GF,Jly 20)
Night Hero (USA) 55 (8f,San,G,May 29)
Night Time 38 (10f,Wnd,GF,Jly 10)
Night Wink (USA) 68 (8f,Red,F,Oct 24)
Nijo 81 (8f,Asc,GF,Jun 20)
Niknaks Nephew 35 (12f,Goo,F,Jly 29)
Nine Barrow Down (IRE) 43 (12f,Thi,GF,May 6)
Nineacres 33 (5f,Ayr,GF,May 10)
Ninette (USA) 51 (9f,Nwm,GF,Oct 13)
Ninety-Five 47 (5f,Pon,GF,Spt 21)
Ninia (USA) 49 (7½f,Bev,GF,Aug 24)
Nite-Owl Dancer 39 (5f,Yor,GF,Aug 16)
No Comebacks 58 (11f,Ayr,G,Spt 16)
No Extras (IRE) 72 (6f,Goo,GF,Aug 26)
No Pattern 47 (12f,Fol,G,Oct 16)
No Speeches (IRE) 57 (10f,Nwm,GF,May 7)
Nobby Barnes 32 (9f,Yor,G,Oct 7)
Noble Kingdom 55 (7f,Nwm,G,May 5)
Noble Neptune 37 (10f,Lei,F,Oct 24)
Noble Rose (IRE) 71 (12f,Yor,GF,Aug 16)
Noble Sprinter (IRE) 62 (9f,Yor,G,Oct 7)
Noeprob (USA) 33 (8f,Bat,F,Jly 1)
Non Vintage (IRE) 43 (14½f,Don,GF,Oct 20)

Nordan Raider 42 (6f,Don,G,Jun 10)
Nordic Breeze (IRE) 42 (7f,Chs,GF,Jun 28)
Nordic Doll (IRE) 54 (7f,Don,GF,Oct 20)
Nordic Mine (IRE) 30 (10½f,Hay,GS,Jun 9)
Nordico Princess 51 (5f,Fol,G,Mar 27)
Nordinex (IRE) 50 (8f,Nwm,GF,Jly 13)
Norling (FR) 32 (6f,Sal,GF,Aug 17)
Nornax Lad (USA) 48 (11f,Ham,F,Aug 9)
Norsong 31 (7f,Nwb,GF,May 21)
North Ardar 45 (12f,Rip,GF,Jly 31)
North Reef (IRE) 41 (10f,Goo,F,Jly 25)
Northern Celadon (IRE) 57 (8f,War,GS,Oct 3)
Northern Fan (IRE) 37 (7f,Fol,GF,Apr 10)
Northern Grey 31 (5f,Thi,GF,Spt 2)
Northern Law 41 (16f,Thi,F,Aug 25)
Northern Spark 40 (7f,Nwc,GF,Oct 30)
Northern Trove (USA) 39 (8f,Thi,GF,May 19)
Northern Union (CAN) 69 (10f,Wnd,G,Jun 12)
Not in Doubt (USA) 41 (14f,Nwm,GF,Apr 18)
Nothing Doing (IRE) 31 (11½f,Wnd,GF,Jly 17)
Nottash (IRE) 44 (7f,San,GF,Aug 25)
Noufari (FR) 58 (20f,Asc,GF,Jun 20)
Noyan 41 (13f,Ham,GF,May 20)
Nuriva (USA) 68 (6f,Nwb,G,Jly 15)
Nwaamis 84 (8f,Nwm,G,May 6)
Oakbury (IRE) 44 (10f,Kem,GF,Aug 2)
Oare Sparrow 59 (6f,Fol,G,Oct 16)
Obelos (USA) 36 (10f,Pon,GF,Apr 19)
Ocean Park 51 (10f,Red,F,Oct 24)
Ochos Rios (IRE) 49 (7½f,Bev,G,Jun 7)
Office Hours 45 (8f,Nwb,G,Apr 22)
Oggi 40 (6f,Goo,G,Spt 9)
Okavango (USA) 48 (9f,San,G,Jun 17)
Okay Baby (IRE) 30 (7f,Nwm,GF,Jly 29)
Old Comrades 34 (6f,Not,GF,Jun 26)
Old Hickory (IRE) 71 (10f,San,G,Jly 7)
Old Provence 36 (12f,Nwm,G,Spt 28)
Old Red (IRE) 56 (18f,Nwm,GF,Oct 14)
Old Rouvel (USA) 77 (16½f,San,G,May 29)
Old Swinford (IRE) 46 (14f,Not,GF,Jly 24)
On a Pedestal (IRE) 32 (12f,Crl,G,Apr 28)
Once More for Luck (IRE) 57 (10½f,Hay,GF,Aug 11)
One Off the Rail (USA) 36 (12f,Kem,GF,Jun 14)
One for Jeannie 36 (5f,Chs,GF,May 9)
Only Royale (IRE) 60 (7f,Nwm,G,May 5)
Ooh Ah Cantona 57 (10f,Red,F,Aug 5)
Opera Buff (IRE) 46 (14f,Not,GF,Oct 19)
Opera Fan (IRE) 32 (9f,Ham,F,Jly 29)
Opera Lover (IRE) 48 (12f,Asc,GS,Spt 24)
Options Open 65 (7f,Asc,GF,Jun 21)
Opus One 47 (12f,Crl,F,Jly 8)
Orchestra Stall 38 (10f,Lei,S,Mar 30)
Oriental Air (IRE) 34 (5f,Edi,GF,Jly 4)

Orthorhombus 45 (6f,Nwm,G,May 6)
Ottavio Farnese 40 (10f,Bri,G,Oct 1)
Otterbourne (IRE) 49 (7f,Nwm,GF,Apr 18)
Our Bessie 47 (12f,Sal,GF,Jly 6)
Our Kris 49 (14f,Nwm,GF,Oct 13)
Our Main Man 47 (10f,Red,F,Aug 5)
Our Rita 56 (8f,San,G,Apr 28)
Our Robert 30 (8f,Lei,G,Oct 9)
Out on a Promise (IRE) 61 (10f,Don,GF,Spt 6)
Outstayed Welcome 39 (14f,Not,GF,Aug 21)
Overbrook 67 (5f,Sal,F,Aug 9)
Overbury (IRE) 81 (9f,Nwm,GF,Apr 19)
Overpower 40 (8f,Nwm,G,Jun 3)
Owdbetts (IRE) 46 (7f,Lei,G,Jly 19)
Owington 83 (5f,Nwm,G,May 6)
Ozubeck (USA) 32 (10½f,Hay,G,Spt 22)
Pab's Choice 42 (7½f,Chs,GF,May 11)
Pacific Spirit 31 (6f,Wol,Std,May 4)
Paddy's Return (IRE) 50 (10f,Bat,GF,May 22)
Paddy's Rice 57 (8f,Lin,GF,Aug 12)
Padre Mio (IRE) 47 (8f,Asc,GF,Jly 22)
Pageboy 53 (5f,Nwm,GF,Jly 11)
Painted Desert 56 (5f,Eps,GF,Aug 28)
Painted Hall (USA) 37 (12f,Hay,GF,Aug 4)
Painter's Row (IRE) 73 (8f,Nwm,G,May 6)
Pakol (IRE) 31 (6f,Thi,F,Jly 29)
Palacegate Episode (IRE) 46 (5f,Thi,GF,Apr 21)
Palacegate Jack (IRE) 53 (5f,Cat,G,Jun 2)
Palacegate Touch 67 (6f,Rip,GS,Apr 5)
Palatial Style 56 (10f,Don,GS,Spt 9)
Paley Prince (USA) 34 (5f,Goo,GF,Aug 25)
Pallium (IRE) 52 (5f,Edi,GF,Jly 4)
Palo Blanco 59 (6f,Hay,GS,Oct 11)
Pampas Breeze (IRE) 38 (12f,Nwm,G,Spt 28)
Panther (IRE) 46 (6f,Thi,F,Jly 29)
Paper Cloud 45 (11½f,Yar,G,Spt 12)
Paradise Navy 63 (14f,Hay,GF,May 8)
Paradise Waters 42 (14f,Nwm,G,Spt 29)
Paris Babe 54 (6f,Yor,GF,Jly 14)
Parliament Piece 58 (7f,Nwm,GF,Aug 5)
Parthian Springs 73 (12f,Nwm,GF,May 7)
Pash 31 (8f,Chp,GS,Oct 10)
Pass Mark 52 (12f,Nwm,GF,Oct 27)
Pat's Splendour 32 (12f,Cat,GF,Oct 13)
Pater Noster (USA) 73 (8f,Nwm,G,Spt 28)
Patsy Grimes 49 (6f,Nwc,F,Jly 1)
Patto (USA) 61 (6f,Ayr,G,Spt 16)
Pay Homage 74 (8f,Goo,F,Jly 25)
Pc's Cruiser (IRE) 41 (7½f,Bev,GF,May 13)
Peace Envoy 69 (7f,Yor,GF,Aug 17)
Peaches Polly 48 (11½f,San,GF,Jun 16)
Pearl Dawn (IRE) 56 (5f,Bri,G,Oct 1)
Pearl Venture 55 (8f,Asc,S,Oct 6)
Pearly River 31 (12f,Fol,F,Aug 15)

Pedraza 67 (16f,Asc,GF,Jun 21)
Pelleman 54 (6f,Thi,GF,Apr 21)
Pembridge Place 57 (12f,Kem,G,Jun 3)
Pendolino (IRE) 38 (10f,Pon,G,Jun 12)
Pengamon 55 (7f,Kem,G,Jun 3)
Penmar 43 (8f,Edi,S,Nov 2)
Pennekamp (USA) 94 (8f,Nwm,G,May 6)
Penny Dip 57 (6f,Nwb,G,Jly 15)
Penny a Day (IRE) 66 (10½f,Yor,GF,Aug 16)
Penny's Wishing 39 (6f,Thi,GF,Apr 21)
Pennycairn 41 (8f,San,GF,Aug 18)
Pentire 84 (12f,Asc,F,Jun 23)
Pentre Ffynnon (IRE) 48 (5f,Nwc,GF,Jly 24)
Percy Braithwaite (IRE) 64 (9f,Yor,GF,Jun 17)
Perfect Brave 43 (6f,Goo,GF,Jun 16)
Perfect World 36 (5f,Not,GF,Apr 17)
Perilous Plight 37 (7f,Chp,GF,Jun 15)
Perryston View 54 (6f,Nwm,G,Jun 3)
Persian Affair (IRE) 50 (7f,Bri,F,May 11)
Persian Bud (IRE) 34 (14f,Not,GF,Aug 12)
Persian Conquest (IRE) 35 (11½f,Wnd,GF,Jun 26)
Persian Elite (IRE) 61 (12f,Kem,G,Spt 2)
Persian Fayre 44 (7f,Ayr,F,Jun 24)
Persian Saint (IRE) 58 (12f,Bat,Hd,Spt 4)
Persian Smoke 31 (12f,Nwm,GF,Oct 27)
Persiansky (IRE) 34 (12f,Crl,Hd,Aug 16)
Persuasive 42 (13f,Ham,F,Jun 14)
Pete Afrique (IRE) 34 (5f,Cat,GF,Jly 19)
Petit Poucet 51 (7f,Asc,GF,Jun 21)
Petite-D-Argent 38 (5f,Ayr,G,Jly 17)
Petomi 48 (6f,Not,GS,Spt 19)
Petraco (IRE) 52 (6f,Fol,S,Spt 27)
Peutetre 35 (10f,Asc,GF,Jly 21)
Phantom Gold 53 (12f,Asc,GF,Jun 22)
Pharamineux 41 (12f,Lei,GF,Aug 14)
Pharaoh's Dancer 42 (7f,Bri,G,Oct 1)
Pharazini 33 (8½f,Bev,GF,May 13)
Pharly Dancer 38 (12f,Ham,G,Spt 25)
Pharsical 50 (6f,Bat,F,Jly 1)
Phase One (IRE) 40 (7f,Crl,F,Jun 29)
Phil's Time 36 (17f,Bat,F,Jly 19)
Phylian 44 (10f,Pon,G,Jun 12)
Piccolo 87 (5f,Asc,F,Jun 23)
Pilsudski (IRE) 70 (12f,Asc,S,Spt 24)
Pine Essence (USA) 40 (10f,Red,F,Aug 5)
Pine Ridge Lad (IRE) 45 (8f,Red,F,Oct 24)
Pinkerton Polka 32 (12f,Lei,F,Oct 24)
Pinkerton's Pal 69 (8f,Yor,G,May 17)
Pinzon (USA) 57 (7f,Nwb,GF,May 21)
Pipe Major (IRE) 86 (8f,Nwm,G,May 6)
Piquant 50 (8f,Red,F,Oct 24)
Pirates Gold (IRE) 32 (6f,Bri,F,Jly 20)
Pistol (IRE) 49 (8f,Asc,GF,May 3)

Pistol River (IRE) 72 (16f,Asc,G,Spt 23)
Pitcroy 52 (10f,San,G,Apr 28)
Pleasant Memories 33 (8f,Ham,F,Aug 3)
Pleasure Trick (USA) 52 (8f,Pon,GF,Jly 28)
Plinth 44 (10f,Bat,Hd,Jly 10)
Plum First 46 (6f,War,F,May 8)
Polar Queen 47 (7f,Sal,F,Aug 10)
Polish Consul 45 (14f,Hay,GS,Jun 9)
Polly Particular 52 (5f,Yor,G,Oct 4)
Polly Peculiar 47 (8f,War,G,May 27)
Polo Kit (IRE) 58 (16½f,San,G,Apr 28)
Polonez Prima 51 (8f,Bat,GF,Jun 17)
Poltarf (USA) 66 (16f,Asc,GF,May 3)
Poly Road 34 (12½f,War,F,May 8)
Polydamas 50 (10f,San,GF,Aug 9)
Pomorie (IRE) 33 (13f,Ham,GF,May 11)
Pop to Stans 32 (8f,San,GF,Jly 19)
Poppy Carew (IRE) 53 (10f,Nwm,GF,Spt 30)
Portelet 63 (5f,Don,GF,Nov 4)
Portend 37 (5f,Don,G,Mar 23)
Portite Sophie 32 (11f,Ham,F,Aug 3)
Posidonas 52 (12f,Goo,G,Spt 8)
Posing (IRE) 34 (10f,Sal,F,Aug 9)
Positivo 48 (8f,Chp,GF,Jly 2)
Poyle Jezebelle 39 (6f,Not,GS,Spt 11)
Prague Spring 30 (10f,Sal,G,May 18)
Precede 30 (10f,Sal,GF,May 4)
Premier Dance 38 (13f,Ham,F,Jun 14)
Premium Gift 46 (5f,Don,G,Jun 10)
Prenonamoss 54 (10f,Don,G,Mar 24)
Presenting 79 (12f,Eps,GF,Jun 10)
Preston Guild (IRE) 34 (12f,Don,GF,May 9)
Pretoria Dancer 52 (14f,Hay,G,Spt 23)
Prickwillow (USA) 50 (10f,San,GS,Spt 13)
Pride of Hayling (IRE) 45 (6f,Bri,F,Jly 20)
Pride of May (IRE) 44 (14f,Nwm,G,May 19)
Pride of Pendle 62 (9f,Yor,GF,Jun 17)
Prima Cominna 46 (5f,Nwm,GF,Jun 30)
Prima Silk 58 (6f,Don,G,Jun 10)
Prime Match (IRE) 44 (6f,Red,G,May 29)
Primo Lara 47 (7f,Cat,GF,Oct 14)
Primula Bairn 34 (5f,Pon,G,Spt 21)
Prince Arthur (IRE) 54 (7f,Nwm,GF,Apr 20)
Prince Belfort 45 (5f,Cat,GF,Jly 19)
Prince Danzig (IRE) 57 (12f,Bri,G,Spt 20)
Prince of Andros (USA) 65 (10f,San,GF,Jly 8)
Prince of India 72 (7f,Nwm,GF,Jly 1)
Prince of Spades 35 (8f,Nwm,GF,Jly 1)
Prince's Feather (IRE) 44 (7f,Kem,GF,Jun 14)
Princess Danielle 32 (9f,Nwm,GF,Oct 27)
Princess Maxine (IRE) 45 (8f,Thi,G,Apr 22)
Princess Oberon (IRE) 74 (5f,Nwm,G,Jly 22)
Princess Sadie 33 (5f,Nwc,GF,Oct 30)
Printers Quill 35 (10f,Bat,GF,Spt 25)

Private Fixture (IRE) 31 (8f,War,G,Jun 7)
Private Line (USA) 50 (8f,Kem,GF,Jun 28)
Prize Pupil (IRE) 38 (10f,Nwb,GF,Aug 11)
Prizefighter 47 (8f,San,GF,Aug 9)
Profit Release (IRE) 41 (8f,San,G,May 30)
Progression 69 (12f,Yor,GF,Aug 17)
Prolific Lady (IRE) 53 (6f,Lin,GF,Jun 27)
Promise Fulfilled (USA) 57 (7f,Chs,G,Jun 8)
Prophets Honour 52 (8f,Nwm,GF,Apr 19)
Proton 71 (12f,Eps,GF,Aug 28)
Proud Destiny 50 (7f,Kem,GF,Aug 2)
Proud Image 44 (8f,Lin,GS,Jly 30)
Provence 53 (14f,Hay,GF,May 8)
Prudent Princess 31 (6f,Nwm,GF,Aug 5)
Prussian Blue (USA) 54 (10f,Nwm,GF,Apr 18)
Pumice 56 (12f,Yor,GF,Aug 17)
Pure Grain 69 (12f,Yor,GF,Aug 16)
Purple Fling 54 (6f,Bat,F,Jly 1)
Purple Splash 83 (16f,Nwb,GS,Oct 19)
Pursuit of Glory 34 (10f,Sal,F,Aug 9)
Pusey Street Boy 44 (8f,War,F,Jly 7)
Pyramus (USA) 51 (7f,Cat,GF,Jly 19)
Q Factor 53 (6f,Kem,GF,Jun 28)
Quandary (USA) 71 (10f,Yar,G,Spt 13)
Quango 47 (10½f,Yor,GF,Jun 17)
Queenbird 45 (7f,Yor,GF,Jly 15)
Queenfisher 54 (8f,Nwm,GF,May 7)
Queens Consul (IRE) 63 (8f,Pon,G,Apr 25)
Queens Stroller (IRE) 45 (10f,Not,G,Apr 24)
Quest Again 56 (14f,Not,GF,Oct 26)
Quilling 59 (7f,Nwm,GF,Oct 28)
Quillon Rose 43 (8f,Lin,GF,Aug 12)
Quintus Decimus 55 (8f,Yor,G,May 18)
Quinwood (USA) 53 (8f,Yar,GS,Jun 15)
Quivira 67 (12f,Rip,GF,Aug 19)
Quiz Time 69 (5f,Nwm,GF,Aug 26)
Raah Algharb (USA) 65 (7f,Nwb,GF,Aug 11)
Raayaat (USA) 34 (8f,Nwm,GF,Apr 19)
Racing Brenda 42 (8½f,Bev,G,Spt 13)
Racing Telegraph 31 (7f,Yar,G,Spt 13)
Rad 40 (7f,Crl,F,Jun 29)
Rahy Zoman (USA) 55 (10f,San,GF,Jun 16)
Rainbow Walk (IRE) 39 (8f,Don,GF,Mar 25)
Rainfest (FR) 49 (14f,Hay,G,Spt 22)
Raise the Stakes 56 (9f,Goo,F,Jly 27)
Rakis (IRE) 40 (7f,San,GF,Aug 30)
Rambo's Hall 63 (10f,Rip,GF,Aug 29)
Rambold 51 (6f,War,GF,Jly 15)
Ramborette 32 (5f,Edi,F,Jly 10)
Rambrino 55 (10½f,Chs,GF,May 11)
Ramsdens (IRE) 53 (9f,Nwm,GF,Oct 27)
Random 52 (6f,Goo,G,Jly 28)
Ranosh (USA) 41 (10f,San,GF,Aug 9)
Rapier Point (IRE) 43 (6f,Thi,GF,Apr 21)

Rapporteur (USA) 48 (10f,Don,G,Mar 24)
Rasas (IRE) 69 (6f,Lin,GF,Jly 30)
Rasayel (USA) 50 (10½f,Yor,GF,Aug 31)
Rasmi (CAN) 45 (7f,Kem,GF,Apr 17)
Reach for Glory 35 (16f,Cat,G,Jun 2)
Reaganesque (USA) 33 (10f,Not,GS,Spt 19)
Real Madrid 38 (8f,War,GS,Oct 3)
Realities (USA) 94 (8f,Goo,GF,Aug 26)
Rebeccas Secret (IRE) 30 (12f,Rip,F,Jun 21)
Red Admiral 46 (6f,Fol,F,Aug 11)
Red Azalea 38 (10f,Wnd,GF,Jun 26)
Red Bishop 79 (10f,San,GF,Jly 8)
Red Bustaan 57 (14f,Goo,F,Jly 27)
Red Carnival (USA) 67 (8f,Nwm,G,Spt 28)
Red Dragon 32 (10f,San,GF,Jun 16)
Red Rita (IRE) 47 (6f,Fol,GF,Jly 12)
Red Spectacle 38 (9f,Ham,F,Jly 14)
Red Valerian 53 (10½f,Chs,G,Jly 15)
Redstella (USA) 57 (10½f,Hay,G,Jun 10)
Reed My Lips (IRE) 35 (8f,Edi,G,May 22)
Reem Dubai (IRE) 39 (12f,Chs,GF,Aug 19)
Regal Chimes 47 (5f,Nwb,GF,Apr 21)
Regal Fanfare (IRE) 35 (10f,Lei,G,Spt 5)
Reimei 54 (12f,Asc,S,Oct 6)
Reported (IRE) 40 (12f,Chs,GF,Jun 28)
Reprehend 63 (7f,Don,GF,Oct 20)
Requested 46 (14f,Not,GF,May 2)
Resolute Bay 36 (9f,Ham,F,Aug 14)
Restructure (IRE) 80 (10½f,Yor,GF,Aug 16)
Retender (USA) 46 (10f,Bev,GF,Apr 7)
Reverand Thickness 62 (8f,Nwm,G,Jly 22)
Revere (IRE) 74 (10f,Goo,GS,Spt 30)
Rhythmic Dancer 39 (5f,Cat,GF,Jly 19)
Rich Glow 47 (5f,Hay,GF,Aug 5)
Richard of York 84 (12f,Asc,G,Spt 23)
Richelieu (IRE) 46 (12f,Hay,GS,Oct 11)
Ridgewood Ben 73 (8f,San,G,Apr 28)
Ridgewood Pearl 94 (8f,Asc,GF,Jun 21)
Right Win (IRE) 63 (13f,Nwb,GF,Aug 12)
Ringmaster (IRE) 57 (12f,Asc,S,Spt 24)
Rinus Manor (IRE) 38 (6f,Lei,S,Spt 18)
Riparius (USA) 58 (12f,Lei,G,Jly 19)
Rise Up Singing 45 (7f,Nwm,GF,Jly 1)
Rising Dough (IRE) 47 (8f,Goo,GF,Jun 16)
Rising Spray 39 (8f,Goo,G,Spt 8)
Risk Master 44 (9f,Nwb,GF,May 21)
Risky 42 (5f,Chs,G,Jly 15)
Risky Romeo 44 (8f,War,F,Aug 28)
Risky Tu 41 (12f,Don,G,Mar 23)
Rival Bid (USA) 53 (10f,Nwm,GF,May 7)
River Board 41 (8½f,Bev,GF,May 23)
River Keen (IRE) 54 (12f,Asc,S,Oct 6)
River North (IRE) 45 (12f,Nwb,G,Apr 22)
Riyadian 80 (12f,Asc,G,Spt 23)

Roadsweeper (FR) 32 (10f,Ayr,GF,Jun 2)
Robellion 58 (5f,Nwm,GF,Aug 26)
Roberty Lea 44 (17f,Pon,GF,Oct 2)
Robingo (IRE) 59 (16½f,San,GF,Jly 8)
Robo Magic (USA) 30 (6f,Lei,G,Aug 23)
Robsera (IRE) 46 (8f,War,GS,Oct 3)
Rock Symphony 69 (6f,Nwc,F,Jly 1)
Rock The Barney (IRE) 36 (11½f,San,GF,Jun 16)
Rocketeer (IRE) 61 (6f,Thi,G,Jly 21)
Rockforce 47 (9f,Kem,GF,Apr 15)
Rockstine (IRE) 39 (8f,Goo,GF,Aug 27)
Rocky Forum 36 (16f,Lin,Std,Aug 5)
Rocky Two 38 (5f,Fol,G,Mar 27)
Rocky Waters (USA) 37 (6f,Goo,G,Jly 28)
Rocquaine Bay 31 (12f,Sal,GF,May 4)
Roderick Hudson 62 (7f,San,G,Jly 7)
Roger the Butler (IRE) 54 (6f,Lin,G,Jun 3)
Roi de la Mer (IRE) 54 (8f,Goo,G,Spt 8)
Roisin Clover 54 (12f,Eps,GF,Aug 28)
Roka 32 (6f,Lin,GF,May 20)
Rokeby Bowl 68 (12f,Yor,GF,Aug 31)
Roll a Dollar 43 (12f,Don,GS,Spt 8)
Rolling (IRE) 42 (6f,Thi,GF,Apr 21)
Rolling Waters 50 (16f,Lin,Std,Aug 5)
Rolling the Bones (USA) 38 (16½f,Fol,G,Jun 7)
Romalito 32 (14f,Not,F,Jly 8)
Roman Reel (USA) 51 (8f,Chp,GF,Jly 2)
Romansh 41 (10f,San,GF,Aug 19)
Romanzof 55 (8f,San,GF,Aug 9)
Romios (IRE) 59 (10½f,Hay,G,Jun 10)
Ron's Secret 48 (8f,Lei,G,Oct 10)
Rood Music 36 (8f,Hay,GF,Aug 11)
Rory 64 (9f,Yor,G,Oct 7)
Rosa Bonheur 33 (6f,Sal,G,Jly 27)
Rose of Glenn 39 (16f,Not,GS,Spt 11)
Roseate Lodge 46 (6f,Pon,G,Apr 25)
Rosebud 55 (7f,Nwb,GF,May 20)
Rosie Sweetheart (IRE) 36 (12f,Rip,GF,Jly 10)
Rossini Blue 60 (7f,Ayr,G,Spt 16)
Rosy Hue (IRE) 42 (9f,Kem,G,Jun 3)
Roufontaine 49 (12f,Thi,GF,Jly 28)
Roving Minstrel 61 (7f,Asc,GF,May 3)
Roy Boy 51 (6f,Thi,GF,Apr 21)
Royal Ballerina (IRE) 75 (12f,Yor,GF,Aug 16)
Royal Carlton (IRE) 33 (6f,Lin,GF,Jun 27)
Royal Circle 60 (12f,Don,GF,Nov 4)
Royal Citizen (IRE) 33 (14f,Not,GF,May 2)
Royal Comedian 40 (7f,Ayr,GF,May 10)
Royal Dome (IRE) 63 (5f,Nwm,G,Spt 28)
Royal Hill 65 (7f,Asc,GF,May 3)
Royal Philosopher 33 (8f,Kem,GF,May 27)
Royal Rabbit 30 (14f,Cat,G,Spt 16)
Royal Rebuke 65 (8f,Goo,F,Jly 27)
Royal Scimitar (USA) 76 (12f,Don,GF,Nov 4)

Royal Solo (IRE) 53 (10½f,Chs,GF,May 9)
Royal York 40 (12f,Yor,GF,Aug 17)
Royale Figurine (IRE) 78 (5f,Kem,G,Jun 3)
Rubadub 33 (10f,Bat,GF,May 22)
Ruby Heights 51 (12f,Nwm,GF,Oct 27)
Ruby Venture 33 (10½f,Hay,GF,May 8)
Ruddigore 37 (8f,War,GS,Oct 3)
Rug 31 (7f,Thi,GF,May 6)
Running Green 38 (9f,Ham,S,Apr 12)
Runs in the Family 34 (6f,Not,G,Apr 24)
Rushaway 44 (10f,Lei,S,Mar 30)
Rushen Raider 40 (7½f,Bev,GF,May 13)
Russian Heroine 54 (7½f,Bev,G,Jly 18)
Russian Maid 54 (7f,Don,G,Spt 7)
Rymer's Rascal 36 (5f,Pon,G,Spt 21)
Saafi (IRE) 38 (12f,Sal,G,May 24)
Sacrament 57 (12f,Nwm,G,May 5)
Saddlehome (USA) 52 (5f,Chs,GF,Aug 19)
Sadler's Image (IRE) 56 (13f,Nwb,GF,May 20)
Sadler's Pearl 31 (7f,Nwb,GF,Apr 21)
Sadler's Walk 66 (10½f,Yor,G,Oct 4)
Safety Factor (USA) 42 (6f,Sal,G,Jly 27)
Safey Ana (USA) 60 (7f,Nwb,G,Jly 14)
Sagebrush Roller 72 (7f,Ayr,G,Spt 16)
Sahil (IRE) 37 (10f,Bev,GF,May 12)
Saifan 58 (8f,Asc,GF,May 3)
Sailormaite 43 (6f,Don,G,Mar 24)
Saint Express 74 (5f,Nwm,GS,Jun 3)
Sakharov 48 (8f,Rip,GF,Jly 10)
Salaman (FR) 45 (18f,Nwm,GF,Oct 14)
Saleel (IRE) 65 (14f,Yor,GF,Aug 15)
Salinger 35 (12f,Cat,GF,Aug 11)
Sally Slade 55 (6f,Yar,G,Jun 7)
Sally Weld 36 (6f,Wnd,GF,May 15)
Salmon Ladder (USA) 69 (10½f,Yor,G,May 17)
Salska 43 (14f,Hay,G,Spt 23)
Salt Lake 76 (10f,San,G,Jly 7)
Saltando 40 (8f,Goo,G,Spt 29)
Saltis (IRE) 45 (8f,Nwm,GF,Aug 5)
Samah 66 (7f,Nwm,GF,Spt 30)
Samaka Hara (IRE) 33 (8½f,Bev,G,Jly 18)
Samba Sharply 56 (7f,Lin,F,Spt 5)
Samsolom 54 (6f,Bri,F,Aug 2)
Samsonesque 51 (11f,Ayr,GF,May 10)
Samwar 39 (6f,Lin,GF,May 20)
San Pietra (IRE) 37 (10f,Nwb,G,Jly 14)
Sandmoor Chambray 61 (7½f,Bev,GF,Apr 7)
Sandmoor Denim 46 (8f,War,GS,Oct 3)
Sanmartino (IRE) 71 (14f,Yor,GF,Aug 16)
Sanoosea (USA) 60 (10½f,Chs,GF,May 11)
Santa Fan (IRE) 41 (10f,Nwb,G,Jly 14)
Santana Lady (IRE) 48 (12f,Rip,GF,Aug 19)
Santella Boy (USA) 39 (12f,Fol,GF,Aug 11)
Sapphire Son (IRE) 33 (7f,Sal,G,May 18)

Sarasota Storm 39 (8f,Nwm,G,Jly 22)
Sarawat 51 (14f,Yor,G,May 17)
Sariyaa 47 (12f,Thi,GF,Jly 28)
Sarmatian (USA) 55 (8f,Ham,F,Aug 9)
Saseedo (USA) 77 (6f,Nwm,G,May 6)
Saucy Maid (IRE) 36 (10f,Wnd,GF,Jly 10)
Saxon Maid 81 (12f,Asc,GS,Spt 24)
Sayeh (IRE) 48 (10f,Eps,G,Spt 6)
Sayyed Alraqs (USA) 35 (10f,Pon,GF,Jun 19)
Sayyedati 100 (8f,Goo,F,Jly 26)
Scalp 'em (IRE) 32 (16f,Not,GF,Jun 26)
Scaraben 56 (8f,Ayr,G,Spt 15)
Scenic Dancer 37 (11½f,Yar,G,Spt 12)
Scharnhorst 43 (7f,Sal,GF,Jun 13)
Scissor Ridge 30 (7f,Don,GF,Oct 20)
Scorpius 40 (7f,Nwm,GF,Aug 5)
Scotsky (IRE) 47 (8f,Rip,G,Aug 28)
Scottish Bambi 32 (10f,Not,GF,May 2)
Sea Devil 34 (7f,Lei,G,Apr 6)
Sea Freedom 60 (16f,Goo,G,Spt 9)
Sea Spouse 30 (8f,Chp,GS,Oct 10)
Sea Thunder 56 (6f,Nwm,G,Jly 21)
Sea Victor 53 (18f,Pon,F,Oct 16)
Sea-Ayr (IRE) 35 (7½f,Bev,GF,Apr 7)
Sea-Deer 64 (6f,Asc,F,Jun 23)
Seasonal Splendour (IRE) 80 (16f,Goo,GS,Spt 30)
Sebastian 83 (12f,Sal,G,May 18)
Seckar Vale (USA) 56 (10f,Don,GF,Spt 6)
Second Chance (IRE) 63 (8f,Goo,F,Jly 29)
Second Colours (USA) 60 (9f,Yor,GF,Aug 30)
Secret Aly (CAN) 75 (8f,Goo,F,Jly 25)
Secret Miss 42 (5f,Lin,S,Spt 14)
Secret Service (IRE) 58 (12f,Don,GF,Nov 4)
Secret Spring (FR) 39 (7f,Fol,GF,Apr 10)
Segala (IRE) 54 (9f,Ham,G,Spt 24)
Segovia 56 (12f,Yor,GF,Aug 17)
Seigneurial 58 (6f,Red,F,Oct 31)
Seize the Day (IRE) 50 (14f,Not,GF,Apr 17)
Self Expression 43 (10f,Bev,GF,Jly 8)
Self Reliance 43 (7f,Goo,F,Jly 28)
Selhurstpark Flyer (IRE) 64 (6f,Nwm,G,May 6)
Senorita Dinero (USA) 67 (10½f,Hay,GF,Aug 4)
Sense of Priority 42 (6f,Thi,GF,Jly 28)
Seren Quest 55 (12f,Nwb,G,May 19)
Sergeyev (IRE) 72 (7f,Asc,GF,Jun 21)
Serious 64 (10½f,Hay,G,Spt 23)
Serious Hurry 47 (5f,Crl,Hd,Aug 21)
Serious Option (IRE) 53 (8f,San,G,May 30)
Set Table (USA) 48 (6f,Don,GF,May 9)
Set the Fashion 49 (8f,Asc,GF,May 3)
Seventeens Lucky 52 (9f,Yor,G,Oct 7)
Shaarid (USA) 44 (10f,Fol,GF,Apr 10)
Shabanaz 50 (12f,Chp,GF,Jly 13)

Shadirwan (IRE) 64 (20f,Asc,GF,Jun 20)
Shadow Jury 58 (5f,Ayr,G,Jly 17)
Shadow Leader 69 (12f,Asc,GF,Jun 21)
Shady Deed 34 (8f,Bat,Hd,Aug 8)
Shaft of Light 65 (12f,Sal,GF,Jly 6)
Shahid 74 (8f,Goo,GF,Aug 26)
Shakiyr (FR) 53 (12f,Chs,GF,May 11)
Shamanic 58 (6f,Eps,G,Spt 6)
Shambo 77 (13¹/₂f,Chs,GF,May 11)
Shamshadal (IRE) 41 (14f,Not,GF,May 2)
Shandine (USA) 39 (7f,Nwb,GF,Jun 15)
Shanghai Venture (USA) 52 (8f,San,G,Apr 28)
Sharazi (USA) 54 (12f,Thi,GF,May 6)
Sharkashka (IRE) 36 (12f,Rip,F,Jun 21)
Sharp 'n Smart 35 (6f,Fol,F,Jun 30)
Sharp Consul (IRE) 44 (7f,Lin,S,Spt 28)
Sharp Falcon (IRE) 69 (10f,Nwm,GF,May 7)
Sharp Holly (IRE) 30 (6f,Lin,GF,Jun 27)
Sharp Imp 38 (6f,Fol,F,Aug 15)
Sharp N' Smooth 38 (7f,Edi,G,Apr 10)
Sharp Point (IRE) 61 (5f,Yor,GF,Aug 17)
Sharp Prod (USA) 66 (6f,Don,GF,Mar 25)
Sharp Prospect 57 (8f,Don,GF,Mar 24)
Sharp Rebuff 57 (7f,Nwb,G,Jly 14)
Sharpical 57 (8f,Goo,G,Spt 8)
Shashi (IRE) 54 (5f,Lin,GF,Jly 1)
Shayim (USA) 52 (7¹/₂f,Bev,GF,May 23)
She's Dynamite (IRE) 45 (7f,Chs,GF,Aug 18)
Sheama (USA) 36 (8f,Chp,GF,Jly 2)
Sheer Danzig (IRE) 68 (10¹/₂f,Yor,G,Oct 4)
Shefoog 68 (7f,San,GF,Jun 16)
Shemaq (USA) 58 (8f,Yor,GF,Jly 14)
Shen Yang (USA) 41 (6f,Lin,GF,Jly 30)
Shepherd Market (IRE) 52 (7f,Chp,GS,Oct 10)
Sheppard's Cross 51 (7f,Nwm,G,May 19)
Sheraz (IRE) 34 (10f,Lei,G,Spt 5)
Sheriff 36 (12f,Hay,GF,Jly 7)
Sherman (IRE) 75 (10¹/₂f,Yor,G,May 18)
Sherqy (IRE) 53 (12f,Cat,G,Spt 16)
Shift Again (IRE) 41 (7f,Chs,GF,May 10)
Shifting Moon 67 (8f,Goo,F,Jly 29)
Shikari's Son 76 (7f,Eps,GF,Jly 5)
Shinerolla 58 (8f,Nwm,GF,Oct 14)
Shining Dancer 33 (9f,Kem,G,Jun 3)
Shining Edge 37 (8¹/₂f,Bev,G,Jly 18)
Shining Example 55 (9f,Nwm,GF,Oct 27)
Shining High 51 (12f,Sal,GF,Jun 13)
Shirley's Train (USA) 34 (12f,Sal,GF,Jly 6)
Shonara's Way 82 (16f,Goo,GS,Spt 30)
Shoofk 33 (10f,Fol,GF,Apr 10)
Shot At Love (IRE) 46 (9f,Goo,GF,Jly 26)
Show Faith (IRE) 34 (8f,Nwb,G,Jly 15)
Showery 51 (6f,Hay,G,May 26)
Shrewd Alibi 53 (20f,Asc,GF,Jun 20)

Shujan (USA) 32 (19f,Chs,GF,May 10)
Shuttlecock 33 (10f,Not,GF,Jun 12)
Sicarian 43 (10¹/₂f,Hay,G,Spt 22)
Sigama (USA) 36 (5f,Nwc,G,May 24)
Sight'n Sound 34 (12f,Sal,GF,May 4)
Signs 59 (7f,Goo,F,Jly 28)
Silca Blanka (IRE) 65 (8f,Nwm,G,May 6)
Silence in Court (IRE) 70 (16f,Hay,G,Apr 15)
Silent Expression 62 (7f,Sal,GF,Aug 31)
Silently 57 (10f,Bat,Hd,Jly 4)
Silk Cottage 49 (5f,Pon,G,Spt 21)
Silktail (IRE) 40 (12f,Yor,GF,Aug 17)
Silver Groom (IRE) 51 (10f,Nwb,GS,Oct 19)
Silver Hunter (USA) 62 (10f,Nwm,GF,May 7)
Silver Singer 47 (10¹/₂f,Hay,G,Spt 22)
Silver Sting 36 (7f,Don,G,Mar 24)
Silver Tzar 37 (6f,Bri,F,Jly 24)
Silver Wedge (USA) 74 (12f,Asc,G,Spt 23)
Silvicolous (USA) 42 (8f,Ayr,GF,Jun 3)
Simafar (IRE) 54 (20f,Asc,GF,Jun 20)
Simand 33 (8f,Crl,Hd,Aug 16)
Simposa (IRE) 30 (11f,Red,G,Spt 22)
Sinclair Lad (IRE) 32 (10f,Not,GF,Jun 12)
Sing With the Band 45 (5f,Pon,G,Spt 21)
Singing Rock (IRE) 33 (7f,San,G,May 29)
Singspiel (IRE) 73 (10f,San,GF,Jly 8)
Sir Arthur Hobbs 48 (8f,Ham,F,Jun 15)
Sir Joey (USA) 71 (6f,Nwm,GF,Jun 3)
Sir Tasker 42 (5f,Edi,F,Jly 10)
Sison (IRE) 39 (6f,Yar,GS,Jun 15)
Six for Luck 32 (5f,Nwc,GF,Oct 30)
Sizzling 49 (6f,Lei,F,Oct 23)
Sky Music 61 (7f,Nwm,GF,Jly 13)
Slaney Project (IRE) 39 (14f,Hay,S,Spt 30)
Slapy Dam 37 (12f,Fol,S,Spt 27)
Slasher Jack (IRE) 54 (10f,San,G,Jly 7)
Slivovitz 43 (6f,Nwc,GF,Oct 30)
Slmaat 60 (12f,Lei,G,Apr 6)
Smart Generation 69 (10f,Nwb,G,May 19)
Smart Guest 58 (7f,Nwm,GF,Apr 19)
Smocking 32 (12f,Cat,GF,Aug 11)
Smolensk (USA) 90 (8f,Asc,GF,Jun 21)
Smuggler's Point (USA) 34 (15¹/₂f,Fol,GF,Spt 7)
Smuggling 68 (20f,Asc,GF,Jun 20)
Snipe Hall 59 (6f,Nwm,GF,May 7)
Snow Princess (IRE) 68 (12f,Nwm,GF,Oct 27)
Snow Valley 45 (12f,Rip,G,May 21)
Snowing 54 (5f,Nwm,GF,Oct 14)
Snowtown (IRE) 69 (12f,Asc,GS,Spt 24)
Snowy Petrel (IRE) 55 (12f,Rip,GF,Aug 19)
So Amazing 38 (7f,Don,GF,Oct 20)
So Factual (USA) 84 (6f,Asc,GF,Jun 22)
So Intrepid (IRE) 62 (5f,War,GF,Jun 17)
Soaking 53 (7f,Kem,GF,Jly 12)

Soba Up 66 (12f,Chs,GF,Jly 14)
Sobering Thoughts 40 (6f,Crl,F,May 12)
Solar Flight 59 (8f,Nwm,GF,Apr 19)
Soldier Cove (USA) 52 (5f,San,G,Spt 12)
Soldier's Leap (FR) 48 (10f,Wnd,G,Jun 12)
Solianna 33 (7f,Cat,GF,Jly 5)
Solomon's Dancer (USA) 54 (14f,Hay,GF,May 8)
Sombreffe 43 (7f,Red,G,Spt 23)
Somerton Boy (IRE) 47 (7f,Don,GF,Nov 3)
Sommersby (IRE) 30 (12f,Yor,GF,Oct 5)
Son of Sharp Shot (IRE) 88 (14f,Yor,GF,Aug 16)
Song of Tara (IRE) 43 (12f,Chp,G,May 29)
Song of Years (IRE) 46 (12f,Nwm,GF,Jly 28)
Sonic Boy 75 (10¹⁄₂f,Hay,GF,Aug 5)
Soojama (IRE) 41 (16¹⁄₂f,Fol,G,Jun 7)
Sooty Tern 58 (8f,Kem,G,Jun 3)
Sophism (USA) 37 (12f,Nwm,G,Jun 10)
Sotoboy (IRE) 57 (7f,Chs,GF,Aug 18)
Souperficial 44 (6f,Nwm,G,Jly 21)
Source of Light 94 (12f,Asc,GF,Jun 21)
South Eastern Fred 36 (8¹⁄₂f,Bev,GF,May 13)
South Rock 66 (6f,Nwm,GF,Oct 14)
South Sea Bubble (IRE) 39 (10f,Not,GF,Oct 26)
Southern Dominion 45 (6f,Hay,G,Spt 22)
Southern Memories (IRE) 52 (8f,Goo,GF,Aug 27)
Southern Power (IRE) 58 (10f,Bev,GF,Apr 7)
Sovereign Page (USA) 80 (10f,Nwm,GF,May 7)
Sovereigns Parade 43 (10f,Nwm,G,Spt 26)
Soviet Bride (IRE) 44 (10f,Kem,GF,Aug 16)
Soviet Line (IRE) 88 (8f,Goo,F,Jly 26)
Spaniards Close 58 (5f,San,G,Spt 12)
Spanish Stripper (USA) 47 (7f,Fol,G,Jun 7)
Spanish Verdict 58 (8f,Crl,F,Jun 28)
Spara Tir 37 (6f,Thi,GF,Jun 20)
Sparrowhawk (IRE) 48 (14f,Nwm,G,Spt 29)
Special Beat 37 (13f,Bat,Hd,Spt 4)
Special Dawn (IRE) 71 (10f,San,GF,Jun 16)
Special-K 44 (7¹⁄₂f,Bev,GF,Aug 24)
Spectacle Jim 35 (6f,Fol,F,Aug 15)
Spectrum (IRE) 80 (10f,Nwm,GF,Oct 14)
Speed to Lead (IRE) 43 (12f,Lei,F,Oct 23)
Speedybird (IRE) 40 (7f,War,GF,Apr 27)
Spencer's Revenge 51 (7f,Yar,F,Oct 18)
Spender 56 (5f,Nwm,GF,Aug 26)
Spirituelle 31 (7¹⁄₂f,Bev,GF,Apr 8)
Splintercat (USA) 52 (7f,Chs,GF,Aug 19)
Spot Prize (USA) 44 (12f,Yor,GF,Jun 17)
Spout 75 (12f,Asc,GS,Spt 24)
Spread The Word 32 (11¹⁄₂f,Lin,S,Spt 28)
Squire Corrie 57 (5f,Nwm,G,Spt 28)
St Louis Lady 39 (7f,Yar,GF,Aug 17)
Stage Struck (IRE) 47 (12f,Kem,GF,Aug 16)
Stalled (IRE) 54 (12f,Sal,GF,Jly 6)
Stand Tall 33 (6f,Nwc,GF,Oct 30)

Star Manager (USA) 65 (8f,Yor,GF,Jly 14)
Star Performer (IRE) 32 (9f,Red,F,Aug 5)
Star Player 46 (20f,Asc,GF,Jun 20)
Star Rage (IRE) 58 (14f,Yor,G,Oct 7)
Star Talent (USA) 63 (7f,Lei,GF,Apr 29)
Star of Gold 40 (7f,San,GF,Aug 30)
Star of Persia (IRE) 41 (10f,San,GF,Jun 16)
Star of Zilzal (USA) 62 (8f,Asc,GF,Jun 20)
Starry Eyed 54 (7f,Asc,G,Aug 23)
Stash the Cash (IRE) 46 (9f,Ham,S,Apr 12)
Statajack (IRE) 63 (10f,Kem,GF,May 27)
State Law 64 (10f,Nwm,G,Spt 29)
Stately Home (IRE) 40 (15f,War,GF,Jly 15)
Statistician 52 (6f,Cat,GF,Jly 6)
Statius 64 (5f,Pon,F,Oct 16)
Steady Ready Go (IRE) 40 (8f,Thi,F,May 20)
Stelvio 70 (16f,Asc,GF,Jun 21)
Step Aloft 63 (12f,Don,GF,Oct 21)
Stephensons Rocket 48 (5f,Rip,G,May 21)
Stevie's Wonder (IRE) 50 (14f,Sal,GS,Spt 27)
Sticks and Stones (IRE) 52 (10¹⁄₂f,Nwm,G,Jun 10)
Stiffelio (IRE) 65 (10¹⁄₂f,Hay,GF,Aug 5)
Stiletto Blade 66 (10¹⁄₂f,Yor,G,May 17)
Stinging Reply 48 (9f,San,G,Jun 17)
Stolen Kiss (IRE) 50 (5f,Ayr,G,Spt 14)
Stolen Melody 30 (7f,Nwm,GF,Oct 14)
Stone Ridge (IRE) 62 (8f,Nwm,GF,Oct 14)
Stoney Valley 55 (16¹⁄₂f,San,G,Apr 28)
Stoppes Brow 57 (6f,Fol,G,Oct 16)
Storiths (IRE) 82 (8f,Yor,G,May 17)
Storm Bid (USA) 48 (6f,Yar,G,Jun 14)
Stormaway (ITY) 39 (10f,Kem,GF,Apr 17)
Strat's Legacy 39 (12f,Chp,GF,Jly 20)
Strategic Choice (USA) 84 (12f,Asc,GF,Jly 22)
Straw Thatch 50 (10f,Ayr,GF,Jun 2)
Streaky Hawk (USA) 40 (10f,Kem,GF,Aug 2)
Striffolino 45 (9f,Red,F,Jun 24)
Struggler 72 (5f,Asc,F,Jun 23)
Strumming (IRE) 54 (8f,San,GS,Spt 13)
Strutting (IRE) 41 (12f,Asc,GF,Jun 22)
Stuffed 47 (6f,Nwc,GF,Oct 30)
Stylish Ways (IRE) 63 (6f,Nwm,GF,Oct 14)
Subya 56 (8f,Kem,GF,Apr 15)
Subzero 56 (6f,Chp,GS,Oct 10)
Sudden Spin 38 (12f,Cat,GF,Aug 11)
Sue Me (IRE) 54 (6f,Hay,G,Spt 2)
Sue's Artiste 68 (10f,Don,GS,Spt 9)
Sue's Return 52 (8f,Yor,GF,Aug 17)
Sugar Mill 60 (14f,Hay,G,Spt 23)
Sujud (IRE) 43 (14f,Not,GF,Oct 19)
Sulb (USA) 68 (8f,Goo,F,Jly 26)
Summer Retreat (USA) 46 (7f,San,GS,Spt 13)
Summerhill Special (IRE) 38 (10f,Nwb,GS,Oct 19)

Summertown (USA) 34 (7f,Kem,GF,Apr 17)
Summit 37 (12f,Lei,G,Jun 17)
Sun of Spring 53 (18f,Nwm,GF,Oct 14)
Sunday News'n'echo (USA) 41 (11f,Ayr,GF,May 10)
Sunderland Echo 52 (12½f,Nwc,F,Jly 1)
Sunshack 58 (12f,Eps,GF,Jun 10)
Super Benz 33 (7f,Don,GF,Nov 3)
Super High 41 (10f,Fol,S,Spt 27)
Super Park 41 (5f,Nwc,G,Spt 27)
Super Rocky 49 (5f,Fol,GF,Jly 12)
Super Serenade 36 (8f,Sal,GF,Aug 17)
Superbit 34 (5f,Not,GF,Aug 2)
Superluminal 70 (10f,Nwm,GF,May 7)
Superoo 58 (8f,War,G,May 27)
Superpride 46 (5f,Thi,G,Jun 5)
Supertop 45 (11f,Ham,GF,May 5)
Supreme Star (USA) 58 (16f,Asc,G,Spt 23)
Supreme Thought 48 (7f,Kem,G,Jun 3)
Sure Care 53 (10f,Bat,GF,May 22)
Surprise Mission 43 (7f,Not,GF,Jun 12)
Surrey Dancer 45 (12f,Thi,G,Apr 22)
Suvalu (USA) 32 (10f,Goo,GF,Aug 25)
Sveltana 37 (10f,Nwm,G,Spt 29)
Swallows Dream (IRE) 70 (12f,Asc,GF,Jly 22)
Swan At Whalley 39 (5f,Edi,GF,Jun 19)
Sweet Allegiance 33 (7f,San,GF,Aug 25)
Sweet Glow (FR) 60 (20f,Asc,GF,Jun 20)
Sweet Magic 70 (5f,Nwm,G,Jly 22)
Sweet Mate 30 (7f,Red,F,Oct 3)
Sweet Mignonette 56 (10½f,Yor,G,Oct 4)
Sweet Pavlova (USA) 49 (10f,Bat,Hd,Aug 3)
Sweet Supposin (IRE) 49 (7f,Fol,G,Jun 7)
Sweet Trentino (IRE) 48 (10½f,Hay,GS,Jun 9)
Swinging Sixties (IRE) 50 (8f,Lei,G,Oct 9)
Swinging Tich 32 (8f,War,F,Jly 7)
Swiss Bank 38 (7f,Sal,F,Aug 10)
Swivel 45 (16½f,San,GF,Aug 18)
Sword Master 33 (14f,Nwm,GF,Apr 18)
Swordking (IRE) 36 (14f,Not,GF,Apr 17)
Sycamore Lodge (IRE) 60 (7f,Don,G,May 27)
Sylvandra 45 (8f,Chp,GF,Jly 8)
Syrian Queen 38 (10f,Lei,G,Spt 5)
Tabook (IRE) 65 (6f,Yar,GF,Aug 10)
Tadellai (IRE) 45 (10f,San,G,May 29)
Tadjoni 42 (10f,Kem,GF,Apr 17)
Tael of Silver 48 (6f,Not,GS,Spt 11)
Tafahhus 60 (6f,Lin,GF,Jun 27)
Taffeta Silk (USA) 49 (6f,Wnd,GF,Jly 24)
Taipan (IRE) 65 (10½f,Hay,G,Jun 10)
Tajannub (USA) 65 (6f,Asc,F,Jun 23)
Tajar (USA) 41 (8½f,Bev,GF,Jly 18)
Takadou (IRE) 66 (5f,San,GF,Jun 17)
Takeshi (IRE) 38 (7f,Chp,GF,Jly 13)

Takhlid (USA) 59 (8½f,Eps,GS,Spt 19)
Taklif (IRE) 48 (12f,Yor,GF,Jun 16)
Talented Ting (IRE) 59 (8f,Ham,F,Aug 9)
Tamarpour (USA) 42 (16f,Not,GF,Aug 2)
Tamayaz (CAN) 68 (8f,Goo,F,Jly 29)
Tamure (IRE) 80 (12f,Eps,GF,Jun 10)
Tanah Merah (IRE) 34 (12f,Ham,Hy,Mar 31)
Tanami 53 (6f,Asc,GF,Jun 22)
Tappeto 39 (12f,Chp,GS,Oct 10)
Tarawa (IRE) 67 (8f,Nwm,GF,Oct 28)
Tarhhib 62 (7f,Nwb,GF,Apr 21)
Tart and a Half 66 (5f,Nwm,GF,Jun 30)
Tartan Gem (IRE) 34 (9f,Nwm,GF,Spt 30)
Tarthooth (IRE) 49 (20f,Asc,GF,Jun 20)
Tatika 55 (7½f,Bev,GF,Apr 7)
Taufan's Melody 89 (12f,Asc,GF,Jun 21)
Tawafij (USA) 64 (7f,Nwm,GF,Aug 5)
Taylord 45 (6f,Bri,F,May 11)
Te Amo (IRE) 51 (8½f,Eps,GS,Spt 19)
Tedburrow 58 (5f,San,GF,Jly 20)
Tee Tee Too (IRE) 39 (5f,Ham,GF,May 11)
Teen Jay 65 (10f,Don,G,Mar 24)
Teetotaller (IRE) 47 (6f,Kem,G,Apr 26)
Telopea 59 (10f,Not,G,Apr 24)
Temora (IRE) 44 (10f,Pon,GF,Jly 11)
Ten Past Six 67 (10½f,Yor,G,May 17)
Tenor 52 (5f,Ayr,GF,Jun 3)
Tenorio 73 (12f,Yor,GF,Jly 14)
Tertium (IRE) 55 (8f,Red,F,Oct 12)
Tessajoe 52 (10½f,Hay,S,Spt 30)
Tethys (USA) 62 (12f,Don,GS,Spt 8)
Thabit (USA) 55 (8f,San,G,May 29)
Thaleros 43 (10f,Pon,GF,Aug 3)
Thaljanah (IRE) 46 (12f,Rip,G,May 21)
Thames Side 46 (10f,Lei,F,Oct 24)
Tharwa (IRE) 42 (5f,Nwb,F,Jun 29)
That Man Again 80 (5f,Hay,GF,Aug 5)
That Old Feeling (IRE) 41 (10f,Wnd,GF,Jun 26)
Thatched (IRE) 45 (8f,Crl,Hd,Aug 21)
Thatcher's Era (IRE) 35 (8f,Lei,G,Oct 9)
Thatcherella 59 (6f,Chp,G,May 29)
Thatchmaster (IRE) 38 (8f,Goo,G,Spt 8)
The Fed 40 (5f,Not,GF,Aug 2)
The Flying Phantom 76 (16½f,San,G,May 29)
The French Friar (IRE) 64 (12f,Kem,G,Jun 3)
The Happy Fox (IRE) 51 (5f,Don,GF,Oct 21)
The Happy Loon (IRE) 36 (6f,Ayr,G,Jly 16)
The Institute Boy 34 (5f,Edi,GF,Jly 4)
The Jotter 69 (6f,Yar,G,Spt 12)
The Kings Ransom 58 (5f,Pon,GF,Jly 28)
The Lone Dancer 35 (10f,Pon,F,May 1)
The Old Chapel 40 (6f,Lei,GF,Apr 29)
The Premier Expres 33 (12f,Ham,Hy,Mar 31)
The Scythian 48 (5f,San,GF,Jly 20)

The Stager (IRE) 51 (7½f,Bev,GF,Apr 8)
Thick as Thieves 31 (5f,Rip,GF,Apr 20)
Thisonesforalice 33 (12f,Edi,GF,Jly 3)
Thousla Rock (IRE) 54 (6f,Nwb,G,Jly 15)
Three Arch Bridge 48 (7½f,Bev,GF,May 13)
Three Stops (USA) 61 (7f,Goo,F,Jly 28)
Threshfield (USA) 31 (8f,Yar,GF,Oct 18)
Thrower 36 (14f,Hay,G,Spt 23)
Thunder River (IRE) 52 (7f,Yar,G,Spt 13)
Thunderheart 52 (16f,Thi,GF,May 19)
Thwaab 30 (7f,Nwc,GF,Oct 30)
Tibetan 42 (16f,Nwb,G,Jly 14)
Tidal Reach (IRE) 36 (10½f,Hay,G,Apr 15)
Tiheros 37 (6f,Fol,GF,Mar 27)
Tikkanen (USA) 63 (12f,Nwm,G,May 5)
Tilaal (USA) 45 (8f,Pon,GF,Aug 22)
Tiler (IRE) 64 (7f,Chs,GF,Aug 18)
Tillandsia (IRE) 52 (10½f,Hay,GF,May 8)
Tilty (USA) 40 (14f,Not,GF,Oct 26)
Time Leader 43 (8f,Nwm,GF,Jun 23)
Time Star (USA) 67 (12f,Asc,F,Jun 23)
Time for Action (IRE) 66 (12f,Don,GF,Nov 4)
Timeless 45 (8f,Yar,GF,Oct 18)
Tinashaan (IRE) 66 (10f,Don,G,May 29)
Tinker Osmaston 53 (5f,Chp,GS,Oct 10)
Tino Tere 37 (5f,Nwc,G,May 25)
Tip the Dove 39 (16f,Hay,G,Apr 15)
Tira Heights (USA) 48 (12f,Sal,G,May 18)
Tirolette (IRE) 44 (12f,Nwm,GF,Oct 27)
To the Roof (IRE) 48 (5f,Chp,GS,Oct 10)
Tolls Choice (IRE) 42 (7½f,Bev,GF,Aug 24)
Tom Morgan 47 (7f,Ayr,G,Jly 17)
Tomal 31 (8f,War,F,Aug 28)
Tommy Cooper 32 (16f,Not,GS,Spt 11)
Tondres (USA) 61 (10f,San,G,May 29)
Tonka 40 (11½f,San,GS,Spt 12)
Tonnerre 42 (12f,Hay,S,Oct 1)
Tony's Fen 65 (12½f,Nwc,F,Jly 1)
Tony's Mist 36 (10f,Bev,GF,Jly 8)
Tonys Gift 44 (8f,Lei,F,Oct 24)
Top Banana 73 (5f,Nwb,F,Jun 29)
Top Cees 69 (18f,Nwm,GF,Oct 14)
Top Guide (USA) 49 (8f,Kem,GF,May 8)
Top Lady (IRE) 52 (12f,Chs,GF,Aug 19)
Top Pet (IRE) 48 (11½f,Lin,GF,Jun 24)
Top Prize 33 (14f,Not,GF,Aug 12)
Top Shop 48 (10½f,Hay,GF,May 8)
Top Show (IRE) 33 (7f,Red,G,May 29)
Topanga 38 (12f,Kem,GF,Jun 14)
Toraja 47 (12½f,Nwc,GF,Apr 17)
Torch Vert (IRE) 60 (13f,Ayr,G,Spt 16)
Torreglia (IRE) 40 (14f,Hay,G,Spt 23)
Torrential (USA) 55 (9f,Rip,GS,Apr 5)
Toskano 31 (10f,Not,GF,Aug 12)

Total Joy (IRE) 52 (12f,Bri,F,Jly 20)
Total Rach (IRE) 44 (8f,Yar,GF,Oct 18)
Total Stranger 56 (5f,Chs,GF,May 9)
Totality 55 (12f,Lei,G,Jun 17)
Touch Above 33 (10f,Nwc,G,Aug 26)
Touch a Million (USA) 45 (8f,Nwm,GF,Jly 13)
Toujours Riviera 69 (8f,Yar,GF,Jly 16)
Toy Princess (USA) 33 (14½f,Don,GF,May 8)
Trade Wind 52 (12f,Kem,G,Jun 3)
Traikey (IRE) 66 (10f,Don,G,May 27)
Tranquillity 45 (9f,San,G,Jun 17)
Trans Siberia 60 (14f,Nwm,G,May 19)
Transom (USA) 47 (16f,Asc,GF,May 3)
Trazl (IRE) 45 (15f,War,GF,Jly 15)
Tregaron (USA) 64 (8f,Asc,GF,May 3)
Tremendisto 39 (12f,Cat,GF,Oct 13)
Templin (IRE) 49 (10f,San,GF,Apr 29)
Triarius (USA) 61 (9f,Yor,GF,Aug 31)
Tribal Peace (IRE) 39 (10½f,Hay,G,Apr 15)
Trimming (IRE) 32 (7f,Nwm,GF,Apr 18)
Triple Joy 70 (6f,Nwc,F,Jly 1)
Triquetti (IRE) 54 (10f,Goo,F,Jly 28)
Tropical Jungle (USA) 43 (10f,Rip,GF,Apr 29)
True Bird (IRE) 40 (16f,Cat,GF,Oct 13)
Trumble 30 (14f,Cat,G,Spt 16)
Try-Haitai (IRE) 36 (6f,Lin,GF,May 20)
Tryphosa (IRE) 43 (10f,San,GF,Jly 8)
Tshusick 39 (6f,Nwb,GF,May 20)
Tu Opes 65 (16f,Red,F,Jly 13)
Tudor Island 61 (14f,Yor,G,Oct 7)
Tuigamala 35 (7f,Bri,F,Aug 2)
Tukano (CAN) 35 (14f,Yar,GF,Jly 5)
Tulu 63 (10f,Ayr,G,Spt 15)
Turnpole (IRE) 59 (12f,Pon,GF,Oct 2)
Turquoise Sea (USA) 53 (16f,Nwb,GS,Oct 19)
Tuscan Dawn 49 (5f,Eps,G,Jly 26)
Twice Purple (IRE) 42 (8f,Lei,G,Oct 9)
Twice as Sharp 61 (5f,Nwc,G,Spt 27)
Twice in Bundoran (IRE) 37 (5f,Nwc,G,May 25)
Twice the Groom (IRE) 56 (12f,Chs,GF,Jly 14)
Twilight Patrol 68 (7f,Goo,GF,Jly 28)
Twilight Sleep (USA) 49 (8f,Don,GF,Mar 25)
Twin Creeks 48 (9f,Ham,F,Jly 14)
Two O'Clock Jump (IRE) 52 (8f,Kem,GF,Apr 15)
Tykeyvor (IRE) 69 (12f,Don,GF,Oct 21)
Typhoon Eight (IRE) 52 (12f,Don,GS,Spt 8)
Tyrian Purple (IRE) 36 (5f,Fol,GF,Jly 12)
Tyrone Flyer 45 (6f,Fol,G,Oct 16)
Ultimate Warrior 36 (10f,Wnd,GF,May 15)
Ultra Beet 43 (5f,Nwm,G,Spt 28)
Un Parfum de Femme (IRE) 35 (11½f,Yar,GF,Jly 16)
Unchanged 49 (17f,Pon,GF,Oct 2)
Uncharted Waters 42 (12f,Sal,GF,Jun 13)

Uncle Doug 44 (14f,Yor,G,May 17)
Uncle Oswald 67 (10f,Wnd,G,Jun 12)
Unforgiving Minute 58 (10f,Don,GS,Spt 9)
Unfuwaanah 50 (5f,Yar,G,Spt 12)
United Force (IRE) 40 (10f,Goo,GF,Aug 25)
United Front 31 (10f,Red,F,May 15)
Unprejudice 48 (8f,Pon,G,Apr 25)
Up in Flames (IRE) 60 (8f,Don,GF,Jly 2)
Upper Mount Clair 47 (18f,Yar,G,Spt 14)
Urania 32 (10f,Fol,GF,Spt 7)
Utr (USA) 32 (5f,Pon,G,Spt 21)
Vain Prince 38 (13f,Ham,F,Aug 9)
Valiant Toski 49 (12f,Bri,F,Jly 20)
Vanborough Lad 42 (8f,Hay,GF,Jly 8)
Varnishing Day (IRE) 50 (7f,Sal,F,Jun 28)
Varvarka 39 (8f,Don,GF,Jly 26)
Vaugrenier (IRE) 53 (11f,Red,F,Oct 31)
Veloce (IRE) 59 (7f,San,GF,Jun 16)
Vena (IRE) 62 (9f,Goo,F,Jly 27)
Venice Beach 42 (8f,Yor,GF,Jun 17)
Venture Capitalist 95 (6f,Asc,F,Jun 23)
Verde Luna 49 (7½f,Bev,GF,May 23)
Verzen (IRE) 81 (8f,Yor,G,Oct 4)
Vettori (IRE) 81 (8f,Asc,GF,Jun 20)
Veuve Hoornaert (IRE) 48 (6f,Yar,G,Spt 12)
Viardot (IRE) 35 (12f,Nwm,G,Spt 28)
Victory Team (IRE) 34 (8f,Nwm,GF,Aug 26)
Vindaloo 72 (12f,Yor,GF,Aug 17)
Vintage Crop 68 (20f,Asc,GF,Jun 22)
Virkon Venture (IRE) 31 (12f,Ham,Hy,Mar 31)
Virtual Reality 63 (10f,Nwb,G,May 19)
Viyapari (IRE) 32 (8f,Lei,G,Apr 6)
Vizard (IRE) 30 (14f,Yar,G,Jun 14)
Volunteer (IRE) 32 (10f,Sal,GS,Spt 27)
Waders Dream (IRE) 35 (6f,Fol,F,Aug 15)
Waikiki Beach (USA) 41 (8f,San,G,May 29)
Waiting 55 (12f,Eps,GF,Jun 9)
Wakeel (USA) 45 (10f,Don,G,May 27)
Waldo 57 (8½f,Eps,GS,Spt 19)
Walk the Beat 49 (6f,Ayr,GF,Aug 5)
Walnut Burl (IRE) 37 (6f,Bri,F,Aug 2)
Walsham Whisper (IRE) 44 (12f,Nwm,GF,Apr 19)
Wandering Minstrel (IRE) 37 (7f,Yar,GF,Aug 17)
Wannaplantatree 49 (14f,Hay,G,Spt 22)
Wardara 30 (7f,Lin,S,Spt 14)
Warm Spell 49 (12f,Eps,G,Spt 6)
Warning Order 62 (10f,Nwm,GF,Oct 12)
Warning Shadows (IRE) 84 (8f,Asc,GF,Jun 21)
Warning Shot 59 (7f,Kem,G,Jun 3)
Warning Star 57 (7f,San,G,Jly 8)
Warwick Warrior (IRE) 33 (6f,Kem,G,Apr 26)
Wasblest 38 (5f,Edi,F,Jly 10)
Watch the Clock 61 (10½f,Yor,G,May 17)
Wathbat Mtoto 55 (12f,Hay,GF,Aug 4)

Wave Hill 46 (8f,Goo,F,Jly 29)
Wavian 78 (5f,Lin,GF,Aug 24)
Wayfarers Way (USA) 55 (10f,San,GF,Aug 19)
Wayne County (IRE) 74 (12f,Asc,G,Spt 23)
We're Joken 36 (6f,Cat,G,Jun 2)
Weather Break 47 (7f,San,GF,Jun 16)
Weaver Bird 68 (8f,Lei,GF,May 29)
Well Arranged (IRE) 56 (14f,Yor,G,May 17)
Well Beloved 49 (14f,Nwm,GF,Apr 18)
Wells Whisper (FR) 46 (10f,Yar,GF,Aug 10)
Wellsian (USA) 52 (10f,Don,GF,Jly 26)
Wellsy Lad (USA) 33 (8f,Edi,GS,Mar 30)
Welsh Mill (IRE) 38 (12f,Hay,G,Spt 22)
Welsh Mist 74 (6f,Yor,GF,Jly 14)
Welshman 41 (16f,Chs,GF,Aug 18)
Welton Arsenal 62 (7f,Yor,G,May 18)
Wentbridge Lad (IRE) 51 (10f,Pon,GF,Aug 3)
Wessam Prince 69 (6f,Asc,GF,Jun 22)
Westcourt Princess 39 (10f,Rip,G,Aug 28)
Western Fame (USA) 58 (8f,Nwm,GF,Oct 28)
Western General 70 (10½f,Hay,G,Jun 10)
Western Reel (USA) 52 (8f,Asc,F,Jun 24)
Western Sal 35 (7f,Yar,G,Jun 14)
Westminster (IRE) 34 (12f,Rip,GF,Apr 20)
Wet Patch (IRE) 45 (10f,Kem,GF,Aug 16)
What a Nightmare (IRE) 35 (7f,Cat,GF,Aug 1)
What's the Verdict (IRE) 42 (10f,Ayr,GF,Jun 3)
Whatever's Right (IRE) 62 (7f,San,GF,Aug 30)
Whispering Loch (IRE) 30 (11½f,Wnd,GF,Jly 17)
White Palace 41 (8f,Not,GF,May 2)
White Sorrel 51 (5f,Chs,G,Jun 8)
White Willow 44 (16f,Bev,GF,Apr 7)
Whitechapel (USA) 73 (12f,Don,GF,Nov 4)
Whittle Woods Girl 33 (6f,Hay,G,Apr 15)
Wigberto (IRE) 48 (8f,Chp,S,Oct 17)
Wijara (IRE) 57 (9f,Nwm,GF,Oct 13)
Wilcuma 57 (8f,Hay,G,Spt 22)
Wild Palm 44 (8f,War,GS,Oct 3)
Wild Rice 70 (7f,Chs,GF,Aug 18)
Wild Rita 49 (12f,Bri,G,Spt 20)
Wild Rose of York 32 (11f,Ham,F,Aug 9)
Wild Strawberry 54 (12f,Eps,GF,Jun 11)
Wildfire (SWI) 30 (12f,Kem,GF,Jun 14)
Willie Conquer 53 (7f,Nwm,GF,Spt 30)
Willshe Gan 32 (7f,Cat,G,Jun 3)
Wind in Her Hair (IRE) 76 (12f,Yor,GF,Aug 16)
Windmachine (SWE) 41 (6f,Nwm,GF,Apr 18)
Windrush Boy 52 (5f,Fol,G,Jun 7)
Windrush Lady 60 (10f,Nwb,G,Jly 15)
Winged Love (IRE) 72 (12f,Asc,GF,Jly 22)
Wings Cove 59 (14f,Not,G,Apr 24)
Winsome Wooster 49 (6f,Wnd,GF,Jly 24)
Winter Scout (USA) 49 (7f,Red,G,May 29)
Wishing (USA) 58 (12f,Goo,F,Jly 28)

Witchfinder (USA) 51 (10½f,Hay,G,Spt 22)
With Intent 33 (7f,Kem,G,Jun 3)
With the Fairies 53 (6f,Nwb,G,Jly 15)
Witney-de-Bergerac (IRE) 34 (11½f,Wnd,GF,Jly 29)
Wizard King 76 (8f,Asc,GF,Jly 22)
Wonderful Day 54 (12½f,Nwc,GF,Jly 24)
Woodcrest 54 (13f,Ayr,G,Spt 16)
Woodrising 39 (10f,Yar,GF,Aug 3)
Worldnews Extra (USA) 46 (8½f,Eps,GF,Jly 5)
Wot-If-We (IRE) 67 (16f,Asc,GF,Jun 21)
Wottashambles 30 (12f,Chp,GF,Jly 13)
Ya Malak 90 (5f,Kem,G,Jun 3)
Yaa Wale 45 (8f,Bri,G,Spt 20)
Yarn (IRE) 60 (11½f,Chs,GF,May 10)
Yarrow (IRE) 48 (10f,Nwm,G,Spt 26)
Yeast 56 (7f,Red,G,Spt 23)
Yet More Roses 51 (5f,Ayr,F,Jun 23)
Yo Kiri-B 38 (8f,War,F,Jly 7)
Yosif (IRE) 31 (7f,Nwb,GF,May 21)
Youdontsay 57 (6f,Kem,GF,Jun 28)
Yougo 46 (16f,Cat,GF,Oct 13)
Young Benson 46 (7½f,Bev,GF,May 23)
Young Buster (IRE) 87 (10½f,Hay,GF,Aug 5)
Young Clifford (USA) 30 (12f,Chp,G,May 29)
Young Duke (IRE) 49 (8f,War,F,Jun 26)

Young Ern 93 (7f,Lei,GF,Apr 29)
Yoush (IRE) 60 (10f,San,G,Jly 7)
Yoxall Lodge 42 (7½f,Bev,GF,Apr 7)
Yubralee (USA) 48 (8f,San,G,May 30)
Zaaheyah (USA) 35 (13f,Ham,G,May 4)
Zacaroon 54 (10f,Don,GF,May 9)
Zahid (USA) 47 (10f,San,GF,Aug 19)
Zahran (IRE) 41 (9f,Ham,F,Aug 14)
Zahwa 48 (6f,Nwm,G,Jly 21)
Zajko (USA) 62 (8f,Nwb,GF,May 21)
Zalament 35 (12f,Kem,GF,Jun 14)
Zamalek (USA) 40 (10½f,Yor,GF,Jun 17)
Zamhareer (USA) 41 (14f,Hay,G,Spt 23)
Zaralaska 84 (12f,Asc,GF,Jun 21)
Zeb (IRE) 63 (6f,Hay,GS,May 27)
Zeetaro 58 (10f,Rip,GF,Aug 19)
Zelda Zonk 42 (7f,Nwm,GF,Oct 28)
Zermatt (IRE) 58 (8f,Nwm,G,Jly 22)
Zidac 35 (10f,Wnd,GF,May 15)
Zifta (USA) 44 (7f,Red,F,May 15)
Ziggy's Dancer (USA) 64 (5f,Bev,GF,May 23)
Zilayah (USA) 37 (7f,San,G,May 29)
Zilzal Zaaman (USA) 75 (13½f,Chs,GF,May 11)
Zingibar 36 (8f,Hay,G,Spt 2)
Zuiena (USA) 45 (15½f,Fol,GF,Spt 7)
Zygo (USA) 33 (8f,Don,GF,May 9)

THREE YEAR-OLDS AND UPWARDS - Sand

A Million Watts 46 (8f,Sou,Std,Mar 3)
Able Choice (IRE) 47 (12f,Lin,Std,Mar 16)
Absalom's Pillar 49 (12f,Sou,Std,May 11)
Abu Simbel (USA) 32 (8f,Sou,Std,Mar 20)
Achilles Heel 34 (10f,Lin,Std,Feb 28)
Admiral Hood (USA) 39 (10f,Lin,Std,Feb 28)
Admirals Flame (IRE) 31 (10f,Lin,Std,Feb 9)
African Chimes 43 (5f,Lin,Std,Mar 16)
Aitch N'Bee 55 (9½f,Wol,Std,Mar 4)
Aljawab (USA) 53 (9½f,Wol,Std,May 27)
Allemande (IRE) 36 (8½f,Wol,Std,Mar 8)
Allinson's Mate (IRE) 30 (7f,Wol,Std,Feb 15)
Almuhtaram 53 (10f,Lin,Std,Dec 15)
Alzoomo (IRE) 37 (12f,Wol,Std,Dec 9)
Anistop 44 (8f,Sou,Std,Nov 16)
Anita's Contessa (IRE) 44 (6f,Wol,Std,Spt 2)
Anjou 43 (16f,Lin,Std,Dec 15)
Another Batchworth 49 (6f,Wol,Std,Oct 28)
Another Episode (IRE) 40 (5f,Lin,Std,Jan 31)
Another Jade 47 (6f,Wol,Std,Apr 1)
Anzio (IRE) 49 (7f,Lin,Std,Nov 21)

Apollo Red 32 (7f,Lin,Std,Mar 25)
Aquado 37 (7f,Sou,Std,Apr 3)
Arc Bright (IRE) 47 (16f,Lin,Std,Feb 14)
Arc Lamp 31 (6f,Wol,Std,Jan 11)
Arcatura 40 (9½f,Wol,Std,Dec 9)
Arctic Guest (IRE) 41 (16f,Lin,Std,Jan 24)
Argyle Cavalier (IRE) 58 (16f,Lin,Std,Jan 24)
Armston 35 (15f,Wol,Std,Jly 3)
Art Form (USA) 63 (16f,Lin,Std,Jan 24)
Ashgore 45 (6f,Wol,Std,Nov 11)
Ashover 60 (11f,Sou,Std,Feb 27)
Ashtina 38 (5f,Lin,Std,Dec 6)
Asmarina 30 (9½f,Wol,Std,Jly 8)
At Liberty (IRE) 42 (12f,Wol,Std,Dec 2)
At the Savoy (IRE) 53 (6f,Sou,Std,Apr 26)
Atherton Green (IRE) 30 (11f,Sou,Std,Jan 16)
Awesome Power 36 (10f,Lin,Std,Nov 2)
Awestruck 39 (12f,Wol,Std,Feb 15)
Ayunli 52 (9½f,Wol,Std,Aug 19)
Backview 40 (12f,Wol,Std,Jly 17)
Bag of Tricks (IRE) 34 (12f,Lin,Std,Jan 14)

Bagshot 46 (8f,Sou,Std,Dec 1)
Ballymac Girl 42 (15f,Wol,Std,Nov 27)
Ballynakelly 55 (12f,Lin,Std,Nov 29)
Band on the Run 30 (9¹/₂f,Wol,Std,Dec 2)
Barahin (IRE) 30 (10f,Lin,Std,Mar 31)
Bardon Hill Boy (IRE) 47 (9¹/₂f,Wol,Std,May 22)
Barti-Ddu 46 (11f,Sou,Std,Feb 27)
Battle Colours (IRE) 43 (7f,Sou,Std,Feb 3)
Be Warned 62 (7f,Sou,Std,Nov 24)
Beauman 31 (8f,Sou,Std,Nov 6)
Beaumont (IRE) 41 (11f,Sou,Std,Dec 1)
Beautete 49 (16f,Lin,Std,Jan 14)
Bella Parkes 59 (8f,Sou,Std,Mar 3)
Belleminette (IRE) 41 (9¹/₂f,Wol,Std,Mar 1)
Bellesonnette (IRE) 36 (7f,Sou,Std,Apr 3)
Bells of Longwick 33 (5f,Sou,Std,May 11)
Bencher Q C (USA) 32 (7f,Lin,Std,Mar 29)
Benfleet 49 (10f,Lin,Std,Nov 21)
Benjamins Law 48 (9¹/₂f,Wol,Std,Nov 13)
Bentico 58 (8f,Lin,Std,Nov 2)
Berge (IRE) 57 (6f,Sou,Std,Nov 24)
Bernard Seven (IRE) 38 (8f,Lin,Std,Dec 14)
Beveled Edge 37 (6f,Sou,Std,Apr 11)
Birequest 59 (10f,Lin,Std,Feb 9)
Blue Sioux 33 (10f,Std,Oct 14)
Blurred Image (IRE) 35 (10f,Lin,Std,Feb 9)
Bogart 30 (7f,Sou,Std,Feb 6)
Bold Aristocrat (IRE) 35 (6f,Sou,Std,Aug 4)
Bold Effort (FR) 39 (5f,Lin,Std,Jan 26)
Bold Habit 43 (10f,Lin,Std,Nov 2)
Bold Street (IRE) 52 (6f,Wol,Std,Nov 27)
Bon Secret (IRE) 30 (12f,Lin,Std,Jan 14)
Brackenthwaite 45 (9¹/₂f,Wol,Std,Jan 11)
Brave Princess 51 (9¹/₂f,Wol,Std,Spt 30)
Brave Spy 43 (16f,Lin,Std,Jun 17)
Braveboy 38 (10f,Lin,Std,Jan 17)
Broadstairs Beauty (IRE) 59 (5f,Sou,Std,Nov 16)
Broom Isle 35 (15f,Wol,Std,Mar 18)
Broughtons Formula 48 (13f,Lin,Std,Dec 19)
Broughtons Turmoil 42 (8f,Lin,Std,Feb 25)
Buckley Boys 30 (11f,Sou,Std,Nov 20)
Buddy's Friend (IRE) 33 (8f,Lin,Std,Mar 2)
Bures (IRE) 37 (12f,Lin,Std,Feb 18)
Busy Banana 32 (10f,Lin,Std,Apr 7)
C-Yer-Simmie (IRE) 32 (5f,Sou,Std,Spt 4)
Caddy's First 32 (7f,Wol,Std,Jly 21)
Calder King 47 (11f,Sou,Std,Dec 1)
Call Me Albi (IRE) 31 (16f,Lin,Std,Dec 15)
Call Me Blue 32 (10f,Lin,Std,Feb 28)
Callonescy (IRE) 36 (9¹/₂f,Wol,Std,Feb 15)
Camden's Ransom (USA) 42 (11f,Sou,Std,Feb 13)
Can Can Charlie 49 (9¹/₂f,Wol,Std,Aug 19)
Canary Falcon 42 (9¹/₂f,Wol,Std,Nov 27)

Canovas Heart 42 (5f,Sou,Std,Jun 8)
Canton Venture 45 (12f,Wol,Std,Spt 16)
Capias (USA) 60 (9¹/₂f,Wol,Std,Dec 2)
Captain Marmalade 40 (8¹/₂f,Wol,Std,May 13)
Carlowitz (USA) 32 (13f,Lin,Std,Jan 10)
Carpathian 52 (12f,Wol,Std,Oct 14)
Carte Blanche 34 (8f,Lin,Std,Feb 25)
Cashmere Lady 42 (7f,Wol,Std,Dec 2)
Castel Rosselo 55 (7f,Wol,,Mar 1)
Cavers Yangous 42 (6f,Sou,Std,Jun 22)
Cavina 46 (16f,Lin,Std,Jun 17)
Cedez le Passage (FR) 44 (12f,Wol,Std,Jan 18)
Cee-Jay-Ay 41 (8¹/₂f,Wol,Std,Jly 22)
Celestial Choir 55 (8¹/₂f,Wol,Std,Nov 11)
Celestial Key (USA) 34 (9¹/₂f,Wol,Std,Dec 2)
Certain Way (IRE) 37 (9¹/₂f,Wol,Std,Dec 9)
Chadwell Hall 49 (5f,Sou,Std,Jun 8)
Chahaya Timor (IRE) 31 (12f,Wol,Std,Aug 5)
Chairmans Choice 64 (9¹/₂f,Wol,Std,Nov 13)
Charlie Bigtime 34 (12f,Wol,Std,Spt 16)
Chatham Island 64 (9¹/₂f,Wol,Std,Jan 11)
Cheeky Chappy 33 (5f,Lin,Std,Dec 6)
Chewit 45 (6f,Lin,Std,Nov 25)
Chez Catalan 34 (16f,Lin,Std,Dec 15)
Chimborazo 39 (15f,Wol,Std,May 13)
Claireswan (IRE) 34 (16f,Lin,Std,Aug 24)
Cliburnel News (IRE) 30 (13f,Lin,Std,Jan 17)
Cloette 40 (7f,Sou,Std,Aug 4)
Coleridge 39 (16f,Lin,Std,Nov 29)
Conspicuous (IRE) 32 (9¹/₂f,Wol,Std,Feb 1)
Cool Tactician 41 (6f,Wol,Std,Spt 16)
Cretan Gift 60 (6f,Wol,Std,Dec 12)
Croft Pool 66 (6f,Sou,Std,Jan 2)
Crown Prosecutor 44 (12f,Sou,Std,Jan 9)
Crystal Heights (FR) 46 (6f,Lin,Std,Feb 28)
Crystal Loop 38 (7f,Wol,Std,Feb 8)
Cuango (IRE) 47 (15f,Wol,Std,Nov 11)
Dahiyah (USA) 31 (8f,Lin,Std,Mar 16)
Daleria 40 (11f,Sou,Std,Spt 4)
Dance So Suite 33 (10f,Lin,Std,Nov 8)
Dancing Diamond (IRE) 39 (13f,Lin,Std,Feb 11)
Dancing Heart 49 (7f,Lin,Std,Nov 8)
Dancing Lawyer 49 (8f,Lin,Std,Nov 25)
Dangerous Guest (IRE) 49 (9¹/₂f,Wol,Std,May 22)
Dark Shot (IRE) 49 (6f,Wol,Std,Spt 16)
Dashing Dancer (IRE) 44 (6f,Lin,GF,Aug 5)
David James' Girl 37 (6f,Wol,Std,Nov 27)
Dawalib (USA) 44 (6f,Sou,Std,Jan 30)
Daytona Beach (IRE) 51 (8¹/₂f,Wol,Std,Jly 22)
Deeply Vale (IRE) 55 (6f,Wol,Std,Dec 9)
Desert Invader (IRE) 55 (6f,Wol,Std,Spt 16)
Dia Georgy 31 (10f,Lin,Std,Aug 12)
Digpast (IRE) 54 (8f,Lin,Std,Mar 29)
Disco Boy 34 (6f,Wol,Std,May 13)

Distant Dynasty 43 (5f,Lin,Std,Jan 31)
Dolly Face 42 (5f,Lin,Std,Mar 16)
Donia (USA) 30 (9½f,Wol,Std,Feb 4)
Double Rush (IRE) 36 (10f,Lin,Std,Nov 14)
Douce Maison (IRE) 49 (9½f,Wol,Std,Aug 19)
Dragonflight 32 (9½f,Wol,Std,Mar 18)
Dream Carrier (IRE) 36 (7f,Sou,Std,Jan 16)
Duello 41 (8½f,Wol,Std,Apr 16)
Duke Valentino 56 (8f,Lin,Std,Nov 14)
Dune River 61 (8f,Lin,Std,Mar 4)
Dvorak (IRE) 32 (12f,Lin,Std,Feb 9)
Eastleigh 40 (8f,Lin,Std,Mar 29)
Easy Choice (USA) 46 (8f,Lin,Std,Nov 29)
Efficacy 38 (6f,Wol,Std,Jun 30)
El Atrevido (FR) 42 (10f,Lin,Std,Mar 29)
El Bailador (IRE) 32 (8f,Lin,Std,Jun 24)
El Nido 38 (14f,Sou,Std,Mar 3)
El Volador 47 (12f,Wol,Std,Dec 9)
Elburg (IRE) 57 (16f,Lin,Std,Jan 14)
Elementary 50 (12f,Lin,Std,Nov 2)
Elpida (USA) 36 (15f,Wol,Std,Spt 16)
Elton Ledger (IRE) 34 (6f,Sou,Std,Jan 16)
Emphatic Candidate (IRE) 34 (9½f,Wol,Std,Aug 5)
Encore M'Lady (IRE) 57 (6f,Wol,Std,Dec 9)
Environmentalist (IRE) 39 (12f,Wol,Std,Spt 30)
Epica 31 (7f,Wol,Std,Apr 29)
Eqtesaad (USA) 43 (8½f,Wol,Std,Apr 1)
Equerry 47 (8½f,Wol,Std,Jly 22)
Ertlon 61 (8f,Lin,Std,Mar 4)
Evening Falls 43 (6f,Wol,Std,Aug 11)
Everset (FR) 48 (7f,Wol,Std,Jan 4)
Exclusive Assembly 31 (7f,Sou,Std,Aug 4)
Exhibit Air (IRE) 48 (12f,Lin,Std,Oct 23)
Explosive Power 33 (10f,Lin,Std,Dec 18)
Faez 35 (6f,Sou,Std,Jan 2)
Fair and Fancy (FR) 35 (14f,Sou,Std,Nov 16)
Fairey Firefly 33 (6f,Wol,Std,Dec 9)
Far Ahead 43 (8½f,Wol,Std,Nov 11)
Farfelu 34 (5f,Lin,Std,Jan 12)
Father Dan (IRE) 42 (10f,Lin,Std,Feb 28)
Fearless Wonder 39 (11f,Sou,Std,Feb 20)
Featherstone Lane 52 (6f,Wol,Std,Spt 16)
Fen Terrier 31 (12f,Sou,Std,Jly 22)
Field of Vision (IRE) 34 (7f,Lin,Std,Dec 15)
Finlaggan 54 (12f,Lin,Std,Oct 23)
First Century (IRE) 32 (9½f,Wol,Std,Feb 4)
First Gold 33 (7f,Sou,Std,Jly 22)
Five to Seven (USA) 32 (14f,Sou,Std,Nov 6)
Flashfeet 35 (9½f,Wol,Std,Apr 15)
Flashman 33 (16f,Wol,Std,Jly 21)
Flowing Ocean 49 (7f,Sou,Std,Feb 24)
Folly Finnesse 35 (8f,Wol,Std,Feb 8)
Forzair 41 (7f,Wol,Std,Jly 3)

Four of Spades 53 (6f,Wol,Std,Spt 2)
Freckles Kelly 31 (5f,Sou,Std,Jly 22)
Friendly Brave (USA) 49 (5f,Lin,Std,Nov 10)
Frisky Miss (IRE) 40 (6f,Wol,Std,Jan 11)
Gallery Artist (IRE) 35 (9½f,Wol,Std,Mar 8)
Ginger Jim 32 (12f,Lin,Std,Feb 9)
Global Dancer 54 (12f,Lin,Std,Oct 23)
Go Hever Golf 58 (6f,Wol,Std,Feb 1)
Gold Blade 48 (11f,Sou,Std,Jan 13)
Gold Surprise (IRE) 45 (16f,Lin,Std,Jan 14)
Grand Selection (IRE) 37 (8f,Wol,Std,Feb 18)
Greatest 37 (7f,Lin,Std,Feb 28)
Greek Gold (IRE) 41 (11f,Sou,Std,Jan 20)
Green's Bid 42 (3f,Lin,Std,Mar 16)
Greenwich Again 38 (8f,Lin,Std,Dec 15)
Grey Charmer (IRE) 38 (6f,Sou,Std,Aug 4)
Guest Alliance (IRE) 31 (16f,Lin,Std,Dec 15)
Gulf Shaadi 52 (8f,Sou,Std,May 11)
H'Ani 39 (12f,Lin,Std,Nov 29)
Half Tone 35 (5f,Lin,Std,Dec 6)
Halliard 34 (5f,Lin,Std,Feb 18)
Handmaiden 33 (12f,Sou,Std,Jan 9)
Hannah's Usher 42 (5f,Wol,Std,Feb 15)
Hard Love 31 (9½f,Wol,Std,Dec 9)
Harlequin Walk (IRE) 30 (12f,Lin,Std,Feb 23)
Harpoon Louie (USA) 45 (8f,Lin,Std,Dec 14)
Hattaafeh (IRE) 36 (13f,Lin,Std,Feb 4)
Hawaii Storm (FR) 46 (7f,Lin,Std,Dec 14)
Hawwam 47 (8f,Sou,Std,Mar 3)
Head Turner 42 (16f,Lin,Std,Mar 2)
Heart Broken 53 (7f,Sou,Std,Aug 4)
Heathyards Lady (USA) 47 (8½f,Wol,Std,Nov 11)
Heathyards Magic (IRE) 33 (6f,Wol,Std,Apr 4)
Heathyards Rock 53 (9½f,Wol,Std,May 22)
Heboob Alshemaal (IRE) 32 (10f,Lin,Std,Nov 21)
Herr Trigger 44 (10f,Lin,Std,Mar 25)
Hever Golf Star 51 (5f,Sou,Std,Nov 16)
High Premium 30 (7f,Wol,Std,Spt 2)
Highborn (IRE) 37 (7f,Wol,,Mar 1)
Hillzah (USA) 49 (12f,Wol,Std,Mar 8)
Hong Kong Dollar 38 (6f,Wol,Std,Jly 3)
How's it Goin (IRE) 35 (14f,Wol,Std,Feb 15)
Hydrofoil 30 (15f,Wol,Std,Spt 16)
I'm Your Lady 36 (5f,Sou,Std,Nov 16)
Ibsen 44 (16f,Lin,Std,Feb 25)
Ijab (CAN) 41 (14f,Sou,Std,Nov 16)
Ikhtiraa (USA) 51 (12f,Lin,Std,Feb 21)
Imperial Bid (FR) 37 (11f,Sou,Std,Jan 23)
In a Moment (USA) 32 (11f,Sou,Std,Feb 13)
In the Money (IRE) 42 (12f,Lin,Std,Feb 18)
Inchkeith 38 (9½f,Wol,Std,Feb 15)
Indian Serenade 38 (8f,Lin,Std,Mar 16)
Inherent Magic (IRE) 52 (6f,Wol,Std,Nov 11)
Insider Trader 37 (5f,Sou,Std,Nov 16)

Instantaneous 33 (12f,Wol,Std,Spt 16)
Intention 32 (13f,Lin,Std,Jan 12)
Invocation 42 (7f,Lin,Std,Nov 8)
Ionio (USA) 66 (10f,Lin,Std,Mar 4)
Iota 46 (14f,Wol,Std,Jan 4)
Iron N Gold 30 (13f,Lin,Std,Dec 19)
Ism 49 (6f,Wol,Std,Spt 2)
Jalmaid 39 (9¹/₂f,Wol,Std,Dec 9)
Jamaica Bridge 40 (6f,Wol,Std,Spt 16)
Jaraab 52 (16f,Lin,Std,Nov 8)
Jemima Puddleduck 37 (11f,Sou,Std,Nov 20)
Jersey Belle 31 (6f,Wol,Std,Jly 3)
Jigsaw Boy 52 (6f,Wol,Std,Oct 28)
Johnnie the Joker 56 (7f,Sou,Std,Nov 24)
Johns Act (USA) 45 (12f,Wol,Std,Mar 8)
Jon's Choice 35 (9¹/₂f,Wol,Std,Spt 2)
Joseph's Wine (IRE) 68 (11f,Sou,Std,Jan 9)
Joyful (IRE) 32 (7f,Lin,Std,Nov 2)
Just Harry 49 (8f,Sou,Std,Jan 2)
Just-Mana-Mou (IRE) 46 (12f,Lin,Std,Nov 29)

Kaafih Homm (IRE) 51 (8f,Lin,Std,Nov 29)
Kadiri (IRE) 49 (16f,Lin,Std,Jan 14)
Kalamata 39 (12f,Wol,Std,Nov 11)
Kalar 54 (5f,Lin,Std,Mar 2)
Katy's Lad 43 (9¹/₂f,Wol,Std,Jun 2)
Kedwick (IRE) 42 (8f,Lin,Std,Mar 29)
Kellaire Girl (IRE) 33 (8f,Lin,Std,Nov 21)
Kenyatta (USA) 35 (12f,Lin,Std,Dec 18)
Kierchem (IRE) 30 (15f,Wol,Std,Jly 17)
Killick 35 (11f,Sou,Std,Jan 13)
Killing Time 35 (11f,Sou,Std,Jan 20)
King Parrot (IRE) 36 (8f,Lin,Std,Feb 25)
King Rambo 52 (6f,Wol,Std,Spt 30)
King Rat (IRE) 46 (9¹/₂f,Wol,Std,Dec 2)
Kinnegad Kid 56 (9¹/₂f,Wol,Std,Mar 18)
Kintwyn 54 (9¹/₂f,Wol,Std,Mar 1)
Kirov Protege (IRE) 32 (8¹/₂f,Wol,Std,Feb 22)
Knotally Wood (USA) 45 (12f,Lin,Std,Nov 30)
Komiamaite 32 (9¹/₂f,Wol,Std,May 27)
Komreyev Dancer 37 (8f,Wol,Std,Jan 7)
La Brief 49 (14f,Sou,Std,Nov 16)
La Petite Fusee 35 (5f,Sou,Std,Nov 16)
La Residence 34 (8f,Lin,Std,Mar 31)
Lady Reema 35 (10f,Lin,Std,Feb 28)
Lady Sheriff 31 (5f,Sou,Std,Nov 16)
Lady Silk 30 (6f,Wol,Std,Oct 28)
Lady Williams (IRE) 32 (8f,Lin,Std,Mar 2)
Landlord 37 (9¹/₂f,Wol,Std,Spt 30)
Langtonian 35 (6f,Sou,Std,Jan 2)
Larn Fort 37 (11f,Sou,Std,Dec 1)
Last Corner 35 (15f,Wol,Std,Spt 16)
Lear Dancer (USA) 42 (16f,Lin,Std,Nov 29)
Legal Fiction 58 (9¹/₂f,Wol,Std,Mar 1)

'Legally Delicious 33 (8f,Sou,Std,May 11)
Legatee 35 (7f,Wol,Std,Jly 3)
Leigh Crofter 56 (8f,Sou,Std,Mar 3)
Let's Get Lost 40 (11f,Sou,Std,Jan 23)
Letsbeonestaboutit 31 (6f,Sou,Std,Feb 20)
Level Edge 34 (9¹/₂f,Wol,Std,Aug 5)
Lift Boy (USA) 39 (6f,Wol,Std,Jan 11)
Little Ibnr 63 (6f,Wol,Std,Dec 12)
Little Saboteur 52 (5f,Lin,Std,Mar 31)
Live Project (IRE) 48 (8f,Lin,Std,Nov 14)
Lochon 34 (5f,Lin,Std,Dec 6)
Lochore 30 (11f,Sou,Std,May 15)
Locorotondo (IRE) 44 (12f,Wol,Std,Jly 3)
Loki (IRE) 57 (12f,Lin,Std,Oct 23)
Long Furlong 34 (12f,Lin,Std,Jan 5)
Lord Jim (IRE) 50 (12f,Wol,Std,Dec 2)
Lord Sky 49 (5f,Sou,Std,Nov 16)
Love Legend 30 (8¹/₂f,Wol,Std,Apr 13)
Loveyoumillions (IRE) 57 (7f,Sou,Std,Nov 16)
Lyford Law (IRE) 68 (8¹/₂f,Wol,Std,Nov 11)
Mad Militant (IRE) 46 (12f,Wol,Std,Mar 8)
Magic Junction (USA) 47 (10f,Lin,Std,Nov 8)
Mahool (USA) 58 (7f,Wol,,Mar 1)
Maid Welcome 40 (7f,Lin,Std,Dec 14)
Majal (IRE) 37 (12f,Lin,Std,Feb 7)
Major Mouse 47 (8f,Sou,Std,Jun 22)
Malibu Man 42 (6f,Wol,Std,Aug 19)
Mam'zelle Angot 46 (9¹/₂f,Wol,Std,Jly 8)
Mamma's Due 38 (5f,Sou,Std,Jun 8)
Manful 38 (12f,Lin,Std,Dec 18)
Maple Bay (IRE) 48 (6f,Wol,Std,Spt 16)
Maradonna (USA) 42 (16f,Lin,Std,Mar 29)
Maralinga (IRE) 62 (9¹/₂f,Wol,Std,Dec 2)
Marco Magnifico (USA) 61 (16f,Lin,Std,Jan 14)
Marowins 43 (8¹/₂f,Wol,Std,Apr 13)
Mary's Case (IRE) 36 (8f,Sou,Std,Spt 4)
Masnun (USA) 64 (10f,Lin,Std,Nov 2)
Masrah Dubai (USA) 30 (12f,Lin,Std,Feb 9)
Master Beveled 41 (9¹/₂f,Wol,Std,Mar 1)
Master Millfield (IRE) 39 (7f,Wol,Std,Feb 8)
Matthew David 34 (6f,Sou,Std,Jan 2)
Md Thompson 31 (7f,Wol,Std,Spt 16)
Meant to Be 54 (14f,Wol,Std,Jan 4)
Mentalasanythin 62 (8f,Lin,Std,Feb 7)
Merit (IRE) 49 (12f,Lin,Std,Oct 23)
Metal Storm (FR) 45 (8f,Lin,Std,Feb 11)
Milngavie (IRE) 35 (14f,Wol,Std,Jan 4)
Milos 41 (7f,Lin,Std,Nov 8)
Miroswaki (USA) 58 (16f,Lin,Std,Nov 29)
Mislemani (IRE) 38 (8f,Sou,Std,Nov 16)
Mister Fire Eyes (IRE) 56 (6f,Sou,Std,Dec 1)
Mixed Mood 33 (6f,Wol,Std,Jly 17)
Mizyan (IRE) 48 (14f,Sou,Std,Apr 11)
Modest Hope (USA) 38 (11f,Sou,Std,Jan 13)

Monarch 33 (11f,Sou,Std,Apr 11)
Monis (IRE) 35 (6f,Wol,Std,Dec 12)
Montague Dawson (IRE) 47 (6f,Wol,Std,Spt 16)
Montanelli (FR) 41 (8f,Lin,Std,Feb 28)
Montone (IRE) 47 (10f,Lin,Std,Nov 2)
Moon Strike (FR) 47 (7f,Lin,Std,Jan 26)
Moscow Road 57 (5f,Lin,Std,Jan 31)
Most Uppitty 33 (5f,Sou,Std,Jun 16)
Moujeeb (USA) 45 (5f,Sou,Std,Jun 8)
Mowlaie 48 (10f,Lin,Std,Nov 2)
Mr Bean 42 (11f,Sou,Std,Apr 3)
Mr Bergerac (IRE) 67 (7f,Sou,Std,Nov 16)
Mr Frosty 49 (8f,Lin,Std,Nov 14)
Mr Martini (IRE) 44 (9½f,Wol,Std,Dec 2)
Mr Nevermind (IRE) 50 (8f,Lin,Std,Nov 29)
Mr Rough 35 (8f,Lin,Std,Nov 2)
Mr Towser 50 (11f,Sou,Std,Feb 13)
Mullitover 37 (8f,Sou,Std,Jan 2)
My Cherrywell 37 (5f,Sou,Std,May 11)
My Gallery (IRE) 37 (7f,Wol,Std,Jly 3)
My Handy Man 43 (11f,Sou,Std,Jan 9)
My Minnie 45 (9½f,Wol,Std,Apr 13)
Nadwaty (IRE) 36 (5f,Sou,Std,Mar 20)
Name the Tune 43 (5f,Sou,Std,Nov 16)
Nashaat (USA) 60 (7f,Sou,Std,Nov 24)
Nessun Doro 37 (8f,Sou,Std,Jun 16)
Neuwest (USA) 47 (8f,Lin,Std,Nov 25)
Newbury Coat 37 (5f,Sou,Std,Spt 4)
Nick the Biscuit 35 (12f,Wol,Std,Jan 18)
Nineacres 38 (5f,Lin,Std,Jan 17)
Ninety-Five 30 (5f,Sou,Std,Spt 4)
Nirvana Prince 31 (12f,Wol,Std,Feb 8)
No Pattern 34 (8f,Lin,Std,Feb 9)
No Speeches (IRE) 53 (10f,Lin,Std,Nov 2)
No Submission (USA) 53 (7f,Sou,Std,May 11)
Non Vintage (IRE) 38 (11f,Sou,Std,Jan 9)
Nordan Raider 39 (6f,Sou,Std,Jan 16)
Nordic Doll (IRE) 33 (8f,Lin,Std,Nov 29)
Nordic Sun (IRE) 38 (12f,Wol,Std,Dec 9)
Nordico Princess 57 (5f,Lin,Std,Mar 16)
North Esk (USA) 35 (8f,Lin,Std,Nov 14)
North Reef (IRE) 41 (10f,Lin,Std,Jly 14)
Northern Celadon (IRE) 43 (9½f,Wol,Std,Jan 11)
Noufari (FR) 50 (12f,Wol,Std,Mar 8)
Ocean Park 66 (9½f,Wol,Std,Nov 13)
Ochos Rios (IRE) 44 (7f,Sou,Std,Nov 24)
Off'n'away (IRE) 35 (10f,Lin,Std,Apr 7)
Oggi 47 (6f,Wol,Std,Spt 2)
Old Hook (IRE) 42 (8f,Lin,Std,Nov 25)
Old Provence 38 (12f,Wol,Std,Nov 27)
Old Rouvel (USA) 33 (12f,Lin,Std,Feb 16)
One Off the Rail (USA) 52 (12f,Lin,Std,Mar 16)
One for Jeannie 39 (6f,Wol,Std,May 4)
Oneoftheoldones 38 (8f,Sou,Std,Jun 16)

Opera Buff (IRE) 62 (13f,Lin,Std,Nov 25)
Orthorhombus 46 (7f,Sou,Std,Apr 3)
Our Eddie 32 (12f,Lin,Std,Feb 2)
Our Shadee (USA) 39 (6f,Lin,Std,Feb 28)
Our Tom 42 (9½f,Wol,Std,Dec 9)
Outstayed Welcome 33 (13f,Lin,Std,Dec 6)
Owdbetts (IRE) 43 (10f,Lin,Std,Dec 15)
Pageboy 34 (6f,Lin,Std,Feb 7)
Palacegate Jo (IRE) 45 (12f,Sou,Std,May 11)
Palacegate Touch 53 (6f,Wol,Std,Jun 24)
Panther (IRE) 32 (6f,Sou,Std,Mar 20)
Pc's Cruiser (IRE) 31 (6f,Sou,Std,Feb 10)
Pearly River 35 (12f,Lin,Std,Feb 7)
Peggy Spencer 50 (6f,Sou,Std,Nov 20)
Pengamon 42 (8f,Lin,Std,Nov 25)
Penmar 42 (7f,Wol,Std,Spt 16)
Perfect Brave 32 (5f,Lin,Std,Nov 10)
Perfect Ending 33 (13f,Lin,Std,Jly 1)
Perfect World 30 (7f,Sou,Std,May 11)
Perilous Plight 49 (7f,Lin,Std,Feb 25)
Persian Conquest (IRE) 40 (12f,Wol,Std,Jly 3)
Petomi 42 (6f,Wol,Std,Aug 11)
Pharaoh's Dancer 31 (7f,Lin,Std,Nov 8)
Pharly Dancer 50 (12f,Sou,Std,Jan 13)
Philgun 31 (12f,Sou,Std,Feb 13)
Philmist 34 (14f,Sou,Std,Nov 16)
Pillow Talk (IRE) 45 (9½f,Wol,Std,Jan 4)
Pine Ridge Lad (IRE) 57 (9½f,Wol,Std,Dec 9)
Pirates Gold (IRE) 31 (7f,Lin,Std,Mar 25)
Pistols At Dawn (USA) 45 (12f,Wol,Std,Dec 12)
Polish Consul 35 (12f,Wol,Std,Jly 3)
Pontynyswen 39 (12f,Wol,Std,Feb 18)
Portend 42 (8f,Sou,Std,Mar 3)
Posted Abroad (IRE) 36 (6f,Sou,Std,Feb 10)
Power 37 (12f,Sou,Std,Mar 3)
Premier Dance 46 (7f,Wol,Std,Apr 29)
Present Situation 57 (8f,Lin,Std,Nov 2)
Press the Bell 37 (5f,Lin,Std,Jan 12)
Pretoria Dancer 31 (11f,Sou,Std,Spt 4)
Pride of May (IRE) 57 (16f,Lin,Std,Jan 14)
Prima Silk 57 (7f,Sou,Std,Nov 24)
Primula Bairn 32 (5f,Wol,Std,Jan 18)
Prince Danzig (IRE) 54 (12f,Lin,Std,Mar 16)
Prince of Andros (USA) 75 (9½f,Wol,Std,Dec 2)
Princely Gait 54 (12f,Lin,Std,Feb 18)
Prizefighter 41 (8f,Lin,Std,Dec 6)
Profit Release (IRE) 35 (8f,Sou,Std,Feb 10)
Promise Fulfilled (USA) 45 (9½f,Wol,Std,Mar 1)
Proposing (IRE) 35 (10f,Lin,Std,Apr 7)
Prudent Pet 35 (8f,Sou,Std,Spt 4)
Prudent Princess 37 (7f,Wol,Std,Spt 16)
Purbeck Centenary 32 (6f,Lin,Std,Feb 28)
Purple Fling 41 (6f,Sou,Std,Jun 22)
Pursuance (IRE) 50 (6f,Wol,Std,Spt 16)

Q Factor 36 (8¹/₂f,Wol,Std,Nov 11)
Quadrant 30 (13f,Lin,Std,Feb 11)
Queens Stroller (IRE) 53 (9¹/₂f,Wol,Std,Mar 4)
Quillwork (USA) 32 (12f,Lin,Std,Jly 22)
Quinzii Martin 44 (7f,Sou,Std,Feb 6)
Racing Hawk (USA) 33 (12f,Wol,Std,Jly 17)
Rakis (IRE) 40 (7f,Wol,Std,Dec 12)
Rambo Waltzer 52 (8¹/₂f,Wol,Std,Nov 11)
Rambo's Hall 48 (8f,Sou,Std,Dec 1)
Rambold 30 (6f,Lin,GF,Aug 5)
Random 40 (5f,Lin,Std,Feb 23)
Rawya (USA) 35 (10f,Lin,Std,Jan 24)
Red Admiral 39 (6f,Lin,GF,Aug 5)
Red Indian 41 (11f,Sou,Std,Feb 27)
Red Phantom (IRE) 40 (9¹/₂f,Wol,Std,Aug 5)
Red Valerian 40 (8f,Lin,Std,Jan 21)
Red Whirlwind 49 (7f,Wol,Std,Apr 29)
Renown 45 (8f,Lin,Std,Nov 14)
Reported (IRE) 48 (9¹/₂f,Wol,Std,Jun 2)
Respectable Jones 30 (7f,Lin,Std,Jan 12)
Retender (USA) 43 (12f,Lin,Std,Nov 30)
Rhythmic Dancer 34 (5f,Sou,Std,Spt 4)
Risky Romeo 40 (8f,Lin,Std,Nov 29)
Risky Tu 34 (16f,Lin,Std,Mar 2)
Rival Bid (USA) 32 (10f,Lin,Std,Dec 18)
River Keen (IRE) 59 (12f,Wol,Std,Dec 2)
Roar on Tour 44 (8f,Sou,Std,Feb 10)
Robellion 32 (5f,Lin,Std,Nov 2)
Robo Magic (USA) 39 (5f,Lin,Std,Dec 6)
Robsera (IRE) 34 (8¹/₂f,Wol,Std,Jly 8)
Rocketeer (IRE) 43 (7f,Wol,Std,Jan 4)
Rockstine (IRE) 41 (9¹/₂f,Wol,Std,Jan 4)
Rocky Waters (USA) 34 (6f,Lin,Std,Mar 31)
Rolling Waters 49 (15f,Wol,Std,Jly 3)
Roman Reel (USA) 47 (10f,Lin,Std,Nov 2)
Rood Music 64 (9¹/₂f,Wol,Std,Nov 13)
Rose of Glenn 33 (16f,Lin,Std,Jan 3)
Roseberry Topping 39 (11f,Sou,Std,Dec 1)
Rossini Blue 45 (5f,Lin,Std,Mar 16)
Rousitto 43 (12f,Wol,Std,Dec 12)
Royal Acclaim 30 (9¹/₂f,Wol,Std,Mar 4)
Royal Citizen (IRE) 41 (11f,Sou,Std,Jan 16)
Russian Heroine 30 (6f,Sou,Std,Jan 20)
Saddlehome (USA) 44 (5f,Wol,Std,Mar 8)
Sadly Sober (IRE) 44 (8f,Lin,Std,Nov 14)
Sailormaite 69 (7f,Sou,Std,Nov 16)
Sakharov 37 (6f,Wol,Std,Apr 4)
Salbus 39 (9¹/₂f,Wol,Std,Feb 18)
Sally Slade 34 (5f,Lin,Std,Mar 31)
Saltando (IRE) 35 (8f,Sou,Std,Nov 20)
Samson-Agonistes 33 (5f,Wol,Std,Jan 18)
Samwar 37 (7f,Lin,Std,Dec 19)
Sand Star 59 (7f,Wol,Std,Dec 2)
Sandmoor Denim 44 (8¹/₂f,Wol,Std,Nov 11)

Sarasi 53 (9¹/₂f,Wol,Std,Dec 9)
Sariyaa 39 (12f,Wol,Std,Spt 30)
Saseedo (USA) 62 (7f,Sou,Std,Nov 24)
Scalp 'em (IRE) 44 (16f,Wol,Std,Jly 21)
Scharnhorst 32 (8f,Lin,Std,Nov 2)
Sea Devil 48 (6f,Sou,Std,May 11)
Sea Spouse 40 (9¹/₂f,Wol,Std,Dec 9)
Sea Victor 42 (12f,Wol,Std,Dec 2)
Second Chance (IRE) 48 (9¹/₂f,Wol,Std,Jan 11)
Second Colours (USA) 53 (8f,Lin,Std,Dec 15)
Secret Aly (CAN) 62 (10f,Lin,Std,Feb 9)
Secret Serenade 45 (16f,Wol,Std,Jan 18)
Segala (IRE) 59 (8¹/₂f,Wol,Std,Jly 22)
Self Expression 35 (8f,Sou,Std,Mar 3)
Sense of Priority 49 (6f,Wol,Std,Jly 17)
Set the Fashion 60 (8f,Lin,Std,Nov 2)
Seventeens Lucky 55 (10f,Lin,Std,Dec 15)
Shabanaz 38 (11f,Sou,Std,Jun 22)
Shadow Jury 58 (5f,Sou,Std,Jly 22)
Shaft of Light 34 (10f,Lin,Std,Mar 4)
Shakiyr (FR) 49 (7f,Wol,Std,Apr 29)
Shanghai Venture (USA) 62 (9¹/₂f,Wol,Std,Spt 2)
Shared Risk 34 (12f,Sou,Std,Jly 13)
Sharp 'n Smart 32 (8f,Lin,Std,Nov 29)
Sharp Conquest 46 (8f,Wol,Std,Jan 18)
Sharp Imp 36 (5f,Lin,Std,Dec 6)
Sheer Danzig (IRE) 33 (8f,Sou,Std,Mar 20)
Sheltered Cove (IRE) 33 (16f,Lin,Std,Feb 14)
Shen Yang (USA) 32 (7f,Lin,Std,Mar 29)
Shining Example 40 (11f,Sou,Std,Spt 4)
Ship of the Line 34 (8f,Wol,Std,Jan 18)
Shuttlecock 38 (8f,Sou,,Feb 27)
Sieve of Time (USA) 60 (9¹/₂f,Wol,Std,Feb 1)
Sigama 34 (5f,Lin,Std,Mar 2)
Silent Expression 43 (6f,Lin,Std,Jan 10)
Silk Cottage 36 (5f,Wol,Std,Oct 14)
Sing With the Band 59 (6f,Wol,Std,Oct 14)
Sir Norman Holt (IRE) 44 (10f,Lin,Std,Dec 15)
Sir Tasker 53 (6f,Lin,Std,Mar 25)
Sison (IRE) 40 (5f,Lin,Std,Feb 23)
Sleeptite (FR) 50 (12f,Lin,Std,Feb 21)
Slip a Coin 41 (9¹/₂f,Wol,Std,Mar 1)
Slmaat 47 (11f,Sou,Std,Jan 30)
So Discreet (USA) 30 (13f,Lin,Std,Feb 2)
Soaking 36 (7f,Lin,Std,Mar 16)
Soldier's Leap (FR) 34 (9¹/₂f,Wol,Std,Feb 8)
Sombreffe 32 (7f,Lin,Std,Nov 2)
Sommersby (IRE) 48 (12f,Wol,Std,Spt 30)
Souperficial 47 (6f,Wol,Std,Aug 19)
South Eastern Fred 63 (10f,Lin,Std,Nov 8)
South Forest (IRE) 42 (6f,Sou,Std,Apr 3)
Southern Dominion 35 (6f,Lin,Std,Nov 30)
Spaniards Close 65 (5f,Sou,Std,Spt 4)
Spanish Stripper (USA) 40 (7f,Sou,Std,Feb 10)

Speedy Classic (USA) 49 (5f,Lin,Std,Nov 30)
Spencer's Revenge 53 (8f,Lin,Std,Dec 15)
Spender 62 (5f,Lin,Std,Jan 31)
Spitfire Bridge (IRE) 43 (12f,Lin,Std,Nov 29)
Squire Corrie 46 (5f,Lin,Std,Nov 2)
Stalled (IRE) 47 (12f,Lin,Std,Dec 18)
Stand Tall 37 (6f,Lin,Std,Nov 29)
Star Fighter 36 (10f,Lin,Std,Nov 2)
Star Quest 36 (16f,Lin,Std,Jan 3)
Stevie's Wonder (IRE) 55 (12f,Wol,Std,Oct 14)
Stoppes Brow 47 (6f,Wol,Std,Nov 11)
Stoproveritate 31 (12f,Sou,Std,Jly 22)
Strat's Legacy 31 (12f,Lin,Std,Nov 30)
Sudden Spin 52 (9½f,Wol,Std,Spt 30)
Suivez 45 (11f,Sou,Std,Feb 27)
Super Benz 44 (7f,Sou,Std,Jan 2)
Super Rocky 46 (5f,Lin,Std,Dec 19)
Superoo 36 (7f,Lin,Std,Nov 29)
Supreme Star (USA) 37 (16f,Lin,Std,Nov 29)
Sure Pride (USA) 35 (16f,Lin,Std,Jun 17)
Surprise Guest (IRE) 32 (13f,Lin,Std,Jan 17)
Sushi Bar (IRE) 38 (11f,Sou,Std,May 15)
Sweet Mate 39 (6f,Wol,Std,Nov 27)
Sweet Supposin (IRE) 49 (7f,Wol,Std,Aug 11)
Swordking (IRE) 34 (15f,Wol,Std,May 13)
T O O Mamma's (IRE) 35 (9½f,Wol,Std,Feb 18)
Tadellal (IRE) 57 (10f,Lin,Std,Nov 2)
Talented Ting (IRE) 33 (13f,Lin,Std,Dec 14)
Tapis Rouge (IRE) 38 (9½f,Wol,Std,Jan 4)
Tarawa (IRE) 62 (9½f,Wol,Std,Dec 2)
Taroudant 44 (16f,Wol,Std,Jan 18)
Tartan Gem (IRE) 48 (9½f,Wol,Std,Dec 9)
Tatika 51 (8½f,Wol,Std,Mar 8)
Tee Tee Too (IRE) 40 (6f,Sou,Std,Jan 6)
Tee-Emm 42 (5f,Lin,Std,Jan 31)
Teen Jay 42 (12f,Wol,Std,Oct 14)
Tempering 45 (11f,Sou,Std,Jan 13)
Tenor 47 (5f,Lin,Std,Feb 23)
Tervel (USA) 32 (12f,Lin,Std,Feb 9)
Tethys (USA) 70 (12f,Lin,Std,Nov 30)
Thaleros 45 (12f,Sou,Std,Feb 3)
That Man Again 38 (5f,Lin,Std,Mar 31)
The Institute Boy 37 (5f,Lin,Std,Feb 23)
The Little Ferret 32 (7f,Lin,Std,Feb 18)
The Old Chapel 54 (6f,Wol,Std,May 13)
The Real Whizzbang (IRE) 33 (5f,Sou,Std,Jly 22)
Three Arch Bridge 32 (7f,Sou,Std,Apr 11)
Tiger Shoot 46 (12f,Sou,Std,May 11)
To the Roof (IRE) 42 (6f,Wol,Std,Aug 11)
Todd (USA) 42 (12f,Lin,Std,Nov 29)

Tommy Tempest 34 (5f,Lin,Std,Jly 14)
Total Rach (IRE) 31 (10f,Lin,Std,Nov 2)
Toujours Riviera 53 (8f,Lin,Std,Dec 14)
Tovarich 52 (12f,Wol,Std,Spt 16)
Toy Princess (USA) 31 (8f,Lin,Std,Mar 25)
Tremendisto 32 (12f,Wol,Std,Spt 30)
Tribal Peace (IRE) 56 (10f,Lin,Std,Dec 15)
Triple Joy 62 (6f,Lin,Std,Feb 14)
Tristan's Comet 34 (12f,Sou,Std,Jan 9)
Tropical Jungle (USA) 36 (10f,Lin,Std,Spt 5)
Tu Opes 58 (9½f,Wol,Std,Mar 18)
Tuigamala 34 (7f,Lin,Std,Nov 29)
Twin Creeks 52 (7f,Sou,Std,Feb 10)
Tyrian Purple (IRE) 39 (6f,Lin,Std,Feb 23)
Tyrone Flyer 36 (6f,Wol,Std,May 13)
Ultimate Warrior 35 (10f,Lin,Std,Aug 12)
Ultra Beet 48 (5f,Lin,Std,Feb 25)
Upper Mount Clair 35 (16f,Lin,Std,Nov 8)
Valiant Toski 33 (13f,Lin,Std,Jly 1)
Verzen (IRE) 65 (9½f,Wol,Std,Dec 2)
View From Above 36 (13f,Lin,Std,Feb 16)
Vindaloo 49 (12f,Lin,Std,Jly 22)
Waikiki Beach (USA) 40 (8f,Lin,Std,Nov 2)
Waldo 41 (10f,Lin,Std,Feb 9)
Walk the Beat 40 (6f,Wol,Std,Jan 11)
Wannaplantatree 37 (14f,Sou,Std,Aug 4)
Warhurst (IRE) 35 (9½f,Wol,Std,Feb 18)
Warluskee 30 (12f,Sou,Std,Mar 3)
Warm Spell 52 (13f,Lin,Std,Feb 28)
Warwick Warrior (IRE) 47 (6f,Sou,Std,Jan 30)
Well and Truly 34 (16f,Wol,Std,Jan 18)
Wentbridge Lad (IRE) 49 (9½f,Wol,Std,May 13)
Wet Patch (IRE) 41 (10f,Lin,Std,Dec 18)
Whatever's Right (IRE) 40 (8f,Lin,Std,May 12)
White Sorrel 69 (6f,Wol,Std,Mar 8)
Whittingham Girl 32 (6f,Wol,Std,Feb 1)
Wild Strawberry 44 (16f,Lin,Std,Feb 25)
Wildfire (SWI) 36 (11f,Sou,Std,Dec 1)
Windrush Boy 31 (5f,Lin,Std,Nov 30)
Winn's Pride (IRE) 31 (11f,Sou,Std,Feb 20)
Words of Wisdom (IRE) 36 (7f,Wol,Std,Apr 29)
World Traveller 49 (7f,Sou,Std,May 11)
Yet More Roses 40 (6f,Wol,Std,Aug 19)
Yougo 47 (13f,Lin,Std,Nov 25)
Young Freeman (USA) 68 (10f,Lin,Std,Mar 25)
Zacaroon 37 (8f,Lin,Std,Feb 14)
Zahran (IRE) 43 (8f,Lin,Std,Mar 31)
Ziggy's Dancer (USA) 52 (6f,Wol,Std,Mar 8)
Zuno Noelyn 38 (10f,Lin,Std,Jan 12)

RACEFORM FASTEST PERFORMERS

5f - 6f

1. Lake Coniston (IRE) 96
2. Venture Capitalist 95
3. Ya Malak 90
4. Alzianah......................................89
5. Brave Edge.................................89
6. Hard to Figure 88
7. Piccolo..87
8. Lucky Parkes 84
9. So Factual (USA) 84
10. Eveningperformance 83
11. Owington....................................83
12. Astrac (IRE)................................83
13. Montendre 80
14. That Man Again 80
15. Double Blue 79
16. Lord High Admiral (CAN).............78
17. Master Planner 78
18. Royale Figurine (IRE)..................78
19. Wavian 78
20. Don't Worry Me (IRE) 77

7f - 9f

1. Sayyedati....................................100
2. Darnay..99
3. Bahri (USA) 95
4. Celtic Swing................................94
5. Harayir (USA) 94
6. Pennekamp (USA) 94
7. Realities (USA) 94
8. Ridgewood Pearl 94
9. Emperor Jones (USA) 93
10. Young Ern 93
11. Smolensk (USA)..........................90
12. Fraam...89
13. Nicolotte 88
14. Soviet Line (IRE) 88
15. Pipe Major (IRE).........................86
16. Diffident (FR) 85

17. Cap Juluca (IRE) 84
18. Celestial Key (USA)......................84
19. Mistle Cat (USA)..........................84
20. Nwaamis (USA)............................84

10f - 12f

1. Muhtarram (USA) 97
2. Source of Light 94
3. Marsoom (CAN) 90
4. Needle Gun (IRE).........................90
5. Just Happy (USA).........................89
6. Taufan's Melody 89
7. Halling (USA)...............................88
8. Son of Sharp Shot (IRE)...............88
9. Young Buster (IRE) 87
10. Classic Cliche (IRE) 85
11. Cotteir Chief (IRE) 85
12. Annus Mirabilis (FR).....................84
13. Blushing Flame (USA)...................84
14. Capias (USA) 84
15. Pentire 84
16. Richard of York............................84
17. Strategic Choice (USA) 84
18. Zaralaska....................................84
19. Aljazzaf 83
20. Balanchine (USA).........................83

13f and upwards

1. Son of Sharp Shot (IRE) 88
2. Double Trigger (IRE) 86
3. Diaghilef (IRE) 85
4. Purple Splash 83
5. Shonara's Way 82
6. Misbelief 81
7. Linney Head (USA) 80
8. Seasonal Splendour (IRE)............80
9. Classic Cliche (IRE) 79

10.	Benfleet	77
11.	Celeric	77
12.	Harlestone Brook	77
13.	Istabraq (IRE)	77
14.	Old Rouvel (USA)	77
15.	Shambo	77
16.	The Flying Phantom	76
17.	Further Flight	75
18.	Halkopous	75
19.	Minds Music (USA)	75
20.	Zilzal Zamaan (USA)	75

TWO-YEAR-OLDS

5f - 6f

1.	Royal Applause	71
2.	Blue Duster (USA)	71
3.	Cayman Kai (IRE)	66
4.	Lucky Lionel (USA)	65
5.	My Branch	64
6.	Mubhij (IRE)	64
7.	Russian Revival (USA)	63
8.	Midnight Blue	62
9.	South Salem (USA)	62
10.	Tadeo	61
11.	Kahir Almaydan (IRE)	61
12.	Woodborough (USA)	60
13.	Pivotal	59
14.	Mutamanni (USA)	59

15.	King of Peru	59
16.	Polaris Flight (USA)	59
17.	Tamnia	59
18.	World Premier	59
19.	Music Gold (IRE)	58
20.	Some Horse (IRE)	58

7f and upwards

1.	Bosra Sham (USA)	85
2.	Bint Shadayid (USA)	78
3.	Mons	72
4.	Matiya (IRE)	71
5.	Rouge Rancon (USA)	63
6.	Shawanni	62
7.	More Royal (USA)	62
8.	Rio Duvida	62
9.	Jack Jennings	61
10.	Tumbleweed Ridge	61
11.	Busy Flight	60
12.	Beauchamp King	60
13.	Brandon Magic	59
14.	Alhaarth (IRE)	59
15.	Storm Trooper (USA)	58
16.	Ruznama (USA)	58
17.	Sil Sila (IRE)	57
18.	Shaamit (IRE)	57
19.	Sketchbook	57
20.	Prince of My Heart	57

Owners names are shown against their horses where this information is available. In the case of Partnerships and Syndicates, the nominated owner is given alongside the horse with other owners listed below the team.

DATES OF PRINCIPAL RACES

(Subject to alteration)

JANUARY

NEW YEAR'S DAY HURDLE (Windsor) .... Mon. 1
NEWTON CHASE (Haydock) .... Sat. 6
MILDMAY CAZALET MEMORIAL CHASE (Sandown) .... Sat. 6
ING BARINGS TOLWORTH HURDLE (Sandown) .... Sat. 6
SLANEY HURDLE (Naas) .... Sat. 6
TOWTON NOVICES CHASE (Wetherby) .... Thur. 11
PML LIGHTNING NOVICES' CHASE (Ascot) .... Fri. 12
VICTOR CHANDLER CHASE (Ascot) .... Sat. 13
THE LADBROKE (Leopardstown) .... Sat. 13
GV MALCOMSON CHASE (Fairyhouse) .... Wed. 17
HAYDOCK PARK CHAMPION HURDLE TRIAL (Haydock) .... Sat. 20
PREMIER LONG DISTANCE HURDLE (Haydock) .... Sat. 20
PETER MARSH CHASE (Haydock) .... Sat. 20
BIC RAZOR LANZAROTE HANDICAP HURDLE (Kempton) .... Sat. 20
A. I. G. EUROPE CHAMPION HURDLE (Leopardstown) .... Sun. 21
CLEEVE HURDLE (Cheltenham) .... Sat. 27
PILLAR PROPERTY INVESTMENTS CHASE (Cheltenham) .... Sat. 27
GREAT YORKSHIRE HANDICAP CHASE (Doncaster) .... Sat. 27

FEBRUARY

BORDERS CHAMPION HURDLE (Kelso) .... Fri. 2
MARSTON MOOR HANDICAP CHASE (Wetherby) .... Sat. 3
JOHN HUGHES GRAND NATIONAL TRIAL (Chepstow) .... Sat. 3
AGFA DIAMOND CHASE (Sandown) .... Sat. 3
HENNESSY GOLD CUP (Leopardstown) .... Sun. 4
COMET CHASE (Ascot) .... Wed. 7
PREMIERE 'NH' AUCTION NOVICES' HURDLE (Wincanton) .... Thur. 8
TOTE GOLD TROPHY HURDLE (Newbury) .... Sat. 10
MITSUBISHI SHOGUN GAME SPIRIT CHASE (Newbury) .... Sat. 10
PZ POWER CHASE (Thurles) .... Thur. 15
FAIRLAWNE CHASE (Windsor) .... Sat. 17
PERSIAN WAR PATTERN HURDLE (Chepstow) .... Sat. 17
TOTE EIDER CHASE (Newcastle) .... Sat. 17
GAIN NATIONAL TRIAL CHASE (Punchestown) .... Sun. 18
K. J. PIKE AND SONS KINGWELL PATTERN HURDLE (Wincanton) ...... Thur. 22
JIM FORD CHASE (Wincanton) .... Thur. 22
RACING POST CHASE (Kempton) .... Sat. 24
RENDLESHAM HURDLE (Kempton) .... Sat. 24
GREENALLS GRAND NATIONAL TRIAL CHASE (Haydock) .... Sat. 24
JOHNSTOWN EBF HURDLE (Naas) .... Sat. 24
NAS NA RIOGH EBF NOVICES' CHASE (Naas) .... Sat. 24
NEWLANDS CHASE (Naas) .... Sat. 24
EBF NOVICE CHASE FINAL (Fairyhouse) .... Sun. 25

MARCH

HENNESSY COGNAC HURDLE (Kelso) .... Fri. 1
SUNDERLANDS IMPERIAL CUP (Sandown) .... Sat. 9
BET WITH THE TOTE CHASE FINAL (Chepstow) .... Sat. 9
SMURFIT CHAMPION HURDLE (Cheltenham) .... Tue. 12
CITROEN SUPREME NOVICE HURDLE (Cheltenham) .... Tue. 12
GUINNESS ARKLE CHALLENGE TROPHY CHASE (Cheltenham) .... Tue. 12
RITZ CLUB GRAND ANNUAL CHASE (Cheltenham) .... Tue. 12

ASTEC VODAFONE GOLD CARD HANDICAP HURDLE (Cheltenham)..............................Tue. 12
FULKE WALWYN HANDICAP CHASE (Cheltenham)...Tue. 12
SUN ALLIANCE CHASE (Cheltenham)..Wed. 13
SUN ALLIANCE HURDLE (Cheltenham)..Wed. 13
QUEEN MOTHER CHAMPION CHASE (Cheltenham)...Wed. 13
CORAL CUP HURDLE (Cheltenham)...Wed. 13
MILDMAY OF FLETE HANDICAP CHASE (Cheltenham)..Wed. 13
BROMSGROVE INDUSTRIES FESTIVAL BUMPER (Cheltenham)...Wed. 13
TOTE CHELTENHAM GOLD CUP CHASE (Cheltenham)...Thur. 14
DAILY EXPRESS TRIUMPH HURDLE (Cheltenham)..Thur. 14
BONUSPRINT STAYERS HURDLE (Cheltenham)...Thur. 14
CHRISTIE'S FOXHUNTER CHASE (Cheltenham)...Thur. 14
NATIONAL HUNT HANDICAP CHASE (Cheltenham)...Thur. 14
COUNTY HANDICAP HURDLE (Cheltenham)..Thur. 14
CATHCART CHASE (Cheltenham)...Thur. 14
LINGFIELD GOLD CUP (Lingfield)..Sat. 16
TETLEY BITTER MIDLANDS NATIONAL (Uttoxeter)...Sat. 16
BET WITH THE TOTE NOVICE CHASE FINAL (Uttoxeter)..Sat. 16
TATTERSALLS MARES ONLY NOVICE CHASE FINAL (Uttoxeter)......................................Sat. 16
LADBROKE HANDICAP HURDLE (Uttoxeter)...Sat. 16
DONCASTER MILE (Doncaster)...Thur. 21
HOECHST PANACUR HURDLE FINAL (Newbury)...Sat. 23
WILLIAM HILL LINCOLN HANDICAP (Doncaster)..Sat. 23
CAMMIDGE TROPHY (Doncaster)...Sat. 23
DUBAI WORLD CUP (Nad Al Sheba)..Wed. 27
MARTELL CUP CHASE (Aintree)...Thur. 28
SEAGRAM TOP NOVICE HURDLE (Aintree)..Thur. 28
GLENLIVET HURDLE (Aintree)..Thur. 28
SANDEMAN MAGHULL NOVICE CHASE (Aintree)..Thur. 28
MUMM MELLING CHASE (Aintree)...Fri. 29
MUMM MILDMAY NOVICES CHASE (Aintree)..Fri. 29
MARTELL MERSEY NOVICE HURDLE (Aintree)...Fri. 29
ODDBINS HANDICAP HURDLE (Aintree)..Fri. 29
BELLE EPOQUE SEFTON NOVICE HURDLE (Aintree)..Fri. 29
MARTELL FOXHUNTER CHASE (Aintree)..Fri. 29
PERRIER JOUET HANDICAP CHASE (Aintree)...Fri. 29
MARTELL GRAND NATIONAL CHASE (Aintree)..Sat. 30
MARTELL AINTREE CHASE (Aintree)...Sat. 30
MARTELL AINTREE HURDLE (Aintree)...Sat. 30
IRISH LINCOLNSHIRE (The Curragh)..Sun. 31

APRIL

DAILY TELEGRAPH NOVICES CHASE (Ascot)...Wed. 3
KENTUCKY DERBY TRIAL (Lingfield)...Thur. 4
BONUSPRINT EASTER STAKES (Kempton)...Sat. 6
BONUSPRINT MASAKA STAKES (Kempton)..Sat. 6
FIELD MARSHAL STAKES (Haydock)...Sat. 6
WETHERBY HANDICAP CHASE (Wetherby)..Mon. 8
WESTMINSTER TAXI INSURANCE ROSEBERY HANDICAP (Kempton)...............................Mon. 8
M & N WELSH CHAMPION HURDLE (Chepstow)..Mon. 8
JAMESON IRISH GRAND NATIONAL (Fairyhouse)...Mon. 8
POWER GOLD CUP CHASE (Fairyhouse)...Tue. 9
D. L. MOORE HANDICAP CHASE (Fairyhouse)...Wed. 10
EBF NH NOVICES' RACE FINAL HURDLE (Cheltenham)...Thur. 11
SILVER TROPHY CHASE (Cheltenham)...Thur. 11
GLADNESS STAKES (The Curragh)...Sat. 13
LETHEBY & CHRISTOPHER LONG DISTANCE HURDLE (Ascot)..Sat. 13
SHADWELL STUD NELL GWYN STAKES (Newmarket)...Tue. 16
ABERNANT STAKES (Newmarket)...Tue. 16
NGK SPARK PLUGS EUROPEAN FREE HANDICAP (Newmarket)...Wed. 17
EARL OF SEFTON STAKES (Newmarket)...Wed. 17

CRAVEN. STAKES (Newmarket) .... Thur. 18
FEILDEN STAKES (Newmarket) .... Thur. 18
GAINSBOROUGH STUD FRED DARLING STAKES (Newbury) .... Fri. 19
ARLINGTON INTERNATIONAL RACECOURSE STAKES (Newbury) .... Fri. 19
LANES END JOHN PORTER STAKES (Newbury) .... Sat. 20
TRIPLEPRINT GREENHAM STAKES (Newbury) .... Sat. 20
LADBROKE SPRING CUP (Newbury) .... Sat. 20
STAKIS CASINOS SCOTTISH NATIONAL (Ayr) .... Sat. 20
DAILY MAIL SCOTTISH CHALLENGE CUP (Ayr) .... Sat. 20
COUNTRY PRIDE CHAMPION NOVICE HURDLE (Punchestown) .... Tue. 23
BMW HANDICAP CHASE (Punchestown) .... Tue. 23
HEINEKEN GOLD CUP (Punchestown) .... Wed. 24
WOODCHESTER CREDIT LYONNAIS HURDLE (Punchestown) .... Wed. 24
MURPHY IRISH STOUT CHAMPION HURDLE (Punchestown) .... Thur. 25
DAVENPORT TIPPERKEVIN 3M HURDLE (Punchestown) .... Thur. 25
SANDOWN MILE (Sandown) .... Fri. 26
LEXUS TETRARCH STAKES (The Curragh) .... Sat. 27
GORDON RICHARDS EBF STAKES (Sandown) .... Sat. 27
WHITBREAD GOLD CUP CHASE (Sandown) .... Sat. 27
THRESHER CLASSIC TRIAL (Sandown) .... Sat. 27
LEICESTERSHIRE STAKES (Leicester) .... Sat. 27

MAY

INSULPAK VICTORIA CUP (Ascot) .... Wed. 1
INSULPAK SAGARO STAKES (Ascot) .... Wed. 1
JOCKEY CLUB STAKES (Newmarket) .... Fri. 3
NEWMARKET STAKES (Newmarket) .... Fri. 3
SPRING TROPHY (Haydock) .... Sat. 4
2000 GUINEAS STAKES (Newmarket) .... Sat. 4
DUBAI RACING CLUB PALACE HOUSE STAKES (Newmarket) .... Sat. 4
LADBROKE HANDICAP (Newmarket) .... Sat. 4
KENTUCKY DERBY (Churchill Downs) .... Sat. 4
1000 GUINEAS STAKES (Newmarket) .... Sun. 5
PRETTY POLLY STAKES (Newmarket) .... Sun. 5
JUBILEE HANDICAP (Kempton) .... Mon. 6
CROWTHER HOMES SWINTON HURDLE (Haydock) .... Mon. 6
CHESTER VASE (Chester) .... Tue. 7
CHESTER CUP (Chester) .... Wed. 8
ORMONDE STAKES (Chester) .... Thur. 9
BNFL INTERNATIONAL DEE STAKES (Chester) .... Thur. 9
DERBY TRIAL (Lingfield) .... Sat. 11
OAKS TRIAL (Lingfield) .... Sat. 11
DERRINSTOWN STUD DERBY TRIAL (Leopardstown) .... Sat. 11
DUBAI POULE D'ESSAI DES POULICHES (Longchamp) .... Sun. 12
DUBAI POULE D'ESSAI DES POULAINS (Longchamp) .... Sun. 12
PRIX LUPIN (Longchamp) .... Sun. 12
TATTERSALLS MUSIDORA STAKES (York) .... Tue. 14
SHEPHERD TROPHY (York) .... Tue. 14
PAUL CADDICK AND MACGAY SPRINT (York) .... Tue. 14
HOMEOWNERS DANTE STAKES (York) .... Wed. 15
HOMEOWNERS SPRINT (York) .... Wed. 15
YORKSHIRE CUP (York) .... Thur. 16
DUKE OF YORK STAKES (York) .... Thur. 16
WILLIAM HILL STAKES (York) .... Thur. 16
KING CHARLES II STAKES (Newmarket) .... Fri. 17
VODAFONE GROUP FILLIES TRIAL STAKES (Newbury) .... Fri. 17
QUANTEL ASTON PARK STAKES (Newbury) .... Sat. 18
LONDON GOLD CUP (Newbury) .... Sat. 18
JUDDMONTE LOCKINGE STAKES (Newbury) .... Sat. 18
WESTMINSTER TAXI INSURANCE PREAKNESS STAKES (Pimlico) .... Sat. 18
PREDOMINATE STAKES (Goodwood) .... Tue. 21

TRIPLEPRINT LUPE STAKES (Goodwood) .... Wed. 22
FESTIVAL STAKES (Goodwood) .... Thur. 23
CRAWLEY WARREN HERON STAKES (Kempton) .... Sat. 25
SANDY LANE STAKES (Haydock) .... Sat. 25
AIRLIE/COOLMORE IRISH 1000 GUINEAS .... Sat. 25
FIRST NATIONAL BUILDING SOCIETY IRISH 2000 GUINEAS .... Sun. 26
TRIPLEPRINT TEMPLE STAKES (Sandown) .... Mon. 27
BONUSPRINT HENRY II STAKES (Sandown) .... Mon. 27
ZETLAND GOLD TROPHY (Redcar) .... Mon. 27
SPILLERS BRIGADIER GERARD STAKES (Sandown) .... Tue. 28
WINALOT NATIONAL STAKES (Sandown) .... Tue. 28

JUNE

LEISURE STAKES (Lingfield) .... Sat. 1
CORAL SPRINT HANDICAP (Newmarket) .... Sat. 1
CHARLOTTE FILLIES' STAKES (Newmarket) .... Sat. 1
PRIX DU JOCKEY CLUB (Chantilly) .... Sun. 2
VODAPHONE OAKS STAKES (Epsom) .... Fri. 7
JOHN OF GAUNT STAKES (Haydock) .... Sat. 8
VODAPHONE DERBY STAKES (Epsom) .... Sat. 8
VODAFONE CORONATION CUP (Epsom) .... Sat. 8
JOHN OF GAUNT STAKES (Haydock) .... Sat. 8
GALLINULE STAKES (The Curragh) .... Sat. 8
BELMONT STAKES (Belmont Park) .... Sat. 8
PRIX DE DIANE (Chantilly) .... Sun. 9
BALLYMACOLL STUD STAKES (Newbury) .... Thur. 13
INNOVATIVE MARKETING SPRINT (York) .... Fri. 14
WILLIAM HILL TROPHY (York) .... Sat. 15
MERCURY STAKES (Leicester) .... Sat. 15
ST. JAMES'S PALACE STAKES (Royal Ascot) .... Tue. 18
PRINCE OF WALES'S STAKES (Royal Ascot) .... Tue. 18
COVENTRY STAKES (Royal Ascot) .... Tue. 18
CORONATION STAKES (Royal Ascot) .... Wed. 19
JERSEY STAKES (Royal Ascot) .... Wed. 19
QUEENS VASE STAKES (Royal Ascot) .... Wed. 19
QUEEN MARY STAKES (Royal Ascot) .... Wed. 19
ROYAL HUNT CUP HANDICAP (Royal Ascot) .... Wed. 19
GOLD CUP (Royal Ascot) .... Thur. 20
CORK AND ORRERY STAKES (Royal Ascot) .... Thur. 20
RIBBLESDALE STAKES (Royal Ascot) .... Thur. 20
NORFOLK STAKES (Royal Ascot) .... Thur. 20
HARDWICKE STAKES (Royal Ascot) .... Fri. 21
KINGS STAND STAKES (Royal Ascot) .... Fri. 21
WOKINGHAM HANDICAP (Royal Ascot) .... Fri. 21
KING EDWARD VII STAKES (Royal Ascot) .... Fri. 21
LADBROKE HANDICAP (Ascot) .... Sat. 22
GALA STAKES (Kempton) .... Wed. 26
NORTHERN ROCK GOSFORTH PARK CUP HANDICAP (Newcastle) .... Fri. 28
INDEPENDENT NEWSPAPERS PRETTY POLLY STAKES (Curragh) .... Sat. 29
NORTHUMBERLAND PLATE (Newcastle) .... Sat. 29
VAN GEEST CRITERION STAKES (Newmarket) .... Sat. 29
EMPRESS STAKES (Newmarket) .... Sat. 29
FRED ARCHER STAKES (Newmarket) .... Sat. 29
INDEPENDENT NEWSPAPERS PRETTY POLLY STAKES (Curragh) .... Sat. 29
BUDWEISER IRISH DERBY (The Curragh) .... Sun. 30
THE SUNDAY STAKES (Chepstow) .... Sun. 30

JULY

HONG KONG JOCKEY CLUB CUP (Sandown) .... Fri. 5
CORAL-ECLIPSE STAKES (Sandown) .... Sat. 6
JULY TROPHY (Haydock) .... Sat. 6

LANCASHIRE OAKS (Haydock) .... Sat. 6
OLD NEWTON CUP (Haydock) .... Sat. 6
PRINCESS OF WALES'S STAKES (Newmarket) .... Tue. 9
HILLSDOWN HOLDINGS CHERRY HINTON STAKES (Newmarket) .... Tue. 9
FALMOUTH STAKES (Newmarket) .... Wed. 10
SBK GROUP JULY STAKES (Newmarket) .... Wed. 10
H. E. LIMITED DUKE OF CAMBRIDGE HANDICAP (Newmarket) .... Wed. 10
LADBROKE BUNBURY CUP (Newmarket) .... Thur. 11
DARLEY JULY CUP (Newmarket) .... Thur. 11
BAHRAIN TROPHY (Newmarket) .... Thur. 11
BLACK DUCK STAKES (York) .... Fri. 12
JOHN SMITH'S MAGNET CUP (York) .... Sat. 13
SILVER TROPHY (Lingfield) .... Sat. 13
KILDANGAN STUD IRISH OAKS (The Curragh) .... Sun. 14
TENNENTS SCOTTISH CLASSIC (Ayr) .... Mon. 15
HACKWOOD STAKES (Newbury) .... Fri. 19
WEATHERBYS SUPER SPRINT (Newbury) .... Sat. 20
DONCASTER BLOODSTOCK SALES ROSE BOWL STAKES (Newbury) .... Sat. 20
FOOD BROKERS TROPHY (Newmarket) .... Sat. 20
GOLDEN PAGES HANDICAP (Leopardstown) .... Sat. 20
DAFFODIL STAKES (Chepstow) .... Thur. 25
BEESWING STAKES (Newcastle) .... Sat. 27
THE KING GEORGE VI AND QUEEN ELIZABETH DIAMOND STAKES (Ascot) ...... Sat. 27
PRINCESS MARGARET STAKES (Ascot) .... Sat. 27
MELD STAKES (The Curragh) .... Sat. 27
WILLIAM HILL CUP (Goodwood) .... Tue. 30
WESTMINSTER TAXI INSURANCE GORDON STAKES (Goodwood) .... Tue. 30
OAK TREE STAKES (Goodwood) .... Tue. 30
KING GEORGE STAKES (Goodwood) .... Tue. 30
SUSSEX STAKES (Goodwood) .... Wed. 31
TOTE GOLD TROPHY STAKES (Goodwood) .... Wed. 31
COUNTRY CLUB HOTELS GOODWOOD STAKES (Goodwood) .... Wed. 31
LANSON CHAMPAGNE VINTAGE STAKES (Goodwood) .... Wed. 31

AUGUST

RICHMOND STAKES (Goodwood) .... Thur. 1
GOODWOOD CUP (Goodwood) .... Thur. 1
SCHWEPPES GOLDEN MILE (Goodwood) .... Thur. 1
MOLECOMB STAKES (Goodwood) .... Fri. 2
SCHRODERS GLORIOUS STAKES (Goodwood) .... Fri. 2
VOLVO TRUCKS FINANCE SPITFIRE STAKES (Goodwood) .... Fri. 2
VODAFONE NASSAU STAKES (Goodwood) .... Sat. 3
VODAC STEWARDS CUP (Goodwood) .... Sat. 3
HERO NURSERY HANDICAP (Newmarket) .... Sat. 3
JOE McGRATH SPRINT .... Mon. 5
PLATINUM LISTED RACE (Fairyhouse) .... Wed. 7
ROSE OF LANCASTER STAKES (Haydock) .... Sat. 10
CORAL HANDICAP (Haydock) .... Sat. 10
NEW ZEALAND HANDICAP (Newmarket) .... Sat. 10
ENZA SWEET SOLERA STAKES (Newmarket) .... Sat. 10
HEINZ 57 PHOENIX STAKES (Leopardstown) .... Sun. 11
HUNGERFORD STAKES (Newbury) .... Fri. 16
WASHINGTON SINGER STAKES (Newbury) .... Fri. 16
TRIPLEPRINT GEOFFREY FREER STAKES (Newbury) .... Sat. 17
SWETTENHAM STUD ST HUGH'S STAKES (Newbury) .... Sat. 17
WILLIAM HILL GREAT ST. WILFRID HANDICAP (Ripon) .... Sat. 17
ROYAL WHIP STAKES (The Curragh) .... Sat. 17
DESMOND STAKES (The Curragh) .... Sat. 17
PRIX MORNY (Deauville) .... Sun. 18
JUDDMONTE INTERNATIONAL STAKES (York) .... Tue. 20
GREAT VOLTIGEUR STAKES (York) .... Tue. 20

YORKSHIRE OAKS (York)..Wed. 21
TOTE EBOR HANDICAP (York)..Wed. 21
SCOTTISH EQUITABLE GIMCRACK STAKES (York)........................Wed. 21
BRADFORD AND BINGLEY HANDICAP (York).............................Thur. 22
NUNTHORPE STAKES (York)...Thur. 22
STAKIS CASINOS LOWTHER STAKES (York)..................................Thur. 22
HOPEFUL STAKES (Newmarket)..Fri. 23
BOADICEA NURSERY HANDICAP (newmarket)................................Sat. 24
TRIPLEPRINT CELEBRATION MILE (Goodwood)............................Sat. 24
SPORT ON 5 MARCH STAKES (Goodwood)....................................Sat. 24
WINTER HILL STAKES (Windsor)...Sat. 24
MAGNA CARTA STAKES (Windsor)...Sat. 24
CROWSON PRESTIGE STAKES (Goodwood)...................................Sun. 25
BONUSPRINT CHAMPION 2-Y-O TROPHY (Ripon).........................Mon. 26
RIPON ROWELS HANDICAP (Ripon)..Mon. 26
MOET AND CHANDON SILVER MAGNUM STAKES (Epsom)..........Mon. 26
SOLARIO STAKES (Sandown)...Fri. 30
CHESTER RATED STAKES (Chester)..Sat. 31
HORNBLOWER STAKES (Ripon)...Sat. 31
TATTERSALLS BREEDERS STAKES (The Curragh)..........................Sat. 31

SEPTEMBER

LAWRENCE BATLEY RATED STAKES (York)....................................Wed. 4
SUN LIFE OF CANADA GARROWBY STAKES (York)......................Thur. 5
FAMOUS GROUSE STRENSALL STAKES (York)...............................Thur. 5
BONUSPRINT SEPTEMBER STAKES (Kempton)................................Sat. 7
SPRINT CUP (Haydock)..Sat. 7
MOYGLARE STUD STAKES (The Curragh).....................................Sun. 8
PARK HILL STAKES (Doncaster)...Wed. 11
TOTE PORTLAND HANDICAP (Doncaster)......................................Wed. 11
DONCASTER CUP (Doncaster)...Thur. 12
KIVETON PARK STAKES (Doncaster)..Thur. 12
MAY HILL STAKES (Doncaster)..Thur. 12
LAURENT PERRIER CHAMPAGNE STAKES (Doncaster)..................Fri. 13
SCHRODER INVESTMENT MANAGEMENT STAKES (Goodwood).......Fri. 13
BELLWAY HOMES STARDOM STAKES (Goodwood)........................Fri. 13
FLYING CHILDERS STAKES (Doncaster)...Sat. 14
TELECONNECTION ST LEGER STAKES (Doncaster).......................Sat. 14
GUINNESS CHAMPION STAKES (Leopardstown)..............................Sat. 14
SHADWELL ESTATES FIRTH OF CLYDE STAKES (Ayr)..................Fri. 20
LADBROKES AYR GOLD CUP (Ayr)..Sat. 21
BONUSPRINT MILL REEF STAKES (Newbury)................................Sat. 21
TOTE AUTUMN CUP (Newbury)...Sat. 21
COURAGE STAKES (Newbury)...Sat. 21
JEFFERSON SMURFIT MEMORIAL ST. LEGER (The Curragh).........Sat. 21
CHARLTON HUNT SUPREME STAKES (Goodwood).........................Thur. 26
ROA FOUNDATION STAKES (Goodwood)..Thur. 26
STANLEY LEISURE HANDICAP (Haydock)......................................Fri. 27
SALE FILLIES' CONDITIONS STAKES (Haydock)...........................Sat. 28
QUEEN ELIZABETH II STAKES (Ascot)...Sat. 28
CUMBERALND LODGE STAKES (Ascot)..Sat. 28
TOTE FESTIVAL HANDICAP (Ascot)...Sat. 28
DIADEM STAKES (Ascot)..Sat. 28
FILLIES MILE (Ascot)..Sun. 29
ROYAL LODGE STAKES (Ascot)...Sun. 29
TOTE SUNDAY SPECIAL HANDicap (Ascot)..................................Sun. 29
MAIL ON SUNDAY MILE HANDICAP FINAL (Ascot)....................Sun. 29

OCTOBER

TATTERSALLS HOUGHTON SALES STAKES (Newmarket)................Tue. 1
SHADWELL STUD CHEVELEY PARK STAKES (Newmarket)............Tue. 1

ROUS STAKES (Newmarket) .... Thur. 3
MIDDLE PARK STAKES (Newmarket) .... Thur. 3
RACING POST GODOLPHIN STAKES (Newmarket) .... Fri. 4
SOMERVILLE TATTERSALL STAKES (Newmarket) .... Fri. 4
JOCKEY CLUB CUP (Newmarket) .... Sat. 5
SUN CHARIOT STAKES (Newmarket) .... Sat. 5
TOTE CAMBRIDGESHIRE HANDICAP (Newmarket) .... Sat. 5
IRISH CESAREWITCH (The Curragh) .... Sat. 5
MERCEDES BENZ CHASE (Chepstow) .... Sat. 5
FREE HANDICAP HURDLE (Chepstow) .... Sat. 5
FORTE PRIX DE L'ARC DE TRIOMPHE (Longchamp) .... Sun. 6
MAISONS LAFFITTE HANDICAP (Haydock) .... Sun. 6
NEWINGTON HOTEL HANDICAP (York) .... Wed. 9
ALLIED DUNBAR HANDICAP (York) .... Thur. 10
BONUSPRINT OCTOBER STAKES (Ascot) .... Fri. 11
PRINCESS ROYAL STAKES (Ascot) .... Sat. 12
WILLMOTT DIXON CORNWALLIS STAKES (Ascot) .... Sat. 12
EAST COAST ROCKINGHAM STAKES (York) .... Sat. 12
CORAL SPRINT TROPHY (York) .... Sat. 12
DERRINSTOWN STUD BIRDCATCHER NURSERY (Naas) .... Sun. 13
ALI RETZA & MAMADI SOUDAVAR GARNET RACE (Naas) .... Sun. 13
GRAND CRITERIUM (Longchamp) .... Sun. 13
KINGS REGIMENT STAKES (Haydock) .... Wed. 16
CHALLENGE STAKES (Newmarket) .... Thur. 17
TWO-YEAR-OLD TROPHY (Redcar) .... Thur. 17
DEWHURST STAKES (Newmarket) .... Fri. 18
ROCKFEL STAKES (Newmarket) .... Fri. 18
BARING INTERNATIONAL DARLEY STAKES (Newmarket) .... Fri. 18
DUBAI CHAMPION STAKES (Newmarket) .... Sat. 19
TOTE CESAREWITCH HANDICAP (Newmarket) .... Sat. 19
ROTHMANS ROYALS NORTH SOUTH FINAL (Newmarket) .... Sat. 19
CHARISMA GOLD CUP (Kempton) .... Sat. 19
JUDDMONTE BERESFORD STAKES (The Curragh) .... Sat. 19
VODAFONE HORRIS HILL STAKES (Newbury) .... Thur. 24
PERPETUAL ST. SIMON STAKES (Newbury) .... Sat. 26
NEWGATE STUD RADLEY STAKES (Newbury) .... Sat. 26
BREEDERS' CUP (Woodbine) .... Sat. 26
RACING POST TROPHY (Doncaster) .... Sat. 26
DESERT ORCHID S. W. PATTERN CHASE (Wincanton) .... Sun. 27

NOVEMBER

JAMES SEYMOUR STAKES (Newmarket) .... Fri. 1
GEORGE STUBBS STAKES (Newmarket) .... Fri. 1
LADBROKE AUTUMN HANDICAP (Newmarket) .... Sat. 2
UNITED HOUSE CONSTRUCTION HANDICAP CHASE (Ascot) .... Sat. 2
CHARLIE HALL CHASE (Wetherby) .... Sat. 2
CHARLIE HALL CHASE (Wetherby) .... Sat. 2
WEST YORKSHIRE HURDLE (Wetherby) .... Sat. 2
WENSLEYDALE JUVENILE HURDLE (Wetherby) .... Sat. 2
ASKO APPLIANCES ZETLAND STAKES (Newmarket) .... Sat. 2
ASKO APPLIANCES MARSHALL STAKES (Newmarket) .... Sat. 2
IRISH FIELD CHASE (Punchestown) .... Sat. 2
MELBOURNE CUP (Flemington) .... Tue. 5
HALDON GOLD CUP CHASE (Exeter) .... Tue. 5
GAMEKEEPERS HANDICAP CHASE (Haydock) .... Wed. 6
TOTE SILVER TROPHY (Chepstow) .... Sat. 9
WILLIAM HILL NOVEMBER HANDICAP (Doncaster) .... Sat. 9
REMEMBRANCE DAY STAKES (Doncaster) .... Sat. 9
RISING STARS PATTERN CHASE (Chepstow) .... Sat. 9
BADGER BEER CHASE (Wincanton) .... Sat. 9

TANGLEFOOT ELITE HURDLE (Wincanton) .... Sat. 9
NOVEMBER HANDICAP (Leopardstown) .... Sun. 10
MACKESON GOLD CUP CHASE (Cheltenham) .... Sat. 16
SEAN GRAHAM MOTHERWELL CHASE (Ayr) .... Sat. 16
MMI CHASE (Punchestown) .... Sat. 16
EDWARD HANMER HANDICAP CHASE (Haydock) .... Wed. 20
COOPERS & LYBRAND HURDLE (Ascot) .... Fri. 22
BECHER CHASE (Aintree) .... Sat. 23
FIRST NATIONAL BANK GOLD CUP CHASE (Ascot) .... Sat. 23
SEAN GRAHAM BROWN LAD HURDLE (Naas) .... Sat. 23
JAPAN CUP (Tokyo) .... Sun. 24
HENNESSY COGNAC GOLD CUP CHASE (Newbury) .... Sat. 30
BONUSPRINT GERRY FEILDEN HURDLE (Newbury) .... Sat. 30
AKZO LONG DISTANCE HURDLE (Newbury) .... Sat. 30
TIM MOLONY CHASE (Haydock) .... Sat. 30
BELLWAY FIGHTING FIFTH HURDLE (Newcastle) .... Sat. 30

DECEMBER

HATTONS GRACE HURDLE (Fairyhouse) .... Sun. 1
ROYAL BOND NOVICE HURDLE (Fairyhouse) .... Sun. 1
ESB DRINMORE CHASE (Fairyhouse) .... Sun. 1
HINCHCLIFFE CHAMPION CHASE (Kelso) .... Mon. 2
MITSUBISHI SHOGUN TINGLE CREEK CHASE (Sandown) .... Sat. 7
WILLIAM HILL HANDICAP HURDLE (Sandown) .... Sat. 7
REHEARSAL CHASE (Chepstow) .... Sat. 7
LOWNDES LAMBERT NOVICES' CHASE (Lingfeild) .... Sat. 14
SUMMIT JUNIOR HURDLE (Lingfield) .... Sat. 14
TOMMY WHITTLE CHASE (Haydock) .... Sat. 14
TRIPLEPRINT GOLD CUP (Cheltenham) .... Sat. 14
BULA HURDLE (Cheltenham) .... Sat. 14
BETTERWARE CUP CHASE (Ascot) .... Sat. 21
LONG WALK HURDLE (Ascot) .... Sat. 21
ST HELENS HANDICAP CHASE (Haydock) .... Sat. 21
KING GEORGE VI TRIPLEPRINT CHASE (Kempton) .... Thur. 26
ROWLAND MEYRICK HANDICAP CHASE (Wetherby) .... Thur. 26
DENNYS CHASE (Leopardstown) .... Thur. 26
THE MID-SEASON CHASE (Wincanton) .... Thur. 26
CASTLEFORD CHASE (Wetherby) .... Fri. 27
BONUSPRINT CHRISTMAS HURDLE (Kempton) .... Fri. 27
FINALE JUNIOR HURDLE (Chepstow) .... Fri. 27
CORAL WELSH NATIONAL (Chepstow) .... Fri. 27
GRUNWICK CHAMPIONSHIP NH FLAT RACE (Chepstow) .... Fri. 27
PADDY POWER CHASE (Leopardstown) .... Fri. 27
ERICSSON CHASE (Leopardstown) .... Sat. 28
LADBROKE GOLD CUP (Newbury) .... Mon. 30
CHALLOW HURDLE (Newbury) .... Mon. 30

Teams which have arrived too late for inclusion in Horses In Training 1996 will be published in the Raceform Update at the end of April.

THE VODAFONE DERBY STAKES (CLASS A)
EPSOM, SATURDAY, JUNE 8th

HORSE	TRAINER
Absolute Utopia (USA)	E. A. L. Dunlop
Abstract View (USA)	D. K. Weld
Acharne	C. E. Brittain
Ahkaam (USA)	D. K. Weld
Air Quest	R. Charlton
Ajaad Aljaree (IRE)	A. C. Stewart
Ajlaan	H. Thomson Jones
Alambar (IRE)	P. T. Walwyn
Albada (USA)	J. E. Hammond
Alhaarth (IRE)	Major W. R. Hern
Alhalal	R. W. Armstrong
Alkami (USA)	A. de Royer Dupre
Almaty (IRE)	C. Collins
Alpine	
Al's Money (USA)	R. Collet
Alzanti	P. F. I. Cole
Alzeus (IRE)	C. A. Horgan
Amazing Sail (IRE)	D. K. Weld
Ambassador (USA)	B. W. Hills
Ameer Jumairah (IRE)	
American Renaisans (IRE)	T. Stack
Amfortas (IRE)	C. E. Brittain
Anchor Venture	S. P. C. Woods
Ancient China (IRE)	M. Kauntze
Ancient Quest	N. A. Callaghan
Ansias (USA)	
Answered Prayer	Mrs C. Head
Apicella	R. Boss
Arbatrax (IRE)	P. Bary
Arctiid (USA)	J. H. M. Gosden
Areed Al Ola (USA)	A. C. Stewart
Arktikos (IRE)	J. H. M. Gosden
Arnhem	C. E. Brittain
Ashbal (USA)	K. Prendergast
Astor Place (IRE)	P. W. Chapple-Hyam
Athenry	J. Pearce
Attaproffitt	
Axford (USA)	P. W. Chapple-Hyam
Babinda	C. E. Brittain
Backdrop (IRE)	P. W. Chapple-Hyam
Backtrack	
Bahamian Knight (CAN)	D. R. Loder
Balios (IRE)	M. Johnston
Ballet High (IRE)	I. A. Balding
Battle Dore (USA)	A. Fabre
Battle Green	
Battle Spark (USA)	C. A. Cyzer
Baylakan (IRE)	A. de Royer Dupre
Bechstein	J. L. Dunlop
Beneficent (FR)	J. H. M. Gosden
Berkeley (FR)	A. Fabre
Berlin Blue	
Beyond Bering (USA)	
Bianca Stella (USA)	
Bint Salsabil (USA)	J. L. Dunlop
Blue Hibiscus (USA)	A. Fabre
Blue Saddle (IRE)	A. Fabre
Boat O'Brig	J. R. Fanshawe
Bold Buster	I. A. Balding
Bon Laron (FR)	
Bourbon Dynasty (FR)	A. Fabre
Bourbonist (FR)	L. M. Cumani
Brentability (IRE)	G. Lewis
Bright Eclipse (USA)	J. W. Hills
Bright Heritage (IRE)	D. R. Loder
Bright Water	H. R. A. Cecil
Brilliant Red	P. F. I. Cole
Burnt Offering	C. E. Brittain
Busy Flight	B. W. Hills
Buttermere	J. E. Hammond
Callaloo	Mrs J. Cecil
Candle Smoke (USA)	G. Harwood
Canyon Creek (IRE)	J. H. M. Gosden
Censor	H. R. A. Cecil
Centre Stalls (IRE)	R. F. Johnson Houghton
Chabrol (CAN)	H. R. A. Cecil
Charming Admiral (IRE)	C. F. Wall
Charnwood Jack (USA)	R. Harris
Chief Contender (IRE)	P. W. Chapple-Hyam
Chirico (USA)	J. H. M. Gosden
Chocolate Ice	C. A. Cyzer
Circus Star	Sir Mark Prescott
City of Stars (FR)	H. R. A. Cecil
Classic Colours (USA)	S. C. Williams
Classic Eag'e	S. C. Williams
Classic Find (USA)	S. C. Williams
Classic Mix (USA)	Mrs C. Head
Clerkenwell (USA)	M. R. Stoute
Code Red	J. W. Hills
Cohiba	T. Stack
Coldstream	
Comic's Future (USA)	P. W. Chapple-Hyam
Committal (IRE)	J. H. M. Gosden
Congo Man	M. R. Stoute
Cope With Reality (IRE)	M. R. Stoute
Copper Cello (BEL)	
Coronation Gold (USA)	
Count Julian	
Coup de Feu (FR)	A. de Royer Dupre
Crackernat (IRE)	
Crandon Boulevard	Lord Huntingdon
Crown Court (USA)	L. M. Cumani
Culvern	
Dance Finale (USA)	A. Fabre
Dances (USA)	
Dancing Cormorant	
Dancing Fred (USA)	D. K. Weld
Danesman (FR)	
Danish Circus (IRE)	M. J. Heaton-Ellis
Dankeston (USA)	M. Bell
Darazari (IRE)	A. de Royer Dupre
Daring Bid (IRE)	A. Fabre
Dark Sound (IRE)	A. B. Mulholland
Dark Waters (IRE)	M. R. Stoute
Darleith	L. M. Cumani
Dasharan (IRE)	J. Oxx
Daydreamer (USA)	J. H. M. Gosden
Deed of Love (USA)	J. S. Bolger
Delta Dancer	
Derby Darbak (USA)	J. H. M. Gosden
Desert Boy (IRE)	P. W. Chapple-Hyam
Desert Dunes	N. A. Graham
Devil's Dance (FR)	M. R. Stoute
Deynawari (IRE)	J. Oxx
Diamond For King (FR)	A. Fabre
Dilazar (USA)	J. R. Fanshawe
Diliapour (IRE)	A. de Royer Dupre
Diminutive (USA)	J. W. Hills
Dirab	T. D. Barron
Disciple of War (USA)	
D'Nain (IRE)	W. J. Haggas
Docklands Limo	B. J. McMath
Doctor Bravious (IRE)	M. Bell
Don Bosio (USA)	M. R. Stoute
Don Vito	R. Charlton
Double Agent	M. Johnston

Horse	Trainer	Horse	Trainer
Double Dash (IRE)	M. Johnston	Hammerstein	M. R. Stoute
Double Diamond (IRE)	M. Johnston	Hanbitooh (USA)	E. A. L. Dunlop
Double Leaf	M. R. Stoute	Handsome Dancer	A. Fabre
Dr Massini (IRE)	M. R. Stoute	Hansi (IRE)	A. de Royer Dupre
Dubai College (IRE)	C. E. Brittain	Harbet House (FR)	C. A. Cyzer
Duel At Dawn	J. H. M. Gosden	Hareb (USA)	J. W. Hills
Dushyantor (USA)	H. R. A. Cecil	Harghar (USA)	J. Oxx
East Wood	A. Fabre	Hariapour (IRE)	A. de Royer Dupre
Egyptoman	Mrs C. Head	Harim	J. E. Hammond
Ela Agapi Mou (USA)		Have A Memory (USA)	
Elashath (USA)	J. H. M. Gosden	Hayaain	Major W. R. Hern
Ela-Yie-Mou (IRE)	L. M. Cumani	Helicon (IRE)	
Elmi Elmak (IRE)	L. M. Cumani	Heron Island (IRE)	P. W. Chapple-Hyam
El Penitente (IRE)	D. R. Loder	He's Got Wings (IRE)	C. D. Broad
Energy Man	M. Dods	Hever Golf Classic	T. J. Naughton
Escamillo (IRE)	M. Kauntze	High Baroque (IRE)	P. W. Chapple-Hyam
Espiel (IRE)	M. Kauntze	Highly Finished (IRE)	J. H. M. Gosden
Etterby Park (USA)	Mrs J. R. Ramsden	Hisar (IRE)	J. Oxx
Even Handed	Mrs M. Bollack-Badel	Hoist To Heaven (USA)	Mrs C. Head
Even Top (IRE)	M. H. Tompkins	Homme de Coeur	A. Fabre
Everyone Can Dream		Hoofprints (IRE)	G. Harwood
Ewar Bold	C. E. Brittain	House of Riches	L. M. Cumani
Exalted (IRE)	Sir Mark Prescott	How Long	L. M. Cumani
Extremely Friendly	N. C. Wright	Humool (USA)	Mrs C. Head
Ezanak (IRE)	J. Oxx	Humourless	L. M. Cumani
Faateq	J. L. Dunlop	Icy Cape (USA)	
Failed To Hit	Sir Mark Prescott	Illuminate	J. A. R. Toller
Fairhonor (FR)	E. Lellouche	Indian Sunset	C. R. Egerton
Fantassin		Indian Twist (IRE)	A. Fabre
Farasan (IRE)	H. R. A. Cecil	Infamous (USA)	P. F. I. Cole
Farmost	Sir Mark Prescott	Influence Pedler	C. E. Brittain
Fatal Desire (USA)		Inner Guard	
Fernhill Blaze (IRE)		Insiyabi (USA)	J. L. Dunlop
First Island	A. Fabre	Jack Jennings	B. A. McMahon
Flaming Feather	D. K. Weld	Jackson Hill	R. Charlton
Flocheck (USA)	J. L. Dunlop	Jamaican Flight (USA)	J. W. Hills
Florentino (IRE)	B. W. Hills	Jan's Pal (IRE)	A. De Moussac
Flyfisher (IRE)	G. Lewis	Jaseur (IRE)	J. H. M. Gosden
Flying Pegasus (IRE)	A. Fabre	Jelali (IRE)	D. J. G. Murray Smith
Flyway (FR)	N. Clement	Jiyush	H. Thomson Jones
Fog City	W. Jarvis	J. J. Baboo (IRE)	D. K. Weld
Foreign Judgement (USA)	W. Musson	Johann Strauss (IRE)	K. Prendergast
Forest Buck (USA)	H. R. A. Cecil	Johnny Jones (USA)	
Fort de France (USA)		Kabalevsky (USA)	J. H. M. Gosden
Fort Nottingham (USA)	J. E. Hammond	Kala Noire	
Freeloader		Karakam (IRE)	J. Oxx
Freequent	L. M. Cumani	Karanpour (IRE)	A. de Royer Dupre
Fursan (USA)	N. A. Graham	Kass Alhawa	M. R. Stoute
Future's Trader	R. Hannon	Kassel	
Galapino	C. E. Brittain	Kazawari (USA)	A. de Royer Dupre
Gallante		Kelemar (IRE)	A. de Royer Dupre
General Shabba	R. Harris	Keltoi	L. M. Cumani
Genereux		Khalikhoum (IRE)	J. Oxx
Generosus (FR)	H. R. A. Cecil	Khasib (IRE)	K. Prendergast
Gentilhomme	P. F. I. Cole	King Alex	R. Charlton
Germano	G. Wragg	King Jade	W. Jarvis
Get Away With It (IRE)	M. R. Stoute	King Rufus	J. R. Arnold
Ginger Fox (USA)	H. R. A. Cecil	King's Academy (IRE)	H. R. A. Cecil
Give And Take	Lord Huntingdon	Kings Clover (USA)	
Go Cahoots (USA)		King's Enthraller (IRE)	
Going Green (USA)	Mrs C. Head	King's Flame	
Gold Lance (USA)	M. R. Stoute	Kings Witness (USA)	W. J. Haggas
Gold Spats (USA)	M. R. Stoute	Kingswood (USA)	
Goodwood Rocket	J. L. Dunlop	Kota	J. Wharton
Goult (FR)	A. Fabre	Krailling	
Go With The Wind	M. Bell	Krantz (USA)	
Grand Blanc (USA)	A. Fabre	Kupe (FR)	J. Cunnington Jun.
Grape Tree Road	A. Fabre	Kutman (USA)	M. R. Stoute
Greenstead (USA)	J. H. M. Gosden	Labeed (USA)	Major W. R. Hern
Guignol (USA)	A. Fabre	Lagan	C. E. Brittain
Gympie		Lake Alfred	
Hal Hoo Yaroom	Major W. R. Hern	Lakeline Legend (IRE)	M. A. Jarvis
Hal's Pal	D. R. Loder	Lallans (IRE)	M. Johnston
Hamad (IRE)	D. K. Weld	L'Ami Louis (USA)	J. H. M. Gosden
		Landler	N. Clement

Land of Heroes (USA)	
Land Ride (USA)	J. E. Hammond
Lascases (IRE)	Mrs C. Head
Latin Reign (USA)	P. W. Chapple-Hyam
Lazali (USA)	E. A. L. Dunlop
Leatherneck (IRE)	A. Fabre
Legal Right (USA)	P. W. Chapple-Hyam
Lelari (IRE)	A. de Royer Dupre
Le Pirate (FR)	P. Bary
Le Triton (USA)	Mrs C. Head
Light Reflections	B. W. Hills
Lionize	P. W. Chapple-Hyam
Lippi (IRE)	A. Fabre
Lituus (USA)	J. H. M. Gosden
Llyswen	J. H. M. Gosden
Lord Chamberlain	
Lord of Men	J. H. M. Gosden
Loup Solitaire (USA)	A. Fabre
Lucky Archer	C. E. Brittain
Ludgrove	C. Collins
Lydenburg (IRE)	A. Fabre
Machagai	
Machalini	J. S. Bolger
Macmorris (USA)	P. F. I. Cole
Magellan (USA)	
Magic Galop (USA)	
Magic Lahr (GER)	I. A. Balding
Maiden Castle	J. H. M. Gosden
Mainer Hero (USA)	
Majdak Jereeb (IRE)	Major W. R. Hern
Mallooh	J. H. M. Gosden
Mambo Drummer (IRE)	A. Fabre
Manninamix	A. Fabre
Maori King (USA)	A. Fabre
Marley's Song (IRE)	M. J. Heaton-Ellis
Master Lynx (USA)	G. Lewis
Mattawan	M. Johnston
Mawared (IRE)	J. L. Dunlop
Mawwal (USA)	R. W. Armstrong
Max's Magic (USA)	J. W. Hills
Mayshiel (IRE)	J. E. Hammond
Mazamet (USA)	J. Oxx
Mazurek	P. W. Chapple-Hyam
Meltemison	C. E. Brittain
Meribel (IRE)	P. W. Chapple-Hyam
Metal Badge (IRE)	M. Johnston
Mick's Love (IRE)	
Migwar	L. M. Cumani
Minnisam	J. L. Dunlop
Minsterbeach	
Misky Bay	J. H. M. Gosden
Misolidix	A. Fabre
Mister Aspecto (IRE)	M. Johnston
Mithali	H. Thomson Jones
Mixed Opinion (IRE)	D. K. Weld
Mohannad (IRE)	J. W. Hills
Mohawk River (IRE)	M. R. Stoute
Mons	L. M. Cumani
Mont D'Arbois (USA)	A. Fabre
Montecristo	R. Guest
Monte Felice (IRE)	G. Harwood
Moon Mischief	Lady Herries
Mourne Mountains	H. Candy
Mr Wild (USA)	B. Hanbury
Mubarhin (USA)	J. L. Dunlop
Muhtadi (IRE)	J. L. Dunlop
Mukeed	J. H. M. Gosden
Mukhlles (USA)	Major W. R. Hern
Multicoloured (IRE)	M. R. Stoute
Munketh (USA)	
Mushahid (USA)	J. L. Dunlop
Musick House (IRE)	P. W. Chapple-Hyam
Mustang	C. W. Thornton
Mutabarik (USA)	
Mutahassin (USA)	R. W. Armstrong

Mutanassib (IRE)	A. C. Stewart
Mutarrattab	Major W. R. Hern
Mystic Knight	R. Charlton
Nabhaan (IRE)	D. Morley
Nador	D. R. Loder
Nafsari (IRE)	A. de Royer Dupre
Namoodaj	
Naninja (USA)	A. Fabre
Narrow Focus (USA)	D. K. Weld
Nascimento (USA)	C. O'Brien
Nash House (IRE)	P. W. Chapple-Hyam
Nashkapour (IRE)	A. de Royer Dupre
Nasrudin (USA)	D. R. Loder
Naval Games	M. Bell
Navigate (USA)	R. Hannon
Nayib	D. Morley
Nereus	B. W. Hills
New York New York (FR)	J. E. Hammond
Night Silence	
Night Watch (FR)	A. Fabre
No-Aman	Major W. R. Hern
Noble Impulse (IRE)	
Noblesse Oblige	J. E. Pease
Nocksky (IRE)	L. Browne
Nomadic Welcome	P. Bary
North Cyclone (USA)	C. E. Brittain
Northern Judge	B. Hanbury
Northern Motto	Mrs J. R. Ramsden
Northern Order (FR)	A. de Royer Dupre
Northern Soul (USA)	M. Johnston
Noukari (IRE)	J. Oxx
Nuzu (IRE)	B. W. Hills
Oblomov	G. Lewis
Old Irish	L. M. Cumani
Ood Dancer (USA)	L. M. Cumani
Orinoco River (USA)	P. W. Chapple-Hyam
Owners Hope	
Palamon (USA)	R. Charlton
Palaverix (IRE)	A. Fabre
Party Poll (USA)	D. K. Weld
Passing Strangers (USA)	P. W. Harris
Pasternak	Sir Mark Prescott
Peace Prize (IRE)	D. K. Weld
Pearl Anniversary (IRE)	
Pep Talk (USA)	H. R. A. Cecil
Percy Park (USA)	M. W. Easterby
Petrolio (IRE)	L. M. Cumani
Philosopher (IRE)	R. Hannon
Poetic Dance (USA)	J. L. Dunlop
Polar Lights (CAN)	A. Fabre
Polinesso	B. W. Hills
Polish Legion	J. H. M. Gosden
Polonaise Prince (USA)	R. Akehurst
Pommard (IRE)	J. H. M. Gosden
Pomme Secret (FR)	J. E. Pease
Portuguese Lil	D. Nicholls
Power Moves (IRE)	D. K. Weld
Power Play	J. Oxx
Precious Ring (USA)	Mrs C. Head
Predapio	J. Oxx
Prefect	T. J. Naughton
Present Arms (USA)	P. F. I. Cole
Primo Secundus (IRE)	
Prince Kinsky	Lord Huntingdon
Princely Sword (USA)	
Prince Montelimar (IRE)	Patrick J. Smyth
Prince of Corinth (USA)	
Prince of My Heart	B. W. Hills
Priolo Prima	Sir Mark Prescott
Private Audience (USA)	H. R. A. Cecil
Prize Giving	G. Wragg
Province	G. Lewis
Pure Swing	N. Clement
Quinze	Sir Mark Prescott
Quorum	A. Fabre

Horse	Trainer
Radiant Star	G. Wragg
Raed	P. T. Walwyn
Ragsak Jameel (USA)	Major W. R. Hern
Raise A Prince (FR)	R. W. Armstrong
Raiyoun (IRE)	J. Oxx
Ravello (IRE)	P. Bary
Rayner (IRE)	
Red Raja	P. Mitchell
Red Tie Affair (USA)	M. Bell
Regal Eagle	I. A. Balding
Resonator (FR)	J. E. Pease
Restless Carl (IRE)	A. Fabre
Reticent	J. H. M. Gosden
Rhum Dancer (IRE)	D. K. Weld
Rio Duvida	D. R. Loder
River Bay (USA)	J. E. Hammond
River Dyle (USA)	A. Fabre
Robamaset (IRE)	L. M. Cumani
Rocky Oasis (USA)	M. R. Stoute
Roushan	J. G. M. O'Shea
Royal Action	J. E. Banks
Royal Applause	B. W. Hills
Royal Canaska	D. R. Loder
Royal Court (IRE)	P. W. Chapple-Hyam
Russian Revival (USA)	
Sabrak (IRE)	M. A. Jarvis
Sacho (IRE)	J. H. M. Gosden
Sadler's Realm	M. R. Stoute
Saharan (USA)	Mrs C. Head
Samakaan (IRE)	J. Oxx
Samim (USA)	J. L. Dunlop
Sandhurst King (USA)	A. Fabre
Sandy Floss (IRE)	H. R. A. Cecil
Santiliana (USA)	J. H. M. Gosden
Sasuru	G. Wragg
Scottish Hero	N. C. Wright
Sea Leopard	J. S. Bolger
Seattle Alley (USA)	Mrs J. R. Ramsden
Seattle Saga	D. R. Loder
Second Barrage	L. M. Cumani
Secondment	L. M. Cumani
Select Few	L. M. Cumani
Separatiste (IRE)	A. de Royer Dupre
Serenus (USA)	Lord Huntingdon
Serif (USA)	
Serious Trust	Sir Mark Prescott
Set Adrift	H. R. A. Cecil
Setting Sun	A. Fabre
Seven Crowns (USA)	R. Hannon
Sevres Rose (IRE)	A. de Royer Dupre
Shady Wells (IRE)	
Shahrur (USA)	A. C. Stewart
Shanab (IRE)	A. de Royer Dupre
Shanaladee	M. R. Stoute
Shantou (USA)	J. H. M. Gosden
Sharaf (IRE)	J. L. Dunlop
Shawkey (IRE)	Major W. R. Hern
Shenango (IRE)	G. Wragg
Sherpas (IRE)	H. R. A. Cecil
Sherwood Lad	
Siglo	T. Stack
Sign From Heaven	
Sihafi (USA)	E. A. L. Dunlop
Silent Guest (IRE)	Sir Mark Prescott
Silver Border	
Silver Dome (USA)	H. R. A. Cecil
Silver Prey (USA)	E. A. L. Dunlop
Silverstorm (FR)	Mrs C. Head
Sir Andrews (FR)	A. Fabre
Sir Oracle	T. Stack
Si Seductor (USA)	A. Fabre
Ski Academy (IRE)	P. W. Chapple-Hyam
Sky Dome (IRE)	M. H. Tompkins
Smart Play (USA)	Mrs J. Cecil
Soaked	J. Fanshawe
Sofyaan (USA)	K. Prendergast
Song of The Sword	M. Kauntze
Sourire (USA)	A. Fabre
Southern Host	
Sovereign Crest (IRE)	C. A. Horgan
Spanking Roger	
Spartan Heartbeat	
Special Reef	C. E. Brittain
Speed Fine (IRE)	Mrs C. Head
Sprong (FR)	C. Laffon-Parias
Squandamania	J. de Roualle
Stage Pass	P. F. I. Cole
Stark Lomond (USA)	N. Clement
Star of Ring (IRE)	H. R. A. Cecil
Star Performance (USA)	M. J. Heaton-Ellis
Star Village (FR)	J. E. Hammond
State Theatre (IRE)	A. Fabre
Steamroller Stanly	P. W. Chapple-Hyam
Stepneyev (IRE)	C. A. Cyzer
Stereo Dancer	Mrs C. Head
Sticks McKenzie	Mrs M. Bollack-Badel
St Mawes (FR)	J. L. Dunlop
Stonecutter	
Stone Temple (USA)	J. E. Hammond
Stoop To Conquer	
Storm Trooper (USA)	H. R. A. Cecil
Stornello (USA)	
Straight Thinking (USA)	P. F. I. Cole
Stretarez (FR)	A. Fabre
Suitor	W. Jarvis
Summer Spell (USA)	R. Charlton
Supreme Commander (FR)	A. Fabre
Swan Hunter	J. H. M. Gosden
Taal Almada	L. M. Cumani
Taarish (USA)	D. K. Weld
Taharqa (IRE)	J. H. M. Gosden
Talamone (USA)	A. Fabre
Ta Matete (IRE)	A. Fabre
Tarakhel (USA)	J. Oxx
Tarator (USA)	A. Fabre
Tasdid	
Tassili (IRE)	G. Wragg
Tawafek (USA)	D. Morley
Tawkil (USA)	B. W. Hills
Tax Reform (USA)	D. K. Weld
Terdad (USA)	M. R. Stoute
Thaki	E. A. L. Dunlop
Tiger Lake	
Tiutchev	
Tomba La Bomba (USA)	R. Charlton
Topup	P. A. Kelleway
Torch Ochre (USA)	
Tormount (USA)	
Touch Judge (USA)	Lord Huntingdon
Tria Kemata	D. K. Weld
Triple Leap	J. L. Dunlop
Trivellino (FR)	J. H. M. Gosden
Trojan Risk	
Troysend	G. Lewis
Trudeau (IRE)	A. P. O'Brien
Trying Times (IRE)	A. Fabre
Twentyforten (IRE)	P. F. I. Cole
Unitus (IRE)	M. R. Stoute
Unreflected (USA)	H. R. A. Cecil
Upper Gallery (IRE)	P. W. Chapple-Hyam
Val d'Oa (FR)	P. Bary
Valedictory	H. R. A. Cecil
Van Gurp	B. A. McMahon
Vaporetto (USA)	A. Fabre
Vautour Rouge (USA)	J. E. Hammond
Velmez	R. Guest
Velvet Jones	G. F. H. Charles-Jones
Verulam (FR)	J. R. W. Jenkins
Village Home (FR)	
Village Native (FR)	K. O. Cunningham-Brown

Vireo (IRE)	
Waadilgore (USA)	
Wahab	R. W. Armstrong
Wakilamix (IRE)	A. Fabre
Washington Reef (USA)	J. H. M. Gosden
Water Poet (IRE)	A. Fabre
Waterwave (USA)	J. H. M. Gosden
Wedding Gallery	
Wee Hope (USA)	M. R. Stoute
Welcome Parade	H. R. A. Cecil
Welcome Royale (IRE)	M. H. Tompkins
Well Drawn	H. Candy
Well Walpi	Mrs C. Head
White Settler	R. Hannon
Winged Hussar	A. Fabre
Winter Quarters (USA)	
World Premier	C. E. Brittain

Yalta (IRE)	R. Charlton
Yipsilanti	Lady Herries
Yom Jameel (IRE)	M. R. Stoute
Zabari (IRE)	J. Oxx
Zaforum	L. Montague Hall
Zaynal (IRE)	J. Oxx
Zurs (IRE)	J. A. R. Toller
ex Beau Dada (IRE)	L. Browne
ex Bold Tango (FR)	
ex Geraldville	
ex Hakas (USA)	
ex Howa Queen (JPN)	
ex La Meilleure	
ex Noble Tiara (USA)	
ex Sharmood (USA)	
ex Upper Sister	
ex Welcome Jaja (JPN)	

EUROPEAN FREE HANDICAP
NEWMARKET, CRAVEN MEETING 1996 (ON THE DEWHURST STAKES COURSE)
WEDNESDAY, APRIL 17th

The NGK Spark Plugs European Free Handicap (Class A) (Listed race) with £25,000 added for two-years old only of 1995 (including all two-years-old in the 1995 International Classification), to run as three-year-olds; lowest weight 7st 7lb; highest weight 9st 7lb. Penalty for winner after December 31, 1995, 5lb.
Seven furlongs.

Rating		st	lb	SF
126	Alhaarth (IRE)	9	7	52
124	Royal Applause	9	5	68
120	Danehill Dancer (IRE)	9	1	58
119	Blue Duster (USA)	9	0	78
	Rio Duvida	9	0	69
118	Lord Of Men	8	13	60
	Loup Solitaire (USA)	8	13	
117	Manninamix	8	12	
	Miss Tahiti (IRE)	8	12	
	Tagula (IRE)	8	12	69
116	Almaty (IRE)	8	11	71
	Woodborough (USA)	8	11	73
115	Beauchamp King	8	10	75
	Eternity Range	8	10	
	Kahir Almaydan (IRE)	8	10	76
	Le Triton (USA)	8	10	
	Mons	8	10	87
114	Bosra Sham (USA)	8	9	102
	Shake The Yoke	8	9	
113	Allied Forces (USA)	8	8	75
	Ashkalani (IRE)	8	8	
	Barricade (USA)	8	8	
	Bint Salsabil (USA)	8	8	67
	Cayman Kai (IRE)	8	8	85
	Even Top (IRE)	8	8	71
	Mawwal (USA)	8	8	70
	Occupandiste (IRE)	8	8	
	Spinning World (USA)	8	8	
	Tumbleweed Ridge	8	8	80
	With Fascination (USA)	8	8	
112	Lucky Lionel (USA)	8	7	86
	Mezzogiorno	8	7	76
	My Branch	8	7	78
	Polaris Flight (USA)	8	7	80
	Russian Revival (USA)	8	7	80
	Solar Crystal (IRE)	8	7	77
	South Salem (USA)	8	7	83
	Storm Trooper (USA)	8	7	79
	Titus Livius (FR)	8	7	
	Winter Quarters (USA)	8	7	59
	World Premier	8	7	80
111	Astor Place (IRE)	8	6	63
	Cliptomania (USA)	8	6	
	Committal (IRE)	8	6	76
	Glory of Dancer	8	6	
	Mubhij (IRE)	8	6	87
	Ragmar (FR)	8	6	
110	Applaud (USA)	8	5	65
	Bijou d'Inde	8	5	81
	Dance Design (IRE)	8	5	
	Dance Sequence (IRE)	8	5	80
	Dark Nile (USA)	8	5	
	Deed Of Love (USA)	8	5	
	Force Of Will (USA)	8	5	
	Go Between (FR)	8	5	
	Like A Hawk (USA)	8	5	79
	Mick's Love (IRE)	8	5	72
	Oliviero (FR)	8	5	
	Priory Belle (IRE)	8	5	
	Take A Left	8	5	79
109	Battle Dore (USA)	8	4	72
	Blue Iris	8	4	
	Blusing Gleam	8	4	87
	Busy Flight	8	4	
	Contare	8	4	
	Darling Flame (USA)	8	4	83
	Heron Island (IRE)	8	4	76
	Kings Witness (USA)	8	4	75
	Luna Wells (IRE)	8	4	
	Mayoumbe (FR)	8	4	
	More Royal (USA)	8	4	89
	Quorum	8	4	
	Radevore	8	4	
	Raisonnable	8	4	
	Restless Carl (IRE)	8	4	
	Ruznama (USA)	8	4	85
	Sovereign's Crown (USA)	8	4	77
	Trivellino (FR)	8	4	
108	Brandon Magic	8	3	
	Galtero (FR)	8	3	
	Honest Guest (IRE)	8	3	79
	Iamus	8	3	83
	Inchrory	8	3	85
	Lavirco (GER)	8	3	
	Mark of Esteem (IRE)	8	3	74
	Martiniquais (IRE)	8	3	
	My Melody Parkes	8	3	78

	Name	st	lb	rating
	Parrot Jungle (IRE)	8	3	66
	Resounder (USA)	8	3	79
	Shining Molly (FR)	8	3	
	Sweet Robin (IRE)	8	3	80
	Wedding Gift (FR)	8	3	
	Yarob (IRE)	8	3	76
107	Bint Shadayid (USA)	8	2	109
	Brighstone	8	2	64
	Jack Jennings	8	2	92
	Kafhar	8	2	
	Kuantan (USA)	8	2	82
	Latin Reign (USA)	8	2	74
	Line Dancer	8	2	77
	Lomberto	8	2	
	Papaha (FR)	8	2	81
	Prevail (USA)	8	2	
	Rupert (FR)	8	2	
	Starmaniac (USA)	8	2	
	Tamnia	8	2	90
	Wood Magic	8	2	74
106	Al Abraq (USA)	8	1	81
	Bahamian Knight (CAN)	8	1	85
	Catch A Glimpse (USA)	8	1	
	Coldstream	8	1	72
	Danesman (IRE)	8	1	73
	Dismissed (USA)	8	1	80
	Double Leaf	8	1	70
	Flying Squaw	8	1	75
	Lidanna	8	1	
	Maid For The Hills	8	1	76
	Media Nox	8	1	
	Myrtle	8	1	81
	Najiya	8	1	89
	Quakers Field	8	1	90
	Red Robbo (CAN)	8	1	64
	Sasuru	8	1	76
	Scarlet Plume	8	1	72
	Sketch Book	8	1	90
	Warning Time	8	1	78
	Zuhair	8	1	74
105	Ahkaam (USA)	8	0	
	Amazing Bay	8	0	72
	Anthelia	8	0	75
	Bright Heritage (IRE)	8	0	83
	Desert Boy (IRE)	8	0	80
	Esquive	8	0	
	Flame of Athens (IRE)	8	0	
	Gentilhomme	8	0	80
	Gothenberg (IRE)	8	0	79
	Harghar (USA)	8	0	
	Helicon (IRE)	8	0	90
	Henry The Fifth	8	0	72
	Konic (ITY)	8	0	
	Leonine (IRE)	8	0	80
	Nashcash (IRE)	8	0	
	Night Watch (USA)	8	0	71
	Polska (USA)	8	0	75
	Premier de Cordee (FR)	8	0	
	Shen Da Shi (FR)	8	0	
	Staffin	8	0	82
	Story Line	8	0	66
	Tarte Aux Pommes (FR)	8	0	
	Tawkil (USA)	8	0	85
	Thracian	8	0	
	Wisam	8	0	83
104	Bonarelli (IRE)	7	13	66
	Brilliant Red	7	13	56
	Double Bluff (IRE)	7	13	
	Dovebrace	7	13	67
	Dublin River (USA)	7	13	54
	Eastern Prophets	7	13	72
	Flyfisher (IRE)	7	13	60
	Home Shopping	7	13	66
	Jarah (USA)	7	13	65
	King of the East (IRE)	7	13	64
	Last Second (IRE)	7	13	54
	Masehaab (IRE)	7	13	57
	Mushahid (USA)	7	13	66
	Pivotal	7	13	74
	Projection (USA)	7	13	57
	Rambling Bear	7	13	72
	Ramooz (USA)	7	13	67
	Rouge Rancon (USA)	7	13	78
	Silver Dome (USA)	7	13	
	Silver Prey (USA)	7	13	51
	Singing Patriarch (IRE)	7	13	60
	Thrilling Day	7	13	72
	Tria Kemata	7	13	66
	Westcourt Magic	7	13	67
	Witch of Fife (IRE)	7	13	61

Foaling dates are shown for two-year-olds where these are provided.

THREE-YEAR-OLDS OF 1995

A classification for three-year-olds trained in Great Britain, which ran during 1995 and have been allotted a rating of not less than 100 (7st 2lb).

1¾m plus

119	Classic Cliche (IRE)	8	7
114	Minds Music (USA)	8	2
113	Double Eclipse (IRE)	8	1
110	In Camera (IRE)	7	12
109	Anchor Clever	7	11
107	Diaghilef (IRE)	7	9
106	Stelvio	7	8
104	Grey Shot	7	6
103	Jellaby Askhir	7	5
102	Daraydan (IRE)	7	4
102	Kristal's Paradise (IRE)	7	4
102	Pedraza	7	4
100	Wot-If-We (IRE)	7	2

1m 3f plus

130	Lammtarra (USA)	9	4
126	Pentire	9	0
122	Luso	8	10
122	Singspiel (IRE)	8	10
122	Tamure (IRE)	8	10
120	Riyadian	8	8
119	Annus Mirabilis (FR)	8	7
119	Presenting	8	7
118	Moonshell (IRE)	8	6
118	Pure Grain	8	6
117	Court of Honour (IRE)	8	5
117	Fahal (USA)	8	5
116	Dance A Dream	8	4
116	Posidonas	8	4
115	Citadeed (USA)	8	3
115	Larrocha (IRE)	8	3
114	Don Corleone	8	2
114	Sebastian	8	2
113	Fanjica (IRE)	8	1
113	Kalabo (USA)	8	1
112	Commoner (USA)	8	0
112	Istidaad (USA)	8	0
112	Munwar	8	0
112	Phantom Gold	8	0
111	Ihtiram (IRE)	7	13
111	Song of Tara (IRE)	7	13
110	Musetta (IRE)	7	12
110	Tillandsia (IRE)	7	12
109	Precede	7	11
109	Spout	7	11

108	Balliol Boy	7	10
108	Jural	7	10
107	Diaghilef (IRE)	7	9
107	Inquisitor (USA)	7	9
106	Asterita	7	8
106	Juyush (USA)	7	8
105	Dreamer (USA)	7	7
105	Labibeh (USA)	7	7
104	Bunting	7	6
104	Indian Light	7	6
104	Medaille Militaire	7	6
103	Fire On Ice (IRE)	7	5
103	Jellaby Askhir	7	5
103	Lucky Di (USA)	7	5
102	Snowtown (IRE)	7	4
102	Tenorio	7	4
101	Hagwah (USA)	7	3
101	Naked Welcome	7	3
100	Al Widyan (IRE)	7	2
100	Maralinga (IRE)	7	2
100	Segovia	7	2

9½f plus

125	Pentire	8	13
124	Spectrum (IRE)	8	12
122	Singspiel (IRE)	8	10
120	Eltish (USA)	8	8
120	Flemensfirth (USA)	8	8
120	Riyadian	8	8
119	Annus Mirabilis (FR)	8	7
119	Montjoy (USA)	8	7
117	Fahal (USA)	8	5
116	Torrential (USA)	8	4
115	Larrocha (IRE)	8	3
114	Caramba	8	2
114	Royal Solo (IRE)	8	2
112	Warning Shadows (IRE)	8	0
111	Sonic Boy	7	13
110	Tillandsia (IRE)	7	12
109	Ela-Aristokrati (IRE)	7	11
109	Spout	7	11
106	Poppy Carew (IRE)	7	8
106	Subya	7	8
106	Western Reel (USA)	7	8
105	Dahik	7	7

105	Traikey (IRE)	7	7
104	Murajja (USA)	7	6
104	Sanoosea (USA)	7	6
103	Stiffelio (IRE)	7	5
103	Warning Order	7	5
102	Ludgate (USA)	7	4
100	Baltic Raider	7	2
100	Jumilla (USA)	7	2
100	Llia	7	2
100	Nash Terrace (IRE)	7	2
100	Salmon Ladder (USA)	7	2

7f plus

129	Bahri (USA)	9	3
124	Celtic Swing	8	12
118	Harayir (USA)	8	6
118	Helmsman (USA)	8	6
117	Charnwood Forest (IRE)	8	5
117	Vettori (IRE)	8	5
116	Pipe Major (IRE)	8	4
116	Tamayaz (CAN)	8	4
116	Torrential (USA)	8	4
115	Aqaarid (USA)	8	3
114	Nwaamis (USA)	8	2
113	Didina	8	1
113	Painter's Row (IRE)	8	1
113	Prince Arthur (IRE)	8	1
113	Shahid	8	1
112	Bishop of Cashel	8	0
112	Cap Juluca (IRE)	8	0
112	Gay Gallanta (USA)	8	0
112	Inzar (USA)	8	0
112	Munwar	8	0
111	Myself	7	13
110	Arabride	7	12
110	Sergeyev (IRE)	7	12
109	Hoh Magic	7	11
109	Peace Envoy	7	11
109	Red Carnival (USA)	7	11
108	Epagris	7	10
107	Easy Dollar	7	9
107	First Island (IRE)	7	9
107	Prince of India	7	9
107	Two O'Clock Jump (IRE)	7	9
106	Alami (USA)	7	8
106	Brief Glimpse (IRE)	7	8
106	Lovely Millie (IRE)	7	8

106	Restructure (IRE)	7	8
106	Silca Blanka (IRE)	7	8
105	Decorated Hero	7	7
105	Romanzof	7	7
104	Bin Rosie	7	6
104	Desert Courier	7	6
104	Private Line (USA)	7	6
103	Allemande (IRE)	7	5
103	Cadeaux Tryst	7	5
103	Wijara (IRE)	7	5
102	Baaderah (IRE)	7	4
102	Nagnagnag (IRE)	7	4
102	Options Open	7	4
102	Star of Zilzal (USA)	7	4
102	Tajannub (USA)	7	4
102	Verzen (IRE)	7	4
101	General Monash (USA)	7	3
101	Hiwaya	7	3
101	Louis' Queen (USA)	7	3
100	A La Carte (IRE)	7	2
100	Be Mindful	7	2
100	Felitza (IRE)	7	2
100	Fleet Hill (IRE)	7	2
100	Mandarina (USA)	7	2
100	Moon King (IRE)	7	2

5f plus

119	Mind Games	8	7
113	Chilly Billy	8	1
112	Easy Option (IRE)	8	0
110	Fard (USA)	7	12
110	Millstream (USA)	7	12
109	Art of War	7	11
109	Hoh Magic	7	11
107	Easy Dollar	7	9
107	Raah Algharb (USA)	7	9
106	Nuriva (USA)	7	8
105	Cheyenne Spirit	7	7
103	Leap For Joy	7	5
103	Warning Star	7	5
102	Double Quick (IRE)	7	4
101	Espartero (IRE)	7	3
101	Go Hever Golf	7	3
101	That Man Again	7	3
100	Iktamal (USA)	7	2
100	Loyalize (USA)	7	2
100	Mr Oscar	7	2

FOUR-YEAR-OLDS AND UP OF 1995

A classification for four-year-olds and upwards trained in Great Britain, which ran during 1995 and have been allotted a rating of not less than 100 (7st 2lb).

1¾m plus

120	Strategic Choice (USA) ...	4	8	8
119	Double Trigger (IRE)	4	8	7
119	Moonax (IRE).................	4	8	7
118	Red Bishop (USA)...........	7	8	6
110	Further Flight	9	7	12
109	Khamaseen..................	4	7	11
109	Parthian Springs	4	7	11
108	Admiral's Well (IRE)........	5	7	10
108	Assessor (IRE)	6	7	10
108	Bold Gait	4	7	10
108	Capias (USA).................	4	7	10
106	Cuff Link (IRE)	5	7	8
106	Saxon Maid	4	7	8
105	Noble Rose (IRE)	4	7	7
104	Always Aloof (USA)	4	7	6
104	Misbelief.....................	5	7	6
103	Castle Courageous..........	8	7	5
103	Old Rouvel (USA)............	4	7	5
103	Poltarf (USA)	4	7	5
102	Bahamian Sunshine (USA)	4	7	4
102	Double Dagger...............	4	7	4
102	Golden Ball (IRE)	4	7	4
102	Source of Light	6	7	4
100	Silence In Court (IRE)......	4	7	2

1m 3f plus

121	Strategic Choice (USA) ...	4	8	9
120	Broadway Flyer (USA).....	4	8	8
118	Alderbrook...................	6	8	6
118	Red Bishop (USA)...........	7	8	6
117	Time Star (USA)	4	8	5
116	Beauchamp Hero	5	8	4
116	Only Royale (IRE)	6	8	4
114	Balanchine (USA)...........	4	8	2
114	Magical Retreat (USA).....	5	8	2
114	Midnight Legend	4	8	2
114	Richard of York..............	5	8	2
112	Environment Friend	7	8	0
112	Linney Head (USA)	4	8	0
112	Wind In Her Hair (IRE)	4	8	0
112	Zilzal Zamaan (USA)........	4	8	0
111	Right Win (IRE)..............	5	7	13
111	Shambo.......................	8	7	13
110	Burooj	5	7	12
109	Ionio (USA)...................	4	7	11

108	Capias (USA).................	4	7	10
108	Sacrament....................	4	7	10
107	Blush Rambler (USA).......	5	7	9
107	Sadler's Image (IRE).......	4	7	9
106	Bal Harbour	4	7	8
106	Mack The Knife..............	6	7	8
106	Saxon Maid	4	7	8
106	Taufan's Melody	4	7	8
105	Escarpment (USA)..........	4	7	7
105	Noble Rose (IRE)	4	7	7
105	River North (IRE)	5	7	7
104	Close Conflict (USA)	4	7	6
104	Silver Wedge (USA)	4	7	6
104	Waiting........................	4	7	6
103	Blushing Flame (USA)	4	7	5
103	Totality	4	7	5
102	Cotteir Chief (IRE)..........	4	7	4
102	Source of Light	6	7	4

9½f plus

128	Halling (USA).................	4	9	2
123	Muhtarram (USA)............	6	8	11
121	Pelder (IRE)..................	5	8	9
118	Flagbird (USA)	4	8	6
118	Needle Gun (IRE)	5	8	6
118	Red Bishop (USA)...........	7	8	6
115	Desert Shot	5	8	3
115	Just Happy (USA)	4	8	3
115	La Confederation............	4	8	3
114	Richard of York..............	5	8	2
114	Triarius (USA)................	5	8	2
113	Alriffa	4	8	1
113	Prince of Andros (USA)...	5	8	1
113	Young Buster (IRE)	7	8	1
112	Environment Friend	7	8	0
111	Revere (IRE)	5	7	13
110	Baron Ferdinand.............	5	7	12
110	Captain Horatius (IRE).....	6	7	12
109	Ionio (USA)...................	4	7	11
109	Wayne County (IRE)........	5	7	11
108	Dance Turn...................	4	7	10
108	Del Deya (IRE)...............	5	7	10
107	Florid (USA)..................	4	7	9
105	Brier Creek (USA)	6	7	7
105	Salt Lake	4	7	7

102	Girl From Ipanema	4	7	4
100	Frustration	4	7	2

7f plus

122	Missed Flight	5	8	10
121	Pelder (IRE)	5	8	9
120	Sayyedati	5	8	8
120	Soviet Line (IRE)	5	8	8
116	Darnay	4	8	4
115	Bin Ajwaad (IRE)	5	8	3
114	Heart Lake	4	8	2
114	Wizard King	4	8	2
113	Branston Abby (IRE)	6	8	1
113	Mr Martini (IRE)	5	8	1
113	Nicolotte	4	8	1
112	Emperor Jones (USA)	5	8	0
112	Mutakddim (USA)	4	8	0
112	Overbury (IRE)	4	8	0
111	Mistle Cat (USA)	5	7	13
111	Realities (USA)	4	7	13
110	Erin Bird (FR)	4	7	12
109	Fraam	6	7	11
109	Nijo	4	7	11
108	Dance Turn	4	7	10
107	Green Green Desert (FR)	4	7	9
107	Lap of Luxury	6	7	9
106	Penny Drops	6	7	8
106	Pollen Count (USA)	6	7	8
105	Celestial Key (USA)	5	7	7
105	Foxhound (USA)	4	7	7
105	Port Lucaya	5	7	7
104	Alanees	4	7	6
103	Governor George (USA)	4	7	5
103	Moccasin Run (USA)	4	7	5
103	Storiths (IRE)	5	7	5
102	Airport (USA)	4	7	4
101	Indian Fly	4	7	3
100	Indhar	4	7	2

5f plus

127	Lake Coniston (IRE)	4	9	1
121	Piccolo	4	8	9
119	Hever Golf Rose	4	8	7
119	Young Ern	5	8	7
117	So Factual (USA)	5	8	5
114	Owington	4	8	2
113	Branston Abby (IRE)	6	8	1
113	Cool Jazz	4	8	1
113	Ya Malak	4	8	1
112	Eveningperformance	4	8	0
110	Lavinia Fontana (IRE)	6	7	12
110	Millyant	5	7	12
108	Hard To Figure	9	7	10
108	Montendre	8	7	10
107	Bunty Boo	6	7	9
107	Carranita (IRE)	5	7	9
107	Sharp Prod (USA)	5	7	9
107	Venture Capitalist	6	7	9
105	Blue Siren	4	7	7
105	El Yasaf (IRE)	7	7	7
105	Mistertopogigo (IRE)	5	7	7
104	Double Blue	6	7	6
104	Loch Patrick	5	7	6
104	Palacegate Episode (IRE)	5	7	6
104	Star Talent (USA)	4	7	6
102	Domulla	5	7	4
102	Hello Mister	4	7	4
102	No Extras (IRE)	5	7	4
102	Royale Figurine (IRE)	4	7	4
102	Windmachine (SWE)	4	7	4
101	Kassbaan	5	7	3
100	Croft Pool	4	7	2
100	Roger The Butler (IRE)	5	7	2
100	Saint Express	5	7	2
100	Triple Joy	4	7	2
100	Welsh Mist	4	7	2

Owners names are shown against their horses where this information is available. In the case of Partnerships and Syndicates, the nominated owner is given alongside the horse with other owners listed below the team.

IRISH CLASSIFICATIONS
TWO-YEAR-OLDS OF 1995

For two-year-olds only that ran in 1995 and are assessed by handicappers Ciaran Kennelly and Dermot MacDormott at a rating of 100 (7st 2 lb) or more relative to the International Classification. Horses trained abroad are included if they won, or achieved their rating, in Ireland.

Rating		st	lb		Rating		st	lb
120	Danehill Dancer (IRE)	8	8		104	Last Second (IRE)	7	6
116	Almaty (IRE)	8	4			Rouge Rancon (USA)	7	6
	Woodborough (USA)	8	4			Thrilling Day (GB)	7	6
112	Polaris Flight (USA)	8	0		103	Axford (USA)	7	5
110	Bijou d'Inde (GB)	7	12			Deynawari (IRE)	7	5
	Dance Design (IRE)	7	12			Rithab (GB)	7	5
	Deed of Love (USA)	7	12			Sunset Reigns (IRE)	7	5
	Force of Will (USA)	7	12		102	Sheraka (IRE)	7	4
	Priory Belle (IRE)	7	12			Super Gift (IRE)	7	4
107	Tamnia (GB)	7	9		101	Common Spirit (IRE)	7	3
106	Catch A Glimpse (USA)	7	8			High Target (IRE)	7	3
	Lidanna (GB)	7	8		100	April The Eighth (GB)	7	2
105	Ahkaam (USA)	7	7			Aylesbury (IRE)	7	2
	Flame of Athens (IRE)	7	7			Ceirseach (IRE)	7	2
	Harghar (USA)	7	7			Long Beach (IRE)	7	2
	Nashcash (IRE)	7	7			No Animosity (IRE)	7	2

IRISH CLASSIFICATIONS
THREE-YEAR-OLDS OF 1995

For horses rated 100 (7st 2 lb) or more relative to the 1995 International Classification, which were trained in Ireland in 1995. Horses trained abroad are included if they won, or achieved their rating in Ireland.

1¾m plus

		st	lb				st	lb
117	Oscar Schindler (IRE)	8	5		117	Oscar Schindler (IRE)	8	5
106	Johansson (USA)	7	8		112	Humbel (USA)	8	0
105	Munif (IRE)	7	7			Russian Snows (IRE)	8	0
102	Daraydan (IRE)	7	4		108	Golden Orb (IRE)	7	10
100	Rawy (USA)	7	2			I'm Supossin (IRE)	7	10
					105	Damancher (GB)	7	7
1m 3f plus					100	Bluffing (IRE)	7	2
121	Winged Love (IRE)	8	9					
120	Definite Article (GB)	8	8		**9f plus**			
119	Annus Mirabilis (FR)	8	7		125	Pentire (GB)	8	3
118	Pure Grain (GB)	8	6		123	Timarida (IRE)	8	11

120	Definite Article (GB)	8	8
118	Shemaran (IRE)	8	6
112	Humbel (USA)	8	0
105	Hasainiya (IRE)	7	7
	Viaticum (IRE)	7	7
104	Alisidora (IRE)	7	6
103	Fill The Bill (IRE)	7	5
100	Bluffing (IRE)	7	2
	Radomsko (GB)	7	2
	Rawy (USA)	7	2
	Zabadi (IRE)	7	2

7f plus

126	Ridgewood Pearl (GB)	9	0
120	Spectrum (IRE)	8	8
117	Adjareli (IRE)	8	5
110	Wild Bluebell (IRE)	7	12
109	Khaytada (IRE)	7	11
	Nautical Pet (IRE)	7	11
107	Off'N'Away (IRE)	7	9
	Two O'Clock Jump (IRE)	7	9
106	Mediation (IRE)	7	8

103	Celladonia (IRE)	7	5
102	Eva Luna (IRE)	7	4
	Free To Speak (IRE)	7	4
	Manashar (IRE)	7	4
	Union Decree (USA)	7	4
101	Charillus (GB)	7	3
	Daryabad (IRE)	7	3
	Kayaara (IRE)	7	3
	Park Charger (GB)	7	3
	Storm Ashore (USA)	7	3

5f plus

120	Desert Style (IRE)	8	8
111	Burden of Proof (IRE)	7	13
110	Millstream (USA)	7	12
109	Nautical Pet (IRE)	7	11
	Petite Fantasy (GB)	7	11
106	Mediation (IRE)	7	8
105	Sharp Point (IRE)	7	7
104	Sir Silver Sox (USA)	7	6
101	Ailleacht (USA)	7	3
100	America's Cup (IRE)	7	2

IRISH CLASSIFICATIONS
FOUR-YEAR-OLDS AND UPWARDS

For horses rated 100 (7st 2lb) or more relative to the 1995 International Classification, which were trained in Ireland in 1995. Horses trained abroad are included if they won, or achieved their rating in Ireland.

1¾m plus

Rating		Age	st	lb
120	Strategic Choice (USA)	4	8	8
119	Moonax (IRE)	4	8	7
	Vintage Crop (IRE)	8	8	7
108	Capias (USA)	4	7	10
	Double On (IRE)	4	7	10
107	Mohaajir (USA)	4	7	9
101	Montelado (IRE)	8	7	3
100	Lake Kariba (GB)	4	7	2

1m 3f plus

110	Royal Ballerina (IRE)	5	7	12
107	Ballykett Nancy (IRE)	4	7	9

9f plus

124	Freedom Cry (GB)	4	8	12
118	Flagbird (USA)	4	8	6
	Needle Gun (IRE)	5	8	6
115	Just Happy (USA)	4	8	3
113	Hushang (IRE)	5	8	1
	Prince of Andros (USA)	5	8	1
110	Al Mohaajir (USA)	4	7	12
	Dancing Sunset (IRE)	4	7	12
	Idris (IRE)	5	7	12
109	Ivory Frontier (IRE)	5	7	11

(continued)

105	Akhiyar (IRE)	4	7	7
	Magic Feeling (IRE)	5	7	7
101	State Crystal (IRE)	4	7	3

7f plus

116	Darnay (GB)	4	8	4
115	Bin Ajwaad (IRE)	5	8	3
114	Wizard King (GB)	4	8	2
113	Mr Martini (IRE)	5	8	1
112	Ridgewood Ben (GB)	4	8	0
111	Mistle Cat (USA)	5	7	13
110	Al Mohaajir (USA)	4	7	12
	Idris (IRE)	5	7	12
109	Nijo (IRE)	4	7	11
108	Dance Turn (GB)	4	7	10
107	Lap of Luxury (GB)	6	7	9
106	The Puzzler (IRE)	4	7	8
105	Akhiyar (IRE)	4	7	7
100	Nordic Oak (IRE)	7	7	2

5f plus

110	Millyant (GB)	5	7	12
107	Bunty Boo (GB)	6	7	9
106	The Puzzler (IRE)	4	7	8
	Tourandot (IRE)	4	7	8
104	Dairine's Delight (IRE)	5	7	6
102	Diamond Class (IRE)	5	7	4

Teams which have arrived too late for inclusion in Horses In Training 1996 will be published in the Raceform Update at the end of April.

INTERNATIONAL CLASSIFICATION

For three-year-olds only which, during 1995 have run or been trained in Europe or North America, and have in their respective races been assessed jointly by international classification committee handicappers and North American rating committee racing officials at a rating of 105 (7st 7lb) or above. In the case of North American horses, the minimum rating is 110.

1¾m plus

Rating		st	lb	Trained
119	Classic Cliche (IRE)	8	7	GB
117	Affidavit (USA)	8	5	FR
114	Minds Music (USA)	8	2	GB
113	Double Eclipse (IRE)	8	1	GB
113	Peckinpah's Soul (FR)	8	1	FR
110	In Camera (IRE)	7	12	GB
110	Madalyn (IRE)	7	12	FR
109	Anchor Clover (GB)	7	11	GB
108	First Hello (GER)	7	10	GER
107	Diaghilev (IRE)	7	9	GB
106	Johansson (USA)	7	8	IRE
106	Stelvio (GB)	7	8	GB
105	Munif (IRE)	7	7	IRE
105	Shanawi (IRE)	7	7	FR

1m 3f plus

		st	lb	Trained
130	Lammtarra (USA)	9	4	GB
126	Pentire (GB)	9	0	GB
125	Swain (IRE)	8	13	FR
123	Thunder Gulch (USA)	8	11	USA
122	Luso (GB)	8	10	GB
122	Singspiel (IRE)	8	10	GB
122	Tamure (IRE)	8	10	GB
121	Poliglote (GB)	8	9	FR
121	Winged Love (IRE)	8	9	FR
120	Definite Article (GB)	8	8	IRE
120	Riyadian (GB)	8	8	GB
120	Star Standard (USA)	8	8	USA
119	Annus Mirabilis (FR)	8	7	GB
119	Mecke (USA)	8	7	USA
119	Presenting (GB)	8	7	GB

		st	lb	Trained
119	Solon (GER)	8	7	GER
118	Moonshell (IRE)	8	6	GB
118	Pure Grain (GB)	8	6	GB
117	Carling (FR)	8	5	FR
117	Court of Honour (IRE)	8	5	GB
117	Fahal (USA)	8	5	GB
117	Oscar Schindler (IRE)	8	5	IRE
116	All My Dreams (IRE)	8	4	GER
116	Dance A Dream (GB)	8	4	GB
116	Housamix (FR)	8	4	FR
116	Posidonas (GB)	8	4	GB
115	Citadeed (USA)	8	3	GB/USA
115	Larrocha (IRE)	8	3	GB
115	Valley of Gold (FR)	8	3	FR
114	De Quest (GB)	8	2	GB
114	Don Corleone (GB)	8	2	GB
114	Flitch (USA)	8	2	USA
114	Muncie (IRE)	8	2	FR
114	Rifapour (IRE)	8	2	FR
114	Sebastian (GB)	8	2	GB
113	Dance Partner (JPN)	8	1	JPN/FR
113	Fanjica (IRE)	8	1	GB
113	Kalabo (USA)	8	1	GB
113	Knockadoon (CAN)	8	1	USA
113	Lecroix (GER)	8	1	GER
112	Commoner (USA)	8	0	GB
112	Humbol (USA)	8	0	IRE
112	Istidaad (USA)	8	0	GB
112	Munwar (GB)	8	0	GB
112	Phantom Gold (GB)	8	0	GB
112	Privity (USA)	8	0	FR
112	Russian Snows (IRE)	8	0	IRE
112	Walk On Mix (FR)	8	0	FR

111	Ihtiram (IRE)	7 13	GB
111	Manzoni (GER)	7 13	GER
111	Song of Tara (IRE)	7 13	GB
110	Masterplayer (GER)	7 12	GER
110	Musetta (IRE)	7 12	GB
110	Sir King (GER)	7 12	GER
110	Tillandsia (IRE)	7 12	GB
110	Wild Bluebell (IRE)	7 12	IRE
109	Artan (IRE)	7 11	GER
109	Danefair (GB)	7 11	FR
109	Precede (GB)	7 11	GB
109	Spout (GB)	7 11	GB
108	Balliol Boy (GB)	7 10	GB
108	Centaine (GB)	7 10	GER
108	Golden Orb (IRE)	7 10	IRE
108	I'm Supposin (IRE)	7 10	IRE
108	Jural (GB)	7 10	GB
107	Tzar Rodney (FR)	7 10	FR
107	Daraydala (IRE)	7 9	FR
107	Diaghilef (IRE)	7 9	GB
107	El Tenor (FR)	7 9	FR
107	Inquisitor (GB)	7 9	GB
107	Lord of Appeal (GB)	7 9	FR
107	Tarhelm (IRE)	7 9	ITY
106	Asterita (GB)	7 8	GB
106	Copent Garden (IRE)	7 8	FR
106	Genoveta (USA)	7 8	FR
106	Ice And Glacial (IRE)	7 8	ITY
106	Juyush (USA)	7 8	GB
106	O'Connor (IRE)	7 8	GER
106	Oxford Line (IRE)	7 8	ITY
106	Secret Quest (GB)	7 8	FR
106	Ultra Finesse (USA)	7 8	FR
105	Damancher (GB)	7 7	IRE
105	Dreamer (USA)	7 7	GB
105	Enquiry (FR)	7 7	FR
105	Labibeh (USA)	7 7	GB
105	Maid of Honor (FR)	7 7	FR
105	Oxalagu (GB)	7 7	GER
105	Powder Bowl (USA)	7 7	FR
105	Seattle John (USA)	7 7	ITY

9½f plus

126	Thunder Gulch (USA)	9 0	USA
125	Pentire (GB)	8 13	GB
125	Timber Country (USA)	8 13	USA
124	Spectrum (IRE)	8 12	GB
123	Timarida (IRE)	8 11	IRE
122	Singspiel (IRE)	8 10	GB
121	Tejano Run (USA)	8 9	USA
121	Valanour (FR)	8 9	FR
120	Definite Article (GB)	8 8	IRE
120	Eltish (USA)	8 8	GB
120	Flemensfirth (USA)	8 8	GB
120	Golden Bri (USA)	8 8	USA
120	Jumron (GB)	8 8	USA
120	Riyadian (GB)	8 8	GB
119	Annus Mirabilis (FR)	8 7	GB
119	Diamond Mix (IRE)	8 7	FR
119	Mecke (USA)	8 7	USA
119	Montjoy (USA)	8 7	GB
118	Shemaran (IRE)	8 6	IRE/USA
118	Slicious (GB)	8 6	ITY
117	Angel In My Heart (FR)	8 5	FR
117	Carling (FR)	8 5	FR
117	Fahal (USA)	8 5	GB
117	Matiara (USA)	8 5	FR
117	Oliver's Twist (USA)	8 5	USA
116	Diplomatic Jet (USA)	8 4	USA
116	Pineing Patty (USA)	8 4	USA
116	Torrential (USA)	8 4	GB
116	Unanimous Vote (IRE)	8 4	USA
115	Balanka (IRE)	8 3	FR
115	Hawk Attack (USA)	8 3	USA
115	Larrocha (IRE)	8 3	GB
114	Caramba (GB)	8 2	GB
114	Green Means Go (USA)	8 2	USA
114	Muncie (IRE)	8 2	FR
114	Royal Solo (IRE)	8 2	GB
114	Tryphosa (IRE)	8 2	GER
113	Dancing Beggar (USA)	8 1	FR
113	Garden Rose (IRE)	8 1	FR
113	Gold And Steel (FR)	8 1	FR/USA
112	Humbol (USA)	8 0	IRE
112	Malthus (USA)	8 0	USA

112	Pretty Discreet (USA)	8 0	USA
112	Vaguely Gay (USA)	8 0	FR
112	Warning Shadows (IRE)	8 0	GB
111	East of Heaven (Ire)	7 13	FR
111	Manzoni (GER)	7 13	GER
111	Regal Discovery (CAN)	7 13	CAN
111	Silent Warrior (IRE)	7 13	FR
111	Sonic Boy (GB)	7 13	GB
110	In Character (GB)	7 12	USA
110	Scott's Scoundrel (USA)	7 12	USA
110	Solar One (FR)	7 12	FR
110	Take Liberties (GB)	7 12	FR
110	Tamise (USA)	7 12	FR
110	Tillandsia (IRE)	7 12	GB
109	Angel Falls (FR)	7 11	FR
109	Ela-Aristokrati (IRE)	7 11	GB
109	Marie de Ken (FR)	7 11	FR
109	Pourquoi Pas (IRE)	7 11	ITY
109	Senneville (USA)	7 11	FR
109	Sharpest Image (IRE)	7 11	FR/USA
109	Spout (GB)	7 11	GB
108	Beau Temps (GB)	7 10	FR/USA
108	Olimpia Dukakis (ITY)	7 10	ITY
108	Philanthrop (FR)	7 10	FR
107	Madrileno (IRE)	7 9	SPA
107	Restiv Star (FR)	7 9	FR
106	Irish Wings (IRE)	7 8	FR
106	Marble Falls (IRE)	7 8	FR
106	Poppy Carew (IRE)	7 8	GB
106	Secret Quest (GB)	7 8	FR
106	Subya (GB)	7 8	GB
106	Suivez La (USA)	7 8	GB
106	Western Reel (USA)	7 8	GB
105	Dahik (GB)	7 7	GB
105	Denver County (GER)	7 7	FR
105	Hasainiya (IRE)	7 7	IRE
105	Loretta Gianni (FR)	7 7	FR
105	Parfait Glace (FR)	7 7	FR
105	Tiger Roi (IRE)	7 7	GER
105	Traikey (IRE)	7 7	GB
105	Viaticum (IRE)	7 7	IRE

7f plus

129	Bahri (USA)	9 3	GB
126	Ridgewood Pearl (GB)	9 0	IRE
126	Serena's Song (USA)	9 0	USA
125	Pennekamp (USA)	8 13	FR
124	Celtic Swing (GB)	8 12	GB
124	Perfect Arc (USA)	8 12	USA
122	Peaks And Valleys (USA)	8 10	USA/CAN
122	Urbane (USA)	8 10	USA
121	Larry The Legend (USA)	8 9	USA
121	Miss Satamixa ((FR)	8 9	FR
120	Afternoon Deelites (USA)	8 8	USA
120	Gal In A Rucktus (CAN)	8 8	USA
120	Shaanxi (USA)	8 8	FR
119	Cat's Cradle (USA)	8 7	USA
119	Labeeb (GB)	8 7	FR/USA
119	Pyramid Peak (USA)	8 7	USA
118	Country Cat (USA)	8 6	USA
118	Harayir (USA)	8 6	GB
118	Helmsman (USA)	8 6	GB/USA
117	Adjareli (IRE)	8 5	IRE
117	Charnwood Forest (IRE)	8 5	GB
117	Smolensk (USA)	8 5	FR
117	Vettori (IRE)	8 5	GB
116	Atticus (USA)	8 4	FR
116	Bail Out Becky (USA)	8 4	USA
116	Miss Union Avenue (USA)	8 4	USA
116	Pipe Major (IRE)	8 4	GB
116	Poplar Bluff (GB)	8 4	FR
116	Suave Prospect (USA)	8 4	USA
116	Talkin Man (CAN)	8 4	CAN/USA
116	Tamayaz (CAN)	8 4	GB
116	Torrential (USA)	8 4	GB
115	Aqaarid (USA)	8 3	GB
115	Auriette (IRE)	8 3	USA
115	Hoolie (USA)	8 3	USA
115	Kathie's Colleen (CAN)	8 3	USA
115	Sleep Easy (USA)	8 3	USA
114	Bobinski (GB)	8 2	GB
114	Conquistadoress (USA)	8 2	USA
114	Fandarel Dancer (USA)	8 2	USA
114	Nwaamis (USA)	8 2	GB
114	Western Larla (USA)	8 2	USA

113	Bashaayeash (IRE)	8	1	FR	111	Rose Law Firm (USA)	7	13	USA
113	Class Kris (USA)	8	1	USA	111	Sneaky Quiet (USA)	7	13	USA
113	Composer (USA)	8	1	USA	111	Vadiamixa (FR)	7	13	FR
113	Da Hoss (USA)	8	1	USA	111	Virginia Carnival (USA)	7	13	USA
113	Dazzling Falls (USA)	8	1	USA	110	Arabride (GB)	7	12	GB
113	Didina (GB)	8	1	GB/USA	110	Bene Erit (USA)	7	12	FR
113	Diffident (FR)	8	1	FR	110	Chato (USA)	7	12	GER
113	French Deputy (USA)	8	1	USA	110	Cuzzin Jeb (USA)	7	12	USA
113	Lily Capote (USA)	8	1	USA	110	Dowty (USA)	7	12	USA
113	Painter's Row (IRE)	8	1	GB	110	Favored One (USA)	7	12	USA
113	Petionville (USA)	8	1	USA	110	Forested (USA)	7	12	USA
113	Prince Arthur (IRE)	8	1	GB	110	Gentleman Beau (CAN)	7	12	USA
113	Sea Emperor (USA)	8	1	USA	110	Sergeyev (IRE)	7	12	GB
113	Shahid (GB)	8	1	GB	110	Tabor (USA)	7	12	FR/USA
112	A Magicman ((FR)	8	0	GER	109	Hoh Magic (GB)	7	11	GB
112	Bishop of Cashel (GB)	8	0	GB	109	Khaytada (IRE)	7	11	IRE
112	Blu Tusmani (USA)	8	0	USA	109	Kill The Crab (IRE)	7	11	NOR
112	Cap Juluca (IRE)	8	0	GB	109	Nautical Pet (IRE)	7	11	IRE
112	Claudius (USA)	8	0	USA	109	Peace Envoy (GB)	7	11	GB
112	Debonair Dan (USA)	8	0	USA	109	Red Carnival (USA)	7	11	GB
112	Gay Gallanta (USA)	8	0	GB	108	Almaz (SU)	7	10	SLOV
112	Honky Tonk Tune (CAN)	8	0	CAN	108	Coco Passion (FR)	7	10	FR
112	Inzar (USA)	8	0	GB	108	Epagris (GB)	7	10	GB
112	Leeds (IRE)	8	0	FR	108	Ladoni (GB)	7	10	GER
112	Minister Wife ((USA)	8	0	USA	108	Suresnes (USA)	7	10	FR
112	Munwar (GB)	8	0	GB	107	Anabaa (USA)	7	9	FR
112	Petit Poucet (GB)	8	0	FR	107	Easy Dollar (GB)	7	9	GB
112	Post It (USA)	8	0	USA	107	Fairy Path (USA)	7	9	FR
112	Top Ruhl (USA)	8	0	USA	107	First Island (IRE)	7	9	GB
112	Treasurer (GB)	8	0	USA	107	Ghostly (IRE)	7	9	FR
112	Via Lombardia (IRE)	8	0	USA	107	Kalatos (GER)	7	9	GER
112	Wild Syn (USA)	8	0	USA	107	Lyphard's Honor (FR)	7	9	FR
111	Christmas Gift (USA)	7	13	USA	107	Off n'away (IRE)	7	9	IRE
111	Dirca (IRE)	7	13	FR/USA	107	Prince of India (GB)	7	9	GB
111	Doc's Dilemma (USA)	7	13	USA	107	Tristano (GB)	7	9	GER
111	Flying Chevron (USA)	7	13	USA	107	Two O'Clock Jump (IRE)	7	9	GB
111	Jewel Princess (USA)	7	13	USA	107	Val d'Arbois (FR)	7	9	SPA
111	Kiridashi (CAN)	7	13	CAN	106	Alami (USA)	7	8	GB
111	Lake George (USA)	7	13	USA	106	Brief Glimpse (IRE)	7	8	GB
111	Mia's Hope (USA)	7	13	USA	106	Collecta (FR)	7	8	FR
111	Mr Purple (USA)	7	13	USA	106	Devil River Peek (USA)	7	8	GER
111	Myself (GB)	7	13	GB	106	Hexane (FR)	7	8	FR
111	Pat n Jac (USA)	7	13	USA	106	Kirdoun (FR)	7	8	FR

106	Lovely Millie (IRE)	7 8	GB
106	Mediation (IRE)	7 8	IRE
106	Restructure (IRE)	7 8	GB
106	Silca Blanka (IRE)	7 8	GB
106	Tiroling (IRE)	7 8	FR
105	Chequer (USA)	7 7	FR
105	Decorated Hero (GB)	7 7	GB
105	Palafairia (FR)	7 7	FR
105	Pinfloron (FR)	7 7	FR
105	Romanzof (GB)	7 7	GB
105	Shannjar (FR)	7 7	FR
105	Tibersen (FR)	7 7	FR

5f plus

121	Serena's Song (USA)	8 9	USA
120	Desert Style (IRE)	8 8	IRE
119	Mind Games (GB)	8 7	GB
119	Mr Greeley (USA)	8 7	USA
116	Chaposa Springs (USA)	8 4	USA
114	Fr Stockton (USA)	8 2	USA
114	Lord Carson (USA)	8 2	USA
114	Scotzanna (CAN)	8 2	CAN
113	Chilly Billy (GB)	8 1	GBUSA
113	Struggler (GB)	8 1	FR
112	Dixieland Gold (USA)	8 0	USA
112	Easy Option (IRE)	8 0	GB
112	Lucky Lavender Gal (USA)	8 0	USA

112	Top Account (USA)	8 0	USA
111	Broad Smile (USA)	7 13	USA
111	Burden of Proof (IRE)	7 13	IRE
111	Call Now (USA)	7 13	USA
111	Tereshkova (USA)	7 13	FR
111	Tethra (CAN)	7 13	CAN
111	Valid Wager (USA)	7 13	USA
110	Cat Appeal (USA)	7 12	USA
110	Devious Course (USA)	7 12	USA
110	Fard (IRE)	7 12	GB
110	Macoumba (USA)	7 12	FR
110	Millstream (USA)	7 12	GB
110	Wild Bluebell (IRE)	7 12	IRE
109	Art of War (GB)	7 11	GB
109	Hoh Magic (GB)	7 11	GB
109	Nautical Pet (IRE)	7 11	IRE
109	Petite Fantasy (GB)	7 11	IRE
108	Linoise (FR)	7 10	FR
108	Macanal (USA)	7 10	GER
107	Easy Dollar (GB)	7 9	GB
107	Raah Alghard (USA)	7 9	GB
106	Mediation (IRE)	7 8	IRE
106	Nuriva (USA)	7 8	GB
105	Cheyenne Spirit (GB)	7 7	GB
105	Sharp Point (IRE)	7 7	IRE

INTERNATIONAL CLASSIFICATION

For four-year-olds and upward which, during 1995 have run or been trained in Europe or North America, and have in their respective races been assessed jointly by international classification committee handicappers and North American rating committee racing officials at a rating of 105 (7st 7lb) or above. In the case of North American horses, the minimum rating is 110.

1¾m plus

120	Strategic Choice (USA)	4	8	8	USA
119	Double Trigger (IRE)	4	87		GB
119	Moonax (IRE)	4	8	7	GB
119	Vintage Crop (IRE)	8	8	7	IRE
118	Red Bishop (USA)	7	8	6	UAE/GB
114	Always Earnest (USA)	7	8	2	FR
112	Shrewd Idea (GB)	5	8	0	SPA/FR
111	Nononito (FR)	4	7	13	FR
110	Further Flight (GB)	9	7	12	GB
110	The Little Thief (FR)	4	7	12	FR
109	Khamaseen (GB)	4	7	11	GB
109	Parthian Springs (GB)	4	7	11	GB
109	Sunrise Song (FR)	4	7	11	FR
108	Admiral's Well (IRE)	5	7	10	GB
108	Assessor (IRE)	6	7	10	GB
108	Bold Gait (GB)	4	7	10	GB
108	Capias (USA)	4	7	10	GB
108	Double On (IRE)	4	7	10	IRE
107	Mohaajir (IRE)	4	7	9	IRE
106	Cuff Link (IRE)	5	7	8	GB
106	Epaphos (GER)	5	7	8	FR
106	Saxon Maid (GB)	4	7	8	GB
105	Lac Ladoga (GB)	4	7	7	FR
105	Noble Rose (IRE)	4	7	7	GB

1m 3f plus

129	Northern Spur (IRE)	4	9	3	USA
128	Freedom Cry (GB)	4	9	2	FR
126	Carnegie (IRE)	4	9	0	FR
125	Lando (GER)	5	8	13	GER
121	Germany (USA)	4	8	9	GER
121	Hernando (FR)	5	8	9	FR
121	Millkom (GB)	4	8	9	FR

121	Sandpit (BRZ)	6	8	9	USA
121	Strategic Choice (USA)	4	8	9	GB
120	Broadway Flyer (USA)	4	8	8	GB
120	Lassigny (USA)	4	8	8	USA
120	Sunshack (GB)	4	8	8	FR
119	Monsun (GER)	5	8	7	GER
118	Alderbrook (GB)	6	8	6	GB
118	Red Bishop (USA)	7	8	6	UAE/GB
118	Special Prince (USA)	6	8	6	USA
117	Kaldounevees (FR)	4	8	5	FR
117	Laroche (GER)	4	8	5	GER
117	Partipral (USA)	6	8	5	FR
117	Time Star (USA)	4	8	6	GB
116	Beauchamp Hero (GB)	5	8	4	GB
116	Boyce (USA)	4	8	4	USA
116	Exchange (CAN)	7	8	4	USA
116	Hasten To Add (USA)	5	8	4	CAN/USA
116	Interim (GB)	4	8	4	USA
116	Only Royale (IRE)	6	8	4	GB
116	Signal Tap (USA)	4	8	4	USA
116	Turk Passer (USA)	5	8	4	USA
115	Flag Down (CAN)	5	8	3	USA
115	Gunboat Diplomacy (FR)	4	8	3	FR
115	Misil (USA)	7	8	3	USA
115	Tikkanen (USA)	4	8	3	FR/USA
115	Tuesday's Special (USA)	5	8	3	FR/USA
114	Balanchine (USA)	4	8	2	GB
114	Magical Retreat (USA)	5	8	2	GB
114	Midnight Legend (GB)	4	8	2	GB
114	Richard of York (GB)	5	8	2	FR/GB
114	River Rhythm (USA)	8	8	2	USA
114	Sternkoenig (IRE)	5	8	2	GER
114	Talloires (USA)	5	8	2	USA
113	Square Cut (USA)	6	8	1	USA

113	Tot Ou Tard (IRE)	5	8	1	FR
112	Chelsey Flower (USA)	4	8	0	USA
112	Environment Friend (GB)	7	8	0	GB
112	Jet Freighter (USA)	4	8	0	CAN
112	Kiri's Clown (USA)	6	8	0	USA
112	Kornado (GB)	5	8	0	GER
112	Lindon Lime (USA)	5	8	0	USA
112	Linney Head (USA)	4	8	0	GB
112	Solid Illusion (USA)	4	8	0	FR
112	Wind In Her Hair (IRE)	4	8	0	GB
112	Yenda (GB)	4	8	0	USA
112	Zilzal Zamaan (USA)	4	8	0	GB
111	Caromana (USA)	4	7	13	USA
111	Liyoun (IRE)	7	7	13	USA
111	Protektor (GER)	6	7	13	GER
111	Right Win (IRE)	5	7	13	GB
111	Shambo (GB)	8	7	13	GB
111	Star of Manila (USA)	4	7	13	USA
110	Alywow (CAN)	4	7	12	CAN
110	Burooj (GB)	5	7	12	GB
110	Caballo (GER)	4	7	12	GER
110	King's Theatre (IRE)	4	7	12	USA
110	Royal Ballerina (IRE)	5	7	12	IRE
110	Suave Tern (USA)	4	7	12	FR
109	Ionio (USA)	4	7	11	GB
109	Matarun (IRE)	7	7	11	FR
109	Sand Reef (GB)	4	7	11	FR
109	Sunrise Song (FR)	4	7	11	FR
108	Capias (USA)	4	7	10	GB
108	Rainbow Dancer (FR)	4	7	10	FR
108	Sacrament (GB)	4	7	10	GB
107	Ballykett Nancy (IRE)	4	7	9	IRE
107	Blush Rambler ((USA)	5	7	9	GB
107	Danseur Landais (GB)	4	7	9	FR
107	Guado d'Annibale (IRE)	6	7	9	ITY
107	Sadler's Image (IRE)	4	7	9	GB
107	Scribano (GB)	5	7	9	ITY
106	Bal Harbour (GB)	4	7	8	GB
106	Fanion de Fete (FR)	4	7	8	FR
106	Mack The Knife (GB)	6	7	8	GB
106	Saxon Maid (GB)	4	7	8	GB
106	Taufan's Melody (GB)	4	7	8	GB
105	Escarpment (USA)	4	7	7	GB

105	L'Ile Tudy (IRE)	5	7	7	FR
105	Noble Rose (IRE)	4	7	7	GB
105	Parme (USA)	4	7	7	FR
105	Pay Me Back (IRE)	5	7	7	ITY
105	River North (IRE)	5	7	7	GB

9½f plus

132	Cigar (USA)	5	9	6	USA
128	Halling (USA)	4	9	2	UAE/GB
128	Heavenly Prize (USA)	4	9	2	USA
125	L'Carriere (USA)	4	8	13	USA
123	Muhtarram (USA)	6	8	11	GB
123	Unaccounted For (USA)	4	8	11	USA
122	Awad (USA)	5	8	10	USA
122	Soul of The Matter (USA)	4	8	10	USA
121	Pelder (IRE)	5	8	9	GB
121	Tinners Way (USA)	5	8	9	USA
120	Best Pal (USA)	7	8	8	USA
120	Devil His Due (USA)	6	8	8	USA
119	Dramatic Gold (USA)	4	8	7	USA
119	Duda (USA)	4	8	7	USA
119	The Vid (USA)	5	8	7	USA
118	Alice Springs (USA)	5	8	6	USA
118	Alpride (IRE)	4	8	6	USA
118	Bold Ruritana (CAN)	5	8	6	CAN
118	Flagbird (USA)	4	8	6	UAE/USA
118	Needle Gun (IRE)	5	8	6	GB
118	Red Bishop (USA)	7	8	6	UAE/GB
117	Danish (IRE)	4	8	5	USA
117	Kaldounevees (FR)	4	8	5	FR
116	Dare And Go (USA)	4	8	4	USA
116	Marildo (FR)	8	8	4	FR
116	Market Booster (USA)	6	8	4	USA
116	Northern Emerald (USA)	5	8	4	USA
116	Royal Chariot (USA)	5	8	4	USA
116	Wandesta (GB)	4	8	4	USA
115	Celtic Arms (FR)	4	8	3	USA
115	Desert Shot (GB)	5	8	3	GB
115	Just Happy (USA)	4	8	3	GB
115	La Confederation (GB)	4	8	3	GB
115	Windsharp (USA)	4	8	3	FR/USA
114	Blues Traveller (IRE)	5	8	2	USA
114	Morgana (USA)	4	8	2	USA

114	Plenty of Sugar (CAN)	4	8	2	USA
114	Richard of York (GB)	5	8	2	FR/GB
114	Romy (USA)	4	8	2	USA
114	Triarius (USA)	5	8	2	GB/UAE
114	Urgent Request (IRE)	5	8	2	USA
113	Alriffa (GB)	4	8	1	GB
113	Earl of Barking (IRE)	5	8	1	USA
113	Hushang (IRE)	5	8	1	IRE
113	Key Contender (USA)	7	8	1	USA
113	Memories (IRE)	4	8	1	USA
113	Prince of Andros (USA)	5	8	1	GB
113	Real Connection (USA)	4	8	1	USA
113	Slew of Damascus (USA)	7	8	1	USA
113	Young Buster (IRE)	7	8	1	GB
112	Basquelian (CAN)	4	8	0	CAN
112	Concepcion (GER)	5	8	0	GER
112	Environment Friend (GB)	7	8	0	GB
112	Hollywood Dream (GER)	4	8	0	GER
112	Snake Eyes (USA)	5	8	0	USA
112	Truly A Dream (IRE)	4	8	0	FR
112	Volochine (IRE)	4	8	0	FR
111	Agathe (USA)	4	7	13	FR
111	Hondero (GER)	5	7	13	GER
111	Revere (IRE)	5	7	13	GB
111	Yearly Tour (USA)	4	7	13	USA
110	Al Mohaajir (USA)	4	7	12	IRE
110	Allez Les Trois (USA)	4	7	12	FR/USA
110	Baron Ferdinand (GB)	5	7	12	GB
110	Captain Horatius (IRE)	6	7	12	GB
110	Dancing Sunset (IRE)	4	7	12	IRE
110	Erin Bird (FR)	4	7	12	GB/FR
110	Manilaman (USA)	4	7	12	USA
110	Sylvan Point (GB)	4	7	12	GER
109	Firing Line (IRE)	6	7	11	ITY
109	Ionio (USA)	4	7	11	GB
109	Ivory Frontier (IRE)	5	7	11	IRE
109	Matarun (IRE)	7	7	11	FR
109	Sand Reef (GB)	4	7	11	FR
109	Wayne County (IRE)	5	7	11	USA
108	Dance Turn (GB)	4	7	10	GB
108	Del Deya (IRE)	5	7	10	GB
107	Florid (USA)	4	7	9	GB
107	Guado d'Annibale (IRE)	6	7	9	ITY
107	Lear White (USA)	4	7	9	ITY
107	Solidoun (FR)	4	7	9	FR
106	Dernier Empereur (USA)	5	7	8	FR
106	Upper Heights (GER)	7	7	8	GER
105	Akhiyar (IRE)	4	7	7	IRE
105	Brier Creek (USA)	6	7	7	GB
105	Magic Feeling (IRE)	5	7	7	IRE
105	Salt Lake (GB)	4	7	7	GB

7f plus

132	Cigar (USA)	5	9	6	USA
129	Inside Information (USA)	4	9	3	USA
126	Silver Goblin (USA)	4	9	0	USA
125	Fastness (IRE)	5	8	13	USA
124	Concern (USA)	4	8	12	USA
124	Possibly Perfect (USA)	5	8	12	USA
122	Green Tune (USA)	4	8	10	FR
122	Missed Flight (GB)	5	8	10	GB
121	Mariah's Storm (USA)	4	8	9	USA
121	Pelder (IRE)	5	8	9	GB
121	Romarin (BRZ)	5	8	9	USA
120	Queens Court Queen (USA)	6	8	8	USA
120	Sayyedati (GB)	5	8	8	GB
120	Soviet Line (IRE)	5	8	8	USA
119	Educated Risk (USA)	5	8	7	USA
119	Irish Linnet (USA)	7	8	7	USA
119	Paseana (ARG)	8	8	7	USA
118	Cherokee Rose (IRE)	4	8	6	FR
118	Dove Hunt (USA)	4	8	6	USA
118	Lakeway (USA)	4	8	6	USA
118	Pirate's Revenge (USA)	4	8	6	USA
118	Schossberg (CAN)	5	8	6	CAN
118	Unfinished Symph (USA)	4	8	6	USA
117	Borodislew (USA)	5	8	5	USA
117	Halo America (USA)	4	8	5	USA
117	Jade Flush (USA)	4	8	5	USA
116	Caress (USA)	4	8	4	USA
116	Cox Orange (USA)	5	8	4	USA
116	Darnay (GB)	4	8	4	GB
116	Marildo (FR)	8	8	4	FR
116	Onceinabluemamoon (USA)	4	8	4	USA
116	Silver Wizard (USA)	5	8	4	USA

116	Tossofthecoin (USA)	5	8	4	USA	112	Royal Abjar (USA)	4	8	0	GER
115	Bin Ajwaad (IRE)	5	8	3	GB	112	Thames (FR)	4	8	0	FR
115	Del Mar Dennis (USA)	5	8	3	USA	112	Top Rung (USA)	4	8	0	USA
115	Nec Plus Ultra (FR)	4	8	3	FR	111	Corrazona (USA)	5	7	13	USA
115	Weekend Madness (IRE)	5	8	3	USA	111	Fly Cry (USA)	4	7	13	USA
115	Wekiva Springs (USA)	4	8	3	USA	111	Golden Klair (GB)	5	7	13	USA
114	Avie's Fancy (USA)	4	8	2	USA	111	Holly Regent (CAN)	4	7	13	CAN
114	Blumin Affair (USA)	4	8	2	USA	111	Klassy Kim (USA)	4	7	13	USA
114	Fit To Leed (USA)	5	8	2	USA	111	Laura's Pistolette (USA)	4	7	13	USA
114	Fourstars Allstar (USA)	7	8	2	USA	111	Les Boyer (GB)	4	7	13	ITY
114	Heart Lake (GB)	4	8	2	UAE/GB	111	Little Buckles (CAN)	4	7	13	USA
114	Judge T C (USA)	4	8	2	USA	111	Marvin's Faith (IRE)	4	7	13	USA
114	Megan's Interco (USA)	6	8	2	USA	111	Mistle Cat (USA)	5	7	13	GB
114	Mighty Forum (GB)	4	8	2	USA	111	Pride of Summer (USA)	7	7	13	USA
114	Morgana (USA)	4	8	2	USA	111	Rapan Boy (AUS)	7	7	13	USA
114	Poor But Honest (USA)	5	8	2	USA	111	Ravier (ITY)	4	7	13	ITY
114	Private Persuassion (USA)	4	8	2	USA	111	Realities (USA)	5	7	13	GB
114	River Flyer (USA)	4	8	2	USA	111	Twice The Vice (USA)	4	7	13	USA
114	Savinio (USA)	5	8	2	USA	110	Al Mohaajir (USA)	4	7	12	IRE
114	Ventiquattrofogli (IRE)	5	8	2	USA	110	Calipha (USA)	4	7	12	USA
114	Wizard King (GB)	4	8	2	GB	110	Erin Bird (FR)	4	7	12	FR
114	Work The Crowd (USA)	4	8	2	USA	110	Idris (IRE)	5	7	12	IRE
113	Aube Indienne (FR)	5	8	1	USA	110	Journalism (USA)	7	7	12	USA
113	Branston Abby (IRE)	6	8	1	GB	110	Lyin To The Moon (USA)	6	7	12	USA
113	Cinnamon Sugar (IRE)	4	8	1	USA	110	Lykatill Hil (USA)	5	7	12	USA
113	Dumaani (USA)	4	8	1	UAE/USA	110	Millyant (GB)	5	7	12	GB
113	Mr Martini (IRE)	5	8	1	GB	110	Morigi (GB)	4	7	12	ITY
113	Mysteriously (CAN)	4	8	1	CAN	110	Symphony Lady (USA)	5	7	12	USA
113	Neverneyev (USA)	5	8	1	FR	110	Tarzans Blade (USA)	4	7	12	USA
113	Nicolotte (GB)	4	8	1	GB	110	Words of War (USA)	6	7	12	USA
113	Recoup The Cash (USA)	5	8	1	USA	109	Fraam (GB)	6	7	11	GB
113	Vaudeville (USA)	4	8	1	USA	109	Nijo (GB)	4	7	11	GB
112	Alphabet Soup (USA)	4	8	0	USA	108	Dance Turn (GB)	4	7	10	GB
112	Debutant Trick (USA)	5	8	0	USA	108	Imprevedible (IRE)	5	7	10	ITY
112	Emperor Jones (USA)	5	8	0	UAE/GB	108	Signoretto (FR)	8	7	10	FR/USA
112	Golden Larch (USA)	4	8	0	USA	107	Green Green Desert (FR)	4	7	9	GB
112	Holy Mountain (USA)	4	8	0	USA	107	Lake Storm (IRE)	4	7	9	ITY
112	Lady Affirmed (USA)	4	8	0	USA	107	Lap of Luxury (GB)	6	7	9	GB
112	Mutakdimm (USA)	4	8	0	GB	107	Lear White(USA)	4	7	9	ITY
112	Overbury (IRE)	4	8	0	GB	107	Tres Heureux (GER)	5	7	9	GER
112	Pennyhill Park (CAN)	5	8	0	CAN	107	Welsh Liberty (IRE)	6	7	9	ITY
112	Powerful Punch (USA)	6	8	0	USA	106	Penny Drops (GB)	6	7	8	GB
112	Ridgewood Ben (GB)	4	8	0	IRE	106	Pollen Count (USA)	6	7	8	GB

106	The Puzzler (IRE)	4	7 8	IRE
105	Akhiyar (IRE)	4	7 7	IRE
105	Celestial Key (USA)	5	7 7	GB
105	Foxhound (USA)	4	7 7	UAE/GB
105	Munaaji (USA)	4	7 7	GER
105	Port Lucaya (GB)	5	7 7	GB

5f plus

127	Holy Bull (USA)	4	9 1	USA
127	Lake Coniston (IRE)	4	9 1	GB
122	Cherokee Run (USA)	5	8 10	USA
122	Sky Beauty (USA)	5	8 10	USA
121	Piccolo (GB)	4	8 9	GB
120	Not Surprising (USA)	5	8 8	USA
119	Hever Golf Rose (GB)	4	8 7	GB
119	Our Emblem (USA)	4	8 7	USA
119	You And I (USA)	4	8 7	USA
119	Young Ern (GB)	5	8 7	GB
118	Cherokee Rose (IRE)	4	8 6	FR
118	Lite The Fuse (USA)	4	8 6	USA
117	Desert Stormer (USA)	5	8 5	USA
117	Golden Gear (USA)	4	8 5	USA
117	So Factual (USA)	5	8 5	GB
116	Classy Mirage (USA)	5	8 4	USA
116	Lit de Justice (USA)	5	8 4	USA
115	Friendly Lover (USA)	7	8 3	USA
115	Hollywood Wildcat (USA)	5	8 3	USA
115	Soviet Problem (USA)	5	8 3	USA
115	Twist Afleet (USA)	4	8 3	USA
114	Birdonthewire (USA)	6	8 2	USA
114	Chimes Band (USA)	4	8 2	USA
114	Itaka (USA)	5	8 2	USA
114	Lucky Forever (USA)	6	8 2	USA
114	Owington (GB)	4	8 2	GB
113	Branston Abby (IRE)	6	8 1	GB
113	Cool Jazz (GB)	4	8 1	GB
113	Golden Tent (USA)	6	8 1	USA

113	Dumaani (USA)	4	8 1	UAE/USA
113	Track Gal (USA)	4	8 1	USA
113	Wessam Prince (GB)	4	8 1	FR
113	Ya Malak (GB)	4	8 1	GB
112	Cardmania (USA)	9	8 0	USA
112	Cool Air (CAN)	5	8 0	USA
112	d'Hallevant (USA)	5	8 0	USA
112	Eveningperformance (GB)	4	8 0	GB
112	Key Phrase (USA)	4	8 0	USA
112	Siphon (BRZ)	4	8 0	USA
111	Angi Go (USA)	5	7 13	USA
111	Beat of Drums (GB)	4	7 13	ITY
111	Crafty Dude (USA)	6	7 13	USA
111	Honor The Hero (USA)	7	7 13	USA
111	Marina Park (GB)	5	7 13	USA
111	Recognizable (USA)	4	7 13	USA
111	Who Wouldn't (USA)	6	7 13	USA
110	Concept Win (USA)	5	7 12	USA
110	Finder's Fortune (USA)	6	7 12	USA
110	King Ruckus (CAN)	5	7 12	CAN
110	Lavinia Fontana (IROE)	6	7 12	GB
110	Low Key Affair (USA)	4	7 12	USA
110	Millyant (GB)	5	7 12	GB
110	Spain Lane (USA)	4	7 12	FR
108	Glenlivet (SWE)	7	7 10	SWE
108	Hard To Figure (GB)	9	7 10	GB
108	Imprevedible (IRE)	5	7 10	ITY
108	Montendre (GB)	8	7 10	GB
107	Bunty Boo (GB)	6	7 9	GB
107	Carranita (IRE)	5	7 9	GB
107	Sharp Prod (USA)	5	7 9	USA
107	Venture Capitalist (GB)	6	7 9	GB
107	West Man (USA)	4	7 9	FR
106	The Puzzler (IRE)	4	7 8	IRE
106	Tourandot (IRE)	4	7 8	IRE
106	Way West (FR)	5	7 8	FR
105	Blue Siren (GB)	4	7 7	GB
105	El Yasaf (IRE)	7	7 7	GB
105	Mistertopogigo (IRE)	5	7 7	GB

HIGH-PRICED YEARLINGS OF 1995 AT TATTERSALLS' SALES

The following yearlings realised 50,000 guineas and over at Tattersalls' Sales in 1995:-

Name and Breeding	Vendor	Purchaser	Gns
B.c. Sadler's Wells (USA) — Exclusive Order (USA)	Cheveley Park Stud.	Mr D. O'Byrne	600,000
B.c. Rainbow Quest (USA) — Nearctic Flame.	Cheveley Park Stud.	Gainsborough Stud Mgt.	600,000
Br.c. Caerleon (USA) — Flood (USA)	Mount Coote Stud, Ireland.	Darley Stud Mgt.	550,000
B.c. Sadler's Wells (USA) — Radiant (USA).	Camas Park Stud, Ireland.	Darley Stud Mgt.	550,000
B.c. Lear Fan (USA) — Connecting Link (USA)	Ted Voute, Agent.	Darley Stud Mgt.	500,000
B.c. Miswaki (USA) — Bold Jessie	Cotswold Stud.	Addison Racing Ltd	350,000
B.f. Sadler's Wells (USA) — Milli Princess.	Camas Park Stud, Ireland.	Mr Olin Gentry	340,000
Ch.f. Woodman (USA) — Catopetl (USA).	Camas Park Stud, Ireland.	Darley Stud Mgt.	300,000
B.c. Sadler's Wells (USA) — Maria Waleska	Lanwades & Staffordstown Studs	Darley Stud Mgt.	290,000
B.c. Groom Dancer (USA) — Sonoma (FR)	Haras d'Etreham, France.	Brian Grassick B/S.	290,000
B.c. Rainbow Quest (USA) — Dance By Night.	Woodcote Stud.	Darley Stud Mgt.	250,000
B.f. Sadler's Wells (USA) — Organza.	Corbally Stud, Ireland.	Darley Stud Mgt.	240,000
One So Wonderful B.f. Nashwan (USA) — Someone Special.	Meon Valley Stud.	Mr Guy Armengol.	240,000
Strawberry Roan (IRE) B.f. Sadler's Wells (USA) — Doff The Derby (USA)	Barronstown Stud, Ireland.	Mr D. O'Byrne	240,000
Intellectuelle B.f. Caerleon (USA) — Sarah Georgina	Woodcote Stud.	Horse France.	220,000
B.c. Sadler's Wells (USA) — Colorspin (FR)	Meon Valley Stud.	Darley Stud Mgt.	210,000
B.c. El Gran Senor (USA) — Mystical River (USA).	Ashton House Stud, Ireland.	Darley Stud Mgt.	210,000
Summer Dance B.f. Sadler's Wells (USA) — Hyabella (GB)	Meon Valley Stud.	Cheveley Park Stud.	205,000
Ch.c. Royal Academy (USA) — Final Farewell (USA).	Camas Park Stud, Ireland.	Addison Racing Ltd	200,000
B.c. Woodman (USA) — Opera Queen (IRE)	Camas Park Stud, Ireland.	Addison Racing Ltd	200,000
B.f. Riverman (USA) — Trolley Song (USA)	Partridge Close Stud.	Darley Stud Mgt.	200,000
B.f. Rainbow Quest (USA) — Hatton Gardens	Crimbourne Stud.	C. Gordon-Watson B/S.	190,000
Purchasing Power (IRE) B.c. Danehill (USA) — Purchasepaperchase.	Cotswold Stud.	Mr D. O'Byrne	190,000
Moving On Up B.c. Salse (USA) — Thundercloud	Whitsbury Manor Stud.	Mr D. K. Weld	185,000
Dead Aim (IRE) B.c. Sadler's Wells (USA) — Dead Certain.	Crichel Stud.	Mr Gordon Smyth.	180,000
B.f. Sadler's Wells (USA) — Possessive	Genesis Green Stud	Darley Stud Mgt.	180,000
High Roller (IRE) B.c. Generous (IRE) — Helpless Haze (USA).	Camas Park Stud, Ireland.	Mr D. O'Byrne	175,000
B.c. Red Ransom (USA) — River Patrol (GB)	Trickledown Stud.	German Intl B/S.	170,000
Ch.c. Nureyev (USA) — Korveya (USA)	Ted Voute, Agent.	C. Gordon-Watson B/S	170,000
B.c. Rainbow Quest (USA) — Blessed Event	Cheveley Park Stud.	Mead, Goodbody Ltd	165,000
B.c. Sadler's Wells (USA) — Marie de Flandre (FR)	Cotswold Stud.	Mr D. O'Byrne	160,000

Yearling	Vendor	Buyer	Price
Hyde Park (IRE) B.c. Alzao (USA) — Park Elect.	Lodge Park Stud, Ireland.	Sir Mark Prescott.	155,000
B.f. St. Jovite (USA) — Azzurrina.	Mellon Stud, Ireland.	B.B.A. (UK) Ltd.	150,000
B.c. Sadler's Wells (USA) — Before Dawn (USA).	Camas Park Stud, Ireland.	Mr D. O'Byrne.	150,000
B.f. Sadler's Wells (USA) — High Spirited.	Airlie Stud, Ireland.	Mr D. O'Byrne.	150,000
B.f. Sadler's Wells (USA) — Nawara.	Barronstown Stud, Ireland.	Addison Racing Ltd.	145,000
B.c. Sadler's Wells (USA) — Diavolina (USA).	Marston Stud.	Mr D. O'Byrne.	140,000
Gersey Ch.f. Generous (IRE) — River Spey.	Hesmonds Stud.	Mr M. Stoute.	140,000
Guernica B.f. Unfuwain (USA) — Greenvera (USA).	Bloomsbury Stud.	German Intl. B/S.	140,000
B.c. Sadler's Wells (USA) — Millieme.	Ashtown House Stud, Ireland.	Mr John M. Weld.	140,000
Barrow Creek Ch.c. Cadeaux Genereux — Breadcrumb.	Overbury Stud.	German Intl. B/S.	135,000
Dancing Queen (IRE) B.f. Sadler's Wells (USA) — Bay Shade (USA).	Camas Park Stud, Ireland.	Lillingston B/S.	130,000
London Lights B.c. Slip Anchor — Pageantry.	Mount Coote Stud, Ireland.	Mrs A. Skiffington.	125,000
Fly To The Stars B.c. Bluebird (USA) — Rise and Fall.	Bishop's Down Farm.	C. Gordon-Watson B/S.	125,000
Ch.f. Rainbow Quest (USA) — Dreamawhile.	Hesmonds Stud.	Gainsborough Stud Mgt.	120,000
Wira (IRE) Ch.c. Lahib (USA) — Mother Courage.	Landscape Stud, Ireland.	Hugo Lascelles B/S.	110,000
Al Azhar B.c. Alzao (USA) — Upend.	Islanmore Stud, Ireland.	P.F.I. Cole Ltd.	110,000
Jayzan B.c. Selkirk (USA) — Land of Ivory (USA).	Whatton Manor Stud.	Mr Gordon Smyth.	100,000
Ch.c. Caerleon (USA) — Niamh Cinn Oir (IRE).	Cotswold Stud.	Newgate Stud Co.	100,000
B.c. Indian Ridge — Sarcita (GB).	Round Hill Stud, Ireland.	Darley Stud Mgt.	100,000
B.c. Fairy King (USA) — Sronica.	Catridge Farm Stud.	Darley Stud Mgt.	100,000
Jaza B.c. Pursuit of Love (GB) — Nordica.	Cooliney Stud Farm, Ireland.	Mr J. T. Doyle.	98,000
B.c. Sadler's Wells (USA) — Echo Cove (GB).	Overbury Stud.	Shadwell Estate Co.	95,000
B/Br.c. Petong — Petriece.	Glen Andred Stud.	Vendor.	94,000
Magdala (IRE) B.f. Sadler's Wells (USA) — Dalawara (IRE).	Ashtown House Stud, Ireland.	Mr A. O. Nerses.	92,000
B.c. Machiavellian (USA) — Mrs Moonlight (GB).	Bloomsbury Stud.	B.B.A. (UK) Ltd.	90,000
Sandstone (IRE) B.c. Green Desert (USA) — Rose de Thai (USA).	Camas Park Stud, Ireland.	John Ferguson B/S.	90,000
B.f. Green Desert (USA) — Royal Climber.	Marston Stud.	B.B.A. (Ireland) Ltd.	90,000
Puteri Wentworth B.f. Sadler's Wells (USA) — Sweeping.	Cotswold Stud.	C. Gordon-Watson B/S.	90,000
Prince Alex (IRE) B.c. Night Shift (USA) — Finalist.	Burton Agnes Stud.	B.B.A. (UK) Ltd.	89,000
B.c. Arazi (USA) — Shoot Clear.	Partridge Close Stud.	Darley Stud Mgt.	88,000
B.c. Kris — Fern (GB).	Ted Voute, Agent.	German Intl. B/S.	86,000
B.c. Red Ransom (USA) — Fan Mail (USA).	Mellon Stud, Ireland.	C.B.A. Ltd.	85,000
Ch.f. Mutahid (USA) — Rosie Potts.	Kirtlington Stud.	B.B.A. (UK) Ltd.	85,000
Slip The Net (IRE) B.c. Slip Anchor — Circus Ring.	Ashtown House Stud, Ireland.	Mr W. H. Ponsonby.	85,000
Ch.c. Salse (USA) — Key Tothe Minstrel (USA).	Ted Voute, Agent.	B.B.A. (UK) Ltd.	84,000
Kinnino B.c. Polish Precedent (USA) — On Tiptoes (GB).	Limestone Stud.	B.B.A. (UK) Ltd.	84,000
Angellino (IRE) B.c. Danehill (USA) — Commanche Belle.	Ashtown House Stud, Ireland.	Mr J. T. Doyle.	80,000

Yearling	Vendor	Purchaser	Price
Darcy Ch.c. Miswaki (USA) — Princess Accord (USA)	Cheveley Park Stud.	Mr William Haggas.	80,000
Royal Beluga B.f. Soviet Star (USA) — Allegedly Blue (USA)	Grange Stud (UK)	Lillingston B/S.	80,000
Ch.c. Soviet Lad (USA) — Special Meeting	Rathbarry Stud, Ireland	Mr Patrick Prendergast	80,000
B.f. Indian Ridge — Lunaire (GB)	Manor House Stud	Darley Stud Mgt	78,000
Deep Water (USA) B.c. Diesis — Water Course (USA)	Airlie Stud, Ireland	Anthony Penfold B/S	78,000
B.c. Fairy King (USA) — Sable Lake	Ashtown House Stud, Ireland	Darley Stud Mgt	76,000
Kwello B.c. Mtoto — Hug Me (FR)	Whitsbury Manor Stud	Mr Gordon Smyth	75,000
Ch.c. Thatching — Loucoum (FR)	Floors Stud.	Darley Stud Mgt	75,000
Ch.c. Caerleon (USA) — Milligram	Meon Valley Stud.	Mr T. Stack	75,000
Silence Reigns B.c. Sadler's Wells (USA) — Rensaler (USA)	Cheveley Park Stud.	B.B.A. (UK) Ltd	75,000
B.f. Danehill (USA) — Sweet Soprano	Ted Voute, Agent.	B.B.A. (UK) Ltd	75,000
Delilah (IRE) B.f. Bluebird (USA) — Courtesane (USA)	Tullamaine Castle Stud, Ireland.	John Warren B/S.	72,000
La Coramalai (IRE) B.f. Rainbow Quest (USA) — North Telstar	Westerlands Stud	B.B.A. (UK) Ltd	72,000
Lysandros (IRE) B c. Lycius (USA) — Trojan Relation	Corduff Stud, Ireland.	Mr J. Gosden	72,000
Manwal (IRE) B.c. Bluebird (USA) — My My Marie	Islamore Stud, Ireland	Shadwell Estate Co.	72,000
B.c. Shadeed (USA) — Pearl Essence (USA)	Genesis Green Stud.	Bloodhorse Intl Ltd	72,000
Prairie Falcon (IRE) B.c. Alzao (USA) — Sea Harrier	Hilltown Stud, Ireland	B. W. Hills Southbank.	72,000
Alfandango (IRE) B.f. Alzao (USA) — Fandangerina (USA)	Yeomanstown Lodge Stud, Ireland	Hugo Lascelles B/S	70,000
Ultra Fair (USA) Ch.c. Rahy (USA) — La Romania (USA)	Furnace Mill Stud.	Mr J. Ryan.	68,000
Ch.c. Indian Ridge — Souadah (USA)	Kingwood Stud.	Mr A. O. Nerses	68,000
B.c. Primo Dominie — Valika	Cheveley Park Stud.	Darley Stud Mgt	66,000
B.f. Green Desert (USA) — Charming Life	Cotswold Stud.	Mead, Goodbody Ltd	65,000
Enlisted (IRE) B.f. Sadler's Wells (USA) — Impudent Miss.	Mount Coote Stud, Ireland.	Mr N. Greig.	65,000
Tikopia B.c. Saddlers' Hall (IRE) — Shesadelight (GB)	Hesmonds Stud	Mr I. A. Balding	65,000
Other Club Ch.c. Kris — Tura	Crimbourne Stud	B.B.A. (UK) Ltd	64,000
Ch.f. Indian Ridge — Long View	Titthorpe Stud.	Darley Stud Mgt	63,000
Fletcher B.c. Salse (USA) — Ballet Classique (USA)	Warren Park Stud.	Newgate Stud Co	62,000
Ch.c. Caerleon (USA) — Catina	Chippenham Lodge Stud.	John Warren B/S	62,000
B.f. Night Shift (USA) — Fear Naught.	Mount Coote Stud, Ireland.	C. Gordon-Watson B/S	62,000
Hadidi B.c. Alzao (USA) — Sesame	Highclere Stud.	Shadwell Estate Co.	62,000
Ch.c. Don't Forget Me — Julip.	Ashtown House Stud, Ireland	Mr F. Carr.	62,000
B.c. Sheikh Albadou (GB) — One Fine Day (USA).	Landscape Stud, Ireland.	Gainsborough Stud Mgt.	62,000
Papua Ch.c. Green Dancer (USA) — Fairy Tern.	Stradishal Manor.	Mr I. A. Balding.	62,000
Solar Storm Ch.c. Polar Falcon (USA) — Sister Sophie (USA)	Cheveley Park Stud.	Lillingston Bloodstock.	62,000
Get The Point B.c. Sadler's Wells (USA) — Tolmi.	Cliff Stud Ltd.	Mr J. E. Bigg.	60,000
Jalb (IRE) B.c. Robellino (USA) — Adjacent (IRE)	Glenvale Stud, Ireland.	Shadwell Estate Co.	60,000
Gr/Ro.c. With Approval (CAN) — Minga Isle (USA)	Green Ireland Properties Ltd	Darley Stud Mgt.	60,000
B.c. Suave Dancer (USA) — Prima Domina (FR)	Camas Park Stud, Ireland	John Ferguson B/S.	60,000

Yearling	Consignor	Purchaser	Price
B.f. Generous (IRE) — Red Comes Up (USA)	Mount Coote Stud, Ireland	Springfield Farm	60,000
Soleil Bleu (IRE) B.f. Waajib — Sun on the Spey	West Stow Stud	B.B.A. (UK) Ltd.	60,000
B.c. Nashwan (USA) — Chief Celebrity (USA)	Cheveley Park Stud	Mead, Goodbody Ltd	58,000
Hoh Explorer (IRE) Ch.c. Shahrastani (USA) — Heart's Harmony (GB)	Kildara Stud, Ireland	Mr I. A. Balding	58,000
Heritage B.c. Danehill (USA) — Misty Halo	Lofts Hall Stud	John Warren B/S	58,000
Fascinating Rhythm B.f. Slip Anchor — Pick of the Pops	Meon Valley Stud	Peter Doyle B/S	57,000
B.c. Royal Academy (USA) — Atyaaf (USA)	Camas Park Stud, Ireland	B.B.A. (UK) Ltd	56,000
Burundi (IRE) B.c. Danehill (USA) — Sofala	Batsford Stud	B.B.A. (UK) Ltd	56,000
Trooper B.c. Rock Hopper — Silica (USA)	Ted Voute, Agent	Newgate Stud Co	55,000
Sudest (IRE) B/Br.c. Taufan (USA) — Frill	The Forest Stud	Mr I. A. Balding	55,000
B.c. Danehill (USA) — Gracieuse Majeste (FR)	Yeomanstown Lodge Stud, Ireland	Mr J. Dunlop	54,000
Liquid Gold (IRE) B.c. Fairy King (USA) — Heavenward (USA)	Rowanstown Stud, Ireland	Mr R. O'Gorman	54,000
Olivo (IRE) Ch.c. Priolo (USA) — Honourable Sheba (USA)	Campbell Stud	Mr J. Delahooke	54,000
B.c. Green Desert (USA) — Stufida	Cheveley Park Stud	Mead, Goodbody Ltd	54,000
B.c. Polar Falcon (USA) — Troyanos	Cheveley Park Stud	John Ferguson B/S	54,000
B.f. Green Desert (USA) — Vaison La Romaine	Airlie Stud, Ireland	Vendor	54,000
Quws B.c. Robellino (USA) — Fleeting Rainbow (GB)	Deerpark Stud, Ireland	Shadwell Estate Co.	53,000
B.c. Salse (USA) — One Last Glimpse	Burton Agnes Stud	Julie Cecil	53,000
Nicklass B.c. Shirley Heights — Glancing	Heatherwold Stud	B.B.A. (UK) Ltd.	52,000
Hint B.c. Warning — Throw Away Line (USA)	Overbury Stud	John Warren B/S	52,000
Gr.c. Alzao (USA) — Jazz (GB)	Highclere Stud Ltd.	Darley Stud Mgt	52,000
Mystique B.f. Mystiko (USA) — Sound of the Sea	Beechgrove Stud Farm Ltd	B.B.A. (UK) Ltd	52,000
B.c. Fairy King (USA) — Prosperous Lady	Genesis Green Stud	Mr D. O'Byrne	52,000
Mujazi (IRE) Ch.c. Mujtahid (USA) — Leaping Salmon	Camas Park Stud, Ireland	Shadwell Estate Co.	51,000
B.c. Green Dancer (USA) — Baby Diamonds	Airlie Stud, Ireland	Peter Wragg B/S (Ire)	50,000
Barnum Sands B.c. Green Desert (USA) — Circus Plume	Woodland Stud	Vendor	50,000
B.c. Slip Anchor — Compton Lady (USA)	Ted Voute, Agent	Darley Stud Mgt.	50,000
Dancer's Chief Ch.c. Suave Dancer (USA) — Kijafa (USA)	Partridge Close Stud	Mr Gordon Smyth	50,000
B.c. Common Grounds — Dorado Llave (USA)	Yeomanstown Stud, Ireland.	B. W. Hills Southbank	50,000
Grandpa Lex (IRE) Gr.c. Kalaglow — Bustling Nelly	Sandley Stud	Mr I. A. Balding	50,000
Graceful Lass B.f. Sadler's Wells (USA) — Hi Lass	Kirtlington Stud.	Vendor	50,000
Midnight Angel Gr.f. Machiavellian (USA) — Night at Sea	Genesis Green Stud	Darley Stud Mgt	50,000
Ch.f. Cadeaux Genereux — Miss Silca Key	Ted Voute, Agent	Mr G. Lewis	50,000
Raindancing (IRE) B.f. Tirol — Persian Song (GB)	Manor House Stud	Peter Doyle B/S.	50,000
B.c. Suave Dancer (USA) — Regent's Folly (IRE)	Blackdown Stud.	Mead, Goodbody Ltd	50,000
B.c. Sadler's Wells (USA) — Reprocolor	Meon Valley Stud.	Mr D. O'Byrne	50,000
B.f. Sadler's Wells (USA) — Royalefort	Bryanstown House Stud, Ireland.	Mr D. O'Byrne	50,000
B.c. Night Shift (USA) — Veronica	Woodcote Stud.	Darley Stud Mgt	50,000

HIGH – PRICED YEARLINGS OF 1995 AT GOFFS' SALES

The following yearlings realised 50,000 Irish guineas and over at Goffs' Sales in 1995:-

Name and Breeding	Vendor	Purchaser	Ire Gns
Majesty (IRE) B.c Sadler's Wells (USA) — Princesse Timide (USA)	Camas Park Stud	Newgate Stud Company	310,000
Karawan (GB) Ch.f Kris — Sweetly (FR)	Camas Park Stud	Shadwell Estate Co. Ltd.	270,000
Ch.c Caerleon (USA) — Ploy	Kilcarn Stud	Shadwell Estate Co. Ltd.	230,000
B.c Sadler's Wells (USA) — La Dame Du Lac (USA)	Oldtown Stud	Dermot K. Weld, Esq.	230,000
B.c Sadler's Wells (USA) — Fair Of The Furze	Airlie Stud	Darley Stud Management	210,000
B.c Sadler's Wells (USA) — Diamond Field (USA)	Lynn Lodge Stud	D. L. O'Byrne, Esq.	210,000
Star Profile (IRE) B.f Sadler's Wells (USA) — Sandhurst Goddess	Tally-Ho Stud	Dermot K. Weld, Esq.	200,000
B.c Royal Academy (USA) — Hastening	Landscape Stud	D. L. O'Byrne, Esq.	190,000
B.c Danehill (USA) — Sabaah (USA)	Irish National Stud	D. L. O'Byrne, Esq.	175,000
Sturgeon (IRE) Ch.c Caerleon (USA) — Ridge The Times (USA)	Ballyinch Stud.	Paul Cole, Esq.	175,000
B.f. Red Ransom (USA) — Sprite's Ridge (USA)	Camas Park Stud	Silky Green Inc.	170,000
Final Trial (IRE) B.c. Last Tycoon — Perfect Alibi	Westerlands Stud	John Ferguson, Esq.	160,000
B.c. Night Shift (USA) — Sheer Audacity	Iverk House Stud	Charles O'Brien, Esq.	150,000
Anubis (IRE) B. c. Caerleon (USA) — Point Of Honour	Eyrefield Lodge.	D. L. O'Byrne, Esq.	150,000
Jude (GB) B/Br.f. Darshaan — Airuccaba	Staffordstown	Newgate Stud Company	150,000
B.c. Sadler's Wells (USA) — Maiden Concert.	Croom House Stud.	Charles O'Brien, Esq.	145,000
Oriental Style (IRE) Ch.c. Indian Ridge — Bazaar Promise	Oak Tree Stud	J. T. Doyle, Esq.	140,000
B.c Caerleon (USA) — Noble Chick (USA).	Barronstown Stud.	Mr Noel O'Callaghan.	140,000
Intiyati (USA) Ch.c. Chief's Crown (USA) — Native Twine.	Abbeville & Meadow Court.	Shadwell Estate Co. Ltd.	130,000
Plaisir D'Amour (IRE) B.f. Danehill (USA) — Mira Adonde (USA).	Mellon Stud.	D. L. O'Byrne, Esq.	130,000
Rickenbacker (IRE) B.c. Bluebird (USA) — Sodium's Niece	Kilcarn Stud.	D. L. O'Byrne, Esq.	120,000
Mutribah (USA) B.f. Silver Hawk (USA) — Pattimech (USA).	Airlie Stud	Shadwell Estate Co. Ltd.	120,000
B.f. Caerleon (USA) — Steady (USA)	Swordlestown Stud.	Silky Green Inc.	115,000
Gr.c. Caerleon (USA) — Lady Capulet (USA)	Camas Park Stud	M. Patrick Barbe.	110,000
Fallah (GB) B.c. Salse (USA) — Alpine Sunset	Bellewstown Farm Stud.	Shadwell Estate Co. Ltd.	110,000
B.f. Storm Bird (CAN) — Handsewn (USA)	Camas Park Stud.	B.B.A. (Ireland) Ltd.	105,000
Fabled Light (IRE) B.c. Alzao (USA) — Fabled Lifestyle	Glenvale Stud	John Ferguson Bldstck.	100,000
Compton Place Ch.c. Indian Ridge — Nosey.	Trickledown Stud.	Charles Gordon-Watson, Esq.	92,000
B.c. Night Shift (USA) — Massawippi	Landscape Stud	Silky Green Inc.	90,000
B.f. St Jovite (USA) — Highland Ball.	Airlie Stud.	Darley Stud Management	90,000
Br.c. Ela-Mana-Mou — Heaven Knows (USA)	Mellon Stud	Castlemartin Stud	90,000
Amid Albadu (USA) B.c. Sheikh Albadou (GB) — Dream Play (USA)	Airlie Stud	Shadwell Estate Co. Ltd.	90,000
Shi-Ar (IRE) Ch.c. Royal Academy (USA) — Welsh Love	Kilcarn Stud	Shadwell Estate Co. Ltd.	90,000
B.c. Sadler's Wells (USA) — Fleur Royale.	Camas Park Stud.	Dermot K. Weld, Esq.	90,000
Smart Boy (IRE) Ch.c. Polish Patriot (USA) — Bouffant	Rathbarry Stud (Agent)	Paul Cole, Esq.	85,000
B.c. Persian Bold — Ziggy Belle (USA)	Carrowdore Castle	Darley Stud Management	85,000
More's The Pity Ch.c. Cadeaux Genereux — What A Pity	Abbeville & Meadow Court.	Dermot K. Weld, Esq.	82,000

Pedigree	Consignor	Purchaser	Price
Genevra (IRE) B.f. Danehill (USA) — Astra Adastra.	John Troy (Agent)	BBA (IRE)/Stauffenberg.	80,000
B.c. Caerleon (USA) — Go Honey Go	Ballyinch Stud.	J. T. Doyle, Esq.	80,000
Machiavelli (GB) B.c. Machiavellian (USA) — Forest Blossom (USA).	Ballymoney Park Stud.	Newgate Stud Company	80,000
B.c. Sadler's Wells (USA) — Princess Tiara.	Barronstown Stud	John Dunlop, Esq.	75,000
B.c. Pursuit of Love (GB) — Overdue Reaction.	Corbally Stud.	Peter Wragg, Esq.	75,000
Sadlers Grey (IRE) B.f. Sadler's Wells (USA) — Fedora Grey	S.I.B.A. spa.	John Walsh Bloodstock.	75,000
Woodex (USA) Ch.c. Woodman (USA) — Excitable (USA)	S.I.B.A. spa.	John Walsh Bloodstock	75,000
B.c. Last Tycoon — Croglin Water.	Mrs A. Whitehead	John Allan, Esq.	74,000
B.f. Petorius — Sugarbird.	Airlie Stud	Seamus Burns, Esq.	72,000
B.c. Fairy King (USA) — Le Melody	Croom House Stud	Amanda Skiffington Agent	71,000
B.f. Seattle Dancer (USA) — Qui Bid (USA).	Ashtown House Stud	BBA (IRE)/Staffenberg	70,000
B.f. Woodman (USA) — Mozartiana (USA).	Camas Park Stud.	Mr Noel O'Callaghan.	70,000
Bold Oriental (IRE) B.c. Tirol — Miss Java	Landscape Stud.	D. L. O'Byrne, Esq.	70,000
Ch.f. Night Shift (USA) — Dabbing (USA)	Oldtown Stud	Newberry Stud	68,000
Yonkelman (USA) Ch.c. Woodman (USA) — Kafiyah.	Mellon Stud.	John Warren Bloodstock.	66,000
Zaretski (GB) B.c. Pursuit of Love (USA) — Tolstoya.	Round Hill Stud	Clive E. Brittain, Esq.	65,000
Alzaro (IRE) B.c. Alzao (USA) — Merriment (USA).	Mr John Mangan	Cash.	65,000
B.c. Alzao (USA) — Brilleaux	Airlie Stud	Darley Stud Management	65,000
Ch.c. Common Grounds — Unbidden Melody (USA)	Yeomanstown Stud.	Mr Noel O'Callaghan.	62,000
B.c. Night Shift (USA) — Stylish Girl (USA).	Mr John Mangan	Shadwell Estate Co. Ltd.	60,000
Mystical Heights (IRE) B.f. High Estate — Richly Deserved (IRE)	Genesis Green Stud	Henry Cecil, Esq.	60,000
B.f. Royal Academy (USA) — Pu Yi.	Landscape Stud.	Barry W. Hills, Esq.	60,000
B.c. Polish Patriot (USA) — Clanjingle.	Rathbarry Stud (Agent)	Peter Wragg, Esq.	60,000
B.c. Danehill (USA) — Ariadne	Ashtown House Stud	Conti Bloodstock Services.	60,000
Ch.c. Gulch (USA) — Aminata.	Ballyinch Stud.	European Bloodstock Agency.	60,000
Ajnad (IRE) B.c. Efisio — Lotte Lenta.	Yeomanstown Stud.	Shadwell Estate Co. Ltd.	58,000
B.c. Common Grounds — Sadie Jordan (USA)	Yeomanstown Stud	J. T. Doyle, Esq.	55,000
Matrona (USA) B.f. Woodman (USA) — Happy Bride.	Staffordstown.	Peter J. Doyle, Esq.	55,000
Speremm (IRE) B.f. Sadler's Wells (USA) — Forli's Treat (USA)	Camas Park Stud	Darley Stud Management	55,000
Ch.c. Persian Bold — Anjuli.	Corbally Stud.	Cherry-Downes Bloodstock Ltd	55,000
Northern Angel (IRE) B.c. Waajib — Angel Divine.	Yeomanstown Stud.	John Oxx, Esq.	54,000
Wildflower Ridge (GB) Ch.f. Indian Ridge — Guest Singer.	Weylands.	B.B.A. (U.K.).	53,000
B.c. Fairy King (USA) — American Garden (USA).	Pondsfield Stud.	Curragh Bloodstock Agency	52,000
Recondite (IRE) B.c. Polish Patriot (USA) — Recherchee (GB)	Rathbarry Stud (Agent)	Charles Gordon-Watson, Esq.	52,000
Louju (USA) B.f. Silver Hawk (USA) — Secretarial Queen (USA)	Mellon Stud, Agent	Henry Cecil Bloodstock.	52,000
Royal Alibi B.c. Royal Academy (USA) — Excellent Alibi (USA)	Abbeville & Meadow Court	Charles O'Brien, Esq.	52,000
B.c. Common Grounds — Concave.	Yeomancarney Stud	Charles O'Brien, Esq.	50,000
Dr Martens (IRE) B.c. Mtoto — Suyayeb (USA).	Ballymacamey Stud	Amanda Skiffington	50,000
B/Br.c. Riverman (USA) — Rossard (DEN).	Staffordstown.	Newmarket International	50,000
Ch.c. Night Shift (USA) — Rose Garland (USA)	Mellon Stud.	T. M. Clark, Esq.	50,000
Ch.f. Woodman (USA) — Pixie Erin	Camas Park Stud	Shadwell Estate Co. Ltd.	50,000
B.c. Night Shift (USA) — Mosaique Bleue (GB)	Croom House Stud	Charles O'Brien, Esq.	50,000
Ch.f. Thatching — Instinctive Move (USA).	Barronstown Stud.	Mr Noel O'Callaghan.	50,000

WINNERS OF GREAT RACES

LINCOLN HANDICAP
Doncaster—1m

1975	Southwark Star 4-7-3	24
1976	The Hertford 5-8-6	26
1977	Blustery 5-7-11	26
1978	Captains Wings 5-7-10	25
1979	Fair Season 5-8-10	23
1980	King's Ride 4-8-12	18
1981	Saher 5-8-12	19
1982	Kings Glory 4-8-3	26
1983	Mighty Fly 4-8-4	26
1984	Saving Mercy 4-8-9	26
1985	Cataldi 4-9-10	26
1986	K-Battery 5-8-4	25
1987	Star of a Gunner 7-8-8	25
1988	Cuvee Charlie 4-8-1	25
1989	Fact Finder 5-7-9	25
1990	Evichstar 6-7-12	24
1991	Amenable 6-8-1	25
1992	High Low 4-8-0	24
1993	High Premium 5-8-8	24
1994	Our Rita 5-8-5	24
1995	Roving Minstrel 4-8-3	23

GREENHAM STAKES (3y)
Newbury—7f

1975	Mark Anthony 9-1	9
1976	Wollow 9-1	10
1977	He Loves Me 8-10	11
1978	Derrylin 8-10	11
1979	Kris 9-0	9
1980	Final Straw 9-0	9
1981	Another Realm 9-0	6
1982	Cajun 9-0	5
1983	Wassl 9-0	5
1984	Creag-an-Sgor 9-0	8
1985	Bairn 9-0	6
1986	Faustus 9-0	9
1987	Risk Me 9-0	8
1988	Zelphi 9-0	5
1989	Zayyani 9-0	12
1990	Rock City 9-0	6
1991	Bog Trotter 9-0	7
1992	Lion Cavern 9-0	8
1993	Inchinor 9-0	7
1994	Turtle Island 9-0	8
1995	Celtic Swing 9-0	9

JOHN PORTER STAKES
Newbury—1m 4f 5yds

1975	Salado 4-8-10	13
1976	Quiet Fling 4-9-0	11
1977	Decent Fellow 4-8-9	11
1978	Orchestra 4-9-0	10
1979	Icelandic 4-8-11	12
1980	Niniski 4-9-0	16
1981	Pelerin 4-8-8	9
1982	Glint of Gold 4-9-0	11

1983	Diamond Shoal 4-8-8	8
1984	Gay Lemur 4-8-8	13
1985	Jupiter Island 6-8-8	14
1986	Lemhill 4-8-8	8
1987	Rakaposhi King 5-8-10	12
1988	Alwasmi 4-8-10	8
1989	Unfuwain 4-8-13	7
1990	Brush Aside 4-8-10	11
1991	Rock Hopper 4-8-10	10
1992	Saddlers' Hall 4-8-13	11
1993	Linpac West 7-8-12	7
1994	Right Win 4-9-3	10
1995	Strategic Choice 4-8-11	10

EUROPEAN FREE HANDICAP (3y)
Newmarket—7f

1975	Green Belt 8-9	15
1976	Man of Harlech 8-4	19
1977	Mrs McArdy 8-0	19
1978	Remainder Man 7-10	12
1979	Lyric Dance 8-10	14
1980	Moorestyle 8-10	13
1981	Motavato 8-13	13
1982	Match Winner 9-4	13
1983	Boom Town Charlie 8-11	8
1984	Cutting Wind 8-8	17
1985	Over The Ocean 8-11	11
1986	Green Desert 9-7	8
1987	Noble Minstrel 9-7	11
1988	Lapierre 9-1	9
1989	Danehill 9-1	9
1990	Anshan 9-7	10
1991	Mystiko 9-7	11
1992	Pursuit of Love 9-1	9
1993	So Factual 9-6	7
1994	Bluegrass Prince 8-13	10
1995	Diffident 9-5	12

CRAVEN STAKES (3y)
Newmarket—1m

1975	No Alimony 8-10	10
1976	Malinowski 8-10	7
1977	Limone 8-10	9
1978	Admiral's Launch 8-10	10
1979	Lyphard's Wish 8-7	3
1980	Tyrnavos 8-7	9
1981	Kind of Hush 8-7	9
1982	Silver Hawk 8-7	9
1983	Muscatite 8-7	5
1984	Lear Fan 8-12	5
1985	Shadeed 8-7	6
1986	Dancing Brave 8-7	11
1987	Ajdal 9-0	6
1988	Doyoun 8-9	5
1989	Shaadi 8-9	5
1990	Tirol 8-12	6
1991	Marju 8-9	8

1992	Alnasr Alwasheek 8-9	8
1993	Emperor Jones 8-9	9
1994	King's Theatre 9-0	10
1995	Painter's Row 8-12	5

CLASSIC TRIAL (3y)
(Royal Stakes before 1971)
Sandown—1m 2f 7yds

1975	Consol 9-0	9
1976	Riboboy 9-0	7
1977	Artaius 8-9	5
1978	Whitstead 8-11	8
1979	Troy 8-7	5
1980	Henbit 8-7	6
1981	Shergar 8-7	9
1982	Peacetime 8-7	11
1983	Gordian 8-7	7
1984	Alphabatim 9-0	8
1985	Damister 8-7	4
1986	Shahrastani 8-7	4
1987	Gulf King 8-12	8
1988	Galitzin 8-7	5
1989	Old Vic 8-8	3
1990	Defensive Play 8-11	6
1991	Hailsham 8-11	5
1992	Pollen Count 8-11	10
1993	True Hero 8-11	6
1994	Linney Head 8-10	9
1995	Pentire 8-10	8

VICTORIA CUP
Ascot—7f

1975	Rhodomantade 4-8-3	20
1976	Record Token 4-9-4	14
1977	Duke Ellington 4-9-1	16
1978	Private Line 5-8-13	16
1979	The Adrianstan 4-8-6	18
1980	Kampala 4-9-3	16
1981	Columnist 4-9-13	14
1982	Indian King 4-9-3	13
1983	Abandoned	
1984	Mummy's Pleasure 5-8-9	13
1985	Tremblant 4-8-5	22
1986	Ready Wit 5-7-13	14
1987	Fusilier 5-7-9	20
1988	Wing Park 4-9-1	16
1989	Top Dream 4-9-1	23
1990	Lomax 4-9-3	19
1991	Sky Cloud 5-7-11	14
1992	Band on the Run 5-9-0	21
1993	Tender Moment 5-7-7	22
1994	Face North 6-8-1	25
1995	Jawaal 5-8-6	25

JUBILEE HANDICAP
Kempton—1m

1975	Jumpabout 4-7-12	14
1976	Royal Match 5-9-0	11
1977	Lord Helpus 4-9-5	16
1978	Sunday Guest 4-8-12	14
1979	Smartset 4-7-0	12
1980	Blue Refrain 4-9-5	10
1981	Greenwood Star 4-9-2	10

1982	Tugoflove 6-8-3	12
1983	Elmar 4-8-10	12
1984	Larionov 4-9-11	11
1985	Portogon 7-7-11	11
1986	Pennine Walk 4-9-11	23
1987	Turfah 4-8-12	15
1988	Just A Flutter 4-9-3	11
1989	Electric Lady 4-9-8	14
1990	Langtry Lady 4-8-3	12
1991	St Ninian 5-9-3	12
1992	Venus Observed 4-9-1	12
1993	Pay Homage 5-9-1	13
1994	Caleman 5-8-12	14
1995	Desert Green 6-9-4	11

JOCKEY CLUB STAKES
Newmarket—1m 4f

1975	Shebeen 4-8-10	6
1976	Orange Bay 4-9-8	8
1977	Oats 4-9-1	11
1978	Classic Example 4-9-5	7
1979	Obraztsovy 4-8-11	9
1980	More Light 4-8-11	8
1981	Master Willie 4-8-12	6
1982	Ardross 6-8-12	6
1983	Electric 4-8-10	11
1984	Gay Lemur 4-8-7	6
1985	Kirmann 4-8-7	8
1986	Phardante 4-8-7	3
1987	Phardante 5-8-12	7
1988	Almaarad 5-8-10	4
1989	Unfuwain 4-8-10	6
1990	Roseate Tern 4-8-9	7
1991	Rock Hopper 4-8-7	8
1992	Sapience 6-8-12	9
1993	Zinaad 4-8-9	8
1994	Silver Wisp 5-8-9	8
1995	Only Royale 6-8-11	7

CHESTER VASE (3y)
Chester—1m 4f 66yds

1975	Shantallah 8-12	7
1976	Old Bill 8-8	6
1977	Hot Grove 8-12	6
1978	Icelandic 8-12	4
1979	Cracaval 8-8	6
1980	Henbit 8-12	5
1981	Shergar 8-12	10
1982	Super Sunrise 8-12	8
1983	Abandoned	
1984	Kaytu 8-8	7
1985	Law Society 8-12	5
1986	Nomrood 8-12	7
1987	Dry Dock 8-11	8
1988	Unfuwain 8-11	4
1989	Old Vic 8-11	5
1990	Belmez 8-11	3
1991	Toulon 8-11	5
1992	Twist and Turn 8-11	5
1993	Armiger 8-11	6
1994	Broadway Flyer 8-10	6
1995	Luso 8-10	7

CHESTER CUP
Chester—2m 2f 117yds

1975	Super Nova 5-7-7	15
1976	John Cherry 5-9-4	15
1977	Sea Pigeon 7-8-8	15
1978	Sea Pigeon 8-9-7	13
1979	Charlotte's Choice 4-8-4	13
1980	Arapahos 5-9-5	10
1981	Donegal Prince 5-8-4	15
1982	Dawn Johnny 5-8-8	16
1983	Abandoned	
1984	Contester 4-8-2	9
1985	Morgans Choice 8-7-11	16
1986	Western Dancer 5-9-0	22
1987	Just David 4-9-8	13
1988	Old Hubert 7-7-8	17
1989	Grey Salute 6-8-7	14
1990	Travelling Light 4-9-1	16
1991	Star Player 5-8-10	16
1992	Welshman 6-7-8	16
1993	Rodeo Star 7-7-13	18
1994	Doyce 5-7-10	17
1995	Top Cees 5-8-8	18

ORMONDE STAKES
Chester—1m 5f 89yds

1975	Rouser 4-8-4	7
1976	Zimbalon 4-8-6	4
1977	Oats 4-9-0	8
1978	Crow 5-9-0	7
1979	Remainder Man 4-8-10	4
1980	Niniski 4-9-4	10
1981	Pelerin 4-9-4	5
1982	Six Mile Bottom 4-8-10	6
1983	Abandoned	
1984	Teenoso 4-9-4	5
1985	Seismic Wave 4-8-10	8
1986	Brunico 4-8-10	8
1987	Rakaposhi King 5-8-11	5
1988	Mr Pintips 4-8-11	6
1989	Mountain Kingdom 5-8-11	3
1990	Braashee 4-8-11	6
1991	Per Quod 6-8-11	7
1992	Saddlers' Hall 4-9-2	7
1993	Shambo 6-9-2	5
1994	Shambo 7-9-2	8
1995	Zilzal Zamaan 4-8-11	4

OAKS TRIAL (3y fillies)
Lingfield—1m 3f 106yds

1975	Juliette Marny 8-9	7
1976	Heaven Knows 9-0	10
1977	Lucent 9-0	5
1978	Suni 9-0	9
1979	Reprocolor 9-0	7
1980	Gift Wrapped 9-0	7
1981	Leap Lively 9-0	7
1982	Tants 9-0	9
1983	Give Thanks 9-0	12
1984	Out of Shot 9-0	7
1985	Kiliniski 8-9	11
1986	Mill on the Floss 8-9	8
1987	Port Helene 8-9	8

1988	Bahamian 8-9	7
1989	Aliysa 8-9	5
1990	Rafha 9-1	5
1991	Ausherra 8-9	7
1992	User Friendly 8-9	5
1993	Oakmead 8-9	6
1994	Munnaya 8-8	6
1995	Asterita 8-8	5

DERBY TRIAL (3y)
Lingfield—1m 3f 106yds

1975	Patch 9-0	8
1976	Norfolk Air 9-0	8
1977	Caporello 9-0	8
1978	Whitstead 9-0	6
1979	Milford 9-0	8
1980	Ginistrelli 9-0	7
1981	Riberetto 9-0	8
1982	Jalmood 9-0	6
1983	Teenoso 9-0	11
1984	Alphabatim 9-0	5
1985	Slip Anchor 9-0	4
1986	Mashkour 9-0	6
1987	Legal Bid 9-0	8
1988	Kahyasi 9-0	8
1989	Cacoethes 9-0	7
1990	Rock Hopper 9-0	5
1991	Corrupt 9-0	8
1992	Assessor 9-0	5
1993	Bob's Return 9-0	8
1994	Hawker's News 8-7	6
1995	Munwar 8-7	7

CORAL HANDICAP (3y)
(formerly Holsten Diat Pils Handicap)
Newmarket—6f

1981	Sharp Venita 7-3	12
1982	Admirals Princess 9-2	13
1983	Bold Secret 8-6	10
1984	Lovers Bid 7-3	14
1985	Zanata 8-4	12
1986	Latch Spring 7-10	14
1987	Bel Byou 8-4	11
1988	Cadeaux Genereux 8-0	16
1989	Didicoy 8-12	11
1990	Case Law 9-7	11
1991	Arturian 8-3	13
1992	Splice 8-4	13
1993	True Precision 7-10	15
1994	Tabook 9-5	13
1995	Perryston View 8-11	12

MUSIDORA STAKES (3y fillies)
York—1m 2f 85yds

1975	Moonlight Night 9-0	10
1976	Everything Nice 9-0	8
1977	Triple First 9-0	9
1978	Princess of Man 9-0	9
1979	Rimosa's Pet 9-0	10
1980	Bireme 9-0	9
1981	Condessa 9-0	5
1982	Last Feather 9-0	5
1983	Give Thanks 9-0	8

1984	Optimistic Lass 9-0	9
1985	Fatah Flare 9-0	9
1986	Rejuvenate 8-11	7
1987	Indian Skimmer 8-8	3
1988	Diminuendo 8-11	6
1989	Snow Bride 8-8	6
1990	In The Groove 8-8	5
1991	Gussy Marlowe 8-8	5
1992	All At Sea 8-8	5
1993	Marillette 8-10	5
1994	Hawajiss 8-10	7
1995	Pure Grain 8-10	5

DANTE STAKES (3y)
York—1m 2f 85yds

1975	Hobnob 9-0	12
1976	Trasi's Son 9-0	11
1977	Lucky Sovereign 9-0	15
1978	Shirley Heights 9-0	9
1979	Lyphard's Wish 9-0	14
1980	Hello Gorgeous 9-0	8
1981	Beldale Flutter 9-0	6
1982	Simply Great 9-0	6
1983	Hot Touch 9-0	9
1984	Claude Monet 9-0	15
1985	Damister 9-0	5
1986	Shahrastani 9-0	7
1987	Reference Point 9-0	8
1988	Red Glow 9-0	7
1989	Torjoun 9-0	7
1990	Sanglamore 9-0	7
1991	Environment Friend 9-0	8
1992	Alnasr Alwasheek 9-0	7
1993	Tenby 9-0	5
1994	Erhaab 9-0	9
1995	Classic Cliche 8-11	8

YORKSHIRE CUP
York—1m 5f 194yds

1975	Riboson 4-8-5	4
1976	Bruni 4-9-1	5
1977	Bright Finish 4-8-10	7
1978	Smuggler 5-8-10	7
1979	Pragmatic 4-8-7	10
1980	Noble Saint 4-9-1	8
1981	Ardross 5-8-12	6
1982	Ardross 6-9-1	6
1983	Line Slinger 4-8-4	10
1984	Band 4-8-10	9
1985	Ilium 4-8-7	10
1986	Eastern Mystic 4-8-9	7
1987	Verd-Antique 4-8-9	7
1988	Moon Madness 5-9-0	8
1989	Mountain Kingdom 5-8-9	6
1990	Braashee 4-8-9	6
1991	Arzanni 4-8-9	7
1992	Rock Hopper 5-8-13	8
1993	Assessor 4-9-0	8
1994	Key To My Heart 4-8-9	7
1995	Moonax 4-9-0	7

DUKE OF YORK STAKES
York—6f

1975	Steel Heart 3-8-13	7
1976	Three Legs 4-9-7	9
1977	Boldboy 7-9-12	13
1978	Private Line 5-9-4	16
1979	Thatching 4-9-0	9
1980	Flash N'Thunder 3-8-1	7
1981	King of Spain 5-9-0	10
1982	Jester 3-8-2	11
1983	Vorvados 6-9-0	11
1984	Gabitat 6-9-4	10
1985	Chapel Cottage 4-8-11	10
1986	Grey Desire 6-9-0	10
1987	Handsome Sailor 4-9-0	9
1988	Handsome Sailor 5-9-8	13
1989	Indian Ridge 4-9-4	10
1990	Lugana Beach 4-9-4	7
1991	Green Line Express 5-9-4	11
1992	Shalford 4-9-4	9
1993	Hamas 4-9-0	10
1994	Owington 3-8-9	11
1995	Lake Coniston 4-9-4	7

LOCKINGE STAKES
Newbury—1m

1975	Abandoned	
1976	El Rastro 6-9-0	8
1977	Relkino 4-9-0	9
1978	Don 4-9-4	10
1979	Young Generation 3-8-4	10
1980	Kris 4-9-7	7
1981	Belmont Bay 4-9-0	6
1982	Motavato 4-9-0	7
1983	Noalcoholic 6-9-4	10
1984	Cormorant Wood 4-9-5	6
1985	Prismatic 3-7-13	11
1986	Scottish Reel 4-9-1	8
1987	Then Again 4-9-4	9
1988	Broken Hearted 4-9-4	5
1989	Most Welcome 5-9-1	4
1990	Safawan 4-9-0	6
1991	Polar Falcon 4-9-0	4
1992	Selkirk 4-9-5	10
1993	Swing Low 4-9-0	10
1994	Emperor Jones 4-9-0	11
1995	Soviet Line 5-9-0	5

TOTE CREDIT SILVER BOWL (3y)
(Cecil Frail Handicap before 1986)
Haydock—1m 30yds

1975	Rebec 7-12	9
1976	Gunner B 8-8	12
1977	Owen Jones 7-9	11
1978	Fair Top 7-10	11
1979	Bold Owl 8-1	10
1980	Greenwood Star 7-7	13
1981	Silver Season 9-5	12
1982	Spanish Pool 9-6	12
1983	Schuss 8-5	10
1984	Incisive 7-9	10
1985	Trucidator 9-7	11

1986	Al Bashaama 7-10	13
1987	Mohamed Abdu 7-8	8
1988	Jamarj 9-7	15
1989	Safawan 8-11	13
1990	Cashtal Dazzler 7-7	8
1991	Takaddum 9-3	13
1992	Sharpitor 9-0	11
1993	Moorish 8-2	13
1994	Dance Turn 9-0	12
1995	Sonic Boy 9-7	9

HENRY II STAKES
Sandown—2m 78yds

1978	Smuggler 5-9-0	6
1979	Buckskin 6-9-3	6
1980	Billion 6-8-8	8
1981	No race	
1982	Ardross 6-9-3	5
1983	Ore 5-8-11	7
1984	Harly 4-8-11	5
1985	Destroyer 4-8-8	8
1986	Longboat 5-8-11	10
1987	Saronicos 4-8-10	7
1988	Primitive Rising 4-8-10	9
1989	Sadeem 6-9-2	8
1990	Teamster 4-8-13	6
1991	Top of The World 4-8-10	7
1992	Drum Taps 6-9-4	8
1993	Brier Creek 4-8-10	8
1994	My Patriarch 4-8-10	9
1995	Double Trigger 4-8-13	7

PREDOMINATE STAKES (3y)
Goodwood—1m 2f

1975	No Alimony 9-0	6
1976	General Ironside 8-11	6
1977	Royal Blend 8-11	6
1978	English Harbour 8-11	9
1979	Troy 9-0	4
1980	Prince Bee 8-6	8
1981	No race	
1982	Peacetime 9-0	9
1983	Morcon 8-6	6
1984	Ilium 8-6	12
1985	Lanfranco 9-0	8
1986	Allez Milord 8-12	8
1987	Ibn Bey 8-12	9
1988	Minster Son 9-1	7
1989	Warrshan 8-12	8
1990	Razeen 8-12	6
1991	Man From Eldorado 8-12	8
1992	Jeune 8-12	9
1993	Geisway 8-12	6
1994	Opera Score 8-8	5
1995	Pentire 9-0	6

LUPE STAKES (3y)
Goodwood—1m 2f

1975	Misoptimist 8-8	7
1976	Laughing Girl 8-3	9
1977	Western Star 8-8	5

1978	Cistus 8-8	7
1979	Britannias Rule 8-3	5
1980	Vielle 8-8	8
1981	Golden Bowl 8-8	4
1982	Height of Fashion 8-11	4
1983	Current Raiser 8-3	8
1984	Miss Beaulieu 8-8	15
1985	Bella Colora 8-11	6
1986	Tralthee 8-11	6
1987	Scimitarra 8-11	16
1988	Miss Boniface 8-11	4
1989	Lady Shipley 8-11	7
1990	Moon Cactus 9-3	7
1991	Fragrant Hill 8-11	9
1992	Oumaldaaya 8-11	6
1993	Gisarne 8-11	7
1994	Bulaxie 9-0	6
1995	Subya 8-11	9

TEMPLE STAKES
Sandown—5f 6yds

1975	Blue Cashmere 5-9-8	12
1976	Lochnager 4-9-4	8
1977	Vilgora 5-9-0	6
1978	*Oscilight 3-8-2	
	*Smarten Up 3-8-2	15
1979	Double Form 4-8-11	12
1980	Sharpo 3-8-2	10
1981	Abandoned	
1982	Mummy's Game 3-8-2	13
1983	Fearless Lad 4-9-8	11
1984	Petorius 3-8-6	9
1985	Never So Bold 5-9-5	6
1986	Double Schwartz 5-9-3	10
1987	Treasure Kay 4-9-3	9
1988	Handsome Sailor 5-9-3	10
1989	Dancing Dissident 3-8-8	6
1990	Dayjur 3-8-8	8
1991	Elbio 4-9-3	8
1992	Snaadee 5-9-3	9
1993	Paris House 4-9-7	10
1994	Lochsong 6-9-7	9
1995	Mind Games 3-8-8	5

BRIGADIER GERARD STAKES
(Coronation Stakes before 1973)
Sandown—1m 2f 7yds

1975	Rymer 4-8-13	7
1976	Anne's Pretender 4-8-11	6
1977	Jellaby 4-8-8	9
1978	Gunner B 5-8-11	6
1979	Jellaby 6-8-11	7
1980	Gregorian 4-8-11	3
1981	Abandoned	
1982	Kalaglow 4-8-11	8
1983	Stanerra 5-8-5	10
1984	Adonijah 8-8	9
1985	Commanche Run 4-9-3	5
1986	Bedtime 6-8-10	7
1987	Mtoto 4-8-10	8
1988	Highland Chieftain 5-9-1	7

1989	Hibernian Gold 4-8-10	6
1990	Husyan 4-8-10	6
1991	Stagecraft 4-8-10	11
1992	Opera House 4-9-1	3
1993	Red Bishop 5-8-10	5
1994	Chatoyant 4-8-10	14
1995	Alriffa 4-8-10	7

LEISURE STAKES
Lingfield—6f

1978	Gypsy Dancer 3-8-7	6
1979	Absalom 4-9-10	7
1980	The Pug 3-8-3	6
1981	Runnett 4-9-10	7
1982	Sylvan Barbarosa 3-8-3	8
1983	Solimile 3-8-6	7
1984	Habibti 4-9-3	8
1985	Alpine Strings 4-9-4	7
1986	Hallgate 3-8-3	9
1987	Mister Majestic 3-8-3	11
1988	Gallic League 3-8-3	8
1989	Restore 6-9-0	12
1990	Sharp N'Early 4-9-0	8
1991	Polish Patriot 3-8-5	15
1992	Central City 3-7-13	8
1993	Pips Pride 3-8-4	9
1994	Hard to Figure 8-9-0	8
1995	Roger The Butler 5-9-0	9

DIOMED STAKES
Epsom—1m 114yds

1975	All Friends 3-8-2	11
1976	All Friends 4-9-5	7
1977	Gunner B 4-9-6	6
1978	Ovac 5-9-9	9
1979	Spring In Deepsea 4-9-4	11
1980	Hardgreen 4-9-3	5
1981	Saher 5-9-6	6
1982	Prima Voce 3-8-3	8
1983	Lofty 3-8-3	6
1984	Adonijah 4-9-9	7
1985	Scottish Reel 3-8-7	7
1986	Pennine Walk 4-9-9	10
1987	Lauries Warrior 3-8-6	10
1988	Waajib 5-9-9	8
1989	Shining Steel 3-8-7	8
1990	Eton Lad 3-8-6	9
1991	Sylva Honda 3-8-6	11
1992	Zaahi 3-8-5	9
1993	Enharmonic 6-9-7	8
1994	Bluegrass Prince 3-8-6	11
1995	Mr Martini 5-9-4	7

CORONATION CUP
Epsom—1m 4f 10yds

1975	Bustino 4-9-0	6
1976	Quiet Fling 4-9-0	6
1977	Exceller 4-9-0	6
1978	Crow 5-9-0	5
1979	Ile de Bourbon 4-9-0	4
1980	Sea Chimes 4-9-0	4
1981	Master Willie 4-9-0	5

1982	Easter Sun 5-9-0	8
1983	Be My Native 4-9-0	6
1984	Time Charter 5-8-11	6
1985	Rainbow Quest 4-9-0	7
1986	Saint Estephe 4-9-0	10
1987	Triptych 5-8-11	5
1988	Triptych 6-8-11	4
1989	Sheriff's Star 4-9-0	9
1990	In The Wings 4-9-0	6
1991	In The Groove 4-8-11	7
1992	Saddlers' Hall 4-9-0	9
1993	Opera House 5-9-0	8
1994	Apple Tree 5-9-0	11
1995	Sunshack 4-9-0	7

JOHN OF GAUNT STAKES
Haydock—7f 30yds

1976	Record Token 4-9-5	6
1977	Gwent 4-9-5	4
1978	Persian Bold 3-8-10	10
1979	Borzoi 3-8-0	4
1980	Hard Fought 3-8-0	8
1981	Last Fandango 4-9-4	7
1982	Indian King 4-9-4	7
1983	Abandoned	
1984	Mr Meeka 3-8-3	13
1985	Sarab 4-9-4	8
1986	Firm Landing 3-8-0	11
1987	Linda's Magic 3-8-4	5
1988	Wantage Park 4-8-9	9
1989	Weldnaas 3-8-7	13
1990	Palace Street 3-8-3	7
1991	Swordsmith 4-8-12	8
1992	Norton Challenger 5-9-4	8
1993	Celestial Key 3-8-2	4
1994	Eurolink Thunder 4-9-5	8
1995	Mutakddim 4-8-12	8

WILLIAM HILL TROPHY
(HANDICAP) (3y)
York—6f

1975	Be Tuneful 8-12	8
1976	Ubedizzy 8-10	13
1977	Mofida 8-13	10
1978	Emperor's Shadow 7-11	14
1979	Eagle Boy 7-8	17
1980	Optimate 8-0	13
1981	Marking Time 7-9	9
1982	Cyrils Choice 9-1	8
1983	Autumn Sunset 7-8	17
1984	Ashley Rocket 7-4	16
1985	Si Signor 8-9	12
1986	*Governor General 8-12	10
	*Sew High 7-7	12
1987	Dowsing 7-10	15
1988	Cadeaux Genereux 8-5	10
1989	Sure Gold 8-11	10
1990	Katzakeena 8-10	10
1991	Sheikh Albadou 9-3	8
1992	Orthorhombus 9-2	11
1993	Aradanza 9-2	13
1994	Encore M'Lady 7-11	14
1995	Bold Effort 3-8-8	15

QUEEN ANNE STAKES
Ascot—1m

1975	Imperial March 3-7-10	11
1976	Ardoon 6-8-11	9
1977	Jellaby 4-9-8	8
1978	Radetzky 5-9-5	10
1979	Baptism 3-8-5	9
1980	Blue Refrain 4-9-8	11
1981	Belmont Bay 4-9-11	10
1982	Mr Fluorocarbon 3-8-6	10
1983	Valiyar 4-9-5	10
1984	Trojan Fen 3-8-5	6
1985	Rousillon 4-9-5	8
1986	Pennine Walk 4-9-2	9
1987	Then Again 4-9-5	6
1988	Waajib 5-9-2	5
1989	Warning 4-9-8	7
1990	Markofdistinction 4-9-5	9
1991	Sikeston 5-9-8	11
1992	Lahib 4-9-2	9
1993	Alflora 4-9-2	9
1994	Barathea 4-9-8	10
1995	Nicolotte 4-9-2	7

PRINCE OF WALES'S STAKES
Ascot—1m 2f

1975	Record Run 4-9-2	6
1976	Anne's Pretender 4-9-1	7
1977	Lucky Wednesday 4-9-1	5
1978	Gunner B 5-9-1	6
1979	Crimson Beau 4-9-1	7
1980	Ela-Mana-Mou 4-9-4	10
1981	Hard Fought 4-9-4	9
1982	Kind of Hush 4-9-1	7
1983	Stanerra 5-8-12	11
1984	Morcon 4-9-1	5
1985	Bob Back 4-9-7	4
1986	English Spring 4-8-12	9
1987	Mtoto 4-9-4	10
1988	Mtoto 5-9-8	4
1989	Two Timing 3-8-4	8
1990	Batshoof 4-9-5	8
1991	Stagecraft 4-9-3	6
1992	Perpendicular 4-9-3	11
1993	Placerville 3-8-4	11
1994	Muhtarram 5-9-7	11
1995	Muhtarram 6-9-8	6

ST JAMES'S PALACE STAKES (3y)
Ascot—1m

1975	Bolkonski 9-0	8
1976	Radetzky 9-0	8
1977	Don 9-0	7
1978	Jaazeiro 9-0	8
1979	Kris 9-0	5
1980	Posse 9-0	8
1981	To-Agori-Mou 9-0	8
1982	Dara Monarch 9-0	9
1983	Horage 9-0	7
1984	Chief Singer 9-0	8
1985	Bairn 9-0	8
1986	Sure Blade 9-0	7
1987	Half a Year 9-0	5

1988	Persian Heights 9-0	7
1989	Shaadi 9-0	5
1990	Shavian 9-0	8
1991	Marju 9-0	7
1992	Brief Truce 9-0	8
1993	Kingmambo 9-0	4
1994	Grand Lodge 9-0	9
1995	Bahri 9-0	9

COVENTRY STAKES (2y)
Ascot—6f

1975	Galway Bay 8-11	10
1976	Cawston's Clown 8-11	12
1977	Solinus 8-11	17
1978	Lake City 8-11	20
1979	Varingo 8-11	18
1980	Recitation 8-11	13
1981	Red Sunset 8-11	16
1982	Horage 8-11	8
1983	Chief Singer 8-11	14
1984	Primo Dominie 8-11	8
1985	Sure Blade 8-11	12
1986	Cutting Blade 8-11	19
1987	Always Fair 8-13	13
1988	High Estate 8-13	9
1989	Rock City 8-13	16
1990	Mac's Imp 8-13	13
1991	Dilum 8-13	14
1992	Petardia 8-13	12
1993	Stonehatch 8-13	6
1994	Sri Pekan 8-13	16
1995	Royal Applause 8-12	13

KING EDWARD VII STAKES (3y)
Ascot—1m 4f

1975	Sea Anchor 8-10	8
1976	Marquis de Sade 8-10	5
1977	Classic Example 8-10	10
1978	Ile de Bourbon 8-6	10
1979	Ela-Mana-Mou 8-6	9
1980	Light Cavalry 8-6	10
1981	Bustomi 8-6	10
1982	Open Day 8-6	11
1983	Shareef Dancer 8-6	7
1984	Head for Heights 8-6	10
1985	Lanfranco 8-6	10
1986	Bonhomie 8-8	13
1987	Love the Groom 8-8	8
1988	Sheriff's Star 8-8	8
1989	Cacoethes 8-8	6
1990	Private Tender 8-8	8
1991	Saddlers' Hall 8-8	9
1992	Beyton 8-8	12
1993	Beneficial 8-8	8
1994	Foyer 8-8	8
1995	Pentire 8-8	8

JERSEY STAKES (3y)
Ascot—7f

1975	Gay Fandango 8-6	13
1976	Gwent 9-2	12
1977	Etienne Gerard 8-10	13
1978	Camden Town 8-10	17

1979	Blue Refrain 9-2	17
1980	Hard Fought 9-2	13
1981	Rasa Penang 8-10	20
1982	Merlins Charm 8-7	21
1983	Tecorno 8-6	13
1984	Miss Silca Key 8-7	16
1985	Pennine Walk 8-10	19
1986	Cliveden 8-10	20
1987	Midyan 9-1	13
1988	Indian Ridge 8-10	12
1989	Zilzal 8-10	12
1990	Sally Rous 8-7	15
1991	Satin Flower 8-7	14
1992	Prince Ferdinand 9-1	12
1993	Ardkinglass 9-1	15
1994	*Gneiss 8-10	
	*River Deep 8-10	21
1995	Sergeyev 8-10	16

QUEEN MARY STAKES (2y fillies)
Ascot—5f

1975	Rory's Rocket 8-8	18
1976	Cramond 8-8	12
1977	Amaranda 8-8	13
1978	Greenland Park 8-8	21
1979	Abeer 8-8	14
1980	Pushy 8-8	17
1981	Fly Baby 8-8	11
1982	Widaad 8-8	16
1983	Night of Wind 8-8	15
1984	Hi-Tech Girl 8-8	17
1985	Gwydion 8-8	14
1986	Forest Flower 8-8	13
1987	Princess Athena 8-8	15
1988	Gloriella 8-8	12
1989	Dead Certain 8-8	13
1990	On Tiptoes 8-8	12
1991	Marling 8-8	14
1992	Lyric Fantasy 8-8	13
1993	Risky 8-8	11
1994	Gay Gallanta 8-8	16
1995	Blue Duster 8-8	12

CORONATION STAKES (3y fillies)
Ascot—1m

1975	Roussalka 9-0	11
1976	Kesar Queen 9-0	8
1977	Orchestration 9-0	10
1978	Sutton Place 8-8	14
1979	One In A Millon 9-4	13
1980	Cairn Rouge 9-4	8
1981	Tolmi 9-0	10
1982	Chalon 9-0	8
1983	Flame of Tara 9-0	6
1984	Katies 9-4	10
1985	Al Bahathri 9-4	7
1986	Sonic Lady 9-4	7
1987	Milligram 9-0	6
1988	Magic of Life 9-0	8
1989	Golden Opinion 9-0	12
1990	Chimes of Freedom 9-0	7
1991	Kooyonga 9-0	8

1992	Marling 9-0	7
1993	Gold Splash 9-0	5
1994	Kissing Cousin 9-0	10
1995	Ridgewood Pearl 9-0	10

ROYAL HUNT CUP
Ascot—1m

1975	Ardoon 5-8-3	18
1976	Jumping Hill 4-9-7	16
1977	My Hussar 5-8-10	15
1978	Fear Naught 4-8-0	19
1979	Pipedreamer 4-8-5	24
1980	Tender Heart 4-9-0	22
1981	Teamwork 4-8-6	20
1982	Buzzards Bay 4-8-12	20
1983	Mighty Fly 4-9-3	31
1984	Hawkley 4-8-6	18
1985	Come on the Blues 6-8-2	27
1986	Patriach 4-7-12	32
1987	Vague Shot 4-9-5	25
1988	Governorship 4-9-6	26
1989	True Panache 4-9-4	27
1990	Pontenuovo 5-7-7	32
1991	Eurolink The Lad 4-8-9	29
1992	Colour Sergeant 4-7-8	31
1993	Imperial Ballet 4-8-12	30
1994	Face North 6-8-3	32
1995	Realities 5-9-10	32

QUEENS VASE
Ascot—2m 45yds

1975	Blood Royal 3-8-0	20
1976	General Ironside 3-8-5	14
1977	Millionaire 3-8-5	14
1978	Le Moss 3-8-0	12
1979	Buttress 3-8-5	13
1980	Toondra 3-8-0	14
1981	Ore 3-8-0	13
1982	Evzon 4-9-3	14
1983	Santella Man 4-9-8	17
1984	Baynoun 3-8-0	11
1985	Wassl Merbayeh 3-8-0	10
1986	Stavordale 3-7-10	13
1987	Arden 3-8-9	9
1988	Green Adventure 8-9	14
1989	Weld 8-9	11
1990	River God 8-11	11
1991	Jendali 8-11	14
1992	Landowner 8-11	11
1993	Infrasonic 8-11	8
1994	Silver Wedge 8-11	12
1995	Stelvio 8-11	11

CORK AND ORRERY STAKES
Ascot—6f

1975	Swingtime 3-7-8	9
1976	Gentilhombre 3-8-0	11
1977	He Loves Me 3-8-4	15
1978	Sweet Mint 4-8-8	12
1979	Thatching 4-9-0	17
1980	Kearney 3-8-0	20
1981	The Quiet Bidder 3-8-2	16

1982	Indian King 4-9-0 18
1983	Sylvan Barbarosa 4-8-10 17
1984	Committed 4-8-7.....................................15
1985	Dafayna 3-7-11 12
1986	Sperry 3-8-0 10
1987	Big Shuffle 3-8-4 11
1988	Posada 3-7-12..14
1989	Danehill 3-8-0 12
1990	Great Commotion 4-9-0..........................17
1991	Polish Patriot 3-8-2 16
1992	Shalford 4-9-4...17
1993	College Chapel 3-8-10............................19
1994	Owington 3-8-10......................................17
1995	So Factual 5-8-13 11

NORFOLK STAKES (2y)
Ascot—5f

1975	Faliraki 8-11 10
1976	Godswalk 8-11..5
1977	Emboss 8-11...5
1978	Schweppeshire Lad 8-11..........................8
1979	Romeo Romani 8-11................................10
1980	Chummy's Special 8-11 6
1981	Day Is Done 8-11......................................8
1982	Brondesbury 8-11......................................5
1983	Precocious 8-11...5
1984	Magic Mirror 8-11......................................4
1985	Marouble 8-11...6
1986	Sizzling Melody 8-11................................10
1987	Colmore Row 8-13.....................................8
1988	Superpower 8-13......................................10
1989	Petillante 8-8...6
1990	Line Engaged 8-13....................................8
1991	Magic Ring 8-13..9
1992	Niche 8-8..9
1993	Turtle Island 8-13......................................8
1994	Mind Games 8-13......................................6
1995	Lucky Lionel 8-12......................................9

GOLD CUP
Ascot—2m 4f

1975	Sagaro 4-9-0 8
1976	Sagaro 5-9-0 7
1977	Sagaro 6-9-0 6
1978	Shangamuzo 5-9-0 10
1979	Le Moss 4-9-0 6
1980	Le Moss 5-9-0 8
1981	Ardross 5-9-0 4
1982	Ardross 6-9-0 5
1983	Little Wolf 5-9-0 12
1984	Gildoran 4-9-0 9
1985	Gildoran 5-9-0 12
1986	Longboat 5-9-0 11
1987	Paean 4-9-0 8
1988	Sadeem 5-9-0 13
1989	Sadeem 6-9-0 8
1990	Ashal 4-9-0 11
1991	Indian Queen 6-8-13 12
1992	Drum Taps 6-9-2 6
1993	Drum Taps 7-9-2 10
1994	Arcadian Heights 6-9-2.............................9
1995	Double Trigger 4-9-0 7

RIBBLESDALE STAKES (3y fillies)
Ascot—1m 4f

1975	Gallina 8-10 6
1976	Catalpa 8-10 7
1977	Nanticious 8-10 9
1978	Relfo 8-10 12
1979	Expansive 8-7 7
1980	Shoot A Line 8-11 9
1981	Strigida 8-7 9
1982	Dish Dash 8-7 10
1983	High Hawk 8-7 14
1984	Ballinderry 8-7 9
1985	Sally Brown 8-7 10
1986	Gull Nook 8-8 12
1987	Queen Midas 8-8.......................................6
1988	Miss Boniface 8-8 11
1989	Alydaress 8-9 6
1990	Hellenic 8-8 11
1991	Third Watch 8-8 14
1992	Armarama 8-8 8
1993	Thawakib 8-8 8
1994	Bolas 8-8 9
1995	Phantom Gold 8-8 7

HARDWICKE STAKES
Ascot—1m 4f

1975	Charlie Bubbles 4-8-10 11
1976	Orange Bay 4-9-0 5
1977	Meneval 4-9-0 7
1978	Montcontour 4-8-12 8
1979	Obraztsovy 4-8-9 6
1980	Scorpio 4-9-0 7
1981	Pelerin 4-8-12 9
1982	Critique 4-8-9 8
1983	Stanerra 5-8-9 10
1984	Khairpour 5-8-12 7
1985	Jupiter Island 6-8-9 4
1986	Dihistan 4-8-9 10
1987	Orban 4-8-9 4
1988	Almaarad 5-8-12 8
1989	Assatis 4-8-9 4
1990	Assatis 5-9-0 7
1991	Rock Hopper 4-8-12 9
1992	Rock Hopper 5-8-12 5
1993	Jeune 4-8-9 5
1994	Bobzao 5-8-9 11
1995	Beauchamp Hero 5-8-9 6

WOKINGHAM STAKES
Ascot—6f

1975	Boone's Cabin 5-10-0 20
1976	Import 5-9-4 12
1977	Calibina 5-8-5 13
1978	Equal Opportunity 4-7-12 24
1979	Lord Rochford 4-8-8 28
1980	Queen's Pride 4-7-13 29
1981	Great Eastern 4-9-8 29
1982	Battle Hymn 3-7-7 24
1983	Melinda 4-7-5 27
1984	Petong 4-9-6 28
1985	Time Machine 4-7-12 30
1986	Touch of Grey 3-8-8 28
1987	Bel Byou 3-8-3 29

1988	Powder Blue 6-8-5	30
1989	Mac's Fighter 4-9-12	27
1990	Knight of Mercy 4-8-6	28
1991	Amigo Menor 5-8-7	29
1992	Red Rosein 6-8-1	29
1993	Nagida 4-8-7	30
1994	Venture Capitalist 5-8-12	30
1995	Astrac 4-8-7	30

KING'S STAND STAKES
Ascot—5f

1975	Flirting Around 4-9-4	12
1976	Lochnager 4-9-3	13
1977	Godswalk 3-8-9	11
1978	Solinus 3-8-9	8
1979	Double Form 4-9-3	13
1980	African Song 3-8-9	14
1981	Marwell 3-8-6	12
1982	Fearless Lad 3-8-9	14
1983	Sayf El Arab 3-8-9	16
1984	Habibti 4-9-0	11
1985	Never So Bold 5-9-3	15
1986	Last Tycoon 3-8-9	14
1987	Bluebird 3-8-9	12
1988	Chilibang 4-9-3	8
1989	Indian Ridge 4-9-3	15
1990	Dayjur 3-8-10	15
1991	Elbio 4-9-3	10
1992	Sheikh Albadou 4-9-3	10
1993	Elbio 6-9-3	8
1994	Lochsong 6-9-0	8
1995	Piccolo 4-9-6	10

NORTHUMBERLAND PLATE
Newcastle—2m 19yds

1975	Grey God 4-8-9	12
1976	Philominsky 5-8-0	11
1977	Tug of War 4-8-7	15
1978	Tug of War 5-9-2	10
1979	Totowah 5-8-2	11
1980	Mon's Beau 5-7-7	15
1981	Dawn Johnny 4-8-6	18
1982	Abandoned	
1983	Weavers Pin 6-8-8	14
1984	Karadar 6-9-10	19
1985	Trade Line 4-7-10	13
1986	Sneak Preview 6-8-12	15
1987	Treasure Hunter 8-7-7	20
1988	Stavordale 5-9-2	10
1989	Orpheus 3-7-7	12
1990	Al Maheb 4-8-11	12
1991	Tamarpour 4-7-7	14
1992	Witness Box 5-9-9	13
1993	Highflying 7-7-11	18
1994	Quick Ransom 6-8-8	20
1995	Bold Gait 4-9-0	17

VAN GEEST CRITERION STAKES
Newmarket—7f

1981	Dalsaan 4-9-7	8
1982	Noalcoholic 5-9-7	14
1983	Thug 3-8-10	12
1984	Grey Desire 4-9-7	11
1985	Capricorn Belle 4-9-9	12

1986	Mister Wonderful 3-8-5	14
1987	Linda's Magic 3-8-2	5
1988	Cadeaux Genereux 3-8-5	5
1989	Zilzal 3-8-10	4
1990	Rock City 3-9-1	7
1991	La Grange Music 4-9-2	12
1992	Toussaud 3-8-4	7
1993	Inchinor 3-8-12	10
1994	Hill Hopper 3-8-4	6
1995	Pipe Major 3-8-8	8

FOSTER'S SILVER CUP
(formerly Sun Page 3 Silver Cup)
York—1m 7f 195yds
NB: Race distance changed in 1994 to 1m 5f 194yds

1985	Skaramanga 3-8-6	4
1986	Rakaposhi King 4-8-12	6
1987	Lemhill 5-9-4	6
1988	Waterfield 4-8-12	6
1989	Ibn Bey 5-9-5	3
1990	Wajna 3-7-11	4
1991	Great Marquess 4-9-8	7
1992	Tyrone Bridge 6-9-6	7
1993	Brandon Prince 5-8-7	4
1994	Castle Courageous 7-9-5	7
1995	Saxon Maid 4-9-5	5

ECLIPSE STAKES
Sandown—1m 2f 7yds

1975	Star Appeal 5-9-7	16
1976	Wollow 3-8-8	10
1977	Artaius 3-8-8	10
1978	Gunner B 5-9-7	9
1979	Dickens Hill 3-8-8	7
1980	Ela-Mana-Mou 4-9-7	6
1981	Master Willie 4-9-7	7
1982	Kalaglow 4-9-7	9
1983	Solford 3-8-8	9
1984	Sadler's Wells 3-8-8	9
1985	Pebbles 4-9-4	4
1986	Dancing Brave 3-8-8	8
1987	Mtoto 4-9-7	8
1988	Mtoto 5-9-7	8
1989	Nashwan 3-8-8	6
1990	Elmaamul 3-8-10	7
1991	Environment Friend 3-8-10	7
1992	Kooyonga 4-9-4	12
1993	Opera House 5-9-7	8
1994	Ezzoud 5-9-7	8
1995	Halling 4-9-7	8

OLD NEWTON CUP
Haydock—1m 3f 200yds

1975	Fool's Mate 4-9-2	9
1976	Peaceful 5-9-0	8
1977	Mint 3-7-7	11
1978	Move Off 5-9-4	12
1979	St Briavels 5-9-3	7
1980	Shady Nook 5-9-5	10
1981	Dogberry 3-7-5	8
1982	Valentinian 4-10-3	10
1983	Regal Steel 5-8-2	9
1984	Bishop's Ring 3-8-6	6

1985	Clanrallier 5-8-3	10
1986	Rakaposhi King 4-9-7	10
1987	Pipsted 3-8-0	9
1988	Roushayd 4-9-10	9
1989	Nickle Plated 4-9-7	16
1990	Hateel 4-9-6	9
1991	Libk 3-8-11	12
1992	Matador 5-9-2	9
1993	Glide Path 4-8-2	11
1994	Glide Path 5-8-10	11
1995	Lombardic 4-8-12	10

LANCASHIRE OAKS (fillies and mares)
Before 1991 3-year-old fillies only
Haydock—1m 3f 200yds

1975	One Over Parr 8-11	5
1976	Centrocon 8-11	9
1977	Busaca 8-11	5
1978	Princess Eboli 9-1	9
1979	Reprocolor 9-1	5
1980	Vielie 8-11	6
1981	Rhein Bridge 8-11	7
1982	Sing Softly 8-11	8
1983	Give Thanks 9-1	13
1984	Sandy Island 8-11	9
1985	Graecia Magna 8-11	8
1986	Park Express 8-11	9
1987	Three Tails 9-1	6
1988	Andaleeb 8-9	8
1989	Roseate Tern 8-9	8
1990	Pharian 8-9	4
1991	Patricia 3-8-4	11
1992	Niodini 3-8-4	11
1993	Rainbow Lake 3-8-4	8
1994	State Crystal 3-8-4	8
1995	Fanjica 3-8-4	5

CHERRY HINTON STAKES (2y)
Newmarket—6f

1975	Everything Nice 8-13	6
1976	Ampulla 8-10	7
1977	Turkish Treasure 8-10	9
1978	Devon Ditty 8-13	13
1979	Mrs Penny 8-7	10
1980	Nasseem 8-10	11
1981	Travel On 8-10	10
1982	Crime of Passion 8-10	8
1983	Chapel Cottage 8-10	9
1984	Top Socialite 8-10	8
1985	Storm Star 8-10	12
1986	Forest Flower 9-0	10
1987	Diminuendo 8-9	9
1988	Kerrera 8-9	9
1989	Chimes of Freedom 8-9	8
1990	Chicarica 8-12	8
1991	Musicale 8-9	6
1992	Sayyedati 8-9	7
1993	Lemon Souffle 8-9	8
1994	Red Carnival 8-9	7
1995	Applaud 8-9	8

BUNBURY HANDICAP
Newmarket—7f

1975	Penny Post 3-8-2	14
1976	Lottogift 5-8-10	7
1977	Kintore 5-8-0	8
1978	Greenhill God 4-8-5	11
1979	Pipedreamer 4-9-3	14
1980	Steeple Bell 4-7-9	14
1981	Captain Nick 5-9-13	11
1982	Paterno 4-9-1	14
1983	Mummy's Pleasure 4-9-3	19
1984	Mummy's Pleasure 5-8-12	17
1985	Tremblant 4-8-12	18
1986	Patriach 4-9-1	16
1987	Individualist 4-8-5	15
1988	Pinctada 6-8-3	16
1989	Baldomero 4-7-7	18
1990	Fedoria 4-8-3	19
1991	Savoyard 3-9-0	17
1992	Consigliere 4-9-1	20
1993	En Attendant 5-9-4	27
1994	En Attendant 6-9-12	20
1995	Cadeaux Tryst 3-9-1	19

PRINCESS OF WALES'S STAKES
Newmarket—1m 4f

1975	Libra's Rib 3-7-11	10
1976	Smuggler 3-7-11	6
1977	Lord Helpus 4-9-2	8
1978	Pollerton 4-9-2	4
1979	Milford 3-8-2	6
1980	Nicholas Bill 5-9-2	9
1981	Light Cavalry 4-9-9	8
1982	Height of Fashion 3-7-11	4
1983	Quilted 3-8-0	11
1984	Head for Heights 3-8-6	9
1985	Petoski 3-8-0	5
1986	Shardari 4-9-0	9
1987	Celestial Storm 4-9-0	8
1988	Unfuwain 3-8-0	5
1989	Carroll House 4-9-5	5
1990	Sapience 4-9-0	7
1991	Rock Hopper 4-9-3	6
1992	Saddlers' Hall 4-9-5	4
1993	Desert Team 3-8-1	7
1994	Wagon Master 4-9-0	12
1995	Beauchamp Hero 5-9-5	9

FALMOUTH STAKES (fillies)
Before 1974: 3-year-olds only
Newmarket—1m

1975	Sauceboat 3-8-1	6
1976	Duboff 4-9-6	9
1977	River Dane 3-8-5	6
1978	Cistus 3-8-2	10
1979	Rose Above 4-8-10	7
1980	Stumped 3-7-12	9
1981	Star Pastures 3-8-3	10
1982	Chalon 3-8-11	7
1983	Royal Heroine 3-8-5	8
1984	Meis El-Reem 3-8-5	5
1985	Al Bahathri 3-8-11	9

1986	Sonic Lady 8-11	8
1987	Sonic Lady 4-9-10	4
1988	Inchmurrin 3-8-6	7
1989	Magic Gleam 3-8-6	6
1990	Chimes of Freedom 3-8-12	5
1991	Only Yours 3-8-6	6
1992	Gussy Marlowe 4-9-1	7
1993	Niche 3-8-6	11
1994	Lemon Souffle 3-8-6	6
1995	Caramba 3-8-6	5

JULY STAKES (2y)
Newmarket—6f

1975	Super Cavalier 8-6	6
1976	Sky Ship 8-10	6
1977	Royal Harmony 8-10	4
1978	Main Reef 8-13	6
1979	Final Straw 8-10	7
1980	Age Quod Agis 8-10	3
1981	End of the Line 8-10	11
1982	Horage 9-2	7
1983	Superlative 8-10	6
1984	Primo Dominie 9-1	7
1985	Green Desert 8-10	8
1986	Mansooj 8-10	8
1987	Sanquirico 8-10	7
1988	Always Valiant 8-10	4
1989	Rock City 9-1	4
1990	Mujtahid 8-10	4
1991	Showbrook 8-10	4
1992	Wharf 8-10	6
1993	First Trump 8-10	6
1994	Fallow 8-10	6
1995	Tagula 8-10	9

JULY CUP
Newmarket—6f

1975	Lianga 4-9-4	13
1976	Lochnager 4-9-6	10
1977	Gentilhombre 4-9-6	8
1978	Solinus 3-8-11	14
1979	Thatching 4-9-6	11
1980	Moorestyle 3-8-11	14
1981	Marwell 3-8-8	14
1982	Sharpo 5-9-6	16
1983	Habibti 3-8-8	15
1984	Chief Singer 3-8-11	9
1985	Never So Bold 5-9-6	9
1986	Green Desert 3-8-11	5
1987	Ajdal 3-8-11	11
1988	Soviet Star 4-9-6	11
1989	Cadeaux Genereux 4-9-6	11
1990	Royal Academy 3-8-13	9
1991	Polish Patriot 3-8-13	8
1992	Mr Brooks 5-9-6	8
1993	Hamas 4-9-6	12
1994	Owington 3-8-13	9
1995	Lake Coniston 4-9-6	9

MAGNET CUP
York—1m 2f 85yds

1975	Jolly Good 3-7-8	15
1976	Bold Pirate 4-9-3	9
1977	Air Trooper 4-9-6	8

1978	Town and Country 4-8-13	9
1979	Tesoro Mio 4-8-3	9
1980	Fine Sun 3-7-8	12
1981	Amyndas 3-8-5	11
1982	Buzzards Bay 4-9-8	6
1983	Bedtime 3-7-9	9
1984	Straight Man 3-8-11	9
1985	Chaumiere 4-9-7	12
1986	Chaumiere 5-9-5	11
1987	*Brave Dancer 3-8-8	
	*Wolsey 3-8-6	9
1988	Bashful Boy 3-8-2	16
1989	Icona 3-9-8	10
1990	Eradicate 5-9-4	19
1991	Halkopous 5-7-3	12
1992	Mr Confusion 4-8-3	17
1993	Baron Ferdinand 3-8-9	13
1994	Cezanne 5-9-12	16
1995	Naked Welcome 3-8-4	16

PRINCESS MARGARET STAKES (2y)
Ascot—6f

1975	Outer Circle 9-4	4
1976	Al Stanza 9-4	8
1977	Sarissa 9-1	4
1978	Devon Ditty 9-1	4
1979	Luck of the Draw 8-12	4
1980	Tolmi 8-12	7
1981	Circus Ring 8-12	9
1982	Royal Heroine 8-12	6
1983	Desirable 8-12	4
1984	Al Bahathri 8-12	9
1985	Kingscote 8-12	11
1986	Hiaam 8-8	6
1987	Bluebook 8-8	6
1988	Muhbubh 8-8	6
1989	Pharaoh's Delight 8-8	6
1990	Cloche d'Or 8-8	4
1991	Bezelle 8-8	10
1992	Marina Park 8-11	6
1993	A Smooth One 8-8	7
1994	Tajannub 8-8	8
1995	Blue Duster 9-0	7

BEESWING STAKES
Newcastle—7f

1977	In Haste 3-8-5	9
1978	John de Coombe 3-8-5	7
1979	Jeroboam 3-8-5	3
1980	Kampala 4-9-6	7
1981	Milk of the Barley 4-9-0	6
1982	Silly Steven 3-8-5	8
1983	Beaudelaire 3-8-5	7
1984	Major Don 4-9-3	7
1985	Sarab 4-9-6	7
1986	Hadeer 4-9-0	9
1987	Farajullah 4-9-1	8
1988	Salse 3-8-9	6
1989	Great Commotion 3-8-6	4
1990	Savahra Sound 5-9-6	6
1991	Bold Russian 4-9-0	7
1992	Casteddu 3-8-7	7
1993	Eurolink Thunder 3-8-7	9

1994	Gabr 4-9-0	10
1995	Shahid 3-8-7	7

STEWARDS' CUP
Goodwood—6f

1975	Import 4-8-0	21
1976	Jimmy the Singer 3-7-8	17
1977	Calibina 5-8-5	24
1978	Ahonoora 3-8-0	23
1979	Standaan 3-7-10	16
1980	Repetitious 3-7-2	28
1981	Crews Hill 5-9-9	30
1982	Soba 3-8-4	30
1983	Autumn Sunset 3-8-2	23
1984	Petong 4-9-10	26
1985	Al Trui 5-8-1	28
1986	Green Ruby 5-8-12	24
1987	Madraco 4-7-2	30
1988	Rotherfield Greys 6-8-8	28
1989	Very Adjacent 4-7-4	22
1990	Knight of Mercy 4-9-0	30
1991	Notley 4-8-7	29
1992	Lochsong 4-8-0	30
1993	King's Signet 4-9-10	29
1994	For The Present 4-8-3	26
1995	Shikari's Son 8-8-13	27

GORDON STAKES (3y)
Goodwood—1m 4f

1975	Guillaume Tell 8-10	9
1976	Smuggler 8-13	6
1977	Pollerton 8-10	4
1978	Sexton Blake 8-10	5
1979	More Light 8-10	6
1980	Prince Bee 8-10	6
1981	Bustomi 9-2	5
1982	Electric 8-13	6
1983	John French 8-10	6
1984	Commanche Run 8-10	8
1985	Kazaroun 8-10	6
1986	Allez Milord 8-10	5
1987	Love the Groom 9-2	4
1988	Minster Son 8-10	5
1989	Warrshan 8-10	4
1990	Karinga Bay 8-10	6
1991	Stylish Senor 8-10	3
1992	Bonny Scot 8-10	8
1993	Right Win 8-10	8
1994	Broadway Flyer 8-13	9
1995	Presenting 8-10	7

OAK TREE STAKES
Goodwood—7f

1980	Trevita 3-8-5	10
1981	Star Pastures 3-8-11	8
1982	Chalon 3-9-0	5
1983	Fenny Rough 3-8-7	6
1984	Brocade 3-8-5	10
1985	Ever Genial 3-8-5	6
1986	Royal Loft 3-8-7	12
1987	Gayane 3-8-10	6
1988	Ohsomellow 3-8-10	7
1989	Kerita 3-8-7	6

1990	Alidiva 3-8-9	9
1991	Himiko 3-8-7	8
1992	Storm Dove 3-8-7	9
1993	Moon Over Miami 3-8-7	11
1994	Blue Siren 3-8-10	10
1995	Brief Glimpse 3-8-7	10

SUSSEX STAKES
Goodwood—1m

1975	Bolkonski 3-8-10	9
1976	Wollow 3-8-10	9
1977	Artaius 3-8-10	11
1978	Jaazeiro 3-8-10	6
1979	Kris 3-8-10	7
1980	Posse 3-8-10	9
1981	Kings Lake 3-8-10	9
1982	On the House 3-8-7	13
1983	Noalcoholic 6-9-7	11
1984	Chief Singer 3-8-10	5
1985	Rousillon 4-9-7	10
1986	Sonic Lady 3-8-7	5
1987	Soviet Star 3-8-10	7
1988	Warning 3-8-10	7
1989	Zilzal 3-8-10	8
1990	Distant Relative 4-9-7	7
1991	Second Set 3-8-13	8
1992	Marling 3-8-0	8
1993	Bigstone 3-8-13	10
1994	Distant View 3-8-13	9
1995	Sayyedati 5-9-4	6

RICHMOND STAKES (2y)
Goodwood—6f

1975	Stand to Reason 8-11	9
1976	J O Tobin 8-11	5
1977	Persian Bold 8-11	5
1978	Young Generation 8-11	5
1979	Castle Green 8-11	5
1980	Another Realm 8-11	10
1981	Tender King 8-11	7
1982	Gallant Special 8-11	4
1983	Godstone 8-11	9
1984	Primo Dominie 8-11	6
1985	Nomination 8-11	10
1986	Rich Charlie 8-11	8
1987	Warning 8-11	7
1988	Heart of Arabia 9-0	6
1989	Contract Law 8-11	5
1990	Mac's Imp 8-11	7
1991	Dilum 8-11	4
1992	Son Pardo 8-11	6
1993	First Trump 8-11	5
1994	Sri Pekan 8-11	6
1995	Polaris Flight 8-11	6

KING GEORGE STAKES
Goodwood—5f

1975	Auction Ring 3-8-4	8
1976	Music Boy 3-8-5	8
1977	Scarcely Blessed 3-8-2	9
1978	Music Maestro 3-9-1	7
1979	Ahonoora 4-9-3	7

1980	Valeriga 4-9-6 9	1981	Indian Trail 8-3 9
1981	King of Spain 5-9-8 8	1982	Busaco 9-1 10
1982	Tina's Pet 4-9-0 12	1983	Millfontaine 8-13 12
1983	Soba 4-9-0 14	1984	Free Guest 8-6 15
1984	Anita's Prince 3-8-8 13	1985	Fish 'N' Chips 8-3 13
1985	Primo Dominie 3-8-13 11	1986	Chinoiserie 8-11 13
1986	Double Schwartz 5-9-5 14	1987	Broken Hearted 9-3 13
1987	Singing Steven 3-8-13 9	1988	Kazaviyna 7-10 14
1988	Silver Fling 3-8-5 13	1989	Biennial 9-2 8
1989	Statoblest 3-8-8 13	1990	Kawtuban 9-2 8
1990	Argentum 3-9-0 14	1991	Green Danube 8-2 16
1991	Title Roll 3-8-7 15	1992	Party Cited 9-4 18
1992	Freddie Lloyd 3-9-0 11	1993	Western Cape 8-12 18
1993	Lochsong 5-8-11 11	1994	Frustration 8-6 10
1994	Lochsong 6-9-7 15	1995	Jalfrezi 7-10 14
1995	Hever Golf Rose 4-9-5 11		

SCHWEPPES HANDICAP
Goodwood—1m

1987	Waajib 4-9-10 20		
1988	Strike Force 3-8-6 21		
1989	Safawan 3-8-0 14		
1990	March Bird 5-7-8 16		
1991	Sky Cloud 5-8-7 15		
1992	Little Bean 3-8-2 21		
1993	Philidor 4-8-4 19		
1994	Fraam 5-9-9 19		
1995	Khayrapour 5-7-13 21		

SCHRODERS GLORIOUS STAKES
Goodwood—1m 4f

1979	Bohemian Grove 3-8-3 5
1980	Water Mill 3-8-2 7
1981	Capstan 3-7-1 5
1982	Capstan 4-9-1 4
1983	Seymour Hicks 3-8-5 7
1984	Longboat 3-8-2 6
1985	Shernazar 4-9-1 8
1986	Nisnas 3-8-2 8
1987	Knockando 3-8-5 9
1988	Maksud 3-8-2 4
1989	Knoosh 3-8-5 3
1990	Hajade 3-8-6 4
1991	Fly Away Soon 3-8-3 5
1992	Spinning 5-9-2 6
1993	Usaidit 4-8-7 12
1994	Duke of Eurolink 5-8-8 8
1995	Midnight Legend 4-9-7 7

GOODWOOD CUP
Goodwood—2m

1975	Girandole 4-9-0 8
1976	Mr Bigmore 4-9-0 6
1977	Grey Baron 4-9-3 8
1978	Tug of War 5-9-0 5
1979	Le Moss 4-9-7 5
1980	Le Moss 5-9-7 5
1981	Ardross 5-9-7 6
1982	Heighlin 6-9-0 8
1983	Little Wolf 5-9-7 7
1984	Gildoran 4-9-7 4
1985	Valuable Witness 5-9-0......................7
1986	Longboat 5-9-7 5
1987	Sergeyevich 3-7-10 5
1988	Sadeem 5-9-7 6
1989	Mazzacano 4-9-0 5
1990	Lucky Moon 3-7-10............................6
1991	Further Flight 5-9-0..........................10
1992	Further Flight 6-9-5..........................11
1993	Sonus 4-9-3 9
1994	Tioman Island 4-9-5 15
1995	Double Trigger 4-9-5 9

MOLECOMB STAKES (2y)
Goodwood—5f

1975	Hayloft 8-10 8
1976	Be Easy 8-10 7
1977	Hatta 8-10 7
1978	Greenland Park 9-4...........................6
1979	Keep Off 8-10 6
1980	Marwell 8-10 7
1981	Prowess Prince 8-10 6
1982	Kafu 8-10 4
1983	Precocious 9-0 7
1984	Absent Chimes 8-10...........................8
1985	Hotbee 8-7 9
1986	Gemini Fire 8-12 6
1987	Classic Ruler 8-12 7
1988	Almost Blue 8-12 13
1989	Haunting Beauty 8-7 10
1990	Poets Cove 8-12 4
1991	Sahara Star 8-7 7
1992	Millyant 8-7 11
1993	Risky 8-12 5
1994	Hoh Magic 8-10 7
1995	Almaty 9-3 7

SPITFIRE HANDICAP (3y)
(Formerly Extel Handicap and News of the World Handicap before 1970)
Goodwood—1m 2f

1975	Duboff 8-0 12
1976	Il Padrone 8-1 13
1977	Ad Lib Ra 9-0 14
1978	Crimson Beau 8-2 8
1979	Lindoro 9-0 8
1980	Karamita 7-7 10

NASSAU STAKES (fillies)
Before 1975 3-year-olds only.
Goodwood—1m 2f

1975	Roussalka 3-8-8	6
1976	Roussalka 4-9-6	10
1977	Triple First 3-8-5	8
1978	Cistus 3-8-5	7
1979	Connaught Bridge 3-8-5	10
1980	Vielle 3-8-5	7
1981	Go Leasing 3-8-8	11
1982	Dancing Rocks 3-8-5	11
1983	Acclimatise 3-8-5	6
1984	Optimistic Lass 3-8-8	5
1985	Free Guest 4-9-8	11
1986	Park Express 3-8-8	7
1987	Nom de Plume 3-8-7	5
1988	Ela Romara 3-8-6	7
1989	Mamaluna 3-8-6	5
1990	Kartajana 3-8-6	6
1991	Ruby Tiger 4-9-4	5
1992	Ruby Tiger 5-9-1	7
1993	Lyphard's Delta 3-8-6	9
1994	Hawajiss 3-8-6	9
1995	Caramba 3-8-9	6

HUNGERFORD STAKES
Newbury—7f 64yds

1975	Court Chad 3-8-3	14
1976	Ardoon 6-9-4	15
1977	He Loves Me 3-8-11	10
1978	Tannenberg 3-8-6	10
1979	Skyliner 3-8-1	13
1980	Kampala 4-9-0	8
1981	Dalsaan 4-9-0	10
1982	Pas de Seul 3-8-9	9
1983	Salieri 3-8-11	10
1984	Prego 4-9-0	8
1985	Ever Genial 3-8-6	12
1986	Hadeer 4-9-3	11
1987	Abuzz 3-8-3	8
1988	Salse 3-8-9	11
1989	Distant Relative 3-8-11	7
1990	Norwich 3-8-9	7
1991	Only Yours 3-8-11	9
1992	Mojave 3-8-8	10
1993	Inchinor 3-8-11	13
1994	*Young Ern 4-9-3	
	*Pollen Count 5-9-0	12
1995	Harayir 3-8-13	9

GEOFFREY FREER STAKES
Newbury—1m 5f 61yds

1975	Consol 3-8-6	10
1976	Swell Fellow 5-9-0	5
1977	Valinsky 3-8-4	5
1978	Ile de Bourbon 3-8-9	7
1979	Niniski 3-8-1	7
1980	Nicholas Bill 5-9-5	5
1981	Ardross 5-9-8	4
1982	Ardross 6-9-8	9
1983	Khairpour 4-9-0	7
1984	Baynoun 3-8-5	5

1985	Shernazar 4-9-0	5
1986	Bakharoff 3-8-3	6
1987	Moon Madness 4-9-8	4
1988	Top Class 3-8-3	6
1989	Ibn Bey 5-9-8	6
1990	Charmer 5-9-2	5
1991	Drum Taps 5-9-5	7
1992	Shambo 5-9-3	4
1993	Azzilfi 3-8-5	5
1994	Red Route 3-8-5	6
1995	Presenting 3-8-5	6

SOLARIO STAKES (2y)
Sandown—7f 16yds

1975	Over to You 8-11	10
1976	Avgerinos 8-11	10
1977	Bolak 8-11	9
1978	Lyphard's Wish 9-1	6
1979	Rankin 9-4	4
1980	To-Agori-Mou 9-0	4
1981	No race	
1982	The Fort 9-0	6
1983	Falstaff 9-0	4
1984	Oh So Sharp 8-8	9
1985	Bold Arrangement 9-0	5
1986	Shining Water 8-8	11
1987	Sanquirico 9-0	4
1988	High Estate 9-0	6
1989	Be My Chief 9-0	3
1990	Radwell 8-11	9
1991	Chicmond 8-11	7
1992	White Crown 8-11	9
1993	Island Magic 8-11	3
1994	Lovely Millie 8-9	7
1995	Alhaarth 9-2	4

JUDDMONTE INTERNATIONAL STAKES
(Benson & Hedges Gold Cup before 1986)
York—1m 2f 85yds

1975	Dahlia 5-9-4	6
1976	Wollow 3-8-10	7
1977	Relkino 4-9-6	8
1978	Hawaiian Sound 3-8-10	10
1979	Troy 3-8-10	10
1980	Master Willie 3-8-10	12
1981	Beldale Flutter 3-8-10	9
1982	Assert 3-8-10	7
1983	Caerleon 3-8-10	9
1984	Cormorant Wood 4-9-3	9
1985	Commanche Run 4-9-6	6
1986	Shardari 4-9-6	12
1987	Triptych 5-9-3	10
1988	Shady Heights 4-9-6	6
1989	Ile De Chypre 4-9-6	7
1990	In The Groove 3-8-9	9
1991	Terimon 5-9-6	6
1992	Rodrigo de Triano 3-8-12	12
1993	Ezzoud 4-9-6	11
1994	Ezzoud 5-9-6	8
1995	Halling 4-9-6	6

GREAT VOLTIGEUR STAKES
(3y)
York—1m 3f 195yds

1975	Patch 9-0	4
1976	Hawkberry 8-7	7
1977	Alleged 8-11	7
1978	Whitstead 8-7	8
1979	Noble Saint 8-7	5
1980	Prince Bee 8-7	5
1981	Glint of Gold 9-0	6
1982	Electric 8-7	7
1983	Seymour Hicks 8-7	5
1984	Rainbow Quest 8-7	7
1985	Damister 8-11	4
1986	Nisnas 8-7	7
1987	Reference Point 9-0	3
1988	Sheriff's Star 8-12	4
1989	Zalazl 8-9	3
1990	Belmez 9-0	5
1991	Corrupt 8-9	7
1992	Bonny Scot 8-9	6
1993	Bob's Return 8-9	9
1994	Sacrament 8-9	7
1995	Pentire 8-12	4

YORKSHIRE OAKS (fillies and mares)
Before 1991 3-year-old fillies only
York—1m 3f 195yds

1975	May Hill 9-0	5
1976	Sarah Siddons 9-0	13
1977	Busaca 9-0	8
1978	Fair Salinia 9-0	10
1979	Connaught Bridge 9-0	5
1980	Shoot a Line 9-0	7
1981	Condessa 9-0	11
1982	Awaasif 9-0	7
1983	Sun Princess 9-0	6
1984	Circus Plume 9-0	5
1985	Sally Brown 9-0	7
1986	Untold 9-0	11
1987	Bint Pasha 9-0	9
1988	Diminuendo 9-0	6
1989	Roseate Tern 9-0	5
1990	Hellenic 9-0	6
1991	Magnificent Star 3-8-11	7
1992	User Friendly 3-8-11	8
1993	Only Royale 4-9-7	8
1994	Only Royale 5-9-7	7
1995	Pure Grain 3-8-8	8

EBOR HANDICAP
York—1m 5f 194yds

1975	Dakota 4-9-4	18
1976	Sir Montagu 3-8-0	15
1977	Move Off 4-8-1	14
1978	Totowah 4-8-1	22
1979	Sea Pigeon 9-10-0	17
1980	Shaftesbury 4-8-5	16
1981	Protection Racket 3-8-1	22
1982	Another Sam 5-9-2	15
1983	Jupiter Island 4-9-0	16

1984	Crazy 3-8-13	14
1985	Western Dancer 4-8-6	19
1986	Primary 3-8-7	22
1987	Daarkom 4-9-3	15
1988	Kneller 3-8-1	21
1989	Sapience 3-8-4	18
1990	Further Flight 4-8-8	22
1991	Deposki 5-7-3	22
1992	Quick Ransom 4-8-3	22
1993	Sarawat 5-8-2	21
1994	Hasten To Add 4-9-3	21
1995	Sanmartino 3-7-11	21

GIMCRACK STAKES (2y)
York—6f

1975	Music Boy 9-0	14
1976	Nebbiolo 9-0	7
1977	Tumbledownwind 9-0	5
1978	Stanford 9-0	11
1979	Sonnen Gold 9-0	7
1980	Bel Bolide 9-0	9
1981	Full Extent 9-0	8
1982	Horage 9-0	7
1983	Precocious 9-0	6
1984	Doulab 9-0	8
1985	Stalker 9-0	6
1986	Wiganthorpe 9-0	11
1987	Reprimand 9-0	6
1988	Sharp N' Early 9-0	8
1989	Rock City 9-3	5
1990	Mujtahid 9-3	5
1991	River Falls 9-0	5
1992	Splendent 9-0	8
1993	Turtle Island 9-5	8
1994	Chilly Billy 9-0	11
1995	Royal Applause 9-0	5

NUNTHORPE STAKES
York—5f

1975	Bay Express 4-9-7	10
1976	Lochnager 4-9-6	11
1977	Haveroid 3-9-2	8
1978	Solinus 3-9-2	9
1979	Ahonoora 4-9-6	9
1980	Sharpo 3-9-2	11
1981	Sharpo 4-9-0	9
1982	Sharpo 5-9-0	11
1983	Habibti 3-8-7	10
1984	Committed 4-8-11	8
1985	Never So Bold 5-9-0	7
1986	Last Tycoon 3-9-2	8
1987	Ajdal 3-9-2	11
1988	Handsome Sailor 5-9-6	12
1989	Cadeaux Genereux 4-9-6	11
1990	Dayjur 3-9-3	9
1991	Sheikh Albadou 3-9-3	9
1992	Lyric Fantasy 2-7-8	11
1993	Lochsong 5-9-3	10
1994	Piccolo 3-9-3	10
1995	So Factual 5-9-6	8

BRADFORD AND BINGLEY HANDICAP
(Rose of York Handicap before 1983)
York—7f 202yds

1975	Chil the Kite 3-9-2	13
1976	Silver Steel 3-7-13	13
1977	Chukaroo 5-7-11	10
1978	Petronisi 4-8-1	15
1979	Piaffer 4-8-6	9
1980	Miner's Lamp 3-8-7	12
1981	Silver Season 3-9-0	9
1982	Indian Trail 4-8-8	11
1983	Mauritzfontein 4-7-11	14
1984	King of Clubs 3-8-12	17
1985	Lucky Ring 3-8-3	14
1986	Digger's Rest 3-9-4	14
1987	Prince Rupert 3-8-8	15
1988	Kingsfold Flame 5-8-5	15
1989	Known Ranger 3-9-4	16
1990	You Missed Me 4-9-2	17
1991	Pontenuovo 6-9-9	16
1992	Doulab's Image 5-8-11	22
1993	Dawning Street 5-8-13	15
1994	Lap of Luxury 5-8-7	13
1995	Cap Juluca 3-8-11	15

LOWTHER STAKES (2y fillies)
York—6f

1975	Pasty 8-11	7
1976	Icena 8-11	13
1977	Enstone Spark 8-11	9
1978	Devon Ditty 9-0	11
1979	Mrs Penny 9-0	8
1980	Kittyhawk 8-8	5
1981	Circus Ring 8-11	8
1982	Habibti 8-11	8
1983	Prickle 8-11	9
1984	Al Bahathri 8-11	10
1985	Kingscote 8-11	7
1986	Polonia 9-0	9
1987	Ela Romara 8-11	5
1988	Miss Demure 8-11	9
1989	Dead Certain 9-0	6
1990	Only Yours 8-11	9
1991	Culture Vulture 8-11	4
1992	Niche 9-0	6
1993	Velvet Moon 8-11	9
1994	Harayir 8-11	6
1995	Dance Sequence 8-11	9

PRESTIGE STAKES (2y)
(Formerly Waterford Candelabra Stakes)
Goodwood—7f

1981	Stratospheric 8-6	6
1982	Flamenco 8-9	4
1983	Shoot Clear 8-9	8
1984	Bella Colora 8-6	6
1985	Asteroid Field 8-6	6
1986	Invited Guest 8-7	6
1987	Obeah 8-9	6
1988	Life at the Top 8-12	7
1989	Moon Cactus 8-12	7
1990	Jaffa Line 8-9	5
1991	Musicale 9-0	5

1992	Love of Silver 8-9	7
1993	Glatisant 8-9	6
1994	Pure Grain 8-9	9
1995	Bint Shadayid 8-9	6

CELEBRATION MILE
(Formerly Waterford Crystal Mile)
Goodwood—1m

1975	Gay Fandango 3-8-8	8
1976	Free State 3-8-3	6
1977	Be My Guest 3-8-7	6
1978	Captain James 4-8-13	5
1979	Kris 3-8-12	6
1980	Known Fact 3-8-12	6
1981	To-Agori-Mou 3-8-12	8
1982	Sandhurst Prince 3-8-5	8
1983	Montekin 4-8-13	6
1984	Rousillon 3-8-6	5
1985	Abandoned	
1986	Then Again 3-8-7	8
1987	Milligram 3-8-7	4
1988	Prince Rupert 4-9-3	6
1989	Distant Relative 3-8-12	5
1990	Shavian 3-9-0	6
1991	Bold Russian 4-9-0	5
1992	Selkirk 4-9-3	7
1993	Swing Low 4-9-3	6
1994	Mehthaaf 3-8-11	6
1995	Harayir 3-8-12	6

SPRINT CUP
Haydock—6f

1975	Lianga 4-9-7	7
1976	Record Token 4-9-8	8
1977	Boldboy 7-9-8	7
1978	Absalom 3-9-6	14
1979	Double Form 4-9-8	7
1980	Moorestyle 3-8-12	8
1981	Runnett 4-9-3	6
1982	Indian King 4-9-3	9
1983	Habibti 3-8-9	6
1984	Petong 4-9-3	9
1985	Orojoya 3-8-12	8
1986	Green Desert 3-8-12	8
1987	Ajdal 3-9-0	8
1988	Dowsing 4-9-2	10
1989	Danehill 3-9-5	9
1990	Dayjur 3-9-6	9
1991	Polar Falcon 4-9-9	8
1992	Sheikh Albadou 4-9-9	8
1993	Wolfhound 4-9-9	7
1994	Lavinia Fontana 5-8-9	8
1995	Cherokee Rose 4-8-11	6

SEPTEMBER STAKES
Kempton—1m 3f 30yds

1979	Cracaval 3-8-10	9
1980	More Light 4-9-2	7
1981	Kind of Hush 3-8-4	11
1982	Critique 4-9-2	7
1983	Lyphard's Special 3-8-4	6
1984	Bedtime 4-9-0	8
1985	Shernazar 4-9-2	5
1986	Dihistan 4-9-2	7

1987	Knockando 3-8-4	8
1988	Percy's Lass 4-8-11	8
1989	Assatis 4-9-5	5
1990	Lord of the Field 3-8-6	6
1991	Young Buster 3-8-6	5
1992	Jeune 3-8-6	5
1993	Spartan Shareef 4-9-3	9
1994	Wagon Master 4-9-5	5
1995	Burooj 5-9-0	7

MAY HILL STAKES (2y)
Doncaster—1m

1981	Height of Fashion 8-9	4
1982	Bright Crocus 8-7	8
1983	Satinette 8-6	9
1984	Ever Genial 8-6	7
1985	Midway Lady 8-6	6
1986	Laluche 8-9	10
1987	Intimate Guest 8-8	6
1988	Tessla 8-8	11
1989	Rafha 8-8	5
1990	Majmu 8-8	7
1991	Midnight Air 8-8	13
1992	Marillette 8-8	12
1993	Hawajiss 8-8	5
1994	Mamlakah 8-8	11
1995	Solar Crystal 8-9	11

PORTLAND HANDICAP
Doncaster—5f 140yds

1975	Walk By 3-8-10	16
1976	Hei'land Jamie 5-7-13	11
1977	Jon George 3-7-12	12
1978	Goldhills Pride 4-8-10	13
1979	Oh Simmie 4-7-0	21
1980	Swelter 4-8-2	20
1981	Touch Boy 5-8-11	21
1982	Vorvados 5-8-13	14
1983	Out of Hand 4-7-3	15
1984	Dawn's Delight 6-7-8	22
1985	Lochtillum 6-8-1	17
1986	Felipe Toro 3-8-2	23
1987	Dawn's Delight 9-8-13	23
1988	Roman Prose 3-9-3	22
1989	Craft Express 3-8-9	22
1990	Love Legend 5-8-7	21
1991	Sarcita 3-8-6	21
1992	Lochsong 4-8-12	22
1993	Amron 6-9-0	18
1994	Hello Mister 3-8-10	22
1995	Hello Mister 4-8-7	22

PARK HILL STAKES (fillies and mares)
Before 1991 3-year-old fillies only
Doncaster—1m 6f 132yds

1975	May Hill 9-0	7
1976	African Dancer 9-0	9
1977	Royal Hive 9-0	3
1978	Idle Waters 9-0	10
1979	Quay Line 9-0	5
1980	Shoot a Line 9-0	6
1981	Alma Ata 9-0	13

1982	Swiftfoot 9-0	6
1983	High Hawk 9-0	7
1984	Borushka 9-0	13
1985	I Want To Be 9-0	7
1986	Rejuvenate 8-9	12
1987	Trampship 8-9	5
1988	Casey 8-9	9
1989	Lucky Song 8-10	4
1990	Madame Dubois 8-9	8
1991	Patricia 3-8-8	11
1992	Niodini 3-8-5	12
1993	Anna of Saxony 4-9-3	9
1994	Coigach 3-8-5	8
1995	Noble Rose 4-9-3	8

KIVETON PARK STAKES
Doncaster—1m

1978	Green Girl 3-8-4	12
1979	Tap on Wood 3-9-3	7
1980	Known Fact 3-9-3	4
1981	Kittyhawk 3-8-5	6
1982	The Quiet Bidder 4-9-10	9
1983	Annie Edge 3-8-4	8
1984	Sarab 3-8-13	10
1985	Lucky Ring 3-8-13	8
1986	Hadeer 4-9-4	12
1987	Guest Performer 3-8-4	12
1988	Salse 3-8-11	6
1989	Gold Seam 3-8-7	6
1990	Green Line Express 4-9-0	10
1991	Bog Trotter 3-9-0	12
1992	Pursuit of Love 3-9-3	10
1993	Swing Low 4-9-7	6
1994	Soviet Line 4-9-0	9
1995	Bishop of Cashel 3-8-9	8

DONCASTER CUP
Doncaster—2m 2f

1975	Crash Course 4-9-0	3
1976	Sea Anchor 4-9-3	4
1977	Shangamuzo 4-8-12	5
1978	Buckskin 5-9-2	6
1979	Le Moss 4-9-2	5
1980	Le Moss 5-9-2	5
1981	Protection Racket 3-7-6	4
1982	Ardross 6-9-2	8
1983	Karadar 5-8-5	8
1984	Wagoner 4-8-5	4
1985	Spicy Story 4-8-9	8
1986	Longboat 5-9-6	4
1987	Buckley 4-8-13	8
1988	Kneller 3-8-4	4
1989	Weld 3-8-0	3
1990	Al Maheb 4-9-5	10
1991	Great Marquess 4-9-3	8
1992	Further Flight 6-9-3	5
1993	Assessor 4-9-7	4
1994	Arcadian Heights 6-9-7	9
1995	Double Trigger 4-9-7	6

CHAMPAGNE STAKES (2y)
Doncaster—7f

Year	Winner	
1975	Wollow 9-0	8
1976	J. O. Tobin 9-0	6
1977	Sexton Blake 9-0	6
1978	R. B. Chesne 9-0	7
1979	Final Straw 9-0	9
1980	Gielgud 9-0	10
1981	Achieved 9-0	8
1982	Gorytus 9-0	5
1983	Lear Fan 9-0	4
1984	Young Runaway 9-0	6
1985	Sure Blade 9-0	5
1986	Don't Forget Me 9-0	9
1987	Warning 9-0	4
1988	Prince of Dance 8-11	7
1989	Abandoned	
1990	Bog Trotter 8-11	5
1991	Rodrigo de Triano 8-11	5
1992	Petardia 9-0	9
1993	Unblest 8-11	4
1994	Sri Pekan 9-0	7
1995	Alhaarth 9-0	3

FLYING CHILDERS STAKES (2y)
(Norfolk Stakes before 1973)
Doncaster—5f

Year	Winner	
1975	Hittite Glory 9-0	5
1976	Mandrake Major 9-0	9
1977	Music Maestro 9-0	8
1978	Devon Ditty 8-11	7
1979	Abeer 8-11	6
1980	Marwell 8-11	6
1981	Peterhof 9-0	7
1982	Kafu 9-0	5
1983	Superlative 9-0	10
1984	Prince Sabo 9-0	6
1985	Green Desert 9-0	8
1986	Sizzling Melody 9-0	6
1987	Gallic League 8-11	7
1988	Shuttlecock Corner 8-11	8
1989	Abandoned	
1990	Distinctly North 8-11	6
1991	Paris House 8-11	5
1992	Poker Chip 8-6	7
1993	Imperial Bailiwick 8-6	8
1994	Raah Algharb 8-11	8
1995	Cayman Kai 8-12	8

AYR GOLD CUP
Ayr—6f

Year	Winner	
1975	Roman Warrior 4-10-0	23
1976	Last Tango 5-7-5	18
1977	Jon George 3-8-4	25
1978	Vaigly Great 3-9-6	24
1979	Primula Boy 4-7-7	22
1980	Sparkling Boy 3-9-2	24
1981	First Movement 3-7-10	21
1982	Famous Star 3-7-7	14
1983	Polly's Brother 5-8-3	28
1984	Able Albert 4-8-6	29
1985	Camps Heath 4-7-9	25
1986	Green Ruby 5-8-11	29

Year	Winner	
1987	Not So Silly 3-7-10	29
1988	So Careful 5-7-7	29
1989	Joveworth 6-8-0	29
1990	Final Shot 3-8-2	29
1991	Sarcita 3-8-10	28
1992	Lochsong 4-9-0	28
1993	Hard To Figure 7-9-6	29
1994	Daring Destiny 3-8-0	29
1995	Royale Figurine 4-8-9	29

SELECT STAKES
(Formerly Valdoe Stakes)
Goodwood—1m 2f

Year	Winner	
1975	Escapologist 3-7-8	7
1976	Obstacle 3-7-12	8
1977	Balmerino 5-9-9	9
1978	Gunner B 5-9-9	3
1979	Bolide (at Sandown) 3-7-13	6
1980	Welsh Chanter 4-9-3	6
1981	Prince Bee 4-9-9	4
1982	Peacetime 3-8-10	6
1983	Morcon 3-8-7	6
1984	Bob Back 3-8-5	5
1985	Iroko 3-8-4	8
1986	Dancing Brave 3-8-13	6
1987	Most Welcome 3-8-6	6
1988	Mtoto 5-9-9	5
1989	Legal Case 3-8-6	5
1990	Missionary Ridge 3-8-12	5
1991	Filia Ardross 5-8-11	6
1992	Knifebox 4-9-0	10
1993	Knifebox 5-9-3	6
1994	Alderbrook 5-9-0	7
1995	Triarius 5-9-0	6

COURAGE HANDICAP
(Peter Hastings Handicap before 1985)
Newbury—1m 2f 6yds

Year	Winner	
1975	Jolly Good 3-8-11	12
1976	Chil the Kite 4-9-10	9
1977	April 3-8-3	11
1978	Pam's Gleam 5-8-0	8
1979	Effulgence 4-9-4	7
1980	Etching 3-8-5	9
1981	Atlantic Boy 4-9-4	8
1982	Oratavo 4-7-13	13
1983	Mauritzfontein 4-8-2	9
1984	Miss Saint-Cloud 3-8-8	7
1985	Leading Star 3-8-13	15
1986	Power Bender 4-8-1	13
1987	Shabib 3-8-4	9
1988	Ile de Chypre 3-9-3	16
1989	Monastery 3-8-4	16
1990	Lord of Tusmore 3-8-2	10
1991	Palatial Style 4-9-7	11
1992	Montpelier Boy 4-8-0	14
1993	Lindon Lime 3-8-5	14
1994	Green Crusader 3-8-1	8
1995	Kutta 3-9-5	20

MILL REEF STAKES (2y)
Newbury—6f 8yds

Year	Winner	
1975	Royal Boy 8-11	8

1976	Anax 8-11	6
1977	Formidable 8-11	6
1978	King of Spain 8-11	8
1979	Lord Seymour 8-11	7
1980	Sweet Monday 8-11	7
1981	Hays 8-11	8
1982	Salieri 8-11	5
1983	Vacarme 8-11	7
1984	Local Suitor 8-11	12
1985	Luqman 8-11	9
1986	Forest Flower 8-8	9
1987	Magic of Life 8-6	5
1988	Russian Bond 8-11	4
1989	Welney 8-11	7
1990	Time Gentlemen 8-11	7
1991	Showbrook 9-1	5
1992	Forest Wind 8-11	7
1993	Polish Laughter 8-11	5
1994	Princely Hush 8-11	9
1995	Kahir Almaydan 8-12	6

AUTUMN CUP (Handicap)
Newbury—1m 5f 61yds

1975	Coed Cochion 3-8-2	15
1976	John Cherry 5-9-6	4
1977	Nearly a Hand 3-8-4	12
1978	Piccadilly Line 5-8-12	8
1979	Greatham House 3-9-1	13
1980	Castle Keep 3-9-1	10
1981	Telsmoss 5-8-4	10
1982	Fitzpatrick 3-8-6	14
1983	Jupiter Island 4-9-8	16
1984	First Bout 3-7-7	13
1985	Eastern Mystic 3-9-4	16
1986	Broken Wave 3-8-3	13
1987	Aim To Please 3-8-2	14
1988	Green Adventure 3-9-10	17
1989	Braashee 3-9-5	16
1990	First Victory 4-9-6	12
1991	Talos 3-8-8	14
1992	Castoret 6-7-13	18
1993	Castoret 7-9-0	20
1994	Warm Spell 4-8-5	16
1995	Whitechapel 7-9-0	23

CUMBERLAND LODGE STAKES
Ascot—1m 4f

1975	Calaba 5-8-8	15
1976	Bruni 4-9-7	9
1977	Orange Bay 5-9-7	6
1978	Fordham 3-8-2	5
1979	Main Reef 3-8-3	6
1980	Fingal's Cave 3-8-3	5
1981	Critique 3-8-5	8
1982	Lafontaine 5-9-0	7
1983	Band 3-8-5	8
1984	Bedtime 4-9-3	7
1985	Shardari 3-8-6	5
1986	Kazaroun 4-9-3	4
1987	Moon Madness 4-9-7	5
1988	Assatis 3-8-5	6

1989	Tralos 4-9-0	4
1990	Ile de Nisky 4-9-0	7
1991	Drum Taps 5-9-5	5
1992	Opera House 4-9-5	5
1993	Prince of Andros 3-8-6	6
1994	Wagon Master 4-9-5	6
1995	Riyadian 3-8-6	8

THE FILLIES MILE (2y fillies)
Ascot—1m

1975	Icing 9-1	6
1976	Miss Pinkie 9-1	8
1977	Cherry Hinton 9-1	8
1978	Formulate 9-1	9
1979	Quick as Lightning 8-12	9
1980	Leap Lively 8-12	7
1981	Height of Fashion 9-2	8
1982	Acclimatise 8-9	8
1983	Nepula 8-9	8
1984	Oh So Sharp 8-10	8
1985	Untold 8-7	9
1986	Invited Guest 9-0	12
1987	Diminuendo 8-13	7
1988	Tessla 8-13	8
1989	Silk Slippers 8-10	8
1990	Shamshir 8-10	12
1991	Culture Vulture 8-10	7
1992	Ivanka 8-10	8
1993	Fairy Heights 8-10	11
1994	Aqaarid 8-10	9
1995	Bosra Sham 8-10	6

DIADEM STAKES
Ascot—6f

1975	*Roman Warrior 4-9-7	8
	*Swingtime 3-8-13	8
1976	Honeyblest 4-9-7	7
1977	Gentilhombre 4-9-7	6
1978	Creetown 6-9-7	14
1979	Absalom 4-9-7	6
1980	Sovereign Rose 3-9-0	9
1981	Moorestyle 4-9-7	10
1982	Indian King 4-9-7	9
1983	Salieri 3-9-3	12
1984	Never So Bold 4-9-7	9
1985	Al Sylah 3-8-9	8
1986	Hallgate 3-8-12	12
1987	Dowsing 3-8-12	17
1988	Cadeaux Genereux 3-8-12	13
1989	Chummy's Favourite 4-9-2	11
1990	Ron's Victory 3-8-11	14
1991	Shalford 3-8-11	16
1992	Wolfhound 3-8-11	11
1993	Catrail 3-8-11	9
1994	Lake Coniston 3-8-11	11
1995	Cool Jazz 4-9-0	15

QUEEN ELIZABETH II STAKES
Ascot—1m

1975	Rose Bowl 3-8-4	5
1976	Rose Bowl 4-9-4	8
1977	Trusted 4-9-0	7
1978	Homing 3-8-7	11
1979	Kris 3-9-0	7
1980	Known Fact 3-9-0	7
1981	To-Agori-Mou 3-9-0	6
1982	Buzzards Bay 4-9-0	10
1983	Sackford 3-8-7	9
1984	Teleprompter 4-9-0	6
1985	Shadeed 3-9-0	7
1986	Sure Blade 3-8-11	7
1987	Milligram 3-8-8	5
1988	Warning 3-8-11	8
1989	Zilzal 3-8-11	5
1990	Markofdistinction 4-9-4	10
1991	Selkirk 3-9-0	9
1992	Lahib 4-9-4	9
1993	Bigstone 3-9-0	9
1994	Maroof 4-9-4	9
1995	Bahri 3-8-11	6

ROYAL LODGE STAKES (2y)
Ascot—1m

1975	Sir Wimborne 8-11	6
1976	Gairloch 8-11	6
1977	Shirley Heights 8-11	8
1978	Ela-Mana-Mou 8-11	8
1979	Hello Gorgeous 8-11	4
1980	Robellino 8-11	8
1981	Norwick 8-11	9
1982	Dunbeath 8-11	9
1983	Gold and Ivory 8-11	5
1984	Reach 8-11	8
1985	Bonhomie 8-11	7
1986	Bengal Fire 8-11	9
1987	Sanquirico 8-13	10
1988	High Estate 8-13	5
1989	Digression 8-10	9
1990	Mujaazif 8-10	8
1991	Made of Gold 8-10	8
1992	Desert Secret 8-10	10
1993	Mister Baileys 8-10	9
1994	Eltish 8-10	8
1995	Mons 8-11	8

CHEVELEY PARK STAKES (2y fillies)
Newmarket—6f

1975	Pasty 8-11	14
1976	Durtal 8-11	15
1977	Sookera 8-11	10
1978	Devon Ditty 8-11	7
1979	Mrs Penny 8-11	12
1980	Marwell 8-11	8
1981	Woodstream 8-11	13
1982	Ma Biche 8-11	9
1983	Desirable 8-11	12
1984	Park Appeal 8-11	13
1985	Embla 8-11	14
1986	Forest Flower 8-11	5
1987	Ravinella 8-11	8

1988	Pass the Peace 8-11	7
1989	Dead Certain 8-11	11
1990	Capricciosa 8-11	11
1991	Marling 8-11	9
1992	Sayyedati 8-11	4
1993	Prophecy 8-11	6
1994	Gay Gallanta 8-11	10
1995	Blue Duster 8-11	5

MIDDLE PARK STAKES (2y)
Newmarket—6f

1975	Hittite Glory 9-0	8
1976	Tachypous 9-0	11
1977	Formidable 9-0	7
1978	Junius 9-0	10
1979	Known Fact 9-0	7
1980	Mattaboy 9-0	9
1981	Cajun 9-0	13
1982	Diesis 9-0	6
1983	Creag-an-Sgor 9-0	9
1984	Bassenthwaite 9-0	8
1985	Stalker 9-0	6
1986	Mister Majestic 9-0	7
1987	Gallic League 9-0	5
1988	Mon Tresor 9-0	6
1989	Balla Cove 9-0	6
1990	Lycius 9-0	6
1991	Rodrigo de Triano 9-0	6
1992	Zieten 9-0	6
1993	First Trump 9-0	8
1994	Fard 9-0	10
1995	Royal Applause 8-11	5

SUN CHARIOT STAKES (fillies and mares)
Before 1974: 3-year-old fillies only.
Newmarket—1m 2f

1975	Duboff 3-8-7	11
1976	Ranimer 3-8-7	10
1977	Triple First 3-9-0	7
1978	Swiss Maid 3-8-7	9
1979	Topsy 3-8-7	8
1980	Snow 3-8-7	7
1981	Home on the Range 3-8-6	10
1982	Time Charter 3-9-0	10
1983	Cormorant Wood 3-8-5	9
1984	Free Guest 3-8-4	8
1985	Free Guest 4-9-4	5
1986	Dusty Dollar 3-8-7	7
1987	Infamy 3-8-7	6
1988	Indian Skimmer 4-9-6	6
1989	Braiswick 3-8-7	9
1990	Kartajana 3-8-11	7
1991	Ristna 3-8-8	5
1992	Red Slippers 3-8-8	7
1993	Talented 3-8-8	7
1994	La Confederation 3-8-8	7
1995	Warning Shadows 3-8-8	7

CAMBRIDGESHIRE
Newmarket—1m 1f

1975	Lottogift 4-8-2	36
1976	Intermission 3-8-6	29

1977	Sin Timon 3-8-3	27
1978	Baronet 6-9-0	18
1979	Smartset 4-8-8	24
1980	Baronet 8-9-3	19
1981	Braughing 4-8-4	28
1982	Century City 3-9-6	29
1983	Sagamore 4-7-8	30
1984	Leysh 3-8-7	34
1985	Tremblant 4-9-8	31
1986	Dallas 3-9-6	31
1987	Balthus 4-8-1	31
1988	Quinlan Terry 3-8-5	29
1989	Rambo's Hall 4-8-6	34
1990	Risen Moon 3-8-9	40
1991	Mellottie 6-9-1	29
1992	Rambo's Hall 7-9-3	30
1993	Penny Drops 4-7-13	33
1994	Halling 3-8-8	30
1995	Cap Juluca 3-9-10	39

JOCKEY CLUB CUP
Newmarket—2m

1975	Blood Royal 4-9-6	6
1976	Bright Finish 3-8-6	6
1977	Grey Baron 4-9-3	5
1978	Buckskin 5-9-7	6
1979	Nicholas Bill 4-8-11	8
1980	Ardross 4-9-5	5
1981	Centroline 3-8-4	9
1982	Little Wolf 4-9-5	8
1983	Karadar 5-9-3	5
1984	Old Country 5-9-7	4
1985	Tale Quale 3-8-4	10
1986	Valuable Witness 6-9-5	4
1987	Buckley 4-9-3	11
1988	Kneller 3-8-7	5
1989	Weld 3-8-7	3
1990	Great Marquess 3-8-3	7
1991	Further Flight 5-9-3	6
1992	Further Flight 6-9-3	4
1993	Further Flight 7-9-3	6
1994	Further Flight 8-9-3	5
1995	Further Flight 9-9-3	8

SUPREME STAKES
Goodwood—7f

1987	Asteroid Field 4-8-6	10
1988	Fair Judgement 4-8-12	8
1989	Kerita 3-8-5	8
1990	Anshan 3-8-9	6
1991	Osario 4-8-12	13
1992	Hazaam 3-8-9	7
1993	Abandoned	
1994	Soviet Line 4-9-2	9
1995	Inzar 3-8-8	10

PRINCESS ROYAL STAKES
Ascot—1m 4f

1975	Shebeen 4-9-6	9
1976	Abandoned	
1977	Aloft 3-8-9	11

1978	Trillionaire 3-8-6	6
1979	Alia 3-8-3	11
1980	Karamita 3-8-7	8
1981	Flighting 3-8-3	11
1982	Believer 3-8-3	14
1983	Sylph 3-8-3	11
1984	One Way Street 3-8-7	11
1985	Free Guest 4-9-7	15
1986	Tashtiya 3-8-9	6
1987	Abandoned	
1988	Banket 3-8-6	8
1989	Snow Bride 3-8-11	10
1990	Narwala 3-8-6	7
1991	Always Friendly 3-8-6	8
1992	Cunning 3-8-9	9
1993	Abandoned	
1994	Dancing Bloom 4-9-0	7
1995	Labibeh 3-8-6	5

CORNWALLIS STAKES (2y)
Ascot—5f

1975	Western Jewel 8-11	7
1976	Abandoned	
1977	Absalom 9-0	8
1978	Greenland Park 8-11	7
1979	Hanu 9-0	8
1980	Pushy 9-0	7
1981	My Lover 9-0	7
1982	Tatibah 9-0	9
1983	Petorius 9-0	14
1984	Doulab 9-0	11
1985	Hallgate 9-0	13
1986	Singing Steven 8-11	9
1987	Abandoned	
1988	Hadif 8-13	13
1989	Argentum 8-13	10
1990	Mujadil 8-13	11
1991	Magic Ring 9-2	11
1992	Up And At 'Em 8-13	13
1993	Abandoned	
1994	Millstream 8-11	7
1995	Mubhij 8-12	7

DEWHURST STAKES (2y)
Newmarket—7f

1975	Wollow 9-0	7
1976	The Minstrel 9-0	11
1977	Try My Best 9-0	7
1978	Tromos 9-0	6
1979	Monteverdi 9-0	6
1980	Storm Bird 9-0	5
1981	Wind and Wuthering 9-0	9
1982	Diesis 9-0	4
1983	El Gran Senor 9-0	10
1984	Kala Dancer 9-0	11
1985	Huntingdale 9-0	8
1986	Ajdal 9-0	5
1987	Abandoned	
1988	*Prince of Dance 9-0	
	*Scenic 9-0	6
1989	Dashing Blade 9-0	7
1990	Generous 9-0	8
1991	Dr Devious 9-0	9

1992	Zafonic 9-0	11
1993	Grand Lodge 9-0	10
1994	Pennekamp 9-0	7
1995	Alhaarth 9-0	4

ROCKFEL STAKES (2y)
Newmarket—7f

1981	Top Hope 8-8	8
1982	Saving Mercy 8-7	7
1983	Mahogany 8-8	13
1984	Kashi Lagoon 8-5	9
1985	Tralthee 8-6	9
1986	At Risk 8-9	13
1987	Abandoned	
1988	Musical Bliss 8-8	9
1989	Negligent 8-8	12
1990	Crystal Gazing 8-8	6
1991	Musicale 8-11	6
1992	Yawl 8-8	7
1993	Relatively Special 8-8	9
1994	Germane 8-8	8
1995	Bint Salsabil 8-12	8

CHALLENGE STAKES
Newmarket—7f

1975	Be Tuneful 3-8-13	7
1976	Star Bird 3-9-0	8
1977	Boldboy 7-9-6	8
1978	Spence Bay 3-9-2	12
1979	Kris 3-9-2	7
1980	Moorestyle 3-9-2	6
1981	Moorestyle 4-9-6	7
1982	Noalcoholic 5-9-6	8
1983	Salieri 3-9-2	10
1984	Brocade 3-8-13	7
1985	Efisio 3-9-2	8
1986	Lucky Ring 4-9-0	12
1987	Asteroid Field 4-8-11	7
1988	Salse 3-8-10	8
1989	Distant Relative 3-8-13	6
1990	Sally Rous 3-8-8	8
1991	Mystiko 3-9-0	7
1992	Selkirk 4-9-3	8
1993	Catrail 3-8-11	7
1994	Zieten 4-9-0	8
1995	Harayir 3-8-12	8

REDCAR TWO-YEAR-OLD TROPHY (2y)
Redcar—6f

1989	Osario 8-4	25
1990	Chipaya 8-5	19
1991	Casteddu 8-1	25
1992	Pips Pride 8-5	24
1993	Cape Merino 7-7	26
1994	Maid For Walking 7-13	26
1995	Blue Iris 8-2	26

CHAMPION STAKES
Newmarket—1m 2f

1975	Rose Bowl 3-8-7	9
1976	Vitiges 3-8-11	19
1977	Flying Water 4-9-0	8
1978	Swiss Maid 3-8-7	10
1979	Northern Baby 3-8-10	14
1980	Cairn Rouge 3-8-7	13
1981	Vayrann 3-8-10	16
1982	Time Charter 3-8-7	14
1983	Cormorant Wood 3-8-7	10
1984	Palace Music 3-8-10	15
1985	Pebbles 4-9-0	10
1986	Triptych 4-9-0	11
1987	Triptych 5-9-0	11
1988	Indian Skimmer 4-9-0	5
1989	Legal Case 3-8-10	11
1990	In The Groove 3-8-9	10
1991	Tel Quel 3-8-12	12
1992	Rodrigo de Triano 3-8-12	10
1993	Hatoof 4-9-0	12
1994	Dernier Empereur 4-9-4	8
1995	Spectrum 3-8-10	8

CESAREWITCH
Newmarket—2m 2f

1975	Shantallah 3-8-10	17
1976	John Cherry 5-9-13	14
1977	Assured 4-8-4	11
1978	Centurion 3-9-8	17
1979	Sir Michael 3-7-8	25
1980	Popsi's Joy 5-8-6	27
1981	Halsbury 3-8-4	30
1982	Mountain Lodge 3-7-10	28
1983	Bajan Sunshine 4-8-8	28
1984	Tom Sharp 4-7-5	26
1985	Kayudee 5-8-1	21
1986	Orange Hill 4-7-9	25
1987	Private Audition 5-7-9	28
1988	Nomadic Way 3-7-9	24
1989	Double Dutch 5-9-10	22
1990	Trainglot 3-7-12	25
1991	Go South 7-7-11	22
1992	Vintage Crop 5-9-6	24
1993	Aahsaylad 7-8-12	31
1994	Captain's Guest 4-9-9	32
1995	Old Red 5-7-11	21

HORRIS HILL STAKES (2y)
Newbury—7f 64yds

1975	State Occasion 9-0	11
1976	Fair Season 9-0	9
1977	*Derrylin 9-0	
	*Persian Bold 9-0	12
1978	Kris 9-0	9
1979	Super Asset 9-0	4
1980	Kalaglow 9-0	10
1981	Montekin 9-0	8
1982	Abandoned	
1983	Elegant Air 9-0	7
1984	Efisio 9-0	5
1985	Celtic Heir 9-0	12
1986	Naheez 9-0	7
1987	Glacial Storm 8-12	8
1988	Gouriev 8-12	8
1989	Tirol 8-12	9
1990	Sapieha 8-12	9
1991	Lion Cavern 8-12	7

1992	Beggarman Thief 8-12	11
1993	Tatami 8-12	8
1994	Painter's Row 8-12	10
1995	Tumbleweed Ridge 8-9	9

ST SIMON STAKES
Newbury—1m 4f 5yds

1975	Dakota 4-9-0	4
1976	Mart Lane 3-8-7	12
1977	Hot Grove 3-8-10	11
1978	Obraztsovy 3-8-7	6
1979	Main Reef 3-8-10	7
1980	Shining Finish 3-8-7	9
1981	Little Wolf 3-8-7	7
1982	Abandoned	
1983	Jupiter Island 4-9-0	11
1984	Gay Lemur 4-9-6	11
1985	Shardari 3-8-10	8
1986	Jupiter Island 7-8-9	9
1987	Lake Erie 4-9-0	11
1988	Upend 3-8-4	9
1989	Sesame 4-8-11	11
1990	Down The Flag 3-8-7	8
1991	Further Flight 5-9-3	11
1992	Up Anchor 3-8-4	8
1993	Kithanga 3-8-4	11
1994	Persian Brave 4-9-0	9
1995	Phantom Gold 3-8-9	12

RACING POST TROPHY (2y)
(Observer Gold Cup before 1976)
(Formerly The Futurity Stakes)
Doncaster—1m

1975	Take Your Place 9-0	11
1976	Sporting Yankee 9-0	6
1977	Dactylographer 9-0	12
1978	Sandy Creek 9-0	11
1979	Hello Gorgeous 9-0	7
1980	Beldale Flutter 9-0	7

1981	Count Pahlen 9-0	13
1982	Dunbeath 9-0	8
1983	Alphabatim 9-0	9
1984	Lanfranco 9-0	10
1985	Bakharoff 9-0	9
1986	Reference Point 9-0	10
1987	Emmson 9-0	6
1988	Al Hareb 9-0	8
1989	Be My Chief 9-0 (Run at Newcastle)	5
1990	Peter Davies 9-0	4
1991	Seattle Rhyme 9-0	8
1992	Armiger 9-0	10
1993	King's Theatre 9-0	9
1994	Celtic Swing 9-0	8
1995	Beauchamp King 9-0	4

NOVEMBER HANDICAP
Doncaster—1m 4f

1975	Mr Bigmore 3-9-1	12
1976	Gale Bridge 3-8-12	14
1977	Sailcloth 3-7-7	20
1978	Eastern Spring 4-7-10	21
1979	Morse Code 4-8-3	14
1980	Path of Peace 4-8-5	22
1981	Lafontaine 4-8-7	20
1982	*Double Shuffle 3-9-0	
	*Turkoman 3-8-7	17
1983	Asir 3-8-7	25
1984	Abu Kadra 3-8-12	23
1985	Bold Rex 3-8-7	24
1986	Beijing 3-8-4	25
1987	Swingit Gunner 6-8-11	25
1988	Young Benz 4-8-4	22
1989	Firelight Fiesta 4-9-8	19
1990	Azzaam 3-9-8	24
1991	Hieroglyphic 3-8-13	22
1992	Turgenev 3-9-0	25
1993	Quick Ransom 5-8-10	25
1994	Saxon Maid 3-8-9	24
1995	Snow Princess 3-8-2	18

Winners of Principal Races in Ireland

IRISH 2000 GUINEAS (3y)
The Curragh—1m

1975	Grundy 9-0	12
1976	Northern Treasure 9-0	17
1977	Pampapaul 9-0	21
1978	Jaazeiro 9-0	12
1979	Dickens Hill 9-0	9
1980	Nikoli 9-0	13
1981	Kings Lake 9-0	13
1982	Dara Monarch 9-0	14
1983	Wassl 9-0	10
1984	Sadler's Wells 9-0	9
1985	Triptych 8-11	16
1986	Flash of Steel 9-0	6
1987	Don't Forget Me 9-0	8
1988	Prince of Birds 9-0	14

1989	Shaadi 9-0	12
1990	Tirol 9-0	9
1991	Fourstars Allstar 9-0	12
1992	Rodrigo de Triano 9-0	6
1993	Barathea 9-0	11
1994	Turtle Island 9-0	9
1995	Spectrum 9-0	9

IRISH 1000 GUINEAS (3y fillies)
The Curragh—1m

1975	Miralla 9-0	11
1976	Sarah Siddons 9-0	14
1977	Lady Capulet 9-0	14
1978	More So 9-0	17
1979	Godetia 9-0	12
1980	Cairn Rouge 9-0	18

1981	Arctique Royale 9-0	15
1982	Prince's Polly 9-0	24
1983	L'Attrayante 9-0	18
1984	Katies 9-0	23
1985	Al Bahathri 9-0	15
1986	Sonic Lady 9-0	19
1987	Forest Flower 9-0	11
1988	Trusted Partner 9-0	16
1989	Ensconse 9-0	13
1990	In The Groove 9-0	12
1991	Kooyonga 9-0	12
1992	Marling 9-0	9
1993	Nicer 9-0	14
1994	Mehthaaf 9-0	10
1995	Ridgewood Pearl 9-0	10

IRISH DERBY (3y)
The Curragh—1m 4f

1975	Grundy 9-0	13
1976	Malacate 9-0	17
1977	The Minstrel 9-0	15
1978	Shirley Heights 9-0	11
1979	Troy 9-0	9
1980	Tyrnavos 9-0	13
1981	Shergar 9-0	12
1982	Assert 9-0	10
1983	Shareef Dancer 9-0	12
1984	El Gran Senor 9-0	8
1985	Law Society 9-0	13
1986	Shahrastani 9-0	11
1987	Sir Harry Lewis 9-0	8
1988	Kahyasi 9-0	11
1989	Old Vic 9-0	8
1990	Salsabil 8-11	9
1991	Generous 9-0	6
1992	St Jovite 9-0	11
1993	Commander in Chief 9-0	11
1994	Balanchine 8-11	9
1995	Winged Love 9-0	13

IRISH OAKS (3y fillies)
The Curragh—1m 4f

1975	Juliette Marny 9-0	14
1976	Lagunette 9-0	18
1977	Olwyn 9-0	8
1978	Fair Salinia 9-0	12
1979	Godetia 9-0	13
1980	Shoot A Line 9-0	8
1981	Blue Wind 9-0	10
1982	Swiftfoot 9-0	10
1983	Give Thanks 9-0	12
1984	Princess Pati 9-0	11
1985	Helen Street 9-0	9
1986	Colorspin 9-0	8
1987	Unite 9-0	8
1988	*Diminuendo 9-0	
	*Melodist 9-0	9
1989	Alydaress 9-0	5
1990	Knight's Baroness 9-0	10
1991	Possessive Dancer 9-0	10
1992	User Friendly 9-0	9

1993	Wemyss Bight 9-0	11
1994	Bolas 9-0	10
1995	Pure Grain 9-0	10

HEINZ '57' PHOENIX STAKES (2y)
Leopardstown—6f

1975	National Wish 9-0	8
1976	Cloonlara 8-11	7
1977	Perla 8-11	6
1978	Kilijaro 8-11	9
1979	Smokey Lady 8-11	10
1980	Swan Princess 8-11	10
1981	Achieved 9-0	7
1982	Sweet Emma 8-11	11
1983	King Persian 9-0	13
1984	Aviance 8-11	9
1985	Roaring Riva 9-0	13
1986	Minstrella 8-11	12
1987	Digamist 9-0	12
1988	Superpower 9-0	10
1989	Pharaoh's Delight 8-11	10
1990	Mac's Imp 9-0	13
1991	Bradawn Breever 9-0	9
1992	Pips Pride 9-0	9
1993	Turtle Island 9-0	9
1994	Eva Luna 8-11	10
1995	Danehill Dancer 9-0	10

IRISH CHAMPION STAKES
Leopardstown—1m 2f
(Phoenix Champion Stakes before 1991)

1984	Sadler's Wells 3-8-11	12
1985	Commanche Run 4-9-6	11
1986	Park Express 3-8-8	13
1987	Triptych 5-9-3	12
1988	Indian Skimmer 4-9-3	9
1989	Carroll House 4-9-6	9
1990	Elmaamul 3-8-11	9
1991	Suave Dancer 3-8-11	7
1992	Dr Devious 3-8-11	8
1993	Muhtarram 4-9-4	10
1994	Cezanne 5-9-4	8
1995	Pentire 3-8-11	8

IRISH CAMBRIDGESHIRE
The Curragh—1m (Hcap)

1975	Inis-Gloire 3-8-0	31
1976	Floriferous 3-8-10	25
1977	Poacher's Moon 4-10-0	22
1978	Loyal Son 4-7-13	22
1979	Habituate 3-9-3	19
1980	I'm Ready 3-8-3	24
1981	Majestic Nurse 6-8-3	18
1982	Majestic Star 5-9-5	14
1983	Persian Royale 3-7-13	25
1984	Chammsky 5-9-4	21
1985	National Form 4-9-9	24
1986	Any Song 3-9-1	26
1987	Silius 4-7-10	24
1988	Ben's Pearl 3-7-9	30
1989	Smoggy Spray 5-8-10	17
1990	Jonjas Chudleigh 3-9-10	22
1991	Must Hurry 4-8-0	12

1992	Khizarabad 3-8-3	16
1993	Wandering Thoughts 4-8-2	18
1994	Saibot 5-9-0	18
1995	The Bower 6-7-8	15

MOYGLARE STUD STAKES (2y fillies)
The Curragh—7f

1975	Petipa 8-11	10
1976	Regal Ray 8-11	8
1977	Ridaness 8-12	9
1978	Phil's Fancy 8-11	9
1979	Daness 8-11	6
1980	Arctique Royale 8-11	14
1981	Woodstream 8-11	14
1982	Habibti 8-11	15
1983	Gala Event 8-11	20
1984	Park Appeal 8-11	13
1985	Gayle Gal 8-11	15
1986	Minstrella 8-11	8
1987	Flutter Away 8-11	11
1988	Flamenco Wave 8-11	11
1989	Chimes of Freedom 8-11	7
1990	Capricciosa 8-11	8
1991	Twafeaj 8-11	8
1992	Sayyedati 8-11	8
1993	Lemon Souffle 8-11	11
1994	Belle Genius 8-11	8
1995	Priory Belle 8-11	13

NATIONAL STAKES (2y)
The Curragh—7f

1975	Sir Wimborne 9-0	7
1976	Pampapaul 9-0	8
1977	Diamonds Are Trump 9-0	9
1978	Tap on Wood 9-0	10
1979	Monteverdi 9-0	15
1980	Storm Bird 9-0	10
1981	Day Is Done 9-0	11
1982	Glenstal 9-0	9
1983	El Gran Senor 9-0	8
1984	Law Society 9-0	9
1985	Tate Gallery 9-0	9
1986	Lockton 9-0	9
1987	Caerwent 9-0	6
1988	Classic Fame 9-0	12
1989	Dashing Blade 9-0	10
1990	Heart of Darkness 9-0	8
1991	El Prado 9-0	5
1992	Fatherland 9-0	5
1993	Manntari 9-0	6

| 1994 | Definite Article 9-0 | 5 |
| 1995 | Danehill Dancer 9-0 | 7 |

IRISH ST LEGER
Before 1983: 3-year-olds only
The Curragh—1m 6f

1975	Caucasus 9-0	13
1976	Meneval 9-0	11
1977	Transworld 9-0	9
1978	M-Lolshan 9-0	8
1979	Niniski 9-0	10
1980	Gonzales 9-0	8
1981	Protection Racket 9-0	7
1982	Touching Wood 9-0	10
1983	Mountain Lodge 4-9-4	10
1984	Opale 4-9-4	9
1985	Leading Counsel 3-8-12	12
1986	Authaal 3-8-12	6
1987	Eurobird 8-9	8
1988	Dark Lomond 3-8-9	13
1989	Petite Ile 3-8-9	10
1990	Ibn Bey 6-9-8	12
1991	Turgeon 5-9-8	10
1992	Mashaallah 4-9-8	9
1993	Vintage Crop 6-9-8	8
1994	Vintage Crop 7-9-8	8
1995	Strategic Choice 4-9-8	7

IRISH CESAREWITCH
The Curragh—2m (Hcap)

1975	Prominent King 3-8-2	21
1976	Cill Dara 4-8-9	29
1977	Cill Dara 5-9-6	28
1978	Chateau Royal 3-8-8	23
1979	Jack of Trumps 7-8-13	23
1980	Potato Merchant 5-7-8	20
1981	The Neurologist 3-9-3	30
1982	Five Nations 5-8-2	29
1983	Five Nations 6-7-11	20
1984	Jean-Claude 3-7-11	24
1985	Ravaro 5-9-12	30
1986	Orient Rose 3-8-12	23
1987	Try a Brandy 5-8-4	29
1988	Midsummer Gamble 7-8-12	26
1989	Marlion 8-7-8	18
1990	Chirkpar 3-7-4	19
1991	Aiybak 5-7-1	16
1992	Sinntara 3-7-7	17
1993	Cliveden Gail 4-9-3	23
1994	Elupa 3-7-10	22
1995	Montelado 8-8-9	14

Winners of Principal Races in France

PRIX GANAY
Longchamp—1m 2f 110yds

1978	Trillion 4-8-13	8
1979	Frere Basile 4-9-2	8
1980	Le Marmot 4-9-2	6
1981	Argument 4-9-2	9
1982	Bikala 4-9-2	10
1983	Lancastrian 6-9-2	7
1984	Romildo 4-9-2	8
1985	Sagace 5-9-2	7
1986	Baillamont 4-9-2	10
1987	Triptych 5-8-13	10
1988	Saint Andrews 4-9-2	5
1989	Saint Andrews 5-9-2	7
1990	Creator 4-9-2	10
1991	Kartajana 4-8-13	7
1992	Subotica 4-9-2	7
1993	Vert Amande 5-9-2	8
1994	Marildo 7-9-2	8
1995	Pelder 5-9-2	10

POULE D'ESSAI DES POULAINS (3y)
Longchamp—1m

1975	Green Dancer 9-2	12
1976	Red Lord 9-2	11
1977	Blushing Groom 9-2	6
1978	Nishapour 9-2	14
1979	Irish River 9-2	4
1980	In Fijar 9-2	13
1981	Recitation 9-2	10
1982	Melyno 9-2	9
1983	L'Emigrant 9-2	10
1984	Siberian Express 9-2	14
1985	No Pass No Sale 9-2	9
1986	Fast Topaze 9-2	8
1987	Soviet Star 9-2	14
1988	Blushing John 9-2	10
1989	Kendor 9-2	10
1990	Linamix 9-2	7
1991	Hector Protector 9-2	6
1992	Shanghai 9-2	9
1993	Kingmambo 9-2	10
1994	Green Tune 9-2	7
1995	Vettori 9-2	8

POULE D'ESSAI DES POULICHES (3y)
Longchamp—1m

1975	Ivanjica 9-2	10
1976	Riverqueen 9-2	11
1977	Madelia 9-2	8
1978	Dancing Maid 9-2	10
1979	Three Troikas 9-2	7
1980	Aryenne 9-2	6
1981	Ukraine Girl 9-2	10
1982	River Lady 9-2	9
1983	L'Attrayante 9-2	10
1984	Masarika 9-2	11

PRIX LUPIN (3y)
Longchamp—1m 2f 110yds

1978	Acamas 9-2	11
1979	Top Ville 9-2	9
1980	Belgio 9-2	13
1981	No Lute 9-2	9
1982	Persepolis 9-2	10
1983	L'Emigrant 9-2	7
1984	Dahar 9-2	7
1985	Metal Precieux 9-2	8
1986	Fast Topaze 9-2	7
1987	Groom Dancer 9-2	7
1988	Exactly Sharp 9-2	9
1989	Galetto 9-2	6
1990	Epervier Bleu 9-2	7
1991	Cudas 9-2	7
1992	Johann Quatz 9-2	7
1993	Hernando 9-2	5
1994	Celtic Arms 9-2	8
1995	Flemensfirth 9-2	6

PRIX SAINT-ALARY (3y fillies)
Longchamp—1m 2f

1978	Reine de Saba 9-2	10
1979	Three Troikas 9-2	7
1980	Paranete 9-2	8
1981	Tootens 9-2	10
1982	Harbour 9-2	8
1983	Smuggly 9-2	8
1984	Grise Mine 9-2	11
1985	Fitnah 9-2	10
1986	Lacovia 9-2	9
1987	Indian Skimmer 9-2	9
1988	Riviere d'Or 9-2	7
1989	Behera 9-2	7
1990	Air de Rein 9-2	9
1991	Treble 9-2	6
1992	Rosefinch 9-2	11
1993	Intrepidity 9-2	7
1994	Moonlight Dance 9-2	6
1995	Muncie 9-2	5

PRIX GANAY (continued)

1985	Silvermine 9-2	10
1986	Baiser Vole 9-2	8
1987	Miesque 9-2	8
1988	Ravinella 9-2	8
1989	Pearl Bracelet 9-2	16
1990	Houseproud 9-2	14
1991	Danseuse du Soir 9-2	9
1992	Culture Vulture 9-2	8
1993	Madeleine's Dream 9-2	9
1994	East of the Moon 9-2	8
1995	Matiara 9-2	16

PRIX JEAN PRAT (3y)
Longchamp—1m 1f 55yds

1978	Midshipman 4-8-11	9
1979	Campero 6-9-0	8
1980	Hard to Sing 4-9-0	9
1981	Gold River 4-9-1	9
1982	Melyno 3-9-2	5
1983	Kelbomec 7-9-0	9
1984	Magwal 5-8-12	12
1985	Baillamont 9-2	8
1986	Magical Wonder 9-2	9
1987	Risk Me 9-2	9
1988	Lapierre 9-2	8
1989	Local Talent 9-2	6
1990	Priolo 9-2	6
1991	Sillery 9-2	7
1992	Kitwood 9-2	5
1993	Le Balafre 9-2	8
1994	Millkom 9-2	6
1995	Torrential 9-2	7

PRIX D'ISPAHAN
(now run at Longchamp)
Chantilly—1m 1f 55yds

1978	Carwhite 4-9-6	10
1979	Irish River 3-8-9	8
1980	Nadjar 4-9-6	10
1981	The Wonder 3-8-9	11
1982	Al Nasr 4-9-6	6
1983	Crystal Glitters 3-8-9	12
1984	Crystal Glitters 4-9-7	8
1985	Sagace 5-9-6	7
1986	Baillamont 4-9-6	8
1987	Highest Honor 4-9-2	6
1988	Miesque 4-8-13	6
1989	Indian Skimmer 5-8-13	6
1990	Creator 4-9-2	9
1991	Sanglamore 4-9-2	7
1992	Zoman 5-9-2	11
1993	Arcangues 5-9-2	7
1994	Bigstone 4-9-2	7
1995	Green Tune 4-9-2	9

PRIX DU JOCKEY-CLUB (3y)
Chantilly—1m 4f

1975	Val de l'Orne 9-2	11
1976	Youth 9-2	18
1977	Crystal Palace 9-2	14
1978	Acamas 9-2	20
1979	Top Ville 9-2	11
1980	Policeman 9-2	14
1981	Bikala 9-2	12
1982	Assert 9-2	14
1983	Caerleon 9-2	12
1984	Darshaan 9-2	17
1985	Mouktar 9-2	11
1986	Bering 9-2	13
1987	Natroun 9-2	17
1988	Hours After 9-2	16
1989	Old Vic 9-2	12
1990	Sanglamore 9-2	12
1991	Suave Dancer 9-2	7

1992	Polytain 9-2	17
1993	Hernando 9-2	11
1994	Celtic Arms 9-2	15
1995	Celtic Swing 9-2	11

PRIX DE DIANE (3y fillies)
Chantilly—1m 2½f

1975	Abandoned	
1976	Pawneese 9-2	11
1977	Madelia 9-2	13
1978	Reine de Saba 9-2	17
1979	Dunette 9-2	12
1980	Mrs Penny 9-2	14
1981	Madam Gay 9-2	14
1982	Harbour 9-2	14
1983	Escaline 9-2	17
1984	Northern Trick 9-2	15
1985	Lypharita 9-2	10
1986	Lacovia 9-2	14
1987	Indian Skimmer 9-2	11
1988	Resless Kara 9-2	16
1989	Lady in Silver 9-2	14
1990	Rafha 9-2	14
1991	Caerlina 9-2	13
1992	Jolypha 9-2	12
1993	Shemaka 9-2	14
1994	East of the Moon 9-2	9
1995	Carling 9-2	12

GRAND PRIX DE PARIS (3y)
Longchamp—1m 2f
(1m 7f up to 1986)

1978	Galiani 8-11	14
1979	Soleil Noir 8-11	7
1980	Valiant Heart 8-11	14
1981	Glint of Gold 8-11	11
1982	Le Nain Jaune 8-11	11
1983	Yawa 8-11	7
1984	At Talaq 8-12	11
1985	Sumayr 8-11	7
1986	Swink 8-11	9
1987	Risk Me 9-2	9
1988	Fijar Tango 9-2	10
1989	Dancehall 9-2	8
1990	Saumarez 9-2	8
1991	Subotica 9-2	9
1992	Homme de Loi 9-2	10
1993	Fort Wood 9-2	9
1994	Millkom 9-2	12
1995	Valanour 3-9-2	10

GRAND PRIX DE SAINT-CLOUD
Saint-Cloud—1m 4f

1975	Un Kopeck 4-9-8	11
1976	Riverqueen 3-8-6	8
1977	Exceller 4-9-8	10
1978	Guadanini 4-9-8	9
1979	Gay Mecene 4-9-8	13
1980	*Dunette 4-9-5	
	*Shakapour 3-8-9	9
1981	Akarad 3-8-9	10
1982	Glint of Gold 4-9-8	9

1983   Diamond Shoal 4-9-8 9
1984   Teenoso 4-9-9 11
1985   Strawberry Road 6-9-8 7
1986   Acatenango 4-9-8 9
1987   Moon Madness 4-9-8 6
1988   Village Star 5-9-8 10
1989   Sheriff's Star 4-9-8 6
1990   In The Wings 4-9-8 8
1991   Epervier Bleu 4-9-8 12
1992   Pistolet Bleu 4-9-8 7
1993   User Friendly 4-9-5 8
1994   Apple Tree 5-9-8 8
1995   Carnegie 4-9-8 8

PRIX JACQUES LE MAROIS
Deauville—1m

1975   Lianga 3-8-12 11
1976   Gravelines 4-9-2 13
1977   Flying Water 4-8-12..................7
1978   Kenmare 3-8-8.......................10
1979   Irish River 3-8-8 8
1980   Nadjar 4-9-2 9
1981   Northjet 4-9-2 11
1982   The Wonder 4-9-2 9
1983   Luth Enchantee 3-8-7 10
1984   Lear Fan 3-8-9 10
1985   Vin de France 3-8-9..................11
1986   Lirung 4-9-2............................12
1987   Miesque 3-8-6 9
1988   Miesque 4-8-13 6
1989   Polish Precedent 3-8-9 10
1990   Priolo 3-8-9 10
1991   Hector Protector 3-8-9 10
1992   Exit to Nowhere 4-9-4...............14
1993   Sayyedati 3-8-8.........................8
1994   East of the Moon 3-8-8...............9
1995   Miss Satamixa 3-8-8..................9

PRIX MORNY (2y)
Deauville—6f

1975   Vitiges 8-11 13
1976   Blushing Groom 8-11 11
1977   Super Concorde 8-11 10
1978   Irish River 8-11 11
1979   Princess Lida 8-11 10
1980   Ancient Regime 8-8...................7
1981   Green Forest 8-11 5
1982   Deep Roots 8-11.......................6
1983   Siberian Express 8-11.................7
1984   Seven Springs 8-8....................7
1985   Regal State 8-8 11
1986   Sakura Reiko 8-8......................8
1987   First Waltz 8-8.........................8
1988   Tersa 8-8 8
1989   Machiavellian 8-11 7
1990   Hector Protector 8-11................12
1991   Arazi 8-11...............................4
1992   Zafonic 8-11 10
1993   Coup de Genie 8-8 8
1994   Hoh Magic 8-10 6
1995   Tagula 9-0 8

PRIX DU MOULIN DE LONGCHAMP
Longchamp—1m

1975   Delmora 3-8-6 11
1976   Gravelines 4-9-2......................9
1977   Pharly 3-8-11..........................7
1978   Sanedtki 4-8-13 10
1979   Irish River 3-8-11.....................8
1980   Kilijaro 4-8-13........................11
1981   Northjet 4-9-2 9
1982   Green Forest 3-8-11..................9
1983   Luth Enchantee 3-8-8 8
1984   Mendez 3-8-11.........................7
1985   Rousillon 4-9-2.......................12
1986   Sonic Lady 3-8-8 14
1987   Miesque 3-8-8 7
1988   Soviet Star 4-9-2......................7
1989   Polish Precedent 3-8-11 11
1990   Distant Relative 4-9-2................6
1991   Priolo 4-9-2 12
1992   All At Sea 3-8-8 10
1993   Kingmambo 3-8-11 11
1994   Ski Paradise 4-8-13...................7
1995   Ridgewood Pearl 3-8-8..............8

PRIX DE LA SALAMANDRE (2y)
Longchamp—7f

1975   Manado 8-11 13
1976   Blushing Groom 8-11 8
1977   John de Coombe 8-11 8
1978   Irish River 8-11 6
1979   Princesse Lida 8-8 7
1980   Miswaki 8-11 5
1981   Green Forest 8-11 5
1982   *Deep Roots 8-11.......................
       *Maximova 8-8 6
1983   Seattle Song 8-11 5
1984   Noblequest 8-11.........................7
1985   Baiser Vole 8-8 10
1986   Miesque 8-8............................10
1987   Common Grounds 8-11 6
1988   Oczy Czarnie 8-8.......................9
1989   Machiavellian 8-11 6
1990   Hector Protector 8-11...................7
1991   Arazi 8-11................................7
1992   Zafonic 8-11 6
1993   Coup de Genie 8-8 6
1994   Pennekamp 8-11........................8
1995   Lord of Men 8-11.......................7

PRIX VERMEILLE (3y fillies)
Longchamp—1m 4f

1975   Ivanjica 9-2 13
1976   Lagunette 9-2..........................10
1977   Kamicia 9-2.............................18
1978   Dancing Maid 9-2......................12
1979   Three Troikas 9-2......................13
1980   Mrs Penny 9-2 12
1981   April Run 9-2 10
1982   All Along 9-2............................13
1983   Sharaya 9-2 12
1984   Northern Trick 9-2.....................10
1985   Walensee 9-2...........................13

1986	Darara 9-2	8
1987	Bint Pasha 9-2	12
1988	Indian Rose 9-2	8
1989	Young Mother 9-2	7
1990	Salsabil 9-2	9
1991	Magic Night 9-2	14
1992	Jolypha 9-2	10
1993	Intrepidity 9-2	8
1994	Sierra Madre 9-2	9
1995	Carling 9-2	10

PRIX DU CADRAN
Longchamp—2m 4f

1975	Le Bavard 4-9-0	13
1976	Sagaro 5-9-2	10
1977	Buckskin 4-9-2	5
1978	Buckskin 5-9-2	9
1979	El Badr 4-9-2	5
1980	Shafaraz 7-9-2	6
1981	Gold River 4-8-13	6
1982	El Badr 7-9-2	5
1983	Karkour 5-9-2	6
1984	Neustrien 5-9-2	6
1985	Balitou 6-9-2	7
1986	Air de Cour 4-9-2	6
1987	Royal Gait 4-9-2	9
1988	Yaka 5-9-2	5
1989	Trebrook 5-9-2	3
1990	Mercalle 4-8-13	6
1991	Victoire Bleue 4-8-13	7
1992	Sought Out 4-8-13	7
1993	Assessor 4-9-2	11
1994	Molesnes 4-8-13	8
1995	Always Earnest 7-9-2	6

PRIX DE L'ABBAYE DE LONGCHAMP
Longchamp—5f

1975	Lianga 4-9-7	12
1976	*Mendip Man 4-9-10	
	*Gentilhombre 3-9-10	10
1977	Gentilhombre 4-9-11	11
1978	Sigy 2-8-5	7
1979	Double Form 4-9-11	13
1980	Moorestyle 3-9-11	9
1981	Marwell 3-9-8	10
1982	Sharpo 5-9-11	13
1983	Habibti 3-9-7	8
1984	Committed 4-9-7	12
1985	Committed 5-9-7	12
1986	Double Schwartz 5-9-11	13
1987	Polonia 3-9-7	9
1988	Handsome Sailor 5-9-11	10
1989	Silver Fling 4-9-7	16
1990	Dayjur 3-9-11	6
1991	Keen Hunter 4-9-11	14
1992	Mr Brooks 5-9-11	9
1993	Lochsong 5-9-8	11
1994	Lochsong 6-9-7	10
1995	Hever Golf Rose 4-9-7	12

PRIX MARCEL BOUSSAC (2y fillies)
Longchamp—1m
(Criterium des Pouliches before 1980)

1975	Theia 8-9	17
1976	Kamicia 8-9	14
1977	Tarona 8-9	14
1978	Pitasia 8-9	8
1979	Aryenne 8-9	13
1980	Tropicaro 8-9	10
1981	Play It Safe 8-9	8
1982	Goodbye Shelley 8-9	11
1983	Almeira 8-9	7
1984	Triptych 8-9	9
1985	Midway Lady 8-9	15
1986	Miesque 8-9	11
1987	Ashayer 8-9	12
1988	Mary Linoa 8-9	11
1989	Salsabil 8-9	15
1990	Shadayid 8-9	9
1991	Culture Vulture 8-11	14
1992	Gold Splash 8-11	11
1993	Sierra Madre 8-11	8
1994	Macoumba 8-11	6
1995	Miss Tahiti 8-11	11

GRAND CRITERIUM (2y)
Longchamp—1m

1975	Manado 8-11	11
1976	Blushing Groom 8-11	10
1977	Super Concorde 8-11	13
1978	Irish River 8-11	12
1979	Dragon 8-11	8
1980	Recitation 8-11	11
1981	Green Forest 8-11	10
1982	Saint Cyrien 8-11	8
1983	Treizieme 8-8	9
1984	Alydar's Best 8-8	6
1985	Femme Elite 8-8	11
1986	Danishkada 8-8	8
1987	Fijar Tango 8-11	6
1988	Kendor 8-11	9
1989	Jade Robbery 8-11	8
1990	Hector Protector 8-11	5
1991	Arazi 8-11	6
1992	Tenby 8-11	11
1993	Lost World 8-11	7
1994	Goldmark 8-11	4
1995	Loup Solitaire 8-11	7

PRIX DE LA FORET
Longchamp—7f

1975	Roan Star 2-8-0	15
1976	Pharly 2-8-5	8
1977	Sanedtki 3-9-7	10
1978	Sanedtki 4-9-8	10
1979	Producer 3-9-7	14
1980	Moorestyle 3-9-11	9
1981	Moorestyle 4-9-12	9
1982	Pas de Seul 3-9-11	9
1983	Ma Biche 3-9-7	8
1984	Procida 3-9-11	10

1985	Brocade 4-9-8	14
1986	Sarab 5-9-12	16
1987	Soviet Star 3-9-11	14
1988	Salse 3-9-11	13
1989	Gabina 4-9-11	8
1990	Septieme Ciel 3-9-12	10
1991	Danseuse du Soir 3-9-6	7
1992	Wolfhound 3-9-10	8
1993	Dolphin Street 3-9-10	5
1994	Bigstone 4-9-11	12
1995	Poplar Bluff 3-9-0	10

PRIX ROYAL-OAK
Longchamp—1m 7f 110yds
Before 1979: 3-year-olds only

1975	Henri le Balafre 3-9-2	16
1976	Exceller 3-9-2	7
1977	Rex Magna 3-9-2	13
1978	Brave Johnny 3-9-2	8
1979	Niniski 3-8-11	9
1980	Gold River 3-8-8	13
1981	Ardross 5-9-3	7
1982	Denel 3-8-11	13
1983	Old Country 4-9-3	14
1984	Agent Double 3-8-11	11
1985	Mersey 3-8-8	12
1986	El Cuite 3-8-11	10
1987	Royal Gait 4-9-3	11
1988	Star Lift 4-9-3	16
1989	Top Sunrise 4-9-3	9

1990	*Braashee 4-9-3	11
	*Indian Queen 5-9-0	11
1991	Turgeon 5-9-3	8
1992	Assessor 3-8-11	12
1993	Raintrap 3-8-11	8
1994	Moonax 3-8-11	7
1995	Sunshack 4-9-4	7

CRITERIUM DE SAINT-CLOUD (2y)
Saint-Cloud—1m 2f

1975	Kano 8-9	9
1976	Conglomerat 8-11	9
1977	Tarek 8-9	7
1978	Callio 8-11	11
1979	Providential 8-9	13
1980	The Wonder 8-13	10
1981	Bon Sang 9-0	14
1982	Escaline 8-6	12
1983	Darshaan 8-9	12
1984	Mouktar 8-9	14
1985	Fast Topaze 8-9	13
1986	Magistros 8-11	15
1987	Waki River 8-11	9
1988	Miserden 8-11	10
1989	Intimiste 8-11	10
1990	Pistolet Bleu 8-11	9
1991	Glaieul 8-11	9
1992	Marchand de Sable 8-11	8
1993	Sunshack 8-11	7
1994	Poliglote 9-0	9
1995	Polaris Flight 9-0	5

Winners of Principal National Hunt Races

MACKESON GOLD CUP
(H'CAP CHASE)
Cheltenham—2¹/₂m

1971	Gay Trip 9y 11st 3lb	10
1972	Red Candle 8y 10st	11
1973	Skymas 8y 10st 5lb	15
1974	Bruslee 8y 10st 7lb	11
1975	Clear Cut 11y 10st 9lb	13
1976	*Cancello 7y 11st 1lb	13
1977	Bachelor's Hall 7y 10st 6lb	16
1978	Bawnogues 7y 10st 7lb	11
1979	Man Alive 8y 10st 9lb	11
1980	Bright Highway 6y 11st 1lb	15
1981	Henry Kissinger 7y 10st 13lb	11
1982	Fifty Dollars More 7y 11st	11
1983	Pounentes 6y 10st 6lb	9
1984	Half Free 8y 11st 10lb	10
1985	Half Free 9y 11st 10lb	10
1986	Very Promising 8y 11st 13lb	11
1987	Beau Ranger 9y 10st 2lb	14
1988	Pegwell Bay 7y 11st 2lb	13
1989	Joint Sovereignty 9y 10st 4lb	15
1990	Multum In Parvo 7y 11st 2lb	13
1991	Another Coral 8y 10st 1lb	15
1992	Tipping Tim 7y 10st 10lb	16
1993	Bradbury Star 8y 11st 8lb	15
1994	Bradbury Star 9y 12st	14
1995	Dublin Flyer 9y 11st 8lb	12

*Run at Haydock

FIRST NATIONAL BANK GOLD CUP
(H'CAP CHASE)
Ascot—2m 3f 110y
1981 Run as Tote Silver Trophy Chase
1982-1992 Run as H & T Walker Gold Cup

1981	Wayward Lad 6y 11st 10lb	8
1982	Pay Related 8y 11st 2lb	6
1983	The Tsarevich 7y 11st 6lb	6
1984	Cybrandian 6y 10st 9lb	6
1985	Very Promising 7y 11st 7lb	7
1986	Church Warden 7y 10st 7lb	6
1987	Weather the Storm 7y 11st	11
1988	Saffron Lord 6y 11st 3lb	5
1989	Man O'Magic 8y 11st 5lb	11
1990	Blazing Walker 6y 11st 6lb	5
1991	Kings Fountain 8y 11st 1lb	8
1992	Deep Sensation 7y 11st 2lb	10
1993	Abandoned due to frost	
1994	Raymylette 7y 11st 10lb	11
1995	Sound Man (IRE) 7y 12st	5

HENNESSY COGNAC GOLD CUP
(H'CAP CHASE)
Newbury—3¹/₄m 110y

1961	Mandarin 10y 11st 5lb	22
1962	Springbok 8y 10st 8lb	27
1963	Mill House 6y 12st	10

1964	Arkle 7y 12st 7lb	9
1965	Arkle 8y 12st 7lb	8
1966	Stalbridge Colonist 7y 10st	6
1967	Rondetto 11y 10st 1lb	13
1968	Man of the West 7y 10st	11
1969	Spanish Steps 6y 11st 8lb	15
1970	Border Mask 8y 11st 1lb	12
1971	Bighorn 7y 10st 11lb	13
1972	Charlie Potheen 7y 11st 4lb	13
1973	Red Candle 9y 10st 4lb	11
1974	Royal Marshal II 7y 10st	13
1975	April Seventh 9y 11st 2lb	13
1976	Zeta's Son 7y 10st 9lb	21
1977	Bachelor's Hall 7y 10st 10lb	14
1978	Approaching 7y 10st 6lb	8
1979	Fighting Fit 7y 11st 7lb	15
1980	Bright Highway 6y 11st 6lb	14
1981	Diamond Edge 10y 11st 10lb	14
1982	Bregawn 8y 11st 10lb	11
1983	Brown Chamberlin 8y 11st 8lb	12
1984	Burrough Hill Lad 8y 12st	13
1985	Galway Blaze 9y 10st	15
1986	Broadheath 9y 10st 5lb	15
1987	Playschool 9y 10st 8lb	12
1988	Strands Of Gold 9y 10st	12
1989	Ghofar 6y 10st 2lb	8
1990	Arctic Call 7y 11st	13
1991	Chatam (USA) 7y 10st 6lb	15
1992	Sibton Abbey 7y 10st	13
1993	Cogent 9y 10st 1lb	9
1994	One Man (IRE) 6y 10st	16
1995	Couldn't Be Better 8y 10st 8lb	11

TRIPLEPRINT GOLD CUP
(H'CAP CHASE)
Cheltenham—2¹/₂m
Previously run under different titles

1971	Leap Frog 7y 12st 1lb	12
1972	Arctic Bow 7y 10st 12lb	11
1973	Pendil 8y 12st 7lb	8
1974	Garnishee 10y 10st 6lb	9
1975	Easby Abbey 8y 11st 10lb	9
1976	Abandoned because of frost	
1977	Even Melody 8y 11st 2lb	11
1978	The Snipe 8y 10st	14
1979	Father Delaney 7y 10st 10lb	12
1980	Bueche Giorod 9y 10st	15
1981	Abandoned because of snow	
1982	Observe 6y 10st 11lb	15
1983	Fifty Dollars More 8y 11st 10lb	13
1984	Beau Ranger 6y 9st 10lb	10
1985	Combs Ditch 9y 11st 9lb	7
1986	Oregon Trail 6y 10st 7lb	6
1987	Bishop's Yarn 8y 10st 7lb	5
1988	Pegwell Bay 7y 10st 13lb	10
1989	Clever Folly 9y 10st 4lb	6
1990	Abandoned because of snow	

1991	Kings Fountain 8y 11st 10lb.....	8
1992	Another Coral 9y 11st 4lb	10
1993	Fragrant Dawn 9y 10st 2lb	11
1994	Dublin Flyer 8y 10st 2lb	11
1995	Abandoned because of frost	

BONUSPRINT CHRISTMAS HURDLE
Kempton—2m
Previously run under different titles

1971	Coral Diver 6y 12st 5lb.............	4
1972	Canasta Lad 6y 12st 1lb...........	6
1973	Lanzarote 5y 12st 1lb..............	4
1974	Tree Tangle 5y 12st 1lb...........	5
1975	Lanzarote 7y 11st 13lb............	5
1976	Dramatist 5y 11 10lb	6
1977	Beacon Light 6y 11st 10lb	3
1978	Kybo 5y 11st 7lb.....................	6
1979	Bird's Nest 9y 11st 10lb	5
1980	Celtic Ryde 5y 11st 6lb............	7
1981	Abandoned because of frost	
1982	Ekbalco 6y 11st 13lb...............	4
1983	Dawn Run 5y 10st 12lb	4
1984	Browne's Gazette 6y 11st 3lb ...	7
1985	Aonoch 6y 11st 3lb	9
1986	Nohalmdun 5y 11st 3lb.............	8
1987	Osric 4y 11st 3lb	8
1988	Kribensis 4y 11st 3lb	7
1989	Kribensis 5y 11st 3lb...............	8
1990	Fidway 5y 11st 7lb	8
1991	Gran Alba (USA) 5y 11st 7lb	7
1992	Mighty Mogul 5y 11st 7lb.........	8
1993	Muse 5y 11st 7lb	5
1994	Absalom's Lady 6y 11st 2lb	6
1995	Abandoned because of frost	

KING GEORGE VI CHASE
Kempton—3m

1957	Mandarin 6y 12st........................	
1958	Lochroe 10y 11st 7lb	7
1959	Mandarin 8y 11st 5lb.................	9
1960	Saffron Tartan 9y 11st 7lb	10
1961	Abandoned because of frost	
1962	Abandoned because of frost	
1963	Mill House 6y 12st.....................	3
1964	Frenchman's Cove 9y 11st 7lb	2
1965	Arkle 8y 12st.............................	4
1966	Dormant 9y 11st........................	7
1967	Cancelled because of foot and mouth epidemic	
1968	Abandoned because of waterlogged course	
1969	Titus Oates 7y 11st 10lb...........	5
1970	Abandoned because of snow	
1971	The Dikler 8y 11st 7lb...............	10
1972	Pendil 7y 12st............................	6
1973	Pendil 8y 12st............................	4
1974	Captain Christy 7y 12st.............	6
1975	Captain Christy 8y 12st.............	7
1976	Royal Marshall II 9y 11st 7lb ...	11
1977	Bachelor's Hall 7y 11st 7lb	9
1978	Gay Spartan 7y 11st 10lb.......	16
1979	Silver Buck 7y 11st 10lb.........	11

1980	Silver Buck 8y 11st 10lb...........	8
1981	Abandoned because of frost	
1982	Wayward Lad 7y 11st 10lb........	6
1983	Wayward Lad 8y 11st 10lb........	5
1984	Burrough Hill Lad 8y 11st 10lb.	3
1985	Wayward Lad 10y 11st 10lb......	5
1986	Desert Orchid 7y 11st 10lb	8
1987	Nupsala (FR) 8y 11st 10lb........	9
1988	Desert Orchid 9y 11st 10lb	5
1989	Desert Orchid 10y 11st 10lb	6
1990	Desert Orchid 11y 11st 10lb	9
1991	The Fellow (FR) 6y 11st 10lb	8
1992	The Fellow (FR) 7y 11st 10lb	8
1993	Barton Bank 7y 11st 10lb.........	10
1994	Algan (FR) 6y 11st 10lb.............	9
1995	* One Man (IRE) 8y 11st 10lb....	11
	*Run at Sandown in January 1996	

CORAL WELSH
NATIONAL (H'CAP CHASE)
Chepstow—3³⁄₄m
1979-1995 Run in December

1971	Royal Toss 9y 10st 12lb............	13
1972	Charlie H 10y 11st 3lb...............	9
1973	Deblin's Green 10y 9st 12lb...	16
1974	Pattered 8y 10st 2lb	24
1975	Abandoned because of waterlogged course	
1976	Rag Trade 10y 11st 2lb.............	17
1977	Abandoned because of waterlogged course	
1978	Abandoned because of frost	
1979	Peter Scot 8y 10st 2lb..............	15
1980	Narvik 7y 10st 11lb...................	18
1981	Peaty Sandy 7y 10st 3lb	23
1982	Corbiere 7y 10st 10lb...............	10
1983	Burrough Hill Lad 7y 10st 9lb.	18
1984	Righthand Man 7y 11st 5lb	18
1985	Run And Skip 7y 10st 8lb..........	18
1986	Stearsby 7y 11st 5lb.................	17
1987	Playschool 9y 10st 11lb...........	13
1988	Bonanza Boy 7y 10st 1lb	12
1989	Bonanza Boy 8y 11st 11lb........	12
1990	Cool Ground 11y 10st................	9
1991	Carvill's Hill 9y 11st 12lb.........	17
1992	Run For Free 8y 10st 9lb...........	11
1993	Riverside Boy 10y 10st..............	8
*1994	Master Oats 8y 11st 6lb............	8
1995	Abandoned because of frost	
	*Run at Newbury	

LADBROKE H'CAP HURDLE
Leopardstown—2m
1971-1975 Run as Irish Sweeps Hurdle
1976-1980 Run as Sweeps H'cap Hurdle
1981-1986 Run as Irish Sweeps H'cap
Hurdle
1982-1996 Run in January

1971	Kelanne 7y 11st 6lb..................	16
1972	Captain Christy 5y 11st 6lb......	13
1973	Comedy Of Errors 6y 12st	9
1974	Comedy Of Errors 7y 12st	8
1975	Night Nurse 4y 11st 5lb............	9

1976	Master Monday 6y 10st 2lb....	19
1977	Decent Fellow 4y 11st 4lb...	18
1978	Chinrullah 6y 10st 6lb.............	12
1979	Irian 5y 10st..............................	20
1980	Carrig Willy 5y 10st	26
1982	For Auction 6y 10st 10lb........	20
1983	Fredcoteri 7y 10st....................	15
1984	Fredcoteri 8y 10st 4lb	18
1985	Hansel Rag 5y 10st	20
1986	Bonalma 6y 10st 13lb.............	22
1987	Barnbrook Again 6y 11st 8lb..	22
1988	Roark 6y 11st 11lb..................	15
1989	Redundant Pal 6y 10st..........	17
1990	Redundant Pal 7y 11st 5lb....	27
1991	The Illiad 10y 10st 13lb.........	17
1992	How's The Boss 6y 10st 2lb ..	20
1993	Glencloud (IRE) 5y 10st 13lb .	25
1994	Atone 7y 10st 8lb...................	25
1995	Anusha 5y 10st 2lb.................	17
1996	Dance Beat (IRE) 5y 9st 12lb .	22

VICTOR CHANDLER
HANDICAP CHASE
Ascot—2m

1987	Abandoned because of frost	
1988	Abandoned because of fog	
1989	Desert Orchid 10y 12st	5
1990	Blitzkreig 8y 10st 4lb	5
1991	Meikleour 11y 10st	10
1992	Waterloo Boy 9y 11st 10lb	5
1993	Sybillin 7y 10st 10lb	11
1994	*Viking Flagship 7y 10st 10lb	4
1995	Martha's Son 8y 10st 9lb	8
1996	Big Matt (IRE) 8y 10st 4lb	11
	*Run at Warwick	

AGFA DIAMOND
HANDICAP CHASE
Sandown—3m 110y
Previously run under different titles

1970	Spanish Steps 7y 12st	3
1971	Titus Oates 9y 12st	3
1972	Crisp 9y 12st............................	3
1973	Royal Toss 11y 11st 9lb	3
1974	Kilvulgan 7y 10st 9lb	6
1975	Abandoned because of waterlogged course	
1976	Bula 11y 12st	3
1977	Master H 8y 10st 8lb	7
1978	Master H 9 11st 3lb	6
1979	Diamond Edge 8y 11st 3lb ...	11
1980	Diamond Edge 9y 12st	7
1981	Tragus 9y 10st 7lb...................	8
1982	*Bregawn 8y 10st 7lb	9
1983	Observe 7y 11st 3lb	5
1984	Burrough Hill Lad 8y 11st 10lb	5
1985	Burrough Hill Lad 9y 12st .....w.o	
1986	Burrough Hill Lad 10y 12st	6
1987	Desert Orchid 8y 11st 10lb	6
1988	Charter Party 10y 10st 11lb ..	11
1989	Desert Orchid 10y 12st	4
1990	Abandoned because of waterlogged course	

1991	Desert Orchid 12y 12st	4
1992	Espy 9y 10st 7lb	9
1993	Country Member 8y 10st 7lb .	3
1994	Second Schedual 9y 10st 7lb	5
1995	Deep Bramble 8y 11st 10lb ..	11
	*Run at Kempton	

TOTE GOLD TROPHY
(H'CAP HURDLE)
Newbury—2m 110y
1970-1986 Run as Schweppes Gold Trophy

1970	Abandoned because of snow & frost	
1971	Cala Mesquida 7y 10st 9lb.....	23
1972	Good Review 6y 10st 9lb........	26
1973	Indianapolis 6y 10st 6lb.........	26
1974	Abandoned because of waterlogged course	
1975	Tammuz 7y 10st 13lb	28
1976	Irish Fashion 5y 10st 4lb	29
1977	True Lad 7y 10st 4lb...............	27
1978	Abandoned because of frost	
1979	Within The Law 5y 11st 4lb ...	28
1980	Bootlaces 6y 10st 9lb.............	21
1981	Abandoned because of frost	
1982	Donegal Prince 6y 10st 8lb....	27
1983	Abandoned because of snow & frost	
1984	Ra Nova 5y 10st 6lb................	26
1985	Abandoned because of snow	
1986	Abandoned because of snow	
1987	Neblin 8y 10st...........................	21
1988	Jamesmead 7y 10st	19
1989	Grey Salute (CAN) 6y 11st 5lb	10
1990	Deep Sensation 5y 11st 3lb...	17
1991	Abandoned because of frost	
1992	Rodeo Star 6y 10st 10lb.........	15
1993	King Credo 8y 10st...................	16
1994	Large Action 6y 10st 8lb	11
1995	Mysilv 5y 10st 8lb	8

HENNESSY COGNAC
GOLD CUP
Leopardstown—3m
1987-1990 Run as Vincent O'Brien Irish Gold Cup

1987	Forgive 'N Forget 10y 12st	9
1988	Playschool (NZ) 10y 12st	5
1989	Carvill's Hill 7y 12st	9
1990	Nick the Brief 8y 12st.................	6
1991	Nick the Brief 9y 12st.................	6
1992	Carvill's Hill 10y 12st	10
1993	Jodami 8y 12st	7
1994	Jodami 9y 12st	6
1995	Jodami 10y 12st	6

RACING POST HANDICAP CHASE
Kempton—3m

1988	Rhyme 'n' Reason 9y 10st 11lb	12
1989	Bonanza Boy 8y 11st 1lb	11
1990	Desert Orchid 11y 12st 3lb	8
1991	Docklands Express 9y 10st 7lb	9
1992	Docklands Express 10y 11st 10lb	11
1993	Zeta's Lad 10y 10st 10lb.........	12

1994   Antonin (FR) 6y 10st 4lb......... 16
1995   Val D'Alene (FR) 8y 11st 2lb .. 9

SUNDERLANDS IMPERIAL CUP
Sandown 2m 110y

1960   Farmer's Boy 7y 11st 7lb........ 20
1961   Fidus Achates 6y 10st 4lb...... 23
1962   Irish Imp 5y 10st 12lb............ 26
1963   Antiar 5y 11st 2lb................ 21
1964   Invader 6y 11st 4lb................ 15
1965   Kildavin 7y 10st 7lb.............. 19
1966   Royal Sanction 7y 10st 1lb 18
1967   Sir Thopas 6y 11st 8lb 20
1968   Persian Empire 5y 11st 5lb ... 18
1969   Abandoned because of waterlogged
          course
1970   Solomon II 6y 11st 1lb 17
1971   Churchwood 7y 11st 3lb........ 12
1972   Spy Net (FR) 5y 10st............. 18
1973   Lanzarote 5y 12st 4lb............ 14
1974   Flash Imp 5y 10st 9lb............ 17
1975   Abandoned because of
          waterlogged course
1976   Nougat 6y 10st 6lb 11
1977   Acquaint 6y 11st 2lb............. 20
1978   Winter Melody 7y 11st 3lb..... 15
1979   Flying Diplomat 8y 10st 6lb.... 9
1980   Prayukta 5y 11st................... 16
1981   Ekbalco 5y 11st 3lb.............. 14
1982   *Holemoor Star 5y 11st 7lb 7
1983   Desert Hero 9y 9st 8lb 16
1984   Dalbury 6y 9st 12lb.............. 13
1985   Floyd 5y 10st 3lb................. 16
1986   Insular 6y 9st 10lb.............. 19
1987   Inlander 6y 10st 3lb............. 23
1988   Sprowston Boy 5y 10st 11lb.. 15
1989   Travel Mystery 6y 10st 8lb........8
1990   Moody Man 5y 10st 13lb 15
1991   Precious Boy 5y 10st 6lb 13
1992   King Credo 7y 10st 4lb 10
1993   Olympian 6y 10st 15
1994   Precious Boy 8y 11st 7lb 13
1995   Collier Bay 5y 10st 2lb 10
          *Run at Kempton

GUINNESS ARKLE
CHALLENGE TROPHY
(NOVICES CHASE)
Cheltenham—2m

1969   Chatham 5y 11st..................... 10
1970   Soloning 5y 11st 13
1971   Alpheus 6y 11st 8lb.............. 11
1972   Pendil 7y 12st 1lb................ 10
1973   Denys Adventure 8y 12st 1lb. 10
1974   Canasta Lad 8y 11st 11lb.... 10
1975   Broncho II 6y 11st 11lb......... 12
1976   Roaring Wind 8y 11st 8lb...... 16
1977   Tip The Wink 7y 11st 8lb........ 10
1978   Alverton 8y 11st 8lb.............. 10
1979   Chinrullah 7y 11st 8lb.............8
1980   Anaglogs Daughter 7y 11st 8lb 9
1981   Clayside 7y 11st 8lb.............. 13

1982   The Brockshee 7y 11st 8lb 19
1983   Ryeman 6y 11st 8lb.............. 16
1984   Bobsline 8y 11st 8lb.............. 8
1985   Boreen Prince 8y 11st 8lb...... 16
1986   Oregon Trail 6y 11st 8lb........ 14
1987   Gala's Image 7y 11st 8lb....... 19
1988   Danish Flight 9y 11st 8lb...... 12
1989   Waterloo Boy 6y 11st 8lb...... 14
1990   Comandante 8y 11st 8lb...... 14
1991   Remittance Man 7y 11st 8lb... 14
1992   Young Pokey 7y 11st 8lb 11
1993   Travado 7y 11st 8lb...................8
1994   Nakir (FR) 6y 11st 8lb............ 11
1995   Klairon Davis (FR) 6y 11st 8lb ..11

SMURFIT CHAMPION HURDLE
Cheltenham—2m 1f

1955   Clair Soleil 6y 12st.................. 21
1956   Doorknocker 8y 12st 14
1957   Merry Deal 7y 12st................ 16
1958   Bandalore 7y 12st................. 18
1959   Fare Time 8y 12st................. 14
1960   Another Flash 6y 12st 12
1961   Eborneezer 6y 12st............... 17
1962   Anzio 5y 11st 12lb................. 14
1963   Winning Fair 8y 12st.............. 21
1964   Magic Court 6y 12st 24
1965   Kirriemuir 4y 11st 12lb 19
1966   Salmon Spray 8y 12st 17
1967   Saucy Kit 6y 12st................. 23
1968   Persian War 5y 11st 12lb 16
1969   Persian War 6y 12st 17
1970   Persian War 7y 12st 14
1971   Bula 6y 12st...........................9
1972   Bula 7y 12st......................... 12
1973   Comedy Of Errors 6y 12st 8
1974   Lanzarote 6y 12st...................7
1975   Comedy Of Errors 8y 12st 13
1976   Night Nurse 5y 12st.................8
1977   Night Nurse 6y 12st 10
1978   Monksfield 6y 12st 13
1979   Monksfield 7y 12st 10
1980 Distance changed from 2m 200y
1980   Sea Pigeon 10y 12st.............. 9
1981   Sea Pigeon 11y 12st............ 14
1982   For Auction 6y 12st............... 14
1983   Gaye Brief 6y 12st............... 17
1984   Dawn Run 6y 11st 9lb............ 14
1985   See You Then 5y 12st........... 14
1986   See You Then 6y 12st........... 23
1987   See You Then 7y 12st........... 18
1988   Celtic Shot 6y 12st 21
1989   Beech Road 7y 12st 15
1990   Kribensis 6y 12st 19
1991   Morley Street 7y 12st 24
1992   Royal Gait 9y 12st 16
1993   Granville Again 7y 12st 18
1994   Flakey Dove 8y 11st 9lb 15
1995   Alderbrook 6y 12st 14

QUEEN MOTHER CHAMPION CHASE
Cheltenham—2m
1959-1979 Run as National Hunt Two Mile Champion Chase

Year	Winner	
1959	Quita Que 10y 12st	9
1960	Fortria 8y 12st	7
1961	Fortria 9y 12st	5
1962	Piperton 8y 12st	7
1963	Sandy Abbot 8y 12st	5
1964	Ben Stack 7y 12st	5
1965	Dunkirk 8y 12st	6
1966	Flyingbolt 7y 12st	6
1967	Drinny's Double 9y 12st	8
1968	Drinny's Double 10y 12st	5
1969	Muir 10y 12st	11
1970	Straight Fort 7y 12st	6
1971	Crisp 8y 12st	8
1972	Royal Relief 8y 12st	5
1973	Inkslinger 6y 12st	6
1974	Royal Relief 10y 12st	6
1975	Lough Inagh 8y 12st	6
1976	Skymas 11y 12st	7
1977	Skymas 12y 12st	8
1978	Hilly Way 8y 12st	10
1979	Hilly Way 9y 12st	9
1980	Another Dolly 10y 12st	7
1981	Drumgora 9y 12st	9
1982	Rathgorman 10y 12st	9
1983	Badsworth Boy 8y 12st	6
1984	Badsworth Boy 9y 12st	10
1985	Badsworth Boy 10y 12st	5
1986	Buck House 8y 12st	11
1987	Pearlyman 8y 12st	8
1988	Pearlyman 9y 12st	8
1989	Barnbrook Again 8y 12st	8
1990	Barnbrook Again 9y 12st	9
1991	Katabatic 8y 12st	9
1992	Remittance Man 8y 12st	6
1993	Deep Sensation 8y 12st	9
1994	Viking Flagship 7y 12st	8
1995	Viking Flagship 8y 12st	10

SUN ALLIANCE NOVICES' CHASE
Cheltenham—3m 1f

Year	Winner	
1970	Proud Tarquin 7y 11st 12lb	17
1971	Tantalum 7y 11st 7lb	16
1972	Clever Scot 7y 11st 7lb	18
1973	Killiney 7y 11st 3lb	9
1974	Ten Up 7y 11st	12
1975	Pengrail 7y 11st	11
1976	Tied Cottage 8y 11st	15
1977	Gay Spartan 6y 11st 4lb	15
1978	Sweet Joe 6y 11st 4lb	17
1979	Master Smudge 7y 11st 4lb	17
1980	Lacson 8y 11st 4lb	17
1981	Lesley Ann 7y 11st 4lb	17
1982	Brown Chamberlin 7y 11st 4lb	15
1983	Canny Danny 7y 11st 4lb	17
1984	A Kinsman 8y 11st 4lb	18
1985	Antartic Bay 8y 11st 4lb	11
1986	Cross Master 9y 11st 4lb	30
1987	Kildimo 7y 11st 4lb	18

Year	Winner	
1988	The West Awake 7y 11st 4lb..	14
1989	Envopak Token 8y 11st 4lb....	15
1990	Garrison Savannah 7y 11st 4lb....9	
1991	Rolling Ball (FR) 8y 11st 4lb....	20
1992	Miinnehoma 9y 11st 4lb	18
1993	Young Hustler 6y 11st 4lb	8
1994	Monsieur Le Cure 8y 11st 4lb....	18
1995	Brief Gale 8y 10st 13lb	13

DAILY EXPRESS TRIUMPH HURDLE
(4-y-o)
Cheltenham—2m 1f

Year	Winner	
1960	Turpial 10st 10lb	13
1961	Cantab 10st 10lb	15
1962	Beaver II 10st 10lb	11
1963	No Race	
1964	No Race	
1965	Blarney Beacon 11st 4lb	7
1966	Black Ice 11st 4lb	11
1967	Persian War 11st 8lb	13
1968	England's Glory 10st 10lb	16
1969	Coral Diver 11st 4lb	26
1970	Varma 11st 4lb	31
1971	Boxer 11st 3lb	18
1972	Zarib 11st	16
1970	Varma 11st 4lb	31
1971	Boxer 11st 3lb	18
1972	Zarib 11st	16
1973	Moonlight Bay 11st	18
1974	Attivo 11st	21
1975	Royal Epic 11st	28
1976	Peterhof 11st	23
1977	Meladon 11st	30
1978	Connaught Ranger 11st	14
1979	Pollardstown 11st	28
1980 Distance changed from 2m 200y		
1980	Heighlin 11st	26
1981	Baron Blakeney 11st	29
1982	Shiny Copper 11st	29
1983	Saxon Farm 11st	30
1984	Northern Game 11st	30
1985	First Bout 11st	27
1986	Solar Cloud 11st	28
1987	Alone Success 11st	29
1988	Kribensis 11st	26
1989	Ikdam 11st	27
1990	Rare Holiday 11st	30
1991	Oh So Risky 11st	27
1992	Duke of Monmouth 11st	30
1993	Shawiya (IRE) 10st 9lb	25
1994	Mysilv 10st 9lb	28
1995	Kissair (IRE) 11st	26

TOTE CHELTENHAM GOLD CUP
(CHASE)
Cheltenham—3¼m 110y

Year	Winner	
1955	Gay Donald 9y 12st	9
1956	Limber Hill 9y 12st	11
1957	Linwell 9y 12st	13
1958	Kerstin 8y 12st	9
1959	Roddy Owen 10y 12st	11
1960	Pas Seul 7y 12st	12

1961	Saffron Tartan 10y 12st..............11
1962	Mandarin 11y 12st........................ 9
1963	Mill House 6y 12st.....................12
1964	Arkle 7y 12st..............................4
1965	Arkle 8y 12st..............................4
1966	Arkle 9y 12st..............................5
1967	Woodland Venture 7y 12st 8
1968	Fort Leney 10y 12st.................... 5
1969	What A Myth 12y 12st................11
1970	L'Escargot 7y 12st....................12
1971	L'Escargot 8y 12st.................... 8
1972	Glencaraig Lady 8y 12st...........12
1973	The Dikler 10y 12st.....................8
1974	Captain Christy 7y 12st.............. 7
1975	Ten Up 8y 12st...........................8
1976	Royal Frolic 7y 12st..................11
1977	Davy Lad 7y 12st......................13
1978	Midnight Court 7y 12st 10
1979	Alverton 9y 12st.......................14
1980	Tied Cottage 12y 12st (subsequently disqualified on technical grounds and race awarded to Master Smudge 8y 12st).... 15
1981	Little Owl 7y 12st 13
1982	Silver Buck 10y 12st................ 22
1983	Bregawn 9y 12st 11
1984	Burrough Hill Lad 8y 12st........ 12
1985	Forgive'N Forget 8y 12st.......... 15
1986	Dawn Run 8y 11st 9lb............. 11
1987	The Thinker 10y 12st................ 12
1988	Charter Party 10y 12st............. 15
1989	Desert Orchid 10y 12st 13
1990	Norton's Coin 9y 12st 12
1991	Garrison Savannah 8y 12st.......14
1992	Cool Ground 10y 12st.............. 8
1993	Jodami 8y 12st......................... 16
1994	The Fellow 9y 12st 15
1995	Master Oats 9y 12st 15

MARTELL CUP CHASE
Aintree—3m 1f
1984-1988 Run as Chivas Regal Cup Chase

1984	Royal Bond 11y 11st 5lb 4
1985	Wayward Lad 10y 11st 5lb 6
1986	Beau Ranger 8y 11st 5lb 4
1987	Wayward Lad 12y 11st 5lb 6
1988	Desert Orchid 9y 11st 5lb 4
1989	Yahoo 8y 11st 5lb....................8
1990	Toby Tobias 8y 11st 9lb 5
1991	Aquilifer 11y 11st 5lb 5
1992	Kings Fountain 9y 11st 9lb........8
1993	Docklands Express 11y 11st 5lb 4
1994	Docklands Express 12y 11st 5lb 4
1995	Merry Gale (IRE) 7y 11st 9lb .. 6

GLENLIVET ANNIVERSARY HURDLE
(4-y-o)
Aintree—2m 110y
Previously run under different titles

1980	Starfen 11st 20
1981	Broadsword (USA) 11st 3lb 10

1982	Prince Bless 11st....................... 12
1983	Benfen 11st 9
1984	Afzal 11st 17
1985	Humberside Lady 10st 9lb...... 15
1986	Dark Raven 11st 16
1987	Aldino 11st 13
1988	Royal Illusion 11st 14
1989	Vayrua (FR) 11st.......................9
1990	Sybillin 11st 18
1991	Montpelier Lad 11st 5lb........... 14
1992	Salwan (USA) 11st 13
1993	Titled Dancer (IRE) 10st 9lb 8
1994	Tropical Lake 10st 9lb 12
1995	Stompin 4y 11st 18

MARTELL AINTREE CHASE
(LIMITED H'CAP)
Aintree—2m
Previously run under different titles

1976	Menehall 9y 10st 10
1977	Skymas 12y 12st 9
1978	Even Melody 9y 11st 6lb 14
1979	Funny Baby 8y 10st 7lb 8
1980	Drumgora 8y 10st 7lb 10
1981	Western Rose 9y 10st 7lb 11
1982	Little Bay 7y 11st 7lb 12
1983	Artifice 12y 11st 9
1984	Little Bay 9y 11st 7lb 7
1985	Kathies Lad 8y 11st 7lb 8
1986	Kathies Lad 9y 10st 13lb 6
1987	Sea Merchant 10y 10st 7lb 9
1988	Prideaux Boy 10y 10st 7lb 13
1989	Feroda 8y 10st 7lb 9
1990	Nohalmdun 9y 10st 7lb 12
1991	Blitzkreig 8y 10st 13lb 11
1992	Katabatic 9y 12st 4
1993	Boutzdaroff 11y 10st 7lb 6
1994	Uncle Ernie 9y 10st 8lb...........8
1995	Coulton 8y 11st 8lb 12

MUMM MELLING CHASE
Aintree—2½m

1991	Blazing Walker 7y 11st 10lb..... 7
1992	Remittance Man 8y 11st 10lb... 4
1993	Deep Sensation 8y 11st 10lb....4
1994	Katabatic 11y 11st 10lb.............5
1995	Viking Flagship 8y 11st 10lb.....6

MARTELL AINTREE HURDLE
Aintree—2½m
Previously run under different titles

1980	Pollardstown 5y 11st 5lb...........3
1981	Daring Run 6y 11st 9lb............. 7
1982	Daring Run 7y 11st 9lb............. 5
1983	Gaye Brief 6y 11st 9lb.............. 6
1984	Dawn Run 6y 11st 11lb.............. 8
1985	Bajan Sunshine 6y 11st 6lb...... 7
1986	Aonoch 7y 11st 9lb 9
1987	Aonoch 8y 11st 9lb 7
1988	Celtic Chief 5y 11st 6lb 9
1989	Beech Road 7y 11st 9lb........... 12
1990	Morley Street 6y 11st 6lb 6
1991	Morley Street 7y 11st 7lb 9

1992	Morley Street 8y 11st 7lb 6
1993	Morley Street 9y 11st 7lb 6
1994	Danoli (IRE) 6y 11st 7lb........... 9
1995	Danoli (IRE) 7y 11st 7lb........... 6

STAKIS SCOTTISH GRAND NATIONAL (H'CAP CHASE)
Ayr—4m 1f
1978-1992 Run as William Hill Scottish National (H'cap Chase)

1970	The Spaniard 8y 10st 10
1971	Young Ash Leaf 7y 10st 2lb .. 21
1972	Quick Reply 7y 9st 9lb 17
1973	Esban 9y 9st 11lb................. 21
1974	Red Rum 9y 11st 13lb......... 17
1975	Barona 9y 10st................... 17
1976	Barona 10y 10st 2lb 23
1977	Sebastian V 9y 10st 2lb........ 18
1978	King Con 9y 9st 13lb............ 21
1979	Fighting Fit 7y 10st 10lb....... 19
1980	Salkeld 8y 10st................... 23
1981	Astral Charge 8y 9st 10lb..... 21
1982	Cockle Strand 9y 9st 11lb...... 15
1983	Canton 9y 10st 2lb 22
1984	Androma 7y 10st................. 19
1985	Androma 8y 10st................. 18
1986	Hardy Lad 9y 10st 24
1987	Little Polveir 9y 10st 11
1988	Mighty Mark 9y 10st 4lb....... 17
1989	Roll-a-Joint 11y 10st............ 11
1990	Four Trix 9y 10st.................. 28
1991	Killone Abbey 8y 10st........... 18
1992	Captain Dibble 7y 11st........... 21
1993	Run For Free 9y 11st 10lb..... 21
1994	Earth Summit 6y 10st 22
1995	Willsford 12y 10st 12lb 22

WHITBREAD GOLD CUP (H'CAP CHASE)
Sandown—3m 5f 110y
*Run at Newcastle

1959	Done Up 9y 10st 13lb............. 23
1960	Plummers Plain 7y 10st........... 21
1961	Pas Seul 8y 12st................... 23
1962	Frenchman's Cove 7y 11st 3lb.22
1963	Hoodwinked 8y 10st 9lb........ 32
1964	Dormant 7y 9st 7lb................. 11
1965	Arkle 8y 12st 7lb...................... 7
1966	What a Myth 9y 9st 8lb........... 8
1967	Mill House 9y 11st 11lb......... 13
1968	Larbawn 9y 10st 9lb............... 16
1969	Larbawn 10y 11st 4lb............. 18
1970	Royal Toss 8y 10st................ 17
1971	Titus Oates 9y 11st 13lb........ 18
1972	Grey Sombrero 9y 9st 10lb.... 28
1973	*Charlie Potheen 8y 12st......... 21

1974	†The Dikler 11y 11st 13lb......... 16
1975	April Seventh 9y 9st 13lb 13
1976	Otter Way 8y 10st 10lb........... 14
1977	Andy Pandy 8y 10st 12lb 15
1978	Strombolus 7y 10st............... 15
1979	Diamond Edge 8y 11st 11lb... 14
1980	Royal Mail 10y 11st 5lb 12
1981	Diamond Edge 10y 11st 7lb... 18
1982	Shady Deal 9y 10st 9
1983	Drumlargan 9y 10st 10lb........ 15
1984	Special Cargo 11y 11st 2lb.... 13
1985	By The Way 7y 11st 20
1986	Plundering 9y 10st 6lb 16
1987	Lean Ar Aghaidh 10y 10st 10lb... 9
1988	Desert Orchid 9y 11st 11lb ... 12
1989	Brown Windsor 7y 10st.......... 18
1990	Mr Frisk 11y 10st 5lb............. 13
1991	††Docklands Express 9y 10st 3lb 10
1992	Topsham Bay 9y 10st 1lb........11
1993	†††Topsham Bay 10y 10st 1lb.......13
1994	Ushers Island 8y 10st..............12
1995	Cache Fleur (FR) 9y 10st 1lb ..14

(† Proud Tarquin, 11y 10st 3lb came in first, disqualified)

(†† Cahervillahow, 7y 11st 2lb came in first, disqualified)

(††† Givus a Buck, 10y 10st came in first, disqualified)

CROWTHER HOMES SWINTON HANDICAP HURDLE
Haydock—2m
1978-1982 Run as Royal Doulton H'cap Hurdle
1984 Run as Tia Maria H'cap Hurdle
1985-93 Run as Swinton Insurance Brokers Trophy

1978	Royal Gaye 5y 10st 20
1979	Beacon Light 8y 11st 1lb 17
1980	No Bombs 5y 10st 9lb............ 14
1981	Gaye Chance 6y 10st 10lb..... 18
1982	Secret Ballot 8y 10st 3lb 17
1983	Abandoned due to waterlogged course
1984	Bajan Sunshine 5y 10st 13lb . 15
1985	Corporal Clinger 6y 10st 3lb .. 21
1986	Prideaux Boy 8y 11st 2lb 20
1987	Inlander 6y 10st 8lb..................8
1988	Past Glories 5y 11st 9lb 23
1989	State Jester 6y 10st................ 18
1990	Sybillin 4y 10st 1lb 14
1991	Winnie the Witch 7y 10st 2lb... 12
1992	Bitofabanter 5y 11st 11lb 22
1993	Spinning 6y 11st...................... 17
1994	Dreams End 6y 11st 4lb......... 19
1995	Chief Minister (IRE) 6y 11st 6lb 13

1000 GUINEAS STAKES (3y fillies) Newmarket – 1 mile

Year	Owner	Winner and Price	Jockey	Trainer	Second	Third	Ran	Time
1958	F Dupre's	Bella Paola (8/11)	S Boullenger	F Mathet	Amante	Alpine Bloom	11	1 38.75
1959	Aly Khan's	Petite Etoile (8/11)	D Smith	N Murless	Rosalba	Paraguana	14	1 40.36
1960	Mrs H Jackson's	Never Too Late (8/11)	R Poincelet	E Pollet	Lady in Trouble	Running Blue	14	1 39.89
1961	Mrs S Costello's	Sweet Solera (4/1)	W Rickaby	R Day	Ambergris	Indian Melody	14	1 38.14
1962	R More O' Ferrall's	Abermaid (100/6)	W Williamson	H Wragg	Display	West Side Story	14	1 39.36
1963	Mrs P Widener's	Hula Dancer (1/2)	R Poincelet	E Pollet	Spree	Royal Cypher	12	1 42.34
1964	Beatrice, Lady Granard's	Pourparler (11/2)	G Bougoure	P J Prendergast	Gwen	*Petite Gina		
1965	L Holliday's	Night Off (9/2)	W Williamson	W Wharton	Yami	Mabel	18	1 38.82
1966	Mrs J Mills's	Glad Rags (100/6)	P Cook	V O'Brien	Berkeley Springs	Miliza	16	1 45.43
1967	R Boucher's	Fleet (11/2)	G Moore	N Murless	St Pauli Girl	Lacquer	21	1 40.30
1968	Mrs N Murless's	Caergwrle (4/1)	A Barclay	N Murless	Photo Flash	Sovereign	16	1 44.76
1969	R Moller's	Full Dress (7/1)	R Hutchinson	H Wragg	Hecuba	Motionless	14	1 40.38
1970	Jean, Lady Ashcombe's	Humble Duty (3/1)	L Piggott	W Walwyn	Gleam	Black Satin	13	1 44.53
1971	F Hue-Williams's	Altesse Royale (25/1)	Y Saint Martin	N Murless	Super Honey	Catherine Wheel	12	1 42.13
1972	Mrs R Stanley's	Waterloo (8/1)	E Hide	J W Watts	Marisela	Rose Dubarry	18	1 40.90
1973	G Pope's	Mysterious (11/1)	G Lewis	N Murless	Jacinth	Favoletta	18	1 39.49
1974	The Queen's	Highclere (12/1)	J Mercer	R Hern	Polygamy	Mrs Twiggywkle	14	1 42.12
1975	Mrs D O' Kelly's	Nocturnal Spree (14/1)	J Roe	A Penna	Girl Friend	Joking Apart	15	1 40.32
1976	D Wildenstein's	Flying Water (2/1)	Y Saint Martin	A Penna	Konafa	Kesar Queen	16	1 41.65
1977	Mrs E Kettlewell's	Mrs McArdy (16/1)	E Hide	M W Easterby	Freeze the Secret		25	1 37.83
1978	R Bonnycastle's	Enstone Spark (35/1)	E Johnson	B Hills	Fair Salinia	Sanedtki	18	1 40.07
1979	Helena Springfield Ltd's	One in a Million (evens)	J Mercer	H Cecil	Abbeydale	Seraphima	17	1 41.56
1980	O Phipps's	Quick as Lightning (12/1)	B Rouse	J Dunlop	Our Home	Yanuka	23	1 43.06
1981	H Joel's	Fairy Footsteps (6/4)	L Piggott	H Cecil	Tolmi	Mrs Penny	14	1 41.89
1982	Sir P Oppenheimer's	On The House (33/1)	J Reid	H Wragg	Time Charter	Go Leasing	15	1 40.45
1983	Maktoum Al-Maktoum's	Ma Biche (5/2)	F Head	Mme C Head	Favoridge	Dione	14	1 40.43
1984	M Lemos's	Pebbles (8/1)	P Robinson	C Brittain	Meis El-Reem	Habibti	18	1 41.71
1985	Sheikh Mohammed's	Oh So Sharp (2/1)	S Cauthen	H Cecil	Al Bahathri	Desirable	15	1 38.18
1986	H Ranier's	Midway Lady (10/1)	R Cochrane	B Hanbury	Maysoon	Bella Colora	17	1 36.85
1987	S Niarchos's	Miesque (15/8)	F Head	F Boutin	Milligram	Sonic Lady	15	1 41.54
1988	E Aland's	Ravinella (4/5)	G W Moore	Mme C Head	Dabaweya	Interval	14	1 38.48
1989	Sheikh Mohammed's	Musical Bliss (7/2)	W R Swinburn	M Stoute	Kerrera	Diminuendo	12	1 40.88
1990	Hamdan Al-Maktoum's	Salsabil (6/4)	W Carson	J Dunlop	Heart of Joy	Aldbourne	10	1 42.69
1991	Hamdan Al-Maktoum's	Shadayid (4/6)	W Carson	J Dunlop	Kooyonga	Negligent	7	1 38.06
1992	Maktoum Al-Maktoum's	Hatoof (5/1)	W R Swinburn	Mme C Head	Marling	Crystal Gazing	14	1 38.18
1993	Mohamed Obaida's	Sayyedati (4/1)	W R Swinburn	C Brittain	Niche	Kenbu	14	1 39.45
1994	R Sangster's	Las Meninas (12/1)	J Reid	T Stack	Balanchine	Aïfan	12	1 37.34
1995	Hamdan Al-Maktoum's	Harayir (5/1)	R Hills	Major W R Hern	Aqaarid	Coup de Genie	15	1 36.71
						Moonshell	14	1 36.72

2000 GUINEAS STAKES (3y) Newmarket—1 mile

Year	Owner	Winner and Price	Jockey	Trainer	Second	Third	Ran	Time
1958	The Queen's	Pall Mall (20/1)	D Smith	C B Rochfort	Major Portion	Nagami	14	1 39.43
1959	Aly Khan's	Taboun (5/2)	G Moore	A Head	Masham	Carnoustie	13	1 42.42
1960	R Webster's	Martial (18/1)	R Hutchinson	P J Prendergast	Venture	Auroy	17	1 38.33
1961	T Yuill's	Rockavon (66/1)	N Stirk	G Boyd	Prince Tudor	Time Greine	22	1 39.46
1962	G Glover's	Privy Councillor (100/6)	W Rickaby	T Waugh	Romulus	Prince Poppa	19	1 38.74
1963	Miss M Sheriffe's	Only for Life (33/1)	J Lindley	J Tree	Ionian	Corpora	21	1 45.00
1964	Mrs H. Jackson's	Baldric (20/1)	W Pyers	E Fellows	Faberge	Balustrade	27	1 38.44
1965	W Harvey's	Niksar (100/8)	D Keith	W Nightingall	Silly Season	Present	22	1 43.31
1966	P Butler's	Kashmir (7/1)	J Lindley	M Bartholomew	Great Nephew	Celtic Song	25	1 40.63
1967	H Joel's	Royal Palace (100/30)	G Moore	N Murless	Taj Dewan	Missile	18	1 39.37
1968	R Guest's	Sir Ivor (11/8)	L Piggott	M V O'Brien	Petingo	Jimmy Reppin	10	1 39.26
1969	J Brown's	Right Tack (15/2)	G Lewis	J Sutcliffe	Tower Walk	Welsh Pageant	13	1 41.65
1970	C Engelhard's	Nijinsky (4/7)	L Piggott	M V O'Brien	Yellow God	Roi Soleil	14	1 41.54
1971	Mrs J Hislop's	Brigadier Gerard (11/2)	J Mercer	R Hern	Mill Reef	My Swallow	6	1 39.20
1972	Sir J Thorn's	High Top (85/40)	W Carson	B Van Cutsem	Roberto	Sun Prince	12	1 40.82
1973	Mrs B Davis's	Mon Fils (50/1)	F Durr	R Hannon	Noble Decree	Sharp Edge	18	1 42.97
1974	Mme M Berger's	Nonoalco (19/2)	Y Saint Martin	F Boutin	Giacometti	Apalachee	12	1 39.53
1975	C d'Alessio's	Bolkonski (33/1)	G Dettori	H Cecil	Grundy	Dominion	24	1 39.53
1976	C d'Alessio's	Wollow (evens)	G Dettori	H Cecil	Vitiges	Thieving Demon	17	1 38.09
1977	N Schibbye's	Nebbiolo (20/1)	G Curran	K Prendergast	Tachypous	The Minstrel	18	1 38.54
1978	J Hayter's	Roland Gardens (28/1)	F Durr	D Sasse	Remainder Man	Weth Nan	19	1 47.33
1979	A Shead's	Tap On Wood (20/1)	S Cauthen	B Hills	Kris	Young Generation	20	1 43.60
1980	K Abdulla's	Known Fact (14/1)	W Carson	J Tree	Posse	Night Alert	14	1 40.46
	(Nureyev fin first disqualified)							
1981	Mrs A Muinos's	To-Agori-Mou (5/2)	G Starkey	G Harwood	Mattaboy	Bel Bolide	19	1 41.43
1982	G Oldham's	Zino (8/1)	F Head	F Boutin	Wind and Wuthering	Tender King	26	1 37.13
1983	R Sangster's	Lomond (9/1)	Pat Eddery	V O'Brien	Tolomeo	Muscatite	16	1 43.87
1984	R Sangster's	El Gran Senor (15/8)	Pat Eddery	V O'Brien	Chief Singer	Lear Fan	9	1 37.41
1985	Maktoum Al Maktoum's	Shadeed (4/5)	L Piggott	M Stoute	Bairn	Supreme Leader	14	1 37.41
1986	K Abdulla's	Dancing Brave (15/8)	G Starkey	G Harwood	Green Desert	Huntingdale	15	1 36.74
1987	J Horgan's	Don't Forget Me (9/1)	W Carson	R Hannon	Bellotto	Midyan	13	1 41.73
1988	H H Aga Khan's	Doyoun (4/5)	W R Swinburn	M Stoute	Charmer	Danehill	9	1 36.44
1989	Hamdan Al-Maktoum's	Nashwan (3/1)	W Carson	R Hern	Exbourne	Bellefella	14	1 35.84
1990	John Horgan's	Tirol (9/1)	M Kinane	R Hannon	Machiavellian	Anshan	14	1 37.83
1991	Lady Beaverbrook's	Mystiko (13/2)	M Roberts	C Brittain	Lycius	Ganges	16	1 38.37
1992	R Sangster's	Rodrigo de Triano (6/1)	L Piggott	P Chapple-Hyam	Lucky Lindy	Pursuit of Love	14	1 35.32
1993	K Abdulla's	Zafonic (5/6)	Pat Eddery	A Fabre	Barathea	Bin Ajwaad	23	1 35.08
1994	G R Bailey Ltd's	Mister Baileys (16/1)	J Weaver	M Johnston	Grand Lodge	Colonel Collins	11	1 35.16
1995	Sheikh Mohammed's	Pennekamp (9/2)	T Jarnet	A Fabre	Celtic Swing	Bahri		

DERBY STAKES (3y) Epsom – 1 mile 4 furlongs 10 yards

Year	Owner	Winner and Price	Jockey	Trainer	Second	Third	Ran	Time
1957	Sir V Sassoon's	Crepello (6/4)	L Piggott	N Murless	Ballymoss	Pipe of Peace	20	2 35.40
1958	Sir V Sassoon's	Hard Ridden (18/1)	C Smirke	M Rogers	Paddy's Point	Nagami	20	2 41.20
1959	Sir H de Trafford's	Parthia (10/1)	W Carr	C B-Rochfort	Fidalgo	Shantung	20	2 36.00
1960	Sir V Sassoon's	St Paddy (7/1)	L Piggott	N Murless	Alcaeus	Kythnos	17	2 35.80
1961	Mrs A. Plesch's	Psidium (66/1)	R Poincelet	H Wragg	Dicta Drake	Pardao	28	2 36.40
1962	R Guest's	Larkspur (22/1)	N Sellwood	V O'Brien	Arcor	Le Cantilien	26	2 37.60
1963	F Dupre's	Relko (5/1)	Y Saint Martin	F Mathet	Merchant Venturer	Ragusa	26	2 39.40
1964	J Ismay's	Santa Claus (15/8)	A Breasley	M Rogers	Indiana	Dilettante	17	2 41.98
1965	J Ternynck's	Sea-Bird (7/4)	P Glennon	E Pollet	Meadow Court	I Say	22	2 38.41
1966	Lady Z Wernher's	Charlottown (5/1)	A Breasley	G Smyth	Pretendre	Black Prince	25	2 37.63
1967	H Joel's	Royal Palace (7/4)	G Moore	N Murless	Ribocco	Dart Board	22	2 38.36
1968	R Guest's	Sir Ivor (4/5)	L Piggott	V O'Brien	Connaught	Mount Athos	13	2 38.73
1969	A Budgett's	Blakeney (15/2)	E Johnson	A Budgett	Shoemaker	Prince Regent	26	2 40.30
1970	C Engelhard's	Nijinsky (11/8)	L Piggott	V O'Brien	Gyr	Stintino	11	2 34.68
1971	P Mellon's	Mill Reef (100/30)	G Lewis	I Balding	Linden Tree	Irish Ball	21	2 37.14
1972	J Galbreath's	Roberto (3/1)	L Piggott	V O'Brien	Rheingold	Pentland Firth	22	2 36.09
1973	A Budgett's	Morston (25/1)	E Hide	A Budgett	Cavo Doro	Freefoot	25	2 35.92
1974	Mrs N. Phillips's	Snow Knight (50/1)	B Taylor	P Nelson	Imperial Prince	Giacometti	18	2 35.04
1975	Dr C Vittadini's	Grundy (5/1)	Pat Eddery	P Walwyn	Nobiliary	Hunza Dancer	18	2 35.35
1976	N B Hunt's	Empery (10/1)	L Piggott	M Zilber	Relkino	Oats	23	2 35.69
1977	R Sangster's	The Minstrel (5/1)	L Piggott	V O'Brien	Hot Grove	Blushing Groom	22	2 36.44
1978	Lord Halifax's	Shirley Heights (8/1)	G Starkey	J Dunlop	Hawaiian Sound	Remainder Man	25	2 35.30
1979	Sir M Sobell's	Troy (6/1)	W Carson	W Hern	Dickens Hill	Northern Baby	23	2 36.59
1980	Mrs A Plesch's	Henbit (7/1)	W Carson	R Hern	Master Willie	Rankin	24	2 34.77
1981	H H Aga Khan's	Shergar (10/11)	W Swinburn	M Stoute	Glint of Gold	Scintillating Air	18	2 44.21
1982	H H Aga Khan's	Golden Fleece (3/1)	Pat Eddery	V O'Brien	Touching Wood	Silver Hawk	18	2 34.27
1983	E Moller's	Teenoso (9/2)	L Piggott	G Wragg	Carlingford Castle	Shearwalk	21	2 49.07
1984	L Migitti's	Secreto (14/1)	C Roche	D O'Brien	El Gran Senor	Mighty Flutter	17	2 39.12
1985	Lord H. de Walden's	Slip Anchor (9/4)	S Cauthen	H Cecil	Law Society	Damister	14	2 36.23
1986	H H Aga Khan's	Shahrastani (11/2)	W Swinburn	M Stoute	Dancing Brave	Mashkour	17	2 37.13
1987	L Freedman's	Reference Point (6/4)	S Cauthen	H Cecil	Most Welcome	Bellotto	19	2 33.90
1988	H H Aga Khan's	Kahyasi (11/1)	R Cochrane	L Cumani	Glacial Storm	Doyoun	14	2 33.84
1989	Hamdan Al-Maktoum's	Nashwan (5/4)	W Carson	W Hern	Terimon	Cacoethes	12	2 34.90
1990	K Abdulla's	Quest For Fame (7/1)	Pat Eddery	R Charlton	Blue Stag	Elmaamul	18	2 37.26
1991	F Salman's	Generous (9/1)	A Munro	P Cole	Marju	Star of Gdansk	13	2 34.00
1992	Sidney H Craig's	Dr Devious (8/1)	J Reid	P Chapple-Hyam	St Jovite	Silver Wisp	18	2 36.19
1993	K Abdulla's	Commander in Chief (15/2)	M Kinane	H Cecil	Blue Judge	Blues Traveller	16	2 34.51
1994	Hamdan Al-Maktoum's	Erhaab (7/2)	W Carson	J Dunlop	King's Theatre	Colonel Collins	25	2 34.16
1995	Saeed Maktoum Al Maktoum's	Lammtarra (14/1)	W Swinburn	S Bin Suroor	Tamure	Presenting	15	2 32.31

OAKS STAKES (3y fillies) Epsom—1 mile 4 furlongs 10 yards

Year	Owner	Winner and Price	Jockey	Trainer	Second	Third	Ran	Time
1963	Mrs J Olin's	Noblesse (4/11)	G Bougoure	P J Prendergast	Spree	Poupoune	9	2 39.60
1964	Sir F Robinson's	Homeward Bound (100/7)	G Starkey	J Oxley	Windmill Girl	La Bamba	18	2 49.36
1965	J C Brady's	Long Look (100/7)	J Purtell	V O'Brien	Mabel	Ruby's Princess	18	2 39.56
1966	C Clore's	Valoris (11/10)	L Piggott	V O'Brien	Berkeley Springs	Varinia	18	2 39.35
1967	Countess M Batthyany's	Pia (100/7)	E Hide	W Elsey	St Pauli Girl	Ludham	13	2 38.34
1968	H Berlin's	La Lagune (11/8)	J Thiboeuf	F Boutin	Glad One	Pandora Bay	12	2 41.66
1969	Lord Rosebery's	Sleeping Partner (100/6)	J Gorton	D Smith	Frontier	Goddess	14	2 39.94
1970	Mrs S Joel's	Lupe (100/30)	A Barclay	N Murless	State Pension	Myastrid	15	2 41.46
1971	F Hue-Williams's	Altesse Royale (6/4)	G Lewis	N Murless	Maina	Arctic Wave	16	2 36.95
1972	C St George's	Ginevra (8/1)	A Murray	R Price	Regal Exception	La Manille	11	2 39.35
1973	G Pope's	Mysterious (13/8)	G Lewis	N Murless	Where You Lead	Arkadina	17	2 36.95
1974	L Freedman's	Polygamy (3/1)	Pat Eddery	P Walwyn	Furioso	Aureoletta	10	2 36.31
1975	J Morrison's	Juliette Marny (12/1)	L Piggott	J Tree	Val's Girl	Matuta	15	2 39.39
1976	D Wildenstein's	Pawneese (6/5)	Y Saint Martin	A Penna	Roses for the Star	Moonlight Night	12	2 39.10
1977	The Queen's	Dunfermline (6/1)	W Carson	M Stoute	Freeze the Secret	African Dancer	14	2 35.25
1978	S Hanson's	Fair Salinia (8/1)	G Starkey	M Stoute	Dancing Maid	Vaguely Deb	13	2 36.53
1979	J Morrison's	Scintillate (20/1)	Pat Eddery	J Tree	Bonnie Isle	Suni	15	2 36.82
1980	R Hollingsworth's	Bireme (9/2)	W Carson	H Herm	Vielle	Britannia's Rule	14	2 43.74
1981	Mrs B Firestone's	Blue Wind (3/1)	L Piggott	D Weld	Madam Gay	The Dancer	11	2 34.33
1982	R Barnett's	Time Charter (12/1)	W Newnes	H Candy	Slightly Dangerous	Leap Lively	12	2 40.93
1983	Sir M Sobell's	Sun Princess (6/1)	W Carson	R Hern	Acclimatise	Last Feather	13	2 34.21
1984	Sir R McAlpine's	Circus Plume (4/1)	L Piggott	J Dunlop	Media Luna	New Coins	15	2 40.98
1985	Sheikh Mohammed's	Oh So Sharp (6/4)	S Cauthen	H Cecil	Triptych	Poquito Queen	12	2 38.97
1986	H Ranier's	Midway Lady (15/8)	R Cochrane	B Hanbury	Untold	Dubian	15	2 41.37
1987	Sheikh Mohammed's	Unite (11/1)	W R Swinburn	M Stoute	Bourbon Girl	Maysoon	11	2 35.60
1988	Sheikh Mohammed's	Diminuendo (7/4)	S Cauthen	H Cecil	Sudden Love	Three Tails	11	2 38.17
1989	Sheikh Mohammed's	Snow Bride (13/2)	S Cauthen	H Cecil	Roseate Tern	Animatrice	9	2 35.02
	(Aliysa finished first but was disqualified)					Mamaluna		2 34.22
1990	Hamdan Al-Maktoum's	Salsabil (2/1)	W Carson	J Dunlop	Game Plan	Knight's Baroness	8	2 38.70
1991	Maktoum Al-Maktoum's	Jet Ski Lady (50/1)	C Roche	C Bolger	Shamshir	Shadayid	9	2 37.30
1992	W J Gredley's	User Friendly (5/1)	G Duffield	C Brittain	All At Sea	Pearl Angel	7	2 39.77
1993	Sheikh Mohammed's	Intrepidity (5/1)	M Roberts	A Fabre	Royal Ballerina	Oakmead	14	2 34.19
1994	Godolphin's	Balanchine (6/1)	L Dettori	H Ibrahim	Wind In Her Hair	Hawaiis	10	2 40.37
1995	Godolphin's	Moonshell (3/1)	L Dettori	S Bin Suroor	Dance A Dream	Pure Grain	10	2 35.44

ST LEGER STAKES (3y) Doncaster—1 mile 6 furlongs 132 yards

Year	Owner	Winner and Price	Jockey	Trainer	Second	Third	Ran	Time
1957	J McShain's	Ballymoss (8/1)	T P Burns	V O'Brien	Court Harwell	Brioche	16	3 15.60
1958	Sir H de Trafford's	Alcide (4/9)	W Carr	C B-Rochfort	None Nicer	Nagami	10	3 6.40
1959	W Hill's	Cantelo (100/7)	E Hide	C Elsey	Fidalgo	Pindari	10	3 4.60
1960	Sir V Sassoon's	St Paddy (4/6)	L Piggott	N Murless	Die Hard	Vienna	9	3 13.20
1961	Mrs V Lilley's	Aurelius (9/2)	L Piggott	N Murless	Bounteous	Dicta Drake	13	3 6.60
1962	L Holliday's	Hethersett (100/8)	W Carr	R Hern	Monterrico	Miralgo	15	3 10.80
1963	J Mullion's	Ragusa (2/5)	G Bougoure	P Prendergast	Star Moss	Fighting Ship	7	3 5.40
1964	C Engelhard's	Indiana (100/7)	J Lindley	J Watts	Patti	Soderini	15	3 5.40
1965	J Astor's	Provoke (28/1)	J Mercer	R Hern	Meadow Court	Solstice	11	3 18.60
1966	R Sigtia's	Sodium (7/1)	F Durr	G Todd	Charlottown	David Jack	9	3 9.80
1967	C Engelhard's	Ribocco (7/2)	L Piggott	R Houghton	Hopeful Venture	Ruysdael	9	3 5.40
1968	C Engelhard's	Ribero (100/30)	L Piggott	R Houghton	Canterbury	Cold Storage	8	3 19.80
1969	G Oldham's	Intermezzo (7/1)	R Hutchinson	H Wragg	Ribofilio	Prince Consort	11	3 11.80
1970	C Engelhard's	Nijinsky (2/7)	L Piggott	V O'Brien	Meadowville	Politico	6	3 6.40
1971	Mrs J Rogerson's	Athens Wood (5/2)	L Piggott	H T Jones	Homeric	Falkland	8	3 14.90
1972	O Phipps's	Boucher (28/1)	L Piggott	V O'Brien	Our Mirage	Ginevra	7	3 28.71
1973	W Behrens's	Peleid (28/1)	F Durr	W Elsey	Buoy	Duke of Ragusa	13	3 8.21
1974	Lady Beaverbrook's	Bustino (11/10)	J Mercer	R Hern	Giacometti	Riboson	10	3 9.02
1975	C St George's	Bruni (9/1)	A Murray	R Price	King Pellinore	Libra's Rib	12	3 9.02
1976	D Wildenstein's	Crow (6/1)	Y Saint-Martin	A Penna	Secret Man	Scallywag	13	3 13.17
1977	The Queen's	Dunfermline (10/1)	W Carson	R Hern	Alleged	Classic Example	13	3 5.17
1978	M Lemos's	Julio Mariner (28/1)	E Hide	C Brittain	Le Moss	M-Loishan	14	3 4.94
1979	A Rolland's	Son of Love (20/1)	A Lequeux	R Collet	Soleil Noir	Niniski	14	3 9.02
1980	H Joel's	Light Cavalry (3/1)	J Mercer	H Cecil	Water Mill	World Leader	7	3 11.48
1981	Sir J Astor's	Cut Above (28/1)	J Mercer	R Hern	Glint of Gold	Bustomi	7	3 11.60
1982	Maktoum Al Maktoum's	Touching Wood (7/1)	P Cook	H T Jones	Zilos	Diamond Shoal	15	3 3.53
1983	Sir M Sobell's	Sun Princess (7/4)	W Carson	H Cecil	Esprit du Nord	Carlingford Castle	12	3 16.65
1984	I Allan's	Commanche Run (7/4)	L Piggott	H Cecil	Baynoun	Alphabatim	11	3 9.93
1985	Sheikh Mohammed's	Oh So Sharp (8/11)	S Cauthen	H Cecil	Phardante	Lanfranco	8	3 7.13
1986	Duchess of Norfolk's	Moon Madness (9/2)	Pat Eddery	J Dunlop	Celestial Storm	Untold	8	3 5.03
1987	L Freedman's	Reference Point (4/11)	S Cauthen	H Cecil	Mountain Kingdom	Dry Dock	7	3 5.91
1988	Lady Beaverbrook's	Minster Son (15/2)	W Carson	N A Graham	Diminuendo	Sheriff's Star	6	3 6.80
1989	C St George's	Michelozzo (6/4)	S Cauthen	H Cecil	Sapience	Roseate Tern	8	3 20.72
	(Run at Ayr)							
1990	M Arbib's	Snurge (7/2)	T Quinn	P Cole	Hellenic	River God	8	3 8.78
1991	K Abdulla's	Toulon (5/2)	Pat Eddery	A Fabre	Saddlers' Hall	Michelletti	8	3 3.12
1992	W J Gredley's	User Friendly (7/4)	G Duffield	C Brittain	Sonus	Bonny Scot	9	3 5.48
1993	Mrs G A E Smith's	Bob's Return (3/1)	P Robinson	M Tompkins	Armiger	Edbaysaan	7	3 7.85
1994	Sheikh Mohammed's	Moonax (40/1)	Pat Eddery	B Hills	Broadway Flyer	Double Trigger	8	3 4.19
1995	Godolphin's	Classic Cliche (100/30)	L Dettori	S bin Suroor	Minds Music	Istidaad	10	3 9.74

KING GEORGE VI AND QUEEN ELIZABETH STAKES
Ascot—1 mile 4 furlongs

Year	Owner	Winner and Price	Jockey	Trainer	Second	Third	Ran	Time
1959	Sir H de Trafford's	Alcide 4-9-7 (2/1)	W Carr	C B-Rochfort	Gladness	Balbo	11	2 31.39
1960	Sir H Wernher's	Aggressor 5-9-7 (100/8)	J Lindley	J Gosden	Petite Etoile	Kythnos	8	2 35.21
1961	Mme E Couture's	Right Royal 3-8-7 (6/4)	R Poincelet	E Pollet	St Paddy	Rockavon	4	2 40.34
1962	F Dupre's	Match 4-9-7 (9/2)	Y Saint Martin	F Mathet	Aurelius	Arctic Storm	11	2 32.02
1963	J Mullion's	Ragusa 3-8-7 (4/1)	G Bougoure	P J Prendergast	Miralgo	Tarqogan	10	2 33.80
1964	Mrs H Jackson's	Nasram 4-9-7 (100/7)	W Pyers	E Fellows	Santa Claus	Royal Avenue	4	2 33.15
1965	G Bell's	Meadow Court 3-8-7 (6/5)	L Piggott	P J Prendergast	Soderini	Oncidium	7	2 33.27
1966	J Hornung's	Aunt Edith 4-9-4 (7/2)	L Piggott	N Murless	Sodium	Prominer	5	2 35.06
1967	S Joel's	Busted 4-9-7 (4/1)	G Moore	N Murless	Salvo	Ribocco	5	2 33.64
1968	H Joel's	Royal Palace 4-9-7 (7/4)	A Barclay	N Murless	Felicio	Topyo	7	2 33.22
1969	Duke of Devonshire's	Park Top 5-9-4 (9/4)	L Piggott	B Van Cutsem	Crozier	Hogarth	9	2 32.46
1970	C Engelhard's	Nijinsky 3-8-7 (40/85)	L Piggott	V O'Brien	Blakeney	Crepellana	6	2 36.16
1971	P Mellon's	Mill Reef 3-8-7 (8/13)	G Lewis	I Balding	Ortis	Acclimatization	10	2 32.56
1972	Mrs J Hislop's	Brigadier Gerard 4-9-7 (8/13)	J Mercer	R Hern	Parnell	Riverman	10	2 32.91
1973	N B Hunt's	Dahlia 3-8-4 (10/1)	W Pyers	M Zilber	Rheingold	Our Mirage	12	2 30.43
1974	N B Hunt's	Dahlia 4-9-4 (15/8)	L Piggott	M Zilber	Highclere	Dankaro	10	2 33.03
1975	Dr C Vittadini's	Grundy 3-8-7 (4/5)	P Eddery	P Walwyn	Bustino	Dahlia	11	2 26.98
1976	D Wildenstein's	Pawnese 3-8-5 (9/4)	Y Saint Martin	A Penna	Bruni	Orange Bay	11	2 29.36
1977	R Sangster's	The Minstrel 3-8-8 (7/4)	L Piggott	V O'Brien	Orange Bay	Exceller	11	2 30.48
1978	D McCall's	Ile de Bourbon 3-8-8 (12/1)	J Reid	F Houghton	Hawaiian Sound	Montcontour	14	2 30.53
1979	Sir M Sobell's	Troy 3-8-8 (2/5)	W Carson	R Hern	Gay Mecene	Ela-Mana-Mou	7	2 33.75
1980	H H Aga Khan's	Ela-Mana-Mou 4-9-7 (11/4)	W Carson	R Hern	Mrs Penny	Gregorian	10	2 35.39
1981	A Ward's	Shergar 3-8-8 (2/5)	W Swinburn	M Stoute	Madam Gay	Fingals Cave	7	2 35.40
1982	R Barnett's	Kalaglow 4-9-7 (13-2)	G Starkey	M Stoute	Assert	Glint of Gold	10	2 31.58
1983	E Moller's	Time Charter 4-9-4 (5/1)	J Mercer	H Candy	Diamond Shoal	Sun Princess	9	2 30.78
1984	Lady Beaverbrook's	Teenoso 4-9-7 (13/2)	L Piggott	G Wragg	Sadler's Wells	Tolomeo	9	2 27.95
1985	K Abdulla's	Petoski 3-8-8 (12/1)	W Carson	G Harwood	Oh So Sharp	Rainbow Quest	13	2 27.61
1986	L Freedman's	Dancing Brave 3-8-8 (6/4)	Pat Eddery	G Harwood	Shardari	Triptych	9	2 29.49
1987	Sheikh Ahmed Al Maktoum's	Reference Point 3-8-8 (11/10)	S Cauthen	H Cecil	Celestial Storm	Triptych	9	2 34.63
1988	Hamdan Al-Maktoum's	Mtoto 5-9-7 (4/1)	M Roberts	A C Stewart	Unfuwain	Tony Bin	10	2 37.33
1989	Sheikh Mohammed's	Nashwan 3-8-8 (2/9)	W Carson	H Cecil	Cacoethes	Top Class	7	2 32.27
1990	Sheikh Mohammed's	Belmez 3-8-9 (15/2)	M Kinane	H Cecil	Old Vic	Assatis	11	2 30.76
1991	F Salman's	Generous 3-8-9 (4/5)	A Munro	P Cole	Sanglamore	Rock Hopper	9	2 28.99
1992	Mrs V K Payson's	St Jovite 3-8-9 (4/5)	S Craine	J Bolger	Saddlers' Hall	Opera House	8	2 30.85
1993	Sheikh Mohammed's	Opera House 5-9-7 (8/1)	M Roberts	M Stoute	White Muzzle	Commander in Chief	10	2 33.94
1994	Sheikh Mohammed's	King's Theatre 3-8-9 (12/1)	M Kinane	H Cecil	White Muzzle	Wagon Master	12	2 28.92
1995	Saeed Maktoum Al Maktoum's	Lammtarra 3-8-9 (9/4)	L Dettori	S Bin Suroor	Pentire	Strategic Choice	7	2 31.01

PRIX DE L'ARC DE TRIOMPHE Longchamp—1 mile 4 furlongs

Year	Owner	Winner and Price	Jockey	Trainer	Second	Third	Ran	Time
1957	R Meyer's	Oroso 4-9-6 (52/1)	S Boullenger	D Lescalle	Denisy	Balbo	.24	2 33.40
1958	J McShain's	Ballymoss 4-9-6 (39/10)	A Breasley	V O'Brien	Fric	Cherasco	.17	2 37.90
1959	Aly Khan's	Saint Crespin 3-8-10 (17/1)	G Moore	A Head	Midnight Sun	Le Loup Garou	.25	2 33.30
1960	H Aubert's	Puissant Chef 3-8-10 (14/1)	M Garcia	C Bartholomew	Hautain	Point d'Amour	.17	2 43.90
1961	E Verga's	Molvedo 3-8-10 (18/10)	E Camici	A Maggi	Right Royal	Misti	.19	2 38.40
1962	Mme C del Ducca's	Soltikoff 3-8-10 (40/1)	M Depalmas	R Pelat	Monade	Val de Loir	.24	2 30.90
1963	Baron G de Rothschild's	Exbury 4-9-6 (36/10)	J Deforge	G Watson	Le Mesnil	Misti	.15	2 34.90
1964	R Ellsworth's	Prince Royal 3-8-10 (16/1)	R Poincelet	G Bridgland	Santa Claus	La Bamba	.22	2 35.50
1965	J Ternynck's	Sea-Bird 3-8-10 (6/5)	P Glennon	E Pollet	Reliance	Diatome	.20	2 39.80
1966	W Burmann's	Prince Royal 3-8-10 (53/10)	F Head	W Head	Sigebert	Lionel	.24	2 39.60
1967	Mme S Volterra's	Topyo 3-8-10 (82/1)	W Pyers	W Head	Salvo	Ribocco	.30	2 38.20
1968	Mrs W Franklyn's	Vaguely Noble 3-8-10 (5/2)	W Williamson	E Pollet	Sir Ivor	Carmarthen	.17	2 35.20
1969	S McGrath's	Levmoss 4-9-6 (52/1)	W Williamson	S McGrath	Park Top	Grandier	.24	2 35.20
1970	A Plesch's	Sassafras 3-8-10 (19/1)	Y Saint Martin	J Mathet	Nijinsky	Miss Dan	.15	2 29.00
1971	P Mellon's	Mill Reef 3-8-10 (7/10)	G Lewis	I Balding	Pistol Packer	Cambizzia	.18	2 29.70
1972	Countess M Batthyany's	San San 3-8-7 (37/2)	F Head	A Penna	Rescousse	Homeric	.19	2 28.30
1973	H Zeisel's	Rheingold 4-9-6 (77/10)	L Piggott	B Hills	Allez France	Hard to Beat	.27	2 35.80
1974	D Wildenstein's	Allez France 4-9-3 (1/2)	Y Saint Martin	A Penna	Comtesse de Loir	Margouillat	.20	2 36.90
1975	W Zeitelhack's	Star Appeal 5-9-6 (119/1)	G Starkey	T Grieper	On My Way	Comtesse de Loir	.24	2 33.60
1976	A Wertheimer's	Ivanjica 4-9-1 (71/10)	F Head	A Head	Crow	Youth	.20	2 39.40
1977	R Sangster's	Alleged 3-8-11 (38/10)	L Piggott	V O'Brien	Balmerino	Crystal Palace	.26	2 30.60
1978	R Sangster's	Alleged 4-9-4 (7/5)	L Piggott	V O'Brien	Trillon	Dancing Maid	.18	2 36.10
1979	Mme H Head's	Three Troikas 3-8-8 (88/10)	F Head	Mme C Head	Le Marmot	Troy	.22	2 28.90
1980	R Sangster's	Detroit 3-8-8 (67/10)	Pat Eddery	O Douieb	Argument	Ela-Mana-Mou	.20	2 28.00
1981	J Wertheimer's	Gold River 4-9-1 (53/1)	G W Moore	A Head	Bikala	April Run	.24	2 37.00
1982	H H Aga Khan's	Akiyda 3-8-8 (43/1)	Y Saint Martin	F. Mathet	Ardross	Awaasif	.17	2 28.10
1983	D Wildenstein's	All Along 4-9-1 (173/10)	W Swinburn	P Biancone	Sun Princess	Luth Enchantée	.26	2 39.10
1984	D Wildenstein's	Sagace 4-9-4 (29/10)	Y Saint Martin	P Biancone	Northern Trick	All Along	.22	2 29.50
1985	K Abdulla's	Rainbow Quest 4-9-4 (71/10)	Pat Eddery	J Tree	Sagace	Kozana	.15	2 29.50
1986	K Abdulla's	Dancing Brave 3-8-11 (11/10)	Pat Eddery	G Harwood	Bering	Triptych	.15	2 27.70
1987	P de Moussac's	Trempolino 3-8-11 (20/1)	Pat Eddery	A Fabre	Tony Bin	Triptych	.11	2 26.30
1988	Mrs V Gaucci del Bono's	Tony Bin 5-9-4 (14/1)	J Reid	L Camici	Mtoto	Boyatino	.24	2 27.30
1989	A Balzarini's	Carroll House 4-9-4 (19/1)	M Kinane	M Jarvis	Behera	Saint Andrews	.19	2 30.80
1990	B McNall's	Saumarez 3-8-11 (15/1)	G Mosse	N Clement	Epervier Bleu	Snurge	.21	2 29.80
1991	H Chalhoub's	Suave Dancer 3-8-11 (37/10)	C Asmussen	J Hammond	Magic Night	Pistolet Bleu	.14	2 31.40
1992	O Lecerf's	Subotica 4-9-1 (88/10)	T Jarnet	A Fabre	User Friendly	Vert Amande	.18	2 39.00
1993	D Tsui's	Urban Sea 4-9-1 (37/1)	E Saint Martin	J Lesbordes	White Muzzle	Opera House	.23	2 37.90
1994	Sheikh Mohammed's	Carnegie 3-8-11 (3/1)	T Jarnet	A Fabre	Hernando	Apple Tree	.20	2 31.10
1995	Al Maktoum's	Lammtarra 3-8-11 (2/1)	L Dettori	S Bin Suroor	Freedom Cry	Swain	.16	2 31.80

GRAND NATIONAL STEEPLECHASE (Liverpool) —4m 4f

Year	Winner and Price	Age & Weight	Jockey	Second	Third	Ran	Time
1956	E.S.B. (100-7)	11 11 3	D V Dick	Gentle Moya	Royal Tan	29	9 21.40
1957	Sundew (20-1)	11 11 7	F T Winter	Wyndburgh	Tiberetta	35	9 42.40
1958	Mr What (18-1)	8 10 6	A Freeman	Tiberetta	Green Drift	31	10 1.20
1959	Oxo (8-1)	8 10 13	M Scudamore	Wyndburgh	Mr What	34	9 37.20
1960	Merryman II (13-2)	9 10 12	G Scott	Badanloch	Clear Profit	26	9 26.20
1961	Nicolaus Silver (28-1)	9 10 1	H Beasley	Merryman II	O'Malley Point	35	9 22.60
1962	Kilmore (28-1)	12 10 4	F T Winter	Wyndburgh	Mr What	32	9 50.00
1963	Ayala (66-1)	9 10 0	P Buckley	Carrickbeg	Hawa's Song	47	9 35.80
1964	Team Spirit (18-1)	12 10 3	G W Robinson	Purple Silk	Peacetown	33	9 47.00
1965	Jay Trump (100-6)	8 11 5	Mr C Smith, jun.	Freddie	Mr Jones	47	9 30.60
1966	Anglo (50-1)	8 10 0	T Norman	Freddie	Forest Prince	47	9 52.80
1967	Foinavon (100-1)	9 10 0	J Buckingham	Honey End	Red Alligator	44	9 49.60
1968	Red Alligator (100-7)	9 10 0	B Fletcher	Moidore's Token	Different Class	45	9 28.60
1969	Highland Wedding (100-9)	12 10 4	E Harty	Steel Bridge	Rondetto	30	9 30.80
1970	Gay Trip (15-1)	8 11 5	P Taaffe	Vulture	Miss Hunter	28	9 38.00
1971	Specify (28-1)	9 10 13	J Cook	Black Secret	Astbury	38	9 34.20
1972	Well To Do (14-1)	9 10 1	G Thorner	Gay Trip	Black Secret	42	10 8.40
1973	Red Rum (9-1)	8 10 5	B Fletcher	Crisp	L'Escargot	38	9 1.90
1974	Red Rum (11-1)	9 12 0	B Fletcher	L'Escargot	Charles Dickens	42	9 20.30
1975	L'Escargot (13-2)	12 11 3	J Carberry	Red Rum	Spanish Steps	31	9 31.10
1976	Rag Trade (14-1)	10 10 12	J Burke	Red Rum	Eyecatcher	32	9 20.90
1977	Red Rum (9-1)	12 11 8	T Stack	Churchtown Boy	Eyecatcher	42	9 30.30
1978	Lucius (14-1)	9 10 9	B R Davies	Sebastian V.	Drumroan	37	9 33.90
1979	Rubstic (25-1)	10 10 0	M Barnes	Zongalero	Rough & Tumble	34	9 52.90
1980	Ben Nevis (40-1)	12 10 12	Mr C Fenwick	Rough & Tumble	The Pilgarlic	30	10 17.40
1981	Aldaniti (10-1)	11 10 13	R Champion	Spartan Missile	Royal Mail	39	9 47.20
1982	Grittar (7-1)	9 11 5	E Saunders	Hard Outlook	Loving Words	39	9 12.60
1983	Corbiere (13-1)	8 11 4	B de Haan	Greasepaint	Yer Man	41	9 47.04
1984	Hallo Dandy (13-1)	10 10 1	N Doughty	Greasepaint	Corbiere	40	9 21.04
1985	Last Suspect (50-1)	11 10 5	H Davies	Mr Snugfit	Corbiere	40	9 42.70
1986	West Tip (15-2)	9 10 11	R Dunwoody	Young Driver	Classified	40	9 33.00
1987	Maori Venture (28-1)	11 10 13	S C Knight	The Tsarevich	Lean Ar Aghaidh	40	9 19.30
1988	Rhyme n'Reason (10-1)	9 11 0	B Powell	Durham Edition	Monanore	40	9 53.50
1989	Little Polveir (28-1)	12 10 3	J Frost	West Tip	The Thinker	40	10 6.80
1990	Mr Frisk (16-1)	11 10 6	Mr M Armytage	Durham Edition	Rinus	38	8 47.80
1991	Seagram (12-1)	11 10 6	N Hawke	Garrison Savannah	Auntie Dot	40	9 29.90
1992	Party Politics (14-1)	8 10 7	C Llewellyn	Romany King	Laura's Beau	40	9 06.30
1993	Race Void						
1994	Minnehoma (16-1)	11 10 8	R Dunwoody	Just So	Moorcroft Boy	36	10 18.80
1995	Royal Athlete (40-1)	12 10 6	J Titley	Party Politics	Over The Deel	35	9 04.00

1995 TWO-YEAR-OLD RATINGS

Compiled by Walter Glynn (Raceform Private Handicapper)

To find the top rated horse in each race, add one point for each pound carried below 9st, or subtract one point for each pound carried above 9st. The figure in parenthesis is an all-weather rating.

A Likely Tale (USA)..80
A Million At Last (IRE)
...................36
A-Aasem 84
Abbott of Whalley55 (57)
Abduction 45
Abir...................70
Absolutelystunning .42
Abundant 88
Academy of Dance (IRE)
...................74
Acharne 85
Addie Pray (IRE).......69
Admiral Jones (IRE).92
Aerleon Jane 74
Aethra 87
Afisiak...............62 (59)
African Sun (IRE) 44
Again Together 63
Age of Reality (USA)68
Ageeb (IRE) 67
Agent 57 (67)
Agile...................63
Agnella (IRE) 88
Ahkaam (USA)........101
Ailesbury Hill (USA).80
Air Wing 88
Akalim 78
Akansa (IRE)...........38
Al Abraq (IRE) 85
Al Shadeedah (USA)74
Al Shafa 89
Al's Alibi 71
Alakhluki...................58
Alambar (IRE)...........75
Alamein (USA)...........73
Albaha (USA)...........75
Albert The Bear.91 (23)
Alessandra 81
Alfahaal (IRE) 51
Alfayza 65

Alhaarth (IRE).........121
Alhawa (USA) 78
Ali-Royal (IRE)...........87
Alicia (IRE)...............48
Alistover 22 (33)
Alisura...................39
All In Good Time 17
All She Surveys........60
Allied Forces (USA)100
Almaty (IRE) 104
Almushtarak (IRE)....86
Alpine...................58
Alpine Hideaway (IRE).
...................75
Alpine Joker 55
Alpine Twist (USA)...64
Alreeh (IRE) 70
Alsahib (USA)...........67
Altamura (USA) 76
Alwarqa...................32
Always Happy 74
Alzanti...................87
Alzotic (IRE) 48 (80)
Amadour (IRE)...........57
Amanita...................75
Amaniy (USA)...........96
Amaretto Bay (IRE)..91
Amazing Bay 96
Amber Fort 74 (66)
Ameer Alfayaafi (IRE)
...................32
Amelanchier 30
Amington Lass.........49
Amoeba (IRE)....66 (55)
Amy Leigh (IRE)70 (70)
Ancestral Jane 74
Anchor Venture........64
Andsome Boy............38
Angaar (IRE)...........78
Angel Chimes...........77
Angel Face (USA).....53

Angus McCoatup (IRE)
...................63(66)
Animation 40
Ann's Music...........36
Anna Settic........51 (36)
Annaba (IRE) 76
Annaberg (IRE)........76
Annecy (USA)...........70
Another Quarter (IRE)..
...................62
Anotheranniversary.92
Anshan's Deity ...63 (9)
Answers-To-Thomas70
Antarctic Storm........76
Anthelia...................91
Antiguan Jane...33 (62)
Antonias Melody 66
Any Colour 51
Apache Len (USA) ...77
Apartments Abroad .64
...................(64)
Apicella...................61
Appeal Again (IRE) ..55
Applaud (USA) 100
Apple Musashi 89
April The Eighth 95
April's Joy 54 (51)
Arabian Heights 48
Arabian Story 72
Arajaan (USA)...........85
Arc of The Diver (IRE)
...................66
Arcady 66 (43)
Arch Angel (IRE)58 (59)
Arctic Fancy (USA) ..77
Arctic Romancer (IRE).
...................79 (84)
Arctic Zipper (USA)..69
Arctiid (USA) 63
Arlington Lady 66
Arrhythmic (IRE) 69

Bright Water 93
Brighter Byfaah (IRE)50
Brilliant Red..............95
Brockville Bairn 40 (40)
Brogans Brush .45 (34)
Bronhallow 58
Brother Roy 65
Budby.......................69
Budding Annie 56
Buff..........................26
Bullfinch 93
Bullpen Belle....74 (53)
Bumblefoot (IRE)56 (69)
Burj..........................67
Burnt Offering 67
Bursul Lady 14
Busy Flight 99
Butterwick Belle (IRE)
................................66
By A Whisker............60
Ca'd'oro 70
Cabcharge Striker....87
Callaloo....................68
Calypso Run 45
Camionneur (IRE) 59
Camp Follower 61
Candle Smoke (USA)58
Candy Dancer...........36
Candy's Delight........55
Canlubang..........26 (25)
Canon Can (USA)......68
Canons Park.............75
Capilano Princess....68
................................(61)
Capo Bay (IRE)..........11
Capstone 55
Capture The Moment65
Cara Rafaela (USA) 109
Carburton 89
Careful (IRE)..............60
Caribbean Dancer....56
Caribbean Quest......87
Caricature (IRE)........86
Carmarthen Bay56 (81)
Carmentalia........84 (73)
Carmosa (USA).76 (62)
Carwyn's Choice31 (24)
Cascadia (IRE)..........72
Castan (IRE) 67
Castle Governor54 (21)
Catch A Glimpse (USA)

................................96
Catch The Lights75 (75)
Catumbella (USA) 75
Catwalk Girl..............55
Caveat Emptor (IRE) 44
Cawdor Lady.......60 (4)
Caxton Star...............81
Cayman Kai (IRE)...100
Cd Super Targeting (IRE)
................................50
Cebwob....................85
Ceilidh (IRE) 42
Ceilidh Star (IRE) 75
Ceirseach (IRE) 93
Celandine.................83
Censor 83
Centre Stalls (IRE) ...91
Centurion.................73
Cerdan (USA) 67
Cerise (IRE) 52
Chalamont (IRE)........89
Chalcuchima 71 (65)
Chalice.....................72
Chalk Dust (USA)......79
Chamber Music.57 (41)
Champagne Prince ..90
Champagne Warrior (IRE)
................................43
Charisse Dancer 42
Charlie Chang (IRE).55
................................(73)
Charlotte Corday......66
Charlton Imp (USA)..44
Charming Admiral (IRE)
................................36
Charming Bride 54 (33)
Charnwood Nell (USA)
................................52
Charterhouse Xpres 78
................................(71)
Charwelton 76
Chauvelin (IRE) 46
Chavin Point.............16
Cheerful Aspect (IRE)79
Chelsea Classic (IRE)56
Chelsea My Love (USA)
................................29
Chemcast 68 (60)
Cherry Garden (IRE) 60
................................(60)
Chief Mouse 72

Chik's Secret.....49 (52)
Chilibang Bang .49 (62)
Chillam 33 (47)
Chilly Looks 45
China Castle......58 (64)
Cinnamon Stick (IRE)49
................................(44)
Circled (USA)............84
Circus Star...............66
Ciserano (IRE) 73
Civil Liberty 84
Clan Chief 67
Classic Affair (USA).62
Classic Artiste (USA)58
Classic Ballet (FR) ...74
Classic Beauty (IRE)65
Classic Call (IRE)27 (39)
Classic Colours (USA)58
Classic Daisy 49 (54)
Classic Defence (IRE)62
Classic Delight (USA)40
................................(43)
Classic Eagle............85
Classic Flyer (IRE) ...68
Classic Fountain (IRE)
................................87
Classic Leader 76
Classic Look (IRE) ...55
Classic Lover (IRE) ..73
Classic Romance 80
Classic Victory........77
Classy Chief 78
Clemente..................76
Clerkenwell (USA)....64
Clever Dorothy (USA)
................................86
Clincher Club 74
Clint.........................41
Cliptomania (USA) .103
Clouds Hill (FR)........74
Clued Up...........44 (32)
Coastguards Hero....39
Cocoon (IRE)............43
Cold Shoulder (IRE).66
Coldstream...............86
Colour Counsellor45 (56)
Colway Bridge..........55
Comic Fantasy (AUS)86
Commin' Up...............54
Committal (IRE)......104
Commons Wheel (IRE)

Flahuil...............67 (33)
Flamands (IRE)........48
Flame Valley (USA)..64
Flame of Athens (IRE) .
.............................98
Flame of Hope......57
Flaming June (USA).61
Flash In The Pan (IRE)
.............................50
Flighty.....................63
Flint And Steel.........63
Flocheck (USA) 78
Flood's Fancy ...60 (58)
Florentino (IRE)........38
Florrie'm 44
Flower Miller............51
Fly Fishing (USA).....73
Fly Tip (IRE)..............84
Flyfisher (IRE) 84
Flying Flowers.........74
Flying Green (FR).....76
Flying Harold...........67
Flying North (IRE) 79
Flying Pennant (IRE)60
Flying Squaw...........96
Fog City 73 (83)
Fond Embrace..........76
Force of Will (USA) ..99
Foreign Judgement
..................(USA)77
Foreman 66 (48)
Forentia....................92
Forest Boy.......46 (68)
Forest Buck (USA)....94
Forest Fantasy 57
Forest Robin...........79
Forever Noble (IRE) .54
Forgie (IRE) 42
Forliando.................50
Formidable Partner..78
Fort de France (USA)45
Fortuitious (IRE)........52
Forzara.....................36
Four Weddings (USA)
..................49 (44)
Fourdaned (IRE).......82
Fran Godfrey.....65 (60)
Frances Mary 67 (67)
Freedom Flame 78
Freeloader 35
Frezeliere 85

Friday Night (USA)...30
Friendly Forester (USA)
.............................84
Fro 47
Frog 54 (31)
Funky......................67
Fursan (USA)............57
Further Future (IRE).17
Future's Trader 50
Fyors Gift (IRE) 68
Gagajulu 75 (66)
Galaka....................61
Galapino 78
Gallante...................56
Galway Blade 72
Gee Gee Tee 48
Gelsemine................68
Gemolly (IRE) 21
General Equation29 (29)
General Glow............51
General Macarthur ...76
General Rose...........75
Genereux 22
Generosa 69
Generous Present.....45
Gentilhomme...........102
Gentle Friend............57
Germano 90
Get Tough.................64
Ghostly Apparition ..52
..............................(38)
Gi La High 66 (62)
Giddy.......................58
Gildoran Sound........32
Gilling Dancer (IRE).57
Ginger Glint.......61 (15)
Ginger Hodgers........44
Give Me A Ring (IRE)63
Gladys Althorpe (IRE)..
..............................71
Glen Parker (IRE) 72
Glenrazie (IRE) 80
Globe Runner 63
Glorious Sound........13
Glowing Reeds.........19
Go Like West 13
Go Too Moor (IRE)....53
Go With The Wind....63
Go-Go-Power-Ranger43
Gold Disc (USA)........81
Gold Kicker 60 (14)

Golden Attraction (USA)
.............................106
Golden Pond (IRE)...72
Golden Silver...........50
Golden Tyke (IRE)....33
Golden Wedding20 (36)
Goldrill 42
Goldsearch (IRE)64 (47)
Golina (IRE) 32
Good To Talk...........58
Goodwood Rocket...71
Goretski (IRE)...........66
Gothenberg (IRE)....92
Gotla Bird 51
Governors Dream 25
..............................(20)
Gracious Gretclo......67
..............................(53)
Great Intent.............46
Greek Icon 84
Green Barries...........94
Green Bentley (IRE).75
Green Bopper (USA)68
Green Charter...........79
Green Gem (BEL).......51
..............................(71)
Gresham Flyer.........12
Grey Galava.............57
Grey Legend............71
Grimstone Girl ..45 (27)
Gryada 89
Gulf of Siam............69
Gumair (USA) 71
Gun Ballad (IRE) 47
Gunner B Special.....16
..............................(46)
Gwespyr...................78
Gymcrak Gem (IRE).62
Gympie....................58
Hadadabble 42
Hal Hoo Yaroom.....68
Hal's Pal.................80
Halebid....................72
Half An Inch (IRE) ...73
Hallikeld 51
Hamlet (IRE) 73
Hammerstein 89
Hanbitooh (USA)......53
Hank-a-chief............53
Hannahs Bay.....34 (48)
Happy Boy 99

Seattle Alley (USA) ..64
Seattle Special (USA)88
Second Time Lucky
(IRE) 78
Secret Pleasure (IRE)72
Secret Voucher 65
Sedbergh (USA)63 (59)
Seeking Destiny
(IRE)..................37 (41)
Seeking Fortune (USA)
..................................71
Seirenes....................79
Select Few 89
Selenia (IRE)..............61
Semper (IRE) 76
Sepoy (IRE)................84
Serendipity (FR).......77
Serif (USA) 59 (57)
Serious Trust............60
Seven Crowns (USA)65
Shaamit (IRE) 88
Shady Girl (IRE) 67
Shady Link (IRE)........64
Shafir (IRE) 67
Shaha 56
Shake the Yoke 108
Shamand (USA)..........45
Shaniko (IRE) 95
Shanoora (IRE) .57 (60)
Sharaf (IRE)................84
Shareda (IRE) 31
Sharp 'n' Shady 60 (23)
Sharp Monty 69
Sharp Night 49
Sharp Pearl................69
Sharp Shuffle (IRE)..73
Sharp Stock................67
Shaw House 48 (52)
Shawanni 95
She's My Love............76
She's Simply Great
(IRE) 54
Sheath Kefaah..........63
Sheemore (IRE) 39
Sheilana (IRE)............68
Sheilas Dream 39
Shemozzle (IRE)........73
Shepherds Dean (IRE).
..........................12 (28)
Sheraka (IRE) 98
Shermood..........51 (39)

Shernadeed (FR)......66
Shining Cloud 81
Shining Molly (FR) ...96
Ship's Dancer..........75
Shirlaty....................44
Shirley Sue........53 (49)
Shock-A-Lot (IRE)....66
Shontaine 78
Shooting Light (IRE)30
Shu Gaa (IRE)............72
Sibbertoft (IRE)........76
Siberian Henry 43
Siberian Mystic 57
Siege Perilous (IRE).49
Sign From Heaven ...50
Signs R Us (IRE) 26
Sihafi (USA) 74
Sikosarki (USA)........23
Sil Sila (IRE)............101
Silent Guest (IRE)....61
Silent Soprano 54
Silhouette (IRE)........41
Silk Masque (USA)....83
Silver Border 78
Silver Dome (USA)....96
Silver Harrow............78
Silver Prey (USA) 80
Silver Welcome 66
Silver Wing (USA) ...72
Silverdale Knight 84
Simply Miss Chief (IRE)
..........................55 (40)
Simply Silly (IRE)......59
Sing And Dance 37
Singing Patriarch (IRE)
..................................82
Singoalla (IRE) 69
Sinking Sun 65
Sis Garden 54 (62)
Sistar Act 59
Sister Kit (IRE)..........72
Six Clerks (IRE).63 (61)
Sizzling Serenade 29
..............................(31)
Sizzling Symphony ..72
Skelton Countess (IRE)
..........................56 (4)
Sketchbook 96
Ski Academy (IRE)....89
Ski For Gold 65
Skillington (USA) 80

Skram........................58
Sky Dome (IRE)........74
Sleepy Boy 11
Sly's Fancy 25
Smarter Charter 51
Smile Forever (USA) 75
Smilin N Wishin (USA)
..................................79
Smiling Bess 24
Smithereens 72
Snitch 54 (39)
Snow Falcon..............75
Snowpoles................62
So Select..................31
Society Girl..............78
Society Magic (USA) 53
Society Sue (IRE)......44
Solar Crystal (IRE) .101
Soldier Mak..............64
Solo Symphony (IRE)53
Solva Mist........54 (9)
Some Horse (IRE) 99
..............................(21)
Somer Solo 62
Son of Anshan 40
Sondos......................68
Song Song Blue (IRE)26
Songsheet 79
Sonic Mail 78
Sonya Marie..............45
Sooki Sooki (IRE)......92
Sorbie Tower (IRE)...72
Soul Risk 34
Soul of Honour (FR).64
Sound Check............66
South Pagoda (IRE) .70
South Salem (USA) 104
Sovereign's Crown
(USA)........................99
Soviet King (IRE)......65
Soviet Sakti (IRE).....47
Soviet Style (AUS) ...95
Sovitaka (IRE) ...54 (47)
Spa Lane..................44
Spanish Luck 49 (44)
Spanking Roger 59
Spartan Heartbeat....50
Sphinx Levelv (IRE) .52
..............................(55)
Spillo 84
Spinning Mouse48 (46)

Spiral Flyer (IRE)......49
Spirito Libro (USA) ..65
Splicing.....................73
Splinter (IRE) 80
Sporting Fantasy61 (22)
Spotted Eagle...........61
Spring Campaign (IRE)
............................68
Spring Silhouette 34
Squandamania 52
St Adele (USA) 55
St Mawes (FR) 75
Staffin.......................90
Stand Your Ground..45
Standown...................73
Star And Garter 77
Star Finch (FR)..........60
Star of Ring (IRE) 71
Starfida 45
Starmaniac (USA) 96
State Approval ..69 (64)
State Theatre (IRE)...80
State Visitor..............42
State of Caution 71
Stately.............56 (31)
Stately Dancer..........69
Static Love 19 (7)
Statoyork 62
Steal 'Em..................70
Stealth Attack (IRE) .65
Steinway (SWE)........71
Stellar Line (USA) 72
Step On Degas 68
Stereo Dancer 26
Sterling Fellow 45
Sticks Mckenzie 63
Stoleamarch 42
Stolen Music (IRE) ...47
Stoney End (USA) 52
Stoop To Conquer ...63
Stop Play (IRE).........76
Storm Trooper (USA)100
Storm Wind (IRE) 28
Story Line 97
Stotfold Boy (IRE) 17
Straight Thinking (USA)
.....................62 (57)
Strategic Ploy...........53
Streete Dancer (IRE) 73
Stronz (IRE) 71
Stunning Prospect

(USA)........................49
Sualtach (IRE) 87
Subfusk 61 (61)
Subterfuge................78
Subtle One (IRE) 59
Suitor 62
Sunday Maelstrom
..........................(IRE)38
Sunley Secure 76
Sunrise Special (IRE)50
............................(50)
Sunset Harbour (IRE)62
Sunset Reigns (IRE) 90
Supamova (USA)......86
Suparoy 61 (59)
Super Baron 23
Superfrills..........46 (10)
Supergal 29
Superior Force 58
Supermister..............53
Supreme Power 75 (62)
Surtees......................73
Sweet Amoret...........44
Sweet Nature (IRE)...68
............................(74)
Sweet Robin (IRE)....96
Sweet Times 64
Sweetness Herself ...68
Swift Fandango (USA).
..............................82
Swift Maiden.............75
Swifty Nifty (IRE).......41
Swing Mania (IRE)....59
............................(47)
Swingalong Girl 20
Swish 43
Swiss Valley Lady....65
............................(55)
Swynford Dream 84
Sylva Paradise (IRE)77
Sylvan Princess 20
Sylvella.....................59
Szloto 56
Ta Rib (USA).............95
Tablets of Stone (IRE)
..............................43
Tabriz 73
Tadeo 99
Tagula (IRE)............112
Tahya (USA) 62 (60)
Takapuna (IRE) .67 (52)

Take A Left 99
Take Note (IRE).52 (58)
Tallulah Belle 46 (59)
Tamhid (USA)............95
Tamnia 99
Tapintime (USA)........69
Tarf (USA) 95
Tarneem (USA).........83
Tarry 65
Tart......................60 (66)
Tartan Express (IRE)30
............................(20)
Tarte Aux Pommes (FR)
..............................91
Tasdik 75
Tashjir (USA) 55
Tasliya (USA)............71
Taufan Boy........80 (80)
Taurean Fire 52
Tawaaded (IRE)........57
Tawafek (USA)..........69
Tawkil (USA)..............92
Temptress.................36
Terdad (USA)............83
Termon......................63
Texas Tramp.............17
Thai Morning 70
The Barnsley Belle (IRE)
..........................51 (58)
The Black Dubh (IRE)58
The Boozing Brief (USA)
..............................74
The Butterwick Kid ..69
The Clan....................40
The Dilettanti (USA).39
The Frisky Farmer....73
............................(40)
The Frog Princess ...39
The Fullbangladesh .46
............................(59)
The Imps (IRE) ..58 (54)
The Jolly Barmaid (IRE)
..............................30
The Kastarbids (IRE)62
............................(25)
The Legions Pride....65
The Man 86
The Swan 71
The Wad....................56
Thea (USA) 72
Theatre Magic...........60

RACEFORM TOP RATED
TWO-YEAR-OLDS OF 1995

Alhaarth (IRE)	121
Bosra Sham (USA)	118
Danehill Dancer (IRE)	115
Royal Applause	115
Blue Duster (USA)	113
Tagula (IRE)	112
Bint Shadayid (USA)	111
My Flag (USA)	110
Loup Solitaire (USA)	110
Manninamix	110
Cara Rafaela (USA)	109
Kahir Almaydan (IRE)	109
Eternity Range (USA)	108
Le Triton (USA)	108
Shake the Yoke	108
Titus Livius (FR)	108
Lord of Men	108
Mubhij (IRE)	108
Beauchamp King	107
Kuantan (USA)	107
Westcourt Magic	107
Golden Attraction (USA)	106
My Branch	106
Mons	106
Dovebrace	106
Miss Tahiti (IRE)	105
Dance Sequence (USA)	105
Russian Revival (USA)	105
Astor Place (IRE)	104
Matiya (IRE)	104
Almaty (IRE)	104
Committal (IRE)	104
Mazeed (IRE)	104
Even Top (IRE)	104
South Salem (USA)	104
Woodborough (USA)	104
Kalmoss (FR)	103
Dark Nile (USA)	103
Cliptomania (USA)	103
With Fascination (USA)	103
Thracian	103
Marl	103
Gentilhomme	102
Kunucu (IRE)	102
Ahkaam (USA)	101
Sil Sila (IRE)	101
Raisonnable	101
Priory Belle (IRE)	101
Double Leaf	101
Barricade (USA)	101

TURF STATISTICS

LEADING FLAT TRAINERS, 1995

	Races Won	Stakes £	£1 level profit	Last Year
1. J. L. Dunlop	126	2,019,765	-102.92	2
2. S bin Suroor	14	1,879,194	+ 30.91	-
3. M. R. Stoute	73	1,362,759	- 78.05	1
4. R. Hannon	110	1,219,356	-291.12	5
5. J. H. M. Gosden	82	1,105,662	- 66.05	4
6. M. Johnston	97	1,081,559	-128.92	6
7. B. W. Hills	74	994,325	- 94.27	11
8. H. R. A. Cecil	83	975,835	- 44.58	3
9. P. F. I. Cole	75	882,955	- 57.43	7
10. C. E. Brittain	39	748,231	- 52.77	35
11. P. W. Chapple-Hyam	37	640,512	- 95.70	27
12. G. Wragg	30	640,338	+ 51.49	10
13. D. R. Loder	44	590,944	+ 5.31	17
14. L. M. Cumani	39	576,387	- 91.37	8
15. M. R. Channon	68	535,648	-143.48	16
16. Major W. R. Hern	21	525,158	- 33.50	34
17. R. Akehurst	49	523,566	-114.08	14
18. R. Charlton	40	513,220	- 53.30	22
19. I. A. Balding	41	478,567	-128.09	12
20. J. Berry	65	453,669	-346.58	9
21. G. Lewis	37	437,758	- 64.20	24
22. Mrs M. Reveley	60	420,969	-224.12	23
23. Mrs J. R. Ramsden	50	403,807	- 90.34	26
24. Lady Herries	26	367,294	- 18.01	20
25. J. R. Fanshawe	29	360,743	- 27.85	43
26. B. J. Meehan	42	348,453	- 85.50	-
27. B. Hanbury	35	334,490	- 31.02	40
28. M. Bell	38	307,295	-140.33	18
29. A. Fabre,France	3	293,446	+ 7.60	15
30. M. A. Jarvis	16	292,527	+ 3.08	-
31. H. ThomsonJones	36	280,238	- 8.19	25
32. D. Morley	21	278,463	- 17.80	28
33. A. C. Stewart	27	258,877	+ 37.64	36
34. R. W. Armstrong	31	253,934	+ 12.42	13
35. R. Hollinshead	40	237,342	-214.15	-
36. S. Dow	26	228,486	- 72.42	-
37. M. H. Tompkins	22	221,004	- 46.02	39

38. P. T. Walwyn	26	214,544 - 62.85	46
39. Sir Mark Prescott	36	208,060 - 82.88	19
40. B. A. McMahon	18	204,252 - 39.38	49
41. J. Oxx, Ireland	1	204,222 - 0.50	-
42. T. D. Barron	22	194,649 - 2.31	37
43. G. Harwood	9	192,801 - 51.42	32
44. P. J. Makin	24	183,937 - 11.14	-
45. E. A. L. Dunlop	17	183,700 - 86.94	-
46. G. L. Moore	27	182,656 - 40.68	-
47. P. W. Harris	24	178,707 - 41.41	48
48. M. J. Fetherston-Godley	9	177,145 - 14.75	-
49. Lord Huntingdon	15	173,140 - 15.63	30
50. P. C. Haslam	21	162,275 - 24.62	-

LEADING FLAT OWNERS, 1995

	Races Won	Stakes £	Last Year
1. Hamdan Al Maktoum	171	2,616,849	1
2. Sheikh Mohammed	113	1,828,102	2
3. Godolphin	14	966,139	15
4. Saeed Maktoum Al Maktoum	2	783,260	19
5. Maktoum Al Maktoum	42	706,478	3
6. Mr K. Abdullah	39	592,397	4
7. Mollers Racing	9	436,242	-
8. Prince Fahd Salman	33	432,411	11
9. Lord Weinstock & The Hon Simon Weinstock	18	416,338	20
10. Cheveley Park Stud	28	413,408	5
11. Mr George Strawbridge	12	319,621	38
12. Mr P. D. Savill	38	318,433	6
13. Mr R. E. Sangster	28	309,220	7
14. Mr Wafic Said	14	298,568	-
15. Sheikh Ahmed Al Maktoum	30	280,123	14
16. Mr E. Penser	8	256,255	-
17. Mr R. W. Huggins	8	256,221	-
18. Mrs Anne Coughlan	1	204,222	-
19. Mr J. D. Abell	21	193,470	41
20. Maktoum Al Maktoum/Godolphin	1	189,673	-
21. The Queen	16	188,083	44
22. Highclere Thoroughbred Racing Ltd	8	172,110	21
23. Hesmonds Stud	22	169,659	50
24. Mr M. A. Jarvis	4	160,761	-

25. Mr Saeed Manana 7	159,522	-
26. Mr Martin Myers 10	149,560	-
27. Mr R. Barnett 3	137,345	-
28. Mr Mana Al Maktoum.................................9	135,720	-
29. Mr J. C. Smith.......................................12	133,167	8
30. Lord Carnarvon 10	132,139	36
31. Windflower Overseas Holdings Inc 11	117,047	-
32. Mr Mohamed Obaida 1	113,807	-
33. Lady Rothschild.....................................8	111,230	-
34. Mr R. M. Cyzer.....................................5	106,841	-
35. Mr K. Higson 14	105,654	45
36. Mr M. Arbib...4	105,566	-
37. Mr I. A. N. Wight 3	102,435	-
38. Elite Racing Club 12	101,000	-
39. Prince A. A. Faisal 11	100,421	-
40. Lucayan Stud 10	97,646	-
41. Bloomsbury Stud....................................5	97,234	-
42. Mrs E. H. Vestey....................................3	96,798	-
43. Sir Philip Oppenheimer (deceased) 11	96,748	35
44. Mr A. S. Reid 19	94,965	-
45. Mr Robert Hughes 4	93,867	-
46. John White and Partners 1	93,295	-
47. Mr Roy Taiano 1	87,326	-
48. Mr S. S. Niarchos 3	86,105	-

LEADING FLAT JOCKEYS, 1995

	Win £	1st	2nd	3rd	Unpl	Total Mts	Per cent		£1 Level stake
1. L. Dettori	1,977,574	211	164	135	475	985	21.4	-	128.60
2. K. Darley	776,673	148	125	123	516	912	16.2	-	161.66
3. J. Weaver	907,107	144	135	127	552	958	15.0	-	195.32
4. W. Carson	1,708,290	139	91	93	391	714	19.5	-	157.96
5. Pat Eddery	1,188,213	125	79	74	369	647	19.3	-	96.83
6. T. Quinn	657,729	111	97	107	519	834	13.3	-	200.78
7. J. Reid	1,159,222	101	96	84	412	693	14.6	-	130.76
8. R. Cochrane	488,833	98	95	101	493	787	12.5	-	158.55
9. K. Fallon	395,841	91	100	87	357	635	14.3	-	17.82
10. W. Ryan	422,717	87	89	69	318	563	15.5	-	150.87
11. J. Carroll	354,364	76	77	64	394	611	12.4	-	173.44
12. M. Hills	679,071	74	56	62	326	518	14.3	+	56.19
13. D. Holland	488,312	71	81	59	251	462	15.4	+	10.19
14. R. Hills	494,429	70	61	57	289	477	14.7	-	134.78
15. M. Roberts	467,195	64	47	50	277	438	14.6	+	2.22
16. R. Hughes	494,433	64	72	55	309	500	12.8	-	61.14

17. G. Carter	285,117	63	75	76	425	639	9.9	-	287.32
18. B. Doyle	481,186	62	57	62	366	547	11.3	-	63.44
19. D. Harrison	343,737	62	73	77	423	635	9.8	-	220.82
20. W. R. Swinburn	1,617,799	60	68	53	239	420	14.3	-	112.83
21. G. Duffield	242,998	58	57	57	427	599	9.7	-	252.29
22. Paul Eddery	356,878	56	63	69	397	585	9.6	-	238.21
23. S. Sanders	267,012	54	56	56	362	528	10.2	-	57.63
24. T. Ives	219,567	53	57	50	319	479	11.1	-	194.31
25. M. Fenton	191,265	51	54	44	380	529	9.6	-	201.20
26. J. Quinn	225,341	48	72	68	525	713	6.7	-	274.89
27. J. Fortune	184,379	46	55	65	283	449	10.2	-	170.68
28. P. Robinson	253,542	41	55	49	262	407	10.1	-	66.62
29. W. Woods	136,188	41	37	48	253	379	10.8	-	140.98
30. J. Stack	172,893	41	44	31	316	432	9.5	-	194.37
31. T. Williams	138,794	38	51	44	390	523	7.3	-	259.77
32. T. Sprake	143,795	37	24	19	213	293	12.6	+	**95.60**
33. S. Whitworth	144,819	37	32	35	276	380	9.7	-	106.08
34. L. Charnock	184,884	36	37	32	340	445	8.1	-	200.72
35. M. Rimmer	138,501	36	32	23	217	308	11.7	-	69.43
36. D. R. McCabe	173,806	35	31	35	199	300	11.7	-	14.93
37. G. Hind	151,837	34	38	24	239	335	10.2	-	158.58
38. A. Mackay	125,176	34	37	48	376	495	6.9	-	263.91
39. J. Tate	170,164	33	27	37	235	332	9.9	-	118.81
40. Dane O'Neill	196,387	33	42	38	232	345	9.6	-	48.75
41. D. McKeown	112,183	31	28	47	384	490	6.3	-	256.67
42. M. Henry	148,388	30	34	35	196	295	10.2	-	39.47
43. M. J. Kinane	455,969	28	33	25	98	184	15.2	-	46.53
44. A. McGlone	115,120	28	27	20	245	320	8.8	-	166.17
45. B. Thomson	159,529	28	28	32	205	293	9.6	-	78.11
46. G. Bardwell	105,859	28	20	26	345	419	6.7	-	173.50
47. N. Varley	86,515	26	32	43	301	402	6.5	-	160.05
48. C. Rutter	91,309	26	13	24	208	271	9.6	-	84.31
49. P. McCabe	96,490	25	21	23	154	223	11.2	+	**30.58**
50. S. Drowne	106,373	25	26	33	303	387	6.5	-	112.50

Owners names are shown against their horses where this information is available. In the case of Partnerships and Syndicates, the nominated owner is given alongside the horse with other owners listed below the team.

NATIONAL HUNT STATISTICS

WINNING TRAINERS 1994-95

	Races Won	Stakes £	%	Last Year
1. NICHOLSON, D.	96	896,683	25	2
2. PIPE, M. C.	137	846,077	23	1
3. BAILEY, K. C.	72	704,480	23	4
4. TWISTON-DAVIES, N. A.	81	525,999	16	3
5. REVELEY, Mrs M.	100	475,435	27	5
6. SHERWOOD, O.	48	447,985	22	9
7. HOBBS, P. J.	86	433,247	23	7
8. PITMAN, Mrs J.	36	429,319	16	-
9. GIFFORD, J. T.	47	413,264	17	6
10. HENDERSON, N. J.	45	341,801	21	8
11. FORSTER, Capt. T. A.	32	279,360	18	20
12. RICHARDS, G.	43	275,418	15	10
13. KNIGHT, Miss H. C.	44	221,299	20	-
14. HAMMOND, M.	42	211,843	15	19
15. WHITE, J.	52	208,320	16	15
16. JOHNSON, J. H.	32	203,972	13	12
17. ELSWORTH, D. R. C.	13	203,272	14	22
18. BROOKS, C. P. E.	31	199,667	19	-
19. BALDING, G. B.	41	199,568	14	-
20. FITZGERALD, J. G.	37	184,519	20	16

WINNING OWNERS 1994/95

	Wins	Total £	Last Year
1. ROACH FOODS LTD	8	211,601	4
2. MATTHEWS, P. A.	4	180,695	-
3. JOHNSON, G. & L.	1	123,066	-
4. PICK, E.	2	119,315	-
5. PELL-MELL PARTNERS	14	106,373	1
6. KILPATRICK, B. A.	6	101,702	-
7. ST QUINTON, M. G.	5	100,886	-

8. STEWART-BROWN, B. T.	5	93,826	13
9. HARTIGAN, P. J.	5	93,323	-
10. DORE, W. H.	13	91,130	-
11. LLOYD WEBBER, LADY	7	88,675	-
12. HUBBARD, G. A.	10	84,019	-
13. MARTIN PIPE RACING CLUB	21	80,207	-
14. JOSEPH, JACK	21	78,912	-
15. SUMNER, J. B.	3	77,118	-

WINNING JOCKEYS 1994/95

	1st	2nd	3rd	%	Last Year
1. DUNWOODY, R.	160	117	102	21	1
2. MAGUIRE, A.	130	111	106	19	2
3. WILLIAMSON, N.	130	113	93	18	4
4. OSBORNE, J.	111	80	66	22	3
5. NIVEN, P.	106	74	50	27	5
6. BRIDGWATER, D.	78	53	48	17	9
7. McCOY, A. P.	74	63	56	16	-
8. FITZGERALD, M. A.	68	89	91	12	6
9. MARSTON, W.	66	36	46	17	17
10. DWYER, M.	65	77	40	16	12
11. DOBBIN, A.	57	40	43	16	-
12. HOBBS, PETER	53	60	26	15	13
13. McCOURT, G.	47	40	32	16	7
14. LLEWELLYN, C.	45	43	31	16	14
15. GALLAGHER, D.	42	36	27	12	-
16. BRADLEY, G.	41	33	27	15	15
17. McNEILL, S.	40	37	34	12	-
18. GUEST, RICHARD	36	34	28	11	-
19. HIDE, P.	34	36	24	16	-
20. WYER, L.	32	42	29	12	10

LEADING TRAINERS ON THE FLAT: 1896 - 1995

1896	A Hayhoe	1930	H S Persse	1963	P Prendergast
1897	R Marsh	1931	J Lawson	1964	P Prendergast
1898	R Marsh	1932	Frank Butters	1965	P Prendergast
1899	J Porter	1933	F Darling	1966	M V O'Brien
1900	R Marsh	1934	Frank Butters	1967	C F N Murless
1901	J Huggins	1935	Frank Butters	1968	C F N Murless
1902	R S Sievier	1936	J Lawson	1969	A M Budgett
1903	G Blackwell	1937	C Boyd-Rochfort	1970	C F N Murless
1904	P P Gilpin	1938	C Boyd-Rochfort	1971	I Balding
1905	W T Robinson	1939	J L Jarvis	1972	W Hern
1906	Hon G Lambton	1940	F Darling	1973	C F N Murless
1907	A Taylor	1941	F Darling	1974	P Walwyn
1908	C Morton	1942	F Darling	1975	P Walwyn
1909	A Taylor	1943	W Nightingall	1976	H Cecil
1910	A Taylor	1944	Frank Butters	1977	M V O'Brien
1911	Hon G Lambton	1945	W Earl	1978	H Cecil
1912	Hon G Lambton	1946	Frank Butters	1979	H Cecil
1913	R Wootton	1947	F Darling	1980	W Hern
1914	A Taylor	1948	C F N Murless	1981	M Stoute
1915	P P Gilpin	1949	Frank Butters	1982	H Cecil
1916	R C Dawson	1950	C H Semblat	1983	W Hern
1917	A Taylor	1951	J L Jarvis	1984	H Cecil
1918	A Taylor	1952	M Marsh	1985	H Cecil
1919	A Taylor	1953	J L Jarvis	1986	M Stoute
1920	A Taylor	1954	C Boyd-Rochfort	1987	H Cecil
1921	A Taylor	1955	C Boyd-Rochfort	1988	H Cecil
1922	A Taylor	1956	C F Elsey	1989	M Stoute
1923	A Taylor	1957	C F N Murless	1990	H Cecil
1924	R C Dawson	1958	C Boyd-Rochfort	1991	P Cole
1925	A Taylor	1959	C F N Murless	1992	R Hannon
1926	F Darling	1960	C F N Murless	1993	H Cecil
1927	Frank Butters	1961	C F N Murless	1994	M Stoute
1928	Frank Butters	1962	W Hern	1995	J Dunlop
1929	R C Dawson				

CHAMPION JOCKEYS: 1894 - 1995

1894	M Cannon	167	1904	O Madden	161	1914	S Donoghue	129
1895	M Cannon	184	1905	E Wheatley	124	1915	S Donoghue	62
1896	M Cannon	164	1906	W Higgs	149	1916	S Donoghue	43
1897	M Cannon	145	1907	W Higgs	146	1917	S Donoghue	42
1898	O Madden	161	1908	D Maher	139	1918	S Donoghue	66
1899	S Loates	160	1909	F Wootton	165	1919	S Donoghue	129
1900	L Reiff	143	1910	F Wootton	137	1920	S Donoghue	143
1901	O Madden	130	1911	F Wootton	187	1921	S Donoghue	141
1902	W Lane	170	1912	F Wootton	118	1922	S Donoghue	102
1903	O Madden	154	1913	D Maher	115	1923	S Donoghue	89
							C Elliott	89

Year	Jockey	Wins	Year	Jockey	Wins	Year	Jockey	Wins
1924	C Elliott	106	1948	G Richards	224	1972	W Carson	132
1925	G Richards	118	1949	G Richards	261	1973	W Carson	164
1926	T Weston	95	1950	G Richards	201	1974	Pat Eddery	148
1927	G Richards	164	1951	G Richards	227	1975	Pat Eddery	164
1928	G Richards	148	1952	G Richards	231	1976	Pat Eddery	162
1929	G Richards	135	1953	G Richards	191	1977	Pat Eddery	176
1930	F Fox	129	1954	D Smith	129	1978	W Carson	182
1931	G Richards	145	1955	D Smith	168	1979	J Mercer	164
1932	G Richards	190	1956	D Smith	155	1980	W Carson	166
1933	G Richards	259	1957	A Breasley	173	1981	L Piggott	179
1934	G Richards	212	1958	D Smith	165	1982	L Piggott	188
1935	G Richards	217	1959	D Smith	157	1983	W Carson	159
1936	G Richards	174	1960	L Piggott	170	1984	S Cauthen	130
1937	G Richards	216	1961	A Breasley	171	1985	S Cauthen	195
1938	G Richards	206	1962	A Breasley	179	1986	Pat Eddery	176
1939	G Richards	155	1963	A Breasley	176	1987	S Cauthen	197
1940	G Richards	68	1964	L Piggott	140	1988	Pat Eddery	183
1941	H Wragg	71	1965	L Piggott	160	1989	Pat Eddery	171
1942	G Richards	67	1966	L Piggott	191	1990	Pat Eddery	209
1943	G Richards	65	1967	L Piggott	117	1991	Pat Eddery	165
1944	G Richards	88	1968	L Piggott	139	1992	M Roberts	206
1945	G Richards	104	1969	L Piggott	163	1993	Pat Eddery	169
1946	G Richards	212	1970	L Piggott	162	1994	L Dettori	233
1947	G Richards	269	1971	L Piggott	162	1995	L Dettori	211

LEADING OWNERS: 1894 - 1995

Year	Owner	Year	Owner	Year	Owner
1894	Mr H. McCalmont	1916	Mr E Hulton	1939	Ld Rosebery
1895	Ld de Rothschild	1917	Mr "Fairie"	1940	Lord Rothermere
1896	Ld de Rothschild	1918	Lady James Douglas	1941	Ld Glanely
1987	Mr J Gubbins	1919	Ld Glanely	1942	His Majesty
1898	Ld de Rothschild	1920	Sir Robert Jardine	1943	Miss D Paget
1899	Duke of Westminster	1921	Mr S B Joel	1944	H.H. Aga Khan
1900	H.R.H. The Prince of Wales	1922	Ld Woolavington	1945	Ld Derby
1901	Sir G Blundell Maple	1923	Ld Derby	1946	H.H. Aga Khan
1902	Mr R S Sievier	1924	H.H. Aga Khan	1947	H.H. Aga Khan
1903	Sir James Miller	1925	Ld Astor	1948	H.H. Aga Khan
1904	Sir James Miller	1926	Ld Woolavington	1949	H.H. Aga Khan
1905	Col W Hall Walker	1927	Ld Derby	1950	M M Boussac
1906	Ld Derby (late)	1928	Ld Derby	1951	M M Boussac
1907	Col W Hall Walker	1929	H.H. Aga Khan	1952	H. H. Aga Khan
1908	Mr J B Joel	1930	H.H. Aga Khan	1953	Sir Victor Sassoon
1909	Mr "Fairie"	1931	Mr J A Dewar	1954	Her Majesty
1910	Mr "Fairie"	1932	H.H. Aga Khan	1955	Lady Zia Wernher
1911	Ld Derby	1933	Ld Derby	1956	Maj L B Holliday
1912	Mr T Pilkington	1934	H.H. Aga Khan	1957	Her Majesty
1913	Mr J B Joel	1935	H.H. Aga Khan	1958	Mr J McShain
1914	Mr J B Joel	1936	Ld Astor	1959	Prince Aly Khan
1915	Mr L Neumann	1937	H.H. Aga Khan	1960	Sir Victor Sassoon
		1938	Ld Derby	1961	Maj L B Holliday

1962	Maj L B Holliday	1973	Mr N B Hunt	1984	Mr R Sangster
1963	Mr J R Mullion	1974	Mr N B Hunt	1985	Sheikh Mohammed
1964	Mrs H E Jackson	1975	Dr C Vittadini	1986	Sheikh Mohammed
1965	M J Ternynck	1976	Mr D Wildenstein	1987	Sheikh Mohammed
1966	Lady Zia Wernher	1977	Mr R Sangster	1988	Sheikh Mohammed
1967	Mr H J Joel	1978	Mr R Sangster	1989	Sheikh Mohammed
1968	Mr Raymond R Guest	1979	Sir M Sobell	1990	Mr Hamdan Al-Maktoum
1969	Mr D Robinson	1980	S Weinstock	1991	Sheikh Mohammed
1970	Mr C Engelhard	1981	H.H. Aga Khan	1992	Sheikh Mohammed
1971	Mr P Mellon	1982	Mr R Sangster	1993	Sheikh Mohammed
1972	Mrs J Hislop	1983	Mr R Sangster	1994	Mr Hamdan Al-Maktoum
				1995	Mr Hamdan Al-Maktoum

LEADING SIRES: 1894 - 1995

1894	St Simon	1928	Phalaris	1962	Never Say Die
1895	St Simon	1929	Tetratema	1963	Ribot
1896	St Simon	1930	Son-in-Law	1964	Chamossaire
1897	Kendal	1931	Pharos	1965	Court Harwell
1898	Galopin	1932	Gainsborough	1966	Charlottesville
1899	Orme	1933	Gainsborough	1967	Ribot
1900	St Simon	1934	Blandford	1968	Ribot
1901	St Simon	1935	Blandford	1969	Crepello
1902	Persimmon	1936	Fairway	1970	Northern Dancer
1903	St Frusquin	1937	Solario	1971	Never Bend
1904	Gallinule	1938	Blandford	1972	Queen's Hussar
1905	Gallinule	1939	Fairway	1973	Vaguely Noble
1906	Persimmon	1940	Hyperion	1974	Vaguely Noble
1907	St Frusquin	1941	Hyperion	1975	Great Nephew
1908	Persimmon	1942	Hyperion	1976	Wolver Hollow
1909	Cyllene	1943	Fairway	1977	Northern Dancer
1910	Cyllene	1944	Fairway	1978	Mill Reef (USA)
1911	Sundridge	1945	Hyperion	1979	Petingo
1912	Persimmon	1946	Hyperion	1980	Pitcairn
1913	Desmond	1947	Nearco	1981	Great Nephew
1914	Polymelus	1948	Big Game	1982	Be My Guest (USA)
1915	Polymelus	1949	Nearco	1983	Northern Dancer
1916	Polymelus	1950	Fair Trial	1984	Northern Dancer
1917	Bayardo	1951	Nasrullah	1985	Kris
1918	Bayardo	1952	Tehran	1986	Nijinsky (CAN)
1919	The Tetrarch	1953	Chanteur II	1987	Mill Reef (USA)
1920	Polymelus	1954	Hyperion	1988	Caerleon (USA)
1921	Polymelus	1955	Alycidon	1989	Blushing Groom (FR)
1922	Lemberg	1956	Court Martial	1990	Sadler's Wells (USA)
1923	Swynford	1957	Court Martial	1991	Caerleon (USA)
1924	Son-in-Law	1958	Mossborough	1992	Sadler's Wells (USA)
1925	Phalaris	1959	Petition	1993	Sadler's Wells (USA)
1926	Hurry On	1960	Aureole	1994	Sadler's Wells (USA)
1927	Buchan	1961	Aureole	1995	Sadler's Wells (USA)

LEADING BREEDERS: 1909 - 1995

1909 Mr "Fairie"	1940 Mr H E Morriss	1968 Mill Ridge Farm
1910 Mr "Fairie"	1941 Ld Glanely	1969 Lord Rosebery
1911 Ld Derby (late)	1942 National Stud	1970 Mr E P Taylor
1912 Col. W Hall Walker	1943 Miss D Paget	1971 Mr P Mellon
1913 Mr J B Joel	1944 Ld Rosebery	1972 Mr J Hislop
1914 Mr J B Joel	1945 Ld Derby	1973 Claiborne Farm
1915 Mr L Neumann	1946 Lt- Col H Boyd-	1974 Mr N B Hunt
1916 Mr E Hulton	Rochfort	1975 Overbury Stud
1917 Mr "Fairie"	1947 H.H. Aga Khan	1976 Dayton Ltd
1918 Lady James Douglas	1948 H.H. Aga Khan	1977 Mr E P Taylor
1919 Ld Derby	1949 H.H. Aga Khan	1978 Cragwood Estates Inc
1920 Ld Derby	1950 M M Boussac	1979 Ballymacoll Stud
1921 Mr S B Joel	1951 M M Boussac	1980 P Clarke
1922 Ld Derby	1952 H. H. Aga Khan	1981 H.H. Aga Khan
1923 Ld Derby	1953 Mr F Darling	1982 Someries Stud
1924 Lady Sykes	1954 Maj L B Holliday	1983 White Lodge Stud
1925 Ld Astor	1955 Someries Stud	1984 Mr E P Taylor
1926 Ld Woolavington	1956 Maj L B Holliday	1985 Dalham Stud Farms
1927 Ld Derby	1957 Eve Stud	1986 H.H. Aga Khan
1928 Ld Derby	1958 Mr R Ball	1987 Cliveden Stud
1929 Ld Derby	1959 Prince Aly Khan and	1988 H. H. Aga Khan
1930 Ld Derby	the late H.H. Aga Khan	1989 Mr Hamdan Al-
1931 Ld Dewar	1960 Eve Stud Ltd	Maktoum
1932 H.H. Aga Khan	1961 Eve Stud Ltd	1990 Capt. Macdonald-
1933 Sir Alec Black	1962 Maj L B Holliday	Buchanan
1934 H.H. Aga Khan	1963 Mr H F Guggenheim	1991 Barronstown Stud
1935 H.H. Aga Khan	1964 Bull Run Stud	1992 Swettenham Stud
1936 Ld Astor	1965 Mr J Ternynck	1993 Juddmonte Farms
1937 H.H. Aga Khan	1966 Someries Stud	1994 Shadwell Farm &
1938 Ld Derby	1967 Mr H J Joel	Estate Ltd
1939 Ld Rosebery		1995 Shadwell Farm &
		Estate Ltd

Teams which have arrived too late for inclusion in Horses In Training 1996 will be published in the Raceform Update at the end of April.

LEADING SIRES OF 1995 IN GREAT BRITAIN AND IRELAND

STALLION	BREEDING	RNRS	WNRS	WINS	WIN MONEY	PLACES	PLACE MONEY	TOTAL
SADLER'S WELLS (1981)	...by Northern Dancer	89	40	55	491713	130	555711	1047424
INDIAN RIDGE (1985)	...by Ahonoora	51	21	47	472454	97	357247	829701
NIJINSKY (1967)	...by Northern Dancer	8	3	5	801087	2	2001	803088
SALSE (1985)	...by Topsider	59	25	36	576233	85	183430	759663
RAINBOW QUEST (1981)	...by Blushing Groom	59	27	38	575159	92	100513	675672
DANEHILL (1986)	...by Danzig	68	36	57	442205	129	176516	618721
CAERLEON (1980)	...by Nijinsky	61	25	39	387939	86	219649	607587
RIVERMAN (1969)	...by Never Bend	29	13	17	395083	45	202047	597130
WARNING (1985)	...by Known Fact	48	21	34	275150	80	321055	596205
POLISH PRECEDENT (1986)	...by Danzig	37	17	27	415633	48	170667	586300
CADEAUX GENEREUX (1985)	..by Young Generation	62	32	53	343090	121	234755	577845
GREEN DESERT (1983)	...by Danzig	83	31	58	375746	133	179670	555416
IN THE WINGS (1986)	...by Sadler's Wells	27	12	16	411140	25	125591	536730
BE MY GUEST (1974)	...by Northern Dancer	52	11	20	367794	73	162751	530545
MTOTO (1983)	...by Busted	49	19	33	306905	83	205713	512618
NIGHT SHIFT (1980)	...by Northern Dancer	58	26	40	285582	112	218731	504313
TAUFAN (1977)	...by Stop The Music	96	36	55	313978	161	171987	485965
DIESIS (1980)	...by Sharpen Up	40	14	17	391102	57	58091	449193
ELA-MANA-MOU (1976)	...by Pitcairn	41	14	23	363238	56	74057	437296
BLUEBIRD (1984)	...by Storm Bird	61	22	40	281878	123	139876	421755

LEADING BRITISH AND IRISH BASED SIRES OF 1995 (GREAT BRITAIN, IRELAND AND OVERSEAS)

STALLION	BREEDING	DOMESTIC WNRS	DOMESTIC WINS	WIN MONEY	OVERSEAS WNRS	OVERSEAS WINS	WIN MONEY	TOTAL
SADLER'S WELLS (1981)	......by Northern Dancer	40	55	491713	45	66	2483700	2975413
CAERLEON (1980)	......by Nijinsky	25	39	387939	47	69	1450429	1838368
RAINBOW QUEST (1981)	......by Blushing Groom	27	38	575159	32	49	1243266	1818425
LAST TYCOON (1983)	......by Try My Best	18	31	127110	44	79	1350223	1477334
DANEHILL (1986)	......by Danzig	36	57	442205	36	60	702038	1144243
ALZAO (1980)	......by Lyphard	32	39	193323	44	79	855878	1049201
INDIAN RIDGE (1985)	......by Ahonoora	21	47	472454	9	20	575608	1048062
BLUEBIRD (1984)	......by Storm Bird	22	40	281878	46	86	693759	975637
WAAJIB (1983)	......by Try My Best	10	16	249280	34	59	711668	960947
BE MY GUEST (1974)	......by Northern Dancer	11	20	367794	57	98	572693	940487
ROYAL ACADEMY (1987)	......by Nijinsky	26	32	204649	20	30	707001	911650
SALSE (1985)	......by Topsider	25	36	576233	16	22	268898	845131
SHIRLEY HEIGHTS (1975)	......by Mill Reef	23	28	205077	23	38	623112	828190
FAIRY KING (1982)	......by Northern Dancer	26	36	179966	28	46	586046	766011
MACHIAVELLIAN (1987)	......by Mr Prospector	13	16	132376	14	25	610040	742416
TAUFAN (1977)	......by Stop The Music	36	55	313978	38	70	369712	683690
PERSIAN BOLD (1975)	......by Bold Lad (IRE)	23	33	200600	35	65	480725	681325
LAW SOCIETY (1982)	......by Alleged	18	29	137057	44	81	528597	665653
WARNING (1985)	......by Known Fact	21	34	275150	26	55	367890	643040
SHARPO (1977)	......by Sharpen Up	19	21	102898	25	46	514318	617215

LEADING TWO-YEAR-OLD SIRES OF 1995 IN GREAT BRITAIN AND IRELAND

STALLION	BREEDING	RNRS	WNRS	WINS	WIN MONEY	PLACES	PLACE MONEY	TOTAL
DANEHILL (1986)............by Danzig		21	9	14	193002	22	53552	246554
WOODMAN (1983)............by Mr Prospector		17	5	7	132055	24	81781	213836
UNFUWAIN (1985)............by Northern Dancer		10	4	8	189736	10	15520	205256
PETONG (1980)............by Mansingh		28	7	10	184238	37	20975	205212
DISTINCTLY NORTH (1988)....by Minshaanshu Amad		51	12	24	133477	66	70383	203860
WAAJIB (1983)............by Try My Best		10	2	5	176508	13	14530	191039
ALZAO (1980)............by Lyphard		37	16	19	110140	44	58475	168614
DANZIG (1977)............by Northern Dancer		7	2	5	148436	7	8241	156676
NASHWAN (1986)............by Blushing Groom		11	4	8	79662	11	56967	136628
TAUFAN (1977)............by Stop The Music		25	9	13	83507	44	46702	130208
MUJTAHID (1988)............by Woodman		24	6	9	63416	31	59525	122941
DISTANT RELATIVE (1986)....by Habitat		10	4	7	59171	12	63583	122754
DEPLOY (1987)............by Shirley Heights		8	3	5	85743	9	32536	118279
GREEN DESERT (1983)............by Danzig		28	8	12	66762	37	51514	118276
EMARATI (1986)............by Danzig		16	8	16	71648	24	45459	117107
IMPERIAL FRONTIER (1984)....by Lyphard		12	5	7	50820	24	63642	114461
NISHAPOUR (1975)............by Zeddaan		1	1	4	111449	1	633	112082
MT LIVERMORE (1981)............by Blushing Groom		4	3	4	42221	10	68176	110397
INDIAN RIDGE (1985)............by Ahonoora		17	5	8	57132	19	46970	104102
PRIMO DOMINIE (1982)............by Dominion		25	11	14	59545	41	41916	101460

LEADING FIRST CROP SIRES OF 1995 IN GREAT BRITAIN AND IRELAND

STALLION	BREEDING	RNRS	WNRS	WINS	WIN MONEY	PLACES	PLACE MONEY	TOTAL
DISTINCTLY NORTH (1988)	by Minshaanshu Amad	51	12	24	133477	66	70383	203860
MUJTAHID (1988)	by Woodman	24	6	9	63416	31	59525	122941
LYCIUS (1988)	by Mr Prospector	22	10	13	71330	19	20064	91394
POLISH PATRIOT (1988)	by Danzig	31	10	14	62185	37	27032	89218
MARJU (1988)	by Last Tycoon	21	8	9	45064	36	38743	83807
PRIOLO (1987)	by Sovereign Dancer	8	2	3	63894	8	7269	71163
TIMELESS TIMES (1988)	by Timeless Moment	21	10	15	45524	36	21143	66667
CLASSIC MUSIC (1987)	by Northern Dancer	23	7	11	34648	23	18662	53310
TOPANOORA (1987)	by Ahonoora	2	1	2	15097		32206	47303
MAC'S IMP (1988)	by Imp Society	31	5	8	23333	40	22519	45852
POLAR FALCON (1987)	by Nureyev	20	5	7	28841	21	16008	44849
ARCHWAY (1988)	by Thatching	9	4	6	21397	17	19233	40630
ANSHAN (1987)	by Persian Bold	14	4	5	22808	8	10081	32889
GENEROUS (1988)	by Caerleon	17	2	3	19117	13	11670	30787
BATSHOOF (1986)	by Sadler's Wells	12	5	5	18051	10	9300	27350
RON'S VICTORY (1987)	by General Holme	13	4	4	10991	12	8787	19777
SAFAWAN (1986)	by Young Generation	10	3	4	12293	8	5758	18051
NICHOLAS (1986)	by Danzig	2	1	1	4069	5	5760	9829
TWO TIMING (1986)	by Blushing Groom	3	1	1	4128	2	804	4931
ACADEMY AWARD (1986)	by Secretariat	1	1	1	2750	2	1900	4650

STALLIONS EARNINGS FOR 1995

(includes every stallion who sired a winner on the flat in Great Britain and Ireland in 1995).

STALLIONS	RNRS	STARTS	WNRS	WINS	PLACES	TOTAL
ABSALOM	47	273	11	14	70	88296.80
ACADEMY AWARD (USA)	1	4	1	1	2	4649.50
ACCORDION	8	40	2	4	12	26864.49
ADBASS (USA)	8	42	2	2	10	12013.80
ADONIJAH	1	7	1	2	3	6738.00
AFFIRMED (USA)	10	46	3	9	19	54939.07
AFLEET (CAN)	2	18	1	2	3	30600.35
AHONOORA	12	68	4	5	20	63349.62
AJDAL (USA)	1	6	1	1	3	6786.10
AJRAAS (USA)	6	19	1	2	3	78326.74
AKARAD (FR)	3	13	1	2	3	13044.55
AL HAREB (USA)	24	146	5	14	36	66884.09
ALLEGED (USA)	31	113	12	19	39	350667.35
ALLEGING (USA)	8	47	2	3	7	15388.10
ALL SYSTEMS GO	4	21	1	2	3	8300.60
AL NASR (FR)	12	82	7	12	23	143615.98
ALPHABATIM (USA)	3	6	1	1	1	4698.00
ALWASMI (USA)	3	11	1	1	2	5273.25
ALWAYS FAIR (USA)	2	8	1	1	1	4100.60
ALYDAR (USA)	5	12	1	1	1	6420.80
ALYSHEBA (USA)	4	13	1	1	6	6821.88
ALZAO (USA)	86	385	32	39	125	369317.75
ANITA'S PRINCE	8	48	4	5	9	32698.17
ANSHAN	14	37	4	5	8	32888.60
ARAGON	54	283	16	25	75	198361.74
ARCHWAY (IRE)	9	47	4	6	17	40630.05
ARCTIC TERN (USA)	18	107	6	8	42	72436.32
ARDAR	1	11	1	2	4	10960.30
ARDROSS	8	27	1	1	5	5189.20
ARKAN	1	18	1	2	6	10439.10
ARRASAS (USA)	6	38	1	1	7	5796.90
ASCENDANT	1	12	1	2	2	7155.80
ASCOT KNIGHT (CAN)	4	33	3	5	15	31232.00
ASSERT	4	10	1	1	3	5196.78
ASTRONEF	26	138	3	5	19	30578.40
AT THE THRESHOLD (USA)	1	7	1	1	4	5215.50
BACKCHAT (USA)	4	21	1	1	3	5602.60
BAIRN (USA)	35	214	14	19	47	93474.32
BALIDAR	6	40	3	5	13	26502.35
BALLACASHTAL (CAN)	18	118	4	7	38	51350.60
BALLAD ROCK	48	269	14	17	65	138378.25
BATSHOOF	12	46	5	5	10	27350.30
BAY EXPRESS	5	24	1	7	9	27522.60
BELDALE FLUTTER (USA)	8	30	2	2	6	8168.53
BELFORT (FR)	28	175	10	15	47	80541.51
BELLYPHA	7	52	2	3	12	15459.99
BELMEZ (USA)	23	74	5	7	26	133164.95
BE MY CHIEF (USA)	40	193	16	24	80	178465.07
BE MY GUEST (USA)	52	234	11	20	73	530544.81
BE MY NATIVE (USA)	29	98	10	11	20	47378.69
BERING	17	80	7	10	20	166978.93
BEVELED (USA)	51	372	21	31	93	202598.45
BLUEBIRD (USA)	61	324	22	40	123	421754.67
BLUSHING GROOM (FR)	6	49	4	9	18	93976.20
BLUSHING JOHN (USA)	4	13	1	2	4	14458.45

STALLIONS	RNRS	STARTS	WNRS	WINS	PLACES	TOTAL
BOB BACK (USA)	18	74	6	6	16	27803.67
BOLD ARRANGEMENT	26	192	9	14	44	120536.42
BOLD FORT	2	13	1	2	4	7751.10
BOLD OWL	14	74	3	6	18	25116.91
BROKEN HEARTED	16	81	6	10	24	57029.66
BROTHERLY (USA)	3	9	1	2	2	8150.25
BURSLEM	7	34	3	4	7	15942.27
BUSTED	1	10	1	5	4	17469.50
BUSTINO	14	57	4	6	7	29611.60
BUZZARDS BAY	4	14	1	1	3	3291.10
CADEAUX GENEREUX	62	323	32	53	121	577844.96
CAERLEON (USA)	61	251	25	39	86	607587.45
CAMDEN TOWN	5	17	2	2	6	23121.68
CANNONADE (USA)	1	15	1	2	5	10830.80
CAPOTE (USA)	3	12	2	2	3	14741.00
CAPRICORN LINE	2	5	1	1	2	3591.60
CARMELITE HOUSE (USA)	15	46	1	1	12	6456.83
CARO	3	18	1	1	8	20396.10
THE CARPENTER (USA)	1	3	1	1	1	3782.05
CASTLE KEEP	6	21	1	1	6	5121.15
CATALDI	5	29	3	4	8	17096.53
CELESTIAL STORM (USA)	19	109	4	5	36	75396.33
CHARMER	16	87	4	6	22	42113.71
CHIEF'S CROWN (USA)	18	67	6	11	22	144604.93
CHIEF SINGER	29	174	8	15	49	112437.80
CHILIBANG	30	164	7	12	34	56220.80
CHUKAROO	2	16	1	1	2	3320.75
CIGAR	7	50	1	3	6	18245.50
CLANTIME	55	337	19	37	93	223505.28
CLASSIC MUSIC (USA)	23	96	7	11	23	53309.99
CLASSIC SECRET (USA)	25	134	8	14	35	65925.29
CLEVER TRICK (USA)	5	24	2	2	6	8890.84
COLMORE ROW	17	72	2	3	17	17973.50
COMMANCHE RUN	8	36	1	2	14	31096.86
COMMON GROUNDS	40	223	13	17	73	144960.22
COMPLIANCE (USA)	1	6	1	1	1	3648.52
COMRADE IN ARMS	1	6	1	1	0	2550.00
CONQUERING HERO (USA)	11	62	2	4	20	24932.16
CONTRACT LAW	35	189	8	14	55	79077.72
COQUELIN (USA)	4	44	2	5	13	30743.57
CORWYN BAY	1	5	1	1	1	23445.54
COZZENE (USA)	8	31	3	3	16	128930.26
CREE SONG	7	36	1	1	7	56153.00
CRICKET BALL (USA)	2	15	1	6	8	40700.30
CROFTER (USA)	2	17	1	1	2	2903.00
CROFTHALL	15	128	6	13	35	88065.81
CRYSTAL GLITTERS (USA)	4	29	1	3	11	16662.40
CYRANO DE BERGERAC	91	493	25	38	117	232922.89
DAHAR (USA)	4	12	2	2	4	6947.43
DALSAAN	1	16	1	2	2	7836.75
DAMISTER (USA)	28	131	10	12	46	175208.09
DANCE OF LIFE (USA)	17	103	8	11	17	39970.33
DANCING BRAVE (USA)	30	124	11	14	46	222904.03
DANCING DISSIDENT (USA)	38	193	15	21	64	183004.39
DANEHILL	68	342	36	57	129	618720.87
DANZIG (USA)	31	109	11	27	39	368753.65
DANZIG CONNECTION (USA)	8	49	5	13	21	94522.63
DARING MARCH	20	107	4	4	26	48816.90
DARN THAT ALARM (USA)	1	5	1	1	4	8166.00
DARSHAAN	40	172	19	26	67	259719.23
DASHING BLADE	11	71	5	12	25	77426.05

STALLIONS	RNRS	STARTS	WNRS	WINS	PLACES	TOTAL
DAYJUR (USA)	25	94	12	15	57	160804.60
DEEP RUN	2	4	1	1	1	2550.74
DEPLOY	27	144	9	16	53	201121.68
DEVIL'S BAG (USA)	6	24	2	4	7	24662.38
DIESIS	40	131	14	17	57	449192.74
DIGAMIST (USA)	44	205	10	12	47	80951.30
DISTANT RELATIVE	33	186	13	20	60	231658.95
DISTINCTLY NORTH (USA)	51	222	12	24	66	203860.27
DIXIELAND BAND (USA)	14	78	6	8	27	75521.97
DOC MARTEN	5	39	3	4	10	14491.60
DOMINION	68	390	16	28	118	315239.17
DOMINION ROYALE	22	134	5	15	26	152916.03
DOM RACINE (FR)	2	5	1	1	1	1860.14
DOMYNSKY	16	99	6	12	28	62442.40
DON'T FORGET ME	66	344	20	28	100	186181.70
DOUBLE BED (FR)	2	9	1	1	4	4799.60
DOUBLE SCHWARTZ	23	120	9	15	31	86924.93
DOUBLETOUR (USA)	9	54	2	2	14	25026.01
DOULAB (USA)	32	299	14	29	84	163533.41
DOWSING (USA)	55	337	25	44	95	257591.88
DOYOUN	27	113	12	16	40	146583.37
DREAMS TO REALITY (USA)	5	26	1	1	5	5426.50
DRUMALIS	6	35	1	4	8	15530.00
DUNBEATH (USA)	28	166	9	20	39	114187.95
DURGAM (USA)	11	56	3	7	16	25080.82
EASTERN ECHO (USA)	1	6	1	1	1	10195.00
EASY GOER (USA)	5	14	4	7	5	31360.20
EFISIO	65	434	27	40	120	387113.01
ELA-MANA-MOU	41	183	14	23	56	437295.70
EL BABA (USA)	1	13	1	1	6	7029.80
ELEGANT AIR	10	40	4	9	6	38888.22
EL GRAN SENOR (USA)	29	115	11	14	41	102614.94
ELMAAMUL (USA)	21	98	10	16	36	108515.06
EMARATI (USA)	31	185	14	26	50	177915.49
EXACTLY SHARP (USA)	8	50	2	2	16	18094.07
EXECUTIVE MAN	6	38	1	3	11	20828.00
EXECUTIVE PRIDE	1	11	1	3	2	11376.23
EXHIBITIONER	14	80	2	3	23	32321.53
EXODAL (USA)	6	34	2	3	10	14511.40
EXPLODENT (USA)	4	24	3	4	8	37211.62
FAIRY KING (USA)	76	307	26	36	102	298169.18
FALIRAKI	1	11	1	2	4	14561.40
FAR NORTH (CAN)	4	19	2	2	13	37793.86
FAST PLAY (USA)	2	3	1	1	1	7623.00
FAUSTUS (USA)	32	173	8	12	48	69045.49
FAYRUZ	62	323	10	15	82	114977.84
FERDINAND (USA)	3	20	2	6	7	58376.40
FIGHTING FIT (USA)	7	52	3	5	11	20583.30
FLASH N THUNDER (USA)	1	7	1	2	1	8254.90
FLASH OF STEEL	6	37	4	6	16	25653.69
FOOLS HOLME (USA)	17	76	4	5	22	39690.35
FORMIDABLE (USA)	46	262	15	27	84	169564.30
FORTY NINER (USA)	4	14	2	3	5	29603.40
FORZANDO	28	141	5	7	41	53979.85
FULL EXTENT (USA)	10	90	2	5	31	45371.30
FURRY GLEN	3	3	1	1	0	0.00
GABITAT	9	47	2	3	8	32960.70
GALLIC LEAGUE	18	83	2	2	17	13789.77
GENERAL VIEW	2	8	1	1	5	4073.01
GENEROUS (IRE)	17	40	2	3	13	30787.24
GILDORAN	3	5	1	1	1	3852.50

STALLIONS	RNRS	STARTS	WNRS	WINS	PLACES	TOTAL
GLENSTAL (USA)	33	181	10	19	43	79789.20
GLINT OF GOLD	12	65	3	4	18	20192.36
GLOW (USA)	15	85	3	4	21	19924.26
GODSWALK (USA)	3	21	2	2	5	11454.50
GOLD CREST (USA)	2	26	2	3	8	13165.00
GOLDEN ACT (USA)	1	10	1	1	3	5928.10
GONE WEST (USA)	13	56	6	7	22	101137.46
GOOD THYNE (USA)	2	4	1	2	0	4917.08
GOOD TIMES (ITY)	12	58	2	4	11	15571.20
GOVERNOR GENERAL	26	110	2	2	12	14087.35
GRAUSTARK	2	7	1	1	3	3738.00
GREAT COMMOTION (USA)	6	20	1	1	2	4050.43
GREEN DANCER (USA)	15	54	2	3	12	27333.57
GREEN DESERT (USA)	83	377	31	58	133	555415.83
GREEN FOREST (USA)	11	48	4	6	12	28101.28
GREEN RUBY (USA)	11	68	1	2	8	12348.15
GREY DESIRE	16	82	2	4	13	46077.35
GROOM DANCER (USA)	14	65	7	12	20	76296.41
GULCH (USA)	13	68	5	12	34	318012.74
GUNNER B	7	44	2	3	11	15085.90
HABITAT	2	21	2	2	6	12739.35
HADEER	38	206	8	9	52	66216.31
HALLGATE	17	118	5	7	25	45741.00
HANDSOME SAILOR	22	121	4	6	33	51800.95
HARD FOUGHT	9	70	4	7	18	32032.62
HATIM (USA)	10	75	3	8	20	44596.58
HEIGHTS OF GOLD	4	23	2	2	11	13160.50
HELLO GORGEOUS (USA)	2	16	1	2	9	10229.10
HERALDISTE (USA)	9	36	3	6	9	26350.11
HERO'S HONOR (USA)	3	21	2	4	9	42278.36
HIGH ESTATE	31	154	9	13	37	76726.54
HIGHEST HONOR (FR)	5	16	1	3	6	43165.02
HIGH KICKER (USA)	9	58	2	4	14	23907.00
HIGH TOP	4	13	1	2	1	4995.00
HOMEBOY	3	29	2	3	8	18998.59
HOMING	5	23	1	1	7	8558.90
HOMO SAPIEN	2	22	1	2	6	10242.80
HONEST PLEASURE (USA)	1	13	1	1	3	9888.90
HORAGE	13	95	5	8	30	53136.41
HORATIUS (USA)	1	14	1	1	6	5731.10
HOSTAGE (USA)	1	12	1	2	1	7495.80
HOUSTON (USA)	1	8	1	1	4	6777.30
HUBBLY BUBBLY (USA)	13	44	1	2	6	9038.75
ILIUM	4	19	1	2	4	8459.05
IMPERIAL FALCON (CAN)	4	36	2	5	19	28040.60
IMPERIAL FLING (USA)	1	15	1	5	6	16763.70
IMPERIAL FRONTIER (USA)	20	95	9	11	35	137998.12
IMP SOCIETY (USA)	8	27	2	2	6	10422.87
INCA CHIEF (USA)	17	53	2	4	4	23127.10
INDIAN FOREST (USA)	5	26	1	1	5	5271.40
INDIAN RIDGE	51	294	21	47	97	829701.45
INSAN (USA)	6	25	2	4	7	18132.35
INTERREX (CAN)	15	85	4	9	21	69242.66
IN THE WINGS	27	75	12	16	25	536730.21
IRISH RIVER (FR)	8	34	2	3	8	17999.85
IRISH TOWER (USA)	1	6	1	1	2	5448.68
IT'S FREEZING (USA)	2	11	1	1	2	7827.97
JADE HUNTER (USA)	2	6	1	1	2	6596.53
JALMOOD (USA)	24	157	8	12	49	156656.20
JAREER (USA)	34	150	5	6	32	37922.45
JAVA GOLD (USA)	1	8	1	3	2	12303.00

STALLIONS	RNRS	STARTS	WNRS	WINS	PLACES	TOTAL
JESTER	10	43	3	5	7	20153.40
JUPITER ISLAND	14	55	5	6	14	42728.21
KABOUR	11	85	1	3	16	20865.45
KAFU	5	46	2	5	11	24628.81
KAHYASI	29	134	15	24	49	244311.91
KALAGLOW	28	136	10	18	32	172176.42
KALA SHIKARI	7	53	4	7	18	90726.50
KALDOUN (FR)	1	9	1	1	2	18960.70
KAMPALA	4	23	1	1	6	6542.66
K-BATTERY	5	36	3	3	15	23828.80
KEEN	19	96	6	9	33	66196.52
KEFAAH (USA)	29	151	8	18	49	88341.30
KENMARE (FR)	3	8	1	1	1	2734.41
KIND OF HUSH	17	102	4	5	16	24543.00
KING AMONG KINGS	3	30	1	2	6	13894.70
KING OF CLUBS	8	40	1	2	9	14840.98
KING OF SPAIN	8	44	3	6	10	45521.15
KIRCHNER	2	14	1	2	3	7774.25
KNOWN FACT (USA)	18	78	7	12	26	171862.44
KOMAITE (USA)	31	211	13	27	59	156932.92
KRAYYAN	8	51	2	4	7	13991.36
KRIS	51	229	22	25	67	173062.92
LAC OUIMET (USA)	2	5	2	3	2	13657.50
LAFONTAINE (USA)	8	21	3	3	10	33739.07
LASHKARI	3	19	1	3	6	13934.44
LAST TYCOON	61	286	18	31	83	190776.29
LATE ACT (USA)	1	10	1	2	5	11715.10
LAW SOCIETY (USA)	44	223	18	29	73	217216.67
LEAD ON TIME (USA)	14	73	5	9	24	104988.05
LEAR FAN (USA)	23	115	11	15	37	102930.97
LEGEND OF FRANCE (USA)	9	44	3	5	10	25589.05
LIBOI (USA)	1	6	1	1	3	5618.55
LIBRATE	5	21	1	1	1	2568.00
LIDHAME	6	67	2	6	18	36262.50
LIGHTER	2	6	1	2	1	5914.25
LITTLE CURRENT (USA)	1	9	1	2	3	18905.60
LOCAL TALENT (USA)	4	16	1	1	6	14236.95
LOCHNAGER	20	109	4	6	23	41348.15
LOMOND (USA)	26	90	6	8	21	65084.64
LONGLEAT (USA)	1	7	1	1	3	16495.35
LORD BUD	2	19	1	4	11	25115.90
LUGANA BEACH	12	81	6	8	23	41337.00
LYCIUS (USA)	22	63	10	13	19	91394.09
LYPHARD (USA)	20	78	8	13	22	128331.96
LYPHARD'S SPECIAL (USA)	3	21	2	2	7	8372.85
LYPHARD'S WISH (FR)	4	14	2	3	5	23916.12
MACHIAVELLIAN (USA)	24	84	13	16	30	180096.65
MAC'S IMP (USA)	31	147	5	8	40	45852.03
MAELSTROM LAKE	16	120	3	6	31	35556.28
MAGICAL STRIKE (USA)	24	102	6	8	26	37502.13
MAGICAL WONDER (USA)	10	60	4	9	27	89720.95
MAJESTIC SHORE (USA)	2	17	2	3	8	13806.00
MANILA (USA)	7	26	2	2	9	76603.60
MANSINGH (USA)	5	38	1	1	8	8969.40
MANSOOJ	5	47	4	4	20	76733.00
MARCHING ON	3	26	3	4	8	18749.00
MARFA (USA)	1	10	1	1	2	5139.40
MARJU (IRE)	21	76	8	9	36	83806.72
MARTIN JOHN	10	52	2	4	14	21434.91
MASHHOR DANCER (USA)	6	17	1	1	2	5474.83
MASTER WILLIE	17	78	6	9	20	55613.78

STALLIONS	RNRS	STARTS	WNRS	WINS	PLACES	TOTAL
MAZAAD	22	89	1	1	20	19249.26
MAZILIER (USA)	34	227	16	25	64	120867.64
MELDRUM	1	11	1	4	1	27967.50
MELYNO	2	31	2	9	10	31543.70
MERDON MELODY	12	63	2	3	19	24805.85
MIAMI SPRINGS	1	13	1	2	6	14687.35
MIDYAN (USA)	53	242	12	23	73	287481.86
MINING (USA)	1	17	1	4	9	16299.00
MINSHAANSHU AMAD (USA)	3	17	1	4	3	15936.65
MINSTER SON	9	44	1	1	10	8263.20
THE MINSTREL (CAN)	3	17	1	1	4	10112.20
MISTER MAJESTIC	6	47	4	9	11	32087.95
MISWAKI (USA)	8	35	3	5	10	60283.85
MONTELIMAR (USA)	7	25	2	3	6	25728.95
MON TRESOR	14	89	7	9	21	41908.26
MORSTON (FR)	4	20	2	3	10	22975.65
MOSCOW SOCIETY (USA)	2	10	1	2	6	7245.04
MOST WELCOME	49	292	27	37	93	287672.47
MR PROSPECTOR (USA)	20	67	8	10	35	146897.92
MT LIVERMORE (USA)	5	18	3	4	11	110769.47
MTOTO	49	236	19	33	83	512618.40
MUJTAHID (USA)	24	67	6	9	31	122940.92
MULHOLLANDE (USA)	6	30	1	4	5	57064.25
MUMMY'S GAME	7	38	2	2	7	9801.40
MUMMY'S PET	1	13	1	2	6	9353.30
MUSCATITE	3	22	1	2	2	11979.07
MUSIC BOY	26	173	10	18	41	87199.89
MY DAD TOM (USA)	2	19	1	3	3	10412.90
MYJINSKI (USA)	4	52	2	4	10	16400.05
NABEEL DANCER (USA)	11	66	4	8	25	64927.35
NAEVUS (USA)	4	27	2	4	9	31431.97
NALCHIK (USA)	3	14	1	1	1	3583.00
NASHAMAA	24	119	7	10	31	78435.66
NASHWAN (USA)	35	114	11	17	49	310979.42
NESHAD (USA)	3	20	1	1	4	5015.64
NEVER SO BOLD	42	233	12	17	56	110532.33
NEW EXPRESS	2	19	1	1	3	3723.00
NICHOLAS (USA)	2	11	1	1	5	9828.87
NICHOLAS BILL	11	24	1	1	2	7691.80
NIGHT SHIFT (USA)	58	348	26	40	112	504312.69
NIJINSKY (CAN)	8	20	3	5	2	803088.01
NINISKI (USA)	25	112	8	14	41	83279.74
NISHAPOUR (FR)	16	63	4	9	16	203400.06
NOALTO	8	37	2	5	5	47908.21
THE NOBLE PLAYER (USA)	16	88	6	8	27	41379.36
NODOUBLE (USA)	3	16	2	2	7	19306.53
NOMINATION	30	197	12	18	43	84954.12
NO PASS NO SALE	1	17	1	2	7	10744.75
NORDANCE (USA)	11	72	4	8	26	39625.81
NORDICO (USA)	74	428	20	32	133	238720.51
NORTHERN BABY (CAN)	14	42	2	4	14	21438.02
NORTHERN FLAGSHIP (USA)	3	14	2	4	8	82119.74
NORTHERN PROSPECT (USA)	1	6	1	1	0	2243.00
NORTHERN STATE (USA)	22	112	4	4	27	27671.55
NORTHERN TEMPEST (USA)	1	17	1	1	2	4558.40
NORTHFIELDS (USA)	1	9	1	2	2	7630.70
NORTHJET	1	12	1	1	6	12159.05
NORWICK (USA)	6	37	2	3	10	27881.40
NUREYEV (USA)	28	96	12	16	42	182090.73
OGYGIAN (USA)	3	14	1	1	2	4791.00
OLD VIC	24	99	9	12	27	77819.89

STALLION EARNINGS FOR 1995

STALLIONS	RNRS	STARTS	WNRS	WINS	PLACES	TOTAL
ON YOUR MARK	2	11	1	1	1	3330.20
OPENING VERSE (USA)	2	7	1	1	1	3037.60
PENNINE WALK	40	201	13	19	51	151349.02
PERSEPOLIS (FR)	1	12	1	3	3	14345.20
PERSIAN BOLD	57	271	23	33	102	274735.39
PERSIAN HEIGHTS	45	239	13	22	65	138980.36
PETONG	64	428	20	33	97	319720.90
PETORIUS	61	391	22	40	105	225713.28
PETOSKI	30	129	5	5	23	28942.37
PHARDANTE (FR)	13	44	5	6	8	25333.39
PHARLY (FR)	52	276	14	28	84	226010.52
PHONE TRICK (USA)	11	49	1	1	9	10330.66
PICEA	5	17	1	1	0	2537.00
PIRATE ARMY (USA)	2	5	1	1	0	1849.50
PLUGGED NICKLE (USA)	1	11	1	1	5	5553.20
POLAR FALCON (USA)	20	57	5	7	21	44848.55
POLISH NAVY (USA)	2	15	2	3	5	20639.35
POLISH PATRIOT (USA)	31	133	10	14	37	89217.57
POLISH PRECEDENT (USA)	37	135	17	27	48	586299.73
POSEN (USA)	25	147	6	15	43	100697.46
PRAGMATIC	1	11	1	1	5	9472.40
PRECIOUS METAL	2	15	1	2	4	9637.30
PRECOCIOUS	29	166	5	5	48	53866.81
PRESIDIUM	27	171	9	13	39	70098.79
PRIMO DOMINIE	65	406	29	47	122	313186.53
PRINCE DANIEL (USA)	15	65	3	4	9	21201.40
PRINCE RUPERT (FR)	26	154	8	13	55	77175.67
PRINCE SABO	58	306	21	30	96	197318.60
PRIOLO (USA)	8	22	2	3	8	71163.44
PRIONSAA	1	4	1	1	1	3996.25
PRIVATE ACCOUNT (USA)	8	25	4	6	8	53385.10
PROCIDA (USA)	2	6	1	1	4	5731.66
PROJECT MANAGER	20	82	2	3	30	21065.65
PROPER REALITY (USA)	1	5	1	1	4	5647.15
PUISSANCE	38	222	11	23	63	208438.75
RABBI (BEL)	1	1	1	1	0	1279.10
RAHY (USA)	9	36	4	8	14	61691.97
RAINBOW QUEST (USA)	59	269	27	38	92	675672.03
RAKAPOSHI KING	5	54	2	5	11	39107.10
RAMBLING RIVER	1	5	1	1	0	2433.00
RAMBO DANCER (CAN)	54	312	20	31	85	174416.05
RAMPAGE (USA)	1	15	1	2	4	8033.05
RARE PERFORMER (USA)	1	3	1	1	1	3244.50
REACH	2	3	1	1	1	2763.00
REASONABLE (FR)	5	30	1	1	5	7063.80
RED RANSOM (USA)	7	24	4	4	13	37085.53
RED SUNSET	29	159	10	17	37	97628.63
REESH	6	29	1	2	3	8017.50
REFERENCE POINT	29	124	8	13	45	86504.83
REPRIMAND	51	271	18	27	80	184581.42
RHOMAN RULE (USA)	4	39	3	6	9	19585.76
RICH CHARLIE	14	103	3	7	27	43889.60
RISK ME (FR)	81	403	11	17	93	188109.90
RIVERMAN (USA)	29	142	13	17	45	597129.85
ROBELLINO (USA)	37	222	15	21	66	135451.69
ROCK CITY	49	275	25	43	84	236337.56
ROI DANZIG (USA)	34	155	6	14	34	87110.78
RON'S VICTORY (USA)	13	60	4	4	12	19777.37
RORY'S JESTER (AUS)	4	24	4	5	10	34457.65
ROSELIER (FR)	3	10	2	2	4	10810.63
ROUSILLON (USA)	22	132	9	17	45	143404.94

STALLIONS	RNRS	STARTS	WNRS	WINS	PLACES	TOTAL
ROYAL ACADEMY (USA)	60	218	26	32	87	325295.56
ROYAL FOUNTAIN	1	4	1	2	1	10035.90
RUNNETT	5	30	1	1	3	4501.87
RUSTICARO (FR)	3	14	1	1	6	3879.85
SABONA (USA)	2	9	1	1	2	8640.95
SADLER'S WELLS (USA)	89	288	40	55	130	1047423.68
SAFAWAN	10	35	3	4	8	18051.28
SALEM DRIVE (USA)	1	3	1	2	1	12783.50
SALSE (USA)	59	267	25	36	85	759662.76
SALT DOME (USA)	35	224	10	16	71	113859.54
SANDHURST PRINCE	3	28	2	5	10	20928.00
SARAB	3	20	1	2	4	8125.20
SATCO (FR)	5	17	2	2	3	8776.00
SAUMAREZ	3	17	3	7	4	33510.76
SAYF EL ARAB (USA)	25	150	9	17	45	90906.25
SCALLYWAG	1	10	1	4	3	14007.50
SCENIC	29	161	11	13	58	82362.95
SCORPIO (FR)	2	19	1	2	1	9430.75
SCOTTISH REEL	17	87	4	4	13	25596.80
SEATTLE DANCER (USA)	13	38	2	2	14	29844.35
SECRETO (USA)	9	47	3	8	11	49252.55
SEEKING THE GOLD (USA)	7	28	4	4	14	60346.18
SEPTIEME CIEL (USA)	1	7	1	1	3	6193.60
SEYMOUR HICKS (FR)	7	24	1	1	6	8938.75
SHAADI (USA)	42	215	23	32	77	235325.75
SHADEED (USA)	15	103	7	12	34	198044.79
SHAHRASTANI (USA)	17	70	7	9	20	56713.20
SHARDARI	13	61	6	7	11	29077.11
SHAREEF DANCER (USA)	46	200	13	16	61	125788.46
SHARPEN UP	2	9	1	1	3	6227.71
SHARPO	55	264	19	21	72	188264.45
SHARP SHOT	1	8	1	4	3	57282.60
SHARP VICTOR (USA)	7	19	1	1	2	5279.70
SHARROOD (USA)	38	208	12	25	71	214375.04
SHAVIAN	18	96	5	9	24	51711.85
SHERNAZAR	35	113	9	11	33	97943.12
SHIRLEY HEIGHTS	56	199	23	28	81	332938.00
SHY GROOM (USA)	17	96	2	2	22	54329.95
SIBERIAN EXPRESS (USA)	30	226	14	25	62	154780.00
SILLY PRICES	2	23	1	2	4	8514.30
SILVER HAWK (USA)	23	81	9	12	32	290006.89
SIMPLY GREAT (FR)	34	152	7	12	35	90580.75
SIR IVOR	4	15	1	1	6	46764.44
SIZZLING MELODY	22	104	5	12	14	65693.52
SKYLINER	11	45	2	2	9	10640.85
SLEW O' GOLD (USA)	5	19	1	1	6	6767.11
SLIP ANCHOR	45	218	21	29	87	236770.30
SMARTEN (USA)	2	17	1	1	2	4729.00
SMILE (USA)	1	3	1	1	1	4488.60
SMOGGY	1	1	1	1	0	2034.65
SONG	4	60	3	7	16	54011.46
SON OF SHAKA	1	19	1	1	8	10825.30
SOVIET LAD (USA)	24	116	9	12	34	61101.08
SOVIET STAR (USA)	42	149	16	25	53	340592.94
SPARKLING BOY	1	12	1	1	1	5293.90
SPORTIN' LIFE (USA)	1	7	1	4	2	20377.47
SQUILL (USA)	8	41	2	4	12	19270.79
STALKER	4	12	1	1	3	7827.96
STANDAAN (FR)	13	56	2	3	14	43447.89
STARCH REDUCED	1	23	1	3	7	14653.00
STAR DE NASKRA (USA)	1	16	1	3	5	37422.55

STALLIONS	RNRS	STARTS	WNRS	WINS	PLACES	TOTAL
STATOBLEST	39	209	10	16	70	112700.90
STOP THE MUSIC (USA)	1	12	1	1	4	3709.50
STORM BIRD (CAN)	17	58	3	4	21	39992.73
STORM CAT (USA)	11	55	6	6	37	67954.79
STRAWBERRY ROAD (AUS)	3	25	2	3	6	11961.91
STRIKE GOLD (USA)	1	4	1	2	0	7073.50
STRONG GALE	12	26	2	3	8	18562.99
SULAAFAH (USA)	12	45	1	1	9	7837.40
SUNSHINE FOREVER (USA)	8	32	3	3	16	30932.20
SUN VALLEY	1	12	1	1	4	4161.90
SUPERLATIVE	26	162	8	14	37	65051.96
SUPERPOWER	44	273	8	13	64	144026.49
SUPREME LEADER	5	29	2	2	11	20632.94
SURE BLADE (USA)	21	123	8	16	31	118326.50
SWEET MONDAY	3	20	2	4	5	23569.20
SWORD DANCE	2	22	1	2	5	10372.50
SYLVAN EXPRESS	8	48	3	4	13	19967.90
TACHERON	1	12	1	2	2	8760.00
TALE QUALE	1	10	1	1	4	3832.92
TASSO (USA)	2	10	1	1	6	6418.21
TATE GALLERY (USA)	26	146	5	8	39	55380.48
TAUFAN (USA)	96	538	36	55	161	485965.42
TEENOSO (USA)	13	62	2	4	19	70029.70
TEJANO (USA)	5	33	1	3	8	13634.85
TELSMOSS	2	16	1	1	4	17479.50
TENDER KING	6	25	1	1	3	3228.55
THATCHING	79	414	22	33	128	253192.09
THEATRICAL	13	55	3	6	26	98284.28
THEN AGAIN	29	114	3	4	19	42118.65
THORN DANCE (USA)	2	12	1	4	5	23080.20
THOWRA (FR)	13	70	3	4	22	22787.75
TILT UP (USA)	2	15	1	2	4	7817.50
TIME FOR A CHANGE (USA)	1	6	1	1	2	28244.00
TIMELESS MOMENT (USA)	6	35	3	9	10	47738.31
TIMELESS NATIVE (USA)	1	8	1	2	2	10282.90
TIMELESS TIMES (USA)	21	126	10	15	36	66666.92
TINA'S PET	29	178	10	12	32	63260.20
TIROL	42	215	14	23	56	159318.08
TODAY AND TOMORROW	11	41	1	2	4	9321.95
TOM ROLFE	2	9	1	2	1	20123.76
TOPANOORA	2	10	1	2	2	47302.70
TOPSIDER (USA)	17	62	6	8	17	73670.33
TOP VILLE	12	55	3	5	23	79855.13
TOTEM (USA)	4	17	1	1	5	4302.82
TOUCH OF GREY	8	57	2	4	17	30677.70
TOUT ENSEMBLE	5	23	1	1	8	6886.67
TOWN AND COUNTRY	4	13	1	1	2	21511.00
TRAGIC ROLE (USA)	16	89	7	8	34	53964.85
TRAPP MOUNTAIN (USA)	1	8	1	1	3	4673.28
TREASURE KAY	38	211	11	18	57	128121.06
TREMBLANT	3	17	1	1	5	5979.10
TREMPOLINO (USA)	17	72	6	10	19	84416.81
TROJAN FEN	6	32	3	6	11	28529.38
TRY MY BEST (USA)	15	98	7	11	27	69367.40
TWO TIMING (USA)	3	10	1	1	2	4931.25
UNCLE POKEY	1	5	1	1	2	6502.50
UNFUWAIN (USA)	39	187	18	25	72	349622.77
VAGUE SHOT	3	14	1	3	2	13579.50
VAIGLY GREAT	8	77	3	5	18	31695.90
VALIYAR	14	97	3	5	13	42299.60
VILLAGE STAR (FR)	4	18	2	2	7	15232.00

STALLIONS	RNRS	STARTS	WNRS	WINS	PLACES	TOTAL
VIN ST BENET	2	13	1	1	1	5095.58
VISION (USA)	28	172	9	19	60	88109.90
VOUCHSAFE	1	5	1	1	3	4278.00
WAAJIB	51	270	10	16	86	351540.89
WAR (USA)	1	2	1	1	0	2872.00
WARNING	48	230	21	34	80	596204.90
WARRSHAN (USA)	18	88	5	6	28	63972.19
WASSL	7	58	3	9	15	40105.70
WELDNAAS (USA)	28	195	10	15	46	139388.05
WELL DECORATED (USA)	2	20	1	2	4	8305.30
WELSH CAPTAIN	6	31	3	4	8	19701.80
WELSH TERM	2	10	1	1	1	6297.03
WILD AGAIN (USA)	2	13	2	3	8	32904.95
WITH APPROVAL (CAN)	3	4	1	2	1	9415.92
WOLVERLIFE	3	21	1	1	4	3841.70
WOODMAN (USA)	47	176	17	25	74	344284.40
YA ZAMAN (USA)	2	9	2	3	2	16750.00
ZAFFARAN (USA)	1	11	1	1	3	4428.20
ZALAZL (USA)	14	100	5	10	33	80938.40
ZIGGY'S BOY (USA)	1	22	1	6	9	45798.92
ZILZAL (USA)	14	49	6	7	19	77292.93

STATISTICS BY KIND PERMISSION OF WEATHERBYS

If an entry is incorrect or has been omitted, please notify the editor by January 10th, 1997.

This will ensure it appears correctly in the 1997 edition.

TBA

The TBA was established in 1943 to help punters place all bets, including difficult and conditional ones and also for the working of systems. We were first to offer this service to the racing public and we believe we still lead the field.

We are not traditional bookmakers – we earn our income from commission offered by the trade on your turnover, acting as agents between the public and the bookmaker. THERE IS NO CHARGE TO YOU FOR OUR SERVICE.

We specialise in placing conditional bets that would not be accepted by conventional bookmakers. These include straight or conditional first show, first shortening show, second show, starting price stipulations and at-any-time conditions.

WE NEVER CLOSE WINNING ACCOUNTS.

Why? Because you are not winning from us — we are merely agents.